KU-029-827

1770

...mi. Oeder. Zoega Fabricius Brünniche Gunnerus Müller

...mania Jacquin Mygind, Haller. Wilck. Murray Schreber. Wolf. Scopoli
Cramer Layler Necker ...

...gie Burmann Royen, Gronovius, Allemand Hahn ...

...yli Meder ... Elly Hope Browne Hudson Hill Solander

...li Jussieu, Gouan, laTourette Gerard. Cusson Duchesne Cameria, Aub...

...li Allioni, Turra, Cyrillus, Baffi Maratti Arduino

...de Laxman, Lerche, Gmelin Falk

...pani Barnadez, Minuart Ant Capdevila

...tania Vandelli

...dici Koenig Muti, Garden. Solander

...vli la Chenal J. Gesner Schenchzer junior Hallerny

...uard Brison Daubenton
...unichi Gouan
...riry, Schäfer, Geoffroy, Scopoli

Order OUT OF Chaos

The type specimen of *Momordica balsamina* L. in Linnaeus' herbarium at the Linnean Society of London (LINN). The annotations at the base of the sheet are in Linnaeus' handwriting.

Order OUT OF Chaos

Linnaean Plant Names and their Types

Charlie Jarvis

Published by The Linnean Society of London
in association with the Natural History Museum, London

First published by The Linnean Society of London in association with the Natural History Museum, London in 2007.

The Linnean Society of London & the Natural History Museum, London identify Charlie Jarvis as the author of this work. Charlie Jarvis asserts his moral rights.

Design © The Linnean Society of London, 2007.
Text © The Linnean Society of London and the Natural History Museum, London, 2007.
Foreword © The Linnean Society of London and the Natural History Museum, London, 2007. Peter Raven asserts his moral rights.
Prefaces © The Linnean Society of London and the Natural History Museum, London, 2007. David Cutler and Mike Dixon assert their moral rights.

Illustrations: please see picture credits for copyright information.

ISBN 978-0-9506207-7-0

British Library Cataloguing-in-Publication data:
A catalogue record for this book is available from the British Library.

Research and editorial work: Katherine Challis
Production and picture research: Leonie Berwick
Cover design: Heather Oliver
Index: Christopher Hobson

Front cover: *Momordica balsamina*, sheet 1150.1 from Linnaeus' herbarium (LINN) © The Linnean Society of London.
Back cover: Portrait of Linnaeus by Gustav Lundberg ca. 1753 © The Linnaeus Museum, Uppsala, Sweden; *Gorteria rigens*, sheet 1027.3 (LINN); *Euphorbia amygdaloides*, sheet 630.72 (LINN); *Delphinium consolida*, sheet 694.1 (LINN); watermark and paper from Linnaeus' herbarium as background © The Linnean Society of London.
Front inside flap: *Stapelia variegata*, sheet 311.1 (LINN) © The Linnean Society of London.
Back inside flap: photo of Charlie Jarvis © Fiona Wild.

All rights reserved. No part of this publication may be reproduced, stored in a retrieval system, or transmitted in any form or by any means, mechanical, photocopying, recording, or otherwise, without the prior permission of the publishers.

The designation of geographical entities in this book, and the presentation of material, do not imply the expression of any opinions whatsoever on the part of the publishers, the editors, authors, or any other participating organisations concerning the legal status of any country, territory, or area, or of its authorities, or concerning the delimitation of its frontiers or boundaries.

Typeset by Servis Filmsetting, Manchester, UK
Typeface Garamond 12/15pt & 10/13pt.
System QuarkXpress®

Printed and bound by CPI Bath, UK
Printed on acid-free paper compliant with ISO 9706 requirements for permanence of paper

The Linnean Society of London
Burlington House, Piccadilly
London W1V 0BF UK
www.linnean.org

Natural History Museum
Cromwell Road
London SW7 5BD UK
www.nhm.ac.uk

The Linnean Society of London: Charity Reference No. 220509

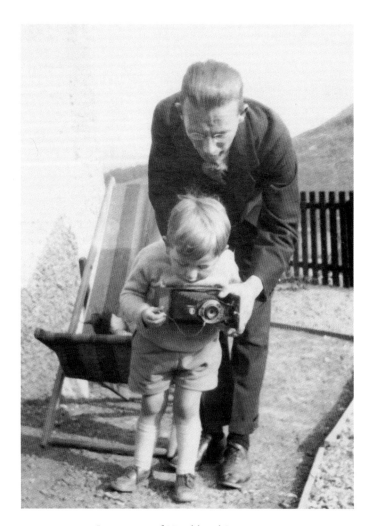

In memory of Harold and Peter Jarvis,
enthusiastic natural historians

This South African specimen from Linnaeus' herbarium is the type of *Ixia crocata* L. (= *Tritonia crocata* (L.) Ker-Gawl.).

CONTENTS

FOREWORD

The published works of the 18th century Swedish naturalist Carl Linnaeus remain important to us today because they include names for more than 9,000 species of plants that we must interpret properly, a task that is very much for specialists. Linnaeus drew both on specimens and on the earlier literature in forming his concepts of species and genera, but he did not select type specimens for them – since the idea of doing so was not to be developed for another 50 years, and not applied to plant names for about another 150 years. To interpret Linnaeus' names properly, both an understanding of the taxa involved and of the literature and attitudes of the 18th century and earlier is necessary. In this book, with contributions from many hundreds of specialists from around the world, the typification of each name proposed by Linnaeus has been fixed as well as it can be after the passage of so many years: a solid basis for the application of these names.

Drawing of an *Erigeron* made by Linnaeus in his Lapland journal

Precise names are important because all of our food and most of our medicines come from plants, directly or indirectly; the ecosystems that they dominate protect our topsoil and regulate our watersheds, determine local climate, and absorb greenhouse gases and other pollutants; and they beautify our lives and stimulate our aesthetic senses. Moreover, we are just starting to understand plants properly at a molecular and cellular level, applications that demand precise ways of naming and understanding them.

We know relatively little about plants, even after so many centuries of study, and we are losing plant species and their genetic diversity thousands of times more rapidly than has been the case historically. We do not even know how many valid species of plant have been named, estimates unbelievably ranging from 235,000 to more than 400,000, with no more than 10 per cent of them reasonably well known; and we estimate that at least 100,000 more await naming, most of them with local distributions in the tropics. The explosive growth of the human population, our growing demands for consumption, and our use of inappropriate technologies are destroying natural habitats all over the world. This drives global warming, and results in the hunting or gathering of selected species of plants and animals, and spreads invasive aliens everywhere, with the result that as many as half of all plant species may be gone from native habitats by the end of this century. For conserving plant species, understanding them, and working with them in any way, the stability of names to which this volume makes such a singular contribution is an absolute necessity. The authorities of the Natural History Museum, London, the Linnean Society of London, Charles Jarvis and his collaborators, and the hundreds of specialists who contributed to the excellence of this volume are to be congratulated on the rich harvest of knowledge that it represents. We are grateful to them for this gift, delivered for all to use on the 300th anniversary of Linnaeus' birth!

Peter H. Raven
President, Missouri Botanical Garden

PREFACE

This major work of Linnaean scholarship is the fruit of an international collaboration between plant taxonomists. It is a most valuable contribution to the botanical literature because it provides a detailed commentary on each of the more than 9,000 botanical names of which Linnaeus was the author. The extensive introductory material updates and expands on the work of generations of botanists, notably the distinguished Linnaean scholar and former President of the Linnean Society, Professor William T. Stearn, whose research laid the foundations for this new study.

The initial three-year grant from the Science and Engineering Research Council to the Society in 1981 launched this great programme with Charlie Jarvis as the principal investigator, under the guidance of the President, William Stearn, with the able support of Norman Robson. Charlie transferred to the Natural History Museum staff at the end of the three years where his research fellows have been variously, and at times irregularly, supported by grants to the Project from the National Science Foundation, the Leverhulme Trust, but mainly from the Society's own resources. The research staff not only contributed typifications themselves, but also maintained a lively correspondence with taxonomic specialists across the world in an effort to reach a stable consensus on the correct application of Linnaean names and their types.

The library, archives and collections of the Linnean Society, which include Linnaeus' original manuscripts, have frequently been consulted by the Project's researchers and testify to the vision of our founder, Sir James Edward Smith, who carefully preserved this unique record of Professor Carl Linnaeus' activities. At the time of writing, a substantial project is under way to prepare scanned digital images of all 14,600 specimens in the principal Linnaean herbarium, normally housed within the Society's rooms and traditionally accessible to researchers only as low-definition monochrome images or by means of a personal visit.

A further element of this project, now completed, was the preparation of a database of Linnaean herbarium specimens based on the catalogue compiled by Mr Spencer Savage, the Linnean Society's former librarian. These data, linked to the bank of scanned images of herbarium sheets, will soon be available online, enabling researchers around the world to examine high-resolution images of authentic Linnaean specimens and searchable associated data, whether or not they have the status of types. The completion of these projects thus marks a major step towards making the Society's collections fully accessible for the first time.

I would like warmly to congratulate Dr Jarvis, his colleagues and associates, the Trustees of the Natural History Museum, and all those involved with the project, for bringing it to a successful conclusion in Linnaeus' anniversary year.

Professor David F. Cutler
President, Linnean Society of London

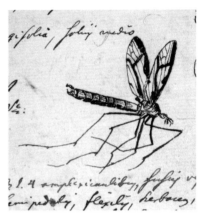

Drawing made by Linnaeus in his Lapland journal

PREFACE

In 1753, the year Linnaeus published *Species Plantarum*, in which he attempted to describe all known species of plant and gave them the binomial names that characterise scientific nomenclature, the London physician Sir Hans Sloane died and his considerable collections were offered to the nation for £20,000, then a substantial sum but much less than their real value. Linnaeus had met Sloane and briefly seen his collections, and used his book *A Voyage to the islands Madera...Jamaica* (1707–1725), as an important source for many tropical plants, such as cocoa and sugar cane, described in *Species Plantarum*. Sloane's collections were the foundation for the British Museum, and subsequent generations added to them so that they grew to fill two Museums – the artefacts in today's British Museum and the objects of nature in the Natural History Museum, which was established in South Kensington in 1881. The 18th and 19th century scientists were committed to describing and cataloguing all of nature, something that is still part of the mission of the Natural History Museum today.

It is fitting that the Linnaean Plant Name Typification Project has had its home in the Museum for the last 25 years. Not only does the Museum hold and care for some key Linnaean plant collections, such as the Clifford and Clayton herbaria, but some of the early proponents of the Linnaean system of binomial nomenclature were based at the Museum. In this scholarly work, Charlie Jarvis traces the complex materials that were used by Linnaeus to describe all species of plant known to him, and also discusses the methods that the Swedish physician used to document and describe nature. Careful and detailed examination of all the materials used by Linnaeus for each species means that a type can be selected, thus tying the name to a particular element and stabilising nomenclature. The type method did not exist in Linnaeus' day, so this retrospective work is critical in allowing today's botanists to apply names consistently.

Consistent naming of plants and animals became more difficult in the 18th century as the known world expanded through exploration. The sentence-long names of organisms became too difficult to remember and to use – the beauty of the two-word naming system Linnaeus first used consistently for plants in 1753 is that it enabled scientists of the day to remember more names of more things. Today, no scientist would hope to remember the names of all organisms, not even of all plants. Linnaeus described some 9,000 species; today we estimate that there are between 250,000 and 500,000 species of plant. New species are discovered every day, and the names chosen for them join the names coined by Linnaeus.

Conservation of naturally occurring diversity is very much a 21st century issue. To even begin this task, we need to know what plants and animals there are, and to communicate about them we need to know their names. This book, the culmination of 25 years of work with Linnaeus and his plants, will allow botanists to apply Linnaean names consistently and enable future generations to concentrate on the conservation of plant diversity for the benefit of all, something with which Linnaeus would have agreed.

Dr Michael Dixon
Director, Natural History Museum, London

Drawing of a fungal fruiting body ("*Amanita*") made by Linnaeus in his Lapland journal

INTRODUCTION

This book, the culmination of more than 20 years' study, brings together for the first time a detailed account of the scientific names applied to the organisms conventionally treated as "plants" coined by the 18th century physician, and great encyclopaedist of the natural world, Carl Linnaeus (1707–1778). Linnaeus is probably best known for three things. The first is his exhaustive attempts to classify the plants and animals, also extended to minerals. The second is his introduction of a new method of naming organisms in which each carries a unique Latin name in two parts: the binomial system of scientific naming. The third is the standardisation of botanical terminology which substantially promoted communication among botanists.

Portrait of Carl Linnaeus by Gustav Lundberg, ca. 1753, oil on canvas

His systems of classification for organisms, dating from the *Systema Naturae* of 1735, though less innovative in the more clearly delimited, larger animal groups, were dramatically different from their predecessors when it came to plants. Fascinated by the variety of reproductive features to be found in flowers, Linnaeus used the number and form of male (stamens) and female (styles and stigmas) parts to construct a numerically-based, though highly artificial, system into which it was very easy to place a previously unknown plant. He created 24 Classes based primarily on the number and arrangement of the stamens (*Monandria* with one, *Pentandria* with five, etc.), culminating in the *Cryptogamia* (plants without proper flowers, and including the ferns, mosses, liverworts, algae and fungi). Each Class, in turn, was subdivided into Orders based on the number and arrangement of the female parts, so a plant such as the potato (*Solanum tuberosum* L.), with five stamens and a single style, would belong in the Class *Pentandria*, Order *Monogynia*.

Georg Dionysius Ehret (1708–1780), a German botanical draughtsman working in Leiden in 1736, designed and printed a plate illustrating Linnaeus' Sexual System which did much to promote the latter in the Netherlands. Johan Gronovius (1690–1762), a Dutch friend and benefactor of Linnaeus, wrote to the English botanist Richard Richardson (quoted below from Blunt 1971) of the activities of a scientific club that met in Leiden:

> "Sometimes we examined minerals, sometimes flowers and plants, insects or fishes. We made such progress that by [Linnaeus's] Tables [his *Systema Naturae*] we can now refer any fish, plant or mineral to its genus, and thus to its species, though

none of us had seen it before. I think these Tables so eminently useful that everyone ought to have them hanging up in his study, like maps. Boerhaave [an eminent physician and botanist] values this work highly and it is his daily recreation".

Linnaeus fully understood that his Sexual System, in using only a few characters to define its groupings, was highly "artificial" (in contrast to natural classifications that attempted to utilise much greater numbers of characters to produce groupings of closely related organisms). However, the utility of Linnaeus' system for rapidly placing plants within a Class and Order, and facilitating identification, was such that it was widely adopted throughout the second half of the 18th century and it only began to wane with a rise in enthusiasm for more natural classifications early in the 19th century. By about 1830 it had been largely discarded, though it lived on in some floristic works such as those of Withering (1858) until later in the 19th century.

Design by Ehret illustrating the *Triandria Monogynia* (C, above) and the *Diadelphia Decandria* (R, below) from Linnaeus' Sexual System

Linnaeus' second innovation was the consistent use of binomial nomenclature and this is the subject of this work. Although, at the time of its introduction, he evidently believed it to be of minor importance, he later claimed it as a major innovation and it has subsequently proved to be perhaps his main legacy. His botanical predecessors grouped their species into genera, as did he, and distinguished the species from one another through the use of short, descriptive, Latin phrases, known as polynomials. As more species became known, the characters required to distinguish one from another increased in number, and so the Latin polynomials (also known as phrase names, diagnoses or *nomina specifica legitima*) became longer and longer. Caspar Bauhin's *Arbutus folio serrato* (Arbutus with saw-toothed leaves) of 1623 had become Linnaeus' *Arbutus caule erecto, foliis glabris serratis, baccis polyspermis* (Arbutus with upright stems, hairless, saw-toothed leaves and many-seeded berries) by 1753.

These diagnoses served a dual function. The first was to list the characters necessary to distinguish each species from every other and the second was to act as a label for that species. Few people, however, could hold such long names in their memories and, for practical purposes, numbers were often substituted. This is what Linnaeus' students did on their botanical excursions, using the species numbers from their Professor's *Flora Suecica* (1745) as, for example, "Achillea no. 5" in place of *Achillea foliis duplicato-pinnatis glabris, laciniis linearibus acute laciniatis* for the plant known in the United Kingdom as milfoil or yarrow. As Stearn (1971: 248), the great Linnaean scholar, has observed, Linnaeus' major contribution was to separate the dual role held by the diagnosis, restricting it to indicating the distinguishing characters for a given species. Linnaeus then added an additional one word specific epithet (*nomen triviale* – trivial name) to the generic name, which served to provide a label for the species in question. In the above case, the binomial was *Achillea millefolium*.

Linnaeus introduced this innovation for plants in his *Species Plantarum* of 1753, which contained accounts of some 5,900 species and varieties, and extended it to animals in the 10th edition of his *Systema Naturae* which appeared five years later. The simplicity and utility of this nomenclatural addition was quickly recognised by many of Linnaeus' contemporaries. Within 10 years, other botanists such as Johannes Burman (1755, 1757), Pehr Osbeck (1757), Nicolaas Laurens Burman (1759), Nicholas Jacquin (1760) and William Hudson (1762) had started to coin their own names in binomial form for species they were describing for the first time. By the 1770s, most botanists had adopted it. Once it was accepted, the number of species that were named using this system grew rapidly and it has been the standard naming method, for at least most groups of plants, ever since. With the adoption in 1905 of an internationally accepted set of rules for botanical nomenclature, Linnaeus' *Species Plantarum* (1753) was formally accepted as the starting point (in the majority of "plants", e.g. including groups such as the fungi which are now not believed to be closely related to the rest of the plants) for the use of these names, with any names published before this date treated as invalid. For animal groups, a similar importance was conferred on Linnaeus' *Systema Naturae*, ed. 10 (1758), which serves as the starting point for zoological nomenclature. *Species Plantarum* contains some 5,900 binomials, which include the names of all the major crop plants and many commercially important ornamentals, as well as numerous common tropical species, medicinally important species, and most of the common wild plants of Europe. Accordingly, Linnaeus' scientific names, recognisable by the familiar letter "L." appended to them, have continuing relevance for biologists. They are also important for those who, often unknowingly, make use of these names which help to maintain clarity about precisely which organism is which.

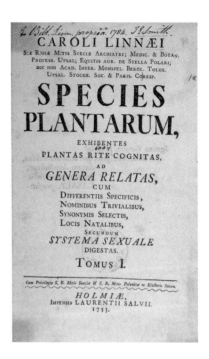

The title page of the first edition of Linnaeus' *Species Plantarum* (1753)

Although the first *International Rules of Botanical Nomenclature* (Briquet 1906) (subsequently re-named the *International Code of Botanical Nomenclature* and hereafter termed the ICBN, or simply "the Code") established the names devised by Linnaeus for genera and species as the starting point, it was some years before agreement was reached that the application of names was to be governed by the use of "types". A type is (usually) a pressed and dried herbarium specimen, and its taxonomic identity governs the way in which the name to which it is attached is to be used. In this way, the "type method" provides a permanent, fixed reference point against which the correct identity of any name can be checked, and if two names are found to apply to the same species, the earlier of them becomes the correct name to use. If not established at the time of publication of a new name, type specimens become fixed only via subsequent publication of a formal typification. Types can be designated in a wide range of different sorts of publication, however, and until now, information on Linnaean type specimens has been widely scattered.

Specimen of *Lathyrus odoratus* L. in Linnaeus' herbarium (LINN)

Opposite: The type specimen of *Delphinium grandiflorum* L. in Linnaeus' herbarium (LINN)

In 1981, the Linnaean Plant Name Typification Project set out to catalogue and establish the correct application of plant names first published by Linnaeus, through a study of the preserved specimens and illustrations that Linnaeus had used. One of the difficulties involved in interpreting these names is that Linnaeus did not work according to this type method. The modern Code (McNeill & al. 2006) requires that, to be validly published, the name of a new species must now be accompanied by the nomination of a type specimen (or an illustration in some groups). However, Linnaeus only rarely provided an explicit reference to any herbarium material when naming a plant species. Instead, in publishing a new name, he usually provided some diagnostic characters, one or more references to earlier illustrated or unillustrated publications (which may or may not be associated with material he had studied), an indication of provenance, and sometimes the name of the source of either material of, or information about, the species in question. In addition, there are a large number of specimens in Linnaeus' own herbarium, now at the Linnean Society of London, and elsewhere which, although he did not cite them, undoubtedly contributed significantly to his concepts of the species he was describing. It follows that the application of Linnaean names is very rarely fixed by what is now termed a holotype (i.e. a single herbarium specimen or illustration, explicitly indicated by its author).

Although Linnaeus at times apparently based his concept of a species on a single source of information, perhaps a herbarium collection received from a remote location like the Kamchatka peninsula in Russia, he more commonly drew on a number of sources. These variously included living plants growing in the University Botanic Garden in Uppsala, dried specimens in his own herbarium (or seen in the collections of others), and published, and unpublished, descriptions, drawings and illustrations. Given that Linnaeus, apart from the time he spent in the Netherlands in 1735–1738, had travelled little outside Sweden, his opportunities for gaining an appreciation of the diversity and variability displayed by plants outside these regions was rather limited. It is therefore not surprising that, stemming from the limited number of specimens, descriptions and illustrations that were available to him from countries unfamiliar to him, his species concepts were generally rather broad in comparison with current thinking. If the taxonomic identity of the herbarium material and the descriptions and illustrations used by Linnaeus for a series of names are studied, it is immediately obvious that, in many cases, more than one species (as recognised by taxonomists today) may be present. At one extreme, there is *Ocimum frutescens* L., in which Linnaeus included what are currently recognised as no fewer than seven different species (from three different genera). However, in other cases he, perhaps surprisingly, distinguished between very similar species recognising, for example, nine

694·7

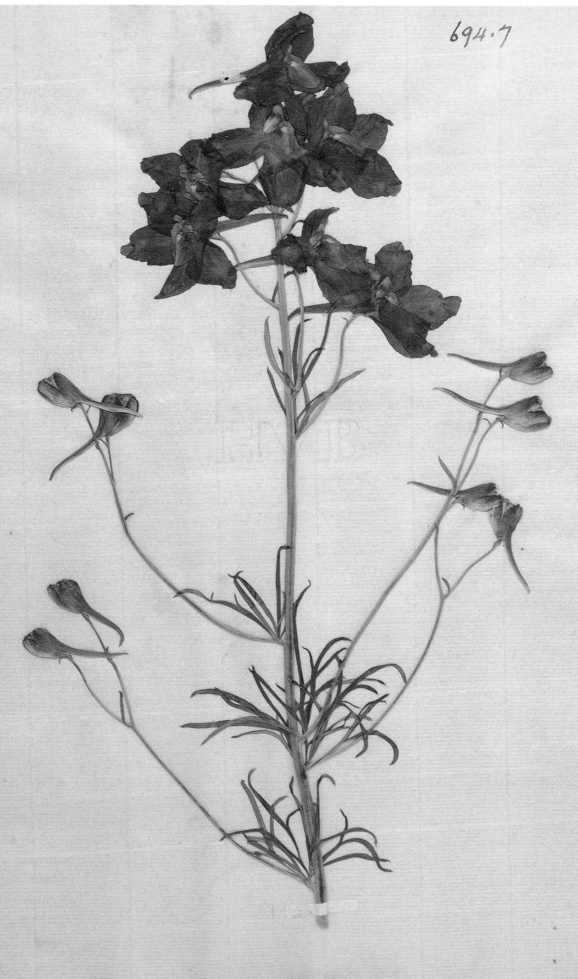

4 grandiflorum

An illustration based on an Ehret drawing of *Kaempferia galanga* L. from Linnaeus' *Hortus Cliffortianus* (t. 3. 1738).

species of *Juniperus* (see Farjon 2005). At the other extreme, he described the species now known as *Silene gallica* L. not only under this name, but also as *S. anglica* L., *S. lusitanica* L., *S. quinquevulnera* L. and *S. rigidula* L.

Without types having been nominated by Linnaeus, and with many of his binomials including more than one species within their original circumscription, how are his names to be applied in a uniform way? The names themselves were, of course, taken up by many of his contemporaries, and continued to be used by several generations of botanists before the type method became established, so usage of the names developed independently of type specimens. The specimens in Linnaeus' herbarium were not generally available to others during his lifetime, and for much of the time that they were in James Edward Smith's (1759–1828) ownership, they were at his family home in Norfolk and inaccessible. Early usage of Linnaeus' names was therefore largely independent of the identity of any of his own collections, and their interpretation was more often based on the illustrations he had cited as synonyms. Although the books in which they appeared were not exactly widely available, they were nevertheless much more accessible than his herbarium specimens. Where several taxa are identifiable within the original elements of a Linnaean name, the one whose identity corresponds with accepted usage is frequently that of a cited illustration rather than that of a herbarium specimen.

Under circumstances such as these (which arise with the binomials published by many 18th century botanists), the Code allows the designation of one element from among the specimens he consulted, and cited and uncited illustrations, to serve as the type – known as a lectotype (see p. 21). However, the designation of lectotypes for Linnaean names is frequently not a straightforward matter. Because of the existence of herbarium collections never owned yet heavily consulted by Linnaeus, it cannot be assumed that the type of a Linnaean name will necessarily be found in his own herbarium, now housed at the Linnean Society of London. There have also been difficulties in dating specimens in this collection, and Linnaeus is known to have given away or destroyed many of his own specimens. A failure to appreciate these, and other complexities, had led to unfortunate type choices being published, resulting in disruption to the usage of a number of well-known scientific names. As, under the Code, the type choice made by the author who first typifies a name is to be followed, it was not always easy to avoid disruption of usage and confusion in the application of Linnaean names (though recent Code changes have ameliorated this). In addition, the absence of any index to such published typifications, widely scattered though the botanical literature, has made it extremely difficult for authors to know if a name had already been typified. This led to duplication of effort in some cases,

Opposite: Maria Sibylla Merian's illustration (from her *Metamorphosis insectorum Surinamensium*: t. 21. 1705) of the plant Linnaeus later named as *Passiflora laurifolia* serves as the type of this name.

J. Mÿnder Sculp

21

and in others to conflicting conclusions being reached with the result that one name could continue in use for different species.

This was the situation under which most taxonomists grappled with Linnaean names until William Stearn, that great Linnaean scholar and a distinguished plant taxonomist, produced a series of erudite papers on Linnaeus' methods of work, his collections, and the factors to be taken into consideration in choosing types. These papers culminated in his exemplary "An Introduction to the Species Plantarum and cognate botanical works of Carl Linnaeus" (Stearn 1957).

Portrait of William T. Stearn, by David Griffiths, 1981

This corpus of knowledge formed an excellent basis for the Linnaean Project when it began in 1981. Given the large body of published, but very scattered, literature on Linnaean names, and the Code's recognition of the priority of type choices, the early stages involved starting an extensive literature search that has continued throughout the Project's life. Any statements related to typification, the doubtful application of Linnaean names, or the identification of any original material for any given name were recorded for each separate binomial (more than 9,000 published in Linnaeus' lifetime). An extensive selection of William Stearn's correspondence on Linnaean names with botanists from around the world, undertaken during his years in the Natural History Museum in London, was also available and proved most informative, as did discussions with him. It was also important to investigate the various Linnaean-linked herbaria still in existence. Some of these (e.g. those of George Clifford, Paul Hermann and John Clayton) are housed at the Natural History Museum. Other herbaria consulted included Linnaeus' Lapland herbarium in the Institut de France, Paris, and the Linnaean herbarium at the Swedish Museum of Natural History in Stockholm. The nearby Bergianska Trädgården holds Linnaean specimens in the Bergius herbarium while a small separate collection of Linnaean specimens exists at the University of Uppsala. The same institute houses the herbaria of Linnaeus' students Fredrik Hasselquist and Pehr Kalm, that of Linnaeus' Professor in Uppsala, Olof Celsius, and that of Joachim Burser, a German student of the great Caspar Bauhin. At the Nationaal Herbarium Nederland in Leiden is the herbarium of Adriaan van Royen, along with a partial duplicate set (of that in London) of Paul Hermann material from Ceylon. There is also a smaller, largely duplicate, set of George Clifford material at the Nationaal Herbarium Nederland in Wageningen.

Material of *Yucca gloriosa* L. from the herbarium of Adriaan van Royen in Leiden (L)

Prior to the start of the Linnaean Project, most typifications of Linnaean names were being undertaken in a rather piecemeal manner, a few names at a time, by individual researchers who may (or may not) have benefitted from Stearn's specific advice. The concept behind the Linnaean Project was therefore to establish for which names typifications appeared to exist, and to subject them to critical review. Untypified names would be studied, with the interpretative knowledge coming from the Project staff, in close collaboration with researchers who would have the necessary detailed taxonomic knowledge, in order to ensure that any new typifications made were based on the best available information.

Enquiries from other botanists were, from the beginning, an important source of taxonomic information and specimen identifications. The Project staff have, in turn, been able to provide information on those specimens and illustrations that represent original material for untypified Linnaean binomials, and have made available thousands of images for consultation. This has allowed stabilising type choices to be made by specialists and the avoidance of unnecessary nomenclatural disruption. One such enquiry led to an early publication on the thorny problem of *Ononis spinosa* L. (universally interpreted from Linnaeus' 1759 concept which was radically different from, and incompatible with, his original 1753 concept). Happily, problems such as this coincided with moves to modify the Code so as to reduce changes in names for purely nomenclatural reasons. In particular, changes allowing the conservation of species names, initially only for taxa of major economic importance, the first significant case being aimed at stabilising the name for bread wheat (Hanelt & al. 1983), provided a means of avoiding unnecessary disruption resulting from typification. The case of *Ononis spinosa*, which, under the rules then operating, was initially proposed for outright rejection (Jarvis & al. 1983) was resolved by new provisions in the Berlin Code (Greuter & al. 1988). These permitted the current application of *O. spinosa* to be maintained by conservation with a conserved type, a specimen that was in conflict with Linnaeus' original diagnosis. In the Tokyo Code (Greuter & al. 1994) all restrictions on conservation of species names were removed, the one criterion being avoidance of disadvantageous nomenclatural change.

The original paper records were supplanted in 1983 by the first of a succession of databases. The most recent version supplies data to the Linnaean Project's website (http://www.nhm.ac.uk/research-curation/projects/linnaean-typification/), which displays a record for every Linnaean binomial. Some are accompanied by images of type specimens or illustrations, and more images and other useful information will be added.

When the Linnaean Project started, it was estimated that approximately 30–40 per cent of Linnaean names were satisfactorily typified, though no list or catalogue of the names and type choices existed. In the intervening years, thousands of type statements scattered through the world's scientific literature have been searched for, located, scrutinised and assessed. Information on specimens, illustrations and manuscripts has been supplied to hundreds of specialists around the world enabling them to clarify the

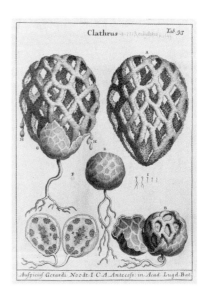

The type illustration of *Clathrus cancellatus* L. (= *Clathrus ruber* Pers.: Pers.) from Micheli's *Nova plantarum genera* (t. 93. 1729)

application of many more Linnaean names. As a result, some 2,175 names have been formally typified under the auspices of the Project. As this book goes to press, well over 80 per cent of the Linnaean binomials for which types can theoretically be designated have been formally typified.

The information drawn together in this book is the result of extensive collaboration with specialists over many years. It has been a rich and rewarding experience, and a privilege to work with so many eminent botanists during this period. Study of Linnaean-linked collections has involved visits to France, the Netherlands, Switzerland, Finland, Italy and, of course, Sweden where there was an opportunity to visit various of Linnaeus' haunts and, perhaps most memorably, to retrace parts of his 1741 exploration of the Baltic islands of Öland and Gotland. Many good friends have been made in the process, a number of whom have been kind enough to comment on an earlier draft version of this book. Their many suggestions and criticisms have greatly improved what would otherwise have appeared here.

The man who, in 18th century Sweden, created order from what he perceived to be botanical chaos, would surely approve. As he himself wrote, "If you do not know the names of things, the knowledge of them is lost too" (*Philosophia Botanica* 1751).

Opposite: A specimen from South Africa, heavily annotated in the distinctive hand of Henry Oldenland, which was brought on loan to Linnaeus by N.L. Burman in 1760. It is original material for *Senecio umbellatus* L.

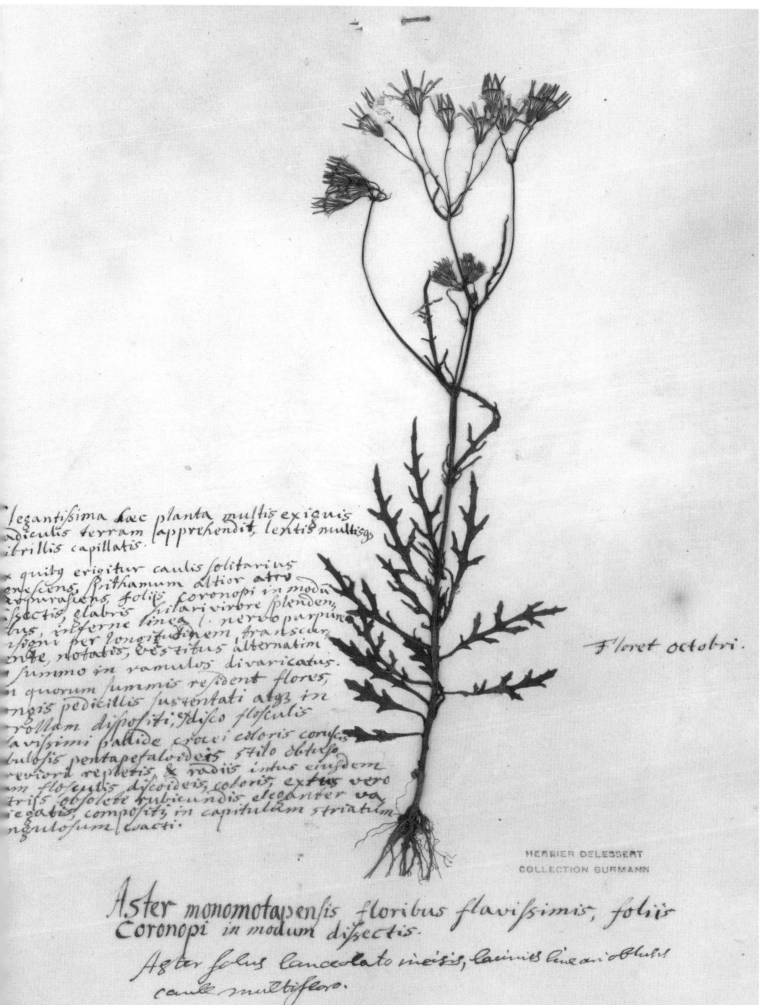

Elegantissima hæc planta multis exiguis
radiculis terram apprehendit, lentis multisq;
fibrillis capillatis.

x quibq erigitur caulis solitarius
senescens, spithamum altior atro
purpurascens, foliis coronopi in modu
dissectis, glabris hilari virore splenden-
bus, inferne linea l. nervo purpure-
scenti per longitudinem transcur-
rente, notatis, vestibus alternatim
summo in ramulos divaricatus.
in quorum summis resident flores,
longis pedicillis sustentati atqz in
rosulam dispositi, disco flosculis
flavissimi pallide croci coloris confertis bulosis pentapetaloideis stilo obtuso
breviori repletis, & radiis intus ejusdem
cum flosculis discoideis coloris, extus vero
purpuris obsolete rubicundis eleganter variegatis, compositis in capitulum striatum
angulosum coacti.

Floret octobri.

HERBIER DELESSERT
COLLECTION BURMANN

Aster monomotapensis floribus flavissimis, foliis
Coronopi in modum dissectis.

Aster foliis lanceolato incisis, laciniis lineari obtusis
caule multifloro.

Chapter 1
THE ART AND SCIENCE OF TYPIFICATION

Introduction

Typification is the process of designating the "type" (see Glossary on p. 60 explaining the many specialist terms used here) of a plant name – usually a dried, pressed specimen in a herbarium collection, but sometimes an illustration. The taxonomic identity of the type determines the group of plants to which the name of the taxon (e.g. a genus, species, subspecies or variety) applies, each name being permanently attached to a single type. It becomes a constant point of reference for the name, to which botanists can refer should doubts arise as to the identity and correct name of a particular taxon. The main focus of this study has been the typification of Linnaean names at the rank of species, along with a small number of names at varietal rank. Typification involves study of the text (termed the protologue) in which the name was published for the first time, in association with the herbarium specimens known to have been used in writing it, and any cited (or otherwise indicated) earlier published descriptions and illustrations. If a type specimen (or illustration) has been designated in accordance with the rules laid down in the International Code of Botanical Nomenclature (ICBN), it cannot be changed other than by the acceptance by an International Botanical Congress (IBC) of a formal proposal to do so, after study by the appropriate Committee nominated by the Nomenclature Section of the previous IBC. This system is aimed at promoting nomenclatural stability and forms part of the architecture for maintaining a logical and comprehensible framework for the naming of plants.

Although the usefulness of Linnaeus' binomial naming system was recognised fairly quickly and had been widely adopted by the 1770s, sets of rules that built on Linnaeus' own *Philosophia Botanica* (1751) for the use of these names developed only gradually, Alphonse de Candolle (1867) being the first to attempt to formalise rules for names of plants. Divergent practices continued, however, with distinctive strands in Europe and North America, and it was only in 1930 that these were unified into a single universally accepted set of International Rules of Botanical Nomenclature (Briquet 1935).

One of the areas of divergence was in the use of types, which was a feature of the 1907 American Code (Arthur & al. 1907), but which was not incorporated into the International Rules until 1930 when the Cambridge

The type specimen of *Calla aethiopica* L. (= *Zantedeschia aethiopica* (L.) Spreng.) in George Clifford's herbarium (BM)

Congress formally agreed that the application of scientific names was to be governed by the use of "types", part of the rapprochement then achieved. Much early controversy had revolved around methods of establishing which species should represent the type of a generic name. Many of Linnaeus' genera contained species that later authors considered to belong in other genera, so in dismembering such a Linnaean genus, it was necessary to decide which part should retain the original name. The identity of the type would establish the way in which the generic name was to be applied.

The type of a generic name is the type of the name of a species. For names of species (and lower ranks such as subspecies, variety etc.), types are usually herbarium specimens either explicitly cited by an author or, in the case of earlier names where such practice was uncommon, known to have been used by him or her. The "type method", however, developed long after binomial nomenclature was accepted, and early authors, including Linnaeus, did not apply it in their own work. Early names can therefore present difficulties when the modern type method is retrospectively applied to them. For an account of the history of the development of botanical nomenclature, see Nicolson (1991) and Knapp & al. (2004).

The rules that govern scientific naming in botany are revised at Nomenclature Section meetings during successive International Botanical Congresses (IBC), which are currently held at six-yearly intervals. A revised edition of the International Code of Botanical Nomenclature (ICBN) results from each meeting, the current version being the Vienna Code (McNeill & al. 2006). The Code is designed to provide a set of rules, together with the necessary guidance, to enable, in most cases, working taxonomists to reach nomenclatural conclusions independently, and without the need to refer to a central body (cf. the International Commission for Zoological Nomenclature). In an important contribution towards maintaining stability in the naming of plants, the Code also includes provisions allowing for the protection of widely used, familiar names whose continued use may be threatened (e.g. because an earlier name for the same species has been found). Such situations allow for a formal proposal, either for conservation, or for the rejection of a threatening name, to be made. This proposal is then assessed and voted upon by one of a series of Committees nominated by the Nomenclature Section, which may recommend acceptance by the subsequent IBC. Names that have been successfully proposed for conservation, or rejection, are listed in Appendices of the ICBN, and a record of all such proposals (including those that were unsuccessful and those that are pending) can be found at http://persoon.si.edu/codes/props/index.cfm.

Opposite: The genus *Pinus* L. was very broadly conceived by Linnaeus in 1753, containing 10 species, many of which had been referred to different genera by other authors. Linnaeus' *Pinus larix* L., which is typified by this plate from Philip Miller's *Catalogus plantarum* (t. 11. 1730), was placed in the genus *Larix* by Miller, and is today known as *Larix decidua* Mill.

Larix folio deciduo Conifera.
Larch Tree.

Huysum pinx.

E. Kirkall fec.

Categories of Types and "Original Material"

A type is defined, as follows, by Art. 7.2 of the ICBN (McNeill & al. 2006): "A nomenclatural type (typus) is that element to which the name of a taxon is permanently attached, whether as a correct name or as a synonym. The nomenclatural type is not necessarily the most typical or most representative element of a taxon".

In describing a new species today, the Code specifies that, for its name to be validly published, a single element, the holotype, which is usually a herbarium specimen but occasionally an illustration, and perhaps (in the case of a specimen) accompanied by duplicates (isotypes), must be specified by its author. However, 18th century scientists did not work according to the type method and were not constrained in this way. Consequently, in order to accommodate earlier names and make the type method applicable to them in retrospect, the Code recognises a number of different categories of type. Because the different sorts of type that exist for a given name can restrict the way in which that name may be typified, each category is discussed below in relation to its occurrence in association with Linnaean binomials.

A **holotype** (Art. 9.1) "is the one specimen or illustration used by the author, or designated by the author as the nomenclatural type. As long as a holotype is extant, it fixes the application of the name concerned".

Given that Linnaeus did not work according to the modern type concept, it follows that he did not explicitly designate holotypes for his names. Similarly, he cites individually recognisable specimens only very rarely and, even then, it is usually very difficult to be sure that such a collection was the only element used by him. Explicitly cited specimens such as those from the Burser herbarium in Uppsala are usually found in protologues where other original material is also indicated. For example, Herb. Burser XI: 126 is cited in the protologue of *Gypsophila repens* L. (1753: 407) but there is also original material (specimens) in LINN and BM, and two cited illustrations. The Burser material is a syntype (see below), but not a holotype. Even where no additional original material is now apparent, it is very difficult to be sure that no other uncited material had been in Linnaeus' possession prior to the publication of the name. Given that it is known that many specimens which were formerly in Linnaeus' herbarium were disposed of or destroyed either by Linnaeus or his son, the current absence of such material from the Linnaean herbarium cannot be taken as a reliable guide that none was ever present. Under these circumstances, very few Linnaean names are interpreted as having holotypes. For some names that, because they are validated only by reference to an earlier description (Art. 7.7), must be typified from the context of their validating publication, there may be an associated illustration or preserved material. However, these cases, too, are best dealt with through lectotypification (see below) with each name being looked at individually given the varying circumstances that can be encountered.

These names are chiefly those published in certain Linnaean dissertations. Binomials from *Herbarium Amboinense* (1754), for example, are usually validated by reference to a plate (or plates) and a description published by Rumphius (1741–1750). In *Flora Anglica* (1754), the binomials are validated by a reference to Ray's *Synopsis Methodica Stirpium Britannicarum* (1724), where the validating account may refer to a mixture of specimens and illustrations. *Calycanthus praecox* L. (1762: 718), however, is arguably an example of a Linnaean name with a holotype because Linnaeus stated that the plant was unknown to him ("*Ignota mihi*"), and cited as the sole source of information a description and illustration (p. 879) from Engelbert Kaempfer's *Amoenitatum Exoticarum* (1712). Kaempfer's illustration is the holotype of this name.

An **isotype** (Art. 9.3) is "any duplicate of a holotype" and is always a specimen.

Given the rarity of holotypes for Linnaean names, isotypes rarely, if ever, exist for Linnaean names.

A **syntype** (Art. 9.4) is "any specimen cited in the protologue when there is no holotype, or any one of two or more specimens simultaneously designated as types", an isosyntype being a duplicate of a syntype. Linnaeus' citing of individually recognisable specimens is uncommon and is generally restricted to those from the Burser herbarium (where the relevant volume and page number is given, e.g. "Burs. XVI. 86" is cited in the protologue of *Saxifraga geranioides* L.), but there were also original or numbered collections received from former students such as Pehr Löfling (e.g. *Ziziphora hispanica* L. where Linnaeus cited "Loefl. 441") and Pehr Kalm ("Kalm. IX. 32" appears in the protologue of *Viscum terrestre* L.). Explicitly cited specimens such as these are significant because they are **syntypes**, which affords them special status when it comes to lectotypification (see **lectotype** below). Accordingly, a syntype of a Linnaean name must almost invariably be the lectotype of its associated binomial. In protologues, Linnaeus commonly indicated, following his "Habitat in . . . " statement, the sources of information (descriptions, dried specimens, seeds etc.) that had reached him. Examples include "*Habitat in* Monspelii. D. *Sauvages*" (*Linum trigynum* L., indicating material or information sent by François Boissier de La Croix de Sauvages (1706–1767)), ". . . in Campechia. *Houst.*" (*Euphorbia ocymoidea* L., for material from Mexico originating with William Houstoun (1695–1733)), ". . . in Virginia, Canada. *Kalm*" (*Anemone quinquefolia* L.) and ". . . in Sibiria. D. *Gmelin. Demidoff.*" (*Bartsia pallida* L., indicating material received from Grigory Akinfievich Demidov (1715–1761)). Although these statements provide further information that should certainly be taken

Following pages:
Left: The type illustration of *Cucumis anguinus* L. (= *Trichosanthes cucumerina* L.) from Rumphius' *Herbarium Amboinense* 5: t. 148 (1747)

Right: Engelbert Kaempfer's account (and this engraving) of the Japanese shrub named *Calycanthus praecox* by Linnaeus (= *Chimonanthus praecox* (L.) Link), was the only source of information available to the Swede about this species.

Tab. CXLVIII.

Obai Robai ロ・クバイ

FVB

into consideration in choosing a lectotype, they do not provide reference to a single identifiable specimen. Consequently, associated material from Sauvages, Houstoun, Kalm or Gmelin is not accepted as having syntype status (though it will, in most cases, be the obvious choice as lectotype from among the original material, assuming it still exists).

A **paratype** (Art. 9.5) is "a specimen cited in the protologue that is neither the holotype nor an isotype, nor one of the syntypes if two or more specimens were simultaneously designated as types". As in the case of holotypes, paratypes are of little, if any, importance for Linnaean names.

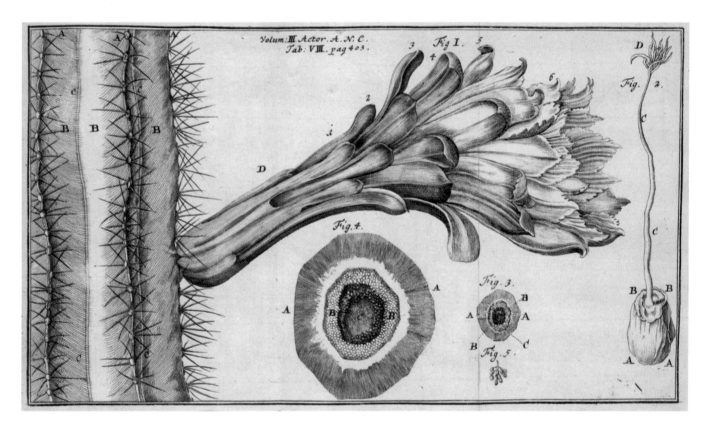

This plate, the work of Ehret, appeared in a short article by Christopher Trew entitled *De cerei plantae charactere generico* (t. 8. 1733) and is the lectotype of *Cactus hexagonus* L. (= *Cereus hexagonus* (L.) Mill.).

Given the rarity of holotypes and syntypes for Linnaean names, other **original material** is particularly important, because it comprises those specimens and illustrations from which a **lectotype** (see below) can be chosen. Original material (Art. 9.2 *Note* 2) consists of "*(a)* those specimens and illustrations (both unpublished and published either prior to or together with the protologue) upon which it can be shown that the description or diagnosis validating the name was based; *(b)* the holotype and those specimens which, even if not seen by the author of the description or diagnosis validating the name, were indicated as types (syntypes or paratypes) of the name at its valid publication; and *(c)* the isotypes or isosyntypes of the name irrespective of whether such specimens were seen by either the author of the validating description or diagnosis, or the author of the name".

Martynia annua, villosa & viscosa, folio subrotunde; Flore magno, rubro   Houstoun.

A **lectotype** (Art. 9.2) is "a specimen or illustration designated from the original material as the nomenclatural type . . . if no holotype was designated at the time of publication, or if it is missing, or if it is found to belong to more than one taxon . . .". Given the rarity of holotypes, the vast majority of Linnaean names are subject to an analysis of the extant herbarium specimens, and cited and uncited illustrations associated with the names, one of which is chosen as the **lectotype** to serve as the nomenclatural type for each name. Art. 9.10 lays down the order in which different sorts of collections must be considered in designating lectotypes and, in the absence of holotypes or isotypes, syntypes (explicitly cited specimens – see **syntype** above) take precedence over other "original material" (uncited specimens, and cited and uncited illustrations). Syntypes, however, are also comparatively rare so, in most cases, Linnaean lectotypes are selected from among all the original material. Where both well-preserved specimens and illustrations are represented in the original material (and they belong to the same taxon), specimens are generally preferred as lectotypes because of their potential ability to provide an enormous range of additional characters (micromorphological, chemical,

This plate from John Martyn's *Historiae plantarum rariorum* (t. 42. 1728) is the lectotype of *Martynia* L., the genus that Linnaeus named in his honour.

molecular) that cannot be matched by illustrations. However, in many cases, herbarium material may be poorly preserved, or sterile, or be identifiable as a species different from that to which the name has traditionally been applied. If a competing illustration lacks any of these flaws, it is likely to prove a better choice of lectotype, particularly if it avoids nomenclatural disruption by allowing the name to continue to be used in its traditional sense. Recognising the desirability of retaining this flexibility in making type choices, the ICBN does not stipulate that, in typification, uncited specimens are to be preferred to illustrations, and some 25 per cent of Linnaean names in fact have illustrations as their types. Some of these were chosen as lectotypes in preference to uncited specimens because the taxonomic identity of the illustrations agreed with the traditional usage of the names involved, while that of the candidate specimens did not.

A **neotype** (Art. 9.6) is "a specimen or illustration selected to serve as nomenclatural type as long as all of the material upon which the name of the taxon was based is missing". Approximately 2.5 per cent of Linnaean names have neotypes, as a result of there being no original material extant. Although Linnaeus had a strong visual memory, and cited published illustrations where they were available, many species were unillustrated. Under the modern Code, descriptions cannot serve as types (Art. 8.1) so neotypes are necessary in cases such as these. In other cases, neotypes have been designated where material likely to have originally been in Linnaeus' herbarium has been lost or destroyed.

An **epitype** (Art. 9.7) "is a specimen or illustration selected to serve as an interpretative type when the holotype, lectotype, or previously designated neotype, or all original material associated with a validly published name, is demonstrably ambiguous and cannot be critically identified for purposes of the precise application of the name of a taxon". The epitype concept is a comparatively recent addition to the ICBN, the need for which first became apparent from recurrent difficulties encountered in the interpretation of Linnaean names (Barrie & al. 1992a). The epitype concept was proposed by Barrie & al. (1992b), approved by the Tokyo Congress in 1993 and first appeared in the Tokyo Code (Greuter & al. 1994). It has proved generally useful and well over 200 Linnaean names currently have designated epitypes. Although originally conceived with the problems of Linnaean and other early binomials in mind, taxonomists have also found it a useful tool in the interpretation of more recent, but similarly problematic, names.

Although it is not a term that appears in the ICBN, **typotype**, a term coined by James Dandy (Stearn 1957: 129), is sometimes applied to the herbarium material from which a type illustration was originally prepared.

"Api", the neotype of *Pyrus malus* var. *epirotica* L. (= *Malus pumila* Mill. 'Pomme d'Api')

Opposite: Particularly among long-cultivated plants, Linnaeus sometimes applied his binomial names to what are now recognised to be cultivated varieties (cultivars). As herbarium material may not show the cultivar's characteristics satisfactorily, where neotypes are required, illustrations are sometimes utilised, as in the case of this plate from Hogg's *Hertfordshire Pomona* (t. 74, f. 2. 1884).

Plate LXXIV

1. Pigeonnet

2. Api

3. Pigeon

4. Colonel Vaughan

5. Cowarne Queening

6. Tyler's Kernel

8. Winter Queening

7. Herefordshire Queening

wyne, Chromolith Brussels

Alice B Ellis + Edith E N
for The Woolhope

For Linnaean names typified by the plates published by Sloane (1707, 1725), the Jamaican herbarium specimens that were the basis for Kickius' drawings, from which the plates in turn were engraved, are typotypes. In cases where there is uncertainty as to the precise identification of an illustration, the existence of such a specimen can be extremely helpful in determining the taxon to which it belongs. Where it is harder to establish such a close relationship between an illustration and specimens believed to be linked (e.g. via collector) with it, the specimens are sometimes termed **voucher specimens**. A typotype or voucher specimen may be suitable for designation as an epitype.

Another term occasionally encountered is **topotype**, used for any gathering of a taxon made at its original type locality (i.e. the place from which its type was either collected, or depicted). For an example, see Stearn (1957: 131). However, while a topotype may prove useful in establishing, for example, the ploidy level of the typical subspecies in a widespread and chromosomally variable species, it has no nomenclatural standing and the term does not appear in the ICBN. If there are no original elements for a name, a topotype collection may be a useful choice as a neotype. Other less commonly seen categories of type are explained in the Glossary at the end of this chapter.

Elements of the Linnaean Protologue

The process of typification involves the formal selection of one element to serve as the type (usually a lectotype; see above) from among those used by Linnaeus in naming a particular taxon (see Stearn, 1957: 125–134). The Linnaean protologue (". . . everything associated with a name at its valid publication, i.e. description or diagnosis, illustrations, references, synonymy, geographical data, citation of specimens, discussion, and comments" – Art. 8A.4, footnote) is the starting point for this process as it is the primary indication of the sources of information that were available at the time.

Linnaean binomials were published in nearly 40 separate publications, and these are listed in Chapter 3, together with a discussion of any sources of information particular to each (e.g. South African material, in Burman's herbarium in Geneva, for Linnaeus' *Plantae Rariores Africanae*). The herbaria in which Linnaean or Linnaean-linked collections can be found are listed in Chapter 5, along with details of the collectors who provided them in Chapter 6. Descriptions of the more important published works by other authors, which provided Linnaeus with information, are given in Chapter 4.

Although the protologues of Linnaean names vary in their extent and complexity depending on the format of the work in which they appeared and whether any earlier synonyms were believed to exist, they are almost always very succinct and can appear disappointingly uninformative on initial scrutiny. Subsequent study sometimes bears out this impression, particularly for names published in works such as the 10th edition of the *Systema Naturae* (1759), where new names are typically accompanied only by a short diagnosis, without reference to illustrations or any indication of provenance. Such extreme succinctness led Baum (1968) to call for 16 names that were not cited in Linnaeus' later works to be rejected as *nomina ambigua* (names of uncertain application). However, it is usually possible to associate herbarium material with binomials newly published there, and some do carry reference to plates published by Browne (1756) and others. In addition, consultation of the subsequent, usually fuller, treatments of these names in the second edition of *Species Plantarum* (1762, 1763) can assist in interpretation, but it is important to remember that additional illustrations etc. that appear only in that later work do not form part of the protologue and are not eligible for selection as lectotypes. Caution must also be exercised because Linnaeus' species concepts were changing, and a 1762–63 account may reflect a very different concept from that used at the time of the same species' original description in 1759. Protologues in some of the dissertations can also be problematic in their brevity, some providing names that are validated solely by reference to earlier publications by other authors (e.g. *Flora Anglica*, 1754; *Herbarium Amboinense*, 1754; *Flora Monspeliensis*, 1759), while others consist of a few character states listed in a concise table (e.g. *De Erica*, 1771).

However, these names are a small minority, most of Linnaeus' binomials having a clear diagnosis (often with a reference to earlier literature, one or more synonyms (often accompanied by reference to illustrations), and an indication of believed provenance, and life form. Descriptions are uncommon, but can be encountered occasionally in some works (e.g. *Species Plantarum*), while they are usual in a few of the dissertations (e.g. *Plantae Rariores Africanae*, 1760).

Variations and idiosyncrasies in other works (chiefly the dissertations) are discussed, and sometimes illustrated, under each separate Linnaean work in Chapter 3. Linnaean protologues have been reproduced and discussed by Stearn (1957: 130; in Blunt 1971: 249) and Heller (1964), and in a number of more recent papers including those of Oost & al. (1989), Knapp & Jarvis (1991) and Jørgensen & al. (1994).

A number of sample protologues, and the procedures involved in typifying the names associated with them, are provided later in this chapter.

The Diagnosis

Linnaean specific names dating from 1753 were numbered within each genus by Linnaeus, unless they belonged to unispecific genera (in which case the separate generic description will form part of the protologue).

Herbarium Codes

BAA	University of Buenos Aires.
BM	Natural History Museum, London.
BM-SL	Natural History Museum, London: Sloane herbarium.
C	University of Copenhagen.
E	Royal Botanic Garden, Edinburgh.
FI	Museum of Natural History, University of Florence.
G	Conservatoire et Jardin botaniques de la Ville de Genève.
GB	University of Gothenberg.
H	University of Helsinki.
K	Royal Botanic Gardens, Kew.
L	Nationaal Herbarium Nederland, Leiden University branch.
LAPP	Institut de France, Paris.
LINN	Linnean Society of London: Carl Linnaeus herbarium.
LINN-SM	Linnean Society of London: J.E. Smith herbarium.
LIV	World Museum, Liverpool.
M	Botanische Staatssammlung, Munich.
MW	Moscow State University.
OXF	University of Oxford.
P	Muséum National d'Histoire Naturelle, Paris.
PH	Academy of Natural Sciences, Philadelphia.
P-JU	Muséum National d'Histoire Naturelle, Paris: Jussieu herbarium.
S	Swedish Museum of Natural History, Stockholm.
SBT	Bergius Foundation, Stockholm.
SI	Instituto de Botánico Darwinion, San Isidro, Buenos Aires.
STU	Staatliches Museum für Naturkunde, Stuttgart.
UPS	Museum of Evolution, University of Uppsala.
US	Smithsonian Institution, Washington DC.

They generally possess a short, diagnostic phrase name (the polynomial, or *nomen specificum legitimum*), appended to the generic name, which serves to distinguish the various species of a particular genus from one another. This is the diagnosis, which acts, therefore, in the same way as a component of a multi-access key and was a tabulation of what Linnaeus believed to be the important distinguishing features of a species.

For example, in the genus *Morus* (Linnaeus 1753: 986), the Latin diagnoses use primarily features of leaf shape and type of indumentum to distinguish the species. Stearn has emphasised the importance of tracing the source of the information contained in the diagnosis, and Linnaeus' own indications of the source of the diagnosis can certainly be valuable in locating relevant specimens.

The diagnoses of both *Morus alba* and *Morus nigra* are cited as coming from Linnaeus' earlier *Hortus Cliffortianus* (1738) account, suggesting that Linnaeus' concept of the taxon had been formed by the time that work was published, and that his concept had not changed significantly since. Any associated material in the Clifford herbarium (BM) would therefore be original material for these names, but so would any other material either in Linnaeus' own herbarium or elsewhere and believed to have been in his possession before 1753. For these two names, Linnaeus adds further references to his own works (*Hortus Upsaliensis, Materia Medica*) and to those of others (van Royen, 1740; Dalibard, 1749) where his *Hortus Cliffortianus* treatment was also cited. Additional references such as these tend to add little of relevance for typification unless accompanied by illustrations, or linked to independent herbarium collections.

The diagnosis of *Morus indica* is cited as having come from Linnaeus' earlier *Flora Zeylanica* (1747), marked with an asterisk to indicate that a good description can be found there, and the Paul Hermann collections (BM) upon which the latter account was based are therefore original material for the name. For each of the remaining four species, the diagnosis is not ascribed to any earlier work and so appears to have been newly coined for *Species Plantarum*. In these (indeed in almost all) cases, material should be sought in Linnaeus' own herbarium (LINN), as well as in those other herbaria in which specimens in Linnaeus' possession prior to 1753, but subsequently dispersed, can be found. The codes of individual herbaria generally follow Holmgren & Holmgren (2007), and those most commonly encountered in this book are listed here.

In the case of *Morus tatarica*, there is a specimen (1112.9, see p. 28) in LINN which was almost certainly collected by Gerber, and which carries, in Linnaeus' hand, "Habitat prope Azof", reflecting Linnaeus' "Habitat ad Assoff" in the published protologue. If no specimens can be traced, it may be that they were among those given away, discarded or destroyed by

Opposite: The account of the genus *Morus* in Linnaeus' *Species Plantarum* (1753: 986)

MORUS.

alba.

1. MORUS foliis oblique cordatis lævibus. *Hort. cliff.*
441. *Hort. upf.* 283 *Roy. lugdb.* 211. *Dalib. parif.* 290.
Morus fructu albo. *Bauh. pin.* 459.
Morus candida. *Dod. pempt.* 810.
Habitat in China. ♄

nigra.

2. MORUS foliis cordatis fcabris. *Hort. cliff.* 441. *Hort.
upf.* 283. *Mat. med.* 422. *Roy. lugdb.* 211. *Dalib.
parif.* 290.
Morus fructu nigro. *Bauh. pin.* 459.
Morus. *Dod. pempt.* 810.
Habitat in Italiæ maritimis. ♄

papyrifera.

3. MORUS foliis palmatis, fructibus hifpidis.
Morus fativa, foliis urticæ mortuæ, cortice papyrifera.
Kæmpf. amœn. 471. *t.* 472.
Morus papyrifera fativa japonica. *Seb. thef.* 1. *p.* 44. *t.*
28. *f.* 3.
Habitat in Japonia. ♄

rubra.

4. MORUS foliis cordatis fubtus villofis, amentis cy-
lindricis.
Morus virginienfis arbor, loti arboris inftar ramofa, foliis ampliffimis. *Pluk. alm.* 253. *t.* 246. *f.* 4.
Habitat in Virginia. ♄
Amenta *longitudine Betulæ albæ.* Folia *recentia fubtus
maxime tomentofa; fæpe etjam palmata funt folia.*

indica.

5. MORUS foliis ovato-oblongis utrinque æqualibus in-
æqualiter ferratis. *Fl. zeyl.* 337. *
Tinda-parua. *Rheed. mal.* 1. *p.* 87. *t.* 49.
Habitat in India. ♄

tatarica.

6. MORUS foliis ovato-oblongis utrinque æqualibus æ-
qualiter ferratis.
Habitat ad Affoff. ♄
*Præcedenti maxime affinis, fed pedunculis petiolisque
longioribus, ferraturis foliorum magis diftinctis; fructus M. nigræ.*

tinctoria.

7. MORUS foliis ovatis hirfutis.
Morus fructu viridi, ligno fulphureo tinctorio. *Sloan.
jam. hift.* 2. *p.* 3. *t.* 158. *f.* 1. *Raj. dendr.* 14.
Zanthoxylum aculeatum, carpini foliis, americanum,
cortice cinereo. *Pluk. alm.* 596. *t.* 239. *f.* 3.
Habitat in Brafilia, Jamaica. ♄

PEN-

1112·9

6 —E. latonica

Linnaeus or his son, or they may never have been present in the first place. This is often true, for example, of plants from the tropics or then little-explored regions such as Japan. There were very few preserved specimens from these areas in Linnaeus' herbarium in 1753 (Hermann's Ceylon collections were only loaned to him for a short period and never formed part of his own collection). Although *Morus papyrifera*, described from Japan, is now represented in LINN by sheet 1112.4, it was a post-1753 addition to the collection and Linnaeus' original concept of the species was shaped by the published accounts of Seba and Kaempfer that he cited. A similar story exists with *Morus tinctoria*, from the New World tropics, where 1112.10 (LINN) was similarly a later addition, and Linnaeus' concept came primarily from accounts published by Sloane and Plukenet.

Occasionally, Linnaeus appends the name of a correspondent or collector to the diagnosis. For example, for *Tilia americana* L., "Tilia floribus nectario instructis" is attributed to "Kalm", and *Leucojum autumnale* L., "Leucojum spatha multiflora, stylo filiformi" is credited to "Loefl." (= Löfling). Authorship of these binomial names, however, is attributable to Linnaeus (Art. 46.2). Where Linnaeus adds the symbol "†" following the diagnosis of a species name (e.g. in *Clutia cascarilla, Clathrus nudus*), this indicates that the taxon was poorly known to him. Confusingly, when Linnaeus used the same symbol in connection with a generic name, it indicates that he had seen herbarium material of it. The symbol "*" appended to a reference (e.g. to Linnaeus' *Flora Zeylanica* under *Malva tomentosa*; to *Iter Gotlandicum* under *Scabiosa columnaria*) indicates that a good description is to be found there.

> 10. RHUS foliis ternatis: foliolis petiolatis lineari-lanceo- *angustifoli-*
> latis integerrimis fubtus tomentofis. *Hort. cliff.* 111. *um.*
> *Roy. lugdb.* 244.
> Rhus africanum trifoliatum majus, foliis fubtus argen-
> teis acutis & margine incifis. *Pluk. alm.* 319. *t.* 219.
> *f.* 6.
> Rhus fruticofum, foliis trifidis linearibus acuminatis.
> *Burm. afric.* 251. *t.* 91. *f.* 1.
> *Habitat in* Æthiopia. ♄

Where a diagnosis accompanying a binomial name is cited as from an earlier work (e.g. *Hortus Cliffortianus*), close comparison frequently shows that the two diagnoses differ. Sometimes this indicates a change in species concept but it is more frequently merely a consequence of the recognition of additional species in the genus and the need to distinguish them adequately. In his treatment of *Rhus*, for example, Linnaeus (1738: 110–111) recognised six species but this had risen to 12 in 1753. Linnaeus cited the 1753 diagnosis of *Rhus angustifolia* ("Rhus foliis ternatis: foliolis lineari-lanceolatis integerrimis subtus tomentosis" – see above) as coming from his earlier *Hortus Cliffortianus* treatment but it is clearly somewhat modified from the original "Rhus foliis ternatis, foliolis

Opposite page: The type specimen of *Morus tatarica* L., almost certainly collected by Traugott Gerber (see p. 26)

> *tomentofum.* 8. RHUS foliis ternatis: foliolis fubpetiolatis rhombeis angulatis fubtus tomentofis.
>
> Rhus foliis ternatis: foliolis ovatis utrinque acutis dentatis: lateralibus petiolatis. *Hort. cliff.* 111.
>
> Rhus foliis ternatis: foliolis petiolatis ovatis acutis dentatis. *Vir. cliff.* 25. *Roy. lugdb.* 244.
>
> Rhus africanum trifoliatum majus, foliis obtufis & incifis hirfutis pubefcentibus. *Pluk. alm.* 319. *t.* 219. *f.* 7.
>
> Vitex trifolia minor indica ferrata. *Comm. hort.* 1. *p.* 179. *t.* 92.
>
> *Habitat ad* Cap. b. Spei. ♄

lineari-lanceolatis, petiolatis integerrimis". For another species, *Rhus tomentosa*, the necessary change in diagnosis (see above) was so great that Linnaeus cited the 1738 version as a synonym rather than as the basis for the 1753 diagnosis.

Apart from references to the *Hortus Cliffortianus* and *Flora Zeylanica* accounts, both of which are linked with independent herbarium collections, there are several other commonly cited works of this type. They include Linnaeus' *Flora Lapponica* (1737), linked with his Lapland herbarium which is now in the Institut de France in Paris (LAPP), Adriaan van Royen's *Florae Leydensis Prodromus* (1740) linked with his herbarium in Leiden, and Gronovius' *Flora Virginica* (1739–43) linked with the John Clayton herbarium (BM). Other works sometimes cited as the original source of diagnoses include Linnaeus' *Flora Suecica* (1745*), Hortus Upsaliensis* (1748), and *Skånska Resa* (1751), but none of these is linked to any independent herbarium collection studied by Linnaeus. Relevant specimens connected with these works should be sought in LINN and the other "general" Linnaean herbaria.

The Synonyms

Linnaeus' intention in compiling *Species Plantarum* was to bring together information on all the plant species then known, and most of his species accounts include a number of synonyms drawn from the work of earlier authors. In the 1753 account of *Morus*, one or two synonyms are cited for all the species except *Morus tatarica* (which Linnaeus believed to be previously undescribed and was probably based exclusively on material collected by Gerber).

Any of the works that are found cited as the source of some diagnosis can also, in other cases, be found cited as the source of synonyms in their own right. Some references are associated with separate herbarium collections that were seen by Linnaeus, though never owned by him. Perhaps the most significant of these are references to Caspar Bauhin's *Pinax Theatri Botanici* (1623), then one of the most important treatments of known European plants and linked to a herbarium prepared by one of Bauhin's students, Joachim Burser. This was arranged according to Bauhin's system and was, fortuitously for Linnaeus, housed in Uppsala. Linnaeus was therefore able to use it as a set of specimens for the interpretation of Bauhin's names, which he cited extensively throughout *Species Plantarum*. Bauhin references are cited as synonyms for both *Morus alba* and *Morus nigra*, and can be linked with material in vol. XXIV: 30 and XXIV: 28 respectively in the Burser herbarium (UPS), specimens which form part of the original material for each name.

Many of the synonyms from other works provide useful descriptions ("*") again indicating a particularly full one) which can aid in the interpretation of Linnaeus' use of a particular binomial. However, as far as typification is concerned, those works which also supplied illustrations are of much greater interest (as descriptions cannot serve as types). As noted in Jarvis (2005), the limited accessibility of Linnaeus' specimens (and the absence of the type method) inevitably made it more likely that early users of his names would try to interpret them via the cited illustrations. While illustrations are generally regarded as less satisfactory than a well-preserved herbarium specimen when a nomenclatural type is needed, it is frequently found that adopting one of these figures as a type serves to maintain what has become established usage of a particular name.

Sir Hans Sloane's specimen, original drawing and published engraving for the Jamaican species that Linnaeus named *Tabernaemontana laurifolia* L.

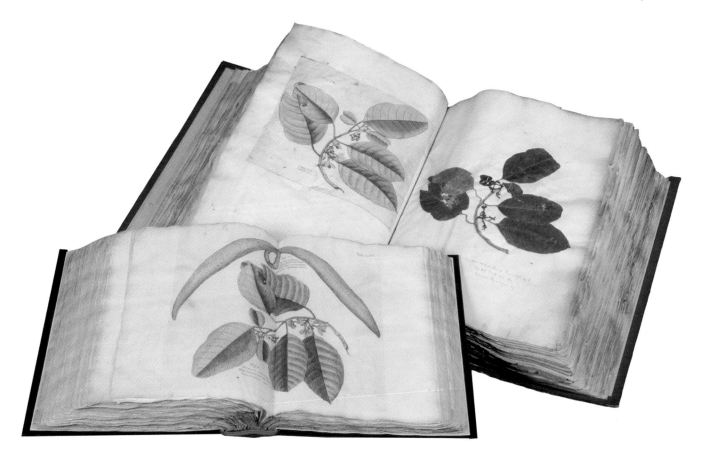

In the case of some of these publications, the identification of the illustrated plants can be assisted by reference to associated herbarium material. The closeness of these associations varies widely. In the case of the engravings published by Sir Hans Sloane (1707, 1725), the specimens he had collected in Jamaica were the starting point for the drawings he commissioned from Everard Kickius, who skilfully and faithfully reproduced the plants. The engravings were produced from Kickius' drawings (the latter still mounted in Sloane's herbarium in BM-SL, adjacent to the plants they depict) and so the relationship between the published plates and the specimens upon which they were based is extremely close. Despite this, it is important to bear in mind that where a Sloane element is original material for a Linnaean name, it is the published engraving that was used by Linnaeus and must be the lectotype. Despite calling on Sloane during his brief visit to London in the summer of 1736 and admiring the scale (if not the method of organisation) of Sloane's herbarium, Linnaeus did not study Sloane's specimens. Consequently, although they can be of immense help in distinguishing between closely related species whose identity perhaps cannot be elucidated from the engraving and description alone, the specimens are not themselves original material for Linnaean binomials. Where such a close relationship between specimen and illustration exists, the term "typotype" (see above and Stearn 1957: 129) has been applied to the specimen. Typotypes are indicated in Chapter 7, where relevant.

A figure (right) published by Leonard Plukenet (*Phytographia*: t. 78, f. 3. 1691) is the type of *Asparagus capensis* L., and there is a specimen (left), from which it was probably prepared in Plukenet's herbarium (in Herb. Sloane 95: 106, BM-SL).

For many other publications, however, the relationship between herbarium material and a published illustration may be much less well defined. For example, the numerous illustrations that appear in Leonard Plukenet's *Phytographia* (1691–1696), though based on herbarium material, are often rather stylised. Faced with a number of candidate specimens in Plukenet's herbarium (BM-SL), it can often be difficult to be certain which (if any) was the basis of the published figure. Similar uncertainties exist with the plates in works by authors such as Johann Jakob Dillenius, Engelbert Kaempfer, Pier Antonio Micheli, Robert Morison and James Petiver and their associated collections. Dried specimens collected by Mark Catesby (BM-SL, OXF etc.) can be associated with taxa described and illustrated by him (Catesby 1731–1747) from the Carolinas and elsewhere, but the original illustrations were apparently prepared from living specimens, before they were pressed, so the link between herbarium material and plate is harder to establish. Under these circumstances, it seems preferable to treat these more loosely associated collections as voucher specimens and, apart from cases where the relationship appears particularly convincing, this is how they are generally listed in Chapter 7. In any case, like typotypes, they were not seen by Linnaeus and cannot be regarded as original material for Linnaean names.

Returning to the *Morus* example, illustrations from Dodoëns (1616) are original material for *Morus alba* and *Morus nigra*, as are plates from Kaempfer (1712) and Seba (1734) for *Morus papyrifera*, from Plukenet (1692) for *Morus rubra* and *Morus tinctoria*, from Rheede tot Draakenstein (1678) for *Morus indica*, and from Sloane (1725) for *Morus tinctoria*.

Provenance, Ecology and Life Form

Any listed synonyms are usually followed by an indication of the location from which Linnaeus believed the plant to originate, usually in the form "Habitat in . . ." [It lives in . . .] followed by a geographical entity. This may be very broad (e.g. in Orbis, America, Asia, Europa, Africa, Indiis, Oriente), an apparently political entity (e.g. Anglia, Aethiopia, Austria, Borussia, Brasilia, Canada, China, Finlandia, Gallia, Germania, Helvetia, Hispania, India, Italia, Jamaica, Japonia, Lusitania, Peru, Suecia, Virginia, Zeylona etc.) or occasionally it may be very specific ("in Lancastria Angliae" [*Lichen ampullaceus*], "in Cappadocia, unde in Europam 1559" [*Tulipa gesneriana*], "in Tau[er]o Radstadiensi" [*Sempervivum hirtum*], or "ad Nursium prope lacum pilati" [*Crepis pygmaea*]. The name of the collector, or supplier, of the material is often appended to the geographical information (e.g. ". . . in Hispania. *Loefling*"; "in Canada. *Kalm*"; ". . . in Sibiria. *Gmelin*"), while an indication of ecological preferences sometimes qualifies the distributional information ("in Virginiae, Canadae *pinetis*"; "in Europae *pratis*"; "*ad ripas petrosas* Danubii"; "in Cambriae *septentrionalis nemorosis*" etc.). In groups of organisms such as the Algae and Fungi, the ecological information sometimes displaces the geographical ("*in Muscis & arborum corticibus*"; "*ad margines Sylvarum*"; "*supra Lapides in rivulis*" etc.).

Linnaeus' geographical names should be interpreted with some caution, and necessarily with some appreciation of the historical context in which they were chosen, as explained very helpfully, and in some detail, by Stearn (1957: 143–150). In particular, it is important to understand how material might have reached Linnaeus from particular areas at this time, and which areas were implied by particular terms. Some of these are far from obvious. For example, Linnaeus' frequent use of "Aethiopia" refers neither to Africa as a whole, nor to the north-east, but rather "to that part of South Africa near the Cape of Good Hope (*Caput bonae spei*) whence the Dutch introduced material to Holland" (Stearn 1957: 143). References to "China" usually indicate only Canton (now Guang Zhou) via Pehr Osbeck, and "Japonia" in reality usually means the Dutch trading post in the harbour at Nagasaki. "Canada" is usually associated with Pehr Kalm, but was used by Linnaeus to indicate the part of eastern North America, from New York and Philadelphia northwards to Quebec (Kalm spent only about 10 weeks of his three-year visit within modern Canada, entirely in Quebec province, cf. Kalm 1966). Stearn provides a useful discussion and a list of some of the less obvious geographical names used by Linnaeus with more modern equivalents.

Lastly, Linnaeus sometimes added one of four symbols to indicate the life form of the plant in question. Each of the species of *Morus*, for example, is accompanied by the symbol (♄) indicating woodiness (i.e. a tree or shrub). The others are "♃" to indicate a perennial, "♂" for a biennial and "☉" for an annual. For information on their origins, and the way in which Linnaeus turned them to his own uses, see Stearn (1957: 162–163).

The Trivial Name or Species Epithet

In *Species Plantarum* and the editions of *Systema Naturae* from 1759, all of which adopted binomial nomenclature, the newly coined specific name (or epithet, or trivial name) appears in the margin, italicised and adjacent to the respective species account. In other works (e.g. dissertations such as *Centuria I Plantarum*), the epithet appeared instead between the generic name and the diagnostic phrase name, often in parentheses and italicised.

Sprague (1955) and Stearn (1957: 73–74) have reviewed the sources used by Linnaeus in choosing his trivial names. Many are drawn from what he felt to be diagnostic, descriptive characters (e.g. *aculeata, acuminata, arborea, coccinea, frutescens, glabra, glauca, glutinosa, herbacea, hirsuta, lutea, multiflora, purpurea, sagittata, scandens, serrata, tomentosa, triflora, variegata*), or from a resemblance to distinctive plants (e.g. *cerastoides,*

Opposite: A specimen, unusually accompanied by a mounted watercolour, of material which Linnaeus annotated as *Primula glutinosa* Wulfen, and which he presumably received from Wulfen in the mid 1770s.

198 · 13

Primula Plutinosa

Xaver wulfen

hypericifolia, myrtifolia, ornithopodioides, pseudo-capsicum, rubioides). Others are geographical (e.g. *armena, canadensis, canariensis, chinensis, cretica, europaea, hispanica, japonica, lapponica, orientalis, pyrenaica*) or indicate habitat (*alpina, arvensis, maritima, montana, palustris, pratensis, sylvatica*). Some allude to their uses or properties, medicinal or otherwise (*aromatica, cathartica, officinalis, tinctoria*), or were taken from earlier generic (e.g. *Pistacia Lentiscus, P. Simaruba* and *P. Terebinthus*) or vernacular names (e.g. *Euphorbia Ipecacuanhae, Fraxinus Ornus, Ulva Linza*), in which case Linnaeus capitalised them. Occasionally, epithets indicated either the collector or the source of information (e.g. *burgessii, burseriana, casabonae, cherleri, gerardii, gmelinii, gronovii, halleri, houstonii, isnardii, jacquini, kalmii, laxmannii, lippii, loeflingii, loeselii, ludwigii, nissolii, osbeckii, plukeneti, plumieri, tournefortii, valerandi* and *vitaliana*). In a small number of cases, they have proved to be somewhat misleading (e.g. *Sibthorpia africana* for an endemic of the Balearic Islands, *Scilla peruviana* for a plant from Portugal, and *Scabiosa cretica* for a plant from the western Mediterranean).

A small number of specific epithets consist of two words (e.g. *Amaryllis* "Bella donna", *Impatiens* "noli tangere", *Narcissus* "Pseudo Narcissus", *Trigonella* "Foenum graecum", *Vitex* "Agnus Castus") and, depending on their linguistic structure, these are either to be hyphenated (e.g. *Impatiens noli-tangere* L.) or treated as a single word (e.g. as *Narcissus pseudonarcissus* L.) under Art. 23.1, Ex. 16, 17.

Two symbols also appear in *Species Plantarum* as part of compound epithets. "∇" indicates water, and epithets such as "Plantago ∇", "Anagall. ∇" and "Nasturtium ∇" have commonly been rendered as "*plantago-aquatica*", "*anagallis-aquatica*" and "*nasturtium-aquaticum*" respectively, and this usage has subsequently been codified (see Art. 23.3, Ex. 2). A second symbol is "♀" (originally indicating Venus, then copper) but treated in epithets such as "umbilicus ♀", "Pecten ♀" and speculum ♀" as "*umbilicus-veneris*", "*pecten-veneris*" and "*speculum-veneris*" respectively. Stearn (1957: 162–163) provides additional information on Linnaeus' use of these and other signs. A further variation is found in Linnaeus' (1753) treatment of the larger genus *Trifolium*, where he divided the species into several groups. The first of these, "*Meliloti leguminibus nudis polyspermis*", contains eight species whose epithets reflect their classification in being preceded by the letter "M"[eliloti] (as "*M. caerulea*", "*M. indica*" etc.). As has been established custom, the "*Melilotus*" is to be ignored, and the accepted form of these names is *Trifolium caeruleum*, *Trifolium indicum* etc. Other, less consistent, situations exist, for example in *Polypodium*, where *P.* "*F. mas*" and *P.* "*F. femina*" are treated as *P. filix-mas* and *P. filix-femina* respectively, but *P.* "*F. fragile*" is treated as *P. fragile* in accordance with historical usage (see Art. 23.8 Ex. 19).

Descriptions and Additional Observations

Descriptions, in contrast to diagnoses, were generally omitted by Linnaeus from his major works, *Species Plantarum* (1753, 1762, 1763) and *Systema Naturae* (1758, 1759, 1767), for these publications were intended to be concise summations of knowledge. There are exceptions in *Species Plantarum*, however, (e.g. the accounts of *Nepeta italica*, *Panicum latifolium*, *Geranium sibiricum*, *Lycopodium nudum* and *Senecio byzantinus*), and particularly in the Appendix (e.g. *Cotyledon hispanica*). Where they appear, such descriptions can be quite long, and usually follow the "Habitat . . ." statement. More frequently, there are short observations that can serve to provide comparisons with other species (e.g. "Vix sufficienter a praecedente distincta" under *Alcea ficifolia*, referring to *A. rosea*), or to clarify sources of information ("Lob. & Dod. figurae bonae sunt. Hoc aevo mihi non visa in Hortis Europaeis" under *Psoralea americana*). For further information, and an extensive dictionary, on the botanical Latin used by Linnaeus, see Stearn (1973).

However, many of Linnaeus' other works were less concise in concept, and often contain quite lengthy descriptions of plants. This is true in many of his floristic works (e.g. *Flora Lapponica* and *Flora Suecica*), some of the post-1753 dissertations (e.g. particularly *Centuria I & II Plantarum*, and *Plantae Rariores Africanae*), as well as later works such as the *Mantissae* (1767, 1771).

The Process of Typifying Linnaean Names

Starting with the protologue of a name, the first step is to establish what original material may be in existence. This can be briefly summarised:

1. Are there any explicitly cited specimens (e.g. Herb. Burser XVI: 8 under *Bupleurum ranunculoides*), i.e. syntypes, and can they be located? If there are two or more, a lectotype must be chosen from among them; if only one, then it must be designated as the lectotype of the name (Art. 9.10).

2. If there are no syntypes, are there any specimens that can be associated with the name in LINN, or the "general" Linnaean herbaria at S, UPS, SBT, MW, G etc?

3. If the diagnosis is cited as having been taken from an earlier publication, or if the publication is cited as a synonym source, are there any specimens in the separate herbaria associated with it? Principal among these are the herbaria linked with publications such as Linnaeus' *Hortus Cliffortianus* (Herb. Clifford, BM), *Flora Zeylanica* (Herb. Hermann, BM), *Flora Lapponica* (Lapland herbarium, Institut de France, Paris), Caspar Bauhin's *Pinax Theatri Botanici* (Herb. Burser, UPS), Gronovius' *Flora Virginica* (Herb. John Clayton, BM) and van Royen's *Florae Leydensis Prodromus* (Herb. van Royen, L).

J. Burman's figure (*Rariorum Africanarum Plantarum*: t. 29. 1738) is the lectotype of *Oxalis pes-caprae* L.

4. Are there any illustrations cited among the synonyms? Note that quite a number of heavily illustrated works (e.g. Bauhin & Cherler 1650–1651) have unnumbered figures scattered through their pages and Linnaeus' references to them consequently lack any tabula, plate or figure number that would alert one to their existence. These should not be overlooked.

5. If specimens are in existence in LINN or any of the "general" Linnaean herbaria, are they annotated by Linnaeus? Is there any evidence to suggest that they were in his possession prior to his publishing the name in question (e.g. presence of a *Species Plantarum* species number written by Linnaeus for a name published in that work)? Many of the collections in LINN are either unannotated by Linnaeus, or reached him after he had described the taxon to which he believed them to belong. For example, Patrick Browne's collections from Jamaica, which Linnaeus did not acquire until 1758, cannot be original material for binomials first published in 1753 (see "Dating of specimens in the Linnaean herbaria" below).

6. What are the taxonomic identities of the specimens and illustrations identified as original material? To what taxon is the Linnaean name generally applied? If the identity of all of the original material corresponds with the usage of the name, then the most complete of the specimens would ordinarily be the obvious choice as lectotype. However, if the most clearly identifiable element is an illustration rather than a specimen, it may act as the lectotype. If more than one species is represented in the original material, a specimen or illustration that corresponds with the current usage of the name should be designated as lectotype, in order to avoid nomenclatural disruption. If the identity of the original material is uncertain (perhaps it is incomplete or poorly preserved or, if an illustration, too generalised for a precise identification to be made), the designation of an epitype in its support may be effective in making its correct application clear. If none of the original material corresponds with usage, an assessment of the history of the application of the name and its importance should be made in order to establish whether it can be typified in a way that will minimise disruption. This might be achieved by allowing it to fall into the synonymy of another name, or nomenclatural stability might be best served by proposing it either for formal conservation with a conserved type, or for outright rejection. Finally, if no original material exists, a neotype can be designated.

It will be clear from the process outlined above that the options available in typifying a Linnaean name will be constrained by the form of the protologue, and the specimens and illustrations that are either cited directly, or are otherwise linked with it. Several protologues are therefore reproduced, and discussed, here to provide examples of some of the different situations that can be encountered.

2. CAMPANULA cauliculis unifloris, foliis caulinis *pulla.*
ovatis crenatis, calycibus cernuis.
Campanula alpina latifolia, flore pullo. *Bauh. pin.* 93.
prodr. 33. *Burf. IV.* 21.
β. Campanula foliis fubrotundis. *Bauh. pin.* 94. *prodr.* 34.
t. 35.
Habitat in Auftria.
Radix *filiformis, repens.* Caules *fpithamæi, erecti, fle-*
xuofi, filiformes, raro ramo uno alterove, eoque flori-
fero. Folia *radicalia & caulina ovata, obtufa, fubcre-*
nata crenis diftantibus, nuda, petiolata. Pedunculus
terminalis. Flos *cernuus, magnitudine* C. *rotundifo-*
liæ, calyce *lævi.* β. *floribus pluribus in fummitate*
caulis variat.

The protologue of **Campanula pulla** L. (*Sp. Pl.* 1: 163. 1753) consists of a
new diagnosis, and a reference to a plant described by Bauhin (1620,
1623) with the addition of "Burs. IV. 21" (indicating material in Herb.
Burser IV: 21 (UPS)). Linnaeus also recognised an unnamed variety based
on a second plant described (and figured) by Bauhin, and the protologue
concludes with an indication that the species grows in "Austria", followed
by quite a detailed description (unusual in this work). Linnaeus' explicit
reference to the precise location of Burser's specimen makes this a syntype
and, as there is only one, it takes precedence over any uncited specimens
and cited and uncited illustrations in the designation of a lectotype (Art.
9.10). Happily, the Burser material (http://www-hotel.uu.se/
evolmuseum/Burser04/Burser-vol04-021.jpg), collected at Schneeberg in
Austria, is identifiable as the plant widely known as *C. pulla*, and it is
formally designated as the lectotype in Chapter 7.

verna. 14. POTENTILLA foliis radicalibus quinatis acute
ferratis, caulinis ternatis, caule declinato. *Fl. fuec.*
419.
Potentilla foliis quinatis incifis, caule affurgente. *Fl.*
lapp. 212. *Hort. cliff.* 194. *Roy. lugdb.* 276.
Potentilla foliis quinatis acute ferratis ora fericea, petalis maculatis. *Hall. helv.* 339. *t.* 6. *f.* 4.
Quinquefolium minus repens alpinum aureum. *Bauh.*
pin. 325.
Habitat in Europæ *pafcuis ficcis, frigidioribus.* ♃

The protologue of **Potentilla verna** L. (*Sp. Pl.* 1: 498. 1753) contains a
diagnosis drawn from Linnaeus' *Flora Suecica* (1745) account, and three
synonyms. No Lapland (LAPP) or Herb. Clifford (BM) material can be
traced, but three specimens and the cited figure of Haller (1740) comprise

original material. Sheet 655.23 (LINN) is identifiable as *P. crantzii* (Crantz) Beck ex Fritsch, the identity of 655.24 (LINN) is uncertain, Herb. Burser XVIII(1): 1 (UPS) belongs to *P. montana* L., and Haller's figure is probably of *P. aurea* L. Aware of these problems, many authors had informally rejected *P. verna* as a *nomen confusum* (see Rico 1998). Designation of either 655.23 (LINN) or the Haller figure as the lectotype would cause nomenclatural disruption because *P. verna* is an earlier name than either *P. crantzii* or *P. aurea*. However, choosing the Burser specimen as lectotype (as was done subsequently by Rico & Martínez Ortega 2002) provides a stabilising solution to the problem because, as *P. verna* and *P. montana* were published simultaneously, *P. verna* can disappear into the synonymy of *P. montana*.

The protologue of **Arum trilobatum** L. (*Sp. Pl.* 2: 965. 1753) takes its diagnosis from Linnaeus' earlier *Flora Zeylanica* (1747) account, which Linnaeus marked with an asterisk (indicating that a good description could be found there). There are also descriptions, from Hermann (1698) and Commelin (1697), with illustrations, cited as synonyms in the protologue. *Flora Zeylanica* was based on material in the Hermann herbarium (now at BM) but, in this case, it is a drawing rather than a specimen that Linnaeus used (and annotated). It is identifiable as the species known as *Typhonium trilobatum* (L.) Schott, and Nicolson & Sivadasan (1981) therefore designated it as the lectotype.

Linnaeus frequently recognised varieties, usually marking them with a Greek letter, in the left margin of the protologue, immediately adjacent to a synonym, the polynomial of which provides the diagnosis for the variety. Although most were not given a name in binomial form, others were formally named, with (in *Species Plantarum*, 1753, 1762–1763) the varietal epithet appearing in the margin beneath the species epithet. In the case of **Scabiosa leucantha** L. (1753: 98), the species has a diagnosis (see below left) cited from Linnaeus' *Hortus Cliffortianus* (1738: 30), with synonyms indicated from Royen (1740), Sauvages (1751) and Bauhin (1623). However, he also named a variety [ß] *spuria* L. for which he provided a diagnosis and also cited a Commelin (1701) description and plate as a synonym. The publication of a variety *spuria* creates an autonymic variety *leucantha* (under Art. 26.3). In this case, Linnaeus italicised those parts of the diagnoses for *S. leucantha* ("foliis pinnatifidis") and var. *spuria* ("foliis lanceolatis serratis") to indicate how the two taxa should be distinguished. He added that while the typical part of the species (var. *leucantha*) came from southern Europe ("in collibus Narbonae"), var. *spuria* came from Africa. The distinction between these two names is therefore very clear, and *S. leucantha* has specimens in the Clifford (BM) and Burser (UPS) herbaria as original material, and the cited Commelin plate is the only original material for var. *spuria*. Wijnands (1983: 93) designated this plate as the lectotype, and the correct name for this taxon at species rank is *Cephalaria rigida* (L.) Roem. & Schult. (based on *Scabiosa rigida* L. 1760). Sprague (1955) and Stearn (1957: 90–94) have provided a review of Linnaeus' handling of varieties in various of his publications.

Dating of Specimens in the Linnaean Herbaria

In assessing whether a particular herbarium collection is part of the original material for a given name, the question of the date of acquisition (for Linnaeus' own herbarium) or the date of study (for specimens that he did not own, or had borrowed from others) is important. Most of the collections that Linnaeus studied which did not end up in his own herbarium (e.g. those of Clayton, Clifford and Hermann) he studied long before he published the associated binomials. Consequently, provided they have appropriate bibliographical or other links (e.g. annotations by Linnaeus), there is little uncertainty about the status of these specimens as original material.

However, it would clearly be wrong for a specimen collected after Linnaeus had described the species to which it belonged to be accepted as original material for that name. The dating of collections in Linnaeus' own herbarium is less straightforward, and has been the subject of differing interpretations in the past. Stearn (1957: 103–115) has given an outline of the history of Linnaeus' own herbarium (now in LINN), recognising a number of phases of acquisition of material, and he lists the important constituent collectors with an indication of when their specimens reached the collection. There are few problems in ascertaining the approximate dates of acquisition where specimens are clearly linked with their collectors (e.g. Brander, Browne, Allioni), as these can often be correlated with other sources of information (e.g. dated letters received by Linnaeus). However, the comparative brevity of annotation on the majority of the specimens in LINN, and the frequent absence of collector information in protologues often makes it difficult to ascertain the provenance of a given specimen with any degree of confidence.

Many authors in the first half of the 20th century followed Jackson (1912), who interpreted marginal marks made by Linnaeus in copies of his works published between 1753 and 1767 as confirmation of the presence or absence of material in the Linnaean herbarium at the time of each "enumeration". However, it is worth quoting Stearn (*in litt.*, 20 May 1983, in a discussion of the relevance of sheet 1071.10 (LINN), material apparently linked with *Aristolochia longa* L.):

> "This, according to Jackson, was in Linnaeus's possession prior to 1753. Linnaean scholars have long known that no reliance whatever can be placed on such a statement by Jackson, which was based on the fact that Linnaeus underlined many specific numbers in his interleaved copy of the *Species Plantarum* (1753). No one really knows why he did this. Linnaeus nowhere stated the intent of this underscoring but Jackson guessed that it referred to the presence of a specimen in his herbarium, for which there is no proof and much difficulty. Even if this were so, it would not necessarily be evidence that the specimen now in the Linnaean Herbarium is the very same specimen Linnaeus had under his eyes when drafting before 1753 the text of the *Species Plantarum*. Modern botanists tend to overlook the fact that Linnaeus lived in the 18th not the 20th century and that a good illustration often provided him with more useful relevant information than a poor specimen. However, as Spencer Savage, a great Linnaean scholar long in charge of the Linnaean Herbarium, at one time Jackson's assistant, later his successor, stated in 1945, "it is mere presumption to suppose that the markings had the intention of registering the presence of specimens in the Herbarium"".

There are numerous examples where Jackson's theory is contradicted by independent evidence. For example, he lists material of *Phyteuma orbicularis* L. as present in the first (1753) enumeration. However, the only material associated with this name (sheet 223.7) carries a numbered (39) label written by Linnaeus' correspondent, Giovanni Scopoli, which corresponds with a specimen listed in a letter, dated 1762, which was sent to Linnaeus by the Italian. Clearly, this specimen could not have been in Linnaeus' possession in 1753.

Refuting Jackson's theory, Stearn instead emphasised the importance of the numbers that Linnaeus often wrote on his herbarium sheets. These typically appear towards the bottom of the sheet, centrally and just below the specimen(s) in question, and are often placed near to the specific epithet, where present. Such numbers almost always link these specimens with the corresponding account in the first edition of *Species Plantarum* (1753). In the case of *Morus*, for example, species number 1 (*Morus alba*) is represented in LINN by sheet 1112.1 which bears both "1" and "alba" near the base, and by 1112.2, which carries just "1". Similarly, for the second species, *Morus nigra*, there is sheet 1112.3 "2 nigra", and for the fourth, *Morus rubra*, 1112.6 "rubra 4" and "K"[alm] indicating the provenance of this North American collection. *Morus tatarica* is the sixth species, represented by sheet 1112.9 "tatarica 6". However, *Morus zanthoxylum*, which was not published until 1759 and is represented by sheet 1112.10, carries no number but only "Xanthoxylon" (deleted), and "tinctoria" in Linnaeus' hand.

The numbers that Linnaeus gave to his species in 1753 were retained in his next worldwide treatment in *Syst. Nat.* ed. 10, 2 in 1759, with species that he was describing as new (or had already described since 1753) intercalated between the existing species and allocated letters rather than numbers. In the 1759 treatment of *Myrtus*, for example, there are six new species, lettered A to E, scattered among the seven species recognised in 1753. The letters often appear on associated herbarium specimens in LINN, as is the case with *Myrtus biflora* ("A" – 637.6), *Myrtus dioica* ("B" – 637.11), *Myrtus chytraculia* ("C" – 637.12) and *Myrtus zuzygium* ("D" – 637.13). By his next global treatment in the second edition of *Species Plantarum* (1762), Linnaeus decided to renumber the species (see below).

Here, *Myrtus biflora* appears as number three, *Myrtus dioica* as six, *Myrtus chytraculia* as seven and *Myrtus zuzygium* as eight. This process was repeated in his last comprehensive treatment of the plants in *Syst. Nat.*, ed. 12, 2 (1767) with the now 12 recognised species again being partially renumbered.

Significantly, it is only the species numbers from the first edition of *Species Plantarum* (or the letters from *Syst. Nat.*, ed. 10) that appear on sheets in this way, and Stearn, from long study of the herbarium specimens and protologues over many years, reached the conclusion that the presence of such a number provided extremely strong evidence that the collection in question was in Linnaeus' possession by 1753.

Stearn (*in litt.*, 20 Mar 1969) wrote:

> "The fact, however, that Linnaeus possessed a specimen of a given taxon in 1753 does not necessarily mean that this same specimen exists in the Linnaean Herbarium today, since Linnaeus sometimes replaced an earlier gathering by a later one conspecific with it in his opinion though not necessarily so, according to ours. Fortunately such substitution, as far as the first edition (1753) of the *Species Plantarum* is concerned, becomes evident through absence of a species number associated with that edition. Conversely, the presence of such a number usually establishes authenticity. Neither Jackson nor Savage appreciated the historical relevance of the numbers on the sheets of the Linnaean herbarium, possibly because working taxonomists and matters of typification of names were not so critically considered in their day. Linnaeus had not hit upon the consistent use of *nomina trivialia* (specific epithets) when he began to prepare the first draft of the *Species Plantarum* and before the introduction of binomial nomenclature for species the only convenient way to designate them concisely was by use of numerals. There is good reason to believe that Linnaeus originally numbered his herbarium sheets using *Species Plantarum* entry numbers, later added specific epithets, then used a number and a specific epithet together on a sheet, then abandoned numbers (since the renumbering of entries in his later works would have necessitated the total renumbering of his herbarium to obviate confusion), and used simply a specific epithet alone. After 1753 Linnaeus gave *Species Plantarum* (1753) entry numbers to the specimens he received from Louis Gérard in 1753, but not, it would appear, to much of any later material. Hence a number on a sheet is fairly good evidence that Linnaeus possessed it in 1753 and examined it for the *Species Plantarum*".

Years of study of Linnaean protologues and collections have not convinced me that Stearn's hypothesis is seriously flawed. As he notes, Gérard's specimens (received by Linnaeus after the publication of *Species Plantarum*), where they represented species already known to Linnaeus, were annotated with the relevant *Species Plantarum* number. For example, *Gérard 13* (sheet 982.8) is annotated *"linosyris 4"* [= *Chrysocoma*] by Linnaeus, and something similar occurred with at least some of the specimens acquired in 1758 from Patrick Browne. However, where we know the provenance and date of acquisition of collections, there is,

Opposite: The lectotype specimen of *Passiflora caerulea* L. is annotated with both the specific epithet and the associated *Species Plantarum* number (i.e. "22") from the 1753 edition, indicating that it was in Linnaeus' possession by 1753.

26

1070.26

22

22 cærulea

generally, a very strong correlation (for 1753 names) on the one hand between presence in the herbarium pre-1753 and a number written on the sheet, and on the other, acquisition post-1753 and the absence of any such number.

For the Linnaean Plant Name Typification Project, in dealing with over 9,000 names, it has been necessary to adopt a consistent approach to the interpretation of what is, and what is not, original material. Based on Stearn's hypothesis, for those names published in 1753, material in LINN (and the collections derived from that herbarium) that lacks a *Species Plantarum* number written on the sheet by Linnaeus is not, in general, accepted as being original material for the name in question. However, if, in individual cases, additional data (e.g. dated specimen lists, geographical information, precise agreement with a description etc.) suggest strongly that an unnumbered sheet was available to Linnaeus, and that he believed it to be identifiable with the name in question, then such sheets have been admitted as original material.

Stearn's account (1957: 125–134) of the typification of Linnaean species names contains a great deal of valuable information and sound advice. However, there are some areas where our approach in typifying Linnaean names differs from that of Stearn. This is partly a result of changes made to the Code over the last 50 years, and partly from a change in general attitudes towards nomenclatural changes that now favours maintenance of existing usage of names where possible. Whereas the rejection of doubtful or ambiguous, confusing names has a long tradition in botanical nomenclature, being sanctioned in pre-1975 editions of the ICBN, formal proposals to reject species names were not provided for prior to the Leningrad Congress in 1975, which also deleted the previous less formal provisions. The possibility of conservation of species names appeared initially only in 1983 with the Sydney Code, and then only for taxa deemed to be of major economic importance. It was expanded to admit all names at species rank at Yokohama in 1993 and since then, there has been a continuing trend towards minimising name changes for purely nomenclatural (rather than taxonomic) causes. Where the Code allows this, we have sought to typify names accordingly.

Chiefly, this is reflected in cases where the identity of the more obvious type candidates (e.g. specimens in the Hermann, Clifford and LINN herbaria) differs from the current application of the name in question. If there are additional elements which are original material for the name (e.g. other specimens, cited illustrations), the identity of which does correspond with usage of the name, then one of these has been designated as the lectotype. This approach avoids the name changes that would result from a less flexible approach to typification and can also, under some circumstances, obviate the need to propose the conservation of long-used and familiar names. Under earlier approaches, the taxonomic identity of a potential lectotype specimen, and the nomenclatural consequences of its designation as type, were often not regarded as of particular importance. The undoubted relevance of the source of the information used in creating the diagnosis was often elevated to the point where only that material believed to have held the primary influence in the creation of the diagnosis was considered for typification purposes. Such collections have been referred to as "obligate lectotypes" and were sometimes designated as such without serious consideration of the nomenclatural consequences, nor any thought as to whether an alternative choice might avoid disruption to the usage of the name in question, and that of other names as well.

At the same time, the laudable aim of maintaining usage of a name was sometimes attempted in ways that were ineffective because they were contrary to provisions of the Code (both then and now). For *Anthericum calyculatum* L. (≡ *Tofieldia calyculata* (L.) Wahlenb.), Stearn (1957: 130–132) provided a very detailed analysis of the protologue, showing that Linnaeus had included four different species within his concept of the name. Current usage of the name is in the sense of a plant from Gotland but no material of this taxon is now extant in any of the Linnaean herbaria. In order to maintain usage of this name, Stearn therefore treated a collection (in K) he himself had made in Gotland (a so-called "topotype") as fixing the application of the name. Because this can only be treated as a neotype, its designation is contrary to Art. 9.11 (because original material for the name is in existence), and the name remains untypified. However, designation of a Séguier plate, cited in the protologue, as the lectotype maintains the desired usage, and this is formalised in Chapter 7.

In the case of some of the other species that Linnaeus had seen in Öland and Gotland in 1741, Stearn (1973b: 7–12) treated the localities given by Linnaeus in his account of his travels there as the type localities for these names. However, there are difficulties with this procedure in that, for some of these names, no original material from the islands is extant. Further, the protologues often include other records and original material from places other than these Baltic islands, and the identification of a type locality must follow the designation of a type, rather than vice versa. For example, Stearn (1973b: 7–9, 11) provided a detailed review of the protologue of *Geranium lucidum* L. ("Habitat in Europae rupibus umbrosis") and discussed Linnaeus' account of finding the plant in Gotland. Stearn treated Torsborgen in Gotland as the restricted type locality, and noted the existence of 858.72 (LINN), but did not refer to it as the type specimen. Although this collection was subsequently designated as the type by Ghafoor (1978: 43), it shows no annotation associating it with Gotland, and it may just as easily have come from somewhere else.

Existing Typifications

The Code states that the author who first designates a lectotype or neotype must be followed (Art. 9.17) and a significant part of this study has involved extensive literature surveys in order to locate relevant statements, and to scrutinise their qualification as type designations. This has been no small task and has fallen into two parts. The first was to assess whether a published statement fulfills the requirements of Art. 7.10–11 (and 9.20–21) (i.e. has the author clearly indicated his or her intention to treat a specimen or illustration as the type?). The second has been to assess whether this choice fulfills other requirements of the Code (e.g. that a proposed lectotype specimen must have been available to the author of the name it typifies when it was published (its duplicates excepted), or that a neotype is not being proposed when original material is in existence).

Statements that could qualify as typifications of Linnaean names are widely scattered through the biological literature, and no previous attempt has been made to catalogue them. While some can be found in the mainstream botanical literature, particularly in monographs and the more specialist taxonomic and nomenclatural literature (e.g. *Taxon*), many can be found in floristic works, some almost monographic in scope (e.g. *Fl. Neotropica*) and others much narrower in their coverage (e.g. *Fl. Valle Tehuacán-Cuicatlán*), and less widely available. Typifications can be found in highly specialist journals (e.g. *Boxwood Bull.*, *Natl. Cact. Succ. J.*), published Abstracts (*9th Pacific Sci. Congr. Abstr.*) and book reviews (e.g. Harley 1982: 86, typifying *Origanum maru* L.), and made in a wide array of languages, both living and dead (e.g. *Flora Iranica*, in Latin).

A number of changes to the Code have tightened the rules connected with typification, making it easier to decide if a typification has been made. Some of the most significant changes were introduced in the Berlin Code (Greuter & al. 1988). Principal among these were the retroactive requirements that a typification had to be effectively published (Art. 8.2 – now 7.10) and that it had to include the use of the term "type" or an equivalent (Art. 8.3 – now 7.11). The latter finally removed the possibility that a name could be typified merely by the exclusion of all but one of its constituent elements (sometimes known as the residue method).

Another new provision in the Berlin Code included the need to specify the place of preservation of a designated lectotype or neotype from 1 January 1990 (now Art. 9.20). The subsequent Tokyo Code (Greuter & al. 1994) introduced the epitype concept. The latter has proved particularly valuable in dealing with older names where type specimens or illustrations are so poor or inadequate as to make a confident identification impossible. Additionally, an earlier provision allowing descriptions to serve as types was deleted. The introduction in the St Louis Code (Greuter & al. 2000) of a provision allowing a type reference to duplicates from a single gathering (several specimens collected simultaneously) to be accepted as a priorable typification (Art. 9.14) has also been beneficial, particularly in dealing with typifications using material in the Hermann herbarium (BM). Some specimens which appear to be part of a single gathering are often scattered through several of four bound volumes of this herbarium, and earlier authors, in treating this material as the lectotype, frequently did not distinguish between individual specimens in different volumes. While their intention was frequently clear, their type designations were often questionable, but Art. 9.14 clarifies the circumstances under which they can be accepted. In addition, clarification on the status of illustrations as types removed any suggestion that uncited specimens should necessarily take precedence over them in typification. The Code now provides explicit guidance to the circumstances under which the incorrect use of terms such as holotype, lectotype and neotype can be corrected. It also rules that, from 1 January 2001, new type designations must use the terms "lectotype" or "neotype" or an equivalent (Art. 9.21), along with the words "designated here" or an equivalent (Art. 7.11), in order to avoid accidental typifications. These new provisions have been immensely helpful in clarifying the nomenclatural soup, and simplifying the Linnaean Project's task.

While the non-retroactive provisions among the innovations are very beneficial for present and future typifications, they cannot help with the interpretation of earlier type statements.

Although the type concept was not admitted to the formal International Rules until 1935, the type concept nevertheless traces its roots back to the 19th century. Consequently, there are numerous 19th century statements by botanists that need to be assessed as possible typifications because the Code does not provide any starting point date for typifications. This has allowed for considerable variability in approach to the acceptance of earlier statements as effecting typification, and this in turn leads to difficulties in establishing priority of choice (as demanded by Art. 9.17). Where competing type choices are taxonomically distinct, serious nomenclatural consequences may follow. Some guidance can be derived from opinions of the relevant Nomenclature Committees of the International Association for Plant Taxonomy (IAPT). The Committee for Spermatophyta (Brummitt 1996: 671), for example, expressed a majority that the hypothetical phrase "*Smith 123* is the basis of the name" is equivalent to "type" for the purposes of Art. 7.11. However, this opinion was formed from a consideration of only a few, hypothetical cases rather than being based on a more general survey involving a large number of real names.

Three of Linnaeus' original herbarium cabinets accommodated in one of the large pieces of furniture that James Edward Smith commissioned to hold them.

James Edward Smith, the first owner of Linnaeus' accumulated library and herbarium, wrote extensively on the collections he had acquired, chiefly in the publications of the Linnean Society of London (of which he was the first President), and later in Rees' *Cyclopedia*, to which he contributed much of the botanical content. Smith's statements regarding Linnaean names and specimens do not amount to formal typification, partly because of the syntax he used, but primarily because he was not using a nomenclatural type concept. For example, although he (Smith 1791) frequently discussed specimens "It appears that Linnaeus described this grass [*Anthoxanthum paniculatum*] from the specimen in Burser's Herbarium only", this is not accepted as a formal typification. In 1815, Smith wrote on *Scutellaria integrifolia* L. [sub *S. teucriifolia*] "Such is the plant intended as his [Linnaeus'] *integrifolia*, which he received from Kalm, along with another specimen, pasted on the same paper", which Reveal (1989: 517) believed to be the earliest typification of that name. However, Smith's statements appear to fall short of formal, modern typification requirements, and the Committee for Spermatophyta (see Brummitt 1993: 695) concluded that Smith had made no formal type choice.

Others also studied the Linnaean collection in this period, including Smith's friend William Dawson Turner; who published very detailed observations on Linnaeus' algal collections (e.g. Turner 1802) but, again, Turner was not working using a modern type concept. While his observations continue to be of interest (e.g. see Spencer & al. in press), they cannot be accepted as typification statements.

After Smith's death, the Linnaean collections (which had been housed at Smith's home in Norwich) returned to London in 1829 following their purchase by the Linnean Society, where they became more readily available to interested scientists. Early visitors who studied parts of the collection included Asa Gray (1840a) who published observations (1840b: 684), for example on *Acer saccharinum* L. ("wholly established by Linnaeus upon a specimen (leaves only) received from Kalm"). Jackson (1922: 27–30) lists a number of publications that appeared between 1825 and 1921 which were based on studies of the Linnaean herbarium.

By the middle of the 19th century, the type method was developing and, in 1865, in a discussion of *Senecio elegans* L., Kippist (1865: 361) clearly referred to one of the Linnaean sheets as "the type specimen" and this appears to be a valid choice, pre-dating that of Belcher (1994: 617), who chose a Clifford sheet (BM).

In the latter part of the 19th century, greater attention was being paid to the application of old names but the syntax of the statements made can cause uncertainty. While the use of "type" or "type specimen" makes a decision easy, because the situation is clear in relation to Art. 7.10, deciding which forms of words are satisfactory as "equivalent" to "type" is a more difficult matter. For example, commenting on *Commelina erecta* L., Clarke (1881: 181) stated "Species hoc loco in figura Dillenii citata . . . stabilita est", while Gray (1881a: t. 6594) stated that *Clematis crispa* L. was "wholly founded upon" another figure from Dillenius' *Hortus Elthamensis*. Britten (1898: 302) subsequently stated that Linnaeus had "established this species [i.e. *Clematis crispa*] on . . . " this figure. Gray (1882) was using expressions such as "wholly characterized . . . upon" (*Aster miser* L.), "is really founded wholly on" (*A. novi-belgii* L.) and "founded wholly on Gronovius' account" (*A. rigidus* L.), while Trimen (1894: 315) contributes "the whole foundation" (*Hedyotis herbacea* L.).

1274.69

Delesseria sinuosa J.Ag.

Caroline Rosenberg

A.

B.

Fucus 21.
A. Frons
B. foliolum cum
Fructificatione

diversus a F. alato.

No. 21.

pinnatus   cristatus   e.et corymbiferus Gmelin

Explicit use of the term "type" now became more common and was employed by authors such as Britton (1891, 1893, 1894), Clarke (1894), Trimen (1895), Howe (1897), Britten (1898) and Greene (1899), but difficulties of interpretation continue well into the 20th century with the use of phrases such as "based on", "partly based on", "mainly based on" and "wholly based on", and "rests on" (Blake 1918: 49) etc. In many cases, expressions such as "based on" are, in any case, purely the author's opinion, and study often shows them to be simply untrue (for example, because additional original material for the name is clearly in existence).

With such a range of expressions used, and in the absence of guidance in the Code, it has been difficult to find a rigorously consistent approach to the interpretation of these earlier type statements. In accordance with Art. 7.10, we have accepted statements using "type" as potential typifications, the earliest of which, at species rank, dates from 1865. However, we have generally not accepted as potential typifications statements that use simply "based on", "founded upon" or "established on". They are capable of such a degree of qualification ("partly", "partially", "mainly", "wholly") as to make them almost impossible to interpret in any consistent way.

Precision of Type Statements

Where authors use the modern family of types (holotype, lectotype, neotype etc.), it is relatively straightforward to understand their intentions (but see below under "Correctability of Type Statements"). While Art. 7.11 makes it clear that the simple use of the term "type" can effect typification, there can be considerable variation in the precision with which type statements refer to the intended specimen or illustration.

Statements such as "Lectotype (designated here by Reveal): *Clayton 549*, Herb. Linn. No. 370.7 (LINN; iso- BM)" (for *Smyrnium integerrimum* L.) leave no doubt as to an intent to typify or the intended specimen (or gathering). However, the Linnaean herbarium (LINN) only comparatively recently acquired the numbering system employed by Savage (1945), and earlier authors clearly would have to find other ways of referring to specimens in the collection. Fawcett & Rendle (1910, 1914, 1920, 1926, 1936), for example, made great use of the LINN, Clifford (BM) and Hermann (BM) collections in their treatment of the *Flora of Jamaica*, and frequently referred to specimens, often in the form "Specimen in BM, Type in Herb. Linn.". Their intent here is clear but leaves the question of whether the intended specimen in LINN can be located. In some cases, more than one specimen may be associated with the name in question, which will generally preclude the statement being accepted as a formal typification. If, however, the candidate collections are part of a single gathering, then such a statement can be accepted as a typification under Art. 9.15 (with the possibility of it being restricted to one sheet or

Opposite: Some herbarium sheets bear diverse material. The lowermost four specimens of *Fucus* (*sensu* Linnaeus) on this sheet (1274.69 LINN) evidently came from König, who mentioned them in his letter to Linnaeus dated 27 Sep 1766 (L3793). Material at the top of the sheet received from Rosenberg was probably added later by J.E. Smith, as was the small watercolour.

3

1140.3

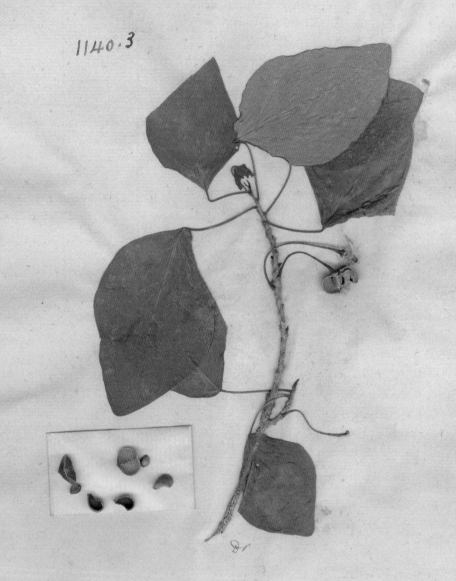

FLORA OF JAMAICA.

Phyllanthus glabellus
Fawc. & Rendle
in Journ. Bot. LVII, 68 (1919)
Det. W. FAWCETT AND A. B. RENDLE.

1919.

croton glabellum

croton 7. Dr. 378

specimen subsequently). In other cases, there may be only a single collection in LINN associated with the name and, under these circumstances, a statement such as Fawcett & Rendle's is accepted as a lectotypification. For example, Ehrendorfer (1962: 16), discussing *Valantia cruciata* L., referred to "das Typus-Exemplar im Herbar LINNÉ" without specifying a sheet number, but as 1219.11(LINN) is the only sheet there associated with this name, his typification statement is accepted.

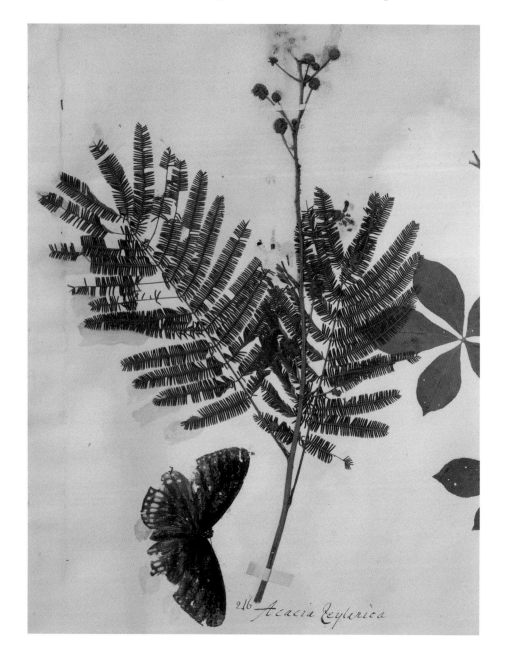

Left: The lectotype of *Mimosa pennata* L. from the herbarium of Paul Hermann (see p. 56)

Opposite page: This Patrick Browne collection from Jamaica was named *Croton "glabellum"* (correctly *"glabellus"*) by Linnaeus, and Fawcett & Rendle (1920: 260) stated "Type in LINN" for this name. As this is the only material in the herbarium associated with *C. glabellus*, their statement is accepted as typifying the name (now referred to *Phyllanthus glabellus* (L.) Fawc. & Rendle).

A similar situation exists with the Swedish Linnaean herbarium (S) and the Clifford herbarium (BM), where the current cataloguing systems are also recent and so omission of specimen numbers should not preclude the acceptance of typification statements, provided it is unambiguously clear which sheet or specimen is intended as the type. This general approach has been extended to all relevant herbaria. In the Hermann herbarium (BM), which comprises four volumes of specimens and one of drawings, a Linnaean name associated with *Flora Zeylanica* may be linked with more than one specimen, often distributed through the pages of separate volumes. Despite this, the material frequently appears to be a part of a single gathering so, where this is believed to be the case, general statements such as "Type in Herb. Hermann" are accepted under Art. 9.15 and are frequently restricted to material on one page, or a single specimen, later. For example, for *Mimosa pennata* L., Brenan & Exell (1957: 101) treated Hermann material from Ceylon (BM) as the type, but did not distinguish between the specimens in vol. 3: 7 and vol. 4: 37. However, as this material appears to be part of a single gathering, these authors are accepted as having typified the name (Art. 9.15), with their original choice restricted to the material in vol. 3 by Nielsen (1981: 66), illustrated on p. 55.

Correctability of Previously Published Type Statements

Terminological difficulties can arise from more recent provisions in the Code. Art. 9.8 is a comparatively recent addition which clarifies the circumstances under which the incorrect usage of a term such as "lectotype" can be corrected to e.g. "neotype". This is undoubtedly generally helpful, and has been utilised extensively in this study, particularly in the correction of "holotype" to "lectotype". However, two potential difficulties arise.

The first involves incorrect statements involving syntypes. Art. 9.8 allows for the correction of terms "defined in the *Code* (Art. 9.1–9.7) as denoting a type" where they have been used incorrectly. Art. 9.4 defines the term "syntype", which is therefore one of these correctable categories. Whereas the terms holotype, lectotype and neotype all indicate the intention of an author to recognise a sole nomenclatural type, a syntype is, by definition, either a cited specimen in the absence of a holotype (i.e. not equivalent to a lectotype, though a candidate for selection as such) or "any one of two or more specimens simultaneously designated as types". As discussed earlier, syntypes are comparatively uncommon for Linnaean names but authors sometimes wrongly indicate as syntypes specimens (and occasionally even illustrations) that are, in fact, part of the original material. Bearing in mind the definition of a syntype, we do not accept such statements as correctable from "syntype" to "lectotype" because we do not believe this can be justified as reflecting the author's intent. We are aware of numerous instances where authors have used "syntype" to indicate authentic material they had seen but which they did not wish, at that point, to formally make a lectotype (often because they had been unable to study other candidate material). For example, in the case of *Teucrium asiaticum* L., Rosselló &

Sáez (2000: 104) incorrectly indicated 722.17 (LINN) as a syntype, rather than part of the original material. As a syntype is not, by definition, the sole type of a name (unlike a holotype, lectotype or neotype), their statement is not accepted as correctable to lectotype under Art. 9.8.

The second area of difficulty arises where an element from the original material for a name is incorrectly stated to be the holotype or just the "type", rather than a lectotype. Prior to 1 January 2001, this would simply be correctable under Art. 9.8. However, since then, under Art. 7.11, lectotypification must be accompanied by the phrase "here designated" or an equivalent, but this is not a statement that is relevant for a holotype (see Art. 7 Note 2). This means that correction of "holotype" to "lectotype" under Art. 9.8 is no longer possible, a point recently clarified in the Vienna Code (Art. 9 Note 4). In accord with this, incorrect indications of holotype of this sort have not been accepted as correctable errors here. For example, Cristóbal (2001: 176) indicated 1074.5 (LINN) (as "1974.5") as the holotype of *Helicteres angustifolia* L. While there do not appear to be grounds for accepting it as a holotype, this collection does appear to be original material for the name and eligible for selection as a lectotype. However, this choice was published after 1 Jan 2001 and so the omission of the phrase "designated here" or an equivalent means that this choice is not effective.

Standard Specimens

We have encountered some difficulty in the interpretation and application of statements made by Epling (1929), reiterated by McClintock & Epling (1942), and adopted by a number of later authors. Epling used the term "standard specimen", deliberately avoiding the word "type". He even stated (1929: 1) that ". . . the identity of historic types is frequently a matter of speculation; their determination frequently impossible" and went on to say that he had sought to ". . . fix upon certain herbarium specimens which may serve as standards, if not always types . . . ". It is quite clear, therefore, that Epling's "standard specimens" were never intended to serve as nomenclatural types and that he was instead attempting to interpret Linnaean names in the sense of an original element correlating with current usage of the name. Consequently Epling's reference to standard specimens is not accepted as effecting typification. The term "standard species", as used by Hitchcock & Green (1929) in the context of establishing the types of Linnaean generic names, is however to be treated as equivalent to "type" (Art. 7.11, Ex. 10).

Problematic Publications

Some publications present difficulties in interpreting the type statements that appear within them. For example, Kerguélen (1975), in a publication dealing with the taxonomy and nomenclature of the members of the Poaceae occurring in France, provided much valuable information on the types of names described by varied authors. However, for the many Linnaean names included, the relevant statement is almost invariably in the form "Type: «in Europae uliginosis». – Europe (LINN)". These statements have not been accepted as putative typifications because it seems clear that they appear in this form irrespective of the number of specimens at LINN that can be associated with the name in question. Indeed, the statement also occurs when there is clearly no material in LINN that can possibly be associated with the name (e.g. in the case of *Poa pilosa* L.). Additionally, he indicates (with the symbol "!") type material that he has seen, and this symbol does not appear associated with material at LINN. Consequently, Kerguélen's Linnaean type statements seem not to comply with Art. 7.11 of the ICBN, in that it seems clear that "the type" was not "definitely accepted as such by the typifying author".

Generic Names

As already mentioned, it was not until 1930 that the Cambridge Congress formally agreed that the application of scientific names was to be governed by the use of "types". Much early controversy had revolved around methods of establishing type species for generic names. Many of Linnaeus' genera contained species that later authors considered to belong in other genera, so in dismembering such a Linnaean genus, it was necessary to decide which part should retain the original name. The identity of the type species would establish the way in which the generic name was to be applied.

Entries in Chapter 7 include an indication of those Linnaean species names that act as types for the 1,313 Linnaean generic names. In most cases, these choices have been uncontroversial but, for 150, choices have been published that conflict, chiefly between those made by Britton and co-workers (e.g. Britton & Brown, 1913) under the American Code and those made by Hitchcock & Green (1929) early in the 20th century (cf. Heller & Stearn 1958: 105, McNeill & al. 1987).

Following a proposal at the Berlin Congress in 1987, a Special Committee on Lectotypification was set up to look at the problems that flowed from the wording of what was then Art. 8. From an analysis of the type choices made by Britton & al., aimed at mitigating the potentially disruptive effects of having to accept either all American Code typifications or none of them, a proposal was made by this Committee for the conservation of 72 generic names, with appropriate conserved types (see Jarvis 1992). These proposals were unfortunately not dealt with directly by the Tokyo Congress (1993), and were eventually referred, via the General Committee, to the relevant Permanent Committees (Bryophyta, Pteridophyta and

Opposite: Pier Antonio Micheli's plate (*Nova plantarum genera*: t. 9. 1729) is the lectotype of *Trichosanthes anguina* L., this binomial (along with the plate) also being the type of the genus *Trichosanthes* L.

Auspiciis Joannis Altovita Patricii Florentini

Spermatophyta respectively). As a result, the proposals relating to *Riccia*, *Lonchitis* and *Trichomanes* were fairly quickly resolved but the numerous Spermatophyte names presented greater difficulties.

In the meantime, changes to Art. 10, Ex. 7 (a "voted example" and therefore binding rather than advisory), in the Saint Louis Code (Greuter & al. 2000) made it clear that American Code choices are to be superseded, making some of the proposals made by Jarvis unnecessary, but others advisable. The General Committee eventually voted on these proposals for conservation immediately prior to the Vienna Congress, and those approved appear in Appendix III of the Vienna Code (McNeill & al. 2006). For a review of the history of these proposals, and their eventual fate, see the relevant report of the General Committee (Barrie 2006).

Glossary

authority – the name of the author (abbreviated following Brummitt & Powell 1992), appended to the *binomial* name which he or she published, e.g. *Lotus mauritanicus* L., "L." indicating Linnaeus. Where two author names appear, as in *Indigofera mauritanica* "(L.) Thunb.", this is an indication that Thunberg transferred an earlier name (*Lotus mauritanicus*), described by the author in parenthesis (Linnaeus), to a different genus (*Indigofera*).

autonym – a name established automatically. For example, the publication of *Lotus corniculatus* var. *tenuifolius* L. (1753) automatically created *Lotus corniculatus* L. var. *corniculatus* to accommodate the "typical" part of the species (see Art. 6.8), even though this varietal name does not appear in *Species Plantarum*.

basionym – a previously published legitimate name or epithet-bringing synonym from which a new name is formed. *Lotus mauritanicus* L. is the basionym of *Indigofera mauritanica* (L.) Thunb.

binomial – the name of a species, composed of two parts in Latin: the name of the genus followed by a single species (specific) name (or *epithet*), e.g. *Lichen caperatus* L.

cytotype – where a species displays significant variation in its chromosome numbers or structures, these different forms may be termed cytotypes. In species such as these, it may be important to establish the cytotype to which the type specimen belongs, in order to apply infraspecific names correctly.

diagnosis – a short phrase, or polynomial, usually in Latin for Linnaean names, giving the characters by which the author believes the taxon can be distinguished. Also known as a diagnostic phrase name, or *nomen specificum legitimum*.

epithet – a single word, usually applied to a species, which when appended to the name of a genus, forms a binomial.

epitype – a specimen or illustration selected to serve as an interpretative type when the identity of the primary type (e.g. the lectotype) cannot be precisely established.

generitype – the type of the name of a genus (which is the type of the name of a species). For purposes of designation or citation of a type, the species name alone suffices, i.e. it is considered as the full equivalent of its type (Art. 10.1).

heterotypic synonym – a synonym based on a type different from that of the accepted name.

holotype – the one specimen or illustration used by an author in publishing a new name.

homonym – a name spelled exactly like another name published for a taxon of the same rank and based on a different type. The later of two such names will be illegitimate.

homotypic synonym – a synonym based on the same type as that of another name at the same rank.

IBC – International Botanical Congress.

ICBN – International Code of Botanical Nomenclature.

iconotype – sometimes used to indicate an illustration that serves as a type.

iso- – indicating a duplicate, hence isolectotype, isoneotype.

isotype – a duplicate of a *holotype*.

L. – authority abbreviation for Linnaeus.

lectotype – a specimen or illustration designated from the original material as the *nomenclatural type* when no holotype was indicated.

monospecific – of a genus, which contains only a single species.

monotypic – see *monospecific*.

neotype – a specimen or illustration selected to serve as a nomenclatural type when all of the material upon which the name was based is missing.

nomenclatural type – see *type*.

nomen specificum legitimum – see *diagnosis*.

nomen ambiguum/nomina ambigua – a name(s) whose application is uncertain or unknown.

original material – those specimens and illustrations from which a *lectotype* can be chosen.

phrase name – see *diagnosis*.

protologue – everything associated with a name at its valid publication, i.e. description or diagnosis, illustrations, references, synonymy, geographical data, citation of specimens, discussion and comments.

rank – any position in a taxonomic hierarchy – order, family, genus, species and variety are examples of different ranks.

single gathering – several specimens collected simultaneously.

superfluous name – a name applied to a taxon circumscribed by its author to include the type of an earlier name (the name of which ought to have been adopted).

syntype – any specimen cited in the protologue when no holotype was designated, or any of two or more specimens simultaneously designated as types (Art. 9.4).

taxon – a taxonomic group at any rank.

topotype – any collection of a taxon made at its type locality.

type – a specimen or illustration to which the name of a taxon is permanently attached.

type method – establishing the correct application of names through the use of types.

typotype – herbarium material from which a type illustration was prepared.

typus – Latin for *type*.

voucher specimen – herbarium material believed to be associated with an illustration, or a specimen preserved when a part of it is used for more detailed study (e.g. micromorphological, chemical, cytological, molecular).

❦ Chapter 2 ❧
A BRIEF LIFE OF LINNAEUS

This chapter provides a chronology of Linnaeus' life but it is not an attempt to repeat the fuller accounts given by Fries (1903, adapted and published in English by Jackson, 1923), Hagberg (1952), Blunt (1971), Stearn (1957) and many others. Rather, while noting the primary events of his life (dates are given in New Style), it concentrates on occasions when he encountered significant scientists or collectors, and studied collections that contributed to his knowledge of the plants he named.

An Early Interest in Natural History

Carl Linnaeus was born on 23 May 1707 at Råshult, near Stenbrohult, in Småland, a province in southern Sweden. He grew up surrounded by wild plants in the marshland and meadows near Lake Möckeln, and evidently developed an early interest in them and their names. His interest was fostered by Johan Stensson Rothman (1684–1763), a local physician, who encouraged him to train as a doctor, and instructed him in botany and the principles of medicine. In particular, Rothman introduced Linnaeus to concepts discussed in a publication (*Sermo de Structura Florum*, 1718) by the Frenchman Sébastien Vaillant (see also Bernasconi & Taiz 2002), who recognised the sexuality of plants. This work had a dramatic effect on Linnaeus' adolescent imagination by revealing that sex comparable to that of animals existed in flowers. It led him to study flowers closely, examining hundreds to discover how they managed procreation. These observations, translated into human terms, formed the basis of his so-called "Sexual System", in which he classified plants into major groups based on the numbers of their genital organs, their stamens and stigmas. His desire to catalogue the natural world manifested itself at an early age.

Lund 1727–1728

Determined to study medicine, Carl Linnaeus entered the University of Lund in August 1727 and, though disappointed by the quality of teaching, was again fortunate in finding a benefactor in Dr Kilian Stobaeus (1690–1742), who offered free bed and board as well as lectures. Stobaeus also gave him access to his fine library, and his natural history collections, which included dried plants, glued and mounted on sheets of paper, something that Linnaeus had never seen before. Linnaeus soon began to make a similar herbarium of his own.

Portrait of Linnaeus as a bridegroom. Copy (1906) by Jean Haagen of a portrait by J.H. Scheffel (1739). Oil on canvas

Uppsala 1728–1735

Transferring to Uppsala University in 1728, Linnaeus found the quality of teaching and the facilities were no better than in Lund. The two elderly professors of medicine, Olof Rudbeck the Younger (1660–1740) and Lars Roberg (1664–1742), were unable to obtain funds to maintain the university hospital; there was no longer any clinical teaching and the university botanic garden was poorly stocked. However, in the spring of 1729, Linnaeus was befriended again, this time by Olof Celsius the Elder (1670–1756), a theologian and naturalist (and uncle to Anders Celsius of thermometer fame) who had been surprised to find a student studying in the botanic garden. He was even more surprised to find that the young man knew the names of the plants. Celsius offered him room and board and the use of his library.

By now, Linnaeus recorded that his own herbarium comprised hundreds of specimens of Swedish plants (Lindberg 1958), and his familiarity with the native flora enabled him to help Celsius with the latter's flora of Uppland, for which Linnaeus contributed herbarium specimens, some of which can now be found in Celsius' own herbarium (UPS, S – see http://www-hotel.uu.se/evolmuseum/fytotek/Celsius/Celdex.htmref.). On New Year's Day, 1730, Linnaeus presented to Celsius a short thesis, written in Swedish, entitled *Praeludia Sponsalia Plantarum* (published much later as a dissertation in 1746), in which the sexual lives of the plants were described, inspired by Vaillant's observations. Much impressed, Celsius evidently showed it to Rudbeck, who decided that Linnaeus should be appointed to give demonstrations in the botanic garden to the students in the summer of 1730. This marked the start of his long teaching career, no fewer than 23 of his own students themselves becoming professors.

In Uppsala in March 1729, Linnaeus had met another medical student, Peter Artedi, who was just as interested in natural history. Artedi was especially interested in fishes, and he and Linnaeus became close friends and colleagues. Together they worked out a plan for studying and documenting the natural world between them, Artedi to deal with fishes, reptiles, amphibians, and the Apiaceae (Umbelliferae) among the plants, and Linnaeus the birds, insects and the plant world in general. Artedi possessed a very thorough, methodical, philosophical and scholarly mind and was educated in modern languages and the classics. There seems little doubt that the methods for the diagnosis, description and naming of organisms (apart from the binomial system of nomenclature) which Linnaeus used were developed by these two young men in co-operation.

Dissatisfied with Tournefort's widely used classification of plants, Linnaeus began to make one of his own, based on numbers of stamens and stigmas. By the age of 24, Linnaeus had laid the foundation for much of his later work, including preparing drafts of the works that would later be published as *Bibliotheca Botanica* (1736), *Critica Botanica* (1737), *Genera Plantarum* (1737) and *Classes Plantarum* (1738).

The Lapland Journey, May–October 1732

As a young man, Rudbeck had travelled in Lapland, but most of his extensive botanical and zoological collections and observations perished in 1702 in the terrible fire which raged across Uppsala and destroyed three-quarters of its buildings. Distraught at the loss, Rudbeck had abandoned his Lapland project, turning instead to philology. However, his descriptions of his Lapland experiences evidently encouraged Linnaeus to make his own exploration of the region.

Setting out alone from Uppsala in May 1732, on horseback, Linnaeus travelled north-east along the coast, taking 11 days to reach Umeå, collecting plants, animals and minerals as he went. On the way, near Gävle, he encountered the plant which he was later to name *Linnaea borealis* in his own honour. At Iggesund, he visited an iron foundry, and met his first Lapland people [Sami]. In Umeå he called on the Provincial Governor, who was himself interested in natural curiosities, and kept caged crossbills and a tame otter.

Turning inland, he explored the area occupied by the Lycksele Sami. He continued collecting and recording whatever aroused his curiosity, despite constant rain. He collected mosses and lichens, and observed that people wore broad collars made of birch bark as protection against the rain. He eventually reached Jokkmokk, on the Arctic Circle, where he studied the nearby pearl fishery – later, he was to investigate ways of improving the low incidence of pearl-bearing mussels. After crossing the watershed into (modern) Norway, he spent a few days on the coast at Rörstad before retracing his steps to Luleå. By the beginning of August he had reached Torneå on what is now the border between Sweden and Finland and spent six weeks in the vicinity, including crossing the Arctic Circle again towards Vittangi. By mid-September, Linnaeus set out for home, travelling down the Finnish seaboard to Turku, from where he sailed back to Sweden.

Linnaeus kept a journal of his Lapland journey but never published it himself. An English translation appeared in 1811, but the Swedish original remained unpublished until 1888. An encyclopedic account of the journey, with maps, is provided by Hellbom & al. (2003) and Fries & al. (2003). The journal itself is full of interesting observations about everything and everyone with whom Linnaeus came into contact. The journey was the most adventurous that he ever made; it has been assessed by his fellow-countrymen as the most fruitful single scientific expedition ever made in Sweden, both for its immediate botanical results and its influence on

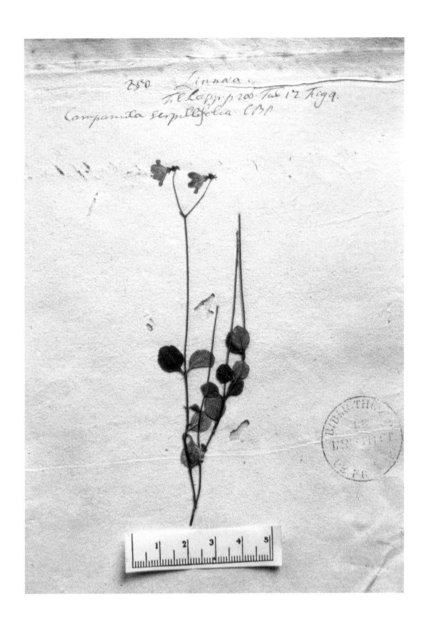

Specimen of *Linnaea borealis* L. (Institut de France, Paris) collected by Linnaeus on his Lapland journey in 1732.

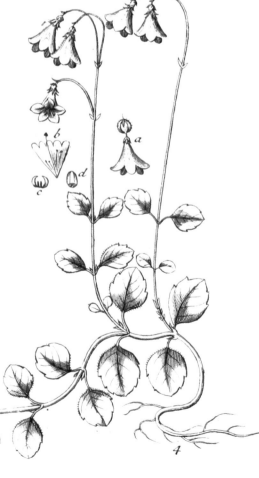

Linnaeus' depiction of the same species in his own *Flora Lapponica* (t. 12, f. 4. 1737).

A woodblock made by R.T. Austin showing the carrying of a boat, commissioned by James Edward Smith and copied from Linnaeus' original drawing, used to illustrate Smith's English translation of Linnaeus' Lapland diary (Smith 1811).

Linnaeus' later career. It led to the publication in 1737 of his *Flora Lapponica* which is of major significance for the nomenclature of Arctic-Alpine species. The Lapland specimens, on which this was based, are still in existence, in Paris.

That Christmas, Linnaeus travelled with fellow student Claes Sohlberg (whose father was a mining inspector) to Falun, where he spent several months, during which he visited the copper and silver mines and the smelters. The Governor of Dalecarlia, Baron Nils Reuterholm, subsequently commissioned Linnaeus to undertake a survey of the Province. Along with seven others, including Sohlberg, the party left Falun in early July 1734 and headed towards Røros in Norway, returning in mid-August. Reluctant to return to Uppsala, Linnaeus remained in Falun teaching until Sohlberg's father suggested that Linnaeus should accompany Claes to the Netherlands in the following year, for which he would be paid a salary of 300 copper dalers. Dutch academia was buoyant and both men would benefit from the experience. Linnaeus gratefully accepted and the two men arrived at the Swedish port of Helsingborg on 18 April 1735.

Linnaeus' signature and seal, dated 2 July 1734, in his journal from the Dalecarlia journey

To the Netherlands, 1735–1738

Sohlberg and Linnaeus reached Hamburg on 27 April, where they spent nearly three weeks. A favourable review of Linnaeus and his works which had appeared in *Hamburgerische Berichte* led to his meeting many local scholars. These included a lawyer, Johann Heinrich von Spreckelsen, who had a large garden with an orangery in which Linnaeus recorded having seen 45 kinds of *Alöe* and 50 different mesembryanthemums (Aizoaceae). He also had a fine library from which Linnaeus was able to borrow a copy of Blair's *Botanick Essays* (1718). The two Swedes reached Amsterdam in late May. They visited the Botanic Garden, and briefly met Johannes Burman, the young Director and Professor of Botany at the University, and Albert Seba, a renowned apothecary who had amassed several cabinets of curiosities and had recently started to publish an account of his collections.

Sohlberg and Linnaeus sailed to the small town of Harderwijk, arriving on 17 June, in order for Linnaeus to obtain a doctor's degree at the accommodating, but now extinct, university. In this fishing town it was possible to obtain a degree within a week, and the day after he arrived, Linnaeus submitted a thesis he had written on "A new hypothesis as to the cause of intermittent fevers". A public defence was made successfully a few days later, and with it the award of Doctor of Medicine.

The time spent in the Netherlands was to prove a highly productive era for Linnaeus, and he was fortunate in his friends, benefactors and contacts. In Leiden he initially failed to get an audience with the great Herman Boerhaave who, though now in his late sixties and semi-retired, was still practising medicine, and lecturing. However, through Johan Gronovius, a local doctor and botanist to whom Linnaeus had shown his manuscript of *Systema Naturae*, he obtained a letter of introduction. After initial mistrust of the somewhat arrogant young Swede, Boerhaave warmed to Linnaeus and invited him to his estate at Oude-Poelgeest, where he had established an extensive arboretum which Linnaeus greatly admired.

In early July, Linnaeus was also delighted to meet again his student friend Peter Artedi who had arrived, almost penniless, in Leiden from London where he had been studying. In Amsterdam, Linnaeus introduced him to Seba, who was then working on the third volume of his *Thesaurus*, a lavishly illustrated work on natural history, which was to include the fishes. Impressed with Artedi's knowledge, Seba agreed to employ him.

Gronovius thought highly of Linnaeus' *Systema Naturae* manuscript and he and Isaac Lawson, a young Scot studying medicine in Leiden, offered to pay for its printing. This slim, and now extremely rare, work which appeared in 1735, was immediately a success, leading to a second edition in 1740, and a succession of ever-expanding editions which continued after Linnaeus' death.

Linnaeus returned to Amsterdam, this time with an introduction to Burman from Boerhaave. Linnaeus now made a more favourable impression and Burman, who was working on his *Thesaurus Zeylanicus*, an account of the plants of Ceylon (1737), persuaded Linnaeus to stay and assist him with this book over the winter. However, within a few months, in late September, Linnaeus had moved to the house of George Clifford, a wealthy Anglo-Dutch banker who owned an enormous estate, the

A plate from Johannes Burman's *Thesaurus Zeylanicus* (t. 80. 1737), the figure to the right (f. 1) being the lectotype of *Ocimum frutescens* L. (= *Perilla frutescens* (L.) Britton)

Hartekamp, near Haarlem. There he became Clifford's physician, and took charge of the huge collection of plants in cultivation in the gardens and glasshouses there. He also had time to complete two more books on which he had been working, *Fundamenta Botanica* (1736) and *Bibliotheca Botanica* (1736), the latter dedicated to Burman.

Tragically, a few days after Linnaeus moved to the Hartekamp, Artedi drowned after falling into a canal at night in Amsterdam. Linnaeus took over the task of ensuring that Artedi's work on fishes should not be lost and, with Clifford's patronage, he edited the surviving manuscripts to publish Artedi's *Ichthyologia* (1738).

Georg Dionysius Ehret, a fine botanical draughtsman, arrived at the Hartekamp just after Linnaeus, and showed Clifford some of his work, resulting in commissions for the plates that were later to appear in the *Hortus Cliffortianus*. He also produced a now famous drawing illustrating Linnaeus' Sexual System.

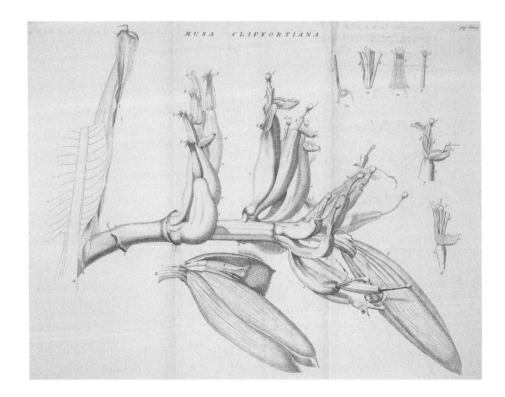

One of the two plates from Linnaeus' *Musa Cliffortiana* (1736), the lectotype of *Musa* × *paradisiaca* L.

Among the exotics growing in Clifford's glasshouses was a banana which Linnaeus, and the gardener Dietrich Nietzel, coaxed into flower – the first time this had been achieved in the Netherlands. Many botanists visited the garden to view this phenomenon, and Linnaeus produced a small book, *Musa Cliffortiana* (1736), illustrated with two plates engraved by A. vander Laan from drawings prepared by M. Hoffman, to mark this achievement.

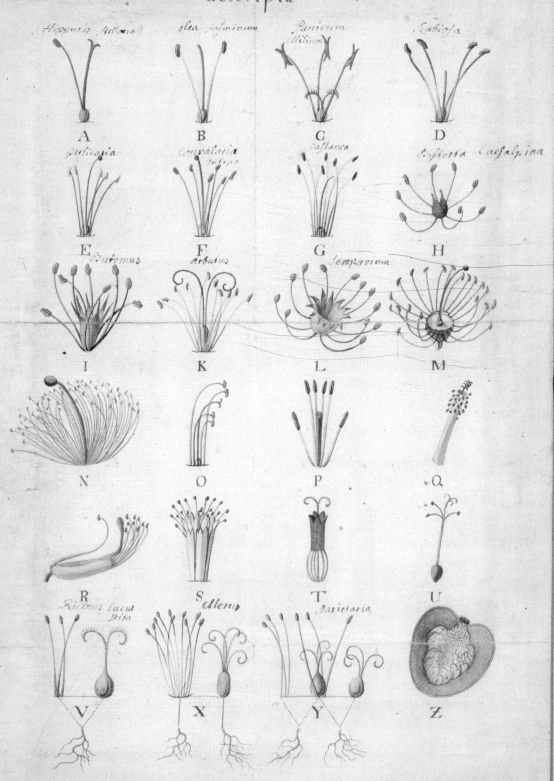

Doct: **LINNÆI**
METHODUS *plantarum* **SEXUALIS**
in **SYSTEMATE NATURÆ**
descripta

G. D. EHRET.
FECIT & EDIDIT
Lugd: bat: 1736.

On 21 July 1736, Linnaeus left for London carrying a letter of introduction to Sir Hans Sloane from Boerhaave. Sloane, now 76, and President of the Royal Society, was a man of wealth and enormous scientific stature, with a huge collection of natural history objects. Linnaeus was impressed with the scale of Sloane's collections, though less so with their organisation, which he described on his return to Holland as "all in chaos". He also visited Philip Miller at Chelsea Physic Garden, from whom he obtained both living plants for Clifford, and dried specimens collected by William Houstoun in Mexico. Linnaeus also met Peter Collinson, a mercer who had strong connections with North America and a lively interest in natural history, through whom many new plants reached England and with whom he was to maintain a correspondence until 1767. John Martyn, Professor of Botany at Cambridge, was also an acquaintance in London.

Linnaeus travelled to Oxford to meet Johann Jakob Dillenius, Sherardian Professor of Botany, a great authority on bryophytes and lichens. After one of Linnaeus' typically difficult initial meetings, Dillenius took to him, presenting him with a copy of his *Hortus Elthamensis* (1732) on his departure. In Oxford, Linnaeus also saw William Sherard's herbarium (though there seems to be little evidence that he studied it), and encountered Thomas Shaw (whose *Catalogus plantarum quas in variis Africae & Asiae partibus* appeared a few years later and from which Linnaeus cited a number of descriptions and illustrations in later works).

By the end of August, Linnaeus was back at the Hartekamp, and starting work on the *Hortus Cliffortianus*. This work, a catalogue of the plants known at the Hartekamp, occupied Linnaeus for nine months. The book is well served by the fine drawings made by Ehret and engravings by Jan Wandelaar. Printed in 1737 (though not distributed until the following year), *Hortus Cliffortianus* joined six other Linnaean books to be published in the Netherlands in that year, including *Genera Plantarum*, *Flora Lapponica* and *Critica Botanica*.

In autumn 1737, Linnaeus was persuaded by Adriaan van Royen, the director of the Botanic Garden in Leiden, to spend the winter of 1737–1738 with him, assisting in preparing a new system for the arrangement of the Hortus. He also helped Gronovius with his study of John Clayton's Virginian collections which were to be the basis of Gronovius' *Flora Virginica*. In May 1738, Linnaeus left for Paris, where he was chiefly in the company of Bernard de Jussieu, who was a demonstrator at the Jardin du Roi. He met Bernard's brother Antoine, who was Professor of Botany and, with Bernard, viewed the herbaria of Tournefort, the Jussieus and Surian. Linnaeus was also able to see the fine library of d'Isnard, and an excursion was made to Fontainebleau where he saw many

Opposite: Ehret's original drawing (1736) illustrating Linnaeus' Sexual System for plants

unfamiliar species, some of which he would encounter later on the Swedish island of Öland. He also met the Court Painter, Claude Aubriet, who had travelled in the Levant with Tournefort and whom Boerhaave had commissioned to make tracings of the original Plumier drawings of plants from the Antilles. Burman later used these as the basis for an edition of drawings. Linnaeus left France for the last time in July, travelling by sea to Helsingborg then on to Falun.

Throughout his life, Linnaeus was helped at crucial moments by offers of bed, board, study facilities and even employment by influential people. He later thanked his benefactors by naming genera after them, assuring them an enduring place in history. Genera named in this way include *Boerhavia, Burmannia, Celsia, Cliffortia, Gronovia, Lawsonia, Milleria, Rothmannia, Royena, Rudbeckia, Sloanea* and *Stobaea*.

Return to Sweden

Back in Sweden after these highly productive years, Linnaeus was dismayed to find himself an object of derision over his Sexual System. Many were shocked by its application to plants and it had been the subject of a particularly vitriolic attack by Johann Siegesbeck, a St Petersburg academician, in a short dissertation published in 1737 which had been widely publicised in Sweden. Other botanists were critical of his abandonment of earlier well-established generic names which he had substituted with ones of his own devising, and were particularly outraged at his re-use of other established names in an entirely new sense.

With no botanical positions available, Linnaeus set up in practice as a physician in Stockholm. Taken up by Count Carl Tessin, a patron of both the arts and sciences, Linnaeus was appointed Physician (Archiater) to the King and his practice flourished. In the same year, Linnaeus was one of the founder members of a new and influential Academy of Sciences "for the investigation of Mathematics, Natural History, Economics, Trade, Useful Arts and Manufacture", and was its first president.

Although medicine had become lucrative, enabling him to marry, Linnaeus' heart still lay with natural history. He had continued to correspond with botanists such as Johann Amman in St Petersburg, and had received many interesting specimens from him in the period between 1738 and 1740. In May 1741, after much wrangling, Linnaeus was appointed Professor of Medicine and Botany at Uppsala University in succession to Lars Roberg.

At the same time, he had been commissioned by the government to undertake a scientific survey of the southern Baltic islands, Öland and Gotland, and particularly to try to find a clay suitable for making porcelain, and plants that could be a source of dyes. Linnaeus and a party of six students set out from Stockholm on 15 May (for maps of the route,

Linnaeus' drawing of a beetle in his *Iter Oelandicum* diary of 1741

see Blunt 1971: 142, 144; Åsberg & Stearn 1973: 204). From Växjö, they moved on to Kalmar, departure point for the nearby island of Öland. The party spent nearly three weeks traversing the island. Öland is a long (130km) and slim (15km) island and geologically remarkable in Sweden in that it is composed of limestone and supports a significantly different flora from that on the igneous and metamorphic rocks of the mainland. A flora of some 1,150 flowering plants can be found there, and Linnaeus was amazed to see, among other things, orchids that he had previously seen only in France (at Fontainebleau) thriving in Sweden. He also found there distinctive Öland species such as the plant he would later name *Potentilla fruticosa* L., and *Helianthemum oelandicum* (L.) DC. (the specimen Linnaeus collected there, 689.40 LINN, is the type of *Cistus oelandicus* L.).

A further month was spent exploring the larger (125km by 52km) island of Gotland, where Linnaeus' party found a number of species that do not occur in Öland, such as those that Linnaeus subsequently named *Lactuca quercina* L. and *Gypsophila fastigiata* L. There are about 30 sheets in LINN annotated by Linnaeus as having been collected on the island, including the type specimens of *Potamogeton marinus* L. (175.13) [= *Potamogeton pectinatus* L.], *Sanicula europaea* L. (333.1*)*, *Scabiosa columbaria* L. (120.17), *Schoenus ferrugineus* L. (68.7) and *Thalictrum minus* L. (713.12).

After his return, Linnaeus moved to Uppsala with his wife and baby son, also Carl. It was another four years before an account (*Öländska och Gothländska Resa*, 1745) of the expedition appeared, but it had proved rewarding. Although there was no china clay and no dye plant, Linnaeus pointed out in his Preface that he had found a new and valuable crop plant on Gotland (*Medicago falcata* L.), reported on the use of grasses to prevent sand-drifting, and on a sedge (*Cladium mariscus* (L.) Pohl) used in thatching. He also described how seals were caught, duck snared and cod and flounders taken, rock formations, quicksands, methods of farming and local remedies for diseases. Characteristically, he concluded "Altogether by this journey I have discovered in the field of natural history more than anyone could have believed possible".

Life in Uppsala

Linnaeus gave his inaugural professorial lecture on 27 October 1741, and a little later was able to redistribute responsibilities with Nils Rosén (who had succeeded Rudbeck in the second Chair of Medicine) such that Linnaeus took over Botany and the supervision of the Botanic Garden. Linnaeus set about renovating the garden, and obtained funds for the building of an orangery. The problem of finding a capable Head Gardener was simply solved by poaching Dietrich Nietzel, gardener to Linnaeus' former benefactor in the Netherlands, George Clifford – although he was never forgiven by the Clifford family. The garden, however, thrived under its new management and, whereas fewer than 300 species had been

1

333·1

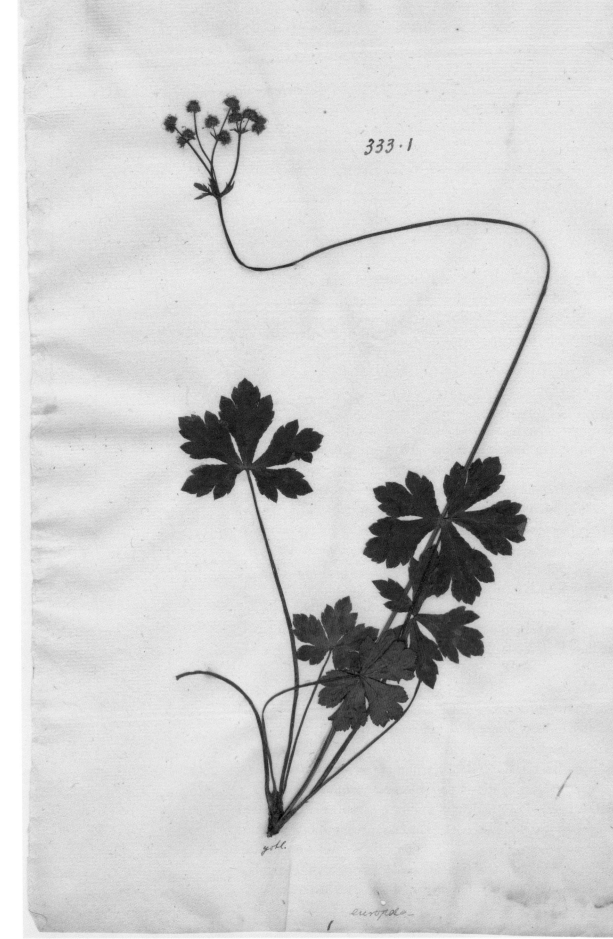

gotl.

europd.

cultivated there in 1739, this had increased to around 3,000 by 1748. Linnaeus also introduced a number of exotic animals into the Garden, including peacocks and parrots, several species of monkey, and a racoon named Sjupp.

In 1744, Linnaeus received on loan from the Danish Apothecary Royal four volumes of specimens and one of drawings that had been assembled by Paul Hermann (1646–1695). Hermann had worked in Ceylon (modern-day Sri Lanka) as a physician with the Dutch East India Company between 1670 and 1677 and this collection provided Linnaeus with a glimpse of the diversity of the tropics, and formed the basis for his later *Flora Zeylanica* (1747). Other interesting collections were reaching him from correspondents such as J.G. Gmelin, who was sending his own material from Russia.

In 1745, Linnaeus published *Flora Suecica*, an account of the plants of Sweden drawn from his own, by now extensive, knowledge of the flora, as well as his account of the Öland and Gotland jouney. In June 1746, he set out on another provincial tour, this time to Västergötland. Travelling south-west (for a map of the itinerary, see Blunt 1971: 161), Linnaeus skirted Lake Vänern to the south, heading towards the coast at Gothenburg. In Gothenberg he met Nicolaus Sahlgren (1701–1776), Director of the Swedish East India Company, and acquired new zoological and mineralogical specimens for his collection. Turning north along the coast, Linnaeus travelled through Bohuslän before turning east to meet Lake Vänern again, this time travelling to its north and eventually returning to Fellingsbro which he had passed through on the first part of his trip. He finally reached Uppsala again in mid-August. Linnaeus' account of this journey was published the following year (1747) as *Wästgöta-Resa*.

Species Plantarum

On his return, Linnaeus started on a new project, an ambitious attempt to catalogue the distinguishing features of all known plant species. Organised following his Sexual System of Classes and Orders, it was eventually to appear as *Species Plantarum* in 1753. Although it had its earliest beginnings in 1733 in two small notebooks, it commenced in earnest in September 1746. Apart from his own Scandinavian collections, which he had correlated with existing literature in order to write *Flora Lapponica* and *Flora Suecica*, he had seen many new plants in the Netherlands – in Clifford's garden, but also Clayton's North American plants that were in Gronovius' possession. In Uppsala he had access to Joachim Burser's herbarium of over 3,000, mostly central European, plants arranged according to Caspar Bauhin's *Pinax Theatri Botanici* (1623) – then still one of the most widely used systems to accommodate such species. As well as Paul Hermann's Ceylon herbarium, he examined specimens collected in

One of Paul Hermann's specimens (3: 12, BM), the lectotype of Linnaeus' *Ptelea viscosa* (= *Dodonaea viscosa* Jacq.)

Opposite: The type specimen of *Sanicula europaea* L. was collected by Linnaeus on Gotland (see "Gotl." written by him near the base of the specimen).

the Kamchatka peninsula by Steller, and in the Volga and Don regions by Gerber, which reached him via Demidoff in 1748. In 1749 he was to receive a significant collection from Provence from his friend Sauvages. He had already developed his generic concepts for plants, in his *Genera Plantarum* (ed. 2, 1742), and he had access to a large number of publications by earlier authors.

By late 1748, this work had proceeded as far as the Tetradynamia (more than halfway through the task). Other tasks, and fatigue, caused Linnaeus to cease any further writing for a while. The manuscript (now at the Linnean Society in London) shows that Linnaeus was including extensive lists of synonyms for each name (similar to the format he had adopted in *Hortus Cliffortianus*), where these were available, and that the marginal specific epithets that were to be such a notable feature of the eventual published work were absent.

Skåne

In 1749 Linnaeus accepted a request from the King for him to undertake a survey of the southwestern province of Skåne. Taking with him a student, Olof Söderberg, as amanuensis, he left Uppsala in late April, before heading for Kristianstad and the coast at Åhus (for a map of the itinerary, see Blunt 1971: 195). He then turned inland and headed for Lund, finding it much changed from his student days. He recorded changes in the flora of the city's walls, noting in particular the frequency of the species he would later name *Inula pulicaris* L. [= *Pulicaria vulgaris* Gaertn.], *Carduus nutans* L. and *Anagallis arvensis* L.

After an exploration of the south-western corner of Skåne, Linnaeus turned northwards again, travelling along the coast towards Helsingborg. After visiting Kullen on its spectacular promontory, Linnaeus turned east and, travelling via Ängelholm and Rossholm, he rejoined his outward route at Kristianstad. During a detour to Ryssby, he encountered quillwort, *Isoëtes lacustris* L., the first time it had been seen in Sweden (see Fuchs 1962). Specimens in Linnaeus' herbarium (LINN) that are annotated as having been collected in Skåne include the type specimens of *Anthericum liliago* L. (432.8), *Astragalus arenarius* L. (926.37), *Athamanta oreoselinum* L. [= *Peucedanum oreoselinum* (L.) Moench] (345.6); *Carex arenaria* L. (1100.9), *Cerastium arvense* L. (603.9), *Cochlearia danica* L. (826.2), *Crepis biennis* L. (955.14), *Hypochaeris radicata* L. (959.5), *Osmunda spicant* L. [= *Blechnum spicant* (L.) Roth] (1244.14), *Senecio paludosus* L. (996.57) and *Sisymbrium nasturtium-aquaticum* L. [= *Rorippa nasturtium-aquaticum* (L.) Hayek] (836.1).

During 1750, Linnaeus was busy with university duties and preparing the text of the *Skånska Resa* and the *Philosophia Botanica*, both of which appeared in 1751. However, in June 1751, apparently enthused by the return from North America of his student Pehr Kalm with hundreds of new plants, Linnaeus resumed work on *Species Plantarum*. He decided, however, to start again from the beginning, using the earlier draft as a basis but including many fewer synonyms, and this allowed far more rapid progress to be made. He also, crucially, added a single specific epithet in the margin of each entry. Letters to his great friend Abraham Bäck chart his progress. By March 1752 he was three-quarters of the way through the book, and by early June had completed the draft. In the same month another of Linnaeus' students, Pehr Osbeck, returned from China and as *Species Plantarum* contains a number of new species described from Osbeck's collections, Linnaeus must have subsequently reworked his manuscript in order to incorporate them, as noted by Stearn (1957: 72). New species collected by other students, Hasselquist in the eastern Mediterranean, and Löfling (who was now in Spain), were also included. The first volume of *Species Plantarum*, dedicated to the King and Queen of Sweden, was published in May 1753, and the second in August (though for purposes of nomenclature they are deemed to have been published simultaneously on 1 May 1753). Together they contained accounts of some 5,900 species of plant and, in the following year, was published another (the fifth) edition of *Genera Plantarum* (which is deemed, for formal nomenclatural purposes, to be linked with the corresponding *Species Plantarum* accounts).

Reception of *Species Plantarum*

Among those who adopted Linnaeus' Sexual System to arrange their descriptions of new and known species were Patrick Browne (1756) and Philip Miller (1759), though they continued to use polynomial names. However, others were struck by the usefulness of the new binomial names and people including Johannes Burman (1755), Pehr Osbeck (1757), Nicolaas Laurens Burman (1759), Nicholas Jacquin (1760), Carlo Allioni (1760–1761), William Hudson (1762), Antoine Gouan (1762), Pietro Arduino (1764), Antonio Turra (1765), Johann Schreber (1766), Philip Miller (1768), Giovanni Antonio Scopoli (1769) and Domenico Vandelli (1771) all adopted this method of naming in their own publications.

Collections from Abroad

In July 1755, Linnaeus received collections and a travel diary made in the eastern Mediterranean by his student, Fredrik Hasselquist. Six years earlier, just before Linnaeus had returned from his tour of Skåne, Hasselquist had sailed from Stockholm for Turkey. Though an enthusiastic botanist, Hasselquist's health was poor, and his resources for the trip inadequate. The following year, in Egypt, his money ran out and only financial support from friends in Sweden (including Linnaeus) enabled him to continue through Palestine, Syria, Cyprus, Rhodes and Chios. He reached Turkey again but was now very ill, and died near Izmir in February 1752, very heavily in debt. His rich collections were eventually repatriated thanks to the Queen of Sweden, who settled the debts. At least some of Hasselquist's specimens had reached Linnaeus in time for him to incorporate a number of new species in *Species Plantarum* but the bulk of the collection, and Hasselquist's travel journal, were not available to Linnaeus until 1755. He published the latter, as *Iter Palaestinum*, in 1757, and it was translated into a number of languages, including an English edition (Hasselquist 1766).

Still more collections became available for Linnaeus to study. In 1756 he was cataloguing the Royal Collections, and those of Count Tessin, and he also received specimens from Erik Brander, then consul in Algiers, and from Louis Gérard from Provence. The following year he started to obtain interesting material from Carlo Allioni in Turin, with Mårten Kähler sending him specimens from various parts of the Mediterranean, and in 1758 he bought the Jamaican collections of Patrick Browne. In the same year, he published the edited papers of Pehr Löfling (who died in Venezuela in 1756) as the latter's *Iter Hispanicum*.

In 1758, Linnaeus was created a Knight of the Polar Star, and he purchased a small estate at Hammarby, just outside Uppsala. He planted a garden there, and in 1761 built a new house where he received visitors and students. He planted a number of exotic species, for both scientific and educational purposes, as well as various fruit trees, and between the time of his death and 1879, when the estate became a museum, some of these plants became naturalised. As well as a few surviving shrubs which are believed to have been planted by Linnaeus, some 47 species introduced by him are believed to persist following his original introduction. Among these are *Corydalis nobilis* (L.) Pers., *Scopolia carniolica* Jacq. [= *Hyoscyamus scopolia* L., *nom. illeg.*] and *Leucojum vernum* L. (see Manktelow 2001).

In 1759, Linnaeus published the second volume (containing the plants) of the 10th edition of his *Systema Naturae*. This included all of the species described by Linnaeus since the *Species Plantarum* of 1753, as well as many new ones (e.g. from Browne's Jamaican collections) and also allowed him to make various adjustments to his 1753 treatment.

Linnaeus was ennobled in 1760, taking the name von Linné. In the same year, one of his favourite pupils, Daniel Solander, travelled to England at his suggestion. Identified as his eventual successor by Linnaeus, Solander, however, subsequently declined his offer of the Chair of Botany at St Petersburg and decided to remain in England, much to Linnaeus' disappointment. However, one of Linnaeus' supporters in England, William Hudson, sent him material (chiefly of grasses) ahead of the publication of Hudson's own *Flora Anglica* (1762). The later loss of Hudson's own herbarium to fire makes the existence of these specimens at the Linnean Society in London of particular interest.

Opposite, top: Wallpaper in Linnaeus' house at Hammarby composed of illustrations, chiefly proof copies of plates by Ehret, Plumier and others

Opposite, bottom: Proof (left), mounted as wallpaper, of an Ehret plate depicting a species of *Musa*, along with the published version (right) of the same plate from Christopher Trew's *Plantae selectae quarum imagines* (t. 23. 1752). The plate is the lectotype of *Musa × sapientum* L.

MVSÆ fructu breviori spadicis fructiferi verticilli tres priores in magnitudine naturali, cum fructib, nonullis ex maturitate dehiscentibus.

MVSÆ fructu breviori spadicis fructiferi verticilli tres priores in magnitudine naturali, cum fructib, nonullis ex maturitate dehiscentibus.

In 1761, the results of his experiments in seeding mussels to induce them to produce pearls allowed him to sell the patent to the State Chamber of Commerce for 3,000 plåtar, a large sum that eliminated the debts he had taken on in purchasing Hammarby. Later, new collections of specimens arrived from Spain (through Clas Alströmer), Italy (through Arduino and Scopoli) and Johan König (South Africa and parts of South-East Asia).

Species Plantarum Revisited

The first volume of a second edition of *Species Plantarum* appeared in 1762, followed by volume two a year later. In 1766, a large fire in Uppsala caused Linnaeus to hurriedly evacuate his collections to a barn on the outskirts for fear of their loss, and he decided then to construct a building at Hammarby to house them. This was started in 1767, but the fear of fire meant it contained no fireplace, and it proved a damp and damaging repository for specimens. This was also the year of the publication of the botanical volume of the 12th edition of the *Systema Naturae* and its accompanying *Mantissa Plantarum*.

Four years later, they were followed by the *Mantissa Plantarum Altera*, the last substantial botanical work that Linnaeus would publish himself. In the same year, he received seeds of 130 plants and some living specimens from Louis XV of France via Count Carl Scheffer. King Adolf Fredrik (who was on the Swedish throne between 1751 and 1771) died and was succeeded by King Gustav III who, like his father, was to be a supporter of Linnaeus in the latter's declining years.

Last Years

By 1772, Linnaeus' health was declining, not helped by a heavy university workload. Plants from his students continued to reach him, however, notably from Thunberg and Sparrman from South Africa, and from Mútis from Colombia. In 1774, one of his former students, J.A. Murray, published in Göttingen a revised edition of the *Systema Naturae* based on an annotated, interleaved copy of the 12th edition given to him for the purpose by Linnaeus. At the end of the year, Linnaeus received a fine gift from King Gustav – 16 chests of plants from Surinam, collected by Dahlberg, much of it preserved in spirit. Among them were many new genera and species, and Linnaeus was moved to prepare a short dissertation, *Plantae Surinamenses* (1775), describing these novelties. To show his gratitude to the King, among them was a new genus named *Gustavia*.

Although he wrote a number of additional dissertations (notably one on *Hypericum* which was published in November 1776), his health was by now extremely poor and he died on 10 January 1778, aged 70. He was buried in Uppsala cathedral.

A flower of *Gustavia augusta* L., collected by Carl Dahlberg in Surinam, now in the Linnaean collection (sheet 290.17) at the Swedish Museum of Natural History in Stockholm (S)

Chapter 3
MAJOR BOTANICAL PUBLICATIONS OF LINNAEUS, THE DISSERTATIONS AND THE AMOENITATES ACADEMICAE

Although the *Systema Naturae* (1735), for example, is rightly regarded as a landmark in Linnaeus' scientific development, those works that are relevant to the introduction and deployment of binomial nomenclature, rather than his classification system, are the focus of this study. For those in search of a comprehensive list of Linnaeus' publications, they have been enumerated in the bibliographies of Hulth (1907) and Soulsby (1933), and a modern union catalogue is in preparation under the auspices of the Linnaeus Link Project (http://www.nhm.ac.uk/research-curation/projects/linnaeus-link/). Stearn (1957: 17–23) provided a list of Linnaeus' major botanical publications and also (*l.c.*: 51–64) dealt with the question of the authorship of the dissertations defended by his students, outlining their publication history and also their subsequent inclusion in the *Amoenitates Academicae*.

There are many differences in style and content across these Linnaean publications. Some of them (e.g. *Flora Zeylanica*, *Plantae Rariores Africanae*) were heavily based on certain collections available to Linnaeus only at a particular time. Others (e.g. *Herbarium Amboinense*) gave binomial names to the descriptions of species published by a single earlier author, while his most famous compilatory works (e.g. *Species Plantarum*) drew together information from a wide variety of different sources. It follows that the interpretation of names published in these varied works benefits from an understanding of the sources of information on which they were based and it therefore seems desirable to provide some notes for each.

Although Linnaeus' major works are well-known, many significant contributions to knowledge, and the first publication of many species names, appeared in the dissertations of Linnaeus' students. Although defended in public disputation by a student, these dissertations were usually the work of Linnaeus himself, as Stearn (1957: 51–64) has discussed. During the time that Linnaeus was a Professor in Uppsala, 186 dissertations in the realms of natural history and medicine were published

The title page for the Linnaean dissertation *Centuria I Plantarum*, defended by Abraham Juslenius on 20 February, 1755

Some of Linnaeus' copies of his own published books in his Library at the Linnean Society of London

(each at a student's expense) between 1743 and 1776, and duly defended. They were also collected together and re-published in 10 volumes comprising Linnaeus' *Amoenitates Academicae* (1749–1790), compared with which the original versions may be either identical, or slightly (or even radically) changed. To confuse matters further, there are several different editions of the *Amoenitates Academicae*. Stearn (1957: 56–63) lists the dissertations, and the dates and editions of the *Amoenitates Academicae*, and Kiger & al. (1999) provide an index to the names of organisms they contain. In *Species Plantarum* (1753, 1762, 1763), Linnaeus variously cited original theses and the reprinted accounts. As there can be significant differences between apparently identical accounts of a given species, it is most important, in matters of typification, to consult the version cited by Linnaeus while being alert to the possibility of the existence of an earlier version which may have its own nomenclatural significance.

The major botanical publications fall into four chronological periods (following Stearn) – "pre-Linnaean" between 1735 and 1752, the nomenclaturally important period from 1753 to 1769, the "period of decline" from 1770 to 1776, and the posthumous period from 1781 onwards. Although it is the second of these that is of most interest here, many of these publications draw in turn on works published during the first period, so these will also be considered.

In addition, two short works published by Linnaeus' son, Carl (often known as "Linnaeus filius") are included. Appearing in 1762 and 1763, they together describe and illustrate 20 rare species grown in the botanic garden in Uppsala. However, 11 of these names had already appeared in works published by his father, and to whom they are attributable. As the remaining nine new names were taken up by Linnaeus in *Species Plantarum*, ed. 2 (1762–1763), these few names are included here. However, the numerous new names attributable to Linnaeus filius that he published in *Supplementum Plantarum* (1782) and elsewhere are beyond the scope of this study.

The most relevant publications are listed below, and are arranged chronologically irrespective of whether they are books or dissertations.

1736. **Musa Cliffortiana.** 46 pp.; 2 cprpl. Leiden.
Linnaeus' first botanical monograph, this slim work was hastily published to mark the first successful flowering and fruiting in Europe of a banana, at George Clifford's garden, the Hartekamp, near Haarlem in the Netherlands. The account, which included two large engravings made by A. vander Laan based on illustrations by M. Hoffman (see Blunt 1971: 107–108), was the basis of Linnaeus' account of the banana in *Species Plantarum* (1753), and one of the 1736 engravings is the type of *Musa paradisiaca* L. A facsimile edition of this work, accompanied by an English translation of the text, is in preparation (Freer, in press).

1737. **Genera Plantarum.** 384 pp. Leiden.
This, the first of many editions of his account of the plant genera he recognised, was one of the manuscripts that Linnaeus had prepared in Sweden and which he took with him to the Netherlands for publication there.

1737. **Flora Lapponica.** 372 pp.; 12 cprpl. Amsterdam.
This substantial work was the result of Linnaeus' Lapland journey, undertaken between May and September in 1732. In it, he accounted for and described 534 different species, publishing illustrations of a small number of them (see p. 85), and also citing many herbarium specimens. He took the manuscript of this book with him to the Netherlands in 1735, where it was published in April 1737. The specimens upon which this account was based were given to Johannes Burman by Linnaeus; they are now in Paris (see Chapter 5).

1737. **Viridarium Cliffortianum.** 104 pp. Amsterdam.
This was a concise listing of the plants that were growing in George Clifford's garden at the Hartekamp in the Netherlands at the time that Linnaeus was in Clifford's employ. The book is unillustrated but was frequently cited by Linnaeus in subsequent works, usually in association with the much more extensive species accounts in *Hortus Cliffortianus* (1738).

1738. **Hortus Cliffortianus.** 502 pp.; 36 col. cprpl. Amsterdam.
The *Hortus Cliffortianus* was, from a typographic point of view, the most lavish publication that Linnaeus ever produced. In folio format, it contained detailed accounts (with extensive synonymy) of the plants grown in Clifford's garden at the Hartekamp, his estate near Haarlem in the Netherlands. The book ran to 502 pages and also contained 36 copperplate engravings, two depicting leaf-form terminology and the remainder showing notable species. These were drawn by Georg Dionysius Ehret (1707–1770) and Jan Wandelaar (1690–1759), and engraved by the latter. There is also an elaborate frontispiece by Wandelaar in which Linnaeus is portrayed as the young Apollo, bringing light to banish the shroud of darkness, equalling ignorance, encircling the goddess Mother Earth (see Callmer & Gertz 1954). Clifford himself paid for the publication of the book but was reluctant to sell it, preferring to make gifts of it to suitable recipients. The book is rare but a facsimile edition was published by Cramer in 1968. Stearn (1957: 44–50) provides much information on the work as a whole, and also formally treats 34 of the engravings as the types of binomials subsequently published by Linnaeus in

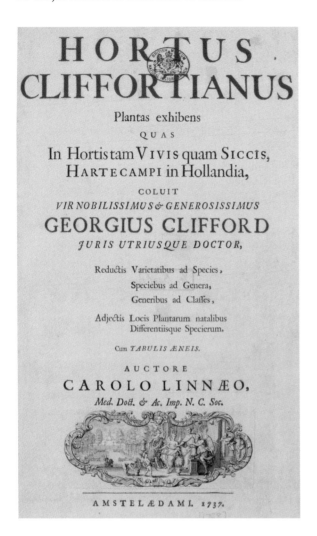

1753. These include the types of *Cliffortia ilicifolia* L., *Collinsonia canadensis* L. and *Lobelia cliffortiana* L.

Clifford's extensive herbarium from this period is extant and is housed at the Natural History Museum in London (BM). A smaller collection, with some duplication of material, also exists in the Nationaal Herbarium Nederland at Wageningen (WAG) (see Chapters 5, 6).

1740. **Species orchidum et affinium plantarum.** *Acta Societas Regia Scientiarum Upsaliensis* 1740: 1–37.

For many of the orchid species treated in *Species Plantarum* (1753), Linnaeus cited the diagnoses as having been drawn directly from this account, which therefore served as a precursor to his later taxonomic concepts in orchids.

1741. **Samling af et hundrade wäxter upfundne på Gothland, Öland och Småland.** *Kongl. Swenska Wetenskaps Academiens Handlingar* 2: 179–210.

This is an account of new and interesting plants from Linnaeus' Öland and Gotland journey which he published in advance of the *Öländska och Gothländska Resa* (1745). Some of the species accounts are cited directly in *Species Plantarum* (e.g. in the protologue of *Geranium lucidum* L.; p. 682), and others are cited indirectly via *Flora Suecica* (Linnaeus 1745).

1741. **Lobelia.** *Acta Societas Regia Scientiarum Upsaliensis* 1741: 23–26, 2 pl.

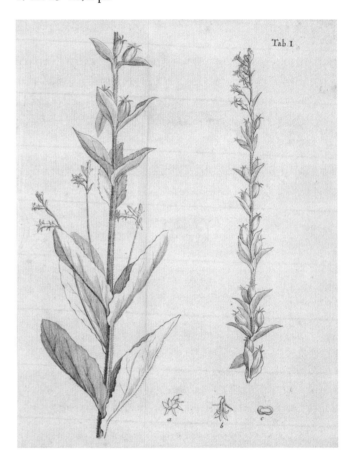

Linnaeus subsequently referred to this illustrated account (see plate above) in the protologue of *Lobelia inflata* L.

1743. ***Betula Nana.*** [Dissertation of L.M. Klase]. Stockholm. An account of the species later formally named *B. nana* L., accompanied by a single copperplate showing habit and leaf morphology. Most of the early dissertations published between 1743 and 1747 were cited by Linnaeus, in *Species Plantarum* (1753), from their reprinted versions in *Amoenitates Academicae* 1 (1751) rather than the originals (though the two versions are often not identical).

1744. ***Ficus, ejusque historia naturalis & medica.*** [Dissertation of G.M.C. Hegardt]. Uppsala. An account of the genus *Ficus*, cited in *Species Plantarum* (1753) from the reprinted version in *Amoen. Acad.* 1: 23–54 (1751) rather than the original.

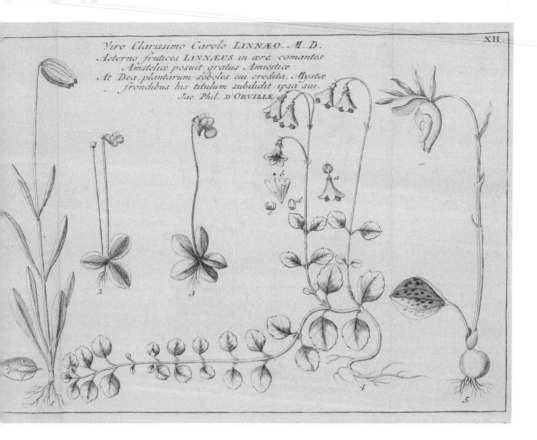

XII.

Viro Clarissimo Carolo LINNÆO. *M. D.*
Aeterno frutices LINNÆUS *in ære comantes*
Amstelæ posuit gratus Amicitiæ.
At Dea, plantarum soboles cu credita, Mystæ
frondibus his titulum subdidit ipsa sui.
Jac. Phil. D'ORVILLE

Left: A plate from Linnaeus' *Flora Lapponica* (1737: t. 12) showing the species that he would later name *Lychnis apetala* L. (f. 1), *Pinguicula villosa* L. (f. 2), *Pinguicula alpina* L. (f. 3), *Linnaea borealis* L. (f. 4) and *Cypripedium bulbosum* L. (f. 5).

TAB: XXIX.

Right: A plate from Linnaeus' *Hortus Cliffortianus* (1738: t. 29), drawn by Ehret and engraved by Wandelaar, is the lectotype of the African tree species, *Kiggelaria africana* L.

1745. *Flora Suecica.* 419 pp. Stockholm.

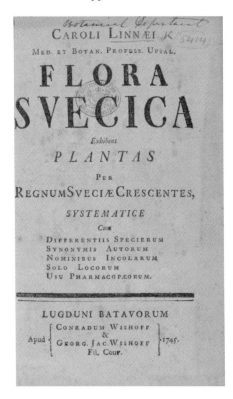

Linnaeus' first complete regional flora drew on his own knowledge of the plants of Sweden, as well as that of others, notably Olof Rudbeck (both father and son), and Olof Celsius. Each species is accompanied by an extensive synonymy, and notes on distribution, ecology and vernacular names. Although this work is extensively cited by Linnaeus in *Species Plantarum* (1753), it is usually difficult to match any herbarium material directly with accounts in *Flora Suecica*. The exception lies with Linnaeus' lichen specimens, where the consecutively numbered accounts (e.g. "976" for the species subsequently named *Lichen cornutus* L.) from *Flora Suecica* can often be found written on the corresponding sheet by Linnaeus. A detailed study of Linnaeus' lichen names is provided by Jørgensen & al. (1994).

1745. *Öländska och Gothländska Resa.* 344 pp.; 1 pl. Stockholm and Uppsala.

An account of Linnaeus' 1741 journey to the Baltic islands of Öland and Gotland. Stearn (in Åsberg & Stearn 1973: 1–17) has provided a detailed description of the book and its significance. He also attributed restricted type localities to the names of 19 plant species that are linked with the islands. However, it is often difficult to associate extant herbarium specimens with such provenances, and specimens are, in any case, often simply missing. Even when specimens do exist, Stearn does not refer to any of them as type material. However, the account of the journey is cited quite frequently in *Flora Suecica* (1745), and occasionally in *Species Plantarum* (1753).

The index is of interest because it shows an early stage in the development of Linnaeus' later introduction of the use of binomial names (see Stearn 1957: 67). Åsberg & Stearn (1973: 19–220) provide an English translation of the Swedish original.

1745. *Plantae Martin-Burserianae explicatae.* [Dissertation of R. Martin]. Uppsala.

This thesis was a study of 240 specimens in the herbarium of Joachim Burser (1583–1639), which Linnaeus had the opportunity to study in Uppsala. The value of the 23 volumes comprising Burser's herbarium was that it was arranged according to the *Pinax Theatri Botanici* (1623) of Caspar Bauhin, with whom Burser had corresponded. The *Pinax* was an extremely important work for Linnaeus, dealing as it did with all the plants described by western botanists to that date, and it is heavily cited throughout Linnaeus' works. Burser's specimens therefore allowed Linnaeus to interpret Bauhin not only through what were often very short polynomials or descriptions, but also through well-correlated material. Linnaeus later prepared a manuscript identifying Burser's specimens with his own new binomials. However, it was not published at the time. It is now at the Linnean Society of London and has been transcribed by Savage (1937a).

It can be difficult to correlate the specimen accounts in the thesis with the intended specimens as Linnaeus did not attribute volume and page numbers to them (though they are listed following the volume arrangement; see Juel 1923, 1936). The dissertation was reprinted in *Amoen. Acad.* 1: 299–332 (Camper ed., 1749); 1: 141–171 (Linnaeus ed., 1749), from where Linnaeus cited it in *Species Plantarum* (1753).

1745. **Passiflora.** [Dissertation of J.G. Hallman fil.]. Stockholm.

The original dissertation is cited in *Species Plantarum* (1753) from its reprinted version in *Amoen. Acad.* 1: 211–242 (1749). It is accompanied by a single copperplate showing leaf forms and floral structure (see above) in *Passiflora*.

1745. *Anandria.* [Dissertation of E.Z. Tursén]. Uppsala.

A detailed account of the plant subsequently described as *Tussilago anandria* L., cited in *Species Plantarum* (1753) from the reprinted version in *Amoen. Acad.* 1: 243–259 (1751) rather than the original, and accompanied by a single copperplate.

1745. *Acrostichum.* [Dissertation of J.B. Heiligtag]. Uppsala. An account of the fern genus *Acrostichum*, cited in *Species Plantarum* (1753) from its reprinted version in *Amoen. Acad.* 1: 260–271 (1749). It is accompanied by a single copperplate.

1746. Limnia, en obekant vext. *Kongliga Swenska Wetenskaps Academiens Handlingar* 7: 130–134, pl. 5. Linnaeus subsequently referred to this illustrated account in the protologue of *Claytonia sibirica* L., and Linnaeus' plate 5 is the lectotype of this binomial.

1747. *Wästgöta-Resa . . . förrättad År 1746.* 284 pp., 5 pl. Stockholm. Linnaeus' account of his tour through Västergötland (see Chapter 2; Blunt 1971: 160–165) contained numerous references to plants, some of which were cited in *Species Plantarum* (1753). Plate IV depicts the seagrass, *Zostera marina* L., which Linnaeus found at Marstrand, and described in some detail (pp. 166–168).

1747. *Nova Plantarum Genera.* [Dissertation of C.M. Dassow]. Stockholm. This dissertation described 43 new genera, though later reference to them in *Species Plantarum* (1753) is to its reprinted version in *Amoen. Acad.* 1: 381–417 (1749).

1747. *Flora Zeylanica.* 240 pp., 4 cprpl. Amsterdam. This work was heavily based on the collections of Paul Hermann (1646–1695), who made one of the earliest scientific collections of plant specimens from Ceylon (now Sri Lanka), where he was Medical Officer to the Dutch East India Company between 1672 and 1677. After his return to Europe, Hermann took up the Chair of Botany at the University of Leiden (1679) where he spent the rest of his life. Subsequently, his notes reached William Sherard (1659–1728) in Oxford, who edited them to produce a catalogue published as *Musaeum Zeylanicum* (1717), with a second edition in 1726. The herbarium and drawings were loaned to Linnaeus who used them, along with the information in *Musaeum Zeylanicum*, to prepare his *Flora Zeylanica* (1747). For more information on Hermann and his herbarium, see Chapters 5, 6.

1748. *Hortus Upsaliensis.* 306 pp.; 3 cprpl. Stockholm. The *Hortus Upsaliensis* provided an account of the plants in cultivation at the University Botanic Garden in Uppsala between 1742 and 1748, including information on synonymy, believed origin, and cultivation requirements. This work, too, is

Plate 3 in *Flora Zeylanica* depicts the plant Linnaeus would later name *Hedysarum strobiliferum* L. (= *Flemingia strobilifera* (L.) W.T. Aiton).

frequently cited in *Species Plantarum*, and quite a number of specimens in the Linnaean herbaria carry the letters "H.U.", written by Linnaeus, indicating that they were grown in the Hortus Upsaliensis. However, it is often more difficult to associate specimens with the publication as Linnaeus' abbreviation evidently indicated garden provenance over many years, rather than a bibliographic reference to this 1748 book.

1749. *Materia Medica.* 252 pp. Stockholm. As a medical doctor, Linnaeus was heavily reliant on plant-based medicines and drugs and therefore understandably interested in the species from which they were derived. In the main catalogue in this book, Linnaeus organised the species following his hierarchy of classes and orders, providing for each

Following page (88): Plate 2 from *Hortus Upsaliensis* is of the North American *Mimulus ringens* L.

This was the first volume of the *Amoenitates Academicae* to appear, and contained 19 of the dissertations, unchanged from the originals, that Linnaeus had written in the years 1743–1748. Published in Leiden (and known as the Camper edition), Linnaeus was unhappy with aspects of it and arranged for a revised version, with the dissertations in a different order and incorporating some changes and corrections, to be published in Stockholm and Leipzig later in the same year.

1749. *Amoenitates Academicae.* Vol. 1. 563 pp.; 17 cprpl. Stockholm and Leipzig.
This revised Linnaeus edition (see Camper edition above) is the one that is cited in *Species Plantarum* (1753), the pagination between the two being different. The significant dissertations as far as plant names are concerned are the following: *Betula Nana* (pp. 1–22), *Ficus* (pp. 23–54), *Plantae Martino-Burserianae* (pp. 141–171), *Passiflora* (pp. 211–242), *Anandria* (pp. 243–259), *Acrostichum* (pp. 260–271) and *Genera Plantarum Nova* (pp. 381–417).

1749. *Gemmae Arborum.* [Dissertation of P. Löfling]. Uppsala.
An account of the varying forms of bud displayed by a range of different tree species and, unusually, one where the student is thought to have written the content. In *Species Plantarum* (1753), descriptions are cited from the reprinted version of the dissertation in *Amoen. Acad.* 2: 182–224 (1751). Along with *Pan Suecicus* (1749), it shows an early stage in the development of Linnaeus' use of binomial names (see Stearn 1957: 68–70).

1749. *Pan Suecicus.* [Dissertation of N.L. Hesselgren]. Uppsala.

species a diagnostic phrase name, limited synonymy and known occurrence, followed by the pharmacological names for the parts of the plant, and the uses and methods of dispensing to be followed. Although not generally linkable with specific herbarium collections, Linnaeus cited this work consistently throughout *Species Plantarum* (1753) and other publications.

1749. *Radix Senega.* [Dissertation of G.M.J. Kiernander]. Stockholm.
This contained descriptions of a number of species of *Polygala* (*sensu* Linnaeus), together with an illustration of the plant he later named *P. senega*, and a discussion of its medicinal properties. These accounts were cited in *Species Plantarum* from the reprinted version in *Amoen. Acad.* 2: 126–153 (1751).

1749. *Amoenitates Academicae.* Vol. 1. 610 pp.; 15 cprpl. Leiden.

82			Boves	Capræ	Oves	Equi	Sues
FLORA SVECICA							
I. MONANDRIA							
1	Salicornia	maritima	o	-	o	o	1
2	Hippuris	aquatica	o	1	o	o	o
3	Callitriche	paluftris	-	-	-	-	-
II. DIANDRIA							
4	Liguftrum	vulgare	1	1	1	o	-
5	Circæa	utraque	-	-	1	-	-
6	Veronica	ternifolia	1	1	1	o	o
7	- -	fpicata	1	o	1	o	-
8	- -	mas	-	1	1	1	-
9	- -	fcutellata	1	1	1	1	-
10	- -	Beccab. oblong.	1	1	-	1	o
11	- - -	- rotund.	1	1	o	o	o
12	-	Pfeudo Chamædrys	1	1	1	-	o
13	- -	alpina	-	-	-	-	-
14	- -	femina	-	1	-	-	-
15	- -	clinopodifolia	-	-	-	-	-
16	- -	caulic. adhærent.	1	1	1	-	-

An account of observations of the palatability to various domesticated animals of different forage plant species (see above), *Pan Suecicus* is of particular interest because it too shows an early stage in the development of Linnaeus' later introduction of the use of binomial names (see Stearn 1957: 68–70).

1750. ***Plantae Rariores Camschatcenses.*** [Dissertation of J.P. Halenius]. Uppsala.

This dissertation was based on a collection of specimens sent to Linnaeus by Grigory Demidov (1715–1761), an enthusiastic amateur Russian botanist whose family included important businessmen, philanthropists and patrons. He developed his botanical interests at a Botanic Garden near Solikamsk in the Urals (now Perm Province), then an important industrial and trading centre on the route connecting European Russia with Siberia and Central Asia. Demidov started corresponding with Linnaeus and the two men exchanged seeds from their respective gardens. Demidov, however, also sent on loan to Linnaeus herbarium material that he had obtained from Steller (from the Second Kamchatka Expedition), from T. Gerber (from Volga and Don), from J.G. Gmelin (from Siberia) and from J. Lerche (from Astrakhan and Ghilan [south-east Azerbaijan]). There was evidently some confusion on Linnaeus' part as to the geographical origin of parts of this collection, and some species that are unknown in Kamchatka were included in the dissertation. For further information on Demidov and these collections, see Sokoloff & al. (2002: 163–169).

There are some changes between the original dissertation and its reprinting in volume 2 of *Amoenitates Academicae* (Linnaeus 1751: 333–364), but these chiefly relate to the provenance of specimens, as Linnaeus had discovered that only Krascheninnikov and Steller had visited Kamchatka. Both versions contain detailed descriptions of 26 new species, most of which were subsequently given binomials in 1753, e.g. *Astragalus physodes* L. (see Jarvis & al. 2002).

1751. **Scabiosa flosculis quadrifidis, folis pinnatifidis: laciniis lateralibus erectisculis and Penthorum.** *Acta Societatis Regiae Scientiarum Upsaliensis* 1749–1750: 11–14, 2 pl.

Linnaeus subsequently referred to the illustrated account of *Scabiosa* (see plate above, right) in the protologue of *S. tatarica* L. (1753), and to that of *Penthorum* in the protologue of *Penthorum sedoides* L. (1753).

1751. ***Skånska Resa.*** 434 pp., 6 cprpl. Stockholm.

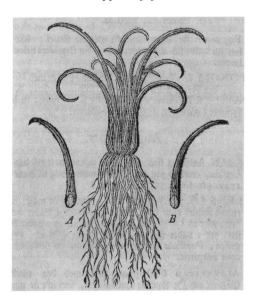

This is an account of Linnaeus' tour through the province of Skåne in 1749, in which there are numerous botanical observations, some of which are cited in *Species Plantarum* (1753). Among them was his discovery, for the first time in Sweden, of *Isoëtes lacustris* L. (quillwort), which is also illustrated (see p. 89).

1751. *Nova Plantarum Genera.* (Dissertation of L.J. Chenon]. Uppsala.
Linnaeus described 37 new genera in this dissertation, continuing the numbering sequence that he had started in the second edition of *Genera Plantarum* (1742). This dissertation includes the genera numbered from 1074–1111 and his later citations of genera from this work always refer to the genus number rather than the page number. This work includes a single copperplate comprising seven figures, one of which (f. 6), is the type of *Gaultheria procumbens* L. The dissertation was reprinted with only minor modification in *Amoen. Acad.* 3: 1–27, 1 cprpl. (1756).

1751. *Plantae Hybridae.* [Dissertation of J.J. Haartmann]. Uppsala.
This discussion of a number of apparent hybrid plants acquired nomenclatural significance when it was reprinted (in *Amoen. Acad.* 3: 28–62. 1756) with the addition of binomials.

1751. *Amoenitates Academicae.* Vol. 2. 478 pp., 4 cprpl. Stockholm.
The most notable dissertation in this collection is that of *Plantae Camschatcenses Rariores* (pp. 332–364, t. 4), a slightly modified reprint of the original *Plantae Rariores Camschatcenses* (1750), but it also contains versions of *Radix Senega* (pp. 126–153), *Gemmae Arborum* (pp. 182–224) and *Pan Suecicus* (pp. 225–262). Where these are referred to in *Species Plantarum*, it is the *Amoen. Acad.* reprint that is cited, rather than the original version.

1752. *Euphorbia, ejusque Historia naturalis et medica.* [Dissertation of J. Wiman]. Uppsala.
Cited extensively under the *Euphorbia* species named in *Species Plantarum* (1753), the references there utilise the species number in the dissertation (e.g. "Diss. euph. 6") rather than the page number.

1753. *Species Plantarum.* (Vol. 1, May; vol. 2, Aug). Stockholm.
Undoubtedly the single most important Linnaean botanical publication, it is also the best known. This was Linnaeus' attempt at accounting for all known plants within his own systematic framework (the Sexual System). It was also accompanied by what seemed at first a minor, largely editorial

innovation: the introduction of the species name or specific epithet forming, with the generic name, the modern scientific species name. Although binomial naming systems were old and widespread, the scientific names for organisms were based around using a generic name in conjunction with a descriptive phrase name or diagnosis. This phrase name, of up to about 12 words (known as a polynomial), indicated the characters distinguishing that species from other members of the genus, and so provided a key enabling the identification of a species once its generic position was known. Linnaeus' idea was to provide a single epithet in the margin next to each species account, intended as a sort of shorthand *aide-mémoire* for the full polynomial name (which Linnaeus nevertheless still conceived to be the real name of the plant; see Stafleu 1971: 103–112). Although some binomial forms had been used by authors such as Bauhin (1623), they were essentially contracted polynomials used where two or more species in a genus could be adequately distinguished by a single, clear character. However, Linnaeus' innovation was the consistent use of a binomial name for all species, and this was gradually adopted by other botanists who saw the utility and used it in their own works, including Burman (1755), Osbeck (1757), Jacquin (1760), Allioni (1760–1761), Hudson (1762) and Miller (1768).

In 1905, in Vienna, the first edition of *Species Plantarum* was adopted as the starting point for binomial nomenclature in plants, with the recognition of the need for an internationally agreed set of rules for the naming of plants. Although the two volumes that comprise the work were not published simultaneously, they are, for nomenclatural purposes, both deemed to have been published on 1 May 1753 (Art. 13.5 of the Code). The generic names therein are also to be associated with their subsequent descriptions published in Linnaeus' *Genera Plantarum*, ed. 5 (1754) under Art. 13.4, i.e. the generic names are considered to be validly published in *Species Plantarum*, even though validating descriptions may not have appeared until the following year.

There have, since then, been some modifications to the groups of organisms for which Linnaean names continue to provide the starting point date. Under Art. 13 of the ICBN (McNeill & al. 2006), the Spermatophyta, Pteridophyta, Hepaticae, Musci (Sphagnaceae only), Fungi and some of the Algae have 1753 as the starting date (except for suprageneric names of Spermatophyta and Pteridophyta, for which it is 1789). Other groups with later starting dates are the Musci (1801, but excluding the Sphagnaceae), some of the Algae

Opposite: Linnaeus' own annotated copy of the first volume of *Species Plantarum* (1753), "Emended by the Author" (see detail below)

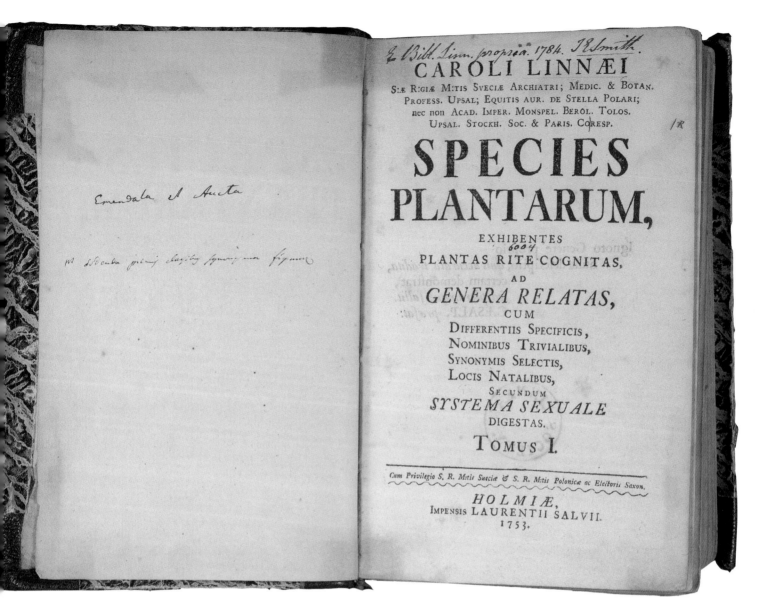

Ex Bibl. Linn. propriâ. 1784. J E Smith.

Emendata et Aucta

D Addenda primis classibus synonyma figuras

CAROLI LINNÆI

S:æ R:giæ M:tis Sveciæ Archiatri; Medic. & Botan.
Profess. Upsal; Equitis aur. de Stella Polari;
nec non Acad. Imper. Monspel. Berol. Tolos.
Upsal. Stockh. Soc. & Paris. Coresp.

SPECIES
PLANTARUM,

EXHIBENTES
PLANTAS RITE COGNITAS,
AD
GENERA RELATAS,
CUM
DIFFERENTIIS SPECIFICIS,
NOMINIBUS TRIVIALIBUS,
SYNONYMIS SELECTIS,
LOCIS NATALIBUS,
SECUNDUM
SYSTEMA SEXUALE
DIGESTAS.

TOMUS I.

Cum Privilegio S. R. M:tis Sueciæ & S. R. M:tis Polonicæ ac Electoris Saxon.

HOLMIÆ,
IMPENSIS LAURENTII SALVII.
1753.

(Nostocaceae Homocysteae – 1802; Nostocaceae Heterocysteae – 1886; Desmidiaceae – 1848; Oedogoniaceae – 1900), and fossil plants in all groups (1820). In addition, the names of most groups of fungi are subject to "sanctioning" (Art. 15), a process by which their usage by either Persoon (1801) or Fries (1821) is protected against divergent occurrences by earlier authors (including Linnaeus).

Species Plantarum (1753) provides some 5,900 binomial names and is therefore the single most important contribution to the approximately 9,100 names that are now attributed to Linnaeus. Much has been written about *Species Plantarum*, and Stearn (1957) and Heller & Stearn (1959) provide a still unrivalled introduction to all aspects of its importance and interpretation. Two versions of volume one exist as a result of Linnaeus having revised and replaced pages 75, 89 and 260 shortly after the volume was printed. The original version is rare but the cancelled entries have no nomenclatural standing (see Stearn 1957: 135–142 for further details).

1753. *Demonstrationes Plantarum in Horto Upsaliensi 1753.* [Dissertation of J.C. Höjer]. (Oct) Uppsala.
This dissertation appeared in October 1753 and contained a list of the plants growing in the Uppsala Botanic Garden, arranged in Linnaeus' system and using the new Linnaean binomials that had just been introduced in *Species Plantarum*. In addition, 22 new binomials that had not been included in that work were also validly published here. The dissertation was reprinted, with minor modification, in *Amoen. Acad.* 3: 394–424 (1756). Stearn (1959a: 81–92) gives a detailed account of this dissertation, and reproduces the validating text for the new taxa, as well as the additional information provided for species already included in *Species Plantarum*.

1754. *Flora Anglica.* [Dissertation of I.O. Grufberg]. (Apr) Uppsala.
This dissertation provided a comparison of aspects of the British and Swedish floras based on the third edition of John Ray's *Synopsis Methodica Stirpium Britannicarum* which was edited by J.J. Dillenius and had appeared in 1724, 19 years after Ray's death. Stearn (1973a: 42–68) has provided a detailed review of the dissertation and its relationship to Ray's works.

The main part of the dissertation attempted to provide Linnaean binomials (and trinomials for varieties) for the polynomials used by Ray, the latter being referred to, in a very succinct way, by a page and species number reference alone (see text sample, above right). Although most of the binomials needed had already been described in *Species Plantarum*, a few new names were required, and these are accepted as validly published by virtue of the corresponding reference to Ray, which is generally clear. For example, the new name *Carex remota* L. (*Fl. Angl.*: 24) is accompanied by "424–11", which

links it with Ray's "*Gramen cyperoides angustifolium, spicis parvis sessilibus in foliorum alis*" which is species number 11 on page 424 of the *Synopsis*. Ray's account provides the validating diagnosis for the name and, in accordance with Art. 7.7 (see Ex. 8) of the Code, typification of Linnaean names published in the dissertation is to be undertaken from the context of Ray's work rather than by using material in Linnaeus' herbarium.

There are significant differences between the original dissertation and the reprinted version in *Amoen. Acad.* 4: 88–111 (1759), as noted by Stearn (1973a: 63). For example, *Carex remota* L. (1754) was replaced with *C. axillaris* L. (1759), and some names from the 1754 dissertation were relegated to the synonymy of species named earlier in *Species Plantarum* (e.g. *Papaver medium* L. (1754) was reduced to the synonymy of *P. dubium* L. (1753) in the reprint). Other names (e.g. *Hypericum elodes* L.) did not appear in the original dissertation but made their first appearance in the reprint.

Further difficulties have arisen from differences in interpretation of apparent typographical errors in this, and other, dissertations. Stearn (1973a: 68) provided a list of what he regarded as either slips of the pen or typographical errors in this dissertation which should not be treated as new names (e.g. "*Parietaria officinarum*" for *P. officinalis* L. 1753). He also noted that Rothmaler (1940) had wrongly attributed a number of new binomials to Grufberg (defender of the dissertation), including *Primula acaulis* (L.) Grufb. and *P. elatior* (L.) Grufb. More recently, Greuter (1989: 566) argued that *P. acaulis* was a new combination made by Linnaeus in 1754, based on *P. veris* var. *acaulis* L. (1753), and therefore pre-dated the usual name for the primrose, *P. vulgaris* Huds. However, Brummitt & Meikle (1993: 181–183) argued that there are typographical variants of the thesis which make it unreasonable to interpret the 1754 name as a new combination.

Stearn (1973: 63–68) also provided a detailed treatment of those names that were newly published in either the original dissertation or the later reprint.

1754. *Herbarium Amboinense.* [Dissertation of O. Stickman]. (May) Uppsala.

TOMUS IV.

1. Leleba.   *Arundo arbor indica procera ver-*
   Arundarbor *eratium.*   *ticillata.Pluk.mant.28.*
   Arundarbor *spiculorum.*
   Arundarbor *vasaria.* Arundo *arbor.*
2. Arundarbor *aspera.*
3. Arundarbor *spinosa.*
4. Arundarbor *fera.*
5. Canna *palustris.*   *Arundo vallatoria Pluk.*
6. Arundo *farcta.*
7. Arundastrum.
8. Flos *festalis.*   Hibiscus *Rosa chinensis.*
9. Flos *horarius.*   Hibiscus *mutabilis.*
10. Abutilon *hirsutum.*   Sida *Abutilon β.*
11. Abutilon *læve.*   Sida *Abutilon α.*
12. Gossypium *Capas.*   Gossypium *herbaceum.*

This dissertation attempted to provide Linnaean binomials for some of the taxa described by Georg Eberhard Rumphius (1627–1702) in the first six (of seven) volumes of his *Herbarium Amboinense* (1741–1755). Rumphius' work included descriptions of over 1,600 taxa, nearly 700 of which were illustrated, from Amboina, a small island in the Moluccas, now part of Indonesia. The work was cited in the synonymy of only 19 species in *Species Plantarum* (1753), as Linnaeus did not acquire a copy until his manuscript was all but complete. This 1754 dissertation included some 30 new binomials (excluding some orthographic variants of earlier names). The reprinted version (in *Amoen. Acad.* 4: 112–143. 1759) also contained some changes to names that had first appeared in the original, as well as adding new names for species described in the *Auctuarium* (a Supplement to Rumphius' six volumes that was published only in 1755). For many of these names, Rumphius' account was the only one that Linnaeus would have seen (no herbarium material yet being available to him from this area), and many of Rumphius' illustrations are therefore types for the corresponding Linnaean names. A detailed account of Rumphius' book, together with the relationship of

Linnaeus' publications to it, is provided by Merrill (1917). Confusion on the part of some recent authors led to Art. 34 Ex. 2. being added to the Code in order to make it clear that the designations in the left-hand column of the dissertation related to Rumphius' names and were not to be interpreted as binomials accepted by Linnaeus (see sample of text, left).

1754. *Genera Plantarum*, ed. 5. (Aug) Stockholm.
The first, two-volume edition of *Species Plantarum* (1753) provides the starting point for binomial nomenclature in plants and the two volumes are deemed to have been published on 1 May 1753 (Art. 13.5). The generic names in *Species Plantarum* are to be associated with the descriptions of the corresponding generic names published in Linnaeus' *Genera Plantarum*, ed. 5 (1754), under Art. 13.4. The generic protologue can therefore be particularly important where only one species is included in the genus (i.e. it is monospecific) because no diagnostic phrase name will be found in *Species Plantarum* (the features of the species being those of the genus).

The Appendix, however, also contains four new binomials: *Cambogia gummi-gutta* L., *Cyanella hyacinthoides* L., *Delima s(p)armentosa* L. and *Lygeum spartum* L. Stearn (1959b: 92–93) reproduces the protologues of each, and discusses each name.

1755. *Centuria I Plantarum* [Dissertation of A.D. Juslenius]. (Feb) Uppsala.
This dissertation contained the descriptions of 101 new species from a variety of sources but included names based on material received from his "apostles" Pehr Kalm, Pehr Osbeck, Pehr Löfling and Fredrik Hasselquist. The later reprint (in *Amoen. Acad.* 4: 261–296. 1759) contained significant changes to some of the names employed, and these have been listed by Nordenstam (1961).

1755. *Flora Suecica*, ed. 2. (Oct) Stockholm.
An expanded version of the first edition (Linnaeus 1745), this second edition was distinguished by the use of binomials, 26 of which appear here for the first time. A useful Swedish "facsimile" version of this work, with much additional interpretation, appeared as "Svensk Flora" by Carl von Linné, prepared by Broberg & al. (1986).

1756. *Flora Palaestina* [Dissertation of B.J. Strand]. (Mar) Uppsala.
This dissertation was based on the plants collected by Fredrik Hasselquist, one of Linnaeus' "apostles", during an ill-fated journey in the Near East (Stearn 1957: 114–115). In late 1749, Hasselquist had travelled to western Turkey, then went to Egypt and Palestine, returning to Turkey via Lebanon, Cyprus, Rhodes and Chios. Sadly, he died near Smyrna [modern Izmir]

in February 1752, and his many debts made it difficult for his collections and effects to be released until the intervention of Queen Lovisa Ulrika of Sweden. Hasselquist's manuscripts and specimens reached Sweden in 1755, with Linnaeus receiving some duplicate specimens from the Queen in the following year. Six new binomials were published in the dissertation, and it was reprinted in *Amoen. Acad.* 4: 443–467 (1759).

1756. ***Centuria II Plantarum*** [Dissertation of E. Torner]. (Jun) Uppsala.
This dissertation, containing a further 100 new species, followed the *Centuria I Plantarum* of 1755. The new species were numbered consecutively from 101 to 200 and, as before, came from a variety of places. In his Introduction, Linnaeus mentions, in particular, material from Monte Baldo [Veneto, Italy] sent to him by Séguier, from Montpellier sent by Sauvages, as well as material from central America via Philip Miller, and specimens from "India orientalis" from a variety of sources. As in the case of *Centuria I Plantarum*, the later reprint (in *Amoen. Acad.* 4: 297–332. 1759) of this dissertation also included some significant changes, and these have been listed by Nordenstam (1961).

1756. ***Flora Monspeliensis*** [Dissertation of T.E. Nathorst]. (Jun) Uppsala.
This dissertation provided binomial names for the plants described by Pierre Magnol in his *Botanicum Monspeliense* (1676, 1686, 1688). However, this was done in a cryptic way, with an unexplained number appended to each Linnaean binomial. As there is no indication of how these numbers should be interpreted, new binomials in the 1756 version of the dissertation are *nomina ambigua*. In the reprinted version (in *Amoen. Acad.* 4: 468–495. 1759), Linnaeus added a sentence (p. 475) indicating that the user should number consecutively the entries in Magnol's book (as Linnaeus had done in his own copy). This established the necessary link between the new binomials and Magnol's descriptions and these names are therefore accepted as validly published in the 1759 reprint. However, many of the names appearing there (in November 1759) had by then already been published in *Systema Naturae*, ed. 10 (May–Jun 1759). The number of binomials validly published in the reprint of this dissertation is therefore few. Stearn (1974) accepts 16 and provides an exhaustive study of the two versions of the dissertation, their relationship with Magnol's book, and the consequent nomenclatural complications. Because of the provisions of Art. 7.7, Linnaean names published in this work are to be typified from the context of Magnol's work. This can result in types being specimens in Magnol's herbarium in MPU (e.g. *Geranium foetidum* L.).

1756. ***Amoenitates Academicae.*** Vol. 3. (Aug) Stockholm.
There are two reprints of notable dissertations in this collection. The first is *Plantae Hybridae* (pp. 28–62, t. 2), a reprint of the original 1751 dissertation significantly modified by the addition of binomial names. Although most of the names used had already appeared in *Species Plantarum* (1753), five are newly published here.

The second (pp. 394–424) is a reprint of *Demonstrationes Plantarum in Horto Upsaliensi 1753* (1753), with some modifications, the most significant of which is probably the transfer of *Bryonia punctata* L. (1753) to *Trichosanthes* (as *T. punctata* (L.) L. 1756).

1758. ***Petri Loefling . . . Iter Hispanicum eller Resa till spanska länderna uti Europa och America.*** 316 pp., 2 cprpl. Stockholm.
Löfling was one of Linnaeus' favourite apostles, and one of the most talented. Linnaeus edited information from the letters that Löfling had sent to him, first from Spain, where he had collected extensively, and then from South America (Löfling died in 1756 after joining an expedition to Venezuela). Linnaeus was also able to obtain some of Löfling's own papers and, from these sources, produced *Iter Hispanicum*. Although there are a number of binomials published here and attributed to Löfling, they can present difficulties, and the loss of Löfling's South American collections makes the interpretation of those names even more difficult. As they are not attributable to Linnaeus, they are beyond the scope of this study and have not been included. For more information on Löfling and his collections, see Chapter 6.

1758. ***Opera Varia.*** Lucca.
This is a reprint, apparently unauthorised, of Linnaeus' *Fundamenta Botanica*, ed. 2 (1740), *Sponsalia Plantarum* (1746), and *Systema Naturae*, ed. 4 (1744), in the *Regnum Vegetabile* portion of which (pp. 195–274) 14 Linnaean generic names (including *Achyronia*, *Aruncus*, *Dalea*, *Mitreola* and *Struthia*) were validated for the first time (see Dandy 1967).

1758. ***Systema Naturae***, ed. 10, vol. 1. Stockholm.
Linnaeus' *Systema Naturae* made its first appearance as a slim volume of 11 pages in 1735, but it grew steadily in size in later years until, with the addition of binomials in the 10th edition, it reached 1,384 pages, spread across two volumes. The first volume of the 10th edition was devoted to the animal kingdom, and now supplies the starting point for zoological nomenclature. However, in a small number of cases, species that Linnaeus believed to be "animal" are treated under the Botanical, rather than the Zoological, Code. Notable among these are a number of coralline algae, whose appearance led

Linnaeus to include them in his genera *Corallina*, *Eschara*, *Madrepora* and *Volvox*. Consequently, there are 12 binomials relating to algae first published here. They are *Corallina corniculata* L., *C. fragilissima* L., *C. officinalis* L., *C. opuntia* L., *C. penicillus* L., *C. rubens* L., *C. spermaphoros* L., *C. squamata* L., *Eschara divaricata* L., *E. fragilis* L., *Madrepora acetabulum* L. and *Volvox globator* L. These, and Linnaeus' other algal names, are the subject of a study by Spencer & al. (in press).

1759. ***Plantae Tinctoriae.*** [Dissertation of E. Jörlin]. (16 May) Uppsala.
This dissertation, dealing with dye plants, includes one new binomial, *Rhamnus minor* L. (p. 14). There is some doubt as to its valid publication, for although the epithet is italicised in the same way as for other previously published binomials listed in this work, the name is attributed to Bauhin. Linnaeus questioned whether the species might perhaps be only a variety of the preceding *R. catharticus* L. *Rhamnus minor* does not appear in any of Linnaeus' later works, with the exception of the reprint of this dissertation in *Amoen. Acad.* 5: 325 (1760).

1759. ***Systema Naturae***, ed. 10, vol. 2. (May–Jun) Stockholm.

The second volume of this edition of the *Systema Naturae* contains the plants, and there are some idiosyncrasies in the way in which the species are arranged and numbered. In earlier editions of the *Systema Naturae*, and in *Species Plantarum*, the species are numbered consecutively within each genus. However, in the 10th edition, rather than doing this again to reflect the number of species recognised in 1759, Linnaeus retained for each species the number it had carried in *Species Plantarum* (1753). Rather than leave unnumbered the names of those new species described either between 1753 and 1758 or

in the *Systema Naturae* itself, Linnaeus allocated letters to them. For example, in *Arenaria* (1759: 1033–1034; see below left), the species numbered one to five are the same as those in *Species Plantarum* (1753: 423), but the sixth (*A. montana* L.) was published in 1755 and carries "A". The next species, *A. rubra* L. was the sixth in 1753 and therefore carries "6" here too, but the next, *A. bavarica* L., was published in 1756 and so carries "B". Other lettered species are *A. striata* L. (1756), carrying "C" and inserted between species numbers "10" and "11", and *A. grandiflora* L., newly published and placed at the end of the genus, and carrying "D".

The necessarily concise nature of the diagnoses (with few synonyms or illustrations being cited) has occasionally caused difficulties in typifying names first published in this work, of which there are 625. Baum (1968) analysed the names involved, concluding that, where they lacked synonyms but were subsequently treated in the second edition of *Species Plantarum* (1762, 1763), usually with expanded synonymies etc., the names should be typified from the context of the later treatment. However, this is not tenable. While the later accounts can certainly be informative, they do not form part of the protologue and, for example, illustrations cited in 1762–1763, but missing from a 1759 protologue, are not original material for such names, and are hence ineligible as lectotypes. It cannot be assumed, either, that Linnaeus' opinions remained unchanged between 1759 and 1762–1763 for, as listed by Baum, 29 names present in 1759 do not appear in the later work.

1759. ***Amoenitates Academicae.*** Vol. 4. (Nov) Stockholm.
There are reprints of six notable dissertations in this collection. Some of the changes that occurred between the original dissertations and their reprints result in new names dating from the latter, but these are fewer than might be anticipated because many of the changes had already been incorporated into the second volume of *Systema Naturae*, ed. 10 (published earlier in May–June 1759).

Flora Anglica (1754) is reprinted (pp. 88–111) with, as noted by Stearn (1973a: 63), significant differences from the original dissertation. For example, *Carex remota* L. (1754) was replaced with *C. axillaris* L. (1759), and some 1754 names were relegated to the synonymy of species named earlier in *Species Plantarum* (e.g. *Papaver medium* L. (1754) was reduced to the synonymy of *P. dubium* L. (1753) in the reprint). Other names (e.g. *Hypericum elodes* L.) did not appear in the original dissertation but made their first appearance in the reprint, which contains eight nomenclatural novelties.

Herbarium Amboinense (1754) is reprinted (pp. 112–143) with some changes to, or replacements of names that had first appeared in the original, as well as adding new names for species described in the *Auctuarium* (a Supplement to Rumphius' six volumes that was published only in 1755). There are seven nomenclatural novelties published here.

Centuria I Plantarum (1755) is similarly reprinted (pp. 261–296) with significant changes. However, all seven of the new names, listed by Nordenstam (1961), had already been published elsewhere by the time the reprint appeared. *Dianthus superbus* L. had been published in *Fl. Suecica*, ed. 2 (1755), and the remaining six names were published in *Syst. Nat.*, ed. 10, 2 (May–Jun 1759).

The reprint (pp. 297–332) of *Centuria II Plantarum* (1756) also contains changes from the original, with three nomenclatural novelties, *Gratiola monnieri* (L.) L., *Dianthus monspessulanus* L. and *Anthyllis asphaltoides* L. (noted by Nordenstam 1961).

Flora Palaestina (1756) is reprinted (pp. 443–467) with no nomenclatural novelties.

Flora Monspeliensis (1756) is reprinted (pp. 468–495) and, as explained above, Linnaeus included a sentence (p. 475), missing from the original, indicating that the user should number the entries in Magnol's *Botanicum Monspeliense* (as Linnaeus had done in his own copy). The new binomials in the 1756 version, all of which are *nomina nuda* (names without a description or diagnosis), are validly published here (cf. ICBN Art. 45 Ex. 1). However, many of the names appearing here (in November 1759), had by then already been published in *Syst. Nat.*, ed. 10 (May–Jun 1759). The number of binomials validly published in the 1759 reprint is therefore few. Stearn (1974) accepts 16, and compares the two versions of the dissertation, their relationship with Magnol's book, and the consequent nomenclatural complications.

1759. ***Plantarum Jamaicensium Pugillus.*** [Dissertation of G. Elmgren]. (Nov) Uppsala.
This dissertation provided binomials for 129 taxa either collected, or described, by Patrick Browne (1720–1790). Linnaeus had a copy of Browne's *A Civil and Natural History of Jamaica* (1756), which described and illustrated hundreds of Jamaican plants, but which did not employ binomials. Linnaeus also acquired Browne's herbarium in 1758. As with the names in several other dissertations, many of those used in this thesis had already been published some months earlier in the second volume of *Syst. Nat.*, ed. 10 (1759), and there are only six new names published here. The dissertation was

reprinted in *Amoen. Acad.* 5: 389–413 (1760) with the title modified as "*Pugillus Jamaicensium Plantarum*".

1759. ***Flora Jamaicensis.*** [Dissertation of C.G. Sandmark]. (Dec) Uppsala.

This dissertation, although covering some of the same ground as *Plantarum Jamaicensium Pugillus*, published a month earlier (see above), was an attempt at providing binomial names for all of the species described by Patrick Browne in his *The Civil and Natural History of Jamaica* (1756). As with other dissertations that did the same for other, similar, publications, the format of the main part of the thesis was very succinct (see sample text above). For example, on p. 22, appears "Mimosa I Gigas 362" where 362 is the page number in Browne (1756), "I" the description intended (in this case, of "Gigalobium I"), and "*Mimosa Gigas*" is the binomial proposed for Browne's description. Where species had previously been treated in *Plantarum Jamaicensium Pugillus*, Linnaeus also provided an additional cross-reference, e.g. on p. 20, appending "E.120" to *Clutia cascarilla*. This indicated species No. 120 from the dissertation *Plantarum Jamaicensium Pugillus*, defended by Gabriel Elmgren ("E"). *Flora Jamaicensis* contains 46 nomenclatural novelties, although a significant proportion have been interpreted either as orthographic variants of earlier names, or are illegitimate. The reprint of this thesis (*Amoen. Acad.* 5: 371–388. 1760) contains some changes, and six nomenclatural novelties appear there.

1760. *Amoenitates Academicae.* Vol. 5 (Sep) Stockholm.
There are reprints of three notable dissertations in this collection.

Plantae Tinctoriae (1759) is reprinted (pp. 314–342) without significant change.

Flora Jamaicensis (1759) is reprinted (pp. 371–388) with six nomenclaturally significant differences from the original dissertation. The new names are *Achras tomentosa* L. (p. 378), *Loranthus altissima* L. (p. 377), *Schinus melicoccus* L. (p. 379), "*Spathalea sorbifolia*", nom. inval. (p. 377) and *Ximenia inermis* L. (p. 378), with *Peplis tetrandra* L. published simultaneously in the reprints of both this (p. 378) and *Plantarum Jamaicensium Pugillus* (p. 413).

Plantarum Jamaicensium Pugillus (1759) is reprinted (pp. 389–413), with the title modified as *Pugillus Jamaicensium Plantarum*, and with some change to the contents. The only nomenclatural novelty is *Peplis tetrandra* L., published simultaneously in the reprints of both this (p. 413) and *Flora Jamaicensis* (p. 378).

1760. *Plantae Rariores Africanae.* [Dissertation of J. Printz]. (Dec) Stockholm.
This dissertation provides descriptions and binomials for 102 species of plant from South Africa, mainly from the Cape of Good Hope (Cape Province). Although many of the new names have synonyms cited for them from the works of authors such as Breyn, Burman, Commelin, Hermann and Plukenet, the names are unusual for a Linnaean work in each being accompanied by a detailed description. This was possible because Linnaeus did not have to rely solely on published works – he also had rich South African collections, made by Oldenland and others, available to him through the Burmans. Originally acquired by Johannes Burman, these collections were brought to Uppsala by his son, Nicolaas Laurens Burman, who studied with Linnaeus during 1760.

The collections were subsequently returned to the Netherlands and never formed part of Linnaeus' own herbarium. Burman's collections were later acquired by Delessert, who bequeathed them to the Conservatoire et Jardin botaniques de la Ville de Genève on his death. Many of the collections believed to have been used by Linnaeus have been traced there, and designated as lectotypes. More detailed information on this material can be found in Chapters 5 and 6.

Most of the 102 species are new, but some are new combinations. The reprint (in *Amoen. Acad.* 6: 77–115. 1763) contained a number of changes and these have been listed by Nordenstam (1961: 278–279).

1761. **Florae Sueciae Novitiae.** *In: Fauna Suecica*, ed. 2, pp. 557–558. Stockholm.
These two pages of botanical notes list new records for 31 plants, together with the places where they were found and their collectors. His student Falk (sometimes Falck), for example, is credited with noting six species from Gotland (during his visit in 1759), including "*Crataegus hybrida*" (p. 557), an apparent novelty but, as it lacks a diagnosis, it is a *nomen nudum*.

1762. *Planta Alströmeria.* [Dissertation of J.P. Falck]. (Jun) Uppsala.
This dissertation was an account of the genus *Alstroemeria*, named by Linnaeus for his apostle, Clas Alströmer. The generic name, and three species, *A. ligtu* L., *A. pelegrina* L. and *A. salsilla* L. were all newly published here.

1762. **Linnaeus, C. filius.** *Decas Prima Plantarum Rariorum Horti Upsaliensis* (Apr–Jul) Stockholm.
This is one of Linnaeus filius' earliest publications, which provided detailed descriptions, accompanied by engravings, for each of 10 species that had been cultivated in the botanic garden in Uppsala. Nine of the names are new (*Astragalus chinensis* L. f., *Ethulia conyzoides* L. f., *Hedysarum junceum* L. f. (typified by the accompanying plate), *Lithospermum dispermum* L. f., *Mercurialis ambigua* L. f., *Nolana prostrata* L. f., *Senecio varicosus* L. f., *Solanum radicans* L. f. and *Zygophyllum album* L. f.). However, *Tripsacum hermaphroditum* L. had been described in 1759. As only a few new species were described here by Linnaeus filius, and because they were taken up in later works by his father, we have included these names within our study.

A second, similar publication (see *Dec. Secunda Pl. Rar. Horti Upsal.* 1763) followed.

1762. *Species Plantarum*, ed. 2, vol. 1. (Sep) Stockholm.
The second edition of *Species Plantarum* followed the same format as the first edition but contained significantly more species, incorporating as it did the new taxa that Linnaeus had described since 1753. In addition, other authors were beginning to adopt the Linnaean method and this second edition therefore included generic names attributable to authors such as Patrick Browne (1758), and binomial names published by Osbeck (1757), Burman (1759), Jacquin (1760, 1762, 1763), William Hudson (1762) and Linnaeus' son (Linnaeus filius 1762). As in 1753, the two volumes were published separately, volume two of the second edition appearing more than a year after volume one.

Changes in Linnaeus' generic and species concepts since 1753, along with the description of further new species, resulted in the two volumes together providing 712 nomenclatural novelties.

In his previous attempt to account for all the plants then known, in *Systema Naturae*, ed. 10, vol. 2 (1759), Linnaeus had retained the species numbers from 1753, giving letters to any species described since then. However, in the second edition of *Species Plantarum*, he re-numbered all the species and eliminated the use of letters.

The guide given by Heller (1959) to the abbreviated references used by Linnaeus in 1753 is also relevant here, with those published after 1753 being listed by Stearn (1961: xviii–xxii).

1763. *Lignum Quassiae.* [Dissertation of G.M.C.M. Blom]. (28 May) Uppsala.

This botanico-medical dissertation on the uses of "Lignum Quassiae" (amargo, a bark with quinine-like uses) contained a detailed description of the plant from which it was derived, which Linnaeus (pp. 6–7) described as *Quassia amara* L. This binomial name first appeared in *Sp. Pl.*, ed. 2, 1: 553 (1762). The dissertation (28 May 1763) pre-dates a further short account of the species in *Sp. Pl.*, ed. 2, 2: 1679 (Oct 1763).

1763. *Species Plantarum*, ed. 2, vol. 2. (Oct) Stockholm.

Volume two of the second edition of *Species Plantarum* was published a full year after the first volume appeared (see additional information above). However, unlike the first edition (where the ICBN rules that, for nomenclatural purposes, both volumes are deemed to have been published simultaneously), priority for names in the second edition dates from September 1762 (vol. 1) and October 1763 (vol. 2) respectively.

The guide (Heller 1959) to the abbreviated references used by Linnaeus in 1753 is also relevant here, with those published after 1753 being listed by Stearn (1961: xviii–xxii).

1763. *Amoenitates Academicae.* Vol. 6. (Oct) Stockholm.

This volume contains reprints of three notable dissertations.

Plantae Rariores Africanae (1760) is reprinted (pp. 77–115) with a number of changes from the original which were listed by Nordenstam (1961: 278–279). The only nomenclatural novelty is "*Orchis satyroides*", nom. illeg. (p. 109).

Planta Alströmeria (1762) is reprinted (pp. 247–262) without significant changes from the original.

Lignum Quassiae (1763) is reprinted (pp. 416–429), also without significant changes from the original.

1763. *Decas Secunda Plantarum Rariorum Horti Upsaliensis* (post-Oct) Stockholm.

This is a second publication (see *Dec. Prima Pl. Rar. Horti Upsal.* 1762) by Linnaeus filius containing descriptions and illustrations of another 10 species grown in the Hortus at Uppsala. However, this evidently appeared after volume two of the second edition of *Species Plantarum* (to which page references are made), and none of the 10 names is newly described here by Linnaeus filius.

1764. *Genera Plantarum*, ed. 6. (Jun) Stockholm.

As in the case of the first edition of *Species Plantarum* (1753) and the fifth edition of *Genera Plantarum* (1754), the names of the genera introduced in the second edition (1762–1763) of the former are associated with the descriptions in the sixth edition of the latter (Art. 13.4). The Appendix, however, also contains a number of new species names. They are "*Asplenium rhizophorum*", nom. illeg., *Cistus villosus* L., *Cytinus hypocistis* (L.) L., *Ambrosina bassii* L., "*Grielum tenuifolium*", nom. illeg., "*Schwenckia americana*", nom. illeg., "*Perilla ocymoides*", nom. illeg., and *Roridula dentata* L.

1764. *Opobalsamum Declaratum.* [Dissertation of W. Le Moine]. (Dec) Uppsala.

This primarily medical dissertation contains descriptions of three new species, *Amyris opobalsamum* L., *A. gileadensis* L. and *Forsskaolea tenacissima* L. It was reprinted, without significant change, in *Amoen. Acad.* 7: 55–73 (1769).

1764. *Species Plantarum*, ed. 3. 3 vols, Vienna.

Although described as a third edition, this is essentially a reprint of the second edition (1762–1763) with Linnaeus' errata incorporated into the main text. Its publication was probably arranged by Linnaeus' supporter N.J. Jacquin (Lack 2005: 35). It contains no nomenclatural novelties.

1767. *Systema Naturae*, ed. 12, vol. 1(2). Stockholm.

As in the case of the 10th edition of the *Systema Naturae*, names of algal taxa can appear among the animals in the second part of volume one (part 1 appeared in 1766). *Lichen cinereus* L., *Millepora coriacea* L., *M. polymorpha* L., *Tubularia acetabulum* (L.) L. and *T. fragilis* (L.) L. are the new names applicable to taxa treated under the ICBN to appear here.

1767. *Systema Naturae*, ed. 12, vol. 2, *Regnum Vegetabile* (Oct) Stockholm.

By its 12th edition, the *Systema Naturae* had grown so large that it extended to three volumes and, for the first time, volume two (which dealt with the plants) was paginated independently from volume one. Increasing numbers of other authors were by now adopting Linnaeus' binomial nomenclature and, in addition to the names of Burman, Hudson, Jacquin and Linnaeus filius that had been included in the second edition of *Species Plantarum* (1762–1763), Linnaeus also adopted binomials that had been published by Arduino (1764), Turra (1765) and Bergius (1767).

Volume two also contains 508 nomenclatural novelties, 370 of which bear a cross-reference, usually in the form "Mant. 72", to Linnaeus' simultaneously published *Mantissa Plantarum [Prima]*. While the *Systema Naturae* accounts for each species are usually restricted to a diagnosis, the parallel *Mantissa* accounts are usually more detailed, often including synonyms, descriptions and information on provenance and distribution. It follows that new species appearing in both works have a protologue that encompasses both accounts (Stearn 1961: vii). An anonymously published index to this work, probably attributable to N.J. Jacquin (Lack 2000: 331), is in existence (Anon. 1770).

1767. *Mantissa Plantarum [Prima]*. (Oct) Stockholm.
The relationship between the *Mantissa Plantarum [Prima]* and *Systema Naturae*, ed. 12, 2 has been referred to above under the latter work. A detailed account has been provided by Stearn (1961) and, as he explains, there are nomenclatural complications arising from other publications that appeared at about the same time.

Bergius' *Descriptiones Plantarum* (Sep 1767) narrowly pre-dates the *Mantissa*, and includes a number of the same Cape species that Linnaeus was describing, but with different names, much to Linnaeus' irritation. For example, *Corymbium scabridum* P. J. Bergius and *C. scabrum* L. (see Sprague 1940) referred to the same species (though they were based on entirely different material). Where they compete in this way, Bergius' names are earlier and have priority over those of Linnaeus.

There are also some complications in relation to Burman's *Flora Indica* (Apr 1768) in that about 20 of the 241 binomials published by Burman also appeared earlier in the *Mantissa* (Merrill 1921), while another 25 species appeared in both works but were given different binomials by Linnaeus. Stearn (1961: viii–x) explains the reasons for this but, where these names compete, those of Linnaeus have priority. Merrill (1921) provides a detailed analysis of the names appearing in these two works. The abbreviated references used by Linnaeus that were not elucidated by Heller (1959), i.e. those published after 1753, are listed by Stearn (1961: xviii–xxii).

Although most of the new names that appeared in the *Mantissa* were simultaneously published in the *Systema*, there are four names, *Brabyla capensis* L., *Cotula pyrethraria* L., *Cotula spilanthes* L. and *Portlandia hexandra* L., that can be found only in the *Mantissa*.

1768. *Systema Naturae*, ed. 12, vol. 3. Stockholm.
The third volume of the 12th edition of the *Systema* contains predominantly mineralogical descriptions but there is also a botanical appendix (pp. 229–236) containing descriptions and names of 20 new species, along with two new combinations.

1769. *Amoenitates Academicae*, vol. 7. Stockholm.
This volume contains reprints of only one notable dissertation, that of ***Opobalsamum declaratum*** (1764) on pp. 55–73. The volume contains no nomenclatural novelties.

1770. *Calceolaria pinnata*, En rar Váxt, beskrifven af Carl v. Linné. *Kongliga Vetenskaps Academiens Handlingar* 31: 286–292. (Oct–Dec).
This short article contains a detailed description of *Calceolaria*, along with the binomials *C. pinnata* L. (p. 288) and *C. integrifolia* L. (p. 289).

1770. *Münchhausen*, O. von. *Der Hausvater* 5: 5(1): 357.
A single Linnaean name, *Munchausia speciosa* L. (p. 357) appeared in this work.

1770. *Erica*. [Dissertation of J.A. Dahlgren]. (Dec) Uppsala.
This dissertation dealt with the whole of the genus *Erica*, and included 17 new species, mostly from South Africa. These names have presented difficulties in some cases, partly as a result of the format of the dissertation. This was unusual in that the characters for each species were presented in tabular form, resulting in diagnoses/descriptions that are often very generalised. Some of these names have been the subject of a detailed study by Oliver & Oliver (2002). *Erica petiveri* L. is typified by an illustration (f. 50 in the illustration reproduced here on p. 100) in this dissertation. The dissertation was reprinted in *Amoen. Acad.* 8: 46–62 (1785).

1771. *Mantissa Plantarum Altera*. (Oct) Stockholm.
This represents a second part (see Stearn 1961: x–xviii) of the *Mantissa Plantarum [Prima]*, published in 1767, the pagination of this later section (pp. 143–687) following that of the earlier part (pp. 1–142). Pages 143–169 describe new genera, and new species and some new combinations are described or created on pages 170–314. The remainder of the book comprises "Observationes in Species Plantarum cum Emendationibus et Animadversionibus". However, nomenclatural novelties, 430 in all, can be found scattered throughout the book. Binomials published by Burman (1768) and Vandelli (1771) are also included here. The abbreviated references used by Linnaeus that were not elucidated by Heller (1959), i.e. those published after 1753, are listed by Stearn (1961: xviii–xxii).

Following page: Plate from Linnaeus' dissertation on the genus *Erica* (1770) showing the range of floral variation encountered

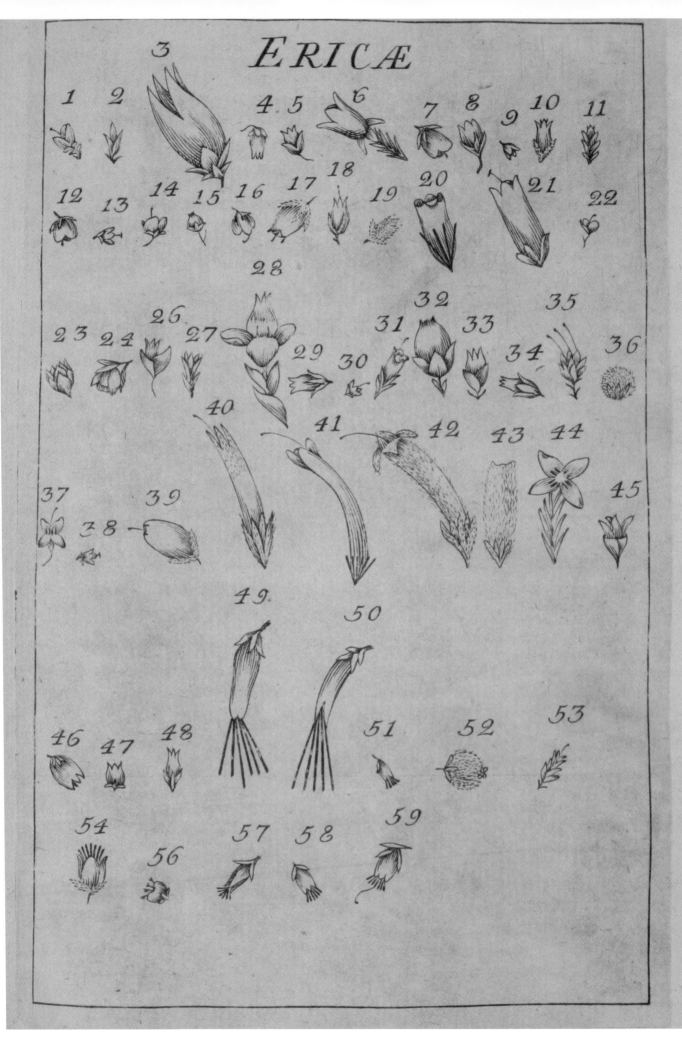

ERICÆ

1774. *Systema Vegetabilium*, ed. 13 [Murray, J.A. (ed.)]. (spring) Göttingen & Gotha.
As noted by Stearn (1957: 23), this was a revised edition of the botanical part of *Systema Naturae*, ed. 12 (1767), published by J.A. Murray and based on Linnaeus' annotated copy of the earlier work which Murray had borrowed from Linnaeus. It contains 66 nomenclatural novelties, attributable to Linnaeus rather than Murray.

1775. *Plantae Surinamenses . . .* [Dissertation of J. Alm]. (Jun) Uppsala.
This dissertation was based primarily on plants that had been collected in Surinam by Carl Gustaf Dahlberg (d. 1775), and 34 new species (some of the names of which, however, are illegitimate) were described for the first time. The thesis was reprinted, and published posthumously, in *Amoenitates Academicae* 8: 249–267 (1785). *Gustavia augusta* L. was one of the species described here and named for the new King, Gustav III, and was evidently based on a number of sheets of material. There are three sheets extant in the herbarium at the Linnean Society of London, and another three in Stockholm (S: 290.13, 290.15, and probably 290.17). One of the latter (see p. 102) bears a label written by P.J. Beurling which says "Surinam: herbar. Prof. Alm, qui specimen accepit a Linneo patre, sub cuius praesidiode arbore haec magnifica academice disseruit". Jacob Alm was the student who had defended this dissertation.

1776. *Planta Aphyteia.* [Dissertation of E. Acharius]. (Jun) Uppsala.
Just one nomenclatural novelty, *Aphyteia hydnora* L. (a superfluous name for *Hydnora africana* Thunb. (1775) and therefore illegitimate), appears in this dissertation. The thesis was reprinted, and published posthumously, in *Amoen. Acad.* 8: 310–317 (1785).

1776. *Hypericum.* [Dissertation of C.N. Hellenius]. (Nov) Uppsala.
Two new species, *Hypericum guineense* L. and *H. mexicanum* L. were published in this dissertation. The thesis was reprinted in *Amoen. Acad.* 8: 318–332 (1785).

Next page: Material of *Gustavia augusta* L. in the Linnaean herbarium in Stockholm

1776. *A Catalogue of the Birds, Beasts, Fishes, Insects, Plants &c. Contained in Edwards's Natural History, in seven volumes, with their Latin Names by Sir C. Linnaeus.* London.

Published by the London bookseller, Jacob Robson, this work gave binomials, supplied by Linnaeus, for the species described in Edwards' seven-volume work (see p. 127). These are predominantly animals, but there are a few plants, and *Gentiana autumnalis* L. (p. 11) is newly published here, validated by the associated description included by the naturalist Edwards, which came originally from William Bartram in North America. The associated plate (see above) is the lectotype of this Linnaean name.

1782. *Supplementum Plantarum Systematis Vegetabilium editum a Carolo a Linné [Fil.].* Brunswick.
Although names published in the *Supplementum Plantarum* are attributed to Linnaeus filius, it is clear that names and descriptions for a significant number of them were originally prepared by Linnaeus in the years between 1771 and his death. However, the names published in the *Supplementum Plantarum* are numerous, are to be attributed to Linnaeus filius, and are beyond the scope of this study.

Gustavia augusta Linn.

(*Pirigara superba* H.B.K.)

Surinam: herbar. Prof. Alm, qui speçi=
men accepit a Linnaeo patre, sub cujus pre=
sidio de arbone hac magnifica açademi-
çe disseruit.

} manu P. J. Beurling.

L. Am. ac. VIII.
266.
("Planta surinamensis)
Suppl. plant. 313

Monadelp.
Polyand.

SOG-14961

Chapter 4
Sources of Information – Literature used by Linnaeus

It seems desirable to devote some space to the important publications used, and cited, by Linnaeus that formed his species concepts. A complete list of such works would be very large indeed and, as this has already been covered in a general way by others, this commentary will concentrate on those published works that have particular significance in the typification of Linnaean names. Under the ICBN, types may be specimens or illustrations (but not descriptions). Consequently, the works considered here are predominantly those containing figures, whether woodcuts or copperplates, as illustrations (on sheets also imprinted on the back) or plates (the backs of which are blank). While most are pre-Linnaean works, post-1753 publications are included, some using binomial nomenclature, where they are significant. More detailed bibliographic information on most of these works can be found elsewhere (e.g. Richter 1840, Pritzel 1871–1877). However, direct references are included here to Stafleu & Cowan's *Taxonomic Literature*, ed. 2 (1976–1988) and to its supplements (Stafleu & Mennega 1992–2000) abbreviated as "TL-2", to Heller's *Index auctorum et librorum a Linnaeo* (Species Plantarum, *1753) citatorum* (1959), abbreviated to "Heller", and to Stearn's *Introductory Notes on Linnaeus's Mantissa Plantarum* (1961), abbreviated as "Stearn". Heller's extremely useful study provides a key to the various abbreviations employed by Linnaeus to indicate the publications that were cited in the first edition of *Species Plantarum* (1753). Stearn (1971) deals in a similar way with later publications that were cited in the *Mantissa Plantarum* (1767) and the *Mantissa Plantarum Altera* (1771), as well as in intervening Linnaean publications. Linnaeus' own library forms part of the collections of the Linnean Society of London, and many of his own copies contain annotations which can be helpful in interpreting his species concepts and identifications. The figures and/or plates in some illustrated works (e.g. Patrick Browne's *Civil and Natural History of Jamaica* of 1756) often bear binomial names written by Linnaeus and the works annotated in this way have been listed by Savage (1940). The following list is in alphabetical order by author, with the name in Latinised form first.

Plate from Patrick Browne's *Civil and Natural History of Jamaica* (t. 11. 1756), the lectotype of *Portlandia grandiflora* L.

Aldinus. Tobia Aldini (fl. 1625).

1625. *Exactissima descriptio . . . plantarum . . . in horto Farnesiano*. Rome. Heller: 11.

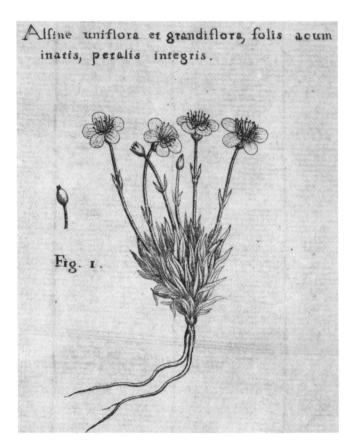

In this account of plants cultivated in the Farnese Gardens in Rome, Aldini provided a number of detailed descriptions, along with 22 copperplate illustrations, several of which were cited as synonyms by Linnaeus. One of these formed the basis for *Mimosa farnesiana* L., and Aldini's plate 4 is the lectotype of that name. Bernardi (1984) and Jarvis (1993) both reproduce this illustration, and Jarvis provides further information on Aldini's work. This work is sometimes attributed to Pietro Castelli (1590–1656).

Allioni. Carlo Allioni (1725–1804).

1755. *Rariorum Pedemontii Stirpium Specimen primum*. Turin. TL-2: 19.053a.

This work contained detailed descriptions of 32 species from what is now north-western Italy, each of which was illustrated in one of the 12 plates. Caramiello & Forneris (2004) have published a facsimile edition, accompanied by a

detailed commentary which includes modern identifications of each plant. Linnaeus cited a number of Allioni's descriptions, and plate 10, f. 1 is the type of *Arenaria grandiflora* L. (see above). For information on Allioni's specimens, see Chapter 6.

Alpinus. Prospero Alpino (or Alpini) (1553–1617).

1627. *De plantis exoticis libri duo Prosperi Alpini . . .* Venice. Heller: 11.

Turland (1995) has provided an overview of this work, with its 145 copperplate illustrations, particularly in relation to the flora of Crete. Eight of the figures are types for Linnaean names, including those of *Serratula chamaepeuce* (p. 76; see opposite, upper left), *Nymphaea lotus* (p. 213) and *Verbascum spinosum* (p. 36).

1640. *Prosperi Alpini De Plantis Aegypti liber, cum . . . notis Ioannis Veslingii . . .* , ed. 2. Padova. Heller: 11.

This account of plants from the Middle East included 73 woodcut illustrations, many of which were cited by Linnaeus. A number of Linnaean names are typified by figures published in this edition (e.g. *Ximenia aegyptiaca* L., *Dolichos lablab* L.). The additional portion attributed to Vesling, which though dated 1638, was probably published in 1640, includes the type of *Convolvulus cairicus* L. (p. 74).

such as *Cymbaria daurica* L., *Gentiana aquatica* L., *Leonurus sibiricus* L., *Rhododendron dauricum* L. and *Stellera chamaejasme* L. (see above) are typified by Amman's plates.

1741 ["1736"]. Quinque nova plantarum genera.
Commentarii Academiae Scientiarum Imperialis Petropolitanae 8: 211–219, pl. 13–18. Heller: 51.
Amman's description of five new genera was accompanied by six plates. His "*Leontopetaloides*" appears to have been the sole basis for *Leontice leontopetaloides* L. (1753), and Amman's plate is the type of the latter. It has been reproduced by Merrill (1945: 90, pl. II A, B).

1744 ["1737"]. De Betula pumila. *Commentarii Academiae Scientiarum Imperialis Petropolitanae* 9: 314–315, pl. 14. Heller: 52.
Amman's description and plate were cited in the synonymy of *Betula nana* L. (1753), though this is not the type of that name. For information on Amman's specimens, see Chapter 6.

Arduino. Pietro Arduino (1728–1805).
1764 ["1763"]. Animadversionum Botanicarum Specimen Alterum. Venice. TL-2: 160.
Stearn (*in notula*, BM copy) notes evidence from the correspondence between Arduino and Linnaeus that this

1719. *Prosperi Alpini . . . Medicina Aegyptiorum: accedunt . . . libri De balsamo & Rhapontico.* Leiden. Heller: 11.
The single copperplate in this work was cited in the synonymy of *Rheum rhaponticum* L. (1753: 371–372), although it is not the type of the name.

1735. *Prosperi Alpini . . . Historiae naturalis Aegypti pars secunda, sive De plantis Aegypti liber auctus et emendatus . . . cum notis Joannis Veslingii.* Leiden. Heller: 11.
This is an emended and expanded edition of Alpinus (1640), with copperplates replacing the woodcuts of that edition. This work includes, among others, the type of *Euphorbia viminalis* L.

Ammanus. Johann Amman (1707–1741).
1739. *Stirpium rariorum in Imperio Rutheno sponte provenientium icones et descriptiones collectae ab Ioanne Ammano.* St Petersburg. TL-2: 114; Heller: 11.
Amman's descriptions of species were accompanied by 35 copperplates, many of which were cited by Linnaeus. Names

Barrelierus. Jacques Barrelier (1606–1673).
1714. *Plantae per Galliam, Hispaniam et Italiam observatae*. Paris. Heller: 12.

Lotus siliquosa maritima lutea Cytisi facie

This work, covering plants from France, Spain and parts of what is now Italy, contains 334 copperplates comprising 1,324 figures, which are numbered consecutively. They were cited fairly extensively by Linnaeus, and at least 12 serve as types for Linnaean names, including *Arum proboscideum* L. (reproduced by Forneris 2004: 129, III), *Achillea macrophylla* L., *Cynosurus durus* L., *Lotus cytisoides* L. (see above) and *Oxalis barrelieri* L.

Bartholinus. Thomas Bartholin (1616–1680).
1671–1672. Obs. 59, dn. Olai Borrichii, Plantae in planis silicibus enatae. *Acta Medica & Philosophica Hafniensia* 1671–1672: 118–119, 1 plate. Heller: 12. This figure was cited in the synonymy of *Fucus filum* L. (1753).

work was probably published in 1764, rather than 1763 as dated. It contains detailed descriptions of a number of species, illustrated by 20 copperplates (see that of *Buphthalmum speciosissimum* above). Arduino gave binomial names to these species, some of which are the earliest for the taxa in question (e.g. *Salvia ceratophylloides* Ard.). Linnaeus generally included them in *Systema Naturae*, ed. 12 (1767), but sometimes coined superfluous names of his own for them (e.g. *Cacalia suffruticosa* L. (1767), *nom. illeg.* is a replacement name for *C. linifolia* Ard.). For information on Arduino's specimens, see Chapter 6.

Bannister. John Banister (1654–1692).
1688. *E catalogo . . . quem composuit d. Johannes Bannister plantarum . . . in Virginia observatarum. In:* Ray, J., *Historia Plantarum* 2: 1926–1928). TL-2: 8701; Heller: 12, 48. Although there are no accompanying illustrations, Linnaeus did occasionally cite this work (e.g. for *Orontium aquaticum* L.).

1673. Obs. 130, dn. Petri Kyllingii, Plantae quaedam domesticae rarae. *Acta Medica & Philosophica Hafniensia* 2: 345–347, 1 plate. Heller: 12.

The figure was cited in the synonymy of *Linnaea borealis* L.

1674–1675. Obs. 81, Joh. Val Willii, Rara quaedam in plantis observata. *Acta Medica & Philosophica Hafniensia* 3: 143–147, 7 illustrations. Heller: 12.

One of the figures (t. 143) was cited in the synonymy of *Cochlearia groenlandica* L. (1753) and has been discussed by Elven & Nordal (2002), and reproduced by Jarvis (2005).

1676. Obs. 1, De herba thée Asiaticorum, ex epistula dn. Andreae Clyers . . . script . . . 1674 . . . ad d.d. Simonem Paulli. *Acta Medica & Philosophica Hafniensia* 4: 1–2, 1 plate. Heller: 12.

The figure was cited in the synonymy of *Thea sinensis* L. (1753).

Bauhinus, C. Caspar Bauhin (1560–1624), brother of Johann Bauhin (1541–1612).

1620. *Prodromus theatri botanici Caspari Bauhini.* Frankfurt am Main. TL-2: 366; Heller: 13.

An important work, containing 138 woodcut illustrations, many cited by Linnaeus. Some serve as lectotypes for Linnaean names, notably *Cardamine resedifolia* L. (see below left), *Fagonia cretica* L. and *Peucedanum alsaticum* L.

1623. *Pinax theatri botanici Caspari Bauhini.* Basel. TL-2: 367, Heller: 13.

A reprint was published in 1671. Although lacking figures, this was an extremely important work to Linnaeus. Firstly, Bauhin's taxonomic system, laid out in the *Pinax*, was at this time still in widespread use in Europe, so it was important for Linnaeus to account for Bauhin's names both in his own new system and in the synonymy of individual species. Secondly, there was in Uppsala the extensive herbarium of Joachim Burser (1583–1639), which was arranged and named according to the *Pinax*, Burser having been a correspondent of Caspar Bauhin. Linnaeus was able to use Burser's herbarium as a voucher collection for the interpretation of Bauhin's names, and it contains many Linnaean type specimens.

1658. *Caspari Bauhini . . . Theatri botanici . . . liber primus.* Basel. Heller: 13.

This contains 254 woodcut illustrations, many of which appear in the synonymy of Linnaean binomials. *Cyperus esculentus* L. (see p. 107, right) and *Phalaris utriculata* L., for example, are typified by illustrations from this work.

Bauhinus, J. Johann Bauhin (1541–1612), brother of Caspar Bauhin (1560–1624).

1650–1651. *Historia Plantarum Universalis, auctoribus Johanne Bauhino . . . Joh. Henrico Cherlero.* Yverdon. TL-2: 368; Heller: 13.

An enormous work by Bauhin & Cherler containing 3,577 woodcut illustrations. Though usually small, and sometimes difficult to interpret, many are cited by Linnaeus. At least 20 figures serve as types for Linnaean binomials, including *Phyteuma pinnatum* L. (see Turland 2006: 305, f. 2), *Pinus*

pinea L., *Quercus aegilops* L. and *Sisymbrium asperum* L. (see below left).

Bellonius. Pierre Belon (1517–1564).

1553. *De arboribus coniferis.* Paris. Heller: 13. Some of the eight woodcut illustrations were cited by Linnaeus, notably for *Pinus cembra* L.

1605. *Plurimarum . . . rerum in Graecia, Asia . . . ab ipso conspectarum observationes . . .* 242 pp. *In*: Clusius, C. *Exoticorum libri decem . . .* Leiden. TL-2: 1150; Heller: 18.

This work supplies the type of *Pinus cedrus* L.

Beslerus. Basilius Besler (1561–1629).

1613. *Hortus Eystettensis.* Nuremberg. TL-2: 497; Heller: 13.

This famous folio work contains 367 copperplates, a number of which were cited as synonyms by Linnaeus (the central figure reproduced above is from the synonymy of *Scilla italica* L.). Schwertschläger (1890) attempted to correlate Besler's names with Linnaean nomenclature. *Aconitum lycoctonum* L. is typified by a figure from Besler's work.

Blair. Patrick Blair (1666–1728).

1718. *Miscellaneous Observations . . . in Botany.* London. Heller: 14.

Blair's work contains only two copperplates, one of which was cited by Linnaeus in the synonymy of *Rumex digynus* L.

Boccone. Paolo (later Silvio) Boccone (1633–1704).

1674. *Icones et Descriptiones Rariorum Plantarum Siciliae, Melitae, Galliae, & Italiae, &c.* Oxford. Heller: 14.

Boccone's descriptions and 52 copperplate illustrations (often comprising several different figures) of plants from southern Europe were a valuable source of information from an area less well known to Linnaeus, and the accounts are frequently cited by him. A number of Boccone's figures are types for Linnaean names, notably for *Campanula dichotoma* L., *Datura ferox* L., *Erigeron siculus* L., *Glinus lotoides* L. (see f. IIB above) and *Iberis semperflorens* L. A significant amount of Boccone's herbarium material is still in existence in BOLO, GE, L, LY, OXF, P and W. However, none of it was studied by Linnaeus, and it is the cited illustrations, rather than any unseen material, that must be taken into consideration for typification purposes. The Boccone plate cited in the synonymy of *Silene fruticosa* L. is reproduced by Lack (2003: 454, Abb. 7), along with voucher material from the Austrian National Academy in Vienna (as Abb. 8).

1697. *Museo di Piante Rare della Sicilia.* Venice. Heller: 14.

This later work contained more than 130 additional copperplates of southern (and some eastern, e.g. *Campanula saxatilis* L. from Crete) Mediterranean plants, some of which are types (e.g. for *Daucus gingidium* L., *Geum reptans* L. and *Solidago linifolia* L.). The types of *Arum proboscideum* L. (t. 50) and *Campanula saxatilis* (ad t. 64) are reproduced by Forneris (2004: 129) and Turland (2006: 304, f. 1) respectively.

1697. *Museo di fisica e di esperienze variato, e decorato di osservazioni naturali: . . .* Venice.

One of the 18 cited plates is cited in the synonymy of *Fucus filum* L. (1753).

Boerhaave. Herman Boerhaave (1668–1738).

1720. *Index Alter Plantarum quae in Horto Academico Lugduno-Batavo aluntur.* Leiden. TL-2: 593; Heller: 14.

Most of the 40 copperplates in this account of plants growing at the Botanic Garden in Leiden were cited by Linnaeus, and several are types of names of South African species in the Proteaceae, including *Leucadendron cancellatum* L., *L. conocarpodendron* L. (see above), *L. cucullata* L., *L. hypophyllocarpodendron* L. and *L. repens* L.

Boissier de la Croix de Sauvages – see **Sauvages**.

Bontius – see **Piso**.

Bradley. Richard Bradley (1688–1732).
  **1716–1727. *Historia Plantarum Succulentarum.* Decas
  I–V.** London. TL-2: 699; Heller: 15.

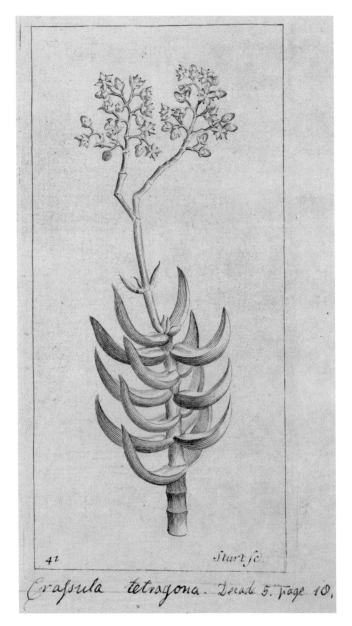

An important work in the history of the study of succulent
plants; some of the 50 plates were cited by Linnaeus. Rowley
(1954) provides modern nomenclature for Bradley's names
(see also Preston & Sell 1989: 228), and *Crassula fruticulosa*
L. is typified by one of the illustrations (see above).

Breynius. Jakob Breyn(e) (1637–1697); Johann Philipp
Breyn(e) (1680–1764).
  1678. *Exoticarum . . . Plantarum Centuria Prima.*
  Danzig. TL-2: 751; Heller: 15.

Just over a hundred copperplates accompanied Breyn's text,
and many were cited by Linnaeus. Among them are the types
of *Gomphrena brasiliana* L., *Mimosa sensitiva* L., *Poinciana
pulcherrima* L. (see above) and *Tulipa breyniana* L.
  1680. *Prodromus Fasciculi Rariorum Plantarum.* Danzig.
  TL-2: 752; Heller: 15. See Breyn (1739) opposite.
  **1689. *Prodromus Fasciculi Rariorum Plantarum
  Secundus.*** Danzig. TL-2: 752; Heller: 15. See Breyn (1739)
  opposite.
  1719. Obs. 2. De balsamo Carpathico. *Acta Physico-
  Medica Academiae Caesareae Leopoldino-Carolinae Naturae
  Curiosorum exhibentia Ephemerides ... (Nürnberg)* Cent. 7:
  4–8, pl. 1. Heller: 39.
  Breyn's plate (see opposite, left), accompanying a detailed
description, is the lectotype of *Pinus cembra* L.

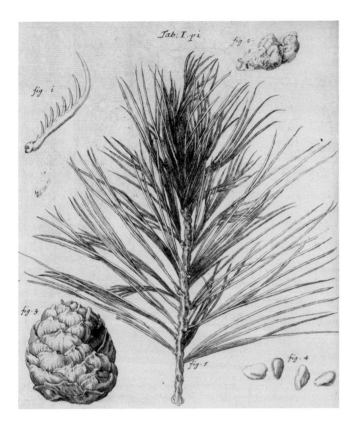

1739. *Prodromi Fasciculi Rariorum Plantarum Primus et Secundus . . . Nova Hac Editione.* Danzig. TL-2: 753; Heller: 15.

A second edition of Jakob Breyn's two *Prodromi* (1680, 1689), edited by his son Johann Philipp, with additional material and copperplates. Among names typified by figures published here are *Hyacinthus orchioides* L., *Xeranthemum imbricatum* L. and *X. proliferum* L.

Browne. Patrick Browne (1720–1790).
1756. *The Civil and Natural History of Jamaica.* London. TL-2: 842, Stearn: xix.

For *Species Plantarum* (1753), Linnaeus had relied upon the published work of Sir Hans Sloane (1707, 1725) for information on the plants of Jamaica. However, in 1756, Patrick Browne published this book, with detailed descriptions, 49 copperplates, and numerous new genera (see Oswald & Nelson 2000 for a list), though he did not adopt binomial nomenclature for species. Linnaeus acquired both the book, and Browne's own herbarium (in 1758), and this resulted in Linnaeus being able to provide binomials for the many new species that Browne had described or collected (see Nelson 1997). These new names were variously published in the 10th edition of *Systema Naturae* (May–Jun 1759), and the dissertations *Plantarum Jamaicensium Pugillus* (Nov 1759) and *Flora Jamaicensis* (Dec 1759), with some additional nomenclatural novelties appearing in the reprints

of these theses in *Amoenitates Academicae* 5: 371–413 (1760). Browne's figures designated as types of Linnaean names include those for *Cedrela odorata* L., *Ixora occidentalis* L., *Justicia assurgens* L. and *Portlandia grandiflora* L. (see plate on p. 103). Nelson (2000) gives further information on Browne; for information on his specimens, see Chapter 6.

Brunfelsius. Otto Brunfels (1488–1534).
1530. *Herbarium Vivum Eicones.* Strassburg. TL-2: 852; Heller: 15.

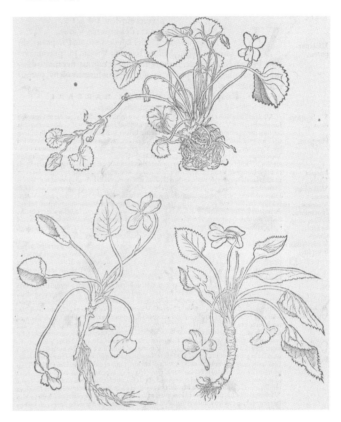

Brunfels' Herbal contains 86 woodcut illustrations, many of which were cited by Linnaeus. Among these, the illustrations associated with *Ophrys spiralis* L. and *Viola hirta* L. (see above, lower, right figure) are the types of those names. Sprague (1928) discusses the work in some detail and provides binomial nomenclature for Brunfels' names.

Buettnerus. David S. A. Büttner (1724–1768).
1750. *Enumeratio Methodica Plantarum Carmine. In:* Cuno, *Ode über seinen Garten . . . zweite Auflage,* pp. 209–230, 1 pl. Amsterdam. Heller: 16.

Following page (112): Plate from Patrick Browne's *Civil and Natural History of Jamaica* (t. 6. 1756), the upper part (f. 2) of which is the lectotype of *Ixora occidentalis* L. (= *Faramea occidentalis* (L.) A. Rich.)

Tab. 6

Fig. 2.

Fig. 1.

B. Ehret delin.

J. Noual Sculp.

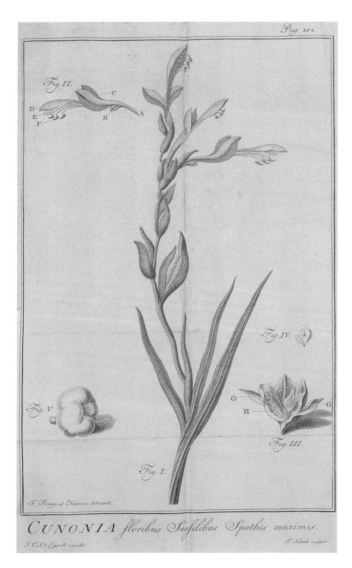

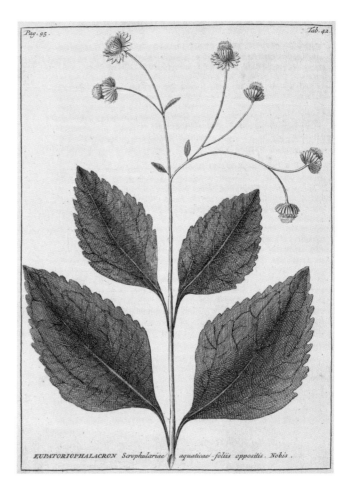

The single plate (see above) included in Büttner's publication was cited by Linnaeus in the synonymy of *Antholyza cunonia* L., of which it is also the lectotype.

Burmannus. Johannes Burman (1707–1779). Father of Nicolaas Laurens Burman (1734–1793).

1737. *Thesaurus Zeylanicus.* Amsterdam. TL-2: 928; Heller: 16.

Burman's work on Ceylonese plants contains 110 copperplates, many of which were cited by Linnaeus. The collection of specimens upon which this was based is now to be found in the Library of the Institut de France, Paris, a detailed account of which is provided by Lourteig (1966). That rather few of Burman's figures are types is probably a result of Linnaeus subsequently having access to Paul Hermann's Ceylon herbarium, which was the primary basis of Linnaeus' own *Flora Zeylanica* (1747). However, Burman's figures are types for names that include *Bauhinia tomentosa* L., *Hedysarum biarticulatum* L., *Rhamnus oenopolia* L. and *Verbesina lavenia* L. (see above right).

In an appendix, Burman included two short catalogues, one of which lists plants named by Paul Hermann. Some of these polynomials can be matched with annotations by Linnaeus to specimens in the Hermann herbarium (BM). An example is *Campanula fruticosa* L., from South Africa, where the polynomial and reference, written by Linnaeus, can be found annotating three specimens in Hermann's herbarium (vol. 4: 16, BM). They clearly represent original material for Linnaeus' name which has been designated as the lectotype by Adamson (1953: 157).

1738–1739. *Rariorum Africanarum Plantarum.* Amsterdam. TL-2: 929; Heller: 16.

This account of South African plants was accompanied by 100 fine copperplates which were heavily cited by Linnaeus and about a third of which are types for Linnaean names. They include *Arctopus echinatus* L. (the type reproduced in Jarvis 2005: 30, f. 5), *Asclepias arborescens* L., *Brunia abrotanoides* L., *Bupleurum villosum* L., *Euphorbia caput-medusae* L. (see p. 114), *Ixia africana* L. and *Oxalis pes-caprae* L. Voucher material associated with some of these

Following page (114): Plate from Johannes Burman's *Rariorum Africanarum Plantarum* (t. 8. 1738), the lectotype of *Euphorbia caput-medusae* L.

Tab. 8.

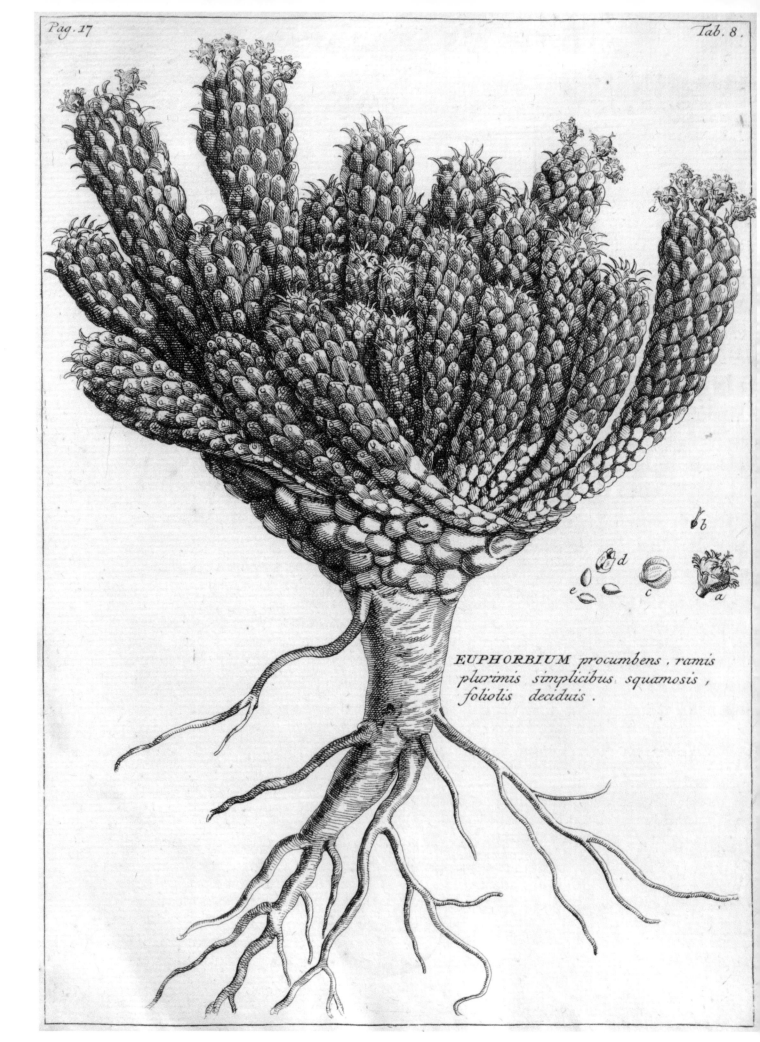

EUPHORBIUM *procumbens, ramis plurimis simplicibus squamosis, foliolis deciduis.*

illustrations can be found in Burman's main herbarium collection, now at G (see Chapters 5 and 6).

1761. Ferrariae Character. *Nova Acta Academia Caesarea Leopoldino–Carolina Germanica Naturae Curiosorum* 2: 198–202, t. 3.

T. 3, f. 1 of this article is the type of *Ferraria crispa* Burm. (and of *F. undulata* L. (1763), *nom. illeg.*).

Burmannus. Nicolaas Laurens Burman (1734–1793), son of Johannes Burman (1706–1779).

1759. *Specimen Botanicum de Geraniis.* Leiden. TL-2: 934; Stearn: xix.

Apart from two works by his father (J. Burman 1755, 1757), this work is one of the first by an author other than Linnaeus in which binomial nomenclature was adopted. It was published in August and therefore post-dated Linnaeus' *Systema Naturae*, ed. 10, 2 (May–Jun). Linnaeus took up Burman's new names in his subsequent works (e.g. *Geranium incanum* Burm. f. in *Pl. Rar. Afr.*: 13. 1760, and *G. alceoides* Burm. f. in *Sp. Pl.*, ed. 2, 2: 948. 1762).

1768. *Flora Indica; cum accedit Series Zoophytorum Indicorum nec non Prodromus Florae Capensis.* Amsterdam. TL-2: 935; Stearn: xx.

This work contains 67 copperplates, among which are the types of *Aquilicia sambucina* L., *Antirrhinum papilionaceum* L., *Cometes alternifolia* L., *C. surattensis* L., *Corchorus tridens* L., *Hedysarum crinitum* L. (see below left) and *H. prostratum* L. The book was published early in 1768 and therefore post-dates Linnaeus' *Mantissa Plantarum* (1767). There is, however, a close relationship between the two, for Johannes Burman and Linnaeus were close friends and corresponded regularly. Indeed, Burman evidently sent to Linnaeus a set of proofs of the plates for his son's *Flora Indica* well ahead of their eventual publication and this accounts for their occasional citation by Linnaeus in 1767. Stearn (1971: viii–x) provides a detailed explanation of this relationship, and Merrill (1921: 329–388) provides a concordance for the names published in Burman's *Flora Indica*, and Linnaeus' *Mantissae* (1767, 1771). For further information on Burman specimens, see Chapter 6.

Buxbaum. Johann Christian Buxbaum (1693–1730).

1721. *Enumeratio Plantarum . . . in agro Hallensi . . . crescentium.* Halle. Heller: 16.

This contained two copperplates, cited by Linnaeus in the synonymy of *Chenopodium urbicum* L. and *Hydnum auriscalpium* L.

1728–1740. *Plantarum Minus Cognitarum Centuria I–V.* St Petersburg. Heller: 17.

HEDYSARUM crinitum.

Buxbaum's book was a significant source of information for Linnaeus about plants from Asia. The five fascicles contain 276 plates and 44 illustrations, much cited by Linnaeus, some of them types of Linnaean names. These include those of Buxbaum's figures cited for *Azalea pontica* L., *Nepeta sibirica* L., *Ophrys catholica* L., *Orchis bicornis* L. (see p. 115, right), *Symphytum orientale* L. and *Veronica multifida* L.

Camerarius. Joachim Camerarius (1534–1598). See also **Matthiolus** and **Thalius**.

1588. *Hortus Medicus et Philosophicus.* Frankfurt am Main. Heller: 17.

This includes a small number of woodcut plates, of which those cited under *Hyoscyamus reticulatus* L. and *Satyrium repens* L. serve as lectotypes for those names.

Castelli. Pietro Castelli (1590–1656) – see **Aldinus**.

Catesby. Mark Catesby (1682–1749).

1731–1747. *The Natural History of Carolina, Florida and the Bahama Islands.* TL-2: 1057; Heller: 17.

Although perhaps best known for the animals (particularly the birds) depicted in the 220 coloured copperplates of this work, Catesby did not neglect the plants even if they played a supporting (often quite literally) role in the artwork. Linnaeus cited almost all of the plates in *Species Plantarum* (1753) and about 40 of them are lectotypes, including those associated with *Annona triloba* L., *Catesbaea spinosa* L., *Dodecatheon meadia* L., *Ipomoea carolina* L. and *Sarracenia flava* L. (see below). Howard & Staples (1983) provided identifications for almost all of the plates, also correlating with them the extant material collected by Catesby (now in Herb. Sloane, BM-SL and elsewhere; see Chapters 5 and 6). Wilbur (1990) has provided a supplement to Howard & Staples' paper.

Celsius. Olof Celsius, the Elder (1670–1756).

1732. Plantarum circa Upsaliam sponte nascentium catalogus. *Acta Societatis Regiae Scientiarum Upsaliensis* 1732: 9–45.

Although unillustrated, this was an important publication because Linnaeus used it in conjunction with Celsius' herbarium (to which he evidently had access; see Chapter 5).

Cherlerus. Johann Heinrich Cherler (1570–1610). See **Bauhinus, J.**

Chomel. Pierre Jean-Baptiste Chomel (1671–1740).

1705. *Conyza montana* . . . *Mémoires de l'Académie Royale des Sciences* 1705: 387–392 [511–517], pl. 8. Heller: 42.

This description and plate is cited in the synonymy of *Solidago montana* L. (1754), of which it appears to be the only extant original element.

1705. *Limodorum montanum* . . . *Mémoires de l'Académie Royale des Sciences* 1705: 392–395 [517–520], pl. 8. Heller: 42.

This account is cited in the synonymy of *Satyrium albidum* L.

Clusius. Charles de l'Escluse (1525–1609).

1576. *Rariorum aliquot stirpium per Hispanias observatarum historiae.* Antwerp. TL-2: 1145; Heller: 18.

Although less frequently cited by Linnaeus than several of Clusius' later works, some of the 233 woodcut illustrations that it contains appear as synonyms (e.g. for *Narcissus serotinus* L.).

1583. *Rariorum aliquot stirpium per Pannoniam* . . . *observatarum historia.* Antwerp. TL-2: 1147; Heller: 18.

Opposite: Plate from the second volume of Mark Catesby's *Natural History of Carolina, Florida and the Bahama Islands* (t. 93. 1743). The image of the upright, white flowered shrub is the lectotype of *Plumeria obtusa* L., and that of the pink flowered plant climbing through it was cited in the synonymy of Linnaeus' *Passiflora cupraea*.

Some of the 766 woodcut illustrations and their associated descriptions of plants from Hungary were cited as synonyms by Linnaeus with, for example, that cited in the synonymy of *Carduus mollis* L. being the lectotype of that name.

1601. *Rariorum plantarum historia.* Antwerp. TL-2: 1149; Heller: 18.

This work contained more than a thousand woodcut illustrations, and many were cited in Linnaean works. More than 20 have been designated as lectotypes for Linnaean names, including *Dracaena draco* (L.) L. (see opposite, below), *Echium maculatum* L., *Erica pallidopurpurea* L., *Iris sisyrinchium* L. and *Ranunculus bullatus* L. See **Pona** for a supplement to this work.

1605. *Exoticorum libri decem . . . ex officina Plantiniana Raphelengi* [Leiden]. TL-2: 1150; Heller: 18.

A further 239 woodcut illustrations were published in this book, among which those cited by Linnaeus in the synonymy of *Cactus melocactus* L. and *Vicia amphicarpa* L. serve as types for those names. See also **Bellonius**.

1611. *Curae posteriore, seu . . . Novae descriptiones . . . ex officina Plantiniana Raphelengi* [Leiden]. TL-2: sub 1150; Heller: 18.

This slimmer volume, published posthumously, contains nearly 50 woodcut illustrations and folios, many of which were cited by Linnaeus. Among these, *Narcissus triandrus* L. is typified by its corresponding Clusius illustration in the *Appendix Altera* of this work.

Colden. Cadwallader Colden (1688–1776).

1743. Plantae Coldenghamiae in provincia Noveboracensi Americes sponte crescentes . . . *Acta Societatis Regiae Scientiarum Upsaliensis* 1743: 81–136.

1744–1750. Plantae Coldenghamiae . . . pars secunda. *Acta Societatis Regiae Scientiarum Upsaliensis* 1744–1750: 47–81. Heller: 58.

Although unillustrated, this was an interesting publication on North American plants for Linnaeus, and Colden's species accounts (237 in all) are often cited by him.

Columna. Fabio Colonna (1567–1650).

1606. *Minus cognitarum stirpium aliquot . . . Ekphrasis.* Rome. Heller: 19.

1616. *Minus cognitarum . . . stirpium Ekphrasis.* Rome. Heller: 19.

Colonna's account of southern Italian (and some eastern Mediterranean) plants, accompanied by 112 copperplate illustrations in the first edition, and 131 depicting 247 plants in the second, supplied information on many plants otherwise unfamiliar to Linnaeus, and the work is frequently cited. Colonna's illustrations provide the types for names such as *Allium chamaemoly* L. (see above, right), *Malva moschata* L., *Scorzonera hirsuta* L. and *Serapias lingua* L. from

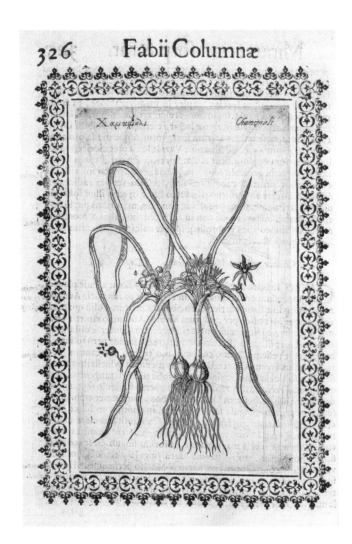

1606, and *Saxifraga androsacea* L. from 1616. For more information on Colonna, see Balsamo (1913: 44). Epitypes can sometimes be useful in cases where Colonna's figures are lectotypes, as in the case of *Malva moschata* L. (Jonsell & Jarvis 2002).

Commelinus. Caspar Commelin (1668–1731). Also known as "Commelijn". Nephew of Jan Commelin.

1701. *Horti medici Amstelodamensis rariorum . . . plantarum . . . auctore Casparo Commelino . . . pars altera.* Amsterdam. TL-2: 1187; Heller: 19.

An earlier, posthumous part was by Jan Commelin, published by his nephew, Caspar. Both it and this second part contained detailed descriptions and fine copperplate illustrations of plants cultivated in Amsterdam. Along with the first part of this work (see **Commelinus, J.**), it was heavily cited by Linnaeus and more than 60 illustrations from the two volumes are lectotypes of Linnaean names. These include *Aloë disticha* L., *Euphorbia canariensis* L. and *Ornithogalum capense* L. from this 1701 volume. For further information on both Commelin, and this work, see Wijnands (1983).

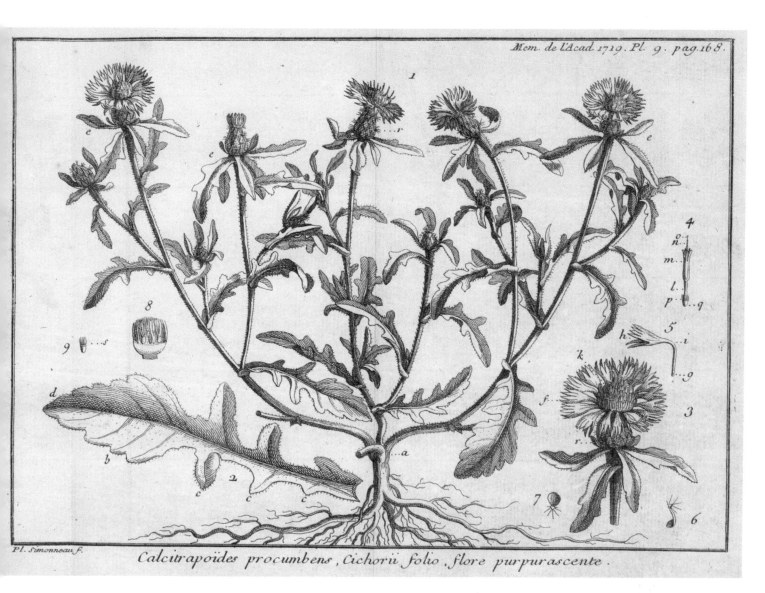

Mem. de l'Acad. 1719. Pl. 9. pag. 168.

Pl. Simonneau. f.

Calcitrapoïdes procumbens, Cichorii folio, flore purpurascente.

Above: Plate from an account by Antoine Tristan Danty D'Isnard (1719) of a new species that Linnaeus subsequently named *Centaurea isnardii* L. (= *C. aspera* L.) in its describer's honour.

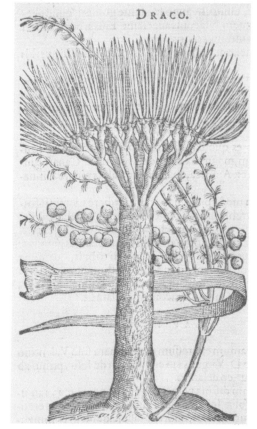

DRACO.

Right: This figure of the Canary Islands dragon tree, from Clusius' *Rariorum plantarum historia* (p. 1. 1601), is the lectotype of *Asparagus draco* L. (= *Dracaena draco* (L.) L.).

Frontispiece from Caspar Commelin's *Horti medici Amstelodamensis rariorum* (1701)

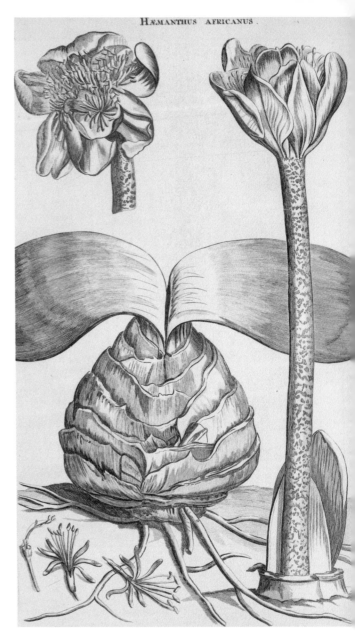

Plate t. 64 from the same work (Commelin 1701) is the lectotype of *Haemanthus coccineus* L. from South Africa.

1703. *Praeludia Botanica.* Leiden. TL-2: 1185; Heller: 20. This is a further volume, with 33 copperplates (see Wijnands 1983), most of which were cited by Linnaeus. Among lectotypes found in this publication are those for *Aloë variegata* L., *Euphorbia mammillaris* L. and *Geranium pinnatum* L.

1706. *Horti medici Amstelaedamensis plantae rariores* . . . Leiden. TL-2: 1186; Heller: 20.
This last volume contains a further 48 copperplates, among which are the types for *Arctotis acaulis* L., *Chironia frutescens* L. (see opposite, above right) and *Momordica operculata* L. The publications of the Commelins have been the subject of detailed study by Wijnands (1983), who also looked at their relationship with Linnaean names, typifying many of the latter in the process.

Commelinus. Jan Commelin (1629–1692). Also known as Commelijn. Uncle of Caspar Commelin.

1697. *Horti medici Amstelodamensis rariorum . . . plantarum . . . auctore Joanne Commelino . . . opus posthumum.* Amsterdam. TL-2: 1187; Heller: 19.
Jan Commelin's posthumous work was published by his nephew, Caspar. It contained detailed descriptions and fine copperplate illustrations of plants cultivated in Amsterdam (see p. 121 for a plate cited by Linnaeus under *Cactus mammillaris* L.). For further information, see Wijnands (1983). Along with the second part of this work (see **Commelinus, C.**), it was heavily cited by Linnaeus and more than 60 illustrations from the two volumes are lectotypes of Linnaean names. These include *Antholyza ringens* L., *Cactus mammillaris* L. and *Erythrina corallodendron* L. from the 1697 volume.

ALOE AMERICANA POLYGONA *Fig. 9*

Condamine. Charles Marie de la Condamine (1701–1744).

1738. Sur l'arbre du quinquina. *Mémoires de l'Académie Royale des Sciences* 1738: 226–243 [319–346], two plates. Heller: 44.

Condamine's account of *Cinchona* appears to have been the sole basis of Linnaeus' knowledge of the species, and one of Condamine's illustrations is the type of *Cinchona officinalis* L.

Cordus. Valerius Cordus (1515–1544).

1561. *Annotationes in . . . Dioscoridis . . . De medica materia . . .* Strassburg. TL-2: 1231; Heller: 20.

Some of the many woodcut illustrations are cited by Linnaeus. Sprague & Sprague (1939) have provided a commentary on the work, as well as modern names.

Cornut. Jacques-Philippe Cornut (1606–1651).

1635. *Canadensium plantarum . . . historia.* Paris. TL-2: 1233; Heller: 20.

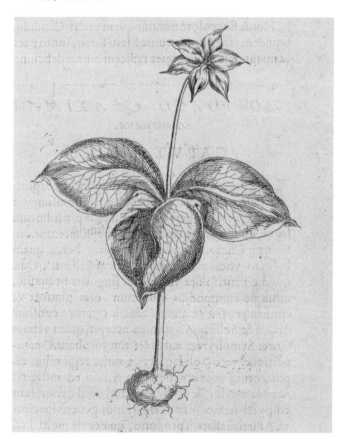

Cornut's book contains many copperplate illustrations of eastern North American plants. Among those serving as lectotypes for Linnaean names are those that Linnaeus associated with *Convallaria stellata* L. and *Trillium erectum* L. (see above).

Dalechamps. Jacques Daléchamps (1513–1588).

1586–1587. *Historia generalis plantarum.* Leiden. TL-2: 1297; Heller: 20.

Another work containing numerous woodcut illustrations. Some were cited by Linnaeus, and one is the type of *Pinus sylvestris* L.

Dillenius. Johann Jakob (or John Jacob) Dillenius (1684–1747).

1719. *Catalogus plantarum ponte circa Gissam nascentium . . .* Frankfurt am Main. TL-2: 1470; Heller: 21.

Although some of the 18 copperplates were cited by Linnaeus, none appears to be a type.

1732. *Hortus Elthamensis.* Oxford. TL-2: 1471; Heller: 21.

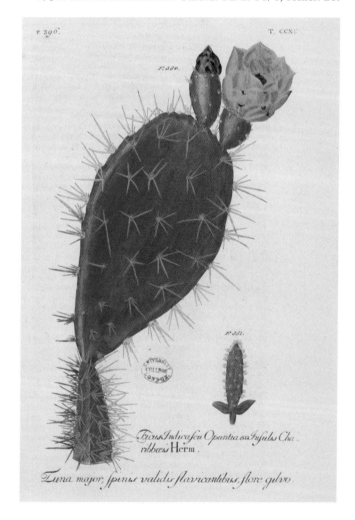

A lavishly illustrated (324 copperplates) account of plants in cultivation at the garden at Eltham Palace, owned by James Sherard (brother of William Sherard, who endowed a Chair of Botany at Oxford for Dillenius), this work was heavily used by Linnaeus. Almost all of Dillenius' plates are cited in the synonymy of Linnaean names, and well over a hundred

Following pages (124–125): These plates, from the first volume of Dillenius' *Hortus Elthamensis* (1732), are the types of *Cacalia papillaris* L. (= *Tylecodon papillaris* (L.) G.D. Rowley) (t. 55, f. 63, left) and *Cassine maurocenia* L. (= *Maurocenia frangula* Mill.) (t. 121, f. 147, right).

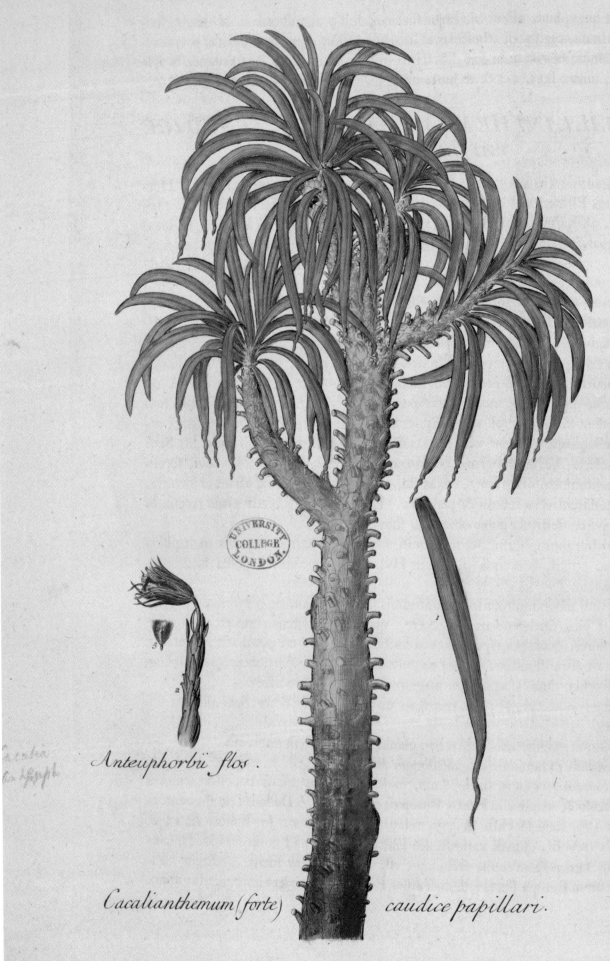

Anteuphorbii flos.

Cacalianthemum (forte) caudice papillari.

UNIVERSITY COLLEGE LONDON.

UNIVERSITY COLLEGE LONDON.

Frangula sempervirens, folio rigido subrotundo.

Cassine Maurocenia

of them serve as lectotypes. They include many South
African species of Aizoaceae (e.g. *Mesembryanthemum
barbatum* L.), as well as species from other geographical areas
such as northern Europe (*Saxifraga groenlandica* L.),
southern Europe (*Iberis gibraltarica* L.), North America
(*Cactus tuna* L. – see p. 123, right, *Erigeron carolinianus* L.)
and South America (*Lepidium bonariense* L.).

Linnaeus' own annotated copy of this work is not with the
rest of his library at the Linnean Society of London, having
been sold by James Edward Smith. It is now in Jena
(Germany), in the University Library, and has been described
by Schmidt (1965).

Much of Dillenius' material is in existence at OXF,
including some voucher material for the published plates (see
Chapter 5). His herbarium was catalogued by Druce &
Vines (1907); see additional observations by Rendle (1934,
1936) and Stearn (1957: 115–116). More recently, the
herbarium has been photographed and is now available in a
microfiche edition (see Marner 1996).

1741. *Historia Muscorum.* Oxford. TL-2: 1472; Heller: 21.

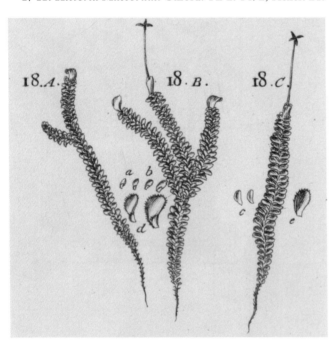

Linnaeus did not have particularly strong interests in the
cryptogamic groups of plants and consequently relied heavily
upon the works of other authors (though this did not
restrain him from "improving upon" their classifications).
Principal among these works was Dillenius' *Historia
Muscorum* which Linnaeus invariably cited in the synonymy
of his names of bryophytes (see above), algae, lichens and
fungi. There are many illustrations from this work
designated as lectotypes for lichen names (see, in particular,
Jørgensen & al. 1994), and the existence of much voucher
material in OXF often allows the interpretation of what
might otherwise be rather uninformative illustrations.

Dodonaeus. Rembert Dodoëns (1518–1585).
1583. *Stirpium historiae pemptades sex libri XXX.*
Antwerp. TL-2: 1489; Heller: 22.

**1616. *Stirpium historiae pemptades sex libri XXX, varie
ab auctore . . . emendati.*** Antwerp. TL-2: 1489; Heller: 22.
Linnaeus' references generally fit the pagination of the 1616
edition, from which types include illustrations of *Allium
porrum* L., *Asplenium adiantum-nigrum* L. and *Cypripedium
calceolus* L. (see above).

Donati. Vitaliano Donati (1717–1762).
**1750. *Della storia naturale marina dell'Adriatico; . . . un
nuovo genere di piante terrestri.*** Venice. TL-2: 1500;
Heller: 22.

Donati described several taxa from the Adriatic coast. The plant that Donati described and figured as *"Vitaliana"* particularly interested Linnaeus, who gave it the name *Primula vitaliana* L. This binomial is typified by Donati's plate.

Douglas. James Douglas (1675–1742).
1725. *Lilium Sarniense, or A description of the Guernsay-lily.* London. Heller: 22.
Douglas' illustrated account was cited by Linnaeus in the synonymy of *Amaryllis sarniense* L., with Linnaeus apparently adopting Douglas' descriptive epithet.

Duhamel du Monceau. Henri Louis Duhamel du Monceau (1700–1782).
1760. *Des semis et plantations des Arbres, et leur culture, &c. : (Additions pour le Traité des Arbres et Arbustes (Additions et Corrections pour le traité de La Physique des Arbres).* Paris.

Plate 27, f. 2 in this work is the type of *Rhodora canadensis* L. (see below left).

Edwards. George Edwards (1694–1773).
1758. Gleanings of Natural History, exhibiting figures of Quadrupeds, birds, Insects, Plants, &c. Vol. 1. London.
Plate t. 255 (see p. 101) is the type of *Gentiana autumnalis* L. (see Fernald 1950: 68–69) for more on this work and its relationship to this binomial.

Ehret. Georg Dionysius Ehret (1710–1770).
1748–1759. *Plantae et papiliones rariores depictae et aeri incisae.* Heidelberg. TL-2: 1644; Heller: 22.
Of the 15 coloured copperplates in this publication, one (t. 1, f. 2) is the lectotype of *Craniolaria annua* L.
1750–1773. *Plantae selectae quarum imagines . . .* Nuremberg. TL-2: 15.131; Heller: 22. For information on this work, see **Trew**.

Ellis. John Ellis (1711–1776).
1755. An essay towards a natural history of the Corallines, . . . London. TL-2: 1661.

Tab. XL.

Plate from Trew and Ehret's
Plantae selectae quarum imagines
(t. 40. 1754), the lectotype of
Antholyza meriana L. (= *Watsonia
meriana* (L.) Mill.)

MERIANA flore rubello.

a. Corolla dissecta ab interna facie, b. b. ejus sex segmenta, c. c. c. tria stamina, d. ovarium, e. stylus, f. ejus extremum trifidum, g. stigma singularum divisionum bifidum et reflexum, i. spatha anduplex, i. x. l. m. n. eadem partes in magnitudine aucta, o. ovarium transverse sectum cum tribus loculis, p. bulbus, q. recens bulbus ex caule propullulans.

Tab.1

Plantae et Papiliones rariores, depictae et aeri incisae
a GEORGIO DIONYSIO EHRET, Palat. Heidelb.
1748.

Plate from Ehret's *Plantae
et papiliones rariores* (t. 1.
1748), the white flowered
plant (f. 2) of which is the
lectotype of *Craniolaria
annua* L.

1. MARTYNIA *annua, villofa et vifcofa, folio fubrotundo, flore magno, rubro.* Houft.
2. MARTYNIA *annua, villofa et vifcofa, aceris folio flore albo tubo longiffimo.* Houft.
3. CYTISUS *procumbens Americanus flore luteo ramofiffimus qui Anil fuppeditat apud Barbadenfium colonos.* Pluk. Alm. p.129. T.6.f.

Although this work, which included 42 plates, dealt mostly with animal groups, a few coralline taxa subsequently recognised to be algae were also included. They include the type of *Corallina squamata* L. (see p. 127, right).

Ferrarius. Giovanni Battista Ferrari (1584–1655).
1646. *Hesperide, sive De malorum aureorum cultura et usu . . .* Rome. Heller: 23.

Few of the delightful copperplates in this volume were cited by Linnaeus. However, one of them is the lectotype of the lemon, named *Citrus medica* var. *limon* by Linnaeus (see above).

Feuillée. Louis Econches Feuillée (1660–1732).
1714. *Journal des observations . . . faites . . . sur les côtes orientales de l'Amérique meridionale . . . tome seconde.* Paris. TL-2: 1767; Heller: 23.
A French clergyman and explorer, Feuillée made many early observations in Peru and Chile, including a study of medicinal plants (pp. 503–767) accompanied by 50 copperplates. Most of these were cited by Linnaeus and

many of them are types, including plates depicting *Alstroemeria ligtu* L., *Datura arborea* L., *Lobelia tupa* L. and *Momordica pedata* L. (see above).
1725. *Journal des observations . . . faites . . . sur les côtes orientales de l'Amérique meridionale . . . tome troisième.* Paris. TL-2: 1767; Heller: 23.
This is a third volume containing further copperplates, among which are the types of *Calceolaria integrifolia* L. and *Solanum montanum* L. (the plate of which is reproduced by Knapp & Jarvis 1991: 344, f. 14).

Franciscus. Erasmus Francisci (1627–1694).
1668. *Ost- und west-indischer wie auch sinesischer Lust- und Stats-garten.* Nuremberg. Heller: 23.
This work contains 66 copperplates, some cited by Linnaeus (e.g. for *Dioscorea aculeata* L. – see opposite, above).

Fuchsius. Leonhart Fuchs (1501–1566).
1542. *De historia stirpium commentarii insignes.* Basel. TL-2: 1909; Heller: 23.
The 512 woodcut illustrations provided by Fuchs are liberally cited by Linnaeus, and the types of e.g. *Corylus avellana* L. and *Orchis morio* L. (see opposite, lower left)

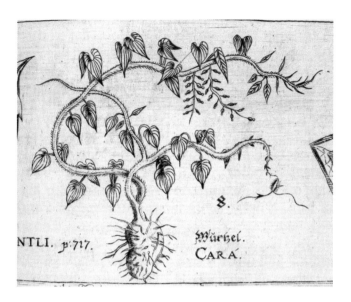

Garcin. Laurent Garcin (1683–1752).

   1733–1734. The settling of a new genus of plants called after the Malayans, Mangostans. *Philosophical Transactions of the Royal Society, London* 36(415): 232–242, pl. 1 (unnum.). Heller: 23, 34.

   Linnaeus named Garcin's new genus after its describer, and the plate accompanying Garcin's account is the lectotype of *Garcinia mangostana* L., the mangosteen.

Garidel. Pierre Joseph Garidel (1658–1737).

   1715. *Histoire des Plantes . . . de la Provence.* Aix. Heller: 24.

can be found among them. Sprague & Nelmes (1931) provided a commentary on the work, along with modern names for the taxa described, and a comprehensive account of Fuchs' work is given by Baumann & al. (2001).

Some of the 100 copperplates were cited by Linnaeus (e.g. in the synonymy of *Inula bifrons* L. – see above), and he named the genus *Garidella* L. for this author. Garidel's plate 39 is cited in the protologue of *G. nigellastrum* L. (although it is not its type).

Gerard. John Gerard (1545–1612).

 1597. ***The herball, or General historie of plants, gathered by John Gerarde***. London. TL-2: 1993.

The binomials published in the Linnaean dissertation, *Flora Anglica* (1754), are validated by references to descriptions in Ray (1724) in which the first edition of Gerard's *Herball* had been used by its author. A few of Gerard's plates from this edition are thereby types of Linnaean names, e.g. *Lolium annuum* L. (see above) and *Borago hortensis* L. (p. 653).

 1636. ***The herball, or General historie of plants, gathered by John Gerarde*, ed. 2.** Heller: 24.

Those of Gerard's numerous woodcut illustrations that were directly cited by Linnaeus in *Species Plantarum* and later works come from this reprint of the second edition.

Gérard. Louis Gérard (1733–1819).

 1761. ***Flora Gallo-Provincialis.*** Paris. TL-2: 1995; Stearn: xx.

Of the 19 copperplates published by Gérard, three are types of Linnaean names – *Alyssum alpestre*, *Anthyllis gerardii* and *Festuca phoenicoides*. Gérard was a correspondent of Linnaeus, and there are some 50 of his specimens in Linnaeus' herbarium (LINN) (see Chapter 6). Burtez (1899) published a catalogue of Gérard's own herbarium (now at Draguignan, France).

Gleditsch. Johann Gottlieb Gleditsch (1714–1786).

 1753. ***Methodus fungorum.*** Berlin. TL-2: 2031; Heller: 24.

Of the six copperplates included in this work, Linnaeus cited plate 1 in the synonymy of *Byssus aurea* L.

Gmelin. Johann Georg Gmelin (1709–1755).

 1747–1752. ***Flora Sibirica, sive Historia plantarum Sibiriae.*** 2 vols. St Petersburg. TL-2: 2047; Heller: 25; Stearn: xx.

The first two volumes of this work contained detailed descriptions of plants from Siberia, accompanied by 148 copperplates which were widely cited by Linnaeus. Two later volumes, published posthumously and edited by Gmelin's

Tab. LXXIV.

Plate from the second volume of
Gmelin's *Flora Sibirica* (t. 74. 1752),
the type of *Cineraria glauca* L.
(= *Ligularia glauca* (L.) O. Hoffm.)

nephew, Samuel Gottlieb Gmelin (1745–1774), appeared in 1768 and 1769 respectively and are sometimes cited in the *Mantissa Plantarum Altera* (1771), e.g. in the case of *Andromeda bryantha* L. Gmelin was a correspondent of Linnaeus and sent the Swede a set of Russian specimens (see Chapter 6). Although the latter are often types for Linnaean names for taxa from "Russia" (*sensu* Linnaeus), around 20 of Gmelin's plates serve as types for Linnaean names, including *Andromeda bryantha*, *Cnicus uniflorus* (see p. 132, right), *Orchis cucullata*, *Scorzonera purpurea* and *Tanacetum sibiricum*. For further information on Gmelin and Linnaeus, see Sokoloff & al. (2002).

Grew. Nehemiah Grew (1641–1712).
   1681. *Musaeum Regalis Societatis, or a catalogue of . . . rarities belonging to the Royal Society.* London. Heller: 25.

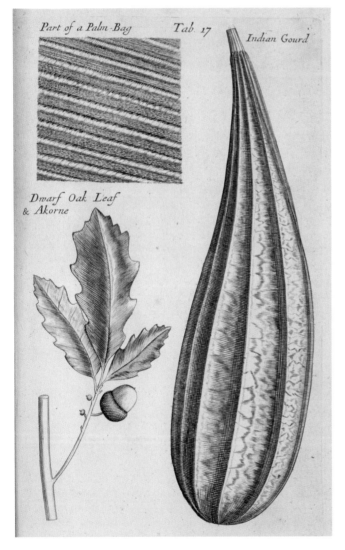

Some of the 31 copperplates published in this work were cited by Linnaeus, notably an unnumbered plate (see above, "Indian Gourd") associated with *Cucumis acutangulus* L.

Gronovius. Johan Frederik Gronovius (1686–1762).
   1739–1743. *Flora Virginica, exhibens plantas quas v. c. Johannes Clayton in Virginia observavit atque collegit . . .* Leiden. TL-2: 2189; Heller: 25.
   Gronovius' account of the plants of Virginia was based on the collections made there by John Clayton (1686–1773). They had been received by Gronovius who was working with them at the time of Linnaeus' visit to the Netherlands (1735–1738), and Linnaeus assisted his great friend in their study. *Flora Virginica* was published in two parts, the first (pp. 1–128) in 1739 and the second (pp. 129–206) in 1743. Linnaeus cites these species accounts throughout and, although the work lacks illustrations, Clayton's specimens are explicitly cited (often with a number) by Gronovius, providing a link between the Clayton specimens (now at BM) and the Gronovian species accounts cited in synonymy by Linnaeus. Clayton specimens provide types for many Linnaean names and images of the BM collection of this herbarium are available at http://www.nhm.ac.uk/research-curation/projects/clayton-herbarium/index.html; see also Chapter 5.
   1755. *Flora Orientalis.* Leiden. TL-2: 2190; Stearn: xx.
   This work was based on a collection made in the near East between 1573 and 1575 by Leonhard Rauwolf, and Gronovius' descriptions are sometimes cited in later Linnaean works. However, Gronovius' book lacks illustrations and, as Linnaeus did not apparently study Rauwolf's herbarium, no lectotypes of Linnaean names are found there.

Hallerus. Albrecht von Haller (1708–1777).
   1742. *Enumeratio methodica stirpium Helvetiae indigenarum.* Göttingen. TL-2: 2306; Heller: 27.
   This work on the plants of Switzerland contains 24 copperplates, and *Androsace halleri* L., *Cherleria sedoides* L. (see opposite, left) and *Pedicularis recutita* L. are typified by plates published here.
   1749. *Opuscula sua botanica . . . retractavit.* Göttingen. TL-2: 2308; Heller: 27.
   This is an edited and revised edition of some of Haller's earlier works. It was evidently not available to Linnaeus when preparing the first edition of *Species Plantarum*. *Arabis halleri* L. is named for Haller, and is typified by the corresponding plate in this work.
   1768. *Historia Stirpium indigenarum Helvetiae inchoata.* 3 vols. Berne. TL-2: 2311.
   Among the 48 copperplates published in this book, one (t. 30) is the lectotype of a Linnaean name (*Orchis pallens* L.).

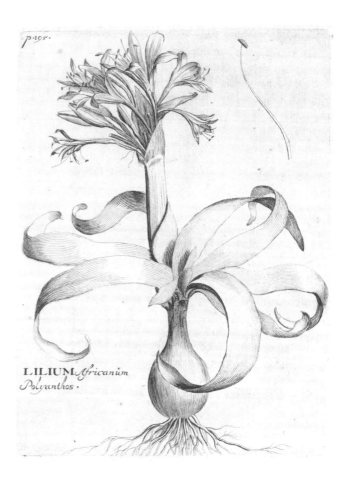

Hasselquist. Fredrik Hasselquist (1722–1752).

1757. *Fredric Hasselquists . . . Iter Palæstinum, eller Resa til Heliga Landet förrättad ifrån År 1749 til 1752, med beskrifningar, rön, anmärkningar, öfver de märkvärdigaste Naturalier.* Stockholm. TL-2: 2459.

This is the travel journal of one of the apostles, Fredrik Hasselquist, who died in Turkey in 1752 (see Chapter 2), which Linnaeus edited and arranged to be published. It was translated into a number of languages, including an English edition (Hasselquist 1766). His collections are mainly in LINN and UPS (see Chapters 5 and 6).

Hermannus. Paul Hermann (1646–1695).

1687. *Horti academici Lugduno-Batavi catalogus.* Leiden. TL-2: 2684; Heller: 27.

Approaching a fifth of the 106 copperplate illustrations in this work on plants cultivated in the botanic garden at Leiden are types of Linnaean names, including those associated with *Crinum asiaticum* L., *Geranium gibbosum* L. and *Lonicera sempervirens* L.

1698. *Paradisus batavus . . . cui accessit Catalogus plantarum quas . . . delineandus curaverat Paulus Hermannus.* Leiden. TL-2: 2687; Heller: 28.

As with Hermann's earlier work, Linnaeus evidently found this very valuable, citing many species accounts in synonymy, and about a fifth of the 111 copperplates are types of Linnaean names. The latter include *Amaryllis longifolia* L. (see above right), *Dracontium polyphyllum* L., *Cheiranthus lacerus* L. and *Orchis susannae* L.

1717. *Musaeum Zeylanicum, sive Catalogus plantarum*

in Zeylana sponte nascentium . . . descriptarum a . . . Paulo Hermanno. Leiden. TL-2: 2688; Heller: 28.

Along with Hermann's Ceylon herbarium (see Chapters 5 and 6), this was part of the basis of Linnaeus' *Flora Zeylanica* (1747 – see Chapter 3).

Hudson. William Hudson (1730–1792).

1762. *Flora Anglica.* London. TL-2: 3108; Stearn: xx.

As it was unillustrated, Hudson's Flora supplies no types for Linnaean names. However, Hudson was a correspondent of Linnaeus, sending him specimens (notably of grasses – see Chapter 6) and was one of the earliest botanists to adopt binomial nomenclature in print.

Isnard. Antoine Tristan Danty D'Isnard (?–1743).

1719. Description de deux nouvelles plantes. *Mémoires de l'Académie Royale des Sciences* 1719: 164–173 [214–226], pl. 9, 10. Heller: 43.

Isnard's descriptions and plates appear to have been the primary basis for Linnaeus' concepts of *Centaurea isnardii* L. (see p. 119) and *C. lippii* L. respectively.

Following page (136): Plate from Paul Hermann's *Paradisus batavus* (p. 217. 1698), the type of *Dioscorea bulbifera* L.

RIZOPHORA
Zeÿlanica.

1720. Etablissement d'un genre de plante appellé Euphorbe. *Mémoires de l'Académie Royale des Sciences* 1720: 384–399 [499–518], pl. 10, 11. Heller: 43.

One of Isnard's plates published here is the type of *Euphorbia cereiformis* L.

Jacquin. Nicolas Joseph (1727–1817).

1760. *Enumeratio Systematica Plantarum quas in Insulis Caribaeis vicinaque Americes continente detexit novas, aut jam cognitas emendavit.* Theodorum Haak, Leiden. TL-2: 3241.

Jacquin was one of the earliest botanists to embrace Linnaeus' binomial nomenclature and this slim volume contains numerous new binomials, as well as a number of new generic names, chiefly for plants from the Caribbean. There were no illustrations but many of Jacquin's names were taken up by Linnaeus in the second edition of *Species Plantarum* (1762, 1763).

1762. *Enumeratio Stirpium pleraque quo sponte crescunt in Agro Vindobonensi.* J.P. Kraus, Leiden. TL-2: 3242; Stearn: xx.

This account of plants from the area surrounding Vienna was published (probably in May 1762) before the first volume of the second edition of Linnaeus' *Species Plantarum* (September 1762) (see Balle & al. 1960). Some of Jacquin's new binomials were subsequently re-combined by Linnaeus

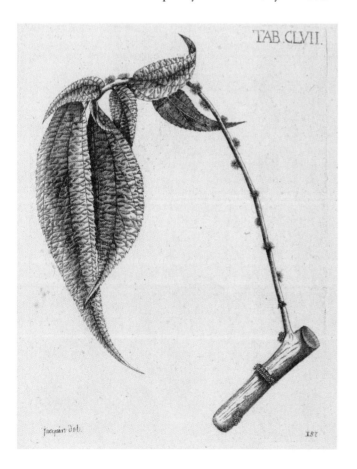

(e.g. *Hieracium austriacum* Jacq. became *H. pyrenaicum* var. *austriacum* (Jacq.) L. 1767, Jacquin's t. 5 being their type).

1763. *Selectarum Stirpium Americanarum Historia.* J.P. Kraus, Leiden. TL-2: 3243; Stearn: xx.

The 185 plates of plants from the New World tropics published here include the types of *Cocos guineensis* L., and the combinations *Callisia repens* (Jacq.) L. and *Caturus ramiflorus* (Jacq.) L. (see below left). There are some Jacquin specimens in LINN (see Chapter 6).

Jussieu. Bernard de Jussieu (1699–1777).

1740. Histoire du Lemma. *Mémoires de l'Académie Royale des Sciences* 1740: 263–275 [375–393], pl. 15. Heller: 44.

Jussieu's plate is original material for *Marsilea quadrifolia* L. (see p. 138).

1742. Observation nouvelle sur les fleurs d'une espèce de plaintain. *Mémoires de l'Académie Royale des Sciences* 1742: 131–138 [177–186], pl. 7. Heller: 44.

Jussieu's plate is original material for *Plantago uniflora* L.

1744. Description d'une plante de Mexique . . . Contrayerva. *Mémoires de l'Académie Royale des Sciences* 1744: 373–383 [511–520], pl. 18. Heller: 44.

Jussieu's plate is the type of *Psoralea pentaphylla* L.

Kaempfer. Engelbert Kaempfer (1651–1716).

1712. *Amoenitatum Exoticarum . . . fasciculi V, quibus continentur variae relationes, observationes & descriptiones rerum Persicarum & ulteriores Asiae.* Lemgo. TL-2: 3483; Heller: 29.

Kaempfer was one of the earliest collectors to bring scientific material from Japan to the west, and his descriptions and illustrations of plants were therefore of great interest to Linnaeus. Nearly all of the copperplates depicting plants were cited by Linnaeus, and many of them, including those appearing in the synonymies of *Camellia japonica* L. (reproduced in Jarvis 2005: 29, f. 4), *Dolichos soja* L. and *Illicium anisatum* L., are types. Kaempfer's herbarium was acquired by Sir Hans Sloane and comprises volumes 211 and 213 of the Sloane herbarium (BM-SL). A recent study by Hinz (2001) provides a catalogue, with modern identifications, of this material, some of which can be linked to a manuscript held in the British Library (described in detail by Hoppe 2003) and the published copperplates. Although these specimens were never studied by Linnaeus, they can nevertheless sometimes be helpful in interpreting the illustrations.

Lobel. Matthias de l'Obel (1538–1616) – see **Plantin.**

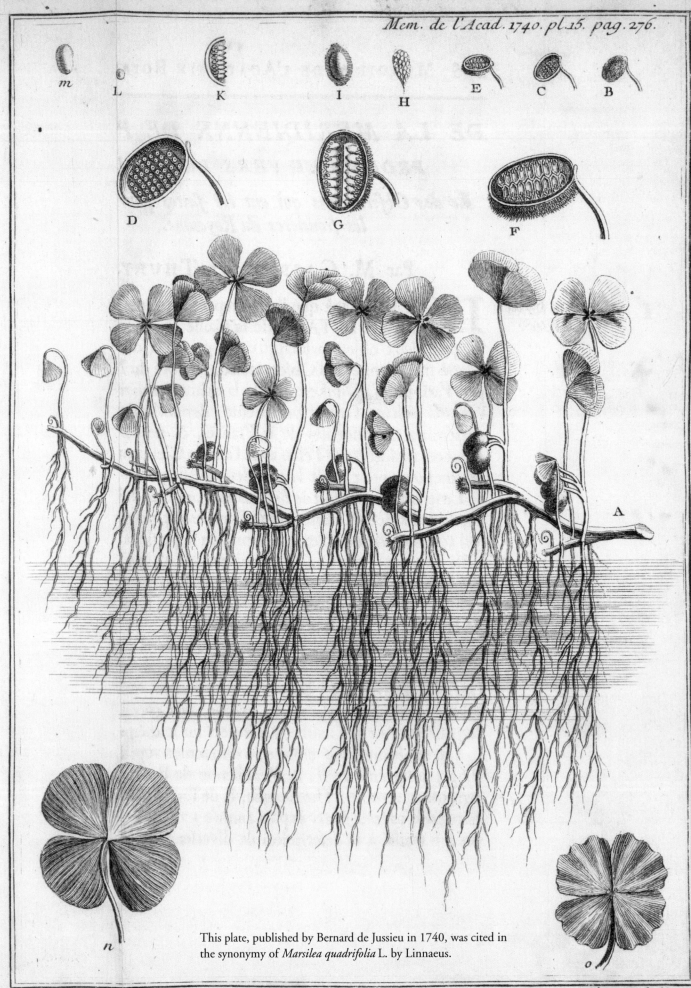

This plate, published by Bernard de Jussieu in 1740, was cited in
the synonymy of *Marsilea quadrifolia* L. by Linnaeus.

M. Basseporte del.

Simonneau Sculp.

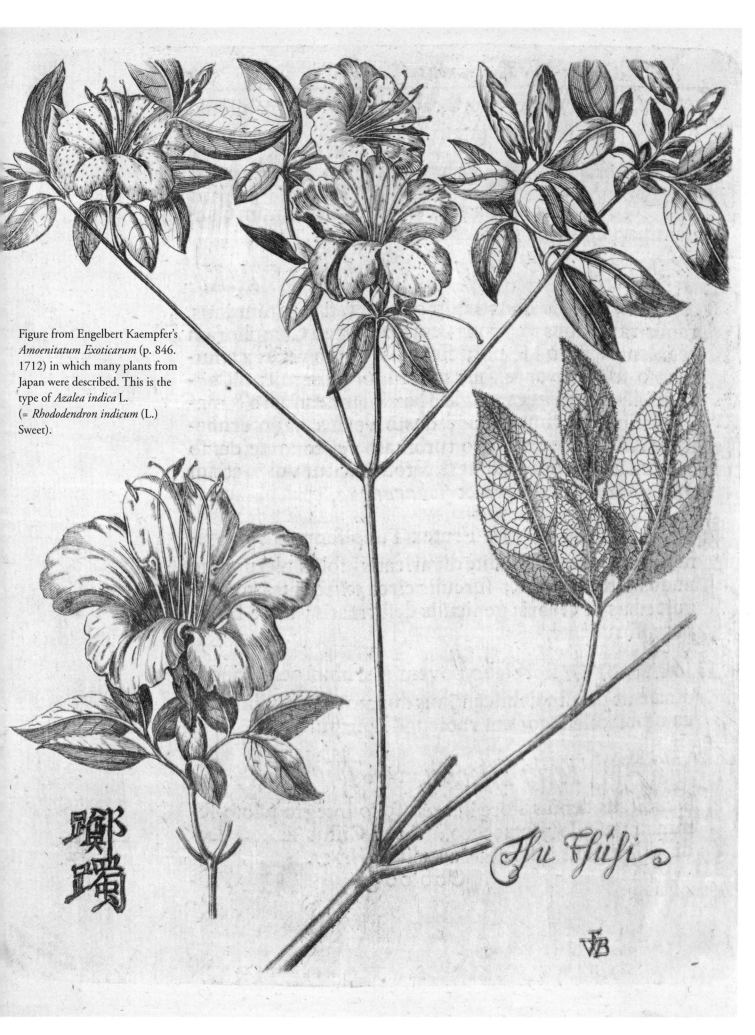

Figure from Engelbert Kaempfer's *Amoenitatum Exoticarum* (p. 846. 1712) in which many plants from Japan were described. This is the type of *Azalea indica* L. (= *Rhododendron indicum* (L.) Sweet).

Loefling. Pehr Löfling (1729–1756).

Löfling was one of the Linnaean apostles who travelled to the Iberian peninsula in 1751, from where he sent material and extensive descriptions back to Linnaeus (see Chapter 6). In 1754, he joined a Spanish expedition to Venezuela, where he died.

1758. *Iter Hispanicum, eller resa til Spanska länderna uti Europa och America . . . utgifven . . . af Carl Linnaeus.* Stockholm. TL-2: 4921.

Linnaeus edited Löfling's manuscripts and arranged for their publication as *Iter Hispanicum* after Löfling's death. In *Species Plantarum* (1753), Linnaeus was forced to refer to unpublished materials (e.g. "Loefl. epist." under *Minuartia dichotoma* L.), but in the second edition (1762–1763) he was able to cite *Iter Hispanicum* for the corresponding names. Most of the nomenclatural novelties that appear in this work have traditionally been attributed to Löfling rather than Linnaeus, and they therefore do not feature in this study.

Loeselius. Johannes Loesel (1607–1655).

1703. *Flora Prussica.* Kalingrad. TL-2: 4933; Heller: 34.

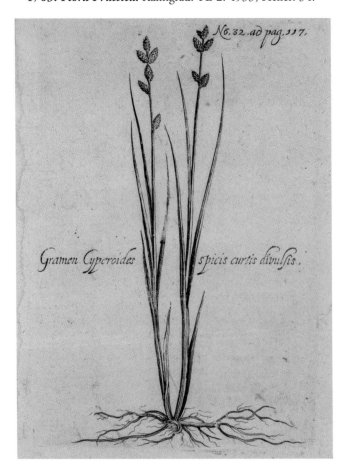

Quite a few of the 83 copperplates from Loesel's work were cited by Linnaeus, one of which is the type of *Carex canescens* L. (see above).

Magnol. Pierre Magnol (1683–1715). See Chapter 6 concerning his specimens.

1676. *Botanicum Monspeliense.* Leiden. TL-2: 5230; Heller: 35.

Linnaeus cited this work in *Species Plantarum* (1753) and, later, it was the basis of the Linnaean dissertation *Flora Monspeliensis* (1756), where Linnaeus provided binomials for the plants described by Magnol in what was an important source of information on the plants of the South of France (Stearn 1974). As explained elsewhere (see Chapter 3), Linnaeus' names in 1756 are not validly published, though most were subsequently validly published in one or the other of two of Linnaeus' works in 1759. However, Linnaeus also cited this work in *Species Plantarum* (1753). *Botanicum Monspeliense* contains 19 copperplate illustrations, among which are the types for *Allium roseum* L., *Statice echioides* L. and *Trifolium tomentosum* L.

1697. *Hortus regius Monspeliensis.* Montpellier. TL-2: 5232; Heller: 35.

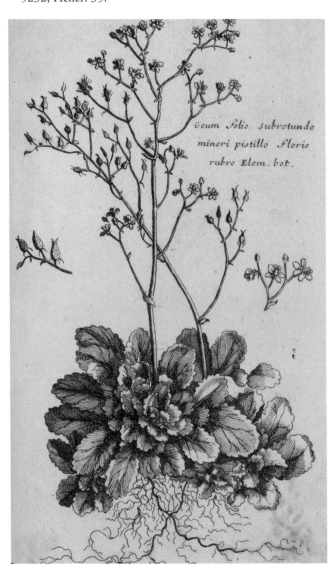

Magnol's later work contains a further 21 copperplates, and among them can be found the types of *Astragalus vesicarius* L., *Ononis tridentata* L. and *Saxifraga umbrosa* L. (see opposite, below right).

Malpighius. Marcello Malpighi (1628–1694).
1679. ***Anatomes plantarum pars altera.*** London. Heller: 35.
Among the 39 copperplates in this work, Linnaeus cited one in the synonymy of *Mucor mucedo* L., for which it is the lectotype (see Kirk 1986).

Marcgravius. Georg Marggraf (1610–1644) – see **Piso.**

Martyn. John Martyn (1699–1768).
1728. ***Historiae plantarum rariorum centuriae primae decas I–V.*** London. TL-2: 5563; Heller: 35.
Martyn's work contains 50 coloured copperplates, most of which were cited by Linnaeus. Types selected from among them include the plates corresponding with *Gronovia scandens* L., *Martynia annua* L. and *Milleria quinqueflora* L.

Matthiolus. Pier Andrea Mattioli (1500–1577).
1586. ***De plantis epitome utilissima Petri Andreae Matthioli . . . aucta & locupletata, a d. Ioachimo Camerario.*** Frankfurt am Main. Heller: 36.
The numerous woodcut illustrations are sparingly cited by Linnaeus but are the types of, among others, *Brassica oleracea* var. *botrytis* L., *Brassica rapa* L. (see right), *Orchis morio* L. and *Pinus abies* L. Oost & al. (1989) reproduce a number of Mattioli's woodcuts associated with *Brassica*.

Mentzelius. Christian Mentzel (1622–1701).
1682. ***Index nominum plantarum universalis . . . accessit . . . Pugillus plantarum rariorum.*** Berlin. Heller: 36.
Most of the images among the 11 copperplates were cited by Linnaeus, and that for *Anemone apennina* L. (t. 8, f. 2) is the lectotype of that name.

Merian. Maria Sibylla Merian (1647–1717).
1705. ***Metamorphosis insectorum Surinamensium.*** Amsterdam. Heller: 36.
Although Merian's principal interest was in depicting the insects of Surinam, her thoroughness in including their developmental stages meant that she also illustrated their food plants in some detail. Linnaeus cited many of the 60 copperplates in the original edition and those associated, for example, with *Costus arabicus* L. (see p. 142), *Passiflora laurifolia* L. and *Spondias mombin* L. are the types of those binomials. Stearn (1982) and Adams (1987) give modern names for Merian's plants, and Rice (1999: 90–119) provides a popular account, reproducing a number of Merian's original drawings.

R A P V M   L O N G V M.

Micheli. Pier Antonio Micheli (1679–1737).
1729. ***Nova plantarum genera.*** Florence. TL-2: 5974; Heller: 37.
Micheli was greatly interested in cryptogamic plants and is regarded as the father of modern mycology (Hawksworth 1976). The 108 copperplates (frequently with numerous figures to each plate) that illustrate this work concentrate particularly on bryophytes, fungi and lichens, and Micheli is second only to Dillenius (1741) in the frequency with which Linnaeus cites his work in these taxonomic groups. However, Micheli also illustrated many spermatophytes. Dozens of Micheli's illustrations are types of Linnaean names, including those associated with *Jungermannia viticulosa*, *Lichen pyxidatus*, *Phallus impudicus* and *Ruta patavina*. Micheli's extensive herbarium at FI is extant, and it is often possible to associate material with Micheli's published species accounts (see Mazzi 1985, Mazzi & Moggi 1991).

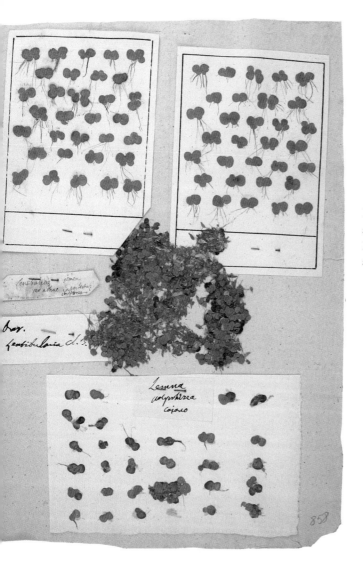

Plate (below) from Micheli's *Nova plantarum genera* (t. 11. 1729) showing various species of *Lemna* L., and (left) a sheet from Micheli's herbarium (FI) showing carefully mounted *Lemna* specimens

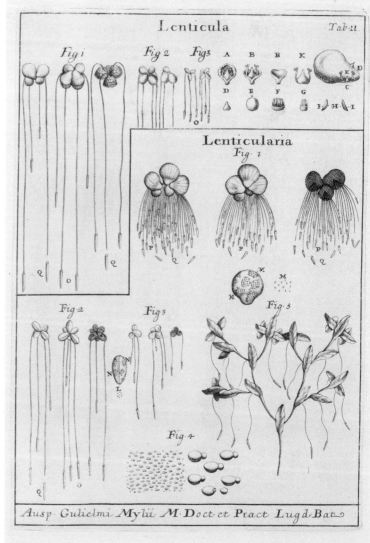

Opposite page: Plate from Maria Sibylla Merian's *Metamorphosis insectorum Surinamensium* (t. 36. 1705), the lectotype of *Costus arabicus* L.

Miller. Philip Miller (1691–1771).

> **1730.** *Catalogus plantarum . . . A catalogue of trees, shrubs, plants and flowers . . . for sale in the gardens near London . . . by a Society of Gardeners.* London. TL-2: 6036; Heller: 34.

This folio volume, containing 21 coloured copperplates, is believed to have been edited by Miller (Ardagh 1934). Most of them are cited by Linnaeus, and *Pinus larix* L. and *Glycine frutescens* L. are typified by plates from this work.

> **1755–1760.** *Figures of the most beautiful, useful and uncommon Plants described in the Gardeners Dictionary.* 2 vols. London. TL-2: 6059; Stearn: xxi.

Illustrations for this work by the engraver John Sebastian Miller often included detailed dissections to show floral and fruiting details (see Jarvis 2005: 26, f. 1). At least 25 are types for Linnaean names, including *Arduina bispinosa*, *Gladiolus recurvus*, *Moraea vegeta* (see above) and *Vinca rosea*. Some material from Philip Miller is in LINN (see Chapter 6).

Morison. Robert Morison (1620–1683).

> **1680.** *Plantarum historiae universalis Oxoniensis pars secunda.* Oxford. TL-2: 6334; Heller: 38.
> **1699.** *Plantarum historiae universalis Oxoniensis pars tertia.* Oxford. TL-2: 6334; Heller: 38.

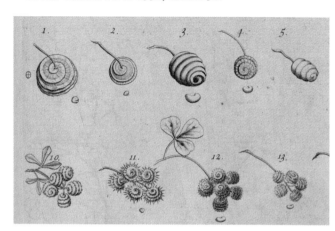

Together, these two volumes contain 289 copperplates with 3,586 figures, many of which were cited by Linnaeus. It is probably not surprising that some 40 Linnaean names are typified by Morison figures, including *Convolvulus cneorum*, *Medicago polymorpha* var. *scutellata* (see above, f. 3) and *Pancratium maritimum* (all 1680), and *Centaurea moschata*, *Polypodium virginianum* and *Serapias helleborine* var. *palustris* (all 1699). Morison's herbarium at OXF (see Chapter 5), though not studied by Linnaeus, has been enumerated by Vines & Druce (1914) and is available on microfiche (see Marner 1996). It can yield voucher material aiding in the interpretation of the published illustrations.

Münchhausen. *O. von Münchhausen* – see **Linnaeus**, 1770 (Chapter 3).

Muntingius. Abraham Munting (1626–1683).

> **1696.** *Naauwkeurige beschryving der aardgewassen.* Leiden and Utrecht. Heller: 39.

A number of the 243 copperplates were cited by Linnaeus: *Chenopodium fruticosum* L. is typified by the corresponding Munting plate.

Nissole. Guillaume Nissole (1647–1734).

> **1730.** *Phaseolus peregrinus. Mémoires de l'Académie Royale des Sciences* 1730: 577–580 [821–824], pl. 42. Heller: 44.

A short article, with an accompanying plate which is the lectotype of *Phaseolus farinosus* L.

Osbeck. Pehr Osbeck (1723–1805).

> **1757.** *Dagbok öfwer en Ostindisk Resa.* Stockholm. TL-2: 7121; Stearn: xxi.

A German translation of an account of his travels by Osbeck (one of Linnaeus' apostles) appeared in 1765, and contains a number of new binomials. An English translation was published by Forster (1771) (see Merrill (1916) for a commentary). Additional information on Osbeck and the specimens in the Linnaean herbarium (see Chapter 6) is supplied by Hansen & Fox Maule (1973), and on *Lichen chinensis* Osbeck by Hawksworth (2004).

Parkinson. John Parkinson (1567–1650).

1629. *Paradisi in sole paradisus terrestris, or A garden of . . . flowers.* London. Heller: 44.
Some of Parkinson's 110 woodcut illustrations were cited by Linnaeus, and *Allium triquetrum* L. is typified by one of them (t. 143, f. 6 – see right).

1640. ***Theatrum botanicum.*** London. Heller: 44.
Parkinson's much larger *Theatrum botanicum* was also cited occasionally by Linnaeus, and *Medicago polymorpha* var. *tornata* L. is typified by one of Parkinson's woodcuts.

Petiver. James Petiver (ca. 1663–1718).

1695–1703. *Musei Petiveriani centuria prima (–decima).* London. Heller: 45.
Among the figures on one of the two folded copperplates is the type of *Roella reticulata* L.

1702–1709. *Gazophylacii naturae & arti decas prima (–decima).* London. Heller: 45.
This two-volume work contains 100 copperplates, many of which are cited by Linnaeus. Designated types include the illustrations associated with *Adiantum philippense* L., *Epidendrum carinatum* L. (see p. 146) and *Sagittaria trifolia* L.

1712. *Pteri-graphia Americana, icones continens . . . filicum variarum specierum . . . nec non muscos, lichenes.* London. Heller: 45.
This is a re-issue of the part of the *Gazophylacii naturae* dealing with the pteridophytes and relatives. However, Linnaeus frequently cited the descriptions and plates from this publication rather than from the original, and more than 20 Linnaean names, including *Acrostichum sorbifolium*, *Asplenium obtusifolium* and *Polypodium crispatum* (see p. 147), find their types here.

Petiver's extensive herbarium collection now comprises 106 volumes of the Sloane herbarium (BM-SL – see Dandy 1958: 175–182; Stearn 1957: 121). It is often difficult to correlate published illustrations with material in his herbarium.

Following page (146): Plate from James Petiver's *Gazophylacii naturae & arti* (t. 44. 1702–1709) with f. 10 being the lectotype of *Epidendrum carinatum* L. (= *Dendrobium carinatum* (L.) Willd.).

Following page (147): Plate from James Petiver's *Pteri-graphia Americana* (t. 13. 1712) with engravings of two ferns that are the types of Linnaean names. *Acrostichum crinitum* L. (= *Elaphoglossum crinitum* (L.) Christ) is typified by f. 14, and *Polypodium crispatum* L. by f. 12 (though the taxonomic identity of the latter is uncertain).

Fig 1

8

2 3

Tab. XL. IV

12

7

10

9

4

12

5 8 6

13

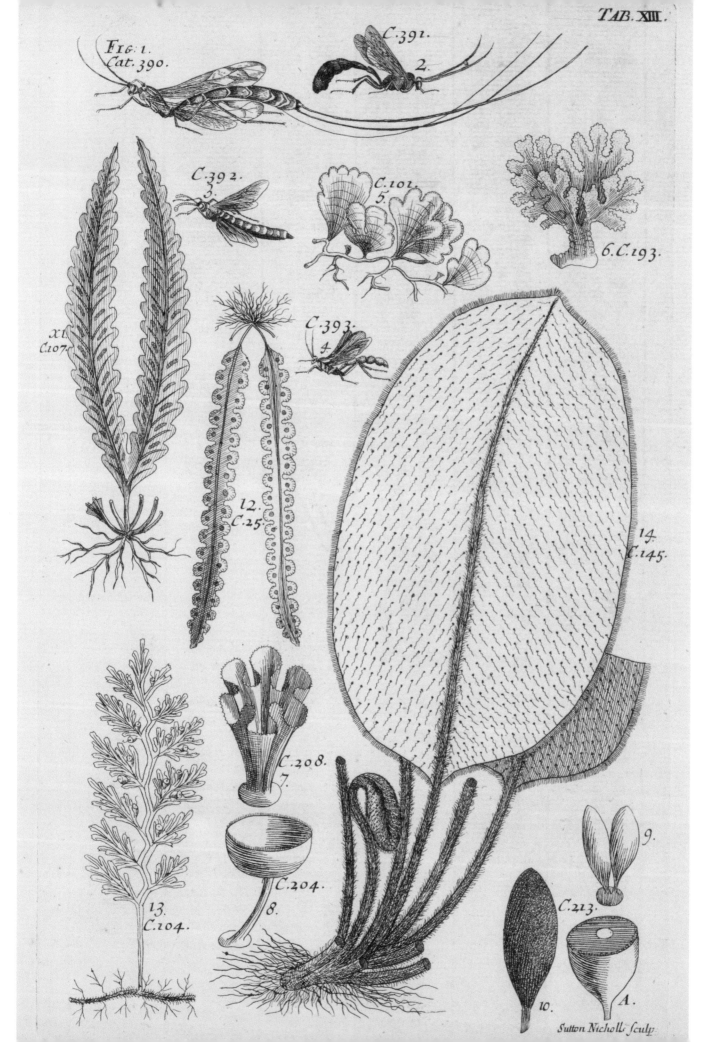

TAB. XIII.

FIG: 1.
Cat. 390.

C. 391.
2.

C. 392.
3.

C. 101.
5.

6. C. 193.

x1.
C. 107.

C. 393.
4.

12.
C. 25.

14.
C. 145.

C. 208.
7.

C. 204.
8.

13.
C. 104.

9.

C. 213.

10.

A.

Sutton Nicholls Sculp

Piso. Willem Piso (1611–ca. 1658) and **Marcgravius.** Georg Marggraf (1610–1644).

> **1648.** ***Gulielmi Pisonis . . . De Medicina Brasilensi libri IV . . . et Georgi Marcgravi . . . Historiae rerum naturalium Brasiliae libri VIII.*** Leiden. Heller: 45.

Some of the many woodcut illustrations in this work were cited by Linnaeus, and those associated with *Baccharis brasiliana* L., *Fevillea trilobata* L. and *Genipa americana* L. (see above) serve as their types.

> **1658.** ***Gulielmi Pisonis . . . De Indiae utriusque re naturali et medica libri XIV.*** Amsterdam. Heller: 45.

This is a later edition of the above, with significant additions. Some of the woodcut illustrations were cited by Linnaeus, notably that for *Solanum paniculatum* L., for which it is the type (see Knapp & Jarvis 1991: 347, f. 15, 16, who reproduce Piso's woodcut). As these authors note, voucher material from Marggraf's herbarium (C) can sometimes be associated with the published woodcuts.

Plantin. Christophe Plantin (1514–1589).

> **1581.** ***Plantarum seu stirpium icones.*** Antwerp. TL-2: 4909; Heller: 33.

Linnaeus made some use of the more than 2,000 woodcut illustrations in this work, and at least 15 of them serve as types for Linnaean binomials, including *Allium carinatum* (see above), *Echinops ritro*, *Ophrys insectifera* var. *arachnites*, *O. nidus-avis*, *Orchis coriophora*, and *Origanum syriacum*. The figures of the orchids among these have been reproduced by Baumann & al. (1989). Although often credited to Lobel, this work is to be attributed to Plantin according to Louis (1957).

Plot. Robert Plot (1640–1696).

> **1677.** ***The natural history of Oxford-shire.*** Oxford. Heller: 46.

From the few copperplates included in this work, that associated with *Tormentilla reptans* is the type of this Linnaean binomial.

Plukenetius. Leonard Plukenet (1641–1706).

Plukenet's publications describe plants from all areas of the then explored world and include several thousand species. He also published 454 copperplates, each comprising a number of separate figures and these were much cited by Linnaeus. The text and the copperplates were not, however, published simultaneously. Plates 1–328 were published in three parts between 1691 and 1694 and form the *Phytographia*. In 1696, a fourth part (*Almagestum botanicum*) appeared containing the descriptions associated with these 328 plates, followed by a fifth part (the *Mantissa*) in 1700, containing plates 329–350 and their associated descriptions. The sixth and last part, *Amaltheum botanicum*, containing the remaining plates (numbered 351–454) and their associated descriptions, appeared in 1705, shortly before Plukenet's death.

Plukenet's large herbarium was acquired in 1710 from the Bishop of Norwich, by Sir Hans Sloane and it forms volumes 83–85, 87–105 (see Dandy 1958: 183–187) of Sloane's herbarium (BM-SL). Many of the specimens from which the engravings were prepared can be traced, and they can prove extremely helpful in interpreting Plukenet's neat, but sometimes stylised illustrations. Approximately 150 of Plukenet's copperplates are types for Linnaean names (see below).

1691–1694. *Phytographia sive Stirpium . . . icones.* London. TL-2: 8064; Heller: 46.

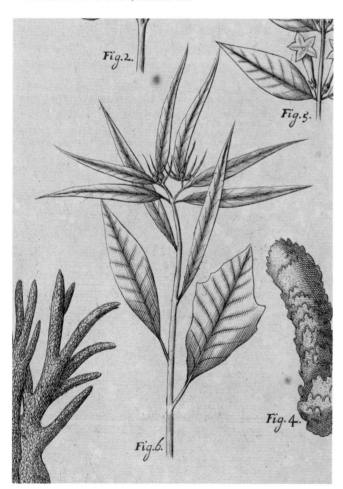

Names typified by plates from these first three parts include *Adiantum reniforme* L., *Cactus triangularis* L., *Carex pilulifera* L. and *Euphorbia heterophylla* L. (see type illustration, left, and voucher specimen, above).

1696. *Almagestum botanicum sive Phytographiae Pluknetianae onomasticon.* London. TL-2: 8064; Heller: 46.

1700. *Almagesti botanici mantissa . . . cum indice totius operis.* London. TL-2: 8064; Heller: 46.

Names typified by plates from this fifth part include those corresponding with *Echium laevigatum* L., *Erica plukenetii* L. and *Mimosa vaga* L.

1705. *Amaltheum botanicum.* London. TL-2: 8064; Heller: 46.

Names typified by plates from this sixth and last part include *Aspalathus astroites* L., *Kalmia latifolia* L. and *Menispermum hirsutum* L.

Plumier. Charles Plumier (1646–1704).

Along with Sloane's (1707–1725) account of the plants of Jamaica, Plumier's works were the primary source of information for Linnaeus, in 1753, on the plants of the Antilles. Plumier collected extensively in Haiti and Martinique during three trips between 1689 and 1697. His species descriptions were generally (except in *Nova plantarum Americanum genera*) detailed, and frequently accompanied by accurate copperplates. Approximately 200 of Plumier's figures serve as types for Linnaean names.

1693. *Description de plantes de l'Amérique.* Paris. TL-2: 8066; Heller: 46.

This folio work contains 108 copperplates, most of which were cited by Linnaeus. Types for Linnaean names include the plates associated with *Aristolochia bilobata*, *Asplenium serratum* and *Banisteria angulosa*. Jarvis (2005: 28, f. 2) reproduces Plumier's type plate for *Polypodium reticulatum* L.

1703. *Nova plantarum Americanum genera.* Paris. TL-2: 8067; Heller: 46.

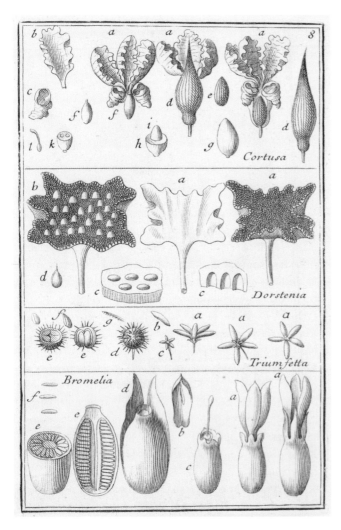

The new genera described here by Plumier are accompanied by 40 copperplates (often with multiple figures) illustrating the floral and/or fruiting features of each. Each generic description is followed by a brief list of included species (carrying Plumier's polynomials). Linnaeus sometimes cites these species in synonymy. However, unless a species in this work is the only one cited by Plumier for the genus, the generic plate cannot be assumed to be original material for that species name, as it cannot be tied to any one of the

included species and might even prove to be a composite drawn from several different taxa. As a consequence, fewer of these plates than might be expected serve as types of Linnaean names. However, those that do include *Achras zapota*, *Dorstenia contrajerva* (see *Dorstenia* left) and *Rheedia lateriflora*.

1705. *Tractatus de filicibus Americanis (Traité des fougères de l'Amérique).* Paris. TL-2: 8068; Heller: 47.

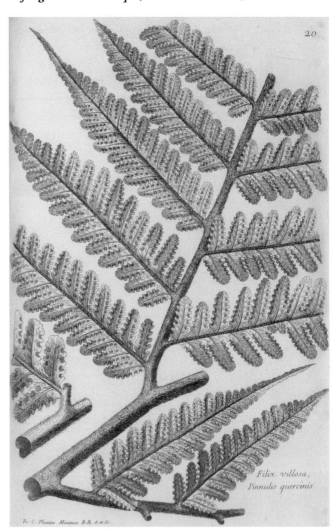

This is a rich source of information on tropical pteridophytes. Plumier's folio work contains 172 fine copperplates, which were heavily cited by Linnaeus. At least a quarter of them are types for their corresponding Linnaean names, including those representing *Acrostichum citrifolium*, *Lonchitis hirsuta* (see above), *Lycopodium linifolium* and *Osmunda hirsuta*. Lellinger & Proctor (1983) provide modern names for these plates.

1755–1760. *Plantarum Americanum fasciculus primus (–decimus), continens plantas quas olim Carolus Plumierus . . . depinxit, has edidit . . . Joannes*

Burmannus. Amsterdam. TL-2: 8069; Heller: 47.

Plumier left 1,219 original drawings (now at P) and, in the years after his death in 1704, several sets of tracings were prepared (312 at BM, many at K). Herman Boerhaave (1668–1738) was keen to acquire a set, and commissioned Claude Aubriet to prepare tracings of the originals. After Boerhaave's death, they passed to Johannes Burman. Aware that many were still unpublished, Burman had engravings prepared, and published them in a series of fascicles between 1755 and 1760. Urban (1920) provides an indispensable guide to this work.

Although these did not begin to be published until after *Species Plantarum* (1753) appeared, it is clear that Linnaeus used the information from many of these plates in forming his concepts for species named in 1753. This was possible because his close friend Burman had been sending Linnaeus proof copies of the plates (which the Swede, doubtless after due scrutiny, had used as wallpaper for the walls of his study at his country estate at Hammarby). Consequently, a significant number of these plates serve as types for Linnaean names published in 1753 including, for instance, *Mentzelia aspera*, *Mimosa latisiliqua* (see Polhill & Stearn 1976) and *Thalia geniculata*. The plates are also cited in the synonymy of post-1753 names and appear, more conventionally, as the types of later names such as *Epidendrum caudatum* L. (1759), *Gentiana exaltata* L. (1762) and *Eupatorium macrophyllum* L. (1763). In a few cases, authors have designated the original Aubriet tracings (now at the University Library in Groningen) as lectotypes (e.g. for *Aristolochia peltata* L., *Begonia obliqua* L., *Caesalpinia brasiliensis* L., *Duranta erecta* L. and *Epidendrum cochleatum* L.). A few Plumier specimens are extant in Jussieu's herbarium (P-JU): see Tryon (1964: 225) concerning material of *Acrostichum citrifolium* L.

Pococke. Richard Pococke (1704–1765).

1743–1745. *A description of the East and some other countries.* London. Heller: 47.

Although this work contains many copperplates, very few are of botanical interest. However, the plates cited by Linnaeus in the synonymy of *Crataegus azarolus* var. *aronia* L., and *Corypha thebaica* L. (see above, right) both serve as the types of those binomials.

Pona. Giovanni Pona (fl. 1595–1608).

1617. *Monte Baldo descritto da Giovanni Pona.* Venice. Heller: 47.

A later, Italian edition of a work originally included (in Latin) as part of Clusius' *Rariorum plantarum historia* (1601). Some of the 91 woodcut illustrations are cited by Linnaeus.

Raius (Rajus). John Ray (1627–1705).

1724. *Synopsis methodica stirpium Britannicarum . . . ; editio tertia.* London. TL-2: 8703; Heller: 48.

John Ray's influence on Linnaeus, chiefly through the former's *Historia Plantarum* (1686, 1688, 1704), was enormous. That work was, however, unillustrated and this 1724 work is the only one of Ray's cited by Linnaeus to contain copperplates. Although edited by Dillenius and published long after Ray's death, it was an important work for Linnaeus and was used as the basis for the Linnaean dissertation, *Flora Anglica* (1754), where Linnaean binomials were applied to the plants described by Ray. Although most of the British taxa described by Ray had already been given binomials in 1753, some new names were published in the dissertation (see Chapter 3). *Mentha piperita* L. and *Ligusticum cornubiense* L. are typified by figures from Ray's work.

Rauwolf. Leonhard Rauwolf (ca. 1535–1596).

1583. *Aigentliche Beschreibung der Raiss . . . in die Morgenländer.* Laugingen. Heller: 49.

Some of the 42 botanical woodcut illustrations are cited by Linnaeus (see example above); one is the type of *Hedysarum alhagi* L. Rauwolf's herbarium is in L (see Legré 1900), appears to contain at least some voucher specimens for the illustrations, and was mentioned by Linnaeus (1736c: 157). However, he does not appear to have studied the specimens in it.

Renealmus. Paul de Reneaulme (ca. 1560–1624).

1611. *Specimen historiae plantarum.* Paris. TL-2: 9073; Heller: 49.

There are 25 copperplate illustrations, some of which are cited by Linnaeus, and among them are the lectotypes of *Ornithogalum umbellatum* L. (see above, right) and *Spartium sphaerocarpum* L.

Rheede. Hendrik Adriaan van Rheede tot Draakenstein (ca. 1560–1624).

1678–1693. *Hortus Indicus Malabaricus.* Amsterdam. TL-2: 9123; Heller: 49.

This is an extremely important source of information for Linnaeus for plants from India. Rheede's detailed account of the plants of Malabar runs to 12 volumes and contains a total of 794 copperplates. About half of these were cited by Linnaeus and around 100 serve as types for Linnaean names, including those for *Amomum cardamomum*, *Bombax pentandrum*, *Cycas circinalis* (see pp. 154–155), and *Strychnos nux-vomica*.

The modern identity of the plants described by Rheede has been investigated in detail by Nicolson & al. (1988), and more recently summarised by Manilal & al. (2003). The latter identify 16 names where Linnaeus took his epithet from Malayalam plant names provided by Rheede.

Rivinus. August Quirinus Rivinus (1652–1723).

1690. *Ordo plantarum quae sunt flore irregulari monopetalo.* Leipzig. TL-2: 9267; Heller: 49.

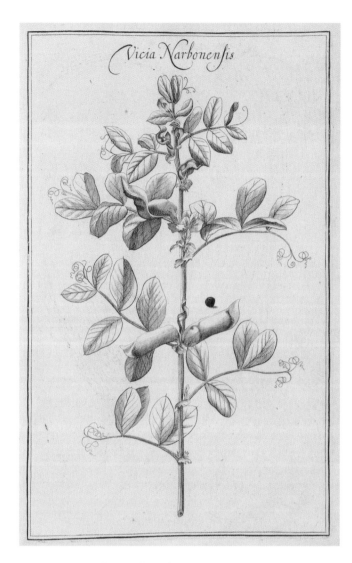

Vicia Narbonensis

Linnaeus worked with van Royen on this new arrangement for the Hortus in Leiden before leaving the Netherlands for Sweden in 1738. Linnaeus cited this work throughout *Species Plantarum* (1753), but it is unillustrated and therefore contributes no type illustrations. However, Linnaeus did have access to van Royen's collections during this period, and there are lectotypes of Linnaean names in the van Royen herbarium (L) which is described more fully elsewhere (see Chapter 5).

Rudbeck. Olof Rudbeck, the Elder (1630–1702); Olof Rudbeck, the Younger (1660–1740).

1701. *Campi Elysii liber secundus, opera Olai Rudbeckii patris & filii editus.* Uppsala. Heller: 50.

The *Campi Elysii* was conceived as an illustrated, de luxe edition of Caspar Bauhin's *Pinax* (1623, 1671), but most of the stock of the two then published volumes, and all of the woodblocks and manuscripts for the projected later volumes, were destroyed in the devastating Uppsala fire of 1702. Quite a number of the approximately 700 woodcut illustrations that had been published were cited by Linnaeus, and those associated with *Narcissus calathinus* L. and *Ornithogalum comosum* L. are the lectotypes of these names.

Rumphius. Georg Eberhard Rumpf (1627–1702).

1741–1750. *Herbarium Amboinense . . . pars prima (–sexta).* Amsterdam. TL-2: 9784; Heller: 51.

1755. *Herbarii Amboinensis Auctuarium.* TL-2: 9785.

This detailed account, in seven volumes, of the plants of the island of Amboina, then a Dutch colony in the Moluccas, appears to have reached Linnaeus only shortly before he completed the text for *Species Plantarum*. Rumphius' book contained much that was new, yet Linnaeus cited only 19 of the accounts in his synonymies in 1753, and those that were included came only from volumes one to four. However, as soon as he could, Linnaeus made a more detailed study of Rumphius' work, the result of which was the dissertation *Herbarium Amboinense* (May 1754), which attempted to provide Linnaean binomials for some of the taxa described in the first six volumes. Rumphius' work includes descriptions of over 1,600 taxa, nearly 700 of which were illustrated in fine copperplates. The 1754 dissertation included some 30 new binomials (excluding some orthographic variants of earlier names). The reprinted version (in *Amoen. Acad.* 4: 112–143. 1759) also contained some changes to names that had first appeared in the original, as well as adding new names for species described in the *Auctuarium* (a Supplement to Rumphius' six volumes that was published only in 1755). For many of these names, Rumphius' account was the only one that Linnaeus would have seen (no herbarium material yet

Linnaeus cited a number of the 125 copperplates in this volume, and those cited in the synonymy of *Scutellaria hastifolia* L. and *Lycopsis variegata* L. are the types of those binomials.

1691. *Ordo plantarum quae sunt flore irregulari tetrapetalo.* Leipzig. TL-2: 9268; Heller: 49.

This volume, with 119 copperplates, supplies the types of *Vicia narbonensis* L. (see above), *V. sativa* var. *angustifolia* L. and *V. sativa* var. *nigra* L.

1699. *Ordo plantarum quae sunt flore irregulari pentapetalo.* Leipzig. TL-2: 9269; Heller: 49.

The last volume, with 140 copperplates, supplies the type of *Seseli carvifolia* L.

Royen. Adriaan van Royen (1704–1779).

1740. *Florae Leydensis prodromus, exhibens plantas quae in horto academico Lugduno-Batavo aluntur.* Leiden. TL-2: 9730; Heller: 50.

Following pages (154–155): Plate from the third volume of Rheede tot Draakenstein's *Hortus Indicus Malabaricus* (t. 19. 1682), the lectotype of *Cycas circinalis* L.

Tab. 19.

Todda-panna. Lat.

Sct. C.

F. E. D.

being available to him from this area), and approaching 100 of Rumphius' illustrations are therefore types for the corresponding Linnaean names, including those of *Cynometra cauliflora, Erythrina variegata* (see above), *Menispermum flavum* and *Psidium cujavus*. A detailed account of Rumphius' book, together with the relationship of Linnaeus' publications to it, and identifications of the plants described there is provided by Merrill (1917), with supplements by de Wit (1959), Boedijn (1959) and Zaneveld (1959).

Ruppius. Heinrich Bernhard Ruppius (1688–1719).
1745. *Flora Jenensis*, ed. 3. Jena. TL-2: 9790; Heller: 51. This work contains six copperplates, one of which (t. 5) serves as the type of *Chaerophyllum aureum* L.

Sauvages. François Boissier de La Croix de Sauvages

(1706–1767).
1751. *Methodus foliorum, seu Plantae florae Monspeliensis.* La Haye. TL-2: 10.368; Heller: 53. Sauvages was a valued correspondent of Linnaeus, who presented his own herbarium of plants from the Montpellier area to the Swede (see Chapter 6). Sauvages' book was cited consistently by Linnaeus, though the absence of illustrations means that there are no Linnaean types directly associated with it.

Scheuchzerus. Johann Scheuchzer (1684–1738); Johann Jacob Scheuchzer (1672–1733).
1708. *Agrostographiae Helveticae Prodromus.* Zürich. TL-2: 10.574.

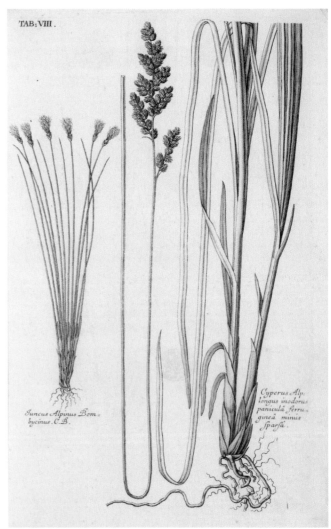

Among the eight copperplates published in this book are the types of *Aira spicata* L., *Carex paniculata* L. (see above, right figure) and *Poa nemoralis* L.
1719. *Agrostographia sive Graminum . . . historia.*

Zürich. TL-2: 10.576; Heller: 53.

This detailed study of grasses and sedges is accompanied by 19 copperplates, each composed of numerous figures depicting inflorescence structures. A number of these serve as the types of Linnaean names, including those associated by Linnaeus with *Aegilops ovata*, *Carex elongata* and *Milium lendigerum*.

1723. ***Uresifoetes Helveticus, sive Itinera per Helvetiae alpinas regiones . . . illustrata a Johanne Jacobo Scheuchzero.*** Leiden. Heller: 53.

This work on Swiss alpine plants contains numerous scattered copperplates, one of which is the type of *Astragalus alpinus* L.

Seba. Albert Seba (1665–1736).

1734–1735. ***Locupletissimi rerum naturalium thesauri accurata descriptio.*** Amsterdam. Heller: 54.

This two-volume folio work contains 125 copperplates, among which can be found the types of *Adiantum lancea* L., *Borbonia tomentosa* L., *Erica abietina* L. (see p. 158) and *Erica coccinea* L.

Seguierus. Jean François Séguier (1703–1784).

1745. ***Plantae Veronenses.*** Verona. TL-2: 11.626; Heller: 54.

Among the 17 copperplates published in volume two of this work on plants from the environs of Verona are types of the Linnaean names *Arenaria ciliata*, *Dianthus caryophyllus* var. *inodorus* (see right, f. 3), and *Sagina procumbens*.

1754. ***Plantae Veronenses . . . volumen tertium.*** Verona. TL-2: 11.626; Heller: 54.

A further eight copperplates were published in this third volume which supplies the types of *Festuca serotina* L. and *Cyperus glaber* L.

For information on Séguier's specimens in LINN, see Chapter 6.

Shavius. Thomas Shaw (1692–1751).

1738. ***Catalogus plantarum quas in variis Africae & Asiae partibus.*** Oxford. Heller: 54.

Shaw, an explorer who had travelled in Africa and the Middle East, had met Linnaeus briefly when the latter visited Oxford (where Shaw was Professor of Greek) in 1736. Among the figures cited by Linnaeus from the seven copperplates published by Shaw are the types of *Centaurea acaulis* L., *Fagonia arabica* L. and *Teucrium mauritanum* L. (see p. 159, f. 575). There are voucher specimens associated with Shaw's account in OXF in at least some cases (see Beier 2005: 229; Serena Marner, pers. comm.).

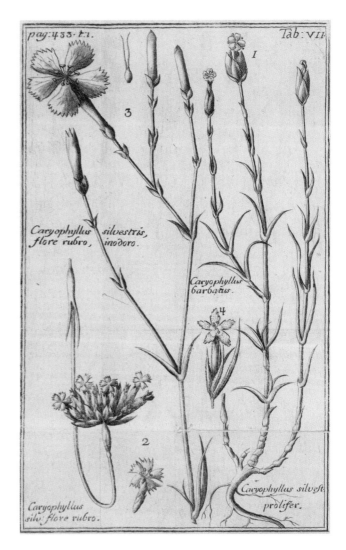

Sloane. Hans Sloane (1660–1753).

1707–1725. ***A voyage to the islands Madera . . . and Jamaica, with the natural history of the herbs and trees . . . &c. of the last of those islands.*** 2 vols. London. TL-2: 12.104; Heller: 54.

Along with the works of Charles Plumier, this two-volume work by Sloane was one of the primary sources of information on the plants of the Antilles available to Linnaeus at the time he produced *Species Plantarum* (1753). Sloane provided detailed accounts of the natural history of the plants he described, though the morphological characters are often more sketchy. These descriptions were accompanied by 274 double-page copperplates, many (though by no means all) of which are botanical. They were heavily cited by Linnaeus and about 100 of them serve as types for Linnaean names, including those associated with *Adiantum trapeziforme*, *Chrysophyllum cainito*, *Grias cauliflora*, *Laurus persea*, *Theobroma cacao* and *Tillandsia lingulata* (see pp. 160–162). The drawings from which the plates were engraved were executed mostly by Everard Kickius, and were

LOCUPLETISSIMI
RERUM
NATURALIUM
THESAURI
ACCURATA DESCRIPTIO,
ET
ICONIBUS ARTIFICIOSISSIMIS
EXPRESSIO,
PER
UNIVERSAM PHYSICES HISTORIAM.
OPUS,
CUI, IN HOC RERUM GENERE, NULLUM PAR EXSTITIT.
EX TOTO TERRARUM ORBE COLLEGIT,
DIGESSIT, DESCRIPSIT, ET DEPINGENDUM CURAVIT
ALBERTUS SEBA,
ETZELA OOSTFRISIUS,
ACADEMIÆ CÆSAREÆ LEOPOLDINO CAROLINÆ NATURÆ CURIOSORUM
COLLEGA XENOCRATES DICTUS; SOCIETATIS REGIÆ ANGLICANÆ,
ET INSTITUTI BONONIENSIS, SODALIS.
TOMUS II.

AMSTELAEDAMI,
Apud JANSSONIO-WAESBERGIOS,
& J. WETSTENIUM, & GUL. SMITH.
MDCCXXXV.

Left: The frontispiece of the second volume of Albert Seba's
Locupletisimi rerum naturalium thesauri accurata descriptio (1735)

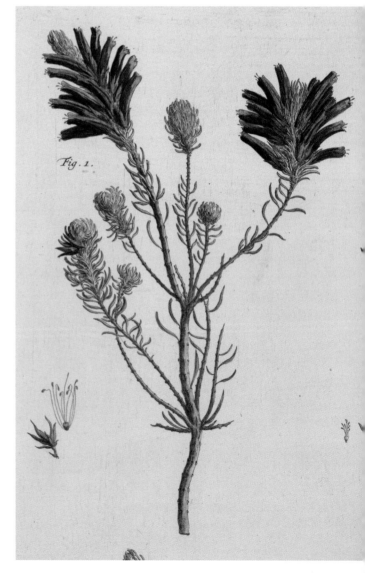

Right: The type of *Erica abietina* L. (1: t. 21, f. 1. 1734)

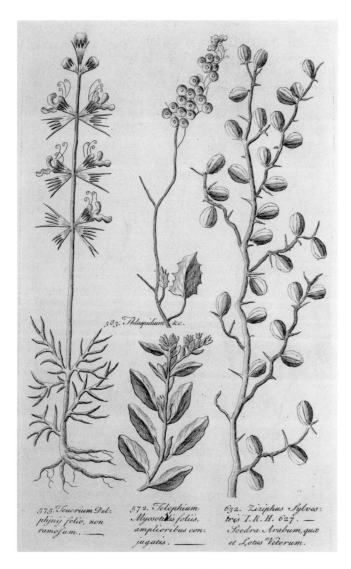

583. *Phlagulum* &c.

575. *Teucrium Del-phinij folie, non ramosum.*   572. *Telephium Myosotidis foliis, amplioribus conjugatis.*   632. *Ziziphus Sylves-tres I.R.H. 627. — Seedra Arabum, quæ et Lotus Veterum.*

Tabernaemontanus. Jacobus Theodorus aus Bergzabern (ca. 1520–1590).

1590. *Eicones plantarum.* Frankfurt am Main. Heller: 56. This work contains 2,255 woodcut illustrations, numbers of which were cited by Linnaeus. Among them are the types of *Clypeola maritima* L., *Lichen subulatus* L. and *Rosa eglanteria* L.

1664. *New vollkommenlich Kräuter-buch . . . jetzt widerumb auffs newe übersehen.* Basel. Heller: 56. This later work contains 2,472 woodcut illustrations. Among them are the types of *Cynara cardunculus* L., *Helianthus indicus* L. and *Salvia hispanica* L.

Thalius. Johannes Thal (1542–1583). See also **Camerarius**.

1588. *Sylva Hercynia, sive Catalogus plantarum.* Frankfurt am Main. TL-2: 14.006; Heller: 17. Published bound with Camerarius' *Hortus Medicus et Philosophicus.*

Among the nine woodcut plates can be found the type of *Arabis thaliana* L., the specific epithet of which was chosen by Linnaeus in honour of Thal.

Tilli. Michelangelo Tilli (1665–1740).

1723. *Catalogus plantarum horti Pisani.* Florence. Heller: 57.

The 50 copperplates that accompany this work were extensively cited by Linnaeus. Jarvis (1993) provides a concordance between them and the Linnaean binomials for which they are original material. Much further information on this, and the relationship between the published engravings and the original watercolours now held at the Natural History Museum in London (Banks ms. 111; see p. 163) is provided by Garbari & al. (1991, 2002). Among the plates are the lectotypes of *Antirrhinum cirrhosum* L., *Cynara acaulis* L. and *Mediola asparagoides* L.

Tournefort. Joseph Pitton de Tournefort (1656–1708).

1717. *Relation d'un voyage du Levant . . . enrichie de descriptions & de figures d'un grand nombre de plantes rares.* 2 vols. Paris. Heller: 57.

Tournefort's account of his travels in the Levant was very popular and several editions appeared rapidly after its first publication, including English and Dutch translations. As noted by Heller, Linnaeus' citations do not all fit the original (Paris) edition, some matching the 1717 Lyon edition instead. The second volume contains numerous

prepared directly from Sloane's herbarium specimens after Sloane returned to England in 1689. They are remarkably faithful to the specimens and are mounted with them in Sloane's herbarium (BM-SL). This close association can make the specimens, though never studied by Linnaeus (and so ineligible as lectotypes), valuable in the interpretation of the plates, particularly where floral details are lacking. Where a particular plate has been designated as a lectotype of a binomial, the associated specimen is often treated as a typotype, or voucher material. Images of Sloane's Jamaican collections are available online (http://www.nhm.ac.uk/research-curation/projects/sloane-herbarium/), together with a searchable database and a detailed guide contributed by C.D. Adams.

Following pages (160–161): To the right, Sloane's Jamaican herbarium specimen (Herb. Sloane 3: 101, BM-SL) of the bromeliad that Linnaeus subsequently named *Tillandsia lingulata* L. (= *Guzmania lingulata* (L.) Mez). It was the basis of the drawing (to the left) that Everard Kickius prepared, from which, in turn, the published engraving (see p. 162) was made.

101.

101.

Tillandsia lingulata, Linn.

Viscum caryophylloides maximum capitulis
in summitate conglomeratis. cat. Jam. p. 77. Raji
189. Raij. Hist. t. 3. p. 405.

Tab. 120.

Viscum cariophylloides maximum
capitulis in summitate conglomeratis.

M. V. gucht Sculp:

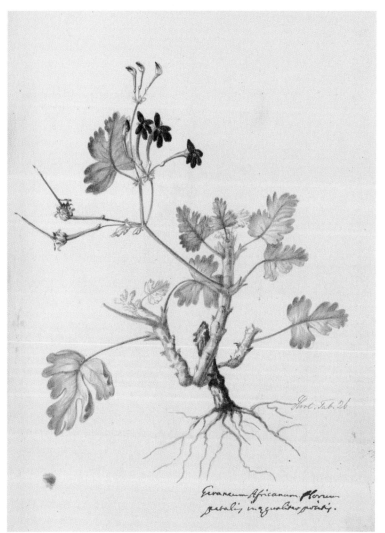

Opposite page: The published engraving, from the first volume of Sloane's *A voyage to the islands Madera...and Jamaica* (t. 120. 1707), of the bromeliad that Linnaeus named *Tillandsia lingulata* L. (= *Guzmania lingulata* (L.) Mez).

Above: Original watercolour of *Geranium fulgidum* L. from Banks ms. 111 (vol. 3, fol. 165, BM).

Tab 26

anium Surianense Chelidonii folio flore coccineo petalis inequalibus

Left: Published plate in Tilli's *Catalogus plantarum horti Pisani* (t. 26. 1723), cited by Linnaeus in the protologue of *Geranium fulgidum* L.

Tom. 2. pag. 245.

Ranunculus Orientalis, Aconiti Lycoctoni folio, flore magno albo Coroll. Inst. Rei herb. 20.

copperplates, often cited by Linnaeus, and Linnaean names such as *Anemone fasciculata* (see above), *Astragalus christianus, Campanula heterophylla, Campanula laciniata, Catananche graeca* and *Daphne pontica* are typified by their corresponding Tournefort plates. Burtt (2001, 2002) gives a popular account of Tournefort's travels in Turkey. Tournefort's own specimens, which often serve as typotypes or voucher specimens for these plates, are at P-TRF.

Trew. Christopher Jacob Trew (1695–1769). See also **Ehret**.
1733. Obs. 129. De cerei plantae charactere generico.
Acta Physico-Medica Academiae Caesareae Leopoldino-Carolinae Naturae Curiosorum exhibentia Ephemerides . . . (Nürnberg) 3: 393–410, pl. 7–8. Heller: 39.
One of the two plates in this article is the designated lectotype of *Cactus hexagonus* L.
1750–1773. *Plantae selectae quarum imagines . . .*
Nuremberg. TL-2: 15.131; Heller: 22.
This lavish work was initiated by Trew, with the intention of

publishing 100 of Georg Dionysius Ehret's finest drawings of plants (see Nickelsen 2006: 39–68 for more details of this work). The copperplates, engraved by Johann Jacob Haid, were hand-coloured and were published in parts, only the first of which was available to Linnaeus before 1753. However, Linnaeus cited many of the plates in his later works, and *Antholyza meriana* L. (see p. 128) and *Indigofera disperma* L. are among the Linnaean names typified by plates from here.

Triumfetti. Giovanni Battista Trionfetti (1658–1708).
1685. *Observationes . . . cum novarum stirpium historia iconibus illustrata.* Rome. Heller: 39.

Phaseolus Indicus cochleato flore

This work contains 17 copperplates, most of which were cited by Linnaeus and two of which are the types of *Phaseolus caracalla* L. (see above) and *Salvia haematodes* L. The type of the latter is reproduced by Del Carratore & al. (1998: 172, f. 2).

Turra. Antonio Turra (1730–1796).

1765. Farsetia, *novum Genus: accedunt Animadversiones quaedam botanicae.* Venice. TL-2: 15.390; Stearn: xxiii. For bibliographic comments on this work, see Baldini (2002: 377). Some of Turra's specimens are in LINN (see Chapter 6).

Vaillant. Sébastien Vaillant (1669–1722).

1719a. Caractères de quatorze genres de plantes. *Mémoires de l'Académie Royale des Sciences* 1719: 9–47 [11–63], pl. 1–4. Heller: 43.

One of the figures from Vaillant's plate 2 is the lectotype of *Ceratophyllum submersum* L.

1719b. Suite . . . de plantes à fleurs composées. *Mémoires de l'Académie Royale des Sciences* 1719: 277–339 [357–439], pl. 20. Heller: 43.

One of the figures from Vaillant's plate 20 is the lectotype of *Ethulia sparganophora* L.

1727. Botanicon Parisiense, ou Dénoubrement . . . des plantes. Leiden & Amsterdam. TL-2: 15.748; Heller: 59.

This work of Vaillant's was accompanied by 33 copperplates which were extensively cited by Linnaeus. Figures from them acting as types for Linnaean names include those associated with *Geranium molle*, *Lycoperdon aurantium* (see f. 9, 10, above) and *Satyrium hircinum.*

Volckamerus. Johann Christoph Volckamer (1644–1720).

1708. *Nürnbergische Hesperides, oder Gründliche Beschreibung der edlen Citronat-, Citronen-, und Pomerantzen-früchte.* Nuremberg. Heller: 59.

Linnaeus cited a number of the 117 copperplates scattered through this book, including those associated with *Mesembryanthemum barbatum* L., and a particularly striking illustration cited in the synonymy of *Cactus grandiflorus* L., reproduced by Hunt (1989: 95).

Volckamerus. Johann Georg Volckamer (1662–1744).

1700. *Flora Noribergensis.* Nuremberg. Heller: 59.

Volckamer's book contains 25 copperplates, a number of which are cited by Linnaeus. Among them, that of *Gnaphalium helianthemifolium* L. (see above) serves as the type of this name.

1715. Obs. 160. De caryophyllo spicam frumenti referenti. *Acta Physico-Medica Academiae Caesareae Leopoldino-Carolinae Naturae Curiosorum exhibentia Ephemerides . . . (Nürnberg)* Cent. 4: 368–370, pl. 9. Heller: 39.

The plate in this article is the designated lectotype of *Dianthus caryophyllus* var. *imbricatus* L.

Waltherus. Augustin Friedrich Walther (1688–1746).

1735. ***Designatio plantarum.*** Leipzig. TL-2: 16.615; Heller: 59.

Many of the 24 copperplates included in this volume were cited by Linnaeus, for example in connection with *Lysimachia ciliata* L. and *Stachys cretica* L. For the latter, t. 19 is the type.

Zannichelli. Gian Girolamo Zannichelli (1662–1729).

1735. ***Istoria delle piante che nascono ne'lidi intorno a Venezia.*** Venice. TL-2: 18.598; Heller: 60.

This account of the plants growing within Venice's lagoon contains 311 copperplates, among which t. 91 appears notable as an important element in Linnaeus' concept of his own *Hibiscus pentacarpos* L., which he described as growing "*in paludosis* Venetiae".

Zanoni. Giacomo Zanoni (1615–1682).

1675. ***Istoria botanica.*** Bologna. Heller: 60.

Zanoni's book contains 80 copperplates, and Jarvis (1993) has provided a concordance between the cited plates and their corresponding Linnaean binomials. Among those that are types of Linnaean names are the plates corresponding with *Agrostemma flos-jobis*, *Aspalathus cretica* and *Fragaria muricata* (see below, left), *Sanguisorba media* and *Sium siculum*. For a detailed account of the work and its history, see Guglielmone (in Forneris 2004: 277–297).

Chapter 5
SOURCES OF INFORMATION – LINNAEAN AND LINNAEAN-LINKED HERBARIA

On his introduction to collections of dried plants by his mentor Kilian Stobaeus in Lund in 1727, Linnaeus had immediately seen their value in facilitating the investigation, at any time, of the features of different taxa. He quickly set about making a herbarium of his own and emphasised, in his *Fundamenta Botanica* (1736) and *Philosophia Botanica* (1751), the importance of such collections in Aphorism 11: "A Herbarium is better than any picture, and necessary for every botanist". This he followed with detailed instructions for preparing herbarium specimens and, in the *Memoranda* of the latter (see Freer 2003: 328–330), he illustrated a suitable herbarium cabinet with notes on its construction and the organisation of specimens within it.

Linnaeus' own herbarium numbers some 14,600 specimens, and it remains the largest individual herbarium used in the interpretation of Linnaean names. Now housed at the Linnean Society of London, it contains not only specimens collected by Linnaeus himself, but also many more supplied by other collectors at various times. This is also true of the other "general" Linnaean herbaria (at H, S, UPS etc.). Linnaeus also had access, at various times, to collections owned by others. These included those of Joachim Burser, George Clifford, Paul Hermann, and many more which provided him with information about species that grew far beyond those parts of northern Europe that Linnaeus knew first-hand. This chapter deals with the various herbaria that contain specimens that Linnaeus was able to study. Chapter 6 provides an alphabetical list of the more significant collectors of such specimens.

Two of Linnaeus' original herbarium cabinets

Part of Linnaeus' herbarium and library at the Linnean Society of London

Linnaean Herbaria

Stearn (1957: 103–124) provides an invaluable guide to the main herbaria comprising specimens that Linnaeus either owned or consulted directly, and much of what Stearn described will not be repeated here in any detail. However, some significant additions and studies on various of these collections have been made in the intervening period and these, and other points, are noted below. The names of institutes and their acronyms follow those adopted by *Index Herbariorum* (Holmgren & Holmgren 2007) except for the Institut de France in Paris which houses Linnaeus' Lapland herbarium and for which the code "LAPP" has been adopted.

The Linnaean Herbarium at the Linnean Society of London (LINN)

Linnaeus' own herbarium, now long in the possession of the Linnean Society of London, is undoubtedly the single most important Linnaean collection, as well as the largest. Although most of its predecessors in the 17th and early 18th centuries were what had been known as Horti Sicci, bound volumes in which the specimens were mounted, often many to a page, Linnaeus held a clear view of how a herbarium should be prepared and organised (Linnaeus 1751a: No. 11), and this involved mounting specimens singly on unbound sheets of paper. This method dispensed with the need for the sorts of potentially complicated indexes that were often necessary in bound collections, and also allowed for the easy incorporation of new material, as well as for substantial reorganisation should that prove either desirable or necessary.

Linnaeus started to make his herbarium in 1727, and it grew steadily in size, not only through specimens he had collected himself, but also through acquisitions from friends, students and correspondents. Stearn identified five periods in its development between 1727 and the present.

The first (Stearn 1957: 105–108) covers the period from its inception until 1752 when Linnaeus completed his manuscript of *Species Plantarum*. Starting with the plants he had collected himself around Stenbrohult, Lund and Uppsala, Linnaeus augmented these with his own Lapland specimens in 1732 (though they were soon to be given to Burman), and with duplicates from Clifford's garden and from Clayton's Virginian collection (given to him by Gronovius) during Linnaeus' stay in the Netherlands in 1735–1738. Plants from Mexico (from Houstoun), the South of France (Magnol and Boissier de Sauvages), Russia (Amman, Gerber), Siberia (Gmelin), Kamchatka (Steller), China (Osbeck) and eastern North America (Kalm) followed, and this was the herbarium, supplemented by that of Burser which he could consult in Uppsala, that supplied Linnaeus with much of the specimen-based information that he used in producing *Species Plantarum*.

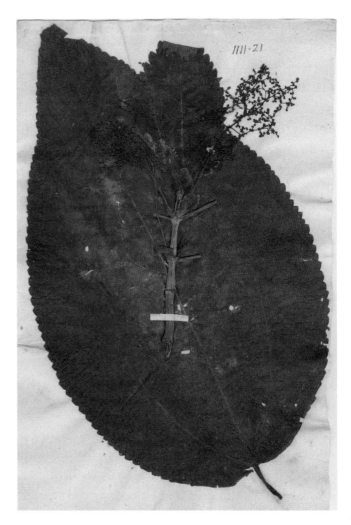

The type of *Urtica grandifolia* L., a specimen, now in LINN, collected by Patrick Browne in Jamaica.

The second period (Stearn 1957: 108–109) runs from 1753 until Linnaeus' death in 1778 and was characterised by the steady addition of more material, often sent by former students (main geographical source in parentheses) such as Forsskål (Egypt, Arabia), Hasselquist (Middle East), Löfling (Spain and Portugal), Rolander (Surinam), Sparrman (South Africa) and Thunberg (South Africa, Japan), but also from correspondents like Allamand (Surinam), Allioni (Italy), Alströmer (Spain), Arduino (Italy and Brazil), Brander (Algeria), the Burmans (South Africa), Dahlberg (Surinam), Gérard (South of France), Gouan (South of France), Hudson (England), Jacquin (various), Kähler (Mediterranean), König (South Africa, India), Mútis (Colombia), David van Royen (various), Schreber (South Africa), Scopoli (Italy), Séguier (South of France), Swartz (Caribbean), Tulbagh (South Africa), Turra (Italy) and Vandelli

Opposite page: Specimen of the South African species *Protea lepidocarpodendron* (L.) L. in Linnaeus' herbarium (LINN)

34

116.34

Lepidocarpodendron   speciosa

(Portugal). Linnaeus had bought Patrick Browne's Jamaican herbarium in 1758 (see p. 168: the type of *Urtica grandifolia* L.). However, as well as acquisition, the discarding of specimens was also a feature in this period. Linnaeus' son, in a letter to his father's great friend Abraham Bäck in 1779, wrote "my late father weeded out his herbarium while he was able to work and seems to have burned all the duplicates, why, no one knows" (Stearn 1957: 108). Linnaeus had moved his collections, in haste, out of Uppsala at the time of the city's 1766 fire and subsequently housed them in a small, unheated museum that he had built in the grounds of his country estate at Hammarby. More of the supposed "duplicates" (specimens merely believed to be conspecific, rather than of the same provenance and/or gathering) were given away to Swedish friends and colleagues such as Alströmer, Bäck, Bergius, Montin, Retzius, Solander and Wahlbom. Such specimens comprise most of the Linnaean herbarium in S, and others are at UPS.

The third period (Stearn 1957: 109) runs from Linnaeus' death in 1778 to that of his son in November 1783. Linnaeus had bequeathed his collections to his wife, Sara Lisa, explicitly prohibiting his son from having access to them, a seemingly harsh judgement. They therefore remained locked away at Hammarby while Sara Lisa tried to sell them but when this failed, she reluctantly allowed her son to remove them to Uppsala where he spent much time trying to restore the damage caused to them by the damp, verminous conditions they had endured. However, he apparently discarded the most badly damaged sheets.

The fourth period (Stearn 1957: 109–111) runs from Linnaeus filius' sudden death in late 1783 until that of J.E. Smith in 1828. Sara Lisa again attempted to sell the collection, which was offered to Sir Joseph Banks in the light of his earlier interest in buying the collection after Linnaeus' death. Banks was apparently not in a position to do so but recommended to the young James Edward Smith, with whom he was breakfasting when the letter from Sweden arrived, that he should secure the collection himself. Not without some difficulty, Smith eventually persuaded his father to provide the money for the purchase and, in October 1784, the entire collection arrived in England. After study and comparison by Smith, Dryander and Banks with Banks' herbarium (then at his home in Chelsea), Smith disposed of a number of supposed duplicates from the Linnaean plant collection. These included 85 to Banks (enumerated by Savage 1937b: 10), which are now kept as a separate collection at BM (and which includes the lectotype of *Arabis capensis* L.), as well as smaller gifts to Davall (see de Beer, 1947), Hosack (taken to New York but now believed lost, see Robbins 1960) and Roscoe (now at LIV, listed by Stearn 1957: 111). Stearn reviews the subsequent history of the collection, through the founding of the Linnean Society of

London in 1788 (of which Smith was the first President), the sale by Smith of the mineral collection in 1796, and the transfer of the library and collections to Smith's home in Norwich where they remained, comparatively inaccessible, until after his death in 1828.

The fifth and final period (Stearn 1957: 111–113) follows Smith's death. Despite his claim in his first Presidential address to the Linnean Society that, as far as the Linnaean collections were concerned, Smith considered himself "a trustee of the public", holding them "only for the purpose of making them useful to the world and natural history in general, and particularly to this society", he did not bequeath them to the Society in his will. Instead the Society was forced to borrow money (only managing to pay off the debt in 1861) to purchase them from the executor of Smith's estate.

The Linnean Society of London's Rooms at Burlington House, the Tower Rooms and the Archway, viewed from the courtyard, ca. 1870. Line and watercolour on paper by Charles Barry Jr (1823–1900).

After their acquisition by the Society, the plant collections were quite frequently consulted (see Jackson 1922: 27–30) for a list of publications in which various specimens featured), the first attempt at a published index to the botanical collection was that of Jackson (1912). Useful though this was, it has been supplanted by the much more detailed catalogue prepared by Savage (1945), which provided transcriptions of the annotations for each sheet and also introduced, for the first time, a numbering system for the collection as a whole. Jackson also interpreted annotations in a series of lists at LINN as indicating whether a particular specimen was present in the herbarium in 1753, 1755 and 1767. Savage (1945: xi) opined, however, that this interpretation was "mere presumption", and Jackson's "dating" is frequently at odds with information drawn, for example, from Linnaeus' correspondence, and cannot be relied upon (see Gage & Stearn 1988: 179). Unfortunately, some later authors have been misled by Jackson's hypothesis into making inappropriate or disruptive type choices.

In 1939, the collections were evacuated from London first to Woburn Abbey, then the Tring Zoological Museum before returning to Burlington House in 1946. During this period, the sheets were numbered by Savage to facilitate their being systematically microfilmed, and his 1945 Catalogue was prepared to accompany the images. However, copies of the microfilm were distributed only to the University of Uppsala and the Arnold Arboretum, Massachusetts and were never widely available.

As Stearn has noted, the Linnaean herbarium (LINN) remains substantially as it was when the Society acquired it in 1829, although there have been what he refers to as "fragmentary" losses since then. Small samples removed from selected specimens can now be found in the collections of the Smithsonian Institution, Washington (US), the Field Museum, Chicago (F), the Gray herbarium at Harvard University (GH), the Universidad de Buenos Aires (BAA) and the Instituto de Botánica Darwinion, San Isidro (SI). Further details are given below under each herbarium.

In 1959, a microfiche edition of the Linnaean herbarium was prepared, and subsequently marketed by Inter Documentation Centre (IDC), and copies of this have become quite widely distributed in larger herbaria and botanical libraries. However, the microfiche provides only low resolution images, making close study difficult. With the advent of the possibility of providing web-based online herbaria, new opportunities have developed. In 2003, the Linnaeus' Plant Name Typification Project's website (http://www.nhm.ac.uk/research-curation/projects/linnaean-typification/) made available digital images of several hundred specimens from LINN that are the type material for Linnaeus' generic names. Recognising the utility of this sort of approach, the Linnean Society has recently

Part of Linnaeus' herbarium and library at LINN

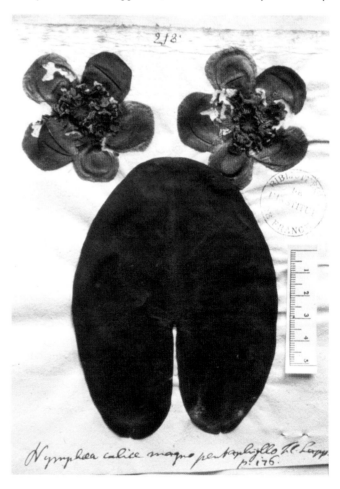

Linnaeus' Lapland specimen of *Nymphaea lutea* L. at LAPP

embarked on the Computer Access to the Records of the Linnean Society (CARLS) Project, one of the first products of which will be the production of high-quality digital images of all the specimens in the Linnaean herbarium (due for completion in 2007). Lower resolution images of these will be freely viewable via the Linnean Society's website.

One slightly puzzling feature of Linnaeus' herbarium is the comparatively small amount of Swedish material that it contains (see Lindberg 1958, Gage & Stearn 1988: 178). That it lacks all but a few of the collections that Linnaeus made in Lapland in 1732 is no surprise, as these were given to Johannes Burman and are still extant in the Institut de France in Paris (see, for example, the type of *Nymphaea lutea* L., p. 171). However, Linnaeus collected extensively in other parts of Sweden too, yet there seem to be surprisingly few of these specimens in LINN. An exception can be found among the lichen collections, where many specimens were annotated by Linnaeus with the corresponding account number from *Flora Suecica* (1745). This work utilised a single number sequence through the entire volume, with the members of *Lichen* numbered from 936 to 991 (e.g. "959" appears on sheet 1273.125 LINN, corresponding with the entry for the species subsequently named *Lichen prunastri* L. (see opposite)). A detailed study of Linnaeus' lichen names and their associated specimens and illustrations has been provided by Jørgensen & al. (1994).

Elsewhere in the collection, there are occasional specimens that carry geographical information written by Linnaeus that confirms their origin as Swedish. From their annotations, some may well have been collected by Linnaeus himself, e.g. *Alisma ranunculoides* L. (473.6: "Gotland"), *Agrostis pumila* L. (84.28: "Hammarby"), *Astragalus alpinus* L. (926.41: "Lapp."), *Veronica hybrida* L. (26.14: "in insula Maelari", "Fläsklösan"), *Cistus oelandicus* L. (689.40: "Oel." [= Öland] (see above)), *Carex arenaria* L. (1100.9: "Scania") and *Pulmonaria angustifolia* L. (184.1: "Scara Wgothia": see above, right). However, others (e.g. "Jemtia" [= Jämtland] (*Satyrium nigrum* L., 1055.4) refer to places that Linnaeus never visited, so these specimens must have been collected by others.

Stearn (*in litt.* 16 Mar 1966) wrote: ". . . most of the

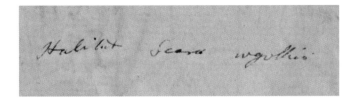

Swedish specimens known once to have been in Linnaeus's possession are missing from the Linnaean herbarium, as Swedes long ago noted, but unfortunately nothing is known of their fate; they may have been taken out for a special purpose and then destroyed as a whole either accidentally or deliberately, as Linnaeus burned a large number of specimens in his old age".

The Linnaean Herbarium at the Swedish Museum of Natural History, Stockholm (S)

This is the largest collection of Linnaean specimens in existence after Linnaeus' own herbarium, now in London, and, as explained above, this Swedish herbarium contains mostly specimens that were at one time in Linnaeus' possession but which were given away by him or his son. These went mostly to friends and students and were already dispersed by the time that the main collection left for England. As a result, these specimens remained in Sweden and, although initially in various private hands, were gradually brought together, forming another Linnaean herbarium, at the Royal Swedish Academy of Sciences, later becoming the nucleus of the Swedish Museum of Natural History's early collections. Lindman (1908, 1910) started to publish what was to be an incomplete catalogue of this herbarium, but also discussed its origins, concluding that the primary sources were Linnaeus filius (1741–1783), Clas Alströmer (1736–1794), Lars Montin (1723–1785) and Daniel Solander (1733–1782). Apart from having been a formidable collector himself, Alströmer acquired Linnaeus filius' own herbarium which had been pledged in exchange for the funds that enabled the younger Linnaeus to visit England in 1781. Alströmer had also received plants direct from Linnaeus. With the acquisition of plants from Anders Dahl (a student of Linnaeus), still more of the Linnaean specimens came into Alströmer's possession. Lars Montin acquired further specimens from Linnaeus along with others received from Osbeck, Kalm and Löfling, and Solander appears to have contributed duplicates from Patrick Browne's Jamaican herbarium.

The herbarium comprises about 4,000 specimens, and was photographed by the Inter Documentation Company (IDC) and marketed in a microfiche edition accompanied by a rudimentary index. The position of the image on a given fiche (e.g. "139.17" for image 17, counting left to right and top to bottom of fiche no. 139) now serves as a reference number for

125

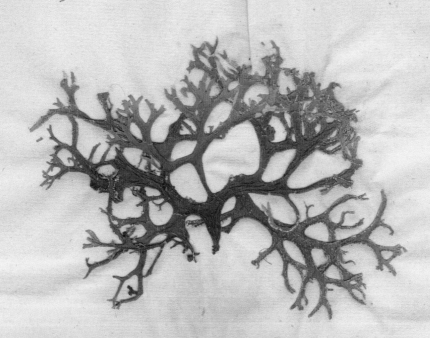

1273·125

95·4

TYPE OF <i>Lichen prunastri</i>

DESCRIBED by Linnaeus

SEE

The type sheet of *Lichen prunastri* L. in LINN (see p. 172)

39 35 prunastri

LECTOTYPUS

Eupatorium altissimum L.
selected by:
Reveal Taxon 47 : 360 (1998)
Herbarium number
S-G-10427

Eupatorium foliis lanceolatis nervosis inferioribus extimo sub
serratis, caule suffruticoso. Linn. Spec. plant. 847. 8.

Habitat in Pensylvania unde femina collegi in Hortum a
theologo nostro Dylandro, mox ibi mortua.

Linnaeus
scripsit

Hort.

Verso views of herbarium sheets in the Linnaean herbarium at the Swedish Museum of Natural History (S). Left: sheet 335.17, the lectotype of *Eupatorium altissimum* L.; the lower annotation "Habitat in Pensylvania…" is by Linnaeus. Above, upper: sheet 346.15, the neotype of *Senecio trilobus* L., heavily annotated by Lars Montin. Above, lower: sheet 373.1 collected by Pehr Osbeck, the lectotype of *Epidendrum amabile* L. (= *Phalaenopsis amabilis* (L.) Blume, annotated by Linnaeus (above) and by Johan Wikström (below).

sheets in the herbarium (leading, in this case, to a specimen of *Fritillaria meleagris* L.). The images are low in resolution, however. In 1997, the Swedish Museum of Natural History itself started to photograph this collection and to make it available on its website (http://linnaeus.nrm.se/botany/fbo/) with particularly high quality digital images. In January 2007, images of 3,658 specimens could be studied, together with informative images of handwriting samples of significant contributors to, or interpreters of, the collection. Images of a number of the symbols used by Linnaeus, and others, are also presented.

Although Linnaeus tended to be comparatively sparing with annotations on the verso of his own herbarium sheets, no such reserve was shown by some of his successors through whose hands the Linnaean sheets that are now at S passed (see pp. 174–175). In particular, those that belonged to Montin typically bear something approaching a protologue of the binomial with which the specimen is associated. For instance, in the case of the type specimen of *Senecio aegyptius* L. (Herb. Linn. No. 346.17, S), there is a full Linnaean diagnosis ("*Senecio (Aegyptius) corollis revolutis, foliis amplexicaulibus pinnatis, squamis calycinis brevioribus integris sphacelatis*"), cited from *Syst. Nat.*, ed. 13 of 1774), a statement of geographical origin ("Habitat in Aegypto"), a statement of provenance (Specimen ex horto Upsal: communicavit Hortulanus Nietzel) and "Herb. Montin". Nietzel had originally been George Clifford's Gardener at his estate near Haarlem but Linnaeus, impressed by his horticultural talents, had persuaded him to leave the Netherlands for a similar post in Uppsala. Broberg is another Head Gardener at Uppsala occasionally mentioned in this way on sheets in the collection (see Herb. Linn. No. 415.7 – *Polypodium arboreum* L.; Herb. Linn. No. 415.3 – *P. parasiticum* L.).

Despite its size, this herbarium contains only about 60 designated lectotypes for Linnaean binomials. This is partly a reflection of the comparatively small proportion of original material present, but also its relative neglect by researchers in comparison with its much better known sister collection in London.

Museum of Evolution, Botany Section, (Fytoteket), Uppsala University (UPS)

There is a small collection in Uppsala of specimens which, like many of those in S, appear to have once formed part of Linnaeus' herbarium. Juel (1931a) lists 83 specimens which came via several different herbaria, including those of Abraham Bäck, Johan Gustav Wahlbom and Carl Peter Thunberg. Among them are the types of *Asclepias pubescens* L., *Clematis virginiana* L., *Cyperus papyrus* L., *Hartogia capensis* L. and *Scirpus acicularis* L. For information on the Celsius herbarium at UPS, see p. 182.

Bergius Foundation, Stockholm (SBT)

Linnaeus gave a small collection of specimens to his friend and former student, Peter Jonas Bergius (1730–1790) and more than 100 sheets (listed by Fries 1935) now at SBT carry Linnaean annotations (see also Stearn 1957: 113). About 10 of them are types for Linnaean names, including those of *Crassula glomerata, Erica denticulata* (from Bergius), *Genista candicans, Holosteum umbellatum* and *Teucrium capitatum* (a Löfling collection).

Botanical Museum, University of Helsinki (H)

Kukkonen & Viljamaa (1973) list and discuss 82 specimens that are believed to have either been in Linnaeus' herbarium at one time, or to be annotated by him. The collection includes the type (reproduced by Kukkonen & Viljamaa 1973: 319, f. 1) of *Salvia glutinosa* L.

Institut de France, Paris (LAPP)

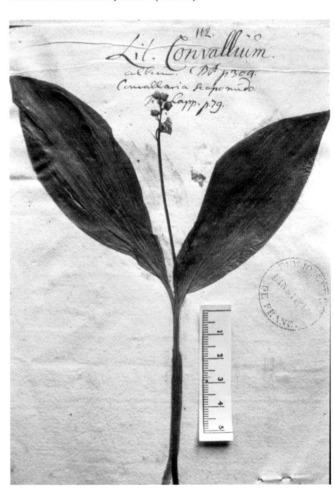

The specimens that Linnaeus collected during his Lapland journey in 1732 are, with a few exceptions, not to be found in Linnaeus' own herbarium in London. This is because he gave them to Johannes Burman, whose generosity and friendship during Linnaeus' stay in the Netherlands in 1735–1738 did much to make it possible for him to remain there for an extended period. The specimens are mounted on small sheets of paper, annotated by Linnaeus with the running species number used in his *Flora Lapponica* (1737), in turn pasted into a larger bound volume which was treated as a book after the death of Delessert, who had acquired Burman's library and collections. The Lapland specimens thereby found their way to the Institut de France in Paris with the library materials, rather than to Geneva where the rest of Burman's collections are now to be found (see Stearn 1957: 115). Fries (1862) provided a first catalogue of this material (see also Alston 1957, who obtained a microfilm of the specimens). Through the kindness of the Institut during a visit in 1982, I was able to prepare colour transparencies (see left) of the specimens (sets in BM, UPS) to allow their study by specialists. Jonsell (2003) provided a more recent review, also reproducing images (pp. 374–375) of specimens of *Andromeda polifolia* L. (the type of that name), and *Rubus arcticus* L. from the collection. Jarvis & Jonsell (2003) have provided a detailed catalogue of the herbarium, correlating the specimens with the associated Linnaean binomials (with their modern equivalents, and Swedish vernacular names), and also providing identifications of the specimens. There are about 250 sheets in this collection, some 10 per cent of which are types for Linnaean names, including *Arbutus alpina*, *Azalea procumbens*, *Linnaea borealis*, *Nymphaea lutea* and *Viola canina*. A few of these distinctive Lapland sheets can be found elsewhere, including Stockholm (sheet no. 172.11 is associated with *Saxifraga stellaris* L.), Geneva (G), Moscow (MW), Oxford (OXF) and London (LINN).

The Herbarium, Biological Faculty, Moscow State University (MW)

There are more than 50 specimens of Linnaean interest in Moscow University, having reached there principally through the collections of Ehrhart, who had been one of Linnaeus' students, and Goldbach, who obtained material collected by J. Lerche from the Lower Volga and by J.G. Gmelin and G.W. Steller from the Second Kamchatka Expedition. For preliminary descriptions of the collection, see Karavaev & Barsukova (1968) and Karavaev & Gubanov (1981), along with the more detailed account of Balandin & al. (2001), which includes specimen images on CD-Rom, and those of Sokoloff & al. (2001), and the wider ranging Sokoloff & al. (2002). One of the Moscow specimens is the lectotype of *Astragalus physodes* L. (see Jarvis & al. 2002).

Botanische Staatssammlung München (M)

This herbarium contains several specimens that evidently came originally from Linnaeus' herbarium, presumably through Schreber. Hertel & Schreiber (1998: 347) noted that five

Linnaean specimens (relating to *Andromeda tetragona* L., *Dianthus plumarius* L., *Salix caprea* L., *Saxifraga oppositifolia* L. and *Scandix cerefolium* L.) were present. Esser (pers. comm.) has located additional specimens annotated by Linnaeus that are clearly original material for *Salvia hispanica* L. and *Pedicularis hirsuta* L.

Göteborg University (GB)

There is a single Linnaean sheet in Göteborg, a collection of *Festuca rubra* L. that was designated as the lectotype of that name (and illustrated) by Jarvis & al. (1987).

Herbier National de Paris, Muséum National d'Histoire Naturelle (P)

Stearn (1957: 105) stated that there are specimens present in Albrecht von Haller's herbarium (P-HA) that were sent to him by Linnaeus. Given the extensive correspondence that existed between the two men (61 letters are known between 1737 and 1766), exchange of material would not be surprising. However, there are very few specimens in Linnaeus' herbarium identifiable as having come from Haller.

Staatliches Museum für Naturkunde, Stuttgart (STU)

There appears to be a duplicate specimen of Gmelin material which may well be original material of *Cortusa gmelinii* L. (Wörz, pers. comm.).

Natural History Museum, London (BM)

There are some 85 specimens, originally from Linnaeus' herbarium, which Smith gave to Banks as "duplicates" after the Linnaean herbarium reached London from Sweden. The specimens were enumerated by Savage (1937b: 10) and they are now kept as a separate collection at BM. The lectotype of *Arabis capensis* L. is among them. This Museum also houses other Linnaean-linked herbaria, notably those of George Clifford (see p. 178), Paul Hermann (see p. 181) and John Clayton (see p. 182).

University of Oxford (OXF)

Linnaeus also gave a small number of Lapland specimens to Dillenius in 1742, and to Sibthorp in 1748. These are extant, and are listed by Stearn (1957: 126). An *Isopyrum* sheet from Amman presumably reached OXF by the same route.

Royal Botanic Garden, Edinburgh (E)

Hedge (1967) described the specimens in Edinburgh of the German physician, Paul Dietrich Giseke (1745–1796), a correspondent of Linnaeus. Among them are a few specimens that apparently originated with Linnaeus (e.g. one associated with the name *Conium rigens* L., noted by Burtt 1988: 92).

Naturhistorisches Museum, Wien (W)

Wagenitz (1976: 221) records a Clayton collection belonging to the *Filago germanica* L. group in the General Herbarium at Vienna (W).

Museo di Storia Naturale dell'Universitá, Firenze (FI)

A small, bound volume, presented to Filippo Parlatore during a visit to Sweden in 1851, now in Florence, contains nine herbarium sheets from the herbaria of Linnaeus, Linnaeus filius, Swartz, Thunberg and Acharius, and includes original material of *Leucojum vernum* L. This collection has been described, and illustrated, in Jarvis (1991).

Academy of Natural Sciences, Philadelphia (PH)

There is a Linnaean specimen of *Convolvulus cantabrica* L. in the herbarium of Henry Muhlenberg at PH, but this is not a recently removed fragment from the London herbarium as are most of the other specimens now in the New World. This specimen was sent to Muhlenberg by J.C.D. Schreber and carries a label in the latter's hand: "Circa Upsaliam; hoc specimen a b. Linneo ipso accepi" (A.E. Schuyler, pers. comm.). An image of this specimen is reproduced by Smith (1962: 444, f. 2). There is also a Kalm specimen of *Caltha palustris* L. present.

Field Museum of Natural History, Chicago (F)

Wheeler (1941: 98) credited Millspaugh with having accumulated "invaluable fragments of types" (though he also added that Millspaugh's work was "notable for the number of worthless new species that he proposed"). It seems likely that the fragment of *Euphorbia chamaesyce* L. taken from a Browne specimen (630.17 LINN) that was noted by Wheeler (p. 269), and that of *Euphorbia corollata* L. taken from 630.56 (LINN) noted by Park (1998: 181), arrived in F via Millspaugh.

Harvard University Herbaria (GH)

St John (1915: 74) reported a fragment of *Rumex persicarioides* L. in GH, annotated by Asa Gray as having come from the Linnaean herbarium (presumably from 464.9 LINN).

United States National Herbarium, Smithsonian Institution, Washington (US)

Many small samples of specimens of Linnaeus' New World grasses are now in US as a result of Hitchcock's studies in London early in the 20th century. Hitchcock (1905: 13) stated (of the foreign herbaria he had visited): "In examining the types I took photographs and in some cases was allowed to take a few spikelets". Most of these are from LINN (e.g. fragments of *Agrostis radiata* L, *Andropogon nutans* L., *Bromus purgans* L., *Elymus virginicus* L., *Festuca fluitans* L., *Panicum dichotomum* L., *Stipa avenacea* L., *Triticum caninum* L. etc.), though a few

appear to be from BM (e.g. a fragment of *Clayton 454* (BM) relating to *Panicum capillare* L., noted by Zuloaga 1989: 315). Janzen (1974: 26) also reported a fragment of the type of *Mimosa cornigera* L. at US.

Universidad de Buenos Aires (BAA)

Molina & Rúgolo de Agrasar (2004: 369) report that a fragment of the type of *Andropogon barbatus* L. (1211.28 LINN) is in BAA.

Instituto de Botánica Darwinion, San Isidro, Buenos Aires (SI)

Peterson & al. (2004: 576) note that there is a fragment of 84.36 (LINN), *Clayton 460B* which is the type of *Agrostis indica* L., in SI.

Linnaean-Linked Herbaria

The specimens discussed above were chiefly those that, at one time or another, formed part of Linnaeus' own herbarium. However, Linnaeus had the opportunity to study a number of other important herbarium collections even though he never owned them. Several of them are linked with specific Linnaean publications, e.g. Paul Hermann's Ceylon herbarium (BM) with Linnaeus' *Flora Zeylanica* (1737), or with the publications of others, e.g. Adriaan van Royen's herbarium (L) with his *Florae Leydensis Prodromus* of 1740. Joachim Burser's extensive herbarium was arranged according to Caspar Bauhin's influential *Pinax* (1623), thereby providing Linnaeus with a set of voucher specimens for Bauhin's names. Herbaria studied by Linnaeus are listed below.

George Clifford Herbarium (BM)

In 1709 George Clifford III's father, George Clifford II (1657–1727), bought the Hartekamp, a large estate with a mansion, formal garden and conservatory, in the coastal area near the university town of Haarlem; this garden was to become his son's passion. The youngest George considerably expanded the garden and added a menagerie, aviary, orangery and four tropical houses. Clifford's enthusiasm for plants and his garden was inspired by botanical contemporaries such as Herman Boerhaave (1668–1739). Specimens of newly introduced species, as well as living plants and seeds, from Virginia to the East Indies and Europe to the Cape of Good Hope, were acquired via other active botanists such as Adriaan van Royen (1705–1779) and Johan Gronovius (1690–1762), and the Hartekamp became part of a highly active Dutch tradition of exchanging plants and herbarium specimens between gardens and the botanists who worked in them.

In 1735, Johannes Burman (1706–1779) visited Clifford at the Hartekamp taking Linnaeus, who was then living and

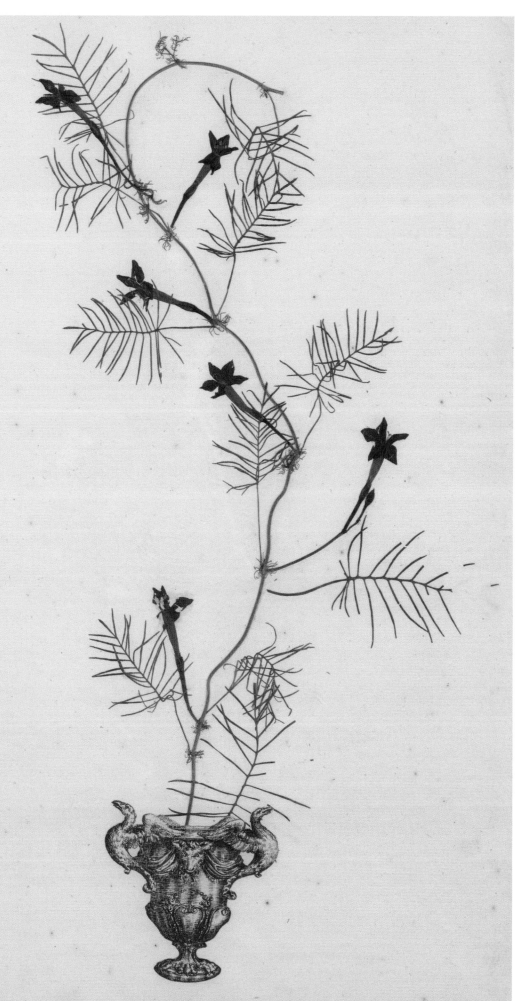

Material from George Clifford's
herbarium (Herb. Clifford: 66,
Ipomoea 1, BM), the lectotype of
Ipomoea quamoclit L.

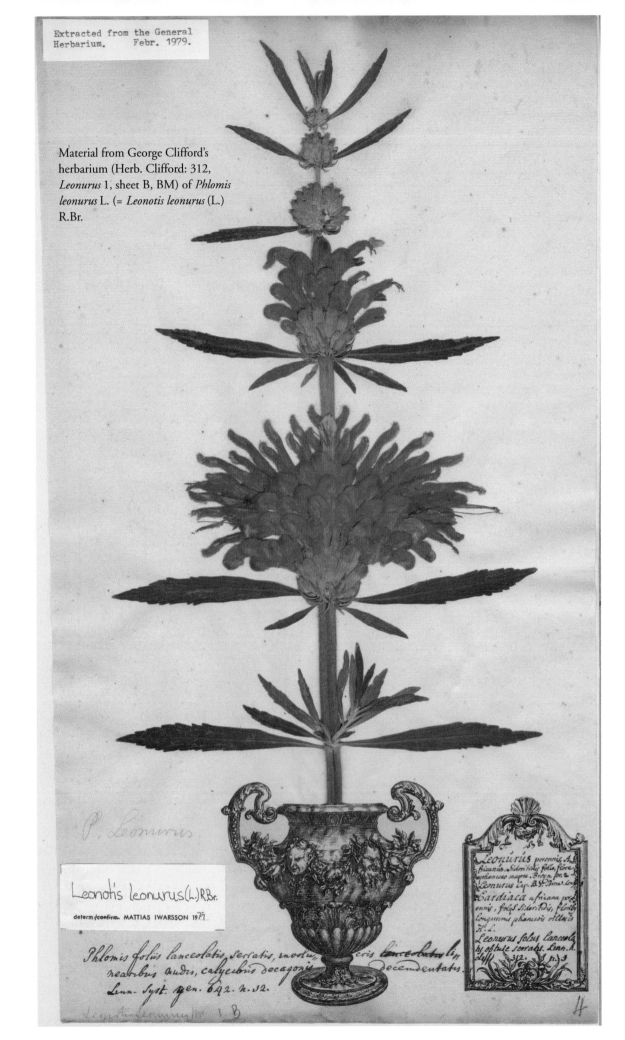

Extracted from the General
Herbarium.   Febr. 1979.

Material from George Clifford's
herbarium (Herb. Clifford: 312,
Leonurus 1, sheet B, BM) of *Phlomis
leonurus* L. (= *Leonotis leonurus* (L.)
R.Br.

working at Burman's house, along with him. Clifford was greatly impressed by the Swede's botanical knowledge, as was Linnaeus by Clifford's garden, glasshouses, rich collections of living and preserved plants, and facilities. Clifford accordingly persuaded Burman to allow Linnaeus' employment at the Hartekamp (with the inducement of the gift of the second volume of Sir Hans Sloane's *Voyage to the islands Madera. . . Jamaica*). Linnaeus was accordingly installed as Clifford's personal physician and horticulturist in September 1735 with a generous salary and almost unimaginable resources. He supervised the hothouses and ordered Clifford's herbarium, and was also charged with producing an account of the plants at the Hartekamp, the *Hortus Cliffortianus*, which was eventually published in 1738. This lavish work is discussed in Chapter 3.

It seems likely that George Clifford established the herbarium at the Hartekamp in the 1720s, building it up with plants not only from his own garden but also from those of others, and from collectors around the world. Unfortunately Clifford's descendants did not share his enthusiasm for the garden and its collections and, in 1788, the Hartekamp was sold. The main part of Clifford's herbarium was bought in 1791 by Sir Joseph Banks (1743–1820) who added it to his own housed at Soho Square, London (Stearn 1957: 118–119). It subsequently passed into the collections of the British Museum, the botanical part of which passed to what is now the Natural History Museum, in South Kensington, in 1881. Later in the 19th century, Clifford's specimens were dispersed by incorporating them in the main herbarium collection, but they were separated out again early in the 20th century.

Many of the specimens are mounted such that they appear to be growing out of highly decorative, engraved paper urns, and are held down by paper ribbons, and with their names inscribed on ornate cartouches (see pp. 179–180). This style of preparation and presentation is characteristic of Dutch herbaria of the 1730s, and can also be seen, for example, in sheets in Adriaan van Royen's herbarium, now at the Nationaal Herbarium Nederland in Leiden. There are few direct indications of the source of any given sheet, as was common in this period. However, the origins of some of the sheets can sometimes be deduced, for instance, from clues from handwriting, the style of labels, watermarks of the mounting paper etc. (see Wijnands & Heniger, 1991).

Clifford's herbarium consists of nearly 3,500 sheets and its importance derives from its association with Linnaeus' *Hortus Cliffortianus* (1738) and the frequency with which Linnaeus cited species accounts from that work in the synonymy of accounts in the later *Species Plantarum* (1753), with its new binomial nomenclature. As a result, Clifford's herbarium is very rich in type specimens for Linnaean names, Jarvis (2005) recording that nearly 10 per cent of those that have been

typified have Clifford specimens as their types. In 2003, the whole of the Clifford herbarium was digitised and it, along with much additional information, can be viewed at http://www.nhm.ac.uk/research-curation/projects/clifford-herbarium/.

A much smaller collection of Clifford specimens exists at the Nationaal Herbarium Nederland, Wageningen University branch (WAG). It has been described briefly by Sosef & Bruin (1996) who reproduced a typical sheet (p. 30, f. 10), as have Brandenburg & al. (1997: 354, f. 2) in a discussion of the typification of *Clematis integrifolia* L.

Linnaeus acquired a number of sheets from Clifford's herbarium and incorporated them into his own. However, as the sheets on which the specimens were mounted in the latter are rather smaller than those used by Clifford, it was necessary for Linnaeus to trim Clifford's sheets. This usually resulted in the loss of the characteristic pots and cartouches that adorned them, but the remains of the tops of the pot are usually enough to confirm the source of such sheets (e.g. see p. 199). They can be found in the Linnaean herbarium in S (e.g. 300.14 – *Robinia pseudacacia* L.) as well as in LINN.

The Ceylon Herbarium of Paul Hermann (BM)

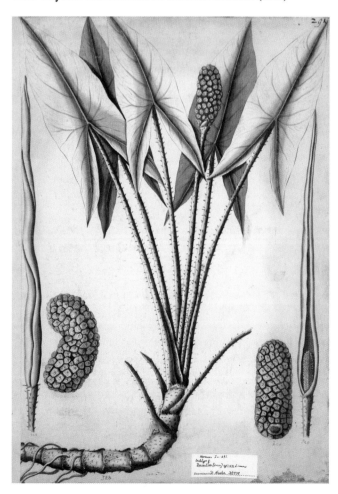

Paul Hermann (1646–1695) was to make one of the earliest scientific collections of plant specimens from Ceylon (now Sri Lanka) between 1672 and 1677. The four volumes of specimens (e.g. see below – the type of *Justicia betonica* L.) and one of drawings (e.g. see p. 181 – the type of *Dracontium spinosum* L. (= *Lasia spinosa* (L.) Thwaites)) were studied by Linnaeus and formed the basis for his *Flora Zeylanica* (1747). As this was, in turn, the basis for most of Linnaeus' accounts of Sri Lankan species in *Species Plantarum*, Hermann's herbarium is very rich in type specimens. See Chapter 3 for details of *Flora Zeylanica*, and Chapter 6 for further information on Hermann's collections.

The Herbarium of Joachim Burser (UPS)

The herbarium of Joachim Burser (1583–1639) is a separate herbarium bound in 23 volumes (see specimen of *Eranthis hyemalis* (L.) Salisb. above), which was studied by Linnaeus in Uppsala and was of particular importance in the interpretation of the plants described by Caspar Bauhin in his *Pinax* (1623). However, it never formed part of Linnaeus' own herbarium and is described separately in Chapter 6.

The Herbarium of John Clayton (BM)
John Clayton's collections from Virginia (see opposite for an example), the basis of Johan Gronovius' *Flora Virginica* (1739–43) were seen by Linnaeus during his stay in the Netherlands and, along with the specimens brought back by Pehr Kalm, were a very significant source of information on eastern North American plants. For more information on this collection, see Chapter 6.

The Celsius Herbarium (UPS; S)
An early Uppsala benefactor of the young Linnaeus, Olof Celsius had made an extensive herbarium collection of the plants of Uppland, a task with which Linnaeus assisted.

Opposite page: John Clayton (no. 94, BM) material from Virginia, the lectotype of *Dioscorea villosa* L.

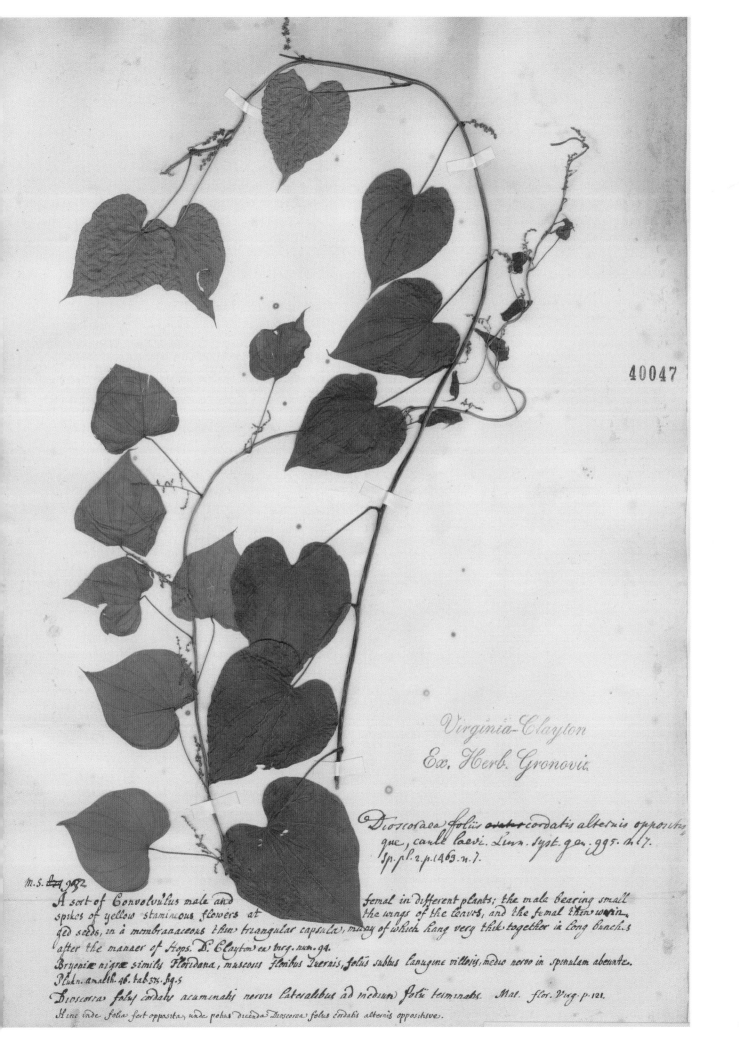

40047

Virginia-Clayton
Ex. Herb. Gronovii.

Dioscorea foliis ~~ovato~~ cordatis alternis oppositis-
que, caule laevi. Linn. syst. gen. 995. n. 7.
sp. pl. 2. p. 1463. n. 7.

m.s. ~~A~~ 972

A sort of Convolvulus male and femal in different plants; the male bearing small
spikes of yellow stamineous flowers at the wings of the leaves, and the femal thin wing-
ged seeds, in a membranaceous thin triangular capsula, many of which hang very thick together in long bunches
after the manner of Hops. D. Clayton ex mss. num. 94.

Bryoniae nigrae similis Floridana, muscosis floribus duernis, foliis subtus lanugine villosis, medio nervo in spinulam abeunte.
Pluk. amalth. 46. tab. 373. fig. 5

Dioscorea folii cordatis acuminatis nervis lateralibus ad medium folii terminatis. Mat. flor. Virg. p. 121.

Hinc inde folia fert opposita, unde potius dicenda Dioscorea foliis cordatis alternis oppositisve.

Linnaeus was certainly familiar with the contents of the herbarium, now in Uppsala, and the types of *Scirpus maritimus* L. and *Veronica agrestis* L. can be found here. For more information on the collection, and a catalogue of the specimens it contains, see http://www-hotel.uu.se/evolmuseum/fytotek/ Celsius/Celdex.htm. A second set of specimens associated with Celsius' *Flora Uplandica*, which was presented to Queen Ulrika Eleonora (1688–1741), is now at the Swedish Museum of Natural History in Stockholm.

The Hasselquist Herbarium (UPS)

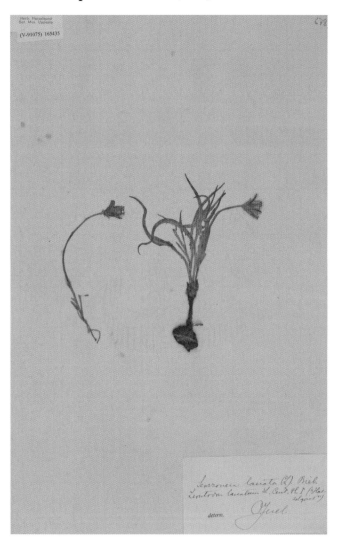

There is a set of specimens in Uppsala (see example above – duplicate of the lectotype of *Leontodon lanatus* L.) collected by Linnaeus' "apostle" Fredrik Hasselquist in the Near East, with

another set in Linnaeus' own herbarium in LINN. Hasselquist died in Smyrna in 1752, and his collections and manuscripts were purchased by Queen Lovisa Ulrika, reaching her at the Royal Palace at Drottningholm in 1755. Although some duplicates were given to Linnaeus (who had previously received some material independently from his former student), the main part of this collection remained at Drottningholm, in the Queen's collection, until 1803, when it was transferred to Uppsala. It has been described by Juel (1918) and runs to 816 specimens. This and the collection of Hasselquist specimens in LINN are discussed in more detail in Chapter 6.

The Kalm Herbarium (UPS)

There appear to have been three separate Kalm collections originally: that given to Linnaeus by Kalm (mostly in LINN), that of Kalm himself (apparently lost by fire in Åbo [now Turku in Finland] in 1827), and a third which Kalm prepared and presented to Queen Lovisa Ulrika in 1754. Along with the Hasselquist herbarium, it reached Uppsala in 1803. It contains about 380 specimens, mounted on heavy, gold-edged paper and with unusually extensive information written by Kalm (in Swedish) on the verso indicating the place and date of collection, sometimes accompanied by ecological observations. The collection has been described and catalogued by Juel (1921) and Juel & Harshburger (1929), and Kalm's annotations have recently been transcribed, and translated into English by Lundqvist & Moberg (1993). Many of the specimens are duplicates of lectotypes of Linnaean names. For further information on Kalm's collections, see Chapter 6.

The van Royen Herbaria (L)

During his visit to the Netherlands, Linnaeus spent the winter of 1737–1738 working with Adriaan van Royen on a new arrangement for the botanic garden in Leiden, while van Royen was working on his *Florae Leydensis Prodromus* (1740). Material annotated by van Royen and associated with this work is present in L (see example opposite, the type of *Gladiolus communis* L.). Adriaan's successor as director of the garden was his nephew, David van Royen, with whom Linnaeus corresponded for many years. For more information on the material of both Adriaan and David, see Chapter 6.

Opposite: A typical sheet from the herbarium of Adriaan van Royen; this is the lectotype of *Gladiolus communis* L.

HERB. LUGD. BAT. | №904,137—228

Rijksherbarium Leiden
L 0052829

900440

IN HERB. LUGD. BAT.
● SUB NOMINE:

coll.000 H.L.B.
GLADIOLUS
communis

Cm

Gladiolus caule simplicissimo, foliis ensiformibus. Roy. prodr. 19. (floribus secundis.)
Gladiolus afer angustifolius, floribus rubro-purpureis minoribus uno versu dispositis. Boerh. mss.

Herb. de Gorter

—

Chapter 6

SOURCES OF INFORMATION – COLLECTORS, SUPPLIERS OF PROPAGULES, INTERMEDIARIES AND RECIPIENTS

This chapter provides an alphabetical list of the more significant collectors or suppliers of the specimens to which Linnaeus had access at one time or another. As an indication of the period during which each was in direct contact with Linnaeus (where relevant), the span of dates and the extent of any known correspondence is recorded. Where there appears to be no extant correspondence between Linnaeus and individuals who were his contemporaries, this is noted. However, for entries relating to people who either pre-dated Linnaeus entirely (e.g. Tournefort) or whose dates overlap only slightly (e.g. Petiver), reference to correspondence is omitted. This information is drawn from the very informative Linnaean Letters Project website (http://linnaeus.c18.net/) and, where individual letters are referred to, the catalogue number is cited from here (e.g. "L2218" for Linnaeus' letter of 2 July 1757). Information on Linnaeus' various students is drawn from Sandermann Olsen (1997). Examples of significant or otherwise interesting specimens are given for each collector. Unless otherwise stated, these specimens are from Linnaeus' own herbarium at the Linnean Society of London (LINN). Herbarium codes follow Holmgren & Holmgren (2007), and those most frequently encountered in this work are listed on p. 252. A question mark appended to the catalogue number of a specimen indicates that the suspected provenance is not confirmed by an explicit annotation on the herbarium sheet.

A painting of the plant named by Linnaeus *Amaryllis formosissima* L. (= *Sprekelia formosissima* (L.) Herb.), sent to him by Otto Brümmers, and now in the Linnaean library and manuscript collection (shown below) at the Linnean Society of London.

Adanson, Michel (1727–1806). French. Botanist in Paris. Travelled in Senegal.

Correspondence: three letters (28 Jun 1754–2 Oct 1758). Seeds collected by Adanson in Senegal were apparently sent to Linnaeus by Bernard de Jussieu (Stearn 1961: xi). Linnaeus referred to Adanson in the protologue of *Mimosa senegal* L. (1753: 521) – "Mimosa aculeata, floribus polyandris spicatis, legumine compresso laevi elliptico. *Adanson, ex B. Jussieu.*" This material seems to have been lost, leading Ross (1975: 451) to designate duplicate material in Adanson's own herbarium (P) as a neotype.

Allamand, Frédéric-Louis (1736–1803?). Swiss. Botanist and physician.

Correspondence: five letters (3 Nov 1770–23 Jun 1776). Allamand's earlier letters were sent from the Low Countries; the last from St Petersburg. The first letter was accompanied by a short manuscript "Genera Plantarum Americanum nova 30 eorumque characteres naturales et species 37". Allamand had visited Surinam and Guiana as a physician in the Dutch navy and brought back specimens, and detailed descriptions and drawings, at least some of which he sent to Linnaeus. He is mentioned in the protologue of *Plinia rubra* L. (1771) "Hab. in Brasilia, Surinamo. *Allemand.*" and about 15 sheets survive in LINN. Some of these carry Allamand's manuscript names (e.g. 47.11b "*Piper cephalicum*") that were apparently never taken up. Some (e.g. 80.70 "*Narthex herbaceus*" and 850.26 "*Seris trifoliata*") are referred to in one of Allamand's letters (L4424), as noted by Jackson (1916a, b). In the case of *Urena typhalaea* L., the specific epithet was taken from one of Allamand's proposed new generic names, and in 1771 Linnaeus gave the generic name *Allamanda* to a new genus that had been given the name "Galarips" in Allamand's manuscript (see above).

Allioni, Carlo (1725–1804). Italian. Professor of Botany, Turin.

Correspondence: 21 letters (13 Feb 1757–8 Nov 1774). Allioni was an enthusiastic promoter of the Linnaean

method, and took up binomial nomenclature in 1760–61. There are about 60 specimens in the Linnaean herbarium (LINN) that Linnaeus received from Allioni. A letter (L2218) written by Linnaeus, and sent to Allioni on 2 July 1757, provided binomial names for specimens that Allioni had sent to the Swede. About half of the mentioned specimens are in LINN, and include examples of *Iberis rotundifolia* L. (827.4), *Cardamine asarifolia* L. (835.3) and *Bupleurum stellatum* L. (335.1). Allioni was explicitly mentioned by Linnaeus in connection with the names *Sedum atratum* L. and *Silene vallesia* L. Allioni collections in LINN are the lectotypes of *Campanula barbata* L. (221.57), *C. cenisia* L. (221.1) (see Pistarino & al. 2002) and *C. elatines* L. (221.76, see Linnaeus' annotation above), and several of his specimens have found their way to S (e.g. *Androsace villosa* L. (73.11), *Inula montana* L. (352.2) and *Silene vallesia* L. (85.1)). Allioni's own herbarium is at TO (see Dal Vesco 1985–1986; Dal Vesco & al. 1987–1988).

Alm, Jacob (1754–1821). Swedish. Student of Linnaeus; defender of the dissertation *Plantae Surinamenses* in 1775.

Two specimens in S are explicitly associated with Alm: material (290.17) of *Gustavia augusta* L., a name first published in the dissertation he defended under Linnaeus (see Chapter 3), and a specimen of *Lactuca quercina* L. (327.11).

Alströmer, Clas (1736–1794). Swedish. Industrialist.

Correspondence: 37 letters (7 Nov 1759–23 Mar 1774). Alströmer sent plants and specimens to Linnaeus from his travels abroad, primarily from Spain in the period 1760–1764. Two manuscript lists of specimens (see Savage (1945: Addendum) exist, one (*Plantae Hispanicae Alströmii*) at LINN dating from 1761, and a second dated 1762 and now at the Royal University Library, Uppsala. Some of Alströmer's specimens are numbered and can be correlated with manuscript materials, and usually carry "Alstr." written by Linnaeus (see below).

Alströmer was frequently cited in Linnaean protologues, and his name is associated, for example, with *Anagallis linifolia* L. (208.4), *Anthyllis heterophylla* L. (*Alströmer 103a*, 897.10), *Avena sterilis* L. (95.12), *Biscutella sempervirens* L. (831.8), *Briza virens* L., *Campanula mollis* L. (221.63), *Cheiranthus fruticulosus* L., *Daphne villosa* L. (500.5), *Genista linifolia* L. (892.5), *Gentiana quadrifolia* L. (494.3), *Orchis papilionacea* L., *Panicum repens* L. (80.47), *Physalis peruviana* L. (247.7), *Phytolacca dioica* L. (607.5), *Plantago lusitanica* L., *Polygala microphylla* L. (882.21), *Rhamnus oleoides* L. (262.4), *Rhododendron ponticum* L. (562.5), *Rumex tingitanus* L. (464.28), *Santolina anthemoides* L. (985.4), *Senecio nebrodensis* L., *Sideritis incana* L. (729.9), and *Statice ferulacea* L. (395.20), with many of the associated specimens being types.

Although not explicitly mentioned in their respective protologues, additional names typified by Alströmer's material in LINN include *Antirrhinum pedunculatum* L. (767.55), *Biscutella lyrata* L. (831.3), *Chrysanthemum pectinatum* L. (1012.18), *Erica australis* L. (498.50), *Euphorbia canescens* L. (630.16), *Serapias cordigera* L. (1057.8) and *Triticum maritimum* L. (104.11).

Linnaeus evidently gave Alströmer some of his own "duplicate" specimens with more received via Dahl, and Alströmer acquired Linnaeus filius' "herbarium parvum" after the latter's death in November 1783. All of this now forms a major part of the Linnaean collection in the Natural History Museum in Stockholm (S). Examples of Alströmer's own specimens in S include *Convolvulus althaeoides* L. (*Alstr. 49*, 77.19), *Erica ciliaris* L. (*Alstr. 79*, 155.19) and *Ranunculus lanuginosus* L. (*Alstr. 111*, 228.3).

Amman, Johann (1707–1741). Swiss. Curator of Hans Sloane's collections (1730–1733); later Professor of Botany and founder of the Botanic Garden of the Academy of Sciences at St Petersburg (1733–1741).

Correspondence: seven letters (15 Sep 1736–29 Sep 1740). Bryce (2005) explores Amman's role as a conduit of botanical (and other) information between Russia and both Hans Sloane and Linnaeus, with both of whom he corresponded. Amman was critical of Linnaeus' system in a letter to Sloane in 1736, and also in a letter to Linnaeus himself (both quoted in Dandy 1958: 82). Sloane's herbarium contains specimens collected by Amman (Herb. Sloane 296: 68–70; 316: 49–59, BM-SL), as well as material supplied by him but collected by others (e.g. possibly Messerschmidt – see p. 221, and Bryce 2005). For information on Amman's publications, see Chapter 4.

Linnaeus cited Amman in connection with *Gentiana aquatica* L. ("Habitat in Sibiria. D. Amman"), and at least 70 specimens from Amman are in LINN. Many of these carry labels written by Amman and they are often numbered. There were many species new to Linnaeus among them, and Amman specimens which are types for Linnaean names probably total about 30. They include material associated with *Agrostis arundinacea* (84.7), *Arabis pendula* (842.13), *Allium lineare* (419.1), *Avena sibirica* (95.1), *Cicuta virosa* (361.1), *Fumaria spectabilis* (881.2), *Pharnaceum cervaria* (387.1), *Poa angustifolia* (87.12), *Polypodium fragile* (1251.51), *P. fragrans* (1251.32, see label above), *Primula cortusoides* (198.18), *Salix pentandra* (1158.5), *S. triandra* (1158.4), *Sibbaldia procumbens* (401.1), *Sparganium natans* (1095.2), *Spiraea sorbifolia* (651.14) and *Stellaria dichotoma* (584.2). *Isopyrum* material from Amman, which Linnaeus gave to either Dillenius or Sibthorp, is now at OXF (Stearn 1957: 116).

Arduino, Pietro (1728–1805). Italian. Professor of Economy, Padua.

Correspondence: 11 letters (25 Mar 1761–23 Apr 1765). There are three separate lists relating to specimens sent to Linnaeus by Arduino. Lists 1 and 2 accompanied a letter from Arduino dated 15 Aug 1761 (L3509) and are at LINN. List 3 accompanied a letter sent to Arduino by Linnaeus, dated 2 Aug 1763 (L3290), and contains Linnaeus' determinations of a numbered set of specimens (1–69) that Arduino had evidently sent earlier. Savage (1945) indicates

238·2

83

eupatorium.

with which list any particular Arduino specimen in LINN can be associated.

Arduino (1764) himself adopted binomial nomenclature (see Chapter 4) and, in some cases, Linnaeus coined new binomials for species already named by Arduino. A number of Linnaean binomials are illegitimate as a consequence (e.g. *Cacalia suffruticosa* L. 1767 [*Arduino 20*, 976.2 LINN] for *C. linifolia* Ard. 1764; *Melica papilionacea* L. 1767 [*Arduino 11*, 86.4 LINN] for *M. brasiliana* Ard. 1764).

Arduino was mentioned by Linnaeus in connection with more than 20 names including *Chaerophyllum coloratum* L. (365.11 LINN), *Chrysanthemum italicum* L. (1012.21 LINN), *Campanula alpini* L. (221.19 LINN is from Turra, possibly received via Arduino), *Galium laevigatum* L. (no material), *Malva sherardiana* L. (?870.20 LINN), *Perilla ocymoides* L. (731.2 LINN), *Polygala aspalatha* L. (882.2 LINN), *Pulmonaria suffruticosa* L., (no material), *Rhus laevigata* L. (378.23 LINN is from Turra, possibly received via Arduino), *Sisyrinchium palmifolium* L. (1064.3 LINN) and *Tordylium peregrinum* L. (337.3 LINN). Arduino collections that are lectotypes include those associated with *Cornucopiae alopecuroides* L. (*Arduino 52*, 76.4 LINN), *Cucubalus pumilio* L. (*Arduino 24*, 582.23 LINN), *Kuhnia eupatorioides* L. (*Arduino 53*, 238.2 LINN), *Marrubium crispum* L. (*Arduino s.n.*, 738.7 LINN, see opposite), *Perdicium brasiliense* L. (*Arduino 17*, 1003.4 LINN), *Polygala brasiliensis* L. (*Arduino 16*, 882.3 LINN), *Potentilla pensylvanica* L. (*Arduino 13*, 655.12 LINN), *Psoralea glandulosa* L. (*Arduino s.n.*, 928.20 LINN), *Salvia serotina* L. (42.9 LINN, "semina ex Italia"), *Sinapis chinensis* L. (*Arduino s.n.*, 845.9 LINN), *S. pubescens* L. (*Arduino 50*, 845.7 LINN), *Stachys palaestina* L. (*Arduino s.n.*, 736.9 LINN), *Teucrium arduinoi* L. (*Arduino s.n.*, 722.18 LINN) and *Turnera sidoides* L. (*Arduino 19*, 384.5 LINN). There are a few Arduino specimens in S, e.g. the lectotype of *Inula squarrosa* L. (*Arduino 62*, 351.5), and specimens of *Bidens bullata* L. (334.14) and *Oenanthe pimpinelloides* L. (122.15). See comments under Turra (p. 232) concerning the relationship between Arduino, Linnaeus and Turra.

Argillander, Abraham (1722–1800). Swedish.
Correspondence: four letters (14 Jun 1751–26 Jul 1753). A single specimen (1267.48 LINN) of *Jungermannia*.

Opposite page: A specimen (238.2 LINN), numbered "53", listed in a letter dated 1761 that was sent to Linnaeus by his Italian correspondent Pietro Arduino. This material is the lectotype of *Kuhnia eupatorioides* L. (= *Brickellia eupatorioides* (L.) Shinners).

Bäck, Abraham (1713–1795). Swedish. Physician, President of the Collegium Medicum, Stockholm. Close friend of Linnaeus.
Correspondence: 541 letters (17 May 1741–5 Dec 1776). Bäck was one of those to whom Linnaeus gave away supposed duplicate specimens. They, and some of Bäck's own specimens (along with others from Wahlbom and Thunberg), are at UPS, and have been listed by Juel (1931a).

Bäck is mentioned by Linnaeus in the protologues of *Galium rubioides* and *Poa eragrostis*, and about 15 specimens in LINN appear to have come from him. They include the types of *Antirrhinum bellidifolium* (767.65), *Aristolochia rotunda* (1071.9), *Cestrum nocturnum* (258.1), *Eryngium maritimum* (331.8) and *Poa eragrostis* (87.23). A sheet in S (340.19, *Gnaphalium eximia* L.) carries an annotation by Montin indicating that it came from Bäck.

Banks, Joseph (1743–1820). British naturalist, President of the Royal Society (1778–1820). With Daniel Solander, took part in the circumnavigation of the globe on Cook's *Endeavour* (1768–1771).
Correspondence: three letters: (31 Dec 1771–8 Jul 1772). Banks had unsuccessfully attempted to buy the Linnaean collections after Linnaeus' death in 1778. After Linnaeus filius' unexpected demise in 1783, Banks was offered the collection and recommended that J.E. Smith buy it. When the collection arrived in London, Smith, Banks and Dryander made careful comparison of the Linnaean and Banksian herbaria. Smith gave 85 supposedly duplicate specimens to Banks in February 1785 (listed by Savage (1937c: 10), which are now maintained as a separate collection in BM.

Although a small number of specimens in LINN are annotated by Smith as having come from Herb. Banks ("HB"), it seems clear that these were added after Linnaeus' death, and probably after the collection reached London. Indeed, some sheets appear to bear Banks' own handwriting (e.g. 989.33, 1014.26).

Barnades, Miguel (?–1771). Spanish botanist and physician to King Carlos III in Madrid.
Correspondence: five letters (14 Aug 1756–26 Mar 1759). Some 10 specimens in LINN have been, with some doubt, associated with Barnades by Savage (1945). They include sheets 120.45 (see handwriting sample on p. 193), 131.3, 241.2, 247.16, 464.39, 689.74, 698.75, 775.9, 1030.37 and 1037.65. One of them (775.9) appears to be original material for *Digitalis obscura* L.

Bartram, John (1699–1777). American. Botanist living in Pennsylvania and Delaware.

Correspondence: five letters (30 Jun 1748–30 Jun 1769). Bartram was mentioned by Linnaeus in connection with a number of species, including *Eupatorium album* L. ("in Pensylvania. Barthram" – 978.5, see Linnaeus' annotation above), *Helonias asphodeloides* L. (471.2), and *Matricaria asteroides* L. 1767 (1013.6). For *Athamanta chinense* L., Linnaeus stated "Hab. – Chinensem dixit Barthram, qui semina misit ex Virginia.", and the type of this name is 345.11 (LINN), a plant cultivated in the Hortus in Uppsala from Bartram's seeds. Gray (1881b: 325) suggests that the seeds sent by Bartram came from Genesee (W. part of New York State), which Linnaeus inadvertently changed to "chinense". The types of *Aconitum uncinatum* (695.9) and *Hydrastis canadensis* (720.1) also appear to have come from Bartram.

Bartsch, Johann (1708–1738). German naturalist whom Linnaeus met in the Netherlands. Bartsch travelled to Surinam as doctor to the Dutch Company there after Linnaeus declined Boerhaave's offer of the post. He sent Linnaeus many letters but died six months after his arrival. Linnaeus named the genus *Bartsia* for him.

Correspondence: 47 letters (8 Apr 1736–26 Jan 1738). Bartsch is cited by Linnaeus in connection with *Hypericum lasianthus* ("in Carolina, Surinamo. J. Bartsch"), and *Melastoma grossularioides* ("in Surinamo. D. Bartsch.") but there do not seem to be any specimens extant.

Bassi, Ferdinando (ca. 1710–1774). Italian. Director of the botanical garden in Bologna.

Correspondence: nine letters (15 Mar 1763–14 Jun 1773). Linnaeus mentioned Bassi in connection with *Betonica hirsuta* L., and material in Bassi's own herbarium (BOLO), in the absence of any in LINN, serves as the neotype of this name (Cristofolini 2001). A small number of Bassi specimens can be found in LINN, including sheets 285.3 (*Claytonia portulacaria* (L.) L.), 308.1 (along with notable

pencil drawings (*Cynanchum viminale* (L.) Bassi, see opposite), 473.9 (*Alisma parnassifolia* L.), 669.4 (*Papaver alpinum* L.), 733.2 (*Lamium garganicum* L.) and 1078.1 ("*Ambrosinia*").

Baster, Job (1711–1775). Dutch. Medical doctor in Leiden.

Correspondence: 17 letters (29 Nov 1751–30 Jun 1769). Baster is cited by Linnaeus in connection with *Clerodendrum calamitosum* from Java, and sheet 207.4 (sub *Lysimachia*) is annotated by Linnaeus with Baster's name.

Bergius, Petter Jonas (1730–1790). Swedish. One of Linnaeus' students and later Professor at Collegium Medicum, Stockholm.

Correspondence: 30 letters (29 Jun 1752–21 Oct 1774). Bergius is one of those to whom Linnaeus gave away supposed duplicate specimens. These, of which 82 are annotated by Linnaeus, are now in SBT, and are listed by Fries (1935). Stearn (1957: 113–114) reported a total of 328 sheets with a Linnaean connection. He also noted that the specimen of *Rudbeckia triloba* L. given to Bergius by Linnaeus is a duplicate of the wild-collected *Clayton 657* (BM) from Virginia, and that Linnaeus retained in his own herbarium (1025.3) a cultivated specimen from the Uppsala Botanic Garden of much less historical interest than the specimen he gave away. Among type specimens present in this collection are those of *Genista candicans* L. (Herb. Linn. No. 53, SBT), *Holosteum umbellatum* L. (Herb. Linn. No. 2, SBT) and *Teucrium capitatum* L. (Herb. Linn. No. 28, SBT).

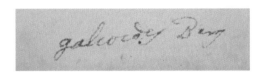

Bergius is cited by Linnaeus in connection with *Erica denticulata* ("ad Cap. b. Spei. D. Bergius communicavit") and *Sedum reflexum* ("in Gotlandia. DD. Bergius") but corresponding material in LINN cannot be definitely linked with Bergius. About 20 specimens from Bergius are in LINN, several from Gotland (e.g. 92.29, 95.14, 473.6) and most of the rest from South Africa (e.g. 498.101, 498.121, 522.7, 893.13, 893.24, 893.53 (see label above), 1048.2). These are often associated with Bergius', rather than Linnaeus', binomials.

Berlin, Andreas (1746–1773). Swedish. One of Linnaeus' students 1765–1766, and secretary to Joseph Banks 1770–1773. Died in Delos, Guinea.

Correspondence: six letters (20 Oct 1771–15 Apr 1774).

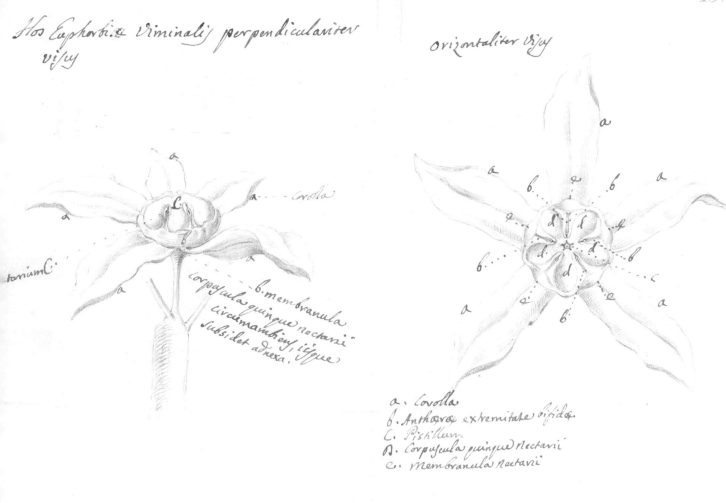

Flos Euphorbiæ viminalis perpendiculariter visus

orizontaliter visus

a ---- Corolla

b. membranula
corpuscula quinque Nectarii
Circummambiens, iisque
Subsidet adnexa.

tonium C.

a. Corolla
b. Antheræ extremitate bifidæ
C. Pistillum
D. Corpuscula quinque Nectarii
c. membranula Nectarii

Drawings of the floral structure of *Euphorbia viminalis* L.
(= *Sarcostemma viminale* (L.) W.T. Aiton) prepared by Ferdinando
Bassi and sent to Linnaeus

Handwriting sample from Miguel Barnades from the verso of an
unnamed *Scabiosa* sheet (120.45 LINN)

Scabiosa corollulis quinquifidis, folis divectis, receptaculis floris Subrotundis Linn. Hort. Cliffort. 31.
Upsal. 28. Spec. plantar. pag. 100 nº 11. Variet. 2ª Flor. Luodb. 143.

Scabiosa stellata, folio laciniato minor, sive maritima C. B. Pin. 465. Journ. I. H. 465.

Scabiosa cum pulchro semine J. Bauh. hist. ..... Ray. hist. general. pl. p. 375.

Berlin is mentioned by Linnaeus in connection with *Hypericum guineense* L. Although no specimens are extant in LINN, material collected in West Africa by Henry Smeathman, to whom Berlin was an assistant, is extant in BM and MPU. Sheet 1030.77 (LINN), associated with "*Centaurea ciliaris*", apparently came from Berlin.

Bielke, Sten Carl (1709–1753). Swedish Baron, government official, patron of science, and naturalist. One of the founders of the Royal Swedish Academy of Sciences. Close friend of Pehr Kalm, whose voyage to America he supported financially. In 1744, Kalm had travelled through Russia and part of the Ukraine with Bielke. Because of restrictions on the export of scientific material, Bielke obtained material clandestinely for Linnaeus.

Correspondence: 14 letters (28 Feb 1744–23 Apr 1750). Few specimens are annotated as having come from Bielke but an exception is the type specimen of *Hyoscyamus physalodes* L. in S (88.9) – "Plantam e Russia misit L.B. Car. Bielke".

Bladh, Pehr Johan (1746–1816). Swedish. Worked for the Swedish East India Company – supercargo for Canton 1766–1783. (See www.ub.gu.se/samlingar/handskrift/ostindie).

There seems to be no preserved correspondence between Bladh and Linnaeus, but some 30 specimens in LINN carry his name. The majority are from South Africa but one is from Java (322.2) and two are from India (Indet.: 142, Indet.: 197). Not very many are associated with names described by Linnaeus, but some carry epithets for names that were described by Linnaeus filius, e.g. *Asclepias carnosa* L. f. (310.43), *Heliophila pinnata* L. f. (840.11, see annotation above), *Ixia fruticosa* L. f. (58.1), *Melanthium ciliatum* L. f. (467.14) and *Pteronia cephalotes* L. f. (980.14). Still others carry manuscript names that seem never to have been validly published, such as "*Erigeron pinnatum*" (994.29), "*Ixia trimaculata*" (58.36), "*Melanthium virides*" (467.6), "*Oederia aliena*" (1047.3) and "*Pharnaceum pennatum*" (387.7).

Blom, Carl Magnus (1737–1815). Swedish. One of Linnaeus' students and later a physician in Dalecarlia.

Correspondence: 13 letters (5 Oct 1759–30 Jun 1766). Blom supplied Linnaeus with material of *Hydrangea arborescens* L. (573.1 LINN), and he is mentioned in the protologue of *Lycoperdon pisiforme* L.

Boerhaave, Herman (1668–1738). Dutch. Professor of Medicine at Leiden – a hugely influential scientist. Linnaeus visited him during his stay in the Netherlands.

Correspondence: three letters (16 Jul 1735–13 Jan 1737). In the opinion of Wijnands & Heniger (1991), some of the handwriting in the Clifford herbarium is probably by Boerhaave. For information on publications, see Chapter 3.

Braad, Christopher Henrik (1728–1781). Swedish. Senior official with the Swedish East India Company.

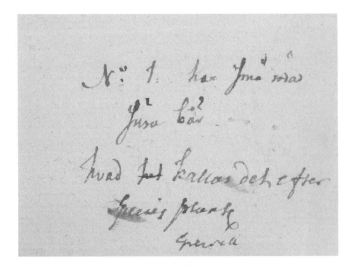

Correspondence: four letters (15 Mar–8 Nov 1763). Linnaeus' letter to Braad of 18 Aug 1763 contains references to seven numbered specimens that Linnaeus had received. The first is a new species of *Grewia* (1076.3) which Linnaeus named *G. asiatica*, mentioning Braad (see Braad's label above). The second is *Sapindus saponaria* L. (514.4), the third *Phyllanthus emblica* L. (not traced), the fourth uncertain (not traced), the fifth *Ocimum tenuiflorum* L. (749.8), the sixth *Hibiscus rosa-sinensis* L. (875.16) and the seventh *Poinciana pulcherrima* L. (529.2). Linnaeus also mentioned Braad in connection with *Baccharis indica* L. (?992.8) and *Convolvulus muricatus* L. (218.18). See Franks (2005) for a broad perspective on Braad, and observations on Torén's (see p. 231) status as a Linnaean apostle.

Brander, Erik (1722–1814). Swedish consul in Algiers, Head of the Swedish Board of Trade. Also known as Skjöldebrand.

Correspondence: eight letters (24 Apr 1754–6 Feb 1761). Linnaeus cited Brander in connection with *Anchusa lanata* L. (182.6 LINN) and *Antirrhinum reflexum* L. (767.54 LINN), for each of which Brander's specimen is the lectotype, and also *Plantago serraria* L. (144.23 LINN, see "Algir" above, written by Linnaeus). There is a manuscript list, "Algerica Branderi", prepared around 1756 by Solander of Brander specimens. The lectotype of *Cotula grandis* L. (1012.28 LINN) also came from Brander, as did a further 20 or so specimens that carry "Brander" on their sheets. In S, material associated with *Mollugo tetraphylla* L. (49.3) and *Ornithogalum pyrenaicum* L. (140.1), marked "Algir", may well have also been sent by Brander.

Breyn, Johann Philipp (1680–1764). German/Polish. Physician in Danzig. Son of Jacob Breyn.
Correspondence: nine letters (23 Sep 1739–10 Mar 1747). At least one specimen (112.1) is in Linnaeus' herbarium in LINN, and another in the University Library at Uppsala (Lack & Wagner 1984: 451). For information on Breyn's publications, see Chapter 4.

Browne, Patrick (1720–1790). Irish. Botanist who made six voyages to the West Indies.
Correspondence: 11 letters (13 Oct 1755–15 May 1771). In 1756 Browne published *The Civil and Natural History of Jamaica* (see Chapter 4) and, two years later, Linnaeus purchased Browne's herbarium, annotating the sheets with the letters "Br", usually close to the base of the mounted specimen (e.g. as in the case of the type of *Erigeron jamaicensis* L., shown above, right). However, the specific epithets were usually added by his pupil Daniel Solander. At the time that he published *Species Plantarum* in 1753, Linnaeus had relied upon Sloane's account (1707, 1725) of the natural history of Jamaica for information on its plants. However, the acquisition of a copy of Browne's book, followed by his collections, must have made Linnaeus realise that there were many new species there that Sloane had not encountered. The Linnaean herbarium in LINN appears to contain nearly 300 of Browne's specimens, about a third of which are types for Linnaean names.

When Solander travelled to London in 1760, he apparently carried with him some duplicates of Browne's specimens, though Stearn (1957: 113) reports that these were returned to Sweden after Solander's death in 1782. There are Browne specimens reported in BM and it may be that these found their way into Banks' herbarium via Solander. There are also specimens in S, including material of *Cassia glandulosa* L. (166.5), *Hemionitis lanceolata* L. (413.3), *Olyra latifolia* L. (377.19), *Piper obtusifolium* L. (13.9), *Psychotria asiatica* L. (84.1), and *Trichomanes membranaceum* L. (416.11).

Burgess, John (?–1805). Scottish. Clergyman.
Correspondence: one letter (20 May 1771).
As he noted in his letter, Burgess sent a small number of specimens to Linnaeus, including 1273.91 LINN, the lichen collection upon which Linnaeus based *Lichen burgessii* L. Jørgensen & al. (1994: 281) discuss and illustrate both it and the relevant portion of the accompanying letter as their f. 9 and 10.

Burman, Johannes (1707–1779). Dutch. Botanist, Professor of Medicine in Amsterdam. Close friend of Linnaeus.

Correspondence: 115 letters (27 Sep 1735–30 Oct 1773).

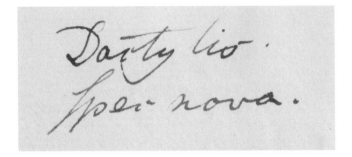

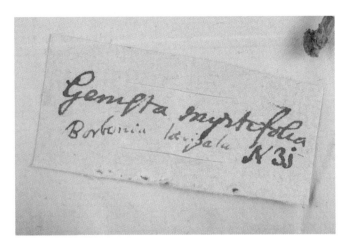

Throughout their long friendship, Linnaeus and Johannes Burman exchanged information and opinions, and loaned each other specimens. Among the Linnaean binomials with which Burman is explicitly associated are *Anthemis fruticosa*, *Anthericum graecum*, *Antirrhinum papilionaceum*, *Aster polifolius*, *Chironia caryophylloides*, *Cineraria cymbalariifolia* (G), *Cotula stricta*, *Crassula punctata*, *Dactylis lagopoides* (90.5 LINN, see Burman's annotation above), *Diosma crenulata*, *Geranium arduinum*, *Geranium scabrum*, *Gladiolus alopecuroides*, *Haemanthus ciliaris*, *Hedysarum lineatum*, *Hottonia indica*, *Hyacinthus viridis*, *Ixia plicata*, *Justicia bivalvis* (28.25 LINN), *Leonurus indicus*, *Nigrina viscosa*, *Ophira stricta*, *Passerina sericea*, *Polygonum perfoliatum* (510.35 LINN), *Santolina pubescens*, *Santolina squarrosa*, *Scirpus antarcticus* (71.54 LINN), *Scorzonera tomentosa*, *Selago rapunculoides*, *Selago tomentosa*, *Senecio longifolius*, *Senecio populifolius*, *Sisymbrium barbareae*, *Tradescantia papilionacea*, *Trigonella laciniata* and *Uniola mucronata*. However, as indicated above, for very few of these names can material that clearly came from Burman be found in LINN. It may well be that many of these specimens were loaned to Linnaeus, and returned to Burman after study, rather than simply being sent as a gift. This is certainly what happened with the South African material that formed the basis for Linnaeus' thesis, *Plantae Rariores Africanae* (1760), and this may well have been a general pattern.

At least a further 30 specimens in LINN carry Burman labels or annotations, and these include the types of *Buchnera capensis* L. (790.9), *Commelina cucullata* L. (65.16), *Hedysarum renifolium* L. (921.8), *Justicia infundibuliformis* L. (28.6), *Salvia acetabulosa* L. (42.42), *Scirpus antarcticus* L. (71.54) and *Stipa arguens* L. (94.10). For information on Burman's publications, see Chapter 4.

Burman, Nicolaas Laurens (1734–1793). Dutch. Professor of Botany and son of Johannes Burman. Linnaeus' pupil in Uppsala in 1760.

Correspondence: 45 letters (15 Jan 1759–10 Sep 1773).

At least 30 specimens in LINN carry annotations by Nicolaas Laurens Burman [cf. previous entry]. These include the type of *Borbonia laevigata* L. (890.4 LINN, see Burman's label and Linnaeus' annotation above) and specimens such as 58.19 (LINN), linked to *Ixia* and mentioned in Burman's letter of 23 Oct 1762. Burman is mentioned by Linnaeus as having sent him seed of what was subsequently described as *Zinnia multiflora* L., and the letters show that many other seed collections were sent from Amsterdam. Lewis & Obermeyer (1972: 110) discuss Linnaeus' correspondence with Burman concerning what is now the type specimen (59.11 LINN) of *Gladiolus undulatus* L. For information on Burman's publications, see Chapter 4.

Burser, Joachim (1583–1639). Danish. Professor of Medicine and Botany in Sorö.

The 23 volumes of specimens brought together by Joachim Burser (now at UPS) form a very important collection for the interpretation and typification of Linnaean names, as has long been realised (see Juel, 1923, 1931b, 1936; Savage, 1936, 1937a; Stearn 1957: 116–118). Burser was Professor of Medicine and Botany in Sorö, Denmark from 1625 to 1639 and, after his death, his herbarium was seized by the Swedes in the war of 1657–1658. As a result, it eventually reached Uppsala, where Linnaeus was able to consult it extensively. The volumes are numbered from I to XXV. Volumes II and V were lost in the great Uppsala fire of 1702, having been borrowed by Rudbeck so that they perished with most of the copies, and the woodblocks, of Rudbeck's *Campus Elysii*. Burser's herbarium contains predominantly central European plants, many of them wild-collected, and is arranged according to Caspar Bauhin's *Pinax* (1623), which was the main comprehensive work dealing with central European plants available at that time. For Linnaeus, the herbarium therefore served as an authoritative voucher collection for the work of Bauhin (with whom Burser had been a correspondent). Although most of the material it contains is from central Europe, there are also specimens from the South of France (e.g. VIII: 72, *Seseli tortuosum* L.) and the Pyrenees (e.g. XVI(1): 75, the type of *Androsace carnea* L.). A few were originally thought to have come from Brazil but are, in fact, North American (see Juel 1931b). Images of the specimens in the Burser herbarium have been available in a microfiche edition published by IDC, but since early 2005, good quality digital images of the whole collection have become freely available by searching for the relevant binomial at http://www-hotel2.uu.se:8888/cgi-bin/wwwdrive.fytotek/beginner.

As Stearn (1957: 116) describes, Linnaeus entered his identifications of the Burser specimens into his copy of the *Pinax* (now at LINN), and in 1745 he published some of his conclusions in a dissertation on 240 of Burser's specimens entitled "*Dissertatio botanica qua Plantae Martino-Burserianae explicantur*". This was reprinted in *Amoenitates Academicae* 1: 141–171 (1749), from where individual accounts were cited in *Species Plantarum* (1753). In the protologue of *Primula vitaliana* L., for example, Linnaeus cited material in Herb. Burser XIII: 154, collected in the Pyrenees, via his account of this collection in *Amoenitates Academicae* 1: 160. Occasionally, Linnaeus also cited Burser specimens explicitly in protologues, e.g. *Aquilegia alpina* (VII: 108), *Bupleurum ranunculoides* (XVI: 8), *Hedysarum caput-galli* (XIX: 135) and *Saxifraga geranioides* (XVI: 86). These instances are particularly significant. As Linnaeus very rarely makes explicit reference to specimens, his binomials do not generally have holotypes, nor are there usually any syntypes. This means that lectotypes are generally required (see Chapter 2), and that these are selected from among the uncited specimens believed to have been available to him at the time a name was published, and the cited illustrations. However, where a specimen is explicitly cited, it is a syntype (Art. 9.4) and therefore (under Art. 9.10) must be chosen as lectotype in preference to any uncited material or illustrations. This effectively turns cited Burser specimens into obligate lectotypes for Linnaean names and the five names given above are all typified by the corresponding Burser specimens. Even where they are not explicitly cited, it is clear that Linnaeus drew heavily on Burser's specimens in interpreting Bauhin's names and deciding where the latter should fall in compiling synonymy. This is supported by the existence of a manuscript at LINN in which Linnaeus provided binomials for many of the specimens in the Burser herbarium. Though unpublished at the time, it was transcribed and published with a commentary by Savage (1937a). Linnaeus' manuscript goes only as far as vol. XXII. However, some of the specimens in later volumes (e.g. XXV: 6) carry determinations by Linnaeus which he wrote directly on Burser's own labels ("Rhamnus catharticus" in this case).

Uncited Burser specimens associated with a cited Bauhin polynomial are therefore accepted as seen by Linnaeus, and are available as potential lectotypes along with any other original material.

In some cases, Linnaeus clearly obtained his geographical information from the labels on Burser's specimens, even though they were not otherwise cited (either directly or indirectly) in the protologue. For *Aretia alpina* L., for example, Linnaeus (1753: 141) made no reference to Bauhin (1623) or a Burser specimen but stated "Habitat in Vallesiae monte Loch dicto", which could only have come from the label on Herb. Burser XVI(1): 77 "In altissimo Vallesiae, im Loch dicto" (see De Beer 1955).

As Burser's material is frequently of good quality, and often localised (see Stearn 1957: 117 for modern equivalents of geographical names appearing on Burser's labels), it

The lectotype of *Delphinium ajacis* L. in Burser's herbarium.

provides well over 300 lectotypes of Linnaean names, including those of *Arnica scorpioides* L., *Briza eragrostis* L., *Cornus canadensis* L., *Delphinium ajacis* L. (see p. 197), *Erica arborea* L., *Fucus foeniculaceus* L., *Gnaphalium stoechas* L., *Heracleum alpinum* L., *Inula oculus-christi* L., *Juniperus oxycedrus* L., *Lycopodium selago* L., *Mespilus pyracantha* L., *Nigella sativa* L., *Osmunda regalis* L., *Paris quadrifolia* L., *Quercus robur* L., *Rosa villosa* L., *Scrophularia sambucifolia* L., *Thymus alpinus* L. and *Viola canadensis* L.

Capeller, Maurice Antonio de (1685–1769). Swiss. Author of a work (1767) on Mount Pilatus (Switzerland).
Correspondence: none recorded.

Although Jackson (1922) believed that specimens in LINN annotated "Capell." came from Gabriel (see p. 204), Savage (1945: vi) has suggested that it is much more likely that they came from the collection of M.A. Capeller, perhaps through J. Gesner. Specimens in LINN annotated in this way include 473.8, 575.52, 655.35, 828.23 (see above) and 896.16, the lectotype of *Ononis cenisia* L.

Catesby, Mark (1682–1749). English. Collector in Virginia, the Carolinas, Georgia, Florida and the Bahamas.
Correspondence: two letters from Catesby to Linnaeus (undated; 6 Apr 1745).
Specimens collected by Catesby and associated with his *The Natural History of Carolina, Florida and the Bahama Islands* (1730–1747) (see Chapter 4) can be found in the Sloane herbarium (BM-SL) and elsewhere (see Stearn 1957: 121–122; Dandy 1958: 110–113). Howard & Staples (1983) provided identifications for almost all of the plates, also correlating with them the extant herbarium material collected by Catesby. Wilbur (1990) has provided a supplement to Howard & Staples' paper. A few

of Catesby's specimens (e.g. 80.55, *Panicum* sp.) are to be found in LINN.

Celsius, Olof, the Elder (1670–1756). Swedish. Orientalist and theologian, Professor at Uppsala. Botanist and plant collector, benefactor of Linnaeus.
Correspondence: eight letters (12 Jan 1730–4 Sep 1739). Celsius had prepared an extensive herbarium from Uppland with which the young Linnaeus assisted (see Chapter 5). There are separate collections at both UPS and S, and the Linnaean herbarium in S also contains two specimens (290.20, *Fumaria bulbosa* L. and 146.16, *Juncus bufonius* L.) linked with Celsius.

Clayton, John (1694–1773). British. County Clerk, and botanist, in Virginia. Correspondence: one letter to Linnaeus (21 Oct 1748).

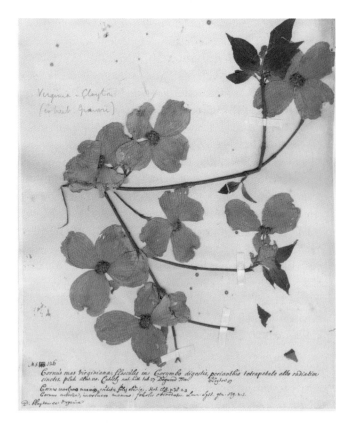

John Clayton was one of the early collectors of plant specimens in Virginia, where he was Clerk to the Court of Gloucester County. Although he published almost nothing himself, Clayton's specimens have considerable nomenclatural importance. Having reached Europe and the hands of Johan Gronovius (1690–1762) by 1735, Linnaeus was able to study many of them and they were some of the earliest North American specimens that he had seen.

Gronovius prepared and published *Flora Virginica* (1739–1743), based on a manuscript of Clayton's and his specimens (see Chapter 4). Along with the specimens from Kalm, Linnaeus' knowledge of North American species was based heavily on Clayton's material, and there are nearly 150 types among them (see *Clayton 57*, opposite, the type of *Cornus florida* L.).

The specimens that Gronovius had studied were bought in 1794 by Sir Joseph Banks (1743–1820). They subsequently passed, with the rest of Banks' collections, to BM. Until the mid 1990s, the specimens were dispersed through the General Herbarium but were then extracted and are now conserved as a separate herbarium. Images of the approximately 600 sheets can be studied at http://www.nhm.ac.uk/research-curation/projects/clayton-herbarium/index.html, where much additional information, including a bibliography, on both Clayton and the specimens can be found. Stearn (1957: 118) and Reveal (1992: 40–44) provide useful background information, and Reveal (1983: 48–58) correlates the Clayton collections cited by Gronovius with their corresponding Linnaean binomials in *Species Plantarum* (1753).

Linnaeus obtained some duplicates of Clayton's specimens, chiefly via Gronovius and Peter Collinson (Stearn 1957: 108). About 100 sheets, now in LINN, carry labels in Gronovius' hand and most of those represent North American taxa originally collected by Clayton. In some cases, they are duplicates of material at BM (e.g. 926.23 LINN; *Hedysarum canadense* L.), but in others the LINN sheets appear to be unicate specimens (e.g. 1237.4; *Panax trifolius* L.). At least 25 of them are lectotypes for Linnaean names. Some Clayton specimens that were originally in Linnaeus' herbarium can now be found in S (e.g. 49.5, *Mollugo verticillata* L. and 158.9, *Polygonum maritimum* L.). Wagentiz (1976: 221) mentions a Clayton sheet in W, and Peterson & al. (2004: 576) report a fragment of the type of *Agrostis indica* L. (84.36 LINN, *Clayton 460B*) in SI.

Clifford, George (1685–1760). Anglo-Dutch. Banker in Amsterdam and a Director of the Dutch East India Company. Owner of the Hartekamp estate, with its extensive gardens and glasshouses, near Haarlem. A major benefactor of Linnaeus in the Netherlands.

Correspondence: eight letters from Clifford to Linnaeus (19 Oct 1737–8 Feb 1741).

Clifford's herbarium at BM, linked with the *Hortus Cliffortianus* (see Chapter 3), consists of 3,461 sheets and has been described in Chapter 5. It is very rich in Linnaean type specimens. In 2003, the whole of the Clifford herbarium was digitised and it, along with much additional information,

can be viewed online at http://www.nhm.ac.uk/research-curation/projects/clifford-herbarium/.

Although Clifford's main herbarium is at BM, a smaller set of specimens is at WAG, and there are also some 140 sheets, formerly in Clifford's herbarium, that he gave to Linnaeus and which are now in LINN. These are quite easily identified as it was necessary for Linnaeus to cut down Clifford's large and characteristically decorated sheets in order to accommodate them in his own herbarium, for which he had used much smaller sheets (41–45 x 26–28cm). Consequently, the remnants of Clifford's elaborate urns and cartouches can often be seen at the edge of these sheets. More than 50 of the LINN sheets are lectotypes for Linnaean names, and they include, for example, 39.3 (*Ziziphora tenuior*), 42.38 (*Salvia aurea*), 116.21 (*Protea conifera*), 248.5 (*Solanum diphyllum*, see above), 1024.7 (*Helianthus strumosus*), 1127.3 (*Poterium spinosum*) and 1192.1 (*Coriaria myrtifolia*). Smaller numbers of Clifford sheets can also be found in the herbaria containing specimens given away by Linnaeus, for example in S where material associated with the names *Ambrosia trifida* L. (383.7 S), *Biscutella lyrata* L. (269.19 S), *Cleome dodecandra* L. (278.11 S), *Cytisus argenteus* L. (307.13 S), *Eupatorium ageratoides* L. f. (336.15 S), *Hyoseris radiata* L. (329.7 S), *Juniperus bermudiana* L. (402.7 S), *Lantana camara* L. (258.15 S), *Lepidium draba* L. (266.17 S), *Liriodendron tulipifera* L. (222.1 S), *Lotus hirsutus* L. (321.19 S), *Malva capensis* L. (287.3 S), *Ocimum tenuiflorum* L. (250.3 S), *Perilla ocymoides* L. (250.3 S), *Robinia pseudoacacia* L. (300.14 S), *Seseli annuum* L. (124.9 S), *Sisymbrium bursifolium* L. (272.7 S) and *Swertia perennis* L. (112.3 S) originated in Clifford's herbarium.

Collinson, Peter (1694–1768). British. Merchant and amateur naturalist in London, corresponded with many scientists. Made Linnaeus and his works widely known.

Correspondence: 59 letters (24 May 1739–20 Apr 1767).

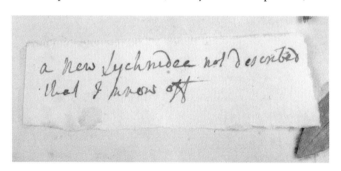

Collinson is mentioned in the protologues of *Phlox paniculata* L., *Rhododendron maximum* L. and *Silphium laciniatum* L. Seeds of *S. laciniatum* were probably sent to Linnaeus by Collinson, and 1032.1 and 1032.2 are the resulting specimens in LINN from the Hortus in Uppsala. Two sheets of *Phlox ovata* L. (217.10 – see above, and 217.11 LINN) carry Collinson labels.

Commerson, Philibert (1727–1773). French explorer and naturalist.

Correspondence: none recorded.

A few lichen specimens (1273.164, 1273.257, 1273.280, 1273.307) are in LINN, evidently acquired via Linnaeus filius. However, more specimens are in Smith's herbarium (LINN-SM).

Dahl, Anders (1751–1789). Student of Linnaeus in Uppsala in 1770. Later Associate Professor of Botany in Åbo (Turku).

Correspondence: none recorded.

Some 25 sheets in LINN bear Dahl's handwriting, the most significant of which appears to be 1164a.4, the type of *Elegia juncea* L. Dahl received specimens from both Linnaeus and his son, and also made his own collections in the Uppsala

Botanic Garden. Many of these are now to be found in the Linnaean collection at S, annotated with a characteristic form on the verso of each sheet, and often with the words "Dahl a Linne P.", added by him.

Dahlberg, Carl Gustaf (? – 1775). Swedish. Colonel, and owner of a plantation in Surinam. Daniel Rolander (see p. 225) went to Surinam to serve as tutor for Dahlberg's children.

Correspondence: two letters from Dahlberg to Linnaeus (18 Jan 1755; 20 Jan 1756), the first prior to his departure from Amsterdam, and the second after his arrival in Surinam. Dahlberg was cited by Linnaeus in the protologues of *Epidendrum pusillum* L., *Glycine subterranea* L. and *Quassia amara* L., and also appears under *Aegopricum betulinum* L. f., as "Dalberg" (inviting confusion with Nils Ericsson Dalberg; see below), but no material in LINN can be confidently associated with these four binomials. However, there appear to be about 35 sheets of material from Dahlberg in LINN linked with other names. The specimens appear to have been the basis of Linnaeus' dissertation, *Plantae Surinamenses*, which was defended by Jacob Alm in June 1775 (see Chapter 3). The dissertation (and a manuscript at LINN) lists numbered specimens, but fewer specimens seem to be extant than might be expected. Dahlberg material in LINN providing lectotypes includes *Anguria lobata* L. (1092.2), *Coronilla monilis* L. (*Dahlberg 157*, 911.1), *Gustavia augusta* L. (863.2), *Hibiscus cancellatus* L. (*Dahlberg 140*, 875.8), *Malpighia bannisterioides* L. (*Dahlberg 33*, 588.13), *Pontederia rotundifolia* L. (*Dahlberg 137*, 407.2), *Sagittaria pugioniformis* L. (*Dahlberg 36*, 1124.7), *Solanum scandens* L. (*Dahlberg 72*, 248.24) and *Sophia carolina* L. (*Dahlberg 27*, 865.1).

There are also about 50 of Dahlberg's specimens in S, including material of *Gustavia augusta* (290.17) that bears a label written by P. J. Beurling which says "Surinam: herbar. Prof. Alm, qui specimen accepit a Linneo patre, sub cuius praesidiode arbore haec magnifica academice disseruit". Alm was the student who defended the dissertation *Plantae Surinamenses* in 1775.

Dalberg, Nils Ericsson (1736–1820). Student of Linnaeus in 1755; later personal physician to King Gustav III.

Correspondence: six letters (24 Oct 1771–10 Jan 1775). Possibly a few specimens in LINN (e.g. 928.23). However, plants from Surinam apparently linked with Dalberg (e.g. in the protologue of *Aegopricum betulinum* L. f.; 887.2 and 887.3 LINN) should almost certainly be associated with Carl Gustaf Dahlberg (see above).

Davall, Edmond (1763–1798). French. Friend of J.E. Smith. After his acquisition of the Linnaean collections, J.E. Smith gave some Linnaean specimens to Davall and one of them (*Diapensia lapponica* L.) is now in G (see Becherer 1945: 142).

Demidov, Grigory Akinfievich (1715–1761). Russian. Nobleman. Accompanied by his brother, Prokofy Akinfievich, he was Linnaeus' student in Uppsala in 1760–1761.

On good terms with Gerber, Gmelin and Steller, the family botanic garden in Solikamsk became home to the living collections that Steller had acquired from remote areas in Russia. Demidov also possessed herbarium material from these botanists, and started to correspond with Linnaeus in 1748, and sent him specimens (also from Lerche) and seeds. See Sokoloff & al. (2002: 161–169) for a review.

Demidov (as "Demidoff") is mentioned in the protologues of *Allium ramosum* L., *Bartsia pallida* L., *Fumaria spectabilis* L., *Pedicularis resupinata* L., *Sophora lupinoides* L., *Thalictrum contortum* L. and *Tiarella trifoliata* L. Additionally, some specimens are annotated as having been grown from seed supplied by Demidov (e.g. 210.7 S, *Potentilla grandiflora* L., bears "ex Horto Upsaliensi e sem. Demidoffii" written by Linnaeus, and 394.15 S, *Cucumis acutangulus* L. is similarly annotated).

Demidov, Prokofy Akinfievich (1710–1786). Russian. Nobleman. Together with his brother Grigory he was Linnaeus' student in Uppsala in 1760–1761. He created a large private garden in Moscow and corresponded with many botanists including Amman, Gerber, Jacquin and Pallas.

Dick, Johann Jakob (1742–1775). Swiss clergyman and botanist.

Correspondence: none recorded.

There are 35 sheets in LINN (e.g. 84.18, 87.74, 575.3, 585.44, 1266.27), none known to have any nomenclatural significance.

Dillenius, Johann Jakob (1684–1747). German. Studied at Giessen. Sherardian Professor of Botany at Oxford.

Correspondence: 13 letters (1733?–21 Feb 1746). Much of Dillenius' own material is in existence at OXF, including some voucher material for the plates published in his *Hortus Elthamensis* (see Chapter 4). His herbarium was catalogued by Druce & Vines (1907); see additional observations by Rendle (1934, 1936) and Stearn (1957: 115–116). More recently, the herbarium has been photographed and is now available in a microfiche edition (see Marner 1996).

There appear to be about 50 specimens in LINN that came from Dillenius. About half of these are bryophytes, with the remainder representing various genera of algae,

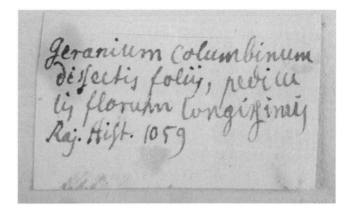

fungi and lichens. There are six sheets of phanerogams, including the types of *Salix caprea* L. (1158.88 LINN) and *Geranium columbinum* L. (858.79 LINN, see Dillenius' label above).

Linnaeus also gave some specimens to Dillenius in 1742, and a few more to Dillenius' successor, Sibthorp (1712–1797), in 1748. Stearn (1957: 116) lists 21 of these, which are at OXF. They are chiefly from Lapland.

Dombey, Joseph (1742–1794). French botanist.

Correspondence: none recorded.

A few lichen specimens (1273.157–159), said to be from Dombey's herbarium, are in LINN.

Duchesne, Antoine Nicolas (1747–1827). French. Horticulturalist at Versailles.

Correspondence: 28 letters (10 Nov 1764–17 Mar 1773). Duchesne was mentioned by Linnaeus in connection with the name *Limonia trifoliata* L. (550.5 LINN), but most of the 20 or so Duchesne specimens in LINN are of *Fragaria*, in which Duchesne was particularly interested (see Staudt 2003). Sheet 654.12 (LINN) is the neotype of both *F. vesca* var. *pratensis* L. and var. *sativa* L.

Ehrhart, Jacob Friedrich (1742–1795). Swiss/German. Botanist. Studied under Linnaeus in Uppsala 1773–1776. Became botanist to the Prince of Brunswick-Lüneburg.

Correspondence: none recorded.

More than 60 specimens in LINN carry annotations by Ehrhart. The majority of these are bryophytes, lichens, algae and fungi, but the few angiosperms include the types of

Gratiola hyssopioides L. (30.6, see Ehrhart's and Linnaeus' annotations on p. 201) and *Justicia fastuosa* L. (28.7 – see Wood & al. 1983); König was mentioned in the protologues of both.

Ekeberg, Carl Gustaf (1716–1784). Swedish. Sea captain with the Swedish East India Company.

Correspondence: three letters from Linnaeus (18 Aug 1763–28 Jun 1771).

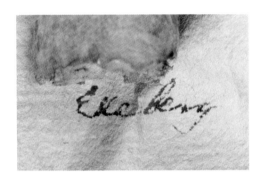

There are a few of Ekeberg's specimens in LINN, including the type of *Gnaphalium eximium* L. (989.1, see annotation above, and the whole sheet opposite). A sheet in S (340.13, *Artemisia chinensis*) bears the statement "e Cantona China. Ekeberg".

Ellis, John (1711–1776). British merchant and naturalist.

Correspondence: 77 letters (31 Dec 1756–13 Aug 1772). Ellis' main interests lay in bryozoans, and most of the Ellis specimens in the herbarium in LINN are found in the genus *Sertularia* (1290), though there are others (219.2, and perhaps 995.6 and 995.7). It follows that his collections have little importance for Linnaeus' botanical names.

Escallón, Antonio y Flórez (fl. 1760–1803). Doctor in Colombia.

Correspondence: none recorded.

Nearly 20 sheets in LINN carry Escallón's name written by Linnaeus filius, almost all of which are also annotated by José Celestino Mútis (e.g. 327.6, 801.3, 943.25). Savage (1945: Abbrev.) notes that Escallón collected plants for his friend, Mútis (see p. 223), in Colombia.

Fabricius, Johan Christian (1745–1808). Danish. Professor of economics and natural history in Kiel. Linnaeus' pupil 1762–1764, and best known as an entomologist.

Correspondence: 11 letters from Fabricius to Linnaeus (22 Dec 1764–14 Apr 1773).

The few specimens in LINN that apparently came from Fabricius include 316.7, 328.30, 429.14, 467.10/12, 772.2

and 893.47, but none is known to have any nomenclatural significance.

Fagraeus, Jonas Theodor (1729–1797). Swedish physician.

Correspondence: two letters from Fagraeus to Linnaeus (13 Jun 1763; 10 Feb 1770).

Sheet 27.4 (LINN) appears to be from Fagraeus.

Falck, Johan Peter (1732–1774). Swedish. Professor of botany and curator of the botanical garden at St Petersburg (also as "Falk").

Correspondence: 14 letters (11 Oct 1763–12 Aug 1772). Falck was mentioned by Linnaeus in the protologue of *Bunias myagroides* L. (1767), and it seems likely that 847.9 (LINN), its lectotype, was cultivated in the Hortus in Uppsala from seed received from Falck. Other Falck specimens are 644.3 (collected in Gotland in 1759, and the type of *Sorbus hybrida* L.) and 824.21 (both LINN).

Forsskål, Pehr (1732–1763). Swedish. Naturalist and explorer. Linnaeus' student; professor in Denmark in 1759. Joined a Danish expedition to Egypt and Arabia in 1761. Died at Jerîm, Arabia.

Correspondence: 28 letters from Forsskål to Linnaeus (10 Dec 1753– 9 Jun 1763).

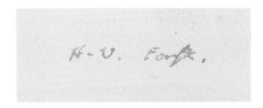

Forsskål's own herbarium is at C (see Hepper & Friis 1994) but his correspondence with Linnaeus resulted in some of his collections finding their way into the Linnaean herbaria. Although few specimens in LINN are explicitly annotated with Forsskål's name (e.g. 999.15, the type of *Inula undulata* L., see above), there are many more that were grown in the Hortus in Uppsala that were probably grown from seed provided by Forsskål. In particular, Linnaeus mentioned Forsskål in the protologues of more than 20 of his own newly described species and, for many of them, there is corresponding material in LINN annotated with "H.U." [= Hortus Upsaliensis], sometimes accompanied by "aegypt" (e.g. *Salvia spinosa* L. – 42.56) or "arabica" (e.g. *Statice incana* L. – 395.7) written by Linnaeus. Other names where

Opposite page: A specimen acquired in South Africa and given to Linnaeus by Ekeberg. It is the lectotype of *Gnaphalium eximium* L. (= *Syncarpha eximia* (L.) B. Nord.).

989·1

Forsskål is mentioned by Linnaeus (with corresponding specimens in LINN in parentheses) include *Ammi copticum* L. (341.4), *Bromus triflorus* L., *Conyza rupestris* L. (993.8), *Corchorus trilocularis* L. (691.2), *Crucianella aegyptia* L., *Delphinium aconiti* L., *Dianthus pomeridianus* L. (581.10), *Hyoseris lucida* L. (957.3), *Illecebrum arabicum* L. (290.19), *Inula arabica* L., *Knautia propontica* L. (121.3), *Lotus arabicus* L. (931.10), *Panicum coloratum* L. (80.46), *Pergularia tomentosa* L., *Phalaris paradoxa* L. (78.6), *Psoralea tetragonoloba* L., *Salvia forskahlei* L. (42.56), *Scabiosa ucranica* L., *Tanacetum monanthos* L. (987.8) and *Zygophyllum simplex* L.

Fothergill, John (1712–1780). British. Collector of natural history objects; established a garden at Upton, near Stratford.
Correspondence: two letters from Fothergill (29 Oct 1758–4 Apr 1774).
Linnaeus cited Fothergill in the protologue of *Acrostichum punctatum* L. but no material associated with this name has been traced in any of the Linnaean herbaria.

Gabriel, Frère (fl. 1757–1768). A Capuchin brother who collected in Provence.
Correspondence: 11 letters (21 Jan 1757–20 Jan 1768).

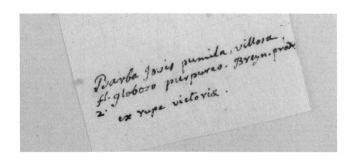

Savage (1945: App.) notes Linnaeus' letter of 24 Mar 1757 in which he provides determinations of 14 plants sent to him by Gabriel. These are now not readily traceable in LINN, except 897.4 (*Anthyllis montana* L., see above) and 759.7 (*Euphrasia linifolia* L.), both of which carry labels attributed to Gabriel. Under *Polypodium fragrans* (Mant. Pl. Alt.: 307. 1771), Linnaeus mentioned "Baro Capucinus", which is presumably Gabriel, with a corresponding specimen (1251.34 LINN).

Jackson (1922) believed that specimens in LINN annotated "Capell." came from Gabriel, but Savage (1945: vi) has suggested that it is much more likely that they came from the collection of M.A. Capeller (1685–1769) (see p. 198), perhaps through J. Gesner. Specimens in LINN annotated in this way include 473.8, 575.52, 655.35, 828.23 and 896.16, the last serving as the lectotype of *Ononis cenisia* L.

Garden, Alexander (1730–1791). Doctor of Medicine, South Carolina.
Correspondence: 22 letters (15 Mar 1755–15 May 1773).
Linnaeus mentioned Garden in the protologues of three names: *Cyrilla racemiflora* L. (272.1), *Sideroxylon tenax* L., and *Stillingia sylvatica* L. (1147.1). The material in LINN associated with these names probably came from Garden but is not explicitly annotated as such.

Gérard, Louis (1733–1819). French botanist in Provence.
Correspondence: Six letters (30 Nov 1755–1 Oct 1757).
There are about 50 Gérard specimens in LINN, most of them numbered in accordance with a list sent to Linnaeus as a part of a letter dated 15 Aug 1756. Most of the specimens are of taxa that Linnaeus had already described in 1753. However, Gérard is mentioned by Linnaeus in connection with a number of names, some of which can be associated with material in LINN (indicated in parentheses). The names are *Arenaria balearica* L., *Centaurea fruticosa* L. (981.4; lectotype), *Convolvulus pentapetaloides* L. (218.41 ex Latourette), *Genista humifusa* L. (892.17; lectotype), *Hedysarum cornutum* L. and *H. spinosum* L. (921.71; lectotype), *Iberis linifolia* L. (827.9; lectotype), *Lagurus cylindricus* (?96.2; lectotype), *Rubia cordifolia* L., *Saxifraga cuneifolia* L. (575.28; lectotype, see opposite) and *Teucrium lucidum* L. For information on Gérard's 1761 publication, see Chapter 4.

Burtez (1899) provided a catalogue of the material in Gérard's own herbarium (in Draguignan), and Tison (2000: 30) states that it contains a well-preserved duplicate of the lectotype of *Iberis linifolia* L.

Gerber, Traugott (1710–1743). German. Botanist.
Correspondence: none recorded.
Demidov (see p. 201) acquired and sent on loan in 1748–1750 to Linnaeus material collected by Gerber in the Volga and Don regions, with permission to keep the duplicates. It seems likely that these were accompanied by a manuscript, "TRAUGOTT GERBERI flora tanaensis per provinciam Woronicensium a Tawrow ad Taniam major", a copy of which, in Linnaeus' hand, is at LINN. The original was presumably returned to Demidov with Gerber's top set of specimens (see Sokoloff & al. 2002: 133–135; 163–169).

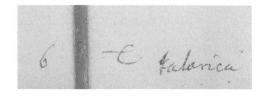

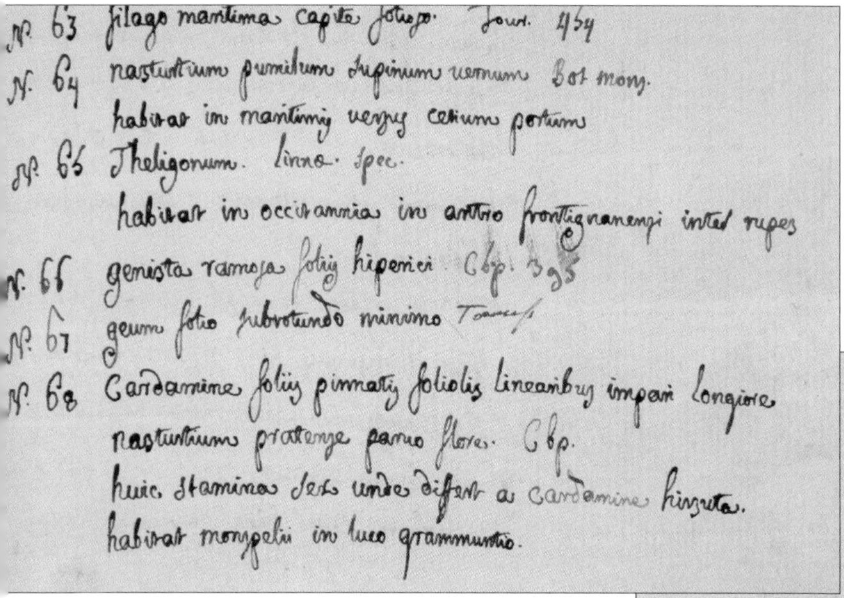

No 63 filago maritima capite foliofo. Tour. 454
N. 64 nasturtium pumilum supinum vernum Bot mons.
habitat in maritimis versus cetium portum
No 65 Theligonum. linno. spec.
habitat in occitannia in antreo frontignanensi inter rupes
No 66 genista ramosa foliis hiperici. C.b.p. 395
No 67 geum folio subrotundo minimo Tournef
No 68 Cardamine foliis pinnatis foliolis linearibus impari longiore.
nasturtium pratense parvo flore. C.b.p.
huic stamina sex unde differt a Cardamine hirsuta.
habitat monspelii in luco grammuntio.

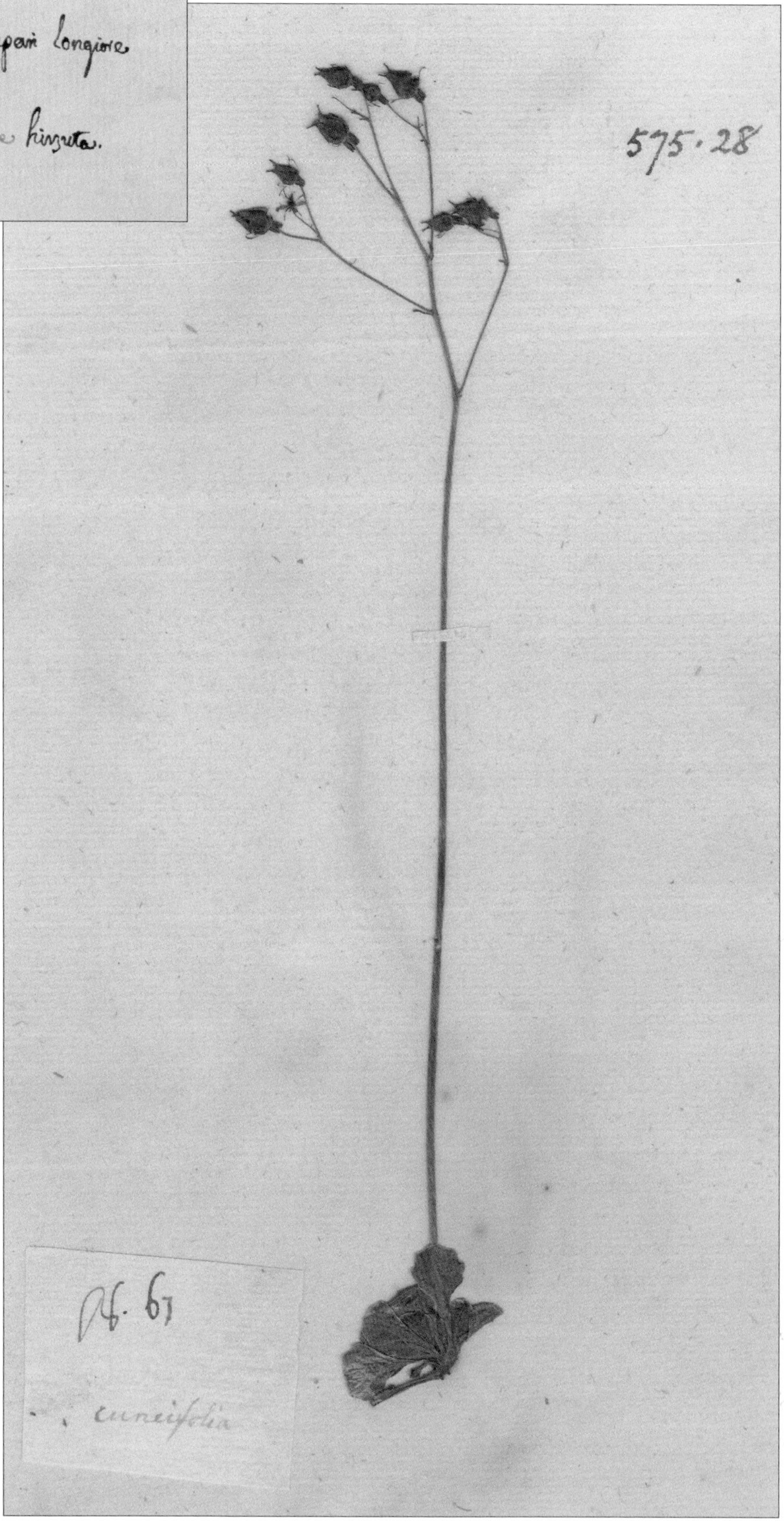

575·28

A. 67

cuneifolia

Above: An extract from Louis Gérard's letter of 15 Aug 1756, with specimen No. 67 listed as "Geum folio subrotundo minimo", to which Linnaeus has appended "Tournef[ort]".
Right: The corresponding specimen (575.28 LINN) carries a small label numbered "67" by Gérard and, at the base of the sheet, "A" and "cuneifolia" written by Linnaeus. This specimen is the lectotype of *Saxifraga cuneifolia* L.

The symbol associated by Stearn (1957: 106) with specimens from the western edge of Asia, and with Gerber (see p. 204), is found on nearly 200 sheets in LINN. Some of these sheets also bear more detailed localities drawn from the manuscript, and specimens carrying localities such as Azof (or Azov or Assoff, see below), Tawrow, Simbirska, Saratoff, Kamischenka, Czaritzin, Tanain, Tula, Woroniz and Bielgrod seem almost certain to have been collected by Gerber. These are sometimes reflected in Linnaeus' choice of geographical epithets (e.g. "caspica", "tatarica" and "ucranica", or his "Habitat" statements (e.g. "in Assoff" for *Morus tatarica* L.; "in Tataria" for *Lonicera tatarica* L.; "in desertis Tacorow; inter Woroniz & Bielgrod" for *Cucubalus sibiricus* L.; "in Tanain prope oppidum Cavilnense" for *Xeranthemum erucifolium* L. etc.).

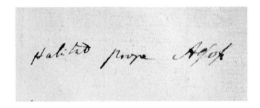

However, it seems unlikely that all of the sheets carrying this symbol came from Gerber. Quite a few specimens in LINN appear to have been understood by Linnaeus to have come from Gmelin. This includes material (187.1) of *Onosma simplicissima* L. ("Habitat in Sibiria. *Gmelin*.").

Despite some uncertainties over precise provenance, well over 50 specimens in LINN carrying this symbol are types for names from this part of the world, including *Centaurea splendens* L. (1030.39), *Hyssopus lophanthus* L. (725.3), *Morus tatarica* L. (1112.9), *Veratrum album* L. (1210.1) and *Veronica incana* L. (26.7), as well as a number in S (e.g. *Hesperis matronalis* L., 274.7 S, *Inula salicina* L., 351.13 S, *Lathyrus latifolius* L., 304.19 S, *Sisymbrium irio* L., 272.5 S, *Senecio nemorensis* L., 347.17 S and *Statice tatarica* L., 132.1).

Gesner, Johann (1709–1790).
Correspondence: none recorded.
Stearn (1957: 108) records the presence of Gesner specimens in LINN but it is difficult to identify individual sheets as from this source. A sheet of *Achillea* (1017.15) may be an exception.

Giseke, Paul Dietrich (1745–1796). German. Spent the spring and summer of 1771 with Linnaeus in Uppsala. Later, Professor of Natural Science in Hamburg.
Correspondence: 22 letters (8 Nov 1767–18 Mar 1777).
A few Giseke specimens are in LINN (e.g. 475.1 – *Disandra*; 722.33 – *Teucrium*).

Hedge (1967: 79) listed 28 specimens acquired by Giseke during his period in Sweden, including seven with an explicit Linnaean connection ("dedit Linnaeus" or "ex dono Linnaei" or "ex Herb. Linnaei"). They are associated with the names *Cornus suecica* L., *Fumaria nobilis* L., *Gladiolus angustus* L., *Protea divaricata* (P.J. Bergius) L., *Tussilago alpina* L., *Veronica sibirica* L. and *Xeranthemum imbricatum* L. Burtt (1988: 92) noted a further specimen (annotated "H.U.") associated with *Conium rigens* L. (= *Dasispermum suffruticosum* (P.J. Bergius) B.L. Burtt).

Gleditsch, Johann Gottlieb (1714–1786). German. Botanist in Berlin.
Correspondence: nine letters from Gleditsch to Linnaeus (21 Mar 1739–20 Aug 1764).
Although Stearn (1957: 108) records the presence of Gleditsch specimens in LINN, it is difficult to identify individual sheets as coming from this source.

Gmelin, Johann Georg (1709–1755). German. Participant in the Second Kamchatka Expedition, travelling through Siberia (1733–1743); later (1749) Professor of Botany and Chemistry in Tübingen.
Correspondence: 46 letters (28 Feb 1744–14 May 1751). Gmelin, Steller and Krascheninnikov were among those undertaking the botanical survey on the Second Kamchatka Expedition (1733–1743) and between them, many collections were made. The Expedition covered an enormous area, mapping and describing the northern and eastern coasts of Russia, from Arkahangel'sk in Europe to the Kuril Islands in the Far East (Sokoloff & al. 2002). Gmelin did not reach Kamchatka (unlike Steller and Krascheninnikov) but he travelled very extensively in Siberia. On his return to St Petersburg in 1743, Gmelin started to prepare his *Flora Sibirica* (see Chapter 4) and his extensive correspondence with Linnaeus started at this time, with the help of Baron Bielke.

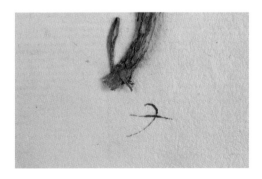

The Russian Academy of Sciences had strict rules over the release of scientific information to foreigners, and Linnaeus was therefore somewhat circumspect about revealing the sources of these specimens. This manifested itself in the use, in his herbarium, of a series of symbols correlated with the broad geographical areas from which the specimens had been obtained (see Stearn 1957: 106).

The symbol associated with Siberia (see opposite, below right), and hence with Gmelin, is found on nearly 200 sheets in LINN, Gmelin having given many duplicates of his own Siberian collections to Linnaeus. However, many more than this passed through Gmelin's hands on their way to Linnaeus, and among them were also specimens from other collectors such as Gerber and Steller. Material from the latter two collectors also reached Linnaeus via Demidov and, as a result, it can sometimes be difficult to ascertain the original collector of some of this material.

Protologues of nearly 50 Linnaean names provide a reference to Gmelin, usually in the form "Habitat in Sibiria. *D. Gmelin*". In many cases it is possible to locate associated material in LINN (indicated in parentheses in the list below). However, comparison of protologues and specimens also shows discrepancies that introduce the uncertainties of provenance mentioned above. For example, the protologue of *Anemone sibirica* L. indicates Siberia, and Gmelin, as to provenance, but the type specimen (710.17 LINN) carries Linnaeus' symbol for Kamchatka (rather than Siberia), so it almost certainly came originally from Steller (though possibly via Gmelin). The protologue of *Bartsia pallida* L. states "*Habitat in* Sibiria. *D. Gmelin. Demidoff.*" yet the associated specimen in LINN (756.2) carries Linnaeus' symbol associated with collections made west of the Urals by Gerber. For *Primula cortusioides* L., the type specimen (198.18 LINN) clearly carries a label written by Amman whereas the protologue mentions only Gmelin, and for *Swertia rotata* L., material in LINN (327.3) appears to be originally from Krascheninnikov.

Other names where Gmelin is mentioned in the protologue include *Antirrhinum genistifolium* L. (767.40, ex Gerber), *Astragalus grandiflorus* L. (921.53), *Astragalus uliginosus* L. (?926.11), *Bunias cornuta* L. (847.1), *Cacalia hastata* L., *Campanula sibirica* L. (?221.61), *Cardamine nudicaulis* L. (835.4), *Centaurea capillata* L. (1030.8, ex Gerber), *C. sibirica* L. (1030.27, ex Gerber), *Cerastium maximum* L. (603.22), *Cortusa gmelinii* L. (199.5 LINN, STU), *Cotyledon spinosa* L., *Dracocephalum pinnatum* L. ("*Habitat in* Jerkatsch. *Steller, D. Gmelin.*", 746.4), *Erigeron gramineus* L. (?994.25), *Hieracium lyratum* L. (954.27), *Lychnis sibirica* L. (602.5), *Onosma simplicissima* L. (187.1, ex Gerber), *Othonna helenitis* L., *Pedicularis resupinata* L. (?763.7), *Polygala sibirica* L. (882.11), *Polygonum ocreatum* L. (510.8), *Sempervivum globiferum* L. (632.1, ex Gerber),

Serratula multiflora L. (965.10 ex Gerber), *Sibbaldia erecta* L. (401.2, ex Amman), *Spergula laricina* L. (604.5), *Spergula saginoides* L. (604.6), *Spinacia fera* L. (1174.2), *Spiraea chamaedryfolia* L. (?651.6), *Statice suffruticosa* L. (395.17), *Stellera chamaejasme* L., *Swertia corniculata* L. (327.4), *Swertia dichotoma* L. (327.5) and *Thalictrum sibiricum* L.

A number of Gmelin specimens are also in S, including *Atriplex sibirica* L. (409.1), *Axyris hybrida* L. (380.5), *Cineraria palustris* (L.) L. (352.4) and *Geranium palustre* L. (282.11).

Gordon, James (fl. 1761–1772). British. Horticulturalist at Mile End, London.

Correspondence: six letters from Gordon to Linnaeus (16 Aug 1761–30 Sep 1772).

Gordon is mentioned by Linnaeus in connection with the maidenhair tree, *Ginkgo biloba* L. (1771) "*Habitat in* Japonia. *Gordon Hortul. angl. vivam arborem dedit.*". Gordon evidently sent the plant to Linnaeus in 1769 (see letter of 26 Oct) and a specimen preserved from it (1292B.2 LINN, see Linnaeus' annotation above) once it was established in the Hortus in Uppsala is the lectotype. Linnaeus also mentions Gordon in connection with *Geranium cotyledonis* L., and other Gordon specimens are at 497.12, 497.13 (*Vaccinium*), 563.8, 563.16 (*Andromeda*), and 685.3, 685.4 (*Thea*).

Gorter, David de (1707 or 1717–1783). Dutch. Botanist and personal physician, in St Petersburg, to Empress Elisabeth of Russia.

Correspondence: 20 letters from de Gorter to Linnaeus (27 May 1747–12 Mar 1773).

Linnaeus mentions de Gorter in connection with the names *Paeonia tenuifolia* L. (?692.4) and *Rheum palmatum* (?520.3). However, it is difficult to be certain that the material now in LINN under these names came from de Gorter, though that for *R. palmatum* may well have been supplied to Linnaeus as seeds.

Gouan, Antoine (1733–1821). French. Student of Sauvages in Montpellier, Director of the Botanic Garden there.

Correspondence: 134 letters (2 Sep 1758–16 Oct 1774).

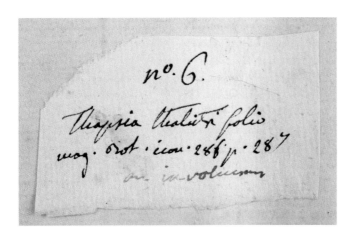

Linnaeus mentions Gouan (with corresponding specimens in LINN in parentheses) in connection with the names *Agrostis bromoides* L. (?84.4), *Arenaria fasciculata* L. (?585.50), *Astragalus stella* L. (926.23), *Erigeron gouanii* L. (994.15), *Festuca spadicea* L. (?92.37), *Milium lendigerum* L., *Ranunculus pyrenaeus* L. (715.7), *Silene porrigens* L. (?580.5), *Stipa aristella* L. (94.6) and *Thapsia garganica* L. (368.2, see label above). A total of about 60 specimens in LINN are annotated by Linnaeus as having come from Gouan and these include the types of *Allium pallens* L. (419.20), *Bunias balearica* L. (847.13), *Ononis pubescens* L. (896.10) and *Scilla hyacinthoides* L. (429.10).

Gronovius, Johan Frederik (1690–1762). Dutch. Naturalist. Linnaeus' benefactor and friend. Published *Flora Virginica* (1739, 1743, 1762) – see Chapter 4.

Correspondence: 120 letters (?1734–6 May 1756). Gronovius was in possession of an extensive collection of Virginian material collected by John Clayton, the basis for Gronovius' *Flora Virginica*. When Linnaeus was in the Netherlands in 1735–1738, he was able to study much of Clayton's material but acquired only a selection of duplicates for his own herbarium, chiefly via Gronovius and Peter Collinson (Stearn 1957: 108). The Clayton herbarium of Gronovius was acquired by Banks in 1794 and it is now at BM.

Linnaeus mentioned Gronovius in connection with the names *Ammannia ramosior* L. (165.2), *Hibiscus palustris* L., *Ipomoea nyctelea* L. (?206.1), *Marchantia tenella* L., *Orchis spectabilis* L. (1054.44, lectotype), *Passerina dodecandra* L. 1755, *Sagina virginica* L. (177.4) and *Silphium solidaginoides* L. (?1032.7). About 100 sheets in LINN carry labels in Gronovius' hand and most of those represent North American taxa originally collected by Clayton. In some cases,

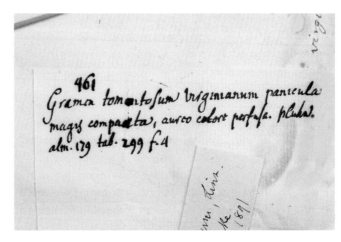

thcy are duplicates of material at BM (e.g. 926.23 LINN; *Hedysarum canadense* L.) but in others the LINN sheets appear to be unicates (e.g. 1237.4 LINN; *Panax trifolius* L.). At least 25 of them are lectotypes for Linnaean names, including *Eriophorum virginicum* L. (72.3, see label written by Gronovius above), *Hedysarum marilandicum* L. (921.35), *Osteospermum uvedalia* L. (1033.3), *Smilax herbacea* L. (1182.12) and *Stewartia malacodendron* L. (876.1). There are also scattered specimens in S (e.g. *Cicuta maculata* L., 122.19) that carry Gronovius' handwriting.

Gundelsheimer, Andreas von (1668–1715). German. Accompanied Joseph Pitton de Tournefort on his travels in the Orient.

Sheet 585.27 (LINN), the type of *Arenaria gypsophiloides* L., carries a label that may be in Gundelsheimer's hand. The material was evidently received by Linnaeus from Schreber whose name appears both on the sheet, and in the protologue.

Gunnerus, Johan Ernst (1718–1773). Norwegian. Bishop of Trondheim and author of *Flora Norwegica* (1766–1776).

Correspondence: 42 letters (24 Apr 1761–2 Jun 1772). Linnaeus mentions Gunnerus in connection with the names *Fucus esculentus* L. (?1274.63) and *F. hirsutus* L. (1274.18). However, it is difficult to be certain that the material now in LINN associated with these names came from Gunnerus as it carries no annotations to confirm this.

Haller, Albrecht von (1708–1777). Swiss. Professor of medicine, botany, anatomy and surgery at Göttingen 1736–1753.

Correspondence: 61 letters (27 Mar 1737–10 Apr 1766). Two specimens in LINN carry labels that Savage believed might be in the hand of Haller. The first, sheet 129.4, is the type of *Galium montanum* L.; the second is sheet 1017.27 (*Achillea*). For information on publications by Haller, see Chapter 4.

Hallman, Daniel Zaccharias (1722–1782). Swedish. Student of Linnaeus, 1744–1746, later a clergyman.

Correspondence: 31 letters from Hallman to Linnaeus (25 Aug 1753–5 Sep 1757).

Hallman is mentioned by Linnaeus in connection with *Lysimachia monnieri* L. but no associated material appears to be extant in any of the Linnaean herbaria. A specimen in S (95.7, *Rhamnus paliurus* L.) has "Hispania. Doct. Hallman" written on its verso.

Hasselquist, Fredrik (1722–1752). Swedish. Physician and naturalist, explorer. Studied under Linnaeus and Lars Roberg 1741–1749. Went to Egypt, Syria, Palestine, Cyprus, Rhodes and the island of Chios. Died near Smyrna on 9 February 1752.

Correspondence: 22 letters (27 Dec 1749–31 Dec 1751). Hasselquist died with considerable debts, his expedition having been severely underfunded, and his assets (chiefly his collections and manuscripts) were therefore seized. Through Linnaeus' influence, they were successfully returned to Sweden after their purchase by Queen Lovisa Ulrika, arriving at the Royal Palace at Drottningholm in 1755. At this point, the Queen gave Linnaeus some duplicates of Hasselquist's specimens which were to form the primary basis for the dissertation *Flora Palaestina* (1756; see Chapter 3) which contained six new Linnaean binomials: *Allium ascalonicum* (419.24 LINN), *Briza bipinnata* (89.2 LINN), *Bromus distachyos* (93.48 LINN; Herb. Hasselquist 70, UPS), *Galium hierosolymitanum* (129.18 LINN), *Parietaria judaica* (1220.3 LINN; Herb. Hasselquist 790, 791, UPS) and *Sideritis lanata* (729.17 LINN; Herb. Hasselquist 478, UPS), for each of which the specimen in LINN is the lectotype with, in some cases, duplicates in UPS (relevant specimens noted in parentheses). Hasselquist's account of his travels was edited and published by Linnaeus in the following year.

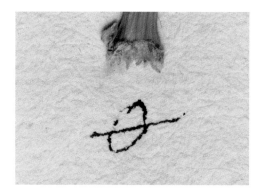

Hasselquist had evidently himself managed to send some specimens and seeds to Linnaeus because his name is mentioned by Linnaeus in the protologues of the 1753

names *Cornucopiae cucullatum* L. (76.2; Herb. Hasselquist 39, UPS), *Cucubalus aegyptiacus* L. (?582.10), *Cucumis dudaim* L. (?1152.11), *Mimosa lebbek* L. (1228.1; 1228.2; Herb. Hasselquist 418, UPS), *M. nilotica* L. ("unde semina per D. Hasselquist"; 1228.28 LINN; 214.7 S), *Myagrum aegyptium* L. (819.16) and *Rhamnus spina-christi* L. (262.36). The Hasselquist material in Linnaeus' own herbarium in LINN often carries a symbol (see below, left) written by Linnaeus that has been interpreted to be geographical, denoting the Near East. The main Hasselquist collection remained at Drottningholm in the Queen's collection until 1803, when it was transferred to Uppsala. It is now at UPS, comprises 816 specimens, and has been described by Juel (1918). For further information on Hasselquist and his travels, see Uggla (1953) and Bodenheimer & Uggla (1953).

The importance of Hasselquist's collections to Linnaeus is indicated by the number of protologues of new species in which the explorer was mentioned. In addition to the names listed above, these include the following, published from 1755 onwards: *Artemisia nilotica* L. (1014.3; 1014.6; Herb. Hasselquist 673, UPS), *Baccharis dioscoridis* L. (992.6; Herb. Hasselquist 674, 676, UPS), *Centaurea calcitrapoides* L. (1030.57), *Centaurea pumilio* (1030.74), *Centaurea verutum* (1030.69; Herb. Hasselquist 702, UPS), *Cerinthe orientalis* L. (Herb. Hasselquist 137, UPS), *Cistus arabicus* L. (689.67, 689.68; Herb. Hasselquist 441, UPS), *Cleome arabica* L. (?850.20; Herb. Hasselquist 542, UPS), *Cucumis chate* L. (?1152.8), *Dianthus pomeridianus* L. (581.10), *Gnaphalium sanguineum* L. (989.51; Herb. Hasselquist 681, UPS), *Hasselquistia aegyptiaca* L. (348.2, see p. 210; Herb. Hasselquist 251, UPS), *Hieracium sanctum* L. (954.18; Herb. Hasselquist 675, UPS), *Hypericum repens* L. (943.19; Herb. Hasselquist 664, UPS), *Hypericum scabrum* L. (943.18; Herb. Hasselquist 662, UPS), *Iberis arabica* L. (827.10), *Knautia palaestina* L. (121.4; Herb. Hasselquist 107, UPS), *Leontodon lanatus* L. (946.9; Herb. Hasselquist 678, UPS), *Salix aegyptiaca* L. (1158.91; Herb. Hasselquist 44, UPS), *Salvia syriaca* L. (42.15; Herb. Hasselquist 471, 472, UPS), *Scabiosa palaestina* L. (?120.36; Herb. Hasselquist 102, UPS), *Scorzonera orientalis* L. (?947.9; Herb. Hasselquist 672, UPS), *Sedum libanoticum* L. (595.4; Herb. Hasselquist 370, UPS), *Smyrnium aegyptiacum* L. (370.2; Herb. Hasselquist 250, UPS), *Trifolium alexandrinum* L. (930.49; Herb. Hasselquist 623, 624, UPS)

Following page (210): Specimen of the genus that Linnaeus named *Hasselquistia* to commemorate his apostle Fredrik Hasselquist. This material (348.2 LINN) is the lectotype of *Hasselquistia aegyptiaca* L.

348·2

and *Trigonella hamosa* L. (932.5; Herb. Hasselquist 580, 581, UPS).

Linnaeus' own collection of Hasselquist specimens in LINN probably exceeds 150 in number, among which there are at least 40 types. Designated lectotypes in the UPS collection are fewer but include the material associated with *Cerinthe orientalis* L., *Salix aegyptiaca* L. and *Scorzonera orientalis* L. There are also at least 20 of Hasselquist's specimens in S, including *Lathyrus amphicarpos* L. (303.5), *Oxalis corniculata* L. (193.3), *Rhamnus spina-cristi* L. (96.1), *Statice pruinosa* L. (133.3) and *Thuja aphylla* L. (390.1).

Hermann, Paul (1646–1695). German. Botanist, physician at Batavia, Professor of Botany at Leiden.

Paul Hermann (1646–1695) was to make one of the earliest scientific collections of plant specimens from Ceylon (now Sri Lanka), where he was Medical Officer to the Dutch East India Company between 1672 and 1677. Although largely restricted to plants from the area around Colombo, and including a number of foreign introductions in gardens, the collection is nevertheless of great scientific importance. After his return to Europe, Hermann took up the Chair of Botany at the University of Leiden in 1679 where he spent the rest of his life. Subsequently, his notes reached William Sherard (1659–1728) in Oxford, who edited them to produce a catalogue published as *Musaeum Zeylanicum* (1717), with a second edition in 1726.

The collection itself, comprising four bound volumes containing pressed plants and a few similarly preserved insects, and a volume of drawings, seems to have disappeared from sight until 1744, when it was in the possession of the Danish Apothecary-Royal, August Günther. He loaned these five volumes to Linnaeus, who set about describing and identifying the many new plants they contained, and the result was his *Flora Zeylanica* (1747; see Chapter 3). Linnaeus numbered the species consecutively, writing these numbers next to Hermann's specimens and drawings as appropriate (see p. 212), and thereby making an explicit link between descriptions and specimens. When, in 1753, Linnaeus published *Species Plantarum*, most of the Sri Lankan taxa he described were based on the corresponding *Flora Zeylanica* accounts and Hermann's herbarium is therefore very rich in Linnaean type material.

After studying them, Linnaeus had returned the volumes to Günther in Copenhagen, from whom they passed to Count Adam Gottlob Moltke. At his death, they were bought by Professor Hermann Treschow of Copenhagen, from whom they were purchased by Sir Joseph Banks in 1793 for £75. The volumes subsequently reached the British Museum with the rest of Banks' collections and are now housed at the Natural History Museum. Hermann's

herbarium has been studied by many botanists, notably by Trimen (1887), who provided identifications for the Sri Lankan specimens (there are also some from South Africa) and drawings. Recently, this interesting herbarium has been photographed and images of the specimens made available, together with a searchable database (see http://www.nhm.ac.uk/research-curation/projects/hermann-herbarium/).

There is another substantial collection of Hermann's Sri Lankan material, now at the Rijksherbarium in Leiden which, although not studied directly by Linnaeus, undoubtedly contains many duplicates of lectotype specimens for Linnaean names. A detailed description of this collection, with determinations, is provided by van Ooststroom (1937), and images of the specimens have been published (IDC microfiche 8302/1). However, this collection was not seen by Linnaeus and it consequently lacks the detailed annotations that distinguish the set in BM. A third collection, now at Erfurt, has been described by Rauschert (1970). Another Sri Lankan collection, the basis for Johannes Burman's *Thesaurus Zeylanicus* (1737), is at the Institut de France in Paris (Lourteig 1966). Hermann's Cape collections, e.g. in the Sloane herbarium (Dandy 1958), and at Oxford, among others, are also of considerable significance.

In an appendix to his *Thesaurus Zeylanicus* (1737), Johannes Burman included two short catalogues, one of which listed plants named by Paul Hermann. Occasionally, these polynomials can be matched with annotations made by Linnaeus to specimens in the Hermann herbarium (BM). An example is *Campanula fruticosa* L., from South Africa, where the polynomial and reference, written by Linnaeus, can be found annotating material in Hermann's herbarium (vol. 4: 16, BM). It is clearly original material for Linnaeus' name and was designated as the lectotype by Adamson (1953).

Holm, Jörgen Tyge (1726–1759). Danish. Student of Linnaeus 1750–1751, 1754–1757. Professor of Economy and Natural History, Copenhagen. Also known as Georg Tycho Holm.

Following page (212): Part of a page (vol. 3: 6, BM) from Paul Hermann's Ceylon herbarium showing a specimen of the plant subsequently named *Croton tiglium* L. by Linnaeus. Near the base of the specimen, Hermann wrote the name he was using for this plant ("Lignum moluccense sive Pavana"), adding some synonyms and the vernacular names of the species concerned. Just above this, Linnaeus added "Croton", and "343", the latter corresponding with the number of the account of this species in Linnaeus' *Flora Zeylanica* (1747). In this way, individual specimens can be closely associated with descriptions in *Flora Zeylanica*, and hence to the corresponding accounts in *Species Plantarum* (1753).

Croton   343

Lignum Mo   luccense five
Narava   Gurg. ab Hort.
Ricinus arbor Indica caustica
purgans. Pinus Indica C.Bauh.
pinei nuclei malucani Chr. à Cost.
c.57.
Grana Tiglia Officinar.
Ricinus Americana Cluff. in
Monard.
ஸ்வே Gajapala.
Ricinocarpos indica, folio subdo. fr. glabro
Burm. zeyl. 250.

Correspondence: three letters from Holm to Linnaeus (18 Sep 1751–1 Jul 1759).

The few lichen specimens received by Linnaeus from Holm include the lectotype of *Lichen saccatus* L. (1273.197 LINN), reproduced by Jørgensen & al. (1994: 353, f. 56). The other Holm specimens are the adjacent 1273.195 and 1273.196.

Hope, John (1725–1786). British. Doctor of Medicine, Professor of Botany, Edinburgh.

Correspondence: nine letters from Hope to Linnaeus (21 Mar 1765–18 Apr 1776).

Hope was mentioned by Linnaeus in the protologue of *Anemone canadensis* L. but no corresponding material has been traced. However, Hope specimens can be found at 176.2 (*Ruppia*), 198.8 (*Primula*) and 210.3 (*Spigelia*). An interesting account of Hope is provided by Morton (1986).

Hosack, David (1769–1835). American. Physician.

After his acquisition of the Linnaean collections, J.E. Smith gave some of the specimens to his friend David Hosack. Hosack returned to New York in 1794 with the material but after being in the Lyceum of Natural History of New York in the 1830s, it disappeared from sight and was probably destroyed by fire in 1866 (Robbins 1960).

Houstoun, William (1695–1733). British. Surgeon. Studied at Leiden under Boerhaave. Went with the South Sea Company to Central America and the West Indies.

Correspondence: none recorded.

Houstoun corresponded with Philip Miller at Chelsea Physic Garden and sent him much material from Mexico. Linnaeus was given some duplicates of these by Miller when Linnaeus visited England in 1736. Linnaeus mentioned him in connection with a number of names, including *Euphorbia ocymoidea* L., for which Houstoun material from Miller's herbarium (BM) was designated as the neotype by Webster & Huft (1988) in the absence of any original material.

Hudson, William (1730–1792). British. Pharmacist in Westmoreland.

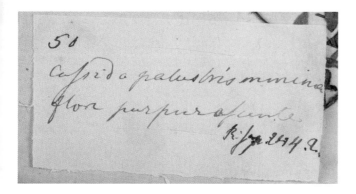

Correspondence: one letter from Hudson to Linnaeus (3 Jul 1760).

Hudson wrote to Linnaeus ahead of the publication of *Flora Anglica* (1762), sending him a number of specimens, notably of grasses. As Hudson's own herbarium was later destroyed by a fire at his house, this is a small but potentially important remnant of the few Hudson specimens known to be extant. There are about 30 sheets in LINN, among which are what appears to be original material for *Bromus erectus* Huds. (93.39) and *Scutellaria minor* Huds. (751.8, see below, left for Hudson's label). A few of Hudson's specimens in LINN are types for Linnaean names, including those of *Alopecurus agrestis* (82.2) and *Bromus racemosus* (93.31).

Jacquin, Nicolaus Joseph, Baron von (1727–1817). Dutch. Botanist. In 1755, at the order of Emperor Francis I , he went to the Antilles and South America. In 1763 he became Professor of Mineralogy and Chemistry at Schemnitz [Banská Štiavnica], later Professor of Botany at Vienna, and advisor to the Botanical Garden at Schönbrunn.

Correspondence: 186 letters (1 Aug 1759–11 Sep 1776).

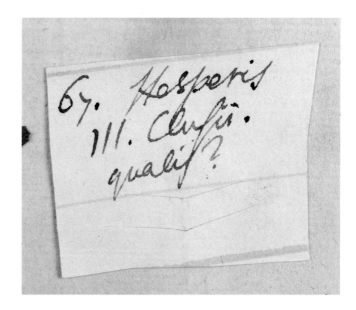

During the course of their long correspondence, Linnaeus received many specimens and seeds from Jacquin. Some 200 specimens in LINN carry labels written by Jacquin, and they came from a variety of places. A significant proportion carry names that Jacquin had either published or was to publish himself (e.g. 70.43 – *Cyperus pannonicus* Jacq.). Many of the labels are numbered, and some of these can be correlated with manuscript materials, notably a list of specimens (e.g. *Linum viscosum* L. – 396.10; *Juncus jacquinii* L. – 449.30) sent to Linnaeus by Jacquin in 1768. Unusually, a coloured engraving from Jacquin is included in Linnaeus' herbarium (see p. 214). Linnaeus mentioned Jacquin in connection with a number of species, among them *Agrostis mexicana* L. (84.33), *Ajuga alpina* L. (?721.3), *Androsace elongata* L. (197.3), *Avena sesquitertia* L. (?95.26), *Carex tomentosa* L., *Cassia atomaria* L. (528.17), *Cheiranthus alpinus* L. (839.5), *Daphne pubescens* L. (500.4), *Euphorbia epithymoides* L., *Laserpitium simplex* L., *Lichen usnea* L. (1273.278), *Petiveria octandra* L. (472.2) and *Sida triquetra* L. (?866.9). Jacquin specimens in LINN supply the types of names such as *Hesperis inodora* L. (841.4, see p. 213 for Jacquin's label) and *Trifolium messanense* L. (930.11). A few can also be found in S, including *Holcus sorghum* L. (406.7), *Inula spiraeifolia* L. (351.3) and *Lepidium alpinum* L. (265.13). For information on Jacquin's publications, see Chapter 4.

A coloured engraving in LINN (652.4) of *Rosa bicolor*, sent by Jacquin

Jussieu, Bernard de (1699–1777). French. Professor of Botany, brother of Antoine and Joseph de Jussieu. Demonstrator at the Jardin des Plantes, Paris. Sébastien Vaillant's successor.

Correspondence: 32 letters (8 Jun 1737–1 Mar 1763).

Stearn (1957: 106) says Linnaeus received "many" specimens from Bernard de Jussieu in Paris in 1738, while returning to Sweden, "which may have included some collected by J.D. Surian (d. 1691) in Haiti". Bernard apparently sent seeds (e.g. of *Atropa physalodes* L.) collected in Peru by his brother Joseph, to Linnaeus, and also seeds collected by Adanson in Senegal (Stearn 1961). However, it is difficult to know which specimens may have come from Jussieu as there are no explicit annotations that might indicate this. Jussieu was mentioned in the protologues of a number of Linnaean names, and the types of several of these are in LINN, represented by specimens that were cultivated in the Hortus in Uppsala, and annotated as such by Linnaeus with "H.U.". It therefore seems very likely that Jussieu was the source of the type material of *Atropa physalodes* L. (246.3), *Cardamine lunaria* L. (833.1), *Nicotiana glutinosa* L. (245.5), *Solanum peruvianum* L. (248.17) and *S. quercifolium* L. (248.8). Jussieu was also mentioned by Linnaeus in connection with *Chrysogonum peruvianum* L., *Cistus aegyptiacus* L. (689.50), *Hypericum aegypticum* L., *Iva annua* L. (?1116.1), *Malva peruviana* L. (870.5) and *Polemonium rubrum* L. For information on Jussieu's publications, see Chapter 4.

Jussieu, Joseph de (1704–1779). French. Botanist, mathematician, explorer. Member of the French Expedition to South America in 1735. Brother of Bernard and Antoine de Jussieu. Seeds he collected in Peru were apparently sent to Linnaeus by his brother, Bernard.

Kähler, Mårten (1728–1773). Swedish. Physician, orator and poet. Studied under Linnaeus and Nils Rosén von Rosenstein. Served as Physician to the Admiralty at Karlskrona. Between 1753 and 1757 he travelled to Bordeaux, then Marseilles, and later Naples, from where he sent letters and specimens to Linnaeus.

Correspondence: six letters from Kähler to Linnaeus (28 Aug 1753–12 Jun 1756).

There are more than 50 sheets of mostly Mediterranean species in LINN that Linnaeus received from Kähler, many of which can be correlated with a manuscript list "Italica Koehleri" in LINN, thought to date from 1757. Among Kähler's material can be found the types of *Anthemis peregrina* L. (1016.11) and *Sonchus maritimus* L. (949.1, see Linnaeus' mark "Kh" above), and his specimens can also be found in S (e.g. *Centaurea sphaerocephala* L., (362.9), *Euphorbia paralias* L. (199.13), *Platanus orientalis* L. (388.15), *Polygala monspeliaca* (291.17), *Rhamnus paliurus* L. (95.10) and *Sinapis erucoides* L. (276.11).

Kaempfer, Engelbert (1651–1716). German. Physician, botanist and explorer. Travelled in Asia. Known for his works on Japan and Japanese natural history.

Kaempfer was one of the earliest collectors to bring scientific material from Japan to the west, and his descriptions and illustrations of plants were therefore of great interest to Linnaeus. Nearly all of the copperplates in his *Amoenitatum Exoticarum* (1712) depicting plants were cited by Linnaeus. Kaempfer's herbarium was acquired by Sir Hans Sloane (see Stearn 1957: 120–121; Dandy 1958: 144–145) and comprises volumes 211 and 213 of the Sloane herbarium (BM-SL). A recent study by Hinz (2001) provides a catalogue, with modern identifications. Although these specimens were never studied by Linnaeus, they can nevertheless sometimes be helpful in interpreting the illustrations. See also Chapter 4.

Kalm, Pehr (1716–1779). Swedish botanist and traveller; one of Linnaeus' most distinguished disciples; later Professor of Natural History at Åbo (now Turku, Finland).

Correspondence: 42 letters (26 Aug 1742–12 Oct 1758). Kalm became a student in Uppsala in 1741 under Linnaeus, and the records of plants he had found on his travels were acknowledged by Linnaeus in his *Flora Suecica* (1745). In 1744, Kalm had travelled through Russia and part of the Ukraine with Bielke, but in the autumn of 1747, he was commissioned by the Government and the Academy of Sciences to visit North America, "for the purpose of describing the natural productions of that part of the world, and of introducing from thence into Sweden such useful plants as might be expected to thrive in the North of Europe". After arriving in Philadelphia in September 1748, Kalm explored Pennsylvania and New Jersey, New York and southern Canada, and later the eastern Great Lakes. His essential task was the assessment and introduction of useful North American plants into Sweden (e.g. American red mulberry, *Morus rubra*, for silk production), but he was also keen to bring as wide a variety of plants as possible back to Uppsala for Linnaeus.

Kalm's return to Uppsala in June 1751, laden with seeds and dried specimens, did much to re-invigorate Linnaeus and it has been suggested that the desire to incorporate Kalm's new discoveries may have been the spur to Linnaeus returning to work on the draft of *Species Plantarum* which he had abandoned in 1748. Apart from providing additional information for species already known, Kalm is explicitly

mentioned by Linnaeus in *Species Plantarum* (1753), in connection with 75 newly described North American species. However, it is clear that he supplied influential material for many more taxa than this.

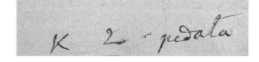

Linnaeus' herbarium in LINN contains approximately 400 Kalm specimens, identifiable by the letter "K" written by Linnaeus either near the base of the specimen or centrally, near the bottom edge of the sheet (see above). It is the primary source of types for Linnaean names based on Kalm's collections, and well over 150 such types can be found here. In the publication of about 90 Linnaean binomials, Kalm's name is explicitly mentioned (see Juel 1920), usually in the form "Habitat in Canada. *Kalm.*" (as in the case of *Prinos glabra* L.) or with the addition or substitution of "Pensylvania" (e.g. *Vaccinium ligustrinum* L.), "Philadelphia" (e.g. *Spiraea tomentosa* L.) or "America septentrionali" (e.g. *Sanguinaria canadensis* L.). Despite the fact that Kalm did not visit Virginia, Linnaeus also linked Kalm's name with this English colony in a few cases (e.g. *Chironia angularis* L). Linnaeus' other main source of information on North American plants came, of course, from John Clayton's Virginia collections which Linnaeus had been able to study in the possession of his friend Johan Gronovius in Leiden. There was inevitably some overlap in species coverage between the two collections, and it is quite common to find both Kalm and Clayton specimens in existence linked to the same Linnaean binomial. Often, the protologues of the names of such taxa will be indicated as "Habitat in Virginia", with Linnaeus not necessarily bothering to modify his geographical statement to accommodate the later Kalm material. However, in other cases, he did just that and "Habitat in Virginia, Canada." is often encountered and usually signals the existence (at least originally) of material from both collectors. Although Linnaeus' own herbarium contains some Clayton duplicates, the main Clayton collection had remained in the Netherlands in 1738 and was not available to Linnaeus for re-consultation when he was preparing *Species Plantarum*.

A second Kalm herbarium, heavily annotated by its collector, was given to Queen Lovisa Ulrika in 1754 and was kept at the Royal Palace at Drottningholm until 1803. It comprises about 390 sheets (see example on p. 216) and is now at UPS (see Juel, 1921; Juel & Harshberger, 1929; Fernald 1931). A more recent account of the UPS collection, with transcriptions and English translations of Kalm's

Pehr Kalm was commissioned to bring back to Sweden, from North America, seed of the American red mulberry (*Morus rubra* L.) as a potential food plant for silkworms, and the possible basis for silk production in Sweden. Two of Kalm's herbarium specimens of this species are extant, in LINN (1112.6, upper left), and in UPS (5: 304, upper right). The collection in UPS had been presented to Queen Lovisa Ulrika in 1754, and was mounted on gold-edged paper and heavily annotated in Swedish on the versos by Kalm (see below).

annotations, is provided by Lundqvist & Moberg (1993). Kalm's own set of specimens was lost in the Åbo fire of 1827.

There are additional scattered Kalm specimens in other herbaria, chiefly as a result of Linnaeus' habit of giving away apparent duplicates to friends and students. As a result there are at least 30 Kalm specimens in S (e.g. *Chrysocoma graminifolia* L. (337.17), *Prenanthes altissima* L. (327.19), *Quercus rubra* L. (387.11) and *Ranunculus abortivus* L. (227.9)). There are also Kalm specimens of *Panax quinquefolius* L. and *Chironia campanulata* L. at BM, and of *Caltha palustris* L. at PH.

Kalm is cited by Linnaeus in the protologues of about 90 names (see Manktelow & Nyberg 2005) and more than 100 Kalm specimens serve as types for Linnaean binomials. They include (all specimens in LINN) *Acer pensylvanicum* (1225.13), *Carex folliculata* (1100.66), *Cupressus thyoides* (1137.4), *Dalibarda repens* (653.24), *Erigeron philadelphicus* (994.13), *Gentiana quinquefolia* (328.31), *Hieracium kalmii* (954.43), *Hypericum kalmianum* (943.2), *Panicum filiforme* (80.38), *Polygonum articulatum* (510.28), *Ribes cynosbati* (278.9), *Smilax rotundifolia* (1182.8), *Thesium umbellatum* (292.11), *Tragopogon virginicus* (946.10), *Vaccinium album* (497.4) and *Viscum terrestre* (1166.1).

Kleynhoff, Christian (fl. 1761–1765, d. 1777). Dutch.
Correspondence: four letters from Kleynhoff to Linnaeus (20 Oct 1761–12 Mar 1765).

Kleynhoff was in Jakarta in 1761, later returning to the Netherlands. He is cited by Linnaeus in connection with the names *Clutia stipularis* L. (1206.13), *Leea aequata* L. (1118.1) and *Prenanthes japonica* L. (952.6), each of which is typified by the corresponding material in LINN. He is also mentioned in the protologues of *Saraca indica* L. and *Sophora japonica* L. (?522.9), and other Kleynhoff specimens are at 279.3 (*Aquilicia*), 921.70 (*Hedysarum*, see p. 218), and 1014.21 (*Cotula*). Further Kleynhoff material is at G.

König, Johan Gerhard (1728–1785). Danish. Physician. Private pupil of Linnaeus in 1757. Visited Iceland. Went to Tranquebar in India, to Ceylon, and Thailand. He died on his way to Tibet.
Correspondence: 19 letters from König to Linnaeus (26 Oct 1763–16 Feb 1776).

Linnaeus mentioned König in connection with some 50 binomials, and there are nearly 300 specimens in LINN either carrying his labels or indicated as having come from him. In fact, there may be many more than this. Much of the material associated with those binomials for which Linnaeus mentions König lacks any annotation to explicitly link it with König. However, in most cases it seems very

unlikely that Linnaeus could also have obtained material from anyone else, bearing in mind the geographical provenance and the lack of time in which this could have occurred.

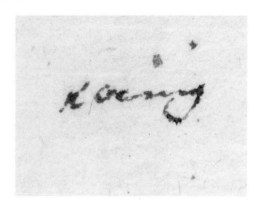

In some cases (e.g. *Agrostis matrella* L.), Linnaeus cited numbered König specimens in the protologue, making these collections (in this case, *König 56*, 84.11 LINN) syntypes. König's plants came from a number of different places. Linnaeus frequently states "Habitat in India orientali", sometimes qualified, e.g. as in the case of *Baccharis arborea* L. (992.3) with "insulae Johannae sylvis". There are also a significant number of specimens from South Africa; e.g. the type (1244.11 LINN, see annotation above) of *Osmunda capensis* L., often with more specific information cited in the protologue – "inter montes Cap. b. spei, inter montem tabularem et Diaboli, ad rivulum". The type (1251.33 LINN) of *Polypodium fragrans* L. (1771, non 1753) is a König specimen from Madeira. Some 20 König specimens can be found in S (e.g. *Achyranthes muricata* L. (101.15), *Gerardia delphinifolia* L. (253.7), *Heliotropium orientale* L. (67.3), *Lobelia plumieri* L. (83.15), *Oldenlandia umbellata* L. (62.15), *Oxalis sensitiva* L. (192.17), *Piper longum* L. (13.5) and *Rhamnus micrantha* L. (95.13)).

Krascheninnikov, Stepan Petrovich (1713–1755). Russian. Professor of Natural History, St Petersburg. Went with Johann Georg Gmelin to Siberia on the Second Kamchatka Expedition reaching Kamchatka, as did Steller.
Correspondence: three letters (24 Oct 1750–24 Jan 1751).

Linnaeus mentioned Krascheninnikov in connection with *Actaea cimicifuga* L. and *Alyssum hyperborea* L. (the type of which is 828.6 LINN). Another specimen is at 327.3 (*Swertia rotata* L.), which apparently reached Linnaeus via Gmelin.

Following page (218): A specimen (921.70 LINN) bearing a label from Christian Kleynhoff, and identified by Linnaeus as *Hedysarum crinitum* L. (= *Uraria crinita* (L.) Desv.).

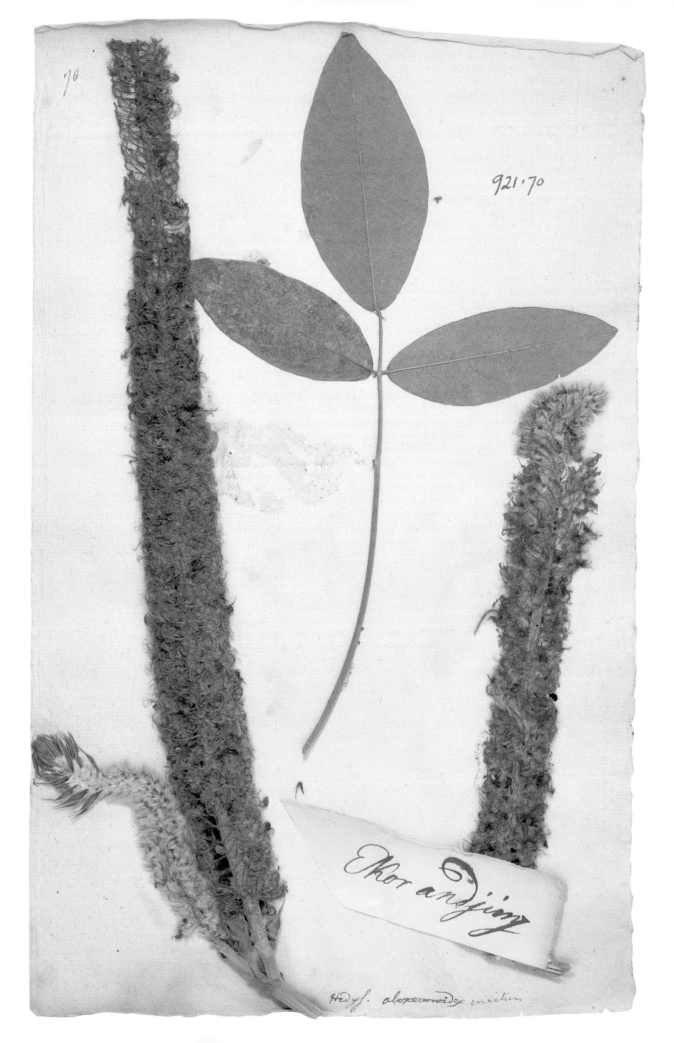

70

921.70

Ekor anjing

Hedys. alexeandes minitum

Kuhn, Adam (1741–1817). American. Physician, Philadelphia. Studied under Linnaeus at Uppsala University in 1762–1763. Linnaeus' only American student.

Correspondence: 15 letters (25 Jun 1764–30 Oct 1773). Although Linnaeus mentioned Kuhn in the protologue of *Kuhnia eupatorioides* L. (1763), the name is based on material apparently supplied by Pietro Arduino (238.2 LINN, see p. 190).

Lagerström, Magnus (1691–1759). Swedish. Director of the Swedish East India Company.

Correspondence: 13 letters from Lagerström to Linnaeus (17 Jul 1748–20 Aug 1757).

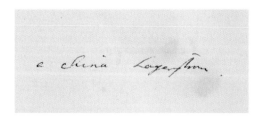

Lagerström supplied Linnaeus with some material "brought by Swedish captains trading with Canton" (Stearn 1957: 106). His name is mentioned by Linnaeus in connection with *Artemisia chinensis* L. (988.45 LINN, see annotation above by Linnaeus) and *A. minima* L. (988.48 LINN), for each of which Lagerström's material in LINN is the type. Other specimens appear to be at 684.2 (*Lagerstroemia*) and 855.8 (*Melochia*).

Latourette, Marc Antoine Louis Claret de Fleurieu de (1729–1793). French. Writer, naturalist and collector.

Correspondence: 14 letters (4 Jul 1770–24 Oct 1774).

Linnaeus mentioned Latourette in the protologue of *Ononis cenisia* L. There is material (896.16) associated with this name in LINN apparently from Capeller. There are nearly 80 specimens in LINN from Latourette, including the type (930.35, see above for Linnaeus' annotation) of *Trifolium ochroleucum* L.

Laxman, Erik (1738–1796). Swedish. Lutheran pastor at the Kolyvanian mines and ironworks in Siberia. Professor and member of the Russian Board of Mines, St Petersburg.

Correspondence: 14 letters (11 Feb 1764–17 Oct 1776). Linnaeus mentioned Laxman in the protologues of a number of binomials, notably *Convolvulus sibiricus* L. (218.5), *Ornithogalum uniflorum* L. (?428.1), *Spiraea laevigata* L. (?651.1), *S. trilobata* L. (?651.11), *Teucrium laxmannii* L. and *Veronica pinnata* L. (?26.18). Although the corresponding specimens in LINN have no annotations by, or reference to, Laxman, it seems very likely that they originated with him, possibly from seed samples (e.g. 108.5 which was cultivated in Uppsala). Further Laxman specimens in LINN are at 93.45 (*Bromus*), 278.7 (*Ribes*), 453.4 (*Berberis*), 514.5 (*Sapindus*), 715.13 (*Ranunculus*) and 768.1 (*Cymbaria*). A much larger collection of Laxman material is at LE.

Leche, Johan (1704–1764). Swedish. Botanist, plant collector and physician. Studied the flora of Skåne. His herbarium was bought by Joseph Banks. Professor of medicine at Åbo.

Correspondence: 17 letters from Leche to Linnaeus (25 Sep 1738–2 Apr 1763).

There are about 20 Leche specimens in LINN, including 100.4 (*Elymus canadensis* L.), 1054.25 (*Orchis militaris* L.), 1135.1 (*Pinus pinea* L.), 1205.4 (*Ruscus hypoglossum* L.) and 1283.2 (*Clathrus nudus* L.), but few, if any, have any nomenclatural importance.

Le Monnier, Louis Guillaume (1717–1799). French. Physician and naturalist. Professor of Botany at the Jardin des Plantes in Paris. Personal physician of Louis XV.

Correspondence: three letters (24 Jun 1746–10 Jan 1754).

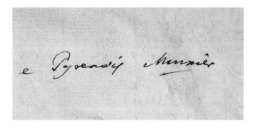

Le Monnier was mentioned by Linnaeus in connection with *Genipa americana* L., *Mirabilis longiflora* L. (?240.3), *Sinapis pyrenaica* L. (?845.5) and *Sonchus plumieri* L. (?949.10). As with Laxman, the associated specimens are not labelled as having come from this source, though the link seems highly likely. Labelled Le Monnier specimens can be seen at 196.4 (*Aretia*), 197.5 (shown above) and 197.12 (*Androsace*), 689.56 and 689.63 (*Cistus*), and 835.2 (*Cardamine*).

Lerche, Johann Jacob (1703–1780). German. Naturalist. Military physician in Russian service at Astrakhan. Travelled in Persia.

Correspondence: 11 letters (5 Nov 1764–11 Apr 1774). Lerche is mentioned by Linnaeus in connection with *Artemisia contra* L. (?988.4), *Cheiranthus salinas* L., *Cucurbita ovifera* L. (?1151.2; ?1151.3) and *Holcus bicolor* L. A specimen annotated with Lerche's name by Linnaeus (see above) is 315.11 LINN (*Salsola altissima*), and another is 110.7 S (*S. vermiculata* – "Astracan misit Lerche").

Leysser, Friedrich Wilhelm von (1731–1815). German. Botanist at Halle; author of *Flora Halensis* (1761).
Correspondence: five letters (2 Mar 1757–2 Oct 1764). A few specimens at LINN are from Leysser, including 91.6 (*Cynosurus*), 127.9 (*Asperula*), 1054.22 (*Orchis*) and 1100.90 (*Carex*).

Lidbeck, Eric Gustaf (1724–1803). Swedish. A student of Linnaeus who accompanied him on the Västgöta journey in 1746. Later, Professor of Natural History and Economy at Lund.
Correspondence: 48 letters (14 Jun 1747–3 Oct 1769). The type of *Thalictrum simplex* L. (713.23 LINN) may well be from Lidbeck. Savage attributes to Lidbeck, with doubt, a number of South African specimens in LINN, including 270.17, 270.26 (*Diosma*), and 271.7a, 271.9, 271.15, 271.16 (*Brunia*).

Linnaeus, Carolus (1707–1778).
An outline of the history of Linnaeus' herbarium has been given in Chapter 5.

Linnaeus filius, Carolus (1741–1783). Carl Linnaeus the younger, the only son of Linnaeus.
Correspondence: none recorded.
Linnaeus filius' herbarium contributed a significant number of specimens to the Linnaean herbarium that is now conserved at S. The younger Linnaeus' own collection

contained much material from the University Botanic Garden in Uppsala, as well as some sheets formerly in his father's collection. Termed the "herbarium parvum", Linnaeus filius had pledged it to Alströmer in return for the funds he needed to travel to England in 1781–1782. Consequently, the herbarium went to Alströmer on the younger Linnaeus' death in 1783 and did not form part of the collections purchased by Smith and transported to England.

There are also many sheets in LINN carrying annotations by Linnaeus filius, presumably added mainly during the period after his mother belatedly allowed him access to the herbarium following his father's death in 1778. Linnaeus filius is mentioned by Linnaeus in the protologue of *Lycoperdon radiatum* as the collector of this taxon, and the son's specimen (1287.6 LINN), annotated by Linnaeus "a filio inventis", is the lectotype of the name.

Löfling, Pehr (1729–1756). Swedish. Botanist and explorer. One of Linnaeus' apostles, studying with him from 1743–1749. Went to Spain in May 1751, becoming Professor of Botany at Madrid; travelled in Spain and Portugal and sent frequent letters, with specimens and seeds, to Linnaeus. Löfling took part in the Spanish expedition to Venezuela in 1754, where he died. Much Spanish material is in LINN.
Correspondence: 50 letters (22 Apr 1751–20 Oct 1754).

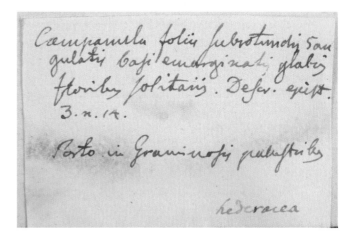

Manktelow & Nyberg (2005: 78) state that Löfling is explicitly mentioned by Linnaeus in the protologues of 50 binomials, and that Löfling sent his teacher specimens of no fewer than 600 species. The number of Löfling specimens now in LINN and S certainly appears rather lower than this, but they are nevertheless numerous, and many types are among them. This material is chiefly from Spain and Portugal (see above for a Löfling label from "Porto"), the material that he collected in South America having been lost. After Löfling's death, Linnaeus edited some of Löfling's manuscripts which were published as *Iter Hispanicum* (1758;

see Chapter 4). The first part of this consisted of Löfling's diaries between 1751 and 1754, followed by descriptions of Spanish and American plants. For details of Löfling's role in the expedition to the Orinoco, see Pelayo López (1990).

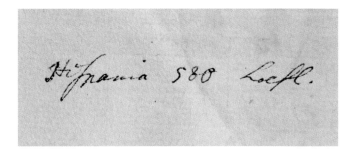

Type specimens from Löfling in LINN include those of *Aira minuta* L. (85.4), *Anthyllis cornicina* L. (897.5, see Linnaeus' annotation above), *Antirrhinum bipunctatum* L. (767.17), *Atractylis humilis* L. (971.2), *Brassica vesicaria* L. (844.20), *Bromus rubens* L. (93.28), *Bupleurum semicompositum* L. (335.13), *Carduus flavescens* L. (966.42), *Genista tridentata* L. (892.8), *Lepidium subulatum* L. (824.12), *Loeflingia hispanica* L. (54.1), *Plantago loeflingii* L. (144.25), *Scorzonera angustifolia* L. (947.6), *Sideritis incana* L. (729.9), *Sisymbrium barrelieri* L. (836.25), *Stipa membranacea* L. (94.9) and *Ziziphora hispanica* L. (39.2). Types in S include material of *Scrophularia auriculata* L. (S 256.12) and *Scirpus palustris* L. (unnumbered).

López González (2003–2004: 429–434) provides an extremely detailed account of Löfling's material and descriptions involved in the treatment of *Minuartia* L. and *Queria* L. by Linnaeus.

Magnol, Pierre (1683–1715). French. Physician and botanist, director of the botanical garden of Montpellier. His herbarium of plants from the South of France reached Linnaeus in 1749, donated by Boissier de Sauvages along with his own herbarium.

About 50 sheets in LINN carry the letter "M" (see above), signifying a specimen, originally from Magnol's herbarium,

that was sent to Linnaeus by Sauvages. Some of these specimens (e.g. 906.14, the type of *Vicia onobrychioides* L.) also carry labels in Sauvages' hand. About half of the Magnol specimens in LINN are types for Linnaean names, and include those of *Acrostichum marantae* L. (1245.12), *Adiantum capillus-veneris* L. (1252.9), *Anthemis altissima* L. (1016.2), *Ervum tetraspermum* L. (907.3), *Inula spiraeifolia* L. (999.21), *Leontodon hispidus* L. (953.9), *Lichen caninus* L. (1273.184), *Ononis pinguis* L. (896.21), *Orchis abortiva* L. (1054.43), *Ornithopus compressus* L. (918.3), *Polygala monspeliaca* L. (882.7), *Santolina annua* L. (986.12), *Thlaspi perfoliatum* L. (825.9), *Trifolium cherleri* L. (930.22), *T. squarrosum* L. (930.31) and *Vicia peregrina* L. (906.28). A few Magnol specimens are in S, including *Linum gallicum* L. (134.3) and *Marrubium hispanicum* L. (244.3). For information on Magnol's publications, see Chapter 4.

Masson, Francis (1741–1805). British. Collector at the Cape of Good Hope in the early 1770s, and was in Madeira in 1776, from where he wrote to Linnaeus, before proceeding to the Canary Islands and the Azores.

Correspondence: two letters from Masson to Linnaeus (28 Dec 1775–6 Aug 1776).

A small number of specimens can be found at LINN, including those at 191.5 (*Echium*), 221.21 and 221.24 (*Campanula*), 290.10 (*Illecebrum*), 315.49 (*Salsola*), 416.2 (*Amaryllis*) and 497.16 (*Vaccinium*).

Messerschmidt, Daniel Gottlieb (1682–1735). German. Traveller and botanist.

As noted by Heller (1959: 12), in the protologue of *Rheum rhabarbarum* L., Linnaeus (1753: 372) refers to "Messerschmidii. Amm. Ruth.", indicating a name taken by Amman (1739) from Messerschmidt, a German botanist "who travelled extensively in Siberia and reached Dauria [Transbaikal] and Chinese Mongolia but never published his numerous observations". Bryce (2005) explores Amman's role as a conduit of botanical (and other) information between Russia and both Hans Sloane (Amman's employer before he left London for St Petersburg in 1733) and Linnaeus. There are 13 specimens in Herb. Sloane 316: 49–58 (BM-SL), collected in Dauria, which Amman sent to Sloane, who received them in 1735. From this early date (Gmelin and Krascheninnikov did not reach Dauria until the summer of 1735), Bryce concludes that the Sloane specimens were probably collected by Messerschmidt in 1724. With Messerschmidt's own collections having been lost in a fire in St Petersburg in 1747, the Sloane specimens may be his only material to have survived, and may well be the earliest known collections of these Daurian species.

Miller, Philip (1691–1771). British. Hortulanus (Curator) at the Chelsea Physic Garden. His own, rich herbarium was sold to Joseph Banks and is now at BM.

Correspondence: 25 letters (20 Jan 1737–12 Jul 1768). Although quite a lot of material was given by Miller to Linnaeus, only about 50 sheets in LINN can be explicitly linked with Miller via annotation. It is likely that many more specimens were raised in Uppsala from seeds that Miller sent to Linnaeus. Miller is mentioned in the protologues of a number of names now typified by what is apparently Miller material in LINN, including *Bidens atriplicifolia* L. (974.4), *Ixia bulbifera* L. (58.16), *Lycium capsulare* L. (259.8), *Mentha exigua* L. (730.17), *Myrtus dioica* L. (637.11), *Nepeta scordotis* L. (726.23) and *Rivina octandra* L. (163.3). Miller's name is also connected with *Coreopsis leucanthema* L. (1026.5), *Geranium bohemicum* L. (?858.69), *Lamium orvala* L., *Malva limensis* L. (?870.6), *Ocimum americanum* L. (749.9), *Rivina paniculata* L., *Sisymbrium bursifolium* L. (?836.15, 836.16) and *Sisymbrium orientale* (?836.43). In addition, the types of *Calycanthus floridus* L. (660.1), *Convolvulus linifolius* L. (393.5), *Mentha verticillata* L. (730.13) and *Viburnum dentatum* L. (379.5) are also from Miller. A few of his specimens can also be found in S, including *Spermacoce hispida* L. (53.17). For information on Miller's publications, see Chapter 4.

Minuart, Juan (1673–1768). Spanish. Botanist and Pharmacist.

Correspondence: none recorded.

Although Stearn (1957: 108) notes that there is material from Minuart in LINN, it is difficult to identify it with confidence. Linnaeus mentioned Minuart in connection with *Galium aristatum* L. ("in monte Ventoso & m. Virginis Neopolitano. *C. G. Minuart.*"; ?56.5 S), *Ortegia hispanica* L. ("in Castilia *Minuart.*") and *Vella pseudocytisus* L. ("in Hispania circa oppidum Aranjuez. *D. Minuart.*").

Monti, Giuseppe (1682–1760). Italian. Professor at Bologna.

Correspondence: one letter from Monti to Linnaeus (5 Jun 1753).

Although Monti was mentioned by Linnaeus in the protologues of *Aldrovanda vesiculosa* L. (?397.1), *Cerinthe maculata* L. (see Edmondson 2004: 800 for a discussion) and *Verbascum phlomoides* L., it has proved difficult to find any material definitely associated with him in LINN. Sheet 1157.2 (*Vallisneria*) may have come from him.

Montin, Lars (1723–1785). Swedish. Physician and botanist. Studied medicine in Uppsala under Linnaeus and Nils Rosén von Rosenstein. Provincial physician of the province of Halland.

Correspondence: seven letters from Montin to Linnaeus (13 Jul 1772–4 Dec 1775).

Montin is mentioned in the protologue of *Lichen cylindricus* L., though it has not been possible to locate any Montin specimen associated with the name. However, a few specimens can be found in LINN, including 178.4 (*Tillaea*) and 309.7 (*Apocynum*), and possibly 297.4 and 297.5 (*Gardenia*) and 1266.4 (*Hypnum*). Linnaeus evidently gave away some supposed duplicate specimens to Montin, whose herbarium now forms part of the Linnaean herbarium in S. Montin also acquired duplicates from Kalm, Löfling and Osbeck.

Moraeus, Johan (1719–1773). Swedish. Accountant at the Swedish Board of Mines. Linnaeus' brother-in-law.

Correspondence: one letter from Moraeus to Linnaeus (18 Nov 1751).

Moraeus accompanied Linnaeus on the visit to Gotland in 1741, and was the collector of *Sanguisorba officinalis* L. (61.7, S) in the eastern part of the island.

Münchhausen, Otto von (1716–1774). German. Chancellor of Göttingen University.

Correspondence: 32 letters (18 Apr 1751–24 Jul 1773).

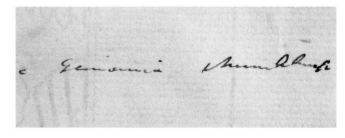

Linnaeus mentioned Münchhausen in connection with the names *Boerhavia diandra* L. (no extant material traced) and *Pyrus pollveria* L. (647.2 LINN). Nearly 20 sheets in LINN appear to have been received by Linnaeus from him, including the type of *Lycopodium complanatum* L. (1257.20, see annotation above).

Murray, Adolf (1751–1803). Swedish. Professor of Anatomy and Surgery in Uppsala. Brother of Johan Andreas Murray.

Correspondence: one letter from Murray to Linnaeus (4 Oct 1772).

A few specimens in LINN, including 315.14 (*Salsola*), 440.4 (*Aletris*), 715.18 (*Ranunculus*) and 842.11 (*Arabis*).

Murray, Johan Andreas (1740–1791). Swedish. Professor of Medicine and Botany, and Director of the Botanical Garden at Göttingen University. Edited the botanical part of the 12th edition of Linnaeus' *Systema Naturae*, publishing it as the 13th edition (1774) under the title *Systema Vegetabilium* (see Chapter 3). Translated Linnaeus' works into German.

Correspondence: 52 letters (24 Nov 1760–5 Aug 1776). Some specimens in LINN, including 28.35 (*Justicia*), 278.2 (*Ribes*), 498.69 (*Erica*), 953.4 (*Leontodon*), 954.56 (*Hieracium*) and 1273.208 (*Lichen*).

Mútis, José Celestino (1732–1808). Spanish. Botanist. Went to South America in 1760 and lived in Bogotá which, thanks to him, became an important centre of learning. His herbarium, manuscripts and watercolour botanical illustrations were sent to Spain after his death.

Correspondence: 12 letters (30 Jun 1761–8 Feb 1777); two between Mútis and Linnaeus filius (30 Jun 1778; 12 Sep 1778).

There are more than 230 Mútis specimens in LINN, and two manuscript lists at LINN relating to them. The first, ca. 1773, is a list by Linnaeus and his son of the first specimens received from "Nova Granada", latter-day Colombia. A second, from ca. 1777, is a partial list, written by Mútis, of a second batch of material sent to Linnaeus. Most of the specimens are numbered and can be correlated with the respective lists.

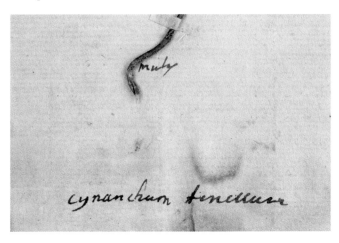

The material contained a enormous number of novelties and it might be thought surprising that Linnaeus did not formally describe more than a few names based on these specimens. Mútis was mentioned by Linnaeus in connection with *Hypericum mexicanum* L. (*Mútis 10*, 943.31 is its type) and *Tradescantia nervosa* L. (406.3). Linnaeus fully recognised the importance of Mútis' collections, as can be seen from his own manuscript annotations on the 1773 list, and on the Mútis sheets in the herbarium. He coined names for many of the new species but by now his health was failing, and there was to be no new edition of the *Systema Naturae* in which such species might have appeared. As it was, it fell to Linnaeus' son to publish many of the new

species in the *Supplementum Plantarum* (1782), several years after his father's death. Study of the specimens and manuscripts shows that many of the names and descriptions published by Linnaeus filius had been chosen and prepared by Linnaeus. For example, 308.11 (LINN) is annotated by Linnaeus with the name "*Cynanchum tenellum*" (see below, left), as is the 1773 manuscript where this specimen, *Mútis 15*, carries the same name, also in Linnaeus' hand. Nevertheless, this name is attributed to Linnaeus filius (1782: 168). However, in other cases it is clear that the names and descriptions are Linnaeus filius' own, particularly those based on specimens sent later, probably in 1777, by which time Linnaeus was much too ill to have taken any serious interest in them. The collection is, accordingly, a rich source of types for the Linnaeus filius names that were based upon them. For further information on Mútis and Linnaeus, see Rydén (1953).

Among the Mútis sheets are specimens from Escallón (see p. 202), a collector employed by Mútis.

Mygind, Franz von (ca. 1710–1789). Danish/Austrian. Counsellor to the Imperial Court in Vienna.

Correspondence: four letters from Mygind to Linnaeus (9 Feb 1771–17 May 1771).

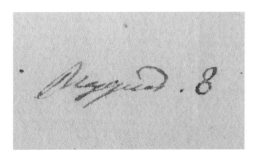

There are about 40 Mygind specimens in LINN. Linnaeus mentioned him in connection with *Rosa rubiginosa* L., and Mygind's material (652.6 LINN (see annotation above)) is the type of that name, as is another specimen (821.3) for *Anastatica syriaca* L.

Nietzel, Diedrich [Dietrich] (1703–1756). German. Skilled horticulturalist to George Clifford whom Linnaeus "poached" with an offer to take over the Botanic Garden in Uppsala.

Correspondence: one letter from Nietzel to Linnaeus (L0281; 9 Apr 1739) in which Nietzel accepts Linnaeus' invitation to leave the Hartekamp for Uppsala.

Specimens in S are often marked as "a hortulanus Nietzel" – e.g. *Potentilla fruticosa* L. (208.9), *Ranunculus aconitifolius* L. (227.11), *Robinia caragana* L. (300.18) and *Rudbeckia laciniata* L. (359.5).

Oldenland, Henry Bernard (fl. 1695). Danish. Physician and botanist. Curator of the Government Garden at the Cape of Good Hope.

In the introduction to the dissertation *Plantae Rariores Africanae* (1960), Linnaeus mentioned Oldenland, some of whose collections had been acquired by the Burmans and which were brought to Uppsala, on loan, by Nicolaas Laurens Burman in 1760. There are probably 100 or more sheets of Cape plants bearing Oldenland's distinctive handwriting at G (see, for example, material linked with *Osmites asteriscoides* L. below). They may at one time have been bound in a volume (see Nordenstam 1968: 92), and the appearance of the paper on which they are mounted (the long, left edge is often cut irregularly) is not inconsistent with this suggestion. In addition, many of the sheets bear, on the verso, a deep imprint of another herbarium specimen and it seems unlikely that this would have been produced via filing or conventional stacking of herbarium sheets.

Some of these specimens are lectotypes for Linnaean binomials published in the dissertation. They include material of *Arnica piloselloides* L., *Hieracium capense* L., *Ophrys circumflexa* L., *Orchis flexuosa* L., *Perdicium capense* L., *Psoralea aphylla* L. and *Psoralea hirta* L. Other Oldenland material is in Herb. Sloane vol. 156 (BM-SL), and Dandy (1958: 173) provides further information on this material and its collector.

Osbeck, Pehr (1722–1805). Swedish. Clergyman, botanist, explorer. Studied at Uppsala under Linnaeus 1745–1750. Chaplain on ships of the Swedish East India Company on voyages to China. Vicar of Hasslöv (Halland).

Correspondence: 71 letters (21 Sep 1750–5 Nov 1773). Pehr Osbeck was the source of most of Linnaeus' Chinese specimens. Osbeck travelled to China as a ship's chaplain in 1750. He returned in June 1752, with his assistant Olof Torén (see p. 231), with collections which arrived in time for Linnaeus to be able to take them into consideration for *Species Plantarum* (1753). Osbeck also brought some specimens from Java (see Hansen & Fox Maule (1973) for an account of the material he collected). Manktelow & Nyberg (2005: 78) state that Osbeck claimed to have furnished Linnaeus with no fewer than 600 species from China. For information on Osbeck's account of his travels, see Chapter 4.

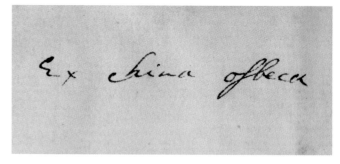

Linnaeus cited Osbeck in the protologues of 42 binomials (Manktelow & Nyberg 2005: 78), for most of which the corresponding material in LINN or S serves as the type (though some specimens are absent). Specimens which are types include those of *Asplenium nidus* L. (1250.6 LINN), *Cassytha filiformis* L. (519.1 LINN), *Croton sebiferum* L. (1140.9 LINN), *Epidendrum amabile* L. (373.1 S), *Lactuca indica* L. ("in Java", 950.8 LINN), *Mammea asiatica* L. ("in Java. Osbeck", 675.2 LINN, see Linnaeus' annotation above), *Rhus javanica* L. (378.4 LINN), *Utricularia bifida* L. (34.7 LINN) and *Verbascum osbeckii* L. (87.17 S).

Pallas, Peter Simon (1741–1811). German. Travelled in Siberia.

Correspondence: one letter to Linnaeus (20 Aug 1776).

There are some 50 specimens from Pallas in LINN, though none seems to have contributed directly to any species described by Linnaeus. Assuming they were received in the late 1770s, Linnaeus' poor health at that time probably accounts for their neglect.

Petiver, James (ca. 1663–1718). British. Apothecary. Collector of natural history specimens.

Petiver's extensive herbarium collection now comprises 106 volumes of the Sloane herbarium (BM-SL – see Dandy 1957: 175–182; Stearn 1957: 121). It is often difficult to correlate published illustrations with material in his herbarium. For information on Petiver's publications, see Chapter 4.

Pott, Johann Friedrich (1738–1805). German. Personal physician to the Duke of Brunswick.

Correspondence: one letter from Pott to Linnaeus (1 Mar 1776).

There are more than 30 sheets in LINN associated with Pott, including 151.14 (*Cornus*), 248.63 (*Solanum*), 335.15 (*Bupleurum*), 449.56 (*Juncus*) and 1135.21 (*Pinus*). None appears to have been used by Linnaeus in describing any species.

Rathgeb, Joseph von (?–1753). Austrian. Imperial Legate at Venice.

Correspondence: 24 letters from Rathgeb to Linnaeus (14 Jul 1747–24 Sep 1751).

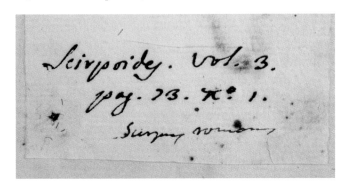

Rathgeb is mentioned by Linnaeus in connection with *Nepeta italica* L. (?726.24), *Salvia hispanica* L. (?42.29) and *Thymus alpinus* L. (744.15). Other specimens can be found at 71.19 (the type of *Scirpus romanus* L., see label above), 71.31 (the type of *S. mucronatus* L.), 80.14 (*Panicum*), 218.63 (*Convolvulus*), 744.15 (*Thymus*), 905.21 (*Lathyrus*), 955.24 (*Crepis*) and 1251.35 (*Polypodium*).

Rolander, Daniel (1725–1793). Swedish. Naturalist and explorer. Studied at Uppsala University under Linnaeus. Went to Surinam in 1755–1756.

Correspondence: six letters (19 Jun 1753–8 Oct 1756).

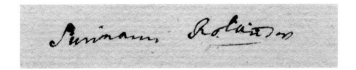

Rolander was mentioned by Linnaeus in connection with both *Myrtus lucida* L. (1759/1762: 637.9 LINN) and *Zygophyllum aestuans* L. (1762). There appear to be about 15 of Rolander's sheets in LINN, including 35.6 (*Verbena*), 210.1 (*Spigelia*), 626.9 (*Lythrum*, see annotation above), 1071.1 (*Aristolochia*), and 384.6, the type of *Turnera cistoides* L. Rolander sold his manuscripts and collections to Friis Rottböll (see below) in Copenhagen.

Roscoe, William (1753–1831). Banker in Liverpool, friend of J.E. Smith.

After his acquisition of the Linnaean collections, James Edward Smith gave a number of Linnaean specimens to Roscoe which, as listed by Stearn, included material of *Epidendrum pusillum* L., *Coronilla coronata* L., *Cytisus glutinosus* L. f., *Atraphaxis* sp. and *Rubus chamaemorus* L., all carrying Smith's handwriting. These collections are now at LIV.

Rosén, Eberhard (1714–1796). Swedish.

Correspondence: none recorded.

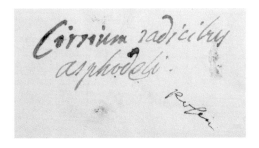

There are at least two sheets from Rosén in LINN, one of which (966.24, see label above) is the type of *Carduus tuberosus* L. Another is at 328.25 (*Gentiana*).

Rottböll, Christian Friis (1727–1797). Danish. Botanist and physician, student of Linnaeus. Professor of Medicine at Copenhagen.

Correspondence: seven letters (29 Aug 1757–31 Dec 1774). There are about 30 sheets in LINN from Rottböll, most of which were referred to the genera *Cyperus* (e.g. 70.19, 70.57, 70.65) and *Scirpus* (71.3, 71.6, 71.34 etc.).

Royen, Adriaan van (1705–1779). Dutch. Professor of Botany and Director of the Botanical Garden in Leiden. Uncle of David van Royen.

Correspondence: 26 letters (23 Feb 1737–3 Aug 1753).

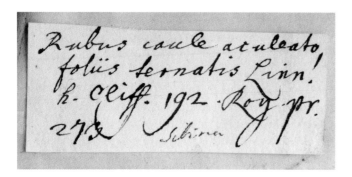

Linnaeus had worked closely with his friend Adriaan van Royen developing a new arrangement for the Botanic Garden in Leiden during the former's stay in the Netherlands. Van Royen's own herbarium is in L, but there are some of his sheets elsewhere, e.g. in Clifford's herbarium (BM). Linnaeus makes only occasional reference to van Royen (aside from bibliographic references to Adriaan's *Florae Leydensis Prodromus*, 1740; see Chapter 4), e.g. in the protologues of the 1753 names *Aspalathus callosa* L. and *Crotalaria triflora* L. Material in LINN from Adriaan is associated with names such as *Rubus caesius* L. (653.7, see label above), *Euphorbia corallioides* L. (630.57) and *E. platyphyllos* L. (630.61).

Royen, David van (1727–1799). Dutch. Nephew of Adriaan van Royen, and his successor as Professor of Botany and Director of the Botanic Garden in Leiden.

Correspondence: 34 letters (18 Mar 1758–18 Apr 1769).

As noted above, reference by Linnaeus to "Royen" in a protologue can lead to uncertainty as to whether Adriaan, or his nephew David, was intended. The date of publication of the name is, however, a strong indicator because Linnaeus' contact with Adriaan declined after 1753, while his correspondence with David ran between 1758 and 1769. It seems to be the case that almost all references to "Royen" in the protologues of post-1756 names refer to David, rather than Adriaan. Among these can be found *Anthyllis aspalathoides* L. (?893.56–58), *Barleria hystrix* L. (?805.5), *Bunias balearica* L. (?847.13–15), *Cassine capensis* L., *Celastrus lucidus* L. (268.8), *Elaeagnus orientalis* L. (?160.2), *Lamium orvala* L., *Leucadendron pinifolium* L. (?116.14), *Pedalium murex* L. (?817.1, ?817.2), *Salvia paniculata* L. (?42.40), *Selago tomentosa* L. (?787.4 LINN; 259.10, S), *Seriphium gnaphaloides* L. (?1049.8), *Verbena indica* L. (?35.1) and *Xeranthemum staehelina* L. (990.16). Binomials

for which David is mentioned in the protologue, and where the corresponding specimens in LINN are the types, include *Royena villosa* L. (570.2), *Septas capensis* L. (480.2), *Sideroxylon melanophleos* L. (261.3) and *Stachys aethiopica* L. (736.13). There are probably at least 70 specimens from David van Royen in LINN (see example of a label, from 736.13 LINN, below, left), with a few also at S (e.g. *Ipomoea triloba* – 79.11 S).

Sauvages, François Boissier de La Croix de (1706–1767). French. Botanist, clergyman and physician, Professor of Medicine at Montpellier.

Correspondence: 114 letters (20 Jun 1737–3 May 1765).

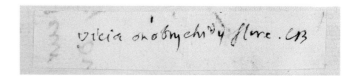

Nyström (2005: 67–68) discusses some aspects of the long correspondence between Sauvages and Linnaeus. Sauvages gave his herbarium of plants from southern France to Linnaeus in 1749. It included the herbarium of Pierre Magnol. Although not all of the plants carry Sauvages labels, it seems clear that in many cases, where he is mentioned in the protologue, corresponding material in LINN carries "Monsp." and in all likelihood came from him. Some sheets (e.g. 722.11) indicate that seed had been sent ("Habitat Monspelii, unde semina Sauvagesii"). Similarly, Linnaeus seems not to have mentioned Magnol in protologues but to have instead indicated Sauvages (presumably as the conduit for the former's collections). So for *Anthemis altissima* L. ("Habitat in Italiae, Hispaniae, G. Narbonensis agris. D. Sauvages"), the type is a Magnol specimen (1016.2), and a similar situation occurs with *Vicia onobrychioides* L. ("Habitat in Gallia. D. Sauvages"; 906.14, see Sauvages' label above) and *V. peregrina* (906.28).

In addition, Sauvages is mentioned in connection with *Andropogon gryllus* L., *Caucalis daucoides* L. (?338.2–5), *Crucianella maritima* L., *Cunila thymoides* L., *Dianthus monspessulanus* L. (?581.18), *Genista candicans* L., *Iberis saxatilis* L. (?825.3), *Phlomis lychnitis* L., *Salix glauca* L. (1158.53), *Salsola tragus* L. (?315.3, ?315.5), *Scleranthus polycarpos* L. (?578.3), *Sideritis scordioides* L. (?729.12), *Thymus pulegioides* L. (?38.5), *Trifolium tomentosum* L., *Triticum tenellum* L. (?104.14) and *Valeriana echinata* L. (?48.19). Unequivocal Sauvages specimens, linked with protologues, are the types of *Illecebrum cymosum* L. (290.12), *Linum trigynum* L. (396.19), *Moluccella frutescens* L. (741.4) and *Potentilla hirta* L. (655.19). Sauvages specimens also typify *Linum tenuifolium* L. (396.12), *Lithospermum fruticosum* L. (181.9), *Lotus rectus* L. (931.22), *Origanum creticum* L. (743.4), *Spartium complicatum* L. (891.8), *Teucrium creticum* L. (722.11) and *Triticum monococcum* L. (104.4). For information on Sauvages' 1751 publication, see Chapter 4.

Scheuchzer, Johann (1684–1738). Swiss. Botanist, Professor of Physics at Zürich.
Correspondence: two letters from Scheuchzer to Linnaeus (23 Jul 1737; 17 Jun 1738).

Triticum polonicum. Journ. inst. 512.

A few specimens are in LINN. Among them are the types of *Orchis globosa* L. (1054.16) and *Triticum polonicum* L. (104.3, see annotation above).

Schmidel, Casimir Christopher (1718–1792). German. Professor of Medicine at Erlangen.
Correspondence: four letters from Schmidel to Linnaeus (15 Nov 1757–23 May 1761).

? Arenaria strictissi-mo folio verna Rupp. Jen. II. p. 89. an vero magis accedit ad Alsinen papalilem lanais folio minore flore Magn in lapidosis circa Oppidum Velden Franconiae.

Only about 12 specimens are in LINN, but these include the type of *Arenaria verna* L. (585.30, see label above).

Schober, Gottlieb (1670–1739?). German.
Correspondence: none recorded.
Nitraria schoberi L. (1759) was named by Linnaeus for Gottlieb Schober who, in 1717–1718, visited the Lower Volga Region, Caucasus and Persia, and Linnaeus apparently had seeds of this species from him, from the shores of the Caspian Sea.

Schreber, Johann Christian Daniel von (1739–1810). German. Awarded doctorate, after studying under Linnaeus, in 1760. Professor of Botany and Director of the Botanic Garden in Erlangen.
Correspondence: 59 letters, all but one from Schreber to Linnaeus (20 May 1754–1 Apr 1772).

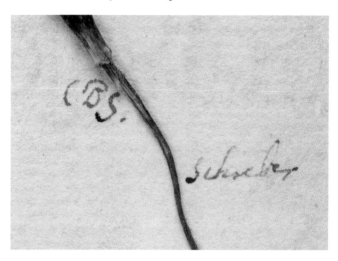

About 40 specimens in LINN appear to have been received from Schreber, about a third of them types for their associated names. Linnaeus mentions him in connection with *Althaea ludwigii* L. (?868.4), *Aristida plumosa* L. (98.6), *Astragalus exscapus* L. (926.55), *Blaeria pusilla* L. (141.4), *Brassica alpina* L. (?844.8), *Bromus ramosus* L., non Huds. (93.40; 93.41), *Cassine barbara* L. (380.4), *Decumaria barbara* L. (?617.2), *Erica hispidula* L., *Galium graecum* L. (129.32), *Lichen divaricatus* L. (1273.277), *Ophrys atrata* L. (1056.31, see annotation above) and *Veronica biloba* L. Sheet 585.27 (LINN), the type of *Arenaria gypsophiloides* L., carries a label that may be in the handwriting of Gundelsheimer (see p. 208). The material was evidently received by Linnaeus from Schreber, whose name appears both on the sheet and in the protologue. Schreber's specimens in LINN also provide types for *Othonna rigens* L. (1027.3), *Teucrium salicifolium* L. (722.15) and *Veronica montana* L. (26.42). Other Schreber collections are in S (e.g. *Selago ericoides* L. (410.15) and *Thesium alpinum* L. (104.11)), and a few Linnaean specimens are in Schreber's herbarium in M (e.g. *Pedicularis hirsuta* L.).

Scopoli, Giovanni Antonio (1723–1788). Italian.
Correspondence: 30 letters (1 Sep 1760–19 Sep 1775).
To judge by the number sequence of the specimens recorded in a manuscript list from 1762, there should be at least 100

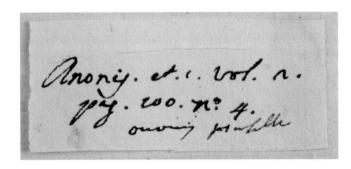

Scopoli specimens in LINN, though fewer than this appear to be present there now. Scopoli was mentioned by Linnaeus in connection with *Arctium carduelis* L. (964.3) and *Melica minuta* L. (86.3), both of which are typified by the associated material in LINN. *Artemisia contra* L. (988.4), *Ononis pusilla* L. (896.6, see label above), *Rosa alpina* L. (652.28) and *Veronica fruticulosa* L. (26.24) are also typified by Scopoli material.

Séguier, Jean François (1703–1784). French. Antiquarian and botanist, Verona and Nîmes. Correspondence: 16 letters (30 Mar 1744–1 Dec 1761).

There appear to be about 50 specimens from Séguier in LINN, almost half of which are types of Linnaean names. Linnaeus mentioned him in connection with a number of names, including *Agrostis serotina* (L.) L. (?84.9), *Andropogon gryllus* L. (1211.2), *Anthemis alpina* L. (?1016.12), *Arenaria bavarica* L. (585.26), *Cerastium manticum* L. (603.28), *Cyperus glomeratus* L. (70.23), *Dianthus monspessulanus* L. (581.17), *Laserpitium peucedanoides* L., *Leontodon aureus* L., *Lepidium alpinum* L. (824.5, see label above), *Potentilla nitida* L. (655.36) and *Pulmonaria suffruticosa* L. (184.3). In addition, *Briza maxima* L. (88.6), *Campanula petraea* L. (221.51), *Erigeron alpinus* L. (994.18), *Geranium argenteum* L. (858.57), *Marsilea natans* L. (1254.1), *Phalaris oryzoides* L. (78.10), *Phleum nodosum* L. (81.2), *Potamogeton densus* L.

(175.4), *Ranunculus thora* L. (715.16) and *Rumex tuberosus* L. (464.37) are all typified by Séguier collections in LINN. For information on Séguier's publications, see Chapter 4.

Sibthorp, Humphrey (1712–1797). British. Sherardian Professor of Botany at Oxford.

Correspondence: six letters from Sibthorp to Linnaeus (21 Nov 1749–6 Nov 1756).

Linnaeus gave a small number of his Lapland specimens to Dillenius in 1742 and to Sibthorp in 1748. These are at OXF and are listed by Stearn (1957: 126).

Skjöldebrand, Erik (1722–1814). See **Brander**.

Sloane, Hans (1660–1753). British. Physician, natural history collector. President of the Royal Society 1727–1741.

Correspondence: three letters (2 Mar 1736–31 Dec 1737). Sloane's enormous herbarium contains various collections that are of interest because they serve as typotypes or voucher specimens for illustrations used by Linnaeus. However, the specimens themselves were not studied by Linnaeus so they do not form original material for his names, and are therefore ineligible for selection as lectotypes. Sloane's own specimens that he collected in Jamaica are the basis for the illustrations prepared by Kickius and later published (Sloane 1707, 1725; see Chapter 4). Stearn (1957: 119–120; 122–123) and Dandy (1958: 204–208) provide a background, and these specimens are viewable online at http://www.nhm.ac.uk/research-curation/projects/sloane-herbarium/.

Apart from his own collections, Sloane managed to acquire, through his long life, an enormous number of specimens from other sources. Among those that have relevance for Linnaean names are voucher specimens collected by Catesby, Kaempfer, Petiver and Plukenet. Bryce (2005) explores Amman's role as a conduit of botanical (and other) information between Russia and both Sloane (Amman's employer before he left London for St Petersburg in 1733) and Linnaeus. Amman himself sent collections that he had made, as well as those of others (e.g. Messerschmidt collections from Dauria – see Bryce, 2005) to Sloane.

Smith, James Edward (1759–1828). British. Purchaser of Linnaeus' collections.

Correspondence: none recorded. On Smith's acquisition of the Linnaean collections, he, Banks and Dryander made careful comparison of the Linnaean and Banksian herbaria. Stearn (1957: 110) reports "their enumeration made by ticking a copy of Murray's 1784 edition of the *Systema Vegetabilium* provides a valuable record of the Linnaean Herbarium as it came into

Smith's hands".

Smith gave a number of supposedly duplicate specimens to some of his colleagues. Savage (1937b) lists 85 specimens given to Banks in February 1785 which are now kept as a separate collection in BM. Smith also gave Linnaean specimens to Davall (e.g. one of *Diapensia lapponica* L. – see Becherer 1945; De Beer 1947: 64; Stearn 1957: 110). Linnaean specimens given to Roscoe, as listed by Stearn, included material of *Epidendrum pusillum* L., *Coronilla coronata* L., *Cytisus glutinosus* L. f., *Atraphaxis* sp., and *Rubus chamaemorus* L., all carrying Smith's handwriting. These specimens are now at LIV. The Linnaean material given by Smith to Hosack went to New York but is apparently lost (see p. 213).

As the first President of the Linnean Society of London (founded in 1788), Smith proclaimed that he held the Linnaean collections "only for the purpose of making them useful to the world and natural history in general, and particularly to this society". However, in 1796, he removed the library and the botanical and zoological collections from London to his family home in Norwich, having sold the mineralogical collection at auction. The remaining collections therefore remained comparatively inaccessible until they returned to London in 1829 when the Society purchased them after Smith's death.

Solander, Daniel (1733–1782). Swedish. Naturalist, explorer. Student in Uppsala under Linnaeus and Johan Gottschalk Wallerius. Went to London in 1760. Curator of natural history collections at the British Museum. Botanist on Cook's first voyage 1768–1771. Joseph Banks' librarian. Correspondence: 38 letters (20 Sep 1753–31 Dec 1764).

In 1758, Linnaeus purchased Patrick Browne's herbarium of Jamaican plants, annotating the sheets with the letters "Br", usually close to the base of the mounted specimen. However, the specific epithets were usually added by his pupil Daniel Solander. When Solander travelled to London in 1760, he apparently carried with him some duplicates of Browne's specimens, though Stearn (1957: 113) reports that these were returned to Sweden after Solander's death in 1782. There are Browne specimens reported in BM and it may be that these found their way into Banks' herbarium via Solander.

Linnaeus mentioned Solander in connection with *Draba*

hirta L. (?823.12), *Gentiana aurea* L. (?328.15), *Hieracium taraxaci* L. ("Habitat in Alpibus Pithoënsi – Lapponicis, lectum 1753 a D. C. Solandro" – 954.4, see label below, left), *Mucor fulvus* L., *M. furfuraceus* L. and *Solandra capensis* L. A number of specimens at LINN (e.g. 1100.30, 1100.48, 1100.50 [*Carex*], 84.19 [*Agrostis*]) evidently came from Solander's Lapland expedition in 1753. A sheet labelled *Stellaria nemorum* L. (185.19 S) has "Sol." and "Alp. Torn." written on the verso).

Sparrman, Anders (1748–1820). Swedish. Explorer and collector. Curator at the Royal Swedish Academy of Sciences. Professor at the Collegium Medicum, Stockholm. Studied at Uppsala 1757–1765, then later (1768) defended a dissertation under Linnaeus after his return from China as a ship's surgeon under Capt. Ekeberg (see p. 202). Stayed at the Cape in 1772 and 1775–1776 and served as physician and naturalist on Cook's second voyage 1772–1775.

Correspondence: eight letters from Sparrman to Linnaeus (11 Dec 1771–26 Apr 1775).

Linnaeus' herbarium at LINN contains some 250 specimens from Sparrman, chiefly from South Africa, and there is a manuscript written by Linnaeus ("Sparmanni Capenses") at LINN, dating from about 1772, that lists many of them. However, few (if any) are associated with new species described by Linnaeus, and the collection has much greater importance for names described by Linnaeus filius, who often mentions Sparrman in protologues. Examples include *Arethusa ciliaris* L. f. (1059.4), *Gladiolus marginatus* L. f. (59.32), *Ophrys bracteata* L. f. (1056.27) and *Orchis draconis* L. f. (1054.10). Specimens are typically annotated by Linnaeus with the letters "Sp.", often followed by a number. Some specimens can also be found in S (e.g. 342.1 – *Gnaphalium sanguineum* L.).

Steller, Georg Wilhelm (1709–1746). German. Voyager, who sailed with Vitus Bering and returned with important collections from Kamchatka.

Correspondence: none recorded.

Demidov acquired and sent on loan in 1748/1750 to Linnaeus material collected by Steller in Kamchatka, with permission to keep the duplicates. See symbols in Stearn (1957: 106).

There appear to be about 30 of Steller's specimens from Kamchatka now at LINN (see the dissertation *Plantae Rariores Camschatcenses* in Chapter 3). Although, in *Species*

Following page (230): A specimen (842.3) believed to have been collected in Kamchatka by Georg Steller, the lectotype of *Arabis grandiflora* L. (= *Parrya nudicaulis* (L.) Regel).

Plantarum, Linnaeus appears to mention Steller directly only in connection with *Dracocephalum pinnatum* L. (sheet 746.4 LINN is its heavily annotated lectotype), these Kamchatka specimens were doubtless of great interest to Linnaeus for, apart from Krascheninnikov, Steller was the earliest collector to bring plant specimens from there. Steller specimens in LINN that typify Linnaean names include those of *Arabis grandiflora* L. (842.3, see opposite), *Arenaria saxatilis* L. (585.29), *Dryas pentapetala* L. (658.1), *Epilobium latifolium* L. (486.2), *Helleborus trifolius* L. (718.8), *Heliotropium orientale* L. (179.12), *Ophrys camschatea* L. (1056.24), *Salsola prostrata* L. (315.15) and *Sophora lupinoides* L. (522.18).

Swartz, Olof (1760–1818). Swedish. Student of Linnaeus filius. Travelled to Lapland, and later to the West Indies. Subsequently Professor of Botany at the Swedish Academy of Sciences.

Correspondence: none recorded.

Some of Swartz's specimens appear to have reached the Linnaean herbarium in LINN after Linnaeus' death, presumably via Linnaeus filius. There are about 70 sheets in all, the majority being lichens, mosses and liverworts. Nordenstam (1991) provides a useful summary of Swartz's life and collections.

Tärnström, Christopher (1711–1746). Swedish. Clergyman and botanist. First of Linnaeus' former students ("apostles") to travel outside Sweden – joined the Swedish East India Company as a chaplain and departed for China in 1746 but died on the island of Pulo Condor (now Con-Dao) in the South China Sea in December of that year, before reaching his destination. Manktelow & Nyberg (2005: 76) report that Tärnström had been able to send Linnaeus only a few unremarkable plants and seeds from Cadiz. For a transcription and analysis of Tärnström's journal, see Söderpalm (2005).

Correspondence: five letters from Tärnström to Linnaeus (Jan 1746–3 May 1746).

Tärnström was not mentioned by Linnaeus in connection with any binomials but three sheets in LINN – 211.1 (*Ophiorrhiza*), 592.4 (*Averrhoa*) and 1184.9 (*Dioscorea*) – appear to have come from him.

Tessin, Carl Gustaf (1695–1770). Swedish. Count, politician and patron of both arts and sciences. A great supporter of Linnaeus.

Correspondence: 112 letters (22 Apr 1740–1 Jan 1770). There appear to be two specimens that probably came from Tessin: 26.14 (the type of *Veronica hybrida* L., see label above, right) and 80.67 (*Panicum*).

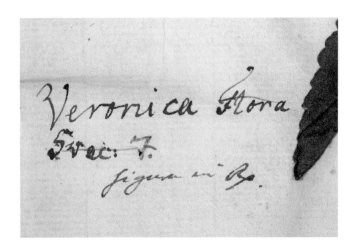

Thoüin, André (1747–1824). French. Botanist. Gardener at the Jardin des Plantes, Paris.

Correspondence: none recorded.

There are about 10 specimens from Thoüin in LINN. Most are also annotated by Linnaeus filius with names that he was to publish later, e.g. *Lycium foetidum* L. f. (259.10), *Salvia coccinea* L. f. (42.41) and *S. triloba* L. f. (42.62).

Thunberg, Carl Peter (1743–1828). Swedish. Botanist, physician, explorer. Professor of Medicine and Botany at Uppsala. Studied medicine under Linnaeus in Uppsala, medicine and surgery in Paris. Travelled in South Africa in 1772–1775, in Japan 1775–1776, Java and Ceylon in 1777–1778.

Correspondence: 29 letters (9 Aug 1770–15 Jun 1775), mostly during Thunberg's stay in Cape Town (see also Karsten 1939).

There are nearly 300 Thunberg specimens in LINN (some of which can be correlated with entries in his letters to Linnaeus), often numbered by Linnaeus. The material is variously annotated by both Linnaeus and Linnaeus filius, but as Linnaeus himself published very little after the *Mantissa Plantarum Altera* in 1771, most of the new species it yielded carry names now attributed to Linnaeus filius from the *Supplementum Plantarum* (1782). Of course, Thunberg also described an enormous number of new species in his own right. In addition, Linnaeus gave a number of specimens from his own herbarium to Thunberg, and some of these are now in the small Linnaean collection in UPS (see Juel 1931a). There are also some Thunberg specimens in the Linnaean herbarium at S (e.g. *Forsskaolea candida* L. f. – 195.13).

Torén, Olof (1718–1753). Swedish. Clergyman, naturalist. Linnaeus' pupil. Went to China in 1748 with another former student, Fredrik Adler, returning the following year with rather disappointing collections (Manktelow & Nyberg 2005: 76).

Torén returned to China and India in 1750, as did Pehr Osbeck (but on a different ship) and arrived back in Sweden in late 1752 (with Osbeck) with much better collections, which Linnaeus was able to take into consideration for *Species Plantarum*. However, Torén was in very poor health, and died in August 1753.

Correspondence: seven letters from Torén to Linnaeus (20 Nov 1752–31 Dec 1754).

Torén was mentioned by Linnaeus in connection with *Conyza chinensis* L. (?993.25), *Justicia nasuta* L. (?28.24) and *Torenia asiatica* L. (770.1). A Torén collection is also the type of *Buchnera asiatica* L. (790.10). See Franks (2005) for some recent observations on Torén and his status as a Linnaean apostle.

Tournefort, Joseph Pitton de (1656–1708). French. Botanist. Travelled extensively in Europe and the Levant.

Linnaeus did not study Tournefort's herbarium (P-TRF) but specimens there can serve as voucher material for Linnaean names typified by illustrations published by Tournefort (see Chapter 4).

Tulbagh, C. Rijk (1699–1771). Dutch. Governor at the Cape. He sent plants, bulbs and seeds to Linnaeus in 1761 and 1769.

Correspondence: three letters (25 Apr 1763–20 Mar 1769). In the only letter (thought to date from 1764, but possibly later) from Linnaeus to Tulbagh known to survive, the Swede acknowledges a gift of "more than 200 specimens of plants, with several birds well-preserved, a very numerous collection of bulbs, and 50 sorts of seeds" sent from the Cape of Good Hope. Linnaeus was evidently greatly impressed with the large number of novelties they contained for he wrote (quoted from the translation of Smith, 1821: 568–570) ". . . I never received a more welcome communication than your last, nor one that gave me more satisfaction, as containing so great a number of rare Cape plants, which I had never before seen. I had thought that the greater part of the vegetable productions of that country, if not all of them, had come under my inspection already; but your collection convinces me that I was previously acquainted with but a small proportion, there being in that collection as many quite unknown to botanists as there are of plants already known. . . . I have carefully dissected and examined the flowers of the dried specimens, and have referred them to their proper genera, with suitable specific distinctions. These, if it please God, may one day be made known to the publick, accompanied with those full descriptions of your own which you have communicated to me and which cannot but redound to your scientific reputation".

The precise number of new species is a little difficult to

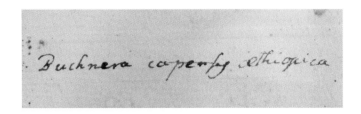

assess for, perhaps surprisingly given Linnaeus' effusive praise in his letter, he does not specifically mention Tulbagh in their protologues. However, these names are mostly to be found in the *Mantissa Plantarum Altera* (1771), with detailed descriptions, indications of provenance including succinct ecological information (e.g. "Habitat in Capitis b. spei campis arenosis"), and the adopted names can be correlated with Tulbagh material and the associated manuscript at LINN. There appear to have been at least 35 new species involved. Those whose names are typified by Tulbagh specimens include *Aspalathus argentea* L. (893.46), *A. canescens* L. (893.40), *A. ciliaris* L. (893.28), *A. laxata* L. (893.45), *A. nigra* L. (893.22), *Buchnera aethiopica* L. (790.6, see annotation above), *B. cernua* L. (790.1), *Cliffortia sarmentosa* L. (1197.3), *Erica albens* L. (498.58), *E. mammosa* L. (498.33), *E. mucosa* L. (498.6), *E. regerminans* L. (498.5), *E. viscaria* L. (498.74), *Gnaphalium maritimum* L. (989.29), *G. repens* L. (989.30), *Gorteria setosa* L. (1027.6), *Indigofera angustifolia* L. (923.18), *I. procumbens* L. (923.5), *Osteospermum corymbosum* L. (1037.15), *O. imbricatum* L. (1037.16), *Phylica stipularis* L. (263.7), *Polygala umbellata* L. (882.13), *Protea parviflora* L. (116.19), *P. totta* L. (116.35), *Psoralea spicata* L. (928.6) and *Spartium contaminatum* L. (891.1), as well as *Tulbaghia capensis* L. (411.1), the type of the genus that Linnaeus named for Tulbagh.

Well over a hundred of the specimens Tulbagh sent to Linnaeus are extant in LINN, many of them numbered. Many of these can be correlated with a numbered manuscript list at LINN, from ca. 1769, reproduced by Jackson (1918).

Turra, Antonio (1730–1796). Italian. Botanist, mineralogist and physician at Vicenza.

Correspondence: 15 letters from Turra to Linnaeus (29 Oct 1762–1 Aug 1772).

Turra is mentioned in connection with the names *Centaurea aegyptiaca* L. (?1030.53), *Convolvulus farinosus* L. (?218.6 LINN) and *Scandix trichosperma* L. (?364.8; ?364.9). He sent quite a number of specimens to Linnaeus and they generally carry labels in Turra's distinctive hand. There was evidently a close relationship between Turra, Pietro Arduino and Linnaeus in that Arduino may be mentioned in a protologue, but the only associated material carries a label

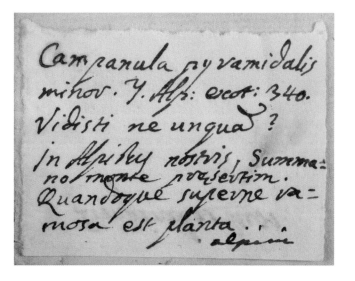

Delphinium aconiti (694.3).

Velez, Cristobal (d. 1753). Spanish. Pharmacist in Madrid.
Correspondence: one letter from Velez to Linnaeus (12 Mar 1753).

Velez is mentioned by Linnaeus in connection with *Ortegia hispanica* L. ("*Habitat in* Castilia *Minuart*. Baetica *Velez*, Salamantica"), and there is also a specimen (326.2, though it is not the lectotype) from Velez of the species for which Linnaeus published (after Löfling) a new genus in his honour – *Velezia*.

Wachendorff, Everhard Jacob van (1702–1758). Dutch. Professor of Medicine, Chemistry and Botany at Utrecht.
Correspondence: six letters from Wachendorff to Linnaeus (15 Dec 1747–10 May 1753).

written by Turra. This is true of both *Rhus laevigata* L. ("Habitat ad Cap. b. Spei. Arduini", typified by 378.23 from Turra) and *Campanula alpini* L. ("Habitat in Summano aliisque Italiae Alpibus. Arduini", typified by 221.19, also from Turra, see his label above). Other names typified by Turra specimens include *Artemisia arborescens* L. (988.10) and *Gossypium religiosum* L. (874.6). For information on Turra's 1765 publication, see Chapter 4.

Vandelli, Domenico (1735–1816). Italian. Physician and botanist. Moved from Padua to Portugal in 1764. Professor at Coimbra and first Director of the Botanic Garden there.

Wachendorff was mentioned in connection with *Gypsophila prostrata* L. ("Habitat – – – semina misit D. Wachendorff") the type of which, 579.4 LINN, was evidently cultivated in the Hortus in Uppsala from the seeds sent by the Dutchman. He was also connected with *Myrtus brasiliana* L. ("Habitat in Brasilia. D. Wachend.") for which corresponding material in LINN (637.5, the lectotype) is annotated "A[rbor] ex Horto Ultrajectino Wachendorff" (see above).

Wahlbom, Johan Gustav (1724–1808). Swedish. Student of Linnaeus. Provincial physician in Kalmar.
Correspondence: 20 letters (2 Nov 1750–18 Jan 1777).
Wahlbom was one of those to whom Linnaeus gave away supposed duplicate specimens (Stearn 1957: 108, 114). Some of these are now at UPS as part of the Linnaean collection there. The specimens in question are listed by Juel (1931a).

Weigel, Christian Ehrenfried (1748–1831). German. Director of the Botanic Garden at Greifswald.
Correspondence: eight letters from Weigel to Linnaeus (17 May 1768–28 Feb 1774).
A few specimens in LINN are from Weigel, including 93.7

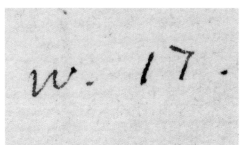

Correspondence: 52 letters (3 Feb 1759–24 Jul 1773).
Vandelli is mentioned in connection with several binomials including *Agrostis australis* L. (?84.6), *Anethum segetum* L., *Anthericum planifolium* L. ("Habitat in Lusitania trans Tagum, prope Capo de Spizel, florens Aprili. D. Vandelli"; 432.4), *Bromus geniculatus* L. (?93.24), *B. rigens* L. (?93.34), *Erythrina crista-galli* L. (888.4, comprising a drawing and a single dried flower – see p. 234), *Poa spicata* L., *Sisymbrium parra* L. and *Ulva labyrinthiformis* L., but annotations providing explicit links with some of the corresponding material in LINN are often lacking. However, other Vandelli specimens typifying Linnaean names include those for *Arenaria biflora* (585.5, see annotation below, left) and

Following page (234): This drawing, unusually mounted on a herbarium sheet along with a single flower, came to Linnaeus from Vandelli. This is the lectotype of *Erythrina crista-galli* L.

4

888·4

vandelli

Erythrina crista galli

and 93.55 (*Bromus*), 449.58 (*Juncus*), 775.6 (*Digitalis*), and 1158.107, 1158.109 and 1158.110 (*Salix*).

Zinn, Johann Gottfried (1727–1759). German. Physician and botanist, Director of the Botanic Garden in Göttingen (1753).

Correspondence: seven letters from Zinn to Linnaeus (26 Feb 1756–6 Sep 1758).

Stearn (1957: 108) reported material in LINN received from Zinn (for whom Linnaeus named the genus *Zinnia*), but it is difficult to identify any particular specimens with this provenance as none appear to be explicitly annotated to indicate such a link.

Zoëga, Johan (1742–1788). Danish. Botanist and economist. A student of Linnaeus, 1762–1764.

Correspondence: 20 letters from Zoëga to Linnaeus (8 Aug 1764–12 Jan 1771).

Zoëga was mentioned by Linnaeus in connection with

Cleome aculeata L. (850.17, see annotation above), *Scandix infesta* L. (?364.10) and *Zoegea leptaura* L. (?1028.1), each of which is typified by the associated material in LINN (given above in parentheses). Names where Zoëga was mentioned, but for which no Zoëga material could be traced, include *Arenaria balearica* L., *Bunias aegyptiaca* L., *Lichen corallinus* L., *Lichen lacteus* L. and *Lichen rupicola* L.

REFERENCES

The references listed below are those that are cited in the Introduction, Chapters 1 to 6, and the opening paragraphs of Chapter 7. In the A–Z section of the latter, and elsewhere in this book, literature references are abbreviated and self-contained.

Adams, C.D. 1987. The last plant name in Merian. *Taxon* 36: 98–99.

Adamson, R.S. 1953. Notes on nomenclature in *Lightfootia*. *J. S. African Bot.* 19: 157–159.

Allioni, C. 1760–1761. Synopsis Methodica Stirpium Horti Taurinensis. *Mélanges Philos. Math. Soc. Roy. Turin* 1760–1761: 48–76.

Alston, A.H.G. 1957. A Linnean Herbarium in Paris. *Proc. Linn. Soc. London* 168: 102–103.

Amman, J. 1739. *Stirpium rariorum in imperio Ruthene sponte provenientium icones et descriptiones.* St Petersburg.

Anonymous. 1770. *Index regni vegetabilis qui continet plantas omnes quae habentur in Linnaeani systematis editione novissima duodecima.* J.P. Kraus, Vienna.

Ardagh, J. 1934. 'Catalogue of Trees, Shrubs [&c.] in the Gardens near London,' 1730. *J. Bot.* 72: 110–111.

Arduino, P. 1764. *Animadversionum botanicarum specimen alterum.* Venice.

Artedi, P. 1738. *Ichthyologia sive opera omnia de Piscibus scilicet.* Leiden.

Arthur, J.C., Barnhart, J.H., Britton, N.L., Clements, F., Cook, O.F., Coville, F.V., Earle, F.S., Evans, A.W., Hazen, T.E., Hoolick, A., Howe, M.A., Knowlton, F.H., Moore, G.T., Rusby, H.H., Shear, C.L., Underwood, L.M., White, D. & Wight, W.F. (Nomenclature Commission). 1907. American Code of Botanical Nomenclature. *Bull. Torrey Bot. Club* 34: 167–178.

Åsborg, M. & Stearn, W.T. 1973. Linnaeus's Öland and Gotland Journey 1741: translated from the Swedish edition 1745. *Biol. J. Linn. Soc.* 5: 1–220.

Balandin, S.A., Gubanov, I.A., Jarvis, C.E., Majorov, S.R., Simenov, S.S., Sokoloff, D.D. & Sukhov, S.V. 2001. *Herbarium Linnaeanum. The Linnaean Collection of the Herbarium of Moscow State University: digital images, comments, historical review.* CD–ROM. Dehlia Co, Moscow.

Baldini, R.M. 2002. Typification in the genus *Rhamnus* L. sectio *Rhamnastrum* Rouy (Rhamnaceae): *R. pumilus* Turra and *R. alpinus* L. *Taxon* 51: 377–380.

Balle, S., Dandy, J.E., Gilmour, J.L.S., Holttum, R.E., Stearn, W.T. & Thoday, D. 1960. *Loranthus. Taxon* 9: 208–210.

Balsamo, F. 1913. Botanici e botanofili napoletani (serie 1). *Bull. Orto Bot. Regia Univ. Napoli* 3: 41–57.

Barrie, F.R. 2006. Report of the General Committee: 9. *Taxon* 55: 795–800.

Barrie, F.R., Jarvis, C.E. & Reveal, J.L. 1992a. The need to change Article 8.3 of the Code. *Taxon* 41: 508–512.

Barrie, F.R., Jarvis, C.E. & Reveal, J.L. 1992b. Two proposals to amend Article 8 of the Code. *Taxon* 41: 600–601.

Bauhin, C. 1620. *Prodromus theatri botanici.* Frankfurt am Main.

Bauhin, C. 1623. *Pinax theatri botanici.* Basel.

Bauhin, C. 1671. *Pinax theatri botanici,* ed. 2. Basel.

Bauhin, J. & Cherler, J.H. 1650–51. *Historia Plantarum Universalis,* 3 vols. Yverdon.

Baum, B.R. 1968. The problem of typifying certain names in Linnaeus's Systema Naturae ed. 10. *Taxon* 17: 507–513.

Baumann, C., Baumann, H. & Baumann-Schleihauf, S. 2001. *Die Kräuterbuchhandschrift des Leonhart Fuchs.* Ulmer, Stuttgart.

Baumann, H., Künkele, S., & Lorenz, R. 1989. Die nomenklatorischen Typen der von Linnaeus veröffentlichten Namen europäischer Orchideen. *Mitteilungsbl. Arbeitskr. Heim. Orchid. Baden-Württemberg* 21: 335–700.

Becherer, A. 1945. Notes sur deux documents linnéens conservés à Genève. *Gesnerus* 2: 141–146.

Beier, B.-A. 2005. A revision of the desert shrub *Fagonia* (Zygophyllaceae). *Syst. Biodivers.* 3: 221–263.

Belcher, R. 1994. *Senecio elegans.* In: *Flora of Australia* 49: 617. Australian Government Publishing Service, Canberra.

Bergius, P.J. 1767. *Descriptiones plantarum ex Capite Bonae Spei: cum differentiis specificis, nominibus trivialibus, et synonymis auctorum justis.* Stockholm.

Bernardi, L. 1984. Contribución a la Dendrología Paraguaya. Primera Parte. *Boissiera* 35: i–xxv, 1–341.

Bernasconi, P. & Taiz, L. 2002. Sebastian Vaillant's 1717 lecture on the structure and function of flowers. *Huntia* 11: 97–128.

Blair, P. 1718. *Botanick Essays.* London.

Blake, S.F. 1918. Notes on the Clayton herbarium. *Rhodora* 20: 21–28.

Blunt, W. 1971. *The Compleat Naturalist. A Life of Linnaeus.* Collins, London.

Bodenheimer, F.S. & Uggla, A.H. 1953. The "Album Itineris" of Frederic Hasselquist. *Svenska Linné-Sällsk. Årsskr.* 35: 18–30.

Boedijn, K.B. 1959. The Fungi in Rumphius's Herbarium Amboinense. In: de Wit, H.C.D. (ed.), *Rumphius Memorial Volume:* 289–294. Baarn.

Brandenburg, W.A., Groendijk-Wilders, N. & Jarvis, C.E. 1997. Lectotypification and description of *Clematis integrifolia* L. (Ranunculaceae). *Bot. J. Linn. Soc.* 125: 351–358.

Brenan, J.P.M. & Exell, A.W. 1957. *Acacia pennata* (L.) Willd. and its relatives in tropical Africa. *Bol. Soc. Brot.* sér. 2, 31: 99–140.

Briquet, J. 1906. *Règles internationales de la nomenclature botaniques adoptées par le Congrès International de Botanique de Vienne 1905.* G. Fischer, Jena.

Briquet, J. 1935. *International rules of botanical nomenclature, adopted by the…Congresses of Vienna, 1905, and Brussels, 1910, revised by the…Congress of Cambridge, 1930.* G. Fischer, Jena.

Britten, J. 1898. Smith's Georgian plants. *J. Bot.* 36: 297–302.

Britton, N.L. 1891. New or noteworthy North American phanerograms. V. *Bull. Torrey Bot. Club* 18: 363–370.

Britton, N.L. 1893. The North American species of the genus *Lespedeza. Trans. New York Acad. Sci.* 12: 57–68.

Britton, N.L. 1894. A revision of the genus *Lechea. Bull. Torrey Bot. Club* 21: 244–253.

Britton, N.L. & Brown, A. 1913. *An illustrated flora of the northern United States, Canada and the British possessions,* ed. 2. 3 vols. Scribner's, New York.

Broberg, G., Kilander, S. & Moberg, R. 1986. *Carl von Linné, Svensk Flora.* Forum, Stockholm.

Browne, P. 1756. *The Civil and Natural History of Jamaica.* London.

Brummitt, R.K. 1993. Report of the Committee for Spermatophyta: 38. *Taxon* 42: 687–697.

Brummitt, R.K. 1996. Report of the Committee for Spermatophyta: 44. *Taxon* 45: 671–681.

Brummitt, R.K. & Meikle, R.D. 1993. The correct Latin names for the primrose and the oxlip, *Primula vulgaris* Hudson and *P. elatior* (L.) Hill. *Watsonia* 19: 181–184.

Bryce, W.J. 2005. Russian collections in the Sloane Herbarium. *Arch. Nat. Hist.* 32: 26–33.

Burman, J. 1737 *Thesaurus Zeylanicus.* Amsterdam.

Burman, J. 1755. Index universalis in sex tomos et auctuarium herbarii Amboinensis Cl. Georgii Everhardi Rumphii. In: Rumphius, G.E., *Herbarii Amboinensis Auctuarium.* Amsterdam.

Burman, J. 1757. *Wachendorfia.* Amsterdam.

Burman, N.L. 1759. *Specimen Botanicum de Geraniis.* Leiden.

Burman, N.L. 1768. *Flora Indica.* Leiden & Amsterdam.

Burtez, A. 1899. *Catalogue des Plantes constituant l'herbier de L. Gérard précédé d'une analyse de l'oeuvre de ce Botaniste.* Draguignan.

Burtt, B.L. 1988. In: Hilliard, O.M. & Burtt, B.L. Notes on some plants of southern Africa chiefly from Natal: XIV. *Notes Roy. Bot. Gard. Edinburgh* 45: 77–94.

Burtt, B.L. 2001. Tournefort in Turkey (1701–1702). *Karaca Arbor. Mag.* 6: 45–62.

Burtt, B.L. 2002. Tournefort in Turkey (1701–1702), Part 2. *Karaca Arbor. Mag.* 6: 137–146.

Burtt, B.L. & Lewis, P. 1949. On the flora of Kuwait: 1. *Kew Bull.* 4: 273–308.

Callmer, C. & Gertz, O. 1954. Om illustrationerna till Hortus Cliffortianus. *Svenska Linné-Sällsk. Årsskr.* 36: 81–88.

Candolle, A.L. de 1867. *Lois de la Nomenclature botanique adoptées par le Congrès…à Paris en Août 1867.* Paris.

Caramiello, R. & Forneris, G. 2004. *Le opere minori di Carlo Allioni dal Rariorum Pedemontii Stirpium all'Auctarium ad Floram Pedemontanam.* Olschki, Florence.

Catesby, M. 1731–47. *The natural history of Carolina, Florida and the Bahama islands &c.* 2 vols, App. London.

Clarke, C.B. 1881. Commelinaceae. In: Candolle, A.L. de & Candolle, A.C.P. de, *Monographiae Phanerogamarum* 3: 113–324. G. Masson, Paris.

Clarke, C.B. 1894. On certain authentic Cyperaceae of Linnaeus. *J. Linn. Soc., Bot.* 30: 299–315.

Commelin, C. 1701. *Horti Medici Amstelodamensis rariorum tam orientalis quam occidentalis Indiae aliarumque peregrinarum Plantarum…descriptio et icones…pars altera.* Amsterdam.

Commelin, J. 1697. *Horti Medici Amstelodamensis rariorum tam orientalis quam occidentalis Indiae aliarumque peregrinarum Plantarum…descriptio et icones…Opus posthumum.* Amsterdam.

Cristóbal, C.L. 2001. Taxonomía del género *Helicteres* (Sterculiaceae). Revisión de las especies Americanas. *Bonplandia* 11: 1–206.

Dal Vesco, G. 1985–1986. Tipi nell'erbario Allioni. *Allionia* 27: 91–99.

Dal Vesco, G., Forneris, G. & Pistarino, A. 1987–88. "Loci classici" e tipi nelle opera e negli erbari di Allioni e di Balbis. *Allionia* 28: 5–20.

Dalibard, T.F. 1749. *Florae Parisiensis Prodromus.* Paris.

Dandy, J.E. 1958. *The Sloane Herbarium. An annotated list of the Horti Sicci composing it: with biographical accounts of the principal contributors.* British Museum (Natural History), London.

Dandy, J.E. 1967. Index of generic names of vascular plants 1753–1774. *Regnum Veg.* 51: 1–130.

De Beer, G.R. 1947. Edmund Davall, F.L.S., an unwritten English chapter in the history of Swiss botany. *Proc. Linn. Soc. London*, sess. 159: 42–65.

De Beer, G.R. 1955. The Dick Herbarium. *J. Linn. Soc., Bot.* 55: 320–332.

Del Carratore, F., Garbari, F. & Jarvis, C. 1998. The application of the Linnaean names *Salvia pratensis, S. agrestis, S. haematodes, S. verbenaca* and *S. clandestina. Pl. Biosystems* 132: 169–176.

de Wit, H.C.D. 1959. A checklist to Rumphius's Herbarium Amboinense. In: de Wit, H.C.D. (ed.), *Rumphius Memorial Volume*: 339–460. Baarn.

Dillenius, J.J. 1732. *Hortus Elthamensis, seu Plantarum rariorum quas in horto suo Elthami in Cantio coluit.* London.

Dillenius, J.J. 1741. *Index Muscorum.* Oxford.

Dodoëns, R. 1616. *Stirpium historiae pemptades sex sive libri xxx.* Antwerp.

Druce, G.C. & Vines, S.H. 1907. *The Dillenian Herbaria: an account of the Dillenian collections in the Herbarium of the University of Oxford, together with a biographical sketch of Dillenius, selections from his correspondence, notes, &c.* Clarendon Press, Oxford.

Edmondson, J. 2004. In Cafferty, S. & Jarvis, C.E. (eds), Typification of Linnaean plant names in Boraginaceae. *Taxon* 53: 799–805.

Ehrendorfer, F. 1962. Notizen zur Systematik und Phylogonie von *Cruciata* Mill. und verwandten Gattungen der Rubiaceae. *Ann. Naturhist. Mus. Wien* 65: 11–20.

Elven, R. & Nordal, I. 2002. *Cochlearia groenlandica.* In: Jonsell, B. & Jarvis, C.E., Lectotypification of Linnaean Names for *Flora Nordica* (Brassicaceae–Apiaceae). *Nordic J. Bot.* 22: 67–86.

Epling, C. 1929. Notes on the Linnean types of American Labiatae. *J. Bot.* 67: 1–12.

Farjon, A. 2005. Conifers in Species Plantarum, an evaluation of taxonomic concepts. *Symb. Bot. Upsal.* 33(3): 92–97.

Farr, E.R. & Zijlstra, G. 2007 (continuously updated). *Index Nominum Genericorum* http://ravenel.si.edu/botany/ing

Fawcett, W. & Rendle, A.B. 1910. *Flora of Jamaica: containing descriptions of the flowering plants known from the island*, vol. 1. British Museum (Natural History), London.

Fawcett, W. & Rendle, A.B. 1914. *Flora of Jamaica: containing descriptions of the flowering plants known from the island*, vol. 3. British Museum (Natural History), London.

Fawcett, W. & Rendle, A.B. 1920. *Flora of Jamaica: containing descriptions of the flowering plants known from the island*, vol. 4. British Museum (Natural History), London.

Fawcett, W. & Rendle, A.B. 1926. *Flora of Jamaica: containing descriptions of the flowering plants known from the island*, vol. 5. British Museum (Natural History), London.

Fawcett, W. & Rendle, A.B. 1936. *Flora of Jamaica: containing descriptions of the flowering plants known from the island*, vol. 7. British Museum (Natural History), London.

Fernald, M.L. 1931. *Potentilla canadensis* and *P. simplex. Rhodora* 33: 180–191.

Fernald, M.L. 1950. A small fascicle of novelties. *Rhodora* 52: 61–71.

Fischer, E. 1997. Notulae ad Floram Germanicam II. *Feddes Repert.* 108: 111–117.

Forneris, G. 2004. *L'Erbario dell'Università di Torino. Pagine di storia e di iconografia nelle collezioni botaniche.* Università degli Studi di Torino, Torino.

Forster, J.R. 1771. *A Voyage to China and the East Indies &c.* [by Peter Osbeck]. Benjamin White, London.

Franks, J. 2005. Reports to the Swedish East India Company: the Indian and eastern years (1748–62) of Christopher Henrik Braad. *Linnean* 21(1): 30–33; 21(2): 17–20; 21(3): 35–41.

Freer, S. 2003. *Linnaeus' Philosophia botanica.* Oxford University Press, Oxford.

Fries, E.M. 1821. *Systema Mycologicum: sistens Fungorum ordines, genera et species huc usque cognitas, &c.* Lund & Greifswald.

Fries, I., Fries, S. & Jacobsson, R. 2003. Carl Linnaeus. Iter Lapponicum. Lappländska resan 1732. II. Kommentardel. *Acta Regiae Societatis Skytteanae* 54(B): 1–532.

Fries, R.E. 1935. Linné-växter i Bergii herbarium. *Svenska Linné-Sällsk. Årsskr.* 18: 109–123.

Fries, S. & Jacobsson, R. 2005. Carl Linnaeus. Iter Lapponicum. Lappländska resan 1732. III. Facsimileutgåva. *Acta Regiae Societatis Skytteanae* 54(C): 1–146.

Fries, T.M. 1862. Anteckningar rörande en i Paris befintlig Linneanska herbarium. *Öfversigt Kongl. Vetensk. Akad. Förh.* 18: 255–272.

Fries, T.M. 1903. *Linné: Lefnadsteckning af T.M. Fries.* Fahlcrantz & Co., Stockholm.

Fuchs, H.P. 1962. Nomenklatur, Taxonomie und Systematik der Gattung *Isoëtes* Linnaeus in geschichtlicher Betrachtung. *Beih. Nova Hedwigia* 3: 1–130.

Gage, A.T. & Stearn, W.T. 1988. *A bicentenary history of the Linnean Society of London.* Academic Press, London.

Garbari, F., Tongiorgi Tomasi, L. & Tosi, A. 1991. *Giardino dei Semplici: l'Orto Botanico di Pisa dal XVI al XX secolo.* Cassa di Risparmio, Pisa.

Garbari, F., Tongiorgi Tomasi, L. & Tosi, A. 2002. *Giardino dei Semplici. Garden of Simples.* Edizioni Plus, Pisa.

Ghafoor, A. 1978. In: Jafri, S.M.H. & El-Gadi, A. (eds). *Flora of Libya* 63: 1–59. Department of Botany, Al Faateh University, Tripoli.

Gouan, A. 1762. *Hortus Regius Monspeliensis.* Lyon.

Gray, A. 1840a. Notices of European herbaria, particularly those most interesting to the North American botanist. *North Amer. Sci.* 40: 1–9.

Gray, A. 1840b. In: Torrey, J. & Gray, A., *A Flora of North America*, vol. 1. New York.

Gray, A. 1881a. *Clematis coccinea. Curtis's Bot. Mag.* 107: t. 6594.

Gray, A. 1881b. A Chinese puzzle by Linnaeus. *J. Bot.* 19: 325–326.

Gray, A. 1882. Contributions to North American botany. *Proc. Amer. Acad. Arts* 16: 163–230.

Greene, E.L. 1899. Early specific types in *Chamaecrista. Pittonia* 4: 25–32.

Greuter, W. 1989. *Primula acaulis, Primula elatior* and the "Flora Anglica" of Linnaeus. *Candollea* 44: 562–567.

Greuter, W., Barrie, F.R., Burdet, H.M., Chaloner, W.G., Demoulin, V., Hawksworth, D.L., Jørgensen, P.M., Nicolson, D.H., Silva, P.C., Trehane, P. & McNeill, J. 1994. International Code of Botanical Nomenclature (Tokyo Code). *Regnum Veg.* 131: 1–389.

Greuter, W., Burdet, H.M., Chaloner, W.G., Demoulin, V., Grolle, R., Hawksworth, D.L., Nicolson, D.H., Silva, P.C., Stafleu, F.A., Voss, E.G. & McNeill, J. 1988. International Code of Botanical Nomenclature (Berlin Code). *Regnum Veg.* 118: 1–328.

Greuter, W., McNeill, J., Barrie, F.R., Burdet, H.M., Demoulin, V., Filgueiras, T.S., Nicolson, D.H., Silva, P.C., Skog, J.E., Trehane, P., Turland, N.J. & Hawksworth, D.L. 2000. International Code of Botanical Nomenclature (Saint Louis Code). *Regnum Veg.* 138: 1–474.

Gronovius, J.F. 1739. *Flora Virginica.* Leiden.

Gronovius, J.F. 1743. *Flora Virginica*, Pars Secunda. Leiden.

Hagberg, K. 1952. *Carl Linnaeus.* Jonathan Cape, London.

Haller, A. 1740. *Iter Helveticum.* Göttingen.

Hanelt, P., Schultze-Motel, J. & Jarvis, C.E. 1983. Proposal to conserve *Triticum aestivum* L. (1753) against *Triticum hybernum* L. (1753) (Gramineae). *Taxon* 32: 492–498.

Hansen, C. & Fox Maule, A. 1973. Pehr Osbeck's collections and Linnaeus's Species Plantarum (1753). *Bot. J. Linn. Soc.* 67: 189–212.

Harley, R.M. 1982. A taxonomic revision of the genus *Origanum* (Labiatae) [book review]. *Watsonia* 14: 86–87.

Hasselquist, F. 1757. *Iter Palaestinum, eller Resa til Heliga Landet förrättad ifrån År 1749 til 1752 &c.* Stockholm.

Hasselquist, F. 1766. *Voyages and travels in the Levant &c.* London.

Hawksworth, D.L. 1976. Introduction. In: Micheli, P. *Nova Plantarum Genera.* Facsimile edition. Richmond Publishing Co. Ltd, Richmond, Surrey.

Hawksworth, D.L. 2004. Rediscovery of the original material of Osbeck's *Lichen chinensis* and the re-instatement of the name *Parmotrema perlatum* (Parmeliaceae). *Herzogia* 17: 37–44.

Hedge, I.C. 1967. The specimens of Paul Dietrich Giseke in the Edinburgh Herbarium. *Notes Roy. Bot. Gard. Edinburgh* 28: 73–86.

Hellbom, A., Fries, S. & Jacobsson, R. 2003. Carl Linnaeus. Iter Lapponicum. Lappländska resan 1732. I. Dagboken. *Acta Regiae Societatis Skytteanae* 54(A): i–xviii, 1–200.

Heller, J.L. 1959. Index auctorum et librorum a Linnaeo (Species Plantarum, 1753) citatorum. In: Linnaeus, C., *Species Plantarum, A Facsimile of the first edition, 1753*, vol. 2: 3–60. Ray Society, London.

Heller, J.L. 1964. The early history of binomial nomenclature. *Huntia* 1: 33–70.

Heller, J.L. & Stearn, W.T. 1959. An Appendix to the Species Plantarum of Carl Linnaeus. In: Linnaeus, C., *Species Plantarum, A Facsimile of the first edition, 1753*, vol. 2: 1–148. Ray Society, London.

Hepper, F.N. & Friis, I. 1994. The plants of Per Forsskal's 'Flora Aegyptiaco-Arabica' : collected on the Royal Danish Expedition to Egypt and the Yemen 1761–63. Royal Botanic Gardens, Kew and Botanical Museum, Copenhagen.

Hermann, P. 1698. *Paradisus Batavus, continens plus centum plantas...aere incisas & descriptionibus illustratas.* Leiden.

Hermann, P. 1717. *Musaeum Zeylanicum, sive Catalogus plantarum in Zeylana sponte nascentium observatarum & descriptarum.* Leiden.

Hermann, P. 1726. *Musaeum Zeylanicum, sive Catalogus plantarum in Zeylana sponte nascentium observatarum & descriptarum.* Leiden.

Hertel, H. & Schreiber, A. 1988. Die botanische Staatssammlung München 1813–1988. (Eine Übersicht über die Sammlungsbestande). *Mitt. Bot. Staatssamml. München* 26: 81–512.

Hinz, P.-A. 2001. The Japanese plant collection of Engelbert Kaempfer (1651–1716) in the Sir Hans Sloane Herbarium at The Natural History Museum, London. *Bull. Nat. Hist. Mus. London, Bot.* 31: 27–34.

Hitchcock, A.S. 1905. North American species of *Agrostis. Bull. Bur. Pl. Industr. U.S.D.A.* 68: 1–68.

Hitchcock, A.S. & Green, M.L. 1929. Standard-species of Linnean genera of Phanerogamae (1753–54). In: *International Botanical Congress. Cambridge (England), 1930: Nomenclature. Proposals by British botanists*: 110–199. H.M.S.O., London.

Holmgren, P.K. & Holmgren, N.H. 2007 (continuously updated). *Index Herbariorum*. New York Botanical Garden. http://sweetgum.nybg.org/ih/

Hoppe, B. 2003. *Zeichnungen japanischer Pflanzen (Originalmanuskript in der British Library, London, Signatur 2914)*. Engelbert Kaempfer Werke, Band 3. Iudicium, München.

Howard, R.A. & Staples, G.W. 1983. The modern names for Catesby's plants. *J. Arnold Arbor.* 64: 511–546.

Howe, M.A. 1897. The North American species of *Porella*. *Bull. Torrey Bot. Club* 24: 512–528.

Hudson, W. 1762. *Flora Anglica*. London.

Hulth, J.M. 1907. *Bibliographia Linnaeana: matériaux pour servir à une bibliographie Linnéenne*. Almqvist & Wiksell, Uppsala.

Hunt, D. 1989. Notes on *Selenicereus* (A. Berger) Britton and Rose and *Aporocactus* Lemaire (Cactaceae: Hylocereinae). *Bradleya* 7: 89–96.

Jackson, B.D. 1912. Index to the Linnean Herbarium with indication of the types of species marked by Carl von Linné. *Proc. Linn. Soc. London*, sess. 124: Suppl., 1–152.

Jackson, B.D. 1916a. An unpublished letter to Linné. *J. Bot.* 54: 360.

Jackson, B.D. 1916b. Bref och skrifvelser af och till Carl von Linné [book review]. *J. Bot.* 54: 372–373.

Jackson, B.D. 1918. Correspondence between Carl von Linné and C. Rijk Tulbagh. *Proc. Linn. Soc. London*, sess. 130: Suppl., 1–13.

Jackson, B.D. 1922. Notes on a catalogue of the Linnean herbarium. *Proc. Linn. Soc. London*, sess. 134: 1–38.

Jackson, B.D. 1923. *Linnaeus (afterwards Carl von Linné): the story of his life, adapted from the Swedish of Theodor Magnus Fries*. H.F. & G. Witherby, London.

Jacquin, N.J. 1760. *Enumeratio systematica plantarum, quas in Insulis Caribaeis vicinaque Americes continente detexit novas, aut jam cognitas emendavit*. Leiden.

Jacquin, N.J. 1762. *Enumeratio Stirpium plerarumque, quae sponte crescunt in agro Vindobonensi, montibusque confinibus: accedunt observationum centuria et appendix de paucis exoticis*. Vienna.

Jacquin, N.J. 1763. *Selectarum stirpium Americanarum historia &c.* Vienna.

Janzen, D.H. 1974. Swollen-thorn Acacias of Central America. *Smithsonian Contr. Bot.* 13: 1–131.

Jarvis, C.E. 1991. An undescribed Hortus Siccus of eighteenth century Swedish herbarium material in the Museo Botanico, Università di Firenze. *Webbia* 45: 103–115.

Jarvis, C.E. 1992. Art. 7.15 and the lectotypification of Linnaean names – a reply to Heath. *Taxon* 41: 63–64.

Jarvis, C.E. 1993. The influence of some Italian Botanic Gardens on Linnaeus' knowledge of the world's flora. *Museol. Sci.* 9: 155–169.

Jarvis, C.E. 2005. From Siberia to South Africa; Surinam to Sri Lanka – Linnaean names and their types. *Symb. Bot. Upsal.* 33(3): 23–33.

Jarvis, C.E., Ivimey-Cook, R.B. & Cannon, P.F. 1983. Proposal to reject *Ononis spinosa* Linnaeus (Leguminosae). *Taxon* 32: 314–316.

Jarvis, C.E. & Jonsell, B. 2003. Förteckning över växterna i Linnés lapplandsherbarium. In: Fries, I., Fries, S. & Jacobsson, R., Carl Linnaeus. Iter Lapponicum. II. Kommentardel. *Acta Regiae Societatis Skytteanae* 54(B): 377–391.

Jarvis, C.E., Majorov, S., Sokoloff, D., Balandin, S., Gubanov, I.A. & Simonov, S.S. 2002 [2001]. The typification of *Astragalus physodes* L. based on material in the Herbarium of Moscow University (MW), and the discovery of an isolectotype of *Phlox sibirica* L. *Taxon* 50: 1129–1135.

Jarvis, C.E., Stace, C.A. & Wilkinson, M.J. 1987. Typification of *Festuca rubra* L., *F. ovina* L. and *F. ovina* var. *vivipara* L. *Watsonia* 16: 299–302.

Jonsell, B. 2003. Linnés lapplandsherbarium. In: Fries, I., Fries, S. & Jacobsson, R., Carl Linnaeus. Iter Lapponicum. II. Kommentardel. *Acta Regiae Societatis Skytteanae* 54(B): 373–376.

Jonsell, B. & Jarvis, C.E. 2002. Lectotypification of Linnaean Names for Flora Nordica (Brassicaceae–Apiaceae). *Nordic J. Bot.* 22: 67–86.

Jørgensen, P.M., James, P.W. & Jarvis, C.E. 1994. The typification of the lichen names described by Linnaeus. *Bot. J. Linn. Soc.* 115: 261–405.

Juel, H.O. 1918. Bemerkungen über Hasselquist's Herbarium. *Svenska Linné-Sällsk. Årsskr.* 1: 95–125.

Juel, H.O. 1920. Early Investigations of North American Flora, with special reference to Linnaeus and Kalm. *Svenska Linné-Sällsk. Årsskr.* 3: 61–79.

Juel, H.O. 1921. A Revision of Kalm's Herbarium in Upsala. *Svenska Linné-Sällsk. Årsskr.* 4: 16–23.

Juel, H.O. 1923. Studien in Burser's Hortus siccus. *Nova Acta Regiae Soc. Sci. Upsal.*, ser. 4, 5(7): i–xvi, 1–144.

Juel, H.O. 1931a. Förteckning över i Uppsala förvarade herbarieexemplar med påskrifter av Linnés hand. *Svenska Linné-Sällsk. Årsskr.* 14: 12–16.

Juel, H.O. 1931b. The French Apothecary's plants in Burser's herbarium. *Rhodora* 33: 177–179.

Juel, H.O. 1936. Joachim Burser's Hortus Siccus. *Symb. Bot. Upsal.* 2(1): 1–187.

Juel, H.O. & Harshberger, J.W. 1929. New light on the collection of North American Plants by Peter Kalm. *Proc. Acad. Nat. Sci. Philadelphia* 81: 297–303.

Kaempfer, E. 1712. *Amoenitarum exoticarum politico-physico-medicarum fasciculi V, quibus continentur variae relationes, observationes & descriptiones rerum Persicarum et ulterioris Asiae, &c.* Lemgo.

Kalm, P. 1966. *The America of 1750. Peter Kalm's travels in North America: the English version of 1770 revised from the original Swedish and edited by Adolph B. Benson.* Dover Publications, New York.

Karavaev, M.N. & Barsukova, A.V. 1968. Friedrich Ehrhart's botanical collections in the Moscow University. *Byull. Moskovsk. Obshch. Isp. Prir., Otd. Biol.* 73(3): 137–139. [In Russian].

Karavaev, M.N. & Gubanov, I.A. 1981. Reliquiae of Karl Linné in the Herbarium of the Moscow University. *Byull. Moskovsk. Obshch. Isp. Prir., Otd. Biol.* 86(3): 79–85. [In Russian].

Kerguélen, M. 1975. Les Gramineae (Poaceae) de la flore française. Essai de mise point taxonomique et nomenclaturale. *Lejeunia,* n.s., 75: 1–343.

Kiger, R.W., Tancin, C.A. & Bridson, G.D.R. 1999. *Index to Scientific Names of Organisms Cited in the Linnaean Dissertations together with a Synoptic Bibliography of the Dissertations and a Concordance for Selected Editions.* Hunt Institute for Botanical Documentation, Carnegie Mellon University, Pittsburgh.

Kippist, R. 1865. *Senecio elegans.* In: Harvey, W.H. & Sonder, O.W., *Flora Capensis* 3: 361. Hodges, Smith & Co, Dublin.

Kirk, P.M. 1986. (815) Proposal to conserve *Mucor* Fresenius over *Mucor* Micheli ex L. and (816) Proposal to conserve *Rhizopus* Ehrenberg over *Ascophora* Tode (Fungi) with notes on the nomenclature and taxonomy of *Mucor, Ascophora, Hydrophora* and *Rhizopus. Taxon* 35: 371–377.

Knapp, S. & Jarvis, C.E. 1991. The typification of the names of New World *Solanum* species described by Linnaeus. *Bot. J. Linn. Soc.* 104: 325–367.

Knapp, S., Lamas, G., Nic Lughadha, E. & Novarino, G. 2004. Stability or stasis in the names of organisms: the evolving codes of nomenclature. *Phil. Trans. Roy. Soc. London,* Ser. B, 359: 611–622.

Kukkonen, I. & Viljamaa, K. 1973. Linnaean specimens in the Botanical Museum of the University of Helsinki. *Ann. Bot. Fenn.* 10: 309–336.

Lack, H.W. 2000. *A Garden for Eternity: the Codex Liechtenstein.* Benteli, Bern.

Lack, H.W. 2003. Zwei wenig bekannte Herbarien von Silvio Boccone OCist in der Österreichischen Nationalbibliothek. *Ann. Naturhist. Mus. Wien* 104 B: 443–462.

Lack, H.W. 2005. Species Plantarum – the grand syntheses from Linnaeus to Engler. *Symb. Bot. Upsal.* 33(3): 35–46.

Lack, H.W. & Wagner, D. 1984. Das Herbar Ullepitsch. *Willdenowia* 14: 417–433.

Legré, L. 1900. *La Botanique en Provence au XVIe siècle.* Marseille.

Lellinger, D.B. & Proctor, G.R. 1983. The ascriptions of Plumier's fern plates. *Taxon* 32: 565–571.

Lewis, G.J. & Obermeyer, A.A. 1972. *Gladiolus,* a revision of the South African species. *J. S. African Bot.,* Suppl. 10: 1–316.

Lindberg, H. 1958. Växter, kända från Norden, i Linnés herbarium. Plantae e septentrione cognitae in herbario Linnaei. *Acta Bot. Fenn.* 60: 1–133.

Lindman, C.A.M. 1908. A Linnaean herbarium in the Natural History Museum in Stockholm. I. Monandria–Tetrandria. *Ark. Bot.* 7(3): 1–57.

Lindman, C.A.M. 1910. A Linnaean herbarium in the Natural History Museum in Stockholm. II. Pentandria. *Ark. Bot.* 9(6): 1–50.

Linnaeus, C. 1735. *Systema Naturae.* Leiden.

Linnaeus, C. 1736. *Musa Cliffortiana.* Leiden.

Linnaeus, C. 1736. *Fundamenta Botanica.* Amsterdam.

Linnaeus, C. 1736. *Bibliotheca Botanica.* Amsterdam.

Linnaeus, C. 1737. *Flora Lapponica.* Amsterdam.

Linnaeus, C. 1737. *Critica Botanica.* Leiden.

Linnaeus, C. 1737. *Genera Plantarum.* Leiden.

Linnaeus, C. 1738. *Hortus Cliffortianus.* Amsterdam.

Linnaeus, C. 1738. *Classes Plantarum.* Leiden.

Linnaeus, C. 1740. *Systema Naturae,* ed. 2. Stockholm.

Linnaeus, C. 1742. *Genera Plantarum,* ed. 2. Leiden.

Linnaeus, C. 1745. *Flora Suecica.* Stockholm.

Linnaeus, C. 1745. *Öländska och Gothländska Resa.* Stockholm & Uppsala.

Linnaeus, C. 1746. *Sponsalia Plantarum* [dissertation of J.G. Wahlbom]. Stockholm.

Linnaeus, C. 1747. *Flora Zeylanica.* Amsterdam.

Linnaeus, C. 1747. *Wästgöta Resa.* Stockholm.

Linnaeus, C. 1747. *Flora Zeylanica.* Amsterdam.

Linnaeus, C. 1748. *Hortus Upsaliensis.* Stockholm.

Linnaeus, C. 1749. *Materia Medica.* Stockholm.

Linnaeus, C. 1749. *Pan Suecicus* [dissertation of N.L. Hesselgren]. Uppsala.

Linnaeus, C. 1749–1790. *Amoenitates Academicae,* 10 vols.

Linnaeus, C. 1750. *Plantae Rariores Camschatcenses* [dissertation of J.P. Halenius]. Uppsala.

Linnaeus, C. 1751a. *Philosophia Botanica.* Stockholm.

Linnaeus, C. 1751b. *Skånska Resa.* Stockholm.

Linnaeus, C. 1753. *Species Plantarum.* Stockholm.

Linnaeus, C. 1754. *Flora Anglica* [dissertation of I.O. Grufberg]. Uppsala.

Linnaeus, C. 1754. *Genera Plantarum,* ed. 5. Stockholm.

Linnaeus, C. 1754. *Herbarium Amboinense* [dissertation of O. Stickman]. Uppsala.

Linnaeus, C. 1755. *Centuria I Plantarum* [dissertation of A.D. Juslenius]. Uppsala.

Linnaeus, C. 1755. *Flora Suecica*, ed. 2. Stockholm.

Linnaeus, C. 1756. *Centuria II Plantarum* [dissertation of E. Torner]. Uppsala.

Linnaeus, C. 1756. *Flora Palaestina* [dissertation of B.J. Strand]. Uppsala.

Linnaeus, C. 1756. *Flora Monspeliensis* [dissertation of T.E. Nathorst]. Uppsala.

Linnaeus, C. 1758. *Systema Naturae*, ed. 10, vol. 1. Stockholm.

Linnaeus, C. 1759a. *Systema Naturae*, ed. 10, vol. 2. Stockholm.

Linnaeus, C. 1759b. Flora Monspeliensis. *Amoenitates Academicae* 4: 468–495. Stockholm.

Linnaeus, C. 1759c. *Plantarum Jamaicensium Pugillus* [dissertation of G. Elmgren]. Uppsala.

Linnaeus, C. 1759d. *Flora Jamaicensis* [dissertation of C.G. Sandmark]. Uppsala.

Linnaeus, C. 1760. *Plantae Rariores Africanae* [dissertation of J. Printz]. Stockholm.

Linnaeus, C. 1762. *Species Plantarum*, ed. 2, vol. 1. Uppsala.

Linnaeus, C. 1763. *Species Plantarum*, ed. 2, vol. 2. Uppsala.

Linnaeus, C. 1767a. *Systema Naturae*, ed. 12, vol. 2. Stockholm.

Linnaeus, C. 1767b. *Mantissa Plantarum [Prima]*. Stockholm.

Linnaeus, C. 1770. *De Erica* [dissertation of J.A. Dahlgren Ebbeson]. Uppsala.

Linnaeus, C. 1771. *Mantissa Plantarum Altera*. Stockholm.

Linnaeus, C. 1774. *Systema Vegetabilium*, ed. 13 [Murray, J.A. (ed.)]. Göttingen & Gotha.

Linnaeus, C. 1775. *Plantae Surinamenses* [dissertation of J. Alm]. Uppsala.

Linnaeus, C. 1776. *Hypericum* [dissertation of C.N. Hellenius]. Uppsala.

Linnaeus filius, C. 1762. *Decas prima plantarum rariorum Horti Upsaliensis, sistens descriptiones & figuras plantarum minus cognitarum*. Stockholm.

Linnaeus filius, C. 1782. *Supplementum plantarum systematis vegetabilium editionis decimae tertiae, Generum plantarum editionis sextae, et Specierum plantarum editionis secundae*. Braunschweig.

Löfling, P. 1758. *Iter Hispanicum, eller Resa til Spanska Länderna uti Europa och America, förrättad ifrån år 1751 til år 1756, med Beskrifningar och rön öfver de märkvärdigaste Växter*. Stockholm.

López González, G. 2003–2004. Los géneros *Minuartia* Loefl. ex L. y *Queria* Loefl. ex L. (Caryophyllaceae). *Anales Jard. Bot. Madrid* 60: 429–434

Louis, A. 1957. Biografische gegevens over de botanicus Matthias de l'Obel. *Biol. Jaarb.* 24: 183–206.

Lourteig, A. 1966. L'herbier de Paul Hermann, base du Thesaurus Zeylanicus de Johan Burman. *Taxon* 15: 23–33.

Lundqvist, S. & Moberg, R. 1993. The Pehr Kalm Herbarium in UPS, a collection of North American plants. *Thunbergia* 19: 1–62.

Magnol, P. 1676. *Botanicum Monspeliense*. Lyon.

Magnol, P. 1686. *Botanicum Monspeliense*. Lyon.

Magnol, P. 1688. *Botanicum Monspeliense*. Lyon.

Manktelow, M. 2001. Linnés Hammarby – ett blommande kulturarv. *Svensk Bot. Tidskr.* 95: 251–313.

Manktelow, M. & Nyberg, K. 2005. Linnaeus' Apostles and the development of the Species Plantarum. *Symb. Bot. Upsal.* 33(3): 73–80.

Marner, S. 1996. Herbaria, Department of Plant Sciences, University of Oxford, on microfiche. *Taxon* 45: 409–410.

Mazzi, G. 1985. Note sull'Erbario Micheli e sul suo valore scientifico. *Webbia* 48: 85–96.

Mazzi, G. & Moggi, G. 1991. L'Erbario di Pier Antonio Micheli: saggio di analisi critica. *Museol. Sci.* 7: 59–98.

McClintock, E. & Epling, C. 1942. A review of the genus *Monarda* (Labiatae). *Univ. California Publ. Bot.* 20: 147–194.

McNeill, J., Barrie, F.R., Burdet, H.M., Demoulin, V., Hawksworth, D.L., Marhold, K., Nicolson, D.H., Prado, J., Silva, P.C., Skog, J.E., Wiersema, J.H. & Turland, N.J. 2006. International Code of Botanical Nomenclature (Vienna Code). *Regnum Veg.* 146: 1–568.

McNeill, J., Odell, E.A., Consaul, L.L. & Katz, D.S. 1987. American Code and later lectotypifications of Linnaean generic names dating from 1753: a case study of discrepancies. *Taxon* 36: 350–401.

Merrill, E.D. 1916. Osbeck's Dagbok öfwer en Ostindsk Resa. *Amer. J. Bot.* 3: 571–588.

Merrill, E.D. 1917. *An interpretation of Rumphius's Herbarium Amboinense*. Manila.

Merrill, E.D. 1921. A review of the new species of plants proposed by N.L. Burman in his Flora Indica. *Philipp. J. Sci.* 19: 329–388.

Merrill, E.D. 1945. On the underground parts of *Tacca pinnatifida* J.R. & G. Forst. (1776) = *Tacca leontopetaloides* (Linn.) O. Kuntze. *J. Arnold Arbor.* 26: 85–92, pl. I, II.

Miller, P. 1759. *The Gardeners Dictionary*, ed. 7. London.

Miller, P. 1768. *The Gardeners Dictionary*, ed. 8. London.

Molina, A.M. & Rúgolo de Agrasar, Z.E. 2004. Revision taxonomíca de las especies del género *Chloris* (Poaceae: Chloridoideae) en Sudamerica. *Candollea* 59: 347–428.

Morton, A.G. 1986. *John Hope, 1725–1786: Scottish botanist*. Edinburgh Botanic Garden (Sibbald) Trust, Edinburgh.

Nelson, E.C. 1997. Patrick Browne's The civil and natural history of Jamaica (1756, 1789). *Arch. Nat. Hist.* 24: 327–336.

Nelson, E.C. 2000. Patrick Browne (ca. 1720–1790), Irish physician, historian and Caribbean botanist: a brief biography with an account of his lost medical dissertations. *Huntia* 11: 5–16.

Nickelsen, K. 2006. Draughtsmen, botanists and nature: the construction of eighteenth-century botanical illustrations. *Archimedes* 15: 1–295.

Nicolson, D.H. 1991. A history of botanical nomenclature. *Ann. Missouri Bot. Gard.* 78: 33–56.

Nicolson, D.H. & Sivadasan, M. 1981. Four frequently confused species of *Typhonium* Schott (Araceae). *Blumea* 27: 483–497.

Nicolson, D.H., Suresh, C.R. & Manilal, K.S. 1988. An interpretation of Van Rheede's Hortus Malabaricus. *Regnum Veg.* 119: 1–378.

Nielsen, I. 1981. In: Aubréville, A. & Leroy, J.-F., *Flore du Cambodge du Laos et du Viêt-Nam* 19: 1–159.

Nordenstam, B. 1961. Notes on some Linnaean dissertations. *Bot. Not.* 114: 276–280.

Nordenstam, B. 1968. The genus *Euryops*. Part 1. Taxonomy. *Opera Bot.* 20: 1–409.

Nordenstam, B. 1991. Olof Swarz. In: Jonsell, B. (ed.), *Bergianska botanister. Berginska stiftelsen och dess professorer under första seklet*: 23–43. Atlantis, Stockholm.

Nyström, E. 2005. Species Plantarum and Linnaeus' correspondence network. *Symb. Bot. Upsal.* 33(3): 61–71.

Oliver, E.G.H. & Oliver, I.M. 2002. The genus *Erica* (Ericaceae) in southern Africa: taxonomic notes 1. *Bothalia* 32: 37–61.

Oost, E.H., Brandenburg, W.A. & Jarvis, C.E. 1989. Typification of *Brassica oleracea* L. (Cruciferae) and its Linnaean varieties. *Bot. J. Linn. Soc.* 100: 329–345.

Ortega Olivencia, A. & Devesa Alcaraz, J.A. 1993. Revision del género *Scrophularia* L. (Scrophulariaceae) en la Península Ibérica e Islas Baleares. *Ruizia* 11: 1–157.

Osbeck, P. 1757. *Dagbok öfver en Ostindisk Resa &c.* Stockholm.

Oswald, P.H. & Nelson, E.C. 2000. Jamaican plant genera named by Patrick Browne (ca. 1720–1790): a checklist with an attempt at an etymology. *Huntia* 11: 17–30.

Park, K. 1998. Monograph of *Euphorbia* sect. *Tithymalopsis* (Euphorbiaceae). *Edinburgh J. Bot.* 55: 161–208.

Pelayo López, F. (ed.) 1990. *Pehr Löfling y la Expedición al Orinoco 1754–1761.* Turner, Madrid.

Persoon, C.H. 1801. *Synopsis methodica Fungorum, sistens enumerationem omnium huc usque detectarum specierum, cum brevibus descriptionibus nec non synonymis et observationibus selectis.* Göttingen.

Peterson, P.M., Valdes Reyna, J. & Ortiz Diaz, J.J. 2004. *Sporobolus* (Poaceae: Chloridoideae: Cynodonteae: Zoysieae: Sporobolinae) from northeastern Mexico. *Sida* 21: 553–589.

Pistarino, A., Forneris, G. & Jarvis, C. 1992. Lectotypification of *Campanula barbata* L. and *C. cenisia* L. (Campanulaceae). *Taxon* 51: 547–550.

Plukenet, L. 1691–1696. *Phytographia sive stirpium illustriorum & miniis cognitarum icones tabulis aeneis summa diligentia elaboratae.* London.

Plukenet, L. 1692. *Phytographia sive stirpium illustriorum & miniis cognitarum icones tabulis aeneis summa diligentia elaboratae. Pars tertia.* London.

Polhill, R.M. & Stearn, W.T. 1976. Linnaeus's notes on Plumier drawings with special reference to *Mimosa latisiliqua. Taxon* 25: 323–325.

Preston, C.D. & Sell, P.D. 1989. The Aizoaceae naturalized in the British Isles. *Watsonia* 17: 217–245.

Pritzel, G.A. 1871–1877. *Thesaurus Literaturae Botanicae omnium gentium inde a rerum botanicarum initiis ad nostra usque tempora, &c.* Leipzig.

Rauschert, S. 1970. Das Herbarium von Paul Hermann (1646–1695) in der Forschungsbibliothek Gotha. *Hercynia* N.F., 7: 301–328.

Ray, J. 1724. *Synopsis methodica stirpium britannicarum,* ed. 3. London.

Rendle, A.B. 1934. Linnaean species of *Spermacoce. J. Bot.* 72: 329–333.

Rendle, A.B. 1936. Notes on the Flora of Jamaica. *J. Bot.* 74: 337–346.

Reveal, J.L. 1983. Significance of pre-1753 botanical explorations in temperate North America on Linnaeus' first edition of Species Plantarum. *Phytologia* 53: 1–96.

Reveal, J.L. 1989. (954–956) Proposals to conserve the names and types of three North American Linnaean species. *Taxon* 38: 515–519.

Reveal, J.L. 1992. *Gentle Conquest: the botanical discovery of North America with illustrations from the Library of Congress.* Starwood Publishing, Washington, DC.

Rheede tot Drakenstein, H.A. van, 1678. *Hortus Indicus Malabaricus,* vol. 1. Amsterdam.

Rice, A.L. 1999. *Voyages of discovery: three centuries of natural history exploration.* Scriptum Editions, London.

Richter, H.E.F. 1840. *Caroli Linnaei Systema, genera, species plantarum uno volumine. Editio critica, adstricta, conferta, sive, Codex botanicus linnaeanus &c.* Otto Wiegand, Leipzig.

Rico, E. 1998. *Potentilla* subgenus *Potentilla*. Pp. 96–130 in: Muñoz Garmendia, F. & Navarro, C. (eds), *Flora Iberica*, vol. 6. Real Jardín Botánico, CSIC, Madrid.

Rico, E. & Martínez Ortega, M. 2002. In: Cafferty, S. & Jarvis, C.E. (eds), Typification of Linnaean plant names in Rosaceae. *Taxon* 51: 539–545.

Robbins, C.C. 1960. David Hosack's herbarium and its Linnaean specimens. *Proc. Amer. Philos. Soc.* 104: 293–313.

Ross, J.H. 1975. The typification of *Mimosa senegal*. *Bothalia* 11: 449–451.

Rosselló, J.A. & Sáez, L. 2000. Index Balaearicum: an annotated check-list of the vascular plants described from the Balearic Islands. *Collect. Bot.* 25: 3–203.

Rothmaler, W. 1940. Nomenklatorisches, meist aus dem westlichen Mittelmeergebiet. II. *Repert. Spec. Nov. Regni Veg.* 49: 272–281.

Rowley, G.D. 1954. Richard Bradley and his "History of Succulent Plants" (1716–1727). *Cact. Succ. J. Gr. Brit.* 16: 30–31, 54–55, 78–81.

Royen, A. van, 1740. *Florae Leydensis Prodromus.* Leiden.

Rumphius, G.E. 1741–1750. *Herbarium Amboinense…pars prima–sexta.* Amsterdam.

Rydén, S. 1953. José Celestino Mutis och hans förbindelser med Linné och hans krets. *Svenska Linné-Sällsk. Årsskr.* 35: 31–38.

St John, H. 1915. *Rumex persicarioides* and its allies in North America. *Rhodora* 17: 73–83.

Sandermann Olsen, S.-E. 1997. *Bibliographia Discipuli Linnaei: bibliographies of the 331 pupils of Linnaeus.* Bibliotheca Linnaeana Danica, Copenhagen.

Sauvages, P.A.B.C. 1751. *Methodus Foliorum, seu Plantae Florae Monspeliensis.* La Haye.

Savage, S. 1936. Caspar Bauhin's Pinax and Burser's herbarium. *Proc. Linn. Soc. London,* sess. 148: 16–26.

Savage, S. 1937a. *Caroli Linnaei determinationes in hortum siccum Joachimi Burseri.* London.

Savage, S. 1937b. Studies in Linnaean synonymy. 2. Sir James Edward Smith and the Linnaean herbarium. *Proc. Linn. Soc. London,* sess. 149: 6–10.

Savage, S. 1940. *Synopsis of the annotations by Linnaeus and his contemporaries in his library of printed books.* London.

Savage, S. 1945. *A Catalogue of the Linnaean Herbarium.* Taylor & Francis, London.

Schreber, J.C.D. von, 1766. *Icones et descriptiones plantarum minus cognitarum.* Halle.

Schwertschläger, J. 1890. *Der botanische Garten der Fürstbischöfe von Eichstätt.* Ph. Brönner, Eichstätt.

Scopoli, G.A. 1769. *Annus II historico-naturalis.* Leipzig.

Seba, A. 1734. *Locupletissimi rerum naturalium thesauri accurata descriptio, et iconibus artificiosissimis expressio, per universam physices historiam, &c.,* vol. 1. Amsterdam

Shaw, T. 1738. *Catalogus plantarum quas in variis Africae & Asiae partibus collegit.* Oxford.

Sloane, H. 1707. *A Voyage to the islands Madera, Barbados, Nieves, S. Christophers and Jamaica,* vol. 1. London.

Sloane, H. 1725. *A Voyage to the islands Madera, Barbados, Nieves, S. Christophers and Jamaica,* vol. 2. London.

Smith, C.E. 1962. Henry Muhlenberg – Botanical Pioneer. *Proc. Amer. Philos. Soc.* 106: 443–460.

Smith, J.E. 1791. On the *Festuca spadicea,* and *Anthoxanthum paniculatum,* of Linnaeus. *Trans. Linn. Soc.* 1: 111–117, t. 10.

Smith, J.E. 1811. *Lachesis Lapponica, or A tour in Lapland, now first published from the original manuscript journal of the celebrated Linnaeus.* London.

Smith, J.E. 1815. *Scutellaria.* In Rees, A., *Cyclopaedia.* London.

Söderpalm, K. 2005. *Christopher Tärnström's Journal: en res mellan Europa och sydostasien ar 1746.* IK Foundation & Company Ltd, London.

Sokoloff, D.D., Balandin, S.A., Gubanov, I.A., Jarvis, C.E., Majorov, S.R., Simonov, S.S. & Sukhov, S.V. 2001. Plant specimens related to C. Linnaeus in the Herbarium of Moscow University (MW). *Byull. Moskovsk. Obshch. Isp. Prir., Otd. Biol.* 106(1): 38–48. [In Russian].

Sokoloff, D.D., Balandin, S.A., Gubanov, I.A., Jarvis, C.E., Majorov, S.R. & Simonov, S.S. 2002. The history of botany in Moscow and Russia in the 18th and early 19th centuries in the context of the Linnaean Collection at Moscow University (MW). *Huntia* 11: 129–191.

Sosef, M.S.M. & de Bruin, J. 1996. Historical collections. In: Breteler, F.J. & Sosef, M.S.M. (eds), Herbarium Vadense 1896–1996. *Wageningen Agricultural University Papers* 96–2: 29–33.

Soulsby, B.H. 1933. *A catalogue of the works of Linnaeus (and publications more immediately relating thereto) preserved in the libraries of the British Museum (Bloomsbury) and the British Museum (Natural History) (South Kensington),* ed. 2. British Museum, London.

Spencer, M., Irvine, L.M. & Jarvis, C.E. Typification of Linnaean names relevant to algal nomenclature. *Taxon,* in press.

Sprague, T.A. 1928. The Herbal of Otto Brunfels. *J. Linn. Soc., Bot.* 48: 79–124.

Sprague, T.A. 1940. The type of *Corymbium africanum* L. *Bull. Misc. Inform. Kew* 1940: 163–166.

Sprague, T.A. 1955. The plan of the Species Plantarum. *Proc. Linn. Soc. London* 165: 151–156.

Sprague, T.A. & Nelmes, E. 1931. The herbal of Leonhart Fuchs. *J. Linn. Soc., Bot.* 48: 545–642.

Sprague, T.A. & Sprague, M.S. 1939. The herbal of Valerius Cordus. *J. Linn. Soc., Bot.* 52: 1–113.

Stafleu, F.A. 1971. Linnaeus and the Linnaeans. The spreading of their ideas in systematic botany, 1735–1789. *Regnum Veg.* 79: xvi + 1–386.

Stafleu, F.A. & Cowan, R.S. 1976–1988. *Taxonomic Literature,* ed. 2, vols 1–7. Bohn, Scheltema & Holkema, Utrecht.

Stafleu, F.A. & Mennega, E.A. 1992–2000. *Taxonomic Literature,* ed. 2, supplements 1–6. Koeltz Scientific Books, Königstein.

Staudt, G. 2003. *Les dessins d'A.N. Duchesne pour son Histoire naturelle des fraisiers.* Muséum national d'Histoire naturelle, Paris.

Stearn, W.T. 1957. An Introduction to the Species Plantarum and cognate botanical works of Carl Linnaeus. In: Linnaeus, C., *Species Plantarum, A Facsimile of the first edition, 1753,* vol. 1: i–xiv, 1–176. Ray Society, London.

Stearn, W.T. 1959a. Demonstrationes Plantarum. In: Heller, J.L. & Stearn, W.T., *An Appendix to the Species Plantarum of Carl Linnaeus*: 82–88. (See also Heller, J.L. & Stearn, W.T. in reference list for further information).

Stearn, W.T. 1959b. Genera Plantarum, fifth edition. In: Heller, J.L. & Stearn, W.T., *An Appendix to the Species Plantarum of Carl Linnaeus*: 92–93. (See also Heller, J.L. & Stearn, W.T. in reference list for further information).

Stearn, W.T. 1961. Introductory notes on Linnaeus's 'Mantissa Plantarum'. In: *Carl Linnaeus Mantissa Plantarum. Facsimile*: v–xxv. J. Cramer, Weinheim.

Stearn, W.T. 1971. Linnaean classification, nomenclature and method. In: Blunt, W., *The Compleat Naturalist. A Life of Linnaeus*: 242–249. Collins, London.

Stearn, W.T. 1973a. Ray, Dillenius, Linnaeus and the Synopsis methodica Stirpium Britannicarum. In: Ray, J., *Synopsis methodica Stirpium Britannicarum, Editio Tertia, 1724; Carl Linnaeus, Flora Anglica 1754 & 1759. Facsimiles with an Introduction by William T. Stearn*: 3–90. Ray Society, London.

Stearn, W.T. 1973b. Linnaeus's Öland and Gotland Journey 1741. Introduction. *Biol. J. Linn. Soc.* 5: 1–17.

Stearn, W.T. 1973c. *Botanical Latin: History, Grammar, Syntax, Terminology and Vocabulary*, ed. 2. David & Charles, Newton Abbot.

Stearn, W.T. 1974. Magnol's Botanicum Monspeliense and Linnaeus's Flora Monspeliensis. In: Geck, E. & Pressler, G. (eds), *Festschrift für Claus Nissen*: 612–650. Guide Pressler, Wiesbaden.

Stearn, W.T. 1982. Maria Sibylla Merian (1647–1717) as a botanical artist. *Taxon* 31: 529–534.

Tison, J.-M. 2000. Sur la typification de deux *Iberis* critiques. *Monde Pl.* 468: 30.

Trimen, H. 1887. Hermann's Ceylon herbarium and Linnaeus's Flora Zeylanica. *J. Linn. Soc., Bot.* 24: 129–155.

Trimen, H. 1894. *A Hand-Book to the Flora of Ceylon*, vol. 2. Dulau & Co, London.

Trimen, H. 1895. *A Hand-Book to the Flora of Ceylon*, vol. 3. Dulau & Co, London.

Tryon, R. 1964. The ferns of Peru. Polypodiaceae (Dennstaedtieae to Oleandreae). *Contr. Gray Herb.* 194: 1–253.

Turland, N. 1995. Linnaeus's interpretation of Prospero Alpino's De plantis exoticis, with special emphasis on the flora of Crete. *Bull. Nat. Hist. Mus. London, Bot.* 25: 127–159.

Turland, N. 2006. Lectotypification of *Campanula saxatilis, Phyteuma pinnatum* and *Verbascum arcturus*, Linnaean names of three taxa endemic to Crete. *Willdenowia* 36: 303–309.

Turner, D. 1802. *A Synopsis of the British Fuci*, 2 vols. F. Bush, London.

Turra, A. 1765. *Farsetia, novum genus: accedunt animadversiones quaedam botanicae.* Venice.

Uggla, A.H. 1953. Fredric Hasselquist. Ett tvåhundraårsminne. *Svenska Linné-Sällsk. Årsskr.* 35: 5–17.

Urban, I. 1920. Plumiers Leben und Schriften nebst einem Schlüssel zu seinen Blütenpflanzen. *Repert. Spec. Nov. Regnum Veg.* 5: 1–196.

Vaillant, S. 1718. *Sermo de structura florum.* Leiden.

Vandelli, D. 1771. *Fasciculus plantarum, cum novis generibus et speciebus.* Lisbon.

van Ooststroom, S.J. 1937. Hermann's collection of Ceylon plants in the Rijksherbarium (National Herbarium) at Leyden. *Blumea* Suppl. 1: 193–209.

Vines, S.H. & Druce, G.C. 1914. *An account of the Morisonian Herbarium in the possession of the University of Oxford, together with biographical and critical sketches of Morison and the two Bobarts and their works and the early history of the Physic Garden 1619–1720, &c.* Oxford.

Wagenitz, G. 1976. Two species of the "Filago germanica" group (Compositae–Inuleae) in the United States. *Sida* 6: 221.

Webster, G.L. & Huft, M.J. 1988. Revised synopsis of Panamanian Euphorbiaceae. *Ann. Missouri Bot. Gard.* 75: 1087–1144

Wheeler, L.C. 1941. *Euphorbia* subgenus *Chamaesyce* in Canada and the United States exclusive of Southern Florida. *Rhodora* 43: 97–154, 168–205, 223–286.

Wijnands, D.O. 1983. *The Botany of the Commelins.* Balkema, Rotterdam.

Wijnands, D.O. & Heniger, J. 1991. The origins of Clifford's herbarium. *Bot. J. Linn. Soc.* 106: 129–146.

Wilbur, R.L. 1990. Identification of the plants illustrated and described in Catesby's Natural History of the Carolinas, Florida and the Bahamas. *Sida* 14: 29–48.

Withering, W. 1858. *A systematic arrangement of British plants…corrected and condensed; preceded by an Introduction to botany by William MacGillivray*, ed. 10. London.

Wood, J.R.I., Hillcoat, D. & Brummitt, R.K. 1983. Notes on the types of some names of Arabian Acanthaceae in the Forsskal herbarium. *Kew Bull.* 38: 429–456.

Zaneveld, J.S. 1959. An identification of the Algae mentioned by Rumphius. In: de Wit, H.C.D. (ed.), *Rumphius Memorial Volume*: 277–280. Baarn.

Zuloaga, F.O. 1989. El genero *Panicum* (Poaceae: Paniceae) en la republica Argentina. III. *Darwiniana* 29: 289–370.

Chapter 7

LINNAEAN PLANT NAMES AND THEIR TYPES

Scope

All the plant names that were validly published by Linnaeus at the ranks of species and variety are listed here. While these are mainly new species names, they also include re-combinations (post-1753) by Linnaeus of names that he had published previously, as well as re-combinations of binomial names published by other authors (e.g. N.L. Burman, Jacquin, Arduino etc.), and new names intended to replace them. Where Linnaean names that were not validly published have entered the botanical literature, these too may be listed. However, Linnaean names that are clearly applicable to taxa that have a later starting date (e.g. Musci, excluding the Sphagnaceae: 1 January 1801) are not included. In addition, a few non-linnaean binomials are included where they are types of Linnaean generic names (and are homotypic with other Linnaean binomials), e.g. *Anacampseros telephiastrum* DC.

Linnaeus' son, Carl (often known as "Linnaeus filius" or "Linnaeus the Younger") described nine new species grown in the botanic garden in Uppsala in 1762. As they were taken up by Linnaeus in *Species Plantarum*, ed. 2 (1762–1763), these few names are included here. However, the numerous new names attributable to the younger Linnaeus that he published later (Linnaeus filius 1782) are excluded.

The type specimen of *Butomus umbellatus* L. from the herbarium of Adriaan van Royen in Leiden (L)

Organisation of Entries

Each Linnaean name is listed alphabetically under genus, together with the place and date of its original publication. If it is a conserved (*nom. cons.*), rejected (*nom. rej.*), not validly published (*nom. inval.*) or an illegitimate (*nom. illeg.*) name, this is noted.

The stated provenance is quoted as in the protologue: it is placed in square brackets if this information was absent in the protologue itself but appeared in a later Linnaean publication. In the case of replacement names (*nomina nova*) or new combinations, the provenance, if known, is quoted from the protologue of the replaced synonym or basionym, i.e. from an earlier work.

Following page (248): The lectotype of *Cheiranthus incanus* L. (= *Matthiola incana* (L.) R. Br.) in Linnaeus' herbarium at LINN (839.17).

17

839.17

4   incana

"RCN" indicates the catalogue number for the binomial in Richter's *Codex Botanicus Linnaeanus* (1840), where a detailed account of the synonyms cited in each of the Linnaean works in which the name appeared, can be found. The absence of any RCN information indicates that the name was not listed by Richter.

Where a name is a replacement for an earlier one, the latter is indicated as "replaced synonym". If the listed name is a new combination involving an earlier name, the latter is indicated as the "basionym". The reciprocal relationship is indicated by the expressions "replaced synonym of" and "basionym of" respectively.

The category of type (e.g. lectotype, neotype, conserved type etc.), and the name of the typifying author and the publication, with date, in which the typification appeared, follows, and the type specimen (or illustration) is indicated. The herbaria where type specimens are conserved are listed by their codes which, in general, follow Holmgren & Holmgren (2007). Those codes that are commonly encountered in this catalogue, together with various abbreviations, are listed below on pp. 251–252.

If a type has not been designated, the original material for the name is listed beneath the statement "Type not designated". However, no original material has been listed for replacement names or re-combinations made by Linnaeus which are based on names described by others. These include replaced names and basionyms described by Jacquin, N.L. Burman and others. Obtaining information on the original material for these names has generally been beyond the scope of this study.

If a binomial is the type of a generic name described by Linnaeus, this is indicated, together with a reference to the place and date of typification. This information has been largely drawn from the *Index Nominum Genericorum* (Farr & Zijlstra 2007). A few non-Linnaean names are also included where they are types of Linnaean generic names.

A current binomial (with infraspecific and cultivar name where appropriate), and family name is also provided. Space has prevented the listing of extensive synonymy and, consequently, taxa from groups where there is continuing taxonomic reorganisation across several genera (with several different classifications possible) will have only one of these options listed.

Under the heading "*Note:*" can be found additional information relevant to the typification of some names. Constraints of space prevent extensive discussion for every name so comments are generally restricted to those names where either marked complexities exist, or where earlier published type statements exist but have, for one reason or another, not been accepted. In the latter instance, the justification for the acceptance or

A plate from the third volume of Georg Rumphius' *Herbarium Amboinense* (t. 57. 1743) is the type of *Casuarina equisetifolia* L.

Following page (250): A plate from Jan Commelin's *Horti medici Amstelodamensis…* (t. 37. 1697) is the lectotype of *Amaryllis zeylanica* L. (= *Crinum zeylanicum* (L.) L.).

LILIO-NARCISSVS CEYLANICVS LATIFOLIVS FLORE NIVEO, EXTERNE LINEA PVRPVREA STRIATO. *Fig. 37.*

rejection of competing statements is discussed. In general, later divergent type choices are not mentioned (unless such a typification has been adopted by some authors resulting in significant nomenclatural consequences). For example, in the case of *Scrophularia vernalis* L., Ortega & Devesa (1993: 120) designated Clifford material (BM) as lectotype. Subsequently, Fischer (1997: 115) designated a different specimen, Herb. Linn. No. 773.13 (LINN), as lectotype. However, as Ortega & Devesa's choice clearly pre-dates Fischer's, the latter is not mentioned here. If the typifier of a name provides a review of earlier typification statements, the discussion is not generally repeated here. Unless otherwise indicated, all references to Articles of the International Code of Botanical Nomenclature (ICBN) refer to the Vienna Code (McNeill & al. 2006).

Glossary

basionym – a previously published legitimate name or epithet-bringing synonym from which a new name is formed. *Lotus mauritanicus* L. is the basionym of *Indigofera mauritanica* (L.) Thunb.

epithet – a single word, usually applied to a species, which when appended to the name of a genus, forms a binomial.

epitype – a specimen or illustration selected to serve as an interpretative type when the identity of the primary type (e.g. the *lectotype*) cannot be precisely established.

generitype – the type of the name of a genus (which is the type of the name of a species). For purposes of designation or citation of a type, the species name alone suffices, i.e. it is considered as the full equivalent of its type (Art. 10.1).

heterotypic synonym – a synonym based on a type different from that of the accepted name.

holotype – the one specimen or illustration used by an author in publishing a new name.

homonym – a name spelled exactly like another name published for a taxon of the same rank and based on a different type. The later of two such names will be illegitimate.

homotypic synonym – a synonym based on the same type as that of another name at the same rank.

ICBN – International Code of Botanical Nomenclature.

iconotype – sometimes used to indicate an illustration that serves as a type.

illegitimate name – see *nomen illegitimum*.

iso- – indicating a duplicate, hence iso-*lectotype*, iso-*neotype* etc.

isotype – a duplicate of a *holotype*.

L. – authority abbreviation for Linnaeus.

l.c. – (= *loco citato*) in a literature citation, indicates that the book or periodical being cited is the same as has already been given in full earlier in the same species entry.

lectotype – a specimen or illustration designated from the *original material* as the *nomenclatural type* when no holotype was indicated.

L. f. – (Linnaeus filius) – author abbreviation for Carl Linnaeus the Younger.

monospecific – of a genus, which contains only a single species.

monotypic – see *monospecific*.

neotype – a specimen or illustration selected to serve as a nomenclatural type when all of the material upon which the name was based is missing.

nom. ambig. – *nomen ambiguum* – a term (no longer appearing in the ICBN) indicating a name whose application is uncertain or unknown.

nom. confusum – *nomen confusum* – a term (no longer appearing in the ICBN) indicating a name whose application and usage is confused.

nom. cons. – *nomen conservandum* – a conserved name (which is listed in the Appendices of the ICBN).

nom. cons. prop. – *nomen conservandum propositum* – a name that has been proposed for conservation, the outcome of which is pending.

nom. dub. – *nomen dubium* – see *nomen ambiguum*.

nom. et orth. cons. – a conserved name, the spelling of which is also conserved.

nom. illeg. – *nomen illegitimum* – an illegitimate name.

nom. inval. – *nomen invalidum* – an invalid name, i.e. one that was not validly published (and therefore without nomenclatural significance).

nom. nov. – *nomen novum* – a replacement for an older name.

nom. nud. – *nomen nudum* – a name published without a description or diagnosis – it is not validly published and has no nomenclatural significance.

nom. rej. – *nomen rejiciendum* – a name ruled as rejected in favour of a name conserved under Art. 14, or a name rejected under Art. 56 (listed in the Appendices of the ICBN).

nom. superfl. – *nomen superfluum* – a superfluous renaming of an earlier name: it is illegitimate.

nom. utique rej. – *nomen utique rejiciendum* – a name rejected against all competing names (listed in the Appendices of the ICBN).

nomenclatural type – see *type*.

nomen illegitimum – an illegitimate name, i.e. one that is contrary to the ICBN's rules, either because it is the same as an earlier name that was based on a different type (a *homonym*), or because it is a superfluous name. For example, *Linum gallicum* L. (1762) is illegitimate because it is a replacement name for the earlier *Linum trigynum* L. (1753).

nomen incertae sedis – a name of uncertain application.

nomen non satis nota – a name that is insufficiently known for it to be applied.

nomen specificum legitimum – see *diagnosis*.

original material – those specimens and illustrations from which a *lectotype* can be chosen.

orth. cons. – a name conserved (and listed in the ICBN) with a particular spelling.

orth. var. – orthographic variant – various spelling, compounding and inflectional forms of a name or its epithet, only one nomenclatural type being involved.

phrase name – see *diagnosis*.

protologue – everything associated with a name at its valid publication, i.e. description or diagnosis, illustrations, references, synonymy, geographical data, citation of specimens, discussion and comments.

rank – any position in a taxonomic hierarchy – order, family, genus, species and variety are examples of different ranks.

RCN – Richter's Codex Number – a number given to a Linnaean name by Richter, 1840. *Codex Botanicus Linnaeanus*.

species incertae sedis – a species of uncertain identity.

superfluous name – a name applied to a *taxon* circumscribed by its author to include the type of an earlier name (the name of which ought to have been adopted).

taxon – a taxonomic group at any *rank*.

topotype – any collection of a taxon made at its type locality.

type – a specimen or illustration to which the name of a taxon is permanently attached.

typotype – herbarium material from which a type illustration was prepared.

typus – Latin for *type*.

voucher specimen – herbarium material believed to be associated with an illustration, or a specimen preserved when a part of it is used for more detailed study (e.g. micromorphological, chemical, cytological, molecular).

Herbarium Codes

BAA – University of Buenos Aires.

BM – Natural History Museum, London.

BM-SL – Natural History Museum, London: Sloane herbarium.

C – University of Copenhagen.

E – Royal Botanic Garden, Edinburgh.

FI – Museum of Natural History, University of Florence.

G – Conservatoire et Jardin botaniques de la Ville de Genève.

GB – University of Gothenberg.

H – University of Helsinki.

K – Royal Botanic Gardens, Kew.

L – Nationaal Herbarium Nederland, Leiden University branch.

LAPP – Institut de France, Paris.

LINN – Linnean Society of London: Carl Linnaeus herbarium.

LINN-SM – Linnean Society of London: J.E. Smith herbarium.

LIV – World Museum, Liverpool.

M – Botanische Staatssammlung, Munich.

MPU – University of Montpellier.

MW – Moscow State University.

OXF – University of Oxford.

P – Muséum National d'Histoire Naturelle, Paris.

PH – Academy of Natural Sciences, Philadelphia.

P-JU – Muséum National d'Histoire Naturelle, Paris: Jussieu herbarium.

P-TOURN – Muséum National d'Histoire Naturelle, Paris: Tournefort herbarium.

S – Swedish Museum of Natural History, Stockholm.

SBT – Bergius Foundation, Stockholm.

SI – Instituto de Botánico Darwinion, San Isidro, Buenos Aires.

STU – Staatliches Museum für Naturkunde, Stuttgart.

UPS – Museum of Evolution, University of Uppsala.

US – Smithsonian Institution, Washington DC.

A–Z OF LINNAEAN NAMES

A

Abrus precatorius Linnaeus, *Systema Naturae,* ed. 12, 2: 472. 1767. ["Habitat in Indiis, Aegypto."] Sp. Pl. 2: 753 (1753). RCN: 5168.
Replaced synonym: *Glycine abrus* L. (1753).
Lectotype (Fawcett & Rendle, *Fl. Jamaica* 4: 43. 1920): Herb. Hermann 2: 6, No. 284 (BM-000621515).
Current name: ***Abrus precatorius*** L. (Fabaceae: Faboideae).
Note: The generitype of *Abrus* Adanson.

Acaena elongata Linnaeus, *Mantissa Plantarum Altera*: 200. 1771. "Habitat in Mexico." RCN: 1005.
Neotype (Barrie in Jarvis & al., *Regnum Veg.* 127: 14. 1993): Herb. Mútis No. 774, specimen labelled *"Acaena"* (MA; iso- MA).
Generitype of *Acaena* Linnaeus.
Current name: ***Acaena elongata*** L. (Rosaceae).

Acalypha australis Linnaeus, *Species Plantarum* 2: 1004. 1753. "Habitat in America meridionali." RCN: 7265.
Lectotype (Airy Shaw in *Kew Bull.* 35: 584. 1980): Herb. Linn. No. 1139.5 (LINN).
Current name: ***Acalypha australis*** L. (Euphorbiaceae).
Note: See discussion by Forster (in *Austrobaileya* 4: 211. 1994).

Acalypha indica Linnaeus, *Species Plantarum* 2: 1003. 1753. "Habitat in Indiis ad fimeta." RCN: 7264.
Lectotype (Coode in Bosser & al., *Fl. Mascareignes* 160: 78. 1982): Herb. Linn. No. 1139.3 (LINN).
Current name: ***Acalypha indica*** L. (Euphorbiaceae).

Acalypha virgata Linnaeus, *Systema Naturae,* ed. 10, 2: 1275. 1759. ["Habitat in Jamaica."] Sp. Pl. ed. 2, 2: 1424 (1763). RCN: 7263.
Lectotype (Fawcett & Rendle, *Fl. Jamaica* 4: 310. 1920): *Browne,* Herb. Linn. No. 1139.2 (LINN; iso- BM?).
Current name: ***Acalypha virgata*** L. (Euphorbiaceae).

Acalypha virginica Linnaeus, *Species Plantarum* 2: 1003. 1753, *nom. cons.*
"Habitat in Zeylona, Virginia." RCN: 1262.
Conserved type (Reveal & al. in *Taxon* 39: 361. 1990): *Clayton 201* (BM-000038872).
Generitype of *Acalypha* Linnaeus (vide Green, *Prop. Brit. Bot.*: 189. 1929).
Current name: ***Acalypha virginica*** L. (Euphorbiaceae).

Acanthus dioscoridis Linnaeus, *Centuria II Plantarum*: 23. 1756. "Habitat in Libano." RCN: 4648.
Type not designated.
Original material: none traced.
Current name: ***Acanthus dioscoridis*** L. (Acanthaceae).

Acanthus ilicifolius Linnaeus, *Species Plantarum* 2: 639. 1753. "Habitat in India." RCN: 4649.

Lectotype (Barker in *J. Adelaide Bot. Gard.* 9: 68. 1986): Herb. Linn. No. 816.6 (LINN).
Current name: ***Dilivaria ilicifolia*** (L.) Juss. (Acanthaceae).

Acanthus maderaspatensis Linnaeus, *Species Plantarum* 2: 639. 1753. "Habitat in India." RCN: 4650.
Neotype (Malik & Ghafoor in Nasir & Ali, *Fl. Pakistan* 188: 7. 1988): Herb. Linn. No. 816.10 (LINN).
Current name: ***Blepharis maderaspatensis*** (L.) Roth (Acanthaceae).
Note: Napper (in *Kew Bull.* 24: 324. 1970) indicated material in LINN as holotype but did not distinguish between 816.10 and 816.11 (LINN). There appear to be no original elements for the name, the two LINN sheets both being post-1753 additions to the herbarium. However, Malik & Ghafoor's indication of 816.10 (LINN) as "holotype" is here treated as correctable under Art. 9.8, and the collection is accepted as a neotype.

Acanthus mollis Linnaeus, *Species Plantarum* 2: 639. 1753. "Habitat in Italiae, Siciliae, humentibus, duris." RCN: 4646.

Lectotype (Brummitt in Jarvis & al., *Regnum Veg.* 127: 14. 1993):
Herb. Clifford: 326, *Acanthus* 1 (BM-000646246).
Generitype of *Acanthus* Linnaeus (vide Green, *Prop. Brit. Bot.*: 170.
1929).
Current name: ***Acanthus mollis*** L. (Acanthaceae).
Note: The type choice has been attributed to Hossain (in Davis,
Fl. Turkey 7: 27. 1982) by some authors (e.g. Wasshausen &
Wood in *Contr. U. S. Natl. Herb.* 49: 10. 2004). However, this is
incorrect as Hossain notes the existence not only of Clifford but
also of LINN (sheet 816.1) material, and refers to neither as the
type.

Acanthus spinosus Linnaeus, *Species Plantarum* 2: 639. 1753.
"Habitat in Italiae humentibus." RCN: 4647.
Type not designated.
Original material: Herb. Burser XXI: 48 (UPS); Herb. Clifford: 327,
Acanthus 2 (BM); [icon] in Dodoëns, Stirp. Hist. Pempt., ed. 2:
719. 1616.
Current name: ***Acanthus spinosus*** L. (Acanthaceae).

Acer campestre Linnaeus, *Species Plantarum* 2: 1055. 1753.
"Habitat in Scania & australiori Europa." RCN: 7640.
Lectotype (Brown, *English Botany,* ed. 3, suppl.: 57. 1892): Herb.
Linn. No. 1225.14 (LINN).
Current name: ***Acer campestre*** L. (Aceraceae).

Acer creticum Linnaeus, *Species Plantarum,* ed. 2, 2: 1497. 1763,
nom. illeg.
"Habitat in Oriente." RCN: 7642.
Replaced synonym: *Acer orientale* L. (1759).
Neotype (Turland in *Taxon* 44: 599. 1995): Turkey. Adana District,
Bahçe (N Amanus), between Haruniye & Fevzipasa, 1,150m, 18
May 1957, *Davis & Hedge sub Davis 26773* (BM).
Current name: ***Acer monspessulanum*** L. subsp. ***oksalianum*** Yalt.
(Aceraceae).
Note: An illegitimate replacement name for *A. orientale* L. (1759).

Acer monspessulanum Linnaeus, *Species Plantarum* 2: 1056.
1753.
"Habitat Monspelii & in Creta." RCN: 7641.
Lectotype (Murray in *Kalmia* 9: 13. 1979): Herb. Linn. No. 1225.15
(LINN).
Current name: ***Acer monspessulanum*** L. subsp. ***monspessulanum***
(Aceraceae).

Acer negundo Linnaeus, *Species Plantarum* 2: 1056. 1753.
"Habitat in Virginia." RCN: 7643.
Lectotype (Murray in *Kalmia* 7: 6. 1975): Herb. Linn. No. 1225.17
(LINN; iso- BM).
Current name: ***Acer negundo*** L. var. ***negundo*** (Aceraceae).

Acer orientale Linnaeus, *Systema Naturae,* ed. 10, 2: 1310. 1759.
["Habitat in Oriente."] Sp. Pl., ed. 2, 2: 1497 (1763). RCN: 7642.
Replaced synonym of: *Acer creticum* L. (1763), *nom. illeg.*
Neotype (Turland in *Taxon* 44: 599. 1995): Turkey. Adana District,
Bahçe (N Amanus), between Haruniye & Fevzipasa, 1,150m, 18
May 1957, *Davis & Hedge sub Davis 26773* (BM).
Current name: ***Acer monspessulanum*** L. subsp. ***oksalianum*** Yalt.
(Aceraceae).

Acer pensylvanicum Linnaeus, *Species Plantarum* 2: 1055. 1753.
"Habitat in Pensylvania. Kalm." RCN: 7639.
Lectotype (Murray in *Kalmia* 7: 9. 1975): *Kalm,* Herb. Linn. No.
1225.13 (LINN; iso- UPS).
Current name: ***Acer pensylvanicum*** L. (Aceraceae).

Acer platanoides Linnaeus, *Species Plantarum* 2: 1055. 1753.
"Habitat in Europa boreali." RCN: 7638.
Lectotype (Murray in *Kalmia* 9: 28. 1979): Herb. Linn. No. 1225.11
(LINN).
Current name: ***Acer platanoides*** L. (Aceraceae).

Acer pseudoplatanus Linnaeus, *Species Plantarum* 2: 1054. 1753.
"Habitat in Helvetiae, Austriae montanis." RCN: 7635.
Lectotype (Murray in *Kalmia* 9: 31. 1979): Herb. Linn. No. 1225.5
(LINN).
Generitype of *Acer* Linnaeus (vide Green, *Prop. Brit. Bot.*: 193.
1929).
Current name: ***Acer pseudoplatanus*** L. (Aceraceae).

Acer rubrum Linnaeus, *Species Plantarum* 2: 1055. 1753.
"Habitat in Virginia, Pensylvania." RCN: 7636.
Lectotype (Murray in *Kalmia* 7: 9. 1975): *Kalm,* Herb. Linn. No.
1225.7 (LINN; iso- UPS).
Current name: ***Acer rubrum*** L. (Aceraceae).

Acer saccharinum Linnaeus, *Species Plantarum* 2: 1055. 1753.
"Habitat in Pensylvania. Kalm." RCN: 7637.
Lectotype (Murray in *Kalmia* 7: 13. 1975): *Kalm,* Herb. Linn. No.
1225.10 (LINN; iso- UPS).
Current name: ***Acer saccharinum*** L. (Aceraceae).

Acer sempervirens Linnaeus, *Systema Naturae,* ed. 12, 2: 674;
Mantissa Plantarum: 128. 1767.
"Habitat in Oriente." RCN: 7633.
Neotype (Turland in *Bull. Nat. Hist. Mus. London, Bot.* 25: 129, f. 1.
1995): Crete. Omalos, 10 Jun 1938, *Ogilvie-Grant 25* (K).
Current name: ***Acer sempervirens*** L. (Aceraceae).

Acer tataricum Linnaeus, *Species Plantarum* 2: 1054. 1753.
"Habitat in Tataria." RCN: 7634.
Type not designated.
Original material: *Gerber,* Herb. Linn. No. 1225.3 (LINN); Herb.
Linn. No. 1225.4 (LINN); Herb. Linn. No. 1225.2? (LINN);
[icon] in Krascheninnikov in Novi Comment. Acad. Sci. Imp.
Petrop. 2: 285, t. 13. 1751 [1749].
Current name: ***Acer tataricum*** L. (Aceraceae).
Note: Murray (*Monogr. Aceraceae*: 239. 1970; in *Kalmia* 9: 35. 1979)
designated 1225.2 (LINN) as type, but this sheet carries no *Species
Plantarum* number (i.e. "1"), and was a post-1753 addition to the
herbarium, and not original material for the name.

Achillea abrotanifolia Linnaeus, *Species Plantarum* 2: 897. 1753.
"Habitat in Oriente." RCN: 6495.
Neotype (Podlech in Rechinger, *Fl. Iranica* 158: 108. 1986): Herb.
Tournefort No. 4721 (P-TOURN).
Current name: ***Tanacetum abrotanifolium*** (L.) Druce
(Asteraceae).
Note: No original material appears to exist for this name. Although it
was not available to Linnaeus, a Tournefort collection was treated as
the type by Podlech, and this is accepted as a neotypification (under
Art. 9.8).

Achillea aegyptiaca Linnaeus, *Species Plantarum* 2: 900. 1753.
"Habitat in Aegypto & Oriente." RCN: 6497.
Lectotype (Humphries in Jarvis & Turland in *Taxon* 47: 351. 1998):
Herb. Linn. No. 1017.6 (LINN).
Current name: ***Achillea aegyptiaca*** L. (Asteraceae).

Achillea ageratum Linnaeus, *Species Plantarum* 2: 897. 1753.
"Habitat in G. Narbonensi, Hetruria." RCN: 6491.

Lectotype (Thornton-Wood in Jarvis & Turland in *Taxon* 47: 351. 1998): Herb. Clifford: 413, *Achillea* 6 (BM-000647158).
Current name: ***Achillea ageratum*** L. (Asteraceae).

Achillea alpina Linnaeus, *Species Plantarum* 2: 899. 1753.
"Habitat in Alpibus Sibiriae." RCN: 6502.
Lectotype (Botschantzev in Schischkin & Bobrov, *Fl. U.R.S.S.* 26: 120. 1961): Herb. Linn. No. 1017.13 (LINN).
Current name: ***Achillea alpina*** L. (Asteraceae).

Achillea atrata Linnaeus, *Species Plantarum* 2: 899. 1753.
"Habitat in Alpibus Helvetiae, Vallesiae, Austriae." RCN: 6503.
Lectotype (Valant-Vetschera in *Feddes Repert.* 106: 54, f. 2. 1995): Herb. Burser VII(1): 16 (UPS).
Current name: ***Achillea atrata*** L. (Asteraceae).

Achillea bipinnata Linnaeus, *Species Plantarum* 2: 900. 1753.
"Habitat in Oriente." RCN: 6496.
Type not designated.
Original material: Herb. Clifford: 413, *Achillea* 9 (BM).
Current name: ***Tanacetum polycephalum*** Sch. Bip. subsp. ***argyrophyllum*** (K. Koch) Podlech (Asteraceae).

Achillea clavennae Linnaeus, *Species Plantarum* 2: 898. 1753.
"Habitat in Alpibus Austriae, Pannoniae, Corinthiae." RCN: 6500.
Lectotype (Franzén in *Willdenowia* 16: 23. 1986): Herb. Linn. No. 1017.10 (LINN).
Current name: ***Achillea clavennae*** L. (Asteraceae).

Achillea cretica Linnaeus, *Species Plantarum* 2: 899. 1753.
"Habitat in Creta." RCN: 6509.
Lectotype (Valant-Vetschera in *Taxon* 44: 95, f. 2. 1995): Herb. Burser VII(1): 71 (UPS).
Current name: ***Achillea cretica*** L. (Asteraceae).
Note: Huber-Morath (in *Ber. Schweiz. Bot. Ges.* 84: 149. 1975) indicated unspecified Tournefort material as type but such material (assuming it was at P) would not have been studied by Linnaeus and would not be original material for the name.

Achillea falcata Linnaeus, *Species Plantarum* 2: 897. 1753.
"Habitat in Oriente." RCN: 6492.
Lectotype (Huber-Morath in *Ber. Schweiz. Bot. Ges.* 84: 137. 1975): Herb. Clifford: 412, *Achillea* 4 (BM-000647153).
Current name: ***Achillea falcata*** L. (Asteraceae).
Note: Huber-Morath indicated material in "Hb. Cliff. 412" as type, and as there is only one collection there associated with this name, this is accepted as a formal choice of type. Subsequently, Valant-Vetschera (in *Bot. J. Linn. Soc.* 121: 164–167. 1996) provided a detailed study of the typification of the name, reproducing the protologue and her chosen type (her f. 2), the same as Huber-Morath's.

Achillea impatiens Linnaeus, *Species Plantarum* 2: 898. 1753.
"Habitat in Sibiria." RCN: 6499.
Type not designated.
Original material: Herb. Linn. No. 1017.9 (LINN); [icon] in Gmelin, Fl. Sibirica 2: 197, t. 83, f. 1. 1752.
Current name: ***Achillea impatiens*** L. (Asteraceae).

Achillea inodora Linnaeus, *Species Plantarum* 2: 900. 1753.
"Habitat in Africa." RCN: 6110.
Neotype (Humphries in Jarvis & Turland in *Taxon* 47: 351. 1998): Algeria. Miliana to Teniet El Had, 30 May 1975, *Davis 58434* (BM-000576309; iso- E).
Current name: ***Lonas annua*** (L.) Vines & Druce (Asteraceae).

Achillea macrophylla Linnaeus, *Species Plantarum* 2: 898. 1753.
"Habitat in Alpibus Helvetiae, Italiae." RCN: 6498.
Lectotype (Thornton-Wood in Jarvis & Turland in *Taxon* 47: 351. 1998): [icon] *"Tanacetum inodor. leucanth. Alpin."* in Barrelier, Pl. Galliam: 101, t. 991. 1714.
Current name: ***Achillea macrophylla*** L. (Asteraceae).

Achillea magna Linnaeus, *Species Plantarum*, ed. 2, 2: 1267. 1763.
"Habitat in Europa australi." RCN: 6505.
Type not designated.
Original material: Herb. Linn. No. 1017.18 (LINN); Herb. Burser VII(1): 67 (UPS).
Current name: ***Achillea sp.*** (Asteraceae).
Note: This name appears not to be in use. The identity of some of the original material suggests the name should fall within the *A. millefolium* L. group, but the name needs critical assessment.

Achillea millefolium Linnaeus, *Species Plantarum* 2: 899. 1753.
"Habitat in Europae pascuis pratisque." RCN: 6506.
Lectotype (Huber-Morath in *Ber. Schweiz. Bot. Ges.* 84: 154. 1975): Herb. Linn. No. 1017.20 (LINN).
Generitype of *Achillea* Linnaeus (vide Green, *Prop. Brit. Bot.*: 182. 1929).
Current name: ***Achillea millefolium*** L. (Asteraceae).
Note: Achillea santolina was treated as the generitype of *Achillea* by Britton & Brown (*Ill. Fl. N. U. S.*, ed. 2, 3: 514. 1913; see McNeill & al. in *Taxon* 36: 356. 1987). However, under Art. 10.5, Ex. 7 (a voted example) of the Vienna Code, this is a type choice made under the American Code and is to be replaced under Art. 10.5b by Green's choice (*Prop. Brit. Bot.*: 182. 1929) of *A. millefolium*. Dabrowska (in *Acta Univ. Wratislav., Prace Bot.* 24: plate XI. 1982) illustrates the type.

Achillea nana Linnaeus, *Species Plantarum* 2: 899. 1753.
"Habitat in Alpibus Helvetiae, Vallesiae." RCN: 6504.
Lectotype (Valant-Vetschera in *Feddes Repert.* 106: 56, f. 3. 1995): Herb. Burser VII(1): post 6 (UPS).
Current name: ***Achillea nana*** L. (Asteraceae).

Achillea nobilis Linnaeus, *Species Plantarum* 2: 899. 1753.
"Habitat in Helvetia, Misnia, Bohemia, G. Narbonensi, Tataria." RCN: 6507.
Lectotype (Thornton-Wood in Jarvis & Turland in *Taxon* 47: 351. 1998): Herb. Burser VII(1): 3 (UPS).
Current name: ***Achillea nobilis*** L. (Asteraceae).
Note: Dabrowska (in *Acta Univ. Wratislav., Prace Bot.* 24: plate VI. 1982) both illustrated 1017.23 (LINN), and indicated it as type. However, the sheet lacks the *Species Plantarum* number (i.e. "15") and is a post-1753 addition to the collection, and not original material for the name. Aware of this, Thornton-Wood subsequently designated Burser material as lectotype.

Achillea odorata Linnaeus, *Systema Naturae*, ed. 10, 2: 1225. 1759.
["Habitat in Helvetica, Narbona, Hispania."] Sp. Pl. ed. 2, 2: 1268. 1763. RCN: 6508.
Lectotype (Thornton-Wood in Jarvis & Turland in *Taxon* 47: 351. 1998): Herb. Linn. No. 1017.25 (LINN).
Current name: ***Achillea odorata*** L. (Asteraceae).

Achillea pallescens Linnaeus, *Systema Naturae*, ed. 10, 2: 1225. 1759. RCN: 6497.
Type not designated.
Original material: none traced.
Note: The name does not appear to be in use, and no original elements have been traced. Linnaeus did not take up the name in the second edition of *Species Plantarum* (1763).

Achillea ptarmica Linnaeus, *Species Plantarum* 2: 898. 1753.
"Habitat in Europa temperata." RCN: 6501.
Lectotype (Dabrowska in *Acta Univ. Wratislav., Prace Bot.* 24: 31, pl. II. 1982): Herb. Linn. No. 1017.11 (LINN).
Current name: ***Achillea ptarmica*** L. (Asteraceae).
Note: Rico (in *Taxon* 47: 351. 1988) independently chose the same type as Dabrowska.

Achillea pubescens Linnaeus, *Species Plantarum* 2: 897. 1753.
"Habitat in Oriente." RCN: 6494.
Type not designated.
Original material: Herb. Clifford: 413, *Achillea* 11, 2 sheets (BM).
Current name: ***Achillea sp.*** (Asteraceae).
Note: The name has apparently been little used in the past, and has now fallen out of use.

Achillea santolina Linnaeus, *Species Plantarum* 2: 896. 1753.
"Habitat in Oriente." RCN: 6490.
Lectotype (Humphries in Jarvis & al., *Regnum Veg.* 127: 14. 1993): Herb. Clifford: 412, *Achillea* 3 (BM-000647152).
Current name: ***Achillea santolina*** L. (Asteraceae).
Note: This was treated as the generitype of *Achillea* by Britton & Brown, *Ill. Fl. N. U. S.*, ed. 2, 3: 514. 1913 (see McNeill & al. in *Taxon* 36: 356. 1987). However, under Art. 10.5, Ex. 7 (a voted example) of the Vienna Code, this is a type choice made under the American Code and is to be replaced under Art. 10.5b by Green's choice (*Prop. Brit. Bot.*: 182. 1929) of *A. millefolium*.
  See extensive discussion by Valant-Vetschera in *Bot. J. Linn. Soc.* 121: 159–164 (1996), who also illustrated the type (as f. 1). She concludes that the name is synonymous with what has been called *A. tenuifolia* Lam.

Achillea tomentosa Linnaeus, *Species Plantarum* 2: 897. 1753.
"Habitat in G. Narbonensi, Vallesia, Tataria." RCN: 6493.
Lectotype (Dabrowska in *Acta Univ. Wratislav., Prace Bot.* 24: pl. IX. 1982): Herb. Linn. No. 1017.3 (LINN).
Current name: ***Achillea tomentosa*** L. (Asteraceae).
Note: Valant-Vetschera (in *Feddes Repert.* 106: 50. 1995) independently chose the same type as Dabrowska, illustrating it as her f. 1.

Achras mammosa Linnaeus, *Species Plantarum*, ed. 2, 1: 469. 1762, *nom. illeg.*
"Habitat in America meridionali." RCN: 2549.
Replaced synonym: *Achras zapota* L. (1753).
Lectotype (Gilly in *Trop. Woods* 73: 5. 1943): [icon] *"Sapota"* in Plumier, Nov. Pl. Amer.: 43, t. 4. 1703.
Current name: ***Manilkara zapota*** (L.) P. Royen (Sapotaceae).
Note: A superfluous name for *A. mammosa* L. (1753).

Achras salicifolia Linnaeus, *Species Plantarum*, ed. 2, 1: 470. 1762.
"Habitat in America meridionali." RCN: 2551.
Lectotype (Gutiérrez Amaro in Greuter & al., *Fl. Republ. Cuba, ser. A*, 6(4): 26. 2002): [icon] *"Salicis folio lato splendente, arbor, floribus parvis pallide luteis pentapetalis, e ramulorum lateribus confertim exeuntibus"* in Sloane, Voy. Jamaica 2: 98, t. 206, f. 2. 1725. – Typotype: Herb. Sloane 7: 16 (BM-SL).
Current name: ***Sideroxylon salicifolium*** (L.) Lam. (Sapotaceae).
Note: Howard (*Fl. Lesser Antilles* 6: 69. 1989) and Pennington (*Fl. Neotropica* 52: 149. 1990) both treated material in Herb. Sloane (BM-SL) as the type. However, it was not seen by Linnaeus and is not original material for the name.

Achras sapota Linnaeus, *Species Plantarum*, ed. 2, 1: 470. 1762, *nom. illeg.*

"Habitat in America meridionali." RCN: 2550.
Replaced synonym: *Sloanea emarginata* L. (1753).
Lectotype (Dandy, *Sloane Herbarium*: 112. 1958): [icon] *"Anona foliis Laurinis, in summitate incisis; fructu compresso scabro fusco, in medio acumine longo"* in Catesby, Nat. Hist. Carolina 2: 87, t. 87. 1743. – Typotype: Herb. Sloane 232: 15 (BM-SL).
Current name: ***Manilkara bahamensis*** (Baker) H.J. Lam & A. Meeuse (Sapotaceae).
Note: A superfluous name for *Sloanea emarginata* L. (1753).

Achras tomentosa Linnaeus, *Amoenitates Academicae* 5: 378. 1760.
"Habitat [in Jamaica.]"
Type not designated.
Original material: [icon] in Browne, Civ. Nat. Hist. Jamaica: 201, t. 17, f. 4. 1756; [icon] in Plukenet, Amalth. Bot.: 23, t. 360, f. 4. 1705 – Typotype: Herb. Sloane 94: 153 (BM-SL); [icon] in Sloane, Voy. Jamaica 2: 98, t. 206, f. 2. 1725 – Typotype: Herb. Sloane 7: 16 (BM-SL).
Current name: ***Sideroxylon salicifolium*** (L.) Lam. (Sapotaceae).

Achras zapota Linnaeus, *Species Plantarum* 2: 1190. 1753.
"Habitat in Jamaica." RCN: 2550.
Replaced synonym of: *Achras mammosa* L. (1762), *nom. illeg.*
Lectotype (Gilly in *Trop. Woods* 73: 5. 1943): [icon] *"Sapota"* in Plumier, Nov. Pl. Amer.: 43, t. 4. 1703.
Generitype of *Achras* Linnaeus, *nom. rej.*
Current name: ***Manilkara zapota*** (L.) P. Royen (Sapotaceae).
Note: Achras Linnaeus, *nom. rej.* in favour of *Manilkara* Adans.
  See a detailed discussion by Tirel (in *Adansonia*, sér. 2, 7: 103–107. 1967), who reproduced (as pl. 1) the Plumier type illustration, as did Cook (in *Contr. U. S. Natl. Herb.* 16: 279, pl. 100. 1913).

Achyranthes alternifolia Linnaeus, *Systema Naturae*, ed. 12, 2: 186; *Mantissa Plantarum*: 50. 1767.
"Habitat in Aegypto, Arabia." RCN: 1657.
Lectotype (Townsend in Polhill, *Fl. Trop. E. Africa, Amaranthaceae*: 37. 1985): Herb. Linn. No. 287.7 (LINN).
Current name: ***Digera muricata*** (L.) Mart. (Amaranthaceae).

Achyranthes aspera Linnaeus, *Species Plantarum* 1: 204. 1753, *typ. cons.*
"Habitat in Sicilia, Zeylona, Jamaica." RCN: 1654.
Conserved type (Townsend in Nasir & Ali, *Fl. W. Pakistan* 71: 35. 1974): Herb. Hermann 2: 69, No. 105 (BM-000621744).
Generitype of *Achyranthes* Linnaeus, *nom. cons.*
Current name: ***Achyranthes aspera*** L. (Amaranthaceae).
Note: Achyranthes aspera was proposed as conserved type of the genus by Jarvis (in *Taxon* 41: 555. 1992) and this was eventually approved by the General Committee (see review of the history of this proposal by Barrie, *l.c.* 55: 795–796. 2006).
  Although Townsend (in Dassanayake & Fosberg, *Revised Handb. Fl. Ceylon* 1: 38. 1980) restricted his original type choice (1974) to one of the specimens on p. 69, his earlier unrestricted choice appeared in the conservation proposal and the conserved type is therefore listed in the Vienna Code (2006) in this way.

Achyranthes aspera Linnaeus var. **indica** Linnaeus, *Species Plantarum* 1: 204. 1753.
RCN: 1654.
Type not designated.
Original material: Herb. Linn. No. 101.1 (S); Herb. Linn. No. 287.1 (LINN); [icon] in Plukenet, Phytographia: t. 10, f. 4. 1691; Almag. Bot.: 26. 1696; [icon] in Burman, Thes. Zeylan.: 16, t. 5, f. 3. 1737.

Current name: ***Achyranthes indica*** (L.) Mill. (Amaranthaceae).
Note: Although some authors (e.g. Fawcett & Rendle, *Fl. Jamaica* 3: 136. 1914; Townsend in Polhill, *Fl. Trop. E. Africa, Amaranthaceae*: 102. 1985) treat the type as from the Hermann herbarium (BM), and therefore homotypic with var. *aspera* L., var. *indica* has as the source of its diagnosis a Burman description and figure. In addition, although some authors treat *A. indica* (L.) Mill. as synonymous with *A. aspera*, others do not.

Achyranthes aspera Linnaeus var. **sicula** Linnaeus, *Species Plantarum* 1: 204. 1753.
RCN: 1654.
Type not designated.
Original material: Herb. Linn. No. 287.1 (LINN); [icon] in Boccone, Icon. Descr. Rar. Pl. Siciliae: 16, 17, t. 9. 1674; [icon] in Plukenet, Phytographia: t. 260, f. 2. 1694; Almag. Bot.: 26. 1696.
Current name: ***Achyranthes sicula*** (L.) All. (Amaranthaceae).
Note: Townsend (in Bosser & al., *Fl. Mascareignes* 142: 21. 1994) stated "Type: Amaranthus radice perpetua, t. 9 in Herb. Boccone (P. holo.: photo.!)" but it is unclear if this is a copy of Boccone's published figure (in which case it can be the type), or a specimen (which would not have been seen by Linnaeus and therefore cannot be the type).

Achyranthes brachiata Linnaeus, *Systema Naturae*, ed. 12, 2: 186; *Mantissa Plantarum*: 50. 1767.
"Habitat in Suratte." RCN: 1670.
Basionym of: *Illecebrum brachiatum* (L.) L. (1771).
Lectotype (Townsend in Nasir & Ali, *Fl. W. Pakistan* 71: 32. 1974): Herb. Linn. No. 290.1 (LINN).
Current name: ***Nothosaerva brachiata*** (L.) Wight (Amaranthaceae).

Achyranthes corymbosa Linnaeus, *Species Plantarum* 1: 205. 1753.
"Habitat in Zeylona." RCN: 1658.
Lectotype (Turrill in Turrill & Milne-Redhead, *Fl. Trop. E. Africa, Caryophyllaceae*: 8. 1956): Herb. Hermann 3: 3, No. 100 (BM-000621797).
Current name: ***Polycarpaea corymbosa*** (L.) Lam. (Caryophyllaceae).

Achyranthes dichotoma Linnaeus, *Systema Naturae*, ed. 12, 2: 186; *Mantissa Plantarum*: 51. 1767.
"Habitat in Virginia." RCN: 1659.
Lectotype (Chaudhri, *Rev. Paronychiinae*: 139. 1968): Herb. Linn. No. 287.11 (LINN; iso- BM).
Current name: ***Paronychia virginica*** Spreng. (Caryophyllaceae).

Achyranthes lanata Linnaeus, *Species Plantarum* 1: 204. 1753.
"Habitat in India." RCN: 1672.
Basionym of: *Illecebrum lanatum* (L.) L. (1771).
Type not designated.
Original material: [icon] in Burman, Thes. Zeylan.: 60, t. 26, f. 1. 1737; [icon] in Rheede, Hort. Malab. 10: 57, t. 29. 1690; [icon] in Plukenet, Phytographia: t. 75, f. 8. 1691; Almag. Bot.: 27. 1696.
Current name: ***Aerva lanata*** (L.) Schult. (Amaranthaceae).
Note: Although Townsend (in Nasir & Ali, *Fl. W. Pakistan* 71: 31. 1974) indicated 290.6 (LINN) as holotype, the sheet lacks a *Species Plantarum* number (i.e. "3") and was a post-1753 addition to the herbarium, and is not original material for the name. With other original material in existence, it cannot be treated as neotype.

Achyranthes lappacea Linnaeus, *Species Plantarum* 1: 204. 1753.
"Habitat in India." RCN: 1655.
Lectotype (Townsend in *Kew Bull.* 34: 135. 1979): Herb. Hermann 1: 2, No. 103, lower specimen (BM-000621231).
Current name: ***Pupalia lappacea*** (L.) A. Juss. (Amaranthaceae).

Note: Although Townsend (in Nasir & Ali, *Fl. W. Pakistan* 71: 25. 1974) indicated 287.4 (LINN) as holotype, the sheet lacks a *Species Plantarum* number (i.e. "2") and was a post-1753 addition to the herbarium, and is not original material for the name. The same author subsequently designated Hermann material as type.

Achyranthes muricata Linnaeus, *Species Plantarum,* ed. 2, 1: 295. 1762.
"Habitat in India." RCN: 1656.
Lectotype (Townsend in Nasir & Ali, *Fl. W. Pakistan* 71: 23. 1974): Herb. Linn. No. 287.6 (LINN).
Current name: ***Digera muricata*** (L.) Mart. (Amaranthaceae).

Achyranthes prostrata Linnaeus, *Species Plantarum,* ed. 2, 1: 296. 1762.
"Habitat in India." RCN: 1660.
Lectotype (Townsend in Dassanayake & Fosberg, *Revised Handb. Fl. Ceylon* 1: 136. 1980): Herb. Linn. No. 287.13 (LINN).
Current name: ***Cyathula prostrata*** (L.) Blume (Amaranthaceae).
Note: Although Fawcett & Rendle (*Fl. Jamaica* 3: 134. 1914) indicated material in LINN as type, they did not distinguish between sheets 287.12 and 287.13 (which are evidently not part of a single gathering, so Art. 9.15 does not apply).

Achyranthes repens Linnaeus, *Species Plantarum* 1: 205. 1753.
"Habitat in Turcomannia." RCN: 1681.
Replaced synonym of: *Illecebrum achyranthum* L. (1762), *nom. illeg.*
Type not designated.
Original material: [icon] in Dillenius, Hort. Eltham. 1: 8, t. 7, f. 7. 1732 – Typotype: Herb. Sherard (OXF).
Current name: ***Alternanthera pungens*** (L.) Kunth (Amaranthaceae).
Note: Melville (in *Kew Bull.* 13: 173. 1958) designated a cultivated specimen in the Sherard herbarium (OXF) as the holotype but this would not have been seen by Linnaeus and is not original material for the name.

Achyranthes sanguinolenta Linnaeus, *Species Plantarum,* ed. 2, 1: 294. 1762.
"Habitat in India." RCN: 1671.
Basionym of: *Illecebrum sanguinolentum* (L.) L. (1771).
Lectotype (Townsend in Nasir & Ali, *Fl. W. Pakistan* 71: 30. 1974): Herb. Linn. No. 290.3 (LINN).
Current name: ***Aerva sanguinolenta*** (L.) Blume (Amaranthaceae).

Acnida cannabina Linnaeus, *Species Plantarum* 2: 1027. 1753.
"Habitat in Virginiae paludibus salsis." RCN: 7429.
Lectotype (Sauer in *Madroño* 13: 11. 1955; Reveal in Jarvis & al., *Regnum Veg.* 127: 14. 1993): *Clayton 599*, Herb. Linn. No. 1176.1 (LINN; iso- BM).
Generitype of *Acnida* Linnaeus.
Current name: ***Acnida cannabina*** L. (Amaranthaceae).
Note: Sauer (1955) indicated *Clayton 599* as the type but did not distinguish between the collections in LINN and BM. He is accepted as having typified the name, with Reveal (1993) having restricted the lectotype choice to the material in LINN.

Aconitum anthora Linnaeus, *Species Plantarum* 1: 532. 1753.
"Habitat in Alpibus Pyrenaeis, Helveticis, Taurinis, Allobrogicis." RCN: 3956.
Type not designated.
Original material: Herb. Clifford: 214, *Aconitum* 4 (BM); Herb. Linn. No. 695.6 (LINN); Herb. Burser X: 12 (UPS); [icon] in Mattioli, Pl. Epit.: 837. 1586.
Current name: ***Aconitum anthora*** L. (Ranunculaceae).

Aconitum cammarum Linnaeus, *Species Plantarum,* ed. 2, 1: 751. 1762.
"Habitat in Stiria, Taurero." RCN: 1958.
Type not designated.
Original material: [icon] in Clusius, Rar. Pl. Hist. 2: 97. 1601; [icon] in Clusius, Rar. Pl. Hist. 2: 95. 1601; [icon] in Clusius, Rar. Pl. Hist. 2: 96. 1601.
Current name: ***Aconitum × cammarum*** L. (Ranunculaceae).
Note: Muntz (in *Gentes Herb.* 6: 466. 1945) noted that, in the cited references of the protologue, at least three different taxa were included, and that there was no material in LINN. Mitka (*Genus Aconitum Poland*: 57. 2003) designated an epitype "Flora Suecica, Västergötland, Toarp s:n, St Bygd, Myrlkra, 24 Aug 1889, *A.O. Olsen s.n.* (KRA 011242)" but without there being a lectotype. He cites (p. 58) Karlsson (in Jonsell in *Nordic J. Bot.* 20: 520. 2000) as saying there are no relevant specimens extant, and that the cited Clusius plates do not depict the garden hybrid. Mitka's epitypification cannot be corrected and accepted as a neotypification (Art. 9.8) because of the existence of original material (the problematic Clusius plates).

Aconitum lycoctonum Linnaeus, *Species Plantarum* 1: 532. 1753.
"Habitat in Alpibus Lapponiae, Helvetiae, Austriae, Italiae." RCN: 3953.
Lectotype (Starmühler in Wisskirchen & Haeupler, *Standardliste Farn-Blütenpfl. Deutschl.*: 41. 1998): [icon] *"Aconitum lycoctonum flore luteo"* in Besler, Hort. Eystett. aest.: ord. 1, fol. 11, f. 2. 1613.
Current name: ***Aconitum lycoctonum*** L. (Ranunculaceae).
Note: Tamura & Lauener (in *Notes Roy. Bot. Gard. Edinburgh* 37: 459. 1979) regarded this as a *nomen ambiguum*. See also discussion of the name and material by Molero & Blanché (in *Anales Jard. Bot. Madrid* 41: 211. 1984) and Skalický (in *Preslia* 57: 136–137. 1985). Although Starmühler attributed the typification to Warncke (*Die europ. Sippen* Aconitum lycoctonum *Gruppe*. 1964), this appears to be an unpublished thesis, so effective typification is therefore attributed to Starmühler.

Aconitum napellus Linnaeus, *Species Plantarum* 1: 532. 1753.
"Habitat in Helvetia, Bavaria, Gallia." RCN: 3954.
Lectotype (Seitz in *Feddes Repert.* 80: 24, t. 1. 1969): Herb. Clifford: 214, *Aconitum* 3, sheet A (BM-000628795).
Generitype of *Aconitum* Linnaeus.
Current name: ***Aconitum napellus*** L. (Ranunculaceae).
Note: Aconitum napellus, with the type designated by Seitz (but in the proposal erroneously attributed to Molero & Blanché in *Anales Jard. Bot. Madrid* 41: 212. 1984), was proposed as conserved type of the genus by Jarvis (in *Taxon* 41: 555. 1992). However, the proposal was eventually ruled unnecessary by the General Committee (see Barrie, *l.c.* 55: 795–796. 2006 for a review of the history of this and related proposals).
    Seitz's choice of the Clifford sheet as type was rejected by Skalický (in *Preslia* 54: 117. 1982), on the grounds of geographical conflict with the protologue, and a neotype chosen. Despite being followed by Starmühler (in Wisskirchen & Haeupler, *Standardliste Farn-Blütenpfl. Deutschl.*: 41. 1998), this is in any case invalid because original elements are in existence.

Aconitum pyrenaicum Linnaeus, *Species Plantarum* 1: 532. 1753.
"Habitat in Sibiria, Tataria, Pyrenaeis." RCN: 3955.
Lectotype (Tamura & Lauener in *Notes Roy. Bot. Gard. Edinburgh* 37: 447. 1979): Herb. Linn. No. 695.4 (LINN).
Current name: ***Aconitum pyrenaicum*** L. (Ranunculaceae).
Note: Tamura & Lauener, in typifying the name, suggested that it should be rejected and *A. barbatum* Pers. used in its place. However, no formal rejection proposal has been made.

Aconitum uncinatum Linnaeus, *Species Plantarum,* ed. 2, 1: 750. 1762.
"Habitat in Philadelphia." RCN: 3959.
Lectotype (Hardin in *Brittonia* 16: 90. 1964): *Bartram*, Herb. Linn. No. 695.9 (LINN; iso- BM).
Current name: ***Aconitum uncinatum*** L. var. ***uncinatum*** (Ranunculaceae).

Aconitum variegatum Linnaeus, *Species Plantarum* 1: 532. 1753.
"Habitat in Italiae, Bohemiae montibus." RCN: 3957.
Lectotype (Götz in *Feddes Repert.* 76: 33. 1967): Herb. Linn. No. 695.8 (LINN).
Current name: ***Aconitum variegatum*** L. (Ranunculaceae).
Note: Starmühler (in *Taxon* 47: 747. 1998) proposed *A. variegatum* as the conserved type of *Aconitum*, but this was not recommended by the Committee for Spermatophyta (in *Taxon* 49: 274. 2000).

Acorus calamus Linnaeus, *Species Plantarum* 1: 324. 1753.
"Habitat α in Europae, β in Indiae fossis paludosis." RCN: 2527.
Lectotype (Suresh & al. in *Taxon* 32: 130. 1983): Herb. Linn. No. 447.1 (LINN).
Generitype of *Acorus* Linnaeus.
Current name: ***Acorus calamus*** L. (Acoraceae).

Acorus calamus Linnaeus var. **verus** Linnaeus, *Species Plantarum* 1: 324. 1753.
"Habitat in Indiae fossis paludosis." RCN: 2527.
Lectotype (Nicolson & al., *Interpret. Van Rheede's Hort. Malab.*: 274. 1988): [icon] *"Vaembu"* in Rheede, Hort. Malab. 11: 99, t. 48. 1692.
Current name: ***Acorus calamus*** L. (Acoraceae).

Acorus calamus Linnaeus var. **vulgaris** Linnaeus, *Species Plantarum* 1: 324. 1753.
"Habitat in Europae, fossis paludosis." RCN: 2527.
Type not designated.
Original material: Herb. Clifford: 137, *Acorus* 1 (BM); [icon] in Morison, Pl. Hist. Univ. 3: 246, s. 8, t. 13, f. 4. 1699.
Current name: ***Acorus calamus*** L. (Acoraceae).

Acrostichum aculeatum Linnaeus, *Systema Naturae,* ed. 10, 2: 1320. 1759.
["Habitat in Jamaica."] Sp. Pl. ed. 2, 2: 1530 (1763). RCN: 7790.
Type not designated.
Original material: Herb. Linn. No. 1245.16 (LINN); [icon] in Sloane, Voy. Jamaica 1: 99, t. 61. 1707 – Typotype: Herb. Sloane 1: 157 (BM-SL).
Current name: ***Pityrogramma chrysophylla*** (Sw.) Link (Pteridaceae).
Note: See discussion by Proctor (in Howard, *Fl. Lesser Antilles* 2: 170. 1977). Despite sharing Sloane's t. 61 (1707) as a cited synonym, this name and *Adiantum aculeatum* L. (1753) are independent names.

Acrostichum areolatum Linnaeus, *Species Plantarum* 2: 1069. 1753.
"Habitat in Virginia, Marilandia." RCN: 7779.
Lectotype (Reveal & al. in *Huntia* 7: 223. 1987): *Clayton 683*, pl. 1 (BM-000062955).
Current name: ***Woodwardia areolata*** (L.) T. Moore (Blechnaceae).

Acrostichum aureum Linnaeus, *Species Plantarum* 2: 1069. 1753.
"Habitat in Jamaicae, Dominicae humentibus." RCN: 7776.
Lectotype (Schelpe in *Contr. Bolus Herb.* 1: 45. 1969): Herb. Clifford: 475, *Acrostichum* 1 (BM-000647610).
Generitype of *Acrostichum* Linnaeus (vide Mirbel, *Dict. Sci. Nat.* 1: 244. 1816; Smith, *Hist. Fil.*: 146. 1875).

Current name: ***Acrostichum aureum*** L. (Pteridaceae).
Note: Although Tardieu-Blot (in Aubréville, *Fl. Gabon* 8: 100. 1964) stated "Type: herb. Linné, 1767" it is unclear whether this refers to LINN (where 1245 would be the generic number). Schelpe's choice of Clifford material as type therefore appears to be the earliest explicit choice although 1245.5 (LINN) was treated as the lectotype by Proctor (in Howard, *Fl. Lesser Antilles* 2: 152. 1977), as was a Plumier plate (by Proctor, *Ferns Jamaica*: 281. 1985).

Acrostichum barbarum Linnaeus, *Species Plantarum* 2: 1072. 1753.
"Habitat in Africa." RCN: 7792.
Type not designated.
Original material: Herb. Clifford: 476, *Acrostichum* 4 (BM); [icon] in Plukenet, Phytographia: t. 181, f. 5. 1692; Almag. Bot.: 156. 1696 – Voucher: Herb. Sloane 96: 44 (BM-SL).
Current name: ***Todea barbara*** (L.) T. Moore (Osmundaceae).
Note: Schelpe & Anthony (in Leistner, *Fl. Southern Africa, Pteridophyta*: 45. 1986) indicated Adair material in Herb. Sloane (presumably linked to the cited Plukenet plate) as the holotype. However, this collection was never seen by Linnaeus and is not original material for the name.

Acrostichum calomelanos Linnaeus, *Species Plantarum* 2: 1072. 1753.
"Habitat in America meridionali." RCN: 7788.
Lectotype (Schelpe in *Contr. Bolus Herb.* 1: 50. 1969): Herb. Linn. No. 1245.19 (LINN).
Current name: ***Pityrogramma calomelanos*** (L.) Link (Pteridaceae).
Note: See discussion by Tryon (in *Contr. Gray Herb.* 189: 60. 1962; 194: 68. 1964) who did not, however, designate a type. Although Tardieu-Blot (in Aubréville, *Fl. Cameroun* 3: 134. 1964) stated "Type: herb. L." it is unclear whether this was intended to refer to Leiden (L), or LINN.

Acrostichum citrifolium Linnaeus, *Species Plantarum* 2: 1067. 1753.
"Habitat in America meridionali." RCN: 7766.
Lectotype (Tryon in *Contr. Gray Herb.* 194: 225. 1964): [icon] *"Lingua Cervina scandens, citrei foliis minor"* in Plumier, Traité Foug. Amér.: 101, t. 116. 1705. – Typotype: *Plumier*, Herb. Jussieu 991 (P-JUSS).
Current name: ***Anetium citrifolium*** (L.) Splitg. (Vittariaceae).

Acrostichum crinitum Linnaeus, *Species Plantarum* 2: 1068. 1753.
"Habitat – – – – –" RCN: 7768.
Lectotype (Proctor in Howard, *Fl. Lesser Antilles* 2: 216. 1977): [icon] *"Phyllitis crinita latissimo fol."* in Petiver, Pteri-graphia Amer.: 145, t. 13, f. 14. 1712 (see p. 147).
Current name: ***Elaphoglossum crinitum*** (L.) Christ (Lomariopsidaceae).

Acrostichum cruciatum Linnaeus, *Species Plantarum* 2: 1072. 1753.
"Habitat in America meridionali." RCN: 7790.
Lectotype (Proctor & Lourteig in *Bradea* 5: 385. 1990): [icon] *"Lonchitis pulverulenta, pinnulis obtuse dentatis"* in Plumier, Traité Foug. Amér.: 37, t. 48, f. B. 1705.
Current name: ***Thelypteris sancta*** (L.) Ching (Thelypteridaceae).

Acrostichum dichotomum Linnaeus, *Species Plantarum* 2: 1068. 1753.
"Habitat in China." RCN: 7772.
Lectotype (Holttum in van Steenis, *Fl. Malesiana*, ser. II, 1: 41. 1959): [icon] *"Cochine branched Comb Fern"* in Petiver, Gazophyl. Nat.: 7, t. 70, f. 12. 1702–1709. – Typotype: Herb. Sloane 163: 43 (BM-SL).
Current name: ***Schizaea dichotoma*** (L.) Sm. (Schizaeaceae).

Note: Stearn (*Introd. Linnaeus' Sp. Pl.* (Ray Soc. ed.): 129. 1957) treated a Cuningham specimen in Petiver's herbarium (BM-SL) as the type but this was not seen by Linnaeus and is not original material for the name.

Acrostichum digitatum Linnaeus, *Species Plantarum* 2: 1068. 1753.
"Habitat in Zeylona." RCN: 7773.
Lectotype (Holttum in van Steenis *Fl. Malesiana*, ser. II, 1: 41. 1959): Herb. Hermann 2: 73, No. 379 (BM-000621756).
Current name: ***Schizaea digitata*** (L.) Wall. (Schizaeaceae).

Acrostichum ebeneum Linnaeus, *Species Plantarum* 2: 1071. 1753.
"Habitat in Jamaicae sepibus humidiusculis." RCN: 7788.
Lectotype (Tryon in *Contr. Gray Herb.* 189: 60. 1962): [icon] *"Filix non ramosa minima, caule nigro, surculis raris pinnulis angustis, raris, brevibus, acutis, subtus niveis"* in Sloane, Voy. Jamaica 1: 92, t. 53, f. 1. 1707.
Current name: ***Pityrogramma calomelanos*** (L.) Link (Pteridaceae).
Note: Tryon (in *Contr. Gray Herb.* 189: 60. 1962) designated the Sloane plate as lectotype, but subsequent study has shown that this belongs to the taxon known as *Pityrogramma calomelanos* (L.) Link, into the synonymy of which *A. ebeneum* should fall. However, Proctor (in *Brit. Fern Gaz.* 9: 220. 1965; *Mem. New York Bot. Gard.* 53: 125. 1989) rejected Tryon's typification in favour of 1245.14 (LINN), a specimen of *P. tartarea* (Cav.) Maxon. As *P. ebenea* (L.) Proctor has been adopted for the latter in some works, Tryon (in *Taxon* 46: 339. 1997) proposed *A. ebeneum* for rejection. However, the Committee for Pteridophyta (in *Taxon* 54: 831. 2005) did not recommend rejection, confirmed by the General Committee (in *Taxon* 55: 800. 2006).

Acrostichum ferruginosum Linnaeus, *Species Plantarum*, ed. 2, 2: 1525. 1763.
"Habitat in America." RCN: 7774.
Lectotype (designated here by Reveal): [icon] *"Filici-folia s. Polypodium tenuifolium minus Virginianum"* in Plukenet, Phytographia: t. 89, f. 9. 1691; Almag. Bot.: 153. 1696. – Typotype: Herb. Sloane 96: 39 (BM-SL).
Current name: ***Polypodium polypodioides*** (L.) Watts var. ***michauxiana*** Weath. (Polypodiaceae).
Note: See comments by Weatherby (in *Contr. Gray Herb.* 74: 24. 1939).

Acrostichum furcatum Linnaeus, *Systema Naturae*, ed. 10, 2: 1321. 1759.
["Habitat in Jamaica."] Sp. Pl., ed. 2, 2: 1529 (1763). RCN: 7789.
Lectotype (Proctor in Howard, *Fl. Lesser Antilles* 2: 62. 1977): [icon] *"Filix furcata, pinnulis longiusculis, non dentatis"* in Plumier, Descr. Pl. Amér.: 13, t. 20. 1693.
Current name: ***Gleichenia furcata*** (L.) Spreng. (Gleicheniaceae).
Note: See Underwood (in *Bull. Torrey Bot. Club* 34: 243, 257. 1907), who wrongly stated that Plumier's 1703 plate 28 "was taken by Linnaeus...in 1759 as the type of *Acrostichum furcatum*".

Acrostichum heterophyllum Linnaeus, *Species Plantarum* 2: 1067. 1753.
"Habitat in Malabaria, Zeylona, Africa." RCN: 7767.
Lectotype (Sledge in *Bull. Brit. Mus. (Nat. Hist.), Bot.* 2: 135. 1960): Herb. Hermann 3: 57; 4: 29, No. 378 (BM-000628016).
Current name: ***Pyrrosia heterophylla*** (L.) M.G. Price (Polypodiaceae).
Note: In designating a type, Sledge did not distinguish between the material mounted in volumes 3 and 4 of the Hermann herbarium. However, as the material appears to be part of a single gathering, Art. 9.15 applies and this is accepted as a formal typification.

Acrostichum ilvense Linnaeus, *Species Plantarum* 2: 1071. 1753.
"Habitat in Europae frigidissimae rupibus." RCN: 7787.
Lectotype (Copeland in *Univ. Calif. Publ. Bot.* 16: 57. 1929): *Amman 51*, Herb. Linn. No. 1245.13 (LINN).
Current name: **Woodsia ilvensis** (L.) R. Br. (Dryopteridaceae).
Note: See Pichi Sermolli (in *Webbia* 12: 182. 1956) who confirmed the identity of 1245.13 (LINN) but suggested that it is not an original element. This seems doubtful, however, and later authors (e.g. Bobrov in *Novosti Sist. Vyssh. Rast.* 21: 7. 1984; Jonsell & Jarvis in *Nordic J. Bot.* 14: 149. 1994) designated the same specimen as lectotype.

Acrostichum lanceolatum Linnaeus, *Species Plantarum* 2: 1067. 1753.
"Habitat in India." RCN: 7765.
Lectotype (Tardieu-Blot in Aubréville, *Fl. Gabon* 8: 201. 1964): Herb. Hermann 1: 3, No. 380 (BM-000621235).
Current name: **Pyrrosia lanceolata** (L.) Farw. (Polypodiaceae).

Acrostichum marantae Linnaeus, *Species Plantarum* 2: 1071. 1753.
"Habitat in Europa australi." RCN: 7786.
Lectotype (Schelpe in *Contr. Bolus Herb.* 1: 73. 1969): *Magnol*, Herb. Linn. No. 1245.12 (LINN).
Current name: **Notholaena marantae** (L.) Desv. (Pteridaceae).

Acrostichum marginatum Linnaeus, *Flora Jamaicensis*. 22. 1759.
["Habitat in Jamaica."] Sp. Pl., ed. 2, 2: 1526 (1763). RCN: 7780.
Type not designated.
Original material: [icon] in Sloane, Voy. Jamaica 1: 84, t. 40. 1707.
Current name: **Pteris grandifolia** L. (Pteridaceae).

Acrostichum nodosum Linnaeus, *Species Plantarum* 2: 1070. 1753.
"Habitat in Dominica." RCN: 7836.
Basionym of: *Asplenium nodosum* (L.) L. (1763).
Lectotype (Underwood in *Bull. Torrey Bot. Club* 29: 671. 1902): [icon] *"Lingua Cervina nodosa major"* in Plumier, Traité Foug. Amér.: 90, t. 108. 1705.
Current name: **Danaea nodosa** (L.) Sm. (Marattiaceae).

Acrostichum pectinatum Linnaeus, *Species Plantarum* 2: 1068. 1753.
"Habitat in Aethiopia." RCN: 7771.
Lectotype (Schelpe & Anthony in Leistner, *Fl. Southern Africa, Pteridophyta*: 51. 1986): Herb. Linn. No. 1245.2 (LINN).
Current name: **Schizaea pectinata** (L.) Sw. (Schizaeaceae).
Note: Verdcourt (in Beentje, *Fl. Trop. E. Africa, Schizaeaceae*: 2. 2000) rejected the type choice of Schelpe & Anthony because they incorrectly referred to 1245.2 (LINN) as the holotype, and designated a Morison plate in its place. However, under Art. 9.8, their type statement is correctable to lectotype, and their choice has priority.

Acrostichum platyneuron Linnaeus, *Species Plantarum* 2: 1069. 1753.
"Habitat in Virginia." RCN: 7782.
Lectotype (Fernald in *Rhodora* 37: 383. 1935): *Clayton 14* (BM-000062962).
Current name: **Asplenium platyneuron** (L.) Britton & al. var. **platyneuron** (Aspleniaceae).
Note: Specific epithet spelled "platyneuros" in the protologue.

Acrostichum polypodioides Linnaeus, *Species Plantarum* 2: 1068. 1753.
"Habitat in Virginia, Jamaica." RCN: 7775.
Lectotype (Verdcourt in Beentje, *Fl. Trop. E. Africa, Polypodiaceae*: 31. 2001): [icon] *"Filix Polypodium dicta minima, Jamaicensis, foliis aversa parte, ferrugineo pulvere Asplenii ritu, circumquaque respersis"*

in Plukenet, Phytographia: t. 289, f. 1. 1694; Almag. Bot.: 153. 1696. – Typotype: Herb. Sloane 129: 29 (BM-SL).
Current name: **Marginaria polypodioides** (L.) Tidestr. var. **polypodioides** (Polypodiaceae).
Note: Weatherby (in *Contr. Gray Herb.* 124: 28. 1939), followed by later authors, treated material in Plukenet's herbarium as the type but this was not seen by Linnaeus and is not original material for the name.

Acrostichum pulchrum Linnaeus, *Species Plantarum* 2: 1072. 1753.
"Habitat Monspelii, inque Harcynia." RCN: 7794.
Type not designated.
Original material: Herb. Burser XX: 12 (UPS); Herb. Linn. No. 1245.20 (LINN).
Current name: **Asplenium adiantum-nigrum** L. (Aspleniaceae).

Acrostichum punctatum Linnaeus, *Species Plantarum*, ed. 2, 2: 1524. 1763.
"Habitat in China. J. Fothergill." RCN: 7769.
Type not designated.
Original material: none traced.
Current name: **Microsorum punctatum** (L.) Copel. (Polypodiaceae).
Note: Many authors since Schelpe & Anthony (in Leistner, *Fl. Southern Africa, Pteridophyta*: 163. 1986) have noted the absence of original material in LINN, and the name appears to need a neotype.

Acrostichum rufum Linnaeus, *Systema Naturae*, ed. 10, 2: 1320. 1759.
["Habitat in America."] Sp. Pl., ed. 2, 2: 1526 (1763). RCN: 7777.
Lectotype (Tryon in *Contr. Gray Herb.* 194: 82. 1964): [icon] *"Filix minor ruffa lanugine tota obducta, in pinnas tantum divisa, raras, non crenatas subrotundas"* in Sloane, Voy. Jamaica 1: 87, t. 45, f. 1. 1707. – Typotype: Herb. Sloane 1: 96 (BM-SL).
Current name: **Hemionitis rufa** (L.) Sw. (Pteridaceae).
Note: Although treated as a new combination based on *Pteris rufa* L. (1753) by some authors, this is unjustified as there is no direct reference to the earlier name in the protologue of *A. rufum*, and *P. rufa* also appears in the same work (1759), as noted by Tryon & Stolze (in *Fieldiana, Bot.* 22: 47. 1989). Linnaeus did, however, treat the two names as synonymous in 1763. See also Lellinger (in *Mem. New York Bot. Gard.* 23: 9. 1972) who indicated what is evidently 1245.6 (LINN, though cited from BM) as the type. This choice is, however, pre-dated by that of Tryon.

Acrostichum sanctum Linnaeus, *Systema Naturae*, ed. 10, 2: 1320. 1759.
["Habitat in Jamaica."] Sp. Pl., ed. 2, 2: 1526 (1763). RCN: 7781.
Lectotype (Proctor in Howard, *Fl. Lesser Antilles* 2: 277. 1977): [icon] *"Filicula non ramosa minima, surculis crebris, pinnulis brevissimis, angustis"* in Sloane, Voy. Jamaica 1: 91, t. 49, f. 2. 1707. – Typotype: Herb. Sloane 1: 115 (BM-SL).
Current name: **Thelypteris sancta** (L.) Ching (Thelypteridaceae).

Acrostichum septentrionale Linnaeus, *Species Plantarum* 2: 1068. 1753.
"Habitat in Europae fissuris rupium." RCN: 7770.
Lectotype (Jonsell & Jarvis in *Nordic J. Bot.* 14: 150. 1994): Herb. Burser XX: 37 (UPS).
Current name: **Asplenium septentrionale** (L.) Hoffm. (Aspleniaceae).

Acrostichum siliquosum Linnaeus, *Species Plantarum* 2: 1070. 1753.
"Habitat in Zeylona." RCN: 7784.
Lectotype (Pichi Sermolli in *Webbia* 12: 651. 1957): Herb. Hermann 2: 59, No. 376 (BM-000621706).
Current name: **Ceratopteris thalictroides** (L.) Brongn. (Pteridaceae).

Acrostichum sorbifolium Linnaeus, *Species Plantarum* 2: 1069. 1753.
"Habitat in Jamaica, Domingo." RCN: 7778.
Lectotype (Proctor in Howard, *Fl. Lesser Antilles* 2: 222. 1977): [icon] *"Lonchitis Calamifera, pinnis serratis"* in Petiver, Pteri-graphia Amer.: 153, t. 9, f. 8. 1712.
Current name: *Lomariopsis sorbifolium* (L.) Fée (Lomariopsidaceae).
Note: Although Underwood (in *Bull. Torrey Bot. Club* 33: 600. 1906) indicated Plumier's t. 117 as type, it does not form part of the protologue so is not original material for the name.

Acrostichum thalictroides Linnaeus, *Species Plantarum* 2: 1070. 1753.
"Habitat in Zeylonae aquosis." RCN: 7785.
Lectotype (Pichi Sermolli in *Webbia* 12: 650. 1957): Herb. Hermann 3: 42, No. 377 (BM-000594684).
Current name: *Ceratopteris thalictroides* (L.) Brongn. (Pteridaceae).

Acrostichum thelypteris Linnaeus, *Species Plantarum* 2: 1071. 1753.
"Habitat in Europae septentrionalioris paludibus." RCN: 7897.
Basionym of: *Polypodium thelypteris* (L.) L. (1774).
Type not designated.
Original material: [icon] in Bauhin & Cherler, Hist. Pl. Univ. 3(2): 738. 1651.
Current name: *Thelypteris palustris* Schott (Thelypteridaceae).

Acrostichum trifoliatum Linnaeus, *Species Plantarum* 2: 1070. 1753.
"Habitat in Jamaica." RCN: 7738.
Lectotype (Proctor, *Ferns Jamaica*: 203. 1985): [icon] *"Phyllitis ramosa trifida"* in Sloane, Voy. Jamaica 1: 88, t. 45, f. 2. 1707. – Typotype: Herb. Sloane 1: 99 (BM-SL).
Current name: *Pityrogramma trifoliatum* (L.) Tryon (Pteridaceae).

Actaea cimicifuga Linnaeus, *Species Plantarum* 1: 504. 1753.
"Habitat in Sibiria. D. Krashenninnikof." RCN: 3962.
Replaced synonym of: *Cimicifuga foetida* L. (1767).
Lectotype (Compton & Jury in *Taxon* 44: 604. 1995): Herb. Linn. No. 220.17 (S).
Generitype of *Cimicifuga* Wernisch.
Current name: *Actaea cimicifuga* L. (Ranunculaceae).

Actaea racemosa Linnaeus, *Species Plantarum* 1: 504. 1753.
"Habitat in Florida, Virginia, Canada." RCN: 3831.
Lectotype (Compton & al. in *Taxon* 47: 614. 1998): Herb. Linn. No. 665.3 (LINN).
Current name: *Actaea racemosa* L. (Ranunculaceae).

Actaea spicata Linnaeus, *Species Plantarum* 1: 504. 1753.
"Habitat in nemoribus Europae." RCN: 3830.
Lectotype (Jonsell & Jarvis in Jarvis & al., *Regnum Veg.* 127: 14. 1993): Herb. Linn. No. 665.1 (LINN).
Generitype of *Actaea* Linnaeus (vide Huth in *Bot. Jahrb. Syst.* 16: 308. 1892).
Current name: *Actaea spicata* L. (Ranunculaceae).
Note: Jonsell & Jarvis (in *Nordic J. Bot.* 14: 160. 1994) provide more details concerning their formal 1993 typification.

Actaea spicata Linnaeus var. **alba** Linnaeus, *Species Plantarum* 1: 504. 1753, *nom. utique rej.*
"Habitat in nemoribus Europae." RCN: 3830.
Type not designated.
Original material: Herb. Burser X: 11? (UPS); [icon] in Cornut, Canad. Pl. Hist.: 76, 77. 1635; [icon] in Morison, Pl. Hist. Univ. 2: 8, s. 1, t. 2, f. 7. 1680.
Current name: *Actaea spicata* L. (Ranunculaceae).

Actaea spicata Linnaeus var. **nigra** Linnaeus, *Species Plantarum* 1: 504. 1753.
"Habitat in nemoribus Americae." RCN: 3830.
Lectotype (Compton & al. in *Taxon* 47: 617. 1998): Herb. Linn. No. 665.1 (LINN).
Current name: *Actaea spicata* L. (Ranunculaceae).

Adansonia bahobab Linnaeus, *Species Plantarum,* ed. 2, 2: 960. 1763, *nom. illeg.*
"Habitat in Senegal, Aegypto." RCN: 5003.
Replaced synonym: *Adansonia digitata* L. (1759).
Lectotype (Robyns in Dassanayake & Fosberg, *Revised Handb. Fl. Ceylon* 1: 67. 1980): Herb. Linn. No. 862.1 (LINN).
Current name: *Adansonia digitata* L. (Bombacaceae).
Note: This name is nomenclaturally superfluous as it is based on all the original elements of the earlier *A. digitata* L. (1759).

Adansonia digitata Linnaeus, *Systema Naturae,* ed. 10, 2: 1144. 1759.
["Habitat in Senegal, Aegypto."] Sp. Pl., ed. 2, 2: 960 (1763). RCN: 5003.
Replaced synonym of: *Adansonia bahobab* L. (1763), *nom. illeg.*
Lectotype (Robyns in Dassanayake & Fosberg, *Revised Handb. Fl. Ceylon* 1: 67. 1980): Herb. Linn. No. 862.1 (LINN).
Generitype of *Adansonia* Linnaeus.
Current name: *Adansonia digitata* L. (Bombacaceae).

Adelia acidoton Linnaeus, *Systema Naturae,* ed. 10, 2: 1298. 1759.
["Habitat in Jamaica."] Sp. Pl., ed. 2, 2: 1472 (1763). RCN: 7522.
Lectotype (Fawcett & Rendle, *Fl. Jamaica* 4: 226. 1920): Browne, Herb. Linn. No. 1201.4 (LINN).
Current name: *Flueggia acidoton* (L.) G.L. Webster (Euphorbiaceae).

Adelia bernardina Linnaeus, *Systema Naturae,* ed. 10, 2: 1298. 1759.
["Habitat in America."] Sp. Pl., ed. 2, 2: 1472 (1763). RCN: 7520.
Type not designated.
Original material: Herb. Linn. No. 1201.1 (LINN).
Current name: *Bernardia dichotoma* (Willd.) Müll. Arg. (Euphorbiaceae).

Adelia ricinella Linnaeus, *Systema Naturae,* ed. 10, 2: 1298. 1759, *typ. cons.*
["Habitat in Jamaica."] Sp. Pl., ed. 2, 2: 1473. 1763. RCN: 7521.
Lectotype (Fawcett & Rendle, *Fl. Jamaica* 4: 292. 1920): Herb. Linn. No. 1201.2 (LINN).
Generitype of *Adelia* Linnaeus, *nom. cons.*
Current name: *Adelia ricinella* L. (Euphorbiaceae).
Note: Adelia Linnaeus, *nom. cons.* against *Adelia* P. Browne.

Adenanthera falcata Linnaeus, *Herbarium Amboinense*: 14. 1754.
["Habitat in India."] Sp. Pl., ed. 2, 1: 550 (1762). RCN: 3025.
Lectotype (Merrill, *Interpret. Rumph. Herb. Amb.*: 33, 248. 1917): [icon] *"Clypearia alba"* in Rumphius, Herb. Amboin. 3: 176, t. 111. 1743.
Current name: *Albizia falcata* (L.) Backer (Fabaceae: Mimosoideae).
Note: Linnaeus originally based this name on two Rumphius plates (*Herb. Amb.* 3: t. 111; t. 112. 1743). In 1759 (*Syst. Nat.*, ed. 10, 2: 1020), Linnaeus cited only t. 112, and then in 1762 (*Sp. Pl.*, ed. 2, 1: 550) *Ad. falcata* did not appear, but *Ad. falcataria* L. (which has essentially the same diagnosis as *Ad. falcata* in 1759, though with Rumphius' t. 111 now the only synonym) was described. In 1767, Linnaeus reverted from "falcataria" to "falcata" with t. 112 again reinstated, as in the 1759 account.
  Complications have arisen because of disagreements over the typification of the name, and over the identity of the two illustrations. Merrill (*Interpret. Rumph. Herb. Amb.*: 33, 248. 1917)

treated t. 111 as the type, and *Ad. falcataria* as a homotypic synonym (of *Albizia falcata* (L.) Backer). However, Fosberg (in *Reinwardtia* 7: 88–90. 1965) instead regarded t. 112 (which he identified as a species of *Pithecellobium*) as the type of *Ad. falcata*, and therefore took up *Al. falcataria* (L.) Fosberg instead, typified by t. 111. Kostermans (in *Ceylon J. Sci., Biol. Sci.* 13: 256–257. 1979) followed Fosberg, and made the combination *P. falcatum* (L.) Kosterm. for *Ad. falcata* (with t. 112 as type). However, Nielsen (in Nielsen & al., *Opera Bot.* 76: 53. 1985), while accepting t. 112 as type, has argued that the identity of the plate is uncertain and that *Ad. falcata* (and *P. falcatum*) should be treated as *nomina dubia*. He accepted *Archidendron clypearia* (Jack) Nielsen as the current name (and described *A. falcatum* Nielsen to preclude any future transfer of *Ad. falcata*).

Despite some confusion on Merrill's part over Linnaeus' 1759 treatment of the two plates (noted by Kostermans), t. 111 was original material for *Ad. falcata* and Merrill was therefore entitled to choose it as the type. Indeed, his decision to treat *Ad. falcata* and *Ad. falcataria* as homotypic seems not unreasonable bearing in mind that Linnaeus seems to have treated the latter as a substitute name for the former in 1762, then reverted once more to *Ad. falcata* in 1767. Later authors have not justified the rejection of Merrill's typification, which results in *Al. falcata* being the correct name. *Albizia falcataria* (syn. *Paraserianthes falcataria* (L.) Nielsen; *Falcataria moluccana* (Miquel) Barneby & Grimes), however, appears to be in wider current use.

Adenanthera falcataria Linnaeus, *Species Plantarum*, ed. 2, 1: 550. 1762.
"Habitat in India." RCN: 3025.
Lectotype (Merrill, *Interpret. Rumph. Herb. Amb.*: 250. 1917): [icon] *"Clypearia alba"* in Rumphius, Herb. Amboin. 3: 176, t. 111. 1743.
Current name: ***Albizia falcata*** (L.) Backer (Fabaceae: Mimosoideae).
Note: See discussion under *Adenanthera falcata* L.

Adenanthera pavonina Linnaeus, *Species Plantarum* 1: 384. 1753.
"Habitat in India." RCN: 3024.
Lectotype (Fawcett & Rendle, *Fl. Jamaica* 4: 128. 1920): Herb. Hermann 2: 30, No. 160 (BM-000594593).
Generitype of *Adenanthera* Linnaeus.
Current name: ***Adenanthera pavonina*** L. (Fabaceae: Mimosoideae).

Adiantum aculeatum Linnaeus, *Species Plantarum* 2: 1096. 1753.
"Habitat in Jamaica, Dominica." RCN: 7939.
Lectotype (Maxon in *Contr. U. S. Natl. Herb.* 17: 161. 1913): [icon] *"Adiantum frutescens, spinosum et repens"* in Plumier, Traité Foug. Amér.: 77, t. 94. 1705.
Current name: ***Odontosoria aculeata*** (L.) J. Sm. (Pteridaceae).
Note: Despite sharing Sloane's t. 61 (1707) as a cited synonym, this name and *Acrostichum aculeatum* L. (1759) are independent names.

Adiantum aethiopicum Linnaeus, *Systema Naturae*, ed. 10, 2: 1329. 1759.
["Habitat ad Cap. b. spei."] Sp. Pl., ed. 2, 2: 1560 (1763). RCN: 7943.
Lectotype (Pichi Sermolli in *Webbia* 12: 695. 1957): Herb. Linn. No. 1252.15 (LINN).
Current name: ***Adiantum aethiopicum*** L. (Pteridaceae).

Adiantum capillus-veneris Linnaeus, *Species Plantarum* 2: 1096. 1753.
"Habitat in Europa australi." RCN: 7932.
Lectotype (Pichi Sermolli in *Webbia* 12: 678. 1957): *Magnol*, Herb. Linn. No. 1252.9 (LINN).
Generitype of *Adiantum* Linnaeus (vide Smith, *Hist. Fil.* 274. 1875).
Current name: ***Adiantum capillus-veneris*** L. (Pteridaceae).

Adiantum caudatum Linnaeus, *Mantissa Plantarum Altera*: 308. 1771.
"Habitat in India orientali." RCN: 7928.
Type not designated.
Original material: Herb. Linn. No. 1252.6 (LINN); [icon] in Burman, Thes. Zeylan.: 8, t. 5, f. 1. 1737.
Current name: ***Adiantum caudatum*** L. (Pteridaceae).
Note: Pichi Sermolli (in *Webbia* 12: 674. 1957) noted that 1252.6 (LINN) is from China and argued that it should be excluded from consideration as a type because of conflict with Linnaeus' "Hab. in India orientali". He added that the cited Burman plate, which "very accurately represents *A. caudatum* in the form which is common in Ceylon" might be the type if Burman's own material in G proved to have been lost.

Adiantum chusanum Linnaeus, *Species Plantarum* 2: 1095. 1753.
"Habitat in China." RCN: 7931.
Type not designated.
Original material: none traced.
Current name: ***Sphenomeris chinensis*** (L.) Maxon (Dennstaedtiaceae).
Note: See discussion by Fosberg (in *Taxon* 18: 596–598. 1969).

Adiantum clavatum Linnaeus, *Species Plantarum* 2: 1096. 1753.
"Habitat in Dominica." RCN: 7938.
Lectotype (Underwood in *Bull. Torrey Bot. Club* 33: 200. 1906): [icon] *"Adiantum minus, foliis in summitate retusis"* in Plumier, Traité Foug. Amér.: 75, t. 101, f. B. 1705.
Current name: ***Sphenomeris clavata*** (L.) Maxon (Dennstaedtiaceae).

Adiantum cristatum Linnaeus, *Systema Naturae*, ed. 10, 2: 1328. 1759.
["Habitat in America meridionali."] Sp. Pl., ed. 2, 2: 1558 (1763). RCN: 7935.
Lectotype (Proctor, *Ferns Jamaica*: 237. 1985): [icon] *"Adiantum ramosum, foliis Trapeziis, dentatis"* in Plumier, Descr. Pl. Amér.: 31, t. 46. 1693.
Current name: ***Adiantum pyramidale*** (L.) Willd. (Pteridaceae).

Adiantum flabellulatum Linnaeus, *Species Plantarum* 2: 1095. 1753.
"Habitat in China. Osbeck." RCN: 7929.
Type not designated.
Original material: Herb. Linn. No. 1252.7 (LINN); [icon] in Plukenet, Phytographia: t. 4, f. 3. 1691; Almag. Bot.: 11. 1696 – Typotype: Herb. Sloane 90: 6 (BM-SL).
Current name: ***Adiantum flabellulatum*** L. (Pteridaceae).

Adiantum hexagonum Linnaeus, *Species Plantarum* 2: 1097. 1753.
"Habitat in America." RCN: 7941.
Lectotype (Proctor, *Ferns Jamaica*: 264. 1985): [icon] *"Adiantum pinnis hexagonis furcatis"* in Petiver, Pteri-graphia Amer.: 94, t. 10, f. 2. 1712.
Current name: ***Anopteris hexagona*** (L.) C. Chr. (Pteridaceae).

Adiantum lancea Linnaeus, *Species Plantarum*, ed. 2, 2: 1557. 1763.
"Habitat Surinami." RCN: 7925.
Lectotype (Kramer in *Acta Bot. Neerl.* 6: 247. 1957): [icon] *"Adiantum album, maximum, Americanum"* in Seba, Locupl. Rer. Nat. Thes. 2: 65, t. 64, f. 7, 8. 1735.
Current name: ***Lindsaea lancea*** (L.) Bedd. (Dennstaedtiaceae).

Adiantum pedatum Linnaeus, *Species Plantarum* 2: 1095. 1753.
"Habitat in Canada, Virginia." RCN: 7924.
Lectotype (designated here by Reveal): [icon] *"Adianthum fruticos. American. summis ramulis reflexis et in orbem expansis"* in Plukenet,

Phytographia: t. 124, f. 2. 1692; Almag. Bot.: 10. 1696. –
Typotype: Herb. Sloane 93: 10 (BM-SL).
Current name: *Adiantum pedatum* L. var. *pedatum* (Pteridaceae).

Adiantum philippense Linnaeus, *Species Plantarum* 2: 1094. 1753.
"Habitat in Philippinis." RCN: 7922.
Lectotype (Pichi Sermolli in *Webbia* 12: 665. 1957): [icon] *"Adiantum
Philippense, folio rotundo laciniato"* in Petiver, Gazophyl. Nat.: 8, t.
4, f. 4. 1702–1709.
Current name: *Adiantum philippense* L. (Pteridaceae).
Note: Some authors (e.g. Morton in *Contr. U. S. Natl. Herb.* 38: 370.
1974) have regarded the type as unidentifiable and so have treated
the name as dubious.

Adiantum pteroides Linnaeus, *Systema Naturae*, ed. 12, 2: 695;
Mantissa Plantarum: 130. 1767.
"Habitat ad Cap. b. spei." RCN: 7942.
Lectotype (Anthony in *Contr. Bolus Herb.* 11: 227. 1984): Herb. Linn.
No. 1252.14 (LINN).
Current name: *Pellaea pteroides* (L.) Prantl (Pteridaceae).

Adiantum pulverulentum Linnaeus, *Species Plantarum* 2: 1096.
1753.
"Habitat in America." RCN: 7934.
Lectotype (Lellinger in *Mem. New York Bot. Gard.* 23: 15. 1972):
[icon] *"Adiantum nigrum, ramosum, pulverulentum et falcatum"* in
Plumier, Descr. Pl. Amér.: 32, t. 47. 1693.
Current name: *Adiantum pulverulentum* L. (Pteridaceae).

Adiantum radiatum Linnaeus, *Species Plantarum* 2: 1094. 1753.
"Habitat in Jamaica, Domingo." RCN: 7923.
Replaced synonym of: *Adiantum radicans* L. (1759), *nom. illeg.*
Lectotype (Lellinger in *Mem. New York Bot. Gard.* 23: 179. 1972):
Herb. Linn. No. 1252.1 (LINN).
Current name: *Adiantopsis radiata* (L.) Fée (Pteridaceae).

Adiantum radicans Linnaeus, *Flora Jamaicensis*: 23. 1759, *nom. illeg.*
"Habitat [in Jamaica.]"
Replaced synonym: *Adiantum radiatum* L. (1753).
Lectotype (Lellinger in *Mem. New York Bot. Gard.* 23: 179. 1972):
Herb. Linn. No. 1252.1 (LINN).
Current name: *Adiantopsis radiata* (L.) Fée (Pteridaceae).
Note: This appears to be a superfluous name for *A. radiatum* L. (1753).

Adiantum reniforme Linnaeus, *Species Plantarum* 2: 1094. 1753.
"Habitat in Madera." RCN: 7921.
Lectotype (Verdcourt in Beentje, *Fl. Trop. E. Africa, Adiantaceae*: 52.
2002): [icon] *"Filix Hemionitis dicta Maderensis pediculis
splendentibus nigris, crenatis foliis Asari rotundioribus crenarum
segmentis oblongo quadratis, ob semina adnascentia per ambitum
circumcirca reflexis"* in Plukenet, Phytographia: t. 287. f. 5. 1694;
Almag. Bot.: 155. 1696. – Typotype: Herb. Sloane 100: 51 (BM-
SL).
Current name: *Adiantum reniforme* L. (Pteridaceae).
Note: See comments on the Plukenet figure and voucher by
Francisco-Ortega & al. (in *Bull. Nat. Hist. Mus. London (Bot.)* 24:
12, f. 6, 7. 1994). Roux (*Consp. Southern African Pteridophyta*: 77.
2001) indicated material in Herb. Sloane as the lectotype, but it
was not studied by Linnaeus and is not original material for the
name.

Adiantum serrulatum Linnaeus, *Species Plantarum* 2: 1095. 1753.
"Habitat in Jamaica." RCN: 7927.
Lectotype (Proctor, *Ferns Jamaica*: 242. 1985): [icon] *"Trichomanes
majus nigrum, pinnis leviter dentatis, trapezii figura"* in Sloane, Voy.

Jamaica 1: 81, t. 35, f. 2. 1707. – Voucher: Herb. Sloane 1: 75
(BM-SL).
Current name: *Adiantum pulverulentum* L. var. *caudatum* Jenman
(Pteridaceae).
Note: Lellinger (in *Mem. New York Bot. Gard.* 23: 14. 1972) indicated
unspecified and unseen material in Herb. Sloane (BM-SL) as type
but this would in any case not have been seen by Linnaeus and
could not be original material for the name.

Adiantum trapeziforme Linnaeus, *Species Plantarum* 2: 1097.
1753.
"Habitat in America meridionali." RCN: 7940.
Lectotype (Lellinger in *Proc. Biol. Soc. Washington* 89: 704. 1977):
[icon] *"Adiantum nigrum ramosum maximum, foliis majoribus
trapezii in modum figuratis"* in Sloane, Voy. Jamaica 1: 98, t. 59.
1707. – Typotype: Herb. Sloane 1: 153 (BM-SL).
Current name: *Adiantum trapeziforme* L. (Pteridaceae).

Adiantum trifoliatum Linnaeus, *Species Plantarum* 2: 1095. 1753.
"Habitat in America." RCN: 7930.
Lectotype (Proctor & Lourteig in *Bradea* 5: 386. 1990): [icon]
"Adiantum clavatum triphyllum" in Petiver, Pteri-graphia Amer.: 99,
t. 11, f. 4. 1712.
Current name: *Hymenophyllum trifoliatum* (L.) Proctor & Lourteig
(Hymenophyllaceae).

Adiantum trilobum Linnaeus, *Species Plantarum* 2: 1095. 1753.
"Habitat in America." RCN: 7926.
Lectotype (Lellinger & Proctor in *Taxon* 32: 568. 1983): [icon]
"Adiantulum triphyllum repens" in Petiver, Pteri-graphia Amer.: 100,
t. 11, f. 9. 1712.
Current name: *Adiantum capillus-veneris* L. (Pteridaceae).

Adiantum villosum Linnaeus, *Systema Naturae*, ed. 10, 2: 1328.
1759.
["Habitat in Jamaica."] Sp. Pl., ed. 2, 2: 1559 (1763). RCN: 7933.
Type not designated.
Original material: Herb. Linn. No. 1252.10 (LINN); [icon] in
Plukenet, Phytographia: t. 253, f.1. 1694.
Current name: *Adiantum villosum* L. (Pteridaceae).
Note: Tryon (in *Contr. Gray Herb.* 194: 152. 1964) treated 1252.10
(LINN) as the type but Proctor (in Howard, *Fl. Lesser Antilles* 2:
185. 1977) argued that both it and the cited Plukenet plate
conflicted with Linnaeus' diagnosis and so designated a neotype
from Herb. Sloane (1: 127, BM-SL). The material in LINN is
apparently identifiable as *A. pulverulentum* L., while the Plukenet
plate is said to depict *A. kendalii* Jenman (Proctor, *Ferns Jamaica*:
241. 1985). However, despite its apparently unfortunate identity,
the Plukenet element forms part of the protologue and therefore
cannot be deemed to conflict with it. It is original material for the
name, and so Proctor's designation of a neotype is contrary to Art.
7.11. The name may be a candidate for conservation with a
conserved type.

Adonis aestivalis Linnaeus, *Species Plantarum*, ed. 2, 1: 771. 1762.
"Habitat inter segetes Europae australis." RCN: 4055.
Lectotype (Shlangena in *Novosti Sist. Vyssh. Rast.* 12: 208. 1975):
Herb. Linn. No. 714.1 (LINN).
Current name: *Adonis aestivalis* L. (Ranunculaceae).
Note: Bobrov (in Komarov, *Fl. U.R.S.S.* 7: 537. 1937) stated "Type in
the Linnaean herbarium" (rather than the far commoner, and
ineffective, "Type in London"). There are, however, two sheets at
LINN associated with this name, so this is not an effective type
choice (and 714.1 and 714.2 are not part of a single gathering so
Art. 9.15 does not apply). Although Reidl (in *Ann. Naturhist. Mus.*

Wien 66: 55. 1963) discussed the protologue, he did not designate a type. Steinberg (in *Webbia* 25: 305. 1971) reproduced the protologue and (p. 310) indicated Bauhin material in BAS as type but, as this was never seen by Linnaeus, it is not original material for the name.

Adonis annua Linnaeus, *Species Plantarum* 1: 547. 1753, *typ. cons.*
"Habitat inter segetes Europae australis." RCN: 4056.
Replaced synonym of: *Adonis autumnalis* L. (1762), *nom. illeg.*
Conserved type (Jarvis in *Taxon* 41: 555. 1992): Herb. Linn. No. 714.3 (LINN).
Generitype of *Adonis* Linnaeus, *nom. cons.*
Current name: ***Adonis annua*** L. (Ranunculaceae).
Note: Adonis annua was proposed as conserved type of the genus by Jarvis (in *Taxon* 41: 555. 1992) and this was eventually approved by the General Committee (see review of the history of the proposal by Barrie, *l.c.* 55: 795–796. 2006).

Adonis annua Linnaeus var. **atrorubens** Linnaeus, *Species Plantarum* 1: 547. 1753.
"Habitat inter segetes Europae australis." RCN: 4056.
Lectotype (Rico in Jarvis & al. in *Taxon* 54: 468. 2005): [icon] *"Flos Adonis vulgo"* in Clusius, Rar. Pl. Hist. 1: 335, 336. 1601. – Epitype (Rico in Jarvis & al. in *Taxon* 54: 468. 2005): France. Tour du Valat, Le Sambuc; SE of the irrigation canal, 11 Jun 1968, *Kendrick & Moyes 215* (BM).
Current name: ***Adonis annua*** L. (Ranunculaceae).
Note: Rico gives a detailed review of earlier type statements.

Adonis annua Linnaeus var. **phoenicea** Linnaeus, *Species Plantarum* 1: 547. 1753.
"Habitat inter segetes Europae australis." RCN: 4055.
Lectotype (Rico in Jarvis & al. in *Taxon* 54: 468. 2005): [icon] *"Adonis flore pallido"* in Mattioli, Pl. Epit.: 648. 1586. – Epitype (Rico in Jarvis & al. in *Taxon* 54: 468. 2005): Serbia & Montenegro. 20 miles W of Belgrade on Autoput. Waste place on road verge. Between 2–300ft, 7 Jun 1955, *W. Sladen 6/5/40* (BM).
Current name: ***Adonis aestivalis*** L. (Ranunculaceae).
Note: Steinberg (in *Webbia* 25: 302. 1971) reproduced the protologue, and discussed what he believed to be the original elements, including several Bauhin collections in BAS which were never seen by Linnaeus and cannot be considered original material. Rico rejected Steinberg's choice in favour of a cited Mattioli plate.

Adonis apennina Linnaeus, *Species Plantarum* 1: 548. 1753.
"Habitat in Sibiria, Apenninis." RCN: 4058.
Lectotype (Wang in *Bull. Bot. Res., Harbin* 14: 107. 1994): Herb. Linn. No. 714.5 (LINN), see above, right.
Current name: ***Adonis apennina*** L. (Ranunculaceae).

Adonis autumnalis Linnaeus, *Species Plantarum,* ed. 2, 1: 771. 1762, *nom. illeg.*
"Habitat inter segetes Europae australis." RCN: 4056.
Replaced synonym: *Adonis annua* L. (1753).
Lectotype (Bobrov in Komarov, *Fl. U.R.S.S.* 7: 539. 1937): Herb. Linn. No. 714.3 (LINN).
Current name: ***Adonis annua*** L. (Ranunculaceae).
Note: Bobrov stated "Type in the Linnaean herbarium" (rather than the far commoner, and ineffective, "Type in London"). 714.3 (LINN) is the only sheet there that can be associated with this name so this choice is accepted as the type. Steinberg (in *Webbia* 25: 305. 1971) reproduced the protologue and treated the name as a *nomen ambiguum* (rather than as a *nomen illegitimum*). Jarvis (in *Taxon* 41: 555. 1992) independently reached the same conclusion as Bobrov.

The lectotype of *Adonis apennina* L.

Adonis capensis Linnaeus, *Species Plantarum* 1: 548. 1753.
"Habitat ad Cap. b. spei." RCN: 4059.
Lectotype (Rasmussen in *Opera Bot.* 53: 16. 1979): Herb. Linn. No. 714.6 (LINN).
Current name: ***Knowltonia capensis*** (L.) Huth (Ranunculaceae).

Adonis vernalis Linnaeus, *Species Plantarum* 1: 547. 1753.
"Habitat in Oelandiae, Borussiae, Bohemiae collibus apricis." RCN: 4057.
Lectotype (Jonsell & Jarvis in *Nordic J. Bot.* 14: 160. 1994): Herb. Linn. No. 714.4 (LINN).
Current name: ***Adonis vernalis*** L. (Ranunculaceae).
Note: Sennikov (in *Novosti Sist. Vyssh. Rast.* 31: 83. 1998) provides an extensive review of the original elements for this name.

Adoxa moschatella Linnaeus, *Flora Anglica*: 15. 1754, *orth. var.*
RCN: 2907.
Lectotype (Nasir in Nasir & Ali, *Fl. Pakistan* 151: 3. 1983): Herb. Linn. No. 516.1 (LINN).
Current name: ***Adoxa moschatellina*** L. (Adoxaceae).
Note: An orthographic variant of *A. moschatellina* L. (1753), as noted by Stearn (*Introd. Ray's Syn. Meth. Stirp. Brit.* (Ray Soc. ed.): 68. 1973).

Adoxa moschatellina Linnaeus, *Species Plantarum* 1: 367. 1753.
"Habitat in Europae nemoribus." RCN: 2907.
Lectotype (Nasir in Nasir & Ali, *Fl. Pakistan* 151: 3. 1983): Herb.
Linn. No. 516.1 (LINN).
Generitype of *Adoxa* Linnaeus.
Current name: ***Adoxa moschatellina*** L. (Adoxaceae).

Aegilops caudata Linnaeus, *Species Plantarum* 2: 1051. 1753.
"Habitat in Creta." RCN: 7591.
Lectotype (Greuter in *Boissiera* 13: 172–173. 1967): Herb. Linn. No.
1218.6 (LINN).
Current name: ***Aegilops caudata*** L. (Poaceae).
Note: Scholz & van Slageren (in *Taxon* 43: 393. 1994) reviewed the
history of the name and proposed it for conservation with a
conserved type, as all original elements belonged to taxa other than
that to which the name had been generally applied. However, the
Committee for Spermatophyta (in *Taxon* 45: 675. 1996) did not
recommend conservation.

Aegilops exaltata Linnaeus, *Mantissa Plantarum Altera*: 575. 1771.
"Habitat in Malabaria ad fossas agrorum." RCN: 7595.
Neotype (Simon in *Taxon* 31: 564. 1982): Herb. Linn. No. 1218.15
(LINN).
Current name: ***Ophiuros exaltatus*** (L.) Kuntze (Poaceae).
Note: Simon (*l.c.*) proposed the rejection of the name in his proposal
for the conservation of *Rottboellia exaltata* L. f. However, this was
declined by the Committee for Spermatophyta (in *Taxon* 34: 659.
1985).

Aegilops incurva Linnaeus, *Species Plantarum* 2: 1051. 1753.
"Habitat in Oriente. Tournefort." RCN: 7594.
Neotype (Cuccuini in Cafferty & al. in *Taxon* 49: 242. 2000): Herb.
Linn. No. 1218.11 (LINN).
Current name: ***Parapholis incurva*** (L.) C.E. Hubb. (Poaceae).
Note: Hubbard (in *Proc. Linn. Soc. London* 148: 112. 1936) provided
an extensive discussion of the elements involved in this name but
did not formally choose a type. Cuccuini (2000) designated
1218.11 (LINN) as the lectotype, but doubts over the material's
status as an original element later led him (in *Webbia* 57: 18–19.
2002) to treat it instead as a neotype.

Aegilops incurvata Linnaeus, *Species Plantarum*, ed. 2, 2: 1490. 1763,
orth. var.
"Habitat in Angliae, Hispaniae, Italiae paludibus maritimis." RCN:
7594.
Neotype (Cuccuini in Cafferty & al. in *Taxon* 49: 242. 2000): Herb.
Linn. No. 1218.11 (LINN).
Current name: ***Parapholis incurva*** (L.) C.E. Hubb. (Poaceae).
Note: Rather than treat this as an illegitimate replacement name for *A.
incurva* L. (1753), it seems preferable to regard it as an orthographic
variant. *Aegilops incurvata* included the elements originally included
in *Nardus articulata* L. (1753), the latter name having been placed
into the synonymy of *A. incurva* by Linnaeus in 1759.

Aegilops ovata Linnaeus, *Species Plantarum* 2: 1050. 1753.
"Habitat in Europa australi." RCN: 7590.
Lectotype (Greuter in *Boissiera* 13: 171. 1967): [icon] *"Gramen
spicatum durioribus & crassioribus Locustis, spica brevi"* in
Scheuchzer, Agrostographia: 11, t. 1, f. 2 A, B, C. 1719.
Current name: ***Aegilops neglecta*** Req. ex Bertol. (Poaceae).
Note: This name has been used in the sense of *A. geniculata* Roth by
most authors for the last 200 years, but the type is identifiable as *A.
neglecta* Req. ex Bertol. Lambinon (in *Taxon* 30: 361. 1981)
therefore proposed the name for rejection. The Committee for
Spermatophyta (in *Taxon* 35: 557–558. 1986), however, was

uncertain over the typification of the name, and declined to accept
the proposal. The Committee nevertheless stated "Rejection of the
proposal should not be construed as recommendation that the name
A. ovata should be taken up in the sense of *A. neglecta*". *Aegilops
ovata* seems subsequently to have dropped out of use – see e.g. van
Slageren (*Wild Wheats, Monogr.* Aegilops *&* Amblyopyrum: 6 [note
3], 281–282 [note 2]. 1994). Greuter's typification seems to have
been generally accepted. However, the legal basis for the
abandonment of *A. ovata* remains unclear. The name is not formally
rejected, and Art. 57 seems not to apply in that a proposal to reject
the name has been made, and ruled upon.

Aegilops squarrosa Linnaeus, *Species Plantarum* 2: 1051. 1753.
"Habitat in Oriente. Tournefort." RCN: 7593.
Lectotype (Bowden in *Canad. J. Genet. Cytol.* 8: 133. 1966): Herb.
Linn. No. 1218.9 (LINN).
Current name: ***Aegilops triuncialis*** L. (Poaceae).

Aegilops triuncialis Linnaeus, *Species Plantarum* 2: 1051. 1753, *typ.
cons.*
"Habitat in Monspelii, Massiliae, Smyrnae aridis." RCN: 7592.
Conserved type (Bowden in *Canad. J. Bot.* 37: 675. 1959): *Löfling
701 β*, Herb. Linn. No. 1218.8 (LINN).
Generitype of *Aegilops* Linnaeus, *nom. cons.*
Current name: ***Aegilops triuncialis*** L. (Poaceae).
Note: Aegilops triuncialis, with the type designated by Bowden, was
proposed as conserved type of the genus by Jarvis (in *Taxon* 41: 555.
1992). This was eventually approved by the General Committee
(see review of the history of this proposal by Barrie, *l.c.* 55:
795–796. 2006).

Aeginetia indica Linnaeus, *Species Plantarum* 2: 632. 1753.
"Habitat in Malabaria." RCN: 4595.
Replaced synonym of: *Orobanche aeginetia* L. (1763), *nom. illeg.*
Lectotype (Parnell in *Thai Forest Bull., Bot.* 29: 73. 2001): [icon]
"Tsjem-cumulu" in Rheede, Hort. Malab. 11: 97, t. 47. 1692.
Generitype of *Aeginetia* Linnaeus.
Current name: ***Aeginetia indica*** L. (Orobanchaceae).

Aegopodium podagraria Linnaeus, *Species Plantarum* 1: 265. 1753.
"Habitat in Europa ad sepes inque pomariis." RCN: 2111.
Lectotype (Reduron & Jarvis in Jarvis & al., *Regnum Veg.* 127: 15.
1993): Herb. Clifford: 107, *Aegopodium* 1 (BM-000558399).
Generitype of *Aegopodium* Linnaeus.
Current name: ***Aegopodium podagraria*** L. (Apiaceae).

Aegopricum betulinum Linnaeus filius, *Supplementum Plantarum*:
413. 1782.
"Habitat in Surinamo. Dalberg."
Lectotype (designated here by Esser): *Dahlberg*, Herb. Thunberg Cat.
No. 21673 (UPS).
Generitype of *Aegopricum* Linnaeus, Pl. Surinamensis: 15. 1775.
Current name: ***Maprounea guianensis*** Aubl. (Euphorbiaceae).
Note: Believing there to be no extant original material, Radcliffe-Smith
(in Jarvis & al., *Regnum Veg.* 127: 15. 1993) designated *Hostmann
996* ["966"] ex Herb. Bentham (K) as a neotype. However, Esser
has located Dalberg material in UPS, which is original material for
the name, and designates it as a lectotype in place of Radcliffe-
Smith's neotype.

Aeschynomene americana Linnaeus, *Species Plantarum* 2: 713.
1753.
"Habitat in Jamaica." RCN: 5489.
Lectotype (Howard, *Fl. Lesser Antilles* 4: 443. 1988): [icon]
"Hedysarum caule hirsuto, mimosae foliis alatis, pinnis acutis minimis

gramineis" in Sloane, Voy. Jamaica 1: 186, t. 118, f. 3. 1707. –
Typotype: Herb. Sloane 3: 90 (BM-SL).
Current name: ***Aeschynomene americana*** L. (Fabaceae: Faboideae).
Note: Although some authors (e.g. Fawcett & Rendle, *Fl. Jamaica* 4:
27. 1920; Rudd in *Contr. U. S. Natl. Herb.* 32: 24. 1955) have
treated Sloane material (BM) as the type, it was not seen by
Linnaeus and is not original material for the name. Howard appears
to have been the first to explicitly treat Sloane's illustration as the
type (which is, however, linked to Sloane's specimen).

Aeschynomene arborea Linnaeus, *Species Plantarum* 2: 713.
1753.
"Habitat – – – –" RCN: 5487.
Neotype (Pedley in Turland & Jarvis in *Taxon* 46: 462. 1997): Sri
Lanka. North of Trincomalie, 1 Sep 1931, *Simpson 8516* (BM).
Current name: ***Desmodium umbellatum*** (L.) DC. (Fabaceae:
Faboideae).

Aeschynomene aspera Linnaeus, *Species Plantarum* 2: 713. 1753.
"Habitat in India." RCN: 5488.
Lectotype (Ali in Nasir & Ali, *Fl. W. Pakistan* 100: 339. 1977): Herb.
Linn. No. 922.3 (LINN).
Generitype of *Aeschynomene* Linnaeus (vide Green, *Prop. Brit. Bot.*:
174. 1929).
Current name: ***Aeschynomene aspera*** L. (Fabaceae: Faboideae).
Note: Although Rudd (in *Reinwardtia* 5: 30. 1959) stated "Type
collected by P. Hermann?", her expressed doubt means that Ali's
choice of material in LINN as type has priority.

Aeschynomene grandiflora (Linnaeus) Linnaeus, *Species Plantarum*,
ed. 2, 2: 1060. 1763.
"Habitat in India." RCN: 5486.
Basionym: *Robinia grandiflora* L. (1753).
Lectotype (Ali in Nasir & Ali, *Fl. W. Pakistan* 100: 87. 1977): Herb.
Linn. No. 922.1 (LINN).
Current name: ***Sesbania grandiflora*** (L.) Pers. (Fabaceae:
Faboideae).
Note: Although Fawcett & Rendle (*Fl. Jamaica* 4: 24. 1920) indicated
material in LINN as type, they did not distinguish between sheets
922.1 and 922.2 (which are evidently not part of a single gathering,
so Art. 9.15 does not apply). Ali appears to have been the first to
make an unequivocal choice.

Aeschynomene indica Linnaeus, *Species Plantarum* 2: 713. 1753.
"Habitat in India." RCN: 5490.
Lectotype (Verdcourt in Milne-Redhead & Polhill, *Fl. Trop. E. Africa,
Leguminosae* 3: 373. 1971): [icon] *"Neli-tali"* in Rheede, Hort.
Malab. 9: 31, t. 18. 1689.
Current name: ***Aeschynomene indica*** L. (Fabaceae: Faboideae).
Note: Although Rudd (in *Contr. U. S. Natl. Herb.* 32: 59. 1955) says
that the type specimen is unknown and that Rheede's 9: t. 18
"...presumably, represents the type", her uncertainty makes this
difficult to accept as a formal typification, but Verdcourt clearly
formalised this choice.

Aeschynomene pumila Linnaeus, *Species Plantarum*, ed. 2, 2: 1061.
1763.
"Habitat in India." RCN: 5492.
Type not designated.
Original material: [icon] in Rheede, Hort. Malab. 9: 35, t. 20.
1689.
Current name: ***Aeschynomene indica*** L. (Fabaceae: Faboideae).
Note: Rudd (in Dassanayake & Fosberg, *Revised Handb. Fl. Ceylon* 7:
163. 1991) indicated "Hermann s.n. (BM)" as lectotype but it has
not proved possible to locate this specimen in either Hermann's

Ceylonese herbarium, or among his specimens in Herb. Sloane. She
has treated the name as a synonym of *A. indica* L. The cited Rheede
plate is identifiable as *Neptunia prostrata* (Lam.) Baill. (see Nicolson
& al., *Interpret. Van Rheede's Hort. Malab.*: 139. 1988).

Aeschynomene sesban Linnaeus, *Species Plantarum* 2: 714. 1753.
"Habitat in Aegypti sepibus." RCN: 5491.
Lectotype (Gillett in Milne-Redhead & Polhill, *Fl. Trop. E. Africa,
Leguminosae* 3: 339. 1971): *Hasselquist*, Herb. Linn. No. 922.12
(LINN).
Current name: ***Sesbania sesban*** (L.) Merr. (Fabaceae: Faboideae).
Note: Although Fawcett & Rendle (*Fl. Jamaica* 4: 23. 1920) indicated
material in LINN as type, they did not distinguish between sheets
922.11, 922.12 and 922.13 (which are evidently not part of a single
gathering so Art. 9.15 does not apply). Cufodontis (in *Bull. Jard.
Bot. État Bruxelles* 25: 288. 1955) stated "Typus: Hasselquist (in
Aegypti sepibus)" but did not indicate a specimen. Gillett (in *Kew
Bull.* 17: 112. 1963) wrongly indicated 922.13 (LINN), a collection
from König that was not received by Linnaeus until 1777, as the
holotype.

Aesculus hippocastanum Linnaeus, *Species Plantarum* 1: 344. 1753.
"Habitat in Asia septentrionaliore, unde in Europam 1550." RCN:
2638.
Lectotype (Barrie in Jarvis & al., *Regnum Veg.* 127: 15. 1993): Herb.
Clifford: 142, *Aesculus* 1 (BM-000558599).
Generitype of *Aesculus* Linnaeus (vide Hitchcock, *Prop. Brit. Bot.*: 149.
1929).
Current name: ***Aesculus hippocastanum*** L. (Hippocastanaceae).

Aesculus pavia Linnaeus, *Species Plantarum* 1: 344. 1753.
"Habitat in Carolina, Brasilia." RCN: 2639.
Lectotype (designated here by Reveal): Herb. Clifford: 143, *Aesculus* 1,
sheet A (BM-000558600).
Current name: ***Aesculus pavia*** L. var. ***pavia*** (Hippocastanaceae).
Note: Hardin (in *Brittonia* 9: 194. 1957) suggested 467.2 (LINN) as
type but this collection lacks the relevant *Species Plantarum* number
(i.e. "2") and was a post-1753 addition to the herbarium, and is not
original material for the name.

Aethusa bunius (Linnaeus) Linnaeus, *Systema Vegetabilium*, ed. 13:
236. 1774.
RCN: 2052.
Basionym: *Carum bunias* L. (1767).
Lectotype (Reduron & Jarvis in Jarvis & al. in *Taxon* 55: 210. 2006):
[icon] *"Saxifraga Petroselini vel Coriandri folio"* in Morison, Pl. Hist.
Univ. 3: 274, s. 9, t. 2, f. 16. 1699.
Current name: ***Ptychotis saxifraga*** (L.) Loret & Barrandon
(Apiaceae).

Aethusa cynapium Linnaeus, *Species Plantarum* 1: 256. 1753.
"Habitat inter Europae olera." RCN: 2051.
Lectotype (Rechinger, *Fl. Iranica* 162: 345. 1987): Herb. Linn. No.
362.1 (LINN).
Generitype of *Aethusa* Linnaeus.
Current name: ***Aethusa cynapium*** L. (Apiaceae).

Aethusa meum (Linnaeus) Linnaeus, *Systema Vegetabilium*, ed. 13:
237. 1774.
["Habitat in Alpibus Italiae, Hispaniae, Helvetiae."] Sp. Pl. 1: 245
(1753). RCN: 1972.
Basionym: *Athamanta meum* L. (1753).
Lectotype (Jarvis & Knees in *Taxon* 37: 474. 1988): Herb. Clifford:
93, *Athamanta* 1 (BM-000558252).
Current name: ***Meum athamanticum*** Jacq. (Apiaceae).

Agaricus alneus Linnaeus, *Species Plantarum* 2: 1176. 1753.
"Habitat in Alno." RCN: 8463.
Type not designated.
Original material: none traced.
Current name: ***Schizophyllum commune*** Fr.: Fr. (Schizophyllaceae).

Agaricus androsaceus Linnaeus, *Species Plantarum* 2: 1175. 1753.
"Habitat in foliis dejectis Pini." RCN: 8412.
Type not designated.
Original material: [icon] in Vaillant, Bot. Paris.: 69, t. 11, f. 21, 22,
23. 1727; [icon] in Boccone, Mus. Piante Rar. Sicilia: 143, t. 104.
1697.
Current name: ***Marasmius androsaceus*** (L.: Fr.) Fr. (Marasmiaceae).

Agaricus betulinus Linnaeus, *Species Plantarum* 2: 1176. 1753.
"Habitat in Betulis." RCN: 8465.
Type not designated.
Original material: none traced.
Current name: ***Lenzites betulina*** (L.: Fr.) Fr. (Polyporaceae).

Agaricus campanulatus Linnaeus, *Species Plantarum* 2: 1175. 1753.
"Habitat in Pratis." RCN: 8432.
Lectotype (Gerhardt in *Biblioth. Bot.* 147: 117. 1996): [icon] *"Fungus
multiplex, obtuse conicus, colore griseo murino"* in Vaillant, Bot. Paris.:
71, t. 12, f. 1, 2. 1727.
Current name: ***Panaeolus campanulatus*** (L.: Fr.) Quél.
(Bolbitiaceae).
Note: Gerhardt treated this as a *nomen dubium* as it evidently differs
from the sanctioned *A. campanulatus* Fr. (1821).

Agaricus campestris Linnaeus, *Species Plantarum* 2: 1173. 1753, *typ.
cons.*
"Habitat in Pratis." RCN: 8422.
Type not designated.
Original material: [icon] in Bauhin & Cherler, Hist. Pl. Univ. 3(2):
824. 1651.
Generitype of *Agaricus* Linnaeus: Fr., *nom. cons.*
Current name: ***Agaricus campestris*** L.: Fr. (Agaricaceae).

Agaricus chantarellus Linnaeus, *Species Plantarum* 2: 1171. 1753.
"Habitat in Pratis." RCN: 8426.
Type not designated.
Original material: [icon] in Vaillant, Bot. Paris.: 60, t. 11, f. 9–15.
1727.
Current name: ***Cantharellus cibarius*** Fr.: Fr. (Cantharellaceae).

Agaricus cinnamomeus Linnaeus, *Species Plantarum* 2: 1173. 1753.
"Habitat in Sylvis." RCN: 8424.
Type not designated.
Original material: none traced.
Current name: ***Cortinarius cinnamomeus*** (L.: Fr.) Fr.
(Cortinariaceae).
Note: Høiland (in *Opera Bot.* 71: 82. 1984) noted that the Linnaean
name probably relates to *Cortinarius croceus* (Schaeff.) Gray.

Agaricus clavus Linnaeus, *Species Plantarum* 2: 1175. 1753.
"Habitat in Nemoribus, inter folia decidua." RCN: 8442.
Type not designated.
Original material: [icon] in Vaillant, Bot. Paris.: 76, t. 11, f. 19, 20.
1727.
Current name: ***Collybia clavus*** (L.: Fr.) Bull. (Tricholomataceae).

Agaricus clypeatus Linnaeus, *Species Plantarum* 2: 1174. 1753.
"Habitat in pratis sylvaticis." RCN: 8435.
Type not designated.

Original material: none traced.
Current name: ***Entoloma clypeatum*** (L.: Fr.) P. Kumm.
(Entolomataceae).

Agaricus crinitus Linnaeus, *Systema Naturae*, ed. 10, 2: 1349. 1759.
["Habitat in America meridionali. Rolander."] Sp. Pl., ed. 2, 2: 1644
(1763). RCN: 8455.
Type not designated.
Original material: Herb. Linn. No. 1279.1 (LINN); [icon] in Browne,
Civ. Nat. Hist. Jamaica: 78, t. 15, f. 1. 1756.
Current name: ***Lentinus crinitus*** (L.: Fr.) Fr. (Polyporaceae).

Agaricus deliciosus Linnaeus, *Species Plantarum* 2: 1172. 1753.
"Habitat in Montibus, sterilibus, sylvosis." RCN: 8430.
Type not designated.
Original material: none traced.
Current name: ***Lactarius deliciosus*** (L.: Fr.) Gray (Russulaceae).

Agaricus dentatus Linnaeus, *Species Plantarum* 2: 1172. 1753.
"Habitat in Sylvis." RCN: 8425.
Type not designated.
Original material: none traced.
Current name: ***Agaricus dentatus*** L. (Agaricaceae).

Agaricus equestris Linnaeus, *Species Plantarum* 2: 1173. 1753.
"Habitat in Pascuis, Sylvis." RCN: 8438.
Type not designated.
Original material: none traced.
Current name: ***Tricholoma equestre*** (L.: Fr.) P. Kumm.
(Tricholomataceae).

Agaricus extinctorius Linnaeus, *Species Plantarum* 2: 1174. 1753.
"Habitat in fimetis & ad pagos." RCN: 8415.
Type not designated.
Original material: none traced.
Current name: ***Macrolepiota procera*** (Scop.: Fr.) Singer
(Agaricaceae).
Note: For an extensive review of the varied applications of this name,
see Redhead & al. (in *Taxon* 50: 209–211. 2001). Linnaeus' name
was not accepted by Fries in 1821 and is therefore not sanctioned.

Agaricus fimetarius Linnaeus, *Species Plantarum* 2: 1174. 1753.
"Habitat in Fimetis." RCN: 8434.
Type not designated.
Original material: [icon] in Sterbeeck, Theatr. Fung.: 218, t. 22, f. J,
K, L. 1675; [icon] in Buxbaum, Pl. Minus Cognit. Cent. 4: 16, t.
27, f. 1. 1733.
Current name: ***Agaricus fimetarius*** L. (Agaricaceae).

Agaricus fragilis Linnaeus, *Species Plantarum* 2: 1175. 1753, *nom.
illeg.*
"Habitat ad ambulacra." RCN: 8431.
Type not designated.
Original material: [icon] in Vaillant, Bot. Paris.: 60, t. 11, f. 16, 17,
18. 1727.
Current name: ***Bolbitius tibitans*** (Bull.: Fr.) Fr. (Bolbitiaceae).
Note: Index Fungorum observes that this is a homonym of *A. fragilis*
Batsch: Fr. 1789, nec Pers.: Fr. 1801, and therefore illegitimate.

Agaricus georgii Linnaeus, *Species Plantarum* 2: 1173. 1753.
"Habitat in Sylvis." RCN: 8429.
Type not designated.
Original material: [icon] in Sterbeeck, Theatr. Fung.: 63, t. 4, f. C.
1675.
Current name: ***Calocybe gambosa*** (Fr.: Fr.) Donk (Tricholomataceae).

Agaricus integer Linnaeus, *Species Plantarum* 2: 1171. 1753.
"Habitat in Sylvis." RCN: 8450.
Type not designated.
Original material: [icon] in Buxbaum, Pl. Minus Cognit. Cent. 4: 12, t. 19. 1733.
Current name: ***Russula integra*** (L.) Fr. (Russulaceae).

Agaricus lactifluus Linnaeus, *Species Plantarum* 2: 1172. 1753.
"Habitat in Sylvis." RCN: 8448.
Type not designated.
Original material: none traced.
Current name: ***Lactarius volemus*** (Fr.) Fr. (Russulaceae).

Agaricus mammosus Linnaeus, *Species Plantarum* 2: 1174. 1753.
"Habitat in Sylvis." RCN: 8437.
Type not designated.
Original material: [icon] in Buxbaum, Pl. Minus Cognit. Cent. 4: 13, t. 21, f. 1. 1733.
Current name: ***Entoloma mammosum*** (L.) Hesler (Entolomataceae).

Agaricus muscarius Linnaeus, *Species Plantarum* 2: 1172. 1753.
"Habitat in Pratis." RCN: 8456.
Type not designated.
Original material: [icon] in Clusius, Rar. Pl. Hist. 2: 280. 1601.
Current name: ***Amanita muscaria*** (L.: Fr.) Hook. (Pluteaceae).
Note: Taking the view that "taxonomists are under no obligation to reach into pre-Linnaean literature for selection of type material, type locality etc.", Jenkins & Petersen (in *Mycologia* 68: 463–469. 1976) designated a neotype from Sweden (Ångermanland: Nordingrå Parish, Summer 1974, R.H. Petersen, TENN 39847) for this name. As a name sanctioned by Fries (Art. 13.1(d)), typification "may be effected in the light of anything associated with the name in that work" (Art. 7.8). However, as in this case that includes the Clusius plate cited in the protologue of *A. muscarius* L. (1753), which is therefore original material for the name, their neotypification appears to be contrary to Art. 9.11.

Agaricus piperatus Linnaeus, *Species Plantarum* 2: 1173. 1753.
"Habitat in Pascuis, Sylvis." RCN: 8414.
Type not designated.
Original material: none traced.
Current name: ***Lactarius piperatus*** (L.: Fr.) Pers. (Russulaceae).

Agaricus quercinus Linnaeus, *Species Plantarum* 2: 1176. 1753.
"Habitat in Quercubus." RCN: 8462.
Type not designated.
Original material: [icon] in Buxbaum, Pl. Minus Cognit. Cent. 5: 3, t. 4, f. 1. 1740.
Current name: ***Daedalea quercina*** (L.: Fr.) Pers. (Fomitopsidaceae).
Note: This is the generitype of *Agaricus* L. ex Murrill (non *Agaricus* L. ex Fr., 1821).

Agaricus quinquepartitus Linnaeus, *Species Plantarum* 2: 1171. 1753.
"Habitat in Pratis." RCN: 8441.
Type not designated.
Original material: none traced.
Current name: ***Agaricus quinquepartitus*** L. (Agaricaceae).

Agaricus separatus Linnaeus, *Species Plantarum* 2: 1175. 1753.
"Habitat in Stercoratis." RCN: 8439.
Neotype (Gerhardt in *Biblioth. Bot.* 147: 23. 1996): Finland. Lappfjord, Ostrobottnia Australis, 23 Jun 1859. *Karsten 2306* (H).
Current name: ***Panaeolus semiovatus*** (Sowerby : Fr.) S. Lundell & Nannf. (Coprinaceae).

Agaricus umbelliferus Linnaeus, *Species Plantarum* 2: 1175. 1753.
"Habitat inter Folia congesta, semiputrida." RCN: 8411.
Lectotype (Jørgensen & Ryman in *Taxon* 38: 307, f. 1. 1989): [icon] Drawing annotated by C.J. Hartman in Rudbeck, Iter Lapponicum (University Library, Uppsala). – Epitype (Jørgensen & Ryman in *Taxon* 43: 254. 1994): Fungi Exs. Suec. 1753 (UPS).
Current name: ***Lichenomphalia umbellifera*** (L.: Fr.) Redhead & al. (Tricholomataceae).
Note: Redhead & Kuyper (in Laursen & al., *Arctic Alpine Mycol.* 2: 326. 1987) selected the cited Micheli plate as lectotype but this choice was rejected by Jørgensen & Ryman (1989) in favour of a Rudbeck drawing because the Micheli element was excluded by Fries, the sanctioning author. Redhead & Kuyper (in *Taxon* 42: 447. 1993) argued that Jørgensen & Ryman's choice was ineligible but Jørgensen & Ryman (*l.c.* 43: 253–255. 1994) refuted this argument and designated an epitype in support of their own type choice (the Rudbeck figure).

Agaricus violaceus Linnaeus, *Species Plantarum* 2: 1173. 1753.
"Habitat ad margines Sylvarum." RCN: 8446.
Type not designated.
Original material: [icon] in Buxbaum, Pl. Minus Cognit. Cent. 4: 7, t. 11. 1733; [icon] in Micheli, Nov. Pl. Gen.: 149, t. 74, f. 1. 1729.
Current name: ***Cortinarius violaceus*** (L.: Fr.) Gray (Cortinariaceae).
Note: Brandrud (in *Nordic J. Bot.* 3: 587. 1983) selected Herb. Moser 74/208 (S) from Sweden (Halland) as a neotype, but original elements are in existence which, under Art. 9.11, preclude the selection of a neotype.

Agaricus viscidus Linnaeus, *Species Plantarum* 2: 1173. 1753.
"Habitat in Sylvis." RCN: 8449.
Type not designated.
Original material: none traced.
Current name: ***Gomphidius viscidus*** (L.) Fr. (Gomphidiaceae).

Agave americana Linnaeus, *Species Plantarum* 1: 323. 1753.
"Habitat in America calidiore." RCN: 2518.
Lectotype (Howard, *Fl. Lesser Antilles* 3: 486. 1979): Herb. Linn. No. 443.1, flowers only (LINN).
Generitype of *Agave* Linnaeus (vide Hitchcock, *Prop. Brit. Bot.*: 147. 1929).
Current name: ***Agave americana*** L. (Agavaceae).

Agave foetida Linnaeus, *Species Plantarum* 1: 323. 1753.
"Habitat in Curacao." RCN: 2521.
Lectotype (Marais & Coode in Bosser & al., *Fl. Mascareignes* 180: 9. 1978): [icon] *"Aloe Americ. viridi rigidissimo et foetido folio piet dicta"* in Commelin, Hort. Med. Amsteled. Pl. Rar. 2: 35, t. 18. 1701.
Current name: ***Furcraea foetida*** (L.) Haw. (Agavaceae).

Agave virginica Linnaeus, *Species Plantarum* 1: 323. 1753.
"Habitat in Virginia." RCN: 2519.
Type not designated.
Original material: none traced.
Current name: ***Manfreda virginica*** (L.) Salisb. ex Rose (Agavaceae).
Note: Thiede (in Eggli, *Ill. Handb. Succ. Pl., Monocots*: 71. 2001) indicated *Clayton 498* (LINN, iso- BM) as type but this choice was published after 1 Jan 2001 and so the omission of the phrase "designated here" or an equivalent (Art. 7.11) means that the choice is not effective.

Agave vivipara Linnaeus, *Species Plantarum* 1: 323. 1753.
"Habitat in America." RCN: 2519.
Lectotype (Wijnands, *Bot. Commelins*: 35. 1983): [icon] *"Aloe Americana Polygona"* in Commelin, Praeludia Bot.: 65, t. 15. 1703 (see p. 121).
Current name: ***Agave vivipara*** L. var. ***vivipara*** (Agavaceae).

Ageratum altissimum Linnaeus, *Species Plantarum* 2: 839. 1753.
"Habitat in Canada, Virginia." RCN: 6075.
Lectotype (Reveal in Jarvis & Turland in *Taxon* 47: 351. 1998): Herb.
  Clifford: 396, *Eupatorium* 3 (BM-000646950).
Current name: ***Ageratina altissima*** (L.) R.M. King & H. Rob.
  (Asteraceae).
Note: Clewell & Wooten (in *Brittonia* 23: 133–134. 1971) claimed the
  name was "based" on the cited reference from Cornut (1635), but
  as these authors discussed only some of the other possible elements
  and did not use the term type or an equivalent, this does not
  constitute effective typification.

Ageratum ciliare Linnaeus, *Species Plantarum* 2: 839. 1753.
"Habitat in Bisnagaria." RCN: 6074.
Lectotype (Robinson in Jarvis & Turland in *Taxon* 47: 351. 1998):
  [icon] *"Centaurium ciliare minus, Bisnagaricum, Origani foliis
  amplioribus, floribus in Umbellis"* in Plukenet, Phytographia: t. 81, f.
  4. 1691; Almag. Bot.: 93. 1696. – Epitype (Robinson in Jarvis &
  Turland in *Taxon* 47: 351. 1998): India. Karnataka, Hassan
  District, Hassan, 21 Sep 1971. *K.N. Gandhi HFP 2103* (US-
  2792681).
Current name: ***Ageratum conyzoides*** L. (Asteraceae).

Ageratum conyzoides Linnaeus, *Species Plantarum* 2: 839. 1753.
"Habitat in America." RCN: 6073.
Lectotype (Grierson in Dassanayake & Fosberg, *Revised Handb. Fl.
  Ceylon* 1: 141. 1980): Herb. Clifford: 396, *Ageratum* 1 (BM-
  000646956).
Generitype of *Ageratum* Linnaeus (vide Green, *Prop. Brit. Bot.*: 180.
  1929).
Current name: ***Ageratum conyzoides*** L. (Asteraceae).
Note: The earliest effective typification appears to be by Grierson (in
  Dassanayake & Fosberg, *Revised Handb. Fl. Ceylon* 1: 141. 1980),
  who indicated Clifford material (BM) as type. As discussed by
  Barrie & al. (in *Taxon* 41: 510. 1992), this material is identifiable as
  Eclipta prostrata (L.) L. There are no grounds for rejecting the
  typification. Reveal (in Jarvis & al., *Regnum Veg.* 127: 15. 1993)
  indicated a Hermann illustration (*Parad. Bat.*: ic. 161. 1698), which
  does agree with current usage of the name, as lectotype. However,
  this later typification does not have priority. It appears that, to avoid
  disruption to the generic names *Eclipta* and *Ageratum*, a
  conservation proposal will be necessary (although the application of
  these names may be temporarily protected by Art. 57.1).

Agrimonia agrimonoides Linnaeus, *Species Plantarum* 1: 448.
  1753.
"Habitat in Italiae nemoribus umbrosis humentibus." RCN: 3480.
Lectotype (Theurillat in Cafferty & Jarvis in *Taxon* 51: 541. 2002):
  Herb. Linn. No. 628.3 (LINN).
Current name: ***Aremonia agrimonoides*** (L.) DC. (Rosaceae).

Agrimonia eupatoria Linnaeus, *Species Plantarum* 1: 448. 1753.
"Habitat in Europae pratis apricis argillaceis." RCN: 3478.
Lectotype (Skalický in *Novit. Bot. Inst. Horto Bot. Univ. Carol. Prag.*
  1972: 15. 1973): Herb. Linn. No. 628.1 (LINN).
Generitype of *Agrimonia* Linnaeus (vide de Candolle, *Prodr.* 2: 588.
  Nov 1825; Green, *Prop. Brit. Bot.*: 157. 1929).
Current name: ***Agrimonia eupatoria*** L. (Rosaceae).

Agrimonia repens Linnaeus, *Systema Naturae*, ed. 10, 2: 1046.
  1759.
["Habitat in Oriente."] Sp. Pl., ed. 2, 1: 643 (1762). RCN: 3479.
Lectotype (Skalický in *Novit. Bot. Inst. Horto Bot. Univ. Carol. Prag.*
  1972: 16. 1973): Herb. Linn. No. 628.2 (LINN).
Current name: ***Agrimonia repens*** L. (Rosaceae).

Agrostemma coeli-rosa Linnaeus, *Species Plantarum* 1: 436. 1753.
"Habitat in Sicilia." RCN: 3387.
Lectotype (Talavera & Muñoz Garmendia in *Anales Jard. Bot. Madrid*
  45: 425. 1989): Herb. Linn. No. 601.3 (LINN).
Current name: ***Silene coeli-rosa*** (L.) Godr. (Caryophyllaceae).
Note: Specific epithet spelled "Coelirosa" in the protologue.

Agrostemma coronaria Linnaeus, *Species Plantarum* 1: 436. 1753.
"Habitat in Italia." RCN: 3385.
Lectotype (Ghazanfar & Nasir in Nasir & Ali, *Fl. Pakistan* 175: 55.
  1986): Herb. Linn. No. 601.2 (LINN).
Current name: ***Silene coronaria*** (L.) Clairv. (Caryophyllaceae).

Agrostemma flos-jovis Linnaeus, *Species Plantarum* 1: 436. 1753.
"Habitat in Helvetia." RCN: 3386.
Lectotype (Greuter in Cafferty & Jarvis in *Taxon* 53: 1050. 2004):
  [icon] *"Licnide umbellifora"* in Zanoni, Istoria Bot.: 128, t. 51.
  1675.
Current name: ***Silene flos-jovis*** (L.) Clairv. (Caryophyllaceae).
Note: The Zanoni plate designated as the lectotype of this name was
  omitted from the listing of Zanoni plates cited by Linnaeus that was
  published by Jarvis (in *Museol. Sci.* 9: 162. 1993).

Agrostemma githago Linnaeus, *Species Plantarum* 1: 435. 1753.
"Habitat inter Europae segetes." RCN: 3384.

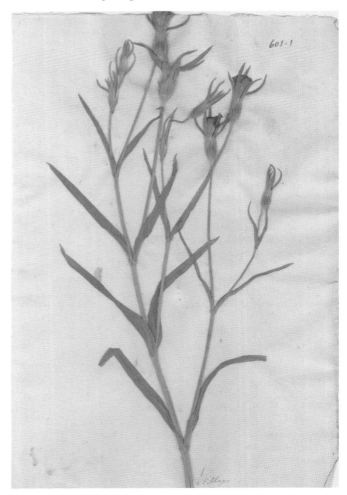

Lectotype (Ghafoor in Jafri & El-Gadi, *Fl. Libya* 59: 56. 1978): Herb.
  Linn. No. 601.1 (LINN).

Generitype of *Agrostemma* Linnaeus (vide Green, *Prop. Brit. Bot.*: 156. 1929).
Current name: ***Agrostemma githago*** L. (Caryophyllaceae).

Agrostis alba Linnaeus, *Species Plantarum* 1: 63. 1753.
"Habitat in Europae nemoribus." RCN: 542.
Lectotype (Widén, *Fl. Fennica* 5: 101. 1971): Herb. A. van Royen No. 913.62–84 (L).
Current name: ***Poa nemoralis*** L. (Poaceae).
Note: Hitchcock (in *Bot. Gaz.* 38: 141. 1904) noted that Linnaeus had confused two species, *A. stolonifera* L. and *A. alba* L. Hitchcock (in *U.S.D.A. Bur. Pl. Ind. Bull.* 68: 25. 1905) considered what is evidently 84.23 (LINN) as the type, but this is a collection from Hudson which was received by Linnaeus long after 1753. Widén (in *Bot. Not.* 120: 508. 1967) regarded *A. alba* as a *nomen ambiguum*, but subsequently resolved the problem by typifying the name using van Royen material, allowing it to fall into the synonymy of *Poa nemoralis* L.

Agrostis arundinacea Linnaeus, *Species Plantarum* 1: 61. 1753.
"Habitat in Europae monticulis sylvosis glareosis juniperitis." RCN: 533.
Lectotype (Veldkamp in Cafferty & al. in *Taxon* 49: 243. 2000): *Amman 26*, Herb. Linn. No. 84.7 (LINN).
Current name: ***Deyeuxia pyramidalis*** (Host) Veldkamp (Poaceae).
Note: The epithet "arundinacea" is pre-occupied in *Deyeuxia* by *D. arundinacea* P. Beauv., and *D. pyramidalis* (Host) Veldkamp is therefore the correct name in that genus. In *Calamagrostis*, however, it remains *C. arundinacea* (L.) Roth.

Agrostis australis Linnaeus, *Systema Naturae,* ed. 12, 2: 90; *Mantissa Plantarum*: 30. 1767.
"Habitat in Lusitania. Vandelli." RCN: 532.
Lectotype (Scholz in Cafferty & al. in *Taxon* 49: 243. 2000): Herb. Linn. No. 84.6 (LINN).
Current name: ***Gastridium phleoides*** (Nees & Meyen) C.E. Hubb. (Poaceae).

Agrostis bromoides Linnaeus, *Systema Naturae,* ed. 12, 2: 90; *Mantissa Plantarum*: 30. 1767.
"Habitat Monspelii. D. Gouan." RCN: 531.
Lectotype (Vázquez & al. in *Anales Jard. Bot. Madrid* 52: 183. 1995): Herb. Linn. No. 84.4 (LINN).
Current name: ***Stipa bromoides*** (L.) Dörfl. (Poaceae).
Note: Freitag (in *Notes Roy. Bot. Gard. Edinburgh* 42: 401. 1985) designated 94.6 (LINN) as lectotype but Vázquez & al. argued persuasively that his choice was not original material for the name.

Agrostis calamagrostis Linnaeus, *Systema Naturae,* ed. 10, 2: 872. 1759.
["Habitat in Helvetiae, Veronae alpinis."] Sp. Pl., ed. 2, 1: 92 (1762). RCN: 534.
Lectotype (Vázquez & al. in *Anales Jard. Bot. Madrid* 52: 184. 1995): [icon] *"Arista recta prodeunte ex ipso alterutrius glumae apice, Folliculo longiore villoso"* in Scheuchzer, Agrostographia: 146, t. 3, f. 11 A, B. 1719.
Current name: ***Stipa calamagrostis*** (L.) Wahlenb. (Poaceae).

Agrostis canina Linnaeus, *Species Plantarum* 1: 62. 1753, *typ. cons.*
"Habitat in Europae pascuis humidiusculis." RCN: 538.
Conserved type (Widén, *Fl. Fennica* 5: 29, f. 25. 1971): Herb. Burser I: 3 (UPS).
Generitype of *Agrostis* Linnaeus, *nom. cons.*
Current name: ***Agrostis canina*** L. (Poaceae).
Note: Agrostis canina, with the type designated by Widén, was

proposed as conserved type of the genus by Jarvis (in *Taxon* 41: 556. 1992) and this was eventually approved by the General Committee (see review of the history of this proposal by Barrie, *l.c.* 55: 795–796. 2006).

Agrostis capillaris Linnaeus, *Species Plantarum* 1: 62. 1753.
"Habitat in Europae pratis." RCN: 540.
Lectotype (Widén, *Fl. Fennica* 5: 65, f. 27. 1971): Herb. A. van Royen No. 912.356–69, left specimen (L).
Current name: ***Agrostis capillaris*** L. (Poaceae).
Note: Problems with the identity of some of the material associated with this name led some authors (e.g. Malte in *Ann. Rep. Natl. Mus. Canada* 50: 116. 1928; Rauschert in *Feddes Repert.* 88: 318. 1977) to treat it as ambiguous. However, Widén's typification has established the usage of the name and seems to have been accepted by later authors. See detailed reviews by Widén (*l.c.*: 68–71) and Edgar & Forde (in *New Zealand J. Bot.* 29: 154. 1991).

Agrostis cruciata Linnaeus, *Systema Naturae,* ed. 10, 2: 873. 1759.
["Habitat in Jamaica."] Sp. Pl., ed. 2, 1: 94 (1762). RCN: 549.
Lectotype (Hitchcock in *Contr. U. S. Natl. Herb.* 12: 120. 1908): *Browne*, Herb. Linn. No. 84.39 (LINN).
Current name: ***Chloris cruciata*** (L.) Sw. (Poaceae).

Agrostis indica Linnaeus, *Species Plantarum* 1: 63. 1753.
"Habitat in India." RCN: 547.
Lectotype (Baaijens & Veldkamp in *Blumea* 35: 422. 1991): *Clayton 460b*, Herb. Linn. No. 84.36 (LINN).
Current name: ***Sporobolus indicus*** (L.) R. Br. (Poaceae).
Note: Hitchcock (in *Contr. U. S. Natl. Herb.* 12: 120. 1908) designated 84.35 (LINN) as the type, but this is a Patrick Browne collection that was not acquired by Linnaeus until 1758, and so cannot be original material for the name. Parham (in Smith, *Fl. Vitiensis Nova* 1: 308. 1979) stated "Apparently a Sloane specimen from Jamaica is the principal basis of Linnaeus' species" but Linnaeus did not study this material, and Parham's statement in any case falls short of formal typification.

Agrostis interrupta Linnaeus, *Systema Naturae,* ed. 10, 2: 872. 1759.
["Habitat in Gallia, Italia."] Sp. Pl., ed. 2, 1: 92 (1762). RCN: 529.
Neotype (Cope in Cafferty & al. in *Taxon* 49: 243. 2000): France. Loire, Orleans, May–Jun 1902–1903, *Giraudias s.n.*, Kneucker Gramineae Exsiccatae. XVII Lieferung, 1905, No. 497 (BM-000576279).
Current name: ***Apera interrupta*** (L.) P. Beauv. (Poaceae).

Agrostis matrella Linnaeus, *Mantissa Plantarum Altera*: 185. 1771.
"Habitat in Malabariae arenosis. Koenig. 56." RCN: 537.
Lectotype (Goudswaard in *Blumea* 26: 171. 1980): *König 56*, Herb. Linn. No. 84.11 (LINN; iso- Herb. A. van Royen 909.67–176, L).
Current name: ***Zoysia matrella*** (L.) Merr. (Poaceae).

Agrostis mexicana Linnaeus, *Systema Naturae,* ed. 12, 2: 91; *Mantissa Plantarum*: 31. 1767.
"Habitat in America calidiore. D. Jacquin." RCN: 546.
Lectotype (Fernald in *Rhodora* 45: 225, pl. 751. 1943): Herb. Linn. No. 84.33 (LINN; iso- US, fragm.).
Current name: ***Muhlenbergia mexicana*** (L.) Trin. (Poaceae).
Note: Fernald's pl. 751, f. 1, 2. makes it clear that he regards 84.33 (LINN) as the type, rather than 84.34 (LINN).

Agrostis miliacea Linnaeus, *Species Plantarum* 1: 61. 1753.
"Habitat in Europa." RCN: 530.
Lectotype (Meikle, *Fl. Cyprus* 2: 1794. 1985): Herb. Linn. No. 84.2 (LINN).

Current name: ***Piptatherum miliaceum*** (L.) Coss. subsp. ***miliaceum*** (Poaceae).

Agrostis minima Linnaeus, *Species Plantarum* 1: 63. 1753.
"Habitat in Gallia." RCN: 544.
Lectotype (Scholz in Cafferty & al. in *Taxon* 49: 243. 2000): Herb. Burser I: 12 (UPS).
Current name: ***Mibora minima*** (L.) Desv. (Poaceae).

Agrostis paradoxa Linnaeus, *Species Plantarum* 1: 62. 1753.
"Habitat in Galloprovincia, G. Narbonensi." RCN: 526.
Basionym of: *Milium paradoxum* (L.) L.
Lectotype (Freitag in Cafferty & al. in *Taxon* 49: 243. 2000): [icon] *"Gram. paniculat. Gallo-provinciale Aquilegiae semine"* in Plukenet, Phytographia: t. 32, f. 2. 1691; Almag. Bot.: 174. 1696. – Voucher: Herb. Sloane 96: 70 (BM-SL).
Current name: ***Piptatherum paradoxum*** (L.) P. Beauv. (Poaceae).

Agrostis pumila Linnaeus, *Systema Naturae*, ed. 12, 2: 91; *Mantissa Plantarum*: 31. 1767.
"Habitat in Suecia, Islandia, Helvetia." RCN: 543.
Lectotype (Philipson in *J. Bot.* 73: 71. 1935): Herb. Linn. No. 84.28 (LINN).
Current name: ***Agrostis capillaris*** L. (Poaceae).
Note: Philipson (in *J. Bot.* 73: 70. 1935) identified 84.28 (LINN) as a specimen of *A. tenuis* Sibth. infected with the fungus *Tilletia decipiens* (Pers.) Körn. and concluded (*l.c.*: 72) that the name could not be retained since it was based on a diseased type. Widén (in *Fl. Fennica* 5: 71. 1971) followed Philipson in rejecting the name as invalid (under Art. 71, dealing with monstrosities) but attributed the infection to *T. sphaerococca* A.A. Fisch. Waldh. Art. 71 was deleted by the Leningrad Congress in 1975, resulting in *A. pumila* becoming valid. However, its type (and *A. tenuis*) is now recognised by many authors (e.g. Romero García & al. in *Ruizia* 7: 105. 1988; Edgar & Forde in *New Zealand J. Bot.* 29: 154. 1991) as a specimen of the variable *A. capillaris* L. (1753), into the synonymy of which *A. pumila* therefore falls.

Agrostis radiata Linnaeus, *Systema Naturae*, ed. 10, 2: 873. 1759.
["Habitat in Indiis."] Sp. Pl., ed. 2, 1: 94 (1762). RCN: 548.
Lectotype (Hitchcock in *Contr. U. S. Natl. Herb.* 12: 120. 1908): *Browne*, Herb. Linn. No. 84.38 (LINN; iso- US).
Current name: ***Chloris radiata*** (L.) Sw. (Poaceae).

Agrostis rubra Linnaeus, *Species Plantarum* 1: 62. 1753.
"Habitat in Europae arenosis subhumidis." RCN: 536.
Type not designated.
Original material: Herb. Linn. No. 46 (LAPP); [icon] in Scheuchzer, Agrostographia: 148, t. 3, f. 11 C. 1719.
Current name: ***Agrostis mertensii*** Trin. (Poaceae).
Note: This name has been widely treated as a *nomen dubium* (e.g. by Hitchcock in *Bot. Gaz.* 38: 141–143. 1904; Widén in *Fl. Fennica* 5: 54–56. 1971 and Rauschert in *Feddes Repert.* 88: 318. 1977). However, it has not been formally proposed for rejection.

Agrostis sepium Linnaeus, *Systema Naturae,* ed. 10, 2: 872. 1759.
RCN: 528.
Lectotype (Romero García in Cafferty & al. in *Taxon* 49: 243. 2000): *Löfling s.n.*, Herb. Linn. No. 84.3 (LINN).
Current name: ***Piptatherum miliaceum*** (L.) Coss. (Poaceae).

Agrostis serotina (Linnaeus) Linnaeus, *Systema Naturae,* ed. 12, 2: 90; *Mantissa Plantarum*: 30. 1767.
"Habitat Veronae. Seguier." RCN: 535.
Basionym: *Festuca serotina* L. (1759).

Lectotype (Scholz in Cafferty & al. in *Taxon* 49: 251. 2000): [icon] *"Gramen loliaceum serotinum, panicula dispansa"* in Séguier, Pl. Veron. 3: 146, 83, t. 3, f. 2. 1754.
Current name: ***Cleistogenes serotina*** (L.) Keng (Poaceae).

Agrostis spica-venti Linnaeus, *Species Plantarum* 1: 61. 1753.
"Habitat in Europa inter segetes." RCN: 527.
Lectotype (Cope in Cafferty & al. in *Taxon* 49: 243. 2000): Herb. A. van Royen No. 912.356–53 (L).
Current name: ***Apera spica-venti*** (L.) P. Beauv. (Poaceae).
Note: Although Kerguélen (in *Lejeunia*, n.s., 75: 84. 1975) stated "Type: ...LINN", this is not accepted as a formal typification, for the reasons explained by Cafferty & al. (in *Taxon* 49: 240. 2000).

Agrostis stolonifera Linnaeus, *Species Plantarum* 1: 62. 1753.
"Habitat in Europa." RCN: 539.
Lectotype (Widén, *Fl. Fennica* 5: 77, f. 28. 1971): Herb. A. van Royen No. 912.356–55 (L).
Current name: ***Agrostis stolonifera*** L. (Poaceae).
Note: Hitchcock (in *Bot. Gaz.* 38: 141. 1904; *U.S.D.A. Bur. Pl. Ind. Bull.* 68: 24. 1905) treated 84.20 (LINN) as the type but the sheet lacks a *Species Plantarum* number (i.e. "7"), was a post-1753 addition to the herbarium and is not original material for the name. Philipson (in *J. Linn. Soc., Bot.* 51: 95. 1937) rejected the material from consideration while Breistroffer (in *Bull. Soc. Bot. France*, 1963 (89th Sess. Extr.): 57. 1966) said the name should be treated as a *nomen ambiguum*. Widén (*Fl. Fennica* 5: 508. 1967) rejected Hitchcock's type choice in favour of van Royen material which he designated as lectotype. There is further discussion by Kurchenko (in *Bot. Zhurn.* 87(5): 115–119. 2002).

Agrostis virginica Linnaeus, *Species Plantarum* 1: 63. 1753.
"Habitat in Virginia." RCN: 545.
Lectotype (Hitchcock in *Contr. U. S. Natl. Herb.* 12: 119. 1908): *Clayton 507*, Herb. Linn. No. 84.30 (LINN; iso- BM, US).
Current name: ***Sporobolus virginicus*** (L.) Kunth (Poaceae).

Agyneia impubes Linnaeus, *Mantissa Plantarum Altera*: 296. 1771.
"Habitat in China." RCN: 7352.
Type not designated.
Original material: Herb. Linn. No. 1145.1 (LINN).
Current name: ***Glochidion puberum*** (L.) Hutch. (Euphorbiaceae).

Agyneia pubera Linnaeus, *Mantissa Plantarum Altera*: 296. 1771.
"Habitat in China." RCN: 7353.
Lectotype (Radcliffe-Smith in Jarvis & al., *Regnum Veg.* 127: 16. 1993): Herb. Linn. No. 1145.2 (LINN).
Generitype of *Agyneia* Linnaeus, nom. rej.
Current name: ***Glochidion puberum*** (L.) Hutch. (Euphorbiaceae).
Note: Agyneia Linnaeus, nom. rej. in favour of *Glochidion* J.R. Forst. & G. Forst.

Aira alpina Linnaeus, *Species Plantarum* 1: 65. 1753.
"Habitat in alpibus Lapponicis, Germania." RCN: 558.
Neotype (Cope in Cafferty & al. in *Taxon* 49: 243. 2000): Sweden. Torne Lappmark, Abisko, Mt. Nuolja, ca. 700–800m, 25 Jul 1950, *N.D. Simpson 50133* (BM-000649414).
Current name: ***Deschampsia cespitosa*** (L.) P. Beauv. subsp. ***alpina*** (L.) Hook. f. (Poaceae).

Aira aquatica Linnaeus, *Species Plantarum* 1: 64. 1753.
"Habitat in Europae pascuis aquosis." RCN: 553.
Lectotype (Sherif & Siddiqi in El-Gadi, *Fl. Libya* 145: 84. 1988): Herb. Linn. No. 85.6 (LINN).
Current name: ***Catabrosa aquatica*** (L.) P. Beauv. (Poaceae).

Note: Although Kerguélen (in *Lejeunia*, n.s., 75: 115. 1975) stated "Type: ...LINN", this is not accepted as a formal typification, for the reasons explained by Cafferty & al. (in *Taxon* 49: 240. 2000).

Aira arundinacea Linnaeus, *Species Plantarum* 1: 64. 1753.
"Habitat in Oriente." RCN: 551.
Neotype (Renvoize in Cafferty & al. in *Taxon* 49: 244. 2000): Turkey. Aras Valley, 19 Jul 1966, 1,100–1,200m, *Davis 46876* (K; iso- E).
Current name: ***Eragrostis collina*** Trin. (Poaceae).
Note: Bor (in Townsend & al., *Fl. Iraq* 9: 442. 1968) stated that Linnaeus based this name on a Tournefort specimen in BM. This material has not been traced. Although Linnaeus cites a Tournefort reference in synonymy, there is no accompanying illustration, and Linnaeus appears not to have studied Tournefort's collections. Renvoize therefore designated a neotype.

Aira caerulea Linnaeus, *Species Plantarum* 1: 63. 1753.
"Habitat in Europae pascuis aquosis." RCN: 550.
Basionym of: *Melica caerulea* (L.) L. (1774).
Lectotype (Trist & Sell in *Watsonia* 17: 154. 1988): Herb. Linn. No. 85.1 (LINN).
Current name: ***Molinia caerulea*** (L.) Moench (Poaceae).
Note: Although Kerguélen (in *Lejeunia*, n.s., 75: 213. 1975) stated "Type: ...LINN", this is not accepted as a formal typification, for the reasons explained by Cafferty & al. (in *Taxon* 49: 240. 2000).

Aira canescens Linnaeus, *Species Plantarum* 1: 65. 1753.
"Habitat in Scania & australioris Europae arvis." RCN: 559.
Lectotype (Cope in Cafferty & al. in *Taxon* 49: 244. 2000): Herb. Linn. No. 85.16 (LINN).
Current name: ***Corynephorus canescens*** (L.) P. Beauv. (Poaceae).
Note: Although Kerguélen (in *Lejeunia*, n.s., 75: 121. 1975) stated "Type: ...LINN", this is not accepted as a formal typification, for the reasons explained by Cafferty & al. (in *Taxon* 49: 240. 2000).

Aira caryophyllea Linnaeus, *Species Plantarum* 1: 66. 1753.
"Habitat in Angliae, Germaniae, Galliae glareosis." RCN: 561.
Lectotype (Clayton in Milne-Redhead & Polhill, *Fl. Trop. E. Africa, Gramineae* 1: 84. 1970): Herb. Linn. No. 85.22 (LINN).
Current name: ***Aira caryophyllea*** L. (Poaceae).

Aira cespitosa Linnaeus, *Species Plantarum* 1: 64. 1753.
"Habitat in Europae partis cultis & fertilibus." RCN: 555.
Lectotype (Clayton in Milne-Redhead & Polhill, *Fl. Trop. E. Africa, Gramineae* 1: 92. 1970): Herb. Linn. No. 85.8 (LINN).
Current name: ***Deschampsia cespitosa*** (L.) P. Beauv. (Poaceae).

Aira cristata Linnaeus, *Species Plantarum* 1: 63. 1753.
"Habitat in Angliae, Galliae, Helvetiae siccioribus." RCN: 589.
Basionym of: *Poa cristata* (L.) L. (1767).
Lectotype (Humphries in Cafferty & al. in *Taxon* 49: 244. 2000): Herb. A. van Royen No. 913.62–99 (L). – Epitype (Humphries in Cafferty & al. in *Taxon* 49: 244. 2000): France. Jura, Bas-Bugey, Montagny de Ste Claire sur Brioguier, 400–500m, 3 Jun 1929, *Briquet 6737* (BM-000576281; iso- G).
Current name: ***Koeleria macrantha*** (Ledeb.) Schult. (Poaceae).
Note: This name has been discussed by a number of authors including Domin (in *Biblioth. Bot.* 65: 142. 1907) and Arnow (in *Syst. Bot.* 19: 7. 1994). *Koeleria cristata* Pers. (1805) is not a combination based on *A. cristata* L. and this epithet is therefore pre-occupied in *Koeleria*. Humphries' typification confirms the identity of *A. cristata*, and its correct name in *Koeleria* is *K. macrantha* (Ledeb.) Schult.

Aira flexuosa Linnaeus, *Species Plantarum* 1: 65. 1753.
"Habitat in Europae petris, rupibus." RCN: 556.
Lectotype (Clayton in Milne-Redhead & Polhill, *Fl. Trop. E. Africa, Gramineae* 1: 94. 1970): Herb. Linn. No. 85.11 (LINN).
Current name: ***Deschampsia flexuosa*** (L.) Trin. (Poaceae).
Note: Although Kerguélen (in *Lejeunia*, n.s., 75: 129. 1975) stated "Type: ...LINN", this is not accepted as a formal typification, for the reasons explained by Cafferty & al. (in *Taxon* 49: 240. 2000).

Aira indica Linnaeus, *Species Plantarum* 1: 63; *Species Plantarum* 2: 1231. 1753.
"Habitat in India." RCN: 485.
Basionym of: *Panicum indicum* (L.) L. (1771), nom. illeg.; *P. conglomeratum* L. (1771).
Neotype (Renvoize in Cafferty & al. in *Taxon* 49: 244. 2000): Sri Lanka. Sabaragamuwa Province, Ratnagsura District, 22 Oct 1974, *Davidse 7871* (K; iso- MO).
Current name: ***Sacciolepis indica*** (L.) Chase (Poaceae).
Note: Specific epithet corrected to "indicum" [sic] from "spicata" in Errata of *Sp. Pl.* 2: 1231 (1753).

Aira minuta Linnaeus, *Species Plantarum* 1: 64. 1753.
"Habitat in Hispania. Loefling." RCN: 552.
Lectotype (Scholz in Cafferty & al. in *Taxon* 49: 244. 2000): *Löfling s.n.*, Herb. Linn. No. 85.4 (LINN).
Current name: ***Molineriella minuta*** (L.) Rouy (Poaceae).
Note: Although Kerguélen (in *Lejeunia*, n.s., 75: 224. 1975) stated "Type: ...LINN", this is not accepted as a formal typification, for the reasons explained by Cafferty & al. (in *Taxon* 49: 240. 2000).

Aira montana Linnaeus, *Species Plantarum* 1: 65. 1753.
"Habitat in Europae alpinis." RCN: 557.
Lectotype (Cope in Cafferty & al. in *Taxon* 49: 244. 2000): [icon] *"Gramen Avenaceum paniculatum alpinum, foliis capillaceis, brevibus, Locustis purpureo-argenteis, splendentibus & aristatis"* in Scheuchzer, Agrostographia: 216, t. 4, f. 16 A, B, C. 1719. – Epitype (Cope in Cafferty & al. in *Taxon* 49: 244. 2000): Germany. Hessen, bei Weilburg, Blessenbach, Rand eines Kiefernwaldes, 28 Jun 1981, 245m, *Conert s.n.* (BM-000576282; iso- FR).
Current name: ***Deschampsia flexuosa*** (L.) Trin. (Poaceae).
Note: Although Kerguélen (in *Lejeunia*, n.s., 75: 130. 1975) stated "Type: ...LINN", this is not accepted as a formal typification, for the reasons explained by Cafferty & al. (in *Taxon* 49: 240. 2000).

Aira praecox Linnaeus, *Species Plantarum* 1: 65. 1753, *typ. cons.*
"Habitat in Europae australis campis arenosis inundatis." RCN: 560.
Conserved type (Cope in *Taxon* 41: 556. 1992): Herb. Linn. No. 85.21 (LINN).
Generitype of *Aira* Linnaeus, *nom. cons.*
Current name: ***Aira praecox*** L. (Poaceae).
Note: Aira praecox, with the type designated by Cope, was proposed as conserved type of the genus by Jarvis (in *Taxon* 41: 556. 1992) and this was eventually approved by the General Committee (see review of the history of this proposal by Barrie, *l.c.* 55: 795–796. 2006).

Aira spicata Linnaeus, *Species Plantarum* 1: 63. 1753, *nom. inval.*
"Habitat in India." RCN: 485.
Type not relevant.
Current name: ***Sacciolepis indica*** (L.) Chase (Poaceae).
Note: Linnaeus accidentally gave the epithet "spicata" to two species of *Aira* in 1753, *Aira* no. 1 (p. 63) and *Aira* no. 7 (p. 64). Realising this, he corrected the first of these to *indica* ["indicum"] on p. 1231 of vol. 2 of the same work (Errata).

Aira spicata Linnaeus, *Species Plantarum* 1: 64. 1753.
"Habitat in Lapponiae alpibus." RCN: 554.
Replaced synonym of: *Aira subspicata* L. (1759), *nom. illeg.*
Lectotype (Louis-Marie in *Rhodora* 30: 238. 1928): [icon] *"Gramen Avenaceum paniculatum Alp. humile, locustis in spicam collectis varicoloribus aristatis"* in Scheuchzer, Agrostographia Helv. Prodr.: 24, t. 6. 1708.
Current name: ***Trisetum spicatum*** (L.) K. Richt. (Poaceae).
Note: Linnaeus accidentally gave the epithet "spicata" to two species of *Aira* in 1753, *Aira* no. 1 (p. 63) and *Aira* no. 7 (p. 64). Realising this, he corrected the first of these to *indica* ["indicum"] on p. 1231 of vol. 2 of the same work (Errata). Hitchcock (in *Contr. U. S. Natl. Herb.* 12: 120. 1908) noted this and discussed material in LINN. Louis-Marie (1928) typified the name using the Scheuchzer plate, though Mackenzie (in *Rhodora* 31: 194. 1929) questioned the "doubtful correctness" of this. Edgar (in *New Zealand J. Bot.* 36: 556. 1998) indicated Herb. Linn. 85.7 (LINN) as the holotype, with an isotype, previously reproduced by Hultén (in *Svensk Bot. Tidskr.* 53: 207, f. 1. 1959), in S. Although Edgar's choice has been followed by some later authors, that of Louis-Marie has priority, and does not appear to cause any nomenclatural disruption.

Aira subspicata Linnaeus, *Systema Naturae,* ed. 10, 2: 873. 1759, *nom. illeg.*
["Habitat in Lapponiae alpibus."] Sp. Pl. 1: 64 (1753). RCN: 554.
Replaced synonym: *Aira spicata* L. (1753).
Lectotype (Louis-Marie in *Rhodora* 30: 238. 1928): [icon] *"Gramen Avenaceum paniculatum Alp. humile, locustis in spicam collectis varicoloribus aristatis"* in Scheuchzer, Agrostographia Helv. Prodr.: 24, t. 6. 1708.
Current name: ***Trisetum spicatum*** (L.) K. Richt. (Poaceae).
Note: An illegitimate renaming of *A. spicata* L. (1753: 64 non 1753: 63).

Aizoon canariense Linnaeus, *Species Plantarum* 1: 488. 1753.
"Habitat in Canariis." RCN: 3714.
Lectotype (Burtt & Lewis in *Kew Bull.* 7: 350. 1952): Herb. Linn. No. 650.1 (LINN).
Generitype of *Aizoon* Linnaeus (vide Green, *Prop. Brit. Bot.*: 159. 1929).
Current name: ***Aizoon canariense*** L. (Aizoaceae).

Aizoon hispanicum Linnaeus, *Species Plantarum* 1: 488. 1753.
"Habitat in Hispania." RCN: 3715.
Lectotype (Peruzzi & al. in *Taxon* 53: 541, f. 1. 2004): [icon] *"Ficoidea Hispanica annua, folio longiore Vaill."* in Dillenius, Hort. Eltham. 1: 143, t. 117, f. 143. 1732.
Current name: ***Aizoanthemum hispanicum*** L.) H.E.K. Hartmann (Aizoaceae).

Aizoon lanceolatum Linnaeus, *Systema Vegetabilium,* ed. 13: 392. 1774, *nom. illeg.*
["Habitat in Africa."] Sp. Pl. 1: 488 (1753). RCN: 3716.
Replaced synonym: *Aizoon paniculatum* L. (1753).
Neotype (Adamson in *J. S. African Bot.* 25: 40. 1959): *Sparrman 109,* Herb. Linn. No. 650.6 (LINN).
Current name: ***Aizoon paniculatum*** L. (Aizoaceae).
Note: Aizoon lanceolatum appeared for the first time in 1774 where it was the third species of *Aizoon,* a position earlier occupied by *A. paniculatum* L. (1753). As the two names also share an identical diagnosis, *A. lanceolatum* is evidently a superfluous name for *A. paniculatum.*

Aizoon paniculatum Linnaeus, *Species Plantarum* 1: 488. 1753.
"Habitat in Africa." RCN: 3716.
Replaced synonym of: *Aizoon lanceolatum* L. (1774), *nom. illeg.*

Neotype (Adamson in *J. S. African Bot.* 25: 40. 1959): *Sparrman 109,* Herb. Linn. No. 650.6 (LINN).
Current name: ***Aizoon paniculatum*** L. (Aizoaceae).
Note: Although the Sparrman collection indicated as the type by Adamson was not received by Linnaeus before 1772, the absence of any original material for this name allows Adamson's choice to be treated as a neotype.

Ajuga alpina Linnaeus, *Systema Naturae,* ed. 12, 2: 387; *Mantissa Plantarum:* 80. 1767.
"Habitat in Alpibus Helveticis, Austriacis. Jacquin." RCN: 4115.
Lectotype (Ball in Jarvis & al. in *Taxon* 50: 510. 2001): Herb. Linn. No. 721.3 (LINN).
Current name: ***Ajuga genevensis*** L. (Lamiaceae).

Ajuga genevensis Linnaeus, *Species Plantarum* 2: 561. 1753.
"Habitat in Europa australiori." RCN: 4116.
Lectotype (Hedge in Jarvis & al. in *Taxon* 50: 510. 2001): Herb. Linn. No. 721.8 (LINN).
Current name: ***Ajuga genevensis*** L. (Lamiaceae).
Note: Davis (*Fl. Turkey* 9: 44. 1982) refers to Herb. Linn. No. 721.8 without selecting a type.

Ajuga orientalis Linnaeus, *Species Plantarum* 2: 561. 1753.
"Habitat in Oriente." RCN: 4113.
Lectotype (Hedge in Jarvis & al. in *Taxon* 50: 510. 2001): Herb. Linn. No. 721.1 (LINN).
Current name: ***Ajuga orientalis*** L. (Lamiaceae).

Ajuga pyramidalis Linnaeus, *Species Plantarum* 2: 561. 1753.
"Habitat in Suecia, Helvetia, Germania." RCN: 4114.
Lectotype (Ball in Jarvis & al. in *Taxon* 50: 510. 2001): Herb. Linn. No. 721.2 (LINN).
Generitype of *Ajuga* Linnaeus (vide Green, *Prop. Brit. Bot.*: 164. 1929).
Current name: ***Ajuga pyramidalis*** L. (Lamiaceae).
Note: Ajuga reptans L. was treated as the generitype of *Ajuga* by Britton & Brown, *Ill. Fl. N. U. S.,* ed. 2, 3: 101. 1913 (see McNeill & al. in *Taxon* 36: 358. 1987). However, under Art. 10.5, Ex. 7 (a voted example) of the Vienna Code, this is a type choice made under the American Code and is to be replaced under Art. 10.5b by Green's choice (*Prop. Brit. Bot.*: 164. 1929) of *A. pyramidalis.*

Ajuga reptans Linnaeus, *Species Plantarum* 2: 561. 1753.
"Habitat in Europa australiori." RCN: 4117.
Lectotype (Hedge in Jarvis & al., *Regnum Veg.* 127: 16. 1993): Herb. Linn. No. 721.10 (LINN).
Current name: ***Ajuga reptans*** L. (Lamiaceae).
Note: This was treated as the generitype of *Ajuga* by Britton & Brown, *Ill. Fl. N. U. S.,* ed. 2, 3: 101. 1913 (see McNeill & al. in *Taxon* 36: 358. 1987). However, under Art. 10.5, Ex. 7 (a voted example) of the Vienna Code, this is a type choice made under the American Code and is to be replaced under Art. 10.5b by Green's choice (*Prop. Brit. Bot.*: 164. 1929) of *A. pyramidalis* L.

Albuca major Linnaeus, *Species Plantarum,* ed. 2, 1: 438. 1762, *nom. illeg.*
"Habitat ad Cap. b. Spei." RCN: 2408.
Replaced synonym: *Ornithogalum canadense* L. (1753).
Lectotype (Müller-Doblies in Jarvis & al., *Regnum Veg.* 127: 16. 1993): Herb. Linn. No. 140.5 (S).
Generitype of *Albuca* Linnaeus (vide Phillips, *Gen. S. African Fl. Pl.,* ed. 2: 188. 1951).
Current name: ***Albuca canadensis*** (L.) F.M. Leight. (Liliaceae/Hyacinthaceae).
Note: A superfluous name for *Ornithogalum canadense* L. (1753).

Albuca minor Linnaeus, *Species Plantarum*, ed. 2, 1: 438. 1762.
"Habitat ad Cap. b. Spei." RCN: 2409.
Lectotype (Müller-Doblies in *Feddes Repert.* 105: 368. 1994): [icon]
   "Ornithogalum Africanum" in Hermann, Parad. Bat.: 209. 1698.
Current name: ***Albuca sp.*** (Liliaceae/Hyacinthaceae).
Note: Müller-Doblies (in *Feddes Repert.* 105: 368. 1994) regards
   Hermann's plate as the type, and the name as a *nomen dubium*, as
   the type is "not sufficiently characteristic for a satisfactory
   identification, possibly = *A. flaccida* [Jacq.] or *A. paradoxa* [Dinter]".

Alcea ficifolia Linnaeus, *Species Plantarum* 2: 687. 1753.
"Habitat – – – –" RCN: 5036.
Type not designated.
Original material: Herb. Burser XVIII(1): 13 (UPS); Herb. Linn. No.
   869.2 (LINN); [icon] in Tabernaemontanus, New Vollk. Kräuterb.:
   1148, 1149. 1664.
Current name: ***Alcea rosea*** L. (Malvaceae).

Alcea rosea Linnaeus, *Species Plantarum* 2: 687. 1753.
"Habitat – – – –" RCN: 5035.
Lectotype (Abedin in Nasir & Ali, *Fl. W. Pakistan* 130: 50. 1979):
   Herb. Linn. No. 869.1 (LINN).
Generitype of *Alcea* Linnaeus (vide Green, *Prop. Brit. Bot.*: 172. 1929).
Current name: ***Alcea rosea*** L. (Malvaceae).

Alchemilla alpina Linnaeus, *Species Plantarum* 1: 123. 1753.
"Habitat in Alpibus Europae." RCN: 1016.
Lectotype (Jonsell & Jarvis in *Nordic J. Bot.* 22: 73. 2002): Herb.
   Linn. No. 67 (LAPP).
Current name: ***Alchemilla alpina*** L. (Rosaceae).

Alchemilla alpina Linnaeus var. **hybrida** Linnaeus, *Species Plantarum*
   1: 123. 1753.
"Habitat in Alpibus Europae." RCN: 1016.
Basionym of: *Alchemilla hybrida* (L.) L. (1756).
Lectotype (Fröhner in Cafferty & Jarvis in *Taxon* 51: 541. 2002):
   [icon] *"Alchimilla alpina pubescens minor"* in Plukenet,
   Phytographia: t. 240, f. 2. 1692; Almag. Bot.: 18. 1696. –
   Typotype: Herb. Sloane 95: 22 (BM-SL).
Current name: ***Alchemilla hybrida*** (L.) L. (Rosaceae).
Note: Bradshaw & al. (in *Watsonia* 5: 261, f. 1, pl. 11a. 1962) treated
   Plukenet material in Herb. Sloane vol. 95: 22 (BM) as the holotype,
   incorrectly, as it was neither seen by Linnaeus nor was it the sole
   element. However, the material is the basis for the cited Plukenet
   illustration, and the latter was formally designated as lectotype by
   Fröhner.

Alchemilla hybrida (Linnaeus) Linnaeus, *Amoenitates Academicae* 3:
   49. 1756.
"Habitat Locus natalis omnium sunt Alpes." RCN: 1016.
Basionym: *Alchemilla alpina* L. var. *hybrida* L. (1753).
Lectotype (Fröhner in Cafferty & Jarvis in *Taxon* 51: 541. 2002):
   [icon] *"Alchimilla alpina pubescens minor"* in Plukenet,
   Phytographia: t. 240, f. 2. 1692; Almag. Bot.: 18. 1696. –
   Typotype: Herb. Sloane 95: 22 (BM-SL).
Current name: ***Alchemilla hybrida*** (L.) L. (Rosaceae).

Alchemilla pentaphyllea Linnaeus, *Species Plantarum* 1: 123. 1753.
"Habitat in monte Canisio, Furca, Gotthardo." RCN: 1017.
Lectotype (Fröhner in Cafferty & Jarvis in *Taxon* 51: 541. 2002):
   Herb. Burser XVIII(1): 66 (UPS).
Current name: ***Alchemilla pentaphyllea*** L. (Rosaceae).

Alchemilla vulgaris Linnaeus, *Species Plantarum* 1: 123. 1753.
"Habitat in Europae pascuis." RCN: 1015.

Lectotype (Purohit & Panigrahi, *Fam. Rosaceae India* 1: 185. 1991):
   Herb. Linn. No. 166.1 (LINN).
Generitype of *Alchemilla* Linnaeus (vide Hitchcock, *Prop. Brit. Bot.*:
   126. 1929).
Current name: ***Alchemilla vulgaris*** L. (Rosaceae).
Note: Fröhner (in *Gleditschia* 14: 51–67. 1986) discussed the
   typification of this name in some detail, but appeared to select an
   ineligible David van Royen (see his f. 4) specimen (sheet
   908.190–1281, L) as lectotype. Purohit & Panigrahi (in *Fam.
   Rosaceae India* 1: 185. 1991) explicitly treated 166.1 (LINN) as the
   type and, recognising that it is a mixture of two taxa, called it a
   nomen confusum. They say they are using it as a "neutral" aggregate
   name. Many authors have treated *A. vulgaris* as a *nomen ambiguum*.

Aldrovanda vesiculosa Linnaeus, *Species Plantarum* 1: 281. 1753.
"Habitat in Italiae & Indiae paludosis. D. Monti." RCN: 2226.
Lectotype (Walters in Jarvis & al., *Regnum Veg.* 127: 16. 1993): Herb.
   Linn. No. 397.1 (LINN).
Generitype of *Aldrovanda* Linnaeus.
Current name: ***Aldrovanda vesiculosa*** L. (Droseraceae).

Aletris capensis Linnaeus, *Systema Naturae*, ed. 10, 2: 985. 1759.
["Habitat ad Cap. b. spei."] Sp. Pl., ed. 2, 1: 456 (1762). RCN: 2503.
Lectotype (Obermeyer in Dyer, *Fl. Pl. Africa* 34: t. 1356. 1961): Herb.
   Linn. No. 440.2 (LINN).
Current name: ***Veltheimia capensis*** (L.) DC.
   (Liliaceae/Hyacinthaceae).

Aletris farinosa Linnaeus, *Species Plantarum* 1: 319. 1753.
"Habitat in America septentrionali." RCN: 2502.
Lectotype (Reveal in Jarvis & al., *Regnum Veg.* 127: 16. 1993): Herb.
   Linn. No. 440.1 (LINN; iso- BM).
Generitype of *Aletris* Linnaeus.
Current name: ***Aletris farinosa*** L. (Liliaceae/Melanthiaceae).

Aletris fragrans Linnaeus, *Species Plantarum*, ed. 2, 1: 456. 1762.
"Habitat in Africa." RCN: 2505.
Lectotype (Wijnands, *Bot. Commelins*: 130. 1983): [icon] *"Aloe
   Africana arborescens floribus albicantibus fragrantissimis"* in
   Commelin, Hort. Med. Amstelod. Pl. Rar. 2: 7, t. 4, f. 2. 1701.
Current name: ***Dracaena fragrans*** (L.) Ker-Gawl.
   (Agavaceae/Dracaenaceae).
Note: Coode (in Bosser & al., *Fl. Mascareignes* 183: 21. 1978) treated
   440.4 (LINN) as the type but this is a later addition to the
   collection annotated only by Linnaeus filius, and not original
   material for the name (see Bos in *Misc. Pap. Landbouwhoogeschool*
   84–1: 73. 1984).

Aletris hyacinthoides (Linnaeus) Linnaeus, *Species Plantarum*, ed. 2,
   1: 456. 1762.
"Habitat α in Zeylona, β in Guinea." RCN: 2504.
Basionym: *Aloë hyacinthoides* L. (1753).
Lectotype (Stearn, *Cat. Bot. Books Miller Hunt* 2(1): liii. 1961): [icon]
   "Aloe Guineensis radice geniculata fol. variegato" in Commelin,
   Praeludia Bot.: 84, t. 33. 1703.
Current name: ***Sansevieria hyacinthoides*** (L.) Druce
   (Agavaceae/Liliaceae).

Aletris hyacinthoides (Linnaeus) Linnaeus var. **guineensis** (Linnaeus)
   Linnaeus, *Species Plantarum*, ed. 2, 1: 456. 1762.
"Habitat in Guinea." RCN: 2504.
Basionym: *Aloë hyacinthoides* L. var. *guineensis* L. (1753).
Lectotype (Stearn, *Cat. Bot. Books Miller Hunt* 2(1): liii. 1961): [icon]
   "Aloe Guineensis radice geniculata fol. variegato" in Commelin,
   Praeludia Bot.: 84, t. 33. 1703.

Current name: ***Sansevieria hyacinthoides*** (L.) Druce
(Agavaceae/Liliaceae).

Aletris hyacinthoides Linnaeus var. **zeylanica** (Linnaeus) Linnaeus,
Species Plantarum, ed. 2, 1: 456. 1762.
"Habitat in Zeylona." RCN: 2504.
Basionym: *Aloë hyacinthoides* L. var. *zeylanica* L. (1753).
Lectotype (Wijnands in *Taxon* 22: 109. 1973): [icon] *"Aloe Zeylanica
pumila foliis variegatis"* in Commelin, Hort. Med. Amsteled. Pl.
Rar. 2: 41, t. 21. 1701.
Current name: ***Sansevieria zeylanica*** (L.) Willd. (Agavaceae/Liliaceae).

Aletris orchidioides Linnaeus, *Mantissa Plantarum Altera*: 367. 1771,
nom. nud.
RCN: 2500.
Type not relevant.
Note: The statement accompanying this name, "excluso Buxbaumii
synonymo ultimo" is not a validating description, and the name is a
nomen nudum.

Aletris uvaria (Linnaeus) Linnaeus, *Systema Vegetabilium,* ed. 13: 277.
1774.
["Habitat ad Cap. b. Spei."] Sp. Pl. 1: 323 (1753). RCN: 2506.
Basionym: *Aloë uvaria* L. (1753).
Lectotype (Codd in Dyer, *Fl. Pl. Africa* 33: t. 1289. 1959): Herb.
Clifford: 133, *Aloë* 14 (BM-000558546).
Current name: ***Kniphofia uvaria*** (L.) Oken
(Liliaceae/Asphodelaceae).

Alisma cordifolia Linnaeus, *Species Plantarum* 1: 343. 1753.
"Habitat in Virginia." RCN: 2631.
Lectotype (Haynes & Holm-Nielsen in *Brittonia* 38: 329. 1986):
[icon] *"Sagittaria Virginiana obtusiore lato folio floribus minoribus
albis"* in Morison, Pl. Hist. Univ. 3: 618, s. 15, t. 4, f. 6. 1699.
Current name: ***Echinodorus cordifolius*** (L.) Griseb. (Alismataceae).
Note: Fernald (in *Rhodora* 49: 108. 1947) cited an unspecified LINN
sheet as "type", presumably the post-1753, 473.4 (LINN) from
Patrick Browne.

Alisma damasonium Linnaeus, *Species Plantarum* 1: 343. 1753.
"Habitat in Angliae, Galliae aquosis." RCN: 2630.
Lectotype (Siddiqi & Ghafoor in Jafri & El-Gadi, *Fl. Libya* 85: 2.
1980): Herb. Linn. No. 473.3 (LINN).
Current name: ***Damasonium alisma*** Mill. (Alismataceae).
Note: See discussion by Rich & Nicholls-Vuille (in *Edinburgh J. Bot.*
58: 50. 2001).

Alisma flava Linnaeus, *Species Plantarum* 1: 343. 1753.
"Habitat in America meridionali." RCN: 2629.
Lectotype (Howard, *Fl. Lesser Antilles* 3: 19. 1979): [icon] *"Butomus
foliis cordato-ovatis"* in Plumier in Burman, Pl. Amer.: 105, t. 115.
1757.
Current name: ***Limnocharis flava*** (L.) Buchenau (Alismataceae).

Alisma natans Linnaeus, *Species Plantarum* 1: 343. 1753.
"Habitat in Galliae, Sueciae fossis." RCN: 2632.
Type not designated.
Original material: Herb. Linn. No. 473.5 (LINN); [icon] in Vaillant
in Mém. Acad. Roy. Sci. Paris 1719: 27, t. 4, f. 8. 1719.
Current name: ***Luronium natans*** (L.) Raf. (Alismataceae).
Note: García Adá & al. (in *Candollea* 51: 378. 1996) noted 473.5
(LINN) as original material but did not designate a type.

Alisma parnassifolia Linnaeus, *Systema Naturae,* ed. 12, 3: 230. 1768.
"Habitat in Apenniniorum paludibus." RCN: 2635.

Type not designated.
Original material: *Cappeller,* Herb. Linn. No. 437.8? (LINN); *Bassi,*
Herb. Linn. No. 473.9? (LINN); [icon] in Bassi, Comment. Acad.
Inst. Sci. Art. Bonon. 6: 13, t. 1. 1768; [icon] in Tilli, Cat. Pl.
Hort. Pisani: 145, t. 46, f. 1. 1723.
Current name: ***Caldesia parnassifolia*** (Bassi ex L.) Parl.
(Alismataceae).

Alisma plantago-aquatica Linnaeus, *Species Plantarum* 1: 342. 1753.
"Habitat in Europae aquosis & ad ripas fluviorum, lacunum." RCN:
2628.
Lectotype (Carter in Hubbard & Milne-Redhead, *Fl. Trop. E. Africa,
Alismataceae*: 5. 1960): Herb. Linn. No. 473.1 (LINN).
Generitype of *Alisma* Linnaeus (vide Hitchcock, *Prop. Brit. Bot.*: 149.
1929).
Current name: ***Alisma plantago-aquatica*** L. (Alismataceae).

Alisma ranunculoides Linnaeus, *Species Plantarum* 1: 343. 1753.
"Habitat in Gotlandiae, Belgii, Angliae, Galliae fossis." RCN: 2633.
Lectotype (designated here by Jonsell): *Bergius, s.n.,* Herb. Linn. No.
473.6 (LINN).
Current name: ***Baldellia ranunculoides*** (L.) Parl. (Alismataceae).
Note: The material in LINN (473.6 and 473.7) was collected in
Gotland, as indicated on the sheets, and agrees with the current
usage of this name. The material on 473.7 was apparently collected
on Linnaeus' journey to Gotland in 1741 but no specific epithet is
written upon it. On sheet 473.6 is written (on the reverse)
"Gotlandia Bergius", which means that it was collected by Linnaeus'
student Peter Jonas Bergius on Gotland in 1752. It should have
reached Linnaeus, together with some other Bergius specimens from
Gotland, later the same year, when *Species Plantarum* was still in
preparation, though at an advanced stage. The epithet, together
with the *Species Plantarum* number "6", is written on the front of
the sheet, and this sheet is therefore selected here as the lectotype.

Alisma subulata Linnaeus, *Species Plantarum* 1: 343. 1753.
"Habitat in Virginia." RCN: 2634.
Lectotype (Bogin in *Mem. New York Bot. Gard.* 9: 204. 1955): *Clayton
723* (BM-000051818).
Current name: ***Sagittaria subulata*** (L.) Buchenau (Alismataceae).

Allamanda cathartica Linnaeus, *Mantissa Plantarum Altera*: 146, 214.
1771.
"Habitat per totam Guianam, juxta fluvios." RCN: 1710.
Neotype (Leeuwenberg in Jarvis & al., *Regnum Veg.* 127: 16. 1993):
Herb. Linn. No. 298.1 (LINN).
Generitype of *Allamanda* Linnaeus.
Current name: ***Allamanda cathartica*** L. (Apocynaceae).
Note: Linnaeus spelled the generic name "Allamanda" in *Mant. Pl.
Altera*: 146, where its description appears, but on p. 214 of the same
work, *A. cathartica* was described, with the genus spelled
"Allemanda".

Allionia incarnata Linnaeus, *Systema Naturae,* ed. 10, 2: 890. 1759,
typ. cons.
["Habitat in Cumanae arenosis."] Sp. Pl., ed. 2, 1: 147 (1762). RCN:
832.
Type not designated.
Original material: none traced.
Generitype of *Allionia* Linnaeus, *nom. cons.*
Current name: ***Allionia incarnata*** L. (Nyctaginaceae).
Note: Allionia Linnaeus 1759, *nom. cons.* against *Allionia* Loefl. 1758.
Although Turner (in *Phytologia* 77: 52. 1994) indicated Löfling
material in LINN, from Venezuela, as the holotype, no such
material exists there and the name appears to need a neotype.

Allionia violacea Linnaeus, *Systema Naturae,* ed. 10, 2: 890. 1759. ["Habitat in Cumana Americes."] Sp. Pl., ed. 2, 1: 147 (1762). RCN: 831.
Type not designated.
Original material: none traced.
Generitype of *Allionia* Loefl., *nom. rej.*
Current name: **Mirabilis violacea** (L.) Choisy (Nyctaginaceae).

Allium ampeloprasum Linnaeus, *Species Plantarum* 1: 294. 1753, *nom. cons.*
"Habitat in Oriente, inque insula Holms Angliae." RCN: 2344.
Lectotype (de Wilde-Duyfjes in *Taxon* 22: 59. 1973): England. Steep Holm Is., *Newton* in Petiver, Hort. Sicc. Angl. (Herb. Sloane 152: 153) (BM-SL).
Current name: **Allium ampeloprasum** L. (Liliaceae/Alliaceae).

Allium angulosum Linnaeus, *Species Plantarum* 1: 300. 1753.
"Habitat in Sibiriae humidiusculis." RCN: 2370.
Lectotype (Hanelt in Wisskirchen in *Feddes Repert.* 108: 103. 1997): Herb. Linn. No. 419.28 (LINN).
Current name: **Allium angulosum** L. (Liliaceae/Alliaceae).

Allium arenarium Linnaeus, *Species Plantarum* 1: 297. 1753.
"Habitat in Thuringia; in Falstria Scaniae." RCN: 2356.
Lectotype (Mathew, *Rev.* Allium *sect.* Allium: 140. 1996): Herb. Linn. No. 419.13 (LINN).
Current name: **Allium vineale** L. (Liliaceae/Alliaceae).

Allium ascalonicum Linnaeus, *Flora Palaestina*: 17. 1756.
["Habitat in Palaestina. Hasselquist."] Sp. Pl., ed. 2, 1: 429 (1762). RCN: 2368.
Lectotype (de Wilde-Duyfjes in *Taxon* 22: 61. 1973): *Hasselquist,* Herb. Linn. No. 419.24, left specimen (LINN).
Current name: **Allium hierochuntinum** Boiss. (Liliaceae/Alliaceae).
Note: See discussion by Mathew (*Rev.* Allium *Sect.* Allium: 144. 1996), who acknowledges that, because of its type, *A. ascalonicum* L. is the earliest name for *A. hierochuntinum* Boiss. Following Stearn (in *Bull. Brit. Mus. (Nat. Hist.), Bot.* 2: 181. 1960), he informally rejected the former because it has been applied more or less continuously since 1762 to a well-known cultivar of *A. cepa* L. However, no formal rejection proposal has been made.

Allium canadense Linnaeus, *Species Plantarum* 2: 1195. 1753.
"Habitat in Canada. Kalm." RCN: 2373.
Type not designated.
Original material: none traced.
Current name: **Allium canadense** L. var. **canadense** (Liliaceae/Alliaceae).

Allium carinatum Linnaeus, *Species Plantarum* 1: 297. 1753.
"Habitat in Germania." RCN: 2357.
Lectotype (de Wilde-Duyfjes in *Meded. Landbouwhoogeschool* 76–11: 108. 1976): [icon] *"Ampeloprasson proliferum"* in Plantin, Pl. Stirp. Icon.: 156. 1581 (see p. 148).
Current name: **Allium carinatum** L. (Liliaceae/Alliaceae).
Note: Stearn (in *Herbertia* 11: 17, f. 118, left. 1944) reproduces the cited Clusius plate.

Allium cepa Linnaeus, *Species Plantarum* 1: 300. 1753.
"Habitat – – – –" RCN: 2376.
Lectotype (de Wilde-Duyfjes in *Taxon* 22: 64. 1973): Herb. A. van Royen No. 908.105–610 (L).
Current name: **Allium cepa** L. (Liliaceae/Alliaceae).
Note: Although de Wilde-Duyfjes treated her chosen type as a neotype, the van Royen material is original material for the name and so is a lectotype (Art. 9.8).

Allium chamaemoly Linnaeus, *Species Plantarum* 1: 301. 1753.
"Habitat in Italia." RCN: 2383.
Lectotype (Stearn in *Ann. Mus. Goulandris* 4: 146. 1978): [icon] *"Chamaemoli"* in Colonna, Ekphr.: 325, 326. 1606 (see p. 118).
Current name: **Allium chamaemoly** L. (Liliaceae/Alliaceae).
Note: De Wilde-Duyfjes (in *Taxon* 22: 60. 1973) incorrectly designated material in Herb. Bauhin, "IX Chamaemoly Columna" (BAS), not seen by Linnaeus, as lectotype. Stearn (in *Ann. Mus. Goulandris* 4: 146. 1978) therefore rejected this choice, designating a Colonna illustration as the lectotype. Pastor & Valdés (in *Revis. Gen. Allium Penins. Iber. Islas Baleares*: 98. 1983) follow Stearn while noting the existence of material in Herb. Burser (III: 110).

Allium descendens Linnaeus, *Species Plantarum* 1: 298. 1753.
"Habitat in Helvetia." RCN: 2360.
Type not designated.
Original material: Herb. Linn. No. 419.15 (LINN); [icon] in Haller, De Allii Genere: 23, t. 1, f. 1. 1745; [icon] in Rudbeck, Campi Elysii 2: 160, f. 20. 1701; [icon] in Rudbeck, Campi Elysii 2: 165, f. 13. 1701.
Current name: **Allium sphaerocephalon** L. subsp. **sphaerocephalon** (Liliaceae/Alliaceae).
Note: This name has been widely treated as a *nomen ambiguum* by authors such as Kollmann (in *Taxon* 19: 789. 1970), Stearn & Özhatay (in *Ann. Mus. Goulandris* 3: 46. 1977) and Mathew (*Rev. Allium Sect.* Allium: 119. 1996). However, no formal proposal for rejection has been made.

Allium fistulosum Linnaeus, *Species Plantarum* 1: 301. 1753.
"Habitat – – – –" RCN: 2378.
Type not designated.
Original material: [icon] in Dodoëns, Stirp. Hist. Pempt., ed. 2: 687. 1616.
Current name: **Allium fistulosum** L. (Liliaceae/Alliaceae).
Note: A neotype (139.7, S) was designated by de Wilde-Duyfjes (in *Taxon* 22: 67. 1973) but, given the existence of original material (a cited Dodoëns figure), this is contrary to Art. 9.11.

Allium flavum Linnaeus, *Species Plantarum* 1: 298. 1753.
"Habitat in Pannonia." RCN: 2362.
Lectotype (de Wilde-Duyfjes in *Taxon* 22: 68. 1973): Herb. Linn. No. 419.16 (LINN).
Current name: **Allium flavum** L. (Liliaceae/Alliaceae).

Allium lineare Linnaeus, *Species Plantarum* 1: 295. 1753.
"Habitat in Sibiria." RCN: 2346.
Lectotype (Dal Vesco & al. in *Webbia* 58: 404. 2003): *Amman 7,* Herb. Linn. No. 419.1 (LINN).
Current name: **Allium lineare** L. (Liliaceae/Alliaceae).

Allium magicum Linnaeus, *Species Plantarum* 1: 296. 1753, *nom. rej.*
"Habitat – – – – –" RCN: 2350.
Lectotype (Seisums in *Taxon* 47: 712. 1998): Herb. Burser III: 106 (UPS).
Current name: **Allium nigrum** L. (Liliaceae/Alliaceae).
Note: Allium magicum is rejected with respect to *A. nigrum* L.

Allium moly Linnaeus, *Species Plantarum* 1: 301. 1753.
"Habitat in Hungaria, Baldo, Monspelii." RCN: 2377.
Lectotype (de Wilde-Duyfjes in *Taxon* 22: 69. 1973): Herb. Linn. No. 419.36 (LINN).
Current name: **Allium moly** L. (Liliaceae/Alliaceae).

Allium moschatum Linnaeus, *Species Plantarum* 1: 298. 1753.
"Habitat in GalloProvinciae, Narbonae, Hispaniae apricis elevatis." RCN: 361.

Lectotype (Pastor & Valdés, *Revis. Gen.* Allium *Penins. Iber. Islas Baleares*: 98. 1983): Herb. Burser III: 111, right specimen (UPS).
Current name: ***Allium moschatum*** L. (Liliaceae/Alliaceae).
Note: De Wilde-Duyfjes (in *Taxon* 22: 70. 1973) incorrectly designated material in Herb. Bauhin, "Moly moschatum capillaceo folio" (BAS), not seen by Linnaeus, as lectotype. Pastor & Valdés (in *Rev. Gen.* Allium *Penins. Iber. Islas Balear.*: 98. 1983) therefore rejected this choice, designating Burser material as the lectotype instead. However, López González (in *Anales Jard. Bot. Madrid* 57: 195–197 1999) demonstrates rather convincingly, based on correspondence between Löfling and Linnaeus, that the name was predominantly based on *Löfling 253* (now lost). He argues that Burser III: 111 conflicts with the diagnosis that Linnaeus attributed to Löfling, and cannot be its type. He concludes that *A. pallens* L. (1762) is a synonym of *A. moschatum* L., and that *A. capillare* Cav. is the correct name for *A. moschatum* L. (1762), non Loefl. ex L. (1753). He suggests that usage of *A. moschatum* could be maintained by a conservation proposal based on Burser III: 111.

Allium nigrum Linnaeus, *Species Plantarum*, ed. 2, 1: 430. 1762, *nom. cons.*
"Habitat in Algiriae inque Galloprovincia." RCN: 2371.
Conserved type (Seisums in *Taxon* 47: 745. 1998): Cyprus. 1–2km NE of Lyso, 10km SE of Polis (Akmas), 450m, 14 Apr 1979, *Edmondson & McClintock 2822* (K; iso- E).
Current name: ***Allium nigrum*** L. (Liliaceae/Alliaceae).

Allium nutans Linnaeus, *Species Plantarum* 1: 299. 1753.
"Habitat in Sibiria." RCN: 2367.
Type not designated.
Original material: *Amman 6*, Herb. Linn. No. 419.23 (LINN); Herb. Linn. No. 138.14 (S); [icon] in Gmelin, Fl. Sibirica 1: 55, t. 12. 1747.
Current name: ***Allium nutans*** L. (Liliaceae/Alliaceae).

Allium obliquum Linnaeus, *Species Plantarum* 1: 296. 1753.
"Habitat in Sibiria." RCN: 2351.
Lectotype (Friesen in *Feddes Repert.* 106: 74. 1995): Herb. Linn. No. 419.7 (LINN).
Current name: ***Allium obliquum*** L. (Liliaceae/Alliaceae).

Allium odorum Linnaeus, *Systema Naturae,* ed. 12, 2: 239; *Mantissa Plantarum*: 62. 1767.
"Habitat in Europa australi." RCN: 2372.
Type not designated.
Original material: none traced.
Current name: ***Allium ramosum*** L. (Liliaceae/Alliaceae).
Note: See comments by Stearn (in *Herbertia* 11: 229. 1946).

Allium oleraceum Linnaeus, *Species Plantarum* 1: 299. 1753.
"Habitat in Suecia, Germania." RCN: 2366.
Lectotype (de Wilde-Duyfjes in *Meded. Landbouwhoogeschool* 76–11: 108. 1976): Herb. Linn. No. 419.22 (LINN).
Current name: ***Allium oleraceum*** L. (Liliaceae/Alliaceae).

Allium pallens Linnaeus, *Species Plantarum*, ed. 2, 1: 427. 1762.
"Habitat in Italia, Hispania, Monspelii, Pannonia." RCN: 2363.
Lectotype (Brullo & al. in *Bocconea* 16: 558, 562. 2003): *Gouan 8*, Herb. Linn. No. 419.20 (LINN).
Current name: ***Allium pallens*** L. (Liliaceae/Alliaceae).
Note: De Wilde-Duyfjes (in *Taxon* 22: 74. 1973) designated Hasselquist material (Herb. Linn. No. 139.9, S) as lectotype, but this choice was rejected by Brullo & al. on the grounds that, having been collected in the Middle East, it conflicted with the geographical elements of the protologue. Brullo & al. designated material sent to Linnaeus by Gouan as lectotype instead.

Allium paniculatum Linnaeus, *Systema Naturae,* ed. 10, 2: 978. 1759. ["Habitat in Sibiria, Italia, Austria, Oriente."] Sp. Pl., ed. 2, 1: 428 (1762). RCN: 2364.
Lectotype (de Wilde-Duyfjes in *Taxon* 22: 75. 1973): *Gerber?*, Herb. Linn. No. 419.21, right specimen (LINN).
Current name: ***Allium paniculatum*** L. (Liliaceae/Alliaceae).

Allium parviflorum Linnaeus, *Species Plantarum*, ed. 2, 1: 427. 1762.
"Habitat in Europa australi." RCN: 2359.
Lectotype (de Wilde-Duyfjes in *Taxon* 22: 76. 1973): Herb. Linn. No. 419.14 (LINN).
Current name: ***Allium parviflorum*** L. (Liliaceae/Alliaceae).

Allium porrum Linnaeus, *Species Plantarum* 1: 295. 1753, *nom. rej.*
"Habitat – – – –" RCN: 2345.
Lectotype (de Wilde-Duyfjes in *Taxon* 22: 77. 1973): [icon] *"Porrum"* in Dodoëns, Stirp. Hist. Pempt., ed. 2: 688. 1616.
Current name: ***Allium porrum*** L. (Liliaceae/Alliaceae).
Note: Allium porrum is rejected against *A. ampeloprasum* L.

Allium ramosum Linnaeus, *Species Plantarum* 1: 296. 1753.
"Habitat in Sibiria. G. Demidoff." RCN: 2352.
Lectotype (Friesen in *Feddes Repert.* 106: 75. 1995): *Gmelin*, Herb. Linn. No. 419.8/9 (LINN).
Current name: ***Allium ramosum*** L. (Liliaceae/Alliaceae).

Allium roseum Linnaeus, *Species Plantarum* 1: 296. 1753.
"Habitat Monspelii in vineis." RCN: 2353.

Lectotype (Seisums in *Taxon* 47: 715. 1998): [icon] *"Allium silvestre sive moly minus roseo amplo flore"* in Magnol, Bot. Monspel.: 11, 10. 1676.

Current name: ***Allium roseum*** L. (Liliaceae/Alliaceae).

Note: De Wilde-Duyfjes (in *Taxon* 22: 78. 1973) designated Herb. Linn. 419.10 (LINN) as lectotype. However, Seisums (in *Taxon* 47: 715. 1998) argued that de Wilde-Duyfjes' typification must be rejected as the specimen conflicts with the protologue (and is a specimen of *A. narcissiflorum* Vill.). He designated a Magnol plate (see p. 277) as lectotype in its place.

Allium rotundum Linnaeus, *Species Plantarum*, ed. 2, 1: 423. 1762.

"Habitat in Europa australiori." RCN: 2347.

Type not designated.

Original material: Herb. Burser III: 104 (UPS); [icon] in Micheli, Nov. Pl. Gen.: 25, t. 24, f. 1. 1729.

Current name: ***Allium rotundum*** L. (Liliaceae/Alliaceae).

Note: De Wilde-Duyfjes (in *Taxon* 22: 80. 1973) treated a Haller collection (P) as the lectotype but this collection was not studied by Linnaeus and is not original material for the name. Pastor & Valdés (*Revis. Gen.* Allium *Penins. Iber. Islas Baleares*: 53–54. 1983) consequently rejected this choice and discussed the other original elements but failed to find one that would make a satisfactory type as they appear to belong to other taxa.

Allium sativum Linnaeus, *Species Plantarum* 1: 296. 1753.

"Habitat in Sicilia." RCN: 2354.

Lectotype (de Wilde-Duyfjes in *Taxon* 22: 81. 1973): Herb. Burser III: 90 (UPS).

Generitype of *Allium* Linnaeus (vide Hitchcock, *Prop. Brit. Bot.*: 145. 1929).

Current name: ***Allium sativum*** L. (Liliaceae/Alliaceae).

Note: Although de Wilde-Duyfjes indicated the Burser material as a neotype, it is in fact original material for the name so her choice is accepted as a lectotypification under Art. 9.8.

Allium schoenoprasum Linnaeus, *Species Plantarum* 1: 301. 1753.

"Habitat in alpestribus Sibiriae, Oelandiae locis rupestribus." RCN: 2379.

Lectotype (de Wilde-Duyfjes in *Taxon* 22: 82. 1973): Herb. Linn. No. 419.37 (LINN).

Current name: ***Allium schoenoprasum*** L. subsp. ***schoenoprasum*** (Liliaceae/Alliaceae).

Allium scorodoprasum Linnaeus, *Species Plantarum* 1: 297. 1753.

"Habitat in Oelandia, Dania, Pannonia." RCN: 2355.

Lectotype (de Wilde-Duyfjes in *Taxon* 22: 83. 1973): Herb. Linn. No. 419.12, left specimen (LINN).

Current name: ***Allium scorodoprasum*** L. (Liliaceae/Alliaceae).

Note: Stearn (in *Biol. J. Linn. Soc.* 5: 9. Mar 1973), in an account of Linnaeus' Öland and Gotland journey of 1741, treats Öland as the restricted type locality, and noted the existence of 419.12 (LINN). In this paper, he attributed restricted type localities irrespective of whether any material existed in LINN and, where specimens do exist, he does not refer to any of them as type specimens. The collection previously designated as the type by de Wilde-Duyfjes (28 Feb 1973) shows no annotation expressly associating it with Öland. Lee (in *Bull. Korea Pl. Res.* 1: 2. 2000) illustrated the type (as plate 1A). Stearn (in *Herbertia* 11: 17, f. 118, right. 1944) had earlier reproduced the cited Clusius plate.

Allium senescens Linnaeus, *Species Plantarum* 1: 299. 1753.

"Habitat in Sibiria, Sicilia." RCN: 2369.

Lectotype (Friesen in *Feddes Repert.* 106: 68. 1995): Herb. Linn. No. 419.25 (LINN).

Current name: ***Allium senescens*** L. (Liliaceae/Alliaceae).

Note: Stearn (in *Herbertia* 11: 32. 1946) stated that the cited Gmelin plate "is usually regarded as the type" but did not formally indicate

it as such himself. Although Hanelt & van Raamsdonk (in Wisskirchen & Haeupler, *Standardliste Farn- Blütenpfl. Deutschl.*: 58. 1998) interpreted this as formal typification, Friesen's choice of material in LINN as type pre-dates their publication.

Allium sibiricum Linnaeus, *Mantissa Plantarum Altera*: 562. 1771.

"Habitat in Sibiria." RCN: 2381.

Type not designated.

Original material: Herb. Linn. No. 419.38? (LINN).

Current name: ***Allium schoenoprasum*** L. subsp. ***sibiricum*** (L.) Čelak. (Liliaceae/Alliaceae).

Note: See notes by Friesen (in *Candollea* 51: 469. 1996).

Allium sphaerocephalon Linnaeus, *Species Plantarum* 1: 297. 1753.

"Habitat in Italia, Sibiria, Helvetia." RCN: 2358.

Lectotype (Stearn & Özhatay in *Ann. Mus. Goulandris* 3: 46. 1977): [icon] *"Allium seu Moly montanum V"* in Clusius, Rar. Pl. Hist. 1: 195. 1601.

Current name: ***Allium sphaerocephalon*** L. subsp. ***sphaerocephalon*** (Liliaceae/Alliaceae).

Note: Although de Wilde-Duyfjes (in *Taxon* 22: 84. 1973) treated a Micheli collection (FI) as the lectotype, this collection was not studied by Linnaeus and is not original material for the name. Consequently, Stearn & Özhatay's subsequent choice of a Clusius plate as type is accepted here.

Allium subhirsutum Linnaeus, *Species Plantarum* 1: 295. 1753.

"Habitat in Africa, Italia, Hispania." RCN: 2349.

Lectotype (Pastor & Valdés, *Revis. Gen.* Allium *Penins. Iber. Islas Baleares*: 124. 1983): Herb. Burser III: 109 (UPS).

Current name: ***Allium subhirsutum*** L. (Liliaceae/Alliaceae).

Note: De Wilde-Duyfjes (in *Taxon* 22: 85. 1973) incorrectly designated the post-1753 419.3 (LINN) as lectotype. Pastor & Valdés (in *Revis. Gen.* Allium *Penins. Iber. Islas Baleares*: 124–125. 1983) therefore rejected this choice, designating Burser material as the lectotype instead. See Stearn (in *Herbertia* 11: 14. 1946), who reproduces Clusius' cited plate (Stearn's f. 117, left).

Allium tenuissimum Linnaeus, *Species Plantarum* 1: 301. 1753.

"Habitat in Sibiria." RCN: 2382.

Lectotype (Friesen in *Feddes Repert.* 106: 69. 1995): *Gmelin*, Herb. Linn. No. 419.43 (LINN).

Current name: ***Allium tenuissimum*** L. (Liliaceae/Alliaceae).

Allium triquetrum Linnaeus, *Species Plantarum* 1: 300. 1753.

"Habitat in Hispania." RCN: 2375.

Lectotype (Nordenstam in *Taxon* 27: 372, f. 1. 1978): [icon] *"Moly caule & foliis triangularibus"* in Parkinson, Parad. Sole Parad. Terr.: 142, 143, f. 6. 1629 (see p. 145).

Current name: ***Allium triquetrum*** L. (Liliaceae/Alliaceae).

Note: De Wilde-Duyfjes (in *Taxon* 22: 86. 1973) incorrectly designated a post-1753 Alströmer collection (419.3 LINN) as lectotype, and Nordenstam (in *Taxon* 27: 372. 1978) rejected it in favour of the cited Parkinson plate. However, it seems there may be some disagreement as to its taxonomic identity; Pastor & Valdés (in *Revis. Gen.* Allium *Penins. Iber. Islas Baleares*: 141. 1983) question whether it represents *A. triquetrum*.

Allium ursinum Linnaeus, *Species Plantarum* 1: 300. 1753.

"Habitat in Europae septentrionalioris nemorosis." RCN: 2374.

Lectotype (Pastor & Valdés, *Revis. Gen.* Allium *Penins. Iber. Islas Baleares*: 144. 1983): Herb. Linn. No. 419.34, left specimen (LINN).

Current name: ***Allium ursinum*** L. (Liliaceae/Alliaceae).

Allium veronense Linnaeus, *Systema Naturae,* ed. 10, 2: 978. 1759.
RCN: 2363.
Type not designated.
Original material: none traced.
Current name: ***Allium paniculatum*** L. (Liliaceae/Alliaceae).
Note: See discussion by de Wilde-Duyfjes (in *Taxon* 22: 87. 1973).

Allium victorialis Linnaeus, *Species Plantarum* 1: 295. 1753.
"Habitat in Alpibus Helvetiae, Italiae." RCN: 2348.
Lectotype (de Wilde-Duyfjes in *Meded. Landbouwhoogeschool* 76–11:
    212. 1976): Herb. Linn. No. 419.2 (LINN).
Current name: ***Allium victorialis*** L. (Liliaceae/Alliaceae).

Allium vineale Linnaeus, *Species Plantarum* 1: 299. 1753.
"Habitat in Germania." RCN: 2365.
Neotype (de Wilde-Duyfjes in *Taxon* 22: 88. 1973): Herb. Bauhin,
    "Porrum sylvestre gemino capite" (BAS).
Current name: ***Allium vineale*** L. (Liliaceae/Alliaceae).
Note: There appear to be no original elements and so de Wilde-
    Duyfjes' choice of a neotype (though she termed it a lectotype) is
    correctable under Art. 9.8 and is accepted as valid. Pastor & Valdés
    (in *Revis. Gen.* Allium *Penins. Iber. Islas Baleares*: 743. 1983)
    correctly point out that the Bauhin material is ineligible as a
    lectotype because Linnaeus never saw it, and discuss the absence of
    relevant Burser material. They appear to accept a Haller plate as the
    type but there is in fact no figure corresponding with the cited
    polynomial, only a similar one relating to a species described by
    Haller on p. 23 (not p. 11) of his *Allium* account.

Allophylus zeylanicus Linnaeus, *Species Plantarum* 1: 348. 1753.
"Habitat in Zeylona." RCN: 2674.
Lectotype (Leenhouts in Jarvis & al., *Regnum Veg.* 127: 16. 1993):
    Herb. Hermann 3: 54, No. 140 (BM-000628001).
Generitype of *Allophylus* Linnaeus.
Current name: ***Allophylus cobbe*** (L.) Raeusch. (Sapindaceae).

Aloë disticha Linnaeus, *Species Plantarum* 1: 321. 1753.
"Habitat in Africae rupibus." RCN: 2513.
Lectotype (Wijnands, *Bot. Commelins*: 132. 1983): [icon] *"Aloe Afric.
    flore rubro, fol. maculis ab utraque parte albicantib. notato"* in
    Commelin, Hort. Med. Amstelod. Pl. Rar. 2: 15, t. 8. 1701.
Current name: ***Gasteria disticha*** (L.) Haw. (Liliaceae/Asphodelaceae).
Note: Van Jaarsveld (*Gasterias S. Africa*: 9. 1994) reproduces the type
    figure.

Aloë disticha Linnaeus var. **plicatilis** Linnaeus, *Species Plantarum* 1:
    321. 1753.
"Habitat in Africae rupibus." RCN: 2513.
Lectotype (Wijnands, *Bot. Commelins*: 125. 1983): [icon] *"Aloe Afric.
    arborescens montana non spinosa, folio longiss. plicatili, flore rubro"* in
    Commelin, Hort. Med. Amstelod. Pl. Rar. 2: 5, t. 3. 1701.
Current name: ***Aloë plicatilis*** (L.) Mill. (Liliaceae/Asphodelaceae).

Aloë hyacinthoides Linnaeus, *Species Plantarum* 1: 321. 1753.
"Habitat α in Zeylona, β. in Guinea." RCN: 2504.
Basionym of: *Aletris hyacinthoides* (L.) L. (1762).
Lectotype (Stearn, *Cat. Bot. Books Miller Hunt* 2(1): liii. 1961): [icon]
    "Aloe Guineensis radice geniculata fol. variegato" in Commelin,
    Praeludia Bot.: 84, t. 33. 1703.
Current name: ***Sansevieria hyacinthoides*** (L.) Druce
    (Agavaceae/Liliaceae).

Aloë hyacinthoides Linnaeus var. **guineensis** Linnaeus, *Species
    Plantarum* 1: 321. 1753.
"Habitat β. in Guinea." RCN: 2504.

Basionym of: *Aletris hyacinthoides* (L.) L. var. *guineensis* (L.) L.
    (1762).
Lectotype (Stearn, *Cat. Bot. Books Miller Hunt* 2(1): liii. 1961): [icon]
    "Aloe Guineensis radice geniculata fol. variegato" in Commelin,
    Praeludia Bot.: 84, t. 33. 1703.
Current name: ***Sansevieria hyacinthoides*** (L.) Druce
    (Agavaceae/Liliaceae).
Note: Wijnands (in *Taxon* 22: 109–114. 1973) argued that var.
    guineensis, not var. *zeylanica*, was the typical variety of *A.
    hyacinthoides*, an argument accepted by the Committee for
    Spermatophyta (in *Taxon* 23: 823. 1973). Consequently, *Sansevieria
    hyacinthoides* (L.) Druce was accepted as the correct name for what
    Stearn called *Aloë guineensis* (L.) Jacq., listed as the type of
    Sansevieria Thunb. in App. III of the ICBN.

Aloë hyacinthoides Linnaeus var. **zeylanica** Linnaeus, *Species
    Plantarum* 1: 321. 1753.
"Habitat α in Zeylona." RCN: 2504.
Basionym of: *Aletris hyacinthoides* (L.) L. var. *zeylanica* (L.) L.
    (1753).
Lectotype (Wijnands in *Taxon* 22: 109. 1973): [icon] *"Aloe Zeylanica
    pumila foliis variegatis"* in Commelin, Hort. Med. Amstelod. Pl.
    Rar. 2: 41, t. 21. 1701.
Current name: ***Sansevieria zeylanica*** (L.) Willd.
    (Agavaceae/Liliaceae).

Aloë perfoliata Linnaeus, *Species Plantarum* 1: 319. 1753.
"Habitat in Aethiopia." RCN: 2511.
Lectotype (Reynolds, Aloes *S. Africa*: 89, f. 69. 1950): Herb. Linn.
    No. 442.1 (LINN).
Generitype of *Aloë* Linnaeus (vide Hitchcock, *Prop. Brit. Bot.*: 146.
    1929).
Current name: ***Aloë perfoliata*** L. (Liliaceae/Asphodelaceae).
Note: The lectotype, while clearly an *Aloë*, apparently cannot be
    identified to species. Wijnands (*Bot. Commelins*: 124. 1983)
    provided current names for each unnamed variety listed in the
    original description, as did Newton (in Eggli, *Ill. Handb. Succ. Pl.,
    Monocots*: 133. 2001). The latter appears to treat this name as
    synonymous with *A. ferox* Mill.

Aloë perfoliata Linnaeus var. **humilis** Linnaeus, *Species Plantarum* 1:
    320. 1753.
"Habitat in Aethiopia." RCN: 2511.
Lectotype (Wijnands, *Bot. Commelins*: 124. 1983): [icon] *"Aloe Afric.
    humilis spin. et verrucis obsita"* in Commelin, Praeludia Bot.: 77, t.
    26. 1703.
Current name: ***Aloë humilis*** (L.) Mill. (Liliaceae/Asphodelaceae).

Aloë perfoliata Linnaeus var. **vera** Linnaeus, *Species Plantarum* 1: 320.
    1753.
"Habitat in Indiis." RCN: 2511.
Lectotype (Wijnands, *Bot. Commelins*: 127. 1983): [icon] *"Kadanaku
    aut Catevala"* in Rheede, Hort. Malab. 11: 7, t. 3. 1692.
Current name: ***Aloë vera*** (L.) Burm. f. (Liliaceae/Asphodelaceae).

Aloë pumila Linnaeus, *Species Plantarum* 1: 322. 1753.
"Habitat in Aethiopiae campestribus." RCN: 2517.
Lectotype (Scott in *Aloe* 16: 45, f. 1. 1978): [icon] *"Aloe Afric. folio in
    summitate triangulari margaritifera, flore subviridi"* in Commelin,
    Hort. Med. Amstelod. Pl. Rar. 2: 19, t. 10. 1701.
Current name: ***Haworthia margaritifera*** (L.) Haw.
    (Liliaceae/Asphodelaceae).
Note: Scott's lectotype designation made this name homotypic with
    Aloë pumila var. *margaritifera* L., over which, as the autonym, it has
    statutory priority.

Aloë pumila Linnaeus var. **arachnoidea** Linnaeus, *Species Plantarum* 1: 322. 1753.
"Habitat in Aethiopiae campestribus." RCN: 2517.
Lectotype (Scott in *Cact. Succ. J. (Los Angeles)* 49: 205, f. 1. 1977): [icon] *"Aloe Africana humilis arachnoidea"* in Commelin, Praeludia Bot.: 78, t. 27. 1703. – Epitype (Breuer & Metzing in *Taxon* 46: 4. 1997): South Africa. Buitenstekloof, Langvlei, 1971, *M.B. Bayer 153* (NBG No. 110455) (NBG).
Current name: ***Haworthia arachnoidea*** (L.) Duval (Liliaceae/Asphodelaceae).

Aloë pumila Linnaeus var. **margaritifera** Linnaeus, *Species Plantarum* 1: 322. 1753.
"Habitat in Aethiopiae." RCN: 2517.
Lectotype (Wijnands, *Bot. Commelins*: 13. 1983): [icon] *"Aloe Afric. folio in summitate triangulari margaritifera, flore subviridi"* in Commelin, Hort. Med. Amstelod. Pl. Rar. 2: 19, t. 10. 1701. – Epitype (Breuer & Metzing in *Taxon* 46: 9. 1997): South Africa. Karoo Garden ground, Worcester, 1946, *R.H. Compton 18963* (NBG-68120).
Current name: ***Haworthia margaritifera*** (L.) Haw. (Liliaceae/Asphodelaceae).
Note: See comments under *Aloë pumila* L.

Aloë retusa Linnaeus, *Species Plantarum* 1: 322. 1753.
"Habitat in Africae argillosis." RCN: 2515.
Lectotype (Wijnands, *Bot. Commelins*: 136. 1983): [icon] *"Aloe Africana brevissimo crassissimoque folio flore subviridi [excluding inflorescence]"* in Commelin, Hort. Med. Amstelod. Pl. Rar. 2: 11, t. 6. 1701. – Epitype (Breuer & Metzing in *Taxon* 46: 11. 1997): South Africa. Blikbonnie, 2km E of Riversdale, 1971, *J. Dekenah s.n.* (NBG-144772).
Current name: ***Haworthia retusa*** (L.) Duval (Liliaceae/Asphodelaceae).

Aloë spiralis Linnaeus, *Species Plantarum* 1: 322. 1753.
"Habitat in Africae campestribus." RCN: 2514.
Lectotype (Wijnands, *Bot. Commelins*: 128. 1983): [icon] *"Aloe Afr. erecta rotunda &c. Comm."* in Dillenius, Hort. Eltham. 1: 16, t. 13, f. 14. 1732.
Current name: ***Astroloba spiralis*** (L.) Uitewaal (Liliaceae/Asphodelaceae).

Aloë uvaria Linnaeus, *Species Plantarum* 1: 323. 1753.
"Habitat ad Cap. b. Spei." RCN: 2506.
Basionym of: *Aletris uvaria* (L.) L. (1774).
Lectotype (Codd in Dyer, *Fl. Pl. Africa* 33: t. 1289. 1959): Herb. Clifford: 133, *Aloë* 14 (BM-000558546).
Current name: ***Kniphofia uvaria*** (L.) Oken (Liliaceae/Asphodelaceae).

Aloë variegata Linnaeus, *Species Plantarum* 1: 321. 1753.
"Habitat in Aethiopiae argillosis." RCN: 2512.
Lectotype (Wijnands, *Bot. Commelins*: 127. 1983): [icon] *"Aloe Afric. humilis fol. ex albo et viridi variegato"* in Commelin, Hort. Med. Amstelaed. Pl. Rar.: 47, t. 47. 1706.
Current name: ***Aloë variegata*** L. (Liliaceae/Asphodelaceae).

Aloë viscosa Linnaeus, *Species Plantarum* 1: 322. 1753.
"Habitat in Aethiopiae campestribus." RCN: 2516.
Lectotype (Scott in *Natl. Cact. Succ. J.* 36: 98, f. 1. 1981): [icon] *"Aloe Afric. erecta triangularis et viscosa"* in Commelin, Praeludia Bot.: 82, t. 31. 1703. – Epitype (Breuer & Metzing in *Taxon* 46: 13. 1997): South Africa. Blackburn Valley, Calitzdorp, 1947, *W.F. Barker 5073* (NBG-68204).

Current name: ***Haworthia viscosa*** (L.) Haw. (Liliaceae/Asphodelaceae).

Aloë vivipara Linnaeus, *Herbarium Amboinense*: 21. 1754.
RCN: 2519.
Type not designated.
Original material: [icon] in Rumphius, Herb. Amboin. 5: 273, t. 94. 1747.
Current name: ***Agave cantala*** Roxb. ex Salm-Dyck (Agavaceae).

Alopecurus agrestis Linnaeus, *Species Plantarum*, ed. 2, 1: 89. 1762.
"Habitat in Europa australi." RCN: 515.
Lectotype (Cope in Cafferty & al. in *Taxon* 49: 245. 2000): *Hudson 29*, Herb. Linn. No. 82.2 (LINN).
Current name: ***Alopecurus myosuroides*** Huds. (Poaceae).
Note: The relationship between this and *A. myosuroides* Huds. was noted by Pryor (in *J. Bot.* 19: 74. 1881). Hudson's name (Jan–Jun) was published earlier than Linnaeus' (Sep) in 1762.

Alopecurus geniculatus Linnaeus, *Species Plantarum* 1: 60. 1753.
"Habitat in Europae uliginosis." RCN: 516.
Lectotype (Cope in Cafferty & al. in *Taxon* 49: 245. 2000): Herb. Burser I: 26 (UPS).
Current name: ***Alopecurus geniculatus*** L. (Poaceae).
Note: Bor (in Rechinger, *Fl. Iranica* 70: 285. 1970) indicated a specimen at LINN as the type, as did Dogan (in *Turkish J. Bot.* 23: 250. 1999). However there is no relevant material at LINN eligible for typification and Cope designated Burser material as lectotype.

Alopecurus hordeiformis Linnaeus, *Species Plantarum* 1: 60. 1753.
"Habitat in India." RCN: 517.
Lectotype (Renvoize in Cafferty & al. in *Taxon* 49: 245. 2000): Herb. Linn. No. 82.5 (LINN).
Current name: ***Pennisetum alopecuroides*** (L.) Spreng. (Poaceae).

Alopecurus indicus Linnaeus, *Systema Vegetabilium*, ed. 13: 92. 1774, *nom. illeg.*
["Habitat in China."] Sp. Pl. 1: 55 (1753). RCN: 472.
Replaced synonym: *Panicum alopecuroides* L. (1753).
Lectotype (Veldkamp in Cafferty & al. in *Taxon* 49: 253. 2000): Herb. Linn. No. 80.1 (LINN).
Current name: ***Pennisetum alopecuroides*** (L.) Spreng. (Poaceae).
Note: An illegitimate replacement name in *Alopecurus* for *Panicum alopecuroides* L. (1753).

Alopecurus monspeliensis Linnaeus, *Species Plantarum* 1: 61. 1753.
"Habitat Monspelii." RCN: 518.
Lectotype (Scholz in Cafferty & al. in *Taxon* 49: 245. 2000): Herb. Linn. No. 82.6 (LINN).
Current name: ***Polypogon monspeliensis*** (L.) Desf. (Poaceae).
Note: Although Hubbard (in Milne-Redhead & Polhill, *Fl. Trop. E. Africa, Gramineae* 1: 100. 1970) indicated unspecified material at LINN as type, the two sheets (82.6 and 82.7) which could have been intended are clearly not part of a single gathering, so Art. 9.15 does not apply. Although Scholz, in typifying the name, stated that he was restricting Hubbard's earlier choice, the typification is solely Scholz's.

Alopecurus paniceus (Linnaeus) Linnaeus, *Species Plantarum*, ed. 2, 1: 90. 1762.
"Habitat in Europae cultis aridis." RCN: 519.
Basionym: *Cynosurus paniceus* L. (1753).
Lectotype (Scholz in Cafferty & al. in *Taxon* 49: 250. 2000): Herb. Linn. No. 82.8 (LINN).
Current name: ***Polypogon monspeliensis*** (L.) Desf. (Poaceae).

Alopecurus pratensis Linnaeus, *Species Plantarum* 1: 60. 1753.
"Habitat in Europae pratis." RCN: 514.
Lectotype (Cope in Jarvis & al., *Regnum Veg.* 127: 17. 1993): Herb. Linn. No. 82.1 (LINN).
Generitype of *Alopecurus* Linnaeus (vide Hitchcock, *Prop. Brit. Bot.*: 119. 1929).
Current name: ***Alopecurus pratensis*** L. (Poaceae).
Note: Although Kerguélen (in *Lejeunia*, n.s., 75: 79. 1975) stated "Type: ...LINN", this is not accepted as a formal typification, for the reasons explained by Cafferty & al. (in *Taxon* 49: 240. 2000).

Alpinia racemosa Linnaeus, *Species Plantarum* 1: 2. 1753.
"Habitat in America calidiore." RCN: 9.
Lectotype (Gagnepain in *Bull. Soc. Bot. France* 50: 190. 1903): [icon] *"Alpinia"* in Plumier in Burman, Pl. Amer.: 11, t. 20. 1755.
Generitype of *Alpinia* Linnaeus, *nom. rej.*
Current name: ***Renealmia racemosa*** (L.) A. Rich. (Zingiberaceae).
Note: Alpinia Linnaeus, *nom. rej.* in favour of *Alpinia* Roxb.

Alsine media Linnaeus, *Species Plantarum* 1: 272. 1753.
"Habitat in Europae cultis." RCN: 2166.
Lectotype (Turrill in Turrill & Milne-Redhead, *Fl. Trop. E. Africa, Caryophyllaceae*: 24. 1956): Herb. Linn. No. 388.1 (LINN).
Generitype of *Alsine* Linnaeus (vide Hitchcock, *Prop. Brit. Bot.*: 143. 1929).
Current name: ***Stellaria media*** (L.) Vill. (Caryophyllaceae).
Note: Although Fawcett & Rendle (*Fl. Jamaica* 3: 178. 1914) indicated material in LINN as type, they did not distinguish between sheets 388.1 and 388.2 (which are evidently not part of a single gathering so Art. 9.15 does not apply).

Alsine mucronata (Linnaeus) Linnaeus, *Species Plantarum,* ed. 2, 1: 389. 1762.
"Habitat in Helvetia." RCN: 2168.
Basionym: *Arenaria mucronata* L. (1753).
Type not designated.
Original material: as basionym.
Current name: ***Arenaria mucronata*** L. (Caryophyllaceae).

Alsine segetalis Linnaeus, *Species Plantarum* 1: 272. 1753.
"Habitat Parisiis." RCN: 2167.
Lectotype (Ratter in Cafferty & Jarvis in *Taxon* 53: 1050. 2004): [icon] *"Alsine segetalis, gramineis foliis unum latus spectantibus"* in Vaillant, Bot. Paris.: 8, t. 3, f. 3. 1727.
Current name: ***Spergularia segetalis*** (L.) G. Don (Caryophyllaceae).

Alstroemeria ligtu Linnaeus, *Planta Alstromeria*: 10. 1762.
"Habitat in Chili ad ripas fluviorum, uti ad flumen Civitate Conceptionis percurrens." RCN: 2523.
Lectotype (Bayer in *Mitt. Bot. Staatssamml. München* 24: 110. 1987): [icon] *"Hemerocallis floribus purpurascentibus, striatis, vulgo Ligtu"* in Feuillée, J. Obs. 2: 710, t. 4. 1714.
Current name: ***Alstroemeria ligtu*** L. (Liliaceae/Alstroemeriaceae).

Alstroemeria pelegrina Linnaeus, *Planta Alstromeria*: 10. 1762.
"Habitat in Peru." RCN: 2522.
Lectotype (Bayer in *Mitt. Bot. Staatssamml. München* 24: 258. 1987): Herb. Linn. No. 444.1 (LINN).
Generitype of *Alstroemeria* Linnaeus (vide Bullock in *Kew Bull.* 14: 40. 1960).
Current name: ***Alstroemeria pelegrina*** L. (Liliaceae/Alstroemeriaceae).

Alstroemeria salsilla Linnaeus, *Planta Alstromeria*: 10. 1762.
"Habitat in Chili in declivitate montis cujusdam." RCN: 2524.

Lectotype (designated here by Hofreiter): [icon] *"Hemerocallis scandens floribus purpureis, vulgo salsilla"* in Feuillée, J. Obs. 2: 713, t. 6. 1714. – Epitype (designated here by Hofreiter): Chile. Concepcion, Küstenkordillere zwischen Santa Juana und Coronel, 21 Dec 1968, *Merxmüller s.n.* (M).
Current name: ***Bomarea salsilla*** (L.) Mirb. (Liliaceae/Alstroemeriaceae).
Note: Hofreiter (in *Feddes Repert.* 117: 391, f. 1A. 2006) treated a plate cited from Feuilleé as the type, and designated a Merxmüller collection (M) from Chile as an epitype. However, this lectotype choice was published after 1 Jan 2001 and so the omission of the phrase "designated here" or an equivalent (Art. 7.11) means that the choice is not effective. However, this lectotype choice, and that of the dependent epitype, is formalised here.

Althaea cannabina Linnaeus, *Species Plantarum* 2: 686. 1753.
"Habitat in Hungaria, Italia, G. Narbonensi." RCN: 5032.
Lectotype (Riedl in Rechinger, *Fl. Iranica* 120: 38. 1976): Herb. Linn. No. 868.2 (LINN).
Current name: ***Althaea cannabina*** L. (Malvaceae).

Althaea hirsuta Linnaeus, *Species Plantarum* 2: 687. 1753.
"Habitat in Gallia, Italia, Hispania." RCN: 5033.
Lectotype (Riedl in Rechinger, *Fl. Iranica* 120: 37. 1976): Herb. Linn. No. 868.3 (LINN).
Current name: ***Althaea hirsuta*** L. (Malvaceae).

Althaea ludwigii Linnaeus, *Systema Naturae,* ed. 12, 2: 459; *Mantissa Plantarum*: 98. 1767.
"Habitat in Sicilia. D. Schreber." RCN: 5034.
Lectotype (Riedl in Rechinger, *Fl. Iranica* 120: 38. 1976): *Schreber?,* Herb. Linn. No. 868.4 (LINN).
Current name: ***Althaea ludwigii*** L. (Malvaceae).

Althaea officinalis Linnaeus, *Species Plantarum* 2: 686. 1753.
"Habitat in Hollandiae, Angliae, Galliae, Sibiriae subhumidis." RCN: 5031.
Lectotype (Riedl in Rechinger, *Fl. Iranica* 120: 39. 1976): Herb. Linn. No. 868.1 (LINN).
Generitype of *Althaea* Linnaeus (vide Green, *Prop. Brit. Bot.*: 172. 1929).
Current name: ***Althaea officinalis*** L. (Malvaceae).

Alyssum alpestre Linnaeus, *Systema Naturae,* ed. 12, 2: 436; *Mantissa Plantarum*: 92. 1767.
"Habitat in Alpibus Galloprovinciae versus Italiam." RCN: 4730.
Lectotype (Polatschek in Cafferty & Jarvis in *Taxon* 51: 530. 2002): [icon] *"Alyssum caulibus fruticulosis, diffusis, foliis subrotundis, incanis"* in Gérard, Fl. Gallo-Provincialis: 352, t. 13, f. 2. 1761.
Current name: ***Alyssum alpestre*** L. (Brassicaceae).

Alyssum alyssoides (Linnaeus) Linnaeus, *Systema Naturae,* ed. 10, 2: 1130. 1759.
["Habitat in Austria, Gallia."] Sp. Pl. 2: 652 (1753). RCN: 4734.
Basionym: *Clypeola alyssoides* L. (1753).
Lectotype (Dudley in *J. Arnold Arbor.* 45: 63. 1964): Herb. Clifford: 329, *Clypeola* 2 (BM-000646255).
Current name: ***Alyssum alyssoides*** (L.) L. (Brassicaceae).

Alyssum calycinum Linnaeus, *Species Plantarum,* ed. 2, 2: 908. 1763, *nom. illeg.*
"Habitat in Austria, Gallia, Germania." RCN: 4734.
Replaced synonym: *Clypeola alyssoides* L. (1753).
Lectotype (Dudley in *J. Arnold Arbor.* 45: 63. 1964): Herb. Clifford: 329, *Clypeola* 2 (BM-000646255).

Current name: ***Alyssum alyssoides*** (L.) L. (Brassicaceae).
Note: As noted by Dudley (in *J. Arnold Arbor.* 45: 65. 1964), this is an illegitimate replacement name for *Clypeola alyssoides* L. (1753). However, Botschantzev (in *Novosti Sist. Vyssh. Rast.* 15: 150–151. 1985) incorrectly treats it as the correct name for *C. alyssoides* and *C. campestris* L. (1753), both of which he treats as ambiguous. See further notes on this name by German (in *Turczaninowia* 6(1): 53–55. 2003).

Alyssum campestre (Linnaeus) Linnaeus, *Systema Naturae,* ed. 10, 2: 1130. 1759.
["Habitat in Gallia."] Sp. Pl. 2: 652 (1753). RCN: 4736.
Basionym: *Clypeola campestris* L. (1753).
Neotype (Polatschek in Cafferty & Jarvis in *Taxon* 51: 532. 2002): France. Montpellier, Herb. Endl. Alyssum calycinum, *Endlicher s.n.* (W).
Current name: ***Alyssum alyssoides*** (L.) L. (Brassicaceae).
Note: Dudley (in *J. Arnold Arbor.* 45: 64. 1964) regarded Sauvages' description itself as the basis of the basionym but this would be contrary to Art. 8.1. *Alyssum campestre* L., *Sp. Pl.,* ed. 2, 2: 909 (1763) is evidently not the same taxon as *A. campestre* (L.) L. (1759), and this has caused confusion, leading to "*A. campestre*" being informally rejected as ambiguous by some authors (e.g. Turrill in *J. Bot.* 73: 261. 1935; Botschantzev in *Novosti Sist. Vyssh. Rast.* 15: 150–151. 1985). In the absence of original material, Polatschek designated a neotype, confirming the position of *A. campestre* (1759) as a synonym of *A. alyssoides*, in agreement with the treatment of Dudley.

Alyssum campestre Linnaeus, *Species Plantarum,* ed. 2 2: 909. 1763, *nom. illeg.*
"Habitat in Gallia."
Note: Alyssum campestre L., *Sp. Pl.,* ed. 2, 2: 909 (1763) is evidently not the same taxon as *A. campestre* (L.) L. (1759), and this has caused confusion, leading to "*A. campestre*" being informally rejected as ambiguous by some authors (e.g. Turrill in *J. Bot.* 73: 261. 1935; Botschantzev in *Novosti Sist. Vyssh. Rast.* 15: 150–151. 1985).

Alyssum clypeatum Linnaeus, *Species Plantarum* 2: 651. 1753.
"Habitat in Europa australi." RCN: 4737.
Lectotype (Phitos in Strid & Kit Tan, *Fl. Hellenica* 2: 224. 2002): Herb. Burser XI: 29 (UPS).
Current name: ***Fibigia clypeata*** (L.) Medik. (Brassicaceae).

Alyssum creticum Linnaeus, *Species Plantarum* 2: 651. 1753.
"Habitat in Creta." RCN: 4739.
Lectotype (Turland in *Bull. Nat. Hist. Mus. London, Bot.* 25: 142, f. 14. 1995): [icon] "*Leucoium luteum utriculato semine*" in Alpino, Pl. Exot.: 119, 118. 1627. – Epitype (Turland in *Bull. Nat. Hist. Mus. London, Bot.* 25: 142, f. 15. 1995): Bickerich sub Rechinger 15302 (BM; iso- W?).
Current name: ***Alyssoides cretica*** (L.) Medik. (Brassicaceae).

Alyssum deltoideum Linnaeus, *Species Plantarum,* ed. 2, 2: 908. 1763.
"Habitat in Oriente." RCN: 4744.
Lectotype (Al-Shehbaz & Turland in Cafferty & Jarvis in *Taxon* 51: 530. 2002): Herb. Linn. No. 828.25 (LINN).
Current name: ***Aubrieta deltoidea*** (L.) DC. (Brassicaceae).

Alyssum gemonense Linnaeus, *Systema Naturae,* ed. 12, 2: 437; *Mantissa Plantarum:* 92. 1767, *nom. illeg.*
RCN: 4741.
Type not designated.
Original material: Herb. Linn. No. 828.21 (LINN); [icon] in Arduino, Animadv. Bot. Spec. Alt.: 30, t. 14. 1764.

Current name: ***Aurinia petraea*** (Ard.) Schur (Brassicaceae).
Note: In the protologue, Linnaeus referred to "Alyssum" from "Ard. Spec. 2. p. t. 10". No page number was given, but t. 10 in *Animadv. Bot. Spec. Alt.* (1764) is an *Arenaria*. However, Linnaeus' diagnosis is a close match for the text on p. 30, and the illustration at t. 14, both associated with *Alyssum petraeum* Ard., a valid binomial. Ball & Dudley (in Tutin & al., *Fl. Europaea* 1: 299. 1964) have treated the two names as synonymous, and *A. gemonense* appears to be illegitimate.

Alyssum halimifolium Linnaeus, *Species Plantarum* 2: 650. 1753.
"Habitat in Europae australis aridis." RCN: 4728.
Lectotype (Borgen in *Opera Bot.* 91: 84. 1987): Herb. Clifford: 333, *Alyssum* 4 (BM-000646290).
Current name: ***Lobularia maritima*** (L.) Desv. (Brassicaceae).

Alyssum hyperboreum Linnaeus, *Species Plantarum* 2: 651. 1753.
"Habitat in America septentrionali. D. Krascheninnikof." RCN: 4731.
Lectotype (Berkutenko in *Linzer Biol. Beitr.* 27: 1116. 1995): Herb. Linn. No. 828.6 (LINN; iso- LE).
Current name: ***Schivereckia hyperborea*** (L.) Berkut. (Brassicaceae).
Note: Berkutenko concluded from her study that 828.6 (LINN) and the Krasheninnikov plate both belong to what had been called *Schivereckia podolica* (Bess.) Andrz., a plant from E Russia, N Ukraine, and NE Romania, and not to the Pacific plant long known as *Draba hyperborea* (L.) Desv. She made the new combination *S. hyperborea* (L.) Berkut., and took up *D. grandis* Langsd. as the correct name for the *Draba* species.

Alyssum incanum Linnaeus, *Species Plantarum* 2: 650. 1753.
"Habitat in Europae septentrionalioris arenosis, apricis." RCN: 4732.
Lectotype (Jonsell & Jarvis in *Nordic J. Bot.* 22: 67. 2002): Herb. Linn. No. 828.7 (LINN).
Current name: ***Berteroa incana*** (L.) DC. (Brassicaceae).

Alyssum minimum Linnaeus, *Species Plantarum* 2: 651. 1753.
"Habitat in Hispania." RCN: 4733.
Lectotype (Borgen in Cafferty & Jarvis in *Taxon* 51: 530. 2002): Herb. Linn. No. 828.8 (LINN).
Current name: ***Lobularia maritima*** (L.) Desv. (Brassicaceae).

Alyssum montanum Linnaeus, *Species Plantarum* 2: 650. 1753.
"Habitat in Helvetia." RCN: 4735.
Lectotype (Dudley in *J. Arnold Arbor.* 45: 358. 1964): Herb. Linn. No. 828.12 (LINN).
Generitype of *Alyssum* Linnaeus (vide Green, *Prop. Brit. Bot.:* 171. 1929).
Current name: ***Alyssum montanum*** L. (Brassicaceae).

Alyssum saxatile Linnaeus, *Species Plantarum* 2: 650. 1753.
"Habitat in Creta." RCN: 4729.
Type not designated.
Original material: Herb. A. van Royen No. 901.212–211 (L).
Current name: ***Aurinia saxatilis*** (L.) Desv. subsp. ***saxatilis*** (Brassicaceae).
Note: Dudley (in *J. Arnold Arbor.* 45: 393. 1964) referred to a van Royen sheet (L) as the holotype, but gave its geographical code, not the unique sheet number. Two van Royen sheets of this taxon were borrowed by Dudley, and annotated as holotypes (Veldkamp, pers. comm.). Only one of these (no. 901.212–211) is annotated by Adriaan van Royen and would be the obvious choice as lectotype. The other (no. 901.212–215) is annotated by David van Royen. However, as Dudley did not distinguish between these sheets, the name remains untypified at present.

Alyssum sinuatum Linnaeus, *Species Plantarum* 2: 651. 1753.
"Habitat in Hispaniae incultis, ad vias." RCN: 4738.
Lectotype (López González in Cafferty & Jarvis in *Taxon* 51: 530.
2002): Herb. Burser XI: 30, right specimen (UPS).
Current name: ***Aurinia sinuata*** (L.) Griseb. (Brassicaceae).
Note: López González (in *Anales Jard. Bot. Madrid* 53: 125–127.
1995) mentioned the original elements, and illustrated Clusius'
figure (as f. 1), but did not choose a type.

Alyssum spinosum Linnaeus, *Species Plantarum* 2: 650. 1753.
"Habitat in Hispaniae, Galliae cautibus." RCN: 4727.
Lectotype (Dudley in *J. Arnold Arbor.* 45: 365. 1964): Herb. Clifford:
332, *Alyssum* 1 (BM-000646287).
Current name: ***Alyssum spinosum*** L. (Brassicaceae).

Alyssum utriculatum Linnaeus, *Systema Naturae*, ed. 12, 2: 437;
Mantissa Plantarum: 92. 1767.
"Habitat in Oriente." RCN: 4742.
Lectotype (Al-Shehbaz & Turland in Cafferty & Jarvis in *Taxon* 51:
531. 2002): Herb. Linn. No. 828.22 (LINN).
Current name: ***Alyssoides utriculata*** (L.) Medik. (Brassicaceae).

Alyssum vesicaria Linnaeus, *Species Plantarum* 2: 651. 1753.
"Habitat in Oriente." RCN: 4743.
Lectotype (Al-Shehbaz & Turland in Cafferty & Jarvis in *Taxon* 51:
531. 2002): [icon] *"Vesicaria Orientalis foliis dentatis"* in Tournefort,
Rel. Voy. Levant (Paris ed.) 2: 252. 1717.
Current name: ***Coluteocarpus vesicaria*** (L.) Holmboe (Brassicaceae).
Note: Hedge (in Hedge & Rechinger, *Fl. Iranica* 57: 97. 1968)
indicated unspecified Tournefort material as type. However, as
Linnaeus did not have the opportunity to study Tournefort's
specimens, this is not an original element for Linnaeus' name.

Amaranthus albus Linnaeus, *Systema Naturae*, ed. 10, 2: 1268. 1759.
["Habitat in Philadelphiae maritimis."] Sp. Pl., ed. 2, 2: 1404 (1763).
RCN: 7165.
Lectotype (Raus in Strid & Kit Tan, *Fl. Hellenica* 1: 143. 1997): Herb.
Linn. No. 1117.1 (LINN).
Current name: ***Amaranthus albus*** L. (Amaranthaceae).

Amaranthus blitum Linnaeus, *Species Plantarum* 2: 990. 1753.
"Habitat in Europa temperatiore." RCN: 7175.
Lectotype (Fillias & al. in *Taxon* 29: 150. 1980): Herb. Linn. No.
1117.14, right specimen (LINN).
Current name: ***Amaranthus blitum*** L. (Amaranthaceae).
Note: Brenan & Townsend (in *Taxon* 29: 695. 1980) proposed the
rejection of *A. blitum*. However, the Committee for Spermatophyta
(in *Taxon* 33: 298. 1984) declined to recommend the proposal.

Amaranthus caudatus Linnaeus, *Species Plantarum* 2: 990. 1753.
"Habitat in Peru, Persia, Zeylona." RCN: 7187.
Lectotype (Townsend in Nasir & Ali, *Fl. W. Pakistan* 71: 10. 1974):
Herb. Linn. No. 1117.26 (LINN).
Generitype of *Amaranthus* Linnaeus (vide Green, *Prop. Brit. Bot.*: 188.
1929).
Current name: ***Amaranthus caudatus*** L. (Amaranthaceae).

Amaranthus cruentus Linnaeus, *Systema Naturae*, ed. 10, 2: 1269.
1759.
["Habitat in China."] Sp. Pl., ed. 2, 2: 1406 (1763). RCN: 7186.
Lectotype (Townsend in Nasir & Ali, *Fl. W. Pakistan* 71: 12. 1974):
Herb. Linn. No. 1117.25 (LINN).
Current name: ***Amaranthus cruentus*** L. (Amaranthaceae).
Note: Stevels (in *Wageningen Agric. Univ. Pap.* 90–1: 106. 1990) gave
an extensive review, but wrongly attributed the typification to Sauer

(in *Ann. Missouri Bot. Gard.* 54: 122. 1967), who discussed the
specimen but did not treat it as the type.

Amaranthus deflexus Linnaeus, *Mantissa Plantarum Altera*: 295.
1771.
RCN: 7178.
Lectotype (Aellen in Rechinger, *Fl. Iranica* 91: 7. 1972): Herb. Linn.
No. 1117.18 (LINN).
Current name: ***Amaranthus deflexus*** L. (Amaranthaceae).

Amaranthus flavus Linnaeus, *Systema Naturae*, ed. 10, 2: 1269. 1759.
["Habitat in India."] Sp. Pl., ed. 2, 2: 1406 (1763). RCN: 7184.
Type not designated.
Original material: Herb. Linn. No. 1117.23 (LINN).
Current name: ***Amaranthus hypochondriacus*** L. (Amaranthaceae).
Note: Sauer (in *Ann. Missouri Bot. Gard.* 54: 111. 1967) described
Linnaeus' diagnosis as ambiguous, and noted the existence of
1117.23 (LINN) but without explicitly treating it as the type.

Amaranthus gangeticus Linnaeus, *Systema Naturae,* ed. 10, 2: 1268.
1759.
["Habitat in India."] Sp. Pl. ,ed. 2, 2: 1404 (1763). RCN: 7170.
Type not designated.
Original material: Herb. Linn. No. 386.5 (S); Herb. Linn. No. 1117.9
(LINN).
Current name: ***Amaranthus tricolor*** L. (Amaranthaceae).

Amaranthus graecizans Linnaeus, *Species Plantarum* 2: 990. 1753.
"Habitat in Virginia." RCN: 7166.
Lectotype (Fernald in *Rhodora* 47: 139, pl. 887. 1945): *Clayton 442*
(BM-000051563).
Current name: ***Amaranthus graecizans*** L. (Amaranthaceae).
Note: Although some (e.g. Burtt & Lewis in *Kew Bull.* 7: 352. 1952)
have treated this as a *nomen confusum*, most recent authors have not.
Fernald's type choice of a Clayton collection appears to be the
earliest, although many later authors have followed Dandy &
Melderis (in Fernandes, *Bol. Soc. Brot.*, sér. 2, 31: 191. 1957) in
accepting 1117.3 (LINN) as the type.

Amaranthus hybridus Linnaeus, *Species Plantarum* 2: 990. 1753.
"Habitat in Virginia." RCN: 7180.
Lectotype (Townsend in Nasir & Ali, *Fl. W. Pakistan* 71: 19. 1974):
Herb. Linn. No. 1117.19 (LINN).
Current name: ***Amaranthus hybridus*** L. (Amaranthaceae).
Note: The name and its original elements were discussed by Brenan (in
Watsonia 4: 267. 1961) and Sauer (in *Ann. Missouri Bot. Gard.* 54:
108. 1967). Although Soó (in *Acta Bot. Hungarica* 15: 342. 1969)
treated it as *nomen dubium*, most recent authors use the name and
Townsend (1974) appears to have been the first to typify it.

Amaranthus hypochondriacus Linnaeus, *Species Plantarum* 2: 991.
1753.
"Habitat in Virginia." RCN: 7185.
Lectotype (Townsend in Polhill, *Fl. Trop. E. Africa, Amaranthaceae*:
25. 1985): Herb. Linn. No. 1117.24 (LINN).
Current name: ***Amaranthus hypochondriacus*** L. (Amaranthaceae).
Note: Sauer (in *Ann. Missouri Bot. Gard.* 54: 111. 1967) discussed the
original material for the name but did not designate a type.

Amaranthus lividus Linnaeus, *Species Plantarum* 2: 990. 1753.
"Habitat in Virginia." RCN: 7173.
Type not designated.
Original material: [icon] in Bauhin & Cherler, Hist. Pl. Univ. 2: 966.
1651.
Current name: ***Amaranthus blitum*** L. (Amaranthaceae).

Note: The typification of this name is somewhat complicated. Aellen (in Rechinger, *Fl. Iranica* 91: 8. 1972) indicated 1174.14 (LINN) as type, but this sheet is annotated in such a way as to link it with *A. blitum* L., of which it is the type. Various authors have therefore rejected Aellen's choice as having been ineligible (i.e. not original material for the name), and most have followed a neotypification by Townsend (in Nasir & Ali, *Fl. W. Pakistan* 71: 17. 1974). However, Linnaeus' third synonym is an account by Bauhin and Cherler, accompanied by an illustration. While Linnaeus did qualify the inclusion of this illustration with a "?", this cannot justify its exclusion from the protologue, and its existence (as an original element) precludes the designation of a neotype.

Amaranthus mangostanus Linnaeus, *Centuria I Plantarum*: 32. 1755.
"Habitat in India." RCN: 7171.
Type not designated.
Original material: Herb. Linn. No. 1117.10 (LINN).
Current name: ***Amaranthus tricolor*** L. (Amaranthaceae).

Amaranthus melancholicus Linnaeus, *Species Plantarum* 2: 989. 1753.
"Habitat in India." RCN: 7167.
Lectotype (Townsend in Bosser & al., *Fl. Mascareignes* 142: 11. 1994): Herb. Linn. No. 1117.4 (LINN).
Current name: ***Amaranthus tricolor*** L. (Amaranthaceae).

Amaranthus oleraceus Linnaeus, *Species Plantarum*, ed. 2, 2: 1403. 1763.
"Habitat in India." RCN: 7174.
Lectotype (Fillias & al. in *Taxon* 29: 150. 1980): Herb. Linn. No. 1117.13 (LINN).
Current name: ***Amaranthus blitum*** L. (Amaranthaceae).
Note: See discussion by Stevels (in *Wageningen Agric. Univ. Pap.* 90–1: 106–107. 1990).

Amaranthus paniculatus Linnaeus, *Species Plantarum*, ed. 2, 2: 1406. 1763.
"Habitat in America." RCN: 7181.
Lectotype (El Hadidi & El Hadidy in *Taeckholmia, Addit. Ser.* 1: 37. 1981): Herb. Linn. No. 1117.20 (LINN).
Current name: ***Amaranthus cruentus*** L. (Amaranthaceae).
Note: The name and its original material were discussed by Brenan (in *Watsonia* 4: 269. 1961) and Sauer (in *Ann. Missouri Bot. Gard.* 54: 122. 1967).

Amaranthus polygamus Linnaeus, *Centuria I Plantarum*: 32. 1755.
"Habitat in India." RCN: 7169.
Type not designated.
Original material: Herb. Linn. No. 1117.9 (LINN).
Current name: ***Amaranthus tricolor*** L. (Amaranthaceae).

Amaranthus polygonoides Linnaeus, *Plantarum Jamaicensium Pugillus*: 27. 1759.
["Habitat in Jamaica, Zeylona."] Sp. Pl., ed. 2, 2: 1405 (1763). RCN: 7179.
Lectotype (Hendrickson in *Sida* 18: 797. 1999): [icon] *"Blitum polygonoides viride seu ex viridi et albo variegatum polyanthos"* in Sloane, Voy. Jamaica 1: 144, t. 92, f. 2. 1707. – Typotype: Herb. Sloane 2: 116 (BM-SL).
Current name: ***Amaranthus polygonoides*** L. (Amaranthaceae).
Note: Kellogg (in Howard, *Fl. Lesser Antilles* 4: 160. 1985) indicated voucher material in Herb. Sloane as the type but this was not seen by Linnaeus and is not original material for the name. It is, however, typotype material for the plate subsequently designated as lectotype by Hendrickson.

Amaranthus retroflexus Linnaeus, *Species Plantarum* 2: 991. 1753.
"Habitat in Pensylvania. Kalm." RCN: 7183.
Lectotype (Townsend in Nasir & Ali, *Fl. W. Pakistan* 71: 12. 1974): Herb. Linn. No. 1117.22 (LINN).
Current name: ***Amaranthus retroflexus*** L. (Amaranthaceae).
Note: Brenan (in *Watsonia* 4: 271. 1961) discussed the material in LINN but did not typify the name.

Amaranthus sanguineus Linnaeus, *Species Plantarum*, ed. 2, 2: 1407. 1763.
"Habitat in Bahama." RCN: 7182.
Type not designated.
Original material: Herb. Linn. No. 1117.21 (LINN); [icon] in Miller, Fig. Pl. Gard. Dict. 1: 15, t. 22. 1755.
Current name: ***Amaranthus cruentus*** L. (Amaranthaceae).
Note: See comments by Sauer (in *Ann. Missouri Bot. Gard.* 54: 122. 1967).

Amaranthus spinosus Linnaeus, *Species Plantarum* 2: 991. 1753.
"Habitat in Indiis." RCN: 7188.
Lectotype (Fawcett & Rendle, *Fl. Jamaica* 3: 130. 1914): Herb. Linn. No. 1117.27 (LINN).
Current name: ***Amaranthus spinosus*** L. (Amaranthaceae).

Amaranthus tricolor Linnaeus, *Species Plantarum* 2: 989. 1753.
"Habitat in India." RCN: 7168.
Lectotype (Townsend in Nasir & Ali, *Fl. W. Pakistan* 71: 14. 1974): Herb. Linn. No. 1117.7 (LINN).
Current name: ***Amaranthus tricolor*** L. (Amaranthaceae).
Note: Townsend gave the number of the type sheet as "117.7" but this is clearly a typographical error for "1117.7".

Amaranthus tristis Linnaeus, *Species Plantarum* 2: 989. 1753.
"Habitat in China." RCN: 7172.
Type not designated.
Original material: Herb. Linn. No. 1117.10 (LINN); Herb. Linn. No. 1117.11 (LINN).
Current name: ***Amaranthus tricolor*** L. (Amaranthaceae).
Note: Townsend (in Polhill, *Fl. Trop. E. Africa, Amaranthaceae*: 28. 1985) incorrectly designated 1117.12 (LINN) as lectotype, a specimen with no very obvious link with this name, and which is not part of the original material.

Amaranthus viridis Linnaeus, *Species Plantarum*, ed. 2, 2: 1405. 1763.
"Habitat in Europa, Brasilia." RCN: 7177.
Lectotype (Fawcett & Rendle, *Fl. Jamaica* 3: 131. 1914): Herb. Linn. No. 1117.15 (LINN).
Current name: ***Amaranthus viridis*** L. (Amaranthaceae).

Amaryllis atamasca Linnaeus, *Species Plantarum* 1: 292. 1753.
"Habitat in Virginia." RCN: 2332.
Lectotype (designated here by Reveal): Herb. Clifford: 135, *Amaryllis* 4 (BM).
Current name: ***Zephyranthes atamasca*** (L.) Herb. (Liliaceae/Amaryllidaceae).

Amaryllis belladonna Linnaeus, *Species Plantarum* 1: 293. 1753, *nom. & typ. cons.*
"Habitat in Caribaeis, Barbados, Surinama." RCN: 2334.
Conserved type (Sealy in *Bull. Misc. Inform. Kew* 1939: 60. 1939): Herb. Clifford: 135, *Amaryllis* 2 (BM-000558561).
Generitype of *Amaryllis* Linnaeus, *nom. cons.*
Current name: ***Amaryllis belladonna*** L. (Liliaceae/Amaryllidaceae).
Note: See extensive review by Sealy (in *Bull. Misc. Inform. Kew* 1939: 49–68. 1939).

Amaryllis capensis Linnaeus, *Plantae Rariores Africanae*: 10. 1760. ["Habitat ad Cap. b. Spei."] Sp. Pl., ed. 2, 1: 420 (1762). RCN: 2330.
Type not designated.
Original material: none traced.
Current name: ***Spiloxene capensis*** (L.) Garside (Liliaceae/Hypoxidaceae).
Note: Garside (in *J. Bot.* 74: 267. 1936) noted specimens in Burman's herbarium (G) believed to be annotated by Linnaeus and which "are undoubtedly the type specimens". Although there are seven sheets in G associated with this name, none is annotated by Linnaeus and the name remains untypified at present.

Amaryllis ciliaris Linnaeus, *Species Plantarum*, ed. 2, 1: 422. 1762, *nom. illeg.*
"Habitat in Aethiopia." RCN: 2340.
Replaced synonym: *Amaryllis guttata* L. (1753).
Neotype (Müller-Doblies & Müller-Doblies in *Feddes Repert.* 105: 357. 1994): South Africa. Cape, Worcester, Chavonnes, near railway station, 14 Mar 1979, *U. & D. Müller-Doblies 79132a* (K; iso- B, BTU, M, MO, PRE, S, Z).
Current name: ***Boophone guttata*** (L.) Herb. (Liliaceae/Amaryllidaceae).
Note: A superfluous name for *Amaryllis guttata* L. (1753).

Amaryllis formosissima Linnaeus, *Species Plantarum* 1: 293. 1753.
"Habitat in America meridionali." RCN: 2333.
Type not designated.
Original material: Herb. Linn. No. 416.4 (LINN); [icon] in Dillenius, Hort. Eltham. 1: 195, t. 162, f. 196. 1732; [icon] in Linnaeus in Kongl. Swenska Wetensk. Acad. Handl. 3: 93, t. 6. 1742; [icon] in Rudbeck, Campi Elysii 2: 89, f. 10. 1701.
Current name: ***Sprekelia formosissima*** (L.) Herb. (Liliaceae/Amaryllidaceae).

Amaryllis guttata Linnaeus, *Species Plantarum* 1: 294. 1753.
"Habitat in Aethiopia." RCN: 2340.
Replaced synonym of: *Amaryllis ciliaris* L. (1762), *nom. illeg.*
Neotype (Müller-Doblies & Müller-Doblies in *Feddes Repert.* 105: 357. 1994): South Africa. Cape, Worcester, Chavonnes, near railway station, 14 Mar 1979, *U. & D. Müller-Doblies 79132a* (K; iso- B, BTU, M, MO, PRE, S, Z).
Current name: ***Boophone guttata*** (L.) Herb. (Liliaceae/Amaryllidaceae).

Amaryllis longifolia Linnaeus, *Species Plantarum* 1: 293. 1753.
"Habitat in Aethiopia." RCN: 2338.
Lectotype (Wijnands, *Bot. Commelins*: 38. 1983): [icon] *"Lilium Africanum Polyanthos"* in Hermann, Parad. Bat.: 195. 1698 (see p. 135).
Current name: ***Cybistetes longifolia*** (L.) Milne-Redh. & Schweick. (Liliaceae/Amaryllidaceae).
Note: Milne-Redhead & Schweickert (in *J. Linn. Soc., Bot.* 52: 159, f. 1. 1939) reproduced Hermann's illustration.

Amaryllis lutea Linnaeus, *Species Plantarum* 1: 292. 1753.
"Habitat in Hispania, Italia, Thracia." RCN: 2331.
Type not designated.
Original material: Herb. A. van Royen No. 897.324–58 (L); Herb. Burser III: 78 (UPS); [icon] in Clusius, Rar. Pl. Hist. 1: 164. 1601.
Current name: ***Sternbergia lutea*** (L.) Ker-Gawl. ex Spreng. (Liliaceae/Amaryllidaceae).
Note: Mathew (in Davis, *Fl. Turkey* 8: 361. 1984) indicated 416.1 (LINN) as the type, and has been followed by later authors including Kamari & Artelari (in *Willdenowia* 19: 375. 1990), and also Morales & Castillo (in *Anales Jard. Bot. Madrid* 61: 124. 2004),

who restricted the choice to the central leaf and flower. However, this collection, from Kähler, did not reach Linnaeus until 1757 and is not original material for the name.

Amaryllis orientalis Linnaeus, *Species Plantarum* 1: 293. 1753.
"Habitat in India." RCN: 2339.
Type not designated.
Original material: [icon] in Sweerts, Florilegium: t. 31. 1612; [icon] in Morison, Pl. Hist. Univ. 2: 368, s. 4, t. 10, f. 35. 1680.
Current name: ***Brunsvigia orientalis*** (L.) Aiton ex Eckl. (Liliaceae/Amaryllidaceae).

Amaryllis reginae Linnaeus, *Systema Naturae*, ed. 10, 2: 977. 1759. ["Habitat in Caribaeis."] Sp. Pl., ed. 2, 1: 421 (1762). RCN: 2335.
Type not designated.
Original material: Herb. Linn. No. 416.5 (LINN); [icon] in Hermann, Parad. Bat.: 194. 1698; [icon] in Miller, Fig. Pl. Gard. Dict. 1: 16, t. 24. 1755.
Current name: ***Hippeastrum reginae*** (L.) Herb. (Liliaceae/Amaryllidaceae).

Amaryllis sarniensis Linnaeus, *Species Plantarum* 1: 293. 1753.
"Habitat in Japonia, nunc in Sarniae insula Angliae." RCN: 2337.
Type not designated.
Original material: [icon] in Cornut, Canad. Pl. Hist.: 157, 158. 1635; [icon] in Douglas, Lilium Sarniense: t. 1, 2. 1725; [icon] in Rudbeck, Campi Elysii 2: 23, f. 14. 1701.
Current name: ***Nerine sarniensis*** (L.) Herb. (Liliaceae/Amaryllidaceae).

Amaryllis undulata Linnaeus, *Systema Naturae*, ed. 12, 2: 237. 1767.
"Habitat – – –" RCN: 2336.
Type not designated.
Original material: Herb. Linn. No. 137.11 (S); Herb. Linn. No. 416.6 (LINN).
Current name: ***Nerine undulata*** (L.) Herb. (Liliaceae/Amaryllidaceae).
Note: See Fuchs (in *Acta Bot. Neerl.* 11: 76. 1962), who appears to argue that Linnaeus had no material of this when he published the name, but that as the description came from David van Royen, an illustration of the plant from Leiden, published later by Meerburg, should be an isotype.

Amaryllis zeylanica Linnaeus, *Species Plantarum* 1: 293. 1753.
"Habitat in Zeylona." RCN: 2327.
Basionym of: *Crinum zeylanicum* (L.) L. (1767).
Lectotype (Dassanayake in *Taxon* 30: 481. 1981): [icon] *"Lilio-Narcissus Ceylanicus latifolius flore niveo, externe linea purpurea striato"* in Commelin, Hort. Med. Amstelod. Pl. Rar. 1: 73, t. 37. 1697 (see p. 250).
Current name: ***Crinum zeylanicum*** (L.) L. (Liliaceae/Amaryllidaceae).
Note: Dassanayake rejects Nordal's typification (in *Norweg. J. Bot.* 24: 189. 1977; *Adansonia*, sér. 2, 20: 187. 1980; *Fl. Gabon* 28: 38. 1986) on an Ehret plate cited by Linnaeus under the unnamed var. β because Linnaeus questions whether or not it belongs to *A. zeylanicum*. See also Wijnands (in *Bot. Commelins*: 37. 1983, "The epithet 'zeylanica' and the habitat 'Zeylona' also indicate that Ehret's plate of an African plant did not contribute to Linnaeus' concept of *A. zeylanica*.

Ambrosia artemisiifolia Linnaeus, *Species Plantarum* 2: 988. 1753.
"Habitat in Virginia, Pensylvania." RCN: 7159.
Lectotype (Hind in Bosser & al., *Fl. Mascareignes* 109: 214. 1993): Herb. Linn. No. 1114.4 (LINN).

Current name: ***Ambrosia artemisiifolia*** L. var. ***artemisiifolia***
(Asteraceae).

Ambrosia elatior Linnaeus, *Species Plantarum* 2: 987. 1753.
"Habitat in Virginia, Canada." RCN: 7158.
Lectotype (Reveal in Jarvis & Turland in *Taxon* 47: 351. 1998): Herb.
   Linn. No. 1114.3 (LINN).
Current name: ***Ambrosia artemisiifolia*** L. var. ***elatior*** (L.) Descourt.
   (Asteraceae).

Ambrosia maritima Linnaeus, *Species Plantarum* 2: 988. 1753.
"Habitat in Hetruriae, Cappadociae maritimis arenosis." RCN: 7160.
Lectotype (Alavi in Jafri & El-Gadi, *Fl. Libya* 107: 120. 1983): Herb.
   Clifford: 443, *Ambrosia* 1 (BM-000647392).
Generitype of *Ambrosia* Linnaeus (vide Green, *Prop. Brit. Bot.*: 188.
   1929).
Current name: ***Ambrosia maritima*** L. (Asteraceae).

Ambrosia trifida Linnaeus, *Species Plantarum* 2: 987. 1753.
"Habitat in Virginia, Canada." RCN: 7157.
Lectotype (Reveal in Jarvis & Turland in *Taxon* 47: 351. 1998): Herb.
   Linn. No. 1114.1 (LINN).
Current name: ***Ambrosia trifida*** L. (Asteraceae).

Ambrosina bassii Linnaeus, *Genera Plantarum*, ed. 6: 579. 1764.
"Habitat Panormi." RCN: 7982.
Type not designated.
Original material: Herb. Linn. No. 1078.1 (LINN); [icon] in
   Boccone, Icon. Descr. Rar. Pl. Siciliae: 50, 51, t. 26, f. 1. 1674.
Generitype of *Ambrosina* Bassi.
Current name: ***Ambrosina bassii*** L. (Araceae).
Note: Generic name spelled "Ambrosinia" in the original publication
   but this has been treated as an orthographic variant. See discussion
   (with a reproduction of the cited Boccone plate) by Forneris
   (*L'Erbario Univ. Torino*: 118. 2004).

Amellus lychnitis Linnaeus, *Systema Naturae*, ed. 10, 2: 1225. 1759,
   typ. cons.
["Habitat ad Cap. b. spei."] Sp. Pl. ed. 2, 2: 1276. 1763. RCN: 6511.
Type not designated.
Original material: Herb. Linn. No. 1023.1 (LINN).
Generitype of *Amellus* Linnaeus, *nom. cons.*
Current name: ***Amellus asteroides*** (L.) Druce (Asteraceae).
Note: Amellus Linnaeus, *nom. cons.* against *Amellus* P. Browne.

Amellus umbellatus Linnaeus, *Systema Naturae*, ed. 10, 2: 1225. 1759.
["Habitat in Jamaica."] Sp. Pl. ed. 2, 2: 1276. 1763. RCN: 6512.
Lectotype (Moore in Fawcett & Rendle, *Fl. Jamaica* 7: 267. 1936):
   Herb. Linn. No. 1023.3 (LINN).
Current name: ***Liabum umbellatum*** (L.) Sch. Bip. (Asteraceae).

Amethystea coerulea Linnaeus, *Species Plantarum* 1: 21. 1753.
"Habitat in Sibiriae montis." RCN: 168.
Lectotype (Press in Jarvis & al., *Regnum Veg.* 127: 17. 1993): Herb.
   Linn. No. 37.1 (LINN).
Generitype of *Amethystea* Linnaeus.
Current name: ***Amethystea coerulea*** L. (Lamiaceae).

Ammannia baccifera Linnaeus, *Species Plantarum* 1: 120. 1753.
"Habitat in China. Osbeck." RCN: 988.
Lectotype (Graham in *J. Arnold Arbor.* 66: 405. 1985): Herb. Linn.
   No. 156.4 (LINN).
Current name: ***Ammannia baccifera*** L. (Lythraceae).
Note: Chamberlain (in Davis, *Fl. Turkey* 4: 180. 1972) indicated 156.3
   (LINN) as the type but this collection lacks the relevant *Species*

Plantarum number (i.e. "3") and was a post-1753 addition to the
   herbarium, and is not original material for the name. See Hansen &
   Fox Maule (in *Bot. J. Linn. Soc.* 67: 207. 1973) for comments on
   Osbeck material.

Ammannia latifolia Linnaeus, *Species Plantarum* 1: 119. 1753.
"Habitat in Caribaeis, locis humidis." RCN: 986.
Lectotype (Graham in *J. Arnold Arbor.* 66: 411. 1985): Herb. Linn.
   No. 156.1 (LINN).
Generitype of *Ammannia* Linnaeus (vide Hitchcock, *Prop. Brit. Bot.*:
   126. 1929).
Current name: ***Ammannia latifolia*** L. (Lythraceae).

Ammannia ramosior Linnaeus, *Species Plantarum* 1: 120. 1753.
"Habitat in Virginia. D. Gronovius." RCN: 987.
Lectotype (Fernald & Griscom in *Rhodora* 37: 169. 1935): *Clayton
   774* (BM-000051788; iso- LINN 156.2).
Current name: ***Rotala ramosior*** (L.) Koehne (Lythraceae).

Ammi copticum Linnaeus, *Systema Naturae*, ed. 12, 2: 206; *Mantissa
   Plantarum*: 56. 1767.
"Habitat in Aegypto. Forskåhl." RCN: 1950.
Lectotype (Townsend in Polhill, *Fl. Trop. E. Africa, Umbelliferae*: 45.
   1989): Herb. Linn. No. 341.4 (LINN).
Current name: ***Trachyspermum ammi*** (L.) Sprague (Apiaceae).

Ammi glaucifolium Linnaeus, *Species Plantarum* 1: 243. 1753.
"Habitat in Gallia." RCN: 1951.
Neotype (Reduron in Jarvis & al. in *Taxon* 55: 208. 2006): France.
   "Bagneux. Juillet 1853, *L. Gouas s.n.*" in Herb. S. Buchet (P).
Current name: ***Ammi majus*** L. var. ***glaucifolium*** (L.) Mérat
   (Apiaceae).

Ammi majus Linnaeus, *Species Plantarum* 1: 243. 1753.
"Habitat in Europa australi." RCN: 1949.
Lectotype (Jafri in Jafri & El-Gadi, *Fl. Libya* 117: 87. 1985): Herb.
   Linn. No. 341.2 (LINN).
Generitype of *Ammi* Linnaeus (vide Hitchcock, *Prop. Brit. Bot.*: 139.
   1929).
Current name: ***Ammi majus*** L. (Apiaceae).

Amomum cardamomum Linnaeus, *Species Plantarum* 1: 1. 1753.
"Habitat in India." RCN: 6.
Lectotype (Burtt & Smith in *Notes Roy. Bot. Gard. Edinburgh* 31: 182.
   1972): [icon] *"Elettari"* in Rheede, Hort. Malab. 11: 9, t. 6. 1692.
Current name: ***Elettaria cardamomum*** (L.) Maton (Zingiberaceae).

Amomum grana-paradisi Linnaeus, *Species Plantarum* 1: 2. 1753.
"Habitat in Madagascar, Guinea." RCN: 7.
Type not designated.
Original material: none traced.
Current name: ***Aframomum melegueta*** (Roscoe) K. Schum.
   (Zingiberaceae).
Note: Gagnepain (in *Bull. Soc. Bot. France* 50: 357. 1903) discussed
   the name and Hepper (in *Kew Bull.* 21: 130. 1967) informally
   rejected it, a course of action supported by Burtt & Smith (in *Notes
   Roy. Bot. Gard. Edinburgh* 31: 180. 1972). However, no formal
   proposal for the rejection of the name has been made.

Amomum zerumbet Linnaeus, *Species Plantarum* 1: 1. 1753.
"Habitat in India." RCN: 5.
Type not designated.
Original material: Herb. Hermann 5: 94, No. 2 [icon] (BM); Herb.
   Clifford: 3, *Amomum* 2, 3 sheets (BM); [icon] in Hermann, Hort.
   Lugd.-Bat. Cat.: 636, 637. 1687.

Current name: ***Zingiber zerumbet*** (L.) Sm. (Zingiberaceae).
Note: Thielade (in *Gard. Bull. Singapore* 48: 228. 1998) wrongly designated material at K as lectotype, the existence of original material precluding the designation of what would be a neotype (Art. 9.11).

Amomum zingiber Linnaeus, *Species Plantarum* 1: 1. 1753.
"Habitat in Indiis inter tropicos." RCN: 4.
Lectotype (Burtt in Jarvis & al., *Regnum Veg.* 127: 17. 1993): Herb. Hermann 4: 7, No. 3 (BM-000594706).
Generitype of *Amomum* Linnaeus, *nom. rej.*
Current name: ***Zingiber officinale*** Roscoe (Zingiberaceae).
Note: Amomum Linnaeus *nom. rej.* in favour of *Amomum* Roxb. and *Zingiber* Boehm.
  Jansen (*Spices, Condiments Med. Pl. Ethiopia*: 124. 1981) incorrectly designated a Rheede plate, not cited in the protologue, as the lectotype.

Amorpha fruticosa Linnaeus, *Species Plantarum* 2: 713. 1753.
"Habitat in Carolina." RCN: 5245.
Lectotype (Stearn, *Introd. Linnaeus' Sp. Pl.* (Ray Soc. ed.): 47. 1957): [icon] *"Amorpha"* in Linnaeus, Hort. Cliff.: 353, t. 19. 1738. – Voucher: Herb. Clifford: 353, *Amorpha* 1 (BM).
Generitype of *Amorpha* Linnaeus.
Current name: ***Amorpha fruticosa*** L. (Fabaceae: Faboideae).

Amygdalus communis Linnaeus, *Species Plantarum* 1: 473. 1753.
"Habitat in Mauritaniae sepibus." RCN: 3619.
Lectotype (Jafri in Jafri & El-Gadi, *Fl. Libya* 31: 12. 1977): Herb. Clifford: 186, *Amygdalus* 2 (BM-000628608).
Generitype of *Amygdalus* Linnaeus (vide Green, *Prop. Brit. Bot.*: 158. 1929).
Current name: ***Prunus dulcis*** (Mill.) D.A. Webb (Rosaceae).

Amygdalus nana Linnaeus, *Species Plantarum* 1: 473. 1753.
"Habitat in Asia septentrionali?" RCN: 3621.
Lectotype (Majorov & Sokoloff in Cafferty & Jarvis in *Taxon* 51: 541. 2002): *Gerber*, Herb. Linn. No. 639.6 (LINN).
Current name: ***Prunus tenella*** Batsch (Rosaceae).

Amygdalus persica Linnaeus, *Species Plantarum* 1: 472. 1753.
"Habitat – – – –" RCN: 3618.
Lectotype (Blanca & Díaz de la Guardia in Cafferty & Jarvis in *Taxon* 51: 541. 2002): Herb. Linn. No. 639.2 (LINN).
Current name: ***Prunus persica*** (L.) Batsch (Rosaceae).
Note: Blanca & Díaz de la Guardia provided a review of earlier type observations for this name.

Amygdalus pumila Linnaeus, *Systema Naturae*, ed. 12, 2: 341; *Mantissa Plantarum*: 74. 1767.
"Habitat in Africa." RCN: 3620.
Lectotype (Bartholomew in Cafferty & Jarvis in *Taxon* 51: 541. 2002): Herb. Linn. No. 639.4 (LINN).
Current name: ***Prunus tenella*** Batsch (Rosaceae).

Amyris balsamifera Linnaeus, *Systema Naturae*, ed. 10, 2: 1000. 1759.
["Habitat in Jamaica."] Sp. Pl., ed. 2, 1: 496 (1762). RCN: 2687.
Lectotype (designated here by Gereau): *Browne*, Herb. Linn. No. 490.2 (LINN).
Current name: ***Amyris balsamifera*** L. (Rutaceae).

Amyris elemifera Linnaeus, *Systema Naturae*, ed. 10, 2: 1000. 1759.
["Habitat in Carolina."] Sp. Pl., ed. 2, 1: 495 (1762). RCN: 2680.
Lectotype (Howard, *Fl. Lesser Antilles* 4: 557. 1988): [icon] *"Frutex*

trifolius resinosus; floribus tetra-petalis albis racemosis" in Catesby, Nat. Hist. Carolina 2: 33, t. 33. 1734.
Current name: ***Amyris elemifera*** L. (Rutaceae).

Amyris gileadensis Linnaeus, *Opobalsamum Declaratum*: 13. 1764.
"Habitat in Arabia felici." RCN: 2683.
Type not designated.
Original material: none traced.
Current name: ***Commiphora gileadensis*** (L.) C. Chr. (Burseraceae).
Note: Specific epithet spelled "giliadensis" in the protologue.

Amyris opobalsamum Linnaeus, *Opobalsamum Declaratum*: 14. 1764.
"Habitat in Arbia [sic]" RCN: 2684.
Type not designated.
Original material: [icon] in Alpino, De Plantis Aegypti: 48, 60. 1640.
Current name: ***Commiphora opobalsamum*** (L.) Engl. (Burseraceae).

Amyris protium Linnaeus, *Systema Naturae*, ed. 12, 2: 266; *Mantissa Plantarum*: 65. 1767.
"Habitat in India orientali." RCN: 3686.
Type not designated.
Original material: [icon] in Rumphius, Herb. Amboin. Auct.: 54, t. 23, f. 1. 1755.
Current name: ***Protium javanicum*** Burm. f. (Burseraceae).

Amyris toxifera Linnaeus, *Systema Naturae*, ed. 10, 2: 1000. 1759.
["Habitat in Carolina."] Sp. Pl., ed. 2, 1: 496 (1762). RCN: 2685.
Lectotype (Howard, *Fl. Lesser Antilles* 5: 99. 1989): [icon] *"Toxicodendron foliis alatis fructu purpureo Pyri formi sparso"* in Catesby, Nat. Hist. Carolina 1: 40, t. 40. 1730.
Current name: ***Metopium toxiferum*** (L.) Krug & Urb. (Anacardiaceae).

Anabasis aphylla Linnaeus, *Species Plantarum* 1: 223. 1753.
"Habitat ad maris Caspii litora." RCN: 1832.
Lectotype (Hedge in Jarvis & al., *Regnum Veg.* 127: 18. 1993): *Gmelin s.n.*, Herb. Linn. No. 316.1 (LINN).
Generitype of *Anabasis* Linnaeus (vide Hitchcock, *Prop. Brit. Bot.*: 137. 1929).
Current name: ***Anabasis aphyllus*** L. (Chenopodiaceae).

Anabasis foliosa Linnaeus, *Species Plantarum* 1: 223. 1753.
"Habitat ad maris Caspii litora." RCN: 1833.
Type not designated.
Original material: *Gmelin*, Herb. Linn. No. 316.3 (LINN); [icon] in Buxbaum, Pl. Minus Cognit. Cent. 1: 12, t. 19, f. 1. 1728.
Current name: ***Salsola foliosa*** (L.) Schrad. (Chenopodiaceae).
Note: Botschantzev (in *Novosti Sist. Vyssh. Rast.* 13: 99. 1976) indicated 316.3 and 316.4 (LINN) as type material. However, these collections do not appear to be part of a single gathering, so Art. 9.15 does not apply and the name is not yet typified.

Anabasis tamariscifolia Linnaeus, *Systema Naturae*, ed. 10, 2: 949. 1759.
["Habitat in Hispania."] Sp. Pl., ed. 2, 1: 324 (1762). RCN: 1834.
Lectotype (Castroviejo & Luceño in *Anales Jard. Bot. Madrid* 45: 370. 1988): Herb. Linn. No. 316.5 (LINN).
Current name: ***Salsola vermiculata*** L. (Chenopodiaceae).

Anacampseros americana Linnaeus, *Flora Jamaicensis*: 17. 1759.
"Habitat [in Jamaica.]"
Type not designated.
Original material: none traced.
Note: The application of this name appears uncertain.

Anacampseros telephiastrum A.P. de Candolle, *Cat. Pl. Horti Monsp.*: 77. 1813.
Replaced synonym: *Portulaca anacampseros* L. (1753).
Lectotype (Wijnands, *Bot. Commelins*: 175. 1983): [icon] "*Telephiastrum folio globoso*" in Dillenius, Hort. Eltham. 2: 375, t. 281, f. 363. 1732.
Generitype of *Anacampseros* Linnaeus, *nom. cons.*
Current name: ***Anacampseros telephiastrum*** DC. (Portulacaceae).
Note: Anacampseros Linnaeus, *Opera Varia*: 232 (1758), *nom. cons.* against *Anacampseros* Mill.

Anacardium occidentale Linnaeus, *Species Plantarum* 1: 383. 1753.
"Habitat in Indiis." RCN: 2922.
Lectotype (Fawcett & Rendle, *Fl. Jamaica* 5: 6. 1926): Herb. Hermann 3: 50, No. 165 (BM-000621986).
Generitype of *Anacardium* Linnaeus.
Current name: ***Anacardium occidentale*** L. (Anacardiaceae).

Anacyclus aureus Linnaeus, *Mantissa Plantarum Altera*: 287. 1771.
"Habitat in Europa australi et oriente. H.U." RCN: 6469.
Type not designated.
Original material: Herb. Burser VII: 29 (UPS); [icon] in Bauhin & Cherler, Hist. Pl. Univ. 3(1): 119. 1651; [icon] in Plantin, Pl. Stirp. Icon.: 771. 1581.
Current name: ***Chamaemelum nobile*** (L.) All. (Asteraceae).

Anacyclus creticus Linnaeus, *Species Plantarum* 2: 892. 1753.
"Habitat in Creta." RCN: 6467.
Lectotype (Humphries in Jarvis & Turland in *Taxon* 47: 351. 1998): Herb. Linn. No. 1015.1 (LINN).
Current name: ***Anthemis rigida*** Boiss. ex Heldr. (Asteraceae).

Anacyclus orientalis Linnaeus, *Species Plantarum* 2: 892. 1753.
"Habitat in Oriente." RCN: 6468.
Lectotype (Franzén in Strid & Kit Tan, *Mountain Fl. Greece* 2: 428. 1991): Herb. Clifford: 417, *Anacyclus* 3 (BM-000647223).
Current name: ***Anthemis orientalis*** (L.) Degen (Asteraceae).
Note: Grierson (in *Notes Roy. Bot. Gard. Edinburgh* 33: 213. 1974), on the basis of the identity of Clifford material, rejected the name as a *nomen confusum* and (in Davis, *Fl. Turkey* 5: 193. 1975) consequently took up *Anthemis pectinata* (Bory & Chaub.) Boiss. & Reut. as the correct name. However, more recent authors have continued to use *Anthemis orientalis*.

Anacyclus valentinus Linnaeus, *Species Plantarum* 2: 892. 1753.
"Habitat ad Reg. Valentini agros & vias." RCN: 6470.
Lectotype (Humphries in *Bull. Brit. Mus. (Nat. Hist.), Bot.* 7: 109. 1979): Herb. Clifford: 417, *Anacyclus* 1 (BM-000647221).
Generitype of *Anacyclus* Linnaeus (vide Green, *Prop. Brit. Bot.*: 182. 1929).
Current name: ***Anacyclus valentinus*** L. (Asteraceae).

Anagallis arvensis Linnaeus, *Species Plantarum* 1: 148. 1753.
"Habitat in Europae arvis." RCN: 1180.
Lectotype (Dyer in Dyer & al., *Fl. Southern Africa* 26: 14. 1963): Herb. Linn. No. 208.1 (LINN).
Generitype of *Anagallis* Linnaeus (vide Hitchcock, *Prop. Brit. Bot.*: 129. 1929).
Current name: ***Anagallis arvensis*** L. (Primulaceae).
Note: Although Taylor (in Hubbard & Milne-Redhead, *Fl. Trop. E. Africa, Primulaceae*: 10. 1958) indicated 208.1 (LINN) as a syntype (which is not, by definition, the sole type of a name, unlike a holotype, lectotype or neotype), this statement is not accepted as correctable to lectotype under Art. 9.8.

Anagallis caerulea Linnaeus, *Amoenitates Academicae* 4: 479. 1759.
Neotype (Burtt in Kollmann & Feinbrun in *Notes Roy. Bot. Gard. Edinburgh* 28: 174, 185. 1968): [icon] "*Anagallis foemina*" in Dodoëns, Stirp. Hist. Comment. Imag.: 61. 1553.
Current name: ***Anagallis arvensis*** L. subsp. ***arvensis*** var. ***caerulea*** (L.) Gouan (Primulaceae).
Note: As noted by Stearn (in Geck & Pressler, *Festschr. Claus Nissen*: 635. 1974), this name is validated by reference to Magnol's *Botanicum Monspeliense*. As Burtt's chosen type is not directly cited by Magnol, his type choice is treated as a neotypification.

Anagallis capensis Linnaeus, *Species Plantarum* 1: 149. 1753.
"Habitat ad Caput b. spei." RCN: 104.
Type not designated.
Original material: none traced.
Current name: ***Diascia capensis*** (L.) Britten (Scrophulariaceae).
Note: Britten (in *J. Bot.* 47: 44. 1909) says that "Linnaeus based [this] on *Anagallis purpurea, bursae pastoris foliis minoribus* Pet. Mus. 245 (*recte* 345), of which Petiver's original specimen, received from Oldenland, is in Herb. Sloane, vol. 156, f. 157". He evidently interpreted the name via this specimen, though he did not refer to it as the type.

Anagallis latifolia Linnaeus, *Species Plantarum* 1: 149. 1753.
"Habitat in Hispania. Loefl." RCN: 1182.
Type not designated.
Original material: Herb. Linn. No. 208.3 (LINN); [icon] in Barrelier, Pl. Galliam: 17, t. 584. 1714.
Current name: ***Anagallis arvensis*** L. (Primulaceae).

Anagallis linifolia Linnaeus, *Species Plantarum*, ed. 2, 1: 212. 1762.
"Habitat in Lusitania, Hispania. Claud. Alstroemer." RCN: 1183.
Type not designated.
Original material: Herb. Linn. No. 208.5 (LINN); *Alströmer s.n.* Herb. Linn. No. 208.4 (LINN).
Current name: ***Anagallis monelli*** L. (Primulaceae).

Anagallis monelli Linnaeus, *Species Plantarum* 1: 148. 1753.
"Habitat – – – –" RCN: 1181.
Type not designated.
Original material: Herb. Clifford: 52, *Anagallis* 2 (BM).
Current name: ***Anagallis monelli*** L. (Primulaceae).
Note: Ali (in Ali & Jafri, *Fl. Libya* 1: 10. 1976) indicated 208.2 (LINN) as the type but this collection lacks the relevant *Species Plantarum* number (i.e. "2"). It was a post-1753 addition to the herbarium, and is not original material for the name.

Anagallis tenella (Linnaeus) Linnaeus, *Systema Vegetabilium*, ed. 13: 165. 1774.
["Habitat in Galliae, Angliae humidis."] Sp. Pl. 1: 148 (1753). RCN: 1184.
Basionym: *Lysimachia tenella* L. (1753).
Type not designated.
Original material: as basionym.
Current name: ***Anagallis tenella*** (L.) L. (Primulaceae).

Anagyris foetida Linnaeus, *Species Plantarum* 1: 374. 1753.
"Habitat in Italiae, Siciliae, Hispaniae montibus." RCN: 2944.
Lectotype (Jafri in Jafri & El-Gadi, *Fl. Libya* 86: 9. 1980): Herb. Linn. No. 523.1 (LINN).
Generitype of *Anagyris* Linnaeus.
Current name: ***Anagyris foetida*** L. (Fabaceae: Faboideae).

Anastatica hierochuntica Linnaeus, *Species Plantarum* 2: 641. 1753.
"Habitat in littoribus maris rubri." RCN: 4665.

Lectotype (Hedge in Jarvis & al., *Regnum Veg.* 127: 18. 1993): Herb. Clifford: 328, *Anastatica* 1 (BM-000646249).
Generitype of *Anastatica* Linnaeus.
Current name: ***Anastatica hierochuntica*** L. (Brassicaceae).

Anastatica syriaca Linnaeus, *Species Plantarum*, ed. 2, 2: 895. 1763.
"Habitat in Syriae tectis, ruderibus." RCN: 4666.
Lectotype (Hedge in Cafferty & Jarvis in *Taxon* 51: 531. 2002): *Mygind s.n.*, Herb. Linn. No. 821.3 (LINN).
Current name: ***Euclidium syriacum*** (L.) W.T. Aiton (Brassicaceae).
Note: Jafri (1973: 103) indicated both 821.2 and 821.3 (LINN) as "type" and, as they are evidently not part of a single gathering, Art. 9.15 does not apply.

Anchusa angustifolia Linnaeus, *Species Plantarum* 1: 133. 1753.
"Habitat in Italia, Germania." RCN: 1076.
Lectotype (Selvi in Cafferty & Jarvis in *Taxon* 53: 800. 2004): Herb. Linn. No. 182.2 (LINN).
Current name: ***Anchusa officinalis*** L. (Boraginaceae).

Anchusa lanata Linnaeus, *Systema Naturae*, ed. 10, 2: 914. 1759.
["Habitat in Algiriae. Brander."] Sp. Pl., ed. 2, 1: 192 (1762). RCN: 1080.
Lectotype (Mill in Cafferty & Jarvis in *Taxon* 53: 800. 2004): *Brander*, Herb. Linn. No. 182.6 (LINN).
Current name: ***Pardoglossum lanatum*** (L.) E. Barbier & Mathez (Boraginaceae).

Anchusa officinalis Linnaeus, *Species Plantarum* 1: 133. 1753.
"Habitat ad Europae ruderata, vias, agros." RCN: 1075.
Lectotype (Selvi & al. in *Taxon* 45: 306. 1996): Herb. Clifford: 46, *Anchusa* 1, sheet A (BM-000557910).
Generitype of *Anchusa* Linnaeus (vide Hitchcock, *Prop. Brit. Bot.*: 127. 1929).
Current name: ***Anchusa officinalis*** L. (Boraginaceae).

Anchusa orientalis Linnaeus, *Species Plantarum* 1: 133. 1753.
"Habitat in Oriente." RCN: 1071.
Basionym of: *Lithospermum orientale* (L.) L. (1767).
Lectotype (Güner & Duman in Cafferty & Jarvis in *Taxon* 53: 800. 2004): Herb. Clifford: 47, *Anchusa* 2 (BM-000557914).
Current name: ***Alkanna orientalis*** (L.) Boiss. (Boraginaceae).

Anchusa sempervirens Linnaeus, *Species Plantarum* 1: 134. 1753.
"Habitat in Anglia, Hispania." RCN: 1081.
Lectotype (Selvi & Bigazzi in *Pl. Biosystems* 132: 129. 1998): Herb. Burser XIV(2): 21 (UPS).
Current name: ***Pentaglottis sempervirens*** (L.) Tausch ex L.H. Bailey (Boraginaceae).

Anchusa tinctoria (Linnaeus) Linnaeus, *Species Plantarum*, ed. 2, 1: 192. 1762.
"Habitat monspelii." RCN: 1078.
Basionym: *Lithospermum tinctorium* L. (1753).
Lectotype (Selvi & al. in Cafferty & Jarvis in *Taxon* 53: 802. 2004): [icon] *"Anchusa monspeliana"* in Bauhin & Cherler, Hist. Pl. Univ. 3(2): 584. 1651. – Epitype (Selvi in Cafferty & Jarvis in *Taxon* 53: 802. 2004): France. Montpellier, May 1861, *G. Watson-Taylor 465* (FI).
Current name: ***Alkanna tuberculata*** (Forrsk.) Meikle (Boraginaceae).

Anchusa undulata Linnaeus, *Species Plantarum* 1: 133. 1753.
"Habitat in Hispaniae, Lusitaniae pratis." RCN: 1077.
Lectotype (Valdés in *Lagascalia* 10: 107. 1981): *Löfling 144a*, Herb. Linn. No. 182.3 (LINN).
Current name: ***Anchusa undulata*** L. (Boraginaceae).

Anchusa virginiana Linnaeus, *Species Plantarum* 1: 133. 1753.
"Habitat in Virginia." RCN: 1079.
Lectotype (Reveal in Cafferty & Jarvis in *Taxon* 53: 800. 2004): *Clayton 304* (BM-000040285; iso- BM).
Current name: ***Lithospermum canescens*** (Michx.) Lehm. (Boraginaceae).

Andrachne fruticosa Linnaeus, *Species Plantarum* 2: 1014. 1753.
"Habitat in China. Osbeck." RCN: 7351.
Lectotype (designated here by Esser): Herb. Linn. No. 1155.2 (LINN).
Current name: ***Breynia fruticosa*** (L.) Müll. Arg. (Euphorbiaceae).
Note: See notes by Hansen & Fox Maule (in *Bot. J. Linn. Soc.* 67: 207. 1973).

Andrachne telephioides Linnaeus, *Species Plantarum* 2: 1014. 1753.
"Habitat in Italia, Graecia, Media." RCN: 7350.
Lectotype (Radcliffe-Smith in Meikle, *Fl. Cyprus* 2: 1448. 1985): Herb. Linn. No. 1155.1 (LINN).
Generitype of *Andrachne* Linnaeus (vide Green, *Prop. Brit. Bot.*: 190. 1929).
Current name: ***Andrachne telephioides*** L. (Euphorbiaceae).

Andromeda arborea Linnaeus, *Species Plantarum* 1: 394. 1753.
"Habitat in Virginia, Carolina." RCN: 3103.
Lectotype (Vander Kloet in Cafferty & Jarvis in *Taxon* 51: 752. 2003 [2002]): *Clayton 613* (BM-000553923).
Current name: ***Oxydendrum arboreum*** (L.) DC. (Ericaceae).

Andromeda bryantha Linnaeus, *Mantissa Plantarum Altera*: 238. 1771.
"Habitat in Camtschatca cum Empetro in rupibus." RCN: 3098.
Lectotype (Mazurenko in Cafferty & Jarvis in *Taxon* 51: 752. 2003 [2002]): [icon] *"Bryanthus"* in Gmelin, Fl. Sibirica 4: 133, t. 57, f. 3. 1769.
Current name: ***Bryanthus gmelinii*** D. Don (Ericaceae).

Andromeda caerulea Linnaeus, *Species Plantarum* 1: 393. 1753.
"Habitat in Lapponiae Alpibus." RCN: 3095.
Lectotype (Jonsell in Cafferty & Jarvis in *Taxon* 51: 752. 2003 [2002]): Herb. Linn. No. 563.3 (LINN).
Current name: ***Phyllodoce caerulea*** (L.) Babc. (Ericaceae).

Andromeda calyculata Linnaeus, *Species Plantarum* 1: 394. 1753.
"Habitat in Virginia, Canada, Sibiria." RCN: 3104.
Lectotype (Majorov & Sokoloff in Cafferty & Jarvis in *Taxon* 51: 752. 2003 [2002]): *Gerber?*, Herb. Linn. No. 563.17, right specimen (LINN).
Current name: ***Chamaedaphne calyculata*** (L.) Moench var. ***calyculata*** (Ericaceae).

Andromeda daboecii Linnaeus, *Systema Naturae*, ed. 12, 2: 300. 1767, *nom. illeg.*
["Habitat in Hiberniae Gallovidia in montibus Mayo, solo caespitoso."] Sp. Pl., ed. 2, 1: 509 (1762). RCN: 3099.
Replaced synonym: *Erica daboecii* L. (1762), *nom. illeg.*
Lectotype (Nelson in *Watsonia* 23: 55, f. 1. 2000): [icon] *"Erica Hibernica fol. Myrti pilosis subtus incanis"* in Petiver, Gazophyl. Nat.: 42, t. 27, f. 4. 1702–1709.
Current name: ***Daboecia cantabrica*** (Huds.) K. Koch (Ericaceae).
Note: This is based on *Erica daboecii* L. (1762), an illegitimate renaming of *Vaccinium cantabricum* Huds. (1762).

Andromeda droseroides Linnaeus, *Mantissa Plantarum Altera*: 239. 1771, *nom. illeg.*

"Habitat ad. Cap. b. spei." RCN: 3100.
Replaced synonym: *Erica glutinosa* P.J. Bergius (1767).
Type not designated.
Current name: ***Erica glutinosa*** P.J. Bergius (Ericaceae).

Andromeda hypnoides Linnaeus, *Species Plantarum* 1: 393. 1753.
"Habitat in Alpibus Lapponicis." RCN: 3094.
Lectotype (Stone & Stone in Cafferty & Jarvis in *Taxon* 51: 752. 2003 [2002]): [icon] *"Andromeda foliis aciformibus confertis"* in Linnaeus, Fl. Lapponica: 128, t. 1, f. 3. 1737. – Epitype (Stone & Stone in Cafferty & Jarvis in *Taxon* 51: 752. 2003 [2002]): Sweden. Torne lappmark, Jukkasjärvi s:n., Vassitjåkko, 17 Jul 1948, *Melderis s.n.* (BM-000576312).
Current name: ***Cassiope hypnoides*** (L.) D. Don (Ericaceae).

Andromeda mariana Linnaeus, *Species Plantarum* 1: 393. 1753.
"Habitat in Virginia." RCN: 3096.
Lectotype (Judd in *J. Arnold Arbor.* 62: 198. 1981): *Kalm*, Herb. Linn. No. 563.5 (LINN; iso- UPS).
Current name: ***Lyonia mariana*** (L.) D. Don (Ericaceae).
Note: See extensive review by Reveal & al. (in *Huntia* 7: 213. 1987).

Andromeda paniculata Linnaeus, *Species Plantarum* 1: 394. 1753.
"Habitat in Virginia." RCN: 3101.
Lectotype (Judd in *J. Arnold Arbor.* 62: 198. 1981): *Kalm*, Herb. Linn. No. 563.14, flowering specimen (LINN).
Current name: ***Leucothoë racemosa*** (L.) A. Gray (Ericaceae).

Andromeda polifolia Linnaeus, *Species Plantarum* 1: 393. 1753.
"Habitat in Europae frigidioris paludibus turfosis." RCN: 3097.
Lectotype (Jarvis & McClintock in *Taxon* 39: 517. 1990): Herb. Linn. No. 163 (LAPP).
Generitype of *Andromeda* Linnaeus (vide Hitchcock, *Prop. Brit. Bot.*: 153. 1929).
Current name: ***Andromeda polifolia*** L. (Ericaceae).
Note: Nelson & Oswald (in *Huntia* 12: 5–11. 2005), in exploring the origin of the epithet "polifolia", reproduce Linnaeus' protologue (p. 7).

Andromeda racemosa Linnaeus, *Species Plantarum* 1: 394. 1753.
"Habitat in Pensylvania. Kalm." RCN: 3102.
Lectotype (Howard & Staples in *J. Arnold Arbor.* 64: 524. 1983): *Kalm*, Herb. Linn. No. 563.15 (LINN).
Current name: ***Leucothoë racemosa*** (L.) A. Gray (Ericaceae).

Andromeda tetragona Linnaeus, *Species Plantarum* 1: 393. 1753.
"Habitat in Alpibus Lapponicis." RCN: 3093.
Lectotype (Stone & Stone in Cafferty & Jarvis in *Taxon* 51: 752. 2003 [2002]): Herb. Linn. No. 166, left specimen (LAPP; iso- G).
Current name: ***Cassiope tetragona*** (L.) D. Don (Ericaceae).

Andropogon alopecuroides Linnaeus, *Species Plantarum* 2: 1045. 1753.
"Habitat in America septentrionaliore." RCN: 7551.
Lectotype (Hitchcock in *Contr. U. S. Natl. Herb.* 12: 125. 1908): *Clayton 601*, Herb. Linn. No. 1211.9 (LINN; iso- BM, US).
Current name: ***Erianthus alopecuroides*** (L.) Elliott (Poaceae).
Note: Fernald (in *Rhodora* 45: 251. 1943) appears to have regarded the material in BM as the type (rather than that in LINN) and illustrated it in pl. 761, f. 1, 2.

Andropogon barbatus Linnaeus, *Systema Naturae*, ed. 10, 2: 1305. 1759.
["Habitat in Jamaica."] Sp. Pl., ed, 2, 2: 1483 (1763). RCN: 7563.
Replaced synonym of: *Andropogon polydactylos* L. (1763), *nom. illeg.*

Lectotype (Hitchcock in *Contr. U. S. Natl. Herb.* 12: 126. 1908): *Browne*, Herb. Linn. No. 1211.28 (LINN).
Current name: ***Chloris dandyana*** C.D. Adams (Poaceae).
Note: Specific epithet spelled "barbatum" in the protologue.
      The existence of *A. barbatus* L. (1771) has resulted in some nomenclatural complexities. *Andropogon barbatus* (1759) relates to a perennial species, recombined in *Chloris* as *C. barbata* (L.) Nash (1898), a later homonym of the annual *C. barbata* Sw. (1797) (which was itself based on the illegitimate *A. barbatus* L. 1771, non 1759). The correct name is *C. dandyana* C.D. Adams (1971), since the only other possible name in *Chloris*, *C. polydactyla* Sw. (1788), is based on *A. polydactylos* L. (1763), an illegitimate renaming of *A. barbatus* L. (1759).

Andropogon barbatus Linnaeus, *Mantissa Plantarum Altera*: 302. 1771, *nom. illeg.*
"Habitat in India orientali." RCN: 7558.
Lectotype (Judziewicz in Görts-van Rijn, *Fl. Guianas*, ser. A, 8: 136. 1990): Herb. Linn. No. 1211.21 (LINN).
Current name: ***Chloris barbata*** Sw. (Poaceae).
Note: A later homonym of *A. barbatus* L. (1759) and hence illegitimate. Although Fosberg (in *Taxon* 25: 325. 1976) argued that *A. barbatus* L. (1771) is merely a modification of *A. barbatus* L. (1759), it seems clear that this is not the case. In *Syst. Nat.*, ed. 13: 759. 1774, both this and the species described in 1759 (though named as *A. polydactylos* L. (1763), *nom. illeg.*) were recognised.

Andropogon bicornis Linnaeus, *Species Plantarum* 2: 1046. 1753, *nom. cons.*
"Habitat in Brasilia, Jamaica." RCN: 7555.
Conserved type (Davidse & Turland in *Taxon* 48: 573. 1999): Puerto Rico. "Mayagüez, between Monte Mesa and the sea", 27 Oct 1913, A. Chase in Amer. Gr. Nat. Herb. No. 247 (MO; iso- BM, F, NY, US).
Current name: ***Andropogon bicornis*** L. (Poaceae).
Note: Specific epithet spelled "bicorne" in the protologue.

Andropogon caricosus Linnaeus, *Species Plantarum*, ed. 2, 2: 1480. 1763.
"Habitat in India." RCN: 7543.
Type not designated.
Original material: [icon] in Rumphius, Herb. Amboin. 6: 17, t. 7, f. 2 A. 1750.
Current name: ***Dichanthium caricosum*** (L.) A. Camus (Poaceae).
Note: Specific epithet spelled "caricosum" in the protologue.
      The description in the protologue refers to a taxon quite different from the only extant original material, the cited Rumphius plate. The latter has been identified as *Imperata cylindrica* (L.) P. Beauv. (by Merrill, *Interpret. Rumph. Herb. Amb.*: 85. 1917), or possibly a species of *Pennisetum* or *Setaria*. Munro (in *J. Proc. Linn. Soc., Bot.* 6: 53. 1862) equated the description with *Andropogon serratus* Retz. Some authors (e.g. Judziewicz in *Fl. Guianas*, ser. A, 8: 168. 1990) have treated unseen Burman material as the probable type. However, even if traced, this seems unlikely to be original material for the name and it appears that a conservation proposal may be necessary.

Andropogon contortus Linnaeus, *Species Plantarum* 2: 1045. 1753.
"Habitat in India." RCN: 7544.
Lectotype (Cope in Nasir & Ali, *Fl. Pakistan* 143: 312. 1982): [icon] *"Gram. Secalinum, Indicum, spica gracili, tomentoso, aristis longioribus, ad se invicem intortis"* in Plukenet, Phytographia: t. 191, f. 5. 1692; Almag. Bot.: 173. 1696. – Voucher: Herb. Sloane 92: 78; 96: 69 (BM-SL).
Current name: ***Heteropogon contortus*** (L.) Roem. & Schult. (Poaceae).

Note: Specific epithet spelled "contortum" in the protologue.

Cope's type choice (Jun 1982) narrowly pre-dates the same choice made by Clayton & Renvoize (in Polhill, *Fl. Trop. E. Africa, Gramineae* 3: 827. Nov 1982).

Andropogon cymbarius Linnaeus, *Mantissa Plantarum Altera*: 303. 1771.

"Habitat in India orientali. Koenig." RCN: 7549.

1211·6

Lectotype (Clayton in *Kew Bull., Addit. Ser.* 2: 110. 1969): Herb. Linn. No. 1211.6 (LINN).

Current name: ***Hyparrhenia cymbaria*** (L.) Stapf (Poaceae).

Note: Specific epithet spelled "cymbarium" in the protologue.

Andropogon distachyos Linnaeus, *Species Plantarum* 2: 1046. 1753, *typ. cons.*

"Habitat in Helvetia. Burser." RCN: 7552.

Conserved type (Clayton & Renvoize in Polhill, *Fl. Trop. E. Africa, Gramineae* 3: 770. 1982): Herb. Burser I: 120 (UPS).

Generitype of *Andropogon* Linnaeus, *nom. cons.*

Current name: ***Andropogon distachyos*** L. (Poaceae).

Note: Specific epithet spelled "distachyon" in the protologue.

Andropogon distachyos, with the type designated by Clayton & Renvoize, was proposed as conserved type of the genus by Jarvis (in *Taxon* 41: 556. 1992). This was eventually approved by the General Committee (see review of the history of this proposal by Barrie, *l.c.* 55: 795–796. 2006).

Andropogon divaricatus Linnaeus, *Species Plantarum* 2: 1045. 1753.

"Habitat in Virginia." RCN: 7545.

Lectotype (Hitchcock in *Contr. U. S. Natl. Herb.* 12: 125. 1908): Herb. Linn. No. 1211.1 (LINN).

Current name: ***Erianthus alopecuroides*** (L.) Elliott (Poaceae).

Note: Specific epithet spelled "divaricatum" in the protologue.

See also Fernald (in *Rhodora* 45: 252. 1943), who illustrates both the lectotype (pl. 761, f. 3, 4) and *Clayton 600* (pl. 761, f. 5).

Andropogon fasciculatus Linnaeus, *Species Plantarum* 2: 1047. 1753.

"Habitat in Indiis." RCN: 7562.

Lectotype (Henrard in *Blumea* 3: 454. 1940; Cope in Cafferty & al. in *Taxon* 49: 245. 2000): Herb. Linn. No. 1211.27, lower central specimen (LINN).

Current name: ***Microstegium fasciculatum*** (L.) Henrard (Poaceae).

Note: Specific epithet spelled "fasciculatum" in the protologue.

Munro (in *J. Proc. Linn. Soc., Bot.* 6: 53. 1862) noted the existence of two species associated with this name in LINN, and Hitchcock (in *Contr. U. S. Natl. Herb.* 12: 126. 1908) provided an extensive discussion. However, Henrard (in *Blumea* 3: 454. 1940) clearly accepted the sheet now numbered as 1211.27 (LINN) as the type, though the material it bears is a mixed collection. Henrard's type choice was therefore restricted by Cope to the lower, central specimen, in accordance with Art. 9.15.

Andropogon gryllus Linnaeus, *Centuria II Plantarum*: 33. 1756.

"Habitat in Rhaetia, Helvetia, Veronae, Sauvages, Seguier." RCN: 7546.

Lectotype (Meikle, *Fl. Cyprus* 2: 1863. 1985): *Séguier*, Herb. Linn. No. 1211.2 (LINN).

Current name: ***Chrysopogon gryllus*** (L.) Trin. (Poaceae).

Note: Although Kerguélen (in *Lejeunia*, n.s., 75: 120. 1975) stated "Type: ...LINN", this is not accepted as a formal typification, for the reasons explained by Cafferty & al. (in *Taxon* 49: 240. 2000).

Andropogon hirtus Linnaeus, *Species Plantarum* 2: 1046. 1753.

"Habitat in Lusitania, Sicilia, Smyrnae." RCN: 7556.

Lectotype (Clayton in *Kew Bull., Addit. Ser.* 2: 75. 1969): Herb. Burser I: 119 (UPS).

Current name: ***Hyparrhenia hirta*** (L.) Stapf (Poaceae).

Note: Specific epithet spelled "hirtum" in the protologue.

Although Kerguélen (in *Lejeunia*, n.s., 75: 196. 1975) stated "Type: ...LINN", this is not accepted as a formal typification, for the reasons explained by Cafferty & al. (in *Taxon* 49: 240. 2000). Romero Zarco (in *Lagascalia* 14: 122. 1986) subsequently chose 1211.15 (LINN) as lectotype but Clayton's choice has priority. See López González (in *Anales Jard. Bot. Madrid* 51: 313. 1993), who discusses various aspects of the typification of this name.

Andropogon insularis Linnaeus, *Systema Naturae*, ed. 10, 2: 1304. 1759.

["Habitat in Jamaica."] Sp. Pl., ed. 2, 2: 1481 (1763). RCN: 7557.

Lectotype (Hitchcock in *Contr. U. S. Natl. Herb.* 12: 126. 1908): *Browne*, Herb. Linn. No. 1211.20 (LINN).

Current name: ***Digitaria insularis*** (L.) Fedde (Poaceae).

Note: Specific epithet spelled "insulare" in the protologue.

Baum (in *Canad. J. Bot.* 45: 1850. 1967) argued that Hitchcock's typification was incorrect, proposing instead that Sloane's cited t. 14, f. 2 (1707) should be the type (with the consequence that *A. insularis* would fall into the synonymy of *A. nutans* L. 1753). However, the material designated as type was evidently original material for *A. insularis*, and Hitchcock's choice has priority and is to be adopted, as concluded by later authors such as Veldkamp (in *Taxon* 33: 95–97. 1984).

Andropogon ischaemum Linnaeus, *Species Plantarum* 2: 1047. 1753.
"Habitat in Europae australioris aridis." RCN: 7561.
Lectotype (Marchi & Longhi-Wagner in *Bol. Inst. Bioci. Univ. Fed. Rio Grande do Sul* 57: 41. 1998): Herb. Linn. No. 1211.26 (LINN).
Current name: ***Bothriochloa ischaemum*** (L.) Keng (Poaceae).
Note: Although Kerguélen (in *Lejeunia*, n.s., 75: 94. 1975) stated "Type: ...LINN", this is not accepted as a formal typification, for the reasons explained by Cafferty & al. (in *Taxon* 49: 240. 2000). Unfortunately, the taxonomic identity of Marchi & Longhi-Wagner's designated type appears to correspond with *A. gerardii* Vitm., as noted by Fernald & Chase (in *Rhodora* 50: 154. 1948). Unaware of this typification but aware of the identity of the material in LINN, Scholz (in Cafferty & al. in *Taxon* 49: 245. 2000) designated Herb. Burser I: 101 (UPS) as the lectotype. Although it does not correspond with the traditional usage of *B. ischaemum*, Marchi & Longhi-Wagner's typification has priority. It seems that a conservation proposal will be necessary if the traditional usage of this name is to be maintained.

Andropogon muticus Linnaeus, *Species Plantarum*, ed. 2, 2: 1482. 1763.
"Habitat ad Cap. b. spei." RCN: 7560.
Type not designated.
Original material: none traced.
Note: Specific epithet spelled "muticum" in the protologue.
     As noted by Nowak (in *Bull. Mus. Natl. Hist. Nat., B, Adansonia*, sér. 4, 17: 54. 1995), there appear to be no extant original elements, and the application of the name is uncertain.

Andropogon nardus Linnaeus, *Species Plantarum* 2: 1046. 1753.
"Habitat in India." RCN: 7559.
Lectotype (Clayton & Renvoize in Polhill, *Fl. Trop. E. Africa, Gramineae* 3: 764. 1982): Herb. Hermann 2: 66, No. 45 (BM-000594628).
Current name: ***Cymbopogon nardus*** (L.) Rendle (Poaceae).
Note: Although Stapf (in *Bull. Misc. Inform. Kew* 1906: 314. 1906) refers to Hermann's specimen at BM "on which the species finally rests", and (p. 354) "based on Hermann's specimen of 'Pengriman.' – Original at the British Museum", this is not accepted as formal typification, and nor is Soenarko's statement (in *Reinwardtia* 9: 349. 1977) "Type: Ceylon, Hermann's specimen", due to the absence of any indicated herbarium. The earliest explicit choice appears to be that of Clayton & Renvoize.

Andropogon nutans Linnaeus, *Species Plantarum* 2: 1045. 1753.
"Habitat in Virginia, Jamaica." RCN: 7547.
Lectotype (Hitchcock in *Contr. U. S. Natl. Herb.* 12: 125. 1908): *Kalm*, Herb. Linn. No. 1211.3 (LINN; iso- US).
Current name: ***Sorghastrum nutans*** (L.) Nash (Poaceae).
Note: Baum (in *Canad. J. Bot.* 45: 1850. 1967) rejected Hitchcock's typification, proposing instead that Sloane's cited t. 14, f. 2 (1707) should be the type. However, the material designated as type was evidently original material for *A. nutans*, and so Hitchcock's choice has priority. Later authors concurring with Hitchcock's choice include Voss (in *Michigan Bot.* 11: 31. 1972), McVaugh, (*Fl. Novo-Galiciana* 14: 142. 1983) and Veldkamp (in *Taxon* 33: 97. 1984).

Andropogon nutans Linnaeus, *Mantissa Plantarum Altera*: 303. 1771, *nom. illeg.*
RCN: 7548.
Replaced synonym of: *Andropogon quadrivalis* L. (1774).
Lectotype (Cope in Cafferty & al. in *Taxon* 49: 246. 2000): Herb. Linn. No. 1211.5 (LINN).
Current name: ***Themeda quadrivalvis*** (L.) Kuntze (Poaceae).
Note: A later homonym of *A. nutans* L. (1753) and hence illegitimate.

In 1774 (*Syst. Veg.*, ed. 13: 758), Linnaeus stated that "nutans" was a typographic error and that "quadrivalvis" was the intended epithet.

Andropogon polydactylos Linnaeus, *Species Plantarum*, ed. 2, 2: 1483. 1763, *nom. illeg.*
"Habitat in Jamaica." RCN: 7563.
Replaced synonym: *Andropogon barbatus* L. (1759).
Lectotype (Hitchcock in *Contr. U. S. Natl. Herb.* 12: 124. 1908): *Browne*, Herb. Linn. No. 1211.28 (LINN).
Current name: ***Chloris dandyana*** C.D. Adams (Poaceae).
Note: Specific epithet spelled "polydactylon" in the protologue.
     The protologue of this name included an explicit reference to the earlier *Amoen. Acad.* 5: 412 (1760) (a reprint of *Pl. Jamaic. Pugillus*) where *A. barbatus* L. (1759) was the binomial used. *Andropogon polydactylos* is therefore illegitimate.

Andropogon prostratus Linnaeus, *Mantissa Plantarum Altera*: 304. 1771.
"Habitat in India orientali. Koenig." RCN: 7550.
Lectotype (Renvoize in Cafferty & al. in *Taxon* 49: 246. 2000): Herb. Linn. No. 1211.8 (LINN).
Current name: ***Iseilema prostratum*** (L.) Andersson (Poaceae).
Note: Specific epithet spelled "prostratum" in the protologue.

Andropogon quadrivalvis Linnaeus, *Systema Vegetabilium*, ed. 13: 758. 1774.
RCN: 7548.
Replaced synonym: *Andropogon nutans* L. (1771), *nom. illeg.*, non L. (1753).
Lectotype (Cope in Cafferty & al. in *Taxon* 49: 246. 2000): Herb. Linn. No. 1211.5 (LINN).
Current name: ***Themeda quadrivalvis*** (L.) Kuntze (Poaceae).
Note: A *nomen novum* for *A. nutans* L. (1771) which is an illegitimate homonym of *A. nutans* L. (1753). In the protologue of *A. quadrivalvis*, Linnaeus explained that the use of "nutans" in 1771 had been a typographic error, and that "quadrivalvis" was the intended epithet.

Andropogon ravennae Linnaeus, *Species Plantarum*, ed. 2, 2: 1481. 1763.
"Habitat in Italia." RCN: 454.
Basionym of: *Saccharum ravennae* (L.) L. (1774).
Lectotype (Cope in Cafferty & al. in *Taxon* 49: 246. 2000): Herb. Linn. No. 77.4 (LINN).
Current name: ***Saccharum ravennae*** (L.) L. (Poaceae).
Note: Although Kerguélen (in *Lejeunia*, n.s., 75: 145. 1975) stated "Type: ...LINN", this is not accepted as a formal typification, for the reasons explained by Cafferty & al. (in *Taxon* 49: 240. 2000). Sherif & Siddiqi (in El-Gadi, *Fl. Libya* 145: 325. 1988) indicated Herb. Linn. 77.4 (LINN) and Zanoni, *Istoria Botanica*: t. 24 (1675) as "type" but this is not a single gathering (Art. 9.15) so no effective choice was made.

Andropogon schoenanthus Linnaeus, *Species Plantarum* 2: 1046. 1753.
"Habitat in India, Arabia." RCN: 7553.
Lectotype (Renvoize in Cafferty & al. in *Taxon* 49: 246. 2000): [icon] *"Gramen dactylon, aromatic., multiplici panicula, spicis brevibus tomento candicantibus, ex eodem pediculo binis"* in Plukenet, Phytographia: t. 190, f. 1. 1692; Almag. Bot.: 175. 1696. – Voucher: Herb. Sloane 96: 72 (BM-SL). – Epitype (Renvoize in Cafferty & al. in *Taxon* 49: 246. 2000): Saudi Arabia. Jebel Daalm, 19 May 1947, *Fitzgerald s.n.*, M.E.A.L.U. Herbarium No. 16950/1. (BM-000609396).
Current name: ***Cymbopogon schoenanthus*** (L.) Spreng. (Poaceae).

Andropogon virginicus Linnaeus, *Species Plantarum* 2: 1046. 1753.
"Habitat in America." RCN: 7554.
Lectotype (Hitchcock in *Contr. U. S. Natl. Herb.* 12: 125. 1908):
Herb. Linn. No. 1211.12 (LINN).
Current name: ***Andropogon virginicus*** L. (Poaceae).
Note: Specific epithet spelled "virginicum" in the protologue.

Androsace carnea Linnaeus, *Species Plantarum* 1: 142. 1753.
"Habitat in alpibus Pyrenais, Helveticis." RCN: 1149.
Lectotype (Kress, *Primulaceen-Studien* 6(1): 48. 1984): Herb. Burser
XVI(1): 75 (UPS).
Current name: ***Androsace carnea*** L. (Primulaceae).

Androsace elongata Linnaeus, *Species Plantarum,* ed. 2, 2: 1668.
1763.
"Habitat in Austria. Jacquin." RCN: 1145.
Type not designated.
Original material: *Jacquin,* Herb. Linn. No. 197.3 (LINN).
Current name: ***Androsace elongata*** L. (Primulaceae).

Androsace halleri Linnaeus, *Species Plantarum* 1: 142. 1753.
"Habitat in alpibus Helvetiae." RCN: 1149.
Lectotype (Kress, *Primulaceen-Studien* 6(1): 29, 59, Abb. 7. 1984):
[icon] *"Androsace angusto nervoso folio multiflora"* in Haller, Enum.
Meth. Stirp. Helv. 1: 486, 376, t. 7. 1742.
Current name: ***Androsace carnea*** L. subsp. ***rosea*** (Jord. & Fourr.)
Rouy (Primulaceae).
Note: Although Kress treats Haller's protologue as the type, this
includes Haller's figure (t. 7) which is therefore accepted as the type.

Androsace lactea Linnaeus, *Species Plantarum* 1: 142. 1753.
"Habitat in Austriae alpibus." RCN: 1148.
Lectotype (Kress, *Primulaceen-Studien* 11: 4. 1993): Herb. Burser
XVI(1): 73 (UPS). – Epitype (Kress, *Primulaceen-Studien* 11: 4.
1993): Austria. Oberösterreich, Traunstein am Ostufer des
Traunsees, von Westen zum Gipfel, ca. 1,100m, 28 Aug 1952
(Herb. Kress).
Current name: ***Androsace lactea*** L. (Primulaceae).

Androsace maxima Linnaeus, *Species Plantarum* 1: 141. 1753.
"Habitat inter Austriae segetes." RCN: 1144.
Lectotype (Ali in Ali & Jafri, *Fl. Libya* 1: 8. 1976): Herb. Linn. No.
197.1 (LINN).
Current name: ***Androsace maxima*** L. (Primulaceae).
Note: This was treated as the generitype of *Androsace* by Britton &
Brown, *Ill. Fl. N. U. S.,* ed. 2, 3: 709. 1913 (see McNeill & al. in
Taxon 36: 358. 1987). However, under Art. 10.5, Ex. 7 (a voted
example) of the Vienna Code, this is a type choice made under the
American Code and is to be replaced under Art. 10.5b by
Hitchcock's choice (*Prop. Brit. Bot.*: 128. 1929) of *A. septentrionalis*
L.

Androsace scabra Linnaeus, *Mantissa Plantarum Altera*: 335. 1771.
RCN: 1149.
Type not designated.
Original material: none traced.
Note: The application of this name appears uncertain.

Androsace septentrionalis Linnaeus, *Species Plantarum* 1: 142. 1753.
"Habitat in alpibus Lapponiae, Russiae apricis glareosis." RCN: 1146.
Lectotype (Nasir in Nasir & Ali, *Fl. Pakistan* 157: 75. 1984): Herb.
Linn. No. 197.4 (LINN).
Generitype of *Androsace* Linnaeus (vide Hitchcock, *Prop. Brit. Bot.*:
128. 1929).
Current name: ***Androsace septentrionalis*** L. (Primulaceae).

Note: Androsace maxima L. was treated as the generitype of *Androsace*
by Britton & Brown, *Ill. Fl. N. U. S.,* ed. 2, 3: 709. 1913 (see
McNeill & al. in *Taxon* 36: 358. 1987). However, under Art. 10.5,
Ex. 7 (a voted example) of the Vienna Code, this is a type choice
made under the American Code and is to be replaced under Art.
10.5b by Hitchcock's choice (*Prop. Brit. Bot.*: 128. 1929) of *A.
septentrionalis* L.

Androsace villosa Linnaeus, *Species Plantarum* 1: 142. 1753.
"Habitat in alpibus Rheticis, Pyrenaeis." RCN: 1147.
Type not designated.
Original material: *Gmelin,* Herb. Linn. No. 197.6 (LINN); Herb.
Burser XVI(1): 72 (UPS); *Le Monnier,* Herb. Linn. No. 197.5
(LINN); [icon] in Clusius, Rar. Pl. Hist. 2: 62. 1601.
Current name: ***Androsace villosa*** L. (Primulaceae).

Andryala integrifolia Linnaeus, *Species Plantarum* 2: 808. 1753.
"Habitat in Gallia, Sicilia." RCN: 5894.
Lectotype (House in Jarvis & al., *Regnum Veg.* 127: 18. 1993): Herb.
Burser VI: 57 (UPS).
Generitype of *Andryala* Linnaeus (vide Green, *Prop. Brit. Bot.*: 178.
1929).
Current name: ***Andryala integrifolia*** L. (Asteraceae).

Andryala integrifolia Linnaeus var. **sinuata** (Linnaeus) Linnaeus,
Systema Naturae, ed. 12, 2: 525. 1767.
["Habitat Monspelii, inque Sicilia."] Sp. Pl. 2: 808. 1753. RCN:
5894.
Basionym: *Andryala sinuata* L. (1753).
Lectotype (House in Jarvis & Turland in *Taxon* 47: 351. 1998): Herb.
Clifford: 387, *Andryala* 1 (BM-000646869).
Current name: ***Andryala integrifolia*** L. (Asteraceae).

Andryala lanata Linnaeus, *Systema Naturae,* ed. 10, 2: 1196. 1759,
nom. illeg.
RCN: 5896.
Replaced synonym: *Hieracium tomentosum* L. (1755).
Type not designated.
Original material: as replaced synonym.
Current name: ***Hieracium tomentosum*** L. (Asteraceae).
Note: An illegitimate renaming of *Hieracium tomentosum* L. (1755), as
noted by Nordenstam (in *Bot. Not.* 114: 277. 1961). Although also
published in a revised version of the original thesis in *Amoen. Acad.*
4: 288 (Nov 1759), *A. lanata* was first published some months
earlier in *Syst. Nat.,* ed. 10, 2: 1196 (May–Jun 1759).

Andryala ragusina Linnaeus, *Species Plantarum,* ed. 2, 2: 1136. 1763.
"Habitat in insulis Archipelagi." RCN: 5895.
Lectotype (House in Jarvis & Turland in *Taxon* 47: 351. 1998): Herb.
Linn. No. 956.4 (LINN).
Current name: ***Andryala ragusina*** L. var. ***ragusina*** (Asteraceae).

Andryala sinuata Linnaeus, *Species Plantarum* 2: 808. 1753.
"Habitat Monspelii, inque Sicilia." RCN: 5894.
Basionym of: *Andryala integrifolia* L. var. *sinuata* (L.) L. (1767).
Lectotype (House in Jarvis & Turland in *Taxon* 47: 351. 1998): Herb.
Clifford: 387, *Andryala* 1 (BM-000646869).
Current name: ***Andryala integrifolia*** L. (Asteraceae).

Anemone alpina Linnaeus, *Species Plantarum* 1: 539. 1753.
"Habitat in Alpibus Styriacis, Helveticis." RCN: 4006.
Type not designated.
Original material: Herb. Burser IX: 81, syntype (UPS); Herb. Burser
IX: 80, syntype (UPS); [icon] in Plantin, Pl. Stirp. Icon.: 282.
1581; [icon] in Clusius, Rar. Pl. Hist. 1: 244, 245. 1601.

Current name: ***Anemone alpina*** L. subsp. ***alpina*** (Ranunculaceae).
Note: Aichele & Schwegler (in *Feddes Repert.* 60: 40, t. II,1. 1957) designated a neotype, but as original material is in existence, their choice is contrary to Art. 9.10 and 9.11.

Anemone apennina Linnaeus, *Species Plantarum* 1: 541. 1753.
"Habitat in Apenninis, Anglia." RCN: 4019.
Lectotype (Jonsell & Jarvis in *Nordic J. Bot.* 14: 160. 1994): [icon] *"Ranunculus nemorosus fl. caeruleo duplex Apennini montis"* in Mentzel, Ind. Nom. Pl.: 257, t. 8. 1682.
Current name: ***Anemone apennina*** L. (Ranunculaceae).

Anemone baldensis Linnaeus, *Systema Naturae,* ed. 12, 2: 375; *Mantissa Plantarum*: 78. 1767.
"Habitat in Baldo." RCN: 4002.
Lectotype (Baldini in Jarvis & al. in *Taxon* 54: 468. 2005): Italy. "Venetia, Prov. Verona, M. Baldo ad la Colona delle Busete, sol. calc., 2,000m, 2 Jul 1913", *G. Rigo s.n.* (BM).
Current name: ***Anemone baldensis*** L. (Ranunculaceae).

Anemone canadensis Linnaeus, *Systema Naturae,* ed. 12, 3: 231. 1768.
"Habitat in Pensylvania. D. Hope." RCN: 4014.
Neotype (Reveal & al. in *Bartonia* 57: 29. 1992): Herb. Linn. No. 710.22 (LINN).
Current name: ***Anemone canadensis*** L. (Ranunculaceae).

Anemone coronaria Linnaeus, *Species Plantarum* 1: 539. 1753, *typ. cons.*
"Habitat in Oriente, Constantinopoli allata." RCN: 4007.
Conserved type (Qaiser in Ali & El-Gadi, *Fl. Libya* 108: 7. 1984): Herb. Linn. No. 710.9 (LINN).
Generitype of *Anemone* Linnaeus, *nom. cons.*
Current name: ***Anemone coronaria*** L. (Ranunculaceae).
Note: Anemone coronaria, with the type designated by Qaiser, was proposed as conserved type of the genus by Jarvis (in *Taxon* 41: 557. 1992). This was eventually approved by the General Committee (see review of the history of this proposal by Barrie, *l.c.* 55: 795–796. 2006).

Anemone dichotoma Linnaeus, *Species Plantarum* 1: 540. 1753.
"Habitat in Canada, Sibiria." RCN: 4015.
Lectotype (Britton in *Ann. New York Acad. Sci.* 6: 228. 1891): Herb. Linn. No. 710.23 (LINN).
Current name: ***Anemone dichotoma*** L. (Ranunculaceae).
Note: See discussion of other choices of type by Reveal & al. (in *Bartonia* 57: 28. 1992).

Anemone fasciculata Linnaeus, *Species Plantarum* 1: 542. 1753.
"Habitat in Oriente." RCN: 4022.
Lectotype (Dutton & al. in *Taxon* 44: 422. 1995): [icon] *"Ranunculus Orientalis, Aconiti Lycoctoni folio, flore magno albo"* in Tournefort, Rel. Voy. Levant (Paris ed.) 2: 245. 1717 (see p. 164).
Current name: ***Anemone narcissiflora*** L. (Ranunculaceae).

Anemone hepatica Linnaeus, *Species Plantarum* 1: 538. 1753.
"Habitat in Europae nemoribus lapidosis." RCN: 3999.
Lectotype (Jonsell & Jarvis in *Nordic J. Bot.* 14: 160. 1994): Herb. Linn. No. 710.1 (LINN).
Current name: ***Anemone hepatica*** L. (Ranunculaceae).
Note: Although Britton (in *Ann. New York Acad. Sci.* 6: 234. 1891) indicated as type "a European plant in the Linnaean herbarium", this does not distinguish between sheets 710.1 and 710.2 which are evidently not part of a single gathering so Art. 9.15 does not apply.

Anemone hortensis Linnaeus, *Species Plantarum* 1: 540. 1753.
"Habitat in Rhenum & in Italia." RCN: 4008.
Lectotype (Strid in Jarvis & al. in *Taxon* 54: 469. 2005): Herb. Clifford: 224, *Pulsatilla* 4, sheet A (BM-000628826).
Current name: ***Anemone hortensis*** L. subsp. ***hortensis*** (Ranunculaceae).

Anemone malvifolia Linnaeus, *Species Plantarum* 2: 1197. 1753.
"Habitat in Hispania ad vias." RCN: 4009.
Type not designated.
Original material: Herb. Burser IX: 59 (UPS); [icon] in Clusius, Rar. Pl. Hist. 1: 248. 1601.
Current name: ***Anemone palmata*** L. (Ranunculaceae).

Anemone narcissiflora Linnaeus, *Species Plantarum* 1: 542. 1753, *nom. & orth. cons.*
"Habitat in Alpibus Austriae, Helvetiae, Sibiriae." RCN: 4021.
Lectotype (Dutton & al. in *Taxon* 44: 421. 1995): Herb. Linn. No. 710.31 (LINN).
Current name: ***Anemone narcissiflora*** L. (Ranunculaceae).
Note: Although Britton (in *Ann. New York Acad. Sci.* 6: 234. 1891) indicated a type in LINN, he did not distinguish between the several sheets there associated with this name. They are evidently not part of a single gathering so Art. 9.15 does not apply. Skalický (in *Novit. Bot. Univ. Carol.* 2: 101–110. 1985) discussed the name and original material but did not designate a type, and Luferov (in *Byull. Glavn. Bot. Sada* 183: 84. 2002) wrongly indicated a Tournefort plate (which was not cited in the protologue) as lectotype. The epithet first appeared as "uarcissifolia" but has been conserved as "narcissiflora".

Anemone nemorosa Linnaeus, *Species Plantarum* 1: 541. 1753.
"Habitat in Europae asperis, duris, nemoribus." RCN: 4018.
Lectotype (Sell in Reveal & al. in *Bartonia* 57: 30. 1992): Herb. Clifford: 224, *Anemone* 3 (BM-000628830).
Current name: ***Anemone nemorosa*** L. (Ranunculaceae).

Anemone palmata Linnaeus, *Species Plantarum* 1: 538. 1753.
"Habitat in Lusitania ad Tagum." RCN: 4009.
Type not designated.
Original material: Herb. Burser IX: 59 (UPS); Herb. Linn. No. 710.16 (LINN); [icon] in Clusius, Rar. Pl. Hist. 1: 248. 1601; [icon] in Morison, Pl. Hist. Univ. 2: 425, s. 4, t. 25, f. 3. 1680.
Current name: ***Anemone palmata*** L. (Ranunculaceae).

Anemone patens Linnaeus, *Species Plantarum* 1: 538. 1753.
"Habitat in Toboliko Sibiriae, Lusatiae inferiore." RCN: 4000.
Lectotype (Jonsell & Jarvis in *Nordic J. Bot.* 14: 160. 1994): Herb. Burser IX: 93 (UPS).
Current name: ***Anemone patens*** L. (Ranunculaceae).
Note: Skalický (in *Preslia* 25: 141. 1985) rejected the neotypification of Aichele & Schwegler (in *Feddes Repert.* 60: 72. 1957) and provided a detailed discussion of the protologue and original elements. He concluded that the Amman element and Herb. Linn. 710.3 (LINN) should be excluded, and suggested that a different neotype, either from northern Poland (cf. the Breyn element) or from Lausitz (the Bauhin element), should be designated. However, as original elements are in existence, a neotype cannot be chosen, and Jonsell & Jarvis' choice of the Burser material (which was not considered by Skalický) as lectotype is accepted here.

Anemone pensylvanica Linnaeus, *Mantissa Plantarum Altera*: 247. 1771.
"Habitat in Canada." RCN: 4014.
Neotype (Reveal & al. in *Bartonia* 57: 29. 1992): Herb. Linn. No. 710.22 (LINN).

Current name: ***Anemone canadensis*** L. (Ranunculaceae).
Note: Through typification, this name is homotypic with *A. canadensis* L. and falls into its synonymy.

Anemone pratensis Linnaeus, *Species Plantarum* 1: 539. 1753.
"Habitat in Scaniae, Germaniae campis pratensibus apricis aridis." RCN: 4005.
Lectotype (Jonsell & Jarvis in *Nordic J. Bot.* 14: 160. 1994): Herb. Linn. No. 710. 6 (LINN).
Current name: ***Anemone pratensis*** L. (Ranunculaceae).

Anemone pulsatilla Linnaeus, *Species Plantarum* 1: 539. 1753.
"Habitat in campis sylvestribus exaridis collibusque apricis Europae borealis." RCN: 4004.

Lectotype (Sell in Jarvis & al. in *Taxon* 54: 469. 2005): Herb. Linn. No. 710.5 (LINN).
Current name: ***Anemone pulsatilla*** L. (Ranunculaceae).
Note: Sprague (in *J. Linn. Soc., Bot.* 48: 90. 1928) argued that a Brunfels illustration, which was not cited in the protologue, should be the type and Aichele & Schwegler (in *Feddes Repert.* 60: 199. 1957) designated a neotype (illustrated as t. XXIX, f. 1). Neither choice can be accepted because original material is in existence.

Anemone quinquefolia Linnaeus, *Species Plantarum* 1: 541. 1753.
"Habitat in Virginia, Canada. Kalm." RCN: 4017.
Lectotype (Reveal & al. in *Bartonia* 57: 29. 1992): [icon] *"Ranunculus Nemorum Fragariae foliis Virginianus"* in Plukenet, Phytographia: t. 106, f. 3. 1691; Almag. Bot.: 310. 1696.
Current name: ***Anemone quinquefolia*** L. (Ranunculaceae).

Anemone ranunculoides Linnaeus, *Species Plantarum* 1: 541. 1753.
"Habitat in Europae borealis pratis nemorosis." RCN: 4020.
Lectotype (Jonsell & Jarvis in *Nordic J. Bot.* 14: 160. 1994): Herb. Linn. No. 710.30 (LINN).
Current name: ***Anemone ranunculoides*** L. (Ranunculaceae).

Anemone sibirica Linnaeus, *Species Plantarum* 1: 541. 1753.
"Habitat in Sibiria. D. Gmelin." RCN: 4010.
Lectotype (Yuzepchuk in Komarov, *Fl. U.R.S.S.* 7: 279. 1937): *Steller*, Herb. Linn. No. 710.17 (LINN).
Current name: ***Anemone sibirica*** L. (Ranunculaceae).

Anemone sulphurea Linnaeus, *Systema Naturae*, ed. 12, 2: 375; *Mantissa Plantarum*: 78. 1767.
"Habitat in Helvetia." RCN: 4001.
Type not designated.
Original material: [icon] in Mattioli, Pl. Epit.: 393. 1586; [icon] in Haller, Enum. Meth. Stirp. Helv. 1: 332, t. 6. 1742.
Current name: ***Pulsatilla vernalis*** (L.) Mill. subsp. ***vernalis*** var. ***alpestris*** Aichele & Schwegler (Ranunculaceae).
Note: Aichele & Schwegler (in *Feddes Repert.* 60: 50. 1957) provided some nomenclatural notes but did not typify the name.

Anemone sylvestris Linnaeus, *Species Plantarum* 1: 540. 1753.
"Habitat in Germania." RCN: 4011.
Lectotype (Jonsell & Jarvis in *Nordic J. Bot.* 14: 160. 1994): Herb. Clifford: 224, *Anemone* 1 (BM-000628828).
Current name: ***Anemone sylvestris*** L. (Ranunculaceae).

Anemone thalictroides Linnaeus, *Species Plantarum* 1: 542. 1753.
"Habitat in Virginia, Canada." RCN: 4023.
Lectotype (Britton in *Ann. New York Acad. Sci.* 6: 238. 1891): *Kalm*, Herb. Linn. No. 710.35 (LINN; iso- UPS).
Current name: ***Anemonella thalictroides*** (L.) Spach (Ranunculaceae).

Anemone trifolia Linnaeus, *Species Plantarum* 1: 540. 1753.
"Habitat in Gallia." RCN: 4016.
Lectotype (Britton in *Ann. New York Acad. Sci.* 6: 226. 1891): Herb. Linn. No. 710.24 (LINN).
Current name: ***Anemone trifolia*** L. (Ranunculaceae).
Note: Ubaldi & Puppi (in *Candollea* 44: 141. 1989) provided a detailed discussion and designated a Clifford sheet as lectotype, but this choice post-dates that of Britton, based on material in LINN.

Anemone vernalis Linnaeus, *Species Plantarum* 1: 538. 1753.
"Habitat in Sueciae, Helvetiae sylvis sterilissimis." RCN: 4003.
Lectotype (Jonsell & Jarvis in *Nordic J. Bot.* 14: 160. 1994): Herb. Linn. No. 710.4 (LINN).
Current name: ***Pulsatilla vernalis*** (L.) Mill. (Ranunculaceae).

Anemone virginiana Linnaeus, *Species Plantarum* 1: 540. 1753.
"Habitat in Virginia." RCN: 4012.
Lectotype (Britton in *Ann. New York Acad. Sci.* 6: 223. 1891): Herb. Linn. No. 710.19 (LINN).
Current name: ***Anemone virginiana*** L. (Ranunculaceae).
Note: See discussion by Reveal & al. (in *Bartonia* 57: 31. 1992).

Anethum foeniculum Linnaeus, *Species Plantarum* 1: 263. 1753.
"Habitat in Narbonae, Aremoriae, Maderae rupibus cretaceis." RCN: 2100.
Lectotype (Jansen, *Spices, Condiments Med. Pl. Ethiopia*: 25. 1981): Herb. Clifford: 106, *Anethum* 2 β (BM-000558385).
Current name: ***Foeniculum vulgare*** Mill. (Apiaceae).

Anethum graveolens Linnaeus, *Species Plantarum* 1: 263. 1753. "Habitat inter Lusitaniae & Hispaniae segetes." RCN: 2098.
Lectotype (Jansen, *Spices, Condiments Med. Pl. Ethiopia*: 34. 1981): Herb. Linn. No. 371.1 (LINN).
Generitype of *Anethum* Linnaeus (vide Hitchcock, *Prop. Brit. Bot.*: 141. 1929).
Current name: ***Anethum graveolens*** L. (Apiaceae).
Note: Although Tardieu-Blot (in Aubréville, *Fl. Cambodge Laos Vietnam* 5: 29. 1967) stated "TYPE: herb. Linné, Hort. Ups. 66", no herbarium is explicitly indicated, and a sheet in LINN shows no link with the *Hortus Upsaliensis*. Consequently, this statement is not accepted as a valid typification, and Jansen is accepted as the typifier.

Anethum segetum Linnaeus, *Mantissa Plantarum Altera*: 219. 1771. "Habitat in Lusitania. D. Vandelli." RCN: 2099.
Neotype (Reduron in Jarvis & al. in *Taxon* 55: 208. 2006): "*Anethum segetum* Grisley, foetidum; *Anethum segetum*. V. Lusit. / *Foeniculum lusitanicum*, minus, annuum, *Anethi odore* I. r. h. 312", Herb. Vaillant (P).
Current name: ***Anethum graveolens*** L. (Apiaceae).

Angelica archangelica Linnaeus, *Species Plantarum* 1: 250. 1753. "Habitat in Alpibus Lapponiae, ad rivulos." RCN: 2016.
Lectotype (Reduron in Jonsell & Jarvis in *Nordic J. Bot.* 22: 83. 2002): Herb. Linn. No. 354.1 (LINN).
Current name: ***Angelica archangelica*** L. (Apiaceae).

Angelica atropurpurea Linnaeus, *Species Plantarum* 1: 251. 1753. "Habitat in Canada." RCN: 2019.
Lectotype (Reveal in Jarvis & al. in *Taxon* 55: 209. 2006): [icon] "*Angelica atropurpurea Canadensis*" in Cornut, Canad. Pl. Hist.: 198, 199. 1635. – Epitype (Reveal in Jarvis & al. in *Taxon* 55: 209. 2006): Canada. London, Ontario, low grounds, 31 Jul 1882 (fr.), *Burgess 871* (BM).
Current name: ***Angelica atropurpurea*** L. (Apiaceae).

Angelica lucida Linnaeus, *Species Plantarum* 1: 251. 1753. "Habitat in Canada." RCN: 2020.
Lectotype (Reveal in Jarvis & al. in *Taxon* 55: 209. 2006): Herb. Clifford: 97, *Angelica* 3 (BM-000558299).
Current name: ***Angelica lucida*** L. (Apiaceae).

Angelica sylvestris Linnaeus, *Species Plantarum* 1: 251. 1753. "Habitat in Europae frigidioris subhumidis sylvaticis." RCN: 2017.
Lectotype (Gutiérrez Bustillo in *Lazaroa* 3: 146. 1981): Herb. Linn. No. 354.3 (LINN).
Generitype of *Angelica* Linnaeus (vide Hitchcock, *Prop. Brit. Bot.*: 140. 1929).
Current name: ***Angelica sylvestris*** L. (Apiaceae).
Note: *Angelica sylvestris*, with Herb. Clifford: 97, *Angelica* 2 (BM) as the type, was proposed as conserved type of the genus by Reduron & Jarvis (in *Taxon* 41: 557. 1992). However, the proposal was eventually ruled unnecessary by the General Committee (see Barrie, *l.c.* 55: 795–796. 2006 for a review of the history of this and related proposals). When Reduron & Jarvis (*l.c.* 41: 557. 1992) proposed the Clifford sheet as a conserved type, they were unaware of the earlier typification made by Gutiérrez Bustillo (1981) based on 354.3 (LINN). Unfortunately, this specimen is identifiable as *A. montana* Brot. (sometimes recognised as a subspecies of *A. sylvestris*). With the failure of the generitype proposal, the type of *A. sylvestris* is now 354.3 (LINN). While Art. 57 provides some protection to the usage of *A. sylvestris* in its traditional sense, it seems that a proposal for its conservation with a conserved type is now necessary.

Angelica verticillaris Linnaeus, *Mantissa Plantarum Altera*: 217. 1771. "Habitat in Italia?" RCN: 2018.
Lectotype (Reduron & al. in Jarvis & al. in *Taxon* 55: 209. 2006): Herb. Linn. No. 354.6 (LINN).
Current name: ***Tommasinia verticillare*** (L.) Bertol. (Apiaceae).

Anguria lobata Linnaeus, *Plantae Surinamenses*: 15. 1775. "Habitat [in Surinamo.]" RCN: 7037.
Lectotype (Pruski in *Brittonia* 51: 329, f. 1. 1999): *Dahlberg s.n.*, Herb. Linn. No. 1092.2 (LINN).
Current name: ***Gurania lobata*** (L.) Pruski (Cucurbitaceae).

Anguria trifoliata Linnaeus, *Species Plantarum*, ed. 2, 2: 1376. 1763. "Habitat in Domingo." RCN: 7039.
Type not designated.
Original material: [icon] in Plumier, Descr. Pl. Amér.: 85, t. 99. 1693.
Current name: ***Psiguria trifoliata*** (L.) Alain (Cucurbitaceae).

Annona africana Linnaeus, *Species Plantarum* 1: 537. 1753. "Habitat in Aethiopia." RCN: 3996.
Type not designated.
Original material: none traced.
Note: The application of this name appears uncertain.

Annona asiatica Linnaeus, *Species Plantarum* 1: 537. 1753. "Habitat in Zeylona." RCN: 3995.
Lectotype (designated here by Rainer): Herb. Hermann 5: 74, No. 225 [icon] (BM).
Current name: ***Annona squamosa*** L. (Annonaceae).

Annona glabra Linnaeus, *Species Plantarum* 1: 537. 1753. "Habitat in Carolina." RCN: 3993.
Lectotype (Dandy, *Sloane Herbarium*: 112. 1958): [icon] "*Anona maxima, foliis latis fructu maximo luteo conoide, cortice glabro*" in Catesby, Nat. Hist. Carolina 2: 64, t. 64. 1738.
Current name: ***Annona glabra*** L. (Annonaceae).

Annona muricata Linnaeus, *Species Plantarum* 1: 536. 1753. "Habitat in America calidiore." RCN: 3989.
Lectotype (Khatoon in Nasir & Ali, *Fl. Pakistan* 167: 11. 1985): [icon] "*Anona maxima, foliis latis splendentibus, fructo maximo viridi conoide, tuberculis seu spinulis innocentibus aspero*" in Sloane, Voy. Jamaica 2: 166, t. 225. 1725. – Typotype: Herb. Sloane 7: 90 (BM-SL).
Generitype of *Annona* Linnaeus (vide Green, *Prop. Brit. Bot.*: 163. 1929).
Current name: ***Annona muricata*** L. (Annonaceae).
Note: Le Thomas (in Aubréville, *Fl. Gabon* 16: 324. 1969) indicated unspecified material in LINN as the type. However, she did not distinguish between the four sheets (708.1–708.4) there associated with this name, none of which in any case appears to be original material for the name.

Annona palustris Linnaeus, *Species Plantarum*, ed. 2, 1: 757. 1762. "Habitat in America ad aquas." RCN: 3992.
Lectotype (designated here by Rainer): [icon] "*Anonae aquaticae foliis laurinis atrovirentibus, fructu minore conoide, luteo, cortice glabro in areolas distincto, semina*" in Sloane, Voy. Jamaica 2: 169, t. 228, f. 1. 1725. – Typotype: Herb. Sloane 7: 99 (BM-SL).
Current name: ***Annona glabra*** L. (Annonaceae).

Annona reticulata Linnaeus, *Species Plantarum* 1: 537. 1753. "Habitat in America meridionali." RCN: 3991.
Lectotype (designated here by Rainer): [icon] "*Anona maxima, foliis oblongis angustis, fructu maximo luteo conoide, cortice glabro in areolas*

distincto" in Sloane, *Voy. Jamaica* 2: 167, t. 226. 1725. – Typotype: Herb. Sloane 7: 95 (BM-SL).
Current name: ***Annona reticulata*** L. (Annonaceae).
Note: Fawcett & Rendle (*Fl. Jamaica* 3: 198. 1914) indicated unspecified material in BM as the type but any material in Herb. Sloane would not have been seen by Linnaeus and is not original material for the name. Although Le Thomas (in Aubréville, *Fl. Gabon* 16: 327. 1969) indicated unspecified material in LINN as the type, there does not appear to be any material there associated with this name.

Annona squamosa Linnaeus, *Species Plantarum* 1: 537. 1753.
"Habitat in America meridionali." RCN: 3990.
Lectotype (designated here by Rainer): [icon] *"Anona, foliis odoratis minoribus, fructu conoide squammoso parvo dulci"* in Sloane, Voy. Jamaica 2: 168, t. 227, excl. leaves/branch. 1725. – Typotype: Herb. Sloane 7: 96 (BM-SL).
Current name: ***Annona squamosa*** L. (Annonaceae).
Note: Although Fawcett & Rendle (*Fl. Jamaica* 3: 197. 1914) and later authors including Keraudren-Aymonin (in Bosser & al., *Fl. Mascareignes* 34: 2. 1980) treated material in Herb. Sloane as type, this would not have been seen by Linnaeus and is not original material for the name. Le Thomas (in Aubréville, *Fl. Gabon* 16: 325. 1969) indicated unspecified material in LINN as the type but the only sheet there associated with this name (708.6) lacks the relevant *Species Plantarum* number (i.e. "3") and was a post-1753 addition to the herbarium, and is also not original material for the name. Smith (*Fl. Vitiensis Nova* 2: 40. 1981) suggested that the cited Sloane plate would perhaps be the most suitable choice of type and this is now formalised here.

Annona triloba Linnaeus, *Species Plantarum* 1: 537. 1753.
"Habitat in Carolina." RCN: 3994.

Lectotype (Dandy, *Sloane Herbarium*: 112. 1958): [icon] *"Anona fructu lutescente, laevi, scrotum Arietis referente"* in Catesby, Nat. Hist. Carolina 2: 85, t. 85. 1743.
Current name: ***Asimina triloba*** (L.) Dunal (Annonaceae).

Anthemis afra Linnaeus, *Systema Naturae,* ed. 10, 2: 1223. 1759.
RCN: 6570.
Lectotype (Bremer in *Bot. Not.* 125: 30. 1972): Herb. Linn. No. 1029.3 (LINN).
Current name: ***Osmitopsis afra*** (L.) K. Bremer (Asteraceae).

Anthemis alpina Linnaeus, *Centuria II Plantarum*: 31. 1756.
"Habitat in alpibus Tyroli, Baldo. Seguier." RCN: 6478.
Lectotype (Vetschera in Jarvis & Turland in *Taxon* 47: 352. 1998): Herb. Linn. No. 1016.12 (LINN).
Current name: ***Achillea oxyloba*** (DC.) Sch. Bip. (Asteraceae).

Anthemis altissima Linnaeus, *Species Plantarum* 2: 893. 1753.
"Habitat in Italiae, Hispaniae, G. Narbonensis agris. D. Sauvages." RCN: 6472.
Lectotype (Humphries in Jarvis & Turland in *Taxon* 47: 352. 1998): *Magnol*, Herb. Linn. No. 1016.2 (LINN).
Current name: ***Cota altissima*** (L.) J. Gay (Asteraceae).
Note: Although Iranshahr (in Rechinger, *Fl. Iranica* 158: 23. 1986) indicated 1016.3 (LINN) as "typus", this material lacks a *Species Plantarum* number (i.e. "2") and is a later addition to the herbarium, and not original material for the name. Recognising this, Humphries designated a different collection at LINN as lectotype.

Anthemis americana Linnaeus, *Species Plantarum* 2: 895. 1753.
"Habitat in Jamaicae, Caribaearum pratis humidiusculis." RCN: 6487.
Replaced synonym of: *Verbesina mutica* L. (1763), *nom. illeg.*
Lectotype (D'Arcy in Woodson & Schery in *Ann. Missouri Bot. Gard.* 62: 1184. 1975): Herb. Clifford: 414, *Buphthalmum* 5 (BM-000647176).
Current name: ***Chrysanthellum americanum*** (L.) Vatke (Asteraceae).

Anthemis arabica Linnaeus, *Species Plantarum* 2: 896. 1753.
"Habitat in Arabia." RCN: 6489.
Lectotype (Stearn, *Introd. Linnaeus' Sp. Pl.* (Ray Soc. ed.): 47. 1957): [icon] *"Buphthalmum caule decomposita, calycibus ramiferis"* in Linnaeus, Hort. Cliff.: 413, t. 24. 1738.
Current name: ***Cladanthus arabicus*** (L.) Cass. (Asteraceae).
Note: Humphries (in *Taxon* 47: 352. 1998) designated 1016.24 (LINN) as type but this choice is pre-dated by that of Stearn.

Anthemis arvensis Linnaeus, *Species Plantarum* 2: 894. 1753.
"Habitat in Europae, praesertim Sueciae agris." RCN: 6481.
Lectotype (Fernandes in *Anales Inst. Bot. Cavanilles* 32: 1472. 1975): Herb. Linn. No. 1016.15 (LINN).
Generitype of *Anthemis* Linnaeus (vide Green, *Prop. Brit. Bot.*: 182. 1929).
Current name: ***Anthemis arvensis*** L. (Asteraceae).
Note: Anthemis maritima was treated as the generitype of *Anthemis* by Britton & Brown, *Ill. Fl. N. U. S.*, ed. 2, 3: 516. 1913 (see McNeill & al. in *Taxon* 36: 359. 1987). However, under Art. 10.5, Ex. 7 (a voted example) of the Vienna Code, this is a type choice made under the American Code and is to be replaced under Art. 10.5b by Green's choice (*Prop. Brit. Bot.*: 182. 1929) of *A. arvensis* L. See extensive discussion of Green's generitype choice by Oberprieler (in *Bocconea* 9: 107. 1998), which he adopts.

Anthemis bellidiastrum Linnaeus, *Systema Naturae*, ed. 10, 2: 1223. 1759, *nom. illeg.*
["Habitat in Aethiopia. Burmannus."] Cent. II Pl.: 31. 1756. RCN: 6568.
Replaced synonym: *Anthemis fruticosa* L. (1756).
Replaced synonym of: *Osmites bellidiastrum* L. (1760), *nom. inval.*
Lectotype (Bremer in *Taxon* 25: 207. 1976): Herb. Linn. No. 1029.1 (LINN).
Current name: ***Relhania fruticosa*** (L.) K. Bremer (Asteraceae).
Note: An illegitimate replacement name for *Anthemis fruticosa* L. (1756).

Anthemis chia Linnaeus, *Species Plantarum* 2: 894. 1753.
"Habitat in Chio." RCN: 6479.
Lectotype (Grierson & Yavin in Davis, *Fl. Turkey* 5: 207. 1975): Herb. Clifford: 415, *Anthemis* 4 (BM-000647189).
Current name: ***Anthemis chia*** L. (Asteraceae).
Note: See also Fernandes (in *Revista Biol. (Lisbon)* 12: 413. 1984).

Anthemis cota Linnaeus, *Species Plantarum* 2: 893. 1753.
"Habitat in Italiae arvis." RCN: 6471.
Lectotype (Humphries in Jarvis & Turland in *Taxon* 47: 352. 1998): [icon] *"Chamaemelum annuum flore maximo capitulis spinosis"* in Morison, Pl. Hist. Univ. 3: 36, s. 6, t. 8, f. 11. 1699.
Current name: ***Cota altissima*** (L.) J. Gay (Asteraceae).

Anthemis cotula Linnaeus, *Species Plantarum* 2: 894. 1753.
"Habitat in Europae ruderatis, praecipue in Ucrania." RCN: 6482.
Lectotype (Yavin in *Israel J. Bot.* 19: 145. 1970): *Gerber*, Herb. Linn. No. 1016.16 (LINN).
Current name: ***Anthemis cotula*** L. (Asteraceae).
Note: Fernandes (in *Revista Biol. (Lisbon)* 12: 410. 1983) gives an extensive discussion on the original material for this name.

Anthemis cretica Linnaeus, *Species Plantarum* 2: 895. 1753.
"Habitat in Creta?" RCN: 6483.
Replaced synonym of: *Anthemis montana* L. (1763), *nom. illeg.*
Lectotype (Grierson & Yavin in Davis in *Notes Roy. Bot. Gard. Edinburgh* 33: 212. 1974): Herb. Clifford: 415, *Anthemis* 2 (BM-000647187).
Current name: ***Anthemis cretica*** L. (Asteraceae).
Note: Fernandes (in *Anales Inst. Bot. Cavanilles* 32: 1433. 1975) independently made the same type choice as Grierson & Yavin, and also illustrated this Clifford sheet (as t. 8).

Anthemis fruticosa Linnaeus, *Centuria II Plantarum*: 31. 1756.
"Habitat in Aethiopia. Burmannus." RCN: 6568.
Replaced synonym of: *Anthemis bellidiastrum* L. (1759), *nom. illeg.*; *Osmites bellidiastrum* L. (1760), *nom. inval.*
Lectotype (Bremer in *Taxon* 25: 207. 1976): Herb. Linn. No. 1029.1 (LINN).
Current name: ***Relhania fruticosa*** (L.) K. Bremer (Asteraceae).

Anthemis italica Linnaeus, *Systema Naturae*, ed. 10, 2: 1223. 1759.
RCN: 6473.
Type not designated.
Original material: none traced.
Note: The name is not in use and there appear to be no extant original elements.

Anthemis leucantha Linnaeus, *Plantae Rariores Africanae*: 23. 1760.
["Habitat ad Cap. b. Spei."] Sp. Pl. ed. 2, 2: 1261 (1763). RCN: 6569.
Basionym of: *Osmites camphorina* L. var. *leucantha* (L.) L. (1771).

Lectotype (Bremer in *Bot. Not.* 125: 30. 1972): Herb. Linn. No. 1029.3 (LINN).
Current name: ***Osmitopsis afra*** (L.) K. Bremer (Asteraceae).

Anthemis maritima Linnaeus, *Species Plantarum* 2: 893. 1753.
"Habitat Monspelii, inque Italia." RCN: 6474.
Lectotype (Fernandes in *Anales Inst. Bot. Cavanilles* 32: 1460. 1975): Herb. Burser VII(1): 18 (UPS).
Current name: ***Anthemis maritima*** L. (Asteraceae).
Note: This was treated as the generitype of *Anthemis* by Britton & Brown, *Ill. Fl. N. U. S.*, ed. 2, 3: 516. 1913 (see McNeill & al. in *Taxon* 36: 359. 1987). However, under Art. 10.5, Ex. 7 (a voted example) of the Vienna Code, this is a type choice made under the American Code and is to be replaced under Art. 10.5b by Green's choice (*Prop. Brit. Bot.*: 182. 1929) of *A. arvensis* L. See extensive discussion of Green's generitype choice by Oberprieler (in *Bocconea* 9: 107. 1998), which he adopts.
  Humphries (in Jarvis & al., *Regnum Veg.* 127: 19. 1993) independently chose the same type as Fernandes.

Anthemis millefolia Linnaeus, *Species Plantarum* 2: 896. 1753.
"Habitat in Sibiria." RCN: 6446.
Replaced synonym of: *Chrysanthemum millefoliatum* L. (1767), *nom. illeg.*
Lectotype (Humphries in Jarvis & Turland in *Taxon* 47: 352. 1998): *Gerber*, Herb. Linn. No. 1012.22 (LINN).
Current name: ***Tanacetum millefolium*** (L.) Tzvelev (Asteraceae).
Note: Although Tzvelev (in Schischkin & Bobrov, *Fl. U.R.S.S.* 26: 349. 1961) stated that the cited Gmelin drawing was "probably" the type specimen, this is not accepted as a formal type choice (Art. 7.11).

Anthemis mixta Linnaeus, *Species Plantarum* 2: 894. 1753.
"Habitat in Italia, Gallia." RCN: 6477.
Lectotype (Humphries in Jarvis & Turland in *Taxon* 47: 352. 1998): [icon] *"Anthemis maritima, lanuginosa, annua, foliis crassis, Pyrethri sapore, semiflosculis albis, juxta discum luteis"* in Micheli, Nov. Pl. Gen.: 32, t. 30, f. 1. 1729.
Current name: ***Cladanthus mixtus*** (L.) Chevall (Asteraceae).
Note: Alavi (in Jafri & El-Gadi, *Fl. Libya* 107: 143. 1983) indicated Herb. Linn. 1016.18 (LINN) as type but as this is annotated "pyrethrum 12" by Linnaeus, it cannot be original material for *Anthemis mixta*. Benedí González (in *Collect. Bot. (Barcelona)* 17: 62. 1987) indicated 1016.8 (LINN) as the lectotype but this is a collection unannotated by Linnaeus apart from an indication that it came from Löfling ("L"). Neither is eligible for designation as lectotype, and Humphries therefore chose the Micheli plate in their place.

Anthemis montana Linnaeus, *Species Plantarum*, ed. 2, 2: 1261. 1763, *nom. illeg.*
"Habitat in Italia, Helvetia." RCN: 6483.
Replaced synonym: *Anthemis cretica* L. (1753).
Lectotype (Grierson & Yavin in Davis in *Notes Roy. Bot. Gard. Edinburgh* 33: 212. 1974): Herb. Clifford: 415, *Anthemis* 2 (BM-000647187).
Current name: ***Anthemis cretica*** L. (Asteraceae).
Note: See discussion by Fernandes (in *Anales Inst. Bot. Cavanilles* 23: 1433. 1975).

Anthemis nobilis Linnaeus, *Species Plantarum* 2: 894. 1753.
"Habitat in Europae pascuis apricis." RCN: 6480.
Lectotype (Humphries in Jarvis & Turland in *Taxon* 47: 352. 1998): Herb. Clifford: 415, *Anthemis* 1 (BM-000647185).
Current name: ***Chamaemelum nobile*** (L.) All. (Asteraceae).

Anthemis peregrina Linnaeus, *Systema Naturae,* ed. 10, 2: 1223. 1759.
RCN: 6475.
Lectotype (Georgiou-Karavata, *Fl. Medit.* 7: 101. 1997): *Kähler,* Herb. Linn. No. 1016.11 (LINN).
Current name: ***Anthemis peregrina*** L. (Asteraceae).
Note: Fernandes (in *Revista Biol. (Lisbon)* 12: 393. 1984) discussed this, and a number of specimens in LINN, in some detail, concluding that it is a name which is difficult, if not impossible, to identify. However, Georgiou-Karavata typified the name in a thesis published in 1990, reiterated subsequently (in *Fl. Medit.* 7: 101. 1997).

Anthemis pyrethrum Linnaeus, *Species Plantarum* 2: 895. 1753.
"Habitat in Arabia, Syria, Creta, Apulia, Thuringia." RCN: 6484.
Lectotype (Humphries in *Bull. Brit. Mus. (Nat. Hist.), Bot.* 7: 111. 1979): Herb. Linn. No. 1016.18 (LINN).
Current name: ***Anacyclus pyrethrum*** (L.) Lag. (Asteraceae).

Anthemis repanda Linnaeus, *Species Plantarum* 2: 895. 1753.
"Habitat in Hispania." RCN: 6486.
Neotype (Humphries in Jarvis & Turland in *Taxon* 47: 352. 1998): Portugal. Porto, dans les montagnes, Jun 1917, *Mário de Castro s.n.* [Sennen, Pl. Espagne No. 3303] (BM-000576305).
Current name: ***Lepidophorum repandum*** (L.) DC. (Asteraceae).

Anthemis tinctoria Linnaeus, *Species Plantarum* 2: 896. 1753.
"Habitat in Sueciae, Germaniae apricis pratis siccis." RCN: 6488.
Lectotype (Iranshahr in Rechinger, *Fl. Iranica* 158: 18. 1986): Herb. Clifford: 414, *Buphthalmum* 2 (BM-000647172).
Current name: ***Cota tinctoria*** (L.) J. Gay (Asteraceae).

Anthemis tinctoria Linnaeus var. **triumfeti** Linnaeus, *Species Plantarum* 2: 896. 1753.
RCN: 6488.
Type not designated.
Original material: Herb. Linn. No. 72 (SBT); [icon] in Trionfetti, Obs. Ortu Veg. Pl.: 79, unnumbered plate. 1685.
Current name: ***Anthemis triumfeti*** (L.) All. (Asteraceae).
Note: The varietal epithet was spelled "triumfelti" in the protologue on p. 896, but corrected to "triumfeti" in the Errata. Iranshahr (in Rechinger, *Fl. Iranica* 158: 19. 1986) indicated 355.13 (LINN) as type but this is clearly an error as genus no. 355 is *Sium,* in which there is no specimen no. 13.

Anthemis tomentosa Linnaeus, *Species Plantarum* 2: 893. 1753.
"Habitat in Graeciae maritimis." RCN: 6476.
Lectotype (Fernandes in *Revista Biol. (Lisbon)* 12: 390, f. 1. 1984): Herb. Clifford: 415, *Anthemis* 3 (BM-000647188).
Current name: ***Anthemis tomentosa*** L. (Asteraceae).
Note: Humphries (in *Taxon* 47: 352. 1998) independently chose the same type as Fernandes.

Anthemis valentina Linnaeus, *Species Plantarum* 2: 895. 1753.
"Habitat in G. Narbonensi." RCN: 6485.
Lectotype (Humphries in *Bull. Brit. Mus. (Nat. Hist.), Bot.* 7: 120. 1979): Herb. Clifford: 414, *Buphthalmum* 3, sheet A (BM-000647174).
Current name: ***Anacyclus radiatus*** Loisel. (Asteraceae).

Anthericum alooides Linnaeus, *Species Plantarum* 1: 311. 1753.
"Habitat ad Cap. b. Spei." RCN: 2450.
Type not designated.
Original material: [icon] in Dillenius, Hort. Eltham. 2: 312, t. 232, f. 299. 1732.

Current name: ***Bulbine alooides*** (L.) Willd. (Liliaceae/Asphodelaceae).
Note: Wijnands (*Bot. Commelins*: 129. 1983) stated that the Dillenius plate "might serve as the type", but his uncertainty prevents this being accepted as a formal typification. Kativu (in *Kirkia* 16: 48. 1997) indicated Clifford material (BM) as the holotype but this appears to be a Gronovius collection now excluded from the Clifford herbarium, and not original material for the name. Subsequently, Van Jaarsveld & Forster (in Eggli, *Ill. Handb. Succ. Pl., Monocots*: 233. 2001) indicated the Dillenius plate as type but as this choice was published after 1 Jan 2001, their omission of the phrase "designated here" or an equivalent (Art. 7.11) means that the choice is not effective.

Anthericum annuum Linnaeus, *Species Plantarum* 1: 311. 1753.
"Habitat in Aethiopia." RCN: 2452.
Type not designated.
Original material: none traced.
Current name: ***Bulbine annua*** (L.) Willd. (Liliaceae/Asphodelaceae).
Note: See comments by Wijnands (*Bot. Commelins*: 129. 1983).

Anthericum asphodeloides Linnaeus, *Species Plantarum* 1: 311. 1753.
"Habitat in Aethiopia." RCN: 2457.
Lectotype (Kativu in *Kirkia* 16: 44. 1996): Herb. Linn. No. 432.11 (LINN).
Current name: ***Bulbine asphodeloides*** (L.) Spreng. (Liliaceae/Asphodelaceae).

Anthericum calyculatum Linnaeus, *Species Plantarum* 1: 311. 1753.
"Habitat in alpibus Helvetiae, Lapponiae, Sibiriae." RCN: 2455.
Lectotype (designated here by Jonsell): [icon] *"Phalangium alpinum, palustre, Iridis folio"* in Séguier, Pl. Veron. 2: 61, t. 14. 1745.
Current name: ***Tofieldia calyculata*** (L.) Wahlenb. (Liliaceae/Tofieldiaceae).
Note: Linnaeus' concept of *A. calyculatum* was broad, and included what are now recognised as four distinct species. Stearn (in *J. Linn. Soc., Bot.* 53: 194–204. 1947; *Introd. Linnaeus' Sp. Pl.* (Ray Soc. ed.): 130–132. 1957; in *Biol. J. Linn. Soc.* 5: 9. 1973) has provided a detailed analysis of this problem, concluding that the name should, in accordance with long usage, be restricted to the species known to Linnaeus from Gotland. Stearn treated Hau, in Gotland, as the restricted type locality, nominating topotype material, but did not designate either a specimen (none of the original specimens belongs to this species) or an illustration as lectotype. Stearn (1947: 197, f. 3B) reproduced the cited *Fl. Lapponica* (1737: t. 10, f. 3) illustration. However, the cited Séguier plate, depicting material from Monte Baldo in northern Italy, corresponds with traditional usage of the name and is designated as the lectotype by Jonsell.

Anthericum frutescens Linnaeus, *Species Plantarum* 1: 310. 1753.
"Habitat ad Cap. b. Spei." RCN: 2449.
Type not designated.
Original material: Herb. Clifford: 122, *Bulbine* 1 (BM); [icon] in Dillenius, Hort. Eltham. 2: 310, t. 231, f. 298. 1732.
Current name: ***Bulbine frutescens*** (L.) Willd. (Liliaceae/Asphodelaceae).
Note: Van Jaarsveld (in Eggli, *Ill. Handb. Succ. Pl., Monocots*: 238. 2001) indicated the cited Dillenius plate as type but as this choice was published after 1 Jan 2001, the omission of the phrase "designated here" or an equivalent (Art. 7.11) means that the choice is not effective.

Anthericum graecum Linnaeus, *Species Plantarum*, ed. 2, 1: 444. 1762.
"Habitat in Oriente. Burmannus." RCN: 2442.
Lectotype (Greuter in *Israel J. Bot.* 19: 159. 1970): Herb. Linn. No. 432.3 (LINN).
Current name: ***Gagea graeca*** (L.) A. Terracc. (Liliaceae).

Anthericum hispidum Linnaeus, *Species Plantarum*, ed. 2, 1: 446. 1762.
"Habitat ad Cap. b. Spei." RCN: 2453.
Type not designated.
Original material: [icon] in Miller, Fig. Pl. Gard. Dict. 1: 38, t. 56. 1755.
Current name: ***Trachyandra hispida*** (L.) Kunth (Liliaceae/Asphodelaceae).
Note: Obermeyer (in *Bothalia* 7: 732. 1962) incorrectly indicated 432.23 and 432.24 (LINN) as syntypes but they do not appear to be even original material for the name.

Anthericum liliago Linnaeus, *Species Plantarum* 1: 310. 1753.
"Habitat in Helvetia, Germania, Gallia." RCN: 2446.
Lectotype (Küpfer in *Boissiera* 23: 99. 1974): Herb. Linn. No. 432.8 (LINN).
Current name: ***Anthericum liliago*** L. (Liliaceae/Anthericaceae).

Anthericum liliastrum (Linnaeus) Linnaeus, *Species Plantarum*, ed. 2, 1: 445. 1762.
"Habitat in Alpibus Helveticis, Allobrogicis." RCN: 2447.
Basionym: *Hemerocallis liliastrum* L. (1753).
Type not designated.
Original material: as basionym.
Current name: ***Paradisea liliastrum*** (L.) Bertol. (Liliaceae/Asphodelaceae).

Anthericum ossifragum Linnaeus, *Species Plantarum* 1: 311. 1753.
"Habitat in Europae borealis uliginosis." RCN: 2454.
Type not designated.
Original material: Herb. Linn. No. 432.13 (LINN); Herb. A. van Royen No. 913.18–49 (L); [icon] in Gmelin, Fl. Sibirica 1: 73, t. 18, f. 2. 1747; [icon] in Dodoëns, Stirp. Hist. Pempt., ed. 2: 208. 1616; [icon] in Moehring in Acta Phys.-Med. Acad. Caes. Leop.-Carol. Nat. Cur. 6: 384, t. 5, f. 4. 1742.
Current name: ***Narthecium ossifragum*** (L.) Huds. (Liliaceae/Melanthiaceae).

Anthericum planifolium Linnaeus, *Mantissa Plantarum Altera*: 224. 1771.
"Habitat in Lusitania trans Tagum, prope Capo de Spizel, florens Aprili. D. Vandelli." RCN: 2443.
Type not designated.
Original material: Herb. Linn. No. 432.4 (LINN).
Current name: ***Simethis mattiazzii*** (Vand.) Sacc. (Liliaceae/Asphodelaceae).

Anthericum ramosum Linnaeus, *Species Plantarum* 1: 310. 1753.
"Habitat in Europae australioris rupibus calcareis." RCN: 2445.
Lectotype (Mathew in Jarvis & al., *Regnum Veg.* 127: 19. 1993): Herb. Linn. No. 432.6 (LINN).
Generitype of *Anthericum* Linnaeus (vide Hitchcock, *Prop. Brit. Bot.*: 146. 1929).
Current name: ***Anthericum ramosum*** L. (Liliaceae/Anthericaceae).

Anthericum revolutum Linnaeus, *Species Plantarum* 1: 310. 1753.
"Habitat – – – –" RCN: 2444.
Neotype (Obermeyer in *Bothalia* 7: 737. 1962): South Africa. Cape, Hermanus, *Galpin 12898* (PRE).

Current name: ***Trachyandra revoluta*** (L.) Kunth (Liliaceae/Asphodelaceae).

Anthericum serotinum (Linnaeus) Linnaeus, *Species Plantarum*, ed. 2, 1: 444. 1762.
"Habitat in alpibus Angliae, Helvetiae, Taureri rastadiensis, Wallaesiae." RCN: 2441.
Basionym: *Bulbocodium serotinum* L. (1753).
Type not designated.
Original material: as basionym.
Current name: ***Lloydia serotina*** (L.) Rchb. (Liliaceae).

Anthericum spirale Linnaeus, *Mantissa Plantarum Altera*: 224. 1771.
"Habitat sub montis Leonis Capitis b. spei, locis glareosis. Koenig." RCN: 2448.
Lectotype (Perry in *Contr. Bolus Herb.* 17: 74. 1994): *König 45*, Herb. Linn. No. 432.10 (LINN).
Current name: ***Eriospermum spirale*** K. Bergius ex Schult. f. (Liliaceae/Eriospermaceae).
Note: Perry treats *Eriospermum spirale* K. Bergius ex Schult. f. (1830) and *Anthericum spirale* L. (1771) as heterotypic, the former preventing the transfer of the latter to *Eriospermum*.

Anthoceros laevis Linnaeus, *Species Plantarum* 2: 1139. 1753.
"Habitat in Europa & America boreali." RCN: 8154.
Lectotype (Proskauer in *Rabenhorst's Kryptogamen-Flora*, ed. 3, 6: 1315. 1958): [icon] *"Anthoceros major"* in Micheli, Nov. Pl. Gen.: 11, t. 7, f. 1. 1729.
Current name: ***Phaeoceros laevis*** (L.) Prosk. (Anthocerotaceae).
Note: Proskauer (in *Ann. Bot.* 12: 259. 1948; *Bull. Torrey Bot. Club* 78: 343. 1951) initially indicated 1272.2 (LINN) as the type but, recognising that this sheet was a post-1753 addition to the collection, rejected this choice in favour of the Micheli plate. Hässel de Menéndez (in *Cryptog. Bryol. Lichénol.* 5: 202. 1984) illustrates the Dillenian material extant at OXF.

Anthoceros multifidus Linnaeus, *Species Plantarum* 2: 1140. 1753.
"Habitat in Germania." RCN: 8155.
Lectotype (Bonner, *Index Hepaticarum* 2: 207. 1962): [icon] *"Anthoceros folio tenuissimo multifido"* in Dillenius, Hist. Musc.: 477, t. 68, f. 4. 1741. – Voucher: Herb. Dillenius (OXF).
Current name: ***Riccardia multifida*** (L.) Gray (Aneuraceae).
Note: Hässel de Menéndez (in *Cryptog. Bryol. Lichénol.* 5: 202. 1984) illustrates the Dillenian voucher material extant at OXF.

Anthoceros punctatus Linnaeus, *Species Plantarum* 2: 1139. 1753.
"Habitat in Angliae, Italiae, uliginosis, umbrosis." RCN: 8153.
Type not designated.
Original material: [icon] in Dillenius, Hist. Musc.: t. 68, f. 1. 1741; [icon] in Micheli, Nov. Pl. Gen.: 11, t. 7, f. 2. 1729.
Generitype of *Anthoceros* Linnaeus (vide Evans in Britton, *Fl. Bermuda* 469. 28 Feb 1918).
Current name: ***Anthoceros punctatus*** L. (Anthocerotaceae).
Note: Stotler & Crandall-Stotler (in *Taxon* 51: 628. 2003) proposed the conservation of *Anthoceros*, with *A. punctatus* as conserved type, in the belief that Schuster (in *J. Hattori Bot. Lab.* 26: 299. 1963) must be accepted as having designated *A. laevis* L. as the generitype. However, the proposal made no reference to Evans' (1918), or later, generitype choices of *A. punctatus*, and the proposal was subsequently withdrawn (see Zijlstra in *Taxon* 54: 525. 2005).
    Proskauer (in *Rabenhorst's Kryptogamen-Flora*, 3, 6: 1307. 1958) and later authors have treated material in Dillenius' herbarium (OXF) as the type, but this was not studied by Linnaeus and, despite its apparent association with the cited Dillenian illustration, is not original material for the name. Isoviita (in *Acta*

Bot. Fenn. 89: 16. 1970) noted duplicate material in H, and a review, with illustrations, is provided by Hässel de Menéndez (in *Cryptog. Bryol. Lichénol.* 5: 201–209. 1984).

Antholyza aethiopica Linnaeus, *Systema Naturae*, ed. 10, 2: 863. 1759. ["Habitat in Aethiopia."] Sp. Pl., ed. 2, 1: 54 (1762). RCN: 312.
Lectotype (de Vos in *S. African J. Bot.* 51: 256. 1985): Herb. Linn. No. 60.3 (LINN).
Current name: ***Chasmanthe aethiopica*** (L.) N.E. Br. (Iridaceae).
Note: Goldblatt & al. (*Crocosmia Chasmanthe*: 14, 53. 2004) give some historical background, and (p. 50) follow de Vos as to type.

Antholyza cepacea Linnaeus, *Mantissa Plantarum Altera*: 176. 1771. "Habitat ad Cap. b. spei." RCN: 316.
Type not designated.
Original material: [icon] in Breyn, Exot. Pl. Cent.: 88, t. 38. 1678.
Current name: ***Antholyza cepacea*** L. (Iridaceae).

Antholyza cunonia Linnaeus, *Species Plantarum* 1: 37. 1753. "Habitat ad Cap. b. spei." RCN: 311.
Lectotype (Goldblatt in Jarvis & al., *Regnum Veg.* 127: 19. 1993): [icon] *"Cunonia floribus sessilibus spathis maximis"* in Büttner, Enum. Meth.: 211, t. 1. 1750 (see p. 113).
Generitype of *Antholyza* Linnaeus (vide Hitchcock in *Amer. J. Bot.* 10: 514. 1923).
Current name: ***Gladiolus cunonia*** (L.) Gaertn. (Iridaceae).
Note: There has been considerable confusion over the type choice for *Antholyza*. The earlier choice (Hitchcock in *Amer. J. Bot.* 10: 514. 1923; *Prop. Brit. Bot.*: 118. 1929) is of *Anth. cunonia* (now recognised as a species of *Gladiolus*) into which *Antholyza* falls as a synonym. However, if *Anth. cunonia* is treated as the generitype, but as *Anomalesia cunonia* (L.) R. Br., the latter genus would be displaced by *Antholyza*. A later choice is *Anth. ringens* (by Brown in *Trans. Roy. Soc. S. Africa* 20: 266. 1932), sometimes accepted in this genus but more recently (Goldblatt in *S. African J. Bot.* 56: 580. 1990) transferred to *Babiana* Ker Gawl. Goldblatt does not accept *Anth. ringens* as the generitype of *Antholyza* so there is no disruption. However, *Index Nominum Genericorum* (ING), noting Linnaeus' comments in 1753 that *Anth. cunonia* probably belongs to a genus distinct from *Antholyza*, argues that it conflicts with the generic protologue, and accepts *Anth. ringens* as generitype. If this is accepted, and *Anth. ringens* is treated as a species of *Babiana*, *Antholyza* becomes the correct name for *Babiana* (as the latter is conserved only against *Beverna* Adans. 1763).

Antholyza maura Linnaeus, *Mantissa Plantarum Altera*: 175. 1771. "Habitat in Capitis b. spei montium latera nemorosa, florens Majo." RCN: 315.
Lectotype (Goldblatt, *Woody Iridaceae*: 118. 1993): Herb. Linn. No. 67.1 (LINN).
Current name: ***Witsenia maura*** (L.) Thunb. (Iridaceae).

Antholyza meriana Linnaeus, *Systema Naturae*, ed. 10, 2: 863. 1759. ["Habitat ad Cap. b. spei?"] Sp. Pl., ed. 2, 1: 54 (1762). RCN: 313.
Lectotype (Roux in *J. S. African Bot.* 46: 368. 1980): [icon] *"Meriana flore rubello"* in Trew, Pl. Select.: 11, t. 40. 1754 (see p. 128).
Current name: ***Watsonia meriana*** (L.) Mill. (Iridaceae).

Antholyza meriana Linnaeus var. **minor** Linnaeus, *Systema Naturae*, ed. 12, 2: 77. 1767.
RCN: 313.
Type not designated.
Original material: [icon] in Miller, Fig. Pl. Gard. Dict. 2: 198, t. 297, f. 2. 1760.
Current name: ***Watsonia meriana*** (L.) Mill. (Iridaceae).

Antholyza merianella Linnaeus, *Systema Vegetabilium*, ed. 13: 77. 1774.
RCN: 314.
Type not designated.
Original material: Herb. Linn. No. 60.7 (LINN); [icon] in Miller, Fig. Pl. Gard. Dict. 2: 198, t. 297, f. 2. 1760.
Current name: ***Homoglossum merianella*** (Thunb.) Baker (Iridaceae).
Note: This name has been treated as illegitimate by some authors (see Milne-Redhead in *Bot. Mag.* 160: t. 9510. 1938; de Vos in *J. S. African Bot.* 42: 333–334. 1976). However, this does not seem to be the case because Linnaeus did not cite *Watsonia humilis* Mill. (1768) as a synonym of *A. merianella* and Miller did not cite his own t. 279, f. 2 (1760) in publishing *W. humilis* (while Linnaeus did). Matters are complicated by the existence of the heterotypic *Gladiolus merianellus* Thunb. (1784) – see Roux (in *J. S. African Bot.* 46: 366. 1980).

Antholyza ringens Linnaeus, *Species Plantarum* 1: 37. 1753. "Habitat in Aethiopia." RCN: 310.
Lectotype (Wijnands, *Bot. Commelins*: 110. 1983): [icon] *"Gladiolo Aethiopico similis planta angustifolia, caule hirsuto, flore rubicundissimo"* in Commelin, Hort. Med. Amsteld. Pl. Rar. 1: 81, t. 41. 1697.
Current name: ***Babiana ringens*** (L.) Ker-Gawl. (Iridaceae).
Note: There has been considerable confusion over the type choice for *Antholyza* – see discussion under *A. cunonia*.

Anthospermum aethiopicum Linnaeus, *Species Plantarum* 2: 1058. 1753.
"Habitat in Aethiopia." RCN: 7704.
Lectotype (Stearn, *Introd. Linnaeus' Sp. Pl.* (Ray Soc. ed.): 47. 1957): [icon] *"Anthospermum mas"* in Linnaeus, Hort. Cliff.: 455, t. 27. 1738. – Voucher: Herb. Clifford: 455, *Anthospermum* 1 (BM).
Generitype of *Anthospermum* Linnaeus.
Current name: ***Anthospermum aethiopicum*** L. (Rubiaceae).

Anthospermum ciliare Linnaeus, *Species Plantarum*, ed. 2, 2: 1512. 1763, *nom. utique rej.*
"Habitat ad Cap. b. spei." RCN: 7705.
Lectotype (Puff in *Taxon* 31: 759. 1982): Herb. Linn. No. 1233.4 (LINN).
Current name: ***Anthospermum galioides*** Rchb. (Rubiaceae).

Anthoxanthum indicum Linnaeus, *Species Plantarum* 1: 28. 1753. "Habitat in India." RCN: 228.
Lectotype (Clayton in Polhill, *Fl. Trop. E. Africa, Gramineae* 2: 395. 1974): Herb. Hermann 1: 29, No. 25 (BM-000621332).
Current name: ***Perotis indica*** (L.) Kuntze (Poaceae).

Anthoxanthum odoratum Linnaeus, *Species Plantarum* 1: 28. 1753. "Habitat in Europae pratis." RCN: 227.
Lectotype (Cope in Jarvis & al., *Regnum Veg.* 127: 19. 1993): Herb. Linn. No. 46.1 (LINN).
Generitype of *Anthoxanthum* Linnaeus (vide Hitchcock, *Prop. Brit. Bot.*: 117. 1929).
Current name: ***Anthoxanthum odoratum*** L. (Poaceae).
Note: Although Kerguélen (in *Lejeunia*, n.s., 75: 82. 1975) stated "Type: …LINN", this is not accepted as a formal typification, for the reasons explained by Cafferty & al. (in *Taxon* 49: 240. 2000).

Anthoxanthum paniculatum Linnaeus, *Species Plantarum* 1: 28. 1753.
"Habitat in Europa australiore." RCN: 229.
Lectotype (Stearn, *Introd. Linnaeus' Sp. Pl.* (Ray Soc. ed.): 128. 1957): Herb. Burser I: 46 (UPS).

Current name: *Festuca paniculata* (L.) Schinz & Thell. subsp.
paniculata (Poaceae).
Note: See early observations on this name by Smith (in *Trans. Linn.
Soc. London* 1: 111–117, f. 10. 1791), with a copy of Rudbeck's
cited plate reproduced there.

Anthyllis aspalathoides Linnaeus, *Systema Naturae*, ed. 10, 2: 1160.
1759.
["Habitat in Aethiopia. Royenus."] Cent. II Pl.: 27 (1756). RCN:
5237.
Replaced synonym: *Anthyllis lotoides* L. (1756), *nom. illeg.*, non L.
(1753).
Lectotype (Dahlgren in *Opera Bot.* 4: 114. 1960): Herb. Linn. No.
893.56 (LINN).
Current name: *Aspalathus aspalathoides* (L.) Rothm. (Fabaceae:
Faboideae).
Note: Specific epithet spelled "aspalatoides" in the protologue.
As noted by Dahlgren (in *Opera Bot.* 4: 114. 1960) and
Nordenstam (in *Bot. Not.* 114: 278. 1961), this is a *nomen novum*
for the illegitimate *A. lotoides* L. (1756), a later homonym of *A.
lotoides* L. (1753).

Anthyllis asphaltoides Linnaeus, *Amoenitates Academicae* 4: 326.
1759, *orth. var.*
"Habitat in Aethiopia. Royenus." RCN: 5237.
Lectotype (Dahlgren in *Opera Bot.* 4: 114. 1960): Herb. Linn. No.
893.56 (LINN).
Current name: *Aspalathus aspalathoides* (L.) Rothm. (Fabaceae:
Faboideae).
Note: As noted by Nordenstam (in *Bot. Not.* 114: 278. 1961), this was
a *nomen novum* provided for the illegitimate *A. lotoides* L. (1756) in
the reprint of *Cent. II Pl.* (Nov 1759). However, it post-dates *A.
aspalathoides* L. (May–Jun 1759), of which it has been treated as an
orthographic variant.

Anthyllis barba-jovis Linnaeus, *Species Plantarum* 2: 720. 1753.
"Habitat in Helvetia." RCN: 5298.
Lectotype (Jafri in Jafri & El-Gadi, *Fl. Libya* 86: 116. 1980): Herb.
Linn. No. 897.9 (LINN).
Current name: *Anthyllis barba-jovis* L. (Fabaceae: Faboideae).

Anthyllis cornicina Linnaeus, *Species Plantarum* 2: 719. 1753.
"Habitat in Hispania. Loefl." RCN: 5293.
Lectotype (Lassen in Turland & Jarvis in *Taxon* 46: 462. 1997):
Löfling 588, Herb. Linn. No. 897.5 (LINN), see p. 221.
Current name: *Hymenocarpos cornicina* (L.) Lassen (Fabaceae:
Faboideae).

Anthyllis cytisoides Linnaeus, *Species Plantarum* 2: 720. 1753.
"Habitat in Hispania." RCN: 5300.
Lectotype (Benedí González in *Anales Jard. Bot. Madrid* 56: 281.
1998): Herb. Linn. No. 897.12 (LINN).
Current name: *Anthyllis cytisoides* L. (Fabaceae: Faboideae).

Anthyllis erinacea Linnaeus, *Species Plantarum* 2: 720. 1753.
"Habitat in Hispania." RCN: 5302.
Lectotype (Polhill in Turland & Jarvis in *Taxon* 46: 462. 1997):
Löfling s.n., Herb. Linn. No. 897.15 (LINN).
Current name: *Erinacea anthyllis* Link subsp. *anthyllis* (Fabaceae:
Faboideae).

Anthyllis gerardii Linnaeus, *Systema Naturae,* ed. 12, 2: 480;
Mantissa Plantarum: 100. 1767.
"Habitat in Galloprovinciae maritimis versus S. Tropes sub Pinubus."
RCN: 5295.

Lectotype (Sokoloff in Turland & Jarvis in *Taxon* 46: 463. 1997):
[icon] *"Anthyllis herbacea, foliis pinnatis inaequalibus, pedunculis
axillaribus folio longioribus, capitulis nudis"* in Gérard, Fl. Gallo-
Provincialis: 490, t. 18. 1761.
Current name: *Dorycnopsis gerardii* (L.) Boiss. (Fabaceae:
Faboideae).
Note: Specific epithet spelled "gerardi" in the protologue.

Anthyllis hermanniae Linnaeus, *Species Plantarum* 2: 720. 1753.
"Habitat in Graecia." RCN: 5301.
Lectotype (Turland in Turland & Jarvis in *Taxon* 46: 463. 1997):
Herb. Linn. No. 897.14 (LINN).
Current name: *Anthyllis hermanniae* L. (Fabaceae: Faboideae).

Anthyllis heterophylla Linnaeus, *Species Plantarum*, ed. 2, 2: 1013.
1763.
"Habitat in Lusitania, Hispania. Alstroemer." RCN: 5299.
Type not designated.
Original material: *Alströmer 103a*, Herb. Linn. No. 897.10 (LINN).
Current name: *Anthyllis sp.* (Fabaceae: Faboideae).
Note: It appears that this is probably based on *Alströmer 103a*, Herb.
Linn. No. 897.10 (LINN). However, the taxonomic identity of this
collection is uncertain (but may be potentially disruptive) and no
type designation has yet been made. Tikhomirov & Sokoloff (in
Feddes Repert. 108: 340. 1997) state that the LINN material is
dissimilar to *Dorycnopsis gerardii* Boiss.

Anthyllis involucrata (P.J. Bergius) Linnaeus, *Mantissa Plantarum
Altera*: 265. 1771.
"Habitat ad Cap. b. spei." RCN: 5296.
Basionym: *Ononis involucrata* P.J.Bergius (1767).
Lectotype (Van Wyk in *Contr. Bolus Herb.* 14: 223. 1991): *Grubb*,
Herb. Bergius 236.51 (SBT).
Current name: *Lotononis involucrata* (P.J. Bergius) Benth. subsp.
involucrata (Fabaceae: Faboideae).

Anthyllis linifolia Linnaeus, *Mantissa Plantarum Altera*: 265. 1771.
"Habitat ad Cap. b. spei rupibus." RCN: 5297.
Type not designated.
Original material: none traced.
Current name: *Aspalathus linearifolia* (Burm. f.) DC. (Fabaceae:
Faboideae).
Note: This has been treated as either unidentifiable (Dahlgren in *Opera
Bot.* 4: 165. 1960) or as a *nomen dubium* questionably synonymous
with *A. linearifolia* (Burm. f.) DC. (Dahlgren in Leistner, *Fl.
Southern Africa* 16(3:6): 45. 1988).

Anthyllis lotoides Linnaeus, *Species Plantarum* 2: 720. 1753.
"Habitat in Hispania. Loefl." RCN: 5294.
Lectotype (Lassen in Turland & Jarvis in *Taxon* 46: 463. 1997): Herb.
Linn. No. 897.6 (LINN).
Current name: *Hymenocarpos hispanicus* Lassen (Fabaceae:
Faboideae).
Note: López González (in *Anales Jard. Bot. Madrid* 55: 161. 1997)
discussed the original elements for the name but did not designate a
type. There have been complications surrounding the correct
name for this taxon – see Lassen (in *Willdenowia* 16: 111. 1986;
16: 443. 1987) and Benedí (in *Anales Jard. Bot. Madrid* 56: 182.
1998).

Anthyllis lotoides Linnaeus, *Centuria II Plantarum*: 27. 1756, *nom.
illeg.*
"Habitat in Aethiopia. Royenus." RCN: 5237.
Replaced synonym of: *Anthyllis aspalathoides* L. (1759); *Aspalathus
anthylloides* L. (1763), *nom. illeg.*

Lectotype (Dahlgren in *Opera Bot.* 4: 114. 1960): Herb. Linn. No. 893.56 (LINN).
Current name: ***Aspalathus aspalathoides*** (L.) Rothm. (Fabaceae: Faboideae).
Note: As noted by Dahlgren (in *Opera Bot.* 4: 114. 1960) and Nordenstam (in *Bot. Not.* 114: 278. 1961), this is a later homonym of *A. lotoides* L. (1753), and therefore illegitimate. In 1759, Linnaeus published *A. aspalathoides* as a *nomen novum* for *A. lotoides* L. (1756).

Anthyllis montana Linnaeus, *Species Plantarum* 2: 719. 1753.
"Habitat in Helvetia, G. Narbonensi, Galloprovincia." RCN: 5292.
Lectotype (Sokoloff in *Taxon* 48: 57. 1999): Herb. Burser XIX: 147 (UPS).
Current name: ***Anthyllis montana*** L. subsp. ***montana*** (Fabaceae: Faboideae).
Note: Benedí (in *Anales Jard. Bot. Madrid* 56: 285. 1998) designated 897.4 (LINN) as lectotype but this was a 1757 addition to the herbarium from Gabriel (see p. 204) and therefore not original material for the name.

Anthyllis tetraphylla Linnaeus, *Species Plantarum* 2: 719. 1753.
"Habitat in Italia, Sicilia." RCN: 5290.
Lectotype (Jafri in Jafri & El-Gadi, *Fl. Libya* 86: 119. 1980): Herb. Linn. No. 897.1 (LINN).
Current name: ***Tripodion tetraphyllum*** (L.) Fourr. (Fabaceae: Faboideae).

Anthyllis vulneraria Linnaeus, *Species Plantarum* 2: 719. 1753.
"Habitat in pratis Europae borealioris." RCN: 5291.
Lectotype (Miniaev & Kloczkova in *Novosti Sist. Vyssh. Rast.* 14: 148. 1977): Herb. Linn. No. 897.2 (LINN).
Generitype of *Anthyllis* Linnaeus (vide Green, *Prop. Brit. Bot.*: 174. 1929).
Current name: ***Anthyllis vulneraria*** L. subsp. ***vulneraria*** (Fabaceae: Faboideae).
Note: Cullen (in *Notes Roy. Bot. Gard. Edinburgh* 35: 9. 1976) indicated both 897.2 and 897.3 (LINN) as type material but as they are evidently not part of a single gathering, Art. 9.15 does not apply.

Anthyllis vulneraria Linnaeus var. **alba** Linnaeus, *Flora Suecica*, ed. 2: 250. 1755.
"Habitat in pratis exsuccis apricis passim, Gotlandia 227. copiose." RCN: 5291.
Type not designated.
Original material: [icon] in Tabernaemontanus, Eicones Pl.: 524. 1590.
Current name: ***Anthyllis vulneraria*** L. (Fabaceae: Faboideae).

Anthyllis vulneraria Linnaeus var. **coccinea** Linnaeus, *Flora Suecica*, ed. 2: 250. 1755.
"Habitat in pratis exsuccis apricis passim, in Oelandia 54. 71. prope tummulum lapillosum Borckholmensem." RCN: 5291.
Lectotype (Kerguélen & al. in *Lejeunia*, n.s., 120: 46. 1987): [icon] *"Vulneraria supina, flore coccineo Lhwyd."* in Dillenius, Hort. Eltham. 2: 431, t. 320, f. 413. 1732.
Current name: ***Anthyllis vulneraria*** L. var. ***coccinea*** L. (Fabaceae: Faboideae).

Anthyllis vulneraria Linnaeus var. **lutea** Linnaeus, *Flora Suecica*, ed. 2: 250. 1755.
"Habitat in pratis exsuccis apricis passim, in Scania, Uplandia." RCN: 5291.

Type not designated.
Original material: Herb. Burser XVIII(2): 84 (UPS); [icon] in Tabernaemontanus, Eicones Pl.: 525. 1590; [icon] in Plantin, Pl. Stirp. Icon. 2: 87. 1581.
Current name: ***Anthyllis vulneraria*** L. (Fabaceae: Faboideae).

Anthyllis vulneraria Linnaeus var. **rubra** Linnaeus, *Flora Suecica*, ed. 2: 250. 1755.
"Habitat in pratis exsuccis apricis passim, in Oelandia campestri ubique." RCN: 5291.
Type not designated.
Original material: none traced.
Current name: ***Anthyllis vulneraria*** L. (Fabaceae: Faboideae).

Antichorus depressus Linnaeus, *Systema Naturae*, ed. 12, 2: 264; *Mantissa Plantarum*: 64. 1767.
"Habitat in Arabia." RCN: 2670.
Lectotype (Ghafoor in Ali & Jafri, *Fl. Libya* 19: 4. 1977): Herb. Linn. No. 487.1 (LINN).
Generitype of *Antichorus* Linnaeus.
Current name: ***Corchorus depressus*** (L.) Stocks (Tiliaceae).

Antidesma alexiteria Linnaeus, *Species Plantarum* 2: 1027. 1753.
"Habitat in India." RCN: 25.
Lectotype (Mandal & Panigrahi in *J. Econ. Taxon. Bot.* 4: 257. 1983): [icon] *"Noeli-tali"* in Rheede, Hort. Malab. 4: 115, t. 56. 1683.
Generitype of *Antidesma* Linnaeus.
Current name: ***Antidesma alexiteria*** L. (Euphorbiaceae).
Note: Philcox (in Jarvis & al., *Regnum Veg.* 127: 19. 1993), followed by Chakrabarty & Gangopadhyay (in *J. Econ. Taxon. Bot.* 24: 1, 11. 2000), designated a Hermann collection (vol. 2: 67, No. 357, BM) as lectotype. However, Philcox's choice appears to be preceded by that of Mandal & Panigrahi (in *J. Econ. Taxon. Bot.* 4: 257. 1983) who treated Rheede's cited t. 56 as the "iconotype". A further complication may be the identity of the plate – Nicolson & al. (*Regnum Veg.* 119: 105. 1988) identify it as *A. menasu* (Tulasne) Müll.-Arg.

Antirrhinum aegyptiacum Linnaeus, *Species Plantarum* 2: 613. 1753.
"Habitat in Aegypto." RCN: 4431.
Neotype (Wickens in *Kew Bull.* 30: 11. 1975): *Lippi* (P).
Current name: ***Kickxia aegyptiaca*** (L.) Nábelek (Scrophulariaceae).
Note: Although Sutton (*Revis. Tribe Antirrhineae*: 117. 1988) indicated 767.7 (LINN) as a syntype, it is not original material for the name. As there is, in fact, no original material in existence, Wickens' earlier treatment of a Lippi collection in P as the holotype is here accepted as correctable to a neotypification under Art. 9.8.

Antirrhinum alpinum Linnaeus, *Species Plantarum* 2: 615. 1753.
"Habitat in Helvetia, Austria, Baldo." RCN: 4448.
Lectotype (Fischer in *Feddes Repert.* 108: 112. 1997): Herb. Burser XII: 32 (UPS).
Current name: ***Linaria alpina*** (L.) Mill. (Scrophulariaceae).
Note: Valdés (*Revis. Esp. Eur. Linaria*: 204. 1970) suggested that a type might be found in van Royen's herbarium, and Sutton (*Revis. Tribe Antirrhineae*: 183. 1988) incorrectly indicated Herb. Burser XII: 32 (UPS) as a syntype. Neither statement effects typification, and Fischer was the first to do this.

Antirrhinum arvense Linnaeus, *Species Plantarum* 2: 614. 1753.
"Habitat in Angliae, Galliae, Italiae arvis." RCN: 4442.
Lectotype (Sutton, *Revis. Tribe Antirrhineae*: 331. 1988): Herb. A. van Royen No. 908.228–413 (L).
Current name: ***Linaria arvensis*** (L.) Desf. (Scrophulariaceae).

Antirrhinum asarina Linnaeus, *Species Plantarum* 2: 612. 1753.
"Habitat in rupibus Veganio conterminis Genevae." RCN: 4465.
Lectotype (designated here by Sutton): Herb. Clifford: 323,
   Antirrhinum 2 (BM-000646219).
Current name: ***Asarina procumbens*** Mill. (Scrophulariaceae).

Antirrhinum bellidifolium Linnaeus, *Species Plantarum* 2: 617.
   1753.
"Habitat in agris inter Lugdunum & Viennam, interque Lugdunum et
   Gratianopolin." RCN: 4467.
Lectotype (Fischer in *Feddes Repert.* 108: 111. 1997): Herb. Linn. No.
   767.65 (LINN).
Current name: ***Anarrhinum bellidifolium*** (L.) Willd.
   (Scrophulariaceae).
Note: Sutton (*Revis. Tribe Antirrhineae*: 134. 1988) incorrectly
   indicated 767.65 (LINN) as a syntype. This is not correctable under
   Art. 9.8 and Fischer appears to have been the first to make a clear
   type choice.

Antirrhinum bicorne Linnaeus, *Plantae Rariores Africanae*: 11.
   1760.
["Habitat ad Cap. b. Spei."] Sp. Pl., ed. 2, 2: 857 (1763). RCN:
   4449.
Lectotype (designated here by Sutton): [icon] *"Linaria foliis copiosis,
   oblongis, dentatis, capsula corniculata, reflexa"* in Burman, Rar. Afric.
   Pl.: 211, t. 75, f. 3. 1739. – Epitype (designated here by Sutton):
   Herb. Burman, sheet 6919/67 (G).
Current name: ***Nemesia bicornis*** (L.) Pers. (Scrophulariaceae).

Antirrhinum bipunctatum Linnaeus, *Species Plantarum* 2: 614.
   1753.
"Habitat in Hispania. Loefling." RCN: 4439.
Lectotype (Valdés, *Revis. Esp. Eur.* Linaria: 241. 1970): *Löfling 448*,
   Herb. Linn. No. 767.17 (LINN).
Current name: ***Antirrhinum bipunctatum*** L. (Scrophulariaceae).

Antirrhinum canadense Linnaeus, *Species Plantarum* 2: 618. 1753.
"Habitat in Virginia, Canada." RCN: 4468.
Lectotype (Pennell in *Torreya* 19: 151. 1919): *Kalm*, Herb. Linn. No.
   767.69 (LINN; iso- UPS).
Current name: ***Nuttallanthus canadensis*** (L.) D.A. Sutton
   (Scrophulariaceae).

Antirrhinum chalepense Linnaeus, *Species Plantarum* 2: 617. 1753.
"Habitat in Italia." RCN: 4459.
Lectotype (Sutton in *Bot. J. Linn. Soc.* 81: 173. 1980): Herb. Linn.
   No. 767.53 (LINN).
Current name: ***Linaria chalepensis*** (L.) Mill. (Scrophulariaceae).

Antirrhinum cirrhosum Linnaeus, *Mantissa Plantarum Altera*: 249.
   1771.
"Habitat in Aegypto." RCN: 4430.
Lectotype (Sutton, *Revis. Tribe Antirrhineae*: 116, fiche. 1988): [icon]
   "Linaria supina villosa fol. sagitto fl. luteo vix conspicuo" in Tilli,
   Cat. Pl. Hort. Pisani: 101, t. 38, f. 2. 1723.
Current name: ***Kickxia cirrhosa*** (L.) Fritsch (Scrophulariaceae).

Antirrhinum cymbalaria Linnaeus, *Species Plantarum* 2: 612.
   1753.
"Habitat in rupibus & muris antiquis Basileae, Parisiis, Harlemi."
   RCN: 4426.
Lectotype (Pennell in *Monogr. Acad. Nat. Sci. Philadelphia* 1: 316.
   1935): Herb. Linn. No. 767.1 (LINN).
Current name: ***Cymbalaria muralis*** Gaertn. & al. (Scrophulariaceae).
Note: See also Sutton (*Revis. Tribe Antirrhineae*: 159. 1988).

Antirrhinum dalmaticum Linnaeus, *Species Plantarum* 2: 616. 1753.
"Habitat in Creta." RCN: 4453.
Lectotype (Alex in *Canad. J. Bot.* 40: 297, f. 1. 1962): Herb. Burser
   XII: 10 (UPS).
Current name: ***Linaria dalmatica*** (L.) Mill. (Scrophulariaceae).

Antirrhinum elatine Linnaeus, *Species Plantarum* 2: 612. 1753.
"Habitat in Germaniae, Angliae, Galliae, Italiae arvis." RCN: 4428.
Lectotype (Pennell in *Monogr. Acad. Nat. Sci. Philadelphia* 1: 313.
   1935): Herb. Linn. No. 767.2 (LINN).
Current name: ***Kickxia elatine*** (L.) Dumort. (Scrophulariaceae).

Antirrhinum genistifolium Linnaeus, *Species Plantarum* 2: 616.
   1753.
"Habitat in Sibiria. D. Gmelin." RCN: 4455.
Lectotype (Davis, *Fl. Turkey* 6: 659. 1978): Herb. Linn. No. 767.40
   (LINN).
Current name: ***Linaria genistifolia*** (L.) Mill. (Scrophulariaceae).

Antirrhinum glaucum Linnaeus, *Systema Naturae*, ed. 10, 2: 1111.
   1759.
["Habitat in Hispania."] Cent. I Pl.: 16 (1755). RCN: 447.
Replaced synonym: *Antirrhinum molle* L. (1755), *nom. illeg.*, non L.
   (1753).
Type not designated.
Original material: as replaced synonym.
Current name: ***Linaria glauca*** (L.) Chaz. (Scrophulariaceae).
Note: A *nomen novum* for *A. molle* L. (1755), *nom. illeg.* (non 1753).

Antirrhinum hirtum Linnaeus, *Species Plantarum* 2: 616. 1753.
"Habitat in Hispania." RCN: 4454.
Lectotype (Viano in *Candollea* 33: 248. 1978): *Löfling 456*, Herb.
   Linn. No. 767.39 (LINN).
Current name: ***Linaria hirta*** (L.) Moench (Scrophulariaceae).

Antirrhinum hybridum Linnaeus, *Flora Anglica*: 19. 1754.
"Habitat [in Anglia.]"
Type not designated.
Original material: none traced.
Current name: ***Kickxia spuria*** (L.) Dumort. (Scrophulariaceae).
Note: Stearn (*Introd. Ray's Syn. Meth. Stirp. Brit.* (Ray Soc. ed.): 64.
   1973) identified this with *K. spuria* on the basis of the cited Bauhin
   synonym but he did not designate a type.

Antirrhinum junceum Linnaeus, *Systema Naturae*, ed. 10, 2: 1112.
   1759.
["Habitat in Lusitania."] Cent. I Pl.: 17 (1755). RCN: 4456.
Replaced synonym: *Antirrhinum spartum* L. (1755), *nom. illeg.*, non *A.*
   sparteum L. (1753).
Type not designated.
Original material: as replaced synonym.
Current name: ***Linaria spartea*** (L.) Chaz. (Scrophulariaceae).
Note: A *nomen novum* for *A. spartum* L. (1755), *nom. illeg.*, (non *A.*
   sparteum L. 1753), as noted by Nordenstam (in *Bot. Not.* 114: 277.
   1961).

Antirrhinum linaria Linnaeus, *Species Plantarum* 2: 616. 1753.
"Habitat in Europae ruderatis." RCN: 4457.
Lectotype (Valdés, *Revis. Esp. Eur.* Linaria: 44. 1970): Herb. Linn. No.
   767.46 (LINN).
Current name: ***Linaria vulgaris*** Mill. (Scrophulariaceae).
Note: Although Pennell (in *Monogr. Acad. Nat. Sci. Philadelphia* 1:
   300. 1935) indicated material in LINN as type, there are six sheets
   linked with this name and as they are evidently not all part of a
   single gathering, Art. 9.15 does not apply.

Antirrhinum linarioides Linnaeus, *Species Plantarum,* ed. 2, 2: 853. 1763.
"Habitat in Europa australi." RCN: 4438.
Type not designated.
Original material: Herb. Linn. No. 767.16 (LINN).
Current name: ***Linaria vulgaris*** Mill. (Scrophulariaceae).
Note: Sutton (*Revis. Tribe Antirrhineae*: 275. 1988) stated that the name is apparently based on depauperate material in LINN, but he did not formally indicate it as type.

Antirrhinum linifolium Linnaeus, *Species Plantarum,* ed. 2, 2: 858. 1763.
"Habitat in Italiae maritimis." RCN: 4458.
Type not designated.
Original material: Herb. Burser XII: 11 (UPS); *Kähler,* Herb. Linn. No. 767.52 (LINN); [icon] in Buxbaum, Pl. Minus Cognit. Cent. 1: 16, t. 25, f. 2 "mala". 1728.
Current name: ***Linaria genistifolia*** (L.) Mill. (Scrophulariaceae).
Note: Sutton (*Revis. Tribe Antirrhineae*: 316. 1988) stated that Herb. Burser XII: 11 "would be a suitable lectotype" but did not designate the collection as such.

Antirrhinum majus Linnaeus, *Species Plantarum* 2: 617. 1753.
"Habitat in Europae australis maceriis, sepibus." RCN: 4462.
Lectotype (Sutton in Jarvis & al., *Regnum Veg.* 127: 19. 1993): Herb. Linn. No. 767.58 (LINN).
Generitype of *Antirrhinum* Linnaeus (vide Green, *Prop. Brit. Bot.:* 167. 1929).
Current name: ***Antirrhinum majus*** L. (Scrophulariaceae).
Note: Sutton (*Revis. Tribe Antirrhineae*: 92. 1988) indicated 767.58 (LINN) as a syntype, subsequently (in Jarvis & al., *Regnum Veg.* 127: 19. 1993) explicitly treating it as the lectotype. As the material in question was not a syntype, the type choice dates from 1993.

Antirrhinum minus Linnaeus, *Species Plantarum* 2: 617. 1753.
"Habitat in glareosis Europae." RCN: 4452.
Lectotype (Speta in *Stapfia* 7: 9. 1980): Herb. Linn. No. 767.38 (LINN).
Current name: ***Chaenorhinum minus*** (L.) Lange (Scrophulariaceae).
Note: Pennell (in *Monogr. Acad. Nat. Sci. Philadelphia* 1: 318. 1935) discussed the original elements but did not choose a type. Although Sutton (*Revis. Tribe Antirrhineae*: 118. 1988) indicated Herb. Clifford: 324, *Antirrhinum* 10 (BM) as lectotype, Speta's choice of 767.38 (LINN) has priority.

Antirrhinum molle Linnaeus, *Species Plantarum* 2: 1198. 1753.
"Habitat in Hispania." RCN: 4466.
Lectotype (designated here by Sutton): Herb. Linn. No. 767.64 (LINN).
Current name: ***Antirrhinum molle*** L. (Scrophulariaceae).
Note: Sutton (*Revis. Tribe Antirrhineae*: 118. 1988) incorrectly indicated 767.64 (LINN) as a syntype but as this is not a correctable error under Art. 9.8, it is designated here as the lectotype.

Antirrhinum molle Linnaeus, *Centuria I Plantarum*: 16. 1755, *nom. illeg.*
"Habitat in Hispania." RCN: 4466.
Replaced synonym of: *Antirrhinum glaucum* L. (1759).
Type not designated.
Original material: [icon] in Buxbaum, Pl. Minus Cognit. Cent. 4: 23, t. 37. 1733.
Current name: ***Linaria glauca*** (L.) Chaz. (Scrophulariaceae).
Note: A later homonym of *A. molle* L. (1753) and hence illegitimate. Linnaeus subsequently realised his error in giving the same name to two different species, renaming this later one as *A. glaucum* L. (1759).

Antirrhinum monspeliense Linnaeus, *Amoenitates Academicae* 4: 486. 1759, *orth. var.*
RCN: 4436.
Lectotype (Sutton, *Revis. Tribe Antirrhineae*: 331. 1988): Herb. Linn. No. 767.15 (LINN).
Current name: ***Linaria repens*** (L.) Mill. (Scrophulariaceae).
Note: As noted by Stearn (in Geck & Pressler, *Festschr. Claus Nissen:* 632. 1974), this is an orthographic variant of *A. monspessulanum* L. (1753), and therefore homotypic with it.

Antirrhinum monspessulanum Linnaeus, *Species Plantarum* 2: 616. 1753.
"Habitat in Gallia." RCN: 4436.
Lectotype (Sutton, *Revis. Tribe Antirrhineae*: 331. 1988): Herb. Linn. No. 767.15 (LINN).
Current name: ***Linaria repens*** (L.) Mill. (Scrophulariaceae).

Antirrhinum multicaule Linnaeus, *Species Plantarum* 2: 615. 1753.
"Habitat in Sicilia." RCN: 4456.
Lectotype (Sutton, *Revis. Tribe Antirrhineae*: 445. 1988): Herb. Clifford: 324, *Antirrhinum* 7, sheet A (BM-000646226).
Current name: ***Linaria multicaulis*** (L.) Mill. (Scrophulariaceae).
Note: Valdés (*Revis. Esp. Eur.* Linaria: 185. 1970) provided an extensive discussion.

Antirrhinum origanifolium Linnaeus, *Species Plantarum* 2: 615. 1753.
"Habitat Massiliae in muris vetustis, inque Pyrenaeis major." RCN: 4451.
Lectotype (Fernandes in *Bot. J. Linn. Soc.* 64: 216. 1971): Herb. Burser XII: 8 (UPS).
Current name: ***Chaenorhinum origanifolium*** (L.) Fourr. (Scrophulariaceae).

Antirrhinum orontium Linnaeus, *Species Plantarum* 2: 617. 1753.
"Habitat in Europae agris & arvis." RCN: 4463.
Lectotype (Fischer in *Feddes Repert.* 108: 113. 1997): Herb. Clifford: 324, *Antirrhinum* 11 (BM-000646231).
Current name: ***Misopates orontium*** (L.) Raf. (Scrophulariaceae).
Note: Sutton (*Revis. Tribe Antirrhineae*: 146. 1988) indicated the type as "probably LINN 767.61" but this statement is too imprecise to effect typification.

Antirrhinum papilionaceum Linnaeus, *Systema Naturae,* ed. 12, 2: 411; *Mantissa Plantarum*: 86. 1767.
"Habitat in Persia. D. Burmannus." RCN: 4464.
Neotype (Miller & al. in *Notes Roy. Bot. Gard. Edinburgh* 40: 28. 1982): [icon] *"Antirrhinum papilionaceum"* in Burman, Fl. Indica: 131, t. 39, f. 2. 1768.
Current name: ***Schweinfurthia papilionacea*** (L.) Boiss. (Scrophulariaceae).

Antirrhinum pedunculatum Linnaeus, *Species Plantarum,* ed. 2, 2: 857. 1763.
"Habitat in Hispania." RCN: 4461.
Lectotype (Viano in *Candollea* 33: 125. 1978): *Alströmer 125,* Herb. Linn. No. 767.55 (LINN).
Current name: ***Linaria pedunculata*** (L.) Chaz. (Scrophulariaceae).

Antirrhinum pelisserianum Linnaeus, *Species Plantarum* 2: 615. 1753.
"Habitat in Gallia." RCN: 4443.
Lectotype (Davis, *Fl. Turkey* 6: 672. 1978): Herb. Linn. No. 767.22 (LINN).
Current name: ***Linaria pelisseriana*** (L.) Mill. (Scrophulariaceae).

Note: As Valdés (*Revis. Esp. Eur.* Linaria: 77. 1970) cited both 767.22 (LINN) and (p. 72) 767.11 (LINN) as lectotype, neither choice is effective. Davis appears to have been the first to make a clear choice.

Antirrhinum purpureum Linnaeus, *Species Plantarum* 2: 613. 1753.
"Habitat ad radices Vesuvii." RCN: 4434.
Lectotype (Viano in *Candollea* 33: 255. 1978): Herb. Linn. No. 767.13 (LINN).
Current name: ***Linaria purpurea*** (L.) Mill. (Scrophulariaceae).

Antirrhinum reflexum Linnaeus, *Systema Naturae,* ed. 10, 2: 1112. 1759.
["Habitat in Barbaria. Brander."] Sp. Pl., ed. 2, 2: 857 (1763). RCN: 4460.
Lectotype (Viano in *Candollea* 33: 225. 1978): *Brander,* Herb. Linn. No. 767.54 (LINN).
Current name: ***Linaria reflexa*** (L.) Desf. (Scrophulariaceae).

Antirrhinum repens Linnaeus, *Species Plantarum* 2: 614. 1753.
"Habitat in Anglia, Gallia." RCN: 4435.
Lectotype (Fischer in *Feddes Repert.* 108: 112. 1997): [icon] *"Linaria angustifolia, flore cinereo striato"* in Dillenius, Hort. Eltham. 1: 198, t. 163, f. 197. 1732.
Current name: ***Linaria repens*** (L.) Mill. (Scrophulariaceae).
Note: Sutton (*Revis. Tribe Antirrhineae*: 331. 1988) indicated 767.14 (LINN) as a possible syntype but it is an Alströmer collection which was a post-1753 addition to the herbarium, and not original material for the name.

Antirrhinum saxatile Linnaeus, *Centuria I Plantarum*: 16. 1755.
"Habitat in Hispania." RCN: 4444.
Lectotype (Valdés, *Revis. Esp. Eur.* Linaria: 252. 1970): Herb. Linn. No. 767.23 (LINN).
Current name: ***Linaria saxatilis*** (L.) Chaz. (Scrophulariaceae).

Antirrhinum sparteum Linnaeus, *Species Plantarum* 2: 1197. 1753.
"Habitat in Hispania. Loefling." RCN: 4437.
Neotype (Viano in *Candollea* 33: 51. 1978): Herb. Linn. No. 767.20 (LINN).
Current name: ***Linaria spartea*** (L.) Chaz. (Scrophulariaceae).
Note: The sheet indicated as type by Viano is evidently a later, cultivated addition to the herbarium. However, as there are no extant original elements, this is accepted as a neotypification under Art. 9.8.

Antirrhinum spartum Linnaeus, *Centuria I Plantarum*: 17. 1755, *nom. illeg.*
"Habitat in Lusitania." RCN: 4456.
Replaced synonym of: *Antirrhinum junceum* L. (1759).
Type not designated.
Original material: none traced.
Current name: ***Linaria spartea*** (L.) Chaz. (Scrophulariaceae).
Note: This name has been mostly treated as a later homonym of *A. sparteum* L. (1753) and hence illegitimate, though Rickett (in *Lloydia* 18: 58. 1955) had doubts as to whether it should be treated in this way. As noted by Nordenstam (in *Bot. Not.* 114: 277. 1961), Linnaeus replaced *A. spartum* with *A. junceum* in the reprint of *Cent. I Pl.* (in *Amoen. Acad.* 4: 277. 1759), though the latter name was actually first published in *Syst. Nat.*, ed. 10 (May–Jun 1759).

Antirrhinum spurium Linnaeus, *Species Plantarum* 2: 613. 1753.
"Habitat in Germaniae, Angliae, Galliae, Italiae arvis." RCN: 4429.
Lectotype (Pennell in *Monogr. Acad. Nat. Sci. Philadelphia* 1: 313. 1935): Herb. Linn. No. 767.3 (LINN).
Current name: ***Kickxia spuria*** (L.) Dumort. (Scrophulariaceae).

Antirrhinum supinum Linnaeus, *Species Plantarum* 2: 615. 1753.
"Habitat in Galliae, Hispaniae arenosis." RCN: 4441.
Lectotype (designated here by Sutton): Herb. Burser XII: 29 (UPS).
Current name: ***Linaria supina*** (L.) Chaz. (Scrophulariaceae).
Note: Valdés (*Revis. Esp. Eur.* Linaria: 123. 1970) suggested that van Royen material might, if extant, be a suitable lectotype while Sutton (*Revis. Tribe Antirrhineae*: 363. 1988) incorrectly indicated Herb. Burser XII: 29 (UPS) as a syntype (though it is original material). The latter is designated as the lectotype here.

Antirrhinum triornithophorum Linnaeus, *Species Plantarum* 2: 613. 1753.
"Habitat in Lusitania, America." RCN: 4433.
Lectotype (Valdés, *Revis. Esp. Eur.* Linaria: 82. 1970): Herb. Linn. No. 767.11 (LINN).
Current name: ***Antirrhinum triornithophorum*** L. (Scrophulariaceae).

Antirrhinum triphyllum Linnaeus, *Species Plantarum* 2: 613. 1753.
"Habitat in umbrosis montibus Valentinis & Hylbaeis circa Syracusas." RCN: 4432.
Lectotype (Qaiser in Jafri & El-Gadi, *Fl. Libya* 88: 47. 1982): Herb. Linn. No. 767.9 (LINN).
Current name: ***Linaria triphylla*** (L.) Mill. (Scrophulariaceae).
Note: The type choice made by Qaiser is stated to have been published on 1 June 1982 which therefore narrowly pre-dates the choice of Herb. Clifford: 324, *Antirrhinum* 5 (BM) made by Viano (in *Candollea* 37: 223) and published on 31 July 1982.

Antirrhinum triste Linnaeus, *Species Plantarum* 2: 613. 1753.
"Habitat Gibraltariae." RCN: 4440.
Lectotype (Valdés, *Revis. Esp. Eur.* Linaria: 140, 146. 1970): [icon] *"Linaria tristis Hispanica"* in Dillenius, Hort. Eltham. 1: 201, t. 164, f. 199. 1732.
Current name: ***Linaria tristis*** (L.) Mill. (Scrophulariaceae).

Antirrhinum villosum Linnaeus, *Species Plantarum,* ed. 2, 2: 852. 1763.
"Habitat in Hispania." RCN: 4450.
Lectotype (designated here by Sutton): [icon] *"Antirrhinum Saxat. minus Origani folio viscoso et villoso flore albo amplo"* in Barrelier, Pl. Galliam: 21, t. 597. 1714.
Current name: ***Chaenorhinum villosum*** (L.) Lange (Scrophulariaceae).
Note: Fernandes (in *Bot. J. Linn. Soc.* 64: 221. 1971) treated 767.35 (LINN), an Alströmer collection, as the type but it was determined by Linnaeus as *A. origanifolium* L. (1753), so it cannot be original material for either name.

Antirrhinum viscosum Linnaeus, *Centuria II Plantarum*: 21. 1756.
"Habitat in Hispania." RCN: 4445.
Lectotype (designated here by Sutton): Herb. Linn. No. 767.24 (LINN).
Current name: ***Linaria viscosa*** (L.) Chaz. (Scrophulariaceae).
Note: Viano (in *Candollea* 33: 57. 1978) wrongly indicated both 767.24 and 767.25 (LINN) as syntypes.

Aphanes arvensis Linnaeus, *Species Plantarum* 1: 123. 1753.
"Habitat in Europae arvis." RCN: 1018.
Lectotype (Kalheber & Lippert in Jarvis & al., *Regnum Veg.* 127: 19. 1993): Herb. Burser VII(2): 47 (UPS).
Generitype of *Aphanes* Linnaeus.
Current name: ***Alchemilla arvensis*** (L.) Scop. (Rosaceae).

Aphyllanthes monspeliensis Linnaeus, *Species Plantarum* 1: 294. 1753.
"Habitat Monspelii, prope Castelneuf locis montosis saxosis sterilibus." RCN: 2343.
Type not designated.
Original material: Herb. Burser XI: 97 (UPS); Herb. Linn. No. 418.1 (LINN); [icon] in Morison, Pl. Hist. Univ. 2: 562, s. 5, t. 25, f. 12. 1680; [icon] in Lobel, Stirp. Adversaria: 190. 1570.
Generitype of *Aphyllanthes* Linnaeus.
Current name: **Aphyllanthes monspeliensis** L. (Liliaceae/Aphyllanthaceae).

Aphyteia hydnora Linnaeus, *Planta Aphyteia*: 10. 1776, *nom. illeg.*
"Habitat ad Caput bonae spei, pone montes sic dictos Bāckfāldtenses."
Replaced synonym: *Hydnora africana* Thunb. (1775).
Lectotype (Musselman in Jarvis & al., *Regnum Veg.* 127: 20. 1993): Herb. Thunberg No. 15452 (UPS).
Generitype of *Aphyteia* Linnaeus.
Current name: **Hydnora africana** Thunb. (Hydnoraceae).

Apium graveolens Linnaeus, *Species Plantarum* 1: 264. 1753.
"Habitat in Europae humectis, praesertim maritimis." RCN: 2110.
Lectotype (Tardieu-Blot in Aubréville, *Fl. Cambodge Laos Vietnam* 5: 44. 1967): Herb. Linn. No. 374.3 (LINN).
Generitype of *Apium* Linnaeus.
Current name: **Apium graveolens** L. (Apiaceae).
Note: Apium graveolens, with the type designated by Reduron & Jarvis (Herb. Clifford: 107, *Apium* 1, BM), was proposed as conserved type of the genus by Jarvis (in *Taxon* 41: 557. 1992). However, the proposal was eventually ruled unnecessary by the General Committee (see Barrie, *l.c.* 55: 795–796. 2006 for a review of the history of this and related proposals). The type designated by Reduron & Jarvis is, however, pre-dated by the choice of 374.3 (LINN) by Tardieu-Blot (1967). With the failure of the conservation proposal, this collection becomes the correct choice as type.

Apium petroselinum Linnaeus, *Species Plantarum* 1: 264. 1753.
"Habitat in Sardinia, juxta scaturigines." RCN: 2109.
Lectotype (Jafri in Jafri & El-Gadi, *Fl. Libya* 117: 82. 1985): Herb. Clifford: 108, *Apium* 2 (BM-000558405).
Current name: **Petroselinum crispum** (Mill.) Fuss (Apiaceae).

Apluda aristata Linnaeus, *Centuria II Plantarum*: 7. 1756.
"Habitat in India." RCN: 7577.
Lectotype (Renvoize in Cafferty & al. in *Taxon* 49: 246. 2000): Herb. Linn. No. 1213.4 (LINN).
Current name: **Apluda mutica** L. (Poaceae).

Apluda mutica Linnaeus, *Species Plantarum* 1: 82. 1753.
"Habitat in India." RCN: 7576.
Lectotype (Cope in Jarvis & al., *Regnum Veg.* 127: 20. 1993): Herb. Linn. No. 1213.1 (LINN).
Generitype of *Apluda* Linnaeus.
Current name: **Apluda mutica** L. (Poaceae).

Apluda zeugites Linnaeus, *Systema Naturae*, ed. 10, 2: 1306. 1759.
["Habitat in Jamaica."] Sp. Pl., ed. 2, 2: 1487 (1763). RCN: 7578.
Lectotype (Hitchcock in *Contr. U. S. Natl. Herb.* 12: 127. 1908): *Browne*, Herb. Linn. No. 1213.5 (LINN).
Current name: **Zeugites americana** Willd. (Poaceae).

Apocynum androsaemifolium Linnaeus, *Species Plantarum* 1: 213. 1753.
"Habitat in Virginia, Canada." RCN: 1763.

Lectotype (Boivin in *Naturaliste Canad.* 93: 114. 1966): Herb. Clifford: 80, *Apocynum* 1 (BM-000558176).
Generitype of *Apocynum* Linnaeus (vide Hitchcock, *Prop. Brit. Bot.*: 136. 1929).
Current name: **Apocynum androsaemifolium** L. (Apocynaceae).
Note: The specific epithet appeared as "fol. androsaemi" in the protologue but is to be corrected to "androsaemifolium" (Art. 23.7, Ex. 18).

Apocynum cannabinum Linnaeus, *Species Plantarum* 1: 213. 1753.
"Habitat in Canada, Virginia." RCN: 1764.
Lectotype (designated here by Reveal): Herb. Linn. No. 309.4 (LINN).
Current name: **Apocynum cannabinum** L. var. **cannabinum** (Apocynaceae).

Apocynum frutescens Linnaeus, *Species Plantarum* 1: 213. 1753.
"Habitat in Zeylona." RCN: 1766.
Lectotype (Huber in Abeywickrama, *Revised Handb. Fl. Ceylon* 1(1): 27. 1973): Herb. Hermann 3: 29, No. 114 (BM-000621912).
Current name: **Ichnocarpus frutescens** (L.) W.T. Aiton (Apocynaceae).

Apocynum reticulatum Linnaeus, *Species Plantarum* 1: 214. 1753.
"Habitat in India." RCN: 1767.
Type not designated.
Original material: none traced.
Current name: **Parsonsia sp.** (Apocynaceae).
Note: The application of this name is uncertain.

Apocynum venetum Linnaeus, *Species Plantarum* 1: 213. 1753.
"Habitat in Adriatici maris insulis." RCN: 1765.
Type not designated.
Original material: Herb. Clifford: 80, *Apocynum* 2 (BM); Herb. Burser XVI(2): 43 (UPS); [icon] in Lobel, Pl. Stirp. Hist.: 201. 1576.
Current name: **Trachomitum venetum** (L.) Woodson (Apocynaceae).

Aquilegia alpina Linnaeus, *Species Plantarum* 1: 533. 1753.
"Habitat in Helvetia." RCN: 3965.
Lectotype (Nardi in Jarvis & al. in *Taxon* 54: 469. 2005): Herb. Burser VII(1): 108 (UPS).
Current name: **Aquilegia alpina** L. (Ranunculaceae).

Aquilegia canadensis Linnaeus, *Species Plantarum* 1: 533. 1753.
"Habitat in Virginia, Canada." RCN: 3966.
Lectotype (Munz in *Gentes Herb.* 7: 118. 1946): Herb. Linn. No. 699.7 (LINN), see opposite, above left.
Current name: **Aquilegia canadensis** L. var. **canadensis** (Ranunculaceae).
Note: A Kalm collection of this taxon in UPS is illustrated by Lundqvist & Moberg (in *Thunbergia* 19: 5, f. 1. 1993).

Aquilegia vulgaris Linnaeus, *Species Plantarum* 1: 533. 1753.
"Habitat in Europae nemoribus saxosis." RCN: 3964.
Lectotype (Jonsell & Jarvis in Jarvis & al., *Regnum Veg.* 127: 20. 1993): Herb. Clifford: 215, *Aquilegia* 1, sheet A (BM-000628801).
Generitype of *Aquilegia* Linnaeus (vide Green, *Prop. Brit. Bot.*: 162. 1929).
Current name: **Aquilegia vulgaris** L. (Ranunculaceae).
Note: Jonsell & Jarvis (in *Nordic J. Bot.* 14: 160. 1994) discussed the reasons for their earlier (1993) choice of lectotype, which pre-dates Vassiljeva's type choice (in *Novosti Sist. Vyssh. Rast.* 30: 15. 1996) of 699.5 (LINN).

The lectotype of *Aquilegia canadensis* L.

Aquilicia sambucina Linnaeus, *Mantissa Plantarum Altera*: 211. 1771, *nom. illeg.*
"Habitat in Java." RCN: 1636.
Replaced synonym of: *Staphylea indica* Burm. f. (1768).
Lectotype (Smith, *Fl. Vitiensis Nova* 3: 715. 1985): [icon] "*Staphylea indica*" in Burman, Fl. Indica: 75, t. 24, f. 2. 1768.
Generitype of *Aquilicia* Linnaeus.
Current name: ***Leea indica*** (Burm. f.) Merr. (Leeaceae).
Note: A superfluous name for *Staphylea indica* Burm. f. (1768).

Arabis alpina Linnaeus, *Species Plantarum* 2: 664. 1753.
"Habitat in Alpibus Helveticis, Lapponicis." RCN: 4835.
Lectotype (Jonsell in Jarvis & al., *Regnum Veg.* 127: 20. 1993): Herb. Clifford: 335, *Arabis* 1 (BM-000646327).
Generitype of *Arabis* Linnaeus (vide Green, *Prop. Brit. Bot.*: 171. 1929).
Current name: ***Arabis alpina*** L. (Brassicaceae).
Note: Jonsell (in Polhill, *Fl. Trop. E. Africa, Cruciferae*: 47. 1982) wrongly indicated the post-1753 842.1 (LINN) as lectotype, and Talavera & Velayos (in *Anales Jard. Bot. Madrid* 50: 146. 1992) restricted this to the central of the three specimens on the sheet. However, none of these specimens is original material for the name

and Jonsell (1993) therefore rejected his earlier choice, replacing it with a Clifford sheet.

Arabis canadensis Linnaeus, *Species Plantarum* 2: 665. 1753.
"Habitat in America septentrionali." RCN: 4842.
Lectotype (Reveal in Cafferty & Jarvis in *Taxon* 51: 531. 2002): *Clayton 400*, Herb. Linn. No. 842.12, left specimen (LINN; iso- BM).
Current name: ***Boechera canadensis*** (L.) Al-Shehbaz (Brassicaceae).

Arabis capensis Linnaeus, *Systema Naturae*, ed. 10, 2: 1135. 1759. RCN: 4826.
Lectotype (Jordaan in Cafferty & Jarvis in *Taxon* 51: 531. 2002): ex Herb. Linn. "Arabis capensis" (BM-000576299).
Current name: ***Heliophila pusilla*** L. f. var. ***pusilla*** (Brassicaceae).
Note: The lectotype chosen by Jordaan is one of the specimens given by J.E. Smith to Sir Joseph Banks from the Linnaean herbarium (as a supposed duplicate) after its purchase from Linnaeus' widow.

Arabis grandiflora Linnaeus, *Species Plantarum* 2: 665. 1753.
"Habitat in Sibiria." RCN: 4836.
Lectotype (Marhold in Cafferty & Jarvis in *Taxon* 51: 531. 2002): *Steller*, Herb. Linn. No. 842.3 (LINN), see p. 230.
Current name: ***Parrya nudicaulis*** (L.) Regel (Brassicaceae).

Arabis halleri Linnaeus, *Species Plantarum*, ed. 2, 2: 929. 1763.
"Habitat in Harcynia ad Clausthal, locis humectis." RCN: 4841.
Lectotype (Al-Shehbaz in Cafferty & Jarvis in *Taxon* 51: 531. 2002): [icon] "*Sisymbrium palustre album foliis imis Barbareae reliquis integris*" in Haller, Opusc. Bot.: 152, unnumbered plate. 1749. – Epitype (Al-Shehbaz in Cafferty & Jarvis in *Taxon* 51: 531. 2002): Herb. Linn. No. 842.11 (LINN).
Current name: ***Arabidopsis halleri*** (L.) O'Kane & Al-Shehbaz (Brassicaceae).
Note: O'Kane & Al-Shehbaz (in *Novon* 7: 325. 1997) incorrectly indicated Herb. Linn. No. 842.11 (LINN) as the holotype. However, the material is unannotated by Linnaeus and cannot be considered original material for the name. Al-Shehbaz subsequently rejected this choice, designating a Haller illustration as lectotype in its place, with the LINN sheet as epitype.

Arabis hispida Linnaeus, *Systema Vegetabilium*, ed. 13: 501. 1774.
"Habitat in Austria." RCN: 4840.
Type not designated.
Original material: Herb. Linn. No. 842.9 (LINN); Herb. Linn. No. 274.17 (S).
Current name: ***Cardaminopsis*** sp. (Brassicaceae).
Note: The application of this name is uncertain.

Arabis lyrata Linnaeus, *Species Plantarum* 2: 665. 1753.
"Habitat in Canada. D. Kalm." RCN: 4839.
Lectotype (O'Kane & Al-Shehbaz in *Novon* 7: 325. 1997): *Kalm*, Herb. Linn. No. 842.8 (LINN).
Current name: ***Arabidopsis lyrata*** (L.) O'Kane & Al-Shehbaz (Brassicaceae).

Arabis pendula Linnaeus, *Species Plantarum* 2: 665. 1753.
"Habitat in Sibiria." RCN: 4843.
Lectotype (Botschantzeva in *Bot. Zhurn.* 82(8): 116. 1997): *Amman 19*, Herb. Linn. No. 842.13 (LINN).
Current name: ***Catolobus pendulus*** (L.) Al-Shehbaz (Brassicaceae).

Arabis thaliana Linnaeus, *Species Plantarum* 2: 665. 1753.
"Habitat in Europae septentrionalioris sabulosis." RCN: 4837.
Lectotype (Anon in *Haussknechtia, Beih.* 8: 43. 1997): [icon] "*Pilosella siliquata*" in Thal, Sylv. Herc.: 84, t. 7, f. D. 1588.

Current name: ***Arabidopsis thaliana*** (L.) Heynh. (Brassicaceae).
Note: Franchetti (in *Webbia* 14: 207. 1958) stated that the type should
be a Clifford specimen, if in existence, or the Thal plate if not.
Jonsell (in Polhill, *Fl. Trop. E. Africa, Cruciferae*: 45. 1982) chose
842.5 (LINN) as lectotype. This sheet lacks a *Species Plantarum*
number (i.e. "3") and, coming from Löfling, is not believed to be
original material for the name. However, the Thal plate has
subsequently been formally designated as lectotype (by an unknown
author).

Arabis turrita Linnaeus, *Species Plantarum* 2: 665. 1753.
"Habitat in Helvetia, Hungaria, Gallia, Sicilia." RCN: 4844.
Lectotype (Al-Shehbaz & Turland in Cafferty & Jarvis in *Taxon* 51:
531. 2002): [icon] *"Brassica syl. albido flore nutante siliqua"* in
Boccone, Mus. Piante Rar. Sicilia: 81, t. 72. 1697. – Epitype (Al-
Shehbaz & Turland in Cafferty & Jarvis in *Taxon* 51: 531. 2002):
Italy. Toscana, La Verna, 27 May 1956, *Corradi s.n.* (FI).
Current name: ***Pseudoturritis turrita*** (L.) Al-Shehbaz (Brassicaceae).
Note: Although Talavera & Velayos (in *Anales Jard. Bot. Madrid* 50:
147. 1992) designated 842.14 (LINN) as lectotype, the sheet lacks
the *Species Plantarum* number (i.e. "7") and was evidently a post-
1753 addition to the collection and not original material for the
name.

Arachis hypogaea Linnaeus, *Species Plantarum* 2: 741. 1753.
"Habitat in Brasilia, Peru." RCN: 5303.
Lectotype (Krapovickas & Gregory in *Bonplandia* 8: 148. 1994):
Herb. Clifford: 353, *Arachis* 2 (BM-000646534).
Generitype of *Arachis* Linnaeus.
Current name: ***Arachis hypogaea*** L. (Fabaceae: Faboideae).
Note: Many authors, from Krapovickas & Rigoni in *Rev. Inv. Agric.*
14: 197–228 (1960, *n.v.*) onwards, have wrongly treated the post-
1753 Herb. Linn. 909.1 (LINN) as type. Krapovickas &
Gregory were the first to choose one of the original elements as
lectotype.

Aralia arborea Linnaeus, *Systema Naturae,* ed. 10, 2: 967. 1759.
["Habitat in Jamaica."] Sp. Pl., ed. 2, 1: 392 (1762). RCN: 2180.
Type not designated.
Original material: *Browne*, Herb. Linn. No. 394.1 (LINN); [icon] in
Plumier in Burman, Pl. Amer.: 139, t. 148. 1757.
Current name: ***Dendropanax arboreus*** (L.) Decne. & Planch.
(Araliaceae).

Aralia chinensis Linnaeus, *Species Plantarum* 1: 273. 1753.
"Habitat in China. Osbeck." RCN: 2182.
Lectotype (Grushvitzky & al. in *Novosti Sist. Vyssh. Rast.* 22: 188.
1985): *Osbeck s.n.*, Herb. Linn. No. 394.4 (LINN).
Current name: ***Aralia chinensis*** L. (Araliaceae).
Note: See also the discussion by Wen & Reveal (in *Taxon* 41: 71.
1992).

Aralia nudicaulis Linnaeus, *Species Plantarum* 1: 274. 1753.
"Habitat in Virginia, simillima (forte eadem) in Iava." RCN: 2184.
Lectotype (Wen & Reveal in *Taxon* 41: 72. 1992): Herb. Clifford:
113, *Aralia* 2 (BM-000558452).
Current name: ***Aralia nudicaulis*** L. (Araliaceae).

Aralia racemosa Linnaeus, *Species Plantarum* 1: 273. 1753.
"Habitat in Canada." RCN: 2183.
Lectotype (Wen & Reveal in *Taxon* 41: 72. 1992): Herb. Linn. No.
394.6 (LINN).
Generitype of *Aralia* Linnaeus (vide Hitchcock, *Prop. Brit. Bot.*: 143.
1929).
Current name: ***Aralia racemosa*** L. (Araliaceae).

Aralia spinosa Linnaeus, *Species Plantarum* 1: 273. 1753.
"Habitat in Virginia." RCN: 2181.
Lectotype (Wen & Reveal in *Taxon* 41: 73. 1992): Herb. Clifford:
113, *Aralia* 1 (BM-000558451).
Current name: ***Aralia spinosa*** L. (Araliaceae).
Note: Although Wijnands (*Bot. Commelins*: 47. 1983) treated material
in the Clifford herbarium as the lectotype, it is not clear which of
the several specimens there he intended. As they are evidently not
part of a single gathering, Art. 9.15 does not apply.

Arbutus acadiensis Linnaeus, *Species Plantarum* 1: 395. 1753.
"Habitat in Acadia." RCN: 3109.
Type not designated.
Original material: none traced.
Note: The application of this name is uncertain.

Arbutus alpina Linnaeus, *Species Plantarum* 1: 395. 1753.
"Habitat in Alpibus Lapponiae, Helvetiae, Sibiriae." RCN: 3110.
Lectotype (Wallace in Cafferty & Jarvis in *Taxon* 51: 752. 2003
[2002]): Herb. Linn. No. 161 (LAPP).
Current name: ***Arctous alpina*** (L.) Nied. (Ericaceae).

Arbutus andrachne Linnaeus, *Systema Naturae,* ed. 10, 2: 1024. 1759.
["Habitat in Oriente."] Sp. Pl., ed. 2, 1: 566 (1762). RCN: 3108.
Neotype (Turland & Cafferty in Cafferty & Jarvis in *Taxon* 51: 752.
2003 [2002]): Greece. Fl. Graeca Exsiccata, "in monte Pentelico
Atticae", April, *Orphanides 78* (BM-000576313).
Current name: ***Arbutus andrachne*** L. (Ericaceae).

Arbutus unedo Linnaeus, *Species Plantarum* 1: 395. 1753.
"Habitat in Europa australi." RCN: 3107.
Lectotype (Chamberlain in Jarvis & al., *Regnum Veg.* 127: 20. 1993):
Herb. Clifford: 163, *Arbutus* 1 (BM-000628452).
Generitype of *Arbutus* Linnaeus (vide Hitchcock, *Prop. Brit. Bot.*: 154.
1929).
Current name: ***Arbutus unedo*** L. (Ericaceae).

Arbutus uva-ursi Linnaeus, *Species Plantarum* 1: 395. 1753.
"Habitat in Europa frigida, Canada." RCN: 3111.
Lectotype (Wallace in Cafferty & Jarvis in *Taxon* 51: 752. 2003
[2002]): Herb. Linn. No. 566.8 (LINN).
Current name: ***Arctostaphylos uva-ursi*** (L.) Spreng. (Ericaceae).

Arctium carduelis Linnaeus, *Systema Naturae,* ed. 12, 2: 528;
Mantissa Plantarum: 108. 1767.
"Habitat in Alpibus Carneolae superioris. D. Scopoli." RCN: 5928.
Lectotype (Duistermaat in *Gorteria*, suppl., 3: 128. 1996): *Scopoli s.n.*,
Herb. Linn. No. 964.3 (LINN).
Current name: ***Carduus carduelis*** (L.) Gren. (Asteraceae).

Arctium lappa Linnaeus, *Species Plantarum* 2: 816. 1753.
"Habitat in Europae cultis ruderatis." RCN: 5926.
Lectotype (Duistermaat in *Taxon* 52: 851. 2003): [icon] *"Bardana, sive
Lappa maior"* in Dodoëns, Stirp. Hist. Pempt., ed. 2: 38. 1616. –
Epitype (Duistermaat in *Taxon* 52: 851. 2003): France. S of Macon,
roadside, 30 Jul 1990, *H. Duistermaat & J.J. Vermeulen 137* (L).
Generitype of *Arctium* Linnaeus (vide Green, *Prop. Brit. Bot.*: 179.
1929).
Current name: ***Arctium lappa*** L. (Asteraceae).
Note: Duistermaat (in *Gorteria*, suppl., 3: 76, 80. 1996) noted that
964.1 (LINN) is identifiable as *A. tomentosum* Mill. Subsequently,
Duistermaat (2003) provided a detailed assessment of the identities
of all available elements, designating a Dodoëns plate as lectotype
supported by an epitype (illustrated in *Gorteria*, suppl., 3: 77, f.
18.2. 1996).

Arctium personata Linnaeus, *Species Plantarum* 2: 816. 1753.
"Habitat in Alpibus Helvetiae, Genevae, Taurero Austriae." RCN: 5927.
Type not designated.
Original material: Herb. Burser XXI: 13, syntype (UPS); [icon] in Gmelin, Fl. Sibirica 2: 62, t. 24. 1752; [icon] in Haller, Enum. Meth. Stirp. Helv. 2: 678, t. 19. 1742.
Current name: ***Carduus personata*** (L.) Jacq. (Asteraceae).
Note: Duistermaat (in *Gorteria*, suppl., 3: 128. 1996) incorrectly indicated 964.2 (as 946.2) LINN as "type". However, the sheet is annotated only by Linnaeus filius and is not original material for the name. Furthermore, a syntype (Herb. Burser XXI: 13, UPS) exists and takes precedence over any original material (Art. 9.10).

Arctopus echinatus Linnaeus, *Species Plantarum* 2: 1058. 1753.
"Habitat in Aethiopia." RCN: 7708.
Proposed conserved type (Van Wyk & al. in *Taxon* 55: 541. 2006): South Africa. Western Cape Province, Cape Town, Signal Hill, near Kramat, *Manning & Reeves 2845* (NBG).
Generitype of *Arctopus* Linnaeus.
Current name: ***Arctopus echinatus*** L. (Apiaceae).
Note: Burtt (in *Edinburgh J. Bot.* 48: 184. 1991) indicated material in the Clifford herbarium as a likely type, but no relevant specimen exists there. The same author subsequently designated a Burman copperplate (*Rar. Afr. Pl.* 1: t. 1. 1738, reproduced by Jarvis in *Symb. Bot. Upsal.* 33(3): 30, f. 5. 2005) as lectotype. Unfortunately, this is identifiable, not as *A. echinatus*, but rather as *A. monacanthus* Sonder. Van Wyk & al. (in *Taxon* 55: 541. 2006) therefore proposed the conservation of *A. echinatus* with a conserved type.

Arctotis acaulis Linnaeus, *Species Plantarum*, ed. 2, 2: 1306. 1763.
"Habitat ad Cap. b. spei." RCN: 6680.
Lectotype (Wijnands, *Bot. Commelins*: 67. 1983): [icon] "*Anemonospermos Afr. fol. plantaginis flore sulph.*" in Commelin, Hort. Med. Amstelaed. Pl. Rar.: 35, t. 35. 1706.
Current name: ***Arctotis acaulis*** L. (Asteraceae).

Arctotis angustifolia Linnaeus, *Species Plantarum* 2: 923. 1753.
"Habitat in Aethiopia." RCN: 6673.
Lectotype (Nordenstam in Jarvis & al., *Regnum Veg.* 127: 20. 1993): Herb. Clifford: 412, *Arctotis* 2 (BM-000647143).
Generitype of *Arctotis* Linnaeus (vide Green, *Prop. Brit. Bot.*: 183. 1929).
Current name: ***Arctotis angustifolia*** L. (Asteraceae).

Arctotis anthemoides Linnaeus, *Systema Naturae*, ed. 10, 2: 1234. 1759.
["Habitat ad Cap. b. spei."] Sp. Pl. ed. 2, 2: 1307 (1763). RCN: 6678.
Lectotype (Prassler in *Mitt. Bot. Staatssamml. München* 6: 428. 1967): Herb. Linn. No. 1036.22 (LINN).
Current name: ***Ursinia anthemoides*** (L.) Poir. (Asteraceae).

Arctotis aspera Linnaeus, *Species Plantarum* 2: 922. 1753.
"Habitat in Aethiopia." RCN: 6674.
Lectotype (Wijnands, *Bot. Commelins*: 67. 1983): Herb. Linn. No. 1036.10 (LINN).
Current name: ***Arctotis aspera*** L. (Asteraceae).

Arctotis calendula Linnaeus, *Species Plantarum* 2: 922. 1753.
"Habitat in Aethiopia." RCN: 6670.
Lectotype (Wijnands, *Bot. Commelins*: 66. 1983): Herb. Linn. No. 1036.7 (LINN).
Current name: ***Arctotheca calendula*** (L.) Levyns (Asteraceae).

Arctotis calendula Linnaeus var. **coruscans** Linnaeus, *Systema Naturae*, ed. 12, 2: 578. 1767.
RCN: 6671.
Type not designated.
Original material: none traced.
Current name: ***Arctotheca calendula*** (L.) Levyns (Asteraceae).

Arctotis calendula Linnaeus var. **hypochondriaca** Linnaeus, *Systema Naturae*, ed. 12, 2: 578. 1767.
RCN: 6671.
Type not designated.
Original material: none traced.
Current name: ***Arctotheca calendula*** (L.) Levyns (Asteraceae).

Arctotis calendula Linnaeus var. **superba** (Linnaeus) Linnaeus, *Systema Naturae*, ed. 12, 2: 578. 1767.
["Habitat in Aethiopia."] Cent. II Pl.: 32 (1756). RCN: 6671.
Basionym: *Arctotis superba* L. (1756).
Type not designated.
Original material: as basionym.
Current name: ***Arctotheca calendula*** (L.) Levyns (Asteraceae).

Arctotis calendula Linnaeus var. **tristis** (Linnaeus) Linnaeus, *Systema Naturae*, ed. 12, 2: 578. 1767.
["Habitat in Aethiopia."] Sp. Pl. 2: 922 (1753). RCN: 6671.
Basionym: *Arctotis tristis* L. (1753).
Type not designated.
Original material: as basionym.
Current name: ***Arctotheca calendula*** (L.) Levyns (Asteraceae).

Arctotis calendulacea Linnaeus, *Systema Naturae*, ed. 12, 2: 578. 1767, *orth. var.*
["Habitat in Aethiopia."] Sp. Pl. 2: 922 (1753). RCN: 6671.
Lectotype (Wijnands, *Bot. Commelins*: 66. 1983): Herb. Linn. No. 1036.7 (LINN).
Current name: ***Arctotheca calendula*** (L.) Levyns (Asteraceae).
Note: An orthographic variant of *A. calendula* L. (1753).

Arctotis dentata Linnaeus, *Plantae Rariores Africanae*: 25. 1760.
["Habitat ad Cap. b. spei."] Sp. Pl. ed. 2, 2: 1307 (1763). RCN: 6677.
Lectotype (Prassler in *Mitt. Bot. Staatssamml. München* 6: 400. 1967): Herb. Linn. No. 1036.20 (LINN).
Current name: ***Ursinia dentata*** (L.) Poir. (Asteraceae).

Arctotis paleacea Linnaeus, *Plantae Rariores Africanae*: 25. 1760.
["Habitat ad Cap. b. spei."] Sp. Pl., ed. 2, 2: 1307 (1763). RCN: 6676.
Lectotype (Wijnands, *Bot. Commelins*: 86. 1983): Herb. Linn. No. 1036.17 (LINN).
Current name: ***Ursinia paleacea*** (L.) Moench (Asteraceae).
Note: Prassler (in *Mitt. Bot. Staatssamml. München* 6: 411–416. 1967) rejected this as a *nomen ambiguum* but Wijnands disagreed, typifying the name and taking it up in *Ursinia* (see also Wijnands in *Taxon* 34: 311. 1985).

Arctotis paradoxa Linnaeus, *Centuria II Plantarum*: 32. 1756.
"Habitat in Aethiopia. Ascanius." RCN: 6675.
Type not designated.
Original material: Herb. Linn. No. 1036.14 (LINN); Herb. Linn. No. 1036.16 (LINN); Herb. Linn. No. 1036.13? (LINN); *Oldenland*, Herb. Burman (G); [icon] in Burman, Rar. Afric. Pl.: 175, t. 64. 1739.
Current name: ***Ursinia anthemoides*** (L.) Poir. (Asteraceae).

Arctotis plantaginea Linnaeus, *Species Plantarum,* ed. 2, 2: 1306.
1763.
"Habitat ad Cap. b. spei." RCN: 6672.
Type not designated.
Original material: none traced.
Note: The application of this name seems to be uncertain, and there
appear to be no original elements.

Arctotis radicans Linnaeus, *Mantissa Plantarum Altera*: 479. 1771.
RCN: 6673.
Type not designated.
Original material: none traced.
Current name: ***Arctotis angustifolia*** L. (Asteraceae).

Arctotis superba Linnaeus, *Centuria II Plantarum*: 32. 1756.
"Habitat in Aethiopia." RCN: 6668.
Basionym of: *Arctotis calendula* L. var. *superba* (L.) L. (1767).
Type not designated.
Original material: Herb. Linn. No. 1036.1 (LINN); [icon] in
Volckamer, Fl. Noriberg.: 224. 1700.
Current name: ***Arctotheca calendula*** (L.) Levyns (Asteraceae).

Arctotis tenuifolia Linnaeus, *Mantissa Plantarum Altera*: 288. 1771.
"Habitat in Cap. b. spei littore maritimo." RCN: 6679.
Lectotype (Prassler in *Mitt. Bot. Staatssamml. München* 6: 409. 1967):
Herb. Linn. No. 1036.24 (LINN).
Current name: ***Ursinia tenuifolia*** (L.) Poir. subsp. ***tenuifolia***
(Asteraceae).

Arctotis tristis Linnaeus, *Species Plantarum* 2: 922. 1753.
"Habitat in Aethiopia." RCN: 6669.
Basionym of: *Arctotis calendula* L. var. *tristis* (L.) L. (1767).
Type not designated.
Original material: Herb. A. van Royen No. 900.255–167? (L); Herb.
Linn. No. 1036.1 (LINN); Herb. A. van Royen No. 900.255–159?
(L); [icon] in Breyn, Prodr. Fasc. Rar. Pl.: 27, t. 15, f. 1. 1739.
Current name: ***Arctotheca calendula*** (L.) Levyns (Asteraceae).

Arduina bispinosa Linnaeus, *Systema Naturae,* ed. 12, 2: 180;
Mantissa Plantarum: 52. 1767.
"Habitat ad Cap. b. spei." RCN: 1587.
Lectotype (Codd in *Bothalia* 7: 450. 1961): [icon] *"Lycium foliis
cordato-ovatis oppositis sessilibus perennantibus, spinis crassis bigeminis
floribus confertis"* in Miller, Fig. Pl. Gard. Dict. 2: 200, t. 300. 1760.
Generitype of *Arduina* Linnaeus, non Adans. (1763), *nom. rej.*
Current name: ***Carissa bispinosa*** (L.) Brenan (Apocynaceae).

Areca catechu Linnaeus, *Species Plantarum* 2: 1189. 1753.
"Habitat in India." RCN: 8548.
Lectotype (Moore & Dransfield in *Taxon* 28: 67, f. 7. 1979): [icon]
"Pinanga" in Rumphius, Herb. Amboin. 1: 26, t. 4. 1741.
Generitype of *Areca* Linnaeus.
Current name: ***Areca catechu*** L. (Arecaceae).

Arenaria balearica Linnaeus, *Systema Naturae,* ed. 12, 3: 230. 1768.
"Habitat insul. Balearibus. Gerard. Zoega." RCN: 3289.
Neotype (Diana-Corrias in *Boll. Soc. Sarda Sci. Nat.* 20: 294. 1981):
Herb. Linn. No. 585.12 (LINN).
Current name: ***Arenaria balearica*** L. (Caryophyllaceae).
Note: The material indicated as lectotype by Diana-Corrias carries
"Arenaria lucida HU" written by Linnaeus, though the fact that it
matches the protologue of *A. balearica* well, presumably led Smith
to add "balearica" to the sheet. Given the doubts as to whether this
is original material for the name, the collection is accepted as a
neotype (Art. 9.8).

Arenaria bavarica Linnaeus, *Centuria II Plantarum*: 17. 1756.
"Habitat in Bavaria, Baldo. Seguier." RCN: 3295.
Lectotype (Sauer in *Bot. Jahrb. Syst.* 84: 278. 1965): *Séguier*, Herb.
Linn. No. 585.26 (LINN).
Current name: ***Moehringia bavarica*** (L.) Gren. (Caryophyllaceae).

Arenaria biflora Linnaeus, *Systema Naturae,* ed. 12, 2: 312; *Mantissa
Plantarum*: 71. 1767.
"Habitat in Europae australis Alpinis." RCN: 3284.
Lectotype (López González in Cafferty & Jarvis in *Taxon* 53: 1050.
2004): *Vandelli 17*, Herb. Linn. No. 585.5 (LINN), see p. 233.
Current name: ***Arenaria biflora*** L. (Caryophyllaceae).

Arenaria cerastoides Linnaeus, *Amoenitates Academicae* 4: 483. 1759,
nom. nud.
Type not relevant.
Note: As noted by Stearn (in Geck & Pressler, *Festschr. Claus Nissen*:
632. 1974), this "name" appeared without reference to Magnol's
Botanicum Monspeliense and is a *nomen nudum*.

Arenaria ciliata Linnaeus, *Species Plantarum* 1: 425. 1753.
"Habitat in Alpibus Helveticis, Pyrenaeis." RCN: 3287.
Replaced synonym of: *Arenaria multicaulis* L. (1759), *nom. illeg.*
Lectotype (López González in Cafferty & Jarvis in *Taxon* 53: 1050.
2004): [icon] *"Alsine serpilli folio, multicaulis et multiflora"* in
Séguier, Pl. Veron. 1: 420, 417, t. 5, f. 2. 1745.
Current name: ***Arenaria ciliata*** L. (Caryophyllaceae).
Note: Gutermann (in *Phyton (Horn)* 17: 32–33. 1975) indicated that
the name should probably be typified by the Séguier plate but fell
short of explicitly designating it as type, stating that the problem
needed further study.

Arenaria fasciculata Linnaeus, *Systema Naturae,* ed. 12, 2: 733. 1767.
"Habitat Monspelii. D. Gouan." RCN: 3304.
Lectotype (McNeill in Cafferty & Jarvis in *Taxon* 53: 1050. 2004):
Herb. Linn. No. 585.50 (LINN).
Current name: ***Minuartia montana*** L. (Caryophyllaceae).

Arenaria grandiflora Linnaeus, *Systema Naturae,* ed. 10, 2: 1034.
1759.
["Habitat in Alpibus Valdensium, Cenisii."] Sp. Pl., ed. 2, 1: 608
(1762). RCN: 3305.
Lectotype (Bechi in *Webbia* 52: 179. 1998): [icon] *"Alsine uniflora et
grandiflora, foliis acuminatis, petalis integris"* in Allioni, Rar. Pedem.
Stirp.: 49, t. 10, f. 1. 1755 (see p. 104).
Current name: ***Arenaria grandiflora*** L. (Caryophyllaceae).

Arenaria gypsophiloides Linnaeus, *Systema Naturae,* ed. 12, 2: 313;
Mantissa Plantarum: 71. 1767.
"Habitat in Oriente. DD. Schreber." RCN: 3296.
Lectotype (McNeill in Davis, *Fl. Turkey* 2: 32. 1967): *Gundelsheimer?*,
Herb. Linn. No. 585.27 (LINN).
Current name: ***Arenaria gypsophiloides*** L. (Caryophyllaceae).

Arenaria hispida Linnaeus, *Species Plantarum* 1: 425. 1753.
"Habitat Monspelii in monte calcaris." RCN: 3299.
Lectotype (López González in Cafferty & Jarvis in *Taxon* 53: 1050.
2004): Herb. Linn. No. 585.34 (LINN).
Current name: ***Arenaria hispida*** L. (Caryophyllaceae).

Arenaria juniperina Linnaeus, *Systema Naturae,* ed. 12, 2: 313;
Mantissa Plantarum: 72. 1767.
RCN: 3300.
Lectotype (Rechinger, *Fl. Iranica* 163: 40. 1988): Herb. Linn. No.
585.35 (LINN).

Current name: ***Minuartia juniperina*** (L.) Maire & Petitm. (Caryophyllaceae).

Arenaria laricifolia Linnaeus, *Species Plantarum* 1: 424. 1753.
"Habitat in montosis Helvetiae, Genevae, Parisiorum, Monspelii."
RCN: 3302.
Type not designated.
Original material: Herb. Linn. No. 585.42 (LINN).
Current name: ***Minuartia laricifolia*** (L.) Schinz & Thell. (Caryophyllaceae).

Arenaria lateriflora Linnaeus, *Species Plantarum* 1: 423. 1753.
"Habitat in Sibiria." RCN: 3285.
Lectotype (Jonsell & Jarvis in *Nordic J. Bot.* 14: 156. 1994): Herb. Linn. No. 585.6 (LINN).
Current name: ***Moehringia lateriflora*** (L.) Fenzl (Caryophyllaceae).

Arenaria liniflora Linnaeus, *Systema Vegetabilium*, ed. 13: 355. 1774.
"Habitat in Europa australi." RCN: 3306.
Type not designated.
Original material: Herb. Linn. No. 585.55 (LINN).
Note: The application of this name appears uncertain.

Arenaria media Linnaeus, *Species Plantarum*, ed. 2, 1: 606. 1762.
"Habitat in Germania, Gallia." RCN: 3294.
Lectotype (Rossbach in *Rhodora* 42: 121. 1940): *Schmidel*, Herb. Linn. No. 585.23 (LINN).
Current name: ***Spergularia media*** (L.) C. Presl (Caryophyllaceae).
Note: A number of authors, from Fernald & Wiegand (in *Rhodora* 12: 159. 1910) to Rauschert (in *Feddes Repert.* 88: 312. 1977) informally rejected this name as a persistent source of confusion, and Lambinon (in *Taxon* 30: 364. 1981) made a formal proposal for its rejection. However, this was not approved by the Committee for Spermatophyta (in *Taxon* 35: 562. 1986).

Arenaria montana Linnaeus, *Centuria I Plantarum*: 12. 1755.
"Habitat in Galliae australis montibus." RCN: 3292.
Lectotype (López González in Cafferty & Jarvis in *Taxon* 53: 1050. 2004): Herb. Linn. No. 585.19 (LINN).
Current name: ***Arenaria montana*** L. (Caryophyllaceae).

Arenaria mucronata Linnaeus, *Species Plantarum* 1: 424. 1753.
"Habitat in Helvetia." RCN: 2168.
Basionym of: *Alsine mucronata* (L.) L. (1762).
Type not designated.
Original material: [icon] in Haller, Enum. Meth. Stirp. Helv. 1: 389, t. 7. 1742.
Current name: ***Arenaria sp.*** (Caryophyllaceae).
Note: This name has been treated by a number of authors (e.g. McNeill in *Notes Roy. Bot. Gard. Edinburgh* 24: 398. 1963; Breistroffer in *Bull. Soc. Bot. France* 1963, 89 sess. extr.: 117. 1966) as a *nomen ambiguum* and its application appears uncertain.

Arenaria multicaulis Linnaeus, *Systema Naturae*, ed. 10, 2: 1034. 1759, *nom. illeg.*
["Habitat in Alpibus Helvetiae, Pyrenaeis."] Sp. Pl. 1: 425 (1753). RCN: 3288.
Replaced synonym: *Arenaria ciliata* L. (1753).
Lectotype (López González in Cafferty & Jarvis in *Taxon* 53: 1050. 2004): [icon] *"Alsine serpilli folio, multicaulis et multiflora"* in Séguier, Pl. Veron. 1: 420, 417, t. 5, f. 2. 1745.
Current name: ***Arenaria moehringioides*** Murr. (Caryophyllaceae).
Note: As noted by López González (in *Anales Jard. Bot. Madrid* 42: 258. 1985), this is an illegitimate replacement name for *A. ciliata* L. (1753).

Arenaria peploides Linnaeus, *Species Plantarum* 1: 423. 1753.
"Habitat ad littora maris Europaei borealia." RCN: 3282.
Lectotype (Jonsell & Jarvis in *Nordic J. Bot.* 14: 156. 1994): Herb. Linn. No. 585.1 (LINN).
Current name: ***Honkenya peploides*** (L.) Ehrh. (Caryophyllaceae).

Arenaria rubra Linnaeus, *Species Plantarum* 1: 423. 1753.
"Habitat α in Europae arenosis collibus, β. in litoribus marinis." RCN: 3293.
Lectotype (Rossbach in *Rhodora* 42: 109. 1940): Herb. Linn. No. 585.20 (LINN).
Current name: ***Spergularia rubra*** (L.) J. Presl & C. Presl (Caryophyllaceae).

Arenaria rubra Linnaeus var. **campestris** Linnaeus, *Species Plantarum* 1: 423. 1753.
"Habitat in Europae arenosis collibus." RCN: 3293.
Lectotype (Ratter in Cafferty & Jarvis in *Taxon* 53: 1050. 2004): Herb. Burser XIV(1): 79 (UPS).
Current name: ***Spergularia rubra*** (L.) J. Presl & C. Presl (Caryophyllaceae).

Arenaria rubra Linnaeus var. **marina** Linnaeus, *Species Plantarum* 1: 423. 1753.
"Habitat in litoribus marinis." RCN: 3293.
Lectotype (Rossbach in *Rhodora* 42: 135, pl. 591. 1940): Herb. Clifford: 173, *Arenaria* 3, sheet B (BM-000628543).
Current name: ***Spergularia salina*** J. Presl & C. Presl (Caryophyllaceae).
Note: Fernald & Wiegand (in *Rhodora* 12: 158. 1910) argued for the rejection of this name as a *nomen confusum*. Following Rossbach's typification, the correct name at the rank of species is *Spergularia salina* J. Presl & C. Presl.

Arenaria saxatilis Linnaeus, *Species Plantarum* 1: 424. 1753.
"Habitat in Germania, Helvetia, Gallia, Sibiria." RCN: 3297.
Lectotype (Lazkov in Cafferty & Jarvis in *Taxon* 53: 1051. 2004): *Steller*, Herb. Linn. No. 585.29 (LINN).
Current name: ***Arenaria saxatilis*** L. (Caryophyllaceae).
Note: Although Ikonnikov (in *Novosti Sist. Vyssh. Rast.* 9: 155–156. 1972) indicated that the type should be material from Linnaeus' herbarium marked as being from the Kamchatka peninsula, he did not formally choose a type. However, his suggestion was later formalised by Lazkov.

Arenaria serpyllifolia Linnaeus, *Species Plantarum* 1: 423. 1753.
"Habitat in Europae sylvis glareosis." RCN: 3290.
Lectotype (Jonsell & Jarvis in Jarvis & al., *Regnum Veg.* 127: 21. 1993): Herb. Clifford: 173, *Arenaria* 2 (BM-000628541).
Generitype of *Arenaria* Linnaeus (vide Green, *Prop. Brit. Bot.*: 155. 1929).
Current name: ***Arenaria serpyllifolia*** L. subsp. ***serpyllifolia*** (Caryophyllaceae).
Note: Jonsell & Jarvis (in *Nordic J. Bot.* 14: 156. 1994) discuss their formal (1993) typification in more detail.

Arenaria striata Linnaeus, *Centuria II Plantarum*: 17. 1756.
"Habitat in alpibus Austriae & montibus vallis augustae." RCN: 3303.
Type not designated.
Original material: Herb. Burser XI: 129, syntype (UPS); Herb. Linn. No. 585.48? (LINN).
Current name: ***Minuartia laricifolia*** (L.) Schinz & Thell. (Caryophyllaceae).

Arenaria tenuifolia Linnaeus, *Species Plantarum* 1: 424. 1753.
"Habitat in Helvetia, Gallia, Anglia, Italia." RCN: 3301.
Type not designated.
Original material: Herb. Linn. No. 188.11 (S); Herb. Linn. No.
585.36 (LINN); Herb. Linn. No. 585.37 (LINN); Herb. Linn. No.
188.19? (S); [icon] in Séguier, Pl. Veron. 1: 418, t. 6, f. 2. 1745;
[icon] in Vaillant, Bot. Paris.: 7, t. 3, f. 1. 1727; [icon] in Bauhin &
Cherler, Hist. Pl. Univ. 3(2): 364. 1651.
Current name: *Minuartia hybrida* (Vill.) Schischk.
(Caryophyllaceae).

Arenaria tetraquetra Linnaeus, *Species Plantarum* 1: 423. 1753.
"Habitat in Pyrenaeis." RCN: 3283.
Lectotype (Goyder in *Bot. J. Linn. Soc.* 97: 17. 1988): Herb. Burser
XI: 135 (UPS).
Current name: *Arenaria tetraquetra* L. (Caryophyllaceae).

Arenaria triflora Linnaeus, *Mantissa Plantarum Altera*: 240. 1771.
"Habitat in Europa australi." RCN: 3291.
Lectotype (López González in Cafferty & Jarvis in *Taxon* 53: 1051.
2004): Herb. Linn. No. 585.15 (LINN).
Current name: *Arenaria triflora* L. (Caryophyllaceae).

Arenaria trinervia Linnaeus, *Species Plantarum* 1: 423. 1753.
"Habitat in Europae sylvis." RCN: 3286.
Lectotype (Rechinger, *Fl. Iranica* 163: 59. 1988): Herb. Linn. No.
585.7 (LINN).
Current name: *Moehringia trinervia* (L.) Clairv. (Caryophyllaceae).
Note: Although Rechinger indicated sheet no. 588.7 (LINN) as the
type, it seems clear that this was a typographic error for 585.7.

Arenaria verna Linnaeus, *Systema Naturae*, ed. 12, 2: 313; *Mantissa
Plantarum*: 72. 1767.
"Habitat in Alpibus Europae australioris." RCN: 3298.
Lectotype (Halliday in *Feddes Repert.* 69: 12. 1964): *Schmidel*, Herb.
Linn. No. 585.30 (LINN), see p. 227.
Current name: *Minuartia verna* (L.) Hiern subsp. *verna*
(Caryophyllaceae).
Note: As noted by Dvoráková (in *Preslia* 60: 2. 1988), Halliday erred
in citing the generic number of the type as "580", rather than
"585", but it is clear that this is a simple error (there is no specimen
numbered "580.30").

Arethusa bulbosa Linnaeus, *Species Plantarum* 2: 950. 1753.
"Habitat in Virginia, Canada." RCN: 6871.
Lectotype (Reveal & al. in *Huntia* 7: 224. 1987): *Kalm*, Herb. Linn.
No. 1059.1 (LINN; iso- UPS).
Generitype of *Arethusa* Linnaeus (vide Green, *Prop. Brit. Bot.*: 185.
1929).
Current name: *Arethusa bulbosa* L. (Orchidaceae).

Arethusa capensis Linnaeus, *Plantae Rariores Africanae*: 28.
1760.
["Habitat ad Cap. b. spei."] Sp. Pl. ed. 2, 2: 1346 (1763). RCN:
6874.
Lectotype (Manning in Cafferty & Jarvis in *Taxon* 48: 46. 1999):
"*Orchis Afric. flore singulari herbaceo. D. Oldenl. Mus. Petiv. 280,
Raj. tom. 3. p. 286*", Herb. Burman (G).
Current name: *Disperis capensis* (L.) Sw. (Orchidaceae).

Arethusa divaricata Linnaeus, *Species Plantarum* 2: 951. 1753.
"Habitat in Americae borealis paludosis." RCN: 6872.
Lectotype (Catling & Gregg in *Lindleyana* 7: 70. 1992): *Clayton 635*,
Herb. Linn. No. 1059.3 (LINN; iso- BM).
Current name: *Cleistes divaricata* (L.) Ames (Orchidaceae).

Arethusa ophioglossoides Linnaeus, *Species Plantarum* 2: 951.
1753.
"Habitat in Virginia, Canada." RCN: 6872.
Lectotype (Sheviak in Cafferty & Jarvis in *Taxon* 48: 47. 1999): *Kalm*,
Herb. Linn. No. 1059.2 (LINN).
Current name: *Pogonia ophioglossoides* (L.) Ker-Gawl.
(Orchidaceae).

Aretia alpina Linnaeus, *Species Plantarum* 1: 141. 1753.
"Habitat in Vallesiae monte Loch dicto." RCN: 1142.
Type not designated.
Original material: Herb. Burser XVI(1): 77 (UPS); [icon] in Haller,
Enum. Meth. Stirp. Helv. 2: 486, t. 8. 1742.
Generitype of *Aretia* Linnaeus.
Current name: *Androsace alpina* (L.) Lam. (Primulaceae).
Note: De Beer (in *J. Linn. Soc., Bot.* 55: 328. 1955) demonstrated that
Linnaeus clearly obtained his geographical information about this
species from Burser's specimen (XVI(1): 77) even though it was not
otherwise cited in the protologue.

Aretia helvetica (Linnaeus) Linnaeus, *Systema Vegetabilium*, ed. 13:
162. 1774.
["Habitat in alpibus Helveticis Gemmi & Pyndtnerberg."] Sp. Pl. 1:
141 (1753). RCN: 1141.
Basionym: *Diapensia helvetica* L. (1753).
Type not designated.
Original material: as basionym.
Current name: *Androsace helvetica* (L.) All. (Primulaceae).

Aretia vitaliana (Linnaeus) Linnaeus, *Systema Vegetabilium*, ed. 13:
162. 1774.
["Habitat in alpibus Pyrenaeis & Italicis."] Sp. Pl. 1: 143 (1753).
RCN: 1143.
Basionym: *Primula vitaliana* L. (1753).
Lectotype (Ferguson in *Taxon* 18: 302. 1969): [icon] "*Vitaliana*" in
Donati, Stor. Nat. Adriat.: 75, unnumbered plate. 1750.
Current name: *Androsace vitaliana* (L.) Lapeyr. (Primulaceae).

Argemone armeniaca Linnaeus, *Species Plantarum* 1: 509. 1753.
"Habitat in Armenia." RCN: 3849.
Neotype (Kadereit in *Edinburgh J. Bot.* 50: 127. 1993): *Tournefort*,
"Papaver orientale, hypecoi folio, fructu minimo" (BM).
Current name: *Papaver armeniaca* (L.) DC. (Papaveraceae).

Argemone mexicana Linnaeus, *Species Plantarum* 1: 508. 1753.
"Habitat in Mexico, Jamaica, Caribaeis, nunc in Europa australi."
RCN: 3848.
Lectotype (Fawcett & Rendle, *Fl. Jamaica* 3: 222. 1914): Herb. Linn.
No. 670.1 (LINN).
Generitype of *Argemone* Linnaeus (vide Green, *Prop. Brit. Bot.*: 160.
1929).
Current name: *Argemone mexicana* L. (Papaveraceae).

Argemone pyrenaica Linnaeus, *Species Plantarum* 1: 509. 1753.
"Habitat in Pyrenaeis. Tournefort." RCN: 3850.
Type not designated.
Original material: none traced.
Current name: *Papaver pyrenaica* (L.) Willd. (Papaveraceae).

Aristida adscensionis Linnaeus, *Species Plantarum* 1: 82. 1753.
"Habitat in Insula Adscensionis. Osbeck." RCN: 688.
Lectotype (Hitchcock in *Contr. U. S. Natl. Herb.* 22: 541. 1924):
Herb. Linn. No. 98.1 (LINN).
Generitype of *Aristida* Linnaeus.
Current name: *Aristida adscensionis* L. (Poaceae).

Aristida americana Linnaeus, *Systema Naturae*, ed. 10, 2: 879. 1759. ["Habitat in Jamaica."] Sp. Pl., ed. 2, 1: 122 (1762). RCN: 689.
Lectotype (Hitchcock in *Contr. U. S. Natl. Herb.* 12: 123. 1908; Davidse in Cafferty & al. in *Taxon* 49: 247. 2000): *Browne*, Herb. Linn. No. 98.2 (LINN; iso- US).
Current name: ***Bouteloua americana*** (L.) Scribn. (Poaceae).
Note: Hitchcock (in *Contr. U. S. Natl. Herb.* 12: 123. 1908) designated a Browne specimen at LINN as type but did not specify which of the two Browne specimens he intended. Griffiths (in *Contr. U. S. Natl. Herb.* 14: 407. 1912) made a similar statement while Judziewicz (in Görts-van Rijn, *Fl. Guianas,* ser. A, 8: 50. 1990) indicated 98.2 and 98.3 (LINN) as syntypes. None of these statements is an effective typification in its own right, so sheet 98.2 (LINN) was formally chosen as lectotype by Davidse, a restriction of Hitchcock's original choice under Art. 9.15 of the Code.

Aristida arundinacea Linnaeus, *Mantissa Plantarum Altera*: 186. 1771.
"Habitat in India orientali. Koenig." RCN: 691.
Lectotype (Hubbard in Milne-Redhead & Polhill, *Fl. Trop. E. Africa, Gramineae* 1: 133. 1970): Herb. Linn. No. 98.8 (LINN).
Current name: ***Neyraudia arundinacea*** (L.) Henrard (Poaceae).

Aristida plumosa Linnaeus, *Species Plantarum*, ed. 2, 2: 1666. 1763.
"Habitat in America. D. Schreber." RCN: 690.
Lectotype (Henrard in *Meded. Rijks-Herb.* 54A: 451. 1927): *Schreber*, Herb. Linn. No. 98.6 (LINN; iso- M).
Current name: ***Stipagrostis plumosa*** (L.) T. Anderson (Poaceae).

Aristolochia arborescens Linnaeus, *Species Plantarum* 2: 960. 1753.
"Habitat in America." RCN: 6954.
Type not designated.
Original material: [icon] in Plukenet, Phytographia: t. 78, f. 1. 1691; Almag. Bot.: 50. 1696 – Typotype: Herb. Sloane 95: 105 (BM-SL).
Current name: ***Aristolochia serpentaria*** L. (Aristolochiaceae).

Aristolochia baetica Linnaeus, *Species Plantarum* 2: 961. 1753.
"Habitat in Hispania, Creta, arbores scandens." RCN: 6959.
Lectotype (designated here by De Groot, Wanke & Neinhuis): [icon] *"Aristolochia Clematitis Baetica"* in Clusius, Rar. Pl. Hist. 2: 71. 1601.
Current name: ***Aristolochia baetica*** L. (Aristolochiaceae).
Note: De Groot & al. (in *Bot. J. Linn. Soc.* 151: 225, 236. 2006) wrongly indicated 1071.5 (LINN) as the holotype. This collection lacks the relevant *Species Plantarum* number (i.e. "6") and was a post-1753 addition to the herbarium, and is not original material for the name.

Aristolochia bilabiata Linnaeus, *Species Plantarum,* ed. 2, 2: 1361. 1763.
"Habitat in America." RCN: 6951.
Lectotype (Rankin in Manitz & Gutjahr, *Fl. Republ. Cuba,* ser. A, 1(2): 25. 1998): [icon] *"Aristolochia foliis ovato-oblongis, obtusis"* in Plumier in Burman, Pl. Amer.: 22, t. 32, f. 1. 1756. – Epitype (Rankin & Greuter in *Taxon* 48: 680. 1999): Hispaniola. Haiti, Massif de la Selle, gr. Morne des Commissaires, Anses-à-Pitre, road to Banane, at Riv. Pedernales, ca. 150m, 25 Aug 1926, *Ekman H6740* (S; iso- G, MO, US).
Current name: ***Aristolochia bilabiata*** L. (Aristolochiaceae).
Note: Rankin & Greuter (in *Taxon* 48: 680. 1999) treat this as a *nomen confusum*, and informally reject it under Art. 57 in favour of *A. oblongata* Jacq.

Aristolochia bilobata Linnaeus, *Species Plantarum* 2: 960. 1753.
"Habitat in Dominica." RCN: 6946.

Lectotype (Rankin & Greuter in *Taxon* 48: 683. 1999): [icon] *"Aristolochia longa, scandens, foliis, ferri equini effigie"* in Plumier, Descr. Pl. Amér.: 91, t. 106. 1693. – Epitype (Rankin & Greuter in *Taxon* 48: 683. 1999): Hispaniola. Haiti, Vicinity of St Raphael, Département du Nord, flowers purple veined on whitish, vining on shrubs, arid foot hills, ca. 350m, 3 Dec 1925, *Leonard 7686* (GH; iso- NY).
Current name: ***Aristolochia bilobata*** L. (Aristolochiaceae).

Aristolochia clematitis Linnaeus, *Species Plantarum* 2: 962. 1753.
"Habitat in Gallia, Tataria." RCN: 6965.

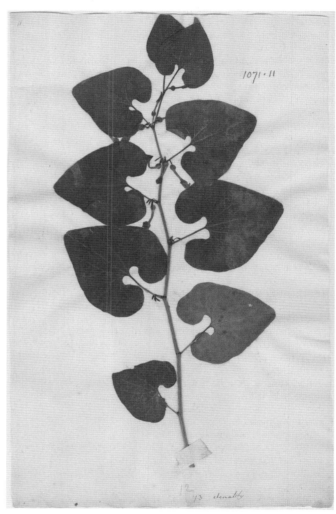

Lectotype (Pfeifer in *Ann. Missouri Bot. Gard.* 53: 174. 1966): Herb. Linn. No. 1071.11 (LINN).
Current name: ***Aristolochia clematitis*** L. (Aristolochiaceae).

Aristolochia cordata Linnaeus, *Flora Jamaicensis*: 20. 1759.
"Habitat [in Jamaica.]"
Type not designated.
Original material: [icon] in Hernandez, Rer. Med. Nov. Hisp.: 162. 1651; [icon] in Sloane, Voy. Jamaica 1: 162, t. 104, f. 1. 1707 – Typotype: Herb. Sloane 3: 32 (BM-SL).
Note: The application of this name is uncertain.

Aristolochia erecta Linnaeus, *Species Plantarum,* ed. 2, 2: 1362. 1763.
"Habitat in Vera Cruce." RCN: 6952.

Lectotype (Pfeifer, *Taxon. Revis. Pentandr. Sp.* Aristolochia: 58. 1970): *Houstoun* (BM; iso- A, NY).
Current name: ***Aristolochia erecta*** L. (Aristolochiaceae).

Aristolochia hirsuta Linnaeus, *Systema Naturae,* ed. 12, 2: 601. 1767, *nom. illeg.*
RCN: 6966.
Replaced synonym: *Aristolochia hirta* L. (1753).
Neotype (Nardi in *Webbia* 45: 35. 1991): [icon] *"Aristolochia subhirsuta chia longa folio oblongo, flore maximo"* in Tournefort, Rel. Voy. Levant (Paris ed.) 1: 386. 1717.
Current name: ***Aristolochia hirta*** L. (Aristolochiaceae).

Aristolochia hirta Linnaeus, *Species Plantarum* 2: 961. 1753.
"Habitat in Chio." RCN: 6966.
Lectotype (Davis & Khan in *Notes Roy. Bot. Gard. Edinburgh* 23: 529. 1961): [icon] *"Aristolochia subhirsuta chia longa folio oblongo, flore maximo"* in Tournefort, Rel. Voy. Levant (Paris ed.) 1: 386. 1717.
Current name: ***Aristolochia hirta*** L. (Aristolochiaceae).

Aristolochia indica Linnaeus, *Species Plantarum* 2: 960. 1753.
"Habitat in India." RCN: 6958.
Lectotype (designated here by Neinhuis): Herb. Hermann 4: 26, No. 323 (BM; iso- Herb. Hermann 1: 46 (BM)).
Current name: ***Aristolochia indica*** L. (Aristolochiaceae).

Aristolochia longa Linnaeus, *Species Plantarum* 2: 962. 1753, *nom. utique rej.*
"Habitat in Hispania, Italia." RCN: 6964.
Lectotype (Nardi in *Taxon* 32: 654. 1983): Herb. Linn. No. 1071.10 (LINN).
Current name: ***Aristolochia fontanesii*** Boiss. & Reut. (Aristolochiaceae).
Note: Nardi (in *Taxon* 37: 978. 1988) proposed the rejection of the name and the Committee for Spermatophyta eventually (*l.c.* 54: 1093. 2005) recommended this, confirmed by the General Committee (*l.c.* 55: 800. 2006). As a result, the correct name for *A. longa* becomes *A. fontanesii* Boiss. & Reut.; see De Groot & al. (in *Bot. J. Linn. Soc.* 151: 223. 2006).

Aristolochia maurorum Linnaeus, *Species Plantarum,* ed. 2, 2: 1363. 1763.
"Habitat circa Halepum." RCN: 6957.
Type not designated.
Original material: [icon] in Morison, Pl. Hist. Univ. 3: 510, s. 12, t. 17, f. 11. 1699; [icon] in Rauwolf, Aigent. Beschr. Morgenl.: 121, t. 121. 1583.
Current name: ***Aristolochia maurorum*** L. (Aristolochiaceae).

Aristolochia odoratissima Linnaeus, *Species Plantarum,* ed. 2, 2: 1362. 1763.
"Habitat in America." RCN: 6955.
Lectotype (Kellogg in Howard, *Fl. Lesser Antilles* 4: 125. 1988): [icon] *"Aristolochia scandens odoratissima, floris labello purpureo, semine cordato. Contrayerva"* in Sloane, Voy. Jamaica 1: 162, t. 104, f. 1. 1707. – Typotype: Herb. Sloane 3: 32 (BM-SL).
Current name: ***Aristolochia odoratissima*** L. (Aristolochiaceae).

Aristolochia peltata Linnaeus, *Species Plantarum* 2: 960. 1753.
"Habitat in America meridionali." RCN: 6949.
Lectotype (Rankin in Manitz & Gutjahr, *Fl. Republ. Cuba,* ser. A, 1(2): 15. 1998): [icon] *"Aristolochia asari folia, umbillicato, flore longissimo, radice repente"* in Plumier, Codex Boerhaavianus 1: t. 84. (University Library, Groningen). – Epitype (Rankin & Greuter in *Taxon* 48: 684. 1999): Hispaniola. Haiti, Massif du Nord. Ennery,

slope of hill north of town, 400m, 12 Jun 1927, *Ekman H8401* (S; iso- US).
Current name: ***Aristolochia peltata*** L. (Aristolochiaceae).

Aristolochia pistolochia Linnaeus, *Species Plantarum* 2: 962. 1753.
"Habitat in Hispania, G. Narbonensi." RCN: 6962.
Lectotype (designated here by De Groot, Wanke & Neinhuis): *Löfling 658a,* Herb. Linn. No. 1071.8 (LINN).
Current name: ***Aristolochia pistolochia*** L. (Aristolochiaceae).
Note: De Groot & al. (in *Bot. J. Linn. Soc.* 151: 221, 237. 2006) wrongly indicated 1071.8 (LINN) as the holotype. While it is part of the original material for the name, and eligible for designation as the lectotype, this statement was published after 1 Jan 2001 and so the omission of the phrase "designated here" or an equivalent (Art. 7.11) means that this choice was not effective.

Aristolochia rotunda Linnaeus, *Species Plantarum* 2: 962. 1753.
"Habitat in Italia, Hispania, G. Narbonensi." RCN: 6963.
Lectotype (Nardi in *Webbia* 38: 242. 1984): Herb. Linn. No. 1071.9 (LINN).
Generitype of *Aristolochia* Linnaeus (vide Green, *Prop. Brit. Bot.*: 186. 1929).
Current name: ***Aristolochia rotunda*** L. (Aristolochiaceae).

Aristolochia sempervirens Linnaeus, *Species Plantarum* 2: 961. 1753.
"Habitat in Creta." RCN: 6960.
Lectotype (Davis & Khan in *Notes Roy. Bot. Gard. Edinburgh* 23: 522. 1961): Herb. Clifford: 432, *Aristolochia* 2 (BM-000647336).
Current name: ***Aristolochia sempervirens*** L. (Aristolochiaceae).

Aristolochia serpentaria Linnaeus, *Species Plantarum* 2: 961. 1753.
"Habitat in Virginia." RCN: 6961.
Lectotype (Pfeifer in *Ann. Missouri Bot. Gard.* 53: 128. 1966): *Kalm,* Herb. Linn. No. 1071.7 (LINN).
Current name: ***Aristolochia serpentaria*** L. (Aristolochiaceae).

Aristolochia smilacea Linnaeus, *Systema Naturae,* ed. 10, 2: 1249. 1759.
Type not designated.
Original material: none traced.
Note: There is no original material extant, and the application of the name appears uncertain.

Aristolochia trilobata Linnaeus, *Species Plantarum* 2: 960. 1753.
"Habitat in America meridionali." RCN: 6947.
Type not designated.
Original material: [icon] in Marggraf, Hist. Rer. Nat. Bras.: 15. 1648.
Current name: ***Aristolochia trilobata*** L. (Aristolochiaceae).
Note: Pfeifer (in *Ann. Missouri Bot. Gard.* 53: 144. 1966) indicated 1071.1 LINN as type, and was followed by e.g. González (in *Fl. Colombia* 12: 127. 1990), Feuillet & Poncy (in *Fl. Guianas,* ser. A, 10: 17. 1998) and Rankin (in *Fl. Republ. Cuba,,* ser. A, 1(2): 18. 1998). However, Rankin & Greuter (in *Taxon* 48: 686–687. 1999) conclude that both specimens on the sheet are post-1753 additions (one from von Rohr, the other from Rolander) and hence ineligible as types. Overlooking the existence of Marggraf's illustration, they designate a neotype (having dismissed Pfeifer's statement as a neotypification because he did not distinguish between the two specimens on the sheet). However, their choice is inadmissible.

Arnica caffra Linnaeus, *Systema Naturae,* ed. 10, 2: 1219. 1759.
RCN: 6403.
Lectotype (Hansen in Jarvis & Turland in *Taxon* 47: 352. 1998): Herb. Linn. No. 1001.7 (LINN).
Current name: ***Gerbera crocea*** (L.) Kuntze (Asteraceae).

Arnica coronopifolia Linnaeus, *Species Plantarum* 2: 885. 1753.
"Habitat in Aethiopia." RCN: 6405.
Type not designated.
Original material: none traced.
Current name: ***Gerbera linnaei*** Cass. (Asteraceae).
Note: Hansen (in *Opera Bot.* 78: 9. 1985) stated that the type was lost
and suggested that the name is probably synonymous with *A.
gerbera* L. If this is confirmed, "coronopifolia" would become an
earlier epithet for what is now called *Gerbera linnaei* Cass., which
might make a rejection proposal desirable.

Arnica crocea Linnaeus, *Species Plantarum* 2: 885. 1753.
"Habitat in Aethiopia." RCN: 6402.
Lectotype (Hansen in Jarvis & Turland in *Taxon* 47: 353. 1998):
[icon] *"Gerbera foliis planis, dentatis, flore purpureo"* in Burman, Rar.
Afric. Pl.: 157, t. 56, f. 2. 1739.
Current name: ***Gerbera crocea*** (L.) Kuntze (Asteraceae).
Note: Hansen (in *Opera Bot.* 78: 13. 1985) indicates Herb. Linn.
1001.7 (LINN) as holotype. However, this collection lacks the
Species Plantarum number (in this case, "4") written by Linnaeus
and was a later addition to the herbarium, and not original material
for the name. Recognising this, Hansen subsequently designated a
Burman plate as lectotype in its place.

Arnica gerbera Linnaeus, *Species Plantarum* 2: 885. 1753, *typ. cons.*
"Habitat in Aethiopia." RCN: 6404.
Lectotype (Hansen in *Opera Bot.* 78: 9. 1985): Herb. Linn. No.
1001.8 (LINN).
Current name: ***Gerbera linnaei*** Cass. (Asteraceae).
Note: A. gerbera is the basionym of *Gerbera linnaei* Cass., the conserved
type of *Gerbera* L.

Arnica maritima Linnaeus, *Species Plantarum* 2: 884. 1753.
"Habitat in Kamschatka & America septentrionali." RCN: 6401.
Neotype (Barkley in Jarvis & Turland in *Taxon* 47: 353. 1998):
Canada. Labrador, HMS Niger Expedition, 1766, *John Williams s.n.*
(BM-000576308).
Current name: ***Senecio pseudoarnica*** Less. (Asteraceae).
Note: Jeffrey & Chen (in *Kew Bull.* 39: 358. 1984) indicated the
Gmelin phrase name as the holotype. However, this is contrary to
Art. 8.1, and Barkley therefore designated a neotype.

Arnica montana Linnaeus, *Species Plantarum* 2: 884. 1753.
"Habitat in Alpibus & pratis Europae frigidioris." RCN: 6398.
Type not designated.
Original material: Herb. Burser X: 20 (UPS); [icon] in Mattioli,
Comment. Dioscoridis: 934. 1565; [icon] in Reneaulme, Specim.
Hist. Pl.: 118, 119. 1611.
Generitype of *Arnica* Linnaeus (vide Green, *Prop. Brit. Bot.*: 182. 1929).
Current name: ***Arnica montana*** L. (Asteraceae).

Arnica montana Linnaeus var. **alpina** Linnaeus, *Species Plantarum* 2:
884. 1753.
RCN: 6398.
Type not designated.
Original material: [icon] in Tabernaemontanus, Eicones Pl.: 336.
1590.
Current name: ***Arnica angustifolia*** Vahl subsp. ***alpina*** (L.) I.K.
Ferguson (Asteraceae).

Arnica piloselloides Linnaeus, *Plantae Rariores Africanae*: 22. 1760.
["Habitat in Aethiopia."] Sp. Pl. ed. 2, 2: 1246 (1763). RCN: 6399.
Lectotype (Hansen in *Opera Bot.* 78: 19. 1985): *Oldenland*, Herb.
Burman (G).
Current name: ***Gerbera piloselloides*** (L.) Cass. (Asteraceae).

Arnica scorpioides Linnaeus, *Species Plantarum* 2: 884. 1753.
"Habitat in Helvetia." RCN: 6400.
Lectotype (Álvarez in Jarvis & Turland in *Taxon* 47: 353. 1998): Herb.
Burser X: 16 (UPS).
Current name: ***Doronicum pardalianches*** L. (Asteraceae).

Artedia muricata Linnaeus, *Species Plantarum* 1: 242. 1753.
"Habitat in Mauritania." RCN: 1948.
Basionym of: *Daucus muricatus* (L.) L. (1762).
Lectotype (Reduron & al. in Jarvis & al. in *Taxon* 55: 209. 2006):
[icon] *"Echinophora Tingitana"* in Rivinus, Ordo Pl. Fl. Pentapetal.:
t. 27. 1699.
Current name: ***Daucus muricatus*** (L.) L. (Apiaceae).

Artedia squamata Linnaeus, *Species Plantarum* 1: 242. 1753.
"Habitat in Libano." RCN: 1943.
Lectotype (Reduron & Jarvis in Jarvis & al., *Regnum Veg.* 127: 21.
1993): Herb. Clifford: 89, *Artedia* 1 (BM-000558239).
Generitype of *Artedia* Linnaeus (vide Hitchcock, *Prop. Brit. Bot.*: 139.
1929).
Current name: ***Artedia squamata*** L. (Apiaceae).

Artemisia abrotanum Linnaeus, *Species Plantarum* 2: 845. 1753.
"Habitat in Syriae, Galatiae, Cappadociae montibus apricis." RCN:
6127.
Lectotype (Ling in Jarvis & Turland in *Taxon* 47: 353. 1998): Herb.
Clifford: 403, *Artemisia* 4 (BM-000647022).
Current name: ***Artemisia abrotanum*** L. (Asteraceae).
Note: Gabrielian & Chandjian (in *Novosti Sist. Vyssh. Rast.* 23: 208.
1986), treated both 988.7 and 988.8 (LINN) as the type. As
these sheets do not appear to be part of a single gathering, Art. 9.15
does not apply, and Ling's type choice of Clifford material is
accepted.

Artemisia absinthium Linnaeus, *Species Plantarum* 2: 848. 1753.
"Habitat in Europae ruderatis aridis." RCN: 6139.
Lectotype (Ling in Jarvis & Turland in *Taxon* 47: 353. 1998): Herb.
Clifford: 404, *Artemisia* 7 (BM-000647029).
Current name: ***Artemisia absinthium*** L. (Asteraceae).
Note: Dillon (in *Fieldiana, Bot.*, n.s., 7: 3. 1981), and a number of
more recent authors, indicated 988.40 (LINN) as type. However,
this collection is not from Europe, and also appears to be a post-
1753 addition to the collection. It is not accepted as original
material for the name (which is fortunate as it is identifiable as *A.
sieversiana* Willd.) and Ling therefore designated a Clifford
collection as lectotype in its place.

Artemisia aethiopica Linnaeus, *Species Plantarum* 2: 845. 1753.
"Habitat in Aethiopia." RCN: 6125.
Type not designated.
Original material: Herb. Linn. No. 988.3 (LINN).
Current name: ***Artemisia herba-alba*** Asso (Asteraceae).
Note: The only original material appears identifiable as *A. herba-alba*
Asso (1779), into the synonymy of which a number of authors (e.g.
Ouyahya in Hind & al., *Adv. Compositae Syst.*: 345. 1995) place the
Linnaean name. A formal proposal may be necessary to formalise
this treatment.

Artemisia ambigua Linnaeus, *Species Plantarum*, ed. 2, 2: 1190.
1763.
"Habitat ad Cap. b. spei." RCN: 6732.
Basionym of: *Seriphium ambiguum* (L.) L. (1774).
Lectotype (Hilliard & Burtt in *Notes Roy. Bot. Gard. Edinburgh* 31: 23.
1971): Herb. Linn. No. 988.55 (LINN).
Current name: ***Ifloga ambigua*** (L.) Druce (Asteraceae).

Artemisia annua Linnaeus, *Species Plantarum* 2: 847. 1753.
"Habitat in Sibiriae montosis." RCN: 6137.
Lectotype (Dillon in *Fieldiana, Bot.*, n.s., 7: 4. 1981): Herb. Linn. No. 988.33 (LINN).
Current name: ***Artemisia annua*** L. (Asteraceae).

Artemisia arborescens Linnaeus, *Species Plantarum*, ed. 2, 2: 1188. 1763.
"Habitat in Italia, Oriente." RCN: 6128.
Lectotype (Ling in Jarvis & Turland in *Taxon* 47: 353. 1998): *Turra*, Herb. Linn. No. 988.10 (LINN).
Current name: ***Artemisia arborescens*** L. (Asteraceae).
Note: Alavi (in Jafri & El-Gadi, *Fl. Libya* 107: 180. 1983) indicated three collections, 988.9, 988.9a and 988.10 (LINN) as type. These collections are not part of a single gathering, so Art. 9.15 does not apply, and the first typification appears to be that of Ling.
  Greuter & al. (in *Taxon* 54: 155. 2005) interpret this name as a new combination based on *Absinthium arborescens* Vaill. (1754), invoking Art. 33.3. If this view is accepted, the name is untypified.

Artemisia caerulescens Linnaeus, *Species Plantarum* 2: 848. 1753.
"Habitat in Europae australis littoribus maris." RCN: 6142.
Lectotype (Persson in *Opera Bot.* 35: 173. 1974): Herb. Clifford: 403, *Artemisia* 3, sheet 5 (BM-000647019).
Current name: ***Artemisia caerulescens*** L. (Asteraceae).

Artemisia campestris Linnaeus, *Species Plantarum* 2: 846. 1753.
"Habitat in Europae campis apricis, aridis." RCN: 6130.
Lectotype (Alavi in Jafri & El-Gadi, *Fl. Libya* 107: 184. 1983): Herb. Linn. No. 988.16 (LINN).
Current name: ***Artemisia campestris*** L. (Asteraceae).

Artemisia chinensis Linnaeus, *Species Plantarum* 2: 849. 1753.
"Habitat in China, Lagerström. Sibiria." RCN: 6144.
Lectotype (Hind in Bosser & al., *Fl. Mascareignes* 109: 128. 1993): *Lagerström*, Herb. Linn. No. 988.45 (LINN), see p. 219.
Current name: ***Crossostephium chinense*** (L.) Makino (Asteraceae).

Artemisia contra Linnaeus, *Mantissa Plantarum Altera*: 282. 1771.
"Habitat in Persia. D. Lerche." RCN: 6126.
Lectotype (Ling in Jarvis & Turland in *Taxon* 47: 353. 1998): *Scopoli 93*, Herb. Linn. No. 988.4 (LINN).
Current name: ***Artemisia judaica*** L. (Asteraceae).

Artemisia crithmifolia Linnaeus, *Species Plantarum* 2: 846. 1753.
"Habitat in Lusitaniae, littoribus arenosis. Loefling." RCN: 6132.
Lectotype (Ling in Jarvis & Turland in *Taxon* 47: 353. 1998): *Löfling 32*, Herb. Linn. No. 988.19 (LINN).
Current name: ***Artemisia campestris*** L. subsp. ***maritima*** Arcang. (Asteraceae).

Artemisia dracunculus Linnaeus, *Species Plantarum* 2: 849. 1753.
"Habitat in Sibiria, Tataria." RCN: 6143.
Lectotype (Leonova in *Novosti Sist. Vyssh. Rast.* 24: 187. 1987): Herb. Linn. No. 988.44 (LINN).
Current name: ***Artemisia dracunculus*** L. (Asteraceae).
Note: Hind (in Bosser & al., *Fl. Mascareignes* 109: 126. 1993) indicated Clifford material as the type, but this choice is pre-dated by that of Leonova.

Artemisia glacialis Linnaeus, *Species Plantarum*, ed. 2, 2: 1187. 1763.
"Habitat in Helvetia, Veletia." RCN: 6134.
Lectotype (Ling in Jarvis & Turland in *Taxon* 47: 353. 1998): Herb. Linn. No. 988.24 (LINN).
Current name: ***Artemisia glacialis*** L. (Asteraceae).

Artemisia integrifolia Linnaeus, *Species Plantarum* 2: 848. 1753.
"Habitat in Sibiria." RCN: 6141.
Lectotype (Ling in Jarvis & Turland in *Taxon* 47: 353. 1998): Herb. Linn. No. 988.43 (LINN).
Current name: ***Artemisia integrifolia*** L. (Asteraceae).

Artemisia judaica Linnaeus, *Systema Naturae*, ed. 10, 2: 1208. 1759.
["Habitat in Judaea, Arabia, Numidia."] Mant. Pl.: 112 (1767). RCN: 3300.
Lectotype (Ling in Jarvis & Turland in *Taxon* 47: 353. 1998): Herb. Linn. No. 340.17 (S).
Current name: ***Artemisia judaica*** L. (Asteraceae).

Artemisia maderaspatana Linnaeus, *Species Plantarum* 2: 849. 1753.
"Habitat in India." RCN: 6145.
Lectotype (Fayed in *Mitt. Bot. Staatssamml. München* 15: 452. 1979): Herb. Linn. No. 988.47 (LINN).
Current name: ***Grangea maderaspatana*** (L.) Poir. (Asteraceae).

Artemisia maritima Linnaeus, *Species Plantarum* 2: 846. 1753.
"Habitat in Europae septentrionalioris littoribus maris." RCN: 6133.
Lectotype (Persson in *Opera Bot.* 35: 134. 1974): Herb. Linn. No. 988.20 (LINN).
Current name: ***Artemisia maritima*** L. (Asteraceae).
Note: Leonova (in *Novosti Sist. Vyssh. Rast.* 7: 282. 1971) indicated unspecified material in LINN as type but this did not distinguish between sheets 988.20 and 988.21, which are not part of the same gathering so Art. 9.15 does not apply. Persson's type choice is accepted here.

Artemisia minima Linnaeus, *Species Plantarum* 2: 849. 1753.
"Habitat in China. Lagerström." RCN: 6146.
Lectotype (Grierson in Dassanayake & Fosberg, *Revised Handb. Fl. Ceylon* 1: 236. 1980): *Lagerström*, Herb. Linn. No. 988.48 (LINN).
Current name: ***Centipeda minima*** (L.) A. Braun & Asch. (Asteraceae).

Artemisia nilotica Linnaeus, *Centuria I Plantarum*: 27. 1755.
"Habitat in Aegypto. D. Hasselquist." RCN: 6456.
Lectotype (Humphries in Jarvis & Turland in *Taxon* 47: 354. 1998): *Hasselquist*, Herb. Linn. No. 1014.6 (LINN; iso- LINN 1014.3, UPS).
Current name: ***Cotula anthemoides*** L. (Asteraceae).

Artemisia palustris Linnaeus, *Species Plantarum* 2: 846. 1753.
"Habitat in Sibiria." RCN: 6131.
Lectotype (Ling in Jarvis & Turland in *Taxon* 47: 354. 1998): Herb. Linn. No. 988.18 (LINN).
Current name: ***Artemisia palustris*** L. (Asteraceae).

Artemisia pontica Linnaeus, *Species Plantarum* 2: 847. 1753.
"Habitat in Hungaria interiore, Pannonia, Thracia, Mysia." RCN: 6136.
Lectotype (Leonova in *Novosti Sist. Vyssh. Rast.* 24: 180. 1987): Herb. Linn. No. 988.31 (LINN).
Current name: ***Artemisia pontica*** L. (Asteraceae).
Note: Leonova treated unspecified material in LINN as "Typus" and as there is only one collection there associated with this name, sheet 988.31 is accepted as the lectotype. Ling (in *Taxon* 47: 354. 1998) independently made the same choice of type.

Artemisia rupestris Linnaeus, *Species Plantarum* 2: 847. 1753.
"Habitat in Sibiria, Oelandiae rupibus calcareis." RCN: 6135.
Lectotype (Ling in Jarvis & Turland in *Taxon* 47: 354. 1998): Herb. Linn. No. 988.25 (LINN).

Current name: ***Artemisia rupestris*** L. (Asteraceae).

Note: Stearn (in *Biol. J. Linn. Soc.* 5: 9. 1973), in an account of Linnaeus' Öland and Gotland journey of 1741, treated Stora Karlsö off Gotland as the restricted type locality, and noted the existence of 988.25 (LINN). In his paper, he attributed restricted type localities irrespective of whether any material existed in LINN and, where specimens do exist, he does not refer to any of them as type specimens. Leonova (in *Novosti Sist. Vyssh. Rast.* 24: 186. 1987) indicated unspecified material in LINN as "Typus" but this does not distinguish between the four sheets (which are not part of a single gathering) associated with this name. Ling's subsequent explicit type choice of 988.25 (LINN), accepted here, shows no annotation expressly associating it with Gotland.

Artemisia santonicum Linnaeus, *Species Plantarum* 2: 845. 1753.
"Habitat in Tataria, Persia &c." RCN: 6129.
Lectotype (Leonova in *Novosti Sist. Vyssh. Rast.* 7: 286. 1971): Herb. Linn. No. 988.11 (LINN).
Current name: ***Artemisia santonicum*** L. (Asteraceae).
Note: Leonova indicated unspecified material in LINN as type but as 988.11 is the only sheet there associated with this name, it is accepted as an effective type choice. Leonova (in *Novosti Sist. Vyssh. Rast.* 24: 198. 1987) subsequently explicitly indicated sheet 988.11 as lectotype, and attributed the choice as having been made in the 1971 publication.

Artemisia tanacetifolia Linnaeus, *Species Plantarum* 2: 848. 1753.
"Habitat in Sibiria." RCN: 6138.
Lectotype (Leonova in *Novosti Sist. Vyssh. Rast.* 24: 181. 1987): Herb. Linn. No. 988.36 (LINN).
Current name: ***Artemisia tanacetifolia*** L. (Asteraceae).
Note: The type designated by Leonova (and independently by Ling in *Taxon* 47: 354. 1998) unfortunately appears to be identifiable as *A. armeniaca* Lam. *Artemisia tanacetifolia* L. may therefore be a candidate for conservation with a conserved type.

Artemisia vermiculata Linnaeus, *Mantissa Plantarum Altera*: 281. 1771.
"Habitat ad Cap. b. spei." RCN: 6123.
Lectotype (Koekemoer in Jarvis & Turland in *Taxon* 47: 354. 1998): Herb. Linn. No. 988.1 (LINN).
Current name: ***Stoebe plumosa*** (L.) Thunb. (Asteraceae).

Artemisia vulgaris Linnaeus, *Species Plantarum* 2: 848. 1753.
"Habitat in Europae cultis, ruderatis." RCN: 6140.
Lectotype (Gabrielian & Chandjian in *Novosti Sist. Vyssh. Rast.* 23: 206. 1986): Herb. Linn. No. 988.41 (LINN).
Generitype of *Artemisia* Linnaeus (vide Green, *Prop. Brit. Bot.*: 180. 1929).
Current name: ***Artemisia vulgaris*** L. (Asteraceae).
Note: Vallés-Xirau (in Jarvis & al., *Regnum Veg.* 127: 21. 1993) independently made the same choice of type as Gabrielian & Chandjian.

Arum arborescens Linnaeus, *Species Plantarum* 2: 967. 1753.
"Habitat in America meridionali." RCN: 7001.
Lectotype (Howard in *J. Arnold Arbor.* 60: 286. 1979): [icon] *"Arum arborescens, sagittariae foliis"* in Plumier, Descr. Pl. Amér.: 44, t. 51, f. G, t. 60. 1693.
Current name: ***Montrichardia arborescens*** (L.) Schott (Araceae).

Arum arisarum Linnaeus, *Species Plantarum* 2: 966. 1753.
"Habitat in Mauritaniae, Italiae, Lusitaniae, Hispaniae, Galloprovinciae nemoribus." RCN: 6998.
Type not designated.

Original material: Herb. Burser X: 143 (UPS); [icon] in Plantin, Pl. Stirp. Icon.: 598. 1581; [icon] in Clusius, Rar. Pl. Hist. 2: 73. 1601.
Current name: ***Arisarum vulgare*** O. Targ. Tozz. (Araceae).
Note: Boyce (in *Kew Mag.* 7: 20. 1990) incorrectly indicated a Brander specimen (1079.10 LINN), which was not received by Linnaeus until after 1753, as holotype.

Arum auritum Linnaeus, *Systema Naturae*, ed. 10, 2: 1251. 1759.
["Habitat in America."] Sp. Pl., ed. 2, 2: 1372 (1763). RCN: 7005.
Lectotype (Croat in *Ann. Missouri Bot. Gard.* 68: 609. 1982): *Browne*, Herb. Linn. No. 1079.18 (LINN).
Current name: ***Syngonium auritum*** (L.) Schott (Araceae).
Note: Croat indicated sheet 1079.17 (LINN) as the type but this material is annotated as "A. lingulatum", and the number Croat gives is clearly a typographic error for sheet 1079.18, the only collection there associated with *A. auritum*.

Arum cannifolium Linnaeus, *Plantae Surinamenses*: 15. 1775.
"Habitat [in Surinamo.]" RCN: 7008.
Type not designated.
Original material: Herb. Linn. No. 1079.15 (LINN).
Current name: ***Philodendron linnaei*** Kunth (Araceae).

Arum colocasia Linnaeus, *Species Plantarum* 2: 965. 1753.
"Habitat in Cretae, Cypri, Syriae, Aegypti aquosis." RCN: 6987.
Lectotype (Nicolson in Smith, *Fl. Vitiensis Nova* 1: 457. 1979): Herb. Linn. No. 1079.4 (LINN).
Current name: ***Colocasia esculenta*** (L.) Schott var. ***antiquorum*** (Schott) F.T. Hubb. & Rehder (Araceae).

Arum divaricatum Linnaeus, *Species Plantarum* 2: 966. 1753.
"Habitat in India." RCN: 6992.
Lectotype (Nicolson & Sivadasan in *Blumea* 27: 485. 1981): [icon] *"Nelenschena major"* in Rheede, Hort. Malab. 11: 39, t. 20. 1692.
Current name: ***Typhonium flagelliforme*** (Lodd.) Blume (Araceae).

Arum dracontium Linnaeus, *Species Plantarum* 2: 964. 1753.
"Habitat in America." RCN: 6984.
Neotype (Reveal & al. in *Bartonia* 56: 15. 1990): [icon] *"Arum, s. Arisarum Virginianum, Dracontii foliis, pene viridi, longo, acuminato"* in Plukenet, Phytographia: t. 271, f. 1. 1694; Almag. Bot.: 52. 1696. – Typotype: Herb. Sloane 95: 106 (BM-SL).
Current name: ***Arisaema dracontium*** (L.) Schott (Araceae).

Arum dracunculus Linnaeus, *Species Plantarum* 2: 964. 1753.
"Habitat in Europa australi." RCN: 6983.
Type not designated.
Original material: Herb. Burser X: 136 (UPS); Herb. A. van Royen No. 898.88–461? (L); Herb. A. van Royen No. 898.88–457 (L); Herb. A. van Royen No. 898.88–458? (L); [icon] in Morison, Pl. Hist. Univ. 3: 548, s. 13, t. 5, f. 46. 1699; [icon] in Dodoëns, Stirp. Hist. Pempt., ed. 2: 329. 1616.
Current name: ***Dracunculus vulgaris*** Schott (Araceae).

Arum esculentum Linnaeus, *Species Plantarum* 2: 965. 1753.
"Habitat in America." RCN: 6988.
Lectotype (Howard, *Fl. Lesser Antilles* 3: 382. 1979): [icon] *"Arum minus nympheae foliis esculentum"* [leaf only] in Sloane, Voy. Jamaica 1: 167, t. 106, f. 1. 1707. – Typotype: Herb. Sloane 3: 39 (BM-SL).
Current name: ***Colocasia esculenta*** (L.) Schott (Araceae).
Note: Bogner (in Leroy, *Fl. Madagascar* 31: 32. 1975) indicated 1079.5 (LINN) as type but this collection was received by Linnaeus long after 1753 and is not original material for the name.

Arum lingulatum Linnaeus, *Systema Naturae,* ed. 10, 2: 1251. 1759. ["Habitat in America."] Sp. Pl., ed. 2, 2: 1371 (1763). RCN: 7004.
Lectotype (Howard, *Fl. Lesser Antilles* 3: 392. 1979): [icon] *"Arum caulescens, radicans, foliis cordatis"* in Plumier in Burman, Pl. Amer.: 26, t. 37. 1756.
Current name: ***Philodendron lingulatum*** (L.) K. Koch (Araceae).

Arum macrorrhizon Linnaeus, *Species Plantarum* 2: 965. 1753. "Habitat in Zeylona." RCN: 6990.
Lectotype (Furtado in *Gard. Bull. Straits Settlem.* 11: 246, 252. 1941): [icon] *"Arum Zeylanicum maximum"* in Hermann, Parad. Bat.: 73. 1698.
Current name: ***Alocasia macrorrhizos*** (L.) G. Don (Araceae).
Note: For the spelling of the epithet, see Hay & Wise (in *Blumea* 35: 533. 1991), who also provide illustrations of the Hermann drawing in Herb. Hermann (BM) and the Rumphius plate (f. 14a, b).

Arum maculatum Linnaeus, *Species Plantarum* 2: 966. 1753. "Habitat in Europa australiore." RCN: 6995.
Lectotype (Boyce, *Genus* Arum: 61. 1993): Herb. Linn. No. 1079.8 (LINN).
Generitype of *Arum* Linnaeus (vide Green, *Prop. Brit. Bot.*: 186. 1929).
Current name: ***Arum maculatum*** L. (Araceae).
Note: Boyce cited the type specimen as "1078.8" (LINN), a non-existent collection and clearly an error for 1079.8 (LINN).

Arum ovatum Linnaeus, *Species Plantarum* 2: 967. 1753. "Habitat in India." RCN: 6999.
Lectotype (Nicolson in *Smithsonian Contr. Bot.* 1: 5. 1969): [icon] *"Karin-pola"* in Rheede, Hort. Malab. 11: 45, t. 23. 1692.
Current name: ***Lagenandra ovata*** (L.) Thwaites (Araceae).
Note: See also a detailed review by de Wit (in *Meded. Landbouwhoogeschool* 78–11: 5–8. 1978) in which the type figure is illustrated (f. 1, 2).

Arum pentaphyllum Linnaeus, *Species Plantarum* 2: 964. 1753. "Habitat in India." RCN: 6985.
Type not designated.
Original material: [icon] in Zanoni, Istoria Bot.: 170, t. 78. 1675; [icon] in Morison, Pl. Hist. Univ. 3: 549, s. 13, t. 5, f. 27. 1699.
Current name: ***Arisaema pentaphyllum*** (L.) Schott (Araceae).

Arum peregrinum Linnaeus, *Species Plantarum* 2: 966. 1753. "Habitat in America." RCN: 6991.
Type not designated.
Original material: none traced.
Current name: ***Alocasia macrorrhizos*** (L.) G. Don (Araceae).

Arum proboscideum Linnaeus, *Species Plantarum* 2: 966. 1753. "Habitat in Apenninis." RCN: 6997.
Lectotype (Galán de Mera & Castroviejo in *Taxon* 53: 1047. 2004): [icon] *"Arisarum latifo. min. rep. cespit."* in Barrelier, Pl. Galliam: 19, t. 1150. 1714.
Current name: ***Arisarum proboscideum*** (L.) Savi (Araceae).
Note: The type figure is reproduced by Forneris (*L'Erbario Univ. Torino*: 129, III. 2004).

Arum sagittifolium Linnaeus, *Species Plantarum* 2: 966. 1753. "Habitat in Brasilia, Jamaica, Barbados." RCN: 6994.
Lectotype (Howard in *J. Arnold Arbor.* 60: 288. 1979): [icon] *"Arum minus esculentum, sagittariae foliis viridi-nigricantibus"* in Sloane, Voy. Jamaica 1: 167, t. 106, f. 2. 1707. – Typotype: Herb. Sloane 3: 40 (BM-SL).

Current name: ***Xanthosoma sagittifolium*** (L.) Schott (Araceae).
Note: Specific epithet spelled "sagittaefolium" in the protologue.

Arum tenuifolium Linnaeus, *Species Plantarum* 2: 967. 1753. "Habitat in Dalmatia, Romae, Monspelii." RCN: 7000.
Type not designated.
Original material: Herb. Burser X: 144 (UPS); Herb. A. van Royen No. 898.88–266 (L); Herb. Clifford: 435, *Arum* 9 (BM); [icon] in Clusius, Rar. Pl. Hist. 2: 74. 1601; [icon] in Morison, Pl. Hist. Univ. 3: 545, s. 13, t. 6, f. 21. 1699.
Current name: ***Biarum tenuifolium*** (L.) Schott (Araceae).
Note: Boyce (in *Aroideana* 29: 7. 2006) indicated 1079.13 and 1079.14 (LINN) as syntypes but these are König collections received by Linnaeus long after 1753 and are not original material for the name.

Arum trilobatum Linnaeus, *Species Plantarum* 2: 965. 1753. "Habitat in Zeylona." RCN: 6993.
Lectotype (Nicolson & Sivarajan in *Blumea* 27: 488. 1981): Herb. Hermann 5: 177, No. 326 [icon] (BM-000594954).
Current name: ***Typhonium trilobatum*** (L.) Schott (Araceae).

Arum trilobum Linnaeus, *Herbarium Amboinense*: 22. 1754, *orth. var.* "Habitat [in Amboina.]"
Lectotype (Wijnands, *Bot. Commelins*: 46. 1983): Herb. Hermann 5: 177, No. 326 [icon] (BM-000594954).
Current name: ***Typhonium trilobatum*** (L.) Schott (Araceae).
Note: An orthographic variant of *A. trilobatum* L. (1753).

Arum triphyllum Linnaeus, *Species Plantarum* 2: 965. 1753. "Habitat in Virginia, Brasilia." RCN: 6986.

Lectotype (Fernald in *Rhodora* 42: 249. 1940): Herb. Linn. No. 1079.2 (LINN).

Current name: ***Arisaema triphyllum*** (L.) Schott (Araceae).
Note: Reveal & al. (in *Huntia* 7: 213. 1987) believed that Fernald's type choice is identifiable as subsp. *pusillum* (Peck) Huttleston, and not subsp. *triphyllum*. Reveal & al. (in *Taxon* 39: 355. 1990) therefore proposed *Clayton 66* as a conserved type in its place. However, this was not recommended by the Committee for Spermatophyta (in *Taxon* 42: 875. 1993), although resubmission in a clearer form was invited.

Arum virginicum Linnaeus, *Species Plantarum* 2: 966. 1753.
"Habitat in Virginia." RCN: 6996.
Lectotype (Blackwell & Blackwell in *J. Elisha Mitchell Sci. Soc.* 90: 138. 1974): *Clayton 228* (BM-000042222).
Current name: ***Peltandra virginica*** (L.) Schott & Endl. (Araceae).

Arundo arenaria Linnaeus, *Species Plantarum* 1: 82. 1753.
"Habitat in Europa ad maris litora arenosa." RCN: 687.
Lectotype (Cope in Cafferty & al. in *Taxon* 49: 247. 2000): Herb. Linn. No. 97.17 (LINN).
Current name: ***Ammophila arenaria*** (L.) Link subsp. ***arenaria*** (Poaceae).
Note: Although Kerguélen (in *Lejeunia*, n.s., 75: 80. 1975) stated "Type: ...LINN", this is not accepted as a formal typification, for the reasons explained by Cafferty & al. (in *Taxon* 49: 240. 2000). Meikle (*Fl. Cyprus* 2: 1789. 1985) indicated unspecified material at LINN as type but did not distinguish between the two sheets present there, which are not a single gathering (Art. 9.15).

Arundo bambos Linnaeus, *Species Plantarum* 1: 81. 1753.
"Habitat in India utraque." RCN: 682.
Lectotype (Judziewicz in Görts-van Rijn, *Fl. Guianas,* ser. A, 8: 50. 1990): [icon] *"Ily"* in Rheede, Hort. Malab. 1: 25, t. 16. 1678.
Current name: ***Bambusa bambos*** (L.) Voss (Poaceae).
Note: McClure (in *Blumea, Suppl.* 3: 109. 1946) discussed the name and the cited Rheede figure but did not make an unequivocal type statement. Although Holttum (in *Taxon* 5: 28, 67. 1956) recommended the rejection of the name as a *nomen confusum*, this has never been formally proposed. Judziewicz (in Görts-van Rijn, *Fl. Guianas,* ser. A, 8: 50. 1990) clearly indicated Rheede's t. 16 as the type, and this choice has priority over that of Xia & Stapleton (in *Kew Bull.* 52: 697, f. 1. 1997), who chose a Hermann specimen in Leiden (L) as the lectotype.

Arundo calamagrostis Linnaeus, *Species Plantarum* 1: 82. 1753.
"Habitat in Europae paludibus graminosis." RCN: 686.
Lectotype (Cope in Cafferty & al. in *Taxon* 49: 247. 2000): Herb. Linn. No. 97.14 (LINN).
Current name: ***Calamagrostis canescens*** (F.H. Wigg.) Roth (Poaceae).
Note: See comments on the cited Scheuchzer element by Vickery (in *Contr. New South Wales Herb.* 1: 44. 1940).

Arundo donax Linnaeus, *Species Plantarum* 1: 81. 1753.
"Habitat in Hispania, Galloprovincia." RCN: 683.
Lectotype (Renvoize in Jarvis & al., *Regnum Veg.* 127: 21. 1993): Herb. A. van Royen No. 912.356–93 (L).
Generitype of *Arundo* Linnaeus (vide Hitchcock, *Prop. Brit. Bot.*: 121. 1929).
Current name: ***Arundo donax*** L. (Poaceae).
Note: Although a number of authors including Meikle (*Fl. Cyprus* 2: 1838. 1985) and Sherif & Siddiqi (in El-Gadi, *Fl. Libya* 145: 206. 1988) indicated material in LINN as type, none of the three sheets (97.3, 97.4 and 97.5) there is original material for the name, and Renvoize's choice therefore has priority.

Arundo epigejos Linnaeus, *Species Plantarum* 1: 81. 1753.
"Habitat in Europae collibus aridis." RCN: 685.
Lectotype (Hubbard in Milne-Redhead & Polhill, *Fl. Trop. E. Africa, Gramineae* 1: 102. 1970): Herb. Linn. No. 97.11 (LINN).
Current name: ***Calamagrostis epigejos*** (L.) Roth (Poaceae).

Arundo phragmites Linnaeus, *Species Plantarum* 1: 81. 1753.
"Habitat in Europae lacubus fluviis." RCN: 684.
Lectotype (Clayton in Milne-Redhead & Polhill, *Fl. Trop. E. Africa, Gramineae* 1: 118. 1970): Herb. Linn. No. 97.6 (LINN).
Current name: ***Phragmites australis*** (Cav.) Trin. ex Steud. (Poaceae).

Arundo vallatoria Linnaeus, *Herbarium Amboinense*: 15. 1754, *nom. inval.*
Type not relevant.
Current name: ***Phragmites karka*** (Retz.) Steud. (Poaceae).
Note: Veldkamp (in *Blumea* 37: 232–233. 1992) has argued that "Arundo vallatoria Pluk.", from the right-hand column of names in the thesis *Herbarium Amboinense* (1754: 15), is a valid Linnaean binomial based on Rumphius' 4: t. 5, and an earlier name for the plant known as *Phragmites karka* Retz. He therefore made a new combination for it as *P. vallatoria* (Pluk. ex L.) Veldk. However, it seems clear that Linnaeus was merely citing "A. vallatoria, Pluk., Mant. 28" as a synonym of Rumphius' plant, the binomial form of Plukenet's name being merely a coincidence. Apart from the reprint of the thesis (*Amoen. Acad.* 4: 115. 1759), Linnaeus never used the name again, and it is in any case invalid (see Art. 34.1, Ex. 2).

Asarum canadense Linnaeus, *Species Plantarum* 1: 442. 1753.
"Habitat in Canada." RCN: 3424.
Type not designated.
Original material: *Kalm*, Herb. Linn. No. 608.2 (LINN); [icon] in Cornut, Canad. Pl. Hist.: 24, 25. 1635; [icon] in Morison, Pl. Hist. Univ. 3: 511, s. 13, t. 7, f. 2. 1699.
Current name: ***Asarum canadense*** L. (Aristolochiaceae).

Asarum europaeum Linnaeus, *Species Plantarum* 1: 442. 1753.
"Habitat in Europae nemoribus." RCN: 3423.
Lectotype (Jonsell & Jarvis in Jarvis & al., *Regnum Veg.* 127: 21. 1993): Herb. Linn. No. 608.1 (LINN).
Generitype of *Asarum* Linnaeus (vide Green, *Prop. Brit. Bot.*: 157. 1929).
Current name: ***Asarum europaeum*** L. (Aristolochiaceae).
Note: Jonsell & Jarvis (in *Nordic J. Bot.* 14: 153. 1994) provide additional information on their formal 1993 type choice.

Asarum hypocistis Linnaeus, *Species Plantarum* 1: 442. 1753.
"Habitat in Hispania, Lusitania parasitica cisti." RCN: 6975.
Basionym of: *Cytinus hypocistis* (L.) L. (1764).
Lectotype (Labani in Jafri & El-Gadi, *Fl. Libya* 71: 3. 1980): Herb. Linn. No. 1075.1 (LINN).
Current name: ***Cytinus hypocistis*** (L.) L. (Rafflesiaceae).

Asarum virginicum Linnaeus, *Species Plantarum* 1: 442. 1753.
"Habitat in Virginia, terra Mariana, Carolina." RCN: 3425.
Lectotype (Reveal & al. in *Huntia* 7: 214. 1987): *Clayton 704* (BM-000051752).
Current name: ***Hexastylis virginicum*** (L.) Small (Aristolochiaceae).

Asclepias amoena Linnaeus, *Species Plantarum* 1: 214. 1753.
"Habitat in America septentrionali." RCN: 1774.
Lectotype (Reveal & al. in *Huntia* 7: 155. 1987): [icon] *"Apocynum floribus amoene purpureis, corniculis surrectis"* in Dillenius, Hort. Eltham. 1: 31, t. 27, f. 30. 1732. – Typotype: Herb. Sherard No. 569 (OXF).

Current name: ***Asclepias purpurascens*** L. (Asclepiadaceae).
Note: See Gray (in *Proc. Amer. Acad. Arts* 12: 67. 1876) and Britten (in
J. Bot. 36: 298. 1898) who both use the expression "founded upon"
(which is not accepted as equivalent to "type") in connection with
the cited Dillenius plate.

Asclepias arborescens Linnaeus, *Mantissa Plantarum Altera*: 216. 1771.
"Habitat ad Cap. b. Spei. montibus." RCN: 1784.
Lectotype (Goyder & Nicholas in *Kew Bull.* 56: 804. 2001): [icon]
*"Apocynum frutescens, latis & undulatis foliis; floribus umbellatis, fructu
gemino sulcato, spinoso"* in Burman, Rar. Afric. Pl.: 31, t. 13. 1738.
Current name: ***Gomphocarpus cancellatus*** (Burm. f.) Bruyns
(Asclepiadaceae).

Asclepias curassavica Linnaeus, *Species Plantarum* 1: 215. 1753.
"Habitat in Curassao." RCN: 1777.
Lectotype (Woodson in *Ann. Missouri Bot. Gard.* 41: 59. 1954): Herb.
Linn. No. 310.19 (LINN).
Current name: ***Asclepias curassavica*** L. (Asclepiadaceae).
Note: Rendle (in *Proc. Linn. Soc. London* 148: 64. 1935) clearly treated
material in LINN as the type, noting that the description
"…corresponds to the specimen, a poor one with a simple umbel".
This fails, however, to distinguish between 310.18 and 310.19,
which do not appear to be part of a single gathering (so Art. 9.15
does not apply). Wijnands (*Bot. Commelins*: 48. 1983) and others
concluded that Rendle intended 310.18 (LINN) as the type, and
accepted him as having typified the name. However, this does not
seem justified, and Woodson appears to have been the first to make
an explicit type choice (of 310.19).

Asclepias decumbens Linnaeus, *Species Plantarum* 1: 216. 1753.
"Habitat in Virginia." RCN: 1780.
Lectotype (designated here by Reveal): *Clayton 83* (BM).
Current name: ***Asclepias tuberosa*** L. var. ***tuberosa*** (Asclepiadaceae).

Asclepias exaltata Linnaeus, *Demonstr. Pl. Horto Upsaliensi*: 7. 1753.
RCN: 1773.
Basionym of: *Asclepias syriaca* L. var. *exaltata* (L.) L. (1762).
Type not designated.
Original material: none traced.
Current name: ***Asclepias exaltata*** L. (Asclepiadaceae).

Asclepias fruticosa Linnaeus, *Species Plantarum* 1: 216. 1753.
"Habitat in Aethiopia." RCN: 1785.
Lectotype (Woodson in *Ann. Missouri Bot. Gard.* 41: 151. 1954):
Herb. Linn. No. 310.33 (LINN). – Epitype (Goyder & Nicholas in
Kew Bull. 56: 782. 2001): South Africa. Northern Cape, Bloeddrif,
12 Sep 1968, *Hardy 2562* (K; iso- PRE, WIND).
Current name: ***Gomphocarpus fruticosus*** (L.) W.T. Aiton
(Asclepiadaceae).
Note: Woodson cited the sheet number of the type as "310.23" (which
relates to *A. incarnata* L.) but this appears to have been a simple
error for "310.33".

Asclepias gigantea Linnaeus, *Species Plantarum* 1: 214. 1753.
"Habitat in India, Aegypto." RCN: 1772.
Lectotype (Huber in Abeywickrama, *Revised Handb. Fl. Ceylon* 1(1):
35. 1973): Herb. Hermann 2: 74, No. 112 (BM-000621762).
Current name: ***Calotropis gigantea*** (L.) R. Br. (Asclepiadaceae).

Asclepias incarnata Linnaeus, *Species Plantarum* 1: 215. 1753.
"Habitat in Canada, Virginia." RCN: 1779.
Lectotype (Woodson in *Ann. Missouri Bot. Gard.* 41: 50. 1954): Herb.
Linn. No. 310.25 (LINN).
Current name: ***Asclepias incarnata*** L. (Asclepiadaceae).

Note: Rendle (in *Proc. Linn. Soc. London* 148: 64. 1935) indicated
material in LINN as the type, but did not distinguish between
sheets 310.23–310.26.

Asclepias lactifera Linnaeus, *Species Plantarum* 1: 216. 1753.
"Habitat in Zeylona." RCN: 1781.
Lectotype (Huber in Abeywickrama, *Revised Handb. Fl. Ceylon* 1(1):
45. 1973): Herb. Hermann 2: 11, No. 111 (BM-000621538).
Current name: ***Gymnema lactiferum*** (L.) R. Br. ex Schult.
(Asclepiadaceae).

Asclepias nigra Linnaeus, *Species Plantarum* 1: 216. 1753.
"Habitat Monspelii in collibus." RCN: 1783.
Type not designated.
Original material: Herb. Burser XVII: 54 (UPS); Herb. Linn. No.
310.30 (LINN); [icon] in Mattioli, Pl. Epit.: 560. 1586.
Current name: ***Vincetoxicum nigrum*** (L.) Moench (Asclepiadaceae).

Asclepias nivea Linnaeus, *Species Plantarum* 1: 215. 1753.
"Habitat in Virginia & America calidiore." RCN: 1778.
Lectotype (Rendle in *Proc. Linn. Soc. London* 148: 64. 1936): [icon]
"Apocynum Persicariae mitis folio, corniculis lacteis" in Dillenius,
Hort. Eltham. 1: 33, t. 29, f. 32. 1732. – Typotype: Herb. Sherard
No. 577 (OXF).
Current name: ***Asclepias nivea*** L. (Asclepiadaceae).
Note: Rendle (in *J. Bot.* 74: 339. 1936) subsequently indicated Sherard
material in OXF as the type but his earlier choice of the Dillenius
plate is correct.

Asclepias pubescens Linnaeus, *Mantissa Plantarum Altera*: 215. 1771.
"Habitat ad Cap. b. spei. H.U." RCN: 1771.
Lectotype (Goyder & Nicholas in *Kew Bull.* 56: 803. 2001): Herb.
Linn. No. 19: *Asclepias pubescens* (UPS).
Current name: ***Gomphocarpus cancellatus*** (Burm. f.) Bruyns
(Asclepiadaceae).

Asclepias purpurascens Linnaeus, *Species Plantarum* 1: 214. 1753.
"Habitat in Carolina." RCN: 1775.
Lectotype (designated here by Reveal): [icon] *"Apocynum floribus
obsolete purpureis, corniculis resupinis"* in Dillenius, Hort. Eltham. 1:
32, t. 28, f. 31. 1732. – Voucher: Herb. Sherard No. 569 (OXF).
Current name: ***Asclepias purpurascens*** L. (Asclepiadaceae).
Note: See Gray (in *Proc. Amer. Acad. Arts* 12: 67. 1876) and Britten (in
J. Bot. 36: 298. 1898), who both use the expression "founded upon"
(which is not acceptable as equivalent to "type") in connection with
the cited Dillenius plate.

Asclepias rubra Linnaeus, *Species Plantarum* 1: 217. 1753.
"Habitat in Virginia." RCN: 1788.
Lectotype (designated here by Reveal): *Clayton 263* (BM-000040313).
Current name: ***Asclepias rubra*** L. (Asclepiadaceae).
Note: See Gray (in *Proc. Amer. Acad. Arts* 12: 90. 1876), who used the
expression "founded upon" (which is not acceptable as equivalent to
"type") in connection with *Clayton 263* (BM). Woodson (in *Ann.
Missouri Bot. Gard.* 41: 80. 1954) indicated 310.39 (LINN) as the
type but the sheet lacks the *Species Plantarum* number (i.e. "17")
and was a post-1753 addition to the herbarium, and not original
material for the name.

Asclepias sibirica Linnaeus, *Species Plantarum* 1: 217. 1753.
"Habitat in Sibiria." RCN: 1786.
Lectotype (Grubov in *Novosti Sist. Vyssh. Rast.* 32: 138. 2000): *Gmelin
s.n.*, Herb. Linn. No. 310.35 (LINN).
Current name: ***Cynanchum thesioides*** (Freyn) K. Schum.
(Asclepiadaceae).

Asclepias syriaca Linnaeus, *Species Plantarum* 1: 214. 1753.
"Habitat in Virginia." RCN: 1773.
Lectotype (Woodson in *Ann. Missouri Bot. Gard.* 41: 105. 1954):
  Herb. Linn. No. 310.14 (LINN).
Generitype of *Asclepias* Linnaeus (vide Hitchcock, *Prop. Brit. Bot.*:
  136. 1929).
Current name: ***Asclepias syriaca*** L. (Asclepiadaceae).

Asclepias syriaca Linnaeus var. **exaltata** (Linnaeus) Linnaeus, *Species
Plantarum*, ed. 2, 1: 313. 1762.
RCN: 1773.
Basionym: *Asclepias exaltata* L. (1753).
Type not designated.
Original material: as basionym.
Current name: ***Asclepias exaltata*** L. (Asclepiadaceae).

Asclepias tuberosa Linnaeus, *Species Plantarum* 1: 217. 1753.
"Habitat in America boreali." RCN: 1789.
Lectotype (Woodson in *Ann. Missouri Bot. Gard.* 41: 74. 1954): *Kalm,*
  Herb. Linn. No. 310.41 (LINN; iso- UPS).
Current name: ***Asclepias tuberosa*** L. (Asclepiadaceae).

Asclepias undulata Linnaeus, *Species Plantarum* 1: 214. 1753.
"Habitat in Africa." RCN: 1768.
Lectotype (Wijnands, *Bot. Commelins*: 48. 1983): [icon] *"Apocynum
  Afric. lapathi folio"* in Commelin, Hort. Med. Amstelaed. Pl. Rar.:
  16, t. 16. 1706.
Current name: ***Asclepias undulata*** L. (Asclepiadaceae).

Asclepias variegata Linnaeus, *Species Plantarum* 1: 215. 1753.
"Habitat in America boreali." RCN: 1776.
Lectotype (Rendle in *Proc. Linn. Soc. London* 148: 63. 1936): [icon]
  *"Apocynum American. erectum, tuberosa radice non incanum, foliis
  rigidioribus, latis, subrotundis, floribus alb. intus purpureis, summo
  cauli Corymbum magnum efformantibus"* in Plukenet, Phytographia:
  t. 77, f. 1. 1691; Almag. Bot.: 34. 1696. – Typotype: Herb. Sloane
  95: 57 (BM-SL).
Current name: ***Asclepias variegata*** L. (Asclepiadaceae).
Note: Although Woodson (in *Ann. Missouri Bot. Gard.* 41: 62, 118.
  1954) indicated 310.20 (LINN) as the type, Rendle's choice has
  priority.

Asclepias verticillata Linnaeus, *Species Plantarum* 1: 217. 1753.
"Habitat in Virginia." RCN: 1787.
Lectotype (Britten in *J. Bot.* 36: 265. 1898): *Clayton 216* (BM-
  000051173).
Current name: ***Asclepias verticillata*** L. (Asclepiadaceae).
Note: See extensive review by Reveal & al. (in *Huntia* 7: 212–213.
  1987).

Asclepias vincetoxicum Linnaeus, *Species Plantarum* 1: 216. 1753.
"Habitat in Europae glareosis." RCN: 1782.
Type not designated.
Original material: Herb. Clifford: 78, *Asclepias* 1, 6 sheets (BM);
  Herb. Burser XVII: 52 (UPS); Herb. Linn. No. 310.27 (LINN);
  Herb. Linn. No. 310.29 (LINN); [icon] in Dodoëns, Stirp. Hist.
  Pempt., ed. 2: 407. 1616.
Current name: ***Vincetoxicum hirudinaria*** Medik. (Asclepiadaceae).
Note: Jagtap & Singh (in *Fasc. Fl. India* 24: 59. 1999) indicated
  310.28 (LINN) as type but this sheet lacks the *Species Plantarum*
  number (i.e. "12") and was a post-1753 addition to the herbarium,
  and not original material for the name.

Ascyrum crux-andreae Linnaeus, *Species Plantarum* 2: 787. 1753.
"Habitat in Virginia." RCN: 5773.

Neotype (Robson in *Taxon* 29: 272. 1980): Herb. Linn. No. 944.1
  (LINN).
Current name: ***Hypericum crux-andreae*** (L.) Crantz (Clusiaceae).
Note: See additional notes by Reveal & al. (in *Huntia* 7: 226.
  1987).

Ascyrum hypericoides Linnaeus, *Species Plantarum* 2: 788. 1753.
"Habitat in Virginia." RCN: 5774.
Lectotype (Robson in *Taxon* 29: 267, 272. 1980): [icon]
  "Hypericoides" in Plumier, Nov. Pl. Amer.: 51, t. 7. 1703.
Generitype of *Ascyrum* Linnaeus.
Current name: ***Hypericum hypericoides*** (L.) Crantz (Clusiaceae).
Note: Fernald (in *Rhodora* 38: 432. 1936) discussed various of the
  original elements, interpreting the name "as to Plumier's plant" but
  this falls short of formal typification. Adams (in *Rhodora* 59: 81.
  1957) adopted a similar line but also designated Browne's specimen
  (944.4 LINN) as a neotype (unacceptable in the presence of
  original material). Robson's choice is followed here. See further
  comments by Reveal & al. (in *Huntia* 7: 226. 1987) and Robson (in
  Bull. Nat. Hist. Mus. London, Bot. 26: 129–130. 1996).

Ascyrum villosum Linnaeus, *Species Plantarum* 2: 788. 1753.
"Habitat in Virginia." RCN: 5775.
Lectotype (Robson in *Taxon* 29: 273. 1980): [icon] *"Hypericum
  Virginianum frutescens pilosissimum"* in Plukenet, Phytographia: t.
  245, f. 6. 1694; Almag. Bot.: 189. 1696.
Current name: ***Hypericum setosum*** L. (Clusiaceae).

Aspalathus albens Linnaeus, *Mantissa Plantarum Altera*: 261. 1771.
"Habitat ad Cap. b. spei." RCN: 5219.
Lectotype (Dahlgren in *Opera Bot.* 21: 24. 1968): Herb. Linn. No.
  893.11 (LINN).
Current name: ***Aspalathus albens*** L. (Fabaceae: Faboideae).

Aspalathus anthylloides Linnaeus, *Species Plantarum*, ed. 2, 2: 1002.
  1763, *nom. illeg.*
"Habitat ad Cap. b. spei." RCN: 5237.
Replaced synonym: *Anthyllis lotoides* L. (1756), *nom. illeg.*, non L.
  (1753); *Anthyllis aspalathoides* L. (1759).
Lectotype (Dahlgren in *Opera Bot.* 4: 114. 1960): Herb. Linn. No.
  893.56 (LINN).
Current name: ***Aspalathus aspalathoides*** (L.) Rothm. (Fabaceae:
  Faboideae).
Note: This is an illegitimate renaming in *Aspalathus* of *Anthyllis
  asphaltoides* L. (Nov 1759), itself usually treated as an orthographic
  variant of the earlier *An. aspalathoides* L. (May–Jun 1759). It in turn
  was a new name for *An. lotoides* L. (1756), *nom. illeg.*, non L.
  (1753).

Aspalathus araneosa Linnaeus, *Species Plantarum* 2: 712. 1753.
"Habitat in Aethiopia." RCN: 5229.
Lectotype (Dahlgren in Leistner, *Fl. Southern Africa* 16(3:6): 161.
  1988): [icon] *"Genista Aethiopica flore flavo, foliolis inflexis, &
  araneosa lanugine fimbriatis, summo ramulo, circa flores glomeratis"* in
  Plukenet, Amalth. Bot.: t. 414, f. 4. 1705; Almag. Mant.: 87. 1700.
  – Typotype: Herb. Sloane 102: 197 (BM-SL) ["4: 197"].
Current name: ***Aspalathus araneosa*** L. (Fabaceae: Faboideae).

Aspalathus argentea Linnaeus, *Species Plantarum* 2: 713. 1753.
"Habitat in Aethiopia." RCN: 5239.
Neotype (Dahlgren in *Opera Bot.* 4: 285. 1960): *Tulbagh 150*, Herb.
  Linn. No. 893.46 (LINN).
Current name: ***Aspalathus argentea*** L. (Fabaceae: Faboideae).
Note: Dahlgren (in *Opera Bot.* 4: 285. 1960) discussed elements
  apparently associated with the name and, aware that a number of

taxa were involved, designated Tulbagh material (LINN) as a neotype, and applied the name in that sense. However, he subsequently had second thoughts (*Opera Bot.* 9(1): 7. 1963; in Leistner, *Fl. Southern Africa* 16(3:6): 51. 1988) and rejected it as a *nomen obscurum et (vel) ambiguum*. Noting that it included elements belonging to *A. sericea* P.J. Bergius, *A. altissima* R. Dahlgren and *A. caledonensis* R. Dahlgren, he took up the latter name in its place, and this seems to have been followed by later authors. Dahlgren's original typification, however, appears sound, and no rejection proposal has been made for *A. argentea*.

Aspalathus astroites Linnaeus, *Species Plantarum* 2: 711. 1753.
"Habitat in Aethiopia." RCN: 5217.
Lectotype (Dahlgren in *Opera Bot.* 21: 11, 176. 1968): [icon] *"Genista Astroites, Juniperinis pungentibus foliis, Aethiopica, floribus saturate luteis"* in Plukenet, Amalth. Bot.: t. 413, f. 2. 1705; Almag. Mant.: 88. 1700.
Current name: ***Aspalathus astroites*** L. (Fabaceae: Faboideae).
Note: Although Dahlgren indicated Herb. Sloane 92: 72 (BM-SL) as the probable typotype, the material in question does not resemble the plate.

Aspalathus callosa Linnaeus, *Species Plantarum* 2: 713. 1753.
"Habitat in Aethiopia. D. Royenus plurimas has Achyronias amicissime communicavit." RCN: 5240.
Lectotype (Dahlgren in *Opera Bot.* 11(1): 53. 1966): [icon] *"Cytisus trifoliatus, Juniperinis foliis, floribus luteis, in spicam densiorem adactis"* in Plukenet, Almag. Mant.: 63, t. 345, f. 4. 1700. – Typotype: Herb. Sloane 92: 54 (BM-SL).
Generitype of *Achyronia* Linnaeus (vide Reveal in Jarvis & al., *Regnum Veg.* 127: 14. 1993).
Current name: ***Aspalathus callosa*** L. (Fabaceae: Faboideae).

Aspalathus canescens Linnaeus, *Mantissa Plantarum Altera*: 262. 1771.
"Habitat ad Cap. b. spei montosis." RCN: 5230.
Lectotype (Dahlgren in *Opera Bot.* 10(1): 168. 1965): *Tulbagh 41*, Herb. Linn. No. 893.40 (LINN).
Current name: ***Aspalathus laricifolia*** P.J. Bergius subsp. ***canescens*** (L.) R. Dahlgren (Fabaceae: Faboideae).

Aspalathus capitata Linnaeus, *Plantae Rariores Africanae*: 14. 1760. ["Habitat ad Cap. b. spei."] Sp. Pl., ed. 2, 2: 1000 (1763). RCN: 5216.
Type not designated.
Original material: Herb. Burman (3 sheets?) (G); Herb. Linn. No. 893.5 (LINN).
Current name: ***Aspalathus capitata*** L. (Fabaceae: Faboideae).
Note: Dahlgren (in *Opera Bot.* 11(1): 30. 1966) designated a specimen in S (Herb. Linn. No. 295.7) as lectotype but it is unannotated by Linnaeus and is not original material for the name.

Aspalathus chenopoda Linnaeus, *Species Plantarum* 2: 711. 1753.
"Habitat in Aethiopia." RCN: 5218.
Lectotype (Polhill in Jarvis & al., *Regnum Veg.* 127: 21. 1993): Herb. Linn. No. 893.10 (LINN).
Generitype of *Aspalathus* Linnaeus (vide Green, *Prop. Brit. Bot.*: 174. 1929).
Current name: ***Aspalathus chenopoda*** L. (Fabaceae: Faboideae).
Note: Dahlgren (in *Opera Bot.* 8(1): 36; 9(1): 33. 1963; in Leistner, *Fl. Southern Africa* 16(3:6): 165. 1988) indicated two different Hermann specimens in Herb. Sloane (vol. 75: 33, BM-SL) as lectotype. However, as neither is original material for the name, Polhill's choice provides the first valid typification.

The lectotype of *Aspalathus chenopoda* L.

Aspalathus ciliaris Linnaeus, *Mantissa Plantarum Altera*: 262. 1771.
"Habitat ad Cap. b. spei campis arenosis." RCN: 5224.
Lectotype (Dahlgren in *Opera Bot.* 8(1): 63. 1963): *Tulbagh 191*, Herb, Linn. No. 893.28 (LINN).
Current name: ***Aspalathus ciliaris*** L. (Fabaceae: Faboideae).

Aspalathus cretica Linnaeus, *Species Plantarum* 2: 712. 1753.
"Habitat in Aethiopia." RCN: 5233.
Lectotype (Turland in Turland & Jarvis in *Taxon* 46: 463. 1997): [icon] *"Genestra arborea di Candia con foglie perpetue"* in Zanoni, Istoria Bot.: 99, t. 39. 1675.
Current name: ***Anthyllis hermanniae*** L. (Fabaceae: Faboideae).

Aspalathus ebenus Linnaeus, *Systema Naturae*, ed. 10, 2: 1158. 1759. ["Habitat in America meridionali."] Sp. Pl., ed. 2, 2: 1001 (1763). RCN: 5232.
Lectotype (Rico in Turland & Jarvis in *Taxon* 46: 463. 1997): Herb. Linn. No. 893.44 (LINN).
Current name: ***Brya ebenus*** (L.) DC. (Fabaceae: Faboideae).
Note: Wijnands (*Bot. Commelins*: 186. 1983) stated that the type "probably is LINN 893.44" but his uncertainty means this statement cannot be accepted as a formal typification.

Aspalathus ericifolia Linnaeus, *Species Plantarum* 2: 711. 1753.
"Habitat in Aethiopia." RCN: 5221.
Lectotype (Dahlgren in Leistner, *Fl. Southern Africa* 16(3:6): 178. 1988): Herb. Linn. No. 893.15 (LINN).
Current name: ***Aspalathus ericifolia*** L. (Fabaceae: Faboideae).
Note: Specific epithet spelled "ericefolia" in the protologue. Dahlgren (in *Opera Bot.* 10(1): 25. 1965) indicated 893.15 (LINN) only as "orig. coll.", but clarified this to "type" in 1988.

Aspalathus genistoides Linnaeus, *Mantissa Plantarum Altera*: 261. 1771.
"Habitat ad Cap. b. spei, e fissuris rupium." RCN: 5225.
Lectotype (Schrire in Turland & Jarvis in *Taxon* 46: 463. 1997): *Tulbagh 29*, ex Herb. Linn. (BM).
Current name: ***Aspalathus corrudifolia*** P.J. Bergius (Fabaceae: Faboideae).
Note: Dahlgren (in *Opera Bot.* 21: 213. 1968; in Leistner, *Fl. Southern Africa* 16(3:6): 316. 1988) stated that the name was based on *Tulbagh 29*, which he could not locate. He therefore designated 893.30 (LINN) as a neotype. He was evidently unaware of the existence of Tulbagh's specimen (which supports current usage) among the small number of Linnaean sheets at BM and, moreover, appeared to overlook 893.31 (LINN), annotated with "genistoides" by Linnaeus which, although it does not support current usage, cannot be dismissed as not being original material.

Aspalathus indica Linnaeus, *Species Plantarum* 2: 712. 1753.
"Habitat in India." RCN: 5231.
Lectotype (Rudd in Dassanayake & Fosberg, *Revised Handb. Fl. Ceylon* 7: 121. 1991): Herb. Hermann 4: 76, No. 271 (BM-000628400).
Current name: ***Indigofera aspalathoides*** DC. (Fabaceae: Faboideae).

Aspalathus laxata Linnaeus, *Mantissa Plantarum Altera*: 263. 1771.
"Habitat in Cap. b. spei rupibus." RCN: 5238.
Lectotype (Van Wyk in *Contr. Bolus Herb.* 14: 223. 1991): *Tulbagh 35*, Herb. Linn. No. 893.45 (LINN).
Current name: ***Lotononis involucrata*** (P.J. Bergius) Benth. subsp. ***involucrata*** (Fabaceae: Faboideae).

Aspalathus nigra Linnaeus, *Mantissa Plantarum Altera*: 262. 1771.
"Habitat ad Cap. b. spei montibus." RCN: 5222.
Lectotype (Dahlgren in Leistner, *Fl. Southern Africa* 16(3:6): 193. 1988): *Tulbagh 151*, Herb. Linn. No. 893.22 (LINN).
Current name: ***Aspalathus nigra*** L. (Fabaceae: Faboideae).
Note: Dahlgren (in *Opera Bot.* 6(2): 41. 1961) indicated 893.22 (LINN) only as "orig. coll.", but clarified this to "type" in 1988.

Aspalathus orientalis Linnaeus, *Mantissa Plantarum Altera*: 263. 1771.
"Habitat in Oriente." RCN: 5241.
Type not designated.
Original material: none traced.
Current name: ***Aspalathus orientalis*** L. (Fabaceae: Faboideae).
Note: Dahlgren (in *Opera Bot.* 9(1): 252. 1963) indicates this as a *nomen dubium*.

Aspalathus pilosa Linnaeus, *Mantissa Plantarum Altera*: 263. 1771.
"Habitat ad Cap. b. spei." RCN: 5236.
Type not designated.
Original material: none traced.
Current name: ***Aspalathus sp.*** (Fabaceae: Faboideae).
Note: Specific epithet spelled "pilosus" in the protologue. Dahlgren (in *Opera Bot.* 4: 214. 1960) noted the absence of original material and later (in *Opera Bot.* 9(1): 252. 1963; in Leistner, *Fl.*

Southern Africa 16(3:6): 37. 1988) treated this as a *nomen dubium*. Its application is uncertain.

Aspalathus pinnata Linnaeus, *Plantae Rariores Africanae*: 14. 1760.
["Habitat ad Cap. b. spei."] Sp. Pl., ed. 2, 2: 1003 (1763). RCN: 5242.
Type not designated.
Original material: none traced.
Note: Dahlgren (*Opera Bot.* 9(1): 253. 1983) excluded this from *Aspalathus* but, in the absence of any original material, the application of this name is uncertain.

Aspalathus quinquefolia Linnaeus, *Plantae Rariores Africanae*: 14. 1760.
["Habitat ad Cap. b. spei."] Sp. Pl., ed. 2, 2: 1002 (1763). RCN: 5234.
Lectotype (Schrire in Turland & Jarvis in *Taxon* 46: 463. 1997): *"Aspalathus 5 folia"*, Herb. Burman (G).
Current name: ***Aspalathus quinquefolia*** L. (Fabaceae: Faboideae).
Note: Dahlgren (in Leistner, *Fl. Southern Africa* 16(3:6): 31. 1988) indicated Herb. Linn. No. 295.19 (S) as the lectotype, but this is not original material as it lacks any annotation by Linnaeus.

Aspalathus retroflexa Linnaeus, *Species Plantarum* 2: 712. 1753.
"Habitat in Aethiopia." RCN: 5227.
Neotype (Dahlgren in *Opera Bot.* 21: 86. 1968): Herb. Linn. No. 893.53 (LINN).
Current name: ***Aspalathus retroflexa*** L. (Fabaceae: Faboideae).

Aspalathus spinosa Linnaeus, *Species Plantarum*, ed. 2, 2: 1000. 1763.
"Habitat ad Cap. b. spei." RCN: 5214.
Lectotype (Dahlgren in Leistner, *Fl. Southern Africa* 16(3:6): 255. 1988): Herb. Linn. No. 893.2 (LINN).
Current name: ***Aspalathus spinosa*** L. (Fabaceae: Faboideae).
Note: Dahlgren (in *Opera Bot.* 11(1): 197. 1966) indicated 893.2 (LINN) only as "orig. coll.", but clarified this to "type" in 1988.

Aspalathus thymifolia Linnaeus, *Species Plantarum* 2: 711. 1753.
"Habitat in Aethiopia." RCN: 5220.
Type not designated.
Original material: [icon] in Plukenet, Amalth. Bot.: t. 413, f. 1. 1705; Almag. Mant.: 88. 1700 – Typotype: Herb. Sloane 92: 72 (BM-SL).
Current name: ***Aspalathus cymbiformis*** DC. (Fabaceae: Faboideae).
Note: Dahlgren (in *Opera Bot.* 8(1): 133. 1963) found that this was probably based on a poorly drawn Plukenet illustration, nevertheless identifiable (via a typotype specimen in Herb. Sloane 92: 72. BM-SL) as *A. cymbiformis* DC. As Linnaeus' name was later used by him for *A. carnosa* P.J. Bergius, and by other botanists mostly for *A. hispida* Thunb., Dahlgren treated *A. thymifolia* as a *nomen ambiguum et dubium* in the synonymy of *A. cymbiformis*. No formal rejection proposal appears to have been made.

Aspalathus tridentata Linnaeus, *Species Plantarum* 2: 712. 1753.
"Habitat in Aethiopia." RCN: 5235.
Neotype (Dahlgren in *Opera Bot.* 4: 213. 1960): Herb. Thunberg "Aspalathus tridentata" (UPS).
Current name: ***Aspalathus tridentata*** L. (Fabaceae: Faboideae).
Note: Dahlgren designated a Thunberg collection, which was not original material for Linnaeus' name, as lectotype. However, as there is no extant original material this is accepted as a neotypification (Art. 9.8).

Aspalathus uniflora Linnaeus, *Species Plantarum* 2: 712. 1753.
"Habitat in Aethiopia." RCN: 5228.

Type not designated.

Original material: [icon] in Plukenet, Amalth. Bot.: t. 413, f. 7. 1705; Almag. Mant.: 88. 1700 – Voucher: Herb. Sloane 102: 197 (BM-SL).

Current name: ***Aspalathus uniflora*** L. (Fabaceae: Faboideae).

Note: Although Dahlgren (in *Opera Bot.* 10(1): 85. 1965) indicated Herb. Linn. 295.13 (S) as the type, it is unannotated by Linnaeus and is not original material for the name. Dahlgren added that 893.34 (LINN), variously annotated with the epithets *coronopifolia*, *ericifolia* and *uniflora*, did not fit the protologue (though it is a good match for Linnaeus' much-changed account of the species in *Sp. Pl.*, ed. 2, 2: 1001. 1763), and that both the cited Plukenet illustration and its voucher material in Herb. Sloane 102: 197 (BM-SL) belong to *A. macrantha* Harv. As *A. uniflora* is in currrent use, it may be that a conservation proposal will be necessary.

Aspalathus verrucosa Linnaeus, *Species Plantarum* 2: 712. 1753.

"Habitat in Aethiopia." RCN: 5215.

Type not designated.

Original material: none traced.

Current name: ***Aspalathus*** sp. (Fabaceae: Faboideae).

Note: Dahlgren (in *Opera Bot.* 9(1): 20, 252. 1963; 11: 120. 1966; in Leistner, *Fl. Southern Africa* 16(3:6): 239. 1988) treated this as a *nomen dubium*. No rejection proposal appears to have been made.

Asparagus acutifolius Linnaeus, *Species Plantarum* 1: 314. 1753.

"Habitat in Lusitania, Hispania." RCN: 2467.

Type not designated.

Original material: Herb. Burser XXV: 72 (UPS); [icon] in Mattioli, Pl. Epit.: 260. 1586.

Current name: ***Asparagus acutifolius*** L. (Liliaceae/Asparagaceae).

Note: Although El-Gadi (in Jafri & El-Gadi, *Fl. Libya* 57: 75. 1978) indicated 434.9 (LINN) as type, it is an Alströmer collection that was not received by Linnaeus until after 1753. It is not original material for the name.

Asparagus aethiopicus Linnaeus, *Systema Naturae*, ed. 12, 2: 245; *Mantissa Plantarum*: 63. 1767.

"Habitat ad Cap. b. spei." RCN: 2464.

Lectotype (Jessop in *Bothalia* 9: 68. 1966): Herb. Linn. No. 434.6 (LINN).

Current name: ***Protasparagus aethiopicus*** (L.) Oberm. (Liliaceae/Asparagaceae).

Note: Although Jessop believed the designated type to have been unavailable to Linnaeus in 1767, it appears, in fact, to be original material for the name, and is therefore accepted as a lectotype (under Art. 9.8).

Asparagus albus Linnaeus, *Species Plantarum* 1: 314. 1753.

"Habitat in Lusitania, Hispania." RCN: 2466.

Lectotype (Valdés in *Anales Inst. Bot. Cavanilles* 32: 1090. 1975): *Löfling? s.n.*, Herb. Linn. No. 434.7, larger fragment (LINN).

Current name: ***Asparagus albus*** L. (Liliaceae/Asparagaceae).

Asparagus aphyllus Linnaeus, *Species Plantarum* 1: 314. 1753.

"Habitat in Sicilia, Hispania, Lusitania." RCN: 2469.

Lectotype (Valdés in *Anales Inst. Bot. Cavanilles* 32: 1091. 1975): Herb. Linn. No. 434.11 (LINN).

Current name: ***Asparagus aphyllus*** L. (Liliaceae/Asparagaceae).

Asparagus asiaticus Linnaeus, *Species Plantarum* 1: 313. 1753.

"Habitat in Asia." RCN: 2465.

Lectotype (Kamble in *J. Econ. Taxon. Bot.* 15: 708. 1991): Herb. Clifford: 122, *Asparagus* 4 (BM).

Current name: ***Asparagus asiaticus*** L. (Liliaceae/Asparagaceae).

Note: See Jessop (in *Bothalia* 9: 50. 1966), who discussed a Plukenet plate cited only indirectly via the cited *Hortus Cliffortianus* account, as a possible type.

Asparagus capensis Linnaeus, *Species Plantarum* 1: 314. 1753.

"Habitat ad Caput b. Spei." RCN: 2470.

Lectotype (Obermeyer & Immelman in Leistner, *Fl. Southern Africa* 5(3): 23. 1992): [icon] *"Asparagus aculeatus triplice spina"* in Plukenet, Phytographia: t. 78, f. 3. 1691; Almag. Bot.: 54. 1696. – Voucher: Herb. Sloane 95: 108 (BM-SL); see p. 32.

Current name: ***Asparagus capensis*** L. (Liliaceae/Asparagaceae).

Note: Jessop (in *Bothalia* 9: 44. 1966) treated Plukenet material in Herb. Sloane as the holotype but this was not studied by Linnaeus and is not original material for the name.

Asparagus declinatus Linnaeus, *Species Plantarum* 1: 313. 1753.

"Habitat in Africa." RCN: 2461.

Lectotype (Obermeyer in *Bothalia* 15: 86, f. 14. 1984): Herb. A. van Royen No. 913.62–567 (L).

Current name: ***Asparagus declinatus*** L. (Liliaceae/Asparagaceae).

Asparagus draco Linnaeus, *Species Plantarum,* ed. 2, 1: 451. 1762.

"Habitat in India orientali." RCN: 2473.

Basionym of: *Dracaena draco* (L.) L. (1767).

Lectotype (Bos in Jarvis & al., *Regnum Veg.* 127: 43. 1993): [icon] *"Draco"* in Clusius, Rar. Pl. Hist. 1: 1. 1601 (see p. 119).

Current name: ***Dracaena draco*** (L.) L. (Agavaceae/Dracaenaceae).

Note: Bos (in *Misc. Pap. Landbouwhoogeschool* 84–1: 16. 1984) and Ramón-Laca Menéndez de Luarca (in *Anales Jard. Bot. Madrid* 55: 422, f. 2. 1997) both reproduce the Clusius type figure.

Asparagus falcatus Linnaeus, *Species Plantarum* 1: 313. 1753.

"Habitat in Zeylona." RCN: 2462.

Lectotype (Jessop in *Bothalia* 9: 70. 1966): [icon] *"Asparagus foliis falcatis, ex uno puncto numerosis"* in Burman, Thes. Zeylan.: 36, t. 13, f. 2. 1737.

Current name: ***Asparagus falcatus*** L. (Liliaceae/Asparagaceae).

Asparagus graminifolius Linnaeus, *Species Plantarum,* ed. 2, 1: 450. 1762.

"Habitat in Asia." RCN: 2477.

Basionym of: *Dracaena graminifolia* (L.) L. (1767).

Type not designated.

Original material: Herb. Linn. No. 435.5 (LINN).

Current name: ***Liriope graminifolia*** (L.) Baker (Liliaceae/Convallariaceae).

Asparagus horridus Linnaeus, *Systema Vegetabilium,* ed. 13: 274. 1774.

RCN: 2468.

Type not designated.

Original material: Herb. Linn. No. 434.10? (LINN).

Current name: ***Asparagus stipularis*** Forssk. (Liliaceae/ Asparagaceae).

Note: This name may threaten *A. stipularis* Forssk. (*Fl. Aegypt.-Arab.*: 71. 1775).

Asparagus officinalis Linnaeus, *Species Plantarum* 1: 313. 1753.

"Habitat in Europae arenosis." RCN: 2460.

Lectotype (Valdés in *Anales Inst. Bot. Cavanilles* 32: 1079. 1975): Herb. Linn. No. 434.1 (LINN).

Generitype of *Asparagus* Linnaeus (vide Hitchcock, *Prop. Brit. Bot.*: 146. 1929).

Current name: ***Asparagus officinalis*** L. (Liliaceae/Asparagaceae).

Asparagus officinalis Linnaeus var. **altilis** Linnaeus, *Species Plantarum* 1: 313. 1753.
"Habitat in Europae arenosis." RCN: 2460.
Lectotype (Marais & Coode in Bosser & al., *Fl. Mascareignes* 183: 8. 1978): Herb. Linn. No. 434.1 (LINN).
Current name: ***Asparagus officinalis*** L. subsp. ***officinalis*** (Liliaceae/Asparagaceae).

Asparagus officinalis Linnaeus var. **maritimus** Linnaeus, *Species Plantarum* 1: 313. 1753.
RCN: 2460.
Lectotype (Valdés in *Anales Inst. Bot. Cavanilles* 32: 1080. 1975): Herb. Burser XXV: 71, lower specimen (UPS).
Current name: ***Asparagus maritimus*** (L.) Mill. (Liliaceae/Asparagaceae).

Asparagus retrofractus Linnaeus, *Species Plantarum* 1: 313. 1753.
"Habitat in Africa." RCN: 2463.
Lectotype (Jessop in *Bothalia* 9: 58. 1966): Herb. Linn. No. 434.4 (LINN).
Current name: ***Asparagus retrofractus*** L. (Liliaceae/Asparagaceae).

Asparagus sarmentosus Linnaeus, *Species Plantarum* 1: 314. 1753.
"Habitat in Zeylona." RCN: 2471.
Type not designated.
Original material: [icon] in Hermann, Hort. Lugd.-Bat. Cat.: 62, 650. 1687; [icon] in Herb. Hermann 5: 237, No. 124. BM; [icon] in Herb. Hermann 5: 385, No. 124. BM.
Current name: ***Asparagus falcatus*** L. (Liliaceae/Asparagaceae).
Note: Trimen (*Handb. Fl. Ceylon* 4: 286. 1898) suggested that the name be abandoned. Van Ooststroom (in *Blumea* Suppl. 1: 195. 1937) concluded that, as there are only drawings in the BM set of Hermann materials, a specimen in Leiden (fol. 12), identifiable as *A. falcatus* L., should be accepted as the type. However, Linnaeus never saw this collection and it is not original material for the name. Jessop (in *Bothalia* 9: 66. 1966) treated the Hermann drawings (ic. 237, 385, BM) as types but did not distinguish between them. More recently, Kamble (in *J. Econ. Taxon. Bot.* 20: 270, 1996) indicated cultivated material in G as a (neo)type but this is contrary to Art. 9.11 because original material is in existence.

Asparagus terminalis Linnaeus, *Species Plantarum,* ed. 2, 1: 450. 1762, *nom. illeg.*
"Habitat in India." RCN: 2475.
Replaced synonym: *Convallaria fruticosa* L. (1754).
Replaced synonym of: *Dracaena terminalis* L. (1767).
Lectotype (Merrill, *Interpret. Rumph. Herb. Amb.*: 33, 137. 1917): [icon] *"Terminalis alba"* in Rumphius, Herb. Amboin. 4: 79, t. 34, f. 1. 1743.
Current name: ***Cordyline fruticosa*** (L.) A. Chev. (Agavaceae/Dracaenaceae).
Note: A superfluous name for *Convallaria fruticosa* L. (1754), as noted by Brummitt & Marais (in *Taxon* 30: 825. 1981).

Asparagus verticillatus Linnaeus, *Species Plantarum,* ed. 2, 1: 450. 1762.
"Habitat in Oriente, cira (sic) Derbertum & alibi." RCN: 2472.
Type not designated.
Original material: [icon] in Buxbaum, Pl. Minus Cognit. Cent. 5, App.: 47, t. 37. 1740.
Current name: ***Asparagus verticillatus*** L. (Liliaceae/Asparagaceae).

Asperugo aegyptiaca (Linnaeus) Linnaeus, *Species Plantarum,* ed. 2, 1: 198. 1762.
"Habitat in Aegypto." RCN: 1112.

Basionym: *Lycopsis aegyptiaca* L. (1753).
Neotype (Mill in Cafferty & Jarvis in *Taxon* 53: 802. 2004): Jordan. Petra, 15 Mar 1974, *L. Boulos & D. Al-Eisawi (with W. Jallad) 6290* (E; iso- IABH).
Current name: ***Anchusa aegyptiaca*** (L.) DC. (Boraginaceae).

Asperugo procumbens Linnaeus, *Species Plantarum* 1: 138. 1753.
"Habitat in Europae ruderatis pinguibus." RCN: 1111.
Lectotype (Moberg & Jonsell in Cafferty & Jarvis in *Taxon* 53: 800. 2004): Herb. Burser XIV(2): 28 (UPS).
Generitype of *Asperugo* Linnaeus.
Current name: ***Asperugo procumbens*** L. (Boraginaceae).
Note: Several authors including Kazmi (in *J. Arnold Arbor.* 52: 118. 1971) and Qaiser (in Jafri & El-Gadi, *Fl. Libya* 68: 7. 1979) have indicated Herb. Linn. 189.1 (LINN), a post-1753 addition to the herbarium, as the type. However, this is not original material for the name and is ineligible as lectotype.

Asperula arvensis Linnaeus, *Species Plantarum* 1: 103. 1753, *typ. cons.*
"Habitat in Gallia, Flandria, Germanica, Anglia." RCN: 848.
Lectotype (Jafri in Jafri & El-Gadi, *Fl. Libya* 65: 30. 1979): Herb. Linn. No. 127.2 (LINN).
Generitype of *Asperula* Linnaeus, *nom. cons.*
Current name: ***Asperula arvensis*** L. (Rubiaceae).

Asperula crassifolia Linnaeus, *Systema Naturae,* ed. 12, 2: 116; *Mantissa Plantarum*: 37. 1767.
"Habitat in Creta, Oriente." RCN: 850.
Type not designated.
Original material: Herb. Linn. No. 127.4 (LINN).
Current name: ***Asperula crassifolia*** L. (Rubiaceae).

Asperula cynanchica Linnaeus, *Species Plantarum* 1: 104. 1753.
"Habitat in Europae pratis aridis." RCN: 853.
Type not designated.
Original material: Herb. Linn. No. 127.9? (LINN); Herb. Linn. No. 55.7 (S); Herb. Burser XIX: 8 (UPS); [icon] in Colonna, Ekphr.: 296, 297. 1606; [icon] in Bauhin & Cherler, Hist. Pl. Univ. 3(2): 723. 1651; [icon] in Tabernaemontanus, New Vollk. Kräuterb.: 433. 1664.
Current name: ***Asperula cynanchica*** L. (Rubiaceae).

Asperula laevigata Linnaeus, *Systema Naturae,* ed. 12, 2: 116; *Mantissa Plantarum*: 38. 1767.
"Habitat in Barbaria, Lusitania." RCN: 854.
Lectotype (Ehrendorfer in *Österr. Bot. Zeitschr.* 99: 629, 630. 1952): Herb. Linn. No. 127.12 (LINN).
Current name: ***Asperula laevigata*** L. (Rubiaceae).

Asperula odorata Linnaeus, *Species Plantarum* 1: 103. 1753.
"Habitat in Sueciae, Germaniae umbrosis." RCN: 847.
Lectotype (Natali & Jeanmonod in Jeanmonod, *Compl. Prodr. Fl. Corse, Rubiaceae*: 109. 2000): Herb. Linn. No. 127.1 (LINN).
Current name: ***Galium odoratum*** (L.) Scop. (Rubiaceae).

Asperula pyrenaica Linnaeus, *Species Plantarum* 1: 104. 1753.
"Habitat in Pyrenaeis versus Hispaniam & prope Valentiam Gallorum." RCN: 852.
Type not designated.
Original material: Herb. Burser XIX: 9, syntype (UPS).
Current name: ***Asperula pyrenaica*** L. (Rubiaceae).

Asperula rotundifolia (Linnaeus) Linnaeus, *Mantissa Plantarum Altera*: 330. 1771.
["Habitat in Helvetiae, Styriae."] Sp. Pl. 1: 108 (1753). RCN: 879.

Basionym: *Galium rotundifolium* L. (1753).
Lectotype (Natali & Jeanmonod in Jeanmonod, *Compl. Prodr. Fl. Corse, Rubiaceae*: 53. 2000): Herb. Burser XIX: 13 (UPS).
Current name: ***Galium rotundifolium*** L. (Rubiaceae).

Asperula taurina Linnaeus, *Species Plantarum* 1: 103. 1753.
"Habitat in Helvetiae, Italiae." RCN: 849.
Type not designated.
Original material: none traced.
Current name: ***Asperula taurina*** L. (Rubiaceae).
Note: Schönbeck-Temesy & Ehrendorfer (in Rechinger, *Fl. Iranica* 176: 151. 2005) indicated 127.3 (LINN) as type but without "designated here" or an equivalent (Art. 7.11), so this cannot be accepted as a formal typification.

Asperula tinctoria Linnaeus, *Species Plantarum* 1: 104. 1753.
"Habitat in Sueciae, Tyringiae, Galliae, Sibiriae collibus aridis saxosis." RCN: 851.
Type not designated.
Original material: none traced.
Current name: ***Asperula tinctoria*** L. (Rubiaceae).

Asphaltus ebenus Linnaeus, *Flora Jamaicensis*: 19. 1759, *orth. var.*
"Habitat [in Jamaica.]" RCN: 5232.
Lectotype (Rico in Turland & Jarvis in *Taxon* 46: 463. 1997): Herb. Linn. No. 893.44 (LINN).
Current name: ***Brya ebenus*** (L.) DC. (Fabaceae: Faboideae).
Note: Evidently an orthographic variant of *Aspalathus ebenus* L. (1759); see Rico (*l.c.*).

Asphodelus capensis Linnaeus, *Systema Naturae,* ed. 10, 2: 982. 1759. RCN: 2453.
Lectotype (Obermeyer in *Bothalia* 7: 694. 1962): [icon] *"Asphodelus foliis planis caule ramoso floribus sparsis"* in Miller, Fig. Pl. Gard. Dict. 1: 38, t. 56. 1755.
Current name: ***Chlorophytum capense*** (L.) Voss (Liliaceae/Asphodelaceae).

Asphodelus fistulosus Linnaeus, *Species Plantarum* 1: 309. 1753.
"Habitat in Gallo-Provincia, Hispania, Creta." RCN: 2439.
Lectotype (El-Gadi in Jafri & El-Gadi, *Fl. Libya* 57: 16. 1978): *Löfling s.n.*, Herb. Linn. No. 431.2 (LINN).
Current name: ***Asphodelus fistulosus*** L. (Liliaceae/Asphodelaceae).
Note: See Díaz Lifante & Valdés (in *Boissiera* 52: 140. 1996) who follow El-Gadi but provide a detailed discussion of the protologue elements.

Asphodelus luteus Linnaeus, *Species Plantarum* 1: 309. 1753.
"Habitat in Sicilia." RCN: 2438.
Type not designated.
Original material: Herb. Linn. No. 431.1 (LINN); Herb. A. van Royen No. 908.105–1550 (L); Herb. Clifford: 127, *Asphodelus* 1 (BM); [icon] in Mattioli, Pl. Epit.: 372. 1586.
Current name: ***Asphodeline lutea*** (L.) Rchb. (Liliaceae/Asphodelaceae).

Asphodelus ramosus Linnaeus, *Species Plantarum* 1: 310. 1753.
"Habitat in Narbona, Lusitania, Hispania, Italia." RCN: 2440.
Lectotype (Díaz Lifante & Valdés in *Taxon* 43: 249. 1994): Herb. Linn. No. 431.4, inflorescence only (LINN).
Generitype of *Asphodelus* Linnaeus (vide Hitchcock, *Prop. Brit. Bot.*: 146. 1929).
Current name: ***Asphodelus ramosus*** L. (Liliaceae/Asphodelaceae).
Note: See detailed discussion by Díaz Lifante & Valdés on the usage of this name.

Asplenium adiantum-nigrum Linnaeus, *Species Plantarum* 2: 1081. 1753.
"Habitat in Europa australiore." RCN: 7846.
Lectotype (Fernandes in *Bol. Soc. Brot.,* sér. 2, 56: 64. 1983): [icon] *"Dryopteris nigra"* in Dodoëns, Stirp. Hist. Pempt., ed. 2: 466. 1616.
Current name: ***Asplenium adiantum-nigrum*** L. (Aspleniaceae).
Note: Although Hedberg (in *Symb. Bot. Upsal.* 15(1): 28. 1957) noted the existence of 1250.19 (LINN), it was not treated as the type.

Asplenium bifolium Linnaeus, *Species Plantarum* 2: 1079. 1753.
"Habitat in America meridionali." RCN: 7833.
Lectotype (Lellinger & Proctor in *Taxon* 32: 570. 1983): [icon] *"Lingua Cervina geminato folio"* in Plumier, Traité Foug. Amér.: 116, t. 133. 1705.
Note: Lellinger & Proctor regard this as "an unknown and dubious species".

Asplenium ceterach Linnaeus, *Species Plantarum* 2: 1080. 1753.
"Habitat in Walliae, Italiae fissuris rupium." RCN: 7834.
Lectotype (Reichstein in *Bot. Helv.* 92: 41. 1982): Herb. Clifford: 474, *Asplenium* 4 (BM-000647590).
Current name: ***Asplenium ceterach*** L. (Aspleniaceae).

Asplenium cultrifolium Linnaeus, *Species Plantarum* 2: 1081. 1753.
"Habitat in Martinica." RCN: 7841.
Lectotype (Proctor in *Mem. New York Bot. Gard.* 53: 227. 1989): [icon] *"Lonchitis latifolia, pediculis lucidis glabris et nigris"* in Plumier, Traité Foug. Amér.: 45, t. 59. 1705.
Current name: ***Asplenium sp.*** (Aspleniaceae).
Note: Morton (in *Contr. U. S. Natl. Herb.* 38: 292. 1974) regarded the cited Plumier plate to be so stylised as to be more or less unidentifiable. Lellinger & Proctor (in *Taxon* 32: 567. 1983) stated incorrectly that it "is the entire protologue" before Proctor (1989) treated it explicitly as the type.

Asplenium dentatum Linnaeus, *Species Plantarum* 2: 1080. 1753.
"Habitat in America meridionali." RCN: 7839.
Lectotype (Morton & Lellinger in *Mem. New York Bot. Gard.* 15: 25. 1966): [icon] *"Trichomanes latifolium dentatum"* in Plumier, Traité Foug. Amér.: 58, t. 101 C. 1705.
Current name: ***Asplenium dentatum*** L. (Aspleniaceae).
Note: Under Art. 23.8, Ex. 19 of the Vienna Code, *A. Trich. dentatum* L. (1753: 1080) is to be treated as *A. dentatum* L. (1753). Although Linnaeus published *A. dentatum* only in *Syst. Nat.* ed. 10, 2: 1323 (1759), this name now dates from 1753.

Asplenium emarginatum Linnaeus, *Flora Jamaicensis*: 23. 1759, *orth. var.*
"Habitat [in Jamaica.]" RCN: 7848.
Lectotype (Proctor, *Ferns Jamaica*: 390. 1985): [icon] *"Phyllitis ramosa, margine membranaceo"* in Petiver, Pteri-graphia Amer.: 108, t. 12, f. 2. 1712.
Current name: ***Hemidictyum marginatum*** (L.) C. Presl (Dryopteridaceae).
Note: An orthographic variant of *A. marginatum* L. (1753).

Asplenium erosum Linnaeus, *Systema Naturae,* ed. 10, 2: 1324. 1759.
["Habitat in India occidentali."] Sp. Pl., ed. 2, 2: 1540 (1763). RCN: 7851.
Lectotype (Underwood in *Bull. Torrey Bot. Club* 33: 196. 1906): [icon] *"Lonchitis major, pinnis angustioribus leviter denticulatis superiori latere auriculatis"* in Sloane, Voy. Jamaica 1: 78, t. 33, f. 2. 1707.
Current name: ***Asplenium erosum*** L. (Aspleniaceae).

Note: Underwood clearly designated the cited Sloane plate as the type, pre-dating the choice made by Weatherby (in *Contr. Gray Herb.* 114: 20. 1936) of 1250.22 (LINN). Unfortunately, Sloane's plant appears to be identifiable as *A. auritum* Sw. rather than *A. erosum* though most authors have adopted Weatherby's type choice. However, Underwood's choice has priority, and it appears that a proposal for the conservation of *A. erosum*, with a conserved type, may be necessary.

Asplenium hemionitis Linnaeus, *Species Plantarum* 2: 1078. 1753.
"Habitat in Italia, Hispania." RCN: 7828.
Lectotype (Reichstein in *Bot. Helv.* 91: 104. 1981): *Löfling s.n.*, Herb. Linn. No. 1250.2 (LINN).
Current name: ***Asplenium hemionitis*** L. (Aspleniaceae).

Asplenium marginatum Linnaeus, *Species Plantarum* 2: 1082. 1753.
"Habitat in America." RCN: 7848.
Lectotype (Proctor, *Ferns Jamaica*: 390. 1985): [icon] *"Phyllitis ramosa, margine membranaceo"* in Petiver, Pteri-graphia Amer.: 108, t. 12, f. 2. 1712.
Current name: ***Hemidictyum marginatum*** (L.) C. Presl (Dryopteridaceae).

Asplenium marinum Linnaeus, *Species Plantarum* 2: 1081. 1753.
"Habitat in Anglia, insulis Stoechadum. Burs." RCN: 7840.
Type not designated.
Original material: Herb. Linn. No. 1250.14 (LINN); Herb. Clifford: 474, *Asplenium* 3 (BM); Herb. Burser XX: 39, syntype (UPS); [icon] in Morison, Pl. Hist. Univ. 3: 573, s. 14, t. 3, f. 25. 1699.
Generitype of *Asplenium* Linnaeus (vide Smith, *Hist. Fil.*: 316. 1875).
Current name: ***Asplenium marinum*** L. (Aspleniaceae).
Note: Reichstein (in *Bot. Helv.* 91: 105. 1981) has variously treated material in LINN (evidently sheet 1250.14) and (*l.c.* 92: 41. 1982) Herb. Clifford: 474, *Asplenium* 3 (BM) as the lectotype. However, unusually, Linnaeus explicitly cited a Burser collection (identifiable as Herb. Burser XX: 39 by Linnaeus' "Habitat in ... insulis Stoechadum") in the protologue. As a syntype, it must take precedence over original material in the designation of a lectotype (Art. 9.10). This formal choice has apparently not yet been made.

Asplenium monanthes Linnaeus, *Systema Naturae*, ed. 12, 2: 690; *Mantissa Plantarum*: 130. 1767.
"Habitat ad Cap. b. spei." RCN: 7844.
Lectotype (Morton & Lellinger in *Mem. New York Bot. Gard.* 15: 34. 1966): Herb. Linn. No. 1250.17 (LINN).
Current name: ***Asplenium monanthes*** L. (Aspleniaceae).

Asplenium nidus Linnaeus, *Species Plantarum* 2: 1079. 1753.
"Habitat in Javae summis arboribus. Osbeck." RCN: 7830.
Lectotype (Holttum in *Gard. Bull. Singapore* 27: 147. 1974): *Osbeck 49*, Herb. Linn. No. 1250.6 (LINN).
Current name: ***Asplenium nidus*** L. (Aspleniaceae).
Note: See Hansen & Fox Maule (in *Bot. J. Linn. Soc.* 67: 205. 1973) for comments on Osbeck material.

Asplenium nodosum (Linnaeus) Linnaeus, *Species Plantarum*, ed. 2, 2: 1539. 1763.
"Habitat in America meridionali." RCN: 7836.
Basionym: *Acrostichum nodosum* L. (1753).
Lectotype (Underwood in *Bull. Torrey Bot. Club* 29: 671. 1902): [icon] *"Lingua Cervina nodosa major"* in Plumier, Traité Foug. Amér.: 90, t. 108. 1705.
Current name: ***Danaea nodosa*** (L.) Sm. (Marattiaceae).

Asplenium obtusifolium Linnaeus, *Species Plantarum* 2: 1080. 1753.
"Habitat in America." RCN: 7835.
Lectotype (Morton & Lellinger in *Mem. New York Bot. Gard.* 15: 11. 1966): [icon] *"Adiantum alis latioribus"* in Petiver, Pteri-graphia Amer.: 117, t. 2, f. 14. 1712.
Current name: ***Asplenium obtusifolium*** L. (Aspleniaceae).

Asplenium onopteris Linnaeus, *Species Plantarum* 2: 1081. 1753.
"Habitat in Italia, Gallia." RCN: 7846.
Lectotype (Fernandes in *Bol. Soc. Brot.*, sér. 2, 56: 66. 1983): Herb. Burser XX: 12 (UPS).
Current name: ***Asplenium onopteris*** L. (Aspleniaceae).

Asplenium plantagineum Linnaeus, *Species Plantarum*, ed. 2, 2: 1537. 1763, *nom. illeg.*
"Habitat in Jamaica." RCN: 7831.
Replaced synonym of: *Asplenium plantaginifolium* L. (1759).
Neotype (Proctor, *Ferns Jamaica*: 394. 1985): Jamaica. Parish of St Catherine, Hollymount, Mt Diablo, *Maxon 1949* (US-428301; iso-BM).
Current name: ***Diplazium plantaginifolium*** (L.) Urb. (Dryopteridaceae).
Note: This has been treated as a superfluous name for *A. plantaginifolium* L. (1759) by authors such as Tryon & Stolze (in *Fieldiana, Bot.* 27: 86. 1991).

Asplenium plantaginifolium Linnaeus, *Systema Naturae*, ed. 10, 2: 1323. 1759.
["Habitat in Jamaica."] Sp. Pl., ed. 2, 2: 1537 (1763). RCN: 7831.
Replaced synonym of: *Asplenium plantagineum* L. (1763).
Neotype (Proctor, *Ferns Jamaica*: 394. 1985): Jamaica. Parish of St Catherine, Hollymount, Mt Diablo, *Maxon 1949* (US-428301; iso-BM).
Current name: ***Diplazium plantaginifolium*** (L.) Urb. (Dryopteridaceae).

Asplenium pygmaeum Linnaeus, *Systema Naturae*, ed. 10, 2: 1323. 1759.
["Habitat in Jamaica."] Sp. Pl., ed. 2, 2: 1540 (1763). RCN: 7842.
Lectotype (Morton & Lellinger in *Mem. New York Bot. Gard.* 15: 25. 1966): Herb. Linn. No. 1250.15 (LINN).
Current name: ***Asplenium dentatum*** L. (Aspleniaceae).

Asplenium radicans Linnaeus, *Systema Naturae*, ed. 10, 2: 1323. 1759.
RCN: 7843.
Replaced synonym of: *Asplenium rhizophyllum* L. (1763), *nom. illeg.*
Lectotype (Morton & Lellinger in *Mem. New York Bot. Gard.* 15: 38. 1966): Herb. Linn. No. 1250.16, right frond (LINN).
Current name: ***Asplenium radicans*** L. (Aspleniaceae).

Asplenium ramosum Linnaeus, *Species Plantarum* 2: 1082. 1753, *nom. rej.*
"Habitat in Arvorniae rupibus." RCN: 7847.
Lectotype (Jermy & Jarvis in *Bot. J. Linn. Soc.* 109: 321. 1992): Herb. Burser XX: 16 (UPS).
Current name: ***Asplenium viride*** Huds. (Aspleniaceae).

Asplenium rhizophorum Linnaeus, *Genera Plantarum*, ed. 6: Emendanda. 1764, *nom. illeg.*
"Habitat in India occidentalis." RCN: 7843.
Replaced synonym: *Asplenium rhizophyllum* L. (1763).
Lectotype (Morton & Lellinger in *Mem. New York Bot. Gard.* 15: 37. 1966): Herb. Linn. No. 1250.16, right frond (LINN).
Current name: ***Asplenium radicans*** L. (Aspleniaceae).

Note: A replacement name for the illegitimate *A. rhizophyllum* L. (1763: 1540, non 1763: 1536, which is *A. rhizophyllum* L. 1753). However *A. rhizophorum* is still a superfluous name for *A. radicans* L. (1759) and therefore illegitimate.

Asplenium rhizophyllum Linnaeus, *Species Plantarum* 2: 1078. 1753.
"Habitat in Jamaica, Virginia, Canada, Sibiria." RCN: 7827.
Lectotype (designated here by Reveal): Kalm, Herb. Linn. No. 1250.1 (LINN; iso- BM).
Current name: ***Asplenium rhizophyllum*** L. (Aspleniaceae).
Note: Maxon (in *Contr. U. S. Natl. Herb.* 10: 482–484. 1908) discussed the original material and concluded that the name should apply to the element from Virginia. While noting the existence of Kalm material (1250.1 LINN), he did not refer to it as the type. Ewan (in *Amer. Fern. J.* 53: 141. 1963) noted that a Banister description and drawing contributed to Linnaeus' knowledge of this taxon (and reproduced the original drawing and Plukenet's copy, as his pl. 10).

Asplenium rhizophyllum Linnaeus, *Species Plantarum,* ed. 2, 2: 1540. 1763, *nom. illeg.*
"Habitat in India occidentalis."
Replaced synonym: *Asplenium radicans* L. (1753).
Lectotype (Morton & Lellinger in *Mem. New York Bot. Gard.* 15: 37. 1966): Herb. Linn. No. 1250.16, right frond (LINN).
Current name: ***Asplenium radicans*** L. (Aspleniaceae).
Note: A superfluous name for *A. radicans* L. (1759), and a later homonym of *A. rhizophyllum* L. (1753).

Asplenium ruta-muraria Linnaeus, *Species Plantarum* 2: 1081. 1753.
"Habitat in Europa ex rupium fissuris." RCN: 7845.
Lectotype (Reichstein, *Bot. Helvetica* 91: 105. 1981): Herb. Linn. No. 1250.18 (LINN).
Current name: ***Asplenium ruta-muraria*** L. subsp. ***ruta-muraria*** (Aspleniaceae).

Asplenium salicifolium Linnaeus, *Species Plantarum* 2: 1080. 1753.
"Habitat in Antillis." RCN: 7837.
Lectotype (Morton & Lellinger in *Mem. New York Bot. Gard.* 15: 23. 1966): [icon] *"Lonchitis glabra, major"* in Plumier, Traité Foug. Amér.: 46, t. 60. 1705.
Current name: ***Asplenium salicifolium*** L. (Aspleniaceae).

Asplenium scolopendrium Linnaeus, *Species Plantarum* 2: 1079. 1753.
"Habitat in Europae umbrosis, nemorosis, saxosis." RCN: 7829.
Lectotype (Reichstein in *Bot. Helv.* 91: 106. 1981): *Löfling s.n.*, Herb. Linn. No. 1250.3 (LINN).
Current name: ***Phyllitis scolopendrium*** (L.) Newman (Aspleniaceae).

Asplenium serratum Linnaeus, *Species Plantarum* 2: 1079. 1753.
"Habitat in America calidiore." RCN: 7832.
Lectotype (Proctor in Howard, *Fl. Lesser Antilles* 2: 313. 1977): [icon] *"Lingua Cervina longo, lato, serratoque folio"* in Plumier, Descr. Pl. Amér.: 27, t. 39. 1693.
Current name: ***Asplenium serratum*** L. (Aspleniaceae).
Note: Morton & Lellinger (in *Mem. New York Bot. Gard.* 15: 9. 1966) wrongly indicated a Sloane description as type (there is no illustration). This choice (which is contrary to Art. 8.1) was rejected by Proctor in favour of a Plumier plate.

Asplenium squamosum Linnaeus, *Species Plantarum* 2: 1082. 1753.
"Habitat in America." RCN: 7849.
Lectotype (Morton & Lellinger in *Mem. New York Bot. Gard.* 15: 27.

1966): [icon] *"Lonchitis ramosa, caule squamosa"* in Petiver, Pterigraphia Amer.: 112, t. 5, f. 2. 1712.
Current name: ***Asplenium squamosum*** L. (Aspleniaceae).

Asplenium striatum Linnaeus, *Species Plantarum* 2: 1082. 1753.
"Habitat in America." RCN: 7850.
Lectotype (Proctor in Howard, *Fl. Lesser Antilles* 2: 267. 1977): [icon] *"Filix striata pinnis crenatis, major et minor"* in Petiver, Pteri-graphia Amer.: 113, 114, t. 3, f. 3, 4. 1712.
Current name: ***Diplazium striatum*** (L.) C. Presl (Dryopteridaceae).

Asplenium trichomanes Linnaeus, *Species Plantarum* 2: 1080. 1753.
"Habitat in Europae fissuris rupium." RCN: 7838.
Lectotype (Bobrov in *Novosti Sist. Vyssh. Rast.* 21: 15. 1984): Herb. Linn. No. 1250.12 (LINN).
Current name: ***Asplenium trichomanes*** L. subsp. ***trichomanes*** (Aspleniaceae).
Note: See discussion by Viane (in *Nordic J. Bot.* 14: 150. 1994), who designated a Burser collection as lectotype but this choice is pre-dated by that of Bobrov.

Asplenium trichomanes-dentatum Linnaeus, *Species Plantarum* 2: 1080. 1753.
"Habitat in America meridionali." RCN: 7839.
Lectotype (Morton & Lellinger in *Mem. New York Bot. Gard.* 15: 25. 1966): [icon] *"Trichomanes latifolium dentatum"* in Plumier, Traité Foug. Amér.: 58, t. 101 C. 1705.
Current name: ***Asplenium dentatum*** L. (Aspleniaceae).
Note: Under Art. 23.8, Ex. 19 of the Vienna Code, *A. trich. dentatum* L. is to be treated as *A. dentatum* L. (1753).

Asplenium trichomanes-ramosum Linnaeus, *Species Plantarum* 2: 1082. 1753, *nom. rej.*
"Habitat in Arvorniae rupibus." RCN: 7847.
Lectotype (Jermy & Jarvis in *Bot. J. Linn. Soc.* 109: 321. 1992): Herb. Burser XX: 16 (UPS).
Current name: ***Asplenium viride*** Huds. (Aspleniaceae).
Note: Under Art. 23.8, Ex. 19 of the Vienna Code, *A. Trich. ramosum* L. is to be treated as *A. ramosum* L. (1753), though the latter is now a rejected name.

Asplenium trichomanoides Linnaeus, *Systema Naturae,* ed. 12, 2: 690. 1767, *nom. illeg.*
RCN: 7838.
Basionym: *Asplenium trichomanes* L. (1753).
Lectotype (Bobrov in *Novosti Sist. Vyssh. Rast.* 21: 15. 1984): Herb. Linn. No. 1250.12 (LINN).
Current name: ***Asplenium trichomanes*** L. (Aspleniaceae).
Note: A superfluous name for *A. trichomanes* L. (1753).

Aster acris Linnaeus, *Species Plantarum,* ed. 2, 2: 1228. 1763, *nom. illeg.*
"Habitat in Hungaria interamni, Hispania, Monspelii." RCN: 6326.
Replaced synonym: *Aster sedifolius* L. (1753).
Type not designated.
Original material: as replaced synonym.
Current name: ***Galatella sedifolius*** (L.) Greuter (Asteraceae).
Note: An illegitimate replacement name for *A. sedifolius* L. (1753).

Aster alpinus Linnaeus, *Species Plantarum* 2: 872. 1753.
"Habitat in Austria, Vallesia, Helvetia, Pyrenaeis." RCN: 6315.
Lectotype (Grierson in Rechinger, *Fl. Iranica* 154: 4. 1982): Herb. Linn. No. 997.10 (LINN).
Current name: ***Aster alpinus*** L. (Asteraceae).

Aster amellus Linnaeus, *Species Plantarum* 2: 873. 1753.
"Habitat in Europae australis asperis collibus." RCN: 6318.
Lectotype (Semple in *Sida* 22: 1088. 2006): Herb. Linn. No. 997.16 (LINN).
Generitype of *Aster* Linnaeus (vide Green, *Prop. Brit. Bot.*: 181. 1929).
Current name: ***Aster amellus*** L. (Asteraceae).
Note: Semple (in Jarvis & Turland, *Taxon* 47: 354. 1998) designated 997.18 (LINN) as lectotype but subsequent study has shown this material to conflict with the diagnosis (and be identifiable as a member of the *Galatella* Cass./*Crinitaria* Cass. complex, rather than *Aster*). Semple (2006) therefore rejected his earlier typification in favour of 997.16 (LINN).

Aster annuus Linnaeus, *Species Plantarum* 2: 875. 1753.
"Habitat in Canada." RCN: 6334.
Lectotype (Scott in Bosser & al., *Fl. Mascareignes* 109: 106. 1993): Herb. Clifford: 408, *Aster* 13 (BM-000647093).
Current name: ***Erigeron annuus*** (L.) Pers. (Asteraceae).

Aster aurantius Linnaeus, *Species Plantarum* 2: 877. 1753.
"Habitat in Vera Cruce." RCN: 6345.
Type not designated.
Original material: Herb. Clifford: 407, *Aster* 1 (BM); [icon] in Houstounia Gen. Pl. Amer.: t. 24. 1736 (LINN).
Current name: ***Dyssodia aurantia*** (L.) Druce (Asteraceae).

Aster chinensis Linnaeus, *Species Plantarum* 2: 877. 1753.
"Habitat in China?" RCN: 6344.
Type not designated.
Original material: Herb. Clifford: 407, *Aster* 2 (BM); Herb. Linn. No. 997.52 (LINN); [icon] in Dillenius, Hort. Eltham. 1: 38, t. 34, f. 38. 1732.
Current name: ***Callistephus chinensis*** (L.) Nees (Asteraceae).

Aster concolor Linnaeus, *Species Plantarum* 2: 874. 1753.
"Habitat in Virginia." RCN: 6327.
Lectotype (Reveal in Jarvis & Turland in *Taxon* 47: 354. 1998): *Clayton 607*, Herb. Linn. No. 997.31 (LINN; iso- BM).
Current name: ***Aster concolor*** L. (Asteraceae).

Aster cordifolius Linnaeus, *Species Plantarum* 2: 875. 1753.
"Habitat in America & Asia septentrionali." RCN: 6332.
Lectotype (Reveal in Hoffmann in *Feddes Repert.* 107: 182. 1996): Herb. Clifford: 408, *Aster* 9 (BM-000647087).
Current name: ***Aster cordifolius*** L. (Asteraceae).
Note: The type choice intended for publication by Reveal (in Jarvis & Turland, *Taxon* 47: 354. 1998) was published inadvertently by Hoffmann in 1996, who attributed it to "JARVIS et al., pers. comm., design. ined.". Confirmation that the choice is attributable to Reveal is provided in the 1998 paper.

Aster crinitus Linnaeus, *Plantae Rariores Africanae*: 21. 1760.
["Habitat ad Cap. b. spei."] Sp. Pl. ed. 2, 2: 1225 (1763). RCN: 6311.
Lectotype (Kroner in *Mitt. Bot. Staatssamml. München* 16: 85. 1980): Herb. Linn. No. 997.5, left specimen (LINN).
Current name: ***Athrixia crinita*** (L.) Druce (Asteraceae).

Aster divaricatus Linnaeus, *Species Plantarum* 2: 873. 1753.
"Habitat in Virginia." RCN: 6319.
Lectotype (Lamboy & Jones in *Brittonia* 39: 290. 1987): Herb. Linn. No. 997.19 (LINN).
Current name: ***Aster divaricatus*** L. (Asteraceae).
Note: Although Gray (in *Proc. Amer. Acad. Arts* 17: 164. 1882) stated that this was "founded...on" material in LINN, this wording is not accepted as effecting typification.

Aster dumosus Linnaeus, *Species Plantarum* 2: 873. 1753.
"Habitat in America septentrionali." RCN: 6321.
Lectotype (Semple in Hoffmann in *Feddes Repert.* 107: 182. 1996): Herb. Clifford: 408, *Aster* 10 (BM-000647088).
Current name: ***Aster dumosus*** L. (Asteraceae).
Note: The type choice intended for publication by Semple (in Jarvis & Turland, *Taxon* 47: 354. 1998) was published inadvertently by Hoffmann in 1996, who attributed it to "JARVIS et al., pers. comm., design. ined.". Confirmation that the choice is attributable to Semple is provided in the 1998 paper.

Aster ericoides Linnaeus, *Species Plantarum* 2: 875. 1753.
"Habitat in America septentrionali." RCN: 6322.
Lectotype (Jones in *Rhodora* 80: 328. 1978): *Clayton 194* (BM-000038864).
Current name: ***Aster ericoides*** L. var. ***ericoides*** (Asteraceae).

Aster fruticosus Linnaeus, *Species Plantarum* 2: 872. 1753.
"Habitat ad Cap. b. Spei in saxosis." RCN: 6312.
Lectotype (Jones & Hiepko in *Willdenowia* 11: 345. 1981): Herb. Clifford: 409, *Aster* 17 (BM-000647099).
Current name: ***Felicia fruticosa*** (L.) G. Nicholson (Asteraceae).
Note: Grau (in *Mitt. Bot. Staatssamml. München* 9: 275. 1973) indicated both 997.6 and 997.7 (LINN) as types. These collections do not form part of a single gathering (so Art. 9.15 does not apply) and Wijnands (*Bot. Commelins*: 75. 1983) was correct to reject this as an ineffective type choice. Jones & Hiepko appear to have been the first to make an explicit type choice.

Aster grandiflorus Linnaeus, *Species Plantarum* 2: 877. 1753.
"Habitat in America septentrionali." RCN: 6331.
Lectotype (Semple in Hoffmann in *Feddes Repert.* 107: 182. 1996): *Clayton 244* (BM-000051177).
Current name: ***Aster grandiflorus*** L. (Asteraceae).
Note: The type choice intended for publication by Semple (in Jarvis & Turland, *Taxon* 47: 354. 1998) was published inadvertently by Hoffmann in 1996, who attributed it to "JARVIS et al., pers. comm., design. ined.". Confirmation that the choice is attributable to Semple is provided in the 1998 paper.

Aster hyssopifolius Linnaeus, *Systema Naturae*, ed. 12, 2: 554; *Mantissa Plantarum*: 114. 1767.
"Habitat in America septentrionali." RCN: 6320.
Lectotype (Reveal in Jarvis & Turland in *Taxon* 47: 354. 1998): Herb. Linn. No. 997.21 (LINN).
Current name: ***Galatella sedifolia*** (L.) Greuter (Asteraceae).

Aster imbricatus Linnaeus, *Plantae Rariores Africanae*: 21. 1760.
["Habitat ad Cap. b. spei."] Sp. Pl. ed. 2, 2: 1225 (1763). RCN: 6310.
Replaced synonym of: *Aster reflexus* L. (1763).
Type not designated.
Original material: Herb. Linn. No. 997.3 (LINN); Herb. Linn. No. 997.2 (LINN); Herb. Burman (4 sheets) (G).
Current name: ***Polyarrhena reflexa*** (L.) Cass. (Asteraceae).
Note: See comments under *Aster reflexus* L.

Aster indicus Linnaeus, *Species Plantarum* 2: 876. 1753.
"Habitat in China." RCN: 6336.
Lectotype (Grierson in *Notes Roy. Bot. Gard. Edinburgh* 26: 158. 1964): Herb. Linn. No. 997.42 (LINN).
Current name: ***Boltonia indica*** (L.) Benth. (Asteraceae).

Aster laevis Linnaeus, *Species Plantarum* 2: 876. 1753.
"Habitat in America septentrionali. Kalm." RCN: 6337.

Lectotype (Scott in Bosser & al., *Fl. Mascareignes* 109: 111. 1993): *Kalm*, Herb. Linn. No. 997.44 (LINN).
Current name: **Aster laevis** L. (Asteraceae).
Note: Although Gray (in *Proc. Amer. Acad. Arts* 17: 166. 1882) stated that this was "described wholly from his [Kalm's] specimen", this wording is not effective in typifying the name.

Aster linariifolius Linnaeus, *Species Plantarum* 2: 874. 1753.
"Habitat in America septentrionali." RCN: 6324.
Lectotype (Reveal & al. in *Huntia* 7: 215. 1987): *Kalm*, Herb. Linn. No. 997.27 (LINN).
Current name: **Aster linariifolius** L. (Asteraceae).

Aster linifolius Linnaeus, *Species Plantarum* 2: 874. 1753.
"Habitat in America septentrionali." RCN: 6325.
Lectotype (designated here by Reveal): Herb. Clifford: 408, *Aster* 15, sheet "21" (BM-000647095).
Current name: **Aster sedifolius** L. (Asteraceae).
Note: Although Gray (in *Proc. Amer. Acad. Arts* 17: 165. 1882) noted the existence of Clifford material, he did not indicate it as the type.

Aster macrophyllus Linnaeus, *Species Plantarum,* ed. 2, 2: 1232. 1763.
"Habitat in America septentrionali." RCN: 6343.

Lectotype (Lamboy & Jones in *Brittonia* 39: 292. 1987): Herb. Linn. No. 997.51 (LINN).
Current name: **Aster macrophyllus** L. (Asteraceae).

Aster miser Linnaeus, *Species Plantarum* 2: 877. 1753.
"Habitat in America septentrionali." RCN: 6342.
Lectotype (Gray in *Proc. Amer. Acad. Arts* 17: 168. 1882): [icon] *"Aster ericoides, Meliloti agrariae umbone"* in Dillenius, Hort. Eltham. 1: 39, t. 35, f. 39. 1732. – Typotype: Herb. Sherard No. 1780 (OXF).
Current name: **Aster dumosus** L. (Asteraceae).

Aster mutabilis Linnaeus, *Species Plantarum* 2: 876. 1753.
"Habitat in America septentrionali." RCN: 6338.
Lectotype (Reveal in Jarvis & Turland in *Taxon* 47: 354. 1998): [icon] *"Aster caeruleus Americanus non fruticosus serotinus angustifolius, humilis flore amplo, floribundus"* in Plukenet, Phytographia: t. 326, f. 1. 1694; Almag. Bot.: 56. 1696. – Epitype (Reveal in Jarvis & Turland in *Taxon* 47: 354. 1998): Herb. Clifford: 408, *Aster* 10 (BM-000647088).
Current name: **Aster dumosus** L. (Asteraceae).

Aster novae-angliae Linnaeus, *Species Plantarum* 2: 875. 1753.
"Habitat in Nova Anglia." RCN: 6329.
Lectotype (Semple in Hoffmann in *Feddes Repert.* 107: 181. 1996): Herb. Clifford: 408, *Aster* 7 *"novae angliae"* (BM-000647084).
Current name: **Aster novae-angliae** L. (Asteraceae).
Note: The type choice intended for publication by Semple (in Jarvis & Turland, *Taxon* 47: 354. 1998) was published inadvertently by Hoffmann in 1996, who attributed it to "JARVIS et al., pers. comm., design. ined.". Confirmation that the choice is attributable to Semple is provided in the 1998 paper.

Aster novi-belgii Linnaeus, *Species Plantarum* 2: 877. 1753.
"Habitat in Virginia, Pensylvania." RCN: 6340.
Lectotype (Shinners in *Rhodora* 45: 348. 1943): [icon] *"Aster Novae Belgiae latifolius, umbellatus, floribus dilute violaceis"* in Hermann, Hort. Lugd.-Bat. Cat.: 66, 69. 1687.
Current name: **Aster novi-belgii** L. (Asteraceae).

Aster oppositifolius Linnaeus, *Systema Naturae,* ed. 10, 2: 1216. 1759.
RCN: 6372.
Type not designated.
Original material: [icon] in Miller, Fig. Pl. Gard. Dict. 1: 51, t. 76, f. 2. 1756.
Current name: **Felicia cymbalariae** (Aiton) Bolus & Wolley-Dod (Asteraceae).

Aster polifolius Linnaeus, *Species Plantarum,* ed. 2, 2: 1224. 1763.
"Habitat ad Cap. b. Spei. Burmannus." RCN: 6394.
Replaced synonym of: *Inula caerulea* L. (1771), *nom. illeg.*
Type not designated.
Original material: Herb. Linn. No. 997.57 (LINN).
Current name: **Printzia polifolia** (L.) Hutch. (Asteraceae).
Note: Bullock (in *Kew Bull.* 3: 54. 1948) discussed this name in detail and clearly regarded a sheet at LINN as "the Linnean type". However, his text does not distinguish between sheets 997.56 and 997.57, which are evidently not part of a single gathering (so Art. 9.15 does not apply). Kroner (in *Mitt. Bot. Staatssamml. München* 16: 111. 1980) explicitly treated sheet 997.56 as the lectotype, but it is a Tulbagh collection, sent to Linnaeus only in 1769 and which cannot therefore have been original material for the name.

Aster puniceus Linnaeus, *Species Plantarum* 2: 875. 1753.
"Habitat in America septentrionali." RCN: 6333.

Lectotype (Semple in Hoffmann in *Feddes Repert.* 107: 183. 1996):
   Herb. Clifford: 408, *Aster* 6 (BM-000647083).
Current name: ***Aster puniceus*** L. (Asteraceae).
Note: The type choice intended for publication by Semple (in Jarvis &
   Turland, *Taxon* 47: 354. 1998) was published inadvertently by
   Hoffmann in 1996, who attributed it to "JARVIS et al., pers.
   comm., design. ined.". Confirmation that the choice is attributable
   to Semple is provided in the 1998 paper.

Aster reflexus Linnaeus, *Species Plantarum* 2: 877. 1753.
"Habitat in Aethiopia." RCN: 6310.
Lectotype (Hilliard & Burtt in *Bot. J. Linn. Soc.* 82: 250. 1981): [icon]
   "Aster Africanus frutescens splendentibus parvis et reflexis foliis" in
   Commelin, Hort. Med. Amstelod. Pl. Rar. 2: 55, t. 28. 1701.
Current name: ***Polyarrhena reflexa*** (L.) Cass. (Asteraceae).
Note: See notes under *Aster reflexus* L. (1763).

Aster reflexus Linnaeus, *Species Plantarum,* ed. 2, 2: 1225. 1763, *nom.
   illeg.*
"Habitat ad Cap. b. spei." RCN: 6310.
Replaced synonym: *Aster imbricatus* L. (1760).
Type not designated.
Original material: as replaced synonym.
Current name: ***Polyarrhena reflexa*** (L.) Cass. (Asteraceae).
Note: Nordenstam (in *Bot. Not.* 114: 279. 1961) stated that *A.
   imbricatus* is a superfluous renaming of *A. reflexus* L. (1753) but this
   is incorrect. The protologue of *A. imbricatus* consists only of a
   phrase name and a short description and has no elements explicitly
   in common with the protologue of *A. reflexus* (which includes a
   Commelin plate). The confusion has arisen because in the reprint of
   Plantae Rariores Africanae in Amoen. Acad. 6: 68, no. 68 (1763),
   Linnaeus substituted the name "A. reflexus" for *A. imbricatus*. In
   Species Plantarum, ed. 2, 2: 1225 (1763), Linnaeus' account of *A.
   reflexus* refers only to the *Amoen. Acad.* account. The diagnoses
   of the 1753 and 1763 names are not particularly similar, though they
   seem to describe some similar features. Nordenstam in any case
   concluded that *A. imbricatus* and *A. reflexus* (1753) are
   synonymous.

Aster rigidus Linnaeus, *Species Plantarum* 2: 874. 1753.
"Habitat in Virginia." RCN: 6328.
Lectotype (Reveal & al. in *Huntia* 7: 214–215. 1987): *Clayton* 9 (BM-
   000032174).
Current name: ***Aster linariifolius*** L. (Asteraceae).
Note: See extensive review by Reveal & al. (*l.c.*).

Aster sedifolius Linnaeus, *Species Plantarum* 2: 874. 1753.
"Habitat in Hungaria interamni, Hispania, Monspelii." RCN: 6326.
Replaced synonym of: *Aster acris* L. (1763), *nom. illeg.*
Type not designated.
Original material: Herb. Burser XV(1): 62 (UPS); [icon] in Plantin,
   Pl. Stirp. Icon.: 349. 1581; [icon] in Plukenet, Phytographia: t. 271,
   f. 3. 1694; Almag. Bot.: 56. 1696.
Current name: ***Galatella sedifolius*** (L.) Greuter (Asteraceae).

Aster sibiricus Linnaeus, *Species Plantarum* 2: 872. 1753.
"Habitat in Sibiria." RCN: 6316.
Lectotype (Semple in Jarvis & Turland in *Taxon* 47: 354. 1998): Herb.
   Linn. No. 997.13 (LINN).
Current name: ***Aster sibiricus*** L. (Asteraceae).
Note: Gray (in *Proc. Amer. Acad. Arts* 17: 164. 1882) noted two
   Gmelin collections (997.12 and 997.13) in LINN, and Jones &
   Hiepko (in *Willdenowia* 11: 350. 1981) referred to the lectotype
   being in LINN but without distinguishing between the two sheets.
   Semple's appears to be the first explicit type choice.

Aster tardiflorus Linnaeus, *Species Plantarum,* ed. 2, 2: 1231. 1763.
"Habitat in America septentrionali." RCN: 6341.
Lectotype (Jones in *Phytologia* 55: 385. 1984): Herb. Linn. No.
   997.48 (LINN).
Current name: ***Aster novi-belgii*** L. subsp. ***tardiflorus*** (L.) A.G. Jones
   (Asteraceae).
Note: Gray (in *Proc. Amer. Acad. Arts* 17: 167. 1882) noted material in
   LINN that had been cultivated in the Uppsala Botanic Garden. There
   are three sheets (997.48, 997.49 and 997.50 LINN) but they are
   evidently not part of a single gathering, so Art. 9.15 could not apply.

Aster taxifolius Linnaeus, *Plantae Rariores Africanae*: 22. 1760.
["Habitat ad Cap. b. spei."] Sp. Pl. ed. 2, 2: 1225 (1763). RCN: 6309.
Type not designated.
Original material: Herb. Burman (4 sheets) (G); Herb. Linn. No.
   997.1 (LINN).
Current name: ***Mairia taxifolia*** (L.) DC. (Asteraceae).

Aster tenellus Linnaeus, *Plantae Rariores Africanae*: 21. 1760.
["Habitat ad Cap. b. spei."] Sp. Pl. ed. 2, 2: 1225 (1763). RCN: 6314.
Lectotype (Grau in *Mitt. Bot. Staatssamml. München* 9: 413. 1973):
   Herb. Linn. No. 997.8, lower specimen (LINN).
Current name: ***Felicia tenella*** (L.) Nees (Asteraceae).

Aster tenuifolius Linnaeus, *Species Plantarum* 2: 873. 1753.
"Habitat in America septentrionali." RCN: 6323.
Type not designated.
Original material: Herb. Linn. No. 997.26 (LINN); [icon] in
   Plukenet, Phytographia: t. 78, f. 5. 1691; Almag. Bot.: 56. 1696 –
   Voucher: Herb. Sloane 95: 109 (BM-SL).
Current name: ***Aster tenuifolius*** L. (Asteraceae).

Aster tradescantii Linnaeus, *Species Plantarum* 2: 876. 1753.
"Habitat in Virginia." RCN: 6339.
Lectotype (Jones in *Phytologia* 55: 383. 1984): Herb. Clifford: 408,
   Aster 12 (BM-000647091).
Current name: ***Aster lateriflorus*** (L.) Britton var. ***hirsuticaulis***
   (Lindl.) Porter (Asteraceae).
Note: See a detailed discussion by Gray (in *Proc. Amer. Acad. Arts* 17:
   166–167. 1882). Jones & Hiepko (in *Willdenowia* 11: 351. 1981)
   referred to "the Linnaean type" without saying what they believed it
   to be, and Hoffmann (in *Feddes Repert.* 107: 175. 1996) also
   discussed the application of the name.

Aster tripolium Linnaeus, *Species Plantarum* 2: 872. 1753.
"Habitat in Europae littoribus maritimis & ad Sibiriae lacus salsos."
   RCN: 6317.
Lectotype (Brandenburg in Jarvis & Turland in *Taxon* 47: 355. 1998):
   Herb. Linn. No. 997.14 (LINN).
Current name: ***Tripolium pannonicum*** (Jacq.) Schur subsp.
   tripolium (L.) Greuter (Asteraceae).
Note: Grierson (in Rechinger, *Fl. Iranica* 154: 6. 1982) indicated
   997.15 (LINN) as type but this sheet lacks the relevant *Species
   Plantarum* number (i.e. "4") and is a later addition to the
   herbarium, and not original material for the name. Brandenburg
   therefore designated a different sheet as lectotype.

Aster undulatus Linnaeus, *Species Plantarum* 2: 875. 1753.
"Habitat in America septentrionali." RCN: 6330.
Lectotype (designated here by Reveal): *Kalm*, Herb. Linn. No. 997.32
   (LINN).
Current name: ***Aster undulatus*** L. (Asteraceae).
Note: Gray (in *Proc. Amer. Acad. Arts* 17: 165. 1882) noted the Kalm
   specimen (997.32 LINN) and the Hermann figure but did not
   choose a type.

Aster vernus Linnaeus, *Species Plantarum* 2: 876. 1753.
"Habitat in Virginia." RCN: 6335.
Lectotype (Reveal in Jarvis & Turland in *Taxon* 47: 355. 1998):
Clayton 391 (BM-000051202; iso- BM).
Current name: ***Erigeron vernus*** (L.) Torr. & A. Gray (Asteraceae).

Aster zephyrinus Linnaeus, *Systema Naturae,* ed. 10, 2: 1216. 1759.
RCN: 6394.
Type not designated.
Original material: none traced.
Note: There appear to be no extant original elements, and Linnaeus did not use the name in *Species Plantarum*, ed. 2 (1763). It does not appear to be in use.

Astragalus alopecuroides Linnaeus, *Species Plantarum* 2: 755. 1753.
"Habitat in Sibiria, Hispania." RCN: 5575.
Lectotype (Podlech in Turland & Jarvis in *Taxon* 46: 463. 1997):
Löfling 544a, Herb. Linn. No. 926.1 (LINN).
Current name: ***Astragalus alopecuroides*** L. subsp. ***alopecuroides*** (Fabaceae: Faboideae).
Note: Pampanini (in *Nuovo Giorn. Bot. Ital.,* n.s., 14: 327–481. 1907) provided an extensive discussion and excluded the Spanish element from his concept of the species. He considered the various original elements (reproducing two Clifford sheets as his f. IX and X) but did not formally designate a type. Although Becht (in *Phanerog. Monogr.* 10: 75. 1978) stated: "Typus: In Hispania (BM)", it is unclear what material may have been intended (there are Gronovius and Clifford sheets) so this cannot be accepted as a formal typification. Podlech subsequently designated material from Spain as the lectotype.

Astragalus alpinus Linnaeus, *Species Plantarum* 2: 760. 1753.
"Habitat in Alpibus Lapponicis, Helveticis." RCN: 5605.
Lectotype (Podlech in Turland & Jarvis in *Taxon* 46: 463. 1997):
[icon] *"Astragalus alpinus, foliis viciae ramosus, & procumbens flore glomerato, oblongo, albo coeruleo"* in Scheuchzer, Uresifoetes Helveticus: 509, inter 508–509, f. 7. 1723. – Epitype (Podlech in Turland & Jarvis in *Taxon* 46: 463. 1997): Switzerland. Joch-Alpe near Churwalden, 6,000ft, Jul 1863, *C. Brügger s.n.* [F. Schultz, Herbarium Normale, nov. ser. Cent. 18. No. 1756] (BM).
Current name: ***Astragalus alpinus*** L. (Fabaceae: Faboideae).

Astragalus arenarius Linnaeus, *Species Plantarum* 2: 759. 1753.
"Habitat in Angliae, Scaniae arena mobili." RCN: 5576.
Lectotype (Podlech in Turland & Jarvis in *Taxon* 46: 463. 1997):
Herb. Linn. No. 926.37 (LINN).
Current name: ***Astragalus arenarius*** L. (Fabaceae: Faboideae).

Astragalus austriacus N.J. Jacquin var. **sulcatus** (Linnaeus) Linnaeus, *Systema Vegetabilium,* ed. 13: 566. 1774.
["Habitat in Sibiria."] Sp. Pl. 2: 756 (1753). RCN: 5601.
Basionym: *Astragalus sulcatus* L. (1753).
Lectotype (Podlech in Turland & Jarvis in *Taxon* 46: 465. 1997):
Herb. Linn. No. 926.5, right specimen (LINN).
Current name: ***Astragalus sulcatus*** L. (Fabaceae: Faboideae).

Astragalus biflorus Linnaeus, *Mantissa Plantarum Altera*: 273. 1771, *nom. inval.*
"Habitat in Insula s. Johannae. Koenig. H.U." RCN: 5257.
Type not relevant.
Current name: ***Crotalaria angulata*** Mill. (Fabaceae: Faboideae).
Note: Linnaeus cited this name as a synonym of the newly described *Crotalaria biflora* L., Mant. Pl. Alt.: 570 (1771). As it was not accepted by the author in the original publication, *A. biflorus* is an invalid name.

Astragalus boeticus Linnaeus, *Species Plantarum* 2: 758. 1753.
"Habitat in Sicilia, Lusitania, Hispania." RCN: 5591.
Lectotype (Podlech in *Sendtnera* 2: 109. 1994): Herb. Linn. No. 926.22 (LINN).
Current name: ***Astragalus boeticus*** L. (Fabaceae: Faboideae).

Astragalus campestris Linnaeus, *Species Plantarum* 2: 761. 1753.
"Habitat in Oelandia, Germania, Helvetia." RCN: 5612.
Lectotype (Welsh in *Great Basin Naturalist* 51: 381. 1991): Herb. Linn. No. 926.51 (LINN).
Current name: ***Oxytropis campestris*** (L.) DC. subsp. ***campestris*** (Fabaceae: Faboideae).
Note: Stearn (in *Biol. J. Linn. Soc.* 5: 9–10. 1973), in an account of Linnaeus' Öland and Gotland journey of 1741, treated Räpplinge in Öland as the restricted type locality, and noted the existence of 926.51 (LINN), annotated by Linnaeus as from Öland. In his paper, Stearn attributed restricted type localities irrespective of whether any material existed in LINN and, where specimens do exist, he does not refer to any of them as type specimens. Jonsell & Jarvis (in *Nordic J. Bot.* 22: 77. 2002) subsequently made a formal type choice of this material, unaware that Welsh had already done so.

Astragalus canadensis Linnaeus, *Species Plantarum* 2: 757. 1753.
"Habitat in Virginia, Canada." RCN: 5585.
Lectotype (Reveal in Turland & Jarvis in *Taxon* 46: 464. 1997):
Clayton 565 (BM-000051646; iso- LINN 926.13).
Current name: ***Astragalus canadensis*** L. var. ***canadensis*** (Fabaceae: Faboideae).

Astragalus capitatus Linnaeus, *Species Plantarum* 2: 755. 1753, *nom. utique rej.*
"Habitat in Oriente." RCN: 5577.
Type not designated.
Original material: Herb. Clifford: 361, *Astragalus* 2 (BM).
Current name: ***Astragalus echinatus*** Murray (Fabaceae: Faboideae).

Astragalus caprinus Linnaeus, *Species Plantarum,* ed. 2, 2: 1071. 1763.
"Habitat in Barbaria." RCN: 5608.
Lectotype (Podlech in Turland & Jarvis in *Taxon* 46: 464. 1997):
[icon] *"Astragalus perennis foliis hirsutis caule recto aphyllo flore ochroleuco odoratissimo"* in Morison, Pl. Hist. Univ. 2: 203, s. 2, t. 24, central figure. 1680. – Epitype (Podlech in Turland & Jarvis in *Taxon* 46: 464. 1997): Algeria. Hauts plateaux oranais env. de Bedeau Broussailles, 1,100m, 30 May 1925, *A. Faure s.n.* (BM).
Current name: ***Astragalus caprinus*** L. subsp. ***caprinus*** (Fabaceae: Faboideae).
Note: Podlech (in *Mitt. Bot. Staatssamml. München* 25: 135. 1988) designated as lectotype Linnaeus' diagnosis from the protologue but this is not an acceptable choice (Art. 8.1). He also reproduced (as Abb. 9) the Morison illustration that he later designated as lectotype.

Astragalus carolinianus Linnaeus, *Species Plantarum* 2: 757. 1753.
"Habitat in Carolina." RCN: 5584.
Lectotype (Barneby in *Mem. New York Bot. Gard.* 13: 604. 1964):
[icon] *"Astragalus procerior non repens, flore e viridi flavescente"* in Dillenius, Hort. Eltham. 1: 45, t. 39, f. 45. 1732. – Typotype: Herb. Sherard No. 1557 (OXF).
Current name: ***Astragalus canadensis*** L. var. ***canadensis*** (Fabaceae: Faboideae).

Astragalus chinensis Linnaeus filius, *Dec. Prima Pl. Horti Upsal.*: 5. 1762.

Lectotype (Podlech in Turland & Jarvis in *Taxon* 46: 464. 1997): Herb. Linn. No. 926.7 (LINN).
Current name: ***Astragalus chinensis*** L. f. (Fabaceae: Faboideae).

Astragalus christianus Linnaeus, *Species Plantarum* 2: 755. 1753.
"Habitat in Oriente." RCN: 5576.
Lectotype (Podlech in Jarvis & al., *Regnum Veg.* 127: 22. 1993): [icon] *"Astragalus Orientalis, maximus, incanus, erectus caule ab imo ad summum florido"* in Tournefort, Rel. Voy. Levant (Paris ed.) 2: 253, 254. 1717.
Generitype of *Astragalus* Linnaeus (vide Rydberg in *Bull. Torrey Bot. Club* 32: 658. 1905; Green, *Prop. Brit. Bot.*: 176. 1929).
Current name: ***Astragalus christianus*** L. (Fabaceae: Faboideae).
Note: Agerer-Kirchhoff (in *Boissiera* 25: 84. 1976) indicated a Tournefort collection (sheet 3636, P) as lectotype but this choice is ineligible as it is not original material for the name. Burtt (in *Karaca Arbor. Mag.* 6: 142. 2002) discusses Tournefort's account of this plant.

Astragalus cicer Linnaeus, *Species Plantarum* 2: 757. 1753.
"Habitat in Austria, Helvetia, Italia." RCN: 5586.
Lectotype (Chamberlain & Matthews in Davis, *Fl. Turkey* 3: 78. 1970): Herb. Clifford: 362, *Astragalus* 5 (BM-000646609).
Current name: ***Astragalus cicer*** L. (Fabaceae: Faboideae).

Astragalus contortuplicatus Linnaeus, *Species Plantarum* 2: 758. 1753.
"Habitat in Sibiria." RCN: 5590.
Lectotype (Ali in *Biologia (Lahore)* 7: 26. 1961): Herb. Linn. No. 926.21 (LINN).
Current name: ***Astragalus contortuplicatus*** L. (Fabaceae: Faboideae).

Astragalus depressus Linnaeus, *Centuria II Plantarum*: 29. 1756.
"Habitat in alpinis Europae." RCN: 5613.
Lectotype (Podlech in Turland & Jarvis in *Taxon* 46: 464. 1997): Herb. Linn. No. 926.53 (LINN).
Current name: ***Astragalus depressus*** L. subsp. ***depressus*** (Fabaceae: Faboideae).

Astragalus epiglottis Linnaeus, *Species Plantarum* 2: 759. 1753.
"Habitat in Hispania." RCN: 5594.
Lectotype (Jafri in Jafri & El-Gadi, *Fl. Libya* 86: 48. 1980): Herb. Clifford: 362, *Astragalus* 4 (BM-000646608).
Current name: ***Astragalus epiglottis*** L. subsp. ***epiglottis*** (Fabaceae: Faboideae).

Astragalus exscapus Linnaeus, *Mantissa Plantarum Altera*: 275. 1771.
"Habitat in Thuringia. D. Schreber Profess. Erlangens." RCN: 5615.
Lectotype (Podlech in *Mitt. Bot. Staatssamml. München* 25: 111. 1988): *Schreber*, Herb. Linn. No. 926.55 (LINN; iso- M?).
Current name: ***Astragalus exscapus*** L. subsp. ***exscapus*** (Fabaceae: Faboideae).

Astragalus galegiformis Linnaeus, *Species Plantarum* 2: 756. 1753.
"Habitat in Sibiria." RCN: 5580.
Lectotype (Podlech in Turland & Jarvis in *Taxon* 46: 464. 1997): Herb. Linn. No. 926.6 (LINN).
Current name: ***Astragalus galegiformis*** L. (Fabaceae: Faboideae).

Astragalus glaux Linnaeus, *Species Plantarum* 2: 759. 1753.
"Habitat in Hispania." RCN: 5599.
Lectotype (Podlech in Turland & Jarvis in *Taxon* 46: 464. 1997): *Löfling 544*, Herb. Linn. No. 926.38 (LINN).
Current name: ***Astragalus glaux*** L. (Fabaceae: Faboideae).

Astragalus glycyphyllos Linnaeus, *Species Plantarum* 2: 758. 1753.
"Habitat in Europae nemoribus." RCN: 5588.
Lectotype (Podlech in Turland & Jarvis in *Taxon* 46: 464. 1997): Herb. Linn. No. 926.18 (LINN).
Current name: ***Astragalus glycyphyllos*** L. (Fabaceae: Faboideae).

Astragalus grandiflorus Linnaeus, *Species Plantarum* 2: 761. 1753.
"Habitat in Sibiria. D. Gmelin." RCN: 5530.
Replaced synonym of: *Hedysarum argenteum* L. (1774), *nom. illeg.*
Type not designated.
Original material: *Gmelin*, Herb. Linn. No. 921.53 (LINN).
Current name: ***Hedysarum grandiflorum*** Pall. (Fabaceae: Faboideae).

Astragalus hamosus Linnaeus, *Species Plantarum* 2: 758. 1753.
"Habitat Messanae, Monspelii." RCN: 5589.
Lectotype (Ali in Nasir & Ali, *Fl. W. Pakistan* 100: 209. 1977): Herb. Linn. No. 926.19 (LINN).
Current name: ***Astragalus hamosus*** L. (Fabaceae: Faboideae).

Astragalus hedysaroides Linnaeus, *Species Plantarum* 2: 756. 1753.
"Habitat in Sibiria, Helvetia." RCN: 5532.
Replaced synonym of: *Hedysarum obscurum* L. (1759), *nom. illeg.*
Type not designated.
Original material: Herb. Linn. No. 921.56 (LINN); [icon] in Haller, Enum. Meth. Stirp. Helv. 2: 567, t. 14, left figure. 1742.
Current name: ***Hedysarum hedysaroides*** (L.) Schinz & Thell. (Fabaceae: Faboideae).

Astragalus hypoglottis Linnaeus, *Mantissa Plantarum Altera*: 274. 1771.
"Habitat in Hispania." RCN: 5596.
Neotype (Lacaita in *J. Bot.* 50: 224. 1912): *Gérard 28*, Herb. Linn. No. 926.31 (LINN).
Current name: ***Astragalus hypoglottis*** L. subsp. ***hypoglottis*** (Fabaceae: Faboideae).

Astragalus incanus Linnaeus, *Systema Naturae, ed. 10*, 2: 1175. 1759.
["Habitat in Galloprovincia."] Sp. Pl., ed. 2, 2: 1072 (1763). RCN: 5611.
Neotype (Podlech in Turland & Jarvis in *Taxon* 46: 464. 1997): Spain. Teruel, in locis aridis prope "Valacloche", 800m, May 1893, *Reverchon s.n.* in Dörfler, Herb. Norm. No. 3832 (M; iso- BM).
Current name: ***Astragalus incanus*** L. subsp. ***incanus*** (Fabaceae: Faboideae).

Astragalus microphyllus Linnaeus, *Species Plantarum* 2: 757. 1753.
"Habitat in Sibiria." RCN: 5587.
Lectotype (Podlech in *Sendtnera* 1: 271. 1993): Herb. Linn. No. 926.17 (LINN).
Current name: ***Astragalus cicer*** L. (Fabaceae: Faboideae).

Astragalus monspessulanus Linnaeus, *Species Plantarum* 2: 761. 1753.
"Habitat Monspelii." RCN: 5610.
Lectotype (Podlech in Turland & Jarvis in *Taxon* 46: 464. 1997): Herb. Linn. No. 926.50 (LINN).
Current name: ***Astragalus monspessulanus*** L. subsp. ***monspessulanus*** (Fabaceae: Faboideae).

Astragalus montanus Linnaeus, *Species Plantarum* 2: 760. 1753.
"Habitat in Helvetia, Vallesia." RCN: 5605.
Type not designated.
Original material: Herb. van Royen, sheet no. 913.55–591 (L); Herb. Burser XIX: 143 (UPS); [icon] in Bauhin & Cherler, Hist. Pl. Univ. 2: 339. 1651; [icon] in Clusius, Rar. Pl. Hist. 2: 240. 1601.

Current name: **Oxytropis sp.** (Fabaceae: Faboideae).
Note: Gutermann & Merxmüller (in *Mitt. Bot. Staatssamml. München* 4: 231–232. 1961) treated this as a *nomen ambiguum* relating to *Oxytropis amethystea* Arvet-Touvet and *O. jacquinii* Bunge.

Astragalus onobrychis Linnaeus, *Species Plantarum* 2: 760. 1753.
"Habitat in Austria." RCN: 5582.
Lectotype (Chamberlain & Matthews in Davis, *Fl. Turkey* 3: 211. 1970): *Gerber*, Herb. Linn. No. 926.8 (LINN).
Current name: **Astragalus onobrychis** L. (Fabaceae: Faboideae).

Astragalus pentaglottis Linnaeus, *Mantissa Plantarum Altera*: 274. 1771, *nom. illeg.*
"Habitat in Hispania." RCN: 5594.
Replaced synonym: *Astragalus echinatus* Murray (1770).
Type not designated.
Current name: **Astragalus echinatus** Murray (Fabaceae: Faboideae).
Note: Linnaeus included *A. echinatus* Murray (1770) within his protologue so *A. pentaglottis* is illegitimate. See discussion by Lacaita (in *J. Bot.* 50: 220. 1912) on the confusion between this and *A. epiglottis* L. (1753).

Astragalus physodes Linnaeus, *Species Plantarum* 2: 760. 1753.
"Habitat in Sibiria." RCN: 5607.
Lectotype (Jarvis & al. in *Taxon* 50: 1129, f. 1, 2. 2002 [2001]): Astrachan, *Lerche s.n.* (MW No. 463).
Current name: **Astragalus physodes** L. (Fabaceae: Faboideae).
Note: Podlech (in *Taxon* 46: 464. 1997), believing there to be no original elements extant for the name, designated Pallas material (BM) as a neotype. However, original material was subsequently found in MW, and Jarvis & al. (in *Taxon* 50: 1129. 2002) consequently rejected Podlech's choice in favour of the MW material. Greuter (in *OPTIMA Newsl.* 36: 44. 2002) argued that the typification was, in fact, effected earlier, by Jarvis & al., *Herb. Linnaeanum*: 11 (2001), but this is erroneous because the phrase "designated here", or an equivalent (necessary under Art. 7.11), did not appear there.

Astragalus pilosus Linnaeus, *Species Plantarum* 2: 756. 1753.
"Habitat in Sibiria, Thuringia." RCN: 5578.
Lectotype (Jonsell & Jarvis in *Nordic J. Bot.* 22: 77. 2002): Herb. Burser XIX: 105 (UPS).
Current name: **Oxytropis pilosa** (L.) DC. var. **pilosa** (Fabaceae: Faboideae).

Astragalus sesameus Linnaeus, *Species Plantarum* 2: 759. 1753.
"Habitat in G. Narbonensi, Italia." RCN: 5593.
Lectotype (designated here by Podlech): [icon] *"Astragalus annuus foliis & siliquis hirsutis, plurimis in foliorum alis sessilibus"* in Plukenet, Phytographia: t. 79, f. 3. 1691; Almag. Bot.: 60. 1696. – Voucher: Herb. Sloane 99: 137 (BM-SL).
Current name: **Astragalus sesameus** L. (Fabaceae: Faboideae).
Note: Gazer (in *Sendtnera* 1: 122. 1993) designated 926.24 (LINN) as lectotype, but the sheet lacks the relevant *Species Plantarum* number (i.e. "17"), was a post-1753 addition to the herbarium and is not original material for the name. This name was considered by Turland & Jarvis (in *Taxon* 46: 464. 1997) where it was to have been typified by Podlech using a Plukenet illustration. However, the omission of any reference to "type" rendered this ineffective. This type choice is validated here.

Astragalus sesamoides Linnaeus, *Amoenitates Academicae* 4: 489. 1759, *orth. var.*
["Habitat in G. Narbonensi, Italia."] Sp. Pl. 2: 759 (1753).
Lectotype (designated here by Podlech): [icon] *"Astragalus annuus foliis*

& siliquis hirsutis, plurimis in foliorum alis sessilibus" in Plukenet, Phytographia: t. 79, f. 3. 1691; Almag. Bot.: 60. 1696. – Voucher: Herb. Sloane 99: 137 (BM-SL).
Current name: **Astragalus sesameus** L. (Fabaceae: Faboideae).
Note: Astragalus sesamoides L. (*Amoen. Acad.* 4: 489. 1759) was regarded by Stearn (in Geck & Pressler, *Festschr. Claus Nissen*: 632. 1974) as an orthographic variant of *A. sesameus* L. (*Sp. Pl.* 2: 759. 1753). This seems perfectly plausible, because the phrase name used by Magnol (*Bot. Monsp.*: 194. 1676), "Ornithopodio affinis hirsuta stella leguminosa", cited (only slightly altered) from Bauhin (*Pinax*: 350. 1623), was treated as a synonym of *A. sesameus* by Linnaeus in 1753. Moreover, *A. sesamoides* never appears again in later works, whereas *A. sesameus* does (see Turland & Jarvis in *Taxon* 46: 464. 1997).

Astragalus sinicus Linnaeus, *Systema Naturae*, ed. 12, 2: 499; *Mantissa Plantarum*: 103. 1767.
"Habitat in China." RCN: 5600.
Lectotype (Nguyên Van Thuân in Morat, *Fl. Cambodge Laos Viêtnam* 23: 176. 1987): Herb. Linn. No. 926.39 (LINN).
Current name: **Astragalus sinicus** L. (Fabaceae: Faboideae).
Note: Podlech (in *Taxon* 46: 465. 1997), unaware of Thuân's typification, independently made the same type choice.

Astragalus stella Linnaeus, *Systema Naturae*, ed. 12, 2: 734. 1767.
"Habitat in Europae australis potissimum maritimis. D. Gouan." RCN: 5592.
Lectotype (Podlech in Turland & Jarvis in *Taxon* 46: 465. 1997): *Gouan s.n.*, Herb. Linn. No. 926.23 (LINN).
Current name: **Astragalus stella** L. (Fabaceae: Faboideae).
Note: The authorship of this name has been sometimes incorrectly attributed to Gouan (*Illustr. Obs. Bot.*: 50. 1773).

Astragalus sulcatus Linnaeus, *Species Plantarum* 2: 756. 1753.
"Habitat in Sibiria." RCN: 5579.
Basionym of: *Phaca sulcata* (L.) L. (1759); *Astragalus austriacus* Jacq. var. *sulcatus* (L.) L. (1774).
Lectotype (Podlech in Turland & Jarvis in *Taxon* 46: 465. 1997): *Gerber*, Herb. Linn. No. 926.5, right specimen (LINN).
Current name: **Astragalus sulcatus** L. (Fabaceae: Faboideae).

Astragalus syriacus Linnaeus, *Species Plantarum* 2: 759. 1753.
"Habitat in Sibiria." RCN: 5597.
Lectotype (Podlech in Turland & Jarvis in *Taxon* 46: 465. 1997): *Gerber*, Herb. Linn. No. 926.36 (LINN).
Current name: **Astragalus syriacus** L. (Fabaceae: Faboideae).

Astragalus tenuifolius Linnaeus, *Species Plantarum*, ed. 2, 2: 1065. 1763.
"Habitat in Sibiria." RCN: 5582.
Lectotype (Podlech in *Sendtnera* 1: 271. 1993): *Gmelin s.n.*, Herb. Linn. No. 926.10 (LINN).
Current name: **Astragalus austriacus** Jacq. (Fabaceae: Faboideae).

Astragalus tragacantha Linnaeus, *Species Plantarum* 2: 762. 1753.
"Habitat in littore Massiliensi, Aethna, Olympo." RCN: 5617.
Lectotype (Podlech in Turland & Jarvis in *Taxon* 46: 465. 1997): Herb. Clifford: 361, *Tragacantha* 1 (BM-000646604).
Current name: **Astragalus tragacantha** L. (Fabaceae: Faboideae).

Astragalus tragacanthoides Linnaeus, *Species Plantarum* 2: 762. 1753.
"Habitat in Sibiria, Armenia." RCN: 5616.
Lectotype (Podlech in *Sendtnera* 1: 271. 1993): *Gmelin s.n.*, Herb. Linn. No. 926.61 (LINN).

Current name: ***Astragalus tragacanthoides*** L. (Fabaceae: Faboideae).
Note: Chater (in *Feddes Repert.* 79: 48. 1968) noted that the identity of this name was uncertain but that its description matched material in LINN which was neither a member of sect. *Myobroma,* nor a European species. With its subsequent typification by Podlech, *A. tragacanthoides* became the correct name for the species previously known as *A. fruticans* Pall. (1800).

Astragalus trimestris Linnaeus, *Species Plantarum* 2: 761. 1753.
"Habitat in Aegypto." RCN: 5603.
Lectotype (Podlech in Turland & Jarvis in *Taxon* 46: 465. 1997): Herb. Linn. No. 926.43 (LINN). – Epitype (Podlech in Turland & Jarvis in *Taxon* 46: 465. 1997): Egypt. Dünen oberhalb Rosetta am linken Nilufer bei Schech Mantur, 9 May 1902, *Anonymous* (BM).
Current name: ***Astragalus trimestris*** L. (Fabaceae: Faboideae).

Astragalus uliginosus Linnaeus, *Species Plantarum* 2: 757. 1753.
"Habitat in Sibiriae pratis subhumidis. D. Gmelin." RCN: 5583.
Lectotype (Podlech in Turland & Jarvis in *Taxon* 46: 465. 1997): Herb. Linn. No. 926.11 (LINN).
Current name: ***Astragalus uliginosus*** L. (Fabaceae: Faboideae).

Astragalus uncatus Linnaeus, *Species Plantarum,* ed. 2, 2: 1072. 1763.
"Habitat in Aleppo. Russel." RCN: 5614.
Lectotype (Podlech in Turland & Jarvis in *Taxon* 46: 465. 1997): Herb. Linn. No. 926.54 (LINN).
Current name: ***Astragalus trimestris*** L. (Fabaceae: Faboideae).

Astragalus uralensis Linnaeus, *Species Plantarum* 2: 761. 1753.
"Habitat in Sibiria." RCN: 5609.
Lectotype (Knjasev in *Bot. Zhurn.* 90: 417, 418. 2006): *Gerber?*, Herb. Linn. No. 926.46 (LINN).
Current name: ***Oxytropis uralensis*** (L.) DC. (Fabaceae: Faboideae).

Astragalus verticillaris Linnaeus, *Mantissa Plantarum Altera*: 275. 1771.
"Habitat in Sibiria." RCN: 5604.
Type not designated.
Original material: [icon] in Amman, Stirp. Rar. Ruth.: 113, t. 19, f. 2. 1739; [icon] in Amman, Stirp. Rar. Ruth.: 111, t. 19, f. 1. 1739.
Current name: ***Oxytropis myriophylla*** (Pall.) DC. (Fabaceae: Faboideae).

Astragalus vesicarius Linnaeus, *Species Plantarum* 2: 760. 1753.
"Habitat in Delphinatu." RCN: 5606.
Lectotype (Podlech in Turland & Jarvis in *Taxon* 46: 465. 1997): [icon] *"Astragalus Alpinus Tragacanthae folio vesicarius"* in Magnol, Hort. Reg. Monspel.: 27, unnumbered plate. 1697.
Current name: ***Astragalus vesicarius*** L. subsp. ***vesicarius*** (Fabaceae: Faboideae).

Astrantia major Linnaeus, *Species Plantarum* 1: 235. 1753.
"Habitat in alpibus Helvetiae, Hetruriae, Pyrenaeis." RCN: 1908.
Lectotype (Reduron & Jarvis in Jarvis & al., *Regnum Veg.* 127: 22. 1993): Herb. Linn. No. 334.1 (LINN).
Generitype of *Astrantia* Linnaeus (vide Hitchcock, *Prop. Brit. Bot.:* 138. 1929).
Current name: ***Astrantia major*** L. (Apiaceae).

Astrantia minor Linnaeus, *Species Plantarum* 1: 235. 1753.
"Habitat in Alpibus Helvetiae." RCN: 1909.
Lectotype (Reduron in Jarvis & al. in *Taxon* 55: 209. 2006): Herb. Burser X: 35 (UPS).
Current name: ***Astrantia minor*** L. (Apiaceae).

Athamanta annua Linnaeus, *Species Plantarum* 1: 245. 1753.
"Habitat in Creta." RCN: 1970.
Neotype (Jarvis & Knees in *Taxon* 37: 473. 1988): *"Myrrhis tenuifolia annua cretica, semine lanugine alba pubescente"* in Herb. Morison (OXF).
Current name: ***Athamanta cretensis*** L. (Apiaceae).

Athamanta cervaria (Linnaeus) Linnaeus, *Systema Naturae,* ed. 10, 2: 956. 1759.
["Habitat in Helvetiae, Sabaudiae, Genevae, Alsatiae, Galloprovinciae montibus."] Sp. Pl. 2: 1194 (1753). RCN: 1964.
Basionym: *Selinum cervaria* L. (1753).
Lectotype (Jarvis & Knees in *Taxon* 37: 476. 1988): Herb. Burser VII(2): 30 (UPS).
Current name: ***Peucedanum cervaria*** (L.) Lapeyr. (Apiaceae).

Athamanta chinensis Linnaeus, *Species Plantarum* 1: 245. 1753.
"Habitat – – – Chinensem dixit Barthram, qui semina misit ex Virginia." RCN: 1971.
Lectotype (Jarvis & Knees in *Taxon* 37: 473. 1988): Herb. Linn. No. 345.11 (LINN).
Current name: ***Conioselinum chinense*** (L.) Britton & al. (Apiaceae).

Athamanta condensata Linnaeus, *Species Plantarum* 2: 1195. 1753.
"Habitat in Sibiria." RCN: 1966.
Lectotype (Jarvis & Knees in *Taxon* 37: 474. 1988): Herb. Linn. No. 345.5 (LINN).
Current name: ***Seseli condensatum*** (L.) Rchb. f. (Apiaceae).

Athamanta cretensis Linnaeus, *Species Plantarum* 1: 245. 1753.
"Habitat in Helvetia." RCN: 1969.
Lectotype (Reduron & Jarvis in Jarvis & al., *Regnum Veg.* 127: 22. 1993): Herb. Burser VII(2): 22 (UPS).
Generitype of *Athamanta* Linnaeus (vide Hitchcock, *Prop. Brit. Bot.:* 139. 1929).
Current name: ***Athamanta cretensis*** L. (Apiaceae).
Note: Jarvis & Knees (in *Taxon* 37: 474. 1988) chose as type a Clifford sheet which was subsequently found to conflict with Linnaeus' diagnosis. This choice was therefore rejected by Reduron & Jarvis (1993), who designated material in Herb. Burser to replace it.

Athamanta libanotis Linnaeus, *Species Plantarum* 1: 244. 1753.
"Habitat in Sueciae, Germaniae pratis siccis apricis." RCN: 1963.
Lectotype (Pardo in *Lagascalia* 3: 168. 1981): Herb. Linn. No. 345.1 (LINN).
Current name: ***Libanotis pyrenaica*** (L.) Schwarz (Apiaceae).
Note: See detailed account by Jarvis & Knees (in *Taxon* 37: 474. 1988) who independently reached the same conclusion as Pardo.

Athamanta meum Linnaeus, *Species Plantarum* 1: 245. 1753.
"Habitat in Alpibus Italiae, Hispaniae, Helvetiae." RCN: 1969.
Basionym of: *Aethusa meum* (L.) L. (1774).
Lectotype (Jarvis & Knees in *Taxon* 37: 474. 1988): Herb. Clifford: 93, *Athamanta* 1 (BM-000558252).
Current name: ***Meum athamanticum*** Jacq. (Apiaceae).

Athamanta oreoselinum Linnaeus, *Species Plantarum* 1: 244. 1753.
"Habitat in Germaniae, Galliae, Angliae collibus apricis." RCN: 1967.
Lectotype (Jarvis & Knees in *Taxon* 37: 475. 1988): Herb. Linn. No. 345.6 (LINN).
Current name: ***Peucedanum oreoselinum*** (L.) Moench (Apiaceae).

Athamanta sibirica Linnaeus, *Species Plantarum* 1: 244. 1753.
"Habitat in Sibiria." RCN: 1965.
Neotype (Jarvis & Knees in *Taxon* 37: 475. 1988): Herb. Linn. No. 345.4 (LINN).

Current name: **Seseli sibiricum** (L.) Garcke (Apiaceae).
Note: See discussion by Pimenov (in *Kew Bull.* 48: 781–785. 1993) on the usage of the name.

Athamanta sicula Linnaeus, *Species Plantarum* 1: 244. 1753.
"Habitat in Sibiria." RCN: 1968.
Lectotype (Jarvis & Knees in *Taxon* 37: 475. 1988): Herb. Linn. No. 345.7 (LINN).
Current name: **Athamanta sicula** L. (Apiaceae).
Note: Heath (in *Taxon* 40: 94. 1991) argued that Jarvis & Knees' type choice is invalid but this was refuted by Jarvis (*l.c.* 41: 62–63. 1992).

Athanasia annua (Linnaeus) Linnaeus, *Species Plantarum,* ed. 2, 2: 1182. 1763.
"Habitat in Africa." RCN: 6110.
Basionym: *Santolina annua* L. (1753).
Lectotype (Humphries in Jarvis & Turland in *Taxon* 47: 365. 1998): *Magnol,* Herb. Linn. No. 986.12 (LINN).
Current name: **Lonas annua** (L.) Vines & Druce (Asteraceae).

Athanasia capitata (Linnaeus) Linnaeus, *Species Plantarum,* ed. 2, 2: 1181. 1763.
"Habitat in Aethiopia." RCN: 6106.
Basionym: *Santolina capitata* L. (1760).
Lectotype (Wijnands, *Bot. Commelins*: 69. 1983): Herb. Burman (G).
Current name: **Athanasia capitata** (L.) L. (Asteraceae).

Athanasia crenata (Linnaeus) Linnaeus, *Species Plantarum,* ed. 2, 2: 1180. 1763.
"Habitat in Aethiopia." RCN: 6105.
Basionym: *Santolina crenata* L. (1753).
Lectotype (Wijnands in *Taxon* 32: 302, f. 1. 1983): Herb. Clifford: 398, *Santolina* 6 (BM-000646973).
Current name: **Athanasia crenata** (L.) L. (Asteraceae).

Athanasia crithmifolia (Linnaeus) Linnaeus, *Species Plantarum,* ed. 2, 2: 1181. 1763.
"Habitat in Aethiopia." RCN: 6113.
Basionym: *Santolina crithmifolia* L. (1753).
Lectotype (Bremer & Wijnands in *Taxon* 31: 544. 1982): Herb. Linn. No. 986.16 (LINN).
Generitype of *Athanasia* Linnaeus (vide Bremer & Wijnands in *Taxon* 31: 545. 1982).
Current name: **Athanasia crithmifolia** (L.) L. (Asteraceae).

Athanasia dentata (Linnaeus) Linnaeus, *Species Plantarum,* ed. 2, 2: 1181. 1763.
"Habitat in Aethiopia." RCN: 6111.
Basionym: *Santolina dentata* L. (1753).
Lectotype (Wijnands, *Bot. Commelins*: 69. 1983): Herb. Clifford: 398, *Santolina* 5 (BM-000646972).
Current name: **Athanasia dentata** (L.) L. (Asteraceae).

Athanasia genistifolia Linnaeus, *Systema Naturae,* ed. 12, 2: 540. 1767.
["Habitat ad Cap. b. spei."] Mant. Pl. Alt.: 464 (1771). RCN: 6108.
Lectotype (Bremer in Jarvis & Turland in *Taxon* 47: 355. 1998): Herb. Linn. No. 986.6 (LINN).
Current name: **Oedera genistifolia** (L.) Anderb. & K. Bremer (Asteraceae).
Note: Bremer (in *Opera Bot.* 40: 39. 1976) designated 986.5 (LINN) as lectotype, a specimen from Tulbagh which Linnaeus did not receive until 1769 and is consequently not original material for the name. Bremer subsequently chose a different lectotype.

Athanasia laevigata (Linnaeus) Linnaeus, *Species Plantarum,* ed. 2, 2: 1181. 1763.
"Habitat ad Cap. b. spei." RCN: 6111.
Basionym: *Santolina laevigata* L. (1760).
Lectotype (Källersjö in Jarvis & Turland in *Taxon* 47: 365. 1998): *"Helychrys. afric. ericoides umbellatum Breyn. in Herm. cat. p. 7",* Herb. Burman (G).
Current name: **Athanasia dentata** (L.) L. (Asteraceae).

Athanasia maritima (Linnaeus) Linnaeus, *Species Plantarum,* ed. 2, 2: 1182. 1763.
"Habitat in Europae australis marisque Mediterranei maritimis." RCN: 6107.
Basionym: *Filago maritima* L. (1753).
Lectotype (Alavi in Jafri & El-Gadi, *Fl. Libya* 107: 162. 1983): Herb. Clifford: 398, *Santolina* 7 (BM-000646974).
Current name: **Achillea maritima** (L.) Ehrend. & Y.P. Guo (Asteraceae).

Athanasia parviflora Linnaeus, *Systema Vegetabilium,* ed. 13: 617. 1774.
RCN: 6114.
Replaced synonym: *Tanacetum crithmifolium* L. (1753).
Lectotype (Wijnands, *Bot. Commelins*: 70. 1983): Herb. Linn. No. 986.17 (LINN).
Current name: **Hymenolepis crithmifolia** (L.) Greuter & al. (Asteraceae).
Note: A *nomen novum* for *Tanacetum crithmifolium* L. (1753), the epithet being pre-occupied in *Athanasia* by *A. crithmifolia* (L.) L. (1763), based on *Santolina crithmifolia* L. (1753) (as noted by Wijnands, *Bot. Commelins*: 70. 1983). While the correct name for this taxon in *Athanasia* is *A. parviflora* L., in *Hymenolepis,* it is correctly *H. crithmifolia* (L.) Greuter & al. (see Greuter & al. in *Taxon* 54: 155. 2005).

Athanasia pubescens (Linnaeus) Linnaeus, *Species Plantarum,* ed. 2, 2: 1182. 1763.
"Habitat in Aethiopia." RCN: 6109.
Basionym: *Santolina pubescens* L. (1756).
Lectotype (Wijnands, *Bot. Commelins*: 70. 1983): *"Afr. austr...Athanasia pubescens",* Herb. Burman (G).
Current name: **Athanasia pubescens** (L.) L. (Asteraceae).

Athanasia squarrosa (Linnaeus) Linnaeus, *Species Plantarum,* ed. 2, 2: 1180. 1763.
"Habitat ad Cap. b. spei." RCN: 6104.
Basionym: *Santolina squarrosa* L. (1756).
Lectotype (Bremer in *Opera Bot.* 40: 42. 1976): Herb. Linn. No. 986.1 (LINN).
Current name: **Oedera squarrosa** (L.) Anderb. & K. Bremer (Asteraceae).

Athanasia trifurcata (Linnaeus) Linnaeus, *Species Plantarum,* ed. 2, 2: 1181. 1763.
"Habitat in Aethiopia." RCN: 6112.
Basionym: *Santolina trifurcata* L. (1753).
Lectotype (Wijnands, *Bot. Commelins*: 70. 1983): Herb. Linn. No. 986.13 (LINN).
Current name: **Athanasia trifurcata** (L.) L. (Asteraceae).

Atractylis cancellata Linnaeus, *Species Plantarum* 2: 830. 1753.
"Habitat in Hispaniae, Siciliae, Cretae agris." RCN: 6001.
Lectotype (Petit in Turland in *Bull. Nat. Hist. Mus. London, Bot.* 25: 150, f. 22. 1995): Herb. Clifford: 395, *Atractylis* 1 (BM-000646943).

Current name: ***Atractylis cancellata*** L. subsp. ***cancellata*** (Asteraceae).
Note: Alavi (in Jafri & El Gadi, *Fl. Libya* 107: 212. 1983) indicated
971.4 (LINN) as the type, and Petit (in *Bull. Mus. Natl. Hist. Nat.,
B, Adansonia,* 9: 425. 1987) also treated it as a syntype. However,
this specimen was received by Linnaeus from Allioni only in 1757,
and is not original material for the name.

Atractylis ciliaris Linnaeus, *Systema Naturae,* ed. 10, 2: 1202. 1759.
["Habitat in Aethiopia."] Sp. Pl. ed. 2, 2: 1284 (1763). RCN: 6575.
Basionym of: *Gorteria ciliaris* (L.) L. (1763).
Lectotype (Roessler in *Mitt. Bot. Staatssamml. München* 3: 280. 1959):
Herb. Linn. No. 1027.7 (LINN).
Current name: ***Cullumia reticulata*** (L.) Greuter & al. (Asteraceae).
Note: See Greuter & al. (in *Taxon* 54: 155. 2005) for an explanation of
the correct name for this taxon.

Atractylis fruticosa Linnaeus, *Species Plantarum* 2: 829. 1753.
"Habitat in Aethiopia." RCN: 6576.
Basionym of: *Gorteria fruticosa* (L.) L. (1763); *Atractylis oppositifolia* L.
(1771), *nom. illeg.*
Lectotype (Roessler in *Mitt. Bot. Staatssamml. München* 3: 131. 1959):
Herb. Clifford: 395, *Atractylis* 2 (BM-000646944).
Current name: ***Berkheya fruticosa*** (L.) Ehrh. (Asteraceae).

Atractylis gummifera Linnaeus, *Species Plantarum* 2: 829. 1753.
"Habitat in Creta, Italia." RCN: 5999.
Lectotype (Petit in *Bull. Mus. Natl. Hist. Nat., B, Adansonia* 9: 412.
1988 [1987]): Herb. Linn. No. 971.1 (LINN).
Current name: ***Carlina gummifera*** (L.) Less. (Asteraceae).

Atractylis humilis Linnaeus, *Species Plantarum* 2: 829. 1753.
"Habitat Madritii in collibus. Loefl. VII: 35." RCN: 6000.
Lectotype (Petit in Jarvis & Turland in *Taxon* 47: 355. 1998): *Löfling
s.n.,* Herb. Linn. No. 971.2 (LINN).
Generitype of *Atractylis* Linnaeus (vide Cassini, *Dict. Sci. Nat.* 47: 510.
Mai 1827; Lessing, *Syn. Gen. Comp.* 13. Jul–Aug 1832).
Current name: ***Atractylis humilis*** L. (Asteraceae).

Atractylis oppositifolia Linnaeus, *Mantissa Plantarum Altera*: 477.
1771, *nom. illeg.*
RCN: 6576.
Replaced synonym: *Atractylis fruticosa* L. (1753).
Lectotype (Roessler in *Mitt. Bot. Staatssamml. München* 3: 131. 1959):
Herb. Clifford: 395, *Atractylis* 2 (BM-000646944).
Current name: ***Berkheya fruticosa*** (L.) Ehrh. (Asteraceae).

Atragene alpina Linnaeus, *Species Plantarum* 1: 542. 1753.
"Habitat in Helvetia, Baldo, Sibiria." RCN: 4025.
Lectotype (Serov & Jarvis in *Taxon* 37: 168. 1988): Herb. Burser
XVII: 39 (UPS).
Generitype of *Atragene* Linnaeus (vide Green, *Prop. Brit. Bot.*: 163.
1929).
Current name: ***Clematis alpina*** (L.) Mill. (Ranunculaceae).
Note: Pringle (in *Brittonia* 23: 363. 1971) stated that the holotype was
in LINN but did not distinguish between sheets 711.1 and 711.2.
However, as these collections are not duplicates, Art. 9.15 does not
apply and Serov & Jarvis' subsequent type choice of Burser material
is correct.

Atragene capensis Linnaeus, *Species Plantarum* 1: 543. 1753.
"Habitat ad Cap. b. Spei." RCN: 4026.
Lectotype (Oliver in Codd, *Fl. Pl. Africa* 40: t. 1569. 1969): [icon]
"Pulsatilla foliis trifidis, dentatis, flore incarnato, pleno" in Burman,
Rar. Afric. Pl.: 148, t. 52. 1739.
Current name: ***Anemone capensis*** (L.) Lam. (Ranunculaceae).

Atragene sibirica Linnaeus, *Species Plantarum* 1: 543. 1753.
"Habitat in Sibiriae subhumidis ubique." RCN: 4027.
Lectotype (Stearn, *Introd. Linnaeus' Sp. Pl.* (Ray Soc. ed.): 82. 1957):
Herb. Linn. No. 711.7 (LINN).
Current name: ***Clematis alpina*** (L.) Mill. subsp. ***sibirica*** (Mill.)
Kuntze (Ranunculaceae).
Note: Stearn says that this is "a new species described from a specimen
(711.7) in his [Linnaeus'] herbarium", and Serov & Jarvis (in *Taxon*
37: 167. 1988) accept it as the type, but treat the name as
ambiguous. They did not propose the name for rejection because
Clematis sibirica Mill. is a new species, not a recombination of the
Linnaean epithet, which prevents the use of the latter in *Clematis.*
Traditional usage is therefore not threatened.

Atragene zeylanica Linnaeus, *Species Plantarum* 1: 542. 1753.
"Habitat in Zeylona." RCN: 4024.
Lectotype (Dassanayake in Dassanayake & Clayton, *Revised Handb.
Fl. Ceylon* 10: 353. 1996): Herb. Hermann 2: 64; 3: 41; 4: 55, No.
226 (BM).
Current name: ***Naravelia zeylanica*** (L.) DC. (Ranunculaceae).
Note: Dassanayake did not distinguish between material of this taxon
in three different volumes of the Hermann herbarium. However, as
they appear to be part of a single gathering, this is an effective
typification under Art. 9.15.

Atraphaxis spinosa Linnaeus, *Species Plantarum* 1: 333. 1753.
"Habitat in Media ad urbem Hansen locis glareosis juxta fluvios."
RCN: 2575.
Type not designated.
Original material: Herb. Linn. No. 462.1 (LINN); [icon] in
Buxbaum, Pl. Minus Cognit. Cent. 1: 19, t. 30. 1728; [icon] in
Dillenius, Hort. Eltham. 1: 47, t. 40, f. 47. 1732.
Generitype of *Atraphaxis* Linnaeus (vide Hitchcock, *Prop. Brit. Bot.*:
148. 1929).
Current name: ***Atraphaxis spinosa*** L. (Polygonaceae).
Note: Although Qaiser (in Ali & Qaiser, *Fl. Pakistan* 205: 172. 2001)
indicated 462.1 (LINN) as type, his choice was published after 1
Jan 2001 and so the omission of the phrase "designated here" or an
equivalent (Art. 7.11) means that this choice is not effective.

Atraphaxis undulata Linnaeus, *Species Plantarum* 1: 333. 1753.
"Habitat in Aethiopia." RCN: 2576.
Type not designated.
Original material: Herb. Clifford: 137, *Atraphaxis* 1 (BM); Herb.
Linn. No. 462.3 (LINN); [icon] in Dillenius, Hort. Eltham. 1: 36,
t. 32, f. 36. 1732.
Current name: ***Polygonum undulatum*** (L.) P.J. Bergius
(Polygonaceae).

Atriplex glauca Linnaeus, *Centuria I Plantarum*: 34. 1755.
"Habitat in Gallia australi & Hispaniae maritimis." RCN: 7614.
Lectotype (Castroviejo in *Anales Jard. Bot. Madrid* 43: 474. 1987):
[icon] *"Atriplex maritima Hispan. frutescens & procumbens Tourn."* in
Dillenius, Hort. Eltham. 1: 46, t. 40, f. 46. 1732.
Current name: ***Atriplex glauca*** L. (Chenopodiaceae).

Atriplex halimus Linnaeus, *Species Plantarum* 2: 1052. 1753.
"Habitat in Hispaniae, Lusitaniae, Virginiae sepibus maritimis." RCN:
7612.
Lectotype (Brenan in Turrill & Milne-Redhead, *Fl. Trop. E. Africa,
Chenopodiaceae*: 14. 1954): Herb. Linn. No. 1221.1 (LINN).
Current name: ***Atriplex halimus*** L. (Chenopodiaceae).

Atriplex hastata Linnaeus, *Species Plantarum* 2: 1053. 1753, *nom.
utique rej.*

"Habitat in Europa frigidiori." RCN: 7620.
Lectotype (Rauschert in *Feddes Repert.* 85: 643. 1974): Herb. Linn.
   No. 1221.17 (LINN).
Current name: ***Atriplex calotheca*** (Raf.) Fr. (Chenopodiaceae).

Atriplex hortensis Linnaeus, *Species Plantarum* 2: 1053. 1753, *typ.
   cons.*
"Habitat in Tataria." RCN: 7618.
Conserved type (McNeill & al. in *Taxon* 32: 552. 1983): Herb.
   Clifford: 469, *Atriplex* 1 (BM-000647538).
Generitype of *Atriplex* Linnaeus, *nom. cons.*
Current name: ***Atriplex hortensis*** L. (Chenopodiaceae).
Note: Atriplex hortensis, with the type designated by McNeill & al., was
   proposed as conserved type of the genus by Jarvis (in *Taxon* 41: 558.
   1992). This was eventually approved by the General Committee
   (see review of the history of this proposal by Barrie, *l.c.* 55:
   795–796. 2006).

Atriplex laciniata Linnaeus, *Species Plantarum* 2: 1053. 1753.
"Habitat ad Europae & Virginiae septentrionalis littora marina."
   RCN: 7619.
Lectotype (Taschereau in *Canad. J. Bot.* 50: 1591. 1972): Herb.
   Clifford: 469, *Atriplex* 3 (BM-000647540).
Current name: ***Atriplex laciniata*** L. (Chenopodiaceae).

Atriplex littoralis Linnaeus, *Species Plantarum* 2: 1054. 1753.
"Habitat in Europae septentrionalis litoribus maris." RCN: 7622.
Lectotype (Jonsell & Jarvis in *Nordic J. Bot.* 14: 154. 1994): Herb.
   Linn. No. 1221.22 (LINN).
Current name: ***Atriplex littoralis*** L. (Chenopodiaceae).

Atriplex marina Linnaeus, *Mantissa Plantarum Altera*: 300. 1771,
   nom. illeg.
"Habitat in Angliae, Sueciae litoribus marinis." RCN: 7623.
Replaced synonym: *Atriplex serrata* Huds. (1762).
Type not designated.
Current name: ***Atriplex littoralis*** L. (Chenopodiaceae).
Note: An illegitimate replacement name for *Atriplex serrata* Huds.
   (1762).

Atriplex maritima Linnaeus, *Flora Anglica*: 25. 1754.
"Habitat [in Anglia.]"
Type not designated.
Original material: none traced.
Current name: ***Atriplex laciniata*** L. (Chenopodiaceae).
Note: See Stearn (*Introd. Ray's Syn. Meth. Stirp. Brit.* (Ray Soc. ed.): 64.
   1973), who treats this as a valid name synonymous with *A.
   laciniata.*

Atriplex patula Linnaeus, *Species Plantarum* 2: 1053. 1753.
"Habitat in Europae cultis, ruderatis." RCN: 7621.
Lectotype (Taschereau in *Canad. J. Bot.* 50: 1574. 1972): Herb. Linn.
   No. 1221.19 (LINN).
Current name: ***Atriplex patula*** L. (Chenopodiaceae).
Note: See notes on the varietal identity of the type by Hansen &
   Pedersen (in *Bot. Tidsskr.* 63: 217. 1968).

Atriplex pedunculata Linnaeus, *Flora Anglica*: 25. 1754.
"Habitat [in Anglia.]" RCN: 7624.
Lectotype (Jonsell & Jarvis in *Nordic J. Bot.* 14: 155. 1994): Herb.
   Linn. No. 1221.24 (LINN).
Current name: ***Halimione pedunculata*** (L.) Aellen
   (Chenopodiaceae).
Note: See notes by Stearn (*Introd. Ray's Syn. Meth. Stirp. Brit.* (Ray Soc.
   ed.): 64. 1973).

Atriplex portulacoides Linnaeus, *Species Plantarum* 2: 1053. 1753.
"Habitat in Oceani: Europae septentrionali littoribus." RCN: 7613.
Lectotype (Jafri & Rateeb in Jafri & El-Gadi, *Fl. Libya* 58: 40. 1978):
   Herb. Linn. No. 1221.4 (LINN).
Current name: ***Atriplex portulacoides*** L. (Chenopodiaceae).

Atriplex rosea Linnaeus, *Species Plantarum*, ed. 2, 2: 1493. 1763.
"Habitat in Europa australiore." RCN: 7615.
Neotype (McNeill & al. in *Taxon* 32: 553. 1983): *"Semen a Zinnio sub
   nomine Atriplex seminis capsula aculeata..."* in Herb. Haller (P-HA).
Current name: ***Atriplex rosea*** L. (Chenopodiaceae).

Atriplex sibirica Linnaeus, *Species Plantarum*, ed. 2, 2: 1493. 1763.
"Habitat in Sibiria." RCN: 7616.
Type not designated.
Original material: Herb. Linn. No. 409.1 (S); Herb. Linn. No. 1221.8
   (LINN); Herb. Linn. No. 1221.7 (LINN).
Current name: ***Atriplex sibirica*** L. (Chenopodiaceae).

Atriplex tatarica Linnaeus, *Species Plantarum* 2: 1053. 1753.
"Habitat in Tataria." RCN: 7617.
Lectotype (Hedge in Rechinger, *Fl. Iranica* 172: 75. 1997): Herb.
   Linn. No. 1221.10 (LINN).
Current name: ***Atriplex tatarica*** L. (Chenopodiaceae).
Note: Although Castroviejo (in *Anales Jard. Bot. Madrid* 43: 475.
   1987) indicated 1221.10 and 1221.12 (LINN) as type material,
   these collections do not appear to be part of a single gathering so
   Art. 9.15 does not apply.

Atropa arborescens Linnaeus, *Centuria II Plantarum*: 10. 1756.
"Habitat in America meridionali." RCN: 1442.
Type not designated.
Original material: none traced.
Current name: ***Acnistus arborescens*** (L.) Schltr. (Solanaceae).
Note: Although Howard (*Fl. Lesser Antilles* 6: 265. 1989) indicated the
   "Plum. Spec. 1" reference as "type", this is not accompanied directly
   by an illustration. While the same polynomial is figured by Burman
   as his t. 46, f. 1, Howard cannot be deemed to have made a formal
   typification.

Atropa belladonna Linnaeus, *Species Plantarum* 1: 181. 1753.
"Habitat in Austriae, Angliae montibus sylvosis." RCN: 1439.
Lectotype (Schönbeck-Temesy in Rechinger, *Fl. Iranica* 100: 70.
   1972): Herb. Linn. No. 246.2 (LINN).
Generitype of *Atropa* Linnaeus (vide Hitchcock, *Prop. Brit. Bot.*: 132.
   1929).
Current name: ***Atropa belladonna*** L. (Solanaceae).

Atropa frutescens Linnaeus, *Species Plantarum* 1: 182. 1753.
"Habitat in Hispania." RCN: 1443.
Type not designated.
Original material: Herb. Linn. No. 246.6 (LINN); [icon] in Barrelier,
   Pl. Galliam: 1, t. 1173. 1714.
Current name: ***Withania frutescens*** (L.) Pauquy (Solanaceae).

Atropa mandragora Linnaeus, *Systema Naturae*, ed. 10, 2: 933. 1759,
   nom. illeg.
["Habitat in Hispaniae, Italiae, Cretae, Cycladum apricis."] Sp. Pl. 1:
   181 (1753). RCN: 1438.
Replaced synonym: *Mandragora officinarum* L. (1753).
Lectotype (Knapp in Jarvis & al., *Regnum Veg.* 127: 64. 1993): Herb.
   Burser IX: 26 (UPS).
Current name: ***Mandragora officinarum*** L. (Solanaceae).
Note: An illegitimate replacement name for *Mandragora officinarum* L.
   (1753).

Atropa physalodes Linnaeus, *Species Plantarum* 1: 181. 1753.
"Habitat in Peru. D.B. Jussieu." RCN: 1440.
Lectotype (Schönbeck-Temesy in Rechinger, *Fl. Iranica* 100: 2. 1972): Herb. Linn. No. 246.3 (LINN).
Current name: ***Nicandra physalodes*** (L.) Gaertn. (Solanaceae).

Atropa solanacea Linnaeus, *Mantissa Plantarum Altera*: 205. 1771, *nom. illeg.*
["Habitat in Guinea."] Sp. Pl. 1: 184 (1753). RCN: 1441.
Replaced synonym: *Solanum guineense* L. (1753).
Lectotype (Wijnands, *Bot. Commelins*: 193. 1983): Herb. Linn. No. 246.4 (LINN).
Current name: ***Solanum guineense*** L. (Solanaceae).
Note: An illegitimate replacement name for *Solanum guineense* L. (1753).

Avena elatior Linnaeus, *Species Plantarum* 1: 79. 1753.
"Habitat in Europae maritimis & apricis." RCN: 665.
Lectotype (Romero Zarco in *Acta Bot. Malac.* 10: 130. 1985): Herb. Linn. No. 95.2 (LINN).
Current name: ***Arrhenatherum elatius*** (L.) J. Presl & C. Presl (Poaceae).
Note: Although Kerguélen (in *Lejeunia*, n.s., 75: 85. 1975) stated "Type: ...LINN", this is not accepted as a formal typification, for the reasons explained by Cafferty & al. (in *Taxon* 49: 240. 2000).

Avena fatua Linnaeus, *Species Plantarum* 1: 80. 1753.
"Habitat in Europae agris inter segetes." RCN: 671.

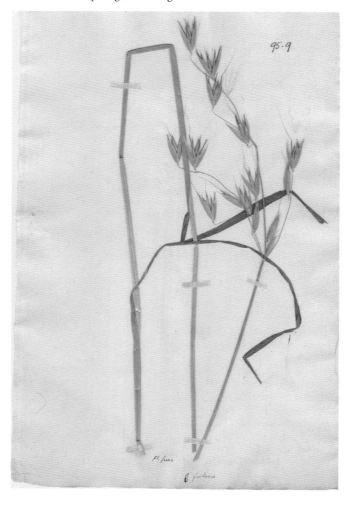

Lectotype (Hubbard in Milne-Redhead & Polhill, *Fl. Trop. E. Africa, Gramineae* 1: 82. 1970): Herb. Linn. No. 95.9 (LINN).
Current name: ***Avena fatua*** L. (Poaceae).
Note: Baum (in *Taxon* 40: 132–134, 1991) proposed the conservation of the name with a conserved type but the Committee for Spermatophyta (in *Taxon* 43: 114. 1994) declined to recommend this. *Avena fatua* was incorrectly indicated as the generitype by Jarvis & al. (in *Regnum Veg.* 127: 22. 1993): the generitype is *A. sativa* L.

Avena flavescens Linnaeus, *Species Plantarum* 1: 80. 1753.
"Habitat in Germania, Anglia, Gallia." RCN: 673.
Lectotype (Cope in Cafferty & al. in *Taxon* 49: 247. 2000): Herb. A. van Royen No. 913.7–458 (L).
Current name: ***Trisetum flavescens*** (L.) P. Beauv. (Poaceae).

Avena fragilis Linnaeus, *Species Plantarum* 1: 80. 1753.
"Habitat in Lusitania, Hispania. Loefl." RCN: 674.
Lectotype (Scholz in Cafferty & al. in *Taxon* 49: 247. 2000): Herb. Linn. No. 43.19 (S).
Current name: ***Gaudinia fragilis*** (L.) P. Beauv. (Poaceae).
Note: Although Kerguélen (in *Lejeunia*, n.s., 75: 184. 1975) stated "Type: ...LINN", this is not accepted as a formal typification, for the reasons explained by Cafferty & al. (in *Taxon* 49: 240. 2000). Sherif & Siddiqi (in El-Gadi, *Fl. Libya* 145: 156. 1988) indicated Herb. Linn. 95.16 (LINN) as type. However, this sheet is a post-1753 addition to the herbarium, and was therefore rejected by Scholz in favour of a Löfling collection in S, annotated by Linnaeus.

Avena loeflingiana Linnaeus, *Species Plantarum* 1: 79. 1753.
"Habitat in Hispania." RCN: 668.
Lectotype (Scholz in Cafferty & al. in *Taxon* 49: 247. 2000): *Löfling s.n.*, Herb. Linn. No. 95.4, upper row of specimens (excl. specimen at bottom left) (LINN).
Current name: ***Trisetaria loeflingiana*** (L.) Paunero (Poaceae).

Avena nuda Linnaeus, *Demonstr. Pl. Horto Upsaliensi*: 3. 1753.
["Habitat – – – – –"] Sp. Pl., ed. 2, 2: 118 (1762). RCN: 670.
Lectotype (Cope in Cafferty & al. in *Taxon* 49: 247. 2000): Herb. Linn. No. 95.8 (LINN).
Current name: ***Avena nuda*** L. (Poaceae).
Note: Although Kerguélen (in *Lejeunia*, n.s., 75: 88. 1975) stated "Type: ...LINN", this is not accepted as a formal typification, for the reasons explained by Cafferty & al. (in *Taxon* 49: 240. 2000). Baum (in *Taxon* 23: 581. 1974; *Oats Wild & Cult.*: 184. 1977) designated a specimen from the Stockholm herbarium as lectotype. However this material is unannotated by Linnaeus and therefore ineligible for designation as the type, and the choice was consequently rejected by Cope.

Avena pensylvanica Linnaeus, *Species Plantarum* 1: 79. 1753.
"Habitat in Pensylvania. Kalm." RCN: 667.
Lectotype (Hitchcock in *Contr. U. S. Natl. Herb.* 12: 123. 1908): *Kalm*, Herb. Linn. No. 95.3 (LINN; iso- BM?, UPS).
Current name: ***Sphenopholis pensylvanica*** (L.) Hitchc. (Poaceae).

Avena pratensis Linnaeus, *Species Plantarum* 1: 80. 1753.
"Habitat in Europae pascuis siccis apricis." RCN: 677.
Lectotype (Röser in *Taxon* 44: 397. 1995): Herb. Linn. No. 44.5 (S).
Current name: ***Helictotrichon pratense*** (L.) Besser (Poaceae).
Note: Holub (in *Acta Mus. Nat. Pragae* 17B(5): 215. 1961) discussed this name, and its original material, in some detail but did not indicate a type. Gervais (in *Denkschr. Schweiz. Naturf. Ges.* 88: 95. 1973) proposed a neotype for this name but this is contrary to Art. 9.11 because original material is in existence. Kerguélen (in

Lejeunia, n.s., 75: 30. 1975) correctly argued that 95.19 (LINN) was not original material, but Romero Zarco (in *Lagascalia* 13: 83. 1984) incorrectly designated the left-hand specimen on 95.17 (LINN), which is also not original material, as lectotype. Röser's typification is therefore accepted here.

Avena sativa Linnaeus, *Species Plantarum* 1: 79. 1753.
"Habitat – – –" RCN: 669.
Lectotype (Baum in *Taxon* 23: 579, f. 1. 1974): Herb. Clifford: 25, *Avena* 1 (BM-000557678).
Generitype of *Avena* Linnaeus (vide Hitchcock, *Prop. Brit. Bot.*: 121. 1929).
Current name: ***Avena sativa*** L. (Poaceae).

Avena sesquitertia Linnaeus, *Systema Naturae*, ed. 12, 2: 99; *Mantissa Plantarum*: 34. 1767.
"Habitat in Helvetia, Austria. Jacquin." RCN: 675.
Lectotype (Cope in Cafferty & al. in *Taxon* 49: 247. 2000): Herb. Linn. No. 95.26 (LINN).
Current name: ***Helictotrichon pubescens*** (Huds.) Pilg. (Poaceae).

Avena sibirica Linnaeus, *Species Plantarum* 1: 79. 1753.
"Habitat in Sibiria." RCN: 664.
Lectotype (Scholz in Cafferty & al. in *Taxon* 49: 248. 2000): *Amman 27*, Herb. Linn. No. 95.1 (LINN).
Current name: ***Stipa sibirica*** (L.) Lam. (Poaceae).

Avena spicata Linnaeus, *Species Plantarum* 1: 80. 1753.
"Habitat in Pensylvania." RCN: 679.
Lectotype (Hitchcock in *Contr. U. S. Natl. Herb.* 12: 123. 1908): *Kalm*, Herb. Linn. No. 95.21 (LINN; iso- 95.22 LINN).
Current name: ***Trisetum spicatum*** (L.) K. Richt. (Poaceae).
Note: See Baum (in *Canad. J. Bot.* 45: 1850. 1967) on the eligibility of the Kalm material as a lectotype. Questions of this sort can now frequently be resolved by the provisions of Art. 9.8.

Avena sterilis Linnaeus, *Species Plantarum*, ed. 2, 1: 118. 1762.
"Habitat in Hispania. Alströmer." RCN: 672.
Lectotype (Hubbard in Milne-Redhead & Polhill, *Fl. Trop. E. Africa, Gramineae* 1: 84. 1970): *Alströmer 7*, Herb. Linn. No. 95.12 (LINN).
Current name: ***Avena sterilis*** L. (Poaceae).
Note: Hubbard (in Milne-Redhead & Polhill, *Fl. Trop. E. Africa, Gramineae* 1: 84. 1970) treats the Alström specimen at LINN (i.e. 95.12) as the type ["Type: ... Alstroemer (LINN-holo!)"]. Unfortunately, it appears to be identifiable as the species long called *Stipa gigantea* Link (see Vázquez & al. in *Anales Jard. Bot. Madrid* 52: 185–6. 1995). Another specimen in LINN (95.11), illustrated by Baum (*Oats Wild & Cult.*: 344, f. 309. 1977), was designated by him (in *Taxon* 23: 582. 1974) as the lectotype (and followed by Romero Zarco in *Lagascalia* 17: 292. 1994). This collection belongs to the taxon understood as *A. sterilis* but it was received by Linnaeus from David van Royen after 1762, probably with a letter dated 7 June 1763 (the specimen is annotated "R. 93" by Linnaeus and corresponds with a list at LINN prepared by D. van Royen, in which specimen no. 93 is determined by Linnaeus as *A. sterilis*). It therefore cannot, in any case, be original material for this name. There seem to be no grounds for rejecting Hubbard's choice of type, so if this name is to continue to be used in its traditional sense, it appears that a conservation proposal will be needed.

Avena stipiformis Linnaeus, *Systema Naturae*, ed. 12, 2: 99; *Mantissa Plantarum*: 34. 1767.
"Habitat ad Cap. b. spei." RCN: 666.
Type not designated.

Original material: none traced.
Note: The application of this name is apparently unknown, with no extant original material. Baum (*Oats Wild & Cult.*: 436. 1977) suggested the genera *Pentaschistis*, *Danthonia* or *Chaetobromus* as a possible home for this name.

Averrhoa acida Linnaeus, *Species Plantarum* 1: 428. 1753.
"Habitat in India." RCN: 3334.
Type not designated.
Original material: Herb. Hermann 5: 306, No. 179? [icon] (BM); [icon] in Rheede, Hort. Malab. 3: 57, t. 47, 48. 1682.
Current name: ***Phyllanthus acidus*** (L.) Skeels (Euphorbiaceae).
Note: Webster (in *J. Arnold Arbor.* 38: 68. 1957), followed by later authors, treated 592.3 (LINN) as type, but it is annotated only by Linnaeus filius and is not original material for the name.

Averrhoa bilimbi Linnaeus, *Species Plantarum* 1: 428. 1753.
"Habitat in India." RCN: 3332.
Lectotype (Nasir in Nasir & Ali, *Fl. W. Pakistan* 11: 3. 1971): Herb. Hermann 2: 20, No. 177 (BM-000621574).
Generitype of *Averrhoa* Linnaeus (vide Green, *Prop. Brit. Bot.*: 156. 1929).
Current name: ***Averrhoa bilimbi*** L. (Oxalidaceae).

Averrhoa carambola Linnaeus, *Species Plantarum* 1: 428. 1753.
"Habitat in India." RCN: 3333.
Lectotype (Nasir in Nasir & Ali, *Fl. W. Pakistan* 11: 3. 1971): Herb. Hermann 2: 6; 4: 70, No. 178 (BM-000594769).
Current name: ***Averrhoa carambola*** L. (Oxalidaceae).
Note: Lourteig (in *Ann. Missouri Bot. Gard.* 67: 825. 1980) indicated Hermann material in BM (but wrongly associated with *Flora Zeylanica* number 178) as type, and (in *Phytologia* 56: 386. 1984) indicated material in both BM and Institut de France, Paris as lectotype. Neither statement restricts Nasir's earlier choice of Hermann material in BM as type.

Avicennia officinalis Linnaeus, *Species Plantarum* 1: 110. 1753.
"Habitat in India." RCN: 4642.
Lectotype (Stearn in *Kew Bull.* 13: 35. 1958): [icon] *"Oepata"* in Rheede, Hort. Malab. 4: 95, t. 45. 1683.
Generitype of *Avicennia* Linnaeus.
Current name: ***Avicennia officinalis*** L. (Avicenniaceae).

Axyris amaranthoides Linnaeus, *Species Plantarum* 2: 979. 1753.
"Habitat in Dauria." RCN: 3097.
Lectotype (Jonsell & Jarvis in Jarvis & al., *Regnum Veg.* 127: 23. 1993): Herb. Linn. No. 1101.4 (LINN).
Generitype of *Axyris* Linnaeus (vide Green, *Prop. Brit. Bot.*: 187. 1929).
Current name: ***Axyris amaranthoides*** L. (Chenopodiaceae).

Axyris ceratoides Linnaeus, *Species Plantarum* 2: 979. 1753.
"Habitat in Tataria, Moravia." RCN: 7096.
Lectotype (Hedge in Rechinger, *Fl. Iranica* 172: 88. 1997): *Gerber*, Herb. Linn. No. 1101.1 (LINN).
Current name: ***Krascheninnikovia ceratoides*** (L.) Gueldenst. (Chenopodiaceae).

Axyris hybrida Linnaeus, *Species Plantarum* 2: 980. 1753.
"Habitat in Sibiria." RCN: 7098.
Lectotype (Suchorukow in *Feddes Repert.* 116: 175. 2005): Herb. Linn. No. 1101.5 (LINN).
Current name: ***Axyris hybrida*** L. (Chenopodiaceae).
Note: Freitag & al. (in Ali & Qaiser, *Fl. Pakistan* 204: 77. 2001) indicated 1101.5 (LINN) as type, but their omission of "designated

here" or an equivalent (Art. 7.11) precluded this from being a valid choice. However, Suchorukow subsequently validated this typification, with "h.l." (= *hoc loco*) used to confirm the intention to typify the name.

Axyris prostrata Linnaeus, *Species Plantarum* 2: 980. 1753.
"Habitat in Sibiria." RCN: 7099.
Lectotype (Suchorukow in *Feddes Repert.* 116: 175. 2005): Herb. Linn. No. 1101.6 (LINN).
Current name: ***Axyris prostrata*** L. (Chenopodiaceae).
Note: Suchorukow's typification statement includes "h.l." (= *hoc loco*) which confirms his intention to typify the name (Art. 7.11).

Ayenia magna Linnaeus, *Systema Naturae,* ed. 10, 2: 1247. 1759.
["Habitat in Cumana."] Sp. Pl., ed. 2, 2: 1354 (1763). RCN: 6916.
Type not designated.
Original material: *Browne,* Herb. Linn. No. 1069.2 (LINN).
Current name: ***Ayenia magna*** L. (Sterculiaceae).
Note: Cristóbal (in *Opera Lilloana* 4: 63. 1960) noted 1069.2 (LINN) and confirmed its identity but did not refer to it as the type.

Ayenia pusilla Linnaeus, *Systema Naturae,* ed. 10, 2: 1247. 1759.
["Habitat in Jamaica, Cumana. Peru."] Sp. Pl., ed. 2, 2: 1354 (1763). RCN: 6914.
Lectotype (Cristóbal in *Opera Lilloana* 4: 190, 193. 1960): Herb. Linn. No. 1069.1 (LINN).
Generitype of *Ayenia* Linnaeus (vide Cristóbal in *Opera Lilloana* 4: 7. 1960).
Current name: ***Ayenia pusilla*** L. (Sterculiaceae).

Ayenia tomentosa Linnaeus, *Systema Naturae,* ed. 10, 2: 1247. 1759.
["Habitat in Cumana."] Sp. Pl., ed. 2, 2: 1354 (1763). RCN: 6915.
Type not designated.
Original material: none traced.
Current name: ***Ayenia tomentosa*** L. (Sterculiaceae).

Azalea indica Linnaeus, *Species Plantarum* 1: 150. 1753.
"Habitat in India." RCN: 1195.
Lectotype (Chamberlain in Cafferty & Jarvis in *Taxon* 51: 752. 2003 [2002]): [icon] *"Tsutsusi"* in Kaempfer, Amoen. Exot. Fasc.: 845, 846. 1712. – Voucher: Herb. Sloane 211: 8 (BM-SL) (see p. 139).
Current name: ***Rhododendron indicum*** (L.) Sweet (Ericaceae).

Azalea lapponica Linnaeus, *Species Plantarum* 1: 151. 1753.
"Habitat in Alpibus Lapponiae." RCN: 1198.

Lectotype (Jonsell in Cafferty & Jarvis in *Taxon* 51: 753. 2003 [2002]): Herb. Linn. No. 215.6, right specimen (LINN).
Current name: ***Rhododendron lapponicum*** (L.) Wahlenb. (Ericaceae).

Azalea lutea Linnaeus, *Species Plantarum* 1: 150. 1753.
"Habitat in Virginia." RCN: 1196.
Replaced synonym of: *Azalea nudiflora* L. (1762), *nom. illeg.*
Lectotype (Blake in *Rhodora* 20: 54. 1918): Herb. Clifford: 69, *Azalea* 1 (BM-000558098).
Current name: ***Rhododendron periclymenoides*** (Michx.) Shinners (Ericaceae).

Azalea nudiflora Linnaeus, *Species Plantarum,* ed. 2, 1: 214. 1762, *nom. illeg.*
"Habitat in Virginiae siccis." RCN: 1196.
Replaced synonym: *Azalea lutea* L. (1753).
Lectotype (Blake in *Rhodora* 20: 54. 1918): Herb. Clifford: 69, *Azalea* 1 (BM-000558098).
Current name: ***Rhododendron periclymenoides*** (Michx.) Shinners (Ericaceae).
Note: As noted by Shinners (in *Castanea* 27: 94–95. 1962), this is an illegitimate renaming of *A. lutea* L. (1753).

Azalea pontica Linnaeus, *Species Plantarum* 1: 150. 1753.
"Habitat in Ponto, Trapezunte." RCN: 1194.
Lectotype (Kron in *Edinburgh J. Bot.* 50: 315. 1993): [icon] *"Chamaerhododendros Pontica maxima, Mespili folio, flore luteo"* in Buxbaum, Pl. Minus Cognit. Cent. 5: 36, t. 69. 1740.
Current name: ***Rhododendron luteum*** Sweet (Ericaceae).

Azalea procumbens Linnaeus, *Species Plantarum* 1: 151. 1753.
"Habitat in Alpibus Europae." RCN: 1199.
Lectotype (Chamberlain in Jarvis & al., *Regnum Veg.* 127: 23. 1993): Herb. Linn. No. 90 (LAPP).
Generitype of *Azalea* Linnaeus, *nom. rej.*
Current name: ***Loiseleuria procumbens*** (L.) Desv. (Ericaceae).
Note: Azalea Linnaeus, *nom. rej.* in favour of *Loiseleuria* Desv.

Azalea viscosa Linnaeus, *Species Plantarum* 1: 151. 1753.
"Habitat in Virginia." RCN: 1197.
Lectotype (Kron in *Edinburgh J. Bot.* 50: 329. 1993): *Kalm,* Herb. Linn. No. 215.4 (LINN; iso- UPS).
Current name: ***Rhododendron viscosum*** (L.) Torr. var. ***viscosum*** (Ericaceae).

B

Baccharis arborea Linnaeus, *Mantissa Plantarum Altera*: 284. 1771.
"Habitat in Ind. orient. insulae Johannae sylvis. Koenig." RCN: 6211.
Lectotype (Brenan in *Kew Bull.* 21: 427. 1967): Herb. Linn. No. 992.3 (LINN).
Current name: ***Vernonia colorata*** (Willd.) Drake (Asteraceae).

Baccharis brasiliana Linnaeus, *Species Plantarum,* ed. 2, 2: 1205. 1763.
"Habitat in Brasilia." RCN: 6215.
Lectotype (Keeley in Jarvis & Turland in *Taxon* 47: 355. 1998): [icon] *"Tremate Brasiliensibus"* in Marggraf, Hist. Rer. Nat. Bras.: 81. 1648.
Current name: ***Vernonia brasiliana*** (L.) Druce (Asteraceae).

Baccharis dioscoridis Linnaeus, *Centuria I Plantarum*: 27. 1755.
"Habitat in Syria, Aegypto. D. Hasselquist." RCN: 6213.
Lectotype (King-Jones in *Willdenowia* 29: 211. 1999): *Hasselquist,* Herb. Linn. No. 992.6 (LINN; iso- UPS-HASSELQ 674, 676).
Current name: ***Pluchea dioscoridis*** (L.) DC. (Asteraceae).
Note: Although King-Jones (1999, and in *Englera* 23: 69. 2001) refers to the type specimen as "Herb. Linn. 992" (omitting the sheet number), her mention of Hasselquist makes it clear that she intends 992.6 rather than 992.7, and this choice is accepted here.

Baccharis foetida Linnaeus, *Species Plantarum* 2: 861. 1753.
"Habitat in Virginia." RCN: 6216.
Lectotype (Godfrey in *J. Elisha Mitchell Sci. Soc.* 68: 262. 1952): *Clayton 159* (BM).
Current name: ***Pluchea foetida*** (L.) DC. (Asteraceae).
Note: There are two Clayton sheets extant, "Clayton 159" and "Clayton 159/451" (both BM). The type designation does not distinguish between these sheets, but as they appear to be part of a single gathering, Art. 9.15 applies and the typification is effective. At some point, it may be desirable to restrict this choice to one or other sheet.

Baccharis halimifolia Linnaeus, *Species Plantarum* 2: 860. 1753, *typ. cons.*
"Habitat in Virginia." RCN: 6212.
Lectotype (Reveal in Jarvis & al., *Regnum Veg.* 127: 23. 1993): Herb. Linn. No. 992.4 (LINN).
Generitype of *Baccharis* Linnaeus, *nom. cons.*
Current name: ***Baccharis halimifolia*** L. (Asteraceae).

Baccharis indica Linnaeus, *Species Plantarum* 2: 861. 1753.
"Habitat in India. Braad." RCN: 6214.
Lectotype (Hunger in *Willdenowia* 27: 221. 1997): Herb. Linn. No. 992.8 (LINN).
Current name: ***Pluchea indica*** (L.) Less. (Asteraceae).

Baccharis ivifolia Linnaeus, *Species Plantarum* 2: 860. 1753.
"Habitat in Virginia, Peru." RCN: 6209.
Lectotype (Reveal in Jarvis & Turland in *Taxon* 47: 355. 1998): Herb. Clifford: 404, *Baccharis* 1 (BM-000647037).
Current name: ***Conyza ivifolia*** (L.) Less. (Asteraceae).
Note: Specific epithet spelled "ivaefolia" in the protologue.

Baccharis neriifolia Linnaeus, *Species Plantarum* 2: 860. 1753.
"Habitat in Aethiopia." RCN: 6210.
Lectotype (Cilliers in *Bothalia* 23: 176. 1993): Herb. Linn. No. 992.2 (LINN).
Current name: ***Brachylaena neriifolia*** (L.) R. Br. (Asteraceae).

Note: Although Phillips & Schweickerdt (in *Bothalia* 3: 209. 1937) noted that both the LINN and a Herb. Clifford sheet were sterile, they did not choose either as sole type.

Baccharis tenuifolia Linnaeus, *Species Plantarum* 2: 860. 1753.
"Habitat in Africa." RCN: 6090.
Replaced synonym of: *Chrysocoma scabra* L. (1763), *nom. illeg.*
Type not designated.
Original material: [icon] in Dillenius, Hort. Eltham. 1: 104, t. 88, f. 103. 1732.
Current name: ***Polyarrhena reflexa*** (L.) Cass. (Asteraceae).
Note: Stearn (in Blunt, *Compleat Naturalist*: 249. 1971) discussed the protologue but did not indicate a type.

Baeckea frutescens Linnaeus, *Species Plantarum* 1: 358. 1753.
"Habitat in China. D. D. Abrah. BAECK. S. R. M:tis." RCN: 2847.
Lectotype (Bean in *Telopea* 7: 248. 1997): *Osbeck s.n.*, Herb. Linn. No. 505.1 (LINN).
Generitype of *Baeckea* Linnaeus.
Current name: ***Baeckea frutescens*** L. (Myrtaceae).
Note: See comments on provenance of the type sheet by Hansen & Fox Maule (in *Bot. J. Linn. Soc.* 67: 205. 1973).

Ballota alba Linnaeus, *Flora Suecica*, ed. 2: 206. 1755.
"Habitat in Scania ad pagos." RCN: 4248.
Lectotype (Davis in *Notes Roy. Bot. Gard. Edinburgh* 21: 62. 1952): Herb. Linn. No. 737.2 (LINN).
Current name: ***Ballota nigra*** L. subsp. ***foetida*** (Vis.) Hayek (Lamiaceae).
Note: Ballota alba was erroneously listed as the generitype by Jarvis & al. (*Regnum Veg.* 127: 23. 1993).
See discussion by Patzek (in *Ann. Naturhist. Mus. Wien* 62: 57–58. 1958).

Ballota disticha Linnaeus, *Systema Naturae*, ed. 12, 2: 395; *Mantissa Plantarum*: 83. 1767.
"Habitat in India." RCN: 4252.
Lectotype (Cramer in Dassanayake & Fosberg, *Revised Handb. Fl. Ceylon* 3: 177. 1981): Herb. Linn. No. 737.7 (LINN).
Current name: ***Anisomeles indica*** (L.) Kuntze (Lamiaceae).

Ballota lanata Linnaeus, *Species Plantarum* 2: 582. 1753.
"Habitat in Sibiria." RCN: 4250.
Lectotype (Krestovskaja in *Novosti Sist. Vyssh. Rast.* 28: 143. 1991): Herb. Linn. No. 737.3 (LINN).
Current name: ***Panzerina lanata*** (L.) Soják (Lamiaceae).

Ballota nigra Linnaeus, *Species Plantarum* 2: 582. 1753.
"Habitat in Europae ruderatis." RCN: 4248.
Lectotype (Davis in *Notes Roy. Bot. Gard. Edinburgh* 21: 62. 1952): Herb. Linn. No. 737.1 (LINN).
Generitype of *Ballota* Linnaeus (vide Green, *Prop. Brit. Bot.*: 165. 1929).
Current name: ***Ballota nigra*** L. (Lamiaceae).
Note: Ballota alba was erroneously listed as the generitype by Jarvis & al. (*Regnum Veg.* 127: 23. 1993).
See discussion by Patzek (in *Ann. Naturhist. Mus. Wien* 62: 57–58. 1958).

Ballota suaveolens Linnaeus, *Systema Naturae*, ed. 10, 2: 1100. 1759.
["Habitat in America meridionali."] Sp. Pl. ed. 2, 2: 815 (1763). RCN: 4251.

Lectotype (Epling in *Revista Mus. La Plata, Secc. Bot.*, n.s., 7: 261. 1949): *Browne*, Herb. Linn. No. 737.6 (LINN).
Current name: ***Hyptis suaveolens*** (L.) Poit. (Lamiaceae).

Baltimora recta Linnaeus, *Mantissa Plantarum Altera*: 288. 1771, *typ. cons.*
"Habitat in Marilandia, ad urbem Baltimore. H. U." RCN: 6645.
Conserved type (Reveal & al. in *Taxon* 40: 337. 1991): Vera Cruz. *Houstoun* (BM-000576304).
Generitype of *Baltimora* Linnaeus, *nom. cons.*
Current name: ***Baltimora recta*** L. (Asteraceae).
Note: Reveal & al. (in *Taxon* 40: 336–338. 1991) proposed the conservation of *Baltimora* with a conserved type. The Committee for Spermatophyta (in *Taxon* 43: 116. 1994) initially ruled that the proposed type should be considered a neotype but subsequently (in *Taxon* 47: 863. 1998) recommended acceptance of the original proposal.

Banisteria angulosa Linnaeus, *Species Plantarum* 1: 427. 1753.
"Habitat in America calidiore." RCN: 3321.
Lectotype (Anderson in *Syst. Bot. Monogr.* 51: 122. 1997): [icon] *"Clematis anguloso folio, aceris fructu"* in Plumier, Descr. Pl. Amér.: 77, t. 92. 1693.
Current name: ***Stigmaphyllon angulosum*** (L.) A. Juss. (Malpighiaceae).

Banisteria benghalensis Linnaeus, *Species Plantarum* 1: 427. 1753.
"Habitat in Indiis." RCN: 3324.
Type not designated.
Original material: Herb. Hermann 2: 49, No. 176 (BM); [icon] in Plumier in Burman, Pl. Amer.: 8, t. 14. 1755; [icon] in Plukenet, Phytographia: t. 3, f. 1. 1691; Almag. Bot.: 7. 1696.
Current name: ***Hiptage benghalensis*** (L.) Kurtz (Malpighiaceae).
Note: Friedman (in Bosser & al., *Fl. Mascareignes* 58: 1. 1987) wrongly indicated 589.3 (LINN), a Browne collection received by Linnaeus in 1758, as the type, and Srivastava (in *Candollea* 47: 605. 1992) did the same for 589.1 (LINN), a König collection acquired long after 1753. Neither collection is original material for the name.

Banisteria brachiata Linnaeus, *Species Plantarum* 1: 428. 1753.
"Habitat in America." RCN: 3327.
Lectotype (Anderson in *Contr. Univ. Michigan Herb.* 19: 370. 1993): Herb. Clifford: 169, *Banisteria* 2 (BM-000628497).
Generitype of *Banisteria* Linnaeus, *nom. rej.* (vide Sprague in *Gard. Chron.* ser. 3, 75: 104. 1924).
Current name: ***Heteropterys brachiata*** (L.) DC. (Malpighiaceae).
Note: Banisteria Linnaeus, *nom. rej.* vs. *Heteropterys* Kunth 1822 (*nom. et orth. cons.*).

Banisteria dichotoma Linnaeus, *Species Plantarum* 1: 427. 1753.
"Habitat in America calidiore." RCN: 3325.
Lectotype (Anderson in Howard, *Fl. Lesser Antilles* 4: 625. 1988): Herb. Clifford: 169, *Banisteria* 3 (BM-000628498).
Current name: ***Stigmaphyllon dichotomum*** (L.) Griseb. (Malpighiaceae).

Banisteria fulgens Linnaeus, *Species Plantarum* 1: 427. 1753.
"Habitat in America." RCN: 3326.
Lectotype (Anderson in Howard, *Fl. Lesser Antilles* 4: 626. 1988): Herb. Clifford: 169, *Banisteria* 1 (BM-000628496).
Current name: ***Stigmaphyllon emarginatum*** (Cav.) A. Juss. (Malpighiaceae).

Banisteria laurifolia Linnaeus, *Species Plantarum*, ed. 2, 1: 611. 1762.
"Habitat in Jamaica." RCN: 3323.

Neotype (Fawcett & Rendle, *Fl. Jamaica* 4: 233. 1920): *Houstoun* ex Herb. Miller (BM).
Current name: ***Heteropterys laurifolia*** (L.) A. Juss. (Malpighiaceae).

Banisteria lupuloides Linnaeus, *Species Plantarum* 1: 427. 1753.
"Habitat in Barbados." RCN: 7647.
Replaced synonym of: *Gouania dominguensis* L., *nom. illeg.* (1763).
Type not designated.
Original material: [icon] in Plukenet, Phytographia: t. 201, f. 4. 1692; Almag. Bot.: 229. 1696 – Voucher: Herb. Sloane 96: 158 (BM-SL); [icon] in Plukenet, Phytographia: t. 162, f. 3. 1692; Almag. Bot.: 121. 1696 – Voucher: Herb. Sloane 95: 177 (BM-SL).
Current name: ***Gouania lupuloides*** (L.) Urb. (Rhamnaceae).

Banisteria purpurea Linnaeus, *Species Plantarum* 1: 427. 1753.
"Habitat in America meridionali." RCN: 3322.
Type not designated.
Original material: [icon] in Plumier in Burman, Pl. Amer.: 8, t. 15. 1755.
Current name: ***Heteropterys purpurea*** (L.) Kunth (Malpighiaceae).

Barleria buxifolia Linnaeus, *Species Plantarum* 2: 636. 1753.
"Habitat in Indiis." RCN: 4623.
Type not designated.
Original material: [icon] in Rheede, Hort. Malab. 2: 91, t. 47. 1679.
Current name: ***Barleria buxifolia*** L. (Acanthaceae).

Barleria coccinea Linnaeus, *Species Plantarum* 2: 637. 1753.
"Habitat in America meridionali." RCN: 4625.
Type not designated.
Original material: [icon] in Plumier in Burman, Pl. Amer.: 31, t. 43, f. 1. 1756.
Current name: ***Ruellia coccinea*** (L.) Vahl (Acanthaceae).

Barleria cristata Linnaeus, *Species Plantarum* 2: 636. 1753.
"Habitat in India." RCN: 4624.
Lectotype (Brummitt & Vollesen in *Taxon* 41: 558. 1992): Herb. Linn. No. 805.12 (LINN).
Generitype of *Barleria* Linnaeus.
Current name: ***Barleria cristata*** L. (Acanthaceae).
Note: Barleria cristata, with the type designated by Brummitt & Vollesen, was proposed as conserved type of the genus by Jarvis (in *Taxon* 41: 558. 1992). However, the proposal was eventually ruled unnecessary by the General Committee (see Barrie, *l.c.* 55: 795–796. 2006 for a review of the history of this and related proposals).
  Malik & Ghafoor (in Nasir & Ali, *Fl. Pakistan* 188: 50. 1988) wrongly indicated 805.4 (LINN), a post-1753 collection apparently associated with *B. hystrix* L., as type. It is not original material for *B. cristata*.

Barleria hystrix Linnaeus, *Systema Naturae*, ed. 12, 2: 425; *Mantissa Plantarum*: 89. 1767.
"Habitat in India. D. Dav. Royen." RCN: 4621.
Type not designated.
Original material: none traced.
Current name: ***Barleria prionitis*** L. (Acanthaceae).

Barleria longifolia Linnaeus, *Centuria II Plantarum*: 22. 1756.
"Habitat in India." RCN: 4619.
Type not designated.
Original material: [icon] in Plukenet, Phytographia: t. 133, f. 4. 1692; Almag. Bot.: 30. 1696.
Current name: ***Hygrophila schullii*** (Buch.-Ham.) M.R. Almeida & S.M. Almeida (Acanthaceae).

Barleria prionitis Linnaeus, *Species Plantarum* 2: 636. 1753.
"Habitat in India." RCN: 4622.
Lectotype (Wood & al. in *Kew Bull.* 38: 436. 1983): Herb. Linn. No.
    262.13 (S).
Current name: ***Barleria prionitis*** L. (Acanthaceae).

Barleria solanifolia Linnaeus, *Species Plantarum* 2: 636. 1753.
"Habitat in America australi." RCN: 4620.
Type not designated.
Original material: [icon] in Plumier in Burman, Pl. Amer.: 31, t. 43, f.
    2. 1756.
Current name: ***Barleriola solanifolia*** (L.) Oerst. (Acanthaceae).

Barreria capensis Linnaeus, *Species Plantarum* 1: 274. 1753.
"Habitat in Aethiopia." RCN: 2185.
Type not designated.
Original material: [icon] in Plukenet, Almag. Mant.: 69, t. 346, f. 7.
    1700 – Voucher: Herb. Sloane 92: 59 (BM-SL).
Generitype of *Barreria* Linnaeus.
Note: Neither the generic, nor the specific, name appears to have been
    taken up. The voucher specimen associated with the cited Plukenet
    illustration appears to be a member of the Bruniaceae. Both of these
    names may prove to be a threat to later well-established names.

Bartramia indica Linnaeus, *Species Plantarum* 1: 389. 1753.
"Habitat in India." RCN: 3451.
Replaced synonym of: *Triumfetta bartramii* L. (1759), *nom. illeg.*
Lectotype (Fawcett & Rendle, *Fl. Jamaica* 5: 82. 1926): Herb.
    Hermann 1: 44, No. 174 (BM-000621387).
Generitype of *Bartramia* Linnaeus, *nom. rej.*
Current name: ***Triumfetta rhomboidea*** Jacq. (Tiliaceae).
Note: Bartramia Linnaeus, *nom. rej.* vs. *Bartramia* Hedw. 1801 (*nom.
    cons.*).

Bartsia alpina Linnaeus, *Species Plantarum* 2: 602. 1753, *typ. cons.*
"Habitat in alpibus Lapponicis, Helveticis, Allobrogicis, Baldo,
    Vallicis." RCN: 4371.
Lectotype (Molau in *Opera Bot.* 102: 19. 1990): Herb. Burser XIV(1):
    36 (UPS).
Generitype of *Bartsia* Linnaeus, *nom. cons.*
Current name: ***Bartsia alpina*** L. (Scrophulariaceae).

Bartsia coccinea Linnaeus, *Species Plantarum* 2: 602. 1753.
"Habitat in Virginia, Noveboraco." RCN: 4368.
Lectotype (Pennell in *Torreya* 19: 236. 1920): *Clayton 293* (BM-
    000042242), see above, right.
Current name: ***Castilleja coccinea*** (L.) Spreng. (Scrophulariaceae).
Note: Reveal & al. (in *Huntia* 7: 229. 1987) provided detailed notes.

Bartsia pallida Linnaeus, *Species Plantarum* 2: 602. 1753.
"Habitat in Sibiria. D. Gmelin. Demidoff." RCN: 4369.
Type not designated.
Original material: Herb. Linn. No. 756.2 (LINN).
Current name: ***Castilleja pallida*** (L.) Spreng. (Scrophulariaceae).
Note: See discussion by Pennell (in *Proc. Acad. Nat. Sci. Philadelphia*
    86: 522. 1935) on the descriptions of Gmelin and Steller collections.
    He concluded that the typical form should apply to the former but
    did not associate the name with material in LINN (where he
    appeared to believe, incorrectly, that both collections existed).

Bartsia trixago Linnaeus, *Species Plantarum* 2: 602. 1753.
"Habitat in Italiae maritimis, humentibus." RCN: 4375.
Basionym of: *Rhinanthus trixago* (L.) L. (1759).
Lectotype (Molau in *Opera Bot.* 102: 27. 1990): Herb. Burser XIV(1):
    36 (UPS).

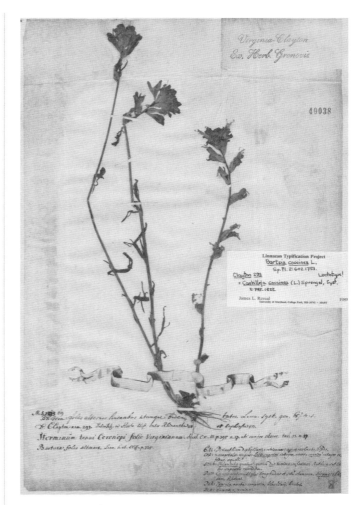

The lectotype of *Bartsia coccinea* L.

Current name: ***Bartsia trixago*** L. (Scrophulariaceae).
Note: Although Qaiser (in Jafri & El-Gadi, *Fl. Libya* 88: 40. 1982)
    indicated 758.3 (LINN) as type, it carries no annotation by
    Linnaeus to link it with this name, and also came from Eastern Asia
    which is at variance with the stated Italian provenance of the
    species. It is not original material for the name.

Bartsia viscosa Linnaeus, *Species Plantarum* 2: 602. 1753.
"Habitat in Angliae, Galliae, Italiae paludibus ad rivulos." RCN:
    4370.
Lectotype (Fischer in *Feddes Repert.* 108: 113. 1997): [icon]
    "*Euphrasia lutea latifolia palustris*" in Plukenet, Phytographia: t. 27,
    f. 5. 1691; Almag. Bot.: 142. 1696.
Current name: ***Parentucellia viscosa*** (L.) Caruel
    (Scrophulariaceae).

Basella alba Linnaeus, *Species Plantarum* 1: 272. 1753.
"Habitat in Syria?" RCN: 2171.
Neotype (Sidwell in *Novon* 9: 563. 1999): Nepal. Mahakali Zone:
    Kanchapur District, 15 miles W of Dhangarhi, 7 Dec 1966,
    Nicolson 2848 (BM; iso- US).
Current name: ***Basella alba*** L. (Basellaceae).
Note: Verdcourt (in Milne-Redhead & Polhill, *Fl. Trop. E. Africa,
    Basellaceae*: 2. 1968), followed by many other authors, treated a

Thran polynomial as the type but this is contrary to Art. 8.1. In the absence of any original material, Sidwell subsequently chose a neotype.

Basella lucida Linnaeus, *Systema Naturae,* ed. 10, 2: 966. 1759. ["Habitat in India."] Sp. Pl. 1: 391 (1753). RCN: 2172.
Neotype (Sidwell in *Novon* 9: 563. 1999): Taiwan. Taipeh, May 1909, *Faurie 109* (BM).
Current name: ***Basella alba*** L. (Basellaceae).

Basella rubra Linnaeus, *Species Plantarum* 1: 272. 1753.
"Habitat in India." RCN: 2170.
Lectotype (Verdcourt in Milne-Redhead & Polhill, *Fl. Trop. E. Africa, Basellaceae*: 2. 1968): Herb. Hermann 5: 207, No. 119 [icon] (BM).
Generitype of *Basella* Linnaeus (vide Hitchcock, *Prop. Brit. Bot.*: 143. 1929).
Current name: ***Basella alba*** L. (Basellaceae).

Bassia longifolia Linnaeus, *Mantissa Plantarum Altera*: 563. 1771.
"Habitat in Malabaria." RCN: 3428.
Lectotype (Pennington in Jarvis & al., *Regnum Veg.* 127: 23. 1993): Herb. Linn. No. 610.1 (LINN).
Generitype of *Bassia* Linnaeus (1771), *nom. illeg.*, non All. (1766).
Current name: ***Madhuca longifolia*** (L.) J.F. Macbr. (Sapotaceae).

Batis americana Linnaeus, *Mantissa Plantarum Altera*: 499. 1771, *nom. inval.*
RCN: 7400.
Type not relevant.
Note: Linnaeus supplied no description for the name, merely the query "Species an distincta a 'Bucephala' Plum?".

Batis maritima Linnaeus, *Systema Naturae,* ed. 10, 2: 1289. 1759. ["Habitat in Jamaica maritimis salsis."] Sp. Pl., ed. 2, 2: 1451 (1763). RCN: 7401.
Neotype (Monro in Cafferty & Monro in *Novon* 9: 490. 1999): Jamaica. Middlesex County, Clarendon Parish, near Tarentum farm, 10ft, 3 Jan 1960, *C.D. Adams 6063* (UCWI).
Generitype of *Batis* P. Browne (1756).
Current name: ***Batis maritima*** L. (Bataceae).

Bauhinia aculeata Linnaeus, *Species Plantarum* 1: 374. 1753.
"Habitat in America calidiore." RCN: 2948.
Lectotype (Stearn, *Introd. Linnaeus' Sp. Pl.* (Ray Soc. ed.): 47. 1957): [icon] *"Bauhinia caule aculeato"* in Linnaeus, Hort. Cliff.: 156, t. 14. 1738. – Voucher: Herb. Clifford: 156, *Bauhinia* 1 (BM).
Current name: ***Bauhinia aculeata*** L. (Fabaceae: Caesalpinioideae).
Note: This was treated as the generitype of *Bauhinia* by Britton & Wilson (*Bot. Porto Rico Virgin Is.* 5: 362. 1924) (see McNeill & al. in *Taxon* 36: 362. 1987). However, under Art. 10.5, Ex. 7 (a voted example) of the Vienna Code, this is a type choice made under the American Code and is to be replaced under Art. 10.5b by Hitchcock's choice (*Prop. Brit. Bot.*: 152. 1929) of *B. divaricata* L.
    Wunderlin (in *Ann. Missouri Bot. Gard.* 63: 47. 1976) indicated Clifford material as type but this choice is pre-dated by that of Stearn.

Bauhinia acuminata Linnaeus, *Species Plantarum* 1: 375. 1753.
"Habitat in Indiis." RCN: 2954.
Lectotype (de Wit in *Reinwardtia* 3: 397. 1956): Herb. Hermann 1: 42, No. 148 (BM-000621378).
Current name: ***Bauhinia acuminata*** L. (Fabaceae: Caesalpinioideae).

Bauhinia divaricata Linnaeus, *Species Plantarum* 1: 374. 1753.
"Habitat in America." RCN: 2949.

Lectotype (Stearn, *Introd. Linnaeus' Sp. Pl.* (Ray Soc. ed.): 47. 1957): [icon] *"Bauhinia foliis quinquenerviis : lobis acuminatis remotissimis"* in Linnaeus, Hort. Cliff.: 156, t. 15. 1738. – Voucher: Herb. Clifford: 156, *Bauhinia* 2 (BM).
Generitype of *Bauhinia* Linnaeus (vide Hitchcock, *Prop. Brit. Bot.*: 152. 1929).
Current name: ***Bauhinia divaricata*** L. (Fabaceae: Caesalpinioideae).
Note: Bauhinia aculeata was treated as the generitype of *Bauhinia* by Britton & Wilson (*Bot. Porto Rico Virgin Is.* 5: 362. 1924) (see McNeill & al. in *Taxon* 36: 362. 1987). However, under 10.5, Ex. 7 (a voted example) of the Vienna Code, this is a type choice made under the *American Code* and is to be replaced under Art. 10.5b by Hitchcock's choice (*Prop. Brit. Bot.*: 152. 1929) of *B. divaricata* L.

Bauhinia purpurea Linnaeus, *Species Plantarum* 1: 375. 1753.
"Habitat in Indiae arenosis." RCN: 2952.
Lectotype (Isely in *Mem. New York Bot. Gard.* 25(2): 189. 1975): [icon] *"Chovanna-mandaru"* in Rheede, Hort. Malab. 1: 59, t. 33. 1678.
Current name: ***Bauhinia purpurea*** L. (Fabaceae: Caesalpinioideae).
Note: De Wit (in *Reinwardtia* 3: 408. 1956) wrongly chose a neotype (original elements are in existence), and so Isely's appears to be the earliest formal type choice.

Bauhinia scandens Linnaeus, *Species Plantarum* 1: 374. 1753.
"Habitat in Malabaria." RCN: 2947.
Lectotype (de Wit in *Reinwardtia* 3: 391. 1956): [icon] *"Naga-valli vel Mandaru-valli"* in Rheede, Hort. Malab. 8: 55, t. 29. 1688.
Current name: ***Bauhinia scandens*** L. (Fabaceae: Caesalpinioideae).
Note: De Wit (in *Reinwardtia* 3: 391. 1956) indicated the cited Rheede plate as the sole basis for this name. Were this not to be accepted as a formal typification, Rudd (in Dassanayake & Fosberg, *Revised Handb. Fl. Ceylon* 7: 41. 1991) explicitly indicated the plate as the type.

Bauhinia tomentosa Linnaeus, *Species Plantarum* 1: 375. 1753.
"Habitat in India." RCN: 2953.
Lectotype (Roti-Michelozzi in *Webbia* 13: 153. 1957): [icon] *"Bauhinia foliis subrotundis, flore flavescente striato"* in Burman, Thes. Zeylan.: 44, t. 18*. 1737. – Typotype: Herb. Burman (G).
Current name: ***Bauhinia tomentosa*** L. (Fabaceae: Caesalpinioideae).
Note: De Wit (in *Reinwardtia* 3: 411. 1956) wrongly chose a neotype (original elements are in existence), and so Roti-Michelozzi's choice of a Burman plate appears to be the earliest. Although other authors (e.g. Isely in *Mem. New York Bot. Gard.* 25(2): 190. 1975; Rudd in Dassanayake & Fosberg, *Revised Handb. Fl. Ceylon* 7: 38. 1991) reached different type solutions, that of Roti-Michelozzi has priority.

Bauhinia ungulata Linnaeus, *Species Plantarum* 1: 374. 1753.
"Habitat in America." RCN: 2950.
Lectotype (Wunderlin in Turland & Jarvis in *Taxon* 46: 466. 1997): Herb. Clifford: 157, *Bauhinia* 3 (BM-000558715).
Current name: ***Bauhinia ungulata*** L. (Fabaceae: Caesalpinioideae).
Note: Wunderlin (in *Ann. Missouri Bot. Gard.* 63: 349. 1976; 70: 124. 1983) indicated an unseen Miller specimen at BM as the lectotype, but this cannot be regarded as original material because Linnaeus did not study these specimens.

Bauhinia variegata Linnaeus, *Species Plantarum* 1: 375. 1753.
"Habitat in Malabariae, Maderae arenosis." RCN: 2951.
Lectotype (Isely in *Mem. New York Bot. Gard.* 25(2): 191. 1975): [icon] *"Chovanna-mandaru"* in Rheede, Hort. Malab. 1: 57, t. 32. 1678.
Current name: ***Bauhinia variegata*** L. (Fabaceae: Caesalpinioideae).

Note: De Wit (in *Reinwardtia* 3: 412. 1956) rejected 535.2 (LINN) as a possible lectotype, but then wrongly chose a neotype (original material was still in existence). Isely rejected de Wit's neotype in favour of the cited Rheede illustration, which is the lectotype.

Befaria aestuans Linnaeus, *Mantissa Plantarum Altera*: 152, 242. 1771, *typ. cons.*
"Habitat in Mexico." RCN: 3438.
Conserved type (Clemants in *Taxon* 43: 473. 1994): Colombia. Santander: road above Río Chicamocha, 60km NNE of Barbosa, 1,700m, 9 May 1979 (fl.), *Luteyn & al. 7616* (NY; iso- COL).
Generitype of *Bejaria* Linnaeus, *orth. cons.*
Current name: ***Bejaria aestuans*** L. (Ericaceae).
Note: Presumably through a misreading of Mútis' handwriting, Linnaeus consistently spelled the name "Befaria". This has been corrected to "Bejaria" through conservation.

Begonia obliqua Linnaeus, *Species Plantarum* 2: 1056. 1753.
"Habitat in America meridionali." RCN: 7205.
Lectotype (Golding in *Phytologia* 45: 245, f. 2. 1980): [icon] *"Begonia nivea maxima, folio aurito"* in Plumier, Codex Boerhaavianus: plate 124. (University Library, Groningen).
Generitype of *Begonia* Linnaeus.
Current name: ***Begonia obliqua*** L. (Begoniaceae).

Bejaria aestuans Linnaeus, *Mantissa Plantarum Altera*: 152, 242. 1771, *typ. cons.*
"Habitat in Mexico." RCN: 3438.
Conserved type (Clemants in *Taxon* 43: 473. 1994): Colombia. Santander: road above Río Chicamocha, 60km NNE of Barbosa, 1,700m, 9 May 1979 (fl.), *Luteyn & al. 7616* (NY; iso- COL).
Generitype of *Bejaria* Linnaeus, *orth. cons.*
Current name: ***Bejaria aestuans*** L. (Ericaceae).
Note: See notes under *Befaria aestuans* L.

Bellis annua Linnaeus, *Species Plantarum* 2: 887. 1753.
"Habitat in Sicilia, Hispania, Monspelii." RCN: 6414.
Lectotype (Alavi in Jafri & El-Gadi, *Fl. Libya* 107: 22. 1983): Herb. Linn. No. 1006.3 (LINN).
Current name: ***Bellis annua*** L. (Asteraceae).

Bellis perennis Linnaeus, *Species Plantarum* 2: 886. 1753.
"Habitat in Europae apricis pascuis." RCN: 6413.
Type not designated.
Original material: Herb. Linn. No. 1006.2 (LINN); Herb. Clifford: 418, *Bellis* 1, 2 sheets (BM); Herb. Burser XIV(2): 69 (UPS); [icon] in Dodoëns, Stirp. Hist. Pempt., ed. 2: 265. 1616.
Generitype of *Bellis* Linnaeus (vide Green, *Prop. Brit. Bot.*: 182. 1929).
Current name: ***Bellis perennis*** L. (Asteraceae).

Bellis perennis Linnaeus var. **hortensis** Linnaeus, *Species Plantarum* 2: 886. 1753.
RCN: 6413.
Type not designated.
Original material: Herb. Linn. No. 1006.1 (LINN); Herb. Burser XIV(2): 71 (UPS).
Current name: ***Bellis perennis*** L. (Asteraceae).

Bellium bellidioides Linnaeus, *Mantissa Plantarum Altera* 2: 285. 1771.
"Habitat in Italiae: Romae aridis, ilim cultis; primo vere. H. U." RCN: 6415.
Lectotype (Greuter in Jarvis & al., *Regnum Veg.* 127: 24. 1993): Herb. Linn. No. 1007.1 (LINN).

Generitype of *Bellium* Linnaeus (vide Greuter in Jarvis & al., *Regnum Veg.* 127: 24. 1993).
Current name: ***Bellium bellidioides*** L. (Asteraceae).

Bellium minutum (Linnaeus) Linnaeus, *Mantissa Plantarum Altera*: 286. 1771.
"Habitat ad orientes fontes." RCN: 6416.
Basionym: *Pectis minuta* L. (1763).
Lectotype (Turland in Jarvis & Turland in *Taxon* 47: 365. 1998): Herb. Linn. No. 1007.2 (LINN).
Current name: ***Bellium minutum*** (L.) L. (Asteraceae).

Bellonia aspera Linnaeus, *Species Plantarum* 1: 172. 1753.
"Habitat in America." RCN: 1356.
Lectotype (Lourteig in *Phytologia* 54: 156. 1983): [icon] *"Bellonia"* in Plumier in Burman, Pl. Amer.: 35, t. 47. 1756.
Generitype of *Bellonia* Linnaeus.
Current name: ***Bellonia aspera*** L. (Gesneriaceae).

Berberis cretica Linnaeus, *Species Plantarum* 1: 331. 1753.
"Habitat in Creta." RCN: 2556.
Lectotype (Turland in *Bull. Nat. Hist. Mus. London, Bot.* 25: 131, f. 5. 1995): [icon] *"Lycium Creticum"* in Alpino, Pl. Exot.: 21, 20. 1627. – Epitype (Turland in *Bull. Nat. Hist. Mus. London, Bot.* 25: 131, f. 6. 1995): *Rechinger 14293* (BM; iso- K, W?).
Current name: ***Berberis cretica*** L. (Berberidaceae).

Berberis vulgaris Linnaeus, *Species Plantarum* 1: 330. 1753.
"Habitat in Europae sylvis." RCN: 2555.
Lectotype (Browicz & Zieliński in Rechinger, *Fl. Iranica* 111: 14. 1975): Herb. Clifford: 122, *Berberis* 1 β (BM-000558505).
Generitype of *Berberis* Linnaeus (vide Hitchcock, *Prop. Brit. Bot.*: 147. 1929).
Current name: ***Berberis vulgaris*** L. (Berberidaceae).

Bergera koenigii Linnaeus, *Mantissa Plantarum Altera*: 563. 1771.
"Habitat in India orientali." RCN: 3023.
Lectotype (Tanaka in *Meded. Rijks-Herb.* 69: 7. 1931; Coode in Bosser & al., *Fl. Mascareignes* 65: 25. 1979): *König s.n.*, Herb. Linn. No. 548.1 (LINN).
Generitype of *Bergera* Linnaeus, *nom. rej.*
Current name: ***Bergera koenigii*** L. (Rutaceae).
Note: Bergera Linnaeus, *nom. rej.* in favour of *Murraya* Linnaeus. Tanaka (in *Meded. Rijks-Herb.* 69: 7. 1931) indicated König material at LINN as type but did not distinguish between sheets 548.1 and 548.2. As these appear to be part of a single gathering (Art. 9.15), typification is attributed to Tanaka, with Coode subsequently restricting the choice to 548.1 (LINN).

Bergia capensis Linnaeus, *Mantissa Plantarum Altera*: 241. 1771.
"Habitat ad Cap. b. spei." RCN: 3365.
Lectotype (Verdcourt in Milne-Redhead & Polhill, *Fl. Trop. E. Africa, Elatinaceae*: 3. 1968): Herb. Linn. No. 597.1 (LINN).
Generitype of *Bergia* Linnaeus.
Current name: ***Bergia capensis*** L. (Elatinaceae).

Besleria cristata Linnaeus, *Species Plantarum* 2: 619. 1753.
"Habitat in America." RCN: 4478.
Lectotype (Leeuwenberg in *Acta Bot. Neerl.* 7: 301. 1958): [icon] *"Besleria pedunculis simplicibus solitariis"* in Plumier in Burman, Pl. Amer.: 37, t. 50. 1756.
Current name: ***Alloplectus cristatus*** (L.) Mart. (Gesneriaceae).

Besleria lutea Linnaeus, *Species Plantarum* 2: 619. 1753.
"Habitat in America." RCN: 4477.

Lectotype (Leeuwenberg in *Acta Bot. Neerl.* 7: 361. 1958): [icon]
"*Besleria pedunculis simplicibus confertis*" in Plumier in Burman, Pl.
Amer.: 36, t. 49, f. 1. 1756.
Generitype of *Besleria* Linnaeus (vide Martius, *Nova Gen. Sp.* 3: 43.
Jan–Jun 1829).
Current name: ***Besleria lutea*** L. (Gesneriaceae).

Besleria melittifolia Linnaeus, *Species Plantarum* 2: 619. 1753.
"Habitat in America." RCN: 4476.
Lectotype (Leeuwenberg in *Acta Bot. Neerl.* 7: 301. 1958): [icon]
"*Besleria pedunculis ramosis*" in Plumier in Burman, Pl. Amer.: 36, t.
48. 1756.
Current name: ***Episcia melittifolia*** (L.) Mart. (Gesneriaceae).

Beta cicla (Linnaeus) Linnaeus, *Systema Naturae*, ed. 12, 2: 195. 1767.
RCN: 1817.
Basionym: *Beta vulgaris* L. var. *cicla* L. (1753).
Lectotype (Letschert in *Wageningen Agric. Univ. Pap.* 93–1: 26, photo
1.2. 1993): Herb. Clifford: 83, *Beta* 1 β (BM-000558195).
Current name: ***Beta vulgaris*** L. subsp. ***vulgaris*** (Chenopodiaceae).

Beta maritima Linnaeus, *Species Plantarum*, ed. 2, 1: 322. 1762.
"Habitat in Angliae, Belgii littoribus maris." RCN: 1818.
Neotype (Letschert in *Wageningen Agric. Univ. Pap.* 93–1: 28, photo
1.3. 1993): Belgium. Nieuwpoort. *Letschert & Fey 137* (WAG).
Current name: ***Beta vulgaris*** L. subsp. ***maritima*** (L.) Arcang.
(Chenopodiaceae).
Note: Hedge (in Rechinger, *Fl. Iranica* 172: 21. 1997) subsequently
indicated 314.3 (LINN) as type, a specimen rejected from
consideration by Letschert on the grounds that it came from
"Aegypto", conflicting with Linnaeus' "…Angliae, Belgii…".

Beta vulgaris Linnaeus, *Species Plantarum* 1: 222. 1753.
"Habitat in Angliae & Belgii littoribus maris." RCN: 1816.
Lectotype (Letschert in *Wageningen Agric. Univ. Pap.* 93–1: 27, photo
1.1. 1993): Herb. A. van Royen No. 889.213–556 (L).
Generitype of *Beta* Linnaeus.
Current name: ***Beta vulgaris*** L. subsp. ***vulgaris*** (Chenopodiaceae).
Note: Larsen (in Morat, *Fl. Cambodge Laos Viêtnam* 24: 91. 1989)
wrongly indicated 314.3 (LINN) as type. It lacks a *Species
Plantarum* number (i.e. "1") and was a post-1753 addition to the
herbarium, and is not original material for the name.

Beta vulgaris Linnaeus var. **cicla** Linnaeus, *Species Plantarum* 1: 222.
1753.
RCN: 1817.
Basionym of: *Beta cicla* (L.) L. (1767).
Lectotype (Letschert in *Wageningen Agric. Univ. Pap.* 93–1: 26, photo
1.2. 1993): Herb. Clifford: 83, *Beta* 1 β (BM-000558195).
Current name: ***Beta vulgaris*** L. subsp. ***vulgaris*** (Chenopodiaceae).

Beta vulgaris Linnaeus var. **perennis** Linnaeus, *Species Plantarum* 1:
222. 1753.
RCN: 1818.
Neotype (Letschert in *Wageningen Agric. Univ. Pap.* 93–1: 28. 1993):
Letschert & Fey 137 (WAG).
Current name: ***Beta vulgaris*** L. subsp. ***maritima*** (L.) Arcang.
(Chenopodiaceae).

Beta vulgaris Linnaeus var. **rubra** Linnaeus, *Species Plantarum* 1: 222.
1753.
RCN: 1816.
Neotype (Letschert in *Wageningen Agric. Univ. Pap.* 93–1: 27, f. 1, 2.
1993): [icon] "*Beta nigra*" in Fuchs, Hist. Stirp.: 804, 806. 1542.
Current name: ***Beta vulgaris*** L. subsp. ***vulgaris*** (Chenopodiaceae).

Betonica alopecuros Linnaeus, *Species Plantarum* 2: 573. 1753.
"Habitat in montibus Sabaudicis, Austriae superioris, Lessanensibus,
Italicis, Galloprovinciae." RCN: 4230.
Lectotype (Hedge in Jarvis & al. in *Taxon* 50: 510. 2001): Herb.
Burser XIII: 119 (UPS).
Current name: ***Stachys alopecuros*** (L.) Benth. (Lamiaceae).
Note: In the protologue, Linnaeus cited "Burs. XIII: 119", an explicit
reference to material in the herbarium of Joachim Burser (UPS),
making it the only syntype and Art. 9.10 states that if syntypes
exist, a lectotype must be chosen from among them. Hedge
therefore designated this material "In montibus GalloProvinciae" as
the lectotype. Hedge noted that the type material belongs to the
western European form sometimes recognised as subsp. *godronii*
(Rouy) Merxm.

Betonica annua Linnaeus, *Species Plantarum* 2: 573. 1753.
"Habitat ad agrorum margines Helvetiae, Germaniae, Galliae." RCN:
4246.
Basionym of: *Stachys annua* (L.) L. (1763).
Lectotype (Nelson in Jarvis & al. in *Taxon* 50: 510. 2001): Herb.
Clifford: 310, *Stachys* 7, sheet A "annua" (BM-000646054).
Current name: ***Stachys annua*** (L.) L. (Lamiaceae).

Betonica annua Linnaeus var. **glabra** Linnaeus, *Species Plantarum* 2:
573. 1753.
RCN: 4246.
Lectotype (Nelson in Jarvis & al. in *Taxon* 50: 510. 2001): Herb.
Burser XIII: 64, right specimen (UPS).
Current name: ***Stachys annua*** (L.) L. (Lamiaceae).

Betonica annua Linnaeus var. **hirsuta** Linnaeus, *Species Plantarum* 2:
574. 1753.
RCN: 4245.
Type not designated.
Original material: Herb. Burser XIII: 61 (UPS); [icon] in Clusius, Rar.
Pl. Hist. 2: 39. 1601.
Current name: ***Stachys annua*** (L.) L. (Lamiaceae).

Betonica heraclea Linnaeus, *Systema Naturae*, ed. 12, 2: 394;
Mantissa Plantarum: 83. 1767.
"Habitat in Oriente." RCN: 4232.
Lectotype (Codd in Leistner, *Fl. Southern Africa* 28(4): 76. 1985):
Herb. Linn. No. 735.7 (LINN).
Current name: ***Stachys aurea*** Benth. (Lamiaceae).
Note: Codd noted that the epithet 'heraclea' is not available in *Stachys*
because it is pre-occupied by *S. heraclea* Col. ex All. (1785).

Betonica hirsuta Linnaeus, *Mantissa Plantarum Altera*: 248.
1771.
"Habitat in Apenninis. D. Bassi hanc rescuscitavit." RCN: 4231.
Neotype (Cristofolini in Jarvis & al. in *Taxon* 50: 510. 2001): Italy.
Apennines. "Betonica foliis hirsutis floribus purpureis amplissimis /
Monti in Zan:46 / Betonica alpina incana purpurea /
Barrel:Ico:340:" *F. Bassi* (BOLO).
Current name: ***Stachys pradica*** (Zanted.) Greuter & Pignatti
(Lamiaceae).
Note: Linnaeus provided a new diagnosis, cited a Mentzel polynomial
in synonymy, and gave an extensive description. He added "Habitat
in Apenninis. D. Bassi hanc rescuscitavit". Herb. Linn. 735.6
(LINN), material from Allioni, is unannotated as to identity by
Linnaeus, although Smith subsequently determined it (*in sched.*) as
B. hirsuta. It is not accepted as original material for the name and,
in the absence of any original elements, material from Fernandino
Bassi's collection (BOLO) was designated as a neotype by
Cristofolini.

The epithet "hirsuta" is not available in *Stachys* because it is pre-occupied by *S. hirsuta* Kunth (1817). The current name was given as *S. monieri* (Gouan) P.W. Ball by Heywood (in *Bot. J. Linn. Soc.* 65: 356. 1972). However, Greuter & Pignatti (in *Giorn. Bot. Ital.* 113: 360–361. 1979) argued that *Betonica monieri* Gouan is a synonym of *Stachys officinalis* (L.) Trevis., not of *B. hirsuta*, based on a study by Lacaita (in *Nuovo Giorn. Bot. Ital.*, n.s., 28: 118–124. 1921). Greuter & Pignatti argued that *B. pradica* Zanted. is the next available name for the latter, and made the necessary combination.

Betonica hirta Linnaeus, *Centuria II Plantarum*: 20. 1756.
"Habitat Monspelii."
Type not designated.
Original material: Herb. Linn. No. 735.5? (LINN); [icon] in Clusius, Rar. Pl. Hist. 2: 39, 40. 1601.
Current name: ***Stachys recta*** L. (Lamiaceae).
Note: As noted by Nordenstam (in *Bot. Not.* 114: 278. 1961), this name is absent from the later edition of this thesis (in *Amoen. Acad.* 4. 1759). *Betonica hirta* L. (1759) evidently relates to a different taxon and is treated as an illegitimate name.

Betonica hirta Linnaeus, *Systema Naturae*, ed. 10, 2: 1097. 1759, *nom. illeg.*
RCN: 4245.
Type not designated.
Original material: none traced.
Current name: ***Stachys* sp.** (Lamiaceae).
Note: Betonica hirta L. (1759) evidently relates to a different taxon from *B. hirta* L. (1756) and is therefore an illegitimate homonym. The application of the name is uncertain.

Betonica officinalis Linnaeus, *Species Plantarum* 2: 573. 1753.
"Habitat in Europa." RCN: 4228.
Lectotype (Press in Jarvis & al., *Regnum Veg.* 127: 24. 1993): Herb. Clifford: 310, *Betonica* 1, sheet 2 (BM-000646062).
Generitype of *Betonica* Linnaeus (vide Green, *Prop. Brit. Bot.*: 164. 1929).
Current name: ***Betonica officinalis*** L. (Lamiaceae).
Note: See Britton & Brown (in *Ill. Fl. N. U. S.* ed. 2. 3: 129. 1913) for a discussion on the generitype.

Betonica orientalis Linnaeus, *Species Plantarum* 2: 573. 1753.
"Habitat in Oriente." RCN: 4229.
Neotype (Hedge in Jarvis & al. in *Taxon* 50: 511. 2001): Turkey. Gümüsane, Erzincan to Kelkit, 1 Aug 1957, *Davis 31895* (E; iso-BM).
Current name: ***Stachys macrostachys*** (Wender.) Briq. (Lamiaceae).
Note: The epithet "orientalis" is not available in *Stachys* because the combination is pre-occupied by *S. orientalis* L. (1753). The current name is based on *Betonica macrostachys* Wender. (1826).

Betula alba Linnaeus, *Species Plantarum* 2: 982. 1753, *nom. rej.*
"Habitat in Europa frigidiore." RCN: 7120.
Lectotype (Holub in *Folia Geobot. Phytotax.* 24: 410. 1989): Herb. Linn. No. 1109.1 (LINN).
Generitype of *Betula* Linnaeus (vide Green, *Prop. Brit. Bot.*: 188. 1929).
Current name: ***Betula pubescens*** Ehrh. (Betulaceae).

Betula alnus Linnaeus, *Species Plantarum* 2: 983. 1753.
"Habitat in Europa." RCN: 7125.
Type not designated.
Original material: Herb. Linn. No. 1109.14? (LINN).
Current name: ***Alnus glutinosa*** (L.) Gaertn. (Betulaceae).

Betula alnus Linnaeus var. **glutinosa** Linnaeus, *Species Plantarum* 2: 983. 1753.
"Habitat in Europa." RCN: 7125.
Basionym of: *Betula glutinosa* (L.) L. (1759).
Lectotype (Jonsell & Jarvis in *Nordic J. Bot.* 14: 152. 1994): Herb. Burser XXIII: 8 (UPS).
Current name: ***Alnus glutinosa*** (L.) Gaertn. (Betulaceae).

Betula alnus Linnaeus var. **incana** Linnaeus, *Species Plantarum* 2: 983. 1753.
"Habitat in Europa." RCN: 7125.
Lectotype (Jonsell & Jarvis in *Nordic J. Bot.* 14: 153. 1994): Herb. Burser XXIII: 9 (UPS).
Current name: ***Alnus incana*** (L.) Moench (Betulaceae).

Betula glutinosa (Linnaeus) Linnaeus, *Systema Naturae*, ed. 10, 2: 1265. 1759.
["Habitat in Europa."] Sp. Pl. 2: 983 (1753). RCN: 7125.
Basionym: *Betula alnus* L. var. *glutinosa* L. (1753).
Lectotype (Jonsell & Jarvis in *Nordic J. Bot.* 14: 152. 1994): Herb. Burser XXIII: 8 (UPS).
Current name: ***Alnus glutinosa*** (L.) Gaertn. (Betulaceae).

Betula lenta Linnaeus, *Species Plantarum* 2: 983. 1753.
"Habitat in Virginia, Canada." RCN: 7122.
Lectotype (designated here by Reveal): Herb. Linn. No. 1109.8 (LINN).
Current name: ***Betula lenta*** L. (Betulaceae).

Betula nana Linnaeus, *Species Plantarum* 2: 983. 1753.
"Habitat in Alpibus Lapponicis; paludibus Sueciae; Russiae." RCN: 7123.
Lectotype (Jonsell & Jarvis in *Nordic J. Bot.* 14: 153. 1994): Herb. Linn. No. 1109.9 (LINN).
Current name: ***Betula nana*** L. (Betulaceae).

Betula nigra Linnaeus, *Species Plantarum* 2: 982. 1753.
"Habitat in Virginia, Canada." RCN: 7121.
Lectotype (designated here by Reveal): Herb. Linn. No. 1109.7 (LINN).
Current name: ***Betula nigra*** L. (Betulaceae).

Betula pumila Linnaeus, *Systema Naturae*, ed. 12, 2: 621; *Mantissa Plantarum*: 124. 1767.
"Habitat in America septentrionali." RCN: 7124.
Lectotype (designated here by Reveal): Herb. Linn. No. 1109.11 (LINN).
Current name: ***Betula pumila*** L. (Betulaceae).

Bidens apiifolia Linnaeus, *Systema Naturae*, ed. 10, 2: 1203. 1759.
["Habitat in America meridionali."] Sp. Pl. ed. 2, 2: 1273 (1763). RCN: 6487.
Type not designated.
Original material: [icon] in Sloane, Voy. Jamaica 1: 263, t. 155, f. 3. 1707.
Current name: ***Chrysanthellum americanum*** (L.) Vatke (Asteraceae).

Bidens atriplicifolia Linnaeus, *Centuria II Plantarum*: 30. 1756.
"Habitat in America meridionali. Miller." RCN: 6014.
Basionym of: *Spilanthes atriplicifolius* (L.) L. (1768).
Lectotype (Keil & Stuessy in *Syst. Bot.* 6: 269. 1981): *Miller*, Herb. Linn. No. 974.4 (LINN).
Current name: ***Isocarpha atriplicifolia*** (L.) DC. (Asteraceae).

Bidens bipinnata Linnaeus, *Species Plantarum* 2: 832. 1753.
"Habitat in Virginia." RCN: 6024.
Lectotype (Mesfin Tadesse in *Kew Bull.* 48: 499. 1993): Herb. Linn. No. 975.12 (LINN).
Current name: ***Bidens bipinnata*** L. (Asteraceae).
Note: Sherff (in *Publ. Field Mus. Nat. Hist., Bot. Ser.* 16: 367. 1937) noted the existence of 975.12 (LINN) but did not typify the name.

Bidens bullata Linnaeus, *Species Plantarum* 2: 833. 1753.
"Habitat in America." RCN: 6028.
Neotype (Jeanmonod in Gamisans & Jeanmonod, *Compl. Prodr. Fl. Corse, Asteraceae I*: 172. 1998): Herb. Linn. No. 975.15 (LINN).
Current name: ***Bidens tripartita*** L. subsp. ***bullata*** (L.) Rouy (Asteraceae).
Note: Sherff (in *Publ. Field Mus. Nat. Hist., Bot. Ser.* 16: 286. 1937) noted the existence of 975.15 (LINN) and concluded that Linnaeus "drew his description either from this specimen or from another identical with it", and that it was a European, not an American, plant. In fact, this collection reached Linnaeus from David van Royen long after 1753, and could not have been the basis for the name.

Bidens cernua Linnaeus, *Species Plantarum* 2: 832. 1753.
"Habitat in Europa ad fontes & fossas." RCN: 6021.
Lectotype (Mesfin Tadesse in Jarvis & Turland in *Taxon* 47: 355. 1998): Herb. Linn. No. 975.5 (LINN).
Current name: ***Bidens cernua*** L. (Asteraceae).
Note: Sherff (in *Publ. Field Mus. Nat. Hist., Bot. Ser.* 16: 302. 1937) stated "Type specimen: A good specimen exists in the Linnean Herbarium [presumably Herb. Linn. 975.5 LINN] but the name *Bidens cernua* traces back by synonymy directly to Caesalpinus 16: 488, cap. XVII". However, the Caesalpinus plate is not cited in the synonymy of Linnaeus' name and is ineligible as type.

Bidens frondosa Linnaeus, *Species Plantarum* 2: 832. 1753.
"Habitat in America septentrionali." RCN: 6022.
Lectotype (Jeanmonod in Gamisans & Jeanmonod, *Compl. Prodr. Fl. Corse, Asteraceae I*: 166. 1998): Herb. Linn. No. 975.6 (LINN).
Current name: ***Bidens frondosa*** L. (Asteraceae).
Note: Greene (in *Pittonia* 4: 246–250. 1901) discussed the pre-Linnaean literature at length, and Sherff (in *Bot. Gaz.* 61: 498. 1916; *Publ. Field Mus. Nat. Hist., Bot. Ser.* 16: 241. 1937) noted 975.6, 975.7 (LINN) and a Clifford sheet (BM), concluding that Linnaeus "clearly had the first or the third specimen, and probably both, in mind when he drew up his description of *B. frondosa* for the *Species Plantarum*". However, Jeanmonod appears to have been the first to designate one of the collections as the type.

Bidens fruticosa Linnaeus, *Species Plantarum* 2: 833. 1753.
"Habitat in America." RCN: 6526.
Basionym of: *Verbesina fruticosa* (L.) L. (1759).
Lectotype (D'Arcy in Woodson & Schery in *Ann. Missouri Bot. Gard.* 62: 1110. 1975): Herb. Clifford: 399, *Bidens* 3 (BM-000646989).
Current name: ***Lasianthaea fruticosa*** (L.) K.M. Becker (Asteraceae).
Note: Blake (in *J. Bot.* 53: 13–14. 1915) discussed the *Hortus Cliffortianus* account and specimen, concluding that *B. fruticosa* was "based on" these two elements. D'Arcy appears to have been the first to explicitly treat the Clifford material as the type.

Bidens nivea Linnaeus, *Species Plantarum* 2: 833. 1753.
"Habitat in Carolina." RCN: 6025.
Lectotype (Parks in *Rhodora* 75: 184. 1973): [icon] *"Bidens scabra flore niveo, folio trilobato"* in Dillenius, Hort. Eltham. 1: 55, t. 47, f. 55. 1732.
Current name: ***Melanthera nivea*** (L.) Small (Asteraceae).

Note: Reveal & al. (in *Bartonia* 56: 19. 1990) have argued that only part of the Dillenius illustration designated as the lectotype by Parks was cited under the supposedly "typical" part of Linnaeus' protologue, arguing for restriction of the type to a single leaf. However, this seems unhelpful and recent authors such as Strother (in Daniel, *Fl. Chiapas* 5: 73. 1999) and Wagner & Robinson (in *Brittonia* 53: 557. 2002) follow Parks.

Bidens nodiflora Linnaeus, *Species Plantarum* 2: 832. 1753.
"Habitat in Benghala." RCN: 6019.
Lectotype (Sherff in *Publ. Field Mus. Nat. Hist., Bot. Ser.* 16: 276. 1937): [icon] *"Bidens nodiflora, Brunellae folio"* in Dillenius, Hort. Eltham. 1: 52, t. 44, f. 52. 1732.
Current name: ***Bidens tripartita*** L. (Asteraceae).
Note: Sherff (in *Bot. Gaz.* 61: 498. 1916) noted material in LINN (evidently sheet 975.3) and the Dillenius plate but did not indicate a type.

Bidens pilosa Linnaeus, *Species Plantarum* 2: 832. 1753.
"Habitat in America." RCN: 6023.
Lectotype (D'Arcy in Woodson & Schery in *Ann. Missouri Bot. Gard.* 62: 1178. 1975): Herb. Linn. No. 975.8 (LINN).
Current name: ***Bidens pilosa*** L. (Asteraceae).
Note: Sherff (in *Publ. Field Mus. Nat. Hist., Bot. Ser.* 16: 414–415. 1937) discussed the original elements for the name but did not designate any one of them as the type. D'Arcy appears to have been the first to make a formal choice of 975.8 (LINN) as type, and this has been followed by many recent authors.

Bidens pilosa Linnaeus var. **chinensis** Linnaeus, *Mantissa Plantarum Altera*: 281. 1771.
"Habitat in India orientali. H. U." RCN: 6023.
Lectotype (Veldkamp & Kreffer in *Blumea* 35: 481. 1991): Herb. Linn. No. 975.10 (LINN).
Current name: ***Bidens pilosa*** L. (Asteraceae).
Note: Sherff (in *Publ. Field Mus. Nat. Hist., Bot. Ser.* 16: 428–429. 1937) regarded Linnaeus' concept as so uncertain that he did not adopt the name.

Bidens scandens Linnaeus, *Species Plantarum* 2: 833. 1753.
"Habitat in Vera Cruce." RCN: 6027.
Lectotype (Blake in *J. Bot.* 53: 197. 1915; Moore in Fawcett & Rendle, *Fl. Jamaica* 7: 241. 1936): Herb. Clifford: 399, *Bidens* 5 (BM-000646991).
Current name: ***Salmea scandens*** (L.) DC. (Asteraceae).
Note: Blake (in *J. Bot.* 53: 197. 1915) referred to Houstoun material from Vera Cruz "in hb. Brit. Mus." as "Linnaeus's types". There is a sheet of wild-collected material from Houstoun annotated by Blake, as well as material in the Clifford herbarium also identified as having originated with Houstoun. Although the latter may have been cultivated, Blake is accepted as having typified the name, with Moore having restricted the choice to the Clifford material.

Bidens tenella Linnaeus, *Plantae Rariores Africanae*: 17. 1760.
["Habitat ad Cap. b. Spei."] Sp. Pl., ed. 2, 2: 1166 (1763). RCN: 6020.
Type not designated.
Original material: Herb. Linn. No. 975.4 (LINN).
Note: The application of this name is uncertain. Sherff (in *Bot. Gaz.* 59: 311. 1915; *Publ. Field Mus. Nat. Hist., Bot. Ser.* 16: 644. 1937), noting 975.4 (LINN) and determinations of two collections on the sheet by Schultz Bipontinus, excluded it from *Bidens*. Although *Felicia* and *Glossocardia* have been suggested as possible generic identities for these collections, original material may well exist in G.

Bidens tripartita Linnaeus, *Species Plantarum* 2: 831. 1753.
"Habitat in Europae inundatis." RCN: 6017.
Lectotype (Sherff in *Publ. Field Mus. Nat. Hist., Bot. Ser.* 16: 271. 1937): Herb. Clifford: 399, *Bidens* 1 α (BM-000646986).
Generitype of *Bidens* Linnaeus (vide Green, *Prop. Brit. Bot.*: 179. 1929).
Current name: **Bidens tripartita** L. (Asteraceae).
Note: Harriman (in *Taxon* 47: 485. 1998) proposed the conservation of the generic name with feminine gender, recommended by the Committee for Spermatophyta (in *Taxon* 49: 272. 2000). However, the General Committee (in *Taxon* 55: 796–797. 2006) referred this back to the Committee for Vascular Plants for reconsideration.

Bidens verticillata Linnaeus, *Species Plantarum* 2: 833. 1753.
"Habitat in Vera Cruce." RCN: 6026.
Lectotype (Blake in *Torreya* 15: 106. 1915): Herb. Clifford: 399, *Bidens* 4 (BM-000646990).
Current name: **Trichospira verticillata** (L.) S.F. Blake (Asteraceae).

Bignonia aequinoctialis Linnaeus, *Species Plantarum* 2: 623. 1753.
"Habitat in Cayenna." RCN: 4511.
Lectotype (Gentry in Harling & Sparre, *Fl. Ecuador* 7: 57. 1977): [icon] *"Bignonia foliis conjugatis, cirrhosis, ternatis"* in Plumier in Burman, Pl. Amer.: 48, t. 58. 1756.
Current name: **Cydista aequinoctialis** (L.) Miers (Bignoniaceae).

Bignonia caerulea Linnaeus, *Species Plantarum* 2: 625. 1753.
"Habitat in Carolina." RCN: 4524.
Lectotype (Dandy, *Sloane Herbarium*: 112. 1958): [icon] *"Arbor Guajaci latiore folio, Bignoniae flore caeruleo, fructu duro in duas partes desiliente, seminibus alatis imbricatim positis"* in Catesby, Nat. Hist. Carolina 1: 42, t. 42. 1730.
Current name: **Jacaranda caerulea** (L.) Griseb. (Bignoniaceae).

Bignonia capreolata Linnaeus, *Species Plantarum* 2: 624. 1753, *typ. cons.*
"Habitat in America." RCN: 4514.
Lectotype (Reveal in Jarvis & al., *Regnum Veg.* 127: 24. 1993): Herb. Clifford: 317, *Bignonia* 2, excl. open flower (BM-000646171).
Generitype of *Bignonia* Linnaeus, *nom. cons.*
Current name: **Bignonia capreolata** L. (Bignoniaceae).

Bignonia catalpa Linnaeus, *Species Plantarum* 2: 622. 1753.
"Habitat in Japonia, Carolina." RCN: 4508.
Lectotype (Reveal & al. in *Bartonia* 56: 17. 1990): [icon] *"Bignonia Urucu foliis flore sordide albo, intus maculis purpureis & luteis asperso, siliqua longissima & angustissima"* in Catesby, Nat. Hist. Carolina 1: 49, t. 49. 1730.
Current name: **Catalpa bignonioides** Walter (Bignoniaceae).

Bignonia crucigera Linnaeus, *Species Plantarum* 2: 624. 1753.
"Habitat in Virginia & australiori America." RCN: 4513.
Lectotype (Barrie & al. in *Ann. Missouri Bot. Gard.* 78: 265. 1991): [icon] *"Pseudo-apocynum folliculis maximis obtusis seminibus amplissimis albis"* in Morison, Pl. Hist. Univ. 3: 612, s. 15, t. 3, f. 16. 1699.
Current name: **Pithecoctenium crucigerum** (L.) A.H. Gentry (Bignoniaceae).

Bignonia indica Linnaeus, *Species Plantarum* 2: 625. 1753.
"Habitat in India." RCN: 4523.
Lectotype (Santisuk & Vidal in Leroy, *Fl. Cambodge Laos Viêtnam* 22: 9. 1985): [icon] *"Palega-pajaneli"* in Rheede, Hort. Malab. 1: 77, t. 43. 1678.
Current name: **Oroxylum indicum** (L.) Benth. ex Kurz (Bignoniaceae).

Bignonia leucoxylon Linnaeus, *Species Plantarum* 2: 624. 1753.
"Habitat in Jamaica, Caribaeis, agris humidioribus, & ad ripas." RCN: 4518.
Replaced synonym of: *Bignonia trifolia* L. (1759), *nom. illeg.*; *Bignonia pentaphylla* L. (1763), *nom. illeg.*
Lectotype (Sandwith in *Kew Bull.* 8: 453. 1953): Herb. Linn. No. 776.4 (LINN).
Current name: **Tabebuia heterophylla** (DC.) Britton (Bignoniaceae).

Bignonia paniculata Linnaeus, *Species Plantarum* 2: 623. 1753.
"Habitat in America calidiore." RCN: 4512.
Lectotype (Howard, *Fl. Lesser Antilles* 6: 317. 1989): [icon] *"Bignonia foliis conjugatis, cirrhosis"* in Plumier in Burman, Pl. Amer.: 46, t. 56, f. 1. 1756.
Current name: **Amphilophium paniculatum** (L.) Kunth (Bignoniaceae).

Bignonia pentaphylla Linnaeus, *Species Plantarum*, ed. 2, 2: 870. 1763, *nom. illeg.*
"Habitat in Jamaica, Caribaeis, agris humidioribus, & ad ripas." RCN: 4517.
Replaced synonym: *Bignonia leucoxylon* L. (1753).
Lectotype (Sandwith in *Kew Bull.* 8: 453. 1953): Herb. Linn. No. 776.4 (LINN).
Current name: **Tabebuia heterophylla** (DC.) Britton (Bignoniaceae).
Note: An illegitimate renaming of *B. leucoxylon* L. (1753).

Bignonia peruviana Linnaeus, *Species Plantarum* 2: 625. 1753.
"Habitat in Peru." RCN: 4522.
Type not designated.
Original material: Herb. Clifford: 317, *Bignonia* 5 (BM).
Current name: **Ampelopsis arborea** (L.) Koehne (Vitaceae).

Bignonia pubescens Linnaeus, *Species Plantarum*, ed. 2, 2: 870. 1763.
"Habitat in Campechia." RCN: 4515.
Neotype (Gentry in Harling & Sparre, *Fl. Ecuador* 7: 41. 1977): *Houstoun* (BM).
Current name: **Arrabidaea pubescens** (L.) A.H. Gentry (Bignoniaceae).

Bignonia radiata Linnaeus, *Species Plantarum* 2: 624. 1753.
"Habitat in Peru." RCN: 4519.
Type not designated.
Original material: [icon] in Feuillée, J. Obs. 2: 731, t. 22. 1714.
Note: The application of this name appears uncertain.

Bignonia radicans Linnaeus, *Species Plantarum* 2: 624. 1753.
"Habitat in America." RCN: 4520.
Lectotype (Dandy, *Sloane Herbarium*: 112. 1958): [icon] *"Bignonia, Fraxini foliis, coccineo flore minore"* in Catesby, Nat. Hist. Carolina 1: 65, t. 65. 1731.
Current name: **Campsis radicans** (L.) Seem. (Bignoniaceae).
Note: See note by Howard & Staples (in *J. Arnold Arbor.* 64: 520. 1983).

Bignonia sempervirens Linnaeus, *Species Plantarum* 2: 623. 1753.
"Habitat in Virginia." RCN: 4509.
Lectotype (Ornduff in *J. Arnold Arbor.* 51: 8. 1970): [icon] *"Syringa volubilis Virginiana Myrti majoris folio, alato semine, florib. odoratis, luteis"* in Plukenet, Phytographia: t. 112, f. 5. 1691; Almag. Bot.: 359. 1696. – Typotype: Herb. Sloane 90: 55 (BM-SL).
Current name: **Gelsemium sempervirens** (L.) J. St.-Hil. (Loganiaceae).

Bignonia stans Linnaeus, *Species Plantarum*, ed. 2, 2: 871. 1763.
"Habitat in America." RCN: 4521.
Lectotype (Gentry in Gómez Pompa, *Fl. Veracruz* 24: 196. 1982): [icon] *"Bignonia foliis pinnatis"* in Plumier in Burman, Pl. Amer.: 44, t. 54. 1756.
Current name: ***Tecoma stans*** (L.) Juss. ex Kunth (Bignoniaceae).

Bignonia trifolia Linnaeus, *Flora Jamaicensis*: 18. 1759, *nom. illeg.*
["Habitat in Jamaica, Caribaeis, agris humidioribus, & ad ripas."] Sp. Pl. 2: 624 (1753).
Replaced synonym: *Bignonia leucoxylon* L. (1753).
Lectotype (Sandwith in *Kew Bull.* 8: 453. 1953): Herb. Linn. No. 776.4 (LINN).
Current name: ***Tabebuia heterophylla*** (DC.) Britton (Bignoniaceae).
Note: An illegitimate replacement name for *B. leucoxylon* L. (1753).

Bignonia triphylla Linnaeus, *Species Plantarum*, ed. 2, 2: 870. 1763.
"Habitat in Vera Cruce." RCN: 4516.
Type not designated.
Original material: none traced.
Note: The application of this name is uncertain.

Bignonia unguis-cati Linnaeus, *Species Plantarum* 2: 623. 1753.
"Habitat in Barbados, Domingo." RCN: 4510.
Lectotype (Nasir in Nasir & Ali, *Fl. W. Pakistan* 131: 18. 1979): [icon] *"Clematis quadrifolia, flore digitalis luteo, claviculis aduncis, siliquis longissimis, semine alato"* in Plumier, Descr. Pl. Amér.: 80, t. 94. 1693.
Current name: ***Macfadyena unguis-cati*** (L.) A.H. Gentry (Bignoniaceae).

Biscutella apula Linnaeus, *Mantissa Plantarum Altera*: 254. 1771, *nom. illeg.*
"Habitat in Italia." RCN: 4751.
Replaced synonym: *Biscutella didyma* L. (1753).
Lectotype (Heywood in *Feddes Repert.* 69: 150. 1964): Herb. Clifford: 329, *Biscutella* 2 (BM-000646258).
Current name: ***Biscutella didyma*** L. (Brassicaceae).
Note: An illegitimate replacement name for *B. didyma* L. (1753).

Biscutella auriculata Linnaeus, *Species Plantarum* 2: 652. 1753.
"Habitat in Italia, Galloprovincia." RCN: 4749.
Lectotype (Raffaelli in *Willdenowia* 22: 21. 1992): Herb. Linn. No. 831.1 (LINN).
Current name: ***Biscutella auriculata*** L. (Brassicaceae).

Biscutella coronopifolia Linnaeus, *Mantissa Plantarum Altera*: 255. 1771.
"Habitat in Hispania, Italia." RCN: 4753.
Lectotype (Raffaelli in *Webbia* 39: 410. 1986): Herb. Linn. No. 831.5 (LINN).
Current name: ***Biscutella coronopifolia*** L. (Brassicaceae).

Biscutella didyma Linnaeus, *Species Plantarum* 2: 653. 1753, *typ. cons.*
"Habitat in Germania, Gallia, Italia." RCN: 4570.
Replaced synonym of: *Biscutella apula* L. (1771).
Conserved type (Heywood in *Feddes Repert.* 69: 150. 1964): Herb. Clifford: 329, *Biscutella* 2 (BM-000646258).
Generitype of *Biscutella* Linnaeus, *nom. cons.*
Current name: ***Biscutella didyma*** L. (Brassicaceae).
Note: Biscutella didyma, with the type designated by Heywood, was proposed as conserved type of the genus by Jarvis (in *Taxon* 41: 558. 1992). This was eventually approved by the General Committee (see review of the history of this proposal by Barrie, *l.c.* 55: 795–796. 2006).

Biscutella laevigata Linnaeus, *Mantissa Plantarum Altera*: 255. 1771.
"Habitat in Italia." RCN: 4754.
Lectotype (Raffaelli & Fiesoli in *Webbia* 47: 75. 1993): *Turra*, Herb. Linn. No. 831.6 (LINN).
Current name: ***Biscutella laevigata*** L. (Brassicaceae).

Biscutella lyrata Linnaeus, *Mantissa Plantarum Altera*: 254. 1771.
"Habitat in Hispania, Sicilia." RCN: 4752.
Lectotype (Raffaelli in *Taxon* 34: 695. 1985): *Alströmer 148*, Herb. Linn. No. 831.3 (LINN).
Current name: ***Biscutella lyrata*** L. (Brassicaceae).
Note: Raffaelli (in *Webbia* 44: 97–105. 1990) provides further discussion relevant to his earlier typification.

Biscutella sempervirens Linnaeus, *Mantissa Plantarum Altera*: 255. 1771.
"Habitat in Oriente, inque Hispania. Cl. Alstroemer." RCN: 4755.
Lectotype (Heywood in *Feddes Repert.* 69: 148. 1964): *Alströmer 149*, Herb. Linn. No. 831.8 (LINN).
Current name: ***Biscutella sempervirens*** L. (Brassicaceae).

Biserrula pelecinus Linnaeus, *Species Plantarum* 2: 762. 1753.
"Habitat in Sicilia, Hispania, Galloprovincia." RCN: 5618.
Lectotype (Gillett in Milne-Redhead & Polhill, *Fl. Trop. E. Africa, Leguminosae* 3: 1059. 1971): Herb. Clifford: 361, *Biserrula* 1 (BM-000646605).
Generitype of *Biserrula* Linnaeus.
Current name: ***Biserrula pelecinus*** L. (Fabaceae: Faboideae).

Bixa orellana Linnaeus, *Species Plantarum* 1: 512. 1753.
"Habitat in America calidiore." RCN: 3859.
Lectotype (Wijnands, *Bot. Commelins*: 51. 1983): Herb. Clifford: 211, *Bixa* 1 (BM-000628766).
Generitype of *Bixa* Linnaeus.
Current name: ***Bixa orellana*** L. (Bixaceae).
Note: Lescot (in Aubréville & Leroy, *Fl. Cambodge Laos Vietnam* 11: 101. 1970) and Villiers (in Aubréville & Leroy, *Fl. Gabon* 22: 62. 1973) indicated 674.1 (LINN) as type but this is a later addition to the herbarium and is not original material for the name. Bridson (in Polhill, *Fl. Trop. E. Africa, Bixaceae*: 1. 1975) wrongly indicated the Clifford sheet as a syntype but as this statement implies no intention to indicate a single nomenclatural type (unlike the use of holotype, lectotype or neotype), this is not regarded as a correctable error.

Blaeria articulata Linnaeus, *Mantissa Plantarum Altera*: 198. 1771.
"Habitat ad Cap. b. spei." RCN: 917.
Lectotype (Oliver in *Contr. Bolus Herb.* 19: 163. 2000): Herb. Linn. No. 141.2 (LINN).
Current name: ***Erica similis*** (N.E. Br.) E.G.H. Oliv. (Ericaceae).

Blaeria ericoides Linnaeus, *Species Plantarum* 1: 112. 1753.
"Habitat ad Cap. b. Spei." RCN: 916.
Lectotype (Oliver in Jarvis & al., *Regnum Veg.* 127: 25. 1993): Herb. Hermann 4: 61, lower right specimen "Blaeria Hort. cliff. 471" (BM-000628310).
Generitype of *Blaeria* Linnaeus.
Current name: ***Erica ericoides*** (L.) E.G.H. Oliv. (Ericaceae).
Note: The material designated as the type by Oliver, though in Paul Hermann's herbarium, was not from Ceylon and so did not feature in Linnaeus' *Flora Zeylanica* (1747). However, this South African collection was directly annotated by Linnaeus and is therefore original material for the name.

Blaeria pusilla Linnaeus, *Systema Naturae,* ed. 12, 2: 121; *Mantissa Plantarum*: 39. 1767.
"Habitat ad Cap. b. spei. D. Schreber." RCN: 918.
Lectotype (designated here by Oliver): *Schreber,* Herb. Linn. No. 141.4 (LINN).
Current name: ***Erica glabella*** Thunb. (Ericaceae).

Blakea trinervia Linnaeus, *Systema Naturae,* ed. 10, 2: 1044. 1759.
["Habitat in Jamaica."] Sp. Pl., ed. 2, 1: 635 (1762). RCN: 3436.
Type not designated.
Original material: *Browne,* Herb. Linn. No. 612.1 (LINN); [icon] in Browne, Civ. Nat. Hist. Jamaica: 323, t. 35. 1756.
Current name: ***Blakea trinervia*** L. (Melastomataceae).

Blakea triplinervia Linnaeus, *Plantae Surinamenses*: 9. 1775.
"Habitat [in Surinamo.]" RCN: 3437.
Type not designated.
Original material: Herb. Linn. No. 612.2 (LINN).
Current name: ***Bellucia grossularioides*** (L.) Triana (Melastomataceae).

Blasia pusilla Linnaeus, *Species Plantarum* 2: 1138. 1753.
"Habitat in Europa ad latera fossarum, solo ex arena sterili." RCN: 8147.
Lectotype (Bonner, *Index Hepaticarum* 3: 420. 1963): [icon] *"Blasia pusilla, Lichenis pyxidati facie"* in Micheli, Nov. Pl. Gen.: 14, t. 7. 1729.
Generitype of *Blasia* Linnaeus.
Current name: ***Blasia pusilla*** L. (Blasiaceae).
Note: See discussion of some of the original elements by Isoviita (in *Acta Bot. Fenn.* 89: 8. 1970) and Grolle (in *Feddes Repert.* 87: 182. 1976).

Blechnum australe Linnaeus, *Systema Naturae,* ed. 12, 2: 688; *Mantissa Plantarum*: 130. 1767.
"Habitat ad Cap. b. Spei." RCN: 7817.
Lectotype (Schelpe in *J. Linn. Soc., Bot.* 53: 508. 1952): Herb. Linn. No. 1247.3 (LINN).
Current name: ***Blechnum australe*** L. (Blechnaceae).

Blechnum occidentale Linnaeus, *Species Plantarum* 2: 1077. 1753.
"Habitat in America meridionali." RCN: 7815.
Lectotype (Proctor in Howard, *Fl. Lesser Antilles* 2: 156. 1977): Herb. Linn. No. 1247.1 (LINN), see above, right.
Generitype of *Blechnum* Linnaeus (vide Smith, *Hist. Fil.*: 300. 1875).
Current name: ***Blechnum occidentale*** L. (Blechnaceae).
Note: Linnaeus evidently transposed the epithets "occidentale" and "orientale" in describing his two species of *Blechnum* in 1753.

Blechnum orientale Linnaeus, *Species Plantarum* 2: 1077. 1753.
"Habitat in China. Osbeck." RCN: 7616.
Type not designated.
Original material: none traced.
Current name: ***Blechnum orientale*** L. (Blechnaceae).
Note: Linnaeus evidently transposed the epithets "occidentale" and "orientale" in describing his two species of *Blechnum* in 1753. See Hansen & Fox Maule (in *Bot. J. Linn. Soc.* 67: 207. 1973) for comments on Osbeck material.

Blechnum radicans Linnaeus, *Mantissa Plantarum Altera*: 307. 1771.
"Habitat in Virginiae et Maderae rimis rupium profundis argillaceis. König." RCN: 7818.
Lectotype (designated here by Reveal): *König s.n.,* Herb. Linn. No. 1247.4 (LINN).
Current name: ***Woodwardia radicans*** (L.) Sm. (Blechnaceae).

The lectotype of *Blechnum occidentale* L.

Blechnum virginicum Linnaeus, *Mantissa Plantarum Altera* 2: 307. 1771.
"Habitat in Virginia." RCN: 7818.
Type not designated.
Original material: none traced.
Current name: ***Woodwardia virginica*** (L.) Sm. (Blechnaceae).

Blitum capitatum Linnaeus, *Species Plantarum* 1: 4. 1753.
"Habitat in Europa praesertim in comit. Tyrolensi." RCN: 34.
Lectotype (Jonsell & Jarvis in Jarvis & al., *Regnum Veg.* 127: 25. 1993): Herb. Linn. No. 14.1 (LINN).
Generitype of *Blitum* Linnaeus (vide Hitchcock, *Prop. Brit. Bot.*: 115. 1929).
Current name: ***Chenopodium capitatum*** (L.) Ach. (Chenopodiaceae).
Note: Jonsell & Jarvis (in *Nordic J. Bot.* 14: 155. 1994) give an explanation of the reasons for their formal 1993 type choice.

Blitum chenopodioides Linnaeus, *Mantissa Plantarum Altera*: 170. 1771.
"Habitat in Tataria; nunc in Svecia. H.V." RCN: 36.
Neotype (Uotila in *Ann. Bot. Fenn.* 38: 96. 2001): Russia. Republic of Dagestan, In fontis Kislar, [early 1800s], *C. Steven* (H-1037202).
Current name: ***Chenopodium chenopodioides*** (L.) Aellen (Chenopodiaceae).

Note: See extensive discussion by Uotila, who rejects 14.3 and 14.4 (LINN) as original material on the grounds that they conflict with the protologue, and designates a neotype. This removes the possibility that the name might be a synonym of *Chenopodium rubrum* L., which had led some authors to informally reject *B. chenopodioides.*

Blitum virgatum Linnaeus, *Species Plantarum* 1: 4. 1753.
"Habitat in Tataria. Hispania." RCN: 35.
Lectotype (Jafri & Rateeb in Jafri & El-Gadi, *Fl. Libya* 58: 11. 1978): *Gerber,* Herb. Linn. No. 14.2 (LINN).
Current name: **Chenopodium foliosum** (Moench) Asch. (Chenopodiaceae).

Bobartia indica Linnaeus, *Species Plantarum* 1: 54. 1753, *typ. cons.*
"Habitat in India." RCN: 449.
Conserved type (Strid in *Taxon* 23: 422. 1974): Herb. Hermann 4: 80, No. 41, top left specimen (BM-000628411).
Generitype of *Bobartia* Linnaeus, *nom. cons.*
Current name: **Bobartia indica** L. (Iridaceae).

Bocconia frutescens Linnaeus, *Species Plantarum* 1: 505. 1753.
"Habitat in Jamaica, Mexico." RCN: 3426.
Lectotype (Howard, *Fl. Lesser Antilles* 4: 276. 1988): Herb. Linn. No. 609.1 (LINN).
Generitype of *Bocconia* Linnaeus.
Current name: **Bocconia frutescens** L. (Papaveraceae).
Note: Although Howard (*Fl. Lesser Antilles* 4: 276. 1988) indicated 609.1 (LINN) as lectotype, this collection lacks the relevant *Species Plantarum* number (i.e. "1") and was a post-1753 addition to the herbarium, and is not original material for the name.

Boerhavia angustifolia Linnaeus, *Systema Naturae,* ed. 12, 2: 51. 1767. RCN: 23.
Type not designated.
Original material: Herb. Linn. No. 9.9 (LINN).
Note: The application of this name is uncertain.

Boerhavia diandra Linnaeus, *Species Plantarum* 2: 1194. 1753.
"Habitat in India. Ott. Munchausen. L.B." RCN: 20.
Type not designated.
Original material: none traced.
Current name: **Boerhavia repens** L. subsp. **diandra** (L.) Maire & Weiller (Nyctaginaceae).

Boerhavia diffusa Linnaeus, *Species Plantarum* 1: 3. 1753, *nom. cons.*
"Habitat in India." RCN: 18.
Conserved type (Whitehouse in *Taxon* 47: 873. 1998): Virgin Islands. St Croix, Teague Bay, West Indies Laboratory, 30 May 1977, *Fosberg 56776* (BM-000593477; iso- B, BISH, GH, K, MO, NSW etc.).
Generitype of *Boerhavia* Linnaeus (vide Hitchcock, *Prop. Brit. Bot.:* 115. 1929).
Current name: **Boerhavia diffusa** L. (Nyctaginaceae).
Note: Boerhavia erecta L. was treated as the generitype of *Boerhavia* by Standley (in *Contr. U. S. Natl. Herb.* 12: 375. 1909). However, under Art. 10.5, Ex. 7 (a voted example) of the Vienna Code, this is a type choice made under the American Code and is to be replaced under Art. 10.5b by Hitchcock's choice (*Prop. Brit. Bot.:* 115. 1929) of *B. diffusa* L.

Boerhavia erecta Linnaeus, *Species Plantarum* 1: 3. 1753.
"Habitat in Vera Cruce." RCN: 17.
Neotype (Fawcett & Rendle, *Fl. Jamaica* 3: 148. 1914): Herb. Linn. No. 9.1 (LINN).

Current name: **Boerhavia erecta** L. (Nyctaginaceae).
Note: This was treated as the generitype of *Boerhavia* by Standley (in *Contr. U. S. Natl. Herb.* 12: 375. 1909). However, under Art. 10.5, Ex. 7 (a voted example) of the Vienna Code, this is a type choice made under the American Code and is to be replaced under Art. 10.5b by Hitchcock's choice (*Prop. Brit. Bot.:* 115. 1929) of *B. diffusa* L.
Gilbert (in Jarvis & al., *Regnum Veg.* 127: 25. 1993) formally designated 9.1 (LINN) as a neotype. However, under Art. 9.8, earlier choices of this post-1753 sheet as lectotype are to be corrected, and that of Fawcett & Rendle appears to be the earliest.

Boerhavia repens Linnaeus, *Species Plantarum* 1: 3. 1753.
"Habitat in Nubia inter Mocho & Tangos." RCN: 22.
Lectotype (Codd in *Bothalia* 9: 121. 1966): Herb. Linn. No. 9.8 (LINN).
Current name: **Boerhavia repens** L. (Nyctaginaceae).

Boerhavia scandens Linnaeus, *Species Plantarum* 1: 3. 1753.
"Habitat in Jamaica ad urbem jago de la vega." RCN: 19.
Lectotype (Kellogg in Howard, *Fl. Lesser Antilles* 4: 178. 1988): [icon] *"Solanum bacciferum Americanum fructu corymboso, ex Insula Jamaicensi"* in Plukenet, Phytographia: t. 226, f. 7. 1692; Almag. Bot.: 349. 1696. – Typotype: Herb. Sloane 98: 51, top left specimen (BM-SL).
Current name: **Boerhavia scandens** L. (Nyctaginaceae).
Note: Fawcett & Rendle (*Fl. Jamaica* 3: 149. 1914) indicated an unspecified type in BM, possibly Plukenet material that was not seen by Linnaeus and is not original material for the name. Meikle (in *Notes Roy. Bot. Gard. Edinburgh* 36: 245. 1978) indicated material in LINN as type but did not distinguish between sheets 9.5 and 9.6, which are not part of a single gathering so Art. 9.15 does not apply. They are, in any case, both post-1753 additions to the herbarium and not original material.

Boletus bovinus Linnaeus, *Species Plantarum* 2: 1177. 1753.
"Habitat in Pratis." RCN: 8477.
Type not designated.
Original material: none traced.
Current name: **Suillus bovinus** (Pers.: Fr.) Rouss. (Suillaceae).

Boletus favus Linnaeus, *Systema Naturae,* ed. 10, 2: 1349. 1759.
"Habitat in China." RCN: 8466.
Type not designated.
Original material: none traced.
Current name: **Hexagonia hirta** (P. Beauv.) Fr. (Polyporaceae).

Boletus fomentarius Linnaeus, *Species Plantarum* 2: 1176. 1753.
"Habitat in Betulis." RCN: 8468.
Type not designated.
Original material: none traced.
Current name: **Fomes fomentarius** (L.: Fr.) J.J. Kickx (Polyporaceae).

Boletus granulatus Linnaeus, *Species Plantarum* 2: 1177. 1753.
"Habitat in Sylvis." RCN: 8478.
Neotype (Palm & Stewart in *Taxon* 33: 711. 1984): *S. Lundell 54* (UPS).
Current name: **Suillus granulatus** (L.: Fr.) Rouss. (Boletaceae).

Boletus igniarius Linnaeus, *Species Plantarum* 2: 1176. 1753.
"Habitat in Betulis aliisque arboribus." RCN: 8469.
Type not designated.
Original material: none traced.
Current name: **Phellinus igniarius** (L.: Fr.) Quél. (Hymenochaetaceae).

Boletus luteus Linnaeus, *Species Plantarum* 2: 1177. 1753.
"Habitat in Sylvis." RCN: 8476.
Type not designated.
Original material: [icon] in Buxbaum, Pl. Minus Cognit. Cent. 5: 7, t. 14. 1740.
Current name: ***Suillus luteus*** (L.: Fr.) Rouss. (Boletaceae).
Note: Palm & Stewart (in *Taxon* 33: 328. 1986) designated *Lundell s.n.*, Fungi Exsiccati Suecici, 553 (UPS) as a neotype. However, a cited plate from Buxbaum is original material for this name, which therefore precludes the designation of a neotype (Art. 9.11).

Boletus perennis Linnaeus, *Species Plantarum* 2: 1177. 1753.
"Habitat in sylvis super terram, subjectis caudicibus arborum putridis." RCN: 8474.
Type not designated.
Original material: [icon] in Vaillant, Bot. Paris.: 61, t. 12, f. 7. 1727.
Current name: ***Coltricia perennis*** (L.: Fr.) Murrill (Hymenochaetaceae).

Boletus sanguineus Linnaeus, *Systema Naturae,* ed. 10, 2: 1350. 1759.
["Habitat Surinami. Rolander."] Sp. Pl., ed. 2, 2: 1646 (1763). RCN: 8470.
Type not designated.
Original material: Herb. Linn. No. 1280.2 (LINN).
Current name: ***Pycnoporus sanguineus*** (L.: Fr.) Murrill (Polyporaceae).

Boletus suaveolens Linnaeus, *Species Plantarum* 2: 1177. 1753.
"Habitat in Salice." RCN: 8472.
Type not designated.
Original material: none traced.
Current name: ***Trametes suaveolens*** (L.: Fr.) Fr. (Polyporaceae).
Note: See Gams (in *Taxon* 41: 103–104. 1992) on Fries' interpretation of this name.

Boletus suberosus Linnaeus, *Species Plantarum* 2: 1176. 1753.
"Habitat in Betulis." RCN: 8467.
Type not designated.
Original material: none traced.
Current name: ***Piptoporus suberosus*** (L.) Murrill (Fomitopsidaceae).

Boletus subsquamosus Linnaeus, *Species Plantarum* 2: 1178. 1753.
"Habitat in Sylvis." RCN: 8480.
Type not designated.
Original material: none traced.
Current name: ***Polyporus subsquamosus*** (L.: Fr.) Fr. (Polyporaceae).

Boletus subtomentosus Linnaeus, *Species Plantarum* 2: 1178. 1753.
"Habitat in sylvis." RCN: 8479.
Type not designated.
Original material: none traced.
Current name: ***Boletus subtomentosus*** L.: Fr. (Boletaceae).

Boletus versicolor Linnaeus, *Species Plantarum* 2: 1176. 1753.
"Habitat ad truncos Arborum antiquarum." RCN: 8471.
Type not designated.
Original material: none traced.
Current name: ***Trametes versicolor*** (L.: Fr.) Lloyd (Polyporaceae).

Boletus viscidus Linnaeus, *Species Plantarum* 2: 1177. 1753.
"Habitat in Sylvis." RCN: 8475.
Type not designated.
Original material: none traced.
Current name: ***Suillus viscidus*** (L.) Fr. (Suillaceae).

Bombax aculeatum Linnaeus, *Systema Naturae,* ed. 10, 2: 1141. 1759, *nom. illeg.*
["Habitat in India utraque."] Sp. Pl. 1: 511 (1753). RCN: 5005.
Replaced synonym: *Bombax ceiba* L. (1753).
Conserved type (Robyns in *Taxon* 10: 160. 1961): [icon] *"Moulelavou"* in Rheede, Hort. Malab. 3: 61, t. 52. 1682.
Current name: ***Bombax ceiba*** L. (Bombacaceae).
Note: A superfluous name for *B. ceiba* L. (1753).

Bombax ceiba Linnaeus, *Species Plantarum* 1: 511. 1753, *typ. cons.*
"Habitat in India utraque." RCN: 5005.
Replaced synonym of: *Bombax aculeatum* L. (1759), *nom. illeg.*
Conserved type (Robyns in *Taxon* 10: 160. 1961): [icon] *"Moulelavou"* in Rheede, Hort. Malab. 3: 61, t. 52. 1682.
Generitype of *Bombax* Linnaeus, *nom. cons.*
Current name: ***Bombax ceiba*** L. (Bombacaceae).

Bombax gossypium Linnaeus, *Systema Naturae,* ed. 12, 2: 457. 1767, *nom. illeg.*
RCN: 5007.
Replaced synonym: *Bombax religiosum* L. (1753).
Lectotype (Nicolson in *Taxon* 28: 368. 1979): Herb. Hermann 3: 18, No. 222 (BM-000594660).
Current name: ***Cochlospermum religiosum*** (L.) Alston (Cochlospermaceae).
Note: A superfluous name for *B. religiosum* L. (1753).

Bombax heptaphyllum Linnaeus, *Species Plantarum,* ed. 2, 2: 960. 1763, *nom. illeg.*
"Habitat in America." RCN: 5006.
Replaced synonym: *Bombax septenatum* Jacq. (1760).
Type not designated.
Current name: ***Pseudobombax septenatum*** (Jacq.) Dugand (Bombacaceae).
Note: A superfluous name for *B. septenatum* Jacq. (1760).

Bombax inerme Linnaeus, *Systema Naturae,* ed. 10, 2: 1141. 1759, *nom. illeg.*
["Habitat in Indiis."] Sp. Pl. 1: 511 (1753). RCN: 5004.
Replaced synonym: *Bombax pentandrum* L. (1753).
Lectotype (Voorhoeve, *Liberian High Forest Trees*: 65, 68. 1965): [icon] *"Panja"* in Rheede, Hort. Malab. 3: 59, t. 50. 1682.
Current name: ***Ceiba pentandra*** (L.) Gaertn. (Bombacaceae).
Note: A superfluous name for *B. pentandrum* L. (1753).

Bombax pentandrum Linnaeus, *Species Plantarum* 1: 511. 1753.
"Habitat in Indiis." RCN: 5004.
Replaced synonym of: *Bombax inerme* L. (1759), *nom. illegit.*
Lectotype (Voorhoeve, *Liberian High Forest Trees*: 65, 68. 1965): [icon] *"Panja"* in Rheede, Hort. Malab. 3: 59, t. 50. 1682.
Current name: ***Ceiba pentandra*** (L.) Gaertn. (Bombacaceae).

Bombax religiosum Linnaeus, *Species Plantarum* 1: 512. 1753.
"Habitat in India." RCN: 5007.
Replaced synonym of: *Bombax gossypium* L. (1767), *nom. illeg.*
Lectotype (Nicolson in *Taxon* 28: 368. 1979): Herb. Hermann 3: 18, No. 222 (BM-000594660).
Current name: ***Cochlospermum religiosum*** (L.) Alston (Cochlospermaceae).
Note: Specific epithet spelled "religiosa" in the protologue.

Bontia daphnoides Linnaeus, *Species Plantarum* 2: 638. 1753.
"Habitat in Barbados." RCN: 4641.

Lectotype (Chinnock in Jarvis & al., *Regnum Veg.* 127: 25. 1993): [icon] *"Bontia Laureolae facie"* in Dillenius, Hort. Eltham. 1: 57, t. 49, f. 57. 1732 (JE).
Generitype of *Bontia* Linnaeus.
Current name: ***Bontia daphnoides*** L. (Myoporaceae).

Bontia germinans Linnaeus, *Systema Naturae,* ed. 10, 2: 1122. 1759. ["Habitat in Indiis."] Sp. Pl., ed. 2, 2: 891 (1763). RCN: 4642.
Lectotype (Stearn in *Kew Bull.* 13: 35. 1958): *Browne,* Herb. Linn. No. 813.2 (LINN).
Current name: ***Avicennia germinans*** (L.) Stearn (Avicenniaceae).
Note: There has been disagreement over the correct name for this taxon – see Little (in *Phytologia* 8: 49–57. 1961) who argued that it should be *A. nitida* Jacq., and Compère (in *Taxon* 12: 150. 1963) who favoured *A. germinans* (L.) L.

Borago africana Linnaeus, *Species Plantarum* 1: 138. 1753.
"Habitat in Aethiopia." RCN: 1108.
Lectotype (Kazmi in *J. Arnold Arbor.* 52: 519. 1971): Herb. Linn. No. 188.4 (LINN).
Current name: ***Trichodesma africanum*** (L.) Sm. (Boraginaceae).

Borago hortensis Linnaeus, *Flora Anglica*: 12. 1754.
"Habitat [in Anglia.]"
Lectotype (Selvi in Cafferty & Jarvis in *Taxon* 53: 800. 2004): [icon] *"Borago hortensis"* in Gerard, Herball: 652, 653. 1597.
Current name: ***Borago officinalis*** L. (Boraginaceae).

Borago indica Linnaeus, *Species Plantarum* 1: 137. 1753.
"Habitat in India Orientali." RCN: 1107.
Lectotype (Kazmi in *J. Arnold Arbor.* 52: 516. 1971): Herb. Linn. No. 188.2 (LINN).
Current name: ***Trichodesma indicum*** (L.) Sm. (Boraginaceae).

Borago officinalis Linnaeus, *Species Plantarum* 1: 137. 1753.
"Habitat hodie in Normannia ad Colbeck & alibi in Europa; venit olim ex Aleppo." RCN: 1106.
Lectotype (Edmondson in Davis, *Fl. Turkey* 6: 435. 1978): Herb. Linn. No. 188.1 (LINN).
Generitype of *Borago* Linnaeus (vide Hitchcock, *Prop. Brit. Bot.*: 128. 1929).
Current name: ***Borago officinalis*** L. (Boraginaceae).

Borago orientalis Linnaeus, *Species Plantarum* 1: 138. 1753.
"Habitat circum Constantinopolin." RCN: 1110.
Lectotype (Edmondson in Cafferty & Jarvis in *Taxon* 53: 800. 2004): Herb. Linn. No. 188.5 (LINN).
Current name: ***Trachystemon orientalis*** (L.) G. Don (Boraginaceae).

Borassus flabellifer Linnaeus, *Species Plantarum* 2: 1187. 1753.
"Habitat in India." RCN: 8542.
Lectotype (Moore & Dransfield in *Taxon* 28: 60, f. 2. 1979): [icon] *"Ampana"* in Rheede, Hort. Malab. 1: 13, t. 10. 1678.
Generitype of *Borassus* Linnaeus.
Current name: ***Borassus flabellifer*** L. (Arecaceae).

Borbonia cordata Linnaeus, *Species Plantarum* 2: 707. 1753.
"Habitat in Aethiopia." RCN: 5185.
Lectotype (Dahlgren in *Bot. Not.* 116: 275. 1963): Herb. Clifford: 494, *Borbonia* 1 (BM-000647673).
Generitype of *Borbonia* Linnaeus (vide Green, *Prop. Brit. Bot.*: 174. 1929).
Current name: ***Aspalathus cordata*** (L.) R. Dahlgren (Fabaceae: Faboideae).
Note: Campbell & Van Wyk (in *S. African J. Bot.* 67: 127. 2001)

appear to treat this name as a synonym of *Rafnia triflora* (L.) Thunb. (syn. *Crotalaria triflora* L.). They cite *B. cordata* as published in 1753, but give the page number as 994 (which corresponds with the *Sp. Pl.,* ed. 2, 2: 994. 1762 account of this species). They quote "e Cap. b. spei" (but both ed. 1 and ed. 2 accounts give "Aethiopia") and state "LINN s.n. (LINN, microfiche, lecto., here designated)". In this, they presumably intend 890.6 (LINN) annotated "Borbonia 3 cordata" by Linnaeus. However, they give no indication of using the ed. 1 and ed. 2 names in different ways, nor of rejecting Dahlgren's choice of type.

Borbonia crenata Linnaeus, *Species Plantarum* 2: 708. 1753.
"Habitat in Aethiopia." RCN: 5186.
Lectotype (Dahlgren in *Opera Bot.* 9: 276. 1963): [icon] *"Planta leguminosa Aethiopica, foliis Rusci"* in Breyn, Exot. Pl. Cent.: 69, t. 28. 1678.
Current name: ***Aspalathus crenata*** (L.) R. Dahlgren (Fabaceae: Faboideae).
Note: Dahlgren (*Opera Bot.* 22: 14, f. 3. 1968) reproduces the Breyn illustration that he had designated as the lectotype.

Borbonia ericifolia Linnaeus, *Plantae Rariores Africanae*: 14. 1760. ["Habitat ad Cap. b. spei."] Sp. Pl., ed. 2, 2: 994 (1763). RCN: 5181.
Lectotype (Schrire in Turland & Jarvis in *Taxon* 46: 466. 1997): *"Genista foliis Ericae brevissimis reris, fl. numeris. Old."*, Herb. Burman (G).
Current name: ***Amphithalea ericifolia*** (L.) Eckl. & Zeyh. (Fabaceae: Faboideae).
Note: Granby (in *Opera Bot.* 80: 28. 1985) designated a neotype, presumably believing that no original material existed for the name. However, two sheets (both confirmed as to their identity by Granby) in Herb. Burman (G) are believed to be relevant original material, and one of them has been designated as lectotype by Schrire.

Borbonia laevigata Linnaeus, *Systema Naturae,* ed. 12, 2: 473; *Mantissa Plantarum*: 100. 1767.
"Habitat ad Cap. b. spei." RCN: 5182.
Lectotype (Schutte & Van Wyk in *Taxon* 43: 579. 1994): *N.L. Burman 31,* Herb. Linn. No. 890.4 (LINN), see p. 196.
Current name: ***Liparia laevigata*** (L.) Thunb. (Fabaceae: Faboideae).

Borbonia lanceolata Linnaeus, *Species Plantarum* 2: 707. 1753.
"Habitat in Aethiopia." RCN: 5184.
Lectotype (Dahlgren in *Opera Bot.* 22: 14, 70. 1968): [icon] *"Frutex Aethiopicus Rusci angusto & minore folio"* in Plukenet, Phytographia: t. 297, f. 4. 1694; Almag. Bot.: 159. 1696. – Typotype: Herb. Sloane 100: 68 (BM-SL).
Current name: ***Aspalathus angustifolia*** (Lam.) R. Dahlgren (Fabaceae: Faboideae).

Borbonia tomentosa Linnaeus, *Species Plantarum* 2: 707. 1753.
"Habitat in Aethiopia." RCN: 5435.
Replaced synonym of: *Liparia villosa* L. (1771), *nom. illeg.*
Lectotype (Schutte & Van Wyk in *Taxon* 42: 47. 1993): [icon] *"Genista, Africana, tomentosa, folio cochleariformi, flore luteo"* in Seba, Locupl. Rer. Nat. Thes. 1: 38, t. 24, f. 1. 1734.
Current name: ***Priestleya tomentosa*** (L.) Druce (Fabaceae: Faboideae).

Borbonia trinervia Linnaeus, *Species Plantarum* 2: 707. 1753.
"Habitat in Aethiopia." RCN: 5183.
Lectotype (Dahlgren in *Opera Bot.* 22: 14, 40. 1968): Herb. Clifford: 494, *Borbonia* 2 (BM-000647690).
Current name: ***Cliffortia ruscifolia*** L. (Rosaceae).

Borbonia umbellata Linnaeus, *Mantissa Plantarum Altera*: 269. 1771. RCN: 5434.
Type not designated.
Original material: none traced.
Current name: ***Liparia laevigata*** (L.) Thunb. (Fabaceae: Faboideae).
Note: Linnaeus gave the alternative name *Liparia umbellata* (seemingly not published elsewhere) in the protologue, and this was repeated in *Syst. Veg.*, ed. 13: 554 (1774). Neither this name nor *L. umbellata* is invalid, having been published pre-1953 (Art. 34.2). Schutte & Van Wyk (in *Taxon* 43: 579. 1994) and Schutte (in *Nordic J. Bot.* 17: 29. 1997) treat this as an illegitimate name, synonymous with *Liparia laevigata* (L.) Thunb.

Bosea yervamora Linnaeus, *Species Plantarum* 1: 225. 1753.
"Habitat in Canariis insulis." RCN: 1844.
Type not designated.
Original material: [icon] in Sloane, Voy. Jamaica 2: 19, t. 158, f. 3. 1725; [icon] in Walther, Design. Pl.: 24, t. 10. 1735.
Generitype of *Bosea* Linnaeus.
Current name: ***Bosea yervamora*** L. (Amaranthaceae).

Brabejum stellatifolium Linnaeus, *Species Plantarum* 1: 121. 1753.
"Habitat in Aethiopia." RCN: 7626.
Lectotype (Weston in Jarvis & al., *Regnum Veg.* 127: 26. 1993): Herb. Clifford: 36, *Brabejum* 1 (BM-000557797).
Generitype of *Brabejum* Linnaeus.
Current name: ***Brabejum stellatifolium*** L. (Proteaceae).

Brabyla capensis Linnaeus, *Mantissa Plantarum*: 137. 1767.
"Habitat ad Cap. b. spei." RCN: 7626.
Type not designated.
Original material: none traced.
Generitype of *Brabyla* Linnaeus (1767), *non Brabila* P. Browne (1756).
Current name: ***Brabejum stellatifolium*** L. (Proteaceae).

Brassica alpina Linnaeus, *Systema Naturae,* ed. 12, 2: 444; *Mantissa Plantarum*: 95. 1767.
"Habitat in Germania...D. Schreber." RCN: 4851.
Lectotype (Greuter & Burdet in *Willdenowia* 13: 283. 1984; Talavera & Velayos in *Anales Jard. Bot. Madrid* 50: 147. 1992): Herb. Linn. No. 844.8, flowering specimen (LINN).
Current name: ***Conringia alpina*** (L.) Link (Brassicaceae).
Note: Greuter & Burdet originally designated 844.8 (LINN) as lectotype, but Talavera & Velayos subsequently restricted this to one of the two specimens on the sheet.

Brassica arvensis Linnaeus, *Systema Naturae,* ed. 12, 2: 444; *Mantissa Plantarum*: 95. 1767.
"Habitat in Europae australis arvis humentibus." RCN: 4850.
Lectotype (Sobrino Vesperinas in Cafferty & Jarvis in *Taxon* 51: 531. 2002): Herb. Linn. No. 844.6 (LINN).
Current name: ***Moricandia arvensis*** (L.) DC. (Brassicaceae).

Brassica campestris Linnaeus, *Species Plantarum* 2: 666. 1753.
"Habitat in agris non argillosis Europae." RCN: 4849.
Lectotype (Bailey in *Gentes Herb.* 2: 247, f. 128. 1930; Oost & al. in *Taxon* 36: 627, f. 3. 1987): Herb. Linn. No. 844.4, right specimen (LINN).
Current name: ***Brassica rapa*** L. subsp. ***campestris*** (L.) A.R. Clapham (Brassicaceae).
Note: Bailey (in *Gentes Herb.* 1: 66. 1922) noted the material in LINN, though he evidently regarded it, erroneously, as a later addition to the collection. He later (1930) treated the same material as the type, and his choice was subsequently restricted to the right-hand specimen on the sheet by Oost & al.

Brassica chinensis Linnaeus, *Centuria I Plantarum*: 19. 1755.
"Habitat in China." RCN: 4855.
Neotype (Oost & al. in *Taxon* 36: 633, f. 5. 1987): "Bok-toy-moy". Seeds from Chinese Garden near New York City, 5 Jul 1891, Herb. L.H. Bailey, sheet BH 441 (BH).
Current name: ***Brassica chinensis*** L. (Brassicaceae).
Note: Bailey (in *Gentes Herb.* 1: 101. 1922; 2: 253. 1930) concluded that there was no type material in LINN, and Oost & al. designated a neotype from his herbarium.

Brassica eruca Linnaeus, *Species Plantarum* 2: 667. 1753.
"Habitat in Helvetia." RCN: 4858.
Lectotype (Gómez-Campo in Cafferty & Jarvis in *Taxon* 51: 531. 2002): Herb. Linn. No. 844.18 (LINN).
Current name: ***Eruca sativa*** Mill. (Brassicaceae).
Note: Although Heath (in *Calyx* 5: 149. 1997) stated that this name is "partly based" on a Bauhin & Cherler element, this does not constitute formal typification.

Brassica erucastrum Linnaeus, *Species Plantarum* 2: 667. 1753.
"Habitat in Europae australioris ruderatis." RCN: 4857.
Lectotype (Sobrino Vesperinas in Cafferty & Jarvis in *Taxon* 51: 531. 2002): *Löfling 486*, Herb. Linn. No. 844.17 (LINN).
Current name: ***Raphanus raphanistrum*** L. (Brassicaceae).
Note: Sobrino Vesperinas (pp. 531–532) reviewed the complications in the application of this name, and typified it such that it fell into the synonymy of *Raphanus raphanistrum* L. (1753).

Brassica napus Linnaeus, *Species Plantarum* 2: 666. 1753.
"Habitat in arenosis maritimis Gotlandiae, Belgii, Angliae." RCN: 4852.
Lectotype (Jonsell in Polhill, *Fl. Trop. E. Africa, Cruciferae*: 7. 1982): Herb. Linn. No. 844.10 (LINN).
Current name: ***Brassica napus*** L. (Brassicaceae).
Note: Bailey (in *Gentes Herb.* 1: 68, 81. 1922; 2: 235. 1930) discussed the Clifford and LINN material but did not designate a type.

Brassica oleracea Linnaeus, *Species Plantarum* 2: 667. 1753.
"Habitat in maritimis Angliae." RCN: 4854.
Neotype (Oost & al. in *Bot. J. Linn. Soc.* 101: 332, f. 2. 1989): *Brassica maritima arborea seu procerior ramosa* Herb. Sloane 123: 4, right specimen (BM-SL).
Generitype of *Brassica* Linnaeus (vide Green, *Prop. Brit. Bot.*: 172. 1929).
Current name: ***Brassica oleracea*** L. (Brassicaceae).

Brassica oleracea Linnaeus var. **botrytis** Linnaeus, *Species Plantarum* 2: 667. 1753.
RCN: 4854.
Lectotype (Oost & al. in *Bot. J. Linn. Soc.* 101: 341, f. 10. 1989): [icon] *"Brassica cauliflora"* in Mattioli, Pl. Epit.: 252. 1586.
Current name: ***Brassica oleracea*** L. (Brassicaceae).

Brassica oleracea Linnaeus var. **capitata** Linnaeus, *Species Plantarum* 2: 667. 1753.
RCN: 4854.
Neotype (Oost & al. in *Bot. J. Linn. Soc.* 101: 333, f. 5. 1989): [icon] *"Brassica capitata albida"* in Dodoëns, Stirp. Hist. Pempt., ed. 2: 623. 1616.
Current name: ***Brassica oleracea*** L. var. ***capitata*** L. (Brassicaceae).

Brassica oleracea Linnaeus var. **gongylodes** Linnaeus, *Species Plantarum* 2: 667. 1753.
RCN: 4854.
Lectotype (Oost & al. in *Bot. J. Linn. Soc.* 101: 344, f. 12. 1989): [icon] *"Caulorapum"* in Mattioli, Pl. Epit.: 251. 1586.
Current name: ***Brassica oleracea*** L. var. ***gongylodes*** L. (Brassicaceae).

Brassica oleracea Linnaeus var. **laciniata** Linnaeus, *Species Plantarum* 2: 667. 1753.
RCN: 4854.
Neotype (Oost & al. in *Bot. J. Linn. Soc.* 101: 337, f. 7. 1989): [icon] *"Brassica Rubra foliis Laciniatis"* in Oellinger, Herbarium Pictum: plate 522. 1553 (University Library, Erlangen).
Current name: **Brassica oleracea** L. (Brassicaceae).

Brassica oleracea Linnaeus var. **napobrassica** Linnaeus, *Species Plantarum* 2: 667. 1753.
RCN: 4854.
Neotype (Oost & al. in *Bot. J. Linn. Soc.* 101: 344, f. 11. 1989): [icon] *"Napus"* in Mattioli, Pl. Epit.: 222. 1586.
Current name: **Brassica napus** L. subsp. **napobrassica** (L.) Jafri (Brassicaceae).

Brassica oleracea Linnaeus var. **rubra** Linnaeus, *Species Plantarum* 2: 667. 1753.
RCN: 4854.
Neotype (Oost & al. in *Bot. J. Linn. Soc.* 101: 333, f. 4. 1989): [icon] *"Brassica rubra capitata"* in Dodoëns, Stirp. Hist. Pempt., ed. 2: 621. 1616.
Current name: **Brassica oleracea** L. convar. **capitata** (L.) Alef. (Brassicaceae).

Brassica oleracea Linnaeus var. **sabauda** Linnaeus, *Species Plantarum* 2: 667. 1753.
RCN: 4854.
Neotype (Oost & al. in *Bot. J. Linn. Soc.* 101: 334, f. 6. 1989): [icon] *"Brassica Sabauda"* in Dodoëns, Stirp. Hist. Pempt., ed. 2: 624. 1616.
Current name: **Brassica oleracea** L. var. **sabauda** L. (Brassicaceae).

Brassica oleracea Linnaeus var. **sabellica** Linnaeus, *Species Plantarum* 2: 667. 1753.
RCN: 4854.
Neotype (Oost & al. in *Bot. J. Linn. Soc.* 101: 340. 1989): [icon] *"Brassica crispa"* in Dodoëns, Stirp. Hist. Pempt., ed. 2: 622. 1616.
Current name: **Brassica oleracea** L. var. **acephala** (DC.) Alef. (Brassicaceae).

Brassica oleracea Linnaeus var. **selenisia** Linnaeus, *Species Plantarum* 2: 667. 1753.
RCN: 4854.
Neotype (Oost & al. in *Bot. J. Linn. Soc.* 101: 339, f. 8. 1989): *"Brassica angusto Apii folio"* in Herb. Morison, M.P.H. 208, no. 14 (OXF).
Current name: **Brassica oleracea** L. convar. **acephala** (DC.) Alef. (Brassicaceae).

Brassica oleracea Linnaeus var. **sylvestris** Linnaeus, *Species Plantarum* 2: 667. 1753.
RCN: 4854.
Neotype (Oost & al. in *Bot. J. Linn. Soc.* 101: 332, f. 2. 1989): *"Brassica maritima arborea seu procerior ramosa"*, Herb. Sloane 123: 4, right specimen (BM-SL).
Current name: **Brassica oleracea** L. (Brassicaceae).

Brassica oleracea Linnaeus var. **viridis** Linnaeus, *Species Plantarum* 2: 667. 1753.
RCN: 4854.
Neotype (Oost & al. in *Bot. J. Linn. Soc.* 101: 333, f. 3. 1989): [icon] *"Brassica vulgaris sativa"* in Dodoëns, Stirp. Hist. Pempt., ed. 2: 621. 1616.
Current name: **Brassica oleracea** L. convar. **acephala** (DC.) Alef. (Brassicaceae).

Brassica orientalis Linnaeus, *Species Plantarum* 2: 666. 1753.
"Habitat in Oriente." RCN: 4858.
Neotype (Jafri in Nasir & Ali, *Fl. W. Pakistan* 55: 49. 1973): Herb. Linn. No. 844.1 (LINN).
Current name: **Conringia orientalis** (L.) Dumort. (Brassicaceae).
Note: In the absence of any original material for the name (844.1 LINN was evidently a post-1753 addition to the herbarium), Jafri's treatment of it as the type is regarded as a correctable error – it is a neotype for the name.

Brassica rapa Linnaeus, *Species Plantarum* 2: 666. 1753.
"Habitat in arvis Angliae, Belgii." RCN: 4853.
Lectotype (Oost & al. in *Taxon* 36: 626, f. 2. 1987): [icon] *"Rapum"* in Mattioli, Pl. Epit.: 219. 1586 (see p. 141).
Current name: **Brassica rapa** L. (Brassicaceae).
Note: See Bailey (in *Gentes Herb.* 1: 67. 1922; 2: 240. 1930) who discusses the Dodoëns and Mattioli plates.

Brassica vesicaria Linnaeus, *Species Plantarum* 2: 668. 1753.
"Habitat in Hispania. Loefling." RCN: 4859.
Lectotype (Gómez-Campo in Cafferty & Jarvis in *Taxon* 51: 532. 2002): Herb. Linn. No. 844.20 (LINN).
Current name: **Eruca vesicaria** (L.) Cav. (Brassicaceae).

Brassica violacea Linnaeus, *Species Plantarum* 2: 667. 1753.
"Habitat in China." RCN: 4856.
Neotype (Al-Shehbaz in Cafferty & Jarvis in *Taxon* 51: 532. 2002): China. Henan Province, Neixang Xian: Baotianman Nat. Reserve Yinghu Gou, 20 May 1994, *Boufford, Liu, Ying, Zhang & Zhu 26131* (A; iso- E, MO).
Current name: **Orychophragmus violaceus** (L.) O.E. Schulz (Brassicaceae).

Breynia indica Linnaeus, *Species Plantarum* 1: 503. 1753.
"Habitat in America calidiore." RCN: 3826.
Replaced synonym of: *Capparis breynia* L. (1759), *nom. illeg.*
Lectotype (Rankin & Greuter in *Willdenowia* 34: 262. 2004): [icon] *"Breynia Elaeagni foliis"* in Breyn, Prodr. Fasc. Rar. Pl.: 13, unnumbered plate. 1739.
Generitype of *Breynia* Linnaeus, *nom. rej.*
Current name: **Capparis indica** (L.) Fawc. & Rendle (Capparaceae).
Note: Breynia Linnaeus (1753), *nom. rej.* vs. *Breynia* J.R. Forst. et G. Forst. (1775), *nom. cons.*
    Al-Shehbaz (in Howard, *Fl. Lesser Antilles* 4: 299. 1985) indicated Plumier's t. 16 (*Nov. Pl. Amer.* 1703) as type (cited erroneously as from 1756). However, as Plumier included two species within his genus, his generic illustration cannot be assumed to apply only to "Breynia eleagni foliis", and is not original material for the name.

Briza bipinnata Linnaeus, *Flora Palaestina*: 12. 1756.
"Habitat in Herjil. Aegypt. Aegypt. frequ. Palaest. rar." RCN: 597.
Basionym of: *Uniola bipinnata* (L.) L. (1762).
Lectotype (Danin in Cafferty & al. in *Taxon* 49: 248. 2000): *Hasselquist*, Herb. Linn. No. 89.2 (LINN).
Current name: **Desmostachya bipinnata** (L.) Stapf (Poaceae).

Briza eragrostis Linnaeus, *Species Plantarum* 1: 70. 1753.
"Habitat in Europa australi ad agrorum versuras." RCN: 595.
Lectotype (Clayton in Polhill, *Fl. Trop. E. Africa, Gramineae* 2: 232. 1974): Herb. Burser I: 10 (UPS).
Current name: **Eragrostis cilianensis** (All.) Vignolo ex Janch. (Poaceae).

Briza maxima Linnaeus, *Species Plantarum* 1: 70. 1753.
"Habitat in Italia, Lusitania." RCN: 594.
Lectotype (Hubbard in Milne-Redhead & Polhill, *Fl. Trop. E. Africa, Gramineae* 1: 53. 1970): *Séguier*, Herb. Linn. No. 88.6 (LINN).
Current name: ***Briza maxima*** L. (Poaceae).

Briza media Linnaeus, *Species Plantarum* 1: 70. 1753.
"Habitat in Europae partis [sic] siccioribus." RCN: 593.
Lectotype (Meikle, *Fl. Cyprus* 2: 1720. 1985): Herb. Linn. No. 88.5 (LINN).
Generitype of *Briza* Linnaeus (vide Hitchcock, *Prop. Brit. Bot.*: 120. 1929).
Current name: ***Briza media*** L. (Poaceae).
Note: Briza minor had been treated as the generitype of *Briza* by Nash (in Britton & Brown, *Ill. Fl. N. U. S.*, ed. 2, 1: 250. 1913) (see McNeill & al. in *Taxon* 36: 362. 1987). However, under Art. 10.5, Ex. 7 (a voted example) of the Vienna Code, this is a type choice made under the American Code and is to be replaced under Art. 10.5b by Hitchcock's choice (*Prop. Brit. Bot.*: 120. 1929) of *B. media* L.

Briza minor Linnaeus, *Species Plantarum* 1: 70. 1753.
"Habitat in Helvetia, Italia." RCN: 591.
Lectotype (Hubbard in Milne-Redhead & Polhill, *Fl. Trop. E. Africa, Gramineae* 1: 53. 1970): Herb. Linn. No. 88.1 (LINN).
Current name: ***Briza minor*** L. (Poaceae).
Note: Conservation of *Briza* with *B. minor* as a conserved type was proposed by Jarvis (in *Taxon* 41: 556. 1992). However, in discussion within the Committee for Spermatophyta, it became clear that the proposed type would conflict with the infrageneric nomenclature adopted by Tzvelev, and so the Committee did not approve conservation (see *Taxon* 44: 612. 1995).
Briza minor had been treated as the generitype of *Briza* by Nash (in Britton & Brown, *Ill. Fl. N. U. S.*, ed. 2, 1: 250. 1913) (see McNeill & al. in *Taxon* 36: 362. 1987). However, under Art. 10.5, Ex. 7 (a voted example) of the Vienna Code, this is a type choice made under the American Code and is to be replaced under Art. 10.5b by Hitchcock's choice (*Prop. Brit. Bot.*: 120. 1929) of *B. media* L.

Briza virens Linnaeus, *Species Plantarum*, ed. 2, 1: 103. 1762.
"Habitat in Oriente, Hispania. Alströmer." RCN: 592.
Lectotype (Hubbard in Milne-Redhead & Polhill, *Fl. Trop. E. Africa, Gramineae* 1: 53. 1970): Herb. Linn. No. 88.3 (LINN).
Current name: ***Briza minor*** L. (Poaceae).

Bromelia acanga Linnaeus, *Systema Naturae*, ed. 12, 2: 232. 1767, *nom. illeg.*
["Habitat in America meridionali."] Sp. Pl. 1: 285 (1753). RCN: 2270.
Replaced synonym: *Bromelia karatas* L. (1753).
Type not designated.
Original material: as replaced synonym.
Current name: ***Bromelia karatas*** L. (Bromeliaceae).
Note: A superfluous name for *B. karatas* L. (1753) – see comments on the identity of the cited synonyms by Smith & Downs (in *Fl. Neotropica* 14: 1678. 1979).

Bromelia ananas Linnaeus, *Species Plantarum* 1: 285. 1753.
"Habitat in nova Hispania, Surinamo." RCN: 2264.
Type not designated.
Original material: [icon] in Commelin, Hort. Med. Amstelod. Pl. Rar. 1: 109, t. 57. 1697; [icon] in Rheede, Hort. Malab. 11: 1, t. 1. 1692.
Current name: ***Ananas comosus*** (L.) Merr. (Bromeliaceae).

Note: Although Smith & Downs (in *Fl. Neotropica* 14: 2062. 1979) stated that this is based on the *Hortus Cliffortianus* account, there are no relevant specimens preserved in the Clifford herbarium. While Ewan (in *Ann. Missouri Bot. Gard.* 78: 58. 1991) reproduced Commelin's cited t. 57 with the caption "...this drawing served as a basionym in the description of the pineapple by Linnaeus in the *Species Plantarum* in 1753", this is not a formal typification.

Bromelia comosa Linnaeus, *Herbarium Amboinense*: 21. 1754.
"Habitat [in Amboina.]"

Lectotype (Merrill, *Interpret. Rumph. Herb. Amb.*: 33, 133. 1917): [icon] *"Anassa domestica"* in Rumphius, Herb. Amboin. 5: 227, t. 81. 1747.
Current name: ***Ananas comosus*** (L.) Merr. (Bromeliaceae).

Bromelia karatas Linnaeus, *Species Plantarum* 1: 285. 1753.
"Habitat in America meridionali." RCN: 2266.
Replaced synonym of: *Bromelia acanga* L. (1767), *nom. illeg.*
Type not designated.
Original material: [icon] in Plumier, Nov. Pl. Amer.: 10, t. 33. 1703.
Generitype of *Bromelia* Linnaeus (vide Regel, *Gartenflora* 17: 67. Mar 1868).
Current name: ***Bromelia karatas*** L. (Bromeliaceae).
Note: Grant & Zijlstra (in *Selbyana* 19: 96. 1998) argue that *B. karatas* is the generitype, the choice having been made by Regel (in *Gartenflora* 17: 67. 1868) which therefore pre-dates the choice of *B.*

pinguin made by Hitchcock (*Prop. Brit. Bot.*: 144. 1929). See discussion of the species name by Smith (in *Phytologia* 15: 173. 1967) who noted that Linnaeus' "panicula diffusa" is not shown by the cited Plumier element to which the name had long been attached. Espejo-Serna & al. (in *Selbyana* 25: 39. 2004) indicated "*C. Plumier s.n.* (LINN)" as the holotype but there is no such material present in LINN.

Bromelia lingulata Linnaeus, *Species Plantarum* 1: 285. 1753.
"Habitat in America meridionali." RCN: 2267.
Lectotype (Howard, *Fl. Lesser Antilles* 3: 405. 1979): [icon] "*Bromelia foliis serrato-spinosis, obtusis*" in Plumier in Burman, Pl. Amer.: 53, t. 64, f. 1. 1756.
Current name: ***Aechmea lingulata*** (L.) Baker (Bromeliaceae).

Bromelia nudicaulis Linnaeus, *Species Plantarum* 1: 286. 1753.
"Habitat in America meridionali." RCN: 2268.
Type not designated.
Original material: [icon] in Plumier in Burman, Pl. Amer.: 51, t. 62. 1756.
Current name: ***Aechmea nudicaulis*** (L.) Griseb. (Bromeliaceae).
Note: Smith & Downs (in *Fl. Neotropica* 14: 1928. 1979) indicated "*Plumier s.n.* (P), West Indies" as type but it is unclear if such a specimen exists at P and, if it does, it would not have been studied by Linnaeus so would not be original material for the name.

Bromelia pinguin Linnaeus, *Species Plantarum* 1: 285. 1753.
"Habitat in Jamaica, Barbados." RCN: 2265.
Lectotype (Smith in *Phytologia* 15: 170. 1967): [icon] "*Pinguin, an Bromelia pyramidata, aculeis nigris Plum.*" in Dillenius, Hort. Eltham. 2: 320, t. 240, f. 311. 1732.
Current name: ***Bromelia pinguin*** L. (Bromeliaceae).
Note: Grant & Zijlstra (in *Selbyana* 19: 96. 1998) argue that *B. karatas* is the generitype, the choice having been made by Regel (in *Gartenflora* 17: 67. 1868) which therefore pre-dates the more widely accepted choice of *B. pinguin*, made by Hitchcock (*Prop. Brit. Bot.*: 144. 1929).

Bromus arvensis Linnaeus, *Species Plantarum* 1: 77. 1753.
"Habitat in Europa ad versuras agrorum." RCN: 640.
Lectotype (Smith in *Notes Roy. Bot. Gard. Edinburgh* 42: 499. 1985): Herb. Linn. No. 93.21 (LINN).
Current name: ***Bromus arvensis*** L. (Poaceae).
Note: Although Kerguélen (in *Lejeunia*, n.s., 75: 99. 1975) stated "Type: ...LINN", this is not accepted as a formal typification, for the reasons explained by Cafferty & al. (in *Taxon* 49: 240. 2000).

Bromus ciliatus Linnaeus, *Species Plantarum* 1: 76. 1753.
"Habitat in Canada; ex semine. D. Kalm." RCN: 638.
Neotype (McNeill in *Taxon* 25: 613. 1976): U.S.A. New York: Essex Co. Huntingdon Wildlife Forest Station, Newcomb, sand pit E. of ranger station, 23 Jul 1939, *Heady 768* (DAO; iso- US).
Current name: ***Bromus ciliatus*** L. (Poaceae).
Note: Hitchcock (in *Contr. U. S. Natl. Herb.* 12: 122. 1908) stated that no type was extant. Baum (in *Canad. J. Bot.* 45: 1849. 1967) referred to a specimen at S, annotated by Linnaeus "H. U. 4 e semine Canadensi" (sheet 40.9), as the "holotype", with sheet "93.10" at LINN (actually 93.12), annotated on the verso by Linnaeus with "e semine canaden.", an "isotype". However, McNeill (in *Taxon* 25: 612–613. 1976) convincingly argued that Baum's typification was unacceptable because the specimens (LINN 93.10, 93.12 & S 40.9) conflict with Linnaeus' diagnosis and, in the absence of any relevant original material, he designated a neotype.

Bromus cristatus Linnaeus, *Species Plantarum* 1: 78. 1753.
"Habitat in Sibiria, Tataria." RCN: 652.
Lectotype (Bowden in *Canad. J. Bot.* 43: 1429. 1965): Herb. Linn. No. 93.44, right specimen (LINN).
Current name: ***Agropyron cristatum*** (L.) Gaertn. (Poaceae).

Bromus distachyos Linnaeus, *Flora Palaestina*: 13. 1756.
"Habitat in H. [= Hasselquist]...Palaestina." RCN: 653.
Lectotype (Schippmann & Jarvis in *Taxon* 37: 158, f. 1. 1988): *Hasselquist*, Herb. Linn. No. 93.48 (LINN; iso- UPS-HASSELQ 70).
Current name: ***Brachypodium distachyon*** (L.) P. Beauv. (Poaceae).
Note: Sherif & Siddiqi (in Jafri & El-Gadi, *Fl. Libya* 145: 87. 1988) wrongly indicated the post-1756 93.46 (LINN) as type, and Meikle (*Fl. Cyprus* 2: 1815. 1985) indicated "Type: ...LINN!" without distinguishing between sheets 93.46 and 93.48. Schippmann & Jarvis designated 93.48 (LINN) as a neotype because they doubted whether it could be regarded as original material for the name. However, as the type is a Hasselquist collection, closely associated with the thesis in which the binomial appeared, it does appear to be original material, and the collection should be treated as a lectotype under Art. 9.8.

Bromus geniculatus Linnaeus, *Systema Naturae*, ed. 12, 2: 97; *Mantissa Plantarum*: 33. 1767.
"Habitat in Lusitania. Vandelli." RCN: 641.
Lectotype (Henrard in *Blumea* 2: 313. 1937): Herb. Linn. No. 93.24 (LINN).
Current name: ***Vulpia geniculata*** (L.) Link (Poaceae).
Note: Henrard's type choice was reiterated by Stace & Jarvis (in *Bot. J. Linn. Soc.* 91: 443. 1985).

Bromus giganteus Linnaeus, *Species Plantarum* 1: 77. 1753.
"Habitat in Europae sylvis siccis." RCN: 643.
Lectotype (Darbyshire in Cafferty & al. in *Taxon* 49: 248. 2000): Herb. A. van Royen No. 913.62–78 (L).
Current name: ***Festuca gigantea*** (L.) Vill. (Poaceae).
Note: Although Kerguélen (in *Lejeunia*, n.s., 75: 149. 1975) stated "Type: ...LINN", this is not accepted as a formal typification, for the reasons explained by Cafferty & al. (in *Taxon* 49: 240. 2000). Kerguélen & Plonka (in *Bull. Soc. Bot. Centre-Ouest*, n.s., num. spéc., 10: 173. 1989) wrongly indicated Herb. Linn. 93.27 (LINN), not original material for the name, as type and Darbyshire therefore rejected their choice in favour of van Royen material.

Bromus hordeaceus Linnaeus, *Species Plantarum* 1: 77. 1753.
"Habitat in Europae collibus aridissimis sabulosis." RCN: 632.
Basionym of: *Bromus secalinus* L. var. *hordeaceus* (L.) L. (1755).
Lectotype (Smith in Cafferty & al. in *Taxon* 49: 248. 2000): [icon] "*Gramen Avenaceum pratense gluma breviore squamosa et villosa*" in Morison, Pl. Hist. Univ. 3: 213, s. 8, t. 7, f. 18. 1699. – Epitype (Smith in Cafferty & al. in *Taxon* 49: 248. 2000): Herb. Linn. No. 93.7 (LINN).
Current name: ***Bromus hordeaceus*** L. (Poaceae).
Note: Lambinon (in *Taxon* 30: 362. 1981) proposed the name for rejection but the Committee for Spermatophyta (in *Taxon* 35: 558. 1986) declined to accept the proposal. Smith (in *Notes Roy. Bot. Gard. Edinburgh* 42: 498. 1985) designated 93.7 (LINN) as a neotype but, in the presence of original material (in this case, an illustration), this choice is contrary to Art. 9.17a of the Vienna Code, and so was subsequently superseded by Smith in 2000.

Bromus inermis Linnaeus, *Mantissa Plantarum Altera*: 186. 1771, *nom. illeg.*

"Habitat in Russiae, Germaniae, Angliae sylvis, sepibus. H. V. [sic]" RCN: 636.
Replaced synonym: *Bromus ramosus* Huds. (1762).
Type not designated.
Current name: ***Bromus ramosus*** Huds. (Poaceae).
Note: An illegitimate replacement name for *B. ramosus* Huds.

Bromus madritensis Linnaeus, *Centuria I Plantarum*: 5. 1755.
"Habitat in Hispania." RCN: 649.
Lectotype (Smith in *Notes Roy. Bot. Gard. Edinburgh* 42: 500. 1985): Herb. Linn. No. 93.35 (LINN).
Current name: ***Bromus madritensis*** L. (Poaceae).
Note: Although Kerguélen (in *Lejeunia*, n.s., 75: 107. 1975) stated "Type: ...LINN", this is not accepted as a formal typification, for the reasons explained by Cafferty & al. (in *Taxon* 49: 240. 2000).

Bromus mollis Linnaeus, *Species Plantarum*, ed. 2, 1: 112. 1762.
"Habitat in Europae australioris siccis." RCN: 633.
Lectotype (Smith in Cafferty & al. in *Taxon* 49: 248. 2000): Herb. Linn. No. 93.6 (LINN).
Current name: ***Bromus hordeaceus*** L. (Poaceae).
Note: See discussion by Smith (in *Watsonia* 6: 328. 1968) and Rauschert (in *Feddes Repert.* 88: 317. 1977).

Bromus pinnatus Linnaeus, *Species Plantarum* 1: 78. 1753.
"Habitat in Europae sylvis montosis asperis." RCN: 651.
Lectotype (Schippmann & Jarvis in *Taxon* 37: 160, f. 3. 1988): Herb. Linn. No. 93.42 (LINN).
Current name: ***Brachypodium pinnatum*** (L.) P. Beauv. (Poaceae).
Note: Although Kerguélen (in *Lejeunia*, n.s., 75: 96. 1975) stated "Type: ...LINN", this is not accepted as a formal typification, for the reasons explained by Cafferty & al. (in *Taxon* 49: 240. 2000). Meikle (*Fl. Cyprus* 2: 1813. 1985) indicated "Type: ...LINN!" without distinguishing between sheets 93.42 and 93.43. Heath (in *Taxon* 40: 94. 1991) argued that Schippmann & Jarvis' type choice is invalid but the argument he used in support of this was refuted by Jarvis (in *Taxon* 41: 63–64. 1992).

Bromus purgans Linnaeus, *Species Plantarum* 1: 76. 1753, *nom. utique rej.*
"Habitat in Canada. Kalm." RCN: 635.
Lectotype (Hitchcock in *Contr. U. S. Natl. Herb.* 12: 122. 1908): *Kalm*, Herb. Linn. No. 93.11 (LINN; iso- US, fragm.).
Current name: ***Bromus kalmii*** A. Gray (Poaceae).

Bromus racemosus Linnaeus, *Species Plantarum*, ed. 2, 1: 114. 1762.
"Habitat in Anglia." RCN: 647.
Lectotype (Smith in *Notes Roy. Bot. Gard. Edinburgh* 42: 499. 1985): *Hudson 34*, Herb. Linn. No. 93.31 (LINN).
Current name: ***Bromus racemosus*** L. (Poaceae).
Note: Although Kerguélen (in *Lejeunia*, n.s., 75: 108. 1975) stated "Type: ...LINN", this is not accepted as a formal typification, for the reasons explained by Cafferty & al. (in *Taxon* 49: 240. 2000).

Bromus ramosus Linnaeus, *Systema Naturae*, ed. 12, 2: 98; *Mantissa Plantarum*: 34. 1767, *nom. illeg.*
"Habitat in Oriente. D. Schreber." RCN: 650.
Lectotype (Schippmann in Cafferty & al. in *Taxon* 49: 248. 2000): *Schreber*, Herb. Linn. No. 93.41 (LINN).
Current name: ***Brachypodium retusum*** (Pers.) P. Beauv. (Poaceae).
Note: A later homonym of *B. ramosus* Huds. (1762) and hence illegitimate.

Bromus rigens Linnaeus, *Systema Naturae,* ed. 12, 2: 97; *Mantissa Plantarum*: 33. 1767.
"Habitat in Lusitania. Vandelli." RCN: 646.
Lectotype (Sales in *Edinburgh J. Bot.* 50: 11. 1993): Herb. Linn. No. 93.34 (LINN).
Current name: ***Bromus scoparius*** L. (Poaceae).

Bromus rubens Linnaeus, *Centuria I Plantarum*: 5. 1755.
"Habitat in Hispania. Loefling." RCN: 644.
Lectotype (Smith in *Notes Roy. Bot. Gard. Edinburgh* 42: 500. 1985): *Löfling 84*, Herb. Linn. No. 93.28 (LINN).
Current name: ***Bromus rubens*** L. (Poaceae).
Note: Although Kerguélen (in *Lejeunia*, n.s., 75: 109. 1975) stated "Type: ...LINN", this is not accepted as a formal typification, for the reasons explained by Cafferty & al. (in *Taxon* 49: 240. 2000).

Bromus scoparius Linnaeus, *Centuria I Plantarum*: 6. 1755.
"Habitat in Hispania." RCN: 645.
Lectotype (Smith in *Notes Roy. Bot. Gard. Edinburgh* 42: 499. 1985): *Löfling 81*, Herb. Linn. No. 93.32 (LINN).
Current name: ***Bromus scoparius*** L. (Poaceae).
Note: Although Kerguélen (in *Lejeunia*, n.s., 75: 110. 1975) stated "Type: ...LINN", this is not accepted as a formal typification, for the reasons explained by Cafferty & al. (in *Taxon* 49: 240. 2000). Meikle (*Fl. Cyprus* 2: 1808. 23 Apr 1985) indicated unspecified material in LINN as type but did not distinguish between sheets 93.32 and 93.33 (which are not part of a single gathering so Art. 9.15 does not apply). Smith's typification from later in 1985 therefore stands.

Bromus secalinus Linnaeus, *Species Plantarum* 1: 76. 1753, *typ. cons.*
"Habitat in Europae agris secalinis arenosis." RCN: 631.
Conserved type (Smith in *Notes Roy. Bot. Gard. Edinburgh* 42: 498. 1985): Herb. Linn. No. 93.1 (LINN).
Generitype of *Bromus* Linnaeus, *nom. cons.*
Current name: ***Bromus secalinus*** L. (Poaceae).
Note: Bromus secalinus, with the type designated by Smith, was proposed as conserved type of the genus by Jarvis (in *Taxon* 41: 559. 1992). This was eventually approved by the General Committee (see review of the history of this proposal by Barrie, *l.c.* 55: 795–796. 2006).

Bromus secalinus Linnaeus var. **hordeaceus** (Linnaeus) Linnaeus, *Flora Suecica*, ed. 2: 33. 1755.
"Habitat β. vero in collibus ad rupes et in glabretis." RCN: 631.
Basionym: *Bromus hordeaceus* L. (1753).
Lectotype (Smith in Cafferty & al. in *Taxon* 49: 248. 2000): [icon] *"Gramen Avenaceum pratense gluma breviore squamosa et villosa"* in Morison, Pl. Hist. Univ. 3: 213, s. 8, t. 7, f. 18. 1699. – Epitype (Smith in Cafferty & al. in *Taxon* 49: 248. 2000): Herb. Linn. No. 93.7 (LINN).
Current name: ***Bromus hordeaceus*** L. (Poaceae).

Bromus squarrosus Linnaeus, *Species Plantarum* 1: 76. 1753.
"Habitat in Gallia, Helvetia, Sibiria." RCN: 634.
Lectotype (Meikle, *Fl. Cyprus* 2: 1809. 1985): *Löfling 79a*, Herb. Linn. No. 93.8 (LINN).
Current name: ***Bromus squarrosus*** L. (Poaceae).
Note: Although Kerguélen (in *Lejeunia*, n.s., 75: 110. 1975) stated "Type: ...LINN", this is not accepted as a formal typification, for the reasons explained by Cafferty & al. (in *Taxon* 49: 240. 2000). Meikle's choice (23 Apr 1985) narrowly pre-dates that of Smith (in *Notes Roy. Bot. Gard. Edinburgh* 42: 500. Oct 1985), who designated the same collection as lectotype.

Bromus sterilis Linnaeus, *Species Plantarum* 1: 77. 1753, *nom. cons.*
"Habitat in Europae australioris agris, sylvis." RCN: 639.
Conserved type (Sales in *Taxon* 41: 584. 1992): *Hubbard 9045* (E; iso-K).
Current name: ***Bromus sterilis*** L. (Poaceae).

Bromus stipoides Linnaeus, *Mantissa Plantarum Altera*: 557. 1771.
"Habitat in Majorca." RCN: 654.
Lectotype (Stace & Jarvis in *Taxon* 34: 443. 1985): Herb. Linn. No. 93.50 (LINN).
Current name: ***Vulpia geniculata*** (L.) Link (Poaceae).

Bromus tectorum Linnaeus, *Species Plantarum* 1: 77. 1753.
"Habitat in Europae collibus siccis et tectis terrestribus." RCN: 642.
Lectotype (Smith in *Notes Roy. Bot. Gard. Edinburgh* 42: 500. 1985): Herb. Linn. No. 93.23 (LINN).
Current name: ***Bromus tectorum*** L. (Poaceae).
Note: Although Kerguélen (in *Lejeunia*, n.s., 75: 111. 1975) stated "Type: ...LINN", this is not accepted as a formal typification, for the reasons explained by Cafferty & al. (in *Taxon* 49: 240. 2000). Meikle (*Fl. Cyprus* 2: 1811. 23 Apr 1985) indicated unspecified material in LINN as type but did not distinguish between sheets 93.23 and 93.25 (which are not part of a single gathering so Art. 9.15 does not apply).

Bromus triflorus Linnaeus, *Species Plantarum*, ed. 2, 1: 115. 1762.
"Habitat in Germaniae, Daniae, nemoribus. Forskåhl." RCN: 648.
Lectotype (Stace in Cafferty & al. in *Taxon* 49: 248. 2000): [icon] *"Gramen Bromoides, panicula sparsa, locustis minoribus, aristatis"* in Scheuchzer, Agrostographia: 511, t. 5, f. 19. 1719. – Epitype (Stace in Cafferty & al. in *Taxon* 49: 248. 2000): Germany. Siebenbäumen between Bad Oldesloe and Ratzeburg, 29 Jul 1969, *Jeppesen & Larsen s.n.* [K. Larsen, Fl. Germ. Exsicc., Schleswig-Holstein, No. 29] (BM-000576272).
Current name: ***Festuca gigantea*** (L.) Vill. (Poaceae).

Brossaea coccinea Linnaeus, *Species Plantarum* 2: 1190. 1753.
"Habitat in America calidiore." RCN: 1403.
Lectotype (Bornstein in Howard, *Fl. Lesser Antilles* 6: 28. 1989): [icon] *"Brossaea"* in Plumier, Nov. Pl. Amer.: 5, t. 17. 1703.
Generitype of *Brossaea* Linnaeus.
Current name: ***Gaultheria dominguensis*** Urb. (Ericaceae).

Browallia alienata Linnaeus, *Systema Naturae*, ed. 10, 2: 1118. 1759. RCN: 4580.
Type not designated.
Original material: [icon] in Miller, Fig. Pl. Gard. Dict. 1: 46, t. 69. 1756.
Current name: ***Ruellia paniculata*** L. (Acanthaceae).
Note: D'Arcy (in *Ann. Missouri Bot. Gard.* 60: 577. 1974) says this name is based on a cited Miller reference but does not explicitly treat it as the type.

Browallia americana Linnaeus, *Species Plantarum* 2: 631. 1753.
"Habitat in America australi." RCN: 4578.
Replaced synonym of: *Browallia demissa* L. (1759), *nom. illeg.*
Lectotype (Stearn, *Introd. Linnaeus' Sp. Pl.* (Ray Soc. ed.): 47. 1957): [icon] *"Browallia"* in Linnaeus, Hort. Cliff.: 319, t. 17. 1738. – Voucher: Herb. Clifford: 319, *Browallia* 1 (BM).
Generitype of *Browallia* Linnaeus.
Current name: ***Browallia americana*** L. (Solanaceae).
Note: Although D'Arcy (in *Ann. Missouri Bot. Gard.* 60: 578. 1974) indicated a Clifford sheet (BM), and Deb (in *J. Econ. Taxon. Bot.* 1: 34. 1980) treated 791.2 (LINN) as the type, both choices are pre-dated by that of Stearn.

Browallia demissa Linnaeus, *Systema Naturae*, ed. 10, 2: 1118. 1759, *nom. illeg.*
["Habitat in America australi."] Sp. Pl. 2: 631 (1753). RCN: 4578.
Replaced synonym: *Browallia americana* L. (1753).
Lectotype (Stearn, *Introd. Linnaeus' Sp. Pl.* (Ray Soc. ed.): 47. 1957): [icon] *"Browallia"* in Linnaeus, Hort. Cliff.: 319, t. 17. 1738. – Voucher: Herb. Clifford: 319, *Browallia* 1 (BM).
Current name: ***Browallia americana*** L. (Solanaceae).
Note: An illegitimate replacement name for *B. americana* L. (1753).

Browallia elata Linnaeus, *Systema Naturae*, ed. 10, 2: 1118. 1759.
["Habitat in Peru."] Sp. Pl., ed. 2, 2: 880 (1763). RCN: 4579.
Lectotype (designated here by Edmonds): Herb. Linn. No. 791.3 (LINN).
Current name: ***Browallia americana*** L. (Solanaceae).

Brunfelsia americana Linnaeus, *Species Plantarum* 1: 191. 1753.
"Habitat in America meridionali." RCN: 1539.
Lectotype (Howard, *Fl. Lesser Antilles* 6: 270. 1989): [icon] *"Brunsfelsia"* in Plumier, Nov. Pl. Amer.: 12, t. 22. 1703.
Generitype of *Brunfelsia* Linnaeus, *orth. cons.*
Current name: ***Brunfelsia americana*** L. (Solanaceae).

Brunia abrotanoides Linnaeus, *Species Plantarum* 1: 199. 1753.
"Habitat in Aethiopia." RCN: 1616.
Lectotype (Powrie in *Taxon* 21: 710. 1972): [icon] *"Brunia foliolis creberrimis, lanceolatis, floribus conglobatis"* in Burman, Rar. Afric. Pl.: 266, t. 100, f. 1. 1739.
Current name: ***Berzelia abrotanoides*** (L.) Brongn. (Bruniaceae).

Brunia ciliata Linnaeus, *Species Plantarum* 1: 199. 1753.
"Habitat in Aethiopia." RCN: 1617.
Type not designated.
Original material: none traced.
Note: The application of this name is uncertain – see discussion by Powrie (in *J. S. African Bot.* 38: 302. 1972).

Brunia cupressina Linnaeus, *Mantissa Plantarum Altera*: 343. 1771, *nom. illeg.*
RCN: 1606.
Replaced synonym: *Diosma dichotoma* P.J. Bergius (1767).
Type not designated.
Current name: ***Thamnea uniflora*** (L.) Sol. ex Brongn. (Bruniaceae).
Note: A superfluous name for *Diosma dichotoma* P.J. Bergius (1767).

Brunia lanuginosa Linnaeus, *Species Plantarum* 1: 199. 1753.
"Habitat in Aethiopia." RCN: 1615.
Lectotype (Powrie in *J. S. African Bot.* 38: 302. 1972): Herb. Clifford: 71, *Brunia* 2 (BM-000558118).
Generitype of *Brunia* Linnaeus, *nom. rej.*
Current name: ***Berzelia lanuginosa*** (L.) Brongn. (Bruniaceae).
Note: Brunia Linnaeus, *nom. rej.* vs. *Brunia* Lam.

Brunia levisanus Linnaeus, *Species Plantarum* 1: 199. 1753.
"Habitat in Aethiopia." RCN: 778.
Basionym of: *Protea levisanus* (L.) L. (1767).
Lectotype (Williams in *Contr. Bolus Herb.* 3: 59. 1972): [icon] *"Brunia foliis oblongis, incanis, florum capitulo ramulum terminante"* in Burman, Rar. Afric. Pl.: 267, t. 100, f. 2. 1738.
Current name: ***Leucadendron levisanus*** (L.) P.J. Bergius (Proteaceae).

Brunia nodiflora Linnaeus, *Species Plantarum* 1: 199. 1753.
"Habitat in Aethiopia." RCN: 1613.
Lectotype (Powrie in *J. S. African Bot.* 38: 303. 1972): Herb. Clifford: 71, *Brunia* 1 (BM-000558117).

Current name: **Widdringtonia nodiflora** (L.) Powrie (Cupressaceae).
Note: See further comments by Powrie (in *Taxon* 21: 711. 1972; 23: 432. 1974) and Farjon (*Monogr. Cupressaceae* Sciadopitys: 471. 2005).

Brunia uniflora Linnaeus, *Species Plantarum* 1: 199. 1753.
"Habitat in Aethiopia." RCN: 1606.
Type not designated.
Original material: Herb. Clifford: 71, *Brunia* 3 (BM); [icon] in Plukenet, Phytographia: t. 279, f. 2. 1694; Almag. Bot.: 136. 1696.
Current name: **Thamnea uniflora** (L.) Sol. ex Brongn. (Bruniaceae).

Bryonia africana Linnaeus, *Species Plantarum* 2: 1013. 1753.
"Habitat in Aethiopia." RCN: 7345.
Type not designated.
Original material: Herb. Linn. No. 395.9 (S); Herb. Linn. No. 1153.9 (LINN); Herb. Clifford: 453, *Bryonia* 4 (BM); [icon] in Hermann, Parad. Bat.: 107, 108. 1698.
Current name: **Kedrostis africana** (L.) Cogn. (Cucurbitaceae).
Note: Meeuse (in *Bothalia* 8: 33. 1962) interpreted the name via a Hermann illustration, which Newton & Njoroge (in Eggli, *Ill. Handb. Succ. Pl., Dicots*: 86. 2002) indicated as the type, but this choice was published after 1 Jan 2001 and so the omission of the phrase "designated here" or an equivalent (Art. 7.11) means that it is not effective.

Bryonia alba Linnaeus, *Species Plantarum* 2: 1012. 1753.
"Habitat in Europa ad pagos & sepes." RCN: 7340.

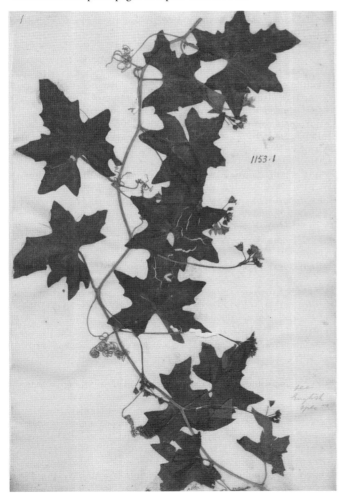

Lectotype (Jeffrey in *Kew Bull.* 23: 455. 1969): Herb. Linn. No. 1153.1 (LINN).
Generitype of *Bryonia* Linnaeus (vide Green, *Prop. Brit. Bot.*: 190. 1929).
Current name: **Bryonia alba** L. (Cucurbitaceae).

Bryonia cordifolia Linnaeus, *Species Plantarum* 2: 1012. 1753.
"Habitat in Zeylona." RCN: 7343.
Lectotype (Jeffrey in Milne-Redhead & Polhill, *Fl. Trop. E. Africa, Cucurbitaceae*: 117. 1967): Herb. Hermann 2: 22, No. 354 (BM-000621582).
Current name: **Mukia maderaspatana** (L.) M. Roem. (Cucurbitaceae).

Bryonia cretica Linnaeus, *Species Plantarum* 2: 1013. 1753.
"Habitat in Creta." RCN: 7346.
Type not designated.
Original material: Herb. Clifford: 453, *Bryonia* 2 (BM).
Current name: **Bryonia cretica** L. subsp. **cretica** (Cucurbitaceae).

Bryonia grandis Linnaeus, *Systema Naturae*, ed. 12, 2: 640; *Mantissa Plantarum*: 126. 1767.
"Habitat in India." RCN: 7342.
Lectotype (Jeffrey in Milne-Redhead & Polhill, *Fl. Trop. E. Africa, Cucurbitaceae*: 68. 1967): Herb. Linn. No. 1153.2 (LINN).
Current name: **Coccinia grandis** (L.) Voigt (Cucurbitaceae).

Bryonia laciniosa Linnaeus, *Species Plantarum* 2: 1013. 1753.
"Habitat in Zeylona." RCN: 7344.
Lectotype (Jeffrey in *Kew Bull.* 15: 346. 1962): Herb. Clifford: 452, *Bryonia* 1 (BM-000647451).
Current name: **Cayaponia laciniosa** (L.) C. Jeffrey (Cucurbitaceae).

Bryonia palmata Linnaeus, *Species Plantarum* 2: 1012. 1753.
"Habitat in Zeylona." RCN: 7341.
Lectotype (Jeffrey in *Kew Bull.* 15: 352. 1962): Herb. Hermann 2: 58, No. 353 (BM-000621700).
Current name: **Diplocyclos palmatus** (L.) C. Jeffrey (Cucurbitaceae).

Bryonia punctata Linnaeus, *Demonstr. Pl. Horto Upsaliensi*: 26. 1753.
"Habitat in India."
Basionym of: *Trichosanthes punctata* (L.) L. (1756).
Lectotype (Wunderlin in Woodson & Schery in *Ann. Missouri Bot. Gard.* 65: 314. 1978): Herb. Linn. No. 1180.1 (LINN).
Current name: **Fevillea cordifolia** L. (Cucurbitaceae).

Bubon galbanus Linnaeus, *Species Plantarum* 1: 253. 1753.
"Habitat in Aethiopia." RCN: 2037.
Lectotype (Van Wyk & Tilney in Jarvis & al. in *Taxon* 55: 209. 2006): Herb. Clifford: 96, *Bubon* 3, sheet A (BM-000558280).
Current name: **Peucedanum galbanum** (L.) Benth. & Hook. f. (Apiaceae).
Note: Specific epithet spelled "galbanum" in the protologue.

Bubon gummiferus Linnaeus, *Species Plantarum* 1: 254. 1753.
"Habitat in Aethiopia." RCN: 2038.
Lectotype (Wijnands, *Bot. Commelins*: 200. 1983): [icon] *"Ferula Africana Galbanifera frutescens myrrhidis foliis"* in Commelin, Hort. Med. Amstelod. Pl. Rar. 2: 115, t. 58. 1701.
Current name: **Peucedanum gummiferum** (L.) Wijnands (Apiaceae).
Note: Specific epithet spelled "gummiferum" in the protologue.

Bubon macedonicum Linnaeus, *Species Plantarum* 1: 253. 1753.
"Habitat in Macedonia." RCN: 2036.
Lectotype (Jarvis & Knees in *Taxon* 37: 475. 1988): Herb. Clifford: 95, *Bubon* 2 (BM-000558277).

Generitype of *Bubon* Linnaeus (vide Bentham & Hooker, *Gen. Pl.* 1: 901. 1867).
Current name: **Athamanta macedonica** (L.) Spreng. (Apiaceae).

Bubon rigidius Linnaeus, *Species Plantarum* 1: 254. 1753.
"Habitat in Sicilia." RCN: 2039.
Type not designated.
Original material: Herb. Clifford: 95, *Bubon* 1 (BM); [icon] in Barrelier, Pl. Galliam: 61, t. 77. 1714; [icon] in Boccone, Mus. Piante Rar. Sicilia: 84, t. 76. 1697.
Note: The application of this name is uncertain but the identity of the original material suggests that *B. rigidius* should be a candidate for formal rejection.

Bucephalon racemosum Linnaeus, *Species Plantarum* 2: 1190. 1753.
"Habitat in America." RCN: 7400.
Lectotype (Burger in Jarvis & al., *Regnum Veg.* 127: 26. 1993): [icon] *"Bucephalon"* in Plumier in Burman, Pl. Amer.: 55, t. 67, f. 1. 1756.
Generitype of *Bucephalon* Linnaeus, nom. rej.
Current name: **Trophis racemosa** (L.) Urb. (Moraceae).
Note: Bucephalon Linnaeus, *nom. rej.* vs *Trophis* P. Browne.
Burger (in *Ann. Missouri Bot. Gard.* 49: 7. 1962) and Berg (in Harling & Andersson, *Fl. Ecuador* 60: 18. 1998) indicated 1165.1 (LINN), a post-1753 addition to the collection, as type. Burger subsequently designated a Plumier plate as lectotype.

Buchnera aethiopica Linnaeus, *Mantissa Plantarum Altera*: 251. 1771.
"Habitat in Capitis b. spei campis arenosis." RCN: 4574.
Lectotype (Hilliard, *Manuleae, Tribe Scrophulariaceae*: 263. 1994): *Tulbagh 171*, Herb. Linn. No. 790.6 (LINN), see p. 232.
Current name: **Sutera aethiopica** (L.) Kuntze (Scrophulariaceae).

Buchnera africana Linnaeus, *Plantae Rariores Africanae*: 12. 1760.
["Habitat in Aethiopia."] Sp. Pl., ed. 2, 2: 879 (1763). RCN: 4376.
Replaced synonym of: *Rhinanthus capensis* L. (1767), *nom. illeg.*
Type not designated.
Original material: [icon] in Plukenet, Phytographia: t. 310, f. 2. 1694; Almag. Bot.: 283. 1696.
Note: The application of this name appears uncertain.

Buchnera americana Linnaeus, *Species Plantarum* 2: 630. 1753.
"Habitat in Virginia, Canada." RCN: 4572.
Lectotype (Pennell in *Torreya* 19: 235. 1919): *Clayton 142* (BM-000038178).
Generitype of *Buchnera* Linnaeus (vide Green, *Prop. Brit. Bot.*: 168. 1929).
Current name: **Buchnera americana** L. (Scrophulariaceae).

Buchnera asiatica Linnaeus, *Species Plantarum* 2: 630. 1753.
"Habitat in Zeylona, China." RCN: 4577.
Lectotype (Hepper in *Rhodora* 76: 46. 1974): *Torén*, Herb. Linn. No. 790.10, branched specimen (LINN).
Current name: **Striga asiatica** (L.) Kuntze (Scrophulariaceae).
Note: Hepper argued that 790.10 (LINN) was collected by Torén in the Comores in 1750 (it is annotated "Ins. Johan."). Saldanha (in *Bull. Bot. Surv. India* 5: 67–68. 1963) reviewed earlier use of the name and concluded that, as it had been applied to several species, it should be rejected under (the then) Art. 69. Cramer (in Dassanayake & Fosberg, *Revised Handb. Fl. Ceylon* 3: 400. 1981) also treated the name as ambiguous. However, Musselman & Hepper (in *Kew Bull.* 41: 207. 1986; *Notes Roy. Bot. Gard. Edinburgh* 45: 44. 1988) accept *S. asiatica*, as do many other authors.

Buchnera canadensis Linnaeus, *Systema Naturae*, ed. 12, 2: 421; *Mantissa Plantarum*: 88. 1767.
"Habitat in Virginia." RCN: 4575.
Lectotype (Moldenke in *Phytologia* 8: 468. 1963): Herb. Linn. No. 790.7 (LINN).
Current name: **Glandularia canadensis** (L.) Nutt. (Verbenaceae).

Buchnera capensis Linnaeus, *Systema Naturae*, ed. 12, 2: 421; *Mantissa Plantarum*: 88. 1767.
"Habitat ad Cap. b. spei." RCN: 4576.
Lectotype (Hilliard, *Manuleae, Tribe Scrophulariaceae*: 402. 1994): *Burman s.n.*, Herb. Linn. No. 790.9 (LINN).
Current name: **Polycarena capensis** (L.) Benth. (Scrophulariaceae).

Buchnera cernua Linnaeus, *Mantissa Plantarum Altera*: 251. 1771.
"Habitat in Cap. b. spei montibus." RCN: 4573.
Lectotype (Moldenke in *Repert. Spec. Nov. Regni Veg.* 45: 314. 1938): *Tulbagh 100*, Herb. Linn. No. 790.1 (LINN).
Current name: **Plexipus cernuus** (L.) R. Fern. (Verbenaceae).

Bucida buceras Linnaeus, *Systema Naturae*, ed. 10, 2: 1025. 1759.
["Habitat in Jamaica."] Sp. Pl., ed. 2, 1: 557 (1762). RCN: 3127.
Lectotype (Fawcett & Rendle, *Fl. Jamaica* 5: 307. 1926): *Browne*, Herb. Linn. No. 556.1 (LINN; iso- BM).
Generitype of *Bucida* Linnaeus, nom. cons.
Current name: **Terminalia buceras** (L.) C. Wright (Combretaceae).
Note: Bucida Linnaeus, *nom. cons.* vs *Buceras* P. Browne.

Buddleja americana Linnaeus, *Species Plantarum* 1: 112. 1753.
"Habitat in Caribaeis ad ripas & torrentes." RCN: 919.
Lectotype (Norman in *Gentes Herb.* 10: 83. 1967): Herb. Clifford: 35, *Buddleja* 1 (BM-000557795).
Generitype of *Buddleja* Linnaeus.
Current name: **Buddleja americana** L. (Loganiaceae/Buddlejaceae).

Buddleja occidentalis Linnaeus, *Species Plantarum*, ed. 2, 1: 162. 1762.
"Habitat in America." RCN: 920.
Lectotype (Norman in *Gentes Herb.* 10: 83. 1967): *Houstoun*, Herb. Miller (BM).
Current name: **Buddleja americana** L. (Loganiaceae/Buddlejaceae).

Bufonia tenuifolia Linnaeus, *Species Plantarum* 1: 123. 1753.
"Habitat in Anglia, Gallia, Hispania." RCN: 1020.
Lectotype (Amich & López González in Jarvis & al., *Regnum Veg.* 127: 27. 1993): *Löfling 138a*, Herb. Linn. No. 168.1 (LINN).
Generitype of *Bufonia* Linnaeus.
Current name: **Bufonia tenuifolia** L. (Caryophyllaceae).

Bufonia tenuissima Linnaeus, *Amoenitates Academicae* 4: 478. 1759, *orth. var.*
["Habitat in Anglia, Gallia, Hispania."] Sp. Pl. 1: 123 (1753). RCN: 1020.
Lectotype (Amich & López González in Jarvis & al., *Regnum Veg.* 127: 27. 1993): *Löfling 138a*, Herb. Linn. No. 168.1 (LINN).
Current name: **Bufonia tenuifolia** L. (Caryophyllaceae).
Note: Bufonia tenuissima L. (Amoen. Acad. 4: 478. 1759) has been treated by Stearn (in Geck & Pressler, *Festschr. Claus Nissen*: 631. 1974) as an orthographic variant of *B. tenuifolia* L. (1753).

Bulbocodium autumnale Linnaeus, *Flora Anglica*: 14. 1754.
"Habitat [in Anglia.]"
Type not designated.
Original material: *Lloyd*, Herb. Sloane 113: 224 (BM-SL); Trigvylchau, June 1700, *Lloyd & Richardson*, Herb. Sloane 152: 1

(BM-SL); [icon] in Ray, Syn. Meth. Stirp. Brit., ed. 3: 374, t. 17, f. 1. 1724.
Current name: ***Lloydia serotina*** (L.) Rchb. (Liliaceae).
Note: See notes by Stearn (*Introd. Ray's Syn. Meth. Stirp. Brit.* (Ray Soc. ed.): 64–65. 1973).

Bulbocodium serotinum Linnaeus, *Species Plantarum* 1: 294. 1753.
"Habitat in Alpibus Helvetiae, Angliae." RCN: 2441.
Basionym of: *Anthericum serotinum* (L.) L. (1762).
Type not designated.
Original material: Herb. A. van Royen No. 908.106–1769 (L); Herb. Burser III: 41 (UPS); [icon] in Ray, Syn. Meth. Stirp. Brit., ed. 3: 374, t. 17, f. 1. 1724; [icon] in Rudbeck, Campi Elysii 2: 64, f. 9. 1701.
Current name: ***Lloydia serotina*** (L.) Rchb. (Liliaceae).
Note: See notes by Stearn (*Introd. Ray's Syn. Meth. Stirp. Brit.* (Ray Soc. ed.): 64–65. 1973).

Bulbocodium vernum Linnaeus, *Species Plantarum* 1: 294. 1753.
"Habitat in Hispania." RCN: 2342.
Lectotype (Mathew & López González in Jarvis & al., *Regnum Veg.* 127: 27. 1993): Herb. Linn. No. 417.1 (LINN).
Generitype of *Bulbocodium* Linnaeus (vide Steudel, *Nom.*, ed. 2, 1: 236. 1840).
Current name: ***Colchicum vernum*** (L.) Stef. (Liliaceae/Colchicaceae).

Bunias aegyptiaca Linnaeus, *Systema Naturae,* ed. 12, 3: 231. 1768.
"Habitat in Aegypto. Zoega." RCN: 4883.
Lectotype (Hedge in Cafferty & Jarvis in *Taxon* 51: 532. 2002): Herb. Linn. No. 847.12 (LINN).
Current name: ***Ochthodium aegyptiacum*** (L.) DC. (Brassicaceae).

Bunias balearica Linnaeus, *Systema Naturae,* ed. 12, 2: 446. 1767.
"Habitat in Balearibus. D. Royen." RCN: 4884.
Lectotype (Rosselló in Cafferty & Jarvis in *Taxon* 51: 532. 2002): *Gouan s.n.*, Herb. Linn. No. 847.13 (LINN).
Current name: ***Succowia balearica*** (L.) Medik. (Brassicaceae).
Note: Rosselló & Sáez (in *Collect. Bot.* 25: 32. 2000) indicated unspecified collections in BM and LINN as syntypes, but this does not constitute typification.

Bunias cakile Linnaeus, *Species Plantarum* 2: 670. 1753.
"Habitat in Europae, Africae, Americae maritimis." RCN: 4881.
Lectotype (Elven in Jonsell & Jarvis in *Nordic J. Bot.* 22: 68. 2002): Herb. Linn. No. 847.5a, right specimen (LINN).
Current name: ***Cakile maritima*** Scop. (Brassicaceae).
Note: Elven provides an extensive discussion along with the formal typification of this name.

Bunias cornuta Linnaeus, *Species Plantarum* 2: 669. 1753.
"Habitat in Sibiria. D. Gmelin." RCN: 4877.
Lectotype (Illarionova in *Komarovia* 1: 36. 1999): Herb. Linn. No. 847.1 (LINN).
Current name: ***Pugionium cornutum*** (L.) Gaertn. (Brassicaceae).

Bunias erucago Linnaeus, *Species Plantarum* 2: 670. 1753.
"Habitat Monspelii in agris humidiusculis." RCN: 4879.
Lectotype (Hedge in Jarvis & al., *Regnum Veg.* 127: 27. 1993): Herb. Clifford: 340, *Bunias* 1 (BM-000646379).
Generitype of *Bunias* Linnaeus (vide Green, *Prop. Brit. Bot.*: 172. 1929).
Current name: ***Bunias erucago*** L. (Brassicaceae).

Bunias myagroides Linnaeus, *Systema Naturae,* ed. 12, 2: 446; *Mantissa Plantarum*: 96. 1767.

"Habitat in Sibiria. J. Falk." RCN: 4882.
Lectotype (Gómez-Campo in Cafferty & Jarvis in *Taxon* 51: 532. 2002): Herb. Linn. No. 847.9 (LINN).
Current name: ***Erucaria hispanica*** (L.) Druce (Brassicaceae).

Bunias orientalis Linnaeus, *Species Plantarum* 2: 670. 1753.
"Habitat in Russia." RCN: 4880.
Lectotype (Jonsell & Jarvis in *Nordic J. Bot.* 22: 68. 2002): Herb. Linn. No. 847.4 (LINN).
Current name: ***Bunias orientalis*** L. (Brassicaceae).

Bunium aromaticum Linnaeus, *Mantissa Plantarum Altera*: 218. 1771.
"Habitat in Creta. Syria." RCN: 1953.
Lectotype (Watson in Jarvis & al. in *Taxon* 55: 208. 2006): Herb. Burser VIII: 43 (UPS).
Current name: ***Trachyspermum copticum*** (L.) Link (Apiaceae).

Bunium bulbocastanum Linnaeus, *Species Plantarum* 1: 243. 1753.
"Habitat in Germania, Anglia, Gallia." RCN: 1952.
Lectotype (Reduron & Jarvis in Jarvis & al., *Regnum Veg.* 127: 27. 1993): Herb. Burser VIII: 78 (UPS).
Generitype of *Bunium* Linnaeus.
Current name: ***Bunium bulbocastanum*** L. (Apiaceae).

Buphthalmum aquaticum Linnaeus, *Species Plantarum* 2: 903. 1753.
"Habitat in Creta, Lusitania, Massiliae." RCN: 6530.
Lectotype (Grierson in Davis, *Fl. Turkey* 5: 51. 1975): Herb. Clifford: 414, *Buphthalmum* 8 (BM-000647179).
Current name: ***Asteriscus aquaticus*** (L.) Less. (Asteraceae).
Note: Buphthalmum aquaticum was incorrectly given as the generitype by Jarvis & al. (*Regnum Veg.* 127: 27. 1993) in error for *B. salicifolium* L., as noted by Greuter (in *Fl. Medit.* 4: 3. 1997).
    Although Davis (*Fl. Turkey* 10: 238. 1988) did not list this as a name typified in the Flora, Grierson (in Davis, *Fl. Turkey* 5: 51. 1975) nevertheless specifically indicated the Clifford material as the type.

Buphthalmum arborescens Linnaeus, *Systema Naturae,* ed. 10, 2: 1227. 1759.
["Habitat in America."] Sp. Pl. ed. 2, 2: 1273 (1763). RCN: 6528.
Lectotype (Howard, *Fl. Lesser Antilles* 6: 533. 1989): [icon] *"Buphthalmum fruticosum foliis fasciculatis"* in Plumier in Burman, Pl. Amer.: 96, t. 106, f. 2. 1757.
Current name: ***Borrichia arborescens*** (L.) DC. (Asteraceae).
Note: Moore (in Fawcett & Rendle, *Fl. Jamaica* 7: 225. 1936) noted the existence of 1022.2 (LINN) and Clifford material (BM) but did not designate a type.

Buphthalmum capense Linnaeus, *Systema Naturae,* ed. 10, 2: 1227. 1759.
["Habitat ad Cap. b. spei."] Sp. Pl. ed. 2, 2: 1274 (1763). RCN: 6715.
Replaced synonym of: *Oedera prolifera* L. (1771), *nom. illeg.*
Lectotype (Anderberg in Jarvis & Turland in *Taxon* 47: 355. 1998): Herb. Linn. No. 1047.1 (LINN).
Current name: ***Oedera capensis*** (L.) Druce (Asteraceae).

Buphthalmum durum Linnaeus, *Species Plantarum,* ed. 2, 2: 1275. 1763.
"Habitat ad Cap. b. spei." RCN: 6532.
Lectotype (designated here by Nordenstam): [icon] *"Chrysanth. African. Asteris facie, imo flore non folioso, capitulis duris"* in Plukenet, Phytographia: t. 21, f. 3. 1691; Almag. Bot.: 101. 1696. – Epitype (designated here by Nordenstam): South Africa. Cape Province, Camps Bay, 8 Oct 1932, *J.P.H. Acock 887* (S).

Current name: ***Osteospermum polygaloides*** L. (Asteraceae).

Note: As some features shown by the lectotype are ambiguous, an epitype is also designated.

Buphthalmum frutescens Linnaeus, *Species Plantarum* 2: 903. 1753.
"Habitat in Jamaica, Virginia." RCN: 6527.
Lectotype (Reveal in Jarvis & Turland in *Taxon* 47: 355. 1998): *Clayton 242* (BM-000040260).
Current name: ***Borrichia frutescens*** (L.) DC. (Asteraceae).

Buphthalmum grandiflorum Linnaeus, *Species Plantarum* 2: 904. 1753.
"Habitat in alpibus Austriae, Italiae, Monspelii." RCN: 6534.
Lectotype (Anderberg in Jarvis & Turland in *Taxon* 47: 356. 1998): Herb. Clifford: 414, *Buphthalmum* 7 (BM-000647178).
Current name: ***Buphthalmum salicifolium*** L. (Asteraceae).

Buphthalmum helianthoides Linnaeus, *Species Plantarum* 2: 904. 1753.
"Habitat in America septentrionali." RCN: 6536.
Lectotype (Reveal in *Taxon* 32: 653. 1983): Herb. Linn. No. 1022.9 (LINN).
Current name: ***Heliopsis helianthoides*** (L.) Sweet (Asteraceae).

Buphthalmum maritimum Linnaeus, *Species Plantarum* 2: 903. 1753.
"Habitat in Massiliae, & in Sicilia ad littora maris." RCN: 6531.
Lectotype (Wiklund in *Nordic J. Bot.* 5: 305. 1985): Herb. Clifford: 414, *Buphthalmum* 9 (BM-000647180).
Current name: ***Asteriscus maritimus*** (L.) Less. (Asteraceae).

Buphthalmum salicifolium Linnaeus, *Species Plantarum* 2: 904. 1753.
"Habitat ad radices Alpium Austriae, Stiriae, Lusatiae, Monspelii." RCN: 6533.
Lectotype (Anderberg in Jarvis & Turland in *Taxon* 47: 356. 1998): Herb. Clifford: 414, *Buphthalmum* 6 (BM-000647177).
Generitype of *Buphthalmum* Linnaeus (vide Green, *Prop. Brit. Bot.*: 183. 1929).
Current name: ***Buphthalmum salicifolium*** L. (Asteraceae).
Note: This is the generitype of *Buphthalmum* but, through an error, *B. aquaticum* was incorrectly listed as the generitype by Jarvis & al. (*Regnum Veg.* 127: 27. 1993), instead of *B. salicifolium* L., as noted by Greuter (in *Fl. Medit.* 7: 43. 1997).

Buphthalmum speciosissimum Linnaeus, *Systema Naturae*, ed. 12, 2: 569; *Mantissa Plantarum*: 117. 1767.
"Habitat in montibus Brixiensibus." RCN: 6535.
Lectotype (Anderberg in Jarvis & Turland in *Taxon* 47: 356. 1998): *Arduino s.n.*, Herb. Linn. No. 1022.7 (LINN).
Current name: ***Telekia speciosissima*** (L.) Less. (Asteraceae).

Buphthalmum spinosum Linnaeus, *Species Plantarum* 2: 903. 1753.
"Habitat in G. Narbonensi, Hispania, Italia, ad margines agrorum." RCN: 6529.
Lectotype (Alavi in Jafri & El-Gadi, *Fl. Libya* 107: 106. 1983): Herb. Clifford: 414, *Buphthalmum* 10 (BM-000647181).
Current name: ***Pallenis spinosa*** (L.) Cass. (Asteraceae).
Note: Wiklund (in *Nordic J. Bot.* 5: 309. 1985) independently made the same choice of type as Alavi.

Bupleurum angulosum Linnaeus, *Species Plantarum* 1: 236. 1753.
"Habitat in Pyrenaeis. β. in Vallesiae alpibus." RCN: 1913.
Lectotype (Neves & Reduron in Jarvis & al. in *Taxon* 55: 209. 2006): Herb. Burser XVI(1): 4 (UPS).
Current name: ***Bupleurum angulosum*** L. (Apiaceae).

Bupleurum difforme Linnaeus, *Species Plantarum* 1: 238. 1753.
"Habitat in Aethiopia (mea aliunde)." RCN: 1924.
Lectotype (Van Wyk & Tilney in Jarvis & al. in *Taxon* 55: 209. 2006): Herb. Linn. No. 335.28, two central leaves (excl. an upper inflorescence and a lower right leaf) (LINN). – Epitype (Van Wyk & Tilney in Jarvis & al. in *Taxon* 55: 209. 2006): South Africa. Cape Province, Robinson Pass, *Allison 50* (PRE; iso- JRAU, K, NBG).
Current name: ***Anginon difforme*** (L.) B.L. Burtt (Apiaceae).

Bupleurum falcatum Linnaeus, *Species Plantarum* 1: 237. 1753.
"Habitat in Misniae, Vallesiae sepibus." RCN: 1915.
Lectotype (Neves & Reduron in Jarvis & al. in *Taxon* 55: 209. 2006): Herb. Burser XVI(1):10 (UPS).
Current name: ***Bupleurum falcatum*** L. (Apiaceae).

Bupleurum fruticescens Linnaeus, *Centuria I Plantarum*: 9. 1755.
"Habitat in Hispaniae collibus altis." RCN: 1923.
Lectotype (Neves & Reduron in Jarvis & al. in *Taxon* 55: 210. 2006): Herb. Linn. No. 335.27 (LINN).
Current name: ***Bupleurum fruticescens*** L. (Apiaceae).

Bupleurum fruticosum Linnaeus, *Species Plantarum* 1: 238. 1753.
"Habitat in Galliae australis saxosis maritimis." RCN: 1922.
Lectotype (Neves & Reduron in Jarvis & al. in *Taxon* 55: 210. 2006): Herb. Clifford: 104, *Bupleurum* 1 (BM-000558357).
Current name: ***Bupleurum fruticosum*** L. (Apiaceae).

Bupleurum junceum Linnaeus, *Species Plantarum*, ed. 2, 1: 343. 1762, *nom. illeg.*
"Habitat in Gallia, Italia." RCN: 1921.
Neotype (Snogerup in Davis, *Fl. Turkey* 4: 408. 1972): [icon] *"Bupleurum angustifolium"* in Dodoëns, Stirp. Hist. Pempt., ed. 2: 632, 633, left figure. 1616.
Current name: ***Bupleurum praealtum*** L. (Apiaceae).
Note: An illegitimate name as it includes the whole basis of *B. praealtum* L. (1759), i.e. the Magnol description and diagnosis. As such it is automatically typified by the type of *B. praealtum*. Stearn (in Geck & Pressler, *Festschr. Claus Nissen*: 65. 1974) reproduces (as his f. 8) the Dodoëns figure that is the type of both names.

Bupleurum longifolium Linnaeus, *Species Plantarum* 1: 237. 1753.
"Habitat Gottingae, inque monte Jura Helvetiae." RCN: 1914.
Lectotype (Neves & Reduron in Jarvis & al. in *Taxon* 55: 210. 2006): Herb. Burser XVI(1): 2 (UPS).
Current name: ***Bupleurum longifolium*** L. (Apiaceae).

Bupleurum odontites Linnaeus, *Species Plantarum* 1: 237. 1753.
"Habitat in alpibus Vallesiae." RCN: 1916.
Lectotype (Reduron in Snogerup & Snogerup in *Willdenowia* 31: 225. 2001): Herb. Linn. No. 335.11 (LINN).
Current name: ***Bupleurum odontites*** L. (Apiaceae).

Bupleurum petraeum Linnaeus, *Species Plantarum* 1: 236. 1753.
"Habitat in alpibus Helvetiae, Baldi." RCN: 1912.
Lectotype (Neves & Reduron in Jarvis & al. in *Taxon* 55: 210. 2006): [icon] *"Sedum petraeum Bupleuri folio"* in Clusius, Rar. Pl. Hist. 2: 347. 1601. – Epitype (Neves & Reduron in Jarvis & al. in *Taxon* 55: 210. 2006): Italy. "Tirolia australis. In rupium fissuris montis Baldi (loc. class.). Flora Exsiccata Austro-Hungarica, No. 120", *Porta s.n.* (P; iso- BM).
Current name: ***Bupleurum petraeum*** L. (Apiaceae).

Bupleurum praealtum Linnaeus, *Amoenitates Academicae* 4: 480. 1759.
Neotype (Snogerup in Davis, *Fl. Turkey* 4: 408. 1972): [icon] *"Bupleurum angustifolium"* in Dodoëns, Stirp. Hist. Pempt., ed. 2: 632, 633, left figure. 1616.
Current name: ***Bupleurum praealtum*** L. (Apiaceae).

Bupleurum ranunculoides Linnaeus, *Species Plantarum* 1: 237. 1753.
"Habitat in Helvetia & Pyrenaeis." RCN: 1918.
Lectotype (Neves & Reduron in Jarvis & al. in *Taxon* 55: 210. 2006): Herb. Burser XVI(1): 8 (UPS). – Epitype (Neves & Reduron in Jarvis & al. in *Taxon* 55: 210. 2006): Herb. Clifford: 104, *Bupleurum* 3 (BM-000558361).
Current name: ***Bupleurum ranunculoides*** L. (Apiaceae).

Bupleurum rigidum Linnaeus, *Species Plantarum* 1: 238. 1753.
"Habitat Monspelii." RCN: 1920.
Lectotype (Reduron & Jarvis in Jarvis & al. in *Taxon* 55: 210. 2006): Herb. Linn. No. 335.19 (LINN).
Current name: ***Bupleurum rigidum*** L. (Apiaceae).

Bupleurum rotundifolium Linnaeus, *Species Plantarum* 1: 236. 1753.
"Habitat inter Europae australis segetes." RCN: 1910.
Lectotype (Rechinger & Snogerup in Rechinger, *Fl. Iranica* 162: 272. 1987): Herb. Linn. No. 335.1 (LINN).
Generitype of *Bupleurum* Linnaeus.
Current name: ***Bupleurum rotundifolium*** L. (Apiaceae).
Note: Bupleurum rotundifolium, with the type designated by Rechinger & Snogerup, was proposed as conserved type of the genus by Jarvis (in *Taxon* 41: 572. 1992). However, the proposal was eventually ruled unnecessary by the General Committee (see Barrie, *l.c.* 55: 795–796. 2006 for a review of the history of this and related proposals).

Bupleurum semicompositum Linnaeus, *Demonstr. Pl. Horto Upsaliensi*: 7. 1753.
"Habitat in Hispania. Loefl." RCN: 1917.
Lectotype (Townsend in *Kew Bull.* 20: 81. 1966): *Löfling s.n.*, Herb. Linn. No. 335.13 (LINN).
Current name: ***Bupleurum semicompositum*** L. (Apiaceae).

Bupleurum stellatum Linnaeus, *Species Plantarum* 1: 236. 1753.
"Habitat in alpibus Helveticis." RCN: 1911.
Lectotype (Neves & Reduron in Jarvis & al. in *Taxon* 55: 210. 2006): Herb. Burser XVI(1): 5 (UPS).
Current name: ***Bupleurum stellatum*** L. (Apiaceae).

Bupleurum tenuifolium Linnaeus, *Amoenitates Academicae* 4: 480. 1759, *orth. var.*
RCN: 1920.
Lectotype (Reduron in Snogerup & Snogerup in *Willdenowia* 31: 264. 2001): Herb. Linn. No. 116.13 (S).
Current name: ***Bupleurum tenuissimum*** L. (Apiaceae).
Note: Stearn (in Geck & Pressler, *Festschr. Claus Nissen*: 631. 1974), regards this as an orthographic error for *B. tenuissimum* L. (1753), with which *B. tenuifolium* is therefore homotypic.

Bupleurum tenuissimum Linnaeus, *Species Plantarum* 1: 238. 1753.
"Habitat in Germania, Anglia, Gallia, Italia." RCN: 1920.
Lectotype (Reduron in Snogerup & Snogerup in *Willdenowia* 31: 264. 2001): Herb. Linn. No. 116.13 (S).
Current name: ***Bupleurum tenuissimum*** L. (Apiaceae).

Bupleurum villosum Linnaeus, *Species Plantarum* 1: 238. 1753.
"Habitat in Aethiopia." RCN: 7649.
Replaced synonym of: *Hermas depauperata* L. (1771), *nom. illeg.*
Lectotype (Burtt in Jarvis & al., *Regnum Veg.* 127: 53. 1993): [icon] *"Perfoliata foliis oblongis, sinuosis, subtus incanis"* in Burman, Rar. Afric. Pl.: 196, t. 71, f. 2. 1739.
Current name: ***Hermas villosa*** (L.) Thunb. (Apiaceae).
Note: Burtt (in *Notes Roy. Bot. Gard. Edinburgh* 48: 213. 1991) suggested that 1227.1 (LINN) was probably the specimen upon which *Hermas depauperata* was based. However, *H. depauperata* is an illegitimate replacement name in *Hermas* for *Bupleurum villosum* L. and homotypic with it. The material in LINN appears to be a post-1753 addition to the collection and not original material for *B. villosum*. For this reason, Burtt (1993) typified the name on the cited Burman illustration (though f. 1, and its corresponding polynomial, was regrettably cited in error for f. 2).

Burmannia biflora Linnaeus, *Species Plantarum* 1: 287. 1753.
"Habitat in Virginiae paludosis." RCN: 2283.
Lectotype (Jonker in *Meded. Bot. Mus. Herb. Rijks Univ. Utrecht* 51: 81. 1938): *Clayton 248* (BM-000040295).
Current name: ***Burmannia biflora*** L. (Burmanniaceae).

Burmannia disticha Linnaeus, *Species Plantarum* 1: 287. 1753.
"Habitat in Zeylonae paludosis." RCN: 2282.
Lectotype (Jonker in *Meded. Bot. Mus. Herb. Rijks Univ. Utrecht* 51: 116. 1938): Herb. Hermann 1: 34, No. 128 (BM-000594465; iso-G-DEL, L).
Generitype of *Burmannia* Linnaeus (vide Hitchcock, *Prop. Brit. Bot.*: 144. 1929).
Current name: ***Burmannia disticha*** L. (Burmanniaceae).

Bursera gummifera Linnaeus, *Species Plantarum*, ed. 2, 1: 471. 1762, *nom. illeg.*
"Habitat in America calidiore." RCN: 2554.
Replaced synonym: *Pistacia simaruba* L. (1753).
Lectotype (Wijnands, *Bot. Commelins*: 55. 1983): [icon] *"Terebinthus major, betulae cortice, fructu triangulari"* in Sloane, Voy. Jamaica 2: 89, t. 199, f. 1, 2. 1725. – Typotype: Herb. Sloane 6: 104, 105 (BM-SL).
Generitype of *Bursera* Linnaeus, *nom. cons.*
Current name: ***Bursera simaruba*** (L.) Sarg. (Burseraceae).
Note: Bursera Linnaeus, *nom. cons.* vs. *Simarouba* Boehm.; *Elaphrium* Jacq.
Bursera gummifera L. is a superfluous name for *Pistacia simaruba* L. (1753).

Butomus umbellatus Linnaeus, *Species Plantarum* 1: 372. 1753.
"Habitat in Europae aquosis." RCN: 2931.
Lectotype (Barrie in Jarvis & al., *Regnum Veg.* 127: 27. 1993): Herb. A. van Royen No. 897.288–115 (L, see p. 247; iso- L).
Generitype of *Butomus* Linnaeus.
Current name: ***Butomus umbellatus*** L. (Butomaceae).
Note: Dandy (in Rechinger, *Fl. Iranica* 79: 1. 1971) indicated 521.1 (LINN) as type but this sheet is unannotated by Linnaeus and cannot be accepted as original material.

Buttneria scabra Linnaeus, *Systema Naturae,* ed. 12, 2: 181. 1767, *orth. var.*
["Habitat in America meridionali."] Sp. Pl. ed. 2, 1: 284 (1762). RCN: 1588.
Type not designated.
Original material: as *Byttneria scabra.*
Current name: ***Byttneria scabra*** L. (Sterculiaceae).
Note: An orthographic variant of *Byttneria scabra* L. (1759).

Buxus sempervirens Linnaeus, *Species Plantarum* 2: 983. 1753.
"Habitat in Europae australis." RCN: 7126.
Lectotype (Fosberg in *Boxwood Bull.* 13(2): 19, f. 1. 1973): Herb.
    Clifford: 441, *Buxus* 1 (BM-000647382).
Generitype of *Buxus* Linnaeus.
Current name: ***Buxus sempervirens*** L. (Buxaceae).

Buxus sempervirens Linnaeus var. **arborescens** Linnaeus, *Species
    Plantarum* 2: 983. 1753.
RCN: 7126.

Lectotype (Fosberg in *Boxwood Bull.* 13(2): 20, f. 2. 1973): Herb.
    Linn. No. 1110.1 (LINN).
Current name: ***Buxus sempervirens*** L. (Buxaceae).

Buxus sempervirens Linnaeus var. **suffruticosa** Linnaeus, *Species
    Plantarum* 2: 983. 1753.
RCN: 7126.
Lectotype (Fosberg in *Boxwood Bull.* 13(2): 21, f. 3. 1973): Herb.
    Linn. No. 1110.2 (LINN).
Current name: ***Buxus sempervirens*** L. (Buxaceae).

Byssus antiquitatis Linnaeus, *Species Plantarum* 2: 1168. 1753.
"Habitat in aedium muris antiquissimis." RCN: 8404.
Type not designated.
Original material: none traced.

Current name: ***Lepraria antiquitatis*** (L.) Ach. (Leprariaceae).
Note: Ross & Irvine (in *Taxon* 16: 185. 1967) stated that the
    application of the name is uncertain. See Laundon (in *Lichenologist*
    24: 340. 1992), who suggested that *B. antiquitatis* L. might be of
    mineral origin.

Byssus aurea Linnaeus, *Species Plantarum* 2: 1168. 1753.
"Habitat in rupibus Arvoniae, Italiae." RCN: 8402.
Lectotype (Irvine in Spencer & al. in *Taxon*, in press): [icon] *"Byssus
    petraea crocea, glomerulis lanuginosis"* in Dillenius, Hist. Musc.: 8, t.
    1, f. 16. 1741. – Voucher: Herb. Dillenius (OXF).
Current name: ***Trentepohlia aurea*** (L.) Mart. (Trentepohliaceae).

Byssus botryoides Linnaeus, *Species Plantarum* 2: 1169. 1753.
"Habitat in terra diutius humida, umbrosa, ut in ollis Hortulanorum."
    RCN: 8408.
Lectotype (Redhead & Kuyper in Laursen & al., *Arctic Alpine Mycol.*
    2: 321. 1987): [icon] *"Byssus botryoides, saturate virens"* in Dillenius,
    Hist. Musc.: 3, t. 1, f. 5. 1741. – Typotype: Herb. Dillenius (OXF).
    – Epitype (Jørgensen & al. in *Bot. J. Linn. Soc.* 115: 270. 1994):
    England. London Borough of Camden, Hampstead Heath, Herb.
    Sherard No. 1995 (OXF).
Current name: ***Omphalina umbellifera*** (L.: Fr.) Quél.
    (Omphalinaceae).
Note: See review by Jørgensen & al. (in *Bot. J. Linn. Soc.* 115: 270,
    371, f. 3. 1994).

Byssus cancellata Linnaeus, *Systema Naturae*, ed. 12, 2: 721.
    1767.
"Habitat in aquis dulcibus; natans tamquam mucor virescenti-luteus."
    RCN: 8398.
Lectotype (John in Spencer & al. in *Taxon*, in press): [icon] *"Etwas
    Schlammmoss"* in Ledermüller, Mikroskop. Gemüths- und Augen-
    Ergötzung: 139, t. 72. 1761.
Current name: ***Hydrodictyon reticulatum*** (L.) Lagerh.
    (Hydrodictyaceae).

Byssus candelaris Linnaeus, *Species Plantarum* 2: 1169. 1753.
"Habitat per omnes quatuor mundi plagas in corticibus arborum,
    parietibus antiquis, tectis diutius vento humido expositis." RCN:
    8407.
Lectotype (Ross & Irvine in *Taxon* 16: 185. 1967): [icon] *"Byssus
    pulverulenta flava, lignis adnascens"* in Dillenius, Hist. Musc.: 3, t. 1,
    f. 4. 1741. – Voucher: Herb. Dillenius (OXF). – Epitype (Jørgensen
    & al. in *Bot. J. Linn. Soc.* 115: 270, 371. 1994): England. London
    Borough of Lewisham, Blackheath, on timber, Herb. J.E. Smith
    (LINN-SM).
Current name: ***Chrysothrix candelaris*** (L.) J.R. Laundon
    (Chrysotrichaceae).
Note: See review by Jørgensen & al. (in *Bot. J. Linn. Soc.* 115: 270,
    371. 1994).

Byssus cryptarum Linnaeus, *Species Plantarum* 2: 1168. 1753.
"Habitat in spelunca rupestri Medelpadiae." RCN: 403.
Lectotype (Ross & Irvine in *Taxon* 16: 185. 1967): Herb. Linn. No.
    1278.5 (LINN).
Current name: ***Trentepohlia aurea*** (L.) Mart. (Trentepohliaceae).
Note: Byssus Linnaeus, *nom. rej.* vs. *Trentepohlia* Mart.

Byssus flos-aquae Linnaeus, *Species Plantarum* 2: 1168. 1753.
"Habitat in Mari & omni aqua, prima aestate; nocte descendit parum,
    die natat fere." RCN: 8397.
Neotype (Pentecost in Spencer & al. in *Taxon*, in press): Rabenhorst,
    Algen Europas No. 1463, *"Sphaerozyga flos aquae* (Linn.)" (BM-
    000769430).

Current name: ***Aphanizomenon flos-aquae*** (L.) Ralfs ex Bornet & Flahault (Nostocaceae).
Note: Although Drouet & Dailey (in *Butler Univ. Bot. Stud.* 12: 145. 1956) attempted to typify the name using 1278.1 (LINN), this collection is annotated only by Linnaeus filius and is evidently a post-1753 addition to the herbarium and not original material for the name. For this reason, Ross & Irvine (in *Taxon* 16: 184. 1967) rejected this type choice.

Byssus incanus Linnaeus, *Species Plantarum* 2: 1169. 1753.
"Habitat solo glareoso, ad latera fossularum, juxta vias publicas." RCN: 8409.
Lectotype (Laundon in *Lichenologist* 24: 333. 1992): [icon] *"Byssus pulverulenta incana, farinae instar strata"* in Dillenius, Hist. Musc.: 3, t. 1, f. 3. 1741. – Voucher: Herb. Dillenius (OXF). – Epitype (Jørgensen & al. in *Bot. J. Linn. Soc.* 115: 271, 371. 1994): Herb. Dillenius Tab. I, No. 3 (OXF).
Current name: ***Lepraria incana*** (L.) Ach. (Leprariaceae).
Note: Specific epithet spelled "incana" in the protologue.
　　See review by Jørgensen & al. (in *Bot. J. Linn. Soc.* 115: 271, 371. 1994).

Byssus jolithus Linnaeus, *Species Plantarum* 2: 1169. 1753.
"Habitat in Europae frigidae sylvis opacis, supra saxa ante unum alterumve annuum eversa & supinata." RCN: 8406.
Lectotype (Irvine in Spencer & al. in *Taxon*, in press): [icon] *"Byssus Germanica, minima, saxatilis, aurea, Violae Martiae odorem spirans"* in Micheli, Nov. Pl. Gen.: 210, t. 89, f. 3. 1729.
Generitype of *Byssus* Linnaeus, nom. rej. (vide Fries, *Stirp. Agri Femsio*: 42. 1825).
Current name: ***Trentepohlia jolithus*** (L.) Wallr. (Trentepohliaceae).
Note: Byssus Linnaeus, *nom. rej.* vs. *Trentepohlia* Mart.
　　See comments by Ross & Irvine (in *Taxon* 16: 185. 1967) and Silva (*l.c.* 29: 144. 1980).

Byssus lacteus Linnaeus, *Species Plantarum* 2: 1169. 1753, *nom. utique rej.*
"Habitat in Muscis & arborum corticibus." RCN: 8410.
Lectotype (Jørgensen & al. in *Taxon* 43: 646. 1994): [icon] *"Byssus candidissima, calcis instar Muscos vestiens"* in Dillenius, Hist. Musc.: 2, t. 1, f. 2. 1741. – Voucher: Herb. Dillenius (OXF).
Note: Jørgensen & al., *Bot. J. Linn. Soc.* 115: 271, f. 3. (1994) discussed the name, concluding it to be a *species non satis nota* which they subsequently (in *Taxon* 43: 646. 1994) successfully proposed for rejection.

Byssus phosphorea Linnaeus, *Species Plantarum* 2: 1168. 1753.
"Habitat in Europae lignis putrescentibus." RCN: 9399.
Lectotype (Ross & Irvine in *Taxon* 16: 184. 1967): [icon] *"Byssus lanuginosa violacea, lignis adnascens"* in Dillenius, Hist. Musc.: 4, t. 1, f. 6. 1741. – Voucher: Herb. Dillenius (OXF).
Current name: ***Terana caerulea*** (Lam.: Fr.) Kuntze (Phanerochaetaceae).

Byssus saxatilis Linnaeus, *Species Plantarum* 2: 1169. 1753.
"Habitat in Saxo omni, diutius aeri exposito, quod perenni cinereo colore obducit, ipsa vix manifesta." RCN: 8405.
Type not designated.
Original material: none traced.
Note: Ross & Irvine (in *Taxon* 16: 185. 1967) noted the absence of any original material while Laundon (in *Lichenologist* 24: 344. 1992) suggested that the name might be applicable to material of mineral origin. The name is of uncertain application and may be a candidate for rejection (see Spencer & al. in *Taxon*, in press).

Byssus septicus Linnaeus, *Systema Naturae*, ed. 12, 3: 235. 1768.
"Habitat in Domibus sub pavimentis, ubi aer mephiticus s. suffocatus, summe septicus corrodit tamquam menstruo naturali domos ligneas, durissimosque truncos, ut fatiscentes cadant damno colonum." RCN: 8396.
Type not designated.
Original material: [icon] in Micheli, Nov. Pl. Gen.: 211, t. 89, f. 9. 1729.
Note: The application of this name is uncertain and the name may be a candidate for rejection (see Spencer & al. in *Taxon*, in press).

Byssus velutina Linnaeus, *Species Plantarum* 2: 1168. 1753.
"Habitat in Terra." RCN: 8401.
Lectotype (Newton in Spencer & al. in *Taxon*, in press): [icon] *"Byssus tenerrima viridis, velutum referens"* in Dillenius, Hist. Musc.: 7, t. 1, f. 14. 1741. – Voucher: Herb. Dillenius (OXF).
Current name: ***Pogonatum aloides*** (Hedw.) P. Beauv. (Polytrichaceae).
Note: According to Druce & Vines (*Dill. Herb.*: 215. 1907), voucher material in the Dillenian herbarium linked with the corresponding cited illustration is identifiable as the moss, *Polytrichum aloides* Hedw. (syn. *Pogonatum aloides* (Hedw.) P. Beauv.).

Byttneria scabra Linnaeus, *Systema Naturae*, ed. 10, 2: 939. 1759.
["Habitat in America meridionali."] Sp. Pl. ed. 2, 1: 284 (1762).
　RCN: 1588.
Type not designated.
Original material: none traced.
Current name: ***Byttneria scabra*** L. (Sterculiaceae).

C

Cacalia alpina Linnaeus, *Species Plantarum* 2: 836. 1753.
"Habitat in Alpibus Helvetiae, Austriae." RCN: 6043.
Lectotype (Jeffrey in Jarvis in *Taxon* 41: 559. 1992): Herb. Burser X: 155 (UPS).
Generitype of *Cacalia* Linnaeus, *nom. rej.* (vide Rydberg in *Bull. Torrey Bot. Club* 51: 370. 1924).
Current name: ***Adenostyles alpina*** (L.) Bluff & Fingerh. (Asteraceae).
Note: Cacalia alpina, with the type designated by Jeffrey, was proposed as conserved type of the genus by Jarvis (in *Taxon* 41: 559. 1992). The Committee for Spermatophyta, however, noting that conservation would result in *Cacalia* displacing *Adenostyles* Cass., voted (see *Taxon* 44: 612. 1995) not to accept the proposal. Wagenitz (in *Taxon* 44: 445. 1995) subsequently proposed the rejection of *Cacalia*, with *C. alpina* as type, recommended by the Committee for Spermatophyta (in *Taxon* 47: 444. 1998).
See comments on the application of *C. alpina* by Wagenitz (in *Phyton (Horn)* 23: 146–147. 1983).

Cacalia anteuphorbium Linnaeus, *Species Plantarum* 2: 834. 1753.
"Habitat in Aethiopia." RCN: 6030.
Lectotype (Halliday in *Hooker's Icon. Pl.* 39(4): 105. 1988): [icon] *"Anteuphorbii flos"* in Dillenius, Hort. Eltham. 1: 63, t. 55, f. 63. 1732.
Current name: ***Kleinia anteuphorbium*** (L.) Haw. (Asteraceae).

Cacalia atriplicifolia Linnaeus, *Species Plantarum* 2: 835. 1753.
"Habitat in Virginia, Canada." RCN: 6042.
Lectotype (Reveal in Jarvis & Turland in *Taxon* 47: 356. 1998): *Kalm*, Herb. Linn. No. 976.17 (LINN).
Current name: ***Arnoglossum atriplicifolium*** (L.) H. Rob. (Asteraceae).

Cacalia cuneifolia Linnaeus, *Systema Naturae,* ed. 12, 2: 535; *Mantissa Plantarum*: 110. 1767.
"Habitat ad Cap. b. spei." RCN: 6031.
Type not designated.
Original material: none traced.
Current name: ***Senecio cuneifolius*** (L.) Sch. Bip. (Asteraceae).

Cacalia ficoides Linnaeus, *Species Plantarum* 2: 834. 1753.
"Habitat in Aethiopia." RCN: 6033.
Lectotype (Wijnands, *Bot. Commelins*: 78. 1983): [icon] *"Senecio Afr. arboresc. ficoidis folio et facie"* in Commelin, Hort. Med. Amstelaed. Pl. Rar.: 40, t. 40. 1706.
Current name: ***Senecio ficoides*** (L.) Sch. Bip. (Asteraceae).

Cacalia hastata Linnaeus, *Species Plantarum* 2: 835. 1753.
"Habitat in Sibiria. D. Gmelin." RCN: 6040.
Type not designated.
Original material: [icon] in Gmelin, Fl. Sibirica 2: 136, t. 66. 1752.
Current name: ***Cacalia hastata*** L. (Asteraceae).

Cacalia incana Linnaeus, *Species Plantarum,* ed. 2, 2: 1169. 1763.
"Habitat in India." RCN: 6038.
Type not designated.
Original material: none traced.
Current name: ***Gynura divaricata*** (L.) DC. (Asteraceae).

Cacalia kleinia Linnaeus, *Species Plantarum* 2: 834. 1753.
"Habitat in Canariis, forte etjam in India." RCN: 6032.
Lectotype (Halliday in *Hooker's Icon. Pl.* 39(4): 109. 1988): Herb. Linn. No. 976.1 (LINN).
Current name: ***Kleinia neriifolia*** Haw. (Asteraceae).

Cacalia papillaris Linnaeus, *Species Plantarum* 2: 834. 1753.
"Habitat in Aethiopia." RCN: 6029.
Lectotype (Rowley in *Natl. Cact. Succ. J.* 34: 34. 1979): [icon] *"Cacalianthemum (forte) caudice papillari"* in Dillenius, Hort. Eltham. 1: 63, t. 55, f. 63 [larger fig.]. 1732 (see p. 124).
Current name: ***Tylecodon papillaris*** (L.) G.D. Rowley (Asteraceae).
Note: Rowley typified the name and took up *Tylecodon papillaris* (L.) G.D. Rowley as the correct name for *T. cacalioides* (L. f.) Tölken. However, Tölken (in Leistner, Fl. Southern Africa 14: 35. 1985) argued that the type illustration (which is figured by Rowley, and also by van Jaarsveld & Koutnik, *Cotyledon and Tylecodon*: 12, f. 14. 2004), being sterile, does not allow a reliable identification to be made, as it could represent either *T. cacalioides* or *T. wallichii* (Harv.) Tölken. Rowley regarded these names as forms of a single species. Tölken concluded that the Linnaean name should be rejected to avoid further confusion, but no formal proposal appears to have been made.

Cacalia porophyllum Linnaeus, *Species Plantarum* 2: 834. 1753.
"Habitat in America." RCN: 6036.
Type not designated.
Original material: Herb. Linn. No. 976.9 (LINN); Herb. Linn. No. 976.8 (LINN); [icon] in Morison, Pl. Hist. Univ. 3: 106, s. 7, t. 17, f. 7. 1699; [icon] in Plukenet, Phytographia: t. 161, f. 1. 1692; Almag. Bot.: 100. 1696 – Typotype: Herb. Sloane 95: 166 (BM-SL).
Current name: ***Porophyllum ruderale*** (Jacq.) Cass. (Asteraceae).
Note: Keil (in *Ann. Missouri Bot. Gard.* 62: 1234. 1975) indicated either Herb. Linn. 976.8 or 976.9 (LINN), neither of which he had seen, as "Type". As these two collections are evidently not part of a single gathering, Art. 9.15 does not apply and the name seems as yet untypified.

Cacalia repens Linnaeus, *Systema Naturae,* ed. 12, 2: 535; *Mantissa Plantarum*: 110. 1767.
"Habitat ad Cap. b. spei." RCN: 6034.
Type not designated.
Original material: none traced.
Current name: ***Senecio serpens*** G.D. Rowley (Asteraceae).

Cacalia saracenica Linnaeus, *Species Plantarum,* ed. 2, 2: 1169. 1763.
"Habitat in Gallia australi." RCN: 6039.
Lectotype (Herborg in *Diss. Bot.* 107: 153. 1987): Herb. Linn. No. 976.12 (LINN).
Current name: ***Senecio cacaliaster*** Lam. (Asteraceae).

Cacalia sonchifolia Linnaeus, *Species Plantarum* 2: 835. 1753.
"Habitat in Zeylona, China." RCN: 6037.
Lectotype (Grierson in Dassanayake & Fosberg, *Revised Handb. Fl. Ceylon* 1: 252. 1980): Herb. Hermann 2: 25; 4: 36; 4: 66, no. 305 (BM).
Current name: ***Emilia sonchifolia*** (L.) DC. ex Wight (Asteraceae).
Note: Although Grierson's choice includes a number of collections, in different volumes of Hermann's herbarium, they appear to form a single gathering (Art. 9.15) so Grierson's type choice is accepted here. This choice pre-dates that of Nicolson (in *Syst. Bot.* 5: 398. 1981) who treated 976.10 (LINN) as the type.

Cacalia suaveolens Linnaeus, *Species Plantarum* 2: 835. 1753.
"Habitat in Virginia, Canada." RCN: 6041.
Lectotype (Reveal in Jarvis & Turland in *Taxon* 47: 356. 1998): Herb. Linn. No. 976.16 (LINN).
Current name: ***Cacalia suaveolens*** L. (Asteraceae).

Cacalia suffruticosa Linnaeus, *Systema Naturae,* ed. 12, 2: 535; *Mantissa Plantarum*: 109. 1767, *nom. illeg.*
"Habitat in Brasilia. Arduini." RCN: 6035.
Replaced synonym: *Cacalia linifolia* Ard. (1764).
Type not designated.
Current name: ***Porophyllum linifolium*** (Ard.) DC. (Asteraceae).
Note: Linnaeus cited, as a synonym, an account of the species published by Arduino in 1764, in which the binomial *C. linifolia* Ard. was adopted. Linnaeus' name is therefore illegitimate. Johnson (in *Univ. Kansas Sci. Bull.* 48: 239. 1968) wrongly cited this as "*Cacalia linifolia* L." as published in *Mant. Pl.*: 109. 1767, though the epithet clearly came from Arduino. Johnson stated that he had seen a photo "of type from Linnean herbarium". Presumably this is likely to have been 976.2 (LINN) – *Arduino 20* – with the epithets "fruticulosa", and "suffruticosa" added by Smith. However, further study would be necessary to establish its link with Arduino's name.

Cachrys libanotis Linnaeus, *Species Plantarum* 1: 246. 1753.
"Habitat in Sicilia, Monspelii." RCN: 1981.
Lectotype (Gruenberg-Fertig & al. in *Taxon* 22: 431, f. 4. 1973): Herb. Burser VIII: 30 (UPS).
Generitype of *Cachrys* Linnaeus.
Current name: ***Cachrys libanotis*** L. (Apiaceae).

Cachrys sicula Linnaeus, *Species Plantarum,* ed. 2, 1: 355. 1762.
"Habitat in Sicilia, Hispania." RCN: 1982.
Lectotype (López González in Jarvis & al. in *Taxon* 55: 210. 2006): Herb. Linn. No. 349.1 (LINN).
Current name: ***Cachrys sicula*** L. (Apiaceae).

Cactus cochenillifer Linnaeus, *Species Plantarum* 1: 468. 1753.
"Habitat in Jamaica & America calidiore." RCN: 3587.
Lectotype (Howard, *Fl. Lesser Antilles* 5: 411. 1989): [icon] *"Tuna mitior flore sanguineo, cochenillifera"* in Dillenius, Hort. Eltham. 2: 399, t. 297, f. 383. 1732.
Current name: ***Nopalea cochenillifera*** (L.) Salm-Dyck (Cactaceae).
Note: Benson (*Cacti U.S. Canada*: 932. 1982) designated a neotype but this is contrary to Art. 9.11 as original material is in existence. See Crook & Mottram (in *Bradleya* 14: 111. 1996) who noted the original elements, and reproduced the type in colour (their f. 18, p. 127).

Cactus curassavicus Linnaeus, *Species Plantarum* 1: 469. 1753.
"Habitat in Curacao." RCN: 3588.
Lectotype (Wijnands, *Bot. Commelins*: 57. 1983): [icon] *"Ficus Indica seu Opuntia Curassavica minima"* in Commelin, Hort. Med. Amstelod. Pl. Rar. 1: 107, t. 56. 1697.
Current name: ***Opuntia curassavica*** (L.) Mill. (Cactaceae).
Note: See comments by Howard & Touw (in *Cact. Succ. J. (Los Angeles)* 54: 173. 1972).

Cactus epidendron Linnaeus, *Plantae Surinamenses*: 10. 1775, *nom. nud.*
RCN: 3581.
Type not relevant.

Cactus ficus-indica Linnaeus, *Species Plantarum* 1: 468. 1753.
"Habitat in America calidiore." RCN: 3585.
Neotype (Leuenberger in *Taxon* 40: 624. 1991): Herb. Linn. No. 201.7 (S).
Current name: ***Opuntia ficus-indica*** (L.) Mill. (Cactaceae).

Cactus flagelliformis Linnaeus, *Species Plantarum* 1: 467. 1753.
"Habitat in America calidiore." RCN: 3580.
Type not designated.

Original material: Herb. Linn. No. 633.2 (LINN); [icon] in Plukenet, Phytographia: t. 158, f. 6. 1692; Almag. Bot.: 148. 1696 – Voucher: Herb. Sloane 95: 156 (BM-SL); [icon] in Ehret, Pl. Papil. Rar.: t. 2, f. 3. 1748.
Current name: ***Disocactus flagelliformis*** (L.) Barthlott (Cactaceae).

Cactus grandiflorus Linnaeus, *Species Plantarum* 1: 467. 1753.
"Habitat in Jamaica, Vera Cruce." RCN: 3579.

Lectotype (Lourteig in *Bradea* 5: 406. 1991): Herb. Clifford: 182, *Cactus* 10 (BM-000628597).
Current name: ***Selenicereus grandiflorus*** (L.) Britton & Rose (Cactaceae).
Note: Benson (*Cacti U.S. Canada*: 935. 1982) indicated 633.1 (LINN) as type but this collection lacks the relevant *Species Plantarum* number (i.e. "11") and was a post-1753 addition to the herbarium, and is not original material for the name. See Hunt (in *Bradleya* 7: 95. 1989) who gives an extensive review of the original elements, and reproduces (p. 96) the striking illustration of Volckamer. Heath (in *Calyx* 2: 76. 1992) wrongly rejected Lourteig's type choice as ineligible, erroneously arguing that the Volckamer plate is the holotype.

Cactus heptagonus Linnaeus, *Species Plantarum* 1: 466. 1753.
"Habitat in America." RCN: 3571.
Type not designated.
Original material: none traced.
Current name: ***Melocactus*** sp. (Cactaceae).

Cactus hexagonus Linnaeus, *Species Plantarum* 1: 466. 1753.
"Habitat Surinami." RCN: 3573.
Lectotype (Leuenberger in *Bot. Jahrb. Syst.* 111: 153, f. 2. 1989):
[icon] *"Cereus Sirinamensis"* in Trew in Acta Phys.-Med. Acad. Caes.
Leop.-Carol. Nat. Cur. 3: 393, t. 8. 1733 (see p. 20).
Current name: ***Cereus hexagonus*** (L.) Mill. (Cactaceae).

Cactus lanuginosus Linnaeus, *Species Plantarum* 1: 467. 1753.
"Habitat in Curacao." RCN: 3576.
Type not designated.
Original material: [icon] in Hermann, Parad. Bat.: 115. 1698.
Current name: ***Pilosocereus lanuginosus*** (L.) Byles & G.D. Rowley
(Cactaceae).

Cactus mammillaris Linnaeus, *Species Plantarum* 1: 466. 1753.
"Habitat in Americae calidioris rupibus." RCN: 3567.
Lectotype (Wijnands, Mammillaria *Index*: 51. 1980): [icon] *"Ficoides
s. Melocactos mamillaris glabra, sulcis carens, fructum suum undiqe
fundens"* in Plukenet, Phytographia: t. 29, f. 1. 1691; Almag. Bot.:
148. 1696.
Generitype of *Cactus* Linnaeus, nom. rej.
Current name: ***Mammillaria mammillaris*** (L.) H. Karst. (Cactaceae).
Note: Cactus Linnaeus, nom. rej., in favour of *Mammillaria* Haw.
For a detailed discussion of this binomial, see Hunt (in *Bradleya*
3: 59. 1985). Mottram (in *Brit. Cactus Succ. J.* 22: 87. 2004)
reproduces the Commelin (f. 1; see also p. 121 in this book),
Plukenet (f. 2) and Hermann (f. 4) illustrations cited by Linnaeus.

Cactus melocactus Linnaeus, *Species Plantarum* 1: 466. 1753.
"Habitat in Jamaica, America calidiore." RCN: 3568.
Lectotype (Heath in *Calyx* 4: 90. 1994): [icon] *"Echinomelocactos"* in
Clusius, Exot. Libri: 92. 1605.
Current name: ***Melocactus caroli-linnaei*** N.P. Taylor (Cactaceae).
Note: Taylor (in *Bradleya* 9: 78. 1991) designated a neotype but this is
contrary to Art. 9.11, as original material is in existence. Mottram
(in *Taxon* 42: 462. 1993) designated a Tournefort plate, not cited by
Linnaeus and hence not original material either, as the lectotype,
and Heath's therefore appears to be the first acceptable type choice.

Cactus moniliformis Linnaeus, *Species Plantarum* 1: 468. 1753.
"Habitat in America calidiore." RCN: 3583.
Lectotype (Mottram in *Bradleya* 20: 88. 2002): [icon] *"Cactus
articulato-prolifer, articulis globosis"* in Plumier in Burman, Pl.
Amer.: 191, t. 198. 1758.
Current name: ***Consolea moniliformis*** (L.) A. Berger (Cactaceae).

Cactus nobilis Linnaeus, *Mantissa Plantarum Altera*: 243. 1771.
"Habitat in Mexico." RCN: 3569.
Type not designated.
Original material: none traced.
Current name: ***Ferocactus nobilis*** (L.) Britton & Rose (Cactaceae).

Cactus opuntia Linnaeus, *Species Plantarum* 1: 468. 1753.
"Habitat in America, Peru, Virginia, nunc in Hispania, Lusitania."
RCN: 3584.
Lectotype (Heath in *Calyx* 2: 74. 1992): [icon] *"Opuntia vulgo
herbariorum"* in Bauhin & Cherler, Hist. Pl. Univ. 1(1): 154. 1650.
Current name: ***Opuntia ficus-indica*** (L.) Mill. (Cactaceae).
Note: Authors including Hunt (in Milne-Redhead & Polhill, *Fl. Trop.
E. Africa, Cactaceae*: 3. 1968), Obermeyer (in Ross, *Fl. Southern
Africa* 22: 153. 1976) and Leuenberger (in *Willdenowia* 16: 498.
1987) interpreted the name via the cited Bauhin & Cherler
illustration but without explicitly treating it as the type. Benson
(*Cacti U.S. Canada*: 923. 1982) wrongly designated 201.7 (S),
material unannotated by Linnaeus and not original material for the

name, as lectotype before Heath (in *Calyx* 2: 74. 1992) formally
made the Bauhin & Cherler figure the type. Leuenberger (in *Taxon*
42: 419, f. 2. 1993), however, rejected Heath's choice in favour of a
Burser collection (UPS) on the grounds that the figure conflicts
with the diagnosis but, as a cited illustration, it cannot be dismissed
in this way as it forms part of the protologue. Crook & Mottram
(in *Bradleya* 22: 73–74. 2004) provide a further review, reproducing
images of the Burser material (f. 106d) and the cited Bauhin &
Cherler type (f. 106c), while following Leuenberger's type choice.

Cactus parasiticus Linnaeus, *Systema Naturae,* ed. 10, 2: 1054. 1759.
["Habitat in America."] Sp. Pl., ed. 2, 1: 668 (1762). RCN: 3581.
Type not designated.
Original material: *Browne*, Herb. Linn. No. 633.3 (LINN); [icon] in
Plumier in Burman, Pl. Amer.: 190, t. 197, f. 2. 1758; [icon] in
Sloane, Voy. Jamaica 2: 160, t. 224, f. 3, 4. 1725.
Note: The name does not appear to be in use. The cited Sloane plate
and the Browne specimen (633.3 LINN), are members of the
Orchidaceae related to *Vanilla, Campylocentrum* or *Dendrophylax,*
and the cited Plumier plate is a *Rhipsalis.* Barthlott & Taylor (in
Bradleya 13: 73. 1995) stated that they intended to propose the
name for rejection but no proposal appears to have been published.

Cactus pentagonus Linnaeus, *Species Plantarum* 1: 467. 1753.
"Habitat in America." RCN: 3574.
Type not designated.
Original material: none traced.
Current name: ***Acanthocereus tetragonus*** (L.) Hummelinck
(Cactaceae).
Note: See notes by Hunt (in *Bradleya* 9: 82. 1991).

Cactus pereskia Linnaeus, *Species Plantarum* 1: 469. 1753.
"Habitat in America calidiore, Jamaica, Margaretha." RCN: 3590.
Lectotype (Wijnands, *Bot. Commelins*: 58. 1983): [icon] *"Pereskia
aculeata, flore albo, fructu flavescente Plumier"* in Dillenius, Hort.
Eltham. 2: 305, t. 227, f. 294. 1732.
Current name: ***Pereskia aculeata*** Mill. (Cactaceae).
Note: See extensive review by Leuenberger (in *Mem. New York Bot.
Gard.* 41: 65. 1986).

Cactus peruvianus Linnaeus, *Species Plantarum* 1: 467. 1753.
"Habitat in Jamaicae, Peru apricis aridis maritimis." RCN: 3577.
Lectotype (Heath in *Calyx* 2: 70. 1992): [icon] *"Euphorbii arbor Cerei
effigie, sive Peruvianus Cereus vulgi"* in Plantin, Pl. Stirp. Icon. 2: 25.
1581.
Current name: ***Cereus peruvianus*** (L.) Mill. (Cactaceae).
Note: Keisling (in *Darwiniana* 24: 444. 1982) provided a neotype for
Cereus peruvianus Mill. (1768). He did not regard this name as a new
combination based on *Cactus peruvianus* L. so did not typify the
latter and, in fact, suggested that it should be rejected as a *nomen
dubium.* Hunt & Taylor (in *Bradleya* 10: 19. 1992), however, rejected
this interpretation, and the name was formally typified by Heath.

Cactus phyllanthus Linnaeus, *Species Plantarum* 1: 469. 1753.
"Habitat in Brasilia, Surinamo, America meridionali." RCN: 3589.
Lectotype (Leuenberger in Görts-Van Rijn & Jansen-Jacobs, *Fl.
Guianas,* ser. A, 18: 17. 1997): [icon] *"Cereus Scolopendrii folio
brachiato"* in Dillenius, Hort. Eltham. 1: 74, t. 64, f. 74. 1732.
Current name: ***Epiphyllum phyllanthus*** (L.) Haw. (Cactaceae).
Note: Wijnands (*Bot. Commelins*: 56. 1983) suggested that the cited
Dillenius plate could be a suitable type but did not formally
designate it as such, while Madsen (in Harling & Andersson, *Fl.
Ecuador,* ser. B, 35: 31. 1989) wrongly treated 633.6 (LINN), a
Browne collection not received by Linnaeus until 1758, as the
holotype.

Cactus portulacifolius Linnaeus, *Species Plantarum* 1: 469. 1753.
"Habitat in America calidiore." RCN: 3591.
Lectotype (Leuenberger in *Mem. New York Bot. Gard.* 41: 93. 1986): [icon] *"Cactus caule tereti, arboreo, spinoso"* in Plumier in Burman, Pl. Amer.: 190, t. 197, f. 1. 1758.
Current name: ***Pereskia portulacifolia*** (L.) DC. (Cactaceae).

Cactus repandus Linnaeus, *Species Plantarum* 1: 467. 1753.
"Habitat in America calidiore." RCN: 3575.
Type not designated.
Original material: none traced.
Current name: ***Cereus repandus*** (L.) Mill. (Cactaceae).
Note: See comments by Hunt & Taylor (in *Bradleya* 10: 19. 1992).

Cactus royenii Linnaeus, *Species Plantarum* 1: 467. 1753.
"Habitat in America." RCN: 3578.
Type not designated.
Original material: none traced.
Current name: ***Pilosocereus royenii*** (L.) Byles & G.D. Rowley (Cactaceae).
Note: Specific epithet spelled "Royeni" in the protologue.

Cactus tetragonus Linnaeus, *Species Plantarum* 1: 466. 1753.
"Habitat in Curacao, America calidiore." RCN: 3572.
Type not designated.
Original material: none traced.
Current name: ***Acanthocereus tetragonus*** (L.) Hummelinck (Cactaceae).
Note: Hummelinck (in *Succulenta* 20: 165. 1938) apparently designated two collections (*Hummelinck 196* (fl.) and *170* (fr.)) as a neotype. The numbering suggests that these may not be part of a single gathering, which presumably renders this choice ineffective.

Cactus triangularis Linnaeus, *Species Plantarum* 1: 468. 1753.
"Habitat in Brasilia, Jamaica." RCN: 3582.
Lectotype (Doweld in *Turczaninowia* 5(1): 12, f. 1. 2002): [icon] *"Ficoid. Americanum s. Cereus erectus cristatus foliis triangularibus profunde canaliculatis"* in Plukenet, Phytographia: t. 29, f. 3. 1691; Almag. Bot.: 147. 1696. – Epitype (Doweld in *Turczaninowia* 5(1): 12. 2002): Jamaica. Manchester, 2,100ft, 31 Aug 1979, *G.R. Proctor 38288* (MO).
Current name: ***Hylocereus triangularis*** (L.) Britton & Rose (Cactaceae).
Note: Hunt (in *Bradleya* 2: 41. 1984) implies this was based on a Plumier plate (t. 200, f. 1) but there is no Plumier element included in the protologue.

Cactus tuna Linnaeus, *Species Plantarum* 1: 468. 1753.
"Habitat in Jamaica & America calidiore." RCN: 3586.
Lectotype (Crook & Mottram in *Bradleya* 22: 61. 2004): [icon] *"Tuna major, spinis validis flavicantibus, flore gilvo"* in Dillenius, Hort. Eltham. 2: 396, t. 295, f. 380. 1732 (see p. 123).
Current name: ***Opuntia tuna*** (L.) Mill. (Cactaceae).

Caesalpinia brasiliensis Linnaeus, *Species Plantarum* 1: 380. 1753.
"Habitat in Jamaicae, Carolinae collibus." RCN: 2996.
Lectotype (Lewis & Reveal in Jarvis & al., *Regnum Veg.* 127: 28. 1993): [icon] *"Caesalpinia polyphylla, aculeis horrida"* in Plumier, Codex Boerhaavianus (University Library, Groningen).
Generitype of *Caesalpinia* Linnaeus (vide Hitchcock, *Prop. Brit. Bot.*: 152. 1929).
Current name: ***Caesalpinia brasiliensis*** L. (Fabaceae: Caesalpinioideae).
Note: Muralt & Chautems (in *Saussurea* 33: 127–132. 2003) provide a detailed review and reproduce (as f. 5) Burman's Plumier illustration.

Caesalpinia crista Linnaeus, *Species Plantarum* 1: 380. 1753.
"Habitat in Zeylona." RCN: 2999.
Lectotype (Skeels in *Science*, n.s., 37: 922. 1913): Herb. Hermann 1: 68, No. 157 (BM-000594500).
Current name: ***Caesalpinia crista*** L. (Fabaceae: Caesalpinioideae).
Note: Dandy & Exell (in *J. Bot.* 76: 176. 1938) provided a detailed discussion and came to the same conclusion as Skeels. Muralt & Chautems (in *Saussurea* 33: 123–127. 2003) also reproduce (as f. 1 and 2) the cited Plukenet and Breyn illustrations.

Caesalpinia crista Linnaeus, *Species Plantarum*, ed. 2, 1: 544. 1762, *nom. illeg.*
"Habitat in Jamaica." RCN: 2999.
Type not designated.
Original material: [icon] in Plumier in Burman, Pl. Amer.: 57, t. 68. 1756; [icon] in Plumier, Codex Boerhaavianus (University Library, Groningen).
Current name: ***Peltophorum brasiliense*** (L.) Urb. (Fabaceae: Caesalpinioideae).
Note: This name has a different diagnostic phrase name, and synonymy, from *C. crista* L. (1753), and is a later, illegitimate, homonym.

Caesalpinia sappan Linnaeus, *Species Plantarum* 1: 381. 1753.
"Habitat in Indiis." RCN: 2998.
Lectotype (Hattink in *Reinwardtia* 9: 51. 1974): Herb. Hermann 4: 31, No. 158 (BM-000628132).
Current name: ***Caesalpinia sappan*** L. (Fabaceae: Caesalpinioideae).

Caesalpinia vesicaria Linnaeus, *Species Plantarum* 1: 381. 1753.
"Habitat in America calidiore." RCN: 2997.
Lectotype (Thulin in Turland & Jarvis in *Taxon* 46: 466. 1997): [icon] *"Sena spuria arborea spinosa, foliis alatis ramosis seu decompositis, flore luteo, siliquis brevibus sulcatis nigris, sabinae odore"* in Sloane, Voy. Jamaica 2: 50, t. 181, f. 2, 3. 1725. – Typotype: Herb. Sloane 6: 40 (BM-SL).
Current name: ***Caesalpinia vesicaria*** L. (Fabaceae: Caesalpinioideae).

Calamus rotang Linnaeus, *Species Plantarum* 1: 325. 1753.
"Habitat in Indiae sylvis juxta fluenta." RCN: 2528.
Type not designated.
Original material: [icon] in Piso, Ind. Nat. Med.: 188. 1658.
Generitype of *Calamus* Linnaeus.
Current name: ***Calamus rotang*** L. (Arecaceae).
Note: Moore & Dransfield (in *Taxon* 28: 59. 1979) designated a Burman specimen in G, linked by Beccari (in *Ann. Roy. Bot. Gard. Calcutta* 11: 272. 1908) with the cited Burman reference, as lectotype. However, Burman did not illustrate the plant and Linnaeus did not see Burman's material so it cannot be original material for the name. As there is a cited Piso illustration in existence, Moore & Dransfield's choice unfortunately cannot be treated as a neotypification under Art. 9.8.

Calceolaria integrifolia Linnaeus, *Kongl. Vetensk. Acad. Handl.* 31: 289. 1770.
"Habitat in Peru." RCN: 139.
Lectotype (Ehrhart in *Sendtnera* 4: 46. 1997): [icon] *"Calceolaria, Salviae folio, vulgo Chachaul"* in Feuillée, J. Obs. 3: 13, t. 7. 1725. – Epitype (Ehrhart in *Sendtnera* 4: 46. 1997): Peru. Concepción-Sta. Juana. *Ehrhart & Sonderegger 95/718* (MSB-32672; iso- BM, F, G, K, NY, P, S etc.).
Current name: ***Calceolaria integrifolia*** L. (Scrophulariaceae).

Calceolaria pinnata Linnaeus, *Kongl. Vetensk. Acad. Handl.* 31: 288. 1770.

"Habitat in Peru." RCN: 138.
Type not designated.
Original material: [icon] in Feuillée, J. Obs. 3: 12, t. 7. 1725.
Generitype of *Calceolaria* Linnaeus, *nom. cons.*
Current name: **Calceolaria pinnata** L. (Scrophulariaceae).
Note: Calceolaria Linnaeus (1770), *nom. cons.* against *Calceolaria* Loefl. (1758).
   Although Molau (in *Fl. Neotropica* 47: 245. 1988) designated 32.1 (LINN) as lectotype, the sheet is unannotated by Linnaeus and is not original material for the name. As a Feuillée illustration, cited in the protologue, exists, Molau's statement is not correctable to a neotype (under Art. 9.8).

Calea amellus (Linnaeus) Linnaeus, *Species Plantarum,* ed. 2, 2: 1179. 1763.
"Habitat in Jamaica." RCN: 6098.
Basionym: *Santolina amellus* L. (1759).
Lectotype (Wussow & al. in *Syst. Bot.* 10: 263. 1985): *Browne,* Herb. Linn. No. 984.3 (LINN).
Current name: **Salmea scandens** (L.) DC. var. **amellus** (L.) Kuntze (Asteraceae).

Calea jamaicensis (Linnaeus) Linnaeus, *Species Plantarum,* ed. 2, 2: 1179. 1763.
"Habitat in Jamaica." RCN: 6096.
Basionym: *Santolina jamaicensis* L. (1759).
Lectotype (Moore in Fawcett & Rendle, *Fl. Jamaica* 7: 260. 1936): *Browne,* Herb. Linn. No. 984.1 (LINN).
Generitype of *Calea* Linnaeus (vide Brown in *Trans. Linn. Soc. London* 12: 106–109. 1818).
Current name: **Calea jamaicensis** (L.) L. (Asteraceae).

Calea oppositifolia (Linnaeus) Linnaeus, *Species Plantarum,* ed. 2, 2: 1179. 1763.
"Habitat in Jamaica." RCN: 6097.
Basionym: *Santolina oppositifolia* L. (1759).
Lectotype (King & Robinson in Woodson & Schery in *Ann. Missouri Bot. Gard.* 62: 958. 1975): *Browne,* Herb. Linn. No. 984.2 (LINN).
Current name: **Isocarpha oppositifolia** (L.) Cass. (Asteraceae).

Calea scoparia (Linnaeus) Linnaeus, *Systema Naturae,* ed. 12, 3: 234. 1768.
"Habitat in Jamaica." RCN: 6099.
Basionym: *Chrysocoma scoparia* L. (1759).
Lectotype (Wussow & al. in *Syst. Bot.* 10: 265. 1985): *Browne,* Herb. Linn. No. 984.4 (LINN).
Current name: **Baccharis scoparia** (L.) Sw. (Asteraceae).

Calendula arvensis Linnaeus, *Species Plantarum,* ed. 2, 2: 1303. 1763.
"Habitat in Europae arvis." RCN: 6660.
Lectotype (Heyn & al. in *Israel J. Bot.* 23: 182. 1974): *Löfling s.n.,* Herb. Linn. No. 1035.1 (LINN).
Current name: **Calendula arvensis** L. (Asteraceae).
Note: Greuter & al. (in *Taxon* 54: 155. 2005) interpret this as a new combination based on *Caltha arvensis* Vaill. (1754), invoking Art. 33.3. If this view is accepted, the name is untypified.

Calendula fruticosa Linnaeus, *Plantae Rariores Africanae*: 25. 1760.
["Habitat ad Cap. b. spei."] Sp. Pl. ed. 2, 2: 1305 (1763). RCN: 6667.
Type not designated.
Original material: Herb. Burman (G); Herb. Linn. No. 1035.9 (LINN).
Current name: **Osteospermum fruticosum** (L.) Norl. (Asteraceae).

Calendula graminifolia Linnaeus, *Species Plantarum* 2: 922. 1753.
"Habitat in Aethiopia." RCN: 6666.
Lectotype (Norlindh, *Stud. Calenduleae* 1: 94. 1943): [icon] *"Bellis Afric. florum pediculis foliosis foliis angustis et integris"* in Commelin, Hort. Med. Amsteled. Pl. Rar. 2: 67, f. 34. 1701.
Current name: **Castalis nudicaulis** (L.) Norl. var. **graminifolia** (L.) Norl. (Asteraceae).

Calendula hybrida Linnaeus, *Species Plantarum* 2: 921. 1753.
"Habitat in Aethiopia." RCN: 6664.
Type not designated.
Original material: Herb. Linn. No. 1035.6 (LINN); [icon] in Trant in Mém. Acad. Roy. Sci. Paris 1724: 39, t. 2. 1724.
Current name: **Dimorphotheca pluvialis** (L.) Norl. (Asteraceae).

Calendula nudicaulis Linnaeus, *Species Plantarum* 2: 922. 1753.
"Habitat in Aethiopia." RCN: 6665.
Lectotype (Norlindh, *Stud. Calenduleae* 1: 89. 1943): [icon] *"Bellis Afric. florum pediculis pene aphyllis foliis incisis"* in Commelin, Hort. Med. Amsteled. Pl. Rar. 2: 66, f. 33. 1701.
Current name: **Castalis nudicaulis** (L.) Norl. (Asteraceae).

Calendula officinalis Linnaeus, *Species Plantarum* 2: 921. 1753.
"Habitat in Europae arvis." RCN: 6662.
Lectotype (Alavi in Jafri & El-Gadi, *Fl. Libya* 107: 195. 1983): Herb. Linn. No. 1035.4 (LINN).
Generitype of *Calendula* Linnaeus (vide Steudel, *Nom.,* ed. 2, 1: 256. 1840).
Current name: **Calendula officinalis** L. (Asteraceae).
Note: Ohle (in *Feddes Repert.* 85: 263. 1974) stated "Typus: Herbar. Linné (BM)" but this appears confused, and does not distinguish between several collections in the Clifford (BM) and Linnaean (LINN) herbaria.

Calendula pluvialis Linnaeus, *Species Plantarum* 2: 921. 1753.
"Habitat in Aethiopia." RCN: 6663.
Type not designated.
Original material: Herb. A. van Royen No. 900.255–493 (L); Herb. Clifford: 425, *Calendula* 2 (BM); Herb. Linn. No. 1035.5 (LINN); Herb. Linn. No. 364.11? (S); [icon] in Breyn, Prodr. Fasc. Rar. Pl.: 26, t. 14, f. 1. 1739; [icon] in Hermann, Hort. Lugd.-Bat. Cat.: 104, 105. 1687; [icon] in Stisser, Bot. Cur.: 59, t. 6. 1697.
Current name: **Dimorphotheca pluvialis** (L.) Norl. (Asteraceae).

Calendula sancta Linnaeus, *Species Plantarum,* ed. 2, 2: 1304. 1763.
"Habitat in Palaestina." RCN: 6661.
Lectotype (Heyn & al. in *Israel J. Bot.* 23: 170. 1974): *Hasselquist,* Herb. Linn. No. 1035.2 (LINN).
Current name: **Calendula sancta** L. (Asteraceae).

Calla aethiopica Linnaeus, *Species Plantarum* 2: 968. 1753.
"Habitat in Aethiopia." RCN: 7014.
Lectotype (Letty in *Bothalia* 11: 9, f. 3. 1973): Herb. Clifford: 435, *Calla* 1 (BM-000647350), see p. 13, opposite.
Current name: **Zantedeschia aethiopica** (L.) Spreng. (Araceae).

Calla orientalis Linnaeus, *Species Plantarum,* ed. 2, 2: 1373. 1763, *nom. utique rej.*
"Habitat Halepi in montosis." RCN: 7016.
Neotype (Govaerts in *Taxon* 45: 545. 1996): Herb. Rauwolff No. 100 (L).
Current name: **Biarum crispidulum** (Schott) Engl. (Araceae).

Calla palustris Linnaeus, *Species Plantarum* 2: 968. 1753.
"Habitat in Europae borealis paludibus." RCN: 7015.

The lectotype of *Calla aethiopica* L.

Lectotype (Lehmann in Jarvis & al., *Regnum Veg.* 127: 28. 1993):
Herb. Clifford: 436, *Calla* 2 (BM-000647351).
Generitype of *Calla* Linnaeus.
Current name: ***Calla palustris*** L. (Araceae).

Callicarpa americana Linnaeus, *Species Plantarum* 1: 111. 1753.
"Habitat in Virginia, Carolina." RCN: 906.
Lectotype (Moldenke in *Repert. Spec. Nov. Regni Veg.* 39: 306. 1936):
Clayton 764, Herb. Linn. No. 136.1 (LINN; iso- BM).
Generitype of *Callicarpa* Linnaeus.
Current name: ***Callicarpa americana*** L. (Verbenaceae).

Callicarpa cana Linnaeus, *Mantissa Plantarum Altera*: 198. 1771.
"Habitat in Java." RCN: 907.
Type not designated.
Original material: none traced.
Current name: ***Callicarpa candicans*** (Burm. f.) Hochr.
(Verbenaceae).
Note: Moldenke (in *Phytologia* 14: 114. 1966) discussed 136.2
(LINN), which he identified as *C. nudiflora* Hook. & Arn., and
136.3 (LINN), annotated as "minima", which he says is "the true *C.
cana* L.". Munir (in *J. Adelaide Bot. Gard.* 6: 19. 1982) indicated an
untraced König collection as type.

Callicarpa lanata Linnaeus, *Mantissa Plantarum Altera*: 331. 1771,
nom. illeg.
["Habitat in India."] Sp. Pl. 1: 118 (1753). RCN: 972.
Replaced synonym: *Tomex tomentosa* L. (1753).
Lectotype (Trimen in *J. Linn. Soc., Bot.* 24: 136. 1887): Herb.
Hermann 1: 64, No. 59 (BM-000594496).
Current name: ***Callicarpa tomentosa*** (L.) L. (Verbenaceae).

Callicarpa tomentosa (Linnaeus) Linnaeus, *Systema Vegetabilium,* ed.
13: 130. 1774.
["Habitat in India."] Sp. Pl. 1: 118 (1753). RCN: 972.
Basionym: *Tomex tomentosa* L. (1753).
Lectotype (Trimen in *J. Linn. Soc., Bot.* 24: 136. 1887): Herb.
Hermann 1: 64, No. 59 (BM-000594496).
Current name: ***Callicarpa tomentosa*** (L.) L. (Verbenaceae).

Calligonum polygonoides Linnaeus, *Species Plantarum* 1: 530.
1753.
"Habitat in monte Ararat." RCN: 3944.
Type not designated.
Original material: Herb. Clifford: 212, *Calligonum* 1 (BM); [icon] in
Tournefort, Rel. Voy. Levant (Paris ed.) 2: 356. 1717.
Generitype of *Calligonum* Linnaeus.
Current name: ***Calligonum polygonoides*** L. (Polygonaceae).
Note: A number of authors, including Cullen (in Davis, *Fl. Turkey* 2:
267. 1967) and Bhopal & Chaudhri (in *Pakistan Syst.* 1(2): 66.
1977) have treated Tournefort material (P-TOURN) as the type but
this was not studied by Linnaeus and is not original material for the
name.

Callisia gnaphalodes Linnaeus, *Plantae Rariores Africanae*: 23.
1760.
["Habitat in Aethiopia."] Sp. Pl. ed. 2, 2: 1249 (1763). RCN: 6420.
Basionym of: *Leysera gnaphalodes* (L.) L. (1763).
Lectotype (Bremer in Jarvis & al., *Regnum Veg.* 127: 28. 1993): *Leysera
gnaphalodes*, fol. A, Herb. Burman (G).
Generitype of *Callisia* Linnaeus, *nom. illeg.*
Current name: ***Leysera gnaphalodes*** (L.) L. (Asteraceae).
Note: Callisia Linnaeus 1760 (Asteraceae), *nom. illeg.*, non *Callisia*
Loefl. 1758 (Commelinaceae).

Callisia repens (N.J. Jacquin) Linnaeus, *Species Plantarum,* ed. 2, 1:
62. 1762.
"Habitat in Americae meridionalis udis depressis umbrosis." RCN:
357.
Basionym: *Hapalanthus repens* Jacq. (1760).
Lectotype (Howard, *Fl. Lesser Antilles* 3: 430. 1979): [icon]
"*Hapalanthus repens*" in Jacquin, Select. Stirp. Amer. Hist.: 11, t. 11.
1763.
Current name: ***Callisia repens*** (Jacq.) L. (Commelinaceae).

Callitriche androgyna Linnaeus, *Centuria I Plantarum*: 31. 1755.
"Habitat in Europae fossis, vere florens." RCN: 32.
Lectotype (Lansdown & Jarvis in *Taxon* 53: 170. 2004): Herb. Linn.
No. 13.1, three lower specimens (LINN).
Current name: ***Callitriche palustris*** L. (Callitrichaceae).
Note: Although not technically a superfluous name, *C. androgyna*
appears to have been intended to replace *C. palustris* var. *minima* L.
(1753) (equivalent to the autonymic variety) so Lansdown & Jarvis
typified *C. androgyna* so as to make it homotypic with *C. palustris*
L. (1753).

Callitriche autumnalis Linnaeus, *Flora Suecica,* ed. 2: 2. 1755, *nom.
illeg.*
"Habitat in aquis quietis, fossis, cum priore; vulgaris." RCN: 33.
Replaced synonym: *Callitriche hermaphroditica* L. (Feb 1755).

Lectotype (Lansdown & Jarvis in *Taxon* 53: 171. 2004): Herb. Linn. No. 13.1, middle two specimens (LINN).

Current name: ***Callitriche hermaphroditica*** L. (Callitrichaceae).

Note: A superfluous name for the earlier *C. hermaphroditica* L. (1755).

Callitriche hermaphroditica Linnaeus, *Centuria I Plantarum*: 31. 1755.

"Habitat in Europae fossis, autumno florens." RCN: 33.

Replaced synonym of: *Callitriche autumnalis* L. (Oct 1755), *nom. illeg.*

Lectotype (Lansdown & Jarvis in *Taxon* 53: 170. 2004): Herb. Linn. No. 13.1, middle two specimens (LINN).

Current name: ***Callitriche hermaphroditica*** L. (Callitrichaceae).

Callitriche palustris Linnaeus, *Species Plantarum* 2: 969. 1753.

"Habitat in Europae fossis paludibus." RCN: 32.

Lectotype (Lansdown & Jarvis in *Taxon* 53: 169. 2004): Herb. Linn. No. 13.1, three lower specimens (LINN).

Generitype of *Callitriche* Linnaeus.

Current name: ***Callitriche palustris*** L. (Callitrichaceae).

Callitriche palustris Linnaeus var. **bifida** Linnaeus, *Species Plantarum* 2: 969. 1753.

RCN: 33.

Type not designated.

Original material: [icon] in Loesel, Fl. Prussica: 140, t. 38. 1703.

Current name: **Stellaria sp.** (Caryophyllaceae).

Note: Lansdown (in Lansdown & Jarvis, *Taxon* 53: 170. 2004) notes that the cited Loesel illustration (which appears to be the only original material for the name) probably depicts a species of *Stellaria* (Caryophyllaceae), rather than a *Callitriche* (Callitrichaceae).

Callitriche palustris Linnaeus var. **minima** Linnaeus, *Species Plantarum* 2: 969. 1753.

RCN: 32.

Lectotype (Lansdown & Jarvis in *Taxon* 53: 170. 2004): Herb. Linn. No. 13.1, three lower specimens (LINN).

Current name: ***Callitriche palustris*** L. (Callitrichaceae).

Callitriche palustris Linnaeus var. **natans** Linnaeus, *Species Plantarum* 2: 969. 1753.

RCN: 32.

Lectotype (Lansdown & Jarvis in *Taxon* 53: 170. 2004): Herb. Burser VII(1): 82, lower left specimen (UPS).

Current name: ***Callitriche platycarpa*** Kütz. (Callitrichaceae).

Callitriche verna Linnaeus, *Flora Suecica*, ed. 2: 2. 1755.

"Habitat in fossis, & aquis quietis; vulgaris." RCN: 32.

Lectotype (Lansdown & Jarvis in *Taxon* 53: 171. 2004): Herb. Linn. No. 13.2 (LINN).

Current name: ***Callitriche palustris*** L. (Callitrichaceae).

Calophyllum calaba Linnaeus, *Species Plantarum* 1: 514. 1753.

"Habitat in Indiis." RCN: 3869.

Lectotype (Stevens in Jarvis & al., *Regnum Veg.* 127: 28. 1993): Herb. Hermann 3: 3, No. 202 (BM-000621800).

Generitype of *Calophyllum* Linnaeus (vide Green, *Prop. Brit. Bot.*: 161. 1929).

Current name: ***Calophyllum calaba*** L. (Clusiaceae).

Note: Furtado (in *Gard. Bull. Straits Settlem.* 11: 258–260. 1941), followed by Howard (in *J. Arnold Arbor.* 43: 397. 1962), argued that the name should be applied to the New World element but did not typify the name. D'Arcy & Keating (in *Ann. Missouri Bot. Gard.*

66: 563. 1969), followed by Lourteig & Fosberg (in *Phytologia* 57: 153–155, f. 1. 1985), designated Plumier, *Nov. Amer. Gen.*: t. 18 (1703) as lectotype but this illustration does not form part of the protologue, so is ineligible. Kostermans (in Dassanayake & Fosberg, *Revised Handb. Fl. Ceylon* 1: 96. 1980) indicated Clifford material (BM, unseen by him and apparently not preserved) as the type. Stevens in *J. Arnold Arbor.* 61: 256. 1980) indicated the several specimens in Herb. Hermann (1: 65; 2: 42, 52; 3: 3, BM) as syntypes, also providing an extensive discussion of the problem in Manilal (*Bot. Hist. Hort. Malab.*: 168–176. 1980). Stevens (in Jarvis & al., *Regnum Veg* 127: 28. 1993) subsequently made an explicit choice of the material in Herb. Hermann 3: 3 (BM) as the lectotype.

Calophyllum inophyllum Linnaeus, *Species Plantarum* 1: 513. 1753.

"Habitat in India." RCN: 3868.

Lectotype (Bamps & al. in Polhill, *Fl. Trop. E. Africa, Guttiferae*: 3. 1978): Herb. Hermann 2: 82, No. 201 (BM-000594641).

Current name: ***Calophyllum inophyllum*** L. (Clusiaceae).

Caltha palustris Linnaeus, *Species Plantarum* 1: 558. 1753.

"Habitat in humidiusculis Europae." RCN: 4111.

Lectotype (Jonsell & Jarvis in Jarvis & al., *Regnum Veg.* 127: 28. 1993): Herb. Burser XV(2): 82 (UPS).

Generitype of *Caltha* Linnaeus.

Current name: ***Caltha palustris*** L. (Ranunculaceae).

Note: See detailed review by Jonsell & Jarvis (in *Nordic J. Bot.* 14: 161. 1994).

Calycanthus floridus Linnaeus, *Systema Naturae,* ed. 10, 2: 1066. 1759.

["Habitat in Carolina."] Sp. Pl., ed. 2, 1: 718 (1762). RCN: 3812.

Lectotype (Nicely in *Castanea* 30: 66. 1965): *Miller,* Herb. Linn. No. 660.1 (LINN; iso- BM).

Generitype of *Calycanthus* Linnaeus, *nom. cons.*

Current name: ***Calycanthus floridus*** L. (Calycanthaceae).

Note: Calycanthus Linnaeus, *nom. cons.* against *Basteria* Mill.

Calycanthus praecox Linnaeus, *Species Plantarum,* ed. 2, 1: 718. 1762.

"Habitat in Japonia." RCN: 3813.

Holotype (Nicely in *Castanea* 30: 74. 1965): [icon] *"Obai seu Robai"* in Kaempfer, Amoen. Exot. Fasc.: 878, 879. 1712 (see p. 19).

Current name: ***Chimonanthus praecox*** (L.) Link (Calycanthaceae).

Cambogia gummi-gutta Linnaeus, *Genera Plantarum,* ed. 5: Appendix. 1754.

"Habitat in Malabaria, Zeylona." RCN: 3851.

Lectotype (Kostermans in *Ceylon J. Sci., Biol. Sci.* 12: 57. 1976): [icon] *"Coddam-pulli"* in Rheede, Hort. Malab. 1: 41, t. 24. 1678.

Generitype of *Cambogia* Linnaeus.

Current name: ***Garcinia gummi-gutta*** (L.) N. Robson (Clusiaceae).

Note: The correct form of the specific epithet is "gummi-gutta" (Art. 23, Ex. 19).

Camellia japonica Linnaeus, *Species Plantarum* 2: 698. 1753.

"Habitat in Japonia, China." RCN: 5111.

Lectotype (Bartholomew in Jarvis & al., *Regnum Veg.* 127: 29. 1993): [icon] *"Tsubaki"* in Kaempfer, Amoen. Exot. Fasc.: 850, 851. 1712. – Voucher: Herb. Sloane 211: 23 (BM-SL).

Generitype of *Camellia* Linnaeus.

Current name: ***Camellia japonica*** L. (Theaceae).

Note: Jarvis (in *Symb. Bot. Upsal.* 33(3): 29, f. 4. 2005) reproduces an image of the Kaempfer lectotype engraving.

Cameraria angustifolia Linnaeus, *Species Plantarum* 1: 210. 1753.
"Habitat in America calidiore." RCN: 1736.
Type not designated.
Original material: [icon] in Plumier in Burman, Pl. Amer.: 61, t. 72, f. 2. 1756.
Current name: ***Cameraria angustifolia*** L. (Apocynaceae).

Cameraria echites (Linnaeus) Linnaeus, *Flora Jamaicensis*: 14. 1759.
["Habitat in Jamaica."] Sp. Pl., ed. 2, 1: 307 (1762).
Basionym: *Tabernaemontana echites* L. (May–Jun 1759).
Type not designated.
Original material: as basionym.
Current name: ***Echites umbellata*** Jacq. (Apocynaceae).

Cameraria latifolia Linnaeus, *Species Plantarum* 1: 210. 1753.
"Habitat in America calidiore." RCN: 1735.
Lectotype (Leeuwenberg in Jarvis & al., *Regnum Veg.* 127: 29. 1993): Herb. Clifford: 76, *Cameraria* 1 (BM-000558143).
Generitype of *Cameraria* Linnaeus (vide Hitchcock, *Prop. Brit. Bot.*: 136. 1929).
Current name: ***Cameraria latifolia*** L. (Apocynaceae).

Camocladia pinnatifolia Linnaeus, *Systema Naturae,* ed. 10, 2: 861. 1759.
"Habitat [in Jamaica.]" RCN: 274.
Type not designated.
Original material: none traced.
Current name: ***Comocladia pinnatifolia*** L. (Anacardiaceae).
Note: Linnaeus spelled the generic epithet "Camocladia" but from his protologue, drawn from Browne (1758), it seems clear that this was an error for *Comocladia* P. Browne.

Campanula alpini Linnaeus, *Species Plantarum*, ed. 2, 2: 1669. 1763.
"Habitat in Summano aliisque Italiae Alpibus. Arduini." RCN: 1306.
Lectotype (Turland in *Bull. Nat. Hist. Mus. London, Bot.* 25: 157, f. 27. 1995): *Turra,* Herb. Linn. No. 221.19 (LINN), see p. 233.
Current name: ***Adenophora liliifolia*** (L.) A. DC. (Campanulaceae).

Campanula americana Linnaeus, *Species Plantarum* 1: 164. 1753.
"Habitat in America." RCN: 1303.
Lectotype (Brummitt in *Taxon* 42: 879. 1993): Herb. Linn. No. 221.13 (LINN).
Current name: ***Campanula americana*** L. (Campanulaceae).
Note: Reveal & al. (in *Taxon* 39: 696. 1990) proposed the conservation of this name with a conserved type but the Committee for Spermatophyta ruled that the collection in question is original material, and is to be accepted as the lectotype.

Campanula barbata Linnaeus, *Systema Naturae,* ed. 10, 2: 926. 1759.
["Habitat in Alpibus Austriae, Helvetiae, Pedemontii. Allioni."] Sp. Pl., ed. 2, 1: 236 (1762). RCN: 1319.
Lectotype (Pistarino & al. in *Taxon* 51: 548, f. 1. 2002): *Allioni,* Herb. Linn. No. 221.57 (LINN).
Current name: ***Campanula barbata*** L. (Campanulaceae).

Campanula bononiensis Linnaeus, *Species Plantarum* 1: 165. 1753.
"Habitat in Baldi Lessinensium jugis, Bononiae." RCN: 1309.
Lectotype (Victorov in *Novosti Sist. Vyssh. Rast.* 34: 202. 2003): [icon] *"Campanula s. Cervicaria Bononiensis"* in Morison, Pl. Hist. Univ. 2: 461, s. 5, t. 4, f. 38. 1680.
Current name: ***Campanula bononiensis*** L. (Campanulaceae).

Campanula canariensis Linnaeus, *Species Plantarum* 1: 168. 1753.
"Habitat in insulis Canariis." RCN: 2568.
Replaced synonym of: *Canarina campanula* L. (1771), *nom. illeg.*

Lectotype (Stearn, *Introd. Linnaeus' Sp. Pl.* (Ray Soc. ed.): 47. 1957): [icon] *"Campanula foliis hastatis dentatis, caule determinato folioso"* in Linnaeus, Hort. Cliff.: 65, t. 8. 1738.
Current name: ***Canarina canariensis*** (L.) Vatke (Campanulaceae).
Note: Francisco-Ortega & al. (in *Bull. Nat. Hist. Mus. London, Bot.* 24: 6, f. 3. 1994) designated Plukenet's t. 276, f. 1 as lectotype, with a voucher in Herb. Sloane 99: 161 (BM-SL). However, this choice is pre-dated by that of Stearn.

Campanula capensis Linnaeus, *Species Plantarum* 1: 169. 1753.
"Habitat ad Caput b. Spei." RCN: 1334.
Lectotype (Wijnands, *Bot. Commelins*: 62. 1983): [icon] *"Campanula Afric. annua hirsuta latis serratisque foliis flor. violaceo"* in Commelin, Hort. Med. Amstelod. Pl. Rar. 2: 69, t. 35. 1701.
Current name: ***Wahlenbergia capensis*** (L.) DC. (Campanulaceae).

Campanula cenisia Linnaeus, *Species Plantarum,* ed. 2, 2: 1669. 1763.
"Habitat in Cenisii alpinis, Ronche dictis. Allion." RCN: 1295.
Lectotype (Pistarino & al. in *Taxon* 51: 549, f. 2. 2002): *Allioni,* Herb. Linn. No. 221.1 (LINN).
Current name: ***Campanula cenisia*** L. (Campanulaceae).

Campanula cervicaria Linnaeus, *Species Plantarum* 1: 167. 1753.
"Habitat in Helvetiae, Sveciae, Germaniae asperis sylvaticis." RCN: 1313.
Lectotype (Victorov in *Novosti Sist. Vyssh. Rast.* 34: 217. 2003): Herb. Linn. No. 221.45 (LINN).
Current name: ***Campanula cervicaria*** L. (Campanulaceae).

Campanula decurrens Linnaeus, *Species Plantarum* 1: 164. 1753.
"Habitat in Finlandia." RCN: 1299.
Type not designated.
Original material: Herb. Linn. No. 221.9 (LINN); Herb. Burser IV: 26 (UPS).
Note: The application of this name is uncertain.

Campanula dichotoma Linnaeus, *Centuria II Plantarum*: 10. 1756.
"Habitat in Sicilia, Syria." RCN: 1317.
Lectotype (Victorov in Victorov & Elenevsky in *Bot. Zhurn.* 83(10): 57. 1998): [icon] *"Campanula hirsuta ocimi folio caulem ambiente, flore pendulo"* in Boccone, Icon. Descr. Rar. Pl. Siciliae: 83, 84, t. 45, f. 1. 1674.
Current name: ***Campanula dichotoma*** L. (Campanulaceae).

Campanula elatines Linnaeus, *Systema Naturae,* ed. 10, 2: 927. 1759.
["Habitat in Alpinis Europae australis. Allioni."] Sp. Pl., ed. 2, 1: 240 (1762). RCN: 1355.
Lectotype (Damboldt in *Bot. Jahrb. Syst.* 84: 336. 1965): *Allioni,* Herb. Linn. No. 221.76 (LINN).
Current name: ***Campanula elatines*** L. (Campanulaceae).

Campanula erinoides Linnaeus, *Systema Naturae,* ed. 12, 2: 162; *Mantissa Plantarum*: 44. 1767.
"Habitat in Africa." RCN: 1337.
Type not designated.
Original material: [icon] in Hermann, Hort. Lugd.-Bat. Cat.: 110, 111. 1687.
Note: The application of this name is uncertain.

Campanula erinus Linnaeus, *Species Plantarum* 1: 169. 1753.
"Habitat in Italia, Galloprovincia, Monspelii." RCN: 1339.
Lectotype (designated here by Pistarino & Jarvis): Herb. Burser IV: 5 (UPS).
Current name: ***Campanula erinus*** L. (Campanulaceae).

Note: Victorov (in *Novosti Sist. Vyssh. Rast.* 34: 204. 2003) designated 221.79 (LINN) as lectotype. However, this is a Gérard collection that did not reach Linnaeus until 1756 so it cannot be original material for the name.

Campanula fruticosa Linnaeus, *Species Plantarum* 1: 168. 1753.
"Habitat ad Caput b. Spei." RCN: 1328.
Lectotype (Adamson in *J. S. African Bot.* 19: 157. 1953): *"Campanula africana, ericae folio, flore coeruleo patulo"*, Herb. Hermann 4: 16, bottom left (BM-000594715).
Current name: ***Prismatocarpus fruticosus*** (L.) L'Hér. (Campanulaceae).
Note: In the protologue, Linnaeus cited a Hermann polynomial published in a supplement by Burman (1737). This polynomial and reference, written by Linnaeus, can be found annotating three specimens in Hermann's herbarium (vol. 4: 16, BM). They are clearly original material for Linnaeus' name and were treated as the type by Adamson.

Campanula glomerata Linnaeus, *Species Plantarum* 1: 166. 1753.
"Habitat in Angliae, Galliae, Sueciae pratis aridis." RCN: 1312.
Lectotype (Victorov in *Novosti Sist. Vyssh. Rast.* 34: 214. 2003): Herb. Linn. No. 221.44 (LINN).
Current name: ***Campanula glomerata*** L. (Campanulaceae).

Campanula graminifolia Linnaeus, *Species Plantarum* 1: 166. 1753.
"Habitat in Italiae montibus, Aprutii Salmone vicinis." RCN: 1310.
Type not designated.
Original material: [icon] in Bauhin & Cherler, Hist. Pl. Univ. 2: 802. 1651; [icon] in Barrelier, Pl. Galliam: 10, t. 332. 1714.
Current name: ***Edraianthus graminifolius*** (L.) DC. (Campanulaceae).
Note: Hartvig (in Strid & Kit Tan, *Mountain Fl. Greece* 2: 395. 1991) indicated 221.36 (LINN) as type but this lacks the relevant *Species Plantarum* number (i.e. "16"), and is a post-1753 addition to the collection, and not original material for the name.

Campanula hederacea Linnaeus, *Species Plantarum* 1: 169. 1753.
"Habitat in Anglia, Gallia, Hispania locis umbrosis humidiusculis." RCN: 1336.
Type not designated.
Original material: *Löfling s.n.*, Herb. Linn. No. 221.77 (LINN); [icon] in Morison, Pl. Hist. Univ. 2: 456, s. 5, t. 2, f. 18. 1680; [icon] in Plukenet, Phytographia: t. 23, f. 1. 1691; Almag. Bot.: 78. 1696.
Current name: ***Wahlenbergia hederacea*** (L.) Rchb. (Campanulaceae).

Campanula heterophylla Linnaeus, *Species Plantarum* 1: 169; *Species Plantarum* 2: Errata. 1753.
"Habitat in Oriente." RCN: 1338.
Lectotype (designated here by Turland): [icon] *"Campanula saxatilis, foliis inferioribus Bellidis, caeteris Nummulariae"* in Tournefort, Rel. Voy. Levant (Paris ed.) 1: 243. 1717. – Voucher: Herb. Tournefort No. 326 (P-TOURN).
Current name: ***Campanula heterophylla*** L. (Campanulaceae).

Campanula hybrida Linnaeus, *Species Plantarum* 1: 168. 1753.
"Habitat in Anglia, Gallia, inter segetes." RCN: 1330.
Type not designated.
Original material: Herb. Linn. No. 221.71 (LINN); [icon] in Morison, Pl. Hist. Univ. 2: 457, s. 5, t. 2, f. 22. 1680.
Current name: ***Legousia hybrida*** (L.) Delarbre (Campanulaceae).

Campanula laciniata Linnaeus, *Species Plantarum* 1: 165. 1753.
"Habitat in Graeciae rupibus." RCN: 1326.
Lectotype (designated here by Turland): [icon] *"Campanula Graeca,*

saxatilis, Jacobeae Foliis" in Tournefort, Rel. Voy. Levant (Paris ed.) 1: 260. 1717. – Typotype: Herb. Tournefort No. 20, p. 3 (P-TOURN).
Current name: ***Campanula laciniata*** L. (Campanulaceae).

Campanula latifolia Linnaeus, *Species Plantarum* 1: 165. 1753.
"Habitat in Angliae, Sueciae montosis, sepibus." RCN: 1307.
Lectotype (Haridasan & Mukherjee in Hajra & Sanjappa in *Fasc. Fl. India* 22: 47. 1996): Herb. Linn. No. 221.29 (LINN).
Generitype of *Campanula* Linnaeus (vide Hitchcock, *Prop. Brit. Bot.*: 131. 1929).
Current name: ***Campanula latifolia*** L. (Campanulaceae).
Note: As there is only a single sheet in LINN annotated as *C. latifolia*, the choice by Haridasan & Mukherjee is accepted here.

Campanula liliifolia Linnaeus, *Species Plantarum* 1: 165. 1753.
"Habitat in Tataria, Sibiria." RCN: 1304.
Lectotype (designated here by Pistarino & Jarvis): *Gerber*, Herb. Linn. No. 221.15 (LINN).
Current name: ***Adenophora liliifolia*** (L.) A. DC. (Campanulaceae).
Note: Specific epithet spelled "lilifolia" in the protologue.

Campanula limoniifolia Linnaeus, *Species Plantarum*, ed. 2, 1: 239. 1762.
"Habitat in Oriente. Burmannus." RCN: 1331.
Lectotype (Damboldt in *Boissiera* 17: 68. 1970): Herb. Linn. No. 221.72 (LINN).
Current name: ***Asyneuma limoniifolium*** (L.) Janch. (Campanulaceae).
Note: Specific epithet spelled "limonifolia" in the protologue.

Campanula linifolia Linnaeus, *Amoenitates Academicae* 4: 479. 1759.
Type not designated.
Original material: [icon] in Magnol, Bot. Monspel.: 46, 45. 1676.
Note: The application of this name is uncertain.

Campanula medium Linnaeus, *Species Plantarum* 1: 167. 1753.
"Habitat in Germaniae, Italiae nemoribus." RCN: 1318.
Lectotype (designated here by Pistarino & Jarvis): Herb. Linn. No. 221.55 (LINN).
Current name: ***Campanula medium*** L. (Campanulaceae).

Campanula mollis Linnaeus, *Species Plantarum*, ed. 2, 1: 237. 1762.
"Habitat in Oriente, Hispania. Alstroemer." RCN: 1322.
Type not designated.
Original material: none traced.
Current name: ***Campanula velutina*** Desf. (Campanulaceae).
Note: López González (in *Bol. Soc. Brot.*, sér. 2, 53: 299–308. 1980) pointed out that the Alströmer specimen (221.63, LINN) conflicts fundamentally with Linnaeus' description, and concluded that the name is best regarded as a *nomen ambiguum*. He informally rejected the name, taking up *C. velutina* Desf. instead.

Campanula patula Linnaeus, *Species Plantarum* 1: 163. 1753.
"Habitat in Angliae, Sueciae arvis." RCN: 1299.
Lectotype (Victorov in *Novosti Sist. Vyssh. Rast.* 34: 228. 2003): [icon] *"Campanula esculentae facie, ramis & flore patulis"* in Dillenius, Hort. Eltham. 1: 68, t. 58, f. 68. 1732.
Current name: ***Campanula patula*** L. (Campanulaceae).

Campanula pentagonia Linnaeus, *Species Plantarum* 1: 169. 1753.
"Habitat in Thracia." RCN: 1332.
Lectotype (Oganesian in *Candollea* 50: 303. 1995): Herb. Clifford: 64, *Campanula* 14 (BM-000558073).
Current name: ***Legousia pentagonia*** (L.) Druce (Campanulaceae).

Campanula peregrina Linnaeus, *Mantissa Plantarum Altera*: 204. 1771.
"Habitat in C.B.S.? inter semina capensia excrevit." RCN: 1314.
Lectotype (Damboldt in Davis, *Fl. Turkey* 6: 63. 1978): Herb. Linn. No. 221.48 (LINN).
Current name: **Campanula peregrina** L. (Campanulaceae).

Campanula perfoliata Linnaeus, *Species Plantarum* 1: 169. 1753.
"Habitat in Virginia." RCN: 1333.
Lectotype (designated here by Reveal): Herb. Linn. No. 221.73 (LINN).
Current name: **Triodanis perfoliata** (L.) Nieuwl. (Campanulaceae).

Campanula persicifolia Linnaeus, *Species Plantarum* 1: 164. 1753.
"Habitat in Europae septentrionalis asperis." RCN: 1301.
Lectotype (Hartvig in Strid & Kit Tan, *Mountain Fl. Greece* 2: 375. 1991): Herb. Linn. No. 221.11 (LINN).
Current name: **Campanula persicifolia** L. (Campanulaceae).
Note: Damboldt (in Davis, *Fl. Turkey* 6: 55. 1978) indicated 221.22 (LINN) as type but that collection is not associated with this name and is not original material for it.

Campanula petraea Linnaeus, *Systema Naturae*, ed. 10, 2: 926. 1759.
["Habitat in Baldo."] Sp. Pl., ed. 2, 1: 236 (1762). RCN: 1316.
Lectotype (designated here by Pistarino & Jarvis): *Séguier*, Herb. Linn. No. 221.51 (LINN).
Current name: **Campanula petraea** L. (Campanulaceae).

Campanula pulla Linnaeus, *Species Plantarum* 1: 163. 1753.
"Habitat in Austria." RCN: 1297.
Lectotype (designated here by Pistarino & Jarvis): Herb. Burser IV: 21 (UPS).
Current name: **Campanula pulla** L. (Campanulaceae).

Campanula pyramidalis Linnaeus, *Species Plantarum* 1: 164. 1753.
"Habitat – – – –" RCN: 1302.
Type not designated.
Original material: Herb. Linn. No. 221.12 (LINN); Herb. Burser IV: 19 (UPS).
Current name: **Campanula pyramidalis** L. (Campanulaceae).

Campanula rapunculoides Linnaeus, *Species Plantarum* 1: 165. 1753.
"Habitat in Helvetia, Gallia." RCN: 1308.
Lectotype (Damboldt in Davis, *Fl. Turkey* 6: 16. 1978): Herb. Linn. No. 221.30 (LINN).
Current name: **Campanula rapunculoides** L. (Campanulaceae).

Campanula rapunculus Linnaeus, *Species Plantarum* 1: 164. 1753.
"Habitat in Helvetia, Anglia, Gallia." RCN: 1300.
Lectotype (designated here by Pistarino & Jarvis): Herb. Burser IV: 4 (UPS).
Current name: **Campanula rapunculus** L. (Campanulaceae).
Note: Although Victorov (in *Novosti Sist. Vyssh. Rast.* 34: 227. 2003) indicated 221.10 (LINN) as type, this was published after 1 Jan 2001 and so the omission of the phrase "designated here" or an equivalent (Art. 7.11) means that this choice is not effective.

Campanula rhomboidalis Linnaeus, *Species Plantarum* 1: 165. 1753.
"Habitat in alpibus Helvetiae, Italiae." RCN: 1305.
Lectotype (designated here by Pistarino & Jarvis): Herb. Linn. No. 221.18, right specimen (LINN).
Current name: **Campanula rhomboidalis** L. (Campanulaceae).

Campanula rotundifolia Linnaeus, *Species Plantarum* 1: 163. 1753.
"Habitat in Europae pascuis." RCN: 1298.

Lectotype (Böcher in *Ann. Bot. Fenn.* 3: 292. 1966): Herb. Linn. No. 221.5 (LINN).
Current name: **Campanula rotundifolia** L. (Campanulaceae).
Note: See also Shetler (in *Phanerog. Monogr.* 11: 55. 1982) for a discussion of the identity of the various elements involved.

Campanula saxatilis Linnaeus, *Species Plantarum* 1: 167. 1753.
"Habitat in Cretae scopulis saxosis." RCN: 1323.
Lectotype (Turland in *Willdenowia* 36: 304, f. 1. 2006): [icon] "*Traicheliu saxat Bellid fol caeruleum creticum*" in Boccone, Mus. Piante Rar. Sicilia: 76, t. 64. 1697.
Current name: **Campanula saxatilis** L. subsp. **saxatilis** (Campanulaceae).
Note: An image of the lectotype is also reproduced by Lack (in *Ann. Naturhist. Mus. Wien* 98B, Suppl.: 195. 1996).

Campanula sibirica Linnaeus, *Species Plantarum* 1: 167. 1753.
"Habitat in Sibiria. D. Gmelin: & Messanae." RCN: 1324.
Type not designated.
Original material: [icon] in Morison, Pl. Hist. Univ. 2: 459, s. 5, t. 3, f. 26. 1680; [icon] in Boccone, Icon. Descr. Rar. Pl. Siciliae: 83, 84, t. 45, f. 1. 1674.
Current name: **Campanula sibirica** L. (Campanulaceae).
Note: Although Victorov (in *Novosti Sist. Vyssh. Rast.* 32: 163. 2000; 34: 217. 2003) indicated 221.59 (LINN) as lectotype, the material came from Scopoli and, as it was not received by Linnaeus until 1762, it cannot be original material for the name.

Campanula speculum-veneris Linnaeus, *Species Plantarum* 1: 168. 1753.
"Habitat inter segetes Europae australis." RCN: 1329.
Lectotype (designated here by Pistarino & Jarvis): Herb. Linn. No. 221.68 (LINN).
Current name: **Legousia speculum-veneris** (L.) Chaix (Campanulaceae).

Campanula spicata Linnaeus, *Species Plantarum* 1: 166. 1753.
"Habitat in Vallesia." RCN: 1320.
Lectotype (designated here by Pistarino & Jarvis): Herb. Burser IV: 37 (UPS).
Current name: **Campanula spicata** L. (Campanulaceae).

Campanula stricta Linnaeus, *Species Plantarum*, ed. 2, 1: 238. 1762.
"Habitat in Syria, Palaestina." RCN: 1327.
Neotype (Damboldt in Davis, *Fl. Turkey* 6: 43. 1978): "*Campanula orientalis, folio oblongo rigido asper, flore sursum spectante*", Herb. Tournefort No. 336 (P-TOURN).
Current name: **Campanula stricta** L. (Campanulaceae).
Note: As there is no original material extant for this name, Damboldt's treatment of a Tournefort collection as "type" is accepted as a neotypification under Art. 9.8.

Campanula thyrsoides Linnaeus, *Species Plantarum* 1: 167. 1753.
"Habitat in alpibus Harcyniae aliisque." RCN: 1315.
Type not designated.
Original material: [icon] in Camerarius, Hort. Med. Phil.: 32, t. 4. 1588; [icon] in Bauhin & Cherler, Hist. Pl. Univ. 2: 809. 1651.
Current name: **Campanula thyrsoides** L. (Campanulaceae).

Campanula trachelium Linnaeus, *Species Plantarum* 1: 166. 1753.
"Habitat in Europae sepibus." RCN: 1311.
Lectotype (Victorov in *Novosti Sist. Vyssh. Rast.* 34: 200. 2003): Herb. Linn. No. 221.41 (LINN).
Current name: **Campanula trachelium** L. (Campanulaceae).

Campanula uniflora Linnaeus, *Species Plantarum* 1: 163. 1753.
"Habitat in alpibus Lapponicis." RCN: 1296.
Type not designated.
Original material: Herb. Linn. No. 79.19? (S); Herb. Linn. No. 221.2 (LINN); [icon] in Linnaeus, Fl. Lapponica: 53, t. 9, f. 5, 6. 1737.
Current name: *Campanula uniflora* L. (Campanulaceae).
Note: Although Victorov (in *Novosti Sist. Vyssh. Rast.* 34: 232. 2003) indicated 221.3 (LINN) as lectotype, the material is unannotated by Linnaeus and cannot be regarded as original material for the name.

Camphorosma acuta Linnaeus, *Species Plantarum* 1: 122. 1753.
"Habitat in Italia, Tataria." RCN: 1012.
Type not designated.
Original material: *Gerber*, Herb. Linn. No. 165.3 (LINN); [icon] in Tabernaemontanus, New Vollk. Kräuterb.: 57. 1664; [icon] in Plantin, Pl. Stirp. Icon.: 404. 1581; [icon] in Daléchamps, Hist. General. Pl. 2: 1150. 1586.
Note: The application of this name appears uncertain.

Camphorosma glabra Linnaeus, *Species Plantarum* 1: 122. 1753.
"Habitat in Helvetia." RCN: 1013.
Type not designated.
Original material: none traced.
Note: The application of this name appears uncertain.

Camphorosma monspeliaca Linnaeus, *Species Plantarum* 1: 122. 1753.
"Habitat in Hispaniae, Narbonae, Tatariae arenosis." RCN: 1011.
Lectotype (Hedge in Jarvis & al., *Regnum Veg.* 127: 29. 1993): Herb. Burser XXV: 55 (UPS).
Generitype of *Camphorosma* Linnaeus (vide Hitchcock, *Prop. Brit. Bot.*: 126. 1929).
Current name: ***Camphorosma monspeliaca*** L. (Chenopodiaceae).
Note: Jafri & Rateeb (in Jafri & El-Gadi, *Fl. Libya* 58: 31. 1978) indicated 165.2 (LINN) as type but as this collection is unannotated by Linnaeus, it is not original material for the name. Their choice is therefore rejected in favour of Hedge's typification.

Camphorosma pteranthus Linnaeus, *Systema Naturae*, ed. 12, 2: 128; *Mantissa Plantarum*: 41. 1767.
"Habitat in Arabia." RCN: 1014.
Type not designated.
Original material: none traced.
Current name: ***Pteranthus dichotomus*** Forssk. (Chenopodiaceae).

Canarina campanula Linnaeus, *Mantissa Plantarum Altera*: 225. 1771, *nom. illeg.*
"Habitat in Canariis." RCN: 2568.
Replaced synonym: *Campanula canariensis* L. (1753).
Lectotype (Stearn, *Introd. Linnaeus' Sp. Pl.* (Ray Soc. ed.): 47. 1957): [icon] *"Campanula foliis hastatis dentatis, caule determinate folioso"* in Linnaeus, Hort. Cliff.: 65, t. 8. 1738.
Generitype of *Canarina* Linnaeus, *nom. cons.*
Current name: ***Canarina canariensis*** (L.) Vatke (Campanulaceae).
Note: Canarina Linnaeus, *nom. cons.* against *Mindium* Adans. Francisco-Ortega & al. (in *Bull. Nat. Hist. Mus. London, Bot.* 24: 6, f. 3. 1994) designated Plukenet's t. 276, f. 1 as lectotype of *Campanula canariensis* L. (the replaced synonym of *Canarina campanula* L.), with a voucher in Herb. Sloane 99: 161 (BM-SL). However, this choice is pre-dated by that of Stearn.

Canarium commune Linnaeus, *Systema Naturae*, ed. 12, 2: 652; *Mantissa Plantarum*: 127. 1767.
"Habitat in India." RCN: 7424.

Lectotype (Merrill, *Interpret. Rumph. Herb. Amb.*: 301. 1917): [icon] *"Canarium Vulgare"* in Rumphius, Herb. Amboin. 2: 145, t. 47. 1741.
Current name: ***Canarium indicum*** L. (Burseraceae).
Note: See comments under *Canarium indicum* L.

Canarium indicum Linnaeus, *Amoenitates Academicae* 4: 143. 1759.
Type not designated.
Original material: [icon] in Rumphius, Herb. Amboin. 2: t. 47–56. 1741.
Generitype of *Canarium* Linnaeus.
Current name: ***Canarium indicum*** L. (Burseraceae).
Note: See comments by Merrill (*Interpret. Rumph. Herb. Amb.*: 301. 1917) who abandoned *C. indicum* on the grounds that Linnaeus had cited under it all the species of *Canarium* figured by Rumphius (t. 47 to t. 56 inclusive), and had later taken up *C. commune* L. (1767) for just one of them. However, Leenhouts (in *Blumea* 9: 329. 1959) accepted *C. indicum* both as a valid name and as the generitype. His designation of a neotype (p. 360), though, is contrary to Art. 9.11 because original material (the cited Rumphius plates) exists.

Canna angustifolia Linnaeus, *Species Plantarum* 1: 1. 1753.
"Habitat inter tropicos Americae: Umbrosis spongiosis." RCN: 2.
Type not designated.
Original material: [icon] in Morison, Pl. Hist. Univ. 3: 250, s. 8, t. 14, f. 6. 1699.
Current name: ***Canna glauca*** L. (Cannaceae).

Canna glauca Linnaeus, *Species Plantarum* 1: 1. 1753.
"Habitat in Carolina?" RCN: 3.
Type not designated.
Original material: Herb. A. van Royen No. 912.356–404 (L); [icon] in Dillenius, Hort. Eltham. 1: 69, t. 59, f. 69. 1732.
Current name: ***Canna glauca*** L. (Cannaceae).
Note: Tanaka (in *Makinoa*, n.s., 1: 53. 2001) designated material cultivated at Chelsea, number 2005 of the Royal Society set (K, iso-BM), as lectotype. However, this is not original material for the name, and the existence of other original elements precludes Tanaka's choice being treated as a neotypification (Art. 9.8).

Canna indica Linnaeus, *Species Plantarum* 1: 1. 1753.
"Habitat inter tropicos Asiae, Africae, Americae." RCN: 1.
Lectotype (Maas in Jarvis & al., *Regnum Veg.* 127: 29. 1993): Herb. A. van Royen No. 912.356–390 (L).
Generitype of *Canna* Linnaeus (vide Hitchcock, *Prop. Brit. Bot.*: 114. 1929).
Current name: ***Canna indica*** L. (Cannaceae).
Note: Siddiqi (in Jafri & El-Gadi, *Fl. Libya* 74: 2. 1970) indicated Herb. Linn. 1.1 (LINN) as type but this collection is a post-1753 addition to the collection and ineligible as type. It is superseded by Maas' type choice.

Cannabis sativa Linnaeus, *Species Plantarum* 2: 1027. 1753.
"Habitat in India." RCN: 7430.
Lectotype (Villiers in Aubréville & Leroy, *Fl. Gabon* 22: 58. 1973): Herb. Linn. No. 1177.2 (LINN).
Generitype of *Cannabis* Linnaeus.
Current name: ***Cannabis sativa*** L. (Cannabaceae).
Note: Qaiser (in Nasir & Ali, *Fl. W. Pakistan* 44: 3. 1973) indicated Herb. Linn. 1177.1 (LINN) as type but, as noted by Stearn (*Bot. Mus. Leafl. Harvard Univ.* 23: 335. 1974), this material is a post-1753 addition to the collection and irrelevant for typification purposes. Stearn himself provided an extensive review (*l.c.*: 325–336), and designated a Clifford collection as the lectotype.

However, his choice was narrowly pre-dated by that of a second specimen in LINN, designated by Villiers. Stearn was evidently unaware of this but agreed that the plant was in Linnaeus' possession in 1753. As such it is original material for the name, along with the Clifford specimens. Images of the specimens in LINN have been published by Schultes (in Joyce & Curry, *Bot. Chem.* Cannabis: 21, f. 1; 22, f. 2. 1970) and by Stearn (*l.c.*: 329, pl. 29; 331, pl. 30).

Capparis baducca Linnaeus, *Species Plantarum* 1: 504. 1753.
"Habitat in India." RCN: 3822.
Lectotype (Jacobs in *Blumea* 12: 435. 1965): [icon] *"Badukka"* in Rheede, Hort. Malab. 6: 105, t. 57. 1686.
Current name: ***Capparis baducca*** L. (Capparaceae).
Note: As discussed by Prado (in *Taxon* 42: 655–660. 1993), uncertainty about the typification of this name (which included both New and Old World elements) has caused some difficulty. In 1965, Jacobs treated the cited Rheede plate (from India) as the type but Prado rejected this choice, based on conflict with Linnaeus' diagnosis, in favour of a Clifford collection (BM) of the New World species otherwise known as *C. frondosa* Jacq. However, as discussed by Rankin & Greuter (in *Willdenowia* 34: 261. 2004), there are no grounds for rejecting Jacobs' typification (as a cited illustration, Rheede's plate is part of the protologue), and *C. baducca* is the correct, if now ambiguous, name for the Indian species. Rankin & Greuter suggest that it may be desirable for it now to be proposed for rejection, allowing *C. rheedei* DC. to replace it.

Capparis breynia Linnaeus, *Systema Naturae,* ed. 10, 2: 1071. 1759, *nom. illeg.*
["Habitat in America calidiore."] Sp. Pl. 1: 503 (1753). RCN: 3826.
Replaced synonym: *Breynia indica* L. (1753).
Lectotype (Rankin & Greuter in *Willdenowia* 34: 262. 2004): [icon] *"Breynia Elaeagni foliis"* in Breyn, Prodr. Fasc. Rar. Pl.: 13, unnumbered plate. 1739.
Current name: ***Capparis indica*** (L.) Fawc. & Rendle (Capparaceae).
Note: A superfluous name in *Capparis* for *Breynia indica* L. (1753), and hence homotypic with it.

Capparis cynophallophora Linnaeus, *Species Plantarum* 1: 504. 1753.
"Habitat in America." RCN: 3823.
Lectotype (Al-Shehbaz in Howard, *Fl. Lesser Antilles* 4: 296. 1988): Herb. Clifford: 204, *Capparis* 2 (BM-000628728).
Current name: ***Capparis cynophallophora*** L. (Capparaceae).
Note: Fawcett & Rendle (in *J. Bot.* 52: 142. 1918) stated that this was based on the *Hortus Cliffortianus* account, and discussed all of the original elements, but did not clearly indicate any one as the type. However, Rankin & Greuter (in *Willdenowia* 34: 262. 2004) disagree and cite Fawcett and Rendle as having typified the name.

Capparis ferruginea Linnaeus, *Systema Naturae,* ed. 10, 2: 1071. 1759.
["Habitat in Jamaica."] Sp. Pl., ed. 2, 1: 722 (1762). RCN: 3821.
Lectotype (Rankin & Greuter in *Willdenowia* 34: 263. 2004): *Browne,* Herb. Linn. No. 664.6 (LINN).
Current name: ***Capparis ferruginea*** L. (Capparaceae).

Capparis flexuosa (Linnaeus) Linnaeus, *Species Plantarum,* ed. 2, 1: 722. 1762.
"Habitat in Jamaica." RCN: 3828.
Basionym: *Morisonia flexuosa* L. (1759).
Lectotype (Fawcett & Rendle, *Fl. Jamaica* 3: 234. 1914): *Browne,* Herb. Linn. No. 664.10 (LINN).
Current name: ***Capparis flexuosa*** (L.) L. (Capparaceae).

Capparis sepiaria Linnaeus, *Systema Naturae,* ed. 10, 2: 1071. 1759.
["Habitat in India."] Sp. Pl., ed. 2, 1: 720 (1762). RCN: 3819.
Lectotype (Jacobs in *Blumea* 12: 489. 1965): Herb. Linn. No. 664.4 (LINN).
Current name: ***Capparis sepiaria*** L. (Capparaceae).
Note: Elffers & al. (in Hubbard & Milne-Redhead, *Fl. Trop. E. Africa, Capparidaceae*: 63. 1964) indicated a König collection (664.5 LINN) as the holotype but this material did not reach Linnaeus until after 1759 and so it is not original material for the name.

Capparis siliquosa Linnaeus, *Systema Naturae,* ed. 10, 2: 1071. 1759.
["Habitat in Jamaica."] Sp. Pl., ed. 2, 1: 721 (1762). RCN: 3829.
Lectotype (Al-Shehbaz in Howard, *Fl. Lesser Antilles* 4: 296. 1988): Herb. Linn. No. 664.8, right specimen (LINN).
Current name: ***Capparis cynophallophora*** L. (Capparaceae).
Note: See comments by Fawcett & Rendle (in *J. Bot.* 52: 142. 1914), who noted that the right specimen, labelled "siliquosa C", is a form of *C. cynophallophora* L.

Capparis spinosa Linnaeus, *Species Plantarum* 1: 503. 1753.
"Habitat in Europae australis arenosis, ruderatis." RCN: 3817.
Lectotype (Burtt & Lewis in *Kew Bull.* 4: 299. 1949): Herb. Clifford: 203, *Capparis* 1 (BM-000628727).
Generitype of *Capparis* Linnaeus (vide Green, *Prop. Brit. Bot.*: 160. 1929).
Current name: ***Capparis spinosa*** L. (Capparaceae).

Capparis zeylanica Linnaeus, *Species Plantarum,* ed. 2, 1: 720. 1762.
"Habitat in Zeylona." RCN: 3818.
Lectotype (Jacobs in *Blumea* 12: 505. 1965): Herb. Hermann 1: 35; 2: 58, No. 210 (BM).
Current name: ***Capparis zeylanica*** L. (Capparaceae).
Note: Jacobs indicated Herb. Hermann material (BM) as type and, although there is material in two volumes, it appears to have been part of a single gathering. Consequently, this is accepted as a formal typification (Art. 9.15).

Capraria biflora Linnaeus, *Species Plantarum* 2: 628. 1753.
"Habitat in Curassao." RCN: 4548.
Lectotype (D'Arcy in Woodson & Schery in *Ann. Missouri Bot. Gard.* 66: 209. 1979): Herb. Linn. No. 785.1 (LINN).
Generitype of *Capraria* Linnaeus.
Current name: ***Capraria biflora*** L. (Scrophulariaceae).
Note: Wijnands (*Bot. Commelins*: 187. 1983), followed by some other authors, treated van Royen material (L) as the lectotype but this choice is pre-dated by that of D'Arcy.

Capraria crustacea Linnaeus, *Systema Naturae,* ed. 12, 2: 419; *Mantissa Plantarum*: 87. 1767.
"Habitat in Amboina; China." RCN: 4550.
Lectotype (Philcox in *Kew Bull.* 22: 17. 1968): Herb. Linn. No. 785.3 (LINN).
Current name: ***Lindernia crustacea*** (L.) F. Muell. (Scrophulariaceae).

Capraria durantifolia Linnaeus, *Systema Naturae,* ed. 10, 2: 1116. 1759.
["Habitat in Jamaicae inundatis."] Sp. Pl., ed. 2, 2: 876 (1763). RCN: 4549.
Type not designated.
Original material: *Browne,* Herb. Linn. No. 785.2 (LINN); [icon] in Sloane, Voy. Jamaica 1: 196, t. 124, f. 2. 1707 – Typotype: Herb. Sloane 3: 113 (BM-SL).
Current name: ***Stemodia durantifolia*** (L.) Sw. (Scrophulariaceae).

Note: See discussion by Nicolson (in *Taxon* 24: 652. 1975), and by Turner & Cowan (in *Phytologia* 74: 73. 1993; 75: 287. 1993), who wrongly treat Sloane material (BM), unseen by Linnaeus, as the lectotype.

Capraria gratioloides Linnaeus, *Systema Naturae*, ed. 10, 2: 1117. 1759, *nom. illeg.*
["Habitat in Virginiae aquosis."] Sp. Pl. 1: 17 (1753). RCN: 4551.
Replaced synonym: *Gratiola dubia* L. (1753).
Lectotype (Pennell in *Torreya* 19: 149. 1919): *Clayton 164* (BM-000038848).
Current name: ***Lindernia dubia*** (L.) Pennell (Scrophulariaceae).
Note: An illegitimate replacement name in *Capraria* for *Gratiola dubia* L. (1753).

Capraria oppositifolia Linnaeus, *Flora Jamaicensis*: 18. 1759.
"Habitat [in Jamaica.]"
Lectotype (designated here by Sutton): [icon] *"Veronica caule hexangulari foliis saturiae ternis, serratis"* in Sloane, Voy. Jamaica 1: 196, t. 124. 1725. – Typotype: Herb. Sloane 3: 113 (BM-SL).
Current name: ***Stemodia durantifolia*** (L.) Sw. (Scrophulariaceae).
Note: This name is validated solely by a reference to the description of "Phaelypea I" in Browne's *Civ. Nat. Hist. Jamaica*: 269 (1756). Turner & Cowan (in *Phytologia* 74: 74. 1993) treated this description as the lectotype but this is contrary to Art. 8.1. Although Browne did not illustrate this plant, he did cite an illustration from Sloane in synonymy and this is now designated here as the lectotype.

Capsicum annuum Linnaeus, *Species Plantarum* 1: 188. 1753.
"Habitat in America meridionali." RCN: 1496.
Lectotype (D'Arcy in Woodson & Schery in *Ann. Missouri Bot. Gard.* 60: 591. 1974): Herb. Clifford: 59, *Capsicum* 1 (BM-000558022).
Generitype of *Capsicum* Linnaeus (vide Hitchcock, *Prop. Brit. Bot.*: 133. 1929).
Current name: ***Capsicum annuum*** L. (Solanaceae).
Note: Although D'Arcy & Eshbaugh (in *Baileya* 19: 98. 1974) discussed the type material, as has been pointed out by Jansen (*Spices, Condiments Med. Pl. Ethiopia*: 38. 1981), there is confusion as to which sheet was intended as type – the authors say that a Clifford sheet is the lectotype but also that it is on the IDC microfiche (i.e. = sheet 249.1 LINN). Jansen rejected both specimens in favour of a van Royen sheet in L. However, D'Arcy's later 1974 type statement is unequivocal, and has priority.

Capsicum baccatum Linnaeus, *Systema Naturae*, ed. 12, 2: 174; *Mantissa Plantarum*: 47. 1767.
"Habitat in Indiis." RCN: 1497.
Lectotype (D'Arcy & Eshbaugh in *Baileya* 19: 95. 1974): Herb. Linn. No. 249.3 (LINN).
Current name: ***Capsicum baccatum*** L. (Solanaceae).

Capsicum frutescens Linnaeus, *Species Plantarum* 1: 189. 1753.
"Habitat in India." RCN: 1499.
Lectotype (Heiser & Pickersgill in *Taxon* 18: 280. 1969): Herb. A. van Royen No. 908.244–150 (L).
Current name: ***Capsicum frutescens*** L. (Solanaceae).

Capsicum fruticosum Linnaeus, *Herbarium Amboinense*: 21. 1754, *orth. var.*
"Habitat [in Amboina.]" RCN: 1499.
Lectotype (Heiser & Pickersgill in *Taxon* 18: 280. 1969): Herb. A. van Royen No. 908.244–150 (L).
Current name: ***Capsicum frutescens*** L. (Solanaceae).
Note: Evidently an orthographic variant of *C. frutescens* L. (1753).

Capsicum grossum Linnaeus, *Systema Naturae,* ed. 12, 2: 175; *Mantissa Plantarum*: 47. 1767.
"Habitat in India." RCN: 1498.
Type not designated.
Original material: Herb. Linn. No. 249.5 (LINN).
Current name: ***Capsicum annuum*** L. (Solanaceae).

Capura purpurata Linnaeus, *Mantissa Plantarum Altera*: 225. 1771.
"Habitat in India." RCN: 2557.
Type not designated.
Original material: none traced.
Generitype of *Capura* Linnaeus, *nom. rej.*
Current name: ***Wikstroemia indica*** (L.) C.A. Mey. (Thymelaeaceae).
Note: Capura Linnaeus, *nom. rej.* in favour of *Wikstroemia* Endl. Rogers & Spencer (in *Taxon* 55: 483. 2006) noted that this name was associated with a particularly complex taxonomic problem, and did not typify it.

Cardamine africana Linnaeus, *Species Plantarum* 2: 655. 1753.
"Habitat in Africa." RCN: 4768.
Lectotype (Marais in Codd & al., *Fl. Southern Africa* 13: 100. 1970): [icon] *"Nasturtium foliis ternis facie Christophorianae"* in Hermann, Parad. Bat.: 202. 1698. – Typotype: Herb. Sherard No. 746 (OXF).
Current name: ***Cardamine africana*** L. (Brassicaceae).
Note: See an extremely detailed review by Marhold (in *Bot. J. Linn. Soc.* 121: 111. 1996), who attributes the typification to Sjöstedt (in *Bot. Not.* 128: 9, 28. 1975), who also discusses Sherard material in OXF. However, Marais appears to have made a still earlier choice of type in 1970.

Cardamine amara Linnaeus, *Species Plantarum* 2: 656. 1753.
"Habitat in Europae pascuis aquosis." RCN: 4775.
Lectotype (Khatri in *Feddes Repert.* 100: 92. 1989): Herb. Linn. No. 835.17 (LINN).
Current name: ***Cardamine amara*** L. subsp. ***amara*** (Brassicaceae).
Note: See detailed review by Marhold (in *Bot. J. Linn. Soc.* 121: 113. 1996).

Cardamine asarifolia Linnaeus, *Species Plantarum* 2: 654. 1753.
"Habitat in Alpibus Italicis." RCN: 4763.
Lectotype (Marhold in *Bot. J. Linn. Soc.* 121: 114. 1996): [icon] *"Nasturtium Montanum Assari folio"* in Hermann, Parad. Bat.: 203. 1698. – Typotype: Herb. Sherard No. 3795 (OXF).
Current name: ***Cardamine asarifolia*** L. (Brassicaceae).

Cardamine bellidifolia Linnaeus, *Species Plantarum* 2: 654. 1753.
"Habitat in Alpibus Lapponiae, Helvetiae, Brittaniae." RCN: 4762.
Lectotype (Khatri in *Feddes Repert.* 101: 442. 1990): Herb. Linn. No. 835.1 (LINN).
Current name: ***Cardamine bellidifolia*** L. subsp. ***bellidifolia*** (Brassicaceae).
Note: See detailed discussion by Marhold (in *Bot. J. Linn. Soc.* 121: 114. 1996).

Cardamine bellifolia Linnaeus, *Flora Anglica*: 19. 1754, *orth. var.*
RCN: 4762.
Lectotype (Khatri in *Feddes Repert.* 101: 442. 1990): Herb. Linn. No. 835.1 (LINN).
Current name: ***Cardamine bellidifolia*** L. (Brassicaceae).
Note: Evidently an orthographic variant of *Cardamine bellidifolia* L. (1753), as noted by Stearn (*Introd. Ray's Syn. Meth. Stirp. Brit.* (Ray Soc. ed.): 68. 1973).

Cardamine chelidonia Linnaeus, *Species Plantarum* 2: 655. 1753.
"Habitat in Sibiria, Italia." RCN: 4769.

Type not designated.
Original material: Herb. Linn. No. 270.7 (S); Herb. Linn. No. 835.8 (LINN); [icon] in Barrelier, Pl. Galliam: 44, t. 156. 1714; [icon] in Hermann, Parad. Bat.: 203. 1698.
Current name: *Cardamine chelidonia* L. (Brassicaceae).
Note: See extensive discussion by Marhold (in *Bot. J. Linn. Soc.* 121: 116–118. 1996), who concludes that the Barrelier plate is the only element corresponding broadly with the use of the name. However, the illustration lacks auriculate petiole bases, and Marhold stated that he intended to propose the name for conservation with a conserved type. However, no formal proposal yet appears to have been made.

Cardamine graeca Linnaeus, *Species Plantarum* 2: 655. 1753.
"Habitat in Sicilia, Corsica, insulis Graeciae." RCN: 4772.
Lectotype (Marhold in *Bot. J. Linn. Soc.* 121: 118, f. 1. 1996): Herb. A. van Royen No. 901.220–60 (L).
Current name: *Cardamine graeca* L. (Brassicaceae).

Cardamine hirsuta Linnaeus, *Species Plantarum* 2: 655. 1753.
"Habitat in Europae areis, hortis, arvis." RCN: 4773.
Lectotype (Fawcett & Rendle, *Fl. Jamaica* 3: 239. 1914): Herb. Linn. No. 835.13 (LINN).
Current name: *Cardamine hirsuta* L. (Brassicaceae).
Note: See extensive discussion by Marhold (in *Bot. J. Linn. Soc.* 121: 120. 1996).

Cardamine impatiens Linnaeus, *Species Plantarum* 2: 655. 1753.
"Habitat in Europae nemoribus ad radices montium." RCN: 4770.

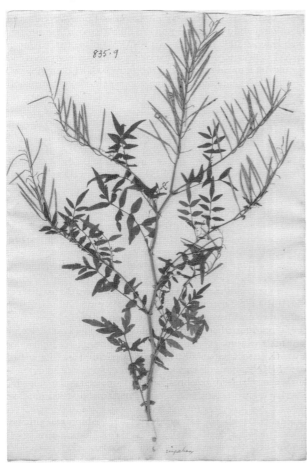

Lectotype (Jafri in Nasir & Ali, *Fl. W. Pakistan* 55: 196. 1973): Herb. Linn. No. 835.9 (LINN).
Current name: *Cardamine impatiens* L. (Brassicaceae).
Note: See extensive discussion by Marhold (in *Bot. J. Linn. Soc.* 121: 120. 1996).

Cardamine lunaria Linnaeus, *Species Plantarum* 2: 656. 1753.
"Habitat in Aegypto. D.B. Jussiaeus." RCN: 4758.
Replaced synonym of: *Ricotia aegyptiaca* L. (1763), *nom. illeg.*
Lectotype (Burtt in Jarvis & al., *Regnum Veg.* 127: 82. 1993): Herb. Linn. No. 833.1, excl. fruiting material (LINN).
Current name: *Ricotia lunaria* (L.) DC. (Brassicaceae).
Note: See extensive discussion by Marhold (in *Bot. J. Linn. Soc.* 121: 121. 1996).

Cardamine nudicaulis Linnaeus, *Species Plantarum* 2: 654. 1753.
"Habitat in Sibiria. D. Gmelin." RCN: 4764.
Lectotype (Botschantzev in *Bot. Zhurn.* 57: 671. 1972): *Gmelin s.n.*, Herb. Linn. No. 835.4 (LINN).
Current name: *Parrya nudicaulis* (L.) Regel (Brassicaceae).
Note: See extensive discussion by Marhold (in *Bot. J. Linn. Soc.* 121: 121–122. 1996).

Cardamine parviflora Linnaeus, *Systema Naturae,* ed. 10, 2: 1131. 1759.
["Habitat in Europa."] Sp. Pl. ed. 2, 2: 914 (1763). RCN: 4771.
Lectotype (Jonsell in Polhill, *Fl. Trop. E. Africa, Cruciferae.* 43. 1982): Herb. Linn. No. 835.10 (LINN).
Current name: *Cardamine parviflora* L. (Brassicaceae).
Note: See extensive discussion by Marhold (in *Bot. J. Linn. Soc.* 121: 122. 1996), who also illustrates the type in his f. 2 (right).

Cardamine petraea Linnaeus, *Species Plantarum* 2: 654. 1753.
"Habitat in Angliae, Arvoniae, Merviniae, Sueciae rupibus excelsis." RCN: 4765.
Lectotype (Marhold in *Bot. J. Linn. Soc.* 121: 122. 1996): Herb. Linn. No. 835.5 (LINN).
Current name: *Arabidopsis petraea* (L.) Kolník & Marhold (Brassicaceae).
Note: O'Kane & Al-Shehbaz (in *Novon* 7: 326. 1997) independently made the same type choice as Marhold.

Cardamine pratensis Linnaeus, *Species Plantarum* 2: 656. 1753.
"Habitat in Europae pascuis aquosis." RCN: 4774.
Lectotype (Khatri in *Feddes Repert.* 100: 92. 1989): Herb. Linn. No. 835.15 (LINN).
Generitype of *Cardamine* Linnaeus (vide Green, *Prop. Brit. Bot.*: 171. 1929).
Current name: *Cardamine pratensis* L. (Brassicaceae).
Note: See extensive discussion by Marhold (in *Bot. J. Linn. Soc.* 121: 124–125. 1996).

Cardamine resedifolia Linnaeus, *Species Plantarum* 2: 656. 1753.
"Habitat in Alpibus Helveticis, Pyrenaeis." RCN: 4766.
Lectotype (Marhold in *Bot. J. Linn. Soc.* 121: 125. 1996): [icon] *"Nasturtium alpinum minus Resedae foliis"* in Bauhin, Prodr. Theatri Bot.: 45. 1620 (see p. 107). – Epitype (Marhold in *Bot. J. Linn. Soc.* 121: 125, f. 3. 1996): France. Porté-Puymorens, Col de Lanoux, ca. 2,400m, 4–17 Aug 1974, *A. Polatschek s.n.* (W).
Current name: *Cardamine resedifolia* L. (Brassicaceae).

Cardamine trifolia Linnaeus, *Species Plantarum* 2: 654. 1753.
"Habitat in Alpibus Helveticis, Lapponicis." RCN: 4767.
Lectotype (Marhold in *Bot. J. Linn. Soc.* 121: 127, f. 2. 1996): Herb. Linn. No. 835.7 (LINN).
Current name: *Cardamine trifolia* L. (Brassicaceae).

Cardamine virginica Linnaeus, *Species Plantarum* 2: 656. 1753.
"Habitat in Virginia." RCN: 4776.
Lectotype (Marhold in *Bot. J. Linn. Soc.* 121: 128. 1996): *Clayton 462* (BM-000042604).
Current name: ***Sibara virginica*** (L.) Rollins (Brassicaceae).

Cardiospermum corindum Linnaeus, *Species Plantarum*, ed. 2, 1: 526. 1762.
"Habitat in Brasilia." RCN: 2901.
Neotype (Leenhouts in Adema & al., *Fl. Malesiana*, ser. I, 11: 484. 1994): Jamaica. *Houstoun, s.n.* (BM).
Current name: ***Cardiospermum corindum*** L. (Sapindaceae).

Cardiospermum halicacabum Linnaeus, *Species Plantarum* 1: 366. 1753.
"Habitat in Indiis." RCN: 2900.
Lectotype (Barrie in Jarvis & al., *Regnum Veg.* 127: 30. 1993): Herb. Clifford: 151, *Cardiospermum* 1 β (BM-000558680).
Generitype of *Cardiospermum* Linnaeus.
Current name: ***Cardiospermum halicacabum*** L. (Sapindaceae).
Note: Croat in *Ann. Missouri Bot. Gard.* 63: 430. 1977) indicated a Patrick Browne specimen, 513.1 (LINN), as type but as this was not received by Linnaeus until 1758, it cannot be original material for the name.

Carduus acanthoides Linnaeus, *Species Plantarum* 2: 821. 1753.
"Habitat in Europae ruderatis." RCN: 5947.
Lectotype (Kazmi in *Mitt. Bot. Staatssamml. München* 5: 356. 1964): Herb. Linn. No. 966.6 ["966.5"] (LINN).
Current name: ***Carduus acanthoides*** L. (Asteraceae).

Carduus acarna Linnaeus, *Species Plantarum* 2: 820. 1753.
"Habitat in Hispania." RCN: 5979.
Basionym of: *Cnicus acarna* (L.) L. (1759).
Lectotype (Turland in Jarvis & Turland in *Taxon* 47: 356. 1998): Herb. Burser XXI: 26 (UPS).
Current name: ***Picnomon acarna*** (L.) Cass. (Asteraceae).

Carduus acaulis Linnaeus, *Species Plantarum* 2: 1199. 1753.
"Habitat in Europae pascuis apricis, depressis." RCN: 5974.
Type not designated.
Original material: Herb. Burser XXI: 31 (UPS); Herb. Linn. No. 966.45 (LINN); [icon] in Bauhin & Cherler, Hist. Pl. Univ. 3(1): 62, 63. 1651.
Current name: ***Cirsium acaule*** (L.) Scop. subsp. ***acaule*** (Asteraceae).
Note: Stearn (in *Biol. J. Linn. Soc.* 5: 10. 1973), in an account of Linnaeus' Öland and Gotland journey of 1741, treated Vible in Gotland as the restricted type locality, and noted the existence of 966.45 (LINN). In his paper, he attributed restricted type localities irrespective of whether any material existed in LINN and, where specimens do exist, he does not refer to any of them as type specimens. This LINN material is not annotated so as to suggest it was collected in Gotland.

Carduus altissimus Linnaeus, *Species Plantarum* 2: 824. 1753.
"Habitat in Carolina." RCN: 5966.
Lectotype (Reveal in Jarvis & Turland in *Taxon* 47: 356. 1998): [icon] *"Cirsium altissimum, laciniato folio, subtus tomentoso"* in Dillenius, Hort. Eltham. 1: 81, t. 69, f. 80. 1732. – Voucher: Herb. Sherard No. 1639 (OXF).
Current name: ***Cirsium altissimum*** (L.) Hill (Asteraceae).

Carduus argentatus Linnaeus, *Mantissa Plantarum Altera*: 280. 1771.
"Habitat in Aegypto." RCN: 5952.

Lectotype (Kazmi in *Mitt. Bot. Staatssamml. München* 5: 453. 1964): Herb. Linn. No. 966.10 (LINN).
Current name: ***Carduus argentatus*** L. (Asteraceae).

Carduus canus Linnaeus, *Systema Naturae*, ed. 12, 2: 529; *Mantissa Plantarum*: 108. 1767.
"Habitat in Austria." RCN: 5955.
Type not designated.
Original material: *Vandelli*, Herb. Linn. No. 966.26 (LINN); [icon] in Bauhin & Cherler, Hist. Pl. Univ. 3(1): 44. 1651.
Current name: ***Cirsium canum*** (L.) All. (Asteraceae).

Carduus casabonae Linnaeus, *Species Plantarum* 2: 823. 1753.
"Habitat – – – –" RCN: 5961.
Lectotype (Greuter in *Boissiera* 22: 144. 1973): Herb. Linn. No. 966.28 (LINN).
Current name: ***Ptilostemon casabonae*** (L.) Greuter (Asteraceae).

Carduus crispus Linnaeus, *Species Plantarum* 2: 821. 1753.
"Habitat in Europae septentrionalioris agris, cultis." RCN: 5948.
Lectotype (Kazmi in *Mitt. Bot. Staatssamml. München* 5: 368. 1964): Herb. Clifford: 393, *Carduus* 6 (BM-000646921).
Current name: ***Carduus crispus*** L. (Asteraceae).

Carduus cyanoides Linnaeus, *Species Plantarum* 2: 822. 1753.
"Habitat in Tataria." RCN: 5954.
Lectotype (Tscherneva in *Bot. Zhurn.* 79(5): 118. 1994): Herb. Linn. No. 966.13 (LINN).
Current name: ***Jurinea cyanoides*** (L.) Rchb. (Asteraceae).

Carduus cyanoides Linnaeus var. **monoclonos** Linnaeus, *Species Plantarum* 2: 822. 1753.
RCN: 5954.
Type not designated.
Original material: Herb. Linn. No. 966.13 (LINN); [icon] in Gmelin, Fl. Sibirica 2: 42, t. 15. 1752.
Current name: ***Jurinea cyanoides*** (L.) Rchb. (Asteraceae).

Carduus cyanoides Linnaeus var. **polyclonos** Linnaeus, *Species Plantarum* 2: 822. 1753.
RCN: 5954.
Type not designated.
Original material: Herb. Linn. No. 966.12 (LINN); [icon] in Gmelin, Fl. Sibirica 2: 44, t. 16. 1752.
Current name: ***Jurinea polyclonos*** (L.) DC. (Asteraceae).

Carduus defloratus Linnaeus, *Systema Naturae*, ed. 10, 2: 1200. 1759.
["Habitat in Helvetiae, Austriae, Monspelii subalpinis."] Sp. Pl. ed. 2, 2: 1152 (1763). RCN: 5957.
Lectotype (Kazmi in *Mitt. Bot. Staatssamml. München* 5: 383. 1964): Herb. Linn. No. 966.23 ["966.13"] (LINN).
Current name: ***Carduus defloratus*** L. subsp. ***defloratus*** (Asteraceae).

Carduus dissectus Linnaeus, *Species Plantarum* 2: 822. 1753.
"Habitat in Anglia, Gallia." RCN: 5953.
Lectotype (Airy Shaw in *Repert. Spec. Nov. Regni Veg.* 43: 312. 1938): [icon] *"Cirsium Anglicum"* in Plantin, Pl. Stirp. Icon.: 583. 1581.
Current name: ***Cirsium dissectum*** (L.) Hill (Asteraceae).

Carduus eriophorus Linnaeus, *Species Plantarum* 2: 823. 1753.
"Habitat in Anglia, Gallia, Hispania, Lusitania." RCN: 5965.
Type not designated.
Original material: Herb. Burser XXI: 38 (UPS); Herb. Linn. No. 966.32 (LINN); [icon] in Plantin, Pl. Stirp. Icon. 2: 9. 1581.
Current name: ***Cirsium eriophorum*** (L.) Scop. (Asteraceae).

Carduus eriophorus Linnaeus var. **spurius** Linnaeus, *Species Plantarum* 2: 824. 1753.
RCN: 5965.
Type not designated.
Original material: none traced.
Current name: ***Cirsium eriophorum*** (L.) Scop. (Asteraceae).

Carduus flavescens Linnaeus, *Species Plantarum* 2: 825. 1753.
"Habitat in Hispania. Loefling." RCN: 5972.
Lectotype (Cantó in *Lazaroa* 6: 61. 1985 [1984]): *Löfling 605a*, Herb. Linn. No. 966.42 (LINN).
Current name: ***Klasea flavescens*** (L.) Holub (Asteraceae).

Carduus helenioides Linnaeus, *Species Plantarum* 2: 825. 1753.
"Habitat in Anglia, Sibiria." RCN: 5969.
Lectotype (Airy Shaw in *Repert. Spec. Nov. Regni Veg.* 43: 306. 1938): Herb. Linn. No. 966.36 (LINN).
Current name: ***Cirsium* × *helenioides*** (L.) Hill (Asteraceae).
Note: Although *Cirsium* × *helenioides* (L.) Hill and *C. heterophyllum* (L.) Hill had been treated as synonymous by many authors, study of the type of *C.* × *helenioides* (966.36 LINN) by Talavera & Valdés (in *Lagascalia* 5: 155–157. 1976) has shown it to be a hybrid between *C. heterophyllum* and *C. rivulare* (Jacq.) All. As *C.* × *helenioides* and *C. heterophyllum* are therefore not synonymous, *C.* × *helenioides* becomes the correct name for the original taxon.

Carduus heterophyllus Linnaeus, *Species Plantarum* 2: 824. 1753.
"Habitat in Europae frigidioris pratis depressis." RCN: 5968.
Lectotype (Talavera & Valdés in *Lagascalia* 5: 156. 1976): Herb. Linn. No. 966.35 (LINN).
Current name: ***Cirsium heterophyllum*** (L.) Hill (Asteraceae).

Carduus lanceolatus Linnaeus, *Species Plantarum* 2: 821. 1753.
"Habitat in Europae cultis ruderatis." RCN: 5945.
Lectotype (Talavera & Valdés in *Lagascalia* 5: 197. 1976): Herb. Linn. No. 966.1 (LINN).
Current name: ***Cirsium vulgare*** (Savi) Ten. (Asteraceae).
Note: Jeffrey (in *Kew Bull.* 22: 129. 1968) indicated material in the Clifford herbarium (BM) as lectotype. However, he did not distinguish between the two sheets preserved there and, as they evidently are not part of a single gathering, Art. 9.15 does not apply. Talavera & Valdés therefore appear to have made the earliest explicit type choice.

Carduus leucographus Linnaeus, *Species Plantarum* 2: 820. 1753.
"Habitat in Campania." RCN: 5944.
Neotype (Turland in Jarvis & Turland in *Taxon* 47: 356. 1998): Italy. Potenza: Basilicate, Lago Negro, 21 Jun 1891, *St-Lager s.n.* (BM-000576307).
Current name: ***Tyrimnus leucographus*** (L.) Cass. (Asteraceae).

Carduus marianus Linnaeus, *Species Plantarum* 2: 823. 1753.
"Habitat in Angliae, Galliae, Italiae aggeribus ruderatis." RCN: 5963.
Lectotype (Jeffrey in *Kew Bull.* 22: 131. 1968): Herb. Clifford: 393, *Carduus* 9 (BM-000646928).
Current name: ***Silybum marianum*** (L.) Gaertn. (Asteraceae).

Carduus mollis Linnaeus, *Centuria II Plantarum*: 30. 1756.
"Habitat in alpibus Austriae." RCN: 5973.
Lectotype (Conti in *Willdenowia* 28: 49, f. 1. 1998): [icon] *"Carduus mollis I"* in Clusius, Rar. Stirp. Pannon.: 661, 662. 1583. – Epitype (Conti in *Willdenowia* 28: 49. 1998): Austria. In collibus apricis prope Vindobonam, 5.1879, *Halacsy s.n.* (G).
Current name: ***Jurinea mollis*** (L.) Rchb. (Asteraceae).
Note: Danin & Davis (in Davis, *Fl. Turkey* 5: 443. 1975) designated

Herb. Linn. 966.43 (LINN) as the lectotype. However, Conti (in *Willdenowia* 28: 47. 1998) rejected this choice on the grounds of conflict with the protologue, the specimen being labelled "Oriente", probably from Turkey, and almost certainly belonging to a different taxon.

Carduus monspessulanus Linnaeus, *Species Plantarum* 2: 822. 1753.
"Habitat Monspelii." RCN: 5958.
Type not designated.
Original material: Herb. Burser XXI: 19 (UPS); [icon] in Dodoëns, Stirp. Hist. Pempt., ed. 2: 737. 1616; [icon] in Bauhin & Cherler, Hist. Pl. Univ. 3(1): 44, 45. 1651.
Current name: ***Cirsium monspessulanum*** (L.) Hill subsp. ***monspessulanum*** (Asteraceae).

Carduus nutans Linnaeus, *Species Plantarum* 2: 821. 1753.
"Habitat in Europa ad pagos." RCN: 5946.
Lectotype (Kazmi in *Mitt. Bot. Staatssamml. München* 5: 323. 1964): Herb. Linn. No. 966.2 (LINN).
Generitype of *Carduus* Linnaeus (vide Green, *Prop. Brit. Bot.*: 179. 1929).
Current name: ***Carduus nutans*** L. (Asteraceae).

Carduus palustris Linnaeus, *Species Plantarum* 2: 822. 1753.
"Habitat in Europae pratis subpaludosis." RCN: 5950.
Lectotype (Talavera & Valdés in *Lagascalia* 5: 188. 1976): *Gmelin s.n.*, Herb. Linn. No. 966.5 (LINN).
Current name: ***Cirsium palustre*** (L.) Scop. (Asteraceae).

Carduus parviflorus Linnaeus, *Mantissa Plantarum Altera*: 279. 1771.
"Habitat in subalpinis australibus." RCN: 5960.
Type not designated.
Original material: none traced.
Current name: ***Cirsium parviflorum*** (L.) DC. (Asteraceae).

Carduus pectinatus Linnaeus, *Mantissa Plantarum Altera*: 279. 1771.
"Habitat [absent] H. U." RCN: 5956.
Type not designated.
Original material: Herb. Linn. No. 966.46? (LINN); Herb. Linn. No. 966.21 (LINN); Herb. Linn. No. 966.23 (LINN).
Current name: ***Carduus defloratus*** L. (Asteraceae).

Carduus polyanthemus Linnaeus, *Systema Naturae,* ed. 12, 2: 529; *Mantissa Plantarum*: 109. 1767.
"Habitat Romae." RCN: 5949.
Type not designated.
Original material: Herb. Linn. No. 966.4 (LINN); Herb. Linn. No. 966.3 (LINN); [icon] in Trionfetti, Obs. Ortu Veg. Pl.: 103, unnumbered plate. 1685.
Current name: ***Carduus crispus*** L. (Asteraceae).

Carduus pycnocephalus Linnaeus, *Species Plantarum,* ed. 2, 2: 1151. 1763.
"Habitat in Europa australi." RCN: 5951.
Lectotype (Kazmi in *Mitt. Bot. Staatssamml. München* 5: 445. 1964): Herb. Linn. No. 966.9 (LINN).
Current name: ***Carduus pycnocephalus*** L. (Asteraceae).

Carduus serratuloides Linnaeus, *Species Plantarum* 2: 825. 1753.
"Habitat in Sibiria, Helvetia, Monspelii." RCN: 5970.
Type not designated.
Original material: Herb. Burser XXI: 18 (UPS); Herb. Linn. No. 331.15 (S); [icon] in Gmelin, Fl. Sibirica 2: 52, t. 22, 23, f. 1. 1752; [icon] in Clusius, Rar. Pl. Hist. 2: 149. 1601.
Current name: ***Cnicus serratuloides*** (L.) Hill (Asteraceae).

Carduus stellatus Linnaeus, *Species Plantarum* 2: 823. 1753.
"Habitat – – – –" RCN: 5962.
Lectotype (Greuter in *Boissiera* 22: 150. 1973): Herb. A. van Royen
No. 900.233–3 (L).
Current name: ***Ptilostemon stellatus*** (L.) Greuter (Asteraceae).
Note: Greuter (in *Boissiera* 22: 150. 1973) designated as "lectotypus"
the description "Carduus spinis ramosis lateralibus, foliis integris
subtus tomentosis" van Royen, *Fl. Leyd. Prodr.*: 133 (1740). He
cited a corresponding specimen in Herb. van Royen (L) as
"typotypus", which is treated here (under Art. 9.8) as interpretable
as a designation of a lectotype.

Carduus syriacus Linnaeus, *Species Plantarum* 2: 823. 1753.
"Habitat in Syria, Creta, Hispania." RCN: 5964.
Lectotype (Kupicha in Davis, *Fl. Turkey* 5: 420. 1975): Herb. Linn.
No. 966.31 (LINN).
Current name: ***Notobasis syriaca*** (L.) Cass. (Asteraceae).

Carduus tataricus Linnaeus, *Species Plantarum* 2: 825. 1753.
"Habitat in Sibiria." RCN: 5971.
Type not designated.
Original material: Herb. Linn. No. 331.17 (S); Herb. Linn. No.
966.51 (LINN).
Current name: ***Cirsium oleraceum*** (L.) Scop. (Asteraceae).

Carduus tuberosus Linnaeus, *Species Plantarum* 2: 824. 1753.
"Habitat Mospelii [sic], Lipsiae, inque Bohemia, Austria, Helvetia."
RCN: 5959.
Lectotype (Talavera & Valdés in *Lagascalia* 5: 145. 1976): *E. Rosén*,
Herb. Linn. No. 966.24 ["866.24"] (LINN), see p. 225.
Current name: ***Cirsium tuberosum*** (L.) All. (Asteraceae).

Carduus virginianus Linnaeus, *Species Plantarum* 2: 824.
1753.
"Habitat in Virginia." RCN: 5967.
Lectotype (Johnson in *Virginia J. Sci.* 25: 156. 1974): *Clayton 193*
(BM-000038863).
Current name: ***Cirsium virginianum*** (L.) Michx. (Asteraceae).

Carex acuta Linnaeus, *Species Plantarum* 2: 978. 1753.
"Habitat in Europa ubique." RCN: 7092.
Lectotype (Egorova, *Sedges Russia*: 446. 1999): Herb. Linn. No.
1100.71 (LINN).
Current name: ***Carex acuta*** L. (Cyperaceae).
Note: Some authors have treated this as a *nomen ambiguum*, and
Luceño & Aedo (in *Bot. J. Linn. Soc.* 114: 197. 1994) suggested
that a conservation proposal was necessary. However, assessment of
the characters shown by 1100.71 (LINN) by Egorova seems to
confirm that the identity of the type is *C. acuta*.

Carex acuta Linnaeus var. **nigra** Linnaeus, *Species Plantarum* 2: 978.
1753.
"Habitat in Europa ubique: in siccioribus." RCN: 7092.
Neotype (Luceño & Aedo in *Bot. J. Linn. Soc.* 114: 207, f. 9. 1994):
Sweden. *C.M. Norman, s.n.*, left specimen (MA).
Current name: ***Carex nigra*** (L.) Rchb. (Cyperaceae).

Carex acuta Linnaeus var. **rufa** Linnaeus, *Species Plantarum* 2: 978.
1753.
"Habitat in Europa ubique: in aquosis." RCN: 7092.
Lectotype (Egorova in Cafferty & Jarvis in *Taxon* 53: 178. 2004):
Herb. Burser I: 68 (UPS).
Current name: ***Carex riparia*** Curtis (Cyperaceae).
Note: Varietal epithet spelled "ruffa" in the protologue.

Carex arenaria Linnaeus, *Species Plantarum* 2: 973. 1753.
"Habitat in Europae arena, praesertim mobili." RCN: 7060.
Lectotype (Egorova, *Sedges Russia*: 507. 1999): Herb. Linn. No.
1100.9 (LINN).
Current name: ***Carex arenaria*** L. (Cyperaceae).
Note: Stearn (in *Biol. J. Linn. Soc.* 5: 10. 1973), in an account of
Linnaeus' Öland and Gotland journey of 1741, treated Grankull in
Öland as the restricted type locality, and noted the existence of
1100.9 (LINN). In his paper, he attributed restricted type localities
irrespective of whether any material existed in LINN and, where
specimens do exist, he does not refer to any of them as type
specimens. This LINN material, formally designated as lectotype by
Egorova, is annotated as having come from Skåne, rather than
Öland.

Carex atrata Linnaeus, *Species Plantarum* 2: 976. 1753.
"Habitat in Alpibus Europae." RCN: 7082.
Lectotype (Marshall in *J. Bot.* 45: 366. 1907): Herb. Linn. No.
1100.52 (LINN).
Current name: ***Carex atrata*** L. (Cyperaceae).
Note: Kukkonen (in *Mem. Soc. Fauna Fl. Fenn.* 56: 151–156. 1980),
followed by Egorova (*Sedges Russia*: 393. 1999), makes a very
detailed study of the original elements (which include several
species), illustrating many of them, and designating a Clifford sheet,
corresponding with usage, as lectotype. However, Kukkonen
overlooked Marshall's unfortunate earlier choice of 1100.52
(LINN), a specimen of *C. atrofusca* Schkuhr. The grounds for
rejecting Marshall's choice appear poor, and a conservation proposal
may be necessary.

Carex axillaris Linnaeus, *Amoenitates Academicae* 4: 107. 1759, *nom.
illeg.*
["Habitat in Europae udis."] Sp. Pl., ed. 2, 2: 1382 (1763). RCN:
7068.
Replaced synonym: *Carex remota* L. (1754, non 1755).
Type not designated.
Original material: as replaced synonym.
Current name: ***Carex remota*** L. (Cyperaceae).
Note: An illegitimate replacement name for *C. remota* L. (1754).

Carex baldensis Linnaeus, *Centuria II Plantarum*: 32. 1756.
"Habitat in Baldo." RCN: 7059.
Lectotype (Egorova in Cafferty & Jarvis in *Taxon* 53: 178. 2004):
[icon] *"Gramen montanum junceum capite squamoso"* in Bauhin,
Prodr. Theatri Bot.: 13. 1620.
Current name: ***Carex baldensis*** L. (Cyperaceae).

Carex brizoides Linnaeus, *Centuria I Plantarum*: 31. 1755.
"Habitat in Europa." RCN: 7064.
Lectotype (Egorova, *Sedges Russia*: 510. 1999): [icon] *"Carex fibrata
radice, angustifolia, caule exquisite triangulari, capitulis pulchellis,
longioribus, & angustioribus, albicantibus, confertim nascentibus"* in
Micheli, Nov. Pl. Gen.: 70, t. 33, f. 17. 1729.
Current name: ***Carex brizoides*** L. (Cyperaceae).

Carex canescens Linnaeus, *Species Plantarum* 2: 974. 1753.
"Habitat in Europa septentrionali." RCN: 7070.
Lectotype (Toivonen in *Ann. Bot. Fenn.* 18: 94, f. 1. 1981): [icon]
"Gramen cyperoides spicis curtis divulsis" in Loesel, Fl. Prussica: 117,
t. 32. 1703 (see p. 140).
Current name: ***Carex canescens*** L. (Cyperaceae).
Note: Marshall (in *J. Bot.* 45: 365. 1907) proposed the abandonment
of this name because of difficulties in establishing its application.
Although some authors took up *C. buxbaumii* Wahlenb. in its place,
most recent authors (e.g. Luceño in *Ruizia* 14: 50. 1994; Egorova,

Sedges Russia: 558. 1999) appear to have adopted Toivonen's typification and are using the Linnaean name in the sense of *C. curta* Good.

Carex capillaris Linnaeus, *Species Plantarum* 2: 977. 1753.
"Habitat in Sueciae pratis humidis." RCN: 7084.
Lectotype (Egorova, *Sedges Russia*: 349. 1999): Herb. Linn. No. 1100.57 (LINN).
Current name: **Carex capillaris** L. (Cyperaceae).

Carex capitata Linnaeus, *Systema Naturae*, ed. 10, 2: 1261. 1759.
["Habitat in Lapponia, Anglia."] Sp. Pl., ed. 2, 2: 1380 (1763). RCN: 7055.
Lectotype (Reinhammer & Bele in *Nordic J. Bot.* 21: 509. 2002 [2001]): *Solander*, Herb. Linn. No. 378.13 (S; iso- LINN?).
Current name: **Carex capitata** L. (Cyperaceae).

Carex cespitosa Linnaeus, *Species Plantarum* 2: 978. 1753.
"Habitat in Europae paludibus turfosis." RCN: 7090.
Lectotype (Marshall in *J. Bot.* 45: 366. 1907): Herb. Linn. No. 1100.69 (LINN).
Current name: **Carex cespitosa** L. (Cyperaceae).

Carex cyperoides Linnaeus, *Systema Vegetabilium*, ed. 13: 703. 1774.
"Habitat in Sibiria, Bohemia." RCN: 7058.
Lectotype (Egorova, *Sedges Russia*: 541. 1999): [icon] *"Carex Bohemica, aquatica, annua, Cyperi facie, caule molli, exquisite trangulari, capitulis in glomeratam spicam digestis, capsulis lanceatis...& in duas veluti aristas attenuatis"* in Micheli, Nov. Pl. Gen.: 70, t. 33, f. 19. 1729.
Current name: **Carex bohemica** Schreb. (Cyperaceae).

Carex digitata Linnaeus, *Species Plantarum* 2: 975. 1753.
"Habitat in Europae nemoribus." RCN: 7075.
Lectotype (Egorova, *Sedges Russia*: 302. 1999): Herb. Linn. No. 1100.41 (LINN).
Current name: **Carex digitata** L. (Cyperaceae).

Carex dioica Linnaeus, *Species Plantarum* 2: 972. 1753.
"Habitat in Europae pratis humidis." RCN: 7054.
Lectotype (Egorova in Cafferty & Jarvis in *Taxon* 53: 178. 2004): [icon] *"Cyperoides parvum, caulibus, & foliis tenuissimis, triangularibus, spica subrotunda, capsulis oblongis, in angustum collum, vix bifidum attenuatis"* in Micheli, Nov. Pl. Gen.: 56, t. 32, f. 2. 1729. – Epitype (Egorova in Cafferty & Jarvis in *Taxon* 53: 178. 2004): England. North Yorkshire, Dentdale, small stony flush low on Weather Ling Hill to northwest of road, ca. 1,000ft, N 53/68, 8 Jun 1968, *G. Halliday s.n.* (LE).
Current name: **Carex dioica** L. (Cyperaceae).
Note: Egorova (*l.c.*) gives a review of the typification of this name.

Carex distans Linnaeus, *Systema Naturae*, ed. 10, 2: 1263. 1759.
["Habitat in Europae australioris paludibus."] Sp. Pl., ed. 2, 2: 1388 (1763). RCN: 7091.
Lectotype (Erteeb & Sherif in Jafri & El-Gadi, *Fl. Libya* 120: 10. 1985): [icon] *"Gramen Cyperoides palustre spicis tribus subrotundis vix aculeatis spatio distantibus"* in Morison, Pl. Hist. Univ. 3: 243, s. 8, t. 12, f. 18. 1699.
Current name: **Carex distans** L. (Cyperaceae).

Carex elongata Linnaeus, *Species Plantarum* 2: 974. 1753.
"Habitat in Europa." RCN: 7069.
Lectotype (Egorova, *Sedges Russia*: 550. 1999): [icon] *"Cyperoides polystachyon, spicis laxis paniculam veluti componentibus"* in Scheuchzer, Agrostographia: 487, t. 11, f. 4. 1719.
Current name: **Carex elongata** L. (Cyperaceae).

Carex filiformis Linnaeus, *Species Plantarum* 2: 976. 1753.
"Habitat in Europae nemoribus." RCN: 7079.
Lectotype (Nelmes in *Watsonia* 2: 252. 1951): [icon] *"Cyperoides sylvaticum, angustifolium, spicis parvis, tenuibus, spadiceo-viridibus"* in Scheuchzer, Agrostographia: 425, t. 10, f. 11. 1719.
Current name: **Carex filiformis** L. (Cyperaceae).

Carex flava Linnaeus, *Species Plantarum* 2: 975. 1753.
"Habitat in Europae paludibus." RCN: 7073.
Lectotype (Schmid in *Watsonia* 14: 312. 1983): Herb. Linn. No. 1100.40 (LINN).
Current name: **Carex flava** L. (Cyperaceae).

Carex folliculata Linnaeus, *Species Plantarum* 2: 978. 1753.
"Habitat in Canada. Kalm." RCN: 7088.
Lectotype (Reveal & al. in *Huntia* 7: 224. 1987): *Kalm*, Herb. Linn. No. 1100.66 (LINN).
Current name: **Carex folliculata** L. (Cyperaceae).

Carex globularis Linnaeus, *Species Plantarum* 2: 976. 1753.
"Habitat in Europa frigidiore." RCN: 7078.
Lectotype (Nelmes in *Watsonia* 2: 250. 1951): *Amman 32*, Herb. Linn. No. 1100.45 (LINN).
Current name: **Carex globularis** L. (Cyperaceae).

Carex hirta Linnaeus, *Species Plantarum* 2: 975. 1753.
"Habitat in Europae sabulosis." RCN: 7094.
Lectotype (Kukkonen in Jarvis in *Taxon* 41: 559. 1992): Herb. A. van Royen No. 901.336–595 (L).
Generitype of *Carex* Linnaeus.
Current name: **Carex hirta** L. (Cyperaceae).
Note: Carex hirta, with the type designated by Kukkonen, was proposed as conserved type of the genus by Jarvis (in *Taxon* 41: 559. 1992. However, the proposal was eventually ruled unnecessary by the General Committee (see Barrie, *l.c.* 55: 795–796. 2006 for a review of the history of this and related proposals).

Carex indica Linnaeus, *Mantissa Plantarum Altera*: 574. 1771.
"Habitat in India orientalis." RCN: 7072.
Lectotype (Nguyen Khac Khoi in *Novosti Sist. Vyssh. Rast.* 16: 68. 1979): Herb. Linn. No. 1100.39 (LINN).
Current name: **Carex indica** L. (Cyperaceae).
Note: Although Nelmes (in *Reinwardtia* 1: 273. 1951) referred to a Linnaean specimen and described its androgynaceous spike, he did not refer to it as the type. Simpson (in *Taxon* 53: 178. 2004) independently reached the same conclusion as Nguyen Khac Khoi.

Carex leporina Linnaeus, *Species Plantarum* 2: 973. 1753.
"Habitat in Europae pratis udis." RCN: 7063.
Lectotype (Egorova, *Sedges Russia*: 545. 1999): [icon] *"Gr. Cyp. palustre majus spica divisa"* in Morison, Pl. Hist. Univ. 3: 244, s. 8, t. 12, f. 29. 1699.
Current name: **Carex leporina** L. (Cyperaceae).
Note: Turland (in *Taxon* 46: 341. 1997) proposed the rejection of *C. leporina* against *C. lachenalii* Schkuhr but this was not recommended by the Committee for Spermatophyta (in *Taxon* 48: 367. 1999) because of uncertainty over its typification. The type proposed by Nelmes (in *Rep. Bot. Soc. Exch. Club Brit. Isles* 13: 337. 1948), 1100.19 (LINN), is identifiable as *C. lachenalii* but Egorova (*Sedges Russia*: 543. 1999) rejected this type choice on the grounds of conflict with the protologue, and typified the name instead using the cited Morison plate, identifiable with what has been called *C. ovalis* Good. The Committee for Spermatophyta (in *Taxon* 54:

1095. 2005) subsequently reconsidered the proposal and, accepting Egorova's typification, found that rejection as proposed was unnecessary. *Carex leporina* is therefore the correct name for what has been known as *C. ovalis*.

Carex limosa Linnaeus, *Species Plantarum* 2: 977. 1753.
"Habitat in Europae frigidae paludibus sylvaticis." RCN: 7083.
Lectotype (Egorova, *Sedges Russia*: 359. 1999): Herb. Linn. No. 1100.56 (LINN).
Current name: ***Carex limosa*** L. (Cyperaceae).

Carex lithosperma (Linnaeus) Linnaeus, *Systema Naturae*, ed. 12, 2: 618. 1767.
["Habitat in India."] Sp. Pl. 1: 51 (1753). RCN: 7095.
Basionym: *Scirpus lithospermus* L. (1753).
Lectotype (Camelbeke & Goetghebeur in *Taxon* 49: 295. 2000): [icon] *"Kaden-pullu"* in Rheede, Hort. Malab. 12: 89, t. 48. 1693.
Current name: ***Scleria lithosperma*** (L.) Sw. (Cyperaceae).

Carex loliacea Linnaeus, *Species Plantarum* 2: 974. 1753.
"Habitat in Suecia." RCN: 7067.
Lectotype (Egorova, *Sedges Russia*: 564. 1999): Herb. Linn. No. 1100.29 (LINN).
Current name: ***Carex loliacea*** L. (Cyperaceae).

Carex montana Linnaeus, *Species Plantarum* 2: 975. 1753.
"Habitat in Europae montanis apricis." RCN: 7076.

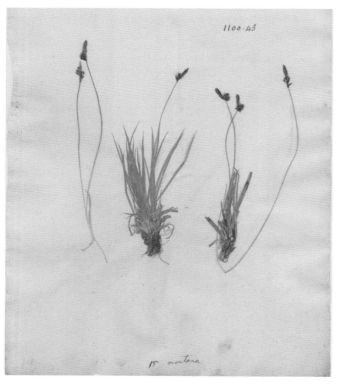

Lectotype (Egorova, *Sedges Russia*: 146. 1999): Herb. Linn. No. 1100.43 (LINN).
Current name: ***Carex montana*** L. (Cyperaceae).

Carex muricata Linnaeus, *Species Plantarum* 2: 974. 1753.
"Habitat in Europae nemoribus humentibus." RCN: 7066.
Lectotype (Marshall in *J. Bot.* 45: 364. 1907): Herb. Linn. No. 1100.26 (LINN).

Current name: ***Carex muricata*** L. (Cyperaceae).
Note: A number of authors, including Soó (in *Feddes Repert.* 83: 148. 1972), have treated this as a *nomen confusum*, and Lambinon (in *Taxon* 30: 362. 1981) proposed the formal rejection of the name. However, the Committee for Spermatophyta (in *Taxon* 35: 558. 1986) declined to support the proposal.

Carex pallescens Linnaeus, *Species Plantarum* 2: 977. 1753.
"Habitat in Europae paludibus." RCN: 7085.
Lectotype (Egorova, *Sedges Russia*: 305. 1999): Herb. Linn. No. 1100.60 (LINN).
Current name: ***Carex pallescens*** L. (Cyperaceae).
Note: See comments on the material in LINN, and the protologue, by Luceño (in *Ruizia* 14: 90. 1994).

Carex panicea Linnaeus, *Species Plantarum* 2: 977. 1753.
"Habitat in Europae uliginosis." RCN: 7087.
Lectotype (Marshall in *J. Bot.* 45: 366. 1907): Herb. Linn. No. 1100.63 (LINN).
Current name: ***Carex panicea*** L. (Cyperaceae).

Carex paniculata Linnaeus, *Centuria I Plantarum*: 32. 1755.
"Habitat in Europae australioribus uliginosis." RCN: 7071.
Lectotype (Egorova, *Sedges Russia*: 483. 1999): [icon] *"Cyperus Alp. longus inodorus panicula ferruginea minus sparsa"* in Scheuchzer, Agrostographia Helv. Prodr.: 27, t. 8. 1708 (see p. 156).
Current name: ***Carex paniculata*** L. (Cyperaceae).

Carex pedata Linnaeus, *Species Plantarum*, ed. 2, 2: 1384. 1763, *nom. utique rej.*
"Habitat in Helvetia, Anglia, Lapponia." RCN: 7074.
Type not designated.
Original material: [icon] in Micheli, Nov. Pl. Gen.: 65, t. 32, f. 14. 1729;

Carex pilulifera Linnaeus, *Species Plantarum* 2: 976. 1753.
"Habitat in Europa." RCN: 7080.
Lectotype (Egorova, *Sedges Russia*: 313. 1999): [icon] *"Gramen cyperoides tenuifolium, spicis ad summum caulem sessilibus, globulorum aemulis"* in Plukenet, Phytographia: t. 91, f. 8. 1691; Almag. Bot.: 178. 1696. – Epitype (Egorova, *Sedges Russia*: 313. 1999): Denmark. Zealand, Southern part of Steenstrup Lyng, W of Nykøbing, 13 Jun 1970, *N. Jacobsen s.n.* (Pl. Vasc. Dan. Exs. No. 261) (LE).
Current name: ***Carex pilulifera*** L. (Cyperaceae).

Carex pseudocyperus Linnaeus, *Species Plantarum* 2: 978. 1753.
"Habitat in Europae fossis." RCN: 7089.
Lectotype (Egorova, *Sedges Russia*: 199. 1999): Herb. Linn. No. 1100.68 (LINN).
Current name: ***Carex pseudocyperus*** L. (Cyperaceae).

Carex pulicaris Linnaeus, *Species Plantarum* 2: 972. 1753.
"Habitat in Europae paludibus limosis." RCN: 7056.
Lectotype (Egorova, *Sedges Russia*: 596. 1999): Herb. Linn. No. 1100.3 (LINN).
Current name: ***Carex pulicaris*** L. (Cyperaceae).

Carex remota Linnaeus, *Flora Anglica*: 24. 1754.
"Habitat [in Anglia.]" RCN: 7068.
Replaced synonym of: *Carex axillaris* L. (1759), *nom. illeg.*
Type not designated.
Original material: [icon] in Plukenet, Phytographia: t. 34, f. 3. 1691; Almag. Bot.: 178. 1696; [icon] in Morison, Pl. Hist. Univ. 3: 243, s. 8, t. 12, f. 17. 1699.

Current name: **Carex remota** L. (Cyperaceae).
Note: In 1754, Linnaeus described *C. remota* in *Fl. Anglica* where it is validated by a reference to Ray's *Syn. Meth. Stirp. Brit.* (1724: 424). The latter account includes, among other elements, synonyms from Morison (*Pl. Hist. Univ.* 3: 243, s. 8, t. 12, f. 17. 1699) and Plukenet (*Almag. Bot.*: 178. 1696; *Phytogr.*: t. 34, f. 3. 1691). A year later, in another thesis (*Cent. I Pl.*: 31. 1755), Linnaeus gave a second account of *C. remota*, this time with a new diagnosis and with synonyms taken from works by Guettard, Dalibard, Scheuchzer and Ray, as well as the Morison and Plukenet accounts cited previously in 1754. In *Syst. Nat.,* ed. 10, 2: 1262 (May–Jun 1759), Linnaeus recognised a single *C. remota* (cited as from 1755), but in a later edition of *Fl. Anglica* (in *Amoen. Acad.* 4: 107. Nov 1759), he substituted *C. axillaris* for *C. remota* (1754). Perhaps most significantly, in *Sp. Pl.,* ed. 2. 1763), Linnaeus recognised both *C. axillaris* (p. 1382) and *C. remota* (p. 1383). Despite Linnaeus later (*Syst. Nat.,* ed. 12, 2: 617. 1767) explicitly uniting *C. remota* and *C. axillaris* under the former name, *C. remota* (1754) and *C. remota* (1755) must be treated as independent names, with the latter an illegitimate homonym of the former. Although some authors (e.g. Chater in Tutin & al., *Fl. Europaea* 5: 300. 1980) regard the name as dating from 1754, others (e.g. Egorova, *Sedges of Russia*: 539. 1999) treat it as appearing first in 1755. Egorova also typified *C. remota* (1755), using the Morison illustration.

Carex remota Linnaeus, *Centuria I Plantarum*: 31. 1755, *nom. illeg.*
"Habitat in Europae umbrosis subhumidis." RCN: 7068.
Lectotype (Egorova, *Sedges Russia*: 539. 1999): [icon] *"Gramen Cyperoides paniculis pluribus sessilibus in foliorum alis"* in Morison, Pl. Hist. Univ. 3: 243, s. 8, t. 12, f. 17. 1699.
Current name: **Carex remota** L. (Cyperaceae).
Note: A later homonym of *C. remota* L. (1754), and therefore illegitimate. See notes under this earlier name.

Carex saxatilis Linnaeus, *Species Plantarum* 2: 976. 1753.
"Habitat in Europae alpibus." RCN: 7081.
Lectotype (Marshall in *J. Bot.* 45: 366. 1907): Herb. Linn. No. 1100.51 (LINN).
Current name: **Carex saxatilis** L. (Cyperaceae).

Carex squarrosa Linnaeus, *Species Plantarum* 2: 973. 1753.
"Habitat in Canada. Kalm." RCN: 7057.
Lectotype (Reznicek in Cafferty & Jarvis in *Taxon* 53: 178. 2004): *Kalm*, Herb. Linn. No. 1100.5 (LINN).
Current name: **Carex squarrosa** L. (Cyperaceae).

Carex tomentosa Linnaeus, *Systema Naturae,* ed. 12, 2: 617; *Mantissa Plantarum*: 123. 1767.
"Habitat in Austria. D. Jacquin." RCN: 7077.
Neotype (Nilsson in Davis, *Fl. Turkey* 9: 140. 1985): *Jacquin s.n.* (W; iso- BM?).
Current name: **Carex tomentosa** L. (Cyperaceae).

Carex uliginosa Linnaeus, *Species Plantarum* 2: 973. 1753, *nom. utique rej.*
"Habitat in Sueciae paludibus sylvaticis." RCN: 7061.
Type not designated.
Original material: Herb. Linn. No. 1100.16 (LINN); Herb. Linn. No. 1100.17 (LINN).

Carex vesicaria Linnaeus, *Species Plantarum* 2: 979. 1753.
"Habitat in Europae udis sylvaticis." RCN: 7093.
Lectotype (Marshall in *J. Bot.* 45: 397. 1907): Herb. Linn. No. 1100.74 (LINN).
Current name: **Carex vesicaria** L. (Cyperaceae).

Carex vulpina Linnaeus, *Species Plantarum* 2: 973. 1753.
"Habitat in Europae paludibus nemorosis." RCN: 7065.
Lectotype (Nelmes in *J. Bot.* 77: 265. 1939): Herb. Linn. No. 1100.22 (LINN). – Epitype (Foley in *Watsonia* 26: 29. 2006): England. Gloucestershire, v.c. 33, near Haw Bridge, 15 Jun 2004, *M.J.Y. Foley 2020* (BM; iso- E, FI, G, LE).
Current name: **Carex vulpina** L. (Cyperaceae).
Note: Foley provided an extensive discussion of the original elements involved in Linnaeus' concept of this taxon, concluding that doubts about the identity of the lectotype were best resolved by the designation of an epitype.

Carica papaya Linnaeus, *Species Plantarum* 2: 1036. 1753.
"Habitat in Indiis." RCN: 7475.
Lectotype (Moreno in Gómez Pompa, *Fl. Veracruz* 10: 7. 1980): Herb. Linn. No. 1190.1 (LINN).
Generitype of *Carica* Linnaeus (vide Green, *Prop. Brit. Bot.*: 192. 1929).
Current name: **Carica papaya** L. (Caricaceae).

Carica posoposa Linnaeus, *Species Plantarum* 2: 1036. 1753.
"Habitat Surinami." RCN: 7476.
Type not designated.
Original material: [icon] in Petiver, Gazophyl. Nat.: 68, t. 43, f. 2. 1704; [icon] in Plukenet, Phytographia: t. 278, f. 2?. 1694; Almag. Bot.: 146. 1696; [icon] in Feuillée, J. Obs. 3: 52, t. 39. 1725.
Current name: **Carica papaya** L. (Caricaceae).

Carissa carandas Linnaeus, *Systema Naturae,* ed. 12, 2: 189; *Mantissa Plantarum*: 52. 1767.
"Habitat in India." RCN: 1704.
Lectotype (Huber in Abeywickrama, *Revised Handb. Fl. Ceylon* 1(1): 9. 1973): [icon] *"Carandas"* in Rumphius, Herb. Amboin. Auct.: 57, t. 25. 1755.
Generitype of *Carissa* Linnaeus, *nom. cons.*
Current name: **Carissa carandas** L. (Apocynaceae).
Note: Carissa Linnaeus, *nom. cons.* against *Carandas* Adans.

Carissa spinarum Linnaeus, *Mantissa Plantarum Altera*: 559. 1771.
"Habitat in India orientali." RCN: 1705.
Lectotype (Huber in Abeywickrama, *Revised Handb. Fl. Ceylon* 1(1): 9. 1973): Herb. Linn. No. 295.2 (LINN).
Current name: **Carissa spinarum** L. (Apocynaceae).

Carlina acaulis Linnaeus, *Species Plantarum* 2: 828. 1753.
"Habitat in Italiae, Germaniae montibus." RCN: 5992.
Lectotype (Meusel & Kästner in *Denkschr. Österr. Akad. Wiss., Math.-Naturwiss. Kl.* 128: 285. 1994): Herb. Clifford: 395, *Carlina* 1 (BM-000646945).
Current name: **Carlina acaulis** L. (Asteraceae).

Carlina atractyloides Linnaeus, *Plantae Rariores Africanae*: 17. 1760.
["Habitat ad Cap. b. spei."] Sp. Pl. ed. 2, 2: 1161 (1763). RCN: 5998.
Type not designated.
Original material: Herb. Burman (G); Herb. Linn. No. 970.9 (LINN); [icon] in Plukenet, Phytographia: t. 273, f. 4. 1694; Almag. Bot.: 86. 1696 – Typotype: Herb. Sloane 99: 172 (BM-SL).
Current name: **Berkheya atractyloides** (L.) Schltr. (Asteraceae).
Note: Roessler (in *Mitt. Bot. Staatssamml. München* 3: 267. 1959) treated this as a *"species dubium"*.

Carlina corymbosa Linnaeus, *Species Plantarum* 2: 828, 1231. 1753.
"Habitat in Italia." RCN: 5994.
Lectotype (Meusel & Kästner in *Feddes Repert.* 83: 221. 1972): [icon] *"Acarna Apula umbellata"* in Colonna, Ekphr.: 28, 27. 1606.

Current name: **Carlina corymbosa** L. (Asteraceae).
Note: The trivial names of *Carlina corymbosa* and *C. vulgaris* were erroneously transposed on p. 828 of *Species Plantarum*. Linnaeus corrected this in the errata on p. 1231, so that no. 3 and its protologue is *C. corymbosa*, not *C. vulgaris*, and no. 4 and its protologue is *C. vulgaris*, not *C. corymbosa*.

Carlina lanata Linnaeus, *Species Plantarum* 2: 828. 1753.
"Habitat in Italia, G. Narbonensi." RCN: 5993.
Lectotype (Meusel & Kästner in *Denkschr. Österr. Akad. Wiss., Math.-Naturwiss. Kl.* 128: 121. 1994): Herb. Burser XXI: 24 (UPS).
Current name: **Carlina lanata** L. (Asteraceae).
Note: Although Rechinger (*Fl. Iranica* 139a: 102. 1979) indicated Herb. Linn. 970.3 (LINN) (as "370.3") as a syntype, the sheet lacks a *Species Plantarum* number (i.e. "2") written by Linnaeus and is a post-1753 addition to the collection, and not original material for the name.

Carlina pyrenaica Linnaeus, *Species Plantarum* 2: 829. 1753.
"Habitat in Pyrenaeis versus Hispaniam copiose." RCN: 5997.
Type not designated.
Original material: Herb. Burser XXI: 43, syntype (UPS).
Current name: **Carduus pyrenaicus** (L.) Kazmi (Asteraceae).

Carlina racemosa Linnaeus, *Species Plantarum* 2: 829. 1753.
"Habitat in Hispaniae desertis." RCN: 5996.
Lectotype (Petit in *Bull. Mus. Natl. Hist. Nat., B, Adansonia* 9: 418. 1988 [1987]): *Löfling s.n.*, Herb. Linn. No. 970.7 (LINN).
Current name: **Carlina racemosa** L. (Asteraceae).

Carlina vulgaris Linnaeus, *Species Plantarum* 2: 828, 1231. 1753.
"Habitat in Europae montosis, aridis, sabulosis." RCN: 5995.
Lectotype (Kästner & Meusel in Jarvis & al., *Regnum Veg.* 127: 30. 1993): Herb. Linn. No. 970.5 (LINN).
Generitype of *Carlina* Linnaeus (vide Green, *Prop. Brit. Bot.*: 179. 1929).
Current name: **Carlina vulgaris** L. (Asteraceae).
Note: The trivial epithets of *Carlina corymbosa* and *C. vulgaris* were erroneously transposed on p. 828 of *Species Plantarum*. Linnaeus corrected this in the errata on p. 1231, so that *Carlina* species no. 3 and its protologue is *C. corymbosa* (not *C. vulgaris*) and *Carlina* species no. 4 and its protologue is *C. vulgaris* (not *C. corymbosa*).

Carpesium abrotanoides Linnaeus, *Species Plantarum* 2: 860. 1753.
"Habitat in China. Osbeck." RCN: 6208.
Lectotype (Rechinger, *Fl. Iranica* 145: 127. 1980): *Osbeck 50*, Herb. Linn. No. 991.2 (LINN).
Current name: **Carpesium abrotanoides** L. (Asteraceae).
Note: Jarvis & al. (*Regnum Veg.* 127: 30. 1993) wrongly listed this name as the generitype. *Carpesium cernuum* L. is the generitype.

Carpesium cernuum Linnaeus, *Species Plantarum* 2: 859. 1753.
"Habitat in Italia." RCN: 6207.
Lectotype (Grierson in Dassanayake & Fosberg, *Revised Handb. Fl. Ceylon* 1: 201. 1980): Herb. Linn. No. 991.1 (LINN).
Generitype of *Carpesium* Linnaeus (vide Green, *Prop. Brit. Bot.*: 181. 1929).
Current name: **Carpesium cernuum** L. (Asteraceae).
Note: Jarvis & al. (*Regnum Veg.* 127: 30. 1993) wrongly listed *C. abrotanoides* L. as the generitype. *Carpesium cernuum* is the generitype.
   Grierson's typification was published in February 1980, pre-dating the same choice made by Rechinger (*Fl. Iranica* 145: 127) in April 1980.

Carpinus betulus Linnaeus, *Species Plantarum* 2: 998. 1753.
"Habitat in Europa, Canada." RCN: 7231.
Lectotype (Browicz in Rechinger, *Fl. Iranica* 97: 3. 1972): Herb. Linn. No. 1131.1 (LINN).
Generitype of *Carpinus* Linnaeus (vide Green, *Prop. Brit. Bot.*: 189. 1929).
Current name: **Carpinus betulus** L. (Betulaceae).

Carpinus ostrya Linnaeus, *Species Plantarum* 2: 998. 1753.
"Habitat in Italia, Virginia." RCN: 7232.
Type not designated.
Original material: Herb. Linn. No. 1131.4 (LINN); Herb. Clifford: 447, *Carpinus* 2 (BM); [icon] in Plukenet, Phytographia: t. 156, f. 1. 1692; Almag. Bot.: 7. 1696; [icon] in Micheli, Nov. Pl. Gen.: 223, t. 104, f. 1, 2. 1729.
Current name: **Ostrya carpinifolia** Scop. (Betulaceae).
Note: See comments by Reveal (in *Taxon* 39: 357, 359. 1990).

Carthamus arborescens Linnaeus, *Species Plantarum* 2: 831. 1753.
"Habitat in Hispania." RCN: 6010.
Lectotype (Hanelt in Jarvis & Turland in *Taxon* 47: 356. 1998): Herb. A. van Royen No. 900.191–368 (L). – Epitype (Hanelt in Jarvis & Turland in *Taxon* 47: 356. 1998): Herb. Linn. No. 973.8 (LINN).
Current name: **Carthamus arborescens** L. (Asteraceae).
Note: Hanelt (in *Feddes Repert.* 67: 66. 1963) indicated Herb. Linn. 973.8 (LINN) as the holotype but the sheet lacks a *Species Plantarum* number (i.e. "6"), was a post-1753 addition to the herbarium and is not original material for the name. Hanelt subsequently designated van Royen material as lectotype, retaining 973.8 (LINN) as an epitype.

Carthamus caeruleus Linnaeus, *Species Plantarum* 2: 830. 1753.
"Habitat in agro Tingitano & Hispalensi inter segetes." RCN: 6006.
Lectotype (Turland in Jarvis & Turland in *Taxon* 47: 356. 1998): Herb. Clifford: 394, *Carthamus* 2 (BM-000646937).
Current name: **Carthamus caeruleus** L. (Asteraceae).

Carthamus carduncellus Linnaeus, *Species Plantarum* 2: 831. 1753.
"Habitat Monspelii." RCN: 6008.
Type not designated.
Original material: Herb. Burser XXI: 68 (UPS); Herb. A. van Royen No. 900.130–248 (L); [icon] in Plantin, Pl. Stirp. Icon. 2: 20. 1581.
Current name: **Carthamus carduncellus** L. (Asteraceae).

Carthamus corymbosus (Linnaeus) Linnaeus, *Species Plantarum*, ed. 2, 2: 1164. 1763.
"Habitat in Apuliae, Hellesponti, Lemni, Thraciae campis." RCN: 6009.
Basionym: *Echinops corymbosus* L. (1753).
Lectotype (Turland in Jarvis & Turland in *Taxon* 47: 360. 1998): Herb. Clifford: 391, *Echinops* 2, sheet 26 (BM-000646905).
Current name: **Cardopatium corymbosum** (L.) Pers. (Asteraceae).

Carthamus creticus Linnaeus, *Species Plantarum*, ed. 2, 2: 1163. 1763.
"Habitat in Creta." RCN: 6004.
Lectotype (Hanelt in *Feddes Repert.* 67: 144. 1963): Herb. Linn. No. 973.3 (LINN).
Current name: **Carthamus creticus** L. (Asteraceae).

Carthamus lanatus Linnaeus, *Species Plantarum* 2: 830. 1753.
"Habitat in Gallia, Italia, Creta." RCN: 6003.
Lectotype (Hanelt in *Feddes Repert.* 67: 136. 1963): *Löfling 610a*, Herb. Linn. No. 973.2 (LINN).
Current name: **Carthamus lanatus** L. subsp. **lanatus** (Asteraceae).

Carthamus mitissimus Linnaeus, *Species Plantarum* 2: 831. 1753.
"Habitat circa Parisios." RCN: 6007.
Type not designated.
Original material: none traced.
Current name: ***Carthamus mitissimus*** L. (Asteraceae).

Carthamus tinctorius Linnaeus, *Species Plantarum* 2: 830. 1753.
"Habitat in Aegypto." RCN: 6002.
Lectotype (Rechinger, *Fl. Iranica* 139b: 434. 1980): Herb. Clifford: 394, *Carthamus* 1 (BM-000646936).
Generitype of *Carthamus* Linnaeus (vide Green, *Prop. Brit. Bot.*: 179. 1929).
Current name: ***Carthamus tinctorius*** L. (Asteraceae).
Note: Hanelt (in *Feddes Repert.* 67: 90. 1963) designated an illustration in Fuchs (*Hist. Stirp.*: 410. 1542) as the type, but as this did not form part of the protologue, it cannot be an original element for the name.

Carthamus tingitanus Linnaeus, *Species Plantarum*, ed. 2, 2: 1163. 1763.
"Habitat in Agro tingitano, Algiriae." RCN: 6005.
Type not designated.
Original material: *Alströmer 201*, Herb. Linn. No. 973.5 (LINN); [icon] in Morison, Pl. Hist. Univ. 3: 159, s. 7, t. 34, f. 19. 1699.
Current name: ***Carthamus caeruleus*** L. (Asteraceae).

Carum bunius Linnaeus, *Systema Naturae,* ed. 12, 2: 733. 1767.
"Habitat in Pyrenaeis." RCN: 2052.
Basionym of: *Aethusa bunius* (L.) L. (1774).
Lectotype (Reduron & Jarvis in Jarvis & al. in *Taxon* 55: 210. 2006): [icon] *"Saxifraga Petroselini vel Coriandri folio"* in Morison, Pl. Hist. Univ. 3: 274, s. 9, t. 2, f. 16. 1699.
Current name: ***Ptychotis saxifraga*** (L.) Loret & Barrandon (Apiaceae).

Carum carvi Linnaeus, *Species Plantarum* 1: 263. 1753.
"Habitat in Europae borealis pratis." RCN: 2101.
Lectotype (Reduron & Jarvis in Jarvis & al., *Regnum Veg.* 127: 30. 1993): Herb. Clifford: 106, *Carum* 1 (BM-000558386).
Generitype of *Carum* Linnaeus.
Current name: ***Carum carvi*** L. (Apiaceae).
Note: Jafri (in Jafri & El-Gadi, *Fl. Libya* 117: 93. 1985) indicated 372.1 (LINN) as type but this is a post-1753 addition to the herbarium and not original material for the name.

Carum carvi Linnaeus var. **peregrinum** Linnaeus, *Demonstr. Pl. Horto Upsaliensi*: 8. 1753, *nom. inval.*
RCN: 2101.
Type not relevant.
Note: The protologue consists of the name "Carum peregrinum", or possibly "Carum carvi var. peregrinum" – the epithet is not absolutely in alignment in the column with the previous epithet, i.e. "carvi", which led Rickett (in *Lloydia* 18: 54. 1955) to query this. The epithet "peregrinum" is followed by "(u)", which provides a link to a footnote which reads as follows:
"(u) Carvi peregrinum difficile determinatur; duplo majus est Carvo Carvi dicto, ex australibus terris allatum.".
There is nothing in the footnote that could serve as a validating description, and *Carum peregrinum* (or *C. carvi* var. *peregrinum*) must therefore be regarded as a *nomen nudum*.

Carum peregrinum Linnaeus, *Demonstr. Pl. Horto Upsaliensi*: 8. 1753, *nom. inval.*
RCN: 2101.
Type not relevant.
Note: See discussion under *C. carvi* var. *peregrinum*.

Caryocar nuciferum Linnaeus, *Mantissa Plantarum Altera*: 247. 1771.
"Habitat in Berbices & Essequebo." RCN: 3961.
Type not designated.
Original material: none traced.
Generitype of *Caryocar* Linnaeus.
Current name: ***Caryocar nucifera*** L. (Caryocaraceae).
Note: This name was evidently based on an Allemand description, but Linnaeus may never have seen a specimen (see Prance in *Fl. Neotropica* 12: 34. 1973).

Caryophyllus aromaticus Linnaeus, *Species Plantarum* 1: 515. 1753.
"Habitat in Moluccis solo aridissimo." RCN: 3884.
Lectotype (McVaugh in Howard, *Fl. Lesser Antilles* 5: 528. 1989): Herb. Clifford: 207, *Caryophyllus* 1 (BM-000628747).
Generitype of *Caryophyllus* Linnaeus, *nom. rej.*
Current name: ***Syzygium aromaticum*** (L.) Merr. & L.M. Perry (Myrtaceae).
Note: Caryophyllus Linnaeus, *nom. rej.* in favour of *Syzygium* Gaertn.

Caryota urens Linnaeus, *Species Plantarum* 2: 1189. 1753.
"Habitat in India." RCN: 8551.
Lectotype (Moore & Dransfield in *Taxon* 28: 70, f. 8. 1979): [icon] *"Schunda-pana"* in Rheede, Hort. Malab. 1: 15, t. 11. 1678.
Generitype of *Caryota* Linnaeus.
Current name: ***Caryota urens*** L. (Arecaceae).

Cassia absus Linnaeus, *Species Plantarum* 1: 376. 1753.
"Habitat in India, Aegypto." RCN: 2958.
Lectotype (de Wit in *Webbia* 11: 280. 1956): Herb. Linn. No. 528.4 (LINN).
Current name: ***Chamaecrista absus*** (L.) H.S. Irwin & Barneby (Fabaceae: Caesalpinioideae).
Note: Fawcett & Rendle (*Fl. Jamaica* 4: 111. 1920) indicated that the type was in Herb. Hermann (BM) but as the elements preserved there include both specimens and drawings, this is not an effective type choice. De Wit appears to have been the next to indicate a type, and chose material in LINN (as "holotype"). Although he was followed by some authors (e.g. Symon in *Trans. Roy. Soc. S. Australia* 90: 131. 1966), Ali (in Nasir & Ali, *Fl. W. Pakistan* 54: 20. 1973) indicated a Hermann collection (BM) as lectotype, and was followed by many authors. These include Irwin & Barneby (in *Mem. New York Bot. Gard.* 30: 281. 1978) who rejected de Wit's choice on the grounds that Linnaeus' account was based primarily on his *Flora Zeylanica* (1747) treatment. However, the collection in LINN does form part of the original material for the name, and de Wit's choice has priority.

Cassia alata Linnaeus, *Species Plantarum* 1: 378. 1753.
"Habitat in America calidiore." RCN: 2976.
Lectotype (Isely in *Mem. New York Bot. Gard.* 25(2): 197. 1975): Herb. Clifford: 158, *Cassia* 3 (BM-000558725).
Current name: ***Senna alata*** (L.) Roxb. (Fabaceae: Caesalpinioideae).
Note: As noted by Isely (in *Mem. New York Bot. Gard.* 25: 197. 1975), de Wit (in *Webbia* 11: 232. 1956) wrongly designated a Patrick Browne collection in LINN, not received by Linnaeus until 1758, as lectotype. Brenan (in Milne-Redhead & Polhill, *Fl. Trop. E. Africa, Leguminosae* 2: 64 (1967) indicated Clifford material (BM) as a syntype. Most later authors have accepted the Clifford material as lectotype and Isely's is the earliest formal typification.

Cassia atomaria Linnaeus, *Systema Naturae,* ed. 12, 2: 289; *Mantissa Plantarum*: 68. 1767.
"Habitat in America. Dr. Jacquin." RCN: 2969.

Lectotype (Irwin & Barneby in *Mem. New York Bot. Gard.* 35: 588. 1982): *Jacquin s.n.*, Herb. Linn. No. 528.17 (LINN).
Current name: ***Senna atomaria*** (L.) H.S. Irwin & Barneby (Fabaceae: Caesalpinioideae).

Cassia auriculata Linnaeus, *Species Plantarum* 1: 379. 1753.
"Habitat in India." RCN: 2980.
Lectotype (Reveal in Turland & Jarvis in *Taxon* 46: 466. 1997): Herb. Hermann 4: 20, No. 151 (BM-000628088).
Current name: ***Senna auriculata*** (L.) Roxb. (Fabaceae: Caesalpinioideae).
Note: De Wit (in *Webbia* 11: 235. 1956) designated a neotype, overlooking that Hermann material (BM) was original material for the name. Brenan (in Milne-Redhead & Polhill, *Fl. Trop. E. Africa, Leguminosae* 2: 76 (1967) and Rudd (in Dassanayake & Fosberg, *Revised Handb. Fl. Ceylon* 7: 79. 1991) treated the Hermann material (distributed over three pages in two volumes) as syntypes, and Reveal subsequently designated one of them as lectotype.

Cassia bicapsularis Linnaeus, *Species Plantarum* 1: 376. 1753.
"Habitat in India." RCN: 2962.
Lectotype (de Wit in *Webbia* 11: 236. 1956): Herb. Linn. No. 528.10 (LINN).
Current name: ***Senna bicapsularis*** (L.) Roxb. (Fabaceae: Caesalpinioideae).
Note: Fawcett & Rendle (*Fl. Jamaica* 4: 103. 1920) noted the existence of 528.10 (LINN), but did not refer to it as the type. De Wit's treatment of this collection as the holotype is accepted as a lectotypification (Art. 9.8).

Cassia biflora Linnaeus, *Species Plantarum* 1: 378. 1753, *nom. rej.*
"Habitat in Indiis." RCN: 2972a.
Neotype (de Wit in *Webbia* 11: 239. 1956): *Browne*, Herb. Linn. No. 528.21 (LINN).
Current name: ***Senna angustisiliqua*** (Lam.) H.S. Irwin & Barneby var. ***fulgens*** (Macfad.) H.S. Irwin & Barneby (Fabaceae: Caesalpinioideae).

Cassia chamaecrista Linnaeus, *Species Plantarum* 1: 379. 1753, *nom. rej.*
"Habitat in Jamaica, Barbados, Virginia." RCN: 2982.
Lectotype (Irwin & Barneby in *Brittonia* 28: 439. 1977 [1976]): Herb. Linn. No. 528.30 (LINN).
Current name: ***Chamaecrista fasciculata*** (Michx.) Greene (Fabaceae: Caesalpinioideae).

Cassia diphylla Linnaeus, *Species Plantarum* 1: 376. 1753.
"Habitat in India." RCN: 2957.
Lectotype (Irwin & Barneby in *Mem. New York Bot. Gard.* 35: 891. 1982): Herb. Linn. No. 528.1 (LINN).
Current name: ***Chamaecrista diphylla*** (L.) Greene (Fabaceae: Caesalpinioideae).
Note: Irwin & Barneby's use of "holotype" is accepted as a lectotypification under Art. 9.8.

Cassia emarginata Linnaeus, *Species Plantarum* 1: 376. 1753.
"Habitat in Caribaeis." RCN: 2963.
Lectotype (Irwin & Barneby in *Mem. New York Bot. Gard.* 35: 402. 1982): [icon] *"Cassia minor fruticosa hexaphylla senae foliis"* in Sloane, Voy. Jamaica 2: 44, t. 180, f. 1, 2, 3, 4. 1725. – Typotype: Herb. Sloane 6: 28 (BM-SL).
Current name: ***Senna bicapsularis*** (L.) Roxb. (Fabaceae: Caesalpinioideae).
Note: Fawcett & Rendle (*Fl. Jamaica* 4: 108. 1920) treated Sloane's specimen as the type but this was never seen by Linnaeus and is not original material for the name.

Cassia falcata Linnaeus, *Species Plantarum* 1: 377. 1753.
"Habitat in America." RCN: 2965.
Neotype (Reveal in Turland & Jarvis in *Taxon* 46: 466. 1997): *Browne*, Herb. Linn. No. 528.13 (LINN).
Current name: ***Senna occidentalis*** (L.) Link (Fabaceae: Caesalpinioideae).
Note: A specimen in Herb. Linn. (No. 528.12, LINN), identifiable as *C. fistula* L., although annotated "falcata" by Linnaeus, lacks glands at the bases of the petioles and is thereby fundamentally at odds with Linnaeus' *nomen specificum legitimum* which states "glandula baseos petiolorum". This specimen could not possibly have been that upon which the validating diagnosis was based and is therefore not original material for *C. falcata*. In the absence of any other original material, Reveal designated a neotype.

Cassia fistula Linnaeus, *Species Plantarum* 1: 377. 1753, *typ. cons.*
"Habitat in India, Aegypto." RCN: 2968.
Lectotype (Fawcett & Rendle, *Fl. Jamaica* 4: 102. 1920; Larsen & Larsen in Aubréville & Leroy, *Fl. Cambodge Laos Viêt-Nam* 18: 79. 1980): Herb. Hermann 2: 29, No. 149 (BM-000594592).
Generitype of *Cassia* Linnaeus, *nom. cons.*
Current name: ***Cassia fistula*** L. (Fabaceae: Caesalpinioideae).

Cassia flexuosa Linnaeus, *Species Plantarum* 1: 379. 1753.
"Habitat in Brasilia." RCN: 2985.
Lectotype (Greene in *Pittonia* 4: 27. 1899): [icon] *"Chamaecrista Pavonis Brasiliana, siliqua singulari"* in Breyn, Exot. Pl. Cent.: 64, t. 23. 1678.
Current name: ***Chamaecrista flexuosa*** (L.) Greene (Fabaceae: Caesalpinioideae).

Cassia galegifolia Linnaeus, *Systema Naturae*, ed. 10, 2: 1017. 1759, *nom. rej.*
RCN: 2972b.
Lectotype (Irwin & Barneby in *Mem. New York Bot. Gard.* 35: 56. 1982): [icon] *"Cassia foliolis quinque jugatis"* in Plumier in Burman, Pl. Amer.: 69, t. 78, f. 1. 1756.
Current name: ***Senna occidentalis*** (L.) Link (Fabaceae: Caesalpinioideae).

Cassia glandulosa Linnaeus, *Systema Naturae*, ed. 10, 2: 1017. 1759.
["Habitat in Jamaica."] Sp. Pl., ed. 2, 1: 543 (1762). RCN: 2983.
Lectotype (Fawcett & Rendle, *Fl. Jamaica* 4: 114. 1920): *Browne*, Herb. Linn. No. 528.32 (LINN).
Current name: ***Chamaecrista glandulosa*** (L.) Greene (Fabaceae: Caesalpinioideae).

Cassia hirsuta Linnaeus, *Species Plantarum* 1: 378. 1753.
"Habitat in America." RCN: 2973.
Lectotype (Brenan in Milne-Redhead & Polhill, *Fl. Trop. E. Africa, Leguminosae* 2: 80. 1967): Herb. Clifford: 159, *Cassia* 4 (BM-000558726).
Current name: ***Senna hirsuta*** (L.) H.S. Irwin & Barneby var. ***hirsuta*** (Fabaceae: Caesalpinioideae).

Cassia javanica Linnaeus, *Species Plantarum* 1: 379. 1753.
"Habitat in India." RCN: 2981.
Lectotype (de Wit in *Webbia* 11: 215. 1956): [icon] *"Cassia fistula Javanica flore carneo"* in Commelin, Hort. Med. Amstelod. Pl. Rar. 1: 217, t. 111. 1697.
Current name: ***Cassia javanica*** L. subsp. ***javanica*** (Fabaceae: Caesalpinioideae).
Note: De Wit (in *Webbia* 11: 215. 1956) indicated the cited Commelin plate as the type. No specimens were available for typification and de Wit (*l.c.*: 219–220), believing that the

Amsterdam Code then in force might preclude the use of illustrations as types, also designated a neotype for this (and other) names "for pre-Linnaean descriptions when type material (Art. 18) proved to be absent". This procedure is not dissimilar to the use of epitypes, introduced much later, but de Wit's intention that the primary type was the Commelin illustration seems clear, and is accepted here.

Cassia ligustrina Linnaeus, *Species Plantarum* 1: 378. 1753, *nom. cons.*
"Habitat in Virginia, Bahama." RCN: 2975.
Conserved type (Reveal in *Taxon* 41: 137. 1992): [icon] *"Senna Ligustri folio Plumier"* in Dillenius, Hort. Eltham. 2: 350, t. 259, f. 338. 1732. – Typotype: Herb. Sherard No. 839 (OXF).
Current name: **Senna ligustrina** (L.) H.S. Irwin & Barneby (Fabaceae: Caesalpinioideae).

Cassia marilandica Linnaeus, *Species Plantarum* 1: 378. 1753.
"Habitat in Virginia, Marilandia." RCN: 2977.
Lectotype (Fernald in *Rhodora* 39: 410. 1937): Herb. Linn. No. 528.27 (LINN).
Current name: **Senna marilandica** (L.) Link (Fabaceae: Caesalpinioideae).
Note: See extensive review by Reveal & al. (in *Huntia* 7: 215–216. 1987).

Cassia mimosoides Linnaeus, *Species Plantarum* 1: 379. 1753.
"Habitat in Zeylona." RCN: 2984.
Lectotype (Larsen & Larsen in Aubréville & Leroy, *Fl. Cambodge Laos Viêt-Nam* 18: 105. 1980): Herb. Hermann 2: 13, No. 154 (BM-000594576).
Current name: **Chamaecrista mimosoides** (L.) Greene (Fabaceae: Caesalpinioideae).
Note: Although de Wit (in *Webbia* 11: 284. 1956) stated that the type was "to be based on a Ceylon specimen preserved in the Bibliothèque at Paris", he appears to have made no formal type choice. Brenan (in Milne-Redhead & Polhill, *Fl. Trop. E. Africa, Leguminosae* 2: 100. 1967) treated the Hermann material (distributed over two pages) as syntypes, and Larsen & Larsen subsequently designated one of them as the lectotype.

Cassia nictitans Linnaeus, *Species Plantarum* 1: 380. 1753.
"Habitat in Virginia." RCN: 2986.
Lectotype (Pennell in *Bull. Torrey Bot. Club* 44: 356. 1917): [icon] *"Cassia calycibus acutis, floribus pentandris"* in Linnaeus, Hort. Cliff.: 497, t. 36. 1738.
Current name: **Chamaecrista nictitans** (L.) Moench (Fabaceae: Caesalpinioideae).
Note: In order to distinguish between this name and *Chamaecrista nictitans* Moench (non (L.) Moench), Reveal (in *Taxon* 41: 135. 1992) proposed the conservation of the Moench name with the same type as the Linnaean name. However, this was not recommended by the Committee for Spermatophyta (in *Taxon* 43: 273. 1994) who voted that *Ch. nictitans* be treated as a new combination based on *C. nictitans* L., the proposal therefore being unnecessary.

Cassia obtusifolia Linnaeus, *Species Plantarum* 1: 377. 1753.
"Habitat in Cuba." RCN: 2964.
Lectotype (Brenan in *Kew Bull.* 13: 251. 1958): [icon] *"Cassia foetida, foliis Sennae Italicae"* in Dillenius, Hort. Eltham. 1: 71, t. 62, f. 72. 1732. – Typotype: Herb. Sherard No. 831 (OXF; iso- G).
Current name: **Senna obtusifolia** (L.) H.S. Irwin & Barneby (Fabaceae: Caesalpinioideae).
Note: Prain (in *J. Asiatic Soc. Bengal* 66(2): 475. 1897) felt (wrongly)

that the cited Dillenius plate could not be the type, and de Wit (in *Webbia* 11: 251. 1956) chose 528.11 (LINN), a sterile specimen of doubtful identity, as a neotype. Brenan argued that this material conflicts with the diagnosis, and rejected de Wit's choice in favour of the Dillenius plate. However, Reveal (in *Taxon* 41: 138. 1992) proposed the name, and the type accepted by Brenan and others, for conservation. The Committee for Spermatophyta (in *Taxon* 43: 273. 1994) did not recommend this, accepting Brenan's choice of type as valid. Conservation was therefore felt to be unnecessary.

Cassia occidentalis Linnaeus, *Species Plantarum* 1: 377. 1753.
"Habitat in Jamaica." RCN: 2966.
Lectotype (Reveal in *Phytologia* 71: 453, 454. 1991): Herb. Clifford: 159, *Cassia* 7, sheet 10 (BM-000558727).
Current name: **Senna occidentalis** (L.) Link (Fabaceae: Caesalpinioideae).
Note: De Wit (in *Webbia* 11: 257. 1956) indicated 528.13 (LINN) as the holotype but it is a Patrick Browne collection, not received by Linnaeus until 1758 and not original material for the name. Others, including Wijnands (*Bot. Commelins*: 60. 1983), treated this collection as a neotype but this is unacceptable because original elements are in existence. Brenan (in Milne-Redhead & Polhill, *Fl. Trop. E. Africa, Leguminosae* 2: 78 (1967), followed by many authors, treated a Clifford sheet (BM) as a syntype, but in any case did not distinguish between the two sheets that exist. Some authors have attributed a formal type choice to Brenan (e.g. Irwin & Barneby in *Mem. New York Bot. Gard.* 35: 436. 1982. as "lectoholotypus") but still fail to distinguish between the sheets. Reveal subsequently provided a detailed review, and designated one of them as the lectotype.

Cassia pilosa Linnaeus, *Systema Naturae*, ed. 10, 2: 1017. 1759.
["Habitat in Jamaica."] Sp. Pl., ed. 2, 1: 540 (1762). RCN: 2970.
Lectotype (Fawcett & Rendle, *Fl. Jamaica* 4: 111. 1920): *Browne*, Herb. Linn. No. 528.18 (LINN).
Current name: **Chamaecrista pilosa** (L.) Greene (Fabaceae: Caesalpinioideae).
Note: Isely (in *Mem. New York Bot. Gard.* 25(2): 207. 1975) provides further information on the type.

Cassia planisiliqua Linnaeus, *Species Plantarum* 1: 377. 1753.
"Habitat in America calidiore." RCN: 2967.
Lectotype (Irwin & Barneby in *Mem. New York Bot. Gard.* 35: 437. 1982): [icon] *"Cassia foliolis quinque jugatis"* in Plumier in Burman, Pl. Amer.: 68, t. 77. 1756.
Current name: **Senna occidentalis** (L.) Link (Fabaceae: Caesalpinioideae).
Note: De Wit (in *Webbia* 11: 271. 1956) failed to locate relevant van Royen material, and Irwin & Barneby concluded that a Plumier plate was the type. The relationship between the tracings of the Plumier plates (made by Aubriet and published by Burman between 1755 and 1760) and Plumier polynomials cited by Linnaeus has been explored by Gillis & Stearn (in *Taxon* 23: 185–191. 1974) and Polhill & Stearn (in *Taxon* 25: 323–325. 1976).

Cassia procumbens Linnaeus, *Species Plantarum* 1: 380. 1753.
"Habitat in Indiis." RCN: 2987.
Lectotype (Reveal in *Taxon* 41: 136. 1992): *Kalm*, Herb. Linn. No. 528.34 (LINN).
Current name: **Chamaecrista procumbens** (L.) Greene (Fabaceae: Caesalpinioideae).
Note: The type belongs to the taxon treated by Reveal as *Chamaecrista nictitans* Moench. He therefore (in *Taxon* 41: 136. 1992) proposed the Linnaean name for rejection, also providing a detailed historical review. However, the Committee for Spermatophyta (in *Taxon* 43:

277. 1994) voted heavily against the proposal under the Berlin Code but agreed that the case should be reconsidered under the Tokyo Code. The Committee subsequently (in *Taxon* 54: 1093. 2005) did not recommend the name for rejection.

Cassia senna Linnaeus, *Species Plantarum* 1: 377. 1753.
"Habitat in Aegypto." RCN: 2971.
Lectotype (Valenti in *Webbia* 26: 62. 1971): [icon] *"Senna Alexandrina sive foliis acutis"* in Morison, Pl. Hist. Univ. 2: 201, s. 2, t. 24, f. 1. 1680.
Current name: *Senna alexandrina* Mill. (Fabaceae: Caesalpinioideae).
Note: Brenan (in Milne-Redhead & Polhill, *Fl. Trop. E. Africa, Leguminosae* 2: 65. 1967) stated that the type was uncertain but that Morison's plant agreed with usage of the name. Valenti was the first to make a formal type choice.

Cassia serpens Linnaeus, *Systema Naturae*, ed. 10, 2: 1018. 1759.
["Habitat in Jamaica."] Sp. Pl., ed. 2, 1: 541 (1762). RCN: 2974.
Lectotype (Fawcett & Rendle, *Fl. Jamaica* 4: 112. 1920): *Browne*, Herb. Linn. No. 528.24 (LINN).
Current name: *Chamaecrista serpens* (L.) Greene (Fabaceae: Caesalpinioideae).

Cassia sophera Linnaeus, *Species Plantarum* 1: 379. 1753.
"Habitat in India." RCN: 2979.
Lectotype (Fawcett & Rendle, *Fl. Jamaica* 4: 105. 1920): Herb. Hermann 4: 79, No. 150 (BM-000594778).
Current name: *Senna sophera* (L.) Roxb. (Fabaceae: Caesalpinioideae).

Cassia tagera Linnaeus, *Species Plantarum* 1: 376. 1753.
"Habitat in India." RCN: 2960.
Lectotype (Nicolson & al., *Interpret. Van Rheede's Hort. Malab.*: 132. 1988): [icon] *"Tagera"* in Rheede, Hort. Malab. 2: 103, t. 53. 1679.
Current name: *Senna tora* (L.) Roxb. (Fabaceae: Caesalpinioideae).
Note: Irwin & Barneby (in *Brittonia* 28: 435–437. 1976) discussed this name in some detail, illustrating the cited Rheede figure as their f. 1. They concluded that the name should be discarded as a *nomen ambiguum*. However, Nicolson & al. subsequently disagreed, and designated the Rheede plate as lectotype.

Cassia tenuissima Linnaeus, *Species Plantarum* 1: 378. 1753, *nom. rej.*
"Habitat in Havana." RCN: 2978.
Neotype (Reveal in *Taxon* 41: 132. 1992): Jamaica. Near Kingston, *Houstoun s.n.* (BM).
Current name: *Senna pallida* (Vahl) H.S. Irwin & Barneby (Fabaceae: Caesalpinioideae).

Cassia tora Linnaeus, *Species Plantarum* 1: 376. 1753.
"Habitat in India." RCN: 2961.
Lectotype (Brenan in *Kew Bull.* 13: 250. 1958): Herb. Hermann 4: 79, No. 152 (BM-000628410).
Current name: *Senna tora* (L.) Roxb. (Fabaceae: Caesalpinioideae).
Note: Fawcett & Rendle (*Fl. Jamaica* 4: 106. 1920) indicated Hermann elements (BM) as type but this did not distinguish between the specimens and illustrations in this collection. De Wit (in *Webbia* 11: 277. 1956) wrongly indicated 528.9 (LINN) as the holotype: it is a Patrick Browne collection not received by Linnaeus until 1758, and not original material for the name. Brenan appears to have made the earliest explicit type choice.

Cassia viminea Linnaeus, *Systema Naturae*, ed. 10, 2: 1016. 1759.
["Habitat in Jamaica."] Sp. Pl., ed. 2, 1: 537 (1762). RCN: 2959.
Lectotype (Fawcett & Rendle, *Fl. Jamaica* 4: 102. 1920): *Browne*, Herb. Linn. No. 528.6 (LINN).

Current name: *Senna viminea* (L.) H.S. Irwin & Barneby (Fabaceae: Caesalpinioideae).

Cassine barbara Linnaeus, *Mantissa Plantarum Altera*: 220. 1771, *nom. cons.*
"Habitat ad Cap. b. spei. D. Schreber." RCN: 2140.
Conserved type (Archer & Van Wyk in *Taxon* 44: 435. 1995): South Africa. Rhenosterkop, *Schlechter 10574* (PRE; iso- BM, GRA, K, MO, P, S, Z).
Current name: *Cassine peragua* L. subsp. *barbara* (L.) R.H. Archer (Celastraceae).

Cassine capensis Linnaeus, *Mantissa Plantarum Altera*: 220. 1771.
"Habitat ad Cap. b. spei. Dav. Royenus." RCN: 2138.
Lectotype (Archer & Van Wyk in *S. African J. Bot.* 63: 149. 1997): [icon] *"Phillyrea Capensis, folio Celastri"* in Dillenius, Hort. Eltham. 2: 315, t. 236, f. 305. 1732.
Current name: *Cassine peragua* L. subsp. *peragua* (Celastraceae).

Cassine maurocenia Linnaeus, *Species Plantarum* 1: 269. 1753.
"Habitat in Aethiopia." RCN: 2141.
Lectotype (Archer & Van Wyk in *Bothalia* 28: 8. 1998): [icon] *"Frangula sempervirens, folio rigido subrotundo"* in Dillenius, Hort. Eltham. 1: 146, t. 121, f. 147. 1732 (see p. 125).
Current name: *Maurocenia frangula* Mill. (Celastraceae).

Cassine peragua Linnaeus, *Species Plantarum* 1: 268. 1753, *typ. cons.*
"Habitat in Aethiopia, Carolina." RCN: 2139.
Conserved type (Robson in Jarvis in *Taxon* 41: 559. 1992): [icon] *"Phillyrea Capensis, folio Celastri"* in Dillenius, Hort. Eltham. 2: 315, t. 236, f. 305. 1732.
Generitype of *Cassine* Linnaeus, *nom. cons.*
Current name: *Cassine peragua* L. (Celastraceae).
Note: Cassine peragua, with the type designated by Robson, was proposed as conserved type of the genus by Jarvis (in *Taxon* 41: 559. 1992). This was eventually approved by the General Committee (see review of the history of this proposal by Barrie, *l.c.* 55: 795–796. 2006).

Cassytha filiformis Linnaeus, *Species Plantarum* 1: 35. 1753.
"Habitat in India." RCN: 2924.
Lectotype (Imkhanitskaya in *Novosti Sist. Vyssh. Rast.* 11: 208. 1974): *Osbeck s.n.*, Herb. Linn. No. 519.1 (LINN).
Generitype of *Cassytha* Linnaeus.
Current name: *Cassytha filiformis* L. (Lauraceae).
Note: Weber (in *J. Adelaide Bot. Gard.* 3: 229. 1981) designated *Acatsja-valli* Rheede, *Hort. Malab.* 7: 83, t. 44 (1688) as type but this choice is pre-dated by that of Imkhanitskaya.

Casuarina equisetifolia Linnaeus, *Amoenitates Academicae* 4: 143. 1759.
RCN: 7514.
Lectotype (Merrill, *Interpret. Rumph. Herb. Amb.*: 180. 1917): [icon] *"Casuarina Litorea"* in Rumphius, Herb. Amboin. 3: 86, t. 57. 1743 (see p. 249).
Generitype of *Casuarina* Linnaeus.
Current name: *Casuarina equisetifolia* L. (Casuarinaceae).
Note: Much has been written about *Casuarina*, chiefly concerning its date of publication (1759) and the status of *C. equisetifolia* L. (valid from 1759) and "*C. litorea* L." (not validly published; Art. 34.1, Ex. 2.(a)). See discussion by Friis (in *Taxon* 29: 499. 1980) and Fosberg (*l.c.* 30: 218. 1981).

Catananche caerulea Linnaeus, *Species Plantarum* 2: 812. 1753.
"Habitat in G. Narbonensi." RCN: 5918.

Lectotype (designated here by Blackmore): Herb. Clifford: 390, *Catananche* 1 (BM-000646896).
Current name: **Catananche caerulea** L. (Asteraceae).
Note: Alavi (in Jafri & El-Gadi, *Fl. Libya* 107: 324. 1983) indicated both Herb. Linn. 961.1 and 961.2 (LINN) as types. As these are evidently not part of a single gathering, Art. 9.15 does not apply and this is not an effective typification.

Catananche graeca Linnaeus, *Species Plantarum* 2: 813. 1753.
"Habitat in Graeciae maritimis." RCN: 5920.
Lectotype (Turland in Jarvis & Turland in *Taxon* 47: 356. 1998): [icon] *"Scorzonera Graeca saxatilis et maritima, foliis varie laciniatis"* in Tournefort, Rel. Voy. Levant (Paris ed.) 1: 223. 1717.
Current name: **Hymenonema graecum** (L.) DC. (Asteraceae).

Catananche lutea Linnaeus, *Species Plantarum* 2: 812. 1753.
"Habitat in Creta." RCN: 5919.
Lectotype (Alavi in Jafri & El-Gadi, *Fl. Libya* 107: 326. 1983): Herb. Linn. No. 961.3 (LINN).
Generitype of *Catananche* Linnaeus (vide Green, *Prop. Brit. Bot.*: 178. 1929).
Current name: **Catananche lutea** L. (Asteraceae).

Catesbaea spinosa Linnaeus, *Species Plantarum* 1: 109. 1753.
"Habitat in Providentia." RCN: 896.
Lectotype (Dandy, *Sloane Herbarium*: 112. 1958): [icon] *"Frutex Spinosus Buxi foliis, plurimis simul nascentibus; flore tetrapetaloide, pendulo, sordide flavo, tubo longissimo; fructu ovali croceo, semina parva continente"* in Catesby, Nat. Hist. Carolina 2: 100, t. 100. 1743. – Voucher: Herb. Sloane 232: 21 (BM-SL).
Generitype of *Catesbaea* Linnaeus.
Current name: **Catesbaea spinosa** L. (Rubiaceae).

Caturus ramiflorus (N.J. Jacquin) Linnaeus, *Systema Naturae,* ed. 12, 2: 650; *Mantissa Plantarum*: 127. 1767.
"Habitat in Martinica ad ripas." RCN: 7399.
Basionym: *Boehmeria ramiflora* Jacq. (1760).
Lectotype (Berg in Görts-van Rijn, *Fl. Guianas,* ser. A, 11: 126. 1992): [icon] *"Boehmeria ramiflora"* in Jacquin, Select. Stirp. Amer. Hist.: 246, t. 157. 1763 (see p. 137).
Current name: **Boehmeria ramiflora** Jacq. (Urticaceae).

Caturus spiciflorus Linnaeus, *Systema Naturae,* ed. 12, 2: 650; *Mantissa Plantarum*: 127. 1767.
"Habitat in India orient." RCN: 7398.
Lectotype (Radcliffe-Smith in Jarvis & al., *Regnum Veg.* 127: 31. 1993): Herb. Linn. No. 1163.1 (LINN).
Generitype of *Caturus* Linnaeus.
Current name: **Acalypha hispida** Burm. f. (Euphorbiaceae).

Caucalis daucoides Linnaeus, *Species Plantarum* 1: 241. 1753.
"Habitat Monspelii. D. Sauvages." RCN: 1936a.
Lectotype (Fernandes in *Bol. Soc. Brot.,* sér. 2, 41: 398, pl. 1. 1967): Herb. Linn. No. 118.1 (S).
Generitype of *Caucalis* Linnaeus (vide Hitchcock, *Prop. Brit. Bot.*: 139. 1929).
Current name: **Orlaya grandiflora** (L.) Hoffm. (Apiaceae).
Note: There have been difficulties in the application of this name and Heywood (in *Agron. Lusit.* 22: 13. 1960) discussed the various elements and concluded that the name should be rejected as a *nomen ambiguum,* taking up *Orlaya kochii* Heyw. instead. However, no formal proposal has ever been made. Fernandes (in *Bol. Soc. Brot.,* sér. 2, 41: 398. 1967) typified the name on a Linnaean collection in S, identifiable as *O. grandiflora* (L.) Hoffm., into the synonymy of which *C. daucoides* would consequently fall. Greuter

(in *Boissiera* 13: 93. 1967) designated a neotype for the name, which would have made *O. daucoides* (L.) Greuter the correct name for what has been called *O. platycarpos* auctt. However, this neotypification is invalid as original material for the name is in existence (Art. 9.11). Nevertheless, what is clear is that *C. daucoides,* the generitype of *Caucalis,* is identified with the genus *Orlaya* Hoffm. (1814) which it pre-dates. Both generic names are in use and priority would dictate that *Caucalis* should therefore replace *Orlaya,* with *Nigera* Bubani (1899) apparently the next available name for *Caucalis.* Proposing *C. platycarpos* as the conserved type of *Caucalis* could stabilise the application of the two generic names involved.

Caucalis daucoides Linnaeus, *Systema Naturae,* ed. 12, 2: 205. 1767, *nom. illeg.*
["Habitat in Italia, Monspelii."] Sp. Pl. 1: 241 (1753). RCN: 1936b.
Replaced synonym: *Caucalis platycarpos* L. (1753).
Lectotype (Heywood in *Agron. Lusit.* 22: 11. 1960): Herb. Clifford: 91, *Caucalis* 3 (BM-000558249).
Current name: **Caucalis platycarpos** L. (Apiaceae).
Note: Both a replacement name for *C. platycarpos* L. (1753) and a later homonym of *C. daucoides* L. (1753).

Caucalis grandiflora Linnaeus, *Species Plantarum* 1: 240. 1753.
"Habitat in Europa australiori inter segetes." RCN: 1935.
Lectotype (Fernandes in *Bol. Soc. Brot.,* sér. 2, 41: 401. 1967): Herb. Burser VII(2): 54 (UPS).
Current name: **Orlaya grandiflora** (L.) Hoffm. (Apiaceae).

Caucalis latifolia Linnaeus, *Systema Naturae,* ed. 12, 2: 205. 1767.
RCN: 1937.
Lectotype (Reduron & Jarvis in Jarvis & al. in *Taxon* 55: 210. 2006): Herb. Linn. No. 338.7 (LINN).
Current name: **Turgenia latifolia** (L.) Hoffm. (Apiaceae).

Caucalis leptophylla Linnaeus, *Species Plantarum* 1: 242. 1753.
"Habitat in Gallia, Italia." RCN: 1942.
Type not designated.
Original material: Herb. Burser XIV(2): 55 (UPS); [icon] in Colonna, Ekphr.: 96, 97. 1606.
Current name: **Torilis leptophylla** (L.) Rchb. f. (Apiaceae).
Note: There are some difficulties with this name. While usually applied to a species of *Torilis,* the diagnosis suggests a true *Caucalis,* as do the associated Burser material and cited Colonna element. The name may be in need of conservation with a conserved type.

Caucalis mauritanica Linnaeus, *Species Plantarum* 1: 241. 1753.
"Habitat in Mauritania." RCN: 1938.
Type not designated.
Original material: Herb. Linn. No. 338.7 (LINN).
Current name: **Caucalis sp.** (Apiaceae).
Note: The application of this name is uncertain. As there is no original material, and the name appears not to be in use, it may be a candidate for rejection.

Caucalis orientalis Linnaeus, *Species Plantarum* 1: 241. 1753.
"Habitat in Oriente." RCN: 1941.
Lectotype (Watson in Jarvis & al. in *Taxon* 55: 210. 2006): Herb. A. van Royen No. 908.259–1690 (L).
Current name: **Astrodaucus orientalis** (L.) Drude (Apiaceae).

Caucalis platycarpos Linnaeus, *Species Plantarum* 1: 241. 1753.
"Habitat in Italia, Monspelii." RCN: 1939.
Replaced synonym of: *Caucalis daucoides* L. (1767), *nom. illeg.,* non L. (1753).

Lectotype (Heywood in *Agron. Lusit.* 22: 11. 1960): Herb. Clifford: 91, *Caucalis* 3 (BM-000558249).
Current name: ***Caucalis platycarpos*** L. (Apiaceae).
Note: Greuter (in Greuter & Rechinger in *Boissiera* 13: 92. 1967) provides an extensive discussion.

Caucalis pumila Linnaeus, *Systema Naturae,* ed. 10, 2: 955. 1759.
RCN: 1940.
Neotype (Jury & al. in Jarvis & al. in *Taxon* 55: 210. 2006): Spain. "Flora Calpensis. Catalan Bay, 22 May 1912, Ex. Herb. A.H. Wolley-Dod. No. 1136". (BM).
Current name: ***Pseudorlaya pumila*** (L.) Grande (Apiaceae).

Ceanothus africanus Linnaeus, *Species Plantarum* 1: 196. 1753.
"Habitat in Aethiopia." RCN: 1586.
Lectotype (Wijnands, *Bot. Commelins*: 180. 1983): Herb. Linn. No. 264.5 (LINN).
Current name: ***Noltea africana*** (L.) Endl. (Rhamnaceae).

Ceanothus americanus Linnaeus, *Species Plantarum* 1: 195. 1753.
"Habitat in Virginia, Carolina." RCN: 1584.
Lectotype (Wijnands, *Bot. Commelins*: 180. 1983): *Kalm*, Herb. Linn. No. 264.1 (LINN; iso- UPS).
Generitype of *Ceanothus* Linnaeus (vide Hitchcock, *Prop. Brit. Bot.*: 134. 1929).
Current name: ***Ceanothus americanus*** L. (Rhamnaceae).

Ceanothus asiaticus Linnaeus, *Species Plantarum* 1: 196. 1753.
"Habitat in Zeylona." RCN: 1585.
Lectotype (Fawcett & Rendle, *Fl. Jamaica* 5: 70. 1926; Johnston in *Brittonia* 23: 47. 1971): Herb. Hermann 2: 11, No. 98 (BM-000621540).
Current name: ***Colubrina asiatica*** (L.) Brongn. (Rhamnaceae).
Note: Fawcett & Rendle indicated Herb. Hermann material (BM) as type. Although there is material mounted on several pages in volume 2, it appears to have been part of a single gathering. Consequently, theirs is accepted as the first typification (Art. 9.15), with the choice subsequently restricted by Johnston.

Cecropia peltata Linnaeus, *Systema Naturae,* ed. 10, 2: 1286. 1759.
["Habitat in Jamaicae calidioris sylvis."] Sp. Pl., ed. 2, 2: 1450 (1763). RCN: 7356.
Type not designated.
Original material: Herb. Linn. No. 1159.1 (LINN); *Browne*, Herb. Linn. No. 1159.2 (LINN).
Current name: ***Cecropia peltata*** L. (Urticaceae).
Note: Berg (in Görts-van Rijn, *Fl. Guianas*, ser. A, 11: 101. 1992) indicated material in LINN as holotype but this does not distinguish between sheets 1159.1 and 1159.2 (which do not appear to be part of a single gathering, so Art. 9.15 does not apply).

Cedrela mahagoni Linnaeus, *Systema Naturae,* ed. 10, 2: 940. 1759.
RCN: 3030.
Lectotype (Dandy, *Sloane Herbarium*: 112. 1958): [icon] *"Arbor foliis pinnatis, nullo impari Alam claudente, nervo ad latus unum excurrente, fructu anguloso magno, semine alato instar Pinus"* in Catesby, Nat. Hist. Carolina 2: 81, t. 81. 1743.
Current name: ***Swietenia mahagoni*** (L.) Jacq. (Meliaceae).
Note: The type, the Catesby plate, is reproduced in colour by Keay (in *Bot. J. Linn. Soc.* 122(1): frontispiece. 1996).

Cedrela odorata Linnaeus, *Systema Naturae,* ed. 10, 2: 940. 1759.
["Habitat in America meridionali."] Sp. Pl., ed. 2, 1: 289 (1762). RCN: 1623.

Lectotype (Smith in *Fieldiana, Bot.* 29: 298. 1960): [icon] *"Cedrela foliis majoribus pinnatis, floribus laxe racemosis, ligno levi odorato"* in Browne, Civ. Nat. Hist. Jamaica: 158, t. 10, f. 1. 1756.
Current name: ***Cedrela odorata*** L. (Meliaceae).

Celastrus bullatus Linnaeus, *Species Plantarum* 1: 196. 1753.
"Habitat in Virginia." RCN: 1591.
Lectotype (designated here by Reveal): [icon] *"Euonymus Virginianus rotundifolius capsulis coccineis eleganter bullatis"* in Plukenet, Phytographia: t. 28, f. 5. 1691; Almag. Bot.: 139. 1696.
Current name: ***Celastrus scandens*** L. (Celastraceae).

Celastrus buxifolius Linnaeus, *Species Plantarum* 1: 197. 1753.
"Habitat in Aethiopia." RCN: 1594.
Lectotype (designated here by Robson): Herb. Clifford: 72, *Celastrus* 2, sheet A (BM-000558125).
Current name: ***Maytenus heterophylla*** (Eckl. & Zeyh.) N. Robson (Celastraceae).
Note: Sebsebe (in *Symb. Bot. Upsal.* 25(2): 88. 1985) indicated Clifford material as lectotype but did not distinguish between the two sheets there that are associated with this name. As they do not appear to be part of a single gathering, Art. 9.15 does not apply.

Celastrus lucidus Linnaeus, *Systema Naturae,* ed. 12, 2: 181; *Mantissa Plantarum*: 49. 1767.
"Habitat ad Cap. b. spei. D.D. Royen." RCN: 1596.
Lectotype (designated here by Robson): *D. van Royen s.n.*, Herb. Linn. No. 268.8 (LINN).
Current name: ***Maytenus lucida*** (L.) Loes. (Celastraceae).
Note: See discussion by Fuchs (in *Acta Bot. Neerl.* 11: 76. 1962).

Celastrus myrtifolius Linnaeus, *Species Plantarum* 1: 196. 1753.
"Habitat in Virginia, Jamaica." RCN: 1593.
Lectotype (Urban in *Symb. Antill.* 5: 93. 1904): [icon] *"Myrti folio arbor, foliis latis subrotundis, flore albo racemoso"* in Sloane, Voy. Jamaica 2: 79, t. 193, f. 1. 1725.
Current name: ***Prunus myrtifolia*** (L.) Urb. (Rosaceae).

Celastrus pyracanthus Linnaeus, *Species Plantarum* 1: 197. 1753.
"Habitat in Aethiopia." RCN: 1595.
Lectotype (Wijnands, *Bot. Commelins*: 64. 1983): Herb. Linn. No. 268.6 (LINN; iso- S-LINN 97.14).
Current name: ***Putterlickia pyracantha*** (L.) Szyszyl. (Celastraceae).

Celastrus scandens Linnaeus, *Species Plantarum* 1: 196. 1753.
"Habitat in Canada." RCN: 1592.
Lectotype (Reveal in Jarvis & al., *Regnum Veg.* 127: 31. 1993): Herb. Linn. No. 268.2 (LINN; iso- BM).
Generitype of *Celastrus* Linnaeus, *gend. masc. cons.* (vide Hitchcock, *Prop. Brit. Bot.*: 134. 1929).
Current name: ***Celastrus scandens*** L. (Celastraceae).

Celosia argentea Linnaeus, *Species Plantarum* 1: 205. 1753.
"Habitat in America." RCN: 1661.
Lectotype (Townsend in Nasir & Ali, *Fl. W. Pakistan* 71: 5. 1974): Herb. Linn. No. 288.1 (LINN).
Generitype of *Celosia* Linnaeus (vide Hitchcock, *Prop. Brit. Bot.*: 135. 1929).
Current name: ***Celosia argentea*** L. (Amaranthaceae).

Celosia castrensis Linnaeus, *Species Plantarum,* ed. 2, 1: 297. 1762.
"Habitat in India." RCN: 1666.
Type not designated.
Original material: [icon] in Mattioli, Pl. Epit.: 792. 1586; [icon] in Rumphius, Herb. Amboin. 5: 236, t. 84. 1747; [icon] in Boccone,

Mus. Piante Rar. Sicilia: 77, t. 66. 1697; [icon] in Barrelier, Pl. Galliam: 46, t. 1195. 1714.
Current name: **Celosia cristata** L. (Amaranthaceae).

Celosia coccinea Linnaeus, *Species Plantarum*, ed. 2, 1: 297. 1762.
"Habitat in India." RCN: 1665.
Lectotype (Townsend in Bosser & al., *Fl. Mascareignes* 142: 4. 1994): Herb. Linn. No. 288.6 (LINN).
Current name: **Celosia argentea** L. (Amaranthaceae).

Celosia cristata Linnaeus, *Species Plantarum* 1: 205. 1753.
"Habitat in Asia." RCN: 1663.
Type not designated.
Original material: Herb. Clifford: 43, *Celosia* 2, 7 sheets (BM); Herb. Linn. No. 288.6? (LINN); [icon] in Mattioli, Pl. Epit.: 792. 1586.
Current name: **Celosia argentea** L. (Amaranthaceae).
Note: Townsend (in Nasir & Ali, *Fl. W. Pakistan* 71: 5. 1974) indicated 288.4 (LINN) as the holotype but this sheet lacks the *Species Plantarum* number (i.e. "2") and is a post-1753 addition to the collection and not original material for the name. Smith (*Fl. Vitiensis Nova* 2: 285. 1981) stated that the Clifford reference "suggests the suitable lectotype", but there are seven sheets (evidently not from a single gathering) associated with this name in the Clifford herbarium, so this is not an effective choice.

Celosia lanata Linnaeus, *Species Plantarum* 1: 205. 1753.
"Habitat in Zeylona." RCN: 1668.
Lectotype (Townsend in Polhill, *Fl. Trop. E. Africa, Amaranthaceae*: 84. 1985): Herb. Hermann 4: 52, No. 102, left specimen (BM-000628251).
Current name: **Aerva javanica** (Burm. f.) Juss. (Amaranthaceae).

Celosia margaritacea Linnaeus, *Species Plantarum*, ed. 2, 1: 297. 1762.
"Habitat in America." RCN: 1662.
Type not designated.
Original material: Herb. Linn. No. 288.1 (LINN); [icon] in Martyn, Hist. Pl. Rar.: 7, t. 7. 1728.
Current name: **Celosia argentea** L. (Amaranthaceae).

Celosia nodiflora Linnaeus, *Species Plantarum* 1: 205. 1753.
"Habitat in Zeylonia." RCN: 1669.
Lectotype (Townsend in Dassanayake & Fosberg, *Revised Handb. Fl. Ceylon* 1: 7. 1980): Herb. Hermann 1: 2, No. 101 (BM-000621232).
Current name: **Allmania nodiflora** (L.) Wight (Amaranthaceae).

Celosia paniculata Linnaeus, *Species Plantarum* 1: 206. 1753.
"Habitat in America septentrionali." RCN: 1665.
Replaced synonym of: *Iresine celosia* L. (1759), *nom. illeg.*; *Iresine celosioides* L. (1763), *nom. illeg.*
Lectotype (Reveal & Nicolson in *Taxon* 38: 504. 1989): *Clayton 576* (BM-000051634).
Current name: **Iresine rhizomatosa** Standl. (Amaranthaceae).

Celosia trigyna Linnaeus, *Mantissa Plantarum Altera*: 212. 1771.
"Habitat in Senegallia." RCN: 1667.
Neotype (Townsend in *Hooker's Icon. Pl.* 38(2): 30. 1975): Herb. Linn. No. 102.19 (S).
Current name: **Celosia trigyna** L. (Amaranthaceae).
Note: Although Townsend treated material in S as the holotype, there appears to be no original material for this name so his choice is accepted as a neotype (Art. 9.8).

Celsia cretica Linnaeus, *Systema Vegetabilium*, ed. 13: 470. 1774.
RCN: 4498.
Type not designated.
Original material: *Latourette*, Herb. Linn. No. 774.3 (LINN); Herb. Linn. No. 774.4 (LINN); Herb. Linn. No. 774.5 (LINN).
Current name: **Verbascum creticum** (L.) Cav. (Scrophulariaceae).

Celsia orientalis Linnaeus, *Species Plantarum* 2: 621. 1753.
"Habitat in Cappodocia, Armenia." RCN: 4496.
Lectotype (Sutton in Jarvis & al., *Regnum Veg.* 127: 31. 1993): Herb. Linn. No. 774.1 (LINN).
Generitype of *Celsia* Linnaeus.
Current name: **Celsia orientalis** L. (Scrophulariaceae).

Celtis australis Linnaeus, *Species Plantarum* 2: 1043. 1753.
"Habitat in Europa australi & Africa citeriore." RCN: 7644.

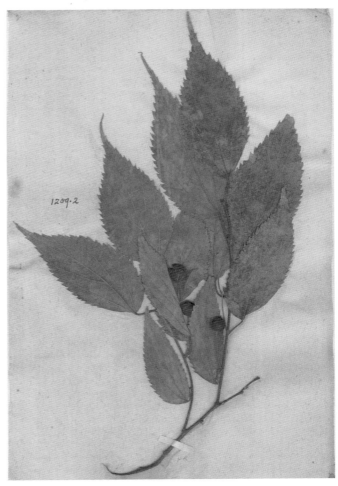

Lectotype (Zieliński in Rechinger, *Fl. Iranica* 142: 12. 1979): Herb. Linn. No. 1209.2 (LINN).
Generitype of *Celtis* Linnaeus (vide Green, *Prop. Brit. Bot.*: 193. 1929).
Current name: **Celtis australis** L. (Ulmaceae).

Celtis occidentalis Linnaeus, *Species Plantarum* 2: 1044. 1753.
"Habitat in Virginia." RCN: 7645.
Lectotype (Fernald & Schubert in *Rhodora* 50: 158, pl. 1097. 1948): *Kalm*, Herb. Linn. No. 1209.4 (LINN).
Current name: **Celtis occidentalis** L. (Ulmaceae).

Celtis orientalis Linnaeus, *Species Plantarum* 2: 1044. 1753.
"Habitat in Indiis." RCN: 7646.
Lectotype (Soepadmo & Edi Hamli in Soepadmo, *Tree Fl. Sabah Sarawak* 2: 399. 1996): Herb. Hermann 2: 2; 4: 71, No. 369 (BM).
Current name: ***Trema orientalis*** (L.) Blume (Ulmaceae).
Note: Polhill (in *Kew Bull.* 19: 143. 1964), and some later authors, have indicated material in Herb. Hermann 2: 2; 4: 71 (BM) as syntypes but as the use of this term implies no intention to indicate a single nomenclatural type (unlike the use of holotype, lectotype or neotype), this is not regarded as a correctable error. Soepadmo & Edi Hamli, however, indicated the same material simply as "type". Although there is material in two volumes, it appears to have been part of a single gathering, so their statement is accepted as the first typification (Art. 9.15).

Cenchrus capitatus Linnaeus, *Species Plantarum* 2: 1049. 1753.
"Habitat in G. Narbonensi, Italia." RCN: 7584.
Lectotype (Meikle, *Fl. Cyprus* 2: 1729. 1985): *Löfling 105*, Herb. Linn. No. 1217.6 (LINN).
Current name: ***Echinaria capitata*** (L.) Desf. (Poaceae).
Note: Although Kerguélen (in *Lejeunia*, n.s., 75: 137. 1975) stated "Type: ...LINN", this is not accepted as a formal typification, for the reasons explained by Cafferty & al. (in *Taxon* 49: 240. 2000).

Cenchrus ciliaris Linnaeus, *Mantissa Plantarum Altera*: 302. 1771.
"Habitat ad Cap. b. spei margines agrorum et in dunis. Koenig." RCN: 7587.
Lectotype (Clayton & Renvoize in Polhill, *Fl. Trop. E. Africa, Gramineae* 3: 691. 1982): *König s.n.*, Herb. Linn. No. 1217.9 (LINN).
Current name: ***Cenchrus ciliaris*** L. (Poaceae).
Note: Although Kerguélen (in *Lejeunia*, n.s., 75: 119. 1975) stated "Type: ...LINN", this is not accepted as a formal typification, for the reasons explained by Cafferty & al. (in *Taxon* 49: 240. 2000).

Cenchrus echinatus Linnaeus, *Species Plantarum* 2: 1050. 1753.
"Habitat in Jamaica, Curassao." RCN: 7585.
Lectotype (Veldkamp in Jarvis & al., *Regnum Veg.* 127: 31. 1993): Herb. A. van Royen No. 912.356–116 (L).
Generitype of *Cenchrus* Linnaeus (vide Green, *Prop. Brit. Bot.*: 193. 1929).
Current name: ***Cenchrus echinatus*** L. (Poaceae).
Note: Hitchcock (in *Contr. U. S. Natl. Herb.* 12: 127. 1908) and a number of later authors treated 1217.7 (LINN) as the type but this collection is a post-1753 addition to the herbarium and ineligible as type. Clayton & Renvoize (in Polhill, *Fl. Trop. E. Africa, Gramineae* 3: 695. 1982) indicated a Dickinson collection from Bermuda (Herb. Sloane, BM) as a syntype, but it was not seen by Linnaeus and cannot be original material for the name.

Cenchrus frutescens Linnaeus, *Species Plantarum* 2: 1050. 1753.
"Habitat in America." [recte "Armenia" in Sp. Pl., ed. 2, 2: 1489. 1763] RCN: 7589.
Type not designated.
Original material: [icon] in Alpino, Pl. Exot.: 105, 104. 1627.
Current name: ***Phragmites australis*** (Cav.) Trin. ex Steud. (Poaceae).
Note: Turland (in *Taxon* 44: 419. 1995) proposed the name for rejection but Greuter & Scholz (in *Taxon* 45: 522. 1996) described the Cretan plant figured by Alpino as a new species, *Phragmites frutescens* Scholz, thereby blocking the possibility of a transfer of the Linnaean epithet, and making the proposal unnecessary. The Committee for Spermatophyta (in *Taxon* 47: 863. 1998) therefore did not recommend acceptance of the proposal.

Cenchrus granularis Linnaeus, *Mantissa Plantarum Altera*: 575. 1771.
"Habitat in India orientali." RCN: 7588.
Lectotype (Clayton & Renvoize in Polhill, *Fl. Trop. E. Africa, Gramineae* 3: 849. 1982): Herb. Linn. No. 1217.12 (LINN).
Current name: ***Hackelochloa granularis*** (L.) Kuntze (Poaceae).

Cenchrus lappaceus Linnaeus, *Species Plantarum*, ed. 2, 2: 1488. 1763.
"Habitat in India." RCN: 7582.
Neotype (Monod de Froideville in *Blumea* 19: 59. 1971): Herb. Linn. No. 1212.15 (LINN; iso- BM).
Current name: ***Centotheca latifolia*** (Osbeck) Trin. (Poaceae).
Note: The material treated as the type by Monod de Froideville is unannotated by Linnaeus and there is no clear link with this binomial. However, in the absence of any relevant original material, the collection is accepted as a neotype (Art. 9.8). Fragmentary material in BM (sheet 000592761), annotated by J.E. Smith as derived from LINN, is a probable iso-neotype.

Cenchrus muricatus Linnaeus, *Mantissa Plantarum Altera*: 302. 1771.
"Habitat in India orientali. Koenig." RCN: 7583.
Neotype (Renvoize in Cafferty & al. in *Taxon* 49: 249. 2000): India. Madras, Tamil Nadu, South Arcot, Chidambarum, Kille, Anuvampattu, Venugopal in RHT No. 21360 (K; iso- RHT).
Current name: ***Trachys muricata*** (L.) Trin. (Poaceae).
Note: Gould (in Dassanayake & al., *Revised Handb. Fl. Ceylon* 8: 441. 1994) stated "Type from India. Koenig", but indicated no specimen location. Herb. Linn. No. 1217.4 is annotated "Cenchrus muricatus" by Linnaeus, and is also a König collection. However, it is dated "1777", post-dating publication of the name for which it therefore cannot be original material. In the absence of any extant original material, a neotype was chosen by Renvoize.

Cenchrus racemosus Linnaeus, *Species Plantarum* 2: 1049. 1753.
"Habitat in Europae australioris maritimis." RCN: 7581.
Lectotype (Scholz in Cafferty & al. in *Taxon* 49: 249. 2000): Herb. Burser I: 5 (UPS).
Current name: ***Tragus racemosus*** (L.) All. (Poaceae).
Note: Sherif & Siddiqi (in Jafri & El-Gadi, *Fl. Libya* 145: 336. 1988) stated: "Type: 1217/183 (LINN)", presumably in error for "1217.1–3". However, none of these three sheets bears original material for this name.

Cenchrus tribuloides Linnaeus, *Species Plantarum* 2: 1050. 1753.
"Habitat in Virginiae maritimis." RCN: 7586.
Lectotype (Hitchcock in *Contr. U. S. Natl. Herb.* 12: 127. 1908): *Kalm*, Herb. Linn. No. 1217.8 (LINN; iso- UPS-KALM 27).
Current name: ***Cenchrus tribuloides*** L. (Poaceae).
Note: Baum (in *Canad. J. Bot.* 45: 1851. 1967) attempted to reject Hitchcock's choice of a Kalm specimen as type, arguing that it was ineligible because Linnaeus had not cited it explicitly. However, Linnaeus commonly omitted explicit reference to Kalm when North American taxa were also known to him from other (e.g. Clayton) collections, and the absence of a reference does not prevent appropriately annotated Kalm collections from being original material for such names.

Centaurea acaulis Linnaeus, *Species Plantarum* 2: 914. 1753.
"Habitat in Arabia." RCN: 6602.
Lectotype (Greuter & Aghababian in Greuter & Raab-Straube in *Willdenowia* 35: 228. 2005): [icon] *"Jacea &c. sive Toffs Arabum"* in Shaw, Cat. Pl. Afr. As.: 42, f. 342. 1738. – Epitype (Greuter & Aghababian in Greuter & Raab-Straube in *Willdenowia* 35: 229.

2005): Tunisia. Governorat de Sililiana: Dorsale Tunisienne, Forêt de Kesra, track no. 764 between Kesra and Djebel Balloula, ca. 3km NE Kesra, 1,030–1,100m, 18 May 1994, *Vogt & Oberprieler 7816* (B).
Current name: ***Centaurea acaulis*** L. (Asteraceae).

Centaurea aegyptiaca Linnaeus, *Systema Naturae,* ed. 12, 2: 574; *Mantissa Plantarum*: 118. 1767.
"Habitat in Aegypto. Turra." RCN: 6623.
Type not designated.
Original material: Herb. Linn. No. 1030.53 (LINN).
Current name: ***Centaurea aegyptiaca*** L. (Asteraceae).

Centaurea alba Linnaeus, *Species Plantarum* 2: 914. 1753.
"Habitat in Hispania." RCN: 6608.
Lectotype (Talavera in *Lagascalia* 12: 247. 1984): Herb. Linn. No. 1030.37 (LINN).
Current name: ***Centaurea alba*** L. (Asteraceae).
Note: Lacaita (in *Nuovo Giorn. Bot. Ital.*, n.s., 30: 203. 1923) discussed this taxon in detail, and noted 1030.37 LINN which he concluded to have come from Löfling (although it is not annotated as such), from the Madrid region. However, like López González (in *Anales Jard. Bot. Madrid* 37: 98. 1980), he did not treat it as the type.

Centaurea alpina Linnaeus, *Species Plantarum* 2: 910. 1753.
"Habitat in Baldo." RCN: 6582.
Type not designated.
Original material: Herb. Clifford: 421, *Centaurea* 6 (BM); [icon] in Bauhin, Prodr. Theatri Bot.: 56. 1620; [icon] in Cornut, Canad. Pl. Hist.: 69, 70. 1635; [icon] in Morison, Pl. Hist. Univ. 3: 132, s. 7, t. 25, f. 5. 1699.
Current name: ***Centaurea alpina*** L. (Asteraceae).

Centaurea amara Linnaeus, *Species Plantarum,* ed. 2, 2: 1292. 1763.
"Habitat in Italia, Monspelii." RCN: 6607.
Lectotype (Barbo & al. in Jarvis & Turland in *Taxon* 47: 357. 1998): [icon] *"Cyanus repens"* in Plantin, Pl. Stirp. Icon.: 548. 1581. – Epitype (Barbo & al. in Jarvis & Turland in *Taxon* 47: 357. 1998): Italy. Bononia in collibus di Zolla pradosa in rure meo, Sep 1852, *Bertoloni s.n.* (BOLO).
Current name: ***Centaurea amara*** L. subsp. ***amara*** (Asteraceae).

Centaurea argentea Linnaeus, *Species Plantarum* 2: 912. 1753.
"Habitat in Creta." RCN: 6597.
Lectotype (Turland in Jarvis & Turland in *Taxon* 47: 357. 1998): Herb. Clifford: 422, *Centaurea* 14 (BM-000647265).
Current name: ***Centaurea argentea*** L. (Asteraceae).
Note: Wijnands & Heniger (in *Bot. J. Linn. Soc.* 106: 136, f. 3. 1991) provide a photograph of the collection subsequently designated as the lectotype.

Centaurea aspera Linnaeus, *Species Plantarum* 2: 916. 1753.
"Habitat Monspelii, inque Hetruria, Lusitania." RCN: 6620.
Type not designated.
Original material: [icon] in Bauhin & Cherler, Hist. Pl. Univ. 3(1): 33. 1651.
Current name: ***Centaurea aspera*** L. subsp. ***aspera*** (Asteraceae).

Centaurea babylonica (Linnaeus) Linnaeus, *Mantissa Plantarum Altera*: 460. 1771.
["Habitat in Oriente."] Sp. Pl., ed. 2, 2: 1149 (1763). RCN: 6611.
Basionym: *Serratula babylonica* L. (1759).
Type not designated.
Original material: as basionym.
Current name: ***Centaurea babylonica*** (L.) L. (Asteraceae).

Centaurea behen Linnaeus, *Species Plantarum* 2: 914. 1753.
"Habitat in Asia minore, Libano." RCN: 6604.
Type not designated.
Original material: [icon] in Bauhin & Cherler, Hist. Pl. Univ. 3(1): 36, 37. 1651; [icon] in Rauwolf, Aigent. Beschr. Morgenl.: 288, t. 288. 1583.
Current name: ***Centaurea behen*** L. (Asteraceae).

Centaurea benedicta (Linnaeus) Linnaeus, *Species Plantarum,* ed. 2, 2: 1296. 1763.
"Habitat in Chio, Lemno, Hispania ad versuras." RCN: 6621.
Basionym: *Cnicus benedictus* L. (1753).
Lectotype (Jeffrey in *Kew Bull.* 22: 138. 1968): Herb. Clifford: 394, *Cnicus* 1 (BM-000646941).
Current name: ***Centaurea benedicta*** (L.) L. (Asteraceae).

Centaurea calcitrapa Linnaeus, *Species Plantarum* 2: 917. 1753.
"Habitat in Helvetia, Anglia & Europa australiori secus vias." RCN: 6624.
Lectotype (Jeffrey in *Kew Bull.* 22: 137. 1968): Herb. Linn. No. 1030.55 (LINN).
Current name: ***Centaurea calcitrapa*** L. (Asteraceae).

Centaurea calcitrapoides Linnaeus, *Centuria I Plantarum*: 29. 1755.
"Habitat Monspelii, & in Palaestina. D. Hasselquist." RCN: 6625.
Type not designated.
Original material: *Hasselquist*, Herb. Linn. No. 1030.57 (LINN).
Current name: ***Centaurea calcitrapoides*** L. (Asteraceae).

Centaurea capillata Linnaeus, *Species Plantarum* 2: 910. 1753.
"Habitat in Sibiria. Gmelinus." RCN: 6585.
Type not designated.
Original material: Herb. Linn. No. 1030.8 (LINN); [icon] in Gmelin, Fl. Sibirica 2: 98, t. 43. 1752; [icon] in Haller in Comment. Soc. Regiae Sci. Gott. 1: 202, t. 6. 1752.
Note: Greuter & al. (in *Taxon* 50: 1204. 2002) note that this name "has never been used in recent times".

Centaurea centaurium Linnaeus, *Species Plantarum* 2: 910. 1753.
"Habitat in Alpibus Gargano, Baldo, Tataria." RCN: 6583.
Lectotype (Dittrich in Jarvis & al., *Regnum Veg.* 127: 31. 1993): Herb. Clifford: 421, *Centaurea* 7 (BM-000647256).
Current name: ***Rhaponticoides centaurium*** (L.) M.V. Agad. & Greuter (Asteraceae).
Note: In order to prevent *Cnicus* L. from becoming the correct name for *Centaurea* L., *sensu stricto*, Greuter & al. (in *Taxon* 50: 1201. 2002) successfully proposed the conservation of *Centaurea* with *C. paniculata* L. as its conserved type, in place of *C. centaurium*.

Centaurea centauroides Linnaeus, *Species Plantarum* 2: 918. 1753.
"Habitat in Italia." RCN: 6629.
Lectotype (designated here by Baldini): [icon] *"Iacea laevis maxima centauroides lutea Apula"* in Colonna, Ekphr.: 33, 35. 1606.
Current name: ***Centaurea centauroides*** L. (Asteraceae).

Centaurea cichoracea Linnaeus, *Systema Naturae,* ed. 10, 2: 1231. 1759.
["Habitat in monte argentario Italiae."] Sp. Pl. ed. 2, 2: 1299 (1763). RCN: 6634.
Neotype (Baldini in Jarvis & Turland in *Taxon* 47: 357. 1998): Italy. Toscana (GR), M.te Argentario, Salenda al Convento dei Padri Passionisti, 26 Jun 1991, *R.M. Baldini & Z. Abrahao da Silva, s.n.* (FI).
Current name: ***Klasea flavescens*** (L.) Holub subsp. ***cichoracea*** (L.) Greuter & Wagenitz (Asteraceae).

Note: Jarvis (in *Museol. Sci.* 9: 167–168, f. 3, 4. 1983) reproduced an illustration by Tilli that, while omitted from the protologue, was cited in synonymy by Linnaeus in 1763.

Centaurea cineraria Linnaeus, *Species Plantarum* 2: 912. 1753.
"Habitat in Italia." RCN: 6596.
Lectotype (Cela Renzoni & Viegi in *Atti Soc. Tosc. Sci. Nat. Mem.,* ser. B, 89: 105. 1983 [1982]): Herb. Linn. No. 1030.22 (LINN).
Current name: ***Centaurea cineraria*** L. (Asteraceae).

Centaurea collina Linnaeus, *Species Plantarum* 2: 918. 1753.
"Habitat in Italia, Hispania." RCN: 6631.
Lectotype (Jeanmonod & al. in Jeanmonod, *Compl. Prodr. Fl. Corse, Asteraceae II*: 145. 2004): Herb. Burser XV(2): 35 (UPS).
Current name: ***Centaurea collina*** L. (Asteraceae).

Centaurea conifera Linnaeus, *Species Plantarum* 2: 915. 1753.
"Habitat Monspelii in saxosis glareosis." RCN: 6613.
Lectotype (Jeanmonod & al. in Jeanmonod, *Compl. Prodr. Fl. Corse, Asteraceae II*: 209. 2004): Herb. Linn. No. 1030.43 (LINN).
Current name: ***Rhaponticum coniferum*** (L.) Greuter (Asteraceae).

Centaurea crocodylium Linnaeus, *Species Plantarum* 2: 919. 1753.
"Habitat in Syria." RCN: 6639.
Type not designated.
Original material: Herb. Linn. No. 1070.73 (LINN); [icon] in Barrelier, Pl. Galliam: 83, t. 503. 1714.
Current name: ***Centaurea crocodylium*** L. (Asteraceae).

Centaurea crupina Linnaeus, *Species Plantarum* 2: 909. 1753.
"Habitat in Hetruria, G. Narbonensi." RCN: 6578.
Lectotype (Jeanmonod & al. in Jeanmonod, *Compl. Prodr. Fl. Corse, Asteraceae II*: 196. 2004): Herb. Clifford: 420, *Centaurea* 1 (BM).
Current name: ***Crupina vulgaris*** Cass. (Asteraceae).

Centaurea cyanus Linnaeus, *Species Plantarum* 2: 911. 1753.
"Habitat inter Europae segetes biennes." RCN: 6592.
Lectotype (Wagenitz in Rechinger, *Fl. Iranica* 139b: 418. 1980): Herb. Linn. No. 1030.16 (LINN).
Current name: ***Cyanus segetum*** Hill (Asteraceae).
Note: Jeffrey (in *Kew Bull.* 22: 137. 1968) designated material ("200") in the Clifford herbarium (BM) as lectotype, but there are three sheets associated with species number 20 (Herb. Clifford: 422, *Centaurea* 20 [2 sheets] and 20 δ – 1 sheet). They are not part of a single gathering so Art. 9.15 does not apply, and Wagenitz's appears to be the first explicit type choice.

Centaurea eriophora Linnaeus, *Species Plantarum* 2: 916. 1753.
"Habitat in Lusitania." RCN: 6622.
Type not designated.
Original material: Herb. Clifford: 423, *Centaurea* 27 (BM); Herb. Linn. No. 1030.52 (LINN).
Current name: ***Centaurea eriophora*** L. (Asteraceae).

Centaurea erucifolia Linnaeus, *Species Plantarum* 2: 909. 1753.
"Habitat – – –" RCN: 6580.
Type not designated.
Original material: none traced.
Current name: ***Serratula erucifolia*** (L.) Druce (Asteraceae).

Centaurea fruticosa Linnaeus, *Systema Naturae,* ed. 10, 2: 1229. 1759.
["Habitat in Creta, Oriente. Gerard."] Sp. Pl. ed. 2, 2: 1286 (1763). RCN: 6081.
Basionym of: *Staehelina fruticosa* (L.) L. (1767).

Lectotype (Dittrich in *Boissiera* 51: 75. 1996): *Gérard 11*, Herb. Linn. No. 981.4 (LINN).
Current name: ***Hirtellina fruticosa*** (L.) Dittrich (Asteraceae).

Centaurea galactites Linnaeus, *Species Plantarum* 2: 919. 1753.
"Habitat in Europa australi." RCN: 6642.
Lectotype (Turland in Jarvis & Turland in *Taxon* 47: 357. 1998): Herb. Burser XXI: 42 (UPS).
Current name: ***Galactites tomentosa*** Moench (Asteraceae).

Centaurea glastifolia Linnaeus, *Species Plantarum* 2: 915. 1753.
"Habitat in Oriente, Sibiria." RCN: 6612.
Lectotype (Wagenitz in Jarvis & Turland in *Taxon* 47: 357. 1998): Herb. Clifford: 421, *Centaurea* 8, sheet A (BM-000647258).
Current name: ***Chartolepis glastifolia*** (L.) Cass. (Asteraceae).
Note: Wagenitz (in Davis, *Fl. Turkey* 5: 523. 1975; in Rechinger, *Fl. Iranica* 139b: 353. 1980) and Wijnands (*Bot. Commelins*: 71. 1983) indicated Clifford material as the type but did not distinguish between the three sheets associated with Herb. Clifford: 421, *Centaurea* 8 (BM). The material is not part of a single gathering so Art. 9.15 does not apply, but Wagenitz subsequently designated one of the three as lectotype.

Centaurea isnardii Linnaeus, *Species Plantarum* 2: 916. 1753.
"Habitat in Europa australi?" RCN: 6618.
Type not designated.
Original material: [icon] in Isnard in *Mém. Acad. Roy. Sci. Paris* 1719: 164, t. 9. 1719 (see p. 119).
Current name: ***Centaurea aspera*** L. subsp. *aspera* (Asteraceae).

Centaurea jacea Linnaeus, *Species Plantarum* 2: 914. 1753.
"Habitat in Europa septentrionali." RCN: 6606.
Lectotype (Marsden-Jones & Turrill, *Brit. Knapweeds*: 14, pl. 2. 1954): Herb. Linn. No. 1030.36 (LINN).
Current name: ***Centaurea jacea*** L. (Asteraceae).
Note: Barbo & al. (in *Taxon* 47: 356. 1998) chose a Clifford sheet as type, unaware of the earlier choice made by Marsden-Jones & Turrill.

Centaurea linifolia Linnaeus, *Systema Naturae,* ed. 12, 2: 572; *Mantissa Plantarum*: 117. 1767.
"Habitat in Hispania, Italia." RCN: 6587.
Lectotype (designated here by Baldini): *Scopoli 100*, Herb. Linn. No. 1030.10 (LINN).
Current name: ***Centaurea linifolia*** L. (Asteraceae).

Centaurea lippii Linnaeus, *Species Plantarum* 2: 910. 1753.
"Habitat in Aegypto inter Alexandriam & Rosette." RCN: 6581.
Type not designated.
Original material: [icon] in Isnard in *Mém. Acad. Roy. Sci. Paris* 1719: 169, t. 10. 1719.
Current name: ***Volutaria lippii*** (L.) Cass. ex Maire (Asteraceae).
Note: Although Jeffrey (in *Kew Bull.* 22: 133. 1968) indicated Herb. Linn. 1030.4 (LINN) as the holotype, the sheet is not annotated with the *Species Plantarum* number (i.e. "4"), was a later addition to the herbarium and is not original material for the name. With the existence of other original material (the Isnard illustration), Jeffrey's statement cannot be treated as correctable to a neotypification (Art. 9.8).

Centaurea melitensis Linnaeus, *Species Plantarum* 2: 917. 1753.
"Habitat in Melita." RCN: 6627.
Lectotype (Dillon in *Fieldiana, Bot.,* n.s., 10: 2. 1982): Herb. Linn. No. 1030.62 (LINN).
Current name: ***Centaurea melitensis*** L. (Asteraceae).

Centaurea montana Linnaeus, *Species Plantarum* 2: 911. 1753.
"Habitat in Alpibus Helveticis." RCN: 6591.
Type not designated.
Original material: Herb. A. van Royen No. 900.193–77 (L); Herb.
Burser XV(2): 56 (UPS); Herb. Clifford: 422, *Centaurea* 19, 2
sheets (BM); Herb. Linn. No. 1030.15 (LINN); Herb.
Burser XV(2): 29, syntype (UPS); [icon] in Plantin, Pl. Stirp. Icon.:
548. 1581; [icon] in Boccone, Mus. Piante Rar. Sicilia: 20, t. 2.
1697.
Current name: ***Centaurea montana*** L. (Asteraceae).

Centaurea moschata Linnaeus, *Species Plantarum* 2: 909. 1753.
"Habitat in Tataria." RCN: 6579.
Lectotype (Gabrielian & Jarvis in *Taxon* 45: 214. 1996): [icon]
"Cyanus Orientalis foliis magis dissectis flo. rubro et albo" in Morison,
Pl. Hist. Univ. 3: 135, s. 7, t. 25, f. 5. 1699.
Current name: ***Amberboa moschata*** (L.) DC. (Asteraceae).

Centaurea moschata Linnaeus var. **amberboi** Linnaeus, *Species
Plantarum* 2: 909. 1753.
"Habitat in Tataria." RCN: 6579.
Lectotype (Gabrielian & Jarvis in *Taxon* 45: 215. 1996): [icon]
"Cyanus Orientalis foliis minus dissectis flore luteo" in Morison, Pl.
Hist. Univ. 3: 135, s. 7, t. 25, f. 9. 1699.
Current name: ***Amberboa amberboi*** (L.) Tzvelev (Asteraceae).

Centaurea muricata Linnaeus, *Species Plantarum* 2: 918. 1753.
"Habitat in Hispania." RCN: 6635.
Type not designated.
Original material: Herb. Burser XV(2): 38 (UPS); [icon] in Dodoëns,
Stirp. Hist. Pempt., ed. 2: 251. 1616.
Current name: ***Volutaria muricata*** (L.) Maire (Asteraceae).

Centaurea napifolia Linnaeus, *Species Plantarum* 2: 916. 1753.
"Habitat in Creta." RCN: 6619.
Lectotype (Jeanmonod & al. in Jeanmonod, *Compl. Prodr. Fl. Corse,
Asteraceae II*: 155. 2004): Herb. Linn. No. 1030.46 (LINN).
Current name: ***Centaurea napifolia*** L. (Asteraceae).

Centaurea nigra Linnaeus, *Species Plantarum* 2: 911. 1753.
"Habitat in Anglia, Helvetia, Austria." RCN: 6589.
Lectotype (Marsden-Jones & Turrill, *Brit. Knapweeds*: 13, pl. 4. 1954):
Herb. Linn. No. 1030.13 (LINN).
Current name: ***Centaurea nigra*** L. (Asteraceae).

Centaurea nudicaulis Linnaeus, *Systema Naturae*, ed. 10, 2: 1232.
1759.
["Habitat in Italia, rupe victoriae Galloprovinciae."] Sp. Pl. ed. 2, 2:
1300 (1763). RCN: 6638.
Type not designated.
Original material: Herb. Linn. No. 1030.72 (LINN).
Current name: ***Klasea nudicaulis*** (L.) Fourr. (Asteraceae).
Note: Cantó (in *Lazaroa* 6: 23. 1984) designated a Barrelier figure,
cited by Linnaeus in *Species Plantarum*, ed. 2, 2: 1300 (1763) but
not in the protologue in 1759, as type. It is consequently not an
original element for the name and, as original material appears to
exist (1030.72 LINN), Cantó's choice is not effective.

Centaurea orientalis Linnaeus, *Species Plantarum* 2: 913. 1753.
"Habitat in Sibiria." RCN: 6603.
Type not designated.
Original material: Herb. Linn. No. 1030.33 (H); *Gerber*, Herb. Linn.
No. 1030.33 (LINN); [icon] in Haller in Philos. Trans. 43(472):
94, t. 4. 1744.
Current name: ***Centaurea orientalis*** L. (Asteraceae).

Centaurea paniculata Linnaeus, *Species Plantarum* 2: 912. 1753, *typ.
cons.*
"Habitat in G. Narbonensi, Austria, Hispania, Verona, Sibiria." RCN:
6593.
Lectotype (Greuter & al. in *Taxon* 50: 1205. 2002 [2001]): [icon]
"Centaurii majoris species tenuifolia" in Bauhin & Cherler, Hist. Pl.
Univ. 3(1): 31. 1651. – Epitype (Greuter & al. in *Taxon* 50: 1205.
2002 [2001]): France. Rhône, Pommiers, sommet du mont de
Buisante, alt. 350m, 15 Aug 1882, C. Michaud in Magnier, Flora
Selecta Exsiccata No. 320 (B; iso- widely distributed).
Generitype of *Centaurea* Linnaeus, *nom. cons.*
Current name: ***Centaurea paniculata*** L. (Asteraceae).

Centaurea pectinata Linnaeus, *Species Plantarum*, ed. 2, 2: 1287.
1763.
"Habitat in Gallia Narbonensi, Galloprovincia." RCN: 6588.
Type not designated.
Original material: *Magnol*, Herb. Linn. No. 1030.12 (LINN); Herb.
Burser XV(2): 41 (UPS); Herb. Burser XV(2): 42 (UPS); Herb.
Linn. No. 1030.11 (LINN); [icon] in Bauhin & Cherler, Hist. Pl.
Univ. 3(1): 29. 1651; [icon] in Bauhin, Prodr. Theatri Bot.: 128.
1620.
Current name: ***Centaurea pectinata*** L. (Asteraceae).

Centaurea peregrina Linnaeus, *Species Plantarum* 2: 918. 1753.
"Habitat in Europa australi." RCN: 6636.
Type not designated.
Original material: Herb. Clifford: 423, *Centaurea* 26, 2 sheets (BM).
Current name: ***Centaurea peregrina*** L. (Asteraceae).

Centaurea phrygia Linnaeus, *Species Plantarum* 2: 910. 1753.
"Habitat in Helvetia, Austria, Finlandia." RCN: 6584.
Type not designated.
Original material: Herb. Linn. No. 1030.7 (LINN); Herb. Burser
XV(2): 30 (UPS); Herb. Burser XV(2): 31 (UPS); Herb. Clifford:
422, *Centaurea* 12 (BM); Herb. Burser XV(2): 32 (UPS); [icon] in
Clusius, Rar. Pl. Hist. 2: 6, 7. 1601.
Current name: ***Centaurea phrygia*** L. (Asteraceae).

Centaurea pullata Linnaeus, *Species Plantarum* 2: 911. 1753.
"Habitat in G. Narbonensi, Hispania." RCN: 6590.
Lectotype (Talavera in *Lagascalia* 12: 272. 1984): Herb. Linn. No.
1030.14 (LINN).
Current name: ***Centaurea pullata*** L. (Asteraceae).

Centaurea pumilio Linnaeus, *Centuria I Plantarum*: 30. 1755, *nom.
& orth. cons.*
"Habitat in Aegypto. D. Hasselquist." RCN: 6640.
Conserved type (Turland in *Taxon* 44: 643. 1995): Egypt. Alexandria,
Sidi-Gaber, 8 Apr 1908, *Bornmüller 10781* (B).
Current name: ***Centaurea pumilio*** L. (Asteraceae).
Note: Turland (in *Taxon* 44: 643. 1995) proposed a conserved
type (and spelling for the epithet) for *C. pumilio* (variously
spelled "pumilis", "pumilio" and "pumila" by Linnaeus),
subsequently approved by the Committee for Spermatophyta (in
Taxon 47: 867. 1998) and the General Committee (in *Taxon* 48:
376. 1999).

Centaurea radiata Linnaeus, *Systema Naturae*, ed. 12, 2: 575. 1767.
RCN: 6637.
Replaced synonym: *Xeranthemum erucifolium* L. (1753).
Type not designated.
Original material: as replaced synonym.
Current name: ***Klasea erucifolia*** (L.) Greuter & Wagenitz
(Asteraceae).

Centaurea ragusina Linnaeus, *Species Plantarum* 2: 912. 1753.
"Habitat in Creta, Epidauro." RCN: 6595.
Lectotype (Turland in Jarvis & Turland in *Taxon* 47: 357. 1998):
    Herb. Clifford: 422, *Centaurea* 17 (BM-000647268).
Current name: ***Centaurea ragusina*** L. (Asteraceae).

Centaurea repens Linnaeus, *Species Plantarum,* ed. 2, 2: 1293. 1763.
"Habitat in Oriente." RCN: 6605.
Type not designated.
Original material: Herb. Linn. No. 1030.34 (LINN).
Current name: ***Acroptilon repens*** (L.) DC. (Asteraceae).

Centaurea rhapontica Linnaeus, *Species Plantarum* 2: 915. 1753.
"Habitat in Alpibus Helveticis, Veronae." RCN: 6610.
Lectotype (Dittrich in *Candollea* 39: 49. 1984): Herb. Clifford: 421,
    Centaurea 9 (BM-000647261).
Current name: ***Rhaponticum scariosum*** Lam. subsp. ***rhaponticum***
    (L.) Greuter (Asteraceae).
Note: Greuter (in Greuter & Raab-Straube in *Willdenowia* 35:
    237–238. 2005) discusses both the name and the form of the
    specific epithet.

Centaurea romana Linnaeus, *Species Plantarum* 2: 916. 1753.
"Habitat in Campania Romana." RCN: 6616.
Lectotype (designated here by Baldini): Herb. Clifford: 423, *Centaurea*
    23 (BM).
Current name: ***Centaurea napifolia*** L. (Asteraceae).

Centaurea rupestris Linnaeus, *Species Plantarum,* ed. 2, 2: 1298.
    1763.
"Habitat in Italia." RCN: 6630.
Lectotype (designated here by Baldini): [icon] *"Iacea montana lutea
    minima tenuifolia"* in Colonna, Ekphr.: 35. 1606.
Current name: ***Centaurea rupestris*** L. (Asteraceae).

Centaurea salmantica Linnaeus, *Species Plantarum* 2: 918. 1753.
"Habitat in Europa australi." RCN: 6633.
Lectotype (Jeanmonod & al. in Jeanmonod, *Compl. Prodr. Fl. Corse,
    Asteraceae II*: 212. 2004): Herb. Clifford: 421, *Centaurea* 5 (BM).
Current name: ***Mantisalca salmantica*** (L.) Briq. & Cavill.
    (Asteraceae).

Centaurea scabiosa Linnaeus, *Species Plantarum* 2: 913. 1753.
"Habitat in Europae septentrionalis pratis." RCN: 6600.
Type not designated.
Original material: Herb. Burser XV(2): 7 (UPS); Herb. Linn. No.
    1030.32 (LINN); [icon] in Daléchamps, Hist. General. Pl. 1: 1066.
    1587.
Current name: ***Centaurea scabiosa*** L. (Asteraceae).

Centaurea sempervirens Linnaeus, *Species Plantarum* 2: 913. 1753.
"Habitat in Lusitania." RCN: 6599.
Lectotype (Wagenitz in Jarvis & Turland in *Taxon* 47: 357. 1998):
    Herb. Clifford: 422, *Centaurea* 13 (BM-000647264).
Current name: ***Cheirolophus sempervirens*** (L.) Pomel (Asteraceae).

Centaurea seridis Linnaeus, *Species Plantarum* 2: 915. 1753.
"Habitat in Hispania." RCN: 6615.
Type not designated.
Original material: Herb. Linn. No. 362.7? (S); Herb. Linn. No. 362.5?
    (S); [icon] in Bauhin & Cherler, Hist. Pl. Univ. 3(1): 33. 1651.
Current name: ***Centaurea seridis*** L. (Asteraceae).

Centaurea sessiliflora Linnaeus, *Species Plantarum* 2: 912. 1753.
"Habitat in G. Narbonensi." RCN: 6589.

Type not designated.
Original material: none traced.
Current name: ***Centaurea sp.*** (Asteraceae).

Centaurea sibirica Linnaeus, *Species Plantarum* 2: 913. 1753.
"Habitat in Sibiria. D. Gmelin." RCN: 6598.
Type not designated.
Original material: Herb. Linn. No. 361.15 (S); Herb. Linn. No.
    1030.27 (LINN); [icon] in Gmelin, Fl. Sibirica 2: 96, t. 42, f. 2.
    1749.
Current name: ***Centaurea sibirica*** L. (Asteraceae).

Centaurea sicula Linnaeus, *Species Plantarum* 2: 918. 1753.
"Habitat in Sicilia." RCN: 6628.
Type not designated.
Original material: Herb. Linn. No. 1030.64 (LINN); Herb. Linn. No.
    1030.63 (LINN); [icon] in Morison, Pl. Hist. Univ. 3: 144, s. 7, t.
    28, f. 26. 1699.
Current name: ***Centaurea solstitialis*** L. (Asteraceae).

Centaurea solstitialis Linnaeus, *Species Plantarum* 2: 917. 1753.
"Habitat in Gallia, Anglia, Italia." RCN: 6626.
Lectotype (Jeffrey in *Kew Bull.* 22: 136. 1968): Herb. Linn. No.
    1030.59 (LINN).
Current name: ***Centaurea solstitialis*** L. (Asteraceae).

Centaurea sonchifolia Linnaeus, *Species Plantarum* 2: 915. 1753.
"Habitat in maritimis maris Mediterranei." RCN: 6614.
Lectotype (Turland in Jarvis & Turland in *Taxon* 47: 357. 1998):
    [icon] *"Jacea laciniata Sonchi folio"* in Hermann, Hort. Lugd.-Bat.
    Cat.: 331, 675. 1687.
Current name: ***Centaurea seridis*** L. subsp. ***sonchifolia*** (L.) Greuter
    (Asteraceae).

Centaurea sphaerocephala Linnaeus, *Species Plantarum* 2: 916. 1753.
"Habitat in Mauritania." RCN: 6617.
Lectotype (Jeanmonod & al. in Jeanmonod, *Compl. Prodr. Fl. Corse,
    Asteraceae II*: 166. 2004): Herb. Linn. No. 1030.45 (LINN).
Current name: ***Centaurea sphaerocephala*** L. (Asteraceae).

Centaurea spinosa Linnaeus, *Species Plantarum* 2: 912. 1753.
"Habitat in Creta." RCN: 6594.
Lectotype (Turland in *Bull. Nat. Hist. Mus. London, Bot.* 25:
    146, f. 17. 1995): Herb. Clifford: 422, *Centaurea* 15 (BM-
    000647266).
Current name: ***Centaurea spinosa*** L. subsp. ***spinosa*** (Asteraceae).

Centaurea splendens Linnaeus, *Species Plantarum* 2: 914. 1753.
"Habitat in Helvetia, Hispania, Sibiria." RCN: 6609.
Lectotype (Greuter in *Willdenowia* 33: 56. 2003): *Gerber*, Herb. Linn.
    No. 1030.39 (LINN).
Current name: ***Centaurea margaritacea*** Ten. (Asteraceae).
Note: Lacaita (in *Nuovo Giorn. Bot. Ital.*, n.s., 30: 205–209. 1923)
    discussed the taxonomically diverse original elements in some detail,
    identifying material on sheets 1030.39 and 1030.40 (LINN) as *C.
    margaritacea* Ten., and that on 1030.38 as *C. deusta* Ten. He
    followed earlier authors, including Boissier, in discarding the name
    as a *nomen confusum*. Greuter (*l.c.*) subsequently designated
    1030.39 (LINN) as lectotype, noting its identity and concluding
    that Art. 57 prevents the use of *C. splendens* in the sense of its type,
    or any other sense. No formal proposal has been made for the
    rejection of the name.

Centaurea stoebe Linnaeus, *Species Plantarum* 2: 914. 1753.
"Habitat in Austria." RCN: 6601.

Neotype (Greuter in *Willdenowia* 33: 56. 2003): Austria. "*Centaurea Rhenana* Bor., Niederösterreich. Felsen in der Mödlinger Klause", 13 Jul 1908, *Korb* (W No. 5875).
Current name: ***Centaurea stoebe*** L. (Asteraceae).
Note: This name has been treated as of doubtful application (see Holub in *Preslia* 49: 314. 1977; Greuter & al. in *Taxon* 50: 1204. 2002) although others (e.g. Ochsmann in *Diss. Bot.* 324: 65. 2000) have used the name. Ochsmann noted the absence of original material, and Greuter (in *Willdenowia* 33: 56. 2003) designated a neotype.

Centaurea strepens Linnaeus, *Amoenitates Academicae* 4: 491. 1759, *nom. nud.*
Type not relevant.
Current name: ***Centaurea alba*** L. (Asteraceae).

Centaurea tingitana Linnaeus, *Species Plantarum,* ed. 2, 2: 1300. 1763.
"Habitat in Agro Tingitano." RCN: 6641.
Type not designated.
Original material: [icon] in Haller, Brev. Enum. Stirp. Hort. Gott.: 370. 1743; [icon] in Hermann, Hort. Lugd.-Bat. Cat.: 162, 163. 1687.
Current name: ***Carthamus caeruleus*** L. (Asteraceae).

Centaurea uniflora Linnaeus, *Systema Naturae,* ed. 12, 2: 572; *Mantissa Plantarum*: 118. 1767, *nom. illeg.*
"Habitat in Alpibus Europae australis." RCN: 6586.
Type not designated.
Original material: [icon] in Boccone, Mus. Piante Rar. Sicilia: 20, t. 2. 1697.
Current name: ***Centaurea uniflora*** Turra (Asteraceae).
Note: A later homonym of *Centaurea uniflora* Turra (*Farsetia Nov. Pl. Gen.*: 12. 1765), and hence illegitimate.

Centaurea verutum Linnaeus, *Centuria I Plantarum*: 30. 1755.
"Habitat in Palaestina. D. Hasselquist." RCN: 6632.
Type not designated.
Original material: *Hasselquist*, Herb. Linn. No. 1030.69 (LINN).
Current name: ***Centaurea verutum*** L. (Asteraceae).

Centella glabrata Linnaeus, *Species Plantarum,* ed. 2, 2: 1393. 1763.
"Habitat ad Cap. b. Spei." RCN: 7116.
Lectotype (Schubert & Van Wyk in Jarvis & al. in *Taxon* 55: 210. 2006): Herb. Linn. No. 332.11 (LINN).
Current name: ***Centella glabrata*** L. (Apiaceae).
Note: As noted by Burtt (in *Notes Roy. Bot. Gard. Edinburgh* 48: 195. 1991), although the binomial appears first in *Pl. Rar. Afr.*: 28. 1760, the generic name was not validated until the publication of *Gen. Pl.* ed. 6 (1763, by association with *Sp. Pl.,* ed. 2), so *C. glabrata* dates from 1763.

Centella villosa Linnaeus, *Species Plantarum,* ed. 2, 2: 1393. 1763.
"Habitat ad Cap. b. Spei." RCN: 7115.
Lectotype (Burtt in Jarvis & al., *Regnum Veg.* 127: 31. 1993): Herb. Linn. No. 332.9 (LINN).
Generitype of *Centella* Linnaeus (vide Coulter & Rose in *Contr. U. S. Natl. Herb.* 7: 30. 1900).
Current name: ***Centella villosa*** L. (Apiaceae).
Note: As noted by Burtt (in *Notes Roy. Bot. Gard. Edinburgh* 48: 199. 1991), although the binomial appears first in *Pl. Rar. Afr.*: 28 (1760), the generic name was not validated until the publication of *Gen. Pl.,* ed. 6 (1763, by association with *Sp. Pl.* ed. 2), so *C. villosa* dates from 1763.

Centunculus minimus Linnaeus, *Species Plantarum* 1: 116. 1753.
"Habitat in Italiae, Galliae, Germaniae, Scaniae arenosis." RCN: 948.
Lectotype (designated here by Bizzarri): Herb. Linn. No. 147.1 (LINN).
Generitype of *Centunculus* Linnaeus.
Current name: ***Centunculus minimus*** L. (Primulaceae).
Note: Bizzarri (in *Webbia* 24: 670–671. 1970) discussed the typification of the name but did not eventually choose between the LINN sheet and the Dillenian material and illustrations, though concluding that all are taxonomically the same.

Cephalanthus occidentalis Linnaeus, *Species Plantarum* 1: 95. 1753.
"Habitat in America septentrionali." RCN: 793.
Lectotype (Reveal in Jarvis & al., *Regnum Veg.* 127: 31. 1993): Herb. Linn. No. 118.1 (LINN).
Generitype of *Cephalanthus* Linnaeus (vide Merrill in *J. Wash. Acad. Sci.* 5: 532. 1915; Hitchcock, *Prop. Brit. Bot.*: 123. 1929).
Current name: ***Cephalanthus occidentalis*** L. (Rubiaceae).
Note: Ridsdale (in *Blumea* 23: 180. 1976) indicated 118.1 and 118.2 (LINN) as types but as the two sheets do not appear to be a single gathering, Art. 9.15 does not apply and Ridsdale's statement does not constitute a valid typification.

Cephalanthus orientalis Linnaeus, *Species Plantarum* 1: 95. 1753.
"Habitat in India & Africa." RCN: 1350.
Basionym of: *Nauclea orientalis* (L.) L. (1762).
Lectotype (Merrill in *J. Washington Acad. Sci.* 5: 533. 1915): Herb. Hermann 5: 338, No. 53 [icon] (BM).
Current name: ***Nauclea orientalis*** (L.) L. (Rubiaceae).
Note: Bakhuizen van den Brink (in *Taxon* 19: 473. 1970) rejected Merrill's typification in favour of 226.1 (LINN). However, the General Committee (*l.c.* 22: 155. 1973) ruled that Merrill's typification was reasonable and not to be set aside. See also Hansen & Fox Maule (in *Bot. J. Linn. Soc.* 67: 202, pl. 5. 1973) on the material in LINN and its provenance.

Cerastium alpinum Linnaeus, *Species Plantarum* 1: 438. 1753.
"Habitat in Alpibus Europae." RCN: 3402.
Lectotype (Jonsell & Jarvis in *Nordic J. Bot.* 14: 156. 1994): Herb. Linn. No. 192 (LAPP).
Current name: ***Cerastium alpinum*** L. (Caryophyllaceae).
Note: Hultén (in *Svensk Bot. Tidskr.* 50: 436, f. 3. 1956) applied the name to the common plant of the Scandinavian mountains, and illustrated the material on sheet 603.12 (LINN), though without referring to it as the type. Möschl (in *Mitt. Naturwiss. Vereines Steiermark* 103: 146. 1973) evidently regarded material in LINN as the type but did not distinguish between sheets 603.12–603.15. As these are evidently not part of a single gathering, Art. 9.15 does not apply.

Cerastium aquaticum Linnaeus, *Species Plantarum* 1: 439. 1753.
"Habitat ad littora lacuum Europae." RCN: 3407.
Lectotype (Larsen in Morat, *Fl. Cambodge Laos Viêtnam* 24: 83. 1989): Herb. Linn. No. 603.23 (LINN).
Current name: ***Stellaria aquatica*** (L.) Scop. (Caryophyllaceae).
Note: Jonsell & Jarvis (in *Nordic J. Bot.* 14: 156. 1994) independently made the same type choice as Larsen, but with a short discussion.

Cerastium arvense Linnaeus, *Species Plantarum* 1: 438. 1753.
"Habitat in Scania & australiori Europa." RCN: 3400.
Lectotype (Ugborogho in *Phyton (Buenos Aires)* 35: 177, f. 4. 1977): Herb. Linn. No. 603.9 (LINN).
Generitype of *Cerastium* Linnaeus.
Current name: ***Cerastium arvense*** L. (Caryophyllaceae).
Note: Möschl (in *Mem. Soc. Brot.* 17: 24. 1964; *Mitt. Naturwiss.*

Vereines Steiermark 103: 147. 1973) indicated unspecified material in LINN as type but he did not distinguish between 603.9 and 603.10. These do not appear to be part of a single gathering so Art. 9.15 does not apply, and Ugborogho's choice is the earliest valid typification.

Cerastium dichotomum Linnaeus, *Species Plantarum* 1: 438. 1753.
"Habitat inter segetes Hispaniae." RCN: 3401.
Lectotype (Ghazanfar & Nasir in Nasir & Ali, *Fl. Pakistan* 175: 37. 1986): Herb. Linn. No. 603.11 (LINN).
Current name: ***Cerastium dichotomum*** L. (Caryophyllaceae).
Note: Möschl (in *Mem. Soc. Brot.* 17: 51. 1964) indicated unspecified material in LINN as type but did not distinguish between sheets 603.11 and 603.13, which were evidently not part of a single gathering so Art. 9.15 does not apply. Ghafoor (in Jafri & Ali, *Fl. Libya* 59: 40. 1978) wrongly indicated 603.1 (LINN), which is not original material, as type.

Cerastium latifolium Linnaeus, *Species Plantarum* 1: 439. 1753.
"Habitat in Alpibus Helvetiae." RCN: 3408.
Lectotype (Bechi in Cafferty & Jarvis in *Taxon* 53: 1051. 2004): Herb. Burser XI: 114 (UPS).
Current name: ***Cerastium latifolium*** L. (Caryophyllaceae).
Note: Möschl (in *Mitt. Naturwiss. Vereines Steiermark* 103: 156. 1973) indicated material in LINN as the type but did not distinguish between sheets 603.24 and 603.25. As these sheets bear material of different gatherings, Art. 9.15 does not apply.

Cerastium manticum Linnaeus, *Centuria II Plantarum*: 18. 1756.
"Habitat Veronae. Seguier." RCN: 3410.
Lectotype (Strid in Strid & Kit Tan, *Fl. Hellenica* 1: 215. 1997): *Séguier*, Herb. Linn. No. 603.28 (LINN).
Current name: ***Moenchia mantica*** (L.) Bartl. subsp. ***mantica*** (Caryophyllaceae).

Cerastium maximum Linnaeus, *Species Plantarum* 1: 439. 1753.
"Habitat in Sibiria. D. Gmelin." RCN: 3406.
Lectotype (Lazkov in Cafferty & Jarvis in *Taxon* 53: 1051. 2004): *Gmelin s.n.*, Herb. Linn. No. 603.22 (LINN), see right.
Current name: ***Cerastium maximum*** L. (Caryophyllaceae).

Cerastium pentandrum Linnaeus, *Species Plantarum* 1: 438. 1753.
"Habitat in Hispania." RCN: 3399.
Lectotype (Sell & Whitehead in *Feddes Repert.* 69: 21. 1964): Herb. Linn. No. 603.8 (LINN).
Current name: ***Cerastium semidecandrum*** L. (Caryophyllaceae).

Cerastium perfoliatum Linnaeus, *Species Plantarum* 1: 437. 1753.
"Habitat in Graecia." RCN: 3395.
Lectotype (Möschl in *Sitzungsber. Österr. Akad. Wiss., Math.-Naturwiss. Kl., Abt. 1, Biol.* 175: 194. 1966): Herb. Linn. No. 603.1 (LINN).
Current name: ***Cerastium perfoliatum*** L. (Caryophyllaceae).

Cerastium repens Linnaeus, *Species Plantarum* 1: 439. 1753.
"Habitat in Gallia, Italia." RCN: 3403.
Lectotype (Bechi in Cafferty & Jarvis in *Taxon* 53: 1051. 2004): [icon] *"Myosotis, polygoni folio canescente"* in Vaillant, Bot. Paris.: 141, t. 30, f. 5. 1727.
Current name: ***Cerastium arvense*** L. (Caryophyllaceae).
Note: Khalaf & Stace (in *Watsonia* 23: 482. 2001) said that the name is "of uncertain application. No type specimen has been traced: the specimen in LINN is not a type" and is identifiable as *C. arvense*. They noted the occasional usage of *C. repens* in the sense of *C. tomentosum* L. and *C. biebersteinii* DC. The only extant original

The lectotype of *Cerastium maximum* L.

element is the Vaillant illustration, also identifiable as *C. arvense*, and Bechi's formal designation of it as lectotype resulted in *C. repens* falling into the synonymy of *C. arvense*.

Cerastium semidecandrum Linnaeus, *Species Plantarum* 1: 438. 1753.
"Habitat in campis apricis sterilissimis Europae borealis." RCN: 3398.
Lectotype (Möschl in *Mem. Soc. Brot.* 5: 10, f. 40. 1949): Herb. Linn. No. 603.7 (LINN).
Current name: ***Cerastium semidecandrum*** L. (Caryophyllaceae).

Cerastium strictum Linnaeus, *Species Plantarum* 1: 439. 1753.
"Habitat in Alpibus Austriacis, Helveticis." RCN: 3404.
Lectotype (Bechi in *Webbia* 52: 176, f. 2. 1998): Herb. Burser XI: 119 (UPS).
Current name: ***Arenaria grandiflora*** L. (Caryophyllaceae).
Note: Möschl (in *Mitt. Naturwiss. Vereines Steiermark* 103: 161. 1973) designated 603.21 (LINN) as type. Despite not indicating the sheet number, it is the only sheet associated with this name, and Ugborogho (in *Phyton (Buenos Aires)* 35: 175, f. 3. 1977) illustrated this collection. However, this material conflicts with the diagnosis in a number of characters and it is also identifiable as *Arenaria*

montana L. (1755). Another collection, Herb. Burser XI: 119 (UPS), is an explicitly cited specimen and is therefore a syntype, taking precedence for lectotypification purposes (Art. 9.10) over uncited material such as 603.21 (LINN). It matches the protologue well, is a specimen of *Arenaria grandiflora* L., and Bechi (in *Webbia* 52: 176, f. 2. 1998) therefore designated it as the lectotype. Fortunately, *C. strictum* L. (1753) cannot displace *A. grandiflora* L. (1759) because of the existence of *A. strictum* Michx., so *C. strictum* falls into the synonymy of *A. grandiflora*.

Cerastium suffruticosum Linnaeus, *Species Plantarum* 1: 439. 1753.
"Habitat in Europa australi." RCN: 3405.
Neotype (Bechi in *Webbia* 52: 186, f. 1. 1998): Italy. Toscana, Apennino, bordo della strada statale 12, loc. "Pian dei Sisi" (PT), 810m, 9 Jul 1995, *N. Bechi & F. Cesati* (FI; iso- PI).
Current name: ***Cerastium suffruticosum*** L. (Caryophyllaceae).

Cerastium tomentosum Linnaeus, *Species Plantarum* 1: 440. 1753.
"Habitat in Granada." RCN: 3409.
Lectotype (Buschmann in *Repert. Spec. Nov. Regni Veg.* 43: 136. 1938): *Scopoli s.n.*, Herb. Linn. No. 603.27 (LINN).
Current name: ***Cerastium tomentosum*** L. (Caryophyllaceae).
Note: Lacaita (in *Bull. Orto Bot. Napoli* 3: 273–274. 1913) discussed the identity of the name, and its protologue, and described 603.27 (LINN) in some detail, but remained uncertain of its identity.

Cerastium viscosum Linnaeus, *Species Plantarum* 1: 437. 1753, *nom. utique rej.*
"Habitat in Europae pratis macilentis." RCN: 3397.
Type not designated.
Original material: Herb. Burser XIV: 93 (UPS); Herb. Linn. No. 603.4 (LINN); Herb. Linn. No. 603.3 (LINN); Herb. Clifford 174, *Cerastium* 4 (BM); Herb. Linn. No. 193 (LAPP); [icon] in Vaillant, Bot. Paris.: 142, t. 30, f. 1. 1727.
Current name: ***Cerastium* sp.** (Caryophyllaceae).

Cerastium vulgatum Linnaeus, *Flora Suecica,* ed. 2: 158. 1755, *nom. utique rej.*
"Habitat in areis, hortis & ruderatis, imprimis Scaniae." RCN: 3396.
Type not designated.
Original material: Herb. Linn. No. 603.6? (LINN); [icon] in Vaillant, Bot. Paris.: 142, t. 30, f. 3. 1727; [icon] in Bauhin & Cherler, Hist. Pl. Univ. 3(2): 359. 1651.
Current name: ***Cerastium* sp.** (Caryophyllaceae).

Ceratocarpus arenarius Linnaeus, *Species Plantarum* 2: 969. 1753.
"Habitat in Tatariae arenosis." RCN: 7028.
Lectotype (Hedge in Jarvis & al., *Regnum Veg.* 127: 32. 1993): *Gerber*, Herb. Linn. No. 1086.1 (LINN).
Generitype of *Ceratocarpus* Linnaeus.
Current name: ***Ceratocarpus arenarius*** L. (Chenopodiaceae).

Ceratonia siliqua Linnaeus, *Species Plantarum* 2: 1026. 1753.
"Habitat in Apulia, Sicilia, Creta, Cypro, Syria, Palaestina." RCN: 7715.
Lectotype (Jafri in Jafri & El-Gadi, *Fl. Libya* 60: 5. 1978): Herb. Linn. No. 1239.1 (LINN).
Generitype of *Ceratonia* Linnaeus.
Current name: ***Ceratonia siliqua*** L. (Fabaceae: Caesalpinioideae).
Note: Both Roti-Michelozzi (in *Webbia* 13: 178. 1957) and Isely (in *Mem. New York Bot. Gard.* 25(2): 210. 1975) noted specimens at LINN, but neither explicitly indicated a type.

Ceratophyllum demersum Linnaeus, *Species Plantarum* 2: 992. 1753.
"Habitat in Europae fossis majoribus sub aqua." RCN: 7196.

Lectotype (Aziz in Nasir & Ali, *Fl. W. Pakistan* 70: 3. 1974): Herb. Clifford: 446, *Ceratophyllum* 1 (BM-000647413).
Generitype of *Ceratophyllum* Linnaeus.
Current name: ***Ceratophyllum demersum*** L. (Ceratophyllaceae).

Ceratophyllum submersum Linnaeus, *Species Plantarum,* ed. 2, 2: 1409. 1763.
"Habitat in Europae aquis." RCN: 7197.
Lectotype (Wilmot-Dear in *Kew Bull.* 40: 264. 1985): [icon] "*Hydroceratophyllon folio laevi, octo cornibus donato*" in Vaillant in Mém. Acad. Roy. Sci. Paris 1719: 16, t. 2, f. 2. 1719.
Current name: ***Ceratophyllum submersum*** L. (Ceratophyllaceae).

Cerbera ahouai Linnaeus, *Species Plantarum* 1: 208. 1753, *typ. cons.*
"Habitat in Brasilia." RCN: 1706.
Conserved type (Leeuwenberg in Jarvis & al., *Regnum Veg.* 127: 94. 1993): Herb. Clifford: 76, *Plumeria* 1, branch, fruit and lower right flower (BM-000558144).
Generitype of *Thevetia* Linnaeus, *nom. cons.*
Current name: ***Thevetia ahouai*** (L.) DC. (Apocynaceae).
Note: Thevetia Linnaeus, *nom. cons.* against *Ahouai* Mill. *Cerbera ahouai* is the basionym of the generitype, *Thevetia ahouai* (L.) DC.

Cerbera manghas Linnaeus, *Species Plantarum* 1: 208. 1753.
"Habitat in Indiis ad aquas." RCN: 1707.
Lectotype (Huber in Abeywickrama, *Revised Handb. Fl. Ceylon* 1(1): 18. 1973): Herb. Hermann 5: 70, No. 106 [icon] (BM).
Generitype of *Cerbera* Linnaeus.
Current name: ***Cerbera mangas*** L. (Apocynaceae).
Note: Cerbera manghas, with Herb. Linn. No. 298.2 (LINN) as the type, was proposed as conserved type of the genus by Jarvis (in *Taxon* 41: 560. 1992). However, the proposal was eventually ruled unnecessary by the General Committee (see Barrie, *l.c.* 55: 795–796. 2006 for a review of the history of this and related proposals). Huber's (1973) type choice of a Hermann drawing, however, pre-dates that of 298.2 (LINN) by Leeuwenberg (in Jarvis, *l.c.* 41: 560. 1992) and becomes the correct choice with the failure of the conservation proposal.

Cerbera thevetia Linnaeus, *Species Plantarum* 1: 209. 1753.
"Habitat in America calidiore." RCN: 1708.
Lectotype (Lippold in *Feddes Repert.* 91: 52. 1980): [icon] "*Cerbera foliis linearibus, longissimus*" in Plumier, Codex Boerhaavianus (University Library, Groningen).
Current name: ***Thevetia peruviana*** (Pers.) K. Schum. (Apocynaceae).

Cercis canadensis Linnaeus, *Species Plantarum* 1: 374. 1753.
"Habitat in Virginia." RCN: 2946.
Lectotype (Reveal in Turland & Jarvis in *Taxon* 46: 466. 1997): *Kalm*, Herb. Linn. No. 524.2 (LINN).
Current name: ***Cercis canadensis*** L. (Fabaceae: Caesalpinioideae).
Note: Although Isely (in *Mem. New York Bot. Gard.* 25(2): 210. 1975) noted specimens in both LINN and BM, either of which he felt would be a reasonable choice as lectotype, he made no formal choice himself.

Cercis siliquastrum Linnaeus, *Species Plantarum* 1: 374. 1753.
"Habitat in Italia, Hispania, Narbona." RCN: 2945.
Lectotype (Polhill in Jarvis & al., *Regnum Veg.* 127: 32. 1993): *Löfling 275a,* Herb. Linn. No. 524.1 (LINN).
Generitype of *Cercis* Linnaeus (vide Hitchcock, *Prop. Brit. Bot.*: 152. 1929).
Current name: ***Cercis siliquastrum*** L. subsp. ***siliquastrum*** (Fabaceae: Caesalpinioideae).
Note: Although Isely (in *Mem. New York Bot. Gard.* 25(2): 211. 1975)

indicated that he had seen the protologue and a fiche of material at LINN, he did not formally designate a type. Menéndez de Luarca (in *Anales Jard. Bot. Madrid* 55: 423. 1997) discusses a Clusius work as a source of information for this species.

Cerinthe echioides Linnaeus, *Species Plantarum* 1: 137. 1753.
"Habitat in Austriae, Pannoniae, Helvetiae, Galliae, Italiae rupibus." RCN: 1105.
Basionym of: *Onosma echioides* (L.) L. (1762).
Lectotype (Lacaita in *Nuovo Giorn. Bot. Ital.*, n.s., 31: 24. 1924): [icon] *"Anchusa echioides lutea, cerinthoides mont."* in Colonna, Ekphr.: 182, 183. 1606.
Current name: ***Onosma echioides*** (L.) L. (Boraginaceae).

Cerinthe maculata Linnaeus, *Species Plantarum* 1: 137. 1753.
"Habitat in montanis Europae australis. D. Monti." RCN: 1101.
Neotype (Edmondson in Cafferty & Jarvis in *Taxon* 53: 800. 2004): Italy. Potenza: Monte Pollino, Cóppola di Paola towards Col di Dragone, ca. 1,500m, 21 Jun 1979, *P. Davis, D. Sutton & S.D. Sutton 65757* (BM-000576310; iso- E).
Current name: ***Cerinthe minor*** L. (Boraginaceae).

Cerinthe major Linnaeus, *Species Plantarum* 1: 136. 1753.
"Habitat in Europa australi." RCN: 1100.
Lectotype (Verdcourt in Jarvis & al., *Regnum Veg.* 127: 32. 1993): Herb. Clifford: 48, *Cerinthe* 2 ζ (BM-000557935).
Generitype of *Cerinthe* Linnaeus (vide Hitchcock, *Prop. Brit. Bot.*: 128. 1929).
Current name: ***Cerinthe major*** L. (Boraginaceae).
Note: Qaiser (in Jafri & El-Gadi, *Fl. Libya* 68: 52. 1979) and Valdés (in *Lagascalia* 10: 100. 1981) both indicated 186.1 (LINN) as type. However, this is a Brander collection from North Africa which was not received by Linnaeus until after 1753 and therefore cannot be original material for the name.

Cerinthe minor Linnaeus, *Species Plantarum* 1: 137. 1753.
"Habitat in Austriae, Styriae agris." RCN: 1102.
Lectotype (Edmondson in Cafferty & Jarvis in *Taxon* 53: 801. 2004): Herb. Burser XIV(2): 35 (UPS).
Current name: ***Cerinthe minor*** L. (Boraginaceae).

Cerinthe orientalis Linnaeus, *Centuria I Plantarum*: 7. 1755.
"Habitat in Aegypto. b.m. D. Hasselquist." RCN: 1104.
Basionym of: *Onosma orientalis* (L.) L. (1762).
Lectotype (Edmondson in Cafferty & Jarvis in *Taxon* 53: 801. 2004): Herb. Hasselquist No. 137 (UPS).
Current name: ***Onosma orientalis*** (L.) L. (Boraginaceae).

Ceropegia biflora Linnaeus, *Species Plantarum* 1: 211. 1753.
"Habitat in Zeylona." RCN: 1744.
Lectotype (Ansari in Jain & al. in *Fasc. Fl. India* 16: 12. 1984): Herb. Hermann 5: 296, No. 110 [icon] (BM).
Current name: ***Ceropegia candelabrum*** L. var. ***biflora*** (L.) Ansari (Asclepiadaceae).
Note: Trimen (*Handb. Fl. Ceylon* 3: 167. 1895) noted the existence of the Hermann drawing, but did not explicitly treat it as the type.

Ceropegia candelabrum Linnaeus, *Species Plantarum* 1: 211. 1753.
"Habitat in Malabaria." RCN: 1743.
Lectotype (Trimen, *Handb. Fl. Ceylon* 3: 167. 1895): [icon] *"Njota-njodien-valli"* in Rheede, Hort. Malab. 9: 27, t. 16. 1689.
Generitype of *Ceropegia* Linnaeus (vide Hitchcock, *Prop. Brit. Bot.*: 136. 1929).
Current name: ***Ceropegia candelabrum*** L. (Asclepiadaceae).
Note: The type is illustrated by Walker (in *Asklepios* 71: 27. 1997).

Ceropegia sagittata Linnaeus, *Mantissa Plantarum Altera*: 215. 1771.
"Habitat in Capitis b. spei. arenosis." RCN: 1745.
Lectotype (Wanntorp in *Opera Bot.* 98: 39. 1988): Herb. Linn. No. 305.1 (LINN).
Current name: ***Microloma sagittata*** (L.) R. Br. (Asclepiadaceae).

Ceropegia tenuifolia (Linnaeus) Linnaeus, *Mantissa Plantarum Altera*: 215, 346. 1771.
["Habitat ad Cap. b. spei dunis."] Sp. Pl. 1: 212 (1753). RCN: 1746.
Basionym: *Periploca tenuifolia* L. (1753).
Lectotype (Wanntorp in *Opera Bot.* 98: 50, f. 34. 1988): [icon] *"Cynanchum radice glandulosa, foliis angustis, sinuatis, floribus urceolatis, miniatis"* in Burman, Rar. Afric. Pl.: 36, t. 15. 1738.
Current name: ***Microloma tenuifolia*** (L.) K. Schum. (Asclepiadaceae).

Cestrum diurnum Linnaeus, *Species Plantarum* 1: 191. 1753.
"Habitat in Chilli, Havana." RCN: 1505.
Lectotype (Howard, *Fl. Lesser Antilles* 6: 274. 1989): Herb. Linn. No. 258.4 (LINN).
Current name: ***Cestrum diurnum*** L. (Solanaceae).

Cestrum nocturnum Linnaeus, *Species Plantarum* 1: 191. 1753.
"Habitat in Jamaica, Chilli." RCN: 1503.
Lectotype (Deb in *J. Econ. Taxon. Bot.* 1: 36. 1980): *Baeck s.n.*, Herb. Linn. No. 258.1 (LINN).
Generitype of *Cestrum* Linnaeus (vide Hitchcock, *Prop. Brit. Bot.*: 133. 1929).
Current name: ***Cestrum nocturnum*** L. (Solanaceae).
Note: D'Arcy (in *Ann. Missouri Bot. Gard.* 60: 607. 1974) and Scott (in Bosser & al., *Fl. Mascareignes* 128: 3. 2000) indicated unseen Clifford material as type; but in fact there is no material of this species preserved in the Clifford herbarium.

Cestrum vespertinum Linnaeus, *Mantissa Plantarum Altera*: 206. 1771.
"Habitat in America." RCN: 1504.
Lectotype (Benítez & D'Arcy in *Ann. Missouri Bot. Gard.* 85: 281. 1998): Herb. Linn. No. 258.2 (LINN).
Current name: ***Cestrum alternifolium*** (Jacq.) O.E. Schulz (Solanaceae).
Note: Benítez & D'Arcy (*l.c.*) treat a footnote to the account of *Chiococca racemosa* L. in *Syst. Nat.* ed. 12, 2: 165. 1767) as a new binomial, *Chiococca alternifolia* L. (a taxonomic synonym of *Cestrum alternifolium* (Jacq.) O.E. Schultz). However, it is far from clear that this was accepted as a valid name by Linnaeus, and it is not accepted as such here.

Chaerophyllum arborescens Linnaeus, *Species Plantarum* 1: 259. 1753.
"Habitat in Virginia." RCN: 2072.
Lectotype (Reveal & Spencer in Jarvis & al. in *Taxon* 55: 210. 2006): Herb. Linn. No. 365.12 (LINN).
Current name: ***Conium maculatum*** L. (Apiaceae).

Chaerophyllum aromaticum Linnaeus, *Species Plantarum* 1: 259. 1753.
"Habitat in Lusatia, Misnia." RCN: 2069.
Lectotype (Watson in Jarvis & al. in *Taxon* 55: 211, 560. 2006): Herb. Clifford: 102, *Chaerophyllum* 6, sheet B (BM-000558348).
Current name: ***Chaerophyllum aromaticum*** L. (Apiaceae).
Note: Watson (in Jarvis & al. in *Taxon* 55: 211. 2006) designated Clifford material (BM) as the type but did not distinguish between two sheets (which are evidently not part of a single gathering so Art. 9.15 does not apply). However, this omission was corrected in *Taxon* 55: 560 (2006), from where the typification dates.

Chaerophyllum aureum Linnaeus, *Species Plantarum,* ed. 2, 1: 370. 1762.
"Habitat in Germania." RCN: 2071.
Lectotype (Reduron & Jarvis in Jarvis & al. in *Taxon* 55: 211. 2006): [icon] *"Myrrhis perennis alba minor foliis hirsutis semina aureo"* in Ruppius, Fl. Jen.: 282, t. 5. 1745. – Epitype (Reduron & Jacquemoud in Jarvis & al. in *Taxon* 55: 211. 2006): "640. Chaerophyllum maculatum. W. / RCHB. Fl. germ. n. 1901. Bei Chemnitz: M. Weicker." Herb. Boissier (G).
Current name: ***Chaerophyllum aureum*** L. (Apiaceae).

Chaerophyllum bulbosum Linnaeus, *Species Plantarum* 1: 258. 1753.
"Habitat in Alsatia, Hungaria, Helvetia." RCN: 2066.
Lectotype (Hedge & Lamond in Rechinger, *Fl. Iranica* 162: 91. 1987): Herb. Linn. No. 365.2 (LINN).
Current name: ***Chaerophyllum bulbosum*** L. (Apiaceae).

Chaerophyllum coloratum Linnaeus, *Systema Naturae,* ed. 12, 2: 214; *Mantissa Plantarum*: 57. 1767.
"Habitat in Illyria. D. Arduini." RCN: 2070.
Lectotype (Jury in Jarvis & al. in *Taxon* 55: 211. 2006): Herb. Linn. No. 365.11 (LINN).
Current name: ***Chaerophyllum coloratum*** L. (Apiaceae).

Chaerophyllum hirsutum Linnaeus, *Species Plantarum* 1: 258. 1753.
"Habitat in Alpibus Helvetiae." RCN: 2068.
Lectotype (Reduron & Jarvis in Jarvis & al. in *Taxon* 55: 211. 2006): Herb. Clifford: 101, *Chaerophyllum* 2 (BM-000558342).
Current name: ***Chaerophyllum hirsutum*** L. (Apiaceae).

Chaerophyllum sylvestre Linnaeus, *Species Plantarum* 1: 258. 1753.
"Habitat in Europae pomariis & cultis." RCN: 2065.
Lectotype (Hedge & Lamond in Rechinger, *Fl. Iranica* 162: 85. 1987): Herb. Linn. No. 365.1 (LINN).
Current name: ***Anthriscus sylvestris*** (L.) Hoffm. (Apiaceae).
Note: See detailed discussions by Spalik & Jarvis (in *Taxon* 38: 292, f. 3. 1989) and Reduron & Spalik (in *Acta Bot. Gallica* 142: 75. 1995).

Chaerophyllum temulentum Linnaeus, *Flora Suecica,* ed. 2: 94. 1755, *nom. illeg.*
["Habitat ad Europae arvos, vias & sepes."] Sp. Pl. 1: 258 (1753). RCN: 2067.
Replaced synonym: *Chaerophyllum temulum* L. (1753).
Lectotype (Reduron & Jarvis in *Taxon* 41: 560. 1992): Herb. Linn. No. 365.3 (LINN).
Current name: ***Chaerophyllum temulum*** L. (Apiaceae).
Note: An illegitimate replacement name for *C. temulum* L. (1753).

Chaerophyllum temulum Linnaeus, *Species Plantarum* 1: 258. 1753.
"Habitat ad Europae arvos, vias & sepes." RCN: 2067.
Replaced synonym of: *Chaerophyllum temulentum* L. (1755), *nom. illeg.*
Lectotype (Reduron & Jarvis in *Taxon* 41: 560. 1992): Herb. Linn. No. 365.3 (LINN).
Generitype of *Chaerophyllum* Linnaeus.
Current name: ***Chaerophyllum temulum*** L. (Apiaceae).
Note: Chaerophyllum temulum, with the type designated by Reduron & Jarvis, was proposed as conserved type of the genus by Jarvis (in *Taxon* 41: 560. 1992). However, the proposal was eventually ruled unnecessary by the General Committee (see Barrie, *l.c.* 55: 795–796. 2006 for a review of the history of this and related proposals).

Chalcas paniculata Linnaeus, *Systema Naturae,* ed. 12, 2: 293; *Mantissa Plantarum*: 68. 1767.
"Habitat in India, ubi colitur in hortis ob flores fragantissimos." RCN: 3021.
Lectotype (Nair in Jarvis & al., *Regnum Veg.* 127: 32. 1993): [icon] *"Camunium"* in Rumphius, Herb. Amboin. 5: 26, t. 17. 1747.
Generitype of *Chalcas* Linnaeus.
Current name: ***Murraya paniculata*** (L.) Jack (Rutaceae).
Note: Tanaka (in *J. Bot.* 68: 229. 1930) referred to what is presumably 539.2 (LINN) as a "Suppl. Type", later (in *Meded. Rijks-Herb.* 69: 7. 1931) indicating unspecified material (which sheet is intended is unclear) in LINN as type. Other authors (e.g. Porter & Elias in *Ann. Missouri Bot. Gard.* 66: 144. 1979; Stone in Dassanayake & Fosberg, *Revised Handb. Fl. Ceylon* 5: 459. 1985; Smith, *Fl. Vitiensis Nova* 3: 513. 1985) give similar statements, all of which are too imprecise to effect formal typification.

Chamaerops humilis Linnaeus, *Species Plantarum* 2: 1187. 1753.
"Habitat in Europa australi, praesertim Hispania." RCN: 8540.
Lectotype (Moore & Dransfield in *Taxon* 28: 60, f. 1. 1979): Herb. Clifford: 482, *Chamaerops* 1 (BM-000647651).
Generitype of *Chamaerops* Linnaeus.
Current name: ***Chamaerops humilis*** L. (Arecaceae).

Chara flexilis Linnaeus, *Species Plantarum* 2: 1157. 1753.
"Habitat in Europae maritimis." RCN: 7033.
Neotype (Wood in *Trans. Amer. Microscop. Soc.* 79: 224. 1960): England. Suffolk, Henly, near Ipswich, *Buddle* in Herb. Sloane 117: 10 (BM-SL).
Current name: ***Nitella flexilis*** (L.) C. Agardh (Characeae).

Chara hispida Linnaeus, *Species Plantarum* 2: 1156. 1753.
"Habitat in Europae maritimis." RCN: 7032.
Lectotype (Wood in *Trans. Amer. Microscop. Soc.* 79: 220, pl. I, II. 1960): Herb. Linn. No. 1088.4 (LINN).
Current name: ***Chara hispida*** L. (Characeae).

Chara tomentosa Linnaeus, *Species Plantarum* 2: 1156. 1753.
"Habitat in Europae stagnis, mari, lacubus." RCN: 7030.
Lectotype (Wood in *Trans. Amer. Microscop. Soc.* 79: 220, pl. I, III. 1960): Herb. Linn. No. 1088.1 (LINN).
Current name: ***Chara tomentosa*** L. (Characeae).

Chara vulgaris Linnaeus, *Species Plantarum* 2: 1156. 1753.
"Habitat in Europae aquis pigris." RCN: 7031.
Lectotype (Wood in *Trans. Amer. Microscop. Soc.* 79: 220, pl. I, II. 1960): *Löfling 757*, Herb. Linn. No. 1088.3 (LINN).
Generitype of *Chara* Linnaeus (vide Robinson in *Bull. New York Bot. Gard.* 4: 254. 1906).
Current name: ***Chara vulgaris*** L. (Characeae).

Cheiranthus africanus Linnaeus, *Plantae Rariores Africanae*: 13. 1760.
["Habitat in Cap. b. spei, locis saxosis incultis."] Sp. Pl., ed. 2, 2: 926 (1763). RCN: 4826.
Replaced synonym of: *Heliophila integrifolia* L. (1763), *nom. illeg.*
Lectotype (Marais in Codd & al., *Fl. Southern Africa* 13: 55. 1970): [icon] *"Leucojum Africanum coeruleo flore, latifolium hirsutum"* in Hermann, Hort. Lugd.-Bat. Cat.: 364, 365. 1687.
Current name: ***Heliophila africana*** (L.) Marais (Brassicaceae).

Cheiranthus alpinus Linnaeus, *Systema Naturae,* ed. 12, 2: 441; *Mantissa Plantarum*: 93. 1767.
"Habitat in alpinis montibus Italiae; in rupe Victoriae Galloprov. D. Jaquin." RCN: 4811.

Lectotype (Polatschek in Cafferty & Jarvis in *Taxon* 51: 532. 2002): *Jacquin 61*, Herb. Linn. No. 839.5 (LINN).
Current name: ***Erysimum sylvestre*** (Crantz) Scop. (Brassicaceae).

Cheiranthus annuus Linnaeus, *Species Plantarum* 2: 662. 1753.
"Habitat in Europae australis maritimis." RCN: 4819.
Lectotype (Gowler in Cafferty & Jarvis in *Taxon* 51: 532. 2002): Herb. Burser XI: 18 (UPS).
Current name: ***Matthiola incana*** (L.) R. Br. (Brassicaceae).

Cheiranthus cheiri Linnaeus, *Species Plantarum* 2: 661. 1753.
"Habitat in Angliae, Helvetiae, Galliae, Hispaniae muris, tectis." RCN: 4812.
Lectotype (Snogerup in *Opera Bot.* 13: 64. 1967): Herb. Linn. No. 839.12 (LINN).
Generitype of *Cheiranthus* Linnaeus (vide Green in *Bull. Misc. Inform. Kew* 1925: 55. 1925).
Current name: ***Erysimum cheiri*** (L.) Crantz (Brassicaceae).

Cheiranthus chius Linnaeus, *Species Plantarum* 2: 661. 1753.
"Habitat in Chio." RCN: 4814.
Lectotype (Stork in *Opera Bot.* 33: 18. 1972): [icon] *"Hesperis siliquis hirsutis, flore parvo rubello Boerh."* in Dillenius, Hort. Eltham. 1: 180, t. 148, f. 178. 1732.
Current name: ***Malcolmia chia*** (L.) DC. (Brassicaceae).

Cheiranthus erysimoides Linnaeus, *Species Plantarum* 2: 661. 1753.
"Habitat in Hungaria, Gallia." RCN: 4810.
Lectotype (Polatschek in Cafferty & Jarvis in *Taxon* 51: 532. 2002): Herb. Linn. No. 839.1 (LINN).
Current name: ***Erysimum odoratum*** Ehrh. (Brassicaceae).

Cheiranthus farsetia Linnaeus, *Systema Naturae,* ed. 12, 2: 442; *Mantissa Plantarum*: 94. 1767, *nom. illeg.*
"Habitat in Aegypto, Arabia." RCN: 4825.
Replaced synonym: *Farsetia aegyptia* Turra (1765).
Lectotype (Jonsell in *Symb. Bot. Upsal.* 25(3): 40. 1986): [icon] *"Ramulus Farsetiae aegyptiae floribus, fructibusque onustus"* in Turra, Farsetia [quarto version]: 5, f. 1. 1765.
Current name: ***Farsetia aegyptia*** Turra (Brassicaceae).
Note: As noted by Jonsell (in *Symb. Bot. Upsal.* 25(3): 40. 1986), this is an illegitimate replacement name for *Farsetia aegyptia* Turra (1765).

Cheiranthus fenestralis Linnaeus, *Species Plantarum* 2: 1198. 1753.
"Habitat – – – –" RCN: 4818.
Neotype (Gowler in Cafferty & Jarvis in *Taxon* 51: 532. 2002): France. Schistes argileux du Bord de mer à Toulon (Var), 10 May 1860, *Fl. Galliae et Germaniae exsiccata de C. Billot No. 3009. Rec. par A. Huet* (BM-000576298).
Current name: ***Matthiola incana*** (L.) R. Br. (Brassicaceae).

Cheiranthus fruticulosus Linnaeus, *Species Plantarum* 2: 662. 1753.
"Habitat in Hispania, Italia, Monspelii." RCN: 4821.
Replaced synonym of: *Cheiranthus tristis* L. (1759), *nom. illeg.*
Lectotype (Meikle, *Fl. Cyprus* 1: 156. 1977): *Löfling 484*, Herb. Linn. No. 839.23 (LINN).
Current name: ***Matthiola fruticulosa*** (L.) Maire (Brassicaceae).

Cheiranthus fruticulosus Linnaeus, *Systema Naturae,* ed. 12, 2: 441; *Mantissa Plantarum*: 94. 1767, *nom. illeg.*
"Habitat in Hispania. Cl. Alstroemer." RCN: 4813.
Lectotype (Meikle in *Curtis's Bot. Mag.* 177: t. 535. 1969): Herb. Linn. No. 839.14 (LINN).
Current name: ***Erysimum helveticum*** (Jacq.) DC. (Brassicaceae).
Note: A later homonym of *C. fruticulosus* L. (1753) and therefore illegitimate.

Cheiranthus incanus Linnaeus, *Species Plantarum* 2: 662. 1753.
"Habitat in Hispaniae maritimis." RCN: 4817.

Lectotype (Jafri in Nasir & Ali, *Fl. W. Pakistan* 55: 200. 1973): Herb. Linn. No. 839.17 (LINN), see also p. 248.
Current name: ***Matthiola incana*** (L.) R. Br. (Brassicaceae).

Cheiranthus lacerus Linnaeus, *Species Plantarum* 2: 662. 1753.
"Habitat in Lusitania." RCN: 4834.
Basionym of: *Hesperis lacera* (L.) L. (1774).
Lectotype (Ball in Cafferty & Jarvis in *Taxon* 51: 532. 2002): [icon] *"Leucoium Lusitanicum purpureum"* in Hermann, Parad. Bat.: 193. 1698. – Epitype (Ball in Cafferty & Jarvis in *Taxon* 51: 532. 2002): Portugal. Abundant in sandy places by the Douro, about Pinhão, 10 Jun 1889, *R.P. Murray s.n.* (BM-000576294).
Current name: ***Malcolmia lacera*** (L.) DC. (Brassicaceae).

Cheiranthus littoreus Linnaeus, *Species Plantarum,* ed. 2, 2: 925. 1763.
"Habitat in Maris Mediterranei littoribus." RCN: 4820.
Lectotype (Ball in Cafferty & Jarvis in *Taxon* 51: 532. 2002): Herb. Linn. No. 839.16 (LINN).
Current name: ***Malcolmia littorea*** (L.) R. Br. (Brassicaceae).

Cheiranthus maritimus Linnaeus, *Centuria I Plantarum*: 19. 1755.
"Habitat in Europae australis maritimis." RCN: 4815.
Lectotype (Stork in *Opera Bot.* 33: 26. 1972): Herb. Linn. No. 839.21 (LINN).
Current name: ***Malcolmia maritima*** (L.) W.T. Aiton (Brassicaceae).

Cheiranthus salinus Linnaeus, *Systema Naturae,* ed. 12, 2: 441; *Mantissa Plantarum*: 93. 1767.
"Habitat in Sibiriae, Tatariae salinas. D.D. Lerche." RCN: 4816.
Type not designated.
Original material: none traced.
Note: The application of this name is uncertain; it is apparently not in current use and may well be a candidate for rejection.

Cheiranthus sinuatus Linnaeus, *Amoenitates Academicae* 4: 487. 1759.
["Habitat in Hispaniae, Monspelii maritimis."] Sp. Pl., ed. 2, 2: 926 (1763). RCN: 4824.
Neotype (Jafri in Ali & Jafri, *Fl. Libya* 23: 149. 1977): Herb. Linn. No. 839.28 (LINN).
Current name: ***Matthiola sinuata*** (L.) R. Br. (Brassicaceae).
Note: Although cited by some authors as if first published in *Sp. Pl.,* ed. 2, 2: 926 (1763), the name was in fact validated in the *Amoen. Acad.* reprint of *Fl. Monspeliensis* published in 1759, as noted by Stearn (in Geck & Pressler, *Festschr. Claus Nissen*: 637. 1974). The name is therefore validated solely by reference to a pre-Starting Point description from Magnol. As Magnol's publication does not have an illustration of this plant, the type choice of 839.28 (LINN) as "type" by Jafri is accepted as a neotypification (Art. 9.8).

Cheiranthus tricuspidatus Linnaeus, *Species Plantarum* 2: 663. 1753.
"Habitat in Europae australis maritimis?" RCN: 4823.
Lectotype (Gowler in Cafferty & Jarvis in *Taxon* 51: 532. 2002): Herb. Clifford: 335, *Cheiranthus* 6 (BM-000646319).
Current name: ***Matthiola tricuspidata*** (L.) R. Br. (Brassicaceae).
Note: Jafri (in Ali & Jafri, *Fl. Libya* 23: 158. 1977) wrongly indicated Kähler material (Herb. Linn. No. 839.26, LINN), received by Linnaeus only in 1757, as "type", and Meikle (*Fl. Cyprus* 1: 158. 1977) indicated unspecified material in BM as "type". Neither statement can be accepted as an effective typification.

Cheiranthus trilobus Linnaeus, *Species Plantarum* 2: 662. 1753.
"Habitat in Hispania & prope insulas Stoechadum." RCN: 4822.
Lectotype (López González in *Anales Jard. Bot. Madrid* 42: 319. 1986): Herb. Linn. No. 839.24 (LINN).
Current name: ***Malcolmia triloba*** (L.) Spreng. (Brassicaceae).

Cheiranthus tristis Linnaeus, *Systema Naturae,* ed. 10, 2: 1134. 1759, *nom. illeg.*
["Habitat in Hispania, Italia, Monspelii."] Sp. Pl., ed. 2, 2: 925 (1763). RCN: 4821.
Replaced synonym: *Cheiranthus fruticulosus* L. (1753).
Lectotype (Meikle, *Fl. Cyprus* 1: 156. 1977): *Löfling 484*, Herb. Linn. No. 839.23 (LINN).
Current name: ***Matthiola fruticulosa*** (L.) Maire (Brassicaceae).

Chelidonium corniculatum Linnaeus, *Species Plantarum* 1: 506. 1753.
"Habitat in Hungaria, Bohemia, Monspelii." RCN: 3837.
Lectotype (Jafri in Jafri & El-Gadi, *Fl. Libya* 40: 6. 1977): Herb. Linn. No. 668.4 (LINN).
Current name: ***Glaucium corniculatum*** (L.) Rudolph subsp. ***corniculatum*** (Papaveraceae).

Chelidonium glaucium Linnaeus, *Species Plantarum* 1: 506. 1753.
"Habitat in Angliae, Helvetiae, Galliae, Italiae, Virginiae arenosis." RCN: 3836.
Lectotype (Grey-Wilson in *Kew Mag.* 6: 151. 1989): Herb. Linn. No. 668.3 (LINN).
Current name: ***Glaucium flavum*** Crantz (Papaveraceae).
Note: Jonsell & Jarvis (in *Nordic J. Bot.* 14: 162. 1994), unaware of Grey-Wilson's earlier choice, designated Herb. Burser IX: 47 (UPS) as lectotype.

Chelidonium hybridum Linnaeus, *Species Plantarum* 1: 506. 1753.
"Habitat in Europa australiore." RCN: 3838.
Lectotype (Jafri & Qaiser in Nasir & Ali, *Fl. W. Pakistan* 61: 6. 1974): Herb. Linn. No. 668.6 (LINN).
Current name: ***Roemeria hybrida*** (L.) DC. subsp. ***hybrida*** (Papaveraceae).

Chelidonium majus Linnaeus, *Species Plantarum* 1: 505. 1753.
"Habitat in Europae ruderatis." RCN: 3835.
Lectotype (Jonsell & Jarvis in Jarvis & al., *Regnum Veg.* 127: 33. 1993): Herb. Linn. No. 668.1 (LINN).
Generitype of *Chelidonium* Linnaeus (vide Adanson, *Fam.* 2: 432. 1763).
Current name: ***Chelidonium majus*** L. (Papaveraceae).
Note: Jonsell & Jarvis (in *Nordic J. Bot.* 14: 162. 1993) provided further information concerning their 1993 type choice.

Chelone glabra Linnaeus, *Species Plantarum* 2: 611. 1753.
"Habitat in Virginia, Canada." RCN: 4419.
Lectotype (Reveal & al. in *Huntia* 7: 220. 1987): *Kalm*, Herb. Linn. No. 765.1 (LINN; iso- UPS).
Generitype of *Chelone* Linnaeus (vide Pennell in *Proc. Acad. Nat. Sci. Philadelphia* 82: 20. 1930).
Current name: ***Chelone glabra*** L. (Scrophulariaceae).

Chelone hirsuta Linnaeus, *Species Plantarum* 2: 611. 1753, *nom. cons.*
"Habitat in Virginia." RCN: 4421.
Conserved type (Barrie & Reveal in *Taxon* 44: 637. 1995): U.S.A. Maryland, Montgomery County, along River Road 0.9 miles west of the junction of West Willard Road, 9 Jun 1995, *J.L. Reveal 7413* (BM; iso- MARY etc.).
Current name: ***Penstemon hirsutus*** (L.) Willd. (Scrophulariaceae).

Chelone obliqua Linnaeus, *Systema Naturae,* ed. 12, 2: 408. 1767. RCN: 4420.
Lectotype (designated here by Sutton): [icon] *"Chelone foliis ovato-lanceolatis serratis floribus rubris"* in Miller, Fig. Pl. Gard. Dict. 1: 62, t. 93. 1756.
Current name: ***Chelone obliqua*** L. (Scrophulariaceae).
Note: Pennell (in *Monogr. Acad. Nat. Sci. Philadelphia* 1: 182. 1935) says this is "based primarily upon a plant described in Miller's gardeners' Dictionary, the type of which has been seen in Herb. British Museum (Natural History) at London". However, this material was not seen by Linnaeus and is not original material for the name.

Chelone penstemon Linnaeus, *Species Plantarum* 2: 612. 1753.
"Habitat in Virginia." RCN: 4420.
Neotype (Crosswhite in *Taxon* 17: 49–50. 1968): Herb. Linn. No. 765.2 (LINN).
Current name: ***Penstemon laevigatus*** Sol. (Scrophulariaceae).
Note: In the absence of any original material, Crosswhite's designation of 765.2 (LINN) as lectotype is accepted as correctable to neotype (Art. 9.8).

Chenopodium album Linnaeus, *Species Plantarum* 1: 219. 1753.
"Habitat in agris Europae." RCN: 1804.
Lectotype (Brenan in Turrill & Milne-Redhead, *Fl. Trop. E. Africa, Chenopodiaceae*: 6. 1954): Herb. Linn. No. 313.8 (LINN).
Generitype of *Chenopodium* Linnaeus (vide Hitchcock, *Prop. Brit. Bot.*: 137. 1929).
Current name: ***Chenopodium album*** L. (Chenopodiaceae).
Note: Chenopodium rubrum L. was treated as the generitype of *Chenopodium* by Britton & Brown, *Ill. Fl. N. U. S.,* ed. 2, 2: 9. 1913 (see McNeill & al. in *Taxon* 36: 365. 1987). However, under

Art. 10.5, Ex. 7 (a voted example) of the Vienna Code, this is a type choice made under the American Code and is to be replaced under Art. 10.5b by Hitchcock's choice (*Prop. Brit. Bot.*: 137. 1929) of *C. album*.

Aellen (in *Verh. Naturf. Ges. Basel* 51(2): 43–65. 1930) discussed the name in some detail and illustrated (p. 50) sheet 313.8 (LINN), but did not appear to choose it explicitly as the type. See notes on the varietal identity of the type by Hansen & Pedersen (in *Bot. Tidsskr.* 63: 226. 1968).

Chenopodium altissimum Linnaeus, *Species Plantarum* 1: 221. 1753.
"Habitat in Astracanum, ad salinas saxonicas inque Italia." RCN: 1824.
Basionym of: *Salsola altissima* (L.) L. (1762).
Lectotype (designated here by Freitag): Herb. Linn. No. 315.10, right specimen (LINN).
Current name: ***Salsola altissima*** (L.) L. (Chenopodiaceae).

Chenopodium ambrosioides Linnaeus, *Species Plantarum* 1: 219. 1753.
"Habitat in Mexico, Lusitania." RCN: 1807.
Lectotype (Brenan in Turrill & Milne-Redhead, *Fl. Trop. E. Africa, Chenopodiaceae*: 10. 1954): Herb. Linn. No. 313.13 (LINN).
Current name: ***Chenopodium ambrosioides*** L. (Chenopodiaceae).

Chenopodium anthelminticum Linnaeus, *Species Plantarum* 1: 220. 1753.
"Habitat in Pensylvania, Bonaria." RCN: 1809.
Type not designated.
Original material: Herb. Linn. No. 313.15 (LINN); [icon] in Dillenius, Hort. Eltham. 1: 77, t. 66, f. 76. 1732 – Voucher: Herb. Sherard No. 592 (OXF).
Current name: ***Chenopodium ambrosioides*** L. (Chenopodiaceae).
Note: Kellogg (in Howard, *Fl. Lesser Antilles* 4: 140. 1988) indicated 313.15 and 313.16 (LINN) as types but as they are evidently not part of a single gathering, Art. 9.15 does not apply.

Chenopodium aristatum Linnaeus, *Species Plantarum* 1: 221. 1753.
"Habitat in Sibiria." RCN: 1815.
Type not designated.
Original material: Herb. Linn. No. 313.24 (LINN).
Current name: ***Chenopodium aristatum*** L. (Chenopodiaceae).

Chenopodium bonus-henricus Linnaeus, *Species Plantarum* 1: 218. 1753.
"Habitat in Europae ruderatis." RCN: 1798.
Lectotype (Jonsell & Jarvis in *Nordic J. Bot.* 14: 155. 1994): Herb. Linn. No. 313.1 (LINN).
Current name: ***Chenopodium bonus-henricus*** L. (Chenopodiaceae).

Chenopodium botrys Linnaeus, *Species Plantarum* 1: 219. 1753.
"Habitat in Europae australis arenosis." RCN: 1806.
Lectotype (Jafri & Rateeb in Jafri & El-Gadi, *Fl. Libya* 58: 13. 1978): Herb. Linn. No. 313.12 (LINN).
Current name: ***Chenopodium botrys*** L. (Chenopodiaceae).

Chenopodium fruticosum Linnaeus, *Species Plantarum* 1: 221. 1753.
"Habitat in Galliae, Hispaniae maritimis." RCN: 1830.
Basionym of: *Salsola fruticosa* (L.) L. (1762).
Lectotype (Heath in *Calyx* 2: 78. 1992): [icon] *"Sedum minus arborescens"* in Munting, Naauwk. Beschryv. Aardgew.: 469, t. 469. 1696 (see above, right).
Current name: ***Suaeda vera*** Forssk. ex J.F. Gmel. (Chenopodiaceae).
Note: As noted by Schenk & Ferren (in *Taxon* 50: 859. 2001), Heath was incorrect in arguing that *Suaeda fruticosa* (L.) Dumort. is the

SEDUM MINUS ARBORESCENS.

correct name for this taxon because it is a later homonym of *S. fruticosa* Forssk. ex J.F. Gmel. Schenk & Ferren also suggest that Heath's type choice is flawed under Art. 9.1, and that the Munting plate is otherwise unsatisfactory. However, there seem to be no grounds for rejecting this choice (and Heath's incorrect use of the term holotype is correctable under Art. 9.8).

Chenopodium glaucum Linnaeus, *Species Plantarum* 1: 220. 1753.
"Habitat ad Europae fimeta." RCN: 1810.
Lectotype (Uotila in *Ann. Bot. Fenn.* 30: 190. 1993): Herb. Linn. No. 313.17 (LINN).
Current name: ***Chenopodium glaucum*** L. (Chenopodiaceae).
Note: Boulos (in *Kew Bull.* 46: 304. 1991) wrongly indicated 313.17 (LINN) as a syntype but as this statement implies no intention to indicate a single nomenclatural type (unlike the use of holotype, lectotype or neotype), this is not regarded as a correctable error.

Chenopodium hirsutum Linnaeus, *Species Plantarum* 1: 221. 1753.
"Habitat Monspelii in maritimis." RCN: 1826.
Basionym of: *Salsola hirsuta* (L.) L. (1762).
Lectotype (Jonsell & Jarvis in *Nordic J. Bot.* 14: 155. 1994): Herb. Burser XVI(2): 19 (UPS).
Current name: ***Bassia hirsuta*** (L.) Asch. (Chenopodiaceae).

Chenopodium hybridum Linnaeus, *Species Plantarum* 1: 219. 1753.
"Habitat in Europae cultis." RCN: 1805.

C

Lectotype (Larsen in Morat, *Fl. Cambodge Laos Viêtnam* 24: 95. 1989): Herb. Linn. No. 313.11 (LINN).
Current name: **Chenopodium hybridum** L. (Chenopodiaceae).

Chenopodium maritimum Linnaeus, *Species Plantarum* 1: 221. 1753.
"Habitat in Europae maritimis." RCN: 1814.
Lectotype (Pedrol & Castroviejo in *Anales Jard. Bot. Madrid* 45: 98. 1988): Herb. Linn. No. 313.21, left specimen (LINN).
Current name: **Suaeda maritima** (L.) Dumort. (Chenopodiaceae).

Chenopodium multifidum Linnaeus, *Species Plantarum* 1: 220. 1753.
"Habitat in Bonaria." RCN: 1808.
Type not designated.
Original material: Herb. Linn. No. 313.14 (LINN); [icon] in Dillenius, Hort. Eltham. 1: 78, t. 66, f. 77. 11732.
Current name: **Chenopodium multifidum** L. (Chenopodiaceae).

Chenopodium murale Linnaeus, *Species Plantarum* 1: 219. 1753.
"Habitat in Europae muris aggeribusque." RCN: 1801.
Lectotype (Brenan in Turrill & Milne-Redhead, *Fl. Trop. E. Africa, Chenopodiaceae*: 7. 1954): Herb. Linn. No. 313.6 (LINN).
Current name: **Chenopodium murale** L. (Chenopodiaceae).

Chenopodium polyspermum Linnaeus, *Species Plantarum* 1: 220. 1753.
"Habitat in Europae cultis." RCN: 1812.
Lectotype (Larsen in Morat, *Fl. Cambodge Laos Viêtnam* 24: 95. 1989): Herb. Linn. No. 313.19 (LINN).
Current name: **Chenopodium polyspermum** L. (Chenopodiaceae).

Chenopodium rubrum Linnaeus, *Species Plantarum* 1: 218. 1753.
"Habitat in Europae cultis, ruderatis." RCN: 1800.
Lectotype (Uotila in *Ann. Bot. Fenn.* 30: 190. 1993): Herb. Linn. No. 313.5 (LINN).
Current name: **Chenopodium rubrum** L. (Chenopodiaceae).
Note: This was was treated as the generitype of *Chenopodium* by Britton & Brown, *Ill. Fl. N. U. S.*, ed. 2, 2: 9. 1913 (see McNeill & al. in *Taxon* 36: 365. 1987). However, under Art. 10.5, Ex. 7 (a voted example) of the Vienna Code, this is a type choice made under the American Code and is to be replaced under Art. 10.5b by Hitchcock's choice (*Prop. Brit. Bot.*: 137. 1929) of *C. album* L.

Chenopodium salsum Linnaeus, *Species Plantarum* 1: 221. 1753.
"Habitat ad Astracanum." RCN: 1825.
Basionym of: *Salsola salsa* (L.) L. (1762).
Lectotype (Freitag & Lomonosova in *Willdenowia* 36: 25, f. 3. 2006): Herb. Linn. No. 315.12 (LINN). – Epitype (Freitag & Lomonosova in *Willdenowia* 36: 25, f. 4. 2006): Russia. Astrakhan prov., northern part of Astrakhan city, near bus station Novostroi, 7 Oct 2004, *M. Lomonosova 716* (NS; iso- AA, ALTB, B, C etc.).
Current name: **Suaeda salsa** (L.) Pall. (Chenopodiaceae).
Note: Freitag & Lomonosova provide an extensive discussion on the original material associated with this name, and the confusion between *S. salsa*, *S. crassifolia* Pall. and *S. prostrata* Pall.

Chenopodium scoparia Linnaeus, *Species Plantarum* 1: 221. 1753.
"Habitat in Graecia, Japonia." RCN: 1813.
Lectotype (Jafri & Rateeb in Jafri & El-Gadi, *Fl. Libya* 58: 26. 1978): Herb. Linn. No. 313.20 (LINN).
Current name: **Bassia scoparia** (L.) A.J. Scott (Chenopodiaceae).

Chenopodium serotinum Linnaeus, *Centuria II Plantarum*: 12. 1756.
"Habitat in Hispania, Anglia, Monspelii." RCN: 1802.

Lectotype (Uotila in *Ann. Bot. Fenn.* 14: 197. 1977): Herb. Linn. No. 313.7 (LINN).
Current name: **Atriplex tatarica** L. (Chenopodiaceae).

Chenopodium urbicum Linnaeus, *Species Plantarum* 1: 218. 1753.
"Habitat in Europae borealis plateis." RCN: 1799.
Lectotype (Uotila in *Ann. Bot. Fenn.* 30: 190. 1993): Herb. Linn. No. 313.2 (LINN).
Current name: **Chenopodium urbicum** L. (Chenopodiaceae).

Chenopodium virginicum Linnaeus, *Species Plantarum* 1: 222. 1753.
"Habitat in Virginia?" RCN: 1815.
Lectotype (designated here by Reveal): Herb. Linn. No. 313.25 (LINN).
Current name: **Chenopodium aristatum** L. (Chenopodiaceae).

Chenopodium viride Linnaeus, *Species Plantarum* 1: 219. 1753.
"Habitat in Europae cultis oleraceis." RCN: 1804.
Lectotype (Uotila in *Acta Bot. Fenn.* 108: 29. 1978): Herb. Linn. No. 313.9 (LINN).
Current name: **Chenopodium album** L. (Chenopodiaceae).
Note: Uotila provided an extensive discussion on the earlier difficulties with this name (often rejected as a *nomen ambiguum*) and, in typifying it, reduced it to a synonym of *C. album*.

Chenopodium vulvaria Linnaeus, *Species Plantarum* 1: 220. 1753.
"Habitat in Europae cultis oleraceis." RCN: 1811.
Lectotype (Jafri & Rateeb in Jafri & El-Gadi, *Fl. Libya* 58: 15. 1978): Herb. Linn. No. 313.18 (LINN).
Current name: **Chenopodium vulvaria** L. (Chenopodiaceae).

Cherleria sedoides Linnaeus, *Species Plantarum* 1: 425. 1753.
"Habitat in Alpibus Helvetiae, Valesiae, Gotthardo." RCN: 3307.
Lectotype (López González in Jarvis & al., *Regnum Veg.* 127: 33. 1993): [icon] *"Cherleria"* in Haller, Enum. Meth. Stirp. Helv. 1: 391, 333, t. 6. 1742 (see p. 135).
Generitype of *Cherleria* Linnaeus.
Current name: **Minuartia sedoides** (L.) Hiern (Caryophyllaceae).
Note: Majumdar & Giri (in *Candollea* 38: 348. 1983) indicated two sheets in LINN (586.1; 586.2) as "type", neither of which is original material for the name.

Chiococca racemosa Linnaeus, *Systema Naturae*, ed. 10, 2: 917. 1759, *nom. illeg.*
["Habitat in Jamaica, Barbados locis confragosis."] Sp. Pl. 1: 175 (1753). RCN: 1368.
Replaced synonym: *Lonicera alba* L. (1753).
Type not designated.
Original material: as replaced synonym.
Current name: **Chiococca alba** (L.) Hitchc. (Rubiaceae).
Note: An illegitimate replacement name for *Lonicera alba* L. (1753).

Chionanthus virginicus Linnaeus, *Species Plantarum* 1: 8. 1753.
"Habitat in America septentrionali." RCN: 56.
Lectotype (Reveal in Jarvis & al., *Regnum Veg.* 127: 33. 1993): Herb. Linn. No. 21.1 (LINN).
Generitype of *Chionanthus* Linnaeus (vide Hitchcock, *Prop. Brit. Bot.*: 115. 1929).
Current name: **Chionanthus virginicus** L. (Oleaceae).

Chionanthus zeylonicus Linnaeus, *Species Plantarum* 1: 8. 1753.
"Habitat in Zeylona." RCN: 57.
Lectotype (Green in Dassanayake & Fosberg, *Revised Handb. Fl. Ceylon* 6: 268. 1987): Herb. Hermann 2: 36; 3: 22, No. 14 (BM).
Current name: **Chionanthus zeylonicus** L. (Oleaceae).

Note: Green indicated Herb. Hermann material (BM) as type and although there is material in more than one volume, it appears to have been part of a single gathering. Consequently, this is accepted as the first typification (Art. 9.15). See discussion by Reveal & al. (in *Huntia* 7: 156. 1987).

Chironia angularis Linnaeus, *Species Plantarum* 1: 190. 1753.
"Habitat in Virginia. Kalm." RCN: 1517.
Lectotype (Wilbur in *Rhodora* 57: 20. 1955): *Kalm*, Herb. Linn. No. 252.5 (LINN).
Current name: ***Sabatia angularis*** (L.) Pursh (Gentianaceae).

Chironia baccifera Linnaeus, *Species Plantarum* 1: 190. 1753.
"Habitat in Aethiopia." RCN: 1519.
Lectotype (Wijnands, *Bot. Commelins*: 105. 1983): [icon] *"Centaurium minus Afric. arborescens pulpiferum"* in Commelin, Hort. Med. Amstelaed. Pl. Rar.: 9, t. 9. 1706.
Current name: ***Chironia baccifera*** L. (Gentianaceae).

Chironia campanulata Linnaeus, *Species Plantarum* 1: 190. 1753.
"Habitat in Canada. Kalm." RCN: 1516.
Lectotype (Blake in *Rhodora* 17: 52. 1915): *Kalm*, Herb. Linn. No. 252.4 (LINN; iso- BM?).
Current name: ***Sabatia campanulata*** (L.) Torr. (Gentianaceae).

Chironia caryophylloides Linnaeus, *Centuria II Plantarum*: 12. 1756.
"Habitat ad Cap. B. Spei. Burmannus." RCN: 1520.
Type not designated.
Original material: [icon] in Burman, Rar. Afric. Pl.: 205, t. 74, f. 1. 1739.
Current name: ***Orphium frutescens*** (L.) E. Mey. (Gentianaceae).

Chironia dodecandra Linnaeus, *Species Plantarum* 1: 190. 1753.
"Habitat in Virginia." RCN: 2695.
Basionym of: *Chlora dodecandra* (L.) L. (1767).
Lectotype (Wilbur in *Rhodora* 57: 86. 1955): *Clayton 120* (BM-000038166).
Current name: ***Sabatia dodecandra*** (L.) Britton & al. (Gentianaceae).

Chironia frutescens Linnaeus, *Species Plantarum* 1: 190. 1753.
"Habitat in Aethiopia." RCN: 1520.
Lectotype (Marais & Verdoorn in Dyer & al., *Fl. Southern Africa* 26: 236. 1963): [icon] *"Centaurium minus Afric. arborescens"* in Commelin, Hort. Med. Amstelaed. Pl. Rar.: 8, t. 8. 1706 (see p. 121).
Current name: ***Orphium frutescens*** (L.) E. Mey. (Gentianaceae).
Note: For a more detailed discussion, see Wijnands (*Bot. Commelins*: 106. 1983).

Chironia jasminoides Linnaeus, *Plantae Rariores Africanae*: 9. 1760.
["Habitat ad Cap. b. spei."] Sp. Pl., ed. 2, 1: 272 (1762). RCN: 1514.
Type not designated.
Original material: Herb. Burman, 3 sheets (G).
Current name: ***Chironia jasminoides*** L. (Gentianaceae).
Note: Marais & Verdoorn (in Dyer & al., *Fl. Southern Africa* 26: 224. 1963) stated that the type was "based on Burmann's specimens from the Cape, seen by Linnaeus and evidently not preserved but specimens in Burmann's herbarium fit the description".

Chironia linoides Linnaeus, *Species Plantarum* 1: 189. 1753.
"Habitat in Capitis b. Spei herbidis." RCN: 1518.
Lectotype (Verdoorn in *Bothalia* 7: 459. 1961): Herb. Clifford: 54, *Chironia* 1 (BM-000557978).

Generitype of *Chironia* Linnaeus (vide Hitchcock, *Prop. Brit. Bot.*: 133. 1929).
Current name: ***Chironia linoides*** L. (Gentianaceae).
Note: See the detailed discussion of the original elements given by Prain (in *Kew Bull.* 1908: 352–353. 1908) who, however, did not designate a type.

Chironia trinervia Linnaeus, *Species Plantarum* 1: 189. 1753.
"Habitat in Zeylona." RCN: 1513.
Lectotype (Cramer in Dassanayake & Fosberg, *Revised Handb. Fl. Ceylon* 3: 58. 1981): Herb. Hermann 3: 26, No. 90 (BM-000594668).
Current name: ***Exacum trinervium*** (L.) Druce (Gentianaceae).

Chlora dodecandra (Linnaeus) Linnaeus, *Systema Naturae,* ed. 12, 2: 267. 1767.
["Habitat in Virginia."] Sp. Pl. 1: 190 (1753). RCN: 2695.
Basionym: *Chironia dodecandra* L. (1753).
Lectotype (Wilbur in *Rhodora* 57: 86. 1955): *Clayton 120* (BM-000038166).
Current name: ***Sabatia dodecandra*** (L.) Britton & al. (Gentianaceae).

Chlora perfoliata (Linnaeus) Linnaeus, *Systema Naturae,* ed. 12, 2: 267. 1767.
["Habitat in Gallia, Anglia, Hispania."] Sp. Pl. 1: 232 (1753). RCN: 2693.
Basionym: *Gentiana perfoliata* L. (1753).
Type not designated.
Original material: as basionym.
Current name: ***Blackstonia perfoliata*** (L.) Huds. (Gentianaceae).

Chlora quadrifolia (Linnaeus) Linnaeus, *Systema Naturae,* ed. 12, 2: 267. 1767.
["Habitat in Europa australi. Cl. Alstroemer."] Sp. Pl., ed. 2, 2: 1671 (1763). RCN: 2694.
Basionym: *Gentiana quadrifolia* L. (1763).
Lectotype (López González & Jarvis in *Anales Jard. Bot. Madrid* 40: 343. 1984): Herb. Linn. No. 494.3 (LINN).
Current name: ***Centaurium quadrifolium*** (L.) G. López & C.E. Jarvis (Gentianaceae).

Chondrilla crepoides Linnaeus, *Systema Vegetabilium,* ed. 13: 595. 1774.
RCN: 5826.
Type not designated.
Original material: none traced.
Note: This name does not appear to be in use, and its application is uncertain.

Chondrilla juncea Linnaeus, *Species Plantarum* 2: 796. 1753.
"Habitat in Germannia, Helvetia, Gallia ad agrorum margines." RCN: 5825.
Lectotype (Lack in Rechinger, *Fl. Iranica* 122: 285. 1977): Herb. Clifford: 383, *Chondrilla* 1 (BM-000646838).
Generitype of *Chondrilla* Linnaeus.
Current name: ***Chondrilla juncea*** L. (Asteraceae).

Chondrilla nudicaulis Linnaeus, *Mantissa Plantarum Altera*: 278. 1771, *nom. cons.*
"Habitat in America septentrionali; ad pyramides aegypti." RCN: 5827.
Conserved type (Kilian in *Taxon* 43: 297. 1994): Egypt. "Kairo, in palmetis ad El Marg", 27 Apr 1908, *Bornmüller 10830* (JE; iso- G, LD, LE).

Current name: **Launaea nudicaulis** (L.) Hook. f. (Asteraceae).
Note: Fernald & Schubert (in *Rhodora* 50: 176. 1948) noted that this
was not an American plant, but the Mediterranean species *Launaea
nudicaulis* (L.) Hook. f. Jeffrey (in *Kew Bull.* 18: 470. 1966)
designated 951.6 (LINN) as lectotype but this collection turned out
to be identifiable as *Lactuca intybacea* Jacq. Kilian (in *Taxon* 41:
297. 1994) successfully proposed the conservation of the name with
a conserved type in order to maintain its usage.

Chrysanthemum achilleae Linnaeus, *Systema Naturae,* ed. 12, 2: 562.
1767.
"Habitat in Italia." RCN: 6438.
Type not designated.
Original material: [icon] in Micheli, Nov. Pl. Gen.: 34, t. 29. 1729. –
Voucher: Herb. Micheli 2809, III: 584, sub *Pyrethrum*, 2810 (FI).
Current name: **Tanacetum corymbosum** (L.) Sch. Bip. subsp.
achilleae (L.) Greuter (Asteraceae).
Note: The Micheli reference, an original element for this name, was
also cited in the synonymy of *C. italicum* L., *Mant. Pl.*: 116 (1767),
but not in that part of its protologue published simultaneously in
Syst. Nat., ed. 12, 2: 563 (1767).

Chrysanthemum alpinum Linnaeus, *Species Plantarum* 2: 889. 1753.
"Habitat in Alpibus Helvetiae ad Thermas Piperinas." RCN: 6431.
Lectotype (Humphries in Jarvis & Turland in *Taxon* 47: 357. 1998):
Herb. Burser VII(1): 33 (UPS).
Current name: **Leucanthemopsis alpina** (L.) Heywood (Asteraceae).
Note: Polatschek (in *Österr. Bot. Zeitschr.* 113: 120. 1966) discussed
the identity of 1012.5 and 1012.6 (LINN), both of which are,
however, post-1753 additions to the herbarium (from Allioni), and
not original material for the name.

Chrysanthemum arcticum Linnaeus, *Species Plantarum* 2: 889. 1753.
"Habitat in Kamtschatca, America septentrionali." RCN: 6441.
Lectotype (Tzvelev in Schischkin & Bobrov, *Fl. U.R.S.S.* 26: 387.
1961): [icon] *"Pyrethrum foliis longe petiolatis, palmatis, supra dilatatis,
ultimis laciniis trilobis"* in Gmelin, Fl. Sibirica 2: 203, t. 84. 1752.
Current name: **Arctanthemum arcticum** (L.) Tzvelev (Asteraceae).
Note: Humphries (in *Taxon* 47: 357. 1998) designated a Gmelin
collection, 1012.16 (LINN) as type, but this choice is pre-dated by
that of Tzvelev, who formally chose Gmelin's plate as type.

Chrysanthemum balsamita Linnaeus, *Species Plantarum*, ed. 2, 2:
1252. 1763.
"Habitat in Oriente." RCN: 6436.
Lectotype (Humphries in Jarvis & Turland in *Taxon* 47: 357. 1998):
Herb. Linn. No. 1012.11 (LINN).
Current name: **Tanacetum balsamita** L. subsp. **balsamitoides** (Sch.
Bip.) Grierson (Asteraceae).
Note: This name is independent of *Tanacetum balsamita* L. (1753).

Chrysanthemum bipinnatum Linnaeus, *Species Plantarum* 2: 890.
1753.
"Habitat in Sibiria." RCN: 6447.
Lectotype (Tzvelev in Schischkin & Bobrov, *Fl. U.R.S.S.* 26: 325.
1961): [icon] *"Pyrethrum foliis duplicato pinnatis, pinnulis incisis,
pedunculis unifloris, caule erecto"* in Gmelin, Fl. Sibirica 2: 205, t.
85, f. 1. 1752.
Current name: **Tanacetum bipinnatum** (L.) Sch. Bip. (Asteraceae).
Note: Humphries (in *Taxon* 47: 358. 1998) designated Herb. Linn.
1012.24 (LINN) as type, but this choice is pre-dated by that of
Tzvelev.

Chrysanthemum coronarium Linnaeus, *Species Plantarum* 2: 890.
1753, *nom. cons.*

"Habitat in Creta, Sicilia." RCN: 6448.
Conserved type (Turland in *Taxon* 53: 1072. 2004): Greece. Kriti
(Crete): Nomos Irakliou, Eparhia Kenourgiou, 500m E of
Gangales, E side of road to Vali, 250m, 13 Apr 2003, *Kyriakopoulos
& Turland sub Turland 1166* (UPA; iso- B, BM, MO).
Current name: **Glebionis coronaria** (L.) Cass. ex Spach (Asteraceae).
Note: Chrysanthemum coronarium had long been treated as the
generitype until Trehane (in *Taxon* 44: 439. 1995) proposed the
conservation of *Chrysanthemum* with *C. indicum* L. as the conserved
type, in order to restrict the generic name to the florists'
chrysanthemum. The proposal was successful, resulting in *Glebionis*
Cass. becoming the correct generic name for *C. segetum* L. and *C.
coronarium*.
   The earliest typification of *C. coronarium* was published by
Dillon (in *Fieldiana, Bot.*, n.s., 7: 5. 1981), who designated 1012.25
(LINN) as the type. Unfortunately, this specimen is identifiable as
Glebionis segetum (L.) Fourr. (syn. *C. segetum* L.). Turland (in *Taxon*
53: 1072. 2004) successfully proposed the conservation of *C.
coronarium* with a conserved type.

Chrysanthemum corymbiferum Linnaeus, *Amoenitates Academicae* 4:
491. 1759, *orth. var.*
["Habitat in Thuringia, Bohemia, Helvetia, Sibiria."] Sp. Pl. 2: 890
(1753). RCN: 6439.
Lectotype (Humphries in Jarvis & Turland in *Taxon* 47: 358. 1998):
Herb. Linn. No. 1012.13 (LINN).
Current name: **Tanacetum corymbosum** (L.) Sch. Bip. var.
corymbosum (Asteraceae).
Note: Although published in the *Amoen. Acad.* reprint of the thesis
Flora Monspeliensis, this name is evidently an orthographic variant
of *C. corymbosum* L. (1753), as noted by Stearn (in Geck & Pressler,
Festschr. Claus Nissen: 632. 1974). In *Sp. Pl.*, ed. 2, 2: 1251 (1763),
Linnaeus again used the epithet "corymbiferum", but in
conjunction with the same diagnosis and synonyms associated with
C. corymbosum in 1753. In *Syst. Nat.*, ed. 12, 2: 562 (1767), he
again used the same diagnosis, but reverted to the use of
"corymbosum".

Chrysanthemum corymbosum Linnaeus, *Species Plantarum* 2: 890.
1753.
"Habitat in Thuringia, Bohemia, Helvetia, Sibiria." RCN: 6439.
Lectotype (Humphries in Jarvis & Turland in *Taxon* 47: 358. 1998):
Gerber, Herb. Linn. No. 1012.13 (LINN).
Current name: **Tanacetum corymbosum** (L.) Sch. Bip. var.
corymbosum (Asteraceae).

Chrysanthemum flosculosum Linnaeus, *Species Plantarum* 2: 890.
1753.
"Habitat in Africa." RCN: 6449.
Lectotype (Turland in *Bull. Nat. Hist. Mus. London, Bot.* 25: 157, f.
26. 1995): Herb. Clifford: 417, *Chrysanthemum* 6 (BM-
000647218).
Current name: **Plagius flosculosus** (L.) Alavi & Heywood
(Asteraceae).

Chrysanthemum frutescens Linnaeus, *Species Plantarum* 2: 887.
1753.
"Habitat in Canariis insulis." RCN: 6428.
Lectotype (Humphries in *Bull. Brit. Mus. (Nat. Hist.), Bot.* 5: 181.
1976): Herb. Clifford: 417, *Chrysanthemum* 5 (BM-000647217).
Current name: **Argyranthemum frutescens** (L.) Sch. Bip.
(Asteraceae).
Note: Francisco-Ortega & Santos-Guerra (in *Archives Nat. Hist.* 26:
261. 1999) reproduce the Plukenet plate cited in the
protologue.

Chrysanthemum graminifolium Linnaeus, *Species Plantarum* 2: 888. 1753.
"Habitat Monspelii." RCN: 6434.
Lectotype (Humphries in Jarvis & Turland in *Taxon* 47: 358. 1998): Herb. Linn. No. 1012.9 (LINN).
Current name: ***Leucanthemum graminifolium*** (L.) Lam. (Asteraceae).

Chrysanthemum indicum Linnaeus, *Species Plantarum* 2: 889. 1753, *typ. cons.*
"Habitat in India." RCN: 6440.
Lectotype (Humphries in Jarvis & Turland in *Taxon* 47: 358. 1998): Herb. Linn. No. 1012.15 (LINN).
Generitype of *Chrysanthemum* Linnaeus, *nom. cons.*
Current name: ***Chrysanthemum indicum*** L. (Asteraceae).
Note: Chrysanthemum coronarium L. had long been treated as the generitype until Trehane (in *Taxon* 44: 439. 1995) proposed the conservation of *Chrysanthemum* with *C. indicum* as the conserved type, in order to restrict the generic name to the florists' chrysanthemum. The proposal was successful, resulting in *Glebionis* Cass. becoming the correct generic name for *C. segetum* L. and *C. coronarium* L.

Chrysanthemum inodorum (Linnaeus) Linnaeus, *Species Plantarum*, ed. 2, 2: 1253. 1763.
"Habitat in ruderatis Sveciae & praestantioris Europae." RCN: 6437.
Basionym: *Matricaria inodora* L. (1755).
Lectotype (Humphries in Jarvis & Turland in *Taxon* 47: 364. 1998): Herb. Linn. No. 1012.12 (LINN).
Current name: ***Tripleurospermum maritimum*** (L.) W.D.J. Koch subsp. ***inodorum*** (L.) Appleq. (Asteraceae).
Note: Rauschert (in *Folia Geobot. Phytotax.* 9: 249–260. 1974) argued (incorrectly) that *M. inodora* L. (the basionym of *C. inodorum*) was a superfluous *nomen novum* for *M. chamomilla* L. (1753). Applequist (in *Taxon* 51: 760. 2003) gives a detailed review of the nomenclature associated with this name, accepting Humphries' typification and concluding that the correct name for the scentless mayweed is either *Tripleurospermum inodorum* (L.) Sch. Bip. at species rank, or *T. maritimum* subsp. *inodorum* (L.) Appleq. at subspecific rank.

Chrysanthemum italicum Linnaeus, *Systema Naturae*, ed. 12, 2: 563; *Mantissa Plantarum*: 116. 1767.
"Habitat in Italia. Arduini." RCN: 6445.
Type not designated.
Original material: *Arduino 69*, Herb. Linn. No. 1012.21 (LINN); [icon] in Micheli, Nov. Pl. Gen.: 34, t. 29. 1729. –Voucher: Herb. Micheli 2809, III: 584, sub *Pyrethrum*, 2810 (FI).
Current name: ***Tanacetum corymbosum*** (L.) Sch. Bip. var. ***tenuifolium*** (Willd.) Briq. & Cavill. (Asteraceae).
Note: The Micheli reference, an original element for this name, was also cited simultaneously in the synonymy of *C. achilleae* L., *Syst. Nat.*, ed. 12, 2: 562 (1767).

Chrysanthemum leucanthemum Linnaeus, *Species Plantarum* 2: 888. 1753.
"Habitat in pratis Europae." RCN: 6432.
Lectotype (Böcher & Larsen in *Watsonia* 4: 15, t. 6, f. 1. 1957): Herb. Clifford: 416, *Chrysanthemum* 3 (BM-000647215).
Current name: ***Leucanthemum vulgare*** Lam. (Asteraceae).
Note: See Greuter & al. (in *Taxon* 54: 162. 2005) for an argument that *Leucanthemum vulgare* Lam. is actually a new combination based on *Bellidioides vulgaris* Vaill. (1754).

Chrysanthemum millefoliatum Linnaeus, *Systema Naturae*, ed. 12, 2: 563. 1767, *nom. illeg.*
["Habitat in Sibiria."] Sp. Pl. 2: 896 (1753). RCN: 6446.
Replaced synonym: *Anthemis millefolia* L. (1753).
Lectotype (Humphries in Jarvis & Turland in *Taxon* 47: 352. 1998): *Gerber*, Herb. Linn. No. 1012.22 (LINN).
Current name: ***Tanacetum millefolium*** (L.) Tzvelev (Asteraceae).
Note: Because Tzvelev (in Schischkin & Bobrov, *Fl. U.R.S.S.* 26: 349. 1961) stated that the cited Gmelin drawing was only "probably" the type specimen (of *Anthemis millefolium* L.), this is not accepted as a formal type choice (Art. 7.11).

Chrysanthemum monspeliense Linnaeus, *Species Plantarum* 2: 889. 1753.
"Habitat Monspelii." RCN: 6435.
Type not designated.
Original material: none traced.
Current name: ***Leucanthemum monspeliense*** (L.) H.J. Coste (Asteraceae).

Chrysanthemum montanum Linnaeus, *Species Plantarum* 2: 888. 1753.
"Habitat Monspelii." RCN: 6433.
Type not designated.
Original material: [icon] in Bauhin & Cherler, Hist. Pl. Univ. 3(1): 115. 1651.
Current name: ***Leucanthemum adustum*** (W.D.J. Koch) Gremli (Asteraceae).
Note: This name seems to have been informally abandoned and treated as a synonym of either *L. adustum* (W.D.J. Koch) Gremli, *L. heterophyllum* (Willd.) DC. or *L. graminifolium* (L.) Lam.

Chrysanthemum myconis Linnaeus, *Species Plantarum*, ed. 2, 2: 1254. 1763.
"Habitat in Lusitaniae, Hispaniae, Italiae, agris." RCN: 6444.
Lectotype (Grierson in Davis, *Fl. Turkey* 5: 256. 1975): Herb. Linn. No. 1012.20 (LINN).
Current name: ***Coleostephus myconis*** (L.) Rchb. f. (Asteraceae).
Note: Humphries (in *Taxon* 47: 358. 1998), unaware of Grierson's earlier choice, independently chose the same type.

Chrysanthemum pectinatum Linnaeus, *Species Plantarum*, ed. 2, 2: 1255. 1763.
"Habitat in Hispania, Italia." RCN: 6442.
Lectotype (López González & Jarvis in *Anales Jard. Bot. Madrid* 40: 343. 1984): *Alströmer 167b*, Herb. Linn. No. 1012.18 (LINN).
Current name: ***Leucanthemopsis pectinata*** (L.) G. López & C.E. Jarvis (Asteraceae).

Chrysanthemum segetum Linnaeus, *Species Plantarum* 2: 889. 1753.
"Habitat in Scaniae, Germaniae, Belgii, Angliae, Galliae agris." RCN: 6443.
Lectotype (Grierson in Dassanayake & Fosberg, *Revised Handb. Fl. Ceylon* 1: 237. 1980): Herb. Clifford: 416, *Chrysanthemum* 2 (BM-000647213).
Current name: ***Glebionis segetum*** (L.) Fourr. (Asteraceae).
Note: Chrysanthemum coronarium L. had long been treated as the generitype until Trehane (in *Taxon* 44: 439. 1995) proposed the conservation of *Chrysanthemum* with *C. indicum* L. as the conserved type, in order to restrict the generic name to the florists' chrysanthemum. The proposal was successful, resulting in *Glebionis* Cass. becoming the correct generic name for *C. segetum* L. and *C. coronarium.*

Chrysanthemum serotinum Linnaeus, *Species Plantarum* 2: 888. 1753.
"Habitat forte in America septentrionali? cum sero floreat." RCN: 6429.
Lectotype (Humphries in Jarvis & Turland in *Taxon* 47: 358. 1998): Herb. Clifford: 416, *Chrysanthemum* 4 (BM-000647216).
Current name: ***Leucanthemella serotina*** (L.) Tzvelev (Asteraceae).

Chrysitrix capensis Linnaeus, *Mantissa Plantarum Altera*: 304. 1771.
"Habitat ad Cap. b. Spei. Koenig." RCN: 7714.
Neotype (Simpson in Jarvis & al., *Regnum Veg.* 127: 33. 1993): Herb. Linn. No. 1238.1 (LINN).
Generitype of *Chrysitrix* Linnaeus.
Current name: ***Chrysitrix capensis*** L. (Cyperaceae).

Chrysobalanus icaco Linnaeus, *Species Plantarum* 1: 513. 1753.
"Habitat in Jamaica, Brasilia, Barbiches, Surinamo." RCN: 3639.
Lectotype (Prance & Sothers, *Sp. Pl. – Fl. World* 9: 5. 2003): [icon] *"Icaco"* in Plumier, Nov. Pl. Amer.: 43, t. 5. 1703. – Epitype (Prance & Sothers, *Sp. Pl. – Fl. World* 9: 5. 2003): U.S.A. Florida, Indian River, *A.H. Curtiss 728* (P; iso- A, F, GH, K, NY, US).
Generitype of *Chrysobalanus* Linnaeus.
Current name: ***Chrysobalanus icaco*** L. (Chrysobalanaceae).
Note: None of the material in LINN is original for the name so Vidal's type statement (in Aubréville, *Fl. Cambodge Laos Vietnam* 6: 195. 1968) is not an effective choice. Prance (in Görts-van-Rijn, *Fl. Guianas*, ser. A, 2: 6. 1986) indicated 641.1 (LINN) as a neotype, but as there are original elements in existence, this too cannot be accepted. Purohit & Panigrahi, *Fam. Rosaceae India* 1: 260–261. 1991) indicated Plumier's t. 158 as "iconotype" on p. 260, and 641.1 LINN as holotype on p. 261, so neither is effective.

Chrysocoma biflora Linnaeus, *Species Plantarum* 2: 841. 1753.
"Habitat in Sibiria." RCN: 6092.
Type not designated.
Original material: *Gerber*, Herb. Linn. No. 982.11 (LINN); *Gerber*, Herb. Linn. No. 982.10 (LINN); [icon] in Gmelin, Fl. Sibirica 2: 190, t. 82, f. 1. 1752.
Current name: ***Aster dracunculoides*** Lam. (Asteraceae).

Chrysocoma cernua Linnaeus, *Species Plantarum* 2: 840. 1753.
"Habitat in Aethiopia." RCN: 6087.
Lectotype (Bayer in *Mitt. Bot. Staatssamml. München* 17: 285. 1981): Herb. Linn. No. 982.3 ["983.3"] (LINN).
Current name: ***Chrysocoma cernua*** L. (Asteraceae).
Note: See discussion by Wijnands (*Bot. Commelins*: 73. 1983), who concluded that the cited Commelin plate was probably a sparsely leaved specimen of *C. coma-aurea* L.

Chrysocoma ciliata Linnaeus, *Species Plantarum* 2: 841. 1753.
"Habitat in Aethiopia." RCN: 6088.
Lectotype (Wijnands, *Bot. Commelins*: 72. 1983): Herb. Linn. No. 982.4 (LINN).
Current name: ***Chrysocoma ciliata*** L. (Asteraceae).

Chrysocoma coma-aurea Linnaeus, *Species Plantarum* 2: 840. 1753.
"Habitat in Aethiopia." RCN: 6085.
Lectotype (Bayer in *Mitt. Bot. Staatssamml. München* 17: 290. 1981): Herb. Linn. No. 982.2 (LINN).
Generitype of *Chrysocoma* Linnaeus (vide Green, *Prop. Brit. Bot.*: 180. 1929).
Current name: ***Chrysocoma coma-aurea*** L. (Asteraceae).

Chrysocoma graminifolia Linnaeus, *Species Plantarum* 2: 841. 1753.
"Habitat in Canada. Kalm." RCN: 6093.

Lectotype (Sieren in *Rhodora* 83: 563. 1981): *Kalm*, Herb. Linn. No. 337.17 (S).
Current name: ***Euthamia graminifolia*** (L.) Nutt. (Asteraceae).

Chrysocoma linosyris Linnaeus, *Species Plantarum* 2: 841. 1753.
"Habitat in Europa temperatiore." RCN: 6091.
Type not designated.
Original material: Herb. Linn. No. 982.4 (LINN); Herb. Burser XII: 18 (UPS); Herb. Clifford: 396, *Chrysocoma* 1 (BM); [icon] in Clusius, Rar. Pl. Hist. 1: 325. 1601; [icon] in Lobel, Pl. Stirp. Hist.: 223. 1576; [icon] in Colonna, Ekphr.: 81, 82. 1606.
Current name: ***Aster linosyris*** (L.) Bernh. (Asteraceae).

Chrysocoma oppositifolia Linnaeus, *Plantae Rariores Africanae*: 18. 1760.
["Habitat ad Cap. b. Spei."] Sp. Pl., ed. 2, 2: 1177 (1763). RCN: 6084.
Lectotype (Lowrey in Jarvis & Turland in *Taxon* 47: 358. 1998): Herb. Linn. No. 982.1 (LINN).
Current name: ***Pteronia divaricata*** Less. (Asteraceae).

Chrysocoma scabra Linnaeus, *Species Plantarum*, ed. 2, 2: 1177. 1763, *nom. illeg.*
"Habitat in Aethiopia." RCN: 6090.
Replaced synonym: *Baccharis tenuifolia* L. (1753).
Type not designated.
Original material: as replaced synonym.
Current name: ***Polyarrhena reflexa*** (L.) Cass. subsp. ***reflexa*** (Asteraceae).
Note: An illegitimate renaming in *Chrysocoma* of *Baccharis tenuifolia* L. (1753).

Chrysocoma scoparia Linnaeus, *Systema Naturae,* ed. 10, 2: 1206. 1759.
["Habitat in Jamaica."] Syst. Nat., ed. 12, 3: 234 (1768). RCN: 6099.
Basionym of: *Calea scoparia* (L.) L. (1768).
Lectotype (Wussow & al. in *Syst. Bot.* 10: 265. 1985): *Browne*, Herb. Linn. No. 984.4 (LINN).
Current name: ***Baccharis scoparia*** (L.) Sw. (Asteraceae).

Chrysocoma tomentosa Linnaeus, *Systema Naturae*, ed. 12, 2: 539. 1767.
RCN: 6089.
Lectotype (Bayer in *Mitt. Bot. Staatssamml. München* 17: 281. 1981): Herb. Linn. No. 982.5 (LINN).
Current name: ***Chrysocoma tomentosa*** L. (Asteraceae).

Chrysocoma villosa Linnaeus, *Species Plantarum* 2: 841. 1753.
"Habitat in Sibiria, Tataria." RCN: 6094.
Type not designated.
Original material: Herb. Linn. No. 982.12 (LINN); [icon] in Gmelin, Fl. Sibirica 2: 192, t. 82, f. 2. 1752.
Current name: ***Aster oleifolius*** (Lam.) Wagenitz (Asteraceae).

Chrysogonum peruvianum Linnaeus, *Species Plantarum* 2: 920. 1753.
"Habitat in Peru. D. Jussieu." RCN: 6423.
Type not designated.
Original material: [icon] in Feuillée, J. Obs. 2: 766, t. 50. 1714.
Note: The only extant original element is the Feuillée plate which appears to be "a wedelioid plant and definitely not a *Zinnia*" (Jeffrey, pers. comm., 15 Oct 1992). The name is not the basionym of *Zinnia peruviana* L. (1759).

Chrysogonum virginianum Linnaeus, *Species Plantarum* 2: 920. 1753.
"Habitat in Virginia." RCN: 6657.
Lectotype (Stuessy in *Rhodora* 79: 193. 1977): *Clayton 298* (BM-000051186; iso- BM?).
Generitype of *Chrysogonum* Linnaeus (vide Lessing, *Syn. Comp.* 220. 1832).
Current name: ***Chrysogonum virginianum*** L. (Asteraceae).
Note: See extensive review by Reveal & al. (in *Huntia* 7: 218. 1987). Herb. Clifford: 424, *Chrysogonum* 1 (BM) may be a duplicate of *Clayton 298* and, perhaps, an isolectotype.

Chrysophyllum cainito Linnaeus, *Species Plantarum* 1: 192. 1753.
"Habitat in America calidiore." RCN: 1540.
Lectotype (Howard, *Fl. Lesser Antilles* 6: 57. 1989): [icon] *"Anona, foliis subtus ferrugineis, fructu rotundo majore, laevi, purpureo, semine nigro, partim rugoso, partim glabro"* in Sloane, *Voy. Jamaica* 2: 170, t. 229. 1725. – Typotype: Herb. Sloane 7: 101 (BM-SL).
Generitype of *Chrysophyllum* Linnaeus.
Current name: ***Chrysophyllum cainito*** L. (Sapotaceae).
Note: Although Malik (in Nasir & Ali, *Fl. Pakistan* 163: 3. 1984) indicated 260.1 (LINN) as type, it is a Patrick Browne specimen not received by Linnaeus until after 1753 and hence not original material for the name.

Chrysophyllum maliforme Linnaeus, *Systema Naturae,* ed. 10, 2: 937. 1759.
["Habitat in America calidiore."] Sp. Pl., ed. 2, 1: 278 (1762). RCN: 1540.
Type not designated.
Original material: none traced.
Current name: ***Chrysophyllum cainito*** L. (Sapotaceae).

Chrysophyllum oliviforme Linnaeus, *Systema Naturae,* ed. 10, 2: 937. 1759.
RCN: 1540.
Lectotype (Vink in *Blumea* 9: 28. 1958): [icon] *"Chrysophyllum"* in Plumier in Burman, Pl. Amer.: 57, t. 69. 1756.
Current name: ***Chrysophyllum oliviforme*** L. (Sapotaceae).

Chrysosplenium alternifolium Linnaeus, *Species Plantarum* 1: 398. 1753.
"Habitat in Sueciae, Germanniae, Angliae opacis humentibus." RCN: 3137.
Lectotype (Jonsell & Jarvis in *Nordic J. Bot.* 22: 72. 2002): Herb. Clifford: 149, *Chrysosplenium* 1 (BM-000558661).
Current name: ***Chrysosplenium alternifolium*** L. (Saxifragaceae).

Chrysosplenium oppositifolium Linnaeus, *Species Plantarum* 1: 398. 1753.
"Habitat in Belgio, Anglia, Canada locis umbrosis humentibus." RCN: 3138.
Lectotype (Gornall in Jarvis & al., *Regnum Veg.* 127: 33. 1993): [icon] *"Saxifraga aurea"* in Dodoëns, Stirp. Hist. Pempt., ed. 2: 316. 1616.
Generitype of *Chrysosplenium* Linnaeus (vide Hitchcock, *Prop. Brit. Bot.*: 154. 1929).
Current name: ***Chrysosplenium oppositifolium*** L. (Saxifragaceae).

Cicca disticha Linnaeus, *Systema Naturae,* ed. 12, 2: 621; *Mantissa Plantarum*: 124. 1767.
"Habitat in India." RCN: 7119.
Lectotype (Radcliffe-Smith in Polhill, *Fl. Trop. E. Africa, Euphorbiaceae*: 37. 1987): Herb. Linn. No. 1108.1 (LINN).
Generitype of *Cicca* Linnaeus.
Current name: ***Phyllanthus acidus*** (L.) Skeels (Euphorbiaceae).

Cicer arietinum Linnaeus, *Species Plantarum* 2: 738. 1753.
"Habitat inter Hispaniae, Italiae segetes." RCN: 5430.
Lectotype (Verdcourt in Milne-Redhead & Polhill, *Fl. Trop. E. Africa, Leguminosae* 4: 1065. 1971): Herb. Clifford: 370, *Cicer* 1 α (BM-000646701).
Generitype of *Cicer* Linnaeus.
Current name: ***Cicer arietinum*** L. (Fabaceae: Faboideae).

Cichorium endivia Linnaeus, *Species Plantarum* 2: 813. 1753.
"Habitat – – – –" RCN: 5922.
Lectotype (Alavi in Jafri & El-Gadi, *Fl. Libya* 107: 320. 1983): Herb. Linn. No. 962.3 (LINN).
Current name: ***Cichorium endivia*** L. (Asteraceae).

Cichorium intybus Linnaeus, *Species Plantarum* 2: 813. 1753.
"Habitat in Europa ad margines agrorum viarumque." RCN: 5921.
Lectotype (Lack in Rechinger, *Fl. Iranica* 122: 6. 1977): Herb. Linn. No. 962.1 (LINN).
Generitype of *Cichorium* Linnaeus (vide Green, *Prop. Brit. Bot.*: 178. 1929).
Current name: ***Cichorium intybus*** L. (Asteraceae).

Cichorium spinosum Linnaeus, *Species Plantarum* 2: 813. 1753.
"Habitat in Cretae, Siciliae collibus arenosis maritimis." RCN: 5923.
Lectotype (Alavi in Jafri & El-Gadi, *Fl. Libya* 107: 322. 1983): Herb. Linn. No. 962.4 (LINN).
Current name: ***Cichorium spinosum*** L. (Asteraceae).

Cicuta bulbifera Linnaeus, *Species Plantarum* 1: 255. 1753.
"Habitat in Virginia, Canada." RCN: 2049.
Lectotype (Mulligan in *Canad. J. Bot.* 58: 1760. 1980): *Kalm,* Herb. Linn. No. 361.2 (LINN).
Current name: ***Cicuta bulbifera*** L. (Apiaceae).

Cicuta maculata Linnaeus, *Species Plantarum* 1: 256. 1753.
"Habitat in Virginiae aquosis." RCN: 2050.
Lectotype (Fernald in *Rhodora* 41: 441. 1939): *Kalm,* Herb. Linn. No. 361.3 (LINN).
Current name: ***Cicuta maculata*** L. (Apiaceae).

Cicuta virosa Linnaeus, *Species Plantarum* 1: 255. 1753.
"Habitat in paludibus Europae sterilibus." RCN: 2048.
Lectotype (Hedge & Lamond in Davis, *Fl. Turkey* 4: 425. 1972): *Amman s.n.,* Herb. Linn. No. 361.1 (LINN), see opposite.
Generitype of *Cicuta* Linnaeus (vide Hitchcock, *Prop. Brit. Bot.*: 140. 1929).
Current name: ***Cicuta virosa*** L. (Apiaceae).

Cimicifuga foetida Linnaeus, *Systema Naturae,* ed. 12, 2: 659. 1767.
["Habitat in Sibiria. D. Kraschenninnikof."] Sp. Pl. 1: 504 (1753). RCN: 3962.
Replaced synonym: *Actaea cimicifuga* L. (1753).
Lectotype (Compton & Jury in *Taxon* 44: 604. 1995): Herb. Linn. No. 220.17 (S).
Current name: ***Cimicifuga foetida*** L. (Ranunculaceae).

Cinchona herbacea Linnaeus, *Mantissa Plantarum Altera*: 338. 1771, *nom. illeg.*
RCN: 1361.
Replaced synonym: *Cinchona caribaea* Jacq. (1760).
Type not designated.
Current name: ***Exostema caribaeum*** (Jacq.) Roem. & Schult. (Rubiaceae).
Note: An illegitimate renaming of *C. caribaea* Jacq. (1760), as noted by Andersson (in *Mem. New York Bot. Gard.* 80: 64. 1998).

The lectotype of *Cicuta virosa* L.

Cinchona officinalis Linnaeus, *Species Plantarum* 1: 172. 1753.
"Habitat in Loxa Peruviae." RCN: 1360.
Lectotype (Jarvis & al., *Regnum Veg.* 127: 34. 1993): [icon]
"*Quinquina*" in Condamine in Mém. Acad. Roy. Sci. Paris 1738:
226, t. 5. 1738. – Voucher: *Herb. Jussieu 9899+B* (P-JU). – Epitype
(Andersson in *Mem. New York Bot. Gard.* 80: 55. 1998): *Herb.
Jussieu 9899+B* (P-JU).
Generitype of *Cinchona* Linnaeus.
Current name: ***Cinchona officinalis*** L. (Rubiaceae).
Note: From correspondence between Linnaeus and Mútis in 1764
(quoted by Jaramillo-Arongo, *The Conquest of Malaria*: 82. 1950),
it is clear that Linnaeus' original 1753 concept was based solely on
Condamine's account of 1738. Jarvis & al. (in *Regnum Veg.* 127: 34.
1993) indicated Condamine's t. 5 as the holotype which was
incorrect in that a second plate, t. 6, also formed part of the
protologue. However, this statement is correctable under Art. 9.8,
leaving t. 5 as the lectotype, a choice also accepted by Andersson (in
Harling & Andersson, *Fl. Ecuador* 50: 51. 1994) and others.
  The type figure is reproduced by Jaramillo-Arongo (*l.c.*: t. 23),
along with a drawing (t. 25) made by Santisteban which Mútis sent
to Linnaeus.

Cineraria alpina (Linnaeus) Linnaeus, *Species Plantarum,* ed. 2, 2:
1243. 1763.

"Habitat in Alpibus Pyrenaeis, Helveticis, Austriacis, Monspelii,
Sibiricis." RCN: 6366.
Basionym: *Solidago alpina* L. (1753).
Lectotype (Kadereit in Jarvis & Turland in *Taxon* 47: 367. 1998):
[icon] "*Jacobaea alpina foliis rotundis serratis*" in Bauhin, Prodr.
Theatri Bot.: 70, 69. 1620.
Current name: ***Jacobaea alpina*** (L.) Moench (Asteraceae).

Cineraria alpina (Linnaeus) Linnaeus var. **alata** (N.J. Jacquin)
Linnaeus, *Species Plantarum,* ed. 2, 2: 1243. 1763.
RCN: 6366.
Basionym: *Solidago alpina* L. var. *alata* Jacq. (1762).
Type not designated.
Current name: ***Senecio* sp.** (Asteraceae).

Cineraria alpina (Linnaeus) Linnaeus var. **helenitis** (Linnaeus)
Linnaeus, *Species Plantarum,* ed. 2, 2: 1244. 1763.
["Habitat in Sibiria. D. Gmelin. Gallia."] Sp. Pl. 2: 925 (1753). RCN:
6366.
Basionym: *Othonna helenitis* L. (1753).
Type not designated.
Original material: as basionym.
Current name: ***Tephroseris helenitis*** (L.) B. Nord. (Asteraceae).

Cineraria alpina (Linnaeus) Linnaeus var. **integrifolia** (Linnaeus)
Linnaeus, *Species Plantarum,* ed. 2, 2: 1243. 1763.
["Habitat in Alpibus Pyrenaicis, Helveticis, Austriacis, Sibiricis."] Sp.
Pl. 2: 925 (1753). RCN: 6366.
Basionym: *Othonna integrifolia* L. (1753).
Type not designated.
Original material: as basionym.
Current name: ***Tephroseris integrifolia*** (L.) Holub subsp. ***integrifolia***
(Asteraceae).

Cineraria amelloides Linnaeus, *Species Plantarum,* ed. 2, 2: 1245.
1763.
"Habitat ad Cap. b. spei." RCN: 6372.
Lectotype (Riley & Levyns in *J. S. African Bot.* 29: 35. 1963): Herb.
Linn. No. 1000.27 (LINN).
Current name: ***Felicia amelloides*** (L.) Voss (Asteraceae).

Cineraria aurea Linnaeus, *Species Plantarum,* ed. 2, 2: 1244. 1763.
"Habitat in Sibiria." RCN: 6367.
Lectotype (Marhold & al. in *Ann. Bot. Fenn.* 40: 377. 2003): Herb.
Linn. No. 1000.22 (LINN).
Current name: ***Senecio paludosus*** L. subsp. ***lanatus*** Holub
(Asteraceae).

Cineraria canadensis Linnaeus, *Species Plantarum,* ed. 2, 2: 1244.
1763.
"Habitat in Canada. Kalm." RCN: 6369.
Replaced synonym: *Othonna cineraria* L. (1753).
Lectotype (Reveal in Jarvis & Turland in *Taxon* 47: 365. 1998): Herb.
Linn. No. 1000.25 (LINN).
Current name: ***Jacobaea maritima*** (L.) Pelser & Meijden subsp.
maritima (Asteraceae).
Note: A *nomen novum* for *Othonna cineraria* L. (1753).

Cineraria cymbalarifolia (Linnaeus) Linnaeus, *Species Plantarum,* ed.
2, 2: 1242. 1763.
"Habitat ad Cap. b. spei. Burmannus." RCN: 6361.
Basionym: *Othonna cymbalarifolia* L. (1760).
Type not designated.
Original material: as basionym.
Current name: ***Senecio cymbalarifolius*** (L.) Less. (Asteraceae).

Cineraria geifolia (Linnaeus) Linnaeus, *Species Plantarum*, ed. 2, 2: 1242. 1763.
"Habitat ad Cap. b. spei." RCN: 6360.
Basionym: *Othonna geifolia* L. (1753).
Lectotype (Wijnands, *Bot. Commelins*: 73. 1983): Herb. Clifford: 410, *Solidago* 7 (BM-000647123).
Generitype of *Cineraria* Linnaeus (vide Phillips, *Gen. S. African Fl. Pl.*, ed. 2: 833. 1951).
Current name: ***Cineraria geifolia*** (L.) L. (Asteraceae).

Cineraria glauca Linnaeus, *Species Plantarum*, ed. 2, 2: 1242. 1763.
"Habitat in Sibiria." RCN: 6363.
Lectotype (Nordenstam & Illarionova in *Taxon* 54: 143, f. 6. 2005): [icon] *"Solidago floribus spicatis, foliis subcordatis, glaberrimis, glaucis, oblonge ellipticis, amplexicaulibus"* in Gmelin, Fl. Sibirica 2: 166, t. 74. 1752 (see p. 133).
Current name: ***Ligularia glauca*** (L.) O. Hoffm. (Asteraceae).

Cineraria linifolia (Linnaeus) Linnaeus, *Species Plantarum*, ed. 2, 2: 1244. 1763.
"Habitat ad Cap. b. spei." RCN: 6370.
Basionym: *Othonna linifolia* L. (1760).
Type not designated.
Original material: as basionym.
Current name: ***Euryops linifolius*** (L.) DC. (Asteraceae).

Cineraria maritima (Linnaeus) Linnaeus, *Species Plantarum*, ed. 2, 2: 1244. 1763.
"Habitat ad maris inferi littora." RCN: 6368.
Basionym: *Othonna maritima* L. (1753).
Lectotype (Peruzzi & al. in *Taxon* 55: 1003, f. 2A. 2006): Herb. Clifford: 410, *Solidago* 11 (BM-000647125).
Current name: ***Jacobaea maritima*** (L.) Pelser & Meijden subsp. ***maritima*** (Asteraceae).

Cineraria othonnites Linnaeus, *Species Plantarum*, ed. 2, 2: 1244. 1763.
"Habitat in Africa." RCN: 6699.
Replaced synonym of: *Othonna frutescens* L. (1771).
Type not designated.
Original material: Herb. Linn. No. 1038.22 (LINN); [icon] in Commelin, Hort. Med. Amstelod. Pl. Rar. 2: 147, t. 74. 1701.
Current name: ***Othonna othonnites*** (L.) Druce (Asteraceae).
Note: Wijnands (*Bot. Commelins*: 79. 1983) suggested that this name was probably based on 1038.22 (LINN) but did not formally choose it as type.

Cineraria palustris (Linnaeus) Linnaeus, *Species Plantarum*, ed. 2, 2: 1243. 1763.
"Habitat in Europae caespitosis, aquosis." RCN: 6365.
Basionym: *Othonna palustris* L. (1753).
Lectotype (Jeffrey & Chen in *Kew Bull.* 39: 284. 1984): Herb. Linn. No. 1000.13 (LINN).
Current name: ***Senecio congestus*** (R. Br.) DC. (Asteraceae).

Cineraria purpurata Linnaeus, *Mantissa Plantarum Altera*: 285. 1771.
"Habitat ad Cap. b. spei." RCN: 6371.
Lectotype (Cron & al. in *Kew Bull.* 61: 529. 2007 (2006)): *Tulbagh 44*, Herb. Linn. No. 1000.26 (LINN).
Note: The application of this name is uncertain.

Cineraria sibirica (Linnaeus) Linnaeus, *Species Plantarum*, ed. 2, 2: 1242. 1763.
"Habitat in Sibiria, Oriente." RCN: 6362.

Basionym: *Othonna sibirica* L. (1753).
Lectotype (Nordenstam & Illarionova in *Taxon* 54: 141, f. 2. 2005): Herb. Linn. No. 348.13 (S).
Current name: ***Ligularia sibirica*** (L.) Cass. (Asteraceae).

Cineraria sonchifolia (Linnaeus) Linnaeus, *Species Plantarum*, ed. 2, 2: 1243. 1763.
"Habitat ad Cap. b. spei." RCN: 6364.
Basionym: *Othonna sonchifolia* L. (1753).
Type not designated.
Original material: as basionym.
Note: The application of this name is uncertain.

Cinna arundinacea Linnaeus, *Species Plantarum* 1: 5. 1753.
"Habitat in Canada, unde semina per D. Kalm." RCN: 37.
Neotype (Hitchcock in *Contr. U. S. Natl. Herb.* 12: 115. 1908): Herb. Linn. No. 15.1 (LINN).
Generitype of *Cinna* Linnaeus.
Current name: ***Cinna arundinacea*** L. (Poaceae).
Note: Doubts as to whether 15.1 (LINN) was in Linnaeus' possession in 1753 cause this collection to be treated as a neotype (there is no other original material extant).

Circaea alpina Linnaeus, *Species Plantarum* 1: 9. 1753.
"Habitat ad radices montium in frigidis Europae." RCN: 65.
Lectotype (Jonsell & Jarvis in *Nordic J. Bot.* 22: 82. 2002): Herb. Burser IX: 24, right specimen (UPS).
Current name: ***Circaea alpina*** L. (Onagraceae).

Circaea lutetiana Linnaeus, *Species Plantarum* 1: 9. 1753.
"Habitat in Europae & Americae borealis nemoribus." RCN: 64.
Lectotype (Boufford in *Ann. Missouri Bot. Gard.* 69: 879. 1983): Herb. Linn. No. 25.1 (LINN).
Generitype of *Circaea* Linnaeus (vide Hitchcock, *Prop. Brit. Bot.*: 116. 1929).
Current name: ***Circaea lutetiana*** L. var. ***lutetiana*** (Onagraceae).

Circaea lutetiana Linnaeus var. **canadensis** Linnaeus, *Species Plantarum* 1: 9. 1753.
RCN: 64.
Neotype (Boufford in *Ann. Missouri Bot. Gard.* 69: 854. 1983): Herb. Linn. No. 4.9 (S).
Current name: ***Circaea lutetiana*** L. var. ***canadensis*** L. (Onagraceae).
Note: Although Boufford treated 4.9 (S) as the lectotype, there are some doubts as to whether this collection was available to Linnaeus in 1753. However, in the absence of any original material, this is treated as a neotype.

Circaea minima Linnaeus, *Mantissa Plantarum Altera*: 316. 1771.
RCN: 65.
Type not designated.
Original material: none traced.
Current name: ***Circaea alpina*** L. (Onagraceae).
Note: Boufford (in *Ann. Missouri Bot. Gard.* 69: 931. 1983) treated *C. minima* as an error for *C. alpina* L. (1753). It is unclear if this is the case.

Cissampelos caapeba Linnaeus, *Species Plantarum* 2: 1032. 1753.
"Habitat in America meridionali." RCN: 7516.
Type not designated.
Original material: none traced.
Current name: ***Cissampelos pareira*** L. (Menispermaceae).

Cissampelos pareira Linnaeus, *Species Plantarum* 2: 1031. 1753.
"Habitat in America meridionali." RCN: 7515.

Lectotype (Troupin in *Bull. Jard. Bot. État Bruxelles* 25: 140. 1955): [icon] *"Clematis baccifera, glabra et villosa, rotundo et umbilicato folio"* in Plumier, Descr. Pl. Amér.: 78, t. 93. 1693.

Generitype of *Cissampelos* Linnaeus (vide Green, *Prop. Brit. Bot.*: 191. 1929).

Current name: ***Cissampelos pareira*** L. (Menispermaceae).

Cissampelos smilacina Linnaeus, *Species Plantarum* 2: 1032. 1753.
"Habitat in Carolina." RCN: 7517.
Lectotype (Howard & Staples in *J. Arnold Arbor.* 64: 532. 1983): [icon] *"Smilax (forte) lenis, folio anguloso hederaceo"* in Catesby, Nat. Hist. Carolina 1: 51, t. 51. 1730.
Current name: ***Cocculus carolinus*** (L.) DC. (Menispermaceae).

Cissus acida Linnaeus, *Species Plantarum,* ed. 2, 1: 170. 1762, *nom. illeg.*
"Habitat in America." RCN: 956.
Replaced synonym: *Sicyos trifoliata* L. (1753).
Lectotype (Lombardi in *Taxon* 44: 203. 1995): [icon] *"Bryonia alba triphylla geniculata, foliis crassis acidis"* in Sloane, Voy. Jamaica 1: 233, t. 142, f. 5, 6. 1707. – Typotype: Herb. Sloane 4: 87, 88 (BM-SL).
Current name: ***Cissus trifoliata*** (L.) L. (Vitaceae).
Note: A superfluous name for *Sicyos trifoliata* L. (1753).

Cissus cordifolia Linnaeus, *Species Plantarum,* ed. 2, 1: 170. 1762.
"Habitat in America." RCN: 953.
Lectotype (Lombardi in *Taxon* 44: 195. 1995): [icon] *"Vitis foliis cordato-orbiculatis"* in Plumier in Burman, Pl. Amer.: 258, t. 259, f. 3. 1760.
Current name: ***Cissus verticillata*** (L.) Nicolson & C.E. Jarvis (Vitaceae).

Cissus laciniata (Linnaeus) Linnaeus, *Systema Naturae,* ed. 10, 2: 897. 1759.
["Habitat in America calidiori."] Sp. Pl. 2: 1013 (1753). RCN: 7348.
Basionym: *Sicyos laciniata* L. (1753).
Lectotype (Lombardi in *Taxon* 46: 430. 1997): [icon] *"Sicyos foliis laciniatis"* in Plumier in Burman, Pl. Amer.: 239, t. 243, f. 1. 1760.
Current name: ***Sicyos laciniata*** L. (Cucurbitaceae).

Cissus quadrangularis Linnaeus, *Systema Naturae,* ed. 12, 2: 124; *Mantissa Plantarum*: 39. 1767.
"Habitat in Arabia, India." RCN: 955.
Lectotype (Nasir & Ali in Nasir & Ali, *Fl. Pakistan* 147: 18. 1982): Herb. Linn. No. 149.3 (LINN).
Current name: ***Cissus quadrangularis*** L. (Vitaceae).

Cissus sicyoides Linnaeus, *Systema Naturae,* ed. 10, 2: 897. 1759.
["Habitat in Jamaica."] Sp. Pl., ed. 2, 1: 170 (1762). RCN: 954.
Lectotype (Nicolson & Jarvis in *Taxon* 33: 726. 1984): [icon] *"Irsiola scandens, foliis oblongo-ovatis ad margines denticulis setaceis refertis"* in Browne, Civ. Nat. Hist. Jamaica: 147, t. 4, f. 1, 2. 1756.
Current name: ***Cissus verticillata*** (L.) Nicolson & C.E. Jarvis (Vitaceae).

Cissus trifoliata (Linnaeus) Linnaeus, *Systema Naturae,* ed. 10, 2: 897. 1759.
["Habitat in Jamaica."] Sp. Pl. 2: 1013 (1753). RCN: 956.
Basionym: *Sicyos trifoliata* L. (1753).
Lectotype (Lombardi in *Taxon* 44: 203. 1995): [icon] *"Bryonia alba triphylla geniculata, foliis crassis acidis"* in Sloane, Voy. Jamaica 1: 233, t. 142, f. 5, 6. 1707. – Typotype: Herb. Sloane 4: 87, 88 (BM-SL).
Current name: ***Cissus trifoliata*** (L.) L. (Vitaceae).

Cissus trifoliata Linnaeus, *Species Plantarum,* ed. 2, 1: 170. 1762, *nom. illeg.*
"Habitat in Jamaica." RCN: 957.
Lectotype (Lombardi in *Taxon* 44: 203. 1995): [icon] *"Bryonia alba triphylla maxima"* in Sloane, Voy. Jamaica 1: 233, t. 144, f. 2. 1707.
Current name: ***Cissus microcarpa*** Vahl (Vitaceae).
Note: A later homonym of *C. trifoliata* (L.) L. (1759).

Cissus vitiginea Linnaeus, *Species Plantarum* 1: 117. 1753.
"Habitat in India." RCN: 952.
Lectotype (Shetty & Singh in *Kew Bull.* 44: 473. 1989): Herb. Hermann 2: 35, No. 60 (BM-000594598).
Generitype of *Cissus* Linnaeus.
Current name: ***Cissus vitiginea*** L. (Vitaceae).

Cistus aegyptiacus Linnaeus, *Species Plantarum* 1: 527. 1753.
"Habitat in Aegypto. B. Jussieus." RCN: 3913.
Lectotype (Jafri in Jafri & El-Gadi, *Fl. Libya* 48: 33. 1977): Herb. Linn. No. 689.50 (LINN).
Current name: ***Helianthemum aegyptiacum*** (L.) Mill. (Cistaceae).

Cistus albidus Linnaeus, *Species Plantarum* 1: 524. 1753.
"Habitat in G. Narbonensi, Hispania." RCN: 3894.
Type not designated.
Original material: Herb. Burser XXIV: 49 (UPS); Herb. Linn. No. 689.11 (LINN); [icon] in Clusius, Rar. Pl. Hist. 1: 68. 1601; [icon] in Bauhin & Cherler, Hist. Pl. Univ. 2: 3. 1651.
Current name: ***Cistus albidus*** L. (Cistaceae).
Note: Specific epithet spelled "albida" in the protologue.

Cistus anglicus Linnaeus, *Mantissa Plantarum Altera*: 245. 1771, *nom. illeg.*
"Habitat in quibusdam Angliae locis." RCN: 3905.
Replaced synonym: *Cistus hirsutus* Huds. (1762).
Type not designated.
Note: A superfluous name for *Cistus hirsutus* Huds. (1762), the application of which appears uncertain.

Cistus apenninus Linnaeus, *Species Plantarum* 1: 529. 1753.
"Habitat in Apenninis, Italiae montibus." RCN: 3925.
Lectotype (López González in *Anales Jard. Bot. Madrid* 50: 47. 1992): Herb. Linn. No. 689.65 (LINN).
Current name: ***Helianthemum apenninum*** (L.) Mill. (Cistaceae).
Note: See also comments by Raynal (in *J. Bot. Soc. Bot. France* 5: 141. 1998) who reproduces a later edition of the protologue and also accepts the sheet in LINN as the type.

Cistus arabicus Linnaeus, *Centuria I Plantarum*: 14. 1755.
"Habitat in Arabica. D. Hasselquist." RCN: 3927.
Type not designated.
Original material: *Hasselquist*, Herb. Linn. No. 689.67 (LINN); *Hasselquist*, Herb. Linn. No. 689.68 (LINN).
Current name: ***Fumana arabica*** (L.) Spach (Cistaceae).

Cistus calycinus Linnaeus, *Mantissa Plantarum Altera*: 565. 1771.
"Habitat in Europa australi." RCN: 3900.
Lectotype (López González in *Anales Jard. Bot. Madrid* 42: 322. 1986): Herb. Linn. No. 689.28 (LINN).
Current name: ***Halimium calycinum*** (L.) K. Koch (Cistaceae).

Cistus canadensis Linnaeus, *Species Plantarum* 1: 526. 1753.
"Habitat in Canada. Kalm." RCN: 3909.
Lectotype (designated here by Reveal): *Kalm*, Herb. Linn. No. 689.46 (LINN).
Current name: ***Helianthemum canadense*** (L.) Michx. (Cistaceae).

Cistus canus Linnaeus, *Species Plantarum* 1: 525. 1753.
"Habitat in G. Narbonensi, Hispania." RCN: 3902.
Lectotype (López González in *Anales Jard. Bot. Madrid* 50: 52. 1992):
 Herb. Burser XXIV: 67 (UPS).
Current name: *Helianthemum oelandicum* (L.) DC. subsp. *incanum*
 (Willk.) G. López (Cistaceae).
Note: Janchen (in *Österr. Bot. Zeitschr.* 59: 225. 1909) published a
 photograph (Abb. 2) of a specimen of *Cistus canus* from the
 Linnaean herbarium (689.35, LINN) which he described as "Ein
 Originalexemplar". Kupatadze (in *Novosti Sist. Vyssh. Rast.* 16: 142.
 1979) treated this collection as the lectotype, but it lacks a *Species
 Plantarum* number (i.e. "12"), and is a post-1753 addition to the
 herbarium, and not original material for the name. See extensive
 comments on the elements involved in this name by López
 González (*l.c.*: 52–53).

Cistus canus Linnaeus var. **lusitanicus** Linnaeus, *Mantissa Plantarum
 Altera*: 403. 1771.
RCN: 3902.
Type not designated.
Original material: none traced.
Current name: *Helianthemum lasianthum* (Lam.) Spach (Cistaceae).
Note: Varietal epithet spelled "lusitanica" in the protologue.
 See note by López González (in *Anales Jard. Bot. Madrid* 50: 53.
 1992).

Cistus canus Linnaeus var. **seguieri** Linnaeus, *Mantissa Plantarum
 Altera*: 403. 1771.
RCN: 3902.
Type not designated.
Original material: Herb. Linn. No. 689.34 (LINN); Herb. Linn. No.
 689.35 (LINN).
Current name: *Helianthemum oelandicum* (L.) DC. subsp. *alpestre*
 (Jacq.) Ces. (Cistaceae).
Note: Varietal epithet spelled "seguierii" in the protologue.
 See note by López González (in *Anales Jard. Bot. Madrid* 50: 53.
 1992).

Cistus capensis Linnaeus, *Species Plantarum*, ed. 2, 1: 736. 1762.
"Habitat ad Cap. b. Spei." RCN: 3885.
Type not designated.
Original material: none traced.
Note: The application of this name is uncertain.

Cistus creticus Linnaeus, *Systema Naturae*, ed. 10, 2: 1077. 1759.
["Habitat in Creta, Syria."] Sp. Pl., ed. 2, 1: 738 (1762). RCN: 3893.
Lectotype (Jafri in Jafri & El-Gadi, *Fl. Libya* 48: 4. 1977): *Hasselquist*,
 Herb. Linn. No. 689.17 (LINN; iso- UPS?).
Current name: *Cistus creticus* L. subsp. *creticus* (Cistaceae).
Note: Specific epithet spelled "cretica" in the protologue.

Cistus crispus Linnaeus, *Species Plantarum* 1: 524. 1753.
"Habitat in Lusitania." RCN: 3895.
Type not designated.
Original material: Herb. Burser XXIV: 53 (UPS); *Löfling s.n.*, Herb.
 Linn. No. 689.19 (LINN); [icon] in Clusius, Rar. Pl. Hist. 1: 69.
 1601.
Generitype of *Cistus* Linnaeus (vide Green, *Prop. Brit. Bot.*: 162.
 1929).
Current name: *Cistus crispus* L. (Cistaceae).

Cistus fumana Linnaeus, *Species Plantarum* 1: 525. 1753.
"Habitat in Gallia, Gotlandia, Helvetia." RCN: 3901.
Type not designated.
Original material: Herb. Burser XXIV: 75? (UPS); Herb. Linn. No.

689.29 (LINN); [icon] in Bauhin & Cherler, Hist. Pl. Univ. 2: 18.
 1651.
Current name: *Fumana procumbens* (Dunal) Gren. & Godr.
 (Cistaceae).

Cistus glutinosus Linnaeus, *Mantissa Plantarum Altera*: 246. 1771.
"Habitat in Europa australi." RCN: 3919.
Type not designated.
Original material: [icon] in Barrelier, Pl. Galliam: 50, t. 415. 1714;
 [icon] in Bauhin & Cherler, Hist. Pl. Univ. 2: 19. 1651.
Current name: *Fumana thymifolia* (L.) Spach ex Webb (Cistaceae).

Cistus guttatus Linnaeus, *Species Plantarum* 1: 526. 1753.
"Habitat in G. Narbonensi, Italia." RCN: 3908.
Lectotype (Jafri in Jafri & El-Gadi, *Fl. Libya* 48: 39. 1977): Herb.
 Linn. No. 689.44 (LINN).
Current name: *Tuberaria guttata* (L.) Fourr. (Cistaceae).

Cistus halimifolius Linnaeus, *Species Plantarum* 1: 524. 1753.
"Habitat in Lusitaniae maritimis." RCN: 3896.
Type not designated.
Original material: Herb. Linn. No. 689.22 (LINN); [icon] in Clusius,
 Rar. Pl. Hist. 1: 71. 1601; [icon] in Clusius, Rar. Pl. Hist. 1: 71.
 1601.
Current name: *Fumana halimifolia* (L.) Willk. (Cistaceae).
Note: Specific epithet spelled "halimifolium" in the protologue.

Cistus helianthemum Linnaeus, *Species Plantarum* 1: 528. 1753.
"Habitat in Europae pascuis siccis." RCN: 3923.
Type not designated.
Original material: Herb. Burser XXIV: 64 (UPS); Herb. Linn. No.
 689.59 (LINN); Herb. Clifford: 206, *Cistus* 9 (BM); [icon] in
 Loesel, Fl. Prussica: 43, t. 8. 1703; [icon] in Mattioli, Pl. Epit.: 501.
 1586.
Current name: *Helianthemum nummularium* (L.) Mill. (Cistaceae).

Cistus hirtus Linnaeus, *Species Plantarum* 1: 528. 1753.
"Habitat in Hispania, Narbona." RCN: 3924.
Lectotype (Jafri in Jafri & El-Gadi, *Fl. Libya* 48: 19. 1977): Herb.
 Linn. No. 689.61 (LINN).
Current name: *Helianthemum hirtum* (L.) Mill. (Cistaceae).

Cistus hirtus Linnaeus, *Centuria I Plantarum*: 14. 1755, *nom. illeg.*
"Habitat Monspelii."
Type not designated.
Original material: Herb. Linn. No. 689.9 (LINN); Herb. Linn. No.
 689.10 (LINN); [icon] in Clusius, Rar. Pl. Hist.: 79, 78. 1601.
Note: Specific epithet spelled "hirta" in the protologue.
 A later homonym of *Cistus hirtus* L. (1753) and therefore
 illegitimate (as noted by Nordenstam in *Bot. Not.* 114: 277. 1961).

Cistus incanus Linnaeus, *Species Plantarum* 1: 524. 1753.
"Habitat in Hispania, G. Narbonensi." RCN: 3892.
Type not designated.
Original material: Herb. Clifford: 205, *Cistus* 4 (BM); Herb. Linn.
 No. 689.14 (LINN); [icon] in Clusius, Rar. Pl. Hist. 1: 69. 1601.
Current name: *Cistus creticus* L. (Cistaceae).
Note: Specific epithet spelled "incana" in the protologue.
 This name has been treated as a *nomen confusum* by some, and
 informally rejected in favour of the later *C. creticus* L. (1759).
 However, no formal proposal for rejection appears to have been
 made.

Cistus indicus Linnaeus, *Systema Naturae*, ed. 12, 2: 367. 1767, *nom.
 illeg.*

Cistus 421

C

["Habitat in Italia."] Sp. Pl., ed. 2, 1: 740 (1762). RCN: 3903.
Replaced synonym: *Cistus italicus* L. (1759).
Type not designated.
Original material: as replaced synonym.
Current name: ***Helianthemum oelandicum*** (L.) DC. subsp. ***italicum*** (L.) Font Quer & Rothm. (Cistaceae).
Note: This appears to have been an error for *C. italicus* L. (1759). The diagnosis is identical for both names, and *C. italicus* does not appear in *Syst. Nat.*, ed. 12 (1767). *Cistus indicus* is treated as entirely including the earlier name, and is therefore illegitimate.

Cistus italicus Linnaeus, *Systema Naturae*, ed. 10, 2: 1078. 1759.
["Habitat in Italia."] Sp. Pl., ed. 2, 1: 740 (1762). RCN: 3903.
Replaced synonym of: *Cistus indicus* L. (1767), *nom. illeg.*
Type not designated.
Original material: Herb. Linn. No. 689.36 (LINN).
Current name: ***Helianthemum oelandicum*** (L.) DC. subsp. ***italicum*** (L.) Font Quer & Rothm. (Cistaceae).

Cistus ladanifer Linnaeus, *Species Plantarum* 1: 523. 1753.
"Habitat in Hispania, Lusitaniae collibus." RCN: 3889.
Type not designated.
Original material: Herb. Clifford: 205, *Cistus* 2, 2 sheets (BM); Herb. Linn. No. 689.5 (LINN); [icon] in Clusius, Rar. Pl. Hist. 1: 77. 1601.
Current name: ***Cistus ladanifer*** L. (Cistaceae).
Note: Specific epithet spelled "ladanifera" in the protologue.
Carazo Román & Jiménez Albarrán (in *Bot. Complut.* 14: 111. 1989) wrongly designated 689.6 (LINN), a specimen annotated only by Linnaeus filius and not original material for the name, as lectotype.

Cistus laevipes Linnaeus, *Centuria I Plantarum*: 14. 1755.
"Habitat Monspelii." RCN: 3899.
Type not designated.
Original material: [icon] in Bauhin & Cherler, Hist. Pl. Univ. 2: 18. 1651.
Current name: ***Fumana laevipes*** (L.) Spach (Cistaceae).

Cistus laurifolius Linnaeus, *Species Plantarum* 1: 523. 1753.
"Habitat in Hispania." RCN: 3888.
Lectotype (Carazo Román & Jiménez Albarrán in *Bot. Complut.* 14: 111. 1989): Herb. Linn. No. 689.4 (LINN).
Current name: ***Cistus laurifolius*** L. (Cistaceae).
Note: Specific epithet spelled "laurifolia" in the protologue.

Cistus ledifolius Linnaeus, *Species Plantarum* 1: 527. 1753.
"Habitat Monspelii." RCN: 3910.
Lectotype (Burtt & Lewis in *Kew Bull.* 4: 305. 1949): Herb. Linn. No. 689.47 (LINN).
Current name: ***Helianthemum ledifolium*** (L.) Mill. (Cistaceae).

Cistus libanotis Linnaeus, *Systema Naturae,* ed. 10, 2: 1077. 1759.
["Habitat in Hispania. Loefling."] Sp. Pl., ed. 2, 1: 739 (1762). RCN: 3897.
Lectotype (Heywood in *Feddes Repert.* 79: 60. 1968): Herb. Linn. No. 689.24 (LINN).
Current name: ***Cistus libanotis*** L. (Cistaceae).

Cistus lippii Linnaeus, *Mantissa Plantarum Altera*: 245. 1771.
"Habitat in Aegypto." RCN: 3915.
Lectotype (Burtt & Lewis in *Kew Bull.* 4: 306. 1949): Herb. Linn. No. 689.53 (LINN).
Current name: ***Helianthemum lippii*** (L.) Dum. Cours. (Cistaceae).
Note: Specific epithet spelled "lippi" in the protologue.

Cistus marifolius Linnaeus, *Species Plantarum* 1: 526. 1753.
"Habitat Massiliae." RCN: 3904.
Lectotype (López González in *Anales Jard. Bot. Madrid* 50: 54. 1992): Herb. Burser XXIV: post 57 (UPS).
Current name: ***Helianthemum marifolium*** (L.) Mill. (Cistaceae).

Cistus monspeliensis Linnaeus, *Species Plantarum* 1: 524. 1753.
"Habitat in Narbonensi & Regno Valentino." RCN: 3890.
Type not designated.
Original material: Herb. Burser XXIV: 79 (UPS); Herb. Burser XXIV: 76 (UPS); Herb. Clifford: 205, *Cistus* 3 (BM); [icon] in Clusius, Rar. Pl. Hist. 1: 79. 1601; [icon] in Daléchamps, Hist. General. Pl. 1: 230. 1587.
Current name: ***Cistus monspeliensis*** L. (Cistaceae).

Cistus niloticus Linnaeus, *Mantissa Plantarum Altera*: 246. 1771.
"Habitat in Aegypto." RCN: 3912.
Type not designated.
Original material: none traced.
Current name: ***Helianthemum ledifolium*** (L.) Mill. (Cistaceae).

Cistus nummularius Linnaeus, *Species Plantarum* 1: 527. 1753.
"Habitat Monspelii." RCN: 3917.
Lectotype (López González in *Anales Jard. Bot. Madrid* 50: 46. 1992): Herb. Linn. No. 689.54 (LINN).
Current name: ***Helianthemum nummularium*** (L.) Mill. (Cistaceae).

Cistus oelandicus Linnaeus, *Species Plantarum* 1: 526. 1753.
"Habitat in rupibus apricis Oelandiae." RCN: 3906.
Lectotype (López González in *Anales Jard. Bot. Madrid* 50: 51. 1992): Herb. Linn. No. 689.40 (LINN), see p. 172.
Current name: ***Helianthemum oelandicum*** (L.) DC. (Cistaceae).
Note: Stearn (in *Biol. J. Linn. Soc.* 5: 10. 1973), in an account of Linnaeus' Öland and Gotland journey of 1741, treated Resmo in Öland as the restricted type locality, and noted the existence of 689.40 (LINN), annotated by Linnaeus as from Öland. In his paper, he attributed restricted type localities irrespective of whether any material existed in LINN and, where specimens do exist, he does not refer to any of them as type specimens. This LINN material was formally designated as lectotype by López González.

Cistus pilosus Linnaeus, *Species Plantarum* 1: 528. 1753.
"Habitat Monspelii." RCN: 3921.
Type not designated.
Original material: Herb. Burser XXIV: 66 (UPS); [icon] in Clusius, Rar. Pl. Hist. 1: 74. 1601.
Current name: ***Helianthemum violaceum*** (Cav.) Pers. (Cistaceae).
Note: Jafri (in Jafri & El-Gadi, *Fl. Libya* 48: 22. 1977) indicated 689.55 (LINN) as type but this collection lacks the relevant *Species Plantarum* number (i.e. "25") and was a post-1753 addition to the herbarium, and is not original material for the name. López González (in *Anales Jard. Bot. Madrid* 50: 40, 45. 1990) argued that *Helianthemum pilosum* Mill. is not based on *C. pilosus* L., making *H. pilosum* (L.) Pers. a later homonym of Miller's name. He follows Sampaio (in *Bol. Soc. Brot.*, sér. 2, 7: 132. 1931) in regarding the correct name for Linnaeus' plant to be *H. violaceum* (Cav.) Pers. There are also problems in that at least some of the original material is identifiable as *Fumana*.

Cistus populifolius Linnaeus, *Species Plantarum* 1: 523. 1753.
"Habitat in Lusitania." RCN: 3926.
Type not designated.
Original material: Herb. Burser XXIV: 78 (UPS); Herb. Clifford: 205, *Cistus* 1 (BM); Herb. Burser XXIV: 77 (UPS); [icon] in Clusius, Rar. Pl. Hist. 1: 78. 1601.

Current name: ***Cistus populifolius*** L. (Cistaceae).
Note: Specific epithet spelled "populifolia" in the protologue.

Cistus racemosus Linnaeus, *Systema Naturae*, ed. 12, 2: 368; *Mantissa Plantarum*: 76. 1767.
"Habitat in Hispania." RCN: 3922.
Type not designated.
Original material: *le Monnier*, Herb. Linn. No. 689. 56 (LINN); [icon] in Barrelier, Pl. Galliam: 52, t. 293. 1714.
Current name: ***Helianthemum racemosum*** (L.) Pau (Cistaceae).

Cistus salicifolius Linnaeus, *Species Plantarum* 1: 527. 1753.
"Habitat in Lusitania, Hispania." RCN: 3911.
Lectotype (Jafri in Jafri & El-Gadi, *Fl. Libya* 48: 33. 1977): Herb. Linn. No. 689.48 (LINN).
Current name: ***Helianthemum salicifolium*** (L.) Mill. (Cistaceae).
Note: Although Burtt & Lewis (in *Kew Bull.* 4: 306. 1949) indicated material in LINN as type, they did not distinguish between 689.48 and 689.49 (LINN), which do not appear to be part of a single gathering so Art. 9.15 does not apply.

Cistus salviifolius Linnaeus, *Species Plantarum* 1: 524. 1753.
"Habitat in Italia, Sicilia, Narbona." RCN: 3891.
Type not designated.
Original material: Herb. Clifford: 205, *Cistus* 5 (BM); Herb. Burser XXIV: 54 (UPS); [icon] in Clusius, Rar. Pl. Hist. 1: 70. 1601.
Current name: ***Cistus salviifolius*** L. (Cistaceae).
Note: Specific epithet spelled "salvifolia" in the protologue.
Jafri (in Jafri & El-Gadi, *Fl. Libya* 48: 8. 1977) indicated 689.11 (LINN) as type, but this collection was received from Alströmer long after 1753 so it cannot be original material for the name.

Cistus serpillifolius Linnaeus, *Species Plantarum* 1: 527. 1753.
"Habitat in Alpibus Austriae, Stiriae." RCN: 3918.
Type not designated.
Original material: Herb. Burser XXIV: 72 (UPS); [icon] in Bauhin & Cherler, Hist. Pl. Univ. 2: 17. 1651.
Current name: ***Helianthemum oelandicum*** (L.) DC. subsp. **alpestre** (Jacq.) Ces. (Cistaceae).

Cistus squamatus Linnaeus, *Species Plantarum* 2: 1196. 1753.
"Habitat in Hispania. Loefl." RCN: 3914.
Type not designated.
Original material: *Löfling 384a*, Herb. Linn. No. 689.51 (LINN).
Current name: ***Helianthemum squamatum*** (L.) Pers. (Cistaceae).

Cistus surrejanus Linnaeus, *Species Plantarum* 1: 527. 1753.
"Habitat in Angliae comitatu Surrejano prope Croydon." RCN: 3916.
Type not designated.
Original material: [icon] in Dillenius, Hort. Eltham. 1: 177, t. 145, f. 174. 1732.
Current name: ***Helianthemum nummularium*** (L.) Mill. (Cistaceae).

Cistus thymifolius Linnaeus, *Species Plantarum* 1: 528. 1753.
"Habitat in G. Narbonensi, Hispania." RCN: 3920.
Lectotype (Molero & Rovira in *Candollea* 42: 519. 1987): Herb. Linn. No. 216.15 (S).
Current name: ***Fumana thymifolia*** (L.) Spach ex Webb (Cistaceae).

Cistus tubararia Linnaeus, *Species Plantarum* 1: 526. 1753.
"Habitat in Galloprovincia, Hispania, Pisis." RCN: 3907.
Type not designated.
Original material: *Löfling s.n.*, Herb. Linn. No. 689.42 (LINN); Herb. Burser XXIV: 55 (UPS); [icon] in Bauhin & Cherler, Hist. Pl. Univ.

2: 12. 1651; [icon] in Bauhin & Cherler, Hist. Pl. Univ. 2: 12, 13. 1651.
Current name: ***Xolantha tubararia*** (L.) M.J. Gallego & al. (Cistaceae).

Cistus umbellatus Linnaeus, *Species Plantarum* 1: 525. 1753.
"Habitat in Gallia, Hispania." RCN: 3898.
Type not designated.
Original material: Herb. Linn. No. 689.25 (LINN); [icon] in Clusius, Rar. Pl. Hist. 1: 81. 1601.
Current name: ***Halimium umbellatum*** (L.) Spach (Cistaceae).

Cistus villosus Linnaeus, *Genera Plantarum*, ed. 6: Emendanda. 1764.
"Habitat in Italia, Hispania." RCN: 3886.
Lectotype (Greuter in Greuter & Rechinger in *Boissiera* 13: 54. 1967): Herb. Linn. No. 689.3 (LINN).
Current name: ***Cistus villosus*** L. (Cistaceae).

Citharexylum caudatum Linnaeus, *Flora Jamaicensis*: 18. 1759.
["Habitat in Jamaica."] Sp. Pl., ed. 2, 2: 872 (1763). RCN: 4528.
Lectotype (Howard, *Fl. Lesser Antilles* 6: 218. 1989): *Browne*, Herb. Linn. No. 777.5 (LINN).
Current name: ***Citharexylum caudatum*** L. (Verbenaceae).
Note: The generic name appears as "Citharexylon" in the protologue.

Citharexylum cinereum Linnaeus, *Species Plantarum*, ed. 2, 2: 872. 1763, *nom. illeg.*
"Habitat in America meridionali." RCN: 4527.
Replaced synonym: *Citharexylum spinosum* L. (1753).
Lectotype (Howard in *Bot. J. Linn. Soc.* 79: 82. 1979): [icon] *"Citharexylum Americanum alterum, foliis ad marginem dentatis"* in Plukenet, Phytographia: t. 161, f. 5. 1692; Almag. Bot.: 108. 1696. – Epitype (Méndez Santos & Cafferty in *Taxon* 50: 1137. 2002): Barbados. St Andrew, Sep 1940, *Gooding 228* (BM).
Current name: ***Citharexylum spinosum*** L. (Verbenaceae).
Note: A superfluous name for *C. spinosum* L. (1753) - see discussion by Méndez Santos & Cafferty (in *Taxon* 50: 1137–1138. 2002).

Citharexylum fruticosum Linnaeus, *Systema Naturae*, ed. 10, 2: 1115. 1759, *nom. illeg.*
RCN: 4527.
Replaced synonym: *Citharexylum spinosum* L. (1753).
Lectotype (Howard in *Bot. J. Linn. Soc.* 79: 82. 1979): [icon] *"Citharexylum Americanum alterum, foliis ad marginem dentatis"* in Plukenet, Phytographia: t. 161, f. 5. 1692; Almag. Bot.: 108. 1696. – Epitype (Méndez Santos & Cafferty in *Taxon* 50: 1137. 2002): Barbados. St Andrew, Sep 1940, *Gooding 228* (BM).
Current name: ***Citharexylum spinosum*** L. (Verbenaceae).
Note: A superfluous name for *C. spinosum* L. (1753) - see discussion by Méndez Santos & Cafferty (in *Taxon* 50: 1137–1138. 2002).

Citharexylum spinosum Linnaeus, *Species Plantarum* 2: 625. 1753.
"Habitat in Barbados." RCN: 4526.
Basionym of: *Citharexylum fruticosum* L. (1759), *nom. illeg.*; *Citharexylum cinereum* L. (1763), *nom. illeg.*
Lectotype (Howard in *Bot. J. Linn. Soc.* 79: 82. 1979): [icon] *"Citharexylum Americanum alterum, foliis ad marginem dentatis"* in Plukenet, Phytographia: t. 161, f. 5. 1692; Almag. Bot.: 108. 1696. – Epitype (Méndez Santos & Cafferty in *Taxon* 50: 1137. 2002): Barbados. St Andrew, Sep 1940, *Gooding 228* (BM).
Generitype of *Citharexylum* Linnaeus.
Current name: ***Citharexylum spinosum*** L. (Verbenaceae).
Note: See discussion by Méndez Santos (in *Willdenowia* 31: 420. 2001); Méndez Santos & Cafferty (in *Taxon* 50: 1137–1138. 2002).

Citrus aurantium Linnaeus, *Species Plantarum* 2: 782. 1753.
"Habitat in India." RCN: 5727.
Lectotype (Mabberley in *Telopea* 7: 170. 1997): Herb. Linn. No.
937.2, upper row of leaves (LINN).
Current name: ***Citrus*** × ***aurantium*** L. (Rutaceae).
Note: Tanaka (in *Meded. Rijks-Herb.* 69: 8. 1931) indicated unspecified material at LINN as type, but as there are several sheets there, which are evidently not part of a single gathering, Art. 9.15 does not apply. Coode (in Bosser & al., *Fl. Mascareignes* 65: 29. 1979) indicated 937.2 (LINN) as lectotype and Mabberley has restricted that choice to the upper specimens on the sheet.

Citrus aurantium Linnaeus var. **decumana** Linnaeus, *Species Plantarum*, ed. 2, 2: 1101. 1763, *nom. illeg.*
RCN: 5728.
Replaced synonym: *Citrus aurantium* var. *grandis* L. (1753).
Lectotype (Mabberley in *Telopea* 7: 170. 1997): [icon] *"Malus arantia, fructu rotundo maximo pallescente humanum caput excedente"* in Sloane, Voy. Jamaica 1: 41, t. 12, f. 2, 3. 1707. – Typotype: Herb. Sloane 7: 115 (BM-SL).
Current name: ***Citrus maxima*** (Burm.) Merr. (Rutaceae).
Note: A superfluous renaming of *C.* × *aurantium* var. *grandis* L. as noted by Scora & Nicolson (in *Taxon* 35: 593. 1986).

Citrus aurantium Linnaeus var. **grandis** Linnaeus, *Species Plantarum* 2: 783. 1753.
"Habitat in India." RCN: 5728.
Basionym of: *Citrus aurantium* var. *decumana* L. (1763), *nom. illeg.*; *C. decumana* L. (1767).
Lectotype (Mabberley in *Telopea* 7: 170. 1997): [icon] *"Malus arantia, fructu rotundo maximo pallescente humanum caput excedente"* in Sloane, Voy. Jamaica 1: 41, t. 12, f. 2, 3. 1707. – Typotype: Herb. Sloane 7: 115 (BM-SL).
Current name: ***Citrus maxima*** (Burm.) Merr. (Rutaceae).
Note: Porter & Elias (in *Ann. Missouri Bot. Gard.* 66: 130. 1979) indicated an unseen Osbeck collection in S as type, but there are three collections potentially associated with this name, none of which appears to be from Osbeck (who is also not mentioned in the protologue).

Citrus aurantium Linnaeus var. **sinensis** Linnaeus, *Species Plantarum* 2: 783. 1753.
RCN: 5727.
Lectotype (Mabberley in *Telopea* 7: 170. 1997): Herb. Linn. No. 937.2, lower row of leaves (LINN).
Current name: ***Citrus*** × ***aurantium*** L. (Rutaceae).
Note: Porter & Elias (in *Ann. Missouri Bot. Gard.* 66: 132. 1979) indicated Bauhin material (BAS), unseen by Linnaeus, as the type, but it is not original material for the name.

Citrus decumana Linnaeus, *Systema Naturae*, ed. 12, 2: 508. 1767.
RCN: 5728.
Replaced synonym: *Citrus aurantium* L. var. *decumana* L. (1763), *nom. illeg.*
Lectotype (Mabberley in *Telopea* 7: 170. 1997): [icon] *"Malus arantia, fructu rotundo maximo pallescente humanum caput excedente"* in Sloane, Voy. Jamaica 1: 41, t. 12, f. 2, 3. 1707. – Typotype: Herb. Sloane 7: 115 (BM-SL).
Current name: ***Citrus maxima*** (Burm.) Merr. (Rutaceae).
Note: Specific epithet spelled "decumanus" in the protologue.
A *nomen novum* for the illegitimate *Citrus aurantium* var. *decumana* L. (1763).

Citrus medica Linnaeus, *Species Plantarum* 2: 782. 1753.
"Habitat in Asia, Media, Assyria, Persia." RCN: 5726.

Lectotype (Porter in Jarvis & al., *Regnum Veg.* 127: 34. 1993): [icon] *"Citreum"* in Tournefort, Inst. Rei Herb.: 620, t. 396. 1700.
Generitype of *Citrus* Linnaeus.
Current name: ***Citrus medica*** L. (Rutaceae).

Citrus medica Linnaeus var. **limon** Linnaeus, *Species Plantarum* 2: 782. 1753.
RCN: 5726.
Lectotype (Mabberley in *Telopea* 7: 169. 1997): [icon] *"Limon vulgaris"* in Ferrari, Hesperides: 191, 193. 1646 (see p. 130).
Current name: ***Citrus*** × ***limon*** (L.) Osbeck (Rutaceae).
Note: Porter & Elias (in *Ann. Missouri Bot. Gard.* 66: 131. 1979) indicated unseen material in LINN as the type. However, the only sheet they could have intended (937.1) is linked with *C. medica* L., rather than var. *limon*, and so is not original material for the name.

Citrus trifoliata Linnaeus, *Species Plantarum,* ed. 2, 2: 1101. 1763.
"Habitat in Japonia." RCN: 5729.
Lectotype (Swingle in Webber & Batchelor, *Citrus Industry* 1: 368. 1943): [icon] *"Karatats banna"* in Kaempfer, Amoen. Exot. Fasc.: 801, 802. 1712.
Current name: ***Citrus trifoliata*** L. (Rutaceae).

Clathrus cancellatus Linnaeus, *Species Plantarum* 2: 1179. 1753.
"Habitat in Europa australiori." RCN: 8488.
Lectotype (Greuter & Kuyper in Jarvis & al., *Regnum Veg.* 127: 34. 1993): [icon] *"Clathrus ruber"* in Micheli, Nov. Pl. Gen.: 214, t. 93. 1729 (see p. 9).
Current name: ***Clathrus ruber*** Pers.: Pers. (Clathraceae).

Clathrus denudatus Linnaeus, *Species Plantarum* 2: 1179. 1753.
"Habitat in Europa australiore." RCN: 8489.
Type not designated.
Original material: [icon] in Micheli, Nov. Pl. Gen.: 214, t. 94, f. 1. 1729.
Current name: ***Arcyria denudata*** (L.) Wettst. (Arcyriaceae).
Note: See discussion by Lister (in *J. Bot.* 51: 160–164. 1913), who reproduced the protologue and discussed the identity of putative original material for the name.

Clathrus nudus Linnaeus, *Species Plantarum* 2: 1179. 1753.
"Habitat in Italiae lignis putridis." RCN: 8490.
Type not designated.
Original material: Herb. Linn. No. 1283.1 (LINN); [icon] in Micheli, Nov. Pl. Gen.: 214, t. 94. 1729.
Current name: ***Clathrus nudus*** L. (Phallaceae).
Note: See discussion by Lister (in *J. Bot.* 51: 160–164. 1913), who reproduced the protologue and discussed the identity of putative original material for the name.

Clathrus recutitus Linnaeus, *Flora Suecica*, ed. 2: 456. 1755.
"Habitat in corticibus arborum." RCN: 8491.
Type not designated.
Original material: none traced.
Current name: ***Clathrus recutitus*** L. (Phallaceae).

Clathrus ruber Persoon: Persoon, *Synopsis Methodica Fungorum*: 241. 1801.
Replaced synonym: *Clathrus cancellatus* L. (1753).
Lectotype (Greuter & Kuyper in Jarvis & al., *Regnum Veg.* 127: 34. 1993): [icon] *"Clathrus ruber"* in Micheli, Nov. Pl. Gen.: 214, t. 93. 1729.
Generitype of *Clathrus* Linnaeus: Pers. (vide Greuter & Kuyper in Jarvis & al., *Regnum Veg.* 127: 34. 1993).
Current name: ***Clathrus ruber*** Pers.: Pers. (Clathraceae).

Clavaria coralloides Linnaeus, *Species Plantarum* 2: 1182. 1753.
"Habitat in Sylvis opacis." RCN: 8508.
Type not designated.
Original material: [icon] in Sterbeeck, Theatr. Fung.: 96, t. 11, f. A, B, C, D. 1675; [icon] in Tournefort, Inst. Rei Herb.: 564, t. 332, f. B. 1700; [icon] in Vaillant, Bot. Paris.: 41, t. 8, f. 4. 1727.
Current name: ***Clavulina coralloides*** (L.: Fr.) J. Schröt. (Clavulinaceae).
Note: Donk (in *Reinwardtia* 2: 456. 1954) noted that the cited Vaillant figure is identifiable as *Clavulinopsis corniculata* (Schaeff.: Fr.) Corner.

Clavaria digitata Linnaeus, *Species Plantarum* 2: 1182. 1753.
"Habitat in sylvis australibus." RCN: 8506.
Type not designated.
Original material: none traced.
Current name: ***Xylaria digitata*** (L.: Fr.) Grev. (Xylariaceae).

Clavaria fastigiata Linnaeus, *Species Plantarum* 2: 1183. 1753.
"Habitat in Sylvis." RCN: 8509.
Type not designated.
Original material: [icon] in Ray, Syn. Meth. Stirp. Brit., ed. 3: 479, t. 24, f. 5. 1724.
Current name: ***Clavulinopsis corniculata*** (Schaeff.: Fr.) Corner (Ramariaceae).

Clavaria fragilis Holmskjold: Fries, *Systema Mycologicum* 1: 465. 1821, *nom. cons.*
Type not designated.
Original material: none traced.
Generitype of *Clavaria* Linnaeus: Fr., *nom. cons.*
Current name: ***Clavaria fragilis*** Holmsk.: Fr. (Clavariaceae).

Clavaria hypoxylon Linnaeus, *Species Plantarum* 2: 1182. 1753.
"Habitat in Cellis, navibus, aliisque nunquam sole illustratis." RCN: 8507.
Type not designated.
Original material: [icon] in Brückmann, Epist. Fungo Hypox. Digit.: 12, t. 1, t. 2. 1725.
Current name: ***Xylaria hypoxylon*** (L.: Fr.) Grev. (Xylariaceae).

Clavaria militaris Linnaeus, *Species Plantarum* 2: 1182. 1753.
"Habitat in sylvis australibus." RCN: 8504.
Type not designated.
Original material: [icon] in Vaillant, Bot. Paris.: 39, t. 7, f. 4. 1727.
Current name: ***Cordyceps militaris*** (L.: Fr.) Link (Clavicipitaceae).

Clavaria muscoides Linnaeus, *Species Plantarum* 2: 1183. 1753.
"Habitat inter Muscos." RCN: 8510.
Type not designated.
Original material: [icon] in Ray, Syn. Meth. Stirp. Brit., ed. 3: 16, t. 24, f. 7. 1724.
Current name: ***Clavaria muscoides*** L. (Clavariaceae).

Clavaria ophioglossoides Linnaeus, *Species Plantarum* 2: 1182. 1753.
"Habitat in sylvis australibus." RCN: 8505.
Type not designated.
Original material: [icon] in Vaillant, Bot. Paris.: 39, t. 7, f. 3. 1727.
Current name: ***Geoglossum glabrum*** Pers.: Fr. (Clavicipitaceae).
Note: See discussion by Donk (in *Reinwardtia* 2: 451–452. 1954).

Clavaria pistillaris Linnaeus, *Species Plantarum* 2: 1182. 1753.
"Habitat in Sylvis umbrosis." RCN: 8503.
Type not designated.
Original material: [icon] in Vaillant, Bot. Paris.: 39, t. 7, f. 5. 1727;
[icon] in Boccone, Mus. Fis.: t. 307. 1697; [icon] in Micheli, Nov. Pl. Gen.: 208, t. 87, f. 1. 1729.
Current name: ***Clavariadelphus pistillaris*** (L.: Fr.) Donk (Gomphaceae).

Claytonia portulacaria (Linnaeus) Linnaeus, *Mantissa Plantarum Altera*: 211. 1771.
["Habitat in Aethiopia."] Sp. Pl., ed. 2, 1: 406 (1762). RCN: 1652.
Basionym: *Crassula portulacaria* L. (1762).
Lectotype (Tölken in *J. S. African Bot.* 38: 73. 1972): [icon] "*Crassula Portulacae facie, arborescens*" in Dillenius, Hort. Eltham. 1: 120, t. 101, f. 120. 1732.
Current name: ***Portulacaria afra*** Jacq. (Portulacaceae).

Claytonia sibirica Linnaeus, *Species Plantarum* 1: 204. 1753.
"Habitat in Sibiria." RCN: 1651.
Lectotype (Jonsell & Jarvis in *Nordic J. Bot.* 14: 155. 1994): [icon] "*Limnia*" in Linnaeus in Kongl. Swensk. Wetensk. Acad. Handl. 7: 130, t. 5. 1746.
Current name: ***Claytonia sibirica*** L. (Portulacaceae).
Note: See discussion by Volkova (in *Novosti Sist. Vyssh. Rast.* 1965: 114–117. 1965).

Claytonia virginica Linnaeus, *Species Plantarum* 1: 204. 1753.
"Habitat in Virginia." RCN: 1650.
Lectotype (Lewis & al. in *Ann. Missouri Bot. Gard.* 54: 168. 1967): *Kalm*, Herb. Linn. No. 285.1 (LINN; iso- UPS).
Generitype of *Claytonia* Linnaeus (vide Hitchcock, *Prop. Brit. Bot.*: 135. 1929).
Current name: ***Claytonia virginica*** L. (Portulacaceae).

Clematis cirrhosa Linnaeus, *Species Plantarum* 1: 544. 1753.
"Habitat in Baetica, arbores operiens & deprimens." RCN: 4028.
Lectotype (Brandenburg in Jarvis & al. in *Taxon* 54: 469. 2005): [icon] "*Clematis altera Baetica*" in Clusius, Rar. Pl. Hist. 1: 122, 123. 1601.
Current name: ***Clematis cirrhosa*** L. (Ranunculaceae).
Note: Although Qaiser (in Jafri & El-Gadi, *Fl. Libya* 108: 3. 1984) indicated 712.1 (LINN) as type, and Johnson (*Släktet Klematis*: 371. 1997) took both it and 712.2 (LINN) as "Typ", neither collection appears to be original material for the name. Wang (in *Acta Phytotax. Sinica* 40: 234. 2002) similarly indicated 712.2 (LINN) as type. Sheet 712.1 is probably from Hasselquist, from the Middle East (rather than Portugal), and evidently unavailable to Linnaeus in 1753, and 712.2 is of North African origin. Brandenburg therefore designated a Clusius illustration as lectotype.

Clematis crispa Linnaeus, *Species Plantarum* 1: 543. 1753.
"Habitat in Carolina." RCN: 4031.
Lectotype (Gray in *Curtis's Bot. Mag.* 107: t. 6594. 1881): [icon] "*Clematis flore crispo*" in Dillenius, Hort. Eltham. 1: 86, t. 73, f. 84. 1732.
Current name: ***Clematis crispa*** L. (Ranunculaceae).

Clematis dioica Linnaeus, *Systema Naturae,* ed. 10, 2: 1084. 1759.
["Habitat in America calidiore."] Sp. Pl., ed. 2, 1: 765 (1762). RCN: 4033.
Lectotype (Lourteig in *Mem. Soc. Ci. Nat. "La Salle"* 16: 36. 1956): *Browne*, Herb. Linn. No. 712.8 (LINN).
Current name: ***Clematis dioica*** L. (Ranunculaceae).

Clematis erecta Linnaeus, *Systema Naturae,* ed. 12, 2: 377. 1767, *orth. var.*
["Habitat in collibus Austriae, Pannoniae, Tatariae, Monspelii."] Sp. Pl. 1: 544 (1753). RCN: 4038.

Lectotype (Serov in *Bot. Zhurn.* 73: 1739. 1988): Herb. Linn. No. 712.14 (LINN).
Current name: ***Clematis recta*** L. (Ranunculaceae).
Note: An orthographic variant of *C. recta* L. (1753).

Clematis flammula Linnaeus, *Species Plantarum* 1: 544. 1753.
"Habitat Monspelii, Jenae, inque Rhetiae sepibus." RCN: 4036.
Lectotype (Brandenburg in Jarvis & al. in *Taxon* 54: 469. 2005): [icon] *"Flammula"* in Dodoëns, Stirp. Hist. Pempt., ed. 2: 404. 1616.
Current name: ***Clematis flammula*** L. (Ranunculaceae).
Note: The original elements that contributed to Linnaeus' concept of *C. flammula* were taxonomically diverse, and included *C. vitalba* L., *C. maritima* L., and possibly *C. chinensis* Osbeck, as well as *C. flammula*. Qaiser (in Jafri & El-Gadi, *Fl. Libya* 108: 5. 1984) designated 712.12 (LINN) as the type but unfortunately this collection is identifiable as *C. vitalba*. Brandenburg rejected Qaiser's typification, on the grounds of conflict of the specimen with the protologue, in favour of a Dodoëns plate corresponding with usage of the name.

Clematis integrifolia Linnaeus, *Species Plantarum* 1: 544. 1753.
"Habitat in Hungaria, Tataria." RCN: 4039.
Lectotype (Serov in *Bot. Zhurn.* 73: 1740. 1988): Herb. Linn. No. 712.15 (LINN).
Current name: ***Clematis integrifolia*** L. (Ranunculaceae).
Note: Brandenburg & al. (in *Bot. J. Linn. Soc.* 125: 351–358. 1997) provided an extensive discussion of the typification of this name, illustrating many of the original elements involved. However, they were unaware of Serov's earlier choice of material in LINN as lectotype, which pre-dates their choice of Clifford material (BM).

Clematis maritima Linnaeus, *Species Plantarum,* ed. 2, 1: 767. 1762.
"Habitat ad littora maris Adriatici, Venetiis, Monspelii." RCN: 4037.
Lectotype (Brandenburg in Jarvis & al. in *Taxon* 54: 469. 2005): Herb. Burser XVII: 37 (UPS).
Current name: ***Clematis flammula*** L. var. ***maritima*** (L.) DC. (Ranunculaceae).

Clematis orientalis Linnaeus, *Species Plantarum* 1: 543. 1753.
"Habitat in Oriente." RCN: 4032.
Lectotype (Brandenburg & al. in *Taxon* 36: 119, f. 1. 1987): [icon] *"Flammula scandens, folio Apii glauco"* in Dillenius, Hort. Eltham. 1: 144, t. 119, f. 145. 1732. – Typotype: Herb. Dillenius No. 2868 (OXF).
Current name: ***Clematis orientalis*** L. (Ranunculaceae).

Clematis recta Linnaeus, *Species Plantarum* 1: 544. 1753.
"Habitat in collibus Austriae, Pannoniae, Tatariae, Monspelii." RCN: 4038.
Lectotype (Serov in *Bot. Zhurn.* 73: 1739. 1988): Herb. Linn. No. 712.14 (LINN).
Current name: ***Clematis recta*** L. (Ranunculaceae).

Clematis viorna Linnaeus, *Species Plantarum* 1: 543. 1753.
"Habitat in Virginia, Carolina." RCN: 4030.
Lectotype (Yang & Moore in *Syst. Geogr. Pl.* 68: 299. 1999): *Clayton 411* (BM-000051213).
Current name: ***Clematis viorna*** L. (Ranunculaceae).

Clematis virginiana Linnaeus, *Centuria I Plantarum*: 15. 1755.
"Habitat in Pensylvania." RCN: 4034.
Lectotype (Essig & Jarvis in *Taxon* 38: 277. 1989): Herb. Linn. No. 2: *Clematis virginica* (UPS).
Current name: ***Clematis virginiana*** L. (Ranunculaceae).

Clematis vitalba Linnaeus, *Species Plantarum* 1: 544. 1753.
"Habitat in sepibus Europae australis, Virginiae, Jamaicae." RCN: 4035.
Lectotype (Serov in *Bot. Zhurn.* 73: 1738. 1988): Herb. Burser XVII: 35 (UPS).
Generitype of *Clematis* Linnaeus (vide Green, *Prop. Brit. Bot.*: 163. 1929).
Current name: ***Clematis vitalba*** L. (Ranunculaceae).
Note: Rechinger (in *Fl. Iranica* 171: 231. 1992) indicated the post-1753 Kähler sheet (712.11 LINN) as type, but this is not original material for the name and is ineligible as lectotype. Although Brandenburg (in Jarvis & al., *Regnum Veg.* 127: 35. 1993) designated *Clematis tertia* Mattioli, *Pl. Epit.*: 697 (1586) as lectotype, his choice is pre-dated by that of Serov (despite his chosen type being associated with Linnaeus' unnamed variety γ).

Clematis viticella Linnaeus, *Species Plantarum* 1: 543. 1753.
"Habitat in Italiae, Hispaniae sepibus." RCN: 4029.
Lectotype (Serov in *Bot. Zhurn.* 73: 1740. 1988): Herb. Linn. No. 712.4 (LINN).
Current name: ***Clematis viticella*** L. (Ranunculaceae).
Note: Serov (1988) appears to have made the first formal choice of type but various other type choices have been proposed. Rechinger (in *Fl. Iran.* 171: 230. 1992) indicated 712.3 (LINN) as type, but this material is in any case a later addition to the herbarium and not original material for the name. Johnson (*Släktet Klematis*: 674. 1997) noted various of the original elements but similarly indicated what is presumably 712.3 (LINN) as type. Brandenburg & al. (in *Bot. J. Linn. Soc.* 135: 13–23. 2001) provided an extensive discussion of the typification of this name, illustrating many of the original elements involved. However, they were unaware of Serov's earlier choice of material in LINN as lectotype, which pre-dates their choice of Clifford material (BM).

Cleome aculeata Linnaeus, *Systema Naturae,* ed. 12, 3: 232. 1768.
"Habitat in America. D. Zoega." RCN: 4901.
Lectotype (Al-Shehbaz in Howard, *Fl. Lesser Antilles* 4: 301. 1988): *Zoega*, Herb. Linn. No. 850.17 (LINN), see p. 235.
Current name: ***Capparis aculeata*** L. (Capparaceae).

Cleome arabica Linnaeus, *Centuria I Plantarum*: 20. 1755.
"Habitat in Arabia. D. Hasselquist." RCN: 4906.
Lectotype (Hedge & Lamond in Rechinger, *Fl. Iranica* 68: 27. 1970): *Hasselquist* (SBT).
Current name: ***Cleome arabica*** L. (Capparaceae).

Cleome capensis Linnaeus, *Species Plantarum,* ed. 2, 2: 940. 1763.
"Habitat ad Cap. b. Spei, & in India." RCN: 4908.
Type not designated.
Original material: Herb. Linn. No. 850.23 (LINN).
Note: The application of this name is uncertain – see Codd & Kers (in Codd & al., *Fl. Southern Africa* 13: 74. 1970).

Cleome dodecandra Linnaeus, *Species Plantarum* 2: 672. 1753.
"Habitat in Indiis." RCN: 4899.
Lectotype (Iltis in *Rhodora* 56: 67. 1954): Herb. Linn. No. 850.12 (LINN).
Current name: ***Polanisia dodecandra*** (L.) DC. (Capparaceae).
Note: See further, extensive discussion by Iltis (in *Rhodora* 68: 41–47. 1966).

Cleome fruticosa Linnaeus, *Species Plantarum* 2: 671. 1753.
"Habitat in India." RCN: 4892.
Type not designated.
Original material: Herb. Linn. No. 850.1 (LINN).
Current name: ***Cadaba fruticosa*** (L.) Druce (Capparaceae).

Cleome gigantea Linnaeus, *Systema Naturae,* ed. 12, 3: 232. 1768.
"Habitat in America." RCN: 4900.
Type not designated.
Original material: *Jacquin*, Herb. Linn. No. 850.16 (LINN); [icon] in Jacquin, Observ. Bot. 4: 1, t. 76. 1771.
Current name: ***Cleome gigantea*** L. (Capparaceae).

Cleome gynandra Linnaeus, *Species Plantarum* 2: 671. 1753.
"Habitat in Asiae, Africae, Americae calidissimis." RCN: 4894.
Lectotype (Al-Shehbaz in Howard, *Fl. Lesser Antilles* 4: 302. 1988): [icon] *"Cara-veela"* in Rheede, Hort. Malab. 9: 43, t. 24. 1689.
Current name: ***Cleome gynandra*** L. (Capparaceae).
Note: In the absence of material in LINN, Iltis (in *Brittonia* 12: 284. 1960) interpreted the name via the cited Rheede plate ("in lieu of the type"). Elffers & al. (in Hubbard & Milne-Redhead, *Fl. Trop. E. Africa, Capparidaceae:* 18. 1964) indicated material in Herb. Clifford as the holotype but did not distinguish between two sheets associated with this name. As they are evidently not part of a single gathering, Art. 9.15 does not apply. Codd & Kers (in Codd & al., *Fl. Southern Africa* 13: 138. 1970) indicated 850.4 (LINN), a collection annotated by Linnaeus with the later epithet "pentaphylla" and crucially lacking the relevant *Species Plantarum* number (i.e. "2"). It was evidently a post-1753 addition to the herbarium, and is not original material for the name. Al-Shehbaz, however, clearly indicated the Rheede plate as the type.

Cleome heptaphylla Linnaeus, *Species Plantarum,* ed. 2, 2: 937. 1763.
"Habitat in Indiis." RCN: 4893.
Type not designated.
Original material: none traced.
Current name: ***Cleome spinosa*** Jacq. (Capparaceae).

Cleome icosandra Linnaeus, *Species Plantarum* 2: 672. 1753.
"Habitat in Zeylona." RCN: 4897.
Lectotype (Iltis in *Brittonia* 12: 283. 1960): Herb. Linn. No. 850.10 (LINN).
Current name: ***Cleome viscosa*** L. (Capparaceae).

Cleome monophylla Linnaeus, *Species Plantarum* 2: 672. 1753.
"Habitat in India." RCN: 4907.
Type not designated.
Original material: Herb. Hermann 1: 52 (bis), No. 243 (BM); Herb. Hermann 1: 57, No. 243 (BM); Herb. Hermann 3: 2, No. 243 (BM); [icon] in Rheede, Hort. Malab. 9: 63, t. 34. 1689; [icon] in Burman, Thes. Zeylan.: 217, t. 100, f. 2. 1737.
Current name: ***Cleome monophylla*** L. (Capparaceae).
Note: Codd & Kers (in Codd & al., *Fl. Southern Africa* 13: 121. 1970) wrongly indicated 850.22 (LINN), a König collection not received by Linnaeus until long after 1753, as the type.

Cleome ornithopodioides Linnaeus, *Species Plantarum* 2: 672. 1753.
"Habitat circa Peram in agris." RCN: 4904.
Lectotype (Meikle, *Fl. Cyprus* 1: 174. 1977): Herb. Linn. No. 850.18 (LINN).
Generitype of *Cleome* Linnaeus (vide Green, *Prop. Brit. Bot.*: 172. 1929).
Current name: ***Cleome ornithopodioides*** L. (Capparaceae).
Note: Cleome ornithopodioides, with the type designated by Meikle (believed then to have been first typified by Carlström in *Willdenowia* 14: 121. 1984), was proposed as conserved type of the genus by Jarvis (in *Taxon* 41: 560. 1992). However, the proposal was eventually ruled unnecessary by the General Committee (see Barrie, *l.c.* 55: 795–796. 2006 for a review of the history of this and related proposals).

Cleome pentaphylla Linnaeus, *Flora Jamaicensis*: 18. 1759.
"Habitat [in Jamaica.]" RCN: 4894.

Lectotype (Iltis in *Brittonia* 12: 284. 1960): Herb. Linn. No. 850.4 (LINN).
Current name: ***Cleome gynandra*** L. (Capparaceae).
Note: Although Fawcett & Rendle (*Fl. Jamaica* 3: 229. 1914) indicated material in LINN as type, they did not distinguish between sheets 850.2, 850.3 and 850.4 (which are evidently not part of a single gathering so Art. 9.15 does not apply). Some authors, including Elffers & al. (in Hubbard & Milne-Redhead, *Fl. Trop. E. Africa, Capparidaceae*: 18. 1964), have believed this to be a superfluous name for *C. gynandra* L. (1753), stemming from the mistaken belief that *C. pentaphylla* dated from 1763 (*Sp. Pl.*, ed. 2, 2: 938). The two names are, however, heterotypic synonyms.

Cleome polygama Linnaeus, *Species Plantarum*, ed. 2, 2: 939. 1763.
"Habitat in Jamaica." RCN: 4896.
Lectotype (Fawcett & Rendle, *Fl. Jamaica* 3: 227. 1914): *Browne*, Herb. Linn. No. 850.7 (LINN).
Current name: ***Cleome serrata*** Jacq. (Capparaceae).

Cleome triphylla Linnaeus, *Species Plantarum*, ed. 2, 2: 938. 1763.
"Habitat in Indiis." RCN: 4895.
Type not designated.
Original material: [icon] in Hermann, Hort. Lugd.-Bat. Cat.: 564, 565. 1687.

Current name: ***Cleome gynandra*** L. (Capparaceae).
Note: In the absence of material in LINN, Iltis (in *Brittonia* 12: 288. 1960) interpreted the name via the cited Hermann plate ("in lieu of the type").

Cleome violacea Linnaeus, *Species Plantarum* 2: 672. 1753.
"Habitat in Lusitania." RCN: 4905.
Type not designated.
Original material: Herb. A. van Royen No. 899.54–107 (L); Herb. Clifford: 341, *Cleome* 3 (BM); Herb. Linn. No. 850.19 (LINN); [icon] in Barrelier, Pl. Galliam: 45, 865. 1714; [icon] in Barrelier, Pl. Galliam: 45, 866. 1714.
Current name: ***Cleome violacea*** L. (Capparaceae).

Cleome viscosa Linnaeus, *Species Plantarum* 2: 672. 1753.
"Habitat in Zeylona, Malabaria." RCN: 4898.
Lectotype (Fawcett & Rendle, *Fl. Jamaica* 3: 228. 1914; Du Puy & Telford in George & al., *Fl. Australia* 50: 169. 1998): Herb. Hermann 3: 2, No. 241 (BM-000621795).
Current name: ***Cleome viscosa*** L. (Capparaceae).
Note: Fawcett & Rendle indicated Herb. Hermann material (BM) as type. Although there is material in two volumes, it appears to have been part of a single gathering. Consequently, theirs is accepted as the first typification (Art. 9.15), with the choice subsequently restricted by Du Puy & Telford. The material (850.11, LINN) treated as the type by Iltis (in *Brittonia* 12: 283. 1960) is evidently a post-1753 collection and is not original material for the name.

Cleonia lusitanica (Linnaeus) Linnaeus, *Species Plantarum,* ed. 2, 2: 837. 1763.
"Habitat in Lusitania, Hispania." RCN: 4364.
Basionym: *Prunella lusitanica* L. (1753).
Lectotype (Press in Jarvis & al., *Regnum Veg.* 127: 35. 1993): *Löfling 445,* Herb. Linn. No. 753.1 (LINN).
Generitype of *Cleonia* Linnaeus.
Current name: ***Cleonia lusitanica*** (L.) L. (Lamiaceae).

Clerodendrum calamitosum Linnaeus, *Systema Naturae,* ed. 12, 2: 426; *Mantissa Plantarum*: 90. 1767.
"Habitat in Java. D. Baster." RCN: 4635.
Lectotype (Moldenke in *Phytologia* 57: 404. 1985): Herb. Linn. No. 810.4, upper two specimens (LINN).
Current name: ***Clerodendrum calamitosum*** L. (Verbenaceae).

Clerodendrum fortunatum Linnaeus, *Centuria II Plantarum*: 23. 1756.
"Habitat in India." RCN: 4634.
Type not designated.
Original material: "Clerodendr. fortunatum", Herb. Linn. (UPS); Herb. Linn. No. 810.2 (LINN).
Current name: ***Clerodendrum fortunatum*** L. (Verbenaceae).
Note: Specific epithet spelled "fortunata" in the protologue. Although Moldenke (in *Phytologia* 59: 467. 1986) says this is "based on...810.2 (LINN)" and confirms its identity, this is not accepted as a formal typification.

Clerodendrum infortunatum Linnaeus, *Species Plantarum* 2: 637. 1753.
"Habitat in India." RCN: 4633.
Lectotype (Moldenke & Moldenke in Dassanayake & Fosberg, *Revised Handb. Fl. Ceylon* 4: 461. 1983): Herb. Hermann 4: 46, No. 232 (BM-000594745).
Generitype of *Clerodendrum* Linnaeus.
Current name: ***Clerodendrum infortunatum*** L. (Verbenaceae).
Note: Specific epithet spelled "infortunata" in the protologue.

Clerodendrum paniculatum Linnaeus, *Systema Naturae,* ed. 12, 2: 426; *Mantissa Plantarum*: 90. 1767.
"Habitat in India." RCN: 4636.
Lectotype (Moldenke & Moldenke in Dassanayake & Fosberg, *Revised Handb. Fl. Ceylon* 4: 412. 1983): Herb. Linn. No. 810.5 (LINN).
Current name: ***Clerodendrum paniculatum*** L. (Verbenaceae).

Clethra alnifolia Linnaeus, *Species Plantarum* 1: 396. 1753.
"Habitat in Carolina, Virginia, Pensylvania." RCN: 3112.
Lectotype (Sleumer in *Bot. Jahrb. Syst.* 87: 75. 1967): Herb. Linn. No. 567.1 (LINN).
Generitype of *Clethra* Linnaeus.
Current name: ***Clethra alnifolia*** L. (Clethraceae).

Clibadium surinamense Linnaeus, *Mantissa Plantarum Altera*: 294. 1771.
"Habitat Surinami." RCN: 7164.
Neotype (Hind in Jarvis & al., *Regnum Veg.* 127: 35. 1993): Surinam. *Hostmann 647* (K).
Generitype of *Clibadium* Linnaeus.
Current name: ***Clibadium surinamense*** L. (Asteraceae).
Note: Howard (*Fl. Lesser Antilles* 6: 537. 1989) stated "Type: Surinam, Allemand s.n.", and it is clear from Linnaeus' protologue that he based this on the account of "Clibadium foetidum" in a manuscript that he received from Allemand, and which is preserved at LINN. However, no material from Allemand appears to have been preserved, and Hind therefore chose a neotype from Surinam.

Cliffortia ilicifolia Linnaeus, *Species Plantarum* 2: 1038. 1753.
"Habitat in Aethiopia." RCN: 7494.
Lectotype (Stearn, *Introd. Linnaeus' Sp. Pl.* (Ray Soc. ed.): 47. 1957): [icon] *"Cliffortia foliis dentatis: mas"* in Linnaeus, Hort. Cliff.: 463, t. 30. 1738.
Current name: ***Cliffortia ilicifolia*** L. (Rosaceae).

Cliffortia polygonifolia Linnaeus, *Species Plantarum* 2: 1038. 1753.
"Habitat in Aethiopia." RCN: 7496.
Lectotype (Stearn, *Introd. Linnaeus' Sp. Pl.* (Ray Soc. ed.): 47. 1957): [icon] *"Cliffortia foliis linearibus pilosis: Femina"* in Linnaeus, Hort. Cliff.: 501, t. 32. 1738. – Voucher: Herb. Clifford: 501, *Cliffortia* 3 (BM).
Generitype of *Cliffortia* Linnaeus (vide Green, *Prop. Brit. Bot.*: 192. 1929).
Current name: ***Cliffortia polygonifolia*** L. (Rosaceae).
Note: Oliver & Fellingham (in Jarvis & al., *Regnum Veg.* 127: 35. 1993) designated a Clifford sheet as lectotype, but this choice is pre-dated by that of Stearn. Weimarck (*Monogr.* Cliffortia: 83. 1934) noted the *Hort. Cliff.* illustration as "a good figure" adding "the type specimen has disappeared".

Cliffortia ruscifolia Linnaeus, *Species Plantarum* 2: 1038. 1753.
"Habitat in Aethiopia." RCN: 7495.
Lectotype (Stearn, *Introd. Linnaeus' Sp. Pl.* (Ray Soc. ed.): 47. 1957): [icon] *"Cliffortia foliis lanceolatis integerrimis: Femina"* in Linnaeus, Hort. Cliff.: 463, t. 31. 1738.
Current name: ***Cliffortia ruscifolia*** L. (Rosaceae).
Note: Weimarck (*Monogr.* Cliffortia: 7, 122. 1934) discussed the original material for the name but did not, however, designate a type.

Cliffortia sarmentosa Linnaeus, *Mantissa Plantarum Altera*: 299. 1771.
"Habitat in Capit. b. spei maritimis; florens majo." RCN: 7498.
Lectotype (Fellingham in Cafferty & Jarvis in *Taxon* 51: 541. 2002): *Tulbagh 105,* Herb. Linn. No. 1197.3 (LINN).
Current name: ***Cliffortia hirta*** Burm. f. (Rosaceae).

Cliffortia strobilifera Linnaeus, *Systema Vegetabilium,* ed. 13: 749. 1774.
"Habitat ad Cap. b. spei." RCN: 7499.
Lectotype (Fellingham in *Bothalia* 24: 32. 1994): [icon] *"Cedrus conifera, Juniperinis foliis, racemosa, conis candicantibus, parvis, ex Prom. Bon. Spei"* in Plukenet, Phytographia: t. 275, f. 2. 1694; Almag. Bot.: 91. 1696. – Typotype: Herb. Sloane 99: 179 (BM-SL).
Current name: ***Cliffortia strobilifera*** L. (Rosaceae).

Cliffortia trifoliata Linnaeus, *Species Plantarum* 2: 1038. 1753.
"Habitat in Aethiopia." RCN: 7497.
Lectotype (Fellingham in Cafferty & Jarvis in *Taxon* 51: 541. 2002): [icon] *"Thymelaeae (forte) affinis Aethiopica, foliis tridentatis, & ex omni parte hirsutie pubescentibus"* in Plukenet, Phytographia: t. 319, f. 4. 1694; Almag. Bot.: 367. 1696. – Typotype: Herb. Sloane 107: 7 (BM-SL). – Voucher: Herb. Sloane 94: 108 (BM-SL).
Current name: ***Cliffortia polygonifolia*** L. var. *trifoliata* (L.) Harv. (Rosaceae).
Note: Weimarck (*Monogr.* Cliffortia: 84. 1934) discussed the Plukenet figure but did not, however, designate a type.

Clinopodium incanum Linnaeus, *Species Plantarum* 2: 588. 1753.
"Habitat in Europa boreali." RCN: 4285.
Lectotype (Reveal & al. in *Huntia* 7: 219. 1987): *Kalm,* Herb. Linn. No. 742.4 (LINN; iso- S).
Current name: ***Pycnanthemum incanum*** (L.) Michx. (Lamiaceae).
Note: Although Epling (in *J. Bot.* 67: 9. 1929) and Grant & Epling (in *Univ. Calif. Publ. Bot.* 20: 206. 1943) indicated Herb. Linn. No. 724.4 (LINN) as a standard specimen, this is not equivalent to a type statement (see Jarvis & al. in *Taxon* 50: 508. 2001).

Clinopodium rugosum Linnaeus, *Species Plantarum* 2: 588. 1753.
"Habitat in Carolina, Jamaica, Gallia aequinoctiali." RCN: 4286.
Lectotype (Epling in *Revista Mus. La Plata, Secc. Bot.,* n.s., 7: 464. 1949): [icon] *"Clinopodium rugosum, capitulis scabiosae"* in Dillenius, Hort. Eltham. 1: 88, t. 75, f. 86. 1732. – Typotype: Herb. Sherard No. 1175 (OXF).
Current name: ***Hyptis alata*** (Raf.) Shinners (Lamiaceae).
Note: Epling (in *J. Bot.* 67: 9. 1929) indicated a Dillenius specimen as the "standard" specimen, but this is not equivalent to a type statement (see Jarvis & al. in *Taxon* 50: 508. 2001). The epithet "rugosa" is not available in *Hyptis* because of the existence of *H. rugosa* Benth. (1833).

Clinopodium vulgare Linnaeus, *Species Plantarum* 2: 587. 1753.
"Habitat in rupestribus Europae, Canadae." RCN: 4284.
Lectotype (Hedge in Ali & Nasir, *Fl. Pakistan* 192: 240. 1990): Herb. Linn. No. 742.1 (LINN).
Generitype of *Clinopodium* Linnaeus (vide Green, *Prop. Brit. Bot.*: 165. 1929).
Current name: ***Clinopodium vulgare*** L. (Lamiaceae).
Note: Hedge's type choice is a specimen grown from North American seed and it has been suggested that it may not belong to the typical infraspecific taxon. For this reason, López González (in Jarvis & al., *Regnum Veg.* 127: 35. 1993) designated Herb. Burser XII: 152 (UPS) as lectotype in its place. This publication was conceived as a possible "Names in Current Use" (NCU) List but, with the rejection of the NCU concept, Hedge's choice clearly has priority, despite the possible difficulties.

Clitoria brasiliana Linnaeus, *Species Plantarum* 2: 753. 1753.
"Habitat in Brasilia." RCN: 5367.
Lectotype (Verdcourt in Turland & Jarvis in *Taxon* 46: 466. 1997): Herb. Clifford: 361, *Clitoria* 2 (BM-000646601).
Current name: ***Centrosema brasilianum*** (L.) Benth. (Fabaceae: Faboideae).

Clitoria galactia (Linnaeus) Linnaeus, *Species Plantarum,* ed. 2, 2: 1026. 1763.
"Habitat in Jamaica." RCN: 5371.
Basionym: *Glycine galactia* L. (1759).
Lectotype (Fortunato in Turland & Jarvis in *Taxon* 46: 470. 1997): Herb. Linn. No. 901.24 (LINN).
Current name: ***Galactia pendula*** Pers. (Fabaceae: Faboideae).
Note: Fawcett & Rendle (*Fl. Jamaica* 4: 55. 1920) treated material in Sloane's herbarium (BM-SL) as the type, but this was not seen by Linnaeus and is not original material for the name.

Clitoria lactescens Linnaeus, *Systema Naturae,* ed. 10, 2: 1172. 1759.
RCN: 5371.
Neotype (Fortunato & Greuter in *Taxon* 47: 704. 1998): U.S.A. Georgia: Dalton, dry pine woods, 850ft, 10 Aug 1900, *R.M. Harper 391* (BM).
Current name: ***Galactia regularis*** (L.) Britton & al. (Fabaceae: Faboideae).

Clitoria mariana Linnaeus, *Species Plantarum* 2: 753. 1753.
"Habitat in America septentrionali." RCN: 5370.
Neotype (Nguyên Van Thuân in Aubréville & Leroy, *Fl. Cambodge Laos Viêt-Nam* 17: 48. 1979): Herb. Linn. No. 902.4 (LINN).
Current name: ***Clitoria mariana*** L. (Fabaceae: Faboideae).
Note: There appear to be no original elements extant for this name. Reveal, however (in *Bot. J. Linn. Soc.* 92: 164. 1986), designated *Clayton 108* (BM) as lectotype. Linnaeus did not cite Gronovius' *Flora Virginica* account in the protologue (but later cited an account from *Flora Virginica,* ed. 2: 111. 1762 in the entry for the same species in *Sp. Pl.,* ed. 2, 2: 1026. 1763). The Clayton specimen cannot be an original element since it was not indirectly cited in the protologue. Although it could now be treated as a neotype (Art. 9.8), such a choice is pre-dated by that of Nguyên Van Thuân, whose indication of 902.4 (LINN) as "type" is similarly accepted as a neotypification.

Clitoria ternatea Linnaeus, *Species Plantarum* 2: 753. 1753.
"Habitat in India." RCN: 5366.
Lectotype (Wijnands, *Bot. Commelins*: 161. 1983): Herb. Clifford: 360, *Clitoria* 1 (BM-000646600).
Generitype of *Clitoria* Linnaeus (vide Green, *Prop. Brit. Bot.*: 176. 1929).
Current name: ***Clitoria ternatea*** L. (Fabaceae: Faboideae).
Note: Fawcett & Rendle (*Fl. Jamaica* 4: 47. 1920) treated material in LINN and in Herb. Hermann (BM) as type. Verdcourt (in Milne-Redhead & Polhill, *Fl. Trop. E. Africa, Leguminosae* 4: 515. 1971), followed by several other authors, indicated material in Herb. Hermann 3: 13, 20; 4: 49 (BM) as syntypes, but gave no indication of intending to lectotypify the name. Fantz (in *Ann. Missouri Bot. Gard.* 67: 592. 1980) indicated 902.1 (LINN) as type but this lacks a *Species Plantarum* number (i.e. "1"), was a post-1753 addition to the herbarium, and is not original material for the name. Wijnands (who chose Clifford material) appears to have been the first to make an explicit type choice.

Clitoria virginiana Linnaeus, *Species Plantarum* 2: 753. 1753.
"Habitat in Virginia." RCN: 5369.
Lectotype (Fawcett & Rendle, *Fl. Jamaica* 4: 46. 1920): *Clayton 112* (BM-000038162).
Current name: ***Centrosema virginianum*** (L.) Benth. (Fabaceae: Faboideae).

Clitoria zoophthalmum Linnaeus, *Systema Naturae,* ed. 10, 2: 1172. 1759.
RCN: 5368.

Neotype (Verdcourt in Turland & Jarvis in *Taxon* 46: 466. 1997):
Dominican Republic. Duarte: San Francisco de Macoris at Rio de la
Cuaba, 26 Apr 1929, *Ekman H12311* (K).
Current name: ***Mucuna urens*** (L.) DC. (Fabaceae: Faboideae).

Clusia major Linnaeus, *Species Plantarum* 1: 509. 1753.
"Habitat in Jamaicae & Caribaearum apricis." RCN: 7627.
Lectotype (Bittrich & Stevens in *Taxon* 47: 121. 1998): [icon] Aubriet
copy of unpublished Plumier drawing (Ms. No. 6, Bot. Amer., t.
VI, *"Clusia flore albo, fructu coccineo"*, P) titled *"Clusia foliis aveniis"*,
excl. separately drawn elements; open fl. on branch, in Plumier,
Codex Boerhaavianus (University Library, Groningen).
Generitype of *Clusia* Linnaeus (vide Green, *Prop. Brit. Bot.*: 160.
1929).
Current name: ***Clusia major*** L. (Clusiaceae).
Note: See extensive review and discussion by Bittrich & Stevens.

Clusia minor Linnaeus, *Species Plantarum* 1: 510. 1753.
"Habitat in America meridonali." RCN: 7630.
Holotype (Bittrich & Stevens in *Taxon* 47: 121. 1998): [icon] Aubriet
copy of unpublished Plumier drawing (Ms. No. 6, Bot. Amer., t.
VI, *"Clusia flore roseo minor, fructu e viridi rubra"*, P) titled *"Clusia
foliis venosis"* in Plumier, Codex Boerhaavianus (University Library,
Groningen).
Current name: ***Clusia minor*** L. (Clusiaceae).
Note: See extensive discussion by Bittrich & Stevens.

Clutia alaternoides Linnaeus, *Species Plantarum* 2: 1042. 1753.
"Habitat in Aethiopia." RCN: 7529.
Lectotype (Wijnands, *Bot. Commelins*: 95. 1983): Herb. Clifford: 444,
Clutia 1 (BM-000647328).
Current name: ***Clutia alaternoides*** L. (Euphorbiaceae).
Note: See detailed discussion of the original elements by Prain (in *Bull.
Misc. Inform. Kew* 1913: 375–378. 1913), who applied the name in
the sense of 1206.2 (LINN) and the Clifford sheet, but without
designating a type.

Clutia androgyna Linnaeus, *Systema Naturae,* ed. 12, 2: 663;
Mantissa Plantarum: 128. 1767.
"Habitat in India." RCN: 7351.
Lectotype (van Welzen in *Blumea* 48: 340. 2003): Herb. Linn. No.
1206.14 (LINN).
Current name: ***Sauropus androgynus*** (L.) Merr. (Euphorbiaceae).

Clutia cascarilla Linnaeus, *Species Plantarum* 2: 1042. 1753.
"Habitat in Carolina." RCN: 7267.
Basionym of: *Croton cascarilla* (L.) L. (1763).
Lectotype (Dandy, *Sloane Herbarium*: 112. 1958): [icon] *"An
Ricinoides Aeleagni folio?"* in Catesby, Nat. Hist. Carolina 2: 46, t.
46. 1736. – Voucher: Herb. Sloane 232: 24 (BM-SL).
Current name: ***Croton cascarilla*** (L.) L. (Euphorbiaceae).
Note: See discussion by Howard & Staples (in *J. Arnold Arbor.* 64: 524.
1983).

Clutia eluteria Linnaeus, *Species Plantarum* 2: 1042. 1753.
"Habitat in Indiis." RCN: 7534.
Lectotype (designated here by Berry): Herb. Clifford: 486, *Elutheria* 1
(BM).
Current name: ***Croton eluteria*** (L.) W. Wright (Euphorbiaceae).

Clutia polygonoides Linnaeus, *Species Plantarum,* ed. 2, 2: 1475.
1763.
"Habitat ad Cap. b. spei." RCN: 7530.
Type not designated.
Original material: Herb. Linn. No. 1206.4 (LINN); Herb. Linn. No.

1206.5 (LINN); [icon] in Burman, Rar. Afric. Pl.: 118, t. 43, f. 3.
1739; [icon] in Plukenet, Phytographia: t. 23, f. 7. 1691; Almag.
Bot.: 107. 1696.
Current name: ***Clutia polygonoides*** L. (Euphorbiaceae).
Note: See discussion of the cited Burman figure, and 1206.4 and
1206.5 (LINN) by Prain (in *Bull. Misc. Inform. Kew* 1913:
375–378. 1913).

Clutia pulchella Linnaeus, *Species Plantarum* 2: 1042. 1753.
"Habitat in Aethiopia." RCN: 7531.
Lectotype (Wijnands, *Bot. Commelins*: 96. 1983): Herb. Linn. No.
1206.7 (LINN).
Generitype of *Clutia* Linnaeus (vide Green, *Prop. Brit. Bot.*: 193. 1929).
Current name: ***Clutia pulchella*** L. (Euphorbiaceae).
Note: Prain (in *Bull. Misc. Inform. Kew* 1913: 375–378. 1913)
discussed the original elements for the name in some detail but did
not make a choice of type.

Clutia retusa Linnaeus, *Species Plantarum* 2: 1042. 1753.
"Habitat in India." RCN: 7533.
Lectotype (Radcliffe-Smith in *Kew Bull.* 41: 6. 1986): Herb. Hermann
2: 71, No. 367 (BM-000594633).
Current name: ***Bridelia retusa*** (L.) A. Juss. (Euphorbiaceae).

Clutia stipularis Linnaeus, *Systema Naturae*, ed. 12, 2: 663; *Mantissa
Plantarum*: 127. 1767.
"Habitat in India Kattuko-kelang. Kleinhoff." RCN: 7535.
Lectotype (Dressler in *Blumea* 41: 294. 1996): *Kleynhoff*, Herb. Linn.
No. 1206.13 (LINN).
Current name: ***Bridelia stipularis*** (L.) Blume (Euphorbiaceae).

Clutia tomentosa Linnaeus, *Mantissa Plantarum Altera*: 299. 1771.
"Habitat ad Cap. b. spei arenosis maritimis; florens Majo." RCN:
7532.
Type not designated.
Original material: *Tulbagh 129*, Herb. Linn. No. 1206.9 (LINN).
Current name: ***Clutia tomentosa*** L. (Euphorbiaceae).
Note: See discussion by Prain (in *Bull. Misc. Inform. Kew* 1913:
375–377. 1913).

Clypeola alyssoides Linnaeus, *Species Plantarum* 2: 652. 1753.
"Habitat in Austria, Gallia." RCN: 4734.
Basionym of: *Alyssum alyssoides* (L.) L. (1759).
Lectotype (Dudley in *J. Arnold Arbor.* 45: 63. 1964): Herb. Clifford:
329, *Clypeola* 2 (BM-000646255).
Current name: ***Alyssum alyssoides*** (L.) L. (Brassicaceae).

Clypeola campestris Linnaeus, *Species Plantarum* 2: 652. 1753.
"Habitat in Gallia." RCN: 4736.
Basionym of: *Alyssum campestre* (L.) L. (1759).
Neotype (Polatschek in Cafferty & Jarvis in *Taxon* 51: 532. 2002):
France. Montpellier, Herb. Endl. Alyssum calycinum, *Endlicher s.n.*
(W).
Current name: ***Alyssum alyssoides*** (L.) L. (Brassicaceae).
Note: Dudley (in *J. Arnold Arbor.* 45: 64. 1964) regarded Sauvages'
description itself as the basis of the basionym but this would be
contrary to Art. 8.1. *Alyssum campestre* L., *Sp. Pl.*, ed. 2, 2: 909
(1763) is evidently not the same taxon as *A. campestre* (L.) L.
(1759), and this has caused confusion leading to "*A. campestre*"
being informally rejected as ambiguous by some authors (e.g. Turrill
in *J. Bot.* 73: 261. 1935; Botschantzev in *Novosti Sist. Vyssh. Rast.*
15: 150–151. 1985). In the absence of original material, Polatschek
designated a neotype, confirming the position of *A. campestre*
(1759) as a synonym of *A. alyssoides*, in agreement with the
treatment of Dudley.

Clypeola jonthlaspi Linnaeus, *Species Plantarum* 2: 652. 1753.
"Habitat in Italiae, Narbonae sabulosis." RCN: 4745.
Lectotype (Ball in Jarvis & al., *Regnum Veg.* 127: 35. 1993): Herb. Clifford: 329, *Clypeola* 1 (BM-000646254).
Generitype of *Clypeola* Linnaeus (vide Green, *Prop. Brit. Bot.*: 55. 1929).
Current name: ***Clypeola jonthlaspi*** L. (Brassicaceae).
Note: Jafri (in Nasir & Ali, *Fl. W. Pakistan* 55: 126. 1973) indicated 830.1 (LINN) as type but this is a post-1753 addition to the herbarium and not original material for the name. Although Meikle (*Fl. Cyprus* 1: 144. 1977) stated "Type: …(BM)", he did not indicate any particular collection.

Clypeola maritima Linnaeus, *Species Plantarum* 2: 652. 1753.
"Habitat in G. Narbonensi." RCN: 4747.
Lectotype (Borgen in Cafferty & Jarvis in *Taxon* 51: 533. 2002): [icon] *"Thlaspi Narbonense Centumculi angusti folio"* in Tabernaemontanus, Eicones Pl.: 461. 1590. – Epitype (Borgen in Cafferty & Jarvis in *Taxon* 51: 533. 2002): Herb. Linn. No. 830.3 (LINN).
Current name: ***Lobularia maritima*** (L.) Desv. (Brassicaceae).

Clypeola minor Linnaeus, *Flora Monspeliensis*: 21. 1756, *nom. nud.*
Type not relevant.
Current name: ***Alyssum alyssoides*** (L.) L. (Brassicaceae).
Note: As explained by Stearn (in Geck & Pressler, *Festschr. Claus Nissen*: 625, 632. 1974), names from the original publication of the dissertation *Flora Monspeliensis* (1756) are not valid, as there are no descriptions nor any indication of the significance of the numbers that appear in the right-hand column. "*Clypeola minor*" appeared in the original dissertation (where it is a *nomen nudum*) but Linnaeus substituted *Alyssum alyssoides* (L.) L., (*Syst. Nat.*, ed. 10, 2: 1130. May-Jun 1759) for it in the Nov 1759 reprint. However, some authors (e.g. Meikle, *Fl. Cyprus* 1: 138. 1977; Hartvig in Strid & Kit Tan, *Fl. Hellenica* 2: 204. 2002) have incorrectly used *Alyssum minus* (L.) Rothm. for this taxon.

Cneorum tricoccon Linnaeus, *Species Plantarum* 1: 34. 1753.
"Habitat in Hispaniae, Narbonae glareosis." RCN: 273.
Lectotype (Lobreau-Callen & Jérémie in *Grana* 25: 156. 1986): Herb. Burser XXIV: 38 (UPS).
Generitype of *Cneorum* Linnaeus.
Current name: ***Cneorum tricoccon*** L. (Cneoraceae).

Cnicus acarna (Linnaeus) Linnaeus, *Systema Naturae*, ed. 10, 2: 1201. 1759.
["Habitat in Hispania."] Sp. Pl. 2: 820 (1753). RCN: 5979.
Basionym: *Carduus acarna* L. (1753).
Lectotype (Turland in Jarvis & Turland in *Taxon* 47: 356. 1998): Herb. Burser XXI: 26 (UPS).
Current name: ***Picnomon acarna*** (L.) Cass. (Asteraceae).

Cnicus benedictus Linnaeus, *Species Plantarum* 2: 826. 1753, *typ. cons.*
"Habitat in Chio, Lemno, Hispania ad versuras agrorum." RCN: 6621.
Basionym of: *Centaurea benedicta* (L.) L. (1763).
Lectotype (Jeffrey in *Kew Bull.* 22: 138. 1968): Herb. Clifford: 394, *Cnicus* 1 (BM-000646941).
Generitype of *Cnicus* Linnaeus, *nom. cons.*
Current name: ***Centaurea benedicta*** (L.) L. (Asteraceae).

Cnicus centauroides Linnaeus, *Species Plantarum* 2: 826. 1753.
"Habitat in Pyrenaeis." RCN: 5981.
Lectotype (Dittrich in *Candollea* 39: 46. 1984): Herb. Clifford: 392, *Carduus* 1 (BM-000646916).
Current name: ***Stemmacantha centauroides*** (L.) Dittrich (Asteraceae).

Cnicus cernuus Linnaeus, *Species Plantarum* 2: 826. 1753.
"Habitat in Sibiria." RCN: 5982.
Lectotype (Iljin & Semidel in Bobrov & Czerepanov, *Fl. U.R.S.S.* 28: 41. 1963): [icon] *"Carduus foliis ex cordato lanceolatis, margine serratis et spinosis, squamis calicum membranaceis, laceris, spinosis, capitulis nutantibus"* in Gmelin, Fl. Sibirica 2: 47, t. 19. 1752.
Current name: ***Alfredia cernua*** (L.) Cass. (Asteraceae).

Cnicus erisithales (N.J. Jacquin) Linnaeus, *Species Plantarum*, ed. 2, 2: 1157. 1763.
"Habitat in Austriae, Galliae pratis subalpinis." RCN: 5976.
Basionym: *Carduus erisithales* Jacq. (1762).
Type not designated.
Current name: ***Cirsium erisithales*** (Jacq.) Scop. (Asteraceae).

Cnicus ferox Linnaeus, *Systema Naturae*, ed. 12, 2: 531; *Mantissa Plantarum*: 109. 1767.
"Habitat in Europae australis montosis, sterilibus." RCN: 5977.
Type not designated.
Original material: [icon] in Bauhin & Cherler, Hist. Pl. Univ. 3(1): 58. 1651.
Current name: ***Cirsium ferox*** (L.) DC. (Asteraceae).

Cnicus oleraceus Linnaeus, *Species Plantarum* 2: 826. 1753.
"Habitat in Europae septentrionalioris pratis subnemorosis." RCN: 5975.
Lectotype (Talavera & Valdés in *Lagascalia* 5: 161. 1976): Herb. Linn. No. 967.1 (LINN).
Current name: ***Cirsium oleraceum*** (L.) Scop. (Asteraceae).

Cnicus pygmaeus (N.J. Jacquin) Linnaeus, *Species Plantarum*, ed. 2, 2: 1156. 1763.
"Habitat in Schneeberg Austriae." RCN: 5978.
Basionym: *Carduus pygmaeus* Jacq. (1762).
Type not designated.
Current name: ***Saussurea pygmaea*** (Jacq.) Spreng. (Asteraceae).

Cnicus spinosissimus Linnaeus, *Species Plantarum* 2: 826. 1753.
"Habitat in Alpibus Helvetiae, Austriae." RCN: 5980.
Type not designated.
Original material: Herb. Burser XXI: 32 (UPS); Herb. Linn. No. 967.4 (LINN); [icon] in Haller, Enum. Meth. Stirp. Helv. 2: 679, t. 20. 1742.
Current name: ***Cirsium spinosissimum*** (L.) Scop. (Asteraceae).

Cnicus uniflorus Linnaeus, *Mantissa Plantarum Altera*: 572. 1771.
"Habitat in Sibiria." RCN: 5983.
Lectotype (Dittrich in *Candollea* 39: 149. 1984): [icon] *"Centaurea calicibus membranaceis, foliis pinnatifidis, dentatis"* in Gmelin, Fl. Sibirica 2: 86, t. 38. 1752 (see p. 132).
Current name: ***Stemmacantha uniflora*** (L.) Dittrich (Asteraceae).

Coccoloba excoriata Linnaeus, *Systema Naturae*, ed. 10, 2: 1007. 1759.
["Habitat in America."] Sp. Pl., ed. 2, 1: 525 (1762). RCN: 2881.
Type not designated.
Original material: *Browne*, Herb. Linn. No. 511.2 (LINN).
Current name: ***Coccoloba tenuifolia*** L. (Polygonaceae).
Note: Fawcett & Rendle (in *J. Bot.* 51: 123. 1913; *Fl. Jamaica* 3: 121. 1914) provided an extensive discussion but did not indicate a type. Howard (in *J. Arnold Arbor.* 38: 94. 1957) observed that Linnaeus had based *C. excoriata* on a Patrick Browne specimen in LINN but did not explicitly treat it as the type.

Coccoloba pubescens Linnaeus, *Systema Naturae,* ed. 10, 2: 1007. 1759.
["Habitat in America."] Sp. Pl. ed. 2, 1: 523 (1762). RCN: 2881.
Lectotype (Howard, *Fl. Lesser Antilles* 4: 133. 1988): [icon] *"Scortea arbor Americana, amplissimis foliis, aversa parte nervis extantibus hirsutie ferruginea refertis"* in Plukenet, Phytographia: t. 222, f. 8. 1692; Almag. Bot.: 38. 1696. – Voucher: Herb. Sloane 98: 23; 101: 196 (BM-SL).
Current name: ***Coccoloba pubescens*** L. (Polygonaceae).
Note: Fawcett & Rendle (in *J. Bot.* 51: 123. 1913) provided an extensive discussion but did not indicate a type, but later (*Fl. Jamaica* 3: 118. 1914) indicated a type in BM (presumably material in Herb. Plukenet that was not seen by Linnaeus and is not original material for the name). See discussion by Howard (in *J. Arnold Arbor.* 38: 229. 1957).

Coccoloba punctata Linnaeus, *Species Plantarum,* ed. 2, 1: 523. 1762, *nom. illeg.*
"Habitat in America." RCN: 2882.
Replaced synonym: *Coccoloba venosa* L. (1759).
Lectotype (Howard, *Fl. Lesser Antilles* 4: 135. 1988): [icon] *"Uvifera arbor Americana convolvulacea, fructu punctato Barbadensibus"* in Plukenet, Phytographia: t. 237, f. 4. 1692; Almag. Bot.: 394. 1696. – Typotype: Herb. Sloane 98: 171 (BM-SL).
Current name: ***Coccoloba venosa*** L. (Polygonaceae).
Note: An illegitimate replacement name for *C. venosa* L. (1759).

Coccoloba rubescens Linnaeus, *Species Plantarum,* ed. 2, 1: 523. 1762, *orth. var.*
"Habitat in America." RCN: 2880.
Lectotype (Howard, *Fl. Lesser Antilles* 4: 133. 1988): [icon] *"Scortea arbor Americana, amplissimis foliis, aversa parte nervis extantibus hirsutie ferruginea refertis"* in Plukenet, Phytographia: t. 222, f. 8. 1692; Almag. Bot.: 38. 1696. – Voucher: Herb. Sloane 98: 23; 101: 196 (BM-SL).
Current name: ***Coccoloba pubescens*** L. (Polygonaceae).
Note: An orthographic variant of *C. pubescens* L. (1759).

Coccoloba tenuifolia Linnaeus, *Systema Naturae,* ed. 10, 2: 1007. 1759.
["Habitat in Jamaica."] Sp. Pl., ed. 2, 1: 542 (1762). RCN: 2885.
Lectotype (Fawcett & Rendle, *Fl. Jamaica* 3: 120. 1914): *Browne,* Herb. Linn. No. 511.3 (LINN).
Current name: ***Coccoloba tenuifolia*** L. (Polygonaceae).

Coccoloba uvifera (Linnaeus) Linnaeus, *Systema Naturae,* ed. 10, 2: 1007. 1759.
["Habitat in America."] Sp. Pl., ed. 2, 1: 523 (1762). RCN: 2879.
Basionym: *Polygonum uviferum* L. (1753).
Lectotype (Brandbyge in Harling & Andersson, *Fl. Ecuador* 38: 39. 1989): Herb. Linn. No. 511.1 (LINN).
Current name: ***Coccoloba uvifera*** (L.) L. (Polygonaceae).

Coccoloba venosa Linnaeus, *Systema Naturae,* ed. 10, 2: 1007. 1759.
["Habitat in America."] Sp. Pl., ed. 2, 1: 524 (1762). RCN: 2882.
Replaced synonym of: *Coccoloba punctata* L. (1762), *nom. illeg.*
Lectotype (Howard, *Fl. Lesser Antilles* 4: 135. 1988): [icon] *"Uvifera arbor Americana convolvulacea, fructu punctato Barbadensibus"* in Plukenet, Phytographia: t. 237, f. 4. 1692; Almag. Bot.: 394. 1696. – Typotype: Herb. Sloane 98: 171 (BM-SL).
Current name: ***Coccoloba venosa*** L. (Polygonaceae).
Note: Fawcett & Rendle (in *J. Bot.* 51: 123. 1913) provided an extensive discussion but did not indicate a type.

Cochlearia anglica Linnaeus, *Systema Naturae,* ed. 10, 2: 1128. 1759.
["Habitat in Angliae littoribus marinis."] Sp. Pl., ed. 2, 2: 903 (1763). RCN: 4709.
Lectotype (Jonsell & Jarvis in *Nordic J. Bot.* 22: 68. 2002): Herb. Linn. No. 826.4 (LINN).
Current name: ***Cochlearia officinalis*** L. subsp. ***anglica*** (L.) Asch. & Graebn. (Brassicaceae).

Cochlearia armoracia Linnaeus, *Species Plantarum* 2: 648. 1753.
"Habitat in Europae fossis & ad rivulos." RCN: 4712.
Lectotype (Rich in Cafferty & Jarvis in *Taxon* 51: 533. 2002): Herb. Linn. No. 826.6 (LINN).
Current name: ***Armoracia rusticana*** Gaertn. & al. (Brassicaceae).

Cochlearia coronopus Linnaeus, *Species Plantarum* 2: 648. 1753.
"Habitat in Europae apricis, nudis." RCN: 4711.
Lectotype (Jonsell & Jarvis in *Nordic J. Bot.* 22: 68. 2002): Herb. Linn. No. 826.5 (LINN).
Current name: ***Lepidium coronopus*** (L.) Al-Shehbaz (Brassicaceae).

Cochlearia danica Linnaeus, *Species Plantarum* 2: 647. 1753.
"Habitat in Daniae, Sueciae litoribus marinis." RCN: 4708.
Lectotype (Vogt in *Mitt. Bot. Staatssamml. München* 23: 402. 1987): Herb. Linn. No. 826.2 (LINN).
Current name: ***Cochlearia danica*** L. (Brassicaceae).

Cochlearia draba (Linnaeus) Linnaeus, *Systema Naturae,* ed. 10, 2: 1129. 1759.
["Habitat in Austria, Gallia, Italia ad versuras."] Sp. Pl., ed. 2, 2: 904 (1763). RCN: 4714.
Basionym: *Lepidium draba* L. (1753).
Lectotype (Jonsell & Jarvis in *Nordic J. Bot.* 22: 70. 2002): Herb. Clifford: 331, *Lepidium* 2, sheet 2 (BM-000646273).
Current name: ***Cardaria draba*** (L.) Desv. (Brassicaceae).

Cochlearia glastifolia Linnaeus, *Species Plantarum* 2: 648. 1753.
"Habitat – – – –" RCN: 4713.
Lectotype (Vogt in *Mitt. Bot. Staatssamml. München* 23: 395. 1987): Herb. Linn. No. 826.7 (LINN).
Current name: ***Cochlearia glastifolia*** L. (Brassicaceae).

Cochlearia groenlandica Linnaeus, *Species Plantarum* 2: 647. 1753.
"Habitat in Norvegia, Islandia, Groenlandia." RCN: 4710.
Lectotype (Elven & Nordal in Jonsell & Jarvis in *Nordic J. Bot.* 22: 69. 2002): Herb. Linn. No. 826.3 (LINN). – Epitype (Elven & Nordal in Jonsell & Jarvis in *Nordic J. Bot.* 22: 69. 2002): Greenland. Disko, Mudderbugten, between Alákariaq and Isungua, 24 Jul 1975, *L. Andersen & S. Hanfgarn 135* (O).
Current name: ***Cochlearia groenlandica*** L. (Brassicaceae).

Cochlearia officinalis Linnaeus, *Species Plantarum* 2: 647. 1753.
"Habitat in Europae borealis littoribus marinis." RCN: 4707.
Lectotype (Nordal & Stabbetorp in *Nordic J. Bot.* 10: 261. 1990): Herb. Linn. No. 826.1 (LINN).
Generitype of *Cochlearia* Linnaeus (vide Green, *Prop. Brit. Bot.*: 170. 1929).
Current name: ***Cochlearia officinalis*** L. (Brassicaceae).

Cochlearia saxatilis Linnaeus, *Species Plantarum* 2: 648. 1753.
"Habitat in Alpibus Helvetiae, Monspelii." RCN: 4661.
Basionym of: *Myagrum saxatile* (L.) L. (1759).
Lectotype (Kit Tan in Cafferty & Jarvis in *Taxon* 51: 533. 2002): Herb. Linn. No. 819.13 (LINN).
Current name: ***Kernera saxatilis*** (L.) Sweet (Brassicaceae).

Cocos guineensis Linnaeus, *Systema Naturae,* ed. 12, 2: 730; *Mantissa Plantarum*: 137. 1767.
"Habitat in America meridionali." RCN: 8545.

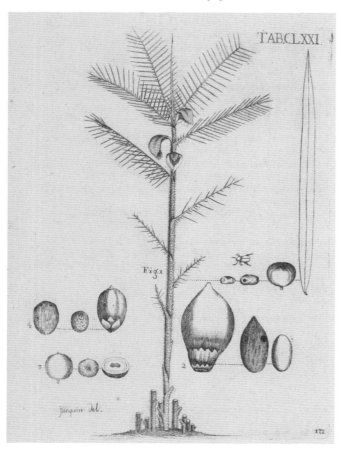

Lectotype (Moore in *Gentes Herb.* 9: 251. 1963): [icon] *"Bactris minor"* in Jacquin, Select. Stirp. Amer. Hist.: 279, t. 171, f. 1. 1763.
Current name: ***Bactris guineensis*** (L.) H.E. Moore (Arecaceae).

Cocos nucifera Linnaeus, *Species Plantarum* 2: 1188. 1753.
"Habitat in Indiae paludosis, umbrosis." RCN: 8544.
Lectotype (Moore & Dransfield in *Taxon* 28: 64, f. 5. 1979): [icon] *"Tenga"* in Rheede, Hort. Malab. 1: 1, t. 1, t. 2, t. 3, t. 4. 1678.
Generitype of *Cocos* Linnaeus.
Current name: ***Cocos nucifera*** L. (Arecaceae).

Codon royenii Linnaeus, *Systema Naturae,* ed. 12, 2: 292. 1767.
RCN: 3012.
Holotype (Jarvis & al., *Regnum Veg.* 127: 36. 1993): Herb. Linn. No. 535.1 [icon] (LINN).
Generitype of *Codon* Linnaeus.
Current name: ***Codon royenii*** L. (Hydrophyllaceae).
Note: The name appears to be based solely on a drawing and description sent to Linnaeus by David van Royen in a letter dated 19 Feb 1767. Linnaeus refers to "Roy. mss", reinforced by his chosen epithet. Royen's drawing is preserved in Linnaeus' herbarium (sheet 535.1), and was consequently referred to as the holotype by Jarvis &. al. Retief & al. (in *Fl. Pl. Africa* 59: 114. 2005) followed Jarvis & al. and suggest that the original material was probably collected by J.A. Auge in 1761–1762 on Hop's expedition to Namaqualand and Southern Namibia.

Coffea arabica Linnaeus, *Species Plantarum* 1: 172. 1753.
"Habitat in Arabia felici." RCN: 1366.
Lectotype (Bridson in Polhill, *Fl. Trop. E. Africa, Rubiaceae* 2: 713. 1988): Herb. Clifford: 59, *Coffea* 1 (BM-000558021).
Generitype of *Coffea* Linnaeus.
Current name: ***Coffea arabica*** L. (Rubiaceae).

Coix dactyloides Linnaeus, *Species Plantarum* 2: 972. 1753.
"Habitat in America." RCN: 7050.
Basionym of: *Tripsacum dactyloides* (L.) L. (1759).
Lectotype (Hitchcock in *Contr. U. S. Natl. Herb.* 12: 124. 1908): Herb. Linn. No. 1097.1 (LINN).
Current name: ***Tripsacum dactyloides*** (L.) L. (Poaceae).

Coix lacryma-jobi Linnaeus, *Species Plantarum* 2: 972. 1753.
"Habitat in Indiis." RCN: 7052.
Lectotype (Clayton & Renvoize in Polhill, *Fl. Trop. E. Africa, Gramineae* 3: 857. 1982): Herb. Linn. No. 1098.1 (LINN).
Generitype of *Coix* Linnaeus (vide Green, *Prop. Brit. Bot.*: 187. 1929).
Current name: ***Coix lacryma-jobi*** L. (Poaceae).
Note: Although Kerguélen (in *Lejeunia*, n.s., 75: 120. 1975) stated "Type: ...LINN", this is not accepted as a formal typification, for the reasons explained by Cafferty & al. (in *Taxon* 49: 240. 2000).

Colchicum autumnale Linnaeus, *Species Plantarum* 1: 341. 1753.
"Habitat in Europae australioris succulentis." RCN: 2620.
Lectotype (Mathew in Jarvis & al., *Regnum Veg.* 127: 36. 1993): Herb. Burser III: 70 (UPS).
Generitype of *Colchicum* Linnaeus (vide Hitchcock, *Prop. Brit. Bot.*: 148. 1929).
Current name: ***Colchicum autumnale*** L. (Liliaceae/Colchicaceae).

Colchicum montanum Linnaeus, *Species Plantarum* 1: 342. 1753.
"Habitat in Hispania, Helvetia." RCN: 2621.
Type not designated.
Original material: Herb. Linn. No. 470.2 (LINN); Herb. Burser III: 75 (UPS); [icon] in Clusius, Rar. Pl. Hist. 1: 200. 1601; [icon] in Clusius, Rar. Stirp. Hispan. Hist.: 266, 267. 1576.
Current name: ***Merendera montana*** (L.) Lange (Liliaceae/Colchicaceae).
Note: See discussion by Lacaita (in *J. Linn. Soc., Bot.* 47: 172–174, f. 3. 1925), who rejected this as a *nomen confusum.* Valdés (in *Bot. J. Linn. Soc.* 76: 313. 1978) treated 472.2 (LINN), which he thought was probably identifiable as *Bulbocodium vernum* L., as the type of *C. montanum* and (in Tutin & al., *Fl. Europaea* 5: 24. 1980) took up *Merendera pyrenaica* (Pourret) Fourn. for the Pyrenean species known alternatively as *M. montana* (L.) Lange. However, Burtt (in *Taxon* 30: 230. 1981) disagreed with Valdés' identification of the type, believing it to be a collection of *C. triphyllum* Kunze. Burtt also rejected Valdés' typification on the grounds that the chosen type was, as indicated by Linnaeus, from Greece, and not original material for the name, and urged the retention of *M. montana,* though without formally proposing an alternative type.

Colchicum variegatum Linnaeus, *Species Plantarum* 1: 342. 1753.
"Habitat in Chio insula." RCN: 2622.
Type not designated.
Original material: [icon] in Morison, Pl. Hist. Univ. 2: 341, s. 4, t. 3, f. 7. 1680.
Current name: ***Colchicum variegatum*** L. (Liliaceae/Colchicaceae).

Coldenia procumbens Linnaeus, *Species Plantarum* 1: 125. 1753.
"Habitat in India." RCN: 1033.
Lectotype (Verdcourt in Polhill, *Fl. Trop. E. Africa, Boraginaceae*: 46. 1991): Herb. Hermann 1: 73, No. 69 (BM-000621476).
Generitype of *Coldenia* Linnaeus.

Current name: ***Coldenia procumbens*** L. (Boraginaceae).
Note: Kazmi (in *J. Arnold Arbor.* 51: 148. 1970) indicated 174.1 (LINN) as type but this appears to be a post-1753 addition to the collection and not original material for the name.

Collinsonia canadensis Linnaeus, *Species Plantarum* 1: 28. 1753.
"Habitat in Virginiae, Canadae sylvis." RCN: 222.
Lectotype (Stearn, *Introd. Linnaeus' Sp. Pl.* (Ray Soc. ed.): 47. 1957): [icon] *"Collinsonia"* in Linnaeus, Hort. Cliff.: 14, t. 5. 1738. – Voucher: Herb. Clifford: 14, *Collinsonia* 1 (BM).
Generitype of *Collinsonia* Linnaeus.
Current name: ***Collinsonia canadensis*** L. (Lamiaceae).
Note: Epling (in *J. Bot.* 67: 6. 1929) termed the Clifford sheet as "standard" but also noted a Kalm sheet in LINN, and Clayton material in BM. Shinners (in *Sida* 1: 80. 1962) regarded Epling as having chosen it as lectotype ("…was designbated lectotype by Epling…(phototype in Gray Herbarium examined)"). However, Epling's standard specimens are not equivalent to types (see Jarvis & al. in *Taxon* 50: 508. 2001). Stearn's choice of the Clifford plate pre-dates Shinners' acceptance of the Clifford sheet as the type.

Columnea longifolia Linnaeus, *Systema Naturae,* ed. 12, 2: 427; *Mantissa Plantarum:* 90. 1767.
"Habitat in India." RCN: 4645.
Lectotype (Cramer in Dassanayake & Fosberg, *Revised Handb. Fl. Ceylon* 3: 404. 1981): [icon] *"Bahel-tsjulli"* in Rheede, Hort. Malab. 9: 169, t. 87. 1689.
Current name: ***Artanema longifolium*** (L.) Vatke (Scrophulariaceae).

Columnea scandens Linnaeus, *Species Plantarum* 2: 638. 1753.
"Habitat in Gallia aequinoctiali." RCN: 4644.
Lectotype (Leeuwenberg in *Acta Bot. Neerl.* 7: 390. 1958): [icon] *"Columnea"* in Plumier in Burman, Pl. Amer.: 77, t. 89, f. 1. 1756.
Generitype of *Columnea* Linnaeus.
Current name: ***Columnea scandens*** L. (Gesneriaceae).
Note: The plate number of the type was cited in error (as "t. 139") by Leeuwenberg, and (as "t. 189") by Jarvis & al. (in *Regnum Veg* 127: 36. 1993).

Colutea arborescens Linnaeus, *Species Plantarum* 2: 723. 1753.
"Habitat in Austria, G. Narbonensi, Italia praecipue ad Vesuvium." RCN: 5457.
Lectotype (Wijnands in Jarvis & al., *Regnum Veg.* 127: 36. 1993): Herb. Linn. No. 914.1 (LINN).
Generitype of *Colutea* Linnaeus (vide Green, *Prop. Brit. Bot.*: 175. 1929).
Current name: ***Colutea arborescens*** L. subsp. ***arborescens*** (Fabaceae: Faboideae).
Note: Browicz (in *Monogr. Bot.* 14: 29. 1963) indicated unspecified and unseen material in LINN as type but did not distinguish between three sheets (914.1–3, LINN) there. They do not appear to be part of a single gathering so Art. 9.15 does not apply. Wijnands (*Bot. Commelins*: 164. 1983) stated "the type is probably LINN 914.1", and formalised this in 1993.

Colutea frutescens Linnaeus, *Species Plantarum* 2: 723. 1753.
"Habitat in Aethiopia." RCN: 5458.
Lectotype (Schrire in Turland & Jarvis in *Taxon* 46: 466. 1997): Herb. Linn. No. 914.4 (LINN).
Current name: ***Lessertia frutescens*** (L.) Goldblatt & J.C. Manning (Fabaceae: Faboideae).

Colutea herbacea Linnaeus, *Species Plantarum* 2: 723. 1753.
"Habitat in Africa." RCN: 5459.
Type not designated.

Original material: [icon] in Commelin, Hort. Med. Amstelod. Pl. Rar. 2: 87, t. 44. 1701.
Current name: ***Lessertia herbacea*** (L.) Druce (Fabaceae: Faboideae).
Note: Wijnands (*Bot. Commelins*: 164. 1983) regarded 914.8 (LINN) as a possible future lectotype (although it does not, in fact, appear to be original material for the name).

Comarum palustre Linnaeus, *Species Plantarum* 1: 502. 1753.
"Habitat in Europae uliginosis." RCN: 811.
Lectotype (Soják in Jarvis & al., *Regnum Veg.* 127: 36. 1993): Herb. Clifford: 195, *Comarum* 1 (BM-000628668).
Generitype of *Comarum* Linnaeus.
Current name: ***Potentilla palustris*** (L.) Scop. (Rosaceae).

Combretum occidentale Linnaeus, *Systema Naturae,* ed. 10, 2: 999. 1759, *nom. illeg.*
RCN: 2671.
Replaced synonym: *Gaura fruticosa* Loefl. (1758).
Type not designated.
Current name: ***Combretum fruticosum*** (Loefl.) Stuntz (Combretaceae).
Note: A superfluous name for *Gaura fruticosa* Loefl. (1758).

Cometes alterniflora Linnaeus, *Systema Naturae,* ed. 12, 2: 127. 1767.
RCN: 996.
Lectotype (Gilbert in Jarvis & al., *Regnum Veg.* 127: 36. 1993): [icon] *"Cometes surattensis"* in Burman, Fl. Indica: 39, t. 15, f. 5. 1768.
Current name: ***Cometes surattensis*** L. (Caryophyllaceae).
Note: In 1767, Linnaeus simultaneously published two different epithets for this taxon: *C. alterniflora* (in *Syst. Nat.* ed. 12, 2: 127) and *C. surattensis* (in *Mant. Pl.*: 39). The latter name has been treated as the generitype, and is the name in current use.

Cometes surattensis Linnaeus, *Mantissa Plantarum*: 39. 1767.
"Habitat in Suratte." RCN: 995.
Lectotype (Gilbert in Jarvis & al., *Regnum Veg.* 127: 36. 1993): [icon] *"Cometes surattensis"* in Burman, Fl. Indica: 39, t. 15, f. 5. 1768.
Generitype of *Cometes* Linnaeus.
Current name: ***Cometes surattensis*** L. (Caryophyllaceae).
Note: In 1767, Linnaeus simultaneously published two different epithets for this taxon: *C. alterniflora* (in *Syst. Nat.*, ed. 12, 2: 127) and *C. surattensis* (in *Mant. Pl.*: 39). The latter name has been treated as the generitype, and is the name in current use. Rechinger (*Fl. Iranica* 144: 23. 1980) indicated Garcin material (G) as type but Linnaeus would not have seen this collection and it is not part of the original material.

Commelina africana Linnaeus, *Species Plantarum* 1: 41. 1753.
"Habitat in Aethiopia." RCN: 347.
Type not designated.
Original material: Herb. A. van Royen No. 899.258–286 (L); Herb. Linn. No. 17.19 (S); Herb. Linn. No. 65.10 (LINN).
Current name: ***Commelina africana*** L. (Commelinaceae).
Note: Brenan (in *Mitt. Bot. Staatssamml. München* 5: 203. 1964) treated 65.3 (LINN) as the type but this collection lacks the relevant *Species Plantarum* number (i.e. "2") and was a post-1753 addition to the herbarium, and is not original material for the name.

Commelina axillaris Linnaeus, *Species Plantarum* 1: 42. 1753.
"Habitat in India." RCN: 2288.
Basionym of: *Tradescantia axillaris* (L.) L. (1771).
Lectotype (Faden in Dassanayake & Clayton, *Revised Handb. Fl. Ceylon* 14: 119. 2000): [icon] *"Ephemerum Phalangoides Maderaspatanum minimum, secundum caulem quasi ex utriculis*

floridium" in Plukenet, Phytographia: t. 174, f. 3. 1692; Almag. Bot.: 135. 1696. – Voucher: Herb. Sloane 96: 16 (BM-SL).
Current name: ***Cyanotis axillaris*** (L.) Sweet (Commelinaceae).

Commelina benghalensis Linnaeus, *Species Plantarum* 1: 41. 1753, *nom. cons.*
"Habitat in Benghala." RCN: 348.
Conserved type (Faden in *Taxon* 41: 341. 1992): Herb. Linn. No. 65.16 (LINN).
Current name: ***Commelina benghalensis*** L. (Commelinaceae).

Commelina communis Linnaeus, *Species Plantarum* 1: 40. 1753.
"Habitat in America." RCN: 346.
Lectotype (Faden & Reveal in Jarvis & al., *Regnum Veg.* 127: 36. 1993): Herb. Linn. No. 65.1 (LINN).
Generitype of *Commelina* Linnaeus (vide Hitchcock, *Prop. Brit. Bot.*: 118. 1929).
Current name: ***Commelina communis*** L. (Commelinaceae).

Commelina cristata Linnaeus, *Species Plantarum* 1: 42. 1753.
"Habitat in Zeylona." RCN: 2289.
Basionym of: *Tradescantia cristata* (L.) L. (1767).
Lectotype (Faden in Dassanayake & Clayton, *Revised Handb. Fl. Ceylon* 14: 123. 2000): Herb. Hermann 5: 152, No. 32 [icon] (BM).
Current name: ***Cyanotis cristata*** (L.) D. Don (Commelinaceae).
Note: Mathew (in Bosser & al., *Fl. Mascareignes* 186: 2. 1978) indicated 406.4 (LINN) as type but this collection lacks the relevant *Species Plantarum* number (i.e. "9") and was a post-1753 addition to the herbarium, and is not original material for the name.

Commelina cucullata Linnaeus, *Mantissa Plantarum Altera*: 176. 1771.
"Habitat in India orientali." RCN: 353.
Lectotype (Faden in *Taxon* 41: 341. 1992): Herb. Linn. No. 65.16 (LINN).
Current name: ***Commelina benghalensis*** L. (Commelinaceae).

Commelina erecta Linnaeus, *Species Plantarum* 1: 41. 1753.
"Habitat in Virginia." RCN: 349.
Lectotype (Clarke in De Candolle in *Monogr. Phanerog.* 3: 181. 1881): [icon] *"Commelina erecta, ampliore subcaeruleo flore"* in Dillenius, Hort. Eltham. 1: 91, t. 77, f. 88. 1732.
Current name: ***Commelina erecta*** L. (Commelinaceae).
Note: Some authors (e.g. Fernald in *Rhodora* 42: 436. 1940) have accepted Clarke (1881) as having typified the name (though this is open to doubt) using the cited Dillenian plate, though Hunt (in McVaugh, *Fl. Novo-Galiciana* 13: 144. 1993) has more recently thrown doubt on the taxonomic identity of this element. Morton (in *Bot. J. Linn. Soc.* 60: 183. 1967) treated 65.6 (LINN) as the type but the identity of this, too, has been questioned (see Rao & al. in *Bot. J. Linn. Soc.* 60: 360. 1968).

Commelina nudiflora Linnaeus, *Species Plantarum* 1: 41. 1753.
"Habitat in India." RCN: 356.
Lectotype (Merrill & Dandy in Merrill in *J. Arnold Arbor.* 18: 64. 1937): Osbeck 2, Herb. Linn. No. 65.12 (LINN).
Current name: ***Murdannia nudiflora*** (L.) Brenan (Commelinaceae).
Note: See Hansen & Fox Maule (in *Bot. J. Linn. Soc.* 67: 200. 1973) for comments on Osbeck material.

Commelina spirata Linnaeus, *Mantissa Plantarum Altera*: 176. 1771.
"Habitat in India orientali ad rivulos locis humentibus. König 56." RCN: 354.

Lectotype (Faden in Dassanayake & Clayton, *Revised Handb. Fl. Ceylon* 14: 157. 2000): Herb. Linn. No. 65.15 (LINN).
Current name: ***Murdannia spirata*** (L.) G. Brückn. (Commelinaceae).

Commelina tuberosa Linnaeus, *Species Plantarum* 1: 41. 1753.
"Habitat in Mexico." RCN: 351.
Lectotype (Hunt in McVaugh, *Fl. Novo-Galiciana* 13: 152. 1993): Herb. Linn. No. 65.8 (LINN).
Current name: ***Commelina tuberosa*** L. (Commelinaceae).

Commelina vaginata Linnaeus, *Mantissa Plantarum Altera*: 177. 1771.
"Habitat in India orientali. König." RCN: 355.
Lectotype (Faden in Dassanayake & Clayton, *Revised Handb. Fl. Ceylon* 14: 165. 2000): Herb. Linn. No. 65.10 (LINN).
Current name: ***Murdannia vaginata*** (L.) G. Brückn. (Commelinaceae).

Commelina virginica Linnaeus, *Species Plantarum*, ed. 2, 1: 61. 1762.
"Habitat in Virginia." RCN: 350.
Lectotype (Hunt in McVaugh, *Fl. Novo-Galiciana* 13: 145. 1993): Herb. Linn. No. 65.7 (LINN).
Current name: ***Commelina virginica*** L. (Commelinaceae).

Commelina zanonia Linnaeus, *Species Plantarum* 1: 41. 1753.
"Habitat in America Galliae aequinoctialis." RCN: 352.
Lectotype (Hunt in Davidse & al., *Fl. Mesoamericana* 6: 161. 1994): [icon] *"Zanonia"* in Plumier, Nov. Pl. Amer.: 38, t. 38. 1703.
Current name: ***Tradescantia zanonia*** (L.) Sw. (Commelinaceae).

Comocladia pinnatifolia Linnaeus, *Systema Naturae*, ed. 10, 2: 861. 1759.
RCN: 274.
Type not designated.
Original material: none traced.
Current name: ***Comocladia pinnatifolia*** L. (Anacardiaceae).
Note: Linnaeus spelled the generic epithet "Camocladia" but from his protologue, drawn from Patrick Browne (1758), it is clear that this was an error for *Comocladia* P. Browne.

Conferva aegagropila Linnaeus, *Species Plantarum* 2: 1167. 1753.
"Habitat in Sueciae lacubus Dannemora, Stockholmiae &c." RCN: 8395.
Lectotype (van den Hoek, *Revis. Eur. Sp.* Cladophora: 51. 1963): Herb. Linn. No. 1277.49 (LINN).
Current name: ***Cladophora aegagropila*** (L.) Trevis. (Cladophoraceae).

Conferva aeruginosa Linnaeus, *Species Plantarum* 2: 1165. 1753.
"Habitat in Angliae fucis." RCN: 8381.
Lectotype (Irvine in Spencer & al. in *Taxon*, in press): [icon] *"Conferva marina capillacea brevis, viridissima mollis"* in Dillenius, Hist. Musc.: 23, t. 4, f. 20. 1741. – Voucher: Herb. Dillenius (OXF).
Current name: ***Spongomorpha aeruginosa*** (L.) C. Hoek (Acrosiphoniaceae).
Note: Van den Hoek (*Revis. Eur. Sp.* Cladophora: 19, 225. 1963), followed by others, treated material in the Dillenius herbarium as the type but as this was not studied by Linnaeus, it cannot be original material.

Conferva amphibia Linnaeus, *Species Plantarum* 2: 1164. 1753.
"Habitat in Europae udis, fossis, umbrosis, ubi aquae vicissitudines servant." RCN: 8379.

Type not designated.

Original material: [icon] in Dillenius, Hist. Musc.: 22, t. 4, f. 17. 1741.

Current name: ***Vaucheria* sp.** (Vaucheriaceae).

Note: For a discussion of the difficulties associated with this name, see Christensen (in *Brit. Phycol. Bull.* 3: 466–467. 1968), who treated it as a *"species minus cognita".* The name may threaten *Vaucheria dillwynii* (F. Weber & Mohr) C. Agardh and may be a candidate for rejection.

Conferva bullosa Linnaeus, *Species Plantarum* 2: 1164. 1753.

"Habitat in Europae aquis stagnantibus." RCN: 8377.

Lectotype (Irvine in Spencer & al. in *Taxon*, in press): [icon] *"Conferva palustris bombycina"* in Dillenius, Hist. Musc.: 18, t. 3, f. 11. 1741. – Voucher: Herb. Dillenius (OXF).

Current name: ***Cladophora glomerata*** (L.) Kütz. var. ***crassior*** (C. Agardh) C. Hoek (Cladophoraceae).

Note: Van den Hoek (*Revis. Eur. Sp.* Cladophora: 179. 1963) designated material in the Dillenius herbarium as the type but as this was not studied by Linnaeus, it cannot be original material.

Conferva canalicularis Linnaeus, *Species Plantarum* 2: 1164. 1753.

"Habitat in Europae rivulis, tubulis, canalibus molendinariis." RCN: 8378.

Lectotype (Christensen in *Brit. Phycol. Bull.* 3: 466. 1968): [icon] *"Conferva rivulorum capillacea, densissime congestis ramulis"* in Dillenius, Hist. Musc.: 21, t. 4, f. 15. 1741. – Voucher: Herb. Dillenius (OXF).

Current name: ***Vaucheria canalicularis*** (L.) T.A. Chr. (Vaucheriaceae).

Note: Van den Hoek (*Revis. Eur. Sp.* Cladophora: 223. 1963) designated material in the Dillenius herbarium as the type but as this was not studied by Linnaeus, it cannot be original material. Christensen (in *Brit. Phycol. Bull.* 3: 465–466. 1968) treated Dillenius' description as the type but clearly included the cited plate as part of this. As a consequence, his statement is accepted as a formal typification of the name.

Conferva cancellata Linnaeus, *Species Plantarum* 2: 1165. 1753.

"Habitat in mari Europaeo." RCN: 8384.

Lectotype (Spencer-Jones in Spencer & al. in *Taxon*, in press): [icon] *"Conferva marina cancellata"* in Dillenius, Hist. Musc.: 24, t. 4, f. 22. 1741. – Voucher: Herb. Dillenius (OXF).

Current name: ***Vesicularia spinosa*** L. (Bryozoa).

Note: The application of this name has been uncertain. Papenfuss (in *J. S. African Bot.* 17: 178. 1952) suggested that the name may relate to a member of the Bryozoa, confirmed by the type choice proposed by Spencer-Jones.

Conferva capillaris Linnaeus, *Species Plantarum* 2: 1166. 1753.

"Habitat in Europae lacubus, stagnis, vadis, fossis." RCN: 8388.

Lectotype (Irvine in Spencer & al. in *Taxon*, in press): [icon] *"Conferva filamentis longis geniculatis simplicibus"* in Dillenius, Hist. Musc.: 25, t. 5, f. 25B. 1741. – Voucher: Herb. Dillenius (OXF).

Current name: ***Cladophora glomerata*** (L.) Kütz. (Cladophoraceae).

Note: See comments by Papenfuss (in *J. S. African Bot.* 17: 178. 1952), van den Hoek (*Revis. Eur. Sp.* Cladophora: 179. 1963), Blair (in *Rhodora* 85: 180. 1983) and Silva & al. (in *Univ. Calif. Publ. Bot.* 79: 936. 1996) on the varied application of this name.

Conferva catenata Linnaeus, *Species Plantarum* 2: 1166. 1753.

"Habitat in Mari Europam australem & Americam meridionalem alluente." RCN: 8390.

Lectotype (Irvine in Spencer & al. in *Taxon*, in press): [icon] *"Conferva ramosa, geniculis longioribus cateniformibus"* in Dillenius,

Hist. Musc.: 27, t. 5, f. 27. 1741. – Voucher: Herb. Dillenius (OXF).

Current name: ***Cladophora catenata*** (L.) Kütz. (Cladophoraceae).

Note: Van den Hoek (*Revis. Eur. Sp.* Cladophora: 19, 123. 1963) designated material in the Dillenius herbarium as the type but as this was not studied by Linnaeus, it cannot be original material for the name.

Conferva corallina Linnaeus, *Systema Vegetabilium,* ed. 13: 818. 1774, *orth. var.*

RCN: 8389.

Lectotype (Irvine in Spencer & al. in *Taxon*, in press): [icon] *"Conferva marina gelatinosa, Corallinae instar geniculata, crassior"* in Dillenius, Hist. Musc.: 33, t. 6, f. 36. 1741. – Voucher: Herb. Dillenius (OXF).

Current name: ***Griffithsia corallinoides*** (L.) Trevis. (Ceramiaceae).

Note: Although some authors (e.g. Silva in *Taxon* 29: 134, 1980) have treated this as a superfluous name for *C. corallinoides* L. (1753), it has also been treated as an orthographic variant (see Spencer & al. in *Taxon*, in press).

Conferva corallinoides Linnaeus, *Species Plantarum* 2: 1166. 1753.

"Habitat in mari Europaeo, colore albo & rubenti." RCN: 8389.

Lectotype (Irvine in Spencer & al. in *Taxon*, in press): [icon] *"Conferva marina gelatinosa, Corallinae instar geniculata, crassior"* in Dillenius, Hist. Musc.: 33, t. 6, f. 36. 1741. – Voucher: Herb. Dillenius (OXF).

Current name: ***Griffithsia corallinoides*** (L.) Trevis. (Ceramiaceae).

Note: Although Irvine (in Maggs & Hommersand, *Seaweeds Brit. Isles* 1(3A): 184. 2001) indicated unspecified material in Herb. Dillenius at OXF as the holotype, this material was not studied by Linnaeus and it is not original material for the name.

Conferva dichotoma Linnaeus, *Species Plantarum* 2: 1165. 1753.

"Habitat in Angliae fossi pratorum." RCN: 8382.

Lectotype (Christensen, *Seaweeds Brit. Isles* 4: 15. 1987): [icon] *"Conferva dichotoma, setis porcinis similis"* in Dillenius, Hist. Musc.: 17, t. 3, f. 9. 1741. – Voucher: Herb. Dillenius (OXF).

Current name: ***Vaucheria dichotoma*** (L.) Mart. (Vaucheriaceae).

Note: See Christensen (in *Brit. Phycol. Bull.* 3: 465. 1968), who discussed Dillenius' description, figures and voucher material in OXF (the latter reproduced as f. 5, 6), stating (p. 463) that the Dillenian material was the type. This, however, was not seen by Linnaeus and is not original material for the name. Christensen (in *Brit. Phycol. J.* 21: 275. 1986) subsequently treated Linnaeus' description as the type but this is contrary to Art. 8.1.

Conferva fluviatilis Linnaeus, *Species Plantarum* 2: 1165. 1753.

"Habitat in Europae fluviis confragosis." RCN: 8386.

Lectotype (Irvine in Spencer & al. in *Taxon*, in press): [icon] *"Conferva fluviatilis lubrica setosa, Equiseti facie"* in Dillenius, Hist. Musc.: 39, t. 7, f. 47. 1741. – Voucher: Herb. Dillenius (OXF).

Current name: ***Lemanea fluviatilis*** (L.) C. Agardh (Lemaneaceae).

Note: See discussion by Silva (in *Univ. Calif. Publ. Bot.* 25: 262. 1952).

Conferva fontinalis Linnaeus, *Species Plantarum* 2: 1164. 1753.

"Habitat in Europae fontibus." RCN: 8376.

Lectotype (Christensen in *Brit. Phycol. Bull.* 3: 465, f. 1–4. 1968): [icon] *"Conferva minima Byssi facie"* in Dillenius, Hist. Musc.: 14, t. 2, f. 3. 1741. – Voucher: Herb. Dillenius (OXF).

Current name: ***Vaucheria fontinalis*** (L.) T.A. Chr. (Vaucheriaceae).

Note: Christensen (in *Brit. Phycol. Bull.* 3: 465. 1968) treated Dillenius' description as the type but clearly included the cited plate as part of this. As a consequence, his statement is accepted as a formal typification for the name.

Conferva gelatinosa Linnaeus, *Species Plantarum* 2: 1166. 1753.
"Habitat in Europae fontibus praestantissimis limpidissimis." RCN: 8387.
Lectotype (Irvine in Spencer & al. in *Taxon*, in press): [icon] *"Conferva fontana nodosa, spermatis ranarum instar lubrica, major & fusca"* in Dillenius, Hist. Musc.: 36, t. 7, f. 42. 1741. – Voucher: Herb. Dillenius (OXF).
Current name: ***Batrachospermum gelatinosum*** (L.) DC. (Batrachospermaceae).
Note: See extensive discussion by Compère (in *Belgian J. Bot.*: 124: 21–26. 1991) who did not, however, make a definitive type choice. Entwisle & Foard (in *Austral. Syst. Bot.* 10: 352. 1997) designated Dillenian material (OXF) as lectotype but this was not seen by Linnaeus and is not original material for the name.

Conferva glomerata Linnaeus, *Species Plantarum* 2: 1167. 1753.
"Habitat in Europae fontibus, fossis, rivulis." RCN: 8393.
Lectotype (Irvine in Spencer & al. in *Taxon*, in press): [icon] *"Conferva fontalis ramosissima, glomeratim congesta"* in Dillenius, Hist. Musc.: 28, t. 5, f. 31. 1741. – Voucher: Herb. Dillenius (OXF).
Current name: ***Cladophora glomerata*** (L.) Kütz. var. ***glomerata*** (Cladophoraceae).
Note: See discussion by Waern (in *Acta Phytogeogr. Suecica* 30: 76. 1952), and by van den Hoek (*Revis. Eur. Sp.* Cladophora: 162. 1963), who treated material in the Dillenius herbarium as the type but, as this was not studied by Linnaeus, it cannot be original material for the name.

Conferva littoralis Linnaeus, *Species Plantarum* 2: 1165. 1753.
"Habitat in Europae marinis rupibus." RCN: 8380.
Lectotype (de Reviers in Spencer & al. in *Taxon*, in press): [icon] *"Conferva marina capillacea longa, ramosissima mollis"* in Dillenius, Hist. Musc.: 23, t. 4, f. 19. 1741. – Voucher: Herb. Dillenius (OXF). – Epitype (Loiseaux & de Reviers in Spencer & al. in *Taxon*, in press): France. Roscoff, Perharidy, mid intertidal, on *Fucus vesiculosus* L., 30 Sep 2002, *A. Peters* (CCAP strain no. 1330/2) (PC-0074126).
Current name: ***Pylaiella littoralis*** (L.) Kjellm. (Acinetosporaceae).
Note: See discussion by Setchell & Gardner (in *Univ. Calif. Publ. Bot.* 8: 403. 1925), Waern (in *Acta Phytogeogr. Suecica* 30: 110. 1952), Dixon & Russell (in *Bot. Notiser* 117: 283. 1964), and Drouet (in *Acad. Nat. Sci. Philadelphia Monogr.* 15: 311. 1968) who treated material in Herb. Dillenius as the type. However, this was not seen by Linnaeus and is not original material for the name.

Conferva polymorpha Linnaeus, *Species Plantarum* 2: 1167. 1753.
"Habitat in Mari Europaeo." RCN: 8391.
Type not designated.
Original material: [icon] in Barrelier, Pl. Galliam: 120, t. 1301. 1714; [icon] in Boccone, Mus. Fis.: 268, 315, t. 5, f. 11; t. 7, f. 1. 1697; [icon] in Dillenius, Hist. Musc.: 32, t. 6, f. 35. 1741; [icon] in Plukenet, Phytographia: t. 47, f. 10. 1691; Almag. Bot.: 119. 1696.
Current name: ***Polysiphonia lanosa*** (L.) Tandy (Rhodomelaceae).
Note: This name is of uncertain identity (see Tandy in *J. Bot.* 69: 225. 1931; Silva & al. in *Univ. Calif. Publ. Bot.* 79: 392. 1996) but potentially threatens *Polysiphonia lanosa* (L.) Tandy and *Ceramium virgatum* Roth, and may prove to be a candidate for rejection.

Conferva reticulata Linnaeus, *Species Plantarum* 2: 1165. 1753.
"Habitat in Europae fluviis ad eorum littora." RCN: 8385.
Lectotype (Irvine in Spencer & al. in *Taxon*, in press): [icon] *"Conferva reticulata"* in Dillenius, Hist. Musc.: 20, t. 4, f. 14. 1741 (see above, right). – Voucher: Herb. Dillenius (OXF).

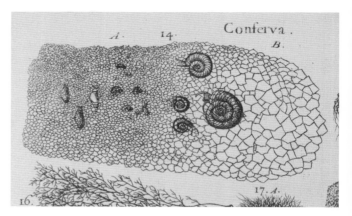

Current name: ***Hydrodictyon reticulatum*** (L.) Lagerh. (Hydrodictyaceae).

Conferva rivularis Linnaeus, *Species Plantarum* 2: 1164. 1753.
"Habitat in Europae rivulis fluviisque pacatioribus." RCN: 8375.
Lectotype (van den Hoek, *Revis. Eur. Sp.* Cladophora: 113. 1963): Herb. A. van Royen No. 910.185–1110 (L).
Current name: ***Cladophora rivularis*** (L.) C. Hoek (Cladophoraceae).

Conferva rupestris Linnaeus, *Species Plantarum* 2: 1167. 1753.
"Habitat in Europae marinis rupibus copiosissima." RCN: 8394a.
Lectotype (Irvine in Spencer & al. in *Taxon*, in press): [icon] *"Conferva marina trichodes ramosior"* in Dillenius, Hist. Musc.: 28, t. 5, f. 29. 1742. – Voucher: Herb. Dillenius (OXF).
Generitype of *Conferva* Linnaeus, *nom. rej.*
Current name: ***Cladophora rupestris*** (L.) Kütz. (Cladophoraceae).
Note: Conferva Linnaeus, *nom. rej.* in favour of *Cladophora* Kütz. Van den Hoek (*Revis. Eur. Sp.* Cladophora: 64. 1963) treated material in the Dillenius herbarium as the type but as this was not studied by Linnaeus, it cannot be original material for the name.

Conferva scoparia Linnaeus, *Species Plantarum* 2: 1165. 1753.
"Habitat in mari Europaeo." RCN: 8383.
Lectotype (Irvine in Spencer & al. in *Taxon*, in press): [icon] *"Conferva marina pennata"* in Dillenius, Hist. Musc.: 24, t. 4, f. 23. 1741. – Voucher: Herb. Dillenius (OXF).
Current name: ***Stypocaulon scoparia*** (L.) Kütz. (Stypocaulaceae).

Conferva vagabunda Linnaeus, *Species Plantarum* 2: 1167. 1753.
"Habitat in Mari Europaeo, libera vagatur in aquarum medio." RCN: 8392.
Lectotype (Irvine in Spencer & al. in *Taxon*, in press): [icon] *"Conferva marina trichodes, lanae instar expansa"* in Dillenius, Hist. Musc.: 30, t. 5, f. 32. 1741. – Voucher: Herb. Dillenius (OXF).
Current name: ***Cladophora vagabunda*** (L.) C. Hoek (Cladophoraceae).
Note: Van den Hoek (*Revis. Eur. Sp.* Cladophora: 144. 1963) treated material in the Dillenius herbarium as the type but as this was not studied by Linnaeus, it cannot be original material for the name.

Conium africanum Linnaeus, *Species Plantarum* 1: 243. 1753.
"Habitat in Africa." RCN: 1956.
Lectotype (Van Wyk & Tilney in Jarvis & al. in *Taxon* 55: 211. 2006): [icon] *"Caucalis; afra; folio minoris Rutae"* in Boerhaave, Index Alter Pl. Hort. Lugdb.-Bat. 1: 63. 1720.
Current name: ***Capnophyllum africanum*** (L.) Gaertn. (Apiaceae).

Conium maculatum Linnaeus, *Species Plantarum* 1: 243. 1753.
"Habitat in Europae cultis, agris, ruderatis." RCN: 1954.

Lectotype (Jafri in Jafri & El-Gadi, *Fl. Libya* 117: 60. 1985): Herb. Linn. No. 343.1 (LINN).

Generitype of *Conium* Linnaeus (vide Hitchcock, *Prop. Brit. Bot.*: 139. 1929).

Current name: ***Conium maculatum*** L. (Apiaceae).

Conium rigens Linnaeus, *Systema Naturae,* ed. 12, 2: 206; *Mantissa Plantarum*: 56. 1767.

"Habitat ad Cap. b. spei." RCN: 1955.

Lectotype (Burtt in *Notes Roy. Bot. Gard. Edinburgh* 45: 93. 1988): Herb. Linn. No. 343.2 (LINN).

Current name: ***Dasispermum suffruticosum*** (P.J. Bergius) B.L. Burtt (Apiaceae).

Conium royenii Linnaeus, *Species Plantarum* 1: 243. 1753.

"Habitat – – – –" RCN: 1957.

Type not designated.

Original material: none traced.

Note: Specific epithet spelled "Royeni" in the protologue.
    The application of this name appears uncertain. As there is no original material, and the name is not in use, it may be a candidate for rejection.

Connarus monocarpos Linnaeus, *Species Plantarum* 2: 675. 1753.

"Habitat in India." RCN: 4930.

Lectotype (Tirvengadum in Dassanayake & Fosberg, *Revised Handb. Fl. Ceylon* 1: 283. 1980): Herb. Hermann 3: 8, No. 248 (BM-000594650).

Generitype of *Connarus* Linnaeus.

Current name: ***Connarus monocarpos*** L. (Connaraceae).

Conocarpus erectus Linnaeus, *Species Plantarum* 1: 176. 1753.

"Habitat in Jamaicae, Bermudensium, Brasiliae maritimis." RCN: 1390.

Lectotype (Wijnands, *Bot. Commelins*: 66. 1983): [icon] *"Alni fructu, laurifolia arbor maritima"* in Sloane, Voy. Jamaica 2: 18, t. 161, f. 2. 1725. – Typotype: Herb. Sloane 5: 63 (BM-SL).

Generitype of *Conocarpus* Linnaeus (vide Steudel, *Nom.*, ed. 2, 1: 404. 1840).

Current name: ***Conocarpus erectus*** L. (Combretaceae).

Note: Specific epithet spelled "erecta" in the protologue.

Conocarpus procumbens Linnaeus, *Species Plantarum* 1: 177. 1753.

"Habitat in Cuba." RCN: 1390.

Type not designated.

Original material: none traced.

Current name: ***Conocarpus erectus*** L. (Combretaceae).

Note: Bornstein (in Howard, *Fl. Lesser Antilles* 5: 457. 1989) stated "Type: Cuba, Ammann Herb. 581 (LE)". If "581" is not taken solely from Linnaeus' synonymy and there is a corresponding specimen present in LE, the latter should be treated as a neotype (although Linnaeus would not have seen it, there is no original material for the name).

Conocarpus racemosus Linnaeus, *Systema Naturae,* ed. 10, 2: 930. 1759.

["Habitat in Jamaicae maritimis."] Sp. Pl., ed. 2, 1: 251 (1762). RCN: 1391.

Lectotype (Stace in Howard, *Fl. Lesser Antilles* 5: 459. 1989): Herb. Linn. No. 237.2 (LINN).

Current name: ***Laguncularia racemosa*** (L.) C.F. Gaertn. (Combretaceae).

Convallaria bifolia Linnaeus, *Species Plantarum* 1: 316. 1753.

"Habitat in Europae borealis pratis depressis asperis." RCN: 2485.

Type not designated.

Original material: Herb. Linn. No. 183.43 (LAPP); Herb. Clifford: 125, *Convallaria* 5 (BM); Herb. Burser XVII: 69 (UPS); Herb. Linn. No. 436.8 (LINN); Herb. Linn. No. 144.1 (S); [icon] in Mattioli, Pl. Epit.: 744. 1586.

Current name: ***Maianthemum bifolium*** (L.) F.W. Schmidt (Liliaceae/Convallariaceae).

Convallaria fruticosa Linnaeus, *Herbarium Amboinense*: 16. 1754.

["Habitat in India."] Sp. Pl., ed. 2, 1: 450 (1762). RCN: 2474.

Replaced synonym of: *Asparagus terminalis* L. (1762), *nom. illeg.*; *Dracaena ferrea* L. (1767), *nom. illeg.*

Lectotype (Merrill, *Interpret. Rumph. Herb. Amb.*: 33, 137. 1917): [icon] *"Terminalis alba"* in Rumphius, Herb. Amboin. 4: 79, t. 34, f. 1. 1743.

Current name: ***Cordyline fruticosa*** (L.) A. Chev. (Agavaceae/Dracaenaceae).

Note: See notes by Brummitt & Marais (in *Taxon* 30: 825. 1981).

Convallaria majalis Linnaeus, *Species Plantarum* 1: 314. 1753.

"Habitat in Europa septentrionali." RCN: 2478.

Lectotype (Mathew in Jarvis & al., *Regnum Veg.* 127: 37. 1993): Herb. Linn. No. 436.1 (LINN).

Generitype of *Convallaria* Linnaeus (vide Rafinesque, *Fl. Tell.* 4: 18. 1838).

Current name: ***Convallaria majalis*** L. (Liliaceae/Convallariaceae).

Convallaria multiflora Linnaeus, *Species Plantarum* 1: 315. 1753.

"Habitat in Europae septentrionalis praecipitiis, rupibus." RCN: 2481.

Type not designated.

Original material: Herb. Linn. No. 436.4 (LINN); Herb. Burser XVII: 57 (UPS); [icon] in Clusius, Rar. Pl. Hist. 1: 275. 1601.

Current name: ***Polygonatum multiflorum*** (L.) All. (Liliaceae/Convallariaceae).

Note: Ali (in Ali & Qaiser, *Fl. Pakistan* 213: 7. 2005) indicated 436.4 (LINN) as the type, but as this choice was published after 1 Jan 2001, the omission of the phrase "designated here" or an equivalent (Art. 7.11) means that the choice is not effective.

Convallaria polygonatum Linnaeus, *Species Plantarum* 1: 315. 1753.

"Habitat in Europae septentrionalis praecipitiis, rupibusque." RCN: 2480.

Lectotype (Jeffrey in *Kew Bull.* 34: 448. 1980): Herb. Linn. No. 436.3 (LINN).

Current name: ***Polygonatum odoratum*** (Mill.) Druce (Liliaceae/Convallariaceae).

Convallaria racemosa Linnaeus, *Species Plantarum* 1: 315. 1753.

"Habitat in Virginia, Canada." RCN: 2482.

Lectotype (LaFrankie in *J. Arnold Arbor.* 67: 421. 1986): Herb. Clifford: 125, *Convallaria* 4, sheet B (BM-000558522).

Current name: ***Maianthemum racemosum*** (L.) Link (Liliaceae/Convallariaceae).

Note: See detailed discussion by Fernald (in *Rhodora* 40: 406. 1938) who treated the two Clifford sheets as the type (though as they are evidently not part of a single gathering, Art. 9.15 does not apply). LaFrankie effectively restricted this to sheet B, figured by Fernald as pl. 512.

Convallaria stellata Linnaeus, *Species Plantarum* 1: 316. 1753.

"Habitat in Canada." RCN: 2483.

Lectotype (LaFrankie in *J. Arnold Arbor.* 67: 430. 1986): [icon] *"Polygonatum spicatum fertile"* in Cornut, Canad. Pl. Hist.: 33, 34. 1635.

Current name: ***Maianthemum stellatum*** (L.) Link
(Liliaceae/Convallariaceae).

Convallaria trifolia Linnaeus, *Species Plantarum* 1: 316. 1753.
"Habitat in Sibiriae sylvis." RCN: 2484.
Lectotype (LaFrankie in *J. Arnold Arbor.* 67: 434. 1986): Herb. Linn.
No. 436.6 (LINN).
Current name: ***Maianthemum trifolium*** (L.) Sloboda
(Liliaceae/Convallariaceae).

Convallaria verticillata Linnaeus, *Species Plantarum* 1: 315. 1753.
"Habitat in Europae septentrionalis saltibus, praecipitiis." RCN: 2479.
Type not designated.
Original material: Herb. Burser XVII: 64 (UPS); Herb. Clifford: 125,
Convallaria 3 (BM); Herb. Linn. No. 436.2 (LINN); Herb. Burser
XVII: 65 (UPS); [icon] in Dodoëns, Stirp. Hist. Pempt., ed. 2: 345.
1616.
Current name: ***Polygonatum verticillatum*** (L.) All.
(Liliaceae/Convallariaceae).
Note: Jeffrey (in *Kew Bull.* 34: 457. 1980) indicated 436.4 (LINN) as
lectotype but this collection is associated with *C. multiflora* L. and is
not original material for *C. verticillata*. Ali (in Ali & Qaiser, *Fl.
Pakistan* 213: 8. 2005) indicated 436.2 (LINN) as the type but as
this choice was published after 1 Jan 2001, the omission of the
phrase "designated here" or an equivalent (Art. 7.11) means that the
choice is not effective.

Convolvulus aculeatus Linnaeus, *Species Plantarum* 1: 155. 1753.
"Habitat in America calidiore." RCN: 1280.
Lectotype (Gunn in *Brittonia* 24: 153. 1972): [icon] *"Convolvulus
Americanus, subrotundis foliis, Viticulis spinosis"* in Plukenet,
Phytographia: t. 276, f. 3. 1694; Almag. Bot.: 115. 1696.
Current name: ***Ipomoea alba*** L. (Convolvulaceae).
Note: Verdcourt (in Hubbard & Milne-Redhead, *Fl. Trop. E. Africa,
Convolvulaceae*: 130. 1963) designated material in Plukenet's
herbarium (now part of Herb. Sloane), never seen by Linnaeus, as
the lectotype. However, it is not original material for the name.

Convolvulus aegyptius (Linnaeus) Linnaeus, *Systema Naturae*, ed. 10,
2: 923. 1759.
["Habitat in America calidiore."] Sp. Pl. 1: 162 (1753). RCN: 1251.
Basionym: *Ipomoea aegyptia* L. (1753).
Lectotype (Austin in Harling & Sparre, *Fl. Ecuador* 16: 84. 1982):
Herb. Linn. No. 218.35 (LINN).
Current name: ***Merremia aegyptia*** (L.) Urb. (Convolvulaceae).

Convolvulus alsinoides Linnaeus, *Species Plantarum* 1: 157.
1753.
"Habitat in Malabaria, Zeylona, Bisnagaria, Bahama." RCN: 2177.
Basionym of: *Evolvulus alsinoides* (L.) L. (1762).
Lectotype (Verdcourt in Hubbard & Milne-Redhead, *Fl. Trop. E.
Africa, Convolvulaceae*: 18. 1963): Herb. Hermann 3: 55, No. 76
(BM-000628009).
Current name: ***Evolvulus alsinoides*** (L.) L. (Convolvulaceae).
Note: Ooststroom (in *Meded. Bot. Mus. Herb. Rijks Univ. Utrecht* 14:
28. 1934) indicated material in LINN (presumably 393.3) as
"type". However, this was a post-1753 addition to the herbarium
and is ineligible as the type. Stearn (in *Taxon* 21: 649. 1972) gives a
detailed appraisal of the typification.

Convolvulus althaeoides Linnaeus, *Species Plantarum* 1: 156. 1753.
"Habitat in Europa meridionali." RCN: 1242.
Lectotype (Sa'ad in *Meded. Bot. Mus. Herb. Rijks Univ. Utrecht* 281:
210. 1967): Herb. Linn. No. 218.26 (LINN).
Current name: ***Convolvulus althaeoides*** L. (Convolvulaceae).

Convolvulus anceps Linnaeus, *Systema Naturae*, ed. 12, 2: 156;
Mantissa Plantarum: 43. 1767.
"Habitat in Zeylona, Java." RCN: 1236.
Neotype (Staples in Staples & Jarvis in *Taxon* 55: 1020. 2006): Java
(West), Tjikao, near waterfall, Jul, *L. Blume 1219* (L 901.163–376;
iso- L 901.184–318).
Current name: ***Operculina turpethum*** (L.) Silva Manso
(Convolvulaceae).

Convolvulus arvensis Linnaeus, *Species Plantarum* 1: 153. 1753.
"Habitat in Europae agris." RCN: 1216.
Lectotype (Meeuse in *Bothalia* 6: 695. 1958): Herb. Linn. No. 218.1
(LINN).
Generitype of *Convolvulus* Linnaeus (vide Hitchcock, *Prop. Brit. Bot.*:
130. 1929).
Current name: ***Convolvulus arvensis*** L. (Convolvulaceae).
Note: Convolvulus arvensis, with the type designated by Meeuse, was
proposed as conserved type of the genus by Jarvis (in *Taxon* 41: 559.
1992). However, the proposal was eventually ruled unnecessary by
the General Committee (see Barrie, *l.c.* 55: 795–796. 2006 for a
review of the history of this and related proposals).

Convolvulus batatas Linnaeus, *Species Plantarum* 1: 154. 1753.
"Habitat in India utraque." RCN: 1229.
Lectotype (Biju in *Taxon* 51: 755. 2003 [2002]): Herb. Linn. No. 77.5
(S).
Current name: ***Ipomoea batatas*** (L.) Lam. (Convolvulaceae).
Note: Verdcourt (in Hubbard & Milne-Redhead, *Fl. Trop. E. Africa,
Convolvulaceae*: 114. 1963) and later authors treated the post-1753
218.12 (LINN) as lectotype, but this choice was rejected by Biju in
favour of original material in S.

Convolvulus biflorus Linnaeus, *Species Plantarum*, ed. 2, 2: 1668.
1763.
"Habitat in China." RCN: 1230.
Neotype (Staples in Staples & Jarvis in *Taxon* 55: 1020. 2006): China.
Hong Kong, haies des jardins à Kennedy-town, 20 Sep 1893, *E.
Bodinier 386* (E; iso- P).
Current name: ***Ipomoea biflora*** (L.) Pers. (Convolvulaceae).
Note: Merrill (in *J. Arnold Arbor.* 19: 361. 1938) points out that the
exact status of this name (and hence *Ipomoea biflora* (L.) Pers.) is
somewhat doubtful. Although some authors have informally
rejected the name, Staples argues for its retention as *I. biflora*.

Convolvulus brasilianus Linnaeus, *Flora Jamaicensis*: 14. 1759, *orth.
var.*
"Habitat [in Jamaica.]" RCN: 7515.
Lectotype (St John, *9th Pacific Sci. Congr. Abstr.*: 66. 1957): [icon]
"Convolvulus marinus catharticus folio rotundo, flore purpureo" in
Plumier, Descr. Pl. Amér.: 89, t. 104. 1693.
Current name: ***Ipomoea pes-caprae*** (L.) R. Br. (Convolvulaceae).
Note: Evidently an orthographic variant of *C. brasiliensis* L. (1753).

Convolvulus brasiliensis Linnaeus, *Species Plantarum* 1: 159. 1753.
"Habitat in Brasiliae, Domingo maritimis." RCN: 1268.
Lectotype (St John, *9th Pacific Sci. Congr. Abstr.*: 66. 1957): [icon]
"Convolvulus marinus catharticus folio rotundo, flore purpureo" in
Plumier, Descr. Pl. Amér.: 89, t. 104. 1693.
Current name: ***Ipomoea pes-caprae*** (L.) R. Br. (Convolvulaceae).

Convolvulus cairicus Linnaeus, *Systema Naturae*, ed. 10, 2: 922. 1759.
["Habitat in Aegypto."] Sp. Pl., ed, 2, 1: 223 (1762). RCN: 1251.
Lectotype (Bosser & Heine in Bosser & al., *Fl. Mascareignes* 127: 32.
2000): [icon] *"Convolvulus Aegyptius"* in Vesling in Alpino, De
Plantis Aegypti: 73, 74. 1640.
Current name: ***Ipomoea cairica*** (L.) Sweet (Convolvulaceae).

Convolvulus canariensis Linnaeus, *Species Plantarum* 1: 155. 1753.
"Habitat in Canariensibus insulis." RCN: 1234.
Lectotype (Sa'ad in *Meded. Bot. Mus. Herb. Rijks Univ. Utrecht* 281:
248. 1967): Herb. Linn. No. 218.17 (LINN).
Current name: ***Convolvulus canariensis*** L. (Convolvulaceae).

Convolvulus cantabrica Linnaeus, *Species Plantarum* 1: 158. 1753.
"Habitat in Italia, Sicilia, Narbona, Verona." RCN: 1257.
Lectotype (Sa'ad in *Meded. Bot. Mus. Herb. Rijks Univ. Utrecht* 281:
124. 1967): Herb. Linn. No. 218.48 (LINN).
Current name: ***Convolvulus cantabrica*** L. (Convolvulaceae).

Convolvulus cantabrica Linnaeus var. **terrestris** (Linnaeus) Linnaeus,
Mantissa Plantarum Altera: 336. 1771.
["Habitat in Europa australi & Africa."] Sp. Pl., ed. 2, 1: 224 (1762).
RCN: 1257.
Basionym: *Convolvulus terrestris* L. (1762).
Lectotype (Sa'ad in *Meded. Bot. Mus. Herb. Rijks Univ. Utrecht* 281:
124. 1967): Herb. Linn. No. 218.49 (LINN).
Current name: ***Convolvulus cantabrica*** L. (Convolvulaceae).

Convolvulus carolinus Linnaeus, *Species Plantarum* 1: 154. 1753.
"Habitat in Carolina." RCN: 1223.
Lectotype (Staples in Staples & Jarvis in *Taxon* 55: 1020. 2006): [icon]
"Convolvulus folio hederaceo, arvensis flore dilute purpureo" in
Dillenius, Hort. Eltham.: t. 84, f. 98. 1732. – Typotype: Herb.
Sherard No. 317 (OXF).
Current name: ***Ipomoea cordatotriloba*** Dennst. (Convolvulaceae).

Convolvulus cneorum Linnaeus, *Species Plantarum* 1: 157. 1753.
"Habitat in Hispaniae, Italiae, Siciliae, Cretae maritimis
campestribus." RCN: 1256.
Lectotype (Sa'ad in *Meded. Bot. Mus. Herb. Rijks Univ. Utrecht* 281:
126. 1967): [icon] *"Convolvulus Creticus rectus s. Dorycnium
quorundam, Ponae"* in Morison, Pl. Hist. Univ. 2: 11, s. 1, t. 3, f. 1.
1680.
Current name: ***Convolvulus cneorum*** L. (Convolvulaceae).
Note: López González (in *Anales Jard. Bot. Madrid* 53: 130. 1995)
reproduces the cited plate from Barrelier (identifiable as *C.
lanuginosus* Desr.).

Convolvulus copticus Linnaeus, *Mantissa Plantarum Altera*: 559. 1771.
"Habitat in Oriente." RCN: 1244.
Lectotype (Verdcourt in Hubbard & Milne-Redhead, *Fl. Trop. E.
Africa, Convolvulaceae*: 128. 1963): Herb. Linn. No. 218.32
(LINN).
Current name: ***Ipomoea coptica*** (L.) Roem. & Schult.
(Convolvulaceae).
Note: Although Meeuse (in *Bothalia* 6: 760. 1958) indicated that one
of the specimens at LINN "is to be taken as the lectotype", he did
not distinguish between sheets 218.32 and 218.33. As they are
evidently not part of a single gathering, Art. 9.15 does not apply.

Convolvulus corymbosus Linnaeus, *Systema Naturae*, ed. 10, 2: 923.
1759.
["Habitat in America."] Sp. Pl., ed. 2, 1: 225 (1762). RCN: 1259.
Lectotype (Stearn in *Cuad. Bot. Canaria* 21: 8. 1974): [icon]
"Convolvulus caule repente, foliis caudatis" in Plumier in Burman, Pl.
Amer.: 78, t. 89, f. 2. 1756.
Current name: ***Turbina corymbosa*** (L.) Raf. (Convolvulaceae).
Note: See extensive review by Stearn (in *Curtis's Bot. Mag.* 181: 59–65,
t. 718. 1976).

Convolvulus dorycnium Linnaeus, *Systema Naturae*, ed. 10, 2: 923.
1759.

["Habitat in Oriente."] Sp. Pl., ed. 2, 1: 224 (1762). RCN: 1258.
Lectotype (Sa'ad in *Meded. Bot. Mus. Herb. Rijks Univ. Utrecht* 281:
90. 1967): *Hasselquist*, Herb. Linn. No. 218.50 (LINN).
Current name: ***Convolvulus dorycnium*** L. (Convolvulaceae).

Convolvulus farinosus Linnaeus, *Mantissa Plantarum Altera*: 203.
1771.
"Habitat – – – – D. Turra." RCN: 1220.
Lectotype (Meeuse in *Bothalia* 6: 684. 1958): Herb. Linn. No. 218.6
(LINN).
Current name: ***Convolvulus farinosus*** L. (Convolvulaceae).

Convolvulus gangeticus Linnaeus, *Centuria II Plantarum*: 9. 1756.
"Habitat in India." RCN: 2177.
Basionym of: *Evolvulus gangeticus* (L.) L. (1762).
Type not designated.
Original material: Herb. Linn. No. 218.46 (LINN); Herb. Linn. No.
130.7 (S).
Current name: ***Cocculus hirsutus*** (L.) Diels (Menispermaceae).

Convolvulus hederaceus Linnaeus, *Species Plantarum* 1: 154. 1753.
"Habitat in Asia, Africa, America." RCN: 1224.
Lectotype (Staples in Staples & Jarvis in *Taxon* 55: 1020. 2006): Herb.
Burser XVII: 6 (UPS).
Current name: ***Ipomoea nil*** (L.) Roth (Convolvulaceae).

Convolvulus hirtus Linnaeus, *Species Plantarum* 1: 159. 1753.
"Habitat in India. Osbeck." RCN: 1265.
Lectotype (Merrill in *Philipp. J. Sci., C*, 7: 245. 1912): *Osbeck 11*,
Herb. Linn. No. 218.56 (LINN).
Current name: ***Merremia hirta*** (L.) Merr. (Convolvulaceae).

Convolvulus jalapa Linnaeus, *Systema Naturae*, ed. 12, 2: 156;
Mantissa Plantarum: 43. 1767.
"Habitat in Mexico, Vera Cruce." RCN: 1239.
Neotype (McDonald in *Taxon* 38: 137. 1989): Mexico. Veracruz,
about 30km SE of Jalapa, occasional in valley between Apazapan
and Jalcomulco, 20 Oct 1987, *McDonald 2430* (BM; iso- K,
MEXU, TEX, XAL).
Current name: ***Ipomoea jalapa*** (L.) Pursh (Convolvulaceae).

Convolvulus jamaicensis Linnaeus, *Flora Jamaicensis*: 14. 1759, *nom.
nud.*
"Habitat [in Jamaica.]" RCN: 1241.
Type not relevant.

Convolvulus lineatus Linnaeus, *Systema Naturae*, ed. 10, 2: 923.
1759.
["Habitat in Hispaniae, Siciliae, Mediterranei maritimis."] Sp. Pl., ed.
2, 1: 224 (1762). RCN: 1255.
Lectotype (Sa'ad in *Meded. Bot. Mus. Herb. Rijks Univ. Utrecht* 281:
128. 1967): *Löfling 163*, Herb. Linn. No. 218.43 (LINN).
Current name: ***Convolvulus lineatus*** L. (Convolvulaceae).

Convolvulus linifolius Linnaeus, *Centuria II Plantarum*: 10. 1756.
"Habitat in Indiis." RCN: 2178.
Basionym of: *Evolvulus linifolius* (L.) L. (1762).
Lectotype (van Ooststroom in *Meded. Bot. Mus. Herb. Rijks Univ.
Utrecht* 14: 36. 1935 [1934]): *Miller*, Herb. Linn. No. 393.5
(LINN).
Current name: ***Evolvulus alsinoides*** (L.) L. (Convolvulaceae).

Convolvulus littoralis Linnaeus, *Systema Naturae*, ed. 10, 2: 924.
1759.
["Habitat in America."] Sp. Pl., ed. 2, 1: 227 (1762). RCN: 1269.

Lectotype (Austin in Woodson & Schery in *Ann. Missouri Bot. Gard.* 62: 199. 1975): [icon] *"Convolvulus foliis obtusis, palmato-lobatis"* in Plumier in Burman, Pl. Amer.: 79, t. 90, f. 2. 1756.

Current name: ***Ipomoea imperati*** (Vahl) Griseb. (Convolvulaceae).

Note: La Valva & Sabato (in *Taxon* 32: 112, f. 3. 1983) also treat the Plumier plate as the type, and reproduce it. Its identity was discussed by these authors, and by Austin & Bianchini (*l.c.* 47: 837. 1998), who argue that it is recognisable as *I. imperati.*

Convolvulus macrocarpus Linnaeus, *Systema Naturae,* ed. 10, 2: 923. 1759.

["Habitat in America."] Sp. Pl., ed. 2, 1: 222 (1762). RCN: 1247.

Lectotype (Staples in Staples & Jarvis in *Taxon* 55: 1021. 2006): [icon] *"Convolvulus foliis palmato-pedatis, pedunculis unifloris"* in Plumier in Burman, Pl. Amer: t. 91, f. 1. 1756.

Current name: ***Operculina macrocarpa*** (L.) Urb. (Convolvulaceae).

Convolvulus macrorhizos Linnaeus, *Systema Naturae,* ed. 10, 2: 923. 1759.

["Habitat in America."] Sp. Pl., ed. 2, 1: 223 (1762). RCN: 1249.

Lectotype (Staples in Staples & Jarvis in *Taxon* 55: 1021. 2006): [icon] *"Convolvulus foliis digitatis, setenis glabris, pedunculis trifloris"* in Plumier in Burman, Pl. Amer: t. 90, f. 1. 1756.

Current name: ***Ipomoea furceyensis*** Urb. (Convolvulaceae).

Convolvulus malabaricus Linnaeus, *Species Plantarum* 1: 155. 1753.

"Habitat in Malabariae arenosis." RCN: 1233.

Lectotype (Suresh in Nicolson & al., *Interpret. Van Rheede's Hort. Malab.*: 88. 1988): [icon] *"Kattu-kelengu"* in Rheede, Hort. Malab. 11: 105, t. 51. 1692.

Current name: ***Hewittia malabarica*** (L.) Suresh (Convolvulaceae).

Convolvulus medium Linnaeus, *Species Plantarum* 1: 156. 1753.

"Habitat in India." RCN: 1221.

Lectotype (Verdcourt in *Kew Bull.* 15: 5. 1961): Herb. Linn. No. 218.7 (LINN).

Current name: ***Merremia medium*** (L.) Hallier f. (Convolvulaceae).

Convolvulus muricatus Linnaeus, *Systema Naturae,* ed. 12, 2: 156; *Mantissa Plantarum*: 44. 1767.

"Habitat in Suratte. Braad." RCN: 1235.

Lectotype (Verdcourt in Hubbard & Milne-Redhead, *Fl. Trop. E. Africa, Convolvulaceae*: 130. 1963): Herb. Linn. No. 218.18 (LINN).

Current name: ***Ipomoea muricata*** (L.) Jacq. (Convolvulaceae).

Convolvulus nil Linnaeus, *Species Plantarum,* ed. 2, 1: 219. 1762.

"Habitat in America." RCN: 1225.

Lectotype (Verdcourt in *Taxon* 6: 232–233. 1957): [icon] *"Convolvulus caeruleus, hederaceo folio, magis anguloso"* in Dillenius, Hort. Eltham. 1: 96, t. 80, f. 91. 1732.

Current name: ***Ipomoea nil*** (L.) Roth (Convolvulaceae).

Convolvulus nummularius Linnaeus, *Species Plantarum* 1: 157. 1753.

"Habitat in Jamaicae & Barbados pratis." RCN: 2175.

Basionym of: *Evolvulus nummularius* (L.) L. (1762).

Lectotype (Verdcourt in Jarvis & al., *Regnum Veg.* 127: 16. 1993): [icon] *"Convolvulus minor repens, nummulariae folio, flore coeruleo"* in Sloane, Voy. Jamaica 1: 157, t. 99, f. 2. 1707. – Typotype: Herb. Sloane 3: 19 (BM-SL).

Current name: ***Evolvulus nummularius*** (L.) L. (Convolvulaceae).

Note: Ooststroom (in *Meded. Bot. Mus. Herb. Rijks Univ. Utrecht* 14: 115, 120. 1934) indicated what is evidently 393.1 (LINN) as type. However, this is not original material for the name, and Verdcourt

(in Hubbard & Milne-Redhead, *Fl. Trop. E. Africa Convolvulaceae*: 16. 1963) and Stearn (in *Taxon* 21: 647. 1972) instead treated material in Sloane's herbarium as the type. Despite the close relationship between Sloane's specimens and his published illustrations, the former were not studied by Linnaeus. Consequently, Verdcourt's (1993) indication of Sloane's illustration as the type is accepted as the earliest typification.

Convolvulus obscurus Linnaeus, *Species Plantarum,* ed. 2, 1: 220. 1762.

"Habitat in China, Batavia, Zeylona, Surinamo." RCN: 1227.

Lectotype (Meeuse in *Bothalia* 6: 746. 1958): [icon] *"Convolvulus flore minore lacteo, fundo atro-rubente"* in Dillenius, Hort. Eltham. 1: 98, t. 83, f. 95. 1732.

Current name: ***Ipomoea obscura*** (L.) Ker-Gawl. (Convolvulaceae).

Convolvulus panduratus Linnaeus, *Species Plantarum* 1: 153. 1753.

"Habitat in Virginiae arenosis." RCN: 1222.

Lectotype (Staples & Austin in Staples & Jarvis in *Taxon* 55: 1021. 2006): *Clayton 641* (BM).

Current name: ***Ipomoea pandurata*** (L.) G. Mey. (Convolvulaceae).

Convolvulus paniculatus Linnaeus, *Species Plantarum* 1: 156. 1753.

"Habitat in Malabariae arenosis." RCN: 1248.

Lectotype (Verdcourt in Hubbard & Milne-Redhead, *Fl. Trop. E. Africa, Convolvulaceae*: 135. 1963): [icon] *"Pal-modecca"* in Rheede, Hort. Malab. 11: 101, t. 49. 1692.

Current name: ***Ipomoea mauritiana*** Jacq. (Convolvulaceae).

Convolvulus peltatus Linnaeus, *Species Plantarum* 2: 1194. 1753.

"Habitat in Amboina." RCN: 1238.

Lectotype (Merrill, *Interpret. Rumph. Herb. Amb.*: 31, 441. 1917): [icon] *"Convolvulus laevis Indicus major"* in Rumphius, Herb. Amboin. 5: 428, t. 157. 1747.

Current name: ***Merremia peltata*** (L.) Merr. (Convolvulaceae).

Convolvulus pentapetaloides Linnaeus, *Systema Naturae,* ed. 12, 3: 229. 1768.

"Habitat in Majorca. Gerard." RCN: 1254.

Lectotype (Sa'ad in *Meded. Bot. Mus. Herb. Rijks Univ. Utrecht* 281: 207. 1967): *Latourette,* Herb. Linn. No. 218.41 (LINN).

Current name: ***Convolvulus pentapetaloides*** L. (Convolvulaceae).

Convolvulus pentaphyllus Linnaeus, *Species Plantarum,* ed. 2, 1: 223. 1762, *nom. illeg.*

"Habitat in America." RCN: 1251.

Replaced synonym: *Ipomoea aegyptia* L. (1753).

Lectotype (Austin in Harling & Sparre, *Fl. Ecuador* 16: 84. 1982): Herb. Linn. No. 218.35 (LINN), opposite above left.

Current name: ***Merremia aegyptia*** (L.) Urb. (Convolvulaceae).

Note: An illegitimate replacement name for *Ipomoea aegyptia* L. (1753).

Convolvulus pentaphyllus Linnaeus var. **serpens** (Linnaeus) Linnaeus, *Species Plantarum,* ed. 2, 1: 223. 1762.

"Habitat in America." RCN: 1251.

Basionym: *Convolvulus serpens* L. (1759).

Lectotype (Staples in Staples & Jarvis in *Taxon* 55: 1022. 2006): [icon] *"Convolvulus foliis digitatis quinis glabris dentatis, caule piloso"* in Plumier in Burman, Pl. Amer.: t. 91, f. 2. 1756.

Current name: ***Merremia quinquefolia*** (L.) Hallier f. (Convolvulaceae).

Convolvulus persicus Linnaeus, *Species Plantarum* 1: 158. 1753.

"Habitat in Persia, ad maris Caspici littus." RCN: 1261.

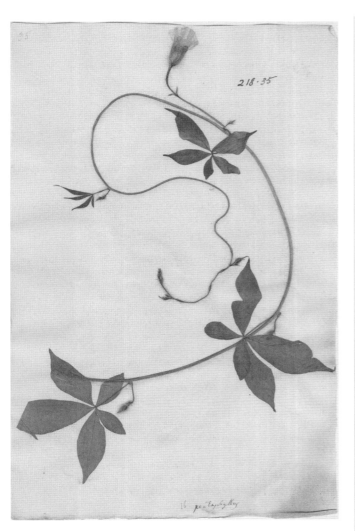

The lectotype of *Convolvulus pentaphyllus* L.

Neotype (Staples in Staples & Jarvis in *Taxon* 55: 1021. 2006): Turkey. "Constantinopel. In arenosis maritimis prope "Kila", Julio 1899", Herbarium Normale ed. I. Dörfler, No. 3865, *G.V. Aznavour s.n.* (BM; iso- B, E, P).
Current name: ***Convolvulus persicus*** L. (Convolvulaceae).

Convolvulus pes-caprae Linnaeus, *Species Plantarum* 1: 159. 1753.
"Habitat in India." RCN: 1267.
Lectotype (St John, *9th Pacific Sci. Congr. Abstr.*: 65. 1957): Herb. Linn. No. 218.59 (LINN).
Current name: ***Ipomoea pes-caprae*** (L.) R. Br. (Convolvulaceae).

Convolvulus purpureus Linnaeus, *Species Plantarum*, ed. 2, 1: 219. 1762.
"Habitat in America." RCN: 1226.
Lectotype (Austin in Woodson & Schery in *Ann. Missouri Bot. Gard.* 62: 193. 1975): [icon] *"Convolvulus folio cordato glabro, flore violaceo"* in Dillenius, Hort. Eltham. 1: 100, t. 84, f. 97. 1732.
Current name: ***Ipomoea purpurea*** (L.) Roth (Convolvulaceae).

Convolvulus quinquefolius (Linnaeus) Linnaeus, *Systema Naturae*, ed. 10, 2: 923. 1759.
["Habitat in America."] Sp. Pl. 1: 162 (1753). RCN: 1250.
Basionym: *Ipomoea quinquefolia* L. (1753).
Lectotype (Austin in Woodson & Schery in *Ann. Missouri Bot. Gard.* 62: 182. 1975): [icon] *"Convolvulus quinquefolius glaber Americanus"* in Plukenet, Phytographia: t. 167, f. 6. 1692; Almag. Bot.: 116. 1696.
Current name: ***Merremia quinquefolia*** (L.) Hallier f. (Convolvulaceae).

Convolvulus repens Linnaeus, *Species Plantarum* 1: 158. 1753.
"Habitat in Americae maritimis." RCN: 1263.
Lectotype (Tryon in *Rhodora* 41: 421. 1939): *Clayton 665* (BM-000051169).
Current name: ***Calystegia sepium*** (L.) R. Br. var. ***repens*** (L.) A. Gray (Convolvulaceae).
Note: Although Brummitt (in *Kew Bull.* 35: 329. 1980) indicated a Plumier plate as type, his choice is pre-dated by that of Tryon.

Convolvulus reptans Linnaeus, *Species Plantarum* 1: 158. 1753.
"Habitat in India." RCN: 1264.
Lectotype (Merrill in *Philipp. J. Sci., C,* 7: 244. 1912): [icon] *"Ballel"* in Rheede, Hort. Malab. 11: 107, t. 52. 1692.
Current name: ***Merremia hirta*** (L.) Merr. (Convolvulaceae).

Convolvulus scammonia Linnaeus, *Species Plantarum* 1: 153. 1753.
"Habitat in Syria, Mysia, Cappadocia." RCN: 1218.
Lectotype (Staples & Jarvis in *Taxon* 55: 1021. 2006): [icon] *"Convolvulus syriacus s. Scammoniaca syriaca"* in Morison, Pl. Hist. Univ. 2: s. 1, t. 3, f. 5. 1680.
Current name: ***Convolvulus scammonia*** L. (Convolvulaceae).

Convolvulus sepium Linnaeus, *Species Plantarum* 1: 153. 1753.
"Habitat in Europae sepibus." RCN: 1217.
Lectotype (Brummitt in Davis, *Fl. Turkey* 6: 220. 1978): Herb. A. van Royen No. 901.138–267 (L).
Current name: ***Calystegia sepium*** (L.) R. Br. (Convolvulaceae).
Note: Meeuse (in *Bothalia* 6: 697. 1958) treated 208.3 (LINN) as the lectotype but it is a Brander collection, not received by Linnaeus until after 1753, and is therefore not original material for the name.

Convolvulus sericeus Linnaeus, *Systema Naturae*, ed. 12, 2: 156; *Mantissa Plantarum*: 43. 1767.
"Habitat in India." RCN: 1240.
Lectotype (Staples in Staples & Jarvis in *Taxon* 55: 1022. 2006): [icon] *"Convolvulus mollis"* in Burman, Fl. Indica: t. 17. 1768. – Typotype: Java, *Kleinhof [Kleynhoff] s.n.*, Herb. Burman (G).
Current name: ***Argyreia mollis*** (Burm. f.) Choisy (Convolvulaceae).

Convolvulus serpens Linnaeus, *Systema Naturae*, ed. 10, 2: 923. 1759.
["Habitat in America."] Sp. Pl., ed. 2, 1: 223 (1762). RCN: 1251.
Basionym of: *Convolvulus pentaphyllus* L. var. *serpens* (L.) L. (1762).
Lectotype (Staples in Staples & Jarvis in *Taxon* 55: 1022. 2006): [icon] *"Convolvulus foliis digitatis quinis glabris dentatis, caule piloso"* in Plumier in Burman, Pl. Amer.: t. 91, f. 2. 1756.
Current name: ***Merremia quinquefolia*** (L.) Hallier f. (Convolvulaceae).

Convolvulus sibiricus Linnaeus, *Mantissa Plantarum Altera*: 203. 1771.
"Habitat in Sibiria. Laxman." RCN: 1219.
Lectotype (Staples in Staples & Jarvis in *Taxon* 55: 1022. 2006): Herb. Linn. No. 218.5 (LINN).
Current name: ***Merremia sibirica*** (L.) Hallier f. (Convolvulaceae).

Convolvulus siculus Linnaeus, *Species Plantarum* 1: 156. 1753.
"Habitat in Sicilia." RCN: 1253.
Lectotype (Verdcourt in Hubbard & Milne-Redhead, *Fl. Trop. E. Africa, Convolvulaceae*: 41. 1963): Herb. Linn. No. 218.40 (LINN).
Current name: *Convolvulus siculus* L. (Convolvulaceae).
Note: The Boccone plate, cited in synonymy, is reproduced by Lack (in *Ann. Naturhist. Mus. Wien* 104B: 456, Abb. 9. 2003), along with voucher material from the Austrian National Academy in Vienna (Abb. 10).

Convolvulus soldanella Linnaeus, *Species Plantarum* 1: 159. 1753.
"Habitat in Angliae, Frisiae littoribus maris." RCN: 1266.
Lectotype (Meeuse in *Bothalia* 6: 697. 1958): Herb. Linn. No. 218.58 (LINN).
Current name: *Calystegia soldanella* (L.) Roem. & Schult. (Convolvulaceae).

Convolvulus spithamaeus Linnaeus, *Species Plantarum* 1: 158. 1753.
"Habitat in Virginia." RCN: 1260.
Lectotype (Tryon in *Rhodora* 41: 417, pl. 557. 1939): *Clayton 553* (BM-000051655).
Current name: *Calystegia spithamaea* (L.) Pursh (Convolvulaceae).
Note: Tryon's pl. 557 clarifies that the "type specimen" is clearly *Clayton 553* (BM).

Convolvulus terrestris Linnaeus, *Species Plantarum*, ed. 2, 1: 224. 1762.
"Habitat in Europa australi & Africa." RCN: 1257.
Basionym of: *Convolvulus cantabrica* L. var. *terrestris* (L.) L. (1771).
Lectotype (Sa'ad in *Meded. Bot. Mus. Herb. Rijks Univ. Utrecht* 281: 124. 1967): Herb. Linn. No. 218.49 (LINN).
Current name: *Convolvulus cantabrica* L. (Convolvulaceae).

Convolvulus tomentosus Linnaeus, *Species Plantarum* 1: 156. 1753.
"Habitat in Jamaica." RCN: 1241.
Lectotype (Staples in Staples & Jarvis in *Taxon* 55: 1022. 2006): [icon] *"Convolvulus folio lanato in tres lacinias divisio, flore oblongo purpureo"* in Sloane, *Voy. Jamaica* 1: t. 98, f. 2. 1707. – Typotype: Herb. Sloane 3: 12 (BM-SL).
Current name: *Ipomoea jamaicensis* G. Don (Convolvulaceae).

Convolvulus tricolor Linnaeus, *Species Plantarum* 1: 158. 1753.
"Habitat in Africa, Mauritania, Hispania, Sicilia." RCN: 1262.
Lectotype (Sa'ad in *Meded. Bot. Mus. Herb. Rijks Univ. Utrecht* 281: 204. 1967): Herb. Clifford: 68, *Convolvulus* 12, sheet A (BM-000558104; iso- BM).
Current name: *Convolvulus tricolor* L. (Convolvulaceae).
Note: Although Sa'ad stated only "Type: in Hort. Sicc. Cliff. (BM)", he annotated one of the two sheets associated with this name as lectotype, and the second as a paratype. The former is accepted as the lectotype.

Convolvulus tridentatus Linnaeus, *Species Plantarum* 1: 157. 1753.
"Habitat in India." RCN: 2179.
Basionym of: *Evolvulus tridentatus* (L.) L. (1762).
Lectotype (Verdcourt in Hubbard & Milne-Redhead, *Fl. Trop. E. Africa, Convolvulaceae*: 51. 1963): [icon] *"Sendera-clandi"* in Rheede, Hort. Malab. 11: 133, t. 65. 1692.
Current name: *Xenostegia tridentata* (L.) D.F. Austin & Staples (Convolvulaceae).

Convolvulus turpethum Linnaeus, *Species Plantarum* 1: 155. 1753.
"Habitat in Zeylona." RCN: 1237.
Lectotype (Verdcourt in Hubbard & Milne-Redhead, *Fl. Trop. E. Africa, Convolvulaceae*: 61. 1963): Herb. Hermann 2: 68, No. 74 (BM-000594630; iso- L).
Current name: *Operculina turpethum* (L.) Silva Manso (Convolvulaceae).

Convolvulus umbellatus Linnaeus, *Species Plantarum* 1: 155. 1753.
"Habitat in Martinica, Domingo, Jamaica." RCN: 1232.
Lectotype (Austin in *Florida Sci.* 42: 221. 1979): [icon] *"Convolvulus Americanus vulgaris folio, capsulis triquetris, numerosis, ex uno puncto longis petiolis propendentibus, semine lanugine ferruginea villoso"* in Plukenet, Phytographia: t. 167, f. 1. 1692; Almag. Bot.: 114. 1696.
Current name: *Merremia umbellata* (L.) Hallier f. (Convolvulaceae).

Convolvulus verticillatus (Linnaeus) Linnaeus, *Species Plantarum*, ed. 2, 1: 220. 1762.
"Habitat in America." RCN: 1231.
Basionym: *Ipomoea verticillata* L. (1759).
Lectotype (Powell & Staples in Howard, *Fl. Lesser Antilles* 6: 170. 1989): *Browne*, Herb. Linn. No. 218.15, lower right part (LINN).
Current name: *Jacquemontia verticillata* (L.) Urb. (Convolvulaceae).

Conyza anthelmintica Linnaeus, *Species Plantarum*, ed. 2, 2: 1207. 1763.
"Habitat in India." RCN: 6230.
Lectotype (Grierson in Dassanayake & Fosberg, *Revised Handb. Fl. Ceylon* 1: 122. 1980): Herb. Hermann 3: 29, No. 418 (BM-000621910).
Current name: *Vernonia anthelmintica* (L.) Willd. (Asteraceae).

Conyza arborescens Linnaeus, *Systema Naturae*, ed. 10, 2: 1213. 1759.
["Habitat in America meridionali."] Sp. Pl., ed. 2, 2: 1209 (1763). RCN: 6236.
Lectotype (Keeley in *Syst. Bot.* 7: 80. 1982): [icon] *"Conyza foliis ovatis"* in Plumier in Burman, Pl. Amer.: 122, t. 130, f. 2. 1757.
Current name: *Vernonia arborescens* (L.) Sw. (Asteraceae).

Conyza asteroides Linnaeus, *Species Plantarum* 2: 861. 1753.
"Habitat in America septentrionali." RCN: 6223.
Lectotype (Reveal & al. in *Huntia* 7: 214. 1987): *Kalm*, Herb. Linn. No. 993.10, the two left specimens (LINN).
Current name: *Sericocarpus asteroides* (L.) Britton (Asteraceae).

Conyza balsamifera Linnaeus, *Species Plantarum*, ed. 2, 2: 1208. 1763.
"Habitat in India." RCN: 6231.
Lectotype (Randeria in *Blumea* 10: 237. 1960): Herb. Linn. No. 993.18 (LINN).
Current name: *Blumea balsamifera* (L.) DC. (Asteraceae).

Conyza bifoliata Linnaeus, *Species Plantarum* 2: 862. 1753.
"Habitat in India." RCN: 6226.
Lectotype (Srivastava & Shukla in Jarvis & Turland in *Taxon* 47: 358. 1998): [icon] *"Eupatoria Conyzoides, integro Jacobaeae folio molli & incano"* in Plukenet, Phytographia: t. 177, f. 1. 1692; Almag. Bot.: 140. 1696.
Current name: *Blumea bifoliata* (L.) DC. (Asteraceae).
Note: Randeria (in *Blumea* 10: 288. 1960) erroneously indicated *Wight 1425* (K) as the "type specimen".

Conyza bifrons Linnaeus, *Species Plantarum* 2: 861. 1753.
"Habitat in Pyrenaeis, Canada." RCN: 6224.
Lectotype (Pruski in *Sida* 21: 2032. 2005): Herb. Clifford: 405, *Conyza* 3 (BM-000647043).

Current name: ***Inula bifrons*** L. (Asteraceae).
Note: Although some authors have assumed that Linnaeus (*Sp. Pl.*, ed. 2, 2: 1236. 1763) subsequently transferred *C. bifrons* to *Inula*, restricting it to the European taxon, it seems clear that this was not the case. On p. 1207 of the same work, Linnaeus also treated *C. bifrons*, with the same diagnosis as in 1753 but with only the previously cited Plukenet polynomial in synonymy. The Hermann reference was transferred to the synonymy of *I. bifrons*, along with three new synonyms. *Inula bifrons* is evidently a new name in *Inula* for the European plant (albeit with the same epithet), and not a new combination in *Inula* of *Conyza bifrons*. See notes by Godfrey (in *J. Elisha Mitchell Sci. Soc.* 68: 264. 1952).

Conyza bifrons Linnaeus var. **flosculosa** Linnaeus, *Species Plantarum* 2: 862. 1753.
"Habitat in Pyrenaeis, Canada." RCN: 6224.
Lectotype (Reveal in Jarvis & Turland in *Taxon* 47: 358. 1998): [icon] *"Eupatoria conyzoides maxima, Canadensis, foliis caulem amplexantibus"* in Plukenet, Phytographia: t. 87, f. 4. 1691; Almag. Bot.: 141. 1696. – Typotype: Herb. Sloane 96: 26 (BM-SL).
Current name: ***Inula bifrons*** L. (Asteraceae).
Note: See comments under *Conyza bifrons*.

Conyza bifrons Linnaeus var. **radiata** Linnaeus, *Species Plantarum* 2: 861. 1753.
"Habitat in Pyrenaeis, Canada." RCN: 6393.
Lectotype (Anderberg in Jarvis & Turland in *Taxon* 47: 358. 1998): [icon] *"Conyza pyraenaica foliis primulae veris"* in Hermann, Parad. Bat.: 127. 1698.
Current name: ***Inula bifrons*** L. (Asteraceae).

Conyza candida Linnaeus, *Species Plantarum* 2: 862. 1753.
"Habitat in Creta." RCN: 6229.
Lectotype (Greuter in *Willdenowia* 33: 242. 2003): [icon] *"Jacobaea Cretica incana integro limonii fol."* in Barrelier, Pl. Galliam: 95, t. 217. 1714. – Epitype (Greuter in *Willdenowia* 33: 243. 2003): Greece. Crete, Gramvousa, Kissamos, in latere austro-orientali arcis veterae, 50–100m, 25 Jul 1973, *Stamatiadou 17335* in Soc. Ech. Pl. Vasc. Eur. Occid. Bassin Médit. No. 7061 (G; iso- widely distributed).
Current name: ***Inula candida*** (L.) Cass. (Asteraceae).
Note: Lacaita (in *Nuovo Giorn. Bot. Ital.*, n.s., 28: 127–132. 1921) provided a detailed discussion of most of the original elements (though he failed to trace the Clifford material), and the confusion resulting from Linnaeus' later (1763) modification of his species concept. Greuter (in *Boissiera* 13: 140. 1967) designated a Tournefort polynomial (acceptable under the Code in force at that time) as lectotype, wrongly interpreted by Kit Tan & al. (in *Taxon* 52: 358. 2003) as a typification using Tournefort material in Paris. Greuter (2003) refuted this interpretation and formally designated a lectotype and epitype.

Conyza chinensis Linnaeus, *Species Plantarum* 2: 862. 1753.
"Habitat in China. Toren." RCN: 6234.
Type not designated.
Original material: *Torén*, Herb. Linn. No. 993.25 (LINN).
Current name: ***Blumea sp.*** (Asteraceae).

Conyza cinerea Linnaeus, *Species Plantarum* 2: 862. 1753.
"Habitat in India." RCN: 6232.
Lectotype (Grierson in Dassanayake & Fosberg, *Revised Handb. Fl. Ceylon* 1: 133. 1980; Jeffrey in *Kew Bull.* 43: 224. 1988): Herb. Hermann 3: 16, No. 419 (BM-000594658).
Current name: ***Vernonia cinerea*** (L.) Less. (Asteraceae).

Conyza decurrens Linnaeus, *Species Plantarum*, ed. 2, 2: 1206. 1763.
"Habitat in India." RCN: 6239.
Lectotype (Cabrera in *Hickenia* 1: 127. 1978): Herb. Linn. No. 993.31 (LINN).
Current name: ***Neojeffreya decurrens*** (L.) Cabrera (Asteraceae).

Conyza fruticosa Linnaeus, *Species Plantarum*, ed. 2, 2: 1209. 1763.
"Habitat in America meridionali." RCN: 6237.
Lectotype (Keeley in *J. Arnold Arbor.* 59: 391. 1978): [icon] *"Conyza foliis ovatis, floribus axillaribus"* in Plumier in Burman, Pl. Amer.: 83, t. 95, f. 1. 1756.
Current name: ***Vernonia fruticosa*** (L.) Sw. (Asteraceae).

Conyza hirsuta Linnaeus, *Species Plantarum* 2: 863. 1753.
"Habitat in China." RCN: 6235.
Lectotype (designated here by Lack): Herb. Linn. No. 993.26 (LINN).
Current name: ***Pluchea hirsuta*** (L.) Less. (Asteraceae).
Note: Stearn (in Blunt, *Compleat Natural.*: 249. 1971) discussed the protologue and noted the existence of 993.26 (LINN), but did not designate a type.

Conyza linifolia Linnaeus, *Species Plantarum* 2: 861. 1753.
"Habitat in America septentrionali." RCN: 6218.
Lectotype (Reveal in Jarvis & Turland in *Taxon* 47: 359. 1998): *Kalm*, Herb. Linn. No. 993.10, right specimen (LINN).
Current name: ***Sericocarpus linifolius*** (L.) Britton (Asteraceae).

Conyza lobata Linnaeus, *Species Plantarum* 2: 862. 1753.
"Habitat in Vera Cruce." RCN: 6225.
Lectotype (Khan & Jarvis in *Taxon* 38: 661. 1989): *Houstoun*, Herb. Clifford: 405, *Conyza* 4 (BM-000647044).
Current name: ***Neurolaena lobata*** (L.) Cass. (Asteraceae).
Note: Although Moore (in Fawcett & Rendle, (*Fl. Jamaica* 7: 269. 1936) indicated Houstoun material in BM as the type (noting duplicate material in the Clifford herbarium), this was not seen by Linnaeus and is not original material for the name. However, the Clifford material was available to Linnaeus, and its choice as type was formalised by Khan & Jarvis (though their attribution of it to Turner (in *Pl. Syst. Evol.* 140: 134. 1982) was incorrect).

Conyza odorata Linnaeus, *Systema Naturae*, ed. 10, 2: 1213. 1759.
["Habitat in America meridionali."] Sp. Pl., ed. 2, 2: 1208 (1763). RCN: 6233.
Lectotype (Britten in *J. Bot.* 36: 54. 1898): [icon] *"Conyza major, odorata seu baccharis, floribus purpureis nudis"* in Sloane, Voy. Jamaica 1: 258, t. 152, f. 1. 1707. – Typotype: Herb. Sloane 5: 18 (BM-SL).
Current name: ***Pluchea odorata*** (L.) Cass. (Asteraceae).

Conyza pubigera Linnaeus, *Systema Naturae*, ed. 12, 2: 548; *Mantissa Plantarum*: 113. 1767.
"Habitat in India." RCN: 6227.
Type not designated.
Original material: Herb. Linn. No. 993.12 (LINN); [icon] in Rumphius, Herb. Amboin. 5: 299, t. 103, f. 2. 1747.
Current name: ***Conyza pubigera*** L. (Asteraceae).

Conyza rupestris Linnaeus, *Systema Naturae*, ed. 12, 2: 547; *Mantissa Plantarum*: 113. 1767.
"Habitat in Arabia. Forskåhl." RCN: 6221.
Lectotype (Lack in Rechinger, *Fl. Iranica* 145: 40. 1980): Herb. Linn. No. 993.8 (LINN).
Current name: ***Phagnalon rupestre*** (L.) DC. (Asteraceae).

Conyza saxatilis (Linnaeus) Linnaeus, *Species Plantarum*, ed. 2, 2: 1206. 1763.
"Habitat in Italia, Istria, Carinthia, Valesia, Palaestina, Cap. b. spei." RCN: 6219.
Basionym: *Gnaphalium saxatile* L. (1753).
Lectotype (Hilliard & Burtt in *Bot. J. Linn. Soc.* 82: 247. 1981): Herb. Clifford: 401, *Gnaphalium* 7 (BM-000647003).
Current name: *Phagnalon saxatile* (L.) Cass. (Asteraceae).

Conyza scabra Linnaeus, *Systema Naturae*, ed. 12, 2: 547; *Mantissa Plantarum*: 113. 1767.
"Habitat in India." RCN: 6222.
Type not designated.
Original material: Herb. Linn. No. 993.9 (LINN).
Current name: *Conyza scabra* L. (Asteraceae).

Conyza sordida (Linnaeus) Linnaeus, *Mantissa Plantarum Altera*: 466. 1771.
["Habitat in G. Narbonensi."] Sp. Pl. 2: 853 (1753). RCN: 6220.
Basionym: *Gnaphalium sordidum* L. (1753).
Lectotype (Hilliard & Burtt in *Bot. J. Linn. Soc.* 82: 247. 1981): Herb. Clifford: 401, *Gnaphalium* 4, sheet C (BM-000647000).
Current name: *Phagnalon sordidum* (L.) Rchb. (Asteraceae).

Conyza squarrosa Linnaeus, *Species Plantarum* 2: 861. 1753.
"Habitat in Germaniae, Belgii, Angliae, Galliae siccis." RCN: 6217.
Lectotype (Rechinger, *Fl. Iranica* 145: 92. 1980): Herb. Clifford: 405, *Conyza* 2 (BM-000647042).
Generitype of *Conyza* Linnaeus, nom. rej.
Current name: *Inula conyzae* (Griess.) Meikle (Asteraceae).
Note: *Conyza* Linnaeus, nom. rej. in favour of *Conyza* Less.

Conyza tortuosa Linnaeus, *Species Plantarum* 2: 862. 1753.
"Habitat in Madagascar, Vera Cruce." RCN: 6228.
Lectotype (Britten in *J. Bot.* 36: 52. 1898): Herb. Clifford: 405, *Conyza* 5 (BM-000647045).
Current name: *Vernonia tortuosa* (L.) S.F. Blake (Asteraceae).

Conyza virgata (Linnaeus) Linnaeus, *Species Plantarum*, ed. 2, 2: 1206. 1763.
"Habitat in Jamaica, Carolina." RCN: 6238.
Basionym: *Gnaphalium virgatum* L. (1759).
Lectotype (D'Arcy in Woodson & Schery in *Ann. Missouri Bot. Gard.* 62: 1048. 1975): *Browne*, Herb. Linn. No. 993.29 (LINN).
Current name: *Pterocaulon virgatum* (L.) DC. (Asteraceae).

Copaifera officinalis (N.J. Jacquin) Linnaeus, *Species Plantarum*, ed. 2, 1: 557. 1762.
"Habitat in Brasilia, Antilles." RCN: 3126.
Basionym: *Copaiva officinalis* Jacq. (1760).
Type not designated.
Generitype of *Copaifera* Linnaeus, nom. cons.
Current name: *Copaifera officinalis* (Jacq.) L. (Fabaceae: Caesalpinioideae).
Note: *Copaifera* Linnaeus, nom. cons. against *Copaiba* Mill. and *Copaiva* Jacq.

Corallina barbata Linnaeus, *Systema Naturae*, ed. 10, 1: 806. 1758.
"Habitat in Oceano Americano."
Lectotype (Irvine in Spencer & al. in *Taxon*, in press): [icon] "*Corallina fistulosa Jamaicensis candida cum internodiis brevissimis, & quasi silo trajectis Plukenet*" in Ellis, Nat. Hist. Corallin.: 54, t. 25, f. C. 1755.
Current name: *Cymopolia barbata* (L.) J.V. Lamour. (Dasycladaceae).

Corallina corniculata Linnaeus, *Systema Naturae*, ed. 10, 1: 806. 1758.
"Habitat in Oceano Europaeo."
Lectotype (Irvine & Johansen in Irvine & Chamberlain, *Seaweeds Brit. Isles* 1(2B): 56. 1994): Herb. Linn. No. 1293.19 (LINN).
Current name: *Jania rubens* (L.) J.V. Lamour. var. *corniculata* (L.) Yendo (Corallinaceae).

Corallina cristata Linnaeus, *Systema Naturae*, ed. 10, 1: 806. 1758.
"Habitat in Oceano Europaeo."
Lectotype (Irvine in Spencer & al. in *Taxon*, in press): [icon] "*Corallina dichotoma, capillis densis, cristatis, spermophoris, fucis minimis teretibus adnascens*" in Ellis, Nat. Hist. Corallin.: 51, t. 24, f. F. 1755.
Current name: *Jania rubens* (L.) J.V. Lamour. (Corallinaceae).

Corallina fragilissima Linnaeus, *Systema Naturae*, ed. 10, 1: 806. 1758.
"Habitat in Indiis."
Lectotype (Johansen in Spencer & al. in *Taxon*, in press): Herb. Linn. No. 1293.20 (LINN).
Current name: *Amphiroa fragilissima* (L.) J.V. Lamour. (Corallinaceae).
Note: Although Manza (in *Philippine J. Sci.* 71: 299. 1940) referred to having seen photographs of "the Linnaean type", he did not indicate what this might be.

Corallina officinalis Linnaeus, *Systema Naturae*, ed. 10, 1: 805. 1758.
"Habitat in O. Europaeo."
Lectotype (Irvine in Jarvis & al., *Regnum Veg.* 127: 37. 1993): Herb. Linn. No. 1293.9 (LINN).
Generitype of *Corallina* Linnaeus (vide Schmitz in *Flora* 72: 455. 1889).
Current name: *Corallina officinalis* L. (Corallinaceae).
Note: Although Manza (in *Philippine J. Sci.* 71: 275. 1940) referred to having seen photographs of "the Linnaean type" and (p. 276) that it was in BM, it is not clear what this might be.

Corallina opuntia Linnaeus, *Systema Naturae*, ed. 10, 1: 805. 1758.
"Habitat in Oceano Europaeo, Americano."
Lectotype (Verbruggen in Spencer & al. in *Taxon*, in press): [icon] "*Corallina tubulata tenera, dichotoma, & pustulosa*" in Ellis, Nat. Hist. Corallin.: 54, t. 25, f. B. 1755.
Current name: *Halimeda opuntia* (L.) J.V. Lamour. (Halimedaceae).

Corallina penicillus Linnaeus, *Systema Naturae*, ed. 10, 1: 807. 1758.
"Habitat in Asia."
Lectotype (Leliaert in Spencer & al. in *Taxon*, in press): Herb. Linn. No. 1293.21 (LINN).
Current name: *Penicillus capitatus* (L.) Lamarck (Udoteaceae).

Corallina rubens Linnaeus, *Systema Naturae*, ed. 10, 1: 806. 1758.
"Habitat in Oceano Europaeo."
Lectotype (Irvine in Irvine & Chamberlain, *Seaweeds Brit. Isles* 1(2B): 56. 1994): Herb. Burser XX: 72 (UPS).
Current name: *Jania rubens* (L.) J.V. Lamour. (Corallinaceae).
Note: Although Manza (in *Philippine J. Sci.* 71: 272. 1940) referred to having seen photographs of "the Linnaean type", it is not clear what this was intended to be.

Corallina spermophoros Linnaeus, *Systema Naturae*, ed. 10, 1: 807. 1758.
"Habitat in Oceano Europaeo."
Lectotype (Irvine in Spencer & al. in *Taxon*, in press): [icon] "*Corallina alba spermophoros, capillis tenuissimis*" in Ellis, Nat. Hist. Corallin.: 51, t. 24, f. G. 1755 (see p. 127).
Current name: *Jania rubens* (L.) J.V. Lamour. (Corallinaceae).

Corallina squamata Linnaeus, *Systema Naturae,* ed. 10, 1: 806. 1758.
"Habitat in Oceano Europaeo."
Lectotype (Irvine & Johansen in Irvine & Chamberlain, *Seaweeds Brit. Isles* 1(2B): 49. 1994): [icon] *"Corallina Anglica erecta, ramulis dense pennatis, lanceolae forma terminantibus, segmentis ad utrumque latus paululum compressis"* in Ellis, Nat. Hist. Corallin.: 49, t. 24, f. C. 1755.
Current name: ***Haliptilon squamatum*** (L.) H.W. Johans. & al. (Corallinaceae).

Corchorus aestuans Linnaeus, *Systema Naturae,* ed. 10, 2: 1079. 1759.
["Habitat in America calidiore."] Sp. Pl., ed. 2, 1: 746 (1762). RCN: 3932.
Lectotype (Fawcett & Rendle, *Fl. Jamaica* 5: 88. 1926): *Browne*, Herb. Linn. No. 691.4 (LINN).
Current name: ***Corchorus aestuans*** L. (Tiliaceae).

Corchorus astuans Linnaeus, *Mantissa Plantarum Altera*: 565. 1771, *orth. var.*
RCN: 3932.
Lectotype (Fawcett & Rendle, *Fl. Jamaica* 5: 88. 1926): *Browne*, Herb. Linn. No. 691.4 (LINN).
Current name: ***Corchorus astuans*** L. (Tiliaceae).
Note: This appears to be an orthographic variant accidentally introduced in 1771 in expanding the description and synonymy of *C. aestuans* L. (1759).

Corchorus capsularis Linnaeus, *Species Plantarum* 1: 529. 1753.
"Habitat in India." RCN: 3933.
Lectotype (Robyns & Meijer in Dassanayake & Fosberg, *Revised Handb. Fl. Ceylon* 7: 420. 1991): Herb. Hermann 5: 261, No. 214 [icon] (BM).
Current name: ***Corchorus capsularis*** L. (Tiliaceae).
Note: Ghafoor (in Nasir & Ali, *Fl. W. Pakistan* 75: 29. 1974) indicated 691.3 (LINN) as the type but this collection lacks the relevant *Species Plantarum* number (i.e. "3") and was a post-1753 addition to the herbarium, and is not original material for the name.

Corchorus caryophylloides Linnaeus, *Systema Naturae,* ed. 10, 2: 1079. 1759.
RCN: 3937.
Type not designated.
Original material: none traced.
Note: The application of this name is uncertain.

Corchorus coreta Linnaeus, *Plantarum Jamaicensium Pugillus*: 14. 1759.
"Habitat [in Jamaica.]" RCN: 3936.
Type not designated.
Original material: none traced.
Current name: ***Corchorus siliquosus*** L. (Tiliaceae).

Corchorus hirsutus Linnaeus, *Species Plantarum* 1: 530. 1753.
"Habitat in America meridionali." RCN: 3934.
Type not designated.
Original material: [icon] in Plumier in Burman, Pl. Amer.: 94, t. 104. 1757.
Current name: ***Corchorus hirsutus*** L. (Tiliaceae).

Corchorus hirtus Linnaeus, *Species Plantarum,* ed. 2, 1: 747. 1762.
"Habitat in America meridionali." RCN: 3935.
Lectotype (Bornstein in Howard, *Fl. Lesser Antilles* 5: 191. 1989): [icon] *"Corchorus caule piloso"* in Plumier in Burman, Pl. Amer.: 93, t. 103, f. 2. 1757.
Current name: ***Corchorus hirtus*** L. (Tiliaceae).

Corchorus olitorius Linnaeus, *Species Plantarum* 1: 529. 1753.
"Habitat in Asia, Africa, America." RCN: 3929.
Lectotype (Wild in Exell & al., *Fl. Zambesiaca* 2: 84. 1963): Herb. Clifford: 209, *Corchorus* 1 (BM-000628760).
Generitype of *Corchorus* Linnaeus (vide Green, *Prop. Brit. Bot.*: 162. 1929).
Current name: ***Corchorus olitorius*** L. (Tiliaceae).

Corchorus siliquosus Linnaeus, *Species Plantarum* 1: 529. 1753.
"Habitat in Jamaica." RCN: 3936.
Type not designated.
Original material: [icon] in Sloane, Voy. Jamaica 1: 145, t. 94, f. 1. 1707 – Voucher: Herb. Sloane 2: 122 (BM-SL).
Current name: ***Corchorus siliquosus*** L. (Tiliaceae).
Note: Jansen-Jacobs & Meijer (in Görts-van Rijn, *Fl. Guianas*, ser. A, 17: 28. 1995) indicated 691.6 (LINN) as the type but it is a Browne collection, received by Linnaeus only in 1758, so not original material for the name. Similarly, although 691.7 (LINN) was treated by McVaugh (*Fl. Novo-Galiciana* 3: 76. 2001) as the type, this collection lacks the relevant *Species Plantarum* number (i.e. "1") and was a post-1753 addition to the herbarium, and is not original material for the name.

Corchorus tridens Linnaeus, *Mantissa Plantarum Altera*: 566. 1771. RCN: 3931.
Lectotype (Stevels in *Wageningen Agric. Univ. Pap.* 90–1: 239. 1990): [icon] *"Corchorus trilocularis"* in Burman, Fl. Indica: 123, t. 37, f. 2. 1768.
Current name: ***Corchorus tridens*** L. (Tiliaceae).
Note: See Wild (in Leistner, *Fl. Southern Africa* 21: 34. 1984) for a discussion of the cited Burman and Plukenet plates.

Corchorus trilocularis Linnaeus, *Systema Naturae,* ed. 12, 2: 369; *Mantissa Plantarum*: 77. 1767.
"Habitat in Arabia. Forskåhl." RCN: 3930.
Lectotype (Ghafoor in Nasir & Ali, *Fl. W. Pakistan* 75: 28. 1974): Herb. Linn. No. 691.2 (LINN).
Current name: ***Corchorus trilocularis*** L. (Tiliaceae).

Cordia bourreria Linnaeus, *Systema Naturae,* ed. 10, 2: 936. 1759.
["Habitat in Jamaica."] Sp. Pl., ed. 2, 1: 275 (1762). RCN: 1530.
Basionym of: *Ehretia bourreria* (L.) L. (1762).
Lectotype (Stearn in *J. Arnold Arbor.* 52: 620. 1971): *Browne*, Herb. Linn. No. 254.2 (LINN).
Current name: ***Bourreria baccata*** Raf. (Boraginaceae).

Cordia callococca Linnaeus, *Flora Jamaicensis*: 14. 1759.
["Habitat in Jamaica."] Sp. Pl., ed. 2, 1: 274 (1762). RCN: 1526.
Neotype (Gaviria in *Mitt. Bot. Staatssamml. München* 23: 141. 1987): Herb. Linn. No. 253.8 (LINN).
Current name: ***Cordia callococca*** L. (Boraginaceae).
Note: As there are no original elements for this name, Gaviria's type choice is accepted as a neotypification under Art. 9.8. Miller (in *Novon* 9: 234. 1999) discusses the complexities of the original publication, reaching the same decision as Gaviria as to the type.

Cordia gerascanthus Linnaeus, *Systema Naturae,* ed. 10, 2: 936. 1759.
["Habitat in Jamaica."] Sp. Pl., ed. 2, 1: 273 (1762). RCN: 1524.
Lectotype (Riedl in Kalkman & al., *Fl. Malesiana,* ser. I, 13: 77. 1997): [icon] *"Gerascanthus foliis ovato-oblongis, utrinque productis, racemis terminalibus"* in Browne, Civ. Nat. Hist. Jamaica: 170, t. 29, f. 3. 1756.
Current name: ***Cordia gerascanthus*** L. (Boraginaceae).

Cordia glabra Linnaeus, *Species Plantarum* 1: 191. 1753.
"Habitat in America meridionali." RCN: 1526.
Neotype (Miller in Cafferty & Jarvis in *Taxon* 53: 801. 2004): Herb.
    Sloane 7: 36, upper specimen (BM-SL).
Current name: ***Bourreria succulenta*** Jacq. (Boraginaceae).

Cordia macrophylla Linnaeus, *Flora Jamaicensis*: 14. 1759.
["Habitat in Jamaica."] Sp. Pl., ed. 2, 1: 274 (1762). RCN: 1525.
Lectotype (Miller in Cafferty & Jarvis in *Taxon* 53: 801. 2004): [icon]
    "Prunus racemosa, foliis oblongis hirsutis maximis, fructu rubro" in
    Sloane, Voy. Jamaica 2: 130, t. 221, f. 1. 1725. – Typotype: Herb.
    Sloane 7: 71, 72 (BM-SL).
Current name: ***Cordia macrophylla*** L. (Boraginaceae).

Cordia myxa Linnaeus, *Species Plantarum* 1: 190. 1753, *typ. cons.*
"Habitat in Aegypto, Malabaria." RCN: 1521.
Conserved type (Warfa in *Compreh. Summ. Uppsala Diss. Fac. Sci.*
    174: 44. 1988): Herb. Linn. No. 94.5 (S).
Generitype of *Cordia* Linnaeus, *nom. cons.*
Current name: ***Cordia myxa*** L. (Boraginaceae).
Note: Cordia myxa, with the type proposed by Warfa (but erroneously
    attributed to Verdcourt), was proposed as conserved type of the
    genus by Jarvis (in *Taxon* 41: 561. 1992). This was eventually
    approved by the General Committee (see review of the history of
    this proposal by Barrie, *l.c.* 55: 795–796. 2006).

Cordia sebestena Linnaeus, *Species Plantarum* 1: 190. 1753.
"Habitat in America calidiore." RCN: 1523.
Lectotype (Miller in Cafferty & Jarvis in *Taxon* 53: 801. 2004): [icon]
    *"Cariophyllus spurius inodorus, folio subrotundo scabro, flore racemoso
    hexapetaloide coccineo speciosissimo"* in Sloane, Voy. Jamaica 2: 20, t.
    164. 1725. – Typotype: Herb. Sloane 5: 71 (BM-SL).
Current name: ***Cordia sebestena*** L. (Boraginaceae).

Cordia spinescens Linnaeus, *Mantissa Plantarum Altera*: 206.
    1771.
"Habitat in India orientali." RCN: 1522.
Lectotype (Johnston in *J. Arnold Arbor.* 30: 104. 1949): Herb. Linn.
    No. 253.2 (LINN).
Current name: ***Cordia spinescens*** L. (Boraginaceae).

Coreopsis alba Linnaeus, *Species Plantarum* 2: 908. 1753.
"Habitat in Insula St. crucis." RCN: 6561.
Type not designated.
Original material: [icon] in Plukenet, Phytographia: t. 160, f. 3. 1692;
    Almag. Bot.: 101. 1696 – Voucher: Herb. Sloane 95: 166; 99: 196
    (BM-SL); [icon] in Hermann, Parad. Bat.: 124. 1698.
Current name: ***Bidens alba*** (L.) DC. (Asteraceae).

Coreopsis alternifolia Linnaeus, *Species Plantarum* 2: 909. 1753.
"Habitat in Virginia, Canada." RCN: 6566.
Lectotype (Reveal in Jarvis & Turland in *Taxon* 47: 359. 1998): Herb.
    Linn. No. 1026.11 (LINN).
Current name: ***Verbesina alternifolia*** (L.) Britton ex Kearney
    (Asteraceae).

Coreopsis angustifolia Linnaeus, *Species Plantarum* 2: 908.
    1753.
"Habitat in Virginia." RCN: 6555.
Basionym of: *Rudbeckia angustifolia* (L.) L. (1763).
Lectotype (Reveal in Jarvis & Turland in *Taxon* 47: 359. 1998):
    Clayton 667 (BM-000051730).
Current name: ***Helianthus angustifolius*** L. (Asteraceae).
Note: As noted by Reveal, Fernald (in *Rhodora* 49: 190, pl. 1084, f. 1.
    1947) treated *Clayton 667* as the type of *Helianthus angustifolius* L.

(1753), a name for which it is not original material. Heiser & al. (in
    Mem. Torrey Bot. Club 22(3): 186. 1969) were aware of this error,
    noting that *Clayton 667* "is apparently the type of *Coreopsis
    angustifolia*". Reveal subsequently formalised this conclusion.

Coreopsis auriculata Linnaeus, *Species Plantarum* 2: 908. 1753.
"Habitat in Virginia." RCN: 6563.
Lectotype (Smith in *Sida* 6: 138. 1976): *Clayton 298* ["290"] (BM-
    000051187).
Current name: ***Coreopsis auriculata*** L. (Asteraceae).
Note: Sherff (in *Publ. Field Mus. Nat. Hist., Bot. Ser.* 11: 357. 1936)
    discussed some of the original elements for the name but did not
    designate a type.

Coreopsis baccata Linnaeus, *Plantae Surinamenses*: 14. 1775.
"Habitat [in Surinamo.]" RCN: 6567.
Lectotype (D'Arcy in Woodson & Schery in *Ann. Missouri Bot. Gard.*
    62: 1170. 1975): Herb. Linn. No. 1026.7 (LINN).
Current name: ***Tilesia baccata*** (L.) Pruski (Asteraceae).

Coreopsis bidens Linnaeus, *Species Plantarum* 2: 908. 1753.
"Habitat ad fossas Europae." RCN: 6565.
Lectotype (Mesfin Tadesse in Jarvis & Turland in *Taxon* 47: 359.
    1998): Herb. Linn. No. 1026.10 (LINN).
Current name: ***Bidens cernua*** L. (Asteraceae).

Coreopsis chrysantha Linnaeus, *Species Plantarum,* ed. 2, 2: 1282.
    1763.
"Habitat in America." RCN: 6559.
Type not designated.
Original material: [icon] in Plumier in Burman, Pl. Amer.: 42, t. 53, f.
    1. 1756.
Current name: ***Bidens chrysantha*** (L.) DC. (Asteraceae).

Coreopsis coronata Linnaeus, *Species Plantarum,* ed. 2, 2: 1281.
    1763.
"Habitat in Virginia." RCN: 6557.
Lectotype (Sherff in *Bot. Gaz.* 59: 314, f. 3. 1915): Herb. Linn. No.
    1026.3 (LINN), see opposite.
Current name: ***Bidens coronata*** (L.) Britton (Asteraceae).
Note: See also Sherff (in *Publ. Field Mus. Nat. Hist., Bot. Ser.* 16: 221,
    pl. LIX, f. m. 1937).

Coreopsis lanceolata Linnaeus, *Species Plantarum* 2: 908. 1753.
"Habitat in Carolina." RCN: 6564.
Lectotype (Smith in *Sida* 6: 141. 1976): [icon] *"Bidens caroliniana,
    florum radiis latissimis, insigniter dentatis, semine alato per
    maturitatem convoluto"* in Martyn, Hist. Pl. Rar.: 26, t. 26. 1728.
Generitype of *Coreopsis* Linnaeus (vide Green, *Prop. Brit. Bot.*: 183.
    1929).
Current name: ***Coreopsis lanceolata*** L. (Asteraceae).
Note: Smith incorrectly described the Martyn plate as a neotype.
    However, as it was an original element for the name, this is a valid
    typification under Art. 9.8, despite the fact that some later authors
    (e.g. Reveal in Jarvis & al., *Regnum Veg.* 127: 37. 1993; Hind in
    Bosser & al., *Fl. Mascareignes* 109: 196. 1993) have indicated a
    Clifford sheet as the lectotype.

Coreopsis leucantha Linnaeus, *Species Plantarum,* ed. 2, 2: 1282.
    1763, *orth. var.*
"Habitat in America." RCN: 6558.
Lectotype (Ballard in *Amer. J. Bot.* 73: 1464. 1986): Herb. Linn. No.
    1026.5 (LINN; iso- BM).
Current name: ***Bidens pilosa*** L. var. ***radiata*** Sch. Bip. (Asteraceae).
Note: An orthographic variant of *Coreopsis leucanthema* L. (1755).

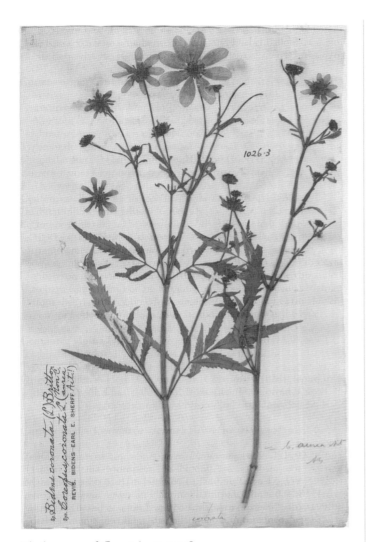

The lectotype of *Coreopsis coronata* L.

Coreopsis leucanthema Linnaeus, *Centuria I Plantarum*: 29. 1755.
"Habitat in America. Miller." RCN: 6558.
Lectotype (Ballard in *Amer. J. Bot.* 73: 1464. 1986): Herb. Linn. No. 1026.5 (LINN; iso- BM).
Current name: ***Bidens pilosa*** L. var. ***radiata*** Sch. Bip. (Asteraceae).
Note: Sherff (in *Publ. Field Mus. Nat. Hist., Bot. Ser.* 16: 437. 1937) discussed the name, noting material in LINN and that Linnaeus had in mind a plant from Philip Miller "perhaps the same specimen that is left today in the Linnaean Herbarium". However, he did not refer to it as the type. Ballard typified the name using this material, and Reveal (in Jarvis & Turland in *Taxon* 47: 359. 1998) noted a duplicate in BM.

Coreopsis reptans Linnaeus, *Systema Naturae*, ed. 10, 2: 1228. 1759.
["Habitat in America."] Sp. Pl., ed. 2, 2: 1281 (1763). RCN: 6562.
Lectotype (Moore in Fawcett & Rendle, *Fl. Jamaica* 7: 252. 1936): *Browne*, Herb. Linn. No. 1026.13 (LINN).
Current name: ***Bidens reptans*** (L.) G. Don (Asteraceae).
Note: Although some authors (e.g. Sherff in *Publ. Field Mus. Nat. Hist., Bot. Ser.* 16: 170. 1937) have treated the cited Sloane plate as the type, Moore's choice of the Browne specimen appears to have priority.

Coreopsis tripteris Linnaeus, *Species Plantarum* 2: 908. 1753.
"Habitat in Virginia." RCN: 6560.
Lectotype (Reveal in Jarvis & Turland in *Taxon* 47: 359. 1998): [icon] *"Chrysanthemum trifoliatum Virginianum folio acutiore laevi"* in Morison, Pl. Hist. Univ. 3: 21, s. 6, t. 3, f. 44. 1699.
Current name: ***Coreopsis tripteris*** L. (Asteraceae).
Note: Smith (in *Sida* 6: 163. 1976) chose a neotype but this is unacceptable as an original element (the cited Morison plate) was in existence. Reveal therefore rejected this choice in favour of Morison's illustration.

Coreopsis verticillata Linnaeus, *Species Plantarum* 2: 907. 1753.
"Habitat in Virginia." RCN: 6556.
Lectotype (Reveal & al. in *Huntia* 7: 218. 1987): *Clayton 308* (BM-000040282).
Current name: ***Coreopsis verticillata*** L. (Asteraceae).
Note: Sherff (in *Publ. Field Mus. Nat. Hist., Bot. Ser.* 11: 401. 1936) suggested that Clayton material, if extant, would be the obvious type. Smith (in *Sida* 6: 177. 1976) indicated Clayton material seen by him at BM as the lectotype but failed to distinguish between three different collections (*Clayton 308; 409; s.n.*). In fact, Smith annotated the last of these sheets as lectotype, and this is the only one of the three that is not original material for the name. Reveal & al. subsequently designated *Clayton 308* (BM) as lectotype.

Coriandrum sativum Linnaeus, *Species Plantarum* 1: 256. 1753.
"Habitat in Italiae agris." RCN: 2053.
Lectotype (Jansen, *Spices, Condiments Med. Pl. Ethiopia*: 60. 1981): Herb. Burser VIII: 38 (UPS).
Generitype of *Coriandrum* Linnaeus (vide Hitchcock, *Prop. Brit. Bot.*: 141. 1929).
Current name: ***Coriandrum sativum*** L. (Apiaceae).

Coriandrum testiculatum Linnaeus, *Species Plantarum* 1: 256. 1753.
"Habitat in Europae australis agris." RCN: 2054.
Lectotype (Jafri in Jafri & El-Gadi, *Fl. Libya* 117: 27. 1985): Herb. Linn. No. 363.2 (LINN).
Current name: ***Bifora testiculata*** (L.) Spreng. ex Schult. (Apiaceae).

Coriaria myrtifolia Linnaeus, *Species Plantarum* 2: 1037. 1753.
"Habitat Monspelii." RCN: 7480.
Lectotype (Ohba in Jarvis & al., *Regnum Veg.* 127: 37. 1993): Herb. Linn. No. 1192.1 (LINN).
Generitype of *Coriaria* Linnaeus (vide Green, *Prop. Brit. Bot.*: 192. 1929).
Current name: ***Coriaria myrtifolia*** L. (Coriariaceae).

Coriaria ruscifolia Linnaeus, *Species Plantarum* 2: 1037. 1753.
"Habitat in Peru." RCN: 7481.
Type not designated.
Original material: [icon] in Feuillée, J. Obs. 3: 17, t. 12. 1725.
Current name: ***Coriaria ruscifolia*** L. (Coriariaceae).
Note: Skog (in *Rhodora* 74: 248. 1972) indicated the cited Feuillée plate as the type, but with a question mark, indicating uncertainty.

Coris monspeliensis Linnaeus, *Species Plantarum* 1: 177. 1753.
"Habitat in Europae australis arenosis maritimis." RCN: 1402.
Lectotype (Ali in Ali & Jafri, *Fl. Libya* 1: 1. 1976): Herb. Clifford: 68, *Coris* 1 (BM-000558097).
Generitype of *Coris* Linnaeus.
Current name: ***Coris monspeliensis*** L. (Primulaceae).
Note: Bizzarri (in *Webbia* 24: 692–693. 1970) discussed the typification of the name but did not eventually choose between the LINN sheet and a Camerarius plate. See comments by Jarvis (in *Webbia* 45: 113. 1991).

Corispermum hyssopifolium Linnaeus, *Species Plantarum* 1: 4. 1753.
"Habitat ad Volgam Tartariae, Gillau Borussiae, Monspelii arenosis."
RCN: 30.
Lectotype (Hedge in Jarvis & al., *Regnum Veg.* 127: 37. 1993): Herb.
Linn. No. 12.1 (LINN).
Generitype of *Corispermum* Linnaeus (vide Hitchcock, *Prop. Brit. Bot.*: 115. 1929).
Current name: ***Corispermum hyssopifolium*** L. (Chenopodiaceae).
Note: Maihle & Blackwell (in *Sida* 7: 385. 1978) stated "(Phototype: Linnaean herbarium, IDC No. 12!)" but as this does not distinguish between sheets 12.1 and 12.2 (LINN), it is not an effective choice. As the two sheets do not appear to be part of a single gathering, Art. 9.15 does not apply.

Corispermum squarrosum Linnaeus, *Species Plantarum* 1: 4.
1753.
"Habitat in Wolgam Tartariae, inque desertis Coffacorum." RCN: 31.
Type not designated.
Original material: *Gmelin*, Herb. Linn. No. 12.3 (LINN); [icon] in Buxbaum, Pl. Minus Cognit. Cent. 3: 30, t. 56. 1729.
Current name: ***Agriophyllum squarrosum*** (L.) Moq.
(Chenopodiaceae).
Note: Although Aellen (in *Feddes Repert.* 69: 144. 1964) says that the type of *C. squarrosum* is identifiable as *Agriophyllum arenarium* M. Bieb., he failed to indicate what collection or illustration he considered to be the type.

Cornucopiae alopecuroides Linnaeus, *Systema Naturae,* ed. 12, 2: 85; *Mantissa Plantarum*: 29. 1767.
"Habitat in Italia. Arduini." RCN: 451.
Lectotype (Scholz in Cafferty & al. in *Taxon* 49: 249. 2000): *Arduino 52*, Herb. Linn. No. 76.4 (LINN).
Current name: ***Cornucopiae alopecuroides*** L. (Poaceae).

Cornucopiae cucullatum Linnaeus, *Species Plantarum* 1: 54.
1753.
"Habitat in Smyrnae. D. Hasselquist." RCN: 450.
Lectotype (Cope in Jarvis & al., *Regnum Veg.* 127: 38. 1993): Herb.
Linn. No. 76.1 (LINN).
Generitype of *Cornucopiae* Linnaeus.
Current name: ***Cornucopiae cucullatum*** L. (Poaceae).

Cornus alba Linnaeus, *Systema Naturae,* ed. 12, 2: 125; *Mantissa Plantarum*: 40. 1767.
"Habitat in Sibiria, Canada." RCN: 962.
Lectotype (Holub in *Zprávy Českoslov. Bot. Společn. Českoslov. Akad. Věd.* 17: 4. 1982): Herb. Linn. No. 151.5 (LINN).
Current name: ***Cornus alba*** L. (Cornaceae).

Cornus canadensis Linnaeus, *Species Plantarum* 1: 118. 1753.
"Habitat in Canada." RCN: 965.
Lectotype (Juel in *Rhodora* 31: 178. 1931): Herb. Burser X: 106 (UPS).
Current name: ***Cornus canadensis*** L. (Cornaceae).

Cornus florida Linnaeus, *Species Plantarum* 1: 117. 1753.
"Habitat in Virginia." RCN: 959.
Lectotype (designated here by Reveal, Barrie & Jarvis): *Clayton 23* (BM), see p. 198 in colour, and above, right.
Current name: ***Cornus florida*** L. (Cornaceae).
Note: Holub (in *Zprávy Českoslov. Bot. Společn. Českoslov. Akad. Věd.* 17:12. 1982) indicated both 151.1 and 151.2 (LINN) as "Typus" but as these are evidently not part of a single gathering, Art. 9.15 does not apply. *Clayton 57* (BM), the lectotype, is reproduced by Gaden (in *Virginia Explorer* 15: 24. 1999).

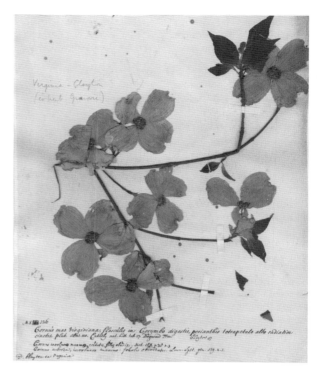

The lectotype of *Cornus florida* L.

Cornus herbacea Linnaeus, *Flora Anglica*: 11. 1754.
"Habitat [in Anglia.]"
Type not designated.
Original material: [icon] in Parkinson, Theatr. Bot.: 1461. 1640; [icon] in Gerard, Herball: 1113. 1597; [icon] in Bauhin & Cherler, Hist. Pl. Univ. 2: 108, 109. 1651.
Current name: ***Cornus suecica*** L. (Cornaceae).
Note: See notes by Stearn (*Introd. Ray's Syn. Meth. Stirp. Brit.* (Ray Soc. ed.): 65. 1973).

Cornus mas Linnaeus, *Species Plantarum* 1: 117. 1753.
"Habitat in sepibus Austriae." RCN: 960.
Lectotype (Holub in *Zprávy Českoslov. Bot. Společn. Českoslov. Akad. Věd.* 17: 7. 1982): Herb. Linn. No. 151.2 (LINN).
Generitype of *Cornus* Linnaeus (vide Rydberg in *Bull. Torrey Bot. Club* 33: 147. 7 Apr 1906).
Current name: ***Cornus mas*** L. (Cornaceae).

Cornus sanguinea Linnaeus, *Species Plantarum* 1: 117. 1753.
"Habitat in Europae, Asiae, Americae borealis dumetis." RCN: 961.
Lectotype (Jonsell & Jarvis in *Nordic J. Bot.* 22: 83. 2002): Herb.
Clifford: 38, *Cornus* 1 (BM-000557822).
Current name: ***Cornus sanguinea*** L. (Cornaceae).
Note: Holub (in *Zprávy Českoslov. Bot. Společn. Českoslov. Akad. Věd.* 17: 22. 1982) noted the need for a neotype based on the poor quality of 151.4 (LINN).

Cornus sericea Linnaeus, *Mantissa Plantarum Altera*: 199. 1771.
"Habitat in America septentrionali." RCN: 963.
Lectotype (Fosberg in *Bull. Torrey Bot. Club* 69: 585. 1942): Herb.
Linn. No. 151.6 (LINN).
Current name: ***Cornus sericea*** L. (Cornaceae).
Note: This name was was based on several elements leading Rickett (in *Rhodora* 36: 272. 1934) to propose its rejection as a *nomen*

ambiguum. However, Fosberg (*l.c.*) disagreed, using the name in the sense of his designated type material in LINN (and *C. stolonifera* Michx.). See also Eyde (in *Bot. Rev.* 54: 255. 1988).

Cornus suecica Linnaeus, *Species Plantarum* 1: 118. 1753.
"Habitat in Suecica, Norvegia, Russia." RCN: 964.
Lectotype (Jonsell & Jarvis in *Nordic J. Bot.* 22: 83. 2002): Herb. Linn. No. 151.12 (LINN).
Current name: ***Cornus suecica*** L. (Cornaceae).

Cornutia pyramidata Linnaeus, *Species Plantarum* 2: 628. 1753.
"Habitat in Caribaeis, Campechia." RCN: 4546.
Lectotype (Howard, *Fl. Lesser Antilles* 6: 224. 1989): Herb. Linn. No. 784.1 (LINN).
Generitype of *Cornutia* Linnaeus.
Current name: ***Cornutia pyramidata*** L. (Verbenaceae).

Coronilla argentea Linnaeus, *Species Plantarum* 2: 743. 1753.
"Habitat in Creta." RCN: 5469.
Lectotype (Greuter in *Ann. Mus. Goulandris* 1: 44. 1973): [icon] *"Colutea Scorpioide odorata"* in Alpino, Pl. Exot.: 17, 16. 1627.
Current name: ***Coronilla valentina*** L. subsp. ***glauca*** (L.) Batt. (Fabaceae: Faboideae).
Note: Turland (in *Bull. Nat. Hist. Mus. London, Bot.* 25: 129, f. 2. 1995) reproduces the type illustration.

Coronilla coronata Linnaeus, *Systema Naturae,* ed. 10, 2: 1168. 1759.
["Habitat in Europa australi."] Sp. Pl., ed. 2, 2: 1047 (1763). RCN: 5467.
Neotype (Lassen in Turland & Jarvis in *Taxon* 46: 467. 1997): *Royen 97,* Herb. Linn. No. 917.9 (LINN).
Current name: ***Coronilla coronata*** L. (Fabaceae: Faboideae).

Coronilla cretica Linnaeus, *Species Plantarum* 2: 743. 1753.
"Habitat in Creta." RCN: 5472.
Lectotype (Lassen in Turland & Jarvis in *Taxon* 46: 467. 1997): Herb. Linn. No. 917.14 (LINN).
Current name: ***Securigera cretica*** (L.) Lassen (Fabaceae: Faboideae).

Coronilla emerus Linnaeus, *Species Plantarum* 2: 742. 1753.
"Habitat Genevae, Monspelii, Salerni, Viennae." RCN: 5463.
Lectotype (Jonsell & Jarvis in *Nordic J. Bot.* 22: 77. 2002): Herb. Clifford: 363, *Coronilla* 4, sheet B (BM-000646626).
Current name: ***Hippocrepis emerus*** (L.) Lassen subsp. ***emerus*** (Fabaceae: Faboideae).

Coronilla glauca Linnaeus, *Centuria I Plantarum*: 23. 1755.
"Habitat in Gallia Narbonensi." RCN: 5466.
Lectotype (Lassen in Turland & Jarvis in *Taxon* 46: 467. 1997): Herb. Linn. No. 917.5 (LINN).
Current name: ***Coronilla valentina*** L. subsp. ***glauca*** (L.) Batt. (Fabaceae: Faboideae).

Coronilla juncea Linnaeus, *Species Plantarum* 2: 742. 1753.
"Habitat Massiliae, Monspelii." RCN: 5464.
Lectotype (Lassen in Turland & Jarvis in *Taxon* 46: 467. 1997): Herb. Burser XIX: 127 (UPS).
Current name: ***Coronilla juncea*** L. subsp. ***juncea*** (Fabaceae: Faboideae).

Coronilla minima Linnaeus, *Centuria II Plantarum*: 28. 1756.
"Habitat in Italia, Gallia australi." RCN: 5468.
Type not designated.

Original material: Herb. Burser XIX: 125 (UPS); Herb. Linn. No. 917.7? (LINN); *Löfling 531b,* Herb. Linn. No. 917.8 (LINN); [icon] in Bauhin & Cherler, Hist. Pl. Univ. 2: 351. 1651.
Current name: ***Coronilla minima*** L. subsp. ***minima*** (Fabaceae: Faboideae).
Note: Although this name is in use, none of the original material appears to correspond with current usage. As noted by Turland & Jarvis (in *Taxon* 46: 467. 1997), *Gérard 50,* Herb. Linn. No. 308.16 (S) is identifiable as *C. minima* but was annotated as *C. coronata* by Linnaeus (and is in any case a post-1753 addition to the herbarium and not original material for *C. minima*). A conservation proposal may prove to be necessary.

Coronilla monilis Linnaeus, *Plantae Surinamenses*: 13. 1775.
"Habitat [in Surinamo.]" RCN: 5474.
Lectotype (Geesink in *Taxon* 33: 743. 1984): *Dahlberg 157,* Herb. Linn. No. 911.1 (LINN).
Current name: ***Lonchocarpus monilis*** (L.) A.M.G. Azevedo (Fabaceae: Faboideae).

Coronilla scandens Linnaeus, *Species Plantarum* 2: 743. 1753.
"Habitat in America calidiore." RCN: 5473.
Lectotype (Rudd in *Contr. U. S. Natl. Herb.* 32: 235. 1958): [icon] *"Coronilla foliolis quinis ovatis"* in Plumier in Burman, Pl. Amer.: 98, t. 107, f. 3. 1757.
Current name: ***Chaetocalyx scandens*** (L.) Urb. (Fabaceae: Faboideae).

Coronilla securidaca Linnaeus, *Species Plantarum* 2: 743. 1753.
"Habitat inter Hispaniae segetes." RCN: 5470.
Lectotype (Lassen in Turland & Jarvis in *Taxon* 46: 467. 1997): Herb. Linn. No. 917.11 (LINN).
Current name: ***Securigera securidaca*** (L.) Degen & Dörfl. (Fabaceae: Faboideae).

Coronilla valentina Linnaeus, *Species Plantarum* 2: 742. 1753, *typ. cons.*
"Habitat in Hispania, Italia." RCN: 5465.
Conserved type (Lassen in Jarvis in *Taxon* 41: 572. 1992): Herb. Linn. No. 917.4 (LINN).
Generitype of *Coronilla* Linnaeus, *nom. cons.*
Current name: ***Coronilla valentina*** L. (Fabaceae: Faboideae).
Note: Coronilla valentina, with the type designated by Lassen, was proposed as conserved type of the genus by Jarvis (in *Taxon* 41: 572. 1992). This was eventually approved by the General Committee (see review of the history of this proposal by Barrie, *l.c.* 55: 795–796. 2006).

Coronilla varia Linnaeus, *Species Plantarum* 2: 743. 1753.
"Habitat in Lusatia, Bohemia, Dania, Gallia." RCN: 5471.
Lectotype (Lassen in Turland & Jarvis in *Taxon* 46: 467. 1997): Herb. Linn. No. 917.12 (LINN).
Current name: ***Securigera varia*** (L.) Lassen (Fabaceae: Faboideae).

Corrigiola litoralis Linnaeus, *Species Plantarum* 1: 271. 1753.
"Habitat in Galliae, Germaniae litoribus arenosis." RCN: 2159.
Lectotype (Chaudhri, *Rev. Paronychiinae*: 37. 1968): Herb. Linn. No. 386.1 (LINN).
Generitype of *Corrigiola* Linnaeus.
Current name: ***Corrigiola litoralis*** L. (Caryophyllaceae).
Note: Jonsell & Jarvis (in Jarvis & al., *Regnum Veg.* 127: 38. 1993) chose Herb. Burser XVI: 44 (UPS) as lectotype, unaware of Chaudhri's earlier choice.

Cortusa gmelinii Linnaeus, *Species Plantarum* 1: 144. 1753.
"Habitat in Sibiria. D. Gmelin." RCN: 1157.
Type not designated.
Original material: *Steller*?, Herb. Linn. No. 199.5 (LINN).
Current name: ***Androsace gmelinii*** (L.) Gaertn. (Primulaceae).
Note: Specific epithet spelled "Gmelini" in the protologue.

Cortusa matthioli Linnaeus, *Species Plantarum* 1: 144. 1753.
"Habitat in alpibus Austriae, Sibiriae." RCN: 1156.
Type not designated.
Original material: Herb. Burser XIII: 155 (UPS); [icon] in Clusius,
Rar. Pl. Hist. 1: 307. 1601.
Generitype of *Cortusa* Linnaeus (vide Hitchcock, *Prop. Brit. Bot.*: 128.
1929).
Current name: ***Cortusa matthioli*** L. (Primulaceae).

Corylus avellana Linnaeus, *Species Plantarum* 2: 998. 1753.
"Habitat in Europae sepibus." RCN: 7238.
Lectotype (Sell in Jarvis & al., *Regnum Veg.* 127: 38. 1993): [icon]
"Avellana nux sylvestris" in Fuchs, Hist. Stirp.: 397, 398. 1542.
Generitype of *Corylus* Linnaeus (vide Green, *Prop. Brit. Bot.*: 189.
1929).
Current name: ***Corylus avellana*** L. (Betulaceae).
Note: Browicz (in Rechinger, *Fl. Iranica* 97: 4. 1972) indicated 1132.1
(LINN) as type but as this is annotated "byzantinus" by Linnaeus,
and appears to be a post-1753 addition to the herbarium, it cannot
be original material for the name.

Corylus colurna Linnaeus, *Species Plantarum* 2: 999. 1753.
"Habitat Byzantii." RCN: 7234.
Lectotype (Browicz in Rechinger, *Fl. Iranica* 97: 5. 1972): Herb. Linn.
No. 1132.4 (LINN).
Current name: ***Corylus colurna*** L. (Betulaceae).

Corymbium africanum Linnaeus, *Species Plantarum* 2: 928. 1753.
"Habitat in Aethopia." RCN: 6735.
Lectotype (Sprague in *Bull. Misc. Inform. Kew* 1940: 165. 1940):
Herb. Clifford: 494, *Corymbium* 1 (BM-000647672).
Generitype of *Corymbium* Linnaeus.
Current name: ***Corymbium africanum*** L. (Asteraceae).
Note: Weitz (in *S. African J. Bot.* 55: 602. 1989) accepted Sprague's
choice and illustrated the type sheet (as f. 1).

Corymbium glabrum Linnaeus, *Systema Naturae*, ed. 12, 2: 582. 1767.
RCN: 6735.
Lectotype (Weitz in *S. African J. Bot.* 55: 615. 1989): [icon] *"Bupleuri
similis Planta umbellata, Aethiopica, ad caulium nodos tomentosa"* in
Plukenet, Phytographia: t. 272, f. 4. 1694; Almag. Bot.: 73. 1696.
Current name: ***Corymbium glabrum*** L. (Asteraceae).

Corymbium scabrum Linnaeus, *Systema Naturae*, ed. 12, 2: 582;
Mantissa Plantarum: 120. 1767.
"Habitat ad Cap. b. spei." RCN: 6734.
Lectotype (Weitz in *S. African J. Bot.* 55: 605. 1989): [icon] *"Bupleuri
folia semine papposo, Valerianoides, Umbellata, cauliculo scabro, ex
Promontor Bon. Spei"* in Plukenet, Phytographia: t. 272, f. 5. 1694;
Almag. Bot.: 73. 1696.
Current name: ***Corymbium africanum*** L. subsp. ***scabridum*** (P.J.
Bergius) Weitz (Asteraceae).

Corypha thebaica Linnaeus, *Species Plantarum* 2: 1187. 1753.
RCN: 8543.
Lectotype (Moore & Dransfield in *Taxon* 28: 60, f. 4. 1979): [icon]
"Palma thebaica" in Pococke, Descr. East 1: 281, t. 73. 1743 (see p.
151).
Current name: ***Hyphaene thebaica*** (L.) Mart. (Arecaceae).

Corypha umbraculifera Linnaeus, *Species Plantarum* 2: 1187. 1753.
"Habitat in India." RCN: 8543.
Lectotype (Moore & Dransfield in *Taxon* 28: 60, f. 3. 1979): [icon]
"Codda-pana" in Rheede, Hort. Malab. 3: 1, t. 2, t. 10. 1682.
Generitype of *Corypha* Linnaeus.
Current name: ***Corypha umbraculifera*** L. (Arecaceae).

Costus arabicus Linnaeus, *Species Plantarum* 1: 2. 1753.
"Habitat in India utraque." RCN: 8.
Lectotype (Nicolson & al., *Interpret. Van Rheede's Hort. Malab.*: 316.
1988): [icon] *"Costus arabicus"* in Merian, Metamorph. Insect.
Surinam.: 36, t. 36. 1705 (see p. 142).
Generitype of *Costus* Linnaeus.
Current name: ***Costus arabicus*** L. (Zingiberaceae/Costaceae).
Note: Maas (in Howard, *Fl. Lesser Antilles* 3: 531. 1979) indicated as
type "a drawing by Ehret of a plant cultivated in the Hortus
Cliffortianus...It is deposited in the library of Sir Joseph Banks
(BM)". It seems most unlikely that Ehret's drawing (it is not cited
by Linnaeus) can be an original element for the name.

Cotula alba (Linnaeus) Linnaeus, *Systema Naturae,* ed. 12, 2: 564.
1767.
["Habitat in Virginia, Surinamo."] Sp. Pl. 2: 902 (1753). RCN: 6513.
Basionym: *Verbesina alba* L. (1753).
Lectotype (D'Arcy in Woodson & Schery in *Ann. Missouri Bot. Gard.*
62: 1102. 1975): Herb. Linn. No. 1020.1 (LINN).
Current name: ***Eclipta prostrata*** (L.) L. (Asteraceae).

Cotula anthemoides Linnaeus, *Species Plantarum* 2: 891. 1753.
"Habitat in Insula Helenae, Hispania." RCN: 6456.
Lectotype (Humphries in Jarvis & Turland in *Taxon* 47: 359. 1998):
Herb. Clifford: 417, *Cotula* 3 (BM-000647227).
Current name: ***Cotula anthemoides*** L. (Asteraceae).

Cotula capensis (Linnaeus) Linnaeus, *Mantissa Plantarum Altera*:
287. 1771.
"Habitat ad Cap. b. spei. H. U." RCN: 6466.
Basionym: *Matricaria capensis* L. (1767).
Type not designated.
Original material: as basionym.
Current name: ***Oncosiphon africanum*** (P.J. Bergius) Källersjö
(Asteraceae).

Cotula coronopifolia Linnaeus, *Species Plantarum* 2: 892. 1753.
"Habitat in Aethiopia, nunc in Frisiae inundatis prope Emdon.
Moehringio teste." RCN: 6459.
Lectotype (Dillon in *Fieldiana, Bot.,* n.s., 7: 6. 1981): Herb. Linn. No.
1014.13 (LINN).
Generitype of *Cotula* Linnaeus (vide Green, *Prop. Brit. Bot.*: 182.
1929).
Current name: ***Cotula coronopifolia*** L. (Asteraceae).
Note: Dillon's choice of type pre-dates that of Humphries (Herb.
Clifford: 417, *Cotula* 2, BM) in Jarvis & al. (*Regnum Veg.* 127: 38.
1993).

Cotula grandis Linnaeus, *Species Plantarum,* ed. 2, 2: 1257. 1763.
"Habitat in Barbaria." RCN: 6460.
Lectotype (Vogt & Oberprieler in *Willdenowia* 36: 62. 2006): *Brander,*
Herb. Linn. No. 1012.28 (LINN).
Current name: ***Plagius grandis*** (L.) Alavi & Heywood (Asteraceae).
Note: In the mistaken belief that no original material was extant,
Humphries (in Jarvis & Turland, *Taxon* 47: 359. 1998) designated a
neotype. However, Vogt & Oberprieler have noted that a Brander
collection from Algeria in LINN is in fact original material for the
name and designated it as the lectotype.

Cotula prostrata (Linnaeus) Linnaeus, *Systema Naturae*, ed. 12, 2: 564. 1767.

["Habitat in India."] Sp. Pl. 2: 902 (1753). RCN: 6514.

Basionym: *Verbesina prostrata* L. (1753).

Lectotype (Wijnands, *Bot. Commelins*: 74. 1983): [icon] *"Chrysanthemum Maderaspatanum, Menthae arvensis folio & facie, floribus bigemellis, ad foliorum alas, pediculis curtis"* in Plukenet, Phytographia: t. 118, f. 5. 1691; Almag. Bot.: 100. 1696. – Typotype: Herb. Sloane 94: 175 (BM-SL).

Current name: ***Eclipta prostrata*** (L.) L. (Asteraceae).

Note: D'Arcy (in *Ann. Missouri Bot. Gard.* 62: 1102. 1975) indicated 1020.4 or 1020.5 (LINN) as the type of the basionym, presumably in error as both are associated with the name "Eclipta latifolia" rather than *V. prostrata*. Neither they, nor 1020.7 (LINN), the post-1753 Patrick Browne collection treated as the lectotype by Kupicha (in Davis, *Fl. Turkey* 5: 46. 1975), are original material for the name. Grierson (in Dassanayake & Fosberg, *Revised Handb. Fl. Ceylon* 1: 212. 1980) treated material in Herb. Plukenet (BM-SL) as "type", but this would not have been seen by Linnaeus and is not original material either. Wijnands' 1983 choice of the Plukenet illustration as lectotype is therefore accepted here.

Cotula pyrethraria Linnaeus, *Mantissa Plantarum*: 116. 1767.

"Habitat in America." RCN: 6465.

Lectotype (Keil & Stuessy in *Syst. Bot.* 6: 284. 1981): Herb. Linn. No. 974.6 (LINN).

Current name: ***Acmella oleracea*** (L.) R.K. Jansen (Asteraceae).

Cotula spilanthes Linnaeus, *Mantissa Plantarum*: 116. 1767, *nom. illeg.*

"Habitat Carthagenae in Arenosis maritimis." RCN: 6011.

Replaced synonym: *Spilanthes urens* Jacq. (1760).

Type not designated.

Current name: ***Spilanthes urens*** Jacq. (Asteraceae).

Note: An illegitimate renaming of *S. urens* Jacq. (1760), as noted by Jansen (in *Syst. Bot.* 6: 253. 1981).

Cotula stricta Linnaeus, *Systema Naturae*, ed. 12, 2: 734. 1767.

"Habitat in Aethiopia. D. Burmannus." RCN: 6458.

Lectotype (Humphries in Jarvis & Turland in *Taxon* 47: 359. 1998): Herb. Linn. No. 1014.12 (LINN).

Current name: ***Lidbeckia pectinata*** P.J. Bergius (Asteraceae).

Cotula tanacetifolia Linnaeus, *Systema Naturae*, ed. 12, 2: 564. 1767, *nom. illeg.*

["Habitat in Aethiopia."] Sp. Pl. 2: 843 (1753). RCN: 6463.

Replaced synonym: *Tanacetum suffruticosum* L. (1753).

Lectotype (Wijnands, *Bot. Commelins*: 80. 1983): Herb. Linn. No. 987.11 (LINN).

Current name: ***Oncosiphon suffruticosum*** (L.) Källersjö (Asteraceae).

Cotula turbinata Linnaeus, *Species Plantarum* 2: 892. 1753.

"Habitat in Aethiopia." RCN: 6462.

Lectotype (Humphries in Jarvis & Turland in *Taxon* 47: 359. 1998): Herb. Clifford: 417, *Cotula* 1 (BM-000647224).

Current name: ***Cotula turbinata*** L. (Asteraceae).

Cotula verbesina Linnaeus, *Systema Naturae*, ed. 10, 2: 1222. 1759.

["Habitat in Jamaica."] Sp. Pl., ed. 2, 2: 1258 (1763). RCN: 6464.

Lectotype (Robinson in Jarvis & Turland in *Taxon* 47: 359. 1998): *Browne*, Herb. Linn. No. 1014.25 (LINN).

Current name: ***Adenostemma verbesina*** (L.) Kuntze (Asteraceae).

Cotula viscosa Linnaeus, *Species Plantarum* 2: 892. 1753.

"Habitat in Vera Cruse [sic]." RCN: 6461.

Lectotype (Nesom in Jarvis & Turland in *Taxon* 47: 359. 1998): Herb. Clifford: 417, *Cotula* 4 (BM-000647228).

Current name: ***Egletes viscosa*** (L.) Less. (Asteraceae).

Cotyledon hemispherica Linnaeus, *Species Plantarum* 1: 429. 1753.

"Habitat in Aethiopia." RCN: 3339.

Lectotype (Smith in *Bothalia* 3: 625. 1939): [icon] *"Cotyledon Capensis, folio semiglobato"* in Dillenius, Hort. Eltham. 1: 112, t. 95, f. 111. 1732.

Current name: ***Adromischus hemisphaericus*** (L.) Lem. (Crassulaceae).

Note: Edmondson & Rowley (in *Bradleya* 16: 15, f. 4. 1998) reproduced the type illustration in colour.

Cotyledon hispanica Linnaeus, *Species Plantarum* 2: 1196. 1753.

"Habitat in Hispania. Loefling." RCN: 3343.

Lectotype (designated here by Castroviejo): Herb. Linn. No. 594.6 (LINN).

Current name: ***Pistorinia hispanica*** (L.) DC. (Crassulaceae).

Note: Although 't Hart (in Eggli, *Ill. Handb. Succ. Pl., Crassulaceae*: 204. 2003) indicated a Löfling collection in LINN (presumably 594.6), the statement lacked the "designated here" (Art. 7.11) necessary since 2001 for typification to be effected.

Cotyledon laciniata Linnaeus, *Species Plantarum* 1: 430. 1753.

"Habitat in Aegypto." RCN: 3342.

Lectotype (Fernandes in *Bol. Soc. Brot.*, sér. 2, 53: 376. 1980): Herb. Clifford: 175, *Cotyledon* 1 (BM-000628567).

Current name: ***Kalanchoë laciniata*** (L.) DC. (Crassulaceae).

Note: Cufodontis (in *Webbia* 19: 734. 1965) stated that Linnaeus received the type from Egypt but did not indicate what he believed the type to be.

Cotyledon orbiculata Linnaeus, *Species Plantarum* 1: 429. 1753, *typ. cons.*

"Habitat ad Cap. b. Spei." RCN: 3337.

Conserved type (Tölken in Jarvis in *Taxon* 41: 561. 1992): [icon] *"Sedum Africanum frutescens incanum orbiculatis foliis"* in Hermann, Hort. Lugd.-Bat. Cat.: 549, 551. 1687.

Generitype of *Cotyledon* Linnaeus, *nom. cons.*

Current name: ***Cotyledon orbiculata*** L. (Crassulaceae).

Note: Cotyledon orbiculata, with the type proposed by Tölken, was proposed as conserved type of the genus by Jarvis (in *Taxon* 41: 561. 1992). This was eventually approved by the General Committee (see review of the history of this proposal by Barrie, *l.c.* 55: 795–796. 2006).

Cotyledon serrata Linnaeus, *Species Plantarum* 1: 429. 1753.

"Habitat in Creta, Sibiria." RCN: 3340.

Type not designated.

Original material: [icon] in Dillenius, Hort. Eltham. 1: 113, t. 95, f. 112. 1732.

Current name: ***Rosularia serrata*** (L.) A. Berger (Crassulaceae).

Note: Eggli (in *Bradleya* 6, Suppl.: 103. 1988) wrongly indicated 595.4 (LINN) as the lectotype, the same sheet he also designated (correctly) as the lectotype of *Sedum libanoticum* L. (1759). Edmondson & Rowley (in *Bradleya* 16: 15, f. 4. 1998) have reproduced the cited Dillenius illustration in colour.

Cotyledon spinosa Linnaeus, *Species Plantarum* 1: 429. 1753.

"Habitat in Sibiria. D. Gmelin." RCN: 2244.

Basionym: *Crassula spinosa* (L.) L. (1771).

Neotype (Byalt in *Novosti Sist. Vyssh. Rast.* 32: 45. 2000): Herb. Linn. No. 400.10 (LINN).

Current name: ***Orostachys spinosa*** (L.) Sweet (Crassulaceae).

Note: In the absence of original material, Byalt's lectotype choice is treated as correctable to a neotype (Art. 9.8).

Cotyledon spuria Linnaeus, *Species Plantarum*, ed. 2, 1: 614. 1762.
"Habitat ad Cap. b. Spei." RCN: 3338.
Lectotype (Tölken in *Bothalia* 12: 619. 1979): [icon] *"Cotyledon Afric. frutesc. folio longo et angusto"* in Commelin, Hort. Med. Amstelaed. Pl. Rar.: 23, t. 23. 1706.
Current name: *Cotyledon orbiculata* (L.) Tölken var. *spuria* (L.) Tölken (Crassulaceae).
Note: The type illustration is figured by van Jaarsveld & Koutnik (Cotyledon *and* Tylecodon: 11, f. 12. 2004).

Cotyledon umbilicus-veneris Linnaeus, *Species Plantarum* 1: 429. 1753.
"Habitat in Lusitania." RCN: 3341.
Type not designated.
Original material: Herb. Linn. No. 594.8? (LINN); Herb. Linn. No. 594.2 (LINN).
Current name: *Umbilicus rupestris* (Salisb.) Dandy (Crassulaceae).
Note: See Fröderstrom (in *Acta Horti Gothob.* 7, App.: 125, pl. LIX. 1932), and Webb (in *Feddes Repert.* 64: 23. 1961), the latter rejecting the name as confused and dubious.

Cotyledon umbilicus-veneris Linnaeus var. **repens** Linnaeus, *Species Plantarum* 1: 429. 1753.
RCN: 3341.
Type not designated.
Original material: [icon] in Mattioli, Pl. Epit.: 858. 1586; [icon] in Dodart, Mém. Acad. Roy. Sci. Paris 1666–1699 4: 265, t. 4. 1731.
Current name: *Umbilicus luteus* (Huds.) Webb & Berthel. (Crassulaceae).
Note: Although some authors have treated *U. erectus* DC. as the correct name for this taxon, it is superfluous as *C. lutea* Huds. (and *C. lusitanica* Lam.) are cited in its protologue (see López González in *Anales Jard. Bot. Madrid* 51: 171. 1993).

Cotyledon umbilicus-veneris Linnaeus var. **tuberosa** Linnaeus, *Species Plantarum* 1: 429. 1753.
RCN: 3341.
Type not designated.
Original material: Herb. Burser XVI: 93 (UPS); [icon] in Clusius, Rar. Pl. Hist. 2: 62, 63. 1601; [icon] in Bauhin & Cherler, Hist. Pl. Univ. 3(2): 683, 684. 1651; [icon] in Morison, Pl. Hist. Univ. 3: 470, s. 12, t. 10, f. 4. 1699.
Current name: *Umbilicus rupestris* (Salisb.) Dandy (Crassulaceae).

Cracca maxima Linnaeus, *Species Plantarum* 2: 752. 1753.
"Habitat in Zeylona." RCN: 5564.
Basionym of: *Galega maxima* (L.) L. (1759).
Lectotype (Gillett in Milne-Redhead & Polhill, *Fl. Trop. E. Africa, Leguminosae* 3: 201. 1971): Herb. Hermann 3: 56, No. 300 (BM-000594698).
Current name: *Tephrosia maxima* (L.) Pers. (Fabaceae: Faboideae).

Cracca purpurea Linnaeus, *Species Plantarum* 2: 752. 1753.
"Habitat in Zeylona." RCN: 5565.
Basionym of: *Galega purpurea* (L.) L. (1759).
Lectotype (Fawcett & Rendle, *Fl. Jamaica* 4: 19. 1920; Ali in *Biologia (Lahore)* 10: 28. 1964): Herb. Hermann 1: 37, No. 301 (BM-000621363).
Generitype of *Cracca* Linnaeus, *nom. rej.*
Current name: *Tephrosia purpurea* (L.) Pers. (Fabaceae: Faboideae).
Note: Cracca villosa was treated as the generitype by Britton & Brown, *Ill. Fl. N. U. S.*, ed. 2, 2: 372. 1913 (see McNeill & al. in *Taxon* 36: 366. 1987). However, under Art. 10.5, Ex. 7 (a voted example) of the Vienna Code, this is a type choice made under the American

Code and is to be replaced under Art. 10.5b by Green's choice (*Prop. Brit. Bot.*: 176. 1929) of *C. purpurea* L.
Fawcett & Rendle (*Fl. Jamaica* 4: 19. 1920) indicated Herb. Hermann material (BM) as type. Although there is material in two separate volumes, it appears to have been part of a single gathering. Consequently, theirs is accepted as the first typification (Art. 9.15), with the choice subsequently restricted by Ali. Although Forbes (in *Bothalia* 4: 974. 1948) designated 924.7 (LINN) as the type, this choice is pre-dated by that of Fawcett & Rendle.

Cracca senticosa Linnaeus, *Species Plantarum* 2: 752. 1753.
"Habitat in Zeylona." RCN: 5568.
Basionym of: *Galega senticosa* (L.) L. (1763); *Galega fruticosa* L. (1759), *nom. illeg.*
Lectotype (Bosman & de Haas in *Blumea* 28: 470. 1983): Herb. Hermann 1: 72, No. 303 (BM-000594504).
Current name: *Tephrosia senticosa* (L.) Pers. (Fabaceae: Faboideae).

Cracca tinctoria Linnaeus, *Species Plantarum* 2: 752. 1753.
"Habitat in Zeylona." RCN: 5567.
Basionym of: *Galega tinctoria* (L.) L. (1759).
Lectotype (Rudd in Dassanayake & Fosberg, *Revised Handb. Fl. Ceylon* 7: 146. 1991): Herb. Hermann 3: 28, No. 302 (BM-000594670).
Current name: *Tephrosia tinctoria* (L.) Pers. (Fabaceae: Faboideae).

Cracca villosa Linnaeus, *Species Plantarum* 2: 752. 1753.
"Habitat in India." RCN: 5563.
Basionym of: *Galega villosa* (L.) L. (1759).
Lectotype (Gillett in *Kew Bull.* 13: 121. 1958; Ali in *Biologia (Lahore)* 10: 25. 1964): Herb. Hermann 1: 31, No. 299 (BM-000621337).
Current name: *Tephrosia villosa* (L.) Pers. (Fabaceae: Faboideae).
Note: Cracca Linnaeus, *nom. rej.* in favour of *Cracca* Benth., but without a listed type.
Cracca villosa was treated as the generitype by Britton & Brown, *Ill. Fl. N. U. S.*, ed. 2, 2: 372. 1913 (see McNeill & al. in *Taxon* 36: 366. 1987). However, under Art. 10.5, Ex. 7 (a voted example) of the Vienna Code, this is a type choice made under the American Code and is to be replaced under Art. 10.5b by Green's choice (*Prop. Brit. Bot.*: 176. 1929) of *C. purpurea* L.
Gillett indicated Herb. Hermann material (BM) as type. Although there is material in two separate volumes, it appears to have been part of a single gathering. Consequently, his is accepted as the first typification (Art. 9.15), with the choice subsequently restricted by Ali.

Cracca virginiana Linnaeus, *Species Plantarum* 2: 752. 1753.
"Habitat in Virginia, Canada." RCN: 5562.
Basionym of: *Galega virginiana* (L.) L. (1759).
Lectotype (Wood in *Rhodora* 51: 267. 1949): *Kalm*, Herb. Linn. No. 924.4 (LINN; iso- UPS).
Current name: *Tephrosia virginiana* (L.) Pers. (Fabaceae: Faboideae).
Note: Britten & Baker (in *J. Bot.* 29: 12–19. 1900) provide a detailed study of the two species included within Linnaeus' concept of this name and present a synonymy (with accepted names subsequently reversed, *l.c.*: 53). However, they did not designate a type.

Crambe hispanica Linnaeus, *Species Plantarum* 2: 671. 1753.
"Habitat in Hispania." RCN: 4891.
Lectotype (Jonsell in Polhill, *Fl. Trop. E. Africa, Cruciferae*: 16. 1982): Herb. Linn. No. 849.5 (LINN).
Current name: *Crambe hispanica* L. (Brassicaceae).

Crambe maritima Linnaeus, *Species Plantarum* 2: 671. 1753.
"Habitat ad littora Oceani septentrionalis." RCN: 4889.

Lectotype (Khalilov in *Bot. Zhurn.* 78(1): 114. 1993): Herb. Linn. No. 849.1 (LINN).

Generitype of *Crambe* Linnaeus (vide Green, *Prop. Brit. Bot.*: 172. 1929).

Current name: ***Crambe maritima*** L. (Brassicaceae).

Note: Hedge (in Jarvis & al., *Regnum Veg.* 127: 38. 1993), unaware of Khalilov's slightly earlier choice, designated Herb. Clifford: 340, *Crambe* 1 (BM) as lectotype.

Crambe orientalis Linnaeus, *Species Plantarum* 2: 671. 1753.

"Habitat in Oriente." RCN: 4890.

Lectotype (Khalilov in *Bot. Zhurn.* 78(1): 112. 1993): Herb. Linn. No. 849.3 (LINN).

Current name: ***Crambe orientalis*** L. (Brassicaceae).

Craniolaria annua Linnaeus, *Species Plantarum* 2: 618. 1753.

"Habitat in America." RCN: 4471.

Lectotype (Barrie in Jarvis & al., *Regnum Veg.* 127: 38. 1993): [icon] *"Martynia annua, villosa et viscosa, Aceris folio flore albo tubo longissimo"* in Ehret, Pl. Papil. Rar.: t. 1, f. 2. 1748 (see p. 129).

Generitype of *Craniolaria* Linnaeus (vide Green, *Prop. Brit. Bot.*: 167. 1929).

Current name: ***Craniolaria annua*** L. (Pedaliaceae).

Craniolaria fruticosa Linnaeus, *Species Plantarum* 2: 618. 1753.

"Habitat in America calidiore." RCN: 4470.

Type not designated.

Original material: none traced.

Current name: ***Gesneria fruticosa*** (L.) Kuntze (Gesneriaceae).

Crassula alternifolia Linnaeus, *Species Plantarum* 1: 283. 1753.

"Habitat – – – – –" RCN: 2253.

Type not designated.

Original material: none traced.

Note: The application of this name is uncertain (see Tölken in *J. S. African Bot.* 38: 68. 1972; in Leistner, *Fl. Southern Africa* 14: 229. 1985).

Crassula caffra Linnaeus, *Mantissa Plantarum Altera*: 222. 1771.

"Habitat ad Cap. b. Spei. H. U." RCN: 2240.

Neotype (Heath in *Calyx* 4: 33. 1993): Herb. Linn. No. 400.6 (LINN).

Current name: ***Crassula tetragona*** L. (Crassulaceae).

Note: Heath's neotypification made *C. caffra* a homotypic synonym of *C. tetragona* L.

Crassula centauroides Linnaeus, *Plantae Rariores Africanae*: 9. 1760.

["Habitat in Aethiopia."] Sp. Pl., ed. 2, 1: 404 (1762). RCN: 2245.

Lectotype (Tölken in *J. S. African Bot.* 38: 75. 1972): *"Crassula dichotoma"*, Herb. Burman (G).

Current name: ***Crassula strigosa*** L. (Crassulaceae).

Note: Heath (in *Calyx* 4: 34. 1993) has treated Tölken's statement as a neotypification.

Crassula ciliata Linnaeus, *Species Plantarum* 1: 283. 1753.

"Habitat in Aethiopia." RCN: 2250.

Lectotype (Tölken in *J. S. African Bot.* 38: 68. 1972): [icon] *"Crassula caulescens, foliis Sempervivi cruciatis"* in Dillenius, Hort. Eltham. 1: 116, t. 98, f. 116. 1732.

Current name: ***Crassula ciliata*** L. (Crassulaceae).

Note: Schonland (in *Trans. Roy. Soc. S. Africa* 17: 264. 1929) treated material in Herb. Sherard (OXF) as the type, but this was not seen by Linnaeus and is not original material for the name.

Crassula coccinea Linnaeus, *Species Plantarum* 1: 282. 1753.

"Habitat in Aethiopia." RCN: 2234.

Lectotype (Tölken in *J. S. African Bot.* 38: 69. 1972): Herb. Clifford: 116, *Crassula* 1 (BM-000558479).

Current name: ***Crassula coccinea*** L. (Crassulaceae).

Note: Heath (in *Calyx* 3: 42. 1993) argued erroneously that the Clifford collection was not original material for the name, and that the cited Commelin plate was the holotype.

Crassula cultrata Linnaeus, *Species Plantarum* 1: 283. 1753.

"Habitat in Aethiopia." RCN: 2243.

Lectotype (Tölken in *J. S. African Bot.* 38: 69. 1972): [icon] *"Crassula Anacampserotis folio"* in Dillenius, Hort. Eltham. 1: 115, t. 97, f. 114. 1732.

Current name: ***Crassula cultrata*** L. (Crassulaceae).

Note: Schonland (in *Trans. Roy. Soc. S. Africa* 17: 270. 1929) treated what is evidently 400.9 (LINN) as the type, but this is annotated only by Linnaeus filius and is evidently a post-1753 addition to the collection and not original material for the name.

Crassula dichotoma Linnaeus, *Plantae Rariores Africanae*: 9. 1760.

["Habitat in Aethiopia."] Sp. Pl., ed. 2, 1: 405 (1762). RCN: 2246.

Lectotype (Tölken in *J. S. African Bot.* 38: 69. 1972): [icon] *"Sedum Africanum annuum, Centaurii minoris facie, flore aureo"* in Hermann, Hort. Lugd.-Bat. Cat.: 550, 553. 1687.

Current name: ***Crassula dichotoma*** L. (Crassulaceae).

Crassula flava Linnaeus, *Systema Naturae*, ed. 12, 2: 225; *Mantissa Plantarum*: 60. 1767.

"Habitat ad Cap. b. spei." RCN: 2236.

Lectotype (Schonland, *Trans. Roy. Soc. S. Africa* 17: 217. 1929): Herb. Linn. No. 400.3 (LINN).

Current name: ***Crassula flava*** L. (Crassulaceae).

Crassula fruticulosa Linnaeus, *Systema Naturae*, ed. 12, 2: 226; *Mantissa Plantarum*: 61. 1767.

"Habitat ad Cap. b. spei." RCN: 2240.

Neotype (Heath in *Calyx* 4: 42. 1994): [icon] *"Cotyledonoidas Afric."* in Bradley, Hist. Pl. Succ. 5: 18, t. 41. 1727 (see p. 110).

Current name: ***Crassula tetragona*** L. (Crassulaceae).

Note: Tölken (in *J. S. African Bot.* 38: 78. 1972; in Leistner, *Fl. Southern Africa* 14: 229. 1985) treated this as insufficiently known (in the absence of type material), but Heath's neotypification makes the name a synonym of *C. tetragona* L. (1753).

Crassula glomerata Linnaeus, *Systema Naturae*, ed. 12, 2: 226; *Mantissa Plantarum*: 60. 1767, *nom. illeg.*

"Habitat ad Cap. b. spei." RCN: 2247.

Type not designated.

Original material: Herb. Linn. No. 400.16 (LINN).

Current name: ***Crassula glomerata*** P.J. Bergius (Crassulaceae).

Note: As noted by Tölken (in *J. S. African Bot.* 38: 70. 1972), *C. glomerata* P.J. Bergius (1767) was published about a month before *C. glomerata* L. Bergius' name is typified by his own material in SBT, and Tölken suggested that Linnaeus' very detailed description was based partly on living material, and partly on material in LINN. *Crasssula glomerata* L. is therefore almost certainly heterotypic with respect to *C. glomerata* P.J. Bergius, and thus a later homonym.

Crassula muscosa Linnaeus, *Plantae Rariores Africanae*: 10. 1760.

["Habitat in Aethiopia."] Sp. Pl., ed. 2, 1: 405 (1762). RCN: 2249.

Lectotype (Tölken in *J. S. African Bot.* 38: 70. 1972): Cape, Herb. Burman (G).

Current name: ***Crassula muscosa*** L. (Crassulaceae).

Crassula nudicaulis Linnaeus, *Species Plantarum* 1: 283. 1753.
"Habitat in Aethiopia." RCN: 2256.
Lectotype (Tölken in *J. S. African Bot.* 38: 71. 1972): [icon] *"Crassula caesposa longifolia"* in Dillenius, Hort. Eltham. 1: 116, t. 98, f. 115. 1732.
Current name: ***Crassula nudicaulis*** L. (Crassulaceae).
Note: Schonland (in *Trans. Roy. Soc. S. Africa* 17: 279. 1929) treated material in Herb. Sherard (OXF) as the type but this was not seen by Linnaeus and is not original material for the name.

Crassula obvallata Linnaeus, *Systema Naturae*, ed. 12, 2: 226; *Mantissa Plantarum*: 61. 1767.
"Habitat ad Cap. b. spei." RCN: 2242.
Type not designated.
Original material: none traced.
Current name: ***Crassula nudicaulis*** L. (Crassulaceae).

Crassula orbicularis Linnaeus, *Species Plantarum* 1: 283. 1753.
"Habitat in Aethiopia." RCN: 2257.

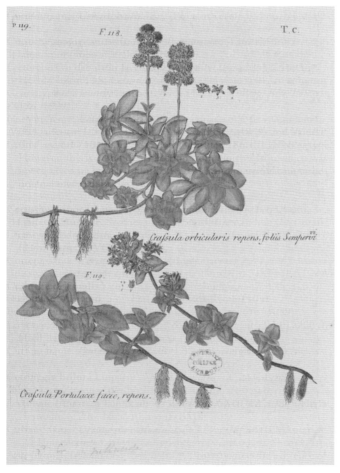

Lectotype (Tölken in *J. S. African Bot.* 38: 71. 1972): [icon] *"Crassula orbicularis repens, foliis Sempervivi"* in Dillenius, Hort. Eltham. 1: 119, t. 100, f. 118. 1732.
Current name: ***Crassula orbicularis*** L. (Crassulaceae).
Note: See notes on specimens in OXF and LINN by Schonland (in *Trans. Roy. Soc. S. Africa* 17: 245. 1929).

Crassula pellucida Linnaeus, *Species Plantarum* 1: 283. 1753.
"Habitat in Aethiopia." RCN: 2258.

Lectotype (Tölken in *J. S. African Bot.* 38: 71. 1972): [icon] *"Crassula Portulacae facie, repens"* in Dillenius, Hort. Eltham. 1: 119, t. 100, f. 119. 1732.
Current name: ***Crassula pellucida*** L. (Crassulaceae).
Note: Schonland (in *Trans. Roy. Soc. S. Africa* 17: 192, 194. 1929) treated material in Herb. Sherard (OXF) as the type. However, this was not studied by Linnaeus and is not original material for the name.

Crassula perfoliata Linnaeus, *Species Plantarum* 1: 282. 1753.
"Habitat in Aethiopia." RCN: 2239.
Lectotype (Wijnands, *Bot. Commelins*: 90. 1983): [icon] *"Crassula altissima perforata"* in Dillenius, Hort. Eltham. 1: 114, t. 96, f. 113. 1732. – Typotype: Herb. Dillenius (OXF).
Generitype of *Crassula* Linnaeus (vide Hitchcock, *Prop. Brit. Bot.*: 143. 1929).
Current name: ***Crassula perfoliata*** L. var. ***perfoliata*** (Crassulaceae).
Note: Schonland (in *Trans. Roy. Soc. S. Africa* 17: 224. 1929) treated material in Herb. Sherard (OXF) as the type, as presumably did Tölken (in *J. S. African Bot.* 38: 71. 1972) (in the Dillenian herbarium). However, this was not studied by Linnaeus and is not original material for the name.

Crassula portulacaria Linnaeus, *Species Plantarum*, ed. 2, 1: 406. 1762.
"Habitat in Aethiopia." RCN: 1652.
Basionym of: *Claytonia portulacaria* (L.) L. (1771).
Lectotype (Tölken in *J. S. African Bot.* 38: 73. 1972): [icon] *"Crassula Portulacae facie, arborescens"* in Dillenius, Hort. Eltham. 1: 120, t. 101, f. 120. 1732.
Current name: ***Portulacaria afra*** Jacq. (Portulacaceae).

Crassula pruinosa Linnaeus, *Systema Naturae*, ed. 12, 2: 226; *Mantissa Plantarum*: 60. 1767.
"Habitat ad Cap. b. spei." RCN: 2237.
Lectotype (Schonland, *Trans. Roy. Soc. S. Africa* 17: 222. 1929): Herb. Linn. No. 400.4 (LINN).
Current name: ***Crassula pruinosa*** L. (Crassulaceae).

Crassula punctata Linnaeus, *Systema Naturae*, ed. 10, 2: 969. 1759.
["Habitat in Aethiopia. Burmannus."] Sp. Pl., ed. 2, 1: 406 (1762). RCN: 2251.
Neotype (Heath in *Calyx* 5: 68. 1995): Herb. Alströmer, *"Crassula punctata"* annot. Dahl (S).
Current name: ***Crassula punctata*** L. (Crassulaceae).
Note: Tölken (in *J. S. African Bot.* 38: 74. 1972; *Contr. Bolus Herb.* 8: 557. 1977; in Leistner, *Fl. Southern Africa* 14: 229. 1985) treated the name as insufficiently known, having been unable to trace any type material. Heath subsequently designated a neotype which is apparently identifiable as *C. capitella* Thunb. subsp. *thyrsiflora* (Thunb.) Tölken, but it does not seem to have been taken up in this sense by Heath, nor proposed for rejection.

Crassula rubens (Linnaeus) Linnaeus, *Systema Naturae*, ed. 10, 2: 969. 1759.
["Habitat in Gallia, Italia."] Sp. Pl. 1: 432 (1753). RCN: 2254.
Basionym: *Sedum rubens* L. (1753).
Lectotype ('t Hart & Jarvis in *Taxon* 42: 405. 1993): Herb. Burser XVI(1): 62 (UPS).
Current name: ***Sedum rubens*** L. (Crassulaceae).

Crassula scabra Linnaeus, *Species Plantarum* 1: 283. 1753.
"Habitat in Africa." RCN: 2238.
Lectotype (Tölken in *J. S. African Bot.* 38: 75. 1972): [icon] *"Crassula Mesembryanthemi facie, foliis longioribus asperis"* in Dillenius, Hort. Eltham. 1: 117, t. 99, f. 117. 1732.

C

Current name: ***Crassula scabra*** L. (Crassulaceae).
Note: Schonland (in *Trans. Roy. Soc. S. Africa* 17: 220. 1929) treated material in Herb. Sherard (OXF) as the type. However, this was not studied by Linnaeus and is not original material for the name.

Crassula spinosa (Linnaeus) Linnaeus, *Mantissa Plantarum Altera*: 388. 1771.
["Habitat in Sibiria. D. Gmelin."] Sp. Pl. 1: 429 (1753). RCN: 2244.
Basionym: *Cotyledon spinosa* L. (1753).
Neotype (Byalt in *Novosti Sist. Vyssh. Rast.* 32: 45. 2000): Herb. Linn. No. 400.10 (LINN).
Current name: ***Orostachys spinosa*** (L.) Sweet (Crassulaceae).

Crassula strigosa Linnaeus, *Plantae Rariores Africanae*: 10. 1760.
["Habitat in Aethiopia."] Sp. Pl., ed. 2, 1: 405 (1762). RCN: 2248.
Lectotype (Tölken in *J. S. African Bot.* 38: 75. 1972): Herb. Burman (G).
Current name: ***Crassula strigosa*** L. (Crassulaceae).

Crassula subulata Linnaeus, *Systema Naturae, ed. 10*, 2: 969. 1759.
["Habitat in Aethiopia."] Sp. Pl., ed. 2, 1: 404 (1762). RCN: 2252.
Lectotype (Tölken in *J. S. African Bot.* 38: 76. 1972): [icon] *"Sedum Africanum umbellatum album"* in Hermann, Hort. Lugd.-Bat. Cat.: 550, 552. 1687.
Current name: ***Crassula subulata*** L. (Crassulaceae).
Note: See Schonland (in *Trans. Roy. Soc. S. Africa* 17: 260. 1929), who suggested that the name be abandoned.

Crassula tetragona Linnaeus, *Species Plantarum* 1: 283. 1753.
"Habitat in Aethiopia." RCN: 2241.
Lectotype (Tölken in *J. S. African Bot.* 38: 78. 1972): Herb. Linn. No. 400.6 (LINN).
Current name: ***Crassula tetragona*** L. (Crassulaceae).

Crassula verticillaris Linnaeus, *Systema Naturae, ed. 12*, 3: 230. 1768.
"Habitat in . . . (enata e variis mictis seminibus)." RCN: 2255.
Type not designated.
Original material: none traced.
Current name: ***Sedum sp.*** (Crassulaceae).
Note: The application of this name is uncertain (see Tölken in Leistner, *Fl. Southern Africa* 14: 229. 1985).

Crataegus aria Linnaeus, *Species Plantarum* 1: 475. 1753.
"Habitat in Europae, Helvetiae, frigidis." RCN: 3640.
Lectotype (Aldasoro & al. in *Syst. Bot. Monogr.* 69: 108. 2004): Herb. Clifford: 187, *Crataegus* 1 (BM).
Current name: ***Sorbus aria*** (L.) Crantz (Rosaceae).

Crataegus aria Linnaeus var. **suecica**, *Species Plantarum* 1: 476. 1753.
"Habitat in Suecia, Anglia." RCN: 3640.
Type not designated.
Original material: none traced.
Current name: ***Sorbus intermedia*** (Ehrh.) Pers. (Rosaceae).

Crataegus azarolus Linnaeus, *Species Plantarum* 1: 477. 1753.
"Habitat Florentiae, Monspelii." RCN: 3648.
Lectotype (Christensen in Cafferty & Jarvis in *Taxon* 51: 541. 2002): Herb. Burser XXIV: 3, excluding lower shoot (UPS).
Current name: ***Crataegus azarolus*** L. var. ***azarolus*** (Rosaceae).
Note: Christensen reviews earlier type statements and provides the rationale for his formal typification, which is accepted here.

Crataegus azarolus Linnaeus var. **aronia** Linnaeus, *Species Plantarum* 1: 477. 1753.
RCN: 3648.
Lectotype (Christensen in *Syst. Bot. Monogr.* 35: 33. 1992): [icon] *"Mespilus Orientalis"* in Pococke, Descr. East 2: 189, t. 85. 1745.
Current name: ***Crataegus azarolus*** L. var. ***aronia*** L. (Rosaceae).

Crataegus coccinea Linnaeus, *Species Plantarum* 1: 476. 1753.
"Habitat in Virginia, Canada." RCN: 3642.
Lectotype (Phipps & al. in *Taxon* 52: 338. 2003): Herb. Clifford: 187, *Crataegus* 3, sheet B (BM-000628618).
Current name: ***Crataegus coccinea*** L. (Rosaceae).
Note: Phipps & al. provide a detailed review of the history of this name.

Crataegus coccinea Linnaeus var. **viridis** (Linnaeus) Linnaeus, *Mantissa Plantarum Altera*: 397. 1771.
["Habitat in Virginia."] Sp. Pl. 1: 476 (1753). RCN: 3643.
Basionym: *Crataegus viridis* L. (1753).
Lectotype (Eggleston in *Rhodora* 10: 83. 1908): *Clayton 526* (BM).
Current name: ***Crataegus viridis*** L. (Rosaceae).

Crataegus crus-galli Linnaeus, *Species Plantarum* 1: 476. 1753.
["Habitat in Virginia."] Sp. Pl., ed. 2, 1: 632 (1762). RCN: 3644.
Lectotype (Phipps in *Bot. J. Linn. Soc.* 96: 365, f. 2. 1988): *Kalm*, Herb. Linn. No. 643.9 (LINN).
Current name: ***Crataegus crus-galli*** L. (Rosaceae).

Crataegus hybrida Linnaeus, *Fauna Suecica*, ed. 2: 557. 1761, *nom. nud.*
RCN: 3650.
Type not relevant.
Note: Hensen (in *Belmontia Hort.* 5(22): 190. 1961) appears to regard *C. hybrida* as a valid name and the basionym of "*Sorbus hybrida* (L.) L." (1762). However, Sell (in *Watsonia* 17: 386. 1989) regards *C. hybrida* as a *nomen nudum*, and *S. hybrida* as a new name dating from 1762.

Crataegus indica Linnaeus, *Species Plantarum* 1: 477. 1753.
"Habitat in India." RCN: 3646.
Lectotype (Vidal in Aubréville, *Fl. Cambodge Laos Vietnam* 5: 85. 1967): Herb. Linn. No. 643.11 (LINN).
Current name: ***Rhaphiolepis indica*** (L.) Ker-Gawl. (Rosaceae).

Crataegus oxyacantha Linnaeus, *Species Plantarum* 1: 477. 1753, *nom. utique rej.*
"Habitat in Europae pratis apricis duris." RCN: 3647.
Lectotype (Dandy in *Rep. Bot. Soc. Exch. Club Brit. Isles* 12: 868. 1946): Herb. Linn. No. 643.12 (LINN).
Generitype of *Crataegus* Linnaeus.
Current name: ***Crataegus rhipidophylla*** Gand. (Rosaceae).

Crataegus tomentosa Linnaeus, *Species Plantarum* 1: 476. 1753.
"Habitat in Virginia." RCN: 3645.
Type not designated.
Original material: *Clayton 55* (BM); *Kalm*, Herb. Linn. No. 643.10 (LINN).
Current name: ***Crataegus calpodendron*** (Ehrh.) Medik. (Rosaceae).
Note: This name has been discussed by Eggleston (in *Rhodora* 10: 78. 1908), Sargent (in *Rhodora* 11: 182. 1909) and Palmer (in *J. Arnold Arb.* 19: 287. 1938), who proposed it should be treated as a *nomen ambiguum*. It appears to be a candidate for rejection.

Crataegus torminalis Linnaeus, *Species Plantarum* 1: 476. 1753.
"Habitat in Anglia, Germania, Helvetia, Burgundia." RCN: 3641.

Lectotype (Jonsell & Jarvis in *Nordic J. Bot.* 22: 74. 2002): Herb. Burser XXIV: 4 (UPS).
Current name: ***Sorbus torminalis*** (L.) Crantz (Rosaceae).

Crataegus viridis Linnaeus, *Species Plantarum* 1: 476. 1753.
"Habitat in Virginia." RCN: 3643.
Basionym of: *Crataegus coccinea* L. var. *viridis* (L.) L. (1771).
Lectotype (Eggleston in *Rhodora* 10: 83. 1908): *Clayton 526* (BM-000051596).
Current name: ***Crataegus viridis*** L. (Rosaceae).

Crateva gynandra Linnaeus, *Species Plantarum*, ed. 2, 1: 636. 1762.
"Habitat in Jamaica." RCN: 3447.
Type not designated.
Original material: [icon] in Plukenet, Phytographia: t. 147, f. 6. 1692; Almag. Bot.: 47. 1696.
Current name: ***Crateva tapia*** L. (Capparaceae).
Note: Although Jacobs (in *Blumea* 12: 189. 1964) treated 619.1 (LINN) as the type, this collection does not appear to be original material for the name, and cannot be accepted as a neotype because of the existence of a cited Plukenet plate.

Crateva marmelos Linnaeus, *Species Plantarum* 1: 444. 1753.
"Habitat in India." RCN: 3449.
Lectotype (Tanaka in *Meded. Rijks-Herb.* 69: 8. 1931): Herb. Hermann 5: 91, No. 212 [icon] (BM).
Current name: ***Aegle marmelos*** (L.) Corrêa (Rutaceae).

Crateva tapia Linnaeus, *Species Plantarum* 1: 444. 1753.
"Habitat in India utraque." RCN: 3448.
Lectotype (Al-Shehbaz in Jarvis & al., *Regnum Veg.* 127: 39. 1993): [icon] *"Apioscorodon s. Arbor Americana triphyllos, Alii odore, poma ferens"* in Plukenet, Phytographia: t. 137, f. 7. 1692; Almag. Bot.: 34. 1696.
Generitype of *Crateva* Linnaeus (vide Corrêa in *Trans. Linn. Soc. London* 5: 222. 1800).
Current name: ***Crateva tapia*** L. (Capparaceae).
Note: Jacobs (in *Blumea* 12: 189. 1964) designated a Plumier illustration as type but as Plumier's work was not cited in the protologue, it is not original material for the name.

Crepis alpina Linnaeus, *Species Plantarum* 2: 806. 1753.
"Habitat in Alpibus Italiae." RCN: 5881.
Lectotype (Babcock in *Univ. Calif. Publ. Bot.* 22: 956, pl.16a. 1947): Herb. Linn. No. 955.4 (LINN).
Current name: ***Crepis alpina*** L. (Asteraceae).

Crepis aspera Linnaeus, *Species Plantarum*, ed. 2, 2: 1132. 1763.
"Habitat in Oriente, Sicilia, Palaestina." RCN: 5884.
Lectotype (Babcock in *Univ. Calif. Publ. Bot.* 22: 879. 1947): Herb. Linn. No. 955.10 (LINN).
Current name: ***Crepis aspera*** L. (Asteraceae).
Note: Although Babcock referred to the type as being in "L" (rather than LINN), it is clear from his f. 291a (which is drawn from the type) that 955.10 (LINN) is the collection he regards as the type.

Crepis barbata Linnaeus, *Species Plantarum* 2: 805. 1753.
"Habitat in Monspelii, Vesuvii, Siciliae, Messanae arenosis maritimis." RCN: 5879.
Lectotype (Jarvis in *Bot. J. Linn. Soc.* 109: 506, f. 1. 1992): Herb. Linn. No. 955.2 (LINN).
Current name: ***Tolpis barbata*** (L.) Gaertn. (Asteraceae).

Crepis biennis Linnaeus, *Species Plantarum* 2: 807. 1753.
"Habitat in Scaniae & Europae australioris apricis." RCN: 5889.

Lectotype (Babcock in *Univ. Calif. Publ. Bot.* 22: 437, 938, 939, pl. 7. 1947): Herb. Linn. No. 955.14 (LINN).
Generitype of *Crepis* Linnaeus (vide Green, *Prop. Brit. Bot.*: 178. 1929).
Current name: ***Crepis biennis*** L. (Asteraceae).
Note: Crepis biennis, with the type designated by Babcock, was proposed as conserved type of the genus by Jarvis (in *Taxon* 41: 561. 1992). However, the proposal was eventually ruled unnecessary by the General Committee (see Barrie, *l.c.* 55: 795–796. 2006 for a review of the history of this and related proposals).

Crepis bursifolia Linnaeus, *Species Plantarum* 2: 805. 1753.
"Habitat in Sicilia." RCN: 5878.
Type not designated.
Original material: [icon] in Boccone, Mus. Piante Rar. Sicilia: 147, t. 106. 1697; [icon] in Boccone, Mus. Piante Rar. Sicilia: 147, t. 112. 1697.
Current name: ***Crepis bursifolia*** L. (Asteraceae).
Note: Babcock (in *Univ. Calif. Publ. Bot.* 22: 906. 1947) noted the cited Boccone plate and said that he had seen authentic Boccone material in M (ex Herb. Schreber), having failed to find "the type" in LINN. However, he did not designate a type.

Crepis dioscoridis Linnaeus, *Species Plantarum*, ed. 2, 2: 1133. 1763.
"Habitat in Gallia." RCN: 5891.
Lectotype (Babcock in *Univ. Calif. Publ. Bot.* 22: 750. 1947): Herb. Linn. No. 955.18 (LINN).
Current name: ***Crepis dioscoridis*** L. (Asteraceae).

Crepis foetida Linnaeus, *Species Plantarum* 2: 807. 1753.
"Habitat in Gallia." RCN: 5883.
Type not designated.
Original material: Herb. A. van Royen? (L); [icon] in Dodoëns, Stirp. Hist. Pempt., ed. 2: 640, 641. 1616; [icon] in Morison, Pl. Hist. Univ. 3: 63, s. 7, t. 4, f. 4. 1699.
Current name: ***Crepis foetida*** L. (Asteraceae).
Note: Babcock (in *Univ. Calif. Publ. Bot.* 22: 688, 691, pl. 17a, 1947) and Lamond (in Davis, *Fl. Turkey* 5: 831. 1975) designated Herb. Linn. 955.6 (LINN) as the type, while Jeffrey (in *Kew Bull.* 18: 462. 1966) did likewise with Herb. Linn. 955.9 (LINN). However, both collections lack the relevant *Species Plantarum* number (i.e. "13") and are evidently post-1753 additions to the herbarium, and not original material.

Crepis hirta Linnaeus, *Species Plantarum* 2: 807. 1753.
"Habitat in Helvetia, Gallia." RCN: 5888.
Type not designated.
Original material: Herb. Burser VI: 59 (UPS); [icon] in Morison, Pl. Hist. Univ. 3: 65, s. 7, t. 5, f. 14. 1699.
Current name: ***Leontodon hirtus*** L. (Asteraceae).

Crepis neglecta Linnaeus, *Systema Naturae*, ed. 12, 2: 525; *Mantissa Plantarum*: 107. 1767.
"Habitat in Italia." RCN: 5893.
Lectotype (Babcock in *Univ. Calif. Publ. Bot.* 22: 782. 1947): Herb. Linn. No. 955.25 (LINN).
Current name: ***Crepis neglecta*** L. (Asteraceae).
Note: Although Babcock referred to the type as being in "L" (rather than LINN), it is clear from his f. 255a (which is drawn from the type) that 955.25 (LINN) is the collection he regards as the type.

Crepis nudicaulis Linnaeus, *Species Plantarum* 2: 805. 1753.
"Habitat in G. Narbonensi, Hispania." RCN: 5843.
Lectotype (Rauschert in *Feddes Repert.* 88: 314. 1977): [icon] *"Hieracium dentis leonis folio hirsutie asperum minus"* in Bauhin, Prodr. Theatri Bot.: 63. 1620.

Current name: **Leontodon crispus** Vill. (Asteraceae).
Note: Finch & Sell (in *Bot. J. Linn. Soc.* 71: 246. 1976) informally proposed the rejection of the name as a *nomen ambiguum*, and this has been accepted by most later authors. If this name is rejected, the correct name for the plant depicted by Bauhin appears to be *Leontodon crispus* Vill. (1779). Fuchs (in *Feddes Repert.* 90: 646–649. 1980) provides an extensive review, and additional comments are provided by Greuter (in *Willdenowia* 33: 235. 2003), who states that the name can no longer be used, citing Art. 57. No formal proposal for the rejection of *C. nudicaulis* has been made.

Crepis pulchra Linnaeus, *Species Plantarum* 2: 806. 1753.
"Habitat in Gallia." RCN: 5892.
Type not designated.
Original material: Herb. Linn. No. 955.23 (LINN); [icon] in Bauhin & Cherler, Hist. Pl. Univ. 2: 1025. 1651.
Current name: **Crepis pulchra** L. (Asteraceae).
Note: Although Babcock (in *Univ. Calif. Publ. Bot.* 22: 664. 1947) referred to "the type specimen of Linnaeus", he did not make clear which element he regarded as the type.

Crepis pygmaea Linnaeus, *Species Plantarum* 2: 805. 1753.
"Habitat in Alpibus Italiae ad Nursiam prope lacum pilati." RCN: 5877.
Lectotype (designated here by Baldini): [icon] *"Hieracium alpinum incanum saxatile Prunellae foliis integris"* in Boccone, Mus. Piante Rar. Sicilia: 33, t. 24. 1697.
Current name: **Crepis pygmaea** L. (Asteraceae).
Note: Babcock (in *Univ. Calif. Publ. Bot.* 22: 241. 1947) said the type is in LINN "and is illustrated in fig. 20a". The only material apparently associated with this name is 955.1 (LINN) but it bears little similarity to Babcock's drawing, and also carries a determination (*in sched.*) of *Crepis nana* Richards. made by Babcock himself in 1925. No other *Crepis* specimen in LINN appears to match Babcock's f. 20a. The material on sheet 955.1 in fact conflicts with the protologue, while Boccone's cited description and plate (from which Linnaeus took the precise locality information) agrees well both with it, and current usage of the name.

Crepis rhagadioloides Linnaeus, *Systema Naturae,* ed. 12, 2: 524; *Mantissa Plantarum*: 108. 1767.
"Habitat . . ." RCN: 5885.
Neotype (Greuter in *Willdenowia* 33: 236. 2003): Herb. Linn. No. 955.26 (LINN).
Current name: **Picris rhagadioloides** (L.) Desf. (Asteraceae).
Note: The application of this name was for many years uncertain. Lack (in *Taxon* 24: 115. 1975) reasoned that, from the description, it could not apply to a species of *Picris*, and excluded it from the genus. However, Greuter (in *Willdenowia* 33: 236. 2003) argues very plausibly that a slip of the pen in Linnaeus' diagnosis was responsible for this. Greuter consequently took up the name in *Picris*, and also typified it.

Crepis rubra Linnaeus, *Species Plantarum* 2: 806. 1753.
"Habitat in Apulia." RCN: 5882.
Lectotype (Babcock in *Univ. Calif. Publ. Bot.* 22: 686. 1947): Herb. Linn. No. 955.5 (LINN).
Current name: **Crepis rubra** L. (Asteraceae).
Note: Although Babcock referred to the type as being in "L" (rather than LINN), sheet 955.5 (LINN) is the only sheet there associated with this name, and is accepted as the lectotype.

Crepis sibirica Linnaeus, *Species Plantarum* 2: 807. 1753.
"Habitat in Sibiria." RCN: 5886.

Lectotype (Babcock in *Univ. Calif. Publ. Bot.* 22: 225. 1947): Herb. Linn. No. 955.11 (LINN).
Current name: **Crepis sibirica** L. (Asteraceae).
Note: Although Babcock referred to the type as being in "L" (rather than LINN), and did not specify a sheet number, sheet 955.11 is the only one associated with this name, and is accepted here as the lectotype.

Crepis tectorum Linnaeus, *Species Plantarum* 2: 807. 1753.
"Habitat in Europae aridis, tectis." RCN: 5887.
Type not designated.
Original material: Herb. Burser VI: 42 (UPS); Herb. Linn. No. 955.12 (LINN); Herb. Linn. No. 955.13 (LINN); [icon] in Tabernaemontanus, Eicones Pl.: 180. 1590; [icon] in Gmelin, Fl. Sibirica 2: 28, t. 11, 12. 1752.
Current name: **Crepis tectorum** L. (Asteraceae).
Note: Although Babcock (in *Univ. Calif. Publ. Bot.* 22: 569. 1947) referred to the type as being in LINN, he failed to distinguish between sheets 995.12 and 995.13. As they are evidently not part of a single gathering, Art. 9.15 does not apply and the name therefore appears to be untypified.

Crepis vesicaria Linnaeus, *Species Plantarum* 2: 805. 1753.
"Habitat α in Helvetia, β in Apulia." RCN: 5880.
Lectotype (Babcock in *Univ. Calif. Publ. Bot.* 22: 828, pl. 30a. 1947): Herb. Linn. No. 955.3 (LINN).
Current name: **Crepis vesicaria** L. (Asteraceae).

Crepis virens Linnaeus, *Species Plantarum,* ed. 2, 2: 1134. 1763, *nom. illeg.*
"Habitat in Helvetiae, Italiae agris." RCN: 5890.
Replaced synonym: *Lapsana capillaris* L. (1753).
Type not designated.
Original material: as replaced synonym.
Current name: **Crepis capillaris** (L.) Wallr. (Asteraceae).
Note: An illegitimate name in *Crepis* for *Lapsana capillaris* L. (1753). Babcock (in *Univ. Calif. Publ. Bot.* 22: 771. 1947) noted the absence of authentic material in LINN.

Crescentia cucurbitina Linnaeus, *Mantissa Plantarum Altera*: 250. 1771, *nom. illeg.*
"Habitat in America calidiore." RCN: 4532.
Replaced synonym: *Crescentia latifolia* Mill. (1768).
Type not designated.
Current name: **Dendrosicus latifolius** (Mill.) A.H. Gentry (Bignoniaceae).
Note: An illegitimate replacement name for *C. latifolia* Mill. (1768).

Crescentia cujete Linnaeus, *Species Plantarum* 2: 626. 1753.
"Habitat in Virginiae, Jamaicae, Brasiliae apricis." RCN: 4531.
Lectotype (Wijnands, *Bot. Commelins*: 50. 1983): [icon] *"Cucurbitifera arbor, subrotundis foliis confertis, fructu ovali, seminibus cordatis, massula nigra inclusis"* in Plukenet, Phytographia: t. 171, f. 2. 1692; Almag. Bot.: 124. 1696. – Typotype: Herb. Sloane 100: 8 (BM-SL).
Generitype of *Crescentia* Linnaeus.
Current name: **Crescentia cujete** L. (Bignoniaceae).
Note: Gentry (in *Ann. Missouri Bot. Gard.* 60: 831. 1974) originally proposed 779.1 (LINN), a Patrick Browne collection not received by Linnaeus until 1758, as type but it is ineligible. Wijnands' 1983 choice of the Plukenet plate was rejected by Reveal (in *Taxon* 41: 145. 1992) as it corresponded with Linnaeus' unnamed var. δ. Reveal argued that the name was based on a Plumier plate depicting *Amphitecna latifolia* (Mill.) A.H. Gentry, and proposed the Linnaean name for conservation with the Browne specimen as

conserved type. However, the Committee for Spermatophyta (in *Taxon* 43: 274. 1994) ruled that Wijnands' type choice was valid, rendering Reveal's proposal unnecessary.

Cressa cretica Linnaeus, *Species Plantarum* 1: 223. 1753.
"Habitat in Cretae litoribus salsis." RCN: 1835.
Lectotype (Verdcourt in Hubbard & Milne-Redhead, *Fl. Trop. E. Africa, Convolvulaceae*: 33. 1963): Herb. Linn. No. 317.1 (LINN).
Generitype of *Cressa* Linnaeus.
Current name: **Cressa cretica** L. (Convolvulaceae).

Crinum africanum Linnaeus, *Species Plantarum* 1: 292. 1753.
"Habitat in Aethiopia." RCN: 2329.
Lectotype (Leighton in *J. S. African Bot., Suppl.* 4: 17, pl. 2. 1965): Herb. Linn. No. 415.6 (LINN).
Current name: **Agapanthus africanus** (L.) Hoffmanns. (Liliaceae/Amaryllidaceae).

Crinum americanum Linnaeus, *Species Plantarum* 1: 292. 1753.
"Habitat in America." RCN: 2328.

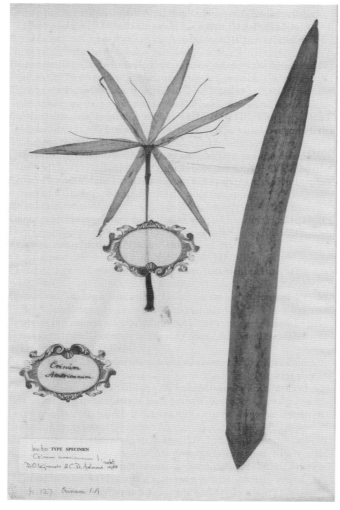

Lectotype (Wijnands, *Bot. Commelins*: 36. 1983): Herb. Clifford: 127, *Crinum* 1, sheet A (BM-000558534).
Generitype of *Crinum* Linnaeus (vide Hitchcock, *Prop. Brit. Bot.*: 145. 1929).
Current name: **Crinum americanum** L. (Liliaceae/Amaryllidaceae).

Note: Lehmiller (in *Herbertia* 49: 58–66. 1994) provided a detailed review but, wrongly, did not admit the Clifford collection as original material, concluding that Commelin's t. 15 must be regarded as the lectotype. Wijnands' choice of the Clifford sheet has priority.

Crinum asiaticum Linnaeus, *Species Plantarum* 1: 292. 1753.
"Habitat in Malabaria, Zeylona." RCN: 2326.
Lectotype (Verdoorn in Killick, *Fl. Pl. Africa* 47: t. 1875. 1983): [icon] *"Lilium Zeylanicum umbelliferum et bulbiferum"* in Hermann, Hort. Lugd.-Bat. Cat.: 682, 683. 1687.
Current name: **Crinum asiaticum** L. (Liliaceae/Amaryllidaceae).
Note: Although Sealy (in *Curtis's Bot. Mag.* 177: t. 528. 1969) noted the contrasting identities of the cited Hermann and Rheede entities, he did not typify the name. Howard (in *J. Arnold. Arbor.* 60: 291. 1979) wrongly treated a plate (t. 1073) in *Curtis's Bot. Mag.* as the lectotype; it is not original material for the name.

Crinum latifolium Linnaeus, *Species Plantarum* 1: 291. 1753.
"Habitat in Asiae arenosis." RCN: 2325.
Type not designated.
Original material: "Crinum latifolium", Herb. Linn. (UPS); [icon] in Rheede, Hort. Malab. 11: 77, t. 39. 1692.
Current name: **Crinum latifolium** L. (Liliaceae/Amaryllidaceae).
Note: See brief comments by Wijnands (*Bot. Commelins*: 37. 1983).

Crinum zeylanicum (Linnaeus) Linnaeus, *Systema Naturae*, ed. 12, 2: 236. 1767.
"Habitat in India orientali." RCN: 2327.
Basionym: *Amaryllis zeylanica* L. (1753).
Lectotype (Dassanayake in *Taxon* 30: 481. 1981): [icon] *"Lilio-Narcissus Ceylanicus latifolius flore niveo, externe linea purpurea striato"* in Commelin, Hort. Med. Amstelod. Pl. Rar. 1: 73, t. 37. 1697.
Current name: **Crinum zeylanicum** (L.) L. (Liliaceae/Amaryllidaceae).
Note: See comments under *Amaryllis zeylanica*.

Crithmum maritimum Linnaeus, *Species Plantarum* 1: 246. 1753.
"Habitat ad oceani Europaei litora." RCN: 1979.
Lectotype (designated here by Reduron): Herb. Clifford: 94, *Crithmum* 1 (BM-000558263).
Generitype of *Crithmum* Linnaeus (vide Hitchcock, *Prop. Brit. Bot.*: 139. 1929).
Current name: **Crithmum maritimum** L. (Apiaceae).
Note: Jafri (in Jafri & El-Gadi, *Fl. Libya* 117: 49. 1985) indicated 347.1 (LINN) as the type but this sheet lacks the relevant *Species Plantarum* number (i.e. "1") and was a post-1753 collection and is not original material for the name. This choice is rejected here, in favour of a Clifford collection.

Crithmum pyrenaicum Linnaeus, *Species Plantarum* 1: 246, Errata. 1753.
"Habitat in pyrenaeis." RCN: 1980.
Neotype (Reduron in Jarvis & al. in *Taxon* 55: 211. 2006): Herb. Linn. No. 347.3 (LINN).
Current name: **Libanotis pyrenaica** (L.) Schwarz (Apiaceae).

Crocus bulbocodium Linnaeus, *Species Plantarum* 1: 36. 1753.
"Habitat in alpibus Italicis." RCN: 286.
Basionym of: *Ixia bulbocodium* (L.) L. (1762).
Lectotype (Labani & El-Gadi in Jafri & El-Gadi, *Fl. Libya* 81: 17. 1980): Herb. Linn. No. 58.4 (LINN).
Current name: **Romulea bulbocodium** (L.) Sebast. & Mauri (Iridaceae).

Crocus sativus Linnaeus, *Species Plantarum* 1: 36. 1753.
"Habitat in Alpibus Helveticis, Pyrenaeis, Lusitanicis, Tracicis." RCN: 284.
Lectotype (Mathew in Jarvis & al., *Regnum Veg.* 127: 39. 1993): Herb. Clifford: 18, *Crocus* 1 (BM-000557641).
Generitype of *Crocus* Linnaeus (vide Hitchcock in *Amer. J. Bot.* 10: 513. 1923).
Current name: ***Crocus sativus*** L. (Iridaceae).
Note: Labani & El-Gadi (in Jafri & El-Gadi, *Fl. Libya* 81: 21. 1980) appear to indicate both Clifford and LINN material as type; this choice is therefore ineffective.

Crocus sativus Linnaeus var. **officinalis** Linnaeus, *Species Plantarum* 1: 36. 1753.
RCN: 284.
Type not designated.
Original material: Herb. Linn. No. 56.1 (LINN); Herb. Burser III: 63 (UPS); [icon] in Morison, Pl. Hist. Univ. 2: 335, s. 4, t. 2, f. 1. 1680.
Current name: ***Crocus sativus*** L. (Iridaceae).

Crocus sativus Linnaeus var. **vernus** Linnaeus, *Species Plantarum* 1: 36. 1753.
RCN: 284.
Type not designated.
Original material: Herb. Burser III: 64–68 (UPS).
Current name: ***Crocus vernus*** (L.) Hill (Iridaceae).

Crotalaria alba Linnaeus, *Species Plantarum* 2: 716. 1753.
"Habitat in Carolina." RCN: 2941.
Basionym of: *Sophora alba* (L.) L. (1767).
Lectotype (Barrie in Turland & Jarvis in *Taxon* 46: 467. 1997): Herb. A. van Royen No. 908.112–704 (L).
Current name: ***Baptisia alba*** (L.) Vent. (Fabaceae: Faboideae).
Note: Isely (in *Mem. New York Bot. Gard.* 25(3): 219. 1981) noted that the name could be traced back to Linnaeus' *Hortus Cliffortianus* (1738) account, "and the associated specimen (BM)", and that material in LINN (evidently sheet 522.7) lacked fruit and could be *Baptisia lactea* (Raf.) Thieret. Turner (in *Syst. Bot.* 7: 351. 1982) was apparently confused about which sheet he had seen, and regarded as the type, suggesting that it was Clifford material at BM (which we have been unable to trace) but, from his description, was evidently 522.7 (LINN). Isely (in *Sida* 11: 434. 1986), assuming Turner to have typified the name using this Clifford material and accepting Turner's determination of 522.7 (LINN), took up *B. alba* in the sense of *B. leucantha* Torr. & A. Gray. However, the material in LINN lacks a *Species Plantarum* number (i.e. "12"), did not reach the herbarium until after 1753, and is not original material for the name. Subsequently, Barrie located original material in L, and designated van Royen material as lectotype, restoring *C. alba* to its traditional usage in the process.

Crotalaria amplexicaulis Linnaeus, *Plantae Rariores Africanae*: 16. 1760.
["Habitat in Aethiopia."] Sp. Pl., ed. 2, 2: 1003 (1763). RCN: 5248.
Lectotype (Campbell & Van Wyk in *S. African J. Bot.* 67: 132. 2001): Herb. Linn. No. 895.5 (LINN).
Current name: ***Rafnia amplexicaulis*** (L.) Thunb. (Fabaceae: Faboideae).

Crotalaria biflora Linnaeus, *Mantissa Plantarum Altera*: 570. 1771.
["Habitat in Insula s. Johannae. Koenig. H.U."] Mant. Pl. Alt.: 273 (1771). RCN: 5257.
Lectotype (Rudd in Dassanayake & Fosberg, *Revised Handb. Fl. Ceylon* 7: 204. 1991): Herb. Linn. No. 895.20 (LINN).

Current name: ***Crotalaria angulata*** Mill. (Fabaceae: Faboideae).
Note: This name appeared in the Appendix of *Mant. Pl. Alt.*, and includes, in its synonymy, *Astragalus biflorus* L. (*Mant. Pl. Alt.*: 273. 1771). As the latter name was not accepted by the author, *A. biflorus* is not validly published, and *C. biflora* is not a new combination based on *A. biflorus*.

Crotalaria chinensis Linnaeus, *Systema Naturae,* ed. 10, 2: 1158. 1759.
["Habitat in China."] Sp. Pl., ed. 2, 2: 1003 (1763). RCN: 5250.
Neotype (Niyomdham in *Thai Forest Bull., Bot.* 11: 129. 1978): Herb. Linn. No. 895.8 (LINN).
Current name: ***Crotalaria chinensis*** L. (Fabaceae: Faboideae).
Note: Niyomdham wrongly indicated 895.8 (LINN) as the holotype (it is not original material for the name). However, in the absence of any original material, this is accepted as a neotypification under Art. 9.8.

Crotalaria cordifolia Linnaeus, *Mantissa Plantarum Altera*: 266. 1771, *nom. illeg.*
"Habitat ad Cap. b. spei rupibus." RCN: 5261.
Replaced synonym: *Spartium sophoroides* P.J. Bergius (1767).
Type not designated.
Current name: ***Hypocalyptus sophoroides*** (P.J. Bergius) Taub. (Fabaceae: Faboideae).
Note: As noted by Dahlgren (in *Bot. Not.* 125: 105. 1972), this is an illegitimate replacement name in *Crotalaria* for *Spartium sophoroides* P.J. Bergius (1767).

Crotalaria imbricata Linnaeus, *Plantae Rariores Africanae*: 16. 1760.
["Habitat ad Cap. b. spei."] Sp. Pl., ed. 2, 2: 1004 (1763). RCN: 5252.
Type not designated.
Original material: Herb. Burman, 4 sheets (G).
Current name: ***Amphithalea imbricata*** (L.) Druce (Fabaceae: Faboideae).
Note: Granby (*Opera Bot.* 80: 16. 1985) selected 890.2 (LINN) as lectotype but the specimen is annotated only with "Borbonia tomentosa" by Linnaeus, and shows no sign of being associated with *C. imbricata*. It is therefore not original material for the name.

Crotalaria incana Linnaeus, *Species Plantarum* 2: 716. 1753.
"Habitat in Jamaica & Caribaeis." RCN: 5262.
Lectotype (Niyomdham in *Thai Forest Bull., Bot.* 11: 135. 1978): [icon] "*Crotalaria trifolia fruticosa foliis rotundis incanis floribus spicatis e viridiluteis fructu pubescente*" in Sloane, Voy. Jamaica 2: 34, t. 179, f. 1. 1725. – Typotype: Herb. Sloane 6: 6, right specimen (BM-SL).
Current name: ***Crotalaria incana*** L. (Fabaceae: Faboideae).

Crotalaria juncea Linnaeus, *Species Plantarum* 2: 714. 1753.
"Habitat in India." RCN: 5251.
Lectotype (Fawcett & Rendle, *Fl. Jamaica* 4: 8. 1920): Herb. Linn. No. 895.11 (LINN).
Current name: ***Crotalaria juncea*** L. (Fabaceae: Faboideae).
Note: Fawcett & Rendle (*Fl. Jamaica* 4: 8. 1920) stated "Type in Herb. Linn." and as there is only a single sheet directly associated with this name, theirs is accepted as the earliest typification. Although some authors (e.g. Polhill in Milne-Redhead & Polhill, *Fl. Trop. E. Africa, Leguminosae* 4: 950. 1971) have treated Clifford material as the type, this choice is pre-dated by that of Fawcett & Rendle.

Crotalaria laburnifolia Linnaeus, *Species Plantarum* 2: 715. 1753.
"Habitat in Asia." RCN: 5260.
Lectotype (Niyomdham in *Thai Forest Bull., Bot.* 11: 139. 1978): Herb. Hermann 4: 1, No. 278 (BM-000628017).

Current name: ***Crotalaria laburnifolia*** L. (Fabaceae: Faboideae).
Note: Polhill (in Milne-Redhead & Polhill, *Fl. Trop. E. Africa, Leguminosae* 4: 856. 1971) indicated two collections in Herb. Hermann (BM) as syntypes but gave no indication of intending to designate a lectotype.

Crotalaria lotifolia Linnaeus, *Species Plantarum* 2: 715. 1753, *typ. cons.*
"Habitat in Jamaica." RCN: 5258.
Conserved type (Fawcett & Rendle, *Fl. Jamaica* 4: 11. 1920): [icon] *"Crotalaria trifolia fruticosa foliis glabris, flore e viridi luteo minore"* in Sloane, Voy. Jamaica 2: 33, t. 176, f. 1, 2. 1725. – Typotype: Herb. Sloane 6: 5 (BM-SL).
Generitype of *Crotalaria* Linnaeus, *nom. cons.*
Current name: ***Crotalaria lotifolia*** L. (Fabaceae: Faboideae).
Note: Crotalaria lotifolia, with the type designated by Fawcett & Rendle, was proposed as conserved type of the genus by Jarvis (in *Taxon* 41: 561. 1992). This was eventually approved by the General Committee (see review of the history of this proposal by Barrie, *l.c.* 55: 795–796. 2006).

Crotalaria lunaris Linnaeus, *Species Plantarum* 2: 715. 1753.
"Habitat in Africa." RCN: 5259.
Lectotype (Schrire in Turland & Jarvis in *Taxon* 46: 467. 1997): Herb. Clifford: 357, *Crotalaria* 5 (BM-000646570).
Current name: ***Argyrolobium lunare*** (L.) Druce (Fabaceae: Faboideae).

Crotalaria perfoliata Linnaeus, *Species Plantarum* 2: 714. 1753.
"Habitat in Carolina." RCN: 5247.
Lectotype (Reveal in Turland & Jarvis in *Taxon* 46: 468. 1997): [icon] *"Crotalaria Perfoliatae folio"* in Dillenius, Hort. Eltham. 1: 122, t. 102, f. 122. 1732. – Typotype: Herb. Sherard No. 1457 (OXF).
Current name: ***Baptisia perfoliata*** (L.) R. Br. (Fabaceae: Faboideae).
Note: Although Isely (in *Mem. New York Bot. Gard.* 25(3): 224. 1981) confirmed the identity of the Dillenius plate, he did not indicate it as the type.

Crotalaria perforata Linnaeus, *Plantae Rariores Africanae*: 15. 1760. ["Habitat ad Cap. b. spei."] Sp. Pl., ed. 2, 2: 1003 (1763). RCN: 5246.
Type not designated.
Original material: none traced.
Current name: ***Aspalathus perforata*** (Thunb.) R. Dahlgren (Fabaceae: Faboideae).
Note: Dahlgren (*Opera Bot.* 22: 28. 1968) treated this as a *nomen dubium.*

Crotalaria quinquefolia Linnaeus, *Species Plantarum* 2: 716. 1753.
"Habitat in India." RCN: 5263.
Lectotype (Niyomdham in *Thai Forest Bull., Bot.* 11: 151. 1978): [icon] *"Wellia-tandale-cotti"* in Rheede, Hort. Malab. 9: 51, t. 28. 1689.
Current name: ***Crotalaria quinquefolia*** L. (Fabaceae: Faboideae).

Crotalaria retusa Linnaeus, *Species Plantarum* 2: 715. 1753.
"Habitat in India." RCN: 5253.
Lectotype (Niyomdham in *Thai Forest Bull., Bot.* 11: 151. 1978): Herb. Hermann 2: 21, No. 276 (BM-000594584).
Current name: ***Crotalaria retusa*** L. (Fabaceae: Faboideae).
Note: Ali (in Nasir & Ali, *Fl. W. Pakistan* 100: 49. 1977) indicated four collections in the Hermann herbarium (BM) as syntypes but gave no indication of intending to typify the name.

Crotalaria sagittalis Linnaeus, *Species Plantarum* 2: 714. 1753.
"Habitat in Brasilia, Virginia." RCN: 5249.
Lectotype (Windler in *Taxon* 21: 545. 1972): *Kalm*, Herb. Linn. No. 895.6 (LINN; iso- UPS).
Current name: ***Crotalaria sagittalis*** L. (Fabaceae: Faboideae).

Crotalaria sessiliflora Linnaeus, *Species Plantarum,* ed. 2, 2: 1004. 1763.
"Habitat in China." RCN: 5254.
Neotype (Niyomdham in *Thai Forest Bull., Bot.* 11: 153. 1978): Herb. Linn. No. 895.9 (LINN).
Current name: ***Crotalaria sessiliflora*** L. (Fabaceae: Faboideae).
Note: Niyomdham wrongly indicated 895.9 (LINN) as the holotype (it is not original material for the name). However, in the absence of any original material, this is accepted as a neotypification under Art. 9.8.

Crotalaria triflora Linnaeus, *Species Plantarum* 2: 715. 1753.
"Habitat in Asia. D. Royen." RCN: 5255.
Neotype (Campbell & Van Wyk in *S. African J. Bot.* 67: 127. 2001): Herb. Linn. No. 895.16 (LINN).
Current name: ***Rafnia triflora*** (L.) Thunb. (Fabaceae: Faboideae).
Note: Campbell & Van Wyk designated 895.16 (LINN) as lectotype, a collection that lacks a *Species Plantarum* number (i.e. "5") and is therefore almost certainly a post-1753 addition to the collection, and not original material for the name. However, in the absence of any original material, their choice is interpreted as a neotypification (Art. 9.8).

Crotalaria verrucosa Linnaeus, *Species Plantarum* 2: 715. 1753.
"Habitat in India." RCN: 5256.
Lectotype (Fawcett & Rendle, *Fl. Jamaica* 4: 8. 1920; Polhill in Milne-Redhead & Polhill, *Fl. Trop. E. Africa, Leguminosae* 4: 959. 1971): Herb. Hermann 3: 4, No. 277 (BM-000621801).
Current name: ***Crotalaria verrucosa*** L. (Fabaceae: Faboideae).
Note: Fawcett & Rendle indicated "Type in Herb. Hermann" but did not distinguish between material and an illustration. This was subsequently clarified by Polhill.

Crotalaria villosa Linnaeus, *Species Plantarum* 2: 715. 1753.
"Habitat in Aethiopia." RCN: 2943.
Type not designated.
Original material: Herb. Clifford: 357, *Crotalaria* 3 (BM); Herb. Clifford: 357, *Crotalaria* 3 α (BM); [icon] in Hermann, Hort. Lugd.-Bat. Cat.: 270, 271. 1687; [icon] in Plukenet, Phytographia: t. 185, f. 2. 1692; Almag. Bot.: 122. 1696 – Typotype: Herb. Sloane 96: 49 (BM-SL) – Voucher: Herb. Sloane 100: 89? (BM-SL).
Current name: ***Podalyria*** sp. (Fabaceae: Faboideae).
Note: The application of this name is uncertain. The Clifford, van Royen, Plukenet and Hermann elements from the protologue all appear in the synonymy of *Sophora biflora* L. (1759) in the later account in *Sp. Pl.,* ed. 2, 1: 534. 1762. Schelpe (in *Veld Fl.* 4: 28. 1974) evidently regarded Herb. Clifford: 357, *Crotalaria* 3 (BM) (a "fake" with flowers of a *Crotalaria* species attached to a *Podalyria*) as the type of *C. villosa,* concluding that it could not be synonymous with *Sophora biflora* L.

Croton argenteus Linnaeus, *Species Plantarum* 2: 1004. 1753.
"Habitat in America." RCN: 7274.
Type not designated.
Original material: Herb. Linn. No. 391.9 (S); Herb. Clifford: 444, *Croton* 2 (BM); Herb. Linn. No. 1140.8 (LINN).
Current name: ***Croton argenteus*** L. (Euphorbiaceae).
Note: Specific epithet spelled "argenteum" in the protologue.

Webster & Huft (in *Ann. Missouri Bot. Gard.* 75: 1124. 1988) indicated possible type material in the Clifford and LINN herbaria. Subsequently, Webster (in *Contr. Univ. Michigan Herb.* 23: 372. 2001) indicated the Clifford material as the holotype, but this choice was published after 1 Jan 2001, so the omission of the phrase "designated here" or an equivalent (Art. 7.11) means that this choice is not effective.

Croton aromaticus Linnaeus, *Species Plantarum* 2: 1005. 1753.
"Habitat in Zeylona." RCN: 7280.
Lectotype (Chakrabarty & Balakrishnan, *Bull. Bot. Survey India* 34: 26. 1992; Webster in Jarvis & al., *Regnum Veg.* 127: 39. 1993): Herb. Hermann 1: 63, No. 345 (BM-000594495).
Current name: *Croton aromaticus* L. (Euphorbiaceae).
Note: Specific epithet spelled "aromaticum" in the protologue.
    Chakrabarty & Balakrishnan indicated both Hermann collections (vol. 1: 63; 4: 21) as the type. As the specimens appear to be part of a single gathering (Art. 9.15), their choice is accepted, with Webster restricting this to the material in vol. 1: 63 shortly afterwards. *Croton tiglium* L., not *C. aromaticus*, is the generitype of *Croton*.

Croton bentzoë Linnaeus, *Mantissa Plantarum Altera*: 297. 1771.
"Habitat in India orientale." RCN: 7268.
Neotype (Wickens in *Kew Bull.* 31: 1. 1976): Herb. Linn. No. 1222.2 (LINN).
Current name: *Terminalia bentzoë* (L.) L. f. (Combretaceae).
Note: Wickens treated what is presumably sheet 1222.2 (LINN) as the holotype but there are no annotations linking the collection to the name. However, in the absence of original material, this choice is treated as a neotypification (Art. 9.8).

Croton cascarilla (Linnaeus) Linnaeus, *Species Plantarum,* ed. 2, 2: 1424. 1763.
"Habitat in America." RCN: 7267.
Basionym: *Clutia cascarilla* L. (1753).
Lectotype (Dandy, *Sloane Herbarium*: 112. 1958): [icon] *"An Ricinoides Aeleagni folio?"* in Catesby, Nat. Hist. Carolina 2: 46, t. 46. 1736. – Voucher: Herb. Sloane 232: 24 (BM-SL).
Current name: *Croton cascarilla* (L.) L. (Euphorbiaceae).

Croton castaneifolius Linnaeus, *Species Plantarum* 2: 1004. 1753.
"Habitat in America meridionali." RCN: 7269.
Type not designated.
Original material: none traced.
Current name: *Caperonia castaneifolia* (L.) A. St.-Hil. (Euphorbiaceae).
Note: Specific epithet spelled "castaneifolium" in the protologue.

Croton flavens Linnaeus, *Systema Naturae,* ed. 10, 2: 1276. 1759.
["Habitat in Jamaica."] Sp. Pl., ed. 2, 2: 1426 (1763). RCN: 7284.
Lectotype (Fawcett & Rendle, *Fl. Jamaica* 4: 279. 1920): *Browne,* Herb. Linn. No. 1140.21 (LINN).
Current name: *Croton flavens* L. (Euphorbiaceae).

Croton glabellus Linnaeus, *Systema Naturae,* ed. 10, 2: 1275. 1759.
["Habitat in Jamaica."] Sp. Pl., ed. 2, 2: 1425 (1763). RCN: 7271.
Lectotype (Fawcett & Rendle, *Fl. Jamaica* 4: 260. 1920): Herb. Linn. No. 1140.3 (LINN), see p. 54.
Current name: *Phyllanthus glabellus* (L.) Fawc. & Rendle (Euphorbiaceae).
Note: Specific epithet spelled "glabellum" in the protologue.

Croton glandulosus Linnaeus, *Systema Naturae,* ed. 10, 2: 1275. 1759.

["Habitat in Jamaica."] Sp. Pl., ed. 2, 2: 1425 (1763). RCN: 7273.
Lectotype (Fawcett & Rendle, *Fl. Jamaica* 4: 285. 1920): *Browne,* Herb. Linn. No. 1140.7 (LINN).
Current name: *Croton glandulosus* L. (Euphorbiaceae).
Note: Specific epithet spelled "glandulosus" in the protologue.

Croton hastatus Linnaeus, *Species Plantarum* 2: 1005. 1753.
"Habitat in India." RCN: 7285.
Type not designated.
Original material: [icon] in Plukenet, Phytographia: t. 220, f. 2. 1694; Almag. Bot.: 320. 1696 – Typotype: Herb. Sloane 97: 163; 94: 69 (BM-SL).
Current name: *Tragia plukenetii* Radcl.-Sm. (Euphorbiaceae).
Note: Specific epithet spelled "hastatum" in the protologue.
    See comments by Prain (in *Bull. Misc. Inform. Kew* 1918: 64. 1918) and Radcliffe-Smith (in Polhill, *Fl. Trop. E. Africa, Euphorbiaceae*: 296. 1987), neither of whom formally typified the name. The only original material appears to be the cited Plukenet plate.

Croton humilis Linnaeus, *Systema Naturae,* ed. 10, 2: 1276. 1759.
["Habitat in Jamaica."] Sp. Pl., ed. 2, 2: 1427 (1763). RCN: 7281.
Lectotype (Fawcett & Rendle, *Fl. Jamaica* 4: 283. 1920): *Browne,* Herb. Linn. No. 1140.19 (LINN).
Current name: *Croton humilis* L. (Euphorbiaceae).
Note: Specific epithet spelled "humile" in the protologue.

Croton laccifer Linnaeus, *Species Plantarum* 2: 1005. 1753.
"Habitat in India." RCN: 7278.
Lectotype (Chakrabarty & Balakrishnan, *Bull. Bot. Survey India* 34: 26. 1992; Philcox in Dassanayake & Clayton, *Revised Handb. Fl. Ceylon* 11: 99. 1997): Herb. Hermann 3: 54, No. 344 (BM-000628006).
Current name: *Croton laccifer* L. (Euphorbiaceae).
Note: Specific epithet spelled "lacciferum" in the protologue.
    Chakrabarty & Balakrishnan indicated more than one Hermann collection (vol. 2: 54; 3: 54; 4: 38, BM) as the type. As the specimens appear to be part of a single gathering (Art. 9.15), their choice is accepted, with Philcox subsequently restricting this to the material in vol. 3: 54.

Croton lobatus Linnaeus, *Species Plantarum* 2: 1005. 1753.
"Habitat in Vera Cruce." RCN: 7286.
Type not designated.
Original material: Herb. Clifford: 445, *Croton* 4 (BM); [icon] in Martyn, Hist. Pl. Rar.: 46, t. 46. 1728.
Current name: *Astraea lobata* (L.) Klotzsch (Euphorbiaceae).
Note: Specific epithet spelled "lobatum" in the protologue.
    Although Webster (in *Contr. Univ. Michigan Herb.* 23: 375. 2001) indicated Houstoun material in the Clifford herbarium as the type, this was published after 1 Jan 2001 and so the omission of the phrase "designated here" or an equivalent (Art. 7.11) means that this choice is not effective.

Croton lucidus Linnaeus, *Systema Naturae,* ed. 10, 2: 1275. 1759.
["Habitat in Jamaica."] Sp. Pl., ed. 2, 2: 1426 (1763). RCN: 7277.
Lectotype (Fawcett & Rendle, *Fl. Jamaica* 4: 281. 1920): Herb. Linn. No. 1140.12 (LINN).
Current name: *Croton lucidus* L. (Euphorbiaceae).
Note: Specific epithet spelled "lucidum" in the protologue.

Croton moluccanus Linnaeus, *Species Plantarum* 2: 1005. 1753.
"Habitat in Zeylona, Moluccis." RCN: 7283.
Lectotype (Prain in *Bull. Misc. Inform. Kew* 1918: 67. 1918): Herb. Hermann 1: 33, No. 346 (BM-000594464).

Current name: ***Givotia moluccana*** (L.) Sreem. (Euphorbiaceae).
Note: Specific epithet spelled "moluccanum" in the protologue.

Croton palustris Linnaeus, *Species Plantarum* 2: 1004. 1753.
"Habitat in Vera Cruce, locis paludosis." RCN: 7270.
Type not designated.
Original material: Herb. Clifford: 445, *Croton* 3 (BM); Herb. Linn.
   No. 1140.2 (LINN).
Current name: ***Caperonia palustris*** (L.) A. St.-Hil. (Euphorbiaceae).
Note: Specific epithet spelled "palustre" in the protologue.

Croton ricinocarpos Linnaeus, *Species Plantarum*, ed. 2, 2: 1427.
   1763.
"Habitat Surinami." RCN: 7282.
Type not designated.
Original material: none traced.
Current name: ***Leidesia procumbens*** (L.) Prain (Euphorbiaceae).

Croton sebifer Linnaeus, *Species Plantarum* 2: 1004. 1753.
"Habitat in Chinae humidis. Osbeck." RCN: 7275.
Lectotype (Radcliffe-Smith in Nasir & Ali, *Fl. Pakistan* 172: 86.
   1986): *Osbeck s.n.*, Herb. Linn. No. 1140.9 (LINN).
Current name: ***Triadica sebifera*** (L.) Small (Euphorbiaceae).
Note: Specific epithet spelled "sebiferum" in the protologue.

Croton spinosus Linnaeus, *Species Plantarum* 2: 1005. 1753.
"Habitat in India." RCN: 7287.
Type not designated.
Original material: Herb. Hermann 5: 361, No. 347 [icon] (BM);
   [icon] in Plukenet, Phytographia: t. 108, f. 3. 1691; Almag. Bot.:
   320. 1696.
Current name: ***Ricinus communis*** L. (Euphorbiaceae).
Note: Specific epithet spelled "spinosum" in the protologue.

Croton subtomentosus Linnaeus, *Systema Naturae,* ed. 10, 2: 1276.
   1759.
RCN: 7281.
Type not designated.
Original material: none traced.
Current name: ***Croton humilis*** L. (Euphorbiaceae).
Note: Specific epithet spelled "subtomentosum" in the protologue.

Croton tiglium Linnaeus, *Species Plantarum* 2: 1004. 1753.
"Habitat in India." RCN: 7276.
Lectotype (Chakrabarty & Balakrishnan in *Bull. Bot. Surv. India* 34:
   72. 1997 [1992]; Philcox in Dassanayake & Clayton, *Revised
   Handb. Fl. Ceylon* 11: 94. 1997): Herb. Hermann 2: 6, No. 343,
   left specimen (BM-000621512), see p. 212.
Generitype of *Croton* Linnaeus (vide Green, *Prop. Brit. Bot.*: 189.
   1929).
Current name: ***Croton tiglium*** L. (Euphorbiaceae).
Note: Chakrabarty & Balakrishnan indicated Hermann material (vol.
   2: 6) as the type, with Philcox subsequently restricting this choice to
   the left specimen.

Croton tinctorius Linnaeus, *Species Plantarum* 2: 1004. 1753.
"Habitat Monspelii." RCN: 7272.
Lectotype (Radcliffe-Smith in Nasir & Ali, *Fl. Pakistan* 172: 50.
   1986): *Löfling s.n.*, Herb. Linn. No. 1140.5 (LINN).
Current name: ***Chrozophora tinctoria*** (L.) A. Juss.
   (Euphorbiaceae).
Note: Specific epithet spelled "tinctorium" in the protologue.
   Prain (in *Bull. Misc. Inform. Kew* 1918: 49. 1918) discusses this
   name and gives (pp. 50–53) an exhaustive account of the pre-
   Linnaean literature. Radcliffe-Smith (in Meikle, *Fl. Cyprus* 2: 1450.

1985) indicated a type at LINN but did not distinguish between
   sheets 1140.5 and 1140.6. As they are evidently not part of a single
   gathering, Art. 9.15 does not apply.

Croton urens Linnaeus, *Species Plantarum* 2: 1005. 1753.
"Habitat in India." RCN: 7288.
Type not designated.
Original material: [icon] in Plukenet, Phytographia: t. 120, f. 6. 1691;
   Almag. Bot.: 320. 1696 .– Typotype: Herb. Sloane 97: 165 (BM-
   SL).
Current name: ***Tragia plukenetii*** Radcl.-Sm. (Euphorbiaceae).
Note: See Radcliffe-Smith (in Polhill, *Fl. Trop. E. Africa,
   Euphorbiaceae*: 296. 1987). The only original material appears to be
   the cited Plukenet plate.

Croton variegatus Linnaeus, *Species Plantarum* 2: 1199. 1753.
"Habitat in India." RCN: 7266.
Lectotype (Merrill, *Interpret. Rumph. Herb. Amb.*: 31, 325. 1917):
   [icon] *"Codiaeum medium Chrysosticon"* in Rumphius, Herb.
   Amboin. 4: 65, t. 25. 1743.
Current name: ***Codiaeum variegatum*** (L.) Blume (Euphorbiaceae).
Note: Specific epithet spelled "variegatum" in the protologue.

Crucianella aegyptiaca Linnaeus, *Systema Naturae,* ed. 12, 2: 119;
   Mantissa Plantarum: 38. 1767.
"Habitat in Aegypto. Forskåhl." RCN: 886.
Type not designated.
Original material: none traced.
Current name: ***Crucianella aegyptiaca*** L. (Rubiaceae).

Crucianella angustifolia Linnaeus, *Species Plantarum* 1: 108. 1753.
"Habitat Monspelii." RCN: 884.
Lectotype (Natali & Jeanmonod in Jeanmonod, *Compl. Prodr. Fl.
   Corse, Rubiaceae*: 18. 2000): Herb. Linn. No. 130.1 (LINN).
Current name: ***Crucianella angustifolia*** L. (Rubiaceae).

Crucianella latifolia Linnaeus, *Species Plantarum* 1: 109. 1753.
"Habitat in Creta & Monspelii." RCN: 885.
Lectotype (Natali in Jarvis & al., *Regnum Veg.* 127: 39. 1993): Herb.
   Clifford: 33, *Crucianella* 2 (BM-000557766).
Generitype of *Crucianella* Linnaeus (vide Hitchcock, *Prop. Brit. Bot.*:
   124. 1929).
Current name: ***Crucianella latifolia*** L. (Rubiaceae).

Crucianella maritima Linnaeus, *Species Plantarum* 1: 109. 1753.
"Habitat in Creta & Monspelii. D. Sauvages." RCN: 888.
Lectotype (Natali & Jeanmonod in Jeanmonod, *Compl. Prodr. Fl.
   Corse, Rubiaceae*: 21. 2000): Herb. Burser XIX: 10 (UPS).
Current name: ***Crucianella maritima*** L. (Rubiaceae).

Crucianella monspeliaca Linnaeus, *Species Plantarum* 1: 109. 1753.
"Habitat Monspelii." RCN: 889.
Type not designated.
Original material: none traced.
Current name: ***Crucianella monspeliaca*** L. (Rubiaceae).

Crucianella patula Linnaeus, *Demonstr. Pl. Horto Upsaliensi*: 4. 1753.
"Habitat in Hispania. Loefl." RCN: 887.
Type not designated.
Original material: none traced.
Current name: ***Crucianella patula*** L. (Rubiaceae).

Cucubalus acaulis Linnaeus, *Species Plantarum* 1: 415. 1753.
"Habitat in Alpibus Lapponicis, Helveticis, Anglicis." RCN: 3272.
Basionym of: *Silene acaulis* (L.) L. (1762).

Lectotype (Talavera & Muñoz Garmendia in *Anales Jard. Bot. Madrid* 45: 445. 1989): Herb. Linn. No. 583.61, upper specimen (LINN).
Current name: ***Silene acaulis*** (L.) Jacq. (Caryophyllaceae).

Cucubalus aegyptiacus Linnaeus, *Species Plantarum* 1: 415. 1753.
"Habitat in Aegypto." RCN: 3228.
Neotype (Hosny in Cafferty & Jarvis in *Taxon* 53: 1051. 2004): Israel. Jerusalem, 17 Mar 1911, *J.E. Dinsmore 618* (CAI).
Current name: ***Silene aegyptiaca*** (L.) L. f. (Caryophyllaceae).
Note: Melzheimer (in Rechinger, *Fl. Iranica* 163: 499. 1988) stated "Typus…Herb. Linn.", but this does not distinguish between sheets 582.8 and 582.10, both of which bear the epithet "aegyptiacus". However, on sheet 582.8 this epithet has been deleted in favour of "5 stellatus" (written by Linnaeus), and the material is a good match for the protologue of *C. stellatus* L., of which name it is the lectotype. Sheet 582.10 bears material received from Latour, lacks a *Species Plantarum* number (i.e. "7"), and was received after 1753. Neither sheet is original material for *C. aegyptiacus*. Linnaeus mentioned Hasselquist in the protologue but, in the absence of any extant material, Hosny designated a neotype.

Cucubalus baccifer Linnaeus, *Species Plantarum* 1: 414. 1753.
"Habitat in Tatariae, Germaniae, Galliae, Italiae nemoribus." RCN: 3223.
Lectotype (Rechinger, *Fl. Iranica* 163: 508. 1988): Herb. Linn. No. 582.1 (LINN).
Generitype of *Cucubalus* Linnaeus (vide Green, *Prop. Brit. Bot.*: 155. 1929).
Current name: ***Silene baccifera*** (L.) Roth (Caryophyllaceae).

Cucubalus behen Linnaeus, *Species Plantarum* 1: 414. 1753.
"Habitat in Europae septentrionalioris pratis siccis." RCN: 3224.
Lectotype (Aeschimann & Bocquet in *Candollea* 38: 204, photo 1. 1983): Herb. Linn. No. 582.4 (LINN).
Current name: ***Silene vulgaris*** (Moench) Garcke subsp. ***vulgaris*** (Caryophyllaceae).

Cucubalus catholicus Linnaeus, *Species Plantarum* 1: 415. 1753.
"Habitat in Italia, Sicilia." RCN: 3232.
Lectotype (Jeanmonod in *Candollea* 40: 30, f. 7. 1985): Herb. Linn. No. 582.18 (LINN).
Current name: ***Silene catholica*** (L.) W.T. Aiton (Caryophyllaceae).

Cucubalus fabarius Linnaeus, *Species Plantarum* 1: 414. 1753.
"Habitat in Sicilia." RCN: 3225.
Neotype (Melzheimer in *Bot. Jahrb. Syst.* 101: 167. 1980): Herb. Tournefort, "Lychnis maritima saxatilis, folio anacampserotis" (P-TOURN).
Current name: ***Silene fabaria*** (L.) Sm. subsp. ***fabaria*** (Caryophyllaceae).

Cucubalus giganteus Linnaeus, *Species Plantarum* 1: 418; *Species Plantarum* 2: Errata. 1753.
"Habitat in Lusitania." RCN: 3250.
Basionym of: *Silene gigantea* (L.) L. (1759).
Lectotype (Greuter in *Willdenowia* 25: 113. 1995): Herb. Linn. No. 583.26 (LINN).
Current name: ***Silene gigantea*** (L.) L. (Caryophyllaceae).
Note: Linnaeus transferred *Silene gigantea* L., *Sp. Pl.* 1: 418 (1753) to *Cucubalus*, as *C. giganteus* L. in the Errata on p. 1231 (1753).

Cucubalus italicus Linnaeus, *Systema Naturae*, ed. 10, 2: 1030. 1759.
["Habitat in Italia."] Sp. Pl., ed. 2, 1: 593 (1762). RCN: 3229.
Lectotype (Ghafoor in Jafri & El-Gadi, *Fl. Libya* 63: 85. 1978): Herb. Linn. No. 582.13 (LINN).

Current name: ***Silene italica*** (L.) Pers. subsp. ***italica*** (Caryophyllaceae).
Note: Greuter (in *Willdenowia* 25: 109. 1995) states that the designated lectotype does not fit the current application of *S. italica* L. subsp. *italica*, and that a proposal for a conserved type will be necessary. However, no formal proposal has yet been published.

Cucubalus mollissimus Linnaeus, *Species Plantarum,* ed. 2, 1: 593. 1762.
"Habitat in Italiae maritimis." RCN: 3233.
Lectotype (Jeanmonod in *Candollea* 39: 228, f. 14. 1984): Herb. Linn. No. 582.20, right specimen (LINN).
Current name: ***Silene mollissima*** (L.) Pers. (Caryophyllaceae).

Cucubalus otites Linnaeus, *Species Plantarum* 1: 415. 1753.
"Habitat in Silesia, Austria, Gallia, Sibiria." RCN: 3234.
Lectotype (Talavera & Muñoz Garmendia in *Anales Jard. Bot. Madrid* 45: 443, 445. 1989): Herb. Burser XI: 69, right flowering specimen (UPS).
Current name: ***Silene otites*** (L.) Wibel (Caryophyllaceae).

Cucubalus pumilio Linnaeus, *Systema Naturae*, ed. 12, 2: 309; *Mantissa Plantarum*: 71. 1767.
"Habitat in Alpibus Italiae, Moraviae. Arduini." RCN: 3247.
Lectotype (Chater in Cafferty & Jarvis in *Taxon* 53: 1051. 2004): *Arduino 24*, Herb. Linn. No. 582.23 (LINN).
Current name: ***Saponaria pumila*** Janch. ex Hayek (Caryophyllaceae).
Note: See Gutermann (in *Phyton (Horn)* 17: 44–45. 1975) on the correct name for this taxon.

Cucubalus quadrifidus Linnaeus, *Species Plantarum* 1: 415. 1753.
"Habitat in Styriae monte ad oppidum Eisenertz." RCN: 3268.
Basionym of: *Silene quadrifida* (L.) L. (1759); *Lychnis quadridentata* L. (1774), *nom. illeg.*
Lectotype (Melzheimer & Polatschek in *Phyton (Horn)* 31: 285. 1992): [icon] *"Caryophyllus minimus humilis alter exoticus flore candido amoeno"* in Plantin, Pl. Stirp. Icon.: 445. 1581.
Current name: ***Silene quadrifida*** (L.) L. (Caryophyllaceae).
Note: Juel (in *Nova Acta Reg. Soc. Sci. Upsal., Ser. IV,* 5(7): 72–73. 1923) provided an extensive discussion around the name, and particularly the Burser material, which was evidently the source of Linnaeus' "Habitat in Styriae monte ad oppidum Eisenertz". However, he does not appear to refer to the Burser material as the type. Walters (in *Feddes Repert.* 69: 47. 1964) stated that Dandy had advised him that the (unspecified) type of *C. quadrifidus* was identifiable as *S. alpestris* Jacq., and Walters therefore recommended that *C. quadrifidus* be rejected as a *nomen ambiguum*. Rauschert (in *Feddes Repert.* 79: 415. 1969) also discussed the name, though apparently without indicating a type himself.
    However, Melzheimer & Polatschek (in *Phyton (Horn)* 31: 284. 1992) subsequently used the name *S. quadrifidus* (L.) L. in the sense of *S. alpestris*, having formally chosen the cited Plantin plate as a neotype. As the plate was cited by Linnaeus, it is in fact a lectotype (treated as a correctable error under Art. 9.8).

Cucubalus reflexus Linnaeus, *Species Plantarum* 1: 416. 1753.
"Habitat Monspelii." RCN: 3235.
Lectotype (Talavera in Cafferty & Jarvis in *Taxon* 53: 1051. 2004): Herb. Linn. No. 582.22 (LINN).
Current name: ***Silene nocturna*** L. (Caryophyllaceae).
Note: Chater & al. (in Tutin & al., *Fl. Europaea*, ed. 2, 1: 217. 1993) stated that the name probably relates to a cleistogamous variant of *S. nocturna* subsp. *nocturna*. In typifying the name, Talavera confirmed this identification and synonymy.

Cucubalus sibiricus Linnaeus, *Systema Naturae,* ed. 10, 2: 1031. 1759.
["Habitat in desertis Tacorow; inter Woroniz & Bielgrod."] Sp. Pl., ed. 2, 1: 592 (1762). RCN: 3231.
Lectotype (Lazkov in *Bot. Zhurn.* 83(5): 93. 1998): [icon] *"Viscago foliis imis petiolatis ovatis floribus paniculatis emarginatis"* in Haller, Brev. Enum. Stirp. Hort. Gott.: 91, unnumbered plate. 1743. – Epitype (Lazkov in Cafferty & Jarvis in *Taxon* 53: 1051. 2004): Herb. Linn. No. 582.16 (LINN).
Current name: ***Silene sibirica*** (L.) Pers. (Caryophyllaceae).

Cucubalus stellatus Linnaeus, *Species Plantarum* 1: 414. 1753.
"Habitat in Virginia, Canada." RCN: 3227.
Lectotype (Rabeler in Cafferty & Jarvis in *Taxon* 53: 1051. 2004): Herb. Linn. No. 582.8 (LINN).
Current name: ***Silene stellata*** (L.) W.T. Aiton (Caryophyllaceae).

Cucubalus tataricus Linnaeus, *Species Plantarum* 1: 415. 1753.
"Habitat in Tataria." RCN: 3230.
Lectotype (Jonsell & Jarvis in *Nordic J. Bot.* 14: 156. 1994): Herb. Linn. No. 582.15 (LINN).
Current name: ***Silene tatarica*** (L.) Pers. (Caryophyllaceae).

Cucubalus viscosus Linnaeus, *Species Plantarum* 1: 414. 1753.
"Habitat in Svecia, Italia, Anglia." RCN: 3226.
Lectotype (Ghazanfar & Nasir in Nasir & Ali, *Fl. Pakistan* 175: 64. 1986): Herb. Linn. No. 582.7 (LINN).
Current name: ***Silene viscosa*** (L.) Pers. (Caryophyllaceae).

Cucumis acutangulus Linnaeus, *Species Plantarum* 2: 1011. 1753.
"Habitat in Tataria, China." RCN: 7332.
Type not designated.
Original material: Herb. Linn. No. 394.15 (S); [icon] in Grew, Mus. Reg. Societ.: 229, t. 17. 1681; [icon] in Plukenet, Phytographia: t. 172, f. 1. 1692; Almag. Bot.: 123. 1696.
Current name: ***Luffa acutangula*** (L.) Roxb. (Cucurbitaceae).
Note: Jeffrey (in *Kew Bull.* 34: 792. 1980), and many later authors have treated 1152.7 (LINN) as the type. However, this collection lacks the relevant *Species Plantarum* number (i.e. "3") and was a post-1753 addition to the herbarium, and is not original material for the name.

Cucumis anguinus Linnaeus, *Systema Naturae,* ed. 10, 2: 1279. 1759.
["Habitat in India."] Sp. Pl., ed. 2, 2: 1438 (1763). RCN: 7337.
Lectotype (Merrill, *Interpret. Rumph. Herb. Amb.*: 494. 1917): [icon] *"Petola Anguina"* in Rumphius, Herb. Amboin. 5: 407, t. 148. 1747 (see p. 18).
Current name: ***Trichosanthes cucumerina*** L. (Cucurbitaceae).

Cucumis anguria Linnaeus, *Species Plantarum* 2: 1011. 1753.
"Habitat in Jamaica." RCN: 7331.
Lectotype (Jeffrey in Stoffers & Lindeman, *Fl. Suriname* 5(1): 486. 1984): Herb. Linn. No. 1152.6 (LINN), see above, right.
Current name: ***Cucumis anguria*** L. (Cucurbitaceae).

Cucumis chate Linnaeus, *Systema Naturae,* ed. 10, 2: 1279. 1759.
["Habitat in Aegypto, Arabia. Hasselquist."] Sp. Pl., ed. 2, 2: 1437 (1763). RCN: 7335.
Lectotype (Jeffrey, *Cucurbitaceae Eastern Asia*: 20. 1980): Herb. Linn. No. 1152.11 (LINN).
Current name: ***Cucumis melo*** L. (Cucurbitaceae).

Cucumis colocynthis Linnaeus, *Species Plantarum* 2: 1011. 1753.
"Habitat – – – –" RCN: 7329.
Type not designated.

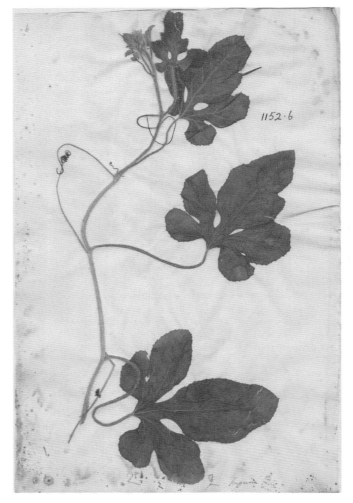

The lectotype of *Cucumis anguria* L.

Original material: Herb. Linn. No. 1152.2 (LINN); [icon] in Mattioli, Pl. Epit.: 982. 1586.
Current name: ***Citrullus colocynthis*** (L.) Schrad. (Cucurbitaceae).
Note: Numerous authors (e.g. Jeffrey in Meikle, *Fl. Cyprus* 1: 676. 1977) have incorrectly treated 1152.1 (LINN) as the type. This collection lacks the relevant *Species Plantarum* number (i.e. "1") and was a post-1753 addition to the herbarium, and is not original material for the name.

Cucumis dudaim Linnaeus, *Species Plantarum* 2: 1011. 1753.
"Habitat in Aegypto, Arabia. Hasselquist." RCN: 7334.
Lectotype (Jeffrey, *Cucurbitaceae Eastern Asia*: 20. 1980): [icon] *"Melo variegatus, Aurantii figura, odoratissimus"* in Dillenius, Hort. Eltham. 2: 223, t. 177, f. 218. 1732. – Typotype: Herb. Dillenius (OXF).
Current name: ***Cucumis melo*** L. (Cucurbitaceae).

Cucumis flexuosus Linnaeus, *Species Plantarum,* ed. 2, 2: 1437. 1763.
"Habitat in India?" RCN: 7338.
Lectotype (Kirkbride, *Biosyst. Monogr.* Cucumis: 104. 1993): [icon] *"Cucumeres longissimi"* in Bauhin & Cherler, Hist. Pl. Univ. 2: 247, 248. 1651.
Current name: ***Cucumis melo*** L. (Cucurbitaceae).

Cucumis maderaspatanus Linnaeus, *Species Plantarum* 2: 1012. 1753.
"Habitat in India." RCN: 7339.
Lectotype (Meeuse in *Bothalia* 8: 14. 1962): [icon] *"Cucumis Maderaspatensis fructu minimo"* in Plukenet, Phytographia: t. 170, f. 2. 1692; Almag. Bot.: 123. 1696. – Typotype: Herb. Sloane 95: 201 (BM-SL).
Current name: ***Mukia maderaspatana*** (L.) M. Roem. (Cucurbitaceae).

Cucumis melo Linnaeus, *Species Plantarum* 2: 1011. 1753.
"Habitat – – – –" RCN: 7333.
Lectotype (Meeuse in *Bothalia* 8: 61. 1962): Herb. Linn. No. 1152.8 (LINN).
Current name: ***Cucumis melo*** L. (Cucurbitaceae).
Note: See notes by Kirkbride (in *Biosyst. Monogr. Cucumis*: 81. 1993).

Cucumis pedatus Linnaeus, *Systema Naturae*, ed. 10, 2: 1279. 1759.
RCN: 7038.
Lectotype (Howard in *J. Arnold Arbor.* 54: 441. 1973): [icon] *"Cucumis foliis pedatis"* in Plumier in Burman, Pl. Amer.: 13, t. 23. 1755.
Current name: ***Psiguria pedata*** (L.) R.A. Howard (Cucurbitaceae).

Cucumis prophetarum Linnaeus, *Centuria I Plantarum*: 33. 1755.
"Habitat in Arabia." RCN: 7330.
Lectotype (Jeffrey in *Kew Bull.* 15: 350. 1962): Herb. Linn. No. 1152.4 (LINN; iso- UPS?).
Current name: ***Cucumis prophetarum*** L. (Cucurbitaceae).

Cucumis sativus Linnaeus, *Species Plantarum* 2: 1012. 1753.
"Habitat – – – –" RCN: 7336.
Lectotype (ten Pas & al. in *Taxon* 34: 290, f. 1–3. 1985): Herb. Burser XVII: 97 (UPS).
Generitype of *Cucumis* Linnaeus (vide Green, *Prop. Brit. Bot.*: 190. 1929).
Current name: ***Cucumis sativus*** L. (Cucurbitaceae).
Note: Jeffrey (in *Kew Bull.* 34: 794 . 1980) designated the *Hortus Cliffortianus* diagnosis as the lectotype but a phrase name cannot serve as a type. Keraudren-Aymonin (in Aubréville & Leroy, *Fl. Cambodge Laos Viêt-Nam* 15: 72 (1975) similarly indicated as type a *Hortus Cliffortianus* illustration ("t. 451") which does not exist.

Cucumis trifoliatus Linnaeus, *Systema Naturae*, ed. 10, 2: 1279. 1759.
RCN: 7039.
Type not designated.
Original material: none traced.
Current name: ***Psiguria trifoliata*** (L.) Alain (Cucurbitaceae).
Note: Pruski (in *Brittonia* 51: 326. 1999) states *Anguria trifoliata* L. (1763) is a new combination for this but the evidence seems purely circumstantial; *C. trifoliatus* disappears in 1763 (when *A. trifoliata* appears) and does not feature in *Syst. Nat.* ed. 12 (1767) either. However, the two names do not have the same diagnosis, and *A. trifoliata* has Plumier *Pl. Amer.*: t. 99 as a synonym, unlike *C. trifoliatus*. There is no explicit link between the names apart from an epithet in common.

Cucumis trilobatus Linnaeus, *Systema Naturae*, ed. 10, 2: 1279. 1759.
RCN: 7036.
Lectotype (Howard in *J. Arnold Arbor.* 54: 442. 1973): [icon] *"Cucumis foliis cordatis, tripartitis"* in Plumier in Burman, Pl. Amer.: 13, t. 22. 1755.
Current name: ***Psiguria trilobata*** (L.) R.A. Howard (Cucurbitaceae).

Cucurbita citrullus Linnaeus, *Species Plantarum* 2: 1010. 1753.
"Habitat in Apulia, Calabria, Sicilia." RCN: 7327.
Type not designated.
Original material: Herb. Burser XVII: 101 (UPS); [icon] in Bauhin & Cherler, Hist. Pl. Univ. 2: 235, 236. 1651.
Current name: ***Citrullus lanatus*** (Thunb.) Mansf. (Cucurbitaceae).
Note: Bailey (in *Gentes Herb.* 2: 79. 1929; 2: 185. 1930) reproduced the protologue, and noted the existence of material in LINN. Jeffrey (in Milne-Redhead & Polhill, *Fl. Trop. E. Africa, Cucurbitaceae*: 47. 1967), followed by some later authors, designated 1151.5 (LINN) as lectotype, but this collection lacks the relevant *Species Plantarum* number (i.e. "5") and was a post-1753 addition to the herbarium, and is not original material for the name. Jeffrey subsequently (in *Kew Bull.* 34: 791. 1980) recognised this, and observed that the LINN sheet should perhaps be regarded as a neotype. However, as original material is in existence, this would be contrary to Art. 9.11.

Cucurbita lagenaria Linnaeus, *Species Plantarum* 2: 1010. 1753.
"Habitat in Americae riguis." RCN: 7322.
Lectotype (Jeffrey in Milne-Redhead & Polhill, *Fl. Trop. E. Africa, Cucurbitaceae*: 51. 1967): Herb. Linn. No. 1151.1 (LINN).
Current name: ***Lagenaria siceraria*** (Molina) Standl. (Cucurbitaceae).
Note: See Bailey (in *Gentes Herb.* 2: 79. 1929), who reproduced the protologue, and noted the existence of material in LINN.

Cucurbita melopepo Linnaeus, *Species Plantarum* 2: 1010. 1753.
"Habitat – – – – –" RCN: 7326.
Type not designated.
Original material: Herb. Burser XVII: 100 (UPS); [icon] in Bauhin & Cherler, Hist. Pl. Univ. 2: 224. 1651.
Current name: ***Cucurbita pepo*** L. var. ***melopepo*** (L.) Alef. (Cucurbitaceae).
Note: See Bailey (in *Gentes Herb.* 2: 79. 1929), who reproduced the protologue, and (as f. 40) the cited Bauhin & Cherler figure.

Cucurbita ovifera Linnaeus, *Systema Naturae*, ed. 12, 2: 639; *Mantissa Plantarum*: 126. 1767.
"Habitat ad Astrachan. DD. Lerche." RCN: 7323.
Lectotype (Bailey in *Gentes Herb.* 2: 88, f. 41. 1929): Herb. Linn. No. 1151.2 (LINN).
Current name: ***Cucurbita pepo*** L. var. ***ovifera*** (L.) Alef. (Cucurbitaceae).
Note: Bailey's illustration of the type sheet (f. 41) confirms that it is sheet no. 1151.2 (LINN) rather than 1151.3.

Cucurbita pepo Linnaeus, *Species Plantarum* 2: 1010. 1753.
"Habitat – – – –" RCN: 7324.
Lectotype (Keraudren-Aymonin in Aubréville & Leroy, *Fl. Cambodge Laos Viêt-Nam* 15: 105. 1975): Herb. Linn. No. 1151.4 (LINN).
Generitype of *Cucurbita* Linnaeus.
Current name: ***Cucurbita pepo*** L. (Cucurbitaceae).
Note: Cucurbita pepo, with Herb. Burser XVII: 103 (UPS) as type, was proposed as conserved type of the genus by Jarvis (in *Taxon* 41: 562. 1992). However, the proposal was eventually ruled unnecessary by the General Committee (see Barrie, *l.c.* 55: 795–796. 2006 for a review of the history of this and related proposals).
   Bailey (in *Gentes Herb.* 2: 79. 1929) reproduced the protologue, and various of the original elements (including a Daléchamps figure and a LINN sheet), and provided an extensive discussion. Keraudren-Aymonin's (1975) type choice of 1151.4 (LINN) has priority over that of the Burser material designated by Jeffrey (in Jarvis, *l.c.* 41: 562. 1992) and becomes the type with the failure of the conservation proposal.

Cucurbita verrucosa Linnaeus, *Species Plantarum* 2: 1010. 1753.
"Habitat – – – –" RCN: 7325.
Type not designated.
Original material: [icon] in Bauhin & Cherler, Hist. Pl. Univ. 2: 222. 1651.
Current name: ***Cucurbita pepo*** L. (Cucurbitaceae).
Note: See Bailey (in *Gentes Herb.* 2: 79. 1929), who reproduced the protologue, and Bauhin & Cherler's cited figure (as f. 39).

Cuminum cyminum Linnaeus, *Species Plantarum* 1: 254. 1753.
"Habitat in Aegypto, Aethiopia." RCN: 2040.
Lectotype (Jansen, *Spices, Condiments Med. Pl. Ethiopia*: 71. 1981): Herb. Linn. No. 358.1 (LINN).
Generitype of *Cuminum* Linnaeus.
Current name: ***Cuminum cyminum*** L. (Apiaceae).

Cunila mariana Linnaeus, *Species Plantarum*, ed. 2, 1: 30. 1762, *nom. illeg.*
"Habitat in Virginia." RCN: 169.
Replaced synonym: *Satureja origanoides* L. (1753).
Lectotype (Reveal & al. in *Huntia* 7: 215. 1987): *Kalm*, Herb. Linn. No. 38.1 (LINN).
Generitype of *Cunila* Royen ex Linnaeus (1759), *nom. cons.*
Current name: ***Cunila origanoides*** (L.) Britton (Lamiaceae).
Note: Cunila van Royen ex Linnaeus (1759), *nom. cons.* against *Cunila* Linnaeus ex P. Miller (1754), *nom. rej.*
        Epling (in *J. Bot.* 67: 7. 1929) indicated *Clayton 197* (BM) as a "standard specimen". This was wrongly indicated as a type choice by Jarvis & al. (*Regnum Veg.* 127: 40. 1993) and is not acceptable as a typification (see Jarvis & al. in *Taxon* 50: 508. 2001).

Cunila pulegioides (Linnaeus) Linnaeus, *Species Plantarum*, ed. 2, 1: 30. 1762.
"Habitat in Virginiae, Canadae siccis." RCN: 170.
Basionym: *Melissa pulegioides* L. (1753).
Lectotype (Irving in *Sida* 8: 288. 1980): *Clayton 514* (BM-000576253).
Current name: ***Hedeoma pulegioides*** (L.) Pers. (Lamiaceae).
Note: Epling (in *J. Bot.* 67: 9. 1929) noted Herb. Linn. No. 38.3 (LINN), a Kalm specimen, as standard but this is not equivalent to a type statement (see Jarvis & al. in *Taxon* 50: 508. 2001).

Cunila thymoides Linnaeus, *Species Plantarum*, ed. 2, 1: 31. 1762.
"Habitat Monspelii. D. Sauvages." RCN: 171.
Replaced synonym: *Thymus pulegioides* L. (1753).
Lectotype (Ronniger in *Heilpfl.-Schriftenr.* 18: 37. 1944): Herb. Linn. No. 38.5 (LINN).
Current name: ***Thymus pulegioides*** L. (Lamiaceae).
Note: This is a legitimate *nomen novum* since, in 1762, Linnaeus simultaneously transferred to *Cunila* both *Melissa pulegioides* L. (1753) (as *C. pulegioides* (L.) L.) and *Thymus pulegioides* L. (1753), only one of which could therefore retain its original epithet.

Cunonia capensis Linnaeus, *Systema Naturae*, ed. 10, 2: 1025. 1759.
["Habitat ad Cap. b. spei."] Sp. Pl., ed. 2, 1: 569 (1762). RCN: 133.
Type not designated.
Original material: Herb. Linn. No. 571.1 (LINN); [icon] in Burman, Rar. Afric. Pl.: 259, t. 96. 1739.
Generitype of *Cunonia* Linnaeus, *nom. cons.*
Current name: ***Cunonia capensis*** L. (Cunoniaceae).
Note: Cunonia Linnaeus, *nom. cons.* against *Cunonia* Mill.

Cupania americana Linnaeus, *Species Plantarum* 1: 200. 1753.
"Habitat in America calidiore." RCN: 7289.
Lectotype (Pennington in Jarvis & al., *Regnum Veg.* 127: 40. 1993):

[icon] *"Cupania"* in Plumier in Burman, Pl. Amer.: 101, t. 110. 1757.
Generitype of *Cupania* Linnaeus.
Current name: ***Cupania americana*** L. (Sapindaceae).

Cupressus disticha Linnaeus, *Species Plantarum* 2: 1003. 1753.
"Habitat in Virginia, Carolina." RCN: 7257.
Lectotype (Wijnands, *Bot. Commelins*: 196. 1983): Herb. Clifford: 449, *Cupressus* 2, sheet A (BM-000647432).
Current name: ***Taxodium distichum*** (L.) A. Rich. (Taxodiaceae).

Cupressus juniperoides Linnaeus, *Species Plantarum*, ed. 2, 2: 1422. 1763.
"Habitat ad Cap. b. spei." RCN: 7259.
Type not designated.
Original material: none traced.
Current name: ***Widdringtonia nodiflora*** (L.) Powrie (Cupressaceae).
Note: The application of this name is uncertain and it was rejected as a *nomen ambiguum* by Marsh (in *Bothalia* 9: 124. 1966). See further comments by Powrie (in *J. S. African Bot.* 38: 303. 1972), and by Farjon (*Monogr. Cupressaceae* Sciadopitys: 469. 2005), who believes *C. juniperoides* is unlikely to relate to a species of *Widdringtonia*.

Cupressus sempervirens Linnaeus, *Species Plantarum* 2: 1002. 1753.
"Habitat in Creta." RCN: 7256.
Lectotype (Silba in *Phytologia* 52: 357, f. 1. 1983): Herb. Clifford: 449, *Cupressus* 1 β (BM-000647431).
Generitype of *Cupressus* Linnaeus (vide Hutchinson in *Bull. Misc. Inform. Kew* 1924: 61. 1924).
Current name: ***Cupressus sempervirens*** L. (Cupressaceae).

Cupressus thyoides Linnaeus, *Species Plantarum* 2: 1003. 1753.
"Habitat in Canada. Kalm." RCN: 7258.
Lectotype (Reveal & al. in *Huntia* 7: 219. 1987): *Kalm*, Herb. Linn. No. 1137.4 (LINN; iso- UPS).
Current name: ***Chamaecyparis thyoides*** (L.) Britton & al. (Cupressaceae).

Curatella americana Linnaeus, *Systema Naturae*, ed. 10, 2: 1079. 1759.
["Habitat in America meridionali."] Sp. Pl., ed. 2, 1: 748 (1762). RCN: 3942.
Neotype (Todzia & Barrie in *Taxon* 40: 488. 1991): Venezuela. Guarico, around San Juan de los Morros, 500m, 29 Nov 1938, *Williams & Alston 97* (LL; iso- BM).
Current name: ***Curatella americana*** L. (Dilleniaceae).

Curcuma longa Linnaeus, *Species Plantarum* 1: 2. 1753, *typ. cons.*
"Habitat in India." RCN: 13.
Type not designated.
Original material: Herb. Hermann 3: 5, No. 7 (BM); Herb. Linn. No. 7.4 (LINN); [icon] in Hermann, Hort. Lugd.-Bat. Cat.: 208, 209. 1687.
Generitype of *Curcuma* Linnaeus, *nom. cons.*
Current name: ***Curcuma longa*** L. (Zingiberaceae).
Note: Although *Curcuma* is conserved, with *C. longa* as its conserved type, the type of *C. longa* is itself uncertain. Merrill (*Interpret. Rumph. Herb. Amb.*: 163. 1917) said that it was "based wholly on *Curcuma radice longa* Herm.", but this comprises an illustration and a specimen, both of which were similarly treated as type by Burtt & Smith (in *Notes Roy. Bot. Gard. Edinburgh* 31: 185. 1972). Burtt & Smith treated *C. longa* as a *nomen dubium* in line with earlier authors such as Valeton, Alston etc., based on difficulties in identification.

Curcuma rotunda Linnaeus, *Species Plantarum* 1: 2. 1753.
"Habitat in India." RCN: 12.
Lectotype (Burtt & Smith in *Notes Roy. Bot. Gard. Edinburgh* 31: 184. 1972): [icon] *"Manja-kua"* in Rheede, Hort. Malab. 11: 19, t. 10. 1692.
Current name: ***Boesenbergia rotunda*** (L.) Mansf. (Zingiberaceae).

Cuscuta americana Linnaeus, *Species Plantarum* 1: 124. 1753.
"Habitat in Virginia." RCN: 1024.
Lectotype (Engelmann in *Trans. Acad. Sci. St. Louis* 1: 482. 1859): Herb. Linn. No. 170.5 (LINN).
Current name: ***Cuscuta americana*** L. (Cuscutaceae).
Note: Believing none of the original elements to correspond with usage, Reveal & al. (in *Taxon* 39: 360. 1990) proposed the name for conservation with a conserved type. The Committee for Spermatophyta, however, ruled that Engelmann had formally chosen (the post-1753) 170.5 (LINN) as lectotype, and (in *Taxon* 42: 876. 1993) "recommends…that this typification be accepted". This rendered the conservation proposal unnecessary and it was not recommended.

Cuscuta epithymum (Linnaeus) Linnaeus, *Amoenitates Academicae* 4: 478. 1759.
RCN: 1023.
Basionym: *Cuscuta europaea* L. var. *epithymum* L. (1753).
Lectotype (García & Cafferty in *Taxon* 54: 478. 2005): Herb. Burser XII: 104 (UPS).
Current name: ***Cuscuta epithymum*** (L.) L. (Cuscutaceae).
Note: Some authors have treated this combination as dating from other publications – see discussion by García & Cafferty (in *Taxon* 54: 477. 2005).

Cuscuta europaea Linnaeus, *Species Plantarum* 1: 124. 1753.
"Habitat in Plantis Europae parasitica." RCN: 1022.
Lectotype (Rajput & Tahir in Nasir & Ali, *Fl. Pakistan* 189: 16. 1988): Herb. Linn. No. 170.1 (LINN).
Generitype of *Cuscuta* Linnaeus (vide Hitchcock, *Prop. Brit. Bot.*: 126. 1929).
Current name: ***Cuscuta europaea*** L. (Cuscutaceae).

Cuscuta europaea Linnaeus var. **epithymum** Linnaeus, *Species Plantarum* 1: 124. 1753.
RCN: 1023.
Basionym of: *Cuscuta epithymum* (L.) L. (1759).
Lectotype (García & Cafferty in *Taxon* 54: 478. 2005): Herb. Burser XII: 104 (UPS).
Current name: ***Cuscuta epithymum*** (L.) L. (Cuscutaceae).
Note: Rajpur & Tahir (in Nair & Ali, *Fl. Pakistan* 189: 14. 1988) erroneously designated 170.4 (LINN), which is not original material, as the type for this name. García & Cafferty rejected this type choice, designating instead Burser material as lectotype.

Cyanella capensis Linnaeus, *Systema Naturae*, ed. 10, 2: 985. 1759, *nom. illeg.*
["Habitat ad Cap. b. spei."] Sp. Pl., ed. 2, 1: 443 (1762). RCN: 2437.
Replaced synonym: *Cyanella hyacinthoides* L. (1754).
Lectotype (Bullock in *Kew Bull.* 8: 553. 1953): Herb. Linn. No. 430.2 (LINN).
Current name: ***Cyanella hyacinthoides*** L. (Liliaceae/Tecophilaeaceae).
Note: A superfluous name for *C. hyacinthoides* L. (1754).

Cyanella hyacinthoides Linnaeus, *Genera Plantarum,* ed. 5: Appendix. 1754.
"Habitat ad Caput b. spei." RCN: 2437.
Replaced synonym of: *Cyanella capensis* L. (1759), *nom. illeg.*

Lectotype (Bullock in *Kew Bull.* 8: 553. 1953): Herb. Linn. No. 430.2 (LINN).
Generitype of *Cyanella* Linnaeus.
Current name: ***Cyanella hyacinthoides*** L. (Liliaceae/Tecophilaeaceae).

Cycas circinalis Linnaeus, *Species Plantarum* 2: 1188. 1753.
"Habitat in India." RCN: 7736.
Lectotype (Stevenson in Jarvis & al., *Regnum Veg.* 127: 40. 1993): [icon] *"Todda-panna"* in Rheede, Hort. Malab. 3: 9, t. 19. 1682 (see pp. 154–155).
Generitype of *Cycas* Linnaeus.
Current name: ***Cycas circinalis*** L. (Cycadaceae).
Note: Stapf (in *Bull. Misc. Inform. Kew* 1916(12): 1–8. 1916) referred to Rheede's t. 13–21 as "the accepted basis of Linnaeus' species". Rheede's nine plates represent a number of different taxa (see Hill in *Taxon* 44: 23–31. 1995) and, for this reason, Stevenson designated Rheede's t. 19 as lectotype.

Cyclamen europaeum Linnaeus, *Species Plantarum* 1: 145. 1753, *nom. rej.*
"Habitat in Austriae, Tatariae, Europae australis nemorosis." RCN: 1160.
Lectotype (Cafferty & Grey-Wilson in *Taxon* 47: 479. 1998): Herb. Burser XVII: 89 (UPS).
Generitype of *Cyclamen* Linnaeus (vide Hitchcock, *Prop. Brit. Bot.*: 129. 1929).
Current name: ***Cyclamen purpurascens*** Mill. (Primulaceae).

Cyclamen indicum Linnaeus, *Species Plantarum* 1: 145. 1753.
"Habitat in Zeylona." RCN: 1161.
Lectotype (Stearn in *Israel J. Bot.* 19: 266, f. 1. 1970): Herb. Hermann 5: 461, No. 401 [icon] (BM).
Note: In typifying the name, Stearn also argued for its rejection as a *nomen ambiguum* under (the then) Art. 71. However, no formal proposal for rejection appears to have been made.

Cymbaria daurica Linnaeus, *Species Plantarum* 2: 618. 1753.
"Habitat in Dauriae montanis, apricis, saxosis." RCN: 4469.
Lectotype (Sutton in Jarvis & al., *Regnum Veg.* 127: 40. 1993): [icon] *"Cymbaria Daurica, pumila, incana, Linariae folio, magno flore luteo, guttato"* in Amman, Stirp. Rar. Ruth.: 36, t. 1, f. 2. 1739.
Generitype of *Cymbaria* Linnaeus.
Current name: ***Cymbaria daurica*** L. (Scrophulariaceae).

Cynanchum acutum Linnaeus, *Species Plantarum* 1: 212. 1753.
"Habitat in Sicilia, Hispania, Astracan." RCN: 1754.
Lectotype (Ali in Nasir & Ali, *Fl. Pakistan* 150: 12. 1983): *Löfling s.n.*, Herb. Linn. No. 308.3 (LINN).
Generitype of *Cynanchum* Linnaeus (vide Meyer, *Comment. Pl. Afr. Austr.*: 216. 1838).
Current name: ***Cynanchum acutum*** L. (Asclepiadaceae).

Cynanchum aphyllum Linnaeus, *Systema Naturae,* ed. 12, 3: 235. 1768, *nom. illeg.*
RCN: 1753.
Replaced synonym: *Euphorbia viminalis* L. (1753).
Lectotype (Liede & Meve in *Bot. J. Linn. Soc.* 112: 2, f. 1. 1993): [icon] *"Felfel Tavil, Piper longum Aegyptium"* in Alpino, De Plantis Aegypti: 190, t. 53. 1735. – Epitype (Liede & Meve in *Bot. J. Linn. Soc.* 118: 47. 1995): *Bassi s.n.* Herb. Linn. No. 308.1 (LINN).
Current name: ***Sarcostemma viminale*** (L.) W.T. Aiton (Asclepiadaceae).
Note: A superfluous renaming of *Euphorbia viminalis* L. The combination *C. viminale*, based on *E. viminalis*, was made by Bassi (in *Comment. Acad. Inst. Sci. Art. Bonon.* 6: 17. 1768) and later taken up by Linnaeus (in *Mant. Pl. Alt.*: 392. 1771).

Cynanchum erectum Linnaeus, *Species Plantarum* 1: 213. 1753.
"Habitat in Syria." RCN: 1762.
Type not designated.
Original material: Herb. Clifford: 79, *Cynanchum* 4 (BM); Herb. Burser XVII: 50 (UPS); Herb. Linn. No. 308.12 (LINN); [icon] in Clusius, Rar. Pl. Hist. 1: 124. 1601.
Current name: ***Cionura erecta*** (L.) Griseb. (Asclepiadaceae).

Cynanchum hirtum Linnaeus, *Species Plantarum* 1: 212. 1753.
"Habitat in America." RCN: 1759.
Type not designated.
Original material: [icon] in Morison, Pl. Hist. Univ. 3: 611, s. 15, t. 3, f. 61. 1699.
Note: The application of this name appears uncertain.

Cynanchum monspeliacum Linnaeus, *Species Plantarum* 1: 212. 1753.
"Habitat in Hispania & Narbonae maritimis." RCN: 1760.
Type not designated.
Original material: Herb. Burser XVII: 2 (UPS); Herb. Clifford: 79, *Cynanchum* 2 (BM); Herb. Linn. No. 308.6 (LINN); [icon] in Clusius, Rar. Pl. Hist. 1: 126. 1601.
Current name: ***Cynanchum acutum*** L. (Asclepiadaceae).

Cynanchum suberosum Linnaeus, *Species Plantarum* 1: 212. 1753.
"Habitat in America calidiore." RCN: 1758.
Lectotype (Reveal & Barrie in *Bartonia* 57: 37. 1992): [icon] *"Periploca Carolinensis, flore minore stellato"* in Dillenius, Hort. Eltham. 2: 308, t. 229, f. 296. 1732.
Current name: ***Gonolobus suberosus*** (L.) R. Br. (Asclepiadaceae).

Cynara acaulis Linnaeus, *Species Plantarum*, ed. 2, 2: 1160. 1763.
"Habitat in Barbaria." RCN: 5991.
Lectotype (Dittrich in *Candollea* 39: 46. 1984): [icon] *"Cinara acaulos, Tunetana, Tafga dicta, magno flore suaviter olente"* in Tilli, Cat. Pl. Hort. Pisani: 41, t. 20, f. 1. 1723.
Current name: ***Rhaponticum acaule*** (L.) DC. (Asteraceae).

Cynara cardunculus Linnaeus, *Species Plantarum* 2: 827. 1753.
"Habitat in Creta." RCN: 5989.
Lectotype (Wiklund in *Bot. J. Linn. Soc.* 109: 113. 1992): [icon] *"Scolymus aculeatus"* in Tabernaemontanus, New Vollk. Kräuterb.: 1075. 1664.
Generitype of *Cynara* Linnaeus (vide Green, *Prop. Brit. Bot.*: 179. 1929).
Current name: ***Cynara cardunculus*** L. (Asteraceae).
Note: Although Wiklund cited an earlier (1590) Tabernaemontanus work as the place of publication of the lectotype figure, the pagination given by Linnaeus makes it clear that he had used a later (1664) work. Wiklund's intention was, however, entirely clear and this is treated as a minor, correctable error.

Cynara humilis Linnaeus, *Species Plantarum* 2: 828. 1753.
"Habitat in agro Tingitano in Baetica." RCN: 5990.
Lectotype (Wiklund in *Bot. J. Linn. Soc.* 109: 90. 1992): Herb. Linn. No. 969.2 (LINN).
Current name: ***Cynara humilis*** L. (Asteraceae).

Cynara scolymus Linnaeus, *Species Plantarum* 2: 827. 1753.
"Habitat in G. Narbonensis, Italiae, Siciliae agris." RCN: 5988.
Lectotype (Kupicha in Davis, *Fl. Turkey* 5: 329. 1975): Herb. Linn. No. 969.1 (LINN).
Current name: ***Cynara scolymus*** L. (Asteraceae).
Note: Although Davis (*Fl. Turkey* 1: 9. 1965; 10: 238. 1988) did not indicate this as a name typified in the Flora of Turkey, Kupicha (in

Davis, *l.c.* 5: 329. 1975) explicitly indicated 969.1 (LINN) as the lectotype, adding "designated here". This typification is accepted here.

Cynoglossum apenninum Linnaeus, *Species Plantarum* 1: 134. 1753.
"Habitat in alpibus Apenninis, Campoclarensibus, umbrosis." RCN: 1086.
Lectotype (Selvi in Cafferty & Jarvis in *Taxon* 53: 801. 2004): [icon] *"Cynoglossa mont. maxima"* in Colonna, Ekphr.: 168, 170. 1606.
Current name: ***Solenanthus apenninus*** (L.) Fisch. & C.A. Mey. (Boraginaceae).

Cynoglossum cheirifolium Linnaeus, *Species Plantarum* 1: 134. 1753.
"Habitat in Creta. Hispania." RCN: 1085.
Lectotype (Mill in Cafferty & Jarvis in *Taxon* 53: 801. 2004): Herb. Burser XIV(2): 32 (UPS).
Current name: ***Pardoglossum cheirifolium*** (L.) Barbier & Mathez subsp. ***cheirifolium*** (Boraginaceae).

Cynoglossum linifolium Linnaeus, *Species Plantarum* 1: 134. 1753.
"Habitat in Lusitania." RCN: 1088.
Lectotype (Selvi in Cafferty & Jarvis in *Taxon* 53: 801. 2004): Herb. Clifford: 47, *Cynoglossum* 3, sheet 2 (BM-000557922).
Current name: ***Omphalodes linifolia*** (L.) Moench (Boraginaceae).

Cynoglossum lusitanicum Linnaeus, *Species Plantarum*, ed. 2, 1: 193. 1762.
"Habitat in Lusitania." RCN: 1089.
Lectotype (Selvi in Cafferty & Jarvis in *Taxon* 53: 802. 2004): Herb. Linn. No. 183.8 (LINN).
Current name: ***Omphalodes nitida*** Hoffmanns. & Link (Boraginaceae).

Cynoglossum montanum Linnaeus, *Demonstr. Pl. Horto Upsaliensi*: 5. 1753.
RCN: 1083.
Lectotype (Lacaita in *Bull. Orto Bot. Regia Univ. Napoli* 3: 291. 1913): [icon] *"Cynoglossa med. mont. rub. flore"* in Colonna, Ekphr.: 176, 175. 1606.
Current name: ***Cynoglossum montanum*** L. (Boraginaceae).

Cynoglossum officinale Linnaeus, *Species Plantarum* 1: 134. 1753.
"Habitat in Europae ruderalis." RCN: 1082.
Lectotype (Verdcourt in Jarvis & al., *Regnum Veg.* 127: 40. 1993): Herb. Clifford: 47, *Cynoglossum* 1 (BM-000557917).
Generitype of *Cynoglossum* Linnaeus (vide Hitchcock, *Prop. Brit. Bot.*: 127. 1929).
Current name: ***Cynoglossum officinale*** L. (Boraginaceae).

Cynoglossum omphaloides Linnaeus, *Species Plantarum* 1: 135. 1753.
"Habitat in Lusitaniae nemorosis." RCN: 1090.
Lectotype (Selvi in Cafferty & Jarvis in *Taxon* 53: 802. 2004): Herb. Clifford: 47, *Cynoglossum* 4 (BM-000557924).
Current name: ***Omphalodes verna*** Moench (Boraginaceae).

Cynoglossum virginianum Linnaeus, *Species Plantarum* 1: 134. 1753.
"Habitat in Virginia." RCN: 1084.
Lectotype (Wells in Cafferty & Jarvis in *Taxon* 53: 802. 2004): *Clayton 257* (BM-000040317).
Current name: ***Cynoglossum virginianum*** L. (Boraginaceae).

Cynometra cauliflora Linnaeus, *Species Plantarum* 1: 382. 1753.
"Habitat in India." RCN: 3010.

Lectotype (Knaap-van Meeuwen in *Blumea* 18: 21. 1970): [icon] *"Cynomorium"* in Rumphius, Herb. Amboin. 1: 163, t. 62. 1741.

Generitype of *Cynometra* Linnaeus (vide Hitchcock, *Prop. Brit. Bot.*: 152. 1929).

Current name: ***Cynometra cauliflora*** L. (Fabaceae: Caesalpinioideae).

Cynometra ramiflora Linnaeus, *Species Plantarum* 1: 382. 1753.
"Habitat in India." RCN: 3011.

Lectotype (Knaap-van Meeuwen in *Blumea* 18: 23. 1970): [icon] *"Cynomorium Silvestre"* in Rumphius, Herb. Amboin. 1: 167, t. 63. 1741.

Current name: ***Cynometra ramiflora*** L. var. ***ramiflora*** (Fabaceae: Caesalpinioideae).

Note: Although Merrill (in *Philipp. J. Sci., C,* 5: 37. 1910) discussed the Rumphius plate, he did not designate it as the type.

Cynomorium coccineum Linnaeus, *Species Plantarum* 2: 970. 1753.
"Habitat in Sicilia, Melita, Mauritania parasiticum terrestre." RCN: 7029.

Type not designated.

Original material: [icon] in Tilli, Cat. Pl. Hort. Pisani: 64, t. 25. 1723; [icon] in Petiver, Gazophyl. Nat.: 60, t. 39, f. 8. 1704; [icon] in Boccone, Icon. Descr. Rar. Pl. Siciliae: 80, 81, t. 81. 1674; [icon] in Micheli, Nov. Pl. Gen.: 17, t. 12. 1729.

Generitype of *Cynomorium* Linnaeus.

Current name: ***Cynomorium coccineum*** L. (Balanophoraceae).

Note: Jafri (in Ali & Jafri, *Fl. Libya* 17: 2. 1977) indicated 1084.1 (LINN) as type, but this collection lacks the relevant *Species Plantarum* number (i.e. "1") and was a post-1753 addition to the herbarium, and is not original material for the name.

Cynosurus aegyptius Linnaeus, *Species Plantarum* 1: 72. 1753.
"Habitat in Africa, Asia, America." RCN: 610.

Lectotype (Kit Tan in Davis, *Fl. Turkey* 9: 578. 1985): Herb. Linn. No. 91.11 (LINN).

Current name: ***Dactyloctenium aegyptium*** (L.) P. Beauv. (Poaceae).

Note: Cope (in Nasir & Ali, *Fl. Pakistan* 143: 106. 1982) indicated two descriptions published by Bauhin, along with a cited Plukenet illustration, as "type", and therefore did not restrict their choice to a single element. Kit Tan appears to have been the first to refer to a single element as the type.

Cynosurus aureus Linnaeus, *Species Plantarum* 1: 73. 1753.
"Habitat in Europa australi." RCN: 613.

Lectotype (Meikle, *Fl. Cyprus* 2: 1727. 1985; Scholz in Cafferty & al. in *Taxon* 49: 249. 2000): Herb. Linn. No. 91.19 (LINN).

Current name: ***Lamarckia aurea*** (L.) Moench (Poaceae).

Note: Although Kerguélen (in *Lejeunia*, n.s., 75: 204. 1975) stated "Type: ...LINN", this is not accepted as a formal typification, for the reasons explained by Cafferty & al. (in *Taxon* 49: 240. 2000). Meikle (*Fl. Cyprus* 2: 1727. 1985) indicated unspecified type material at LINN but did not distinguish between two possible sheets there (91.19 and 91.20). It is difficult to be certain that these did not form part of a single collection, so Meikle's choice is accepted as effective, and was restricted to sheet 91.19 by Scholz, in accordance with Art. 9.15.

Cynosurus caeruleus Linnaeus, *Species Plantarum* 1: 72. 1753.
"Habitat in Europae pascuis uliginosis." RCN: 608.

Lectotype (Rauschert in *Feddes Repert.* 79: 412. 1969): [icon] *"Gramen glumis variis"* in Bauhin, Prodr. Theatri Bot.: 21. 1620. – Epitype (Foggi & al. in *Taxon* 50: 1103. 2002): Herb. Bauhin "Gramen glumis variis. Monspel." (BAS).

Current name: ***Sesleria caerulea*** (L.) Ard. (Poaceae).

Note: See Foggi & al. (in *Taxon* 50: 1101. 2002) for a review of the application of this name. Their acceptance of Rauschert's choice of lectotype (and their own epitypification) fixes the application of the name to the plant of dry grasslands (also known as *S. varia* (Jacq.) Wettst. or *S. albicans* Kit. ex Schult.), leaving *S. uliginosa* Opiz as the correct name for the plant of wet places.

Cynosurus coracanus Linnaeus, *Systema Naturae,* ed. 10, 2: 875. 1759.
["Habitat in India."] Sp. Pl., ed. 2, 1: 107 (1762). RCN: 609.

Lectotype (Phillips in *Kew Bull.* 27: 254. 1972): [icon] *"Gramen dactylon Orientale, majus, frumentaceum, semine Napi"* in Plukenet, Phytographia: t. 91, f. 5. 1691; Almag. Bot.: 174. 1696. – Typotype: Herb. Sloane 96: 74 (BM-SL). – Voucher: Herb. Sloane 93: 189 (BM-SL).

Current name: ***Eleusine coracana*** (L.) Gaertn. (Poaceae).

Cynosurus cristatus Linnaeus, *Species Plantarum* 1: 72. 1753.
"Habitat in Europae pratis." RCN: 604.

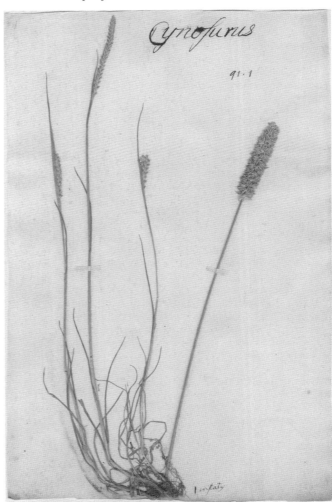

Lectotype (Cope in Jarvis & al., *Regnum Veg.* 127: 41. 1993): Herb. Linn. No. 91.1 (LINN).

Generitype of *Cynosurus* Linnaeus.

Current name: ***Cynosurus cristatus*** L. (Poaceae).

Note: Although Kerguélen (in *Lejeunia*, n.s., 75: 124. 1975) stated "Type: ...LINN", this is not accepted as a valid typification under Art. 7.11 (see justification by Cafferty & al. in *Taxon* 49: 240. 2000).

Cynosurus durus Linnaeus, *Species Plantarum* 1: 72. 1753.
"Habitat in Europa australi." RCN: 607.
Lectotype (Stace & Jarvis in *Bot. J. Linn. Soc.* 91: 438. 1985): [icon] *"Gramen arvense, Polypodii panicula crassiore"* in Barrelier, Pl. Galliam: 111, t. 50. 1714.
Current name: ***Sclerochloa dura*** (L.) P. Beauv. (Poaceae).
Note: Although Kerguélen (in *Lejeunia*, n.s., 75: 253. 1975) stated "Type: ...LINN", this is not accepted as a formal typification, for the reasons explained by Cafferty & al. (in *Taxon* 49: 240. 2000). Meikle (*Fl. Cyprus* 2: 1740. 1985) indicated unspecified material in LINN as type but did not distinguish between sheets 91.5 and 91.6 (which are not part of a single gathering so Art. 9.15 does not apply).

Cynosurus echinatus Linnaeus, *Species Plantarum* 1: 72. 1753.
"Habitat in Europa australiori." RCN: 605.
Lectotype (Veldkamp in Cafferty & al. in *Taxon* 49: 249. 2000): Herb. A. van Royen No. 913.62–79 (L).
Current name: ***Cynosurus echinatus*** L. (Poaceae).
Note: Although Kerguélen (in *Lejeunia*, n.s., 75: 124. 1975) stated "Type: ...LINN", this is not accepted as a formal typification, for the reasons explained by Cafferty & al. (in *Taxon* 49: 240. 2000). Meikle (*Fl. Cyprus* 2: 1726. 1985) indicated unspecified material in LINN as type but did not distinguish between sheets 91.2 and 91.3 (which are not part of a single gathering so Art. 9.15 does not apply).

Cynosurus indicus Linnaeus, *Species Plantarum* 1: 72. 1753.
"Habitat in Indiis." RCN: 611.
Lectotype (Phillips in Cafferty & al. in *Taxon* 49: 249. 2000): [icon] *"Gramen Dactyloides spicis deorsum aristatis"* in Burman, Thes. Zeylan.: 106, t. 47, f. 1. 1737. – Epitype (Phillips in Cafferty & al. in *Taxon* 49: 249. 2000): Sri Lanka. Central Province, Matale District, 5 miles South of Matale on Kandy Road, 1970, *Clayton 5330* (K; iso- PDA, US).
Current name: ***Eleusine indica*** (L.) Gaertn. (Poaceae).
Note: Although Kerguélen (in *Lejeunia*, n.s., 75: 140. 1975) stated "Type: ...LINN", this is not accepted as a formal typification, for the reasons explained by Cafferty & al. (in *Taxon* 49: 240. 2000). Sherif & Siddiqi (in Jafri & El-Gadi, *Fl. Libya* 145: 258. 1988) indicated Herb. Linn. 91.15 (LINN) as type but this specimen was evidently a post-1753 addition to the herbarium and not original material for the name. Phillips (in *Kew Bull.* 27: 256. 1972) and Poilecot (in *Boissiera* 56: 235. 1999) indicated the Burman plate as perhaps the type (i.e. with "?"), which is therefore ineffective. Phillips subsequently formalised this choice, with the additional designation of an epitype.

Cynosurus lima Linnaeus, *Species Plantarum* 1: 72. 1753.
"Habitat in Hispania." RCN: 606.
Lectotype (Hernández Cardona in *Anales Jard. Bot. Madrid* 37: 86. 1980): *Löfling 74a*, Herb. Linn. No. 91.4, central specimen (LINN).
Current name: ***Wangenheimia lima*** (L.) Trin. (Poaceae).

Cynosurus paniceus Linnaeus, *Species Plantarum* 1: 73. 1753.
"Habitat in Europae agris cultis." RCN: 519.
Basionym of: *Alopecurus paniceus* (L.) L. (1762).
Lectotype (Scholz in Cafferty & al. in *Taxon* 49: 250. 2000): Herb. Linn. No. 82.8 (LINN).
Current name: ***Polypogon monspeliensis*** (L.) Desf. (Poaceae).

Cynosurus virgatus Linnaeus, *Systema Naturae*, ed. 10, 2: 876. 1759.
["Habitat in Jamaica."] Sp. Pl., ed. 2, 1: 106 (1762). RCN: 612.
Lectotype (Hitchcock in *Contr. U. S. Natl. Herb.* 12: 122. 1908): *Browne*, Herb. Linn. No. 91.18 (LINN).
Current name: ***Leptochloa virgata*** (L.) P. Beauv. (Poaceae).

Cyperus alternifolius Linnaeus, *Systema Naturae*, ed. 12, 2: 82; *Mantissa Plantarum*: 28. 1767.
"Habitat in Virginia." RCN: 401.
Lectotype (Baijnath in *Kew Bull.* 30: 522. 1975): Herb. Linn. No. 70.40 (LINN).
Current name: ***Cyperus alternifolius*** L. (Cyperaceae).
Note: See further discussion by Kukkonen (in *Ann. Bot. Fenn.* 27: 62. 1990).

Cyperus articulatus Linnaeus, *Species Plantarum* 1: 44. 1753.
"Habitat in Jamaicae rivulis." RCN: 374.
Lectotype (Tucker in *Syst. Bot. Monogr.* 2: 42. 1983): [icon] *"Juncus cyperoides creberrime geniculatus medulla farctus, aquaticus, radice tuberosa, odorata"* in Sloane, Voy. Jamaica 1: 121, t. 81, f. 1. 1707. – Voucher: Herb. Sloane 2: 63 (BM-SL).
Current name: ***Cyperus articulatus*** L. (Cyperaceae).

Cyperus arundinaceus Linnaeus, *Species Plantarum* 1: 44. 1753.
"Habitat in Virginia." RCN: 400.
Replaced synonym of: *Schoenus spathaceus* L. (1762), *nom. illeg.*; *Cyperus spathaceus* L. (1767), *nom. illeg.*
Lectotype (Kukkonen in *Ann. Bot. Fenn.* 27: 65. 1990): Herb. Linn. No. 70.39 (LINN; iso- BM).
Current name: ***Dulichium arundinaceum*** (L.) Britton (Cyperaceae).
Note: Specific epithet spelled "arundinacea" in the protologue.

Cyperus caespitosus Linnaeus, *Flora Jamaicensis*: 12. 1759, *nom. inval.*
"Habitat [in Jamaica.]"
Type not relevant.
Note: The citation "2 caespitosus 126" appears to be an erroneous insertion of a reference to *Scirpus caespitosus* L. (1753), which is repeated six lines below this in the dissertation. "Cyperus caespitosus" was not a name used anywhere else by Linnaeus, and it appears to be an invalid name resulting from a typographical error.

Cyperus compressus Linnaeus, *Species Plantarum* 1: 46. 1753.
"Habitat in Americae septentrionalis pratis arenosis." RCN: 392.
Lectotype (Tucker in *Syst. Bot. Monogr.* 43: 103. 1994): *Clayton 598* (BM-000051698).
Current name: ***Cyperus compressus*** L. (Cyperaceae).
Note: There appear to be problems with this name. Tucker (in *Syst. Bot. Monogr.* 2: 35. 1983) said that the type was "probably based on Sloane's plate". However, later (in *Syst. Bot. Monogr.* 43: 103. 1994) he explicitly recognised *Clayton 598* (BM) as the (holo)type, noting that McVaugh had pointed out his earlier "lapse". Unfortunately, although Sloane's plant is what has been known as *C. compressus*, Clayton's specimen is apparently of *C. rivularis* Kunth, and Tucker (who calls this *C. bipartitus* Torr.) was presumably unaware that *C. compressus* should now displace the latter.

Cyperus difformis Linnaeus, *Centuria II Plantarum*: 6. 1756.
"Habitat in India." RCN: 383.
Lectotype (Tucker in *Syst. Bot. Monogr.* 43: 50. 1994): Herb. Linn. No. 70.10 (LINN).
Current name: ***Cyperus difformis*** L. (Cyperaceae).
Note: Lye (in *Nordic J. Bot.* 1: 57. 1981) stated that the type was in LINN but did not distinguish between sheets 70.10, 70.11 and 70.12. As they are evidently not part of a single gathering, Art. 9.15 does not apply.

Cyperus elatus Linnaeus, *Centuria II Plantarum*: 5. 1756.
"Habitat in India." RCN: 386.
Lectotype (Simpson in Cafferty & Jarvis in *Taxon* 53: 178. 2004): Herb. Linn. No. 70.22 (LINN).
Current name: ***Cyperus elatus*** L. (Cyperaceae).

Cyperus elegans Linnaeus, *Species Plantarum* 1: 45. 1753.
"Habitat in Jamaicae paludosis maritimis." RCN: 389.
Lectotype (Tucker & McVaugh in McVaugh, *Fl. Novo-Galiciana* 13: 292. 1993): [icon] *"Cyperus panicula maxime sparsa, ferruginea, compressa elegantissima"* in Sloane, Voy. Jamaica 1: 117, t. 75, f. 1. 1707.
Current name: **Cyperus elegans** L. (Cyperaceae).

Cyperus esculentus Linnaeus, *Species Plantarum* 1: 45. 1753.
"Habitat Monspelii, inque Italia, Oriente." RCN: 380.
Lectotype (Simpson in Jarvis & al., *Regnum Veg.* 127: 41. 1993): [icon] *"Cyperus rotundus esculentus angustifolius"* in Bauhin, Theatri Bot.: 221, 222. 1658 (see p. 107).
Generitype of *Cyperus* Linnaeus (vide Britton in *Bull. Dept. Agric. Jamaica* 5, Suppl. 1: 6. 1907).
Current name: **Cyperus esculentus** L. (Cyperaceae).
Note: De Vries (in *Econ. Bot.* 45: 32–34. 1991) discusses the early treatment of the species, and reproduces plates from Plantin (as f. 4).

Cyperus flavescens Linnaeus, *Species Plantarum* 1: 46. 1753.
"Habitat in Germaniae, Helvetiae, Galliae paludosis." RCN: 393.
Lectotype (Kukkonen in Cafferty & Jarvis in *Taxon* 53: 178. 2004): Herb. Burser I: 81 (UPS).
Current name: **Pycreus flavescens** (L.) Rchb. (Cyperaceae).

Cyperus fuscus Linnaeus, *Species Plantarum* 1: 46. 1753.
"Habitat in Galliae, Germaniae, Helvetiae pratis humidis." RCN: 394.
Lectotype (Kukkonen in Cafferty & Jarvis in *Taxon* 53: 179. 2004): Herb. Burser I: 82 (UPS).
Current name: **Cyperus fuscus** L. (Cyperaceae).

Cyperus glaber Linnaeus, *Mantissa Plantarum Altera*: 179. 1771.
"Habitat in Veronae humentibus." RCN: 388.
Lectotype (Simpson in Cafferty & Jarvis in *Taxon* 53: 179. 2004): [icon] *"Cyperus parvus, panicula conglobata, spicis compressis, spadiceo-viridibus"* in Séguier, Pl. Veron. 3: 66, 67, t. 2, f. 1. 1754. – Epitype (Simpson in *Taxon* 53: 179. 2004): Italy. Prov. Verona. Brigafatta in pugo vigusio. Aug 1894. *Rigo 3273* (BM).
Current name: **Cyperus glaber** L. (Cyperaceae).

Cyperus glomeratus Linnaeus, *Centuria II Plantarum*: 5. 1756.
"Habitat in Italiae paludosis. Seguvier." RCN: 387.
Lectotype (Kukkonen in Rechinger, *Fl. Iranica* 173: 107. 1998): *Séguier*, Herb. Linn. No. 70.23 (LINN).
Current name: **Cyperus glomeratus** L. (Cyperaceae).

Cyperus haspan Linnaeus, *Species Plantarum* 1: 45. 1753.
"Habitat in India, Aethiopia." RCN: 378.
Lectotype (McGivney in *Biol. Ser. Catholic Univ. Amer.* 26: 45. 1938): Herb. Hermann 2: 43, No. 37 (BM-000621657).
Current name: **Cyperus haspan** L. (Cyperaceae).
Note: See Kartesz & Gandhi (in *Phytologia* 72: 19. 1992) for a discussion on the spelling of *haspan* vs. *halpan*. They conclude it should be "haspan", as does Wilson (in *Telopea* 5: 598. 1994).

Cyperus iria Linnaeus, *Species Plantarum* 1: 45. 1753.
"Habitat in India. Osbeck." RCN: 384.
Lectotype (Tucker in *Syst. Bot. Monogr.* 43: 91. 1994): Herb. Linn. No. 70.16 (LINN).
Current name: **Cyperus iria** L. (Cyperaceae).

Cyperus laevigatus Linnaeus, *Mantissa Plantarum Altera*: 179. 1771.
"Habitat ad Cap. b. spei. I.G. Koenig." RCN: 377.
Lectotype (Tucker & McVaugh in McVaugh, *Fl. Novo-Galiciana* 13: 308. 1993): Herb. Linn. No. 70.13 (LINN).
Current name: **Cyperus laevigatus** L. (Cyperaceae).

Cyperus ligularis Linnaeus, *Systema Naturae,* ed. 10, 2: 867. 1759.
["Habitat in Jamaica."] Sp. Pl., ed. 2, 1: 70 (1762). RCN: 398.
Lectotype (Tucker in *Syst. Bot. Monogr.* 2: 49. 1983): *Browne*, Herb. Linn. No. 70.37 (LINN).
Current name: **Cyperus ligularis** L. (Cyperaceae).

Cyperus longus Linnaeus, *Species Plantarum* 1: 45. 1753.
"Habitat in Italiae, Galliae paludibus." RCN: 379.
Lectotype (Kukkonen in Cafferty & Jarvis in *Taxon* 53: 179. 2004): Herb. A. van Royen No. 909.89–686 (L).
Current name: **Cyperus longus** L. (Cyperaceae).

Cyperus minimus Linnaeus, *Species Plantarum* 1: 44. 1753.
"Habitat in Jamaica, Africa." RCN: 375.
Lectotype (Adams in Cafferty & Jarvis in *Taxon* 53: 179. 2004): Herb. A. van Royen No. 902.88–688 (L).
Current name: **Bulbostylis capillaris** (L.) C.B. Clarke (Cyperaceae).

Cyperus monostachyos Linnaeus, *Mantissa Plantarum Altera*: 180. 1771.
"Habitat in India orientali. König." RCN: 376.
Lectotype (Gordon-Gray in *J. S. African Bot.* 32: 144. 1966): Herb. Linn. No. 70.3 (LINN).
Current name: **Abilgaardia ovata** (Burm. f.) Kral (Cyperaceae).
Note: Nicolson (in *Taxon* 35: 328. 1986) discusses the correct form of the specific epithet.

Cyperus mucronatus Linnaeus, *Systema Naturae,* ed. 10, 2: 866. 1759.
RCN: 390.
Type not designated.
Original material: none traced.
Note: The application of this name is uncertain.

Cyperus odoratus Linnaeus, *Species Plantarum* 1: 46. 1753.
"Habitat in America ad fluviorum ripas." RCN: 391.
Lectotype (Dandy in Exell, *Cat. Vasc. Pl. S. Tomé*: 360. 1944): [icon] *"Cyperus longus odoratus, panicula sparsa, spicis strigosioribus viridibus"* in Sloane, Voy. Jamaica 1: 116, t. 74, f. 1. 1707. – Typotype: Herb. Sloane 2: 46 (BM-SL).
Current name: **Cyperus odoratus** L. (Cyperaceae).

Cyperus papyrus Linnaeus, *Species Plantarum* 1: 47. 1753.
"Habitat in Calabria, Sicilia, Syria, Aegypto." RCN: 399.
Lectotype (Simpson in Cafferty & Jarvis in *Taxon* 53: 179. 2004): Herb. Linn. No. 15: *Papyrus* (UPS).
Current name: **Cyperus papyrus** L. (Cyperaceae).

Cyperus pumilus Linnaeus, *Centuria II Plantarum*: 6. 1756.
"Habitat in India." RCN: 395.
Lectotype (Kukkonen in Cafferty & Jarvis in *Taxon* 53: 179. 2004): Herb. Linn. No. 70.34, right specimen (LINN).
Current name: **Pycreus pumilus** (L.) Nees (Cyperaceae).
Note: Kukkonen provides a review of the typification of this name.

Cyperus rotundus Linnaeus, *Species Plantarum* 1: 45. 1753.
"Habitat in India." RCN: 381.
Lectotype (Tucker in *Syst. Bot. Monogr.* 43: 100. 1994): Herb. Hermann 1: 3, No. 36, 2 specimens (BM).
Current name: **Cyperus rotundus** L. (Cyperaceae).
Note: Tucker's type choice is of material from a single gathering, but comprising two specimens, so the typification is valid under Art. 9.15.

Cyperus spathaceus (Linnaeus) Linnaeus, *Systema Naturae,* ed. 12, 2: 735. 1767, *nom. illeg.*
RCN: 400.
Replaced synonym: *Cyperus arundinaceus* L. (1753); *Schoenus spathaceus* L. (1762), *nom. illeg.*
Lectotype (Kukkonen in *Ann. Bot. Fenn.* 27: 65. 1990): Herb. Linn. No. 70.39 (LINN; iso- BM).
Current name: ***Dulichium arundinaceum*** (L.) Britton (Cyperaceae).
Note: Linnaeus based this on *Schoenus spathaceus* L. (1762), an illegitimate replacement name for *Cyperus arundinaceus* L. (1753).

Cyperus squarrosus Linnaeus, *Centuria II Plantarum*: 6. 1756.
"Habitat in India." RCN: 382.
Lectotype (Kern in *Blumea* 10: 642. 1960): Herb. Linn. No. 70.8, right specimen (LINN).
Current name: ***Mariscus squarrosus*** (L.) C.B. Clarke (Cyperaceae).

Cyperus strigosus Linnaeus, *Species Plantarum* 1: 47. 1753.
"Habitat in paludibus Jamaicae, Virginiae." RCN: 397.
Lectotype (Fernald & Griscom in *Rhodora* 37: 187. 1935): *Kalm,* Herb. Linn. No. 70.36 (LINN).
Current name: ***Cyperus strigosus*** L. (Cyperaceae).

Cyperus triflorus Linnaeus, *Mantissa Plantarum Altera*: 180. 1771.
"Habitat in India orientali. König." RCN: 396.
Lectotype (Gordon-Gray in *Strelitzia* 2: 20. 1995): Herb. Linn. No. 70.35 (LINN).
Current name: ***Abilgaardia triflora*** (L.) Abeyw. (Cyperaceae).

Cypripedium bulbosum Linnaeus, *Species Plantarum* 2: 951. 1753.
"Habitat in Lapponia, Russia, Sibiria." RCN: 6876.
Lectotype (Baumann & al. in *Mitteilungsbl. Arbeitskr. Heim. Orchid. Baden-Württemberg* 21: 441. 1989): Herb. Linn. No. 1061.4 (LINN).
Current name: ***Calypso bulbosa*** (L.) Oakes (Orchidaceae).

Cypripedium calceolus Linnaeus, *Species Plantarum* 2: 951. 1753.
"Habitat in Europae, Asiae, Americae septentrionalibus." RCN: 6875.
Lectotype (Baumann & al. in *Mitteilungsbl. Arbeitskr. Heim. Orchid. Baden-Württemberg* 21: 452. 1989): [icon] *"Calceolus marianus"* in Dodoëns, Stirp. Hist. Pempt., ed. 2: 180, left figure. 1616 (see p. 126).
Generitype of *Cypripedium* Linnaeus (vide Salisbury, *Parad. Lond.* 2: t. 89. 1807).
Current name: ***Cypripedium calceolus*** L. (Orchidaceae).
Note: Baumann & al. designated the original publication of Dodoëns' woodcut (in *Fl. Coronar.*: 77. 1568) as lectotype but this publication was not cited in Linnaeus' protologue. However, as Linnaeus cited the same woodcut from Dodoëns' later *Stirp. Hist. Pempt.*, ed. 2 (1616), and Baumann & al.'s intention is clear, the later illustration has been accepted as the lectotype, while still attributing the choice to Baumann & al. (see Jarvis & al. in *Regnum Veg.* 127: 41. 1993).

Cyrilla racemiflora Linnaeus, *Systema Naturae,* ed. 12, 2: 182; *Mantissa Plantarum*: 50. 1767.
"Habitat in Carolinae pinetis humentibus. D. Garden." RCN: 1620.
Lectotype (Nelson in *Taxon* 39: 665. 1990): *Garden,* Herb. Linn. No. 272.1 (LINN).
Generitype of *Cyrilla* Linnaeus.
Current name: ***Cyrilla racemiflora*** L. (Cyrillaceae).
Note: Thomas (in *Contr. Gray Herb.* 186: 5, 77. 1960) indicated that this was based on material from Garden but neither he nor Bornstein (in Howard, *Fl. Lesser Antilles* 5: 105. 1989) distinguished between 271.1 and 271.2 (LINN).

Cytinus hypocistis (Linnaeus) Linnaeus, *Genera Plantarum*, ed. 6: 576. 1764.
["Habitat in Hispania, Lusitania parasitica cisti."] Sp. Pl. 1: 442 (1753). RCN: 6975.
Basionym: *Asarum hypocistis* L. (1753).
Lectotype (Labani in Jafri & El-Gadi, *Fl. Libya* 71: 3. 1980): Herb. Linn. No. 1075.1 (LINN).
Generitype of *Cytinus* Linnaeus, *nom. cons.*
Current name: ***Cytinus hypocistis*** (L.) L. subsp. ***hypocistis*** (Rafflesiaceae).
Note: Cytinus Linnaeus, *nom. cons.* against *Hypocistis* Mill.

Cytisus aethiopicus Linnaeus, *Species Plantarum* 2: 740. 1753.
"Habitat in Aethiopia." RCN: 5273.
Lectotype (Polhill in Turland & Jarvis in *Taxon* 46: 468. 1997): [icon] *"Cytisus Aethiopicus, subrotundis, incanis minoribus foliis, floribus parvis, luteis"* in Plukenet, Phytographia: t. 278, f. 3. 1694; Almag. Bot.: 128. 1696. – Typotype: Herb. Sloane 100: 15 (BM-SL).
Current name: ***Melolobium aethiopicum*** (L.) Druce (Fabaceae: Faboideae).
Note: Wijnands (*Bot. Commelins*: 165. 1983) provided an extensive discussion of this name but did not designate a type.

Cytisus argenteus Linnaeus, *Species Plantarum* 2: 740. 1753.
"Habitat in G. Narbonensi." RCN: 5447.
Lectotype (Schrire in Turland & Jarvis in *Taxon* 46: 468. 1997): Herb. Burser XVIII(2): 78 (UPS).
Current name: ***Argyrolobium zanonii*** (Turra) P.W. Ball (Fabaceae: Faboideae).

Cytisus austriacus Linnaeus, *Species Plantarum,* ed. 2, 2: 1042. 1763.
"Habitat in Sibiria, Austria, Italia." RCN: 5444.
Lectotype (Cristofolini in Turland & Jarvis in *Taxon* 46: 468. 1997): Herb. Burser XXII: 3, left specimen (UPS).
Current name: ***Cytisus austriacus*** L. (Fabaceae: Faboideae).

Cytisus cajan Linnaeus, *Species Plantarum* 2: 739. 1753.
"Habitat in India." RCN: 5440.
Lectotype (Fawcett & Rendle, *Fl. Jamaica* 4: 71. 1920; Westphal, *Pulses Ethiopia, Taxon. Agric. Signif.*: 64, 68. 1974): Herb. Hermann 1: 14, No. 279 (BM-000594445).
Current name: ***Cajanus cajan*** (L.) Millsp. (Fabaceae: Faboideae).
Note: Fawcett & Rendle (*Fl. Jamaica* 4: 71. 1920) indicated Herb. Hermann material (BM) as type. Although there is material in several volumes, it appears to have been part of a single gathering. Consequently, theirs is accepted as the first typification (Art. 9.15), with the choice subsequently restricted by Westphal in 1974. Verdcourt (in Milne-Redhead & Polhill, *Fl. Trop. E. Africa, Leguminosae* 4: 709. 1971) indicated two collections in Herb. Hermann (BM) as syntypes but gave no indication of intending to designate a lectotype. See extensive discussion of the original elements by van der Maesen (in *Agric. Univ. Wageningen Pap.* 85–4: 13. 1985).

Cytisus graecus Linnaeus, *Species Plantarum* 2: 740. 1753.
"Habitat in Archipelagi insulis." RCN: 5446.
Neotype (Turland in Turland & Jarvis in *Taxon* 46: 468. 1997): Greece. Zakinthos: Mt Skopos, 28 Apr 1926, *Bornmüller 482* (BM; iso- B?).
Current name: ***Anthyllis hermanniae*** L. (Fabaceae: Faboideae).

Cytisus hirsutus Linnaeus, *Species Plantarum* 2: 739. 1753.
"Habitat in Hispania, Sibiria, Austria, Italia." RCN: 5442.
Lectotype (Cristofolini & Jarvis in *Taxon* 40: 497. 1991): Herb. Burser XXII: 5 (UPS).

Current name: ***Chamaecytisus hirsutus*** (L.) Link (Fabaceae: Faboideae).

Note: Skalická (in *Novit. Bot. Univ. Carol.* 1: 55–61. 1982) discussed most of the original material for the name (though not the Burser collection). She concluded that *Cytisus hirsutus* should be interpreted in the sense of the cited Clusius description and illustration, identifiable as *Cytisus villosus* Pourr. As a result, she informally rejected *C. hirsutus.* Although Cristofolini & Jarvis (in *Taxon* 40: 497. 1991) believed Skalická to have made a formal typification (which they rejected in favour of Burser material), this does not seem to be the case. She stated (pp. 63–64) "I have made the typification...so that it could include only one species, which is conformable to the conceptions in Hortus cliffortianus", and "I appoint as the type-locality…ad montium radices circa Calpen et Baeticae maritimis. The type must be elected in convenience with the description of Cytisus III. Clus. Rar. Plant. Hist. 1: 94, 1601 and with the illustration of the species designated as Cytisus III". It seems that Skalická intended that another unspecified collection (a neotype?), agreeing with Clusius' concept and stated locality, should be chosen to serve as the type. However, she did not designate such a collection herself. Consequently, the lectotype designated by Cristofolini & Jarvis, which maintains the usage of the Linnaean name as *Chamaecytisus hirsutus*, is the earliest formal choice.

Cytisus laburnum Linnaeus, *Species Plantarum* 2: 739. 1753.
"Habitat in Helvetia, Sabaudia." RCN: 5437.
Lectotype (Turland in Turland & Jarvis in *Taxon* 46: 468. 1997): Herb. Clifford: 354, *Cytisus* 1 (BM-000646540).
Current name: ***Laburnum anagyroides*** Medik. (Fabaceae: Faboideae).

Cytisus monspessulanus Linnaeus, *Species Plantarum* 2: 740. 1753.
"Habitat in Monspelii." RCN: 5201.
Neotype (Gibbs & Dingwall in *Bol. Soc. Brot.,* sér. 2, 45: 304. 1971): *Arduino 19,* Herb. Linn. No. 892.2 (LINN).
Current name: ***Genista monspessulana*** (L.) L.A.S. Johnson (Fabaceae: Faboideae).
Note: Gibbs & Dingwall wrongly indicated Arduino material (892.2 LINN) as the type (it was not received by Linnaeus until long after 1753). However, in the absence of any original material, this choice is accepted as a neotypification under Art. 9.8.

Cytisus nigricans Linnaeus, *Species Plantarum* 2: 739. 1753.
"Habitat in Austria, Pannonia, Bohemia, Italia." RCN: 5438.
Lectotype (Cristofolini in Turland & Jarvis in *Taxon* 46: 468. 1997): Herb. Burser XXII: 11, left specimen (UPS).
Current name: ***Cytisus nigricans*** L. (Fabaceae: Faboideae).

Cytisus patens Linnaeus, *Systema Vegetabilium,* ed. 13: 555. 1774.
RCN: 5441.
Lectotype (Cristofolini in Turland & Jarvis in *Taxon* 46: 468. 1997): Herb. Linn. No. 912.8 (LINN).
Current name: ***Cytisus striatus*** (Hill) Rothm. (Fabaceae: Faboideae).

Cytisus pinnatus Linnaeus, *Species Plantarum* 2: 741. 1753.
"Habitat in India." RCN: 5452.
Replaced synonym of: *Robinia mitis* L. (1763), *nom. illeg.*
Lectotype (Smith, *Fl. Vitiensis Nova* 3: 170. 1985): [icon] *"Phaseolo affinis Arbor Indica Coral dicta polyphyllos non spinosa, foliis mollibus subhirsutis"* in Plukenet, Phytographia: t. 104, f. 3. 1691; Almag. Bot.: 293. 1696.
Current name: ***Millettia pinnata*** (L.) Panigrahi (Fabaceae: Faboideae).
Note: Merrill (in *Philipp. J. Sci., C,* 5: 101. 1910) took up *Robinia mitis* L. (1763) in place of this name and interpreted *R. mitis* via Herb. Linn. No. 913.3 (LINN). *Robinia mitis* is, however, an illegitimate renaming of *C. pinnatus* and consequently the two names are homotypic. Although annotated with "mitis" by Linnaeus, sheet 913.3 (LINN) is not original material for *C. pinnatus.* Smith appears to have been the first to make a formal choice of type for *C. pinnatus* (and hence *R. mitis*).

Cytisus psoraloides Linnaeus, *Plantae Rariores Africanae*: 15. 1760.
["Habitat ad Cap. b. spei."] Sp. Pl., ed. 2, 2: 1043 (1763). RCN: 5445.
Basionym of: *Indigofera psoraloides* (L.) L. (1767).
Lectotype (Schrire in Turland & Jarvis in *Taxon* 46: 468. 1997): [icon] *"Trifolium Aethiopicum ex alis foliorum spicatum, bituminosi foliis angustioribus, s. Trifolium spicatum tenuifolium"* in Plukenet, Phytographia: t. 320, f. 3. 1694; Almag. Bot.: 375. 1696. – Typotype: Herb. Sloane 102: 91, central specimen (BM-SL).
Current name: ***Indigofera psoraloides*** (L.) L. (Fabaceae: Faboideae).

Cytisus sessilifolius Linnaeus, *Species Plantarum* 2: 739. 1753.
"Habitat in Italia, Galloprovincia." RCN: 5439.
Lectotype (Cristofolini in Turland & Jarvis in *Taxon* 46: 468. 1997): Herb. Clifford: 355, *Cytisus* 4 (BM-000646545).
Generitype of *Cytisus* Linnaeus, *nom. rej.*
Current name: ***Cytisophyllum sessilifolium*** (L.) O. Lang (Fabaceae: Faboideae).
Note: Cytisus Linnaeus, *nom. rej.* in favour of *Cytisus* Desf.

Cytisus supinus Linnaeus, *Species Plantarum* 2: 740. 1753.
"Habitat in Sibiria, Italia, Sicilia, Galloprovincia." RCN: 5443.
Lectotype (Cristofolini & Jarvis in *Taxon* 40: 498. 1991): [icon] *"Cytisus VII"* in Clusius, Rar. Pl. Hist. 1: 96. 1601.
Current name: ***Chamaecytisus supinus*** (L.) Link (Fabaceae: Faboideae).

D

Dactylis ciliaris Linnaeus, *Mantissa Plantarum Altera*: 185. 1771.
"Habitat ad Cap. b. spei." RCN: 602.
Lectotype (Linder & Davidse in *Bot. Jahrb. Syst.* 119: 483. 1997):
  Herb. Linn. No. 90.4 (LINN).
Current name: ***Tribolium obtusifolium*** (Nees) Renvoize (Poaceae).

Dactylis cynosuroides Linnaeus, *Species Plantarum* 1: 71. 1753.
"Habitat in Virginia, Canada, Lusitania." RCN: 600.
Lectotype (Hitchcock in *Contr. U. S. Natl. Herb.* 12: 121. 1908):
  Clayton 577, Herb. Linn. No. 90.1 (LINN; iso- BM, US).
Current name: ***Spartina cynosuroides*** (L.) Roth (Poaceae).

Dactylis glomerata Linnaeus, *Species Plantarum* 1: 71. 1753.
"Habitat in Europae cultis ruderatis." RCN: 601.
Lectotype (Clayton in Milne-Redhead & Polhill, *Fl. Trop. E. Africa*,
  Gramineae 1: 43. 1970): Herb. Linn. No. 90.3 (LINN).
Generitype of *Dactylis* Linnaeus (vide Hitchcock, *Prop. Brit. Bot.*: 120.
  1929).
Current name: ***Dactylis glomerata*** L. subsp. ***glomerata*** (Poaceae).

Dactylis lagopoides Linnaeus, *Systema Naturae*, ed. 12, 2: 95;
  Mantissa Plantarum: 33. 1767.
"Habitat in India. Burmannus." RCN: 603.
Lectotype (Renvoize in Cafferty & al. in *Taxon* 49: 250. 2000): *J.
  Burman s.n.*, Herb. Linn. No. 90.5 (LINN), see p. 196.
Current name: ***Aeluropus lagopoides*** (L.) Trin. ex Thwaites (Poaceae).
Note: Bor (in Rechinger, *Fl. Iranica* 70: 419. 1970) indicated a
  Burman specimen at L as type, but no relevant material has been
  traced there. Meikle (*Fl. Cyprus* 2: 1846. 1985) and Sherif &
  Siddiqi (in Jafri & El-Gadi, *Fl. Libya* 145: 233. 1988) indicated
  material at LINN as type, but as they did not distinguish between
  three possible sheets at LINN, which are not part of a single
  gathering (Art. 9.15), no effective choice of type was made.

Dais cotinifolia Linnaeus, *Species Plantarum*, ed. 2, 1: 556. 1762.
"Habitat ad Cap. b. spei." RCN: 3066.
Lectotype (Peterson in Polhill, *Fl. Trop. E. Africa, Thymelaeaceae*: 16.
  1978): Herb. Linn. No. 554.1 (LINN).
Generitype of *Dais* Linnaeus.
Current name: ***Dais cotinifolia*** L. (Thymelaeaceae).
Note: Fuchs in *Acta Bot. Neerl.* 11: 74. 1962) argued that as Linnaeus'
  description came from David van Royen, an illustration of the plant
  from Leiden, published later by Meerburg, should be the holotype.
  This could have been an effective neotypification (Art. 9.8) but for
  the existence of original material (Herb. Linn. 554.1, LINN),
  subsequently designated as type by Peterson.

Dais octandra Linnaeus, *Systema Naturae*, ed. 12, 2: 297; *Mantissa
  Plantarum*: 69. 1767.
"Habitat in India." RCN: 3067.
Lectotype (Ding Hou in van Steenis, *Fl. Malesiana*, ser. I, 6: 18.
  1960): Herb. Linn. No. 554.2 (LINN).
Current name: ***Phaleria octandra*** (L.) Baill. (Thymelaeaceae).

Dalechampia scandens Linnaeus, *Species Plantarum* 2: 1054. 1753.
"Habitat in America meridionali." RCN: 7261.
Lectotype (Howard, *Fl. Lesser Antilles* 5: 42. 1989): [icon] *"Lupulus
  folio trifido, fructu tricocco et hispido"* in Plumier, Descr. Pl. Amér.:
  87, t. 101. 1693.
Generitype of *Dalechampia* Linnaeus.
Current name: ***Dalechampia scandens*** L. (Euphorbiaceae).
Note: Radcliffe-Smith (in Polhill, *Fl. Trop. E. Africa, Euphorbiaceae*:

287 (1987) wrongly indicated 1138.3 (LINN), a sheet annotated
  only by Linnaeus filius and not original material for the name, as
  holotype. Armbruster (in *Syst. Bot.* 13: 310. 1988) stated the type
  "is presumably in Hortus Cliffortianus Herb. (BM)", but no
  specimen is preserved there.

Dalibarda repens Linnaeus, *Species Plantarum* 1: 491. 1753.
"Habitat in Canada. Kalm." RCN: 3768.
Replaced synonym of: *Rubus dalibarda* L. (1762), nom. illeg.
Lectotype (Reveal in Jarvis & al., *Regnum Veg.* 127: 41. 1993): *Kalm*,
  Herb. Linn. No. 653.24 (LINN).
Generitype of *Dalibarda* Linnaeus.
Current name: ***Dalibarda repens*** L. (Rosaceae).

Damasonium lingua Linnaeus, *Amoenitates Academicae* 4: 492. 1759,
  nom. inval.
Type not relevant.
Note: This "name" resulted from the misplacement of "*Damasonium*"
  within a list of *Serapias* names in a revised version of the 1756
  thesis, *Flora Monspeliensis*. It is not validly published.

Damasonium palustris Linnaeus, *Amoenitates Academicae* 4: 492.
  1759, *nom. inval.*
Type not relevant.
Note: As noted by Stearn (in Geck & Pressler, *Festschr. Claus Nissen*:
  631. 1974, this "name" resulted from the misplacement of
  "*Damasonium*" within a list of *Serapias* names in a revised version
  of the 1756 thesis, *Flora Monspeliensis*. Stearn suggested that
  "Damasonium" was intended as a varietal epithet under *S.
  helleborine*, but this does not seem to have been adopted in any of
  Linnaeus' later works.

Daphne alpina Linnaeus, *Species Plantarum* 1: 356. 1753.
"Habitat in Alpibus Helvetiae, Genevae, Italiae." RCN: 2822.
Lectotype (Urbani in *Taxon* 40: 494. 1991): [icon] *"Chamelaea Alpina
  incana"* in Plantin, Pl. Stirp. Icon.: 370. 1581.
Current name: ***Daphne alpina*** L. (Thymelaeaceae).

Daphne cneorum Linnaeus, *Species Plantarum* 1: 357. 1753.
"Habitat in Helvetia, Hungaria, Pyrenaeis, Baldo." RCN: 2826.
Lectotype (Rogers in Rogers & Spencer in *Taxon* 55: 485. 2006):
  Herb. Burser XXIV: 45 (UPS).
Current name: ***Daphne cneorum*** L. (Thymelaeaceae).

Daphne gnidium Linnaeus, *Species Plantarum* 1: 357. 1753.
"Habitat in Hispania, Italia, G. Narbonensi." RCN: 2827.
Lectotype (Rogers in Rogers & Spencer in *Taxon* 55: 485. 2006):
  Herb. Burser XXIV: 40 (UPS).
Current name: ***Daphne gnidium*** L. (Thymelaeaceae).

Daphne indica Linnaeus, *Species Plantarum* 1: 357. 1753.
"Habitat in China." RCN: 2825.
Lectotype (Townsend in Dassanayake & Fosberg, *Revised Handb. Fl.
  Ceylon* 2: 503. 1981): Herb. Linn. No. 500.11 (LINN).
Current name: ***Wikstroemia indica*** (L.) C.A. Mey. (Thymelaeaceae).

Daphne laureola Linnaeus, *Species Plantarum* 1: 357. 1753.
"Habitat in Anglia, Helvetia, Gallia, Baldo." RCN: 2823.
Lectotype (Mathew in Jarvis in *Taxon* 41: 572. 1992): Herb. Clifford:
  147, *Daphne* 1 (BM-000558637).
Generitype of *Daphne* Linnaeus (vide Meyer in *Bull. Cl. Phys.-Math.
  Acad. Imp. Sci. St.-Pétersbourg* 1: 358. 1843).

Current name: **Daphne laureola** L. (Thymelaeaceae).
Note: Daphne laureola, with the type designated by Mathew, was
proposed as conserved type of the genus by Jarvis (in *Taxon* 41:
572. 1992). However, the proposal was eventually ruled
unnecessary by the General Committee (see Barrie, *l.c.* 55:
795–796. 2006 for a review of the history of this and related
proposals).

Daphne mezereum Linnaeus, *Species Plantarum* 1: 356. 1753.
"Habitat in Europae borealis sylvis." RCN: 2817.
Lectotype (Peterson in Rechinger, *Fl. Iranica* 95: 2. 1972): Herb. Linn.
No. 500.1 (LINN).
Current name: **Daphne mezereum** L. (Thymelaeaceae).

Daphne pontica Linnaeus, *Species Plantarum* 1: 357. 1753.
"Habitat in Ponto." RCN: 2824.
Lectotype (Kit Tan in Davis, *Fl. Turkey* 7: 522. 1982): [icon]
"Thymelaea Pontica Citrei foliis" in Tournefort, Rel. Voy. Levant
(Paris ed.) 2: 179, 180. 1717. – Voucher: Herb. Tournefort No.
5834 (P-TOURN).
Current name: **Daphne pontica** L. (Thymelaeaceae).
Note: Burtt (in *Karaca Arbor. Mag.* 6(2): 46, f. 1. 2001) reproduces the
Tournefort type illustration.

Daphne pubescens Linnaeus, *Systema Naturae,* ed. 12, 2: 271;
Mantissa Plantarum: 66. 1767.
"Habitat in Austria. D. Jacquin." RCN: 2819.
Lectotype (Kit Tan in *Notes Roy. Bot. Gard. Edinburgh* 38: 231. 1980):
Jacquin s.n., Herb. Linn. No. 500.4 (LINN).
Current name: **Thymelaea pubescens** (L.) Meisn. (Thymelaeaceae).

Daphne squarrosa Linnaeus, *Species Plantarum* 1: 358. 1753.
"Habitat in Aethiopia." RCN: 2828.
Lectotype (Rogers in Rogers & Spencer in *Taxon* 55: 485. 2006):
[icon] *"Thymelaea capitata, lanuginosa, foliis creberrimis, minimis,
aculeatis"* in Burman, Rar. Afric. Pl.: 134, t. 49, f. 1. 1738. –
Epitype (Rogers in Rogers & Spencer in *Taxon* 55: 485. 2006):
South Africa. Western Cape Province, Cape Peninsula, Cape Point,
20 Nov 1938, *E. Wall s.n.* (MO-5653217).
Current name: **Gnidia squarrosa** (L.) Druce (Thymelaeaceae).

Daphne tartonraira Linnaeus, *Species Plantarum* 1: 356. 1753.
"Habitat in Galloprovincia." RCN: 2821.
Lectotype (Rogers in Rogers & Spencer in *Taxon* 55: 485. 2006):
Herb. Burser XXIV: 43 (UPS).
Current name: **Thymelaea tartonraira** (L.) All. (Thymelaeaceae).

Daphne thymelaea Linnaeus, *Species Plantarum* 1: 356. 1753.
"Habitat in Hispania & Monspelii in Horto Dei." RCN: 2818.
Lectotype (Kit Tan in *Notes Roy. Bot. Gard. Edinburgh* 38: 233. 1980):
Herb. Linn. No. 500.3 (LINN).
Current name: **Thymelaea sanamunda** All. (Thymelaeaceae).

Daphne villosa Linnaeus, *Species Plantarum,* ed. 2, 1: 510. 1762.
"Habitat in Lusitania, Hispania. Alstroemer." RCN: 2820.
Lectotype (Kit Tan in *Notes Roy. Bot. Gard. Edinburgh* 38: 229. 1980):
Alströmer 235, Herb. Linn. No. 500.5 (LINN).
Current name: **Thymelaea villosa** (L.) Endl. (Thymelaeaceae).

Datisca cannabina Linnaeus, *Species Plantarum* 2: 1037. 1753.
"Habitat in Creta." RCN: 7483.
Lectotype (Turland in *Bull. Nat. Hist. Mus. London, Bot.* 25: 153, f.
24. 1995): Herb. Linn. No. 1196.1 (LINN).
Generitype of *Datisca* Linnaeus.
Current name: **Datisca cannabina** L. (Datiscaceae).

Datisca hirta Linnaeus, *Species Plantarum* 2: 1037. 1753, *nom. utique
rej.*
"Habitat in Philadelphia. Kalm." RCN: 7484.
Lectotype (Britton in *Bull. Torrey Bot. Club* 18: 269. 1891): *Kalm*,
Herb. Linn. No. 1196.5 (LINN).
Current name: **Rhus typhina** L. (Anacardiaceae).

Datura arborea Linnaeus, *Species Plantarum* 1: 179. 1753.
"Habitat in Peru." RCN: 1422.

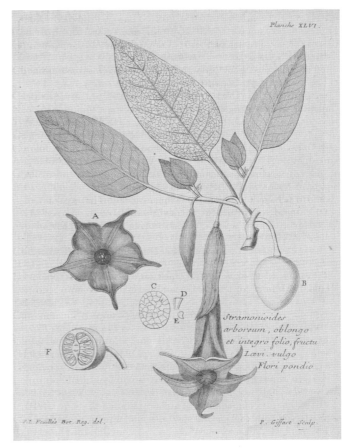

Lectotype (Stearn in *Taxon* 10: 17. 1961): [icon] *"Stramonioides
arboreum, oblongo et integro folio, fructu Laevi, vulgo Flori pondio"* in
Feuillée, J. Obs. 2: 761, t. 46. 1714.
Current name: **Brugmansia arborea** (L.) Pers. (Solanaceae).
Note: See detailed discussion by Hadkins & al. (in *Bot. J. Linn. Soc.*
125: 299–300. 1998), including an illustration of the lectotype (as
f. 6).

Datura fastuosa Linnaeus, *Systema Naturae,* ed. 10, 2: 932. 1759.
["Habitat in Aegypto."] Sp. Pl., ed. 2, 1: 256 (1762). RCN: 1420.
Lectotype (Schönbeck-Temesy in Rechinger, *Fl. Iranica* 100: 46. 1972;
Hadkins & al. in *Bot. J. Linn. Soc.* 125: 304, f. 13. 1998): Herb.
Linn. No. 243.3, left specimen (LINN).
Current name: **Datura metel** L. (Solanaceae).
Note: See detailed discussion by Hadkins & al. (in *Bot. J. Linn. Soc.*
125: 300–304. 1998), who restrict the type choice to the left-hand
specimen on sheet 243.3 (LINN). They also include an illustration
of the lectotype (as f. 13).

Datura ferox Linnaeus, *Demonstr. Pl. Horto Upsaliensi*: 6. 1753.
"Habitat in China." RCN: 1417.

Lectotype (Hammer & al. in *Kulturpflanze* 31: 48. 1983): [icon] *"Stramonium ferox"* in Boccone, Icon. Descr. Rar. Pl. Siciliae: 50, 51, t. 26, f. c, e. 1674.
Current name: **Datura ferox** L. (Solanaceae).
Note: See detailed discussion by Hadkins & al. (in *Bot. J. Linn. Soc.* 125: 300–303. 1998), including an illustration of the lectotype (as f. 9).

Datura metel Linnaeus, *Species Plantarum* 1: 179. 1753.
"Habitat in Asia, Africa." RCN: 1421.
Lectotype (Timmerman in *Pharm. J.* 118: 572. 1927): Herb. Clifford: 55, *Datura* 2 γ (BM-000557992).
Current name: **Datura metel** L. (Solanaceae).
Note: See detailed discussion by Hadkins & al. (in *Bot. J. Linn. Soc.* 125: 298–299. 1998), including an illustration of the lectotype (as f. 4).

Datura stramonium Linnaeus, *Species Plantarum* 1: 179. 1753.
"Habitat in America, nunc vulgaris per Europam." RCN: 1418.
Lectotype (D'Arcy in Woodson & Schery in *Ann. Missouri Bot. Gard.* 60: 624. 1974): Herb. Clifford: 55, *Datura* 1 (BM-000557989).
Generitype of *Datura* Linnaeus (vide Hitchcock, *Prop. Brit. Bot.*: 132. 1929).
Current name: **Datura stramonium** L. (Solanaceae).
Note: Schönbeck-Temesy (in Rechinger, *Fl. Iranica* 100: 45. 1972) indicated 243.1 (LINN) as type, but this is a post-1753 addition to the herbarium and not original material. See detailed discussion by Hadkins & al. (in *Bot. J. Linn. Soc.* 125: 296–298. 1998), including an illustration of the lectotype (as f. 2).

Datura tatula Linnaeus, *Species Plantarum*, ed. 2, 1: 256. 1762.
"Habitat – – – – – – –" RCN: 1419.
Lectotype (Hadkins & al. in *Bot. J. Linn. Soc.* 125: 305, f. 15. 1998): Herb. Linn. No. 243.2 (LINN).
Current name: **Datura stramonium** L. forma **tatula** (L.) Danert (Solanaceae).

Daucus carota Linnaeus, *Species Plantarum* 1: 242. 1753.
"Habitat in Europae campis exaridis." RCN: 1944.
Lectotype (Sáenz Laín in *Anales Jard. Bot. Madrid* 37: 487. 1981): Herb. Linn. No. 340.1 (LINN).
Generitype of *Daucus* Linnaeus (vide Hitchcock, *Prop. Brit. Bot.*: 139. 1929).
Current name: **Daucus carota** L. (Apiaceae).
Note: See Wijnheimer & al. (in *Taxon* 37: 183. 1988) for a detailed account of the typification of this name (though they were unaware that their choice of type had been made earlier). They illustrate the type as their f. 2. Heath (in *Taxon* 40: 94. 1991) argued that this type choice was invalid but this was refuted by Jarvis (in *Taxon* 41: 63–64. 1992).

Daucus gingidium Linnaeus, *Species Plantarum* 1: 242. 1753.
"Habitat Monspelii." RCN: 1947.
Lectotype (Onno in *Beih. Bot. Centralbl.* 56(B): 101. 1936): [icon] *"Pastinaca Oenanthes folio"* in Boccone, Icon. Descr. Rar. Pl. Siciliae: 75, 74, t. 40, f. 3. 1674.
Current name: **Daucus carota** L. subsp. **gummifer** Hook. f. (Apiaceae).

Daucus mauritanicus Linnaeus, *Species Plantarum*, ed. 2, 1: 348. 1762.
"Habitat in Hispania, Italia, Mauritania." RCN: 1945.
Lectotype (Jury & al. in Jarvis & al. in *Taxon* 55: 211. 2006): Herb. Linn. No. 340.2 (LINN).
Current name: **Daucus carota** L. (Apiaceae).

Daucus muricatus (Linnaeus) Linnaeus, *Species Plantarum*, ed. 2, 1: 349. 1762.
"Habitat in Mauritania." RCN: 1948.
Basionym: *Artedia muricata* L. (1753).
Lectotype (Reduron & al. in Jarvis & al. in *Taxon* 55: 209. 2006): [icon] *"Echinophora Tingitana"* in Rivinus, Ordo Pl. Fl. Pentapetal.: t. 27. 1699.
Current name: **Daucus muricatus** (L.) L. (Apiaceae).

Daucus muricatus (Linnaeus) Linnaeus var. **maritimus** Linnaeus, *Species Plantarum*, ed. 2, 1: 349. 1762.
"Habitat in littoribus maris Mediterranei." RCN: 1948.
Lectotype (Reduron & Jarvis in Jarvis & al. in *Taxon* 55: 212. 2006): Herb. Burser VII(2): 59 (UPS).
Current name: **Pseudorlaya pumila** (L.) Grande (Apiaceae).

Daucus visnaga Linnaeus, *Species Plantarum* 1: 242. 1753.
"Habitat in Europa australi." RCN: 1946.
Lectotype (Jafri in Jafri & El-Gadi, *Fl. Libya* 117: 88. 1985): Herb. Clifford: 89, *Daucus* 2 (BM-000558237).
Current name: **Ammi visnaga** (L.) Lam. (Apiaceae).

Decumaria barbara Linnaeus, *Species Plantarum*, ed. 2, 2: 1663. 1763.
"Habitat an in Africa? Schreber." RCN: 3445.
Lectotype (Barrie in Jarvis & al., *Regnum Veg.* 127: 42. 1993): Herb. Linn. No. 617.2 (LINN).
Generitype of *Decumaria* Linnaeus.
Current name: **Decumaria barbara** L. (Hydrangeaceae).

Delima sarmentosa Linnaeus, *Systema Naturae*, ed. 10, 2: 1076. 1759.
["Habitat in Zeylona."] Gen. Pl., ed. 5: Appendix (1754). RCN: 3877.
Lectotype (Stearn, *Four Suppl. Linnaean Publ.*: 93. 1959; Hoogland in Jarvis & al., *Regnum Veg.* 127: 42. 1993): Herb. Hermann 2: 19, No. 205, lower left specimen (BM-000621572).
Current name: **Tetracera sarmentosa** (L.) Vahl (Dilleniaceae).
Note: Hoogland (in *Reinwartia* 2: 190. 1953) treated *D. s(p)armentosa* as a synonym of *Tragia scandens* L. (= *Tetracera scandens* (L.) Merr.) but this was based on the erroneous assumption that the type of *D. sarmentosa* was the unannotated 683.1 (LINN). In 1959, Stearn typified the name using material in Herb. Hermann 2: 19, and Hoogland (1993) subsequently restricted this choice to one of the three specimens on the page. This material belongs not to *Tetracera scandens*, however, but to a different species, *Tetracera asiatica* (Lour.) Hoogl., which is now correctly known as *Tetracera sarmentosa* (L.) Vahl, a change subsequently taken up by Wadhwa (in Dassanayake & Clayton, *Revised Handb. Fl. Ceylon* 10: 117. 1996).

Delima sparmentosa Linnaeus, *Genera Plantarum*, ed. 5: Appendix. 1754, *orth. var.*
"Habitat in Zeylona." RCN: 3877.
Lectotype (Stearn, *Four Suppl. Linnaean Publ.*: 93. 1959; Hoogland in Jarvis & al., *Regnum Veg.* 127: 42. 1993): Herb. Hermann 2: 19, No. 205, lower left specimen (BM-000621572).
Generitype of *Delima* Linnaeus.
Current name: **Tetracera sarmentosa** (L.) Vahl (Dilleniaceae).
Note: Delima sparmentosa L. (1754) is generally treated as a correctable orthographic error. The epithet was corrected to "sarmentosa" by Linnaeus in 1759.

Delphinium aconiti Linnaeus, *Systema Naturae*, ed. 12, 2: 370; *Mantissa Plantarum*: 77. 1767.

"Habitat in Dardanella. Forskåhl." RCN: 3947.
Lectotype (Munz in *J. Arnold Arbor.* 48: 170. 1967): *Vandelli 21*,
Herb. Linn. No. 694.3 (LINN).
Current name: **Consolida aconiti** (L.) Lindl. (Ranunculaceae).

Delphinium ajacis Linnaeus, *Species Plantarum* 1: 531. 1753.
"Habitat – – – –" RCN: 3946.
Lectotype (Molero & Blanché in *Anales Jard. Bot. Madrid* 41: 217.
1984): Herb. Burser VII(1): 83 (UPS), see p. 197.
Current name: **Consolida ajacis** (L.) Schur (Ranunculaceae).
Note: Wilmott (in *J. Bot.* 80: 17. 1942) identified material in LINN
and the Clifford herbarium (BM) as *D. orientale* Gay (*Consolida
orientalis* (Gay) Schrödinger). Keener (in *Castanea* 41: 15. 1976)
reported that Wilmott had concluded that the name was typified by
a Clifford sheet, quoting J.E. Dandy as saying that European
botanists had generally rejected *D. ajacis* as a *nomen ambiguum*,
taking up *D. ambiguum* L. (*C. ambigua* (L.) P.W. Ball & Heywood)
as the name for the garden larkspur. However, no formal
typification was made until Molero & Blanché designated a Burser
collection, overlooked by earlier workers, as the lectotype, and again
took up *C. ajacis*.

Delphinium ambiguum Linnaeus, *Species Plantarum,* ed. 2, 1: 749.
1762.
"Habitat in Mauritania." RCN: 3948.
Lectotype (Munz in *J. Arnold Arbor.* 48: 177. 1967): Herb. Linn. No.
694.4 (LINN).
Current name: **Consolida ajacis** (L.) Schur (Ranunculaceae).
Note: See extensive discussion by Blanché & Molero (in *Bot. J. Linn.
Soc.* 113: 125–133. 1993). They agree with the choice made by
Munz, but argue that De Candolle was the first to select the
lectotype. They conclude that the name is a synonym of *Consolida
ajacis* (L.) Schur. See further comments by Blanché & al. (in
Lagascalia 19: 74. 1997).

Delphinium consolida Linnaeus, *Species Plantarum* 1: 530. 1753.
"Habitat in agris Europae restibilibus." RCN: 3945.
Lectotype (Jonsell & Jarvis in *Nordic J. Bot.* 14: 161. 1994): Herb.
Linn. No. 694.1 (LINN), see above, right.
Current name: **Consolida regalis** Gray (Ranunculaceae).

Delphinium elatum Linnaeus, *Species Plantarum* 1: 531. 1753.
"Habitat in Sibiria." RCN: 3951.
Lectotype (Munz in *J. Arnold Arbor.* 49: 139. 1968): Herb. Clifford:
213, *Delphinium* 4 (BM-000628787).
Current name: **Delphinium elatum** L. (Ranunculaceae).
Note: Warnock (in *Taxon* 42: 453. 1993) proposed the conservation of
Delphinium with *D. elatum* as the conserved type. He also chose a
specimen in UPS as lectotype without commenting on Munz's
earlier choice. The Committee for Spermatophyta (in *Taxon* 44:
609. 1995) did not recommend this proposal. See notes on generic
typification by Blanché & al. (in *Lagascalia* 19: 73. 1997).

Delphinium grandiflorum Linnaeus, *Species Plantarum* 1: 531. 1753.
"Habitat in Sibiria." RCN: 3950.
Lectotype (Munz in *J. Arnold Arbor.* 48: 519. 1967): Herb. Linn. No.
694.7 (LINN), see p. 5.
Current name: **Delphinium grandiflorum** L. (Ranunculaceae).

Delphinium × hybridum Linnaeus, *Demonstr. Pl. Horto Upsaliensi*:
15. 1753.
RCN: 3951.
Type not designated.
Original material: Herb. Linn. No. 218.19 (S); Herb. Linn. No. 694.9
(LINN).

The lectotype of *Delphinium consolida* L.

Current name: **Delphinium cuneatum** Steven ex DC.
(Ranunculaceae).
Note: Burtt (in *Kew Bull.* 9: 68. 1954) stated "The true *D. hybridum*,
of which there is a specimen in the Linnean herbarium, is the same
as *D. cuneatum* Stev.". Subsequently, Chowdhuri & al. (in *Notes
Roy. Bot. Gard. Edinburgh* 22: 404. 1958) stated that "the specimen
in the Linnaean herbarium…must be accepted as the type", but did
not distinguish between 694.9 and 694.10 (LINN). They rejected
the name as a *nomen confusum*. It does not appear to be in use and
should probably be a candidate for formal rejection.

Delphinium monstrosum Linnaeus, *Demonstr. Pl. Horto Upsaliensi*:
14. 1753.
RCN: 3951.
Type not designated.
Original material: Herb. Linn. No. 694.10 (LINN).
Note: The application of this name is uncertain.

Delphinium peregrinum Linnaeus, *Species Plantarum* 1: 531. 1753.
"Habitat in Italia, Sicilia, Melita." RCN: 3949.
Lectotype (Chowdhuri & Davis in *Notes Roy. Bot. Gard. Edinburgh* 22:
410. 1958): Herb. Clifford: 213, *Delphinium* 3 (BM-000628786).

Generitype of *Delphinium* Linnaeus.

Current name: **Delphinium peregrinum** L. (Ranunculaceae).

Note: Delphinium peregrinum, with the type designated by Chowdhuri & Davis, was proposed as conserved type of the genus by Jarvis (in *Taxon* 41: 562. 1992). However, the proposal was eventually ruled unnecessary by the General Committee (see Barrie, *l.c.* 55: 795–796. 2006 for a review of the history of this and related proposals).

Delphinium staphisagria Linnaeus, *Species Plantarum* 1: 531. 1753.

"Habitat in Istria, Dalmatia, Calabria, Apulia, Creta, Galloprovincia." RCN: 3952.

Type not designated.

Original material: none traced.

Current name: **Delphinium staphisagria** L. (Ranunculaceae).

Note: Munz (in *J. Arnold Arbor.* 48: 258. 1967) stated "Type locality: described from Istria, Dalmatia, Calabria, Apulia, S. France (LINN 694/12)", but did not explicitly treat the material as a type specimen. Ilarslan (in *Turk. J. Bot.* 20: 141. 1996) appears to follow him.

Dentaria bulbifera Linnaeus, *Species Plantarum* 2: 653. 1753.

"Habitat in Europa australi ad radices montium umbrosas." RCN: 4760.

Lectotype (Marhold in *Willdenowia* 31: 45. 2001): Herb. Burser XVIII(1): 82 (UPS).

Current name: **Cardamine bulbifera** (L.) Crantz (Brassicaceae).

Dentaria enneaphyllos Linnaeus, *Species Plantarum* 2: 653. 1753.

"Habitat in Austria, Italia." RCN: 4759.

Lectotype (Marhold in *Willdenowia* 31: 44. 2001): Herb. Burser XVIII(1): 83 (UPS).

Current name: **Cardamine enneaphyllos** (L.) R. Br. (Brassicaceae).

Dentaria pentaphyllos Linnaeus, *Species Plantarum* 2: 654. 1753.

"Habitat in Alpibus Helveticis, Allobrogicis, aliisque." RCN: 4761.

Lectotype (Hedge in Jarvis & al., *Regnum Veg.* 127: 42. 1993): Herb. Burser XVIII(1): 80 (UPS).

Generitype of *Dentaria* Linnaeus (vide Green, *Prop. Brit. Bot.*: 171. 1929).

Current name: **Cardamine pentaphyllos** (L.) Crantz (Brassicaceae).

Dialium indum Linnaeus, *Systema Naturae,* ed. 12, 2: 56; *Mantissa Plantarum*: 24. 1767.

"Habitat in India." RCN: 60.

Lectotype (Rojo in Jarvis & al., *Regnum Veg.* 127: 42. 1993): Herb. Linn. No. 23.1 (LINN).

Generitype of *Dialium* Linnaeus.

Current name: **Dialium indum** L. var. **indum** (Fabaceae: Caesalpinioideae).

Dianthera americana Linnaeus, *Species Plantarum* 1: 27. 1753.

"Habitat in Virginia." RCN: 129.

Lectotype (Reveal in Jarvis & al., *Regnum Veg.* 127: 42. 1993): *Clayton 408* (BM-000051211).

Generitype of *Dianthera* Linnaeus.

Current name: **Justicia americana** (L.) Vahl (Acanthaceae).

Dianthera comata Linnaeus, *Systema Naturae,* ed. 10, 2: 850. 1759.

["Habitat in Jamaica."] Sp. Pl., ed. 2, 1: 24 (1762). RCN: 130.

Lectotype (Graham in *Kew Bull.* 43: 618. 1988): *Browne,* Herb. Linn. No. 29.2 (LINN).

Current name: **Justicia comata** (L.) Lam. (Acanthaceae).

Dianthus alpinus Linnaeus, *Species Plantarum* 1: 412. 1753.

"Habitat in Stiria, Austria." RCN: 3218.

Lectotype (Widder in *Ber. Bayer. Bot. Ges.* 37: 83. 1964): Herb. Burser XI: 95 (UPS).

Current name: **Dianthus alpinus** L. (Caryophyllaceae).

Dianthus arboreus Linnaeus, *Species Plantarum* 1: 413. 1753, *nom. utique rej.*

"Habitat in Creta." RCN: 3220.

Lectotype (Greuter in *Candollea* 20: 186. 1965): [icon] *"Betonica coronaria arborea Cretica"* in Bauhin & Cherler, Hist. Pl. Univ. 3(2): 328. 1651. – Typotype: *Benincasa s.n.,* cult. at Montbéliard (BAS).

Current name: **Dianthus juniperinus** Sm. subsp. **bauhinorum** (Greuter) Turland (Caryophyllaceae).

Dianthus arenarius Linnaeus, *Species Plantarum* 1: 412. 1753.

"Habitat in Europae frigidioris arena mobili." RCN: 3217.

Lectotype (Miniaev & Samutina in *Novosti Sist. Vyssh. Rast.* 22: 120. 1985): Herb. Linn. No. 581.23 (LINN).

Current name: **Dianthus arenarius** L. (Caryophyllaceae).

Dianthus armeria Linnaeus, *Species Plantarum* 1: 410. 1753.

"Habitat in sterilibus Gotlandiae, Germaniae, Galliae, Italiae." RCN: 3206.

Lectotype (Jonsell & Jarvis in *Nordic J. Bot.* 14: 156. 1994): Herb. Linn. No. 581.6 (LINN).

Current name: **Dianthus armeria** L. (Caryophyllaceae).

Dianthus barbatus Linnaeus, *Species Plantarum* 1: 409. 1753.

"Habitat in – – – –" RCN: 3203.

Lectotype (Jonsell & Jarvis in *Nordic J. Bot.* 14: 157. 1994): Herb. Clifford: 165, *Dianthus* 6 (BM-000628462).

Current name: **Dianthus barbatus** L. (Caryophyllaceae).

Dianthus carthusianorum Linnaeus, *Species Plantarum* 1: 409. 1753.

"Habitat in Germaniae, Italiae Siciliae sterilibus apricis." RCN: 3204.

Lectotype (Jonsell & Jarvis in *Nordic J. Bot.* 14: 157. 1994): Herb. Burser XI: 92 (UPS).

Current name: **Dianthus carthusianorum** L. (Caryophyllaceae).

Dianthus caryophyllus Linnaeus, *Species Plantarum* 1: 410. 1753.

"Habitat in Italia. Rajus." RCN: 3209.

Lectotype (Ghafoor in Jafri & El-Gadi, *Fl. Libya* 59: 104. 1978): Herb. Linn. No. 581.8 (LINN), see opposite, above left.

Generitype of *Dianthus* Linnaeus (vide Hitchcock, *Prop. Brit. Bot.*: 155. 1929).

Current name: **Dianthus caryophyllus** L. (Caryophyllaceae).

Note: See detailed discussion by Langen & al. (in *Taxon* 33: 717. 1984), who chose a Herb. Clifford sheet (see their f. 1) as lectotype, unaware of Ghafoor's earlier choice. As the Linnaean sheet appears to be original material, Ghafoor's choice is valid and has priority.

Dianthus caryophyllus Linnaeus var. **coronarius** Linnaeus, *Species Plantarum* 1: 410. 1753.

RCN: 3209.

Lectotype (Ghafoor in Jafri & El-Gadi, *Fl. Libya* 59: 104. 1978): Herb. Linn. No. 581.8 (LINN).

Current name: **Dianthus caryophyllus** L. (Caryophyllaceae).

Note: For a discussion of the relationship between this variety and the autonym, see Langen & al. (in *Taxon* 33: 717. 1984).

Dianthus caryophyllus Linnaeus var. **imbricatus** Linnaeus, *Species Plantarum* 1: 410. 1753.

RCN: 3209.

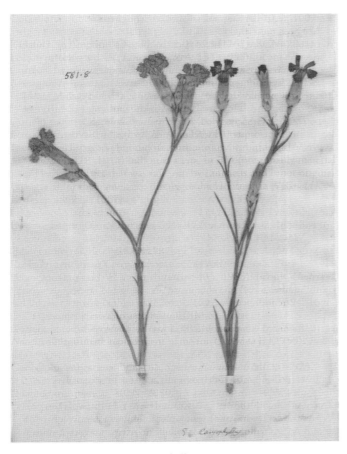

The lectotype of *Dianthus caryophyllus* L.

Lectotype (Langen & al. in *Taxon* 33: 719. 1984): [icon] *"Caryophyllus spicam frumenti referens"* in Volckamer in Acad. Caes.-Leop. Carol. Nat. Cur. Ephem. 4: 368, t. 9. 1715.
Current name: ***Dianthus caryophyllus*** L. (Caryophyllaceae).

Dianthus caryophyllus Linnaeus var. **inodorus** Linnaeus, *Species Plantarum* 1: 410. 1753.
RCN: 3209.
Lectotype (Langen & al. in *Taxon* 33: 719. 1984): [icon] *"Caryophyllus silvestris, flore rubro, inodoro"* in Séguier, Pl. Veron. 1: 435, 433, t. 7, f. 3. 1745 (see p. 157).
Current name: ***Dianthus caryophyllus*** L. (Caryophyllaceae).

Dianthus chinensis Linnaeus, *Species Plantarum* 1: 411. 1753.
"Habitat in China." RCN: 3213.
Lectotype (Langen & al. in *Taxon* 33: 723. 1984): Herb. Linn. No. 581.13 (LINN).
Current name: ***Dianthus chinensis*** L. (Caryophyllaceae).

Dianthus deltoides Linnaeus, *Species Plantarum* 1: 411. 1753.
"Habitat in Europae pratis." RCN: 3211.
Lectotype (Jonsell & Jarvis in *Nordic J. Bot.* 14: 157. 1994): Herb. Linn. No. 581.11 (LINN).
Current name: ***Dianthus deltoides*** L. (Caryophyllaceae).

Dianthus diminutus Linnaeus, *Species Plantarum,* ed. 2, 1: 587. 1762.
"Habitat in Germania." RCN: 3208.

Lectotype (Ball in Cafferty & Jarvis in *Taxon* 53: 1051. 2004): [icon] *"Caryophyllus sylvestris minimus"* in Tabernaemontanus, New Vollk. Kräuterb.: 670, 669. 1664. – Epitype (Ball in Cafferty & Jarvis in *Taxon* 53: 1051. 2004): Germany. Lübeck, Jul 1901, *Kjellberg s.n.* (BM).
Current name: ***Petrorhagia prolifera*** (L.) P.W. Ball & Heywood (Caryophyllaceae).

Dianthus fruticosus Linnaeus, *Species Plantarum* 1: 413. 1753.
"Habitat in Graecia." RCN: 3221.
Lectotype (Runemark in *Bot. Not.* 133: 482. 1980): [icon] *"Caryophyllus Graecus arboreus Leucoii folio peramaro"* in Tournefort, Rel. Voy. Levant (Paris ed.) 1: 183. 1717.
Current name: ***Dianthus fruticosus*** L. subsp. ***fruticosus*** (Caryophyllaceae).

Dianthus glaucus Linnaeus, *Species Plantarum* 1: 411. 1753.
"Habitat in Anglia." RCN: 3212.
Lectotype (Jonsell in Cafferty & Jarvis in *Taxon* 53: 1051. 2004): Herb. Linn. No. 581.12 (LINN).
Current name: ***Dianthus deltoides*** L. (Caryophyllaceae).

Dianthus hyssopifolius Linnaeus, *Centuria I Plantarum*: 11. 1755.
"Habitat in Germania, Gallia Narbonensi."
Lectotype (Laínz & Muñoz Garmendia in *Anales Jard. Bot. Madrid* 44: 572. 1987): Herb. Linn. No. 581.18 (LINN).
Current name: ***Dianthus hyssopifolius*** L. (Caryophyllaceae).

Dianthus monspeliacus Linnaeus, *Systema Naturae,* ed. 10, 2: 1029. 1759.
RCN: 3214.
Lectotype (Bernal Cid in Cafferty & Jarvis in *Taxon* 53: 1051. 2004): *Séguier,* Herb. Linn. No. 581.17 (LINN).
Current name: ***Dianthus hyssopifolius*** L. (Caryophyllaceae).
Note: Rickett (in *Lloydia* 18: 60. 1955) and Nordenstam (in *Bot. Not.* 114: 278. 1961) both noted that *D. monspessulanus* did not feature in *Centuria I Plantarum* (1755) and was a new addition in the later version of that thesis published in the *Amoenitates Academicae* (Nov 1759). Both *D. monspessulanus* and Linnaeus' earlier (May–Jun 1759) *D. monspeliacus* have very similar diagnoses. Sheet 581.17 (LINN) bears material from Séguier annotated "monspeliensis A" by Linnaeus, the "A" associating the material with *D. monspeliacus* (species "A" in *Syst. Nat.*, ed. 10, 2: 1029), and Séguier is mentioned in the protologue of *D. monspessulanus* ("Habitat Monspelii. Sauvages; Veronae. Seguier"). Partly because there has been some usage of *D. monspessulanus* (by e.g. Greuter & al., *Med-Checklist* 1: 199. 1984; Tutin & Walters in Tutin & al., *Fl. Europaea,* ed. 2, 1: 238. 1993), it seems preferable to treat these two as independent, though homotypic, names (rather than orthographic variants). Laínz & Muñoz Garmendia (in *Anales Jard. Bot. Madrid* 44: 571–572. 1987) clarified the typification of *D. hyssopifolius* and they, and Bernal & al. (in Castroviejo & al., *Fl. Iberica* 2: 426–462. 1990) have treated it and *D. monspeliacus* as synonymous. The typifications made by Bernal Cid for both *D. monspeliacus* and *D. monspessulanus* formalise this position.

Dianthus monspessulanus Linnaeus, *Amoenitates Academicae* 4: 313. 1759.
"Habitat Monspelii. Sauvages; Veronae. Seguier." RCN: 3214.
Lectotype (Bernal Cid in Cafferty & Jarvis in *Taxon* 53: 1051. 2004): *Séguier,* Herb. Linn. No. 581.17 (LINN).
Current name: ***Dianthus hyssopifolius*** L. (Caryophyllaceae).
Note: See discussion under *D. monspeliacus* L.

Dianthus plumarius Linnaeus, *Species Plantarum* 1: 411. 1753.
"Habitat in Europae & Canadae pascuis nemorosis." RCN: 3215.
Type not designated.
Original material: Herb. Burser XI: 100 (UPS); Herb. Burser XI: 102 (UPS); Herb. Linn. No. 179.11 (S); Herb. Linn. No. 581.19 (LINN); Herb. Linn. No. 581.22 (LINN).
Current name: *Dianthus plumarius* L. (Caryophyllaceae).

Dianthus pomeridianus Linnaeus, *Species Plantarum,* ed. 2, 2: 1673. 1763.
"Habitat Constantinopoli. Forskåhl; in Palaestina. Hasselquist." RCN: 3210.
Type not designated.
Original material: *Hasselquist,* Herb. Linn. No. 581.10 (LINN); Herb. Linn. No. 180.1 (S).
Current name: *Dianthus* sp. (Caryophyllaceae).
Note: The application of this name is uncertain.

Dianthus prolifer Linnaeus, *Species Plantarum* 1: 410. 1753.
"Habitat in Germaniae & australioris Europae pascuis sterilibus." RCN: 3207.
Lectotype (Thomas in *Bot. J. Linn. Soc.* 87: 73. 1983): Herb. Linn. No. 178.19 (S).
Current name: *Petrorhagia prolifera* (L.) P.W. Ball & Heywood (Caryophyllaceae).

Dianthus pungens Linnaeus, *Mantissa Plantarum Altera*: 240. 1771.
"Habitat in Hispaniae maritimis." RCN: 3222.
Lectotype (Laínz in *Anales Jard. Bot. Madrid* 44: 179. 1987): Herb. Linn. No. 581.27 (LINN).
Current name: *Dianthus pungens* L. (Caryophyllaceae).

Dianthus saxifragus Linnaeus, *Species Plantarum* 1: 413. 1753.
"Habitat in Helvetia, Gallia, Ingolstadii." RCN: 3194.
Basionym of: *Gypsophila saxifraga* (L.) L. (1759).
Lectotype (Jonsell & Jarvis in *Nordic J. Bot.* 14: 157. 1994): Herb. Burser XVI(1): 42 (UPS).
Current name: *Petrorhagia saxifraga* (L.) Link (Caryophyllaceae).

Dianthus superbus Linnaeus, *Flora Suecica,* ed. 2: 146. 1755.
"Habitat in pratis & graminosis Lapponiae; Ostrobothniae, praesertim ad templum Kemi; in prato unico ad Stiernarp Hallandiae..." RCN: 3216.
Lectotype (Jonsell & Jarvis in *Nordic J. Bot.* 14: 157. 1994): Herb. Linn. No. 581.21 (LINN).
Current name: *Dianthus superbus* L. (Caryophyllaceae).

Dianthus virgineus Linnaeus, *Species Plantarum* 1: 412. 1753.
"Habitat Monspelii." RCN: 3219.
Type not designated.
Original material: Herb. Burser XI: 99, syntype (UPS); Herb. Linn. No. 581.25 (LINN); [icon] in Dillenius, Hort. Eltham. 2: 401, t. 298, f. 385. 1732.
Current name: *Dianthus* sp. (Caryophyllaceae).
Note: The application of this name is uncertain.

Diapensia helvetica Linnaeus, *Species Plantarum* 1: 141. 1753.
"Habitat in alpibus Helveticis Gemmi & Pyndtnerberg." RCN: 1141.
Basionym of: *Aretia helvetica* (L.) L. (1774).
Type not designated.
Original material: Herb. Burser XVI: 71 (UPS); [icon] in Haller, Enum. Meth. Stirp. Helv. 1: 486, t. 8. 1742.
Current name: *Androsace helvetica* (L.) All. (Primulaceae).

Diapensia lapponica Linnaeus, *Species Plantarum* 1: 141. 1753.
"Habitat in alpibus Lapponicis." RCN: 1140.
Lectotype (Barrie in Jarvis & al., *Regnum Veg.* 127: 42. 1993): Herb. Linn. No. 195.1 (LINN).
Generitype of *Diapensia* Linnaeus (vide Hitchcock, *Prop. Brit. Bot.*: 128. 1929).
Current name: *Diapensia lapponica* L. (Diapensiaceae).

Dictamnus albus Linnaeus, *Species Plantarum* 1: 383. 1753.
"Habitat in Germania, Gallia, Italia." RCN: 3013.
Lectotype (Nair in Jarvis & al., *Regnum Veg.* 127: 42. 1993): Herb. Clifford: 161, *Dictamnus* 1, sheet A (BM-000558738).
Generitype of *Dictamnus* Linnaeus.
Current name: *Dictamnus albus* L. (Rutaceae).
Note: Townsend (in Rechinger, *Fl. Iranica* 36: 1. 1966) indicated 536.1 (LINN) as type, but this sheet is unannotated by Linnaeus and cannot be original material for the name.

Digitalis canariensis Linnaeus, *Species Plantarum* 2: 622. 1753.
"Habitat in Canariis." RCN: 4507.
Lectotype (Wijnands, *Bot. Commelins*: 188. 1983): Herb. Linn. No. 775.10 (LINN).
Current name: *Digitalis canariensis* L. (Scrophulariaceae).
Note: The Plukenet plate cited by Linnaeus in synonymy and the corresponding voucher material in Herb. Sloane are reproduced by Francisco-Ortega & al. (in *Bull. Nat. Hist. Mus. London, Bot.* 24: 10–11, f. 4, 5. 1994).

Digitalis ferruginea Linnaeus, *Species Plantarum* 2: 622. 1753.
"Habitat in Italia, Constantinopoli." RCN: 4505.
Lectotype (designated here by Sutton): Herb. Burser XIII: 164 (UPS).
Current name: *Digitalis ferruginea* L. (Scrophulariaceae).

Digitalis lutea Linnaeus, *Species Plantarum* 2: 622. 1753.
"Habitat in Galliae, Italiae sabulosis." RCN: 4502.
Lectotype (Fischer in *Feddes Repert.* 108: 111. 1997): Herb. Linn. No. 775.3 (LINN).
Current name: *Digitalis lutea* L. (Scrophulariaceae).

Digitalis minor Linnaeus, *Mantissa Plantarum Altera*: 567. 1771.
"Habitat in Hispania." RCN: 4501.
Lectotype (Wijnands & Belder in *Misc. Pap. Landbouwhoogeschool* 19: 429. 1980): Herb. Linn. No. 775.2 (LINN).
Current name: *Digitalis minor* L. (Scrophulariaceae).
Note: A more detailed discussion is provided by Hinz (in *Candollea* 42: 168. 1987) who also illustrates the type (as f. 2).

Digitalis obscura Linnaeus, *Species Plantarum,* ed. 2, 2: 867. 1763.
"Habitat in Hispania." RCN: 4506.
Lectotype (designated here by Sutton): Herb. Linn. No. 775.9 (LINN).
Current name: *Digitalis obscura* L. (Scrophulariaceae).

Digitalis purpurea Linnaeus, *Species Plantarum* 2: 621. 1753.
"Habitat in Europa australiore." RCN: 4499.
Lectotype (D'Arcy in Woodson & Schery in *Ann. Missouri Bot. Gard.* 66: 216. 1979): Herb. Linn. No. 775.1 (LINN).
Generitype of *Digitalis* Linnaeus (vide Green, *Prop. Brit. Bot.*: 168. 1929).
Current name: *Digitalis purpurea* L. (Scrophulariaceae).
Note: Hinz (in *Candollea* 42: 168. 1987) also accepted 775.1 (LINN) as type, illustrating it as her f. 1.

Digitalis thapsi Linnaeus, *Species Plantarum,* ed. 2, 2: 867. 1763.
"Habitat in Hispania." RCN: 4501.
Type not designated.

Original material: [icon] in Boccone, Mus. Piante Rar. Sicilia: 108, t. 85. 1697; [icon] in Barrelier, Pl. Galliam: 20, t. 1183. 1714.
Current name: ***Digitalis thapsi*** L. (Scrophulariaceae).
Note: Wijnands & Belder (in *Misc. Pap. Landbouwhoogeschool* 19: 429. 1980) state that the Boccone plate (1697: 108, t. 85), cited in synonymy, is not identifiable as *D. thapsi*. Hinz (in *Candollea* 42: 187. 1987) argued that both it and the cited Barrelier plate conflict with the diagnosis and designated a neotype. However, cited plates form part of the protologue and cannot therefore be rejected as being in conflict with it.

Dillenia indica Linnaeus, *Species Plantarum* 1: 535. 1753.
"Habitat in Malabaria." RCN: 3975.
Lectotype (Hoogland in *Blumea* 7: 113. 1952): [icon] *"Syalita"* in Rheede, Hort. Malab. 3: 39, t. 38, t. 39. 1682.
Generitype of *Dillenia* Linnaeus.
Current name: ***Dillenia indica*** L. (Dilleniaceae).

Diodia virginiana Linnaeus, *Species Plantarum* 1: 104. 1753.
"Habitat in Virginiae aquosis." RCN: 855.
Lectotype (Reveal in Jarvis & al., *Regnum Veg.* 127: 42. 1993): *Clayton 277* (BM-000042231).
Generitype of *Diodia* Linnaeus.
Current name: ***Diodia virginiana*** L. (Rubiaceae).

Dioscorea aculeata Linnaeus, *Species Plantarum* 2: 1033. 1753.
"Habitat in Malabaria." RCN: 7455.
Type not designated.
Original material: [icon] in Rheede, Hort. Malab. 7: 71, t. 37. 1688; [icon] in Francisci, Ost- West-Ind. Gart.: 717, t. 25, f. 8. 1668.
Current name: ***Dioscorea aculeata*** L. (Dioscoreaceae).
Note: See discussion by Nicolson & al. (*Interpret. Van Rheede's Hort. Malab.*: 290. 1988) who do not, however, formally typify the name.

Dioscorea alata Linnaeus, *Species Plantarum* 2: 1033. 1753.
"Habitat in Indiis." RCN: 7456.
Lectotype (Howard, *Fl. Lesser Antilles* 3: 506. 1979): Herb. Linn. No. 1184.2 (LINN).
Current name: ***Dioscorea alata*** L. (Dioscoreaceae).

Dioscorea bulbifera Linnaeus, *Species Plantarum* 2: 1033. 1753.
"Habitat in Indiis." RCN: 7457.
Lectotype (Milne-Redhead in Polhill, *Fl. Trop. E. Africa, Dioscoreaceae*: 10. 1975): [icon] *"Rizophora Zeylanica"* in Hermann, Parad. Bat.: 217. 1698 (see p. 136).
Current name: ***Dioscorea bulbifera*** L. (Dioscoreaceae).

Dioscorea oppositifolia Linnaeus, *Species Plantarum* 2: 1033. 1753.
"Habitat in India." RCN: 7460.
Type not designated.
Original material: [icon] in Petiver, Gazophyl. Nat.: 50, t. 31, f. 6. 1704.
Current name: ***Dioscorea oppositifolia*** L. (Dioscoreaceae).
Note: Jayasuriya (in Dassanayake & al., *Revised Handb. Fl. Ceylon* 9: 67. 1995) incorrectly indicated a König collection (1184.7 LINN) received by Linnaeus long after 1753, as the lectotype. He also excluded (p. 65) from synonymy the only original element (a Petiver plate) for the name.

Dioscorea pentaphylla Linnaeus, *Species Plantarum* 2: 1032. 1753.
"Habitat in India." RCN: 7453.
Lectotype (Jayasuriya in Dassanayake & al., *Revised Handb. Fl. Ceylon* 9: 55. 1995): [icon] *"Nuren-kelengu"* in Rheede, Hort. Malab. 7: 67, t. 35. 1688.
Current name: ***Dioscorea pentaphylla*** L. (Dioscoreaceae).

Dioscorea sativa Linnaeus, *Species Plantarum* 2: 1033. 1753, *typ. cons.*
"Habitat in Indiis." RCN: 7458.
Conserved type (McNeill & al. in *Taxon* 36: 369. 1987): [icon] *"Dioscorea foliis cordatis, caule laevi"* in Linnaeus, Hort. Cliff.: 459, t. 28 [stem and leaves]. 1738.
Generitype of *Dioscorea* Linnaeus, *nom. cons.*
Current name: ***Dioscorea villosa*** L. (Dioscoreaceae).
Note: Dioscorea sativa, with the type designated by McNeill & al., was proposed as conserved type of the genus by Jarvis (in *Taxon* 41: 562. 1992). This was eventually approved by the General Committee (see review of the history of this proposal by Barrie, *l.c.* 55: 795–796. 2006).

Dioscorea triphylla Linnaeus, *Species Plantarum* 2: 1032. 1753.
"Habitat in Malabaria." RCN: 7454.
Lectotype (Merrill, *Interpret. Rumph. Herb. Amb.*: 148. 1917): [icon] *"Tsjageri-nuren"* in Rheede, Hort. Malab. 7: 63, t. 33. 1688.
Current name: ***Dioscorea pentaphylla*** L. (Dioscoreaceae).

Dioscorea villosa Linnaeus, *Species Plantarum* 2: 1033. 1753.
"Habitat in Virginia, Florida." RCN: 7459.

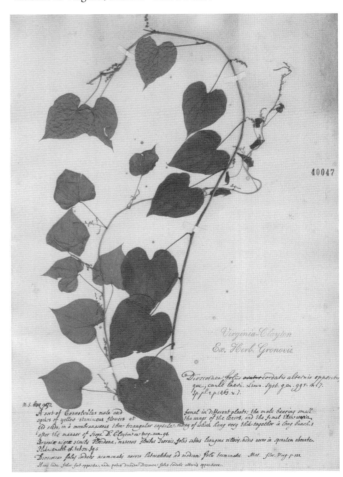

Lectotype (Al-Shehbaz & Schubert in *J. Arnold Arbor.* 70: 70. 1989): *Clayton 94*, staminate plant (BM-000051149) (see also p. 183).
Current name: ***Dioscorea villosa*** L. (Dioscoreaceae).

Diosma capensis (Linnaeus) Linnaeus, *Mantissa Plantarum Altera*: 343. 1771.
"Habitat ad Cap. b. spei." RCN: 1604.

D

Basionym: *Hartogia capensis* L. (1759).
Lectotype (Porter in Jarvis & al., *Regnum Veg.* 127: 52. 1993): Linnaeus in Herb. Wahlbom, No. 25 (UPS).
Current name: ***Agathosma hispida*** Bartl. & H.L. Wendl. (Rutaceae).

Diosma capitata Linnaeus, *Mantissa Plantarum Altera*: 210. 1771.
"Habitat ad Cap. b. spei, florens septembri." RCN: 1605.
Type not designated.
Original material: Herb. Linn. No. 270.15 (LINN).
Current name: ***Audouinia capitata*** (L.) Brongn. (Bruniaceae).

Diosma ciliata Linnaeus, *Species Plantarum* 1: 198. 1753.
"Habitat in Aethiopia." RCN: 1609.
Replaced synonym of: *Hartogia ciliaris* L. (1767).
Type not designated.
Original material: Herb. Linn. No. 270.31 (LINN); [icon] in Plukenet, Amalth. Bot.: 197, t. 411, f. 3. 1705.
Current name: ***Agathosma ciliata*** (L.) Link (Rutaceae).

Diosma crenata Linnaeus, *Systema Naturae*, ed. 10, 2: 940. 1759, *orth. var.*
RCN: 1610.
Type not designated.
Original material: as *Diosma crenulata*.
Current name: ***Agathosma crenulata*** (L.) Pillans (Rutaceae).
Note: An orthographic variant of *D. crenulata* L. (1756).

Diosma crenulata Linnaeus, *Centuria II Plantarum*: 11. 1756.
"Habitat in Aethiopia. Burmannus." RCN: 1610.
Type not designated.
Original material: Herb. Linn. No. 270.34 (LINN).
Current name: ***Agathosma crenulata*** (L.) Pillans (Rutaceae).

Diosma cupressina Linnaeus, *Systema Naturae*, ed. 12, 2: 182; *Mantissa Plantarum*: 50. 1767.
"Habitat in Cap. b. spei." RCN: 1606.
Type not designated.
Original material: Herb. Linn. No. 270.23 (LINN).
Current name: ***Thamnea uniflora*** (L.) Sol. ex Brongn. (Bruniaceae).
Note: See comments by Williams (in *J. S. African Bot.* 48: 370. 1982).

Diosma ericoides Linnaeus, *Species Plantarum* 1: 198. 1753.
"Habitat in Aethiopia." RCN: 1603.
Lectotype (Williams in *J. S. African Bot.* 47: 99. 1981): [icon] "*Ericaeformis, Coridis folio, Aethiopica floribus pentapetalis in apicibus*" in Plukenet, Phytographia: t. 279, f. 5. 1694; Almag. Bot.: 136. 1696.
Current name: ***Diosma hirsuta*** L. (Rutaceae).

Diosma hirsuta Linnaeus, *Species Plantarum* 1: 198. 1753.
"Habitat ad Caput b. Spei." RCN: 1601.
Lectotype (Williams in *J. S. African Bot.* 48: 350. 1982): Herb. Clifford: 71, *Diosma* 1 (BM-000558120; iso- 270.3 LINN).
Current name: ***Diosma hirsuta*** L. (Rutaceae).

Diosma imbricata (Linnaeus) Linnaeus, *Systema Vegetabilium*, ed. 13: 199. 1774.
["Habitat ad Cap. b. spei."] Mant. Pl.: 124 (1767). RCN: 1607.
Basionym: *Hartogia imbricata* L. (1767).
Type not designated.
Original material: as basionym.
Current name: ***Agathosma imbricata*** (L.) Willd. (Rutaceae).

Diosma lanceolata Linnaeus, *Species Plantarum* 1: 198. 1753.
"Habitat in Aethiopia." RCN: 1608.
Basionym of: *Hartogia lanceolata* (L.) L. (1767).
Type not designated.
Original material: none traced.
Current name: ***Agathosma lanceolata*** (L.) Engl. (Rutaceae).

Diosma oppositifolia Linnaeus, *Species Plantarum* 1: 198. 1753.
"Habitat ad Caput b. Spei." RCN: 1600.
Lectotype (Williams in *J. S. African Bot.* 40: 276. 1974): [icon] "*Spiraea Africana foliis cruciatim positis*" in Commelin, Hort. Med. Amstelaed. Pl. Rar.: 1, t. 1. 1706.
Generitype of *Diosma* Linnaeus (vide Hitchcock, *Prop. Brit. Bot.*: 134. 1929).
Current name: ***Diosma oppositifolia*** L. (Rutaceae).
Note: See also notes by Wijnands (*Bot. Commelins*: 185. 1983).

Diosma pulchella Linnaeus, *Systema Naturae*, ed. 10, 2: 940. 1759.
["Habitat in Aethiopia."] Sp. Pl., ed. 2, 1: 289 (1762). RCN: 1612.
Basionym of: *Hartogia pulchella* (L.) L. (1767).
Type not designated.
Original material: Herb. Linn. No. 270.35? (LINN).
Current name: ***Agathosma pulchella*** (L.) Link (Rutaceae).

Diosma rubra Linnaeus, *Species Plantarum* 1: 198. 1753.
"Habitat in Aethiopia." RCN: 1602.
Lectotype (Williams in *J. S. African Bot.* 47: 99. 1981): Herb. Linn. No. 270.4, right specimen ["240.4"] (LINN).
Current name: ***Diosma hirsuta*** L. (Rutaceae).
Note: Williams (in *J. S. African Bot.* 40: 275. 1974) informally rejected the name as it was based on discordant elements but subsequently typified it such that it fell into the synonymy of *D. hirsuta* L.

Diosma uniflora Linnaeus, *Species Plantarum* 1: 198. 1753.
"Habitat in Aethiopia." RCN: 1611.
Lectotype (Strid in *Opera Bot.* 32: 37. 1972): Herb. Linn. No. 270.25, left specimen (LINN).
Current name: ***Adenandra uniflora*** (L.) Willd. (Rutaceae).

Diospyros lotus Linnaeus, *Species Plantarum* 2: 1057. 1753.
"Habitat in G. Narbonensi, Italia, Mauritania." RCN: 7701.
Lectotype (White in Jarvis & al., *Regnum Veg.* 127: 43. 1993): Herb. Burser XXIII: 54 (UPS).
Generitype of *Diospyros* Linnaeus (vide Green, *Prop. Brit. Bot.*: 194. 1929).
Current name: ***Diospyros lotus*** L. (Ebenaceae).
Note: A detailed discussion of the early description of this plant is given by Carder (in *Curtis's Bot. Mag.* 180: 165–168. 1976), who says it is based on a Clifford specimen "and other elements". Ghazanfar (in Nair & Ali, *Fl. W. Pakistan* 116: 3. 1978) stated "Type: LINN 1231.102", presumably in error for "1231.1–2". These two sheets in LINN are not part of the same gathering, so Art. 9.15 does not apply.

Diospyros virginiana Linnaeus, *Species Plantarum* 2: 1057. 1753.
"Habitat in America septentrionali." RCN: 7702.
Lectotype (designated here by Reveal): *Kalm*, Herb. Linn. No. 1231.4 (LINN; iso- UPS).
Current name: ***Diospyros virginiana*** L. (Ebenaceae).
Note: Briand (in *Huntia* 12: 71–89. 2005) provides a history of the American persimmon, and reproduces Linnaeus' protologue (f. 4) and the cited Catesby plate (f. 5).

Dipsacus fullonum Linnaeus, *Species Plantarum* 1: 97. 1753.
"Habitat in Gallia, Anglia, Italia." RCN: 794.

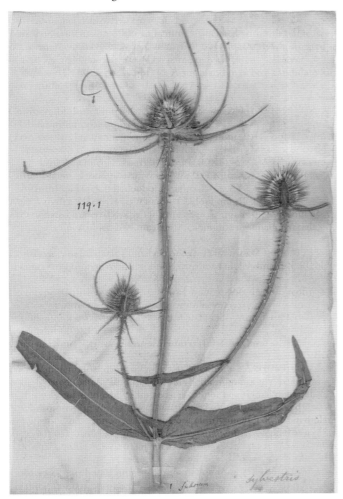

Lectotype (Wilmott in *Rep. Bot. Soc. Exch. Club Brit. Isles* 13: 20.
  1947): Herb. Linn. No. 119.1 (LINN).
Generitype of *Dipsacus* Linnaeus (vide Hitchcock, *Prop. Brit. Bot.*:
  123. 1929).
Current name: ***Dipsacus fullonum*** L. (Dipsacaceae).
Note: Lambinon (in *Taxon* 30: 362. 1981) proposed the rejection of
  the name as a *nomen ambiguum*, but the Committee for
  Spermatophyta (in *Taxon* 35: 559. 1986) declined the proposal.

Dipsacus fullonum Linnaeus var. **sativus** Linnaeus, *Species
  Plantarum,* ed. 2, 2: 1677. 1763.
RCN: 794.
Type not designated.
Original material: none traced.
Current name: ***Dipsacus sativus*** (L.) Honck. (Dipsacaceae).

Dipsacus laciniatus Linnaeus, *Species Plantarum* 1: 97. 1753.
"Habitat in Alsatia, Azow." RCN: 795.
Lectotype (Lack in Rechinger, *Fl. Iranica* 168: 3. 1991): Herb. Linn.
  No. 119.2 (LINN).
Current name: ***Dipsacus laciniatus*** L. (Dipsacaceae).

Dipsacus pilosus Linnaeus, *Species Plantarum* 1: 97. 1753.
"Habitat in Anglia, Gallia." RCN: 796.

Lectotype (Lack in Rechinger, *Fl. Iranica* 168: 6. 1991): Herb. Linn.
  No. 119.4 (LINN).
Current name: ***Dipsacus pilosus*** L. (Dipsacaceae).

Dirca palustris Linnaeus, *Species Plantarum* 1: 358. 1753.
"Habitat in Virginiae paludosis." RCN: 830.
Lectotype (Nevling in *J. Arnold Arbor.* 45: 158. 1964): Herb. Linn.
  No. 501.1 (LINN).
Generitype of *Dirca* Linnaeus.
Current name: ***Dirca palustris*** L. (Thymelaeaceae).

Disandra prostrata Linnaeus, *Systema Vegetabilium,* ed. 13: 290.
  1774, *nom. illeg.*
["Habitat – – – –"] Sp. Pl. 2: 63 (1753). RCN: 2637.
Replaced synonym: *Sibthorpia peregrina* L. (1753).
Lectotype (Hampshire in Jarvis & al., *Regnum Veg.* 127: 43. 1993):
  [icon] *"Planta"* in Plukenet, Phytographia: t. 257, f. 5. 1694.
Generitype of *Disandra* Linnaeus.
Current name: ***Sibthorpia peregrina*** L. (Scrophulariaceae).
Note: An illegitimate replacement name in *Disandra* for *Sibthorpia
  peregrina* L. (1753).

Dodartia indica Linnaeus, *Species Plantarum* 2: 633. 1753.
"Habitat in India." RCN: 4598.
Lectotype (Prijanto in *Reinwardtia* 7: 550. 1969): Herb. Linn. No.
  800.3 (LINN).
Current name: ***Lindenbergia indica*** (L.) Vatke (Scrophulariaceae).

Dodartia orientalis Linnaeus, *Species Plantarum* 2: 633. 1753.
"Habitat in monte Ararat, Tataria." RCN: 4597.
Lectotype (Sutton in Jarvis & al., *Regnum Veg.* 127: 43. 1993): Herb.
  Clifford: 326, *Dodartia* 1 (BM-000646241).
Generitype of *Dodartia* Linnaeus (vide Green, *Prop. Brit. Bot.*: 169.
  1929).
Current name: ***Dodartia orientalis*** L. (Scrophulariaceae).
Note: Although Edmondson (in Davis, *Fl. Turkey* 6: 678. 1978)
  indicated a Tournefort collection as type, this collection is not
  original material for the name as it was unseen by Linnaeus.

Dodecatheon meadia Linnaeus, *Species Plantarum* 1: 144. 1753.
"Habitat in Virginia." RCN: 1159.
Lectotype (Dandy, *Sloane Herbarium*: 112. 1958): [icon] *"Meadia"* in
  Catesby, Nat. Hist. Carolina 2, App.: 1, t. 1. 1747.
Generitype of *Dodecatheon* Linnaeus.
Current name: ***Dodecatheon meadia*** L. (Primulaceae).

Dolichos aristatus Linnaeus, *Species Plantarum,* ed. 2, 2: 1021.
  1763.
"Habitat in America." RCN: 5344.
Neotype (Rudd & Verdcourt in Turland & Jarvis in *Taxon* 46: 468.
  1997): U.S.A. Virginia: near Portsmouth, in fruticetis, Aug 1840,
  Rugel s.n. (K).
Current name: ***Centrosema virginianum*** (L.) Benth. (Fabaceae:
  Faboideae).

Dolichos biflorus Linnaeus, *Species Plantarum* 2: 727. 1753.
"Habitat in India." RCN: 5353.
Lectotype (Brenan in *Mem. New York Bot. Gard.* 8: 416. 1954): Herb.
  A. van Royen No. 908.115–2120 (L).
Current name: ***Vigna unguiculata*** (L.) Walp. (Fabaceae:
  Faboideae).
Note: Westphal (*Pulses Ethiopia, Taxon. Agric. Signif.*: 214, 224. 1974)
  provides an extensive discussion on the typification of this name, as
  does Verdcourt (in Milne-Redhead & Polhill, *Fl. Trop. E. Africa,
  Leguminosae* 4: 643. 1971).

Dolichos bulbosus Linnaeus, *Species Plantarum*, ed. 2, 2: 1021. 1763, *nom. illeg.*
"Habitat in Indiis." RCN: 5342.
Replaced synonym: *Dolichos erosus* L. (1753).
Lectotype (Sørensen in *Nordic J. Bot.* 8: 169, 177. 1988): [icon] *"Phaseolus Nevisensis foliis multangulis, tuberosa radice esculenta"* in Plukenet, Phytographia: t. 52, f. 4. 1691; Almag. Bot.: 292. 1696.
Current name: ***Pachyrhizus erosus*** (L.) Urb. (Fabaceae: Faboideae).
Note: An illegitimate replacement name for *D. erosus* L. (1753).

Dolichos capensis Linnaeus, *Plantae Rariores Africanae*: 17. 1760.
["Habitat ad Cap. b. spei."] Sp. Pl., ed. 2, 2: 1020 (1763). RCN: 5340.
Neotype (Verdcourt in Turland & Jarvis in *Taxon* 46: 468. 1997): South Africa. Knysna between Keurbooms River & Bitou River, 8 Apr 1814, *Burchell 5274* (K).
Current name: ***Rhynchosia capensis*** (Burm. f.) Schinz (Fabaceae: Faboideae).

Dolichos ensiformis Linnaeus, *Species Plantarum* 2: 725. 1753.
"Habitat in Jamaica." RCN: 5350.
Lectotype (Sauer in *Brittonia* 16: 142. 1964): [icon] *"Phaseolus maximus, siliqua ensiformi nervis insignita, et semine albo membranula incluso"* in Sloane, Voy. Jamaica 1: 177, t. 114, f. 1, 2, 3. 1707. – Typotype: Herb. Sloane 3: 67 (BM-SL).
Current name: ***Canavalia ensiformis*** (L.) DC. (Fabaceae: Faboideae).
Note: Fawcett & Rendle (*Fl. Jamaica* 4: 61. 1920) stated "Type in Herb. Mus. Brit. and specimen from Jacquin's Herb." but this cannot be accepted as a formal typification.

Dolichos erosus Linnaeus, *Species Plantarum* 2: 726. 1753.
"Habitat in America." RCN: 5342.
Replaced synonym of: *Dolichos bulbosus* L. (1763), *nom. illeg.*
Lectotype (Sørensen in *Nordic J. Bot.* 8: 169, 177. 1988): [icon] *"Phaseolus Nevisensis foliis multangulis, tuberosa radice esculenta"* in Plukenet, Phytographia: t. 52, f. 4. 1691; Almag. Bot.: 292. 1696.
Current name: ***Pachyrhizus erosus*** (L.) Urb. (Fabaceae: Faboideae).
Note: D'Arcy (in *Ann. Missouri Bot. Gard.* 67: 744. 1980) queried whether 900.11 (LINN) might be the type, but it is not original material for this name.

Dolichos filiformis Linnaeus, *Systema Naturae*, ed. 10, 2: 1163. 1759.
["Habitat in Jamaica."] Sp. Pl., ed. 2, 2: 1021 (1763). RCN: 5345.
Lectotype (Fawcett & Rendle, *Fl. Jamaica* 4: 58. 1920): Herb. Linn. No. 900.13 (LINN).
Current name: ***Galactia parvifolia*** A. Rich. (Fabaceae: Faboideae).

Dolichos lablab Linnaeus, *Species Plantarum* 2: 725. 1753.
"Habitat in Aegypto." RCN: 5329.
Lectotype (Verdcourt in Milne-Redhead & Polhill, *Fl. Trop. E. Africa, Leguminosae* 4: 696. 1971): [icon] *"Phaseolus niger Lablab"* in Alpino, De Plantis Aegypti: 74, 75. 1640.
Current name: ***Lablab purpureus*** (L.) Sweet subsp. ***purpureus*** (Fabaceae: Faboideae).
Note: Fawcett & Rendle (*Fl. Jamaica* 4: 70. 1920) indicated material in LINN as type but 900.1 (LINN) lacks the *Species Plantarum* number (i.e. "1"), was a later addition to the herbarium, and is not original material for the name. Although Westphal (*Pulses Ethiopia, Taxon. Agric. Signif.*: 97. 1974) rejected an earlier type choice of an Alpino illustration made by Verdcourt in favour of Burser material, Verdcourt's choice has priority.

Dolichos lignosus Linnaeus, *Species Plantarum* 2: 726. 1753.
"Habitat – – – –" RCN: 5348.
Lectotype (Stearn, *Introd. Linnaeus' Sp. Pl.* (Ray Soc. ed.): 47. 1957):

[icon] *"Dolichos caule perenni lignoso"* in Linnaeus, Hort. Cliff.: 360, t. 20. 1738.
Current name: ***Dipogon lignosus*** (L.) Verdc. (Fabaceae: Faboideae).
Note: Stirton (in *Bothalia* 13: 327. 1981) designated a Smith illustration as a neotype but a *Hortus Cliffortianus* illustration is original material for the name (and was designated as the type by Stearn in 1957).

Dolichos minimus Linnaeus, *Species Plantarum* 2: 726. 1753.
"Habitat in Jamaica." RCN: 5339.
Lectotype (Stearn, *Introd. Linnaeus' Sp. Pl.* (Ray Soc. ed.): 47. 1957): [icon] *"Dolichos minimus, floribus luteis"* in Linnaeus, Hort. Cliff.: 360, t. 21. 1738.
Current name: ***Rhynchosia minima*** (L.) DC. (Fabaceae: Faboideae).
Note: Verdcourt (in Milne-Redhead & Polhill, *Fl. Trop. E. Africa, Leguminosae* 4: 756. 1971), followed by many authors, treated material in Sloane's herbarium as lectotype. However, these specimens were never studied by Linnaeus and are not original material for the name. Stearn had in any case previously designated a *Hortus Cliffortianus* illustration as type.

Dolichos polystachios Linnaeus, *Species Plantarum* 2: 726. 1753.
"Habitat in Virginia." RCN: 5349.
Lectotype (Fernald in *Rhodora* 40: 438. 1938): *Clayton 568* (BM-000051643).
Current name: ***Phaseolus polystachios*** (L.) Britton & al. var. ***polystachios*** (Fabaceae: Faboideae).

Dolichos pruriens Linnaeus, *Herbarium Amboinense*: 23. 1754. RCN: 5337.
Lectotype (Merrill, *Interpret. Rumph. Herb. Amb.*: 33, 277. 1917): [icon] *"Cacara pruritus"* in Rumphius, Herb. Amboin. 5: 393, t. 142. 1747.
Current name: ***Mucuna pruriens*** (L.) DC. (Fabaceae: Faboideae).

Dolichos pubescens Linnaeus, *Species Plantarum*, ed. 2, 2: 1021. 1763, *nom. utique rej.*
"Habitat in America." RCN: 5360.
Lectotype (Verdcourt in *Taxon* 45: 329. 1996): Herb. Linn. No. 900.18 (LINN).
Current name: ***Macrotyloma uniflorum*** (Lam.) Verdc. (Fabaceae: Faboideae).

Dolichos purpureus Linnaeus, *Species Plantarum*, ed. 2, 2: 1021. 1763.
"Habitat in Indiis." RCN: 5346.
Neotype (Verdcourt in Turland & Jarvis in *Taxon* 46: 469. 1997): France. Loire-Atlantique: Reze near Nantes, hort. C. Renault, 14 Aug 1900, ex Herb. Gadeceau (BM).
Current name: ***Lablab purpureus*** (L.) Sweet subsp. ***purpureus*** (Fabaceae: Faboideae).

Dolichos regularis Linnaeus, *Species Plantarum* 2: 726. 1753.
"Habitat in Virginia." RCN: 5347.
Lectotype (Duncan in *Sida* 8: 173. 1979): *Clayton 121* (BM-000038167).
Current name: ***Galactia regularis*** (L.) Britton & al. (Fabaceae: Faboideae).

Dolichos repens Linnaeus, *Systema Naturae*, ed. 10, 2: 1163. 1759.
["Habitat in Jamaicae maritimis."] Sp. Pl., ed. 2, 2: 1022 (1763). RCN: 5354.
Neotype (Pasquet in Turland & Jarvis in *Taxon* 46: 469. 1997): Herb. Thunberg No. 16775 (UPS).
Current name: ***Vigna luteola*** (Jacq.) Benth. (Fabaceae: Faboideae).

Dolichos scarabaeoides Linnaeus, *Species Plantarum* 2: 726. 1753.
"Habitat in India." RCN: 5341.
Lectotype (van der Maesen in *Agric. Univ. Wageningen Pap.* 85–4: 189. 1985): Herb. Hermann 1: 34, No. 282 (BM-000594465).
Current name: **Cajanus scarabaeoides** (L.) Thouars ex Graham (Fabaceae: Faboideae).

Dolichos sesquipedalis Linnaeus, *Species Plantarum,* ed. 2, 2: 1019. 1763.
"Habitat in America." RCN: 5335.
Neotype (Westphal, *Pulses Ethiopia, Taxon. Agric. Signif.*: 214. 1974): *Westphal 8677* (WAG; iso- K, P).
Current name: **Vigna unguiculata** (L.) Walp. subsp. **sesquipedalis** (L.) Verdc. (Fabaceae: Faboideae).

Dolichos sinensis Linnaeus, *Centuria II Plantarum*: 28. 1756.
"Habitat in India." RCN: 5330.
Lectotype (Merrill, *Interpret. Rumph. Herb. Amb.*: 284. 1917): [icon] *"Dolichus Sinensis"* in Rumphius, Herb. Amboin. 5: 375, t. 134. 1747.
Current name: **Vigna unguiculata** (L.) Walp. subsp. **unguiculata** (Fabaceae: Faboideae).

Dolichos soja Linnaeus, *Species Plantarum* 2: 727. 1753.
"Habitat in India." RCN: 5352.
Lectotype (Verdcourt in Turland & Jarvis in *Taxon* 46: 469. 1997): [icon] *"Daidsu"* in Kaempfer, Amoen. Exot. Fasc.: 837, 838. 1712.
Current name: **Glycine max** (L.) Merr. (Fabaceae: Faboideae).

Dolichos tetragonolobus Linnaeus, *Herbarium Amboinense*: 23. 1754.
["Habitat in India."] Sp. Pl., ed. 2, 2: 1020 (1763). RCN: 5334.
Lectotype (Merrill, *Interpret. Rumph. Herb. Amb.*: 264. 1917): [icon] *"Lobus quadrangularis"* in Rumphius, Herb. Amboin. 5: 374, t. 133. 1747.
Current name: **Psophocarpus tetragonolobus** (L.) DC. (Fabaceae: Faboideae).

Dolichos trilobatus Linnaeus, *Systema Naturae,* ed. 12, 2: 483; *Mantissa Plantarum*: 101. 1767.
"Habitat in India." RCN: 5357.
Lectotype (Verdcourt in *Taxon* 17: 171. 1968): [icon] *"Trifolium Maderaspatan. cauliculis pilosis scandens, Passiflorae modo trilobatum"* in Plukenet, Phytographia: t. 120, f. 7. 1691; Almag. Bot.: 292. 1696. – Typotype: Herb. Sloane 98: 123 (BM-SL).
Current name: **Vigna trilobata** (L.) Verdc. (Fabaceae: Faboideae).

Dolichos trilobus Linnaeus, *Species Plantarum* 2: 726. 1753, *typ. cons.*
"Habitat in India." RCN: 5357.
Lectotype (Verdcourt in *Taxon* 17: 173. 1968): [icon] *"Phaseolus Maderaspatanus, foliis glabris trilobatis, floribus exiguis, longis petiolis ex eodem puncto gemellis"* in Plukenet, Phytographia: t. 214, f. 3. 1692; Almag. Bot.: 292. 1696. – Typotype: Herb. Sloane 97:87 (BM-SL). – Voucher: Herb. Sloane 94: 40 (BM-SL).
Generitype of *Dolichos* Linnaeus, *nom. cons.*
Current name: **Dolichos trilobus** L. (Fabaceae: Faboideae).

Dolichos uncinatus Linnaeus, *Species Plantarum,* ed. 2, 2: 1019. 1763.
"Habitat in America." RCN: 5331.
Lectotype (Verdcourt in *Kew Bull.* 24: 278. 1970): *Browne*, Herb. Linn. No. 900.3 (LINN).
Current name: **Teramnus uncinatus** (L.) Sw. (Fabaceae: Faboideae).

Dolichos unguiculatus Linnaeus, *Species Plantarum* 2: 725. 1753.
"Habitat in Barbados." RCN: 5332.
Neotype (Westphal, *Pulses Ethiopia, Taxon. Agric. Signif.*: 213. 1974): *Westphal 8682* (WAG; iso- K, P).
Current name: **Vigna unguiculata** (L.) Walp. subsp. **unguiculata** (Fabaceae: Faboideae).
Note: Piper (in *Torreya* 12: 190. 1912) interpreted this name via material in LINN (evidently sheet 900.5) identifiable as *Phaseolus antillanus* Urb., for which he substituted *P. unguiculatus* (L.) Piper. However, as queried by Merrill (in *Trans. Amer. Philos. Soc.,* n.s., 24: 215. 1935), this is unannotated by Linnaeus and is not original material for the name. The absence of type material was noted by authors such as Fawcett & Rendle (*Fl. Jamaica* 4: 69. 1920), and this uncertainty led some to reject it informally. See review by Westphal who provided a neotype for the name.

Dolichos urens Linnaeus, *Systema Naturae,* ed. 10, 2: 1162. 1759.
["Habitat in America meridionali."] Sp. Pl., ed. 2, 2: 1020 (1763). RCN: 5338.
Lectotype (Verdcourt in Turland & Jarvis in *Taxon* 46: 469. 1997): [icon] *"Phaseolus Americanus frutescens, foliis glabris, lobis pluribus, villosis, pungentibus, fructu orbiculari, plano, hilo nigro, tanquam annulo, totum fere ambiente"* in Plukenet, Phytographia: t. 213, f. 2. 1692; Almag. Bot.: 292. 1696. – Voucher: Herb. Sloane 97: 86 (BM-SL).
Current name: **Mucuna urens** (L.) DC. (Fabaceae: Faboideae).
Note: Although Howard (*Fl. Lesser Antilles* 4: 510. 1988) indicated Plukenet material in Herb. Sloane as "type", this was never seen by Linnaeus and is not original material for the name.

Doronicum bellidiastrum Linnaeus, *Species Plantarum* 2: 886. 1753.
"Habitat in Alpibus Helveticis, Italicis, Tyrolensibus." RCN: 6408.
Type not designated.
Original material: Herb. Burser XIV(2): 68 (UPS); Herb. Linn. No. 1002.7 (LINN); [icon] in Micheli, Nov. Pl. Gen.: 32, t. 29. 1729; [icon] in Mentzel, Ind. Nom. Pl. Univ.: t. 8. 1682.
Current name: **Bellidiastrum michelii** Cass. (Asteraceae).

Doronicum incanum Linnaeus, *Species Plantarum* 2: 886. 1753.
"Habitat in Alpibus Helveticis, Pyrenaeis." RCN: 6302.
Type not designated.
Original material: Herb. Burser X: 29 (UPS).
Current name: **Senecio doronicum** (L.) L. (Asteraceae).

Doronicum pardalianches Linnaeus, *Species Plantarum* 2: 885. 1753.
"Habitat in Alpibus Helvetiae, Pannoniae, Vallesiae." RCN: 6406.
Lectotype (Llamas & al. in Jarvis & Turland in *Taxon* 47: 360. 1998): Herb. Clifford: 411, *Doronicum* 1 (BM-000647132).
Generitype of *Doronicum* Linnaeus (vide Green, *Prop. Brit. Bot.*: 182. 1929).
Current name: **Doronicum pardalianches** L. (Asteraceae).

Doronicum plantagineum Linnaeus, *Species Plantarum* 2: 885. 1753.
"Habitat in Lusitania, Hispania, Gallia." RCN: 6407.
Lectotype (Llamas & al. in Jarvis & Turland in *Taxon* 47: 360. 1998): Herb. Clifford: 411, *Doronicum* 2 (BM-000647133).
Current name: **Doronicum plantagineum** L. (Asteraceae).

Dorstenia alexiteria Linnaeus, *Systema Naturae,* ed. 10, 2: 899. 1759.
RCN: 993.
Replaced synonym: *Dorstenia contrajerva* L. var. *houstonii* L. (1753).
Type not designated.
Original material: as replaced synonym.
Current name: **Dorstenia contrajerva** L. (Moraceae).
Note: This appears to be a *nomen novum* at specific rank for

D. contrajerva var. *houstonii* L. (1753). Both names appear to have been based on an illustrated account by Houstoun. Although Berg (in Harling & Andersson, *Fl. Ecuador* 60: 116. 1998; *Fl. Neotropica* 83: 198. 2001) indicated *Houstoun s.n.* (BM) as the holotype, it is most unlikely that Linnaeus could have seen this material and, with the existence of a cited illustration as original material, the Houstoun collection cannot serve as a neotype.

Dorstenia caulescens Linnaeus, *Species Plantarum* 1: 121. 1753.
"Habitat in America meridionali." RCN: 994.
Type not designated.
Original material: [icon] in Plumier in Burman, Pl. Amer.: 110, t. 120, f. 1. 1757.
Current name: ***Dorstenia* sp.** (Moraceae).
Note: The application of this name appears to be uncertain.

Dorstenia contrajerva Linnaeus, *Species Plantarum* 1: 121. 1753.
"Habitat in nova Hispania, Mexico, Peru, Vera Cruce, insula Vicentii." RCN: 991.
Lectotype (Berg in Görts-van Rijn, *Fl. Guianas,* ser. A, 11: 34. 1992): [icon] *"Dorstenia"* in Plumier, Nov. Pl. Amer.: 29, t. 8. 1703 (see p. 150).
Generitype of *Dorstenia* Linnaeus (vide Hitchcock, *Prop. Brit. Bot.*: 126. 1929).
Current name: ***Dorstenia contrajerva*** L. (Moraceae).
Note: Barrie's (in Jarvis & al., *Regnum Veg.* 127: 43. 1993) choice of a Houstoun figure as type is pre-dated by Berg's 1992 choice of a Plumier plate.

Dorstenia contrajerva Linnaeus var. **houstonii** Linnaeus, *Species Plantarum* 1: 121. 1753.
["Habitat in Campechia."] Sp. Pl., ed. 2, 1: 176 (1762). RCN: 993.
Basionym of: *Dorstenia alexiteria* L. (1755); *Dorstenia houstonii* (L.) L. (1762), *nom. illeg.*
Type not designated.
Original material: [icon] in Houstoun in Philos. Trans. 37(421): 196, f. 2. 1733.
Current name: ***Dorstenia contrajerva*** L. (Moraceae).
Note: Varietal epithet spelled "houstoni" in the protologue.
    Although Berg (in Harling & Andersson, *Fl. Ecuador* 60: 116. 1998; *Fl. Neotropica* 83: 198. 2001) indicated *Houstoun s.n.* (BM) as the holotype, it is most unlikely that Linnaeus could have seen this material and, with the existence of a cited illustration as original material, the Houstoun collection cannot serve as a neotype.

Dorstenia drakena Linnaeus, *Systema Naturae,* ed. 10, 2: 899. 1759.
["Habitat in Vera Cruce."] Sp. Pl., ed. 2, 1: 176 (1762). RCN: 992.
Type not designated.
Original material: [icon] in Houstoun in Philos. Trans. 37(421): 196, f. 1. 1733.
Current name: ***Dorstenia drakena*** L. (Moraceae).
Note: Although Berg (*Fl. Neotropica* 83: 203. 2001) indicated *Houstoun s.n.* (BM) as the holotype, it is most unlikely that Linnaeus could have seen this material and, with the existence of a cited illustration as original material, the Houstoun collection cannot serve as a neotype.

Dorstenia houstonii (Linnaeus) Linnaeus, *Species Plantarum,* ed. 2, 1: 176. 1762, *nom. illeg.*
"Habitat in Campechia." RCN: 993.
Basionym: *Dorstenia contrajerva* L. var. *houstonii* L. (1753).
Type not designated.
Original material: as basionym.
Current name: ***Dorstenia contrajerva*** L. (Moraceae).

Note: Specific epithet spelled "houstoni" in the protologue.
    As *D. alexiteria* L. (1759) is a *nomen novum* at specific rank for *D. contrajerva* var. *houstonii* L. (1753), *D. houstonii* is a superfluous name for *D. alexiteria* L.

Draba aizoides Linnaeus, *Systema Naturae,* ed. 12, 2: 432; *Mantissa Plantarum*: 91. 1767.
"Habitat in Alpibus Europae." RCN: 4668.
Lectotype (Rich in Cafferty & Jarvis in *Taxon* 51: 533. 2002): Herb. Linn. No. 823.1 (LINN).
Current name: ***Draba aizoides*** L. (Brassicaceae).

Draba alpina Linnaeus, *Species Plantarum* 2: 642. 1753.
"Habitat in Alpibus Europae." RCN: 4670.
Lectotype (Elven in Jonsell & Jarvis in *Nordic J. Bot.* 22: 69. 2002): Herb. Linn. No. 823.5 (LINN).
Current name: ***Draba alpina*** L. (Brassicaceae).

Draba ciliaris Linnaeus, *Systema Naturae,* ed. 12, 2: 432; *Mantissa Plantarum*: 91. 1767.
"Habitat in Alpibus Barcinonensibus." RCN: 4669.
Lectotype (Lakusic in Cafferty & Jarvis in *Taxon* 51: 533. 2002): Herb. Linn. No. 823.3 (LINN).
Current name: ***Draba aizoides*** L. (Brassicaceae).
Note: Although traditionally treated as a synonym of *Draba aizoides* L., Lakusic, who typified the name, recognises it as a distinct species.

Draba hirta Linnaeus, *Systema Naturae,* ed. 10, 2: 1127. 1759.
["Habitat in Alpibus Helveticis, Lapponicis. D. C. Solander."] Sp. Pl., ed. 2, 2: 897 (1763). RCN: 4675.
Type not designated.
Original material: Herb. Linn. No. 823.12 (LINN).
Current name: ***Draba* sp.** (Brassicaceae).
Note: This name appears to have been widely, though informally, rejected as confused or ambiguous.

Draba incana Linnaeus, *Species Plantarum* 2: 643. 1753.
"Habitat in Alpibus & alpinis Europae." RCN: 4676.
Lectotype (Buttler in *Mitt. Bot. Staatssamml. München* 6: 329. 1967): Herb. Linn. No. 823.14 (LINN).
Generitype of *Draba* Linnaeus (vide Green in *Bull. Misc. Inform. Kew* 1925: 51. 1925).
Current name: ***Draba incana*** L. (Brassicaceae).
Note: *Draba incana*, with the type designated by Buttler (but with the choice incorrectly attributed to Rollins), was proposed as conserved type of the genus by Jarvis (in *Taxon* 41: 562. 1992). However, the proposal was eventually ruled unnecessary by the General Committee (see Barrie, *l.c.* 55: 795–796. 2006 for a review of the history of this and related proposals).

Draba muralis Linnaeus, *Species Plantarum* 2: 642. 1753.
"Habitat in Europae nemoribus." RCN: 4673.
Lectotype (Jonsell & Jarvis in *Nordic J. Bot.* 22: 69. 2002): Herb. Linn. No. 823.10 (LINN).
Current name: ***Draba muralis*** L. (Brassicaceae).

Draba nemorosa Linnaeus, *Species Plantarum* 2: 643. 1753.
"Habitat in Sueciae nemoribus." RCN: 4674.
Lectotype (Jafri in Ali & Jafri, *Fl. Libya* 23: 143. 1977): Herb. Linn. No. 823.11 (LINN).
Current name: ***Draba nemorosa*** L. (Brassicaceae).

Draba pyrenaica Linnaeus, *Species Plantarum* 2: 642. 1753.
"Habitat in Pyrenaeis." RCN: 4672.

Lectotype (Villar in Cafferty & Jarvis in *Taxon* 51: 533. 2002): Herb. Linn. No. 823.8 (LINN).
Current name: ***Petrocallis pyrenaica*** (L.) R. Br. (Brassicaceae).

Draba verna Linnaeus, *Species Plantarum* 2: 642. 1753.
"Habitat in Europae aridis." RCN: 4671.
Lectotype (Jafri in Nasir & Ali, *Fl. W. Pakistan* 55: 149. 1973): Herb. Linn. No. 823.7 (LINN).
Current name: ***Draba verna*** L. (Brassicaceae).

Dracaena draco (Linnaeus) Linnaeus, *Systema Naturae,* ed. 12, 2: 246. 1767.
"Habitat in India orientali." RCN: 2473.
Basionym: *Asparagus draco* L. (1762).
Lectotype (Bos in Jarvis & al., *Regnum Veg.* 127: 43. 1993): [icon] *"Draco"* in Clusius, Rar. Pl. Hist 1: 1. 1601 (see p. 119).
Generitype of *Dracaena* Linnaeus (vide Rafinesque, *Fl. Tell.* 4: 17. 1838).
Current name: ***Dracaena draco*** (L.) L. (Agavaceae/Dracaenaceae).
Note: Bos (in *Agric. Univ. Wageningen Pap.* 84–1: 16. 1984) and Ramón-Laca Menéndez de Luarca (in *Anales Jard. Bot. Madrid* 55: 422, f. 2. 1997) both reproduce the Clusius type figure.

Dracaena ensifolia Linnaeus, *Systema Naturae,* ed. 12, 2: 246; *Mantissa Plantarum*: 63. 1767.
"Habitat in India." RCN: 2476.
Lectotype (Henderson in *Taxon* 26: 133. 1977; Coode in Bosser & al., *Fl. Mascareignes* 183: 32. 1978): Herb. Linn. No. 435.3, inflorescence only (LINN).
Current name: ***Dianella ensifolia*** (L.) DC. (Liliaceae/Asparagaceae).
Note: Henderson (1977) indicated 353.3 (LINN) as the type and this choice was subsequently restricted to the inflorescence only, by Coode (1978).

Dracaena ferrea Linnaeus, *Systema Naturae,* ed. 12, 2: 246. 1767, *nom. illeg.*
"Habitat in China." RCN: 2474.
Replaced synonym: *Convallaria fruticosa* L. (1754).
Lectotype (Merrill, *Interpret. Rumph. Herb. Amb.*: 33, 137. 1917): [icon] *"Terminalis alba"* in Rumphius, Herb. Amboin. 4: 79, t. 34, f. 1. 1743.
Current name: ***Cordyline fruticosa*** (L.) A. Chev. (Agavaceae/Dracaenaceae).
Note: A superfluous name for *Convallaria fruticosa* L. (1754).

Dracaena graminifolia (Linnaeus) Linnaeus, *Systema Naturae,* ed. 12, 2: 246. 1767.
"Habitat in Asia." RCN: 2477.
Basionym: *Asparagus graminifolius* L. (1762).
Type not designated.
Original material: as basionym.
Current name: ***Liriope graminifolia*** (L.) Baker (Liliaceae/Convallariaceae).

Dracaena terminalis Linnaeus, *Systema Naturae,* ed. 12, 2: 246. 1767, *nom. illeg.*
RCN: 2475.
Replaced synonym: *Convallaria fruticosa* L. (1754); *Asparagus terminalis* L. (1762), *nom. illeg.*
Lectotype (Merrill, *Interpret. Rumph. Herb. Amb.*: 33, 137. 1917): [icon] *"Terminalis alba"* in Rumphius, Herb. Amboin. 4: 79, t. 34, f. 1. 1743.
Current name: ***Cordyline fruticosa*** (L.) A. Chev. (Agavaceae/Dracaenaceae).
Note: A combination based on *Asparagus terminalis* L. (1762) *nom. illeg.*, itself a superfluous name for *Convallaria fruticosa* L. (1754).

Dracocephalum austriacum Linnaeus, *Species Plantarum* 2: 595. 1753.
"Habitat in Austria." RCN: 4318.
Lectotype (Budantzev in Jarvis & al. in *Taxon* 50: 511. 2001): Herb. Linn. No. 746.6 (LINN).
Current name: ***Dracocephalum austriacum*** L. (Lamiaceae).

Dracocephalum canadense Linnaeus, *Systema Naturae,* ed. 12, 2: 401. 1767, *nom. illeg.*
Replaced synonym: *Dracocephalum canariense* L. (1753).
Lectotype (Wijnands, *Bot. Commelins*: 114. 1983): Herb. Clifford: 308, *Dracocephalum* 5 (BM-000646035).
Current name: ***Cedronella canariense*** (L.) Webb & Berthel. (Lamiaceae).
Note: This has the same phrase name as *D. canariense* L. (1753) and is therefore illegitimate.

Dracocephalum canariense Linnaeus, *Species Plantarum* 2: 594. 1753.
"Habitat in Canariis." RCN: 4315.
Replaced synonym of: *Dracocephalum canadense* L. (1767), *nom. illeg.*
Lectotype (Wijnands, *Bot. Commelins*: 114. 1983): Herb. Clifford: 308, *Dracocephalum* 5 (BM-000646035).
Current name: ***Cedronella canariensis*** (L.) Webb & Berthel. (Lamiaceae).

Dracocephalum canescens Linnaeus, *Species Plantarum* 2: 595. 1753.
"Habitat in Oriente." RCN: 4323.
Lectotype (Wijnands, *Bot. Commelins*: 115. 1983): Herb. Linn. No. 746.14 (LINN).
Current name: ***Lallemantia canescens*** (L.) Fisch. & C.A. Mey. (Lamiaceae).
Note: Wijnands wrongly interpreted Edmondson (in Davis, *Fl. Turkey* 7: 291. 1982) as having typified the name. However, Wijnands' own statement is unequivocal and is accepted here as a formal typification.

Dracocephalum grandiflorum Linnaeus, *Species Plantarum* 2: 595. 1753.
"Habitat in Sibiria." RCN: 4320.
Lectotype (Budantzev in Jarvis & al. in *Taxon* 50: 511. 2001): *Gmelin s.n.*, Herb. Linn. No. 746.8 (LINN).
Current name: ***Dracocephalum grandiflorum*** L. (Lamiaceae).
Note: Tscherneva (in Grubov & al., *Pl. C. Asia* 5: 48–49. 2002) stated "Type in London (Linn.)" and cited Keenan (in *Baileya* 5: 33. 1957) as saying there are three collections in LINN. Two of these were reported to be "typical" (the third is supposed to be *D. stellerianum* Hiltebr.), which Tscherneva stated "were evidently collected from Barguzin and should be treated as type of *D. grandiflorum* L.". Keenan regarded all three as conspecific, but 746.8 (from Gmelin) as the atypical one of the three (with smaller flowers and entire bracts) from which "Linnaeus obviously drew his description". However, neither author made a statement clearly designating any one of these collections as the type.

Dracocephalum moldavica Linnaeus, *Species Plantarum* 2: 595. 1753, *typ. cons.*
"Habitat in Moldavica." RCN: 4322.
Lectotype (Hedge in Jarvis & al., *Regnum Veg.* 127: 43. 1993): Herb. Clifford: 308, *Dracocephalum* 2, sheet 2 (BM-000646031).
Generitype of *Dracocephalum* Linnaeus, *nom. cons.*
Current name: ***Dracocephalum moldavica*** L. (Lamiaceae).
Note: Hedge (in *Notes Roy. Bot. Gard. Edinburgh* 27: 155. 1967) indicated 746.12 (LINN) as type, but this is a post-1753 addition to the herbarium and not original material for the name.

Dracocephalum nutans Linnaeus, *Species Plantarum* 2: 596. 1753.
"Habitat in Sibiria." RCN: 4326.
Lectotype (Hedge in *Notes Roy. Bot. Gard. Edinburgh* 27: 154. 1967): Herb. Linn. No. 746.16 (LINN).
Current name: ***Dracocephalum nutans*** L. (Lamiaceae).

Dracocephalum peltatum Linnaeus, *Species Plantarum* 2: 596. 1753.
"Habitat in Oriente." RCN: 4324.
Lectotype (Hedge in Jarvis & al. in *Taxon* 50: 511. 2001): Herb. Linn. No. 746.15 (LINN).
Current name: ***Lallemantia peltata*** (L.) Fisch. & C.A. Mey. (Lamiaceae).

Dracocephalum peregrinum Linnaeus, *Centuria II Plantarum*: 20. 1756.
"Habitat in Sibiria." RCN: 4317.
Lectotype (Budantzev in Jarvis & al. in *Taxon* 50: 511. 2001): Herb. Linn. No. 746.5 (LINN).
Current name: ***Dracocephalum peregrinum*** L. (Lamiaceae).

Dracocephalum pinnatum Linnaeus, *Species Plantarum* 2: 594. 1753.
"Habitat in Jerkatsch. Steller, D. Gmelin." RCN: 4316.
Lectotype (Budantzev in Jarvis & al. in *Taxon* 50: 511. 2001): *Steller*, Herb. Linn. No. 746.4 (LINN).
Current name: ***Dracocephalum pinnatum*** L. (Lamiaceae).

Dracocephalum ruyschiana Linnaeus, *Species Plantarum* 2: 595. 1753.
"Habitat in Sibiria, Suecia." RCN: 4318.
Lectotype (Budantzev in Jarvis & al. in *Taxon* 50: 511. 2001): Herb. Linn. No. 746.7 (LINN).
Current name: ***Dracocephalum ruyschiana*** L. (Lamiaceae).

Dracocephalum sibiricum (Linnaeus) Linnaeus, *Systema Naturae*, ed. 10, 2: 1104. 1759.
["Habitat in Sibiria."] Sp. Pl. 2: 572 (1753). RCN: 4321.
Basionym: *Nepeta sibirica* L. (1753).
Lectotype (Hedge in Jarvis & al. in *Taxon* 50: 511. 2001): [icon] *"Cataria montana, folio Veronicae pratensis"* in Buxbaum, Pl. Minus Cognit. Cent. 3: 27, t. 50, f. 1. 1729.
Current name: ***Nepeta sibirica*** L. (Lamiaceae).

Dracocephalum thymiflorum Linnaeus, *Species Plantarum* 2: 596. 1753.
"Habitat in Sibiria." RCN: 4327.
Lectotype (Wijnands, *Bot. Commelins*: 115. 1983): Herb. Linn. No. 746.17 (LINN).
Current name: ***Dracocephalum thymiflorum*** L. (Lamiaceae).

Dracocephalum virginianum Linnaeus, *Species Plantarum* 2: 594. 1753.
"Habitat in America septentrionali." RCN: 4314.
Lectotype (Cantino in *Contr. Gray Herb.* 211: 86. 1982): Herb. Linn. No. 746.1 (LINN).
Current name: ***Physostegia virginiana*** (L.) Benth. (Lamiaceae).
Note: Although Epling (in *J. Bot.* 67: 9. 1929) indicated Herb. Linn. No. 746.1 (LINN) as the standard specimen, this is not equivalent to a type statement (see Jarvis & al. in *Taxon* 50: 508. 2001).

Dracontium camtschatcense Linnaeus, *Species Plantarum* 2: 968. 1753.
"Habitat in Sibiria." RCN: 7012.
Type not designated.
Original material: none traced.
Current name: ***Lysichiton camtschatcensis*** (L.) Schott (Araceae).

Dracontium foetidum Linnaeus, *Species Plantarum* 2: 967. 1753.
"Habitat in Virginia." RCN: 7011.
Type not designated.
Original material: *Kalm*, Herb. Linn. No. 1080.2 (LINN); *Clayton 17* (BM).
Current name: ***Symplocarpus foetidus*** (L.) W.P.C. Barton (Araceae).

Dracontium pertusum Linnaeus, *Species Plantarum* 2: 968. 1753.
"Habitat in America meridionali." RCN: 7013.
Lectotype (Madison in *Contr. Gray Herb.* 207: 36, f. 33. 1977): [icon] *"Arum hederaceum, amplis foliis perforatis"* in Plumier, Descr. Pl. Amér.: 40, t. 56, t. 57. 1693.
Current name: ***Monstera adansonii*** Schott (Araceae).

Dracontium polyphyllum Linnaeus, *Species Plantarum* 2: 967. 1753.
"Habitat Surinami." RCN: 7009.
Lectotype (Hay in *Ann. Missouri Bot. Gard.* 79: 189, f. 3. 1992): [icon] *"Arum polyphyllum caule scabro punicante etc."* in Hermann, Parad. Bat.: 93. 1698. – Epitype (Zhu & Grayum in *Taxon* 44: 521. 1995): Cultivated. Missouri Botanical Garden, *Zhu 1462* [originally collected from Saül, French Guiana, *Croat 74210*] (MO; iso- CAY, K, US).
Generitype of *Dracontium* Linnaeus (vide Green, *Prop. Brit. Bot.*: 186. 1929).
Current name: ***Dracontium polyphyllum*** L. (Araceae).

Dracontium spinosum Linnaeus, *Species Plantarum* 2: 967. 1753.
"Habitat in Zeylona." RCN: 7010.
Lectotype (Nicolson in Dassanayake & Fosberg, *Revised Handb. Fl. Ceylon* 6: 35. 1987): Herb. Hermann 5: 29, No. 328 [icon] (BM), see p. 181.
Current name: ***Lasia spinosa*** (L.) Thwaites (Araceae).
Note: The type is illustrated by Hay (in *Blumea* 33: 458, f. 15. 1988).

Drosera capensis Linnaeus, *Species Plantarum* 1: 282. 1753.
"Habitat in Aethiopia." RCN: 2229.
Type not designated.
Original material: [icon] in Burman, Rar. Afric. Pl.: 209, t. 75, f. 1. 1739 – Typotype: Herb. Burman (G).
Current name: ***Drosera capensis*** L. (Droseraceae).
Note: Obermeyer (in Codd & al., *Fl. Southern Africa* 13: 199. 1970) incorrectly indicated 398.4 (LINN) as type, but this collection lacks the relevant *Species Plantarum* number (i.e. "4") and was a post-1753 addition to the herbarium, and is not original material for the name.

Drosera cistiflora Linnaeus, *Plantae Rariores Africanae*: 9. 1760.
["Habitat in Aethiopia."] Sp. Pl., ed. 2, 1: 403 (1762). RCN: 2231.
Lectotype (Obermeyer in Codd & al., *Fl. Southern Africa* 13: 196. 1970): Herb. Linn. No. 398.6 (LINN).
Current name: ***Drosera cistiflora*** L. (Droseraceae).

Drosera indica Linnaeus, *Species Plantarum* 1: 282. 1753.
"Habitat in India." RCN: 2232.
Lectotype (Laundon in Hubbard & Milne-Redhead, *Fl. Trop. E. Africa, Droseraceae*: 2. 1959): Herb. Hermann 5: 227, No. 121 [icon] (BM-000621002).
Current name: ***Drosera indica*** L. (Droseraceae).

Drosera longifolia Linnaeus, *Species Plantarum* 1: 282. 1753, *nom. rej.*
"Habitat in Europa." RCN: 2228.
Lectotype (Heath in *Calyx* 2: 79. 1992): [icon] *"Salsirora, siue Ros solis. 2. faemella, ubique notissima"* in Thal, Sylv. Herc.: 116, t. 9, f. 2. 1588. – Epitype (Heath in *Calyx* 6: 38. 1998): Herb. Linn. No. 398.3 (LINN).

Current name: ***Drosera anglica*** Huds. (Droseraceae).
Note: This name has long been treated as ambiguous, and usually
placed in the synonymy of either *D. anglica* Huds. (1778) or *D.
intermedia* Hayne (1801). Cheek (in *Taxon* 47: 749. 1998)
therefore proposed the name for rejection (stating that Heath's
choice of lectotype could belong to either *D. anglica* or *D.
intermedia*). Heath (in *Calyx* 6: 34. 1998) responded by designating
Herb. Linn. No. 398.3 (LINN), a specimen of *D. anglica*, as an
epitype. However, Cheek's proposal was recommended (see Barrie
in *Taxon* 55: 796. 2006) but the name is listed without a type in
Appendix V of the Vienna Code.

Drosera lusitanica Linnaeus, *Species Plantarum* 1: 282. 1753.
"Habitat in Lusitania." RCN: 2230.
Type not designated.
Original material: [icon] in Morison, Pl. Hist. Univ. 3: 620, s. 15, t. 4,
f. 4. 1699; [icon] in Plukenet, Phytographia: t. 117, f. 2. 1691;
Almag. Bot.: 323. 1696.
Current name: ***Drosophyllum lusitanicum*** (L.) Link
(Droseraceae).

Drosera rotundifolia Linnaeus, *Species Plantarum* 1: 281. 1753.
"Habitat in Europae, Asiae, Americae paludibus." RCN: 2227.
Lectotype (Cheek in Jarvis & al., *Regnum Veg.* 127: 44. 1993): Herb.
Linn. No. 398.2 (LINN).
Generitype of *Drosera* Linnaeus (vide Hitchcock, *Prop. Brit. Bot.*: 143.
1929).
Current name: ***Drosera rotundifolia*** L. (Droseraceae).

Drupina cristata Linnaeus, *Plantae Surinamenses*: 11. 1775.
"Habitat [in Surinamo.]" RCN: 4479.
Type not designated.
Original material: none traced.
Generitype of *Drupina* Linnaeus.
Current name: ***Drupina cristata*** L. (Scrophulariaceae).

Dryas octopetala Linnaeus, *Species Plantarum* 1: 501. 1753.
"Habitat in Alpibus Lapponicis, Helveticis, Austriacis, Sabaudicis,
Hibernicis, Sibiricis." RCN: 3810.
Lectotype (Barrie in Jarvis & al., *Regnum Veg.* 127: 44. 1993): Herb.
Linn. No. 658.3 (LINN).
Generitype of *Dryas* Linnaeus (vide Willdenow in *Ges. Naturf. Freunde
Berlin Mag.* 5: 397. 1811).
Current name: ***Dryas octopetala*** L. (Rosaceae).

Dryas pentapetala Linnaeus, *Species Plantarum* 1: 501. 1753.
"Habitat in Camschatka." RCN: 3809.
Lectotype (Soják in Cafferty & Jarvis in *Taxon* 51: 541. 2002): *Steller,*
Herb. Linn. No. 658.1 (LINN).
Current name: ***Sieversia pentapetala*** (L.) Greene (Rosaceae).

Drypis spinosa Linnaeus, *Species Plantarum* 1: 413. 1753.
"Habitat in Italia, Mauritania." RCN: 2169.
Lectotype (Walters in Jarvis & al., *Regnum Veg.* 127: 44. 1993): [icon]
"*Drypis Italica, aculeata, floribus albis, umbellatim compactis*" in
Micheli, Nov. Pl. Gen.: 24, t. 23. 1729.
Generitype of *Drypis* Linnaeus.
Current name: ***Drypis spinosa*** L. (Caryophyllaceae).
Note: The type illustration is reproduced by Guglielmone in Forneris
(*L'Erbario Univ. Torino*: 289. 2004).

Duranta erecta Linnaeus, *Species Plantarum* 2: 637. 1753.
"Habitat in America." RCN: 4626.
Lectotype (Caro in *Revista Argentina Agron.* 23: 5. 1956): [icon]
"*Duranta inermis*" in Plumier in Burman, Pl. Amer.: t. 79. 1756.
Current name: ***Duranta erecta*** L. (Verbenaceae).
Note: A detailed review is provided by Munir (in *J. Adelaide Bot. Gard.*
16: 7. 1995), who argues that an Aubriet tracing from the Codex
Boerhaavianus in Groningen should be the lectotype rather than the
Plumier plate (published by Burman in 1756) designated as the
type by Caro. As there is evidence that proof copies of Burman's
plates were available to Linnaeus before 1753, Caro's typification is
accepted here.

Duranta repens Linnaeus, *Species Plantarum* 2: 637. 1753.
"Habitat in America." RCN: 4626.
Neotype (Sanders in Howard, *Fl. Lesser Antilles* 6: 225. 1989): Herb.
Linn. No. 806.2 (LINN).
Generitype of *Duranta* Linnaeus (vide Green, *Prop. Brit. Bot.*: 169.
1929).
Current name: ***Duranta erecta*** L. (Verbenaceae).
Note: In the absence of any original elements, Sanders' type statement
(as "type") is correctable to "neotype" under Art. 9.8.

Durio zibethinus Linnaeus, *Systema Vegetabilium*, ed. 13: 581. 1774.
"Habitat in India orientali." RCN: 5732.
Type not designated.
Original material: [icon] in Rumphius, Herb. Amboin. 1: 99, t. 29.
1741.
Current name: ***Durio zibethinus*** L. (Bombacaceae).

E

Ebenus capensis Linnaeus, *Mantissa Plantarum Altera*: 264. 1771, *nom. illeg.*
"Habitat ad Cap. b. spei." RCN: 5305.
Replaced synonym: *Spartium cytisoides* P.J. Bergius (1767).
Type not designated.
Note: The application of this name seems uncertain.

Ebenus cretica Linnaeus, *Species Plantarum* 2: 764. 1753.
"Habitat in Creta." RCN: 5304.
Lectotype (Turland in Jarvis & al., *Regnum Veg.* 127: 44. 1993): Herb. Linn. No. 929.1 (LINN).
Generitype of *Ebenus* Linnaeus.
Current name: ***Ebenus cretica*** L. (Fabaceae: Faboideae).

Echinophora spinosa Linnaeus, *Species Plantarum* 1: 239. 1753.
"Habitat ad litora maris praesertim mediterranei." RCN: 1925.
Lectotype (Reduron & Jarvis in Jarvis & al., *Regnum Veg.* 127: 44. 1993): Herb. Burser XVI(2): 14 (UPS).
Generitype of *Echinophora* Linnaeus (vide Hitchcock, *Prop. Brit. Bot.*: 138. 1929).
Current name: ***Echinophora spinosa*** L. (Apiaceae).

Echinophora tenuifolia Linnaeus, *Species Plantarum* 1: 239. 1753.
"Habitat in Apuliae maritimis apricis, salsis." RCN: 1926.
Lectotype (Jury & Southam in Jarvis & al. in *Taxon* 55: 212. 2006): Herb. Linn. No. 336.2 (LINN).
Current name: ***Echinophora tenuifolia*** L. (Apiaceae).

Echinops corymbosus Linnaeus, *Species Plantarum* 2: 815. 1753.
"Habitat in Apulia, Hellesponto, Lemno, T[h]racia, in campis." RCN: 6009.
Basionym of: *Carthamus corymbosus* (L.) L. (1763).
Lectotype (Turland in Jarvis & Turland in *Taxon* 47: 360. 1998): Herb. Clifford: 391, *Echinops* 2, sheet 26 (BM-000646905).
Current name: ***Cardopatium corymbosum*** (L.) Pers. (Asteraceae).

Echinops fruticosus Linnaeus, *Species Plantarum* 2: 815. 1753.
"Habitat in America meridionali." RCN: 6723.
Lectotype (Howard, *Fl. Lesser Antilles* 6: 595. 1989): [icon] *"Echinops foliis lanceolatis, dentatis, capitulis axillaribus"* in Plumier in Burman, Pl. Amer.: 114, t. 123, f. 1. 1757.
Current name: ***Rolandra fruticosa*** (L.) Kuntze (Asteraceae).

Echinops ritro Linnaeus, *Species Plantarum* 2: 815. 1753.
"Habitat in Gallia, Sibiria." RCN: 6721.
Lectotype (Jeffrey in *Curtis's Bot. Mag.* 180: 78. 1974): [icon] *"Ritro floribus caeruleis"* in Plantin, Pl. Stirp. Icon. 2: 8. 1581.
Current name: ***Echinops ritro*** L. subsp. ***ritro*** (Asteraceae).
Note: Bobrov (in Schischkin & Bobrov, *Fl. U.R.S.S.* 27: 31. 1962; Engl. Transl.: 31. 1998) said that the Gmelin plate associated with the unnamed var. beta "can be considered as the type of the species" but added that this was only a preliminary solution (in maintaining the name for a Russian, rather than a south European plant). He added that to solve the problem, it would be necessary to determine to which species the plant grown in Uppsala "i.e. the formal type specimen" belongs. He clearly did not designate the Gmelin plate as a formal lectotype.

Echinops sphaerocephalus Linnaeus, *Species Plantarum* 2: 814. 1753.
"Habitat in Italia." RCN: 6719.
Lectotype (Arevschatian in *Biol. Zhurn. Armenii* 42: 216. 1989): Herb. Linn. No. 1045.1 (LINN).

Generitype of *Echinops* Linnaeus (vide Green, *Prop. Brit. Bot.*: 179. 1929).
Current name: ***Echinops sphaerocephalus*** L. (Asteraceae).
Note: Arevschatian indicated "628.1" LINN as type (the IDC fiche on which sheet no. 1045.1 appears is fiche no. 628). There is only one collection associated with this name and, despite not using Savage's numbering system, the author's intention is clear and the type choice accepted here. Jeffrey (in Jarvis & al., *Regnum Veg.* 127: 44. 1993) designated Herb. Burser XXI: 35 (UPS) as lectotype but this is pre-dated by Arevschatian's choice.

Echinops spinosus Linnaeus, *Systema Naturae*, ed. 12, 2: 581; *Mantissa Plantarum*: 119. 1767, *nom. illeg.*
"Habitat in Aegypto, Arabia." RCN: 6720.
Type not designated.
Original material: Herb. Linn. No. 1045.2 (LINN); [icon] in Dodoëns, Stirp. Hist. Pempt., ed. 2: 722. 1616.
Current name: ***Echinops*** sp. (Asteraceae).
Note: Linnaeus included *Echinops spinosissimus* Turra (1765) in the synonymy of his name and *E. spinosus* is therefore illegitimate (see Greuter in *Willdenowia* 33: 58. 2003). However, both names appear to be in use for separate taxa (see e.g. Kozuharov in Tutin & al., *Fl. Europaea* 4: 213. 1976).

Echinops strigosus Linnaeus, *Species Plantarum* 2: 815. 1753.
"Habitat in Hispania. Loefl." RCN: 6722.
Lectotype (López González in Jarvis & Turland in *Taxon* 47: 360. 1998): Herb. Linn. No. 1045.4 (LINN).
Current name: ***Echinops strigosus*** L. (Asteraceae).

Echites angularis Linnaeus, *Plantae Surinamenses*: 7. 1775.
"Habitat [in Surinamo.]" RCN: 1729.
Type not designated.
Original material: Herb. Linn. No. 106.3 (S).
Note: The application of this name appears uncertain.

Echites caudata Linnaeus, *Systema Naturae*, ed. 12, 2: 190; *Mantissa Plantarum*: 52. 1767.
"Habitat in India." RCN: 1727.
Lectotype (designated here by Beentje): Herb. Linn. No. 302.1 (LINN).
Current name: ***Strophanthus caudatus*** (L.) Kurz (Apocynaceae).

Echites scholaris Linnaeus, *Systema Naturae*, ed. 12, 2: 190; *Mantissa Plantarum*: 53. 1767.
"Habitat in India." RCN: 1728.
Lectotype (Huber in Abeywickrama, *Revised Handb. Fl. Ceylon* 1(1): 12. 1973): Herb. Linn. No. 302.2 (LINN).
Current name: ***Alstonia scholaris*** (L.) R. Br. (Apocynaceae).
Note: Monachino (in *Pacific Sci.* 3: 147. 1949) provided a somewhat confused type statement, quoting Robert Brown who approved the identity of Rumphius' 1: t. 45 (which was not, however, part of Linnaeus' protologue) and cast doubt on that of Rumphius' 2: t. 82 (which was). Monachino stated that Linnaeus' name was "based on" *Lignum scholare* of Rumphius but noted that t. 82 "diverges widely from *A. scholaris*, but is not adequate for precise identification", while agreeing that there was "strong justification" for Browne's identification of it with *A. spectabilis* R. Br. Despite this, Monachino applied the Linnaean name in its traditional sense, suggesting that he was not accepting Rumphius' t. 82 as the type. Although Forster (in *Austral. Syst. Bot.* 5: 751. 1992) accepted Monachino as having typified the name, the latter's statements seem contrary to Art. 7.11

as the type was not "definitely accepted as such by the typifying author". Huber's 1973 choice of type is therefore accepted here.

Echium capitatum Linnaeus, *Systema Naturae,* ed. 12, 2: 148; *Mantissa Plantarum*: 42. 1767.
"Habitat ad Cap. b. spei." RCN: 1122.
Lectotype (Buys & van der Walt in *Taxon* 45: 515. 1996): Herb. Linn. No. 191.8 (LINN).
Current name: **Lobostemon capitatus** (L.) H. Buek (Boraginaceae).

Echium creticum Linnaeus, *Species Plantarum* 1: 139. 1753.
"Habitat in Creta." RCN: 1128.
Lectotype (Fernandes in *Bol. Soc. Brot.,* sér. 2, 43: 152. 1969): Herb. Linn. No. 191.21 (LINN).
Current name: **Echium creticum** L. (Boraginaceae).
Note: Lacaita (in *J. Linn. Soc., Bot.* 44: 401. 1919) and Klotz (in *Wiss. Z. Martin-Luther-Univ., Halle-Wittenberg, Math.-Naturwiss. Reihe* 11: 293. 1962) argued that the name should be rejected as a *nomen confusum*, but Fernandes (*l.c.*) has formally typified the name (see extensive discussion and a photograph (pl. 1) of the type). It has been taken up in the sense of *E. australe* Lam.

Echium fruticosum Linnaeus, *Species Plantarum* 1: 139. 1753.
"Habitat in Aethiopia." RCN: 1120.
Lectotype (Buys & van der Walt in *Taxon* 45: 515. 1996): [icon] "*Echium Africanum frutescens foliis pilosis*" in Commelin, Hort. Med. Amstelod. Pl. Rar. 2: 107, t. 54. 1701.
Current name: **Lobostemon fruticosus** (L.) H. Buek (Boraginaceae).

Echium italicum Linnaeus, *Species Plantarum* 1: 139. 1753.
"Habitat in Anglia, Italia." RCN: 1125.
Lectotype (Gibbs in *Lagascalia* 1: 48. 1971): Herb. Linn. No. 191.17 (LINN).
Current name: **Echium italicum** L. (Boraginaceae).
Note: Echium italicum was treated as the generitype of *Echium* by Britton & Brown, *Ill. Fl. N. U. S.,* ed. 2, 3: 93. 1913 (see McNeill & al. in *Taxon* 36: 370. 1987). However, under Art. 10.5, Ex. 7 (a voted example) of the Vienna Code, this is a type choice made under the American Code and is to be replaced under Art. 10.5b by Hitchcock's choice (*Prop. Brit. Bot.*: 128. 1929) of *E. vulgare* L.

Echium laevigatum Linnaeus, *Systema Naturae,* ed. 10, 2: 916. 1759. ["Habitat ad Cap. b. spei."] Sp. Pl., ed. 2, 1: 199 (1762). RCN: 1124.
Lectotype (Buys & van der Walt in *Taxon* 45: 516. 1996): [icon] "*Buglossum Africanum Echii folio, flore purpureo*" in Plukenet, Almag. Mant.: 33, t. 341, f. 7. 1700.
Current name: **Lobostemon fruticosus** (L.) H. Buek (Boraginaceae).

Echium lusitanicum Linnaeus, *Species Plantarum* 1: 140. 1753.
"Habitat in Europa australi." RCN: 1130.
Lectotype (Gibbs in Cafferty & Jarvis in *Taxon* 53: 802. 2004): Herb. A. van Royen No. 898.272–471 (L).
Current name: **Echium lusitanicum** L. (Boraginaceae).

Echium lycopsis Linnaeus, *Flora Anglica*: 12. 1754, *nom. utique rej.*
Lectotype (Stearn, *Introd. Ray's Syn. Meth. Stirp. Brit.* (Ray Soc. ed.): 65. 1973): [icon] "*Echii altera species*" in Dodoëns, Stirp. Hist. Pempt., ed. 2: 630, 631. 1616.

Echium maculatum Linnaeus, *Amoenitates Academicae* 4: 478. 1759.
Lectotype (Hilger & Böhle in *Taxon* 49: 744. 2000): [icon] "*Echium rubro flore*" in Clusius, Rar. Pl. Hist. 2: 164. 1601.
Current name: **Pontechium maculatum** (L.) Böhle & Hilger (Boraginaceae).

Echium orientale Linnaeus, *Species Plantarum* 1: 139. 1753.
"Habitat in Oriente." RCN: 1129.
Lectotype (Mill in Cafferty & Jarvis in *Taxon* 53: 802. 2004): [icon] "*Echium Orientale verbasci folio flore maximo, Campanulato*" in Tournefort, Rel. Voy. Levant (Paris ed.) 2: 247, 248. 1717.
Current name: **Echium orientale** L. (Boraginaceae).
Note: Tournefort's description was discussed in some detail by Burtt (in *Karaca Arbor. Mag.* 6: 138–139. 2002) who also (*l.c.* 6: 60, f. 13. 2001) reproduced an illustration of the subsequently designated lectotype.

Echium plantagineum Linnaeus, *Mantissa Plantarum Altera*: 202. 1771.
"Habitat in Italia." RCN: 1123.
Lectotype (Gibbs in *Lagascalia* 1: 58. 1971): [icon] "*Lycopsis lato Plantaginis folio Italica*" in Barrelier, Pl. Galliam: 16, t. 1026. 1714.
Current name: **Echium plantagineum** L. (Boraginaceae).
Note: Lacaita (in *J. Linn. Soc., Bot.* 44: 420. 1919) discussed this name, and Qaiser (in Jafri & El-Gadi, *Fl. Libya* 68: 37. 1979) treated 191.14 (LINN) as the type. Perry & McNeill (in *Taxon* 36: 483–492. 1987) argued that the specimen should take precedence over the Barrelier plate, but the latter is original material for the name, and Gibbs' choice has priority.

Echium violaceum Linnaeus, *Systema Naturae,* ed. 12, 2: 148; *Mantissa Plantarum*: 42. 1767.
"Habitat in Austria." RCN: 1127.
Type not designated.
Original material: Herb. Linn. No. 191.20 (LINN); [icon] in Clusius, Rar. Pl. Hist. 2: 164. 1601.
Current name: **Echium sp.** (Boraginaceae).
Note: Lacaita (in *J. Linn. Soc., Bot.* 44: 423. 1919) discussed this name in some detail, and Piggin (in *Muelleria* 3: 227. 1977) notes that it has been discarded as ambiguous because it is a mixture of *E. rubrum* Jacq. and *E. rosulatum* Lange. It appears to be a candidate for rejection.

Echium vulgare Linnaeus, *Species Plantarum* 1: 139. 1753.
"Habitat in Europa ad vias & agros." RCN: 1126.
Lectotype (Gibbs in *Lagascalia* 1: 54. 1971): Herb. Linn. No. 191.19 (LINN), see p. 492.
Generitype of *Echium* Linnaeus (vide Hitchcock, *Prop. Brit. Bot.*: 128. 1929).
Current name: **Echium vulgare** L. (Boraginaceae).
Note: Echium italicum was treated as the generitype of *Echium* by Britton & Brown, *Ill. Fl. N. U. S.,* ed. 2, 3: 93. 1913 (see McNeill & al. in *Taxon* 36: 370. 1987). However, under Art. 10.5, Ex. 7 (a voted example) of the Vienna Code, this is a type choice made under the American Code and is to be replaced under Art. 10.5b by Hitchcock's choice (*Prop. Brit. Bot.*: 128. 1929) of *E. vulgare* L.

Eclipta erecta Linnaeus, *Mantissa Plantarum Altera*: 286. 1771, *nom. illeg., typ. cons.*
["Habitat in Virginia, Surinamo."] Sp. Pl. 2: 902 (1753). RCN: 6513.
Replaced synonym: *Verbesina alba* L. (1753).
Lectotype (D'Arcy in Woodson & Schery in *Ann. Missouri Bot. Gard.* 62: 1102. 1975): Herb. Linn. No. 1020.1 (LINN).
Generitype of *Eclipta* Linnaeus, *nom. cons.*
Current name: **Eclipta prostrata** (L.) L. (Asteraceae).
Note: Eclipta Linnaeus, *nom. cons.* against *Eupatoriophalacron* Mill. As noted by Grierson (in Dassanayake & Fosberg, *Revised Handb. Fl. Ceylon* 1: 212. 1980), *Eclipta erecta* is an illegitimate replacement name for *Verbesina alba* L. (1753).

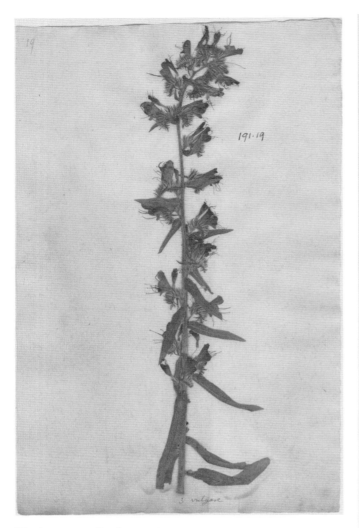

The lectotype of *Echium vulgare* L.

Eclipta prostrata (Linnaeus) Linnaeus, *Mantissa Plantarum Altera*: 286. 1771.
"Habitat in India." RCN: 6514.
Basionym: *Verbesina prostrata* L. (1753).
Lectotype (Wijnands, *Bot. Commelins*: 74. 1983): [icon]
    "*Chrysanthemum Maderaspatanum, Menthae arvensis folio & facie, floribus bigemellis, ad foliorum alas, pediculis curtis*" in Plukenet, Phytographia: t. 118, f. 5. 1691; Almag. Bot.: 100. 1696. – Typotype: Herb. Sloane 94: 175 (BM-SL).
Current name: *Eclipta prostrata* (L.) L. (Asteraceae).
Note: D'Arcy (in *Ann. Missouri Bot. Gard.* 62: 1102. 1975) indicated 1020.4 or 1020.5 (LINN) as the type of the basionym, presumably in error as both are associated with the name "Eclipta latifolia" rather than *V. prostrata*. Neither they, nor 1020.7 (LINN), the post-1753 Patrick Browne collection treated as the lectotype by Kupicha (in Davis, *Fl. Turkey* 5: 46. 1975), are original material for the name. Grierson (in Dassanayake & Fosberg, *Revised Handb. Fl. Ceylon* 1: 212. 1980) treated material in Herb. Plukenet (BM-SL) as "type" but this would not have been seen by Linnaeus and is not original material either. Wijnands' 1983 choice of the Plukenet illustration as lectotype is therefore accepted here.

Eclipta punctata Linnaeus, *Mantissa Plantarum Altera*: 286. 1771, *nom. illeg.*
"Habitat in Domingo et Martinicae inundatis." RCN: 6515.
Replaced synonym: *Bellis ramosa* Jacq. (1760).
Type not designated.
Current name: *Eclipta prostrata* (L.) L. (Asteraceae).
Note: An illegitimate replacement name in *Eclipta* for *Bellis ramosa* Jacq. (1760).

Ehretia bourreria (Linnaeus) Linnaeus, *Species Plantarum*, ed. 2, 1: 275. 1762.
"Habitat in Jamaica." RCN: 1530.
Basionym: *Cordia bourreria* L. (1759).
Lectotype (Stearn in *J. Arnold Arbor.* 52: 620. 1971): *Browne*, Herb. Linn. No. 254.2 (LINN).
Current name: *Bourreria baccata* Raf. (Boraginaceae).

Ehretia tinifolia Linnaeus, *Systema Naturae*, ed. 10, 2: 936. 1759. ["Habitat in Jamaica."] Sp. Pl., ed. 2, 1: 275 (1762). RCN: 1528.
Lectotype (Miller in *Ann. Missouri Bot. Gard.* 76: 1069. 1989): *Browne*, Herb. Linn. No. 254.1 (LINN).
Current name: *Ehretia tinifolia* L. (Boraginaceae).

Elaeagnus angustifolia Linnaeus, *Species Plantarum* 1: 121. 1753.
"Habitat in Bohemia, Hispania, Syria, Cappodocia." RCN: 996.
Lectotype (McKean in Jarvis & al., *Regnum Veg.* 127: 44. 1993): Herb. Clifford: 38, *Elaeagnus* 1 (BM-000557825).
Generitype of *Elaeagnus* Linnaeus (vide Hitchcock, *Prop. Brit. Bot.*: 126. 1929).
Current name: *Elaeagnus angustifolia* L. (Elaeagnaceae).

Elaeagnus latifolia Linnaeus, *Species Plantarum* 1: 121. 1753.
"Habitat in Zeylona." RCN: 999.
Type not designated.
Original material: Herb. Hermann 5: 61, No. 58 [icon] (BM); Herb. Hermann 3: 48, No. 58 (BM); Herb. Linn. No. 160.4 (LINN); Herb. Hermann 1: 43, No. 58 (BM); [icon] in Burman, Thes. Zeylan.: 92, t. 39, f. 2. 1737.
Current name: *Elaeagnus latifolia* L. (Elaeagnaceae).
Note: Specific epithet spelled "latifolio" in the protologue.

Elaeagnus orientalis Linnaeus, *Systema Naturae,* ed. 12, 2: 127; *Mantissa Plantarum*: 41. 1767.
"Habitat in Oriente. D.D. Royen." RCN: 997.
Lectotype (Murray in Rechinger, *Fl. Iranica* 55: 3. 1968): Herb. Linn. No. 160.2 (LINN).
Current name: *Elaeagnus angustifolia* L. (Elaeagnaceae).

Elaeagnus spinosa Linnaeus, *Centuria II Plantarum*: 9. 1756.
"Habitat in Aegypto." RCN: 998.
Type not designated.
Original material: *Hasselquist*, Herb. Linn. No. 160.3 (LINN); [icon] in Rauwolf, Aigent. Beschr. Morgenl.: 112, 276, t. 112. 1583.
Current name: *Elaeagnus spinosa* L. (Elaeagnaceae).

Elaeocarpus serratus Linnaeus, *Species Plantarum* 1: 515. 1753.
"Habitat in India." RCN: 3874.
Lectotype (Tirel & Raynal in *Adansonia*, n.s., 20: 170. 1980): Herb. Hermann 1: 51, No. 206 (BM-000594482).
Generitype of *Elaeocarpus* Linnaeus.
Current name: *Elaeocarpus serratus* L. (Elaeocarpaceae).
Note: Tirel & Raynal's description of the lectotype as comprising two specimens side by side on a single page makes it clear that they intend the material in Herb. Hermann vol. 1: 51. They also illustrated (pl. 1) the cited Burman and Rumphius (3: t. 101) plates.

Elate sylvestris Linnaeus, *Species Plantarum* 2: 1189. 1753.
"Habitat in India." RCN: 8550.
Lectotype (Moore & Dransfield in *Taxon* 28: 67, f. 8. 1979): [icon] *"Katou-indel"* in Rheede, Hort. Malab. 3: 15, t. 22. 1682.
Generitype of *Elate* Linnaeus.
Current name: ***Phoenix sylvestris*** (L.) Roxb. (Arecaceae).

Elaterium trifoliatum Linnaeus, *Systema Naturae,* ed. 12, 2: 614; *Mantissa Plantarum*: 123. 1767.
"Habitat in Virginia." RCN: 7035.
Lectotype (designated here by Reveal): *Clayton 642* (BM).
Current name: ***Nemophila aphylla*** (L.) Brummitt (Hydrophyllaceae).

Elatine alsinastrum Linnaeus, *Species Plantarum* 1: 368. 1753.
"Habitat Aboae, Lipsiae, Parisiis, Monspelii in fossis." RCN: 2909.
Lectotype (Jonsell & Jarvis in *Nordic J. Bot.* 22: 82. 2002): Herb. Linn. No. 161.5 (S).
Current name: ***Elatine alsinastrum*** L. (Elatinaceae).

Elatine hydropiper Linnaeus, *Species Plantarum* 1: 367. 1753.
"Habitat in Europae inundatis." RCN: 2908.
Lectotype (Jonsell & Jarvis in *Nordic J. Bot.* 22: 82. 2002): Herb. Linn. No. 517.2 (LINN).
Generitype of *Elatine* Linnaeus (vide Hitchcock, *Prop. Brit. Bot.*: 151. 1929).
Current name: ***Elatine hydropiper*** L. (Elatinaceae).

Elegia juncea Linnaeus, *Mantissa Plantarum Altera*: 297. 1771.
"Habitat ad Cap. b. spei. Koenig." RCN: 7396.
Replaced synonym of: *Restio elegia* L. (1774), *nom. illeg.*
Neotype (Linder in *Bothalia* 15: 424. 1985): Herb. Linn. No. 1164a.4 (LINN).
Generitype of *Elegia* Linnaeus.
Current name: ***Elegia juncea*** L. (Restionaceae).

Elephantopus scaber Linnaeus, *Species Plantarum* 2: 814. 1753.
"Habitat in Indiis." RCN: 6713.
Lectotype (Jeffrey in Jarvis & al., *Regnum Veg.* 127: 44. 1993): [icon] *"Ana-schovadi"* in Rheede, Hort. Malab. 10: 13, t. 7. 1690.
Generitype of *Elephantopus* Linnaeus (vide Baker in *Trans. Acad. Sci. St. Louis* 12: 45. 1902).
Current name: ***Elephantopus scaber*** L. (Asteraceae).
Note: Philipson (in *J. Bot.* 76: 302. 1938) designated 1043.1 (LINN) as the type, but unfortunately this collection is a post-1753 addition to the herbarium and not original material for the name. Grierson (in Dassanayake & Fosberg, *Revised Handb. Fl. Ceylon* 1: 135. 1980) indicated Clifford material (BM) as type but this was presumably based on the literature reference, as no relevant Clifford material has been either recorded, or found.

Elephantopus tomentosus Linnaeus, *Species Plantarum* 2: 814. 1753.
"Habitat in Virginia." RCN: 6714.
Lectotype (Reveal & al. in *Huntia* 7: 220. 1987): *Clayton s.n.* (probably a duplicate of *Clayton 148*) (BM-000038182; iso- BM).
Current name: ***Elephantopus tomentosus*** L. (Asteraceae).

Ellisia aculeata Linnaeus, *Flora Jamaicensis*: 18. 1759, *nom. illeg.*
"Habitat [in Jamaica.]"
Replaced synonym: *Ellisia acuta* L. (1759).
Type not designated.
Original material: as replaced synonym.
Current name: ***Duranta erecta*** L. (Verbenaceae).
Note: An illegitimate replacement name (published Dec 1759) for *E. acuta* L. (May–Jun 1759).

Ellisia acuta Linnaeus, *Systema Naturae,* ed. 10, 2: 1121. 1759.
RCN: 4627.
Replaced synonym of: *Ellisia aculeata* L. (1759), *nom. illeg.*
Type not designated.
Original material: [icon] in Browne, Civ. Nat. Hist. Jamaica: 262, t. 29, f. 1. 1756.
Current name: ***Duranta erecta*** L. (Verbenaceae).
Note: Méndez Santos (in Greuter & Rankin, *Fl. Cuba,* Ser. A, 7(3): 115. 2003) indicated the cited Browne t. 29, f. 1 as the holotype, which it almost certainly is not. It is, however, original material for the name, but the absence of the phrase "designated here" or an equivalent (Art. 7.11) means that this cannot be accepted as a formal typification.

Ellisia nyctelea (Linnaeus) Linnaeus, *Species Plantarum,* ed. 2, 2: 1662. 1763.
"Habitat in Virginia." RCN: 1169.
Basionym: *Ipomoea nyctelea* L. (1753).
Lectotype (Reveal in Jarvis & al., *Regnum Veg.* 127: 45. 1993): Herb. Linn. No. 206.1 (LINN; iso- BM).
Generitype of *Ellisia* Linnaeus, *nom. cons.*
Current name: ***Ellisia nyctelea*** (L.) L. (Hydrophyllaceae).
Note: Ellisia Linnaeus, *nom. cons.* against *Ellisia* P. Browne.

Elvela mitra Linnaeus, *Species Plantarum* 2: 1180. 1753.
"Habitat in Truncis putridis." RCN: 8492.
Type not designated.
Original material: [icon] in Mentzel, Ind. Nom. Pl. Univ.: t. 6. 1682; [icon] in Micheli, Nov. Pl. Gen.: 204, t. 86, f. 7. 1729.
Current name: ***Helvella crispa*** (Scop.) Fr. (Helvellaceae).
Note: "Elvela" is an orthographic error for "Helvella", to which it was corrected by Linnaeus in 1763.

Elvela pineti Linnaeus, *Species Plantarum* 2: 1180. 1753.
"Habitat in Pinu, Abiete." RCN: 8493.
Type not designated.
Original material: none traced.
Current name: ***Thelephora terrestris*** Ehrh.: Fr. (Thelephoraceae).
Note: "Elvela" is an orthographic error for "Helvella", to which it was corrected by Linnaeus in 1763.

Elymus arenarius Linnaeus, *Species Plantarum* 1: 83. 1753.
"Habitat ad Europae litora marina in arena mobili." RCN: 696.
Lectotype (Bowden in *Canad. J. Bot.* 42: 567. 1964): Herb. Linn. No. 100.1 (LINN).
Current name: ***Leymus arenarius*** (L.) Hochst. (Poaceae).

Elymus canadensis Linnaeus, *Species Plantarum* 1: 83. 1753.
"Habitat in Canada. Kalm." RCN: 699.
Replaced synonym of: *Elymus philadelphicus* L. (1755), *nom. illeg.*
Lectotype (Hitchcock in *Contr. U. S. Natl. Herb.* 12: 124. 1908): Herb. Linn. No. 100.3 (LINN; iso- US, fragm.).
Current name: ***Elymus canadensis*** L. (Poaceae).

Elymus caninus (Linnaeus) Linnaeus, *Flora Suecica,* ed. 2: 39. 1755.
"Habitat ad Hellekis W-gothiae." RCN: 704.
Basionym: *Triticum caninum* L. (1753).
Lectotype (Cope & van Slageren in Cafferty & al. in *Taxon* 49: 258. 2000): Herb. Linn. No. 100.10 (LINN).
Current name: ***Agropyron caninum*** (L.) P. Beauv. (Poaceae).

Elymus caput-medusae Linnaeus, *Species Plantarum* 1: 84. 1753.
"Habitat in Lusitaniae, Hispaniae maritimis." RCN: 702.
Lectotype (Humphries in *Bot. J. Linn. Soc.* 76: 342. 1978): Herb. Linn. No. 100.6 (LINN).

Current name: *Taeniatherum caput-medusae* (L.) Nevski subsp.
  caput-medusae (Poaceae).
Note: Although Humphries indicated the type sheet as "106.6", it
  seems clear that this was simply a typographical error for "100.6".

Elymus europaeus Linnaeus, *Systema Naturae,* ed. 12, 2: 101;
  Mantissa Plantarum: 35. 1767.
"Habitat in Germania." RCN: 705.
Lectotype (Cope in Cafferty & al. in *Taxon* 49: 250. 2000): Herb.
  Linn. No. 100.13 (LINN).
Current name: *Hordelymus europaeus* (L.) Harz (Poaceae).
Note: Although Kerguélen (in *Lejeunia*, n.s., 75: 193. 1975) stated
  "Type: ...LINN", this is not accepted as a formal typification, for
  the reasons explained by Cafferty & al. (in *Taxon* 49: 240. 2000).

Elymus hystrix Linnaeus, *Species Plantarum* 1: 560. 1753.
"Habitat – – – –" RCN: 703.
Lectotype (Hitchcock in *Contr. U. S. Natl. Herb.* 12: 124. 1908):
  Clayton 570, Herb. Linn. No. 100.8 (LINN; iso- BM).
Current name: *Hystrix patula* Moench (Poaceae).

Elymus monococcus Linnaeus, *Systema Naturae,* ed. 10, 2: 879.
  1759.
RCN: 701.
Type not designated.
Original material: none traced.
Note: The application of this name is obscure.

Elymus philadelphicus Linnaeus, *Centuria I Plantarum*: 6. 1755,
  nom. illeg.
"Habitat in Pensylvania. Kalm." RCN: 698.
Replaced synonym: *Elymus canadensis* L. (1753).
Lectotype (Hitchcock in *Contr. U. S. Natl. Herb.* 12: 124. 1908):
  Herb. Linn. No. 100.3 (LINN; iso- US, fragm.).
Current name: *Elymus canadensis* L. (Poaceae).

Elymus sibiricus Linnaeus, *Species Plantarum* 1: 83. 1753.
"Habitat in Sibiria." RCN: 697.
Lectotype (Bowden in *Canad. J. Bot.* 42: 554. 1964): Herb. Linn. No.
  100.2 (LINN).
Generitype of *Elymus* Linnaeus (vide Hitchcock, *Prop. Brit. Bot.*: 121.
  1929).
Current name: *Elymus sibiricus* L. (Poaceae).
Note: Elymus sibiricus, with the type designated by Bowden, was
  proposed as conserved type of the genus by Jarvis (in *Taxon* 41: 572.
  1992). However, the proposal was eventually ruled unnecessary by
  the General Committee (see Barrie, *l.c.* 55: 795–796. 2006 for a
  review of the history of this and related proposals).

Elymus virginicus Linnaeus, *Species Plantarum* 1: 84. 1753.
"Habitat in Virginia." RCN: 700.
Lectotype (Hitchcock in *Contr. U. S. Natl. Herb.* 12: 124. 1908):
  Herb. Linn. No. 100.5 (LINN; iso- US, fragm.).
Current name: *Elymus virginicus* L. (Poaceae).
Note: The lectotype designated by Hitchcock (in *Contr. U.S. Natl.
  Herb. Wash.* 12: 124. 1908), 100.5 (LINN), does not belong to *E.
  virginicus* L. var. *virginicus* as currently understood, and Campbell
  (in *Taxon* 45: 128. 1996) therefore proposed the name for
  conservation with a conserved type. The proposal was eventually
  declined by the Committee for Spermatophyta (in *Taxon* 54: 1094.
  2005) but Campbell (in *Sida* 22: 493. 2006) has indicated a desire
  to revisit the question.

Empetrum album Linnaeus, *Species Plantarum* 2: 1022. 1753.
"Habitat in Lusitania." RCN: 7388.

Type not designated.
Original material: Herb. Linn. No. 1160.1 (LINN); [icon] in Clusius,
  Rar. Pl. Hist. 1: 45. 1601.
Current name: *Corema album* (L.) D. Don (Empetraceae).

Empetrum nigrum Linnaeus, *Species Plantarum* 2: 1022. 1753.
"Habitat in Europae frigidissimae montosis paludosis." RCN: 7389.
Lectotype (Good in *J. Linn. Soc., Bot.* 47: 512. 1927): Herb. Linn.
  No. 1160.2 (LINN).
Generitype of *Empetrum* Linnaeus (vide Green, *Prop. Brit. Bot.*: 191.
  1929).
Current name: *Empetrum nigrum* L. (Empetraceae).

Ephedra distachya Linnaeus, *Species Plantarum* 2: 1040. 1753.
"Habitat in G. Narbonensis, Hispaniae saxosis collibus marinis."
  RCN: 7513.
Lectotype (Nouviant in *Bull. Murith. Soc. Valais. Sci. Nat.* 114: 132, f.
  1. 1996): Herb. Clifford: 465, *Ephedra* 1 (BM-000647523).
Generitype of *Ephedra* Linnaeus (vide Green, *Prop. Brit. Bot.*: 192.
  1929).
Current name: *Ephedra distachya* L. (Ephedraceae).

Ephedra monostachya Linnaeus, *Species Plantarum* 2: 1040. 1753.
"Habitat in Sibiriae montibus apricis, sterilissimis." RCN: 7514.
Lectotype (Nouviant in *Bull. Murith. Soc. Valais. Sci. Nat.* 116: 85, f.
  p. 83. 1999): *Gmelin 17*, Herb. Linn. No. 1200.4 (LINN).
Current name: *Ephedra distachya* L. subsp. *monostachya* (L.) Riedl
  (Ephedraceae).

Epidendrum aloifolium Linnaeus, *Species Plantarum* 2: 953. 1753.
"Habitat in Malabariae arboribus, parasitica." RCN: 6893.
Lectotype (Seth in *Kew Bull.* 37: 399. 1982): [icon] *"Kansjiram-
  maravara"* in Rheede, Hort. Malab. 12: 17, t. 8. 1693.
Current name: *Cymbidium aloifolium* (L.) Sw. (Orchidaceae).

Epidendrum amabile Linnaeus, *Species Plantarum* 2: 953. 1753.
"Habitat in India. Osbeck." RCN: 6898.
Lectotype (Sweet, *Genus* Phalaenopsis: 21. 1980): *Osbeck s.n.*, Herb.
  Linn. No. 373.1 (S), see p. 175.
Current name: *Phalaenopsis amabilis* (L.) Blume (Orchidaceae).

Epidendrum carinatum Linnaeus, *Species Plantarum* 2: 953. 1753.
"Habitat in Insulis Luzonum, parasitica." RCN: 6892.
Lectotype (Cribb in Cafferty & Jarvis in *Taxon* 48: 47. 1999): [icon]
  "Bontiana Luzon, geniculis inferioribus carinulatis" in Petiver,
  Gazophyl. Nat.: 70, t. 44, f. 10. 1702–1709 (see p. 146). – Epitype
  (Cribb in Cafferty & Jarvis in *Taxon* 48: 47. 1999): Philippine
  Islands. 1906, *Loeher 5319* (K).
Current name: *Dendrobium carinatum* (L.) Willd. (Orchidaceae).

Epidendrum caudatum Linnaeus, *Systema Naturae,* ed. 10, 2: 1246.
  1759.
["Habitat in America."] Sp. Pl. ed. 2, 2: 1349 (1763). RCN: 6886.
Lectotype (McLeish & al., *Native Orchids of Belize*: 120. 1995): [icon]
  "Epidendrum foliis radicalibus, lanceolatis" in Plumier in Burman, Pl.
  Amer.: 172, t. 177. 1758.
Current name: *Brassia caudata* (L.) Lindl. (Orchidaceae).

Epidendrum ciliare Linnaeus, *Systema Naturae,* ed. 10, 2: 1246.
  1759.
["Habitat in America."] Sp. Pl. ed. 2, 2: 1349 (1763). RCN: 6888.
Lectotype (Garay & Sweet in Howard, *Fl. Lesser Antilles, Orchidaceae*:
  128. 1974): [icon] *"Epidendrum foliis oblongis, aveniis"* in Plumier in
  Burman, Pl. Amer.: 174, t. 179, f. 2. 1758.
Current name: *Epidendrum ciliare* L. (Orchidaceae).

Epidendrum cochleatum Linnaeus, *Species Plantarum*, ed. 2, 2: 1351. 1763.
"Habitat in America." RCN: 6899.
Lectotype (Garay & Sweet in Howard, *Fl. Lesser Antilles, Orchidaceae*: 116. 1974): [icon] in Plumier, Codex Boerhaavianus (University Library, Groningen).
Current name: ***Encyclia cochleata*** (L.) Dressler (Orchidaceae).

Epidendrum cucullatum Linnaeus, *Species Plantarum*, ed. 2, 2: 1350. 1763.
"Habitat in America." RCN: 6890.
Lectotype (Garay & Sweet in Howard, *Fl. Lesser Antilles, Orchidaceae*: 163. 1974): [icon] *"Epidendrum foliis subulatis, scapis unifloris"* in Plumier in Burman, Pl. Amer.: 173, t. 179, f. 1. 1758.
Current name: ***Brassavola cucullata*** (L.) R. Br. (Orchidaceae).

Epidendrum domesticum Linnaeus, *Species Plantarum* 2: 952. 1753.
"Habitat in Indiae orientalis Bataviae arboribus, parasitica." RCN: 6877.
Lectotype (Garay in *Harvard Pap. Bot.* 2: 49. 1997): [icon] *"Angurek warna"* in Kaempfer, Amoen. Exot. Fasc.: 867, 869. 1712. – Epitype (Goldblatt & Mabberley in *Novon* 15: 129. 2005): *E. Davall* in Herb. J.E. Smith, No. 89.42 (LINN-SM).
Current name: ***Belamcanda chinensis*** (L.) A. DC. (Iridaceae).
Note: The name has been associated with the genus *Vanilla*, probably as a result of Linnaeus reducing it to an unnamed variety of *E. vanilla* (*Sp. Pl.*, ed. 2, 2: 1348. 1763), and is evidently based on the cited Kaempfer reference. However, Garay has recently typified the name using part of Kaempfer's illustration that he identifies as *Belamcanda chinensis* (L.) DC. (Iridaceae). As a consequence, *E. domesticum* falls into the synonymy of the latter. However, if *Belamcanda* is subsumed within *Iris*, as favoured by Goldblatt & Mabberley (in *Novon* 15: 128–132. 2005), the correct name for *E. domesticum* is *I. domestica* (L.) Goldblatt & Mabb.

Epidendrum ensifolium Linnaeus, *Species Plantarum* 2: 954. 1753.
"Habitat in China. Osbeck." RCN: 6902.
Lectotype (Du Puy & Cribb, *Genus* Cymbidium: 156. 1988): *Osbeck s.n.*, Herb. Linn. No. 1062.10 (LINN).
Current name: ***Cymbidium ensifolium*** (L.) Sw. (Orchidaceae).

Epidendrum flos-aeris Linnaeus, *Species Plantarum* 2: 952. 1753.
"Habitat in Java, parasitica." RCN: 6878.
Lectotype (Wood in Cafferty & Jarvis in *Taxon* 48: 47. 1999): [icon] *"Angurek katong' ging"* in Kaempfer, Amoen. Exot. Fasc.: 868, 869. 1712.
Current name: ***Arachnis flos-aeris*** (L.) Rchb. f. (Orchidaceae).

Epidendrum furvum Linnaeus, *Species Plantarum*, ed. 2, 2: 1348. 1763.
"Habitat in India." RCN: 6881.
Lectotype (Smith in Merrill, *Interpret. Rumph. Herb. Amb.*: 178. 1917): [icon] *"Angraecum octavum sive furvum"* in Rumphius, Herb. Amboin. 6: 104, t. 46, f. 1. 1750.
Current name: ***Vanda furva*** (L.) Lindl. (Orchidaceae).

Epidendrum graminifolium Linnaeus, *Species Plantarum*, ed. 2, 2: 1353. 1763.
"Habitat in America." RCN: 6906.
Lectotype (Garay & Sweet in Howard, *Fl. Lesser Antilles, Orchidaceae*: 116. 1974): [icon] *"Convallaria? caule articulato"* in Plumier in Burman, Pl. Amer.: 171, t. 176, f. 1. 1758.
Current name: ***Octomeria graminifolia*** (L.) R. Br. (Orchidaceae).

Epidendrum guttatum Linnaeus, *Species Plantarum* 2: 953. 1753.
"Habitat in Jamaica, parasitica." RCN: 6894.
Lectotype (Stearn, *Introd. Linnaeus' Sp. Pl.* (Ray Soc. ed.): 123. 1957): [icon] *"Viscum delphinii flore albo guttato, minus, radice fibrosa"* in Sloane, Voy. Jamaica 1: 251, t. 148, f. 2. 1707. – Typotype: Herb. Sloane 4: 122 (BM-SL).
Current name: ***Oncidium guttatum*** (L.) Fawc. & Rendle (Orchidaceae).

Epidendrum juncifolium Linnaeus, *Species Plantarum*, ed. 2, 2: 1351. 1763.
"Habitat in America." RCN: 6895.
Lectotype (Cribb in Cafferty & Jarvis in *Taxon* 48: 47. 1999): [icon] *"Epidendrum foliis radicalibus subulatis"* in Plumier in Burman, Pl. Amer.: 179, t. 184, f. 2. 1758.
Current name: ***Oncidium ceboletta*** (Jacq.) Sw. (Orchidaceae).

Epidendrum moniliforme Linnaeus, *Species Plantarum* 2: 954. 1753.
"Habitat in Japoniae rupibus & arboribus parasitica." RCN: 6903.
Lectotype (Merrill in *J. Arnold Arbor.* 19: 330. 1938): [icon] *"Fu Ran"* in Kaempfer, Amoen. Exot. Fasc.: 864, 865. 1712.
Current name: ***Dendrobium moniliforme*** (L.) Sw. (Orchidaceae).

Epidendrum nodosum Linnaeus, *Species Plantarum* 2: 953. 1753.
"Habitat in America meridionali, parasitica." RCN: 6891.
Lectotype (Jones in *Bol. Soc. Brot.*, sér. 2, 41: 16. 1967): [icon] *"Orchidi affinis Epidendron Corassavicum folio crasso Sulcato"* in Hermann, Parad. Bat.: 207. 1698.
Generitype of *Epidendrum* Linnaeus (1753), *nom. rej.*
Current name: ***Brassavola nodosa*** (L.) Lindl. (Orchidaceae).
Note: Epidendrum Linnaeus (1753), *nom. rej.* in favour of *Epidendrum* Linnaeus (1763).
   Cribb (in *Taxon* 48: 47. 1999), unaware of Jones' earlier choice, also designated the Hermann plate as type.

Epidendrum ovatum Linnaeus, *Species Plantarum* 2: 952. 1753.
"Habitat in India." RCN: 6887.
Lectotype (Cribb in Cafferty & Jarvis in *Taxon* 48: 47. 1999): [icon] *"Anantali-maravara"* in Rheede, Hort. Malab. 12: 15, t. 7. 1693. – Epitype (Cribb in Cafferty & Jarvis in *Taxon* 48: 47. 1999): India. Malabar. "Herb. Ind. Dr. Hook. Fil. & Thompson", *Stocks & Law s.n.* (K).
Current name: ***Dendrobium ovatum*** (L.) Kraenzl. (Orchidaceae).

Epidendrum punctatum Linnaeus, *Systema Naturae*, ed. 10, 2: 1246. 1759.
["Habitat in America."] Sp. Pl., ed. 2, 2: 1349 (1763). RCN: 6885.
Lectotype (McVaugh, *Fl. Novo-Galiciana* 16: 77. 1985): [icon] *"Epidendrum racemo floribusque punctatis"* in Plumier in Burman, Pl. Amer.: 182, t. 187. 1758.
Current name: ***Cyrtopodium punctatum*** (L.) Lindl. (Orchidaceae).
Note: The Plumier figure appears to be the sole original element.

Epidendrum pusillum Linnaeus, *Species Plantarum*, ed. 2, 2: 1352. 1763.
"Habitat in Surinami. C. Dahlberg." RCN: 6901.
Lectotype (McLeish & al., *Native Orchids of Belize*: 140. 1995): Herb. Linn. No. 373.3 (S).
Current name: ***Psygmorchis pusilla*** (L.) Dodson & Dressler (Orchidaceae).

Epidendrum retusum Linnaeus, *Species Plantarum* 2: 953. 1753.
"Habitat in India." RCN: 6897.
Lectotype (Majumdar & Bakshi in *Taxon* 28: 354. 1979): [icon] *"Ansjeli-maravara"* in Rheede, Hort. Malab. 12: 1, t. 1. 1693.
Current name: ***Rhynchostylis retusa*** (L.) Blume (Orchidaceae).

Epidendrum scriptum Linnaeus, *Species Plantarum,* ed. 2, 2: 1351. 1763.
"Habitat in India." RCN: 6896.
Lectotype (Wood & Cribb, *Checkl. Orchids Borneo*: 122. 1994): [icon] *"Angraecum scriptum"* in Rumphius, Herb. Amboin. 6: 95, t. 42. 1750.
Current name: ***Grammatophyllum scriptum*** (L.) Blume (Orchidaceae).

Epidendrum spathulatum Linnaeus, *Species Plantarum* 2: 952. 1753.
"Habitat in India." RCN: 6880.
Lectotype (Majumdar & Bakshi in *Taxon* 28: 354. 1979): [icon] *"Ponnampu-maravara"* in Rheede, Hort. Malab. 12: 7, t. 3. 1693.
Current name: ***Vanda spathulata*** (L.) Spreng. (Orchidaceae).

Epidendrum tenuifolium Linnaeus, *Species Plantarum* 2: 952. 1753.
"Habitat in India." RCN: 6879.
Lectotype (Majumdar & Bakshi in *Taxon* 28: 354. 1979): [icon] *"Tsjerou-mau-maravara"* in Rheede, Hort. Malab. 12: 11, t. 5. 1693.
Current name: ***Cymbidium tenuifolium*** (L.) Willd. (Orchidaceae).

Epidendrum terrestre Linnaeus, *Systema Naturae,* ed. 10, 2: 1246. 1759.
RCN: 6900.
Replaced synonym of: *Epidendrum tuberosum* L. (1763), *nom. illeg.*
Lectotype (Ormerod in *Austral. Orchid Rev.* 59: 14. 1994): [icon] *"Angraecum terrestre primum"* in Rumphius, Herb. Amboin. 6: 112, t. 52, f. 1. 1750.
Current name: ***Phaius terrestris*** (L.) Ormerod (Orchidaceae).
Note: Ormerod (*l.c.*) typified the name using the Rumphius plate and made the combination *Phaius terrestris* (L.) Ormerod. Garay (in *Harvard Pap. Bot.* 2: 47, f. 1. 1997) rejected this choice on the grounds that the plate conflicted with the diagnosis and that the Code "always gives preference to existing specimens over cited illustrations". He proposed 1062.19 (LINN) as lectotype instead, a specimen identifiable as a species of *Geodorum* for which the combination *G. terrestre* (L.) Garay was made. Although Ormerod apparently overlooked the material in LINN, he nevertheless designated a cited figure, part of the protologue (with which it cannot therefore be in conflict) and original material for the name, as the type. Uncited specimens and cited illustrations carry equal weight for typification purposes (Art. 9.10) and so Ormerod's choice cannot be overturned in this way.

Epidendrum tuberosum Linnaeus, *Species Plantarum,* ed. 2, 2: 1352. 1763, *nom. illeg.*
"Habitat in Indiis." RCN: 6900.
Replaced synonym: *Epidendrum terrestre* L. (1759).
Lectotype (Ormerod in *Austral. Orchid Rev.* 59: 14. 1994): [icon] *"Angraecum terrestre primum"* in Rumphius, Herb. Amboin. 6: 112, t. 52, f. 1. 1750.
Current name: ***Phaius terrestris*** (L.) Ormerod (Orchidaceae).
Note: An illegitimate renaming of *E. terrestre* L. (1759). See discussion of the application of both names under *E. terrestre*.

Epidendrum vanilla Linnaeus, *Species Plantarum* 2: 952. 1753.
"Habitat in America australi." RCN: 6877.
Lectotype (Cribb in Cafferty & Jarvis in *Taxon* 48: 47. 1999): [icon] *"Volubilis siliquosa Mexicana plantagini folio"* in Catesby, Nat. Hist. Carolina 2, App.: 7, t. 7. 1747.
Current name: ***Vanilla mexicana*** Mill. (Orchidaceae).

Epigaea repens Linnaeus, *Species Plantarum* 1: 395. 1753.
"Habitat in Virginiae, Canadae pinetis." RCN: 3105.
Lectotype (Reveal & al. in *Huntia* 7: 232. 1987): Herb. Linn. No. 564.1 (LINN).

Generitype of *Epigaea* Linnaeus.
Current name: ***Epigaea repens*** L. (Ericaceae).

Epilobium alpinum Linnaeus, *Species Plantarum* 1: 348. 1753, *nom. utique rej.*
"Habitat in Alpibus Helveticis, Lapponicis." RCN: 2669.
Lectotype (Marshall in *J. Bot.* 45: 367. 1907): Herb. Linn. No. 486.8 (LINN).
Current name: ***Epilobium lactiflorum*** Hausskn. (Onagraceae).

Epilobium angustifolium Linnaeus, *Species Plantarum* 1: 347. 1753.
"Habitat in Europae boreali." RCN: 2663.
Lectotype (Raven in *Notes Roy. Bot. Gard. Edinburgh* 24: 186. 1962): Herb. Linn. No. 486.1 (LINN).
Current name: ***Epilobium angustifolium*** L. (Onagraceae).
Note: Specific epithet spelled "angustifolia" in the protologue.

Epilobium hirsutum Linnaeus, *Species Plantarum* 1: 347. 1753.
"Habitat in Europae humidiusculis." RCN: 2665.
Lectotype (Brenan in Turrill & Milne-Redhead, *Fl. Trop. E. Africa, Onagraceae*: 2. 1953): Herb. Linn. No. 486.3 (LINN).
Generitype of *Epilobium* Linnaeus (vide Hitchcock, *Prop. Brit. Bot.*: 149. 1929).
Current name: ***Epilobium hirsutum*** L. (Onagraceae).

Epilobium latifolium Linnaeus, *Species Plantarum* 1: 347. 1753.
"Habitat in Sibiria." RCN: 2664.
Lectotype (Raven in Rechinger, *Fl. Iranica* 7: 5. 1964): *Steller?*, Herb. Linn. No. 486.2 (LINN).
Current name: ***Epilobium latifolium*** L. (Onagraceae).
Note: Specific epithet spelled "latifolia" in the protologue.

Epilobium montanum Linnaeus, *Species Plantarum* 1: 348. 1753.
"Habitat in Europae montosis." RCN: 2666.
Lectotype (Raven in *Notes Roy. Bot. Gard. Edinburgh* 24: 191. 1962): Herb. Linn. No. 486.5 (LINN).
Current name: ***Epilobium montanum*** L. (Onagraceae).

Epilobium palustre Linnaeus, *Species Plantarum* 1: 348. 1753.
"Habitat in Europae humidiusculis. β in Alpibus." RCN: 2668.
Lectotype (Jonsell & Jarvis in *Nordic J. Bot.* 22: 83. 2002): Herb. Linn. No. 486.7 (LINN).
Current name: ***Epilobium palustre*** L. (Onagraceae).

Epilobium tetragonum Linnaeus, *Species Plantarum* 1: 348. 1753.
"Habitat in Europa." RCN: 2667.
Lectotype (Marshall in *J. Bot.* 45: 367. 1907): Herb. Linn. No. 486.6 (LINN).
Current name: ***Epilobium tetragonum*** L. (Onagraceae).

Epimedium alpinum Linnaeus, *Species Plantarum* 1: 117. 1753.
"Habitat in alpinum Euganeorum, Ligurinorum, Pontebarum umbrosis." RCN: 958.
Lectotype (Chamberlain in Jarvis & al., *Regnum Veg.* 127: 45. 1993): Herb. Clifford: 37, *Epimedium* 1 (BM-000557819).
Generitype of *Epimedium* Linnaeus.
Current name: ***Epimedium alpinum*** L. (Berberidaceae).
Note: Stearn (in *J. Linn. Soc., Bot.* 51: 472. 1938) stated that Linnaeus knew this only from garden material and that the Colli Euganei (near Padova, Italy) should be regarded as the type locality. However, he did not designate a type. Stearn (*Genus* Epimedium: 3–4, 155–156. 2002) subsequently provided further comments on Linnaeus' knowledge of this species.

Equisetum arvense Linnaeus, *Species Plantarum* 2: 1061. 1753.
"Habitat in Europae agris, pratis." RCN: 7730.
Lectotype (Jonsell & Jarvis in *Nordic J. Bot.* 14: 148. 1994): *Clayton 341* (BM-000062951).
Current name: ***Equisetum arvense*** L. (Equisetaceae).
Note: Hauke (in *Nova Hedwigia* 13: 106. 1966) indicated *Löfling 713* (1241.4 LINN) as "a type for the name", but he believed that it was a post-1753 addition to the herbarium, and evidently treated it as a neotype. As original material is in existence, designation of a neotype is contrary to Art. 9.11, and Jonsell & Jarvis therefore rejected Hauke's choice in favour of a Clayton collection.

Equisetum fluviatile Linnaeus, *Species Plantarum* 2: 1062. 1753.
"Habitat in Europa ad ripas lacuum, fluviorum." RCN: 7732.
Lectotype (Hauke in *Nova Hedwigia* 30: 423. 1978): Herb. Linn. No. 1241.6 (LINN).
Generitype of *Equisetum* Linnaeus (vide Britton & Brown, *Ill. Fl. N. U. S.*, ed. 2. 1: 39. 1913).
Current name: ***Equisetum fluviatile*** L. (Equisetaceae).
Note: Fernald & Weatherby (in *Rhodora* 23: 43. 1921) stated that the identity of the name "is fixed by the existence in Linnaeus' herbarium of a specimen… labelled by him with the descriptive phrase assigned to *E. fluviatile* in the *Species Plantarum*". No sheet there appears to carry this information so this statement cannot be accepted as a valid type choice.

Equisetum giganteum Linnaeus, *Systema Naturae,* ed. 10, 2: 1318. 1759.
["Habitat in America."] Sp. Pl., ed. 2, 2: 1517 (1763). RCN: 7735.
Lectotype (Hauke in *Beih. Nova Hedwigia* 8: 51. 1963): [icon] *"Equisetum setis simplicissimis spiciferis"* in Plumier in Burman, Pl. Amer.: 115, t. 125. f. 2. 1757.
Current name: ***Equisetum giganteum*** L. (Equisetaceae).

Equisetum hyemale Linnaeus, *Species Plantarum* 2: 1062. 1753.
"Habitat in Europae sylvis, asperis, uliginosis." RCN: 7734.
Type not designated.
Original material: *Clayton 657*, pl. 2 (BM); [icon] in Mattioli, Pl. Epit.: 770, f. A. 1586.
Current name: ***Equisetum hyemale*** L. (Equisetaceae).
Note: Hauke (in *Amer. Fern J.* 52: 59. 1962) designated 1241.7 (LINN) as a neotype but, with the existence of original material, this is contrary to Art. 9.11.

Equisetum limosum Linnaeus, *Species Plantarum* 2: 1062. 1753.
"Habitat in Europae paludibus turfosis, profundis." RCN: 7733.
Type not designated.
Original material: [icon] in Ray, Syn. Meth. Stirp. Brit., ed. 3: 131, t. 5, f. 2. 1724.
Current name: ***Equisetum fluviatile*** L. (Equisetaceae).

Equisetum palustre Linnaeus, *Species Plantarum* 2: 1061. 1753.
"Habitat in Europae aquosis." RCN: 7731.
Type not designated.
Original material: *Amman 60*, Herb. Linn. No. 1241.5 (LINN); [icon] in Ray, Syn. Meth. Stirp. Brit., ed. 3: 131, t. 5, f. 3. 1724.
Current name: ***Equisetum palustre*** L. (Equisetaceae).
Note: Hauke (in *Nova Hedwigia* 13: 106. 1966; 30: 425. 1978) noted that the material on sheet 1241.5 (LINN) belongs to *E. arvense* L. and so designated the diagnosis as the type. However, this is contrary to Art. 8.1.

Equisetum sylvaticum Linnaeus, *Species Plantarum* 2: 1061. 1753.
"Habitat in Europae septentrionalis pratis sylvaticis." RCN: 7729.

Lectotype (Jonsell & Jarvis in *Nordic J. Bot.* 14: 148. 1994): Herb. Linn. No. 1241.1 (LINN).
Current name: ***Equisetum sylvaticum*** L. (Equisetaceae).
Note: Hauke (in *Nova Hedwigia* 30: 438. 1978) indicated both 1241.1 and 1241.2 (LINN) as the type. However, these two collections are evidently not part of a single gathering so Art. 9.15 does not apply.

Eranthemum angustatum Linnaeus, *Mantissa Plantarum Altera*: 171. 1771, *nom. illeg.*
["Habitat in Aethiopia."] Sp. Pl. 2: 629 (1753). RCN: 63.
Replaced synonym: *Selago dubia* L. (1753).
Lectotype (Wijnands, *Bot. Commelins*: 192. 1983): [icon] *"Thymaelea foliis angustissimis linearibus, flosculis spicatis"* in Burman, Rar. Afric. Pl.: 130, t. 47, f. 3. 1739.
Current name: ***Microdon dubius*** (L.) Hilliard (Globulariaceae).

Eranthemum capense Linnaeus, *Species Plantarum* 1: 9. 1753.
"Habitat in Aethiopia." RCN: 61.
Lectotype (Vollesen in Jarvis & al., *Regnum Veg.* 127: 45. 1993): Herb. Hermann 4: 42, No. 15 (BM-000628190).
Generitype of *Eranthemum* Linnaeus.
Current name: ***Eranthemum capense*** L. (Acanthaceae).

Erethia tinifolia Linnaeus, *Flora Jamaicensis*: 14. 1759, *orth. var.*
["Habitat in Jamaica."] Sp. Pl., ed. 2, 1: 275 (1762). RCN: 1528.
Lectotype (Miller in *Ann. Missouri Bot. Gard.* 76: 1069. 1989): Herb. Linn. No. 254.1 (LINN).
Current name: ***Ehretia tinifolia*** L. (Boraginaceae).
Note: An orthographic variant of the earlier *Ehretia tinifolia* L. (1759).

Erica abietina Linnaeus, *Species Plantarum* 1: 355. 1753.
"Habitat in Aethiopia." RCN: 2730, 2809.
Lectotype (designated here by Oliver): [icon] *"Erica, Africana, Abietis folio longiore & tenuiore, floroibus oblongis, saturate rubris"* in Seba, Locupl. Rer. Nat. Thes. 1: 31, t. 21, f. 1. 1734 (see p. 158).
Current name: ***Erica abietina*** L. (Ericaceae).
Note: Salter (in *J. S. African Bot.* 8: 280. 1942) interpreted this name via the cited Seba plate (illustrated as f. 1), but fell short of calling it the type.

Erica absinthoides Linnaeus, *Systema Naturae,* ed. 12, 2: 269; *Mantissa Plantarum*: 66. 1767.
"Habitat ad Cap. b. spei." RCN: 2786.
Lectotype (designated here by Oliver): Herb. Linn. No. 498.63 (LINN).
Current name: ***Erica hispidula*** L. (Ericaceae).

Erica albens Linnaeus, *Diss. Botanicum de Erica*: 10. 1770.
RCN: 2745.
Lectotype (designated here by Oliver): *Tulbagh 39*, Herb. Linn. No. 498.58 (LINN).
Current name: ***Erica albens*** L. (Ericaceae).

Erica arborea Linnaeus, *Species Plantarum* 1: 353, 1200. 1753.
"Habitat in Europa australi." RCN: 2725, 2780.
Lectotype (Jarvis & McClintock in *Taxon* 39: 518. 1990): Herb. Burser XXV: 42 (UPS).
Current name: ***Erica arborea*** L. (Ericaceae).
Note: Pichi Sermolli & Heiniger (in *Webbia* 9: 20–25. 1953) discussed the protologue in some detail but erroneously believed there to be no original material for the name.

Erica articularis Linnaeus, *Systema Naturae,* ed. 12, 2: 269; *Mantissa Plantarum*: 65. 1767.
"Habitat ad Cap. b. spei." RCN: 2737, 2788.

E

Neotype (designated here by Oliver): South Africa. Cape Peninsula, 3418AB, lower eastern slopes of Steenberg, 16 Mar 1936, *Salter 5946* (BOL; iso- SAM).
Current name: ***Erica articularis*** L. (Ericaceae).

Erica australis Linnaeus, *Diss. Botanicum de Erica*: 9. 1770.
RCN: 2741.
Lectotype (Jarvis & McClintock in *Taxon* 39: 518. 1990): *Alströmer 80*, Herb. Linn. No. 498.50 (LINN).
Current name: ***Erica australis*** L. (Ericaceae).

Erica baccans Linnaeus, *Diss. Botanicum de Erica*: 9. 1770.
RCN: 2734.
Lectotype (designated here by Oliver): Herb. Linn. No. 498.37 (LINN).
Current name: ***Erica baccans*** L. (Ericaceae).

Erica bergiana Linnaeus, *Diss. Botanicum de Erica*: 9. 1770.
RCN: 2717.
Lectotype (designated here by Oliver): Herb. Linn. No. 498.7 (LINN).
Current name: ***Erica bergiana*** L. (Ericaceae).

Erica bruniades Linnaeus, *Species Plantarum* 1: 354. 1753.
"Habitat in Aethiopia." RCN: 2764, 2799.
Lectotype (designated here by Oliver): [icon] *"Eriocephalos Bruniades Ericaeformis, Monomotapensis, capitulis globulorum instar, interius cavis & densa lanugine tectis"* in Plukenet, Almag. Mant.: 69, t. 347, f. 9. 1700. – Voucher: Herb. Sloane 102: 180 (BM-SL).
Current name: ***Erica bruniades*** L. (Ericaceae).

Erica caffra Linnaeus, *Species Plantarum* 1: 353. 1753.
"Habitat in Aethiopia." RCN: 2732, 2777.
Lectotype (designated here by Oliver): Herb. Clifford: 148, *Erica* 7 (BM-000558645).
Current name: ***Erica caffra*** L. (Ericaceae).

Erica calycina Linnaeus, *Species Plantarum*, ed. 2, 1: 507. 1762, *nom. cons.*
"Habitat in Aethiopia." RCN: 2738, 2797.
Conserved type (Cafferty & al. in *Taxon* 51: 810. 2003 [2002]): South Africa. Cape Town, 3318CD, Tafelberg [Table Mountain], plateau near reservoir, 28 Nov 1897, *W. Froembling 326* (NBG).
Current name: ***Erica calycina*** L. (Ericaceae).

Erica capitata Linnaeus, *Species Plantarum* 1: 355. 1753.
"Habitat in Aethiopia." RCN: 2747, 2800.
Lectotype (designated here by Oliver): [icon] *"Erica, Africana, calyce lanuginoso, ex viridi luteo, capitulum referente, flosculis concoloribus, extus lanugine obsitis"* in Seba, Locupl. Rer. Nat. Thes. 1: 30, t. 20, f. 1. 1734.
Current name: ***Erica capitata*** L. (Ericaceae).

Erica carnea Linnaeus, *Species Plantarum* 1: 355. 1753, *nom. cons.*
"Habitat in Pannonia, Helvetia." RCN: 2769, 2801.
Lectotype (Ross in *J. Linn. Soc., Bot.* 60: 65. 1967): [icon] *"Erica Coris folio IX"* in Clusius, Rar. Pl. Hist. 1: 44. 1601.
Current name: ***Erica carnea*** L. (Ericaceae).

Erica cerinthoides Linnaeus, *Species Plantarum*, ed. 2, 1: 505. 1762.
"Habitat in Aethiopia." RCN: 2754, 2808.
Lectotype (designated here by Oliver): [icon] *"Erica coris folio hispido, cerinthoides africana"* in Breyn, Exot. Pl. Cent.: 25, t. 13. 1678.
Current name: ***Erica cerinthoides*** L. (Ericaceae).

Erica ciliaris Linnaeus, *Species Plantarum* 1: 354. 1753.
"Habitat in Lusitania." RCN: 2750, 2789.
Lectotype (McClintock in *Bot. J. Linn. Soc.* 80: 207. 1980): Herb. Linn. No. 498.64, smaller specimen (LINN).
Current name: ***Erica ciliaris*** L. (Ericaceae).

Erica cinerea Linnaeus, *Species Plantarum* 1: 352. 1753.
"Habitat in Europa media." RCN: 2739, 2775.
Lectotype (Jarvis & McClintock in *Taxon* 39: 518. 1990): Herb. Linn. No. 498.46 (LINN).
Generitype of *Erica* Linnaeus.
Current name: ***Erica cinerea*** L. (Ericaceae).
Note: Erica cinerea, with the type designated by Jarvis & McClintock, was proposed as conserved type of the genus by Jarvis (in *Taxon* 41: 572. 1992). However, the proposal was eventually ruled unnecessary by the General Committee (see Barrie, *l.c.* 55: 795–796. 2006 for a review of the history of this and related proposals).

Erica coccinea Linnaeus, *Species Plantarum* 1: 355. 1753.
"Habitat in Aethiopia." RCN: 2753, 2805.

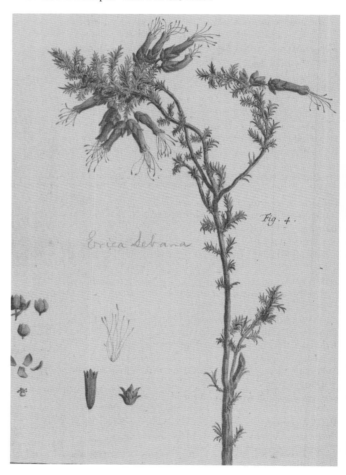

Lectotype (Oliver & al. in Oliver & Oliver in *Bothalia* 32: 38. 2002): [icon] *"Erica, Africana, angustifolia, glabra, floribus longis, tubulosis, dependentibus, coccineis, cum longissimis filamentis, seu appendicibus, concoloribus"* in Seba, Locupl. Rer. Nat. Thes. 1: 32, t. 21, f. 4. 1734.
Current name: ***Erica coccinea*** L. (Ericaceae).
Note: Salter (in *J. S. African Bot.* 8: 280, f. 4. 1942) reproduced the Seba plate subsequently designated as the type.

Erica comosa Linnaeus, *Mantissa Plantarum Altera*: 234. 1771, *nom. illeg.*
"Habitat ad Cap. b. spei." RCN: 2760.
Replaced synonym: *Erica transparens* P.J. Bergius (1767).
Type not designated.
Current name: ***Erica transparens*** P.J. Bergius (Ericaceae).
Note: An illegitimate replacement name for *E. transparens* P.J. Bergius (1767).

Erica corifolia Linnaeus, *Species Plantarum* 1: 355. 1753, *nom. cons.*
"Habitat in Aethiopia." RCN: 2736, 2787.
Conserved type (Cafferty & al. in *Taxon* 51: 810. 2003 [2002]): South Africa. Cape District, Bothasig, (Bosmansdam) 3318DC, 27 Oct 1965, *E. Esterhuysen 31332* (NBG; iso- BOL).
Current name: ***Erica corifolia*** L. (Ericaceae).

Erica cubica Linnaeus, *Diss. Botanicum de Erica*: 10. 1770.
RCN: 2756.
Lectotype (designated here by Oliver): Herb. Linn. "18 Erica cubica" (UPS). – Epitype (designated here by Oliver): South Africa. SW Cape Province, 3320CD, Swellendam State Forest, "Plaat" above Wamakersbos, lower slopes of Langeberg, ca. 1,500ft, fairly frequent, pink, 2 Oct 1979, *Taylor 10032* (NBG; iso- PRE).
Current name: ***Erica cubica*** L. (Ericaceae).

Erica curviflora Linnaeus, *Species Plantarum* 1: 354. 1753.
"Habitat in Aethiopia." RCN: 2752, 2806.
Lectotype (Oliver & Cafferty in Oliver & Oliver in *Bothalia* 35: 128. 2005): Herb. Clifford: 148, *Erica 10* (BM).
Current name: ***Erica curviflora*** L. (Ericaceae).

Erica daboecii Linnaeus, *Species Plantarum*, ed. 2, 1: 509. 1762, *nom. illeg.*
"Habitat in Hiberniae Gallovidia in montibus Mayo, solo caespitoso." RCN: 3099.
Replaced synonym: *Vaccinium cantabricum* Huds. (1762).
Replaced synonym of: *Andromeda daboecii* L. (1767), *nom. illeg.*
Lectotype (Nelson in *Watsonia* 23: 55, f. 1. 2000): [icon] *"Erica Hibernica fol. Myrti pilosis subtus incanis"* in Petiver, Gazophyl. Nat.: 42, t. 27, f. 4. 1702–1709.
Current name: ***Daboecia cantabrica*** (Huds.) K. Koch (Ericaceae).
Note: An illegitimate renaming of *Vaccinium cantabricum* Hudson, *Fl. Anglica*: 143 (Jun 1762), to which Linnaeus refers explicitly in the protologue (Sep 1762). See extensive discussion of the history of this name by Nelson (in *Watsonia* 23: 48–52. 2000).

Erica denticulata Linnaeus, *Mantissa Plantarum Altera*: 229. 1771.
"Habitat ad Cap. b. Spei. D. Bergius communicavit." RCN: 2757.
Lectotype (designated here by Oliver): "Erica denticulata" in Herb. Bergius (SBT).
Current name: ***Erica denticulata*** L. (Ericaceae).

Erica depressa Linnaeus, *Diss. Botanicum de Erica*: 9. 1770.
"Habitat ad Cap. b. spei." RCN: 2718.
Lectotype (designated here by Oliver): Herb. Linn. No. 498.8 (LINN).
Current name: ***Erica depressa*** L. (Ericaceae).

Erica empetrifolia Linnaeus, *Species Plantarum*, ed. 2, 1: 507. 1762, *orth. var.*
"Habitat in Aethiopia." RCN: 2743, 2813.
Neotype (designated here by Oliver): Herb. Linn. No. 498.52 (LINN).
Current name: ***Erica empetrina*** L. (Ericaceae).
Note: An orthographic variant of *E. empetrina* L. (1759).

Erica empetrina Linnaeus, *Systema Naturae*, ed. 10, 2: 1003. 1759.
["Habitat in Aethiopia."] Sp. Pl., ed. 2, 1: 507 (1762). RCN: 2743.
Neotype (designated here by Oliver): Herb. Linn. No. 498.52 (LINN).
Current name: ***Erica empetrina*** L. (Ericaceae).

Erica fastigiata Linnaeus, *Systema Naturae*, ed. 12, 2: 270; *Mantissa Plantarum*: 66. 1767.
"Habitat ad Cap. b. spei." RCN: 2755, 2796.
Lectotype (designated here by Oliver): *N.L. Burman 13*, Herb. Linn. No. 498.72 (LINN).
Current name: ***Erica fastigiata*** L. (Ericaceae).

Erica gnaphaloides Linnaeus, *Species Plantarum* 1: 356. 1753.
"Habitat in Aethiopia." RCN: 2735, 2793.
Neotype (designated here by Oliver): South Africa. Cape Peninsula, 3418AB, Kenilworth Race Course, Wetton Road end, above hollow filled with water in winter, 18 Nov 1970 *Esterhuysen 32538* (BOL; iso- K, NBG).
Current name: ***Erica gnaphaloides*** L. (Ericaceae).

Erica granulata Linnaeus, *Diss. Botanicum de Erica*: 10. 1770.
RCN: 2759.
Lectotype (designated here by Oliver): Herb. Linn. No. 498.77 (LINN).
Current name: ***Erica multumbellifera*** P.J. Bergius (Ericaceae).

Erica halicacaba Linnaeus, *Plantae Rariores Africanae*: 11. 1760.
["Habitat in Aethiopia."] Sp. Pl., ed. 2, 1: 507 (1762). RCN: 2714, 2795.
Neotype (designated here by Oliver): South Africa. Wynberg Division, 3418AB, Karbonkelberg, rocky ledges facing south near The Sentinel, 1,000ft, 14 Sep 1964, *Chater in STE 30095* (NBG).
Current name: ***Erica halicacaba*** L. (Ericaceae).

Erica herbacea Linnaeus, *Species Plantarum* 1: 352. 1753.
"Habitat in Europa australiori." RCN: 2769, 2802.
Lectotype (Ross in *J. Linn. Soc., Bot.* 60: 67. 1967): [icon] *"Erica Coris folio VIII"* in Clusius, Rar. Pl. Hist. 1: 44. 1601.
Current name: ***Erica carnea*** L. (Ericaceae).
Note: See discussion by Rauschert (in *Feddes Repert.* 83: 650. 1972) and McClintock & Wijnands (in *Taxon* 31: 319. 1982). *Erica carnea* is now conserved against *E. herbacea* L. (see *Taxon* 39: 294. 1990).

Erica hispidula Linnaeus, *Species Plantarum*, ed. 2, 2: 1672. 1763.
"Habitat ad Cap. b. spei. Schreber." RCN: 2811.
Lectotype (designated here by Oliver): Herb. Linn. No. 498.65 (LINN).
Current name: ***Erica hispidula*** L. (Ericaceae).

Erica imbricata Linnaeus, *Species Plantarum*, ed. 2, 1: 503. 1762, *nom. cons.*
"Habitat in Aethiopia." RCN: 2765, 2792.
Conserved type (Cafferty & al. in *Taxon* 51: 811. 2003 [2002]): South Africa. Cape Peninsula, 3418AB, Tokai Flats, 1 Oct 1916, *W. Foley 10* (NBG; iso- BM).
Current name: ***Erica imbricata*** L. (Ericaceae).

Erica mammosa Linnaeus, *Diss. Botanicum de Erica*: 9. 1770.
RCN: 2731.
Lectotype (Oliver & al. in Oliver & Oliver in *Bothalia* 32: 45. 2002): *Tulbagh 17*, Herb. Linn. No. 498.33 (LINN).
Current name: ***Erica mammosa*** L. (Ericaceae).

Erica mauritanica Linnaeus, *Systema Naturae*, ed. 10, 2: 1002. 1759. RCN: 2773.
Lectotype (Ross in *J. Linn. Soc., Bot.* 60: 70. 1967): Herb. Linn. No. 498.10 (LINN).
Current name: ***Erica mauritanica*** L. (Ericaceae).

Erica mediterranea Linnaeus, *Diss. Botanicum de Erica*: 10. 1770. RCN: 2771.
Lectotype (Ross in *J. Linn. Soc., Bot.* 60: 67. 1967): Herb. Burser XXV: 44 (UPS).
Current name: ***Erica carnea*** L. (Ericaceae).

Erica melanthera Linnaeus, *Diss. Botanicum de Erica*: 10. 1770. RCN: 2748.
Lectotype (designated here by Oliver): Herb. Linn. No. 498.61 (LINN).
Current name: ***Erica melanthera*** L. (Ericaceae).

Erica mucosa Linnaeus, *Diss. Botanicum de Erica*: 9. 1770. RCN: 2716.
Lectotype (designated here by Oliver): *Tulbagh 12*, Herb. Linn. No. 498.6 (LINN).
Current name: ***Erica ferrea*** P.J. Bergius (Ericaceae).

Erica multiflora Linnaeus, *Species Plantarum* 1: 355. 1753. "Habitat Monspelii." RCN: 2770, 2804.
Lectotype (Jarvis & McClintock in *Taxon* 39: 519. 1990): [icon] *"Erica foliis corios multiflora"* in Bauhin & Cherler, Hist. Pl. Univ. 1(2): 356. 1650.
Current name: ***Erica multiflora*** L. (Ericaceae).

Erica nigrita Linnaeus, *Systema Naturae*, ed. 12, 2: 270; *Mantissa Plantarum*: 65. 1767.
"Habitat ad Cap. b. spei." RCN: 2722, 2803.
Neotype (designated here by Oliver): South Africa. Cape Peninsula (3318CD), Cecilia, E slopes of Table Mtn, 29 Oct 1946, *W.F. Barker 4282* (NBG).
Current name: ***Erica calycina*** L. (Ericaceae).

Erica nudiflora Linnaeus, *Diss. Botanicum de Erica*: 10. 1770. RCN: 2763.
Lectotype (designated here by Oliver): Herb. Linn. No. 498.89 (LINN).
Current name: ***Erica nudiflora*** L. (Ericaceae).

Erica pallidopurpurea Linnaeus, *Species Plantarum* 1: 354. 1753. "Habitat in Europa australi." RCN: 2781.
Replaced synonym of: *Erica purpurascens* L. (1762), *nom. illeg.*
Lectotype (Nelson in Cafferty & Jarvis in *Taxon* 51: 753. 2003 [2002]): [icon] *"Erica Coris folio VII"* in Clusius, Rar. Pl. Hist. 1: 44, 43. 1601.
Current name: ***Erica carnea*** L. (Ericaceae).
Note: Specific epithet spelled "pallido-purpurea" in the protologue.

Erica paniculata Linnaeus, *Species Plantarum*, ed. 2, 1: 508. 1762. "Habitat in Aethiopia." RCN: 2740, 2784.
Lectotype (designated here by Oliver): Herb. Linn. No. 498.49 (LINN).
Current name: ***Erica paniculata*** L. (Ericaceae).

Erica parviflora Linnaeus, *Systema Naturae*, ed. 10, 2: 1002. 1759.
["Habitat ad Cap. b. spei."] Sp. Pl., ed. 2, 1: 506 (1762). RCN: 2729, 2790.
Basionym of: *Erica pubescens* L. var. *parviflora* (L.) L. (1771).
Lectotype (designated here by Oliver): Herb. Linn. No. 498.26 (LINN).
Current name: ***Erica parviflora*** L. (Ericaceae).

Erica pentaphylla Linnaeus, *Species Plantarum*, ed. 2, 1: 506. 1762. "Habitat in Aethiopia." RCN: 2721, 2810.
Lectotype (designated here by Oliver): Herb. Linn. No. 498.11 (LINN).
Current name: ***Erica caffra*** L. (Ericaceae).

Erica persoluta Linnaeus, *Diss. Botanicum de Erica*: 9. 1770. RCN: 2727.
Lectotype (designated here by Oliver): *N.L. Burman 73*, Herb. Linn. No. 498.22 (LINN).
Current name: ***Erica subdivaricata*** P.J. Bergius (Ericaceae).

Erica petiveri Linnaeus, *Diss. Botanicum de Erica*: 10. 1770. RCN: 2762.
Lectotype (Oliver & al. in Oliver & Oliver in *Bothalia* 32: 38. 2002): [icon] *"Erica petiveri"* in Linnaeus, Diss. Bot. Erica: 10, unnumbered plate, f. 50. 1770 (see p. 100).
Current name: ***Erica coccinea*** L. (Ericaceae).

Erica physodes Linnaeus, *Systema Naturae*, ed. 10, 2: 1002. 1759.
["Habitat in Aethiopia."] Sp. Pl., ed. 2, 1: 507 (1762). RCN: 2742, 2794.
Lectotype (designated here by Oliver): Herb. Burman (G).
Current name: ***Erica physodes*** L. (Ericaceae).

Erica pilulifera Linnaeus, *Species Plantarum* 1: 355. 1753. "Habitat in Aethiopia." RCN: 2719, 2798.
Lectotype (designated here by Oliver): Herb. Linn. No. 498.9 (LINN).
Current name: ***Erica pilulifera*** L. (Ericaceae).

Erica planifolia Linnaeus, *Species Plantarum*, ed. 2, 1: 508. 1762. "Habitat in Aethiopia." RCN: 2723, 2785.
Lectotype (designated here by Oliver): Herb. Linn. No. 498.16 (LINN).
Current name: ***Erica planifolia*** L. (Ericaceae).

Erica plukenetii Linnaeus, *Species Plantarum* 1: 356. 1753. "Habitat in Aethiopia." RCN: 2761, 2814.
Lectotype (Oliver & al. in Oliver & Oliver in *Bothalia* 32: 41. 2002): [icon] *"Chamaepitys Aethiopica foliis laete virentibus, flore oblongo, phoeniceo, plusquam eleganti, sive Plusqueneti"* in Plukenet, Almag. Mant.: 45, t. 344, f. 3. 1700. – Voucher: Herb. Sloane 89: 11 (BM-SL).
Current name: ***Erica plukenetii*** L. (Ericaceae).
Note: Specific epithet spelled "plukeneti" in the protologue.

Erica pubescens Linnaeus, *Species Plantarum*, ed. 2, 1: 506. 1762. "Habitat in Aethiopia." RCN: 2729, 2812.
Lectotype (designated here by Oliver): Herb. Linn. No. 498.25 (LINN).
Current name: ***Erica pubescens*** L. (Ericaceae).

Erica pubescens Linnaeus var. **parviflora** (Linnaeus) Linnaeus, *Mantissa Plantarum Altera*: 374. 1771.
["Habitat ad Cap. b. spei."] Sp. Pl., ed. 2, 1: 506 (1762). RCN: 2729, 2790.
Basionym: *Erica parviflora* L. (1759).
Lectotype (designated here by Oliver): Herb. Linn. No. 498.26 (LINN).
Current name: ***Erica parviflora*** L. (Ericaceae).

Erica purpurascens Linnaeus, *Species Plantarum*, ed. 2, 1: 503. 1762, *nom. illeg.*
"Habitat in Europa australi." RCN: 2767, 2781.

Replaced synonym: *Erica pallidopurpurea* L. (1753).
Lectotype (Nelson in Cafferty & Jarvis in *Taxon* 51: 753. 2003 [2002]): [icon] *"Erica Coris folio VII"* in Clusius, Rar. Pl. Hist. 1: 44, 43. 1601.
Current name: ***Erica carnea*** L. (Ericaceae).
Note: An illegitimate replacement name for *E. pallidopurpurea* L. (1753).

Erica ramentacea Linnaeus, *Systema Naturae,* ed. 12, 2: 269; *Mantissa Plantarum*: 65. 1767.
"Habitat ad Cap. b. spei." RCN: 2726, 2782.
Neotype (designated here by Oliver): South Africa. Cape Peninsula, 3418AB, Kenilworth Race course, sandy flats with short restiads, mainly in hollows, 100ft, 18 Dec 1959, *Oliver 382* (NBG).
Current name: ***Erica multumbellifera*** P.J. Bergius (Ericaceae).

Erica regerminans Linnaeus, *Diss. Botanicum de Erica*: 9. 1770.
RCN: 2715.
Lectotype (designated here by Oliver): *Tulbagh 47*, Herb. Linn. No. 498.5 (LINN).
Current name: ***Erica regerminans*** L. (Ericaceae).

Erica scoparia Linnaeus, *Species Plantarum* 1: 353. 1753.
"Habitat Monspelii, in Hispania, & Europa australi." RCN: 2724, 2776.
Lectotype (Jarvis & McClintock in *Taxon* 39: 519. 1990): Herb. Linn. No. 498.17 (LINN).
Current name: ***Erica scoparia*** L. (Ericaceae).

Erica spumosa Linnaeus, *Plantae Rariores Africanae*: 11. 1760.
["Habitat in Aethiopia."] Sp. Pl., ed. 2, 1: 508 (1762). RCN: 2746, 2793.
Lectotype (designated here by Oliver): Herb. Linn. No. 498.59 (LINN).
Current name: ***Erica spumosa*** L. (Ericaceae).

Erica tenuifolia Linnaeus, *Systema Naturae,* ed. 10, 2: 1002. 1759.
["Habitat in Aethiopia."] Sp. Pl., ed. 2, 1: 507 (1762). RCN: 2744, 2783.
Lectotype (designated here by Oliver): Herb. Linn. No. 498.55 (LINN). – Epitype (designated here by Oliver): South Africa. Cape Peninsula, 3318CD, Table Mountain, top of and near the face, on rocks, pale pink, 24 Jan 1929, *Gillet 3351* (NBG; iso- BM).
Current name: ***Erica tenuifolia*** L. (Ericaceae).

Erica tetralix Linnaeus, *Species Plantarum* 1: 353. 1753.
"Habitat in Europae borealis paludibus cespitosis." RCN: 2728, 2779.
Lectotype (McClintock in *Bot. J. Linn. Soc.* 80: 209. 1980): Herb. Linn. No. 498.24 (LINN).
Current name: ***Erica tetralix*** L. (Ericaceae).
Note: The typification of this name was also discussed by Jarvis & McClintock (in *Taxon* 39: 519. 1990).

Erica triflora Linnaeus, *Species Plantarum* 1: 354. 1753.
"Habitat in Aethiopia." RCN: 2733, 2791.
Neotype (designated here by Oliver): Herb. Linn. No. 498.35 (LINN).
Current name: ***Erica triflora*** L. (Ericaceae).

Erica tubiflora Linnaeus, *Species Plantarum,* ed. 2, 1: 505. 1762.
"Habitat in Aethiopia." RCN: 2751, 2807.
Lectotype (designated here by Oliver): Herb. Linn. No. 498.67 (LINN).
Current name: ***Erica curviflora*** L. (Ericaceae).

Erica umbellata Linnaeus, *Species Plantarum* 1: 352. 1753.
"Habitat in Lusitania." RCN: 2766, 2774.
Lectotype (Ross in *J. Linn. Soc., Bot.* 60: 65. 1967): *Löfling s.n.*, Herb. Linn. No. 498.97 (LINN).
Current name: ***Erica umbellata*** L. (Ericaceae).
Note: The typification of this name was also discussed by Jarvis & McClintock (in *Taxon* 39: 519. 1990).

Erica vagans Linnaeus, *Diss. Botanicum de Erica*: 10. 1770, *nom. cons.*
"Habitat in Africa; etiam Tolosae." RCN: 2768.
Conserved type (McClintock in *Taxon* 38: 526. 1989): England. Cornwall, Goonhilly, 12 Jul 1932, *Turrill s.n.* (K).
Current name: ***Erica vagans*** L. (Ericaceae).

Erica viridipurpurea Linnaeus, *Species Plantarum* 1: 353. 1753, *nom. utique rej. prop.*
"Habitat in Lusitania." RCN: 2720, 2778.
Type not designated.
Original material: Herb. Clifford: 148, *Erica* 5? (BM); [icon] in Clusius, Rar. Pl. Hist. 1: 42. 1601.
Current name: ***Erica erigena*** R. Ross (Ericaceae).
Note: Specific epithet spelled "viridi-purpurea" in the protologue. Cafferty & Nelson (in *Taxon* 54: 206. 2005) proposed the rejection of the name as the only available type element is identifiable as *E. erigena* R. Ross (1969), a name in widespread current use.

Erica viscaria Linnaeus, *Diss. Botanicum de Erica*: 10. 1770.
RCN: 2758.
Lectotype (Oliver & al. in Oliver & Oliver in *Bothalia* 32: 56. 2002): *Tulbagh 115*, Herb. Linn. No. 498.74 (LINN).
Current name: ***Erica viscaria*** L. (Ericaceae).

Erica vulgaris Linnaeus, *Species Plantarum* 1: 352. 1753.
"Habitat in Europae campestribus sterilibus frequens." RCN: 2712, 2772.
Lectotype (Jarvis & McClintock in *Taxon* 39: 519. 1990): Herb. Linn. No. 141 (LAPP).
Current name: ***Calluna vulgaris*** (L.) Hull (Ericaceae).

Erigeron acris Linnaeus, *Species Plantarum* 2: 863. 1753.
"Habitat in Europae apricis, siccis." RCN: 6252.
Lectotype (Huber in *Veröff. Geobot. Inst. E.T.H. Stiftung Rübel Zürich* 114: 44. 1993): Herb. Linn. No. 994.16 (LINN).
Current name: ***Erigeron acris*** L. (Asteraceae).
Note: Specific epithet spelled "acre" in the protologue.

Erigeron aegyptiacus Linnaeus, *Systema Naturae,* ed. 12, 2: 549; *Mantissa Plantarum*: 112. 1767.
"Habitat in Sicilia, Aegypto." RCN: 6250.
Type not designated.
Original material: Herb. Linn. No. 994.14 (LINN); [icon] in Morison, Pl. Hist. Univ. 3: 114, s. 7, t. 20, f. 14. 1699; [icon] in Boccone, Icon. Descr. Rar. Pl. Siciliae: 13, 14, t. 7, f. B. 1674.
Current name: ***Conyza aegyptiaca*** (L.) Aiton (Asteraceae).
Note: Specific epithet spelled "aegyptiacum" in the protologue.

Erigeron alpinus Linnaeus, *Species Plantarum* 2: 864. 1753.
"Habitat in Alpibus Helvetiae." RCN: 6253.
Lectotype (Huber in *Veröff. Geobot. Inst. E.T.H. Stiftung Rübel Zürich* 114: 34. 1993): *Séguier*, Herb. Linn. No. 994.18 (LINN).
Current name: ***Erigeron alpinus*** L. (Asteraceae).
Note: Specific epithet spelled "alpinum" in the protologue.

Erigeron bonariensis Linnaeus, *Species Plantarum* 2: 863. 1753.
"Habitat in America australi." RCN: 6247.
Lectotype (D'Arcy in Woodson & Schery in *Ann. Missouri Bot. Gard.* 62: 1021. 1975): Herb. Linn. No. 994.11 (LINN).
Current name: ***Conyza bonariensis*** (L.) Cronquist (Asteraceae).
Note: Specific epithet spelled "bonariense" in the protologue.
    Although Blake (in *Contr. Gray Herb.* 52: 27. 1917) suggested that the name was based on the cited Dillenian plate, this is insufficiently explicit to accept as formal typification. Burtt (in *Kew Bull.* 3: 369. 1948) provided an extensive discussion of the name but did not designate a type.

Erigeron camphoratus Linnaeus, *Species Plantarum* 2: 864. 1753.
"Habitat in Virginia." RCN: 6256.
Lectotype (Fernald in *Rhodora* 41: 461, pl. 569. 1939): *Clayton 165* (BM-000038849).
Current name: ***Pluchea camphorata*** (L.) DC. (Asteraceae).
Note: Specific epithet spelled "camphoratum" in the protologue.

Erigeron canadensis Linnaeus, *Species Plantarum* 2: 863. 1753.
"Habitat in Canada, Virginia, nunc in Europa australi." RCN: 6246.
Lectotype (D'Arcy in Woodson & Schery in *Ann. Missouri Bot. Gard.* 62: 1022. 1975): Herb. Linn. No. 994.10 (LINN).
Current name: ***Erigeron canadensis*** L. (Asteraceae).
Note: Specific epithet spelled "canadense" in the protologue.

Erigeron carolinianus Linnaeus, *Species Plantarum* 2: 863. 1753.
"Habitat in Carolina." RCN: 6245.
Lectotype (Torrey & Gray, *Fl. N. America* 2: 180. 1841): [icon] *"Virga aurea Carol. Linariae Monsp. foliis"* in Dillenius, Hort. Eltham. 2: 412, t. 306, f. 394. 1732. – Typotype: Herb. Sherard No. 1877 (OXF).
Current name: ***Euthamia caroliniana*** (L.) Greene (Asteraceae).
Note: Specific epithet spelled "carolinianum" in the protologue.
    There remains uncertainty about the identity of the plant illustrated by Dillenius (see Fernald in *Rhodora* 46: 323–330. 1944; Reveal in *Taxon* 40: 505–508. 1991).

Erigeron foetidus (Linnaeus) Linnaeus, *Species Plantarum,* ed. 2, 2: 1213. 1763.
"Habitat in Africa." RCN: 6258.
Basionym: *Inula foetida* L. (1759).
Lectotype (Wild in *Bol. Soc. Brot.,* sér. 2, 43: 217. 1969): [icon] *"Senecio, Africanus folio retuso"* in Miller, Fig. Pl. Gard. Dict. 2: 155, t. 233. 1758.
Current name: ***Nidorella foetida*** (L.) DC. (Asteraceae).
Note: Specific epithet spelled "foetidum" in the protologue.
    Linnaeus caused considerable confusion in his *Sp. Pl.,* ed. 2, 2 (1763) treatment by simultaneously recognising both *Inula foetida* (p. 1241), originally published in 1759 linked with an African element but in 1763 said to be from Malta, and *Erigeron foetidus* (p. 1213) from Africa. Interpretation has been complicated because Linnaeus cited the Miller illustration (now the lectotype of *I. foetida*) in the synonymy of both names. However, most authors (e.g. Brullo in *Webbia* 34: 290. 1979) have interpreted *I. foetida* (1759) as homotypic with *E. foetidus* (L.) L. (1763), and the Maltese taxon has been described as *Chiliadenus bocconei* Brullo.

Erigeron glutinosus Linnaeus, *Systema Naturae,* ed. 12, 2: 549; *Mantissa Plantarum*: 112. 1767.
"Habitat in Hispaniae, Galliae australis montosis maritimis." RCN: 6243.

Type not designated.
Original material: Herb. Linn. No. 994.7 (LINN); [icon] in Daléchamps, Hist. General. Pl. 2: 1201. 1586; [icon] in Barrelier, Pl. Galliam: 95, t. 158. 1714.
Note: Specific epithet spelled "glutinosum" in the protologue.
    Brullo (in *Webbia* 34: 290. 1979) stated that the unspecified Linnaean type was of uncertain identification, and that the name should therefore be treated as ambiguous. Linnaeus' name has been treated as the basionym of *Chiliadenus glutinosus* (L.) Fourr. but no original elements corresponding with this usage of the name appear to be in existence.

Erigeron gouanii Linnaeus, *Species Plantarum,* ed. 2, 2: 1212. 1763.
"Habitat – – – – D.D. Gouan." RCN: 6251.
Type not designated.
Original material: Herb. Linn. No. 345.5? (S); Herb. Linn. No. 994.15 (LINN).
Current name: ***Conyza gouanii*** (L.) Willd. (Asteraceae).
Note: Specific epithet spelled "gouani" in the protologue.

Erigeron gramineus Linnaeus, *Species Plantarum* 2: 864. 1753.
"Habitat in Sibiria. D. Gmelin." RCN: 6255.
Type not designated.
Original material: Herb. Linn. No. 994.25 (LINN); [icon] in Gmelin, Fl. Sibirica 2: 174, t. 76, f. 2. 1752.
Current name: ***Arctogeron gramineum*** (L.) DC. (Asteraceae).
Note: Specific epithet spelled "gramineum" in the protologue.

Erigeron graveolens Linnaeus, *Centuria I Plantarum*: 28. 1755.
"Habitat Monspelii." RCN: 6242.
Lectotype (Grierson in Davis, *Fl. Turkey* 5: 72. 1975): *Hasselquist,* Herb. Linn. No. 994.4 (LINN).
Current name: ***Dittrichia graveolens*** (L.) Greuter (Asteraceae).
Note: Although not listed by Davis (*Fl. Turkey* 10: 238. 1988) as a name typified in the Flora, Grierson's statement is clear.

Erigeron jamaicensis Linnaeus, *Systema Naturae,* ed. 10, 2: 1213. 1759.
["Habitat in Jamaica."] Sp. Pl., ed. 2, 2: 1211 (1763). RCN: 6248.
Lectotype (Nesom in Jarvis & Turland in *Taxon* 47: 360. 1998): *Browne,* Herb. Linn. No. 994.12 (LINN), see p. 195.
Current name: ***Erigeron jamaicensis*** L. (Asteraceae).
Note: Specific epithet spelled "jamaicense" in the protologue.

Erigeron obliquus Linnaeus, *Mantissa Plantarum Altera*: 574. 1771.
"Habitat in India orientali." RCN: 6240.
Lectotype (Randeria in *Blumea* 10: 287. 1960): Herb. Linn. No. 994.1 (LINN).
Current name: ***Blumea obliqua*** (L.) Druce (Asteraceae).
Note: Specific epithet spelled "obliquum" in the protologue.

Erigeron philadelphicus Linnaeus, *Species Plantarum* 2: 863. 1753.
"Habitat in Canada. Kalm." RCN: 6249.
Lectotype (Scott in Bosser & al., *Fl. Mascareignes* 109: 106. 1993): *Kalm,* Herb. Linn. No. 994.13 (LINN).
Current name: ***Erigeron philadelphicus*** L. (Asteraceae).
Note: Specific epithet spelled "philadelphicum" in the protologue.

Erigeron siculus Linnaeus, *Species Plantarum* 2: 864. 1753.
"Habitat in Siciliae paludosis." RCN: 6244.
Lectotype (Gamal-Eldin in *Phanerog. Monogr.* 14: 116. 1981): [icon] *"Conyza Sicula annua, lutea, foliis atroviridibus, caule rubente"* in Boccone, Icon. Descr. Rar. Pl. Siciliae: 62, 60, t. 31, f. 4. 1674.

Current name: **Pulicaria sicula** (L.) Moris (Asteraceae).
Note: Specific epithet spelled "siculum" in the protologue.

Erigeron tuberosus Linnaeus, *Species Plantarum* 2: 864. 1753.
"Habitat in Galloprovincia, G. Narbonensi, Syria." RCN: 6257.
Type not designated.
Original material: Herb. Burser VI: 101 (UPS); *Magnol*, Herb. Linn.
No. 994.26 (LINN); [icon] in Morison, Pl. Hist. Univ. 3: 114, s. 7,
t. 20, f. 15. 1699; [icon] in Morison, Pl. Hist. Univ. 3: 114, s. 7, t.
19, f. 20. 1699; [icon] in Morison, Pl. Hist. Univ. 3: 118, s. 7, t.
22, f. 7. 1699.
Current name: **Jasonia tuberosa** (L.) DC. (Asteraceae).
Note: Specific epithet spelled "tuberosum" in the protologue.

Erigeron uniflorus Linnaeus, *Species Plantarum* 2: 864. 1753.
"Habitat in Alpibus Lapponiae, Helvetiae." RCN: 6254.
Lectotype (Huber in Jarvis in *Taxon* 41: 563. 1992): Herb. Linn. No.
994.23 (LINN).
Generitype of *Erigeron* Linnaeus.
Current name: **Erigeron uniflorus** L. (Asteraceae).
Note: Erigeron uniflorus, with the type designated by Huber, was
proposed as conserved type of the genus by Jarvis (in *Taxon* 41: 563.
1992). However, the proposal was eventually ruled unnecessary by
the General Committee (see Barrie, *l.c.* 55: 795–796. 2006 for a
review of the history of this and related proposals).

Erigeron viscosus Linnaeus, *Species Plantarum* 2: 863. 1753.
"Habitat in Narbonensi, Hispania, Italia." RCN: 6241.
Lectotype (Turland in Jarvis & Turland in *Taxon* 47: 360. 1998):
Herb. Clifford: 409, *Aster* 19 (BM-000647101).
Current name: **Dittrichia viscosa** (L.) Greuter subsp. **viscosa**
(Asteraceae).
Note: Specific epithet spelled "viscosum" in the protologue.

Erinus africanus Linnaeus, *Species Plantarum* 2: 630. 1753.
"Habitat in Aethiopia." RCN: 4569.
Lectotype (Hilliard, *Manuleae, Tribe Scrophulariaceae*: 492. 1994):
Herb. A. van Royen No. 908.234–607 (L).
Current name: **Zaluzianskya villosa** F.W. Schmidt (Scrophulariaceae).

Erinus alpinus Linnaeus, *Species Plantarum* 2: 630. 1753.
"Habitat in Alpibus Helveticis, Pyrenaicis, Monspelii." RCN: 4568.
Lectotype (Sutton in Jarvis & al., *Regnum Veg.* 127: 45. 1993): Herb.
Linn. No. 789.1 (LINN).
Generitype of *Erinus* Linnaeus (vide Green, *Prop. Brit. Bot.*: 168.
1929).
Current name: **Erinus alpinus** L. (Scrophulariaceae).

Erinus capensis Linnaeus, *Mantissa Plantarum Altera*: 252. 1771.
"Habitat in Cap. b. spei arenosis." RCN: 4567.
Lectotype (Hilliard & Burtt in *Notes Roy. Bot. Gard. Edinburgh* 41: 26.
1983): Herb. Linn. No. 789.5 (LINN).
Current name: **Zaluzianskya capensis** (L.) Walp. (Scrophulariaceae).

Erinus laciniatus Linnaeus, *Species Plantarum* 2: 630. 1753.
"Habitat in Peru." RCN: 4571.
Type not designated.
Original material: [icon] in Feuillée, J. Obs. 3: 35, t. 25. 1725.
Current name: **Glandularia laciniata** (L.) Schnack & Covas
(Verbenaceae).

Erinus peruvianus Linnaeus, *Species Plantarum* 2: 630. 1753.
"Habitat in Peru." RCN: 4570.
Type not designated.
Original material: [icon] in Feuillée, J. Obs. 3: 36, f. 25. 1725.
Current name: **Verbena peruviana** (L.) Britton (Verbenaceae).

Eriocaulon decangulare Linnaeus, *Species Plantarum* 1: 87. 1753.
"Habitat in Americae septentrionalis paludibus." RCN: 734.
Lectotype (Reveal & al. in *Huntia* 7: 233. 1987): *Clayton 234 & 439*,
Herb. Linn. No. 105.4 (LINN; iso- BM).
Generitype of *Eriocaulon* Linnaeus (vide Hitchcock, *Prop. Brit. Bot.*:
122. 1929).
Current name: **Eriocaulon decangulare** L. (Eriocaulaceae).

Eriocaulon quinquangulare Linnaeus, *Species Plantarum* 1: 87. 1753.
"Habitat in India." RCN: 731.
Type not designated.
Original material: Herb. Hermann 2: 21, No. 48 (BM); [icon] in
Plukenet, Phytographia: t. 221, f. 7. 1692; Almag. Bot.: 336. 1696.
Current name: **Eriocaulon quinquangulare** L. (Eriocaulaceae).

Eriocaulon setaceum Linnaeus, *Species Plantarum* 1: 87. 1753.
"Habitat in India." RCN: 733.
Lectotype (Phillips in Polhill, *Fl. Trop. E. Africa, Eriocaulaceae*: 5.
1998): Herb. Hermann 1: 40, No. 50 (BM-000594471).
Current name: **Eriocaulon setaceum** L. (Eriocaulaceae).

Eriocaulon sexangulare Linnaeus, *Species Plantarum* 1: 87. 1753.
"Habitat in India." RCN: 732.
Lectotype (Trimen in *J. Linn. Soc., Bot.* 24: 136. 1887): Herb.
Hermann 1: 40, No. 49 (BM-000594471).
Current name: **Eriocaulon sexangulare** L. (Eriocaulaceae).

Eriocaulon triangulare Linnaeus, *Species Plantarum*, ed. 2, 1: 128.
1762.
"Habitat in Brasilia." RCN: 730.
Type not designated.
Original material: Herb. Linn. No. 105.1 (LINN); [icon] in Morison,
Pl. Hist. Univ. 3: 259, s. 8, t. 16, f. 17. 1699; [icon] in Breyn, Exot.
Pl. Cent.: 108, t. 50. 1678.
Current name: **Paepalanthus triangularis** (L.) Körn. (Eriocaulaceae).

Eriocephalus africanus Linnaeus, *Species Plantarum* 2: 926. 1753.
"Habitat in Aethiopia." RCN: 6702.
Type not designated.
Original material: Herb. Linn. No. 365.15 (S); [icon] in Dillenius,
Hort. Eltham. 1: 132, t. 110, f. 134. 1732; [icon] in Walther,
Design. Pl.: 1, t. 1. 1735.
Generitype of *Eriocephalus* Linnaeus.
Current name: **Eriocephalus africanus** L. (Asteraceae).
Note: Levyns (in *J. S. African Bot.* 7: 135. 1941) suggested that
Linnaeus' plant was likely to be the one then known as *E.*
umbellulatus Cass., adding "There is a type specimen of *E. africanus*
in the Linnaean herbarium so that at some future date it will be
possible to verify this assumption". However, the material she
presumably intended (1040.1, LINN) lacks a *Species Plantarum*
number (i.e. "1"), is a post-1753 addition to the herbarium, and is
not original material for the name. Müller & al. (in Germishuizen,
Fl. Southern Africa 33(4:1): 23. 2001) treated the Dillenius plate as
one of two iconotypes (the other being the ineligible (post-1753)
Hill t. 79). However, no explicit type choice was made.

Eriocephalus pectinifolius Linnaeus, *Systema Naturae*, ed. 12, 2: 579.
1767, *nom. illeg.*
RCN: 6701.
Replaced synonym: *Tanacetum frutescens* L. (1753).
Lectotype (Wijnands, *Bot. Commelins*: 77. 1983): Herb. Linn. No.
1039.3 (LINN).
Current name: **Hippia frutescens** (L.) L. (Asteraceae).
Note: An illegitimate replacement name in *Eriocephalus* for *Tanacetum*
frutescens L. (1753). In the protologue of *E. pectinifolius*, *T.*
"fruticosum" was cited in error for *T. frutescens*.

Eriocephalus racemosus Linnaeus, *Plantae Rariores Africanae*: 26. 1760.
RCN: 6703.
Type not designated.
Original material: Herb. Burman? (G); Herb. Linn. No. 1040.3 (LINN).
Current name: **Eriocephalus racemosus** L. (Asteraceae).

Eriophorum alpinum Linnaeus, *Species Plantarum* 1: 53. 1753.
"Habitat in Europae alpibus, locisque affinibus." RCN: 443.
Lectotype (Simpson in Cafferty & Jarvis in *Taxon* 53: 179. 2004): Herb. Linn. No. 72.4 (LINN).
Current name: **Scirpus hudsonianus** (Michx.) Fernald (Cyperaceae).

Eriophorum cyperinum Linnaeus, *Species Plantarum*, ed. 2, 1: 77. 1762.
"Habitat in America septentrionali." RCN: 442.
Lectotype (Reveal & al. in *Huntia* 7: 219. 1987): *Clayton 205* (BM-000051167).
Current name: **Scirpus cyperinus** (L.) Kunth (Cyperaceae).

Eriophorum polystachion Linnaeus, *Species Plantarum* 1: 52. 1753, *nom. utique rej.*
"Habitat in Europae uliginosis, turfosis." RCN: 440.
Lectotype (Novoselova in *Bot. Zhurn.* 79(11): 86. 1994): Herb. Linn. No. 72.2, middle specimen (LINN).
Current name: **Eriophorum angustifolium** Roth (Cyperaceae).

Eriophorum vaginatum Linnaeus, *Species Plantarum* 1: 52. 1753.
"Habitat in Europae frigidis sterilibus." RCN: 439.
Lectotype (Simpson in Jarvis & al., *Regnum Veg.* 127: 45–46. 1993): Herb. Burser I: 43 (UPS).
Generitype of *Eriophorum* Linnaeus (vide Hitchcock, *Prop. Brit. Bot.*: 119. 1929).
Current name: **Eriophorum vaginatum** L. (Cyperaceae).
Note: Hartvig (in Strid, *Mountain Fl. Greece* 2: 836. 1991) noted the existence of 72.1 (LINN), which Novoselova (in *Bot. Zhurn.* 79(12): 71. 1994) treated as "type". However, the latter post-dates Simpson's typification.

Eriophorum virginicum Linnaeus, *Species Plantarum* 1: 52. 1753.
"Habitat in Virginia." RCN: 441.
Lectotype (Novoselova in *Bot. Zhurn.* 79(11): 83. 1994): *Clayton 461*, Herb. Linn. No. 72.3 (LINN; iso- BM).
Current name: **Eriophorum virginicum** L. (Cyperaceae).

Erithalis fruticosa Linnaeus, *Systema Naturae,* ed. 10, 2: 930. 1759.
["Habitat in Jamaica."] Sp. Pl., ed. 2, 1: 251 (1762). RCN: 1393.
Type not designated.
Original material: Herb. Linn. No. 86. 9 (S); [icon] in Browne, Civ. Nat. Hist. Jamaica: 165, t. 17, f. 3. 1756.
Current name: **Erithalis fruticosa** L. (Rubiaceae).
Note: Negrón-Ortiz (in *Sida* 21: 1584. 2005) wrongly refers to the cited Browne plate as the holotype (there is also original material in S). Although this could be corrected to lectotype under Art. 9.8, the absence of "designated here" with the type statement (Art. 7.11) means this cannot be accepted as a formal typification (see Art. 9.8, Note 4).

Ervum ervilia Linnaeus, *Species Plantarum* 2: 738. 1753.
"Habitat in Gallia, Italia." RCN: 5429.
Lectotype (Chrtková-Zertová & al. in Rechinger, *Fl. Iranica* 140: 21. 1979): Herb. Linn. No. 907.8 (LINN).
Current name: **Vicia ervilia** (L.) Willd. (Fabaceae: Faboideae).

Ervum hirsutum Linnaeus, *Species Plantarum* 2: 738. 1753.
"Habitat in Europae agris." RCN: 5426.
Lectotype (Ali in *Bot. Not.* 120: 50. 1967): Herb. Linn. No. 907.5 (LINN).
Current name: **Vicia hirsuta** (L.) Gray (Fabaceae: Faboideae).
Note: Jarvis & al. (*Regnum Veg.* 127: 46. 1993) wrongly listed *E. hirstum* as the generitype, in error for *E. tetraspermum.* Some authors (e.g. Verdcourt in Milne-Redhead & Polhill, *Fl. Trop. E. Africa, Leguminosae* 4: 1072. 1971) have treated Herb. Clifford material as the type but the choice made by Ali is the earliest.

Ervum lens Linnaeus, *Species Plantarum* 2: 738. 1753.
"Habitat inter Galliae segetes." RCN: 5424.
Lectotype (Westphal, *Pulses Ethiopia, Taxon. Agric. Signif.*: 109, 112. 1974): Herb. Linn. No. 907.1, left specimen (LINN).
Current name: **Lens culinaris** Medik. (Fabaceae: Faboideae).

Ervum monanthos Linnaeus, *Species Plantarum* 2: 738. 1753.
"Habitat in Asia ruthenica." RCN: 5428.
Type not designated.
Original material: Herb. Linn. No. 907.6 (LINN).
Current name: **Vicia articulata** Hornem. (Fabaceae: Faboideae).

Ervum soloniense Linnaeus, *Centuria II Plantarum*: 28. 1756.
"Habitat in Anglia, Gallia." RCN: 5427.
Lectotype (Lassen in Turland & Jarvis in *Taxon* 46: 469. 1997): [icon] "*Vicia minima*" in Rivinus, Ordo Pl. Fl. Tetrapetal.: t. 55. 1691.
Current name: **Vicia lathyroides** L. (Fabaceae: Faboideae).
Note: Czefranova (in *Novosti Sist. Vyssh. Rast.* 8: 191. 1971) treated this as a *nomen ambiguum.*

Ervum tetraspermum Linnaeus, *Species Plantarum* 2: 738. 1753.
"Habitat inter Europae segetes." RCN: 5425.
Lectotype (Ali in *Bot. Not.* 120: 51. 1967): *Magnol*, Herb. Linn. No. 907.3 (LINN).
Generitype of *Ervum* Linnaeus (vide Green, *Prop. Brit. Bot.*: 175. 1929).
Current name: **Vicia tetrasperma** (L.) Schreb. (Fabaceae: Faboideae).
Note: Jarvis & al. (*Regnum Veg.* 127: 46. 1993) wrongly listed *E. hirsutum* as the generitype, in error for *E. tetraspermum.*

Eryngium alpinum Linnaeus, *Species Plantarum* 1: 233. 1753.
"Habitat in alpibus Helvetiae, Italiae." RCN: 1899.
Lectotype (Reduron in Wörz in *Stuttgarter Beitr. Naturk., A*, 596: 1. 1999): [icon] "*Alpinum caeruleum Genevense*" in Plantin, Pl. Stirp. Icon. 2: 23. 1581.
Current name: **Eryngium alpinum** L. (Apiaceae).
Note: Although there was an indication that the type designation was to be made elsewhere, the wording of Reduron's statement nevertheless means that his type choice dates from this work.

Eryngium amethystinum Linnaeus, *Species Plantarum* 1: 233. 1753.
"Habitat in Styriae montibus." RCN: 1898.
Lectotype (Wörz & al. in Jarvis & al. in *Taxon* 55: 212. 2006): Herb. Linn. No. 331.10 (LINN).
Current name: **Eryngium amethystinum** L. (Apiaceae).

Eryngium aquaticum Linnaeus, *Species Plantarum* 1: 232. 1753.
"Habitat in Virginia." RCN: 1892.
Lectotype (Wörz in *Stuttgarter Beitr. Naturk., A*, 596: 3. 1999): *Clayton 500*, Herb. Linn. No. 331.4 (LINN; iso- BM).
Current name: **Eryngium aquaticum** L. (Apiaceae).

Eryngium campestre Linnaeus, *Species Plantarum* 1: 233. 1753.
"Habitat in Germaniae, Galliae, Hispaniae, Italiae incultis." RCN: 1897.

Lectotype (Reduron & Wörz in Jarvis & al. in *Taxon* 55: 212. 2006): Herb. Linn. No. 331.9 (LINN).
Current name: ***Eryngium campestre*** L. (Apiaceae).

Eryngium foetidum Linnaeus, *Species Plantarum* 1: 232. 1753.
"Habitat in Virginia, Jamaica, Mexico, Canada." RCN: 1891.
Lectotype (Wörz in *Stuttgarter Beitr. Naturk., A,* 596: 19. 1999): [icon] *"Eryngium foliis angustis serratis foetidum"* in Sloane, Voy. Jamaica 1: 264, t. 156, f. 3. 1707. – Typotype: Herb. Sloane 5: 47 (BM-SL).
Current name: ***Eryngium foetidum*** L. (Apiaceae).

Eryngium maritimum Linnaeus, *Species Plantarum* 1: 233. 1753.
"Habitat ad Europae littora arenosa maritima." RCN: 1896.
Lectotype (Reduron & Jarvis in Jarvis & al., *Regnum Veg.* 127: 46. 1993): *Baeck s.n.*, Herb. Linn. No. 331.8 (LINN).
Generitype of *Eryngium* Linnaeus (vide Hitchcock, *Prop. Brit. Bot.*: 138. 1929).
Current name: ***Eryngium maritimum*** L. (Apiaceae).

Eryngium planum Linnaeus, *Species Plantarum* 1: 233. 1753.
"Habitat in Russia, Polonia, Austria, Helvetia." RCN: 1893.
Lectotype (designated here by Jury): Herb. Clifford: 87, *Eryngium* 1, sheet A (labelled "3") (BM-000558216).

Current name: ***Eryngium planum*** L. (Apiaceae).
Note: Jury & Southam (in Jarvis & al. in *Taxon* 55: 212. 2006) indicated "Herb. Clifford: 87, *Eryngium* 1, sheet A (labelled "4")" as the lectotype. Unfortunately, sheet A is labelled "3", and sheet B is labelled "4", making this type choice ineffective. However, a typification is now formalised here.

Eryngium pusillum Linnaeus, *Species Plantarum* 1: 233. 1753.
"Habitat in Hispania." RCN: 1894.
Lectotype (López González in *Anales Jard. Bot. Madrid* 42: 322. 1986): Herb. Clifford: 87, *Eryngium* 4 (BM-000558227).
Current name: ***Eryngium pusillum*** L. (Apiaceae).

Eryngium tricuspidatum Linnaeus, *Demonstr. Pl. Horto Upsaliensi*: 8. 1753.
"Habitat in Hispania, Loefl." RCN: 1895.
Lectotype (Jury & Southam in Jarvis & al. in *Taxon* 55: 212. 2006): Herb. Linn. No. 331.6 (LINN).
Current name: ***Eryngium tricuspidatum*** L. (Apiaceae).

Eryngium trifidum Linnaeus, *Demonstr. Pl. Horto Upsaliensi*: 8. 1753.
"Habitat in Hispania." RCN: 1897.
Type not designated.
Original material: [icon] in Barrelier, Pl. Galliam: 62, t. 36. 1714.
Current name: ***Eryngium* sp.** (Apiaceae).
Note: The application of this name is uncertain and the identity of the only original material, a Barrelier illustration, suggests that *E. trifidum* may be a candidate for rejection.

Erysimum alliaria Linnaeus, *Species Plantarum* 2: 660. 1753.
"Habitat in Europa sepibus, cultis, umbrosis." RCN: 4806.
Lectotype (Hedge in Cafferty & Jarvis in *Taxon* 51: 533. 2002): Herb. Clifford: 338, *Erysimum* 6 (BM-000646355).
Current name: ***Alliaria petiolata*** (M. Bieb.) Cavara & Grande (Brassicaceae).

Erysimum barbarea Linnaeus, *Species Plantarum* 2: 660. 1753.
"Habitat in Europa." RCN: 4805.
Lectotype (Jonsell & Jarvis in *Nordic J. Bot.* 22: 70. 2002): Herb. Linn. No. 837.2 (LINN).
Current name: ***Barbarea vulgaris*** W.T. Aiton (Brassicaceae).

Erysimum cheiranthoides Linnaeus, *Species Plantarum* 2: 661. 1753.
"Habitat ubique in Europae arvis." RCN: 4808.
Lectotype (Polatschek in *Ann. Naturhist. Mus. Wien* 78: 174. 1974): Herb. Linn. No. 837.6 (LINN).
Generitype of *Erysimum* Linnaeus (vide Green in *Bull. Misc. Inform. Kew* 1925: 55. 1925).
Current name: ***Erysimum cheiranthoides*** L. (Brassicaceae).
Note: Ball (in Jarvis & al., *Regnum Veg.* 127: 46. 1993) independently made the same type choice as Polatschek.

Erysimum hieraciifolium Linnaeus, *Centuria I Plantarum*: 18. 1755.
"Habitat in Gallia." RCN: 4809.
Type not designated.
Original material: Herb. Linn. No. 837.9 (LINN); Herb. Burser XI: 36 (UPS); Herb. Linn. No. 837.7 (LINN).
Current name: ***Erysimum hieracifolium*** L. (Brassicaceae).
Note: Specific epithet spelled "hieracifolium" in the protologue.
    This has frequently been treated as an ambiguous name but has been used in some recent treatments (e.g. Ball in Tutin & al., *Fl. Europaea*, ed. 2, 1: 335. 1993). For an extensive discussion, see Wisskirchen (in Wisskirchen & Haeupler, *Standardliste Farn-Blütenpfl. Deutschl.*: 206. 1998).

Erysimum officinale Linnaeus, *Species Plantarum* 2: 660. 1753.
"Habitat in Europae ruderatis." RCN: 4804.
Lectotype (Fawcett & Rendle, *Fl. Jamaica* 3: 240. 1914): Herb. Linn. No. 837.1 (LINN).
Current name: ***Sisymbrium officinale*** (L.) Scop. (Brassicaceae).

Erysimum repandum Linnaeus, *Demonstr. Pl. Horto Upsaliensi*: 17. 1753.
RCN: 4807.
Lectotype (Ebel in Cafferty & Jarvis in *Taxon* 51: 533. 2002): Herb. Linn. No. 837.5 (LINN).
Current name: ***Erysimum repandum*** L. (Brassicaceae).
Note: Polatschek (in *Ann. Naturhist. Mus. Wien* 78: 180. 1974) designated 837.4 (LINN) as lectotype but this is a post-1753 Arduino collection which is not original material for the name. Meikle (*Fl. Cyprus* 1: 162. 1977) indicated unspecified material at LINN as type, but did not distinguish between sheets 837.4 and 837.5, which do not appear to be part of a single gathering so Art. 9.15 does not apply.

Erythrina corallodendrum Linnaeus, *Species Plantarum* 2: 706. 1753.
"Habitat in Indiis." RCN: 5175.
Lectotype (Wijnands, *Bot. Commelins*: 163. 1983): [icon] *"Arbor Coral Americana"* in Commelin, Hort. Med. Amstelod. Pl. Rar. 1: 211, t. 108. 1697 (see p. 122).
Generitype of *Erythrina* Linnaeus (vide Green, *Prop. Brit. Bot.*: 173. 1929).
Current name: ***Erythrina corallodendron*** L. (Fabaceae: Faboideae).
Note: Fawcett & Rendle (*Fl. Jamaica* 4: 50. 1920) stated "Type in Herb. Linn." but they did not distinguish between 888.2 and 888.3 (LINN). As these two collections are not duplicates, Art. 9.15 does not apply and Wijnands' typification stands.

Erythrina corallodendrum Linnaeus var. **occidentalis** Linnaeus, *Species Plantarum* 2: 706. 1753.
RCN: 5175.
Lectotype (Wijnands, *Bot. Commelins*: 163. 1983): [icon] *"Arbor Coral Americana"* in Commelin, Hort. Med. Amstelod. Pl. Rar. 1: 211, t. 108. 1697.
Current name: ***Erythrina corallodendron*** L. (Fabaceae: Faboideae).
Note: Krukoff & Barneby (in *Lloydia* 37: 399–400. 1974) noted the existence of 888.2 and 888.3 (LINN) but did not accept them as original material. They conclude "it seems obvious that Commelin's plate and description should be regarded as representing the plant Linnaeus had in mind when he described var. occidentalis", but did not formally designate it as the type. This was done subsequently by Wijnands. The lectotype is an original element (and the type) of var. *occidentalis*. The autonym therefore has statutory priority over this name.

Erythrina corallodendrum Linnaeus var. **orientalis** Linnaeus, *Species Plantarum* 2: 706. 1753.
RCN: 5175.
Lectotype (Krukoff & Barneby in *Lloydia* 37: 431. 1974): [icon] *"Mouricou"* in Rheede, Hort. Malab. 6: 13, t. 7. 1686.
Current name: ***Erythrina variegata*** L. var. ***orientalis*** (L.) Merr. (Fabaceae: Faboideae).

Erythrina crista-galli Linnaeus, *Systema Naturae*, ed. 12, 2: 473; *Mantissa Plantarum*: 99. 1767.
"Habitat in Brasilia. D. Vandelli." RCN: 5178.
Lectotype (Howard, *Fl. Lesser Antilles* 4: 488. 1988): *Vandelli s.n.*, Herb. Linn. No. 888.4 (LINN), see p. 234.
Current name: ***Erythrina crista-galli*** L. (Fabaceae: Faboideae).

Note: Krukoff (in *Phytologia* 22: 250. 1971) noted seeing 888.5 (LINN) and added "it is clear that this name is correctly interpreted" but this falls short of a formal typification. In any case, this material has the annotation "Erythrina crista 93" – the "93" corresponding with the number cited in *Plantae Surinamenses*: 12 (1775), making it a post-1767 addition to the herbarium. Krukoff & Barneby (in *Lloydia* 37: 343. 1974) noted the existence of 888.4 (LINN), but did not indicate it as the type.

Erythrina herbacea Linnaeus, *Species Plantarum* 2: 706. 1753.
"Habitat in Carolina, Missipi [sic]." RCN: 5174.
Lectotype (Reveal in Turland & Jarvis in *Taxon* 46: 469. 1997): [icon] *"Corallodendron humile, spica florum longissima coccinea, radice crassissimo"* in Catesby, Nat. Hist. Carolina 2: 49, t. 49. 1736.
Current name: ***Erythrina herbacea*** L. (Fabaceae: Faboideae).
Note: Krukoff (in *Phytologia* 22: 255. 1971) and Krukoff & Barneby (in *Lloydia* 37: 343. 1974) noted seeing a photo of 888.1 (LINN), and confirmed its identity but concluded that it was not original material for the name. Ali (in Nasir & Ali, *Fl. W. Pakistan* 100: 236. 1977) designated this material as type but it is a post-1753 addition to the collection, and not original material for the name.

Erythrina picta Linnaeus, *Species Plantarum*, ed. 2, 2: 993. 1763.
"Habitat in India." RCN: 5176.
Type not designated.
Original material: [icon] in Rumphius, Herb. Amboin. 2: 234, t. 77. 1741.
Current name: ***Erythrina variegata*** L. (Fabaceae: Faboideae).

Erythrina piscipula Linnaeus, *Species Plantarum* 2: 707. 1753.
"Habitat in America calidiore." RCN: 5179.
Replaced synonym of: *Piscidia erythrina* L. (1759), *nom. illeg.*
Lectotype (Rudd in *Phytologia* 18: 486. 1969): [icon] *"Coral arbor polyphylla non spinosa, fraxini folio, siliqua alis foliaceis extantibus, rotae molendinariae fluviatilis, vel seminum laserpitii instar, aucta"* in Sloane, Voy. Jamaica 2: 39, t. 176, f. 4, 5. 1725. – Typotype: Herb. Sloane 6: 18 (BM-SL).
Current name: ***Piscidia piscipula*** (L.) Sarg. (Fabaceae: Faboideae).
Note: Although Fawcett & Rendle (*Fl. Jamaica* 4: 84. 1920) stated "Type in Herb. Mus. Brit.", they did not specify which material they intended.

Erythrina planisiliqua Linnaeus, *Systema Naturae*, ed. 10, 2: 1155. 1759.
["Habitat in America."] Sp. Pl., ed. 2, 2: 993 (1763). RCN: 5177.
Type not designated.
Original material: [icon] in Plumier in Burman, Pl. Amer.: 92, t. 102, f. 1. 1757.
Current name: ***Rhodopis planisiliqua*** (L.) Urb. (Fabaceae: Faboideae).

Erythrina variegata Linnaeus, *Herbarium Amboinense*: 10. 1754.
RCN: 5176.
Lectotype (Merrill, *Interpret. Rumph. Herb. Amb.*: 33, 276. 1917): [icon] *"Gelala Alba"* in Rumphius, Herb. Amboin. 2: 234, t. 77. 1741 (see p. 156).
Current name: ***Erythrina variegata*** L. (Fabaceae: Faboideae).

Erythronium dens-canis Linnaeus, *Species Plantarum* 1: 305. 1753.
"Habitat in Liguria, Allobrogibus, Augusta Taurinorum, Sibiria, Virginia." RCN: 2404.
Lectotype (Mathew in *Bot. J. Linn. Soc.* 109: 459. 1992): Herb. Linn. No. 424.1 (LINN).
Generitype of *Erythronium* Linnaeus.
Current name: ***Erythronium dens-canis*** L. (Liliaceae).

Erythroxylon areolatum Linnaeus, *Systema Naturae,* ed. 10, 2: 1035. 1759.
["Habitat in Jamaica."] Sp. Pl., ed. 2, 1: 613 (1762). RCN: 3330.
Type not designated.
Original material: Herb. Linn. No. 591.2 (LINN); *Browne 278*, Herb. Linn. No. 591.1 (LINN); [icon] in Browne, Civ. Nat. Hist. Jamaica: 278, t. 38, f. 2. 1756.
Current name: ***Erythroxylon areolatum*** L. (Erythroxylaceae).
Note: Although Plowman & Hensold (in *Brittonia* 56: 5. 2004) indicated 591.1 (LINN) as type, this choice was published after 1 Jan 2001 and so the omission of the phrase "designated here" or an equivalent (Art. 7.11) means that this choice is not effective.

Eschara divaricata Linnaeus, *Systema Naturae,* ed. 10, 1: 805. 1758.
"Habitat in O. Asiatico."
Lectotype (Huisman & Townsend in *Bot. J. Linn. Soc.* 113: 100, f. 2. 1993): Herb. Linn. No. 1297.4 (LINN).
Current name: ***Galaxaura divaricata*** (L.) Huisman & R.A. Towns. (Galaxauraceae).

Eschara fragilis Linnaeus, *Systema Naturae,* ed. 10, 1: 805. 1758.
"Habitat in Oceano Americano."
Basionym of: *Tubularia fragilis* (L.) L. (1767).
Lectotype (Huisman & Townsend in *Bot. J. Linn. Soc.* 113: 100, f. 1. 1993): Herb. Linn. No. 1297.1, upper specimen (LINN).
Current name: ***Tricleocarpa fragilis*** (L.) Huisman & R.A. Towns. (Galaxauraceae).

Ethulia bidentis Linnaeus, *Systema Naturae,* ed. 12, 2: 536; *Mantissa Plantarum*: 110. 1767.
"Habitat in India?" RCN: 6049.
Lectotype (Howard, *Fl. Lesser Antilles* 6: 566. 1989): Herb. Linn. No. 977.4 (LINN).
Current name: ***Flaveria bidentis*** (L.) Kuntze (Asteraceae).

Ethulia conyzoides Linnaeus filius, *Dec. Prima Pl. Horti Upsal.*: 1. 1762.
RCN: 6045.
Type not designated.
Original material: none traced.
Current name: ***Ethulia conyzoides*** L. f. (Asteraceae).

Ethulia divaricata Linnaeus, *Systema Naturae,* ed. 12, 2: 536; *Mantissa Plantarum*: 110. 1767.
"Habitat in India." RCN: 6047.
Lectotype (Grierson in Dassanayake & Fosberg, *Revised Handb. Fl. Ceylon* 1: 236. 1980): Herb. Linn. No. 988.48 (LINN).
Current name: ***Epaltes divaricata*** (L.) Cass. (Asteraceae).
Note: Grierson (in *Ceylon J. Sci., Biol. Sci.* 11: 15. 1974) argued that Linnaeus' apparent inclusion of *Artemisia minima* L. (1753) in the protologue was a bibliographic confusion resulting from proof copies of Burman's *Fl. Indica*. He argued that Linnaeus corrected this later (in *Mant. Pl. Alt.*: 572. 1771), and that *E. divaricata* L. is not illegitimate.

Ethulia sparganophora Linnaeus, *Species Plantarum,* ed. 2, 2: 1171. 1763.
"Habitat in India." RCN: 6046.
Lectotype (Hind in Jarvis & Turland in *Taxon* 47: 360. 1998): [icon] *"Sparganophoros Virgae aureae folio, floribus e foliorum alis, absque pediculis"* in Vaillant in Mém. Acad. Roy. Sci. Paris 1719: 309, t. 20, f. 35. 1719. – Epitype (Hind in Jarvis & Turland in *Taxon* 47: 360. 1998): Guadeloupe. Basse-Terre, near Grand Etang, 400–425m, 27 Nov 1959, *Proctor 20182* (BM-000576316).
Current name: ***Struchium sparganophorum*** (L.) Kuntze (Asteraceae).

Note: Grierson (in Dassanayake & Fosberg, *Revised Handb. Fl. Ceylon* 1: 120. 1980) indicated as the type material in Vaillant's herbarium (P) which was not seen by Linnaeus, and Jeffrey (in *Kew Bull.* 43: 272. 1988) treated Vaillant's polynomial itself as the type. Neither choice is effective, nor is that of Howard (*Fl. Lesser Antilles* 6: 598. 1989), who indicated as type a Browne plate, originally indicated by Linnaeus as of doubtful relevance, and subsequently (*Mant. Pl. Alt.*: 463. 1771) excluded by him from the synonymy of this name. In the protologue, Linnaeus added "Plantam mihi ignotam ex charactere Vaillantii addidi". Hind designated Vaillant's cited illustration as lectotype, supported by an epitype.

Ethulia tomentosa Linnaeus, *Systema Naturae,* ed. 12, 2: 536; *Mantissa Plantarum*: 110. 1767.
"Habitat in China." RCN: 6048.
Lectotype (Ling & Humphries in Jarvis & Turland in *Taxon* 47: 360. 1998): Herb. Linn. No. 977.3 (LINN).
Current name: ***Crossostephium chinense*** (L.) Makino (Asteraceae).

Euclea racemosa Linnaeus, *Systema Vegetabilium,* ed. 13: 747. 1774.
RCN: 7482.
Lectotype (de Winter in Dyer & al., *Fl. Southern Africa* 26: 97. 1963): [icon] *"Padus foliis subrotundis, fructu racemoso"* in Burman, Rar. Afric. Pl.: 238, t. 84, f. 1. 1739.
Generitype of *Euclea* Linnaeus.
Current name: ***Euclea racemosa*** L. (Ebenaceae).

Eugenia acutangula Linnaeus, *Species Plantarum* 1: 471. 1753.
"Habitat in India." RCN: 3601.
Lectotype (Payens in *Blumea* 15: 231. 1967): Herb. Hermann 4: 50, No. 190 (BM-000594749).
Current name: ***Barringtonia acutangula*** (L.) Gaertn. (Lecythidaceae).

Eugenia jambos Linnaeus, *Species Plantarum* 1: 470. 1753.
"Habitat in India." RCN: 3597.
Lectotype (Fawcett & Rendle, *Fl. Jamaica* 5: 352. 1926): Herb. Hermann 2: 20, No. 188 (BM-000594583).
Current name: ***Syzygium jambos*** (L.) Alston (Myrtaceae).

Eugenia malaccensis Linnaeus, *Species Plantarum* 1: 470. 1753.
"Habitat in India." RCN: 3596.
Type not designated.
Original material: Herb. Hermann 5: 241, No. 187 [icon] (BM); [icon] in Rheede, Hort. Malab. 1: 29, t. 18. 1678.
Current name: ***Syzygium malaccense*** (L.) Merr. & L.M. Perry (Myrtaceae).

Eugenia racemosa Linnaeus, *Species Plantarum* 1: 471. 1753.
"Habitat in India." RCN: 3602.
Type not designated.
Original material: Herb. Hermann 5: 212, 213, 339, No. 191 [icon] (BM); [icon] in Rheede, Hort. Malab. 4: 11, t. 6. 1683.
Current name: ***Barringtonia racemosa*** (L.) Spreng. (Lecythidaceae).
Note: Payens (in *Blumea* 15: 195. 1967) and Sangai (in Milne-Redhead & Polhill, *Fl. Trop. E. Africa, Lecythidaceae*: 4. 1971) indicated drawings in Herb. Hermann 5: 212, 213 and 339 (BM) as syntypes.

Eugenia uniflora Linnaeus, *Species Plantarum* 1: 470. 1753.
"Habitat in India." RCN: 3599.
Lectotype (McVaugh in *Taxon* 5: 140. 1956): [icon] *"Eugenia Indica, Myrti folio, deciduo, flore albo, fructu suave rubente, molli, leviter sulcato, & odoro"* in Micheli, Nov. Pl. Gen.: 226, t. 108. 1729.
Generitype of *Eugenia* Linnaeus (vide Green, *Prop. Brit. Bot.*: 158. 1929).
Current name: ***Eugenia uniflora*** L. (Myrtaceae).

Euonymus americanus Linnaeus, *Species Plantarum* 1: 197. 1753.
"Habitat in Virginia." RCN: 1598.
Lectotype (Wijnands, *Bot. Commelins*: 63. 1983): *Kalm*, Herb. Linn.
No. 269.3 (LINN; iso- UPS).
Current name: ***Euonymus americanus*** L. (Celastraceae).

Euonymus colpoon Linnaeus, *Mantissa Plantarum Altera*: 210. 1771,
nom. illeg.
"Habitat in Cap. b. spei littoribus maritimis. Lepelboom Belgis."
RCN: 1599.
Replaced synonym: *Colpoon compressum* P.J. Bergius (1767).
Type not designated.
Current name: ***Osyris compressa*** (P.J. Bergius) A. DC. (Santalaceae).
Note: Archer & Van Wyk (in *J. S. African Bot.* 63: 149. 1997) treat
this name as a legitimate synonym of *Cassine peragua* L.
(*Celastraceae*), and typify it on the cited Burman plate (*Rar. Afr. Pl.*
t. 86, f. 240. 1739). However, this is clearly incorrect as *Colpoon
compressum* P.J. Bergius (*Santalaceae*) is cited in Linnaeus'
protologue so Linnaeus' name is superfluous and illegitimate, and
homotypic with Bergius' name.

Euonymus europaeus Linnaeus, *Species Plantarum* 1: 197. 1753.
"Habitat in Europae sepibus." RCN: 1597.
Lectotype (Jonsell & Jarvis in *Nordic J. Bot.* 22: 80. 2002): Herb.
Clifford: 38, *Euonymus* 1 (BM-000557820).
Generitype of *Euonymus* Linnaeus, *nom. & orth. cons.*
Current name: ***Euonymus europaeus*** L. (Celastraceae).
Note: Paclt (in *Taxon* 47: 473. 1998) proposed amending the gender of
Euonymus to feminine but this was not recommended by the
Committee for Spermatophyta (in *Taxon* 49: 270. 2000).

Euonymus europaeus Linnaeus var. **latifolius** Linnaeus, *Species
Plantarum* 1: 197. 1753.
"Habitat in Pannonia." RCN: 1597.
Type not designated.
Original material: Herb. Clifford: 38, *Euonymus* 1 α? (BM); [icon] in
Clusius, Rar. Pl. Hist. 1: 56. 1601.
Current name: ***Euonymus latifolius*** (L.) Mill. (Celastraceae).

Euonymus europaeus Linnaeus var. **tenuifolius** Linnaeus, *Species
Plantarum* 1: 197. 1753.
RCN: 1597.
Type not designated.
Original material: Herb. Burser XXIII: 16 (UPS); [icon] in Clusius,
Rar. Pl. Hist. 1: 57. 1601.
Current name: ***Euonymus europaeus*** L. (Celastraceae).
Note: The application of this name appears to be uncertain.

Eupatorium album Linnaeus, *Systema Naturae,* ed. 12, 2: 536;
Mantissa Plantarum: 111. 1767.
"Habitat in Pensylania. Barthram." RCN: 6057.
Lectotype (Reveal in Jarvis & Turland in *Taxon* 47: 360. 1998):
Bartram, Herb. Linn. No. 978.5 (LINN).
Current name: ***Eupatorium album*** L. (Asteraceae).

Eupatorium altissimum Linnaeus, *Species Plantarum* 2: 837. 1753.
"Habitat in Pensylania." RCN: 6060.
Lectotype (Reveal in Jarvis & Turland in *Taxon* 47: 360. 1998): Herb.
Linn. No. 335.17 (S), see p. 174.
Current name: ***Eupatorium altissimum*** L. (Asteraceae).

Eupatorium aromaticum Linnaeus, *Species Plantarum* 2: 839. 1753.
"Habitat in Virginia." RCN: 6068.
Lectotype (Reveal in Jarvis & Turland in *Taxon* 47: 360. 1998):
Clayton 603 (BM-000051683).

Current name: ***Ageratina aromatica*** (L.) Spach (Asteraceae).
Note: Clewell & Wooten (in *Brittonia* 23: 138. 1971) indicated Herb.
Linn. No. 978.22 (LINN) as the type, but the sheet lacks a *Species
Plantarum* number (i.e. "14"), was a later addition to the
herbarium, and is not original material for the name.

Eupatorium cannabinum Linnaeus, *Species Plantarum* 2: 838. 1753.
"Habitat in Europa ad aquas." RCN: 6063.
Lectotype (Rechinger, *Fl. Iranica* 164: 31. 1989): Herb. Clifford: 396,
Eupatorium 2 (BM-000646949).
Generitype of *Eupatorium* Linnaeus (vide Green, *Prop. Brit. Bot.*: 180.
1929).
Current name: ***Eupatorium cannabinum*** L. (Asteraceae).

Eupatorium chinense Linnaeus, *Species Plantarum* 2: 837. 1753.
"Habitat in China. Osbeck." RCN: 6058.
Type not designated.
Original material: none traced.
Current name: ***Eupatorium chinense*** L. (Asteraceae).
Note: Murata & Koyama (in *Acta Phytotax. Geobot.* 33: 292. 1982)
assumed the type to be an Osbeck specimen in S ("Stockform")
which they had not seen. However, no such material has been
traced in S and there appear to be no extant original elements.

Eupatorium coelestinum Linnaeus, *Species Plantarum* 2: 838. 1753.
"Habitat in Carolina, Virginia." RCN: 6067.
Lectotype (Reveal & al. in *Huntia* 7: 221. 1987): Herb. Linn. No.
978.20 (LINN).
Current name: ***Conoclinium coelestinum*** (L.) DC. (Asteraceae).

Eupatorium dalea Linnaeus, *Systema Naturae,* ed. 10, 2: 1204. 1759.
["Habitat in Jamaica."] Sp. Pl., ed. 2, 2: 1171 (1763). RCN: 6050.
Lectotype (Robinson in Jarvis & Turland in *Taxon* 47: 361. 1998):
Browne, Herb. Linn. No. 978.1 (LINN).
Current name: ***Critonia dalea*** (L.) DC. (Asteraceae).

Eupatorium fruticosum Linnaeus, *Systema Naturae,* ed. 10, 2: 1204.
1759.
RCN: 6052.
Type not designated.
Original material: none traced.
Note: This name was published by Linnaeus in 1759 but it does not
appear in any later works and, perhaps not surprisingly, has never
been in use. The absence of any original elements makes its
interpretation difficult and it may well prove to be a candidate for
rejection.

Eupatorium hastatum Linnaeus, *Systema Naturae,* ed. 10, 2: 1204.
1759.
["Habitat in Jamaica."] Sp. Pl., ed. 2, 2: 1172 (1763). RCN: 6061.
Lectotype (Holmes in Jarvis & Turland in *Taxon* 47: 361. 1998):
Browne, Herb. Linn. No. 978.9 (LINN).
Current name: ***Mikania hastata*** (L.) Willd. (Asteraceae).

Eupatorium houstonianum Linnaeus, *Species Plantarum* 2: 836.
1753.
"Habitat in Vera Cruce." RCN: 6054.
Lectotype (King & Robinson in Woodson & Schery in *Ann. Missouri
Bot. Gard.* 62: 973. 1975): Herb. Clifford: 396, *Eupatorium* 6 (BM-
000646954; iso- MW).
Current name: ***Mikania houstoniana*** (L.) B.L. Rob. (Asteraceae).

Eupatorium houstonis Linnaeus, *Systema Naturae,* ed. 10, 2: 1204.
1759, *orth. var.*
RCN: 6054.

Lectotype (King & Robinson in Woodson & Schery in *Ann. Missouri Bot. Gard.* 62: 973. 1975): Herb. Clifford: 396, *Eupatorium* 6 (BM-000646954; iso- MW).

Current name: ***Mikania houstoniana*** (L.) B.L. Rob. (Asteraceae).

Note: Evidently an orthographic variant of *E. houstonianum* L. (1753), having the same Linnaean phrase name, and the same species number (i.e. "3"). *Eupatorium houstonianum* is absent from *Syst. Nat.*, ed. 10.

Eupatorium hyssopifolium Linnaeus, *Species Plantarum* 2: 836. 1753.
"Habitat in Virginia." RCN: 6051.
Lectotype (Reveal & al. in *Huntia* 7: 220. 1987): [icon] *"Eupatorium Virgin. folio angusto, floribus albis Herm."* in Dillenius, Hort. Eltham. 1: 141, t. 115, f. 140. 1732.
Current name: ***Eupatorium hyssopifolium*** L. (Asteraceae).
Note: Specific epithet spelled "hyssopifolia" in the protologue.

Eupatorium ivifolium Linnaeus, *Systema Naturae*, ed. 10, 2: 1205. 1759.
["Habitat in Jamaica."] Sp. Pl., ed. 2, 2: 1174 (1763). RCN: 6070.
Lectotype (King & Robinson in Woodson & Schery in *Ann. Missouri Bot. Gard.* 62: 924. 1975): *Browne*, Herb. Linn. No. 978.28 (LINN).
Current name: ***Chromolaena ivifolia*** (L.) R.M. King & H. Rob. (Asteraceae).
Note: Specific epithet spelled "ivaefolium" in the protologue.
Although Moore (in Fawcett & Rendle, *Fl. Jamaica* 7: 175. 1936) noted the existence of 978.28 (LINN), he did not indicate it as the type. King & Robinson, despite believing that the material might be from Swartz, indicated the same material as the type, and are followed here.

Eupatorium macrophyllum Linnaeus, *Species Plantarum,* ed. 2, 2: 1175. 1763.
"Habitat in America." RCN: 6071.
Lectotype (King & Robinson in Woodson & Schery in *Ann. Missouri Bot. Gard.* 62: 952. 1975): [icon] *"Eupatorium foliis cordato-acuminatis"* in Plumier in Burman, Pl. Amer.: 121, t. 129. 1757.
Current name: ***Hebeclinum macrophyllum*** (L.) DC. (Asteraceae).

Eupatorium maculatum Linnaeus, *Centuria I Plantarum*: 27. 1755.
"Habitat in America septentrionali." RCN: 6065.
Lectotype (Wiegand in *Rhodora* 22: 59. 1920): *Kalm*, Herb. Linn. No. 978.15 (LINN).
Current name: ***Eupatorium maculatum*** L. (Asteraceae).
Note: Although Mackenzie (in *Rhodora* 29: 8. 1927) maintained that this Kalm material could not have been the basis for the name, this seems incorrect and Wiegand's type choice is accepted here. Lamont (in *Mem. New York Bot. Gard.* 72: 36. 1995) recognised *E. maculatum* L. as a species distinct from *E. purpureum* L. He also illustrated the type (as f. 25).

Eupatorium odoratum Linnaeus, *Systema Naturae*, ed. 10, 2: 1205. 1759.
["Habitat in America."] Sp. Pl., ed. 2, 2: 1174 (1763). RCN: 6069.
Lectotype (King & Robinson in Woodson & Schery in *Ann. Missouri Bot. Gard.* 62: 925. 1975): [icon] *"Eupatoria Conyzoides folio molli & incano, capitulis magnis, Americana"* in Plukenet, Phytographia: t. 177, f. 3. 1692; Almag. Bot.: 141. 1696. – Typotype: Herb. Sloane 96: 25 (BM-SL).
Current name: ***Chromolaena odorata*** (L.) R.M. King & H. Rob. (Asteraceae).
Note: Although Moore (in Fawcett & Rendle, *Fl. Jamaica* 7: 175. 1936) noted the existence of 978.27 (LINN), he did not indicate it as the type.

Eupatorium perfoliatum Linnaeus, *Species Plantarum* 2: 838. 1753.
"Habitat in Virginiae aquosis." RCN: 6066.
Lectotype (Reveal & al. in *Huntia* 7: 222. 1987): *Kalm*, Herb. Linn. No. 978.17 (LINN; iso- 336.9 S).
Current name: ***Eupatorium perfoliatum*** L. (Asteraceae).

Eupatorium purpureum Linnaeus, *Species Plantarum* 2: 838. 1753.
"Habitat in America septentrionali." RCN: 6064.
Lectotype (Wiegand & Weatherby in *Rhodora* 39: pl. 466. 1937): Herb. Linn. No. 978.13 (LINN).
Current name: ***Eupatorium purpureum*** L. (Asteraceae).
Note: Wiegand (in *Rhodora* 22: 60. 1920) provided an extensive discussion of the original elements for this name which he applied in a sense different from that of Mackenzie (in *Rhodora* 22: 158–161. 1920; 29: 9. 1927). Mackenzie concluded that "the type...was the plant from which he [Linnaeus] drew his own description, quite probably the Hortus Cliffortianus plant...", which Mackenzie believed to be *E. maculatum* L. See review by Reveal & al. (in *Huntia* 7: 221. 1987). Wiegand & Weatherby's choice appears to be the earliest formal type designation. Lamond (in *Mem. New York Bot. Gard.* 72: 50, f. 29. 1995) also illustrates the type.

Eupatorium rotundifolium Linnaeus, *Species Plantarum* 2: 837. 1753.
"Habitat in Virginia, Canada." RCN: 6059.
Lectotype (Reveal & al. in *Huntia* 7: 221. 1987): *Kalm*, Herb. Linn. No. 978.6 (LINN).
Current name: ***Eupatorium rotundifolium*** L. (Asteraceae).

Eupatorium scandens Linnaeus, *Species Plantarum* 2: 836. 1753.
"Habitat in aquosis virginiae." RCN: 6053.
Lectotype (Holmes in *Sida Bot. Misc.* 5: 34. 1990): Herb. Linn. No. 978.2 (LINN).
Current name: ***Mikania scandens*** (L.) Willd. (Asteraceae).

Eupatorium sessilifolium Linnaeus, *Species Plantarum* 2: 837. 1753.
"Habitat in Virginia." RCN: 6056.
Lectotype (Reveal in Jarvis & Turland in *Taxon* 47: 361. 1998): Herb. Linn. No. 978.4 (LINN; iso- BM?).
Current name: ***Eupatorium sessilifolium*** L. (Asteraceae).

Eupatorium sophiifolium Linnaeus, *Species Plantarum,* ed. 2, 2: 1175. 1763.
"Habitat in America." RCN: 6072.
Lectotype (Robinson in Jarvis & Turland in *Taxon* 47: 361. 1998): [icon] *"Eupatorium foliis pinnato-multifidis"* in Plumier in Burman, Pl. Amer.: 121, t. 128, f. 2. 1757.
Current name: ***Eupatorina sophiifolia*** (L.) R.M. King & H. Rob. (Asteraceae).
Note: Specific epithet spelled "sophiaefolium" in the protologue.

Eupatorium trifoliatum Linnaeus, *Species Plantarum* 2: 837. 1753.
"Habitat in Virginia." RCN: 6062.
Lectotype (Reveal in Jarvis & Turland in *Taxon* 47: 361. 1998): Herb. Linn. No. 336.1 (S).
Current name: ***Eupatorium purpureum*** L. (Asteraceae).
Note: Wiegand (in *Rhodora* 22: 61. 1920) provided an extensive discussion of the original elements for this name. Mackenzie (in *Rhodora* 22: 163–165. 1920; 29: 6. 1927) disputed that *Clayton 620* (BM) played any role in this but neither author designated a type. See review by Reveal & al. (in *Huntia* 7: 221. 1987). Lamond (in *Mem. New York Bot. Gard.* 72: 48. 1995) incorrectly treated 978.11 (LINN), a post-1753 addition to the herbarium, as the holotype.

E

Eupatorium zeylanicum Linnaeus, *Species Plantarum* 2: 837. 1753.
"Habitat in Zeylona." RCN: 6055.
Lectotype (Grierson in Dassanayake & Fosberg, *Revised Handb. Fl. Ceylon* 1: 131. 1980): Herb. Hermann 1: 29; 3: 36; 4: 22, No. 306 (BM).
Current name: *Vernonia zeylanica* (L.) Less. (Asteraceae).

Euphorbia aleppica Linnaeus, *Species Plantarum* 1: 458. 1753.
"Habitat in Creta, Aleppo." RCN: 3537.
Lectotype (Turland in *Bull. Nat. Hist. Mus. London, Bot.* 25: 136, f. 10. 1995): Herb. Linn. No. 630.46 (LINN).
Current name: *Euphorbia aleppica* L. (Euphorbiaceae).

Euphorbia amygdaloides Linnaeus, *Species Plantarum* 1: 463. 1753.
"Habitat in Gallia, Germania." RCN: 3554.
Lectotype (Geltman in *Novosti Sist. Vyssh. Rast.* 34: 106. 2003): Herb. Linn. No. 630.71 (LINN).
Current name: *Euphorbia amygdaloides* L. (Euphorbiaceae).

Euphorbia antiquorum Linnaeus, *Species Plantarum* 1: 450. 1753.
"Habitat in India." RCN: 3493.
Lectotype (Wijnands, *Bot. Commelins*: 97. 1983): Herb. Clifford: 196, *Euphorbia* 1 (BM-000628669).
Generitype of *Euphorbia* Linnaeus (vide Green, *Prop. Brit. Bot.*: 157. 1929).
Current name: *Euphorbia antiquorum* L. (Euphorbiaceae).

Euphorbia apios Linnaeus, *Species Plantarum* 1: 457. 1753.
"Habitat in Crera. [sic]" RCN: 3529.
Lectotype (Khan in *Notes Roy. Bot. Gard. Edinburgh* 25: 102. 1964): [icon] *"Tithymalus tuberosa radice, Ischas"* in Clusius, Rar. Pl. Hist. 2: 190. 1601.
Current name: *Euphorbia apios* L. (Euphorbiaceae).

Euphorbia canariensis Linnaeus, *Species Plantarum* 1: 450. 1753.
"Habitat in Canariis." RCN: 3494.
Lectotype (Wijnands, *Bot. Commelins*: 98. 1983): [icon] *"Tithymalus aizoides fruticosus canariensis quadrangularis etc."* in Commelin, Hort. Med. Amstelod. Pl. Rar. 2: 207, t. 104. 1701.
Current name: *Euphorbia canariensis* L. (Euphorbiaceae).

Euphorbia canescens Linnaeus, *Species Plantarum*, ed. 2, 1: 652. 1762.
"Habitat in Hispania." RCN: 3515.
Lectotype (Benedí González & Orell in *Collect. Bot. (Barcelona)* 22: 149. 1993): *Alströmer 146a*, Herb. Linn. No. 630.16 (LINN).
Current name: *Euphorbia chamaesyce* L. (Euphorbiaceae).

Euphorbia caput-medusae Linnaeus, *Species Plantarum* 1: 452. 1753.
"Habitat in Aethiopia." RCN: 3500.
Lectotype (Wijnands, *Bot. Commelins*: 98. 1983): [icon] *"Euphorbium procumbens, ramis plurimis simplicibus squamosis, foliolis deciduis"* in Burman, Rar. Afric. Pl.: 17, t. 8. 1738 (see p. 114).
Current name: *Euphorbia caput-medusae* L. (Euphorbiaceae).

Euphorbia cereiformis Linnaeus, *Species Plantarum* 1: 451. 1753.
"Habitat in Aethiopia." RCN: 3497.
Lectotype (Wijnands, *Bot. Commelins*: 101. 1983): [icon] *"Euphorbium polygonum, spinosum, Cerei effigie"* in Isnard in Mém. Acad. Roy. Sci. Paris 1720: 385, t. 10. 1720.
Current name: *Euphorbia officinarum* L. (Euphorbiaceae).

Euphorbia chamaesyce Linnaeus, *Species Plantarum* 1: 455. 1753.
"Habitat in Europa australi, Sibiria." RCN: 3516.

Lectotype (Khan in *Notes Roy. Bot. Gard. Edinburgh* 25: 152. 1964): *Löfling 373*, Herb. Linn. No. 630.15 (LINN).
Current name: *Euphorbia chamaesyce* L. (Euphorbiaceae).
Note: Wheeler (in *Rhodora* 43: 265, pl. 668A. 1941) treated 630.17 (LINN) as the type, but this is a Browne specimen from Jamaica that Linnaeus did not receive until 1758 so it is not original material for the name.

Euphorbia characias Linnaeus, *Species Plantarum* 1: 463. 1753.
"Habitat in Gallia, Hispania, Italia." RCN: 3556.

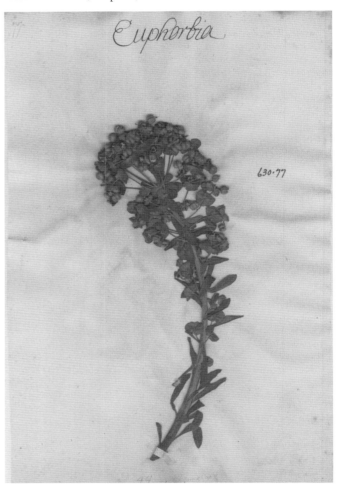

Lectotype (Geltman in *Komarovia* 2: 24. 2002): Herb. Linn. No. 630.77 (LINN).
Current name: *Euphorbia characias* L. (Euphorbiaceae).

Euphorbia corallioides Linnaeus, *Species Plantarum* 1: 460. 1753.
"Habitat in Sicilia, Mauritania, Oriente." RCN: 3544.
Type not designated.
Original material: Herb. Linn. No. 630.57 (LINN).
Current name: *Euphorbia corallioides* L. (Euphorbiaceae).

Euphorbia corollata Linnaeus, *Species Plantarum* 1: 459. 1753.
"Habitat in Virginia, Canada." RCN: 3543.
Lectotype (Reveal & al. in *Huntia* 7: 237. 1987): *Kalm*, Herb. Linn. No. 630.56 (LINN).
Current name: *Euphorbia corollata* L. (Euphorbiaceae).
Note: Park (in *Edinburgh J. Bot.* 55: 181. 1998) noted a fragment of the type at F.

Euphorbia cotinifolia Linnaeus, *Species Plantarum* 1: 453. 1753.
"Habitat in Curacao." RCN: 3505.
Lectotype (Wijnands, *Bot. Commelins*: 99. 1983): Herb. Clifford: 198, *Euphorbia* 11 (BM-000628671).
Current name: ***Euphorbia cotinifolia*** L. (Euphorbiaceae).

Euphorbia cyparissias Linnaeus, *Species Plantarum* 1: 461. 1753.
"Habitat in Misnia, Bohemia, Helvetia, G. Narbonensi." RCN: 3549.
Lectotype (Molero & Rovira in *Collect. Bot. (Barcelona)* 21: 156. 1992): Herb. Linn. No. 630.67 (LINN).
Current name: ***Euphorbia cyparissias*** L. (Euphorbiaceae).

Euphorbia dendroides Linnaeus, *Species Plantarum* 1: 462. 1753.
"Habitat in Italia, Creta, Insulis Staechadum." RCN: 3553.
Lectotype (Molero & Rovira in *Taxon* 54: 472. 2005): Herb. Burser XVI(2): 32 (UPS).
Current name: ***Euphorbia dendroides*** L. (Euphorbiaceae).
Note: Although Carter (in Eggli, *Ill. Handb. Succ. Pl., Dicots*: 132. 2002) indicated 630.89 (LINN) as type, this was published after 1 Jan 2001 and so the omission of the phrase "designated here" or an equivalent (Art. 7.11) means that this choice is not effective. The collection is not, in any case, original material for the name, as noted by Molero & Rovira.

Euphorbia dulcis Linnaeus, *Species Plantarum* 1: 457. 1753.
"Habitat in Gallia, Italia, Germania." RCN: 3533.
Type not designated.
Original material: Herb. Linn. No. 630.38 (LINN); Herb. Linn. No. 630.39 (LINN); Herb. Burser XVI(2): 58 (UPS); [icon] in Plantin, Pl. Stirp. Icon.: 358. 1581.
Current name: ***Euphorbia dulcis*** L. (Euphorbiaceae).

Euphorbia epithymoides Linnaeus, *Species Plantarum,* ed. 2, 1: 656. 1762.
"Habitat in Italia. D. Jacquin." RCN: 3532.
Type not designated.
Original material: Herb. Linn. No. 199.9? (S); *Scopoli s.n.,* Herb. Linn. No. 630.37 (LINN); [icon] in Colonna, Ekphr., ed. 2: 52, 51. 1616.
Current name: ***Euphorbia epithymoides*** L. (Euphorbiaceae).

Euphorbia esula Linnaeus, *Species Plantarum* 1: 461. 1753.
"Habitat in Germania, Belgio, Gallia." RCN: 3548.
Lectotype (Molero & Rovira in *Collect. Bot. (Barcelona)* 21: 158. 1992): Herb. Linn. No. 630.62 (LINN).
Current name: ***Euphorbia esula*** L. (Euphorbiaceae).
Note: See Geltman (in *Bot. Zhurn.* 81(9): 73–77. 1996) for a review.

Euphorbia exigua Linnaeus, *Species Plantarum* 1: 456. 1753.
"Habitat in Lusatia, Gallia, Helvetia, Hispania inter segetes." RCN: 3525.
Lectotype (Jafri & El-Gadi, *Fl. Libya* 89: 39. 1982): Herb. Linn. No. 630.27 (LINN).
Current name: ***Euphorbia exigua*** L. (Euphorbiaceae).

Euphorbia exigua Linnaeus var. **acuta** Linnaeus, *Species Plantarum* 1: 456. 1753.
RCN: 3525.
Lectotype (Jafri & El-Gadi, *Fl. Libya* 89: 39. 1982): Herb. Linn. No. 630.27 (LINN).
Current name: ***Euphorbia exigua*** L. var. ***exigua*** (Euphorbiaceae).
Note: As this varietal epithet is associated with the part of the protologue equivalent to *E. exigua* (rather than the named and unnamed varieties β and γ), it is synonymous with var. *exigua*, and homotypic with it.

Euphorbia exigua Linnaeus var. **retusa** Linnaeus, *Species Plantarum* 1: 456. 1753.
"Habitat Monspelii in saxosis." RCN: 3525.
Type not designated.
Original material: Herb. Linn. No. 630.29 (LINN); Herb. Burser XVI(2): 54 (UPS).
Current name: ***Euphorbia exigua*** L. var. ***retusa*** L. (Euphorbiaceae).
Note: Radcliffe-Smith (in Meikle, *Fl. Cyprus* 2: 1443. 1985) indicated unspecified type material at both LINN (presumably 630.29) and at BM but did not typify the name.

Euphorbia falcata Linnaeus, *Species Plantarum* 1: 456. 1753, *nom. cons.*
"Habitat in Europa australi." RCN: 3524.
Conserved type (Molero in *Taxon* 42: 715. 1993): *Arduino s.n.,* Herb. Linn. No. 630.26, right specimen (LINN).
Current name: ***Euphorbia falcata*** L. (Euphorbiaceae).

Euphorbia helioscopia Linnaeus, *Species Plantarum* 1: 459. 1753.
"Habitat in Europae cultis." RCN: 3540.
Lectotype (Jafri & El-Gadi, *Fl. Libya* 89: 33. 1982): Herb. Linn. No. 630.49 (LINN).
Current name: ***Euphorbia helioscopia*** L. (Euphorbiaceae).

Euphorbia heptagona Linnaeus, *Species Plantarum* 1: 450. 1753.
"Habitat – – – –" RCN: 3495.
Type not designated.
Original material: [icon] in Boerhaave, Index Alter Pl. Hort. Lugdb.-Bat. 1: 258. 1720.
Current name: ***Euphorbia heptagona*** L. (Euphorbiaceae).

Euphorbia heterophylla Linnaeus, *Species Plantarum* 1: 453. 1753.
"Habitat in America calidiore." RCN: 3504.
Lectotype (Radcliffe-Smith in Bosser & al., *Fl. Mascareignes* 160: 94. 1982): [icon] *"Tithymalus Curassavicus, Salicis & Atriplicis foliis variis, caulibus viridantibus"* in Plukenet, Phytographia: t. 112, f. 6. 1691; Almag. Bot.: 369. 1696. – Typotype: Herb. Sloane 98: 108 (BM-SL), see p. 149.
Current name: ***Euphorbia heterophylla*** L. (Euphorbiaceae).
Note: Dressler (in *Ann. Missouri Bot. Gard.* 48: 332. 1961) noted the absence of any material at LINN and interpreted the name via the Plukenet plate, though without expressly treating it as the type.

Euphorbia hirsuta Linnaeus, *Amoenitates Academicae* 4: 483. 1759.
"Habitat [Monspelii.]"
Type not designated.
Original material: none traced.
Current name: ***Euphorbia hirsuta*** L. (Euphorbiaceae).
Note: See Stearn (in Geck & Pressler, *Festschr. Claus Nissen*: 643. 1974), who reproduces the account by Magnol that validates this name. Stearn added that the plant described by Magnol "is evidently the widespread Mediterranean species commonly known as *E. pubescens* Vahl".

Euphorbia hirta Linnaeus, *Species Plantarum* 1: 454. 1753.
"Habitat in India." RCN: 3510.
Lectotype (Wheeler in *Contr. Gray Herb.* 124: 72. 1939): Herb. Linn. No. 630.7 (LINN).
Current name: ***Euphorbia hirta*** L. (Euphorbiaceae).

Euphorbia hyberna Linnaeus, *Species Plantarum* 1: 462. 1753.
"Habitat in Hibernia, Sibiria, Austria, Pyrenaeis." RCN: 3552.
Type not designated.
Original material: Herb. Burser XVI(2): 45 (UPS); Herb. Linn. No. 630.70 (LINN); [icon] in Dillenius, Hort. Eltham. 2: 387, t. 290, f. 374. 1732.
Current name: ***Euphorbia hyberna*** L. (Euphorbiaceae).

Euphorbia hypericifolia Linnaeus, *Species Plantarum* 1: 454. 1753.
"Habitat in India." RCN: 3508.
Lectotype (Fosberg & Mazzeo in *Castanea* 30: 199. 1965): Herb.
   Linn. No. 630.4 (LINN).
Current name: ***Euphorbia hypericifolia*** L. (Euphorbiaceae).
Note: Fosberg & Mazzeo (in *Castanea* 30: 199. 1965) agree with
   Stearn's argument (*in litt.* to Wheeler, 1960) that 630.4 (LINN) is
   the type of this name (and not of *E. maculata* L., as believed by
   Wheeler (in *Contr. Gray Herb.* 127: 76. 1939) and Fosberg (in
   Rhodora 48: 199–200. 1946; 55: 241–242. 1953). Wheeler had
   incorrectly treated 630.3 (LINN), a Browne collection not received
   by Linnaeus until 1758, as the type. Fosberg & Mazzeo clearly
   treated 630.4 as the type themselves, pre-dating the choice of a
   Sloane plate made by Burch (in *Rhodora* 68: 162. 1966).

Euphorbia hyssopifolia Linnaeus, *Systema Naturae*, ed. 10, 2: 1048.
   1759.
["Habitat in America."] Sp. Pl., ed. 2, 1: 651 (1762). RCN: 3512.
Lectotype (Fawcett & Rendle, *Fl. Jamaica* 4: 339. 1920): *Browne*,
   Herb. Linn. No. 630.9 (LINN).
Current name: ***Euphorbia hyssopifolia*** L. (Euphorbiaceae).

Euphorbia ipecacuanhae Linnaeus, *Species Plantarum* 1: 455.
   1753.
"Habitat in Virginia, Canada." RCN: 3520.
Lectotype (designated here by Reveal): *Kalm*, Herb. Linn. No. 630.21
   (LINN).
Current name: ***Euphorbia ipecacuanhae*** L. (Euphorbiaceae).

Euphorbia lathyrus Linnaeus, *Species Plantarum* 1: 457. 1753.
"Habitat in Gallia, Italia ad agrorum margines." RCN: 3527.
Type not designated.
Original material: Herb. Clifford: 198, *Euphorbia* 13 (BM); Herb.
   Burser XVI(2): 64 (UPS); Herb. Linn. No. 630.32 (LINN); [icon]
   in Fuchs, Hist. Stirp.: 454, 455. 1542; [icon] in Mattioli, Pl. Epit.:
   968. 1586.
Current name: ***Euphorbia lathyrus*** L. (Euphorbiaceae).

Euphorbia linifolia Linnaeus, *Amoenitates Academicae* 4: 483. 1759.
Type not designated.
Original material: none traced.
Current name: ***Euphorbia segetalis*** L. var. ***pinea*** (L.) Lange
   (Euphorbiaceae).
Note: See Stearn (in Geck & Pressler, *Festschr. Claus Nissen*: 643.
   1974), who stated that the plant described by Magnol (whose
   description validates Linnaeus' binomial) "is evidently *E. segetalis*
   L.".

Euphorbia maculata Linnaeus, *Species Plantarum* 1: 455. 1753.
"Habitat in America septentrionali." RCN: 3509.
Lectotype (Croizat in *Webbia* 17: 191. 1962): Herb. Linn. No. 630.11
   (LINN).
Current name: ***Euphorbia maculata*** L. (Euphorbiaceae).
Note: Wheeler (in *Contr. Gray Herb.* 127: 75. 1939; *Rhodora* 43: 143,
   pl. 668B. 1941; *Rhodora* 62: 134–141. 1960) attempted to show
   that 630.4 (LINN) was the correct type. The papers which
   contributed to the extensive debate that followed are listed by
   Croizat (in *Webbia* 17: 187–188. 1962), and include Fosberg (in
   Rhodora 48: 197–200. 1946), who illustrated one of the LINN
   specimens and the cited Plukenet plate. However, 630.4 has been
   shown to be the type of *E. hypericifolia* L., and Croizat designated
   630.11 (LINN) as the type of *E. maculata*. This choice has been
   accepted by authors such as Fosberg & Mazzeo (in *Castanea* 30:
   199. 1965), Burch (in *Rhodora* 68: 156–160. 1966) and Benedí &
   Orell (in *Collect. Bot. (Barcelona)* 21: 31. 1992).

Euphorbia mammillaris Linnaeus, *Species Plantarum* 1: 451. 1753.
"Habitat in Aethiopia." RCN: 3496.
Lectotype (Wijnands, *Bot. Commelins*: 100. 1983): [icon] *"Tithymalus
   Afric. aiz. spinis validissimis armato"* in Commelin, Praeludia Bot.:
   59, t. 9. 1703.
Current name: ***Euphorbia mammillaris*** L. (Euphorbiaceae).

Euphorbia mauritanica Linnaeus, *Species Plantarum* 1: 452. 1753.
"Habitat in Africae maritimis." RCN: 3501.
Type not designated.
Original material: [icon] in Dillenius, Hort. Eltham. 2: 384, t. 289, f.
   373. 1732.
Current name: ***Euphorbia mauritanica*** L. (Euphorbiaceae).

Euphorbia myrsinites Linnaeus, *Species Plantarum* 1: 461. 1753.
"Habitat in Calabria, Monspelii." RCN: 3550.
Type not designated.
Original material: Herb. Linn. No. 630.68 (LINN); Herb. Clifford:
   199, *Euphorbia* 18 α (BM); [icon] in Clusius, Rar. Pl. Hist. 2: 189.
   1601.
Current name: ***Euphorbia myrsinites*** L. (Euphorbiaceae).

Euphorbia myrtifolia Linnaeus, *Flora Jamaicensis*: 17. 1759, *orth. var.*
"Habitat [in Jamaica.]" RCN: 3522.
Lectotype (Fawcett & Rendle, *Fl. Jamaica* 4: 337. 1920): *Browne*,
   Herb. Linn. No. 630.23 (LINN).
Current name: ***Euphorbia myrtillifolia*** L. (Euphorbiaceae).
Note: It seems likely that this is an orthographic variant of the earlier
   E. myrtillifolia L. (May–Jun 1759).

Euphorbia myrtillifolia Linnaeus, *Systema Naturae*, ed. 10, 2: 1047.
   1759.
RCN: 3522.
Lectotype (Fawcett & Rendle, *Fl. Jamaica* 4: 337. 1920): *Browne*,
   Herb. Linn. No. 630.23 (LINN).
Current name: ***Euphorbia myrtillifolia*** L. (Euphorbiaceae).

Euphorbia neriifolia Linnaeus, *Species Plantarum* 1: 451. 1753.
"Habitat in India." RCN: 3499.
Lectotype (Radcliffe-Smith in Bosser & al., *Fl. Mascareignes* 160: 93.
   1982): Herb. Linn. No. 630.1 (LINN).
Current name: ***Euphorbia neriifolia*** L. (Euphorbiaceae).
Note: Radcliffe-Smith's type choice of 630.1 (LINN) narrowly pre-
   dates that of Wijnands (*Bot. Commelins*: 100. 1983), who chose a
   Commelin plate.

Euphorbia ocymoidea Linnaeus, *Species Plantarum* 1: 453. 1753.
"Habitat in Campechia. Houst." RCN: 3506.
Neotype (Webster & Huft in *Ann. Missouri Bot. Gard.* 75: 1139.
   1988): *Houstoun* (BM).
Current name: ***Euphorbia ocymoidea*** L. (Euphorbiaceae).
Note: See also McVaugh (in *Contr. Univ. Michigan Herb.* 19: 229. 1993).

Euphorbia officinarum Linnaeus, *Species Plantarum* 1: 451. 1753.
"Habitat in Aethiopia & Africa calidiore." RCN: 3498.
Lectotype (Wijnands, *Bot. Commelins*: 101. 1983): [icon]
   "Euphorbium Cerei effigie" in Commelin, Hort. Med. Amstelod. Pl.
   Rar. 1: 21, t. 11. 1697.
Current name: ***Euphorbia officinarum*** L. (Euphorbiaceae).

Euphorbia orientalis Linnaeus, *Species Plantarum* 1: 460. 1753.
"Habitat in oriente." RCN: 3546.
Lectotype (Croizat in *J. Arnold Arbor.* 19: 98. 1938): Herb. Linn. No.
   630.60 (LINN).
Current name: ***Euphorbia orientalis*** L. (Euphorbiaceae).

Euphorbia origanoides Linnaeus, *Species Plantarum* 1: 453. 1753.
"Habitat in Insula Ascensionis." RCN: 3507.
Type not designated.
Original material: Herb. Linn. No. 630.2 (LINN).
Current name: ***Euphorbia origanoides*** L. (Euphorbiaceae).

Euphorbia palustris Linnaeus, *Species Plantarum* 1: 462. 1753.
"Habitat in Suecia australi, Germania, Belgio." RCN: 3551.
Lectotype (Polatschek in *Ann. Naturhist. Mus. Wien* 75: 190. 1971):
    Herb. Linn. No. 630.69 (LINN).
Current name: ***Euphorbia palustris*** L. (Euphorbiaceae).

Euphorbia paralias Linnaeus, *Species Plantarum* 1: 458. 1753.
"Habitat in Europae arena maritima." RCN: 3536.
Type not designated.
Original material: Herb. Clifford: 200, *Euphorbia* 22 (BM); Herb.
    Linn. No. 199.13 (S); Herb. Burser XVI(2): 39 (UPS); [icon] in
    Mattioli, Pl. Epit.: 962. 1586; [icon] in Dodoëns, Stirp. Hist.
    Pempt., ed. 2: 369, 370. 1616.
Current name: ***Euphorbia paralias*** L. (Euphorbiaceae).
Note: Jafri & El-Gadi (*Fl. Libya* 89: 44. 1982), followed by others,
    indicated both 630.44 and 630.45 (LINN) as "type". As these
    collections are not part of a single gathering, Art. 9.15 does not
    apply.

Euphorbia parviflora Linnaeus, *Systema Naturae*, ed. 10, 2: 1047.
    1759.
["Habitat in India."] Sp. Pl., ed. 2, 1: 652 (1762). RCN: 3514.
Lectotype (Esser & Chayamarit in *Harvard Pap. Bot.* 6: 263. 2001):
    [icon] *"Tithymalus humilis, ramosissimus, hirsutus, foliis Thymi
    serratis"* in Burman, Thes. Zeylan.: 225, t. 105, f. 3. 1737. –
    Epitype (Esser & Chayamarit in *Harvard Pap. Bot.* 6: 263. 2001):
    Sri Lanka. *P. Hartog s.n.* (G).
Current name: ***Euphorbia parviflora*** L. (Euphorbiaceae).
Note: Esser & Chayamarit (in *Harvard Pap. Bot.* 6: 263–265. 2001)
    provide a detailed review of this name and conclude that Philcox (in
    Dassanayake & Clayton, *Revised Handb. Fl. Ceylon* 11: 196. 1997)
    was wrong to recognise Burman's t. 105, f. 2 as the type. They reject
    his choice on the grounds that t. 105, f. 2 was not an original
    element for the name, designating t. 105, f. 3 as lectotype in its
    place.

Euphorbia peplis Linnaeus, *Species Plantarum* 1: 455. 1753.
"Habitat in Narbonae, Hispaniae maritimis." RCN: 3517.
Type not designated.
Original material: [icon] in Clusius, Rar. Pl. Hist.: 187. 1601; [icon]
    in Daléchamps, Hist. General. Pl. 2: 1659. 1586; [icon] in Mattioli,
    Pl. Epit.: 970. 1586.
Current name: ***Euphorbia peplis*** L. (Euphorbiaceae).
Note: El Hadidi (in *Bull. Jard. Bot. Natl. Belg.* 43: 90. 1973) and
    others have treated 630.18 (LINN) as the type but this material was
    sent by Kähler and did not reach Linnaeus until after 1753.

Euphorbia peplus Linnaeus, *Species Plantarum* 1: 456. 1753.
"Habitat in Europae cultis oleraceis." RCN: 3523.
Lectotype (El Hadidi & Fayed in *Taeckholmia* 9: 46. 1978): Herb.
    Linn. No. 630.24 (LINN).
Current name: ***Euphorbia peplus*** L. (Euphorbiaceae).

Euphorbia pilosa Linnaeus, *Species Plantarum* 1: 460. 1753.
"Habitat in Sibiria." RCN: 3545.
Type not designated.
Original material: Herb. Linn. No. 630.59 (LINN); [icon] in
    Barrelier, Pl. Galliam: 5, t. 885. 1714; [icon] in Gmelin, Fl. Sibirica
    2: 226, t. 93. 1752.

Current name: ***Euphorbia pilosa*** L. (Euphorbiaceae).
Note: See Baikov (in *Turczaninowia* 3(4): 39–42. 2001) who identifies
    (and illustrates as f. 1) Gmelin's cited t. 93 as *E. lutescens* Ledeb. He
    also notes 630.59 (LINN).

Euphorbia pilulifera Linnaeus, *Species Plantarum* 1: 454. 1753, *nom.
    rej.*
"Habitat in India." RCN: 3511.
Lectotype (Brown & al. in Oliver, *Fl. Trop. Africa* 6(1): 497–498.
    1911): Herb. Linn. No. 630.8 (LINN).
Current name: ***Euphorbia parviflora*** L. (Euphorbiaceae).

Euphorbia pinea Linnaeus, *Systema Naturae*, ed. 12, 2: 333. 1767.
RCN: 3538.
Type not designated.
Original material: none traced.
Current name: ***Euphorbia pinea*** L. (Euphorbiaceae).

Euphorbia pithyusa Linnaeus, *Species Plantarum* 1: 458. 1753.
"Habitat in arenosis Belgii, Hispaniae, Italiae." RCN: 3534.
Type not designated.
Original material: Herb. Linn. No. 630.42 (LINN); [icon] in
    Daléchamps, Hist. General. Pl. 2: 1652. 1586.
Current name: ***Euphorbia pithyusa*** L. (Euphorbiaceae).

Euphorbia platyphyllos Linnaeus, *Species Plantarum* 1: 460. 1753.
"Habitat in agris Galliae, Angliae, Germaniae." RCN: 3547.
Type not designated.
Original material: Herb. Burser XVI(2): 46 (UPS); Herb. Linn. No.
    630.61 (LINN); [icon] in Fuchs, Hist. Stirp.: 810, 813. 1542.
Current name: ***Euphorbia platyphyllos*** L. (Euphorbiaceae).

Euphorbia polygonifolia Linnaeus, *Species Plantarum* 1: 455. 1753.
"Habitat in Canada, Virginia." RCN: 3518.
Lectotype (Wheeler in *Rhodora* 43: 117. 1941): *Kalm*, Herb. Linn.
    No. 630.19 (LINN).
Current name: ***Euphorbia polygonifolia*** L. (Euphorbiaceae).
Note: See notes by Reveal & al. (in *Huntia* 7: 222. 1987). However,
    Wheeler's type statement clearly complies with Art. 7.11.

Euphorbia portlandica Linnaeus, *Species Plantarum* 1: 458. 1753.
"Habitat in Angliae Devonschire." RCN: 3535.
Type not designated.
Original material: none traced.
Current name: ***Euphorbia portlandica*** L. (Euphorbiaceae).

Euphorbia portulacoides Linnaeus, *Species Plantarum* 1: 456. 1753.
"Habitat in Philadelphia. Kalm." RCN: 3521.
Lectotype (Croizat in *Darwiniana* 6: 183. 1943): [icon] *"Tithymalus
    perennis, Portulacae folio, vulgo Pichua"* in Feuillée, J. Obs. 2: 707, t.
    2. 1714.
Current name: ***Euphorbia portulacoides*** L. (Euphorbiaceae).

Euphorbia segetalis Linnaeus, *Species Plantarum* 1: 458. 1753.
"Habitat in Mauritania." RCN: 3539.
Type not designated.
Original material: [icon] in Morison, Pl. Hist. Univ. 3: 339, s. 10, t. 2,
    f. 3. 1699.
Current name: ***Euphorbia segetalis*** L. (Euphorbiaceae).

Euphorbia serrata Linnaeus, *Species Plantarum* 1: 459. 1753.
"Habitat in Narbona, Hispania." RCN: 3541.
Lectotype (Jafri & El-Gadi, *Fl. Libya* 89: 22. 1982): *Löfling 369*,
    Herb. Linn. No. 630.50 (LINN).
Current name: ***Euphorbia serrata*** L. (Euphorbiaceae).

Euphorbia spinosa Linnaeus, *Species Plantarum* 1: 457. 1753.
"Habitat in Creta." RCN: 3531.
Type not designated.
Original material: Herb. Burser XVI(2): 42 (UPS); Herb. Clifford: 200, *Euphorbia* 24 (BM).
Current name: ***Euphorbia spinosa*** L. (Euphorbiaceae).

Euphorbia stricta Linnaeus, *Systema Naturae,* ed. 10, 2: 1048. 1759.
RCN: 3542.
Lectotype (Radcliffe-Smith in Davis, *Fl. Turkey* 7: 593. 1982): Herb. Linn. No. 630.54 (LINN).
Current name: ***Euphorbia stricta*** L. (Euphorbiaceae).
Note: Dandy (in *Watsonia* 7: 157–178. 1969) treated this as a superfluous name for *E. verrucosa* L. (1753), but Riedl (in *Taxon* 19: 798. 1970) disagreed, noting that both names appeared in the 1759 account of the genus.

Euphorbia sylvatica Linnaeus, *Species Plantarum* 1: 463. 1753.
"Habitat in Germania, Gallia, Hispania, Italia." RCN: 3555.
Lectotype (Geltman in *Komarovia* 2: 23. 2002): Herb. Linn. No. 630.72 (LINN).
Current name: ***Euphorbia amygdaloides*** L. subsp. ***amygdaloides*** (Euphorbiaceae).

Euphorbia terracina Linnaeus, *Species Plantarum,* ed. 2, 1: 654. 1762.
"Habitat in Hispania. Alstroemer." RCN: 3528.
Lectotype (El Hadidi & Fayed in *Taeckholmia* 9: 50. 1978): Herb. Linn. No. 630.33 (LINN).
Current name: ***Euphorbia terracina*** L. (Euphorbiaceae).

Euphorbia thymifolia Linnaeus, *Species Plantarum* 1: 454. 1753.
"Habitat in India." RCN: 3513.
Lectotype (Wheeler in *Rhodora* 43: 253. 1941): Herb. Linn. No. 630.10 (LINN).
Current name: ***Euphorbia thymifolia*** L. (Euphorbiaceae).

Euphorbia tirucalli Linnaeus, *Species Plantarum* 1: 452. 1753.
"Habitat in India." RCN: 3502.
Lectotype (Leach in *Kirkia* 9: 70. 1973): [icon] *"Tithymalus Indicus frutescens"* in Commelin, Hort. Med. Amstelod. Pl. Rar. 1: 27, t. 14. 1697.
Current name: ***Euphorbia tirucalli*** L. (Euphorbiaceae).
Note: See also Wijnands (*Bot. Commelins*: 102. 1983).

Euphorbia tithymaloides Linnaeus, *Species Plantarum* 1: 453. 1753.
"Habitat in Curassao." RCN: 3503.
Type not designated.
Original material: Herb. Clifford: 198, *Euphorbia* 10 (BM).
Current name: ***Euphorbia tithymaloides*** L. (Euphorbiaceae).
Note: Croizat (in *Caldasia* 2: 134. 1943) and Dressler (in *Contr. Gray Herb.* 182: 138, 147. 1957) designated different neotypes for this name but a neotype cannot be designated where original material (in this case, a Clifford sheet) is in existence.

Euphorbia tithymaloides Linnaeus var. **myrtifolia** Linnaeus, *Species Plantarum* 1: 453. 1753.
RCN: 3503.
Lectotype (Dressler in *Contr. Gray Herb.* 182: 138. 1957): [icon] *"Tithymalus Curassavicus Myrti folius"* in Commelin, Hort. Med. Amstelod. Pl. Rar. 1: 31, t. 16. 1697.
Current name: ***Euphorbia tithymaloides*** L. (Euphorbiaceae).

Euphorbia tithymaloides Linnaeus var. **padifolia** Linnaeus, *Species Plantarum* 1: 453. 1753.

"Habitat forte in India." RCN: 3503.
Type not designated.
Original material: [icon] in Dillenius, Hort. Eltham. 2: 383, t. 288, f. 372. 1732.
Current name: ***Euphorbia tithymaloides*** L. subsp. ***padifolia*** (L.) V.W. Steinm. (Euphorbiaceae).

Euphorbia tuberosa Linnaeus, *Species Plantarum* 1: 456. 1753.
"Habitat in Aegypto & Aethiopia." RCN: 3526.
Type not designated.
Original material: [icon] in Buxbaum, Pl. Minus Cognit. Cent. 2: 27, t. 23. 1728; [icon] in Burman, Rar. Afric. Pl.: 9, t. 4. 1738.
Current name: ***Euphorbia tuberosa*** L. (Euphorbiaceae).

Euphorbia verrucosa Linnaeus, *Species Plantarum* 1: 459. 1753.
"Habitat in Gallia, Helvetia." RCN: 3542.
Type not designated.
Original material: Herb. Linn. No. 630.54? (LINN); Herb. Burser XVI(2): 38 (UPS).
Current name: ***Euphorbia verrucosa*** L. (Euphorbiaceae).
Note: Khan (in *Notes Roy. Bot. Gard. Edinburgh* 25: 103. 1964) used the name in the sense of *E. pubescens* Vahl, based on 630.51 (LINN). Dandy (in *Watsonia* 7: 163. 1969) rejected the name as ambiguous, though Riedl (in *Taxon* 19: 798. 1970) argued for its retention. Lambinon (in *Taxon* 30: 363. 1981) proposed its formal rejection but this was declined by the Committee for Spermatophyta (in *Taxon* 35: 559. 1986), partly because 630.51 was a post-1753 addition to Linnaeus' collection and cannot be the type of the name.

Euphorbia viminalis Linnaeus, *Species Plantarum* 1: 452. 1753.
"Habitat in Africae maritimis." RCN: 1753.
Replaced synonym of: *Cynanchum aphyllum* L. (1768), *nom. illeg.*
Lectotype (Liede & Meve in *Bot. J. Linn. Soc.* 112: 2, f. 1. 1993): [icon] *"Felfel Tavil, Piper longum Aegyptium"* in Alpino, De Plantis Aegypti: 190, t. 53. 1735. – Epitype (Liede & Meve in *Bot. J. Linn. Soc.* 118: 47. 1995): *Bassi s.n.* Herb. Linn. No. 308.1 (LINN).
Current name: ***Sarcostemma viminale*** (L.) W.T. Aiton (Asclepiadaceae).

Euphrasia latifolia Linnaeus, *Species Plantarum* 2: 604. 1753.
"Habitat in Apulia, Italia, Monspelii." RCN: 4379.
Lectotype (designated here by Sutton): [icon] *"Euphrasia pratensis Italica latifolia"* in Morison, Pl. Hist. Univ. 3: 431, s. 11, t. 24, f. 8. 1699.
Current name: ***Parentucellia latifolia*** (L.) Caruel (Scrophulariaceae).
Note: Hedge (in Davis in *Notes Roy. Bot. Gard. Edinburgh* 36: 11. 1978) treated 759.1 (LINN) as the type. However, the sheet lacks the relevant *Species Plantarum* number (i.e. "1"), is a post-1753 addition to the collection, and not original material for the name.

Euphrasia linifolia Linnaeus, *Species Plantarum* 2: 604. 1753.
"Habitat in Italia, Helvetia, Gallia." RCN: 4384.
Lectotype (Bolliger in *Willdenowia* 26: 100. 1996): *Gabriel*, Herb. Linn. No. 759.7 (LINN).
Current name: ***Odontites luteus*** (L.) Clairv. (Scrophulariaceae).

Euphrasia lutea Linnaeus, *Species Plantarum* 2: 604. 1753.
"Habitat in Europa australi." RCN: 4383.
Lectotype (Bolliger in *Willdenowia* 26: 100. 1996): Herb. Linn. No. 759.5 (LINN).
Current name: ***Odontites luteus*** (L.) Clairv. (Scrophulariaceae).

Euphrasia odontites Linnaeus, *Species Plantarum* 2: 604. 1753.
"Habitat in Europae arvis pascuisque sterilibus." RCN: 4382.

Lectotype (Snogerup in *Acta Bot. Fenn.* 124: 4. 1983): Herb. Burser XIII: 68 (UPS).
Current name: **Odontites vulgaris** Moench (Scrophulariaceae).

Euphrasia officinalis Linnaeus, *Species Plantarum* 2: 604. 1753.
"Habitat in Europae pascuis aridis." RCN: 4380.
Lectotype (Yeo in *Bot. J. Linn. Soc.* 77: 237. 1978): Herb. Linn. No. 759.2, excl. middle specimen (LINN).
Generitype of *Euphrasia* Linnaeus (vide Green, *Prop. Brit. Bot.*: 167. 1929).
Current name: **Euphrasia officinalis** L. subsp. **officinalis** (Scrophulariaceae).
Note: Some authors (e.g. Pugsley in *Bot. J. Linn. Soc.* 48: 522. 1930; Smejkal in *Biol. Práce* 9(9): 6. 1963; Sell & Yeo in *Bot. J. Linn. Soc.* 63: 201. 1970) have rejected this as a *nomen ambiguum*, as did Yeo (in *Bot. J. Linn. Soc.* 77: 237. 1979), despite designating a lectotype. Silverside (in *Watsonia* 18: 343–346. 1991) accepted Yeo's typification but argued that there are no grounds for rejecting the name, and applied it in the sense of *E. rostkoviana* Hayne var. *fennica* (Kihlman) Jalas.

Euphrasia tricuspidata Linnaeus, *Species Plantarum* 2: 604. 1753.
"Habitat in Italia." RCN: 4381.
Lectotype (Vitek & al., in *Annalen Nat. Hist. Mus. Wien, B,* in press): [icon] *"Eufragia sassatile con foglie larghe lanceolate"* in Zanoni, Rar. Stirp. Hist.: 110, t. 76. 1742. – Epitype (Vitek & al., in *Annalen Nat. Hist. Mus. Wien, B,* in press): Flora Exsiccata Austro-Hungarica 143, uppermost, richly-branched specimen (BM).
Current name: **Euphrasia tricuspidata** L. (Scrophulariaceae).
Note: Yeo (in *Bot. J. Linn. Soc.* 77: 37. 1979) designated 759.3 (LINN) as lectotype but the sheet lacks the relevant *Species Plantarum* number (i.e. "3"), was a post-1753 addition to the herbarium, and is not original material for the name.

Euphrasia viscosa Linnaeus, *Systema Naturae,* ed. 12, 2: 406; *Mantissa Plantarum*: 86. 1767.
"Habitat in Galloprovinciae glareosis sterilibus." RCN: 4385.
Type not designated.
Original material: [icon] in Garidel, Hist. Pl. Prov.: 351, t. 80. 1715.
Current name: **Parentucellia viscosa** (L.) Caruel (Scrophulariaceae).

Evolvulus alsinoides (Linnaeus) Linnaeus, *Species Plantarum,* ed. 2, 1: 392. 1762.
"Habitat in Malabaria, Zeylona, Bisnagaria, Bahama." RCN: 2178.
Basionym: *Convolvulus alsinoides* L. (1753).
Lectotype (Verdcourt in Hubbard & Milne-Redhead, *Fl. Trop. E. Africa, Convolvulaceae*: 18. 1963): Herb. Hermann 3: 55, No. 76 (BM-000628009).
Current name: **Evolvulus alsinoides** (L.) L. (Convolvulaceae).

Evolvulus gangeticus (Linnaeus) Linnaeus, *Species Plantarum,* ed. 2, 1: 391. 1762.
"Habitat in India." RCN: 2176.
Basionym: *Convolvulus gangeticus* L. (1756).
Type not designated.
Original material: as basionym.
Current name: **Cocculus hirsutus** (L.) Diels (Menispermaceae).

Evolvulus linifolius (Linnaeus) Linnaeus, *Species Plantarum,* ed. 2, 1: 392. 1762.
"Habitat in Jamaica." RCN: 2178.

Basionym: *Convolvulus linifolius* L. (1756).
Lectotype (van Oostroom in *Meded. Bot. Mus. Herb. Rijks Univ. Utrecht* 14: 36. 1935 [1934]): *Miller,* Herb. Linn. No. 393.5 (LINN).
Current name: **Evolvulus alsinoides** (L.) L. (Convolvulaceae).

Evolvulus nummularius (Linnaeus) Linnaeus, *Species Plantarum,* ed. 2, 1: 391. 1762.
"Habitat in Jamaicae, Barbados pratis." RCN: 2175.
Basionym: *Convolvulus nummularius* L. (1753).
Lectotype (Verdcourt in Jarvis & al., *Regnum Veg.* 127: 46. 1993): [icon] *"Convolvulus minor repens, nummulariae folio, flore coeruleo"* in Sloane, Voy. Jamaica 1: 157, t. 99, f. 2. 1707. – Typotype: Herb. Sloane 3: 19 (BM-SL).
Generitype of *Evolvulus* Linnaeus.
Current name: **Evolvulus nummularius** (L.) L. (Convolvulaceae).
Note: Oostroom (in *Meded. Bot. Mus. Herb. Rijks Univ. Utrecht* 14: 115, 120. 1934) indicated what is evidently 393.1 (LINN) as type. However, this is not original material for the name, and Verdcourt (in Hubbard & Milne-Redhead, *Fl. Trop. E. Africa, Convolvulaceae*: 16. 1963) and Stearn (in *Taxon* 21: 647. 1972) instead treated material in Sloane's herbarium as the type. Despite the close relationship between Sloane's specimens and his published illustrations, the former were not studied by Linnaeus. Consequently, Verdcourt's (1993) indication of Sloane's illustration as the type is accepted as the earliest typification.

Evolvulus tridentatus (Linnaeus) Linnaeus, *Species Plantarum,* ed. 2, 1: 392. 1762.
["Habitat in India."] Sp. Pl. 1: 157 (1753). RCN: 2179.
Basionym: *Convolvulus tridentatus* L. (1753).
Lectotype (Verdcourt in Hubbard & Milne-Redhead, *Fl. Trop. E. Africa, Convolvulaceae*: 51. 1963): [icon] *"Sendera-clandi"* in Rheede, Hort. Malab. 11: 133, t. 65. 1692.
Current name: **Xenostegia tridentata** (L.) D.F. Austin & Staples (Convolvulaceae).

Exacum pedunculatum Linnaeus, *Species Plantarum* 1: 112. 1753.
"Habitat in India." RCN: 922.
Lectotype (Klackenberg in *Nordic J. Bot.* 3: 367. 1983): [icon] *"Centaurium minus Hypericoides, flore luteo Lini capitulis"* in Plukenet, Almag. Mant.: 43, t. 343, f. 3. 1700.
Current name: **Exacum pedunculatum** L. (Gentianaceae).

Exacum sessile Linnaeus, *Species Plantarum* 1: 112. 1753.
"Habitat in Asia & Africa." RCN: 921.
Lectotype (Cramer in Dassanayake & Fosberg, *Revised Handb. Fl. Ceylon* 3: 65. 1981): Herb. Hermann 3: 42, No. 25 (BM-000621956).
Generitype of *Exacum* Linnaeus (vide Hitchcock, *Prop. Brit. Bot.*: 125. 1929).
Current name: **Exacum sessile** L. (Gentianaceae).

Excoecaria agallocha Linnaeus, *Systema Naturae,* ed. 10, 2: 1288. 1759.
["Habitat in Amboina."] Sp. Pl., ed. 2, 2: 1451. 1763. RCN: 7397.
Lectotype (Merrill, *Interpret. Rumph. Herb. Amb.*: 327. 1917): [icon] *"Arbor Excaecans"* in Rumphius, Herb. Amboin. 2: 237, t. 79. 1741.
Generitype of *Excoecaria* Linnaeus.
Current name: **Excoecaria agallocha** L. (Euphorbiaceae).

F

Fagara octandra Linnaeus, *Systema Naturae,* ed. 12, 2: 125; *Mantissa Plantarum*: 40. 1767, *nom. illeg.*
"Habitat in Curaçao duris." RCN: 970.
Replaced synonym: *Elaphrium tomentosum* Jacq. (1760).
Type not designated.
Current name: ***Bursera tomentosa*** (Jacq.) Triana & Planch. (Burseraceae).
Note: A superfluous name for *Elaphrium tomentosum* Jacq. (1760).

Fagara piperita Linnaeus, *Systema Naturae,* ed. 10, 2: 897. 1759.
["Habitat in Japonia."] Sp. Pl., ed. 2, 1: 172 (1762). RCN: 968.
Lectotype (Murata in *Acta Phytotax. Geobot.* 35: 30, f. 25. 1984): [icon] *"Seo & Sanjo"* in Kaempfer, Amoen. Exot. Fasc.: 892, 893. 1712.
Current name: ***Zanthoxylum piperitum*** (L.) DC. (Rutaceae).

Fagara pterota Linnaeus, *Systema Naturae,* ed. 10, 2: 897. 1759, *typ. cons.*
["Habitat in Jamaica."] Sp. Pl., ed. 2, 1: 172 (1762). RCN: 967.
Lectotype (Adams in Jarvis & al., *Regnum Veg.* 127: 47. 1993): *Browne*, Herb. Linn. No. 152.2 (LINN).
Generitype of *Fagara* Linnaeus, *nom. cons.*
Current name: ***Zanthoxylum fagara*** (L.) Sarg. (Rutaceae).
Note: Fagara Linnaeus, *nom. cons.* against *Fagara* Duhamel.
   Fawcett & Rendle (*Fl. Jamaica* 4: 175. 1920) stated that this was based on a specimen from Browne noting that "a spec. so named in Solander's hand is in Herb. Linn.", implying doubt as to whether this was to be intended as the type. Porter (in *Brittonia* 28: 445. 1977) and Porter & Elias (in *Ann. Missouri Bot. Gard.* 66: 153. 1979) wrongly assumed *F. pterota* to be homotypic with *Schinus fagara* L. (1753) and treated a Sloane illustration, which was not an original element, as the type of *F. pterota*. Adams' explicit type choice is accepted here.

Fagonia arabica Linnaeus, *Species Plantarum* 1: 386. 1753.
"Habitat in Arabia." RCN: 3045.
Lectotype (Beier in *Syst. Biodivers.* 3: 229. 2005): [icon] *"Fagonia Arabica, longissimis aculeis armata"* in Shaw, Cat. Pl. Afr. As.: 41, f. 220. 1738.
Current name: ***Fagonia arabica*** L. (Zygophyllaceae).

Fagonia cretica Linnaeus, *Species Plantarum* 1: 386. 1753.
"Habitat in Creta." RCN: 3043.
Lectotype (El Hadidi in Jarvis & al., *Regnum Veg.* 127: 47. 1993): [icon] *"Trifolium spinosum Creticum"* in Bauhin, Prodr. Theatri Bot.: 142. 1620.
Generitype of *Fagonia* Linnaeus (vide Hitchcock, *Prop. Brit. Bot.*: 153. 1929).
Current name: ***Fagonia cretica*** L. (Zygophyllaceae).
Note: El-Hadidi (in *Candollea* 21: 39. 1966) indicated an unspecified Linnaean collection as type, and (in *Bot. Not.* 125: 531. 1972) clarified this by indicating 546.1 (LINN) as the holotype. Unfortunately, this sheet is a post-1753 addition to the collection and ineligible as the type. Greuter & al. (in *Willdenowia* 14: 295. 1984) stated that Bauhin's polynomial was the basis of the name, and El-Hadidi (1993) subsequently formalised the choice of a Bauhin illustration as the lectotype.

Fagonia hispanica Linnaeus, *Species Plantarum* 1: 386. 1753.
"Habitat in Hispania." RCN: 3044.
Type not designated.
Original material: none traced.
Current name: ***Fagonia cretica*** L. (Zygophyllaceae).

Fagus castanea Linnaeus, *Species Plantarum* 2: 997. 1753.
"Habitat in Italiae & australioris Europae montibus." RCN: 7228.
Type not designated.
Original material: Herb. Clifford: 447, *Fagus* 2 α (BM).
Current name: ***Castanea sativa*** Mill. (Fagaceae).

Fagus pumila Linnaeus, *Species Plantarum* 2: 998. 1753.
"Habitat in America septentrionali." RCN: 7229.
Lectotype (Johnson in *J. Arnold Arbor.* 69: 41. 1988): *Clayton 927* (BM-000098026).
Current name: ***Castanea pumila*** (L.) Mill. (Fagaceae).

Fagus sylvatica Linnaeus, *Species Plantarum* 2: 998. 1753.
"Habitat in Europa." RCN: 7230.
Lectotype (Jonsell & Jarvis in Jarvis & al., *Regnum Veg.* 127: 47. 1993): Herb. Burser XXII: 92 (UPS).
Generitype of *Fagus* Linnaeus (vide Green, *Prop. Brit. Bot.*: 189. 1929).
Current name: ***Fagus sylvatica*** L. (Fagaceae).
Note: Jonsell & Jarvis (in *Nordic J. Bot.* 14: 153. 1994) gave an explanation for their formal (1993) choice of type.

Ferraria undulata Linnaeus, *Species Plantarum,* ed. 2, 2: 1353. 1763, *nom. illeg.*
"Habitat ad Cap. b. spei." RCN: 6910.
Replaced synonym: *Ferraria crispa* Burm. (1761).
Lectotype (de Vos in *J. S. African Bot.* 45: 338. 1979): [icon] *"Ferraria foliis nervosis, ensiformibus, vaginantibus; petalis fimbriatis"* in Burman in Nova Acta Phys.-Med. Acad. Caes. Leop.-Carol. Nat. Cur. 2: 199, t. 3, f. 1. 1761.
Current name: ***Ferraria crispa*** Burm. (Iridaceae).
Note: A superfluous name for *F. crispa* Burm. (1761), cited explicitly in the protologue, as noted by Moore (in *Baileya* 19: 110. 1974).

Ferula assa-foetida Linnaeus, *Species Plantarum* 1: 248. 1753.
"Habitat in Persia." RCN: 1992.
Lectotype (Chamberlain in *Notes Roy. Bot. Gard. Edinburgh* 35: 230. 1977): [icon] *"Hingiseh seu Planta Asae foetidae"* in Kaempfer, Amoen. Exot. Fasc.: 535, 536. 1712.
Current name: ***Ferula assa-foetida*** L. (Apiaceae).

Ferula canadensis Linnaeus, *Species Plantarum* 1: 247. 1753.
"Habitat in Virginia." RCN: 1991.
Lectotype (Reveal in Jarvis & al. in *Taxon* 55: 212. 2006): *Clayton 548* (BM-000051614).
Current name: ***Ligusticum canadense*** (L.) Vail (Apiaceae).

Ferula communis Linnaeus, *Species Plantarum* 1: 246. 1753.
"Habitat in Europa australi." RCN: 1984.
Lectotype (Jafri in Jafri & El-Gadi, *Fl. Libya* 117: 98. 1985): Herb. Clifford: 95, *Ferula* 1 (BM-000558268).
Generitype of *Ferula* Linnaeus (vide Hitchcock, *Prop. Brit. Bot.*: 140. 1929).
Current name: ***Ferula communis*** L. subsp. ***communis*** (Apiaceae).

Ferula ferulago Linnaeus, *Species Plantarum* 1: 247. 1753.
"Habitat in Sicilia." RCN: 1987.
Lectotype (Reduron & Watson in Jarvis & al. in *Taxon* 55: 212. 2006): Herb. Clifford: 95, *Ferula* 4 (BM-000558272).
Current name: ***Ferula communis*** L. subsp. ***communis*** (Apiaceae).

Ferula glauca Linnaeus, *Species Plantarum* 1: 247. 1753.
"Habitat in Sicilia, Italia." RCN: 1985.
Lectotype (Reduron & Watson in Jarvis & al. in *Taxon* 55: 212. 2006): Herb. Clifford: 95, *Ferula* 2 (BM-000558269).
Current name: ***Ferula communis*** L. subsp. ***glauca*** (L.) Rouy & E.G. Camus (Apiaceae).

Ferula meoides Linnaeus, *Species Plantarum* 1: 247. 1753.
"Habitat in Oriente." RCN: 1989.
Lectotype (Watson in Jarvis & al. in *Taxon* 55: 212. 2006): Herb. Clifford: 95, *Ferula* 6 (BM-000558274).
Current name: ***Ferula communis*** L. subsp. ***communis*** (Apiaceae).

Ferula nodiflora Linnaeus, *Species Plantarum* 1: 247. 1753.
"Habitat in Europa australi, Istria." RCN: 1990.
Lectotype (Watson & Reduron in Jarvis & al. in *Taxon* 55: 212. 2006): [icon] *"Panax Asclepium Ferulae facie"* in Plantin, Pl. Stirp. Icon.: 783. 1581.
Current name: ***Ferula communis*** L. subsp. ***communis*** (Apiaceae).

Ferula orientalis Linnaeus, *Species Plantarum* 1: 247. 1753.
"Habitat in Oriente." RCN: 1988.
Lectotype (Watson in Jarvis & al in *Taxon* 55: 212, 560. 2006): Herb. Clifford: 95, *Ferula* 5, sheet A (BM-000558278).
Current name: ***Ferula orientalis*** L. (Apiaceae).
Note: Watson (in Jarvis & al. in *Taxon* 55: 212. 2006) designated Clifford material (BM) as the type, but did not distinguish between two sheets (which are evidently not part of a single gathering so Art. 9.15 does not apply). However, this omission was corrected in *Taxon* 55: 560 (2006), from where the typification dates.

Ferula tingitana Linnaeus, *Species Plantarum* 1: 247. 1753.
"Habitat in Oriente." RCN: 1986.
Lectotype (Reduron in Jarvis & al. in *Taxon* 55: 212. 2006): Herb. Clifford: 95, *Ferula* 3 (BM-000558270).
Current name: ***Ferula tingitana*** L. (Apiaceae).

Festuca amethystina Linnaeus, *Species Plantarum* 1: 74. 1753.
"Habitat in Italia, Gallia, Anglia." RCN: 619.
Lectotype (Kerguélen & Plonka in *Bull. Soc. Bot. Centre-Ouest*, n.s., num. spéc., 10: 117. 1989): [icon] *"Gramen montanum, foliis capillaceis, longioribus, panicula heteromalla, spadicea & veluti Amethystina"* in Scheuchzer, Agrostographia: 276, t. 6, f. 7. 1719. – Epitype (Scholz in Cafferty & al. in *Taxon* 49: 250. 2000): Switzerland. Fribourg au Breitfeld, 670m, 8 Jun 1928, *Jacquet s.n.* (B).
Current name: ***Festuca amethystina*** L. subsp. ***amethystina*** (Poaceae).

Festuca barbata Linnaeus, *Demonstr. Pl. Horto Upsaliensi*: 3. 1753.
"Habitat in Hispania." RCN: 630.
Lectotype (Scholz in Cafferty & al. in *Taxon* 49: 250. 2000): Herb. Linn. No. 92.26 (LINN).
Current name: ***Schismus barbatus*** (L.) Thell. (Poaceae).
Note: Although Kerguélen (in *Lejeunia*, n.s., 75: 253. 1975) stated "Type: ...LINN", this is not accepted as a formal typification, for the reasons explained by Cafferty & al. (in *Taxon* 49: 240. 2000).

Festuca bromoides Linnaeus, *Species Plantarum* 1: 75. 1753.
"Habitat in Anglia, Gallia." RCN: 621.
Lectotype (Stace & Jarvis in *Bot. J. Linn. Soc.* 91: 436. 1985): Herb. A. van Royen No. 912.356–219 (L).
Current name: ***Vulpia bromoides*** (L.) Gray (Poaceae).
Note: Henrard (in *Blumea* 2: 302. 1937) discussed this name, and Hedberg (in *Symb. Bot. Upsal.* 15(1): 38. 1957) noted the existence of 92.14 (LINN) but without treating it as the type.

Festuca cristata Linnaeus, *Species Plantarum* 1: 76. 1753.
"Habitat in Lusitanae collibus sterilibus." RCN: 629.
Lectotype (Sherif & Siddiqi in El-Gadi, *Fl. Libya* 145: 167. 1988): Herb. Linn. No. 92.24 (LINN).
Current name: ***Rostraria cristata*** (L.) Tzvelev (Poaceae).

Festuca decumbens Linnaeus, *Species Plantarum* 1: 75. 1753.
"Habitat in Europae pascuis siccis sterilibus." RCN: 626.
Lectotype (Baeza in Cafferty & al. in *Taxon* 49: 250. 2000): Herb. Linn. No. 92.16 (LINN).
Current name: ***Danthonia decumbens*** (L.) DC. (Poaceae).

Festuca dumetorum Linnaeus, *Species Plantarum*, ed. 2, 1: 109. 1762.
"Habitat in Hispania." RCN: 617.
Lectotype (Howarth in *J. Linn. Soc., Bot.* 46: 326. 1923): Herb. Linn. No. 92.7 (LINN).
Current name: ***Festuca rubra*** L. **agg.** (Poaceae).
Note: This name has been treated in a variety of ways, and by some as a *nomen ambiguum*. There may be grounds for making a formal proposal for rejection.

Festuca duriuscula Linnaeus, *Species Plantarum* 1: 74. 1753.
"Habitat in Europae pratis siccis." RCN: 616.
Lectotype (van der Meijden in Cafferty & al. in *Taxon* 49: 250. 2000): Herb. A. van Royen No. 913.7–451 (L).
Current name: ***Festuca rubra*** L. subsp. ***rubra*** var. ***barbata*** (Schrank) Hack. (Poaceae).
Note: See Howarth (in *J. Linn Soc., Bot.* 46: 325–326. 1923). Kerguélen (in *Lejeunia*, n.s., 75: 171, 173–174. 1975) provided a confused type statement "Type: 'Habitat in Europae pratis siccus' (LINN, holo) 'SCHEUCHZ, 285'", and informally rejected the name as ambiguous. However, no formal proposal was made.

Festuca elatior Linnaeus, *Species Plantarum* 1: 75. 1753, *nom. utique rej.*
"Habitat in Europae pratis fertilissimis." RCN: 627.
Lectotype (Terrell in *Brittonia* 19: 131. 1967): Herb. Linn. No. 92.17 (LINN).
Current name: ***Festuca arundinacea*** Schreb. (Poaceae).

Festuca fluitans Linnaeus, *Species Plantarum* 1: 75. 1753.
"Habitat in Europae fossis & paludibus." RCN: 628.
Lectotype (Kit Tan in Davis, *Fl. Turkey* 9: 537. 1985): Herb. Linn. No. 92.22 (LINN; iso- US, fragm.).
Current name: ***Glyceria fluitans*** (L.) R. Br. (Poaceae).
Note: Although Kerguélen (in *Lejeunia*, n.s., 75: 185. 1975) stated "Type: ...LINN", this is not accepted as a formal typification, for the reasons explained by Cafferty & al. (in *Taxon* 49: 240. 2000).

Festuca fusca Linnaeus, *Systema Naturae*, ed. 10, 2: 876. 1759.
["Habitat in Palaestina."] Sp. Pl., ed. 2, 1: 109 (1762). RCN: 625.
Lectotype (Phillips in Polhill, *Fl. Trop. E. Africa, Gramineae* 2: 281. 1974): *Hasselquist*, Herb. Linn. No. 92.21 (LINN).
Current name: ***Leptochloa fusca*** (L.) Kunth (Poaceae).

Festuca incrassata Linnaeus, *Species Plantarum* 1: 75. 1753, *nom. inval.*
Type not relevant.
Current name: ***Nardus maritimus*** (L.) Murb. (Poaceae).
Note: This name appeared in the rare, original version of *Species Plantarum* (1753) and was replaced by *F. maritima* in the amended version. *Festuca incrassata* is an invalid name (see Stace & Jarvis in *Bot. J. Linn. Soc.* 91: 437. 1985).

Festuca marina Linnaeus, *Amoenitates Academicae* 4: 96. 1759.
"Habitat [in Anglia.]"
Lectotype (Stace & Jarvis in *Bot. J. Linn. Soc.* 91: 440. 1985): *Newton s.n.*, Herb. Sloane 84: 87, verso (BM-SL).
Current name: ***Catapodium marinum*** (L.) C.E. Hubb. (Poaceae).
Note: López González (in *Anales Jard. Bot. Madrid* 53: 266–267. 1995) argued that this name is an orthographic variant of *F. maritima* L. (1753).

Festuca maritima Linnaeus, *Species Plantarum* 1: 75. 1753.
"Habitat in Hispania." RCN: 622.
Lectotype (Hubbard in *Proc. Linn. Soc. London* 148: 110. 1936): Herb. Linn. No. 104.17 (LINN).
Current name: ***Nardurus maritimus*** (L.) Murb. (Poaceae).

Festuca myuros Linnaeus, *Species Plantarum* 1: 74. 1753.
"Habitat in Anglia, Italia." RCN: 620.
Lectotype (Stace & Jarvis in *Bot. J. Linn. Soc.* 91: 436. 1985): Herb. A. van Royen No. 912.356–218 (L).
Current name: ***Vulpia myuros*** (L.) C.C. Gmel. (Poaceae).
Note: Meikle (*Fl. Cyprus* 2: 1733. 23 Apr 1985) indicated unspecified material in LINN as type but did not distinguish between sheets 92.12 and 92.13 (which are not part of a single gathering so Art. 9.15 does not apply).

Festuca ovina Linnaeus, *Species Plantarum* 1: 73. 1753.
"Habitat in Alpibus Lapponicae, Helvetiae, Scotiae." RCN: 614.
Lectotype (Kerguélen in *Lejeunia*, n.s., 75: 150. 1975): Herb. Linn. No. 92.1; Lapland Herb. No. 55 (LINN; iso- LAPP).
Generitype of *Festuca* Linnaeus (vide Hitchcock, *Prop. Brit. Bot.*: 120. 1929).
Current name: ***Festuca ovina*** L. (Poaceae).
Note: A detailed account of the original elements is given by Jarvis & al. (in *Watsonia* 16: 300. 1987) who also illustrated the type (their pl. 2A), though their choice is pre-dated by that of Kerguélen (1975).

Festuca ovina Linnaeus var. **vivipara** Linnaeus, *Flora Suecica*, ed. 2: 31. 1755.
"Habitat in alpibus Lapponicis, ubi nullum gramen magis frequens." RCN: 614.
Lectotype (Jarvis & al. in *Watsonia* 16: 300. 1987): Herb. Linn. No. 92.5 (LINN).
Current name: ***Festuca vivipara*** (L.) Sm. (Poaceae).

Festuca phoenicoides Linnaeus, *Systema Naturae*, ed. 12, 2: 96; *Mantissa Plantarum*: 33. 1767.
"Habitat in Galloprovinciae maritimis arenosis." RCN: 624.
Lectotype (Schippmann & Jarvis in *Taxon* 37: 160, f. 2. 1988): [icon] *"Festuca Spiculis alternis, sub sessilibus, Teretibus, Foliis involutis mucronato-pungentibus"* in Gérard, Fl. Gallo-Provincialis: 95, t. 2, f. 2. 1761 (see above, right).
Current name: ***Brachypodium phoenicoides*** (L.) Roem. & Schult. (Poaceae).
Note: Although Kerguélen (in *Lejeunia*, n.s., 75: 95. 1975) stated "Type: ...LINN", this is not accepted as a formal typification, for the reasons explained by Cafferty & al. (in *Taxon* 49: 240. 2000).

Festuca reptatrix Linnaeus, *Species Plantarum*, ed. 2, 1: 108. 1762.
"Habitat in Arabia, Palaestina." RCN: 615.
Lectotype (Snow in Cafferty & al. in *Taxon* 49: 250. 2000): *Hasselquist*, Herb. Linn. No. 92.20, left specimen (LINN).
Current name: ***Leptochloa fusca*** (L.) Kunth subsp. ***fusca*** (Poaceae).
Note: Although this name first appeared in *Flora Palaestina*: 13 (1756), it was a *nomen nudum* in that work, and therefore invalid. The binomial dates from 1762.

Fig. 2.ᵉ Pag. 95.

1. Poa paniculâ erectâ Spiculis trifloris glabris corollis acuminatis, Calyce duplo longioribus. Pag. 91. N.º 11.
2. Festuca Spiculis alternis sub sessilibus, Teretibus, Foliis involutis mucronato-pungentibus. Pag. 95. N.º 5.

The lectotype of *Festuca phoenicoides* L.

Festuca rubra Linnaeus, *Species Plantarum* 1: 74. 1753.
"Habitat in Europae sterilibus siccis." RCN: 618.
Lectotype (Jarvis & al. in *Watsonia* 16: 302, pl. 2B. 1987): *Linnaeus s.n.* (GB).
Current name: ***Festuca rubra*** L. (Poaceae).

Festuca serotina Linnaeus, *Systema Naturae*, ed. 10, 2: 876. 1759.
["Habitat Veronae. Seguier."] Sp. Pl., ed. 2, 1: 112 (1762). RCN: 535.
Basionym of: *Agrostis serotina* (L.) L. (1767).
Lectotype (Scholz in Cafferty & al. in *Taxon* 49: 251. 2000): [icon] *"Gramen loliaceum serotinum, panicula dispansa"* in Séguier, Pl. Veron. 3: 146, 83, t. 3, f. 2. 1754.
Current name: ***Cleistogenes serotina*** (L.) Keng (Poaceae).

Festuca spadicea Linnaeus, *Systema Naturae*, ed. 12, 2: 732. 1767. "Habitat Monspelii. Gouan." RCN: 623.
Lectotype (Kerguélen & Plonka in *Bull. Soc. Bot. Centre-Ouest*, n.s., num. spéc., 10: 243. 1989): *Gouan s.n.*, Herb. Linn. No. 92.37 (LINN).
Current name: ***Festuca paniculata*** (L.) Schinz & Thell. subsp. ***spadicea*** (L.) Litard. (Poaceae).
Note: Although Kerguélen (in *Lejeunia*, n.s., 75: 181. 1975) stated "Type: ...LINN", this is not accepted as a formal typification, for the reasons explained by Cafferty & al. (in *Taxon* 49: 240. 2000). Kerguélen (in *Lejeunia*, n.s., 110: 4. 1983) suggested that the name should be rejected.

Fevillea cordifolia Linnaeus, *Species Plantarum* 2: 1013. 1753. "Habitat in America calidiore." RCN: 7433.
Replaced synonym of: *Fevillea scandens* L. (1763), *nom. illeg.*
Lectotype (Jeffrey in Jarvis & al., *Regnum Veg.* 127: 47. 1993): [icon] *"Nhandiroba"* in Plumier, Nov. Pl. Amer.: 20, t. 27. 1703.
Current name: ***Fevillea cordifolia*** L. (Cucurbitaceae).
Note: Fevillea cordifolia was treated as the generitype by Britton & Wilson (*Sci. Surv. Porto Rico* 6: 270. 1925) (see McNeill & al. in *Taxon* 36: 371. 1987). However, under Art. 10.5, Ex. 7 (a voted example) of the Vienna Code, this is a type choice made under the American Code and is to be replaced under Art. 10.5b by Green's choice (*Prop. Brit. Bot.*: 190. 1929) of *F. trilobata* L.

Fevillea scandens Linnaeus, *Species Plantarum*, ed. 2, 2: 1457. 1763, *nom. illeg.*
"Habitat in India occidentali." RCN: 7433.
Replaced synonym: *Fevillea cordifolia* L. (1753).
Lectotype (Jeffrey in Jarvis & al., *Regnum Veg.* 127: 47. 1993): [icon] *"Nhandiroba"* in Plumier, Nov. Pl. Amer.: 20, t. 27. 1703.
Current name: ***Fevillea cordifolia*** L. (Cucurbitaceae).
Note: A superfluous name for *F. cordifolia* L. (1753).

Fevillea trilobata Linnaeus, *Species Plantarum* 2: 1014. 1753. "Habitat in Brasilia, Jamaica." RCN: 7434.
Lectotype (Robinson & Wunderlin in *Sida* 21: 1990. 2005): [icon] *"Ghandiroba vel Nhandiroba Brasiliensibus"* in Marggraf, Hist. Rer. Nat. Bras.: 46. 1648.
Generitype of *Fevillea* Linnaeus.
Current name: ***Fevillea trilobata*** L. (Cucurbitaceae).
Note: Fevillea cordifolia was treated as the generitype by Britton & Wilson (*Sci. Surv. Porto Rico* 6: 270. 1925) (see McNeill & al. in *Taxon* 36: 371. 1987). However, under Art. 10.5, Ex. 7 (a voted example) of the Vienna Code, this is a type choice made under the American Code and is to be replaced under Art. 10.5b by Green's choice (*Prop. Brit. Bot.*: 190. 1929) of *F. trilobata* L.

Ficus benghalensis Linnaeus, *Species Plantarum* 2: 1059. 1753. "Habitat in India." RCN: 7721.
Lectotype (Wijnands, *Bot. Commelins*: 153. 1983): [icon] *"Ficus Bengalensis, folio subrotundo, fructu orbiculato"* in Commelin, Hort. Med. Amstelod. Pl. Rar. 1: 119, t. 62. 1697.
Current name: ***Ficus benghalensis*** L. (Moraceae).
Note: See discussion by Corner (in *Gard. Bull. Straits Settlem.* 17: 382. 1960), who interpreted the name via the Rheede element though without formally typifying Linnaeus' name, although Smith (*Fl. Vitiensis Nova* 2: 175. 1981) believed Corner had done so. Wijnands therefore appears to have made the earliest explicit type choice.

Ficus benjamina Linnaeus, *Systema Naturae*, ed. 12, 2: 681; *Mantissa Plantarum*: 129. 1767.
"Habitat in India." RCN: 7720.

Lectotype (Smith, *Fl. Vitiensis Nova* 2: 175. 1981): [icon] *"Itty-alu"* in Rheede, Hort. Malab. 1: 45, t. 26. 1678.
Current name: ***Ficus benjamina*** L. (Moraceae).
Note: Smith wrongly attributed the type choice to Merrill (*Interpret. Rumph. Herb. Amb.*: 195–196. 1917), who merely excluded the cited Rumphius element. Smith's own statement, however, typifies the name, though there appear to be doubts as to the identity of the type. Nicolson & al. (*Interpret. Rheede Hort. Malab.*: 186. 1988) suggest it is probably identifiable as *F. microcarpa* L. f.

Ficus carica Linnaeus, *Species Plantarum* 2: 1059. 1753. "Habitat in Europa australi, Asia." RCN: 7716.
Lectotype (Bhopal & Chaudhri in *Pakistan Syst.* 1(2): 37. 1977): Herb. Linn. No. 1240.1 (LINN).
Generitype of *Ficus* Linnaeus (vide Green, *Prop. Brit. Bot.*: 194. 1929).
Current name: ***Ficus carica*** L. (Moraceae).

Ficus indica Linnaeus, *Species Plantarum* 2: 1060. 1753. "Habitat in Indiis." RCN: 7722.
Type not designated.
Original material: Herb. Linn. No. 1240.8? (LINN); [icon] in Catesby, Nat. Hist. Carolina 2, App.: 18, t. 18. 1747; [icon] in Rheede, Hort. Malab. 3: 73, t. 57. 1682; [icon] in Rheede, Hort. Malab. 3: 85, t. 63. 1682; [icon] in Sloane, Voy. Jamaica 2: 140, t. 223. 1725; [icon] in Tabernaemontanus, New Vollk. Kräuterb.: 1370. 1664; [icon] in Plukenet, Phytographia: t. 178, f. 4. 1692; Almag. Bot.: 144. 1696 – Voucher: Herb. Sloane 96: 34 (BM-SL).
Current name: ***Ficus benghalensis*** L. (Moraceae).
Note: See discussion by Corner (in *Gard. Bull. Straits Settlem.* 17: 382. 1960), who treated this as a synonym of *F. benghalensis* L., though without typifying either name.

Ficus maculata Linnaeus, *Species Plantarum*, ed. 2, 2: 1515. 1763, *nom. illeg.*
"Habitat in America." RCN: 7727.
Replaced synonym: *Ficus serrata* L. (1759).
Type not designated.
Original material: as replaced synonym.
Note: A superfluous name for *F. serrata* L. (1759), the application of which appears uncertain.

Ficus perforata Linnaeus, *Plantae Surinamenses*: 17. 1775, *nom. rej.*
"Habitat [in Surinamo.]" RCN: 7724.
Lectotype (Howard, *Fl. Lesser Antilles* 4: 58. 1988): [icon] *"Ficus foliis ovato-oblongis"* in Plumier in Burman, Pl. Amer.: 124, t. 132, f. 2. 1757.
Current name: ***Ficus americana*** Aubl. (Moraceae).
Note: This name is rejected against *F. americana* Aubl.

Ficus pumila Linnaeus, *Species Plantarum* 2: 1060. 1753. "Habitat in China, Japonia." RCN: 7725.
Type not designated.
Original material: [icon] in Kaempfer, Amoen. Exot. Fasc.: 803, 804. 1712 – Voucher: Herb. Sloane 211: 51.2 (BM-SL).
Current name: ***Ficus pumila*** L. (Moraceae).

Ficus racemosa Linnaeus, *Species Plantarum* 2: 1060. 1753. "Habitat in India." RCN: 7723.
Type not designated.
Original material: [icon] in Rheede, Hort. Malab. 1: 43, t. 25. 1678.
Current name: ***Ficus racemosa*** L. (Moraceae).
Note: See Nicolson & al. (*Interpret. Van Rheede's Hort. Malab.*: 187. 1988) who confirmed the identity of the cited Rheede plate, but did not formally designate a type.

Ficus religiosa Linnaeus, *Species Plantarum* 2: 1059. 1753.
"Habitat in India." RCN: 7719.
Type not designated.
Original material: Herb. Linn. No. 1240.6 (LINN); Herb. Hermann
    4: 40, No. 372 (BM); Herb. Hermann 4: 82, No. 372 (BM); [icon]
    in Rheede, Hort. Malab. 1: 47, t. 27. 1678; [icon] in Plukenet,
    Phytographia: t. 178, f. 2. 1692; Almag. Bot.: 144. 1696 –
    Voucher: Herb. Sloane 93: 160; 96: 33 (BM-SL).
Current name: *Ficus religiosa* L. (Moraceae).
Note: Although Browicz (in Rechinger, *Fl. Iranica* 153: 13. 1982)
    indicated both 1240.4 and 1240.5 (LINN) as "typus", both
    collections lack the relevant *Species Plantarum* number (i.e. "3") and
    were post-1753 additions to the herbarium, and are not original
    material for the name.

Ficus retusa Linnaeus, *Systema Naturae*, ed. 12, 2: 681; *Mantissa
    Plantarum*: 129. 1767.
"Habitat in India." RCN: 7724.
Lectotype (Corner in *Gard. Bull. Straits Settlem.* 17: 393. 1960): Herb.
    Linn. No. 1240.10 (LINN).
Current name: *Ficus retusa* L. (Moraceae).

Ficus serrata Linnaeus, *Systema Naturae*, ed. 10, 2: 1315. 1759.
["Habitat in America."] Sp. Pl., ed. 2, 2: 1515 (1763). RCN: 7727.
Replaced synonym of: *Ficus maculata* L. (1763), *nom. illeg.*
Type not designated.
Original material: [icon] in Plumier in Burman, Pl. Amer.: 122, t.
    131, f. 1. 1757.
Note: The application of this name is uncertain. While apparently
    based primarily on the cited Plumier plate, as noted by Friis (in
    Kew Bull. 38: 460. 1983), the name does not appear to have been
    typified.

Ficus sycomorus Linnaeus, *Species Plantarum* 2: 1059. 1753.
"Habitat in Aegypto." RCN: 7717.
Type not designated.
Original material: [icon] in Bauhin & Cherler, Hist. Pl. Univ. 1(1):
    124. 1650; [icon] in Mattioli, Pl. Epit.: 180, f. 3. 1586; [icon] in
    Plukenet, Phytographia: t. 178, f. 3. 1692; Almag. Bot.: 144. 1696.
Current name: *Ficus sycomorus* L. (Moraceae).
Note: Aweke (in *Meded. Landbouwhoogeschool* 79–3: 75. 1979)
    wrongly designated a post-1753 Jacquin collection (1240.2 LINN)
    as (neo)type, overlooking the existence of original material.

Ficus toxicaria Linnaeus, *Mantissa Plantarum Altera*: 305. 1771, *nom.
    illeg.*
"Habitat in Sumatrae pago Padano." RCN: 7726.
Replaced synonym: *Ficus padana* Burm. f. (1768).
Type not designated.
Current name: *Ficus padana* Burm. f. (Moraceae).
Note: A superfluous name for *F. padana* Burm. f. (1768).

Ficus trigonata Linnaeus, *Plantae Surinamenses*: 17. 1775.
"Habitat [in Surinamo.]" RCN: 7728.
Lectotype (Berg & DeWolf in Lanjouw & Stoffers, *Fl. Suriname* 5(1):
    264. 1975): [icon] *"Ficus foliis ovatis, integerrimis"* in Plumier in
    Burman, Pl. Amer.: 123, t. 132, f. 1. 1757.
Current name: *Ficus trigonata* L. (Moraceae).

Filago acaulis Linnaeus, *Systema Naturae*, ed. 12, 2: 580. 1767, *nom.
    illeg.*
["Habitat in Europa australi."] Sp. Pl. 2: 927 (1753). RCN: 6704.
Replaced synonym: *Filago pygmaea* L. (1753).
Type not designated.
Original material: as replaced synonym.

Current name: *Filago pygmaea* L. (Asteraceae).
Note: An illegitimate replacement name for *F. pygmaea* L. (1753),
    having the same diagnosis as that given for *F. pygmaea* in *Sp. Pl.*, ed.
    2, 2: 1311 (1763). *Filago pygmaea* is absent from *Syst. Nat.*, ed. 12,
    2 (1767).

Filago arvensis Linnaeus, *Species Plantarum* 2: 856, 1230. 1753.
"Habitat in Europae campis aridis, arvisque sabulosis." RCN: 6709.
Neotype (Wagenitz in Rechinger, *Fl. Iranica* 145: 24. 1980): Herb.
    Linn. No. 1041.7 (LINN).
Current name: *Filago arvensis* L. (Asteraceae).
Note: As there are no original elements, Wagenitz's choice of the post-
    1753 sheet 1041.7 (LINN) as the type is accepted here, modified to
    a neotype under Art. 9.8.

Filago gallica Linnaeus, *Species Plantarum* 2: 857, 1230. 1753.
"Habitat in Anglia, Gallia." RCN: 6708.
Lectotype (Alavi in Jafri & El-Gadi, *Fl. Libya* 107: 48. 1983): Herb.
    Linn. No. 1041.6 (LINN).
Current name: *Filago gallica* L. (Asteraceae).

Filago germanica Linnaeus, *Systema Naturae*, ed. 10, 2: 1235. 1759,
    nom. inval.
RCN: 6706.
Type not relevant.
Current name: *Filago pyramidata* L. (Asteraceae).
Note: Although apparently first published in *Syst. Nat.*, ed. 10: 1235.
    1759, the Errata of that work makes it clear that "germanica" is an
    error for "pyramidata", the latter being the third species of *Filago* in
    both the 1753 and 1759 accounts. *Filago germanica* L. therefore
    dates not from 1759, but from 1763, where it is a later homonym
    of *F. germanica* Hudson (1762). This has been elucidated by
    Wagenitz (in *Willdenowia* 4: 48. 1965).

Filago germanica Linnaeus, *Species Plantarum*, ed. 2, 2: 1311. 1763,
    nom. illeg.
"Habitat in Europa." RCN: 6705.
Lectotype (Wagenitz in *Willdenowia* 4: 48. 1965): [icon]
    "Gnaphalium" in Fuchs, Hist. Stirp.: 221, 222. 1542.
Current name: *Filago vulgaris* Lam. (Asteraceae).
Note: A later homonym of *F. germanica* Hudson (1762), and hence
    illegitimate; see Wagenitz (in *Willdenowia* 4: 48. 1965).

Filago leontopodium (Linnaeus) Linnaeus, *Species Plantarum*, ed. 2,
    2: 1312. 1763.
"Habitat in Alpibus Helvetiae, Valesiae, Corinthi, Austriae, Sibiriae."
    RCN: 6710.
Basionym: *Gnaphalium leontopodium* L. (1753).
Type not designated.
Original material: as basionym.
Current name: *Leontopodium nivale* (Ten.) Hand.-Mazz. subsp.
    alpinum (Cass.) Greuter (Asteraceae).

Filago maritima Linnaeus, *Species Plantarum* 2: 927. 1753.
"Habitat in Europae australis, marisque mediterranei littoribus."
    RCN: 6107.
Basionym of: *Athanasia maritima* (L.) L. (1763).
Lectotype (Alavi in Jafri & El-Gadi, *Fl. Libya* 107: 162. 1983): Herb.
    Clifford: 398, *Santolina* 7 (BM-000646974).
Current name: *Achillea maritima* (L.) Ehrend. & Y.P. Guo
    (Asteraceae).

Filago montana Linnaeus, *Species Plantarum* 2: 857, 1230. 1753.
"Habitat in Europae collibus sabulosis." RCN: 6707.
Type not designated.

Original material: Herb. Burser XV(1): 10 (UPS); Herb. Linn. No. 1041.8 (LINN); [icon] in Bauhin & Cherler, Hist. Pl. Univ. 3(1): 159. 1651; [icon] in Plantin, Pl. Stirp. Icon.: 481. 1581.
Current name: **Filago arvensis** L. × **minima** (Sm.) Pers. (Asteraceae).
Note: See comments by Greuter (in *Boissiera* 13: 137. 1967).

Filago pygmaea Linnaeus, *Species Plantarum* 2: 927. 1753.
"Habitat in Europa australi." RCN: 6704.
Replaced synonym of: *Filago acaulis* L. (1767), *nom. illeg.*
Type not designated.
Original material: Herb. Burser XV(1): 12 (UPS); [icon] in Vaillant in Mém. Acad. Roy. Sci. Paris 1719: 314, t. 20, f. 9. 1719; [icon] in Barrelier, Pl. Galliam: 89, t. 127. 1714; [icon] in Bauhin, Prodr. Theatri Bot.: 122. 1620.
Current name: **Filago pygmaea** L. (Asteraceae).
Note: Alavi (in Jafri & El-Gadi, *Fl. Libya* 107: 51. 1983) and Jeanmonod (in Gamisans & Jeanmonod, *Compl. Prodr. Fl. Corse, Asteraceae I*: 97. 1998) wrongly indicated an Allioni collection (1041.1 LINN), not received by Linnaeus until 1757, as type.

Filago pyramidata Linnaeus, *Species Plantarum* 2: 1199, 1230. 1753, *typ. cons.*
"Habitat in Hispania. Loefling. [also "Germania" from Gnaphalium germanicum]" RCN: 6706.
Type not designated.
Original material: Herb. Burser XV(1): 8 (UPS); [icon] in Petiver, Herb. Britannici: 18, t. 18, f. 10. 1713.
Generitype of *Filago* Linnaeus, *nom. cons.*
Current name: **Filago pyramidata** L. (Asteraceae).
Note: In the Addenda to *Species Plantarum*, Linnaeus (*Sp. Pl.* 2: 1230. 1753) adds *Gnaphalium germanicum* L. (p. 857) to the protologue, as a synonym. See Wagenitz (in *Willdenowia* 4: 47, 49. 1965), Dandy (in *Watsonia* 7: 165. 1969) and Greuter (in *Boissiera* 13: 136. 1967).

Flagellaria indica Linnaeus, *Species Plantarum* 1: 333. 1753.
"Habitat in Java, Malabaria, Zeylona." RCN: 2606.
Lectotype (Napper in Milne-Redhead & Polhill, *Fl. Trop. E. Africa, Flagellariaceae*: 3. 1971): Herb. Linn. No. 463.1 (LINN).
Generitype of *Flagellaria* Linnaeus.
Current name: **Flagellaria indica** L. (Flagellariaceae).

Forsskaolea tenacissima Linnaeus, *Opobalsamum Declaratum*: 18. 1764.
"Habitat in Arabia." RCN: 3416.
Lectotype (Friis & Wilmot-Dear in Jarvis & al., *Regnum Veg.* 127: 47. 1993): Herb. Linn. No. 389.7 (S).
Generitype of *Forsskaolea* Linnaeus.
Current name: **Forsskaolea tenacissima** L. (Urticaceae).
Note: Bhopal & Chaudhri (in *Pakistan Syst.* 1(2): 53. 1977) indicated unspecified material in LINN as the holotype, but the only material there associated with this name (605.1, 605.2) is annotated by J.E. Smith alone and is not original material for the name. Friis & Wilmot-Dear (in *Nordic J. Bot.* 8: 35. 1988) noted that material in S would be a suitable lectotype but formalised this choice only in 1993.

Fothergilla gardenii Linnaeus, *Systema Vegetabilium,* ed. 13: 418. 1774.
"Habitat in Carolina." RCN: 3943.
Lectotype (Reveal in Jarvis & al., *Regnum Veg.* 127: 47. 1993): *Garden,* Herb. Linn. No. 693.1 (LINN; iso- BM).
Generitype of *Fothergilla* Linnaeus.
Current name: **Fothergilla gardenii** L. (Hamamelidaceae).

Fragaria muricata Linnaeus, *Species Plantarum* 1: 495. 1753.
"Habitat – – – –" RCN: 3771.
Lectotype (Staudt in Cafferty & Jarvis in *Taxon* 51: 541. 2002): [icon] *"Fragaria Arborea con fiore herbaceo"* in Zanoni, Istoria Bot.: 95, t. 38. 1675 (see p. 166).
Current name: **Fragaria vesca** L. subsp. **vesca** 'Muricata' (Rosaceae).

Fragaria sterilis Linnaeus, *Species Plantarum* 1: 495. 1753.
"Habitat in Anglia." RCN: 3772.
Lectotype (Jonsell & Jarvis in *Nordic J. Bot.* 22: 74. 2002): Herb. Burser XVIII(2): 13 (UPS).
Current name: **Potentilla sterilis** (L.) Garcke (Rosaceae).

Fragaria vesca Linnaeus, *Species Plantarum* 1: 494. 1753.
"Habitat in Europae borealis, sterilibus, duris, apricis." RCN: 3769.
Lectotype (Staudt in *Canad. J. Bot.* 40: 870, pl. 1, f. 1. 1962): Herb. Linn. No. 654.2 (LINN).
Generitype of *Fragaria* Linnaeus.
Current name: **Fragaria vesca** L. subsp. **vesca** (Rosaceae).

Fragaria vesca Linnaeus var. **chiloensis** Linnaeus, *Species Plantarum* 1: 495. 1753.
RCN: 3769.
Lectotype (Mabberley in *Telopea* 9: 797, ic. 2002): [icon] *"Fragaria Chiloensis fructu maximo, foliis carnosis hirsutis Frez."* in Dillenius, Hort. Eltham. 1: 145, t. 120, f. 146. 1732.
Current name: **Fragaria chiloensis** (L.) Mill. subsp. **chiloensis** (Rosaceae).
Note: Staudt (in *Canad. J. Bot.* 40: 881. 1962) designated 654.21 (LINN) as lectotype but this collection is a post-1753 addition to the collection, and not original material for the name. Staudt (in *Univ. Calif. Publ. Bot.* 81: 101, f. 27. 1999) provided a picture of this specimen. Mabberley subsequently rejected Staudt's choice in favour of the cited Dillenius figure.

Fragaria vesca Linnaeus var. **pratensis** Linnaeus, *Species Plantarum,* ed. 2, 1: 709. 1762, *nom. illeg.*
RCN: 3769.
Replaced synonym: *Fragaria vesca* L. var. *sativa* L. (1753).
Neotype (Staudt in Cafferty & Jarvis in *Taxon* 51: 541. 2002): *Duchesne,* Herb. Linn. No. 654.12 (LINN).
Current name: **Fragaria viridis** Duchesne (Rosaceae).
Note: An illegitimate renaming of *F. vesca* var. *sativa* L. (1753).

Fragaria vesca Linnaeus var. **sativa** Linnaeus, *Species Plantarum* 1: 495. 1753.
RCN: 3769.
Replaced synonym of: *Fragaria vesca* L. var. *pratensis* L. (1762), *nom. illeg.*
Neotype (Staudt in Cafferty & Jarvis in *Taxon* 51: 541. 2002): *Duchesne,* Herb. Linn. No. 654.12 (LINN).
Current name: **Fragaria viridis** Duchesne (Rosaceae).

Fragaria vesca Linnaeus var. **sylvestris** Linnaeus, *Species Plantarum* 1: 495. 1753.
RCN: 3769.
Lectotype (Staudt in *Univ. Calif. Publ. Bot.* 81: 38. 1999): Herb. Linn. No. 654.2 (LINN).
Current name: **Fragaria vesca** L. subsp. **vesca** (Rosaceae).

Frankenia hirsuta Linnaeus, *Species Plantarum* 1: 331. 1753.
"Habitat in Apulia, Creta." RCN: 2570.
Type not designated.
Original material: Herb. Linn. No. 457.4 (LINN); Herb. Burser XVI(1): 47 (UPS); [icon] in Micheli, Nov. Pl. Gen.: 23, t. 22, f. 2. 1729.

Current name: ***Frankenia hirsuta*** L. (Frankeniaceae).
Note: Siddiqi (in Jafri & El-Gadi, *Fl. Libya* 64: 4. 1979) designated 457.4 (LINN) as lectotype, but this is a collection from Hasselquist, not originating from either Puglia or Crete and hence not original material. As pointed out by Santos Guerra (in *Anales Jard. Bot. Madrid* 50: 136. 1992), most of the material on this sheet belongs to *F. corymbosa* Desf., of which Siddiqi appears to have been unaware. Santos Guerra noted that the cited Micheli plate and Herb. Burser XVI: 47 (UPS) both correspond with usage, but did not make a formal choice of type.

Frankenia laevis Linnaeus, *Species Plantarum* 1: 331. 1753.
"Habitat in Europae australis maritimis." RCN: 2569.
Lectotype (Whalen in Jarvis & al., *Regnum Veg.* 127: 47. 1993): *Löfling s.n.*, Herb. Linn. No. 457.1 (LINN).
Generitype of *Frankenia* Linnaeus (vide Hitchcock, *Prop. Brit. Bot.*: 147. 1929).
Current name: ***Frankenia laevis*** L. (Frankeniaceae).
Note: Siddiqi (in Jafri & El-Gadi, *Fl. Libya* 64: 6. 1979) indicated both 457.1 and 457.2 (LINN) as types – this statement consequently did not make an effective choice of type. As the two sheets do not appear to be part of a single collection, Art. 9.15 does not apply.

Frankenia pulverulenta Linnaeus, *Species Plantarum* 1: 332. 1753.
"Habitat in Susexiae, Narbonae, Italiae, Apuliae littoribus." RCN: 2571.
Lectotype (Nasir in Nasir & Ali, *Fl. W. Pakistan* 7: 3. 1971): Herb. Linn. No. 457.6 (LINN).
Current name: ***Frankenia pulverulenta*** L. (Frankeniaceae).

Fraxinus americana Linnaeus, *Species Plantarum* 2: 1057. 1753.
"Habitat in Carolina, Virginia." RCN: 7700.
Lectotype (Fernald in *J. Arnold Arbor.* 27: 391, pl. 3. 1946): *Clayton 742*, Herb. Linn. No. 1230.3 (LINN; iso- BM).
Current name: ***Fraxinus americana*** L. (Oleaceae).

Fraxinus excelsior Linnaeus, *Species Plantarum* 2: 1057. 1753.
"Habitat in Europae sepibus." RCN: 7698.
Lectotype (Green in Jarvis & al., *Regnum Veg.* 127: 47. 1993): Herb. Clifford: 469, *Fraxinus* 1 (BM-000647544).
Generitype of *Fraxinus* Linnaeus (vide Green, *Prop. Brit. Bot.*: 194. 1929).
Current name: ***Fraxinus excelsior*** L. (Oleaceae).
Note: Nikolaev (in *Bot. Zhurn.* 66: 1423. 1981) indicated unspecified material in LINN as type but no sheet there is associated with this name.

Fraxinus ornus Linnaeus, *Species Plantarum* 2: 1057. 1753.
"Habitat in Europa australi." RCN: 7699.
Type not designated.
Original material: Herb. Clifford: 470, *Fraxinus* 2 (BM); Herb. Burser XXII: 86 (UPS).
Current name: ***Fraxinus ornus*** L. (Oleaceae).
Note: Although Nikolaev (in *Bot. Zhurn.* 66: 1429. 1981) indicated unspecified material in BM as type, this is too vague to be accepted as a typification.

Fritillaria imperialis Linnaeus, *Species Plantarum* 1: 303. 1753.
"Habitat in Persia? e Constantinopoli venit in Europam circa 1570." RCN: 2393.
Lectotype (Rechinger, *Fl. Iranica* 165: 63. 1990): Herb. Linn. No. 421.1 (LINN).
Current name: ***Fritillaria imperialis*** L. (Liliaceae).

Fritillaria meleagris Linnaeus, *Species Plantarum* 1: 304. 1753.
"Habitat in Gallia, Italia." RCN: 2398.
Lectotype (Turrill in *Lily Year-Book* 15: 100, 114. 1951): Herb. Linn. No. 421.3 (LINN).
Generitype of *Fritillaria* Linnaeus (vide Hitchcock, *Prop. Brit. Bot.*: 145. 1929).
Current name: ***Fritillaria meleagris*** L. (Liliaceae).
Note: Fritillaria pyrenaica L. was treated as the generitype by Britton & Brown, *Ill. Fl. N. U. S.*, ed. 2, 1: 505. 1913 (see McNeill & al. in *Taxon* 36: 372. 1987). However, under Art. 10.5, Ex. 7 (a voted example) of the Vienna Code, this is a type choice made under the American Code and is to be replaced under Art. 10.5b by Hitchcock's choice (*Prop. Brit. Bot.*: 145. 1929) of *F. meleagris* L.

Fritillaria persica Linnaeus, *Species Plantarum* 1: 304. 1753.
"Habitat in Persia? e Susis venit in Europam 1573." RCN: 2396.
Type not designated.
Original material: Herb. A. van Royen No. 913.62–380 (L); Herb. Burser III: 121 (UPS); [icon] in Clusius, Rar. Pl. Hist. 1: 130. 1601.
Current name: ***Fritillaria persica*** L. (Liliaceae).
Note: Although Rechinger (*Fl. Iranica* 165: 68. 1990) indicated unspecified material in LINN as type, there appears to be none there of any relevance.

Fritillaria pyrenaica Linnaeus, *Species Plantarum* 1: 304. 1753.
"Habitat in Pyrenaeis." RCN: 2397.
Type not designated.
Original material: Herb. Linn. No. 421.2 (LINN); Herb. Burser III: 62 (UPS).
Current name: ***Fritillaria pyrenaica*** L. (Liliaceae).
Note: Fritillaria pyrenaica L. was treated as the generitype by Britton & Brown, *Ill. Fl. N. U. S.*, ed. 2, 1: 505. 1913 (see McNeill & al. in *Taxon* 36: 372. 1987). However, under Art. 10.5, Ex. 7 (a voted example) of the Vienna Code, this is a type choice made under the American Code and is to be replaced under Art. 10.5b by Hitchcock's choice (*Prop. Brit. Bot.*: 145. 1929) of *F. meleagris* L.

Fritillaria regia Linnaeus, *Species Plantarum* 1: 303. 1753.
"Habitat ad Cap. b. Spei." RCN: 2394.
Type not designated.
Original material: [icon] in Dillenius, Hort. Eltham. 1: 109, t. 93, f. 109. 1732; [icon] in Dillenius, Hort. Eltham. 1: 109, t. 92, f. 108. 1732.
Current name: ***Eucomis regia*** (L.) L'Hér. (Liliaceae/Hyacinthaceae).
Note: Reyneke (in *J. S. African Bot.* 40: 63. 1974) indicated two illustrations from Dillenius as the type, one of which (t. 92, f. 108) is not explicitly cited in the protologue.

Fuchsia multiflora Linnaeus, *Systema Vegetabilium*, ed. 13: 299. 1774. RCN: 2692.
Type not designated.
Original material: none traced.
Current name: ***Fuchsia sp.*** (Onagraceae).
Note: The application of this name appears to be uncertain.

Fuchsia triphylla Linnaeus, *Species Plantarum* 2: 1191. 1753.
"Habitat in America." RCN: 2691.
Lectotype (Wright in *Plantsman* 1: 181. 1979): [icon] *"Fuchsia"* in Plumier, Nov. Pl. Amer.: 14, t. 14. 1703.
Generitype of *Fuchsia* Linnaeus.
Current name: ***Fuchsia triphylla*** L. (Onagraceae).
Note: Munz (in *Proc. Calif. Acad. Sci.*, ser. 4, 43: 1. 1943) indicated that Linnaeus based this on Plumier's description and figure. Wright (1979) later formalised this as a typification.

Fucus abrotanifolius Linnaeus, *Species Plantarum* 2: 1161. 1753.
"Habitat in mari Anglico." RCN: 8289, 8353.
Lectotype (Roberts in *J. Linn. Soc., Bot.* 60: 252. 1968): *Löfling s.n.*,
Herb. Linn. No. 1274.95 (LINN).
Current name: *Cystoseira foeniculacea* (L.) Grev. (Cystoseiraceae).
Note: Turner (in *Fuci* 4: 134. 1819) cited *F. abrotanifolius* as a variety
of *F. foeniculaceus* L. Goodenough & Woodward (in *Trans. Linn.
Soc.* 3: 127. 1797) noted Löfling's specimen in LINN.

Fucus acinarius Linnaeus, *Species Plantarum* 2: 1160. 1753.
"Habitat in Italia & Oceano australiori." RCN: 8279, 8305.
Type not designated.
Original material: Herb. Linn. No. 1274.172 (LINN); [icon] in
Donati, Stor. Nat. Adriat.: 35, t. 4, f. A. 1750; [icon] in Plantin, Pl.
Stirp. Icon. 2: 256. 1581.
Current name: *Sargassum acinarium* (L.) Setch. (Sargassaceae).
Note: Silva & al. (in *Univ. Calif. Publ. Bot.* 79: 929–931. 1996) gave
an extensive review, suggesting that "the Adriatic plant described
and illustrated by Donati" might be a suitable type. However, it
seems that nomenclatural difficulties might result from this type
choice (see Spencer & al. in *Taxon*, in press).

Fucus aculeatus Linnaeus, *Species Plantarum*, ed. 2, 2: 1632. 1763.
"Habitat inter Angliam & Galliam." RCN: 8302, 8328.
Lectotype (Irvine in Spencer & al. in *Taxon*, in press): Herb. Linn. No.
1274.15 (LINN).
Current name: *Desmarestia aculeata* (L.) J.V. Lamour.
(Desmarestiaceae).

Fucus barbatus Linnaeus, *Species Plantarum* 2: 1161. 1753.
"Habitat in Oceana." RCN: 8285, 8323.
Basionym of: *Fucus foeniculaceus* L. var. *barbatus* (L.) L. (1767).
Lectotype (Irvine in Spencer & al. in *Taxon*, in press): Herb. Burser
XX: 94 (UPS).
Current name: *Cystoseira foeniculacea* (L.) Grev. (Cystoseiraceae).
Note: Although Roberts (in *Bot. J. Linn. Soc.* 60: 257, pl. 4. 1968)
suggested that Herb. Burser XX: 94 (UPS) might be the type, she
did not designate it as such.

Fucus buccinalis Linnaeus, *Mantissa Plantarum Altera*: 312. 1771.
"Habitat in Oceano, extra Cap. b. spei, lapidibus profundissimis
innatus, inde saepe evulsus natat, et ad littora rejicitur. Koenig. 43."
RCN: 3338.
Neotype (Irvine in Spencer & al. in *Taxon*, in press): South Africa.
Cap Agulhas, "*Lessonia nigrescens* Bory", *R.F. Hohenacker No. 162*
(BM-000774387).
Current name: *Ecklonia maxima* (Osbeck) Papenf. (Alariaceae).

Fucus canaliculatus Linnaeus, *Systema Naturae*, ed. 12, 2: 716.
1767.
RCN: 8315, 8274.
Lectotype (Irvine in Spencer & al. in *Taxon*, in press): Herb. Linn. No.
1274.55 (LINN).
Current name: *Pelvetia canaliculata* (L.) Decne. & Thur. (Fucaceae).

Fucus cartilagineus Linnaeus, *Species Plantarum* 2: 1161. 1753.
"Habitat in Oceano australiore." RCN: 8292, 8354.
Lectotype (Dixon in *Blumea* 15: 56. 1967): Herb. A. van Royen No.
910.184–14 (L).
Current name: *Plocamium cartilagineum* (L.) P.S. Dixon
(Plocamiaceae).
Note: Saunders & Lehmkuhl (in *Europ. J. Phycol.* 40: 303. 2005)
provide a discussion concerning the likely provenance of the type
collection and reproduce an image of it (f. 12), and rehydrated
microscopical preparations (f. 13, 14).

Fucus ceranoides Linnaeus, *Species Plantarum* 2: 1158. 1753.
"Habitat in Oceano." RCN: 8267, 8313.
Lectotype (Irvine in Spencer & al. in *Taxon*, in press): Herb. Linn. No.
1274.52 (LINN).
Current name: *Fucus ceranoides* L. (Fucaceae).

Fucus concatenatus Linnaeus, *Species Plantarum* 2: 1160. 1753.
"Habitat in Oceano." RCN: 8277, 8327.
Lectotype (Roberts in *J. Linn. Soc., Bot.* 60: 253, pl. 1, 2a. 1968):
Herb. A. van Royen No. 910.153–1332 (L).
Current name: *Cystoseira foeniculacea* (L.) Grev. (Cystoseiraceae).
Note: Roberts (in *Brit. Phycol. Bull.* 3: 347, f. 1, 2. 1967) discussed the
protologue and figured the van Royen collection but did not refer to
the material as the type. The typification was formalised by her the
following year. Roberts (*l.c.* 3: 556, f. 11. 1968) provided an
additional photograph of a preparation of the type material,
together with a scale bar (missing from the earlier images).

Fucus confervoides Linnaeus, *Species Plantarum*, ed. 2, 2: 1629.
1763, *nom. illeg.*
"Habitat in Mari Anglico." RCN: 8290, 8358.
Lectotype (Steentoft & al. in *Taxon* 40: 663. 1991): Herb. Linn. No.
1274.111, larger, right specimen (LINN).
Current name: *Gracilariopsis longissima* (S.G. Gmel.) Steentoft &
al. (Gracilariaceae).
Note: A later homonym of *Fucus confervoides* Huds. (*Fl. Anglica*: 474.
1762), as noted by Silva & al. (in *Univ. Calif. Publ. Bot.* 79: 917.
1996), and hence illegitimate.

Fucus crispatus Linnaeus, *Systema Naturae*, ed. 12, 2: 718. 1767.
RCN: 8345.
Neotype (Irvine in Spencer & al. in *Taxon*, in press): United Kingdom.
Scarborough, "*F. crispatus*" ex Herb. Hudson (BM-000619664).
Current name: *Cryptopleura ramosa* (Huds.) L. Newton
(Delesseriaceae).

Fucus crispus Linnaeus, *Systema Naturae*, ed. 12, 2: 718; *Mantissa
Plantarum*: 134. 1767, *nom. illeg.*
"Habitat in Oceano Atlantico. Koenig." RCN: 8344.
Lectotype (Brodie in Spencer & al. in *Taxon*, in press): Herb. Linn.
No. 1274.68, top specimen (LINN).
Current name: *Chondrus crispus* Stackh. (Gigartinaceae).
Note: A later homonym of *Fucus crispus* Huds. (*Fl. Anglica*: 472.
1762), and hence illegitimate.

Fucus dentatus Linnaeus, *Systema Naturae*, ed. 12, 2: 718; *Mantissa
Plantarum*: 135. 1767.
"Habitat in Oceano Atlantico." RCN: 8347.
Lectotype (Athanasiadis, *Taxon. Litt. Biogeogr. Skand. Rödalg. Brunalg.*:
129. 1996): Herb. Linn. No. 1274.72 (LINN).
Current name: *Odonthalia dentata* (L.) Lyngb. (Rhodomelaceae).

Fucus discors Linnaeus, *Systema Naturae*, ed. 12, 2: 717. 1767.
RCN: 8331.
Neotype (Roberts in *J. Linn. Soc., Bot.* 60: 252. 1968): Herb. Linn.
No. 1274.21, left specimen (LINN).
Current name: *Cystoseira foeniculacea* (L.) Grev. (Cystoseiraceae).
Note: The material treated as the type by Roberts is annotated only by
Linnaeus filius, rather than his father, and there must be some
doubt as to whether this is original material for the name. However,
in the absence of any other original material, this collection is
accepted as a neotype (Art. 9.8).

Fucus distichus Linnaeus, *Systema Naturae*, ed. 12, 2: 716. 1767.
RCN: 8316.

Lectotype (Powell in *J. Mar. Biol. Assoc. U.K.* 36: 420, pl. 1, f. 2A. 1957): Herb. Linn. No. 1274.56, uppermost specimen (LINN).
Current name: ***Fucus distichus*** L. subsp. ***distichus*** (Fucaceae).

Fucus divaricatus Linnaeus, *Species Plantarum* 2: 1159. 1753.
"Habitat in Anglia, Lusitania." RCN: 8272, 8311.
Lectotype (Fletcher in Spencer & al. in *Taxon*, in press): *Löfling 39*, Herb. Linn. No. 1274.50 (LINN).
Current name: ***Fucus vesiculosus*** L. (Fucaceae).

Fucus elongatus Linnaeus, *Species Plantarum* 2: 1159. 1753.
"Habitat inter Angliam & Hispaniam." RCN: 8273, 8321.
Lectotype (Setchell in *Univ. Calif. Publ. Bot.* 16: 358. 1931): *Löfling s.n.*, Herb. Linn. No. 1274.1 (LINN).
Current name: ***Himanthalia elongata*** (L.) Gray (Himanthaliaceae).

Fucus ericoides Linnaeus, *Species Plantarum*, ed. 2, 2: 1631. 1763.
"Habitat in Oceano Europaeo." RCN: 8301, 8359.
Lectotype (Athanasiadis, *Taxon. Litt. Biogeogr. Skand. Rödalg. Brunalg.*: 219. 1996): Herb. Linn. No. 1274.18 (LINN).
Current name: ***Cystoseira tamariscifolia*** (Huds.) Papenf. (Cystoseiraceae).
Note: Roberts (in *Bot. J. Linn. Soc.* 60: 256. 1968) stated that this was based on a Ray synonym (unaccompanied by an illustration).

Fucus esculentus Linnaeus, *Systema Naturae*, ed. 12, 2: 718; *Mantissa Plantarum*: 135. 1767.
"Habitat in Mari Atlantico. Equis & hominibus esculentus. D. Gunnerus, König." RCN: 8340.
Lectotype (Irvine in Spencer & al. in *Taxon*, in press): Herb. Linn. No. 1274.63 (LINN).
Current name: ***Alaria esculenta*** (L.) Grev. (Alariaceae).

Fucus excisus Linnaeus, *Species Plantarum* 2: 1159. 1753.
"Habitat in Oceano Europaeo." RCN: 8274, 8315.
Type not designated.
Original material: Herb. Linn. No. 1274.143 (LINN); [icon] in Morison, Pl. Hist. Univ. 3: 646, s. 15, t. 8, f. 11. 1699.
Current name: ***Pelvetia canaliculata*** (L.) Decne. & Thur. (Fucaceae).
Note: This name appears to threaten *Pelvetia canaliculata* and may be a candidate for rejection.

Fucus fastigiatus Linnaeus, *Species Plantarum* 2: 1162. 1753.
"Habitat in Oceano Balthico." RCN: 8297, 8335.
Lectotype (Drew in *J. Linn. Soc., Bot.* 55: 363, pl. 62a. 1958): Herb. Linn. No. 1274.24, upper specimen (LINN).
Current name: ***Furcellaria lumbricalis*** (Huds.) J.V. Lamour. (Furcellariaceae).

Fucus filum Linnaeus, *Species Plantarum* 2: 1162. 1753.
"Habitat in Oceano Atlantico." RCN: 8299, 8333.
Lectotype (Irvine in Spencer & al. in *Taxon*, in press): [icon] *"Fucus sive Filum maritimum Germanicum"* in Boccone, Mus. Fis.: 271, t. 7, f. 9. 1697.
Current name: ***Chorda filum*** (L.) Stackh. (Chordariaceae).
Note: See discussion by South & Burrows (in *Brit. Phycol. Bull.* 3: 379–380. 1967).

Fucus foeniculaceus Linnaeus, *Species Plantarum* 2: 1161. 1753.
"Habitat in Oceano." RCN: 8286, 8323.
Lectotype (Roberts in *J. Linn. Soc., Bot.* 60: 252. 1968): Herb. Burser XX: 93 (UPS).
Current name: ***Cystoseira foeniculacea*** (L.) Grev. (Cystoseiraceae).

Note: Goodenough & Woodward (in *Trans. Linn. Soc.* 3: 135. 1797) noted and discussed the material in LINN, and Roberts (in *Brit. Phycol. Bull.* 3: 548. 1968) provided a photograph of the type material.

Fucus foeniculaceus Linnaeus var. **barbatus** (Linnaeus) Linnaeus, *Systema Naturae*, ed. 12, 2: 717. 1767.
["Habitat in Oceana."] Sp. Pl. 2: 1161 (1753). RCN: 8285, 8323.
Basionym: *Fucus barbatus* L. (1753).
Lectotype (Irvine in Spencer & al. in *Taxon*, in press): Herb. Burser XX: 94 (UPS).
Current name: ***Cystoseira foeniculacea*** (L.) C. Agardh (Cystoseiraceae).

Fucus furcellatus Linnaeus, *Species Plantarum*, ed. 2, 2: 1631. 1763.
"Habitat in Oceano Anglico." RCN: 8298, 8336.
Lectotype (Athanasiadis, *Taxon. Litt. Biogeogr. Skand. Rödalg. Brunalg.*: 59. 1996): [icon] *"Fucus parvus segmentis praelongis teretibus acutis"* in Morison, Pl. Hist. Univ. 3: 648, s. 15, t. 9, f. 4. 1699.
Current name: ***Furcellaria lumbricalis*** (Huds.) J.V. Lamour. (Furcellariaceae).
Note: See comments by Waern (in *Acta Phytogeog. Suec.* 30: 185–190. 1952), Drew (in *J. Linn. Soc., Bot.* 55: 749. 1958) and Dixon & Irvine (*Seaweeds Brit. Isles* 1: 181. 1977).

Fucus gigartinus Linnaeus, *Systema Naturae*, ed. 10, 2: 1344. 1759. RCN: 8275, 8355.
Neotype (Irvine in Spencer & al. in *Taxon*, in press): Herb. Linn. No. 1274.102 (LINN).
Current name: ***Gigartina pistillata*** (S.G. Gmel.) Stackh. (Gigartinaceae).
Note: The specific epithet was spelled "gigantinus" in the protologue, subsequently corrected by Linnaeus in *Syst. Nat.* ed. 12 (1767).

Fucus granulatus Linnaeus, *Species Plantarum*, ed. 2, 2: 1629. 1763.
"Habitat in Oceano Indico." RCN: 8284, 8325.
Lectotype (Roberts in *J. Linn. Soc., Bot.* 60: 264, pl. 5. 1968): Herb. Linn. No. 1274.11 (LINN).
Current name: ***Cystoseira usneoides*** (L.) M. Roberts (Cystoseiraceae).
Note: Although Roberts (in *Bot. J. Linn. Soc., Bot.* 60: 260. 1968) believed this to be a superfluous name for *F. usneoides* L. (1759), the protologues of the two names are far from identical, although the annotations to material in LINN suggest that Linnaeus regarded them as conspecific.

Fucus hirsutus Linnaeus, *Systema Naturae*, ed. 12, 2: 71; *Mantissa Plantarum*: 134. 1767.
"Habitat in Pelago. D. Gunnerus." RCN: 8330.
Lectotype (Irvine in Spencer & al. in *Taxon*, in press): Herb. Linn. No. 1274.18 (LINN).
Current name: ***Cladostephus spongiosus*** (Huds.) C. Agardh var. ***verticillatus*** (Lightf.) Prud'homme (Cladostephaceae).

Fucus inflatus Linnaeus, *Species Plantarum* 2: 1159. 1753.
"Habitat in Oceano Atlantico." RCN: 8271, 8312.
Lectotype (Powell in *J. Mar. Biol. Assoc. U.K.* 36: 432, pl. 1, f. 1. 1957): Herb. Linn. No. 1274.51 (LINN).
Current name: ***Fucus vesiculosus*** L. (Fucaceae).

Fucus lacerus Linnaeus, *Species Plantarum*, ed. 2, 2: 1627. 1763.
"Habitat in Oceano Anglico." RCN: 8268, 8313.
Type not designated.
Original material: none traced.
Current name: ***Fucus ceranoides*** L. var. ***lacerus*** (L.) Lightf. (Fucaceae).

Note: This name poses a potential threat to a number of well-established names and may be a candidate for rejection (see Spencer & al. in *Taxon*, in press).

Fucus lanosus Linnaeus, *Systema Naturae,* ed. 12, 2: 718. 1767.
"Habitat in O. Islandico. Koenig." RCN: 8334.
Lectotype (Tandy in *J. Bot.* 69: 227. 1931): *König s.n.,* Herb. Linn. No. 1274.23 (LINN).
Current name: ***Polysiphonia lanosa*** (L.) Tandy (Rhodomelaceae).

Fucus lendigerus Linnaeus, *Species Plantarum* 2: 1160. 1753.
"Habitat ad insulam Adscensionis. Osbeck." RCN: 8280, 8306.
Lectotype (Irvine in Spencer & al. in *Taxon,* in press): Herb. Linn. No. 1274.18 (LINN; iso- BM-000563637).
Current name: ***Sargassum lendigerum*** (L.) C. Agardh (Sargassaceae).
Note: See Hansen & Fox Maule (in *Bot. J. Linn. Soc.* 67: 207. 1973) for comments on Osbeck material.

Fucus loreus Linnaeus, *Systema Naturae,* ed. 12, 2: 716. 1767.
RCN: 8321.
Lectotype (Irvine in Spencer & al. in *Taxon,* in press): *Osbeck s.n.,* Herb. Linn. No. 1274.3 (LINN).
Current name: ***Himanthalia elongata*** (L.) Gray (Himanthaliaceae).

Fucus lycopodioides Linnaeus, *Systema Naturae,* ed. 12, 2: 717. 1767.
RCN: 8329.
Lectotype (Athanasiadis, *Taxon. Litt. Biogeogr. Skand. Rödalg. Brunalg.*: 59. 1996): Herb. Linn. No. 1274.20 (LINN).
Current name: ***Rhodomela lycopodioides*** (L.) C. Agardh (Rhodomelaceae).

Fucus muscoides Linnaeus, *Species Plantarum* 2: 1161. 1753.
"Habitat ad Insulam Adscensionis. Osbeck." RCN: 8291, 8328.
Neotype (de Jong, *Syst. Phylogen. Biogeogr. Stud. Atlantic Seaweeds*: 133. 1998): Brazil. Desfontaines, LD 94/068.9765 (no. 38011) (LD).
Current name: ***Acanthophora muscoides*** (L.) Bory (Rhodomelaceae).

Fucus natans Linnaeus, *Species Plantarum* 2: 1160. 1753.
"Habitat in Pelago libere natans, nec radicatus." RCN: 8278, 8304.
Lectotype (Børgesen, *Mind. Japetus Steenstrups Fødsel Art.* 32: 7. 1914): Herb. Linn. No. 1274.35 (LINN), see above, right.
Current name: ***Sargassum natans*** (L.) Gaillon (Sargassaceae).

Fucus nodosus Linnaeus, *Species Plantarum* 2: 1159. 1753.
"Habitat in Mari Atlantico." RCN: 8276, 8317.
Lectotype (Irvine in Spencer & al. in *Taxon,* in press): Herb. Linn. No. 1274.58 (LINN).
Current name: ***Ascophyllum nodosum*** (L.) Le Jol. (Fucaceae).
Note: Woelkerling (in *Rhodora* 77: 16. 1975) indicated unspecified material in LINN as type but this did not distinguish between sheets 1274.58 and 1274.134. As they do not appear to be part of a single gathering, Art. 9.15 does not apply.

Fucus ornatus Linnaeus, *Mantissa Plantarum Altera*: 312. 1771.
"Habitat ad Cap. b. spei." RCN: 8350.
Lectotype (Papenfuss in *J. S. African Bot.* 17: 173. 1951): *König s.n.,* Herb. Linn. No. 1274.80 (LINN).
Current name: ***Suhria vittata*** (L.) Endl. (Gelidiaceae).

Fucus ovarius Linnaeus, *Systema Naturae,* ed. 12, 2: 714. 1767, *orth. var.*
"Habitat in O. Asiatico." RCN: 8303.
Lectotype (Brodie in Spencer & al. in *Taxon,* in press): Herb. Linn. No. 1274.32 (LINN).

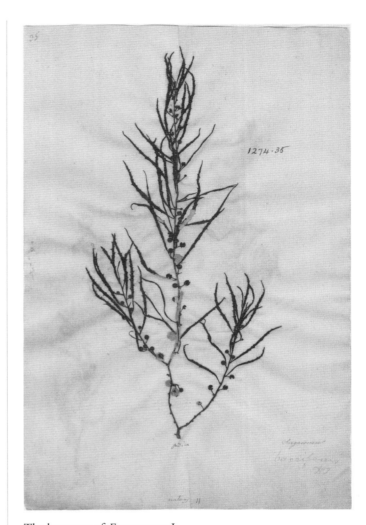

The lectotype of *Fucus natans* L.

Current name: ***Botryocladia uvaria*** (L.) Kylin (Rhodymeniaceae).
Note: This appears to be an orthographic variant of *F. uvarius* L. (1759).

Fucus palmatus Linnaeus, *Species Plantarum* 2: 1162. 1753.
"Habitat in Oceano." RCN: 8294, 8337.
Lectotype (Irvine, *Seaweeds Brit. Isles* 1(2A): 68. 1983): Herb. A. van Royen No. 910.184–2889 (L).
Current name: ***Rhodymenia palmata*** (L.) Grev. (Rhodymeniaceae).

Fucus pavonicus Linnaeus, *Species Plantarum* 2: 1162. 1753.
"Habitat in Mari Europae australis." RCN: 8296, 8360.
Basionym of: *Ulva pavonica* (L.) L. (1767).
Lectotype (De Clerck in Spencer & al. in *Taxon,* in press): Herb. Burser XX: 106 (UPS).
Current name: ***Padina pavonica*** (L.) J.V. Lamour. (Dictyotaceae).

Fucus pavonius Linnaeus, *Species Plantarum,* ed. 2, 2: 1630. 1763, *orth. var.*
"Habitat in Mari Europae australis." RCN: 8296, 8360.
Lectotype (De Clerck in Spencer & al. in *Taxon,* in press): Herb. Burser XX: 106 (UPS).
Current name: ***Padina pavonica*** (L.) J.V. Lamour. (Dictyotaceae).

F

Note: As noted by Price & al. (in *Bull. Brit. Mus. (Nat. Hist.) Bot.* 7: 3. 1979), this appears best accepted as an orthographic error for *F. pavonicus* L. (1753) though some authors (e.g. Silva & al. in *Univ. Calif. Publ. Bot.* 79: 605. 1996) have instead treated it as superfluous, and therefore illegitimate.

Fucus pyriferus Linnaeus, *Mantissa Plantarum Altera*: 311. 1771.
"Habitat in Oceano Aethiopico e profundissimo mari saepe enatans insulasque quasi formans. Koenig. mss. 42." RCN: 8318.
Neotype (Irvine in Spencer & al. in *Taxon*, in press): W. Falkland Islands. King George's Sound, Oct 1910, *Mrs Elinor Vallentin* (BM-000840161).
Current name: ***Macrocystis pyrifera*** (L.) C. Agardh (Lessoniaceae).
Note: Although Womersley (in *Univ. Calif. Publ. Bot.* 27: 113. 1954) discussed possible type material in LINN, the only collection associated with this name is unannotated by Linnaeus and is not original material.

Fucus ramentaceus Linnaeus, *Systema Naturae,* ed. 12, 2: 718. 1767. RCN: 8351.
Lectotype (Irvine in Spencer & al. in *Taxon*, in press): Herb. Linn. No. 1274.82, top left specimen (LINN).
Current name: ***Devaleraea ramentacea*** (L.) Guiry (Palmariaceae).

Fucus rubens Linnaeus, *Species Plantarum* 2: 1162. 1753.
"Habitat in Oceano." RCN: 8295, 8348.
Lectotype (Dixon in *Bot. Not.* 117: 57. 1964): Herb. A. van Royen No. 910.128–1044 (L).
Current name: ***Phycodrys rubens*** (L.) Batters (Delesseriaceae).
Note: See review by Wynne (in *Contr. Univ. Michigan Herb.* 21: 330. 1997), rebutting a suggestion by Silva & al. (in *Univ. Calif. Publ. Bot.* 79: 906. 1996) that the name should be superseded.

Fucus saccharinus Linnaeus, *Species Plantarum* 2: 1161. 1753.
"Habitat in Mari Atlantico." RCN: 8293, 8341.
Lectotype (Lane in Spencer & al. in *Taxon*, in press): Herb. Linn. No. 1274.64 (LINN). – Epitype (Lane in Spencer & al. in *Taxon*, in press): United Kingdom. Cornwall, Looe, Hannafore Point, 24 Jul 2005, *J. Brodie* (BM-000893631).
Current name: ***Saccharina latissima*** (L.) C.E. Lane & al. (Laminariaceae).

Fucus selaginoides Linnaeus, *Systema Naturae,* ed. 12, 2: 717; *Mantissa Plantarum*: 134. 1767.
"Habitat in Oceano Norvegico." RCN: 8287, 8326.
Lectotype (Roberts in *J. Linn. Soc., Bot.* 60: 256. 1968): Herb. Linn. No. 1274.12 (LINN).
Current name: ***Cystoseira tamariscifolia*** (Huds.) Papenf. (Cystoseiraceae).

Fucus serratus Linnaeus, *Species Plantarum* 2: 1158. 1753.
"Habitat in Oceano." RCN: 8265, 8308.
Lectotype (Fletcher in Spencer & al. in *Taxon*, in press): Herb. Linn. No. 1274.46 (LINN).
Current name: ***Fucus serratus*** L. (Fucaceae).

Fucus siliculosus Linnaeus, *Systema Naturae,* ed. 12, 2: 716. 1767. RCN: 8320.
Type not designated.
Original material: none traced.
Note: The application of this name appears to be uncertain, but it may threaten *Hizikia fusiformis* (Harv.) Okamura.

Fucus siliquosus Linnaeus, *Species Plantarum* 2: 1160. 1753.
"Habitat in Oceano." RCN: 8283, 8319.

Lectotype (Irvine in Spencer & al. in *Taxon*, in press): Herb. Linn. No. 1274.60 (LINN).
Current name: ***Halidrys siliquosa*** (L.) Lyngb. (Cystoseiraceae).

Fucus spermophorus Linnaeus, *Systema Naturae,* ed. 12, 2: 719. 1767. RCN: 8357.
Type not designated.
Original material: Herb. Linn. No. 1274.109 (LINN); Herb. Linn. No. 1274.106 (LINN).
Current name: ***Chondrus spermophorus*** (L.) Grev. (Gigartinaceae).
Note: The application of this name is uncertain but it may threaten names in *Gracilaria* Grev. and *Gelidium* J.V. Lamour., and so might prove to be a candidate for rejection.

Fucus spinosus Linnaeus, *Mantissa Plantarum Altera*: 313. 1771, *nom. illeg.*
"Habitat ad Cap. b. spei." RCN: 8356.
Replaced synonym: *Fucus denticulatus* Burm. f. (1768).
Type not designated.
Current name: ***Eucheuma denticulatum*** (Burm. f.) Collins & Herv. (Solieriaceae).
Note: A superfluous name for *F. denticulatus* Burm. f. (1768) and also a later homonym of *F. spinosus* Gmelin (1768). Although Doty (in Abbott, *Taxon. Econ. Seaweeds* 2: 179 1988) treated 1274.104 (LINN) as the type, this shows no connection with *F. denticulatus* and is not original material for that name.

Fucus spiralis Linnaeus, *Species Plantarum* 2: 1159. 1753.
"Habitat in Oceano." RCN: 8270, 8314.
Lectotype (Børgesen in *J. Linn. Soc., Bot.* 39: 119, pl. 9. 1909): Herb. Linn. No. 1274.53 (LINN).
Current name: ***Fucus spiralis*** L. (Fucaceae).
Note: See Powell (in *Brit. Phycol. Bull.* 2: 17. 1960), who mistakenly concluded that Børgesen's chosen type was not original material for the name.

Fucus tendo Linnaeus, *Species Plantarum* 2: 1162. 1753.
RCN: 8300, 8332.
Lectotype (Irvine in Spencer & al. in *Taxon*, in press): [icon] *"Fucus Indicus, teres, setam piscatoriam referens, longissimus"* in Plukenet, Phytographia: t. 184, f. 3. 1692; Almag. Bot.: 160. 1696.
Note: The application of this name is uncertain but is thought to relate to an animal substance (see Spencer & al. in *Taxon*, in press).

Fucus triqueter Linnaeus, *Mantissa Plantarum Altera*: 312. 1771, *nom. illeg.*
"Habitat in Mari Capensi. Koenig." RCN: 8324.
Lectotype (Irvine in Spencer & al. in *Taxon*, in press): Herb. Linn. No. 1274.8 (LINN).
Current name: ***Hormophysa cuneiformis*** (J.F. Gmel.) P.C. Silva (Cystoseiraceae).
Note: A later homonym of *Fucus triqueter* Gmelin (1768), and hence illegitimate (see Spencer & al. in *Taxon*, in press).

Fucus turbinatus Linnaeus, *Species Plantarum* 2: 1160. 1753.
"Habitat in America rupibus marinis." RCN: 8282, 8307.
Lectotype (Irvine in Spencer & al. in *Taxon*, in press): [icon] *"Fucus marinus vesiculas habens membranis extantibus alatas"* in Sloane, Voy. Jamaica 1: 58, t. 20, f. 6. 1707. – Typotype: Herb. Sloane 1: 6 (BM-SL).
Current name: ***Turbinaria turbinata*** (L.) Kuntze (Sargassaceae).

Fucus uranus Linnaeus, *Systema Naturae,* ed. 10, 2: 1345. 1759, *orth. var.*
RCN: 8281.

Lectotype (Brodie in Spencer & al. in *Taxon*, in press): Herb. Linn. No. 1274.32 (LINN).
Current name: ***Botryocladia uvaria*** (L.) Kylin (Rhodymeniaceae).
Note: This appears to be an orthographic variant, corrected by Linnaeus to *F. uvarius* in 1774 (see Spencer & al. in *Taxon*, in press).

Fucus usneoides Linnaeus, *Systema Naturae*, ed. 10, 2: 1345. 1759.
RCN: 8288.
Lectotype (Roberts in *J. Linn. Soc., Bot.* 60: 264, pl. 5. 1968): Herb. Linn. No. 1274.11 (LINN).
Current name: ***Cystoseira usneoides*** (L.) M. Roberts (Cystoseiraceae).

Fucus uvarius Linnaeus, *Systema Naturae*, ed. 12, 2: 714. 1767.
"Habitat in O. Asiatico." RCN: 8303.
Lectotype (Brodie in Spencer & al. in *Taxon*, in press): Herb. Linn. No. 1274.32 (LINN).
Current name: ***Botryocladia uvaria*** (L.) Kylin (Rhodymeniaceae).

Fucus venosus Linnaeus, *Mantissa Plantarum Altera*: 312. 1771.
"Habitat ad Cap. b. spei." RCN: 8349.
Lectotype (Irvine in Spencer & al. in *Taxon*, in press): Herb. Linn. No. 1274.78 (LINN).
Current name: ***Hymenena venosa*** (L.) C. Krauss (Delesseriaceae).

Fucus vesiculosus Linnaeus, *Species Plantarum* 2: 1158. 1753.
"Habitat in Mari atlantico." RCN: 8266, 8310.
Lectotype (Irvine in Spencer & al. in *Taxon*, in press): Herb. Linn. No. 1274.48 (LINN).
Generitype of *Fucus* Linnaeus (vide De Toni in *Flora* 74: 173. 1891).
Current name: ***Fucus vesiculosus*** L. (Fucaceae).
Note: Woelkerling (in *Rhodora* 77: 16. 1975) indicated material in LINN as the type but did not distinguish between several sheets there associated with this name. As they are evidently not part of a single gathering, Art. 9.15 does not apply.

Fucus vittatus Linnaeus, *Systema Naturae*, ed. 12, 2: 718. 1767.
RCN: 8350.
Lectotype (Papenfuss in *J. S. African Bot.* 17: 173. 1951): Herb. Linn. No. 1274.79 (LINN).
Current name: ***Suhria vittata*** (L.) Endl. (Gelidiaceae).

Fucus volubilis Linnaeus, *Systema Naturae*, ed. 10, 2: 1344. 1759.
["Habitat in Mari Mediterraneo."] Sp. Pl., ed. 2, 2: 1627 (1763). RCN: 8269, 8309.
Lectotype (Irvine in Spencer & al. in *Taxon*, in press): Herb. Linn. No. 1274.47 (LINN).
Current name: ***Osmundaria volubilis*** (L.) R.E. Norris (Rhodomelaceae).
Note: See discussion by Norris (in *Bot. J. Linn. Soc.* 106: 15. 1991), who treated unspecified material in L as the holotype. This cannot be traced but is very unlikely to have been original material for the name (see Spencer & al. in *Taxon*, in press).

Fumaria bulbosa Linnaeus, *Species Plantarum* 2: 699. 1753, *nom. rej.*
"Habitat in Europae nemoribus & umbrosis." RCN: 5121.
Conserved type (Lidén in *Taxon* 30: 323. 1981): Herb. Linn. No. 881.5 (LINN).
Current name: ***Corydalis solida*** (L.) Clairv. (Fumariaceae).

Fumaria bulbosa Linnaeus var. **cava** Linnaeus, *Species Plantarum* 2: 699. 1753.
RCN: 5121.
Lectotype (Lidén in *Taxon* 30: 323. 1981): Herb. Linn. No. 881.4 (LINN).

Current name: ***Corydalis cava*** (L.) Schweigg. & Körte (Fumariaceae).
Note: See Bunting (in *Baileya* 14: 43. 1966), who incorrectly concluded that the name should be typified by a Bauhin polynomial.

Fumaria bulbosa Linnaeus var. **intermedia** Linnaeus, *Species Plantarum* 2: 699. 1753.
RCN: 5121.
Lectotype (Greuter in *Taxon* 36: 171. 1987): Herb. Burser VII(1): 102 (UPS).
Current name: ***Corydalis intermedia*** (L.) Mérat (Fumariaceae).

Fumaria bulbosa Linnaeus var. **solida** Linnaeus, *Species Plantarum* 2: 699. 1753.
RCN: 5121.
Lectotype (Jonsell & Jarvis in *Nordic J. Bot.* 14: 162. 1994): Herb. Burser VII(1): 101 (UPS).
Current name: ***Corydalis solida*** (L.) Clairv. (Fumariaceae).

Fumaria capnoides Linnaeus, *Species Plantarum* 2: 700. 1753.
"Habitat in Gallia, Italia, Mauritania." RCN: 5124.
Type not designated.
Original material: Herb. Linn. No. 881.10 (LINN); Herb. Clifford: 352, *Fumaria* 6 α (BM); Herb. Burser VII(1): 97 (UPS); [icon] in Plukenet, Phytographia: t. 90, f. 2. 1691; Almag. Bot.: 162. 1696; [icon] in Daléchamps, Hist. General. Pl. 2: 1294. 1586.
Current name: ***Corydalis capnoides*** (L.) Pers. (Fumariaceae).
Note: Ryberg (in *Acta Horti Berg.* 17: 135. 1955) noted that the identity of 881.10 (LINN) corresponded with usage of the name but did not designate a type.

Fumaria capreolata Linnaeus, *Species Plantarum* 2: 701. 1753.
"Habitat in G. Narbonensi, Anglia." RCN: 5127.
Lectotype (Lidén in *Opera Bot.* 88: 69. 1986): Herb. Burser VII(1): 94 (UPS).
Current name: ***Fumaria capreolata*** L. (Fumariaceae).
Note: Soler (in *Lagascalia* 11: 198. 1983) indicated Herb. Burser VII(1): 92 (UPS) as the type but this collection is associated with *F. officinalis* L. and is not original material for *F. capreolata*.

Fumaria claviculata Linnaeus, *Species Plantarum* 2: 701. 1753.
"Habitat in Angliae locis uliginosis saxosis." RCN: 5129.
Lectotype (Lidén in *Opera Bot.* 88: 39. 1986): Herb. Clifford: 351, *Fumaria* 3 (BM-000646514).
Current name: ***Ceratocapnos claviculata*** (L.) Lidén (Fumariaceae).

Fumaria cucullaria Linnaeus, *Species Plantarum* 2: 699. 1753.
"Habitat in Virginia, Canada." RCN: 5118.
Lectotype (designated here by Reveal): Herb. Linn. No. 881.1 (LINN).
Current name: ***Dicentra cucullaria*** (L.) Bernh. (Fumariaceae).

Fumaria enneaphylla Linnaeus, *Species Plantarum* 2: 700. 1753.
"Habitat in Hispaniae, Siciliae saxosis." RCN: 5125.
Lectotype (Lidén in *Opera Bot.* 88: 36. 1986): Herb. Linn. No. 881.11 (LINN).
Current name: ***Sarcocapnos enneaphylla*** (L.) DC. (Fumariaceae).

Fumaria lutea Linnaeus, *Mantissa Plantarum Altera*: 258. 1771.
"Habitat in Mauritania." RCN: 5123.
Lectotype (Lidén in Jonsell in *Nordic J. Bot.* 20: 522. 2001 [2000]): Herb. Burser VII(1): 97 (UPS).
Current name: ***Pseudofumaria lutea*** (L.) Borkh. (Fumariaceae).
Note: Lidén (in *Opera Bot.* 88: 32. 1986) indicated Herb. Linn. No. 291.11 (S) as lectotype, but this sheet is unannotated by Linnaeus and cannot be accepted as original material. He subsequently designated a Burser specimen as lectotype in its place.

Fumaria nobilis Linnaeus, *Systema Naturae,* ed. 12, 2: 469. 1767. RCN: 5120.
Lectotype (Lidén in Jonsell in *Nordic J. Bot.* 20: 522. 2001 [2000]): Herb. Linn. No. 881.3 (LINN).
Current name: ***Corydalis nobilis*** (L.) Pers. (Fumariaceae).

Fumaria officinalis Linnaeus, *Species Plantarum* 2: 700. 1753.
"Habitat in Europae agris, cultis." RCN: 5126.
Lectotype (Sell in *Feddes Repert.* 68: 178. 1963): Herb. Linn. No. 881.13 (LINN).
Generitype of *Fumaria* Linnaeus (vide Green, *Prop. Brit. Bot.*: 173. 1929).
Current name: ***Fumaria officinalis*** L. (Fumariaceae).
Note: Although Pugsley (in *J. Bot.* 50, Suppl. A: 45. 1912) noted a specimen at LINN, he did not refer to it as a type.

Fumaria sempervirens Linnaeus, *Species Plantarum* 2: 700. 1753.
"Habitat in Canada, Virginia." RCN: 5122.
Lectotype (Lidén in Jonsell in *Nordic J. Bot.* 20: 522. 2001 [2000]): Herb. Linn. No. 881.8 (LINN).
Current name: ***Capnoides sempervirens*** (L.) Borkh. (Fumariaceae).

Fumaria spectabilis Linnaeus, *Species Plantarum* 2: 699. 1753.
"Habitat in Sibiria. D. Demidoff." RCN: 5119.
Lectotype (Lidén in Jonsell in *Nordic J. Bot.* 20: 522. 2001 [2000]): *Amman s.n.,* Herb. Linn. No. 881.2 (LINN).
Current name: ***Lamprocapnos spectabilis*** (L.) Fukuhara (Fumariaceae).

Fumaria spicata Linnaeus, *Species Plantarum* 2: 700. 1753.
"Habitat in Hispania, G. Narbonensi, Veronae ad agros, vias." RCN: 5128.

Lectotype (Lidén in *Opera Bot.* 88: 40. 1986): Herb. Burser VII(1): 96 (UPS).
Current name: ***Platycapnos spicata*** (L.) Bernh. (Fumariaceae).
Note: Stearn (in Geck & Pressler, *Festschr. Claus Nissen*: 639. 1974) stated that this was based on Sauvages' material from Montpellier, but did not formally designate a type.

Fumaria tenuifolia Linnaeus, *Amoenitates Academicae* 4: 487. 1759.
Type not designated.
Original material: none traced.
Current name: ***Platycapnos spicata*** (L.) Bernh. (Fumariaceae).
Note: Stearn (in Geck & Pressler, *Festschr. Claus Nissen*: 639. 1974) noted that this was based on a Magnol description of a plant from Montpellier.

Fumaria vesicaria Linnaeus, *Species Plantarum* 2: 701. 1753.
"Habitat in Aethiopia." RCN: 5130.
Type not designated.
Original material: Herb. Clifford: 351, *Fumaria* 4 (BM); Herb. Linn. No. 881.16 (LINN); [icon] in Boerhaave, Index Alter Pl. Hort. Lugdb.-Bat. 1: 310. 1720; [icon] in Plukenet, Amalth. Bot.: t. 355, f. 3. 1705; Almag. Bot.: 400. 1696.
Current name: ***Cysticapnos vesicaria*** (L.) Fedde (Fumariaceae).
Note: Lidén (in *Opera Bot.* 88: 106. 1986) indicated either 881.16 (LINN) or Clifford material in BM as the type.

Fusanus compressus Linnaeus, *Systema Vegetabilium,* ed. 13: 765. 1774.
RCN: 7632.
Type not designated.
Original material: none traced.
Generitype of *Fusanus* Linnaeus.
Current name: ***Osyris compressa*** (P.J. Bergius) A. DC. (Santalaceae).

G

Galanthus nivalis Linnaeus, *Species Plantarum* 1: 288. 1753.
"Habitat ad radices Alpium Veronae, Tridenti, Viennae." RCN: 2299.
Lectotype (Davis in Jarvis & al., *Regnum Veg.* 127: 48. 1993): Herb.
   Linn. No. 409.1 (LINN).
Generitype of *Galanthus* Linnaeus.
Current name: ***Galanthus nivalis*** L. (Liliaceae/Amaryllidaceae).

Galax aphylla Linnaeus, *Species Plantarum* 1: 200. 1753.
"Habitat in Virginia." RCN: 1622.
Neotype (Reveal in Jarvis & al., *Regnum Veg.* 127: 48. 1993): U.S.A.
   North Carolina, Chatham Co., about 1 mile west of Bynum,
   alluvial woods along How River near U.S. Highway 15–501, 25
   Apr 1960, *Ahles & Radford 53245* (BM).
Generitype of *Galax* Linnaeus, *nom. rej.*
Current name: ***Nemophila aphylla*** (L.) Brummitt (Hydrophyllaceae).
Note: Galax Linnaeus, *nom. rej.* in favour of *Galax* Sims.
   Reveal (in *Taxon* 41: 592. 1992) argued that *Clayton 4* (P-JU), a
   specimen of *Galax urceolata* (Poir.) Brummitt (Diapensiaceae), must
   be the lectotype and therefore proposed the conservation of the
   name with a conserved type. The Committee for Spermatophyta (in
   Taxon 43: 276. 1994) ruled that *Clayton 4* could not be the type of
   G. aphylla because it conflicted with Linnaeus' generic description
   (among other things), and that conservation was unnecessary. The
   Committee ruled that the proposed conserved type was to be
   treated as a neotype. Reveal (1993) explicitly treated it in this way,
   and his typification therefore dates from 1993.

Galega cinerea Linnaeus, *Systema Naturae*, ed. 10, 2: 1172. 1759.
["Habitat in Jamaica."] Sp. Pl., ed. 2, 2: 1062 (1763). RCN: 5559.
Lectotype (Fawcett & Rendle, *Fl. Jamaica* 4: 20. 1920): Herb. Linn.
   No. 924.2 (LINN).
Current name: ***Tephrosia cinerea*** (L.) Pers. (Fabaceae: Faboideae).

Galega fruticosa Linnaeus, *Systema Naturae*, ed. 10, 2: 1172. 1759,
   nom. illeg.
RCN: 5568.
Replaced synonym: *Cracca senticosa* L. (1753).
Lectotype (Bosman & de Haas in *Blumea* 28: 470. 1983): Herb.
   Hermann 1: 72, No. 303 (BM-000594504).
Current name: ***Tephrosia senticosa*** (L.) Pers. (Fabaceae: Faboideae).
Note: An illegitimate replacement name in *Galega* for *Cracca senticosa*
   L. (1753).

Galega littoralis (N.J. Jacquin) Linnaeus, *Systema Naturae*, ed. 12, 2:
   497. 1767.
"Habitat in Carthagenae littoribus arenosis marinis." RCN: 5561.
Basionym: *Vicia littoralis* Jacq. (1760).
Type not designated.
Current name: ***Tephrosia cinerea*** (L.) Pers. (Fabaceae: Faboideae).

Galega maxima (Linnaeus) Linnaeus, *Systema Naturae*, ed. 10, 2:
   1172. 1759.
["Habitat in Zeylona."] Sp. Pl. 2: 752 (1753). RCN: 5564.
Basionym: *Cracca maxima* L. (1753).
Lectotype (Gillett in Milne-Redhead & Polhill, *Fl. Trop. E. Africa,
   Leguminosae* 3: 201. 1971): Herb. Hermann 3: 56, No. 300 (BM-
   000594698).
Current name: ***Tephrosia maxima*** (L.) Pers. (Fabaceae: Faboideae).

Galega officinalis Linnaeus, *Species Plantarum* 2: 714. 1753.
"Habitat in Italia, Hispania, Africa, ad margines agrorum." RCN:
   5559.

Lectotype (Ali in Nasir & Ali, *Fl. W. Pakistan* 100: 91. 1977): Herb.
   Clifford: 362, *Galega* 1 (BM-000646617).
Generitype of *Galega* Linnaeus.
Current name: ***Galega officinalis*** L. (Fabaceae: Faboideae).

Galega purpurea (Linnaeus) Linnaeus, *Systema Naturae,* ed. 10, 2:
   1172. 1759.
["Habitat in Zeylona."] Sp. Pl. 2: 752 (1753). RCN: 5565.
Basionym: *Cracca purpurea* L. (1753).
Lectotype (Fawcett & Rendle, *Fl. Jamaica* 4: 19. 1920; Ali in *Biologia
   (Lahore)* 10: 28. 1964): Herb. Hermann 1: 37, No. 301 (BM-
   000621363).
Current name: ***Tephrosia purpurea*** (L.) Pers. (Fabaceae: Faboideae).
Note: Fawcett & Rendle (*Fl. Jamaica* 4: 19. 1920) indicated Herb.
   Hermann material (BM) as type. Although there is material in two
   separate volumes, it appears to have been part of a single gathering.
   Consequently, theirs is accepted as the first typification (Art. 9.15),
   with the choice subsequently restricted by Ali. Although Forbes (in
   Bothalia 4: 974. 1948) designated 924.7 (LINN) as the type, this
   choice is pre-dated by that of Fawcett & Rendle.

Galega senticosa (Linnaeus) Linnaeus, *Species Plantarum,* ed. 2, 2:
   1063. 1763.
"Habitat in Zeylona." RCN: 5568.
Basionym: *Cracca senticosa* L. (1753).
Lectotype (Bosman & de Haas in *Blumea* 28: 470. 1983): Herb.
   Hermann 1: 72, No. 303 (BM-000594504).
Current name: ***Tephrosia senticosa*** (L.) Pers. (Fabaceae: Faboideae).

Galega tinctoria (Linnaeus) Linnaeus, *Systema Naturae,* ed. 10, 2:
   1172. 1759.
["Habitat in Zeylona."] Sp. Pl. 2: 752 (1753). RCN: 5567.
Basionym: *Cracca tinctoria* L. (1753).
Lectotype (Rudd in Dassanayake & Fosberg, *Revised Handb. Fl.
   Ceylon* 7: 146. 1991): Herb. Hermann 3: 28, No. 302 (BM-
   000594670).
Current name: ***Tephrosia tinctoria*** (L.) Pers. (Fabaceae: Faboideae).

Galega villosa (Linnaeus) Linnaeus, *Systema Naturae,* ed. 10, 2: 1172.
   1759.
["Habitat in India."] Sp. Pl. 2: 752 (1753). RCN: 5563.
Basionym: *Cracca villosa* L. (1753).
Lectotype (Gillett in *Kew Bull.* 13: 121. 1958; Ali in *Biologia
   (Lahore)* 10: 25. 1964): Herb. Hermann 1: 31, No. 299 (BM-
   000621337).
Current name: ***Tephrosia villosa*** (L.) Pers. (Fabaceae: Faboideae).

Galega virginiana (Linnaeus) Linnaeus, *Systema Naturae,* ed. 10, 2:
   1172. 1759.
["Habitat in Virginia, Canada."] Sp. Pl. 2: 752 (1753). RCN: 5562.
Basionym: *Cracca virginiana* L. (1753).
Lectotype (Wood in *Rhodora* 51: 267. 1949): *Kalm,* Herb. Linn. No.
   924.4 (LINN; iso- UPS).
Current name: ***Tephrosia virginiana*** (L.) Pers. (Fabaceae:
   Faboideae).

Galenia africana Linnaeus, *Species Plantarum* 1: 359. 1753.
"Habitat in Africa." RCN: 2849.
Lectotype (Adamson in *J. S. African Bot.* 22: 91. 1956): Herb. Linn.
   No. 507.1 (LINN).
Generitype of *Galenia* Linnaeus.
Current name: ***Galenia africana*** L. (Aizoaceae).

Galeopsis galeobdolon Linnaeus, *Species Plantarum* 2: 580. 1753.
"Habitat in Europae nemoribus." RCN: 4227.
Lectotype (Polatschek in *Österr. Bot. Zeitschr.* 122: 267. 1973): Herb. Linn. No. 734.4 (LINN).
Current name: ***Lamiastrum galeobdolon*** (L.) Ehrend. & Polatschek (Lamiaceae).
Note: See discussion by Gutermann & al. (in *Österr. Bot. Zeitschr.* 122: 266–267. 1973). Mennema (in *Leiden Bot. Ser.* 11: 36. 1989) incorrectly regarded *G. galeobdolon* as the basionym of *Lamium galeobdolon* L. (*Amoen. Acad.* 4: 485. 1759), an invalid name.

Galeopsis hirsuta Linnaeus, *Species Plantarum* 2: 580. 1753.
"Habitat in Hispania." RCN: 4244.
Replaced synonym of: *Sideritis ocymastrum* L. (1759); *Stachys hirta* L. (1763), nom. illeg.
Lectotype (Turland in Jarvis & al. in *Taxon* 50: 511. 2001): Herb. Linn. No. 736.16 (LINN).
Current name: ***Stachys ocymastrum*** (L.) Briq. (Lamiaceae).
Note: Galeopsis hirsuta was transferred to *Sideritis* in 1759 (as *S. ocymastrum* L. because of the existence of *Sideritis hirsuta* L. (1753)), and then appeared as *Stachys hirta* L. in 1763. The use of "hirta" may originally have been an error for "hirsuta" (as *G. hirsuta* is included in its synonymy), but as Linnaeus continued to use "hirta" in later works (*Syst. Nat.*, ed. 12, 2: 395. 1767; *Syst. Nat.*, ed. 13: 447. 1774), *Stachys hirta* is treated as illegitimate.

Galeopsis ladanum Linnaeus, *Species Plantarum* 2: 579. 1753.
"Habitat in Europae arvis & campis sabulosis." RCN: 4225.
Lectotype (Townsend in *Watsonia* 5: 143. 1962): Herb. Linn. No. 734.1 (LINN).
Current name: ***Galeopsis ladanum*** L. (Lamiaceae).

Galeopsis tetrahit Linnaeus, *Species Plantarum* 2: 579. 1753.
"Habitat in Europae segetes & olera." RCN: 4226.
Lectotype (Press in Jarvis & al., *Regnum Veg.* 127: 48. 1993): Herb. Clifford: 314, *Galeopsis* 2 β (BM-000646117).
Generitype of *Galeopsis* Linnaeus (vide Green, *Prop. Brit. Bot.*: 165. 1929).
Current name: ***Galeopsis tetrahit*** L. (Lamiaceae).

Galium aparine Linnaeus, *Species Plantarum* 1: 108. 1753.
"Habitat in Europae cultis & ruderatis." RCN: 882.
Lectotype (Jafri in Jafri & El-Gadi, *Fl. Libya* 65: 15. 1979): Herb. Linn. No. 129.33 (LINN).
Current name: ***Galium aparine*** L. (Rubiaceae).

Galium aristatum Linnaeus, *Species Plantarum*, ed. 2, 1: 152. 1762.
"Habitat in monte Ventoso & m. Virginis Neapolitano. C. G. Minuart." RCN: 872.
Type not designated.
Original material: Herb. Linn. No. 56.5 (S); Herb. Linn. No. 129.16 (LINN); Herb. Linn. No. 129.17 (LINN); [icon] in Barrelier, Pl. Galliam: 12, t. 583. 1714; [icon] in Boccone, Mus. Piante Rar. Sicilia: 83, t. 75. 1697; [icon] in Barrelier, Pl. Galliam: 12, t. 356. 1714.
Current name: ***Galium aristatum*** L. (Rubiaceae).

Galium bermudense Linnaeus, *Species Plantarum* 1: 105. 1753.
"Habitat in Virginia." RCN: 880.
Lectotype (Reveal & al. in *Huntia* 7: 234. 1987): [icon] *"Rubia tetraphyllos glabra latiore folio Bermudensis, seminibus binis atropurpureis"* in Plukenet, Phytographia: t. 248, f. 6. 1692; Almag. Bot.: 324. 1696. – Typotype: *Dickinson s.n.*, Bermuda (32: 82, BM-SL).
Current name: ***Galium bermudense*** L. (Rubiaceae).

Note: Britten (in *J. Bot.* 47: 41–42. 1909) discussed this name in detail, concluding that it should be used in the sense of the Plukenet plate, and making the combination *Relbunium bermudense* (L.) Britten to accompany it. However, he did not explicitly designate a type though Reveal & al. subsequently did so. Weatherby & Blake (in *Rhodora* 18: 193. 1916) proposed that the name be rejected as a *nomen confusum*; see Gillis & Proctor (in *Sida* 6: 59. 1975). Although evidently a mixture with *G. pilosum* Aiton, typification has subsequently established correct usage of the name.

Galium boreale Linnaeus, *Species Plantarum* 1: 108. 1753.
"Habitat in Europae borealis pratis." RCN: 877.
Lectotype (Nazimuddin & Qaiser in Nasir & Ali, *Fl. Pakistan* 190: 70. 1989): Herb. Linn. No. 129.25 (LINN).
Current name: ***Galium boreale*** L. (Rubiaceae).

Galium glaucum Linnaeus, *Species Plantarum* 1: 107. 1753.
"Habitat in Tataria, Helvetia, Austria, Monspelii." RCN: 874.
Lectotype (Krendl in *Ann. Naturhist. Mus. Wien* 104B: 609. 2003): Herb. Linn. No. 129.20 (LINN). – Epitype (Krendl in *Ann. Naturhist. Mus. Wien* 104B: 609. 2003): Austria. Niederösterreich, Waldviertel, W Pulkau, Pulkhaul-N. oberhalb der Hammerschmeide, bei der Einmündung des Passendorfer Baches, ca. 340m, 2n=44, 20 May 1994. *F. Krendl 30112* (W).
Current name: ***Galium glaucum*** L. (Rubiaceae).

Galium graecum Linnaeus, *Systema Naturae*, ed. 12, 2: 118; *Mantissa Plantarum*: 38. 1767.
"Habitat in Insulis Archipelagi. D. Schreber." RCN: 881.
Lectotype (Ehrendorfer & Schönbeck-Temesy in Davis, *Fl. Turkey* 7: 826. 1982): *Schreber*, Herb. Linn. No. 129.32 (LINN).
Current name: ***Galium graecum*** L. subsp. ***graecum*** (Rubiaceae).

Galium hierosolymitanum Linnaeus, *Flora Palaestina*: 13. 1756.
"Habitat in Hierosolym." RCN: 873.
Type not designated.
Original material: *Hasselquist*, Herb. Linn. No. 129.18 (LINN).
Current name: ***Galium hierosolymitanum*** L. (Rubiaceae).

Galium laevigatum Linnaeus, *Species Plantarum*, ed. 2, 2: 1667. 1763.
"Habitat in Italia. Arduini." RCN: 872.
Type not designated.
Original material: [icon] in Boccone, Mus. Piante Rar. Sicilia: 83, t. 75. 1697.
Current name: ***Galium laevigatum*** L. (Rubiaceae).

Galium maritimum Linnaeus, *Systema Naturae*, ed. 12, 2: 118; *Mantissa Plantarum*: 38. 1767.
"Habitat in Oriente." RCN: 878.
Type not designated.
Original material: *Schreber*, Herb. Linn. No. 129.28 (LINN).
Current name: ***Galium maritimum*** L. (Rubiaceae).

Galium minutum Linnaeus, *Species Plantarum* 1: 106. 1753.
"Habitat in Imperio Ruthenico." RCN: 867.
Type not designated.
Original material: none traced.
Current name: ***Galium minutum*** L. (Rubiaceae).

Galium mollugo Linnaeus, *Species Plantarum* 1: 107. 1753.
"Habitat in Europa mediterranea." RCN: 870.
Lectotype (Krendl in *Österr. Bot. Zeitschr.* 114: 528. 1967): Herb. Linn. No. 129.14 (LINN).
Current name: ***Galium mollugo*** L. (Rubiaceae).

Galium montanum Linnaeus, *Species Plantarum,* ed. 2, 1: 155. 1762.
"Habitat in Germania." RCN: 862.
Lectotype (Krendl in *Ann. Naturhist. Mus. Wien* 104B: 609. 2003):
    Herb. Linn. No. 129.4 (LINN).
Current name: ***Galium glaucum*** L. (Rubiaceae).

Galium palustre Linnaeus, *Species Plantarum* 1: 105. 1753.
"Habitat in Europae rivulis limosis." RCN: 860.
Type not designated.
Original material: Herb. Burser XIX: 31 (UPS); Herb. Linn. No.
    129.3 (LINN); Herb. Linn. No. 59 (LAPP).
Current name: ***Galium palustre*** L. (Rubiaceae).

Galium parisiense Linnaeus, *Species Plantarum* 1: 108. 1753.
"Habitat in Anglia, Gallia." RCN: 883.
Lectotype (Natali & Jeanmonod in Jeanmonod, *Compl. Prodr. Fl.*
    Corse, Rubiaceae: 132, f. 34. 2000): Herb. Linn. No. 129.34
    (LINN).
Current name: ***Galium parisiense*** L. (Rubiaceae).

Galium purpureum Linnaeus, *Species Plantarum* 1: 107. 1753.
"Habitat in Italia." RCN: 875.
Type not designated.
Original material: "Galium 14 purpureum", Herb. Linn. (UPS).
Current name: ***Asperula purpurea*** (L.) Ehrend. (Rubiaceae).

Galium pusillum Linnaeus, *Species Plantarum* 1: 106. 1753.
"Habitat in montibus Galloprovinciae." RCN: 868.
Type not designated.
Original material: Herb. Burser XIX: 17 (UPS).
Current name: ***Galium pusillum*** L. (Rubiaceae).

Galium rotundifolium Linnaeus, *Species Plantarum* 1: 108. 1753.
"Habitat in alpibus Helvetiae, Styriae." RCN: 854.
Basionym of: *Asperula rotundifolia* (L.) L. (1771).
Lectotype (Natali & Jeanmonod in Jeanmonod, *Compl. Prodr. Fl.*
    Corse, Rubiaceae: 53. 2000): Herb. Burser XIX: 13 (UPS).
Current name: ***Galium rotundifolium*** L. (Rubiaceae).
Note: See extensive discussion by Ehrendorfer (in *Österr. Bot. Zeitschr.*
    99: 625–631. 1952) who, however, wrongly chose (because original
    material was in existence) a neotype for this name. He was followed
    in this by Fici (in *Fl. Medit.* 2: 102. 1992).

Galium rubioides Linnaeus, *Species Plantarum* 1: 105. 1753.
"Habitat in Europa australi. D. Baeck." RCN: 859.
Type not designated.
Original material: none traced.
Current name: ***Galium rubioides*** L. (Rubiaceae).

Galium rubrum Linnaeus, *Species Plantarum* 1: 107. 1753.
"Habitat in Italia." RCN: 876.
Type not designated.
Original material: Herb. Burser XIX: 30 (UPS); Herb. Clifford: 34,
    Galium 2 (BM); [icon] in Clusius, Rar. Pl. Hist. 2: 175. 1601.
Current name: ***Galium rubrum*** L. (Rubiaceae).

Galium saxatile Linnaeus, *Species Plantarum* 1: 106. 1753.
"Habitat in Hispaniae maritimis lapidosis." RCN: 866.
Type not designated.
Original material: Herb. Linn. No. 129.8 (LINN); Herb. Clifford: 34,
    Galium 8 (BM); [icon] in Jussieu in Mém. Acad. Roy. Sci. Paris
    1714: 380, t. 15. 1714.
Current name: ***Galium saxatile*** L. (Rubiaceae).
Note: Various authors have perceived nomenclatural problems with
    this name, chiefly because current usage does not agree with

Linnaeus' original concept, which was apparently of a Spanish
    plant. Rauschert (in *Feddes Repert.* 79: 420. 1969), for example,
    treated it as a *nomen ambiguum.* The name, however, is in use.

Galium scabrum Linnaeus, *Species Plantarum* 1: 108. 1753.
"Habitat in Europa australi." RCN: 879.
Lectotype (Natali & Jeanmonod in Jeanmonod, *Compl. Prodr. Fl.*
    Corse, Rubiaceae: 146. 2000): [icon] *"Rubia quadrifolia foliis et*
    seminibus hispidis" in Morison, Pl. Hist. Univ. 3: 329, s. 9, t. 21, f.
    5. 1699.
Current name: ***Galium scabrum*** L. (Rubiaceae).

Galium spurium Linnaeus, *Species Plantarum* 1: 106. 1753.
"Habitat in Europae cultis." RCN: 865.
Lectotype (Natali & Jeanmonod in Jeanmonod, *Compl. Prodr. Fl.*
    Corse, Rubiaceae: 53. 2000): Herb. Linn. No. 55.17 (S).
Current name: ***Galium spurium*** L. (Rubiaceae).
Note: Moore (in *Canad. J. Bot.* 53: 881. 1975) provided a description
    of 129.7 (LINN), but made it clear (p. 879) that he was not
    typifying the name (it was in any case not original material).

Galium sylvaticum Linnaeus, *Species Plantarum,* ed. 2, 1: 155. 1762.
"Habitat in Germaniae & Europae australis montibus sylvosis." RCN:
    871.
Type not designated.
Original material: none traced.
Current name: ***Galium sylvaticum*** L. (Rubiaceae).

Galium tinctorium Linnaeus, *Species Plantarum* 1: 106. 1753.
"Habitat in America septentrionali. Kalm." RCN: 863.
Lectotype (Fernald in *Rhodora* 37: 444, pl. 403, f. 1. 1935): *Kalm,*
    Herb. Linn. No. 129.5 (LINN; iso- BM?).
Current name: ***Galium tinctorium*** L. (Rubiaceae).

Galium trifidum Linnaeus, *Species Plantarum* 1: 105. 1753.
"Habitat in Canada. Kalm." RCN: 861.
Lectotype (Fernald in *Rhodora* 37: 443. 1935): Herb. Linn. No.
    129.3a (LINN).
Current name: ***Galium trifidum*** L. (Rubiaceae).

Galium uliginosum Linnaeus, *Species Plantarum* 1: 106. 1753.
"Habitat in Europae pascuis aquosis sterilibus." RCN: 864.
Type not designated.
Original material: Herb. Linn. No. 129.6 (LINN); Herb. Linn. No.
    58 (LAPP).
Current name: ***Galium uliginosum*** L. (Rubiaceae).

Galium verum Linnaeus, *Species Plantarum* 1: 107. 1753.
"Habitat in Europa frequens." RCN: 869.
Lectotype (Nazimuddin & Qaiser in Nasir & Ali, *Fl. Pakistan* 190: 66.
    1989): Herb. Linn. No. 129.13 (LINN).
Generitype of *Galium* Linnaeus.
Current name: ***Galium verum*** L. (Rubiaceae).
Note: Galium verum, with the type designated by Nazimuddin &
    Qaiser, was proposed as conserved type of the genus by Jarvis (in
    Taxon 41: 563. 1992). However, the proposal was eventually ruled
    unnecessary by the General Committee (see Barrie, *l.c.* 55: 795–796.
    2006 for a review of the history of this and related proposals).

Garcinia celebica Linnaeus, *Herbarium Amboinense*: 7. 1754.
RCN: 3441.
Lectotype (Merrill, *Interpret. Rumph. Herb. Amb.*: 373. 1917): [icon]
    "Mangostana Celebica" in Rumphius, Herb. Amboin. 1: 134, t. 44.
    1741.
Current name: ***Garcinia celebica*** L. (Clusiaceae).

G

Garcinia cornea Linnaeus, *Systema Vegetabilium,* ed. 13: 368. 1774. RCN: 3442.
Lectotype (Merrill, *Interpret. Rumph. Herb. Amb.*: 374. 1917): [icon] *"Lignum corneum"* in Rumphius, Herb. Amboin. 3: 55, t. 30. 1743.
Current name: ***Garcinia cornea*** L. (Clusiaceae).

Garcinia mangostana Linnaeus, *Species Plantarum* 1: 443. 1753.
"Habitat in Java." RCN: 3440.
Lectotype (Hammel in Jarvis & al., *Regnum Veg.* 127: 48. 1993): [icon] *"Mangostans"* in Garcin in Philos. Trans. 38(431): 232, unnumbered plate. 1734.
Generitype of *Garcinia* Linnaeus.
Current name: ***Garcinia mangostana*** L. (Clusiaceae).
Note: D'Arcy (in *Ann. Missouri Bot. Gard.* 67: 998. 1981) and Smith (*Fl. Vitiensis Nova* 2: 347. 1981) both suggested unseen Clifford material as a suitable type, but none is in existence.

Gardenia florida Linnaeus, *Species Plantarum,* ed. 2, 1: 305. 1762, *nom. illeg.*
"Habitat in India orientali: Suratte, Amboina, Cap. b. spei." RCN: 1709.
Replaced synonym: *Gardenia jasminoides* J. Ellis (1761).
Replaced synonym of: *Nerium floridum* L. (1771), *nom. illeg.*
Type not designated.
Current name: ***Gardenia jasminoides*** J. Ellis (Rubiaceae).
Note: An illegitimate renaming of *G. jasminoides* J. Ellis (1761).

Garidella nigellastrum Linnaeus, *Species Plantarum* 1: 425. 1753.
"Habitat in Galloprovincia." RCN: 3308.
Lectotype (Zohary in *Pl. Syst. Evol.* 142: 78. 1983): Herb. Linn. No. 587.1 (LINN).
Generitype of *Garidella* Linnaeus.
Current name: ***Nigella nigellastrum*** (L.) Willk. (Ranunculaceae).

Gaultheria procumbens Linnaeus, *Species Plantarum* 1: 395. 1753.
"Habitat in Canadae sterilibus arenosis." RCN: 3106.
Lectotype (Middleton in *Bot. J. Linn. Soc.* 106: 233. 1991): [icon] *"Gaultheria"* in Linnaeus, Nov. Pl. Genera: 20, t. 1, f. 6. 1751.
Generitype of *Gaultheria* Linnaeus.
Current name: ***Gaultheria procumbens*** L. (Ericaceae).

Gaura biennis Linnaeus, *Species Plantarum* 1: 347. 1753.
"Habitat in Virginia, Pensylvania." RCN: 2662.
Lectotype (Raven & Gregory in *Mem. Torrey Bot. Club* 23: 74. 1973): Herb. Linn. No. 485.1 (LINN).
Generitype of *Gaura* Linnaeus.
Current name: ***Gaura biennis*** L. (Onagraceae).

Genipa americana Linnaeus, *Systema Naturae,* ed. 10, 2: 931. 1759.
["Habitat in America meridionali. Monnier."] Sp. Pl., ed. 2, 1: 251 (1762). RCN: 1502.
Lectotype (Howard, *Fl. Lesser Antilles* 6: 413. 1989): [icon] *"Ianipaba"* in Marggraf, Hist. Rer. Nat. Bras.: 92. 1648 (see p. 148).
Generitype of *Genipa* Linnaeus.
Current name: ***Genipa americana*** L. (Rubiaceae).
Note: Although Steyermark (in *Mem. New York Bot. Gard.* 23: 349. 1972) discussed the original elements for the name, he did not formally choose a type.

Genista anglica Linnaeus, *Species Plantarum* 2: 710. 1753.
"Habitat in Angliae ericetis humidiusculis." RCN: 5210.
Lectotype (Gibbs in *Notes Roy. Bot. Gard. Edinburgh* 27: 64. 1966): Herb. Clifford: 355, *Genista* 4 (BM-000646555).
Current name: ***Genista anglica*** L. (Fabaceae: Faboideae).

Genista canariensis Linnaeus, *Species Plantarum* 2: 709. 1753.
"Habitat in Hispania, Canariis." RCN: 5200.
Type not designated.
Original material: Herb. Clifford: 355, *Genista* 6 (BM); Herb. Linn. No. 892.1 (LINN); Herb. Linn. No. 293.19 (S); [icon] in Plukenet, Almag. Bot.: 128, t. 277, f. 6. 1696; [icon] in Commelin, Hort. Med. Amstelod. Pl. Rar. 2: 103, t. 52. 1701; [icon] in Seba, Locupl. Rer. Nat. Thes. 2: 6, t. 4, f. 6, 7. 1735; [icon] in Clusius, Rar. Pl. Hist. 1: 93, 94. 1601.
Current name: ***Genista canariensis*** L. (Fabaceae: Faboideae).
Note: Gibbs & Dingwall (in *Bol. Soc. Brot.,* sér. 2, 45: 275. 1971) indicated both Clifford material and 892.1 (LINN) as types, and Wijnands (*Bot. Commelins*: 168. 1983) stated that the Linnaean sheet "could serve as the type". However, neither statement constitutes formal typification.

Genista candicans Linnaeus, *Centuria I Plantarum*: 22. 1755.
"Habitat Monspelii & in Italia. D. Sauvages." RCN: 5201.
Lectotype (Gibbs in Turland & Jarvis in *Taxon* 46: 469. 1997): Herb. Linn. No. 53 (SBT).
Current name: ***Genista monspessulana*** (L.) L.A.S. Johnson (Fabaceae: Faboideae).

Genista florida Linnaeus, *Systema Naturae,* ed. 10, 2: 1157. 1759.
["Habitat in Hispania."] Sp. Pl., ed. 2, 2: 998 (1763). RCN: 5207.

892·15

Lectotype (Gibbs in *Notes Roy. Bot. Gard. Edinburgh* 27: 43. 1966): Herb. Linn. No. 892.15 (LINN).
Current name: ***Genista florida*** L. (Fabaceae: Faboideae).

Genista germanica Linnaeus, *Species Plantarum* 2: 710. 1753.
"Habitat in Germania." RCN: 5211.
Lectotype (Gibbs in Turland & Jarvis in *Taxon* 46: 470. 1997): Herb.
Burser XXII: 29 (UPS).
Current name: ***Genista germanica*** L. (Fabaceae: Faboideae).
Note: Gibbs (in *Notes Roy. Bot. Gard. Edinburgh* 27: 70. 1966)
simultaneously designated both 892.21 (LINN) and van Royen
material (L) as holotypes – an ineffective choice.

Genista hispanica Linnaeus, *Species Plantarum* 2: 711. 1753.
"Habitat in Hispania, G. Narbonensi." RCN: 5212.
Lectotype (Gibbs in *Notes Roy. Bot. Gard. Edinburgh* 27: 69. 1966):
Herb. Linn. No. 892.24 (LINN).
Current name: ***Genista hispanica*** L. (Fabaceae: Faboideae).

Genista humifusa Linnaeus, *Systema Naturae*, ed. 10, 2: 1157.
1759.
["Habitat in Oriente. D. Gerard."] Sp. Pl., ed. 2, 2: 998 (1763). RCN:
5209.
Lectotype (Gibbs in Turland & Jarvis in *Taxon* 46: 470. 1997): *Gérard
10*, Herb. Linn. No. 892.17 (LINN).
Current name: ***Genista tinctoria*** L. (Fabaceae: Faboideae).

Genista linifolia Linnaeus, *Species Plantarum*, ed. 2, 2: 997. 1763.
"Habitat in Oriente, Hispania. Cl. Alstroemer." RCN: 5202.
Lectotype (Gibbs & Dingwall in *Bol. Soc. Brot.*, sér. 2, 45: 294. 1971):
Alströmer 185, Herb. Linn. No. 892.5 (LINN).
Current name: ***Genista linifolia*** L. (Fabaceae: Faboideae).

Genista lusitanica Linnaeus, *Species Plantarum* 2: 711. 1753.
"Habitat in Lusitania, Hispania." RCN: 5213.
Lectotype (López González in *Anales Jard. Bot. Madrid* 39: 49, f. 1.
1982): *Löfling 26*, Herb. Linn. No. 892.27, left specimen (LINN).
Current name: ***Genista lusitanica*** L. (Fabaceae: Faboideae).
Note: Lacaita (in *J. Bot.* 67: 199–200. 1929) believed that this name
was based entirely on Clusius' plate but this is incorrect, as
demonstrated by López González.

Genista pilosa Linnaeus, *Species Plantarum* 2: 710. 1753.
"Habitat in Pannonia, G. Narbonensi, Germania." RCN: 5208.
Lectotype (Gibbs in *Notes Roy. Bot. Gard. Edinburgh* 27: 50. 1966):
Herb. Clifford: 355, *Genista 3* (BM-000646554).
Current name: ***Genista pilosa*** L. (Fabaceae: Faboideae).

Genista purgans Linnaeus, *Systema Naturae*, ed. 10, 2: 1157. 1759.
["Habitat Monspelii."] Sp. Pl., ed. 2, 2: 999 (1763). RCN: 5192.
Basionym of: *Spartium purgans* (L.) L. (1767).
Lectotype (López González & Jarvis in *Anales Jard. Bot. Madrid* 40:
342. 1984): *Löfling 231b*, Herb. Linn. No. 892.20 (LINN).
Current name: ***Genista scorpius*** (L.) DC. (Fabaceae: Faboideae).
Note: López González (in *Taxon* 45: 699. 1996) proposed the name for
conservation with a conserved type in order to restore the use of the
name in its pre-1984 sense. However, this proposal was not
recommended by the Committee for Spermatophyta (in *Taxon* 48:
364. 1999).

Genista sagittalis Linnaeus, *Species Plantarum* 2: 710. 1753.
"Habitat in Germania, Gallia." RCN: 5203.
Lectotype (Gibbs in Turland & Jarvis in *Taxon* 46: 470. 1997): Herb.
Linn. No. 892.7 (LINN).
Current name: ***Genista sagittalis*** L. subsp. *sagittalis* (Fabaceae:
Faboideae).

Genista sibirica Linnaeus, *Mantissa Plantarum Altera*: 571. 1771.
"Habitat in Sibiria." RCN: 5206.

Lectotype (Gibbs in Turland & Jarvis in *Taxon* 46: 470. 1997): Herb.
Linn. No. 892.11 (LINN).
Current name: ***Genista tinctoria*** L. (Fabaceae: Faboideae).

Genista tinctoria Linnaeus, *Species Plantarum* 2: 710. 1753.
"Habitat in Germania, Anglia." RCN: 5205.
Lectotype (Gibbs in *Notes Roy. Bot. Gard. Edinburgh* 27: 33. 1966):
Herb. Clifford: 355, *Genista 1*, sheet 1 (BM-000646551; iso- BM).
Generitype of *Genista* Linnaeus (vide Green, *Prop. Brit. Bot.*: 174.
1929).
Current name: ***Genista tinctoria*** L. (Fabaceae: Faboideae).

Genista tridentata Linnaeus, *Species Plantarum* 2: 710. 1753.
"Habitat in Lusitania. Loefl." RCN: 5204.
Lectotype (Gibbs in Turland & Jarvis in *Taxon* 46: 470. 1997): *Löfling
s.n.*, Herb. Linn. No. 892.8 (LINN).
Current name: ***Genista tridentata*** L. subsp. *tridentata* (Fabaceae:
Faboideae).

Gentiana acaulis Linnaeus, *Species Plantarum* 1: 228. 1753.
"Habitat in alpibus Helveticis, Austriacis, Pyrenaicis." RCN: 1865.
Type not designated.
Original material: Herb. Burser X: 54 (UPS); Herb. Clifford: 81,
Gentiana 5 (BM); Herb. Linn. No. 328.9 (LINN); [icon] in
Reneaulme, Specim. Hist. Pl.: 70, 68. 1611.
Current name: ***Gentiana acaulis*** L. (Gentianaceae).

Gentiana amarella Linnaeus, *Species Plantarum* 1: 230. 1753.
"Habitat in Europae pratis." RCN: 1882.
Lectotype (Gillett in *Ann. Missouri Bot. Gard.* 44: 249. 1957): Herb.
Linn. No. 328.32 (LINN).
Current name: ***Gentianella amarella*** (L.) Börner (Gentianaceae).

Gentiana aquatica Linnaeus, *Species Plantarum* 1: 229. 1753.
"Habitat in Sibiria. D. Amman." RCN: 1873.
Lectotype (Omer & Qaiser in *Edinburgh J. Bot.* 50: 65. 1993): [icon]
"*Gentiana humilis, aquatica, verna*" in Amman, Stirp. Rar. Ruth.: 4,
t. 1, f. 1. 1739.
Current name: ***Ciminalis aquatica*** (L.) Zuev (Gentianaceae).
Note: Pritchard (in Davis, *Fl. Turkey* 6: 186. 1978) indicated 328.17
(LINN) as type, as did Agrawal (in *J. Econ. Taxon. Bot.* 5: 436.
1984) but the sheet lacks a *Species Plantarum* number (i.e. "12"),
was a post-1753 addition to the herbarium, and is not original
material for the name. It also apparently conflicts with the
protologue and does not belong to the species normally known
under this name. Omer & Qaiser therefore rejected this choice of
type in favour of the cited Amman plate.

Gentiana asclepiadea Linnaeus, *Species Plantarum* 1: 227. 1753.
"Habitat in alpibus Helvetiae, Pannoniae, Mauritaniae." RCN: 1861.
Type not designated.
Original material: Herb. Burser X: 53 (UPS); Herb. Clifford: 80,
Gentiana 2 (BM); [icon] in Reneaulme, Specim. Hist. Pl.: 67, 68.
1611.
Current name: ***Gentiana asclepiadea*** L. (Gentianaceae).
Note: Ho & Liu (in *Worldw. Monogr.* Gentiana: 304. 2001) indicated
328.5 (LINN) as holotype, with 328.6 (LINN) and (evidently) a
Clifford sheet as unspecified sorts of type. However, sheet 328.5 is
not annotated by Linnaeus such as to link it with this name, and it
is not original material for *G. asclepiadea*.

Gentiana aurea Linnaeus, *Systema Naturae*, ed. 10, 2: 951. 1759.
["Habitat in alpibus Burdegalensibus & Lapponiae Norvegicae. D. C.
Solander."] Sp. Pl., ed. 2, 1: 331 (1762). RCN: 1871.
Type not designated.

G

Original material: Herb. Linn. No. 328.15 (LINN); [icon] in
Barrelier, Pl. Galliam: 3, t. 104. 1714.
Current name: **Gentianella aurea** (L.) Harry Sm. ex Hyl.
(Gentianaceae).
Note: Gillett (in *Ann. Missouri Bot. Gard.* 44: 242. 1957) indicated
König material (presumably sheet 328.44 in LINN) as type.
However, no annotation by Linnaeus associates this collection with
the name, and the numerous König collections in LINN were
mostly received well after 1759. This collection is therefore not
accepted as original material for the name.

Gentiana autumnalis Linnaeus, *Cat. Edwards's Nat. Hist.*: 11. 1776.
Lectotype (Pringle in *Brittonia* 19: 2. 1967): [icon] *"The Autumnal
Gentian of the Desert"* in Edwards, Gleanings Nat. Hist. 1: 98, t.
255. 1758 (see p. 101).
Current name: **Gentiana autumnalis** L. (Gentianaceae).
Note: Fernald (in *Rhodora* 52: 68–69. 1950) gives an informative
explanation of the circumstances surrounding the publication of
this name and states that it is based on Edwards' plate and Bartram's
description. Pringle, however, referred to the plate as "the type".

Gentiana bavarica Linnaeus, *Species Plantarum* 1: 229. 1753.
"Habitat in alpibus Helvetiae, Bavaria." RCN: 1870.
Type not designated.
Original material: Herb. Linn. No. 112.15 (S); Herb. Clifford: 81,
Gentiana 6 (BM); [icon] in Camerarius, Hort. Med. Phil.: 65, t. 15
f. 2. 1588.
Current name: **Gentiana bavarica** L. (Gentianaceae).
Note: Ho & Liu (in *Worldw. Monogr.* Gentiana: 270. 2001) indicate
what is evidently a Clifford sheet as holotype (with a specimen in S
as "type"). The Clifford material must therefore be intended as a
lectotype, but the absence of "designated here" (Art. 7.11) appears
to make this an ineffective type choice.

Gentiana campestris Linnaeus, *Species Plantarum* 1: 231. 1753.
"Habitat in Europae pratis siccis." RCN: 1883.
Type not designated.
Original material: Herb. Linn. No. 328.34 (LINN); Herb. Burser X:
60 (UPS); Herb. Linn. No. 94 (LAPP); [icon] in Colonna, Ekphr.:
223, 221. 1606; [icon] in Barrelier, Pl. Galliam: 3, t. 97, f. 2. 1714.
Current name: **Gentianella campestris** (L.) Börner (Gentianaceae).

Gentiana centaurium Linnaeus, *Species Plantarum* 1: 229. 1753.
"Habitat in Europae apricis, praesertim maritimis." RCN: 1876.
Lectotype (Melderis in *Bot. J. Linn. Soc.* 65: 229. 1972): Herb.
Clifford: 81, *Gentiana* 9 (BM-000558187).
Current name: **Centaurium littorale** (Turner) Gilmour (Gentianaceae).
Note: Difficulties between the competing *C. littorale* (Turner) Gilmour
(1937) and *C. minor* Moench (1794) led Pringle (in *Taxon* 36: 482.
1987) to successfully propose the rejection of Moench's name.

Gentiana ciliata Linnaeus, *Species Plantarum* 1: 231. 1753.
"Habitat in Helvetiae, Italiae, Canadae montibus." RCN: 1884.
Lectotype (Hartvig in Strid & Kit Tan, *Mountain Fl. Greece* 2: 7.
1991): *Gmelin s.n.*, Herb. Linn. No. 328.7 (LINN).
Current name: **Gentianella ciliata** (L.) Borkh. (Gentianaceae).
Note: Fernald (in *Rhodora* 25: 85. 1923) discussed the Canadian
element in the protologue, concluding that Kalm must have
collected an endemic species, *G. victorinii* Fernald, in Quebec.

Gentiana cruciata Linnaeus, *Species Plantarum* 1: 231. 1753.
"Habitat in Pannoniae, Apenninorum, Helvetiae montosis apricis."
RCN: 1885.
Lectotype (Hartvig in Strid & Kit Tan, *Mountain Fl. Greece* 2: 5.
1991): Herb. Linn. No. 328.40 (LINN).

Current name: **Gentiana cruciata** L. (Gentianaceae).
Note: In what was clearly a typographic error, Hartvig referred to the
type as sheet "338.40" rather than "328.40".

Gentiana exacoides Linnaeus, *Species Plantarum*, ed. 2, 1: 332. 1762.
"Habitat ad Cap. b. spei." RCN: 1875.
Type not designated.
Original material: [icon] in Plukenet, Phytographia: t. 275, f. 4. 1694;
Almag. Bot.: 94. 1696; [icon] in Seba, Locupl. Rer. Nat. Thes. 1:
35, t. 22, f. 7. 1734; [icon] in Burman, Rar. Afric. Pl.: 208, t. 74, f.
5. 1739.
Current name: **Sebaea exacoides** (L.) Schinz (Gentianaceae).
Note: Marais & Verdoorn (in Dyer & al., *Fl. Southern Africa* 26: 190.
1963) stated "Type: Cape, *Hermann*" but it is unclear what element
may have been intended.

Gentiana exaltata Linnaeus, *Species Plantarum*, ed. 2, 1: 331. 1762.
"Habitat in America." RCN: 1866.
Lectotype (Shinners in *S. W. Naturalist* 2: 40. 1957): [icon] *"Gentiana
foliis sessilibus, lanceolatis"* in Plumier in Burman, Pl. Amer.: 71, t.
81, f. 1. 1756.
Current name: **Eustoma exaltatum** (L.) G. Don (Gentianaceae).

Gentiana filiformis Linnaeus, *Species Plantarum* 1: 231. 1753.
"Habitat in Gallia." RCN: 1887.
Type not designated.
Original material: [icon] in Vaillant, Bot. Paris.: 32, t. 6, f. 3. 1727.
Current name: **Cicendia filiformis** (L.) Delarbre (Gentianaceae).

Gentiana heteroclita Linnaeus, *Mantissa Plantarum Altera*: 560. 1771.
"Habitat in Malabariae agris. D. Koenig." RCN: 1888.
Lectotype (Cramer in Dassanayake & Fosberg, *Revised Handb. Fl.
Ceylon* 3: 73. 1981): *König s.n.*, Herb. Linn. No. 328.43 (LINN;
iso- BM).
Current name: **Canscora heteroclita** (L.) Gilg (Gentianaceae).

Gentiana lutea Linnaeus, *Species Plantarum* 1: 227. 1753.
"Habitat in alpibus Norvegicis, Helveticis, Apenninis, Pyrenaeis,
Tridentinis." RCN: 1858.
Lectotype (Aitken in Jarvis & al., *Regnum Veg.* 127: 49. 1993): Herb.
Clifford: 80, *Gentiana* 1 (BM-000558179).
Generitype of *Gentiana* Linnaeus (vide Hitchcock, *Prop. Brit. Bot.*:
138. 1929).
Current name: **Gentiana lutea** L. (Gentianaceae).

Gentiana maritima Linnaeus, *Systema Naturae*, ed. 12, 2: 200;
Mantissa Plantarum: 55. 1767.
"Habitat in Italiae, Galliae australis maritimis." RCN: 1877.
Replaced synonym: *Gentiana pumila* Gouan (1765), *nom. illeg.*, non
Jacq. (1762).
Type not designated.
Current name: **Centaurium maritimum** (L.) Fritsch (Gentianaceae).
Note: A *nomen novum* for *G. pumila* Gouan (1765), *nom. illeg.*, non
Jacq. (1762). It is homotypic with Gouan's name.

Gentiana nivalis Linnaeus, *Species Plantarum* 1: 229. 1753.
"Habitat in Lapponiae, Helvetiae summis alpibus." RCN: 1872.
Type not designated.
Original material: Herb. Burser X: 61 (UPS); Herb. Linn. No. 95
(LAPP); [icon] in Haller, Enum. Meth. Stirp. Helv. 1: 475, t. 7. 1742.
Current name: **Gentiana nivalis** L. (Gentianaceae).
Note: Ho & Liu (in *Worldw. Monogr.* Gentiana: 224. 2001) incorrectly
indicated 328.16 (LINN) as the holotype, but the sheet in any case
lacks the *Species Plantarum* number (i.e. "11"), was a post-1753
addition to the collection, and is not original material for the name.

Gentiana perfoliata Linnaeus, *Species Plantarum* 1: 232. 1753.
"Habitat in Gallia, Anglia, Hispania." RCN: 2693.
Basionym of: *Chlora perfoliata* (L.) L. (1767).
Type not designated.
Original material: Herb. Burser XVI(1): 15 (UPS); [icon] in
Reneaulme, Specim. Hist. Pl.: 80, 76. 1611; [icon] in Clusius, Rar.
Pl. Hist. 2: 180. 1601; [icon] in Morison, Pl. Hist. Univ. 2: 565, s.
5, t. 26, f. 1, 2. 1680.
Current name: ***Blackstonia perfoliata*** (L.) Huds. (Gentianaceae).

Gentiana pneumonanthe Linnaeus, *Species Plantarum* 1: 228.
1753.
"Habitat in Europae pascuis humidiusculis." RCN: 1862.
Type not designated.
Original material: Herb. Linn. No. 328.7 (LINN); Herb. Clifford: 80,
Gentiana 3, 3 sheets (BM); Herb. Burser X: 67 (UPS); [icon] in
Reneaulme, Specim. Hist. Pl.: 69, 68. 1611.
Current name: ***Gentiana pneumonanthe*** L. (Gentianaceae).
Note: Ho & Liu (in *Worldw. Monogr.* Gentiana: 287. 2001) wrongly
indicated 328.7 (LINN) as holotype (with three other collections as
"type"). The absence of "designated here" (Art. 7.11) precludes the
acceptance of the material in LINN as a lectotype.

Gentiana punctata Linnaeus, *Species Plantarum* 1: 227. 1753.
"Habitat in Helvetia, Sibiria." RCN: 1860.
Type not designated.
Original material: Herb. Burser X: 52 (UPS).
Current name: ***Gentiana punctata*** L. (Gentianaceae).
Note: Although Ho & Liu (in *Worldw. Monogr.* Gentiana: 261. 2001)
indicated 328.4 (LINN) as type, it is a post-1753 collection from
Scopoli and not original material for the name.

Gentiana purpurea Linnaeus, *Species Plantarum* 1: 227. 1753.
"Habitat in alpibus Helveticis." RCN: 1859.
Type not designated.
Original material: Herb. Burser X: 51 (UPS); Herb. Burser X: 50,
syntype (UPS); [icon] in Mattioli, Pl. Epit.: 416. 1586.
Current name: ***Gentiana purpurea*** L. (Gentianaceae).

Gentiana pyrenaica Linnaeus, *Systema Naturae,* ed. 12, 2: 200;
Mantissa Plantarum: 55. 1767.
"Habitat in Pyrenaeis." RCN: 1868.
Type not designated.
Original material: Herb. Linn. No. 328.14 (LINN).
Current name: ***Gentiana pyrenaica*** L. (Gentianaceae).
Note: Although Ho & Liu (in *Worldw. Monogr.* Gentiana: 432. 2001)
incorrectly indicated 328.14 (LINN) as holotype, the absence of
"designated here" (Art. 7.11) precludes the acceptance of this
material as a lectotype.

Gentiana quadrifolia Linnaeus, *Species Plantarum,* ed. 2, 2: 1671.
1763.
"Habitat in Europa australi. Cl. Alstroemer." RCN: 2694.
Basionym of: *Chlora quadrifolia* (L.) L. (1767).
Lectotype (López González & Jarvis in *Anales Jard. Bot. Madrid* 40:
343. 1984): *Alströmer s.n.,* Herb. Linn. No. 494.3 (LINN).
Current name: ***Centaurium quadrifolium*** (L.) G. López & C.E.
Jarvis (Gentianaceae).

Gentiana quinquefolia Linnaeus, *Species Plantarum* 1: 230. 1753.
"Habitat in Pensylvania. Kalm." RCN: 1880.
Lectotype (Gillett in *Ann. Missouri Bot. Gard.* 44: 243. 1957): *Kalm,*
Herb. Linn. No. 328.31 (LINN).
Current name: ***Gentianella quinquefolia*** (L.) Small
(Gentianaceae).

Gentiana saponaria Linnaeus, *Species Plantarum* 1: 228. 1753.
"Habitat in Virginia." RCN: 1863.
Lectotype (Pringle in *Brittonia* 19: 2. 1967): *Kalm,* Herb. Linn. No.
328.8 (LINN).
Current name: ***Gentiana saponaria*** L. (Gentianaceae).
Note: See discussion of the Catesby element by Howard & Staples (in
J. Arnold Arbor. 64: 526. 1983).

Gentiana sessilis Linnaeus, *Species Plantarum* 1: 231. 1753.
"Habitat in Chilli." RCN: 1886.
Type not designated.
Original material: [icon] in Feuillée, J. Obs. 3: 20, t. 14. 1725; [icon]
in Tabernaemontanus, Eicones Pl.: 780. 1590.
Current name: ***Chlora sessilis*** (L.) Willd. (Gentianaceae).

Gentiana spicata Linnaeus, *Species Plantarum* 1: 230. 1753.
"Habitat in montibus Euganeis & Monspelii." RCN: 1878.
Lectotype (Mansion in *Taxon* 53: 726. 2004): Herb. Burser XVI(1):
14 (UPS).
Current name: ***Schenkia spicata*** (L.) G. Mans. (Gentianaceae).

Gentiana utriculosa Linnaeus, *Species Plantarum* 1: 229. 1753.
"Habitat in Alpibus Helvetiae, Italiae." RCN: 1874.
Type not designated.
Original material: [icon] in Barrelier, Pl. Galliam: 3, t. 48. 1714;
[icon] in Colonna, Ekphr.: 220, 221. 1606.
Current name: ***Gentiana utriculosa*** L. (Gentianaceae).
Note: Although Ho & Liu (in *Worldw. Monogr.* Gentiana: 263. 2001)
incorrectly indicated 328.18 (LINN) as holotype, the absence of
"designated here" (Art. 7.11) precludes the acceptance of this
material as a lectotype which, in any case, does not appear to be
original material for the name.

Gentiana verna Linnaeus, *Species Plantarum* 1: 228. 1753.
"Habitat in alpibus Helvetiae." RCN: 1867.
Type not designated.
Original material: Herb. Burser X: 57 (UPS); Herb. Linn. No. 328.12
(LINN); [icon] in Clusius, Rar. Pl. Hist. 1: 315. 1601; [icon] in
Reneaulme, Specim. Hist. Pl.: 75, 68. 1611.
Current name: ***Gentiana verna*** L. (Gentianaceae).
Note: Although Ho & Liu (in *Worldw. Monogr.* Gentiana: 263. 2001)
incorrectly indicated 328.12 (LINN) as holotype, the absence of
"designated here" (Art. 7.11) precludes the acceptance of this
material as a lectotype.

Gentiana verticillata Linnaeus, *Systema Naturae,* ed. 10, 2: 952.
1759.
["Habitat in America."] Sp. Pl., ed. 2, 1: 333 (1762). RCN: 1879.
Lectotype (Raynal in *Adansonia,* n.s., 9: 78, pl. 1. 1969): [icon]
"Centaurium minus ad alas floridum" in Plumier, Codex
Boerhaavianus (University Library, Groningen).
Current name: ***Enicostema verticillatum*** (L.) Engl. ex Gilg
(Gentianaceae).

Gentiana villosa Linnaeus, *Species Plantarum* 1: 228. 1753.
"Habitat in Virginia." RCN: 1864.
Type not designated.
Original material: *Clayton 605* (BM).
Current name: ***Gentiana villosa*** L. (Gentianaceae).
Note: Pringle (in *Ann. Missouri Bot. Gard.* 44: 2. 1967) indicated
unspecified material in BM as the type, while Ho & Liu (in *Worldw.
Monogr.* Gentiana: 302. 2001) indicated Clayton material (BM) as
the holotype (which it is not). Unfortunately, the absence of
"designated here" or an equivalent (Art. 7.11) precludes this
statement from being accepted as a formal typification.

Geranium acaule Linnaeus, *Systema Naturae*, ed. 10, 2: 1143. 1759. RCN: 4962.
Lectotype (designated here by Aedo): Herb. Linn. No. 858.41 (LINN).
Current name: ***Erodium acaule*** (L.) Bech. & Thell. (Geraniaceae).

Geranium acetosum Linnaeus, *Species Plantarum* 2: 678. 1753.
"Habitat in Africa." RCN: 4935.
Lectotype (Wijnands, *Bot. Commelins*: 106. 1983): Herb. Clifford: 345, *Geranium* 13 (BM-000646430).
Current name: ***Pelargonium acetosum*** (L.) Aiton (Geraniaceae).

Geranium alchemilloides Linnaeus, *Species Plantarum* 2: 678. 1753.
"Habitat in Africa." RCN: 4950.
Lectotype (Kokwaro in Milne-Redhead & Polhill, *Fl. Trop. E. Africa, Geraniaceae*: 20. 1971): Herb. Linn. No. 858.24 (LINN).
Current name: ***Pelargonium alchemilloides*** (L.) Aiton (Geraniaceae).
Note: Specific epithet spelled "alchimilloides" in the protologue.

Geranium althaeoides Linnaeus, *Species Plantarum* 2: 679. 1753.
"Habitat in Africa." RCN: 4955.
Type not designated.
Original material: none traced.
Current name: ***Pelargonium althaeoides*** (L.) L'Hér. (Geraniaceae).

Geranium arduinum Linnaeus, *Species Plantarum*, ed. 2, 2: 952. 1763.
"Habitat ad Cap. b. spei. Burmannus." RCN: 4969.
Type not designated.
Original material: none traced.
Current name: ***Erodium sp.*** (Geraniaceae).
Note: The application of this name appears uncertain.

Geranium argenteum Linnaeus, *Centuria II Plantarum*: 25. 1756.
"Habitat in Baldi summis praeruptis rupibus." RCN: 4983.
Lectotype (Aedo in *Syst. Bot. Monogr.* 49: 39. 1996): *Séguier*, Herb. Linn. No. 858.67, right specimen (LINN).
Current name: ***Geranium argenteum*** L. (Geraniaceae).

Geranium auritum Linnaeus, *Species Plantarum* 2: 679. 1753.
"Habitat in Africa." RCN: 4958.
Basionym of: *Geranium prolificum* L. var. *auritum* (L.) L. (1763).
Lectotype (van der Walt & Vorster in *J. S. African Bot.* 46: 285. 1980): [icon] "*Geranium Afric. foliis plerumque auritis, flor. ex rubro purpurascentibus*" in Commelin, Hort. Med. Amstelod. Pl. Rar. 2: 121, t. 61. 1701.
Current name: ***Pelargonium auritum*** (L.) Willd. (Geraniaceae).

Geranium betulinum Linnaeus, *Species Plantarum* 2: 679. 1753.
"Habitat in Africa." RCN: 4940.
Lectotype (van der Walt in *Bothalia* 15: 352. 1985): Herb. Linn. No. 858.9 (LINN).
Current name: ***Pelargonium betulinum*** (L.) L'Hér. (Geraniaceae).

Geranium bohemicum Linnaeus, *Centuria II Plantarum*: 25. 1756.
"Habitat in Bohemia? Miller." RCN: 4986.
Lectotype (Novoselova in *Novosti Sist. Vyssh. Rast.* 31: 150. 1998): Herb. Linn. No. 858.69 (LINN).
Current name: ***Geranium bohemicum*** L. (Geraniaceae).
Note: See also Jonsell & Jarvis (in *Nordic J. Bot.* 22: 79. 2002), who independently chose the same type as Novoselova.

Geranium capitatum Linnaeus, *Species Plantarum* 2: 678. 1753.
"Habitat in Africa." RCN: 4947.
Lectotype (van der Walt in *Bothalia* 15: 353. 1985): Herb. Linn. No. 858.17 (LINN).
Current name: ***Pelargonium capitatum*** (L.) L'Hér. (Geraniaceae).

Geranium carnosum Linnaeus, *Centuria I Plantarum*: 20. 1755.
"Habitat in Aethiopia." RCN: 4942.
Type not designated.
Original material: [icon] in Dillenius, Hort. Eltham. 1: 153, t. 127, f. 154. 1732.
Current name: ***Pelargonium carnosum*** (L.) Aiton (Geraniaceae).
Note: Dyer (in *Fl. Pl. Africa* 29: pl. 1145. 1953) assumed the typical form of the species to be indicated by the cited Dillenian plate but he did not appear to be typifying the name. Albers (in Eggli, *Ill. Handb. Succ. Pl., Dicots*: 251. 2002) indicated the same plate as type but this choice was published after 1 Jan 2001 and so the omission of the phrase "designated here" or an equivalent (Art. 7.11) means that this choice is not effective. Edmondson & Rowley (in *Bradleya* 16: 15, f. 3. 1998) reproduce the plate in colour.

Geranium carolinianum Linnaeus, *Species Plantarum* 2: 682. 1753.
"Habitat in Carolina, Virginia." RCN: 4990.
Lectotype (Fawcett & Rendle, *Fl. Jamaica* 4: 154. 1920): *Clayton 372* (BM-000040264).
Current name: ***Geranium carolinianum*** L. (Geraniaceae).
Note: Fernald (in *Rhodora* 37: 300, pl. 373. 1935) illustrated the cited Dillenian plate and noted that it belongs to *G. langloisii* Greene.

Geranium chium Linnaeus, *Systema Naturae*, ed. 10, 2: 1143. 1759.
["Habitat in Chio."] Sp. Pl., ed. 2, 2: 951 (1763). RCN: 4965.
Lectotype (Venter & Verhoeven in *S. African J. Bot.* 56: 82. 1990): Herb. Linn. No. 858.45 (LINN).
Current name: ***Erodium chium*** (L.) Willd. (Geraniaceae).

Geranium ciconium Linnaeus, *Centuria I Plantarum*: 21. 1755.
"Habitat in Europa australi, Valesia Italiae, Monspelii." RCN: 4971.
Lectotype (Burtt in *Kew Bull.* 9: 401. 1954): Herb. Linn. No. 858.53 (LINN).
Current name: ***Erodium ciconium*** (L.) L'Hér. (Geraniaceae).

Geranium cicutarium Linnaeus, *Species Plantarum* 2: 680. 1753.
"Habitat in Europae sterilibus cultis." RCN: 4963.
Lectotype (Venter & Verhoeven in *S. African J. Bot.* 56: 83. 1990): Herb. Linn. No. 858.43 (LINN).
Current name: ***Erodium cicutarium*** (L.) L'Hér. (Geraniaceae).

Geranium cicutarium Linnaeus var. **moschatum** Linnaeus, *Species Plantarum* 2: 680. 1753.
RCN: 4964.
Basionym of: *Geranium moschatum* (L.) L. (1754).
Lectotype (designated here by Aedo): Herb. Burser XVIII: 58 (UPS).
Current name: ***Erodium moschatum*** (L.) L'Hér. (Geraniaceae).
Note: A number of authors (e.g. Schönbeck-Temesy in Rechinger, *Fl. Iranica* 69: 55. 1970) have treated 858.44 (LINN) as the type but this collection is evidently a post-1753 addition to the herbarium and is not original material for the name.

Geranium columbinum Linnaeus, *Species Plantarum* 2: 682. 1753.
"Habitat in Gallia, Helvetia, Germania." RCN: 4991.
Lectotype (Ghafoor in Jafri & El-Gadi, *Fl. Libya* 63: 47. 1978): *Dillenius?*, Herb. Linn. No. 858.79 (LINN), see p. 201.
Current name: ***Geranium columbinum*** L. (Geraniaceae).

Geranium coriandrifolium Linnaeus, *Species Plantarum*, ed. 2, 2: 949. 1763.
"Habitat in Aethiopia." RCN: 4956.
Lectotype (van der Walt & Boucher in *S. African J. Bot.* 52: 443. 1986): Herb. Clifford: 345, *Geranium* 19 (BM-000646438).
Current name: ***Pelargonium myrrhifolium*** (L.) L'Hér. var. ***coriandrifolium*** (L.) Harv. (Geraniaceae).

Geranium cotyledonis Linnaeus, *Mantissa Plantarum Altera*: 569. 1771.
"Habitat ad Cap. b. spei. Gordon." RCN: 4949.
Neotype (Cronk, *Endemic Fl. St Helena*: 58. 2000): St Helena. *Banks & Solander s.n.* (BM).
Current name: ***Pelargonium cotyledonis*** (L.) L'Hér. (Geraniaceae).

Geranium cucullatum Linnaeus, *Species Plantarum* 2: 677. 1753.
"Habitat in Africa." RCN: 4941.
Lectotype (van der Walt & Forster, *Pelargoniums Southern Africa* 2: 43. 1981): Herb. Clifford: 345, *Geranium* 17 (BM-000646435).
Current name: ***Pelargonium cucullatum*** (L.) L'Hér. (Geraniaceae).
Note: See further discussion of the typification by Volschenk & al. (in *Bothalia* 14: 46, 48, f. 2. 1982).

Geranium dissectum Linnaeus, *Centuria I Plantarum*: 21. 1755.
"Habitat in Europa australiori." RCN: 4993.
Lectotype (Carolin in *Proc. Linn. Soc. New South Wales* 89: 336. 1965): Herb. Linn. No. 858.82 (LINN).
Current name: ***Geranium dissectum*** L. (Geraniaceae).

Geranium foetidum Linnaeus, *Amoenitates Academicae* 4: 487. 1759.
Lectotype (Guittonneau in *Boissiera* 20: 97. 1972): Herb. Magnol (MPU).
Current name: ***Erodium foetidum*** (L.) L'Hér. (Geraniaceae).
Note: Stearn (in Geck & Pressler, *Festschr. Claus Nissen*: 639. 1974) discussed this name, which was published in the 1759 reprint of the dissertation *Flora Monspeliensis*. Linnaeus' name is validated solely by a reference to Magnol's *Botanicum Monspeliense*: 109. 1676, the text of which Stearn reproduces, along with a plate (Magnol's t. 8; Stearn's f. 3). Under Art. 7.7, Linnaeus' binomial must be typified "by an element selected from the context of the validating description or diagnosis", and the type choice made by Guittonneau of Magnol material in MPU is therefore accepted here.

Geranium fulgidum Linnaeus, *Species Plantarum* 2: 676. 1753.
"Habitat in Aethiopia." RCN: 4932.
Lectotype (Albers & al. in *S. African J. Bot.* 66: 39. 2000): [icon] *"Geranium Afric. folio Alceae, flore coccineo fulgidissimo Boerh."* in Dillenius, Hort. Eltham. 1: 156, t. 130, f. 157. 1732.
Current name: ***Pelargonium fulgidum*** (L.) Aiton (Geraniaceae).
Note: The Tilli illustration cited by Linnaeus is figured by Jarvis (in *Museol. Sci.* 9: 164, f. 5, 6. 1993), and here (p. 163).

Geranium fuscum Linnaeus, *Systema Naturae*, ed. 12, 2: 455; *Mantissa Plantarum*: 97. 1767.
"Habitat in Europa Australi." RCN: 4976.
Lectotype (Aedo in *Syst. Bot. Monogr.* 49: 72. 1996): Herb. Linn. No. 858.58 (LINN).
Current name: ***Geranium phaeum*** L. (Geraniaceae).

Geranium gibbosum Linnaeus, *Species Plantarum* 2: 677. 1753.
"Habitat in Africa." RCN: 4943.
Lectotype (Maggs & al. in *S. African J. Bot.* 61: 173, f. 2. 1995): [icon] *"Geranium Africanum, noctu olens, tuberosum et nodosum, Aquilegiae foliis"* in Hermann, Hort. Lugd.-Bat. Cat.: 284, 285. 1687.
Current name: ***Pelargonium gibbosum*** (L.) L'Hér. (Geraniaceae).

Geranium glaucophyllum Linnaeus, *Species Plantarum* 2: 679. 1753.
"Habitat in Aegypto." RCN: 4968.
Lectotype (designated here by Aedo): [icon] *"Geranium Aegypt. glaucophyllum, rostris longissimis plumosis"* in Dillenius, Hort. Eltham. 1: 150, t. 124, f. 150. 1732.
Current name: ***Erodium glaucophyllum*** (L.) L'Hér. (Geraniaceae).

Note: A number of authors (e.g. Schönbeck-Temesy in Rechinger, *Fl. Iranica* 69: 45. 1970) have indicated unspecified van Royen material as the type. However, the only sheet traced in L that can be associated with this name (No. 903.278–317) appears to post-date Adriaan van Royen, and is therefore not original material for the name.

Geranium grandiflorum Linnaeus, *Species Plantarum* 2: 683. 1753.
"Habitat in Aethiopia." RCN: 3367.
Replaced synonym of: *Grielum tenuifolium* L. (1764), *nom. illeg.*
Type not designated.
Original material: [icon] in Burman, Rar. Afric. Pl.: 88, t. 34, f. 1. 1738.
Current name: ***Grielum grandiflorum*** (L.) Druce (Neuradaceae).

Geranium grossularioides Linnaeus, *Species Plantarum* 2: 679. 1753.
"Habitat in Africa." RCN: 4954.
Type not designated.
Original material: [icon] in Hermann, Hort. Lugd.-Bat. Cat.: 287, 289. 1687.
Current name: ***Pelargonium grossularioides*** (L.) L'Hér. (Geraniaceae).

Geranium gruinum Linnaeus, *Species Plantarum* 2: 680. 1753.
"Habitat in Creta." RCN: 4970.
Lectotype (Ghafoor in Jafri & El-Gadi, *Fl. Libya* 63: 36. 1978): Herb. Linn. No. 858.52 (LINN).
Current name: ***Erodium gruinum*** (L.) L'Hér. (Geraniaceae).

Geranium hybridum Linnaeus, *Systema Naturae*, ed. 12, 2: 452; *Mantissa Plantarum*: 97. 1767.
"Habitat ad Cap. b. spei. Filia Ger. inquinantis ex Ger. acetoso." RCN: 4934.
Type not designated.
Original material: [icon] in Dillenius, Hort. Eltham. 1: 152, t. 125, f. 152. 1732.
Note: The application of this name appears uncertain.

Geranium incarnatum Linnaeus, *Systema Naturae*, ed. 10, 2: 1142. 1759.
RCN: 4957.
Type not designated.
Original material: Herb. Linn. No. 43 (SBT); [icon] in Breyn, Exot. Pl. Cent.: 129, t. 59. 1678; [icon] in Hermann, Parad. Bat.: 178. 1698.
Current name: ***Pelargonium incarnatum*** (L.) L'Hér. (Geraniaceae).

Geranium inquinans Linnaeus, *Species Plantarum* 2: 676. 1753.
"Habitat in Africa." RCN: 4933.
Type not designated.
Original material: Herb. Clifford: 345, *Geranium* 18 (BM); [icon] in Dillenius, Hort. Eltham. 1: 151, t. 125, f. 151, 152. 1732; [icon] in Martyn, Hist. Pl. Rar.: 3, t. 3. 1728.
Current name: ***Pelargonium inquinans*** (L.) Aiton (Geraniaceae).

Geranium lobatum N.L. Burman var. **hirsutum** (N.L. Burman) Linnaeus, *Species Plantarum*, ed. 2, 2: 950. 1763.
RCN: 4960.
Basionym: *Geranium hirsutum* Burm. f. (1759).
Type not designated.
Current name: ***Pelargonium*** **sp.** (Geraniaceae).

Geranium lobatum N.L. Burman var. **pinnatifidum** (N.L. Burman) Linnaeus, *Species Plantarum*, ed. 2, 2: 950. 1763.
RCN: 4960.

G

Basionym: *Geranium pinnatifidum* Burm. f. (1759).
Type not designated.
Current name: ***Pelargonium sp.*** (Geraniaceae).

Geranium lucidum Linnaeus, *Species Plantarum* 2: 682. 1753.
"Habitat in Europae rupibus umbrosis." RCN: 4988.
Lectotype (Ghafoor in Jafri & El-Gadi, *Fl. Libya* 63: 43. 1978): Herb.
    Linn. No. 858.72 (LINN).
Current name: ***Geranium lucidum*** L. (Geraniaceae).
Note: Stearn (in *Biol. J. Linn. Soc.* 5: 7–9, 11. 1973) provided a
    detailed review of the protologue, particularly with reference to
    Linnaeus' account of finding the plant in Gotland. In this account
    of Linnaeus' Öland and Gotland journey of 1741, Stearn treated
    Torsborgen in Gotland as the restricted type locality, and noted the
    existence of 858.72 (LINN). In his paper, he attributed restricted
    type localities irrespective of whether any material existed in LINN
    and, where specimens do exist, he does not refer to any of them as
    type specimens. The collection subsequently designated as the type
    by Ghafoor shows no annotation associating it with Gotland.

Geranium macrorrhizum Linnaeus, *Species Plantarum* 2: 680. 1753.
"Habitat – – –" RCN: 4974.
Lectotype (designated here by Aedo): Herb. Clifford: 343, *Geranium* 4
    (BM-000646405).
Current name: ***Geranium macrorrhizum*** L. (Geraniaceae).

Geranium maculatum Linnaeus, *Species Plantarum* 2: 681. 1753.
"Habitat in Carolina, Virginia, Sibiria." RCN: 4984.
Lectotype (Aedo in *Anales Jard. Bot. Madrid* 59: 10. 2001): [icon]
    "*Geranium batrachioides Amer. maculatum, floribus obsolete caeruleis*"
    in Dillenius, Hort. Eltham. 1: 158, t. 132, f. 159. 1732. – Epitype
    (Aedo in *Anales Jard. Bot. Madrid* 59: 10. 2001): U.S.A. Georgia,
    Union County, Chatahoochee National Forest, 9/5/82, *Utrech & al.
    82–030* (BM).
Current name: ***Geranium maculatum*** L. (Geraniaceae).

Geranium malacoides Linnaeus, *Species Plantarum* 2: 680. 1753.
"Habitat in Italiae G. Narbonensis, Angliae maritimis." RCN: 4966.
Lectotype (Ghafoor in Jafri & El-Gadi, *Fl. Libya* 63: 22. 1978): Herb.
    Clifford: 344, *Geranium* 11 (BM-000646425).
Current name: ***Erodium malacoides*** (L.) L'Hér. (Geraniaceae).

Geranium maritimum Linnaeus, *Systema Naturae,* ed. 10, 2: 1143.
    1759.
["Habitat in Angliae maritimis."] Sp. Pl., ed. 2, 2: 952 (1763). RCN:
    4967.
Lectotype (designated here by Aedo): Herb. Linn. No. 858.49
    (LINN).
Current name: ***Erodium maritimum*** (L.) L'Hér. (Geraniaceae).

Geranium molle Linnaeus, *Species Plantarum* 2: 682. 1753.
"Habitat in Europa ad plateas." RCN: 4989.
Lectotype (Carolin in *Proc. Linn. Soc. New South Wales* 89: 332.
    1965): [icon] "*Geranium omnium villosissimum*" in Vaillant, Bot.
    Paris.: 79, t. 15, f. 3. 1727.
Current name: ***Geranium molle*** L. subsp. ***molle*** (Geraniaceae).

Geranium moschatum (Linnaeus) Linnaeus, *Systema Naturae,* ed. 10,
    2: 1143. 1759.
"Habitat [in Anglia.]" RCN: 4964.
Basionym: *Geranium cicutarium* L. var. *moschatum* L. (1753).
Lectotype (designated here by Aedo): Herb. Burser XVIII: 58 (UPS).
Current name: ***Erodium moschatum*** (L.) L'Hér. (Geraniaceae).
Note: Greuter (in *Candollea* 44: 563, f. 2. 1989), citing Rothmaler (in
    Repert. Spec. Nov. Regni Veg. 49: 272–281. 1940) has argued that

this new combination for *G. cicutarium* var. *moschatum* L. (1753)
was first made in *Fl. Anglica*: 20. 1754. However, Stearn (*Introd.
Ray's Syn. Meth. Stirp. Brit.* (Ray Soc. ed.): 56. 1973), in his analysis
of names in *Fl. Anglica*, treated this as a repeat of Linnaeus' use of
moschatum at varietal rank from 1753. Brummitt & Meikle (in
Watsonia 19: 181–183. 1993) have argued (in the context of
"*Primula acaulis* (L.) L.", where there is a similar situation) that
there are typographical variants of the thesis which make it
unreasonable to interpret this as a new combination.

Geranium myrrhifolium Linnaeus, *Species Plantarum* 2: 677. 1753.
"Habitat in Africa." RCN: 4956.
Lectotype (van der Walt & Boucher in *S. African J. Bot.* 52: 441.
    1986): Herb. Clifford: 345 *Geranium* 19 α (BM-000646439).
Current name: ***Pelargonium myrrhifolium*** (L.) L'Hér. (Geraniaceae).

Geranium nodosum Linnaeus, *Species Plantarum* 2: 681. 1753.
"Habitat in Delphinatu." RCN: 4978.
Lectotype (designated here by Aedo): Herb. Linn. No. 858.61
    (LINN).
Current name: ***Geranium nodosum*** L. (Geraniaceae).

Geranium odoratissimum Linnaeus, *Species Plantarum* 2: 679. 1753.
"Habitat in Africa." RCN: 4952.
Lectotype (Ghafoor in Jafri & El-Gadi, *Fl. Libya* 63: 41. 1978): Herb.
    Linn. No. 858.25 (LINN).
Current name: ***Pelargonium odoratissimum*** (L.) Aiton
    (Geraniaceae).

Geranium palustre Linnaeus, *Centuria II Plantarum*: 25. 1756.
"Habitat in Russia, Germania." RCN: 4981.
Lectotype (Novoselova in *Novosti Sist. Vyssh. Rast.* 31: 150. 1998):
    Herb. Linn. No. 858.65 (LINN).
Current name: ***Geranium palustre*** L. (Geraniaceae).
Note: Jonsell & Jarvis (in *Nordic J. Bot.* 22: 79. 2002), unaware of
    Novoselova's earlier choice, designated a collection in the Linnaean
    herbarium in S as lectotype.

Geranium papilionaceum Linnaeus, *Species Plantarum* 2: 676. 1753.
"Habitat in Africa." RCN: 4936.
Type not designated.
Original material: Herb. Clifford: 345, *Geranium* 16 (BM); [icon] in
    Martyn, Hist. Pl. Rar.: 15, t. 15. 1728; [icon] in Dillenius, Hort.
    Eltham. 1: 154, t. 128, f. 155. 1732.
Current name: ***Pelargonium papilionaceum*** (L.) L'Hér.
    (Geraniaceae).
Note: Van der Walt (in *Bothalia* 15: 382. 1985) treated 858.5 (LINN)
    as the lectotype, but the sheet lacks the relevant *Species Plantarum*
    number (i.e. "4") and was a post-1753 addition to the collection,
    and not original material for the name.

Geranium peltatum Linnaeus, *Species Plantarum* 2: 678. 1753.
"Habitat in Africa." RCN: 4944.
Lectotype (Ghafoor in Jafri & El-Gadi, *Fl. Libya* 63: 39. 1978): Herb.
    Linn. No. 858.12 (LINN).
Current name: ***Pelargonium peltatum*** (L.) L'Hér. (Geraniaceae).

Geranium phaeum Linnaeus, *Species Plantarum* 2: 681. 1753.
"Habitat in Alpibus Pannonicis, Helveticis, Styriacis." RCN: 4975.
Lectotype (Aedo in *Syst. Bot. Monogr.* 49: 72. 1996): Herb. Linn. No.
    858.57 (LINN).
Current name: ***Geranium phaeum*** L. (Geraniaceae).

Geranium pinnatum Linnaeus, *Species Plantarum* 2: 677. 1753.
"Habitat in Africa." RCN: 4958.

Basionym of: *Geranium prolificum* L. var. *pinnatum* (L.) L. (1763).
Lectotype (Wijnands, *Bot. Commelins*: 108, t. 3. 1983): [icon]
"*Geranium Afric. astragali folio*" in Commelin, Praeludia Bot.: 53, t.
3. 1703.
Current name: ***Pelargonium pinnatum*** (L.) L'Hér. (Geraniaceae).

Geranium pratense Linnaeus, *Species Plantarum* 2: 681. 1753.
"Habitat in Europae borealis pratis." RCN: 4982.
Lectotype (Novoselova in *Bot. Zhurn.* 81(10): 85. 1996): Herb. Linn.
No. 858.66 (LINN).
Current name: ***Geranium pratense*** L. (Geraniaceae).
Note: The same choice of type was made independently by Jonsell &
Jarvis (in Aedo, *Anales Jard. Bot. Madrid* 59: 20. 2001).

Geranium prolificum Linnaeus, *Species Plantarum,* ed. 2, 2: 949.
1763.
"Habitat ad Cap. b. spei." RCN: 4958.
Type not designated.
Original material: [icon] in Commelin, Hort. Med. Amstelod. Pl. Rar.
2: 125, t. 63. 1701.
Current name: ***Pelargonium rapaceum*** (L.) L'Hér. (Geraniaceae).
Note: This has been considered to be an illegitimate renaming of *G.
rapaceum* L. (1759) by some (e.g. Wijnands, *Bot. Commelins*: 109.
1983), although the phrase names are not particularly similar.

Geranium prolificum Linnaeus var. **auritum** (Linnaeus) Linnaeus,
Species Plantarum, ed. 2, 2: 950. 1763.
["Habitat in Africa."] Sp. Pl. 2: 679 (1753). RCN: 4958.
Basionym: *Geranium auritum* L. (1753).
Lectotype (van der Walt & Vorster in *J. S. African Bot.* 46: 285. 1980):
[icon] "*Geranium Afric. foliis plerumque auritis, flor. ex rubro
purpurascentibus*" in Commelin, Hort. Med. Amstelod. Pl. Rar. 2:
121, t. 61. 1701.
Current name: ***Pelargonium auritum*** (L.) Willd. (Geraniaceae).

Geranium prolificum Linnaeus var. **longifolium** (N.L. Burman)
Linnaeus, *Species Plantarum,* ed. 2, 2: 950. 1763.
"Habitat [ad Cap. b spei.]" RCN: 4958.
Basionym: *Geranium longifolium* Burm. f. (1759).
Type not designated.
Current name: ***Pelargonium longifolium*** (Burm. f.) Jacq.
(Geraniaceae).

Geranium prolificum Linnaeus var. **oxaloides** (N.L. Burman)
Linnaeus, *Species Plantarum,* ed. 2, 2: 950. 1763.
"Habitat [ad Cap. b spei.]" RCN: 4958.
Basionym: *Geranium oxaloides* Burm. f. (1759).
Type not designated.
Current name: ***Pelargonium oxaloides*** (Burm. f.) Willd.
(Geraniaceae).

Geranium prolificum Linnaeus var. **pinnatum** (Linnaeus) Linnaeus,
Species Plantarum, ed. 2, 2: 950. 1763.
["Habitat in Africa."] Sp. Pl. 2: 677 (1753). RCN: 4958.
Basionym: *Geranium pinnatum* L. (1753).
Lectotype (Wijnands, *Bot. Commelins*: 108, t. 3. 1983): [icon]
"*Geranium Afric. astragali folio*" in Commelin, Praeludia Bot.: 53, t.
3. 1703.
Current name: ***Pelargonium pinnatum*** (L.) L'Hér. (Geraniaceae).

Geranium prolificum Linnaeus var. **proliferum** (N.L. Burman)
Linnaeus, *Species Plantarum,* ed. 2, 2: 949. 1763.
"Habitat [ad Cap. b. spei.]" RCN: 4958.
Basionym: *Geranium proliferum* Burm. f. (1759).
Type not designated.

Current name: ***Pelargonium proliferum*** (Burm. f.) Steud.
(Geraniaceae).

Geranium pusillum Linnaeus, *Systema Naturae,* ed. 10, 2: 1144.
1759.
["Habitat in Anglia, Gallia."] Sp. Pl., ed. 2, 2: 957 (1763). RCN:
4995.
Lectotype (Holmgren in Cronquist & al., *Intermountain Fl.* 3A: 332.
1997): Herb. Linn. No. 858.86 (LINN).
Current name: ***Geranium pusillum*** L. (Geraniaceae).

Geranium rapaceum Linnaeus, *Systema Naturae,* ed. 10, 2: 1141.
1759.
RCN: 4958.
Type not designated.
Original material: Herb. Linn. No. 858.37 (LINN); [icon] in
Commelin, Hort. Med. Amstelod. Pl. Rar. 2: 125, t. 63. 1701.
Current name: ***Pelargonium rapaceum*** (L.) L'Hér. (Geraniaceae).
Note: Albers (in Eggli, *Ill. Handb. Succ. Pl., Dicots*: 266. 2002)
indicated the cited Commelin plate as type, but this was published
after 1 Jan 2001 and so the omission of the phrase "designated
here" or an equivalent (Art. 7.11) means that this choice is not
effective.

Geranium reflexum Linnaeus, *Mantissa Plantarum Altera*: 257. 1771.
"Habitat in Italia. H. U." RCN: 4977.
Lectotype (Aedo in *Syst. Bot. Monogr.* 49: 79. 1996): Herb. Linn. No.
282.9 (S).
Current name: ***Geranium reflexum*** L. (Geraniaceae).

Geranium robertianum Linnaeus, *Species Plantarum* 2: 681. 1753.
"Habitat in Europae borealis rupibus." RCN: 4987.
Lectotype (Ghafoor in Jafri & El-Gadi, *Fl. Libya* 63: 44. 1978): Herb.
Linn. No. 858.70 (LINN).
Current name: ***Geranium robertianum*** L. (Geraniaceae).

Geranium rotundifolium Linnaeus, *Species Plantarum* 2: 683. 1753.
"Habitat in Europae cultis." RCN: 4994.
Lectotype (Carolin in *Proc. Linn. Soc. New South Wales* 89: 335.
1965): Herb. Linn. No. 858.83 (LINN).
Current name: ***Geranium rotundifolium*** L. (Geraniaceae).

Geranium sanguineum Linnaeus, *Species Plantarum* 2: 683. 1753.
"Habitat in Europae pratis siccis umbrosis." RCN: 4997.
Lectotype (Jonsell & Jarvis in Aedo in *Anales Jard. Bot. Madrid* 59: 23.
2001): Herb. Clifford: 343, *Geranium* 1, sheet A (BM-000646399).
Current name: ***Geranium sanguineum*** L. (Geraniaceae).

Geranium scabrum Linnaeus, *Systema Naturae,* ed. 10, 2: 1142.
1759.
["Habitat ad Caput bonae spei. Burmannus."] Amoen. Acad. 4: 281
(1759). RCN: 4939.
Type not designated.
Original material: none traced.
Current name: ***Pelargonium scabrum*** (L.) L'Hér. (Geraniaceae).

Geranium sibiricum Linnaeus, *Species Plantarum* 2: 683. 1753.
"Habitat in Sibiria." RCN: 4996.
Lectotype (Yeo in *Edinburgh J. Bot.* 49: 189. 1992): Herb. Linn. No.
858.87 (LINN).
Current name: ***Geranium sibiricum*** L. (Geraniaceae).

Geranium striatum Linnaeus, *Systema Naturae,* ed. 10, 2: 1143.
1759, *nom. illeg.*
["Habitat in Italia."] Cent. I Pl.: 21 (1755). RCN: 4979.

Replaced synonym: *Geranium versicolor* L. (1755).
Lectotype (designated here by Aedo): [icon] *"Geranium Romanum versicolor"* in Morison, Pl. Hist. Univ. 2: 516, s. 5, t. 16, f. 24. 1680. – Epitype (designated here by Aedo): Italy. Sicily Nebrodi, cruce de la carretera con el arroyo Torti, 37º 53'N, 14º 39'E, 1,300m, 8 Jun 2000, *M.A. García & al. 1481* (MA-645561).
Current name: **Geranium versicolor** L. (Geraniaceae).
Note: As noted by Nordenstam (in *Bot. Not.* 114: 277. 1961), this is a superfluous renaming of *G. versicolor* L. (1755). *Geranium striatum* also appears in the slightly later reprint of *Cent. I Pl.* (in *Amoen. Acad.* 4: 282. Nov 1759).

Geranium sylvaticum Linnaeus, *Species Plantarum* 2: 681. 1753.
"Habitat in Europae borealis sylvis." RCN: 4980.
Lectotype (Yeo in Jarvis & al., *Regnum Veg.* 127: 49. 1993): Herb. Linn. No. 858.63 (LINN).
Generitype of *Geranium* Linnaeus (vide Green, *Prop. Brit. Bot.*: 172. 1929).
Current name: **Geranium sylvaticum** L. (Geraniaceae).

Geranium triste Linnaeus, *Species Plantarum* 2: 676. 1753.
"Habitat in Aethiopia & forte in India." RCN: 4960.
Type not designated.
Original material: Herb. Clifford 344: *Geranium* 12 (BM); Herb. Clifford 345: *Geranium* 12 γ, sheet 12 (BM); Herb. Linn. No. 858.39 (LINN); Herb. Clifford 345: *Geranium* 12 γ, sheet 14 (BM); [icon] in Commelin, Hort. Med. Amstelod. Pl. Rar. 2: 123, t. 62. 1701; [icon] in Cornut, Canad. Pl. Hist.: 109, 110. 1635; [icon] in Breyn, Exot. Pl. Cent.: 126, t. 58. 1678.
Current name: **Pelargonium triste** (L.) Aiton (Geraniaceae).
Note: Wijnands (*Bot. Commelins*: 107. 1983) provided an extensive discussion, concluding that material in the Clifford herbarium "344.12 beta" should be the type choice. Unfortunately, it is unclear from his statement (there is no variety beta) which of three possible specimens at BM may have been intended. As they are evidently not part of a single gathering, Art. 9.15 does not apply. Albers (in Eggli, *Ill. Handb. Succ. Pl., Dicots*: 270. 2002) indicated "344.12 (LINN)" as type, but this choice was published after 1 Jan 2001 and so the omission of the phrase "designated here" or an equivalent (Art. 7.11) means that this choice is not effective.

Geranium tuberosum Linnaeus, *Species Plantarum* 2: 680. 1753.
"Habitat in Anglia?" RCN: 4973.
Lectotype (Davis in *Israel J. Bot.* 19: 107. 1970): Herb. Clifford: 343, *Geranium* 3 (BM-000646404).
Current name: **Geranium tuberosum** L. (Geraniaceae).

Geranium versicolor Linnaeus, *Centuria I Plantarum*: 21. 1755.
"Habitat in Italia."
Replaced synonym of: *Geranium striatum* L. (1759), *nom. illeg.*
Lectotype (designated here by Aedo): [icon] *"Geranium Romanum versicolor"* in Morison, Pl. Hist. Univ. 2: 516, s. 5, t. 16, f. 24. 1680. – Epitype (designated here by Aedo): Italy. Calabria, ca. 20km W of Stilo, Passo di Pietra Spoda, 15 Jun 1979, *Davis & Sutton, D. & S. 65221* (BM).
Current name: **Geranium versicolor** L. (Geraniaceae).

Geranium vitifolium Linnaeus, *Species Plantarum* 2: 678. 1753.
"Habitat in Africa." RCN: 4946.
Lectotype (van der Walt in *Bothalia* 15: 355. 1985): Herb. Linn. No. 858.15 (LINN).
Current name: **Pelargonium vitifolium** (L.) L'Hér. (Geraniaceae).

Geranium zonale Linnaeus, *Species Plantarum* 2: 678. 1753.
"Habitat in Africa." RCN: 4945.

858.14

Lectotype (Wijnands, *Bot. Commelins*: 109. 1983): Herb. Linn. No. 858.14 (LINN).
Current name: **Pelargonium zonale** (L.) L'Hér. (Geraniaceae).

Gerardia delphinifolia Linnaeus, *Centuria II Plantarum*: 21. 1756.
"Habitat in India." RCN: 4414.
Lectotype (Cramer in Dassanayake & Fosberg, *Revised Handb. Fl. Ceylon* 3: 394. 1981): Herb. Linn. No. 764.1 (LINN).
Current name: **Sopubia delphinifolia** (L.) G. Don (Scrophulariaceae).

Gerardia flava Linnaeus, *Species Plantarum* 2: 610. 1753.
"Habitat in Virginia, Canada." RCN: 4416.
Lectotype (Pennell in *Bull. Torrey Bot. Club* 40: 409. 1913): *Kalm*, Herb. Linn. No. 764.6 (LINN).
Current name: **Aureolaria flava** (L.) Farw. (Scrophulariaceae).
Note: Blake (in *Rhodora* 20: 67. 1918) chose *Clayton 91* (BM) as lectotype, a specimen of *Aureolaria virginica* (L.) Pennell, into the synonymy of which this name would therefore fall. However, usage follows Pennell (in *Rhodora* 20: 133. 1918), who argued that the Kalm specimen (764.6 LINN) fitted Linnaeus' diagnosis better and should therefore be the type. It is identifiable as *A. flava*. Reveal (in *Taxon* 41: 143. 1992) therefore proposed the conservation of the name with the Kalm sheet as conserved type. However, the Committee for Spermatophyta (in *Taxon* 43: 274. 1994) did not recommend acceptance, arguing that it was unnecessary as Pennell (1913), despite his unclear wording, had typified the name first.

Gerardia glutinosa Linnaeus, *Species Plantarum* 2: 611. 1753.
"Habitat in China." RCN: 4418.
Type not designated.
Original material: Herb. Linn. No. 764.8 (LINN).
Current name: ***Adenosma glutinosa*** (L.) Merr. (Scrophulariaceae).

Gerardia pedicularia Linnaeus, *Species Plantarum* 2: 611. 1753.
"Habitat in Virginia, Canada." RCN: 4417.
Lectotype (designated here by Sutton): *Kalm*, Herb. Linn. No. 764.7 (LINN).
Current name: ***Aureolaria pedicularia*** (L.) Raf. (Scrophulariaceae).
Note: Reveal & al. (in *Huntia* 7: 220. 1987) reported that Pennell (in *Acad. Nat. Sci. Philadelphia Monogr.* 1: 399. 1935) had selected a Kalm specimen (764.7 LINN) as lectotype but this is incorrect; he did not. This collection is, however, original material for the name.

Gerardia purpurea Linnaeus, *Species Plantarum* 2: 610. 1753.
"Habitat in Virginia, Canada." RCN: 4415.
Lectotype (Pennell in *Torreya* 19: 212. 1919): [icon] *"Digitalis Virginiana rubra, folio & facie Antirrhini vulgaris"* in Plukenet, Amalth. Bot.: t. 388, f. 1. 1705; Almag. Mant.: 65. 1700. – Typotype: Herb. Sloane 92: 54 (BM-SL).
Current name: ***Agalinis purpurea*** (L.) Pennell (Scrophulariaceae).

Gerardia tuberosa Linnaeus, *Species Plantarum* 2: 610. 1753.
"Habitat in America calidiore." RCN: 4413.
Type not designated.
Original material: [icon] in Plumier, Nov. Pl. Amer.: 31, t. 12. 1703.
Generitype of *Gerardia* Linnaeus, *nom. rej.*
Current name: ***Stenandrium tuberosum*** (L.) Urb. (Acanthaceae).
Note: *Gerardia* Linnaeus, *nom. rej.* in favour of *Stenandrium* Nees.

Gerbera linnaei Cassini, *Dict. Sci. Nat.* 18: 460. 1821, *typ. cons.*
RCN: 6404.
Replaced synonym: *Arnica gerbera* L. (1753), *typ. cons.*
Lectotype (Hansen in *Opera Bot.* 78: 9. 1985): Herb. Linn. No. 1001.8 (LINN).
Generitype of *Gerbera* Linnaeus, *nom. cons.*
Current name: ***Gerbera linnaei*** Cass. (Asteraceae).
Note: *Arnica gerbera* L. is the basionym of *Gerbera linnaei* Cass., the conserved type of *Gerbera* L.

Geropogon glaber Linnaeus, *Species Plantarum*, ed. 2, 2: 1109. 1763.
"Habitat in Italia." RCN: 5776.
Lectotype (Díaz de la Guardia & Blanca in *Lazaroa* 9: 38. 1988 [1986]): Herb. Linn. No. 945.1 (LINN).
Generitype of *Geropogon* Linnaeus (vide Steudel, *Nom.*, ed. 2, 1: 681. 1840).
Current name: ***Geropogon hybridus*** (L.) Sch. Bip. (Asteraceae).
Note: Specific epithet spelled "glabrum" in the protologue.

Geropogon hirsutus Linnaeus, *Species Plantarum*, ed. 2, 2: 1109. 1763.
"Habitat in Italia." RCN: 5777.
Lectotype (Díaz de la Guardia & Blanca in *Taxon* 46: 761. 1997): [icon] *"Tragopogon gram. fol. suaverubente flore"* in Colonna, Ekphr.: 232, 231. 1606.
Current name: ***Geropogon hybridus*** (L.) Sch. Bip. (Asteraceae).
Note: Specific epithet spelled "hirsutum" in the protologue.

Gesneria acaulis Linnaeus, *Systema Naturae*, ed. 10, 2: 1110. 1759.
["Habitat in Jamaica."] Sp. Pl., ed. 2, 2: 850 (1763). RCN: 4424.
Lectotype (Skog in *Smithsonian Contr. Bot.* 29: 104. 1976): [icon] *"Rapunculo affinis anomala vasculifera, folio oblongo serrato, flore coccineo tubuloso, semine minuto oblongo luteo"* in Sloane, Voy.

Jamaica 1: 159, t. 102, f. 1. 1707. – Typotype: Herb. Sloane 3: 27 (BM-SL).
Current name: ***Gesneria acaulis*** L. (Gesneriaceae).

Gesneria humilis Linnaeus, *Species Plantarum* 2: 612. 1753.
"Habitat in America australi." RCN: 4423.
Neotype (Skog in *Smithsonian Contr. Bot.* 29: 95. 1976): [icon] *"Gesnera"* in Plumier, Nov. Pl. Amer.: 27, t. 9. 1703.
Generitype of *Gesneria* Linnaeus (vide Fritsch in Engler & Prantl, *Nat. Pflanzenfam.* 4(36): 183. 1895).
Current name: ***Gesneria humilis*** L. (Gesneriaceae).
Note: Plumier's plate t. 9 is illustrative for the genus in which he included three species. One of these has a spotted, fimbriate corolla (which t. 9 does not depict) but it is not possible to say which of the two remaining species it applies to. Although it is therefore not original material for this name, in the absence of any other original material, Skog's type choice is accepted as a neotypification.

Gesneria tomentosa Linnaeus, *Species Plantarum* 2: 612. 1753.
"Habitat ad Jamaicae ripas." RCN: 4425.
Type not designated.
Original material: Herb. Clifford: 318, *Gesneria* 1 (BM); [icon] in Sloane, Voy. Jamaica 1: 162, t. 104, f. 2. 1707.
Current name: ***Rhytidophyllum tomentosum*** (L.) Mart. (Gesneriaceae).

Gethyllis afra Linnaeus, *Species Plantarum* 1: 442. 1753.
"Habitat in Africa." RCN: 3427.
Type not designated.
Original material: Herb. Linn. No. 445.1 (LINN).
Generitype of *Gethyllis* Linnaeus.
Current name: ***Gethyllis afra*** L. (Liliaceae/Amaryllidaceae).

Geum montanum Linnaeus, *Species Plantarum* 1: 501. 1753.
"Habitat in Alpibus Helvetiae, Austriae, Delphinatus." RCN: 3807.
Lectotype (Krahulcová & Kirschner in Cafferty & Jarvis in *Taxon* 51: 542. 2002): Herb. Burser XVIII(1): 79 (UPS).
Current name: ***Geum montanum*** L. (Rosaceae).

Geum reptans Linnaeus, *Species Plantarum* 1: 501. 1753.
"Habitat in Helvetia & valle Barsilionensi." RCN: 3808.
Lectotype (Kirschner in Cafferty & Jarvis in *Taxon* 51: 542. 2002): [icon] *"Caryophyllata Alpina tenuifolia"* in Boccone, Mus. Piante Rar. Sicilia: 160, t. 128. 1697. – Epitype (Kirschner & Cafferty in Cafferty & Jarvis in *Taxon* 51: 542. 2002): Italy. Reg. Veneto, Prov. Belluno, ca. 41km west from Cortina d'Ampezzo, Arabba. 2,450m, 23 Jul 1985, *Jury, Watson, Webb & Wyse Jackson 6740* (BM-000576271; iso- DBC, RNG).
Current name: ***Geum reptans*** L. (Rosaceae).

Geum rivale Linnaeus, *Species Plantarum* 1: 501. 1753.
"Habitat in Europae pratis subhumidis." RCN: 3806.
Lectotype (Jonsell & Jarvis in *Nordic J. Bot.* 22: 74. 2002): Herb. Clifford: 195, *Geum* 2 (BM-000628664).
Current name: ***Geum rivale*** L. (Rosaceae).

Geum urbanum Linnaeus, *Species Plantarum* 1: 501. 1753.
"Habitat in Europae umbrosis." RCN: 3805.
Lectotype (Jonsell & Jarvis in *Nordic J. Bot.* 22: 74. 2002): Herb. Clifford: 195, *Geum* 1 (BM-000628662).
Generitype of *Geum* Linnaeus.
Current name: ***Geum urbanum*** L. (Rosaceae).

Geum virginianum Linnaeus, *Species Plantarum* 1: 500. 1753.
"Habitat in Virginia." RCN: 3804.

Lectotype (Fernald in *Rhodora* 37: 292, pl. 368. 1935): Herb. Linn. No. 657.1 (LINN).
Current name: ***Geum virginianum*** L. (Rosaceae).

Ginkgo biloba Linnaeus, *Mantissa Plantarum Altera*: 313. 1771.
"Habitat in Japonia. Gordon Hortul. angl. vivam arborem dedit." RCN: 7239.
Lectotype (Barrie in Jarvis & al., *Regnum Veg.* 127: 49. 1993): *Gordon*, Herb. Linn. No. 1292B.2 (LINN), see p. 207.
Generitype of *Ginkgo* Linnaeus.
Current name: ***Ginkgo biloba*** L. (Ginkgoaceae).

Gisekia pharnacioides Linnaeus, *Mantissa Plantarum Altera*: 562. 1771.
"Habitat in India orientali." RCN: 2233.
Lectotype (Jeffrey in Hubbard & Milne-Redhead, *Fl. Trop. E. Africa, Aizoaceae*: 5. 1961; Hedge & Lamond in Rechinger, *Fl. Iranica* 114: 2. 1975): Herb. Linn. No. 399.1 (LINN).
Generitype of *Gisekia* Linnaeus.
Current name: ***Gisekia pharnacioides*** L. (Molluginaceae).
Note: Jeffrey (in Hubbard & Milne-Redhead, *Fl. Trop. E. Africa, Aizoaceae*: 5. 1961), Tardieu-Blot (in Aubréville, *Fl. Cambodge Laos Vietnam* 5: 91. 1967) and Nasir (in Nasir & Ali, *Fl. W. Pakistan* 41: 10. 1973) all indicated unspecified material at LINN as type. However, these statements are ineffective in distinguishing between sheets 399.1 and 399.2 (LINN). Adamson (in *J. S. African Bot.* 27: 133. 1961) concluded that the type was lost, and selected a neotype from Herb. Montin (S). However, original material exists for the name so neotypification is not possible. The two LINN sheets appear to be duplicates so, under Art. 9.15, Jeffrey (1961) is accepted as having been the first to typify the name, with Hedge & Lamond (1975) restricting his choice to 399.1 (LINN).

Glabraria tersa Linnaeus, *Mantissa Plantarum Altera*: 276. 1771.
"Habitat in India orientali." RCN: 5730.
Lectotype (Kostermans in *Reinwardtia* 4: 536. 1959): Herb. Linn. No. 938.1 (LINN).
Generitype of *Glabraria* Linnaeus, *nom. rej.*
Current name: ***Brownlowia tersa*** (L.) Kosterm. (Tiliaceae).
Note: Glabraria Linnaeus, *nom. rej.* in favour of *Brownlowia* Roxb.

Gladiolus alatus Linnaeus, *Plantae Rariores Africanae*: 8. 1760.
["Habitat ad Cap. b. spei."] Sp. Pl., ed. 2, 1: 53 (1762). RCN: 300.
Lectotype (Lewis & Obermeyer in *J. S. African Bot., Suppl.* 10: 160, f. 31.1. 1972): Herb. Burman (G).
Current name: ***Gladiolus alatus*** L. (Iridaceae).

Gladiolus alopecuroides Linnaeus, *Centuria II Plantarum*: 5. 1756.
"Habitat in Aethiopia. Burmannus." RCN: 306.
Type not designated.
Original material: Herb. Linn. No. 59.14 (LINN); Herb. Linn. No. 59.15 (LINN).
Current name: ***Micranthus alopecuroides*** (L.) Eckl. (Iridaceae).

Gladiolus angustus Linnaeus, *Species Plantarum* 1: 37. 1753.
"Habitat in Africa." RCN: 307.
Lectotype (Stearn, *Introd. Linnaeus' Sp. Pl.* (Ray Soc. ed.): 47. 1957): [icon] *"Gladiolus foliis linearibus"* in Linnaeus, Hort. Cliff.: 20, t. 6. 1738.
Current name: ***Gladiolus angustus*** L. (Iridaceae).
Note: Lewis & Obermeyer (in *J. S. African Bot., Suppl.* 10: 88. 1972) designated 59.16 (LINN) as type, but this choice is pre-dated by that of Stearn.

Gladiolus capitatus Linnaeus, *Species Plantarum* 1: 37. 1753.
"Habitat in Africa." RCN: 309.
Neotype (Goldblatt & al. in *Novon* 12: 191. 2002): South Africa. Western Cape, foot of Du Toit's Kloof, 15 Oct 1949, *W.F. Barker 6075* (NBG; iso- K, MO, PRE).
Current name: ***Aristea capitata*** (L.) Ker-Gawl. (Iridaceae).

Gladiolus communis Linnaeus, *Species Plantarum* 1: 36. 1753.
"Habitat in Europa australi." RCN: 298.
Lectotype (Mathew in Jarvis & al., *Regnum Veg.* 127: 49. 1993): Herb. A. van Royen No. 904.137–228 (L), see p. 185.
Generitype of *Gladiolus* Linnaeus (vide Hitchcock in *Amer. J. Bot.* 10: 513. 1923).
Current name: ***Gladiolus communis*** L. (Iridaceae).

Gladiolus imbricatus Linnaeus, *Species Plantarum* 1: 37. 1753.
"Habitat in Russia citeriore." RCN: 299.
Lectotype (Stearn in *Taxon* 10: 17. 1961): *Gerber*, Herb. Linn. No. 59.2 (LINN).
Current name: ***Gladiolus imbricatus*** L. (Iridaceae).

Gladiolus plicatus (Linnaeus) Linnaeus, *Species Plantarum*, ed. 2, 1: 53. 1762.
"Habitat in Aethiopia." RCN: 301.
Basionym: *Ixia plicata* L. (1756).
Lectotype (Lewis in *J. S. African Bot., Suppl.* 3: 11. 1959): Herb. Linn. No. 59.6, left specimen (LINN).
Current name: ***Babiana villosula*** (J.G. Gmel.) Ker ex Steud. (Iridaceae).

Gladiolus ramosus Linnaeus, *Species Plantarum* 1: 37. 1753.
"Habitat in Africa." RCN: 308.
Type not designated.
Original material: none traced.
Current name: ***Melasphaerula ramosa*** (L.) Klatt ex T. Durand & Schinz (Iridaceae).

Gladiolus recurvus Linnaeus, *Systema Naturae*, ed. 12, 2: 76; *Mantissa Plantarum*: 27. 1767.
"Habitat ad Cap. b. spei." RCN: 304.
Lectotype (Lewis & Obermeyer in *J. S. African Bot., Suppl.* 10: 205. 1972): [icon] *"Gladiolus, foliis linearibus sulcatis, floribus uno versu dispositis, tubo floris longiore"* in Miller, Fig. Pl. Gard. Dict. 2: 157, t. 235, f. 2. 1758.
Current name: ***Gladiolus recurvus*** L. (Iridaceae).

Gladiolus spicatus Linnaeus, *Species Plantarum* 1: 37. 1753.
"Habitat in Africa." RCN: 305.
Type not designated.
Original material: Herb. Linn. No. 59.3 (LINN).
Current name: ***Thereianthus spicatus*** (L.) G.J. Lewis (Iridaceae).
Note: See notes on 59.3 (LINN) by Merrill (in *J. Arnold Arbor.* 19: 329. 1938), and by Lewis (in *J. S. African Bot.* 7: 41. 1941) on confused usage of the name. Manning & Goldblatt (in *Bothalia* 34: 105. 2004) wrongly indicated unspecified material in LINN (presumably sheet 59.3) as the holotype but this choice was published after 1 Jan 2001 and so the omission of the phrase "designated here" or an equivalent (Art. 7.11) means that it is not effective.

Gladiolus tristis Linnaeus, *Species Plantarum*, ed. 2, 1: 53. 1762.
"Habitat in Aethiopia." RCN: 302.
Lectotype (Lewis & Obermeyer in *J. S. African Bot., Suppl.* 10: 191. 1972): Herb. Linn. No. 59.9 (LINN).
Current name: ***Gladiolus tristis*** L. (Iridaceae).

Gladiolus undulatus Linnaeus, *Systema Naturae,* ed. 12, 2: 76; *Mantissa Plantarum*: 27. 1767.
"Habitat in Aethiopia." RCN: 303.
Lectotype (Lewis & Obermeyer in *J. S. African Bot., Suppl.* 10: 110. 1972): Herb. Linn. No. 59.11 (LINN; iso- G).
Current name: ***Gladiolus undulatus*** L. (Iridaceae).

Glaux maritima Linnaeus, *Species Plantarum* 1: 207. 1753.
"Habitat in Europae maritimis, salsis." RCN: 1687.
Lectotype (Nasir in Nasir & Ali, *Fl. Pakistan* 157: 93. 1984): Herb. Linn. No. 291.1 (LINN).
Generitype of *Glaux* Linnaeus.
Current name: ***Glaux maritima*** L. (Primulaceae).

Glechoma arvensis Linnaeus, *Species Plantarum* 2: 578. 1753.
"Habitat in arvis Europae." RCN: 4247.
Basionym of: *Stachys arvensis* (L.) L. (1763).
Lectotype (Turland in Jarvis & al. in *Taxon* 50: 511. 2001): Herb. Burser XIII: 63 (UPS).
Current name: ***Stachys arvensis*** (L.) L. (Lamiaceae).
Note: Codd (in Leistner, *Fl. Southern Africa* 28(4): 70. 1985) indicated Clifford material as type but as the protologue contains no reference to *Hortus Cliffortianus* (1738), such a specimen cannot be original material for the name.

Glechoma belgica Linnaeus, *Species Plantarum* 2: 578. 1753.
"Habitat in Belgii subhumidis." RCN: 4247.
Lectotype (Turland in Jarvis & al. in *Taxon* 50: 511. 2001): [icon] *"Lamium Melissae folio, paludosum Belgicum"* in Hermann, Hort. Lugd.-Bat. Cat.: 351, 353. 1687.
Current name: ***Stachys arvensis*** (L.) L. (Lamiaceae).

Glechoma hederacea Linnaeus, *Species Plantarum* 2: 578. 1753.
"Habitat in Europae septentrionalioris sepibus." RCN: 4216.
Lectotype (Press in Jarvis & al., *Regnum Veg.* 127: 49. 1993): Herb. Clifford: 307, *Glechoma* 1, sheet 2 (BM-000646017).
Generitype of *Glechoma* Linnaeus, *nom. & orth. cons.*
Current name: ***Glechoma hederacea*** L. (Lamiaceae).

Gleditsia inermis Linnaeus, *Systema Naturae,* ed. 10, 2: 1313. 1759.
["Habitat in Java."] Sp. Pl., ed. 2, 2: 1509 (1763). RCN: 7697.
Type not designated.
Original material: [icon] in Plukenet, Phytographia: t. 123, f. 3. 1692; Almag. Bot.: 6. 1696 – Typotype: Herb. Sloane 95: 7 (BM-SL).
Current name: ***Acacia sp.*** (Fabaceae: Mimosoideae).
Note: Bunting (in *Taxon* 16: 469. 1967) and Hernández & Nicolson (in *Taxon* 35: 747. 1986) discussed the basis for this name, the only original element for which is a Plukenet illustration of a single leaf, the identification of which is uncertain. It is a species of *Acacia* (Lourdes Rico, pers. comm.) and, if from Java, may represent *A. leucophloea* (Roxb.) Willd.

Gleditsia triacanthos Linnaeus, *Species Plantarum* 2: 1056. 1753.
"Habitat in Virginia." RCN: 7696.
Lectotype (Reveal in Jarvis & al., *Regnum Veg.* 127: 49. 1993): Herb. Clifford: 489, *Oidea (Caesalpinoides)* 12, sheet A (BM-000647669).
Generitype of *Gleditsia* Linnaeus.
Current name: ***Gleditsia triacanthos*** L. (Fabaceae: Caesalpinioideae).
Note: Isely (in *Mem. New York Bot. Gard.* 25: 214. 1975) noted material in LINN, observing that 1229.1 "would be a reasonable candidate as lectotype", along with (unseen) material in the Clifford herbarium. However, he did not make a choice of type.

Glinus lotoides Linnaeus, *Species Plantarum* 1: 463. 1753.
"Habitat in Sicilia, Hispania ad fossas." RCN: 3557.

Lectotype (Adamson in *J. S. African Bot.* 27: 127. 1961): [icon] *"Alsine Lotoides Sicula"* in Boccone, Icon. Descr. Rar. Pl. Siciliae: 21, 20, t. 11, f. 2 B. 1674 (see p. 109). – Typotype: *Boccone s.n.* (OXF).
Generitype of *Glinus* Linnaeus.
Current name: ***Glinus lotoides*** L. (Molluginaceae).
Note: Jeffrey (in Hubbard & Milne-Redhead), *Fl. Trop. E. Africa, Aizoaceae*: 15 (1961) indicated a Boccone specimen at OXF as "typolectotype". However, despite its links with Boccone's illustration, the material would not have been seen by Linnaeus and is not original material for the name. It is treated here as typotype material.

Globba marantina Linnaeus, *Mantissa Plantarum Altera*: 170. 1771.
"Habitat in India orientali." RCN: 224.
Lectotype (Burtt & Smith in *Notes Roy. Bot. Gard. Edinburgh* 31: 188. 1972): Herb. Linn. No. 45.1 (LINN).
Generitype of *Globba* Linnaeus (vide Burtt & Smith in *Notes Roy. Bot. Gard. Edinburgh* 31: 188. 1972).
Current name: ***Globba marantina*** L. (Zingiberaceae).

Globba nutans Linnaeus, *Mantissa Plantarum Altera*: 170. 1771.
"Habitat in India orientali." RCN: 225.
Lectotype (Smith in *Notes Roy. Bot. Gard. Edinburgh* 34: 160. 1975): [icon] *"Globba silvestris major"* in Rumphius, Herb. Amboin. 6: 140, t. 62, t. 63. 1750.
Current name: ***Alpinia nutans*** (L.) Roscoe (Zingiberaceae).

Globba uviformis Linnaeus, *Mantissa Plantarum Altera*: 171. 1771.
"Habitat in India orientalis." RCN: 226.
Type not designated.
Original material: [icon] in Rumphius, Herb. Amboin. 6: 138, t. 59, f. 2. 1750.
Current name: ***Plagiostachys uviformis*** (L.) Loes. (Zingiberaceae).

Globularia alypum Linnaeus, *Species Plantarum* 1: 95. 1753.
"Habitat Monspelii & in regno Valentino." RCN: 786.
Lectotype (Fayed in *Taeckholmia, Addit. Ser.* 1: 96. 1981): Herb. Linn. No. 117.1 (LINN).
Current name: ***Globularia alypum*** L. (Globulariaceae).
Note: Milletti & Jarvis (in *Taxon* 36: 635–636. 1987) provide a detailed discussion, independently reaching the same conclusion as Fayed. Heath (*l.c.* 40: 94. 1991) argued that this type choice was invalid but this was refuted by Jarvis (*l.c.* 41: 63–64. 1992).

Globularia bisnagarica Linnaeus, *Species Plantarum* 1: 96. 1753.
"Habitat in Bisnagariae sylvis." RCN: 787.
Lectotype (Milletti & Jarvis in *Taxon* 36: 636. 1987): [icon] *"Scabiosa Bisnagarica s. Globularia frutesc. rigidis foliis, ad radicem rotundioribus cordatis, ad caulem autem mucrone praeditis"* in Plukenet, Phytographia: t. 58, f. 5. 1691; Almag. Bot.: 336. 1696. – Voucher: Herb. Sloane 90: 101; 101: 190 (BM-SL).
Current name: ***Globularia bisnagarica*** L. (Globulariaceae).

Globularia cordifolia Linnaeus, *Species Plantarum* 1: 96. 1753.
"Habitat in Pannonia, Austria, Helvetia, Pyrenaeis." RCN: 790.
Lectotype (Milletti & Jarvis in *Taxon* 36: 638. 1987): Herb. Linn. No. 117.3 (LINN).
Current name: ***Globularia cordifolia*** L. (Globulariaceae).

Globularia nudicaulis Linnaeus, *Species Plantarum* 1: 97. 1753.
"Habitat in Pyrenaeis & Austriae montibus." RCN: 791.
Lectotype (Milletti & Jarvis in *Taxon* 36: 638. 1987): Herb. Burser XIV(2): 75 (UPS).
Current name: ***Globularia nudicaulis*** L. (Globulariaceae).

Globularia orientalis Linnaeus, *Species Plantarum* 1: 97. 1753.
"Habitat in Natolia. Biórling." RCN: 792.
Lectotype (Edmondson in Davis, *Fl. Turkey* 7: 28. 1982): Herb. Linn. No. 117.5 (LINN).
Current name: ***Globularia orientalis*** L. (Globulariaceae).
Note: See additional discussion by Milletti & Jarvis (in *Taxon* 36: 639. 1987).

Globularia spinosa Linnaeus, *Species Plantarum* 1: 96. 1753.
"Habitat in Granadae montibus." RCN: 789.
Neotype (Milletti & Jarvis in *Taxon* 36: 639. 1987): Spain. "Grenada, in abruptis calcareis", 1,500m, Jun 1905, *Reverchon s.n.* (FI).
Current name: ***Globularia spinosa*** L. (Globulariaceae).

Globularia vulgaris Linnaeus, *Species Plantarum* 1: 96. 1753.
"Habitat in Europae apricis duris." RCN: 788.

Lectotype (Milletti & Jarvis in *Taxon* 36: 637. 1987): Herb. Linn. No. 117.2 (LINN).
Generitype of *Globularia* Linnaeus (vide Hitchcock, *Prop. Brit. Bot.*: 123. 1929).
Current name: ***Globularia vulgaris*** L. (Globulariaceae).
Note: Stearn (in *Biol. J. Linn. Soc.* 5: 11. 1973), in an account of Linnaeus' Öland and Gotland journey of 1741, treated Resmo in Öland as the restricted type locality, and noted the existence of 117.2 (LINN) (as "116.2"). In his paper, he attributed restricted

type localities irrespective of whether any material existed in LINN and, where specimens do exist, he does not refer to any of them as type specimens. The collection subsequently designated as the type shows no annotation associating it with Öland.

Gloriosa simplex Linnaeus, *Systema Naturae,* ed. 12, 2: 241; *Mantissa Plantarum*: 62. 1767.
"Habitat in Senegal." RCN: 2403.
Type not designated.
Original material: none traced.
Current name: ***Gloriosa superba*** L. (Liliaceae/Colchicaceae).
Note: Field (in *Kew Bull.* 25: 244. 1971) treated this as a *nomen incertae sedis.*

Gloriosa superba Linnaeus, *Species Plantarum* 1: 305. 1753.
"Habitat in Malabaria." RCN: 2402.
Lectotype (Wijnands, *Bot. Commelins*: 133. 1983): Herb. Hermann 3: 31, No. 122 (BM-000594673).
Generitype of *Gloriosa* Linnaeus.
Current name: ***Gloriosa superba*** L. (Liliaceae/Colchicaceae).

Gluta renghas Linnaeus, *Mantissa Plantarum Altera*: 293. 1771.
"Habitat in Java." RCN: 6916.
Type not designated.
Original material: Herb. Linn. No. 1068.1 (LINN).
Generitype of *Gluta* Linnaeus.
Current name: ***Gluta renghas*** L. (Anacardiaceae).

Glycine abrus Linnaeus, *Species Plantarum* 2: 753. 1753.
"Habitat in Indiis, Aegypto." RCN: 5168.
Replaced synonym of: *Abrus precatorius* L. (1767).
Lectotype (Fawcett & Rendle, *Fl. Jamaica* 4: 43. 1920): Herb. Hermann 2: 6, No. 284 (BM-000621515).
Current name: ***Abrus precatorius*** L. (Fabaceae: Faboideae).

Glycine apios Linnaeus, *Species Plantarum* 2: 753. 1753.
"Habitat in Virginia." RCN: 5363.
Lectotype (Reveal in Turland & Jarvis in *Taxon* 46: 470. 1997): *Kalm*, Herb. Linn. No. 901.19 (LINN).
Current name: ***Apios americana*** Medik. (Fabaceae: Faboideae).

Glycine bituminosa Linnaeus, *Species Plantarum* 2: 754. 1753.
"Habitat ad Cap. b. Spei." RCN: 5361.
Lectotype (Schrire in Turland & Jarvis in *Taxon* 46: 470. 1997): [icon] *"Phaseolus Africanus hirsutus bituminosus, siliquis bullatis, flore flavo"* in Hermann, Hort. Lugd.-Bat. Cat.: 492, 493. 1687. – Epitype (Schrire in Turland & Jarvis in *Taxon* 46: 470. 1997): South Africa. Stellenbosch, Jonkershoek, 4 August 1917, *S. Garside 1035* (K; iso-STE?).
Current name: ***Bolusafra bituminosa*** (L.) Kuntze (Fabaceae: Faboideae).

Glycine bracteata Linnaeus, *Species Plantarum* 2: 754. 1753.
"Habitat in Virginia madidis, umbrosis." RCN: 5356.
Replaced synonym of: *Glycine monoica* L. (1763), *nom. illeg.*
Lectotype (Reveal & al. in *Huntia* 7: 230. 1987): *Kalm*, Herb. Linn. No. 901.3 (LINN).
Current name: ***Amphicarpaea bracteata*** (L.) Fernald (Fabaceae: Faboideae).

Glycine comosa Linnaeus, *Species Plantarum* 2: 754. 1753.
"Habitat in Virginia madidis umbrosis." RCN: 5359.
Lectotype (Reveal & al. in *Huntia* 7: 230. 1987): *Clayton 182* (BM-000038856).
Current name: ***Amphicarpaea bracteata*** (L.) Fernald (Fabaceae: Faboideae).

Glycine frutescens Linnaeus, *Species Plantarum* 2: 753. 1753.
"Habitat in Carolina." RCN: 5364.
Lectotype (Reveal in Turland & Jarvis in *Taxon* 46: 470. 1997): [icon] *"Phaseoloides, frutescens Caroliniana foliis pinnatis floribus caeruleis conglomeratis"* in Miller, Cat. Pl.: 55, t. 15. 1730.
Current name: **Wisteria frutescens** (L.) Poir. (Fabaceae: Faboideae).

Glycine galactia Linnaeus, *Systema Naturae*, ed. 10, 2: 1173. 1759.
["Habitat in Jamaica."] Sp. Pl., ed. 2, 2: 1026 (1763). RCN: 5371.
Basionym of: *Clitoria galactia* (L.) L. (1763).
Lectotype (Fortunato in Turland & Jarvis in *Taxon* 46: 470. 1997): Herb. Linn. No. 901.24 (LINN).
Current name: **Galactia pendula** Pers. (Fabaceae: Faboideae).
Note: Fawcett & Rendle (*Fl. Jamaica* 4: 55. 1920) treated material in Sloane's herbarium (BM-SL) as the type but this was not seen by Linnaeus and is not original material for the name.

Glycine javanica Linnaeus, *Species Plantarum* 2: 754. 1753.
"Habitat in India." RCN: 5358.
Lectotype (Verdcourt in *Taxon* 15: 35. 1966): Herb. Linn. No. 901.8 (LINN).
Generitype of *Glycine* Linnaeus, *nom. rej.*
Current name: **Pueraria montana** (Lour.) Merr. (Fabaceae: Faboideae).
Note: Glycine Linnaeus, *nom. rej.* in favour of *Glycine* Willd.

Glycine monoica Linnaeus, *Species Plantarum*, ed. 2, 2: 1023. 1763, *nom. illeg.*
"Habitat in Americae septentrionalis umbrosis madidis." RCN: 5356.
Replaced synonym: *Glycine bracteata* L. (1753).
Lectotype (Reveal & al. in *Huntia* 7: 230. 1987): *Kalm*, Herb. Linn. No. 901.3 (LINN).
Current name: **Amphicarpaea bracteata** (L.) Fernald (Fabaceae: Faboideae).

Glycine monophylla Linnaeus, *Systema Naturae*, ed. 12, 2: 484; *Mantissa Plantarum*: 101. 1767.
"Habitat ad Cap. b. spei." RCN: 5365.
Lectotype (Stirton in *J. S. African Bot.* 50: 461. 1984): Herb. Linn. No. 901.20 (LINN).
Current name: **Psoralea monophylla** (L.) C.H. Stirt. (Fabaceae: Faboideae).

Glycine nummularia Linnaeus, *Mantissa Plantarum Altera*: 571. 1771.
"Habitat in India orientali." RCN: 5362.
Lectotype (Nguyên Van Thuân in Aubréville & Leroy, *Fl. Cambodge Laos Viêt-Nam* 17: 135. 1979): *König s.n.*, Herb. Linn. No. 901.14 (LINN).
Current name: **Rhynchosia nummularia** (L.) DC. (Fabaceae: Faboideae).

Glycine subterranea Linnaeus, *Species Plantarum*, ed. 2, 2: 1023. 1763.
"Habitat in Brasilia, Surinamo. C. Dahlberg." RCN: 5355.
Lectotype (Verdcourt in Milne-Redhead & Polhill, *Fl. Trop. E. Africa, Leguminosae* 4: 668. 1971): Herb. Linn. No. 901.1 (LINN).
Current name: **Voandzeia subterranea** (L.) Thouars subsp. **subterranea** (Fabaceae: Faboideae).

Glycine tomentosa Linnaeus, *Species Plantarum* 2: 754. 1753.
"Habitat in Virginia." RCN: 5360.
Lectotype (Fernald in *Rhodora* 44: 424. 1942): *Clayton 588*, Herb. Linn. No. 901.10 (LINN; iso- BM).
Current name: **Rhynchosia tomentosa** (L.) Hook. & Arn. (Fabaceae: Faboideae).

Glycyrrhiza echinata Linnaeus, *Species Plantarum* 2: 741. 1753.
"Habitat in Gargano Apuliae, in deserto Nagico Tatariae." RCN: 5460.
Lectotype (Chamberlain in Jarvis & al., *Regnum Veg.* 127: 50. 1993): Herb. Linn. No. 916.1 (LINN).
Current name: **Glycyrrhiza echinata** L. (Fabaceae: Faboideae).
Note: Glycyrrhiza echinata was treated as the generitype by Britton & Brown (*Ill. Fl. N. U. S.*, ed. 2, 2: 391. 1913; see McNeill & al. in *Taxon* 36: 373. 1987). However, under Art. 10.5, Ex. 7 (a voted example) of the Vienna Code, this is a type choice made under the American Code and is to be replaced under Art. 10.5b by Green's choice (*Prop. Brit. Bot.*: 175. 1929) of *G. glabra* L.
Chamberlain (in Davis, *Fl. Turkey* 3: 261. 1970) and Nadezhina (in *Novosti Sist. Vyssh. Rast.* 15: 174. 1985) treated material in LINN as type but failed to make an effective choice between 916.1 and 916.2 (LINN).

Glycyrrhiza glabra Linnaeus, *Species Plantarum* 2: 742. 1753.
"Habitat in Franconia, Gallia, Hispania, Italia." RCN: 5461.
Lectotype (Ali in Nasir & Ali, *Fl. W. Pakistan* 100: 97. 1977): Herb. Linn. No. 916.3 (LINN).
Generitype of *Glycyrrhiza* Linnaeus (vide Green, *Prop. Brit. Bot.*: 175. 1929).
Current name: **Glycyrrhiza glabra** L. (Fabaceae: Faboideae).
Note: See comments under *Glycyrrhiza echinata* L.

Glycyrrhiza hirsuta Linnaeus, *Species Plantarum* 2: 742. 1753.
"Habitat in Oriente." RCN: 5462.
Type not designated.
Original material: Herb. Linn. No. 308.3 (S); Herb. Linn. No. 916.4 (LINN).
Current name: **Glycyrrhiza glabra** L. (Fabaceae: Faboideae).

Gmelina asiatica Linnaeus, *Species Plantarum* 2: 626. 1753.
"Habitat in India." RCN: 4533.
Lectotype (Verdcourt in Jarvis & al., *Regnum Veg.* 127: 50. 1993): Herb. Hermann 2: 26, No. 230 (BM-000594589).
Generitype of *Gmelina* Linnaeus.
Current name: **Gmelina asiatica** L. (Verbenaceae).
Note: Moldenke & Moldenke (in Dassanayake & Fosberg, *Revised Handb. Fl. Ceylon* 4: 394. 1988) and Moldenke (in *Phytologia* 55: 480. 1984) indicated 780.2 (LINN) as type, but this sheet is unannotated by Linnaeus and is not original material for the name.

Gnaphalium alpinum Linnaeus, *Species Plantarum* 2: 856. 1753.
"Habitat in Alpibus Lapponiae, Helvetiae." RCN: 6187.
Lectotype (Malte in *Rhodora* 36: 102, pl. 281. 1934): Herb. Linn. No. 989.71 (LINN).
Current name: **Antennaria alpina** (L.) Gaertn. (Asteraceae).

Gnaphalium arborescens Linnaeus, *Plantae Rariores Africanae*: 18. 1760.
["Habitat ad Cap. b. spei."] Sp. Pl., ed. 2, 2: 1191 (1763). RCN: 6148.
Replaced synonym of: *Gnaphalium arboreum* L. (1763), *nom. illeg.*
Neotype (Lundgren in *Opera Bot.* 31: 28. 1972): South Africa. Cape Peninsula, Table Mt., rocky slopes and ledges above Kirstenbosch, 600m, 14 Sep 1952, *Esterhuysen 20389* (BOL; iso- PRE).
Current name: **Anaxeton arborescens** (L.) Less. (Asteraceae).

Gnaphalium arboreum Linnaeus, *Species Plantarum*, ed. 2, 2: 1191. 1763, *nom. illeg.*
"Habitat ad Cap. b. spei." RCN: 6148.
Replaced synonym: *Gnaphalium arborescens* L. (1760).

G

Neotype (Lundgren in *Opera Bot.* 31: 28. 1972): South Africa. Cape Peninsula, Table Mt., rocky slopes and ledges above Kirstenbosch, 600m, 14 Sep 1952, *Esterhuysen 20389* (BOL; iso- PRE).

Current name: ***Anaxeton arborescens*** (L.) Less. (Asteraceae).

Note: An illegitimate replacement name for *G. arborescens* L. (1760), as noted by Hilliard & Burtt (in *Bot. J. Linn. Soc.* 82: 239. 1981).

Gnaphalium arenarium Linnaeus, *Species Plantarum* 2: 854. 1753.

"Habitat in Europae campis arenosis." RCN: 6168.

Lectotype (designated here by Galbany-Casals, Sáez & Benedí): Herb. Linn. No. 989.36 (LINN).

Current name: ***Helichrysum arenarium*** (L.) Moench (Asteraceae).

Note: Hilliard & Burtt (in *Notes Roy. Bot. Gard. Edinburgh* 32: 344. 1973) said that the type was "probably" 989.36 (LINN) and later (in *Bot. J. Linn. Soc.* 82: 239. 1981) noted the existence of this material. The latter statement was misinterpreted by Galbany-Casals & al. (in *Taxon* 55: 491. 2006) as a formal typification but no formal type choice had then been made. This is rectified here.

Gnaphalium arvense Linnaeus, *Species Plantarum* 2: 856. 1753, *nom. inval.*

"Habitat in Europae campis aridis, arvisque sabulosis." RCN: 6709.

Type not relevant.

Current name: ***Filago arvensis*** L. (Asteraceae).

Note: Linnaeus transferred this to *Filago arvensis* L. in the Addenda to his *Species Plantarum* (1753: 1230), and *Gnaphalium arvense* is consequently an invalid name (Greuter in *Boissiera* 13: 136. 1967); Hilliard & Burtt (in *Bot. J. Linn. Soc.* 82: 239. 1981).

Gnaphalium coronatum Linnaeus, *Systema Naturae*, ed. 10, 2: 1210. 1759.

["Habitat ad Cap. b. spei."] Sp. Pl., ed. 2, 2: 1190 (1763). RCN: 6151.

Lectotype (Lundgren in *Bot. Not.* 127: 120. 1974): Herb. Linn. No. 989.6 (LINN).

Current name: ***Petalacte coronata*** (L.) D. Don (Asteraceae).

Gnaphalium crassifolium Linnaeus, *Systema Naturae*, ed. 12, 2: 544; *Mantissa Plantarum*: 112. 1767.

"Habitat ad Cap. b. spei." RCN: 6163.

Lectotype (Hilliard & Burtt in *Notes Roy. Bot. Gard. Edinburgh* 32: 345. 1973): Herb. Linn. No. 989.27 (LINN).

Current name: ***Helichrysum crassifolium*** (L.) D. Don (Asteraceae).

Note: See discussion by Galbany-Casals & al. (in *Taxon* 55: 491. 2006) on the application of this name.

Gnaphalium crispum Linnaeus, *Species Plantarum*, ed. 2, 2: 1197. 1763.

"Habitat ad Cap. b. spei." RCN: 6179.

Lectotype (Hilliard & Burtt in *Bot. J. Linn. Soc.* 82: 241. 1981): [icon] *"Gnaphalium aureum Aethiopicum flore roseo pleno"* in Plukenet, Phytographia: t. 298, f. 3. 1694; Almag. Bot.: 171. 1696. – Typotype: Herb. Sloane 100: 104 (BM-SL).

Current name: ***Helichrysum crispum*** (L.) D. Don (Asteraceae).

Gnaphalium cylindricum Linnaeus, *Species Plantarum*, ed. 2, 2: 1194. 1763, *nom. illeg.*

"Habitat ad Cap. b. spei." RCN: 6166.

Replaced synonym: *Gnaphalium cylindriflorum* L. (1760).

Lectotype (Hilliard & Burtt in Jarvis & Turland in *Taxon* 47: 361. 1998): [icon] *"Gnaphalium Aethiopicum minus, ramosum, capitulis coccineis"* in Plukenet, Phytographia: t. 298, f. 4. 1694; Almag. Bot.: 172. 1696. – Typotype: Herb. Sloane 100: 104 (BM-SL).

Current name: ***Helichrysum cylindriflorum*** (L.) Hilliard & B.L. Burtt (Asteraceae).

Note: An illegitimate replacement name for *G. cylindriflorum* L. (1760), as noted by Hilliard & Burtt (in *Bot. J. Linn. Soc.* 82: 241, 261. 1981).

Gnaphalium cylindriflorum Linnaeus, *Plantae Rariores Africanae*: 19. 1760.

["Habitat ad Cap. b. spei."] Sp. Pl., ed. 2, 2: 1194 (1763). RCN: 6166.

Lectotype (Hilliard & Burtt in Jarvis & Turland in *Taxon* 47: 361. 1998): [icon] *"Gnaphalium Aethiopicum minus, ramosum, capitulis coccineis"* in Plukenet, Phytographia: t. 298, f. 4. 1694; Almag. Bot.: 172. 1696. – Typotype: Herb. Sloane 100: 104 (BM-SL).

Current name: ***Helichrysum cylindriflorum*** (L.) Hilliard & B.L. Burtt (Asteraceae).

Note: Hilliard & Burtt (in *Bot. J. Linn. Soc.* 82: 241. 1981) indicated Plukenet material in Herb. Sloane as type. However, as this was never seen by Linnaeus and is not original material for the name, Hilliard & Burtt (1998) subsequently modified their typification.

Gnaphalium cymosum Linnaeus, *Species Plantarum* 2: 855. 1753.

"Habitat in Africa." RCN: 6171.

Lectotype (Hilliard & Burtt in *Bot. J. Linn. Soc.* 82: 241. 1981): Herb. Clifford: 401, *Gnaphalium* 6 ["7"] (BM-000647002).

Current name: ***Helichrysum cymosum*** (L.) D. Don (Asteraceae).

Gnaphalium decurrens Linnaeus, *Systema Naturae,* ed. 10, 2: 1211. 1759.

RCN: 6239.

Type not designated.

Original material: none traced.

Note: Although Hilliard & Burtt (in *Bot. J. Linn. Soc.* 82: 241. 1981) took the view that this is the basionym of *Conyza decurrens* L. (1763), there is no direct link between the protologues of these two names. *Conyza decurrens* L. (1763) is a new name, and the basionym of *Neojeffreya decurrens* (L.) Cabrera.

Gnaphalium dentatum Linnaeus, *Species Plantarum* 2: 854. 1753.

["Habitat in Aethiopia."] Sp. Pl., ed. 2, 2: 1194 (1763). RCN: 6159.

Lectotype (Hilliard & Burtt in *Bot. J. Linn. Soc.* 82: 241, 259. 1981): Herb. A. van Royen No. 900.365–40 (L).

Current name: ***Pentzia dentata*** (L.) Kuntze (Asteraceae).

Gnaphalium dioicum Linnaeus, *Species Plantarum* 2: 850. 1753.

"Habitat in Europae apricis aridis." RCN: 6186.

Type not designated.

Original material: Herb. A. van Royen No. 900.72–131 (L); Herb. Clifford: 400, *Gnaphalium* 1 β (BM); Herb. A. van Royen No. 900.72–122 (L); Herb. Burser XV(1): 17 (UPS); Herb. Linn. No. 301, lower sheet? (LAPP); Herb. Linn. No. 989.69 (LINN); Herb. Linn. No. 301, upper sheet, right specimen? (LAPP).

Current name: ***Antennaria dioica*** (L.) Gaertn. (Asteraceae).

Note: Williams (in *J. Bot.* 39: 217. 1901) discussed this name and illustrated (as t. 423) sheet 989.69 (LINN). Despite stating "...all the European forms may be grouped in three varieties, inclusive of the type", nowhere is the LINN sheet itself indicated as the intended type specimen. Hilliard & Burtt (in *Bot. J. Linn. Soc.* 82: 241. 1981) also noted the existence of this material.

Gnaphalium dioicum Linnaeus var. **feminum** Linnaeus, *Species Plantarum* 2: 850. 1753.

RCN: 6186.

Type not designated.

Original material: Herb. Linn. No. 301, upper sheet, left specimen? (LAPP); Herb. Burser XV(1): 15 (UPS); [icon] in Dodoëns, Stirp. Hist. Pempt., ed. 2: 68. 1616.

Current name: ***Antennaria dioica*** (L.) Gaertn. (Asteraceae).
Note: Varietal epithet spelled "femina" in the protologue.

Gnaphalium dioicum Linnaeus var. **mas** Linnaeus, *Species Plantarum*
2: 850. 1753.
RCN: 6186.
Type not designated.
Original material: Herb. Burser XV(1): 17 (UPS); Herb. Linn. No.
301, upper sheet, right specimen (LAPP); [icon] in Dodoëns, Stirp.
Hist. Pempt., ed. 2: 68. 1616.
Current name: ***Antennaria dioica*** (L.) Gaertn. (Asteraceae).

Gnaphalium discolorum Linnaeus, *Species Plantarum*, ed. 2, 2: 1191.
1763.
"Habitat ad Cap. b. spei." RCN: 6152.
Lectotype (Lundgren in *Opera Bot.* 31: 28. 1972): Herb. Linn. No.
989.7 (LINN).
Current name: ***Anaxeton arborescens*** (L.) Less. (Asteraceae).

Gnaphalium ericoides Linnaeus, *Plantae Rariores Africanae*: 19.
1760.
["Habitat ad Cap. b. spei."] Sp. Pl., ed. 2, 2: 1193 (1763). RCN:
6154.
Neotype (Hilliard & Burtt in *Bot. J. Linn. Soc.* 82: 242, 252. 1981):
Herb. Linn. No. 989.17 (LINN).
Current name: ***Helichrysum asperum*** (Thunb.) Hilliard & B.L. Burtt
(Asteraceae).

Gnaphalium eximium Linnaeus, *Mantissa Plantarum Altera*: 573.
1771.
"Habitat ad Cap. b. spei." RCN: 6147.
Lectotype (Hilliard & Burtt in *Bot. J. Linn. Soc.* 82: 242, 252. 1981):
Ekeberg, Herb. Linn. No. 989.1 (LINN), see pp. 202, 203.
Current name: ***Syncarpha eximia*** (L.) B. Nord. (Asteraceae).

Gnaphalium foetidum Linnaeus, *Species Plantarum* 2: 851. 1753.
"Habitat in Aethiopia." RCN: 6177.
Lectotype (Hilliard & Burtt in *Bot. J. Linn. Soc.* 82: 242. 1981;
Hilliard & Burtt in Jarvis & Turland in *Taxon* 47: 361. 1998):
Herb. Clifford: 402, *Gnaphalium* 13, sheet 8 (BM-000647008).
Current name: ***Helichrysum foetidum*** (L.) Moench (Asteraceae).
Note: Hilliard & Burtt (in *Bot. J. Linn. Soc.* 82: 242. 1981) designated
Herb. Clifford: 402, *Gnaphalium* 13 as "type", but there are two
sheets, one with white capitula, the other with yellow. These authors
subsequently (1998) restricted this choice to the yellow form.

Gnaphalium fruticans Linnaeus, *Mantissa Plantarum Altera*: 282.
1771.
"Habitat ad Cap. b. spei." RCN: 6150.
Lectotype (Hilliard & Burtt in *Bot. J. Linn. Soc.* 82: 242, 252. 1981):
Herb. Linn. No. 989.5 (LINN).
Current name: ***Helichrysum fruticans*** (L.) D. Don (Asteraceae).

Gnaphalium gallicum Linnaeus, *Species Plantarum* 2: 857. 1753,
nom. inval.
"Habitat in Anglia, Gallia." RCN: 6708.
Type not relevant.
Current name: ***Filago gallica*** L. (Asteraceae).
Note: Linnaeus transferred this to *Filago gallica* ["gallicum"] in the
Addenda to his *Species Plantarum* (1753: 1230). *Gnaphalium
gallicum* is consequently invalid. The associated specimens and cited
figures are original elements for *F. gallica*.

Gnaphalium germanicum Linnaeus, *Species Plantarum* 2: 857. 1753,
nom. inval.

"Habitat in Germania." RCN: 6705.
Type not relevant.
Current name: ***Filago pyramidata*** L. (Asteraceae).
Note: Linnaeus transferred this to *Filago pyramidata* in the Addenda to
his *Species Plantarum* (1753: 1230). *Gnaphalium germanicum* is
consequently invalid. The associated specimens and cited figures are
original elements for *F. pyramidata*.

Gnaphalium glomeratum Linnaeus, *Plantae Rariores Africanae*: 20.
1760.
["Habitat ad Cap. b. spei."] Sp. Pl., ed. 2, 2: 1200 (1763). RCN:
6193.
Lectotype (Hilliard & Burtt in *Bot. J. Linn. Soc.* 82: 200, 243, 254.
1981): Herb. Linn. No. 989.85 (LINN).
Current name: ***Helichrysum tinctum*** (Thunb.) Hilliard & B.L. Burtt
(Asteraceae).

Gnaphalium grandiflorum Linnaeus, *Species Plantarum* 2: 850.
1753.
"Habitat in Aethiopia." RCN: 6149.
Lectotype (Hilliard & Burtt in Jarvis & Turland in *Taxon* 47: 361.
1998): [icon] *"Gnaphalium tomentosum, foliis inferioribus
subrotundis, &c."* in Burman, Rar. Afric. Pl.: 213, t. 76, f. 1. 1739. –
Typotype: Herb. Burman (G).
Current name: ***Helichrysum grandiflorum*** (L.) D. Don (Asteraceae).
Note: Hilliard & Burtt (in *Bot. J. Linn. Soc.* 82: 243. 1981) designated
989.3 (LINN) as lectotype. However, the material lacks the *Species
Plantarum* number (i.e. "4"), is a post-1753 addition to the
herbarium and not original material for the name. Hilliard & Burtt
subsequently designated a Burman plate as lectotype.

Gnaphalium helianthemifolium Linnaeus, *Species Plantarum* 2: 851.
1753.
"Habitat in Aethiopia." RCN: 6180.
Lectotype (Hilliard & Burtt in *Notes Roy. Bot. Gard. Edinburgh* 32:
350. 1973): [icon] *"Gnaphalium Africanum floribus minimis
albicantibus inodorum"* in Volckamer, Fl. Noriberg.: 194. 1700
(see pp. 165, 548).
Current name: ***Helichrysum helianthemifolium*** (L.) D. Don
(Asteraceae).

Gnaphalium ignescens Linnaeus, *Species Plantarum* 2: 854. 1753.
"Habitat – – – –" RCN: 6158.
Lectotype (Hilliard & Burtt in *Bot. J. Linn. Soc.* 82: 243, 252. 1981):
Herb. Linn. No. 989.24 (LINN).
Current name: ***Helichrysum arenarium*** (L.) Moench (Asteraceae).

Gnaphalium imbricatum Linnaeus, *Species Plantarum* 2: 855. 1753.
"Habitat in Aethiopia." RCN: 6170.
Lectotype (Hilliard & Burtt in Jarvis & Turland in *Taxon* 47: 362.
1998): [icon] *"Gnaphalium incanum, angustifolium, calicis squamis
ferrugineis reflexis"* in Burman, Rar. Afric. Pl.: 226, t. 80, f. 2. 1739.
– Typotype: Herb. Burman (G).
Current name: ***Helichrysum cochleariforme*** DC. (Asteraceae).
Note: Hilliard & Burtt (in *Bot. J. Linn. Soc.* 82: 243, 260, 262. 1981)
indicated a specimen in the Burman herbarium at G, unseen by
Linnaeus and not original material for the name, as lectotype.
Hilliard & Burtt subsequently designated a Burman plate as
lectotype.

Gnaphalium indicum Linnaeus, *Species Plantarum* 2: 852. 1753.
"Habitat in India." RCN: 6188.
Lectotype (Grierson in *Notes Roy. Bot. Gard. Edinburgh* 31: 138.
1971): Herb. Hermann 4: 15, No. 307 (BM-000628069).
Current name: ***Helichrysum indicum*** (L.) Grierson (Asteraceae).

The lectotype of *Gnaphalium helianthemifolium* L.

Gnaphalium leontopodium Linnaeus, *Species Plantarum* 2: 855. 1753.
"Habitat in Alpibus Helvetiae, Vallesiae, Corinthi, Austriae, Sibiriae." RCN: 6710.
Basionym of: *Filago leontopodium* (L.) L. (1763).
Type not designated.
Original material: Herb. Burser XV(1): 18 (UPS); [icon] in Dodoëns, Stirp. Hist. Pempt., ed. 2: 68. 1616; [icon] in Bauhin & Cherler, Hist. Pl. Univ. 3(1): 161. 1651; [icon] in Clusius, Rar. Pl. Hist. 1: 328. 1601.
Current name: *Leontopodium nivale* (Ten.) Hand.-Mazz. subsp. *alpinum* (Cass.) Greuter (Asteraceae).

Gnaphalium luteoalbum Linnaeus, *Species Plantarum* 2: 851. 1753.
"Habitat in Helvetia, G. Narbonensi, Hispania, Lusitania." RCN: 6173.
Lectotype (Hilliard & Burtt in *Bot. J. Linn. Soc.* 82: 206, 244. 1981): Herb. A. van Royen No. 900.286–294 (L).
Current name: *Laphangium luteoalbum* (L.) Tzvelev (Asteraceae).
Note: Specific epithet spelled "luteo-album" in the protologue.
Royen (*Alp. Fl. N. Guinea* 4: 3348. 1983) indicated Herb. Linn. 989.45 (LINN) as the holotype but this designation post-dates that of Hilliard & Burtt. The orthography of the specific epithet ("luteo-album" vs. "luteoalbum") was discussed by Brummitt & Taylor (in *Taxon* 39: 303. 1990).

Gnaphalium margaritaceum Linnaeus, *Species Plantarum* 2: 850. 1753.
"Habitat in America septentrionali, kamtschatca. [sic]" RCN: 6184.
Lectotype (Fernald in *Rhodora* 40: 219. 1938): Herb. Clifford: 401, *Gnaphalium* 8 (BM-000647004).
Current name: *Anaphalis margaritacea* (L.) Benth. & Hook. f. (Asteraceae).

Gnaphalium maritimum Linnaeus, *Mantissa Plantarum Altera*: 283. 1771, *nom. illeg.*
"Habitat ad Cap. b. spei littora maris." RCN: 6164.
Lectotype (Hilliard & Burtt in *Bot. J. Linn. Soc.* 82: 200, 244, 252. 1981): *Tulbagh 71*, Herb. Linn. No. 989.29 (LINN).
Current name: *Helichrysum dasyanthum* (Willd.) Sweet (Asteraceae).
Note: A later homonym of *Gnaphalium maritimum* Hill (1769), and hence illegitimate.

Gnaphalium montanum Linnaeus, *Species Plantarum* 2: 857. 1753, *nom. inval.*
"Habitat in Europae collibus sabulosis." RCN: 6707.
Type not relevant.
Current name: *Filago arvensis* L. × *minima* (Sm.) Pers. (Asteraceae).
Note: Linnaeus transferred this to *Filago montana* in the Addenda to his *Species Plantarum* (1753: 1230) so *Gnaphalium montanum* is invalid. The associated specimens and cited figures are original elements for *F. montana*.

Gnaphalium muricatum Linnaeus, *Species Plantarum* 2: 852. 1753.
"Habitat in Aethiopia." RCN: 6153.
Lectotype (Hilliard & Burtt in *Bot. J. Linn. Soc.* 82: 244. 1981): Herb. Clifford: 402, *Gnaphalium* 17 ["18"] (BM-000647013).
Current name: *Metalasia muricata* (L.) D. Don (Asteraceae).
Note: Hilliard & Burtt (in *Bot. J. Linn. Soc.* 82: 244. 1981) indicated *Gnaphalium* sheet no. 18 in Herb. Clifford (BM) as lectotype, presumably in error for no. 17, filed at the end of the genus. Karis (in *Opera Bot.* 99: 121. 1989) noted Hilliard & Burtt's lectotypification, correcting the sheet number from "18" to "17", and pointing out that sheet no. 18 bears material of *Conyza candida* L. (= *Inula candida* (L.) Cass.) and is totally inconsistent with the description of *Metalasia muricata*.

Gnaphalium niveum Linnaeus, *Species Plantarum* 2: 852. 1753.
"Habitat in Aethiopia." RCN: 6728.
Replaced synonym of: *Stoebe gnaphaloides* L. (1774), *nom. illeg.*
Type not designated.
Original material: [icon] in Burman, Rar. Afric. Pl.: 215, t. 77, f. 1. 1739.
Current name: *Helichrysum niveum* (L.) Less. (Asteraceae).
Note: Although Hilliard & Burtt (in *Bot. J. Linn. Soc.* 82: 244, 259. 262. 1981) indicated Plukenet material in Herb. Sloane 100: 24 (BM-SL) as lectotype, this material was never seen by Linnaeus, is not associated with any Plukenet illustration, and is not original material for the name.

Gnaphalium nudifolium Linnaeus, *Plantae Rariores Africanae*: 19. 1760.
["Habitat in Aethiopia."] Sp. Pl., ed. 2, 2: 1196 (1763). RCN: 6172.
Lectotype (Hilliard & Burtt in *Bot. J. Linn. Soc.* 82: 245. 1981): [icon] *"Chrysocome Aethiopica plantaginis folio"* in Breyn, Exot. Pl. Cent.: 143, t. 71. 1678.
Current name: *Helichrysum nudifolium* (L.) Less. (Asteraceae).

Gnaphalium obtusifolium Linnaeus, *Species Plantarum* 2: 851. 1753.
"Habitat in Virginia, Pensylvania." RCN: 6183.
Lectotype (Reveal in Jarvis & Turland in *Taxon* 47: 362. 1998): *Kalm*, Herb. Linn. No. 989.64 (LINN).

Current name: ***Pseudognaphalium obtusifolium*** (L.) Hilliard & B.L. Burtt (Asteraceae).

Note: Blake (in *Rhodora* 20: 72. 1918) discussed this name, as did Hilliard & Burtt (in *Bot. J. Linn. Soc.* 82: 205. 1981), who treated 989.63 and 989.64 (LINN) as syntypes. As these collections are neither syntypes nor part of a single gathering, Art. 9.15 does not apply. Reveal's appears to be the first explicit type choice.

Gnaphalium odoratissimum Linnaeus, *Species Plantarum* 2: 855. 1753.

"Habitat – – –" RCN: 6175.

Lectotype (Hedberg in *Symb. Bot. Upsal.* 15(1): 201. 1957): [icon] "*Elichrysum latifolium villosum, alato caule, odoratissimum*" in Plukenet, Phytographia: t. 173, f. 6. 1692; Almag. Bot.: 134. 1696.

Current name: ***Helichrysum odoratissimum*** (L.) Sweet (Asteraceae).

Note: Hedberg's type choice pre-dates type assessments made by Hilliard & Burtt (in *Notes Roy. Bot. Gard. Edinburgh* 32: 353. 1973), who indicated 989.49, 989.50 and 989.51 (LINN) as types. The same authors (in *Bot. J. Linn. Soc.* 82: 245, 253. 1981) designated 989.48 as lectotype, but this collection lacks the *Species Plantarum* number (i.e. "27"), was a post-1753 addition to the collection, and is not original material for the name.

Gnaphalium orientale Linnaeus, *Species Plantarum* 2: 853. 1753.

"Habitat in Africa." RCN: 6167.

Lectotype (Hilliard & Burtt in *Bot. J. Linn. Soc.* 82: 245. 1981): Herb. Clifford: 402, *Gnaphalium* 9 ["10"] (BM-000647005).

Current name: ***Helichrysum orientale*** (L.) Vaill. (Asteraceae).

Note: Hilliard & Burtt indicated the type as Herb. Clifford: 402, "Gnaphalium 10", evidently in error for sheet no. 9 (sheet no. 10 does not exist), as noted by Wijnands (*Bot. Commelins*: 75. 1983) and Galbany-Casals & al. (in *Taxon* 55: 492. 2006). Although Gaertner has traditionally been accepted as the combining author in *Helichrysum*, Greuter & al. (in *Taxon* 54: 155. 2005) show that this should correctly be Vaillant.

Gnaphalium patulum Linnaeus, *Species Plantarum* 2: 855. 1753.

"Habitat in Aethiopia." RCN: 6161.

Lectotype (Hilliard & Burtt in *Notes Roy. Bot. Gard. Edinburgh* 32: 355. 1973): Herb. Clifford: 402, *Gnaphalium* 15 (BM-000647011).

Current name: ***Helichrysum patulum*** (L.) D. Don (Asteraceae).

Gnaphalium pedunculare Linnaeus, *Mantissa Plantarum Altera*: 284. 1771.

"Habitat ad Cap. b. spei." RCN: 6174.

Lectotype (Hilliard & Burtt in *Notes Roy. Bot. Gard. Edinburgh* 32: 353. 1973): Herb. Linn. No. 989.47 (LINN).

Current name: ***Helichrysum odoratissimum*** (L.) Sweet (Asteraceae).

Gnaphalium petiolatum Linnaeus, *Species Plantarum* 2: 854. 1753.

"Habitat in Aethiopia." RCN: 6162.

Lectotype (Hilliard & Burtt in *Notes Roy. Bot. Gard. Edinburgh* 32: 357, 384. 1973): Herb. Clifford: 402, *Gnaphalium* 16 (BM-000647012).

Current name: ***Staehelina petiolata*** (L.) Hilliard & B.L. Burtt (Asteraceae).

Note: The type is also reproduced by Lack (in *Ann. Naturhist. Mus. Wien* 98B Suppl.: 207. 1996).

Gnaphalium plantagineum Linnaeus, *Systema Naturae*, ed. 12, 2: 545. 1767, *nom. illeg.*

RCN: 6185.

Replaced synonym: *Gnaphalium plantaginifolium* L. (1753).

Lectotype (Robinson in *Rhodora* 3: 13. 1901): *Kalm*, Herb. Linn. No. 989.68 (LINN).

Current name: ***Antennaria plantaginifolia*** (L.) Hook. (Asteraceae).

Note: An illegitimate replacement name for *G. plantaginifolium* L. (1753), as noted by Fernald (in *Rhodora* 47: 240. 1945).

Gnaphalium plantaginifolium Linnaeus, *Species Plantarum* 2: 850. 1753.

"Habitat in Virginia." RCN: 6185.

Replaced synonym of: *Gnaphalium plantagineum* L. (1767), *nom. illeg.*

Lectotype (Robinson in *Rhodora* 3: 13. 1901): *Kalm*, Herb. Linn. No. 989.68 (LINN).

Current name: ***Antennaria plantaginifolia*** (L.) Hook. (Asteraceae).

Note: See discussion by Reveal (in *Taxon* 40: 658–659. 1991), who proposed the name for conservation with *Kalm*, Herb. Linn. No. 989.68 (LINN) as a conserved type. He interpreted Britton (in *J. Bot.* 36: 266. 1898) as being first to typify the name based on *Clayton* 287 (BM), a specimen of *Antennaria solitaria* Rydb. However, Robinson (in *Rhodora* 3: 11–13. 1901) argued that the Clayton material could not have been the basis for the name as it is staminate, and Linnaeus stated that he had seen only the pistillate form. Robinson concluded that the two (Kalm) specimens mounted on sheet 989.68 (LINN), which are pistillate, "must be regarded as the types for the name", although Greene (in *Pittonia* 4: 280–283. 1901) dismissed material in LINN as ever having any relevance to Linnaean names. Fernald (in *Rhodora* 47: 240, pl. 957. 1945) interpreted the name via the Plukenet element, rejecting that of Gronovius (and of Clayton). The Committee for Spermatophyta (in *Taxon* 43: 271. 1994) could not decide which of these competing type choices was valid, and so did not recommend conservation. The Committee recommended that, in the meantime, the name is to be used in its current sense. In the light of this, Robinson's typification is accepted here.

Gnaphalium purpureum Linnaeus, *Species Plantarum* 2: 854. 1753, *nom. cons. prop.*

"Habitat in Carolina, Virginia, Pensylvania." RCN: 6189.

Proposed conserved type (Nesom & Pruski in *Taxon* 54: 1103. 2005): *Clayton* 385 (BM-000051197; iso- BM).

Current name: ***Gamochaeta purpurea*** (L.) Cabrera (Asteraceae).

Note: Nesom & Pruski (in *Taxon* 54: 1103. 2005) identify the type (Herb. A. van Royen, No. 900.286–424, L) designated by Hilliard & Burtt (in *Bot. J. Linn. Soc.* 82: 246. 1981) of *G. purpureum* L. as a collection of *Gamochaeta americana* (Mill.) Wedd. In order to maintain the traditional usage of the Linnaean name, they therefore proposed the name for conservation with a conserved type.

Gnaphalium repens Linnaeus, *Mantissa Plantarum Altera*: 283. 1771.

"Habitat ad Cap. b. spei." RCN: 6165.

Lectotype (Hilliard & Burtt in *Bot. J. Linn. Soc.* 82: 252, 264. 1981): *Tulbagh 101*, Herb. Linn. No. 989.30, upper specimen (LINN).

Current name: ***Ifloga repens*** (L.) Hilliard & B.L. Burtt (Asteraceae).

Gnaphalium rutilans Linnaeus, *Species Plantarum* 2: 854. 1753.

"Habitat in Africa." RCN: 6169.

Lectotype (Hilliard & Burtt in *Bot. J. Linn. Soc.* 82: 263, 247. 1981): Herb. Clifford: 401, *Gnaphalium* 5 ["6"] (BM-000647001).

Current name: ***Helichrysum rutilans*** (L.) D. Don (Asteraceae).

Note: Hilliard & Burtt indicated the type as Herb. Clifford: 401, "Gnaphalium 6", evidently in error for sheet no. 5 (sheet no. 6 is associated with *G. cymosum* L.).

Gnaphalium sanguineum Linnaeus, *Centuria I Plantarum*: 27. 1755.

"Habitat in Palaestina, Aegypto. D. Hasselquist." RCN: 6176.

Lectotype (Hilliard & Burtt in *Bot. J. Linn. Soc.* 82: 247, 253. 1981): *Hasselquist*, Herb. Linn. No. 989.51 (LINN; iso- UPS-HASSELQ 681).
Current name: **Helichrysum sanguineum** (L.) Kostel. (Asteraceae).

Gnaphalium saxatile Linnaeus, *Species Plantarum* 2: 857. 1753.
"Habitat in Italia, Sicilia." RCN: 6219.
Basionym of: *Conyza saxatilis* (L.) L. (1763).
Lectotype (Hilliard & Burtt in *Bot. J. Linn. Soc.* 82: 247. 1981): Herb. Clifford: 401, *Gnaphalium* 7 (BM-000647003).
Current name: **Phagnalon saxatile** (L.) Cass. (Asteraceae).

Gnaphalium scabrum Linnaeus, *Species Plantarum* 2: 855. 1753.
"Habitat in Aethiopia." RCN: 6181.
Replaced synonym of: *Gnaphalium squarrosum* L. (1763), *nom. illeg.*
Lectotype (Hilliard & Burtt in *Bot. J. Linn. Soc.* 82: 199, 247. 1981): Herb. A. van Royen No. 900.346–99 (L).
Current name: **Helichrysum spiralepis** Hilliard & B.L. Burtt (Asteraceae).

Gnaphalium serratum Linnaeus, *Plantae Rariores Africanae*: 19. 1760.
["Habitat in Aethiopia."] Sp. Pl., ed. 2, 2: 1194 (1763). RCN: 6160.
Lectotype (Hilliard & Burtt in *Bot. J. Linn. Soc.* 82: 247, 259. 1981): Herb. Burman, specimen illustrated in Burman, *Rar. Afr. Pl.*: t. 76, f. 3 (G).
Current name: **Helichrysum helianthemifolium** (L.) D. Don (Asteraceae).

Gnaphalium sordidum Linnaeus, *Species Plantarum* 2: 853. 1753.
"Habitat in G. Narbonensi." RCN: 6220.
Basionym of: *Conyza sordida* (L.) L. (1771).
Lectotype (Hilliard & Burtt in *Bot. J. Linn. Soc.* 82: 247. 1981): Herb. Clifford: 401, *Gnaphalium* 4, sheet C (BM-000647000).
Current name: **Phagnalon sordidum** (L.) Rchb. (Asteraceae).

Gnaphalium squarrosum Linnaeus, *Species Plantarum,* ed. 2, 2: 1197. 1763, *nom. illeg.*
"Habitat in Aethiopia." RCN: 6181.
Replaced synonym: *Gnaphalium scabrum* L. (1753).
Lectotype (Hilliard & Burtt in *Bot. J. Linn. Soc.* 82: 199, 247. 1981): Herb. A. van Royen No. 900.346–99 (L).
Current name: **Helichrysum spiralepis** Hilliard & B.L. Burtt (Asteraceae).
Note: An illegitimate replacement name for *G. scabrum* L. (1753), as noted by Hilliard & Burtt.

Gnaphalium stellatum Linnaeus, *Plantae Rariores Africanae*: 19. 1760.
["Habitat in Cap. b. spei."] Sp. Pl., ed. 2, 2: 1198 (1763). RCN: 6182.
Lectotype (Hilliard & Burtt in *Bot. J. Linn. Soc.* 82: 248, 260. 1981): Herb. Burman, specimen illustrated in Burman, *Rar. Afr. Pl.*: t. 80, f. 1 (G).
Current name: **Helichrysum stellatum** (L.) Less. (Asteraceae).

Gnaphalium stoechas Linnaeus, *Species Plantarum* 2: 853. 1753.
"Habitat in Germania, Gallia, Hispania." RCN: 6157.
Lectotype (Galbany-Casals & al. in *Taxon* 55: 492. 2006): Herb. Burser XV(1): 22 (UPS).
Current name: **Helichrysum stoechas** (L.) Moench (Asteraceae).

Gnaphalium supinum Linnaeus, *Systema Naturae*, ed. 12, 3: 234. 1768.
"Habitat in Alpibus Helveticis, Italicis." RCN: 6191.

Lectotype (Grierson in Davis in *Notes Roy. Bot. Gard. Edinburgh* 33: 423. 1975): Herb. Linn. No. 989.81 (LINN).
Current name: **Gnaphalium supinum** L. (Asteraceae).

Gnaphalium sylvaticum Linnaeus, *Species Plantarum* 2: 856. 1753.
"Habitat in Europae sylvis arenosis." RCN: 6190.
Lectotype (Rechinger, *Fl. Iranica* 145: 49. 1980): Herb. Clifford: 402, *Gnaphalium* 12 (BM-000647007).
Current name: **Gnaphalium sylvaticum** L. (Asteraceae).

Gnaphalium teretifolium Linnaeus, *Species Plantarum* 2: 854. 1753.
"Habitat in Aethiopia." RCN: 6155.
Lectotype (Hilliard & Burtt in *Bot. J. Linn. Soc.* 82: 248. 1981): Herb. Clifford: 401, *Gnaphalium* 2 (BM-000646997).
Current name: **Helichrysum teretifolium** (L.) D. Don (Asteraceae).

Gnaphalium uliginosum Linnaeus, *Species Plantarum* 2: 856. 1753.
"Habitat in Europae paludibus, ubi aquae stagnant." RCN: 6192.
Lectotype (Hilliard & Burtt in *Bot. J. Linn. Soc.* 82: 249, 254. 1981): Herb. Linn. No. 989.84 (LINN).
Generitype of *Gnaphalium* Linnaeus (vide Green, *Prop. Brit. Bot.*: 181. 1929).
Current name: **Gnaphalium uliginosum** L. (Asteraceae).
Note: Gnaphalium uliginosum, with the type designated by Hilliard & Burtt, was proposed as conserved type of the genus by Jarvis (in *Taxon* 41: 563. 1992). However, the proposal was eventually ruled unnecessary by the General Committee (see Barrie, *l.c.* 55: 795–796. 2006 for a review of the history of this and related proposals).

Gnaphalium undulatum Linnaeus, *Species Plantarum* 2: 852. 1753.
"Habitat in Africa." RCN: 6178.
Lectotype (Hilliard & Burtt in *Bot. J. Linn. Soc.* 82: 205, 249. 1981): Herb. Clifford: 402, *Gnaphalium* 14 (BM-000647010).
Current name: **Pseudognaphalium undulatum** (L.) Hilliard & B.L. Burtt (Asteraceae).

Gnaphalium virgatum Linnaeus, *Systema Naturae*, ed. 10, 2: 1211. 1759.
["Habitat in Jamaica, Carolina."] Sp. Pl., ed. 2, 2: 1206 (1763). RCN: 6238.
Basionym of: *Conyza virgata* (L.) L. (1763).
Lectotype (D'Arcy in Woodson & Schery in *Ann. Missouri Bot. Gard.* 62: 1048. 1975): *Browne*, Herb. Linn. No. 993.29 (LINN).
Current name: **Pterocaulon virgatum** (L.) DC. (Asteraceae).

Gnetum gnemon Linnaeus, *Systema Naturae*, ed. 12, 2: 637; *Mantissa Plantarum*: 125. 1767.
"Habitat in India." RCN: 7307.
Lectotype (Stevenson in Görts-van Rijn, *Fl. Guianas*, ser. A, 9: 13. 1991): [icon] *"Gnemon Domestica"* in Rumphius, Herb. Amboin. 1: 181, t. 71. 1741.
Generitype of *Gnetum* Linnaeus.
Current name: **Gnetum gnemon** L. (Gnetaceae).
Note: Merrill (in *Interpret. Rumph. Herb. Amb.*: 77. 1917) discussed the Rumphius plates but did not designate a type.

Gnidia oppositifolia Linnaeus, *Species Plantarum* 1: 358. 1753.
"Habitat in Aethiopia." RCN: 2836.
Lectotype (Rogers in Rogers & Spencer in *Taxon* 55: 486. 2006): Herb. Linn. No. 502.8, second specimen from left (LINN).
Current name: **Gnidia oppositifolia** L. (Thymelaeaceae).

Gnidia pinifolia Linnaeus, *Species Plantarum* 1: 358. 1753.
"Habitat in Aethiopia." RCN: 2831.

Lectotype (Rogers in Rogers & Spencer in *Taxon* 55: 485. 2006): [icon] *"Rapunculus foliis nervosis linearibus, floribus argenteis, non galeatis"* in Burman, Rar. Afric. Pl.: 112, t. 41, f. 3. 1739. – Epitype (Rogers in Rogers & Spencer in *Taxon* 55: 486. 2006): South Africa. Western Cape Province, Cape Peninsula, slopes of mountains above Clovelly, ca. 400ft, 24 Sep 1983, *P. Goldblatt 6953* (MO-3116540).
Generitype of *Gnidia* Linnaeus (vide Hitchcock, *Prop. Brit. Bot.*: 150. 1929).
Current name: ***Gnidia pinifolia*** L. (Thymelaeaceae).

Gnidia radiata Linnaeus, *Systema Naturae*, ed. 12, 2: 272; *Mantissa Plantarum*: 67. 1767.
"Habitat ad Cap. b. spei." RCN: 2832.
Lectotype (Rogers in Rogers & Spencer in *Taxon* 55: 486. 2006): Herb. Linn. No. 502.2 (LINN).
Current name: ***Gnidia pinifolia*** L. (Thymelaeaceae).

Gnidia sericea (Linnaeus) Linnaeus, *Systema Naturae,* ed. 12, 2: 272. 1767.
["Habitat in Aethiopia. Burmannus."] Cent. II Pl.: 15 (1756). RCN: 2835.
Basionym: *Passerina sericea* L. (1756).
Lectotype (Rogers in Rogers & Spencer in *Taxon* 55: 487. 2006): *"Passerina (sericea) foliis ovatis tomentosis, caule hirsuto, floribus coronatis..."*, Herb. Burman (G).
Current name: ***Gnidia sericea*** (L.) L. (Thymelaeaceae).

Gnidia simplex Linnaeus, *Systema Naturae*, ed. 12, 2: 272; *Mantissa Plantarum*: 67. 1767.
"Habitat ad Cap. b. spei." RCN: 2833.
Lectotype (Rogers in Rogers & Spencer in *Taxon* 55: 486. 2006): Herb. Linn. No. 502.3 (LINN). – Epitype (Rogers in Rogers & Spencer in *Taxon* 55: 486. 2006): South Africa. Western Cape Province, Houw Hoek, 1,500ft, 24 Nov 1896, *F.R.R. Schlechter 9388* (MO-5473554; iso- US).
Current name: ***Gnidia simplex*** L. (Thymelaeaceae).

Gnidia tomentosa Linnaeus, *Species Plantarum* 1: 358. 1753.
"Habitat in Aethiopia." RCN: 2834.
Neotype (Rogers in Rogers & Spencer in *Taxon* 55: 486. 2006): South Africa. Western Cape Province, Kalk Bay Mountain, Cape Peninsula, above Boyes Drive, 2 Jun 1974, *P. Goldblatt 2024* (MO-2243060).
Current name: ***Gnidia tomentosa*** L. (Thymelaeaceae).
Note: Peterson (in Rechinger, *Fl. Iranica* 95: 473, 476. 1959) noted the existence of three specimens in LINN. However, all are post-1753 additions to the herbarium, and Rogers therefore designated a neotype.

Gomphrena brasiliana Linnaeus, *Centuria II Plantarum*: 13. 1756.
"Habitat in Brasilia." RCN: 1840.
Lectotype (Mears in *Taxon* 29: 91. 1980): [icon] *"Amarantho affinis Brasiliana, glomeratis parvisque flosculis"* in Breyn, Exot. Pl. Cent.: 111, t. 52. 1678.
Current name: ***Alternanthera brasiliana*** (L.) Kuntze (Amaranthaceae).

Gomphrena ficoidea Linnaeus, *Species Plantarum* 1: 225. 1753, *nom. & typ. cons.*
"Habitat in America meridionali." RCN: 1683.
Basionym of: *Illecebrum ficoideum* (L.) L. (1762).
Conserved type (Veldkamp in *Taxon* 38: 299. 1989): Herb. Linn. No. 290.23 (LINN).
Current name: ***Alternanthera ficoidea*** (L.) P. Beauv. (Amaranthaceae).

Gomphrena flava Linnaeus, *Species Plantarum* 1: 224. 1753.
"Habitat in Vera Cruce." RCN: 1843.
Lectotype (Mears in *Taxon* 29: 88. 1980): Herb. Clifford: 87, *Gomphrena* 2 (BM-000558214).
Current name: ***Alternanthera flava*** (L.) Mears (Amaranthaceae).

Gomphrena globosa Linnaeus, *Species Plantarum* 1: 224. 1753.
"Habitat in India." RCN: 1837.
Lectotype (Townsend in Nasir & Ali, *Fl. W. Pakistan* 71: 46. 1974): Herb. Linn. No. 319.1 (LINN).
Generitype of *Gomphrena* Linnaeus (vide Hitchcock, *Prop. Brit. Bot.*: 137. 1929).
Current name: ***Gomphrena globosa*** L. (Amaranthaceae).

Gomphrena hispida Linnaeus, *Species Plantarum*, ed. 2, 1: 326. 1762.
"Habitat in Malabaria." RCN: 1839.
Lectotype (Mears in *Taxon* 29: 92. 1980): [icon] *"Min-angani"* in Rheede, Hort. Malab. 9: 141, t. 72. 1689.
Current name: ***Platostoma hispidum*** (L.) A.J. Paton (Lamiaceae).
Note: See Paton (in *Kew Bull.* 52: 273. 1997) for a discussion of this name.

Gomphrena interrupta Linnaeus, *Species Plantarum* 1: 224. 1753.
"Habitat in America." RCN: 1842.
Lectotype (Veldkamp in *Taxon* 30: 209. 1981): *Houstoun*, Herb. A. van Royen No. 908.260–241 (L; iso- BM).
Current name: ***Froelichia lanata*** (L.) Moq. (Amaranthaceae).
Note: Mears (in *Taxon* 29: 87. 1980) stated that the Royen specimen had been recently lost and designated *Houstoun s.n.* (BM!) as neotype. Veldkamp (in *Taxon* 30: 209. 1981) reported that this was incorrect and rejected Mears' choice in favour of van Royen's sheet (original material for the name).

Gomphrena perennis Linnaeus, *Species Plantarum* 1: 224. 1753.
"Habitat in Bonaria." RCN: 1838.
Lectotype (Mears in *Taxon* 29: 86. 1980): [icon] *"Amaranthoides floribus, stramineis radiatis, perenne"* in Dillenius, Hort. Eltham. 1: 24, t. 20, f. 22. 1732.
Current name: ***Gomphrena perennis*** L. (Amaranthaceae).

Gomphrena polygonoides Linnaeus, *Species Plantarum* 1: 225. 1753.
"Habitat in America meridionali." RCN: 1682.
Basionym of: *Illecebrum polygonoides* (L.) L. (1762).
Type not designated.
Original material: [icon] in Hermann, Parad. Bat.: 17. 1698; [icon] in Sloane, Voy. Jamaica 1: 141, t. 86, f. 2. 1707.
Current name: ***Alternanthera sessilis*** (L.) DC. (Amaranthaceae).
Note: This name had frequently been rejected as a *nomen dubium* (e.g. by Pedersen in *Darwiniana* 17: 438. 1967 and Mears & Gillis in *J. Arnold Arbor.* 58: 62. 1977) before Mears (in *Taxon* 29: 91. 1980) attempted to dispose of the name by typifying it using material in Herb. Sloane 2: 106 (BM-SL), which he stated would make it a synonym of *Alternanthera sessilis* (L.) DC. However, his chosen type is not the material from which Sloane's t. 86, f. 2 (which was cited by Linnaeus) was prepared, which is identifiable as *A. paronychioides* A. St.-Hil. Although Mears' intention was laudable, a neotype cannot be designated when original material exists (Art. 9.11). It appears that formal rejection of the name may be necessary.

Gomphrena serrata Linnaeus, *Species Plantarum* 1: 224. 1753.
"Habitat in America." RCN: 1841.
Neotype (Mears in *Taxon* 29: 86. 1980): Mexico. Vera Cruz, *Houstoun* (BM; iso- BM).
Current name: ***Gomphrena serrata*** L. (Amaranthaceae).

G

Gomphrena sessilis Linnaeus, *Species Plantarum* 1: 225. 1753.
"Habitat in India." RCN: 1684.
Basionym of: *Illecebrum sessile* (L.) L. (1762).
Lectotype (Fawcett & Rendle, *Fl. Jamaica* 3: 140. 1914; Mears in *Taxon* 29: 89. 1980): Herb. Hermann 2: 9, No. 116 (BM-000621528).
Current name: ***Alternanthera sessilis*** (L.) DC. (Amaranthaceae).
Note: Fawcett & Rendle's original indication of the Hermann material as type was restricted by Mears to the material in vol. 2: 9 (BM). Mears' choice (1 Feb 1980) appears to narrowly pre-date that of Townsend (in *Revised Handb. Fl. Ceylon* 1: 49. Feb 1980), who instead chose the material in vol. 2: 78.

Gomphrena vermicularis Linnaeus, *Species Plantarum* 1: 224. 1753.
"Habitat in Brasilia, Curassao." RCN: 1685.
Replaced synonym of: *Illecebrum vermiculatum* L. (1762).
Type not designated.
Original material: [icon] in Hermann, Parad. Bat.: 15. 1698; [icon] in Plukenet, Phytographia: t. 75, f. 9. 1691; Almag. Bot.: 27. 1696.
Current name: ***Blutaparon vermiculare*** (L.) Mears (Amaranthaceae).
Note: Fawcett & Rendle (*Fl. Jamaica* 3: 141. 1914) indicated a type in LINN, but the only material that might be associated with this name (290.26) came from Browne and was a post-1753 addition to the herbarium, and is not original material for the name. Mears (in *Taxon* 29: 88. 1980) designated material in Herb. Sloane vol. 2, fol. 108 (BM-SL, which he erroneously believed to have been collected by Hermann), which Linnaeus never saw, as lectotype. Neither of these choices can be treated as a neotypification because original material is in existence.

Gorteria ciliaris (Linnaeus) Linnaeus, *Species Plantarum*, ed. 2, 2: 1284. 1763.
"Habitat in Aethiopia." RCN: 6575.
Basionym: *Atractylis ciliaris* L. (1759).
Lectotype (Roessler in *Mitt. Bot. Staatssamml. München* 3: 280. 1959): Herb. Linn. No. 1027.7 (LINN).
Current name: ***Cullumia ciliaris*** (L.) R. Br. (Asteraceae).

Gorteria fruticosa (Linnaeus) Linnaeus, *Species Plantarum*, ed. 2, 2: 1284. 1763.
"Habitat in Aethiopia." RCN: 6576.
Basionym: *Atractylis fruticosa* L. (1753).
Lectotype (Roessler in *Mitt. Bot. Staatssamml. München* 3: 131. 1959): Herb. Clifford: 395, *Atractylis* 2 (BM-000646944).
Current name: ***Berkheya fruticosa*** (L.) Ehrh. (Asteraceae).

Gorteria personata Linnaeus, *Systema Naturae*, ed. 10, 2: 1229. 1759.
["Habitat ad Cap. b. spei."] Sp. Pl., ed. 2, 2: 1283 (1763). RCN: 6571.
Lectotype (Roessler in *Mitt. Bot. Staatssamml. München* 3: 321. 1959): Herb. Linn. No. 1027.1 (LINN).
Generitype of *Gorteria* Linnaeus.
Current name: ***Gorteria personata*** L. (Asteraceae).

Gorteria rigens (Linnaeus) Linnaeus, *Species Plantarum*, ed. 2, 2: 1284. 1763.
"Habitat ad Cap. b. spei." RCN: 6572.
Basionym: *Othonna rigens* L. (1760).
Lectotype (Roessler in *Mitt. Bot. Staatssamml. München* 3: 371. 1959): *Schreber*, Herb. Linn. No. 1027.3 (LINN).
Current name: ***Gazania rigens*** (L.) Gaertn. (Asteraceae).
Note: Wijnands (*Bot. Commelins*: 84. 1981) argued that the typification by Roessler should be rejected because the thesis in

which *Othonna rigens* was published was based largely on specimens lent to Linnaeus by Burman. While this is generally true, 1027.3 (LINN, above) is annotated as *Othonna rigens* by Linnaeus, and appears to be original material for both that name and *Gorteria rigens* (L.) L. (1763). Roessler's typification is accepted here.

Gorteria setosa Linnaeus, *Mantissa Plantarum Altera*: 287. 1771.
"Habitat ad Cap. b. spei rupibus maritimis." RCN: 6574.
Lectotype (Roessler in *Mitt. Bot. Staatssamml. München* 3: 282. 1959): *Tulbagh 156*, Herb. Linn. No. 1027.6 (LINN).
Current name: ***Cullumia setosa*** (L.) R. Br. (Asteraceae).

Gorteria squarrosa Linnaeus, *Plantae Rariores Africanae*: 23. 1760.
["Habitat ad Cap. b. spei."] Sp. Pl., ed. 2, 2: 1284 (1763). RCN: 6573.
Lectotype (Roessler in *Mitt. Bot. Staatssamml. München* 3: 297. 1959): Herb. Linn. No. 1027.4 (LINN).
Current name: ***Cullumia squarrosa*** (L.) R. Br. (Asteraceae).
Note: Wijnands (*Bot. Commelins*: 81. 1981) argued that the typification by Roessler should be rejected because the thesis in which the Linnaean name was published was based largely on specimens lent to Linnaeus by Burman. While this is generally true, 1027.4 (LINN) is annotated as *Gorteria squarrosa* by Linnaeus, and appears to be original material for the name. Consequently, Roessler's typification is accepted here.

Gossypium arboreum Linnaeus, *Species Plantarum* 2: 693. 1753.
"Habitat in Indiae arenosis." RCN: 5075.
Lectotype (Fawcett & Rendle, *Fl. Jamaica* 5: 148. 1926): Herb. Linn. No. 874.3 (LINN).
Generitype of *Gossypium* Linnaeus.
Current name: ***Gossypium arboreum*** L. (Malvaceae).
Note: Watt (*Wild Cult. Cotton Pl. World*: 84, pl. 7. 1907) discussed some of the elements involved and, although he concluded that Plukenet's description and plate "... must be accepted as manifesting the type of the species botanically", he also referred (pl. 7) to the LINN specimen as "type". Watt therefore failed to make an effective type choice.

Gossypium barbadense Linnaeus, *Species Plantarum* 2: 693. 1753.
"Habitat in Barbados." RCN: 5078.
Lectotype (Fryxell in *Brittonia* 20: 381. 1968): [icon] *"Gossipium frutescens, annuum, folio trilobato, Barbadense"* in Plukenet, Phytographia: t. 188, f. 1. 1692; Almag. Bot.: 172. 1696. – Typotype: Herb. Sloane 100: 105 (BM-SL).
Current name: ***Gossypium barbadense*** L. (Malvaceae).

Gossypium herbaceum Linnaeus, *Species Plantarum* 2: 693. 1753.
"Habitat in America." RCN: 5074.
Lectotype (Fryxell in *Brittonia* 20: 378. 1968): Herb. Linn. No. 874.1 (LINN).
Current name: ***Gossypium herbaceum*** L. (Malvaceae).
Note: Watt (*Wild Cult. Cotton Pl. World*: 157, pl. 24. 1907) discussed both 874.1 (LINN) and the Clifford material as "types". However, these collections are not part of a single gathering, so Art. 9.15 does not apply, and he did not make a choice of type.

Gossypium hirsutum Linnaeus, *Species Plantarum*, ed. 2, 2: 975. 1763.
"Habitat in America." RCN: 5076.
Type not designated.
Original material: Herb. Linn. No. 874.4 (LINN).
Current name: ***Gossypium hirsutum*** L. (Malvaceae).
Note: Watt (*Wild Cult. Cotton Pl. World*: 184, pl. 29. 1907) indicated a Miller collection in Herb. Sloane 294: 45 (BM-SL) as the type, but this was never studied by Linnaeus and is not original material for the name. It cannot be treated as a neotype because 874.4 (LINN) appears to be original material. Fryxell (in *Brittonia* 20: 382. 1968) regarded Miller's cited description as the protologue but this is contrary to Art. 8.1.

Gossypium religiosum Linnaeus, *Systema Naturae*, ed. 12, 2: 462. 1767.
"Habitat in Indiis." RCN: 5077.
Lectotype (Watt, *Wild Cult. Cotton Pl. World*: 201, 203, pl. 32. 1907): *Turra*, Herb. Linn. No. 874.6 (LINN).
Current name: ***Gossypium hirsutum*** L. (Malvaceae).

Gouania dominguensis Linnaeus, *Species Plantarum*, ed. 2, 2: 1663. 1763, *nom. illeg.*
["Habitat in Barbados, Jamaica."] Sp. Pl., ed. 2, 2: 1663 (1763). RCN: 7647.
Replaced synonym: *Banisteria lupuloides* L. (1753).
Type not designated.
Original material: as replaced synonym.
Current name: ***Gouania lupuloides*** (L.) Urb. (Rhamnaceae).
Note: A superfluous name for *Banisteria lupuloides* L. (1753).

Gratiola dubia Linnaeus, *Species Plantarum* 1: 17. 1753.
"Habitat in Virginiae aquosis." RCN: 4551.
Replaced synonym of: *Capraria gratioloides* L. (1759), *nom. illeg.*; *Lindernia pyxidaria* L. (1771), *nom. illeg.*

Lectotype (Pennell in *Torreya* 19: 149. 1919): *Clayton 164* (BM-000038848).
Current name: ***Lindernia dubia*** (L.) Pennell (Scrophulariaceae).

Gratiola hyssopioides Linnaeus, *Mantissa Plantarum Altera*: 174. 1771.
"Habitat in Tranquebariae agris oryzaceis. D. Koenig." RCN: 134.
Lectotype (Yamazaki in Leroy, *Fl. Cambodge Laos Viêt-Nam* 21: 86. 1985): Herb. Linn. No. 30.6 (LINN), see p. 201.
Current name: ***Lindernia hyssopioides*** (L.) Haines (Scrophulariaceae).
Note: Although Philcox (in *Kew Bull.* 22: 50. 1968) indicated unseen König material as type, it is unclear what material he may have intended, as the only specimens associated with the name in LINN are annotated by Ehrhardt.

Gratiola monnieri (Linnaeus) Linnaeus, *Systema Naturae*, ed. 10, 2: 851. 1759.
["Habitat in America meridionali. Hallman."] Cent. II Pl.: 9 (1756). RCN: 132.
Basionym: *Lysimachia monnieri* L. (1756).
Neotype (Cramer in Dassanayake & Fosberg, *Revised Handb. Fl. Ceylon* 3: 421. 1981): [icon] *"Moniera minima repens, foliis subrotundis, floribus singularibus alaribus"* in Browne, Civ. Nat. Hist. Jamaica: 269, t. 28, f. 3. 1756.
Current name: ***Bacopa monnieri*** (L.) Pennell (Scrophulariaceae).
Note: This has been interpreted as a new combination in *Gratiola* of *Lysimachia monnieri* L. (1756) because the diagnoses of the two are essentially the same, and the latter does not appear in *Syst. Nat.*, ed. 10, 2 (May–Jun 1759). Additionally, Linnaeus (in *Amoen. Acad.* 4: 306. Nov 1959) changed the name *L. monnieri* to *G. "monnieria"* in the reprint of the dissertation in which the former had originally appeared, as noted by Nordenstam (in *Bot. Not.* 114: 278. 1961). Linnaeus' intention therefore seems clear. Cramer designated a Browne figure as type. Although it was not cited in the synonymy of the basionym, there is no original material in existence so this choice is treated as a neotypification under Art. 9.8.

Gratiola monnieria (Linnaeus) Linnaeus, *Amoenitates Academicae* 4: 306. 1759, *orth. var.*
"Habitat in Jamaica." RCN: 132.
Basionym: *Lysimachia monnieri* L. (1756).
Neotype (Cramer in Dassanayake & Fosberg, *Revised Handb. Fl. Ceylon* 3: 42. 1981): [icon] *"Moniera minima repens, foliis subrotundis, floribus singularibus alaribus"* in Browne, Civ. Nat. Hist. Jamaica: 269, 28, f. 3. 1756.
Current name: ***Bacopa monnieri*** (L.) Pennell (Scrophulariaceae).
Note: This has been variously treated as either an orthographic variant of *G. monnieri* (L.) L. (1759), or an independent name. However, the former seems more appropriate, making the name homotypic with *G. monnieri* (L.) L. and its basionym *Lysimachia monnieri* L. (1756).

Gratiola officinalis Linnaeus, *Species Plantarum* 1: 17. 1753.
"Habitat in Lusatia, Gallia & australioribus Europae humidiusculis." RCN: 131.
Lectotype (Sutton in Jarvis & al., *Regnum Veg.* 127: 50. 1993): Herb. Clifford: 9, *Gratiola* 1 (BM-000557556).
Generitype of *Gratiola* Linnaeus (vide Hitchcock, *Prop. Brit. Bot.*: 116. 1929).
Current name: ***Gratiola officinalis*** L. (Scrophulariaceae).

Gratiola peruviana Linnaeus, *Species Plantarum* 1: 17. 1753.
"Habitat in Peru." RCN: 136.
Type not designated.
Original material: [icon] in Feuillée, J. Obs. 3: 23, t. 17. 1725.
Current name: ***Gratiola peruviana*** L. (Scrophulariaceae).

G

Gratiola rotundifolia Linnaeus, *Mantissa Plantarum Altera*: 174. 1771.
"Habitat in Malabariae arenosis." RCN: 133.
Lectotype (Cramer in Dassanayake & Fosberg, *Revised Handb. Fl. Ceylon* 3: 417. 1981): Herb. Linn. No. 30.4 (LINN).
Current name: ***Lindernia rotundifolia*** (L.) Alston (Scrophulariaceae).

Gratiola virginiana Linnaeus, *Species Plantarum* 1: 17. 1753.
"Habitat in Virginia." RCN: 135.
Lectotype (Pennell in *Monogr. Acad. Nat. Sci. Philadelphia* 1: 92. 1935): *Clayton 379* (BM-000051192).
Current name: ***Gratiola virginiana*** L. (Scrophulariaceae).

Grewia asiatica Linnaeus, *Systema Naturae*, ed. 12, 2: 602; *Mantissa Plantarum*: 122. 1767, *nom. illeg.*
"Habitat in Suratte. Braad." RCN: 6980.
Replaced synonym: *Microcos lateriflora* L. (1753).
Type not designated.
Original material: as replaced synonym.
Current name: ***Grewia asiatica*** L. (Tiliaceae).
Note: Although this name is evidently in use, it appears to be a superfluous renaming of *Microcos lateriflora* L. (1753).

Grewia microcos Linnaeus, *Systema Naturae*, ed. 12, 2: 602. 1767, *nom. illeg.*
"Habitat in India." RCN: 6981.
Replaced synonym: *Microcos paniculata* L. (1753).
Lectotype (Panigrahi in *Taxon* 34: 703. 1985): Herb. Hermann 1: 59, No. 207 (BM-000621430).
Current name: ***Microcos paniculata*** L. (Tiliaceae).
Note: A superfluous name for *Microcos paniculata* L. (1753).

Grewia occidentalis Linnaeus, *Species Plantarum* 2: 964. 1753.
"Habitat in Aethiopia, Curacao." RCN: 6978.
Lectotype (Chung in *Taxon* 48: 51. 1999): Herb. Clifford: 433, *Grewia* 1 (BM-000647342).
Generitype of *Grewia* Linnaeus (vide Green, *Prop. Brit. Bot.*: 186. 1929).
Current name: ***Grewia occidentalis*** L. (Tiliaceae).
Note: Wijnands (*Bot. Commelins*: 197. 1983) indicated the post-1753 1076.1 (LINN) as type, and Wild (in Leistner, *Fl. Southern Africa* 21(1): 16. 1984) accepted unspecified material at LINN as the holotype (but failed to distinguish between 1076.1 and 1076.2). Wijnands' choice has been rejected by Chung in favour of Clifford material.

Grewia orientalis Linnaeus, *Species Plantarum* 2: 964. 1753.
"Habitat in India." RCN: 6979.
Lectotype (Chung in *Taxon* 48: 51. 1999): Herb. Hermann 2: 18, No. 324, right specimen (BM-000621568).
Current name: ***Grewia orientalis*** L. (Tiliaceae).

Grias cauliflora Linnaeus, *Systema Naturae*, ed. 10, 2: 1075. 1759.
["Habitat in Jamaica."] Sp. Pl., ed. 2, 1: 732 (1762). RCN: 3867.
Lectotype (Mori, *Fl. Neotropica* 21(1): 200. 1979): [icon] *"Palmis affinis malus Persica maxima caudice non ramoso, foliis longissimis, flore tetrapetalo pallide luteo, fructu ex arboris trunco prodeunte"* in Sloane, Voy. Jamaica 2: 122, t. 216. 1725. – Typotype: Herb. Sloane 7: 56, 57 (BM-SL).
Generitype of *Grias* Linnaeus.
Current name: ***Grias cauliflora*** L. (Lecythidaceae).

Grielum tenuifolium Linnaeus, *Genera Plantarum*, ed. 6: 578. 1764, *nom. illeg.*
["Habitat in Aethiopia."] Sp. Pl. 2: 683 (1753). RCN: 3367.

Replaced synonym: *Geranium grandiflorum* L. (1753).
Type not designated.
Original material: as replaced synonym.
Generitype of *Grielum* Linnaeus.
Current name: ***Grielum grandiflorum*** (L.) Druce (Neuradaceae).

Grislea secunda Linnaeus, *Species Plantarum* 1: 348. 1753.
"Habitat in America calidiore." RCN: 2673.
Lectotype (Rendle in *J. Bot.* 61: 115. 1923): Herb. Clifford: 146, *Grislea* 1 (BM-000558634).
Generitype of *Grislea* Linnaeus, *nom. rej.*
Current name: ***Combretum farinosum*** Kunth (Combretaceae).
Note: Grislea Linnaeus, *nom. rej.* in favour of *Combretum* Loefl.

Gronovia scandens Linnaeus, *Species Plantarum* 1: 202. 1753.
"Habitat in Vera Cruce." RCN: 1635.
Lectotype (Barrie in Jarvis & al., *Regnum Veg.* 127: 51. 1993): [icon] *"Gronovia scandens lappacea, pampinea fronde"* in Martyn, Hist. Pl. Rar.: 40, t. 40. 1728.
Generitype of *Gronovia* Linnaeus.
Current name: ***Gronovia scandens*** L. (Loasaceae).

Guaiacum afrum Linnaeus, *Species Plantarum* 1: 382. 1753.
"Habitat in Aethiopia." RCN: 3009.
Lectotype (Codd in *Bothalia* 6: 518. 1956): Herb. Linn. No. 532.4 (LINN).
Current name: ***Schotia afra*** (L.) Thunb. (Zygophyllaceae).

Guaiacum officinale Linnaeus, *Species Plantarum* 1: 381. 1753.
"Habitat in Hispaniola, Jamaica." RCN: 3007.
Lectotype (El Hadidi in Jarvis & al., *Regnum Veg.* 127: 51. 1993): [icon] *"Lignum Vitae"* in Sloane, Voy. Jamaica 2: 133, t. 222, f. 3, 4, 5, 6. 1725.
Generitype of *Guaiacum* Linnaeus, *nom. & orth. cons.* (vide Hitchcock, *Prop. Brit. Bot.*: 152. 1929).
Current name: ***Guaiacum officinale*** L. (Zygophyllaceae).
Note: "Guaiacum" is the original spelling but has sometimes been treated as an orthographic variant of "Guajacum". The original form, "Guaiacum", is now the conserved spelling.
Ghafoor (in Nasir & Ali, *Fl. W. Pakistan* 76: 3. 1974) indicated 532.1 (LINN) as type but this is a Patrick Browne specimen, received by Linnaeus only in 1758 and therefore not original material for the name.

Guaiacum sanctum Linnaeus, *Species Plantarum* 1: 382. 1753.
"Habitat in Americes insula S. Johannis de Porto Ricco." RCN: 3008.
Lectotype (Wijnands, *Bot. Commelins*: 202. 1983): Herb. Linn. No. 532.2 (LINN).
Current name: ***Guaiacum sanctum*** L. (Zygophyllaceae).

Guarea trichilioides Linnaeus, *Mantissa Plantarum Altera*: 228. 1771, *nom. illeg.*
["Habitat in Brasilia aliisque indiae occidentalis."] Sp. Pl., ed. 2, 1: 551 (1762). RCN: 2679.
Replaced synonym: *Melia guara* Jacq. (1760); *Trichilia guara* (Jacq.) L. (1762).
Type not designated.
Generitype of *Guarea* Linnaeus, *nom. cons.*
Current name: ***Guarea guidonia*** (L.) Sleumer (Meliaceae).
Note: Guarea Linnaeus, *nom. cons.* against *Elutheria* P. Browne.
This name is an illegitimate new name in *Guarea* for *Melia guara* Jacq. (1760), "Guarea guara" not (quite) being a tautonym.

Guettarda speciosa Linnaeus, *Species Plantarum* 2: 991. 1753.
"Habitat in Java." RCN: 7195.

Lectotype (Wong & Verdcourt in *Kew Bull.* 43: 496. 1988; Verdcourt in Polhill, *Fl. Trop. E. Africa, Rubiaceae* 3: 924. 1991): Herb. Linn. No. 1121.1, excl. fruit (LINN).
Generitype of *Guettarda* Linnaeus.
Current name: ***Guettarda speciosa*** L. (Rubiaceae).
Note: Verdcourt (1991) restricted the earlier type choice that he had made with Wong (1988) by excluding the fruiting element mounted on Herb. Linn. No. 1121.1 (LINN).

Guilandina bonduc Linnaeus, *Species Plantarum* 1: 381. 1753.
"Habitat in Indiis." RCN: 3003.
Lectotype (Skeels in *Science*, n.s., 37: 922. 1913; Dandy & Exell in *J. Bot.* 76: 177. 1938): Herb. Hermann 3: 35, No. 156 (BM-000594677).
Generitype of *Guilandina* Linnaeus (vide Hitchcock, *Prop. Brit. Bot.*: 152. 1929).
Current name: ***Caesalpinia bonduc*** (L.) Roxb. (Fabaceae: Caesalpinioideae).
Note: Skeels (*l.c.*), noting Trimen's identifications of Hermann's specimens, treated material associated with *Flora Zeylanica* No. 156 as the type. As the material appears to have been part of a single gathering, but is distributed between three of Hermann's volumes, Dandy & Exell are accepted as having restricted Skeels' original type choice.

Guilandina bonducella Linnaeus, *Species Plantarum*, ed. 2, 1: 545. 1762.
"Habitat in Indiis." RCN: 3003.
Lectotype (Rudd in Dassanayake & Fosberg, *Revised Handb. Fl. Ceylon* 7: 48. 1991): Herb. Hermann 3: 35, No. 156 (BM-000594677).
Current name: ***Caesalpinia bonduc*** (L.) Roxb. (Fabaceae: Caesalpinioideae).
Note: Although Brenan (in Milne-Redhead & Polhill, *Fl. Trop. E. Africa, Leguminosae* 2: 38. 1967) observed that this name was homotypic with *G. bonduc* L., he did not effectively typify the latter, so the typification of *C. bonducella* dates from Rudd's 1991 choice.

Guilandina dioica Linnaeus, *Species Plantarum* 1: 381. 1753.
"Habitat in Canada." RCN: 3006.
Neotype (Reveal in Turland & Jarvis in *Taxon* 46: 470. 1997): U.S.A. Michigan: Ingham Co. East Lansing, 8 Jun 1978, *Gillis 14675* (BM).
Current name: ***Gymnocladus dioicus*** (L.) K. Koch (Fabaceae: Caesalpinioideae).
Note: Although Isely (in *Mem. New York Bot. Gard.* 25: 215. 1975) suggested a possible lectotype might exist at P, and Lee (in *J. Arnold Arbor.* 57: 104. 1976) proposed an interim typification based on a Linnaean generic description, neither made an effective type choice and, in the absence of any original material, Reveal designated a neotype.

Guilandina moringa Linnaeus, *Species Plantarum* 1: 381. 1753.
"Habitat in Zeylona." RCN: 3005.
Lectotype (Keraudren & Gillett in *Bull. Soc. Bot. France* 110: 317. 1963): Herb. Hermann 2: 24, No. 155 (BM-000594587).
Current name: ***Moringa oleifera*** Lam. (Moringaceae).
Note: Vidal (in Tardieu-Blot, *Fl. Cambodge Laos Vietnam* 2: 5. 1962) gives *Burman 18* (G) as type but this would not have been studied by Linnaeus and is not original material for the name. Although Bullock (in *Kew Bull.* 14: 44. 1960) stated that this was "based upon" the Rheede plate, this is only partially correct in that a number of other important elements (notably the Hermann material) contributed to Linnaeus' concept. Bullock's statement does not constitute a formal typification.

Guilandina nuga Linnaeus, *Species Plantarum*, ed. 2, 1: 546. 1762.
"Habitat in Amboina." RCN: 3004.
Lectotype (Merrill, *Interpret. Rumph. Herb. Amb.*: 261. 1917): [icon] *"Nugae silvarum litoreae et terrestres"* in Rumphius, Herb. Amboin. 5: 94, t. 50. 1747.
Current name: ***Caesalpinia crista*** L. (Fabaceae: Caesalpinioideae).

Gundelia tournefortii Linnaeus, *Species Plantarum* 2: 814. 1753.
"Habitat in Armenia, Syria." RCN: 6724.
Lectotype (Vitek & Jarvis in *Annalen Nat. Hist. Mus. Wien, B,* in press): [icon] *"Silybum dioscoridis s. Hacub alcardeg serapionis"* in Rauwolf, Aigent. Beschr. Morgenl.: 74, t. 74. 1583. – Epitype (Vitek & Jarvis in *Annalen Nat. Hist. Mus. Wien, B,* in press): Herb. Rauwolf 4: 81 (L).
Generitype of *Gundelia* Linnaeus.
Current name: ***Gundelia tournefortii*** L. (Asteraceae).
Note: See Burtt (in *Karaca Arbor. Mag.* 6: 59, f. 12. 2001; 6: 139, f. 4. 2002) on Tournefort's account of this plant, including a reproduction of Tournefort's illustration.

Gunnera perpensa Linnaeus, *Systema Naturae,* ed. 12, 2: 597; *Mantissa Plantarum*: 121. 1767.
"Habitat ad Cap. b. spei." RCN: 6907.
Lectotype (Raynal in *Adansonia*, n.s., 6: 538. 1967): Herb. Linn. No. 1063.1 (LINN).
Generitype of *Gunnera* Linnaeus.
Current name: ***Gunnera perpensa*** L. (Gunneraceae).

Gustavia augusta Linnaeus, *Plantae Surinamenses*: 12. 1775.
"Habitat [in Surinamo.]" RCN: 5114.
Lectotype (Mori, *Fl. Neotropica* 21(1): 158. 1979): Herb. Linn. No. 863.2 (LINN).
Generitype of *Gustavia* Linnaeus, *nom. cons.*
Current name: ***Gustavia augusta*** L. (Lecythidaceae).
Note: *Gustavia* Linnaeus, *nom. cons.* against *Japarandiba* Adans.

Gypsophila aggregata Linnaeus, *Species Plantarum* 1: 406. 1753.
"Habitat in monte Vignon Galliae, Monspelii, Pyrenaeis." RCN: 3283.
Lectotype (Goyder in *Bot. J. Linn. Soc.* 97: 23. 1988): Herb. Burser XI: 134 (UPS).
Current name: ***Arenaria tetraquetra*** L. (Caryophyllaceae).
Note: López González & Nieto Feliner (in *Bot. J. Linn. Soc.* 102: 1–8. 1990) argued that Goyder's type choice was inappropriate and that 585.3 (LINN) should have been chosen instead. However, the Burser collection is original material for the name, and Goyder's choice has priority.

Gypsophila altissima Linnaeus, *Species Plantarum* 1: 407. 1753.
"Habitat in Sibiria." RCN: 3188.
Lectotype (Lazkov in Cafferty & Jarvis in *Taxon* 53: 1052. 2004): Herb. Linn. No. 579.10 (LINN).
Current name: ***Gypsophila altissima*** L. (Caryophyllaceae).
Note: Although Barkoudah (in *Wentia* 9: 68. 1962) stated that Herb. Linn. sheets 579.10, 11 and 12 "are [the] only authentic specimens", this statement does not effect typification.

Gypsophila fastigiata Linnaeus, *Species Plantarum* 1: 407. 1753.
"Habitat in Gotlandiae, Borussiae, Helvetiae rupibus." RCN: 3190.
Lectotype (Barkoudah in *Wentia* 9: 71. 1962): Herb. Linn. No. 579.15 (LINN).
Current name: ***Gypsophila fastigiata*** L. (Caryophyllaceae).

Gypsophila muralis Linnaeus, *Species Plantarum* 1: 408. 1753.
"Habitat in Suecia, Germania, Helvetia ad vias." RCN: 3192.

Lectotype (Jonsell & Jarvis in *Nordic J. Bot.* 14: 157. 1994): Herb. Burser XI: 137 (UPS).
Current name: ***Gypsophila muralis*** L. (Caryophyllaceae).
Note: Although Barkoudah (in *Wentia* 9: 145. 1962) noted 579.18 (LINN) as an "authentic specimen", he did not typify the name.

Gypsophila paniculata Linnaeus, *Species Plantarum* 1: 407. 1753.
"Habitat in Sibiriae, Tatariae desertis sabulosis, Tawrow, Bielogrod." RCN: 3186.
Lectotype (Barkoudah in *Wentia* 9: 95. 1962): Herb. Linn. No. 579.5 (LINN).
Current name: ***Gypsophila paniculata*** L. (Caryophyllaceae).

Gypsophila perfoliata Linnaeus, *Species Plantarum* 1: 408. 1753.
"Habitat in Hispania & Oriente." RCN: 3191.
Lectotype (Barkoudah in *Wentia* 9: 104. 1962): Herb. Linn. No. 579.16 (LINN).
Current name: ***Gypsophila perfoliata*** L. (Caryophyllaceae).

Gypsophila prostrata Linnaeus, *Species Plantarum* 2: 1195. 1753.
"Habitat – – – – semina misit D. Wachendorff." RCN: 3185.
Lectotype (Barkoudah in *Wentia* 9: 179. 1962): Herb. Linn. No. 579.4 (LINN).
Current name: ***Gypsophila* sp.** (Caryophyllaceae).
Note: The application of this name is uncertain.

Gypsophila repens Linnaeus, *Species Plantarum* 1: 407. 1753.
"Habitat in Sibiriae, Austriae, Helvetiae montibus." RCN: 3184.
Lectotype (López González in Jarvis & al., *Regnum Veg.* 127: 51. 1993): Herb. Burser XI: 126 (UPS).
Generitype of *Gypsophila* Linnaeus (vide Hitchcock, *Prop. Brit. Bot.*: 154. 1929).

Current name: ***Gypsophila repens*** L. (Caryophyllaceae).
Note: Barkoudah (in *Wentia* 9: 64. 1962) discussed the identity of material in the Clifford and Linnaean herbaria but did not designate a type.

Gypsophila rigida Linnaeus, *Species Plantarum* 1: 408. 1753.
"Habitat Monspelii et forte in Belgio." RCN: 3193.
Lectotype (Jonsell in Cafferty & Jarvis in *Taxon* 53: 1052. 2004): Herb. Linn. No. 579.24 (LINN).
Current name: ***Petrorhagia saxifraga*** (L.) Link (Caryophyllaceae).

Gypsophila saxifraga (Linnaeus) Linnaeus, *Systema Naturae*, ed. 10, 2: 1028. 1759.
["Habitat in Helvetia, Gallia, Ingolstadii."] Sp. Pl. 1: 413 (1753). RCN: 3194.
Basionym: *Dianthus saxifragus* L. (1753).
Lectotype (Jonsell & Jarvis in *Nordic J. Bot.* 14: 157. 1994): Herb. Burser XVI(1): 42 (UPS).
Current name: ***Petrorhagia saxifraga*** (L.) Link (Caryophyllaceae).

Gypsophila struthium Linnaeus, *Systema Naturae*, ed. 10, 2: 1028. 1759.
["Habitat in Hispania."] Sp. Pl., ed. 2, 1: 581 (1762). RCN: 3189.
Type not designated.
Original material: Herb. Linn. No. 579.14 (LINN).
Current name: ***Gypsophila struthium*** L. (Caryophyllaceae).

Gypsophila tomentosa Linnaeus, *Centuria I Plantarum*: 11. 1755.
"Habitat in Hispania." RCN: 3187.
Lectotype (Barkoudah in *Wentia* 9: 105. 1962): Herb. Linn. No. 579.17 (LINN).
Current name: ***Gypsophila tomentosa*** L. (Caryophyllaceae).

H

Haemanthus carinatus Linnaeus, *Species Plantarum,* ed. 2, 1: 413. 1762.
"Habitat ad Cap. b. spei." RCN: 2298.
Type not designated.
Original material: none traced.
Current name: ***Haemanthus coccineus*** L. (Liliaceae/Amaryllidaceae).
Note: Snijman (in *J. S. African Bot., Suppl.* 12: 96. 1984) gives this as a synonym of *H. coccineus* L. but says the type is unknown and possibly not preserved.

Haemanthus ciliaris Linnaeus, *Species Plantarum,* ed. 2, 1: 413. 1762.
"Habitat ad Cap. b. spei. Burmannus." RCN: 2296.
Type not designated.
Original material: Herb. Linn. No. 408.1 (LINN); [icon] in Breyn, Exot. Pl. Cent.: 89, t. 39. 1678.
Current name: ***Boophone guttata*** (L.) Herb. (Liliaceae/Amaryllidaceae).
Note: See Snijman (in *J. S. African Bot., Suppl.* 12: 122. 1984) who notes that 408.1 (LINN) is probably identifiable as *Boophone guttata* (L.) Herb.

Haemanthus coccineus Linnaeus, *Species Plantarum* 1: 325. 1753.
"Habitat ad Cap. b. Spei." RCN: 2295.
Lectotype (Björnstad & Friis in *Norweg. J. Bot.* 19: 190, f. 1. 1972): [icon] *"Haemanthus Africanus"* in Commelin, Hort. Med. Amstelod. Pl. Rar. 2: 127, t. 64. 1701 (see p. 120).
Generitype of *Haemanthus* Linnaeus (vide Hitchcock, *Prop. Brit. Bot.:* 147. 1929).
Current name: ***Haemanthus coccineus*** L. (Liliaceae/Amaryllidaceae).

Haemanthus puniceus Linnaeus, *Species Plantarum* 1: 325. 1753.
"Habitat in Africa." RCN: 2297.
Lectotype (Björnstad & Friis in *Norweg. J. Bot.* 19: 196. 1972): Herb. Linn. No. 408.2 (LINN).
Current name: ***Scadoxus puniceus*** (L.) Friis & Nordal (Liliaceae/Amaryllidaceae).

Haematoxylum campechianum Linnaeus, *Species Plantarum* 1: 384. 1753.
"Habitat in Campeche Americes." RCN: 3019.
Lectotype (Howard & Staples in *J. Arnold Arbor.* 64: 529. 1983): Herb. Linn. No. 538.1 (LINN).
Generitype of *Haematoxylum* Linnaeus.
Current name: ***Haematoxylum campechianum*** L. (Fabaceae: Caesalpinioideae).
Note: Fawcett & Rendle (*Fl. Jamaica* 4: 97. 1920) indicated material in LINN as type but did not distinguish between sheets 538.1 and 538.2. These two collections (one is ex Herb. Clifford) do not appear to be part of a single gathering, so Art. 9.15 does not apply.

Halesia carolina Linnaeus, *Systema Naturae,* ed. 10, 2: 1044. 1759.
RCN: 3443.
Lectotype (Reveal & Seldin in *Taxon* 25: 133. 1976): [icon] *"Halesia"* in Ehret, Commemorative plate of Halesia. 1760 (BM, P-JU).
Generitype of *Halesia* Linnaeus, *nom. cons.*
Current name: ***Halesia carolina*** L. (Styracaceae).
Note: Halesia Linnaeus, *nom. cons.* against Halesia P. Browne.

Halleria lucida Linnaeus, *Species Plantarum* 2: 625. 1753.
"Habitat in Aethiopia." RCN: 4530.

Lectotype (Philcox in Jarvis & al., *Regnum Veg.* 127: 52. 1993): Herb. Clifford: 323, *Halleria* 1 (BM-000646218).
Generitype of *Halleria* Linnaeus.
Current name: ***Halleria lucida*** L. (Scrophulariaceae).

Hamamelis virginiana Linnaeus, *Species Plantarum* 1: 124. 1753.
"Habitat in Virginia." RCN: 1021.
Lectotype (Reveal in Jarvis & al., *Regnum Veg.* 127: 52. 1993): *Kalm,* Herb. Linn. No. 169.1 (LINN).
Generitype of *Hamamelis* Linnaeus.
Current name: ***Hamamelis virginiana*** L. (Hamamelidaceae).
Note: Catesby's illustration, an original element for the name, was reproduced by Venema (in *Belmontia, Hort.* 1(2): 144, f. B. 1957).

Hartogia capensis Linnaeus, *Systema Naturae,* ed. 10, 2: 939. 1759.
["Habitat ad Cap. b. spei."] Sp. Pl., ed. 2, 1: 288 (1762). RCN: 1604.
Basionym of: *Diosma capensis* (L.) L. (1771).
Lectotype (Porter in Jarvis & al., *Regnum Veg.* 127: 52. 1993): Linnaeus in Herb. Wahlbom, No. 25 (UPS).
Generitype of *Hartogia* Linnaeus, *nom. rej.*
Current name: ***Agathosma hispida*** Bartl. & H.L. Wendl. (Rutaceae).
Note: Hartogia Linnaeus, *nom. rej.* in favour of *Agathosma* Willd.

Hartogia capensis Linnaeus, *Species Plantarum,* ed. 2, 1: 288. 1762, *nom. illeg.*
"Habitat in Cap. b. spei." RCN: 1604.
Type not designated.
Original material: none traced.
Current name: ***Cassine schinoides*** (Spreng.) R.H. Archer (Celastraceae).
Note: As noted by Archer & Van Wyk (in *S. African J. Bot.* 63: 155. 1997), this is a later homonym of *H. capensis* L. (1759; Rutaceae), and is therefore illegitimate.

Hartogia ciliaris Linnaeus, *Systema Naturae,* ed. 12, 2: 625. 1767, *nom. illeg.*
["Habitat in Aethiopia."] Sp. Pl. 1: 198 (1753). RCN: 1609.
Replaced synonym: *Diosma ciliata* L. (1753).
Type not designated.
Original material: as replaced synonym.
Current name: ***Agathosma ciliata*** (L.) Link (Rutaceae).

Hartogia imbricata Linnaeus, *Systema Naturae,* ed. 12, 2: 625; *Mantissa Plantarum*: 124. 1767.
"Habitat ad Cap. b. spei." RCN: 1607.
Basionym of: *Diosma imbricata* (L.) L. (1774).
Type not designated.
Original material: Herb. Linn. No. 270.28 (LINN).
Current name: ***Agathosma imbricata*** (L.) Willd. (Rutaceae).

Hartogia lanceolata (Linnaeus) Linnaeus, *Systema Naturae,* ed. 12, 2: 625. 1767.
["Habitat in Aethiopia."] Sp. Pl. 1: 198 (1753). RCN: 1608.
Basionym: *Diosma lanceolata* L. (1753).
Type not designated.
Original material: as basionym.
Current name: ***Agathosma lanceolata*** (L.) Engl. (Rutaceae).

Hartogia pulchella (Linnaeus) Linnaeus, *Systema Naturae,* ed. 12, 2: 625. 1767.
["Habitat in Aethiopia."] Sp. Pl., ed. 2, 1: 289 (1762). RCN: 1612.
Basionym: *Diosma pulchella* L. (1759).

Type not designated.
Original material: as basionym.
Current name: **Agathosma pulchella** (L.) Link (Rutaceae).

Hasselquistia aegyptiaca Linnaeus, *Centuria I Plantarum*: 9. 1755.
"Habitat in Arabia. b.m. Doctor Hasselquist." RCN: 1927.
Replaced synonym of: *Hasselquistia orientalis* L. (1771), nom. illeg.
Lectotype (Meikle, *Fl. Cyprus* 1: 764. 1977): *Hasselquist*, Herb. Linn.
  No. 348.2 (LINN, see p. 210); iso- UPS-HASSELQ 251).
Generitype of *Hasselquistia* Linnaeus.
Current name: **Tordylium aegyptiacum** (L.) Lam. (Apiaceae).

Hasselquistia orientalis Linnaeus, *Mantissa Plantarum Altera*: 217.
  1771, *nom. illeg.*
["Habitat in Arabia. b.m. Doctor Hasselquist."] Cent. Pl. I: 9 (1755).
  RCN: 1927.
Replaced synonym: *Hasselquistia aegyptiaca* L. (1755).
Lectotype (Meikle, *Fl. Cyprus* 1: 764. 1977): *Hasselquist*, Herb. Linn.
  No. 348.2 (LINN).
Current name: **Tordylium aegyptiacum** (L.) Lam. (Apiaceae).
Note: An illegitimate replacement name for *H. aegyptiaca* L. (1755).

Hebenstretia cordata Linnaeus, *Systema Naturae*, ed. 12, 2: 420. 1767.
RCN: 4566.
Lectotype (Roessler in *Mitt. Bot. Staatssamml. München* 15: 37. 1979):
  D. van Royen, Herb. Linn. No. 788.6 (LINN).
Current name: **Hebenstretia cordata** L. (Scrophulariaceae).

Hebenstretia dentata Linnaeus, *Species Plantarum* 2: 629. 1753.
"Habitat in Aethiopia." RCN: 4563.
Lectotype (Roessler in *Mitt. Bot. Staatssamml. München* 15: 43. 1979):
  Herb. Clifford: 326, *Hebenstretia* 1 (BM-000646245).
Generitype of *Hebenstretia* Linnaeus (vide Green, *Prop. Brit. Bot.*: 168.
  1929).
Current name: **Hebenstretia dentata** L. (Scrophulariaceae).
Note: Rolfe (in *J. Linn. Soc., Bot.* 20: 343. 1884) noted the existence of
  several sheets in LINN and stated that the name was founded on
  the Commelin and Burman references. Hedberg (in *Symb. Bot.
  Upsal.* 15(1): 167. 1957) designated 788.2 (LINN) as lectotype, but
  this collection was a post-1753 addition to the herbarium and is not
  original material for the name.

Hebenstretia integrifolia Linnaeus, *Species Plantarum* 2: 629. 1753.
RCN: 4565.
Type not designated.
Original material: none traced.
Current name: **Hebenstretia integrifolia** L. (Scrophulariaceae).

Hedera helix Linnaeus, *Species Plantarum* 1: 202. 1753.
"Habitat in Europae arboribus putrescentibus, inque sepibus." RCN:
  1637.
Lectotype (McAllister & Rutherford in *Watsonia* 18: 40. 1990): Herb.
  Linn. No. 280.2 (LINN).
Generitype of *Hedera* Linnaeus (vide Lamarck, *Tabl. Encycl. (Ill. Gen.)*
  2: 135. 1797).
Current name: **Hedera helix** L. (Araliaceae).
Note: Lawrence & Schultze (in *Gentes Herb.* 6: 131. 1942), on the
  basis of Jackson's Index, treated unspecified material in LINN as the
  type. In fact, there are two sheets (not part of a single gathering so
  Art. 9.15 does not apply) associated with this name, and Browicz
  (in Rechinger, *Fl. Iranica* 102: 2. 1973) designated 280.1 (LINN) as
  type. However, this specimen came from M. Kähler, and was not
  received by Linnaeus until after 1753 so cannot be original material.
  McAllister & Rutherford (in *Watsonia* 18: 14. 1990) chose 280.2
  (LINN) as lectotype, noting that it belongs to the diploid cytotype.

Hedera quinquefolia Linnaeus, *Species Plantarum* 1: 202. 1753.
"Habitat in Canada." RCN: 1638.
Lectotype (designated here by Reveal): *Clayton 116* (BM).
Current name: **Parthenocissus quinquefolia** (L.) Planch. (Vitaceae).
Note: See discussion by Fernald (in *Rhodora* 41: 430. 1939).

Hedyotis auricularia Linnaeus, *Species Plantarum* 1: 101. 1753.
"Habitat in Zeylona." RCN: 834.
Lectotype (Fosberg & Sachet in *Allertonia* 6: 207, 215. 1991): Herb.
  Hermann 1: 27; 3: 35; 4: 36, No. 64 (BM).
Current name: **Hedyotis auricularia** L. (Rubiaceae).
Note: Rogers' statement (in *J. Arnold Arbor.* 68: 154. 1987) that the
  type is "presumably" in the Hermann herbarium is too uncertain to
  effect typification, but that of Fosberg & Sachet is accepted here.
  Although the relevant specimens are scattered through three
  volumes of Hermann's herbarium (BM), they appear to be part of a
  single gathering.

Hedyotis fruticosa Linnaeus, *Species Plantarum* 1: 101. 1753, *typ.
  cons.*
"Habitat in Zeylona." RCN: 833.
Conserved type (Verdcourt in *Taxon* 41: 564. 1992): Herb. Hermann
  1: 18, No. 63 (BM-000621289).
Generitype of *Hedyotis* Linnaeus, *nom. cons.*
Current name: **Hedyotis fruticosa** L. (Rubiaceae).
Note: *Hedyotis fruticosa*, with the type designated by Verdcourt, was
  proposed as conserved type of the genus by Jarvis (in *Taxon* 41: 564.
  1992). This was eventually approved by the General Committee
  (see review of the history of this proposal by Barrie, *l.c.* 55:
  795–796. 2006).

Hedyotis herbacea Linnaeus, *Species Plantarum* 1: 102. 1753.
"Habitat in Zeylona." RCN: 835.
Lectotype (Trimen, *Handb. Fl. Ceylon* 2: 315. 1894): Herb. Hermann
  4: 19, No. 65 (BM).
Current name: **Oldenlandia herbacea** (L.) Roxb. (Rubiaceae).

Hedysarum alhagi Linnaeus, *Species Plantarum* 2: 745. 1753.
"Habitat in Tataria, Persia, Syria, Mesopotamia." RCN: 5493.
Lectotype (Gruenberg-Fertig & Zohary in *Israel J. Bot.* 19: 295.
  1970): [icon] *"Agul"* in Rauwolf, Aigent. Beschr. Morgenl.: 94, t.
  94.173. 1583. – Typotype: Herb. Rauwolf (L). – Epitype (Yakovlev
  & al. in *Bot. Zhurn.* 88(1): 105. 2003): Turkey. "In graminosis
  insularum Tigridid pr. Mossul. 6 Sep 1841. Th. Kotschy, Pl. allep.
  kurd. moss. Ed. Hohenacker. 1843" (LE).
Current name: **Alhagi maurorum** Medik. (Fabaceae: Faboideae).

Hedysarum alpinum Linnaeus, *Species Plantarum* 2: 750. 1753, *typ.
  cons.*
"Habitat α in Sibiria, β in Helvetia." RCN: 5531.
Lectotype (Ali in Nasir & Ali, *Fl. W. Pakistan* 100: 335. 1977): Herb.
  Linn. No. 921.54 (LINN).
Generitype of *Hedysarum* Linnaeus, *nom. cons.*
Current name: **Hedysarum alpinum** L. (Fabaceae: Faboideae).

Hedysarum argenteum Linnaeus, *Systema Vegetabilium*, ed. 13: 562.
  1774, *nom. illeg.*
["Habitat in Sibiria. D. Gmelin."] Sp. Pl. 2: 761 (1753). RCN: 5530.
Replaced synonym: *Astragalus grandiflorus* L. (1753).
Type not designated.
Original material: as replaced synonym.
Current name: **Hedysarum grandiflorum** Pall. (Fabaceae: Faboideae).

Hedysarum barbatum Linnaeus, *Systema Naturae*, ed. 10, 2: 1170.
  1759.

["Habitat in Jamaica."] Sp. Pl., ed. 2, 2: 1055 (1763). RCN: 5527.
Lectotype (Schubert in Milne-Redhead & Polhill, *Fl. Trop. E. Africa, Leguminosae* 3: 477. 1971): Herb. Linn. No. 921.48 (LINN).
Current name: ***Desmodium barbatum*** (L.) Benth. (Fabaceae: Faboideae).

Hedysarum biarticulatum Linnaeus, *Species Plantarum* 2: 747. 1753.
"Habitat in India." RCN: 5511.
Lectotype (Dy Phon in Morat, *Fl. Cambodge Laos Viêtnam* 27: 44. 1994): [icon] *"Hedysarum trifoliatum, siliculis glabris, peltatis, geminis inarticulatis"* in Burman, Thes. Zeylan.: 114, t. 50, f. 2. 1737.
Current name: ***Desmodium biarticulatum*** (L.) F. Muell. (Fabaceae: Faboideae).
Note: Although Pedley (in Dassanayake & Clayton, *Revised Handb. Fl. Ceylon* 10: 167. 1996) indicated Herb. Hermann 1: 25 and 3: 15 (BM) as "type", subsequently restricted to the latter collection (in *Taxon* 46: 471. 1997), Dy Phon's choice (1994) of the Burman plate pre-dates this.

Hedysarum bupleurifolium Linnaeus, *Species Plantarum* 2: 745. 1753.
"Habitat in India." RCN: 5494.
Lectotype (Ali in *Biologia (Lahore)* 12: 33. 1966): [icon] *"Scorpioides Maderaspatana, Graminis Leucanthemi foliis, siliquis nodosis"* in Plukenet, Amalth. Bot.: 189, t. 443, f. 5. 1705.
Current name: ***Alysicarpus bupleurifolius*** (L.) DC. (Fabaceae: Faboideae).

Hedysarum canadense Linnaeus, *Species Plantarum* 2: 748. 1753.
"Habitat in Virginia, Canada." RCN: 5514.
Lectotype (Reveal in Turland & Jarvis in *Taxon* 46: 471. 1997): Herb. Linn. No. 921.32 (LINN).
Current name: ***Desmodium canadense*** (L.) DC. (Fabaceae: Faboideae).

Hedysarum canescens Linnaeus, *Species Plantarum* 2: 748. 1753.
"Habitat in Virginia, Jamaica." RCN: 5515.
Lectotype (Reveal in Turland & Jarvis in *Taxon* 46: 471. 1997): *Clayton 209* (BM-000038877).
Current name: ***Desmodium canescens*** (L.) DC. (Fabaceae: Faboideae).

Hedysarum caput-galli Linnaeus, *Species Plantarum* 2: 751. 1753.
"Habitat in Galloprovinciae littoribus maris." RCN: 5541.
Lectotype (Kit Tan & Strid in Turland & Jarvis in *Taxon* 46: 471. 1997): Herb. Burser XIX: 135 (UPS).
Current name: ***Onobrychis caput-galli*** (L.) Lam. (Fabaceae: Faboideae).
Note: Jafri (in Jafri & El-Gadi, *Fl. Libya* 86: 142. 1980) and Rechinger (*Fl. Iranica* 157: 401. 1984) both treated 921.68 (LINN) as the type. However, this material came from Allioni and was received long after 1753. Kit Tan & Strid designated a specimen from the Burser herbarium, cited explicitly in Linnaeus' protologue (and hence a syntype), as lectotype.

Hedysarum cornutum Linnaeus, *Species Plantarum*, ed. 2, 2: 1060. 1763, *nom. cons.*
"Habitat in Oriente. D. Gerard." RCN: 5544.
Replaced synonym: *Hedysarum spinosum* L. (1759), *nom. rej.*
Lectotype (Ali in Nasir & Ali, *Fl. W. Pakistan* 100: 327. 1977): *Gérard 18*, Herb. Linn. No. 921.71 (LINN).
Current name: ***Onobrychis cornuta*** (L.) Desv. (Fabaceae: Faboideae).
Note: The Tournefort illustration cited in the protologue is reproduced by Burtt (in *Karaca Arbor. Mag.* 6: 62, f. 14. 2001).

Hedysarum coronarium Linnaeus, *Species Plantarum* 2: 750. 1753.
"Habitat in Italiae pratis." RCN: 5533.
Lectotype (Jafri in Jafri & El-Gadi, *Fl. Libya* 86: 139. 1980): Herb. Linn. No. 921.57 (LINN).
Current name: ***Sulla coronaria*** (L.) Medik. (Fabaceae: Faboideae).
Note: Although *H. coronarium* had long been treated as the generitype, Choi & Ohashi (in *Taxon* 47: 877. 1998) successfully proposed *H. alpinum* as the conserved type of *Hedysarum* in its place. This was because *H. coronarium* L. belongs to a small section of the genus which is likely to be segregated from *Hedysarum* in the near future.

Hedysarum crinitum Linnaeus, *Systema Naturae,* ed. 12, 2: 495; *Mantissa Plantarum*: 102. 1767.
"Habitat in India." RCN: 5543.
Lectotype (Dy Phon in Morat, *Fl. Cambodge Laos Viêtnam* 23: 115. 1987): [icon] *"Hedysarum crinitum"* in Burman, Fl. Indica: 169, t. 56. 1768 (see p. 115).
Current name: ***Uraria crinita*** (L.) Desv. (Fabaceae: Faboideae).
Note: Dy Phon & Adema (in *Taxon* 46: 471. 1997 designated 921.70 (LINN) as lectotype. However, Dy Phon (1987) had already designated Burman's cited plate as type, and this earlier choice therefore has priority.

Hedysarum diphyllum Linnaeus, *Species Plantarum* 2: 747. 1753.
"Habitat in Indiis." RCN: 5506.
Lectotype (Dandy & Milne-Redhead in *Kew Bull.* 17: 74. 1963): Herb. Hermann 2: 14, No. 291 (BM-000594577).
Current name: ***Zornia diphylla*** (L.) Pers. (Fabaceae: Faboideae).
Note: Although Fawcett & Rendle (*Fl. Jamaica* 4: 31. 1920) indicated material in BM as type, they did not indicate which material (Sloane's, Hermann's etc.) they intended.

Hedysarum ecastaphyllum Linnaeus, *Systema Naturae,* ed. 10, 2: 1169. 1759.
["Habitat in America meridionali."] Sp. Pl., ed. 2, 2: 1052 (1763). RCN: 5172.
Basionym of: *Pterocarpus ecastaphyllum* (L.) L. (1774).
Lectotype (Fawcett & Rendle, *Fl. Jamaica* 4: 78. 1920): *Browne*, Herb. Linn. No. 887.4 (LINN).
Current name: ***Dalbergia ecastaphyllum*** (L.) Taub. (Fabaceae: Faboideae).
Note: There are evidently differences between Linnaeus' original (1759) account, and that in *Sp. Pl.*, ed. 2, 2: 1052 (1763) – see Carvalho (in *Brittonia* 49: 107. 1997).

Hedysarum flexuosum Linnaeus, *Species Plantarum* 2: 750. 1753.
"Habitat in Asia." RCN: 5534.
Type not designated.
Original material: Herb. Linn. No. 921.58 (LINN).
Current name: ***Hedysarum flexuosum*** L. (Fabaceae: Faboideae).

Hedysarum frutescens Linnaeus, *Species Plantarum* 2: 748. 1753.
"Habitat in Virginia." RCN: 5517.
Lectotype (Britton in *Trans. New York Acad. Sci.* 12: 64. 1893): *Clayton 174* (BM-000038853).
Current name: ***Lespedeza frutescens*** (L.) Hornem. (Fabaceae: Faboideae).
Note: See review by Reveal & Barrie (in *Phytologia* 71: 456–461. 1991), who conclude that the lectotype belongs to what has been known as *L. violacea* (L.) Pers., and that the type of the latter is a specimen of *L. intermedia* Britton. Turland & Jarvis (in *Taxon* 46: 471. 1997) were therefore wrong to indicate *H. frutescens* as a synonym of *L. violacea*, and Akiyama's type choice there is pre-dated by that of Britton, albeit using the same element.

Hedysarum gangeticum Linnaeus, *Species Plantarum* 2: 746. 1753.
"Habitat in India." RCN: 5500.
Lectotype (Fawcett & Rendle, *Fl. Jamaica* 4: 35. 1920): Herb. Linn. No. 921.13 (LINN).
Current name: ***Desmodium gangeticum*** (L.) DC. (Fabaceae: Faboideae).

Hedysarum hamatum Linnaeus, *Systema Naturae*, ed. 10, 2: 1170. 1759.
["Habitat in Jamaica, Zeylona."] Sp. Pl., ed. 2, 2: 1056 (1763). RCN: 5525.
Lectotype (Kirkbride & Kirkbride in *Taxon* 36: 457. 1987): [icon] *"Anonis non spinosa minor, glabra, procumbens, flore luteo"* in Sloane, Voy. Jamaica 1: 187, t. 119, f. 2. 1707. – Typotype: Herb. Sloane 3: 94 (BM-SL).
Current name: ***Stylosanthes hamata*** (L.) Taub. (Fabaceae: Faboideae).
Note: The autonymic varietal epithet was established in *Pl. Jam. Pug*: 20 (1759). Fawcett & Rendle (*Fl. Jamaica* 4: 28. 1920) excluded the Burman element and indicated (unspecified) material in BM as type. It seems likely that they intended Sloane material but this was, in any case, not seen by Linnaeus and is not original material for the name.

Hedysarum hamatum Linnaeus var. **viscosum** Linnaeus, *Plantarum Jamaicensium Pugillus*: 20. 1759.
"Habitat [in Jamaica.]"
Lectotype (Kirkbride & Kirkbride in *Taxon* 36: 456. 1987): [icon] *"Loto pentaphyllo siliquoso villoso similis anonis non spinosa, foliis cisti instar glutinosis & odoratis"* in Sloane, Voy. Jamaica 1: 186, t. 119, f. 1. 1707. – Typotype: Herb. Sloane 3: 93 (BM-SL).
Current name: ***Stylosanthes viscosa*** (L.) Sw. (Fabaceae: Faboideae).
Note: Varietal epithet spelled "viscosia" in the protologue.
    Fawcett & Rendle (*Fl. Jamaica* 4: 29. 1920) indicated (unspecified) material in BM as type; it seems likely that they intended Sloane material (as did Dillon in *Ann. Missouri Bot. Gard.* 67: 776. 1980) but this was, in any case, not seen by Linnaeus and is not original material for the name.

Hedysarum heterocarpon Linnaeus, *Species Plantarum* 2: 747. 1753.
"Habitat in India." RCN: 5512.
Lectotype (Pedley in Dassanayake & Clayton, *Revised Handb. Fl. Ceylon* 10: 168. 1996; Pedley in Turland & Jarvis in *Taxon* 46: 471. 1997): Herb. Hermann 2: 32, No. 294, left specimen (BM-000621619).
Current name: ***Desmodium heterocarpon*** (L.) DC. (Fabaceae: Faboideae).
Note: Although Meeuwen & al. (in *Reinwardtia* 6: 93. 1961) interpreted the name in the sense of the Hermann material, they did not designate a type. Schubert (in Milne-Redhead & Polhill, *Fl. Trop. E. Africa, Leguminosae* 3: 462. 1971) indicated Hermann material in three volumes of the herbarium (BM) as syntypes, and has been followed by authors such as Ohashi (in *J. Jap. Bot.* 66: 17. 1991). Pedley (in Dassanayake & Clayton, *Revised Handb. Fl. Ceylon* 10: 168. 1996) indicated Herb. Hermann material (BM) as "type", without distinguishing between the specimens in different volumes of the collection. However, as it appears to have been part of a single gathering, Pedley's is accepted as the first typification (Art. 9.15), with the choice subsequently restricted by the same author.

Hedysarum hirtum Linnaeus, *Species Plantarum* 2: 748. 1753.
"Habitat in Virginia." RCN: 5519.
Lectotype (Fernald in *Rhodora* 43: 580. 1941; Clewell in *Brittonia* 16: 75. 1964): *Clayton 510*, Herb. Linn. No. 921.39 (LINN; iso- BM).
Current name: ***Lespedeza hirta*** (L.) Hornem. (Fabaceae: Faboideae).
Note: Britton (in *Trans. New York Acad. Sci.* 12: 66. 1893) discussed

both Clayton and Kalm collections, and Fernald (in *Rhodora* 43: 580. 1941) evidently regarded Clayton material as the type, though without distinguishing between the sheets in LINN and BM. They carry the same Clayton number and appear to have been part of a single gathering (Art. 9.15), so Fernald is accepted as having typified the name, with a subsequent restriction to the sheet in LINN being made by Clewell.

Hedysarum junceum Linnaeus filius, *Dec. Prima Pl. Horti Upsal.*: 7. 1762.
Lectotype (Ali in *Biologia (Lahore)* 12: 40. 1966): [icon] *"Hedysarum junceum"* in Linnaeus filius, Dec. Prima Pl. Horti Upsal.: 7, t. 4. 1762.
Current name: ***Lespedeza juncea*** (L. f.) Pers. (Fabaceae: Faboideae).

Hedysarum lagopodioides Linnaeus, *Species Plantarum* 2: 1198. 1753.
"Habitat in China. Osbeck." RCN: 5528.
Neotype (Dy Phon in Morat, *Fl. Cambodge Laos Viêtnam* 23: 103. 1987): Herb. Linn. No. 921.49 (LINN).
Current name: ***Uraria lagopodioides*** (L.) DC. (Fabaceae: Faboideae).
Note: There being no original elements, Dy Phon & Adema (in *Taxon* 46: 471. 1997) designated Chinese material in P as a neotype. However, Dy Phon (1987) had already designated 921.49 (LINN) as type so, under Art. 9.8, this is to be treated as a valid neotypification.

Hedysarum latebrosum Linnaeus, *Mantissa Plantarum Altera*: 270. 1771.
"Habitat in India." RCN: 5502.
Lectotype (Ali in *Taxon* 16: 463. 1967): Herb. Linn. No. 921.15 (LINN).
Note: Ali (in *Taxon* 16: 463. 1967) noted that although the name had been in use as *Heylandia latebrosa* (L.) DC., the identity of its type (in LINN) was "presently obscure" but certainly did not correspond with *Heylandia* DC. (or its synonym *Goniogyna* DC.). The application of this name remains uncertain.

Hedysarum lineatum Linnaeus, *Systema Naturae*, ed. 10, 2: 1170. 1759.
["Habitat in Zeylona. Burmannus."] Sp. Pl., ed. 2, 2: 1054 (1763). RCN: 5508.
Lectotype (Schrire in Turland & Jarvis in *Taxon* 46: 471. 1997): Herb. Linn. No. 311.17 (S).
Current name: ***Flemingia lineata*** (L.) Roxb. (Fabaceae: Faboideae).

Hedysarum maculatum Linnaeus, *Species Plantarum* 2: 746. 1753.
"Habitat in India." RCN: 5501.
Lectotype (Schubert in *J. Arnold Arbor.* 44: 294. 1963): Herb. Linn. No. 921.14 (LINN).
Current name: ***Desmodium gangeticum*** (L.) DC. (Fabaceae: Faboideae).

Hedysarum marilandicum Linnaeus, *Species Plantarum* 2: 748. 1753.
"Habitat in Carolina, Virginia." RCN: 5516.
Lectotype (Reveal & al. in *Huntia* 7: 224. 1987): *Clayton 516*, Herb. Linn. No. 921.35 (LINN; iso- BM).
Current name: ***Desmodium marilandicum*** (L.) DC. (Fabaceae: Faboideae).

Hedysarum moniliferum Linnaeus, *Systema Naturae*, ed. 12, 2: 493; *Mantissa Plantarum*: 102. 1767.
"Habitat in India." RCN: 5496.
Lectotype (Thulin in Turland & Jarvis in *Taxon* 46: 472. 1997): Herb. Linn. No. 310.19 (S).

Current name: ***Alysicarpus monilifer*** (L.) DC. (Fabaceae: Faboideae).
Note: Ali (in *Biologia (Lahore)* 12: 34. 1966; in Nasir & Ali, *Fl. W. Pakistan* 100: 345. 1977), Polhill (in Bosser & al., *Fl. Mascareignes* 80: 111. 1990), and Rechinger & Ali (in Rechinger, *Fl. Iranica* 157: 482. 1984) all indicated a specimen in Herb. Burman (G) as the lectotype, when in fact this was not studied by Linnaeus and only Burman's illustration (t. 52, f. 3), cited by Linnaeus in the protologue, is eligible as such. The specimen at S (which also supports current usage) was preferred by Thulin as a more useful type than the illustration.

Hedysarum nudiflorum Linnaeus, *Species Plantarum* 2: 749. 1753.
"Habitat in Virginia." RCN: 5523.

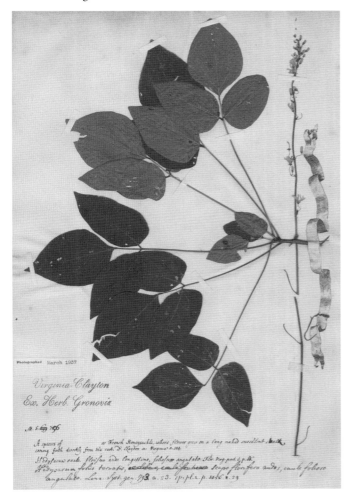

Lectotype (Reveal in Turland & Jarvis in *Taxon* 46: 472. 1997): *Clayton 124* (BM-000038169).
Current name: ***Desmodium nudiflorum*** (L.) DC. (Fabaceae: Faboideae).

Hedysarum nummariifolium Linnaeus, *Species Plantarum* 2: 746. 1753.
"Habitat in India." RCN: 5495.
Lectotype (Merrill in *Philipp. J. Sci., C,* 5: 92. 1910): [icon] *"Onobrychis Madraspat. Nummulariae folio, Ornithopodii siliquis"* in Petiver, Gazophyl. Nat.: 41, t. 26, f. 4. 1702–1709.
Current name: ***Indigofera nummulariifolia*** (L.) Alston (Fabaceae: Faboideae).

Note: Specific epithet spelled "nummularifolium" in the protologue.
Although Fawcett & Rendle (*Fl. Jamaica* 4: 40. 1920), and many later authors, treated Herb. Hermann material (BM) as the type, this choice is pre-dated by Merrill's 1910 designation of a Petiver illustration as type.

Hedysarum obscurum Linnaeus, *Systema Naturae,* ed. 10, 2: 1171. 1759, *nom. illeg.*
["Habitat in Sibiria, Helvetia."] Sp. Pl. 2: 756 (1753). RCN: 5531.
Replaced synonym: *Astragalus hedysaroides* L. (1753).
Type not designated.
Original material: as replaced synonym.
Current name: ***Hedysarum hedysaroides*** (L.) Schinz & Thell. (Fabaceae: Faboideae).

Hedysarum onobrychis Linnaeus, *Species Plantarum* 2: 751. 1753.
"Habitat in Sibiriae, Galliae, Angliae, Bohemiae apricis, cretaceis." RCN: 5539.
Lectotype (Kit Tan & Strid in Turland & Jarvis in *Taxon* 46: 473. 1997): Herb. Clifford: 365, *Hedysarum* 4 α (BM-000646643).
Current name: ***Onobrychis viciifolia*** Scop. (Fabaceae: Faboideae).

Hedysarum paniculatum Linnaeus, *Species Plantarum* 2: 749. 1753.
"Habitat in Virginia." RCN: 5522.
Lectotype (Reveal & al. in *Huntia* 7: 228. 1987): *Clayton 184* (BM-000038857).
Current name: ***Desmodium paniculatum*** (L.) DC. (Fabaceae: Faboideae).

Hedysarum prostratum Linnaeus, *Systema Naturae,* ed. 12, 2: 496; *Mantissa Plantarum*: 102. 1767.
"Habitat in India." RCN: 5549.
Lectotype (Rudd in Dassanayake & Fosberg, *Revised Handb. Fl. Ceylon* 7: 120. 1991): [icon] *"Hedysarum prostratum"* in Burman, Fl. Indica: 168, t. 55, f. 1. 1768.
Current name: ***Indigofera linnaei*** Ali (Fabaceae: Faboideae).
Note: Ali (in *Bot. Not.* 111: 550. 1958) discussed this name, concluding (in Nasir & Ali, *Fl. W. Pakistan* 100: 76. 1977) that the type was material in Plukenet's herbarium (Herb. Sloane 95: 186, BM). Although this choice was followed by several other authors, this collection was not seen by Linnaeus and is not original material for the name.

Hedysarum pulchellum Linnaeus, *Species Plantarum* 2: 747. 1753.
"Habitat in India." RCN: 5507.
Lectotype (Dy Phon in Morat, *Fl. Cambodge Laos Viêtnam* 27: 42. 1994): Herb. Linn. No. 921.24 (LINN).
Current name: ***Desmodium pulchellum*** (L.) Benth. (Fabaceae: Faboideae).

Hedysarum pumilum Linnaeus, *Species Plantarum,* ed. 2, 2: 1059. 1763.
"Habitat in Hispania." RCN: 5538.
Lectotype (Pedley in Turland & Jarvis in *Taxon* 46: 472. 1997): Herb. Linn. No. 921.64 (LINN).
Current name: ***Onobrychis pumila*** (L.) Desv. (Fabaceae: Faboideae).

Hedysarum renifolium Linnaeus, *Systema Naturae,* ed. 10, 2: 1169. 1759.
["Habitat in India."] Sp. Pl., ed. 2, 2: 1051 (1763). RCN: 5498.
Replaced synonym of: *Hedysarum reniforme* L. (1763), *nom. illeg.*
Lectotype (Ohashi in Morat, *Fl. Cambodge Laos Viêtnam* 27: 104. 1994): *J. Burman 29*, Herb. Linn. No. 921.8 (LINN).
Current name: ***Desmodium renifolium*** (L.) Schindl. (Fabaceae: Faboideae).

H

Note: Pedley (in *Taxon* 46: 472. 1997) also designated material in LINN as lectotype but is pre-dated by Ohashi.

Hedysarum reniforme Linnaeus, *Species Plantarum*, ed. 2, 2: 1051. 1763, *nom. illeg.*
"Habitat in India." RCN: 5498.
Replaced synonym: *Hedysarum renifolium* L. (1759).
Lectotype (Ohashi in Morat, *Fl. Cambodge Laos Viêtnam* 27: 104. 1994): *J. Burman 29*, Herb. Linn. No. 921.8 (LINN).
Current name: *Desmodium renifolium* (L.) Schindl. (Fabaceae: Faboideae).
Note: A superfluous name for *H. renifolium* L. (1759), and therefore illegitimate.

Hedysarum repens Linnaeus, *Species Plantarum* 2: 749. 1753.
"Habitat in Virginia." RCN: 5524.
Lectotype (Britton in *Trans. New York Acad. Sci.* 12: 60. 1893): *Clayton 85* (BM-000051143).
Current name: *Lespedeza repens* (L.) W.P.C. Barton (Fabaceae: Faboideae).

Hedysarum retroflexum Linnaeus, *Systema Naturae,* ed. 12, 2: 494; *Mantissa Plantarum*: 103. 1767.
"Habitat in India." RCN: 5509.
Lectotype (Pedley in Turland & Jarvis in *Taxon* 46: 472. 1997): Herb. Linn. No. 921.26 (LINN).
Current name: *Desmodium styracifolium* (Osbeck) Merr. (Fabaceae: Faboideae).

Hedysarum saxatile Linnaeus, *Systema Naturae,* ed. 10, 2: 1171. 1759.
["Habitat in Galloprovincia & in agro Nicaeensi."] Sp. Pl., ed. 2, 2: 1059 (1763). RCN: 5540.
Type not designated.
Original material: *Gérard 77*, Herb. Linn. No. 921.66 (LINN); Herb. Linn. No. 313.5? (S).
Current name: *Onobrychis saxatilis* (L.) Lam. (Fabaceae: Faboideae).

Hedysarum sororium Linnaeus, *Mantissa Plantarum Altera*: 270. 1771, *nom. illeg.*
"Habitat in India orientali." RCN: 5499.
Replaced synonym: *Glycine monophyllos* Burm. f. (1768).
Type not designated.
Current name: *Eleiotis monophyllos* (Burm. f.) DC. (Fabaceae: Faboideae).

Hedysarum spinosissimum Linnaeus, *Species Plantarum* 2: 750. 1753.
"Habitat in Hispania." RCN: 5536.
Lectotype (Jafri in Jafri & El-Gadi, *Fl. Libya* 86: 139. 1980): Herb. Linn. No. 921.62 (LINN).
Current name: *Hedysarum spinosissimum* L. subsp. *spinosissimum* (Fabaceae: Faboideae).
Note: Although the identity of Herb. Linn. No. 921.62 (LINN) was discussed earlier by Heyn (in *Israel J. Bot.* 12: 190. 1963), she did not refer to the specimen as the type (or any equivalent), so Jafri's statement is accepted as the earliest formal choice of type.

Hedysarum spinosum Linnaeus, *Systema Naturae,* ed. 10, 2: 1171. 1759, *nom. rej.*
["Habitat in Oriente. D. Gerard."] Sp. Pl., ed. 2, 2: 1060 (1763). RCN: 5544.
Replaced synonym of: *Hedysarum cornutum* L. (1763), *nom. cons.*
Lectotype (Turland in *Taxon* 45: 331. 1996): *Gérard 18*, Herb. Linn. No. 921.71 (LINN).
Current name: *Onobrychis cornuta* (L.) Desv. (Fabaceae: Faboideae).

Hedysarum strobiliferum Linnaeus, *Species Plantarum* 2: 746. 1753.
"Habitat in India." RCN: 5505.
Lectotype (Fawcett & Rendle, *Fl. Jamaica* 4: 75. 1920): Herb. Hermann 3: 48, No. 289 (BM-000594690).
Current name: *Flemingia strobilifera* (L.) W.T. Aiton (Fabaceae: Faboideae).

Hedysarum triflorum Linnaeus, *Species Plantarum* 2: 749. 1753.
"Habitat in India." RCN: 5526.
Lectotype (Fawcett & Rendle, *Fl. Jamaica* 4: 38. 1920; Pedley in Turland & Jarvis in *Taxon* 46: 472. 1997): Herb. Hermann 1: 21, No. 297 (BM-000594452).
Current name: *Desmodium triflorum* (L.) DC. (Fabaceae: Faboideae).
Note: Schubert (in *J. Arnold Arbor.* 44: 293. 1963), followed by many other authors, indicated Herb. Linn. No. 921.45 (LINN) as the lectotype, but this cannot be regarded as relevant original material because Linnaeus' annotation of the sheet lacks the *Species Plantarum* number (i.e. "25"). Fawcett & Rendle (*Fl. Jamaica* 4: 38. 1920) indicated material in Herb. Hermann (BM) as the lectotype which, although distributed between several volumes, appears to have been part of a single gathering. Consequently, theirs is accepted as the first typification (Art. 9.15), with the choice subsequently restricted by Pedley.

Hedysarum triquetrum Linnaeus, *Species Plantarum* 2: 746. 1753.
"Habitat in India." RCN: 5504.
Lectotype (Fawcett & Rendle, *Fl. Jamaica* 4: 39. 1920; Pedley in Turland & Jarvis in *Taxon* 46: 472. 1997): Herb. Hermann 4: 18, No. 286, left specimen (BM-000628081).
Current name: *Desmodium triquetrum* (L.) DC. (Fabaceae: Faboideae).
Note: Fawcett & Rendle (*Fl. Jamaica* 4: 39. 1920) indicated Herb. Hermann material (BM) as type. Although there is material in more than one volume, it appears to have been part of a single gathering. Consequently, theirs is accepted as the first typification (Art. 9.15), with the choice subsequently restricted by Pedley. The choice of Herb. Linn. 921.20 (LINN) by Dy Phon (in Morat, *Fl. Cambodge Laos Viêtnam* 27: 52. 1994) post-dates that of Fawcett & Rendle.

Hedysarum umbellatum Linnaeus, *Species Plantarum* 2: 747. 1753.
"Habitat in India." RCN: 5510.
Lectotype (Fawcett & Rendle, *Fl. Jamaica* 4: 39. 1920; Pedley in Turland & Jarvis in *Taxon* 46: 473. 1997): Herb. Hermann 2: 26, No. 293 (BM-000621598).
Current name: *Desmodium umbellatum* (L.) DC. (Fabaceae: Faboideae).
Note: Fawcett & Rendle (Fl. *Jamaica* 4: 39. 1920) indicated Herb. Hermann material (BM) as type. Although there is material in more than one volume, it appears to have been part of a single gathering. Consequently, theirs is accepted as the first typification (Art. 9.15), with the choice subsequently restricted by Pedley. The choice of Herb. Linn. 921.28 (LINN) by Dy Phon (in Morat, *Fl. Cambodge Laos Viêtnam* 27: 27. 1994) post-dates that of Fawcett & Rendle.

Hedysarum vaginale Linnaeus, *Species Plantarum* 2: 746. 1753.
"Habitat in India." RCN: 5503.
Lectotype (Verdcourt in Turland & Jarvis in *Taxon* 46: 473. 1997): Herb. Hermann 1: 27, No. 287, upper specimen (BM-000621319).
Current name: *Alysicarpus vaginalis* (L.) DC. (Fabaceae: Faboideae).
Note: Cufodontis (in *Bull. Jard. Bot. État Bruxelles* 25: 303. 1955) indicated an unspecified and unlocalised Burman element as type, but Verdcourt (in Milne-Redhead & Polhill, *Fl. Trop. E. Africa,*

Leguminosae 3: 493. 1971) erroneously indicated material in Herb. Hermann 1: 27 and 1: 59 (BM) as syntypes, and was followed in this by many other authors. He formally designated a lectotype in 1997.

Hedysarum violaceum Linnaeus, *Species Plantarum* 2: 749. 1753.
"Habitat in Virginia." RCN: 5521.
Lectotype (Clewell in *Rhodora* 68: 390, 392. 1966): *Kalm*, Herb. Linn. No. 921.41 (LINN; iso- UPS, BM).
Current name: ***Lespedeza violacea*** (L.) Pers. (Fabaceae: Faboideae).
Note: See extensive discussion by Reveal & Barrie (in *Phytologia* 71: 456–461. 1991) where they conclude that the lectotype belongs to what has been known as *L. intermedia* Britton, for which *L. violacea* becomes the correct name.

Hedysarum virginicum Linnaeus, *Species Plantarum* 2: 750. 1753.
"Habitat in Virginia." RCN: 5537.
Lectotype (Reveal in Turland & Jarvis in *Taxon* 46: 473. 1997): *Clayton 614*, left specimen (BM-000051647; iso- BM).
Current name: ***Aeschynomene virginica*** (L.) Britton & al. (Fabaceae: Faboideae).
Note: Rudd (in *Contr. U. S. Natl. Herb.* 32: 56. 1955) indicated *Clayton 564* and *Clayton 614* (mounted on the same sheet but not part of a single gathering) as syntypes. Reveal subsequently designated the latter as lectotype.

Hedysarum viridiflorum Linnaeus, *Species Plantarum* 2: 748. 1753.
"Habitat in Virginia." RCN: 5518.
Type not designated.
Original material: *Clayton 190* (BM).
Current name: ***Desmodium viridiflorum*** (L.) DC. (Fabaceae: Faboideae).
Note: Although Britton (in *Bull. Torrey Bot. Club* 21: 114. 1894) regarded Clayton 190 (BM) as "the specimen ...on which Linnaeus founded the species", this is not accepted as equivalent to the use of "type".

Hedysarum viscidum Linnaeus, *Species Plantarum* 2: 747. 1753.
"Habitat in India." RCN: 5513.
Lectotype (Rudd in Dassanayake & Clayton, *Revised Handb. Fl. Ceylon* 10: 196. 1996): Herb. Hermann 1: 22, No. 295 (BM-000594453).
Current name: ***Pseudarthria viscida*** (L.) Wight & Arn. (Fabaceae: Faboideae).

Hedysarum volubile Linnaeus, *Species Plantarum* 2: 750. 1753.
"Habitat in America septentrionali." RCN: 5529.
Type not designated.
Original material: [icon] in Dillenius, Hort. Eltham. 1: 173, t. 143, f. 170. 1732 – Voucher: Herb. Sherard (OXF).
Current name: ***Galactia volubilis*** (L.) Britton (Fabaceae: Faboideae).
Note: Torrey & Gray (*Fl. N. Amer.* 1: 365, 1840) stated that the name was "founded upon" Dillenius, *Hort. Eltham.*: t. 143, f. 170 (1732) but this is not accepted as equivalent to the use of "type".

Heisteria pungens P.J. Bergius, *Descr. Pl. Cap.*: 185. 1767.
RCN: 5153.
Replaced synonym: *Polygala heisteria* L. (1753).
Lectotype (Wijnands in Jarvis & al., *Regnum Veg.* 127: 52. 1993): Herb. Clifford: 352, *Heisteria* 1 (BM-000646524).
Generitype of *Heisteria* Linnaeus, *nom. rej.*
Current name: ***Muraltia heisteria*** (L.) DC. (Polygalaceae).
Note: *Heisteria* Linnaeus (1758), *nom. rej.* in favour of *Heisteria* Jacq. (1760) (Olacaceae), *nom. cons.*

Helenium autumnale Linnaeus, *Species Plantarum* 2: 886. 1753.
"Habitat in America septentrionali ["septenttionali"]." RCN: 6412.
Lectotype (Fernald in *Rhodora* 45: 486, pl. 796. 1943): Herb. Linn. No. 1005.1 (LINN; iso- S?).
Generitype of *Helenium* Linnaeus.
Current name: ***Helenium autumnale*** L. (Asteraceae).

Helianthus altissimus Linnaeus, *Species Plantarum*, ed. 2, 2: 1278. 1763.
"Habitat in Pensylvania." RCN: 6545.
Lectotype (Watson in *Pap. Michigan Acad. Sci.* 9: 439, pl. 70. 1929): Herb. Linn. No. 1024.9 (LINN).
Current name: ***Helianthus giganteum*** L. (Asteraceae).

Helianthus angustifolius Linnaeus, *Species Plantarum* 2: 906. 1753.
"Habitat in Virginia." RCN: 6547.
Lectotype (Heiser & al. in *Mem. Torrey Bot. Club* 22(3): 183. 1969): *Clayton 13* (BM-000032582).
Current name: ***Helianthus angustifolius*** L. (Asteraceae).
Note: Watson (in *Pap. Michigan Acad. Sci.* 9: 336. 1929) referred to material at LINN as the type, though it is unclear which sheet was intended. There is no suitably annotated sheet under *Helianthus*, though there is sheet 1025.9 (under *Rudbeckia*). However, this material came from David van Royen, certainly after 1753, and it cannot be original material for the name. Fernald (in *Rhodora* 49: 190. 1947) regarded a Clayton specimen as the type. However, from his illustration (pl. 1084, f. 1) it is clear that he intended *Clayton 667* (which is original material for *Coreopsis angustifolia* L. but not for this), and not *Clayton 13* (which is original material for *H. angustifolius*). Heiser & al. (in *Mem. Torrey Bot. Club* 22(3): 183. 1969) stated "(T: Virginia, Clayton)", adding (p. 186) that the photo they had seen from BM "bearing the annotation as the type of *H. angustifolius* shows a plant with much broader leaves [than Clayton 667]". It seems clear they regarded *Clayton 13* as the type. See Reveal & al. (in *Huntia* 7: 223. 1987), who recognised Fernald's error.

Helianthus annuus Linnaeus, *Species Plantarum* 2: 904. 1753.
"Habitat in Peru, Mexico." RCN: 6537.
Lectotype (Watson in *Pap. Michigan Acad. Sci.* 9: 358. 1929): Herb. Linn. No. 1024.1 (LINN).
Generitype of *Helianthus* Linnaeus (vide Green, *Prop. Brit. Bot.*: 183. 1929).
Current name: ***Helianthus annuus*** L. (Asteraceae).
Note: Jeffrey (in *Curtis's Bot. Mag.* 183: 33. 1978) rejected Watson's choice of type, partly on the grounds that it conflicted with the protologue (it does not show "fol. omnibus cordatis" according to Jeffrey, pers. comm., Oct 1992). However, he rejected 1024.1 (LINN) in favour of "Corona solis I" of Tabernaemontanus (*Eicones Pl.*: 763. 1590), which did not form part of the protologue. This later choice is therefore in conflict with Art. 9.17(b), and Watson's choice stands. This does not appear to cause any nomenclatural difficulties.

Helianthus atrorubens Linnaeus, *Species Plantarum* 2: 906. 1753.
"Habitat in Virginia." RCN: 6549.
Lectotype (Watson in *Pap. Michigan Acad. Sci.* 9: 344. 1929): *Clayton 136*, Herb. Linn. No. 1024.13 (LINN), see p. 564.
Current name: ***Helianthus atrorubens*** L. (Asteraceae).
Note: Although authors such as Fernald (in *Rhodora* 48: 75. 1946) and Heiser (in *Mem. Torrey Bot. Club* 22(3): 196. 1969) treated the Dillenius plate (t. 94, f. 110) as type, Watson's choice has priority.

Helianthus decapetalus Linnaeus, *Species Plantarum* 2: 905. 1753.
"Habitat in Canada ex semine. D. Kalm." RCN: 6541.

The lectotype of *Helianthus atrorubens* L.

Lectotype (Watson in *Pap. Michigan Acad. Sci.* 9: 381. 1929): Herb. Linn. No. 1024.5 (LINN).
Current name: ***Helianthus decapetalus*** L. (Asteraceae).

Helianthus divaricatus Linnaeus, *Species Plantarum* 2: 906. 1753.
"Habitat in America septentrionali." RCN: 6548.
Lectotype (Watson in *Pap. Michigan Acad. Sci.* 9: 383. 1929): Herb. Linn. No. 1024.12 (LINN).
Current name: ***Helianthus divaricatus*** L. (Asteraceae).

Helianthus frondosus Linnaeus, *Centuria I Plantarum*: 28. 1755.
"Habitat in Canada." RCN: 6542.
Lectotype (Reveal in Jarvis & Turland in *Taxon* 47: 362. 1998): Herb. Linn. No. 1024.6 (LINN).
Current name: ***Helianthus decapetalus*** L. (Asteraceae).

Helianthus giganteus Linnaeus, *Species Plantarum* 2: 905. 1753.
"Habitat in Virginia, Canada." RCN: 6544.
Lectotype (Reveal in Jarvis & Turland in *Taxon* 47: 362. 1998): *Clayton 109* (BM-000038159).
Current name: ***Helianthus giganteus*** L. (Asteraceae).
Note: Long (in *Rhodora* 56: 200. 1954) indicated unspecified material in LINN (but presumably Herb. Linn. No. 1024.8) as type, but that sheet lacks a *Species Plantarum* number (i.e. "6"), was a later addition to the herbarium, and is not original material for the name.

Helianthus indicus Linnaeus, *Systema Naturae,* ed. 12, 2: 569; *Mantissa Plantarum*: 117. 1767.
"Habitat culta in Aegypto." RCN: 6538.
Lectotype (Reveal in Jarvis & Turland in *Taxon* 47: 362. 1998): [icon] *"Corona solis minor III"* in Tabernaemontanus, New Vollk. Kräuterb.: 1146, 1147. 1664.
Current name: ***Helianthus annuus*** L. (Asteraceae).

Helianthus laevis Linnaeus, *Species Plantarum* 2: 906. 1753.
"Habitat in Virginia." RCN: 6546.
Lectotype (Sherff in *Publ. Field Mus. Nat. Hist., Bot. Ser.* 16: 315. 1937): *Clayton 195* (BM-000038865).
Current name: ***Bidens laevis*** (L.) Britton (Asteraceae).
Note: Sherff (in *Bot. Gaz.* 61: 504. 1916) stated that he had been unable to find *Clayton 195* at BM, although it had previously been reported as present by Gray. Sherff subsequently designated it as the type.

Helianthus multiflorus Linnaeus, *Species Plantarum* 2: 905. 1753.
"Habitat in Virginia." RCN: 6539.
Lectotype (Reveal in Jarvis & Turland in *Taxon* 47: 362. 1998): Herb. Linn. No. 1024.2 (LINN).
Current name: ***Helianthus* × *multiflorus*** L. (Asteraceae).

Helianthus strumosus Linnaeus, *Species Plantarum* 2: 905. 1753.
"Habitat in Canada." RCN: 6543.
Lectotype (Watson in *Pap. Michigan Acad. Sci.* 9: 460, pl. 83. 1929): Herb. Linn. No. 1024.7 (LINN).
Current name: ***Helianthus strumosus*** L. (Asteraceae).

Helianthus tuberosus Linnaeus, *Species Plantarum* 2: 905. 1753.
"Habitat in Brasilia." RCN: 6540.
Lectotype (Cockerell in *Amer. Naturalist* 53: 188. 1919): [icon] *"Flos Solis Farnesianus, Aster Peruan. tuberosus"* in Colonna, Ekphr., ed. 2: 11, 13. 1616.
Current name: ***Helianthus tuberosus*** L. (Asteraceae).

Heliconia bihai (Linnaeus) Linnaeus, *Mantissa Plantarum Altera*: 211. 1771.
RCN: 1653.
Basionym: *Musa bihai* L. (1753).
Neotype (Maas & De Rooij in Stoffers & Lindeman, *Fl. Suriname* 5(1): 399. 1979): Herb. Linn. No. 286.1 (LINN).
Generitype of *Heliconia* Linnaeus, *nom. cons.*
Current name: ***Heliconia bihai*** (L.) L. (Musaceae).
Note: Heliconia Linnaeus, *nom. cons.* against *Bihai* Mill.

Helicteres angustifolia Linnaeus, *Species Plantarum* 2: 963. 1753.
"Habitat in China. Osbeck." RCN: 6971.
Type not designated.
Original material: Herb. Linn. No. 1074.5 (LINN).
Current name: ***Helicteres angustifolia*** L. (Sterculiaceae).
Note: Cristóbal (in *Bonplandia* 11: 176. 2001) indicated 1074.5 (LINN) (as "1974.5") as the holotype. While there do not appear to be grounds for accepting it as a holotype, this collection does appear to be original material for the name and eligible for selection as a lectotype. However, this choice was published after 1 Jan 2001 and so the omission of the phrase "designated here" or an equivalent (Art. 7.11) means that this choice is not effective.

Helicteres isora Linnaeus, *Species Plantarum* 2: 963. 1753.
"Habitat in Malabaria, Jamaica." RCN: 6970.
Lectotype (Howard in *J. Arnold Arbor.* 54: 454. 1973): [icon] *"Helicteres arbor Ind. Or. siliqua varicosa, & funiculi in modum contortuplicata"* in Plukenet, Phytographia: t. 245, f. 2 [closed fr. only]. 1692; Almag. Bot.: 181. 1696.

Generitype of *Helicteres* Linnaeus (vide Green, *Prop. Brit. Bot.*: 186. 1929).

Current name: **Helicteres isora** L. (Sterculiaceae).

Note: Leach (in Jarvis & al., *Regnum Veg.* 127: 52. 1993) designated the cited Rheede plate as type but this choice is pre-dated by that of Howard, as noted by Cristóbal (in *Bonplandia* 11: 170. 2001).

Helicteres pentandra Linnaeus, *Mantissa Plantarum Altera*: 294. 1771.

"Habitat Surinami." RCN: 6972.

Type not designated.

Original material: none traced.

Current name: **Helicteres pentandra** L. (Sterculiaceae).

Note: Cristóbal (in *Bonplandia* 11: 136. 2001) indicates *Hostmann 240* (K; iso- BM, G, P, W) as a neotype but her wording unfortunately fails to comply with Art. 7.11 (by omitting "designated here" or an equivalent, even though she does use this form of words elsewhere in her revision).

Heliocarpus americanus Linnaeus, *Species Plantarum* 1: 448. 1753.

"Habitat in America meridionali." RCN: 3477.

Lectotype (Stearn, *Introd. Linnaeus' Sp. Pl.* (Ray Soc. ed.): 128. 1957): Herb. Clifford: 211, *Heliocarpus* 1 (BM-000628765).

Generitype of *Heliocarpus* Linnaeus.

Current name: **Heliocarpus americanus** L. (Tiliaceae).

Note: Rose (in *Contr. U. S. Natl. Herb.* 5: 125. 1897) stated that the name was "based upon" Linnaeus' *Hort. Cliff.*: t. 16 (1738), and Baker (in *J. Bot.* 36: 131. 1898) noted the existence of Clifford material at BM. Watson (in *Bull. Torrey Bot. Club* 50: 10. 1923), however, designated a neotype from Venezuela. Sprague (in *J. Bot.* 61: 255. 1923) disagreed, but also argued that the plant in Clifford's herbarium could not serve as the type. Ko Ko Lay (in *Ann. Missouri Bot. Gard.* 36: 528. 1940) indicated that the type was in BM (but gave no indication of what it might be). None of the preceding statements are accepted as valid typifications. Stearn (*Introd. Linnaeus' Sp. Pl.* (Ray Soc. ed.): 47. 1957) included Clifford's t. 16 in a list of the figures to be treated as the types of Linnaean binomials but later (p. 128) in the same publication, he clearly treated the Clifford specimen as the type. The latter has been followed by others (e.g. McVaugh, *Fl. Novo-Galiciana* 3: 77. 2001), and is accepted here.

Heliophila coronopifolia Linnaeus, *Species Plantarum*, ed. 2, 2: 927. 1763.

"Habitat ad Cap. b. spei." RCN: 4827.

Lectotype (Marais in Codd & al., *Fl. Southern Africa* 13: 43. 1970): [icon] *"Leucojum Africanum, coeruleo flore, Coronopi angusto folio, minus"* in Hermann, Hort. Lugd.-Bat. Cat.: 366, 367. 1687.

Current name: **Heliophila coronopifolia** L. (Brassicaceae).

Heliophila integrifolia Linnaeus, *Species Plantarum*, ed. 2, 2: 926. 1763, *nom. illeg.*

"Habitat in Cap. b. spei, locis saxosis incultis." RCN: 4826.

Replaced synonym: *Cheiranthus africanus* L. (1760).

Lectotype (Marais in Codd & al., *Fl. Southern Africa* 13: 55. 1970): [icon] *"Leucojum Africanum coeruleo flore, latifolium hirsutum"* in Hermann, Hort. Lugd.-Bat. Cat.: 364, 365. 1687.

Generitype of *Heliophila* Linnaeus.

Current name: **Heliophila africana** (L.) Marais (Brassicaceae).

Note: As noted by Marais, this is an illegitimate renaming of *Cheiranthus africanus* L. (1760).

Heliotropium arborescens Linnaeus, *Systema Naturae*, ed. 10, 2: 913. 1759.

["Habitat in Peru."] Sp. Pl., ed. 2, 1: 187 (1762). RCN: 1054.

Replaced synonym of: *Heliotropium peruvianum* L. (1762), *nom. illeg.*

Lectotype (Riedl in Kalkman & al., *Fl. Malesiana*, ser. I, 13: 102. 1997): [icon] *"Heliotropium, foliis ovato-lanceolatis, spicis plurimis confertis caule fruticoso"* in Miller, Fig. Pl. Gard. Dict. 1: 96, t. 144. 1757.

Current name: **Heliotropium arborescens** L. (Boraginaceae).

Heliotropium curassavicum Linnaeus, *Species Plantarum* 1: 130. 1753.

"Habitat in Americae calidioris maritimis." RCN: 1060.

Lectotype (Verdcourt in Polhill, *Fl. Trop. E. Africa, Boraginaceae*: 67. 1991): [icon] *"Heliotropium Curassavicum foliis Lini umbilicati"* in Morison, Pl. Hist. Univ. 3: 452, s. 11, t. 31, f. 12. 1699. – Typotype: Herb. Morison? (OXF).

Current name: **Heliotropium curassavicum** L. (Boraginaceae).

Heliotropium europaeum Linnaeus, *Species Plantarum* 1: 130. 1753.

"Habitat in Europa australi." RCN: 1057.

Lectotype (Förther in Jarvis & al., *Regnum Veg.* 127: 53. 1993): Herb. Clifford: 45, *Heliotropium* 1 (BM-000557900).

Generitype of *Heliotropium* Linnaeus (vide Hitchcock, *Prop. Brit. Bot.*: 127. 1929).

Current name: **Heliotropium europaeum** L. (Boraginaceae).

Note: Kazmi (in *J. Arnold Arbor.* 51: 175. 1970) indicated 179.8 (LINN) as type, but this is an Alströmer collection not received by Linnaeus until long after 1753. It is not original material for the name.

Heliotropium fruticosum Linnaeus, *Systema Naturae,* ed. 10, 2: 913. 1759.

["Habitat in Jamaica."] Sp. Pl., ed. 2, 1: 188 (1762). RCN: 1059.

Lectotype (Johnston in *Contr. Gray Herb.* 81: 67. 1928; Nash & Moreno in Gómez Pompa, *Fl. Veracruz* 18: 84. 1981): *Browne,* Herb. Linn. No. 179.10 (LINN).

Current name: **Heliotropium fruticosum** L. (Boraginaceae).

Note: Johnston clearly treated Browne material in LINN as the type but did not distinguish between sheets 179.10 and 179.11. However, they may well be part of a single gathering so Johnson is accepted as having typified the name (Art. 9.15), with Nash & Moreno having restricted the choice to sheet 179.10.

Heliotropium gnaphalodes Linnaeus, *Systema Naturae*, ed. 10, 2: 913. 1759.

["Habitat in Barbados, Jamaicae maritimis."] Sp. Pl., ed. 2, 1: 188 (1762). RCN: 1062.

Lectotype (Howard, *Fl. Lesser Antilles* 6: 189. 1989): [icon] *"Heliotropium Gnaphaloides litoreum, fruticescens, Americanum"* in Plukenet, Phytographia: t. 193, f. 5. 1692; Almag. Bot.: 182. 1696.

Current name: **Heliotropium gnaphalodes** L. (Boraginaceae).

Heliotropium indicum Linnaeus, *Species Plantarum* 1: 130. 1753.

"Habitat in India utraque." RCN: 1055.

Lectotype (Mill in Cafferty & Jarvis in *Taxon* 53: 802. 2004): Herb. Hermann 1: 9, No. 70 (BM-000621256).

Current name: **Heliotropium indicum** L. (Boraginaceae).

Note: Mill provides a summary of earlier type statements for this name.

Heliotropium orientale Linnaeus, *Species Plantarum* 1: 131. 1753.

"Habitat in Asia." RCN: 1061.

Lectotype (Johnston in *Contr. Gray Herb.* 81: 80. 1928): *Steller?,* Herb. Linn. No. 179.12 (LINN).

Current name: **Plagiobothrys orientalis** (L.) I.M. Johnst. (Boraginaceae).

Heliotropium parviflorum Linnaeus, *Mantissa Plantarum Altera*: 201. 1771.
"Habitat in Indiis." RCN: 1056.
Lectotype (Howard, *Fl. Lesser Antilles* 6: 202. 1989): [icon] *"Heliotropium Barbad., Parietariae folio, flore albo minimo"* in Dillenius, Hort. Eltham. 1: 178, t. 146, f. 175. 1732.
Current name: ***Heliotropium angiospermum*** Murray (Boraginaceae).

Heliotropium peruvianum Linnaeus, *Species Plantarum*, ed. 2, 1: 187. 1762, *nom. illeg.*
"Habitat in Peru." RCN: 1054.
Replaced synonym: *Heliotropium arborescens* L. (1759).
Lectotype (Riedl in Kalkman & al., *Fl. Malesiana*, ser. I, 13: 102. 1997): [icon] *"Heliotropium, foliis ovato-lanceolatis, spicis plurimis confertis caule fruticoso"* in Miller, Fig. Pl. Gard. Dict. 1: 96, t. 144. 1757.
Current name: ***Heliotropium arborescens*** L. (Boraginaceae).
Note: An illegitimate replacement name for *H. arborescens* L. (1759) with which it is therefore homotypic.

Heliotropium supinum Linnaeus, *Species Plantarum* 1: 130. 1753.
"Habitat in Salmanticae juxta agros, Monspelii in littore." RCN: 1058.
Lectotype (Verdcourt in *Kew Bull.* 42: 710. 1988): Herb. Burser XIV(2): 2 (UPS).
Current name: ***Heliotropium supinum*** L. (Boraginaceae).

Helleborus foetidus Linnaeus, *Species Plantarum* 1: 558. 1753.
"Habitat in Germania, Helvetia, Gallia." RCN: 4109.
Lectotype (Mathew in Jarvis & al. in *Taxon* 54: 469. 2005): Herb. Linn. No. 718.6 (LINN).
Current name: ***Helleborus foetidus*** L. (Ranunculaceae).
Note: Mathew (*Hellebores*: 55. 1989) indicated unspecified material in LINN as type but this did not distinguish between sheets 718.6 and 718.7 (LINN). They do not appear to form part of a single gathering, and Art. 9.15 therefore does not apply. One of the two sheets was subsequently designated as lectotype by the same author.

Helleborus hyemalis Linnaeus, *Species Plantarum* 1: 557. 1753.
"Habitat in Lombardia, Italia, Apenninis." RCN: 4106.
Lectotype (Sell in Jonsell & Jarvis in *Nordic J. Bot.* 14: 161. 1994): Herb. Clifford: 227, *Helleborus* 4 (BM-000628873).
Current name: ***Eranthis hyemalis*** (L.) Salisb. (Ranunculaceae).
Note: Although Riedl (in Rechinger, *Fl. Iranica* 171: 34. 1992) indicated unspecified material at LINN as type, this does not distinguish between sheets 718.1 and 718.2. As they are evidently not part of a single gathering, Art. 9.15 does not apply.

Helleborus niger Linnaeus, *Species Plantarum* 1: 558. 1753.
"Habitat in Austria, Hetruria, Appeninis." RCN: 4107.
Lectotype (Jonsell & Jarvis in Jarvis & al., *Regnum Veg.* 127: 53. 1993): Herb. Clifford: 227, *Helleborus* 3 (BM-000628872).
Generitype of *Helleborus* Linnaeus (vide Green, *Prop. Brit. Bot.*: 164. 1929).
Current name: ***Helleborus niger*** L. (Ranunculaceae).

Helleborus trifolius Linnaeus, *Species Plantarum* 1: 558. 1753.
"Habitat in Canada, Sibiria." RCN: 4110.
Lectotype (Reveal in Jarvis & al. in *Taxon* 54: 469. 2005): *Steller?*, Herb. Linn. No. 718.8 (LINN).
Current name: ***Coptis trifolia*** (L.) Salisb. (Ranunculaceae).

Helleborus viridis Linnaeus, *Species Plantarum* 1: 558. 1753.
"Habitat in montibus Viennensibus, Euganeis." RCN: 4108.
Lectotype (Mathew, *Hellebores*: 112. 1989): Herb. Linn. No. 718.5 (LINN).

Current name: ***Helleborus viridis*** L. subsp. *viridis* (Ranunculaceae).
Note: Zanotti & Cristofolini (in *Webbia* 49: 7, f. 3a. 1994) designated Herb. Clifford: 227, *Helleborus* 4 (BM) as lectotype. However, their choice is pre-dated by that of Mathew. Although he did not provide a sheet number, there is only one sheet at LINN assocated with this name and (on p. 111), he indicates that Linnaeus' "type specimen" belongs to the larger flowered form found in northern Italy and Austria.

Helonias asphodeloides Linnaeus, *Species Plantarum*, ed. 2, 1: 485. 1762.
"Habitat in Pensylvania. Barthram." RCN: 2624.
Lectotype (designated here by Reveal): *Bartram*, Herb. Linn. No. 471.2 (LINN).
Current name: ***Xerophyllum asphodeloides*** (L.) Nutt. (Liliaceae/Melanthiaceae).

Helonias bullata Linnaeus, *Species Plantarum* 1: 342. 1753.
"Habitat in Pensylvaniae paludosis." RCN: 2623.
Lectotype (Reveal in Jarvis & al., *Regnum Veg.* 127: 53. 1993): *Kalm*, Herb. Linn. No. 471.1 (LINN; iso- BM).
Generitype of *Helonias* Linnaeus.
Current name: ***Helonias bullata*** L. (Liliaceae/Melanthiaceae).

Helonias minuta Linnaeus, *Mantissa Plantarum Altera*: 225. 1771.
"Habitat juxta urbem Cap. b. spei locis glareosis." RCN: 2625.
Type not designated.
Original material: none traced.
Note: The application of this name appears to be uncertain.

Helvella crispa (Scopoli) Fries, *Systema Mycologicum* 2: 13. 1822.
Basionym: *Phallus crispus* Scop. (1772).
Type not designated.
Generitype of *Helvella* Linnaeus : Fr., *orth. sanct.* (vide Dissing in *Dansk Bot. Ark.* 25: 30. 1966).
Current name: ***Helvella crispa*** (Scop.) Fr. (Helvellaceae).

Helvella mitra Linnaeus, *Species Plantarum*, ed. 2, 2: 1649. 1763.
"Habitat in Truncis putridis." RCN: 8492.
Type not designated.
Original material: [icon] in Mentzel, Ind. Nom. Pl. Univ.: t. 6. 1682; [icon] in Micheli, Nov. Pl. Gen.: 204, t. 86, f. 7. 1729.
Current name: ***Helvella crispa*** (Scop.) Fr. (Helvellaceae).
Note: This name first appeared in 1753 as "*Elvela*" *mitra*, the generic spelling used there now being regarded as an orthographic error for "Helvella" to which it was corrected by Linnaeus in 1763.

Helvella pineti Linnaeus, *Species Plantarum*, ed. 2, 2: 1649. 1763.
"Habitat in Pinu, Abiete." RCN: 8493.
Type not designated.
Original material: none traced.
Current name: ***Thelephora terrestris*** Ehrh.: Fr. (Thelephoraceae).
Note: This name first appeared in 1753 as "*Elvela*" *pineti*, the generic spelling used there now being regarded as an orthographic error for "Helvella" to which it was corrected by Linnaeus in 1763.

Hemerocallis flava (Linnaeus) Linnaeus, *Species Plantarum*, ed. 2, 1: 462. 1762, *nom. illeg.*
"Habitat in Sibiriae, Hungariae campis uliginosis." RCN: 2525.
Basionym: *H. lilioasphodelus* L. var. *flava* L. (1753).
Type not designated.
Original material: as basionym.
Current name: ***Hemerocallis lilioasphodelus*** L. (Liliaceae/Hemerocallidaceae).

Note: Linnaeus included the primary phrase name and the complete synonymy for *H. lilioasphodelus,* as well as that for var. *flava* under this name.

Hemerocallis fulva (Linnaeus) Linnaeus, *Species Plantarum,* ed. 2, 1: 462. 1762.
"Habitat in China." RCN: 2526.
Basionym: *Hemerocallis lilioasphodelus* L. var. *fulva* L. (1753).
Type not designated.
Original material: as basionym.
Current name: ***Hemerocallis fulva*** (L.) L. (Liliaceae/Hemerocallidaceae).

Hemerocallis liliastrum Linnaeus, *Species Plantarum* 1: 324. 1753.
"Habitat in Alpibus Helveticis, Allobrogicis." RCN: 2447.
Basionym of: *Anthericum liliastrum* (L.) L. (1762).
Type not designated.
Original material: Herb. Clifford: 128, *Hemerocallis* 2 (BM); Herb. A. van Royen No. 913.18–70 (L); Herb. Linn. No. 432.9 (LINN); Herb. A. van Royen No. 913.18–65 (L); [icon] in Daléchamps, Hist. General. Pl. 1: 852. 1587; [icon] in Clusius, Cur. Post. (App. Alt.): [13]. 1611.
Current name: ***Paradisea liliastrum*** (L.) Bertol. (Liliaceae/Asphodelaceae).

Hemerocallis lilioasphodelus Linnaeus, *Species Plantarum* 1: 324. 1753.
"Habitat α in Hungariae, Sibiriae campis uliginosis, at β. Hybrida & constans, ex India Orientali." RCN: 2526.
Type not designated.
Original material: Herb. Clifford: 128, *Hemerocallis* 1 α (BM); Herb. A. van Royen No. 908.62–564 (L); Herb. A. van Royen No. 908.106–1581 (L).
Generitype of *Hemerocallis* Linnaeus.
Current name: ***Hemerocallis lilioasphodelus*** L. (Liliaceae/Hemerocallidaceae).
Note: Specific epithet spelled "Lilio Asphodelus" in the protologue. Bailey (in *Gentes Herb.* 2: 143. 1930) noted the existence of material at LINN but did not designate a type.

Hemerocallis lilioasphodelus Linnaeus var. **flava** Linnaeus, *Species Plantarum* 1: 324. 1753.
"Habitat α in Hungariae, Sibiriae campis uliginosis." RCN: 2525.
Basionym of: *Hemerocallis flava* (L.) L. (1762), *nom. illeg.*
Type not designated.
Original material: Herb. Burser III: 122 (UPS); Herb. Linn. No. 446.1 (LINN); [icon] in Clusius, Rar. Pl. Hist. 1: 137. 1601.
Current name: ***Hemerocallis lilioasphodelus*** L. (Liliaceae/Hemerocallidaceae).
Note: Varietal epithet spelled "flavus" in the protologue.

Hemerocallis lilioasphodelus Linnaeus var. **fulva** Linnaeus, *Species Plantarum* 1: 324. 1753.
"Habitat β. Hybrida & constans, ex India Orientali." RCN: 2526.
Basionym of: *Hemerocallis fulva* (L.) L. (1762).
Type not designated.
Original material: Herb. Burser III: 123 (UPS); Herb. Linn. No. 446.2 (LINN).
Current name: ***Hemerocallis fulva*** (L.) L. (Liliaceae/Hemerocallidaceae).
Note: Varietal epithet spelled "fulvus" in the protologue.

Hemimeris bonae-spei Linnaeus, *Plantae Rariores Africanae*: 8. 1760.
["Habitat ad Cap. bon. spei."] Sp. Pl., ed. 2, 1: 20 (1762). RCN: 104.

Basionym of: *Paederota bonae-spei* (L.) L. (1762).
Type not designated.
Original material: *Oldenland,* Herb. Burman (G); [icon] in Plukenet, Phytographia: t. 320, f. 5. 1694; Almag. Bot.: 383. 1696.
Generitype of *Hemimeris* Linnaeus, *nom. rej.*
Current name: ***Diascia capensis*** (L.) Britten (Scrophulariaceae).
Note: *Hemimeris* Linnaeus, *nom. rej.* in favour of *Hemimeris* Linnaeus filius.

Hemionitis lanceolata Linnaeus, *Species Plantarum* 2: 1077. 1753.
"Habitat in America meridionali." RCN: 7820.
Lectotype (Proctor, *Ferns Jamaica*: 258. 1985): [icon] *"Lingua Cervina, angustifolia, et reticulata"* in Plumier, Traité Foug. Amér.: 111, t. 127, f. C. 1705.
Current name: ***Polytaenium feei*** (Schaffner ex Fée) Maxon (Vittariaceae).

Hemionitis palmata Linnaeus, *Species Plantarum* 2: 1077. 1753.
"Habitat in America meridionali." RCN: 7822.
Lectotype (Tryon in *Contr. Gray Herb.* 194: 85. 1964): Herb. Linn. No. 1248.3 (LINN).
Generitype of *Hemionitis* Linnaeus (vide Kaulfuss, *Enum. Fil.*: 68, 198. 1824; Smith, *Hist. Fil.*: 150. 1875).
Current name: ***Hemionitis palmata*** L. (Pteridaceae).

Hemionitis parasitica Linnaeus, *Systema Naturae,* ed. 10, 2: 1322. 1759.
["Habitat in Jamaica."] Sp. Pl., ed. 2, 2: 1535 (1763). RCN: 7821.
Lectotype (Proctor, *Ferns Jamaica*: 254. 1985): Herb. Linn. No. 1248.2 (LINN).
Current name: ***Anetium citrifolium*** (L.) Splitg. (Vittariaceae).

Heracleum alpinum Linnaeus, *Species Plantarum* 1: 250. 1753.
"Habitat in Helvetiae Alpibus." RCN: 2008.
Lectotype (Reduron & Watson in Jarvis & al. in *Taxon* 55: 212. 2006): Herb. Burser VIII: 22 (UPS).
Current name: ***Heracleum sphondylium*** L. subsp. **alpinum** (L.) Bonnier & Layens (Apiaceae).

Heracleum angustifolium Linnaeus, *Systema Naturae,* ed. 12, 2: 210; *Mantissa Plantarum*: 57. 1767, *nom. illeg.*
"Habitat in Svecia, Anglia." RCN: 2004.
Lectotype (Reduron in Jarvis & al. in *Taxon* 55: 212. 2006): Herb. Linn. No. 352.2 (LINN).
Current name: ***Heracleum sphondylium*** L. subsp. **sibiricum** (L.) Simonk. (Apiaceae).

Heracleum austriacum Linnaeus, *Species Plantarum* 1: 249. 1753.
"Habitat in Alpibus Austriae." RCN: 2007.
Lectotype (Watson in Jarvis & al. in *Taxon* 55: 212. 2006): Herb. Burser VIII: 21 (UPS).
Current name: ***Heracleum austriacum*** L. (Apiaceae).

Heracleum panaces Linnaeus, *Species Plantarum* 1: 249. 1753.
"Habitat in Apenninis, Sibiria." RCN: 2006.
Lectotype (Reduron & Watson in Jarvis & al. in *Taxon* 55: 212. 2006): Herb. Linn. No. 352.7 (LINN).
Current name: ***Heracleum panaces*** L. (Apiaceae).

Heracleum sibiricum Linnaeus, *Species Plantarum* 1: 249. 1753.
"Habitat in Sibiria." RCN: 2005.
Lectotype (Reduron in Jonsell & Jarvis in *Nordic J. Bot.* 22: 84. 2002): Herb. Linn. No. 352.5 (LINN).
Current name: ***Heracleum sphondylium*** L. subsp. **sibiricum** (L.) Simonk. (Apiaceae).

Heracleum sphondylium Linnaeus, *Species Plantarum* 1: 249. 1753.
"Habitat in Europae nemorosis." RCN: 2003.
Lectotype (Reduron & Jarvis in Jarvis & al., *Regnum Veg.* 127: 53.
  1993): Herb. Clifford: 103, *Heracleum* 1, sheet 3 (BM-000558354).
Generitype of *Heracleum* Linnaeus (vide Hitchcock, *Prop. Brit. Bot.*:
  140. 1929).
Current name: ***Heracleum sphondylium*** L. (Apiaceae).

Hermannia alnifolia Linnaeus, *Species Plantarum* 2: 674. 1753.
"Habitat in Aethiopia." RCN: 4916.
Lectotype (Verdoorn in *Bothalia* 13: 44. 1980): Herb. Linn. No.
  854.5 (LINN).
Current name: ***Hermannia alnifolia*** L. (Sterculiaceae).

Hermannia althaeifolia Linnaeus, *Species Plantarum* 2: 673. 1753.
"Habitat in Aethiopia." RCN: 4914.
Lectotype (Verdoorn in *Bothalia* 13: 29. 1980): Herb. Clifford: 342,
  Hermannia 5 (BM-000646395).
Current name: ***Hermannia althaeifolia*** L. (Sterculiaceae).
Note: Specific epithet spelled "althaeaefolia" in the protologue.

Hermannia grossularifolia Linnaeus, *Species Plantarum* 2: 673. 1753.
"Habitat in Aethiopia." RCN: 4922.
Lectotype (de Winter in *Bothalia* 11: 263. 1974): Herb. Linn. No.
  854.14 (LINN).
Current name: ***Hermannia grossularifolia*** L. (Sterculiaceae).

Hermannia hyssopifolia Linnaeus, *Species Plantarum* 2: 674. 1753.
"Habitat in Aethiopia." RCN: 4917.
Lectotype (Verdoorn in *Bothalia* 13: 35. 1980): Herb. Clifford: 342,
  Hermannia 3 (BM-000646393).
Generitype of *Hermannia* Linnaeus (vide Green, *Prop. Brit. Bot.*: 172.
  1929).
Current name: ***Hermannia hyssopifolia*** L. (Sterculiaceae).

Hermannia lavendulifolia Linnaeus, *Species Plantarum* 2: 674. 1753.
"Habitat in Aethiopia." RCN: 4918.
Lectotype (Verdoorn in *Bothalia* 13: 37. 1980): Herb. Clifford: 342,
  Hermannia 2 (BM-000646392).
Current name: ***Hermannia lavendulifolia*** L. (Sterculiaceae).

Hermannia pinnata Linnaeus, *Species Plantarum* 2: 674. 1753.
"Habitat in Aethiopia." RCN: 2260.
Basionym of: *Mahernia pinnata* (L.) L. (1767).
Lectotype (de Winter in *Bothalia* 11: 264. 1974): Herb. Clifford: 342,
  Hermannia 6 (BM-000646396).
Current name: ***Hermannia pinnata*** L. (Sterculiaceae).

Hermannia trifoliata Linnaeus, *Species Plantarum* 2: 674. 1753.
"Habitat in Aethiopia." RCN: 4920.
Lectotype (Verdoorn in *Bothalia* 13: 25. 1980): Herb. Clifford: 342,
  Hermannia 1 (BM-000646391).
Current name: ***Hermannia trifoliata*** L. (Sterculiaceae).

Hermannia trifurca Linnaeus, *Plantae Rariores Africanae*: 13. 1760.
RCN: 4915.
Lectotype (Verdoorn in *Bothalia* 13: 20. 1980): Herb. Linn. No.
  854.4 (LINN).
Current name: ***Hermannia trifurca*** L. (Sterculiaceae).
Note: Verdoorn indicated a specimen at LINN ("no. 854") as type, but
  he can only have intended 854.4, which is accepted as an effective
  choice.

Hermannia triphylla Linnaeus, *Plantae Rariores Africanae*: 13. 1760.
["Habitat ad Cap. b. spei."] Sp. Pl., ed. 2, 2: 942 (1763). RCN: 4921.

Type not designated.
Original material: none traced.
Note: The application of this name appears uncertain.

Hermas depauperata Linnaeus, *Mantissa Plantarum Altera*: 299.
  1771, *nom. illeg.*
"Habitat ad Cap. b. Spei." RCN: 7649.
Replaced synonym: *Bupleurum villosum* L. (1753).
Lectotype (Burtt in Jarvis & al., *Regnum Veg.* 127: 53. 1993): [icon]
  "Perfoliata foliis oblongis, sinuosis, subtus incanis" in Burman, Rar.
  Afric. Pl.: 196, t. 71, f. 2. 1739.
Generitype of *Hermas* Linnaeus.
Current name: ***Hermas villosa*** (L.) Thunb. (Apiaceae).
Note: Burtt (in *Notes Roy. Bot. Gard. Edinburgh* 48: 213. 1991)
  suggested that 1227.1 (LINN) was probably the specimen upon
  which this was based. However, *H. depauperata* is an illegitimate
  replacement name in *Hermas* for *Bupleurum villosum* L. (1753) and
  homotypic with it. The material in LINN appears to be a post-1753
  addition to the collection and not original material for *B. villosum*.
  For this reason, Burtt (1993) typified the name on the cited
  Burman illustration (though f. 1 and its corresponding polynomial
  was unfortunately cited in error for f. 2).

Hernandia ovigera Linnaeus, *Herbarium Amboinense*: 14. 1754.
["Habitat in India orientali."] Sp. Pl., ed. 2, 2: 1392 (1763). RCN:
  7108.
Lectotype (Merrill, *Interpret. Rumph. Herb. Amb.*: 33, 239. 1917):
  [icon] *"Arbor Ovigera"* in Rumphius, Herb. Amboin. 3: 193, t. 123.
  1743.
Current name: ***Hernandia ovigera*** L. (Hernandiaceae).

Hernandia sonora Linnaeus, *Species Plantarum* 2: 981. 1753.
"Habitat in Indiis." RCN: 7107.
Lectotype (Stearn, *Introd. Linnaeus' Sp. Pl.* (Ray Soc. ed.): 47. 1957):
  [icon] *"Hernandia"* in Linnaeus, Hort. Cliff.: 485, t. 33. 1738.
Generitype of *Hernandia* Linnaeus.
Current name: ***Hernandia sonora*** L. (Hernandiaceae).

Herniaria fruticosa Linnaeus, *Centuria I Plantarum*: 8. 1755.
"Habitat in Hispania." RCN: 1796.
Lectotype (Chaudhri in Cafferty & Jarvis in *Taxon* 53: 1052. 2004):
  Löfling 186a, Herb. Linn. No. 312.4 (LINN).
Current name: ***Herniaria fruticosa*** L. (Caryophyllaceae).
Note: Chaudhri (in *Meded. Bot. Mus. Herb. Rijks Univ. Utrecht* 285:
  386. 1968) stated "Type: Spain: Herb. Linnaeus 312/3–4 (LINN)".
  This did not distinguish between the two cited sheets, the material
  of which does not appear to be part of a single gathering (so Art.
  9.15 does not apply). Chaudhri subsequently designated a Löfling
  collection as the lectotype.

Herniaria glabra Linnaeus, *Species Plantarum* 1: 218. 1753.
"Habitat in Europae apricis, glareosis, siccis." RCN: 1794.
Lectotype (Pugsley in *J. Bot.* 68: 214. 1930): Herb. Linn. No. 312.1
  (LINN).
Generitype of *Herniaria* Linnaeus (vide Hitchcock, *Prop. Brit. Bot.*:
  137. 1929).
Current name: ***Herniaria glabra*** L. (Caryophyllaceae).

Herniaria hirsuta Linnaeus, *Species Plantarum* 1: 218. 1753.
"Habitat in Angliae, Hispaniae, Italiae agris." RCN: 1795.
Lectotype (Hartvig in Strid & Kit Tan, *Fl. Hellenica* 1: 231. 1997):
  Herb. Linn. No. 312.2 (LINN).
Current name: ***Herniaria hirsuta*** L. (Caryophyllaceae).
Note: Chaudhri (in *Pakistan Syst.* 1(2): 30. 1977) indicated unseen
  Bauhin material in BAS as the holotype. However, this collection
  was not seen by Linnaeus and is not original material for the name.

Herniaria lenticulata Linnaeus, *Species Plantarum* 1: 218. 1753.
"Habitat in Hispaniae montibus Escurial, Monspelii." RCN: 1797.
Neotype (designated here by Staples): Herb. Linn. No. 312.5 (LINN).
Current name: ***Cressa cretica*** L. (Convolvulaceae).
Note: Burtt & Lewis (in *Kew Bull.* 7: 337–338. 1952) argued that
although 312.5 (LINN) is identifiable as *Cressa cretica* L.
(Convolvulaceae), it is not original material for *H. lenticulata*,
which should be based instead on material in Herb. Bauhin (BAS).
This, too, would not be original material but Burtt & Lewis
declined to make any formal type choice. Chaudhri (*Rev.
Paronychiinae*: 398. 1968), however, excluded this name from
Herniaria and treated it as a synonym of *Cressa cretica*. In the
absence of original material, this synonymy is formalised by the
designation of 312.5 (LINN) as a neotype.

Hesperis africana Linnaeus, *Species Plantarum* 2: 663. 1753.
"Habitat in Africa." RCN: 4832.
Lectotype (Ball in Cafferty & Jarvis in *Taxon* 51: 533. 2002): Herb.
Clifford: 335, *Hesperis* 3 (BM-000646325).
Current name: ***Malcolmia africana*** (L.) R. Br. (Brassicaceae).
Note: Botschantzev (in *Bot. Zhurn.* 57: 1038. 1972) indicated
unspecified material at LINN (but evidently 841.5) as type, as have
later authors, but the lack of a relevant *Species Plantarum* number
(in this case "4") indicates it is a post-1753 addition to the
herbarium.

Hesperis dentata Linnaeus, *Species Plantarum* 2: 664. 1753.
"Habitat in Sicilia." RCN: 4785.
Type not designated.
Original material: Herb. A. van Royen No. 901.256–327 (L); Herb.
A. van Royen No. 901.256–326? (L); [icon] in Dillenius, Hort.
Eltham. 1: 179, t. 148, f. 177. 1732.
Current name: ***Rorippa dentata*** (L.) O. Bolòs & Vigo (Brassicaceae).

Hesperis inodora Linnaeus, *Species Plantarum*, ed. 2, 2: 927. 1763.
"Habitat Wiennae, Monspelii." RCN: 4831.
Lectotype (Ball in Cafferty & Jarvis in *Taxon* 51: 533. 2002): *Jacquin
67*, Herb. Linn. No. 841.4 (LINN), see p. 213.
Current name: ***Hesperis inodora*** L. (Brassicaceae).

Hesperis lacera (Linnaeus) Linnaeus, *Systema Vegetabilium*, ed. 13:
501. 1774.
["Habitat in Lusitania."] Sp, Pl. 2: 762 (1753). RCN: 4834.
Basionym: *Cheiranthus lacerus* L. (1753).
Lectotype (Ball in Cafferty & Jarvis in *Taxon* 51: 532. 2002): [icon]
"Leucoium Lusitanicum purpureum" in Hermann, Parad. Bat.: 193.
1698. – Epitype (Ball in Cafferty & Jarvis in *Taxon* 51: 532. 2002):
Portugal. Abundant in sandy places by the Douro, about Pinhão, 10
Jun 1889, *R.P. Murray s.n.* (BM).
Current name: ***Malcolmia lacera*** (L.) DC. (Brassicaceae).

Hesperis matronalis Linnaeus, *Species Plantarum* 2: 663. 1753.
"Habitat in Italia." RCN: 4829.
Lectotype (Ball in Jarvis & al., *Regnum Veg.* 127: 54. 1993): Herb.
Clifford: 335, *Hesperis* 2 (BM-000646321).
Generitype of *Hesperis* Linnaeus (vide Green, *Prop. Brit. Bot.*: 171.
1929).
Current name: ***Hesperis matronalis*** L. subsp. ***matronalis***
(Brassicaceae).

Hesperis provincialis Linnaeus, *Species Plantarum* 2: 664. 1753.
"Habitat in Galloprovincia." RCN: 4821.
Lectotype (Gowler in Cafferty & Jarvis in *Taxon* 51: 533. 2002):
Herb. Clifford: 335, *Cheiranthus* 4 (BM-000646317).
Current name: ***Matthiola fruticulosa*** (L.) Maire (Brassicaceae).

Hesperis sibirica Linnaeus, *Species Plantarum* 2: 663. 1753.
"Habitat in Sibiria." RCN: 4830.
Lectotype (Ebel in Cafferty & Jarvis in *Taxon* 51: 533. 2002): Herb.
Linn. No. 841.3 (LINN).
Current name: ***Hesperis matronalis*** L. subsp. ***matronalis***
(Brassicaceae).

Hesperis tristis Linnaeus, *Species Plantarum* 2: 663. 1753.
"Habitat in Hungaria." RCN: 4828.
Lectotype (Ball in Cafferty & Jarvis in *Taxon* 51: 533. 2002): Herb.
Linn. No. 841.1 (LINN).
Current name: ***Hesperis tristis*** L. (Brassicaceae).

Hesperis verna Linnaeus, *Species Plantarum* 2: 664. 1753.
"Habitat in Galloprovinciae maritimis." RCN: 4833.
Lectotype (Meikle, *Fl. Cyprus* 1: 150. 1977): Herb. Linn. No. 841.6
(LINN).
Current name: ***Arabis verna*** (L.) R. Br. (Brassicaceae).

Heuchera americana Linnaeus, *Species Plantarum* 1: 226. 1753.
"Habitat in Virginia." RCN: 1852.
Lectotype (Reveal in Jarvis & al., *Regnum Veg.* 127: 54. 1993): Herb.
Clifford: 82, *Heuchera* 1 (BM-000558190).
Generitype of *Heuchera* Linnaeus.
Current name: ***Heuchera americana*** L. (Saxifragaceae).
Note: Fernald (in *Rhodora* 43: 496. 1941; 44: 39. 1942) discussed
many of the original elements but did not typify the name, and
Wells (in *Syst. Bot. Monogr.* 3: 83, 90. 1984) noted the Clayton and
Clifford sheets but also did not make a typification. Reveal appears
to have been the first to make an unambiguous choice.

Hibiscus abelmoschus Linnaeus, *Species Plantarum* 2: 696. 1753.
"Habitat in Indiis." RCN: 5096.
Lectotype (Borssum Waalkes in *Blumea* 14: 92. 1966): Herb. Clifford:
349, *Hibiscus* 4 (BM-000646497).
Current name: ***Hibiscus abelmoschus*** L. (Malvaceae).

Hibiscus aethiopicus Linnaeus, *Mantissa Plantarum Altera*: 258.
1771.
"Habitat ad Cap. b. spei." RCN: 5103.
Type not designated.
Original material: Herb. Linn. No. 875.37 (LINN); [icon] in
Plukenet, Phytographia: t. 254, f. 2. 1694; Almag. Bot.: 13.
1696.
Current name: ***Hibiscus aethiopicus*** L. (Malvaceae).

Hibiscus brasiliensis Linnaeus, *Species Plantarum*, ed. 2, 2: 977.
1763.
"Habitat in Brasilia." RCN: 5085.
Type not designated.
Original material: [icon] in Plumier in Burman, Pl. Amer.: 153, t.
160, f. 1. 1758.
Current name: ***Hibiscus brasiliensis*** L. (Malvaceae).
Note: This has been treated as a *nomen dubium* by some authors,
including Robyns (in *Ann. Missouri Bot. Gard.* 52: 509. 1966) and
Fryxell (in *Fl. Neotropica* 76: 254. 1999), but no proposal for
rejection has been made. *Hibiscus phoenicea* Jacq. has sometimes
been taken up in its place.

Hibiscus cancellatus Linnaeus, *Plantae Surinamenses*: 12. 1775.
"Habitat [in Surinamo.]" RCN: 5108.
Lectotype (Fryxell in *Syst. Bot. Monogr.* 25: 319. 1988): Herb. Linn.
No. 875.8 (LINN; iso- S?).
Current name: ***Pavonia cancellata*** (L.) Cav. (Malvaceae).

Hibiscus cannabinus Linnaeus, *Systema Naturae*, ed. 10, 2: 1149. 1759.
["Habitat in India."] Sp. Pl., ed. 2, 2: 979 (1763). RCN: 5093.
Neotype (Wijnands, *Bot. Commelins*: 144. 1983): [icon] *"Alcea Bengalensis spinosissima"* in Commelin, Hort. Med. Amstelod. Pl. Rar. 1: 35, t. 18. 1697.
Current name: *Hibiscus cannabinus* L. (Malvaceae).
Note: Following a suggestion by Borssum Waalkes (in *Blumea* 14: 63. 1966), Wijnands treated a Commelin plate as the lectotype. However, this is not cited in the protologue (though it was added in the later account in *Sp. Pl.*, ed. 2, 2: 979. 1763). It is therefore not original material for the name but, in the absence of any original material at all (sheet 875.27 (LINN) is original material for *H. sabdariffa* L.), Wijnands' statement is treated as correctable to a neotypification (Art. 9.8).

Hibiscus clypeatus Linnaeus, *Systema Naturae*, ed. 10, 2: 1149. 1759.
["Habitat in America."] Sp. Pl., ed. 2, 2: 980 (1763). RCN: 5098.
Lectotype (Fryxell in *Syst. Bot. Monogr.* 25: 203. 1988): [icon] *"Hibiscus foliis cordato-angulatis"* in Plumier in Burman, Pl. Amer.: 153, t. 160, f. 2. 1758.
Current name: *Hibiscus clypeatus* L. (Malvaceae).

Hibiscus esculentus Linnaeus, *Species Plantarum* 2: 696. 1753.
"Habitat in Indiis." RCN: 5097.
Lectotype (Borssum Waalkes in *Blumea* 14: 100. 1966): Herb. Linn. No. 875.31 (LINN).
Current name: *Hibiscus esculentus* L. (Malvaceae).
Note: Although Fawcett & Rendle (*Fl. Jamaica* 5: 143. 1926) indicated material in LINN as type, they did not distinguish between sheets 875.31 and 875.32 (which are evidently not part of a single gathering so Art. 9.15 does not apply).

Hibiscus ficulneus Linnaeus, *Species Plantarum* 2: 695. 1753.
"Habitat in Zeylona." RCN: 5091.
Lectotype (Borssum Waalkes in *Blumea* 14: 102. 1966): [icon] *"Ketmia Zeylanica, Fici folio, perianthio oblongo integro"* in Dillenius, Hort. Eltham. 1: 190, t. 157, f. 190. 1732.
Current name: *Hibiscus ficulneus* L. (Malvaceae).

Hibiscus fraternus Linnaeus, *Plantae Surinamenses*: 12. 1775.
"Habitat [in Surinamo.]" RCN: 5105.
Lectotype (Fryxell in *Syst. Bot. Monogr.* 25: 225. 1988): Herb. Linn. No. 875.36 (LINN; iso- S).
Current name: *Hibiscus sabdariffa* L. (Malvaceae).

Hibiscus hirtus Linnaeus, *Species Plantarum* 2: 694. 1753.
"Habitat in India." RCN: 5086.
Lectotype (Borssum Waalkes in *Blumea* 14: 76. 1966): Herb. Linn. No. 875.18 (LINN).
Current name: *Hibiscus hirtus* L. (Malvaceae).

Hibiscus malvaviscus Linnaeus, *Species Plantarum* 2: 694. 1753.
"Habitat in Mexico." RCN: 5088.
Lectotype (Borssum Waalkes in *Blumea* 14: 132. 1966): Herb. Clifford: 349, *Hibiscus* 2 (BM-000646495).
Current name: *Malvaviscus arboreus* Cav. (Malvaceae).

Hibiscus manihot Linnaeus, *Species Plantarum* 2: 696. 1753.
"Habitat in Indiis." RCN: 5095.
Lectotype (Borssum Waalkes in *Blumea* 14: 97. 1966): Herb. Clifford: 350, *Hibiscus* 5 (BM-000646498).
Current name: *Hibiscus manihot* L. (Malvaceae).

Hibiscus moscheutos Linnaeus, *Species Plantarum* 2: 693. 1753.
"Habitat in Canada, Virginia." RCN: 5079.
Lectotype (designated here by Reveal): Herb. Linn. No. 875.1 (LINN).
Current name: *Hibiscus moscheutos* L. (Malvaceae).
Note: See comments by Fernald (in *Rhodora* 44: 270. 1942).

Hibiscus mutabilis Linnaeus, *Species Plantarum* 2: 694. 1753.
"Habitat in India." RCN: 5087.
Lectotype (Fawcett & Rendle, *Fl. Jamaica* 5: 140. 1926): Herb. Linn. No. 875.20 (LINN).
Current name: *Hibiscus mutabilis* L. (Malvaceae).

Hibiscus palustris Linnaeus, *Species Plantarum* 2: 693. 1753.
"Habitat in Virginia. Gronov. Canada. Kalm." RCN: 5080.
Lectotype (designated here by Reveal): Herb. Burser XVIII(1): 21 (UPS).
Current name: *Hibiscus palustris* L. (Malvaceae).

Hibiscus pentacarpos Linnaeus, *Species Plantarum* 2: 697. 1753.
"Habitat in paludosis Venetiae." RCN: 5102.
Type not designated.
Original material: [icon] in Zannichelli, Istoria Piante: 155, t. 91. 1735.
Current name: *Kosteletzkya pentacarpos* (L.) Ledeb. (Malvaceae).

Hibiscus populneus Linnaeus, *Species Plantarum* 2: 694. 1753.
"Habitat in India." RCN: 5081.
Lectotype (Fawcett & Rendle, *Fl. Jamaica* 5: 145. 1926): Herb. Hermann 4: 54, No. 258 (BM-000628263).
Current name: *Thespesia populnea* (L.) Sol. ex Corrêa (Malvaceae).

Hibiscus rosa-sinensis Linnaeus, *Species Plantarum* 2: 694. 1753.
"Habitat in India." RCN: 5084.
Lectotype (Borssum Waalkes in *Blumea* 14: 72. 1966): Herb. Hermann 3: 4, No. 260 (BM-000621802).
Current name: *Hibiscus rosa-sinensis* L. (Malvaceae).
Note: Although Fawcett & Rendle (*Fl. Jamaica* 5: 138. 1926) indicated material in LINN as type, they did not distinguish between sheets 875.15 and 875.16 (which are evidently not part of a single gathering so Art. 9.15 does not apply).

Hibiscus sabdariffa Linnaeus, *Species Plantarum* 2: 695. 1753, *nom. cons.*
"Habitat in India." RCN: 5092.
Conserved type (Fryxell in *Taxon* 50: 929. 2001): Herb. Clifford: 350, *Hibiscus* 6 (BM-000646500).
Current name: *Hibiscus sabdariffa* L. (Malvaceae).

Hibiscus salicifolius Linnaeus, *Plantae Surinamenses*: 12. 1775.
"Habitat [in Surinamo.]" RCN: 5107.
Lectotype (Fryxell, *Fl. Neotropica* 76: 192. 1999): Herb. Linn. No. 875.41 (LINN).
Current name: *Pavonia fruticosa* (Mill.) Fawc. & Rendle (Malvaceae).

Hibiscus simplex Linnaeus, *Species Plantarum*, ed. 2, 2: 977. 1763.
"Habitat in Asia." RCN: 5083.
Type not designated.
Original material: none traced.
Current name: *Firmiana simplex* (L.) W. Wight (Sterculiaceae).
Note: See notes by Ridley (in *Bull. Misc. Inform. Kew* 1934: 215. 1934) and a detailed discussion by Kostermans (in *Reinwardtia* 4: 305–306. 1957), who concluded that 875.12 and 875.13 (LINN) were "the type" of the name. However, these specimens do not

appear to be original material for the name and, as they are not part of a single gathering, Kostermans' statement cannot be accepted as a neotypification (Art. 9.8).

Hibiscus sororius Linnaeus, *Plantae Surinamenses*: 12. 1775.
"Habitat [in Surinamo.]" RCN: 5106.
Lectotype (Fryxell in *Syst. Bot. Monogr.* 25: 226. 1988): Herb. Linn. No. 875.7 (LINN).
Current name: ***Hibiscus sororius*** L. (Malvaceae).

Hibiscus spinifex Linnaeus, *Systema Naturae,* ed. 10, 2: 1149. 1759.
["Habitat in America meridionali."] Sp. Pl., ed. 2, 2: 978 (1763). RCN: 5089.
Lectotype (Fryxell in Howard, *Fl. Lesser Antilles* 5: 243. 1989): [icon] *"Hibiscus foliis cordatis, crenatis"* in Plumier in Burman, Pl. Amer.: 1, t. 1. 1755.
Current name: ***Pavonia spinifex*** (L.) Cav. (Malvaceae).

Hibiscus surattensis Linnaeus, *Species Plantarum* 2: 696, 1200. 1753.
"Habitat in India." RCN: 5094.
Type not designated.
Original material: [icon] in Rumphius, Herb. Amboin. 4: 40, t. 16. 1743.
Current name: ***Hibiscus surattensis*** L. (Malvaceae).
Note: Borssum Waalkes (in *Blumea* 14: 58. 1966) and others have treated 875.29 (LINN) as the type, but the sheet lacks the relevant *Species Plantarum* number (i.e. "12"), and was a post-1753 addition to the collection, and is not original material for the name.

Hibiscus syriacus Linnaeus, *Species Plantarum* 2: 695. 1753, *typ. cons.*
"Habitat in Syria." RCN: 5090.

Lectotype (Abedin in Nasir & Ali, *Fl. W. Pakistan* 130: 13. 1979): Herb. Linn. No. 875.24 (LINN, see below, left; iso- S).
Generitype of *Hibiscus* Linnaeus, *nom. cons.*
Current name: ***Hibiscus syriacus*** L. (Malvaceae).

Hibiscus tiliaceus Linnaeus, *Species Plantarum* 2: 694. 1753.
"Habitat in India." RCN: 5082.
Lectotype (Borssum Waalkes in *Blumea* 14: 31. 1966): Herb. Hermann 3: 51, No. 259 (BM-000594693).
Current name: ***Talipariti tiliaceum*** (L.) Fryxell (Malvaceae).
Note: Borssum Waalkes gave the species number of the type as "258" in error for "259", but as there is no specimen numbered 258 at the given location, this is treated as a correctable error.

Hibiscus trionum Linnaeus, *Species Plantarum* 2: 697. 1753.
"Habitat in Italia, Africa." RCN: 5104.
Type not designated.
Original material: Herb. Burser XVIII(1): 29 (UPS); Herb. A. van Royen No. 908.136–300 (L); [icon] in Plantin, Pl. Stirp. Icon.: 656. 1581.
Current name: ***Hibiscus trionum*** L. (Malvaceae).
Note: Although Fawcett & Rendle (*Fl. Jamaica* 5: 140. 1926) indicated material in LINN as type, they did not distinguish between sheets 875.39 and 875.40, neither of which carries the relevant *Species Plantarum* number (i.e. "20"). Both appear to be post-1753 additions to the collection, and neither is original material for the name.

Hibiscus virginicus Linnaeus, *Species Plantarum* 2: 697. 1753.
"Habitat in Virginiae paludosis salsis." RCN: 5101.
Lectotype (designated here by Reveal): *Clayton 567*, Herb. Linn. 875.35 (LINN; iso- BM).
Current name: ***Kosteletzkya virginica*** (L.) C. Presl ex A. Gray (Malvaceae).

Hibiscus vitifolius Linnaeus, *Species Plantarum* 2: 696. 1753.
"Habitat in India." RCN: 5099.
Lectotype (Brenan & Exell in *Bol. Soc. Brot.,* sér. 2, 32: 70. 1958): Herb. Hermann 4: 39, No. 265 (BM-000628178).
Current name: ***Fioria vitifolia*** (L.) Mattei (Malvaceae).

Hibiscus zeylonicus Linnaeus, *Species Plantarum* 2: 697. 1753.
"Habitat in Zeylona." RCN: 5100.
Lectotype (Abedin in Nasir & Ali, *Fl. W. Pakistan* 130: 98. 1979): Herb. Hermann 4: 81, No. 266 (BM-000594780).
Current name: ***Pavonia zeylonica*** (L.) Cav. (Malvaceae).
Note: Despite two errors in citation ("51" for "81" and "286" for "266"), it is clear which collection Abedin was indicating as the type.

Hieracium alpinum Linnaeus, *Species Plantarum* 2: 800. 1753.
"Habitat in Alpibus Lapponicis, Britannicis." RCN: 5849.
Lectotype (Pugsley in *J. Linn. Soc., Bot.* 54: 40. 1948): Herb. Linn. No. 954.2 (LINN).
Current name: ***Hieracium alpinum*** L. (Asteraceae).

Hieracium amplexicaule Linnaeus, *Species Plantarum* 2: 803. 1753.
"Habitat in Pyrenaeis." RCN: 5869.
Lectotype (Sell in *Watsonia* 16: 336. 1987): Herb. Clifford: 387, *Hieracium* 5 (BM-000646878).
Current name: ***Hieracium amplexicaule*** L. (Asteraceae).

Hieracium aurantiacum Linnaeus, *Species Plantarum* 2: 801. 1753.
"Habitat in Syria, Helvetia." RCN: 5857.
Type not designated.

Original material: Herb. Burser VI: 79 (UPS); Herb. Linn. No. 954.15 (LINN); Herb. Burser VI: 78 (UPS); [icon] in Colonna, Ekphr., ed. 2: 28, 30. 1616; [icon] in Morison, Pl. Hist. Univ. 3: 78, s. 7, t. 8, f. 7. 1699.
Current name: *Hieracium aurantiacum* L. (Asteraceae).
Note: Pugsley (in *J. Linn. Soc., Bot.* 54: 4. 1948) noted that 954.15 (LINN) was available for typification purposes but did not formally choose a type.

Hieracium auricula Linnaeus, *Species Plantarum* 2: 800. 1753.
"Habitat in Europae pratis aridis, juxta agros." RCN: 5854.
Type not designated.
Original material: Herb. Linn. No. 954.10? (LINN); Herb. Burser XV(1): 4? (UPS); Herb. Linn. No. 954.9? (LINN).
Current name: *Hieracium × floribundum* Wimm. & Grab. (Asteraceae).
Note: Sheets 954.9 and 954.10 (LINN) bear specimens belonging to more than one taxon, a situation which led Pugsley (in *J. Linn. Soc., Bot.* 54: 320. 1948) to reject the name as a *nomen confusum*. However, no formal proposal for rejection has been made.

Hieracium blattarioides Linnaeus, *Species Plantarum* 2: 804. 1753.
"Habitat in Pyrenaeis." RCN: 5870.
Basionym of: *Hieracium pyrenaicum* var. *blattarioides* (L.) L. (1767).
Type not designated.
Original material: Herb. Clifford: 387, *Hieracium* 4 (BM).
Current name: *Crepis pyrenaica* (L.) Greuter (Asteraceae).

Hieracium capense Linnaeus, *Plantae Rariores Africanae*: 17. 1760.
RCN: 5861.
Lectotype (Jarvis in *Bot. J. Linn. Soc.* 109: 508, f. 2. 1992): *Oldenland*, Herb. Burman, right specimen (G).
Current name: *Tolpis capensis* (L.) Sch. Bip. (Asteraceae).

Hieracium cerinthoides Linnaeus, *Species Plantarum* 2: 803. 1753.
"Habitat in Pyrenaeis." RCN: 5868.
Type not designated.
Original material: Herb. Linn. No. 954.28 (LINN); Herb. A. van Royen No. 900.316–336 (L).
Current name: *Hieracium cerinthoides* L. (Asteraceae).

Hieracium chondrilloides Linnaeus, *Species Plantarum* 2: 801. 1753.
"Habitat in Sneeberg Austriae inferioris." RCN: 5863.
Type not designated.
Original material: Herb. Burser VI: 87, syntype (UPS); [icon] in Bauhin, Prodr. Theatri Bot.: 64. 1620.
Current name: *Crepis jacquinii* Tausch (Asteraceae).

Hieracium conyzoides Linnaeus, *Amoenitates Academicae* 4: 490. 1759, *nom. nud.*
Type not relevant.
Note: The name is cited without reference to Magnol, *Botanicum Monspeliense* and is therefore a *nomen nudum*.

Hieracium cymosum Linnaeus, *Species Plantarum*, ed. 2, 2: 1126. 1763.
"Habitat in Russia, Dania, Germania, Helvetia." RCN: 5855.
Type not designated.
Original material: Herb. Burser VI: 92? (UPS); Herb. Linn. No. 954.10? (LINN); [icon] in Bauhin & Cherler, Hist. Pl. Univ. 2: 1040. 1651; [icon] in Bauhin, Prodr. Theatri Bot.: 67. 1620.
Current name: *Hieracium cymosum* L. (Asteraceae).

Hieracium dubium Linnaeus, *Species Plantarum* 2: 800. 1753.
"Habitat in Suecia." RCN: 5853.

Type not designated.
Original material: Herb. Linn. No. 954.8 (LINN); Herb. Burser XV(1): 2 (UPS).
Current name: *Hieracium × dubium* L. (Asteraceae).
Note: Pugsley (in *J. Linn. Soc., Bot.* 54: 320. 1948) regarded the name as a *nomen confusum*.

Hieracium glutinosum Linnaeus, *Species Plantarum* 2: 804. 1753.
"Habitat in G. Narbonensi." RCN: 5872.
Type not designated.
Original material: Herb. Burser VI: 49? (UPS).
Current name: *Hieracium glutinosum* L. (Asteraceae).

Hieracium gmelinii Linnaeus, *Species Plantarum* 2: 802. 1753.
"Habitat in Sibiria." RCN: 5859.
Lectotype (Babcock in *Univ. Calif. Publ. Bot.* 22: 962, pl. 19. 1947): *Gmelin s.n.*, Herb. Linn. No. 954.17 (LINN; iso- MW).
Current name: *Crepis gmelinii* (L.) Tausch (Asteraceae).
Note: Specific epithet spelled "Gmelini" in the protologue.

Hieracium gronovii Linnaeus, *Species Plantarum* 2: 802. 1753, *nom. cons.*
"Habitat in Virginia, Pensylania." RCN: 5858.
Conserved type (Reveal in *Taxon* 41: 149. 1992): *Clayton 447* (BM-000051568).
Current name: *Hieracium gronovii* L. (Asteraceae).
Note: Reveal (in *Taxon* 41: 149. 1992) proposed *Clayton 447* (BM) as the conserved type because the lectotype (954.16, LINN), designated by D'Arcy & Tomb (in *Ann. Missouri Bot. Gard.* 62: 1294. 1975) was identifiable as *H. venosum* L. The Committee for Spermatophyta (in *Taxon* 43: 277. 1994) initially voted against the proposal, but later reconsidered the case in the light of changes made to the Code, and subsequently (in *Taxon* 45: 674. 1996) voted unanimously for conservation.

Hieracium hedypnoides Linnaeus, *Species Plantarum* 2: 800. 1753.
"Habitat in Lotharingia, Monspelii." RCN: 5847.
Type not designated.
Original material: [icon] in Clusius, Rar. Pl. Hist. 2: 141, 142. 1601.
Current name: *Hieracium hedypnoides* L. (Asteraceae).

Hieracium incanum Linnaeus, *Species Plantarum* 2: 799. 1753.
"Habitat in Alpibus Danubio imminentibus, Helvetiae, Tauro." RCN: 5846.
Type not designated.
Original material: Herb. Burser VI: 81 (UPS); [icon] in Bauhin & Cherler, Hist. Pl. Univ. 2: 1038. 1651; [icon] in Clusius, Rar. Pl. Hist. 2: 141. 1601.
Current name: *Leontodon incanus* (L.) Schrank (Asteraceae).

Hieracium kalmii Linnaeus, *Species Plantarum* 2: 804. 1753.
"Habitat in Pensylania. Kalm." RCN: 5873.
Lectotype (Lepage in *Naturaliste Canad.* 87: 83. 1960): *Kalm*, Herb. Linn. No. 954.43 (LINN).
Current name: *Hieracium kalmii* L. (Asteraceae).
Note: Reveal (in *Novon* 3: 73. 1993) provides a detailed discussion concerning the type and the application of the name.

Hieracium lyratum Linnaeus, *Species Plantarum* 2: 803. 1753.
"Habitat in Sibiria. D. Gmelin." RCN: 5867.
Lectotype (Babcock in *Univ. Calif. Publ. Bot.* 22: 280, f. 35a. 1947): *Gmelin s.n.*, Herb. Linn. No. 954.27 (LINN).
Current name: *Crepis lyrata* (L.) Froel. (Asteraceae).
Note: Babcock (in *Univ. Calif. Publ. Bot.* 22: f. 35a. 1947) provided a habit drawing stated to be "from type (L)", and also listed a

collection (p. 280) "Siberia: Without locality (L), type of *H. lyratum*". A comparison of Babcock's habit drawing and 954.27 (LINN) shows that the specimen was clearly the model for the sketch. Despite Babcock's use of "L" (rather than "LINN") for the location of the material, it seems clear that this material was his intended type, and this choice is accepted here.

Hieracium murorum Linnaeus, *Species Plantarum* 2: 802. 1753.
"Habitat in Europae apricis duris." RCN: 5865.
Lectotype (Sell in *Watsonia* 16: 368. 1987): Herb. Clifford: 388, *Hieracium* 6, right inflorescence (BM-000646879).
Generitype of *Hieracium* Linnaeus (vide Green, *Prop. Brit. Bot.*: 178. 1929).
Current name: ***Hieracium murorum*** L. (Asteraceae).
Note: Pugsley (in *J. Linn. Soc., Bot.* 54: 4. 1948) noted the existence of 954.22 (LINN) but concluded that the name should be regarded, in its segregate sense, as a *nomen confusum*. However, Sell's subsequent typification has allowed the name to continue in use in its usual sense.

Hieracium murorum Linnaeus var. **pilosissimum** Linnaeus, *Species Plantarum* 2: 803. 1753.
RCN: 5865.
Type not designated.
Original material: Herb. Burser VI: 89 (UPS); [icon] in Daléchamps, Hist. General. Pl. 1: 565. 1587.
Current name: ***Hieracium murorum*** L. (Asteraceae).

Hieracium murorum Linnaeus var. **sylvaticum** Linnaeus, *Species Plantarum* 2: 803. 1753.
RCN: 5865.
Type not designated.
Original material: Herb. Burser VI: 90 (UPS); [icon] in Tabernaemontanus, New Vollk. Kräuterb.: 504. 1664.
Current name: ***Hieracium murorum*** L. (Asteraceae).

Hieracium paludosum Linnaeus, *Species Plantarum* 2: 803. 1753.
"Habitat in Europae borealioris nemoribus paludosis." RCN: 5866.
Lectotype (Babcock in *Univ. Calif. Publ. Bot.* 22: 200, 234. 1947): Herb. Linn. No. 954.25 (LINN).
Current name: ***Crepis paludosa*** (L.) Moench (Asteraceae).
Note: Babcock (*l.c.*) stated there were two sheets in LINN, one of which (evidently 954.25) is typical of this species; the other (954.26) belonging to *C. lapsanoides* (Gouan) Tausch, an identification also noted earlier by Smith (*in sched.*). "There is no question as to which should be accepted as the Linnaean 'type'", Babcock wrote. On p. 234, he says a photo of the type shows young florets and no achenes. From comparison with the LINN material, it seems clear that Babcock's type choice was 954.25 (LINN), and this is accepted here.

Hieracium paniculatum Linnaeus, *Species Plantarum* 2: 802. 1753.
"Habitat in Canada. Kalm." RCN: 5862.
Lectotype (Reveal in Jarvis & Turland in *Taxon* 47: 362. 1998): *Kalm*, Herb. Linn. No. 954.20 (LINN).
Current name: ***Hieracium paniculatum*** L. (Asteraceae).

Hieracium pilosella Linnaeus, *Species Plantarum* 2: 800. 1753.
"Habitat in Europae pascuis aridis." RCN: 5852.
Type not designated.
Original material: Herb. Linn. No. 954.7 (LINN); Herb. Burser XV(1): 1 (UPS); [icon] in Fuchs, Hist. Stirp.: 604, 605. 1542; [icon] in Mattioli, Pl. Epit.: 709. 1586.
Current name: ***Hieracium pilosella*** L. (Asteraceae).

Hieracium porrifolium Linnaeus, *Species Plantarum* 2: 802. 1753.
"Habitat in Alpibus Austriae, Italiae." RCN: 5864.
Type not designated.
Original material: [icon] in Boccone, Mus. Piante Rar. Sicilia: 147, t. 106. 1697.
Current name: ***Hieracium porrifolium*** L. (Asteraceae).

Hieracium praemorsum Linnaeus, *Species Plantarum* 2: 801. 1753.
"Habitat in Helvetia, Harcynia, Uplandia." RCN: 5856.
Lectotype (Babcock in *Univ. Calif. Publ. Bot.* 22: 553. 1947): Herb. Linn. No. 954.14 (LINN).
Current name: ***Crepis praemorsa*** (L.) Walther (Asteraceae).
Note: Although Babcock referred to the type as being in "L" (rather than LINN), sheet 954.14 (LINN) is the only sheet there associated with this name, and is accepted as the lectotype.

Hieracium pumilum Linnaeus, *Mantissa Plantarum Altera*: 279. 1771.
"Habitat in Helvetia, Sabaudia." RCN: 5848.
Type not designated.
Original material: none traced.
Current name: ***Crepis pygmaea*** L. (Asteraceae).

Hieracium pyrenaicum Linnaeus, *Species Plantarum* 2: 804. 1753.
"Habitat in Pyrenaeis. Burs. VI. 74." RCN: 5870.
Lectotype (Greuter in *Exsiccata Genavensia* 1: 15. 1970): Herb. Burser VI: 74 (UPS).
Current name: ***Crepis pyrenaica*** (L.) Greuter (Asteraceae).

Hieracium pyrenaicum Linnaeus var. **austriacum** (N.J. Jacquin) Linnaeus, *Systema Naturae*, ed. 12, 2: 523. 1767.
RCN: 5870.
Basionym: *Crepis austriaca* Jacq. (1762).
Lectotype (Lack in Jarvis & Turland in *Taxon* 47: 362. 1998): [icon] *"Crepis austriaca"* in Jacquin, Enum. Stirp. Vindob.: 270, t. 5. 1762.
Current name: ***Crepis pyrenaica*** (L.) Greuter (Asteraceae).

Hieracium pyrenaicum Linnaeus var. **blattarioides** (Linnaeus) Linnaeus, *Systema Naturae*, ed. 12, 2: 523. 1767.
RCN: 5870.
Basionym: *Hieracium blattarioides* L. (1753).
Type not designated.
Original material: as basionym.
Current name: ***Crepis pyrenaica*** (L.) Greuter (Asteraceae).

Hieracium pyrenaicum Linnaeus var. **helveticum** Linnaeus, *Systema Naturae*, ed. 12, 2: 524. 1767.
RCN: 5870.
Type not designated.
Original material: none traced.

Hieracium pyrenaicum Linnaeus var. **pilosum** Linnaeus, *Systema Naturae*, ed. 12, 2: 523. 1767.
RCN: 5870.
Replaced synonym: *Picris pyrenaica* L. (1753).
Lectotype (Lack in *Taxon* 24: 113. 1975): [icon] *"Hieracium Blattariae folio"* in Hermann, Parad. Bat.: 184. 1698.
Current name: ***Crepis sp.*** (Asteraceae).
Note: A new name in *Hieracium*, at varietal rank, for *Picris pyrenaica* L. (1753).

Hieracium sabaudum Linnaeus, *Species Plantarum* 2: 804. 1753.
"Habitat in Germania." RCN: 5875.
Type not designated.
Original material: Herb. Linn. No. 954.45 (LINN); [icon] in Bauhin & Cherler, Hist. Pl. Univ. 2: 1030. 1651.

Current name: ***Hieracium sabaudum*** L. (Asteraceae).
Note: Pugsley (in *J. Linn. Soc., Bot.* 54: 5. 1948) noted 954.45 (LINN), but wrongly believed it to be a later addition to the collection. Nikolaev (in *Bot. Zhurn.* 75: 560. 1990) also noted its existence but did not explicitly treat it as the type. The material is apparently identifiable as *H. perpropinquum* Druce (Sell, pers. comm.).

Hieracium sanctum Linnaeus, *Centuria II Plantarum*: 30. 1756.
"Habitat in Palaestina. Hasselquist." RCN: 5860.
Type not designated.
Original material: *Hasselquist*, Herb. Linn. No. 954.18 (LINN).
Current name: ***Crepis sancta*** (L.) Babc. (Asteraceae).

Hieracium sprengerianum Linnaeus, *Species Plantarum* 2: 804. 1753.
"Habitat in Lusitania." RCN: 5874.
Lectotype (Alavi in Jafri & El-Gadi, *Fl. Libya* 107: 359. 1983): Herb. Linn. No. 954.44 (LINN).
Current name: ***Hieracium*** sp. (Asteraceae).
Note: Greuter (in *Willdenowia* 33: 235. 2003) notes that Schultz Bipontinus annotated the type material as identifiable as *H. virosum* Pall. and that if, as he suspects, closer scrutiny confirmed this, *H. sprengerianum*, unless it is formally rejected, threatens to displace *H. virosum*, a well-known name of a widespread Asian and SE European species.

Hieracium taraxaci Linnaeus, *Species Plantarum*, ed. 2, 2: 1125. 1763.
Lectotype (designated here by Jonsell): *Solander*, Herb. Linn. No. 954.4 (LINN), see p. 229.
Current name: ***Scorzoneroides autumnalis*** (L.) Moench subsp. ***borealis*** (Ball) Greuter (Asteraceae).

Hieracium tomentosum Linnaeus, *Centuria I Plantarum*: 26. 1755.
"Habitat in Europa australi."
Replaced synonym of: *Andryala lanata* L. (1759), *nom. illeg.*
Type not designated.
Original material: [icon] in Dillenius, Hort. Eltham. 1: 181, t. 150, f. 180. 1732.
Current name: ***Hieracium tomentosum*** L. (Asteraceae).

Hieracium umbellatum Linnaeus, *Species Plantarum* 2: 804. 1753.
"Habitat in Europae pascuis siccis." RCN: 5876.
Lectotype (designated here by Lack): Herb. Clifford: 387, *Hieracium* 2, sheet 24 (BM-000646874).
Current name: ***Hieracium umbellatum*** L. (Asteraceae).
Note: Pugsley (in *J. Linn. Soc., Bot.* 54: 293. 1948) noted that 954.46 (LINN) conflicts with the diagnosis, and Lack (in Rechinger, *Fl. Iranica* 22: 178. 1977) stated "Typus: Hort. Cliff. 387.2, BM". However, he did not distinguish between two Clifford sheets at BM and, as they are not part of a single gathering, Art. 9.15 does not apply. This name is now typified here.

Hieracium venosum Linnaeus, *Species Plantarum* 2: 800. 1753.
"Habitat in Virginia." RCN: 5851.
Lectotype (Reveal & al. in *Huntia* 7: 225. 1987): *Clayton 386* (BM-000051199).
Current name: ***Hieracium venosum*** L. (Asteraceae).
Note: Although Reveal & al. wrongly attributed the choice of lectotype to Fernald (in *Rhodora* 45: 323–325. 1943), they clearly treat *Clayton 386* (BM) as the lectotype and the choice is attributable to them.

Hippia frutescens (Linnaeus) Linnaeus, *Mantissa Plantarum Altera*: 291. 1771.

"Habitat in Aethiopia." RCN: 6701.
Basionym: *Tanacetum frutescens* L. (1753).
Lectotype (Wijnands, *Bot. Commelins*: 77. 1983): Herb. Linn. No. 1039.3 (LINN).
Generitype of *Hippia* Linnaeus.
Current name: ***Hippia frutescens*** (L.) L. (Asteraceae).

Hippocratea volubilis Linnaeus, *Species Plantarum* 2: 1191. 1753.
"Habitat in America calidiori." RCN: 283.
Lectotype (Smith in *Brittonia* 3: 364. 1940): [icon] *"Coa"* in Plumier, Nov. Pl. Amer.: 8, t. 35. 1703.
Generitype of *Hippocratea* Linnaeus.
Current name: ***Hippocratea volubilis*** L. (Celastraceae).

Hippocrepis comosa Linnaeus, *Species Plantarum* 2: 744. 1753.
"Habitat in Germania, Italia, Gallia." RCN: 5481.
Lectotype (Lassen in Turland & Jarvis in *Taxon* 46: 473. 1997): Herb. Burser XIX: 123 (UPS).
Current name: ***Hippocrepis comosa*** L. (Fabaceae: Faboideae).

Hippocrepis multisiliquosa Linnaeus, *Species Plantarum* 2: 744. 1753.
"Habitat in Angliae, G. Narbonensis, Hispaniae, Italiae cretaceis." RCN: 5480.
Lectotype (Domínguez in *Lagascalia* 5: 249. 1976): Herb. Linn. No. 919.3 (LINN).
Current name: ***Hippocrepis multisiliquosa*** L. (Fabaceae: Faboideae).
Note: Although Domínguez gave the sheet number of his chosen type as 919.2 (LINN), it is clear from his discussion that this was an error for 919.3 (LINN), subsequently confirmed by Talavera & Domínguez (in *Anales Jard. Bot. Madrid* 57: 455. 2000).

Hippocrepis unisiliquosa Linnaeus, *Species Plantarum* 2: 744. 1753.
"Habitat in Italia." RCN: 5479.
Lectotype (Domínguez in *Lagascalia* 5: 236. 1976): Herb. Linn. No. 919.1 (LINN).
Generitype of *Hippocrepis* Linnaeus (vide Green, *Prop. Brit. Bot.*: 176. 1929).
Current name: ***Hippocrepis unisiliquosa*** L. subsp. ***unisiliquosa*** (Fabaceae: Faboideae).

Hippomane biglandulosa Linnaeus, *Species Plantarum*, ed. 2, 2: 1431. 1763, *nom. illeg.*
"Habitat in America calidiore." RCN: 7304.
Replaced synonym: *Sapium aucuparium* Jacq. (1763).
Lectotype (Jablonski in *Phytologia* 16: 403. 1968): [icon] *"Sapium aucuparium"* in Jacquin, Select. Stirp. Amer. Hist.: 249, t. 158. 1763.
Current name: ***Sapium glandulosum*** (L.) Morong (Euphorbiaceae).
Note: A superfluous name for *Sapium aucuparium* Jacq. (1763).

Hippomane glandulosa Linnaeus, *Species Plantarum* 2: 1191. 1753.
"Habitat in America calidiore." RCN: 7304.
Lectotype (Croizat in *J. Arnold Arbor.* 24: 176. 1943): [icon] *"Tithym. arbor American. Mali Medicae fol. amplioribus tenuissime crenatis, succo maxime venenato"* in Plukenet, Phytographia: t. 229, f. 8. 1692; Almag. Bot.: 369. 1696. – Typotype: Herb. Sloane 98: 111 (BM-SL).
Current name: ***Sapium glandulosum*** (L.) Morong (Euphorbiaceae).
Note: See detailed discussion and illustrations of types by Kruijt & Zijlstra (in *Taxon* 38: 320–325, f. 1–3. 1989) and by Kruijt (in *Biblioth. Bot.* 146: 44. 1996).

Hippomane mancinella Linnaeus, *Species Plantarum* 2: 1191. 1753.
"Habitat in Caribaeis saepius inundatis." RCN: 7303.

Lectotype (Wijnands, *Bot. Commelins*: 103. 1983): [icon] *"Juglandi affinis arbor julifera, lactescens, venenata pyrifolia, Mançanillo Hispanis dicta"* in Sloane, Voy. Jamaica 2: 3, t. 159. 1725. – Typotype: Herb. Sloane 5: 55 (BM-SL).
Generitype of *Hippomane* Linnaeus (vide Green, *Prop. Brit. Bot.*: 195. 1929).
Current name: ***Hippomane mancinella*** L. (Euphorbiaceae).
Note: Fawcett & Rendle (*Fl. Jamaica* 4: 328. 1920) treated material in LINN (presumably 1146.1) as the type, but this is evidently a post-1753 addition to the collection and not original material for the name.

Hippomane spinosa Linnaeus, *Species Plantarum* 2: 1191. 1753.
"Habitat in America calidiore." RCN: 7305.
Type not designated.
Original material: [icon] in Plukenet, Phytographia: t. 196, f. 3. 1692; Almag. Bot.: 197. 1696 – Voucher: Herb. Sloane 96: 116 (BM-SL); [icon] in Plumier, Nov. Pl. Amer.: 50, t. 30. 1703.
Current name: ***Hippomane spinosa*** L. (Euphorbiaceae).

Hippophaë canadensis Linnaeus, *Species Plantarum* 2: 1024. 1753.
"Habitat in Canada. Kalm." RCN: 7409.
Type not designated.
Original material: *Kalm*, Herb. Linn. No. 1168.2 (LINN).
Current name: ***Shepherdia canadensis*** (L.) Nutt. (Elaeagnaceae).

Hippophaë rhamnoides Linnaeus, *Species Plantarum* 2: 1023. 1753.
"Habitat in Europae maritimis arenosis." RCN: 7408.
Type not designated.
Original material: Herb. Burser XXV: 4 (UPS); [icon] in Mattioli, Pl. Epit.: 81. 1586.
Generitype of *Hippophaë* Linnaeus (vide Green, *Prop. Brit. Bot.*: 191. 1929).
Current name: ***Hippophaë rhamnoides*** L. (Elaeagnaceae).
Note: Rousi (in *Ann. Bot. Fenn.* 8: 201–202, f. 14. 1971) designated *J. F. Sacklén s.n.* [ex Hort. Academ. Upsal.] in S as lectotype (but in reality a neotype). As original material was in existence, this choice is contrary to Art. 9.11. Rousi recognised that Herb. Burser XXV: 4 (UPS) was original material for the name but identified it as subsp. *fluviatilis* Soest. *Hippophaë rhamnoides* remains untypified at present.

Hippuris vulgaris Linnaeus, *Species Plantarum* 1: 4. 1753.
"Habitat in Europae fontibus." RCN: 29.
Lectotype (Nilsson in Jonsell & Jarvis in *Nordic J. Bot.* 22: 83. 2002): Herb. Clifford: 3, *Hippuris* 1 (BM-000557511).
Generitype of *Hippuris* Linnaeus.
Current name: ***Hippuris vulgaris*** L. (Hippuridaceae).

Hirtella americana Linnaeus, *Species Plantarum* 1: 34. 1753.
"Habitat in America meridionali." RCN: 1625.
Lectotype (Sandwith in *Bull. Misc. Inform. Kew* 1931: 376. 1931): Herb. Clifford: 17, *Hirtella* 1 (BM-000557636).
Generitype of *Hirtella* Linnaeus.
Current name: ***Hirtella americana*** L. (Chrysobalanaceae).

Holcus bicolor Linnaeus, *Mantissa Plantarum Altera*: 301. 1771.
"Habitat in Persia. D. Lerche. H. U." RCN: 7565.
Lectotype (Davidse in Cafferty & al. in *Taxon* 49: 251. 2000): Herb. Clifford: 468, *Holcus* 1 (BM-000647533).
Current name: ***Sorghum bicolor*** (L.) Moench (Poaceae).
Note: See exhaustive review by Snowden (*Cult. Races* Sorghum: 7, 106. 1936), who stated that a specimen in LINN (perhaps 1212.6?) "may be the type". This is ineffective. Poilecot (in *Boissiera* 56: 509.

1999) indicated material in LINN as the type of *S. bicolor* (L.) Moench, and a Clifford collection as the lectotype of *H. bicolor* L. Davidse & Turland (in *Taxon* 50: 577. 2001) have, however, accepted Poilecot as having effectively typified the name using the Clifford sheet. This, however, was ineffective, and Davidse's 2000 choice is accepted as typifying the name.

Holcus halepensis Linnaeus, *Species Plantarum* 2: 1047. 1753.
"Habitat in Syria, Mauritania." RCN: 7567.
Lectotype (Meikle, *Fl. Cyprus* 2: 1869. 1985): Herb. Linn. No. 1212.7 (LINN).
Current name: ***Sorghum halepense*** (L.) Pers. (Poaceae).
Note: Snowden (in *J. Linn. Soc., Bot.* 55: 197. 1955) noted the existence of two collections at LINN but did not designate a type.

Holcus lanatus Linnaeus, *Species Plantarum* 2: 1048. 1753.
"Habitat in Europae pascuis arenosis." RCN: 570.
Lectotype (Cope in Jarvis & al., *Regnum Veg.* 127: 54. 1993): Herb. Linn. No. 1212.10 (LINN).
Generitype of *Holcus* Linnaeus, *nom. cons.*
Current name: ***Holcus lanatus*** L. (Poaceae).
Note: Although Kerguélen (in *Lejeunia*, n.s., 75: 193. 1975) indicated unspecified material in LINN as type, this is not accepted as an effective typification (Art. 7.11). See Cafferty & al. (in *Taxon* 49: 240. 2000) for a detailed explanation.

Holcus laxus Linnaeus, *Species Plantarum* 2: 1048. 1753.
"Habitat in Virginia, Canada." RCN: 7571.
Lectotype (Hitchcock in *Contr. U. S. Natl. Herb.* 12: 126. 1908): *Clayton 589*, Herb. Linn. No. 1212.11 (LINN; iso- BM).
Current name: ***Chasmanthium laxum*** (L.) H.O. Yates subsp. ***laxum*** (Poaceae).
Note: Yates (in *S. W. Naturalist* 11: 442, f. 6. 1966) reproduced a photograph of the type.

Holcus mollis Linnaeus, *Systema Naturae*, ed. 10, 2: 1305. 1759.
["Habitat in Europa: in Hallandia. Osbeck."] Sp. Pl., ed. 2, 2: 1485 (1763). RCN: 7569.
Lectotype (Cope in Cafferty & al. in *Taxon* 49: 251. 2000): Herb. Linn. No. 1212.9 (LINN).
Current name: ***Holcus mollis*** L. (Poaceae).
Note: Although Kerguélen (in *Lejeunia*, n.s., 75: 193. 1975) stated "Type: …LINN", this is not accepted as a formal typification, for the reasons explained by Cafferty & al. (in *Taxon* 49: 240. 2000).

Holcus odoratus Linnaeus, *Species Plantarum* 2: 1048. 1753.
"Habitat in Europae frigidioris pascuis humentibus." RCN: 7573.
Lectotype (Weimarck in *Bot. Not.* 124: 136. 1971): Herb. Linn. No. 1212.14, second specimen from left (LINN).
Current name: ***Anthoxanthum nitens*** (Weber) Y. Schouten & Veldkamp (Poaceae).

Holcus pertusus Linnaeus, *Mantissa Plantarum Altera*: 301. 1771.
"Habitat in India orientali." RCN: 7575.
Lectotype (Clayton in *Kew Bull.* 32: 4. 1977): Herb. Linn. No. 1212.16 (LINN).
Current name: ***Dichanthium pertusum*** (L.) Clayton (Poaceae).

Holcus saccharatus Linnaeus, *Species Plantarum* 2: 1047. 1753, *nom. rej.*
"Habitat in India." RCN: 7568.
Type not designated.
Original material: none traced.
Current name: ***Sorghum bicolor*** (L.) Moench (Poaceae).

H

Holcus sorghum Linnaeus, *Species Plantarum* 2: 1047. 1753.
"Habitat in India." RCN: 7566.
Lectotype (Davidse in Cafferty & al. in *Taxon* 49: 251. 2000): Herb.
Clifford: 468, *Holcus* 1 (BM-000647533).
Current name: ***Sorghum bicolor*** (L.) Moench (Poaceae).
Note: Clayton (in Dassanayake & al., *Revised Handb. Fl. Ceylon* 8:
414. 1994), and Judziewicz (in Görts-van Rijn, *Fl. Guianas*, ser. A,
8: 598. 1990) appear to have regarded Herb. Linn. No. 1212.6
(LINN) as the type, but it is a post-1753 specimen, and therefore
not original material for the name.

Holcus spicatus Linnaeus, *Systema Naturae*, ed. 10, 2: 1305. 1759.
["Habitat in India."] Sp. Pl., ed. 2, 2: 1484 (1763). RCN: 7564.
Lectotype (Davidse in Dassanayake & al., *Revised Handb. Fl. Ceylon* 8:
363. 1994): [icon] *"Gr. Alopecuroid. spica max. Ind. Orient."* in
Plukenet, Phytographia: t. 32, f. 4. 1691; Almag. Bot.: 174. 1696.
Current name: ***Pennisetum glaucum*** (L.) R. Br. (Poaceae).
Note: See notes and discussion by Chase (in *Contr. U. S. Natl. Herb.*
22: 216. 1920; *Amer. J. Bot.* 8: 44, 48. 1921) and Terrell (in *Taxon*
25: 297–304. 1976).

Holcus striatus Linnaeus, *Species Plantarum* 2: 1048. 1753.
"Habitat in Virginiae paludibus." RCN: 7572.
Lectotype (Hitchcock in *Contr. U. S. Natl. Herb.* 12: 127. 1908):
Clayton 590, Herb. Linn. No. 1212.12 (LINN; iso- BM).
Current name: ***Sacciolepis striata*** (L.) Nash (Poaceae).

Holosteum cordatum Linnaeus, *Species Plantarum* 1: 88. 1753.
"Habitat in Jamaica, Surinama." RCN: 738.
Lectotype (Burger in Cafferty & Jarvis in *Taxon* 53: 1052. 2004):
[icon] *"Alsine Americana Nummulariae foliis"* in Hermann, Parad.
Bat.: 11. 1698.
Current name: ***Drymaria cordata*** (L.) Roem. & Schult.
(Caryophyllaceae).
Note: Fawcett & Rendle (*Fl. Jamaica* 3: 175. 1914) stated "Type in
Herb. Linn." and Turrill (in Turrill & Milne-Redhead, *Fl. Trop. E.
Africa, Caryophyllaceae*: 11. 1956) made a similar statement. Later,
Mizushima (in *J. Jap. Bot.* 32: 70. 1957) explicitly chose 109.1
(LINN) as lectotype and was followed by others. However, this
sheet, as noted by Howard (*Fl. Lesser Antilles* 4: 211. 1988), is a
post-1753 addition to the Linnaean herbarium, is not original
material, and is not eligible for lectotypification of the name.

Holosteum hirsutum Linnaeus, *Species Plantarum* 1: 88. 1753.
"Habitat in Malabaria." RCN: 740.
Lectotype (van Steenis in *Blumea* 13: 167. 1965): Herb. A. van Royen
No. 899.143–553 (L).
Current name: ***Glinus lotoides*** L. (Molluginaceae).

Holosteum succulentum Linnaeus, *Species Plantarum* 1: 88. 1753.
"Habitat in Noveboraco." RCN: 739.
Type not designated.
Original material: none traced.
Note: Although Fernald (in *Rhodora* 11: 109–115. 1909) concluded
that this was based on a Colden description, the application of
Linnaeus' name is uncertain and *H. succulentum* may be a candidate
for rejection.

Holosteum umbellatum Linnaeus, *Species Plantarum* 1: 88. 1753.
"Habitat in Germaniae, Galliae arvis." RCN: 741.
Lectotype (Jonsell & Jarvis in Jarvis & al., *Regnum Veg.* 127: 54.
1993): Herb. Bergius, sheet bearing "4 umbellatum", lower
specimen (SBT).
Generitype of *Holosteum* Linnaeus (vide Hitchcock, *Prop. Brit. Bot.*:
122. 1929).

Current name: ***Holosteum umbellatum*** L. (Caryophyllaceae).
Note: Although Ghazanfar & Nasir (in Nasir & Ali, *Fl. Pakistan* 175: 33.
1986) indicated syntypes in SBT and UPS, they made no effective
type choice. Jonsell & Jarvis (in *Nordic J. Bot.* 14: 157. 1994)
provided further information on their own formal (1993) type choice.

Hopea tinctoria Linnaeus, *Systema Naturae,* ed. 12, 2: 509; *Mantissa
Plantarum*: 105. 1767.
"Habitat in Carolina." RCN: 1734.
Lectotype (Howard & Staples in *J. Arnold Arbor.* 64: 538. 1983):
Herb. Linn. No. 942.1 (LINN).
Generitype of *Hopea* Linnaeus, *nom. rej.*
Current name: ***Symplocos tinctoria*** (L.) L'Hér. (Symplocaceae).
Note: Hopea Linnaeus, *nom. rej.* in favour of *Hopea* Roxb.

Hordeum bulbosum Linnaeus, *Centuria II Plantarum*: 8. 1756.
"Habitat in Italia, Oriente." RCN: 714.
Lectotype (Jørgensen in *Nordic J. Bot.* 2: 423. 1982): *Hasselquist,*
Herb. Linn. No. 103.3, base only (LINN).
Current name: ***Hordeum bulbosum*** L. (Poaceae).
Note: Although Kerguélen (in *Lejeunia*, n.s., 75: 194. 1975) stated
"Type: ...LINN", this is not accepted as a formal typification, for
the reasons explained by Cafferty & al. (in *Taxon* 49: 240. 2000).

Hordeum distichon Linnaeus, *Species Plantarum* 1: 85. 1753.
"Habitat – – – –" RCN: 712.
Neotype (Cope in Cafferty & al. in *Taxon* 49: 251. 2000): France. "Pl.
de l'Ouest de la France", 29 Jun 1879, *Guadeceau s.n.* (BM-
000576277).
Current name: ***Hordeum distichon*** L. (Poaceae).

Hordeum distichon Linnaeus var. **nudum** Linnaeus, *Species
Plantarum* 1: 85. 1753.
RCN: 712.
Neotype (Cope in Cafferty & al. in *Taxon* 49: 251. 2000): Herb.
Shuttleworth 1806. Hort. "H. distichon nudum var. beta". (BM-
000576278).
Current name: ***Hordeum distichon*** L. (Poaceae).
Note: The varietal epithet was spelled "dist.nudum" ["dist." =
"distichon"] in the protologue. This was later corrected (Linnaeus,
Sp. Pl., ed. 2, 1: 125. 1762) to "nudum". As is established custom,
the "distichon" is to be ignored under Art. 23.8 and Ex. 19.

Hordeum hexastichon Linnaeus, *Species Plantarum* 1: 85. 1753.
"Habitat – – – –" RCN: 711.
Neotype (Cope in Cafferty & al. in *Taxon* 49: 251. 2000): Greece.
Kapujilar, 3 m SE of Salonika, May 1918, *J. Ramsbottom s.n.* (BM-
000576274).
Current name: ***Hordeum vulgare*** L. subsp. ***vulgare*** convar. ***vulgare***
var. ***hexastichon*** (L.) Asch. (Poaceae).

Hordeum jubatum Linnaeus, *Species Plantarum* 1: 85. 1753.
"Habitat in Canada. Kalm." RCN: 717.
Lectotype (Hitchcock in *Contr. U. S. Natl. Herb.* 12: 124. 1908):
Kalm, Herb. Linn. No. 103.10 (LINN).
Current name: ***Hordeum jubatum*** L. (Poaceae).

Hordeum murinum Linnaeus, *Species Plantarum* 1: 85. 1753.
"Habitat in Europae locis ruderatis." RCN: 716.
Lectotype (Baum & Jarvis in *Taxon* 34: 529, f. 1. 1985): Herb.
Clifford: 24, *Hordeum* 3 (BM-000557673).
Current name: ***Hordeum murinum*** L. subsp. ***murinum*** (Poaceae).
Note: Although Kerguélen (in *Lejeunia*, n.s., 75: 195. 1975) stated
"Type: ...LINN", this is not accepted as a formal typification, for
the reasons explained by Cafferty & al. (in *Taxon* 49: 240. 2000).

Hordeum nodosum Linnaeus, *Species Plantarum*, ed. 2, 1: 126. 1762. "Habitat in Italia, Anglia." RCN: 717.
Lectotype (Jørgensen in *Nordic J. Bot.* 2: 423. 1982): Herb. Linn. No. 103.4 (LINN).
Current name: ***Hordeum bulbosum*** L. (Poaceae).
Note: Baum & Jarvis (in *Taxon* 34: 531. 1985) agreed with Jørgensen's choice but provided a more detailed discussion.

Hordeum vulgare Linnaeus, *Species Plantarum* 1: 84. 1753. "Habitat – – – –" RCN: 710.
Lectotype (Bowden in *Canad. J. Bot.* 37: 679. 1959): Herb. Linn. No. 103.1 (LINN).
Generitype of *Hordeum* Linnaeus (vide Hitchcock, *Prop. Brit. Bot.*: 121. 1929).
Current name: ***Hordeum vulgare*** L. (Poaceae).

Hordeum vulgare Linnaeus var. **coeleste** Linnaeus, *Species Plantarum* 1: 85. 1753.
RCN: 710.
Neotype (Cope in Cafferty & al. in *Taxon* 49: 251. 2000): Herb. R.J. Shuttleworth, "H. hexastichon", left specimen (BM-000576276).
Current name: ***Hordeum vulgare*** L. (Poaceae).

Hordeum zeocriton Linnaeus, *Species Plantarum* 1: 85. 1753. "Habitat – – – –" RCN: 713.
Lectotype (Bowden in *Canad. J. Bot.* 37: 680. 1959): Herb. Linn. No. 103.2 (LINN).
Current name: ***Hordeum vulgare*** L. subsp. ***vulgare*** convar. ***distichon*** (L.) Alef. var. ***zeocriton*** (L.) Körn. (Poaceae).

Horminum pyrenaicum Linnaeus, *Species Plantarum* 2: 596. 1753. "Habitat in altis montium Tyrolensium, Pyrenaeorum." RCN: 4328.
Lectotype (Press in Jarvis & al., *Regnum Veg.* 127: 55. 1993): Herb. Clifford: 309, *Horminum* 1 (BM-000646042).
Generitype of *Horminum* Linnaeus (vide Green, *Prop. Brit. Bot.*: 166. 1929).
Current name: ***Horminum pyrenaicum*** L. (Lamiaceae).

Horminum virginicum Linnaeus, *Species Plantarum* 2: 596. 1753. "Habitat in Virginia, Carolina." RCN: 184.
Lectotype (Reveal & al. in *Huntia* 7: 236. 1987): [icon] *"Melissa atrorubens, Bugulae folio"* in Dillenius, Hort. Eltham. 2: 219, t. 175, f. 216. 1732. – Typotype: Herb. Sherard No. 42 (OXF).
Current name: ***Salvia lyrata*** L. (Lamiaceae).
Note: Although Epling (in *J. Bot.* 67: 10. 1929) noted a specimen in LINN as a standard specimen, this is not equivalent to a type statement (see Jarvis & al. in *Taxon* 50: 508. 2001).

Hottonia indica Linnaeus, *Systema Naturae,* ed. 10, 2: 919. 1759. ["Habitat in India. Burmannus."] Sp. Pl., ed. 2, 1: 208 (1762). RCN: 1166.
Lectotype (Philcox in *Kew Bull.* 24: 115. 1970): Herb. Linn. No. 204.2 (LINN).
Current name: ***Limnophila indica*** (L.) Druce (Primulaceae).

Hottonia palustris Linnaeus, *Species Plantarum* 1: 145. 1753. "Habitat in fossis & paludibus Europae borealioris." RCN: 1165.
Type not designated.
Original material: Herb. Burser VII(1): 74 (UPS); Herb. Burser VII(1): 75 (UPS).
Generitype of *Hottonia* Linnaeus.
Current name: ***Hottonia palustris*** L. (Primulaceae).

Houstonia caerulea Linnaeus, *Species Plantarum* 1: 105. 1753. "Habitat in Virginia." RCN: 857.

Lectotype (Reveal & al. in *Huntia* 7: 227. 1987): *Clayton 60* ["63"] (BM-000042705).
Generitype of *Houstonia* Linnaeus (vide Hitchcock, *Prop. Brit. Bot.*: 124. 1929).
Current name: ***Houstonia caerulea*** L. (Rubiaceae).

Houstonia purpurea Linnaeus, *Species Plantarum* 1: 105. 1753. "Habitat in Virginia." RCN: 858.
Lectotype (Reveal & al. in *Huntia* 7: 234. 1987): *Clayton 63* ["506"] (BM-000042707).
Current name: ***Houstonia purpurea*** L. (Rubiaceae).
Note: Terrell (in *Rhodora* 61: 168. 1959) evidently regarded material on 128.2 (LINN) as the type, but this collection was a later addition to the herbarium, and ineligible. Reveal & al. designated what is evidently *Clayton 63* (BM) as lectotype, despite describing it as *Clayton 506*. Subsequently, Terrell (in *Syst. Bot. Monogr.* 48: 50. 1996) has rejected their choice in favour of *Clayton 63*, but it seems clear that both are talking about the same sheet and there has merely been confusion over labelling.

Hudsonia ericoides Linnaeus, *Systema Naturae,* ed. 12, 2: 327; *Mantissa Plantarum*: 74. 1767. "Habitat in Virginia." RCN: 3456.
Lectotype (Reveal in Jarvis & al., *Regnum Veg.* 127: 55. 1993): Herb. Linn. No. 622.1 (LINN; iso- BM).
Generitype of *Hudsonia* Linnaeus.
Current name: ***Hudsonia ericoides*** L. (Cistaceae).
Note: Skog & Nickerson (in *Ann. Missouri Bot. Gard.* 59: 457. 1972) referred to having seen a "photograph of Linnaeus' type species" but are vague as to exactly what this may have been. Reveal's choice, however, is unequivocal.

Hugonia mystax Linnaeus, *Species Plantarum* 2: 675. 1753. "Habitat in India." RCN: 4931.
Lectotype (Barrie in Jarvis & al., *Regnum Veg.* 127: 55. 1993): Herb. Hermann 1: 50, No. 249 (BM-000621401).
Generitype of *Hugonia* Linnaeus.
Current name: ***Hugonia mystax*** L. (Linaceae).
Note: Hajra (in Jain & al., *Fasc. Fl. India* 13: 6. 1983) wrongly indicated post-1753 material from König at LINN as type.

Humulus lupulus Linnaeus, *Species Plantarum* 2: 1028. 1753. "Habitat in Europae sepibus & ad radices montium." RCN: 7431.
Lectotype (Small in *Syst. Bot.* 3: 61. 1978): Herb. Clifford: 458, *Humulus* 1 (BM-000647487).
Generitype of *Humulus* Linnaeus.
Current name: ***Humulus lupulus*** L. (Cannabaceae).
Note: Qaiser (in Nasir & Ali, *Fl. W. Pakistan* 44: 5. 1973) wrongly indicated the post-1753 1178.1 (LINN) as type.

Hura crepitans Linnaeus, *Species Plantarum* 2: 1008. 1753. "Habitat in Mexico, Guayava, Jamaica." RCN: 7308.
Lectotype (Stearn, *Introd. Linnaeus' Sp. Pl.* (Ray Soc. ed.): 47. 1957): [icon] *"Hura"* in Linnaeus, Hort. Cliff.: 486, t. 34. 1738 (see p. 578).
Generitype of *Hura* Linnaeus.
Current name: ***Hura crepitans*** L. (Euphorbiaceae).

Hyacinthus amethystinus Linnaeus, *Species Plantarum* 1: 317. 1753. "Habitat in Hispania." RCN: 2491.
Lectotype (Stearn in *Ann. Mus. Goulandris* 8: 193, f. 6. 1990): Herb. Linn. No. 438.7 (LINN).
Current name: ***Brimeura amethystina*** (L.) Salisb. (Liliaceae/Hyacinthaceae).

The lectotype of *Hura crepitans* L.

Hyacinthus botryoides Linnaeus, *Species Plantarum* 1: 318. 1753.
"Habitat in Italia." RCN: 2498.
Lectotype (Stearn in *Ann. Mus. Goulandris* 8: 206, f. 14. 1990): Herb.
   Linn. No. 438.16 (LINN).
Current name: ***Muscari botryoides*** (L.) Mill.
   (Liliaceae/Hyacinthaceae).

Hyacinthus cernuus Linnaeus, *Species Plantarum* 1: 317. 1753.
"Habitat in Hispania." RCN: 2488.
Lectotype (Stearn in *Ann. Mus. Goulandris* 8: 191, f. 3. 1990): Herb.
   Linn. No. 438.3 (LINN).
Current name: ***Hyacinthoides non-scripta*** (L.) Rothm. **'Rosea'**
   (Liliaceae/Hyacinthaceae).

Hyacinthus comosus Linnaeus, *Species Plantarum* 1: 318. 1753.
"Habitat in Galliae & Europae australis agris." RCN: 2497.
Lectotype (Bentzer in *Bot. Not.* 126: 75. 1973): Herb. Linn. No.
   438.15 (LINN).
Current name: ***Muscari comosum*** (L.) Mill.
   (Liliaceae/Hyacinthaceae).
Note: See extensive discussion by Stearn (in *Ann. Mus. Goulandris* 8:
   204, f. 12. 1980), who independently chose the same type.

Hyacinthus corymbosus Linnaeus, *Mantissa Plantarum Altera*: 223.
   1771.
"Habitat in Cap. b. spei pascuis. Koenig." RCN: 2493.
Neotype (Stearn in *Ann. Mus. Goulandris* 8: 214, f. 19. 1990): Herb.
   Linn. No. 438.9 (LINN).
Current name: ***Polyxena corymbosa*** (L.) Jessop
   (Liliaceae/Hyacinthaceae).

Note: Jessop (in *J. S. African Bot.* 42: 429. 1976) noted that 438.9
   (LINN) was unannotated by Linnaeus and did not appear to have
   come from König so could not be the type. Stearn subsequently
   designated it as a neotype.

Hyacinthus lanatus Linnaeus, *Species Plantarum* 1: 318. 1753.
"Habitat – – – –" RCN: 2501.
Lectotype (Stearn in *Ann. Mus. Goulandris* 8: 210, f. 18. 1990): Herb.
   A. van Royen No. 904.28–47 (L).
Current name: ***Lanaria lanata*** (L.) T. Durand & Schinz
   (Haemodoraceae).

Hyacinthus monstrosus Linnaeus, *Species Plantarum* 1: 318. 1753.
"Habitat – – – primum inventa in agro Papiensi, & juxta Boran
   Galliae." RCN: 2496.
Lectotype (Stearn in *Ann. Mus. Goulandris* 8: 200, f. 11. 1990): Herb.
   Clifford: 126, *Hyacinthus* 5 (BM-000558530).
Current name: ***Muscari comosum*** (L.) Mill. **'Monstrosum'**
   (Liliaceae/Hyacinthaceae).

Hyacinthus muscari Linnaeus, *Species Plantarum* 1: 317. 1753.
"Habitat in Asia ultra Bosphorum, inde in Europam ante 1554."
   RCN: 2495.
Lectotype (Stearn in *Ann. Mus. Goulandris* 8: 198, f. 9. 1990): [icon]
   "Muscari obsoletiore flore" in Clusius, Rar. Pl. Hist. 1: 178. 1601.
Current name: ***Muscari muscarimi*** Medik. (Liliaceae/Hyacinthaceae).

Hyacinthus non-scriptus Linnaeus, *Species Plantarum* 1: 316. 1753.
"Habitat in Anglia, Gallia, Hispania, Italia." RCN: 2487.
Lectotype (Stearn in *Ann. Mus. Goulandris* 8: 188. 1990): Herb. Linn.
   No. 438.1 (LINN).
Current name: ***Hyacinthoides non-scripta*** (L.) Rothm.
   (Liliaceae/Hyacinthaceae).

Hyacinthus orchioides Linnaeus, *Species Plantarum* 1: 318. 1753.
"Habitat in Aethiopia." RCN: 2500.
Lectotype (Stearn in *Ann. Mus. Goulandris* 8: 210, f. 17. 1990): [icon]
   *"Hyacinthus orchioides Africanus, major, bifolius maculatus; flore
   sulphureo, obsoleto, majore"* in Breyn, Prodr. Fasc. Rar. Pl.: 24, t. 11,
   f. 2. 1739.
Current name: ***Lachenalia orchioides*** (L.) Aiton
   (Liliaceae/Hyacinthaceae).

Hyacinthus orientalis Linnaeus, *Species Plantarum* 1: 317. 1753.
"Habitat in Asia, Africa." RCN: 2492.
Lectotype (Stearn in *Ann. Mus. Goulandris* 8: 196, f. 7. 1990): Herb.
   Clifford: 125, *Hyacinthus* 2 (BM-000558527).
Generitype of *Hyacinthus* Linnaeus (vide Hitchcock, *Prop. Brit. Bot.*:
   146. 1929).
Current name: ***Hyacinthus orientalis*** L. (Liliaceae/Hyacinthaceae).

Hyacinthus racemosus Linnaeus, *Species Plantarum* 1: 318. 1753.
"Habitat in Europa australi." RCN: 2499.
Lectotype (Stearn in *Ann. Mus. Goulandris* 8: 208, f. 14. 1990):
   Hasselquist, Herb. Linn. No. 438.17 (LINN).
Current name: ***Muscari neglectum*** Guss. (Liliaceae/Hyacinthaceae).
Note: Stearn took the view (*l.c.*: 206–210) that *Muscari racemosum* Mill.
   (1768) is a new name for *H. muscari* L. (1753), not a new
   combination based on *H. racemosus* L. (1753). Although some had
   previously rejected Linnaeus' name as ambiguous, Stearn's
   interpretation resulted in *M. racemosum* Mill. making *M. racemosum*
   (L.) Medik. a later homonym. Stearn noted that the type of *H.
   racemosus* cannot be identified with certainty – it is very difficult to
   distinguish *M. neglectum* Guss. and *M. atlanticum* Boiss. & Reuter in
   herbarium material (and some authors treat them as synonymous).

Hyacinthus romanus Linnaeus, *Mantissa Plantarum Altera*: 224. 1771.
"Habitat Romae in cultis & hortis sponte." RCN: 2494.
Lectotype (Stearn in *Ann. Mus. Goulandris* 8: 216, f. 20. 1990): Herb. Linn. No. 438.10 (LINN).
Current name: ***Bellevalia romana*** (L.) Sweet (Liliaceae/Hyacinthaceae).

Hyacinthus serotinus Linnaeus, *Species Plantarum* 1: 317. 1753.
"Habitat in Hispania, Mauritania." RCN: 2489.
Lectotype (Stearn in *Ann. Mus. Goulandris* 8: 192, f. 5. 1990): Herb. Linn. No. 438.4 (LINN).
Current name: ***Dipcadi serotinum*** (L.) Medik. (Liliaceae/Hyacinthaceae).
Note: El-Gadi (in Jafri & El-Gadi, *Fl. Libya* 57: 42. 1978) indicated 438.3 (LINN) as type, but this collection is associated with *H. cernuus* L. and is not original material for *H. serotinus*.

Hyacinthus viridis Linnaeus, *Systema Naturae*, ed. 10, 2: 984. 1759.
["Habitat ad Cap. b. spei; vivam aluit D. Burmannus."] Sp. Pl., ed. 2, 1: 454 (1762). RCN: 2490.
Lectotype (Stearn in *Ann. Mus. Goulandris* 8: 219, f. 19. 1990): Herb. Linn. No. 438.6 (LINN).
Current name: ***Dipcadi viride*** (L.) Moench (Liliaceae/Hyacinthaceae).

Hydnum auriscalpium Linnaeus, *Species Plantarum* 2: 1178. 1753.
"Habitat in Sylvis acerosis supra terram, subjacente ramo aut strobilo." RCN: 8484.
Type not designated.
Original material: [icon] in Buxbaum, Pl. Minus Cognit. Cent. 1: 36, t. 57, f. 1. 1728; [icon] in Buxbaum, Enum. Pl. Agro Hall.: 129, unnumbered plate. 1721; [icon] in Micheli, Nov. Pl. Gen.: 132, t. 72, f. 8. 1729.
Current name: ***Auriscalpium vulgare*** Gray (Auriscalpiaceae).

Hydnum imbricatum Linnaeus, *Species Plantarum* 2: 1178. 1753.
"Habitat in Sylvis acerosis." RCN: 8481.
Type not designated.
Original material: [icon] in Micheli, Nov. Pl. Gen.: 132, t. 72, f. 2. 1729.
Current name: ***Sarcodon imbricatus*** (L.: Fr.) P. Karst. (Bankeraceae).

Hydnum parasiticum Linnaeus, *Species Plantarum*, ed. 2, 2: 1648. 1763.
"Habitat in Europae arboribus." RCN: 8485.
Type not designated.
Original material: none traced.
Current name: ***Hydnum parasiticum*** L. (Hydnaceae).

Hydnum repandum Linnaeus, *Species Plantarum* 2: 1178. 1753, *typ. cons.*
"Habitat in Sylvarum desertis." RCN: 8482.
Type not designated.
Original material: [icon] in Micheli, Nov. Pl. Gen.: 132, t. 72, f. 3. 1729.
Generitype of *Hydnum* Linnaeus: Fr., *nom. cons.*
Current name: ***Hydnum repandum*** L.: Fr. (Hydnaceae).

Hydnum tomentosum Linnaeus, *Species Plantarum* 2: 1178. 1753.
"Habitat in Sylvis acerosis." RCN: 8483.
Type not designated.
Original material: none traced.
Current name: ***Phellodon tomentosus*** (L.: Fr.) Banker (Bankeraceae).

Hydrangea arborescens Linnaeus, *Species Plantarum* 1: 397. 1753.
"Habitat in Virginia." RCN: 3132.
Lectotype (Fernald in *Rhodora* 43: 559. 1941): *Clayton 79* (BM-000051139).
Generitype of *Hydrangea* Linnaeus.
Current name: ***Hydrangea arborescens*** L. (Hydrangeaceae).

Hydrastis canadensis Linnaeus, *Systema Naturae*, ed. 10, 2: 1088. 1759.
["Habitat in Canadae aquis."] Sp. Pl., ed. 2, 1: 784. 1762. RCN: 4112.
Lectotype (Reveal in *Phytologia* 71: 464. 1991): *Bartram*, Herb. Linn. No. 720.2 (LINN).
Generitype of *Hydrastis* Linnaeus.
Current name: ***Hydrastis canadensis*** L. (Ranunculaceae).
Note: Jarvis & al. (in *Regnum Veg.* 127: 55. 1993) wrongly reported Reveal to have chosen sheet 720.1 (LINN) as the type. In fact, Reveal had chosen 720.2 (LINN).

Hydrocharis morsus-ranae Linnaeus, *Species Plantarum* 2: 1036. 1753.
"Habitat in Europae fossis limosis." RCN: 7474.
Lectotype (Cook & Lüönd in *Aquatic Bot.* 14: 185. 1982): Herb. Linn. No. 1189.1 (LINN).
Generitype of *Hydrocharis* Linnaeus.
Current name: ***Hydrocharis morsus-ranae*** L. (Hydrocharitaceae).

Hydrocotyle americana Linnaeus, *Species Plantarum* 1: 234. 1753.
"Habitat in America septentrionali. Kalm." RCN: 1902.
Lectotype (Reveal in Jarvis & al. in *Taxon* 55: 212. 2006): Herb. Linn. No. 332.4 (LINN).
Current name: ***Hydrocotyle americana*** L. (Apiaceae).

Hydrocotyle asiatica Linnaeus, *Species Plantarum* 1: 234. 1753.
"Habitat in India." RCN: 1903.
Lectotype (Tardieu-Blot in Aubréville, *Fl. Cambodge Laos Vietnam* 5: 25. 1967): Herb. Linn. No. 332.5 (LINN).
Current name: ***Centella asiatica*** (L.) Urb. (Apiaceae).

Hydrocotyle chinensis Linnaeus, *Species Plantarum* 1: 234. 1753.
"Habitat in China." RCN: 1904.
Lectotype (Affolter in *Syst. Bot. Monogr.* 6: 38. 1985): Herb. Linn. No. 332.7 (LINN; iso- BM).
Current name: ***Lilaeopsis chinensis*** (L.) Kuntze (Apiaceae).

Hydrocotyle umbellata Linnaeus, *Species Plantarum* 1: 234. 1753.
"Habitat in America." RCN: 1901.
Lectotype (Matthias in *Brittonia* 2: 207. 1936): *Clayton 429* (BM-000051557).
Current name: ***Hydrocotyle umbellata*** L. (Apiaceae).

Hydrocotyle vulgaris Linnaeus, *Species Plantarum* 1: 234. 1753.
"Habitat in Europae inundatis." RCN: 1900.
Lectotype (Reduron & Jarvis in Jarvis & al., *Regnum Veg.* 127: 55. 1993): Herb. Linn. No. 332.1 (LINN), see p. 580.
Generitype of *Hydrocotyle* Linnaeus (vide Hitchcock, *Prop. Brit. Bot.*: 138. 1929).
Current name: ***Hydrocotyle vulgaris*** L. (Apiaceae).

Hydrolea spinosa Linnaeus, *Species Plantarum*, ed. 2, 1: 328. 1762.
"Habitat in America meridionali." RCN: 1850.
Neotype (Barrie in Jarvis & al., *Regnum Veg.* 127: 55. 1993): Venezuela. "Chama in paludosis", 1865, *Moritz 1297* (BM-000648925).

H

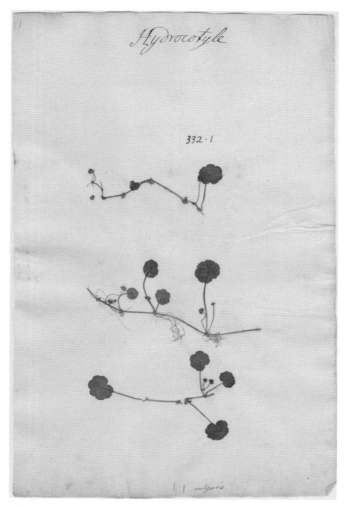

The lectotype of *Hydrocotyle vulgaris* L.

Generitype of *Hydrolea* Linnaeus, *nom. cons.*
Current name: ***Hydrolea spinosa*** L. (Hydrophyllaceae).
Note: Davenport (in *Rhodora* 90: 183. 1988) noted the absence of
material in LINN. Barrie therefore designated a neotype.

Hydrophyllum canadense Linnaeus, *Systema Naturae*, ed. 10, 2: 919.
1759.
["Habitat in Canada."] Sp. Pl., ed. 2, 1: 208 (1762). RCN: 1168.
Lectotype (Beckmann in *Taxon* 29: 276. 1980): *Kalm*, Herb. Linn.
No. 205.3 (LINN; iso- UPS).
Current name: ***Hydrophyllum canadense*** L. (Hydrophyllaceae).

Hydrophyllum virginianum Linnaeus, *Species Plantarum* 1: 146.
1753.
"Habitat in Virginia." RCN: 1167.
Lectotype (Beckmann in *Taxon* 29: 276. 1980): *Clayton 249* (BM-
000042614).
Generitype of *Hydrophyllum* Linnaeus.
Current name: ***Hydrophyllum virginianum*** L. (Hydrophyllaceae).
Note: The type sheet, although it does not carry a Clayton number,
appears from Gronovius (*Fl. Virginica*: 21. 1739) to be likely to be
Clayton 249 (and not 294 as listed by Jarvis & al., *Regnum Veg.* 127:
56. 1993).

Hymenaea courbaril Linnaeus, *Species Plantarum* 2: 1192. 1753.
"Habitat in Brasilia." RCN: 2955.
Lectotype (Lee & Langenheim in *Univ. Calif. Publ. Bot.* 69: 81.
1975): [icon] *"Ceratia diphyllos Antegoana, Ricini majoris, fructu
osseo, siliqua grandi incluso"* in Plukenet, Phytographia: t. 82, f. 3.
1691; Almag. Bot.: 96. 1696.
Generitype of *Hymenaea* Linnaeus.
Current name: ***Hymenaea courbaril*** L. (Fabaceae:
Caesalpinioideae).

Hyobanche sanguinea Linnaeus, *Mantissa Plantarum Altera*: 253.
1771.
"Habitat ad Cap. b. spei, parasitica radicum." RCN: 4596.
Type not designated.
Original material: none traced.
Generitype of *Hyobanche* Linnaeus.
Current name: ***Hyobanche sanguinea*** L. (Scrophulariaceae).

Hyoscyamus albus Linnaeus, *Species Plantarum* 1: 180. 1753.
"Habitat in Europa australi." RCN: 1425.
Lectotype (Schönbeck-Temesy in Rechinger, *Fl. Iranica* 100: 69.
1972): Herb. Linn. No. 244.2 (LINN).
Current name: ***Hyoscyamus albus*** L. (Solanaceae).

Hyoscyamus aureus Linnaeus, *Species Plantarum* 1: 180. 1753.
"Habitat in Creta." RCN: 1426.
Lectotype (Turland in *Bull. Nat. Hist. Mus. London, Bot.* 25: 140, f.
13. 1995): Herb. Clifford: 56, *Hyoscyamus* 3, sheet A (BM-
000558001).
Current name: ***Hyoscyamus aureus*** L. (Solanaceae).

Hyoscyamus muticus Linnaeus, *Systema Naturae*, ed. 12, 2: 170;
Mantissa Plantarum: 45. 1767.
"Habitat in Aegypto, Arabia." RCN: 1427.
Lectotype (Turland in *Bull. Nat. Hist. Mus. London, Bot.* 25: 147, f.
18. 1995): [icon] *"Hyosciamus albus Aegyptius"* in Alpino, Pl. Exot.:
193, 192. 1627. – Epitype (Turland in *Bull. Nat. Hist. Mus.
London, Bot.* 25: 147, f. 19. 1995): Egypt. Suez to Wadi Sudr, 28
Feb 1883, Herb. Postian. 106 (BM).
Current name: ***Hyoscyamus muticus*** L. (Solanaceae).

Hyoscyamus niger Linnaeus, *Species Plantarum* 1: 179. 1753.
"Habitat in Europae ruderatis pinguibus." RCN: 1423.
Lectotype (Schönbeck-Temesy in Rechinger, *Fl. Iranica* 100: 66.
1972): Herb. Linn. No. 244.1 (LINN).
Generitype of *Hyoscyamus* Linnaeus (vide Hitchcock, *Prop. Brit. Bot.*:
132. 1929).
Current name: ***Hyoscyamus niger*** L. (Solanaceae).

Hyoscyamus physalodes Linnaeus, *Species Plantarum* 1: 180.
1753.
"Habitat in Sibiria." RCN: 1429.
Lectotype (Nordenstam in *Fauna & Flora (Uppsala)* 73: 129, f. 1.
1978): Herb. Linn. No. 88.9 (S).
Current name: ***Physalis physalodes*** (L.) G. Don (Solanaceae).

Hyoscyamus pusillus Linnaeus, *Species Plantarum* 1: 180. 1753.
"Habitat in Persia." RCN: 1428.
Lectotype (Schönbeck-Temesy in Rechinger, *Fl. Iranica* 100: 67.
1972): Herb. Linn. No. 244.5 (LINN).
Current name: ***Hyoscyamus pusillus*** L. (Solanaceae).

Hyoscyamus reticulatus Linnaeus, *Species Plantarum*, ed. 2, 1: 257.
1762.
"Habitat in Creta, Syria, Aegypto." RCN: 1424.

Lectotype (Schönbeck-Temesy in Rechinger, *Fl. Iranica* 100: 54. 1972): [icon] *"Hyoscyamus peculiaris"* in Camerarius, Hort. Med. Phil.: 77, t. 22. 1588.
Current name: ***Hyoscyamus reticulatus*** L. (Solanaceae).

Hyoscyamus scopolia Linnaeus, *Systema Naturae,* ed. 12, 2: 171; *Mantissa Plantarum*: 46. 1767, *nom. illeg.*
"Habitat circa Idram in sylvis. Wilke." RCN: 1430.
Replaced synonym: *Scopola carniolica* Jacq. (1764).
Type not designated.
Current name: ***Scopolia carniolica*** Jacq. (Solanaceae).
Note: Evidently an illegitimate replacement name for *Scopola carniolica* Jacq. (1764).

Hyoscyamus vulgaris Linnaeus, *Flora Anglica*: 12. 1754.
"Habitat [in Anglia.]"
Type not designated.
Original material: none traced.
Current name: ***Hyoscyamus niger*** L. (Solanaceae).
Note: As noted by Stearn (*Introd. Ray's Syn. Meth. Stirp. Brit.* (Ray Soc. ed.): 66. 1973), this is a synonym of *H. niger* L.

Hyoseris cretica Linnaeus, *Species Plantarum* 2: 810. 1753.
"Habitat in Creta." RCN: 5905.
Neotype (Nordenstam in Rechinger, *Fl. Iranica* 122: 139. 1977): Herb. Linn. No. 957.11 (LINN).
Current name: ***Hedypnois rhagadioloides*** (L.) F.W. Schmidt (Asteraceae).
Note: Although 957.11 (LINN) lacks a *Species Plantarum* number (i.e. "8") and is believed to have been a later addition to the herbarium, and not original material for the name, Nordenstam treated it as the type. However, as there are no original elements in existence, Nordenstam's type choice is accepted here as correctable to a neotype, under Art. 9.8.
  Greuter (in *Candollea* 31: 230. 1976) argued that the correct name in *Hedypnois* is *H. rhagadioloides* (L.) F.W. Schmidt, regarding Dumont de Courset's preference for "cretica" as not definitely accepted by the author, and so not valid.

Hyoseris foetida Linnaeus, *Species Plantarum* 2: 808. 1753.
"Habitat in Alpibus Italiae, Austriae superioris." RCN: 5897.
Type not designated.
Original material: Herb. Burser VI: 39 (UPS); [icon] in Colonna, Ekphr., ed. 2: 29, 31. 1616; [icon] in Micheli, Nov. Pl. Gen.: 31, t. 28. 1729.
Current name: ***Aposeris foetida*** (L.) Less. (Asteraceae).

Hyoseris hedypnois Linnaeus, *Species Plantarum* 2: 809. 1753.
"Habitat in Europa australi." RCN: 5903.
Lectotype (Turland in Jarvis & Turland in *Taxon* 47: 362. 1998): Herb. Linn. No. 957.8 (LINN).
Current name: ***Hedypnois rhagadioloides*** (L.) F.W. Schmidt (Asteraceae).

Hyoseris lucida Linnaeus, *Systema Naturae,* ed. 12, 2: 525; *Mantissa Plantarum*: 108. 1767.
"Habitat in Oriente. Forskåhl." RCN: 5899.
Lectotype (Garbari & Vangelisti in Jarvis & Turland in *Taxon* 47: 363. 1998): Herb. Linn. No. 957.3 (LINN).
Current name: ***Hyoseris lucida*** L. (Asteraceae).

Hyoseris minima Linnaeus, *Species Plantarum* 2: 809. 1753.
"Habitat in Europae arvis apricis." RCN: 5902.
Type not designated.
Original material: Herb. A. van Royen No. 900.74–407 (L); Herb.

Linn. No. 957.6 (LINN); [icon] in Clusius, Rar. Pl. Hist. 2: 142. 1601; [icon] in Tabernaemontanus, Eicones Pl.: 180. 1590.
Current name: ***Arnoseris minima*** (L.) Schweigg. & Kört. (Asteraceae).

Hyoseris radiata Linnaeus, *Species Plantarum* 2: 808. 1753.
"Habitat in Hispania, G. Narbonensi." RCN: 5898.
Lectotype (Alavi in Jafri & El-Gadi, *Fl. Libya* 107: 334. 1983): Herb. Linn. No. 957.1 (LINN).
Generitype of *Hyoseris* Linnaeus (vide Green, *Prop. Brit. Bot.*: 178. 1929).
Current name: ***Hyoseris radiata*** L. (Asteraceae).

Hyoseris rhagadioloides Linnaeus, *Species Plantarum* 2: 809. 1753.
"Habitat in Europa australi." RCN: 5904.
Lectotype (Nordenstam in Rechinger, *Fl. Iranica* 122: 139. 1977): Herb. Linn. No. 957.9 (LINN).
Current name: ***Hedypnois rhagadioloides*** (L.) F.W. Schmidt (Asteraceae).

Hyoseris scabra Linnaeus, *Species Plantarum* 2: 809. 1753.
"Habitat in Sicilia." RCN: 5900.
Lectotype (Garbari & Vangelisti in Jarvis & Turland in *Taxon* 47: 363. 1998): Herb. Clifford: 386, *Hyoseris* 1 (BM-000646858).
Current name: ***Hyoseris scabra*** L. (Asteraceae).
Note: Alavi (in Jafri & El-Gadi, *Fl. Libya* 107: 332. 1983) indicated Herb. Linn. No. 957.4 (LINN) as type, but this sheet lacks a *Species Plantarum* number (i.e. "3") and was a later addition to the herbarium. It is not original material for the name.

Hyoseris virginica Linnaeus, *Species Plantarum* 2: 809. 1753.
"Habitat in Virginia." RCN: 5901.
Lectotype (Shinners in *Wrightia* 1: 197. 1947): *Clayton 376* (BM-000051190).
Current name: ***Krigia virginica*** (L.) Willd. (Asteraceae).

Hypecoum erectum Linnaeus, *Species Plantarum* 1: 124. 1753.
"Habitat in Dauria." RCN: 1027.
Type not designated.
Original material: [icon] in Amman, Stirp. Rar. Ruth.: 58, t. 9. 1739.
Current name: ***Hypecoum erectum*** L. (Fumariaceae).
Note: Dahl (in *Nordic J. Bot.* 10: 139. 1990) indicated material seen in LINN as the type, but there is no material associated with this name under *Hypecoum* (171.1–5 LINN).

Hypecoum pendulum Linnaeus, *Species Plantarum* 1: 124. 1753.
"Habitat in Galloprovincia." RCN: 1026.
Lectotype (Jafri & Qaiser in Nasir & Ali, *Fl. W. Pakistan* 61: 29. 1974): *Löfling 133,* Herb. Linn. No. 171.4 (LINN).
Current name: ***Hypecoum pendulum*** L. (Fumariaceae).

Hypecoum procumbens Linnaeus, *Species Plantarum* 1: 124. 1753.
"Habitat inter Archipelagi, Narbonae & Salmanticenses segetes." RCN: 1025.
Lectotype (Dahl in *Pl. Syst. Evol.* 163: 251. 1989): Herb. Burser IX: 53 (UPS).
Generitype of *Hypecoum* Linnaeus (vide Hitchcock, *Prop. Brit. Bot.*: 126. 1929).
Current name: ***Hypecoum procumbens*** L. (Fumariaceae).
Note: Jafri (in Jafri & El-Gadi, *Fl. Libya* 44: 7. 1977) indicated 171.4 (LINN) as type, but this collection is clearly associated with *H. pendulum* L., and is not original material for *H. procumbens*.

Hypericum aegypticum Linnaeus, *Species Plantarum* 2: 784. 1753.
"Habitat in Aegypto. D. B. Jussiaeus." RCN: 5748.

Neotype (Robson in *Bull. Nat. Hist. Mus. London, Bot.* 26: 149. 1996): Herb. Jussieu No. 11803, *B. Jussieu* (P-JUS).
Current name: ***Hypericum aegypticum*** L. (Clusiaceae).

Hypericum alium Linnaeus, *Plantae Surinamenses*: 13. 1775.
"Habitat [in Surinamo.]" RCN: 5739.
Type not designated.
Original material: *Dahlberg 52*, Herb. Linn. No. 326.7 (S).
Note: The application of this name is uncertain.

Hypericum androsaemum Linnaeus, *Species Plantarum* 2: 784. 1753.
"Habitat in Angliae, Ilvae sepibus." RCN: 5743.
Lectotype (Robson in *Bull. Brit. Mus. (Nat. Hist.), Bot.* 12: 301, 304. 1985): Herb. Clifford: 380, *Hypericum* 4 (BM-000646805).
Current name: ***Hypericum androsaemum*** L. (Clusiaceae).

Hypericum ascyron Linnaeus, *Species Plantarum* 2: 783. 1753.
"Habitat in Oriente, Sibiria, Canada." RCN: 5741.
Lectotype (Robson in *Bull. Nat. Hist. Mus. London, Bot.* 31: 53. 2001): Herb. Linn. No. 943.9 (LINN).
Current name: ***Hypericum ascyron*** L. (Clusiaceae).

Hypericum bacciferum Linnaeus, *Mantissa Plantarum Altera*: 277. 1771.
"Habitat in Mexico." RCN: 5739.
Lectotype (designated here by Robson): Herb. Linn. No. 326.7 (S).
Current name: ***Vismia baccifera*** (L.) Triana & Planch. (Clusiaceae).

Hypericum balearicum Linnaeus, *Species Plantarum* 2: 783. 1753.
"Habitat in Majorca." RCN: 5736.
Lectotype (Robson in *Bull. Brit. Mus. (Nat. Hist.), Bot.* 12: 203. 1985): Herb. Linn. No. 943.1 (LINN).
Current name: ***Hypericum balearicum*** L. (Clusiaceae).

Hypericum cajense Linnaeus, *Plantae Surinamenses*: 13. 1775.
"Habitat [in Surinamo.]" RCN: 5738.
Type not designated.
Original material: none traced.
Note: The application of this name seems uncertain.

Hypericum calycinum Linnaeus, *Systema Naturae*, ed. 12, 2: 509; *Mantissa Plantarum*: 106. 1767.
"Habitat in America septentrionali?" RCN: 5740.
Lectotype (Robson in *Bull. Brit. Mus. (Nat. Hist.), Bot.* 12: 228. 1985): Herb. Linn. No. 943.7 (LINN).
Current name: ***Hypericum calycinum*** L. (Clusiaceae).
Note: Fernald & Schubert (in *Rhodora* 50: 167. 1948) stated that *H. calycinum* is native to the Old, rather than the New, World and that "the type specimen is matched by a large amount of herbarium-material". However, they gave no indication of what they believed the type to be.

Hypericum canadense Linnaeus, *Species Plantarum* 2: 785. 1753.
"Habitat in Canada. Kalm." RCN: 5754.
Lectotype (Rodríguez Jiménez in *Mem. Soc. Ci. Nat. "La Salle"* 33: 71. 1973): *Kalm*, Herb. Linn. No. 943.26 (LINN).
Current name: ***Hypericum canadense*** L. (Clusiaceae).

Hypericum canariense Linnaeus, *Species Plantarum* 2: 784. 1753.
"Habitat in Canariis." RCN: 5746.
Lectotype (Wijnands, *Bot. Commelins*: 110. 1983): Herb. Clifford: 381, *Hypericum* 9 (BM-000646815).
Current name: ***Hypericum canariense*** L. (Clusiaceae).
Note: The Plukenet plate cited by Linnaeus is reproduced by Francisco-Ortega & Santos-Guerra (in *Archives Nat. Hist.* 26: 259. 1999).

Hypericum chinense Linnaeus, *Systema Naturae*, ed. 10, 2: 1184. 1759, *nom. illeg.*
["Habitat in China."] Sp. Pl., ed. 2, 2: 1107 (1763). RCN: 5772.
Replaced synonym of: *Hypericum monogynum* L. (1763).
Lectotype (Robson in *Taxon* 39: 134. 1990): [icon] *"Hypericum, floribus monogynis, staminibus corolla longioribus, calycibus coloratis caule fruticoso"* in Miller, Fig. Pl. Gard. Dict. 2: 101, t. 151, f. 2. 1757. – Typotype: Herb. Miller (BM).
Current name: ***Hypericum monogynum*** L. (Clusiaceae).
Note: A later homonym of *H. chinense* Osbeck (1757), and hence illegitimate.

Hypericum coris Linnaeus, *Species Plantarum* 2: 787. 1753.
"Habitat in Europa australi." RCN: 5768.
Lectotype (designated here by Robson): [icon] *"Coris lutea, C.B.P. legitima"* in Morison, Pl. Hist. Univ. 2: 469, s. 5, t. 6, f. 4. 1680. – Epitype (designated here by Robson): France. Alpes Maritimes entre Ste Agnès et la Sommet de Col de la Madone de Gorbio, 12 Jul 1972, *Van Assche s.n.* (BM; iso- BR).
Current name: ***Hypericum coris*** L. (Clusiaceae).

Hypericum crispum Linnaeus, *Systema Naturae*, ed. 12, 2: 510; *Mantissa Plantarum*: 106. 1767, *nom. illeg.*
"Habitat in Calabria, Sicilia, Graecia." RCN: 5760.
Replaced synonym: *Hypericum triquetrifolium* Turra (1765).
Type not designated.
Current name: ***Hypericum triquetrifolium*** Turra (Clusiaceae).
Note: A superfluous name for *Hypericum triquetrifolium* Turra (1765).

Hypericum elodes Linnaeus, *Amoenitates Academicae* 4: 105. 1759.
["Habitat in Angliae, Galliae paludosis."] Sp. Pl., ed. 2, 2: 1106 (1763). RCN: 5765.
Lectotype (Robson in *Bull. Nat. Hist. Mus. London, Bot.* 26: 209. 1996): *Buddle*, Herb. Sloane 124: 9 (BM-SL).
Current name: ***Hypericum elodes*** L. (Clusiaceae).
Note: See notes by Stearn (*Introd. Ray's Syn. Meth. Stirp. Brit.* (Ray Soc. ed.): 66. 1973).

Hypericum ericoides Linnaeus, *Species Plantarum* 2: 785. 1753.
"Habitat in Lusitania, Hispania." RCN: 5753.
Lectotype (designated here by Robson): [icon] *"Hypericum Ericoides minimum, foliis cinereis ex Hispania, an Hypericum Francorum, non scriptum, tenuifolium"* in Plukenet, Phytographia: t. 93, f. 5. 1691; Almag. Bot.: 189. 1696.
Current name: ***Hypericum ericoides*** L. (Clusiaceae).

Hypericum guineense Linnaeus, *Hypericum*: 4. 1776.
"Habitat in Guinea. And. Berlin." RCN: 5742.
Lectotype (designated here by Robson): [icon] *"Hypericum floribus pentagynis, subumbellatis, caule fruticoso, ramis teretibus, foliis ovatis, acutis"* in Linnaeus, Hypericum: 4, f. 1. 1776. – Epitype (designated here by Robson): Sierra Leone. *H. Smeathman s.n.* (BM; iso- MPU).
Current name: ***Vismia guineensis*** (L.) Choisy (Clusiaceae).
Note: The only original material is the figure that forms part of the protologue. Linnaeus, however, mentioned Andreas Berlin, a student of his who was latterly employed by Sir Joseph Banks, as the source of material (or possibly information). Berlin was in West Africa as an assistant to Henry Smeathman, and specimens of this species said to have been collected by the latter have been located in BM and MPU. Although it is most unlikely that they were ever seen by Linnaeus, they are chosen as epitypes.

Hypericum hircinum Linnaeus, *Species Plantarum* 2: 784. 1753.
"Habitat in Sicilia, Calabria, Creta." RCN: 5747.

Lectotype (Ramos Nuñez in *Collect. Bot. (Barcelona)* 15: 372. 1984): Herb. Linn. No. 943.16 (LINN).
Current name: ***Hypericum hircinum*** L. (Clusiaceae).
Note: Ramos Nuñez (in *Collect. Bot. (Barcelona)* 15: 372. 1984) wrongly attributed the choice of lectotype to Robson (in Davis, *Fl. Turkey* 2: 372. 1967). However, Ramos Nuñez's use of the term lectotype effects typification ahead of Robson (in *Bull. Brit. Mus. (Nat. Hist.), Bot.* 12: 307, 310. 1985).

Hypericum hirsutum Linnaeus, *Species Plantarum* 2: 786. 1753.
"Habitat in Europae collibus & montibus." RCN: 5761.
Lectotype (Robson in Rechinger, *Fl. Iranica* 49: 15. 1968): Herb. Linn. No. 943.41 (LINN).
Current name: ***Hypericum hirsutum*** L. (Clusiaceae).

Hypericum humifusum Linnaeus, *Species Plantarum* 2: 785. 1753.
"Habitat in Europa australiore." RCN: 5759.
Lectotype (Robson in Jonsell & Jarvis in *Nordic J. Bot.* 22: 81. 2002): Herb. Linn. No. 943.35 (LINN).
Current name: ***Hypericum humifusum*** L. (Clusiaceae).

Hypericum kalmianum Linnaeus, *Species Plantarum* 2: 783. 1753.
"Habitat in Virginia. Kalm." RCN: 5737.
Lectotype (Svenson in *Rhodora* 42: 9. 1940): *Kalm*, Herb. Linn. No. 943.2 (LINN).
Current name: ***Hypericum kalmianum*** L. (Clusiaceae).

Hypericum lasianthus Linnaeus, *Species Plantarum* 2: 783. 1753.
"Habitat in Carolina, Surinamo. J. Bartsch." RCN: 5110.
Lectotype (designated here by Reveal): [icon] *"Alcea Floridana quinque capsularis Laurinis foliis, leviter crenatis, seminibus coniferarum instar alatis"* in Catesby, Nat. Hist. Carolina 1: 44, t. 44. 1730.
Current name: ***Gordonia lasianthus*** (L.) J. Ellis (Theaceae).

Hypericum mexicanum Linnaeus, *Hypericum*: 5. 1776.
"Habitat in nova Granada. Mutis." RCN: 5756.
Lectotype (Robson in *Bull. Brit. Mus. (Nat. Hist.), Bot.* 16: 56. 1987): *Mútis s.n.*, Herb. Linn. No. 943.31 (LINN; iso- BM).
Current name: ***Hypericum mexicanum*** L. (Clusiaceae).

Hypericum monogynum Linnaeus, *Species Plantarum,* ed. 2, 2: 1107. 1763.
"Habitat in China." RCN: 5772.
Replaced synonym: *Hypericum chinense* L. (1759), *nom. illeg.*
Lectotype (Robson in *Blumea* 20: 251. 1972): [icon] *"Hypericum, floribus monogynis, staminibus corolla longioribus, calycibus coloratis caule fruticoso"* in Miller, Fig. Pl. Gard. Dict. 2: 101, t. 151, f. 2. 1757. – Typotype: Herb. Miller (BM).
Current name: ***Hypericum monogynum*** L. (Clusiaceae).
Note: A *nomen novum* for *H. chinense* L. (1759), *nom. illeg.*, non *H. chinense* Osbeck (1757).

Hypericum montanum Linnaeus, *Flora Suecica,* ed. 2: 266. 1755.
"Habitat in montibus Westrogothiae 213. Scaniae." RCN: 5761.
Lectotype (Robson in *Bull. Nat. Hist. Mus. London, Bot.* 26: 196. 1996): Herb. Linn. No. 943.39 (LINN).
Current name: ***Hypericum montanum*** L. (Clusiaceae).

Hypericum mutilum Linnaeus, *Species Plantarum* 2: 787. 1753.
"Habitat in Virginia, Canada." RCN: 5770.
Lectotype (Fernald in *Rhodora* 41: 549. 1939): *Clayton 232* (BM-000042223; iso- BM).
Current name: ***Hypericum mutilum*** L. (Clusiaceae).
Note: See notes by Reveal & al. (in *Huntia* 7: 226. 1987).

Hypericum nummularium Linnaeus, *Species Plantarum* 2: 787. 1753.
"Habitat in Pyrenaeis." RCN: 5767.
Lectotype (designated here by Robson): Herb. Burser XVI(1): 20 (UPS).
Current name: ***Hypericum nummularium*** L. (Clusiaceae).

Hypericum olympicum Linnaeus, *Species Plantarum* 2: 784. 1753.
"Habitat in Pyrenaeis, Olympo." RCN: 5744.
Lectotype (Robson in *Notes Roy. Bot. Gard. Edinburgh* 27: 199. 1967): Herb. Clifford: 380, *Hypericum* 8 (BM-000646814).
Current name: ***Hypericum olympicum*** L. (Clusiaceae).

Hypericum orientale Linnaeus, *Species Plantarum* 2: 785. 1753.
"Habitat in Oriente." RCN: 5749.
Lectotype (designated here by Robson): [icon] *"Hypericum Orientale, Ptarmicae foliis"* in Tournefort, Rel. Voy. Levant (Paris ed.) 2: 220. 1717.
Current name: ***Hypericum orientale*** L. (Clusiaceae).

Hypericum perfoliatum Linnaeus, *Systema Naturae,* ed. 12, 2: 510. 1767.
RCN: 5764.
Lectotype (Burtt in Burtt & Davis in *Kew Bull.* 4: 102. 1949): Herb. Linn. No. 943.44 (LINN).
Current name: ***Hypericum perfoliatum*** L. (Clusiaceae).

Hypericum perforatum Linnaeus, *Species Plantarum* 2: 785. 1753.
"Habitat in Europae pratis." RCN: 5758.
Lectotype (Robson in Rechinger, *Fl. Iranica* 49: 17. 1968): Herb. Linn. No. 943.34 (LINN).
Generitype of *Hypericum* Linnaeus (vide Green, *Prop. Brit. Bot.*: 177. 1929).
Current name: ***Hypericum perforatum*** L. (Clusiaceae).
Note: Robson indicated his type choice as sheet "943.94" (which does not exist), clearly in error for 943.34.

Hypericum petiolatum Linnaeus, *Species Plantarum,* ed. 2, 2: 1102. 1763.
"Habitat in Brasilia." RCN: 5745.
Type not designated.
Original material: none traced.
Current name: ***Vismea sp.*** (Clusiaceae).

Hypericum prolificum Linnaeus, *Systema Naturae,* ed. 12, 2: 510; *Mantissa Plantarum*: 106. 1767.
"Habitat in America septentrionali." RCN: 5752.
Lectotype (Svenson in *Rhodora* 42: 9. 1940): Herb. Linn. No. 943.20 (LINN).
Current name: ***Hypericum prolificum*** L. (Clusiaceae).
Note: Fernald & Schubert (in *Rhodora* 50: 167–168. 1948) agreed that 943.20 (LINN) was the type (illustrated in Plate 1101, f. 1–3), but questioned its identity. However, later authors (e.g. Svenson in *Rhodora* 54: 205. 1952; Robson in *Bull. Nat. Hist. Mus. London, Bot.* 26: 96. 1996) confirm that it belongs to *H. prolificum* of usage.

Hypericum pulchrum Linnaeus, *Species Plantarum* 2: 786. 1753.
"Habitat in Europa australiori." RCN: 5766.
Lectotype (Robson in Jonsell & Jarvis in *Nordic J. Bot.* 22: 81. 2002): [icon] *"Hypericum pulchrum tragi"* in Bauhin & Cherler, Hist. Pl. Univ. 3(2): 383. 1651. – Epitype (Robson in Jonsell & Jarvis in *Nordic J. Bot.* 22: 81. 2002): France. Sur les grès bigarré dans la forêt de l'Arceot, canton de Belfort (Haut-Rhine), 6 Jul 1852, *L. Parisot, s.n.*, Flora Galliae et Germaniae exsiccata de C. Billot, no. 947 (BM).
Current name: ***Hypericum pulchrum*** L. (Clusiaceae).

Hypericum quadrangulum Linnaeus, *Species Plantarum* 2: 785. 1753, *nom. utique rej.*
"Habitat in Europae pratis." RCN: 5757.
Lectotype (Robson in *Taxon* 39: 135. 1990): Herb. Clifford: 380, *Hypericum* 5 (BM-000646806).
Current name: ***Hypericum tetrapterum*** Fr. (Clusiaceae).

Hypericum repens Linnaeus, *Centuria I Plantarum*: 26. 1755.
"Habitat in Palaestina & adjacentibus. D. Hasselquist." RCN: 5751.
Lectotype (Robson in Meikle, *Fl. Cyprus* 1: 298. 1977): *Hasselquist*, Herb. Linn. No. 943.19 (LINN; iso- UPS-HASSELQ 664).
Current name: ***Hypericum repens*** L. (Clusiaceae).

Hypericum scabrum Linnaeus, *Centuria I Plantarum*: 25. 1755.
"Habitat in Arabia. D. Hasselquist." RCN: 5750.
Lectotype (Robson in Nasir & Ali, *Fl. W. Pakistan* 32: 8. 1973): *Hasselquist*, Herb. Linn. No. 943.18 (LINN; iso- UPS-HASSELQ 662).
Current name: ***Hypericum scabrum*** L. (Clusiaceae).

Hypericum setosum Linnaeus, *Species Plantarum* 2: 787. 1753.
"Habitat in Virginia." RCN: 5771.
Lectotype (Rodríguez Jiménez in *Mem. Soc. Ci. Nat. "La Salle"* 33: 133. 1973): *Clayton 153* (BM-000051158).
Current name: ***Hypericum setosum*** L. (Clusiaceae).

Hypericum tomentosum Linnaeus, *Species Plantarum* 2: 786. 1753.
"Habitat in G. Narbonensi, Hispania." RCN: 5763.
Lectotype (Robson in *Bull. Nat. Hist. Mus. London, Bot.* 26: 185. 1996): Herb. Linn. No. 943.43 (LINN).
Current name: ***Hypericum tomentosum*** L. (Clusiaceae).

Hypericum virginicum Linnaeus, *Systema Naturae*, ed. 10, 2: 1184. 1759.
["Habitat in Pensylvania."] Sp. Pl., ed. 2, 2: 1104 (1763). RCN: 5755.
Lectotype (Gillett & Robson in *Publ. Bot. (Ottowa)* 11: 32. 1981): *Kalm*, Herb. Linn. No. 943.27 (LINN).
Current name: ***Triadenum virginicum*** (L.) Raf. (Clusiaceae).

Hypochaeris achyrophorus Linnaeus, *Species Plantarum* 2: 810. 1753.
"Habitat in Creta." RCN: 5907.
Lectotype (Turland in Jarvis & Turland in *Taxon* 47: 363. 1998): Herb. Clifford: 385, *Hypochaeris* 1 (BM-000646854).
Current name: ***Hypochaeris achyrophorus*** L. (Asteraceae).

Hypochaeris glabra Linnaeus, *Species Plantarum* 2: 811. 1753.
"Habitat in Dania, Germania, Belgio." RCN: 5912.
Lectotype (Alavi in Jafri & El-Gadi, *Fl. Libya* 107: 347. 1983): Herb. Linn. No. 959.4 (LINN).
Current name: ***Hypochaeris glabra*** L. (Asteraceae).
Note: Hypochaeris glabra was treated as the generitype by Britton & Brown (*Ill. Fl. N. U. S.*, ed. 2, 3: 309. 1913; see McNeill & al. in *Taxon* 36: 374. 1987). However, under Art. 10.5, Ex. 7 (a voted example) of the Vienna Code, this is a type choice made under the American Code and is to be replaced under Art. 10.5b by Green's choice (*Prop. Brit. Bot.*: 178. 1929) of *H. radicata* L.

Hypochaeris maculata Linnaeus, *Species Plantarum* 2: 810. 1753.
"Habitat in Europae frigidioris pratis asperis." RCN: 5911.
Type not designated.
Original material: Herb. Burser VI: 71 (UPS); Herb. Linn. No. 959.1 (LINN); Herb. Burser VI: 72 (UPS); Herb. A. van Royen No. 900.337–285 (L); Herb. Clifford: 385, *Hypochaeris* 2 (BM); [icon]

in Clusius, Rar. Pl. Hist. 2: 139. 1601; [icon] in Haller, Enum. Meth. Stirp. Helv. 2: 760, t. 24. 1742.
Current name: ***Hypochaeris maculata*** L. (Asteraceae).

Hypochaeris montana Linnaeus, *Species Plantarum* 2: 810. 1753, *orth. var.*
"Habitat in Sabaudiae montibus." RCN: 5910.
Lectotype (Greuter in *Willdenowia* 33: 233. 2003): [icon] *"Hieracium montanum Endiviae folio"* in Boccone, Mus. Piante Rar. Sicilia: 148, t. 113. 1697.
Current name: ***Crepis pontana*** (L.) Dalla Torre (Asteraceae).
Note: See under *Hypochaeris pontana.*

Hypochaeris pontana Linnaeus, *Species Plantarum* 2: 810. 1753.
"Habitat in Sabaudiae montibus." RCN: 5910.
Lectotype (Greuter in *Willdenowia* 33: 233. 2003): [icon] *"Hieracium montanum Endiviae folio"* in Boccone, Mus. Piante Rar. Sicilia: 148, t. 113. 1697.
Current name: ***Crepis pontana*** (L.) Dalla Torre (Asteraceae).
Note: The specific epithet was spelled "pontana" in the protologue, argued by Sell (in *Bot. J. Linn. Soc.* 71: 251. 1975) as an error for "montana". As "montana" was already pre-occupied in *Crepis*, Sell coined *C. bocconei* (as "bocconi") as a *nomen novum.* However, Greuter points out that Linnaeus used "pontana" consistently throughout his works, and this spelling of the epithet was also taken up by many subsequent authors, in several genera. Greuter argues that it cannot be treated as a correctable error, and that *C. pontana* is the correct name.

Hypochaeris radicata Linnaeus, *Species Plantarum* 2: 811. 1753.
"Habitat in Europae cultioris pascuis." RCN: 5913.
Lectotype (Scott in Bosser & al., *Fl. Mascareignes* 109: 28. 1993): Herb. Linn. No. 959.5 (LINN).
Generitype of *Hypochaeris* Linnaeus (vide Green, *Prop. Brit. Bot.*: 178. 1929).
Current name: ***Hypochaeris radicata*** L. (Asteraceae).
Note: Hypochaeris glabra was treated as the generitype by Britton & Brown (*Ill. Fl. N. U. S.*, ed. 2, 3: 309. 1913; see McNeill & al. in *Taxon* 36: 374. 1987). However, under Art. 10.5, Ex. 7 (a voted example) of the Vienna Code, this is a type choice made under the American Code and is to be replaced under Art. 10.5b by Green's choice (*Prop. Brit. Bot.*: 178. 1929) of *H. radicata* L.
Grierson (in Dassanayake & Fosberg, *Revised Handb. Fl. Ceylon* 1: 270. 1980) and Alavi in Jafri & El-Gadi, *Fl. Libya* 107: 348. 1983) both treated unspecified material in Herb. Clifford (BM) as the type. However, there are two sheets associated with this name, evidently not part of a single gathering, and Art. 9.15 therefore does not apply. Consequently, Scott's typification appears to provide the earliest explicit choice.

Hypochaeris urens Linnaeus, *Species Plantarum* 2: 810. 1753.
"Habitat in Sicilia." RCN: 5909.
Basionym of: *Seriola urens* (L.) L. (1763).
Neotype (Turland in Jarvis & Turland in *Taxon* 47: 363. 1998): Italy. Sicilia: Palermo, S. Martino, in pascuis apricis submontosis, *Todaro 1257* [Todaro, Flora Sicula Exsiccata] (BM-000576306).
Current name: ***Hypochaeris cretensis*** (L.) Bory & Chaub. (Asteraceae).

Hypoxis decumbens Linnaeus, *Systema Naturae*, ed. 10, 2: 986. 1759.
["Habitat in America meridionali."] Sp. Pl., ed. 2, 1: 439 (1762). RCN: 2411.
Lectotype (Howard in *J. Arnold Arbor.* 60: 300. 1979): *Browne*, Herb. Linn. No. 427.2 (LINN).
Current name: ***Hypoxis decumbens*** L. (Liliaceae/Hypoxidaceae).

Hypoxis erecta Linnaeus, *Systema Naturae,* ed. 10, 2: 986. 1759, *nom. illeg.*
["Habitat in Virginia, Canada."] Sp. Pl., ed. 2, 1: 439 (1762). RCN: 2410.
Replaced synonym: *Ornithogalum hirsutum* L. (1753).
Lectotype (Stearn in *Ann. Mus. Goulandris* 6: 148. 1983): *Kalm*, Herb. Linn. No. 427.1 (LINN).
Generitype of *Hypoxis* Linnaeus (vide Britton & Brown, *Ill. Fl. N. U. S.*, ed. 2, 1: 534. 1913).
Current name: ***Hypoxis hirsuta*** (L.) Coville (Liliaceae/Hypoxidaceae).
Note: A superfluous name for *Ornithogalum hirsutum* L. (1753).

Hypoxis fasciculatus Linnaeus, *Systema Naturae,* ed. 10, 2: 986. 1759.
["Habitat ad Aleppo."] Sp. Pl., ed. 2, 1: 439 (1762). RCN: 2412.
Type not designated.
Original material: *Solander?*, Herb. Linn. No. 427.3 (LINN); [icon] in Russell, Nat. Hist. Aleppo: t. 34. 1756.
Current name: ***Merendera montana*** (L.) Lange (Liliaceae/Colchicaceae).

Hypoxis sessilis Linnaeus, *Species Plantarum,* ed. 2, 1: 439. 1762.
"Habitat in Carolina." RCN: 2413.
Lectotype (Herndon in *Rhodora* 94: 46. 1992): [icon] *"Ornithogali Virginici facie, Herba tuber. Carolinens."* in Dillenius, Hort. Eltham. 2: 298, t. 220, f. 287. 1732.

Current name: ***Hypoxis sessilis*** L. (Liliaceae/Hypoxidaceae).
Note: See discussion by Herndon (in *Rhodora* 94: 46. 1992), who also treats the Dillenius plate as the type.

Hyssopus lophanthus Linnaeus, *Species Plantarum* 2: 569. 1753.
"Habitat in Sibiria." RCN: 4166.
Lectotype (Hedge in Jarvis & al. in *Taxon* 50: 512. 2001): *Gerber,* Herb. Linn. No. 725.3 (LINN).
Current name: ***Lophanthus chinensis*** Benth. (Lamiaceae).

Hyssopus nepetoides Linnaeus, *Species Plantarum* 2: 569. 1753.
"Habitat in Virginia, Canada." RCN: 4167.
Lectotype (Sanders in Jarvis & al. in *Taxon* 50: 512. 2001): Herb. Clifford: 316, *Brunella* 2 (BM-000646158).
Current name: ***Agastache nepetoides*** (L.) Kuntze (Lamiaceae).
Note: Although Epling (in *J. Bot.* 67: 8. 1929) discussed the original elements for the name, and treated the Clifford element (BM) as the "standard specimen", this is not equivalent to a type statement (see Jarvis & al. in *Taxon* 50: 508. 2001).

Hyssopus officinalis Linnaeus, *Species Plantarum* 2: 569. 1753.
"Habitat in – – – –" RCN: 4165.
Lectotype (Hedge in *Notes Roy. Bot. Gard. Edinburgh* 27: 171. 1967): Herb. Linn. No. 725.1 (LINN).
Generitype of *Hyssopus* Linnaeus (vide Green, *Prop. Brit. Bot.*: 164. 1929).
Current name: ***Hyssopus officinalis*** L. (Lamiaceae).

H

I

Iberis amara Linnaeus, *Species Plantarum* 2: 649. 1753.
"Habitat in Helvetia." RCN: 4721.
Lectotype (Ebel in Cafferty & Jarvis in *Taxon* 51: 533. 2002): Herb. Linn. No. 827.8 (LINN).
Current name: *Iberis amara* L. (Brassicaceae).

Iberis arabica Linnaeus, *Centuria I Plantarum*: 17. 1755.
"Habitat in Cappodicia, Arabia. Hasselquist." RCN: 4724.
Lectotype (Hedge in Cafferty & Jarvis in *Taxon* 51: 533. 2002): *Hasselquist*, Herb. Linn. No. 827.10 (LINN).
Current name: *Aethionema arabicum* (L.) DC. (Brassicaceae).

Iberis badensis Linnaeus, *Centuria I Plantarum*: 17. 1755.
"Habitat in montibus Badensibus, Austriae, Matesii Italiae, inque Helvetiae alpibus."
Lectotype (Marhold & Mártonfi in Cafferty & Jarvis in *Taxon* 51: 533. 2002): [icon] *"Thlaspi montanum II"* in Clusius, Rar. Pl. Hist. 2: 131. 1601.
Current name: *Thlaspi montanum* L. (Brassicaceae).

Iberis cretica Linnaeus, *Species Plantarum* 2: 649. 1753.
"Habitat Monspelii." RCN: 4722a.
Neotype (Moreno in Cafferty & Jarvis in *Taxon* 51: 533. 2002): France. Var, Fréjus, "Bois dans le Malpey", May 1905, Herbier E. Jahandiez (Leg. C. Bertrand) (MA-44808).
Current name: *Iberis umbellata* L. (Brassicaceae).

Iberis gibraltarica Linnaeus, *Species Plantarum* 2: 649. 1753.
"Habitat in Gibraltariam Hispaniae." RCN: 4117.
Lectotype (Moreno in Cafferty & Jarvis in *Taxon* 51: 534. 2002): [icon] *"Thlaspidium Hispan. ampliore flore, folio crasso dentato"* in Dillenius, Hort. Eltham. 2: 382, t. 287, f. 371. 1732. – Epitype (Moreno in Cafferty & Jarvis in *Taxon* 51: 534. 2002): Gibraltar. 19 Apr 1907, *Bicknell & Pollini s.n.*, lower left-hand specimen (MA-44627).
Current name: *Iberis gibraltarica* L. (Brassicaceae).

Iberis linifolia Linnaeus, *Systema Naturae,* ed. 10, 2: 1129. 1759.
["Habitat in Hispania, Lusitania."] Sp. Pl., ed. 2, 2: 906 (1763). RCN: 4722.
Lectotype (Moreno in *Collect. Bot. (Barcelona)* 15: 344. 1984): *Gérard s.n.*, Herb. Linn. No. 827.9 (LINN; iso- Draguignan).
Current name: *Iberis linifolia* L. subsp. *linifolia* (Brassicaceae).
Note: Tison (in *Monde Pl.* 468: 30. 2000) states that there is a well-preserved isotype in Gérard's herbarium in Draguignan.

Iberis nudicaulis Linnaeus, *Species Plantarum* 2: 650. 1753.
"Habitat in Europae arenosis, sylvaticis, nudis, sterilissimis." RCN: 4725.
Lectotype (Moreno in Cafferty & Jarvis in *Taxon* 51: 534. 2002): Herb. Linn. No. 827.11 (LINN).
Current name: *Teesdalia nudicaulis* (L.) R. Br. (Brassicaceae).

Iberis odorata Linnaeus, *Species Plantarum* 2: 649. 1753.
"Habitat in Alpibus Allobrogicis." RCN: 4723.
Lectotype (Meikle, *Fl. Cyprus* 1: 123. 1977): [icon] *"Thlaspi IIII parvum odorato flore"* in Clusius, Rar. Pl. Hist. 2: 132. 1601. – Epitype (Moreno in Cafferty & Jarvis in *Taxon* 51: 534. 2002): Algeria. 8 Apr 1952, *Dubuis & Faurel s.n.*, lower left-hand specimen (MA-562364).
Current name: *Iberis odorata* L. (Brassicaceae).
Note: As noted by Villarrubia & Moreno (in *Acta Bot. Malac.* 17: 127.

1992), Linnaeus believed, on the authority of Clusius, that this taxon came from the Savoie Alps in France, but this is erroneous, the species in fact occurring in Greece, Turkey, Crete and Algeria. Moreno designated an epitype in order to clarify the discrepancy in distribution.

Iberis pinnata Linnaeus, *Centuria I Plantarum*: 18. 1755.
"Habitat in Europae maritimis." RCN: 4726.
Lectotype (Moreno in Cafferty & Jarvis in *Taxon* 51: 534. 2002): Herb. Linn. No. 827.12 (LINN).
Current name: *Iberis pinnata* L. (Brassicaceae).
Note: Although Villarrubia & Moreno (in *Bot. Complut.* 18: 130. 1993) noted the existence of 827.12 and 827.13 (LINN), they did not indicate either as type.

Iberis rotundifolia Linnaeus, *Species Plantarum* 2: 649. 1753.
"Habitat in Helvetia." RCN: 4719.
Type not designated.
Original material: Herb. Linn. No. 827.7? (LINN); [icon] in Barrelier, Pl. Galliam: 38, t. 848. 1714.
Current name: *Thlaspi cepaeifolium* (Wulfen) W.D.J. Koch subsp. *rotundifolium* Greuter & Burdet (Brassicaceae).
Note: Polatschek (in *Ann. Naturhist. Mus. Wien* 70: 32. 1967) treated 827.4 (LINN) as lectotype, but this is an Allioni collection received by Linnaeus only in 1757, so it could not have been original material for the name.

Iberis saxatilis Linnaeus, *Centuria II Plantarum*: 23. 1756.
"Habitat in Italia, Galliaeque australis aridis sabulosis. Sauvages." RCN: 4718.
Lectotype (Franzén in Strid, *Mountain Fl. Greece* 1: 333. 1986): Herb. Linn. No. 825.3 (LINN).
Current name: *Iberis saxatilis* L. (Brassicaceae).

Iberis semperflorens Linnaeus, *Species Plantarum* 2: 648. 1753.
"Habitat in Sicilia, Persia." RCN: 4715.
Lectotype (Moreno in Jarvis & al., *Regnum Veg.* 127: 56. 1993): [icon] *"Thlaspi fruticosum leucojifolio latifolium platycarpon"* in Boccone, Icon. Descr. Rar. Pl. Siciliae: 55, 56, t. 29, f. A-i. 1674.
Generitype of *Iberis* Linnaeus (vide Green in *Bull. Misc. Inform. Kew* 1925: 52. 1925).
Current name: *Iberis semperflorens* L. (Brassicaceae).

Iberis sempervirens Linnaeus, *Species Plantarum* 2: 648. 1753.
"Habitat in Cretae rupestribus." RCN: 4716.
Lectotype (Moreno in Cafferty & Jarvis in *Taxon* 51: 534. 2002): Herb. Clifford: 330, *Iberis* 3 (BM-000646261).
Current name: *Iberis sempervirens* L. (Brassicaceae).

Iberis umbellata Linnaeus, *Species Plantarum* 2: 649. 1753.
"Habitat in Hetruria, Creta." RCN: 4720.
Lectotype (Moreno in Cafferty & Jarvis in *Taxon* 51: 534. 2002): Herb. Linn. No. 827.6 (LINN).
Current name: *Iberis umbellata* L. (Brassicaceae).
Note: Franchetti (in *Webbia* 14: 178. 1958) discussed various options for the typification of this name but did not herself choose a type.

Ilex agrifolium Linnaeus, *Amoenitates Academicae* 4: 478. 1759, *orth. var.*
Lectotype (Pedley in George, *Fl. Australia* 22: 201. 1984): Herb. Linn. No. 173.1 (LINN).
Current name: *Ilex aquifolium* L. (Aquifoliaceae).

Note: As noted by Stearn (in Geck & Pressler, *Festschr. Claus Nissen*: 631. 1974), this is an orthographic variant of *I. aquifolium* L. (1753).

Ilex aquifolium Linnaeus, *Species Plantarum* 1: 125. 1753.
"Habitat in Europa australiori, Japonia, virginia [sic]." RCN: 1028.
Lectotype (Pedley in George, *Fl. Australia* 22: 201. 1984): Herb. Linn. No. 173.1 (LINN).
Generitype of *Ilex* Linnaeus (vide Hitchcock, *Prop. Brit. Bot.*: 126. 1929).
Current name: ***Ilex aquifolium*** L. (Aquifoliaceae).

Ilex asiatica Linnaeus, *Species Plantarum* 1: 125. 1753.
"Habitat in India Asiae." RCN: 1030.
Type not designated.
Original material: none traced.
Note: As noted by Hu (in *J. Arnold Arbor.* 30: 235. 1949), the application of this name appears uncertain.

Ilex cassine Linnaeus, *Species Plantarum* 1: 125. 1753.
"Habitat in Carolina." RCN: 1029.
Lectotype (González Gutiérrez & Sierra Calzado in Greuter & Rankin, *Fl. Republ. Cuba*, ser. A, 9(1): 10. 2004): [icon] *"Agrifolium Carolinense foliis dentatis baccis rubris"* in Catesby, Nat. Hist. Carolina 1: 31, t. 31. 1730.
Current name: ***Ilex cassine*** L. (Aquifoliaceae).
Note: See Edwin (in *Castanea* 28: 49–54. 1963), who discussed the name, and reproduced the Catesby plate (p. 52).

Ilex cuneifolia Linnaeus, *Species Plantarum* 1: 125. 1753.
"Habitat in America meridonali." RCN: 1031.
Lectotype (Pennington, *Fl. Neotropica* 28: 277. 1757): [icon] *"Ilex foliis cuneiformibus"* in Plumier in Burman, Pl. Amer.: 109, t. 118, f. 2. 1757.
Current name: ***Trichilia aquifolia*** P. Wilson (Meliaceae).

Ilex dodonaea Linnaeus, *Species Plantarum* 1: 125. 1753.
"Habitat in America meridonali." RCN: 1032.
Lectotype (Howard, *Fl. Lesser Antilles* 5: 97. 1989): [icon] *"Dodonaea"* in Plumier, Nov. Pl. Amer.: 20, t. 12. 1703.
Current name: ***Comocladia dodonaea*** (L.) Urb. (Aquifoliaceae).

Illecebrum achyranthum Linnaeus, *Species Plantarum*, ed. 2, 1: 299. 1762, *nom. illeg.*
"Habitat in Turcomannia." RCN: 1681.
Replaced synonym: *Achyranthes repens* L. (1753).
Type not designated.
Original material: as replaced synonym.
Current name: ***Alternanthera pungens*** (L.) Kunth (Amaranthaceae).
Note: An illegitimate replacement name for *Achyranthes repens* L. (1753).

Illecebrum alsinifolium Linnaeus, *Systema Naturae,* ed. 12, 2: 188; *Mantissa Plantarum*: 51. 1767.
"Habitat in Hispania." RCN: 1686.
Lectotype (Amich in Cafferty & Jarvis in *Taxon* 53: 1052. 2004): Herb. Linn. No. 290.28 (LINN).
Current name: ***Polycarpon tetraphyllum*** (L.) L. (Caryophyllaceae).

Illecebrum arabicum Linnaeus, *Systema Naturae,* ed. 12, 2: 188; *Mantissa Plantarum*: 51. 1767.
"Habitat in Arabia. Forskåhl." RCN: 1680.
Lectotype (Burtt & Lewis in *Kew Bull.* 7: 336. 1952): Herb. Linn. No. 290.19 (LINN).
Current name: ***Paronychia arabica*** (L.) DC. (Caryophyllaceae).

Illecebrum bengalense Linnaeus, *Mantissa Plantarum Altera*: 213. 1771.
"Habitat in India orientali: Benghala, Java." RCN: 1679.
Type not designated.
Original material: none traced.
Current name: ***Achyranthes*** sp. (Amaranthaceae).
Note: The application of this name is uncertain.

Illecebrum brachiatum (Linnaeus) Linnaeus, *Mantissa Plantarum Altera*: 213. 1771.
"Habitat in India orientali." RCN: 1670.
Basionym: *Achyranthes brachiata* L. (1767).
Lectotype (Townsend in Nasir & Ali, *Fl. W. Pakistan* 71: 32. 1974): Herb. Linn. No. 290.1 (LINN).
Current name: ***Nothosaerva brachiata*** (L.) Wight (Amaranthaceae).

Illecebrum capitatum Linnaeus, *Species Plantarum* 1: 207. 1753.
"Habitat in G. Narbonensis, Hispania." RCN: 1678.
Lectotype (Chaudhri, *Rev. Paronychiinae*: 283. 1968): Herb. Linn. No. 290.17 (LINN).
Current name: ***Paronychia capitata*** (L.) Lam. (Caryophyllaceae).

Illecebrum cymosum Linnaeus, *Species Plantarum* 1: 206. 1753.
"Habitat Monspelii. D. Sauvages." RCN: 1676.
Lectotype (Soriano Martín in Cafferty & Jarvis in *Taxon* 53: 1052. 2004): Herb. Linn. No. 290.12 (LINN).
Current name: ***Chaetonychia cymosa*** (L.) Sweet (Caryophyllaceae).

Illecebrum ficoideum (Linnaeus) Linnaeus, *Species Plantarum*, ed. 2, 1: 300. 1762, *typ. cons.*
"Habitat in marinis littoribus Americae, nunc Hispaniae." RCN: 1683.
Basionym: *Gomphrena ficoidea* L. (1753), *nom. & typ. cons.*
Conserved type (Veldkamp in *Taxon* 38: 299. 1989): Herb. Linn. No. 290.23 (LINN).
Current name: ***Alternanthera ficoidea*** (L.) P. Beauv. (Amaranthaceae).

Illecebrum javanicum (N.L. Burman) Linnaeus, *Systema Vegetabilium,* ed. 13: 206. 1774.
RCN: 1673.
Basionym: *Iresine javanica* Burm. f. (1768).
Type not designated.
Current name: ***Aerva javanica*** (Burm. f.) Juss. (Amaranthaceae).
Note: Specific epithet spelled "javanica" in *Syst. Veg.*, ed. 13.

Illecebrum lanatum (Linnaeus) Linnaeus, *Mantissa Plantarum Altera*: 344. 1771.
["Habitat in India."] Sp. Pl. 1: 204 (1753). RCN: 1672.
Basionym: *Achyranthes lanata* L. (1753).
Type not designated.
Original material: as basionym.
Current name: ***Aerva lanata*** (L.) Schult. (Amaranthaceae).

Illecebrum paronychia Linnaeus, *Species Plantarum* 1: 206. 1753.
"Habitat in Hispania & Narbona." RCN: 1677.
Lectotype (Chaudhri in Cafferty & Jarvis in *Taxon* 53: 1052. 2004): Herb. Clifford: 41, *Herniaria* 2, sheet B (BM-000557848).
Current name: ***Paronychia argentea*** Lam. (Caryophyllaceae).
Note: Chaudhri (in *Meded. Bot. Mus. Herb. Rijks Univ. Utrecht* 285: 211. 1968) stated "Lectotype: Hort. Cliff. 41, Linnaeus Herb. 290/14 (LINN!)". However, this includes three separate collections (two at BM, one at LINN) which are not part of a single gathering, so his statement was not an effective typification.

Illecebrum polygonoides (Linnaeus) Linnaeus, *Species Plantarum,* ed. 2, 1: 300. 1762.
"Habitat in Americae littoribus maris." RCN: 1682.
Basionym: *Gomphrena polygonoides* L. (1753).
Type not designated.
Original material: as basionym.
Current name: ***Alternanthera sessilis*** (L.) DC. (Amaranthaceae).

Illecebrum sanguinolentum (Linnaeus) Linnaeus, *Mantissa Plantarum Altera*: 344. 1771.
["Habitat in India."] Sp. Pl., ed. 2, 1: 294 (1762). RCN: 1671.
Basionym: *Achyranthes sanguinolenta* L. (1762).
Lectotype (Townsend in Nasir & Ali, *Fl. W. Pakistan* 71: 30. 1974): Herb. Linn. No. 290.3 (LINN).
Current name: ***Aerva sanguinolenta*** (L.) Blume (Amaranthaceae).

Illecebrum sessile (Linnaeus) Linnaeus, *Species Plantarum,* ed. 2, 1: 300. 1762.
"Habitat in India Orientali." RCN: 1684.
Basionym: *Gomphrena sessilis* L. (1753).
Lectotype (Fawcett & Rendle, *Fl. Jamaica* 3: 140. 1914; Mears in *Taxon* 29: 89. 1980): Herb. Hermann 2: 9, No. 116 (BM-000621528).
Current name: ***Alternanthera sessilis*** (L.) DC. (Amaranthaceae).
Note: Fawcett & Rendle's original indication of the Hermann material as type was restricted by Mears to the material in vol. 2: 9 (BM).

Illecebrum suffruticosum Linnaeus, *Species Plantarum* 1: 206. 1753.
"Habitat in Hispania." RCN: 1675.
Lectotype (Chaudhri, *Rev. Paronychiinae*: 118. 1968): Herb. Linn. No. 290.11 (LINN).
Current name: ***Paronychia suffruticosa*** (L.) DC. (Caryophyllaceae).

Illecebrum vermiculatum Linnaeus, *Species Plantarum,* ed. 2, 1: 300. 1762, *nom. illeg.*
"Habitat in Brasilia, Curacao." RCN: 1685.
Replaced synonym: *Gomphrena vermicularis* L. (1753).
Type not designated.
Original material: as replaced synonym.
Current name: ***Blutaparon vermiculare*** (L.) Mears (Amaranthaceae).

Illecebrum verticillatum Linnaeus, *Species Plantarum* 1: 206. 1753.
"Habitat in Europae pascuis udis." RCN: 1674.
Lectotype (Jonsell & Jarvis in Jarvis & al., *Regnum Veg.* 127: 56. 1993): Herb. Burser XII: 53 (UPS).
Generitype of *Illecebrum* Linnaeus (vide Hitchcock, *Prop. Brit. Bot.*: 135. 1929).
Current name: ***Illecebrum verticillatum*** L. (Caryophyllaceae).
Note: Jonsell & Jarvis (in *Nordic J. Bot.* 14: 157. 1994) gave further details of their formal (1993) type choice.

Illicium anisatum Linnaeus, *Systema Naturae,* ed. 10, 2: 1050. 1759.
["Habitat in Japonia, China."] Sp. Pl., ed. 2, 1: 664 (1762). RCN: 3976.
Lectotype (Lin in *Acta Phytotax. Sinica* 38: 169. 2000): [icon] *"Skimmi"* in Kaempfer, Amoen. Exot. Fasc.: 880, 881. 1712. – Voucher: Herb. Sloane 211: 51 (BM-SL).
Generitype of *Illicium* Linnaeus.
Current name: ***Illicium anisatum*** L. (Illiciaceae).
Note: While Smith (in *Sargentia* 7: 30. 1947) indicated that the name was based entirely upon Kaempfer's account and plate, this falls short of formal typification which was, however, subsequently effected by Lin.

Impatiens balsamina Linnaeus, *Species Plantarum* 2: 938. 1753.
"Habitat in India." RCN: 6796.
Type not designated.
Original material: Herb. Linn. No. 1053.3 (LINN); Herb. Linn. No. 370.1? (S); Herb. Clifford: 428, *Impatiens* 2, 2 sheets (BM); Herb. Linn. No. 1053.4 (LINN); Herb. Burser XVII: 81 (UPS); [icon] in Dodoëns, Stirp. Hist. Pempt., ed. 2: 671. 1616.
Current name: ***Impatiens balsamina*** L. (Balsaminaceae).

Impatiens chinensis Linnaeus, *Species Plantarum* 2: 937. 1753.
"Habitat in China." RCN: 6792.
Type not designated.
Original material: Herb. Linn. No. 1053.1 (LINN).
Current name: ***Impatiens chinensis*** L. (Balsaminaceae).

Impatiens cornuta Linnaeus, *Species Plantarum* 2: 937. 1753.
"Habitat in Zeylona." RCN: 6795.
Type not designated.
Original material: Herb. Hermann 4: 4, No. 316 (BM); Herb. Hermann 3: 9, No. 316 (BM); [icon] in Burman, Thes. Zeylan.: 41, t. 16, f. 1. 1737.
Current name: ***Impatiens balsamina*** L. (Balsaminaceae).

Impatiens latifolia Linnaeus, *Species Plantarum* 2: 937. 1753.
"Habitat in India." RCN: 6793.
Type not designated.
Original material: Herb. Linn. No. 1053.2 (LINN); [icon] in Rheede, Hort. Malab. 9: 91, t. 48. 1689.
Current name: ***Impatiens latifolia*** L. (Balsaminaceae).
Note: See Manilal & al. (in *Rheedea* 13: 17. 2005), who wrongly claim that this was based solely on the Rheede element.

Impatiens noli-tangere Linnaeus, *Species Plantarum* 2: 938. 1753.
"Habitat in Europae, Canadae nemoribus." RCN: 6798.
Lectotype (Grey-Wilson in Rechinger, *Fl. Iranica* 143: 4. 1979): *Kalm*, Herb. Linn. No. 1053.6 (LINN).
Generitype of *Impatiens* Linnaeus (vide Green, *Prop. Brit. Bot.*: 184. 1929).
Current name: ***Impatiens noli-tangere*** L. (Balsaminaceae).
Note: Grey-Wilson (in Rechinger, *Fl. Iranica* 143: 4. 1979) indicated a Kalm specimen (1053.6 LINN) as type, but the collection is apparently identifiable as *I. capensis* Meerb. (see Barrie & al. in *Taxon* 41: 511. 1992). Reveal (in Jarvis & al., *Regnum Veg.* 127: 57. 1993) therefore designated a Clifford sheet as lectotype against the possible adoption of the latter work as a Names in Current Use (NCU) List. However, Grey-Wilson's choice now has priority and, if the identity of the type is confirmed, a conservation proposal appears to be necessary.

Impatiens oppositifolia Linnaeus, *Species Plantarum* 2: 937. 1753.
"Habitat in Zeylonae arenosis." RCN: 6794.
Lectotype (Grey-Wilson in Dassanayake & Fosberg, *Revised Handb. Fl. Ceylon* 5: 110. 1985): Herb. Hermann 2: 15, No. 314 (BM-000621557).
Current name: ***Impatiens oppositifolia*** L. (Balsaminaceae).

Impatiens triflora Linnaeus, *Species Plantarum* 2: 938. 1753.
"Habitat in Zeylonae paludosis." RCN: 6797.
Lectotype (Grey-Wilson in *Kew Bull.* 35: 218. 1980): Herb. Hermann 3: 35, No. 315 (BM-000621927).
Current name: ***Hydrocera triflora*** (L.) Wight & Arn. (Balsaminaceae).

Imperatoria ostruthium Linnaeus, *Species Plantarum* 1: 259. 1753.
"Habitat ad radices Alpium Helvetiae, Austriae." RCN: 2073.

Lectotype (Reduron & Jarvis in Jarvis & al., *Regnum Veg.* 127: 57.
1993): Herb. Clifford: 103, *Imperatoria* 1 (BM-000558352).
Generitype of *Imperatoria* Linnaeus.
Current name: ***Peucedanum ostruthium*** (L.) W.D.J. Koch (Apiaceae).

Indigofera angustifolia Linnaeus, *Mantissa Plantarum Altera*: 272.
1771.
"Habitat ad Cap. b. spei, locis argillosis." RCN: 5554.
Lectotype (Schrire in Turland & Jarvis in *Taxon* 46: 473. 1997):
Tulbagh 94, Herb. Linn. No. 923.18 (LINN).
Current name: ***Indigofera angustifolia*** L. (Fabaceae: Faboideae).

Indigofera anil Linnaeus, *Mantissa Plantarum Altera*: 272. 1771.
"Habitat in India." RCN: 5555.
Lectotype (Kort & Thijsse in *Blumea* 30: 135. 1985): Herb. Linn. No.
923.20 (LINN).
Current name: ***Indigofera suffruticosa*** Mill. (Fabaceae: Faboideae).
Note: Although Fawcett & Rendle (*Fl. Jamaica* 4: 16. 1920) noted the
existence of 923.20 (LINN), and commented on its identity, they
did not treat it as the type.

Indigofera argentea Linnaeus, *Mantissa Plantarum Altera*: 273. 1771,
nom. illeg.
"Habitat in India." RCN: 5558.
Lectotype (Schrire in Turland & Jarvis in *Taxon* 46: 473. 1997): [icon]
*"Coluteae affinis fruticosa argentea floribus spicatis e viridi purpureis
siliquis falcatis"* in Sloane, Voy. Jamaica 2: 37, t. 176, f. 3. 1725. –
Typotype: Herb. Sloane 6: 8, upper left specimen (BM-SL).
Current name: ***Indigofera tinctoria*** L. (Fabaceae: Faboideae).
Note: A later homonym of *Indigofera argentea* Burm. f. (1768) and
hence illegitimate. See comments by Ali (*Rev. Gen.* Indigofera: 565.
1958).

Indigofera cytisoides (Linnaeus) Linnaeus, *Systema Naturae*, ed. 12,
2: 496. 1767.
["Habitat ad Cap. b. spei."] Sp. Pl., ed. 2, 2: 1076 (1763). RCN: 5552.
Basionym: *Psoralea cytisoides* L. (1763).
Lectotype (Wijnands, *Bot. Commelins*: 163. 1983): Herb. Linn. No.
923.13 (LINN).
Current name: ***Indigofera cytisoides*** (L.) L. (Fabaceae: Faboideae).

Indigofera disperma Linnaeus, *Systema Naturae*, ed. 12, 3: 232.
1768.
"Habitat in Indiis." RCN: 5557.
Lectotype (Lievens in Turland & Jarvis in *Taxon* 46: 473. 1997):
[icon] *"Indigofera scapo infirmo, foliorum pinnis oblongis pallide
virentibus glabris, pedunculis spicae longissimis, floribus laxe dispositis,
leguminibus compressis brevibus gibbosis subasperis dispermis"* in Trew,
Pl. Select.: 24, t. 55. 1759, see above, right.
Current name: ***Indigofera caroliniana*** Mill. (Fabaceae: Faboideae).

Indigofera enneaphylla Linnaeus, *Mantissa Plantarum Altera*: 272.
1771, *nom. illeg.*
"Habitat in India orientali." RCN: 5549.
Replaced synonym: *Psoralea pinnata* L. (1753).
Lectotype (Stirton in *Taxon* 41: 568. 1992): Herb. Clifford: 370,
Dorycnium 1 (BM-000646705).
Current name: ***Psoralea pinnata*** L. (Fabaceae: Faboideae).
Note: As noted by Ali (in *Bot. Not.* 111: 551. 1958) and Kort &
Thijsse (in *Blumea* 30: 125. 1984), this is an illegitimate renaming
in *Indigofera* of *Psoralea pinnata* L. (1753). Although Sanjappa (in
Reinwardtia 10: 225. 1985) indicated material in Herb. Sloane 95:
186 (BM-SL) as the type of *I. linnaei* Ali (thought to be homotypic
with *I. enneaphylla*), the typification of the latter is dependent on
that of *P. pinnata*, which was made by Stirton in 1992.

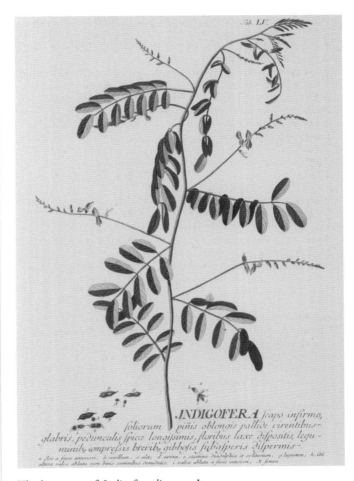

The lectotype of *Indigofera disperma* L.

Indigofera glabra Linnaeus, *Species Plantarum* 2: 751. 1753.
"Habitat in India." RCN: 5551.
Lectotype (Ali in *Bot. Not.* 111: 572. 1958): Herb. Hermann 3: 27,
No. 274 (BM-000621906).
Current name: ***Indigofera glabra*** L. (Fabaceae: Faboideae).

Indigofera hirsuta Linnaeus, *Species Plantarum* 2: 751. 1753.
"Habitat in India." RCN: 5553.
Lectotype (Ali in *Bot. Not.* 111: 560. 1958): Herb. Hermann 1: 60,
No. 272 (BM-000594492).
Current name: ***Indigofera hirsuta*** L. (Fabaceae: Faboideae).

Indigofera pentaphylla Linnaeus, *Systema Vegetabilium*, ed. 13: 564.
1774.
RCN: 5550.
Lectotype (Sanjappa in Turland & Jarvis in *Taxon* 46: 473. 1997):
Herb. Linn. No. 923.12 (LINN).
Current name: ***Indigofera glabra*** L. (Fabaceae: Faboideae).

Indigofera procumbens Linnaeus, *Mantissa Plantarum Altera*: 271.
1771.
"Habitat ad Cap. b. spei montibus." RCN: 5548.
Lectotype (Schrire in Turland & Jarvis in *Taxon* 46: 473. 1997):
Tulbagh 121, Herb. Linn. No. 923.5 (LINN).
Current name: ***Indigofera procumbens*** L. (Fabaceae: Faboideae).

Indigofera psoraloides (Linnaeus) Linnaeus, *Systema Naturae*, ed. 12, 2: 496. 1767.
["Habitat ad Cap. b. spei."] Sp. Pl., ed. 2, 2: 1043 (1763). RCN: 5547.
Basionym: *Cytisus psoraloides* L. (1760).
Lectotype (Schrire in Turland & Jarvis in *Taxon* 46: 468. 1997): [icon] *"Trifolium Aethiopicum ex alis foliorum spicatum, bituminosi foliis angustioribus, s. Trifolium spicatum tenuifolium"* in Plukenet, Phytographia: t. 320, f. 3. 1694; Almag. Bot.: 375. 1696. – Typotype: Herb. Sloane 102: 91, central specimen (BM-SL).
Current name: ***Indigofera psoraloides*** (L.) L. (Fabaceae: Faboideae).

Indigofera racemosa Linnaeus, *Species Plantarum*, ed. 2, 2: 1062. 1763.
"Habitat ad Cap. b. spei." RCN: 5547.
Replaced synonym: *Indigofera trifoliata* L. (1760), *nom. illeg.*, non L. (1756).
Neotype (Schrire in Turland & Jarvis in *Taxon* 46: 474. 1997): South Africa. Cape Peninsula, W of Little Lions Head, slopes near sea, 4 Nov 1933, *T.M. Salter 3967* (K).
Current name: ***Indigofera psoraloides*** (L.) L. (Fabaceae: Faboideae).
Note: A *nomen novum* for the illegitimate *Indigofera trifoliata* L. (1760), non (1756).

Indigofera sericea Linnaeus, *Mantissa Plantarum Altera*: 271. 1771.
"Habitat ad Cap. b. spei campis arenosis, montosis humentibus. H. U." RCN: 5545.
Type not designated.
Original material: *Tulbagh 46 & 116*, Herb. Linn. No. 923.1 (LINN).
Current name: ***Amphithalea ericifolia*** (L.) Eckl. & Zeyh. (Fabaceae: Faboideae).
Note: Although Granby (*Opera Bot.* 80: 28. 1985) indicated both 923.1 and 923.2 (LINN) as types, they are not part of a single gathering and so Art. 9.15 does not apply. The name remains untyped at present.

Indigofera tinctoria Linnaeus, *Species Plantarum* 2: 751. 1753.
"Habitat in India." RCN: 5556.
Lectotype (Fawcett & Rendle, *Fl. Jamaica* 4: 15. 1920): Herb. Hermann 3: 20, No. 273 (BM-000594662).
Generitype of *Indigofera* Linnaeus (vide Green, *Prop. Brit. Bot.*: 176. 1929).
Current name: ***Indigofera tinctoria*** L. (Fabaceae: Faboideae).

Indigofera trifoliata Linnaeus, *Centuria II Plantarum*: 29. 1756.
"Habitat in India." RCN: 5546.
Lectotype (Ali in *Bot. Not.* 111: 552. 1958; Sanjappa in Turland & Jarvis in *Taxon* 46: 474. 1997): Herb. Linn. No. 923.3, right specimen (LINN).
Current name: ***Indigofera trifoliata*** L. (Fabaceae: Faboideae).
Note: Ali (in *Bot. Not.* 111: 552. 1958), followed by other authors, designated the whole sheet 923.3 (LINN) as the type. However, subsequent study has shown this sheet to bear a mixture of materials and Sanjappa therefore restricted Ali's original choice to that part of the material that corresponds with *I. trifoliata* of usage.

Indigofera trifoliata Linnaeus, *Plantae Rariores Africanae*: 15. 1760, *nom. illeg.*
["Habitat ad Cap. b. spei."] Sp. Pl., ed. 2, 2: 1062. 1763.
Replaced synonym of: *Indigofera racemosa* L. (1763).
Neotype (Schrire in Turland & Jarvis in *Taxon* 46: 474. 1997): South Africa. Cape Peninsula, W of Little Lions Head, slopes near sea, 4 Nov 1933, *T.M. Salter 3967* (K).
Current name: ***Indigofera psoraloides*** (L.) L. (Fabaceae: Faboideae).
Note: A later homonym of *Indigofera trifoliata* L. (1756) and hence illegitimate.

Inula aestuans Linnaeus, *Species Plantarum*, ed. 2, 2: 1236. 1763.
"Habitat in America calidiore." RCN: 6392.
Type not designated.
Original material: [icon] in Plumier in Burman, Pl. Amer.: 29, t. 41, f. 2. 1756.
Note: The cited Plumier plate is the only original element and seems to be unidentifiable. The name seems not to have been taken up.

Inula arabica Linnaeus, *Systema Naturae*, ed. 12, 2: 558; *Mantissa Plantarum*: 114. 1767.
"Habitat in Arabia. Forskåhl; India." RCN: 6381.
Lectotype (Lack in Rechinger, *Fl. Iranica* 145: 115. 1980): Herb. Linn. No. 999.20 (LINN).
Current name: ***Pulicaria arabica*** (L.) Cass. subsp. ***arabica*** (Asteraceae).

Inula aromatica Linnaeus, *Plantae Rariores Africanae*: 22. 1760.
["Habitat ad Cap. b. spei."] Sp. Pl., ed. 2, 2: 1241 (1763). RCN: 6395.
Lectotype (Kroner in *Mitt. Bot. Staatssamml. München* 16: 116. 1980): [icon] *"Aster fruticescens luteus, Mauritanicus, folio Staechadis incano, Seriphii facie, & sapore"* in Plukenet, Phytographia: t. 326, f. 2. 1694; Almag. Bot.: 58. 1696. – Typotype: Herb. Sloane 99: 136 (BM-SL).
Current name: ***Printzia aromatica*** (L.) Less. (Asteraceae).

Inula bifrons Linnaeus, *Species Plantarum*, ed. 2, 2: 1236. 1763.
"Habitat in Italia, Galloprovincia, Pyrenaeis." RCN: 6393.
Lectotype (Anderberg in Jarvis & Turland in *Taxon* 47: 363. 1998): Herb. Linn. No. 993.11 (LINN).
Current name: ***Inula bifrons*** L. (Asteraceae).
Note: The Hermann (1698) reference that appeared in synonymy here had previously been cited in the synonymy of *Conyza bifrons* L. (1753), leading many authors to assume that Linnaeus was restricting *C. bifrons* to a European taxon and simultaneously transferring it to *Inula*. However, this is not the case for, in 1763, he continued to recognise *C. bifrons* (*Sp. Pl.*, ed. 2, 2: 1207), instead restricting it to a North American taxon. The correct authority is therefore *I. bifrons* L., rather than *I. bifrons* (L.) L.

Inula britannica Linnaeus, *Species Plantarum* 2: 882. 1753.
"Habitat in Lusatia, Bavaria, Scania." RCN: 6376.
Lectotype (Anderberg in Jarvis & Turland in *Taxon* 47: 363. 1998): Herb. Burser XV(1): 41 (UPS).
Current name: ***Inula britannica*** L. (Asteraceae).
Note: Rechinger (*Fl. Iranica* 145: 90. 1980) indicated Herb. Linn. No. 999.14 (LINN) as the type, presumably in error as this material is not associated with *I. brittanica* and is, in fact, the lectotype of *I. dysenterica* L.

Inula caerulea Linnaeus, *Mantissa Plantarum Altera*: 471. 1771, *nom. illeg.*
RCN: 6394.
Replaced synonym: *Aster polifolius* L. (1763).
Type not designated.
Original material: as replaced synonym.
Current name: ***Printzia polifolia*** (L.) Hutch. (Asteraceae).
Note: An illegitimate replacement name in *Inula* for both *Aster polifolius* L. (1753) and *I. cernua* P.J. Bergius (1767), as noted by Kroner (in *Mitt. Bot. Staatssamml. München* 16: 111. 1980). Kroner also indicated 997.56 (LINN) as lectotype, but this material came from Tulbagh and did not reach Linnaeus until 1769 so it cannot be original material for the name.

Inula crithmoides Linnaeus, *Species Plantarum* 2: 883. 1753.
"Habitat in Angliae, Galliae, Lusitaniae, Hispaniae maritimis." RCN: 6389.

Lectotype (Anderberg in Jarvis & Turland in *Taxon* 47: 363. 1998): Herb. Linn. No. 999.34 (LINN).

Current name: ***Limbarda crithmoides*** (L.) Dumort. (Asteraceae).

Note: Alavi (in Jafri & El-Gadi, *Fl. Libya* 107: 76. 1983) indicated both LINN and Clifford (BM) material as the type, but as these collections are not part of a single gathering, Art. 9.15 does not apply.

Inula dysenterica Linnaeus, *Species Plantarum* 2: 882. 1753.
"Habitat in Europae fossis subhumidis." RCN: 6377.
Lectotype (Lack in Rechinger, *Fl. Iranica* 145: 113. 1980): Herb. Linn. No. 999.14 (LINN).
Current name: ***Pulicaria dysenterica*** (L.) Bernh. (Asteraceae).

Inula ensifolia Linnaeus, *Species Plantarum* 2: 883. 1753.
"Habitat in Austria inferiore." RCN: 6388.
Lectotype (Anderberg in Jarvis & Turland in *Taxon* 47: 363. 1998): Herb. Burser XV(1): 53 (UPS).
Current name: ***Inula ensifolia*** L. (Asteraceae).
Note: Strid & Kit Tan (*Mountain Fl. Greece* 2: 418. 1981) noted the existence of 999.32 (LINN) but did not treat it as the type.

Inula foetida Linnaeus, *Systema Naturae,* ed. 10, 2: 1219. 1759.
["Habitat in Africa."] Sp. Pl., ed. 2, 2: 1213 (1763). RCN: 6397.
Basionym of: *Erigeron foetidus* (L.) L. (1763).
Lectotype (Wild in *Bol. Soc. Brot.,* sér. 2, 43: 217. 1969): [icon] "*Senecio, Africanus folio retuso*" in Miller, Fig. Pl. Gard. Dict. 2: 155, t. 233. 1758.
Current name: ***Nidorella foetida*** (L.) DC. (Asteraceae).
Note: Linnaeus caused considerable confusion in his *Sp. Pl.,* ed. 2, 2 (1763) treatment by simultaneously recognising both *I. foetida* (p. 1241), now from Malta, and *Erigeron foetidus* (p. 1213) from Africa. Interpretation has been complicated because Linnaeus cited the Miller illustration (now the lectotype of *I. foetida*) in the synonymy of both names. However, most authors (e.g. Brullo in *Webbia* 34: 290. 1979) have interpreted *I. foetida* (1753) as homotypic with *E. foetidus* (L.) L. (1763), and the Maltese taxon has been described as *Chiliadenus bocconei* Brullo.

Inula germanica Linnaeus, *Species Plantarum* 2: 883. 1753.
"Habitat in Misnia, Pannonia, Sibiria." RCN: 6387.
Lectotype (Rechinger, *Fl. Iranica* 145: 84. 1980): *Gerber?,* Herb. Linn. No. 999.31 (LINN).
Current name: ***Inula germanica*** L. (Asteraceae).

Inula helenium Linnaeus, *Species Plantarum* 2: 881. 1753.
"Habitat in Anglia, Belgio." RCN: 6373.
Lectotype (Anderberg in Jarvis & al., *Regnum Veg.* 127: 57. 1993): Herb. Linn. No. 999.1 (LINN).
Generitype of *Inula* Linnaeus (vide Green, *Prop. Brit. Bot.*: 182. 1929).
Current name: ***Inula helenium*** L. (Asteraceae).

Inula hirta Linnaeus, *Species Plantarum* 2: 883. 1753.
"Habitat in Bavaria, Gallia, Genevae." RCN: 6385.
Lectotype (Anderberg in Jarvis & Turland in *Taxon* 47: 363. 1998): Herb. Burser XV(1): 48 (UPS).
Current name: ***Inula hirta*** L. (Asteraceae).

Inula indica Linnaeus, *Species Plantarum,* ed. 2, 2: 1237. 1763.
"Habitat in India orientali." RCN: 6379.
Lectotype (Anderberg in *Taxon* 32: 652. 1983): Herb. Linn. No. 999.16 (LINN).
Current name: ***Pentanema indicum*** (L.) Y. Ling (Asteraceae).

Inula mariana Linnaeus, *Species Plantarum,* ed. 2, 2: 1240. 1763.
"Habitat in America septentrionali." RCN: 6386.
Lectotype (Reveal & al. in *Huntia* 7: 214. 1987): *Kalm,* Herb. Linn. No. 999.30 (LINN).
Current name: ***Chrysopsis mariana*** (L.) Elliott (Asteraceae).

Inula montana Linnaeus, *Species Plantarum* 2: 884. 1753.
"Habitat in Alpibus Helvetiae, Vallesiae." RCN: 6391.
Type not designated.
Original material: Herb. Linn. No. 352.2 (S); Herb. Burser XV(1): 54 (UPS); [icon] in Morison, Pl. Hist. Univ. 3: 119, s. 7, t. 21, f. 12. 1699.
Current name: ***Inula montana*** L. (Asteraceae).

Inula myrtifolia Linnaeus, *Systema Naturae,* ed. 10, 2: 1219. 1759.
RCN: 6383.
Type not designated.
Original material: none traced.
Current name: ***Inula spiraeifolia*** L. (Asteraceae).

Inula oculus-christi Linnaeus, *Species Plantarum* 2: 881. 1753.
"Habitat in austria (sic)." RCN: 6375.
Lectotype (Anderberg in Jarvis & Turland in *Taxon* 47: 363. 1998): Herb. Burser XV(1): 31 (UPS).
Current name: ***Inula oculus-christi*** L. (Asteraceae).
Note: Rechinger (*Fl. Iranica* 145: 88. 1980) indicated both LINN and Clifford (BM) material as the type but as these collections are not part of a single gathering, Art. 9.15 does not apply.

Inula odora Linnaeus, *Species Plantarum* 2: 881. 1753.
"Habitat in Italia, Galloprovincia, Narbona." RCN: 6374.
Lectotype (Grierson in Davis in *Notes Roy. Bot. Gard. Edinburgh* 33: 255. 1974): [icon] "*Asteris species, an Baccharis*" in Colonna, Ekphr.: 251, 253. 1606.
Current name: ***Pulicaria odora*** (L.) Rchb. (Asteraceae).
Note: Grierson (in *Notes Roy. Bot. Gard. Edinburgh* 33: 255. 1974) discussed the original elements for the name.

Inula pinifolia Linnaeus, *Plantae Rariores Africanae*: 22. 1760.
["Habitat in Aethiopia."] Sp. Pl., ed. 2, 2: 1241 (1763). RCN: 6396.
Type not designated.
Original material: Herb. Burman (G); [icon] in Breyn, Exot. Pl. Cent.: 136, t. 64. 1678.
Current name: ***Senecio pinifolius*** (L.) Lam. (Asteraceae).

Inula provincialis Linnaeus, *Species Plantarum* 2: 884. 1753.
"Habitat in Collendaneis Galloprovinciae." RCN: 6390.
Type not designated.
Original material: Herb. Burser VI: 123, syntype (UPS).
Current name: ***Senecio provincialis*** (L.) Druce (Asteraceae).

Inula pulicaria Linnaeus, *Species Plantarum* 2: 882. 1753.
"Habitat ad vias & plateas Europae temperatae." RCN: 6380.
Lectotype (Lack in Rechinger, *Fl. Iranica* 145: 114. 1980): Herb. Linn. No. 999.17 (LINN).
Current name: ***Pulicaria vulgaris*** Gaertn. (Asteraceae).

Inula salicina Linnaeus, *Species Plantarum* 2: 882. 1753.
"Habitat in Europae borealis pratis uliginosis asperis." RCN: 6384.
Lectotype (Anderberg in Jarvis & Turland in *Taxon* 47: 363. 1998): Herb. Linn. No. 999.25 (LINN).
Current name: ***Inula salicina*** L. (Asteraceae).

Inula spiraeifolia Linnaeus, *Systema Naturae,* ed. 10, 2: 1219. 1759.
["Habitat in Italia."] Sp. Pl., ed. 2, 2: 1238 (1763). RCN: 6382.

I

Lectotype (Anderberg in Jarvis & Turland in *Taxon* 47: 363. 1998): *Magnol*, Herb. Linn. No. 999.21 (LINN).
Current name: ***Inula spiraeifolia*** L. (Asteraceae).

Inula squarrosa Linnaeus, *Species Plantarum*, ed. 2, 2: 1240. 1763.
"Habitat in Italia, Monspelii." RCN: 6383.
Lectotype (Anderberg in Jarvis & Turland in *Taxon* 47: 363. 1998): *Arduino 62*, Herb. Linn. No. 351.5 ["351.3"] (S).
Current name: ***Inula spiraeifolia*** L. (Asteraceae).
Note: Due to an unfortunate transposition of numbers, Anderberg's type choice of material in S was published as Herb. Linn. No. 351.3 (a sheet which is unannotated by Linnaeus and is not original material for the name) rather than the intended Herb. Linn. No. 351.5.

Inula trixis Linnaeus, *Systema Naturae*, ed. 10, 2: 1219. 1759.
["Habitat in Jamaica."] Sp. Pl., ed. 2, 2: 1248 (1763). RCN: 6410.
Replaced synonym of: *Perdicium radiale* L. (1763), *nom. illeg.*
Lectotype (Anderson in *Brittonia* 23: 349. 1971): *Browne*, Herb. Linn. No. 1003.3 (LINN).
Current name: ***Trixis inula*** Crantz (Asteraceae).
Note: Although Moore (in Fawcett & Rendle, *Fl. Jamaica* 7: 284. 1936) noted the existence of 1003.3 (LINN), he did not indicate it as the type.

Inula undulata Linnaeus, *Systema Naturae*, ed. 12, 2: 558; *Mantissa Plantarum*: 115. 1767.
"Habitat in Aegypto." RCN: 6378.
Lectotype (Lack in Rechinger, *Fl. Iranica* 145: 120. 1980): *Forsskål*, Herb. Linn. No. 999.15 (LINN), see p. 202.
Current name: ***Francoeria undulata*** (L.) Lack (Asteraceae).
Note: Jeffrey & al. (in *Taxon* 29: 694. 1980) proposed the rejection of the name but this was declined by the Committee for Spermatophyta (in *Taxon* 32: 282. 1983). See review of usage by Hind & Boulos (in *Kew Bull.* 57: 495. 2002).

Inula villosa Linnaeus, *Systema Naturae*, ed. 10, 2: 1219. 1759.
["Habitat Wiennae, Monspelii & in Hispaniae."] Sp. Pl., ed. 2, 2: 1241 (1763). RCN: 6391.
Type not designated.
Original material: none traced.
Current name: ***Inula montana*** L. (Asteraceae).

Ipomoea aegyptia Linnaeus, *Species Plantarum* 1: 162. 1753.
"Habitat in America calidiore." RCN: 1251.
Basionym of: *Convolvulus aegyptius* (L.) L. (1759); *Convolvulus pentaphyllus* L. (1767), *nom. illeg.*
Lectotype (Austin in Harling & Sparre, *Fl. Ecuador* 16: 84. 1982): Herb. Linn. No. 218.35 (LINN).
Current name: ***Merremia aegyptia*** (L.) Urb. (Convolvulaceae).

Ipomoea alba Linnaeus, *Species Plantarum* 1: 161. 1753.
"Habitat in Malabariae arenosis, arbores scandens." RCN: 1280.
Replaced synonym of: *Ipomoea bona-nox* L. (1762), *nom. illeg.*
Lectotype (Verdcourt in Hubbard & Milne-Redhead, *Fl. Trop. E. Africa*, Convolvulaceae: 130. 1963): [icon] *"Munda-valli"* in Rheede, Hort. Malab. 11: 103, t. 50. 1692.
Current name: ***Ipomoea alba*** L. (Convolvulaceae).
Note: Meeuse (in *Bothalia* 6: 765. 1958) wrongly treated Rheede's 11: t. 49 as the type but this plate did not form part of the protologue.

Ipomoea bona-nox Linnaeus, *Species Plantarum*, ed. 2, 1: 228. 1762, *nom. illeg.*
"Habitat in Indiae arenosis, arbores scandens." RCN: 1280.
Replaced synonym: *Ipomoea alba* L. (1753).

Lectotype (Verdcourt in Hubbard & Milne-Redhead, *Fl. Trop. E. Africa*, Convolvulaceae: 130. 1963): [icon] *"Munda-valli"* in Rheede, Hort. Malab. 11: 103, t. 50. 1692.
Current name: ***Ipomoea alba*** L. (Convolvulaceae).
Note: An illegitimate replacement name for *I. alba* L. (1753).

Ipomoea campanulata Linnaeus, *Species Plantarum* 1: 160. 1753.
"Habitat in India." RCN: 1281.
Lectotype (Gunn in *Brittonia* 24: 170, f. 2. 1972): [icon] *"Adamboe"* in Rheede, Hort. Malab. 11: 115, t. 56. 1692.
Current name: ***Ipomoea campanulata*** L. (Convolvulaceae).

Ipomoea carolina Linnaeus, *Species Plantarum* 1: 160. 1753.
"Habitat in Carolina." RCN: 1274.
Lectotype (Dandy, *Sloane Herbarium*: 112. 1958): [icon] *"Convolvulus minor Pentaphyllos, flore purpureo minore"* in Catesby, Nat. Hist. Carolina 2: 91, t. 91. 1743.
Current name: ***Ipomoea carolina*** L. (Convolvulaceae).

Ipomoea coccinea Linnaeus, *Species Plantarum* 1: 160. 1753.
"Habitat in Domingo." RCN: 1275.
Lectotype (Wijnands, *Bot. Commelins*: 88. 1983): Herb. Linn. No. 219.3 (LINN).
Current name: ***Ipomoea coccinea*** L. (Convolvulaceae).

Ipomoea digitata Linnaeus, *Systema Naturae*, ed. 10, 2: 924. 1759.
["Habitat in America."] Sp. Pl., ed. 2, 1: 228 (1762). RCN: 1279.
Lectotype (Stearn in *Taxon* 10: 17. 1961): [icon] *"Ipomoea foliis pedatis"* in Plumier in Burman, Pl. Amer.: 81, t. 92, f. 1. 1756.
Current name: ***Ipomoea digitata*** L. (Convolvulaceae).

Ipomoea glaucifolia Linnaeus, *Species Plantarum* 1: 161. 1753, *nom. utique rej. prop.*
"Habitat in Mexico arvis." RCN: 1286.
Lectotype (Staples & al. in *Taxon* 55: 535. 2006): [icon] *"Convolvulus stellatus, arvensis folio glauco"* in Dillenius, Hort. Eltham.: 103, t. 87, f. 101. 1732.
Current name: ***Convolvulus glaucifolius*** (L.) Spreng. (Convolvulaceae).
Note: Staples & al. (in *Taxon* 55: 535. 2006) have proposed the rejection of the name.

Ipomoea hastata Linnaeus, *Mantissa Plantarum Altera*: 204. 1771, *nom. illeg.*
"Habitat in Java." RCN: 1285.
Replaced synonym: *Ipomoea sagittifolia* Burm. f. (1768).
Type not designated.
Current name: ***Xenostegia tridentata*** (L.) D.F. Austin & Staples (Convolvulaceae).

Ipomoea hederifolia Linnaeus, *Systema Naturae*, ed. 10, 2: 925. 1759.
["Habitat in America."] Sp. Pl., ed. 2, 1: 230 (1762). RCN: 1288.
Lectotype (O'Donell in *Lilloa* 29: 48. 1959): [icon] *"Ipomoea foliis cordatis"* in Plumier in Burman, Pl. Amer.: 82, t. 93, f. 2. 1756.
Current name: ***Ipomoea hederifolia*** L. (Convolvulaceae).

Ipomoea hepaticifolia Linnaeus, *Species Plantarum* 1: 161. 1753.
"Habitat in Zeylona." RCN: 1289.
Lectotype (Staples & Jarvis in *Taxon* 55: 1022. 2006): [icon] Herb. Hermann 5: 141, No. 79 (BM).
Current name: ***Ipomoea pes-tigridis*** L. (Convolvulaceae).
Note: Specific epithet spelled "hepaticaefolia" in the protologue.

Ipomoea lacunosa Linnaeus, *Species Plantarum* 1: 161. 1753.
"Habitat in Carolina." RCN: 1276.

Lectotype (Staples in Staples & Jarvis in *Taxon* 55: 1022. 2006):
Current name: ***Ipomoea lacunosa*** L. (Convolvulaceae).

Ipomoea nyctelea Linnaeus, *Species Plantarum* 1: 160. 1753.
"Habitat in Virginia. D. Gronovius." RCN: 1169.
Basionym of: *Ellisia nyctelea* (L.) L. (1763); *Polemonium nyctelea* (L.)
L. (1762).
Lectotype (Reveal in Jarvis & al., *Regnum Veg.* 127: 45. 1993): Herb.
Linn. No. 206.1 (LINN; iso- BM).
Current name: ***Ellisia nyctelea*** (L.) L. (Hydrophyllaceae).

Ipomoea pes-tigridis Linnaeus, *Species Plantarum* 1: 162. 1753, *typ.
cons.*
"Habitat in India." RCN: 1291.
Lectotype (Meeuse in *Bothalia* 6: 744. 1958): Herb. Linn. No. 219.11
(LINN).
Generitype of *Ipomoea* Linnaeus, *nom. cons.*
Current name: ***Ipomoea pes-tigridis*** L. (Convolvulaceae).

Ipomoea quamoclit Linnaeus, *Species Plantarum* 1: 159. 1753.
"Habitat in India." RCN: 1271.

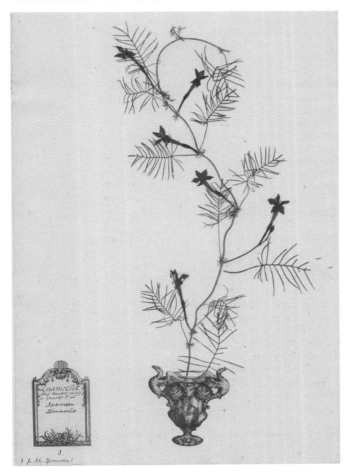

Lectotype (Biju in *Taxon* 51: 755. 2003 [2002]): Herb. Clifford: 66,
Ipomoea 1 (BM-000558077), see also p. 179.
Current name: ***Ipomoea quamoclit*** L. (Convolvulaceae).

Ipomoea quinquefolia Linnaeus, *Species Plantarum* 1: 162. 1753.
"Habitat in America." RCN: 1250.
Basionym of: *Convolvulus quinquefolius* (L.) L. (1759).

Lectotype (Austin in Woodson & Schery in *Ann. Missouri Bot. Gard.*
62: 182. 1975): [icon] *"Convolvulus quinquefolius glaber
Americanus"* in Plukenet, Phytographia: t. 167, f. 6. 1692; Almag.
Bot.: 116. 1696.
Current name: ***Merremia quinquefolia*** (L.) Hallier f. (Convolvulaceae).

Ipomoea rubra (Linnaeus) Linnaeus, *Systema Vegetabilium,* ed. 13:
171. 1774.
["Habitat in Carolinae citerioris arenosis. B. Jussieu."] Sp. Pl. 1: 163
(1753). RCN: 1272.
Basionym: *Polemonium rubrum* L. (1753).
Lectotype (designated here by Reveal): [icon] *"Quamoclit pennatum,
erectum, floribus in thyrsum digestis"* in Dillenius, Hort. Eltham. 2:
321, t. 241, f. 312. 1732.
Current name: ***Ipomopsis rubra*** (L.) Wherry (Polemoniaceae).

Ipomoea serpens Linnaeus, *Flora Jamaicensis*: 13. 1759.
"Habitat [in Jamaica.]"
Lectotype (Staples & Jarvis in *Taxon* 55: 1022. 2006): [icon] *"Pulli-
schovadi"* in Rheede, Hort. Malab. 11: t. 59. 1692.
Current name: ***Ipomoea pes-tigridis*** L. (Convolvulaceae).

Ipomoea solanifolia Linnaeus, *Species Plantarum* 1: 161. 1753.
"Habitat in America." RCN: 1277.
Neotype (Austin in *Ann. Missouri Bot. Gard.* 64: 331. 1978 [1977]):
[icon] *"Ipomoea foliis cordatis"* in Plumier in Burman, Pl. Amer.: 82,
t. 94, f. 1. 1756.
Current name: ***Jacquemontia solanifolia*** (L.) Hallier f.
(Convolvulaceae).

Ipomoea tamnifolia Linnaeus, *Species Plantarum* 1: 162. 1753.
"Habitat in Carolina." RCN: 1290.
Lectotype (Verdcourt, *Fl. Trop. E. Afr., Convolvulaceae*: 35. 1963):
[icon] *"Volubilis Car. Tamni folio subhirsuto"* in Dillenius, Hort.
Eltham. 2: 428, t. 318, f. 410. 1732.
Current name: ***Jacquemontia tamnifolia*** (L.) Griseb.
(Convolvulaceae).

Ipomoea triloba Linnaeus, *Species Plantarum* 1: 161. 1753.
"Habitat in America." RCN: 1287.
Lectotype (Austin in *Bull. Torrey Bot. Club* 105: 127. 1978): [icon]
"Convolvulus pentaphyllos minor, flore purpureo" in Sloane, Voy.
Jamaica 1: 153, t. 97, f. 1. 1707. – Typotype: Herb. Sloane 3: 5
(BM-SL).
Current name: ***Ipomoea triloba*** L. (Convolvulaceae).

Ipomoea tuberosa Linnaeus, *Species Plantarum* 1: 160. 1753.
"Habitat in Jamaica." RCN: 1278.
Lectotype (Austin in Woodson & Schery in *Ann. Missouri Bot. Gard.*
62: 182. 1975): Herb. Linn. No. 219.4 (LINN).
Current name: ***Merremia tuberosa*** (L.) Rendle (Convolvulaceae).

Ipomoea umbellata Linnaeus, *Systema Naturae,* ed. 10, 2: 924. 1759.
["Habitat in America."] Sp. Pl., ed. 2, 1: 227 (1762). RCN: 1273.
Lectotype (Staples & Austin in Staples & Jarvis in *Taxon* 55: 1023.
2006): [icon] *"Ipomoea foliis digitatis, pedunculis umbellatis
brevissimis"* in Plumier in Burman, Pl. Amer.: t. 92, f. 2. 1756.
Current name: ***Ipomoea carolina*** L. (Convolvulaceae).
Note: Often wrongly stated to be the basionym of *Merremia umbellata*
(L.) Hallier f., the latter in fact being based on *Convolvulus
umbellata* L. (1753), an entirely different species.

Ipomoea verticillata Linnaeus, *Systema Naturae,* ed. 10, 2: 924. 1759.
["Habitat in America."] Sp. Pl., ed. 2, 1: 221 (1762). RCN: 1231.
Basionym of: *Convolvulus verticillatus* (L.) L. (1762).

I

Lectotype (Powell & Staples in Howard, *Fl. Lesser Antilles* 6: 170. 1989): *Browne*, Herb. Linn. No. 218.15, lower right part (LINN).
Current name: ***Jacquemontia verticillata*** (L.) Urb. (Convolvulaceae).

Ipomoea violacea Linnaeus, *Species Plantarum* 1: 161. 1753.
"Habitat in America meridionali." RCN: 1282.
Lectotype (Manitz in *Feddes Repert.* 88: 268, t. 34. 1977): [icon] in Plumier, Codex Boerhaavianus: tab. sub. No. 851. (University Library, Groningen).
Current name: ***Ipomoea violacea*** L. (Convolvulaceae).
Note: Shinners (in *Taxon* 14: 104. 1975) stated that the name "must be typified with the plant of Plumier" but without explicitly treating the plate as type. Austin (in Woodson & Schery in *Ann. Missouri Bot. Gard.* 62: 210. 1975) concluded that the typification was obscure, but Manitz's explicit type choice has been accepted by most recent authors.

Iresine celosia Linnaeus, *Systema Naturae,* ed. 10, 2: 1291. 1759, *nom. illeg.*
["Habitat in America septentrionali."] Sp. Pl. 1: 206 (1753). RCN: 7426.
Replaced synonym: *Celosia paniculata* L. (1753).
Lectotype (Reveal & Nicolson in *Taxon* 38: 504. 1989): *Clayton 576* (BM-000051634).
Current name: ***Iresine rhizomatosa*** Standl. (Amaranthaceae).
Note: A new name in *Iresine* for *Celosia paniculata* L. (1753), and therefore illegitimate (see Shinners in *Taxon* 11: 141. 1962).

Iresine celosioides Linnaeus, *Species Plantarum,* ed. 2, 2: 1456. 1763, *nom. illeg.*
"Habitat in Virginia, Jamaica." RCN: 7426.
Replaced synonym: *Celosia paniculata* L. (1753).
Lectotype (Reveal & Nicolson in *Taxon* 38: 504. 1989): *Clayton 576* (BM-000051634).
Current name: ***Iresine rhizomatosa*** Standl. (Amaranthaceae).
Note: Shinners (in *Taxon* 11: 141. 1962) points out that this is a new name for *Iresine celosia* L. (1759), itself an illegitimate renaming of *Celosia paniculata* L. (1753).

Iris aphylla Linnaeus, *Species Plantarum* 1: 38. 1753.
"Habitat – – – –" RCN: 322.
Type not designated.
Original material: none traced.
Current name: ***Iris aphylla*** L. (Iridaceae).
Note: See comments by Dykes (*Genus* Iris: 158. 1913) on 61.4 (LINN) which is, however, not original material for this name.

Iris biflora Linnaeus, *Species Plantarum* 1: 38. 1753.
"Habitat in Lusitaniae rupibus." RCN: 324.
Type not designated.
Original material: Herb. Linn. No. 61.4 (LINN).
Current name: ***Iris biflora*** L. (Iridaceae).
Note: As it included elements identifiable as both *I. pumila* and *I. aphylla*, the name has often been treated as a *nomen confusum*, e.g. by Dykes (*Genus* Iris: 146, 158–159. 1913) and Mathew (*The Iris*: 24. 1981).

Iris florentina Linnaeus, *Systema Naturae,* ed. 10, 2: 863. 1759.
["Habitat in Europa australi-Carniola."] Sp. Pl., ed. 2, 1: 55 (1762). RCN: 318.
Type not designated.
Original material: none traced.
Current name: ***Iris germanica*** L. 'Florentina' (Iridaceae).
Note: Mathew (*The Iris*: 25. 1981) treats this as a cultivar of *I. germanica* L.

Iris foetidissima Linnaeus, *Species Plantarum* 1: 39. 1753.
"Habitat in Gallia, Anglia, Hetruria." RCN: 328.
Type not designated.
Original material: [icon] in Bauhin & Cherler, Hist. Pl. Univ. 2: 731. 1651; [icon] in Dodoëns, Stirp. Hist. Pempt., ed. 2: 247. 1616.
Current name: ***Iris foetidissima*** L. (Iridaceae).

Iris germanica Linnaeus, *Species Plantarum* 1: 38. 1753.
"Habitat in Germaniae editis." RCN: 319.
Lectotype (Mathew in Jarvis & al., *Regnum Veg.* 127: 57. 1993): Herb. Clifford: 18, *Iris* 2 (BM-000557643).
Generitype of *Iris* Linnaeus (vide Hitchcock, *Prop. Brit. Bot.*: 118. 1929).
Current name: ***Iris germanica*** L. (Iridaceae).
Note: See discussion by Dykes (*Genus* Iris: 6, 163, 165. 1913). Labani & El-Gadi (in Ali & Jafri, *Fl. Libya* 81: 7. 1980) indicated the post-1753 sheet 61.6 (LINN) as type, but this is not original material for the name and is ineligible as type.

Iris graminea Linnaeus, *Species Plantarum* 1: 39. 1753.
"Habitat in Austria ad radices montium." RCN: 335.
Type not designated.
Original material: Herb. Clifford: 19, *Iris* 10 (BM); Herb. Linn. No. 17.9 (S); *Amman 4,* Herb. Linn. No. 61.15 (LINN).
Current name: ***Iris graminea*** L. (Iridaceae).
Note: See discussion by Dykes (*Genus* Iris: 6. 1913).

Iris ochroleuca Linnaeus, *Mantissa Plantarum Altera*: 175. 1771.
"Habitat in Oriente -, floret julio." RCN: 334.
Type not designated.
Original material: none traced.
Current name: ***Iris orientalis*** Mill. (Iridaceae).

Iris persica Linnaeus, *Species Plantarum* 1: 40. 1753.
"Habitat in Persia." RCN: 339.
Type not designated.
Original material: Herb. A. van Royen No. 904.138–307 (L).
Current name: ***Iris persica*** L. (Iridaceae).

Iris pseudacorus Linnaeus, *Species Plantarum* 1: 38. 1753.
"Habitat in Europa ad ripas paludum fossarum." RCN: 327.
Type not designated.
Original material: Herb. Linn. No. 61.7 (LINN); Herb. Clifford: 19, *Iris* 6 (BM); [icon] in Bauhin, Theatri Bot.: 633. 1658.
Current name: ***Iris pseudacorus*** L. (Iridaceae).

Iris pumila Linnaeus, *Species Plantarum* 1: 38. 1753.
"Habitat in Austriae, Pannoniae, collibus apricis." RCN: 325.
Type not designated.
Original material: Herb. Clifford: 19, *Iris* 5, 2 sheets (BM); Herb. Linn. No. 61.1 (LINN).
Current name: ***Iris pumila*** L. (Iridaceae).
Note: See discussion by Dykes (*Genus* Iris: 6, 141, 144. 1913).

Iris pyrenaica Linnaeus, *Centuria I Plantarum*: 4. 1755.
"Habitat in Pyrenaeis." RCN: 326.
Type not designated.
Original material: none traced.
Current name: ***Iris pyrenaica*** L. (Iridaceae).
Note: The application of this name appears uncertain (see Dykes, *Genus* Iris: 239. 1913).

Iris sambucina Linnaeus, *Systema Naturae,* ed. 10, 2: 863. 1759.
["Habitat in Europa australi."] Sp. Pl., ed. 2, 1: 55 (1762). RCN: 320.
Type not designated.

Original material: none traced.
Current name: **Iris × *sambucina*** L. (Iridaceae).
Note: This is believed to be a hybrid between *I. variegata* L. and *I. pallida* L. (see Mathew, *The Iris*: 34. 1981).

Iris sibirica Linnaeus, *Species Plantarum* 1: 39. 1753.
"Habitat in Austriae, Helvetiae, Sibiriae pratis." RCN: 329.
Type not designated.
Original material: Herb. Clifford: 19, *Iris* 8 (BM); Herb. Linn. No. 61.20 (LINN); *Amman s.n.*, Herb. Linn. No. 61.19 (LINN); [icon] in Bauhin, Theatri Bot.: 597. 1658.
Current name: **Iris sibirica** L. (Iridaceae).
Note: See discussion by Dykes (*Genus* Iris: 6, 22. 1913).

Iris sisyrinchium Linnaeus, *Species Plantarum* 1: 40. 1753.
"Habitat in Hispania, Lusitania." RCN: 340.
Lectotype (Goldblatt in *Bot. Not.* 133: 254. 1980): [icon] "*Sisyrinchium majus*" in Clusius, Rar. Pl. Hist. 1: 216. 1601.
Current name: **Moraea sisyrinchium** (L.) Ker-Gawl. (Iridaceae).

Iris spuria Linnaeus, *Species Plantarum* 1: 39. 1753.
"Habitat in Germaniae pratis." RCN: 333.
Type not designated.
Original material: Herb. Linn. No. 61.17 (LINN).
Current name: **Iris spuria** L. (Iridaceae).
Note: See discussion by Dykes (*Genus* Iris: 6, 58. 1913).

Iris squalens Linnaeus, *Systema Naturae,* ed. 10, 2: 863. 1759.
["Habitat in Europa australi."] Sp. Pl., ed. 2, 1: 56 (1762). RCN: 321.
Type not designated.
Original material: none traced.
Current name: **Iris × *squalens*** L. (Iridaceae).
Note: This is believed to be a hybrid between *I. variegata* L. and *I. germanica* L. (see Mathew, *The Iris*: 35. 1981).

Iris susiana Linnaeus, *Species Plantarum* 1: 38. 1753.
"Habitat in Oriente; venit constantinopoli in Belgium 1573." RCN: 317.
Type not designated.
Original material: Herb. Linn. No. 61.3 (LINN); [icon] in Bauhin, Theatri Bot.: 579. 1658.
Current name: **Iris susiana** L. (Iridaceae).
Note: See Sealy (in *Curtis's Bot. Mag.* 177: t. 550. 1970) on the history of this taxon.

Iris tuberosa Linnaeus, *Species Plantarum* 1: 40. 1753.
"Habitat in Arabia & Oriente." RCN: 337.
Type not designated.
Original material: Herb. A. van Royen No. 904.138–304 (L); Herb. Burser III: 3 (UPS).
Current name: **Iris tuberosa** L. (Iridaceae).

Iris variegata Linnaeus, *Species Plantarum* 1: 38. 1753.
"Habitat in Hungaria." RCN: 323.
Type not designated.
Original material: none traced.
Current name: **Iris variegata** L. (Iridaceae).

Iris verna Linnaeus, *Species Plantarum* 1: 39. 1753.
"Habitat in Virginia." RCN: 336.
Lectotype (Edwards in *Rhodora* 71: 213. 1969): *Clayton 253* (BM-000040320).
Current name: **Iris verna** L. (Iridaceae).

Iris versicolor Linnaeus, *Species Plantarum* 1: 39. 1753.
"Habitat in Virginia, Marilandia, Pensylvania." RCN: 336.

Type not designated.
Original material: [icon] in Dillenius, Hort. Eltham. 1: 187, t. 155, f. 187. 1732; [icon] in Ehret, Pl. Papil. Rar.: t. 6, f. 2. 1748; [icon] in Dillenius, Hort. Eltham. 1: 188, t. 155, f. 188. 1732.
Current name: **Iris versicolor** L. (Iridaceae).
Note: See discussion by Dykes (*Genus* Iris: 80. 1913).

Iris virginica Linnaeus, *Species Plantarum* 1: 39. 1753.
"Habitat in Virginia." RCN: 331.
Lectotype (Dykes, *Genus* Iris: 80. 1913): *Clayton 259* ["258"] (BM-000040315).
Current name: **Iris virginica** L. (Iridaceae).

Iris xiphium Linnaeus, *Species Plantarum* 1: 40. 1753.
"Habitat in Hispania." RCN: 338.
Type not designated.
Original material: Herb. Clifford: 20, *Iris* 12 (BM).
Current name: **Iris xiphium** L. (Iridaceae).

Isatis aegyptica Linnaeus, *Species Plantarum* 2: 671. 1753.
"Habitat in Aegypto." RCN: 4888.
Type not designated.
Original material: none traced.
Current name: **Cakile sp.** (Brassicaceae).
Note: The application of this name is uncertain.

Isatis armena Linnaeus, *Species Plantarum* 2: 670. 1753.
"Habitat in Armeniae pratis siccioribus ad rivulos." RCN: 4887.
Lectotype (Hedge in Cafferty & Jarvis in *Taxon* 51: 534. 2002): [icon] "*Isatis Orientalis, foliis Brassicae perfoliatae, fructu cordiformi, canescente*" in Buxbaum, Pl. Minus Cognit. Cent. 1: 3, t. 4. 1728.
Current name: **Sameraria armena** (L.) Desv. (Brassicaceae).
Note: Hedge (in Hedge & Rechinger, *Fl. Iranica* 57: 93. 1968) indicated unspecified Tournefort material as type. However, as no Tournefort illustration was cited, and Linnaeus did not have the opportunity to study Tournefort's specimens, this statement (which has been followed by some later authors) cannot be accepted as a valid typification.

Isatis lusitanica Linnaeus, *Species Plantarum* 2: 670. 1753.
"Habitat in Hispania & Oriente." RCN: 4886.
Lectotype (Jafri in Ali & Jafri, *Fl. Libya* 23: 108. 1977): Herb. Linn. No. 848.2 (LINN).
Current name: **Isatis lusitanica** L. (Brassicaceae).

Isatis tinctoria Linnaeus, *Species Plantarum* 2: 670. 1753.
"Habitat ad littora maris Balthici & oceani Europae." RCN: 4885.
Lectotype (Jafri in Nasir & Ali, *Fl. W. Pakistan* 55: 76. 1973): Herb. Linn. No. 848.1 (LINN).
Generitype of *Isatis* Linnaeus (vide Green, *Prop. Brit. Bot.*: 56. 1929).
Current name: **Isatis tinctoria** L. (Brassicaceae).

Ischaemum aristatum Linnaeus, *Species Plantarum* 2: 1049. 1753.
"Habitat in China." RCN: 7580.
Lectotype (Bor in *Kew Bull.* 15: 411. 1962): Herb. Linn. No. 1214.2 (LINN).
Current name: **Ischaemum aristatum** L. (Poaceae).

Ischaemum muticum Linnaeus, *Species Plantarum* 2: 1049. 1753.
"Habitat in India." RCN: 7579.
Lectotype (Renvoize in Jarvis & al., *Regnum Veg.* 127: 57. 1993): Herb. Linn. No. 1214.1 (LINN).
Generitype of *Ischaemum* Linnaeus (vide Green, *Prop. Brit. Bot.*: 193. 1929).
Current name: **Ischaemum muticum** L. (Poaceae).

I

Isnardia palustris Linnaeus, *Species Plantarum* 1: 120. 1753.
"Habitat in Galliae, Alsatiae, Russiae, Virginiae fluviis." RCN: 989.
Lectotype (Raven in Jarvis & al., *Regnum Veg.* 127: 57. 1993): Herb. Linn. No. 157.3 (LINN).
Generitype of *Isnardia* Linnaeus.
Current name: ***Ludwigia palustris*** (L.) Elliott (Onagraceae).
Note: Raven (in *Reinwardtia* 6: 400. 1963) previously indicated 157.1 (LINN) as lectotype, but this collection is unannotated by Linnaeus and not original material for the name.

Isoëtes lacustris Linnaeus, *Species Plantarum* 2: 1100. 1753.
"Habitat in Europae frigidae fundo lacuum." RCN: 7959.
Lectotype (Fuchs in *Beih. Nova Hedwigia* 3: 30, f. 10. 1962): Herb. Linn. No. 1256.1 (LINN).
Generitype of *Isoëtes* Linnaeus.
Current name: ***Isoëtes lacustris*** L. (Isoëtaceae).
Note: Jonsell & Jarvis (in Jarvis & al., *Regnum Veg.* 127: 57. 1993; *Nordic J. Bot.* 14: 148. 1994), unaware of Fuchs' earlier type choice (with its detailed discussion and illustration of many of the original elements), independently reached the same conclusion. Although Fuchs' assumption that the type collection (which has no direct indication of provenance) came from Lake Möcklen (Småland, Sweden, see p. 90) may not be correct, his type choice has priority.

Isopyrum aquilegioides Linnaeus, *Species Plantarum* 1: 557. 1753.
"Habitat in Alpibus Helveticis, Tridentinis, Apenninis." RCN: 4105.
Lectotype (Nardi in *Webbia* 47: 219. 1993): [icon] *"Aquilegia parvo flore Thalictri folio"* in Morison, Pl. Hist. Univ. 3: 458, s. 12, t. 1, f. 5. 1699.
Current name: ***Isopyrum thalictroides*** L. (Ranunculaceae).
Note: De Beer & Stearn (in *Bull. Brit. Mus. (Nat. Hist.), Bot.* 2: 200, f. 3. 1960) designated Herb. Burser VII(1): 109 (UPS), a specimen of *Aquilegia*, as lectotype. Nardi (in *Webbia* 47: 219–221. 1993) argued that the Burser material was not original material for the name – Linnaeus (in ms.) determined it as an *Aquilegia* and it shows no characters of *Isopyrum*. Nardi therefore treated the choice as a neotypification, which he rejected (as original material was in existence) in favour of the cited Morison illustration. The consequence of this is that *I. aquilegioides* is a synonym of *I. thalictroides* L.

Isopyrum fumarioides Linnaeus, *Species Plantarum* 1: 557. 1753.
"Habitat in nemoribus Sibiriae." RCN: 4103.
Lectotype (Nardi in *Webbia* 47: 217. 1993): Herb. Linn. No. 717.1 (LINN).
Current name: ***Leptopyrum fumarioides*** (L.) Rchb. (Ranunculaceae).

Isopyrum thalictroides Linnaeus, *Species Plantarum* 1: 557. 1753, *typ. cons.*
"Habitat in Alpibus Italicis, Grationopoli, inque agro Viennensi." RCN: 4104.
Lectotype (Nardi in *Webbia* 47: 218. 1993): [icon] *"Ranunc. praecox II. Thalictri fol."* in Clusius, Rar. Pl. Hist. 1: 233. 1601.
Generitype of *Isopyrum* Linnaeus, *nom. cons.*
Current name: ***Isopyrum thalictroides*** L. (Ranunculaceae).
Note: Nardi's type choice, published 11 May 1993, pre-dates the same choice made by Jarvis (in Jarvis & al., *Regnum Veg.* 127: 57. 1993), published 25 May 1993.

Itea virginica Linnaeus, *Species Plantarum* 1: 199. 1753.
"Habitat in Virginia." RCN: 1621.
Lectotype (designated here by Reveal): *Clayton 556, n. 2*, Herb. Linn. No. 273.1 (LINN).
Generitype of *Itea* Linnaeus.
Current name: ***Itea virginica*** L. (Iteaceae).

Note: Reveal (in *Huntia* 7: 217. 1987) indicated a Clayton sheet ("Clayton 556, pl. 2 (BM)!") as lectotype, but it has not been possible to locate material in BM annotated in this way. There may have been some confusion with a sheet annotated as *Clayton 114* (BM), but this comprises material of *Clethra alnifolia* L. and cannot be original material for *I. virginica*. There is, however, Clayton material in LINN (sheet 273.1) annotated as "566, pl. 2" by Gronovius, and as "Itea 1 virginica" by Linnaeus, and this is now designated as the lectotype.

Iva annua Linnaeus, *Species Plantarum* 2: 988. 1753.
"Habitat in America meridionali. D. B. Jussieu." RCN: 7163.
Lectotype (Jackson in *Kansas Univ. Sci. Bull.* 41: 808. 1960): Herb. Linn. No. 1116.1 (LINN).
Current name: ***Iva annua*** L. (Asteraceae).
Note: Iva annua was treated as the generitype by Britton & Brown (*Ill. Fl. N. U. S.*, ed. 2, 3: 338. 1913; see McNeill & al. in *Taxon* 36: 375. 1987). However, under Art. 10.5, Ex. 7 (a voted example) of the Vienna Code, this is a type choice made under the American Code and is to be replaced under Art. 10.5b by Green's choice (*Prop. Brit. Bot.*: 188. 1929) of *I. frutescens* L.

Iva frutescens Linnaeus, *Species Plantarum* 2: 989. 1753.
"Habitat in Virginia, Peru." RCN: 7164.
Lectotype (Jackson in *Kansas Univ. Sci. Bull.* 41: 817. 1960): Herb. Linn. No. 1116.3 (LINN).
Generitype of *Iva* Linnaeus (vide Green, *Prop. Brit. Bot.*: 188. 1929).
Current name: ***Iva frutescens*** L. (Asteraceae).
Note: Iva annua was treated as the generitype by Britton & Brown (*Ill. Fl. N. U. S.*, ed. 2, 3: 338. 1913; see McNeill & al. in *Taxon* 36: 375. 1987). However, under Art. 10.5, Ex. 7 (a voted example) of the Vienna Code, this is a type choice made under the American Code and is to be replaced under Art. 10.5b by Green's choice (*Prop. Brit. Bot.*: 188. 1929) of *I. frutescens* L.

Ixia africana Linnaeus, *Species Plantarum* 1: 36. 1753.
"Habitat ad Cap. b. Spei." RCN: 289.
Lectotype (Goldblatt in Jarvis & al., *Regnum Veg.* 127: 57. 1993): [icon] *"Ixia foliis ad radicem nervosis, gramineis, floribus ac fructu &c."* in Burman, Rar. Afric. Pl.: 191, t. 70, f. 2. 1739.
Generitype of *Ixia* Linnaeus (1753), *nom. rej.*
Current name: ***Aristea africana*** (L.) Hoffmanns. (Iridaceae).
Note: Ixia Linnaeus (1753), *nom. rej.* in favour of *Ixia* Linnaeus (1762).

Ixia alba Linnaeus, *Systema Naturae*, ed. 10, 2: 862. 1759.
RCN: 294.
Type not designated.
Original material: none traced.
Current name: ***Sparaxis bulbifera*** (L.) Ker-Gawl. (Iridaceae).

Ixia bulbifera Linnaeus, *Centuria II Plantarum*: 4. 1756.
"Habitat – – – Miller." RCN: 291.
Lectotype (Goldblatt in *J. S. African Bot.* 35: 237. 1969): Herb. Linn. No. 58.16 (LINN).
Current name: ***Sparaxis bulbifera*** (L.) Ker-Gawl. (Iridaceae).

Ixia bulbocodium (Linnaeus) Linnaeus, *Species Plantarum*, ed. 2, 1: 51. 1762.
"Habitat in alpibus Italicis." RCN: 286.
Basionym: *Crocus bulbocodium* L. (1753).
Lectotype (Labani & El-Gadi in Jafri & El-Gadi, *Fl. Libya* 81: 17. 1980): Herb. Linn. No. 58.4 (LINN).
Current name: ***Romulea bulbocodium*** (L.) Sebast. & Mauri (Iridaceae).

Ixia chinensis Linnaeus, *Species Plantarum* 1: 36. 1753.
"Habitat in India." RCN: 290.
Lectotype (Goldblatt & Mabberley in *Novon* 15: 129. 2005): [icon]
   "Belam-canda-schularmani" in Rheede, Hort. Malab. 11: 73, t. 37.
   1692.
Current name: ***Belamcanda chinensis*** (L.) A. DC. (Iridaceae).
Note: The correct name in *Belamcanda* is *B. chinensis* (L.) A. DC.
   However, if *Belamcanda* is subsumed within *Iris,* as favoured by
   Goldblatt & Mabberley (in *Novon* 15: 128–132. 2005), the correct
   name for *Ixia chinensis* is *Iris domestica* (L.) Goldblatt & Mabb.

Ixia corymbosa Linnaeus, *Centuria II Plantarum*: 4. 1756.
"Habitat ad Cap. b. Spei." RCN: 288.
Neotype (Goldblatt & Manning in *S. African J. Bot.* 58: 332. 1992):
   MacOwan, Herb. Norm. Austr. Afr. 268 (SAM; iso- BM, BOL, G).
Current name: ***Lapeirousia corymbosa*** (L.) Ker-Gawl. (Iridaceae).

Ixia crocata Linnaeus, *Species Plantarum,* ed. 2, 1: 52. 1762.
"Habitat ad Cap. b. spei." RCN: 297.

Lectotype (Goldblatt in Codd, *Fl. Pl. Africa* 42: t. 1655. 1972): Herb.
   Linn. No. 58.24 (LINN), see also p. vi.
Current name: ***Tritonia crocata*** (L.) Ker-Gawl. (Iridaceae).

Ixia flexuosa Linnaeus, *Species Plantarum,* ed. 2, 1: 51. 1762.
"Habitat ad Cap. b. spei." RCN: 292.

Lectotype (Lewis in *J. S. African Bot.* 28: 110. 1962): [icon] *"Ixia foliis
   linearibus floribus spicatis sessilibus"* in Miller, Fig. Pl. Gard. Dict. 2:
   104, t. 156, f. 2. 1757.
Current name: ***Ixia flexuosa*** L. (Iridaceae).

Ixia hirsuta Linnaeus, *Systema Naturae,* ed. 12, 2: 76; *Mantissa
   Plantarum:* 27. 1767.
"Habitat ad Cap. b. spei." RCN: 289.
Replaced synonym of: *Wachendorfia umbellata* L. (1774), *nom. illeg.*
Type not designated.
Original material: none traced.
Current name: ***Dilatris corymbosa*** P.J. Bergius (Haemodoraceae).

Ixia maculata Linnaeus, *Species Plantarum,* ed. 2, 2: 1664. 1763.
"Habitat ad Cap. b. spei." RCN: 296.
Lectotype (Lewis in *J. S. African Bot.* 28: 138. 1962): Herb. Linn. No.
   58.21 (LINN).
Current name: ***Ixia maculata*** L. (Iridaceae).

Ixia plicata Linnaeus, *Centuria II Plantarum*: 4. 1756.
"Habitat in Aethiopia. Burmannus." RCN: 301.
Basionym of: *Gladiolus plicatus* (L.) L. (1762).
Lectotype (Lewis in *J. S. African Bot., Suppl.* 3: 11. 1959): Herb. Linn.
   No. 59.6, left specimen (LINN).
Current name: ***Babiana villosula*** (J.G. Gmel.) Ker ex Steud.
   (Iridaceae).
Note: This has a very confused synonymy. Lewis argued that *Babiana
   plicata* Ker is not based on *I. plicata,* so Linnaeus' name is not
   available for use in the genus despite its priority. She was also aware
   that the Sparrman collection on the right of sheet 59.6 (LINN) was
   a later addition to the herbarium and therefore restricted her type
   choice to the specimen to the left.

Ixia polystachya Linnaeus, *Species Plantarum,* ed. 2, 1: 51. 1762, *typ.
   cons.*
"Habitat ad Cap. b. Spei." RCN: 293.
Lectotype (Lewis in *J. S. African Bot.* 28: 103. 1962): [icon] *"Ixia,
   foliis lineari-gladiolatis, floribus alaribus & terminalibus"* in Miller,
   Fig. Pl. Gard. Dict. 2: 104, t. 155, f. 2. 1757.
Generitype of *Ixia* Linnaeus (1762), *nom. cons.*
Current name: ***Ixia polystachya*** L. (Iridaceae).
Note: Ixia Linnaeus (1762), *nom. cons.* against *Ixia* Linnaeus (1753).

Ixia rosea Linnaeus, *Systema Naturae,* ed. 12, 2: 75. 1767.
RCN: 285.
Lectotype (de Vos in *J. S. African Bot., Suppl.* 9: 249. 1972): [icon]
   "Bulbocodium, pedunculis nudis unifloris, foliis subulatis longissimis"
   in Miller, Fig. Pl. Gard. Dict. 2: 160, t. 240. 1758.
Current name: ***Romulea rosea*** (L.) Eckl. (Iridaceae).

Ixia scillaris Linnaeus, *Species Plantarum,* ed. 2, 1: 52. 1762.
"Habitat ad Cap. b. spei." RCN: 295.
Lectotype (Lewis in *J. S. African Bot.* 28: 174. 1962): Herb. Linn. No.
   58.25 (LINN).
Current name: ***Ixia scillaris*** L. (Iridaceae).

Ixia uniflora Linnaeus, *Systema Naturae,* ed. 12, 2: 75; *Mantissa
   Plantarum:* 27. 1767.
"Habitat ad Cap. b. spei. D. von Royen." RCN: 287.
Lectotype (Goldblatt in Germishuisen, *Fl. Southern Africa* 7(2:1): 161.
   1999): Herb. Linn. No. 58.19 (LINN).
Current name: ***Sparaxis grandiflora*** (D. Delaroche) Ker-Gawl.
   (Iridaceae).

Ixora alba Linnaeus, *Species Plantarum* 1: 110. 1753.
"Habitat in India." RCN: 898.

Lectotype (Ridsdale in Manilal, *Bot. Hist. Hort. Malab.*: 132. 1980):
[icon] *"Bem-schetti"* in Rheede, Hort. Malab. 2: 19, t. 14. 1679.
Current name: ***Ixora alba*** L. (Rubiaceae).

Ixora americana Linnaeus, *Systema Naturae,* ed. 10, 2: 893. 1759.
["Habitat in America."] Sp. Pl., ed. 2, 1: 160 (1762). RCN: 899.
Type not designated.
Original material: Herb. Linn. No. 132.3 (LINN).
Current name: ***Ixora americana*** L. (Rubiaceae).

Ixora coccinea Linnaeus, *Species Plantarum* 1: 110. 1753.
"Habitat in India." RCN: 897.
Lectotype (Fosberg & Sachet in *Taxon* 38: 488. 1989): [icon] *"Schetti"*
in Rheede, Hort. Malab. 2: 17, t. 13. 1679.
Generitype of *Ixora* Linnaeus (vide Hitchcock, *Prop. Brit. Bot.*: 124.
1929).
Current name: ***Ixora coccinea*** L. (Rubiaceae).
Note: Bremekamp (in *Bull. Jard. Bot. Buitenz.,* sér. 3, 14: 198. 1937)
designated the type of *Ixora* as "I. coccinea L. in Hb. Hermanni

(Hb. Mus. Brit.)" but as there are both specimens and drawings
present, this is not a single gathering in the sense of Art. 9.15.
Corner (in *Gard. Bull. Straits Settlem.* 11: 185. 1941) stated
(confusingly, as these collections pre-date those of Osbeck) "Type:
Osbeck's specimen of the Flora Zeylandica". Dwyer (in *Ann.
Missouri Bot. Gard.* 67: 258. 1980) indicated "131.1 LINN" (a
specimen of *Rubia*, and not original material for this name) as type.
Fosberg & Sachet (in *Taxon* 38: 486–489. 1989) discussed the
typification of this name in detail, concluding that no valid
typification existed at that point, and designated a Rheede plate as
lectotype, accepted here.

Ixora occidentalis Linnaeus, *Systema Naturae,* ed. 10, 2: 893. 1759.
RCN: 900.
Lectotype (Howard, *Fl. Lesser Antilles* 6: 412. 1989): [icon]
*"Pavetta? foliis oblongo-ovatis oppositis, stipulis setaceis petiolis
interpositis"* in Browne, Civ. Nat. Hist. Jamaica: 142, t. 6, f. 2. 1756
(see p. 112).
Current name: ***Faramea occidentalis*** (L.) A. Rich. (Rubiaceae).

J

Jacquinia ruscifolia N.J. Jacquin, *Enum. Syst. Pl.*: 15. 1760.
"Habitat in Jamaica." RCN: 1511.
Type not designated.
Generitype of *Jacquinia* Linnaeus (1759), *nom. & orth. cons.*
Current name: ***Jacquinia ruscifolia*** Jacq. (Theophrastaceae).

Jambolifera pedunculata Linnaeus, *Species Plantarum* 1: 349. 1753.
"Habitat in India." RCN: 2677.
Lectotype (Hartley in *Taxon* 23: 435. 1974; Nair in Jarvis & al.,
   Regnum Veg. 127: 58. 1993): Herb. Hermann 2: 82, No. 139 (BM-
   000621776).
Generitype of *Jambolifera* Linnaeus, *nom. rej.*
Current name: ***Acronychia pedunculata*** (L.) Miq. (Rutaceae).
Note: Jambolifera Linnaeus, *nom. rej.* in favour of *Acronychia* J. R.
   Forst. & G. Forst.
      Although Merrill (*Interpret. Rumph. Herb. Amb.*: 394. 1917)
   stated that this was based "primarily on" the *Flora Zeylanica* account
   number 139, this does not constitute formal typification. Hartley
   (in *Taxon* 23: 435. 1974) referred to the Hermann element as "type"
   and this is accepted, with Nair subsequently having restricted this
   choice to one of the several specimens involved.

Jasione montana Linnaeus, *Species Plantarum* 2: 928. 1753.
"Habitat in Europae collibus siccissimus." RCN: 6736.
Lectotype (Parnell in Jarvis & al., *Regnum Veg.* 127: 58. 1993): Herb.
   Clifford: 426, *Jasione* 1 (BM-000647299).
Generitype of *Jasione* Linnaeus.
Current name: ***Jasione montana*** L. (Campanulaceae).

Jasminum azoricum Linnaeus, *Species Plantarum* 1: 7. 1753.
"Habitat in India." RCN: 45.
Lectotype (Wijnands, *Bot. Commelins*: 156. 1983): Herb. Clifford: 5,
   Jasminum 2 (BM-000557520).
Current name: ***Jasminum azoricum*** L. (Oleaceae).

Jasminum fruticans Linnaeus, *Species Plantarum* 1: 7. 1753.
"Habitat in Europa australi." RCN: 46.
Lectotype (Green in *Notes Roy. Bot. Gard. Edinburgh* 23: 382. 1961):
   Herb. Clifford: 5, *Jasminum* 3 (BM-000557522).
Current name: ***Jasminum fruticans*** L. (Oleaceae).

Jasminum grandiflorum Linnaeus, *Species Plantarum*, ed. 2, 1: 9.
   1762.
"Habitat in Malabaria." RCN: 44.
Lectotype (D'Arcy in *Ann. Missouri Bot. Gard.* 63: 558. 1977):
   Hasselquist, Herb. Linn. No. 17.2 (LINN).
Current name: ***Jasminum grandiflorum*** L. (Oleaceae).

Jasminum humile Linnaeus, *Species Plantarum* 1: 7. 1753.
"Habitat – – – – –" RCN: 47.
Lectotype (Green in *Notes Roy. Bot. Gard. Edinburgh* 23: 365. 1961):
   Herb. Linn. No. 17.6 (LINN).
Current name: ***Jasminum humile*** L. (Oleaceae).

Jasminum odoratissimum Linnaeus, *Species Plantarum* 1: 7. 1753.
"Habitat in India?" RCN: 48.
Lectotype (Green in *Notes Roy. Bot. Gard. Edinburgh* 23: 374. 1961):
   Herb. Linn. No. 17.7 (LINN).
Current name: ***Jasminum odoratissimum*** L. (Oleaceae).

Jasminum officinale Linnaeus, *Species Plantarum* 1: 7. 1753.
"Habitat in India." RCN: 43.

Lectotype (Green in Jarvis & al., *Regnum Veg.* 127: 58. 1993): Herb.
   Clifford: 5, *Jasminum* 1 (BM-000557518).
Generitype of *Jasminum* Linnaeus (vide Hitchcock, *Prop. Brit. Bot.*:
   115. 1929).
Current name: ***Jasminum officinale*** L. (Oleaceae).

Jatropha curcas Linnaeus, *Species Plantarum* 2: 1006. 1753.
"Habitat in America calidiore." RCN: 7292.
Lectotype (Radcliffe-Smith in Nasir & Ali, *Fl. Pakistan* 172: 81.
   1986): Herb. Clifford: 445, *Jatropha* 3 (BM-000647406).
Current name: ***Jatropha curcas*** L. (Euphorbiaceae).
Note: Fawcett & Rendle (*Fl. Jamaica* 4: 311. 1920) indicated material
   in LINN as type, but did not distinguish between several sheets
   (none of which is original material for the name).

Jatropha gossypiifolia Linnaeus, *Species Plantarum* 2: 1006. 1753,
   typ. cons.
"Habitat in America meridionali." RCN: 7290.
Conserved type (Scott in Bosser & al., *Fl. Mascareignes* 160: 82.
   1982): Herb. Linn. No. 1141.1 (LINN).
Generitype of *Jatropha* Linnaeus, *nom. cons.*
Current name: ***Jatropha gossypiifolia*** L. (Euphorbiaceae).
Note: Specific epithet spelled "gossypifolia" in the protologue.
      Jatropha gossypiifolia, with 1141.1 (LINN) as the type (incorrectly
   attributed to Wijnands, *Bot. Commelins*: 104. 1983) was proposed as
   conserved type of the genus by Jarvis (in *Taxon* 41: 564. 1992). This
   was eventually approved by the General Committee (see review of
   the history of this proposal by Barrie, *l.c.* 55: 795–796. 2006).

Jatropha herbacea Linnaeus, *Species Plantarum* 2: 1007. 1753.
"Habitat in Vera Cruce." RCN: 7297.
Type not designated.
Original material: none traced.
Current name: ***Cnidoscolus herbaceus*** (L.) I.M. Johnst.
   (Euphorbiaceae).

Jatropha janipha Linnaeus, *Systema Naturae*, ed. 12, 2: 636; *Mantissa
   Plantarum*: 126. 1767, *nom. illeg.*
"Habitat in America calidiore." RCN: 7295.
Replaced synonym: *Jatropha carthaginensis* Jacq. (1760).
Type not designated.
Current name: ***Manihot carthaginensis*** (Jacq.) Muell. Arg.
   (Euphorbiaceae).
Note: A superfluous name for *Jatropha carthaginensis* Jacq. (1760).

Jatropha manihot Linnaeus, *Species Plantarum* 2: 1007. 1753.
"Habitat in America australi." RCN: 7294.
Lectotype (Radcliffe-Smith in Polhill, *Fl. Trop. E. Africa,
   Euphorbiaceae*: 367. 1987): Herb. Linn. No. 1141.11 (LINN).
Current name: ***Manihot esculenta*** Crantz (Euphorbiaceae).

Jatropha moluccana Linnaeus, *Species Plantarum* 2: 1006. 1753.
"Habitat in Moluccis, Zeylona." RCN: 7291.
Lectotype (Fawcett & Rendle, *Fl. Jamaica* 4: 315. 1920; Radcliffe-
   Smith in *Kew Bull.* 41: 54. 1986): Herb. Hermann 3: 27, No. 348
   (BM-000621904).
Current name: ***Aleurites moluccana*** (L.) Willd. (Euphorbiaceae).
Note: Fawcett & Rendle indicated Herb. Hermann material (BM) as
   type. Although there is material in several volumes, it appears to
   have been part of a single gathering so theirs is accepted as the first
   typification (Art. 9.15), with the choice subsequently restricted by
   Radcliffe-Smith.

Jatropha multifida Linnaeus, *Species Plantarum* 2: 1006. 1753.
"Habitat in America meridionali." RCN: 7293.
Lectotype (Radcliffe-Smith in Polhill, *Fl. Trop. E. Africa*,
  Euphorbiaceae: 354. 1987): [icon] *"Manihot folio tenuiter diviso"* in
  Dillenius, Hort. Eltham. 2: 217, t. 173, f. 213. 1732.
Current name: ***Jatropha multifida*** L. (Euphorbiaceae).
Note: Fawcett & Rendle (*Fl. Jamaica* 4: 313. 1920) indicated 1141.9
  (LINN) as type but this collection was received by Linnaeus from
  Browne only in 1758, so it cannot be original material for the name.

Jatropha urens Linnaeus, *Species Plantarum* 2: 1007. 1753.
"Habitat in Brasilia." RCN: 7296.
Lectotype (Wijnands, *Bot. Commelins*: 96. 1983): Herb. Linn. No.
  1141.13 (LINN).
Current name: ***Cnidoscolus urens*** (L.) Arthur (Euphorbiaceae).

Juglans alba Linnaeus, *Species Plantarum* 2: 997. 1753.
"Habitat in Virginia." RCN: 7224.
Type not designated.
Original material: *Kalm*, Herb. Linn. No. 1129.2 (LINN); *Clayton*
  466, Herb. Linn. No. 79 (SBT); *Clayton 466* (BM); [icon] in
  Catesby, Nat. Hist. Carolina 1: 38, t. 38. 1730; [icon] in Plukenet,
  Phytographia: t. 309, f. 2. 1694; Almag. Bot.: 264. 1696 –
  Voucher: Herb. Sloane 101: 57 (BM-SL).
Current name: ***Carya tomentosa*** (Poir.) Nutt. (Juglandaceae).
Note: This name was treated as ambiguous by Rehder (in *J. Arnold*
  Arbor. 26: 483. 1945) on the grounds that it was a mixture of *Carya*
  ovata (Mill.) K. Koch – Shagbark Hickory (the Plukenet element)
  and *C. tomentosa* (Poir.) Nutt. – Mockernut Hickory (Gronovius,
  Parkinson, Catesby and Kalm elements). Some (e.g. Howard &
  Staples in *J. Arnold Arbor.* 64: 527. 1983) appear to have used the
  name *C. alba* (L.) K. Koch for *C. tomentosa*, wrongly believing
  Crantz to have effectively typified the name on the Catesby
  element. There may well be a case for rejection. See also comments
  by Wilbur (in *Sida* 14: 36. 1990), who supports this solution.

Juglans baccata Linnaeus, *Systema Naturae,* ed. 10, 2: 1272. 1759.
["Habitat in Jamaica."] Sp. Pl., ed. 2, 2: 1416 (1763). RCN: 7227.
Neotype (Hayden & Reveal in *Taxon* 29: 508. 1980): [icon] *"Nux*
  juglans trifolia, fructu magnitudine nucis moschatae" in Sloane, Voy.
  Jamaica 2: 1, t. 157, f. 1. 1725. – Typotype: Herb. Sloane 5: 49
  (BM-SL).
Current name: ***Picrodendron baccatum*** (L.) Krug & Urb.
  (Euphorbiaceae).

Juglans cinerea Linnaeus, *Systema Naturae,* ed. 10, 2: 1272. 1759.
["Habitat in America septentrionali."] Sp. Pl., ed. 2, 2: 1415 (1763).
  RCN: 7226.
Type not designated.
Original material: none traced.
Current name: ***Juglans cinerea*** L. (Juglandaceae).

Juglans nigra Linnaeus, *Species Plantarum* 2: 997. 1753.
"Habitat in Virginia, Marilandia." RCN: 7225.
Lectotype (Reveal & al. in *Huntia* 7: 226. 1987): Herb. Linn. No.
  1129.5 (LINN).
Current name: ***Juglans nigra*** L. (Juglandaceae).

Juglans regia Linnaeus, *Species Plantarum* 2: 997. 1753.
"Habitat – – – –" RCN: 7223.
Lectotype (Nasir in Nasir & Ali, *Fl. W. Pakistan* 14: 3. 1972): Herb.
  Linn. No. 1129.1 (LINN).
Generitype of *Juglans* Linnaeus (vide Green, *Prop. Brit. Bot.*: 189.
  1929).
Current name: ***Juglans regia*** L. (Juglandaceae).

Juncus acutus Linnaeus, *Species Plantarum* 1: 325. 1753.
"Habitat in Angliae, Galliae, Italiae maritimis paludosis." RCN: 2529.
Lectotype (Snogerup in Davis, *Fl. Turkey* 9: 4. 1985): Herb. Linn. No.
  449.1, left specimen (LINN).
Generitype of *Juncus* Linnaeus (vide Hitchcock, *Prop. Brit. Bot.*: 147.
  1929).
Current name: ***Juncus acutus*** L. (Juncaceae).

Juncus articulatus Linnaeus, *Species Plantarum* 1: 327. 1753.
"Habitat in Europae aquosis." RCN: 2537.
Type not designated.
Original material: Herb. A. van Royen No. 904.145–409 (L); Herb.
  A. van Royen No. 904.145–411 (L); Herb. Burser I: 58 (UPS);
  Herb. A. van Royen No. 904.145–410 (L); Herb. Burser I: 59
  (UPS); [icon] in Bauhin, Prodr. Theatri Bot.: 12. 1620; [icon] in
  Morison, Pl. Hist. Univ. 3: 227, s. 8, t. 9, f. 1. 1699; [icon] in
  Bauhin, Theatri Bot.: 75, 76. 1658; [icon] in Bauhin, Prodr.
  Theatri Bot.: 12. 1620.
Current name: ***Juncus articulatus*** L. (Juncaceae).
Note: Novikov (in *Novosti Sist. Vyssh. Rast.* 15: 90. 1985) treats
  unspecified material in LINN as the type but none of the specimens
  in LINN are original material for this name. Similarly, the specimen
  (449.19 LINN) indicated by Snogerup (in Strid & Kit Tan,
  Mountain Fl. Greece 2: 738. 1991) as a possible lectotype is
  unannotated by Linnaeus and is not original material.

Juncus articulatus Linnaeus var. **aquaticus** Linnaeus, *Systema*
  Naturae, ed. 12, 2: 250. 1767.
RCN: 2537.
Type not designated.
Original material: none traced.
Current name: ***Juncus articulatus*** L. (Juncaceae).

Juncus articulatus Linnaeus var. **sylvaticus** Linnaeus, *Systema*
  Naturae, ed. 12, 2: 250. 1767.
RCN: 2537.
Type not designated.
Original material: none traced.
Current name: ***Juncus sp.*** (Juncaceae).
Note: The application of this name is uncertain.

Juncus biglumis Linnaeus, *Species Plantarum* 1: 328. 1753.
"Habitat in Alpibus Lapponicis." RCN: 2542.
Lectotype (Kirschner in Kirschner & al., *Sp. Pl. – Fl. World* 7: 112.
  2002): Herb. Linn. No. 449.33 (LINN).
Current name: ***Juncus biglumis*** L. (Juncaceae).

Juncus bufonius Linnaeus, *Species Plantarum* 1: 328. 1753.
"Habitat in Europae inundatis." RCN: 2539.
Lectotype (Cope & Stace in *Watsonia* 12: 121. 1978): Herb. A. van
  Royen No. 904.145–433 (L).
Current name: ***Juncus bufonius*** L. (Juncaceae).
Note: Although Carter (in Milne-Redhead & Polhill, *Fl. Trop. E.*
  Africa, Juncaceae: 2 1966), and some later authors, indicated
  unspecified material in LINN as type, they did not distinguish
  between several specimens there associated with the name. As these
  specimens are evidently not part of a single gathering, Art. 9.15
  does not apply.

Juncus bulbosus Linnaeus, *Species Plantarum* 1: 327. 1753.
"Habitat in Europae pascuis sterilibus subhumidis, at γ in Sibiria,
  Virginia." RCN: 2538.
Lectotype (Snogerup in Davis, *Fl. Turkey* 9: 20. 1985; Procków in
  Taxon 51: 551, f. 1. 2002): Herb. Linn. No. 449.27, right specimen
  (LINN).

Current name: ***Juncus bulbosus*** L. (Juncaceae).
Note: Procków restricted Snogerop's earlier type choice of material on sheet 449.27 (LINN) to the right-hand specimen on the sheet (which he illustrates as his f. 1).

Juncus campestris Linnaeus, *Species Plantarum* 1: 329. 1753.
"Habitat in Europae pascuis siccioribus." RCN: 2546.
Lectotype (Carter in Milne-Redhead & Polhill, *Fl. Trop. E. Africa, Juncaceae*: 8. 1966): Herb. Linn. No. 449.44 (LINN).
Current name: ***Luzula campestris*** (L.) DC. (Juncaceae).

Juncus conglomeratus Linnaeus, *Species Plantarum* 1: 326. 1753.
"Habitat in Europae borealis uliginosis." RCN: 2530.
Lectotype (Snogerup in *Bot. Not.* 123: 428. 1970): Herb. A. van Royen No. 904.145–425 (L).
Current name: ***Juncus conglomeratus*** L. (Juncaceae).
Note: Dandy (in *Watsonia* 7:169. 1969) argued that this is a synonym of *J. effusus* and selected an apparently ineligible van Royen specimen of *J. effusus* as the lectotype.

Juncus effusus Linnaeus, *Species Plantarum* 1: 326. 1753.
"Habitat in Europae uliginosis, α in alpibus." RCN: 2531.
Lectotype (designated here by Kirschner): Herb. Linn. No. 449.6 (LINN).
Current name: ***Juncus effusus*** L. (Juncaceae).
Note: Although Carter (in Milne-Redhead & Polhill, *Fl. Trop. E. Africa, Juncaceae*: 2 1966) indicated unspecified material in LINN as type, she did not distinguish between several specimens there associated with the name. As these specimens are evidently not part of a single gathering, Art. 9.15 does not apply. Obermeyer (in Leistner, *Fl. Southern Africa* 4(2): 76. 1985) treated 449.3 (LINN) as the type, but this sheet is unannotated by Linnaeus and is not original material for the name. Kirschner & al. (in *Sp. Pl. – Fl. World* 8: 88. 2002) indicated 449.6 (LINN) as lectotype, apparently following Lye (in Edwards & al., *Fl. Ethiopia Eritrea* 6: 387. 1997) but Lye, like Carter, did not distinguish a single sheet as type. As Kirschner & al.'s type statement is later than 2001, their omission of the phrase "designated here" or an equivalent (Art. 7.11) means that the choice is not effective. However, this is rectified here.

Juncus filiformis Linnaeus, *Species Plantarum* 1: 326. 1753.
"Habitat in Europae uliginoso-paludosis turfosis." RCN: 2533.
Lectotype (Hämet-Ahti in Kirschner & al., *Sp. Pl. – Fl. World* 8: 107. 2002): Herb. Linn. No. 449.9 (LINN).
Current name: ***Juncus filiformis*** L. (Juncaceae).
Note: Novikov (in *Novosti Sist. Vyssh. Rast.* 15: 86. 1985) treated unspecified material in LINN as the type. However, this does not distinguish between sheets 449.9, 449.10 and 449.11 and as they are evidently not part of a single gathering, Art. 9.15 does not apply.

Juncus glomeratus Linnaeus, *Amoenitates Academicae* 4: 481. 1759, *orth. var.*
RCN: 2530.
Lectotype (Snogerup in *Bot. Not.* 123: 428. 1970): Herb. A. van Royen No. 904.145–425 (L).
Current name: ***Juncus conglomeratus*** L. (Juncaceae).
Note: Juncus glomeratus L. (*Amoen. Acad.* 4: 481. 1759) was regarded by Stearn (in Geck & Pressler, *Festschr. Claus Nissen*: 632. 1974) as an orthographic variant of *J. conglomeratus* L. (*Sp. Pl.* 1: 326. 1753). This seems plausible, because the phrase name used by Magnol (*Bot. Monsp.*: 635. 1676) is cited as a synonym of *J. conglomeratus* by Linnaeus in 1753. Moreover, *J. glomeratus* never appears again.

Juncus inflexus Linnaeus, *Species Plantarum* 1: 326. 1753.
"Habitat in Europa australi." RCN: 2532.

Type not designated.
Original material: [icon] in Barrelier, Pl. Galliam: 48, t. 204. 1714; [icon] in Morison, Pl. Hist. Univ. 3: 233, s. 8, t. 10, f. 25. 1699.
Current name: ***Juncus inflexus*** L. (Juncaceae).

Juncus jacquinii Linnaeus, *Systema Naturae,* ed. 12, 2: 251; *Mantissa Plantarum*: 63. 1767.
"Habitat in Schneberg Austriae." RCN: 2541.
Lectotype (Kirschner & al., *Sp. Pl. – Fl. World* 8: 81. 2002): [icon] *"Juncus biglumis"* in Jacquin, Enum. Stirp. Vindob.: 237, t. 4, f. 2. 1762.
Current name: ***Juncus jacquinii*** L. (Juncaceae).
Note: Specific epithet spelled "jacquini" in the protologue.

Juncus niveus Linnaeus, *Systema Naturae,* ed. 10, 2: 987. 1759.
["Habitat in Alpibus Bohemicis, Helveticis, Rhaeticis, Monspelii."] Sp. Pl., ed. 2, 1: 468 (1762). RCN: 2545.
Lectotype (designated here by Kirschner): Herb. Linn. No. 449.41 (LINN).
Current name: ***Luzula nivea*** (L.) DC. (Juncaceae).
Note: Kirschner (in Kirschner & al., *Sp. Pl. – Fl. World* 6: 25. 2002) cited this name from *Amoen. Acad.* 4: 481 (Nov 1759) but gave its publication date as 1756 (i.e. that of the original dissertation, *Flora Monspeliensis*, in which the name did not appear – see Stearn in Geck & Pressler, *Festschr. Claus Nissen*: 629. 1974). The name actually dates from *Syst. Nat.*, ed. 10, 2 (May–Jun 1759) where it is not validated solely by a reference to Magnol (as believed by Kirschner).

Juncus nodosus Linnaeus, *Species Plantarum,* ed. 2, 1: 466. 1762.
"Habitat in America septentrionali." RCN: 2536.
Lectotype (Balslev, *Fl. Neotropica* 68: 128. 1996): Herb. Linn. No. 449.17 (LINN).
Current name: ***Juncus nodosus*** L. (Juncaceae).
Note: Fernald & Schubert (in *Rhodora* 50: 155. 1948) identified 449.16 (LINN) as *J. scopioides* Michx., and 449.17 (LINN) as *J. nodosus*. While not explicitly typifying the name, they indicated that its application should not be changed. Balslev's indication of Kalm material in LINN as the type identifies 449.17 as the intended sheet.

Juncus pilosus Linnaeus, *Species Plantarum* 1: 329. 1753.
"Habitat in Europae sylvis." RCN: 2544.
Type not designated.
Original material: Herb. Burser I: 95 (UPS); Herb. A. van Royen No. 904.145–429 (L); Herb. Linn. No. 124 (LAPP); Herb. Burser I: 91 (UPS); [icon] in Scheuchzer, Agrostographia: 312, t. 6. 1719; [icon] in Bauhin, Theatri Bot. 3: 225, s. 8, t. 9, f. 1. 1699; [icon] in Bauhin, Prodr. Theatri Bot.: 16. 1620; [icon] in Bauhin, Theatri Bot.: 106. 1658; [icon] in Barrelier, Pl. Galliam: 49, t. 748, f. 2. 1714; [icon] in Bauhin, Theatri Bot.: 102. 1658; [icon] in Morison, Pl. Hist. Univ. 3: 225, s. 8, t. 9, f. 3. 1699; [icon] in Morison, Pl. Hist. Univ. 3: 225, s. 8, t. 9, f. 2. 1699.
Current name: ***Luzula pilosa*** (L.) Willd. (Juncaceae).

Juncus spicatus Linnaeus, *Species Plantarum* 1: 330. 1753.
"Habitat in Lapponiae Alpibus." RCN: 2547.
Lectotype (Kirschner in Kirschner & al., *Sp. Pl. – Fl. World* 6: 62. 2002): Herb. Linn. No. 125 (LAPP).
Current name: ***Luzula spicata*** (L.) DC. (Juncaceae).

Juncus squarrosus Linnaeus, *Species Plantarum* 1: 327. 1753.
"Habitat in Europae borealis sespitosis." RCN: 2535.
Lectotype (designated here by Kirschner): Herb. Linn. No. 449.14 (LINN).

Current name: *Juncus squarrosus* L. (Juncaceae).
Note: See Kirschner & al. (in *Sp. Pl. – Fl. World* 8: 9. 2002), who stated that 449.14 (LINN) is "recommendable as the lectotype" but, post-dating 2001, omitted the phrase "designated here" or an equivalent (Art. 7.11) which means that the choice is not effective. This is rectified here.

Juncus stygius Linnaeus, *Systema Naturae,* ed. 10, 2: 987. 1759. ["Habitat in Sveciae, paludibus, caespitosis sylvaticis profundis."] Sp. Pl., ed. 2, 1: 467 (1762). RCN: 2540.
Type not designated.
Original material: Herb. Linn. No. 449.29 (LINN); Herb. Linn. No. 449.28 (LINN); [icon] in Morison, Pl. Hist. Univ. 3: 239, s. 8, t. 11, f. 40. 1699.
Current name: *Juncus stygius* L. (Juncaceae).

Juncus trifidus Linnaeus, *Species Plantarum* 1: 326. 1753.
"Habitat in Alpibus Lapponicis, Helveticis, Pyrenaeis." RCN: 2534.
Lectotype (Kirschner in Kirschner & al., *Sp. Pl. – Fl. World* 8: 43. 2002): Herb. Linn. No. 119 (LAPP).
Current name: *Juncus trifidus* L. (Juncaceae).

Juncus triglumis Linnaeus, *Species Plantarum* 1: 328. 1753.
"Habitat frequens in Alpibus Lapponicis, Tauro Rastadiensi." RCN: 2543.
Lectotype (Jafri in Nasir & Ali, *Fl. Pakistan* 137: 7. 1981): Herb. Linn. No. 449.35 (LINN).
Current name: *Juncus triglumis* L. (Juncaceae).

Jungermannia albicans Linnaeus, *Species Plantarum* 2: 1133. 1753.
"Habitat in Europae umbrosis." RCN: 8119.
Type not designated.
Original material: Herb. Linn. No. 1267.11? (LINN); [icon] in Dillenius, Hist. Musc.: 492, t. 71, f. 20. 1741; [icon] in Vaillant, Bot. Paris.: 100, t. 19, f. 5. 1727.
Current name: *Diplophyllum albicans* (L.) Dumort. (Scapaniaceae).
Note: Isoviita (in *Acta Bot. Fenn.* 89: 8. 1970) thought that 1267.11 (LINN) came from Celsius but he did not treat it as the type. Grolle (in *Feddes Repert.* 87: 191. 1976) designated material in the Dillenius herbarium (OXF) as lectotype (with an isotype in FI), but this material was not studied by Linnaeus and is not original material for the name.

Jungermannia alpina Linnaeus, *Species Plantarum* 2: 1135. 1753.
"Habitat in Alpibus Britanniae, inque rupibus Sueciae." RCN: 8132.
Type not designated.
Original material: [icon] in Dillenius, Hist. Musc.: 506, t. 73, f. 39. 1741.
Note: The application of this name is uncertain, but it seems likely that it applies to a member of the Musci, in which case it is a pre-Starting Point name, and of no nomenclatural significance.

Jungermannia asplenioides Linnaeus, *Species Plantarum* 2: 1131. 1753.
"Habitat in Europae Indiae udis umbrosis." RCN: 8110.
Type not designated.
Original material: Herb. Linn. No. 1267.1 (LINN); [icon] in Dillenius, Hist. Musc.: 482, t. 69, f. 5. 1741; [icon] in Vaillant, Bot. Paris.: 99, t. 19, f. 7. 1729; [icon] in Morison, Pl. Hist. Univ. 3: 627, s. 15, t. 6, f. 42. 1699; [icon] in Micheli, Nov. Pl. Gen.: 7, t. 5, f. 1, 2. 1729; [icon] in Dillenius, Hist. Musc.: 483, t. 69, f. 6. 1741; [icon] in Loesel, Fl. Prussica: 167, t. 45. 1703; [icon] in Micheli, Nov. Pl. Gen.: 8, t. 5, f. 3. 1729.
Current name: *Plagiochila asplenioides* (L.) Dumort. (Plagiochilaceae).

Note: Grolle (in *Trans. Brit. Bryol. Soc.* 5: 279. 1967) provided an extensive discussion of the original material for this name, but designated Dillenian material (OXF) as lectotype (which was not studied by Linnaeus and is not original material for the name).

Jungermannia bicuspidata Linnaeus, *Species Plantarum* 2: 1132. 1753.
"Habitat in Europae umbrosis humidis." RCN: 8115.
Type not designated.
Original material: [icon] in Micheli, Nov. Pl. Gen.: 9, t. 6, f. 17. 1729; [icon] in Dillenius, Hist. Musc.: 488, t. 70, f. 13. 1741.
Current name: *Cephalozia bicuspidata* (L.) Dumort. (Cephaloziaceae).
Note: See notes by Isoviita (in *Acta Bot. Fenn.* 89: 18. 1970) and Grolle (in *Feddes Repert.* 87: 185. 1976).

Jungermannia bidentata Linnaeus, *Species Plantarum* 2: 1132. 1753.
"Habitat in Europae ericetis umbrosis." RCN: 8114.
Type not designated.
Original material: [icon] in Vaillant, Bot. Paris.: 99, t. 19, f. 8. 1727; [icon] in Micheli, Nov. Pl. Gen.: 8, t. 5, f. 12. 1729; [icon] in Dillenius, Hist. Musc.: 487, t. 70, f. 11. 1741; [icon] in Morison, Pl. Hist. Univ. 3: 627, s. 15, t. 6, f. 47. 1699.
Current name: *Lophocolea bidentata* (L.) Dumort. (Geocalycaceae).
Note: See notes by Isoviita (in *Acta Bot. Fenn.* 89: 18. 1970) and Grolle (in *Feddes Repert.* 87: 203. 1976). Vogelpoel (in *Acta Bot. Neerl.* 26: 493. 1977) designated material in the Dillenian herbarium (OXF) as lectotype but this collection was not studied by Linnaeus and it is not original material for the name.

Jungermannia ciliaris Linnaeus, *Species Plantarum* 2: 1134. 1753.
"Habitat in Europa passim." RCN: 8127.
Lectotype (Isoviita in *Acta Bot. Fenn.* 89: 7. 1970): Herb. Linn. No. 1267.29 (LINN).
Current name: *Ptilidium ciliare* (L.) Hampe (Ptilidiaceae).

Jungermannia complanata Linnaeus, *Species Plantarum* 2: 1133. 1753.
"Habitat in Europa ad arborum truncos." RCN: 8123.
Type not designated.
Original material: Herb. Linn. No. 1267.18 (LINN); [icon] in Dillenius, Hist. Musc.: 496, t. 72, f. 26. 1741; [icon] in Micheli, Nov. Pl. Gen.: 7, t. 5, f. 21. 1729.
Current name: *Radula complanata* (L.) Dumort. (Radulaceae).
Note: Grolle (in *Trans. Brit. Bryol. Soc.* 5: 772. 1969) designated material in the Dillenian herbarium (OXF) as lectotype but this collection was not studied by Linnaeus and it is not original material for the name. See also notes by Isoviita (in *Acta Bot. Fenn.* 89: 9. 1970), and Hansen & Fox Maule (in *Bot. J. Linn. Soc.* 67: 200. 1973) for comments on Osbeck material.

Jungermannia dilatata Linnaeus, *Species Plantarum* 2: 1133. 1753.
"Habitat in Europa, America, ad arborum truncos." RCN: 8124.
Type not designated.
Original material: Herb. Linn. 1267.22 (LINN); [icon] in Dillenius, Hist. Musc.: 497, t. 72, f. 27. 1741; [icon] in Micheli, Nov. Pl. Gen.: 10, t. 6, f. 6. 1729; [icon] in Vaillant, Bot. Paris.: 99, t.19, f. 10. 1727.
Current name: *Frullania dilatata* (L.) Dumort. (Frullaniaceae).
Note: Grolle (in *Wiss. Z. Friedrich-Schiller-Univ. Jena, Math.-Naturwiss. Reihe* 19: 316. 1970) designated material in the Dillenian herbarium (OXF) as lectotype but this collection was not studied by Linnaeus and it is not original material for the name. See also notes by Isoviita (in *Acta Bot. Fenn.* 89: 8, 19. 1970).

Jungermannia epiphylla Linnaeus, *Species Plantarum* 2: 1135. 1753.
"Habitat in Europae ripis elatioribus umbrosis udis." RCN: 8134.
Lectotype (Isoviita in *Acta Bot. Fenn.* 89: 9. 1970): Herb. Linn. No. 1267.44 (LINN).
Current name: **Pellia epiphylla** (L.) Corda (Pelliaceae).

Jungermannia furcata Linnaeus, *Species Plantarum* 2: 1136. 1753.
"Habitat in Europa ad truncos, rupes & e terra." RCN: 8137.
Lectotype (Grolle & So in *Cryptog. Bryol.* 23: 119. 2002): [icon] *"Lichenastrum tenuifolium furcatum, thecis globosis pilosis"* in Dillenius, Hist. Musc.: 512, t. 74, f. 45 A, B, C, F, G. 1741. – Voucher: Herb. Dillenius (OXF). – Epitype (Grolle & So in *Cryptog. Bryol.* 23: 120. 2002): Herb. Dillenius fol. 163, No. 45 (OXF; iso- H-SOL).
Current name: **Metzgeria furcata** (L.) Dumort. (Metzgeriaceae).

Jungermannia julacea Linnaeus, *Species Plantarum* 2: 1135, Errata. 1753.
"Habitat in Alpibus Britanniae." RCN: 8129.
Lectotype (Isoviita in *Acta Bot. Fenn.* 89: 21. 1970): [icon] *"Lichenastrum alpinum, Bryi julacei argentei facie"* in Dillenius, Hist. Musc.: 506, t. 73, f. 38. 1741. – Voucher: Herb. Dillenius (OXF).
Current name: **Anthelia julacea** (L.) Dumort. (Antheliaceae).
Note: Orthography of epithet corrected from "gulacea" in Errata.

Jungermannia lanceolata Linnaeus, *Species Plantarum* 2: 1131. 1753, *nom. rej.*
"Habitat in Europae humidis umbrosis." RCN: 8113.
Lectotype (Grolle in *Taxon* 15: 189. 1966): [icon] *"Lichenastrum Trichomanis facie minus, ab extremitate florens"* in Dillenius, Hist. Musc.: 486, t. 70, f. 10 A. 1741. – Voucher: Herb. Dillenius (OXF).
Generitype of *Jungermannia* Linnaeus (vide Müller, *Lebermoose Ergänzungsband*: 164. 1940).
Current name: **Jungermannia atrovirens** Dumort. (Jungermanniaceae).

Jungermannia multifida Linnaeus, *Species Plantarum* 2: 1136. 1753.
"Habitat in Angliae ericetis." RCN: 8136.
Lectotype (Isoviita in *Acta Bot. Fenn.* 89: 21. 1970): [icon] *"Lichenastrum Ambrosiae divisura"* in Dillenius, Hist. Musc.: 511, t. 74, f. 43. 1741. – Voucher: Herb. Dillenius (OXF).
Current name: **Riccardia multifida** (L.) Gray (Aneuraceae).

Jungermannia nemorea Linnaeus, *Systema Naturae*, ed. 10, 2: 1337. 1759.
RCN: 8118a.
Replaced synonym of: *Jungermannia nemorosa* L. (1763).
Neotype (Grolle in *Feddes Repert.* 87: 233. 1976): *Haller* in Herb. Dillenius (OXF; iso- H-SOL).
Current name: **Scapania nemorea** (L.) Grolle (Scapaniaceae).
Note: Grolle (in *Revue Bryol. Lichénol.*, n.s., 32: 160. 1963) and Isoviita (in *Acta Bot. Fenn.* 89: 18. 1970) both treated *J. nemorosa* L. (1763) as a superfluous name for *J. nemorea*, while Stotler & Zehr (in *Taxon* 29: 493. 1980) argued that "nemorea" in 1759 is an orthographic error, corrected to "nemorosa" in 1763. However, Grolle & Isoviita (in *Ann. Bot. Fenn.* 18: 83. 1981) present evidence that "nemorea" is not a variant of "nemorosa". Although Grolle (in *Feddes Repert.* 87: 233. 1976) designated a Haller specimen in Herb. Dillenius (OXF, iso- H-SOL) as the lectotype, this material was not studied by Linnaeus and is not original material for this name. However, in the absence of any original material at all, Grolle's choice is accepted as a neotypification (Art. 9.8).

Jungermannia nemorosa Linnaeus, *Species Plantarum,* ed. 2, 2: 1598. 1763, *nom. illeg.*
"Habitat in Europae sylvis." RCN: 8118a.
Replaced synonym: *Jungermannia nemorea* L. (1759).
Neotype (Grolle in *Feddes Repert.* 87: 233. 1976): *Haller* in Herb. Dillenius (OXF; iso- H-SOL).
Current name: **Scapania nemorea** (L.) Grolle (Scapaniaceae).
Note: Grolle (in *Revue Bryol. Lichénol.*, n.s., 32: 160. 1963) and Isoviita (in *Acta Bot. Fenn.* 89: 18. 1970) both treated this as a superfluous name for *J. nemorea* (1759) while Stotler & Zehr (in *Taxon* 29: 493. 1980) argued that "nemorea" in 1759 is an orthographic error, corrected to "nemorosa" in 1763. However, Grolle & Isoviita (in *Ann. Bot. Fenn.* 18: 83. 1981) presented evidence that "nemorea" is not a variant of "nemorosa", and the latter is therefore treated as illegitimate. Although Bonner (*Index Hepaticarum* 8: 247. 1976) treated a Dillenius figure as the type, this element was not cited in the protologue of *J. nemorea* and so is not original material for either name.

Jungermannia pinguis Linnaeus, *Species Plantarum* 2: 1136. 1753.
"Habitat in Europae paludibus." RCN: 8135.
Type not designated.
Original material: [icon] in Plukenet, Phytographia: t. 42, f. 2. 1691; Almag. Bot.: 216. 1696; [icon] in Dillenius, Hist. Musc.: 509, t. 74, f. 42. 1741; [icon] in Micheli, Nov. Pl. Gen.: 5, t. 4, f. 2. 1729.
Current name: **Aneura pinguis** (L.) Dumort. (Aneuraceae).
Note: Perold (in *Bothalia* 31: 169. 2001) indicated Lichenastrum No. 42 (OXF syn.; H-SOL-isosyn.) as the type but this material was not seen by Linnaeus and is not original material for the name.

Jungermannia platyphylla Linnaeus, *Species Plantarum* 2: 1134. 1753.
"Habitat in Europae & America septentrionalis sylvis." RCN: 8126.
Type not designated.
Original material: Herb. Linn. No. 1267.24? (LINN); [icon] in Dillenius, Hist. Musc.: 501, t. 72, f. 32. 1741; [icon] in Micheli, Nov. Pl. Gen.: 9, t. 6, f. 3, 4. 1729; [icon] in Vaillant, Bot. Paris.: t. 19, f. 9. 1727; [icon] in Morison, Pl. Hist. Univ. 3: 627, s. 15, t. 6, f. 44. 1699.
Current name: **Porella platyphylla** (L.) Pfeiff. (Porellaceae).
Note: See notes by Isoviita (in *Acta Bot. Fenn.* 89: 20. 1970) and Grolle (in *Feddes Repert.* 87: 221. 1976).

Jungermannia polyanthos Linnaeus, *Species Plantarum* 2: 1131. 1753.
"Habitat in Europae palustribus." RCN: 8112.
Type not designated.
Original material: [icon] in Micheli, Nov. Pl. Gen.: 8, t. 5, f. 5. 1729; [icon] in Dillenius, Hist. Musc.: 486, t. 70, f. 9. 1741.
Current name: **Chiloscyphus polyanthos** (L.) Corda (Geocalycaceae).
Note: Although Grolle (in *Taxon* 19: 646. 1970) designated a specimen in the Dillenian herbarium (OXF) as lectotype, this material was not studied by Linnaeus and is not original material for the name.

Jungermannia pusilla Linnaeus, *Species Plantarum* 2: 1136. 1753.
"Habitat in Europae rupibus, ericetis humentibus." RCN: 8138.
Lectotype (Isoviita in *Acta Bot. Fenn.* 89: 22. 1970): [icon] *"Lichenastrum exiguum, capitulis nigris lucidis, e cotylis parvis nascentibus"* in Dillenius, Hist. Musc.: 513, t. 74, f. 46. 1741. – Voucher: Herb. Dillenius (OXF). – Epitype (Stotler & Crandall-Stotler in *J. Bryol.* 27: 73, f. 1D, E, F. 2005): Herb. Dillenius [sheet] CLXIII, n. 46. *L. exiguum, capitulis nigris lucidis,* etc., as *Jungermannia pusilla* (OXF).
Current name: **Fossombronia pusilla** (L.) Nees (Codoniaceae).
Note: See Stotler & Crandall-Stotler (in *J. Bryol.* 27: 71–73. 2005)

J

who provide a detailed analysis of the typification of this name, reproducing the protologue (f. 1A) and, like Isoviita, treat the Dillenius plate (illustrated as f. 1C) as the lectotype. They also designate an epitype from the Dillenian herbarium, illustrating it (f. 1D, E) and reproducing an SEM image of a spore taken from it.

Jungermannia reptans Linnaeus, *Species Plantarum* 2: 1133. 1753.
"Habitat in Europae Ericetis udis." RCN: 8121.
Lectotype (Isoviita in *Acta Bot. Fenn.* 89: 19. 1970): [icon] *"Lichenastrum multifidum exiguum, ad basim florens, per siccitatem imbricatum"* in Dillenius, Hist. Musc.: 494, t. 71, f. 24. 1741. – Voucher: Herb. Dillenius (OXF).
Current name: ***Lepidozia reptans*** (L.) Dumort. (Lepidoziaceae).

Jungermannia resupinata Linnaeus, *Species Plantarum* 2: 1132. 1753.
"Habitat in Europae rupibus." RCN: 8118b.
Type not designated.
Original material: [icon] in Dillenius, Hist. Musc.: 491, t. 71, f. 19. 1741.
Current name: ***Scapania compacta*** (Roth) Dumort. (Scapaniaceae).
Note: Although Isoviita (in *Acta Bot. Fenn.* 89: 18. 1970) referred to the cited Dillenian figure as "probably the lectotype", he also treated the name as ambiguous, following e.g. Evans (in *Rhodora* 8: 42. 1906). *Scapania compacta* (Roth) Dumort. has sometimes been taken up in its place but no formal rejection proposal for *J. resupinata* appears to have been made.

Jungermannia rupestris Linnaeus, *Species Plantarum* 2: 1135. 1753.
"Habitat in Europae frigidis rupibus humentibus." RCN: 8130.
Type not designated.
Original material: [icon] in Dillenius, Hist. Musc.: 507, t. 73, f. 40. 1741.
Current name: ***Andreaea sp.*** (Andreaeaceae).
Note: The application of this name is uncertain, but it seems likely that it applies to a member of the Musci, in which case it would be a pre-Starting Point name, and of no nomenclatural significance.

Jungermannia tamarisci Linnaeus, *Species Plantarum* 2: 1134. 1753.
"Habitat in Europae ad truncos arborum, rupes." RCN: 8125.
Replaced synonym of: *Jungermannia tamariscifolia* L. (1755), *nom. illeg.*
Lectotype (Stotler in *Taxon* 17: 637. 1968): Herb. Linn. No. 1267.24 (LINN).
Current name: ***Frullania tamarisci*** (L.) Dumort. (Frullaniaceae).

Jungermannia tamariscifolia Linnaeus, *Flora Suecica,* ed. 2: 404. 1755, *nom. illeg.*
"Habitat frequens in rupibus & truncis arborum, praesertim Fagi." RCN: 8125.
Replaced synonym: *Jungermannia tamarisci* L. (1753).
Lectotype (Stotler in *Taxon* 17: 637. 1968): Herb. Linn. No. 1267.24 (LINN).
Current name: ***Frullania tamarisci*** (L.) Dumort. (Frullaniaceae).
Note: This has been treated as a superfluous name for *J. tamarisci* L. (1753) by e.g. Isoviita (in *Acta Bot. Fenn.* 89: 20. 1970).

Jungermannia trichophylla Linnaeus, *Species Plantarum* 2: 1135. 1753.
"Habitat in Europae frigidis rupibus." RCN: 8131.
Lectotype (Isoviita in *Acta Bot. Fenn.* 89: 21. 1970): [icon] *"Lichenastrum trichodes minimum, in extremitate florens"* in Dillenius, Hist. Musc.: 505, t. 73, f. 37. 1741. – Voucher: Herb. Dillenius (OXF).
Current name: ***Blepharostoma trichophyllum*** (L.) Dumort. (Pseudolepicoleaceae).

Jungermannia trilobata Linnaeus, *Species Plantarum* 2: 1133. 1753.
"Habitat in Svecia, Anglia, Italia." RCN: 8120.
Type not designated.
Original material: Herb. Linn. No. 1267.13 (LINN); Herb. Linn. No. 1267.11? (LINN); [icon] in Dillenius, Hist. Musc.: 493, t. 71, f. 22. 1741; [icon] in Micheli, Nov. Pl. Gen.: 7, t. 5, f. 10. 1729.
Current name: ***Bazzania trilobata*** (L.) Gray (Lepidoziaceae).
Note: Isoviita (in *Acta Bot. Fenn.* 89: 8, 19. 1970) referred to the Dillenian element as "probably the lectotype" while Grolle (in *Lindenbergia* 1: 197. 1972) designated material in the Dillenius herbarium (OXF) as lectotype, noting a duplicate in H-SOL. However, this material was not seen by Linnaeus and is not original material for the name.

Jungermannia undulata Linnaeus, *Species Plantarum* 2: 1132. 1753.
"Habitat in Europa." RCN: 8117.
Type not designated.
Original material: [icon] in Vaillant, Bot. Paris.: 98, t. 19, f. 6. 1727; [icon] in Dillenius, Hist. Musc.: 490, t. 71, f. 17. 1741.
Current name: ***Scapania undulata*** (L.) Dumort. (Scapaniaceae).
Note: Grolle & al. (in *Taxon* 54: 508. 2005) claimed that the cited Dillenius figure had been previously designated as the lectotype by Grolle (in *Taxon* 22: 691. 1973; *Feddes Repert.* 87: 236. 1976). However, although linked with the published figure, Grolle in both publications clearly treats the herbarium material in OXF as the lectotype. As this material was not studied by Linnaeus, it is not original material for the name. Although Grolle & al. clearly accept Dillenius' figure as the type (and the voucher material in OXF as an epitype), their statement was published after 1 Jan 2001 and so the omission of the phrase "designated here" or an equivalent (Art. 7.11) means that their lectotype choice is not effective and, in the absence of a lectotype, an epitype cannot be designated. The material in OXF is not original for the name, and the name remains untypified at present.

Jungermannia varia Linnaeus, *Species Plantarum* 2: 1135. 1753.
"Habitat in Europae sylvis ericetis." RCN: 8128.
Lectotype (Isoviita in *Acta Bot. Fenn.* 89: 20. 1970): [icon] *"Lichenastrum foliis variis"* in Dillenius, Hist. Musc.: 505, t. 73, f. 36. 1741. – Voucher: Herb. Dillenius (OXF).
Current name: ***Diplophyllum albicans*** (L.) Dumort. (Scapaniaceae).

Jungermannia viticulosa Linnaeus, *Species Plantarum* 2: 1131. 1753.
"Habitat in Europae udis umbrosis sylvis." RCN: 8111.
Lectotype (Evans in *Rhodora* 7: 55. 1905): [icon] *"Jungermannia terrestris, viticulis longis, foliis perexiguis, densissimis, ex rotunditate acuminatis"* in Micheli, Nov. Pl. Gen.: 8, t. 5, f. 4. 1729. – Epitype (Grolle in *Trans. Brit. Bryol. Soc.* 5: 546. 1968): Italy. Tuscany, "Cotto di Maggio...inter Rosina et Stazema" [Jungermannia Ordo 5, No. 3], Herb. Micheli (FI).
Current name: ***Saccogyna viticulosa*** (L.) Dumort. (Geocalycaceae).
Note: Grolle (1968) treated Micheli material in FI, which was not seen by Linnaeus, as the lectotype. However, as it is closely associated with the cited Micheli plate previously designated as the lectotype by Evans, Grolle's statement is treated as correctable to epitype under Art. 9.8.

Juniperus barbadensis Linnaeus, *Species Plantarum* 2: 1039. 1753.
"Habitat in America." RCN: 7501.
Lectotype (Adams & al. in *Taxon* 36: 441, f. 1A. 1987): Herb. Linn. No. 1198.1 (LINN).
Current name: ***Juniperus barbadensis*** L. (Cupressaceae).
Note: Heath (in *Taxon* 40: 94. 1991) argued that Adams & al.'s type choice was invalid but this contention was refuted by Jarvis (*l.c.* 41: 43–44. 1992).

Juniperus bermudiana Linnaeus, *Species Plantarum* 2: 1039. 1753.
"Habitat in America." RCN: 7502.
Type not designated.
Original material: [icon] in Hermann, Hort. Lugd.-Bat. Cat.: 345, 347. 1687.
Current name: ***Juniperus bermudiana*** L. (Cupressaceae).
Note: Adams & al. (in *Taxon* 36: 443. 1987), because of difficulties in identifying a cited Hermann illustration that is the only original material for the name, designated a neotype (Herb. D. van Royen, No. 901.130–394, L) that maintained the traditional usage of the name. However, with the existence of original material, the designation of a neotype is contrary to Art. 9.11.

Juniperus chinensis Linnaeus, *Systema Naturae,* ed. 12, 2: 660; *Mantissa Plantarum*: 127. 1767.
"Habitat in China." RCN: 7503.
Lectotype (Nguyên Tiên Hiêp & Vidal in Morat, *Fl. Cambodge Laos Viêtnam* 28: 87. 1996): Herb. Linn. No. 1198.3 (LINN).
Current name: ***Juniperus chinensis*** L. (Cupressaceae).

Juniperus communis Linnaeus, *Species Plantarum* 2: 1040. 1753.
"Habitat in Europae septentrionalis sylvis." RCN: 7506.
Lectotype (Farjon & Jarvis in Jarvis & al., *Regnum Veg.* 127: 58. 1993): Herb. Clifford: 464, *Juniperus* 1 (BM-000647518).
Generitype of *Juniperus* Linnaeus (vide Green, *Prop. Brit. Bot.*: 192. 1929).
Current name: ***Juniperus communis*** L. subsp. ***communis*** (Cupressaceae).
Note: Although Imkhanitskaya (in *Novosti Sist. Vyssh. Rast.* 27: 7. 1990) indicated 1198.8 (LINN) as type, this is a post-1753 addition to the collection and not original material for the name.

Juniperus lycia Linnaeus, *Species Plantarum* 2: 1039. 1753.
"Habitat in Gallia, Sibiria." RCN: 7509.
Lectotype (designated here by Farjon): Herb. Linn. No. 1198.10 (LINN).
Current name: ***Juniperus phoenicea*** L. (Cupressaceae).
Note: Farjon (*Monogr. Cupressaceae* Sciadopitys: 337. 2005) indicated 1198.10 (LINN) as lectotype, wrongly attributing the choice to Jarvis & al. (in *Regnum Veg.* 127: 58. 1993) where it does not, in fact, appear. As Farjon's statement was published after 1 Jan 2001, the omission of the phrase "designated here" or an equivalent (Art. 7.11) means that the choice was not effective. However, this is rectified here.

Juniperus oxycedrus Linnaeus, *Species Plantarum* 2: 1038. 1753.
"Habitat in Hispania, G. Narbonensi." RCN: 7507.
Lectotype (Christensen in Strid & Kit Tan, *Fl. Hellenica* 1: 12. 1997): Herb. Burser XXV: 67 (UPS).
Current name: ***Juniperus oxycedrus*** L. subsp. ***oxycedrus*** (Cupressaceae).
Note: Imkhanitskaya (in *Novosti Sist. Vyssh. Rast.* 27: 15. 1990) indicated 1198.9 (LINN) as type but this is a 1757 addition, from Kähler, to the collection and not original material for the name.

Juniperus phoenicea Linnaeus, *Species Plantarum* 2: 1040. 1753.
"Habitat in Europa australi, Monspelii." RCN: 7508.
Lectotype (Christensen in Strid & Kit Tan, *Fl. Hellenica* 1: 13. 1997): Herb. Burser XXV: 61 (UPS).
Current name: ***Juniperus phoenicea*** L. (Cupressaceae).

Juniperus sabina Linnaeus, *Species Plantarum* 2: 1039. 1753.
"Habitat in Italia, Sibiria, Olympo, Ararat, Lusitania." RCN: 7504.
Lectotype (Christensen in Strid & Kit Tan, *Fl. Hellenica* 1: 14. 1997): Herb. Burser XXV: 59 (UPS).
Current name: ***Juniperus sabina*** L. (Cupressaceae).

Juniperus thurifera Linnaeus, *Species Plantarum* 2: 1039. 1753.
"Habitat in Hispania." RCN: 7500.
Neotype (Farjon, *Monogr. Cupressaceae* Sciadopitys: 389. 2005): Spain. Aragon: Teruel, Camarena, Mansana, Aug 1892, *E. Reverchon 788* (BM).
Current name: ***Juniperus thurifera*** L. (Cupressaceae).

Juniperus virginiana Linnaeus, *Species Plantarum* 2: 1039. 1753.
"Habitat in Virginia, Carolina." RCN: 7505.
Lectotype (designated here by Farjon): Herb. Linn. No. 1198.7 (LINN).
Current name: ***Juniperus virginiana*** L. (Cupressaceae).
Note: Fernald & Griscom (in *Rhodora* 37: 133. 1935) discussed the original material and treated a Clayton collection, which they called "Clayton 884", as the type. However, it has not proved possible to locate a sheet annotated in this way. There is a collection (BM) from Gronovius annotated "Rode Cedar ex Nova Anglia 1735, febr. no. 32" by him, which may have been the sheet they intended but, if so, it is not original material for the name. Farjon (*Monogr. Cupressaceae* Sciadopitys: 399. 2005) indicated 1198.7 (LINN) as lectotype, wrongly attributing the choice to Jarvis & al. (in *Regnum Veg.* 127: 58. 1993) where it does not, in fact, appear. As Farjon's statement was published after 1 Jan 2001, the omission of the phrase "designated here" or an equivalent (Art. 7.11) means that the choice was not effective, but this is rectified here.

Jussiaea adscendens Linnaeus, *Systema Naturae,* ed. 12, 2: 297; *Mantissa Plantarum*: 69. 1767.
"Habitat in India." RCN: 3058.
Neotype (designated here by Raven, Hoch, Nicolson, Freeland & Wagner): India. Mysore, Hassan district, Belur-Gendehally Road, 17 Sep 1969, *C. Saldanha 15027* (MO-2334663; iso- JSB, K, US).
Current name: ***Ludwigia adscendens*** (L.) H. Hara (Onagraceae).
Note: Raven (in *Reinwardtia* 6: 388. 1963) noted the absence of any type material.

Jussiaea erecta Linnaeus, *Species Plantarum* 1: 388. 1753.
"Habitat in America & forte in Virginia." RCN: 3063.
Lectotype (Fawcett in *J. Bot.* 64: 11–12. 1926): Herb. Linn. No. 552.4 (LINN).
Current name: ***Ludwigia erecta*** (L.) H. Hara (Onagraceae).

Jussiaea peruviana Linnaeus, *Species Plantarum* 1: 388. 1753.
"Habitat in Lima." RCN: 3060.
Lectotype (Raven in *Reinwardtia* 6: 346. 1963): [icon] *"Onagra Laurifolia, flore amplo, pentapetalo"* in Feuillée, J. Obs. 2: 716, t. 9. 1714 (see p. 606).
Current name: ***Ludwigia peruviana*** (L.) H. Hara (Onagraceae).

Jussiaea pubescens Linnaeus, *Species Plantarum,* ed. 2, 1: 555. 1762.
"Habitat in America." RCN: 3061.
Type not designated.
Original material: Herb. Linn. No. 552.3 (LINN).
Current name: ***Ludwigia octovalvis*** (Jacq.) P.H. Raven subsp. ***octovalvis*** (Onagraceae).

Jussiaea purpurea Linnaeus, *Herbarium Amboinense*: 26. 1754, *orth. var.*
RCN: 126.
Lectotype (Stearn in *Taxon* 10: 17. 1961): Herb. Linn. No. 28.26 (LINN).
Current name: ***Justicia purpurea*** L. (Acanthaceae).
Note: The Rumphius plate upon which this name was apparently based is cited in the synonymy of *Justicia purpurea* L. (1753) in

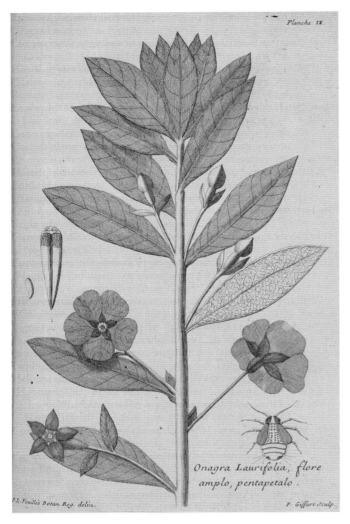

Planche IX.

Onagra Laurifolia, flore amplo, pentapetalo .

P.L. Feuilleé Botan.Reg. delin.   P. Giffart sculp.

The lectotype of *Jussiaea peruviana* L.

Linnaeus' later accounts of that species (*Syst. Nat.*, ed. 10, 2: 850. 1759; *Sp. Pl.*, ed. 2, 1: 23. 1762), suggesting strongly that "Jussiaea" was an error for "Justicia", as noted by Merrill (*Interpret. Rumph. Herb. Amb.*: 476. 1917). "Jussiaea purpurea" was not used by Linnaeus again in 1759 or 1762. It is treated as an orthographic variant of *Justicia purpurea* L.

Jussiaea repens Linnaeus, *Species Plantarum* 1: 388. 1753.
"Habitat in India." RCN: 3058.
Lectotype (Raven in Jarvis & al., *Regnum Veg.* 127: 58. 1993): [icon] "*Nir-carambu*" in Rheede, Hort. Malab. 2: 99, t. 51. 1679.
Generitype of *Jussiaea* Linnaeus (vide Hitchcock, *Prop. Brit. Bot.*: 153. 1929).
Current name: ***Ludwigia adscendens*** (L.) H. Hara (Onagraceae).
Note: Brenan (in Turrill & Milne-Redhead, *Fl. Trop. E. Africa, Onagraceae*: 14. 1953) indicated 552.1 (LINN) as lectotype but this was a post-1753 addition to the herbarium and not original material for the name.

Jussiaea suffruticosa Linnaeus, *Species Plantarum* 1: 388. 1753.
"Habitat in India." RCN: 3062.
Type not designated.

Original material: [icon] in Rheede, Hort. Malab. 2: 95, t. 49. 1679.
Current name: ***Ludwigia octovalvis*** (Jacq.) P.H. Raven subsp. ***sessiliflora*** (Micheli) P.H. Raven (Onagraceae).

Justicia adhatoda Linnaeus, *Species Plantarum* 1: 15. 1753.
"Habitat in Zeylona." RCN: 107.
Lectotype (Manning & Getliffe Norris in *S. African J. Bot.* 51: 483. 1985): Herb. Hermann 2: 43, No. 16 (BM-000621656).
Current name: ***Adhatoda vasica*** Nees (Acanthaceae).

Justicia assurgens Linnaeus, *Systema Naturae*, ed. 10, 2: 850. 1759.
["Habitat in Jamaica."] Sp. Pl., ed. 2, 1: 23 (1762). RCN: 124.
Lectotype (Daniel in Breedlove, *Fl. Chiapas* 4: 29. 1995): [icon] "*Justicia herbacea assurgens, ad alas alternas nodos & summitates florida; foliis paucioribus ovatis petiolis longis incidentibus*" in Browne, Civ. Nat. Hist. Jamaica: 118, t. 2, f. 1. 1756.
Current name: ***Dicliptera sexangularis*** (L.) Juss. (Acanthaceae).

Justicia betonica Linnaeus, *Species Plantarum* 1: 15. 1753.
"Habitat in India." RCN: 109.
Lectotype (Immelman in *Bothalia* 16: 40. 1986): Herb. Hermann 3: 2, No. 18 (BM-000621793).
Current name: ***Justicia betonica*** L. (Acanthaceae).
Note: Although Cufodontis (in *Bull. Jard. Bot. État Bruxelles* 34: 968. 1964) stated "Typus: Rheede (Malabaria)", this is insufficiently precise to effect typification.

Justicia bivalvis Linnaeus, *Systema Naturae*, ed. 10, 2: 850. 1759.
["Habitat in Asia indica. J. Burmannus."] Sp. Pl., ed. 2, 1: 24 (1762). RCN: 127.
Lectotype (Wood & al. in *Kew Bull.* 38: 452. 1983): *J. Burman s.n.*, Herb. Linn. No. 28.25 (LINN).
Current name: ***Peristrophe bivalvis*** (L.) Merr. (Acanthaceae).

Justicia chinensis Linnaeus, *Species Plantarum* 1: 16. 1753.
"Habitat in China." RCN: 120.
Lectotype (Hara in *J. Jap. Bot.* 55: 324. 1980): Herb. Linn. No. 28.19 (LINN).
Current name: ***Dicliptera chinensis*** (L.) Juss. (Acanthaceae).

Justicia ecbolium Linnaeus, *Species Plantarum* 1: 15. 1753.
"Habitat in Malabaria, Zeylona." RCN: 108.
Type not designated.
Original material: [icon] in Rheede, Hort. Malab. 2: 31, t. 20. 1679; [icon] in Burman, Thes. Zeylan.: 7, t. 4, f. 1. 1737; [icon] in Plukenet, Phytographia: t. 171, f. 4. 1692; Almag. Bot.: 126. 1696.
Current name: ***Ecbolium ligustrinum*** (Vahl) Vollesen (Acanthaceae).

Justicia echioides Linnaeus, *Species Plantarum* 1: 16. 1753.
"Habitat in India." RCN: 121.
Lectotype (Stearn ex Cramer in Dassanayake & Clayton, *Revised Handb. Fl. Ceylon* 12: 100. 1998): Herb. Hermann 4: 40, No. 21 (BM-000628183).
Current name: ***Andrographis echioides*** (L.) Nees (Acanthaceae).

Justicia fastuosa Linnaeus, *Mantissa Plantarum Altera*: 172. 1771.
"Habitat in Tranquebaria, Arabia felici. D. Koenig." RCN: 114.
Lectotype (Wood & al. in *Kew Bull.* 38: 455. 1983): Herb. Linn. No. 28.7 (LINN).
Current name: ***Hypoestes* sp.** (Acanthaceae).
Note: Wood & al. were unable to match the Linnaean type with any known species of *Hypoestes*.

Justicia gangetica Linnaeus, *Centuria II Plantarum*: 3. 1756.
"Habitat in India." RCN: 128.
Lectotype (Malik & Ghafoor in Nasir & Ali, *Fl. Pakistan* 188: 68.
1988): Herb. Linn. No. 28.27 (LINN).
Current name: ***Asystasia gangetica*** (L.) T. Anderson (Acanthaceae).
Note: Heine (in Aubréville, *Fl. Gabon* 13: 135. 1966) indicated
unspecified material in LINN as the holotype. However, he did not
distinguish between sheets 28.27 and 28.28 (LINN), not part of a
single gathering, so this is not an effective typification.

Justicia hyssopifolia Linnaeus, *Species Plantarum* 1: 15. 1753.
"Habitat in insulis Fortunatis." RCN: 116.
Lectotype (Wijnands, *Bot. Commelins*: 32. 1983): Herb. Linn. No.
28.10 (LINN).
Generitype of *Justicia* Linnaeus.
Current name: ***Justicia hyssopifolia*** L. (Acanthaceae).
Note: Justicia hyssopifolia, with the type designated by Wijnands, was
proposed as conserved type of the genus by Jarvis (in *Taxon* 41: 564.
1992). However, the proposal was eventually ruled unnecessary by
the General Committee (see Barrie, *l.c.* 55: 795–796. 2006, for a
review of the history of this and related proposals).

Justicia infundibuliformis Linnaeus, *Systema Naturae,* ed. 10, 2: 850.
1759.
["Habitat in India."] Sp. Pl., ed. 2, 1: 21 (1762). RCN: 112.
Lectotype (Malik & Ghafoor in Nasir & Ali, *Fl. Pakistan* 188: 65.
1988): *J. Burman s.n.*, Herb. Linn. No. 28.6 (LINN).
Current name: ***Crossandra infundibuliformis*** (L.) Nees
(Acanthaceae).

Justicia nasuta Linnaeus, *Species Plantarum* 1: 16. 1753.
"Habitat in India. Toren." RCN: 125.
Type not designated.
Original material: *Torén*, Herb. Linn. No. 28.24 (LINN); [icon] in
Rheede, Hort. Malab. 9: 135, t. 69. 1689.
Current name: ***Rhinacanthus nasutus*** (L.) Kurz (Acanthaceae).
Note: Manilal & al. (in *Rheedea* 13: 16. 2005) wrongly claim that this
was based solely on the Rheede element.

Justicia pectinata Linnaeus, *Centuria II Plantarum*: 3. 1756.
"Habitat in India." RCN: 118.
Lectotype (Cramer in Dassanayake & Clayton, *Revised Handb. Fl.
Ceylon* 12: 105. 1998): Herb. Linn. No. 28.17 (LINN).
Current name: ***Rungia pectinata*** (L.) Nees (Acanthaceae).

Justicia picta Linnaeus, *Species Plantarum,* ed. 2, 1: 21. 1762.
"Habitat in Asia." RCN: 111.
Lectotype (Durkee in Woodson & Schery in *Ann. Missouri Bot. Gard.*
65: 199. 1978): Herb. Linn. No. 28.5 (LINN).
Current name: ***Graptophyllum pictum*** (L.) Griff. (Acanthaceae).

Justicia procumbens Linnaeus, *Species Plantarum* 1: 15. 1753.
"Habitat in Zeylona." RCN: 117.
Lectotype (Malik & Ghafoor in Nasir & Ali, *Fl. Pakistan* 188: 37.
1988): Herb. Linn. No. 28.14 (LINN).
Current name: ***Justicia procumbens*** L. (Acanthaceae).
Note: Malik & Ghafoor's type choice (20 Apr 1988) of material in
LINN pre-dates that of Graham (in *Kew Bull.* 43: 597. Nov 1988),
who chose Herb. Hermann vol. 2: 4, No. 19 (BM) as lectotype.

Justicia purpurea Linnaeus, *Species Plantarum* 1: 16. 1753.
"Habitat in Zeylona." RCN: 126.
Lectotype (Stearn in *Taxon* 10: 17. 1961): Herb. Linn. No. 28.26
(LINN).
Current name: ***Justicia purpurea*** L. (Acanthaceae).

Justicia repens Linnaeus, *Species Plantarum* 1: 15. 1753.
"Habitat in Zeylona." RCN: 119.
Type not designated.
Original material: Herb. Hermann 2: 28, No. 20 (BM); [icon] in
Burman, Thes. Zeylan.: 7, t. 3, f. 2. 1737.
Current name: ***Rungia repens*** (L.) Nees (Acanthaceae).

Justicia scorpioides Linnaeus, *Species Plantarum,* ed. 2, 1: 21. 1762.
"Habitat in Vera Cruce." RCN: 110.
Neotype (Daniel in *Taxon* 38: 270, f. 3. 1989): *Houstoun*, Herb.
Sloane 292: 69, left specimen (BM-SL).
Current name: ***Dicliptera sexangularis*** (L.) Juss. (Acanthaceae).

Justicia sexangularis Linnaeus, *Species Plantarum* 1: 16. 1753.
"Habitat in Vera cruce, Jamaica." RCN: 122.
Type not designated.
Original material: Herb. Clifford: 10, *Justicia* 3 (BM); Herb. Linn.
No. 28.22 (LINN); [icon] in Plukenet, Phytographia: t. 279, f. 6.
1694; Almag. Bot.: 142. 1696 – Voucher: Herb. Sloane 100: 35
(BM-SL).
Current name: ***Dicliptera sexangularis*** (L.) Juss. (Acanthaceae).
Note: Daniel (in Breedlove, *Fl. Chiapas* 4: 29. 1995) noted the original
material for the name but did not designate a type.

K

Kaempferia galanga Linnaeus, *Species Plantarum* 1: 2. 1753.
"Habitat in India." RCN: 14.
Lectotype (Stearn, *Introd. Linnaeus' Sp. Pl.* (Ray Soc. ed.): 47. 1957):
[icon] *"Kaempferia"* in Linnaeus, Hort. Cliff.: 2, t. 3. 1738 (see
p. 6).
Generitype of *Kaempferia* Linnaeus (vide Hitchcock in *Amer. J. Bot.*
10: 514. 1923).
Current name: ***Kaempferia galanga*** L. (Zingiberaceae).

Kaempferia rotunda Linnaeus, *Species Plantarum* 1: 3. 1753.
"Habitat in India." RCN: 15.
Type not designated.
Original material: Herb. Hermann 5: 272, No. 9 [icon] (BM).
Current name: ***Kaempferia rotunda*** L. (Zingiberaceae).

Kalmia angustifolia Linnaeus, *Species Plantarum* 1: 391. 1753.
"Habitat in Pensylvania, Nova Caesarea, Noveboraco." RCN: 3084.
Lectotype (Southall & Hardin in *J. Elisha Mitchell Sci. Soc.* 90: 18.
1974; Ebinger in *Rhodora* 76: 367. 1974): Herb. Linn. No. 560.2,
right specimen (LINN).
Current name: ***Kalmia angustifolia*** L. (Ericaceae).
Note: Southall & Hardin (spring 1974) designated the material on
sheet 560.2 (LINN), which comprises three specimens, as the type.
However, later the same year (Sep 1974), Ebinger designated the
right-hand specimen, only, as the lectotype. Ebinger's choice is
therefore treated as a restriction of the original typification made by
Southall & Hardin. Annotations by Kalm on a sheet collected by
him, and now in UPS, are reproduced by Lundqvist & Moberg (in
Thunbergia 19: 7, f. 3. 1993).

Kalmia latifolia Linnaeus, *Species Plantarum* 1: 391. 1753.
"Habitat in Marilandia, Virginia, Pensylvania." RCN: 3083.
Lectotype (Reveal in Jarvis & al., *Regnum Veg.* 127: 58. 1993): [icon]
*"Cistus Chamaerhododendros Mariana, Laurifolia, floribus expansis,
summo ramulo in umbellam plurimis"* in Plukenet, Amalth. Bot.: t.
379, f. 6. 1705; Almag. Mant.: 49. 1700. – Typotype: Herb. Sloane
93: 100 (BM-SL).
Generitype of *Kalmia* Linnaeus (vide Hitchcock, *Prop. Brit. Bot.*: 153.
1929).
Current name: ***Kalmia latifolia*** L. (Ericaceae).
Note: Many authors including Fernald (in *Rhodora* 42: 53. 1940),
Lawrence (in *Baileya* 1: 64. 1953), Southall & Hardin (in *J. Elisha
Mitch. Sci. Soc.* 90: 16. 1974), Reveal & al. (in *Huntia* 7: 19.
1987) regarded the name as partially or wholly based on Herb.
Linn. 560.1 (LINN), and Ebinger (in *Rhodora* 76: 352. 1974)
explicitly restricted the type to the top right-hand specimen on the
sheet. However, the sheet lacks a *Species Plantarum* number and is a
post-1753 addition to the collection and hence ineligible as
lectotype. Annotations by Kalm on a sheet collected by him, and
now in UPS, are reproduced by Lundqvist & Moberg (in
Thunbergia 19: 7, f. 3. 1993).

Kiggelaria africana Linnaeus, *Species Plantarum* 2: 1037. 1753.
"Habitat in Africa." RCN: 7477.
Lectotype (Stearn, *Introd. Linnaeus' Sp. Pl.* (Ray Soc. ed.): 47. 1957):
[icon] *"Kiggelaria: mas"* in Linnaeus, Hort. Cliff.: 462, t. 29. 1738
(see p. 85).
Generitype of *Kiggelaria* Linnaeus.
Current name: ***Kiggelaria africana*** L. (Flacourtiaceae).
Note: Sleumer (in Polhill, *Fl. Trop. E. Africa, Flacourtiaceae*: 31. 1975)
and Killick (in Ross, *Fl. Southern Africa* 22: 62. 1976) both
indicated material in LINN as the type but none of the four sheets

there is original material for the name. Barrie (in Jarvis & al.,
Regnum Veg. 127: 59. 1993) therefore designated Herb. Clifford:
462, *Kiggelaria* 1A (BM) as lectotype, but this choice is pre-dated
by that of Stearn.

Kleinhovia hospita Linnaeus, *Species Plantarum*, ed. 2, 2: 1365.
1763.
"Habitat in India orientali." RCN: 6968.
Lectotype (Verdcourt in Jarvis & al., *Regnum Veg.* 127: 59. 1993):
Herb. Linn. No. 1073.1 (LINN).
Generitype of *Kleinhovia* Linnaeus.
Current name: ***Kleinhovia hospita*** L. (Sterculiaceae).
Note: Merrill (*Interp. Rumph. Herb. Amb.*: 363. 1917), followed by
Smith (*Fl. Vitiensis Nova* 2: 399. 1981), stated that the type is a
Kleynhof specimen but without saying where it was conserved.

Knautia orientalis Linnaeus, *Species Plantarum* 1: 101. 1753.
"Habitat in Oriente." RCN: 827.
Lectotype (Barrie in Jarvis & al., *Regnum Veg.* 127: 59. 1993): Herb.
Clifford: 32, *Knautia* 1 (BM-000557763).
Generitype of *Knautia* Linnaeus.
Current name: ***Knautia orientalis*** L. (Dipsacaceae).

Knautia palaestina Linnaeus, *Mantissa Plantarum Altera*: 197. 1771.
"Habitat in Palaestina. Hasselquist." RCN: 829.
Type not designated.
Original material: *Hasselquist*, Herb. Linn. No. 121.4 (LINN).
Current name: ***Lomelosia brachiata*** (Sm.) Greuter & Burdet
(Dipsacaceae).

Knautia plumosa Linnaeus, *Mantissa Plantarum Altera*: 197. 1771.
"Habitat in Oriente." RCN: 830.
Lectotype (Burtt in *Notes Roy. Bot. Gard. Edinburgh* 22: 281. 1957):
Herb. Linn. No. 121.5 (LINN).
Current name: ***Pterocephalus plumosus*** (L.) Coult. (Dipsacaceae).

Knautia propontica Linnaeus, *Species Plantarum*, ed. 2, 2: 1666.
1763.
"Habitat in Oriente. Forskåhl." RCN: 828.
Type not designated.
Original material: Herb. Linn. No. 121.3 (LINN); [icon] in Tilli, Cat.
Pl. Hort. Pisani: 153, t. 48. 1723.
Current name: ***Scabiosa propontica*** (L.) Lag. (Dipsacaceae).

Knoxia scandens Linnaeus, *Flora Jamaicensis*: 13. 1759.
"Habitat [in Jamaica.]"
Type not designated.
Original material: [icon] in Browne, Civ. Nat. Hist. Jamaica: 140, t. 3,
f. 3. 1756.
Current name: ***Knoxia scandens*** L. (Rubiaceae).

Knoxia zeylanica Linnaeus, *Species Plantarum* 1: 104. 1753.
"Habitat in Zeylona supra truncos arborum putridarum." RCN: 856.
Lectotype (Puff in Jarvis & al., *Regnum Veg.* 127: 59. 1993): Herb.
Hermann 1: 63, No. 400 (BM-000594495).
Generitype of *Knoxia* Linnaeus.
Current name: ***Knoxia zeylanica*** L. (Rubiaceae).

Koenigia islandica Linnaeus, *Systema Naturae*, ed. 12, 2: 104;
Mantissa Plantarum: 35. 1767.
Lectotype (Elkington in Jarvis & al., *Regnum Veg.* 127: 59. 1993):
Herb. Linn. No. 110.1 (LINN).

Generitype of *Koenigia* Linnaeus.
Current name: ***Koenigia islandica*** L. (Polygonaceae).

Krameria ixine Linnaeus, *Systema Naturae,* ed. 10, 2: 899. 1759.
["Habitat in Cumana Americae."] Sp. Pl., ed. 2, 1: 177 (1762). RCN: 1004.
Neotype (Simpson, *Fl. Neotropica* 49: 81. 1989): Venezuela. Sucre, 18km SE of Cumaná on the road to Cumanocoa, 22 Dec 1976, *Simpson 8504* (BM; iso- NY, TEX, US).
Current name: ***Krameria ixine*** L. (Krameriaceae).
Note: This is the generitype of *Krameria* Loefl. (*Iter Hisp.*: 195. 1758). Although some authors (e.g. Simpson in *Fl. Neotropica* 49: 81. 1989) have regarded the binomial as dating from 1758, it

seems clear that "Ixine Loefl." is there intended as a generic synonym of *Krameria*, rather than as a specific epithet to be combined with it.

Kuhnia eupatorioides Linnaeus, *Species Plantarum,* ed. 2, 2: 1662. 1763.
"Habitat in Pensylvania, unde vivam attulit Adam Kuhn." RCN: 1392.
Lectotype (Reveal in Jarvis & al., *Regnum Veg.* 127: 59. 1993): *Arduino 53*, Herb. Linn. No. 238.2 (LINN), see p. 190.
Generitype of *Kuhnia* Linnaeus, *nom. rej.*
Current name: ***Brickellia eupatorioides*** (L.) Shinners (Asteraceae).
Note: Kuhnia Linnaeus, *nom. rej.* in favour of *Brickellia* Elliott.

K

L

Lachnaea conglomerata Linnaeus, *Species Plantarum* 1: 560. 1753,
nom. utique rej.
"Habitat ad Cap. b. spei." RCN: 2846.
Type not designated.
Original material: [icon] in Breyn, Exot. Pl. Cent.: 18, t. 7. 1678.
Current name: ***Phylica stipularis*** L. (Rhamnaceae).

Lachnaea eriocephala Linnaeus, *Species Plantarum* 1: 560. 1753.
"Habitat in Aethiopia." RCN: 2845.
Neotype (Beyers in *Strelitzia* 11: 98. 2001): South Africa. Western
Cape, Simonstown, Hottentots Holland Mts, Sir Lowry's Pass
(3418 BB), 6 Sep 1998, *J. Beyers 270* (NBG; iso- BM, BOL, K,
MO, NY, P, PRE, S, Z).
Generitype of *Lachnaea* Linnaeus (vide Meisner in de Candolle, *Prodr.*
14: 580. 1857).
Current name: ***Lachnaea eriocephala*** L. (Thymelaeaceae).

Lactuca canadensis Linnaeus, *Species Plantarum* 2: 796. 1753.
"Habitat in Canada. Kalm." RCN: 5822.
Lectotype (Fernald in *Rhodora* 40: 481. 1938): *Kalm*, Herb. Linn. No.
950.7 (LINN).
Current name: ***Lactuca canadensis*** L. var. ***canadensis*** (Asteraceae).

Lactuca indica Linnaeus, *Mantissa Plantarum Altera*: 278. 1771.
"Habitat in Java." RCN: 5823.
Lectotype (Merrill in *Bot. Mag. (Tokyo)* 51: 192, pl. 3. 1937): *Osbeck
13*, Herb. Linn. No. 950.8 (LINN).
Current name: ***Pterocypsela indica*** (L.) C. Shih (Asteraceae).

Lactuca perennis Linnaeus, *Species Plantarum* 2: 796. 1753.
"Habitat in Germania, Helvetia, Gallia." RCN: 5824.
Lectotype (van Raamsdonk in Wisskirchen in *Feddes Repert.* 108: 105.
1997): Herb. A. van Royen No. 900.344–36 (L).
Current name: ***Lactuca perennis*** L. (Asteraceae).

Lactuca quercina Linnaeus, *Species Plantarum* 2: 795. 1753.
"Habitat in Insula Carolina Balthici." RCN: 5817.
Lectotype (van Raamsdonk in Wisskirchen in *Feddes Repert.* 108: 105.
1997): Herb. Linn. No. 950.1 (LINN).
Current name: ***Lactuca quercina*** L. (Asteraceae).
Note: Stearn (in *Biol. J. Linn. Soc.* 5: 11. 1973), in an account of
Linnaeus' Öland and Gotland journey of 1741, treated Lilla Karlsö,
near Gotland, as the restricted type locality, and noted the existence
of 950.1 (LINN). In his paper, he attributed restricted type
localities irrespective of whether any material existed in LINN and,
where specimens do exist, he does not refer to any of them as type
specimens. The collection subsequently designated as the type
shows no annotation associating it with Gotland.

Lactuca saligna Linnaeus, *Species Plantarum* 2: 796. 1753.
"Habitat in Gallia, Lipsiae." RCN: 5821.
Lectotype (de Vries & Jarvis in *Taxon* 36: 153, f. 7. 1987): Herb.
Burser VI: 11 (UPS).
Current name: ***Lactuca saligna*** L. (Asteraceae).

Lactuca sativa Linnaeus, *Species Plantarum* 2: 795. 1753.
"Habitat – – – –" RCN: 5818.
Lectotype (Alavi in Jafri & El-Gadi, *Fl. Libya* 107: 403. 1983): Herb.
Linn. No. 950.2 (LINN).
Generitype of *Lactuca* Linnaeus (vide Green, *Prop. Brit. Bot.*: 177.
1929).
Current name: ***Lactuca sativa*** L. (Asteraceae).

Note: De Vries & Jarvis (in *Taxon* 36: 142. 1987) provided a detailed
review of the original elements, illustrating many of them, including
their chosen type (as f. 1), but they were unaware of Alavi's earlier
choice.

Lactuca sativa Linnaeus var. **capitata** Linnaeus, *Species Plantarum* 2:
795. 1753.
RCN: 5818.
Lectotype (de Vries & Jarvis in *Taxon* 36: 145, f. 2. 1987): Herb.
Burser VI: 6 (UPS).
Current name: ***Lactuca sativa*** L. (Asteraceae).

Lactuca sativa Linnaeus var. **crispa** Linnaeus, *Species Plantarum* 2:
795. 1753.
RCN: 5818.
Lectotype (de Vries & Jarvis in *Taxon* 36: 145, f. 3. 1987): Herb.
Burser VI: 7 (UPS).
Current name: ***Lactuca sativa*** L. (Asteraceae).

Lactuca scariola Linnaeus, *Amoenitates Academicae* 4: 489. 1759.
["Habitat in Europa australi."] Sp. Pl., ed. 2, 2: 1119 (1763). RCN:
5819.
Lectotype (de Vries & Jarvis in *Taxon* 36: 151. 1987): [icon] *"Lactuca
silvestris sive Endivia multis dicta, folio laciniato, dorso spinoso"* in
Bauhin & Cherler, Hist. Pl. Univ. 2: 1003. 1651.
Current name: ***Lactuca serriola*** L. (Asteraceae).

Lactuca serriola Linnaeus, *Centuria II Plantarum*: 29. 1756.
"Habitat in Europa australi." RCN: 5819.
Lectotype (Prince & Carter in *Watsonia* 11: 337. 1977): Herb. Linn.
No. 950.3 (LINN).
Current name: ***Lactuca serriola*** L. (Asteraceae).
Note: See extensive discussion of the original elements by De Vries &
Jarvis (in *Taxon* 36: 148. 1987). Oswald (in *Watsonia* 23: 149–159.
2000) discusses early usage of *L. serriola* in England.

Lactuca virosa Linnaeus, *Species Plantarum* 2: 795. 1753.
"Habitat in Europae australioris aggeribus, sepibus." RCN: 5820.
Lectotype (de Vries & Jarvis in *Taxon* 36: 147, f. 5. 1987): Herb. A.
van Royen No. 900.344–163 (L).
Current name: ***Lactuca virosa*** L. (Asteraceae).

Laetia americana Linnaeus, *Systema Naturae,* ed. 10, 2: 1074. 1759.
RCN: 3872.
Type not designated.
Original material: none traced.
Generitype of *Laetia* Linnaeus, *nom. cons.*
Current name: ***Laetia americana*** L. (Flacourtiaceae).
Note: Sleumer (in *Fl. Neotropica* 22: 240. 1980) indicated that this was
based on Löfling material that has not been traced.

Laetia thamnia Linnaeus, *Plantarum Jamaicensium Pugillus*: 31. 1759.
"Habitat [in Jamaica.]" RCN: 3872.
Lectotype (Sleumer, *Fl. Neotropica* 22: 243. 1980): Herb. Linn. No.
680.1 (LINN).
Current name: ***Laetia thamnia*** L. (Flacourtiaceae).

Lagerstroemia chinensis Linnaeus, *Amoenitates Academicae* 4: 137.
1759.
Type not designated.
Original material: [icon] in Rumphius, Herb. Amboin. Auct.: 61, t.
28, f. 1. 1755.
Current name: ***Lagerstroemia indica*** L. (Lythraceae).

Lagerstroemia indica Linnaeus, *Systema Naturae*, ed. 10, 2: 1076. 1759.
["Habitat in China."] Sp. Pl., ed. 2, 1: 734. 1762. RCN: 3881.
Lectotype (Merrill, *Interpret. Rumph. Herb. Amb.*: 381. 1917): [icon] *"Tsjinkin"* in Rumphius, Herb. Amboin. Auct.: 61, t. 28, f. 1. 1755.
Generitype of *Lagerstroemia* Linnaeus.
Current name: ***Lagerstroemia indica*** L. (Lythraceae).

Lagoecia cuminoides Linnaeus, *Species Plantarum* 1: 203. 1753.
"Habitat in Creta, Lemno, Lysia, Galatia." RCN: 1647.
Lectotype (Jafri in Jafri & El-Gadi, *Fl. Libya* 117: 14. 1985): Herb. Linn. No. 282.1 (LINN).
Generitype of *Lagoecia* Linnaeus.
Current name: ***Lagoecia cuminoides*** L. (Apiaceae).

Lagurus cylindricus Linnaeus, *Systema Naturae*, ed. 10, 2: 878. 1759.
["Habitat Monspelii, Creta, Smyrnae. D. Gerardus."] Sp. Pl., ed. 2, 1: 120 (1762). RCN: 681.
Lectotype (Clayton & Renvoize in Polhill, *Fl. Trop. E. Africa, Gramineae* 3: 700. 1982): Herb. Linn. No. 96.2 (LINN).
Current name: ***Imperata cylindrica*** (L.) Raeusch. (Poaceae).
Note: Although Kerguélen (in *Lejeunia*, n.s., 75: 197. 1975) stated "Type: ...LINN", this is not accepted as a formal typification, for the reasons explained by Cafferty & al. (in *Taxon* 49: 240. 2000).

Lagurus ovatus Linnaeus, *Species Plantarum* 1: 81. 1753.
"Habitat in Italia, Gallia, Sicilia, Lusitania." RCN: 680.
Lectotype (Meikle, *Fl. Cyprus* 2: 1788. 1985): Herb. Linn. No. 96.1 (LINN).
Generitype of *Lagurus* Linnaeus.
Current name: ***Lagurus ovatus*** L. (Poaceae).
Note: Although Kerguélen (in *Lejeunia*, n.s., 75: 204. 1975) indicated unspecified material in LINN as type, this is not accepted as an effective typification (Art. 7.11). See Cafferty & al. (in *Taxon* 49: 240. 2000) for a detailed explanation.

Lamium album Linnaeus, *Species Plantarum* 2: 579. 1753.
"Habitat in Europae cultis." RCN: 4221.
Lectotype (Mennema in Rechinger, *Fl. Iranica* 150: 323. 1982): Herb. Linn. No. 733.10 (LINN).
Generitype of *Lamium* Linnaeus (vide Green, *Prop. Brit. Bot.*: 165. 1929).
Current name: ***Lamium album*** L. (Lamiaceae).
Note: Lamium purpureum was treated as the generitype by Britton & Brown (*Ill. Fl. N. U. S.*, ed. 2, 3: 121. 1913; see McNeill & al. in *Taxon* 36: 376. 1987). However, under Art. 10.5, Ex. 7 (a voted example) of the Vienna Code, this is a type choice made under the American Code and is to be replaced under Art. 10.5b by Green's choice (*Prop. Brit. Bot.*: 165. 1929) of *L. album* L. Hedge & Lamond (in *Notes Roy. Bot. Gard. Edinburgh* 28: 90. 1968) indicated unspecified material at LINN as type but this did not distinguish between sheets 733.8, 733.9 and 733.10. They are not part of a single gathering so Art. 9.15 does not apply.

Lamium amplexicaule Linnaeus, *Species Plantarum* 2: 579. 1753.
"Habitat in Europae cultis." RCN: 4223.
Lectotype (Hedge & Lamond in *Notes Roy. Bot. Gard. Edinburgh* 28: 89. 1968): Herb. Linn. No. 733.12 (LINN).
Current name: ***Lamium amplexicaule*** L. (Lamiaceae).

Lamium galeobdolon Linnaeus, *Amoenitates Academicae* 4: 485. 1759, *nom. inval.*
Type not relevant.
Current name: ***Lamiastrum galeobdolon*** (L.) Ehrend. & Polatschek (Lamiaceae).

Note: As noted by Stearn (in Geck & Pressler, *Festschr. Claus Nissen*: 631. 1974), *Lamium galeobdolon* is a typographical error, the generic name *Galeopsis* having been misplaced, with the result that *Galeopsis galeobdolon* L. (1753) appeared as *Lamium galeobdolon*. The latter name did not appear in *Sp. Pl.*, ed. 2 (1763), nor in later Linnaean works. *Lamium galeobdolon* is therefore not a validly published Linnaean name.

Lamium garganicum Linnaeus, *Species Plantarum*, ed. 2, 2: 808. 1763.
"Habitat in Gargano monte ad castrum angeli." RCN: 4219.
Lectotype (Mennema in *Leiden Bot. Ser.* 11: 100. 1989): Herb. Linn. No. 733.4 (LINN).
Current name: ***Lamium garganicum*** L. subsp. ***garganicum*** (Lamiaceae).

Lamium laevigatum Linnaeus, *Species Plantarum*, ed. 2, 2: 808. 1763.
"Habitat in Italia, Sibiria." RCN: 4218.
Lectotype (Mennema in *Leiden Bot. Ser.* 11: 77. 1989): Herb. Linn. No. 733.7 (LINN).
Current name: ***Lamium maculatum*** L. (Lamiaceae).

Lamium maculatum Linnaeus, *Species Plantarum*, ed. 2, 2: 809. 1763.
"Habitat in Italia." RCN: 4220.
Lectotype (Mennema in *Leiden Bot. Ser.* 11: 77. 1989): Herb. Linn. No. 733.6 (LINN).
Current name: ***Lamium maculatum*** L. (Lamiaceae).
Note: Although Mennema wrongly treated this as a new combination based on *L. album* var. *maculatum* L. (1753), a binomial that was not published there, his typification nevertheless stands.

Lamium multifidum Linnaeus, *Species Plantarum* 2: 579. 1753.
"Habitat in Oriente." RCN: 4224.
Lectotype (Wijnands, *Bot. Commelins*: 120. 1983): Herb. Clifford: 315, *Lamium* 4 (BM-000646128).
Current name: ***Wiedemannia multifida*** (L.) Benth. (Lamiaceae).
Note: Mill (in Davis, *Fl. Turkey* 7: 149. 1982) indicated a specimen in Herb. Tournefort (P) as the holotype but Wijnands rejected this in favour of material in the Clifford herbarium, on the grounds that Linnaeus would not have seen the Tournefort collection.

Lamium orvala Linnaeus, *Systema Naturae*, ed. 10, 2: 1099. 1759.
["Habitat in Pannonia, Italia. Miller, D. Royen."] Sp. Pl., ed. 2, 2: 808 (1763). RCN: 4217.
Lectotype (Mennema in *Leiden Bot. Ser.* 11: 132. 1989): Herb. Linn. No. 733.2 (LINN).
Current name: ***Lamium orvala*** L. (Lamiaceae).

Lamium purpureum Linnaeus, *Species Plantarum* 2: 579. 1753.
"Habitat in Europae cultis." RCN: 4222.
Lectotype (Mennema in Rechinger, *Fl. Iranica* 150: 579. 1982): Herb. Linn. No. 733.11 (LINN).
Current name: ***Lamium purpureum*** L. (Lamiaceae).
Note: Lamium purpureum was treated as the generitype by Britton & Brown (*Ill. Fl. N. U. S.*, ed. 2, 3: 121. 1913; see McNeill & al. in *Taxon* 36: 376. 1987). However, under Art. 10.5, Ex. 7 (a voted example) of the Vienna Code, this is a type choice made under the American Code and is to be replaced under Art. 10.5b by Green's choice (*Prop. Brit. Bot.*: 165. 1929) of *L. album* L.

Lantana aculeata Linnaeus, *Species Plantarum* 2: 627. 1753.
"Habitat in America calidiore." RCN: 4543.
Lectotype (Méndez Santos & Cafferty in *Taxon* 50: 1138. 2002

[2001]): [icon] *"Viburnum Americanum odorat. Urticae foliis latioribus, spinosum floribus miniatis"* in Plukenet, Phytographia: t. 233, f. 5. 1692; Almag. Bot.: 385. 1696. – Voucher: Herb. Sloane 98: 143 (BM-SL). – Epitype (Sanders in *Sida* 22: 403, f. 9. 2006): Herb. Sloane 98: 143, bottom, centre specimen (BM-SL).
Current name: ***Lantana camara*** L. var. ***aculeata*** (L.) Moldenke (Verbenaceae).

Lantana africana Linnaeus, *Species Plantarum* 2: 628. 1753.
"Habitat in Aethiopia." RCN: 4545.
Lectotype (Wijnands, *Bot. Commelins*: 190. 1983): Herb. Clifford: 320, *Lantana* 3 (BM-000646196).
Current name: ***Oftia africana*** (L.) Bocq. (Scrophulariaceae).

Lantana annua Linnaeus, *Species Plantarum* 2: 627. 1753.
"Habitat in America calidiore." RCN: 4539.
Type not designated.
Original material: [icon] in Sloane, Voy. Jamaica 2: 82, t. 195, f. 3. 1725; [icon] in Plukenet, Phytographia: t. 114, f. 5. 1691; Almag. Bot.: 386. 1696 – Voucher: Herb. Sloane 98: 141 (BM-SL).
Current name: ***Lantana trifolia*** L. (Verbenaceae).

Lantana bullata Linnaeus, *Species Plantarum* 2: 627. 1753.
"Habitat in Jamaica." RCN: 1536.
Lectotype (Gaviria in *Mitt. Bot. Staatssamml. München* 23: 224. 1987): [icon] *"Salvia Barbadensibus dicta spica florum compactiori"* in Plukenet, Phytographia: t. 221, f. 3. 1692; Almag. Bot.: 329. 1696.
Current name: ***Cordia curassavica*** (Jacq.) Roem. & Schult. (Boraginaceae).

Lantana camara Linnaeus, *Species Plantarum* 2: 627. 1753, *typ. cons.*
"Habitat in America calidiore." RCN: 4541.
Conserved type (Moldenke & Moldenke in Dassanayake & Fosberg, *Revised Handb. Fl. Ceylon* 4: 220. 1983): Herb. Linn. No. 783.4 (LINN).
Generitype of *Lantana* Linnaeus, *nom. cons.*
Current name: ***Lantana camara*** L. (Verbenaceae).
Note: Lantana camara, with the type designated by Moldenke & Moldenke, was proposed as conserved type of the genus by Jarvis (in *Taxon* 41: 564. 1992). This was eventually approved by the General Committee (see review of the history of this proposal by Barrie, *l.c.* 55: 795–796. 2006). Sanders (in *Sida* 22: 381–421. 2006) provided a detailed study of the type (illustrated on p. 384, f. 1), concluding that it belongs to the wild species and not to the cultigen to which the name has also been applied. As a result, he named the latter *L. strigocamara* R.W. Sanders.

Lantana corymbosa Linnaeus, *Species Plantarum* 2: 628. 1753.
"Habitat in Jamaica." RCN: 1532.
Replaced synonym of: *Varronia lineata* L. (1759), *nom. illeg.*
Lectotype (Johnston in *J. Arnold Arbor.* 30: 94. 1949): [icon] *"Ulmi angustifoliae facie Baccifera Jamaicensis foliis superne scabris, subtus villosis, floribus flavis perpusillis, fructu botryoide monospermo"* in Plukenet, Phytographia: t. 328, f. 5. 1694; Almag. Bot.: 393. 1696. – Typotype: Herb. Sloane 102: 132 (BM-SL).
Current name: ***Cordia linnaei*** Stearn (Boraginaceae).
Note: Stearn (in *J. Arnold Arbor.* 52: 630. 1971) argued that the Sloane plate must be taken as the lectotype but the Plukenet plate, previously designated as type by Johnston, is original material and this earlier choice therefore has priority. Taroda & Gibbs (in *Notes Roy. Bot. Gard. Edinburgh* 44: 134. 1986) provide an extensive discussion.

Lantana involucrata Linnaeus, *Centuria II Plantarum*: 22. 1756.
"Habitat in America meridionali." RCN: 4540.

Lectotype (Sanders in Howard, *Fl. Lesser Antilles* 6: 229. 1989): Herb. Linn. No. 783.3 (LINN).
Current name: ***Lantana involucrata*** L. (Verbenaceae).

Lantana mista Linnaeus, *Systema Naturae*, ed. 12, 2: 417. 1767.
RCN: 4537.
Lectotype (Méndez Santos & Cafferty in *Taxon* 50: 1138. 2002 [2001]): [icon] *"Camara Lamii albi folio, flore misto"* in Dillenius, Hort. Eltham. 1: 64, t. 56, f. 64. 1732. – Epitype (Sanders in *Sida* 22: 404, f. 10. 2006): Herb. Sherard No. 1272 (OXF).
Current name: ***Lantana* × *mista*** L. (Verbenaceae).

Lantana odorata Linnaeus, *Systema Naturae*, ed. 12, 2: 418. 1767.
RCN: 4542.
Lectotype (Méndez Santos & Cafferty in *Taxon* 50: 1139. 2002 [2001]): Herb. Linn. No. 783.5 (LINN).
Current name: ***Lantana involucrata*** L. (Verbenaceae).

Lantana salviifolia Linnaeus, *Systema Naturae*, ed. 10, 2: 1116. 1759.
["Habitat in Aethiopia."] Sp. Pl., ed. 2, 2: 875 (1763). RCN: 4544.
Lectotype (Bruce & Lewis in Hubbard & Milne-Redhead, *Fl. Trop. E. Africa, Loganiaceae*: 38. 1960): Herb. Linn. No. 783.7 (LINN).
Current name: ***Buddleja salviifolia*** (L.) Lam. (Loganiaceae/Buddlejaceae).
Note: Specific epithet spelled "salvifol." in the protologue.

Lantana trifolia Linnaeus, *Species Plantarum* 2: 626. 1753.
"Habitat in America calidiore." RCN: 4538.
Lectotype (Verdcourt, *Fl. Trop. E. Africa, Verbenaceae*: 46. 1992): [icon] in Plumier, Codex Boerhaavianus (University Library, Groningen).
Current name: ***Lantana trifolia*** L. (Verbenaceae).

Lapsana capillaris Linnaeus, *Species Plantarum* 2: 812. 1753.
"Habitat in Helvetiae, Italiae agris." RCN: 5890.
Replaced synonym of: *Crepis virens* L. (1763), *nom. illeg.*
Type not designated.
Original material: Herb. Burser VI: 45 (UPS).
Current name: ***Crepis capillaris*** (L.) Wallr. (Asteraceae).

Lapsana chondrilloides Linnaeus, *Species Plantarum* 2: 812. 1753.
"Habitat in Gallia, Italia." RCN: 5892.
Type not designated.
Original material: [icon] in Colonna, Ekphr.: 248, 249. 1606; [icon] in Morison, Pl. Hist. Univ. 3: 68, s. 7, t. 5, f. 37. 1699.
Current name: ***Crepis* sp.** (Asteraceae).
Note: The application of this name appears uncertain.

Lapsana communis Linnaeus, *Species Plantarum* 2: 811. 1753.
"Habitat in Europae cultis." RCN: 5914.
Lectotype (Sell in *Watsonia* 13: 301. 1981): Herb. Clifford: 389, *Lapsana* 1, sheet A (BM-000646889).
Generitype of *Lapsana* Linnaeus (vide Green, *Prop. Brit. Bot.*: 178. 1929).
Current name: ***Lapsana communis*** L. (Asteraceae).

Lapsana rhagadiolus Linnaeus, *Species Plantarum* 2: 812. 1753.
"Habitat in Oriente." RCN: 5917.
Lectotype (Turland in Jarvis & Turland in *Taxon* 47: 364. 1998): Herb. Linn. No. 960.4 (LINN).
Current name: ***Rhagadiolus stellatus*** (L.) Gaertn. (Asteraceae).
Note: Kupicha (in Davis, *Fl. Turkey* 6: 688. 1975) and Meikle (in *Taxon* 28: 136. 1979) indicated Herb. Linn. No. 330.3 (S) as type, but this sheet lacks a *Species Plantarum* number (i.e. "4") and was a later addition to the herbarium. It is not original material for the name. The lectotype designated by Turland is a specimen of

Rhagadiolus stellatus, into the synonymy of which *L. rhagadiolus* therefore falls. Linnaeus' name has generally been treated as a synonym of *R. edulis* Gaertn. (which is often not recognised as distinct from *R. stellatus*), but the present choice of type is not disruptive as the specific epithet "rhagadiolus" cannot in any case be used in *Rhagadiolus*.

Lapsana stellata Linnaeus, *Species Plantarum* 2: 811. 1753.
"Habitat Monspelii, Bononiae." RCN: 5916.
Lectotype (Meikle in *Taxon* 28: 138. 1979): Herb. Linn. No. 960.3 (LINN).
Current name: ***Rhagadiolus stellatus*** (L.) Gaertn. (Asteraceae).

Lapsana zacintha Linnaeus, *Species Plantarum* 2: 811. 1753.
"Habitat in Italia." RCN: 5915.
Lectotype (Turland in Jarvis & Turland in *Taxon* 47: 364. 1998): Herb. Clifford: 390, *Lapsana* 4 (BM-000646895).
Current name: ***Crepis zacintha*** (L.) Loisel. (Asteraceae).

Laserpitium angustifolium Linnaeus, *Species Plantarum* 1: 248. 1753.
"Habitat in Europa australi." RCN: 1996.
Lectotype (Reduron in Jarvis & al. in *Taxon* 55: 213. 2006): [icon] *"Laserpitium angustifol. segmentis indivisis"* in Morison, Pl. Hist. Univ. 3: 321, s. 9, t. 19, f. 9. 1699.
Current name: ***Laserpitium gallicum*** L. (Apiaceae).

Laserpitium chironium Linnaeus, *Species Plantarum* 1: 249. 1753.
"Habitat Monspelii." RCN: 2000.
Lectotype (Reduron & Jarvis in Jarvis & al. in *Taxon* 55: 213. 2006): Herb. Burser VIII: 16 (UPS).
Current name: ***Opopanax chironium*** W.D.J. Koch (Apiaceae).

Laserpitium ferulaceum Linnaeus, *Species Plantarum*, ed. 2, 1: 358. 1762.
"Habitat in Oriente." RCN: 2001.
Lectotype (Herrnstadt & Heyn in *Boissiera* 26: 39. 1977): Herb. Linn. No. 351.14 (LINN).
Current name: ***Prangos ferrulacea*** (L.) Lindl. (Apiaceae).

Laserpitium gallicum Linnaeus, *Species Plantarum* 1: 248. 1753.
"Habitat in Europa australi." RCN: 1995.
Lectotype (Reduron & Jarvis in Jarvis & al., *Regnum Veg.* 127: 60. 1993): Herb. Clifford: 96, *Laserpitium* 5 (BM-000558290).
Generitype of *Laserpitium* Linnaeus (vide Hitchcock, *Prop. Brit. Bot.*: 140. 1929).
Current name: ***Laserpitium gallicum*** L. (Apiaceae).

Laserpitium latifolium Linnaeus, *Species Plantarum* 1: 248. 1753.
"Habitat in Europae nemoribus siccis." RCN: 1993.
Lectotype (Reduron in Jonsell & Jarvis in *Nordic J. Bot.* 22: 84. 2002): Herb. Clifford: 96, *Laserpitium* 1 α (BM-000558283).
Current name: ***Laserpitium latifolium*** L. (Apiaceae).

Laserpitium peucedanoides Linnaeus, *Centuria II Plantarum*: 13. 1756.
"Habitat in Baldi valle vaccariae. Seguier." RCN: 1998.
Lectotype (Jury & Southam in Jarvis & al. in *Taxon* 55: 213. 2006): [icon] *"Laserpitium exoticum, lobis longissimis integris Ammeos quorundam divisuris"* in Plukenet, Phytographia: t. 96, f. 1. 1691; Almag. Bot.: 207. 1696. – Typotype: Herb. Sloane 96: 133 (BM).
Current name: ***Laserpitium peucedanoides*** L. (Apiaceae).

Laserpitium prutenicum Linnaeus, *Species Plantarum* 1: 248. 1753.
"Habitat in Borussia, Lipsiae." RCN: 1997.
Lectotype (Reduron in Jarvis & al. in *Taxon* 55: 213. 2006): [icon] *"Laserpitium daucoides prutenicum viscoso semine"* in Breyn, Exot. Pl.

Cent.: 167, t. 84. 1678. – Epitype (Reduron & Spalik in Jarvis & al. in *Taxon* 55: 213. 2006): Poland. "Königshöhe bei Zoppot, VIII 1861, leg. *Klinggraff 264*" (TRN).
Current name: ***Laserpitium prutenicum*** L. (Apiaceae).

Laserpitium siler Linnaeus, *Species Plantarum* 1: 249. 1753.
"Habitat in Austria, Helvetia, Gallia." RCN: 1999.
Lectotype (Reduron & Jarvis in Jarvis & al. in *Taxon* 55: 213. 2006): Herb. Clifford: 96, *Laserpitium* 3 (BM-000558289).
Current name: ***Laserpitium siler*** L. (Apiaceae).

Laserpitium simplex Linnaeus, *Systema Naturae*, ed. 12, 2: 210; *Mantissa Plantarum*: 56. 1767.
"Habitat in Alpibus austriacis. D. Jacquin." RCN: 2002.
Neotype (Reduron & Jacquemoud in Jarvis & al. in *Taxon* 55: 213. 2006): Austria. Tirolia (Ahrnthal), Aug 1894, *G. Treffer s.n.*, Herb. Normale Dörfler 3411, in Herb. Post (G).
Current name: ***Pachypleurum mutellinoides*** (Crantz) Holub (Apiaceae).

Laserpitium trilobum Linnaeus, *Species Plantarum* 1: 248. 1753.
"Habitat in Gorgano monte." RCN: 1994.
Lectotype (Reduron & Jarvis in Jarvis & al. in *Taxon* 55: 213. 2006): Herb. Burser VIII: 28 (UPS).
Current name: ***Laser trilobum*** (L.) Borkh. (Apiaceae).

Lathraea anblatum Linnaeus, *Species Plantarum* 2: 606. 1753.
"Habitat in Oriente." RCN: 4393.
Type not designated.
Original material: none traced.
Note: The application of this name is uncertain.

Lathraea clandestina Linnaeus, *Species Plantarum* 2: 605. 1753.
"Habitat in umbrosis Galliae, Pyrenaeorum, Italiae." RCN: 4391.
Lectotype (Fischer in Wisskirchen & Haeupler, *Standardliste Farn-Blütenpfl. Deutschl.*: 284. 1998): Herb. Burser III: 155 (UPS).
Current name: ***Lathraea clandestina*** L. (Scrophulariaceae).

Lathraea phelypaea Linnaeus, *Species Plantarum* 2: 606. 1753.
"Habitat in Lusitaniae umbrosis." RCN: 4392.
Neotype (Foley in *Anales Jard. Bot. Madrid* 58: 229. 2000): Herb. Tournefort No. 6443, "Orobanche elegantissima verna flores luteo virid. Lusit. Grisley" (P-TOURN).
Current name: ***Cistanche phelypaea*** (L.) Cout. (Orobanchaceae).

Lathraea squamaria Linnaeus, *Species Plantarum* 2: 606. 1753.
"Habitat in Europae frigidioris umbrosissimis." RCN: 4394.
Lectotype (Sutton in Jarvis & al., *Regnum Veg.* 127: 60. 1993): Herb. Linn. No. 761.3 (LINN).
Generitype of *Lathraea* Linnaeus (vide Green, *Prop. Brit. Bot.*: 167. 1929).
Current name: ***Lathraea squamaria*** L. (Scrophulariaceae).

Lathyrus amphicarpos Linnaeus, *Species Plantarum* 2: 729. 1753.
"Habitat in Syria." RCN: 5387.
Lectotype (Mattatia in *Bot. Not.* 129: 442. 1977): Herb. Linn. No. 905.3 (LINN).
Current name: ***Lathyrus amphicarpos*** L. (Fabaceae: Faboideae).

Lathyrus angulatus Linnaeus, *Species Plantarum* 2: 731. 1753.
"Habitat in Gallia, Hispania, Oriente." RCN: 5392.
Type not designated.
Original material: [icon] in Buxbaum, Pl. Minus Cognit. Cent. 3: 23, t. 42, f. 2. 1729.
Current name: ***Lathyrus angulatus*** L. (Fabaceae: Faboideae).

L

Lathyrus annuus Linnaeus, *Demonstr. Pl. Horto Upsaliensi*: 20. 1753. ["Habitat in Hispania, Monspelii."] Sp. Pl., ed. 2, 2: 1032 (1763). RCN: 5395.
Lectotype (Lassen in Turland & Jarvis in *Taxon* 46: 474. 1997): Herb. Linn. No. 905.22 (LINN).
Current name: ***Lathyrus annuus*** L. (Fabaceae: Faboideae).
Note: Meikle (*Fl. Cyprus* 1: 569. 1977) indicated material at LINN as type, but did not distinguish between sheets 905.22 and 905.23. Other authors (e.g. Jafri in Jafri & El-Gadi, *Fl. Libya* 86: 286. 1980) indicated both of these collections as the type. However, the two collections are evidently not part of a single gathering so Art. 9.15 does not apply, and Lassen's later type choice is therefore the earliest effective typification.

Lathyrus aphaca Linnaeus, *Species Plantarum* 2: 729. 1753.
"Habitat in Italia, Gallia, Anglia inter segetes." RCN: 5385.
Lectotype (Ali in *Biologia (Lahore)* 11(2): 2. 1965): *Löfling s.n.*, Herb. Linn. No. 905.1 (LINN).
Current name: ***Lathyrus aphaca*** L. (Fabaceae: Faboideae).

Lathyrus articulatus Linnaeus, *Species Plantarum* 2: 731. 1753.
"Habitat in Baetica." RCN: 5393.
Lectotype (Lassen in Turland & Jarvis in *Taxon* 46: 474. 1997): Herb. Burser XIX: post 71 (UPS).
Current name: ***Lathyrus articulatus*** L. (Fabaceae: Faboideae).

Lathyrus bithynicus Linnaeus, *Species Plantarum* 2: 731. 1753.
"Habitat in Italiae, Bavariae, arvis." RCN: 5421.
Basionym of: *Vicia bithynica* (L.) L. (1759).
Lectotype (Ali in *Bot. Not.* 120: 48. 1967): Herb. Linn. No. 906.19 (LINN).
Current name: ***Vicia bithynica*** (L.) L. (Fabaceae: Faboideae).

Lathyrus cicera Linnaeus, *Species Plantarum* 2: 730. 1753.
"Habitat in Hispania." RCN: 5388.
Lectotype (Ali in *Biologia (Lahore)* 11(2): 8. 1965): Herb. Linn. No. 905.5 (LINN).
Current name: ***Lathyrus cicera*** L. (Fabaceae: Faboideae).

Lathyrus clymenum Linnaeus, *Species Plantarum* 2: 732. 1753.
"Habitat in Mauritania." RCN: 5397.
Lectotype (Jafri in Jafri & El-Gadi, *Fl. Libya* 86: 288. 1980): Herb. Linn. No. 905.16 (LINN).
Current name: ***Lathyrus clymenum*** L. (Fabaceae: Faboideae).

Lathyrus heterophyllus Linnaeus, *Species Plantarum* 2: 733. 1753.
"Habitat ad radices montium Europae." RCN: 5403.
Lectotype (Jonsell & Jarvis in *Nordic J. Bot.* 22: 77. 2002): Herb. Linn. No. 905.24 (LINN).
Current name: ***Lathyrus heterophyllus*** L. (Fabaceae: Faboideae).

Lathyrus hirsutus Linnaeus, *Species Plantarum* 2: 732. 1753.
"Habitat inter Angliae, Galliae segetes." RCN: 5398.
Lectotype (Ali in *Biologia (Lahore)* 11(2): 8. 1965): Herb. Linn. No. 905.13 (LINN).
Current name: ***Lathyrus hirsutus*** L. (Fabaceae: Faboideae).

Lathyrus inconspicuus Linnaeus, *Species Plantarum* 2: 730. 1753.
"Habitat in Oriente." RCN: 5390.
Lectotype (Ali in *Biologia (Lahore)* 11(2): 3. 1965): Herb. Linn. No. 905.7 (LINN).
Current name: ***Lathyrus inconspicuus*** L. (Fabaceae: Faboideae).

Lathyrus latifolius Linnaeus, *Species Plantarum* 2: 733. 1753.
"Habitat in Europae sepibus." RCN: 5402.

Lectotype (Lassen in Turland & Jarvis in *Taxon* 46: 474. 1997): Herb. Clifford: 367, *Lathyrus* 7 (BM-000646673).
Current name: ***Lathyrus latifolius*** L. (Fabaceae: Faboideae).

Lathyrus nissolia Linnaeus, *Species Plantarum* 2: 729. 1753.
"Habitat in Gallia." RCN: 5386.
Lectotype (Cannon in *Watsonia* 6: 30. 1964): Herb. Linn. No. 905.2 (LINN).
Current name: ***Lathyrus nissolia*** L. (Fabaceae: Faboideae).

Lathyrus odoratus Linnaeus, *Species Plantarum* 2: 732. 1753.
"Habitat α in Sicilia, β in Zeylona." RCN: 5394.

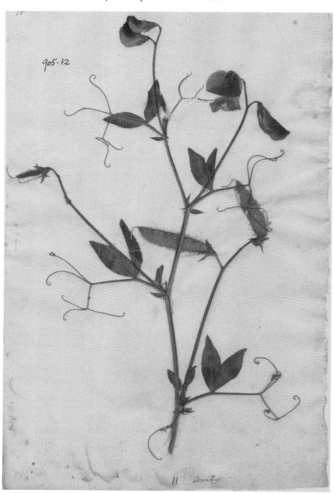

Lectotype (Wijnands, *Bot. Commelins*: 164. 1983): Herb. Linn. No. 905.12 (LINN), see also p. 4.
Current name: ***Lathyrus odoratus*** L. (Fabaceae: Faboideae).

Lathyrus odoratus Linnaeus var. **siculus** Linnaeus, *Species Plantarum* 2: 732. 1753.
"Habitat α in Sicilia." RCN: 5394.
Lectotype (Wijnands, *Bot. Commelins*: 164. 1983): [icon] "*Lathyrus distoplatyphyllus hirsutus mollis et odorus*" in Commelin, Hort. Med. Amstelod. Pl. Rar. 2: 159, t. 80. 1701.
Current name: ***Lathyrus odoratus*** L. (Fabaceae: Faboideae).

Lathyrus odoratus Linnaeus var. **zeylanicus** Linnaeus, *Species Plantarum* 2: 732. 1753.

"Habitat β in Zeylona." RCN: 5394.
Type not designated.
Original material: none traced.
Current name: ***Lathyrus odoratus*** L. (Fabaceae: Faboideae).

Lathyrus palustris Linnaeus, *Species Plantarum* 2: 733. 1753.
"Habitat in Europae borealis pascuis paludosis." RCN: 5404.
Lectotype (Lassen in Turland & Jarvis in *Taxon* 46: 474. 1997): Herb.
    Linn. No. 305.3 (S).
Current name: ***Lathyrus palustris*** L. (Fabaceae: Faboideae).
Note: Thuân (in Morat, *Fl. Cambodge Laos Viêtnam* 23: 190. 1987)
    indicated 905.25 (LINN) as lectotype. However, this collection lacks
    the *Species Plantarum* number (i.e. "20") and was a post-1753
    addition to the herbarium, and is not original material for the name.

Lathyrus pisiformis Linnaeus, *Species Plantarum* 2: 734. 1753.
"Habitat in Sibiria." RCN: 5405.
Lectotype (Valdés Bermejo & López in *Anales Inst. Bot. Cavanilles* 34:
    164. 1977): Herb. Linn. No. 905.27 (LINN).
Current name: ***Lathyrus pisiformis*** L. (Fabaceae: Faboideae).

Lathyrus pratensis Linnaeus, *Species Plantarum* 2: 733. 1753.
"Habitat in Europae pratis." RCN: 5400.
Lectotype (Ali in *Biologia (Lahore)* 11(2): 6. 1965): Herb. Linn. No.
    905.18 (LINN).
Current name: ***Lathyrus pratensis*** L. (Fabaceae: Faboideae).

Lathyrus sativus Linnaeus, *Species Plantarum* 2: 730. 1753.
"Habitat in Hispania, Gallia." RCN: 5389.
Lectotype (Westphal, *Pulses Ethiopia, Taxon. Agric. Signif.*: 104, 106.
    1974): Herb. Clifford: 367, *Lathyrus* 4 (BM).
Current name: ***Lathyrus sativus*** L. (Fabaceae: Faboideae).
Note: Although Ali (in *Biologia (Lahore)* 11(2): 7. 1965) indicated
    905.6 (LINN) as "type", and a Clifford collection (BM) incorrectly
    as an isotype (they are evidently not part of a single gathering),
    905.6 (LINN) lacks the *Species Plantarum* number (i.e. "5") and
    was a post-1753 addition to the herbarium, and is not original
    material for the name. Westphal subsequently designated the
    Clifford material as lectotype.

Lathyrus setifolius Linnaeus, *Species Plantarum* 2: 731. 1753.
"Habitat Monspelii." RCN: 5391.
Lectotype (Lassen in Turland & Jarvis in *Taxon* 46: 474. 1997): Herb.
    Linn. No. 303.13 (S).
Current name: ***Lathyrus setifolius*** L. (Fabaceae: Faboideae).
Note: Jafri (in Jafri & El-Gadi, *Fl. Libya* 86: 281. 1980) and Meikle
    (*Fl. Cyprus* 1: 576. 1977) both indicated material from Allioni,
    Herb. Linn. No. 905.9 (LINN) as the lectotype. However, the
    material was not received by Linnaeus until 1757 and cannot be
    original material for the name.

Lathyrus sylvestris Linnaeus, *Species Plantarum* 2: 733. 1753.
"Habitat in Europae pratis montosis." RCN: 5401.
Lectotype (Goyder in Jarvis in *Taxon* 41: 565. 1992): Herb. Linn. No.
    905.19 (LINN).
Generitype of *Lathyrus* Linnaeus.
Current name: ***Lathyrus sylvestris*** L. (Fabaceae: Faboideae).
Note: Lathyrus sylvestris, with the type designated by Goyder, was
    proposed as conserved type of the genus by Jarvis (in *Taxon* 41: 565.
    1992). However, the proposal was eventually ruled unnecessary by
    the General Committee (see Barrie, *l.c.* 55: 795–796. 2006 for a
    review of the history of this and related proposals).

Lathyrus tingitanus Linnaeus, *Species Plantarum* 2: 732. 1753.
"Habitat in Mauritania." RCN: 5396.

Lectotype (Lassen in Turland & Jarvis in *Taxon* 46: 474. 1997): Herb.
    Linn. No. 905.14 (LINN).
Current name: ***Lathyrus tingitanus*** L. (Fabaceae: Faboideae).

Lathyrus tuberosus Linnaeus, *Species Plantarum* 2: 732. 1753.
"Habitat inter Belgii, Genevae, Tatariae segetes." RCN: 5399.
Lectotype (Chrtková-Zertová & al. in Rechinger, *Fl. Iranica* 140: 71.
    1979): Herb. Clifford: 367, *Lathyrus* 5 (BM-000646671).
Current name: ***Lathyrus tuberosus*** L. (Fabaceae: Faboideae).

Laurus aestivalis Linnaeus, *Species Plantarum* 1: 370. 1753.
"Habitat in Virginia ad ripas rivulorum." RCN: 2919.
Lectotype (Fernald in *Rhodora* 47: 142, pl. 888. 1945): Herb. Linn.
    No. 518.15 (LINN).
Current name: ***Litsea aestivalis*** (L.) Fernald (Lauraceae).

Laurus benzoin Linnaeus, *Species Plantarum* 1: 370. 1753.
"Habitat in Virginia." RCN: 2920.
Lectotype (Fernald in *Rhodora* 47: 141, pl. 889. 1945): Herb. Clifford:
    154, *Laurus* 2 (BM-000558697).
Current name: ***Lindera benzoin*** (L.) Blume (Lauraceae).

Laurus borbonia Linnaeus, *Species Plantarum* 1: 370. 1753.
"Habitat in Carolina, Virginia." RCN: 2918.
Lectotype (Kopp in *Mem. New York Bot. Gard.* 14: 44. 1966): [icon]
    "*Laurus Carolinensis, foliis acuminatis, baccis caeruleis, pediculis longis
    rubris insidentibus*" in Catesby, Nat. Hist. Carolina 1: 63, t. 63. 1731.
Current name: ***Persea borbonia*** (L.) Spreng. (Lauraceae).

Laurus camphora Linnaeus, *Species Plantarum* 1: 369. 1753.
"Habitat in Japonia." RCN: 2912.
Lectotype (Kostermans in Nasir & Ali, *Fl. W. Pakistan* 118: 18. 1978):
    Herb. Linn. No. 518.7 (LINN).
Current name: ***Cinnamomum camphora*** (L.) J. Presl (Lauraceae).

Laurus cassia Linnaeus, *Species Plantarum* 1: 369. 1753.
"Habitat in Malabaria, Sumatra, Java." RCN: 2911.
Type not designated.
Original material: Herb. Hermann 5: 120, No. 146 [icon] (BM);
    Herb. Hermann 4: 11, No. 146 (BM); Herb. Hermann 2: 67, No.
    146 (BM); [icon] in Burman, Thes. Zeylan.: 63, t. 28. 1737; [icon]
    in Rheede, Hort. Malab. 1: 107, t. 57. 1678.
Current name: ***Neolitsea cassia*** (L.) Kosterm. (Lauraceae).
Note: See Wight (in *Hooker's J. Bot.* 2: 340. 1840) for an extensive
    discussion. Kostermans (in *Reinwardtia* 4: 246. 1957) says this
    name is based on Hermann's specimens via Linnaeus' *Fl. Zeylanica*
    no. 146, and that they represent a mixture of *Litsea zeylanica* Nees
    and "the wild *Cinnamomum zeylanicum*". As they are evidently not
    part of a single gathering, Kostermans' subsequent treatment (in
    Dassanayake & al., *Revised Handb. Fl. Ceylon* 9: 164. 1995) of the
    Hermann material as the type does not comply with Art. 9.15 and
    cannot be accepted as a formal typification.

Laurus chloroxylon Linnaeus, *Flora Jamaicensis*: 15. 1759.
["Habitat in Jamaica."] Sp. Pl., ed. 2, 1: 528 (1762). RCN: 2914.
Type not designated.
Original material: *Browne*, Herb. Linn. No. 518.8 (LINN); [icon] in
    Browne, Civ. Nat. Hist. Jamaica: 187, t. 7, f. 1. 1756.
Current name: ***Ziziphus chloroxylon*** (L.) Oliv. (Rhamnaceae).

Laurus cinnamomum Linnaeus, *Species Plantarum* 1: 369. 1753.
"Habitat in Zeylona." RCN: 2910.
Type not designated.
Original material: Herb. Hermann 1: 69, 70; 3: 53; 4: 8, 9, 10, 12,
    13, 14, 15, No. 145 (BM); Herb. Clifford: 154, *Laurus* 6, 2 sheets

L

(BM); Herb. Hermann 5: 117, 118, 119, 121, 122, 123, 124, No. 145 [icon] (BM); Herb. Linn. No. 518.2 (LINN); [icon] in Burman, Thes. Zeylan.: 62, t. 27. 1737; [icon] in Hermann, Hort. Lugd.-Bat. Cat.: 129, 655. 1687.

Current name: ***Cinnamomum verum*** J. Presl (Lauraceae).

Note: Kostermans (in Bosser & al., *Fl. Mascareignes* 153: 14. 1982) indicated 518.1 (LINN) as type but this collection lacks the relevant *Species Plantarum* number (i.e. "1") and was a post-1753 addition to the herbarium, and is not original material for the name. He subsequently (in *Bull. Bot. Surv. India* 25: 126. 1985) treated material in the Clifford herbarium (BM) as the type, but did not distinguish between the two sheets that are associated with the name. As they are evidently not part of a single gathering, Art. 9.15 does not apply. Kostermans (in *Ginkgoana* 6: frontispiece I. 1986) reproduced the Hermann drawing of a Ceylonese cinnamon garden from Herb. Hermann 5: 411 (BM).

Laurus culilaban Linnaeus, *Mantissa Plantarum Altera*: 237. 1771, *orth. var.*
"Habitat in India orientali." RCN: 2913.
Lectotype (Merrill, *Interpret. Rumph. Herb. Amb.*: 232. 1917): [icon] *"Cortex Caryophylloides"* in Rumphius, Herb. Amboin. 2: 65, t. 14 [excl. inflorescence]. 1741. – Epitype (Kostermans in *Ginkgoana* 6: 67. 1986): *de Fretes, H.B. 5557* (L).
Current name: ***Cinnamomum culitlawan*** (L.) Kosterm. (Lauraceae).
Note: Kostermans (in *Ginkgoana* 6: 68. 1986) treats this as an orthographic variant of *L. culitlawan* L. (1754).

Laurus culitlawan Linnaeus, *Herbarium Amboinense*: 9. 1754. RCN: 2913.
Lectotype (Merrill, *Interpret. Rumph. Herb. Amb.*: 232. 1917): [icon] *"Cortex Caryophylloides"* in Rumphius, Herb. Amboin. 2: 65, t. 14 [excl. inflorescence]. 1741. – Epitype (Kostermans in *Ginkgoana* 6: 67. 1986): *de Fretes, H.B. 5557* (L).
Current name: ***Cinnamomum culitlawan*** (L.) Kosterm. (Lauraceae).
Note: See further discussion by Kostermans (in *Ginkgoana* 6: 68, 72–75. 1986).

Laurus indica Linnaeus, *Species Plantarum* 1: 370. 1753.
"Habitat in Virginia." RCN: 2916.
Type not designated.
Original material: Herb. Linn. No. 518.13 (LINN); Herb. Linn. No. 518.12 (LINN); Herb. Clifford: 154, *Laurus* 4 (BM); [icon] in Seba, Locupl. Rer. Nat. Thes. 2: 90, t. 84, f. 6. 1735; [icon] in Plukenet, Phytographia: t. 304, f. 1. 1694; Almag. Bot.: 210. 1696 – Voucher: Herb. Sloane 100: 167 (BM-SL); [icon] in Barrelier, Pl. Galliam: 123, t. 877. 1714.
Current name: ***Persea indica*** (L.) Spreng. (Lauraceae).

Laurus nobilis Linnaeus, *Species Plantarum* 1: 369. 1753.
"Habitat in Italia, Graecia." RCN: 2915.
Lectotype (van der Werff in Jarvis & al., *Regnum Veg.* 127: 60. 1993): Herb. Clifford: 155, *Laurus* 7, sheet 7 (BM-000558704).
Generitype of *Laurus* Linnaeus (vide Hitchcock, *Prop. Brit. Bot.*: 151. 1929).
Current name: ***Laurus nobilis*** L. (Lauraceae).
Note: Jafri (in Jafri & El-Gadi, *Fl. Libya* 12: 2. 1977) indicated 510.10 (LINN) as type, but this is a post-1753 addition to the herbarium and not original material for the name.

Laurus persea Linnaeus, *Species Plantarum* 1: 370. 1753.
"Habitat in America calida." RCN: 2917.
Lectotype (van der Werff in *Novon* 12: 580. 2002): [icon] *"Prunifera arbor, fructu maximo pyriformi viridi, pericarpio esculento butyraceo nucleum unicum maximum nullo ossiculo tectum, cingente"* in Sloane,

Voy. Jamaica 2: 132, t. 222, f. 2. 1725. – Typotype: Herb. Sloane 7: 77 (BM-SL).
Current name: ***Persea americana*** Mill. (Lauraceae).

Laurus sassafras Linnaeus, *Species Plantarum* 1: 371. 1753.
"Habitat in Virginia, Carolina, Florida." RCN: 2921.
Type not designated.
Original material: *Kalm*, Herb. Linn. No. 518.21 (LINN); Herb. Clifford: 156, *Laurus* 1 (BM); [icon] in Plukenet, Phytographia: t. 222, f. 6. 1692; Almag. Bot.: 120. 1696; [icon] in Catesby, Nat. Hist. Carolina 1: 55, t. 55. 1730.
Current name: ***Sassafras albidum*** (Nutt.) Nees (Lauraceae).

Laurus winterana Linnaeus, *Species Plantarum* 1: 371. 1753.
"Habitat in Jamaica, Barbados, Carolina." RCN: 3446.
Replaced synonym of: *Winterana canella* L. (1759).
Type not designated.
Original material: Herb. Clifford: 488, *Winterania* 1 (BM); [icon] in Plukenet, Phytographia: t. 160, f. 7. 1692; Almag. Bot.: 89. 1696 – Voucher: Herb. Sloane 95: 168 (BM-SL); [icon] in Catesby, Nat. Hist. Carolina 2: 50, t. 50. 1736; [icon] in Sloane, Voy. Jamaica 2: 87, t. 191, f. 2. 1725 – Voucher: Herb. Sloane 6: 100 (BM-SL); [icon] in Plukenet, Phytographia: t. 81, f. 1. 1691; Almag. Bot.: 89. 1696.
Current name: ***Canella winterana*** (L.) Gaertn. (Canellaceae).

Lavandula dentata Linnaeus, *Species Plantarum* 2: 572. 1753.
"Habitat in Hispaniae Calape." RCN: 4185.
Lectotype (Upson in Jarvis & al. in *Taxon* 50: 512. 2001): Herb. Clifford: 303, *Lavandula* 3 (BM-000628955).
Current name: ***Lavandula dentata*** L. (Lamiaceae).

Lavandula multifida Linnaeus, *Species Plantarum* 2: 572. 1753.
"Habitat in regione Baetica." RCN: 4184.
Lectotype (Upson in Jarvis & al. in *Taxon* 50: 512. 2001): Herb. Clifford: 303, *Lavandula* 2, sheet A (BM-000628951).
Current name: ***Lavandula multifida*** L. (Lamiaceae).
Note: Siddiqi (in Jafri & El-Gadi, *Fl. Libya* 118: 54. 1985) indicated Herb. Linn. 727.2 (LINN) as type but this specimen lacks the relevant *Species Plantarum* number (i.e. "2") and is not original material for the name. Wijnands (*Bot. Commelins*: 116. 1983) discussed this name in some detail, concluding "its type probably is HSC [Hortus Siccus Cliffortianus] 303.2". Though this was not an effective choice of type (there are in any case two sheets involved), one of the Clifford sheets was subsequently designated as lectotype by Upson.

Lavandula spica Linnaeus, *Species Plantarum* 2: 572. 1753, *nom. utique rej.*
"Habitat in Europa australi." RCN: 4183.
Lectotype (López González in Jarvis & al., *Regnum Veg.* 127: 60. 1993): Herb. Burser XII: 64 (UPS).
Generitype of *Lavandula* Linnaeus (vide Green, *Prop. Brit. Bot.*: 164. 1929).
Current name: ***Lavandula spica*** L. (Lamiaceae).

Lavandula stoechas Linnaeus, *Species Plantarum* 2: 573. 1753.
"Habitat in Europa australi." RCN: 4186.
Lectotype (Upson in Jarvis & al. in *Taxon* 50: 512. 2001): Herb. Burser XII: 60 (UPS).
Current name: ***Lavandula stoechas*** L. (Lamiaceae).
Note: See further discussion by Upson & Andrews (*Genus* Lavandula: 228. 2004).

Lavatera americana Linnaeus, *Systema Naturae*, ed. 10, 2: 1148. 1759.
["Habitat in Jamaica."] Sp. Pl., ed. 2, 2: 973 (1763). RCN: 5065.

Lectotype (Fryxell in *Syst. Bot. Monogr.* 25: 30. 1988): *Browne*, Herb. Linn. No. 871.7 (LINN).

Current name: ***Abutilon abutiloides*** (Jacq.) Garcke ex Hochr. (Malvaceae).

Note: In typifying the name, Fryxell (and in *Lundellia* 5: 82. 2002) incorrectly treated this as the basionym of *Sida americana* (L.) L. 1763. However, there are no cited elements in common, the diagnoses are far from identical and, perhaps crucially, Linnaeus recognises both *L. americana* and *S. americana* in *Sp. Pl.*, ed. 2 (pp. 973 and 963 respectively).

Lavatera arborea Linnaeus, *Species Plantarum* 2: 690. 1753.
"Habitat inter Pisas & Liburnum." RCN: 5060.
Lectotype (Fernandes in *Collect. Bot. (Barcelona)* 7: 427. 1968): Herb. Linn. No. 871.1 (LINN).
Current name: ***Malva dendromorpha*** M.F. Ray (Malvaceae).

Lavatera cretica Linnaeus, *Species Plantarum* 2: 691. 1753.
"Habitat in Creta." RCN: 5067.
Lectotype (Fernandes in *Collect. Bot. (Barcelona)* 7: 429. 1968): Herb. Linn. No. 287.11 (S).
Current name: ***Malva linnaei*** M.F. Ray (Malvaceae).

Lavatera lusitanica Linnaeus, *Species Plantarum* 2: 691. 1753.
"Habitat in Lusitania." RCN: 5064.
Type not designated.
Original material: none traced.
Current name: ***Lavatera triloba*** L. (Malvaceae).
Note: Fernandes (in *Collect. Bot. (Barcelona)* 7: 431, tab. XI, XII. 1968) provided an extensive discussion, concluding that the name is a synonym of *L. triloba* L. (1753).

Lavatera micans Linnaeus, *Species Plantarum* 2: 690. 1753.
"Habitat in Hispania, Lusitania." RCN: 5061.
Type not designated.
Original material: [icon] in Morison, Pl. Hist. Univ. 2: 523, s. 5, t. 17, f. 9. 1680.
Current name: ***Lavatera triloba*** L. (Malvaceae).
Note: Fernandes (in *Collect. Bot. (Barcelona)* 7: 435. 1968) provided an extensive discussion, concluding that the name is a confused synonym of *L. triloba* L. (1753).

Lavatera olbia Linnaeus, *Species Plantarum* 2: 690. 1753.
"Habitat in Olbia insula Galloprovinciae." RCN: 5062.
Lectotype (Stearn, *Introd. Linnaeus' Sp. Pl.* (Ray Soc. ed.): 117. 1957): Herb. Burser XVIII(1): 20 (UPS).
Current name: ***Lavatera olbia*** L. (Malvaceae).
Note: See also Fernandes (in *Collect. Bot. (Barcelona)* 7: 418. 1968).

Lavatera thuringiaca Linnaeus, *Species Plantarum* 2: 691. 1753.
"Habitat in Pannonia, Thuringia, Tataria ad sepes." RCN: 5066.
Lectotype (Fernandes in *Collect. Bot. (Barcelona)* 7: 424. 1968): Herb. Burser XVIII(1): 16 (UPS).
Current name: ***Lavatera thuringiaca*** L. (Malvaceae).

Lavatera triloba Linnaeus, *Species Plantarum* 2: 691. 1753.
"Habitat in Hispania." RCN: 5063.
Lectotype (Fernandes in *Collect. Bot. (Barcelona)* 7: 438. 1968): Herb. Linn. No. 871.3 (LINN).
Current name: ***Lavatera triloba*** L. (Malvaceae).

Lavatera trimestris Linnaeus, *Species Plantarum* 2: 692. 1753.
"Habitat in Syria, Hispania, G. Narbonensi." RCN: 5068.
Lectotype (Fernandes in *Collect. Bot. (Barcelona)* 7: 400. 1968): Herb. Linn. No. 871.11 (LINN).

Generitype of *Lavatera* Linnaeus (vide Green, *Prop. Brit. Bot.*: 173. 1929).
Current name: ***Lavatera trimestris*** L. (Malvaceae).

Lawsonia inermis Linnaeus, *Species Plantarum* 1: 349. 1753.
"Habitat in India, Aegypto." RCN: 2697.
Type not designated.
Original material: [icon] in Rheede, Hort. Malab. 4: 117, t. 57. 1683; [icon] in Walther, Design. Pl.: 3, t. 4. 1735.
Generitype of *Lawsonia* Linnaeus (vide Hitchcock, *Prop. Brit. Bot.*: 150. 1929).
Current name: ***Lawsonia inermis*** L. (Lythraceae).
Note: Dar (in Nasir & Ali, *Fl. W. Pakistan* 78: 5. 1975) and a number of later authors have treated 496.1 (LINN) as the type. However, the material is a post-1753 addition to the collection and not original material for the name.

Lawsonia spinosa Linnaeus, *Species Plantarum* 1: 349. 1753.
"Habitat in India." RCN: 2698.
Type not designated.
Original material: [icon] in Rheede, Hort. Malab. 1: 73, t. 40. 1678; [icon] in Plukenet, Phytographia: t. 220, f. 1. 1692; Almag. Bot.: 318. 1696 – Voucher: Herb. Sloane 97: 151 (BM-SL).
Current name: ***Lawsonia inermis*** L. (Lythraceae).

Lechea major Linnaeus, *Species Plantarum* 1: 90. 1753.
"Habitat in Canadae aridis." RCN: 755.
Lectotype (Blake in *Rhodora* 20: 49. 1918): *Clayton 730* (BM-000051813).
Current name: ***Crocanthemum canadense*** (L.) Britton (Cistaceae).

Lechea minor Linnaeus, *Species Plantarum* 1: 90. 1753.
"Habitat in Canadae sylvis glareosis." RCN: 754.
Lectotype (Britton in *Bull. Torrey Bot. Club* 21: 247. 1894): Herb. Linn. No. 115.5 (LINN).
Generitype of *Lechea* Linnaeus (vide Hitchcock, *Prop. Brit. Bot.*: 122. 1929).
Current name: ***Lechea minor*** L. (Cistaceae).
Note: Reveal (in *Taxon* 38: 516. 1989), regarding Smith (1812) as having typified the name on 115.3 (LINN), a specimen of *L. villosa* Elliot, proposed the name for conservation with 115.5 (LINN) as conserved type. However, the Committee for Spermatophyta decided (in *Taxon* 42: 694. 1993) that Smith had not made an effective typification, but that Britton (*l.c.*) had done so, using 115.5 (LINN). As this is identifiable as *L. minor* of usage, the proposal was declined as unnecessary.

Lecythis ollaria Linnaeus, *Systema Naturae*, ed. 10, 2: 1071. 1759.
["Habitat in America meridionali."] Sp. Pl., ed. 2, 1: 734 (1762). RCN: 3875.
Neotype (Prance & Mori in *Taxon* 26: 216. 1977): Venezuela. Miranda, Carretera Ocumare del Yuy-San Fernando de Yare, 27 Jul 1952 (fl.), *Aristeguieta 839* (VEN).
Current name: ***Lecythis ollaria*** L. (Lecythidaceae).

Ledum palustre Linnaeus, *Species Plantarum* 1: 391. 1753.
"Habitat in Europae septentrionalis paludibus uliginosis." RCN: 3085.
Lectotype (Harmaja in Jarvis & al., *Regnum Veg.* 127: 60. 1993): Herb. Linn. No. 160 (LAPP).
Generitype of *Ledum* Linnaeus.
Current name: ***Rhododendron tomentosum*** Harmaja (Ericaceae).

Leea aequata Linnaeus, *Systema Naturae*, ed. 12, 2: 627; *Mantissa Plantarum*: 124. 1767, *typ. cons.*

L

"Habitat in India orientali. Kleynhoff." RCN: 7189.

Lectotype (Ridsdale in *Blumea* 22: 90. 1974): *Kleynhoff,* Herb. Linn. No. 1118.1 (LINN).

Generitype of *Leea* Linnaeus, *nom. cons.*

Current name: **Leea aequata** L. (Leeaceae).

Note: Leea Linnaeus, *nom. cons.* against *Nalagu* Adans.

Leea crispa Linnaeus, *Systema Naturae,* ed. 12, 2: 627; *Mantissa Plantarum*: 124. 1767.

"Habitat ad Cap. b. spei. Dav. v. Royen." RCN: 7190.

Lectotype (Ridsdale in *Blumea* 22: 89. 1974): *Royen 59,* Herb. Linn. No. 1118.2 (LINN).

Current name: **Leea crispa** L. (Leeaceae).

Lemna arrhiza Linnaeus, *Mantissa Plantarum Altera*: 294. 1771.

"Habitat in Italia, Galliae aquis. Du Chesne." RCN: 7044.

Type not designated.

Original material: [icon] in Micheli, Nov. Pl. Gen.: 16, t. 11, f. 4. 1729.

Current name: **Wolffia arrhiza** (L.) Wimm. (Lemnaceae).

Lemna gibba Linnaeus, *Species Plantarum* 2: 970. 1753.

"Habitat in Europae aquis segnibus." RCN: 7042.

Lectotype (Hashimi & Omer in Nasir & Ali, *Fl. Pakistan* 173: 5. 1986): [icon] *"Lenticula palustris, major, inferne magis convexa, fructu polyspermo"* in Micheli, Nov. Pl. Gen.: 15, t. 11, f. 2. 1729.

Current name: **Lemna gibba** L. (Lemnaceae).

Note: Although Riedl (in Rechinger, *Fl. Iranica* 119: 4. 1976) indicated material in the Clifford herbarium as type, there is none preserved there.

Lemna minor Linnaeus, *Species Plantarum* 2: 970. 1753.

"Habitat in Europae aquis quietis." RCN: 7041.

Lectotype (Hepper in Polhill, *Fl. Trop. E. Africa, Lemnaceae*: 4. 1973): Herb. Linn. No. 1093.2 (LINN).

Generitype of *Lemna* Linnaeus.

Current name: **Lemna minor** L. (Lemnaceae).

Note: Lemna minor, with the type designated by Hepper (incorrectly attributed to Landolt), was proposed as conserved type of the genus by Jarvis (in *Taxon* 41: 565. 1992). However, the proposal was eventually ruled unnecessary by the General Committee (see Barrie, *l.c.* 55: 795–796. 2006 for a review of the history of this and related proposals).

Lemna polyrhiza Linnaeus, *Species Plantarum* 2: 970. 1753.

"Habitat in Europae paludibus fossis." RCN: 7043.

Type not designated.

Original material: [icon] in Ray, Syn. Meth. Stirp. Brit., ed. 3: 129, t. 4, f. 2. 1724; [icon] in Micheli, Nov. Pl. Gen.: 16, t. 11, f. 1. 1729.

Current name: **Spirodela polyrhiza** (L.) Schleid. (Lemnaceae).

Note: Although Riedl (in Rechinger, *Fl. Iranica* 119: 2. 1976) indicated material in the Clifford herbarium as type, there is none preserved there.

Lemna trisulca Linnaeus, *Species Plantarum* 2: 970. 1753.

"Habitat in Europae sub aquis pigris puris." RCN: 7040.

Lectotype (Howard, *Fl. Lesser Antilles* 3: 402. 1979): Herb. Linn. No. 1093.1 (LINN).

Current name: **Lemna trisulca** L. (Lemnaceae).

Lens phaseoloides Linnaeus, *Herbarium Amboinense*: 18. 1754.

"Habitat [in Amboina.]" RCN: 7665.

Lectotype (Merrill, *Interpret. Rumph. Herb. Amb.*: 33, 253. 1917): [icon] *"Faba marina"* in Rumphius, Herb. Amboin. 5: 5, t. 4. 1747.

Current name: **Entada phaseoloides** (L.) Merr. (Fabaceae: Mimosoideae).

Leontice chrysogonum Linnaeus, *Species Plantarum* 1: 312. 1753.

"Habitat inter Graeciae segetes." RCN: 2456.

Lectotype (Phitos & Strid in Strid & Kit Tan, *Fl. Hellenica* 2: 82. 2002): [icon] *"Leontopetalo affinis foliis quernis"* in Morison, Pl. Hist. Univ. 2: 285, s. 3, t. 15, f. 7. 1680. – Epitype (Phitos & Strid in Strid & Kit Tan, *Fl. Hellenica* 2: 82. 2002): Greece. Peloponnisos, Nom. Achaias, ep. Egialias: Road Selinous-Pteri, just NE of the village of Achladea, 350m, 22 May 1987, *Strid & al. 25491* (C; iso- G, RSA, UPA).

Current name: **Bongardia chrysogonum** (L.) Endl. (Berberidaceae).

Leontice leontopetaloides Linnaeus, *Species Plantarum* 1: 313. 1753.

"Habitat in India." RCN: 2459.

Lectotype (Merrill in *J. Arnold Arbor.* 26: 90, pl. 2 A, B. 1945): [icon] *"Leontopetaloides foliis profunde laciniatis, radice tuberosa"* in Amman in Comment. Acad. Sci. Imp. Petrop. 8: 211, t. 13. 1741.

Current name: **Tacca leontopetaloides** (L.) Kuntze (Taccaceae).

Leontice leontopetalum Linnaeus, *Species Plantarum* 1: 312. 1753.

"Habitat in Apulia, Hetruria, Creta." RCN: 2457.

Lectotype (Browicz in Rechinger, *Fl. Iranica* 101: 7. 1973): Herb. Linn. No. 433.1 (LINN).

Generitype of *Leontice* Linnaeus (vide Hitchcock, *Prop. Brit. Bot.*: 146. 1929).

Current name: **Leontice leontopetalum** L. (Berberidaceae).

Leontice thalictroides Linnaeus, *Species Plantarum* 1: 312. 1753.

"Habitat in Virginia." RCN: 2458.

Lectotype (designated here by Reveal): *Clayton 545* (BM).

Current name: **Caulophyllum thalictroides** (L.) Michx. (Berberidaceae).

Note: Stearn (*Genus* Epimedium: 215. 2002) indicated unspecified material in LINN as type. Although sheet 433.2 (LINN) is from Kalm, it is undetermined by Linnaeus, but this questionable choice was in any case published after 1 Jan 2001 and so the omission of the phrase "designated here" or an equivalent (Art. 7.11) means that it is not effective.

Leontodon aureus Linnaeus, *Systema Naturae,* ed. 10, 2: 1193. 1759.

["Habitat in Alpibus Helvetiae, Baldi, Italiae. Seguier."] Sp. Pl., ed. 2, 2: 1122 (1763). RCN: 5839.

Type not designated.

Original material: *J.A. Murray,* Herb. Linn. No. 953.4 (LINN).

Current name: **Crepis aurea** (L.) Cass. (Asteraceae).

Note: Specific epithet spelled "aureum" in the protologue.

Leontodon autumnalis Linnaeus, *Species Plantarum* 2: 798. 1753.

"Habitat in Europae pratis, pascuis, autumno." RCN: 5842.

Lectotype (Sell in Jarvis & Turland in *Taxon* 47: 364. 1998): Herb. Linn. No. 953.8 (LINN).

Current name: **Scorzoneroides autumnalis** (L.) Moench (Asteraceae).

Note: Specific epithet spelled "autumnale" in the protologue.

Leontodon bulbosus Linnaeus, *Species Plantarum* 2: 798. 1753.

"Habitat Monspelii, inque Italia." RCN: 5838.

Lectotype (Turland in Jarvis & Turland in *Taxon* 47: 364. 1998): Herb. Burser VI: 100 (UPS).

Current name: **Sonchus bulbosus** (L.) N. Kilian & Greuter (Asteraceae).

Note: Specific epithet spelled "bulbosum" in the protologue.

Leontodon dandelion Linnaeus, *Species Plantarum* 2: 798. 1753. "Habitat in Virginia." RCN: 5787.
Basionym of: *Tragopogon dandelion* (L.) L. (1763).
Lectotype (Kim & Turner in *Brittonia* 44: 192. 1992): *Clayton 19 & 383*, Herb. Linn. No. 946.8 (LINN).
Current name: ***Krigia dandelion*** (L.) Nutt. (Asteraceae).

Leontodon hastilis Linnaeus, *Species Plantarum*, ed. 2, 2: 1123. 1763. "Habitat in Europa australi." RCN: 5840.
Type not designated.
Original material: none traced.
Current name: ***Leontodon hispidus*** L. subsp. ***hastilis*** (L.) Pawl. (Asteraceae).
Note: Specific epithet spelled "hastile" in the protologue.

Leontodon hirtus Linnaeus, *Systema Naturae*, ed. 10, 2: 1194. 1759. ["Habitat in Helvetia, G. Narbonensi, Hispania."] Sp. Pl., ed. 2, 2: 1124 (1763). RCN: 5843.
Type not designated.
Original material: Herb. Linn. No. 953.10 (H); Herb. Linn. No. 953.10 (LINN); Herb. Linn. No. 953.14 (LINN); *Allioni*, Herb. Linn. No. 953.12 (LINN); Herb. Burser VI: 47 (UPS); [icon] in Bauhin, Prodr. Theatri Bot.: 63. 1620; [icon] in Bauhin & Cherler, Hist. Pl. Univ. 2: 1038. 1651.
Current name: ***Leontodon hirtus*** L. (Asteraceae).
Note: Specific epithet spelled "hirtum" in the protologue.
   This name is based on elements previously treated (in *Sp. Pl.* 2: 799. 1753) as two unnamed varieties of *L. hispidus* L. Although not typified by any of the following authors, the name has been variously interpreted by Britten (in *J. Bot.* 45: 32. 1907), Lacaita (in *J. Bot.* 56: 97. 1918) and Finch & Sell (in *Bot. J. Linn. Soc.* 71: 245. 1976).

Leontodon hispidus Linnaeus, *Species Plantarum* 2: 799. 1753, *typ. cons.*
"Habitat in Europae pratis." RCN: 5844.
Lectotype (Pittoni in Rechinger, *Fl. Iranica* 122: 129. 1977): *Magnol*, Herb. Linn. No. 953.9 (LINN).
Generitype of *Leontodon* Linnaeus, *nom. cons.* (vide Green, *Prop. Brit. Bot.*: 178. 1929).
Current name: ***Leontodon hispidus*** L. (Asteraceae).
Note: Specific epithet spelled "hispidum" in the protologue.
   The number of the lectotype sheet was erroneously given as "53.9" by Jarvis & al. (*Regnum Veg.* 127: 60. 1993).

Leontodon lanatus Linnaeus, *Centuria I Plantarum*: 26. 1755. "Habitat in Arabia. D. Hasselquist." RCN: 5788.
Basionym of: *Tragopogon lanatus* (L.) L. (1763).
Lectotype (Díaz de la Guardia & Blanca in *Taxon* 46: 761. 1997): *Hasselquist*, Herb. Linn. No. 946.9 (LINN; iso- UPS-HASSELQ 678, see p. 184).
Current name: ***Scorzonera czerepanovii*** Kamelin ex Czerep. (Asteraceae).
Note: Specific epithet spelled "lanatum" in the protologue.

Leontodon taraxacum Linnaeus, *Species Plantarum* 2: 798. 1753. "Habitat in Europae pascuis." RCN: 5837.
Lectotype (Richards in *Taxon* 34: 634. 1985): Herb. Linn. No. 280 (LAPP).
Current name: ***Taraxacum officinale*** Weber (Asteraceae).
Note: Although Arevschatian (in *Bot. Zhurn.* 69: 1383. 1984) indicated unspecified material in LINN as the type of *T. officinale*, *L. taraxacum* was not cited in synonymy. Even if the relationship between these two names is inferred, the statement does not distinguish between sheets 953.1 and 953.2 (LINN), which are not

part of a single gathering, so Art. 9.15 does not apply. This is not a valid type choice and Richards' typification appears to be the earliest.

Leontodon tuberosus Linnaeus, *Species Plantarum* 2: 799. 1753. "Habitat in Hetruriae, Galloprovinciae, Narbonae pratis." RCN: 5841.
Lectotype (Alavi in Jafri & El-Gadi, *Fl. Libya* 107: 353. 1983): Herb. Linn. No. 953.5 (LINN).
Current name: ***Leontodon tuberosus*** L. (Asteraceae).
Note: Specific epithet spelled "tuberosum" in the protologue.

Leonurus cardiaca Linnaeus, *Species Plantarum* 2: 584. 1753. "Habitat in Europae ruderatis." RCN: 4263.
Lectotype (Hedge & Lamond in *Notes Roy. Bot. Gard. Edinburgh* 28: 90. 1968): Herb. Linn. No. 739.1 (LINN).
Generitype of *Leonurus* Linnaeus (vide Green, *Prop. Brit. Bot.*: 165. 1929).
Current name: ***Leonurus cardiaca*** L. (Lamiaceae).
Note: Krestovskaja (in *Bot. Zhurn.* 73: 1748. 1988) noted the existence of Herb. Linn. No. 739.5 (LINN). However, this is actually original material for *L. tataricus* and (in *Novosti Sist. Vyssh. Rast.* 27: 141. 1990) it was incorrectly indicated as the lectotype of *L. cardica*. Hedge & Lamond's choice in any case has priority.

Leonurus indicus Linnaeus, *Systema Naturae*, ed. 10, 2: 1101. 1759. ["Habitat in India. Burmannus."] Sp. Pl., ed. 2, 2: 817 (1763). RCN: 4276.
Lectotype (Sebald in *Stuttgarter Beitr. Naturk., A,* 341: 188. 1980): Herb. Linn. No. 739.8 (LINN).
Current name: ***Leucas lavandulifolia*** Sm. (Lamiaceae).
Note: Although Sebald indicated unspecified material that he had seen in LINN as "Typus", this can only be 739.8 (LINN), and this is accepted as a valid type choice. The epithet "indicus" is pre-occupied in *Leucas* R. Br. by *Leucas indica* (L.) R. Br. (based on *Phlomis indica* L. 1753), and the correct name for *Leonurus indicus* in *Leucas* is therefore *Leucas lavandulifolia* Sm.

Leonurus marrubiastrum Linnaeus, *Species Plantarum* 2: 584. 1753. "Habitat in Bohemia, Ucraniae." RCN: 4264.
Lectotype (Krestovskaja in Jarvis & al. in *Taxon* 50: 512. 2001): *Gerber*, Herb. Linn. No. 739.3 (LINN).
Current name: ***Leonurus marrubiastrum*** L. (Lamiaceae).

Leonurus sibiricus Linnaeus, *Species Plantarum* 2: 584. 1753. "Habitat in Sibiria, China." RCN: 4266.
Lectotype (Kuprianova in Schischkin, *Fl. U.R.S.S.* 21: 157. 1954): [icon] *"Ballote inodora, foliis Coronopi"* in Amman, Stirp. Rar. Ruth.: 48, t. 8. 1739 (see p. 620).
Current name: ***Leonurus sibiricus*** L. (Lamiaceae).
Note: Kuprianova (1954) typified the name in the sense of the Siberian taxon, taking up *L. heterophyllus* Sweet for the tropical weed to which the Linnaean name had often been applied. Krestovskaja (in *Novosti Sist. Vyssh. Rast.* 24: 156. 1987; 25: 133. 1988) further clarified the problem, though the choice of 739.7 (LINN) as type, adopted there, is pre-dated by that of Kuprianova using an Amman illustration. Harley & Paton (in *Kew Bull.* 56: 243. 2001) have provided a recent summary.

Leonurus tataricus Linnaeus, *Species Plantarum* 2: 584. 1753. "Habitat in Tataria." RCN: 4265.
Lectotype (Krestovskaja in *Novosti Sist. Vyssh. Rast.* 27: 140. 1990): Herb. Linn. No. 739.5 (LINN).
Current name: ***Leonurus tataricus*** L. (Lamiaceae).
Note: Krestovskaja (in *Bot. Zhurn.* 73: 1748. 1988) noted the existence of Herb. Linn. No. 739.5 (LINN), but did not refer to it as the

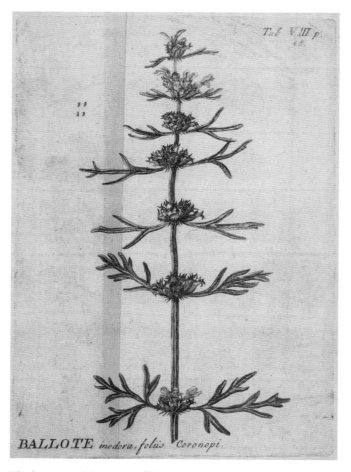

BALLOTE *inodora, foliis Coronopi.*

The lectotype of *Leonurus sibiricus* L.

type. She treats this as a distinct species, not as a synonym of *L. cardiaca* L. as has been done by some other authors.

Lepidium alpinum Linnaeus, *Centuria II Plantarum*: 23. 1756.
"Habitat in alpibus Sneeberg, Tyrolensibus, Saltzburgensibus, Helveticis, Baldi. Seguier." RCN: 4681.
Lectotype (Appel & Al-Shehbaz in *Novon* 7: 339. 1998 [1997]): *Séguier*, Herb. Linn. No. 824.5 (LINN), see p. 228.
Current name: ***Hornungia alpina*** (L.) O. Appel (Brassicaceae).

Lepidium bonariense Linnaeus, *Species Plantarum* 2: 645. 1753.
"Habitat in Bonaria." RCN: 4695.
Lectotype (Marais in Codd & al., *Fl. Southern Africa* 13: 93. 1970): [icon] *"Thlaspi Bonar. multiscissum, flore invisibili"* in Dillenius, Hort. Eltham. 2: 381, t. 286, f. 370. 1732.
Current name: ***Lepidium bonariense*** L. (Brassicaceae).

Lepidium cardamine Linnaeus, *Centuria I Plantarum*: 17. 1755.
"Habitat in Hispania ad margines viarum argillosas & aridas." RCN: 4683.
Lectotype (López González in Cafferty & Jarvis in *Taxon* 51: 534. 2002): *Löfling 468b*, Herb. Linn. No. 824.8 (LINN).
Current name: ***Lepidium cardamine*** L. (Brassicaceae).

Lepidium chalepense Linnaeus, *Centuria II Plantarum*: 23. 1756.
"Habitat in Oriente." RCN: 4696.

Lectotype (Jafri in Nasir & Ali, *Fl. W. Pakistan* 55: 68. 1973): Herb. Linn. No. 824.20 (LINN).
Current name: ***Cardaria chalepense*** (L.) Hand.-Mazz. (Brassicaceae).

Lepidium didymum Linnaeus, *Systema Naturae,* ed. 12, 2: 433; *Mantissa Plantarum*: 92. 1767.
RCN: 4691.
Lectotype (Fawcett & Rendle, *Fl. Jamaica* 3: 244. 1914): Herb. Linn. No. 824.16 (LINN).
Current name: ***Lepidium didymum*** L. (Brassicaceae).

Lepidium draba Linnaeus, *Species Plantarum* 2: 645. 1753.
"Habitat in Germania, praesertim Austria, Gallia, Italia." RCN: 4714.
Basionym of: *Cochlearia draba* (L.) L. (1759).
Lectotype (Jonsell & Jarvis in *Nordic J. Bot.* 22: 70. 2002): Herb. Clifford: 331, *Lepidium* 2, sheet 2 (BM-000646273).
Current name: ***Lepidium draba*** L. (Brassicaceae).

Lepidium graminifolium Linnaeus, *Systema Naturae,* ed. 10, 2: 1127. 1759.
["Habitat in Europa australi."] Sp. Pl., ed. 2, 2: 900 (1763). RCN: 4689.
Lectotype (Hedge in Cafferty & Jarvis in *Taxon* 51: 534. 2002): Herb. Linn. No. 824.15 (LINN).
Current name: ***Lepidium graminifolium*** L. (Brassicaceae).

Lepidium iberis Linnaeus, *Species Plantarum* 2: 645. 1753.
"Habitat in Germania, Gallia, Italia, Sicilia secus vias." RCN: 4694.
Lectotype (Rich in Cafferty & Jarvis in *Taxon* 51: 534. 2002): Herb. Linn. No. 824.19 (LINN).
Current name: ***Lepidium virginicum*** L. (Brassicaceae).
Note: This name had been treated as a synonym of *L. graminifolium* L. (1759) by some authors, e.g. Vasconcellos in Tutin & al., *Fl. Europaea* 1: 333 (1964), despite *L. iberis* pre-dating the latter. Rich's typification avoided an unfortunate change of name, *L. iberis* becoming a synonym of *L. virginicum* L. (1753), rather than an earlier name for the taxon known as *L. graminifolium*.

Lepidium latifolium Linnaeus, *Species Plantarum* 2: 644. 1753.
"Habitat in Galliae, Angliae umbrosis, succulentis." RCN: 4687.
Lectotype (Jafri in Nasir & Ali, *Fl. W. Pakistan* 55: 60. 1973): Herb. Linn. No. 824.11a (LINN).
Generitype of *Lepidium* Linnaeus (vide Green, *Prop. Brit. Bot.*: 170. 1929).
Current name: ***Lepidium latifolium*** L. (Brassicaceae).

Lepidium lyratum Linnaeus, *Species Plantarum* 2: 644. 1753.
"Habitat in Oriente." RCN: 4686.
Lectotype (Hedge in Cafferty & Jarvis in *Taxon* 51: 534. 2002): [icon] *"Lepidium Orientale Nasturtii Crispi folio"* in Tournefort, Rel. Voy. Levant (Paris ed.) 2: 339. 1717.
Current name: ***Lepidium lyratum*** L. (Brassicaceae).

Lepidium nudicaule Linnaeus, *Species Plantarum* 2: 643. 1753.
"Habitat Monspelii." RCN: 4679.
Lectotype (Moreno in Cafferty & Jarvis in *Taxon* 51: 534. 2002): Herb. Linn. No. 824.3 (LINN).
Current name: ***Teesdalia nudicaulis*** (L.) R. Br. (Brassicaceae).
Note: The basionym of *T. nudicaulis* (L.) R. Br. is *Iberis nudicaulis* L. (1753), not *L. nudicaule* L. (1753).

Lepidium perfoliatum Linnaeus, *Species Plantarum* 2: 643. 1753.
"Habitat in Persia, Syria." RCN: 4677.
Lectotype (Jonsell & Jarvis in *Nordic J. Bot.* 22: 70. 2002): Herb. Clifford: 331, *Lepidium* 3 (BM-000646274).
Current name: ***Lepidium perfoliatum*** L. (Brassicaceae).

Lepidium petraeum Linnaeus, *Species Plantarum* 2: 644. 1753.
"Habitat in Lapidosis Oelandiae, Angliae." RCN: 4682.
Lectotype (Jonsell & Jarvis in *Nordic J. Bot.* 22: 70. 2002): Herb.
    Linn. No. 824.7 (LINN).
Current name: ***Hornungia petraea*** (L.) Rchb. (Brassicaceae).
Note: Stearn (in *Biol. J. Linn. Soc.* 5: 11. 1973), in an account of
    Linnaeus' Öland and Gotland journey of 1741, treated Bornholm
    in Öland as the restricted type locality, and noted the existence of
    824.7 (LINN). In his paper, he attributed restricted type localities
    irrespective of whether any material existed in LINN and, where
    specimens do exist, he does not refer to any of them as type
    specimens. The collection subsequently designated as the type
    shows no annotation associating it with Öland.

Lepidium procumbens Linnaeus, *Species Plantarum* 2: 643.
    1753.
"Habitat Monspelii." RCN: 4680.
Lectotype (Hedge in Cafferty & Jarvis in *Taxon* 51: 534. 2002): [icon]
    "Nasturtium pumilum supinum vernum" in Magnol, Bot. Monspel.:
    185, 184. 1676.
Current name: ***Hornungia procumbens*** (L.) Hayek (Brassicaceae).

Lepidium ruderale Linnaeus, *Species Plantarum* 2: 645. 1753.
"Habitat in Europae ruderatis & ad vias." RCN: 4692.
Lectotype (Jonsell & Jarvis in *Nordic J. Bot.* 22: 70. 2002): Herb.
    Linn. No. 824.17 (LINN).
Current name: ***Lepidium ruderale*** L. (Brassicaceae).

Lepidium sativum Linnaeus, *Species Plantarum* 2: 644. 1753.
"Habitat – – – –" RCN: 4685.
Lectotype (Fawcett & Rendle, *Fl. Jamaica* 3: 243. 1914): Herb. Linn.
    No. 824.11 (LINN).
Current name: ***Lepidium sativum*** L. (Brassicaceae).

Lepidium subulatum Linnaeus, *Species Plantarum* 2: 644. 1753.
"Habitat in Hispania. Loefl." RCN: 4688.
Lectotype (López González in Cafferty & Jarvis in *Taxon* 51: 534.
    2002): *Löfling 469*, Herb. Linn. No. 824.12 (LINN).
Current name: ***Lepidium subulatum*** L. (Brassicaceae).

Lepidium suffruticosum Linnaeus, *Systema Naturae*, ed. 12, 2: 433;
    Mantissa Plantarum: 91. 1767.
"Habitat in Hispania." RCN: 4690.
Neotype (López González in Cafferty & Jarvis in *Taxon* 51: 535.
    2002): Spain. "Barcelone, Riera de Vallvidrera, lieux herbeux", 16
    Oct 1924, F. Sennen, Exsicc. Pl. d'Espagne, No. 5025 (specimen on
    the left) (MA-44005; iso- BM).
Current name: ***Lepidium graminifolium*** L. subsp. ***suffruticosum*** (L.)
    P. Monts. (Brassicaceae).

Lepidium vesicarium Linnaeus, *Species Plantarum* 2: 643. 1753.
"Habitat in Iberiae, Mediae aridis." RCN: 4678.
Lectotype (López González in Cafferty & Jarvis in *Taxon* 51: 535.
    2002): [icon] *"Lepidium Orientale, Nasturtii folio, caule vesicario"* in
    Buxbaum, Pl. Minus Cognit. Cent. 1: 17, t. 26. 1728.
Current name: ***Lepidium vesicarium*** L. (Brassicaceae).
Note: Although Hedge (in Hedge & Rechinger, *Fl. Iranica* 57: 66.
    1968) indicated unspecified Tournefort material as type, no
    Tournefort illustration was cited, and Linnaeus did not have the
    opportunity to study Tournefort's specimens. This statement cannot
    therefore be accepted as a formal typification.

Lepidium virginianum Linnaeus, *Flora Jamaicensis*: 18. 1759, *orth.
    var.*
"Habitat [in Jamaica.]" RCN: 4693.

Lectotype (Marais in Codd & al., *Fl. Southern Africa* 13: 94. 1970):
    Herb. Linn. No. 824.18 (LINN).
Current name: ***Lepidium virginicum*** L. (Brassicaceae).
Note: Evidently an orthographic variant of *L. virginicum* L. (1753).

Lepidium virginicum Linnaeus, *Species Plantarum* 2: 645. 1753.
"Habitat in Virginia, Jamaicae glareosis." RCN: 4693.
Lectotype (Marais in Codd & al., *Fl. Southern Africa* 13: 94. 1970):
    Herb. Linn. No. 824.18 (LINN).
Current name: ***Lepidium virginicum*** L. (Brassicaceae).

Lerchea longicauda Linnaeus, *Mantissa Plantarum Altera*: 256. 1771.
"Habitat in India orientali." RCN: 4910.
Lectotype (Axelius in *Blumea* 32: 108. 1987): Herb. Linn. No. 851a.1
    (LINN).
Generitype of *Lerchea* Linnaeus, *nom. cons.*
Current name: ***Lerchea longicauda*** L. (Rubiaceae).
Note: Lerchea Linnaeus, *nom. cons.* against *Lerchia* Zinn.

Leucadendron acaulon Linnaeus, *Species Plantarum* 1: 92. 1753.
"Habitat ad Caput b. spei." RCN: 783.
Type not designated.
Original material: [icon] in Boerhaave, Index Alter Pl. Hort. Lugdb.-
    Bat. 2: 191. 1720.
Current name: ***Protea acaulos*** (L.) Reichard (Proteaceae).

Leucadendron cancellatum Linnaeus, *Species Plantarum* 1: 91. 1753.
"Habitat ad Caput b. spei." RCN: 782.
Lectotype (Rourke in *S. African J. Bot.* 53: 479. 1987): [icon]
    *"Lepidocarpodendron; foliis angustissimis, gramineis; fructu cancellato;
    semine coronato"* in Boerhaave, Index Alter Pl. Hort. Lugdb.-Bat. 2:
    193. 1720.
Current name: ***Aulax cancellata*** (L.) Druce (Proteaceae).

Leucadendron conocarpodendron Linnaeus, *Species Plantarum* 1:
    93. 1753.
"Habitat in Aethiopia." RCN: 785.
Lectotype (Rourke in *J. S. African Bot., Suppl.* 8: 36. 1972): [icon]
    *"Conocarpodendron; folio crasso, nervoso, lanuginoso, supra crenato,
    ibique limbo rubro; flore aureo; cono facile deciduo"* in Boerhaave,
    Index Alter Pl. Hort. Lugdb.-Bat. 2: 196. 1720 (see p. 109).
Current name: ***Leucospermum conocarpodendron*** (L.) H. Buek
    (Proteaceae).

Leucadendron cucullatum Linnaeus, *Species Plantarum* 1: 93. 1753.
"Habitat ad Cap. b. spei locis uliginosis." RCN: 764.
Basionym of: *Protea cucullata* (L.) L. (1771).
Lectotype (Rourke in *J. S. African Bot.* 50: 182. 1984): [icon]
    *"Hypophyllocarpodendron; foliis inferioribus apice trifido, rubro,
    superioribus penitus rubris, glabris"* in Boerhaave, Index Alter Pl.
    Hort. Lugdb.-Bat. 2: 206. 1720.
Current name: ***Mimetes cucullatus*** (L.) R. Br. (Proteaceae).

Leucadendron cyanoides Linnaeus, *Species Plantarum* 1: 93. 1753.
"Habitat ad Cap. b. spei." RCN: 761.
Basionym of: *Protea cyanoides* (L.) L. (1771).
Type not designated.
Original material: [icon] in Plukenet, Almag. Mant.: 61, t. 345, f. 6.
    1700.
Current name: ***Serruria cyanoides*** (L.) R. Br. (Proteaceae).

Leucadendron cynaroides Linnaeus, *Species Plantarum* 1: 92. 1753,
    typ. cons.
"Habitat ad Caput b. spei in humidis mont. Tabularis." RCN: 767.
Basionym of: *Protea cynaroides* (L.) L. (1771).

L

Type not designated.
Original material: [icon] in Boerhaave, Index Alter Pl. Hort. Lugdb.-Bat. 2: 184. 1720.
Generitype of *Protea* Linnaeus (1771), *nom. cons.*
Current name: ***Protea cynaroides*** (L.) L. (Proteaceae).
Note: Specific epithet spelled "cinaroides" in the protologue.

Leucadendron glomeratum Linnaeus, *Species Plantarum, ed. 2, 1:* 137. 1762.
"Habitat ad Cap. b. spei." RCN: 759.
Type not designated.
Original material: [icon] in Burman, Rar. Afric. Pl.: 265, t. 99, f. 2. 1739.
Current name: ***Serruria glomerata*** (L.) R. Br. (Proteaceae).

Leucadendron hirtum Linnaeus, *Plantae Rariores Africanae*: 8. 1760.
["Habitat ad Cap. b. spei."] Sp. Pl., ed. 2, 1: 136 (1762). RCN: 763.
Basionym of: *Protea hirta* (L.) L. (1771).
Lectotype (Rourke in *J. S. African Bot.* 50: 218. 1984): Herb. Linn. No. 116.36 (LINN).
Current name: ***Mimetes hirta*** (L.) Knight (Proteaceae).

Leucadendron hypophyllocarpodendron Linnaeus, *Species Plantarum* 1: 93. 1753.
"Habitat ad Cap. b. spei in campis sabulosis." RCN: 771.
Basionym of: *Protea hypophyllocarpodendron* (L.) L. (1771).
Lectotype (Rourke in *J. S. African Bot., Suppl.* 8: 104. 1972): [icon] "*Conocarpodendron; folio rigido, angusto, apice tridentato rubro; flore aureo*" in Boerhaave, Index Alter Pl. Hort. Lugdb.-Bat. 2: 198. 1720.
Current name: ***Leucospermum hypophyllocarpodendron*** (L.) Druce (Proteaceae).

Leucadendron lepidocarpodendron Linnaeus, *Species Plantarum* 1: 91. 1753.
"Habitat ad Cap. b. spei." RCN: 768.
Basionym of: *Protea lepidocarpodendron* (L.) L. (1771).
Type not designated.
Original material: [icon] in Boerhaave, Index Alter Pl. Hort. Lugdb.-Bat. 2: 189. 1720; [icon] in Boerhaave, Index Alter Pl. Hort. Lugdb.-Bat. 2: 188. 1720.
Generitype of *Leucadendron* Linnaeus, *nom. rej.* (vide Hitchcock, *Prop. Brit. Bot.*: 122. 1929).
Current name: ***Protea lepidocarpodendron*** (L.) L. (Proteaceae).
Note: Leucadendron Linnaeus, *nom. rej.* in favour of *Leucadendron* R. Br.

Leucadendron pinifolium Linnaeus, *Systema Naturae, ed. 12, 2:* 110; *Mantissa Plantarum*: 36. 1767.
"Habitat ad Cap. b. spei. D. Royen." RCN: 756.
Basionym of: *Protea pinifolia* (L.) L. (1771).
Lectotype (Rourke in *S. African J. Bot.* 53: 479. 1987): [icon] *"Pini foliis planta Africana, Cyperi capitulis Herm."* in Burman, Rar. Afric. Pl.: 193, t. 70, f. 3. 1739.
Current name: ***Aulax cancellata*** (L.) Druce (Proteaceae).

Leucadendron proteoides Linnaeus, *Species Plantarum* 1: 91. 1753.
"Habitat ad Cap. b. spei." RCN: 780.
Replaced synonym of: *Protea purpurea* L., *nom. illeg.*
Neotype (Rourke in *J. S. African Bot.* 42: 203. 1976): Herb. Linn. No. 116.16 (LINN).
Current name: ***Diastella proteoides*** (L.) Druce (Proteaceae).
Note: The collection indicated as the type by Rourke lacks the relevant *Species Plantarum* number (i.e. "2") and was a post-1753 addition to the herbarium, and is not original material for the name.

However, in the apparent absence of any original material, this choice is accepted as a neotypification (Art. 9.8).

Leucadendron racemosum Linnaeus, *Species Plantarum* 1: 91. 1753.
"Habitat in Aethiopia." RCN: 757.
Basionym of: *Protea racemosa* (L.) L. (1771).
Neotype (Rourke in *J. S. African Bot., Suppl.* 7: 117, pl. 10. 1969): *Grubb*, Herb. Bergius (SBT).
Current name: ***Spatalla racemosa*** (L.) Druce (Proteaceae).

Leucadendron repens Linnaeus, *Species Plantarum* 1: 91. 1753.
"Habitat ad Caput b. spei." RCN: 766.
Basionym of: *Protea repens* (L.) L. (1771).
Lectotype (Rycroft in *J. S. African Bot.* 27: 191. 1961): [icon] *"Lepidocarpodendron; foliis angustis, brevioribus, salignis; calicis squamis elegantissime ex roseo, aureo, albo, atro-rubro variegatis; florum plumis albis"* in Boerhaave, Index Alter Pl. Hort. Lugdb.-Bat. 2: 187. 1720.
Current name: ***Protea repens*** (L.) L. (Proteaceae).

Leucadendron scolymocephalum Linnaeus, *Species Plantarum* 1: 92. 1753.
"Habitat ad Caput b. spei, in ericetis mont. Tigridis." RCN: 784.
Type not designated.
Original material: [icon] in Boerhaave, Index Alter Pl. Hort. Lugdb.-Bat. 2: 192. 1720.
Current name: ***Protea scolymocephala*** (L.) Reichard (Proteaceae).

Leucadendron serraria Linnaeus, *Species Plantarum* 1: 93. 1753.
"Habitat in Aethiopia." RCN: 760.
Basionym of: *Protea serraria* (L.) L. (1771).
Type not designated.
Original material: [icon] in Burman, Rar. Afric. Pl.: 265, t. 99, f. 2. 1739; [icon] in Seba, Locupl. Rer. Nat. Thes. 2: 64, t. 63, f. 6. 1735; [icon] in Burman, Rar. Afric. Pl.: 264, t. 99, f. 1. 1739; [icon] in Plukenet, Almag. Mant.: 1, t. 329, f. 1. 1700.
Current name: ***Serruria fasciflora*** Knight (Proteaceae).

Leucadendron speciosum Linnaeus, *Systema Naturae, ed. 12, 2:* 110; *Mantissa Plantarum*: 36. 1767.
"Habitat ad Cap. b. spei." RCN: 769.
Basionym of: *Protea speciosa* (L.) L. (1771).
Type not designated.
Original material: [icon] in Boerhaave, Index Alter Pl. Hort. Lugdb.-Bat. 2: 185. 1720.
Current name: ***Protea speciosa*** (L.) L. (Proteaceae).

Leucojum aestivum Linnaeus, *Systema Naturae, ed. 10, 2:* 975. 1759.
["Habitat in Pannonia, Hetruria, Monspelii."] Sp. Pl., ed. 2, 1: 414 (1762). RCN: 2301.
Type not designated.
Original material: Herb. Linn. No. 410.2 (LINN).
Current name: ***Leucojum aestivum*** L. (Liliaceae/Amaryllidaceae).

Leucojum autumnale Linnaeus, *Species Plantarum* 1: 289. 1753.
"Habitat in Lusitania." RCN: 2302.
Type not designated.
Original material: Herb. Linn. No. 410.3 (LINN); Herb. Burser III: 52 (UPS); Herb. Burser III: 50 (UPS); [icon] in Clusius, Rar. Pl. Hist. 1: 170. 1601.
Current name: ***Acis autumnalis*** (L.) Herb. (Liliaceae/Amaryllidaceae).

Leucojum vernum Linnaeus, *Species Plantarum* 1: 289. 1753.
"Habitat in Germaniae, Helvetiae, Italiae umbrosis pratis, ad rivulos." RCN: 2300.
Type not designated.

Original material: Herb. Linn. No. 410.1 (LINN); Herb. Linn. (FI); Herb. Clifford: 135, *Leucojum* 1 (BM); Herb. Burser III: 49 (UPS); [icon] in Reneaulme, Specim. Hist. Pl.: 99, 100. 1611.
Generitype of *Leucojum* Linnaeus (vide Hitchcock, *Prop. Brit. Bot.*: 144. 1929).
Current name: ***Leucojum vernum*** L. (Liliaceae/Amaryllidaceae).
Note: See notes on original material in FI by Jarvis (in *Webbia* 45: 104–108. 1991).

Leysera callicornia Linnaeus, *Mantissa Plantarum Altera*: 286. 1771.
"Habitat ad Cap. b. spei." RCN: 6421.
Replaced synonym: *Callicornia gnaphalodes* Burm. f. (1768).
Type not designated.
Current name: ***Leysera gnaphalodes*** (L.) L. (Asteraceae).
Note: A *nomen novum* in *Leysera* for *Callicornia gnaphalodes* Burm. f. (1768), the existence of *L. gnaphalodes* (L.) L. (1763) preventing the transfer of *C. gnaphalodes*.

Leysera gnaphalodes (Linnaeus) Linnaeus, *Species Plantarum*, ed. 2, 2: 1249. 1763.
"Habitat in Aethiopia." RCN: 6420.
Basionym: *Callisia gnaphalodes* L. (1760).
Lectotype (Bremer in Jarvis & al., *Regnum Veg.* 127: 61. 1993): *Leysera gnaphalodes*, fol. A, Herb. Burman (G).
Generitype of *Leysera* Linnaeus.
Current name: ***Leysera gnaphalodes*** (L.) L. (Asteraceae).

Leysera paleacea Linnaeus, *Systema Naturae*, ed. 12, 2: 561. 1767.
RCN: 6422.
Lectotype (Bremer in *Taxon* 25: 207. 1976): Herb. Linn. No. 1008.6 (LINN).
Current name: ***Relhania fruticosa*** (L.) K. Bremer (Asteraceae).

Lichen ampullaceus Linnaeus, *Species Plantarum* 2: 1146. 1753.
"Habitat in Lancastria Angliae." RCN: 8200.
Lectotype (Jørgensen & al. in *Bot. J. Linn. Soc.* 115: 272, 372, f. 4. 1994): [icon] *"Lichenoides tinctorium glabrum, vesiculosum"* in Dillenius, Hist. Musc.: 188, t. 24, f. 82. 1741. – Voucher: Herb. Dillenius (OXF). – Epitype (Jørgensen & al. in *Bot. J. Linn. Soc.* 115: 272, 372. 1994): United Kingdom. Isles of Scilly, St Martin's, Chapel Down, overlooking Stoney Port, 5 May 1980, *P.W. James s.n.* (BM).
Current name: ***Parmelia omphalodes*** (L.) Ach. (Parmeliaceae).

Lichen aphthosus Linnaeus, *Species Plantarum* 2: 1148. 1753.
"Habitat in Europae Sylvis acerosis sterilibus sub juniperis. terrestris." RCN: 8215.
Lectotype (Howe in *Bull. Torrey Bot. Club* 39: 201. 1912): Herb. Linn. No. 1273.175 (LINN).
Current name: ***Peltigera aphthosa*** (L.) Willd. (Peltigeraceae).
Note: Specific epithet spelled "aphtosus" in the protologue.
See extensive reviews by Jørgensen & al. (in *Bot. J. Linn. Soc.* 115: 273, f. 5. 1994), and by Vitikainen (in *Acta Bot. Fenn.* 152: 26. 1994).

Lichen aquaticus Linnaeus, *Species Plantarum* 2: 1148. 1753.
"Habitat in Suecia sub aqua, in paludibus." RCN: 8212.
Neotype (Jørgensen & al. in *Bot. J. Linn. Soc.* 115: 274, 372. 1994): Sweden. Västergötland, Floda, Nääs, 16 Aug 1919, *H. Magnusson* (Malme Lich. Suec. Exs. 790) (UPS).
Current name: ***Dermatocarpon luridum*** (With.) J.R. Laundon (Verrucariaceae).

Lichen arcticus Linnaeus, *Species Plantarum* 2: 1148. 1753.
"Habitat in Suecia boreali, sub juniperis. terrestris." RCN: 8216.

Lectotype (Howe in *Bull. Torrey Bot. Club* 39: 201. 1912; Jørgensen & al. in *Bot. J. Linn. Soc.* 115: 275, f. 6. 1994): Herb. Linn. No. 1273.183, lowermost specimen (LINN).
Current name: ***Nephroma arcticum*** (L.) Torss. (Nephromataceae).
Note: See review by Jørgensen & al. (in *Bot. J. Linn. Soc.* 115: 275, 372, f. 6. 1994), who restrict Howe's original choice to the lowermost specimen on the sheet.

Lichen articulatus Linnaeus, *Species Plantarum* 2: 1156. 1753.
"Habitat in Europae australis sylvis." RCN: 8255.
Lectotype (Jørgensen & al. in *Bot. J. Linn. Soc.* 115: 277. 1994): [icon] *"Usnea capillacea & nodosa"* in Dillenius, Hist. Musc.: 60, t. 11, f. 4. 1741. – Voucher: Herb. Dillenius (OXF). – Epitype (Jørgensen & al. in *Bot. J. Linn. Soc.* 115: 277, 372. 1994): England. Burnley, *T. Willifell*, Herb. Sherard (OXF).
Current name: ***Usnea articulata*** (L.) Hoffm. (Parmeliaceae).

Lichen atroalbus Linnaeus, *Species Plantarum* 2: 1141. 1753, *nom. utique rej.*
"Habitat in Alpium rupibus." RCN: 8169.
Type not designated.
Original material: none traced.
Note: Specific epithet spelled "atro-albus" in the protologue.
See discussion in Jørgensen & al. (in *Bot. J. Linn. Soc.* 115: 277. 1994), who concluded that this is a *nomen non satis nota* and (in *Taxon* 43: 646. 1994) successfully proposed its rejection.

Lichen atrovirens Linnaeus, *Species Plantarum* 2: 1141. 1753, *nom. utique rej.*
"Habitat in Europae rupibus." RCN: 8158.
Type not designated.
Original material: none traced.
Note: Specific epithet spelled "atro-virens" in the protologue.
See discussion by Jørgensen & al. (in *Bot. J. Linn. Soc.* 115: 277. 1994), who concluded that the name is a *nomen non satis nota* and (in *Taxon* 43: 647. 1994) successfully proposed the rejection of the name.

Lichen barbatus Linnaeus, *Species Plantarum* 2: 1155. 1753.
"Habitat in Europae & Americae septentrionalis sylvis fagetis." RCN: 8246.
Lectotype (Jørgensen & al. in *Bot. J. Linn. Soc.* 115: 280, f. 7. 1994): [icon] *"Usnea barbata, loris tenuibus fibrosis"* in Dillenius, Hist. Musc.: 63, t. 12, f. 6. 1741. – Voucher: Herb. Dillenius (OXF). – Epitype (Jørgensen & al. in *Bot. J. Linn. Soc.* 115: 372. 1994): Sweden. Västmanland, Kila par., torpruin SO om Granmuren, 20 Jul 1982, *I. Nordin s.n.* (UPS).
Current name: ***Usnea barbata*** (L.) Weber ex F.H. Wigg. (Parmeliaceae).

Lichen burgessii Linnaeus, *Systema Vegetabilium*, ed. 13: 807. 1774.
RCN: 8194.
Lectotype (Jørgensen & al. in *Bot. J. Linn. Soc.* 115: 281, f. 10. 1994): *Burgess*, Herb. Linn. No. 1273.91, left specimen (LINN).
Current name: ***Leptogium burgessii*** (L.) Mont. (Collemataceae).

Lichen byssoides Linnaeus, *Systema Naturae*, ed. 12, 2: 709; *Mantissa Plantarum*: 133. 1767, *nom. cons.*
"Habitat in Europae glareosis." RCN: 8159.
Conserved type (Jørgensen & al. in *Taxon* 43: 649. 1994): Herb. Linn. No. 1273.2 (LINN).
Current name: ***Baeomyces rufus*** (Huds.) Rebent. (Baeomycetaceae).
Note: See extensive discussion in Jørgensen & al. (in *Bot. J. Linn. Soc.* 115: 281. 1994). They concluded that all original elements are in conflict with the protologue, but successfully proposed the name for conservation with a conserved type.

Lichen calcareus Linnaeus, *Species Plantarum* 2: 1140. 1753, *nom. cons.*

"Habitat in Europae rupibus marmoreis." RCN: 8167.

Conserved type (Jørgensen & al. in *Taxon* 43: 650. 1994): Sweden. Gotland, Visby, 26 Jun 1918, *Malme*, Lich. Suec. Exsicc. No. 772 (UPS).

Current name: ***Aspicilia calcarea*** (L.) Körb. (Hymeneliaceae).

Note: See discussion by Jørgensen & al. (in *Bot. J. Linn. Soc.* 115: 283. 1994), who concluded that none of the original elements agreed with current usage, and successfully proposed the name for conservation, with a conserved type.

Lichen calicaris Linnaeus, *Species Plantarum* 2: 1146. 1753, *nom. cons.*

"Habitat in Europae arboribus, rupibus." RCN: 8203.

Conserved type (Jørgensen & al. in *Taxon* 43: 650. 1994): Herb. Dillenius t. 23, No. 62B (OXF).

Current name: ***Ramalina calicaris*** (L.) Fr. (Ramalinaceae).

Note: See extensive discussion by Jørgensen & al. (in *Bot. J. Linn. Soc.* 115: 283–285. 1994). Howe (in *Bryologist* 16: 83. 1913) had typified the name on 1273.15 (LINN), a specimen of *Ramalina siliquosa* (Huds.) A.L. Sm. Jørgensen & al. successfully proposed the name for conservation with a conserved type.

Lichen candelarius Linnaeus, *Species Plantarum* 2: 1141. 1753.

"Habitat in Europae parietibus, muris, truncis arborum, praesertim Quercus." RCN: 8175.

Neotype (Santesson in *Thunbergia* 2: 10. 1986): Sweden. Öland, Böda, Mensalvaret, 3 Aug 1983, *R. Santesson & T. Tönsberg* (Lich. Sel. Exs. Ups. 25) (UPS).

Current name: ***Xanthoria candelaria*** (L.) Th. Fr. (Teloschistaceae).

Note: See review by Jørgensen & al. (in *Bot. J. Linn. Soc.* 115: 285, 373. 1994).

Lichen caninus Linnaeus, *Species Plantarum* 2: 1149. 1753.

"Habitat in Europae sylvis, juxta lapides, in terra. terrestris." RCN: 8217.

Lectotype (Howe in *Bull. Torrey Bot. Club.* 39: 201. 1912): *Magnol*, Herb. Linn. No. 1273.184 (LINN).

Current name: ***Peltigera canina*** (L.) Willd. (Peltigeraceae).

Note: Jørgensen & al. (in *Bot. J. Linn. Soc.* 115: 285. 1994) accepted Howe's choice of lectotype but noted that the type (their f. 12) belongs to *Peltigera praetextata* (Flörke ex Sommerf.) Zopf. Accordingly, they stated (pp. 286, 373) that a proposal for the conservation of the name with a conserved type (Germany, Flörke, Deutsche lich. 153 (UPS)) was to be made by Vitikainen in 1994, also noted by the latter (in *Acta Bot. Fenn.* 152: 30. 1994). However, this proposal does not appear to have been published.

Lichen caperatus Linnaeus, *Species Plantarum* 2: 1147. 1753.

"Habitat in Europa & America ad saxa & arbores." RCN: 8208.

Lectotype (Mattsson in *Opera Bot.* 119: 41. 1993): [icon] *"Lichenoides caperatum, rosacee expansum e sulphureo virens"* in Dillenius, Hist. Musc.: 193, t. 25, f. 97. 1741. – Epitype (Jørgensen & al. in *Bot. J. Linn. Soc.* 115: 287, 373. 1994): Herb. Dillenius Tab. XXV, sheet 97B (OXF).

Current name: ***Flavoparmelia caperata*** (L.) Hale (Parmeliaceae).

Note: Jørgensen & al. (in *Bot. J. Linn. Soc.* 115: 286, 373. 1994), unaware of Mattsson's earlier choice, independently designated the same Dillenius illustration as lectotype. However, their epitype choice stands.

Lichen carpineus Linnaeus, *Species Plantarum* 2: 1141. 1753.

"Habitat in Carpini truncis, ramis." RCN: 8172.

Lectotype (Jørgensen & al. in *Bot. J. Linn. Soc.* 115: 287, f. 13. 1994): Herb. Linn. No. 1273.18, largest (lower) specimen (LINN).

Current name: ***Lecanora carpinea*** (L.) Vain. (Lecanoraceae).

Lichen centrifugus Linnaeus, *Species Plantarum* 2: 1142. 1753.

"Habitat in Europae frigidae rupibus. rupestris." RCN: 8182.

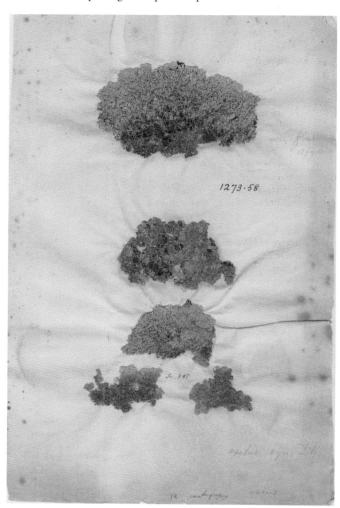

1273·58

Lectotype (Howe in *Bull. Torrey Bot. Club* 39: 201. 1912; Jørgensen & al. in *Bot. J. Linn. Soc.* 115: 288, f. 14. 1994): Herb. Linn. No. 1273.58, upper specimen (LINN).

Current name: ***Arctoparmelia centrifuga*** (L.) Hale (Parmeliaceae).

Note: Jørgensen & al. (in *Bot. J. Linn. Soc.* 115: 288, 373, f. 14. 1994) restricted Howe's original type choice to one of the specimens on the sheet.

Lichen chalybeiformis Linnaeus, *Species Plantarum* 2: 1155. 1753, *nom. cons.*

"Habitat in Europa supra rupes & sepimenta." RCN: 8252.

Conserved type (Jørgensen & al. in *Taxon* 43: 650. 1994): Herb. Linn. No. 1273.291 (LINN).

Current name: ***Bryoria chalybeiformis*** (L.) Brodo & D. Hawksw. (Parmeliaceae).

Note: See discussion by Jørgensen & al. (in *Bot. J. Linn. Soc.* 115: 290, f. 15. 1994). They accepted that Howe (in *Bull. Torrey Bot. Club* 39: 201. 1912) typified the name on 1273.290 (LINN), but as this is a specimen of *B. fuscescens* (Gyeln.) Brodo & D. Hawksw., they successfully proposed the name for conservation with a conserved type.

Lichen chrysophthalmos Linnaeus, *Mantissa Plantarum Altera*: 311. 1771.
"Habitat in Cap. b. spei rupibus." RCN: 8193.
Lectotype (Howe in *Bull. Torrey Bot. Club* 39: 201. 1912): Herb. Linn. No. 1273.89 (LINN).
Current name: *Teloschistes chrysophthalmus* (L.) Th. Fr. (Teloschistaceae).
Note: Specific epithet spelled "chrysophtalmos" in the protologue. See review by Jørgensen & al. (in *Bot. J. Linn. Soc.* 115: 291, 374, f. 16. 1994).

Lichen ciliaris Linnaeus, *Species Plantarum* 2: 1144. 1753.
"Habitat in Europae arboribus. arboreus." RCN: 8195.
Lectotype (Howe in *Bull. Torrey Bot. Club* 39: 201. 1912; Jørgensen & al. in *Bot. J. Linn. Soc.* 115: 292, f. 17. 1994): Herb. Linn. No. 1273.92, upper specimen (LINN).
Current name: *Anaptychia ciliaris* (L.) Körb. (Physciaceae).
Note: Jørgensen & al. (in *Bot. J. Linn. Soc.* 115: 292, 374, f. 17. 1994) restricted Howe's original type choice to one of the specimens on the sheet.

Lichen cinereus Linnaeus, *Systema Naturae,* ed. 12, 2: 709; *Mantissa Plantarum*: 132. 1767.
"Habitat ubique in rupibus, saxis." RCN: 8168.
Neotype (Jørgensen & al. in *Bot. J. Linn. Soc.* 115: 294, 374. 1994): Switzerland. Mount Belpberg, *Schaerer Lich. Helv. Exs. 127* (UPS).
Current name: *Aspicilia cinerea* (L.) Körb. (Hymeneliaceae).

Lichen cocciferus Linnaeus, *Species Plantarum* 2: 1151. 1753.
"Habitat in Europae sylvis sterilibus, ericetis, rupibus." RCN: 8230.
Lectotype (Jørgensen & al. in *Bot. J. Linn. Soc.* 115: 294, 374, f. 18. 1994): Herb. Linn. No. 1273.215, top specimen (LINN).
Current name: *Cladonia coccifera* (L.) Willd. (Cladoniaceae).

Lichen corallinus Linnaeus, *Systema Naturae,* ed. 12, 2: 709; *Mantissa Plantarum*: 131. 1767.
"Habitat in Sveciae rupibus. Zoega." RCN: 8173.
Neotype (Jørgensen & al. in *Bot. J. Linn. Soc.* 115: 296, 374. 1994): Herb. Linn. No. 1273.17 (LINN).
Current name: *Pertusaria corallina* (L.) Arnold (Pertusariaceae).

Lichen cornucopioides Linnaeus, *Species Plantarum* 2: 1151. 1753, *nom. utique rej.*
"Habitat in Lapponiae, Sueciae, Angliae sylvis glareosis." RCN: 8231.
Lectotype (Jørgensen & al. in *Bot. J. Linn. Soc.* 115: 296, f. 19. 1994): Herb. Linn. No. 1273.217, young podetium (LINN).
Current name: *Cladonia cornuta* (L.) Hoffm. (Cladoniaceae).
Note: The lectotype is a young specimen of the difficult *Cladonia cornuta* (L.) Hoffm. complex, and which could have displaced *C. groenlandica* (E. Dahl) Trass. Jørgensen & al. (in *Taxon* 43: 648. 1994) successfully proposed the name for rejection.

Lichen cornutus Linnaeus, *Species Plantarum* 2: 1152. 1753.
"Habitat in Europae ericetis." RCN: 8236.
Lectotype (Ahti in Greuter, *Regnum Veg.* 128: 73. 1993): Herb. Linn. No. 1273.223, lower specimen (LINN).
Current name: *Cladonia cornuta* (L.) Hoffm. (Cladoniaceae).
Note: See discussion by Jørgensen & al. (in *Bot. J. Linn. Soc.* 115: 297–298. 1994), who also illustrate the type (f. 20).

Lichen cristatus Linnaeus, *Species Plantarum* 2: 1143. 1753, *nom. cons.*

"Habitat in Europa australi." RCN: 8189.
Conserved type (Jørgensen & al. in *Taxon* 43: 651. 1994): Italy. Trentino, Cortina d'Ampezzo, Pocol, 1948, *G. Degelius* (UPS).
Current name: *Collema cristatum* (L.) Weber ex F.H. Wigg. (Collemataceae).
Note: Degelius (in *Symb. Bot. Upsal.* 13(2): 308. 1954) designated a neotype (contrary to Art. 9.11 because original material, the Dillenius figure, was in existence). The latter was the sole available element and was therefore designated as lectotype, along with an epitype, by Jørgensen & al. (in *Bot. J. Linn. Soc.* 115: 299. 1994). Unfortunately, the type belongs to *Collema tenax* (Sw.) Ach., so these authors successfully proposed the conservation of the name with Degelius' neotype as the conserved type.

Lichen crocatus Linnaeus, *Mantissa Plantarum Altera*: 310. 1771.
"Habitat in India. Koenig." RCN: 8209.
Lectotype (Howe in *Bull. Torrey Bot. Club* 39: 201. 1912): *König s.n.*, Herb. Linn. No. 1273.137 (LINN).
Current name: *Pseudocyphellaria crocata* (L.) Vain. (Lobariaceae).
Note: See review by Jørgensen & al. (in *Bot. J. Linn. Soc.* 115: 299, f. 21. 1994).

Lichen croceus Linnaeus, *Species Plantarum* 2: 1149. 1753.
"Habitat in Lapponia, Helvetia, Groenlandia. terrestris." RCN: 8222.
Lectotype (Howe, *Bull. Torrey Bot. Club.* 39: 201. 1912): Herb. Linn. No. 1273.189 (LINN).
Current name: *Solorina crocea* (L.) Ach. (Peltigeraceae).
Note: See review by Jørgensen & al. (in *Bot. J. Linn. Soc.* 115: 299–300, f. 22. 1994).

Lichen cylindricus Linnaeus, *Species Plantarum* 2: 1144. 1753, *nom. cons.*
"Habitat in Pensylvania, Lapponia. D. Montin." RCN: 8226.
Conserved type (Jørgensen & al. in *Taxon* 43: 651. 1994): Sweden. ad flumen Kamajock, prope Qvickjock (= Kvikkjokk) Lapponiae Lulensis, 1871, *P.J. & E.V.M. Hellbom* (UPS).
Current name: *Umbilicaria cylindrica* (L.) Delise ex Duby (Umbiliculariaceae).
Note: Jørgensen & al. (in *Bot. J. Linn. Soc.* 115: 301–302. 1994) provided a detailed investigation, and concluded that the only extant original element, that of Dillenius (see their f. 23), is based on material of *Parmotrema perforata* (Jacq.) Hale. They successfully proposed the conservation of the name with a conserved type.

Lichen deformis Linnaeus, *Species Plantarum* 2: 1152. 1753.
"Habitat in Europae ericetis." RCN: 8237.
Lectotype (Jørgensen & al. in *Bot. J. Linn. Soc.* 115: 303, f. 24. 1994): [icon] *"Lichen caule simplici apice acuto aut calice turbinato terminato"* in Linnaeus, Fl. Lapponica: 330, t. 11, f. 5 [right specimen]. 1737. – Epitype (Jørgensen & al. in *Bot. J. Linn. Soc.* 115: 375. 1994): Sweden. Uppland, Värmdön, Hasseludden, 1915, *G.O.A. Malme* (Malme Lich. Suec. Exs. 533) (S).
Current name: *Cladonia deformis* (L.) Hoffm. (Cladoniaceae).

Lichen deustus Linnaeus, *Species Plantarum* 2: 1150. 1753, *nom. cons.*
"Habitat in Sueciae, Galliae rupibus s. cautibus apricis. rupestris." RCN: 8227.
Conserved type (Jørgensen & al. in *Taxon* 43: 651. 1994): Sweden. Närke, Örebro, *Hellbom* in Rabenhorst, Exsicc. No. 812 (UPS).
Current name: *Umbilicaria deusta* (L.) Baumg. (Umbiliculariaceae).
Note: See discussion by Jørgensen & al. (in *Bot. J. Linn. Soc.* 115: 303–304. 1994). Howe (in *Bull. Torrey Bot. Club* 39: 201. 1912) chose 1273.206 (LINN) as lectotype (see Jørgensen & al.: f. 25), but unfortunately this belongs to *Umbilicaria proboscidea* Ach. non

L

L. Wei (in *Suppl. Mycosyst.* 5: 13. 1993) has introduced an illegitimate *nomen novum* for it, and taken up *U. flocculosa* Hoffm. for *U. deusta* auct. Jørgensen & al. successfully proposed the name for conservation with a conserved type.

Lichen digitatus Linnaeus, *Species Plantarum* 2: 1152. 1753, *nom. cons.*
"Habitat in Europae sylvis sterilibus." RCN: 8235.
Conserved type (Jørgensen & al. in *Taxon* 43: 652. 1994): Sweden. Ostrogothia, *Stenhammar* in Lich. Suec. Exsicc. No. 195 (UPS).
Current name: ***Cladonia digitata*** (L.) Hoffm. (Cladoniaceae).
Note: See discussion by Jørgensen & al. (in *Bot. J. Linn. Soc.* 304–305. 1994). The only extant original element is that of Dillenius, which represents *Cladonia floerkiana* (Fr.) Flörke. In order to avoid a change of name, Jørgensen & al. successfully proposed the conservation of the name with a conserved type.

Lichen divaricatus Linnaeus, *Systema Naturae,* ed. 12, 2: 713. 1767.
"Habitat in Helvetiae, Missniae cacuminibus Arborum acifoliarum. D. Schreber." RCN: 8247.
Lectotype (Howe in *Bull. Torrey Bot. Club* 39: 201. 1912; Jørgensen & al. in *Bot. J. Linn. Soc.* 115: 305, f. 26. 1994): *Schreber,* Herb. Linn. No. 1273.277, extreme right specimen (LINN).
Current name: ***Evernia divaricata*** (L.) Ach. (Parmeliaceae).
Note: Jørgensen & al. (in *Bot. J. Linn. Soc.* 115: 305, 375, f. 26. 1994) restricted Howe's original type choice to one of the specimens on the sheet.

Lichen ericetorum Linnaeus, *Species Plantarum* 2: 1141. 1753.
"Habitat in Europae sylvis sterilissimis, glareosis subnudis, uliginosis." RCN: 8174.
Lectotype (Howe in *Bull. Torrey Bot. Club* 39: 201. 1912): Herb. Linn. No. 1273.19 (LINN).
Current name: ***Icmadophila ericetorum*** (L.) Zahlbr. (Icmadophilaceae).
Note: See review by Jørgensen & al. (in *Bot. J. Linn. Soc.* 115: 305, f. 27. 1994).

Lichen fagineus Linnaeus, *Species Plantarum* 2: 1141. 1753, *nom. utique rej.*
"Habitat in Europa, vestiens truncos Fagi." RCN: 8171.
Type not designated.
Original material: none traced.
Note: See Jørgensen & al. (in *Bot. J. Linn. Soc.* 115: 307. 1994) who, noting that the name has been applied to a number of grey, sorediate, crustose species, treated this as a *nomen non satis nota* and successfully proposed (in *Taxon* 43: 647. 1994) it for rejection.

Lichen fahlunensis Linnaeus, *Species Plantarum* 2: 1143. 1753, *nom. utique rej.*
"Habitat in Europae rupibus nudis. rupestris." RCN: 8186.
Lectotype (Jørgensen & al. in *Bot. J. Linn. Soc.* 115: 308. 1994): Herb. Linn. No. 1273.70 (LINN).
Current name: ***Melanelia stygia*** (L.) Essl. (Parmeliaceae).
Note: See discussion by Jørgensen & al. (in *Bot. J. Linn. Soc.* 307–309, f. 28. 1994). The type of this name is a specimen of *Melanelia stygia* (L.) Essl. When combined in the same species, "fahlunensis" has priority over the well-known "stygius". In order to avoid a confusing name change, Jørgensen & al. (in *Taxon* 43: 648. 1994) successfully proposed the rejection of the name.

Lichen farinaceus Linnaeus, *Species Plantarum* 2: 1146. 1753.
"Habitat in Europae arboribus, praesertim Quercetis Fraxinetis." RCN: 8202.

Lectotype (Howe in *Bull. Torrey Bot. Club* 39: 201. 1912; Hawksworth in *Bryologist* 72: 255. 1969): Herb. Linn. No. 1273.110, lowest specimen (LINN).
Current name: ***Ramalina farinacea*** (L.) Ach. (Ramalinaceae).
Note: See discussion by Jørgensen & al. (in *Bot. J. Linn. Soc.* 115: 309, 375, f. 29. 1994). Howe's original type choice was subsequently restricted to one specimen by Hawksworth.

Lichen fascicularis Linnaeus, *Systema Naturae,* ed. 12, 2: 711; *Mantissa Plantarum*: 133. 1767.
"Habitat in Susexia Angliae. Dill. ad Stenbrohult Smolandiae. Filius." RCN: 8211.
Lectotype (Howe in *Bull. Torrey Bot. Club* 39: 201. 1912): Herb. Linn. No. 1273.141 (LINN).
Current name: ***Collema fasciculare*** (L.) Weber ex F.H. Wigg. (Collemataceae).
Note: See discussion by Jørgensen & al. (in *Bot. J. Linn. Soc.* 115: 309, f. 30. 1994).

Lichen fimbriatus Linnaeus, *Species Plantarum* 2: 1152. 1753.
"Habitat in Europae sylvis sterilibus." RCN: 8233.
Lectotype (Ahti in Greuter, *Regnum Veg.* 128: 77. 1993): [icon] *"Coralloides scyphiforme gracile, marginibus serratis"* in Dillenius, Hist. Musc.: 84, t. 14, f. 8. 1741. – Epitype (Jørgensen & al. in *Bot. J. Linn. Soc.* 115: 311, 376. 1994): Herb. Dillenius Tab. XIV, No. 8, lower row, first specimen to the left (OXF).
Current name: ***Cladonia fimbriata*** (L.) Fr. (Cladoniaceae).

Lichen floridus Linnaeus, *Species Plantarum* 2: 1156. 1753.
"Habitat in Europae fagetis." RCN: 8256.
Lectotype (Howe in *Bull. Torrey Bot. Club* 39: 201. 1912; Clerc in *Cryptog. Bryol. Lichénol.* 5: 346. 1984): Herb. Linn. No. 1273.300, lowermost specimen (LINN).
Current name: ***Usnea florida*** (L.) Weber ex F.H. Wigg. (Parmeliaceae).
Note: See discussion by Jørgensen & al. (in *Bot. J. Linn. Soc.* 115: 311, f. 31. 1994). Howe's original type choice was subsequently restricted to one specimen by Clerc.

Lichen fragilis Linnaeus, *Species Plantarum* 2: 1154. 1753.
"Habitat in Europae alpibus alpinisque, per Sueciam in rupibus." RCN: 8243.
Lectotype (Howe in *Bull. Torrey Bot. Club* 39: 201. 1912; Wedin in *Pl. Syst. Evol.* 187: 229, f. 2. 1993): Herb. Linn. No. 1273.261, uppermost specimen (LINN).
Current name: ***Sphaerophorus fragilis*** (L.) Pers. (Sphaerophoraceae).
Note: See review by Jørgensen & al. (in *Bot. J. Linn. Soc.* 115: 312–313, f. 32. 1994). Howe's original type choice was subsequently restricted to one specimen by Wedin.

Lichen fraxineus Linnaeus, *Species Plantarum* 2: 1146. 1753.
"Habitat in Europae Arboribus, praesertim Faxinis. arboreus." RCN: 8204.
Lectotype (Howe in *Bull. Torrey Bot. Club* 39: 201. 1912; Krog & James in *Norweg. J. Bot.* 24: 33. 1977): Herb. Linn. No. 1273.121, specimen B (LINN).
Current name: ***Ramalina fraxinea*** (L.) Ach. (Ramalinaceae).
Note: See discussion by Jørgensen & al. (in *Bot. J. Linn. Soc.* 115: 314, 376, f. 33. 1994). Howe's original type choice was subsequently restricted to one specimen by Krog & James.

Lichen fuciformis Linnaeus, *Species Plantarum* 2: 1147. 1753.
"Habitat in India, Canariis." RCN: 8205.

Lectotype (Jørgensen & al. in *Bot. J. Linn. Soc.* 115: 314. 1994): [icon] *"Lichenoides fuciforme tinctorium, corniculis longioribus & acutioribus"* in Dillenius, Hist. Musc.: 168, t. 22, f. 61. 1741. – Epitype (Jørgensen & al. in *Bot. J. Linn. Soc.* 115: 314, 376. 1994): Herb. Dillenius Tab. XXII, No. 61, central specimen (OXF).
Current name: **Roccella fuciformis** (L.) DC. (Roccellaceae).

Lichen furfuraceus Linnaeus, *Species Plantarum* 2: 1146. 1753.
"Habitat in Europae arboribus. arboreus." RCN: 8199.
Lectotype (Howe in *Bull. Torrey Bot. Club* 39: 201. 1912; Hawksworth & Chapman in *Lichenologist* 4: 51. 1971): Herb. Linn. No. 1273.107, central specimen (LINN).
Current name: **Pseudevernia furfuracea** (L.) Zopf (Parmeliaceae).
Note: See review by Jørgensen & al. (in *Bot. J. Linn. Soc.* 115: 314–317, 376, f. 34. 1994). Howe's original type choice was subsequently restricted to one specimen by Hawksworth & Chapman.

Lichen fuscoater Linnaeus, *Species Plantarum* 2: 1140. 1753.
"Habitat in Europae rupibus." RCN: 8165.
Neotype (Hertel, *Khumbu Himal, Ergebn. Forsch. Nepal Himal.* 6: 244. 1977): Sweden. Uppland, Uppsala, Vårdsätra, NE-SE of the mouth of the river Hågåå, 17 May 1964, *R. Santesson 16299* (UPS).
Current name: **Lecidea fuscoatra** (L.) Ach. (Lecidiaceae).
Note: Specific epithet spelled "fusco-ater" in the protologue.
See review by Jørgensen & al. (in *Bot. J. Linn. Soc.* 115: 317, 376. 1994).

Lichen gelidus Linnaeus, *Systema Naturae,* ed. 12, 2: 709; *Mantissa Plantarum:* 133. 1767.
"Habitat in Islandiae saxis. König." RCN: 8176.
Neotype (Jørgensen & al. in *Bot. J. Linn. Soc.* 115: 317, 376. 1994): Iceland. Kjosarsysla, Reykir, 29 Jun 1937, *B. Lynge* (O).
Current name: **Placopsis gelida** (L.) Linds. (Trapeliaceae).

Lichen geographicus Linnaeus, *Species Plantarum* 2: 1140. 1753.
"Habitat in Europae rupibus altis." RCN: 8157.
Lectotype (Hawksworth & Sowter in *Trans. Leicester Lit. Phil. Soc.* 63: 58. 1969): [icon] *"Lichenoides nigro-flavum, tabulae Geographicae instar pictum"* in Dillenius, Hist. Musc.: 126, t. 18, f. 5. 1741. – Epitype (Jørgensen & al. in *Bot. J. Linn. Soc.* 115: 318, 376. 1994): Herb. Dillenius Tab. XVIII, No. 5 (UPS).
Current name: **Rhizocarpon geographicum** (L.) DC. (Rhizocarpaceae).
Note: See review by Jørgensen & al. (in *Bot. J. Linn. Soc.* 115: 317, 377. 1994).

Lichen glaucus Linnaeus, *Species Plantarum* 2: 1148. 1753.
"Habitat in Europae frigidae, presertim Sueciae, truncis Betulinis. arboreus." RCN: 8210.
Lectotype (Howe in *Bull. Torrey Bot. Club* 39: 201. 1912; Jørgensen & al. in *Bot. J. Linn. Soc.* 115: 318, f. 35. 1994): Herb. Linn. No. 1273.139, lower specimen (LINN).
Current name: **Platismatia glauca** (L.) W.L. Culb. & C.F. Culb. (Parmeliaceae).
Note: Jørgensen & al. (in *Bot. J. Linn. Soc.* 115: 318, 377, f. 35. 1994) restricted Howe's original type choice to one of the specimens on the sheet.

Lichen globiferus Linnaeus, *Systema Naturae,* ed. 12, 2: 713; *Mantissa Plantarum:* 133. 1767, *nom. illeg.*
"Habitat in Tingitana. Pluk. in Anglia. Dill. Stenbrohult Smolandiae. Filius." RCN: 8241.
Replaced synonym: *Lichen globosus* Huds. (1762).

Lectotype (Wedin in *Pl. Syst. Evol.* 187: 230. 1993): [icon] *"Coralloides cupressiforme, capitulis globosis"* in Dillenius, Hist. Musc.: 117, t. 17, f. 35. 1741. – Voucher: Herb. Dillenius (OXF).
Current name: **Sphaerophorus globosus** (Huds.) Vain. (Sphaerophoraceae).
Note: Linnaeus explicitly cited as a synonym the validly published *Lichen globosus* Huds. (1762) in *Syst. Nat.* ed. 12, but not in the *Mantissa* account. This was overlooked by Jørgensen & al. (in *Bot. J. Linn. Soc.* 115: 318, 377, f. 36. 1994), who accepted Howe's typification (in *Bull. Torrey Bot. Club* 39: 201. 1912) using 1273.251 (LINN). However, Linnaeus' name must be homotypic with that of Hudson, which has been typified by Wedin (in *Pl. Syst. Evol.* 187: 230–231. 1993).

Lichen gracilis Linnaeus, *Species Plantarum* 2: 1152. 1753.
"Habitat in Europae ericetis montosis, sylvaticis." RCN: 8234.
Lectotype (Ahti in Greuter, *Regnum Veg.* 128: 79. 1993): [icon] *"Coralloides scyphiforme serratum elatius, caulibus gracilibus glabris"* in Dillenius, Hist. Musc.: 88, t. 14, f. 13. 1741. – Epitype (Jørgensen & al. in *Bot. J. Linn. Soc.* 115: 377. 1994): Herb. Dillenius Tab. XIV, No. 13C (OXF).
Current name: **Cladonia gracilis** (L.) Willd. (Cladoniaceae).
Note: See review by Jørgensen & al. (in *Bot. J. Linn. Soc.* 115: 319, 377. 1994).

Lichen hirtus Linnaeus, *Species Plantarum* 2: 1155. 1753, *nom. cons.*
"Habitat in Europae arboribus, sepimentis." RCN: 8253.
Conserved type (Jørgensen & al. in *Taxon* 43: 652. 1994): Sweden. Fries, Lich. Suec. Exsicc. No. 150 (UPS).
Current name: **Usnea hirta** (L.) Weber ex F.H. Wigg. (Parmeliaceae).
Note: See review by Jørgensen & al. (in *Bot. J. Linn. Soc.* 115: 320–322, 377, f. 37. 1994), who concluded that the only original elements (those of Dillenius) belong to various species of *Usnea*, but none of them to *U. hirta.* The same authors successfully proposed the name for conservation with a conserved type.

Lichen islandicus Linnaeus, *Species Plantarum* 2: 1145. 1753.
"Habitat in Europae sylvis sterilissimis, Pinetis. terrestris." RCN: 8196.
Lectotype (Howe in *Bull. Torrey Bot. Club* 39: 201. 1912; Kärnefelt in *Opera Bot.* 46: 98. 1979): Herb. Linn. No. 1273.97, lowermost specimen (LINN).
Current name: **Cetraria islandica** (L.) Ach. (Parmeliaceae).
Note: See review by Jørgensen & al. (in *Bot. J. Linn. Soc.* 115: 322, 377, f. 38. 1994). Howe's original type choice was subsequently restricted to one specimen by Kärnefelt.

Lichen islandicus Linnaeus var. **tenuissimus** Linnaeus, *Species Plantarum* 2: 1145. 1753.
"Habitat frequens in sterilissimis collibus Sueciae." RCN: 8196.
Lectotype (Howe in *Bull. Torrey Bot. Club* 39: 201. 1912): Herb. Linn. No. 1273.100 (LINN).
Current name: **Coelocaulon aculeatum** (Schreb.) Link (Parmeliaceae).
Note: See review by Jørgensen & al. (in *Bot. J. Linn. Soc.* 115: 322, 377, f. 39. 1994).

Lichen jubatus Linnaeus, *Species Plantarum* 2: 1155. 1753, *nom. utique rej.*
"Habitat in Europae sylvis & rupibus." RCN: 8249.
Lectotype (Hawksworth in *Taxon* 19: 238. 1970): Herb. Linn. No. 1273.281, left specimen (LINN).
Note: The type is a specimen of *Bryoria fremontii* (Tuck.) Brodo & D. Hawksw. which led to the formal rejection of *L. jubatus.* See review by Jørgensen & al. (in *Bot. J. Linn. Soc.* 115: 324, 377, f. 40. 1994).

L

Lichen juniperinus Linnaeus, *Species Plantarum* 2: 1147. 1753, *nom. cons.*
"Habitat in Europae juniperetis. arboreus." RCN: 8207.
Conserved type (Howe in *Bull. Torrey Bot. Club* 39: 201. 1912; Mattsson in *Taxon* 43: 655. 1994): Sweden. Härjedalen, Storsjö, Flatruet W of Falkvålen, 2 Aug 1991, *Mattsson 2340* (LD; iso- H, HMAS, LE, M, O, TNS, US).
Current name: ***Vulpicida juniperina*** (L.) Mattsson & M.J. Lai (Parmeliaceae).
Note: The lectotype (1273.128 LINN) of this name is a specimen of *Vulpicida tubulosus* (Schaer.) Mattsson & Lai; see detailed reviews by Mattsson (in *Opera Bot.* 119: 35–37. 1993) and Jørgensen & al. (in *Bot. J. Linn. Soc.* 115: 324–326, f. 41. 1994.) Mattsson successfully proposed the conservation of the name with a conserved type.

Lichen lacteus Linnaeus, *Systema Naturae,* ed. 12, 2: 709; *Mantissa Plantarum*: 132. 1767.
"Habitat ubique in rupibus, saxis. Zoega." RCN: 8160.
Neotype (Jørgensen & al. in *Bot. J. Linn. Soc.* 115: 326, 378. 1994): Sweden. Västergötland, Mularp, Stommen, 6 Aug 1922, *E.P. Vrang* (Malme Lich. Suec. Exs. 848) (UPS).
Current name: ***Pertusaria lactea*** (L.) Arnold (Pertusariaceae).

Lichen lanatus Linnaeus, *Species Plantarum* 2: 1155. 1753.
"Habitat in Europae frigidae rupibus." RCN: 8250.
Lectotype (Howe in *Bull. Torrey Bot. Club* 39: 201. 1912): *Löfling 89*, Herb. Linn. No. 1273.284 (LINN).
Current name: ***Ephebe lanata*** (L.) Vain. (Lichinaceae).
Note: See detailed review by Jørgensen & al. (in *Bot. J. Linn. Soc.* 115: 326–328, 378, f. 42. 1994).

Lichen leucomelos Linnaeus, *Species Plantarum,* ed. 2, 2: 1613. 1763.
"Habitat in America meridionali." RCN: 8201.
Lectotype (Swinscow & Krog in *Norweg. J. Bot.* 23: 124. 1976): Herb. Linn. No. 1273.109 (LINN).
Current name: ***Heterodermia leucomelaena*** (L.) Poelt (Physciaceae).
Note: See review by Jørgensen & al. (in *Bot. J. Linn. Soc.* 115: 329, 378, f. 43. 1994).

Lichen miniatus Linnaeus, *Species Plantarum* 2: 1149. 1753.
"Habitat in Angliae, Helvetiae, Italiae, rupibus alpinis." RCN: 8223.
Lectotype (Jørgensen & al. in *Bot. J. Linn. Soc.* 115: 330. 1994): [icon] *"Lichenoides coriaceum nebulosum cinereum punctatum, subtus fulvum"* in Dillenius, Hist. Musc.: 223, t. 30, f. 127. 1741. – Epitype (Jørgensen & al. in *Bot. J. Linn. Soc.* 115: 330, 378. 1994): Herb. Dillenius Tab. XXX, No. 127B (OXF).
Current name: ***Dermatocarpon miniatum*** (L.) W. Mann (Verrucariaceae).

Lichen nivalis Linnaeus, *Species Plantarum* 2: 1145. 1753.
"Habitat in Lapponiae, Upsaliae, Gronlandiae alpinis, apricis, siccis, glareosis. terrestris." RCN: 8197.
Lectotype (Howe in *Bull. Torrey Bot. Club* 39: 201. 1912; Jørgensen & al. in *Bot. J. Linn. Soc.* 115: 330, f. 44. 1994): Herb. Linn. No. 1273.101, lower left specimen (LINN).
Current name: ***Cetraria nivalis*** (L.) Ach. (Parmeliaceae).
Note: Jørgensen & al. (in *Bot. J. Linn. Soc.* 115: 330, 378, f. 44. 1994) restricted Howe's original type choice to one of the specimens on the sheet.

Lichen olivaceus Linnaeus, *Species Plantarum* 2: 1143. 1753, *nom. cons.*
"Habitat in Europae rupibus. arboreus & rupestris." RCN: 8185.

Conserved type (Jørgensen & al. in *Taxon* 43: 652. 1994): Sweden. Härjedalen, Fjellnäs, *Vrang* in Crypt. Exsicc. Mus. Hist. Nat. Vindob. No. 3063 (UPS).
Current name: ***Melanohalea olivacea*** (L.) O. Blanco & al. (Parmeliaceae).
Note: Howe (in *Bull. Torrey Bot. Club* 37: 201. 1912) typified the name on 1273.66 (LINN), a collection of *Parmelia pulla* Ach. (see review by Jørgensen & al. in *Bot. J. Linn. Soc.* 115: 332, 378, f. 45. 1994). The same authors successfully proposed the name for conservation with a conserved type.

Lichen omphalodes Linnaeus, *Species Plantarum* 2: 1143. 1753.
"Habitat in Europae rupibus. rupestris & arboreus." RCN: 8184.
Lectotype (Jørgensen & al. in *Bot. J. Linn. Soc.* 115: 333. 1994): [icon] *"Lichenoides saxatile tinctorium, foliis pilosis purpureis"* in Dillenius, Hist. Musc.: 185, t. 24, f. 80 A. 1741. – Epitype (Jørgensen & al. in *Bot. J. Linn. Soc.* 115: 378. 1994): Herb. Dillenius Tab. XXIV, No. 80 (OXF).
Current name: ***Parmelia omphalodes*** (L.) Ach. (Parmeliaceae).

Lichen pallescens Linnaeus, *Species Plantarum* 2: 1142. 1753, *nom. cons.*
"Habitat in Europae corticibus arborum." RCN: 8178.
Conserved type (Jørgensen & al. in *Taxon* 43: 653. 1994): Sweden. Härjedalen, Ramundberget, NE of Kvarbäckstjärn, 27 Jun 1973, *R. Santesson 24384* (UPS).
Current name: ***Ochrolechia pallescens*** (L.) A. Massal. (Pertusariaceae).
Note: See extensive discussion by Jørgensen & al. (in *Bot. J. Linn. Soc.* 115: 333–334. 1994), who concluded that none of the original elements coincided with usage, and chose t. XVIII, f. 17 from Dillenius as lectotype. This represents *Lecanora dispersa* (Pers.) Sommerf., and the same authors successfully proposed the Linnaean name for conservation with a conserved type.

Lichen parellus Linnaeus, *Systema Naturae,* ed. 12, 2: 710; *Mantissa Plantarum*: 132. 1767.
"Habitat in Muris." RCN: 8180.
Lectotype (Jørgensen & al. in *Bot. J. Linn. Soc.* 115: 334. 1994): [icon] *"Lichenoides leprosum tinctorium, scutellis lapidum cancri figura"* in Dillenius, Hist. Musc.: 130, t. 18, f. 10. 1741. – Epitype (Jørgensen & al. in *Bot. J. Linn. Soc.* 115: 379. 1994): Herb. Dillenius Tab. XVIII, No. 10, lower central specimen (OXF).
Current name: ***Ochrolechia parella*** (L.) A. Massal. (Pertusariaceae).

Lichen parietinus Linnaeus, *Species Plantarum* 2: 1143. 1753.
"Habitat in Europae parietibus, rupibus, lignis. arboreus s. rupestris." RCN: 8190.
Lectotype (Jørgensen & al. in *Bot. J. Linn. Soc.* 115: 335, 379. 1994): [icon] *"Lichenoides vulgare sinuosum, foliis & scutellis luteis"* in Dillenius, Hist. Musc.: 180, t. 24, f. 76 A. 1741. – Epitype (Jørgensen & al. in *Bot. J. Linn. Soc.* 115: 379. 1994): Herb. Dillenius Tab. XXIV, f. 76A (OXF).
Current name: ***Xanthoria parietina*** (L.) Th. Fr. (Teloschistaceae).

Lichen paschalis Linnaeus, *Species Plantarum* 2: 1153. 1753.
"Habitat in Helvetiae, Italiae, Cambriae, Lapponiae, Scaniae, Groenlandiae, Pensylvaniae alpestribus." RCN: 8242.
Lectotype (Lamb in *J. Hattori Bot. Lab.* 43: 200. 1977): Herb. Linn. No. 1273.259, lowermost specimen (LINN).
Current name: ***Stereocaulon paschale*** (L.) Hoffm. (Stereocaulaceae).
Note: See extensive review by Jørgensen & al. (in *Bot. J. Linn. Soc.* 115: 335, 379, f. 46. 1994).

Lichen pertusus Linnaeus, *Systema Naturae,* ed. 12, 2: 709; *Mantissa Plantarum*: 131. 1767, *nom. illeg.*
"Habitat in Saxis & arboribus Europae. D. Fagraeus." RCN: 8162.
Replaced synonym: *Lichen verrucosus* Huds. (1762).
Lectotype (Jørgensen & al. in *Bot. J. Linn. Soc.* 115: 337, 379. 1994): [icon] *"Lichenoides verrucosum & rugosum, cinereum, glabrum"* in Dillenius, Hist. Musc.: 128, t. 18, f. 9 [pertusa element]. 1741. – Epitype (Jørgensen & al. in *Bot. J. Linn. Soc.* 115: 379. 1994): Herb. Dillenius Tab. XVIII, No. 9, upper central specimen (OXF).
Current name: ***Pertusaria pertusa*** (Weigel) Tucker (Pertusariaceae).
Note: An illegitimate replacement name for *Lichen verrucosus* Huds. (1762).

Lichen physodes Linnaeus, *Species Plantarum* 2: 1144. 1753.
"Habitat in Europae corticibus Betulae, & Saxis ac rupibus." RCN: 8191.
Lectotype (Howe in *Bull. Torrey Bot. Club* 39: 201. 1912; Jørgensen & al. in *Bot. J. Linn. Soc.* 115: 338, f. 47. 1994): Herb. Linn. No. 1273.77, lower specimen (LINN).
Current name: ***Hypogymnia physodes*** (L.) Nyl. (Parmeliaceae).
Note: Jørgensen & al. (in *Bot. J. Linn. Soc.* 115: 338, 379, f. 47. 1994) restricted Howe's original type choice to one of the specimens on the sheet.

Lichen plicatus Linnaeus, *Species Plantarum* 2: 1154. 1753, *nom. utique rej.*
"Habitat in Europae & Americae borealis sylvis densis umbrosisque fagetis." RCN: 8245.
Lectotype (Jørgensen & al. in *Bot. J. Linn. Soc.* 115: 339, 379. 1994): [icon] *"Usnea vulgaris, loris longis implexis"* in Dillenius, Hist. Musc.: 56, t. 11, f. 1. 1741. – Voucher: Herb. Dillenius (OXF).
Note: The type of this name belongs to *Usnea ceratina* Ach. To avoid an unfortunate name change, Jørgensen & al. (in *Taxon* 43: 648. 1994) successfully proposed the name for rejection.

Lichen polyphyllus Linnaeus, *Species Plantarum* 2: 1150. 1753.
"Habitat in Europae rupibus elatis apricis. rupestris." RCN: 8228.
Lectotype (Jørgensen & al. in *Bot. J. Linn. Soc.* 115: 340, 379. 1994): [icon] *"Lichenoides tenue pullum, foliis utrinque glabris"* in Dillenius, Hist. Musc.: 225, t. 30, f. 129. 1741. – Epitype (Jørgensen & al. in *Bot. J. Linn. Soc.* 115: 340, 379. 1994): Herb. Dillenius Tab. XXX, No. 129B (OXF).
Current name: ***Umbilicaria polyphylla*** (L.) Baumg. (Umbilicariaceae).

Lichen polyrhizos Linnaeus, *Species Plantarum* 2: 1151. 1753.
"Habitat in Arvoniae, Sveciae rupibus apricis elatis. rupestris." RCN: 8229.
Lectotype (Jørgensen & al. in *Bot. J. Linn. Soc.* 115: 340, 379. 1994): [icon] *"Lichenoides pullum superne & glabrum, inferne nigrum & cirrosum"* in Dillenius, Hist. Musc.: 226, t. 30, f. 130. 1741. – Epitype (Jørgensen & al. in *Bot. J. Linn. Soc.* 115: 340, 379. 1994): Herb. Dillenius Tab. XXX, No. 129, largest specimen (OXF).
Current name: ***Umbilicaria polyrhiza*** (L.) Fr. (Umbilicariaceae).

Lichen proboscideus Linnaeus, *Species Plantarum* 2: 1150. 1753, *nom. cons.*
"Habitat in Suecia." RCN: 8226.
Conserved type (Jørgensen & al. in *Taxon* 43: 653. 1994): Sweden. Uppland, Boo, Värmdö, Skepparholmen, 1906, *Malme* in Lich. Suec. Exsicc. No. 56 (UPS).
Current name: ***Umbilicaria proboscidea*** (L.) Schrad. (Umbilicariaceae).
Note: See discussion by Jørgensen & al. (in *Bot. J. Linn. Soc.* 115: 340–341, 379, f. 48. 1994), who conclude that the holotype is

1273.204 (LINN), a collection belonging to *Umbilicaria cylindrica* (L.) Delise ex Duby. They successfully proposed the name for conservation with a conserved type.

Lichen prunastri Linnaeus, *Species Plantarum* 2: 1147. 1753.
"Habitat in Europae arboribus, praesertim in Pruno spinosa. arboreus." RCN: 8206.
Lectotype (Howe in *Bull. Torrey Bot. Club* 39: 201. 1912; Jørgensen & al. in *Bot. J. Linn. Soc.* 115: 342, f. 49. 1994): Herb. Linn. No. 1273.125, central specimen (LINN).
Current name: ***Evernia prunastri*** (L.) Ach. (Parmeliaceae).
Note: Jørgensen & al. (in *Bot. J. Linn. Soc.* 115: 342, 380, f. 49. 1994) restricted Howe's original type choice to one of the specimens on the sheet.

Lichen pubescens Linnaeus, *Species Plantarum* 2: 1155. 1753.
"Habitat in Europa septentrionali, Lapponia, Suecia." RCN: 8251.
Lectotype (Jørgensen & al. in *Bot. J. Linn. Soc.* 115: 343. 1994): [icon] *"Usnea caespitosa exilis, capillacea, atra"* in Dillenius, Hist. Musc.: 66, t. 13, f. 9. 1741. – Voucher: Herb. Dillenius (OXF). – Epitype (Jørgensen & al. in *Bot. J. Linn. Soc.* 115: 343, 380. 1994): Herb. Linn. No. 1273.286 (LINN).
Current name: ***Pseudephebe pubescens*** (L.) M. Choisy (Parmeliaceae).

Lichen pulmonarius Linnaeus, *Species Plantarum* 2: 1145. 1753.
"Habitat in Europae sylvis umbrosis super arbores antiquas, praesertim in Fagis & Quercubus. arboreus." RCN: 8198.
Lectotype (Yoshimura & Hawksworth in *J. Jap. Bot.* 45: 36. 1970): Herb. Linn. No. 1273.103, lower specimen (LINN).
Current name: ***Lobaria pulmonaria*** (L.) Hoffm. (Lobariaceae).
Note: See review by Jørgensen & al. (in *Bot. J. Linn. Soc.* 115: 343, 380. 1994), who illustrate the type (as f. 50; p. 344 as does Jørgensen in *Symb. Bot. Upsal.* 33(3): 88, f. 7. 2005).

Lichen pustulatus Linnaeus, *Species Plantarum* 2: 1150. 1753.
"Habitat in Europae rupibus apricis. rupestris." RCN: 8225.
Lectotype (Howe in *Bull. Torrey Bot. Club* 39: 201. 1912; Jørgensen & al. in *Bot. J. Linn. Soc.* 115: 345, f. 51. 1994): Herb. Linn. No. 1273.201, uppermost specimen (LINN).
Current name: ***Lasallia pustulata*** (L.) Mérat (Umbilicariaceae).
Note: Jørgensen & al. (in *Bot. J. Linn. Soc.* 115: 345, 380, f. 51. 1994) restricted Howe's original type choice to one of the specimens on the sheet.

Lichen pyxidatus Linnaeus, *Species Plantarum* 2: 1151. 1753.
"Habitat in Europae sylvis." RCN: 8232.
Lectotype (Jørgensen & al. in *Bot. J. Linn. Soc.* 115: 347, f. 52. 1994): [icon] *"Lichen pyxidatus, major"* in Micheli, Nov. Pl. Gen.: 82, t. 41, f. 1L [squamulose morphotype]. 1729. – Epitype (Jørgensen & al. in *Bot. J. Linn. Soc.* 115: 347, 380. 1994): Herb. Micheli (FI).
Current name: ***Cladonia pyxidata*** (L.) Hoffm. (Cladoniaceae).
Note: Aptroot & al. (in *Lichenologist* 33: 272, f. 1. 2001) reproduce a (rather poor) photograph of the epitype in FI.

Lichen rangiferinus Linnaeus, *Species Plantarum* 2: 1153. 1753.
"Habitat in Alpibus, Europae frigidae sylvis sterilissimis, Alpestris differt a sylvatico, ut flos plenus a simplici." RCN: 8238.
Lectotype (Nourish & Oliver in *Biol. J. Linn. Soc.* 6: 259. 1974): Herb. Linn. No. 1273. 240 (LINN).
Current name: ***Cladonia rangiferina*** (L.) Weber ex F.H. Wigg. (Cladoniaceae).
Note: See review by Jørgensen & al. (in *Bot. J. Linn. Soc.* 115: 347–349, 380, f. 53. 1994).

L

Lichen rangiferinus Linnaeus var. **alpestris** Linnaeus, *Species Plantarum* 2: 1153. 1753.

"Habitat in Alpibus, Europae frigidae sylvis sterilissimis, Alpestris differt a sylvatico, ut flos plenus a simplici." RCN: 8238.

Lectotype (Pouzar & Vežda in *Preslia* 43: 195. 1971): [icon] *"Coralloides montanum fruticuli specie, ubique candicans varietas retiformis"* in Dillenius, Hist. Musc.: 108, t. 16, f. 29 F. 1741. – Voucher: Herb. Dillenius (OXF). – Epitype (Jørgensen & al. in *Bot. J. Linn. Soc.* 115: 349, 389. 1994): Herb. Dillenius Tab. XVI, No. 29F (OXF).

Current name: ***Cladonia stellaris*** (Opiz) Pouzar & Vežda (Cladoniaceae).

Lichen rangiferinus Linnaeus var. **sylvaticus** Linnaeus, *Species Plantarum* 2: 1153. 1753, *nom. utique rej.*

"Habitat in Alpibus, Europae frigidae sylvis sterilissimis, Alpestris differt a sylvatico, ut flos plenus a simplici." RCN: 8238.

Lectotype (Jørgensen & al. in *Bot. J. Linn. Soc.* 115: 349. 1994): [icon] *"Coralloides fruticuli specie candicans, corniculis rufescentibus"* in Dillenius, Hist. Musc.: 110, t. 16, f. 30. 1741. – Voucher: Herb. Dillenius (OXF).

Note: See review by Jørgensen & al. (in *Bot. J. Linn. Soc.* 115: 349, 380. 1994), who show that the type belongs to *Cladonia portentosa* (Dufour) Coem. As *C. sylvatica* (L.) Hoffm. had already fallen out of use, these authors (in *Taxon* 43: 648. 1994) successfully proposed the name for rejection.

Lichen resupinatus Linnaeus, *Species Plantarum* 2: 1148. 1753.

"Habitat in Europae sylvis. terrestris." RCN: 8213.

Lectotype (Howe in *Bull. Torrey Bot. Club* 39: 201. 1912): Herb. Linn. No. 1273.169 (LINN).

Current name: ***Nephroma resupinatum*** (L.) Ach. (Nephromataceae).

Note: See review by Jørgensen & al. (in *Bot. J. Linn. Soc.* 115: 349, 380, f. 54. 1994).

Lichen roccella Linnaeus, *Species Plantarum* 2: 1154. 1753.

"Habitat in insulis Archipelagi, Canariis, ad rupes marinas." RCN: 8244.

Lectotype (Howe in *Bull. Torrey Bot. Club* 39: 201. 1912; Jørgensen & al. in *Bot. J. Linn. Soc.* 115: 350, f. 55. 1994): Herb. Linn. No. 1273.263, lower specimen (LINN).

Current name: ***Roccella tinctoria*** DC. (Roccellaceae).

Note: Jørgensen & al. (in *Bot. J. Linn. Soc.* 115: 350, 380, f. 55. 1994) restricted Howe's original type choice to one of the specimens on the sheet.

Lichen rugosum Linnaeus, *Species Plantarum* 2: 1140. 1753.

"Habitat in Europae, sylvis supra arborum truncos." RCN: 8163.

Lectotype (Hawksworth & Punithalingam in *Trans. Brit. Mycol. Soc.* 60: 503. 1973): [icon] *"Lichenoides punctatum & rugosum nigrum"* in Dillenius, Hist. Musc.: 125, t. 18, f. 2. 1741. – Epitype (Jørgensen & al. in *Bot. J. Linn. Soc.* 115: 352, 381. 1994): Herb. Dillenius Tab. XVIII, No. 2, top right specimen (OXF).

Current name: ***Ascodichaena rugosa*** (Fr.) Butin (Ascodichaenaceae).

Note: See review by Jørgensen & al. (in *Bot. J. Linn. Soc.* 115: 351, 381. 1994).

Lichen rupicola Linnaeus, *Systema Naturae*, ed. 12, 2: 709; *Mantissa Plantarum*: 132. 1767.

"Habitat supra rupes planiusculas nudas apricas in sylvis. Zoega." RCN: 8161.

Neotype (Leuckert & Poelt in *Nova Hedwigia* 49: 149. 1989): Sweden. Dalarna, Grangärde, Hällön, Lake Rämen, W-side of island, Mar 1959, *R. Santesson 1737a* (BM).

Current name: ***Lecanora rupicola*** (L.) Zahlbr. (Lecanoraceae).

Note: See brief discussion by Jørgensen & al. (in *Bot. J. Linn. Soc.* 115: 352, 381. 1994).

Lichen saccatus Linnaeus, *Flora Suecica*, ed. 2: 419. 1755.

"Habitat in Alpibus Lapponicis; copiose ad latera Norwegiam spectantia Tych. Holm." RCN: 8221.

Lectotype (Almborn in *Bot. Not.* 119: 104. 1966; Jørgensen & al. in *Bot. J. Linn. Soc.* 115: 352, f. 56. 1994): *J.T. Holm*, Herb. Linn. No. 1273.197, lower specimen (LINN).

Current name: ***Solorina saccata*** (L.) Ach. (Peltigeraceae).

Note: Jørgensen & al. (in *Bot. J. Linn. Soc.* 115: 352, 381, f. 56. 1994) restricted Almborn's original type choice to one of the specimens on the sheet.

Lichen sanguinarium Linnaeus, *Species Plantarum* 2: 1140. 1753.

"Habitat in Europae rupibus truncisque arborum." RCN: 8164.

Lectotype (Jørgensen & al. in *Bot. J. Linn. Soc.* 115: 353, f. 57. 1994): Herb. Linn. No. 1273.10 (LINN).

Current name: ***Mycoblastus sanguinarius*** (L.) Norman (Mycoblastaceae).

Lichen saxatilis Linnaeus, *Species Plantarum* 2: 1142. 1753.

"Habitat in Europae rupibus. rupestris." RCN: 8183.

Lectotype (Howe in *Bull. Torrey Bot. Club* 39: 201. 1912; Galloway & Elix in *New Zealand J. Bot.* 21: 405. 1983): Herb. Linn. No. 1273.62, second specimen from bottom (LINN).

Generitype of *Lichen* Linnaeus, *nom. rej.*

Current name: ***Parmelia saxatilis*** (L.) Ach. (Parmeliaceae).

Note: *Lichen* Linnaeus, *nom. rej.* in favour of *Parmelia* Ach.
See discussion by Jørgensen & al. (in *Bot. J. Linn. Soc.* 115: 354, 381, f. 58. 1994). Galloway & Elix restricted Howe's original type choice to one of the specimens on the sheet.

Lichen scriptus Linnaeus, *Species Plantarum* 2: 1140. 1753.

"Habitat in Europae corticibus arborum." RCN: 8156.

Lectotype (Jørgensen & al. in *Bot. J. Linn. Soc.* 115: 356. 1994): [icon] *"Lichenoides crusta tenuissima, peregrinis velut litteris inscripta"* in Dillenius, Hist. Musc.: 125, t. 18, f. 1 B. 1741. – Voucher: Herb. Dillenius (OXF). – Epitype (Jørgensen & al. in *Bot. J. Linn. Soc.* 115: 356, 381. 1994): Sweden. Södermanland, Jernbol, Björkvid, 1895, *G.O.A. Malme* (Malme Lich. Suec. Exs. 47) (UPS).

Current name: ***Graphis scripta*** (L.) Ach. (Graphidaceae).

Lichen stellaris Linnaeus, *Species Plantarum* 2: 1144. 1753.

"Habitat in Europae ramis arborum. arboreus." RCN: 8192.

Lectotype (Howe in *Bull. Torrey Bot. Club* 39: 201. 1912; Jørgensen & al. in *Bot. J. Linn. Soc.* 115: 356, f. 59. 1994): Herb. Linn. No. 1273.81, upper left specimen (LINN).

Current name: ***Physcia stellaris*** (L.) Nyl. (Physciaceae).

Note: Jørgensen & al. (in *Bot. J. Linn. Soc.* 115: 356, 381, f. 59. 1994) restricted Howe's original type choice to one of the specimens on the sheet.

Lichen stygius Linnaeus, *Species Plantarum* 2: 1143. 1753.

"Habitat in Suecia, imprimis in Insula Balthici Blåkulla. rupestris." RCN: 8187.

Neotype (Jørgensen & al. in *Bot. J. Linn. Soc.* 115: 356, 381. 1994): Sweden. Uppland, Värmdö, Hasseludden, Aug 1907, *G.O.A. Malme* (Malme Lich. Suec. Exs. 66) (UPS).

Current name: ***Melanelia stygia*** (L.) Essl. (Parmeliaceae).

Lichen subfuscus Linnaeus, *Species Plantarum* 2: 1142. 1753, *nom. utique rej.*
"Habitat in Europa, arboribus & rupibus innascens." RCN: 8179.
Lectotype (Brodo & Vitikainen in *Mycotaxon* 21: 294. 1984): [icon] *"Lichenoides crustaceum & leprosum, scutellis subfuscis"* in Dillenius, Hist. Musc.: 134, t. 18, f. 16. 1741. – Voucher: Herb. Dillenius (OXF).
Note: See review by Jørgensen & al. (in *Bot. J. Linn. Soc.* 115: 357. 1994).

Lichen subulatus Linnaeus, *Species Plantarum* 2: 1153. 1753.
"Habitat in Europae sylvis ericetis." RCN: 8240.
Lectotype (Jørgensen & al. in *Bot. J. Linn. Soc.* 115: 358, f. 60. 1994): [icon] *"Muscus corniculatus"* in Tabernaemontanus, Eicones Pl.: 809, upper fig. 1590. – Epitype (Jørgensen & al. in *Bot. J. Linn. Soc.* 115: 358, 382. 1994): Herb. Linn. No. 1273.249 (LINN).
Current name: **Cladonia subulata** (L.) Weber ex F.H. Wigg. (Cladoniaceae).
Note: Jørgensen & al. rejected Laundon's earlier choice of 1273.249 (LINN) as lectotype as it is not original material for the name. However, they designated it as an epitype.

Lichen tartareus Linnaeus, *Species Plantarum* 2: 1141. 1753, *nom. cons.*
"Habitat in Europa ad parietes rupium." RCN: 8177.
Conserved type (Jørgensen & al. in *Taxon* 43: 653. 1994): *Burgess,* Herb. Linn. No. 1273.31 (LINN).
Current name: **Ochrolechia tartarea** (L.) A. Massal. (Pertusariaceae).
Note: See extensive discussion by Jørgensen & al. (in *Bot. J. Linn. Soc.* 115: 358, 382. 1994) in which they chose the Dillenius element as lectotype. Neither it, nor any of the other available elements, corresponded with usage and they successfully proposed the name for conservation with a conserved type.

Lichen uncialis Linnaeus, *Species Plantarum* 2: 1153. 1753, *nom. cons.*
"Habitat in Europae ericetis." RCN: 8239.
Conserved type (Jørgensen & al. in *Taxon* 34: 654. 1994): Sweden. Dalarna, Stora Kopparberg, Rotneby, *Stenhammar* in Lich. Suec. Exs., ed. 2, No. 210 (UPS).
Current name: **Cladonia uncialis** (L.) F.H. Wigg. (Cladoniaceae).
Note: See discussion by Jørgensen & al. (in *Bot. J. Linn. Soc.* 115: 360, 382, f. 61. 1994). The lectotype, 1273.246, lower specimen (LINN), belongs to *Cladonia amaurocraea* (Flörke) Schaer and the name was successfully proposed for conservation with a conserved type.

Lichen upsaliensis Linnaeus, *Species Plantarum* 2: 1142. 1753.
"Habitat in summis Jugis supra terram sterilissimam campi polonici, Upsaliae, nec alibi nobis visus." RCN: 8181.
Lectotype (Howe in *Bull. Torrey Bot. Club* 39: 201. 1912; Jørgensen & al. in *Bot. J. Linn. Soc.* 115: 360, f. 63. 1994): Herb. Linn. No. 1273.44, upper right specimen (LINN).
Current name: **Ochrolechia upsaliensis** (L.) A. Massal. (Pertusariaceae).
Note: Jørgensen & al. (in *Bot. J. Linn. Soc.* 115: 360, 382, f. 63. 1994) restricted Howe's original type choice to one of the specimens on the sheet.

Lichen usnea Linnaeus, *Systema Naturae,* ed. 12, 2: 713; *Mantissa Plantarum*: 131. 1767.
"Habitat in arboribus Indiae Or. Ins. Helenae, madagascar, Martinicae. Jacqu." RCN: 8248.

Lectotype (Howe in *Bull. Torrey Bot. Club* 39: 201. 1912): *Jacquin s.n.,* Herb. Linn. No. 1273.278 (LINN).
Current name: **Ramalina usnea** (L.) R. Howe (Ramalinaceae).
Note: See review by Jørgensen & al. (in *Bot. J. Linn. Soc.* 115: 361, 382, f. 62. 1994).

Lichen velleus Linnaeus, *Species Plantarum* 2: 1150. 1753.
"Habitat in alpinis Lapponiae, Sueciae, Angliae. rupestris." RCN: 8224.
Lectotype (Howe in *Bull. Torrey Bot. Club* 39: 201. 1912; Jørgensen & al. in *Bot. J. Linn. Soc.* 115: 364, f. 64. 1994): Herb. Linn. No. 1273.199, right specimen (LINN).
Current name: **Umbilicaria vellea** (L.) Ach. (Umbilicariaceae).
Note: Jørgensen & al. (in *Bot. J. Linn. Soc.* 115: 364, 382, f. 64. 1994) restricted Howe's original type choice to one of the specimens on the sheet.

Lichen venosus Linnaeus, *Species Plantarum* 2: 1148. 1753.
"Habitat in Europa ad margines scrobiculorum in sylvis. terrestris." RCN: 8214.
Lectotype (Vitikainen in *Acta Bot. Fenn.* 152: 84. 1994): Herb. Linn. No. 1273.172, central specimen (LINN).
Current name: **Peltigera venosa** (L.) Hoffm. (Peltigeraceae).
Note: See review by Jørgensen & al. (in *Bot. J. Linn. Soc.* 115: 365, 382, f. 65. 1994).

Lichen ventosus Linnaeus, *Species Plantarum* 2: 1141. 1753.
"Habitat in Alpium rupibus." RCN: 8170.
Neotype (Jørgensen & al. in *Bot. J. Linn. Soc.* 115: 365, 382. 1994): Herb. Linn. No. 1273.15, Ehrhart exs. 30 (LINN).
Current name: **Ophioparma ventosa** (L.) Norman (Ophioparmaceae).

Lichen vernalis Linnaeus, *Systema Naturae,* ed. 12, 3: 234. 1768, *nom. cons.*
"Habitat primo vere in aridissimo colle Polonico Upsaliae & passim in Europa." RCN: 8166.
Conserved type (Jørgensen & al. in *Taxon* 43: 654. 1994): Sweden. Fries, Lich. Suec. Exsicc. No. 224 (UPS).
Current name: **Biatora vernalis** (L.) Fr. (Lecanoraceae).
Note: See review by Jørgensen & al. (in *Bot. J. Linn. Soc.* 115: 365, 382. 1994). They chose a Dillenian figure as lectotype, but it and the other original elements do not correspond with usage. These authors, however, successfully proposed the name for conservation with a conserved type.

Lichen vulpinus Linnaeus, *Species Plantarum* 2: 1155. 1753.
"Habitat in Europae tectis ligneis, muris." RCN: 8254.
Lectotype (Howe in *Bull. Torrey Bot. Club* 39: 201. 1912; Jørgensen & al. in *Bot. J. Linn. Soc.* 115: 367, f. 66. 1994): Herb. Linn. No. 1273.298, upper left specimen (LINN).
Current name: **Letharia vulpina** (L.) Hue (Parmeliaceae).
Note: Jørgensen & al. (in *Bot. J. Linn. Soc.* 115: 367, 383, f. 66. 1994) restricted Howe's original type choice to one of the specimens on the sheet.

Ligusticum austriacum Linnaeus, *Species Plantarum* 1: 250. 1753.
"Habitat in Austriae alpinis." RCN: 2012.
Lectotype (Reduron in Jonsell & Jarvis in *Nordic J. Bot.* 22: 84. 2002): Herb. Burser VIII: 66 (UPS).
Current name: **Pleurospermum austriacum** (L.) Hoffm. (Apiaceae).

Ligusticum balearicum Linnaeus, *Mantissa Plantarum Altera*: 218. 1771.

"Habitat in Balearibus; Romae." RCN: 2015.
Neotype (Rosselló & Sáez in *Collect. Bot. (Barcelona)* 25: 13. 2000): Herb. Linn. No. 353.8 (LINN).
Current name: ***Kundmannia sicula*** (L.) DC. (Apiaceae).

Ligusticum cornubiense Linnaeus, *Centuria II Plantarum*: 13. 1756.
"Habitat in Cornubia." RCN: 2013.
Lectotype (Reduron in Jarvis & al. in *Taxon* 55: 213. 2006): [icon] *"Smyrnium tenuifolium, nostras"* in Ray, Syn. Meth. Stirp. Brit., ed. 3: 209, t. 8. 1724. – Epitype (Reduron in Jarvis & al. in *Taxon* 55: 213. 2006): *"Tragoselinum maximum cornubiense umbella candida N.11"* in Herb. Buddle; Herb. Sloane 120: 37 (BM-SL).
Current name: ***Physospermum cornubiense*** (L.) DC. (Apiaceae).

Ligusticum levisticum Linnaeus, *Species Plantarum* 1: 250. 1753.
"Habitat in Apenninis Liguriae." RCN: 2009.
Lectotype (Reduron in Jarvis & al. in *Taxon* 55: 213. 2006): Herb. Clifford: 97, *Ligusticum* 2 (BM-000558301).
Current name: ***Levisticum officinale*** W.D.J. Koch (Apiaceae).

Ligusticum peleponnesiacum Linnaeus, *Species Plantarum* 1: 250. 1753.
"Habitat in Peleponesiacis & Rheticis montibus nemorosis." RCN: 2011.
Lectotype (Ullmann in *Flora, Morphol. Geobot. Oekophysiol.* 179: 268. 1987): Herb. Burser VIII: 60 (UPS).
Current name: ***Molopospermum peleponnesiacum*** (L.) W.D.J. Koch (Apiaceae).

Ligusticum peregrinum Linnaeus, *Species Plantarum*, ed. 2, 1: 360. 1762.
"Habitat in Lusitania." RCN: 2014.
Type not designated.
Original material: Herb. Linn. No. 353.7 (LINN).
Current name: ***Petroselinum sp.*** (Apiaceae).
Note: It appears that this name probably threatens *Petroselinum crispum* (Mill.) Fuss and is therefore a candidate for rejection.

Ligusticum scothicum Linnaeus, *Species Plantarum* 1: 250. 1753.
"Habitat ad litora Maris in Anglia, Suecia." RCN: 2010.
Lectotype (Reduron & Jarvis in Jarvis & al., *Regnum Veg.* 127: 61. 1993): Herb. Clifford: 97, *Ligusticum* 3 (BM-000558302).
Generitype of *Ligusticum* Linnaeus (vide Hitchcock, *Prop. Brit. Bot.*: 140. 1929).
Current name: ***Ligusticum scothicum*** L. (Apiaceae).
Note: Specific epithet spelled "scothieum" in the protologue.

Ligusticum scoticum Linnaeus, *Systema Naturae*, ed. 10, 2: 958. 1759, *orth. var.*
["Habitat ad litora Maris in Anglia, Suecia."] Sp. Pl. 1: 250 (1753). RCN: 2010.
Lectotype (Reduron & Jarvis in Jarvis & al., *Regnum Veg.* 127: 61. 1993): Herb. Clifford: 97, *Ligusticum* 3 (BM-000558302).
Current name: ***Ligusticum scoticum*** L. (Apiaceae).
Note: Evidently an orthographic variant of *Ligusticum scothicum* L. (1753). The species number and Linnaean polynomial are the same.

Ligustrum vulgare Linnaeus, *Species Plantarum* 1: 7. 1753.
"Habitat in Europae collibus glareosis." RCN: 49.
Lectotype (Green in Jarvis & al., *Regnum Veg.* 127: 61. 1993): Herb. Linn. No. 18.1 (LINN).
Generitype of *Ligustrum* Linnaeus.
Current name: ***Ligustrum vulgare*** L. (Oleaceae).

Lilium bulbiferum Linnaeus, *Species Plantarum* 1: 302. 1753.
"Habitat in Italia, Austria, Sibiria." RCN: 2385.
Type not designated.
Original material: Herb. Burser III: 116? (UPS); Herb. Linn. No. 420.2 (LINN); Herb. A. van Royen No. 916.62–583 (L); Herb. Burser III: 115 (UPS).
Current name: ***Lilium bulbiferum*** L. (Liliaceae).
Note: See extensive discussion of the original literature elements by Woodcock & Stearn (*Lilies World*: 166–167. 1950).

Lilium camschatcense Linnaeus, *Species Plantarum* 1: 303. 1753.
"Habitat in Canada, Camschatca." RCN: 2392.
Type not designated.
Original material: *Kalm*, Herb. Linn. No. 420.7 (LINN).
Current name: ***Fritillaria camschatcensis*** (L.) Ker-Gawl. (Liliaceae).
Note: See notes by Turrill & Sealy (in *Hooker's Icon. Pl.* 39: 298. 1980).

Lilium canadense Linnaeus, *Species Plantarum* 1: 303. 1753.
"Habitat in Canada." RCN: 2390.
Lectotype (Adams & Dress in *Baileya* 21: 172. 1982): *Kalm*, Herb. Linn. No. 420.6 (LINN).
Current name: ***Lilium canadense*** L. (Liliaceae).

Lilium candidum Linnaeus, *Species Plantarum* 1: 302. 1753.
"Habitat in Palaestina, Syria." RCN: 2384.
Type not designated.
Original material: Herb. A. van Royen No. 913.62–563 (L); Herb. Linn. No. 420.1 (LINN); Herb. Burser III: 114 (UPS); Herb. Burser III: 113 (UPS); [icon] in Dodoëns, Stirp. Hist. Pempt., ed. 2: 197. 1616.
Generitype of *Lilium* Linnaeus (vide Hitchcock, *Prop. Brit. Bot.*: 145. 1929).
Current name: ***Lilium candidum*** L. (Liliaceae).
Note: Dasgupta & Deb (in *Candollea* 39: 488. 1984) indicated 421.1 (LINN) as type, but this is material linked with *Fritillaria* and not original material for this name.

Lilium chalcedonicum Linnaeus, *Species Plantarum* 1: 302. 1753.
"Habitat in Persia." RCN: 2387.
Type not designated.
Original material: Herb. Clifford: 120, *Lilium* 4, 3 sheets (BM); Herb. Burser III: 118 (UPS); [icon] in Plantin, Pl. Stirp. Icon.: 169. 1581; [icon] in Clusius, Rar. Pl. Hist. 1: 131. 1601.
Current name: ***Lilium chalcedonicum*** L. (Liliaceae).

Lilium martagon Linnaeus, *Species Plantarum* 1: 303. 1753.
"Habitat in Hungaria, Helvetia, Sibiria, Lipsiae." RCN: 2389.
Type not designated.
Original material: Herb. A. van Royen No. 913.62–570 (L); Herb. Linn. No. 420.5 (LINN); Herb. Burser III: 117 (UPS); [icon] in Dodoëns, Stirp. Hist. Pempt., ed. 2: 201. 1616.
Current name: ***Lilium martagon*** L. (Liliaceae).

Lilium philadelphicum Linnaeus, *Species Plantarum*, ed. 2, 1: 435. 1762.
"Habitat in Canada." RCN: 2391.
Lectotype (designated here by Reveal): *Kalm*, Herb. Linn. No. 420.7 (LINN).
Current name: ***Lilium philadelphicum*** L. (Liliaceae).
Note: Howard & Staples (in *J. Arnold Arbor.* 64: 515. 1983) indicated the cited Miller plate as "presumably" the type but their uncertainty (and the existence of 420.7, LINN) means that this statement is not accepted as formal typification.

Lilium pomponium Linnaeus, *Species Plantarum* 1: 302. 1753.
"Habitat in Pyrenaeis, Sibiria." RCN: 2386.
Type not designated.
Original material: Herb. Clifford: 120, *Lilium* 4, 3 sheets (BM); Herb. Burser III: 119 (UPS); [icon] in Clusius, Rar. Pl. Hist. 1: 133. 1601.
Current name: ***Lilium pomponium*** L. (Liliaceae).
Note: See discussion by Woodcock & Stearn (*Lilies World*: 314. 1950) who state that Linnaeus' concept included a number of different taxa.

Lilium superbum Linnaeus, *Species Plantarum*, ed. 2, 1: 434. 1762.
"Habitat in America septentrionali." RCN: 2388.

LILIVM folis sparsis, fundo aureo, limbo aurantio, pedunculis singulis — multiflorum, floribus reflexis, tio, punctis nigricantibus, unico folio instructis

Lectotype (designated here by Reveal): [icon] *"Lilium foliis sparsis, multiflorum, floribus reflexis, fundo aureo, limbo aurantio, punctis nigricantibus, pedunculis singulis unico folio instructis"* in Trew, Pl. Select.: 2, t. 11. 1751.
Current name: ***Lilium superbum*** L. (Liliaceae).
Note: See discussion by Woodcock & Stearn (*Lilies World*: 345. 1950), whose f. 110 (and see above) is of Trew's illustration which was cited in the protologue. Adams & Dress (in *Baileya* 21: 179. 1982) treated 420.8 (LINN) as the lectotype, but rightly state there is nothing to link this material with the name. It is not original material and is ineligible for designation as the lectotype.

Limeum africanum Linnaeus, *Systema Naturae,* ed. 10, 2: 995. 1759.
["Habitat in Aethiopia."] Sp. Pl., ed. 2, 1: 489 (1762). RCN: 2640.
Neotype (Jeffrey in Jarvis & al., *Regnum Veg.* 127: 61. 1993): *Garcin 11,* Herb. Burman (G).
Generitype of *Limeum* Linnaeus.
Current name: ***Limeum africanum*** L. (Molluginaceae).
Note: Friedrich in *Mitt. Bot. Staatssamml. München* 2: 139. 1955) stated "Typus speciei: Burmann s.Nr. LINN". Although there are two sheets in LINN (477.1, 477.2), they are annotated only by Linnaeus filius, and give no indication of any link with Burman. Consequently they are later additions to the collection and are not original material for the name. They do not appear to be part of the same collection so Art. 9.15 does not apply. Jeffrey has designated a collection in Burman's herbarium (G) as a neotype.

Limodorum altum Linnaeus, *Systema Naturae,* ed. 12, 2: 594. 1767. RCN: 6870.
Lectotype (Fawcett & Rendle, *Fl. Jamaica* 1: 113. 1910): Herb. Linn. No. 1058.2 (LINN).
Current name: ***Eulophia alta*** (L.) Fawc. & Rendle (Orchidaceae).

Limodorum tuberosum Linnaeus, *Species Plantarum* 2: 950. 1753.
"Habitat in America septentrionali." RCN: 6869.
Lectotype (Mackenzie in *Rhodora* 27: 194. 1925): *Clayton 76* (BM-000051136).
Generitype of *Limodorum* Linnaeus, *nom. rej.*
Current name: ***Calopogon tuberosa*** (L.) Britton & al. (Orchidaceae).
Note: Limodorum Linnaeus, *nom. rej.* against *Limodorum* Boehm. *Calopogon* R. Br. is a conserved name.
   Fernald (in *Rhodora* 23: 132. 1921) stated that this "rests chiefly upon and draws its specific name directly from... Martyn t. 50". However, we believe that this is insufficiently precise to be accepted as a valid typification (which is fortunate as the illustration is of *Bletia purpurea* (Lam.) DC.). Luer (*Native Orch. Florida*: 58. 1972) and Boivin (in *Phytologia* 42: 397. 1979) follow Mackenzie.

Limonia acidissima Linnaeus, *Species Plantarum,* ed. 2, 1: 554. 1762.
"Habitat in India." RCN: 3054.
Replaced synonym: *Schinus limonia* L. (1753).
Lectotype (Tanaka in *Meded. Rijks-Herb.* 69: 8. 1931): Herb. Hermann 1: 76, No. 175 (BM-000594508).
Generitype of *Limonia* Linnaeus.
Current name: ***Limonia acidissima*** L. (Rutaceae).
Note: Panigrahi (in *Taxon* 26: 577. 1977) proposed the name for rejection but Stone & Nicolson (in *Taxon* 27: 551. 1979) argued against this. The Committee for Spermatophyta (in *Taxon* 31: 540. 1982) declined Panigrahi's rejection proposal.

Limonia monophylla Linnaeus, *Mantissa Plantarum Altera*: 237. 1771, *typ. cons.*
"Habitat in India orientali." RCN: 3052.
Conserved type (Nair & Barrie in *Taxon* 44: 429. 1995): India. Kerala: Idukki, Chinnar, 10 Oct 1994, *E.S. Santhosh Kumar 17590* (BM; iso- CAL, MH, MO, TBGT).
Current name: ***Atalantia monophylla*** (L.) DC. (Rutaceae).

Limonia trifoliata Linnaeus, *Mantissa Plantarum Altera*: 237. 1771, *nom. illeg.*
"Habitat in India orientali. D. DuChesne." RCN: 3053.
Replaced synonym: *Limonia trifolia* Burm. f. (1768).
Type not designated.
Current name: ***Triphasia trifolia*** (Burm. f.) P. Wilson (Rutaceae).
Note: An illegitimate replacement name for *L. trifolia* Burm. f. (1768).

Limosella aquatica Linnaeus, *Species Plantarum* 2: 631. 1753.
"Habitat in Europae septentrionalis inundatis." RCN: 4583.
Lectotype (Pennell in *Monogr. Acad. Nat. Sci. Philadelphia* 1: 164. 1935): Herb. Linn. No. 794.1 (LINN).
Generitype of *Limosella* Linnaeus.
Current name: ***Limosella aquatica*** L. (Scrophulariaceae).

Limosella diandra Linnaeus, *Mantissa Plantarum Altera*: 252. 1771.
"Habitat ad Cap. b. spei littoribus." RCN: 4584.
Lectotype (Yamazaki in Leroy, *Fl. Cambodge Laos Viêt-Nam* 21: 158. 1985): Herb. Linn. No. 794.2 (LINN).
Current name: ***Glossostigma diandrum*** (L.) Kuntze (Scrophulariaceae).

Linconia alopecuroides Linnaeus, *Mantissa Plantarum Altera*: 216. 1771.
"Habitat in Capitis b. spei montosis aquosis." RCN: 1793.
Lectotype (Hall in Jarvis & al., *Regnum Veg.* 127: 61. 1993): Herb. Linn. No. 323.1 (LINN).
Generitype of *Linconia* Linnaeus.
Current name: ***Linconia alopecuroides*** L. (Bruniaceae).

Lindernia pyxidaria Linnaeus, *Mantissa Plantarum Altera*: 252. 1771, *nom. illeg.*
"Habitat in Virginiae, Alsatiae, Pedemontii paludibus spongiosis inundatis." RCN: 4551.
Replaced synonym: *Gratiola dubia* L. (1753).
Lectotype (Pennell in *Torreya* 19: 149. 1919): *Clayton 164* (BM-000038848).
Current name: ***Lindernia dubia*** (L.) Pennell (Scrophulariaceae).
Note: An illegitimate replacement name in *Lindernia* for *Gratiola dubia* L. (1753).

Linnaea borealis Linnaeus, *Species Plantarum* 2: 631. 1753.
"Habitat in Sueciae, Sibiriae, Helvetiae, Canadae sylvis antiquis, muscosis, acerosis, sterilibus, umbrosis." RCN: 4581.
Lectotype (Jonsell in Jarvis & al., *Regnum Veg.* 127: 61. 1993): Herb. Linn. No. 250 (LAPP), see p. 66.
Generitype of *Linnaea* Linnaeus.
Current name: ***Linnaea borealis*** L. (Caprifoliaceae).

Linum africanum Linnaeus, *Species Plantarum* 1: 280. 1753.
"Habitat in Africa." RCN: 2220.
Neotype (Rogers in *Nordic J. Bot.* 1: 715. 1981): Herb. Linn. No. 396.34 (LINN).
Current name: ***Linum africanum*** L. (Linaceae).
Note: Although the collection indicated by Rogers as the holotype was almost certainly a post-1753 addition to the herbarium, the absence of any original material means that this can be treated as a neotype under Art. 9.8.

Linum arboreum Linnaeus, *Species Plantarum* 1: 279. 1753.
"Habitat in Creta." RCN: 2218.
Lectotype (Turland in *Bull. Nat. Hist. Mus. London, Bot.* 25: 131, f. 3. 1995): [icon] *"Linum Arboreum"* in Alpino, Pl. Exot.: 19, 18. 1627. – Epitype (Turland in *Bull. Nat. Hist. Mus. London, Bot.* 25: 131, f. 4. 1995): *Rechinger 12202* (BM; iso- W?).
Current name: ***Linum arboreum*** L. (Linaceae).

Linum austriacum Linnaeus, *Species Plantarum* 1: 278. 1753.
"Habitat in Austria inferiore." RCN: 2213.
Lectotype (Ockenden in *Watsonia* 8: 210. 1971): Herb. Burser XII: 44 (UPS).
Current name: ***Linum austriacum*** L. (Linaceae).

Linum campanulatum Linnaeus, *Species Plantarum* 1: 280. 1753.
"Habitat in Galloprovinciae montibus, Monspelii in monte lupi." RCN: 2219.
Type not designated.
Original material: Herb. Burser XII: 38 (UPS); [icon] in Bauhin & Cherler, Hist. Pl. Univ. 2: 817. 1651; [icon] in Plantin, Pl. Stirp. Icon.: 414. 1581.
Current name: ***Linum campanulatum*** L. (Linaceae).

Linum catharticum Linnaeus, *Species Plantarum* 1: 281. 1753.
"Habitat in Europae septentrionalis pascuis succulentis." RCN: 2222.
Lectotype (Rogers in *Brittonia* 15: 108. 1963): Herb. Linn. No. 396.37 (LINN).
Current name: ***Linum catharticum*** L. (Linaceae).

Linum flavum Linnaeus, *Species Plantarum* 1: 279. 1753.
"Habitat in Austria." RCN: 2215.
Lectotype (Optasyuk & Jarvis in Optasyuk & Mosyakin, *Ukrainian Bot. J.* 63: 525, f. [525]. 2006): Herb. Burser XII: 37 (LINN).
Current name: ***Linum flavum*** L. (Linaceae).

Linum gallicum Linnaeus, *Species Plantarum*, ed. 2, 1: 401. 1762, *nom. illeg.*
"Habitat Monspelii." RCN: 2210.
Replaced synonym: *Linum trigynum* L. (1753).
Lectotype (Siddiqi in Jafri & El-Gadi, *Fl. Libya* 35: 4. 1977): Herb. Linn. No. 396.19 (LINN).
Current name: ***Linum trigynum*** L. (Linaceae).
Note: A superfluous name for *L. trigynum* L. (1753).

Linum hirsutum Linnaeus, *Species Plantarum* 1: 277. 1753.
"Habitat in Austriae, Tatariae edits graminosis." RCN: 2207.
Lectotype (Optasyuk in Optasyuk & Mosyakin, *Ukrainian Bot. J.* 63: 525, f. [524]. 2006): Gerber, Herb. Linn. No. 396.11 (LINN).
Current name: ***Linum hirsutum*** L. (Linaceae).

Linum maritimum Linnaeus, *Species Plantarum* 1: 280. 1753.
"Habitat in Austria ad Thermas badensis, Monspelii." RCN: 2211.
Type not designated.
Original material: Herb. Linn. No. 396.20 (LINN); Herb. Burser XII: 39 (UPS); Herb. Clifford: 114, *Linum 3* (BM); [icon] in Bauhin & Cherler, Hist. Pl. Univ. 3(2): 454. 1651; [icon] in Dodoëns, Stirp. Hist. Pempt., ed. 2: 534. 1616.
Current name: ***Linum maritimum*** L. (Linaceae).

Linum narbonense Linnaeus, *Species Plantarum* 1: 278. 1753.
"Habitat in Galloprovincia, Monspelii, unde Burserus attulit C. Bauhino." RCN: 2208.
Type not designated.
Original material: Herb. Burser XII: 34, syntype? (UPS).
Current name: ***Linum narbonense*** L. (Linaceae).

Linum nodiflorum Linnaeus, *Species Plantarum* 1: 280. 1753.
"Habitat in Italiae pratis argillosis." RCN: 2221.
Lectotype (Rechinger, *Fl. Iranica* 106: 8. 1974): Herb. Linn. No. 396.36 (LINN).
Current name: ***Linum nodiflorum*** L. (Linaceae).

Linum perenne Linnaeus, *Species Plantarum* 1: 277. 1753.
"Habitat in Sibiria et Cantabrigiae." RCN: 2205.
Lectotype (Ockenden in *Watsonia* 8: 209. 1971): Herb. Linn. No. 396.8 (LINN).
Current name: ***Linum perenne*** L. (Linaceae).

Linum quadrifolium Linnaeus, *Species Plantarum* 1: 281. 1753.
"Habitat in Aethiopia." RCN: 2224.
Lectotype (Rogers in *Nordic J. Bot.* 1: 718. 1981): Herb. Linn. No. 396.39 (LINN).
Current name: ***Linum quadrifolium*** L. (Linaceae).

Linum radiola Linnaeus, *Species Plantarum* 1: 281. 1753.
"Habitat in Europae sabulo inundato." RCN: 2223.
Lectotype (Jonsell & Jarvis in *Nordic J. Bot.* 22: 79. 2002): Herb. Clifford: 114, *Linum* 6 (BM-000558461).
Current name: ***Radiola linoides*** Roth (Linaceae).
Note: Smith (in Hubbard & Milne-Redhead, *Fl. Trop. E. Africa, Linaceae*: 11. 1966) wrongly indicated 396.38 (LINN) as a syntype but as this statement implies no intention to indicate a single nomenclatural type (unlike the use of holotype, lectotype or neotype), this is not regarded as a correctable error.

Linum strictum Linnaeus, *Species Plantarum* 1: 279. 1753.
"Habitat in Monspelii, Hispaniae, Siciliae squalidis." RCN: 2216.
Lectotype (Hajra in Jain & al. in *Fasc. Fl. India* 13: 8. 1983): *Löfling 246a*, Herb. Linn. No. 396.29 (LINN).
Current name: ***Linum strictum*** L. (Linaceae).

Linum suffruticosum Linnaeus, *Species Plantarum* 1: 279. 1753.
"Habitat in Regno Valentino." RCN: 2217.
Neotype (Nicholls in *Bot. J. Linn. Soc.* 91: 486. 1986): Herb. Tournefort No. 3089 (P).
Current name: ***Linum tenuifolium*** L. subsp. ***suffruticosum*** (L.) Litard. (Linaceae).
Note: Although the Tournefort collection was not studied by Linnaeus, and cannot be the holotype as suggested by Nicholls, the absence of any original material for the name means that this collection can be treated as a neotype (under Art. 9.8).

Linum tenuifolium Linnaeus, *Species Plantarum* 1: 278. 1753.
"Habitat in Galliae, Helvetiae aridis herbosis." RCN: 2209.
Lectotype (Nicholls in *Bot. J. Linn. Soc.* 91: 480. 1986 [1985]): Herb. Linn. No. 396.12 (LINN).
Current name: ***Linum tenuifolium*** L. (Linaceae).

Linum trigynum Linnaeus, *Species Plantarum* 1: 279. 1753.
"Habitat in Monspelii. D. Sauvages." RCN: 2210.
Replaced synonym of: *Linum gallicum* L. (1762), *nom. illeg.*
Lectotype (Rechinger, *Fl. Iranica* 106: 9. 1974): Herb. Linn. No. 396.19 (LINN).
Current name: ***Linum trigynum*** L. (Linaceae).

Linum usitatissimum Linnaeus, *Species Plantarum* 1: 277. 1753.
"Habitat hodie inter segetes Europae australis." RCN: 2204.
Lectotype (Seegeler in *Taxon* 38: 278, f. 1. 1989): Herb. Clifford: 114, *Linum* 1 (BM-000558456).
Generitype of *Linum* Linnaeus (vide Hitchcock, *Prop. Brit. Bot.*: 143. 1929).
Current name: ***Linum usitatissimum*** L. (Linaceae).
Note: Kulpa & Danert (in *Kulturpflanze* 3: 342. 1962) indicated a Brander collection (396.1 LINN), not received by Linnaeus until 1756, as type but it cannot be original material for the name. Rechinger (*Fl. Iranica* 106: 17. 1974) indicated Clifford material as "syntypi", but the two sheets preserved at BM are not a single collection so Art. 9.15 does not apply. Seegeler is therefore the first to have made an explicit choice of lectotype.

Linum usitatum Linnaeus, *Flora Anglica*: 14. 1754, *orth. var.*
RCN: 2204.

Lectotype (Seegeler in *Taxon* 38: 278, f. 1. 1989): Herb. Clifford: 114, *Linum* 1 (BM).
Current name: ***Linum usitatissimum*** L. (Linaceae).
Note: An orthographic variant of *L. usitatissimum* L. (1753), as noted by Stearn (*Introd. Ray's Syn. Meth. Stirp. Brit.* (Ray Soc. ed.): 68. 1973).

Linum verticillatum Linnaeus, *Species Plantarum* 1: 281. 1753.
"Habitat in Italia." RCN: 2225.
Type not designated.
Original material: [icon] in Boccone, Mus. Piante Rar. Sicilia: 49, t. 42. 1697; [icon] in Barrelier, Pl. Galliam: 65, t. 1226. 1714.
Note: The application of this name appears to be uncertain.

Linum virginianum Linnaeus, *Species Plantarum* 1: 279. 1753.
"Habitat in Virginia, Pensylvania." RCN: 2214.
Lectotype (Fernald in *Rhodora* 37: 428. 1935): *Kalm*, Herb. Linn. No. 396.24 (LINN).
Current name: ***Linum virginianum*** L. (Linaceae).

Linum viscosum Linnaeus, *Species Plantarum*, ed. 2, 1: 398. 1762.
"Habitat in montibus Bononiensibus, Sumano, Augustae vindelicorum, Ingolstadii." RCN: 2206.
Type not designated.
Original material: none traced.
Current name: ***Linum viscosum*** L. (Linaceae).

Liparia graminifolia Linnaeus, *Mantissa Plantarum Altera*: 268. 1771.
"Habitat ad Cap. b. spei arenosis." RCN: 5432.
Lectotype (Schutte & Van Wyk in *Taxon* 43: 579. 1994): *Tulbagh 5*, Herb. Linn. No. 910.3 (LINN).
Current name: ***Liparia graminifolia*** L. (Fabaceae: Faboideae).

Liparia opposita Linnaeus, *Mantissa Plantarum Altera*: 269. 1771, *nom. illeg.*
["Habitat ad Cap. b. spei."] Sp. Pl., ed. 2, 2: 995 (1763). RCN: 5433.
Replaced synonym: *Spartium capense* L. (1760).
Conserved type (Campbell & al. in *Taxon* 48: 833. 1999): South Africa. Western Cape Province, Cape of Good Hope Nature Reserve, *Campbell & Van Wyk 151* (NBG; iso- K, MO, PRE).
Current name: ***Rafnia capensis*** (L.) Schinz (Fabaceae: Faboideae).
Note: Liparia opposita L. is an illegitimate renaming of *Spartium capense* L., and therefore homotypic with it. Campbell-Young & al. (in *Taxon* 48: 833. 1999) successfully proposed *S. capense* for conservation with a conserved type because all original elements for the name belong to *Rafnia angulata* Thunb.

Liparia sericea Linnaeus, *Mantissa Plantarum Altera*: 269. 1771.
RCN: 5436.
Type not designated.
Original material: none traced.
Current name: ***Amphithalea*** sp. (Fabaceae: Faboideae).
Note: The application of this name is uncertain (see Schutte & Van Wyk in *Taxon* 42: 46. 1993).

Liparia sphaerica Linnaeus, *Mantissa Plantarum Altera*: 268. 1771.
"Habitat ad Cap. b. Spei." RCN: 5431.
Neotype (Schutte & Van Wyk in Jarvis & al., *Regnum Veg.* 127: 62. 1993): Herb. Linn. No. 910.1 (LINN).
Generitype of *Liparia* Linnaeus (vide Hutchinson, *Gen. Fl. Pl.* 1: 367. 1964).
Current name: ***Liparia splendens*** (Burm. f.) Bos & de Wit (Fabaceae: Faboideae).

L

Note: Bos (in *J. S. African Bot.* 33: 270, 281. 1967) noted that two sheets in LINN (910.1, 910.2) were annotated only by Linnaeus filius and post-date the publication of the name. Schutte & Van Wyk subsequently designated one of these sheets as a neotype.

Liparia umbellata Linnaeus, *Mantissa Plantarum Altera*: 269. 1771. RCN: 5182.
Type not designated.
Original material: none traced.
Current name: ***Liparia laevigata*** (L.) Thunb. (Fabaceae: Faboideae).
Note: Linnaeus gave the alternative name *Borbonia umbellata* (seemingly not published elsewhere) in the protologue, and this was repeated in *Syst. Veg.*, ed. 13: 554 (1774). Neither this name nor *B. umbellata* is invalid, having been published pre-1953 (Art. 34.2). Dahlgren (in *Opera Bot.* 22: 101. 1968), however, treated it as invalid ("should not be considered from the point of view of nomenclature"), and Schutte & Van Wyk (in *Taxon* 43: 579. 1994) and Schutte (in *Nordic J. Bot.* 17: 29. 1997) treat this as an illegitimate name, synonymous with *Liparia laevigata* (L.) Thunb.

Liparia villosa Linnaeus, *Mantissa Plantarum Altera*: 269. 1771, *nom. illeg.*
["Habitat in Aethiopia."] Sp. Pl. 2: 707 (1753). RCN: 5435.
Replaced synonym: *Borbonia tomentosa* L. (1753).
Lectotype (Schutte & Van Wyk in *Taxon* 42: 47. 1993): [icon] *"Genista, Africana, tomentosa, folio cochleariformi, flore luteo"* in Seba, Locupl. Rer. Nat. Thes. 1: 38, t. 24, f. 1. 1734.
Current name: ***Priestleya tomentosa*** (L.) Druce (Fabaceae: Faboideae).
Note: An illegitimate renaming of *Borbonia tomentosa* L. (1753) in *Liparia*, as noted by Schutte & Van Wyk.

Lippia americana Linnaeus, *Species Plantarum* 2: 633. 1753.
"Habitat in Vera Cruce." RCN: 4599.
Lectotype (Moldenke in *Phytologia* 12: 76. 1965): Herb. Linn. No. 801.1 (LINN).
Generitype of *Lippia* Linnaeus.
Current name: ***Lippia americana*** L. (Verbenaceae).

Lippia ovata Linnaeus, *Systema Naturae*, ed. 12, 2: 423; *Mantissa Plantarum*: 89. 1767.
"Habitat ad Cap. b. spei." RCN: 4601.
Type not designated.
Original material: Herb. Linn. No. 801.2 (LINN).
Current name: ***Microdon capitatus*** (P.J. Bergius) Levyns (Globulariaceae).
Note: Although Rolfe (in *J. Linn. Soc., Bot.* 20: 347. 1884) noted the existence of 801.2 (LINN), he did not indicate it as type, and Hilliard (*Tribe Selagineae*: 12. 1999) did so, but with doubt ("Type: sheet no. 801.2 herb. LINN?").

Liquidambar aspleniifolia (Linnaeus) Linnaeus, *Species Plantarum*, ed. 2, 2: 1418. 1763.
"Habitat in America septentrionali." RCN: 7238.
Basionym: *Myrica aspleniifolia* L. (1753).
Type not designated.
Original material: as basionym.
Current name: ***Comptonia peregrina*** (L.) J.M. Coult. (Myricaceae).
Note: Specific epithet spelled "asplenifolium" in the protologue.

Liquidambar peregrina Linnaeus, *Species Plantarum* 2: 999. 1753.
"Habitat in Canada." RCN: 7238.
Lectotype (Reveal & al. in *Huntia* 7: 223. 1987): *Kalm*, Herb. Linn. No. 1134.3 (LINN).

Current name: ***Comptonia peregrina*** (L.) J.M. Coult. (Myricaceae).
Note: See discussion by Fernald (in *Rhodora* 40: 411. 1938).

Liquidambar styraciflua Linnaeus, *Species Plantarum* 2: 999. 1753.
"Habitat in Virginia, Mexico." RCN: 7237.
Lectotype (Wijnands, *Bot. Commelins*: 109. 1983): *Kalm*, Herb. Linn. No. 1134.1 (LINN).
Generitype of *Liquidambar* Linnaeus (vide Green, *Prop. Brit. Bot.*: 189. 1929).
Current name: ***Liquidambar styraciflua*** L. (Hamamelidaceae).

Liriodendron liliifera Linnaeus, *Species Plantarum*, ed. 2, 1: 755. 1762.
"Habitat in Amboina." RCN: 3979.
Lectotype (Merrill, *Interpret. Rumph. Herb. Amb.*: 224. 1917): [icon] *"Sampacca montana"* in Rumphius, Herb. Amboin. 2: 204, t. 69. 1741.
Current name: ***Talauma rumphii*** Blume (Magnoliaceae).

Liriodendron tulipifera Linnaeus, *Species Plantarum* 1: 535. 1753.
"Habitat in America septentrionali." RCN: 3978.
Lectotype (Reveal in Jarvis & al., *Regnum Veg.* 127: 62. 1993): Herb. Clifford: 223, *Liriodendron* 1, sheet A (BM-000628821).
Generitype of *Liriodendron* Linnaeus.
Current name: ***Liriodendron tulipifera*** L. (Magnoliaceae).

Lisianthius biflorus Linnaeus, *Flora Jamaicensis*: 14. 1759.
"Habitat [in Jamaica.]"
Replaced synonym of: *Lisianthius cordifolius* L. (1767), *nom. illeg.*
Type not designated.
Original material: [icon] in Browne, Civ. Nat. Hist. Jamaica: 157, t. 9, f. 2. 1756.
Current name: ***Lisianthius cordifolius*** L. (Gentianaceae).
Note: This name appears never to have been taken up. It is validated solely by reference to an account of *Lisianthius* species no. 2 in Browne (*Civ. Nat. Hist. Jamaica*: 157. 1756), which also includes an illustration (t. 9, f. 2). Linnaeus later substituted *L. cordifolius* L. (1767) for it. The latter, although in use, therefore appears to be illegitimate.

Lisianthius cordifolius Linnaeus, *Systema Naturae*, ed. 12, 2: 154; *Mantissa Plantarum*: 43. 1767, *nom. illeg.*
"Habitat in Jamaica." RCN: 1191.
Replaced synonym: *Lisianthius biflorus* L. (1759).
Type not designated.
Original material: as replaced synonym.
Current name: ***Lisianthius cordifolius*** L. (Gentianaceae).
Note: This name appears to be an illegitimate replacement for *L. biflorus* L. (1759). The latter is validated solely by reference to an account of *Lisianthius* species no. 2 in Browne (*Civ. Nat. Hist. Jamaica*: 157. 1756), which also includes an illustration (t. 9, f. 2). Linnaeus later substituted *L. cordifolius* L. (1767) for it. The latter, although in use, therefore appears to be illegitimate.

Lisianthius longifolius Linnaeus, *Systema Naturae*, ed. 12, 2: 154; *Mantissa Plantarum*: 43. 1767.
"Habitat in Jamaicae sylvis." RCN: 1190.
Type not designated.
Original material: [icon] in Sloane, Voy. Jamaica 1: 157, t. 101, f. 1. 1707 – Voucher: Herb. Sloane 3: 22 (BM-SL); [icon] in Browne, Civ. Nat. Hist. Jamaica: 157, t. 9, f. 1. 1756.
Current name: ***Lisianthius longifolius*** L. (Gentianaceae).

Lithospermum arvense Linnaeus, *Species Plantarum* 1: 132. 1753.
"Habitat in Europae agris & arvis." RCN: 1069.

Lectotype (Kazmi in *J. Arnold Arbor.* 52: 356. 1971): Herb. Linn. No. 181.4 (LINN).
Current name: ***Buglossoides arvensis*** (L.) I.M. Johnst. (Boraginaceae).

Lithospermum dispermum Linnaeus filius, *Dec. Prima Pl. Horti Upsal.*: 13. 1762.
"Habitat in Hispania inter Gaditanum & Madritium." RCN: 1074.
Lectotype (Kazmi in *J. Arnold Arbor.* 52: 114. 1971): Herb. Linn. No. 181.11 (LINN).
Current name: ***Rochelia disperma*** (L. f.) K. Koch (Boraginaceae).

Lithospermum fruticosum Linnaeus, *Species Plantarum* 1: 133. 1753.
"Habitat in Gallia, Samo & Europa australi." RCN: 1073.
Lectotype (Turland in *Bull. Nat. Hist. Mus. London, Bot.* 25: 138, f. 11. 1995): Herb. Linn. No. 181.9 (LINN).
Current name: ***Lithodora fruticosa*** (L.) Griseb. (Boraginaceae).

Lithospermum officinale Linnaeus, *Species Plantarum* 1: 132. 1753.
"Habitat in Europae ruderatis." RCN: 1068.
Lectotype (Kazmi in *J. Arnold Arbor.* 52: 358. 1971): Herb. Linn. No. 181.1 (LINN).
Generitype of *Lithospermum* Linnaeus (vide Hitchcock, *Prop. Brit. Bot.*: 127. 1929).
Current name: ***Lithospermum officinale*** L. (Boraginaceae).

Lithospermum orientale (Linnaeus) Linnaeus, *Systema Naturae,* ed. 12, 2: 145. 1767.
["Habitat in Oriente."] Sp. Pl. 1: 133 (1753). RCN: 1071.
Basionym: *Anchusa orientalis* L. (1753).
Lectotype (Güner & Duman in Cafferty & Jarvis in *Taxon* 53: 800. 2004): Herb. Clifford: 47, *Anchusa* 2 (BM-000557914).
Current name: ***Alkanna orientalis*** (L.) Boiss. (Boraginaceae).

Lithospermum purpurocaeruleum Linnaeus, *Species Plantarum* 1: 132. 1753.
"Habitat in Ungariae, Angliae, Galliae nemoribus." RCN: 1072.
Lectotype (Selvi in Cafferty & Jarvis in *Taxon* 53: 802. 2004): Herb. Linn. No. 181.8 (LINN).
Current name: ***Buglossoides purpurocaerulea*** (L.) I.M. Johnst. (Boraginaceae).

Lithospermum tinctorium Linnaeus, *Species Plantarum* 1: 132. 1753.
"Habitat in Oriente, Monspelii." RCN: 1078.
Basionym of: *Anchusa tinctoria* (L.) L. (1762).
Lectotype (Selvi & al. in Cafferty & Jarvis in *Taxon* 53: 802. 2004): [icon] *"Anchusa monspeliana"* in Bauhin & Cherler, Hist. Pl. Univ. 3(2): 584. 1651. – Epitype (Selvi in Cafferty & Jarvis in *Taxon* 53: 802. 2004): France. Montpellier, May 1861, *G. Watson-Taylor 465* (FI).
Current name: ***Alkanna matthioli*** Tausch (Boraginaceae).

Lithospermum virginianum Linnaeus, *Species Plantarum* 1: 132. 1753.
"Habitat in Virginia." RCN: 1070.
Lectotype (Wells in Cafferty & Jarvis in *Taxon* 53: 802. 2004): *Clayton 647* (BM-000051717).
Current name: ***Onosmodium virginianum*** (L.) A. DC. (Boraginaceae).

Littorella lacustris Linnaeus, *Mantissa Plantarum Altera*: 295. 1771, *nom. illeg.*
["Habitat in Europae littora lacuum."] Sp. Pl. 1: 115 (1753). RCN: 7118.

Replaced synonym: *Plantago uniflora* L. (1753).
Type not designated.
Original material: as replaced synonym.
Current name: ***Littorella uniflora*** (L.) Asch. (Plantaginaceae).
Note: A superfluous name for *Plantago uniflora* L. (1753).

Loasa hispida Linnaeus, *Systema Naturae,* ed. 12, 2: 364. 1767, *nom. illeg.*
RCN: 3880.
Replaced synonym: *Loasa urens* Jacq. (1767).
Type not designated.
Current name: ***Loasa urens*** Jacq. (Loasaceae).
Note: Loasa hispida L. (Sep 1767) is a superfluous name for *Loasa urens* Jacq. (Apr 1767).

Lobelia assurgens Linnaeus, *Systema Naturae,* ed. 10, 2: 1237. 1759.
["Habitat in Jamaica."] Sp. Pl., ed. 2, 2: 1321 (1763). RCN: 6748.
Type not designated.
Original material: *Browne,* Herb. Linn. No. 1051.18 (LINN).
Current name: ***Lobelia assurgens*** L. (Campanulaceae).
Note: Although Rendle (in *J. Bot.* 73: 276. 1935) noted the existence of Browne material in LINN, he did not treat it as the type.

Lobelia bulbosa Linnaeus, *Species Plantarum* 2: 933. 1753.
"Habitat in Aethiopia." RCN: 6745.
Type not designated.
Original material: [icon] in Burman, Rar. Afric. Pl.: 99, t. 38, f. 2. 1738.
Current name: ***Cyphia bulbosa*** (L.) P.J. Bergius (Campanulaceae).

Lobelia cardinalis Linnaeus, *Species Plantarum* 2: 930. 1753.
"Habitat in Virginia." RCN: 6749.
Lectotype (McVaugh in *Rhodora* 38: 276. 1936): Herb. Linn. No. 1051.19 (LINN).
Generitype of *Lobelia* Linnaeus (vide Green, *Prop. Brit. Bot.*: 184. 1929).
Current name: ***Lobelia cardinalis*** L. (Campanulaceae).
Note: Lobelia dortmanna was treated as the generitype by Britton & Brown (*Ill. Fl. N. U. S.,* ed. 2, 3: 299. 1913; see McNeill & al. in *Taxon* 36: 377. 1987). However, under Art. 10.5, Ex. 7 (a voted example) of the Vienna Code, this is a type choice made under the American Code and is to be replaced under Art. 10.5b by Green's choice (*Prop. Brit. Bot.*: 184. 1929) of *Lobelia cardinalis* L.

Lobelia cheiranthus Linnaeus, *Species Plantarum* 2: 933. 1753.
"Habitat in Africa." RCN: 4561.
Basionym of: *Manulea cheiranthus* (L.) L. (1767).
Lectotype (Wijnands, *Bot. Commelins*: 189. 1983): [icon] *"Cheiranthos Africana flore luteo"* in Commelin, Hort. Med. Amstelod. Pl. Rar. 2: 83, t. 42. 1701.
Current name: ***Manulea cheiranthus*** (L.) L. (Scrophulariaceae).

Lobelia cliffortiana Linnaeus, *Species Plantarum* 2: 931. 1753.
"Habitat in Virginia, Canada." RCN: 6753.
Lectotype (Stearn, *Introd. Linnaeus' Sp. Pl.* (Ray Soc. ed.): 47. 1957): [icon] *"Lobelia caule erecto, foliis cordatis obsolete dentatis petiolatis, corymbo terminatrice"* in Linnaeus, Hort. Cliff.: 426, t. 26. 1738.
Current name: ***Lobelia cliffortiana*** L. (Campanulaceae).
Note: Rendle (in *J. Bot.* 73: 273. 1935; in Fawcett & Rendle, *Fl. Jamaica* 7: 142. 1936) stated that the name was based on the Clifford plate, also noting good material in the Clifford herbarium (BM). However, he did not explicitly indicate a type.

Lobelia comosa Linnaeus, *Species Plantarum* 2: 933. 1753.
"Habitat in Aethiopia." RCN: 6746.

L

Type not designated.

Original material: none traced.

Current name: **Lobelia comosa** L. (Campanulaceae).

Note: Although Adamson (in *J. S. African Bot.* 8: 274. 1942) stated that this was based on the *Hortus Cliffortianus* account, there are no Clifford collections now associated with this name.

Lobelia cornuta Linnaeus, *Species Plantarum* 2: 930. 1753.

"Habitat in Cayenna." RCN: 6743.

Type not designated.

Original material: none traced.

Current name: **Centropogon cornutus** (L.) Druce (Campanulaceae).

Note: Although Staples (in Howard, *Fl. Lesser Antilles* 6: 498. 1989) stated "Type : Cayenne, Royen, n. v.", the statement is derived from the protologue and does not imply the existence of a specific D. van Royen collection.

Lobelia coronopifolia Linnaeus, *Species Plantarum* 2: 933. 1753.

"Habitat in Aethiopia." RCN: 6762.

Type not designated.

Original material: [icon] in Burman, Rar. Afric. Pl.: 98, t. 38, f. 1. 1738; [icon] in Breyn, Exot. Pl. Cent.: 174, t. 88. 1678.

Current name: **Lobelia coronopifolia** L. (Campanulaceae).

Lobelia dortmanna Linnaeus, *Species Plantarum* 2: 929. 1753.

"Habitat in Europae frigidissimae lacubus & ripis." RCN: 6739.

Lectotype (McVaugh in *Rhodora* 38: 358. 1936): Herb. Linn. No. 1051.5 (LINN).

Current name: **Lobelia dortmanna** L. (Campanulaceae).

Note: Lobelia dortmanna was treated as the generitype by Britton & Brown (*Ill. Fl. N. U. S.*, ed. 2, 3: 299. 1913; see McNeill & al. in *Taxon* 36: 377. 1987). However, under Art. 10.5, Ex. 7 (a voted example) of the Vienna Code, this is a type choice made under the American Code and is to be replaced under Art. 10.5b by Green's choice (*Prop. Brit. Bot.*: 184. 1929) of *Lobelia cardinalis* L.

Lobelia erinoides Linnaeus, *Species Plantarum* 2: 932. 1753.

"Habitat in Aethiopia." RCN: 6758b.

Lectotype (Thulin & al. in *Taxon* 35: 726. 1986): Herb. Clifford: 426, *Lobelia* 4 (BM-000647303).

Current name: **Lobelia erinus** L. (Campanulaceae).

Lobelia erinus Linnaeus, *Species Plantarum* 2: 932. 1753.

"Habitat in Aethiopia." RCN: 6757.

Neotype (Thulin & al. in *Taxon* 35: 726, f. 1. 1986): *Burmester s.n.* (SBT).

Current name: **Lobelia erinus** L. (Campanulaceae).

Lobelia hirsuta Linnaeus, *Species Plantarum* 2: 932. 1753.

"Habitat in Aethiopia." RCN: 6761.

Lectotype (Thulin & al. in *Taxon* 35: 722, f. 1, 2. 1986): [icon] *"Rapuntium foliis subrotundis, hirtis, flore ex alis solitario"* in Burman, Rar. Afric. Pl.: 105, t. 40, f. 2. 1738. – Typotype: Herb. Burman (G).

Current name: **Gnidia hirsuta** (L.) Thulin (Thymelaeaceae).

Lobelia hirta Linnaeus, *Species Plantarum* 2: 932. 1753.

"Habitat in Aethiopia." RCN: 6759.

Type not designated.

Original material: none traced.

Note: The application of this name appears uncertain.

Lobelia inflata Linnaeus, *Species Plantarum* 2: 931. 1753.

"Habitat in Virginia, Canada." RCN: 6752.

Lectotype (designated here by Reveal): [icon] *"Lobelia caule erecto,*

foliis ovatis subserratis pedunculo longioribus, capsulis inflatis" in Linnaeus in Acta Soc. Regiae Sci. Upsal. 1741: 23, t. 1. 1741 (see p. 84).

Current name: **Lobelia inflata** L. (Campanulaceae).

Note: McVaugh (in *Rhodora* 38: 232. 1936) indicated 1051.26 (LINN) as type, but the sheet lacks the relevant *Species Plantarum* number (i.e. "12") and was a post-1753 addition to the collection and is not original material for the name.

Lobelia kalmii Linnaeus, *Species Plantarum* 2: 930. 1753.

"Habitat in Canada." RCN: 6741.

Lectotype (McVaugh in *Rhodora* 38: 355. 1936): *Kalm*, Herb. Linn. No. 1051.8 (LINN).

Current name: **Lobelia kalmii** L. (Campanulaceae).

Lobelia laurentia Linnaeus, *Species Plantarum* 2: 931. 1753.

"Habitat in Italia." RCN: 6756.

Lectotype (Crespo & al. in *Taxon* 45: 117. 1996): [icon] *"Laurentia annua, minima, flore caeruleo"* in Micheli, Nov. Pl. Gen.: 18, t. 14. 1729. – Voucher: Herb. Micheli 779, I: 717 [69: 125] 2 sheets (FI).

Current name: **Solenopsis laurentia** (L.) C. Presl (Campanulaceae).

Lobelia longiflora Linnaeus, *Species Plantarum* 2: 930. 1753.

"Habitat in Jamaica ad ripas." RCN: 6747.

Lectotype (Crespo & al. in *Taxon* 45: 118. 1996): [icon] *"Rapunculus aquaticus foliis cichorii, flore albo, tubulo longissimo"* in Sloane, Voy. Jamaica 1: 158, t. 101, f. 2. 1707. – Typotype: Herb. Sloane 3: 23, upper specimen (BM-SL).

Current name: **Hippobroma longiflora** (L.) G. Don (Campanulaceae).

Note: McVaugh (in *Bull. Torrey Bot. Club* 67: 783. 1940) stated that the material in Herb. Sloane should be regarded as the type, but this was not seen by Linnaeus and is not original material for the name (though it is now its typotype).

Lobelia lutea Linnaeus, *Species Plantarum* 2: 932. 1753.

"Habitat in Aethiopia." RCN: 6760.

Type not designated.

Original material: [icon] in Burman, Rar. Afric. Pl.: 101, t. 39, f. 1. 1738.

Current name: **Monopsis lutea** (L.) Urb. (Campanulaceae).

Lobelia minuta Linnaeus, *Mantissa Plantarum Altera*: 292. 1771.

"Habitat ad Cap. b. spei subaquosis." RCN: 6755.

Neotype (Meikle in *Kew Bull.* 34: 374. 1979): Herb. Tournefort No. 861 (P-TOURN).

Current name: **Solenopsis minuta** (L.) C. Presl subsp. **minuta** (Campanulaceae).

Lobelia obscura Linnaeus, *Plantae Surinamenses*: 14. 1775.

"Habitat [in Surinamo.]" RCN: 6764.

Type not designated.

Original material: none traced.

Current name: **Centropogon cornutus** (L.) Druce (Campanulaceae).

Lobelia paniculata Linnaeus, *Species Plantarum* 2: 930. 1753.

"Habitat in Aethiopia." RCN: 6742.

Type not designated.

Original material: [icon] in Burman, Rar. Afric. Pl.: 100, t. 38, f. 3. 1738.

Note: The application of this name appears uncertain.

Lobelia phyteuma Linnaeus, *Species Plantarum* 2: 930. 1753.

"Habitat in Aethiopia." RCN: 6744.

Type not designated.

Original material: none traced.
Current name: ***Cyphia phyteuma*** (L.) Willd. (Campanulaceae).

Lobelia pinifolia Linnaeus, *Species Plantarum* 2: 929. 1753.
"Habitat in Aethiopia." RCN: 6738.
Type not designated.
Original material: Herb. Linn. No. 1051.2 (LINN); [icon] in Burman, Rar. Afric. Pl.: 111, t. 41, f. 2. 1739; [icon] in Breyn, Exot. Pl. Cent.: 173, t. 87. 1678.
Current name: ***Lobelia pinifolia*** L. (Campanulaceae).

Lobelia plumieri Linnaeus, *Species Plantarum* 2: 929. 1753.
"Habitat in Indiis." RCN: 1359.
Replaced synonym of: *Scaevola lobelia* L. (1771), *nom. illeg.*
Lectotype (Davies in Polhill, *Fl. Trop. E. Africa, Goodeniaceae*: 3. 1978): [icon] *"Lobelia frutescens, Portulacae folio"* in Catesby, Nat. Hist. Carolina 1: 79, t. 79. 1731.
Current name: ***Scaevola plumieri*** (L.) Vahl (Goodeniaceae).
Note: Davies' type choice (9 Aug 1978) narrowly pre-dates that of Guillaumet (in Leroy, *Fl. Madagascar* 188: 30. 10 Oct 1978), who instead designated 229.1 (LINN) as lectotype.

Lobelia simplex Linnaeus, *Mantissa Plantarum Altera*: 291. 1771.
"Habitat ad Cap. b. spei." RCN: 6737.
Lectotype (Barker in *J. S. African Bot.* 50: 136. 1984): Herb. Linn. No. 1051.1 (LINN).
Current name: ***Monopsis simplex*** (L.) Wimm. (Campanulaceae).

Lobelia siphilitica Linnaeus, *Species Plantarum* 2: 931. 1753.
"Habitat in Virginia." RCN: 6750.
Lectotype (McVaugh in *Rhodora* 38: 278. 1936): Herb. Linn. No. 1051.25 (LINN).
Current name: ***Lobelia siphilitica*** L. (Campanulaceae).

Lobelia surinamensis Linnaeus, *Species Plantarum*, ed. 2, 2: 1320. 1763.
"Habitat Surinami." RCN: 6751.
Type not designated.
Original material: none traced.
Current name: ***Centropogon cornutus*** (L.) Druce (Campanulaceae).

Lobelia tenella Linnaeus, *Systema Naturae*, ed. 12, 2: 584; *Mantissa Plantarum*: 120. 1767.
"Habitat ad Cap. b. spei." RCN: 6763.
Lectotype (Phillipson in *Bot. J. Linn. Soc.* 99: 257. 1989): Herb. Linn. No. 1051.50 (LINN).
Current name: ***Wahlenbergia* sp.** (Campanulaceae).
Note: Phillipson, in typifying the name, excluded it from *Monopsis* but stated only that it applied to an unspecified species of *Wahlenbergia*.

Lobelia trapa Linnaeus, *Species Plantarum* 2: 929. 1753 *orth. var.*
"Habitat in Peru." RCN: 6740.
Lectotype (Matthews in *Kew Mag.* 5: 161. 1988): [icon] *"Rapuntium spicatum, foliis acutis, vulgo Tupa"* in Feuillée, J. Obs. 2: 739, t. 29. 1714.
Current name: ***Lobelia tupa*** L. (Campanulaceae).
Note: The specific epithet was drawn from Feuillée's phrase name, misquoted by Linnaeus as "Rap. spicatum, fol. auritis, vulgo Trapa". He corrected the spelling in *Sp. Pl.*, ed. 2, 2: 1318 (1763).

Lobelia triquetra Linnaeus, *Systema Naturae*, ed. 12, 2: 583; *Mantissa Plantarum*: 120. 1767.
"Habitat ad Cap b. spei." RCN: 6746.
Type not designated.
Original material: none traced.
Current name: ***Lobelia comosa*** L. (Campanulaceae).

Lobelia tupa Linnaeus, *Species Plantarum*, ed. 2, 2: 1318. 1763.
"Habitat in Peru." RCN: 6740.
Lectotype (Matthews in *Kew Mag.* 5: 161. 1988): [icon] *"Rapuntium spicatum, foliis acutis, vulgo Tupa"* in Feuillée, J. Obs. 2: 739, t. 29. 1714.
Current name: ***Lobelia tupa*** L. (Campanulaceae).
Note: An orthographic correction by Linnaeus for the earlier "trapa".

Lobelia urens Linnaeus, *Species Plantarum* 2: 931. 1753.
"Habitat in Gallia." RCN: 6754.
Type not designated.
Original material: *Löfling s.n.*, Herb. Linn. No. 1051.32 (LINN); [icon] in Morison, Pl. Hist. Univ. 2: 467, s. 5, t. 5, f. 56. 1680; [icon] in Boccone, Icon. Descr. Rar. Pl. Siciliae: 21, 20, t. 11. 1674.
Current name: ***Lobelia urens*** L. (Campanulaceae).

Lobelia zeylanica Linnaeus, *Species Plantarum* 2: 932. 1753.
"Habitat in China. Osbeck." RCN: 6759.
Type not designated.
Original material: Herb. Linn. No. 1051.42 (LINN); Herb. Linn. No. 1051.41 (LINN); Herb. Linn. No. 368.3 (S); [icon] in Seba, Locupl. Rer. Nat. Thes. 1: 37, t. 22, f. 12. 1734.
Current name: ***Lobelia zeylanica*** L. (Campanulaceae).
Note: Merrill & Perry (in *J. Arnold Arbor.* 22: 386. 1941) stated that "the Osbeck specimen [in LINN] is unquestionably the type" but did not distinguish between (presumably) 1051.41 and 1051.42, neither of which is annotated as having come from Osbeck (see Hansen & Fox Maule in *Bot. J. Linn. Soc.* 67: 198. 1973). There is also an extensive review by Moeliono & Tuyn in van Steenis, *Fl. Malesiana*, ser. I, 6: 129. 1960).

Loeflingia hispanica Linnaeus, *Species Plantarum* 1: 35. 1753.
"Habitat in Hispaniae collibus apricis." RCN: 281.
Lectotype (Burtt & Lewis in *Kew Bull.* 7: 334. 1952): *Löfling s.n.*, Herb. Linn. No. 54.1 (LINN).
Generitype of *Loeflingia* Linnaeus.
Current name: ***Loeflingia hispanica*** L. (Caryophyllaceae).

Loeselia ciliata Linnaeus, *Species Plantarum* 2: 628. 1753.
"Habitat in Vera Cruce." RCN: 4547.
Lectotype (West in Jarvis & al., *Regnum Veg.* 127: 62. 1993): Herb. A. van Royen No. 913.7–269 (L).
Generitype of *Loeselia* Linnaeus.
Current name: ***Loeselia ciliata*** L. (Polemoniaceae).
Note: Turner (in *Phytologia* 77: 321. 1994) wrongly indicated Houstoun material in L, unseen by Linnaeus, as the holotype.

Lolium annuum Linnaeus, *Flora Anglica*: 11. 1754.
"Habitat [in Anglia.]"
Lectotype (Turland in Cafferty & al. in *Taxon* 49: 252. 2000): [icon] *"Lollium album"* in Gerard, Herball: 71. 1597 (see p. 132).
Current name: ***Lolium temulentum*** L. (Poaceae).
Note: In the later *Amoen. Acad.* edition of *Flora Anglica*, Linnaeus (1759: 97) transferred this name to the synonymy of *L. temulentum* L. (1753).

Lolium distachyon Linnaeus, *Mantissa Plantarum Altera*: 187. 1771.
"Habitat in Malabaria. Koenig." RCN: 695.
Lectotype (Terrell, *Taxon. Revis. Genus* Lolium: 59. 1968): Herb. Linn. No. 99.11 (LINN).
Current name: ***Digitaria* sp.** (Poaceae).
Note: Terrell identified the type material as a species of *Digitaria*, and consequently excluded the name from *Lolium*.

L

Lolium perenne Linnaeus, *Species Plantarum* 1: 83. 1753.
"Habitat in Europa ad agrorum versuras solo fertili." RCN: 692.
Lectotype (Terrell, *Taxon. Revis. Genus* Lolium: 7. 1968): Herb. Linn. No. 99.1 (LINN).
Generitype of *Lolium* Linnaeus (vide Hitchcock, *Prop. Brit. Bot.*: 121. 1929).
Current name: ***Lolium perenne*** L. (Poaceae).
Note: See extensive review by Loos & Jarvis (in *Bot. J. Linn. Soc.* 108: 400, f. 1. 1992).

Lolium temulentum Linnaeus, *Species Plantarum* 1: 83. 1753.
"Habitat in Europae agris inter Hordeum, Linum." RCN: 694.
Lectotype (Loos & Jarvis in *Bot. J. Linn. Soc.* 108: 408. 1992): Herb. Burser I: 113 (UPS).
Current name: ***Lolium temulentum*** L. (Poaceae).
Note: Although Kerguélen (in *Lejeunia*, n.s., 75: 209. 1975) stated "Type: ...LINN", this is not accepted as a formal typification, for the reasons explained by Cafferty & al. (in *Taxon* 49: 240. 2000). Loos & Jarvis account for other pre-1992 typification statements.

Lolium tenue Linnaeus, *Species Plantarum,* ed. 2, 1: 122. 1762.
"Habitat in Gallia." RCN: 693.
Lectotype (Terrell, *Taxon. Revis. Genus* Lolium: 46. 1968): Herb. Linn. No. 99.6 (LINN).
Current name: ***Lolium perenne*** L. (Poaceae).

Lonchitis aurita Linnaeus, *Species Plantarum* 2: 1078. 1753.
"Habitat in America meridionali." RCN: 7824.
Lectotype (Proctor in *Brit. Fern Gaz.* 10: 21, f. 1. 1968): [icon] *"Filix latifolia, spinulis mollibus et nigris aculeata"* in Plumier, Traité Foug. Amér.: 14, t. 17. 1705.
Current name: ***Lonchitis aurita*** L. (Dennstaedtiaceae).
Note: Tryon (in *Contr. Gray Herb.* 191: 95. 1962) wrongly regarded the name as illegitimate (as he believed the cited Plumier plate to be a mixture of two species). See additional comments by Morton (in *Contr. U. S. Natl. Herb.* 38(2): 49. 1967).

Lonchitis hirsuta Linnaeus, *Species Plantarum* 2: 1078. 1753.
"Habitat in America meridionali." RCN: 7823.
Lectotype (Tryon in *Contr. Gray Herb.* 191: 95. 1962): [icon] *"Filix villosa, pinnulis quercinis"* in Plumier, Traité Foug. Amér.: 16, t. 20. 1705 (see p. 150).
Generitype of *Lonchitis* Linnaeus (vide Brongniart, *Dict. Class. Hist. Nat.* 9: 490. 1826).
Current name: ***Lonchitis hirsuta*** L. (Dennstaedtiaceae).
Note: Lonchitis hirsuta, with the type designated by Tryon (erroneously attributed to Proctor in Howard, *Fl. Lesser Antilles* 2: 133. 1977), was proposed as conserved type of the genus by Jarvis (in *Taxon* 41: 565. 1992). The Committee for Pteridophyta (in *Taxon* 48: 133. 1999) ruled that the proposal was unnecessary, concluding that *L. hirsuta* is in any case the generitype, as chosen by Brongniart in 1826.

Lonchitis pedata Linnaeus, *Systema Naturae,* ed. 10, 2: 1323. 1759.
["Habitat in Jamaica."] Sp. Pl., ed. 2, 2: 1536 (1763). RCN: 7826.
Lectotype (Proctor, *Ferns Jamaica*: 278. 1985): Herb. Linn. No. 1249.1 (LINN).
Current name: ***Pteris podophylla*** Sw. (Pteridaceae).

Lonchitis repens Linnaeus, *Species Plantarum* 2: 1078. 1753.
"Habitat in America meridionali." RCN: 7825.
Lectotype (Underwood in *Bull. Torrey Bot. Club* 33: 192. 1906): [icon] *"Filix aculeata, repens"* in Plumier, Traité Foug. Amér.: 11, t. 12. 1705.
Current name: ***Hypolepis repens*** (L.) C. Presl (Dennstaedtiaceae).

Lonicera alba Linnaeus, *Species Plantarum* 1: 175. 1753.
"Habitat in Jamaica, Barbados locis confragosis." RCN: 1368.
Replaced synonym of: *Chiococca racemosa* L. (1759), nom. illeg.
Type not designated.
Original material: [icon] in Sloane, Voy. Jamaica 2: 97, t. 188, f. 3. 1725 – Typotype: Herb. Sloane 7: 46 (BM-SL); [icon] in Dillenius, Hort. Eltham. 2: 306, t. 228, f. 295. 1732.
Current name: ***Chiococca alba*** (L.) Hitchc. (Rubiaceae).
Note: Steyermark (in *Mem. New York Bot. Gard.* 23: 381. 1972) wrongly indicated a Browne collection (233.1 LINN) acquired by Linnaeus only in 1758 as the type. Howard (*Fl. Lesser Antilles* 6: 398. 1989) suggested that a specimen in the Sloane herbarium might be an appropriate type (but it was not seen by Linnaeus and is not original material for the name). Lorence (in *Monogr. Syst. Bot. Missouri Bot. Gard.* 73: 33, 97. 1999) noted Howard's suggestion and also suggested that unseen Clifford material might be relevant. The name, however, remains untypified.

Lonicera alpigena Linnaeus, *Species Plantarum* 1: 174. 1753.
"Habitat in Alpibus Helveticis, Pyrenaicis, Allobrogicis." RCN: 1379.
Type not designated.
Original material: Herb. Linn. No. 235.10 (LINN); Herb. Clifford: 58, *Lonicera* 7 (BM); [icon] in Clusius, Rar. Pl. Hist. 1: 59. 1601.
Current name: ***Lonicera alpigena*** L. (Caprifoliaceae).

Lonicera caerulea Linnaeus, *Species Plantarum* 1: 174. 1753.
"Habitat in Helvetia." RCN: 1380.
Type not designated.
Original material: Herb. Linn. No. 235.12 (LINN); [icon] in Clusius, Rar. Stirp. Pannon.: 85, 86. 1583; [icon] in Bauhin & Cherler, Hist. Pl. Univ. 2: 108. 1651.
Current name: ***Lonicera caerulea*** L. (Caprifoliaceae).

Lonicera caprifolium Linnaeus, *Species Plantarum* 1: 173. 1753.
"Habitat in Europa australi." RCN: 1371.
Lectotype (Wijnands in Jarvis & al., *Regnum Veg.* 127: 62. 1993): Herb. Clifford: 58, *Lonicera* 5 (BM-000558014).
Generitype of *Lonicera* Linnaeus (vide Hitchcock, *Prop. Brit. Bot.*: 131. 1929).
Current name: ***Lonicera caprifolium*** L. (Caprifoliaceae).

Lonicera corymbosa Linnaeus, *Species Plantarum* 1: 175. 1753.
"Habitat in Peru." RCN: 1383.
Lectotype (Kuijt in *Syst. Bot. Monogr.* 19: 20. 1988): [icon] *"Periclymenum foliis acutis, floribus profunde dissectis, vulgo y tiu"* in Feuillée, J. Obs. 2: 760, t. 45. 1714.
Current name: ***Tristerix corymbosus*** (L.) Kuijt (Caprifoliaceae).

Lonicera diervilla Linnaeus, *Species Plantarum* 1: 175. 1753.
"Habitat in Acadia, Noveboraco." RCN: 1382.
Lectotype (Stearn, *Introd. Linnaeus' Sp. Pl.* (Ray Soc. ed.): 47. 1957): [icon] *"Diervilla"* in Linnaeus, Hort. Cliff.: 63, t. 7. 1738.
Current name: ***Diervilla lonicera*** Mill. (Caprifoliaceae).

Lonicera dioica Linnaeus, *Systema Naturae,* ed. 12, 2: 165. 1767.
RCN: 1373.
Type not designated.
Original material: Herb. Linn. No. 235.4 (LINN).
Current name: ***Lonicera dioica*** L. (Caprifoliaceae).
Note: The LINN specimen appears to be the sole original element.

Lonicera marilandica Linnaeus, *Species Plantarum* 1: 175. 1753.
"Habitat in Virginia, Marilandia, Carolina." RCN: 1187.
Basionym of: *Spigelia marilandica* (L.) L. (1767).

Lectotype (Reveal & al. in *Huntia* 7: 230. 1987): *Clayton s.n.* (BM-000098044).
Current name: ***Spigelia marilandica*** (L.) L. (Strychnaceae).

Lonicera nigra Linnaeus, *Species Plantarum* 1: 173. 1753.
"Habitat in Delphinatu, Gallia, Helvetia." RCN: 1375.
Type not designated.
Original material: Herb. Burser XXIII: 66 (UPS); [icon] in Bauhin & Cherler, Hist. Pl. Univ. 2: 107. 1651; [icon] in Clusius, Rar. Pl. Hist. 1: 58. 1601.
Current name: ***Lonicera nigra*** L. (Caprifoliaceae).

Lonicera parasitica Linnaeus, *Species Plantarum* 1: 175. 1753.
"Habitat in India orientali." RCN: 2563.
Replaced synonym of: *Loranthus loniceroides* L. (1762), *nom. illeg.*
Type not designated.
Original material: Herb. Hermann 2: 21, No. 83 (BM); [icon] in Plukenet, Phytographia: t. 212, f. 5. 1692; Almag. Bot.: 287. 1696; [icon] in Rheede, Hort. Malab. 7: 55, t. 29. 1688.
Current name: ***Macrosolen parasiticus*** (L.) Danser (Loranthaceae).

Lonicera periclymenum Linnaeus, *Species Plantarum* 1: 173. 1753.
"Habitat in Europa media." RCN: 1374.
Type not designated.
Original material: Herb. Burser XVII: 47 (UPS); [icon] in Miller, Cat. Pl.: 15, t. 6, 8. 1730.
Current name: ***Lonicera periclymenum*** L. (Caprifoliaceae).

Lonicera pyrenaica Linnaeus, *Species Plantarum* 1: 174. 1753.
"Habitat in Pyrenaeis." RCN: 1378.
Type not designated.
Original material: Herb. Linn. No. 235.9 (LINN); [icon] in Magnol, Hort. Reg. Monspel.: unnumbered plate. 1697.
Current name: ***Lonicera pyrenaica*** L. (Caprifoliaceae).

Lonicera sempervirens Linnaeus, *Species Plantarum* 1: 173. 1753.
"Habitat in Virginia, Mexico." RCN: 1372.
Lectotype (Wijnands, *Bot. Commelins*: 63. 1983): [icon] *"Periclymenum perfoliatum Virginianum semper virens et florens"* in Hermann, Hort. Lugd.-Bat. Cat.: 484, 485. 1687.
Current name: ***Lonicera sempervirens*** L. (Caprifoliaceae).

Lonicera symphoricarpos Linnaeus, *Species Plantarum* 1: 175. 1753.
"Habitat in Virginia, Carolina." RCN: 1381.
Type not designated.
Original material: *Clayton 281* (BM); Herb. Linn. No. 85.13 (S); Herb. Clifford: 58, *Lonicera* 2 (BM); *Clayton 201* (BM); Herb. Linn. No. 235.13 (LINN); [icon] in Miller, Cat. Pl.: 85, t. 20. 1730; [icon] in Dillenius, Hort. Eltham. 2: 371, t. 278, f. 360. 1732.
Current name: ***Symphoricarpos orbiculatus*** Moench (Caprifoliaceae).

Lonicera tatarica Linnaeus, *Species Plantarum* 1: 173. 1753.
"Habitat in Tataria." RCN: 1376.
Type not designated.
Original material: *Gerber*, Herb. Linn. No. 235.7 (LINN).
Current name: ***Lonicera tatarica*** L. (Caprifoliaceae).

Lonicera xylosteum Linnaeus, *Species Plantarum* 1: 174. 1753.
"Habitat in Europae frigidioris sepibus." RCN: 1377.
Type not designated.
Original material: Herb. Burser XXIII: 69 (UPS); Herb. Clifford: 58, *Lonicera* 6 (BM); Herb. A. van Royen No. 899.69–21 (L); Herb. Linn. No. 235.8 (LINN); [icon] in Dodoëns, Stirp. Hist. Pempt., ed. 2: 411, 412. 1616.
Current name: ***Lonicera xylosteum*** L. (Caprifoliaceae).

Loranthus altissimus Linnaeus, *Amoenitates Academicae* 5: 377. 1760.
"Habitat [in Jamaica.]"
Type not designated.
Original material: none traced.
Note: Specific epithet spelled "altissima" in the protologue. The application of this name is uncertain.

Loranthus americanus Linnaeus, *Species Plantarum* 1: 331. 1753.
"Habitat in Martinique." RCN: 2560.
Type not designated.
Original material: [icon] in Plumier in Burman, Pl. Amer.: 158, t. 166, f. 1. 1758; [icon] in Plumier, Nov. Pl. Amer.: 17, t. 37. 1703.
Generitype of *Loranthus* Linnaeus, *nom. rej.*
Current name: ***Psitticanthus americanus*** (L.) Mart. (Loranthaceae).
Note: Loranthus Linnaeus, *nom. rej.* in favour of *Loranthus* Jacq.

Loranthus loniceroides Linnaeus, *Species Plantarum*, ed. 2, 1: 472. 1762, *nom. illeg.*
"Habitat in Asiae arboribus." RCN: 2563.
Replaced synonym: *Lonicera parasitica* L. (1753).
Type not designated.
Original material: as replaced synonym.
Current name: ***Macrosolen parasiticus*** (L.) Danser (Loranthaceae).
Note: A superfluous name for *Lonicera parasitica* L. (1753).

Loranthus occidentalis Linnaeus, *Systema Naturae,* ed. 10, 2: 988. 1759.
["Habitat in Americae arboribus."] Sp. Pl., ed. 2, 1: 473 (1762). RCN: 2562.
Type not designated.
Original material: [icon] in Sloane, Voy. Jamaica 2: 92, t. 200, f. 2. 1725 – Voucher: Herb. Sloane 6: 108 (BM-SL).
Current name: ***Oryctanthus occidentalis*** (L.) Eichler (Loranthaceae).
Note: Kuijt (in *Bot. Jahrb. Syst.* 95: 521. 1976) wrongly treated material in Herb. Sloane (6: 108, BM-SL) as the holotype, but this was not studied by Linnaeus and is not original material for the name.

Loranthus pentandrus Linnaeus, *Systema Naturae,* ed. 12, 2: 252; *Mantissa Plantarum*: 63. 1767.
"Habitat in India." RCN: 2565.
Lectotype (Danser, *Bull. Jard. Bot. Buitenzorg,* sér. 3, 11: 419. 1931): Herb. Linn. No. 455.7 (LINN).
Current name: ***Dendrophthoe pentandra*** (L.) Miq. (Loranthaceae).

Loranthus scurrula Linnaeus, *Species Plantarum,* ed. 2, 1: 472. 1762, *nom. illeg.*
"Habitat in China." RCN: 2558.
Replaced synonym: *Scurrula parasitica* L. (1753).
Lectotype (Barlow in Kalkman & al., *Fl. Malesiana,* ser. I, 13: 387. 1997): Herb. Linn. No. 455.1 (LINN).
Current name: ***Scurrula parasitica*** L. (Loranthaceae).
Note: A superfluous name for *Scurrula parasitica* L. (1753).

Loranthus stelis Linnaeus, *Species Plantarum,* ed. 2, 1: 473. 1762.
"Habitat in Cumanae arboribus." RCN: 2564.
Neotype (Kuijt in *Novon* 6: 50. 1996): Panama. Panamá: seaside just W of Vera Cruz, sea level, on *Laguncularia racemosa, Hammel 3298* (MO; iso- LEA).
Current name: ***Phthirusa stelis*** (L.) Kuijt (Loranthaceae).

Lotus angustissimus Linnaeus, *Species Plantarum* 2: 774. 1753.
"Habitat in G. Narbonensi." RCN: 1691.
Lectotype (Heyn in Davis, *Fl. Turkey* 3: 523. 1970): Herb. Clifford: 372, *Lotus* 5 (BM-000646725).

Current name: ***Lotus angustissimus*** L. (Fabaceae: Faboideae).
Note: Heyn (in *Israel J. Bot.* 19: 260. Jun 1970) gives a slightly more detailed account than in Davis, *Fl. Turkey* 3: 523 (16 Apr 1970), the place of her original typification.

Lotus arabicus Linnaeus, *Systema Naturae,* ed. 12, 2: 504; *Mantissa Plantarum*: 104. 1767.
"Habitat in Arabia. D. Forskåhl." RCN: 5692.
Lectotype (Lassen in Turland & Jarvis in *Taxon* 46: 474. 1997): Herb. Linn. No. 931.10 (LINN).
Current name: ***Lotus arabicus*** L. (Fabaceae: Faboideae).
Note: Gillett (in Milne-Redhead & Polhill, *Fl. Trop. E. Africa, Leguminosae* 4: 1048. 1971) indicated the specimen in Herb. Linn. No. 931.11 (LINN) as the lectotype, but this cannot be regarded as relevant original material because there is nothing in Linnaeus' annotation of the sheet to link it with *L. arabicus.*

Lotus conjugatus Linnaeus, *Species Plantarum* 2: 774. 1753.
"Habitat Monspelii." RCN: 5687.
Lectotype (Domínguez & Galiano in *Lagascalia* 8: 204. 1979): Herb. Linn. No. 931.3 (LINN).
Current name: ***Tetragonolobus conjugatus*** (L.) Link (Fabaceae: Faboideae).
Note: Specific epithet spelled "conjugata" in the protologue.

Lotus corniculatus Linnaeus, *Species Plantarum* 2: 775. 1753.
"Habitat in Europa." RCN: 5699.
Lectotype (Chrtková-Zertová in *Rozpr. Cesk. Akad. Ved., Mat. Prír.* 83(4): 28, f. 3. 1973): Herb. Linn. No. 931.23 (LINN).
Generitype of *Lotus* Linnaeus (vide Green, *Prop. Brit. Bot.*: 177. 1929).
Current name: ***Lotus corniculatus*** L. (Fabaceae: Faboideae).
Note: Heyn (in Davis, *Fl. Turkey* 3: 526. 1970) indicated non-fruiting material in the Clifford herbarium as type, but did not distinguish between the two sheets (Herb. Clifford: 372, *Lotus* 6A; 6B) preserved there. As they are evidently not part of the same gathering, Art. 9.15 does not apply. Chrtková-Zertová (in *Ann. Naturhist. Mus. Wien* 75: 34. 1971) identified this material as *L. uliginosus* Schkuhr, and subsequently (1973) made an explicit type choice.

Lotus corniculatus Linnaeus var. **tenuifolius** Linnaeus, *Species Plantarum* 2: 776. 1753.
RCN: 5699.
Lectotype (Heath in *Calyx* 2: 51. 1992): Herb. Burser XVIII(2): 73 (UPS).
Current name: ***Lotus tenuis*** Waldst. & Kit. (Fabaceae: Faboideae).
Note: Specific epithet spelled "corniculata" and varietal epithet "tenuifolia" in the protologue.
   Greuter (in *Taxon* 44: 424. 1995) observes that the cited Burser material is a syntype, which therefore takes precedence over any uncited material or cited illustrations, and concludes that it is the obligate lectotype.

Lotus creticus Linnaeus, *Species Plantarum* 2: 775. 1753.
"Habitat in Syria, Creta." RCN: 5695.
Lectotype (Heyn & Herrnstadt in *Kew Bull.* 21: 300. 1967): Herb. Clifford: 372, *Lotus* 10 (BM-000646731).
Current name: ***Lotus creticus*** L. (Fabaceae: Faboideae).
Note: Specific epithet spelled "cretica" in the protologue.

Lotus cytisoides Linnaeus, *Species Plantarum* 2: 776. 1753.
"Habitat in maritimis Europae australis." RCN: 5700.
Lectotype (Heyn & Herrnstadt in *Kew Bull.* 21: 307. 1967): [icon] *"Lotus siliquosa maritima lutea, Cytisi facie"* in Barrelier, Pl. Galliam: 71, t. 1031. 1714 (see p. 106).
Current name: ***Lotus cytisoides*** L. (Fabaceae: Faboideae).

Lotus dorycnium Linnaeus, *Species Plantarum* 2: 776. 1753.
"Habitat in Hispania, G. Narbonensi, Austria." RCN: 5701.
Lectotype (Lassen in Turland & Jarvis in *Taxon* 46: 474. 1997): Herb. Clifford: 371, *Dorycnium* 3, sheet B (BM-000646710).
Current name: ***Dorycnium pentaphyllum*** Scop. (Fabaceae: Faboideae).

Lotus edulis Linnaeus, *Species Plantarum* 2: 774. 1753.
"Habitat in Italia, Sicilia, Creta." RCN: 5689.
Lectotype (Heyn in Davis, *Fl. Turkey* 3: 520. 1970): Herb. Clifford: 371, *Lotus* 2 (BM-000646722).
Current name: ***Lotus edulis*** L. (Fabaceae: Faboideae).

Lotus erectus Linnaeus, *Species Plantarum* 2: 774. 1753.
"Habitat Monspelii." RCN: 5685.
Replaced synonym of: *Lotus siliquosus* L. (1759), *nom. illeg.*
Lectotype (Lassen in Turland & Jarvis in *Taxon* 46: 475. 1997): Herb. Burser XVIII(2): 79 (UPS).
Current name: ***Lotus maritimus*** L. (Fabaceae: Faboideae).
Note: Specific epithet spelled "erecta" in the protologue.

Lotus fruticosus Linnaeus, *Systema Naturae,* ed. 10, 2: 1179. 1759.
RCN: 5435.
Lectotype (Schutte & Van Wyk in *Taxon* 42: 46. 1993): Herb. Linn. No. 293.5 (S).
Current name: ***Xiphotheca fruticosa*** (L.) A.L. Schutte & B.-E. van Wyk (Fabaceae: Faboideae).

Lotus graecus Linnaeus, *Systema Naturae,* ed. 12, 2: 505; *Mantissa Plantarum*: 104. 1767.
"Habitat in Oriente: in Graecia, Arabia." RCN: 5697.
Lectotype (Lassen in Turland & Jarvis in *Taxon* 46: 475. 1997): Herb. Linn. No. 931.20 (LINN).
Current name: ***Dorycnium graecum*** (L.) Ser. (Fabaceae: Faboideae).

Lotus hirsutus Linnaeus, *Species Plantarum* 2: 775. 1753.
"Habitat in G. Narbonensi, Italia." RCN: 5696.
Lectotype (Jafri in Jafri & El-Gadi, *Fl. Libya* 86: 112. 1980): Herb. Linn. No. 931.16 (LINN).
Current name: ***Dorycnium hirsutum*** (L.) Ser. (Fabaceae: Faboideae).
Note: Specific epithet spelled "hirsuta" in the protologue.

Lotus jacobaeus Linnaeus, *Species Plantarum* 2: 775. 1753.
"Habitat in Insula S. Jacobi." RCN: 5694.
Lectotype (Wijnands, *Bot. Commelins*: 165. 1983): Herb. Clifford: 372, *Lotus* 7 (BM-000646728).
Current name: ***Lotus jacobaeus*** L. (Fabaceae: Faboideae).

Lotus maritimus Linnaeus, *Species Plantarum* 2: 773. 1753.
"Habitat in Europae maritimis." RCN: 5684.
Lectotype (Domínguez & Galiano in *Lagascalia* 8: 197. 1979): Herb. Linn. No. 931.1 (LINN).
Current name: ***Tetragonolobus maritimus*** (L.) Roth (Fabaceae: Faboideae).
Note: Stearn (in *Biol. J. Linn. Soc.* 5: 11. 1973), in an account of Linnaeus' Öland and Gotland journey of 1741, treated Grankulla in Öland as the restricted type locality, and noted the existence of 931.1 (LINN). In his paper, he attributed restricted type localities irrespective of whether any material existed in LINN and, where specimens do exist, he does not refer to any of them as type specimens. The collection subsequently designated as the type shows no annotation associating it with Öland.

Lotus mauritanicus Linnaeus, *Systema Naturae,* ed. 10, 2: 1179. 1759.

L

otus-Lupinus 643

["Habitat ad Cap. b. spei."] Sp. Pl., ed. 2, 2: 1091 (1763). RCN: 5289.
Basionym of: *Ononis mauritanica* (L.) L. (1771).
Lectotype (Schrire in Turland & Jarvis in *Taxon* 46: 475. 1997): Herb. Linn. No. 931.34 (LINN).
Current name: ***Indigofera mauritanica*** (L.) Thunb. (Fabaceae: Faboideae).

Lotus ornithopodioides Linnaeus, *Species Plantarum* 2: 775. 1753.
"Habitat in Sicilia." RCN: 5693.
Lectotype (Heyn in *Israel J. Bot.* 15: 43. 1966): Herb. Clifford: 372, *Lotus* 4 (BM-000646724).
Current name: ***Lotus ornithopodioides*** L. (Fabaceae: Faboideae).

Lotus peregrinus Linnaeus, *Species Plantarum* 2: 774. 1753.
"Habitat in Europa australi." RCN: 5690.
Lectotype (Heyn in *Israel J. Bot.* 15: 40. 1966; Chrtková-Zertová in *Ann. Naturhist. Mus. Wien* 75: 34, f. 1a. 1971): Herb. Clifford: 372, *Lotus* 3, left branch (BM-000646723).
Current name: ***Lotus peregrinus*** L. (Fabaceae: Faboideae).
Note: Heyn (1966) designated the Clifford sheet as the type but her choice was subsequently restricted to the left-hand branch by Chrtková-Zertová in 1972.

Lotus prostratus Linnaeus, *Systema Naturae*, ed. 10, 2: 1179. 1759.
["Habitat ad Cap. b. spei."] Sp. Pl., ed. 2, 2: 1090 (1763). RCN: 5277.
Basionym of: *Ononis prostrata* (L.) L. (1771).
Lectotype (Van Wyk in *Contr. Bolus Herb.* 14: 232. 1991): Herb. Linn. No. 931.35 (LINN).
Current name: ***Lotononis prostrata*** (L.) Benth. (Fabaceae: Faboideae).

Lotus rectus Linnaeus, *Species Plantarum* 2: 775. 1753.
"Habitat in G. Narbonensi, Sicilia, Calabria." RCN: 5698.
Lectotype (Jafri in Jafri & El-Gadi, *Fl. Libya* 86: 113. 1980): Herb. Linn. No. 931.22 (LINN).
Current name: ***Dorycnium rectum*** (L.) Ser. (Fabaceae: Faboideae).
Note: Specific epithet spelled "recta" in the protologue.

Lotus siliquosus Linnaeus, *Systema Naturae*, ed. 10, 2: 1178. 1759, *nom. illeg.*
["Habitat Monspelii."] Sp. Pl. 2: 774 (1753). RCN: 5685.
Replaced synonym: *Lotus erectus* L. (1753).
Lectotype (Lassen in Turland & Jarvis in *Taxon* 46: 475. 1997): Herb. Burser XVIII(2): 79 (UPS).
Current name: ***Lotus maritimus*** L. (Fabaceae: Faboideae).
Note: An illegitimate name for *L. erectus* L. (1753).

Lotus tetragonolobus Linnaeus, *Species Plantarum* 2: 773. 1753.
"Habitat in Siciliae collibus." RCN: 5686.
Lectotype (Domínguez & Galiano in *Lagascalia* 8: 209. 1979): Herb. Linn. No. 931.2 (LINN).
Current name: ***Lotus tetragonolobus*** L. (Fabaceae: Faboideae).

Lotus tetraphyllus Linnaeus, *Systema Vegetabilium*, ed. 13: 575. 1774.
["Habitat in Maiorca."] L. f., Suppl. Pl.: 340 (1782). RCN: 5688.
Lectotype (Lassen in Turland & Jarvis in *Taxon* 46: 475. 1997): Herb. Linn. No. 931.33 (LINN).
Current name: ***Lotus tetraphyllus*** L. (Fabaceae: Faboideae).

Ludwigia alternifolia Linnaeus, *Species Plantarum* 1: 118. 1753.
"Habitat in Virginia." RCN: 975.
Lectotype (Reveal in Jarvis & al., *Regnum Veg.* 127: 62. 1993): *Kalm*, Herb. Linn. No. 154.1 (LINN).

Generitype of *Ludwigia* Linnaeus (vide Hitchcock, *Prop. Brit. Bot.*: 125. 1929).
Current name: ***Ludwigia alternifolia*** L. (Onagraceae).

Ludwigia erigata Linnaeus, *Systema Naturae*, ed. 12, 2: 125; *Mantissa Plantarum*: 40. 1767.
"Habitat in India." RCN: 977.
Lectotype (Raven in *Reinwardtia* 6: 405. 1963): Herb. Linn. No. 154.3 (LINN).
Note: Raven excluded this from the Onagraceae, referring it instead to the Rubiaceae.

Ludwigia oppositifolia Linnaeus, *Systema Naturae*, ed. 12, 2: 125. 1767, *nom. illeg.*
["Habitat in India."] Sp. Pl. 1: 119 (1753). RCN: 976.
Replaced synonym: *Ludwigia perennis* L. (1753).
Lectotype (Brenan in Turrill & Milne-Redhead, *Fl. Trop. E. Africa, Onagraceae*: 13. 1953): Herb. Hermann 2: 9, No. 66 (BM-000594572).
Current name: ***Jussiaea perennis*** (L.) Brenan (Onagraceae).
Note: A superfluous name for *L. perennis* L. (1753).

Ludwigia perennis Linnaeus, *Species Plantarum* 1: 119. 1753.
"Habitat in India." RCN: 976.
Replaced synonym of: *Ludwigia oppositifolia* L. (1767), *nom. illeg.*
Lectotype (Brenan in Turrill & Milne-Redhead, *Fl. Trop. E. Africa, Onagraceae*: 13. 1953): Herb. Hermann 2: 9, No. 66 (BM-000594572).
Current name: ***Jussiaea perennis*** (L.) Brenan (Onagraceae).

Luffa arabum Linnaeus, *Plantae Surinamenses*: 16. 1775.
"Habitat [in Surinamo.]" RCN: 7317.
Type not designated.
Original material: none traced.
Current name: ***Luffa aegyptiaca*** Mill. (Cucurbitaceae).

Lunaria annua Linnaeus, *Species Plantarum* 2: 653. 1753.
"Habitat in Germania." RCN: 4757.
Lectotype (Ball in Jarvis & al., *Regnum Veg.* 127: 62. 1993): Herb. Linn. No. 832.2 (LINN).
Current name: ***Lunaria annua*** L. (Brassicaceae).
Note: Lunaria annua was treated as the generitype by Britton & Brown (*Ill. Fl. N. U. S.*, ed. 2, 2: 190. 1913; see McNeill & al. in *Taxon* 36: 377. 1987). However, under Art. 10.5, Ex. 7 (a voted example) of the Vienna Code, this is a type choice made under the American Code and is to be replaced under Art. 10.5b by Green's choice (*Prop. Brit. Bot.*: 171. 1929) of *L. rediviva* L.

Lunaria rediviva Linnaeus, *Species Plantarum* 2: 653. 1753.
"Habitat in Europa septentrionaliore." RCN: 4756.
Lectotype (Jonsell & Jarvis in *Nordic J. Bot.* 22: 70. 2002): Herb. Clifford: 333, *Lunaria* 1, sheet 1 (BM-000646298).
Generitype of *Lunaria* Linnaeus.
Current name: ***Lunaria rediviva*** L. (Brassicaceae).
Note: Lunaria annua was treated as the generitype by Britton & Brown (*Ill. Fl. N. U. S.*, ed. 2, 2: 190. 1913; see McNeill & al. in *Taxon* 36: 377. 1987). However, under Art. 10.5, Ex. 7 (a voted example) of the Vienna Code, this is a type choice made under the American Code and is to be replaced under Art. 10.5b by Green's choice (*Prop. Brit. Bot.*: 171. 1929) of *L. rediviva* L.

Lupinus albus Linnaeus, *Species Plantarum* 2: 721. 1753.
"Habitat – – – –" RCN: 5307.
Lectotype (Westphal, *Pulses Ethiopia, Taxon. Agric. Signif.*: 118. 1974): Herb. Clifford: 359, *Lupinus* 1, sheet A (BM-000646590).

Generitype of *Lupinus* Linnaeus (vide Green, *Prop. Brit. Bot.*: 174. 1929).
Current name: ***Lupinus albus*** L. subsp. ***albus*** (Fabaceae: Faboideae).
Note: Westphal's type choice of Clifford material (BM) was published in February 1974, and therefore has priority over the competing choice of 898.2 (LINN) made by Gladstones (*Tech. Bull. Dept. Agric. Western Australia* 26: 4) in December 1974.

Lupinus angustifolius Linnaeus, *Species Plantarum* 2: 721, 1200. 1753.
"Habitat – – – – [on p. 1200:] Hispania." RCN: 5311.
Lectotype (Gladstones in *Tech. Bull. Dept. Agric. Western Australia* 26: 9. 1974): Herb. Linn. No. 898.7 (LINN).
Current name: ***Lupinus angustifolius*** L. subsp. ***angustifolius*** (Fabaceae: Faboideae).

Lupinus hirsutus Linnaeus, *Species Plantarum* 2: 721. 1753, *nom. utique rej.*
"Habitat – – – –" RCN: 5309.
Lectotype (Lee & Gladstones in *Taxon* 28: 619. 1979): Herb. A. van Royen No. 908.119–125 (L).
Current name: ***Lupinus*** sp. (Fabaceae: Faboideae).

Lupinus integrifolius Linnaeus, *Plantae Rariores Africanae*: 16. 1760. ["Habitat ad Cap. b. spei."] Sp. Pl., ed. 2, 2: 1016 (1763). RCN: 5313.
Type not designated.
Original material: none traced.
Note: The application of this name is uncertain.

Lupinus luteus Linnaeus, *Species Plantarum* 2: 722. 1753.
"Habitat in Siciliae arenosis." RCN: 5312.

Lectotype (Gladstones in *Tech. Bull. Dept. Agric. Western Australia* 26: 17. 1974): Herb. Linn. No. 898.8 (LINN).
Current name: ***Lupinus luteus*** L. (Fabaceae: Faboideae).

Lupinus perennis Linnaeus, *Species Plantarum* 2: 721. 1753.
"Habitat in Virginia." RCN: 5306.
Type not designated.
Original material: *Kalm*, Herb. Linn. No. 898.1 (LINN); Herb. Kalm No. 246 (UPS); [icon] in Morison, Pl. Hist. Univ. 2: 87, s. 2, t. 7, f. 6. 1680.
Current name: ***Lupinus perennis*** L. (Fabaceae: Faboideae).

Lupinus pilosus Linnaeus, *Systema Vegetabilium*, ed. 13: 545. 1774. RCN: 5310.
Neotype (Plitmann in Turland & Jarvis in *Taxon* 46: 475. 1997): Turkey. Mersin, Anamur, 14 Apr 1956, *Davis & Polunin sub Davis 25950* (BM).
Current name: ***Lupinus pilosus*** L. (Fabaceae: Faboideae).

Lupinus stoloniferus Linnaeus, *Centuria I Plantarum*: 23. 1755.
"Habitat in Sicilia, Archipelago, Arabia."
Type not designated.
Original material: Herb. Linn. No. 898.5? (LINN).
Current name: ***Lupinus*** sp. (Fabaceae: Faboideae).
Note: As noted by Rickett (in *Lloydia* 18: 59. 1955) and Nordenstam (in *Bot. Not.* 114: 277. 1981), this name did not appear in the later version of the thesis (in *Amoen. Acad.* 4. 1759), nor in any later Linnaean works. Its application is uncertain.

Lupinus varius Linnaeus, *Species Plantarum* 2: 721. 1753.
"Habitat Messanae, Monspelii inter segetes." RCN: 5308.
Lectotype (Lee & Gladstones in *Taxon* 28: 617. 1979): Herb. A. van Royen No. 908.119–414 (L).
Current name: ***Lupinus varius*** L. (Fabaceae: Faboideae).
Note: Lee & Gladstones (in *Taxon* 28: 616. 1979) proposed the rejection of the name under the then Art. 69, but this was not recommended by the Committee for Spermatophyta (in *Taxon* 32: 624. 1983).

Lychnis alpina Linnaeus, *Species Plantarum* 1: 436. 1753.
"Habitat in Alpibus Lapponicis, Helveticis, Sibiricis, Pyrenaicis." RCN: 3391.
Lectotype (Ikonnikov in *Novosti Sist. Vyssh. Rast.* 24: 81. 1987): Herb. Linn. No. 602.3 (LINN).
Current name: ***Silene suecica*** (Lodd.) Greuter & Burdet (Caryophyllaceae).
Note: Jonsell & Jarvis (in *Nordic J. Bot.* 14: 157. 1994) designated a Lapland specimen in Paris No. 158, LAPP) as lectotype, but their choice is pre-dated by that of Ikonnikov.

Lychnis apetala Linnaeus, *Species Plantarum* 1: 437. 1753.
"Habitat in Alpibus Lapponicis, Sibiricis." RCN: 3394.
Lectotype (Bocquet in *Candollea* 22: 26. 1967): Herb. Linn. No. 602.9 (LINN).
Current name: ***Silene uralensis*** (Rupr.) Bocquet subsp. ***apetala*** (L.) Bocquet (Caryophyllaceae).

Lychnis chalcedonica Linnaeus, *Species Plantarum* 1: 436. 1753.
"Habitat in Tataria." RCN: 3388.
Lectotype (Jonsell & Jarvis in Jarvis & al., *Regnum Veg.* 127: 63. 1993): Herb. Clifford: 174, *Lychnis* 1 α (BM-000628549).
Generitype of *Lychnis* Linnaeus, *nom. rej.* (vide Green, *Prop. Brit. Bot.*: 156. 1929).
Current name: ***Silene chalcedonica*** (L.) E.H.L. Krause (Caryophyllaceae).

Note: Lychnis Linnaeus, *nom. rej.* in favour of *Silene* Linnaeus, *nom. cons.* Jonsell & Jarvis (in *Nordic J. Bot.* 14: 158. 1994) gave an explanation for their earlier (1993) formal type choice.

Lychnis dioica Linnaeus, *Species Plantarum* 1: 437. 1753.
"Habitat in Europae frigidae pratis succulentis." RCN: 3393.
Lectotype (Talavera & Muñoz Garmendia in *Anales Jard. Bot. Madrid* 45: 453. 1989): Herb. Linn. No. 602.6, female specimen (LINN).
Current name: **Silene dioica** (L.) Clairv. (Caryophyllaceae).

Lychnis flos-cuculi Linnaeus, *Species Plantarum* 1: 436. 1753.
"Habitat in partis [sic] Europae humidiusculis." RCN: 3389.
Lectotype (Sell in Jonsell & Jarvis in *Nordic J. Bot.* 14: 158. 1994): Herb. Clifford: 174, *Lychnis* 2 (BM-000628551).
Current name: **Lychnis flos-cuculi** (L.) Clairv. (Caryophyllaceae).

Lychnis quadridentata Linnaeus, *Systema Vegetabilium,* ed. 13: 362. 1774, *nom. illeg.*
["Habitat in Styriae monte ad oppidum Eisenertz."] Sp. Pl. 1: 415 (1753). RCN: 3268.
Replaced synonym: *Cucubalus quadrifidus* L. (1753).
Lectotype (Melzheimer & Polatschek in *Phyton (Horn)* 31: 285. 1992): [icon] *"Caryophyllus minimus humilis alter exoticus flore candido amoeno"* in Plantin, Pl. Stirp. Icon.: 445. 1581.
Current name: **Silene quadrifida** (L.) L. (Caryophyllaceae).
Note: As noted by Walters (in *Feddes Repert.* 69: 47. 1964), this is an illegitimate replacement name for *Silene quadrifida* (L.) L. (1759), itself based on *Cucubalus quadrifidus* L. (1753).

Lychnis sibirica Linnaeus, *Species Plantarum* 1: 437. 1753.
"Habitat in Sibiria. Gmelin." RCN: 3392.
Lectotype (Lazkov in Cafferty & Jarvis in *Taxon* 53: 1052. 2004): *Gmelin s.n.*, Herb. Linn. No. 602.5, excl. lower left specimen (LINN).
Current name: **Lychnis sibirica** L. (Caryophyllaceae).

Lychnis viscaria Linnaeus, *Species Plantarum* 1: 436. 1753.
"Habitat in Europae septentrionalis pratis siccis." RCN: 3390.
Lectotype (Ikonnikov in *Novosti Sist. Vyssh. Rast.* 24: 80. 1987): Herb. Linn. No. 602.2 (LINN).
Current name: **Lychnis viscaria** L. (Caryophyllaceae).

Lychnis viscosa Linnaeus, *Flora Anglica*: 16. 1754, *orth. var.*
RCN: 3390.
Lectotype (Ikonnikov in *Novosti Sist. Vyssh. Rast.* 24: 80. 1987): Herb. Linn. No. 602.2 (LINN).
Current name: **Lychnis viscaria** L. (Caryophyllaceae).
Note: An orthographic variant of *L. viscaria* L. (1753), as noted by Stearn (*Introd. Ray's Syn. Meth. Stirp. Brit.* (Ray Soc. ed.): 52. 1973).

Lycium afrum Linnaeus, *Species Plantarum* 1: 191. 1753.
"Habitat in Africa & in Regno Valentino." RCN: 1506.
Lectotype (Feinbrun & Stearn in *Israel J. Bot.* 12: 116. 1963): Herb. Clifford: 57, *Lycium* 2 (BM-000558011).
Generitype of *Lycium* Linnaeus (vide Hitchcock, *Prop. Brit. Bot.*: 133. 1929).
Current name: **Lycium afrum** L. (Solanaceae).

Lycium barbarum Linnaeus, *Species Plantarum* 1: 192. 1753.
"Habitat in Asia, Africa?" RCN: 1507.
Lectotype (Feinbrun & Stearn in *Israel J. Bot.* 12: 116. 1963): Herb. Linn. No. 259.6 (LINN).
Current name: **Lycium barbarum** L. (Solanaceae).

Lycium capsulare Linnaeus, *Centuria II Plantarum*: 11. 1756.
"Habitat in Mexico. Miller." RCN: 1509.
Lectotype (Davenport in *Rhodora* 90: 183. 1988): *Miller 5*, Herb. Linn. No. 259.8 (LINN).
Current name: **Hydrolea spinosa** L. (Hydrophyllaceae).

Lycium europaeum Linnaeus, *Species Plantarum* 1: 192. 1753.
"Habitat in Narbona, Hispania, Lusitania, Italia." RCN: 1508.
Lectotype (Feinbrun in *Collect. Bot. (Barcelona)* 7: 363. 1968): Herb. Linn. No. 259.7 (LINN).
Current name: **Lycium europaeum** L. (Solanaceae).

Lycoperdon aurantium Linnaeus, *Species Plantarum* 2: 1184. 1753, *nom. utique rej.*
"Habitat in Gallia." RCN: 8514.
Lectotype (Demoulin in *Bull. Jard. Bot. Natl. Belg.* 37: 297, f. 1. 1967): [icon] *"Lycoperdon, aurantii coloris, ad basin rugosum"* in Vaillant, Bot. Paris.: 123, t. 16, f. 9, 10. 1727 (see p. 165).
Current name: **Scleroderma aurantium** (L.: Pers.) Pers. (Sclerodermataceae).

Lycoperdon bovista Linnaeus, *Species Plantarum* 2: 1183. 1753.
"Habitat in Campis sterilibus." RCN: 8513.
Type not designated.
Original material: none traced.
Current name: **Lycoperdon bovista** L. (Lycoperdaceae).

Lycoperdon carpobolus Linnaeus, *Species Plantarum* 2: 1184. 1753.
"Habitat in Italia." RCN: 8516.
Type not designated.
Original material: [icon] in Micheli, Nov. Pl. Gen.: 221, t. 101. 1729.
Current name: **Sphaerobolus stellatus** (L.: Fr.) Tode (Geastraceae).

Lycoperdon cervinum Linnaeus, *Species Plantarum* 2: 1183. 1753.
"Habitat in Bohemia, Silesia. Vermelandia." RCN: 8512.
Type not designated.
Original material: [icon] in Micheli, Nov. Pl. Gen.: 220, t. 99, f. 4. 1729; [icon] in Bauhin & Cherler, Hist. Pl. Univ. 3(2): 851. 1651.
Current name: **Elaphomyces granulatus** Fr. (Elaphomycetaceae).

Lycoperdon epidendrum Linnaeus, *Species Plantarum* 2: 1184. 1753.
"Habitat in Lignis, Parietibus antiquis." RCN: 8524.
Type not designated.
Original material: none traced.
Generitype of *Lycoperdon* Linnaeus, non Pers. (vide Martin in *Univ. Iowa Stud. Nat. Hist.* 20(8): 23. 1966).
Current name: **Lycogala epidendrum** (L.) Fr. (Lycogalaceae).
Note: Lister (in *J. Bot.* 51: 161. 1913) reproduced the protologue, adding (p. 184), of 1287.11 (LINN), "it is very possible that this may be Linné's type, but we have no proof that it is so". See also Martin (in *Univ. Iowa Stud. Nat. Hist.* 20(8): 23. 1966).

Lycoperdon epiphyllum Linnaeus, *Species Plantarum* 2: 1185. 1753.
"Habitat in dorso foliorum Tussilaginis." RCN: 8525.
Type not designated.
Original material: none traced.
Current name: **Puccinia epiphylla** (L.) Wettst. (Pucciniaceae).

Lycoperdon pedunculatum Linnaeus, *Species Plantarum* 2: 1184. 1753.
"Habitat in Campestribus." RCN: 8518.
Type not designated.
Original material: [icon] in Tournefort, Inst. Rei Herb.: 563, t. 331, f. E, F. 1700.
Current name: **Tulostoma brumale** Pers.: Pers. (Tulostomataceae).

L

Lycoperdon pisiforme Linnaeus, *Systema Naturae*, ed. 12, 2: 726. 1767.
RCN: 8523.
Type not designated.
Original material: none traced.
Current name: ***Nidularia farcta*** (Roth: Fr.) Fr. (Nidulariaceae).
Note: Specific epithet spelled "pisiformis" in the protologue.

Lycoperdon pistillare Linnaeus, *Mantissa Plantarum Altera*: 313. 1771.
"Habitat in India orientali. Koenig." RCN: 8519.
Lectotype (Priest & Lenz in *Austral. Syst. Bot.* 12: 114. 1999): Herb. Linn. No. 1287.7 (LINN).
Current name: ***Podaxis pistillaris*** (L.: Pers.) Morse (Lycoperdaceae).

Lycoperdon radiatum Linnaeus, *Species Plantarum*, ed. 2, 2: 1654. 1763.
Lectotype (Lister in *J. Bot.* 51: 163. 1913): *Linnaeus filius*, Herb. Linn. No. 1287.6 (LINN).
Current name: ***Diderma radiatum*** (L.) Morgan (Didymiaceae).

Lycoperdon stellatum Linnaeus, *Species Plantarum* 2: 1184. 1753.
"Habitat in Collibus." RCN: 8515.
Type not designated.
Original material: [icon] in Micheli, Nov. Pl. Gen.: 220, t. 100, f. 1, 2, 3. 1729; [icon] in Ray, Syn. Meth. Stirp. Brit., ed. 3: 27, t. 1, f. 1. 1724; [icon] in Buxbaum, Pl. Minus Cognit. Cent. 2: 45, t. 49, f. 3. 1728; [icon] in Boccone, Mus. Fis.: t. 305, f. 4. 1697.
Current name: ***Sphaerobolus stellatus*** (L.: Fr.) Tode (Geastraceae).

Lycoperdon truncatum Linnaeus, *Systema Vegetabilium*, ed. 13: 824. 1774.
"Habitat in Fagetis." RCN: 8522.
Type not designated.
Original material: none traced.
Current name: ***Lycoperdon truncatum*** L.: Fr. (Lycoperdaceae).

Lycoperdon tuber Linnaeus, *Species Plantarum* 2: 1183. 1753.
"Habitat sub Terra." RCN: 8512.
Type not designated.
Original material: [icon] in Micheli, Nov. Pl. Gen.: 221, t. 102. 1729; [icon] in Mattioli, Comment. Dioscoridis: 544. 1565.
Current name: ***Elaphomyces* sp.** (Elaphomycetaceae).

Lycoperdon variolosum Linnaeus, *Systema Naturae*, ed. 12, 3: 234. 1768.
"Habitat passim in Arborum ramis emortuis aut moribundis." RCN: 8521.
Type not designated.
Original material: Herb. Linn. No. 1287.10 (LINN); [icon] in Dillenius, Hist. Musc.: 127, t. 18, f. 7. 1741; [icon] in Micheli, Nov. Pl. Gen.: 216, t. 95, f. 2. 1729.
Current name: ***Hypoxylon variolosum*** (L.) J. Kickx f. (Xylariaceae).

Lycopodium alopecuroides Linnaeus, *Species Plantarum* 2: 1102. 1753.
"Habitat in Virginia, Canada." RCN: 7966.
Lectotype (Øllgaard in *Biol. Skr.* 34: 30. 1989): *Kalm*, Herb. Linn. No. 1257.7 (LINN).
Current name: ***Lycopodiella alopecuroides*** (L.) Cranfill (Lycopodiaceae).

Lycopodium alpinum Linnaeus, *Species Plantarum* 2: 1104. 1753.
"Habitat in Alpibus Lapponiae, Helvetiae." RCN: 7974.
Lectotype (Wilce in *Beih. Nova Hedwigia* 19: 132. 1965): Herb. Linn. No. 1257.19 (LINN).
Current name: ***Lycopodium alpinum*** L. (Lycopodiaceae).

Lycopodium annotinum Linnaeus, *Species Plantarum* 2: 1103. 1753.
"Habitat in Europae nemoribus." RCN: 7970.
Lectotype (Jonsell & Jarvis in *Nordic J. Bot.* 14: 147. 1994): [icon] *"Muscus terrestris repens, clavis singularibus, foliosis, erectis"* in Plukenet, Phytographia: t. 205, f. 5. 1692; Almag. Bot.: 258. 1696. – Typotype: Herb. Sloane 97: 3 (BM-SL).
Current name: ***Lycopodium annotinum*** L. (Lycopodiaceae).

Lycopodium apodum Linnaeus, *Species Plantarum* 2: 1105. 1753.
"Habitat in Carolina, Virginia, Pensylvania." RCN: 7979.
Lectotype (Fraile in Davidse & al., *Fl. Mesoamericana* 1: 29. 1995): *Kalm*, Herb. Linn. No. 1257.27 (LINN).
Current name: ***Selaginella apoda*** (L.) Spring (Selaginellaceae).
Note: See Morton (in *Amer. Fern J.* 57: 104–106. 1967) and Rauschert (in *Feddes Repert.* 94: 289. 1983), who discuss the orthography of the epithet.

Lycopodium bryopteris Linnaeus, *Species Plantarum* 2: 1103. 1753.
"Habitat in India." RCN: 7972.
Type not designated.
Original material: [icon] in Morison, Pl. Hist. Univ. 3: 628, s. 15, t. 7, f. 51. 1699; [icon] in Plukenet, Phytographia: t. 100, f. 3. 1691; Almag. Bot.: 257. 1696; [icon] in Dillenius, Hist. Musc.: 472, t. 66, f. 11. 1741.
Current name: ***Selaginella bryopteris*** (L.) Baker (Selaginellaceae).

Lycopodium canaliculatum Linnaeus, *Species Plantarum* 2: 1105. 1753.
"Habitat in Amboina." RCN: 79981.
Lectotype (Alston in *J. Bot.* 69: 253. 1931): [icon] *"Lycopodioides erectum filicinum, pinnulis Acaciae, caule sulcato"* in Dillenius, Hist. Musc.: 469, t. 65, f. 6. 1741. – Voucher: Herb. Dillenius (OXF).
Current name: ***Selaginella canaliculata*** (L.) Spring (Selaginellaceae).

Lycopodium carolinianum Linnaeus, *Species Plantarum* 2: 1104. 1753.
"Habitat in Carolina." RCN: 7976.
Lectotype (Pichi Sermolli in *Webbia* 23: 165. 1968): [icon] *"Lycopodium pinnatum repens, spicis & pediculis singularibus longis"* in Dillenius, Hist. Musc.: 452, t. 62, f. 6. 1741. – Voucher: Herb. Dillenius (OXF).
Current name: ***Lycopodiella caroliniana*** (L.) Pic. Serm. var. ***caroliniana*** (Lycopodiaceae).

Lycopodium cernuum Linnaeus, *Species Plantarum* 2: 1103. 1753.
"Habitat in Indiis." RCN: 7971.
Lectotype (Proctor in Howard, *Fl. Lesser Antilles* 2: 33. 1977): Herb. Linn. No. 1257.13 (LINN).
Current name: ***Lycopodiella cernua*** (L.) Pic. Serm. (Lycopodiaceae).

Lycopodium circinale Linnaeus, *Systema Vegetabilium*, ed. 13: 794. 1774.
RCN: 7984.
Type not designated.
Original material: *Vandelli*, Herb. Linn. No. 1257.34 (LINN); [icon] in Morison, Pl. Hist. Univ. 3: 628, s. 15, t. 7, f. 51. 1699; [icon] in Plukenet, Phytographia: t. 100, f. 3. 1691; Almag. Bot.: 257. 1696; [icon] in Dillenius, Hist. Musc.: 472, t. 66, f. 11. 1741.
Current name: ***Selaginella bryopteris*** (L.) Baker (Selaginellaceae).

Lycopodium clavatum Linnaeus, *Species Plantarum* 2: 1101. 1753.
"Habitat in Europae sylvis muscosis." RCN: 7963.
Lectotype (Jonsell & Jarvis in Jarvis & al., *Regnum Veg.* 127: 63. 1993): Herb. Burser XX: 49 (UPS).

Generitype of *Lycopodium* Linnaeus (vide Britton & Brown, *Ill. Fl. N. U. S.*, ed. 2, 1: 43. 1913).
Current name: ***Lycopodium clavatum*** L. (Lycopodiaceae).
Note: Proctor (in Howard, *Fl. Lesser Antilles* 2: 31. 1977) indicated 1257.2 (LINN) as type, but this is a post-1753 addition to the herbarium and not original material for the name. Although Schelpe & Anthony (in Leistner, *Fl. Southern Africa, Pteridophyta*: 1. 1986) stated "Type:...?Hort. Sicc. Cliff. (?BM, holo)", it is not clear that these authors accepted Clifford material as the type so this is ineffective (Art. 7.11). Jonsell & Jarvis (in *Nordic J. Bot.* 14: 147. 1994) provide a brief explanation of their earlier (1993) formal type choice.

Lycopodium complanatum Linnaeus, *Species Plantarum* 2: 1104. 1753.
"Habitat in Europae & Americae septentrionalis sylvis acerosis." RCN: 7975.
Lectotype (Jermy in *Fern Gaz.* 13: 262. 1989): *Münchhausen*, Herb. Linn. No. 1257.20 (LINN), see p. 222.
Current name: ***Lycopodium complanatum*** L. (Lycopodiaceae).
Note: Löve & Löve (in *Bot. Not.* 114: 34. 1961) suggested this might be a *nomen confusum* but it has remained in use subsequently.

Lycopodium denticulatum Linnaeus, *Species Plantarum* 2: 1106. 1753.
"Habitat in Lusitania, Hispania, Iberia." RCN: 7978.
Type not designated.
Original material: *Löfling s.n.*, Herb. Linn. No. 1257.24 (LINN); Herb. Linn. No. 1257.25 (LINN); [icon] in Dillenius, Hist. Musc.: 462, t. 66, f. 1 A. 1741; [icon] in Clusius, Rar. Pl. Hist. 2: 249. 1601.
Current name: ***Selaginella denticulata*** (L.) Spring (Selaginellaceae).

Lycopodium flabellatum Linnaeus, *Species Plantarum* 2: 1105. 1753.
"Habitat in America calidiore." RCN: 7980.
Lectotype (Proctor in Howard, *Fl. Lesser Antilles* 2: 38. 1977): [icon] *"Muscus squammosus erectus"* in Plumier, Descr. Pl. Amér.: 35, t. 24. 1693.
Current name: ***Selaginella flabellata*** (L.) Spring (Selaginellaceae).

Lycopodium helveticum Linnaeus, *Species Plantarum* 2: 1104. 1753.
"Habitat in Alpibus Helvetiae." RCN: 7977.
Type not designated.
Original material: Herb. Burser XX: 46 (UPS); [icon] in Dillenius, Hist. Musc.: 465, t. 64, f. 2. 1741; [icon] in Morison, Pl. Hist. Univ. 3: 626, s. 15, t. 6, f. 34. 1699.
Current name: ***Selaginella helvetica*** (L.) Spring (Selaginellaceae).

Lycopodium inundatum Linnaeus, *Species Plantarum* 2: 1102. 1753.
"Habitat in Europae inundatis." RCN: 7967.
Lectotype (Jonsell & Jarvis in *Nordic J. Bot.* 14: 147. 1994): Herb. Linn. No. 1257.8 (LINN).
Current name: ***Lycopodiella inundata*** (L.) Holub (Lycopodiaceae).

Lycopodium linifolium Linnaeus, *Species Plantarum* 2: 1100. 1753.
"Habitat in America meridionali." RCN: 7960.
Lectotype (Proctor in Howard, *Fl. Lesser Antilles* 2: 26. 1977): [icon] *"Muscus maximus, Linariae foliis"* in Plumier, Traité Foug. Amér.: 144, t. 166, f. C. 1705.
Current name: ***Lycopodium linifolium*** L. (Lycopodiaceae).

Lycopodium nudum Linnaeus, *Species Plantarum* 2: 1100. 1753.
"Habitat in Indiis." RCN: 7961.
Lectotype (Proctor in Howard, *Fl. Lesser Antilles* 2: 16. 1977): Herb. Linn. No. 1257.1 (LINN).
Current name: ***Psilotum nudum*** (L.) P. Beauv. (Psilotaceae).

Lycopodium obscurum Linnaeus, *Species Plantarum* 2: 1102. 1753.
"Habitat in Philadelphia." RCN: 7969.
Lectotype (Øllgaard in *Biol. Skr.* 34: 59. 1989): *Kalm*, Herb. Linn. No. 1257.12 (LINN).
Current name: ***Lycopodium obscurum*** L. (Lycopodiaceae).

Lycopodium ornithopodioides Linnaeus, *Species Plantarum* 2: 1105. 1753.
"Habitat in India." RCN: 7983.
Type not designated.
Original material: Herb. Hermann 3: 1, No. 388 (BM); [icon] in Dillenius, Hist. Musc.: 464, t. 66, f. 1 B. 1741.
Current name: ***Selaginella ornithopodioides*** (L.) Spring (Selaginellaceae).

Lycopodium phlegmaria Linnaeus, *Species Plantarum* 2: 1101. 1753.
"Habitat in Malabaria, Zeylona." RCN: 7962.
Type not designated.
Original material: Herb. Hermann 4: 5, No. 386 (BM); [icon] in Breyn, Exot. Pl. Cent.: 180, t. 92. 1678; [icon] in Dillenius, Hist. Musc.: 450, t. 61, f. 5. 1741; [icon] in Rheede, Hort. Malab. 12: 27, t. 14. 1693.
Current name: ***Huperzia phlegmaria*** (L.) Rothm. (Lycopodiaceae).
Note: Roux (*Consp. S. African Pteridophyta*: 19. 2001) stated that Dillenius' t. 61, f. 5A, B, C (1741) "is eligible as lectotype", following Øllgaard (in *Biol. Skr.* 34: 61. 1989) but this is not a formal typification. Verdcourt (in Beentje & Ghazanfar, *Fl. Trop. E. Africa, Lycopodiaceae*: 9. 2005) indicated the same illustration as the lectotype but this was published after 1 Jan 2001 and so the omission of the phrase "designated here" or an equivalent (Art. 7.11) means that the choice is not effective.

Lycopodium plumosum Linnaeus, *Species Plantarum* 2: 1105. 1753.
"Habitat in Indiis." RCN: 7982.
Lectotype (Alston in *J. Bot.* 69: 255. 1931): [icon] *"Lycopodioides dentatum dichotomum, rigidum, minus"* in Dillenius, Hist. Musc.: 471, t. 66, f. 10. 1741. – Voucher: Herb. Dillenius (OXF).
Current name: ***Selaginella plumosa*** (L.) C. Presl (Selaginellaceae).

Lycopodium rupestre Linnaeus, *Species Plantarum* 2: 1101. 1753.
"Habitat in Virginia, Canada, Sibiria." RCN: 7964.
Lectotype (Tryon in *Ann. Missouri Bot. Gard.* 42: 64. 1955): *Kalm*, Herb. Linn. No. 1257.4 (LINN).
Current name: ***Selaginella rupestris*** (L.) Spring (Selaginellaceae).

Lycopodium sanguinolentum Linnaeus, *Species Plantarum* 2: 1104. 1753.
"Habitat in Camtschatca." RCN: 7973.
Type not designated.
Original material: Herb. Linn. No. 1257.18 (LINN); [icon] in Linnaeus, Amoen. Acad. 2: 363, t. 4, f. 26. 1751.
Current name: ***Selaginella sanguinolenta*** (L.) Spring (Selaginellaceae).

Lycopodium selaginoides Linnaeus, *Species Plantarum* 2: 1101. 1753.
"Habitat in Europae pascuis muscosis." RCN: 7965.
Lectotype (Jonsell & Jarvis in *Nordic J. Bot.* 14: 147. 1994): Herb. Linn. No. 1257.5, upper specimen (LINN).
Current name: ***Selaginella selaginoides*** (L.) Beauv. ex Schrank & Mart. (Selaginellaceae).

Lycopodium selago Linnaeus, *Species Plantarum* 2: 1102. 1753.
"Habitat in Europae borealis sylvis acerosis." RCN: 7968.

Lectotype (Jonsell & Jarvis in *Nordic J. Bot.* 14: 147. 1994): Herb. Burser XX: 52 (UPS).
Current name: ***Huperzia selago*** (L.) Schrank & Mart. (Lycopodiaceae).

Lycopsis aegyptiaca Linnaeus, *Species Plantarum* 1: 138. 1753.
"Habitat in Aegypto." RCN: 1112.
Basionym of: *Asperugo aegyptiaca* (L.) L. (1763).
Neotype (Mill in Cafferty & Jarvis in *Taxon* 53: 802. 2004): Jordan. Petra, 15 Mar 1974, *L. Boulos & D. Al-Eisawi (with W. Jallad) 6290* (E; iso- IABH).
Current name: ***Anchusa aegyptiaca*** (L.) DC. (Boraginaceae).

Lycopsis arvensis Linnaeus, *Species Plantarum* 1: 139. 1753.
"Habitat in Europae agris." RCN: 1116.
Lectotype (Selvi & al. in *Taxon* 45: 306. 1996): Herb. Burser XIV(2): 26 (UPS).
Generitype of *Lycopsis* Linnaeus (vide Hitchcock, *Prop. Brit. Bot.*: 128. 1929).
Current name: ***Lycopsis arvensis*** L. (Boraginaceae).

Lycopsis echioides Linnaeus, *Species Plantarum,* ed. 2, 1: 199. 1762.
"Habitat in America." RCN: 1117.
Lectotype (Edmondson in *Willdenowia* 8: 23. 1977): Herb. Linn. No. 71.7 (S).
Current name: ***Arnebia pulchra*** (Roem. & Schult.) J.R. Edm. (Boraginaceae).
Note: Edmondson's typification made this the earliest name for what had previously been called *Nonea ventricosa* (Sm.) Griseb. so he (in *Taxon* 27: 126. 1976) proposed the Linnaean name for rejection. This was not approved by the Committee for Spermatophyta (*l.c.* 29: 492. 1980), but as the epithet "echioides" is pre-occupied in the genus *Arnebia* by *A. echioides* DC., the correct name for this taxon is *A. pulchra*. Popova (in *Bot. Zhurn.* 80(9): 96–98. 1995) rejected Edmondson's type choice based only on its identity, and designated Tournefort collections as "lectotype" in its place. However, this is contrary to Art. 9.17.

Lycopsis orientalis Linnaeus, *Species Plantarum* 1: 139. 1753.
"Habitat in Oriente." RCN: 1118.
Neotype (Güner & Duman in Cafferty & Jarvis in *Taxon* 53: 803. 2004): Turkey. B5 Nevsehir: Ürgüp, 1,080m, lake shores, wet places, 22 Jun 1989, *M. Vural 5360 & Ü. Kol, H. Duman, N. Adýgüzel* (GAZI; iso- ISTF, AIBU).
Current name: ***Anchusa arvensis*** (L.) M. Bieb. subsp. ***orientalis*** (L.) Nordh. (Boraginaceae).

Lycopsis pulla Linnaeus, *Systema Naturae,* ed. 10, 2: 916. 1759, *nom. illeg.*
["Habitat in Tataria, Germania."] Sp. Pl. 1: 198 (1753). RCN: 1114.
Lectotype (Kazmi in *J. Arnold Arbor.* 52: 676. 1971): Herb. Linn. No. 190.2 (LINN).
Current name: ***Nonea pulla*** (L.) DC. (Boraginaceae).
Note: There are some difficulties with this name. *Lycopsis pulla* Loefl., *Iter Hispanicum*: 302, 66, 81 (1758) appears to be based on a Löfling collection (190.6 LINN) from Spain (López González & Jarvis in *Anales Jard. Bot. Madrid* 40: 343. 1984), which is not the designated type of *L. pulla* L. (1759). The type of the later name (190.2 LINN) is identifiable as the Central and Eastern European species widely known as *Nonea pulla* which does not occur in Spain. The 1759 name is therefore illegitimate, and a conservation proposal may be necessary to ensure its use in its traditional sense.

Lycopsis variegata Linnaeus, *Species Plantarum* 1: 138. 1753.
"Habitat in Creta." RCN: 1115.

Lectotype (Greuter in *Candollea* 20: 208. 1965): [icon] *"Buglossoides Cretica"* in Rivinus, Ordo Pl. Fl. Monopetal.: 6, t. 9. 1690. – Epitype (Bigazzi & al. in *Pl. Syst. Evol.* 205: 254. 1997): Greece. Crete, Eparchia Kidhonia: Peninsula Akrotiri, 24 Apr 1976, *A. Charpin 11873* (G).
Current name: ***Anchusa variegata*** (L.) Lehm. (Boraginaceae).

Lycopsis vesicaria Linnaeus, *Species Plantarum* 1: 138. 1753.
"Habitat in Europae australi." RCN: 1113.
Lectotype (Qaiser in Jafri & El-Gadi, *Fl. Libya* 68: 26. 1979): Herb. Linn. No. 190.1 (LINN).
Current name: ***Nonea vesicaria*** (L.) Rchb. (Boraginaceae).

Lycopsis virginica Linnaeus, *Species Plantarum* 1: 139. 1753.
"Habitat in Virginia ad vias." RCN: 1119.
Neotype (Miller in Cafferty & Jarvis in *Taxon* 53: 803. 2004): U.S.A. Virginia, Henrico County, border of woods, east of Fulton Hill, 6 Jun 1940. *Fernald & Long 12175* (MO; iso- GH).
Current name: ***Myosotis virginica*** (L.) Britton & al. (Boraginaceae).

Lycopus europaeus Linnaeus, *Species Plantarum* 1: 21. 1753.
"Habitat in Europae ripis humentibus." RCN: 166.
Lectotype (Hedge & Lamond in *Notes Roy. Bot. Gard. Edinburgh* 28: 92. 1968): Herb. Linn. No. 36.1 (LINN).
Generitype of *Lycopus* Linnaeus (vide Hitchcock, *Prop. Brit. Bot.*: 116. 1929).
Current name: ***Lycopus europaeus*** L. (Lamiaceae).

Lycopus virginicus Linnaeus, *Species Plantarum* 1: 21. 1753.
"Habitat in Virginia." RCN: 167.
Lectotype (Reveal in Jarvis & al. in *Taxon* 50: 512. 2001): *Clayton 185* (BM-000038858).
Current name: ***Lycopus virginicus*** L. (Lamiaceae).
Note: Epling (in *J. Bot.* 67: 3. 1929) discussed the original elements for the name, and treated *Clayton 185* (BM) as the "standard specimen" (not the same as the type). However, this does appear to be the obvious choice as type, and it has been designated as such by Reveal.

Lygeum spartum Linnaeus, *Genera Plantarum,* ed. 5: Appendix. 1754.
"Habitat in Hispania." RCN: 448.
Lectotype (Cope in Nasir & Ali, *Fl. Pakistan* 143: 39. 1982): *Löfling 36a*, Herb. Linn. No. 75.1 (LINN).
Generitype of *Lygeum* Linnaeus.
Current name: ***Lygeum spartum*** L. (Poaceae).

Lysimachia atropurpurea Linnaeus, *Species Plantarum* 1: 147. 1753.
"Habitat in Oriente." RCN: 1172.
Lectotype (Wijnands, *Bot. Commelins*: 178. 1983): Herb. Linn. No. 207.5 (LINN).
Current name: ***Lysimachia atropurpurea*** L. (Primulaceae).

Lysimachia ciliata Linnaeus, *Species Plantarum* 1: 147. 1753.
"Habitat in Virginia, Canada." RCN: 1176.
Type not designated.
Original material: [icon] in Walther, Design. Pl.: 32, t. 12. 1735.
Current name: ***Steironema ciliatum*** (L.) Baudo (Primulaceae).
Note: Coffey & Jones (in *Brittonia* 32: 315. 1980) indicated what is presumably 207.11 (LINN) as the holotype, but this collection lacks the relevant *Species Plantarum* number (i.e. "7") and was a post-1753 addition to the herbarium, and is not original material for the name.

Lysimachia ephemerum Linnaeus, *Species Plantarum* 1: 146. 1753.
"Habitat in Media." RCN: 1171.
Type not designated.
Original material: Herb. Linn. (UPS); Herb. Linn. No. 207.3
(LINN); [icon] in Tilli, Cat. Pl. Hort. Pisani: 106, t. 40, f. 2. 1723;
[icon] in Buxbaum, Pl. Minus Cognit. Cent. 1: 22, t. 33. 1728.
Current name: ***Lysimachia ephemerum*** L. (Primulaceae).

Lysimachia linum-stellatum Linnaeus, *Species Plantarum* 1: 148.
1753.
"Habitat in Gallia." RCN: 1177.
Lectotype (Ali in Ali & Jafri, *Fl. Libya* 1: 8. 1976): Herb. Linn. No.
207.12 (LINN).
Current name: ***Asterolinon linum-stellatum*** (L.) Duby (Primulaceae).

Lysimachia monnieri Linnaeus, *Centuria II Plantarum*: 9. 1756.
"Habitat in America meridionali. Hallman." RCN: 132.
Basionym of: *Gratiola monnieri* (L.) L. (1759).
Neotype (Cramer in Dassanayake & Fosberg, *Revised Handb. Fl.
Ceylon* 3: 421. 1981): [icon] *"Moniera minima repens, foliis
subrotundis, floribus singularibus alaribus"* in Browne, Civ. Nat. Hist.
Jamaica: 269, t. 28, f. 3. 1756.
Current name: ***Bacopa monnieri*** (L.) Pennell (Scrophulariaceae).
Note: Gratiola monnieri (L.) L. (1759) has been regarded as a new
combination based on *Lysimachia monnieri* L. (1756) because the
diagnoses of the two are essentially the same, and the latter does not
appear in *Syst. Nat.*, ed. 10, 2 (May–Jun 1759). Additionally,
Linnaeus (in *Amoen. Acad.* 4: 306. Nov 1959) changed the name *L.
monnieri* to *G. "monnieria"* in the reprint of the dissertation in
which the former had originally appeared, as noted by Nordenstam
(in *Bot. Not.* 114: 278. 1961). Linnaeus' intention therefore seems
clear. Cramer designated a Browne figure as type of *G. monnieri*.
Although it was not cited in the synonymy of the basionym, there is
no original material in existence so this choice is treated as a
neotypification under Art. 9.8.

Lysimachia nemorum Linnaeus, *Species Plantarum* 1: 148. 1753.
"Habitat in Germaniae, Galliae, Angliae nemoribus glareosis." RCN:
1178.
Type not designated.
Original material: Herb. Linn. No. 207.13 (LINN); Herb. Clifford:
52, *Lysimachia* 7 (BM); Herb. Burser XIV(1): 96 (UPS); [icon] in
Clusius, Rar. Pl. Hist. 2: 182. 1601; [icon] in Morison, Pl. Hist.
Univ. 2: 569, s. 5, t. 26, f. 5. 1680.
Current name: ***Lysimachia nemorum*** L. (Primulaceae).

Lysimachia nummularia Linnaeus, *Species Plantarum* 1: 148. 1753.
"Habitat in Europa juxta agros & scrobes." RCN: 1179.
Type not designated.
Original material: Herb. Clifford: 52, *Lysimachia* 6 (BM); Herb.
Burser XVII: 95 (UPS); Herb. Linn. No. 207.14 (LINN); [icon] in
Mattioli, Pl. Epit.: 394. 1586.
Current name: ***Lysimachia nummularia*** L. (Primulaceae).

Lysimachia punctata Linnaeus, *Species Plantarum* 1: 147. 1753.
"Habitat in Hollandia inter arundines." RCN: 1175.
Lectotype (designated here by Chater & Preston): Herb. Linn. No.
207.10 (LINN).
Current name: ***Lysimachia punctata*** L. (Primulaceae).

Lysimachia quadrifolia Linnaeus, *Species Plantarum* 1: 147. 1753.
"Habitat in Virginia." RCN: 1174.
Lectotype (Reveal & al. in *Huntia* 7: 212. 1987): *Clayton 419* (BM-
000051554).
Current name: ***Lysimachia quadrifolia*** L. (Primulaceae).

Lysimachia tenella Linnaeus, *Species Plantarum* 1: 148. 1753.
"Habitat in Galliae, Angliae humidis." RCN: 1184.
Basionym of: *Anagallis tenella* (L.) L. (1774).
Type not designated.
Original material: Herb. Burser XVII: 96 (UPS); [icon] in Morison,
Pl. Hist. Univ. 2: 567, s. 5, t. 26, f. 2. 1680.
Current name: ***Anagallis tenella*** (L.) L. (Primulaceae).

Lysimachia thyrsiflora Linnaeus, *Species Plantarum* 1: 147. 1753.
"Habitat in Europa, in paludibus." RCN: 1173.
Type not designated.
Original material: Herb. Linn. No. 207.8 (LINN); Herb. Clifford: 52,
Lysimachia 5 (BM); [icon] in Clusius, Rar. Pl. Hist. 2: 53. 1601.
Current name: ***Lysimachia thyrsiflora*** L. (Primulaceae).

Lysimachia vulgaris Linnaeus, *Species Plantarum* 1: 146. 1753.
"Habitat in Europa ad ripas & paludes." RCN: 1170.
Lectotype (Nasir in Nasir & Ali, *Fl. Pakistan* 157: 84. 1984): Herb.
Linn. No. 207.1 (LINN).
Generitype of *Lysimachia* Linnaeus (vide Hitchcock, *Prop. Brit. Bot.*:
129. 1929).
Current name: ***Lysimachia vulgaris*** L. (Primulaceae).

Lythrum fruticosum Linnaeus, *Systema Naturae*, ed. 10, 2: 1045.
1759.
["Habitat in China."] Sp. Pl., ed. 2, 1: 641 (1763). RCN: 3468.
Lectotype (Dar in Nasir & Ali, *Fl. W. Pakistan* 78: 6. 1975): Herb.
Linn. No. 626.4 (LINN).
Current name: ***Woodfordia fruticosa*** (L.) Kurz (Lythraceae).
Note: Dar gave the number of the type sheet as "62/4" (LINN), clearly
a typographic error for 626.4, and accepted as such by authors such
as Graham (in *Syst. Bot.* 20: 496, 498, 1995), and here.

Lythrum hyssopifolia Linnaeus, *Species Plantarum* 1: 447. 1753.
"Habitat in Germaniae, Helvetiae, Angliae, Galliae inundatis." RCN:
3474.
Lectotype (Lourteig in Harling & Andersson, *Fl. Ecuador* 37: 10.
1989): Herb. Burser XII: 93 (UPS).
Generitype of *Lythrum* Linnaeus (vide Green, *Prop. Brit. Bot.*: 157.
1929).
Current name: ***Lythrum hyssopifolia*** L. (Lythraceae).
Note: Lythrum salicaria was treated as the generitype by Britton &
Brown (*Ill. Fl. N. U. S.*, ed. 2, 2: 580. 1913; see McNeill & al. in
Taxon 36: 377. 1987). However, under Art. 10.5, Ex. 7 (a voted
example) of the Vienna Code, this is a type choice made under the
American Code and is to be replaced under Art. 10.5b by Green's
choice (*Prop. Brit. Bot.*: 157. 1929) of *L. hyssopifolia* L.

Lythrum lineare Linnaeus, *Species Plantarum* 1: 447. 1753.
"Habitat in Virginia." RCN: 3471.
Lectotype (designated here by Reveal): *Clayton 505*, Herb. Linn. No.
626.7 (LINN; iso- BM-000051582).
Current name: ***Lythrum lineare*** L. (Lythraceae).

Lythrum melanium Linnaeus, *Systema Naturae,* ed. 10, 2: 1045. 1759.
["Habitat in Jamaica."] Sp. Pl., ed. 2, 1: 642 (1762). RCN: 3473.
Type not designated.
Original material: none traced.
Current name: ***Cuphea melanium*** (L.) R. Br. ex Steud. (Lythraceae).

Lythrum parsonsia Linnaeus, *Systema Naturae,* ed. 10, 2: 1045. 1759.
["Habitat in Jamaica."] Sp. Pl., ed. 2, 1: 641 (1762). RCN: 3472.
Lectotype (Fawcett & Rendle, *Fl. Jamaica* 5: 293. 1926): *Browne,*
Herb. Linn. No. 626.8 (LINN).
Current name: ***Cuphea parsonsia*** (L.) R. Br. ex Steud. (Lythraceae).

L

Lythrum petiolatum Linnaeus, *Species Plantarum* 1: 446. 1753.
"Habitat in Virginia." RCN: 3470.
Type not designated.
Original material: *Clayton 418* (BM).
Current name: ***Cuphea viscosissima*** Jacq. (Lythraceae).

Lythrum salicaria Linnaeus, *Species Plantarum* 1: 446. 1753.
"Habitat in Europa ad ripas aquarum." RCN: 3466.
Lectotype (Dar in Nasir & Ali, *Fl. W. Pakistan* 78: 7. 1975): Herb.
     Linn. No. 626.1 (LINN).
Current name: ***Lythrum salicaria*** L. (Lythraceae).
Note: Lythrum salicaria was treated as the generitype by Britton &
     Brown (in *Ill. Fl. N. U. S.*, ed. 2, 2: 580. 1913; see McNeill & al.
     in *Taxon* 36: 377. 1987). However, under Art. 10.5, Ex. 7
     (a voted example) of the Vienna Code, this is a type choice made
     under the American Code and is to be replaced under Art.
     10.5b by Green's choice (*Prop. Brit. Bot.*: 157. 1929) of *L.
     hyssopifolia* L.

Lythrum thymifolia Linnaeus, *Species Plantarum* 1: 447. 1753.
"Habitat in Italiae & G. Narbonensis uliginosis." RCN: 3475.
Type not designated.
Original material: Herb. Linn. No. 626.19 (LINN); [icon] in
     Barrelier, Pl. Galliam: 53, t. 773, f. 2. 1714; [icon] in Bauhin &
     Cherler, Hist. Pl. Univ. 3(2): 792. 1651.
Current name: ***Lythrum thymifolia*** L. (Lythraceae).

Lythrum verticillatum Linnaeus, *Species Plantarum* 1: 446. 1753.
"Habitat in Virginia." RCN: 3469.
Lectotype (designated here by Reveal): Herb. Linn. No. 626.6 (LINN).
Current name: ***Decodon verticillatus*** (L.) Elliott (Lythraceae).

Lythrum virgatum Linnaeus, *Species Plantarum* 1: 447. 1753.
"Habitat in Sibiria, Tataria." RCN: 3467.
Type not designated.
Original material: Herb. Linn. No. 626.3 (LINN).
Current name: ***Lythrum virgatum*** L. (Lythraceae).

M

Macrocnemum jamaicense Linnaeus, *Plantarum Jamaicensium Pugillus*: 31. 1759.

["Habitat in Jamaica."] Sp. Pl., ed. 2, 1: 244 (1762). RCN: 1355.

Type not designated.

Original material: *Browne*, Herb. Linn. No. 227.1 (LINN).

Generitype of *Macrocnemum* P. Browne.

Current name: ***Macrocnemum jamaicense*** L. (Rubiaceae).

Madrepora acetabulum Linnaeus, *Systema Naturae*, ed. 10, 1: 793. 1758.

"Habitat in O. Europaeo, Americano."

Basionym of: *Tubularia acetabulum* (L.) L. (1767).

Lectotype (John in Spencer & al. in *Taxon*, in press): [icon] *"Acetabulum"* in Tournefort, Inst. Rei Herb.: 569, t. 338. 1700.

Current name: ***Acetabularia acetabulum*** (L.) P.C. Silva (Dasycladaceae).

Magnolia acuminata (Linnaeus) Linnaeus, *Systema Naturae*, ed. 10, 2: 1081. 1759.

["Habitat in Pensylvania."] Sp. Pl., ed. 2, 1: 756 (1762). RCN: 3983.

Basionym: *Magnolia virginiana* L. var. *acuminata* L. (1753).

Lectotype (Dandy, *Sloane Herbarium*: 112. 1958; Tobe in Hunt, *Magnolias*: 191. 1998): [icon] *"Magnolia flore albo, folio majore acuminato haud albicante"* in Catesby, Nat. Hist. Carolina 2, App.: 15, t. 15, open flower excluded. 1747.

Current name: ***Magnolia acuminata*** (L.) L. (Magnoliaceae).

Note: Tobe (in Hunt, *Magnolias*: 191. 1998) provides an illustration of the lectotype, but argues that it is a chimaera, with the leaves of *M. acuminata* and an open, stylised flower of another species, which he excludes from Dandy's original choice of the whole plate.

Magnolia glauca (Linnaeus) Linnaeus, *Systema Naturae*, ed. 10, 2: 1081. 1759.

["Habitat in Virginia, Pensylvania."] Sp. Pl., ed. 2, 1: 755 (1762). RCN: 3982.

Basionym: *Magnolia virginiana* L. var. *glauca* L. (1753).

Lectotype (Dandy, *Sloane Herbarium*: 112. 1958): [icon] *"Magnolia Lauri folio, subtus albicante"* in Catesby, Nat. Hist. Carolina 1: 39, t. 39. 1730.

Current name: ***Magnolia virginiana*** L. (Magnoliaceae).

Note: Tobe (in Hunt, *Magnolias*: 180. 1998) provides an illustration of the lectotype.

Magnolia grandiflora Linnaeus, *Systema Naturae*, ed. 10, 2: 1082. 1759.

["Habitat in Florida, Carolina."] Sp. Pl., ed. 2, 1: 755 (1762). RCN: 3961.

Lectotype (Vázquez in *Brittonia* 46: 5. 1994): [icon] *"Magnolia, foliis lanceolatis persistentibus, caule erecto arboreo"* in Miller, Fig. Pl. Gard. Dict. 2: 115, t. 172. 1757.

Current name: ***Magnolia grandiflora*** L. (Magnoliaceae).

Note: Tobe (in Hunt, *Magnolias*: 184. 1998) provides an illustration of the lectotype, and one (p. 185) of Catesby's t. 61. Jarvis (in *Symb. Bot. Upsal.* 33(3): 26, f. 1. 2005) also reproduces the lectotype.

Magnolia tripetala (Linnaeus) Linnaeus, *Systema Naturae*, ed. 10, 2: 1081. 1759.

["Habitat in Carolina, rarius in Virginia."] Sp. Pl., ed. 2, 1: 756 (1762). RCN: 3984.

Basionym: *Magnolia virginiana* L. var. *tripetala* L. (1753).

Lectotype (Dandy, *Sloane Herbarium*: 112. 1958): [icon] *"Magnolia, amplissimo flore albo, fructu coccineo"* in Catesby, Nat. Hist. Carolina 2: 80, t. 80. 1738.

Current name: ***Magnolia tripetala*** (L.) L. (Magnoliaceae).

Magnolia virginiana Linnaeus, *Species Plantarum* 1: 535. 1753.

"Habitat in Virginia, Carolina." RCN: 3980.

Lectotype (Dandy in *Curtis's Bot. Mag.* 175: t. 457. 1964): Herb. Clifford: 222, *Magnolia* 1 (BM-000628820).

Generitype of *Magnolia* Linnaeus.

Current name: ***Magnolia virginiana*** L. (Magnoliaceae).

Note: Tobe (in Jarvis & al., *Regnum Veg.* 127: 63. 1993) independently chose the same type as Dandy, and later (in Hunt, *Magnolias*: 180. 1998) provided an illustration of the lectotype.

Magnolia virginiana Linnaeus var. **acuminata** Linnaeus, *Species Plantarum* 1: 536. 1753.

["Habitat in Pensylvania."] Sp. Pl., ed. 2, 1: 756 (1762). RCN: 3980.

Basionym of: *Magnolia acuminata* (L.) L. (1759).

Lectotype (Dandy, *Sloane Herbarium*: 112. 1958; Tobe in Hunt, *Magnolias*: 191. 1998): [icon] *"Magnolia flore albo, folio majore acuminato haud albicante"* in Catesby, Nat. Hist. Carolina 2, App.: 15, t. 15, open flower excluded. 1747.

Current name: ***Magnolia acuminata*** (L.) L. (Magnoliaceae).

Note: Tobe (in Hunt, *Magnolias*: 191. 1998) provides an illustration of the lectotype, but argues that it is a chimaera, with the leaves of *M. acuminata* and an open, stylised flower of another species, which he excludes from Dandy's original choice of the whole plate.

Magnolia virginiana Linnaeus var. **foetida** Linnaeus, *Species Plantarum* 1: 536. 1753.

RCN: 3980.

Type not designated.

Original material: *Clayton 24* (BM); [icon] in Catesby, Nat. Hist. Carolina 2: 61, t. 61. 1738; [icon] in Plumier, Nov. Pl. Amer.: 38, t. 7. 1703.

Current name: ***Magnolia grandiflora*** L. (Magnoliaceae).

Magnolia virginiana Linnaeus var. **glauca** Linnaeus, *Species Plantarum* 1: 535. 1753.

["Habitat in Virginia, Pensylvania."] Sp. Pl., ed. 2, 1: 755 (1762). RCN: 3980.

Basionym of: *Magnolia glauca* (L.) L. (1759).

Lectotype (Dandy, *Sloane Herbarium*: 112. 1958): [icon] *"Magnolia Lauri folio, subtus albicante"* in Catesby, Nat. Hist. Carolina 1: 39, t. 39. 1730.

Current name: ***Magnolia virginiana*** L. (Magnoliaceae).

Note: Tobe (in Hunt, *Magnolias*: 180. 1998) provides an illustration of the lectotype.

Magnolia virginiana Linnaeus var. **grisea** Linnaeus, *Species Plantarum* 1: 536. 1753.

RCN: 3980.

Type not designated.

Original material: none traced.

Current name: ***Magnolia grandiflora*** L. (Magnoliaceae).

Magnolia virginiana Linnaeus var. **tripetala** Linnaeus, *Species Plantarum* 1: 536. 1753.

["Habitat in Carolina, rarius in Virginia."] Sp. Pl., ed. 2, 1: 756 (1762). RCN: 3980.

Basionym of: *Magnolia tripetala* (L.) L. (1759).

Lectotype (Dandy, *Sloane Herbarium*: 112. 1958): [icon] *"Magnolia, amplissimo flore albo, fructu coccineo"* in Catesby, Nat. Hist. Carolina 2: 80, t. 80. 1738.
Current name: ***Magnolia tripetala*** (L.) L. (Magnoliaceae).

Mahernia pinnata (Linnaeus) Linnaeus, *Systema Naturae,* ed. 12, 2: 227. 1767.
["Habitat in Aethiopia."] Sp. Pl. 2: 674 (1753). RCN: 2260.
Basionym: *Hermannia pinnata* L. (1753).
Lectotype (de Winter in *Bothalia* 11: 264. 1974): Herb. Clifford: 342, *Hermannia* 6 (BM-000646396).
Current name: ***Hermannia pinnata*** L. (Sterculiaceae).

Mahernia verticillata Linnaeus, *Systema Naturae,* ed. 12, 2: 227; *Mantissa Plantarum*: 59. 1767.
"Habitat ad Cap. b. spei." RCN: 2259.
Neotype (de Winter in *Bothalia* 11: 264. 1974): Herb. Linn. No. 854.17 (LINN).
Generitype of *Mahernia* Linnaeus.
Current name: ***Hermannia pinnata*** L. (Sterculiaceae).
Note: Winter wrongly referred to the LINN sheet as the holotype but as it is annotated only by Linnaeus filius, and there is no original material for the name, this is treated as a correctable error under Art. 9.8, and accepted as a neotype. Jarvis & al. (*Regnum Veg.* 127: 63. 1993) wrongly gave the sheet number as "634.17".

Malachra capitata (Linnaeus) Linnaeus, *Systema Naturae,* ed. 12, 2: 458. 1767.
"Habitat in Caribaeis, locis paludosis." RCN: 9029.
Basionym: *Sida capitata* L. (1753).
Lectotype (Fawcett & Rendle, *Fl. Jamaica* 5: 124. 1926): Herb. Linn. No. 867.1 (LINN).
Generitype of *Malachra* Linnaeus.
Current name: ***Malachra capitata*** (L.) L. (Malvaceae).

Malachra radiata (Linnaeus) Linnaeus, *Systema Naturae,* ed. 12, 2: 459. 1767.
["Habitat in America."] Sp. Pl., ed. 2, 2: 965 (1763). RCN: 5030.
Basionym: *Sida radiata* L. (1763).
Lectotype (Fryxell in *Syst. Bot. Monogr.* 25: 269. 1988): [icon] *"Sida foliis palmatis, caule hispido"* in Plumier in Burman, Pl. Amer.: 10, t. 19. 1755.
Current name: ***Malachra radiata*** (L.) L. (Malvaceae).

Malope malacoides Linnaeus, *Species Plantarum* 2: 692. 1753.
"Habitat in Hetruriae pratis." RCN: 5069.
Lectotype (designated here by Baldini): Herb. Clifford: 347, *Malope* 1 (BM-000646477).
Generitype of *Malope* Linnaeus.
Current name: ***Malope malacoides*** L. (Malvaceae).

Malpighia angustifolia Linnaeus, *Species Plantarum,* ed. 2, 1: 610. 1762, *nom. illeg.*
"Habitat in America meridionali." RCN: 3313.
Replaced synonym: *Malpighia linearis* Jacq. (1760).
Neotype (Meyer in *Phanerog. Monogr.* 23: 249. 2000): H(ortus) Imp(erialis) Vind(obonensis), s. d., s. coll. (Herb. W. Gerhard, Lips. 1820) (JE).
Current name: ***Malpighia linearis*** Jacq. (Malpighiaceae).
Note: A superfluous name for *M. linearis* Jacq. (1760), with which it is therefore homotypic, and not typified by a Browne collection (588.7, LINN) as suggested by Anderson (in Howard, *Fl. Lesser Antilles* 4: 619. 1988).

Malpighia aquifolia Linnaeus, *Species Plantarum* 1: 426. 1753.
"Habitat in America calidiore." RCN: 3316.

Type not designated.
Original material: [icon] in Plumier in Burman, Pl. Amer.: 161, t. 168, f. 1. 1758.
Current name: ***Malpighia aquifolia*** L. (Malpighiaceae).
Note: Meyer (in *Phanerog. Monogr.* 23: 309. 2000) treated Plumier's 1703 phrase name as the lectotype but this is contrary to Art. 8.1.

Malpighia bannisterioides Linnaeus, *Plantae Surinamenses*: 9. 1775.
"Habitat [in Surinamo.]" RCN: 3320.
Lectotype (Anderson in *Taxon* 41: 328. 1992): Herb. Linn. No. 588.13 (LINN; iso- S-LINN 190.5).
Current name: ***Stigmaphyllon bannisterioides*** (L.) C.E. Anderson (Malpighiaceae).
Note: Generic name spelled "Malpigia" in the protologue.

Malpighia coccigera Linnaeus, *Species Plantarum* 1: 426. 1753.
"Habitat in America calidiore." RCN: 3317.
Lectotype (Anderson in Howard, *Fl. Lesser Antilles* 4: 617. 1988): [icon] in Plumier, Codex Boerhaavianus (University Library, Groningen).
Current name: ***Malpighia coccigera*** L. (Malpighiaceae).

Malpighia coccigrya Linnaeus, *Species Plantarum,* ed. 2, 1: 611. 1762, *orth. var.*
"Habitat in America calidiore." RCN: 3317.
Lectotype (Anderson in Howard, *Fl. Lesser Antilles* 4: 617. 1988): [icon] in Plumier, Codex Boerhaavianus (University Library, Groningen).
Current name: ***Malpighia coccigera*** L. (Malpighiaceae).
Note: Evidently an orthographic variant of *M. coccigera* L. (1753).

Malpighia crassifolia Linnaeus, *Species Plantarum* 1: 426. 1753.
"Habitat in America calidiore." RCN: 3314.
Lectotype (Cuatrecasas & Croat in Woodson & Schery in *Ann. Missouri Bot. Gard.* 67: 872. 1981 [1980]): Herb. Linn. No. 588.8 (LINN).
Current name: ***Byrsonima crassifolia*** (L.) Kunth (Malpighiaceae).

Malpighia glabra Linnaeus, *Species Plantarum* 1: 425. 1753.
"Habitat in Jamaica, Brasilia, Surinamo, Curacao." RCN: 3309.
Lectotype (Anderson in Jarvis & al., *Regnum Veg.* 127: 63. 1993): Herb. Clifford: 169, *Malpighia* 1 (BM-000628495).
Generitype of *Malpighia* Linnaeus (vide Green, *Prop. Brit. Bot.*: 155. 1929).
Current name: ***Malpighia glabra*** L. (Malpighiaceae).
Note: Vivaldi (in *Ann. Missouri Bot. Gard.* 67: 904. 1981) indicated 588.1 (LINN), a post-1753 addition to the herbarium, as type but it is not original material for the name.

Malpighia punicifolia Linnaeus, *Species Plantarum,* ed. 2, 1: 609. 1762.
"Habitat in America meridionali." RCN: 3310.
Lectotype (Vivaldi in *Ann. Missouri Bot. Gard.* 67: 904. 1980): Herb. Linn. No. 588.4 (LINN).
Current name: ***Malpighia glabra*** L. (Malpighiaceae).

Malpighia urens Linnaeus, *Species Plantarum* 1: 426. 1753.
"Habitat in America calidiore." RCN: 3312.
Lectotype (Fawcett & Rendle, *Fl. Jamaica* 4: 227. 1920): Herb. Linn. No. 588.6 (LINN).
Current name: ***Malpighia urens*** L. (Malpighiaceae).

Malpighia verbascifolia Linnaeus, *Species Plantarum* 1: 426. 1753.
"Habitat in America calidiore." RCN: 3315.

Lectotype (Anderson in *Mem. New York Bot. Gard.* 32: 91. 1981): Herb. Linn. No. 588.10 (LINN).
Current name: ***Byrsonima verbascifolia*** (L.) DC. (Malpighiaceae).

Malva abutiloides Linnaeus, *Species Plantarum,* ed. 2, 2: 971. 1763.
"Habitat in Providentia, Bahama." RCN: 5059.
Type not designated.
Original material: [icon] in Dillenius, Hort. Eltham. 1: 1, t. 1, f. 1. 1732.
Current name: ***Phymosia abutiloides*** (L.) Ham. (Malvaceae).

Malva aegyptia Linnaeus, *Species Plantarum* 2: 690. 1753.
"Habitat in Aegypto." RCN: 5058.
Lectotype (Meikle, *Fl. Cyprus* 1: 308. 1977): Herb. Linn. No. 870.32 (LINN).
Current name: ***Malva aegyptia*** L. (Malvaceae).

Malva alcea Linnaeus, *Species Plantarum* 2: 689. 1753.
"Habitat in Germania, Anglia, Gallia." RCN: 5055.
Lectotype (Jonsell & Jarvis in *Nordic J. Bot.* 22: 80. 2002): Herb. Clifford: 347, *Malva* 8, sheet A (BM-000646469).
Current name: ***Malva alcea*** L. (Malvaceae).

Malva americana Linnaeus, *Species Plantarum* 2: 687. 1753.
"Habitat in America." RCN: 5041.
Lectotype (Borssum Waalkes in *Blumea* 14: 154. 1966): Herb. A. van Royen No. 908.139–311 (L; iso- G).
Current name: ***Malvastrum americanum*** (L.) Torr. (Malvaceae).

Malva bryoniifolia Linnaeus, *Species Plantarum* 2: 688. 1753.
"Habitat in Hispania." RCN: 5044.
Lectotype (Bates in *Gentes Herb.* 10: 357. 1969): Herb. Linn. No. 870.7 (LINN).
Current name: ***Anisodontea bryoniifolia*** (L.) D.M. Bates (Malvaceae).
Note: Specific epithet spelled "bryonifolia" in the protologue.

Malva capensis Linnaeus, *Species Plantarum* 2: 688. 1753.
"Habitat in Aethiopia." RCN: 5045.
Lectotype (Bates in *Gentes Herb.* 10: 235, f. 2. 1969): Herb. Clifford: 347, *Malva* 3 (BM-000646461).
Current name: ***Anisodontea capensis*** (L.) D.M. Bates (Malvaceae).

Malva capensis Linnaeus var. **scabrosa** (Linnaeus) Linnaeus, *Species Plantarum,* ed. 2, 2: 967. 1763.
["Habitat in Aethiopia."] Cent. II Pl.: 27 (1756). RCN: 5045.
Basionym: *Malva scabrosa* L. (1756).
Lectotype (Bates in *Gentes Herb.* 10: 239, f. 4. 1969): [icon] "*Malva Africana frutescens flore rubro*" in Commelin, Hort. Med. Amstelod. Pl. Rar. 2: 171, t. 86. 1701.
Current name: ***Anisodontea scabrosa*** (L.) D.M. Bates (Malvaceae).

Malva caroliniana Linnaeus, *Species Plantarum* 2: 688. 1753.
"Habitat in Carolina." RCN: 5046.
Lectotype (Paul & Nayar in *Fasc. Fl. India* 19: 183. 1988): Herb. Linn. No. 870.15 (LINN; iso- S).
Current name: ***Modiola caroliniana*** (L.) G. Don (Malvaceae).
Note: Paul & Nayar's typification (30 Mar 1988) narrowly pre-dates that of Fryxell (in *Syst. Bot. Monogr.* 25: 306. 13 Dec 1988) who chose the same type.

Malva coromandeliana Linnaeus, *Species Plantarum* 2: 687. 1753.
"Habitat in America?" RCN: 5040.
Lectotype (Borssum Waalkes in *Blumea* 14: 152. 1966): Herb. Linn. No. 870.3 (LINN).

Current name: ***Malvastrum coromandelianum*** (L.) Garcke (Malvaceae).
Note: See discussion by Merrill (in *Philipp. J. Sci., C,* 7: 240. 1912) of the Clifford and Plukenet entries, who concluded that the name should stay with *Malvastrum*, though he did not make an explicit typification. The type designated by Borssum Waalkes is illustrated (though the image has been reversed) by Hill (in *Rhodora* 84: 326, f. 64. 1982).

Malva crispa (Linnaeus) Linnaeus, *Systema Naturae,* ed. 10, 2: 1147. 1759.
"Habitat in Syria." RCN: 5054.
Basionym: *Malva verticillata* var. *crispa* L. (1753).
Type not designated.
Original material: as basionym.
Current name: ***Malva crispa*** (L.) L. (Malvaceae).

Malva gangetica Linnaeus, *Species Plantarum,* ed. 2, 2: 967. 1763.
"Habitat in India." RCN: 5039.
Lectotype (Hill in *Rhodora* 84: 187. 1982): [icon] "*Althaea Indica Abutili subrotundo folio, flore luteo, spicato*" in Plukenet, Phytographia: t. 74, f. 6. 1691; Almag. Bot.: 24. 1696.
Current name: ***Malvastrum americanum*** (L.) Torr. (Malvaceae).

Malva hispanica Linnaeus, *Species Plantarum* 2: 689. 1753.
"Habitat in Hispania." RCN: 5052.
Type not designated.
Original material: [icon] in Plukenet, Phytographia: t. 44, f. 3. 1691; Almag. Bot.: 238. 1696 – Voucher: Herb. Sloane 100: 202 (BM-SL).
Current name: ***Malva hispanica*** L. (Malvaceae).

Malva limensis Linnaeus, *Centuria II Plantarum*: 27. 1756.
"Habitat in America. Miller." RCN: 5043.
Lectotype (Krapovickas in *Darwiniana* 10: 629. 1954): Herb. Linn. No. 870.6 (LINN).
Current name: ***Fuertesimalva limensis*** (L.) Fryxell (Malvaceae).

Malva mauritiana Linnaeus, *Species Plantarum* 2: 689. 1753.
"Habitat in Italia, Lusitania, Hispania." RCN: 5051.
Lectotype (Abedin in Nasir & Ali, *Fl. W. Pakistan* 130: 38. 1979): Herb. Linn. No. 870.24 (LINN).
Current name: ***Malva sylvestris*** L. var. ***mauritiana*** (L.) Boiss. (Malvaceae).

Malva moschata Linnaeus, *Species Plantarum* 2: 690. 1753.
"Habitat in Italia, Gallia." RCN: 5056.
Lectotype (Jonsell & Jarvis in *Nordic J. Bot.* 22: 81. 2002): [icon] "*Malva sive Alcea montana*" in Colonna, Ekphr.: 148, 147. 1606. – Epitype (Jonsell & Jarvis in *Nordic J. Bot.* 22: 81. 2002): Italy. Molise, Matese, Selve del Matese, Jul 1873, *A. Jatta s.n.* (RO).
Current name: ***Malva moschata*** L. (Malvaceae).

Malva parviflora Linnaeus, *Demonstr. Pl. Horto Upsaliensi*: 18. 1753. RCN: 5047.
Lectotype (Riedl in Rechinger, *Fl. Iranica* 120: 23. 1976): Herb. Linn. No. 870.17 (LINN).
Current name: ***Malva parviflora*** L. (Malvaceae).
Note: See detailed comments on 870.16 and 870.17 (LINN) by Burtt (in *Kew Bull.* 9: 391. 1954).

Malva peruviana Linnaeus, *Species Plantarum* 2: 688. 1753.
"Habitat in Peru. D. Jussieu." RCN: 5042.
Neotype (Krapovickas in *Darwiniana* 10: 629, lam. VII. 1954): Herb. Linn. No. 870.5 (LINN; iso- P-JU).

M

Current name: **Fuertesimalva peruviana** (L.) Fryxell (Malvaceae).
Note: Krapovickas' choice of type appears to be a later addition to the herbarium and not original material. However, no other original material appears to exist so this choice is accepted as a valid neotypification under Art. 9.8.

Malva rotundifolia Linnaeus, *Species Plantarum* 2: 688. 1753, *nom. utique rej.*
"Habitat in Europae ruderatis, viis, plateis." RCN: 5048.
Lectotype (Riedl in Rechinger, *Fl. Iranica* 120: 26. 1976): Herb. Linn. No. 870.18 (LINN).
Current name: **Malva pusilla** Sm. (Malvaceae).

Malva scabrosa Linnaeus, *Centuria II Plantarum*: 27. 1756.
"Habitat in Aethiopia." RCN: 5045.
Basionym of: *Malva capensis* L. var. *scabrosa* (L.) L. (1763).
Lectotype (Bates in *Gentes Herb.* 10: 239, f. 4. 1969): [icon] *"Malva Africana frutescens flore rubro"* in Commelin, Hort. Med. Amstelod. Pl. Rar. 2: 171, t. 86. 1701.
Current name: **Anisodontea scabrosa** (L.) D.M. Bates (Malvaceae).

Malva sherardiana Linnaeus, *Species Plantarum,* ed. 2, 2: 1675. 1763.
"Habitat in Bithynia. Arduino." RCN: 5049.

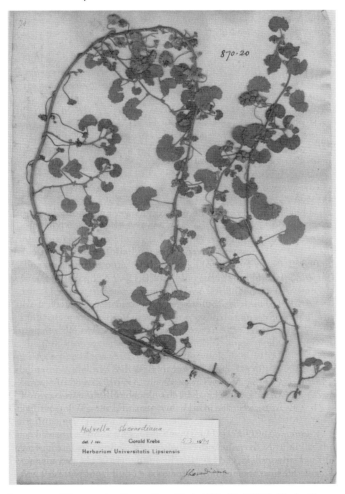

Lectotype (Clement in *Contr. Gray Herb.* 180: 49. 1957): Herb. Linn. No. 870.20 (LINN).
Current name: **Malvella sherardiana** (L.) Fryxell (Malvaceae).
Note: Specific epithet spelled "scherardiana" in the protologue.

Malva spicata Linnaeus, *Systema Naturae,* ed. 10, 2: 1146. 1759.
RCN: 5037.
Lectotype (Borssum Waalkes in *Blumea* 14: 154. 1966): [icon] *"Althaea spicata, betonicae folio villosissimo"* in Sloane, Voy. Jamaica 1: 218, t. 138, f. 1. 1707. – Typotype: Herb. Sloane 5: 55 (BM-SL).
Current name: **Melochia spicata** (L.) Fryxell (Sterculiaceae).
Note: Bates (in *Rhodora* 84: 196. 1982) treated material in Herb. Sloane (apparently in vol. 5: 56, BM-SL), identifiable as *Malvastrum americanum* (L.) Torrey, as the lectotype, but it was never seen by Linnaeus and is not original material for the name. Krapovickas & Cristóbal (in *Bonplandia* 9: 257–258. 1997) argued that the type is 870.1 (LINN), another specimen of the same species, into the synonymy of which *Malva spicata* would then fall. However, the competing Sloane illustration is clearly an original element for the name and was formally chosen as the type by Borssum Waalkes in 1966. Later authors have not provided grounds for rejecting this choice. Sloane's plant is of the species formerly known as *Melochia villosa* (Mill.) Fawc. & Rendle, for which the new combination *Melochia spicata* (L.) Fryxell was made in 1988.

Malva sylvestris Linnaeus, *Species Plantarum* 2: 689. 1753.
"Habitat in Europae campestribus." RCN: 5050.
Lectotype (Ali in Ali & Jafri, *Fl. Libya* 10: 7. 1977): Herb. Linn. No. 870.22 (LINN).
Generitype of *Malva* Linnaeus (vide Green, *Prop. Brit. Bot.*: 173. 1929).
Current name: **Malva sylvestris** L. (Malvaceae).

Malva tomentosa Linnaeus, *Species Plantarum* 2: 687. 1753.
"Habitat in India." RCN: 5038.
Lectotype (Hill in *Brittonia* 32: 466. 1980): Herb. Linn. No. 870.2 (LINN).
Current name: **Malvastrum tomentosum** (L.) S.R. Hill (Malvaceae).
Note: The type is illustrated (though the image has been reversed) by Hill (in *Rhodora* 84: 214, f. 36. 1982).

Malva tournefortiana Linnaeus, *Centuria I Plantarum*: 21. 1755.
"Habitat in Galloprovincia, Hispania. Loefling 509a." RCN: 5057.
Type not designated.
Original material: *Löfling 509a*, Herb. Linn. No. 870.31, syntype (LINN); Herb. Linn. No. 286.13 (S); [icon] in Plukenet, Phytographia: t. 44, f. 4. 1691; Almag. Bot.: 13. 1696 – Voucher: Herb. Sloane 95: 21 (BM-SL).
Current name: **Malva tournefortiana** L. (Malvaceae).

Malva verticillata Linnaeus, *Species Plantarum* 2: 689. 1753.
"Habitat in China, Syria." RCN: 5053.
Lectotype (Abedin in Nasir & Ali, *Fl. W. Pakistan* 130: 45. 1979): Herb. Linn. No. 870.26 (LINN).
Current name: **Malva verticillata** L. (Malvaceae).

Malva verticillata Linnaeus var. **crispa** Linnaeus, *Species Plantarum* 2: 689. 1753.
["Habitat in Syria."] Sp. Pl., ed. 2, 2: 970 (1763). RCN: 5054.
Basionym of: *Malva crispa* (L.) L. (1759).
Type not designated.
Original material: Herb. Burser XVIII(1): 6 (UPS); Herb. Clifford: 347, *Malva* 7 (BM); [icon] in Dodoëns, Stirp. Hist. Pempt., ed. 2: 654, 653. 1616.
Current name: **Malva crispa** (L.) L. (Malvaceae).
Note: Fryxell (in *Syst. Bot. Monogr.* 25: 275. 1988) indicated 870.27 (LINN) as holotype, with an isotype at S (presumably sheet 286.7). However, neither of these collections appears to have been in Linnaeus' possession in 1753, and they are not original material for the name.

Mammea americana Linnaeus, *Species Plantarum* 1: 512. 1753.
"Habitat in Hispaniola, Jamaica." RCN: 3863.
Lectotype (D'Arcy in Woodson & Schery in *Ann. Missouri Bot. Gard.* 67: 1003. 1981 [1980]): Herb. Linn. No. 675.1 (LINN).
Generitype of *Mammea* Linnaeus (vide Green, *Prop. Brit. Bot.*: 161. 1929).
Current name: ***Mammea americana*** L. (Clusiaceae).

Mammea asiatica Linnaeus, *Species Plantarum* 1: 512. 1753.
"Habitat in Java. Osbeck." RCN: 3864.
Lectotype (Payens in *Blumea* 15: 186. 1967): *Osbeck*, Herb. Linn. No. 675.2 (LINN), see p. 224.
Current name: ***Barringtonia asiatica*** (L.) Kurz (Lecythidaceae).

Mandragora officinarum Linnaeus, *Species Plantarum* 1: 181. 1753.
"Habitat in Hispaniae, Italiae, Cretae, Cycladum apricis." RCN: 1438.
Replaced synonym of: *Atropa mandragora* L. (1759), *nom. illeg.*
Lectotype (Knapp in Jarvis & al., *Regnum Veg.* 127: 64. 1993): Herb. Burser IX: 26 (UPS).
Generitype of *Mandragora* Linnaeus.
Current name: ***Mandragora officinarum*** L. (Solanaceae).

Manettia reclinata Linnaeus, *Mantissa Plantarum Altera*: 558. 1771.
"Habitat in Mexico." RCN: 1003.
Type not designated.
Original material: none traced.
Generitype of *Manettia* Linnaeus, *nom. cons.*
Current name: ***Manettia reclinata*** L. (Rubiaceae).
Note: Manettia Linnaeus, *nom. cons.* against *Manettia* Boehm. and *Lygistum* P. Browne.
   Lorence (in *Monogr. Syst. Bot. Missouri Bot. Gard.* 73: 101. 1999) says this was based on Colombian material seen by Mútis (not from Mexico), and that a neotype is needed. However, he did not designate one.

Mangifera indica Linnaeus, *Species Plantarum* 1: 200. 1753.
"Habitat in India." RCN: 1624.
Lectotype (Bornstein in Howard, *Fl. Lesser Antilles* 5: 98. 1989): [icon] *"Mau"* in Rheede, Hort. Malab. 4: 1, t. 1, t. 2. 1683.
Generitype of *Mangifera* Linnaeus.
Current name: ***Mangifera indica*** L. (Anacardiaceae).
Note: Herb. Linn. 276.1 (LINN) has been indicated as the type by a number of authors since Fawcett & Rendle (*Fl. Jamaica* 5: 7. 1926), but it is evidently a later addition to the herbarium and not original material for the name. Although Mukherji (in *Lloydia* 12: 74, 83. 1949) concluded that no type specimen existed, he treated Hermann's description as the basis of the species (which is contrary to Art. 8.1). Kostermans & Bompard (*The Mangoes*: 96, f. 61. 1993) treated an illustration in Herb. Hermann 5: 223 (BM) as the holotype, but their choice is pre-dated by that of Bornstein, which is accepted here.

Manisuris myurus Linnaeus, *Mantissa Plantarum Altera*: 300. 1771.
"Habitat in India." RCN: 596.
Lectotype (Clayton in Cafferty & al. in *Taxon* 49: 252. 2000): Herb. Linn. No. 1215.2 (LINN).
Generitype of *Manisuris* Linnaeus, *nom. rej.*
Current name: ***Manisuris myurus*** L. (Poaceae).
Note: Although *Rottboellia* L. f. (1782) is conserved against *Manisuris* L. (1771), recent treatments now recognise them as distinct genera.

Manulea cheiranthus (Linnaeus) Linnaeus, *Systema Naturae*, ed. 12, 2: 419; *Mantissa Plantarum*: 88. 1767.
"Habitat ad Cap b. spei." RCN: 4561.
Basionym: *Lobelia cheiranthus* L. (1753).

Lectotype (Wijnands, *Bot. Commelins*: 189. 1983): [icon] *"Cheiranthos Africana flore luteo"* in Commelin, Hort. Med. Amstelod. Pl. Rar. 2: 83, t. 42. 1701.
Generitype of *Manulea* Linnaeus, *nom. cons.*
Current name: ***Manulea cheiranthus*** (L.) L. (Scrophulariaceae).
Note: Manulea Linnaeus, *nom. cons.* against *Nemia* Berg.

Manulea tomentosa (Linnaeus) Linnaeus, *Systema Vegetabilium*, ed. 13: 476. 1774.
["Habitat ad Cap. b. spei. David Royen & J. Burmannus."] Sp. Pl., ed. 2, 2: 877 (1763). RCN: 4562.
Basionym: *Selago tomentosa* L. (1760).
Type not designated.
Original material: as basionym.
Current name: ***Manulea tomentosa*** (L.) L. (Scrophulariaceae).

Maranta arundinacea Linnaeus, *Species Plantarum* 1: 2. 1753.
"Habitat in America calidiore." RCN: 10.
Lectotype (Andersson in *Nordic J. Bot.* 6: 739. 1986): Herb. Clifford: 2, *Maranta* 1 (BM-000557503).
Generitype of *Maranta* Linnaeus.
Current name: ***Maranta arundinacea*** L. (Marantaceae).

Maranta galanga Linnaeus, *Species Plantarum*, ed. 2, 1: 3. 1762.
"Habitat in India aquosa." RCN: 11.
Lectotype (Merrill, *Interpret. Rumph. Herb. Amb.*: 153. 1917): [icon] *"Galanga major"* in Rumphius, Herb. Amboin. 5: 143, t. 63. 1747.
Current name: ***Alpinia galanga*** (L.) Willd. (Zingiberaceae).

Marcgravia umbellata Linnaeus, *Species Plantarum* 1: 503. 1753.
"Habitat in America calidiore." RCN: 3814.
Lectotype (Bedell in Howard, *Fl. Lesser Antilles* 5: 303. 1989): [icon] *"Marcgravia"* in Plumier, Nov. Pl. Amer.: 7, t. 29. 1703.
Generitype of *Marcgravia* Linnaeus.
Current name: ***Marcgravia umbellata*** L. (Marcgraviaceae).
Note: See comments on the Plumier elements by Dressler (in *Curtis's Bot. Mag.* 14: 130–131. 1997).

Marchantia androgyna Linnaeus, *Species Plantarum* 2: 1138. 1753.
"Habitat in Italia, Jamaica inter saxorum crepedines." RCN: 8146.
Type not designated.
Original material: Herb. Linn. 1269.11 (LINN).
Current name: ***Mannia androgyna*** (L.) A. Evans (Aytoniaceae).
Note: Grolle (in *Trans. Brit. Bryol. Soc.* 5: 544. 1968; *Feddes Repert.* 87: 208. 1976) treated a Micheli collection in FI as the lectotype but this material was never seen by Linnaeus and is not original material for the name. See comments by Zijlstra (in *Taxon* 39: 291. 1990) on this name in connection with a proposal to conserve *Mannia* Opiz.

Marchantia chenopoda Linnaeus, *Species Plantarum* 2: 1137. 1753.
"Habitat in Martinica." RCN: 8141.
Lectotype (Isoviita in *Acta Bot. Fenn.* 89: 23. 1970): [icon] *"Lichen Anapodocarpon"* in Plumier, Traité Foug. Amér.: 143, t. 142. 1705.
Current name: ***Marchantia chenopoda*** L. (Marchantiaceae).

Marchantia conica Linnaeus, *Species Plantarum* 2: 1138. 1753.
"Habitat in Europae locis umbrosis, ripis elevatis." RCN: 8145.
Lectotype (Proskauer in *Taxon* 7: 126. 1958): [icon] *"Hepatica vulgaris, major, vel officinarum Italiae"* in Micheli, Nov. Pl. Gen.: 3, t. 2, f. 1. 1729 (see p. 656).
Current name: ***Conocephalum conicum*** (L.) Dumort. (Conocephalaceae).

M

The lectotype of *Marchantia conica* L. (t. 2, f. 1)

Marchantia cruciata Linnaeus, *Species Plantarum* 2: 1137. 1753.
"Habitat in Europae umbrosis." RCN: 8142.
Type not designated.
Original material: [icon] in Dillenius, Hist. Musc.: 521, t. 75, f. 5. 1741; [icon] in Micheli, Nov. Pl. Gen.: 4, t. 4. 1729; [icon] in Buxbaum, Pl. Minus Cognit. Cent. 1: 41, t. 62, f. 2. 1728.
Current name: *Lunularia cruciata* (L.) Dumort. (Lunulariaceae).
Note: See notes by Isoviita (in *Acta Bot. Fenn.* 89: 8. 1970) and Grolle (in *Feddes Repert.* 87: 208. 1976).

Marchantia hemisphaerica Linnaeus, *Species Plantarum* 2: 1138. 1753.
"Habitat in Europae paludosis." RCN: 8144.
Type not designated.
Original material: Herb. Linn. No. 1269.8 (LINN); [icon] in Dillenius, Hist. Musc.: 519, t. 75, f. 2. 1741; [icon] in Buxbaum, Pl. Minus Cognit. Cent. 2: 9, t. 5, f. 1. 1728; [icon] in Micheli, Nov. Pl. Gen.: 3, t. 2, f. 2. 1729.
Current name: *Reboulia hemisphaerica* (L.) Raddi (Aytoniaceae).
Note: See notes by Isoviita (in *Acta Bot. Fenn.* 89: 8. 1970) and Grolle (in *Feddes Repert.* 87: 224. 1976).

Marchantia polymorpha Linnaeus, *Species Plantarum* 2: 1137. 1753.
"Habitat in Europa juxta aquas, locis umbrosis." RCN: 8140.
Lectotype (Bischler-Causse & Boisselier-Daubayle in *J. Bryol.* 16: 363. 1991): [icon] *"Lichen fontanus major, stellatus aeque, ac umbellatus,*

& cyathophorus" in Dillenius, Hist. Musc.: 523, t. 76, f. 6 E, F. 1741. – Voucher: Herb. Dillenius (OXF).
Generitype of *Marchantia* Linnaeus (vide Leman, *Dict. Sci. Nat.* 29: 115. 1823).
Current name: *Marchantia polymorpha* L. (Marchantiaceae).
Note: Warncke (in *Bot. Tidsskr.* 63: 359. 1968) referred to material at LINN (evidently sheet 1269.1) as "the type", but as it is associated with the Lapland plant described as the unnamed var. γ, it was rejected from consideration by Isoviita (in *Acta Bot. Fenn.* 89: 7. 1970) and Grolle (in *Feddes Repert.* 87: 210. 1976). Bischler-Causse & Boisselier-Daubayle (1991) have subsequently designated the cited Dillenius illustration as lectotype, and have been followed by e.g. Bischler & Piippo (in *Ann. Bot. Fenn.* 28: 279. 1991) and Perold (in *Fl. Southern Africa, Hepatophyta*: 84. 1999). The latter (p. 87) discusses current names for Linnaeus' unnamed varieties.

Marchantia tenella Linnaeus, *Species Plantarum* 2: 1137. 1753.
"Habitat in Virginia. D. Gronovius." RCN: 8143.
Lectotype (Isoviita in *Acta Bot. Fenn.* 89: 22. 1970): [icon] *"Lichen pileatus parvus carinatus, capitulis fimbriatis"* in Dillenius, Hist. Musc.: 521, t. 75, f. 4. 1741. – Voucher: Herb. Dillenius (OXF).
Current name: *Asterella tenella* (L.) P. Beauv. (Aytoniaceae).

Margaritaria alternifolia Linnaeus, *Plantae Surinamenses*: 16. 1775, *nom. inval.*
"Habitat [in Surinamo.]"
Type not relevant.
Current name: *Margaritaria nobilis* L. f. (Euphorbiaceae).
Note: As the generic name was not validly published until 1782, this binomial is invalid.

Margaritaria oppositifolia Linnaeus, *Plantae Surinamenses*: 16. 1775, *nom. inval.*
"Habitat [in Surinamo.]"
Type not relevant.
Current name: *Margaritaria nobilis* L. f. (Euphorbiaceae).
Note: The generic name was not validly published until 1782 so this binomial is invalid.

Marrubium acetabulosum Linnaeus, *Species Plantarum* 2: 584. 1753.
"Habitat in Creta." RCN: 4262.
Lectotype (Turland in Jarvis & al. in *Taxon* 50: 512. 2001): [icon] *"Dyctamnus falsus Verticillatus Pericarpio choanoide Cret."* in Barrelier, Pl. Galliam: 26, t. 129. 1714.
Current name: *Ballota acetabulosa* (L.) Benth. (Lamiaceae).

Marrubium africanum Linnaeus, *Species Plantarum* 2: 583. 1753.
"Habitat ad Cap. b. Spei." RCN: 4258.
Lectotype (Wijnands, *Bot. Commelins*: 114. 1983): Herb. Clifford: 311, *Marrubium* 2 (BM-000646082).
Current name: *Ballota africana* (L.) Benth. (Lamiaceae).

Marrubium alysson Linnaeus, *Species Plantarum* 2: 582. 1753.
"Habitat in Hispania." RCN: 4253.
Lectotype (Seybold in Jarvis & al. in *Taxon* 50: 512. 2001): Herb. Clifford: 311, *Marrubium* 1 (BM-000646081).
Current name: *Marrubium alysson* L. (Lamiaceae).

Marrubium candidissimum Linnaeus, *Species Plantarum* 2: 583. 1753.
"Habitat in Creta?" RCN: 4255.
Lectotype (Turland in Jarvis & al. in *Taxon* 50: 512. 2001): Herb. Linn. No. 738.4, lower specimen (LINN). – Epitype (Turland in Jarvis & al. in *Taxon* 50: 513. 2001): Greece. Crete, Sfakia. Lefka

Ori, 4km W of summit of Mt. Melindaou, 1,500m, 2 Jul 1994, *Turland 815* (BM-000098230; iso- UPA).

Current name: **Sideritis syriaca** L. subsp. **syriaca** (Lamiaceae).

Note: Lacaita (in *J. Linn. Soc., Bot.* 47: 155–159. 1925) observed that this name had been in use for the taxon subsequently known as *M. incanum* Desr., but that the two Clifford sheets (illustrated by him as f. 2 and 3) are identifiable as *M. globosum* Montbr. & Auch. He identified Herb. Linn. 738.3 (LINN) as a mixture of *M. incanum* and *M. supinum* L., with sheet 738.4 (LINN) a further mixture of a species of *Marrubium*, and *Sideritis syriaca*. Lacaita did not formally choose a type for *M. candidissimum*, which has been associated with a number of different species of *Marrubium* at one time or another. As a result of this confusion, the name has fallen out of use in recent years. Typification of this name using any of the available *Marrubium* elements could have displaced one of the now established later names, and caused considerable confusion. Turland therefore typified the name using the specimen of *S. syriaca*, supported by an epitype, allowing *M. candidissimum* to fall into its synonymy.

Marrubium crispum Linnaeus, *Species Plantarum*, ed. 2, 2: 1674. 1763.

"Habitat in Italia, Hispania. Arduini." RCN: 4259.

Lectotype (Seybold in Jarvis & al. in *Taxon* 50: 513. 2001): *Arduino s.n.*, Herb. Linn. No. 738.7 (LINN).

Current name: **Ballota africana** (L.) Benth. (Lamiaceae).

Marrubium hispanicum Linnaeus, *Species Plantarum* 2: 583. 1753.

"Habitat in Hispania." RCN: 4260.

Lectotype (Heywood in *Agron. Lusit.* 20: 202. 1959): Herb. Clifford: 312, *Marrubium* 7 (BM-000646091).

Current name: **Ballota hispanica** (L.) Benth. (Lamiaceae).

Note: Lacaita (in *J. Linn. Soc., Bot.* 47: 166. 1925) concluded that the name should be abandoned as excessively confused. Heywood (1959) argued that Lacaita was wrong to reject the Clifford material, and that it must be the lectotype, also discussing the possibility that rejection of the name might be necessary. Patzak (in *Ann. Naturhist. Mus. Wien* 63: 58, 67–69. 1959) followed Heywood as to typification, but rejected the name as ambiguous, taking up *B. hirsuta* Benth. for the Spanish plant, and *B. rupestris* (Biv.) Vis. for the Eastern Mediterranean taxon. However, no formal proposal for the rejection of the name has been made.

Marrubium peregrinum Linnaeus, *Species Plantarum* 2: 582. 1753.

"Habitat in Siciliae, Cretae, Austriae siccis." RCN: 4254.

Lectotype (Seybold in Jarvis & al. in *Taxon* 50: 513. 2001): Herb. Clifford: 311, *Marrubium* 3 (BM-000646084).

Current name: **Marrubium peregrinum** L. (Lamiaceae).

Note: Lacaita (in *J. Linn. Soc., Bot.* 47: 159–163. 1925) provided a detailed examination of the different elements associated with this name, but did not formally designate a type.

Marrubium pseudodictamnus Linnaeus, *Species Plantarum* 2: 583. 1753.

"Habitat in Creta." RCN: 4261.

Lectotype (Turland in Jarvis & al. in *Taxon* 50: 513. 2001): Herb. Burser XII: 133 (UPS).

Current name: **Ballota pseudodictamnus** (L.) Benth. subsp. **pseudodictamnus** (Lamiaceae).

Marrubium supinum Linnaeus, *Species Plantarum* 2: 583. 1753.

"Habitat in Hispania, G. Narbonensi." RCN: 4256.

Lectotype (Seybold in Jarvis & al. in *Taxon* 50: 513. 2001): Herb. Clifford: 312, *Marrubium* 6 (BM-000646090).

Current name: **Marrubium supinum** L. (Lamiaceae).

Note: Lacaita (in *J. Linn. Soc., Bot.* 47: 165–166. 1925) provided an examination of the different elements associated with this name but did not formally designate a type.

Marrubium vulgare Linnaeus, *Species Plantarum* 2: 582. 1753.

"Habitat in Europae borealis ruderatis." RCN: 4257.

Lectotype (Press & Hedge in Jarvis & al., *Regnum Veg.* 127: 64. 1993): Herb. Clifford: 312, *Marrubium* 5, sheet A (BM-000646087).

Generitype of *Marrubium* Linnaeus (vide Green, *Prop. Brit. Bot.*: 165. 1929).

Current name: **Marrubium vulgare** L. (Lamiaceae).

Note: Hedge & Lamond (in *Notes Roy. Bot. Gard. Edinburgh* 28: 93. 1968) indicated 738.5 (LINN) as type but this was a post-1753 addition to the herbarium and is not original material for the name. Although Seybold (in *Stuttgarter Beitr. Naturk., A,* 310: 7. 1978) said "Typus: Linne (BM), non vidi", this is inadequate as a typification statement.

Marsilea minuta Linnaeus, *Mantissa Plantarum Altera*: 308. 1771.

"Habitat in India orientali." RCN: 7957.

Lectotype (Launert in *Senckenberg. Biol.* 49: 291. 1968): Herb. Linn. No. 1254.6 (LINN).

Current name: **Marsilea minuta** L. (Marsileaceae).

Marsilea natans Linnaeus, *Species Plantarum* 2: 1099. 1753.

"Habitat in Italiae fossis paludosis stagnantibus lente fluentibus." RCN: 7955.

Lectotype (Bobrov in *Novosti Sist. Vyssh. Rast.* 21: 20. 1984): Herb. Linn. No. 1254.1 (LINN).

Current name: **Salvinia natans** (L.) All. (Salviniaceae).

Note: The cited Micheli plate is reproduced by Johnson (in *Taxon* 37: 484. 1988), who also discusses it in relation to the generic description.

Marsilea quadrifolia Linnaeus, *Species Plantarum* 2: 1099. 1753, *typ. cons.*

"Habitat in Indiae, Sibiriae, Galliae, Alsatiae, fossis." RCN: 7956.

Type not designated.

Original material: [icon] in Mattioli, Pl. Epit.: 853. 1586; [icon] in Morison, Pl. Hist. Univ. 3: 619, s. 15, t. 4, f. 5. 1699; [icon] in Mappus, Hist. Pl. Alsat.: 166, t. 166. 1742; [icon] in Bauhin & Cherler, Hist. Pl. Univ. 3(2): 785. 1651; [icon] in Jussieu in Mém. Acad. Roy. Sci. Paris 1740: 263, t. 15. 1740 (see p. 138).

Generitype of *Marsilea* Linnaeus, *nom. cons.* (vide Christensen, *Index Filicum*: LVII. 1906).

Current name: **Marsilea quadrifolia** L. (Marsileaceae).

Note: Bobrov (in *Novosti Sist. Vyssh. Rast.* 21: 20. 1984) indicated 1254.2 (LINN) as type but this collection lacks the relevant *Species Plantarum* number (i.e. "2") and was a post-1753 addition to the herbarium, and is not original material for the name. Johnson (in *Syst. Bot. Monogr.* 11: 39. 1986) treated a Jussieu collection (No. 1599-A, P-JU) as the lectotype but this material would not have been studied by Linnaeus and is not original material for the name either.

Martynia annua Linnaeus, *Species Plantarum* 2: 618. 1753.

"Habitat in Americes Vera Cruce." RCN: 4473.

Lectotype (Nafday in *Bull. Bot. Soc. Coll. Sci. Nagpur* 4: 65. 1964): [icon] *"Martynia annua, villosa & viscosa, folio subrotundo, flore magno rubro"* in Martyn, Hist. Pl. Rar.: 42, t. 42. 1728 (see p. 21). – Typotype: Miller ex Roy. Soc. No. 476. 1731 (BM-SL).

Generitype of *Martynia* Linnaeus (vide Green, *Prop. Brit. Bot.*: 167. 1929).

Current name: **Martynia annua** L. (Pedaliaceae).

M

Martynia longiflora Linnaeus, *Systema Naturae,* ed. 12, 2: 412. 1767. "Habitat ad Cap b. spei." RCN: 4474.
Type not designated.
Original material: none traced.
Current name: ***Rogeria longiflora*** (L.) J. Gay (Pedaliaceae).

Martynia perennis Linnaeus, *Species Plantarum* 2: 618. 1753. "Habitat in America." RCN: 4472.
Lectotype (Stearn, *Introd. Linnaeus' Sp. Pl.* (Ray Soc. ed.): 47. 1957): [icon] *"Martynia foliis serratis"* in Linnaeus, Hort. Cliff.: 322, t. 18. 1738. – Voucher: Herb. Clifford: 322, *Martynia* 1 (BM).
Current name: ***Gloxinia perennis*** (L.) Fritsch (Gesneriaceae).

Matricaria argentea Linnaeus, *Species Plantarum* 2: 891. 1753. "Habitat in Oriente." RCN: 6454.
Type not designated.
Original material: Herb. Clifford: 415, *Matricaria* 2 (BM).
Current name: ***Tanacetum sericeum*** (Adams) Sch. Bip. (Asteraceae).
Note: Grierson (in Davis, *Fl. Turkey* 5: 270. 1975) discusses Tournefort material in the context of this name.

Matricaria arvensis Linnaeus, *Amoenitates Academicae* 4: 491. 1759, *nom. inval.*
Type not relevant.
Current name: ***Anthemis arvensis*** L. (Asteraceae).
Note: As noted by Stearn (in Geck & Pressler, *Festschr. Claus Nissen*: 631. 1974), this "name" resulted from the omission of the generic name *Anthemis* from a table in a revised version of the 1756 thesis, *Flora Monspeliensis.* It is not validly published.

Matricaria asteroides Linnaeus, *Systema Naturae,* ed. 12, 2: 563; *Mantissa Plantarum*: 116. 1767. "Habitat in Pensylvania. Barthram." RCN: 6455.
Lectotype (Fernald in *Rhodora* 42: 485, pl. 640, f. 1. 1940): Herb. Linn. No. 1013.6 (LINN).
Current name: ***Boltonia asteroides*** (L.) L'Hér. (Asteraceae).

Matricaria capensis Linnaeus, *Systema Naturae,* ed. 12, 2: 563; *Mantissa Plantarum*: 115. 1767. "Habitat ad Cap. b. spei." RCN: 6466.
Basionym of: *Cotula capensis* (L.) L. (1771).
Type not designated.
Original material: Herb. Linn. No. 1014.28 (LINN); Herb. Linn. No. 1014.27a (LINN); Herb. Linn. No. 1013.9 (LINN).
Current name: ***Oncosiphon africanum*** (P.J. Bergius) Källersjö (Asteraceae).

Matricaria chamomilla Linnaeus, *Species Plantarum* 2: 891. 1753. "Habitat in Europae agris, cultis." RCN: 6453.
Lectotype (Grierson in Davis in *Notes Roy. Bot. Gard. Edinburgh* 33: 252. 1974): Herb. Clifford: 415, *Matricaria* 1 (BM-000647192).
Current name: ***Matricaria chamomilla*** L. (Asteraceae).
Note: Applequist (in *Taxon* 51: 757–761. 2003) gives a detailed review of the nomenclatural complexities associated with this name, and accepts Grierson's type choice (a specimen of chamomile). Although both *M. chamomilla* and *M. recutita* L. (which has also been used for the species) date from 1753, Applequist argues that *M. chamomilla* is the correct name, Visiani having been the first to combine the two in 1844.

Matricaria cotula Linnaeus, *Amoenitates Academicae* 4: 491. 1759, *nom. inval.*
Type not relevant.
Current name: ***Anthemis cotula*** L. (Asteraceae).

Note: As noted by Stearn (in Geck & Pressler, *Festschr. Claus Nissen*: 631. 1974), this "name" resulted from the omission of the generic name *Anthemis* from a table in a revised version of the 1756 thesis, *Flora Monspeliensis.* It is not validly published.

Matricaria inodora Linnaeus, *Flora Suecica,* ed. 2: 297. 1755. "Habitat juxta agros, vias, plateas, minus frequens, quam praecedens." RCN: 6437.
Basionym of: *Chrysanthemum inodorum* (L.) L. (1763).
Lectotype (Humphries in Jarvis & Turland in *Taxon* 47: 364. 1998): Herb. Linn. No. 1012.12 (LINN).
Current name: ***Tripleurospermum maritimum*** (L.) W.D.J. Koch subsp. ***inodorum*** (L.) Appleq. (Asteraceae).
Note: Rauschert (in *Folia Geobot. Phytotax.* 9: 249–260. 1974) argued (incorrectly) that *M. inodora* L. (1755) was a superfluous *nomen novum* for *M. chamomilla* L. (1753). Applequist (in *Taxon* 51: 760. 2003) gives a detailed review of the nomenclature associated with this name, accepting Humphries' typification and concluding that the correct name for the scentless mayweed is either *Tripleurospermum inodorum* (L.) Sch. Bip. at species rank, or *T. maritimum* subsp. *inodorum* (L.) Appleq. at subspecific rank.

Matricaria maritima Linnaeus, *Species Plantarum* 2: 891. 1753. "Habitat in Europae septentrionalis littoribus maris." RCN: 6451.
Lectotype (Sell in Jarvis & Turland in *Taxon* 47: 364. 1998): Herb. Linn. No. 1013.2 (LINN).
Current name: ***Tripleurospermum maritimum*** (L.) W.D.J. Koch (Asteraceae).

Matricaria parthenium Linnaeus, *Species Plantarum* 2: 890. 1753. "Habitat in Europae cultis, ruderatis." RCN: 6450.
Type not designated.
Original material: Herb. Clifford: 416, *Matricaria* 3, 4 sheets (BM); Herb. Linn. No. 1013.1 (LINN).
Current name: ***Tanacetum parthenium*** (L.) Sch. Bip. (Asteraceae).
Note: Grierson (in Davis, *Fl. Turkey* 5: 268. 1975) noted the existence of material in the Clifford herbarium but did not indicate it as the type. Dillon (in *Fieldiana, Bot., n.s.,* 7: 19. 1981) indicated unspecified (and unseen) material in BM as type. Alavi (in Jafri & El-Gadi, *Fl. Libya* 107: 168. 1983) also indicated Herb. Clifford: 416, *Matricaria* 3 (BM) as type (as did Jeanmonod in *Compl. Prodr. Fl. Corse, Asteraceae I*: 230. 1998, wrongly attributing the choice to Grierson). In fact there are four sheets in the Clifford herbarium associated with this name. They do not form part of a single gathering and so none of the above statements effects typification (Art. 9.15).

Matricaria pyrethrum Linnaeus, *Amoenitates Academicae* 4: 491. 1759, *nom. nud.*
Type not relevant.
Current name: ***Anacyclus pyrethrum*** (L.) Lag. (Asteraceae).
Note: As noted by Stearn (in Geck & Pressler, *Festschr. Claus Nissen*: 631. 1974), this "name" resulted from the omission of the generic name *Anthemis* from a table in a revised version of the 1756 thesis, *Flora Monspeliensis.* It is not validly published.

Matricaria recutita Linnaeus, *Species Plantarum* 2: 891. 1753, *typ. cons.*
"Habitat in Europa." RCN: 6452.
Replaced synonym of: *Matricaria suaveolens* L. (1755), *nom. illeg.*
Conserved type (Jeffrey in Jarvis in *Taxon* 41: 566. 1992): Czech Rep., in ruderatis ad urbem Brno, ca. 180m, 15 Jun 1925, Podpěra in Fl. Exsicc. Reip. Boh.-Slov. No. 946.II (K).
Generitype of *Matricaria* Linnaeus, *nom. cons.*
Current name: ***Matricaria chamomilla*** L. (Asteraceae).

Note: Matricaria recutita, with the type designated by Jeffrey, was proposed as conserved type of the genus by Jarvis (in *Taxon* 41: 566. 1992). This was eventually approved by the General Committee (see review of the history of this proposal by Barrie, *l.c.* 55: 795–796. 2006).

Applequist (in *Taxon* 51: 757–761. 2003) gives a detailed review of the nomenclature associated with this name, and accepts Jeffrey's type choice. Although both *M. chamomilla* L. and *M. recutita* L. (which has also been used for the species) date from 1753, Applequist argues that *M. chamomilla* is the correct name for chamomile, Visiani having been the first to combine the two in 1844.

Matricaria suaveolens Linnaeus, *Flora Suecica*, ed. 2: 297. 1755, *nom. illeg.*
"Habitat in areis ad pagos Stenbrohult Smolandiae, Flaberg W-gothiae 107." RCN: 6452.
Replaced synonym: *Matricaria recutita* L. (1753).
Lectotype (Jeffrey in Jarvis in *Taxon* 41: 566. 1992): Podpěra in Fl. Exsicc. Reip. Boh.-Slov. No. 946.II (K).
Current name: ***Matricaria chamomilla*** L. (Asteraceae).
Note: An illegitimate replacement name for *M. recutita* L. (1753) as noted by Toman & Starý (in *Taxon* 14: 226. 1965).

Matricaria tinctoria Linnaeus, *Amoenitates Academicae* 4: 491. 1759, *nom. inval.*
Type not relevant.
Current name: ***Anthemis tinctoria*** L. (Asteraceae).
Note: As noted by Stearn (in Geck & Pressler, *Festschr. Claus Nissen*: 631. 1974), this "name" resulted from the omission of the generic name *Anthemis* from a table in a revised version of the 1756 thesis, *Flora Monspeliensis*. It is not validly published.

Matricaria valentina Linnaeus, *Amoenitates Academicae* 4: 491. 1759, *nom. inval.*
Type not relevant.
Current name: ***Anacyclus radiatus*** Loisel. (Asteraceae).
Note: As noted by Stearn (in Geck & Pressler, *Festschr. Claus Nissen*: 631. 1974), this "name" resulted from the omission of the generic name *Anthemis* from a table in a revised version of the 1756 thesis, *Flora Monspeliensis*. It is not validly published.

Matthiola scabra Linnaeus, *Species Plantarum* 2: 1192. 1753.
"Habitat in America." RCN: 1398.
Type not designated.
Original material: [icon] in Plumier, Nov. Pl. Amer.: 16, t. 6. 1703; [icon] in Zanoni, Istoria Bot.: 167, t. 75. 1675.
Generitype of *Matthiola* Linnaeus, *nom. rej.*
Current name: ***Guettarda scabra*** (L.) Lam. (Rubiaceae).
Note: Matthiola Linnaeus, *nom. rej.* in favour of *Matthiola* Aiton.

Medeola aculeata Linnaeus, *Species Plantarum* 1: 339. 1753.
"Habitat in America calidiore." RCN: 1511.
Lectotype (Ståhl in *Nordic J. Bot.* 15: 501. 1996 [1995]): [icon] "*Fruticulus foliis Rusci stellatis*" in Dillenius, Hort. Eltham. 1: 148, t. 123, f.149. 1732.
Current name: ***Jacquinia aculeata*** (L.) Mez (Theophrastaceae).

Medeola asparagoides Linnaeus, *Species Plantarum* 1: 339. 1753.
"Habitat in Aethiopia." RCN: 2616.
Lectotype (Jessop in *Bothalia* 9: 82. 1966): [icon] "*Asparagus Africanus, scandens, Myrti folio et Myrti folio angustiore*" in Tilli, Cat. Pl. Hort. Pisani: 17, t. 12, f. 1, 2. 1723.
Current name: ***Asparagus asparagoides*** (L.) W. Wight (Liliaceae/Asparagaceae).

Note: See Kleinjan & Edwards (in *S. African J. Bot.* 65: 28. 1999) who note that the type figure is inadequate to distinguish between the forms of the taxon that they recognise.

Medeola virginiana Linnaeus, *Species Plantarum* 1: 339. 1753.
"Habitat in Virginia." RCN: 2615.
Lectotype (Reveal in Jarvis & al., *Regnum Veg.* 127: 65. 1993): *Kalm*, Herb. Linn. No. 468.1 (LINN).
Generitype of *Medeola* Linnaeus (vide Hitchcock, *Prop. Brit. Bot.*: 148. 1929).
Current name: ***Medeola virginiana*** L. (Liliaceae/Convallariaceae).

Medicago arborea Linnaeus, *Species Plantarum* 2: 778. 1753.
"Habitat in Rhodo, Neapoli." RCN: 5712.
Lectotype (Heyn in *Bull. Res. Council Israel, Sect. D, Bot.* 7: 161. 1959): Herb. Clifford: 377, *Medicago* 6 (BM-000646774).
Current name: ***Medicago arborea*** L. (Fabaceae: Faboideae).

Medicago circinnata Linnaeus, *Species Plantarum* 2: 778. 1753.
"Habitat in Hispania, Italia." RCN: 5715.
Lectotype (Heyn in *Bull. Res. Council Israel, Sect. D, Bot.* 7: 161. 1959): Herb. Clifford: 377, *Medicago* 7 (BM-000646775).
Current name: ***Hymenocarpos circinnatus*** (L.) Savi (Fabaceae: Faboideae).

Medicago falcata Linnaeus, *Species Plantarum* 2: 779. 1753.
"Habitat in Europae pratis apricis, siccis." RCN: 5717.
Lectotype (Ali in *Taxon* 17: 541. 1968): Herb. Linn. No. 933.8 (LINN).
Current name: ***Medicago falcata*** L. (Fabaceae: Faboideae).
Note: Although Heyn (in *Bull. Res. Council Israel, Sect. D, Bot.* 7: 162. 1959) discussed some of the original material, she did not designate a lectotype.

Medicago lupulina Linnaeus, *Species Plantarum* 2: 779. 1753.
"Habitat in Europae pratis." RCN: 5718.
Lectotype (Ali in *Taxon* 17: 540. 1968): Herb. Linn. No. 933.10 (LINN).
Current name: ***Medicago lupulina*** L. (Fabaceae: Faboideae).
Note: Although Heyn (in *Bull. Res. Council Israel, Sect. D, Bot.* 7: 162. 1959) discussed some of the original material, she did not designate a lectotype. Despite her comments, 933.10 (LINN) is linked with the *Species Plantarum* account by the number ("7") of this species written on the sheet by Linnaeus. It is original material for the name and was designated as the type by Ali.

Medicago marina Linnaeus, *Species Plantarum* 2: 779. 1753.
"Habitat in maris Mediterranei littoribus." RCN: 5719.
Lectotype (Heyn in *Bull. Res. Council Israel, Sect. D, Bot.* 7: 163. 1959): Herb. Clifford: 378, *Medicago* 10 (BM-000646780).
Current name: ***Medicago marina*** L. (Fabaceae: Faboideae).

Medicago minima (Linnaeus) Linnaeus, *Flora Anglica*: 21. 1754, *nom. inval.*
Type not relevant.
Current name: ***Medicago minima*** (L.) Bartal. (Fabaceae: Faboideae).
Note: Shinners (in *Rhodora* 58: 3. 1956) questioned whether the recombination of var. *minima* at species rank was made by Linnaeus (in *Fl. Anglica*: 21. 1754). Shinners suggested that this is an error of interpretation, as Linnaeus subsequently continued to treat the taxon as a variety of *M. polymorpha*. Shinners accepted Bartalini (1776) as the first to make the combination at species rank, as did Stearn (*Introd. Ray's Syn. Meth. Stirp. Brit.* (Ray Soc. ed.): 57. 1973). Greuter (in *Candollea* 44: 563. 1989) disagreed, arguing that the combination dates from 1754. Brummitt & Meikle (in *Watsonia*

M

19: 181–183. 1993) argued, however, that there are typographical variants of the thesis which make it unreasonable to interpret names such as this (though they focussed particularly on two names in *Primula*) as a new combination.

Medicago polymorpha Linnaeus, *Species Plantarum* 2: 779, 1200. 1753.

"Habitat [p. 1200:] Europa australi." RCN: 5720.

Lectotype (Heyn in *Bull. Res. Council Israel, Sect. D, Bot.* 7: 163. 1959): Herb. Clifford: 378, *Medicago* 11 δ (BM-000646786).

Current name: ***Medicago polymorpha*** L. (Fabaceae: Faboideae).

Note: Shinners (in *Rhodora* 58: 5–7. 1956) provided an extensive discussion, concluding "[the name] is here typified by the element later named var. nigra", but he cited no specimen or illustration to serve as the type. Heyn (1959) subsequently designated Clifford material as the type. However, Greuter (in *Boissiera* 13: 80. 1967) argued that an implicit typification by Krocker in 1790 meant that the name must be regarded as a *nomen ambiguum*. Lambinon (in *Taxon* 30: 363. 1981) subsequently proposed the rejection of the name but this was not approved by the Committee for Spermatophyta (in *Taxon* 35: 560. 1986).

Medicago polymorpha Linnaeus var. **arabica** Linnaeus, *Species Plantarum* 2: 780. 1753.

RCN: 5720.

Lectotype (Heyn in *Bull. Res. Council Israel, Sect. D, Bot.* 7: 167. 1959): [icon] *"Medica cochleata minor polycarpos annua capsula majore, alba, folio cordato, macula fusca notato"* in Morison, Pl. Hist. Univ. 2: 154, s. 2, t. 15, f. 12. 1680.

Current name: ***Medicago arabica*** (L.) Huds. (Fabaceae: Faboideae).

Medicago polymorpha Linnaeus var. **ciliaris** Linnaeus, *Species Plantarum* 2: 780. 1753.

RCN: 5720.

Neotype (Lassen in Turland & Jarvis in *Taxon* 46: 475. 1997): France. Aude: Craboules, prés salés et bord des chemins, Jun 1889, *Abbé Pons s.n.* [Magnier Fl. Select. Exsicc. 2353] (LD).

Current name: ***Medicago ciliaris*** (L.) All. (Fabaceae: Faboideae).

Note: Heyn (in *Bull. Res. Council Israel, Sect. D, Bot.* 7: 167. 1959) discussed the name but was unable to locate a suitable type. Lassen subsequently designated a neotype.

Medicago polymorpha Linnaeus var. **coronata** Linnaeus, *Species Plantarum* 2: 780. 1753.

RCN: 5720.

Lectotype (Heyn in *Bull. Res. Council Israel, Sect. D, Bot.* 7: 167. 1959): [icon] *"Medica coronata Cherleri, parva"* in Bauhin & Cherler, Hist. Pl. Univ. 2: 386. 1651.

Current name: ***Medicago coronata*** (L.) Bartal. (Fabaceae: Faboideae).

Medicago polymorpha Linnaeus var. **hirsuta** Linnaeus, *Species Plantarum* 2: 780. 1753.

RCN: 5720.

Lectotype (Heyn in *Bull. Res. Council Israel, Sect. D, Bot.* 7: 168. 1959): [icon] *"Medica echinata hirsuta"* in Bauhin & Cherler, Hist. Pl. Univ. 2: 386. 1651.

Current name: ***Medicago minima*** (L.) L. (Fabaceae: Faboideae).

Medicago polymorpha Linnaeus var. **intertexta** Linnaeus, *Species Plantarum* 2: 780. 1753.

RCN: 5720.

Lectotype (Heyn in *Bull. Res. Council Israel, Sect. D, Bot.* 7: 167. 1959): [icon] *"Medica cochleata spinosa major dicarpos capsula seu spinis longioribus sursum & deorsum tendentibus"* in Morison, Pl. Hist. Univ. 2: 153, s. 2, t. 15, f. 8, 9. 1680.

Current name: ***Medicago intertexta*** (L.) Mill. (Fabaceae: Faboideae).

Medicago polymorpha Linnaeus var. **laciniata** Linnaeus, *Species Plantarum* 2: 781. 1753.

RCN: 5720.

Lectotype (Heyn in *Bull. Res. Council Israel, Sect. D, Bot.* 7: 169. 1959): [icon] *"Trifolium cochleatum spinosum Syriacum, laciniatis foliis"* in Breyn, Exot. Pl. Cent.: 81, t. 34. 1678.

Current name: ***Medicago laciniata*** (L.) Mill. (Fabaceae: Faboideae).

Medicago polymorpha Linnaeus var. **minima** Linnaeus, *Species Plantarum* 2: 780. 1753.

RCN: 5720.

Lectotype (Heyn in *Bull. Res. Council Israel, Sect. D, Bot.* 7: 168. 1959): [icon] *"Medica echinata, minima"* in Bauhin & Cherler, Hist. Pl. Univ. 2: 386. 1651.

Current name: ***Medicago minima*** (L.) Bartal. (Fabaceae: Faboideae).

Note: Shinners (in *Rhodora* 58: 3. 1956) questioned whether the recombination of var. *minima* at species rank was made by Linnaeus (in *Fl. Anglica*: 21. 1754). Shinners suggested that this is an error of interpretation, as Linnaeus subsequently continued to treat the taxon as a variety of *M. polymorpha*. Shinners accepted Bartalini (1776) as the first to make the combination at species rank, as did Stearn (*Introd. Ray's Syn. Meth. Stirp. Brit.* (Ray Soc. ed.): 57. 1973). Greuter (in *Candollea* 44: 563. 1989) disagreed, arguing that the combination dates from 1754. Brummitt & Meikle (in *Watsonia* 19: 181–183. 1993) argued, however, that there are typographical variants of the thesis which make it unreasonable to interpret names such as this (though they focussed particularly on two names in *Primula*) as a new combination.

Medicago polymorpha Linnaeus var. **muricata** Linnaeus, *Species Plantarum* 2: 781. 1753.

RCN: 5720.

Lectotype (Heyn in *Bull. Res. Council Israel, Sect. D, Bot.* 7: 168. 1959): [icon] *"Medica cochleata dicarpos capsula spinosa rotunda minore, rarius spinis crassioribus & brevioribus armata"* in Morison, Pl. Hist. Univ. 2: 153, s. 2, t. 15, f. 18. 1680.

Current name: ***Medicago rigidula*** (L.) All. (Fabaceae: Faboideae).

Medicago polymorpha Linnaeus var. **nigra** Linnaeus, *Mantissa Plantarum Altera*: 454. 1771.

RCN: 5720.

Lectotype (Lassen in Turland & Jarvis in *Taxon* 46: 475. 1997): [icon] *"Medica cochleata minor polycarpos annua capsula nigra hispidiore"* in Morison, Pl. Hist. Univ. 2: 154, s. 2, t. 15, f. 13. 1680. – Epitype (Lassen in Turland & Jarvis in *Taxon* 46: 475. 1997): France. Var, dans les champs argilo-calcaires à Solliès-Toucas, 10 Jun 1892, *A. Albert s.n.* [Magnier Fl. Sel. Exsicc. 2961] (LD).

Current name: ***Medicago polymorpha*** L. (Fabaceae: Faboideae).

Note: The lectotype is Morison's f. 13, not f. 19 as cited by Linnaeus or f. 18 as given by Morison (cf. Heyn (in *Bull. Res. Council Israel, Sect. D, Bot.* 7: 168, 173. 1959).

Medicago polymorpha Linnaeus var. **orbicularis** Linnaeus, *Species Plantarum* 2: 779. 1753.

RCN: 5720.

Lectotype (Heyn in *Bull. Res. Council Israel, Sect. D, Bot.* 7: 164. 1959): [icon] *"Medica cochleata major dicarpos, fructus capsula compressa orbiculata, nigra, plana, oris crispis"* in Morison, Pl. Hist. Univ. 2: 152, s. 2, t. 15, f. 1. 1680.

Current name: ***Medicago orbicularis*** (L.) Bartal. (Fabaceae: Faboideae).

Medicago polymorpha Linnaeus var. **rigidula** Linnaeus, *Species Plantarum* 2: 780. 1753.

RCN: 5720.

Lectotype (Heyn in *Bull. Res. Council Israel, Sect. D, Bot.* 7: 168. 1959): [icon] *"Medica hirsuta echinis rigidioribus"* in Bauhin & Cherler, Hist. Pl. Univ. 2: 385. 1651.
Current name: ***Medicago rigidula*** (L.) All. (Fabaceae: Faboideae).

Medicago polymorpha Linnaeus var. **scutellata** Linnaeus, *Species Plantarum* 2: 779. 1753.
RCN: 5720.
Lectotype (Heyn in *Bull. Res. Council Israel, Sect. D, Bot.* 7: 164. 1959): [icon] *"Medica cochleata major dicarpos fructus capsula rotunda globosa scutellata"* in Morison, Pl. Hist. Univ. 2: 152, s. 2, t. 15, f. 3. 1680 (see p. 144).
Current name: ***Medicago scutellata*** (L.) Mill. (Fabaceae: Faboideae).

Medicago polymorpha Linnaeus var. **tornata** Linnaeus, *Species Plantarum* 2: 780. 1753.
RCN: 5720.
Lectotype (Heyn in *Bull. Res. Council Israel, Sect. D, Bot.* 7: 165. 1959): [icon] *"Medica tornata minoris lenis"* in Parkinson, Theatr. Bot.: 1116. 1640.
Current name: ***Medicago tornata*** (L.) Mill. (Fabaceae: Faboideae).

Medicago polymorpha Linnaeus var. **turbinata** Linnaeus, *Species Plantarum* 2: 780. 1753.
RCN: 5720.
Lectotype (Heyn in *Bull. Res. Council Israel, Sect. D, Bot.* 7: 166. 1959): [icon] *"Medica magna turbinata"* in Bauhin & Cherler, Hist. Pl. Univ. 2: 385. 1651.
Current name: ***Medicago turbinata*** (L.) All. (Fabaceae: Faboideae).

Medicago radiata Linnaeus, *Species Plantarum* 2: 778. 1753.
"Habitat in Italia." RCN: 5714.
Lectotype (Heyn in *Bull. Res. Council Israel, Sect. D, Bot.* 7: 161. 1959): Herb. Clifford: 377, *Medicago* 8 (BM-000646776).
Current name: ***Trigonella radiata*** (L.) Boiss. (Fabaceae: Faboideae).

Medicago sativa Linnaeus, *Species Plantarum* 2: 778. 1753, *typ. cons.*
"Habitat in Hispaniae, Galliae apricis." RCN: 5716.
Lectotype (Heyn in *Bull. Res. Council Israel, Sect. D, Bot.* 7: 162. 1959): [icon] *"Medica falcata sativa siliqua cornuta magis tortili flore violaceo"* in Morison, Pl. Hist. Univ. 2: 158, s. 2, t. 16, f. 2. 1680.
Generitype of *Medicago* Linnaeus, *nom. cons.*
Current name: ***Medicago sativa*** L. subsp. ***sativa*** (Fabaceae: Faboideae).

Medicago virginica Linnaeus, *Species Plantarum* 2: 778. 1753.
"Habitat in Virginia." RCN: 5713.
Lectotype (Britton in *Trans. New York Acad. Sci.* 12: 65. 1893): *Clayton* 191 (BM).
Current name: ***Lespedeza virginica*** (L.) Britton (Fabaceae: Faboideae).

Melaleuca leucadendra (Linnaeus) Linnaeus, *Systema Naturae,* ed. 12, 2: 509; *Mantissa Plantarum*: 105. 1767, *typ. cons.*
"Habitat in India." RCN: 5733.
Basionym: *Myrtus leucadendra* L. (1754), *typ. cons.*
Lectotype (Blake in *Contr. Queensland Herb.* 1: 17. 1968): [icon] *"Arbor alba"* in Rumphius, Herb. Amboin. 2: 72, t. 16. 1741.
Generitype of *Melaleuca* Linnaeus, *nom. cons.*
Current name: ***Melaleuca leucadendra*** (L.) L. (Myrtaceae).
Note: *Melaleuca* Linnaeus, *nom. cons.* against *Kajuputi* Adans.

Melampodium americanum Linnaeus, *Species Plantarum* 2: 921. 1753.
"Habitat in Vera Cruce." RCN: 6658.

Lectotype (Stuessy in *Rhodora* 74: 21. 1972): *Houstoun*, Herb. Clifford: 425, *Melampodium* 1 (BM-000647294).
Generitype of *Melampodium* Linnaeus.
Current name: ***Melampodium americanum*** L. (Asteraceae).

Melampyrum arvense Linnaeus, *Species Plantarum* 2: 605. 1753.
"Habitat in Europae agris." RCN: 4387.
Lectotype (Popova in *Novosti Sist. Vyssh. Rast.* 17: 224. 1980): Herb. Linn. No. 760.2 (LINN).
Current name: ***Melampyrum arvense*** L. (Scrophulariaceae).

Melampyrum cristatum Linnaeus, *Species Plantarum* 2: 605. 1753.
"Habitat in Europae borealis pratis asperis." RCN: 4386.
Lectotype (Popova in *Novosti Sist. Vyssh. Rast.* 17: 227. 1980): Herb. Linn. No. 760.1 (LINN).
Current name: ***Melampyrum cristatum*** L. (Scrophulariaceae).

Melampyrum nemorosum Linnaeus, *Species Plantarum* 2: 605. 1753.
"Habitat in Europae borealis nemoribus." RCN: 4388.
Lectotype (Fischer in *Feddes Repert.* 108: 112. 1997): Herb. Linn. No. 760.3 (LINN).
Current name: ***Melampyrum nemorosum*** L. (Scrophulariaceae).

Melampyrum pratense Linnaeus, *Species Plantarum* 2: 605. 1753.
"Habitat in Europae borealis pratis siccis." RCN: 4389.
Lectotype (Smith in *Watsonia* 5: 366. 1963): Herb. Linn. No. 760.4 (LINN).
Generitype of *Melampyrum* Linnaeus.
Current name: ***Melampyrum pratense*** L. (Scrophulariaceae).
Note: Melampyrum pratense, with the type designated by Smith, was proposed as conserved type of the genus by Jarvis (in *Taxon* 41: 573. 1992). However, the proposal was eventually ruled unnecessary by the General Committee (see Barrie, *l.c.* 55: 795–796. 2006, for a review of the history of this and related proposals).

Melampyrum sylvaticum Linnaeus, *Species Plantarum* 2: 605. 1753.
"Habitat in Europae borealis sylvis." RCN: 4390.
Lectotype (Fischer in *Feddes Repert.* 108: 112. 1997): Herb. Linn. No. 760.5 (LINN).
Current name: ***Melampyrum sylvaticum*** L. (Scrophulariaceae).

Melanthium capense Linnaeus, *Species Plantarum,* ed. 2, 1: 483. 1762, *nom. illeg.*
"Habitat ad Cap. b. spei." RCN: 2613.
Replaced synonym: *Melanthium punctatum* L. (1760).
Type not designated.
Original material: as replaced synonym.
Current name: ***Onixotis punctata*** (L.) Mabb. (Liliaceae/Melanthiaceae).
Note: A superfluous name for *M. punctatum* L. (1760) and therefore illegitimate, though it has been incorrectly used (as *Androcymbium capense* (L.) Krause) by recent authors such as Müller-Doblies & Müller-Doblies (in *Feddes Repert.* 113: 577. 2002), who also treated unspecified material in LINN (presumably either 467.4 or 467.5) as the type.

Melanthium indicum Linnaeus, *Mantissa Plantarum Altera*: 226. 1771.
"Habitat in Tranquebaria. Koenig." RCN: 2614.
Lectotype (MacFarlane in George, *Fl. Australia* 45: 405. 1987): *König s.n.*, Herb. Linn. No. 467.9 (LINN).
Current name: ***Iphigenia indica*** (L.) A. Gray ex Kunth (Liliaceae/Melanthiaceae).

M

Melanthium punctatum Linnaeus, *Plantae Rariores Africanae*: 10. 1760.
["Habitat ad Cap. b. spei."] Sp. Pl., ed. 2, 1: 483 (1762). RCN: 2613.
Replaced synonym of: *Melanthium capense* L. (1762), *nom. illeg.*
Type not designated.
Original material: none traced.
Current name: ***Onixotis punctata*** (L.) Mabb.
   (Liliaceae/Melanthiaceae).

Melanthium sibiricum Linnaeus, *Species Plantarum* 1: 339. 1753.
"Habitat in Sibiria." RCN: 2612.
Type not designated.
Original material: *Steller*?, Herb. Linn. No. 467.3 (LINN); [icon] in Gmelin, Fl. Sibirica 1: 45, t. 8. 1747; [icon] in Linnaeus, Amoen. Acad. 2: 349, t. 4, f. 11. 1751.
Current name: ***Zigadenus sibiricus*** (L.) A. Gray
   (Liliaceae/Melanthiaceae).

Melanthium virginicum Linnaeus, *Species Plantarum* 1: 339. 1753.
"Habitat in Virginia." RCN: 2611.
Lectotype (Reveal in Jarvis & al., *Regnum Veg.* 127: 65. 1993): *Kalm*, Herb. Linn. No. 467.1 (LINN).
Generitype of *Melanthium* Linnaeus (vide Hitchcock, *Prop. Brit. Bot.*: 148. 1929).
Current name: ***Melanthium virginicum*** L. (Liliaceae/Melanthiaceae).

Melastoma acinodendron Linnaeus, *Species Plantarum* 1: 389. 1753.
"Habitat in America calidiore." RCN: 3068.
Lectotype (Howard & Kellogg in *J. Arnold Arbor.* 67: 235. 1986): Herb. Clifford: 162, *Melastoma* 1 (BM-000558744).
Current name: ***Miconia acinodendron*** (L.) D. Don
   (Melastomataceae).

Melastoma asperum Linnaeus, *Species Plantarum* 1: 391. 1753.
"Habitat in India." RCN: 3072.
Lectotype (Hansen in *Ginkgoana* 4: 80. 1977): Herb. Hermann 2: 3, No. 172 (BM-000621501).
Current name: ***Osbeckia aspera*** (L.) Blume (Melastomataceae).
Note: Specific epithet spelled "aspera" in the protologue.

Melastoma crispatum Linnaeus, *Species Plantarum,* ed. 2, 1: 560. 1762.
"Habitat in Amboina." RCN: 3079.
Lectotype (Merrill, *Interpret. Rumph. Herb. Amb.*: 404. 1917): [icon] *"Funis Muraenarum mas"* in Rumphius, Herb. Amboin. 5: 66, t. 35, f. 1. 1747.
Current name: ***Medinilla crispata*** (L.) Blume (Melastomataceae).
Note: Specific epithet spelled "crispata" in the protologue.

Melastoma discolor Linnaeus, *Systema Naturae,* ed. 10, 2: 1022. 1759.
["Habitat in America."] Sp. Pl., ed. 2, 1: 560 (1762). RCN: 3077.
Lectotype (Howard & Kellogg in *J. Arnold Arbor.* 67: 240. 1986): [icon] *"Grossulariae fructu non spinosa, malabrathri foliis subtus niveis, fructu racemoso in umbellae modum disposito"* in Sloane, Voy. Jamaica 2: 86, t. 198, f. 1. 1725. – Voucher: Herb. Sloane 6: 98 (BM-SL).
Current name: ***Tetrazygia discolor*** (L.) DC. (Melastomataceae).

Melastoma grossularioides Linnaeus, *Species Plantarum* 1: 390. 1753.
"Habitat in Surinamo. D. Bartsch." RCN: 3069.
Lectotype (Renner in *Mem. New York Bot. Gard.* 50: 5, 23. 1989): [icon] *"Arbor Americ. latiori & acuminato folio trinervi, utrinque glabro & margine leviter crenato"* in Plukenet, Phytographia: t. 249,

f. 4. 1692; Almag. Bot.: 40. 1696. – Voucher: Herb. Sloane 95: 78 (BM-SL).
Current name: ***Bellucia grossulariodes*** (L.) Triana (Melastomataceae).

Melastoma hirtum Linnaeus, *Species Plantarum* 1: 390. 1753.
"Habitat in America meridionali." RCN: 3071.
Type not designated.
Original material: [icon] in Plukenet, Phytographia: t. 264, f. 1. 1694; Almag. Bot.: 40. 1696 – Typotype: Herb. Sloane 99: 115 (BM-SL).
Current name: ***Clidemia hirta*** (L.) D. Don (Melastomataceae).
Note: Specific epithet spelled "hirta" in the protologue.
   Wickens (in Polhill, *Fl. Trop. E. Africa, Melastomataceae*: 74. 1975) indicated unspecified material in LINN as type, but 559.2 was a 1758 acquisition from Browne, and 559.3 was also received after 1753. Some later authors, too, have accepted one sheet or the other as the type but neither can be accepted as a neotype because original material is in existence.

Melastoma holosericeum Linnaeus, *Species Plantarum* 1: 390. 1753.
"Habitat in Brasilia, Jamaica, Surinamo." RCN: 3073.
Lectotype (Wurdack in Görts-van Rijn, *Fl. Guianas,* ser. A, 13: 202. 1993): Herb. Clifford: 162, *Melastoma* 2 (BM-000558745).
Current name: ***Miconia holosericea*** (L.) DC. (Melastomataceae).
Note: Specific epithet spelled "holosericea" in the protologue.

Melastoma laevigatum Linnaeus, *Systema Naturae,* ed. 10, 2: 1022. 1759.
["Habitat in America."] Sp. Pl., ed. 2, 1: 560 (1762). RCN: 3076.
Lectotype (Fawcett & Rendle, *Fl. Jamaica* 5: 374. 1926): *Browne*, Herb. Linn. No. 559.10 (LINN).
Current name: ***Miconia laevigata*** (L.) D. Don (Melastomataceae).
Note: Specific epithet spelled "laevigata" in the protologue.

Melastoma malabathricum Linnaeus, *Species Plantarum* 1: 390. 1753.
"Habitat in India." RCN: 3075.
Lectotype (Bremer in Dassanayake & Fosberg, *Revised Handb. Fl. Ceylon* 6: 159. 1987; Bremer in Jarvis & al., *Regnum Veg.* 127: 65. 1993): Herb. Hermann 1: 55, No. 171 (BM-000594487).
Generitype of *Melastoma* Linnaeus (vide Hitchcock, *Prop. Brit. Bot.*: 153. 1929).
Current name: ***Melastoma malabathricum*** L. (Melastomataceae).
Note: Bremer (1987) indicated material in Herb. Hermann (BM) in both vol. 1: 55 and 4: 3 as type. Under Art. 9.15, this is a valid typification, later (1993) restricted to that in vol. 1: 55 by the same author.

Melastoma octandrum Linnaeus, *Species Plantarum* 1: 391. 1753.
"Habitat in India." RCN: 3078.
Lectotype (Hansen in *Ginkgoana* 4: 109. 1977): Herb. Hermann 3: 42, No. 173, right specimen (BM-000621953).
Current name: ***Osbeckia octandra*** (L.) DC. (Melastomataceae).
Note: Specific epithet spelled "octandra" in the protologue.

Melastoma scabrosum Linnaeus, *Systema Naturae,* ed. 10, 2: 1022. 1759.
["Habitat in Jamaica."] Sp. Pl., ed. 2, 1: 558 (1762). RCN: 3070.
Lectotype (Fawcett & Rendle, *Fl. Jamaica* 5: 400. 1926): *Browne*, Herb. Linn. No. 559.1 (LINN).
Current name: ***Ossaea scabrosa*** (L.) DC. (Melastomataceae).
Note: Specific epithet spelled "scabrosa" in the protologue.

Melastoma sessilifolium Linnaeus, *Systema Naturae,* ed. 10, 2: 1022. 1759.
["Habitat in Jamaica."] Sp. Pl., ed. 2, 1: 559 (1762). RCN: 3074.

Lectotype (Fawcett & Rendle, *Fl. Jamaica* 5: 395. 1926): *Browne*, Herb. Linn. No. 559.8 (LINN).
Current name: ***Henriettea sessilifolia*** (L.) Alain (Melastomataceae).

Melia azadirachta Linnaeus, *Species Plantarum* 1: 385. 1753.
"Habitat in India." RCN: 3032.
Lectotype (Howard, *Fl. Lesser Antilles* 4: 582. 1988): Herb. Hermann 2: 56, No. 161 (BM-000594618).
Current name: ***Azadirachta indica*** A. Juss. (Meliaceae).
Note: Siddiqi (in Jafri & El-Gadi, *Fl. Libya* 93: 2. 1983) wrongly indicated material in Herb. Hermann 1: 10 (BM) as type, evidently confusing this name with *M. azedarach* L.

Melia azedarach Linnaeus, *Species Plantarum* 1: 384. 1753.
"Habitat in Syria." RCN: 3031.
Lectotype (Abdulla in Nasir & Ali, *Fl. W. Pakistan* 17: 8. 1972): Herb. Hermann 1: 10, No. 162 (BM-000621259).
Generitype of *Melia* Linnaeus (vide Hitchcock, *Prop. Brit. Bot.*: 153. 1929).
Current name: ***Melia azedarach*** L. (Meliaceae).
Note: Mabberley (in *Gard. Bull. Singapore* 37: 63–64. 1984) provided a detailed account of the history of this taxon and its many cultivars, concluding that its type should be a Clifford sheet. However, this choice is pre-dated by that of Abdulla (and followed by several later authors), who chose Hermann material from Sri Lanka as the type. Despite some confusion over the geographical provenance (Syria vs. Ceylon) of *M. azedarach* and its var. *sempervirens* by Linnaeus, his diagnosis for the species name is firmly linked with the *Flora Zeylanica* account, and there seem to be no grounds for rejecting Abdulla's choice. There appear to be no nomenclatural implications at species rank.

Melia azedarach Linnaeus var. **sempervirens** Linnaeus, *Species Plantarum* 1: 384. 1753.
"Habitat in Zeylona." RCN: 3031.
Lectotype (Wijnands, *Bot. Commelins*: 145. 1983): Herb. Clifford: 161, *Melia* 1 α (BM-000558743).
Current name: ***Melia azedarach*** L. (Meliaceae).

Melianthus major Linnaeus, *Species Plantarum* 2: 639. 1753.
"Habitat in Aethiopiae succulentis." RCN: 4652.
Type not designated.
Original material: Herb. Linn. No. 818.2 (LINN); Herb. Linn. No. 818.1 (LINN); [icon] in Hermann, Hort. Lugd.-Bat. Cat.: 414, 415. 1687.
Generitype of *Melianthus* Linnaeus (vide Green, *Prop. Brit. Bot.*: 170. 1929).
Current name: ***Melianthus major*** L. (Melianthaceae).

Melianthus minor Linnaeus, *Species Plantarum* 2: 639. 1753, *nom. utique rej.*
"Habitat in Aethiopia." RCN: 4653.
Lectotype (Wijnands, *Bot. Commelins*: 146. 1983): [icon] *"Melianthus Afric. minor foetidus"* in Commelin, Hort. Med. Amstelaed. Pl. Rar.: 4, t. 4. 1706.
Current name: ***Melianthus comosus*** Vahl (Melianthaceae).

Melica altissima Linnaeus, *Species Plantarum* 1: 66. 1753.
"Habitat in Sibiria, Canada." RCN: 566.
Lectotype (Cope in Cafferty & al. in *Taxon* 49: 252. 2000): Herb. Linn. No. 86.5 (LINN).
Current name: ***Melica altissima*** L. (Poaceae).

Melica caerulea (Linnaeus) Linnaeus, *Systema Vegetabilium*, ed. 13: 97. 1774.

["Habitat in Europae pascuis aquosis."] Sp. Pl. 1: 63 (1753). RCN: 550.
Basionym: *Aira caerulea* L. (1753).
Lectotype (Trist & Sell in *Watsonia* 17: 154. 1988): Herb. Linn. No. 85.1 (LINN).
Current name: ***Molinia caerulea*** (L.) Moench (Poaceae).

Melica ciliata Linnaeus, *Species Plantarum* 1: 66. 1753.
"Habitat in Europae collibus sterilibus saxosis." RCN: 562.
Lectotype (Cope in Cafferty & al. in *Taxon* 49: 252. 2000): Herb. Linn. No. 86.1 (LINN).
Current name: ***Melica ciliata*** L. (Poaceae).
Note: Stearn (in *Biol. J. Linn. Soc.* 5: 11–12. 1973), in an account of Linnaeus' Öland and Gotland journey of 1741, treated Vible in Gotland as the restricted type locality, and noted the existence of 86.1 (LINN). In his paper, he attributed restricted type localities irrespective of whether any material existed in LINN and, where specimens do exist, he does not refer to any of them as type specimens. The collection subsequently designated as the type shows no annotation associating it with Gotland. Although Kerguélen (in *Lejeunia*, n.s., 75: 210. 1975) stated "Type: ...LINN", this is not accepted as a formal typification, for the reasons explained by Cafferty & al. (in *Taxon* 49: 240. 2000).

Melica minuta Linnaeus, *Systema Naturae*, ed. 12, 2: 92; *Mantissa Plantarum*: 32. 1767.
"Habitat in Italia. D. Scopoli." RCN: 564.
Lectotype (Meikle, *Fl. Cyprus* 2: 1750. 1985): *Scopoli 109*, Herb. Linn. No. 86.3 (LINN).
Current name: ***Melica minuta*** L. (Poaceae).
Note: Although Kerguélen (in *Lejeunia*, n.s., 75: 211. 1975) stated "Type: ...LINN", this is not accepted as a formal typification, for the reasons explained by Cafferty & al. (in *Taxon* 49: 240. 2000).

Melica nutans Linnaeus, *Species Plantarum* 1: 66. 1753.
"Habitat in Europae frigidioris rupibus." RCN: 563.
Lectotype (Hempel in Jarvis in *Taxon* 41: 566. 1992): Herb. Linn. No. 86.2 (LINN).
Generitype of *Melica* Linnaeus.
Current name: ***Melica nutans*** L. (Poaceae).
Note: Melica nutans, with the type designated by Hempel, was proposed as conserved type of the genus by Jarvis (in *Taxon* 41: 566. 1992). However, the proposal was eventually ruled unnecessary by the General Committee (see Barrie, *l.c.* 55: 795–796. 2006 for a review of the history of this and related proposals).

Melica papilionacea Linnaeus, *Systema Naturae*, ed. 12, 2: 92; *Mantissa Plantarum*: 31. 1767, *nom. illeg.*
"Habitat in Brasilia. D. Arduinus." RCN: 565.
Replaced synonym: *Melica brasiliana* Ard. (1764).
Type not designated.
Current name: ***Melica brasiliana*** Ard. (Poaceae).
Note: An illegitimate replacement name for *Melica brasiliana* Ard. (1764).

Melicocca bijuga Linnaeus, *Species Plantarum*, ed. 2, 1: 495. 1762, *nom. illeg.*
"Habitat in America meridionali." RCN: 2678.
Replaced synonym: *Melicoccus bijugatus* Jacq. (1760).
Type not designated.
Current name: ***Melicoccus bijugatus*** Jacq. (Sapindaceae).
Note: A superfluous name for *Melicoccus bijugatus* Jacq. (1760).

Melissa calamintha Linnaeus, *Species Plantarum* 2: 593. 1753.
"Habitat in Italiae, Hispaniae, Galliae clivis saxosis." RCN: 4310.

M

Lectotype (Garbari & al. in *Taxon* 40: 500. 1991): Herb. Linn. No. 745.4 (LINN).
Current name: ***Clinopodium nepeta*** (L.) Kuntze (Lamiaceae).

Melissa cretica Linnaeus, *Species Plantarum* 2: 593. 1753.
"Habitat Monspelii." RCN: 4312.
Lectotype (Morales in Jarvis & al. in *Taxon* 50: 513. 2001): Herb. Burser XIII: 17 (UPS).
Current name: ***Clinopodium creticum*** (L.) Kuntze (Lamiaceae).

Melissa fruticosa Linnaeus, *Species Plantarum* 2: 593. 1753.
"Habitat in Hispania." RCN: 4313.
Lectotype (Morales in *Anales Jard. Bot. Madrid* 48: 138. 1991): Herb. Linn. No. 745.9 (LINN).
Current name: ***Clinopodium serpyllifolium*** (M. Bieb.) Kuntze subsp. *fruticosum* (L.) Bräuchler (Lamiaceae).

Melissa grandiflora Linnaeus, *Species Plantarum* 2: 592. 1753.
"Habitat in Hetruriae montosis." RCN: 4309.
Lectotype (Ubera in *Taxon* 46: 542. 1997): Herb. Linn. No. 745.3 (LINN).
Current name: ***Clinopodium grandiflorum*** (L.) Kuntze (Lamiaceae).
Note: Morales & Luque (in *Anales Jard. Bot. Madrid* 55: 272. 28 Nov 1997) independently made the same choice, but later in the year than Ubera (published 15 Aug 1997).

Melissa nepeta Linnaeus, *Species Plantarum* 2: 593. 1753.
"Habitat in Italiae, Galliae, Angliae, Helvetiae aggeribus glareosis." RCN: 4311.
Lectotype (Garbari & al. in *Taxon* 40: 501. 1991): Herb. Linn. No. 745.5 (LINN).
Current name: ***Clinopodium nepeta*** (L.) Kuntze (Lamiaceae).

Melissa officinalis Linnaeus, *Species Plantarum* 2: 592. 1753.
"Habitat in montibus Genevensibus, Allobrogicis, Italicis." RCN: 4308.
Lectotype (Hedge in Jarvis & al., *Regnum Veg.* 127: 65. 1993): Herb. Linn. No. 745.1 (LINN).
Generitype of *Melissa* Linnaeus (vide Green, *Prop. Brit. Bot.*: 166. 1929).
Current name: ***Melissa officinalis*** L. (Lamiaceae).

Melissa pulegioides Linnaeus, *Species Plantarum* 2: 593. 1753.
"Habitat in Virginia, Canada." RCN: 170.
Basionym of: *Cunila pulegioides* (L.) L. (1762).
Lectotype (Irving in *Sida* 8: 288. 1980): *Clayton 514* (BM-000576253).
Current name: ***Hedeoma pulegioides*** (L.) Pers. (Lamiaceae).
Note: Epling (in *J. Bot.* 67: 9. 1929) noted Herb. Linn. No. 38.3 (LINN), a Kalm specimen, as standard, but this is not equivalent to a type statement (see Jarvis & al. in *Taxon* 50: 508. 2001).

Melittis melissophyllum Linnaeus, *Species Plantarum* 2: 597. 1753.
"Habitat in subalpinis Germaniae, Helvetiae, Angliae, Monspelii." RCN: 4329.
Lectotype (Press in Jarvis & al., *Regnum Veg.* 127: 65. 1993): Herb. Clifford: 309, *Melittis* 1, sheet 7 (BM-000646039).
Generitype of *Melittis* Linnaeus.
Current name: ***Melittis melissophyllum*** L. (Lamiaceae).

Melochia concatenata Linnaeus, *Species Plantarum* 2: 675. 1753.
"Habitat in India utraque." RCN: 4927.
Lectotype (Verdcourt in Dassanayake & al., *Revised Handb. Fl. Ceylon* 9: 415. 1995): Herb. Hermann 3: 10, No. 247 (BM-000621830).
Current name: ***Melochia corchorifolia*** L. (Sterculiaceae).

Melochia corchorifolia Linnaeus, *Species Plantarum* 2: 675. 1753, *typ. cons.*
"Habitat in India." RCN: 4928.
Conserved type (Goldberg in *Contr. U. S. Natl. Herb.* 34: 305. 1967): [icon] *"Melochia Corchori folio"* in Dillenius, Hort. Eltham. 2: 221, t. 176, f. 217. 1732. – Typotype: Herb. Dillenius (OXF).
Generitype of *Melochia* Linnaeus, *nom. cons.*
Current name: ***Melochia corchorifolia*** L. (Sterculiaceae).
Note: Melochia corchorifolia, with a Dillenian illustration as the type, was proposed as conserved type of the genus by Jarvis (in *Taxon* 41: 573. 1992). This was eventually approved by the General Committee (see review of the history of this proposal by Barrie, *l.c.* 55: 795–796. 2006).

Melochia depressa Linnaeus, *Species Plantarum* 2: 674. 1753.
"Habitat in Havana." RCN: 4926.
Lectotype (Blanchard & al. in *Gentes Herb.* 11: 356. 1978): Herb. A. van Royen No. 909.64–115 (L).
Current name: ***Kosteletzkya depressa*** (L.) O.J. Blanch. & al. (Malvaceae).

Melochia pyramidata Linnaeus, *Species Plantarum* 2: 674. 1753.
"Habitat in Brasilia." RCN: 4923.
Lectotype (Goldberg in *Contr. U. S. Natl. Herb.* 34: 338. 1967): Herb. Linn. No. 855.1 (LINN).
Current name: ***Melochia pyramidata*** L. (Sterculiaceae).

Melochia supina Linnaeus, *Species Plantarum* 2: 675. 1753.
"Habitat in India." RCN: 4929.
Type not designated.
Original material: [icon] in Plukenet, Phytographia: t. 132, f. 4. 1692; Almag. Bot.: 14. 1696 – Typotype: Herb. Sloane 95: 39 (BM-SL) – Voucher: Herb. Sloane 99: 39 (BM-SL).
Current name: ***Melochia corchorifolia*** L. (Sterculiaceae).

Melochia tomentosa Linnaeus, *Systema Naturae,* ed. 10, 2: 1140. 1759.
["Habitat in America meridionali."] Sp. Pl., ed. 2, 2: 943 (1763). RCN: 4925.
Type not designated.
Original material: Herb. Linn. No. 855.3 (LINN); Herb. Linn. No. 855.2 (LINN); [icon] in Sloane, Voy. Jamaica 1: 220, t. 139, f. 1. 1707.
Current name: ***Melochia tomentosa*** L. (Sterculiaceae).
Note: Goldberg (in *Contr. U. S. Natl. Herb.* 34: 330. 1967) noted the two sheets at LINN but referred to neither as the type. Fryxell (in McVaugh, *Fl. Novo-Galiciana* 3: 136. 2001) indicated 855.2 (LINN) as lectotype, but this choice was published after 1 Jan 2001 and so the omission of the phrase "designated here" or an equivalent (Art. 7.11) means that it is not effective.

Melothria pendula Linnaeus, *Species Plantarum* 1: 35. 1753.
"Habitat in Canada, Virginia, Jamaica." RCN: 277.
Lectotype (Wunderlin in Woodson & Schery in *Ann. Missouri Bot. Gard.* 65: 333. 1978): Herb. Linn. No. 51.1 (LINN).
Generitype of *Melothria* Linnaeus.
Current name: ***Melothria pendula*** L. (Cucurbitaceae).

Memecylon capitellatum Linnaeus, *Species Plantarum* 1: 349. 1753.
"Habitat in Zeylona." RCN: 2699.
Lectotype (Bremer in Dassanayake & Fosberg, *Revised Handb. Fl. Ceylon* 6: 214. 1987): Herb. Hermann 1: 17, No. 136, right specimen (BM-000621286; iso- L).
Generitype of *Memecylon* Linnaeus.
Current name: ***Memecylon capitellatum*** L. (Melastomataceae).

Menais topiaria Linnaeus, *Species Plantarum,* ed. 2, 1: 251. 1762. "Habitat in America meridionali." RCN: 1394.
Type not designated.
Original material: none traced.
Current name: ***Menais topiaria*** L. (Boraginaceae).

Menispermum canadense Linnaeus, *Species Plantarum* 1: 340. 1753.
"Habitat in Virginia, Canada." RCN: 7485.
Lectotype (Reveal in Jarvis & al., *Regnum Veg.* 127: 66. 1993): Herb. Clifford: 140, *Menispermum* 1 (BM-000558591).
Generitype of *Menispermum* Linnaeus (vide Hitchcock, *Prop. Brit. Bot.*: 148. 1929).
Current name: ***Menispermum canadense*** L. (Menispermaceae).

Menispermum carolinum Linnaeus, *Species Plantarum* 1: 340. 1753.
"Habitat in Carolina." RCN: 7487.
Type not designated.
Original material: none traced.
Current name: ***Cocculus carolinus*** (L.) DC. (Menispermaceae).

Menispermum cocculus Linnaeus, *Species Plantarum* 1: 340. 1753.
"Habitat in India." RCN: 7488.
Lectotype (Forman in *Kew Bull.* 32: 330. 1978): [icon] *"Natsjatam"* in Rheede, Hort. Malab. 7: 1, t. 1. 1688.
Current name: ***Anamirta cocculus*** (L.) Wight & Arn. (Menispermaceae).

Menispermum crispum Linnaeus, *Species Plantarum,* ed. 2, 2: 1468. 1763.
"Habitat in Bengala." RCN: 7489.
Lectotype (Forman in *Kew Bull.* 36: 394. 1981): [icon] *"Funis felleus"* in Rumphius, Herb. Amboin. 5: 82, t. 44, f. 1. 1747.
Current name: ***Tinospora crispa*** (L.) Hook. f. & Thomson (Menispermaceae).
Note: See comments by Merrill (*Interpret. Rumph. Herb. Amb.*: 220–221. 1917), who does not, however, make a choice of type.

Menispermum flavum Linnaeus, *Herbarium Amboinense*: 18. 1754.
RCN: 7488.
Lectotype (Merrill, *Interpret. Rumph. Herb. Amb.*: 33, 222. 1917): [icon] *"Tuba flava"* in Rumphius, Herb. Amboin. 5: 38, t. 24. 1747.
Current name: ***Archangelisia flava*** (L.) Merr. (Menispermaceae).

Menispermum hirsutum Linnaeus, *Species Plantarum* 1: 341. 1753.
"Habitat in India." RCN: 7492.
Lectotype (Troupin, *Fl. Trop. E. Africa, Menispermaceae*: 12. 1956): [icon] *"Cocculi Indi altera species minor, scandens Vincae pervincae foliis villosis"* in Plukenet, Amalth. Bot.: 61, t. 384, f. 7. 1705. – Typotype: Herb. Sloane 93: 107 (BM-SL).
Current name: ***Cocculus hirsutus*** (L.) Diels (Menispermaceae).

Menispermum myosotoides Linnaeus, *Species Plantarum* 1: 341. 1753.
"Habitat in India." RCN: 7492.
Type not designated.
Original material: [icon] in Plukenet, Amalth. Bot.: 62, t. 384, f. 3. 1705 – Voucher: Herb. Sloane 94: 182 (BM-SL).
Current name: ***Cocculus hirsutus*** (L.) Diels (Menispermaceae).

Menispermum orbiculatum Linnaeus, *Species Plantarum* 1: 341. 1753.
"Habitat in insula Crocodilorum Asiae." RCN: 7491.
Lectotype (Troupin in *Bull. Jard. Bot. État Bruxelles* 25: 141. 1955): [icon] *"Cocculi Orientalis Frutex, convolvulaceus, orbiculatis foliis, prona parte villosis, ex una de Insulis Crocodilorum"* in Plukenet,

Amalth. Bot.: 61, t. 384, f. 6. 1705. – Typotype: *Cuninghame* in Herb. Sloane 93: 107 (BM-SL).
Current name: ***Cocculus orbiculatus*** (L.) DC. (Menispermaceae).
Note: See Forman (in *Kew Bull.* 22: 349–374. 1968) for comments on the identity of the typotype collection.

Menispermum virginicum Linnaeus, *Species Plantarum* 1: 340. 1753.
"Habitat in Virginiae & Caroliniae maritimis." RCN: 7486.
Lectotype (designated here by Reveal): [icon] *"Menispermum folio hederaceo"* in Dillenius, Hort. Eltham. 2: 223, t. 178, f. 219. 1732.
Current name: ***Cocculus carolinus*** (L.) DC. (Menispermaceae).

Mentha aquatica Linnaeus, *Species Plantarum* 2: 576. 1753.
"Habitat in Europa ad aquas." RCN: 4204.
Lectotype (Tucker & al. in *Taxon* 29: 235, f. 5. 1980): Herb. Clifford: 306, *Mentha* 4 (BM-000646007).
Current name: ***Mentha aquatica*** L. (Lamiaceae).
Note: Graham (in *Watsonia* 3: 109. 1954) provided an extensive appraisal of 730.9 (LINN), concluding that it conflicts with Linnaeus' protologue.

Mentha arvensis Linnaeus, *Species Plantarum* 2: 577. 1753.
"Habitat in Europae agris frequens post messem." RCN: 4208.
Lectotype (Tucker & al. in *Taxon* 29: 236, f. 8. 1980): Herb. Linn. No. 238.11 (S).
Current name: ***Mentha arvensis*** L. (Lamiaceae).

Mentha auricularia Linnaeus, *Systema Naturae,* ed. 12, 2: 391; *Mantissa Plantarum*: 81. 1767.
"Habitat in Indiae aquosis." RCN: 4198.
Lectotype (Tucker & al. in *Taxon* 29: 238, f. 15. 1980): Herb. Hermann 4: 42, No. 411 (BM-000594741).
Current name: ***Pogostemon auricularius*** (L.) Hassk. (Lamiaceae).

Mentha canadensis Linnaeus, *Species Plantarum* 2: 577. 1753.
"Habitat in Canada. Kalm." RCN: 4210.
Lectotype (Tucker & al. in *Taxon* 29: 237, f. 9. 1980): *Kalm*, Herb. Linn. No. 730.18 (LINN).
Current name: ***Mentha canadensis*** L. (Lamiaceae).
Note: Although Epling (in *J. Bot.* 67: 8. 1929) stated that the Linnaean sheet is "probably also the historical type", this falls short of formal typification.

Mentha canariensis Linnaeus, *Species Plantarum* 2: 578. 1753.
"Habitat in Canariis." RCN: 4213.
Lectotype (Tucker & al. in *Taxon* 29: 237, f. 12. 1980): Herb. Clifford: 307, *Mentha* 8, sheet A (BM-000646014).
Current name: ***Bystropogon canariense*** (L.) L'Hér. (Lamiaceae).

Mentha cervina Linnaeus, *Species Plantarum* 2: 578. 1753.
"Habitat Monspelii & ad Rhodanum." RCN: 4212.
Lectotype (Tucker & al. in *Taxon* 29: 237, f. 11. 1980): Herb. Burser XII: 131 (UPS).
Current name: ***Mentha cervina*** L. (Lamiaceae).

Mentha crispa Linnaeus, *Species Plantarum* 2: 576. 1753.
"Habitat in Sibiria." RCN: 4203.
Lectotype (Tucker & al. in *Taxon* 29: 233, f. 1. 1980): Herb. Clifford: 306, *Mentha* 3, sheet 2 (BM-000646005).
Current name: ***Mentha crispa*** L. (Lamiaceae).

Mentha exigua Linnaeus, *Centuria II Plantarum*: 20. 1756.
"Habitat in Anglia. Miller." RCN: 4209.
Lectotype (Tucker & al. in *Taxon* 29: 238, f. 14. 1980): *Miller*, Herb. Linn. No. 730.17 (LINN).
Current name: ***Mentha pulegium*** L. var. ***exigua*** (L.) Huds. (Lamiaceae).

M

Mentha gentilis Linnaeus, *Species Plantarum* 2: 577. 1753.
"Habitat in Europa australiore." RCN: 4207.
Lectotype (Tucker & al. in *Taxon* 29: 236, f. 7. 1980): Herb. Linn. No. 730.14 (LINN).
Current name: ***Mentha arvensis*** L. (Lamiaceae).

Mentha longifolia (Linnaeus) Linnaeus, *Amoenitates Academicae* 4: 485. 1759, *nom. inval.*
Type not relevant.
Current name: ***Mentha longifolia*** (L.) Huds. (Lamiaceae).
Note: As noted by Stearn (in Geck & Pressler, *Festschr. Claus Nissen*: 630. 1974), "Mentha longifolia" is a typographical error for *Mentha spicata* var. *longifolia* L. (1753). The former name did not appear in *Syst. Nat.*, ed. 10 (1759), nor *Sp. Pl.*, ed. 2 (1763) or later Linnaean works. Kerguélen & al. (in *Lejeunia*, n.s., 120: 207. 1987) also cast doubt on the relationship between these two "names". Tucker & al. (in *Taxon* 29: 234, f. 3. 1980) treated *M. longifolia* as a valid recombination based on *M. spicata* var. *longifolia* L. (1753), and typified by Herb. Burser XIII: 9 (UPS).

Mentha perilloides Linnaeus, *Systema Naturae*, ed. 12, 2: 736. 1767, *nom. illeg.*
["Habitat in India."] Sp. Pl. 2: 597 (1753). RCN: 4214.
Replaced synonym: *Ocimum frutescens* L. (1753).
Lectotype (Paton in Jarvis & al., *Regnum Veg.* 127: 74. 1993): [icon] *"Ocymum Zeylanicum perenne, odoratissimum, latifolium"* in Burman, Thes. Zeylan.: 174, t. 80, f. 1. 1737.
Current name: ***Perilla frutescens*** (L.) Britton (Lamiaceae).
Note: An illegitimate replacement name in *Mentha* for *Ocimum frutescens* L. (1753).

Mentha piperita Linnaeus, *Species Plantarum* 2: 576. 1753.
"Habitat in Anglia." RCN: 4205.
Lectotype (Tucker & al. in *Taxon* 29: 235, f. 6. 1980): [icon] *"Mentha spicis brevioribus & habitioribus, foliis Menthae fuscae, sapore fervido Piperis"* in Ray, Syn. Meth. Stirp. Brit., ed. 3: 234, t. 10, f. 2. 1724. – Typotype: Herb. Sherard No. 926 (OXF).
Current name: ***Mentha × piperita*** L. (Lamiaceae).
Note: Graham (in *Watsonia* 2: 31. 1951) wrongly regarded a specimen in Herb. Buddle (which would not have been seen by Linnaeus and is not original material) as "the type".

Mentha pulegium Linnaeus, *Species Plantarum* 2: 577. 1753.
"Habitat in Angliae, Galliae, Helvetiae inundatis." RCN: 4211.
Lectotype (Tucker & al. in *Taxon* 29: 237, f. 10. 1980): Herb. Linn. No. 730.19 (LINN).
Current name: ***Mentha pulegium*** L. (Lamiaceae).

Mentha sativa Linnaeus, *Species Plantarum,* ed. 2, 2: 805. 1763, *nom. illeg.*
"Habitat in Europa australi." RCN: 4206.
Replaced synonym: *Mentha verticillata* L. (1759).
Lectotype (Tucker & al. in *Taxon* 29: 238, f. 14. 1980): *Miller*, Herb. Linn. No. 730.13 (LINN).
Current name: ***Mentha verticillata*** L. (Lamiaceae).
Note: An illegitimate replacement name for *M. verticillata* L. (1759).

Mentha spicata Linnaeus, *Species Plantarum* 2: 576. 1753.
"Habitat in Dania, Germania, Anglia, Gallia." RCN: 4202.
Lectotype (Tucker & al. in *Taxon* 29: 234. 1980): Herb. Clifford: 306, *Mentha* 1 (BM-000646003).
Generitype of *Mentha* Linnaeus (vide Green, *Prop. Brit. Bot.*: 165. 1929).
Current name: ***Mentha spicata*** L. (Lamiaceae).

Mentha spicata Linnaeus var. **longifolia** Linnaeus, *Species Plantarum* 2: 576. 1753.
RCN: 4202.
Replaced synonym of: *Mentha sylvestris* L. (1763), *nom. illeg.*
Lectotype (Tucker & al. in *Taxon* 29: 234, f. 3. 1980): Herb. Burser XIII: 9 (UPS).
Current name: ***Mentha longifolia*** (L.) Huds. (Lamiaceae).
Note: Hedge & Lamond (in *Notes Roy. Bot. Gard. Edinburgh* 28: 95. 1968) indicated unspecified (and unseen) material in the Clifford herbarium (BM) as type but there is no material there associated with this name.

Mentha spicata Linnaeus var. **rotundifolia** Linnaeus, *Species Plantarum* 2: 576. 1753.
RCN: 4201.
Lectotype (Harley in *Bot. J. Linn. Soc.* 65: 251. 1972): Herb. Burser XIII: 8 (UPS).
Current name: ***Mentha rotundifolia*** (L.) Huds. (Lamiaceae).
Note: The type is illustrated by Tucker & al. (in *Taxon* 29: 244, f. 4. 1980).

Mentha spicata Linnaeus var. **viridis** Linnaeus, *Species Plantarum* 2: 576. 1753.
RCN: 4200.
Basionym of: *Mentha viridis* (L.) L. (1763).
Lectotype (Tucker & al. in *Taxon* 29: 234. 1980): Herb. Clifford: 306, *Mentha* 1 (BM-000646003).
Current name: ***Mentha spicata*** L. (Lamiaceae).
Note: Homotypic with, and replaced by, *M. spicata* var. *spicata* which, as the autonym, has statutory priority.

Mentha sylvestris Linnaeus, *Species Plantarum,* ed. 2, 2: 804. 1763, *nom. illeg.*
"Habitat in Dania, Germania, Anglia, Gallia." RCN: 4199.
Replaced synonym: *Mentha spicata* L. var. *longifolia* L. (1753).
Lectotype (Tucker & al. in *Taxon* 29: 234, f. 3. 1980): Herb. Burser XIII: 9 (UPS).
Current name: ***Mentha longifolia*** (L.) Huds. (Lamiaceae).
Note: This is an illegitimate replacement name for *Mentha longifolia* (L.) Hudson (1762), itself based on *Mentha spicata* var. *longifolia* L. (1753).

Mentha verticillata Linnaeus, *Systema Naturae*, ed. 10, 2: 1099. 1759.
["Habitat in Europa australi."] Sp. Pl., ed. 2, 2: 805 (1763). RCN: 4206.
Replaced synonym of: *Mentha sativa* L. (1763), *nom. illeg.*
Lectotype (Tucker & al. in *Taxon* 29: 238, f. 14. 1980): *Miller*, Herb. Linn. No. 730.13 (LINN).
Current name: ***Mentha verticillata*** L. (Lamiaceae).

Mentha viridis (Linnaeus) Linnaeus, *Species Plantarum,* ed. 2, 2: 804. 1763.
"Habitat in Germania, Anglia, Gallia." RCN: 4200.
Basionym: *Mentha spicata* L. var. *viridis* L. (1753).
Lectotype (Tucker & al. in *Taxon* 29: 234. 1980): Herb. Clifford: 306, *Mentha* 1 (BM-000646003).
Current name: ***Mentha spicata*** L. (Lamiaceae).

Mentzelia aspera Linnaeus, *Species Plantarum* 1: 516. 1753.
"Habitat in America." RCN: 3879.
Lectotype (Weigend in *Bot. Jahrb. Syst.* 118: 235. 1996): [icon] *"Mentzelia"* in Plumier in Burman, Pl. Amer.: 167, t. 174, f. 1. 1758.
Generitype of *Mentzelia* Linnaeus.
Current name: ***Mentzelia aspera*** L. (Loasaceae).

Note: Weigend (*l.c.*) noted that Plumier's plate was poor, and that designation of an epitype would be desirable should suitable material from Hispaniola become available.

Menyanthes indica Linnaeus, *Species Plantarum* 1: 145. 1753.
"Habitat in Malabariae, Zeylonae fossi." RCN: 1163.
Lectotype (Marais & Verdoorn in Dyer & al., *Fl. Southern Africa* 26: 243. 1963): [icon] *"Nedel ambel"* in Rheede, Hort. Malab. 11: 55, t. 28. 1692.
Current name: ***Nymphoides indica*** (L.) Kuntze (Menyanthaceae).

Menyanthes nymphoides Linnaeus, *Species Plantarum* 1: 145. 1753.
"Habitat in Belgii, Dantisci fossi majoribus." RCN: 1162.
Type not designated.
Original material: Herb. Burser X: (between 131 & 132) (UPS).
Current name: ***Nymphoides peltata*** (S.G. Gmel.) Kuntze (Menyanthaceae).

Menyanthes trifoliata Linnaeus, *Species Plantarum* 1: 145. 1753.
"Habitat in Europae paludibus." RCN: 1164.
Lectotype (Qaiser in Nasir & Ali, *Fl. W. Pakistan* 111: 3. 1977): Herb. Linn. No. 203.4 (LINN).
Generitype of *Menyanthes* Linnaeus (vide Steudel, *Nom.*, ed. 2, 2: 128. 1841).
Current name: ***Menyanthes trifoliata*** L. (Menyanthaceae).

Mercurialis afra Linnaeus, *Mantissa Plantarum Altera*: 298. 1771.
"Habitat in Cap. b. spei juxta latera montis Leonis. Koenig." RCN: 7473.
Lectotype (Schubert & Van Wyk in Jarvis & al. in *Taxon* 55: 213. 2006): Herb. Linn. No. 332.8 (LINN).
Current name: ***Centella villosa*** L. (Apiaceae).

Mercurialis ambigua Linnaeus filius, *Dec. Prima Pl. Horti Upsal.*: 15. 1762.
RCN: 7470.
Note: The application of this name is uncertain.

Mercurialis annua Linnaeus, *Species Plantarum* 2: 1035. 1753.
"Habitat in Europae temperatae umbrosis." RCN: 7471.
Lectotype (Radcliffe-Smith in Meikle, *Fl. Cyprus* 2: 1451. 1985): Herb. Linn. No. 1188.3 (LINN).
Current name: ***Mercurialis annua*** L. (Euphorbiaceae).

Mercurialis perennis Linnaeus, *Species Plantarum* 2: 1035. 1753.
"Habitat in Europae nemoribus." RCN: 7469.
Lectotype (Radcliffe-Smith in Jarvis & al., *Regnum Veg.* 127: 66. 1993): Herb. Clifford: 461, *Mercurialis* 1 (BM-000647504).
Generitype of *Mercurialis* Linnaeus (vide Green, *Prop. Brit. Bot.*: 192. 1929).
Current name: ***Mercurialis perennis*** L. (Euphorbiaceae).

Mercurialis procumbens Linnaeus, *Species Plantarum* 2: 1036. 1753.
"Habitat in Africa." RCN: 7282.
Neotype (Radcliffe-Smith in *Kew Bull.* 44: 451. 1989): Herb. Linn. No. 1188.5 (LINN).
Current name: ***Leidesia procumbens*** (L.) Prain (Euphorbiaceae).
Note: In the apparent absence of any original material, Radcliffe-Smith's indication of 1188.5 (LINN) as the holotype is taken as correctable to neotype (Art. 9.8).

Mercurialis tomentosa Linnaeus, *Species Plantarum* 2: 1035. 1753.
"Habitat in G. Narbonensi, Hispania." RCN: 7472.

Type not designated.
Original material: Herb. Clifford: 461, *Mercurialis* 3, 2 sheets (BM); [icon] in Clusius, Rar. Pl. Hist. 2: 48. 1601.
Current name: ***Mercurialis tomentosa*** L. (Euphorbiaceae).

Mesembryanthemum acaule Linnaeus, *Systema Naturae,* ed. 10, 2: 1059. 1759, *nom. illeg.*
["Habitat in Africa."] Sp. Pl. 1: 482 (1753). RCN: 3678.
Replaced synonym: *Mesembryanthemum bellidiflorum* L. (1753).
Lectotype (Glen in *Bothalia* 16: 214. 1986): [icon] *"Mesembryanthemum Bellidiflorum"* in Dillenius, Hort. Eltham. 2: 244, t. 189, f. 233. 1732.
Current name: ***Acrodon bellidiflorus*** (L.) N.E. Br. (Aizoaceae).
Note: A superfluous name for *M. bellidiflorum* L. (1753).

Mesembryanthemum acinaciforme Linnaeus, *Species Plantarum* 1: 485. 1753.
"Habitat ad Cap. b. Spei." RCN: 3696.
Lectotype (Preston & Sell in *Watsonia* 17: 238. 1989): [icon] *"Mesembryanthemum acinaciforme, flore amplissimo purpureo"* in Dillenius, Hort. Eltham. 2: 282, t. 211, f. 270. 1732 (OXF).
Current name: ***Carpobrotus acinaciformis*** (L.) L. Bolus (Aizoaceae).
Note: Preston & Sell indicate Dillenius' own, coloured copy of his book at OXF as the lectotype. Jonkers (in *Brit. Cact. Succ. J.* 19: 182, f. 7. 2001) reproduces the type illustration.

Mesembryanthemum acinaciforme Linnaeus var. **flavum** Linnaeus, *Species Plantarum* 1: 485. 1753.
RCN: 3697.
Replaced synonym of: *Mesembryanthemum edule* L. (1759).
Lectotype (Blake in *Contr. Queensland Herb.* 7: 17. 1969): [icon] *"Mesembryanthemum falcatum majus, flore amplo luteo"* in Dillenius, Hort. Eltham. 2: 283, t. 212. f. 272. 1732.
Current name: ***Carpobrotus edulis*** (L.) N.E. Br. (Aizoaceae).
Note: Preston & Sell (in *Watsonia* 17: 238. 1989) note Dillenius' own coloured copy at OXF and (f. 7) reproduce an illustration.

Mesembryanthemum acinaciforme Linnaeus var. **purpureum** Linnaeus, *Species Plantarum* 1: 485. 1753.
RCN: 3696.
Lectotype (Preston & Sell in *Watsonia* 17: 238. 1989): [icon] *"Mesembryanthemum acinaciforme, flore amplissimo purpureo"* in Dillenius, Hort. Eltham. 2: 282, t. 211, f. 270. 1732 (OXF).
Current name: ***Carpobrotus acinaciformis*** (L.) L. Bolus (Aizoaceae).

Mesembryanthemum albidum Linnaeus, *Species Plantarum*, ed. 2, 1: 699. 1762.
"Habitat in Aethiopia." RCN: 3711.
Lectotype (Hartmann, *Ill. Handb. Succ. Pl., Aizoaceae F–Z*: 136. 2001): [icon] *"Mesembryanthemum foliis robustis albicantibus"* in Dillenius, Hort. Eltham. 2: 243, t. 189, f. 232. 1732.
Current name: ***Machairophyllum albidum*** (L.) Schwantes (Aizoaceae).

Mesembryanthemum aureum Linnaeus, *Systema Naturae,* ed. 10, 2: 1060. 1759.
RCN: 3699.
Neotype (Hartmann, *Ill. Handb. Succ. Pl., Aizoaceae F–Z*: 79. 2001): [icon] *"Mesembryanthemum aureum"* in Curtis in Bot. Mag. 8: t. 262. 1794.
Current name: ***Lampranthus aureus*** (L.) N.E. Br. (Aizoaceae).

Mesembryanthemum barbatum Linnaeus, *Species Plantarum* 1: 482. 1753.
"Habitat ad Cap. b. Spei." RCN: 3680.

Lectotype (Niesler in Hartmann, *Ill. Handb. Succ. Pl., Aizoaceae F–Z*: 341. 2001): [icon] *"Mesembryanthemum radiatum, ramulis prolixis, recumbentibus"* in Dillenius, Hort. Eltham. 2: 245, t. 190, f. 234. 1732.
Current name: ***Trichodiadema barbatum*** (L.) Schwantes (Aizoaceae).

Mesembryanthemum bellidiflorum Linnaeus, *Species Plantarum* 1: 482. 1753.
"Habitat in Africa." RCN: 3678.
Replaced synonym of: *Mesembryanthemum acaule* L. (1759), *nom. illeg.*
Lectotype (Glen in *Bothalia* 16: 214. 1986): [icon] *"Mesembryanthemum Bellidiflorum"* in Dillenius, Hort. Eltham. 2: 244, t. 189, f. 233. 1732.
Current name: ***Acrodon bellidiflorus*** (L.) N.E. Br. (Aizoaceae).

Mesembryanthemum bicolor Linnaeus, *Species Plantarum* 1: 485. 1753.
"Habitat in Africa." RCN: 3698.
Lectotype (Hartmann, *Ill. Handb. Succ. Pl., Aizoaceae F–Z*: 79. 2001): [icon] *"Mesembryanthemum tenuifolium fruticescens, flore croceo"* in Dillenius, Hort. Eltham. 2: 267, t. 202, f. 258. 1732.
Current name: ***Lampranthus bicolor*** (L.) N.E. Br. (Aizoaceae).

Mesembryanthemum calamiforme Linnaeus, *Species Plantarum* 1: 481. 1753.
"Habitat ad Cap. b. Spei." RCN: 3677.
Lectotype (Hartmann, *Ill. Handb. Succ. Pl., Aizoaceae A–E*: 180. 2001): [icon] *"Mesembryanthemum calamiforme"* in Dillenius, Hort. Eltham. 2: 239, t. 186, f. 228. 1732.
Current name: ***Cylindrophyllum calamiforme*** (L.) Schwantes (Aizoaceae).

Mesembryanthemum copticum Linnaeus, *Species Plantarum*, ed. 2, 1: 688. 1762.
"Habitat in Aegypto." RCN: 3670.
Lectotype (designated here by Hartmann): *Hasselquist*, Herb. Linn. No. 649.2 (LINN).
Current name: ***Mesembryanthemum nodiflorum*** L. (Aizoaceae).
Note: Gerbaulet (in Hartmann, *Ill. Handb. Succ. Pl., Aizoaceae F–Z*: 151. 2001) indicated a Bauhin description as type, but this is contrary to Art. 8.1.

Mesembryanthemum corniculatum Linnaeus, *Species Plantarum*, ed. 2, 1: 697. 1762.
"Habitat in Africa." RCN: 3703.
Lectotype (Hartmann in *Mitt. Inst. Allg. Bot. Hamburg* 22: 153. 1988): [icon] *"Mesembryanthemum foliis corniculatis longioribus"* in Dillenius, Hort. Eltham. 2: 262, t. 199, f. 253, 254. 1732.
Current name: ***Cephalophyllum corniculatum*** (L.) Schwantes (Aizoaceae).

Mesembryanthemum crassifolium Linnaeus, *Species Plantarum* 1: 484. 1753.
"Habitat in Africa." RCN: 3690.
Lectotype (Preston & Sell in *Watsonia* 17: 228, 230, f. 4. 1989): [icon] *"Mesembryanthemum crassifolium repens, flore purpureo"* in Dillenius, Hort. Eltham. 2: 266, t. 201, f. 257. 1732 (OXF).
Current name: ***Disphyma crassifolium*** (L.) L. Bolus (Aizoaceae).
Note: Preston & Sell reproduce the type illustration (as their f. 4).

Mesembryanthemum crystallinum Linnaeus, *Species Plantarum* 1: 480. 1753.
"Habitat in Africa?" RCN: 3669.

Lectotype (Hartmann & Bittrich in *Bothalia* 20: 156. 1990): [icon] *"Mesembryanthemum crystallinum, Plantaginis folio undulato"* in Dillenius, Hort. Eltham. 2: 231, t. 180, f. 221. 1732.
Current name: ***Mesembryanthemum crystallinum*** L. (Aizoaceae).

Mesembryanthemum deltoides Linnaeus, *Species Plantarum* 1: 482. 1753.
"Habitat in Africa." RCN: 3679.
Lectotype (Glen in *Bothalia* 16: 55. 1986): [icon] *"Mesembryanthemum deltoides, & dorso, & lateribus muricatis, minus"* in Dillenius, Hort. Eltham. 2: 255, t. 195, f. 246. 1732 (OXF). – Typotype: Herb. Dillenius (OXF).
Current name: ***Oscularia deltoides*** (L.) Schwantes (Aizoaceae).
Note: See Preston & Sell (in *Watsonia* 17: 227–229. 1989), who restrict Glen's lectotype choice to Dillenius' own, coloured copy of his book in OXF, and reproduce this figure (their f. 3).

Mesembryanthemum difforme Linnaeus, *Species Plantarum* 1: 487. 1753.
"Habitat in Aethiopia." RCN: 3710.
Lectotype (Hartmann & Gölling in *Bradleya* 11: 41. 1993): [icon] *"Mesembryanthemum foliis difformibus, flore luteo"* in Dillenius, Hort. Eltham. 2: 252, t. 194, f. 241, 242. 1732.
Current name: ***Glottiphyllum difforme*** (L.) N.E. Br. (Aizoaceae).

Mesembryanthemum dolabriforme Linnaeus, *Species Plantarum* 1: 487. 1753.
"Habitat in Africa." RCN: 3709.

Lectotype (Hartmann in *Bradleya* 16: 81. 1998): [icon] *"Mesembryanthemum folio dolabrae-formi"* in Dillenius, Hort. Eltham. 2: 248, t. 191, f. 237. 1732 (see below, left).
Current name: ***Rhombophyllum dolabriforme*** (L.) Schwantes (Aizoaceae).

Mesembryanthemum edule Linnaeus, *Systema Naturae*, ed. 10, 2: 1060. 1759.
["Habitat ad Cap. b. spei."] Sp. Pl., ed. 2, 1: 695 (1762). RCN: 3697.
Replaced synonym: *Mesembryanthemum acinaciforme* L. var. *flavum* L. (1753).
Lectotype (Blake in *Contr. Queensland Herb.* 7: 17. 1969): [icon] *"Mesembryanthemum falcatum majus, flore amplo luteo"* in Dillenius, Hort. Eltham. 2: 283, t. 212, f. 272. 1732.
Current name: ***Carpobrotus edulis*** (L.) N.E. Br. (Aizoaceae).
Note: See Preston & Sell (in *Watsonia* 17: 237–238, f. 7. 1989) and Jonkers (in *Brit. Cact. Succ. J.* 19: 182, f. 6. 2001), who both reproduce the type illustration.

Mesembryanthemum emarginatum Linnaeus, *Species Plantarum*, ed. 2, 1: 692. 1762.
"Habitat ad Cap. b. spei." RCN: 3684.
Lectotype (Liede & Meve in *Bradleya* 8: 39. 1990): [icon] *"Mesembr. purpureum scabrum, staminibus expansis"* in Dillenius, Hort. Eltham. 2: 259, t. 197, f. 250. 1732.
Current name: ***Lampranthus emarginatus*** (L.) N.E. Br. (Aizoaceae).

Mesembryanthemum expansum Linnaeus, *Systema Naturae*, ed. 10, 2: 1059. 1759.
["Habitat ad Cap. b. spei."] Sp. Pl., ed. 2, 1: 697 (1762). RCN: 3675.
Lectotype (designated here by Hartmann): [icon] *"Mesembryanthemum tortuosum, foliis Sempervivi expansis"* in Dillenius, Hort. Eltham. 2: 234, t. 182, f. 223. 1732.
Current name: ***Sceletium expansum*** (L.) L. Bolus (Aizoaceae).
Note: Gerbaulet (in Hartmann, *Ill. Handb. Succ. Pl., Aizoaceae F–Z*: 289. 2001) indicated material in K (ex Herb. Dillenius, OXF) as lectotype but this was not studied by Linnaeus and is not original material for the name.

Mesembryanthemum falcatum Linnaeus, *Species Plantarum* 1: 484. 1753.
"Habitat in Africa." RCN: 3694.
Lectotype (Hartmann, *Ill. Handb. Succ. Pl., Aizoaceae F–Z*: 86. 2001): [icon] *"Mesembryanthemum falcatum minimum, flore purpureo parvo"* in Dillenius, Hort. Eltham. 2: 288, t. 213, f. 276. 1732.
Current name: ***Lampranthus falcatus*** (L.) N.E. Br. (Aizoaceae).

Mesembryanthemum filamentosum Linnaeus, *Systema Naturae*, ed. 10, 2: 1060. 1759.
["Habitat ad Cap. b. Spei."] Sp. Pl., ed. 2, 1: 694 (1762). RCN: 3693.
Lectotype (designated here by Hartmann): [icon] *"Mesembryanthemum falcatum majus, flore purpureo mediocri"* in Dillenius, Hort. Eltham. 2: 285, t. 212, f. 273. 1732.
Current name: ***Ruschia filamentosa*** (L.) L. Bolus (Aizoaceae).

Mesembryanthemum forficatum Linnaeus, *Systema Naturae*, ed. 10, 2: 1060. 1759.
["Habitat ad Cap. b. Spei."] Sp. Pl., ed. 2, 1: 695 (1762). RCN: 3695.
Neotype (Liede in *Beitr. Biol. Pflanzen* 64: 467. 1990 [1989]): *Jacquin s.n.*, Herb. Linn. No. 649.5 (LINN).
Current name: ***Erepsia forficata*** (L.) Schwantes (Aizoaceae).
Note: See Bruyns (in *J. S. African Bot.* 63: 241. 1997) on confusion over the use of this name for a species of *Ruschia* (as *R. forficata* (L.) L. Bolus), and Hartmann (in *Bradleya* 16: 52–53. 1998) on its correct name.

Mesembryanthemum geniculiflorum Linnaeus, *Species Plantarum* 1: 481. 1753.
"Habitat ad Cap. b. Spei." RCN: 3671.
Lectotype (Gerbaulet in *Bot. Jahrb. Syst.* 119: 197. 1997): [icon] *"Mesembryanthemum Capense geniculiflorum, Neapolitanum creditum"* in Dillenius, Hort. Eltham. 2: 271, t. 205, f. 261. 1732.
Current name: ***Aptenia geniculiflora*** (L.) Gerbaulet (Aizoaceae).

Mesembryanthemum glaucum Linnaeus, *Species Plantarum* 1: 486. 1753.
"Habitat in Africa." RCN: 3702.
Lectotype (Hartmann, *Ill. Handb. Succ. Pl., Aizoaceae F–Z*: 88. 2001): [icon] *"Mesembryanthemum scabrum, flore sulphureo convexo"* in Dillenius, Hort. Eltham. 2: 256, t. 196, f. 248. 1732.
Current name: ***Lampranthus glaucus*** (L.) N.E. Br. (Aizoaceae).

Mesembryanthemum glomeratum Linnaeus, *Species Plantarum*, ed. 2, 1: 694. 1762.
"Habitat ad Cap. b. Spei." RCN: 3691.
Lectotype (Hartmann, *Ill. Handb. Succ. Pl., Aizoaceae F–Z*: 89. 2001): [icon] *"Mesembryanthemum falcatum minus, flore carneo minore"* in Dillenius, Hort. Eltham. 2: 287, t. 213, f. 274. 1732.
Current name: ***Lampranthus glomeratus*** (L.) N.E. Br. (Aizoaceae).

Mesembryanthemum hispidum Linnaeus, *Species Plantarum* 1: 482. 1753.
"Habitat ad Cap. b. Spei." RCN: 3681.
Lectotype (Hartmann & Bruckmann in *Bradleya* 18: 97. 2000): [icon] *"Mesembryanthemum pilosum micans, flore saturanter purpureo"* in Dillenius, Hort. Eltham. 2: 289, t. 214, f. 277. 1732.
Current name: ***Drosanthemum hispidum*** (L.) Schwantes (Aizoaceae).

Mesembryanthemum linguiforme Linnaeus, *Species Plantarum* 1: 488. 1753.
"Habitat in Africa." RCN: 3712.
Lectotype (Hartmann & Gölling in *Bradleya* 11: 42. 1993): [icon] *"Mesembryanthemum folio scalprato"* in Dillenius, Hort. Eltham. 2: 235, t. 183, f. 224. 1732.
Current name: ***Glottiphyllum linguiforme*** (L.) N.E. Br. (Aizoaceae).

Mesembryanthemum loreum Linnaeus, *Species Plantarum* 1: 486. 1753.
"Habitat in Africa." RCN: 3692.
Lectotype (Hartmann in *Mitt. Inst. Allg. Bot. Hamburg* 22: 153. 1988): [icon] *"Mesembryanthemum loreum"* in Dillenius, Hort. Eltham. 2: 264, t. 200, f. 255. 1732.
Current name: ***Cephalophyllum loreum*** (L.) Schwantes (Aizoaceae).

Mesembryanthemum micans Linnaeus, *Species Plantarum* 1: 485. 1753.
"Habitat ad Cap. b. Spei." RCN: 3701.
Lectotype (Hartmann & Bruckmann in *Bradleya* 18: 105. 2000): [icon] *"Mesembryanthemum micans, flore phoeniceo, filamentis atris"* in Dillenius, Hort. Eltham. 2: 292, t. 215, f. 282. 1732.
Current name: ***Drosanthemum micans*** (L.) Schwantes (Aizoaceae).
Note: Edmondson & Rowley (in *Bradleya* 16: 15, f. 2. 1998) reproduce the type illustration in colour.

Mesembryanthemum noctiflorum Linnaeus, *Species Plantarum* 1: 481. 1753.
"Habitat in Africa." RCN: 3672.
Lectotype (Gerbaulet in *Bot. Jahrb. Syst.* 118: 48. 1996): [icon] *"Mesembryanthemum noctiflorum, flore intus candido, extus phoeniceo odoratissimo"* in Dillenius, Hort. Eltham. 2: 273, t. 206, f. 262. 1732.
Current name: ***Aridaria noctiflora*** (L.) Schwantes (Aizoaceae).

Mesembryanthemum nodiflorum Linnaeus, *Species Plantarum* 1: 480. 1753, *typ. cons.*
"Habitat in Aegypto, Neapoli." RCN: 3672.
Lectotype (Burtt & Lewis in *Kew Bull.* 7: 351. 1952): *Hasselquist*, Herb. Linn. No. 649.1 (LINN).
Generitype of *Mesembryanthemum* Linnaeus, *nom. cons.*
Current name: ***Mesembryanthemum nodiflorum*** L. (Aizoaceae).

Mesembryanthemum pomeridianum Linnaeus, *Species Plantarum,* ed. 2, 1: 698. 1762.
"Habitat ad Cap. b. Spei." RCN: 3705.
Neotype (Ihlenfeldt & Gerbaulet in *Bot. Jahrb. Syst.* 111: 479. 1990): [icon] *"Mesembryanthemum pomeridianum"* in Linnaeus filius, Dec. Secunda Pl. Horti Upsal.: 25, t. 13. 1763.
Current name: ***Carpanthea pomeridiana*** (L.) N.E. Br. (Aizoaceae).
Note: As there seems to be no original material for the name, Ihlenfeldt & Gerbaulet's choice as lectotype of the plate published by Linnaeus filius is treated as correctable to neotype (Art. 9.8).

Mesembryanthemum pugioniforme Linnaeus, *Species Plantarum* 1: 488. 1753.
"Habitat ad Cap. b. Spei." RCN: 3713.
Lectotype (Ihlenfeldt & Gerbaulet in *Bot. Jahrb. Syst.* 111: 485. 1990): [icon] *"Mesembryanthemum pugioniforme, flore amplo stramineo"* in Dillenius, Hort. Eltham. 2: 280, t. 210, f. 269. 1732.
Current name: ***Conicosia pugioniformis*** (L.) N.E. Br. (Aizoaceae).

Mesembryanthemum ringens Linnaeus, *Species Plantarum* 1: 487. 1753.
"Habitat ad Cap. b. Spei." RCN: 3708.
Lectotype (Hartmann, *Ill. Handb. Succ. Pl., Aizoaceae A–E*: 102. 2001): [icon] *"Mesembryanthemum rictum caninum referens"* in Dillenius, Hort. Eltham. 2: 241, t. 188, f. 231. 1732.
Current name: ***Carruanthus ringens*** (L.) Boom (Aizoaceae).

Mesembryanthemum ringens Linnaeus var. **caninum** Linnaeus, *Species Plantarum* 1: 487. 1753.
RCN: 3708.
Lectotype (Hartmann, *Ill. Handb. Succ. Pl., Aizoaceae A–E*: 102. 2001): [icon] *"Mesembryanthemum rictum caninum referens"* in Dillenius, Hort. Eltham. 2: 241, t. 188, f. 231. 1732.
Current name: ***Carruanthus ringens*** (L.) Boom (Aizoaceae).
Note: This varietal epithet is associated with the typical part of the species (i.e. everything except var. *felinum* L. 1753) and, as such, is equivalent to the autonym with which it is therefore homotypic. See discussion by Boom (in *Succulenta* 11: 141–145. 1959) and Hartmann (*Ill. Handb. Succ. Pl., Aizoaceae A–E*: 102. 2002).

Mesembryanthemum ringens Linnaeus var. **felinum** Linnaeus, *Species Plantarum* 1: 487. 1753.
RCN: 3708.
Lectotype (Groen & van der Maesen in *Bothalia* 29: 39. 1999): [icon] *"Mesembryanthemum rictum felinum repraesentans"* in Dillenius, Hort. Eltham. 2: 240, t. 187, f. 230. 1732.
Current name: ***Faucaria felina*** (Weston) Schwantes ex H. Jacobsen (Aizoaceae).
Note: According to Ingram (in *Baileya* 17: 47–48. 1970), *M. felinum* Weston (1770) was published without reference to Linnaeus, preventing the recombination of Linnaeus' varietal epithet in *Mesembryanthemum*. He gives the correct name as *Faucaria felina* (Weston) Schwantes ex H. Jacobsen.

Mesembryanthemum rostratum Linnaeus, *Species Plantarum* 1: 486. 1753.
"Habitat in Africa." RCN: 3707.

Lectotype (Hartmann & Dehn in *Bot. Jahrb. Syst.* 108: 635. 1987): [icon] *"Mesembryanthemum rostrum Ardeae referens"* in Dillenius, Hort. Eltham. 2: 240, t. 186, f. 229. 1732.
Current name: ***Cheiridopsis rostrata*** (L.) N.E. Br. (Aizoaceae).

Mesembryanthemum scabrum Linnaeus, *Species Plantarum* 1: 483. 1753.
"Habitat in Africa." RCN: 3683.
Lectotype (Liede & Meve in *Bradleya* 8: 39, f. 2. 1990): [icon] *"Mesembryanthemum purpureum scabrum, staminibus collectis"* in Dillenius, Hort. Eltham. 2: 259, t. 197, f. 251. 1732.
Current name: ***Lampranthus scaber*** (L.) N.E. Br. (Aizoaceae).

Mesembryanthemum serratum Linnaeus, *Species Plantarum* 1: 485. 1753.
"Habitat in Africa." RCN: 3700.
Lectotype (Liede in *Beitr. Biol. Pflanzen* 64: 473. 1990 [1989]): [icon] *"Mesembryanthemum serratum, flore acetabuliformi luteo"* in Dillenius, Hort. Eltham. 2: 249, t. 192, f. 238. 1732.
Current name: ***Circandra serrata*** (L.) N.E. Br. (Aizoaceae).

Mesembryanthemum spinosum Linnaeus, *Species Plantarum* 1: 483. 1753.
"Habitat in Africa." RCN: 3700.
Lectotype (Hartmann & Stüber in *Contr. Bolus Herb.* 15: 66. 1993): [icon] *"Mesembryanthemum fruticescens, ramulis triacanthis"* in Dillenius, Hort. Eltham. 2: 276, t. 208, f. 265. 1732.
Current name: ***Ruschia spinosa*** (L.) Dehn (Aizoaceae).
Note: Edmondson & Rowley (in *Bradleya* 16: 15, f. 1. 1998) reproduce the type illustration in colour.

Mesembryanthemum splendens Linnaeus, *Species Plantarum* 1: 486. 1753.
"Habitat ad Cap. b. Spei." RCN: 3673.
Lectotype (designated here by Hartmann): [icon] *"Mesembryanthemum foliis confertis splendentibus, flore pallido"* in Dillenius, Hort. Eltham. 2: 270, t. 204, f. 260. 1732.
Current name: ***Phyllobolus splendens*** (L.) Gerbaulet subsp. ***splendens*** (Aizoaceae).
Note: Gerbaulet (in *Bot. Jahrb. Syst.* 119: 189. 1997) stated "Holotype: Hort. cliff. 220 (OXF; partly K!); Drawing: Dill, Hort. Eltham. 270 t. 204 f. 260", and (in Hartmann, *Ill. Handb. Succ. Pl., Aizoaceae F–Z*: 214. 2001) indicated as type "Hort. Cliff. 220 (OXF, isotype K!)". There does not appear to be any relevant Clifford material at either OXF or K. Any material connected with the *Hortus Elthamensis* account would not have been seen by Linnaeus and so will not be original material for the name.

Mesembryanthemum stipulaceum Linnaeus, *Species Plantarum* 1: 484. 1753.
"Habitat in Africa." RCN: 3689.
Lectotype (Liede in *Beitr. Biol. Pflanzen* 64: 473. 1990 [1989]): [icon] *"Mesembryanthemum frutescens, flore purpureo rariore"* in Dillenius, Hort. Eltham. 2: 279, t. 209, f. 267, 268. 1732.
Current name: ***Lampranthus stipulaceum*** (L.) N.E. Br. (Aizoaceae).

Mesembryanthemum tenuifolium Linnaeus, *Species Plantarum* 1: 484. 1753.
"Habitat in Africa." RCN: 3688.
Lectotype (designated here by Hartmann): Herb. Clifford: 220, *Mesembryanthemum* 26 (BM).
Current name: ***Lampranthus tenuifolius*** (L.) N.E. Br. (Aizoaceae).
Note: Wijnands (*Bot. Commelins*: 149. 1983) noted the presence of a Clifford specimen and indicated the Dillenius element as a

paratype. Hartmann (*Ill. Handb. Succ. Pl., Aizoaceae F–Z*: 105. 2001) states that Wijnands regarded his statement as a formal typification but the meaning of his wording is most unclear. Hartmann therefore makes a formal typification here.

Mesembryanthemum tortuosum Linnaeus, *Species Plantarum* 1: 487. 1753.
"Habitat ad Cap. b. Spei." RCN: 3704.
Lectotype (Gerbaulet in *Bot. Jahrb. Syst.* 118: 20. 1996): [icon] *"Mesembryanthemum tortuosum, foliis Sempervivi congestis"* in Dillenius, Hort. Eltham. 2: 233, t. 181, f. 222. 1732.
Current name: ***Sceletium tortuosum*** (L.) N.E. Br. (Aizoaceae).

Mesembryanthemum tripolium Linnaeus, *Species Plantarum* 1: 481. 1753.
"Habitat in Africa." RCN: 3676.
Lectotype (designated here by Hartmann): [icon] *"Mesembryanthemum Tripolii folio, flore argenteo"* in Dillenius, Hort. Eltham. 2: 230, t. 179, f. 220. 1732.
Current name: ***Skiatophytum tripolium*** (L.) L. Bolus (Aizoaceae).

Mesembryanthemum tuberosum Linnaeus, *Species Plantarum* 1: 484. 1753.
"Habitat in Africa." RCN: 3687.
Lectotype (Glen in *Bothalia* 13: 454. 1981): [icon] *"Mesembryanthemum fruticescens, radice ingenti tuberosa"* in Dillenius, Hort. Eltham. 2: 275, t. 207, f. 264. 1732.
Current name: ***Mestoklema tuberosa*** (L.) N.E. Br. ex Glen (Aizoaceae).

Mesembryanthemum umbellatum Linnaeus, *Species Plantarum* 1: 481. 1753.
"Habitat ad Caput b. Spei." RCN: 3674.
Lectotype (Hartmann in *Bradleya* 17: 70. 1999): [icon] *"Mesembryanthemum frutescens, floribus albis umbellatis"* in Dillenius, Hort. Eltham. 2: 277, t. 208, f. 266. 1732.
Current name: ***Ruschia umbellata*** (L.) Schwantes (Aizoaceae).
Note: Edmondson & Rowley (in *Bradleya* 16: 15, f. 1. 1998) reproduce the type illustration in colour.

Mesembryanthemum uncinatum Linnaeus, *Species Plantarum* 1: 483. 1753.
"Habitat in Africa." RCN: 3685.
Lectotype (Hartmann in *Bradleya* 17: 70. 1999): [icon] *"Mesembryanthemum perfoliatum, foliis minoribus diacanthis"* in Dillenius, Hort. Eltham. 2: 250, t. 193, f. 239. 1732.
Current name: ***Ruschia uncinata*** (L.) Schwantes (Aizoaceae).
Note: As Friedrich (in *Mitt. Bot. Staatssamml. München* 4: 132. 1961) expressed doubt as to whether the Dillenius plate was the type, Hartmann is accepted as the typifier.

Mesembryanthemum verruculatum Linnaeus, *Species Plantarum* 1: 486. 1753.
"Habitat in Africa." RCN: 3706.
Lectotype (Klak in *Bothalia* 30: 39. 2000): [icon] *"Mesembrianthemum foliis veruculiformibus, floribus melinis umbellatis"* in Dillenius, Hort. Eltham. 2: 268, t. 203, f. 259. 1732.
Current name: ***Scopelogena verruculata*** (L.) L. Bolus (Aizoaceae).

Mesembryanthemum villosum Linnaeus, *Species Plantarum* 1: 483. 1753.
"Habitat in Africa." RCN: 3682.
Type not designated.
Original material: none traced.
Current name: ***Mesembryanthemum villosum*** L. (Aizoaceae).

Note: Gerbaulet (in Hartmann, *Ill. Handb. Succ. Pl., Aizoaceae F–Z*: 167. 2001) suggests this may be a species of *Aizoon*, and it shows the greatest similarity with *A. karooicum* Compton. The Linnaean name does not appear to be in use and there is no original material extant.

Mespilus amelanchier Linnaeus, *Species Plantarum* 1: 478. 1753.
"Habitat in Helvetia, Austria, Galloprovincia." RCN: 3656.
Lectotype (Favarger & Stearn in *Bot. J. Linn. Soc.* 87: 97, f. 4. 1983): Herb. Linn. No. 646.11 (LINN).
Current name: ***Amelanchier ovalis*** Medik. (Rosaceae).

Mespilus arbutifolia Linnaeus, *Species Plantarum* 1: 478. 1753.
"Habitat in Virginia." RCN: 3655.
Lectotype (Phipps in Cafferty & Jarvis in *Taxon* 51: 542. 2002): Herb. Linn. No. 646.8 (LINN).
Current name: ***Aronia arbutifolia*** (L.) Pers. (Rosaceae).

Mespilus canadensis Linnaeus, *Species Plantarum* 1: 478. 1753.
"Habitat in Virginia, Canada." RCN: 3658.
Lectotype (Fernald in *Rhodora* 43: 560, pl. 672, f. 1. 1941): *Kalm*, Herb. Linn. No. 646.19 (LINN).
Current name: ***Amelanchier canadensis*** (L.) Medik. (Rosaceae).

Mespilus chamaemespilus Linnaeus, *Species Plantarum* 1: 479. 1753.
"Habitat in Alpibus Austriacis, Pyrenaicis." RCN: 3657.
Lectotype (Aldasoro & al. in *Syst. Bot. Monogr.* 69: 118. 2004): Herb. Burser XXIII: 74 (UPS).
Current name: ***Sorbus chamaemespilus*** (L.) Crantz (Rosaceae).
Note: Specific epithet spelled "Chamae Mespilus" in the protologue.

Mespilus cotoneaster Linnaeus, *Species Plantarum* 1: 479. 1753, *nom. cons.*
"Habitat in Europae frigidioris collibus apricis inque Pyrenaeis, Ararat." RCN: 3659.
Conserved type (Thulin & Ryman in *Taxon* 52: 371. 2003): Sweden. Uppland, Norby lund, at the Linnaean path, 15 Jul 2002, *S. Ryman 9126* (UPS).
Current name: ***Cotoneaster integerrimus*** Medik. (Rosaceae).
Note: Hylmö (in *Svensk Bot. Tidskr.* 87: 327. 1993) designated Herb. Clifford: 189, *Mespilus* 5 (BM) as lectotype, a collection that he identified as belonging to a mainly central European taxon that he regarded as not conspecific with the apomictic Scandinavian taxon to which the name had long been applied. Hylmö described the Scandinavian species as *C. scandinavicus* Hylmö. Thulin & Ryman (in *Taxon* 52: 371. 2003) successfully proposed *M. cotoneaster* for conservation with a conserved type, in order to allow *C. integerrimus* Medik. to continue in use for the Scandinavian taxon whether a narrow or broad species concept is adopted.

Mespilus germanica Linnaeus, *Species Plantarum* 1: 478. 1753.
"Habitat in Europa australi." RCN: 3653.
Lectotype (Phipps in Jarvis & al., *Regnum Veg.* 127: 66. 1993): Herb. Linn. No. 646.1 ["696.1"] (LINN).
Generitype of *Mespilus* Linnaeus (vide Green, *Prop. Brit. Bot.*: 158. 1929).
Current name: ***Mespilus germanica*** L. (Rosaceae).
Note: Phipps' type statement erroneously cited "Herb. Linn. No. 696.1" (a member of the Winteraceae), a typographical error for "Herb. Linn. No. 646.1" (clearly annotated as *Mespilus germanica* by Linnaeus).

Mespilus pyracantha Linnaeus, *Species Plantarum* 1: 478. 1753.
"Habitat in Galloprovinciae, Italiae sepibus." RCN: 3654.
Lectotype (Muñoz Garmendia & Aedo in *Taxon* 47: 171. 1998): Herb. Burser XXIV: 8 (UPS).

M

Current name: ***Pyracantha coccinea*** M. Roem. (Rosaceae).
Note: Muñoz Garmendia & Aedo typified the name in a proposal to conserve *P. coccinea* M. Roem., which is a *nomen novum* based on this Linnaean name.

Messersmidia argusia Linnaeus, *Systema Naturae*, ed. 12, 2: 149; *Mantissa Plantarum*: 42. 1767, *nom. illeg.*
"Habitat in Dauniae [sic] apricis, glareosis, aridis. H. U." RCN: 1131.
Replaced synonym: *Tournefortia sibirica* L. (1753).
Lectotype (Majorov in Cafferty & Jarvis in *Taxon* 53: 804. 2004): *Gerber*, Herb. Linn. No. 192.1 (LINN).
Current name: ***Argusia sibirica*** (L.) Dandy (Boraginaceae).
Note: An illegitimate name in *Messersmidia* for *Tournefortia sibirica* L. (1753).

Messersmidia sibirica (Linnaeus) Linnaeus, *Mantissa Plantarum Altera*: 334. 1771.
["Habitat in Dauriae apricis glareosis aridis."] Sp. Pl. 1: 141 (1753). RCN: 1131.
Basionym: *Tournefortia sibirica* L. (1753).
Lectotype (Majorov in Cafferty & Jarvis in *Taxon* 53: 804. 2004): *Gerber*, Herb. Linn. No. 192.1 (LINN).
Current name: ***Argusia sibirica*** (L.) Dandy (Boraginaceae).

Mesua ferrea Linnaeus, *Species Plantarum* 1: 515. 1753.
"Habitat in India." RCN: 5112.
Lectotype (Maheshwari in *Bull. Bot. Surv. India* 5: 337. 1963): Herb. Hermann 1: 38, No. 203 (BM-000594469).
Generitype of *Mesua* Linnaeus.
Current name: ***Mesua ferrea*** L. (Clusiaceae).
Note: Kostermans (in Dassanayake & Fosberg, *Revised Handb. Fl. Ceylon* 1: 106. 1980) identified the lectotype as material of *M. thwaitesii* Planchon & Triana. However, Stevens (in *Taxon* 35: 353. 1986) refutes this identification.

Michelia champaca Linnaeus, *Species Plantarum* 1: 536. 1753.
"Habitat in India." RCN: 3985.
Lectotype (Nooteboom in *Blumea* 31: 113. 1985): Herb. Hermann 3: 55, No. 144 (BM-000628007).
Generitype of *Michelia* Linnaeus.
Current name: ***Michelia champaca*** L. (Magnoliaceae).

Michelia tsiampacca Linnaeus, *Systema Naturae*, ed. 12, 2: 374; *Mantissa Plantarum*: 78. 1767.
"Habitat in India." RCN: 3986.
Lectotype (Nooteboom in *Blumea* 31: 103. 1985): [icon] *"Sampacca silvestris"* in Rumphius, Herb. Amboin. 2: 202, t. 68. 1741.
Current name: ***Elmerrillia tsiampacca*** (L.) Dandy (Magnoliaceae).

Microcos lateriflora Linnaeus, *Species Plantarum* 1: 514. 1753.
"Habitat in Zeylona." RCN: 6980.
Replaced synonym of: *Grewia asiatica* L. (1767), *nom. illeg.*
Type not designated.
Original material: Herb. Hermann 1: 8, No. 208 (BM).
Current name: ***Grewia asiatica*** L. (Tiliaceae).
Note: Although *Grewia asiatica* L. (1767) appears to be an illegitimate renaming of *Microcos lateriflora* L., the former is evidently in use.

Microcos paniculata Linnaeus, *Species Plantarum* 1: 514. 1753.
"Habitat in India." RCN: 6981.
Replaced synonym of: *Grewia microcos* L. (1767), *nom. illeg.*
Lectotype (Panigrahi in *Taxon* 34: 703. 1985): Herb. Hermann 1: 59, No. 207 (BM-000621430).
Generitype of *Microcos* Linnaeus (vide Green, *Prop. Brit. Bot.*: 161. 1929).

Current name: ***Microcos paniculata*** L. (Tiliaceae).
Note: If treated as a species of *Grewia*, the correct name is *G. nervosa* (Lour.) Panigrahi.

Micropus erectus Linnaeus, *Species Plantarum* 2: Addenda. 1753.
"Habitat in Hispania." RCN: 6712.
Lectotype (López González in *Anales Jard. Bot. Madrid* 55: 480. 1997): *Löfling 652a*, Herb. Linn. No. 1042.2 (LINN).
Current name: ***Bombycilaena erecta*** (L.) Smoljan. (Asteraceae).
Note: It appears that Linnaeus had a mixture of two taxa. 1042.2 (LINN) and Löfling's description refer to *Bombycilaena discolor* (Pers.) Laínz, while the published illustration in Löfling's *Iter* (not an original element) is *B. erecta*. Usage has followed the plate. See López González (in *Anales Jard. Bot. Madrid* 55: 480. 1997), who also typified the name in this contrary sense. Löfling's sheet is the lectotype, making *B. erecta* the correct name for what has been called *B. discolor*.

Micropus supinus Linnaeus, *Species Plantarum* 2: 927. 1753.
"Habitat in Lusitaniae maritimis." RCN: 6711.
Lectotype (Wagenitz in Rechinger, *Fl. Iranica* 145: 10. 1980): Herb. Linn. No. 1042.1 (LINN).
Generitype of *Micropus* Linnaeus.
Current name: ***Micropus supinus*** L. (Asteraceae).

Milium capense Linnaeus, *Mantissa Plantarum Altera*: 185. 1771.
"Habitat ad Cap. b. spei." RCN: 520.
Type not designated.
Original material: none traced.
Current name: ***Achnatherum capense*** (L.) P. Beauv. (Poaceae).

Milium cimicinum Linnaeus, *Mantissa Plantarum Altera*: 184. 1771.
"Habitat in Malabariae et oppidi Johannis plateis. Koenig. 55." RCN: 523.
Neotype (Clayton & Renvoize in Polhill, *Fl. Trop. E. Africa, Gramineae* 3: 617. 1982): Herb. Linn. No. 83.2 (LINN).
Current name: ***Alloteropsis cimicina*** (L.) Stapf (Poaceae).

Milium confertum Linnaeus, *Species Plantarum* 1: 61. 1753.
"Habitat in Helvetiae sylvis." RCN: 525.
Lectotype (Cope in Cafferty & al. in *Taxon* 49: 252. 2000): *Löfling s.n.*, Herb. Linn. No. 83.4 (LINN).
Current name: ***Piptatherum miliaceum*** (L.) Coss. (Poaceae).

Milium effusum Linnaeus, *Species Plantarum* 1: 61. 1753.
"Habitat in Europae nemoribus umbrosis." RCN: 524.
Lectotype (Cope in Jarvis & al., *Regnum Veg.* 127: 66. 1993): Herb. Linn. No. 83.3 (LINN).
Generitype of *Milium* Linnaeus (vide Hitchcock, *Prop. Brit. Bot.*: 119. 1929).
Current name: ***Milium effusum*** L. (Poaceae).
Note: Although Kerguélen (in *Lejeunia*, n.s., 75: 212. 1975) stated "type: ...LINN", this is not accepted as a valid typification under Art. 7.11 (see justification by Cafferty & al. in *Taxon* 49: 240. 2000).

Milium lendigerum Linnaeus, *Species Plantarum*, ed. 2, 1: 91. 1762.
"Habitat in Monspelii. Gouan." RCN: 522.
Lectotype (Scholz in Cafferty & al. in *Taxon* 49: 252. 2000): [icon] *"Arista tortili aliquantisper recurva, prodeunte ex ipso alterutrius glumae apice, folliculo brevissimo parvo"* in Scheuchzer, Agrostographia: 148, t. 3, f. 11 C. 1719. – Epitype (Scholz in Cafferty & al. in *Taxon* 49: 252. 2000): France. Champs des argiles oxfordiennes à Bougon près de La Mothe-Saint-Héray (Deux-Sèvres), 30 Jul 1853, *Sauzé & Maillard s.n.* [C. Billot, Fl. Gall. Germ. Exsicc. No. 1363] (B).

Current name: **Gastridium ventricosum** (Gouan) Schinz & Thell. (Poaceae).

Note: Although Linnaeus (*Sp. Pl.*, ed. 2, 2: 1676. 1763) subsequently placed *Agrostis ventricosa* Gouan (1762) in the synonymy of *M. lendigerum*, Gouan's name was published in April 1762 and consequently has priority over *M. lendigerum* (published on 20 Sep 1762).

Milium paradoxum (Linnaeus) Linnaeus, *Systema Naturae*, ed. 10, 2: 872. 1759.
["Habitat in Galloprovincia, G. Narbonensis."] Sp. Pl. 1: 62 (1753). RCN: 526.
Basionym: *Agrostis paradoxa* L. (1753).
Lectotype (Freitag in Cafferty & al. in *Taxon* 49: 243. 2000): [icon] *"Gram. paniculat. Gallo-provinciale Aquilegiae semine"* in Plukenet, Phytographia: t. 32, f. 2. 1691; Almag. Bot.: 174. 1696. – Voucher: Herb. Sloane 96: 70 (BM-SL).
Current name: **Oryzopsis paradoxa** (L.) Nutt. (Poaceae).

Milium punctatum Linnaeus, *Systema Naturae*, ed. 10, 2: 872. 1759.
["Habitat in Jamaica."] Sp. Pl., ed. 2, 1: 91 (1753). RCN: 521.
Lectotype (Hitchcock in *Contr. U. S. Natl. Herb.* 12: 119. 1908): *Browne*, Herb. Linn. No. 83.1 (LINN).
Current name: **Eriochloa punctata** (L.) Ham. (Poaceae).

Millepora coriacea Linnaeus, *Systema Naturae*, ed. 12, 1(2): 1285. 1767, *nom. illeg.*
Replaced synonym: *Millepora agaraciformis* Pall. (1766).
Type not designated.
Current name: **Mesophyllum lichenoides** (J. Ellis) M. Lemoine (Corallinaceae).
Note: A superfluous name for *Millepora agaraciformis* Pall. (1766).

Millepora polymorpha Linnaeus, *Systema Naturae*, ed. 12, 1(2): 1285. 1767, *nom. illeg.*
Replaced synonym: *Millepora calcarea* Pall. (1766).
Lectotype (Irvine in Spencer & al. in *Taxon*, in press): [icon] *"Corallium pumilum album, fere lapideum, ramosum"* in Ellis, Nat. Hist. Corallin.: 76, t. 27, f. C. 1755. – Epitype (Woelkerling & Irvine in Spencer & al. in *Taxon*, in press): United Kingdom. Cornwall, St Mawes Bank, 11 Dec 1983, BM Box 1626 (BM-000562555).
Current name: **Phymatolithon calcareum** (Pall.) W.H. Adey & D.L. McKibbin (Corallinaceae).
Note: A superfluous name for *M. calcarea* Pall. (1766). Woelkerling & Irvine (in *Brit. Phycol. J.* 21: 58. 1986) designated a neotype for the Pallas (and hence the Linnaean) name, but as Pallas cited numerous illustrations (which are original material), their choice is contrary to Art. 9.11.

Milleria biflora Linnaeus, *Species Plantarum* 2: 919. 1753.
"Habitat in Campechia." RCN: 6644.
Lectotype (Stearn, *Introd. Linnaeus' Sp. Pl.* (Ray Soc. ed.): 47. 1957): [icon] *"Milleria foliis ovatis, pedunculis simplicibus"* in Linnaeus, Hort. Cliff.: 425, t. 25. 1738.
Current name: **Delilia biflora** (L.) Kuntze (Asteraceae).

Milleria quinqueflora Linnaeus, *Species Plantarum* 2: 919. 1753.
"Habitat in Panama, Vera Cruce." RCN: 6643.
Lectotype (Stuessy in Jarvis & Turland in *Taxon* 47: 364. 1998): [icon] *"Milleria annua, erecta, foliis conjugatis, floribus spicatis luteis"* in Martyn, Hist. Pl. Rar.: 41, t. 41. 1728.
Generitype of *Milleria* Linnaeus (vide Lessing, *Syn. Comp.*: 215. 1832).
Current name: **Milleria quinqueflora** L. (Asteraceae).

Note: Stuessy (in *Ann. Missouri Bot. Gard.* 62: 1061. 1975) indicated sheet 1031.1 (LINN) as type, but as it lacks a *Species Plantarum* number and was a later addition to the herbarium, it is not original material for the name. See notes on the possible provenance of early material by Turner & Triplett (in *Phytologia* 81: 351. 1996).

Mimosa arborea Linnaeus, *Species Plantarum* 1: 519. 1753.
"Habitat in Jamaicae & Caribaearum humidis." RCN: 7671.
Lectotype (Barneby & Grimes in *Mem. New York Bot. Gard.* 74(2): 43. 1997): [icon] *"Acacia arborea maxima non spinosa, pinnis majoribus, flore albo, siliqua contorta coccinea ventriosa elegantissima"* in Sloane, Voy. Jamaica 2: 54, t. 182, f. 1, 2. 1725. – Typotype: Herb. Sloane 6: 41 (BM-SL).
Current name: **Cojoba arborea** (L.) Britton & Rose (Fabaceae: Mimosoideae).
Note: Fawcett & Rendle (*Fl. Jamaica* 4: 148. 1920) indicated unspecified material in BM as type, but it is unclear whether Plukenet or Sloane material may have been intended, though neither would be original material for the name.

Mimosa asperata Linnaeus, *Systema Naturae*, ed. 10, 2: 1312. 1759.
["Habitat in Jamaica, Vera cruce."] Sp. Pl., ed. 2, 2: 1507 (1763). RCN: 7687.
Lectotype (Brenan in Hubbard & Milne-Redhead, *Fl. Trop. E. Africa, Leguminosae* 1: 43. 1959): Herb. Linn. No. 1228.32 (LINN).
Current name: **Mimosa pigra** L. (Fabaceae: Mimosoideae).
Note: Brenan treated 1228.32 (LINN) as the holotype, and was followed in this by authors such as Wijnands (*Bot. Commelins*: 151. 1983) and Howard (*Fl. Lesser Antilles* 4: 368. 1988). With this typification, Brenan treated *M. asperata* as a synonym of *M. pigra* L. (1755). However, Barneby (in Tan, *Davis & Hedge Festschr.*: 140. 1989) rejected Brenan's choice in favour of Miller's t. 182, f. 3 (1760), wrongly believing the material to post-date the protologue. There appears to be no evidence for this. The Miller plate is identifiable as *M. berlandieri* A. Gray which, if accepted as the type, would result in *M. asperata* being the earliest name for this taxon, and it is in this sense that Barneby uses *M. asperata*, as does Bässler (in *Feddes Repert.* 96: 599. 1985). There appear to be no grounds for rejecting Brenan's earlier choice of type. However, in a further complication, Barneby (in *Mem. New York Bot. Gard.* 65: 437. 1991) argues that Brenan's type is identifiable as *M. pellita* Humb. & Bonpl., rather than *M. pigra sensu stricto*. While it seems clear that the type of *M. asperata* must be 1228.32 (LINN), differences of opinion over its identity mean that *M. asperata* may be treated either as a synonym of *M. pigra*, or as the correct name for what has been known as *M. pellita*. This is particularly unfortunate because Barneby uses *M. asperata* in a different sense, that of *M. berlandieri*.

Mimosa bigemina Linnaeus, *Species Plantarum* 1: 517. 1753.
"Habitat in India." RCN: 7653.
Lectotype (Kostermans in Dassanayake & Fosberg, *Revised Handb. Fl. Ceylon* 1: 507. 1980): Herb. Hermann 2: 55, No. 218 (BM-000621689).
Current name: **Archidendron bigeminum** (L.) I.C. Nielsen (Fabaceae: Mimosoideae).

Mimosa caesia Linnaeus, *Species Plantarum* 1: 522. 1753.
"Habitat in India." RCN: 7688.
Lectotype (Kostermans in Dassanayake & Fosberg, *Revised Handb. Fl. Ceylon* 1: 481. 1980; Rico in Turland & Jarvis in *Taxon* 46: 475. 1997): Herb. Hermann 2: 50, No. 217 (BM-000594612).
Current name: **Acacia caesia** (L.) Willd. (Fabaceae: Mimosoideae).
Note: Kostermans indicated Hermann material in BM as the type, this choice subsequently being restricted by Rico to one of the four specimens involved.

M

Mimosa casta Linnaeus, *Species Plantarum* 1: 518. 1753.
"Habitat in India." RCN: 7662.
Lectotype (Wijnands, *Bot. Commelins*: 151. 1983): Herb. Clifford:
208, *Mimosa* 2 (BM-000628750).
Current name: ***Mimosa casta*** L. (Fabaceae: Mimosoideae).

Mimosa ceratonia Linnaeus, *Species Plantarum* 1: 523. 1753.
"Habitat in America calidiore." RCN: 7694.
Lectotype (Howard, *Fl. Lesser Antilles* 4: 367. 1988): [icon] *"Mimosa
aculeata, foliis bipinnatis, propriis trijugis"* in Plumier in Burman, Pl.
Amer.: 4, t. 8. 1755.
Current name: ***Mimosa ceratonia*** L. (Fabaceae: Mimosoideae).

Mimosa cineraria Linnaeus, *Systema Naturae,* ed. 10, 2: 1311. 1759.
["Habitat in India."] Sp. Pl., ed. 2, 2: 1500 (1763). RCN: 7661.
Replaced synonym: *Mimosa cinerea* L. (1753: 517, No. 10, non 1753:
520, No. 25).
Lectotype (Rico in Turland & Jarvis in *Taxon* 46: 476. 1997): [icon]
*"Acacia Maderaspat. spinosa Intsiae accedens, cortice cinereo, ramulis
communi pediculo binis"* in Plukenet, Phytographia: t. 2, f. 1. 1691;
Almag. Bot.: 4. 1696. – Epitype (Rico in Turland & Jarvis in *Taxon*
46: 476. 1997): India. Jottian, April 1806, *Wallich 5299a* (K; iso-
BM).
Current name: ***Prosopis cineraria*** (L.) Druce (Fabaceae:
Mimosoideae).
Note: Linnaeus simultaneously published both *Mimosa cinerea* L.
(1753: 517, No. 10) and *M. cinerea* L. (1753: 520, No. 25).
Realising his mistake, he renamed the former as *M. cineraria* L.
(1759) and retained *M. cinerea* for the latter (see Art. 53.6 Ex. 19).
Although the correct name for *M. cinerea* No. 10 in *Prosopis* is *P.
cinerea* (L.) Druce, rather than *P. cineraria* (L.) Druce (Art. 53.6, Ex.
21), the use of *P. cineraria* is widespread, and Ali (in *Taxon* 53: 206.
2004) successfully proposed the rejection of *M. cinerea* (1753: 517,
No. 10) to regularise this usage.

Mimosa cinerea Linnaeus, *Species Plantarum* 1: 517. 1753, *nom.
utique rej.*
"Habitat in India." RCN: 7661.
Replaced synonym of: *Mimosa cineraria* L. (1759).
Lectotype (Rico in Turland & Jarvis in *Taxon* 46: 476. 1997): [icon]
*"Acacia Maderaspat. spinosa Intsiae accedens, cortice cinereo, ramulis
communi pediculo binis"* in Plukenet, Phytographia: t. 2, f. 1. 1691;
Almag. Bot.: 4. 1696. – Epitype (Rico in Turland & Jarvis in *Taxon*
46: 476. 1997): India. Jottian, April 1806, *Wallich 5299a* (K; iso-
BM).
Current name: ***Prosopis cineraria*** (L.) Druce (Fabaceae:
Mimosoideae).
Note: See notes under *Mimosa cineraria.*

Mimosa cinerea Linnaeus, *Species Plantarum* 1: 520. 1753.
"Habitat in India." RCN: 7679.
Lectotype (Ali in Nasir & Ali, *Fl. W. Pakistan* 36: 37. 1973): Herb.
Hermann 2: 44, No. 215 (BM-000621661).
Current name: ***Dichrostachys cinerea*** (L.) Wight & Arn. (Fabaceae:
Mimosoideae).
Note: Linnaeus simultaneously published both *Mimosa cinerea* L.
(1753: 517, No. 10) and *M. cinerea* L. (1753: 520, No. 25).
Realising his mistake, he renamed the former as *M. cineraria* L.
(1759) and retained *M. cinerea* for the latter (see Art. 53.6 Ex. 18).

Mimosa circinalis Linnaeus, *Species Plantarum* 1: 517. 1753.
"Habitat in America calidiore." RCN: 7660.
Lectotype (Barneby & Grimes in *Mem. New York Bot. Gard.* 74(2): 10.
1997): [icon] *"Mimosa spinis ad alas geminis, foliis bipinnatis"* in
Plumier in Burman, Pl. Amer.: 3, t. 5. 1755.

Current name: ***Pithecellobium circinale*** (L.) Benth. (Fabaceae:
Mimosoideae).
Note: Barneby & Grimes (May 1997) indicate the original Aubriet
tracing (rather than the plate published by Burman) as the type but,
confusingly, say it is in Leiden (rather than Groningen). Rico (in
Taxon 46: 476. August 1997) independently came to broadly the
same conclusion, designating the Burman reproduction of the plate
as lectotype. The published image is accepted as the type, but with
the choice attributed to Barneby & Grimes.

Mimosa cornigera Linnaeus, *Species Plantarum* 1: 520. 1753.
"Habitat in Mexico, Cuba." RCN: 7680.
Lectotype (Rudd in *Madroño* 17: 199. 1964): Herb. Clifford: 208,
Mimosa 4 (BM-000628753; iso- US).
Current name: ***Acacia cornigera*** (L.) Willd. (Fabaceae: Mimosoideae).
Note: Janzen (in *Smithsonian Contr. Bot.* 13: 26. 1974) reports a
fragment of the type at US.

Mimosa entada Linnaeus, *Species Plantarum* 1: 518. 1753.
"Habitat in utraque India." RCN: 7666.
Lectotype (Kostermans in Dassanayake & Fosberg, *Revised Handb. Fl.
Ceylon* 1: 464. 1980): [icon] *"Entada"* in Rheede, Hort. Malab. 9:
151, t. 77. 1689.
Current name: ***Entada rheedei*** Spreng. (Fabaceae: Mimosoideae).

Mimosa fagifolia Linnaeus, *Species Plantarum* 1: 516. 1753.
"Habitat in Barbados." RCN: 7651.

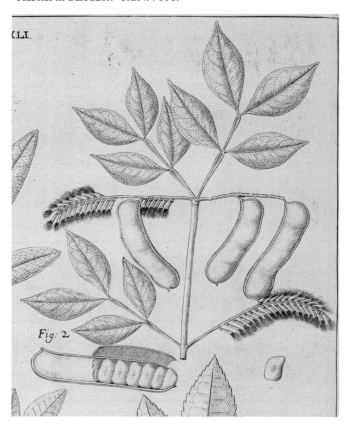

Lectotype (Bässler in *Gleditschia* 20: 4. 1992): [icon] *"Arbor siliquifera
Faginis fol. Americ. fl. comosis"* in Plukenet, Phytographia: t. 141, f.
2. 1692; Almag. Bot.: 44. 1696. – Voucher: Herb. Sloane 95: 96
(BM-SL).
Current name: ***Inga laurina*** (Sw.) Willd. (Fabaceae: Mimosoideae).

Note: Inga fagifolia (L.) Willd. ex Benth., based on *M. fagifolia* L., had been widely used for a Latin American taxon not including its type. Howard (*Fl. Lesser Antilles* 4: 360. 1988) wrongly treated Plukenet material (BM), unseen by Linnaeus, as the type but identified the Plukenet element as *I. laurina* (Sw.) Willd. Bässler (1992) formally typified the name using the Plukenet plate. The existence of *I. fagifolia* G. Don (1832), see Pennington (*Genus Inga*: 371. 1997), prevents the transfer of *M. fagifolia* to *Inga*, meaning that *I. laurina* (Sw.) Willd. is the correct name.

Mimosa farnesiana Linnaeus, *Species Plantarum* 1: 521. 1753.
"Habitat in Domingo." RCN: 7683.
Lectotype (Ross in *Bothalia* 11: 465, 471. 1975): [icon] *"Acaciae indicae folia, flores, et siliquae"* in Aldini, Exact. Descr. Pl. Romae Hort. Farn.: 3, 4. 1625.
Current name: ***Acacia farnesiana*** (L.) Willd. (Fabaceae: Mimosoideae).
Note: The lectotype figure has been much reproduced and can be seen in Ross (in *Bothalia* 11: 472, f. 1. 1975; *l.c.* 13: 102, f. 9. 1980), Bernardi (in *Boissiera* 35: 135. 1984) and Jarvis (in *Museol. Sci.* 9: 156. 1993).

Mimosa gigas Linnaeus, *Flora Jamaicensis*: 22. 1759.
"Habitat [in Jamaica.]"
Neotype (Panigrahi in *Taxon* 34: 714. 1985): Herb. Linn. No. 1228.11 (LINN).
Current name: ***Entada gigas*** (L.) Fawc. & Rendle (Fabaceae: Mimosoideae).
Note: Various authors (e.g. Johnston in *Sargentia* 8: 136. 1949; Brenan in Hubbard & Milne-Redhead, *Fl. Trop. E. Africa, Leguminosae* 1: 11. 1959) have treated either untraced Patrick Browne material, or his published description (*Civ. Nat. Hist. Jamaica*: 362. 1758), as the type. However, Panigrahi (1985) treated what is clearly 1228.11 (LINN), material cultivated in the Botanic Garden in Uppsala, as the type. As *M. gigas* is validated solely by reference to Browne's work, the name should be typified from the context of that publication (Art. 7.7). However, as no relevant Browne material has been traced, and there is no illustration in his book, Panigrahi's choice is accepted as a neotypification (Art. 9.8).

Mimosa glauca Linnaeus, *Species Plantarum* 1: 520. 1753.
"Habitat in America." RCN: 7678.
Lectotype (de Wit in *Taxon* 10: 54. 1961): Herb. A. van Royen No. 908.132–54 (L).
Current name: ***Acacia glauca*** (L.) Moench (Fabaceae: Mimosoideae).

Mimosa horrida Linnaeus, *Species Plantarum* 1: 521. 1753.
"Habitat in India." RCN: 7681.
Lectotype (Hillcoat & Brenan in *Kew Bull.* 13: 39. 1958): [icon] *"Acacia Maderaspatana foliolis parvis, aculeis e regione binis praegrandibus horrida, cortice cinereo"* in Plukenet, Phytographia: t. 121, f. 4. 1692; Almag. Bot.: 3. 1696. – Typotype: Herb. Sloane 95: 3 (BM-SL).
Current name: ***Acacia horrida*** (L.) Willd. (Fabaceae: Mimosoideae).

Mimosa inga Linnaeus, *Species Plantarum* 1: 516. 1753.
"Habitat in Brasilia, Jamaica, Surinamo." RCN: 7650.
Lectotype (Bässler in *Gleditschia* 20: 12, Abb. 4. 1992): [icon] *"Arbor siliquosa brasiliensis, foliis pinnatis, costa media membranulis utrinque extantibus alata"* in Sloane, Voy. Jamaica 2: 58, t. 183, f. 1. 1725. – Typotype: Herb. Sloane 6: 51 (BM-SL).
Current name: ***Inga vera*** Willd. (Fabaceae: Mimosoideae).
Note: Although León (in *Ann. Missouri Bot. Gard.* 53: 335, 337. 1966) discussed the Sloane plate and material, no formal typification was published. Hoc (in *Darwiniana* 30: 241. 1991 [1990]) indicated

Plumier, Nov. Pl. Genera: 13, t. 19. 1703. as "tipo" for *Inga* Mill., with *M. inga* and *I. vera* Willd. as heterotypic synonyms. However, Plumier's plate is not cited in the protologue of *M. inga*, so this statement cannot be interpreted as a typification for this name.

Mimosa intsia Linnaeus, *Species Plantarum* 1: 522. 1753.
"Habitat in India." RCN: 7690.
Lectotype (Rico in Turland & Jarvis in *Taxon* 46: 476. 1997): [icon] *"Intsia"* in Rheede, Hort. Malab. 6: 7, t. 4. 1686.
Current name: ***Acacia intsia*** (L.) Willd. (Fabaceae: Mimosoideae).
Note: Ali (in *Taxon* 16: 237. 1967) indicated a specimen in Herb. Sloane 95: 5 (BM-SL) as the lectotype, when in fact only the corresponding illustration by Plukenet (*Phytographia* t. 122, f. 2. 1692), cited in the protologue, is eligible as such. In fact, this material does not support current usage, and for this reason, Rico designated a Rheede illustration as lectotype.

Mimosa latifolia Linnaeus, *Systema Naturae,* ed. 10, 2: 1310. 1759.
["Habitat in America."] Sp. Pl., ed. 2, 2: 1499 (1763). RCN: 7656.
Lectotype (Howard, *Fl. Lesser Antilles* 4: 376. 1988): [icon] *"Mimosa inermis, foliis conjugatis"* in Plumier in Burman, Pl. Amer.: 5, t. 9. 1755.
Current name: ***Zygia latifolia*** (L.) Fawc. & Rendle (Fabaceae: Mimosoideae).

Mimosa latisiliqua Linnaeus, *Species Plantarum* 1: 519. 1753.
"Habitat in America calidiore." RCN: 7674.
Lectotype (de Wit in *Taxon* 10: 52. 1961): [icon] *"Mimosa inermis, foliis bipinnatis, partialibus quinque jugis"* in Plumier in Burman, Pl. Amer.: 3, t. 6. 1755.
Current name: ***Lysiloma latisiliquum*** (L.) Benth. (Fabaceae: Mimosoideae).
Note: De Wit's 1961 typification, using a Plumier illustration published by Burman in 1755, was rejected by Gillis & Stearn (in *Taxon* 23: 185–191. 1974) in favour of Herb. Linn. 1228.19 (LINN). However, de Wit (in *Taxon* 24: 349, f. 1, 2. 1975) pointed out that this material conflicts with Linnaeus' diagnosis and could not have been the basis of the name. Polhill & Stearn (in *Taxon* 25: 323–325. 1976) re-examined the question and concluded that de Wit's objections were well founded, and that the Plumier element should indeed be the type. However, they treated Aubriet's tracing (at Groningen) of Plumier's original drawing as the type (rather than Burman's published version, which was derived from the tracing).

Mimosa lebbeck Linnaeus, *Species Plantarum* 1: 516. 1753.
"Habitat in Aegypto superiore." RCN: 7672.
Lectotype (Codd in *Bothalia* 7: 81. 1958): Herb. Linn. No. 1228.16 (LINN).
Current name: ***Albizia lebbeck*** (L.) Benth. (Fabaceae: Mimosoideae).
Note: Fawcett & Rendle (*Fl. Jamaica* 4: 145. 1920) indicated unspecified material in BM as "type", but there appears to be no original material for the name preserved there. Codd's is the first explicit type choice.

Mimosa muricata Linnaeus, *Systema Naturae,* ed. 10, 2: 1311. 1759.
["Habitat in America."] Sp. Pl., ed. 2, 2: 1504. 1763. RCN: 7676.
Lectotype (Howard, *Fl. Lesser Antilles* 4: 341. 1988): [icon] *"Mimosa inermis, foliis bipinnatis, partialibus quinque jugis"* in Plumier in Burman, Pl. Amer.: 6, t. 11. 1755.
Current name: ***Acacia muricata*** (L.) Willd. (Fabaceae: Mimosoideae).

M

Mimosa nilotica Linnaeus, *Species Plantarum* 1: 521. 1753.
"Habitat in Aegypto, unde semina per D. Hasselquist." RCN: 7684.
Lectotype (Fawcett & Rendle, *Fl. Jamaica* 4: 140. 1920): *Hasselquist*, Herb. Linn. No. 1228.28 (LINN; iso- 214.7 S).
Current name: ***Acacia nilotica*** (L.) Delile (Fabaceae: Mimosoideae).

Mimosa nodosa Linnaeus, *Species Plantarum* 1: 516. 1753.
"Habitat in Zeylona." RCN: 7652.
Lectotype (Irwin & Barneby in *Mem. New York Bot. Gard.* 35: 113. 1982): [icon] *"Phaseolus arboreus tetraphyllos Zeylanicus"* in Plukenet, Phytographia: t. 211, f. 5. 1692; Almag. Bot.: 294. 1696.
Current name: ***Senna bacillaris*** (L. f.) H.S. Irwin & Barneby (Fabaceae: Caesalpinioideae).

Mimosa pennata Linnaeus, *Species Plantarum* 1: 522. 1753.
"Habitat in Zeylona." RCN: 7689.
Lectotype (Brenan & Exell in *Bol. Soc. Brot.*, sér. 2, 31: 101. 1957; Nielsen in Leroy, *Fl. Cambodge Laos Viêt-Nam* 19: 66. 1981): Herb. Hermann 3: 7, No. 216 (BM-000594649).
Current name: ***Acacia pennata*** (L.) Willd. (Fabaceae: Mimosoideae).
Note: Brenan & Exell (in *Bol. Soc. Brot.*, sér. 2, 31: 101. 1957) treated Hermann material from Ceylon (BM) as the type, but did not distinguish between the specimens in vol. 3: 7 and vol. 4: 37. However, as this material appears to be part of a single gathering, Brenan & Exell are accepted as having typified the name (Art. 9.15), with their original choice restricted to the material in vol. 3 by Nielsen in 1981. Ross (in *Bothalia* 13: 108, f. 17. 1980) reproduces the Burman plate cited by Linnaeus in the protologue.

Mimosa peregrina Linnaeus, *Species Plantarum* 1: 520. 1753.
"Habitat in America." RCN: 7677.
Neotype (Rico in Turland & Jarvis in *Taxon* 46: 476. 1997): Guyana. 1839, *Schomburgk 866* [sheet No. 1] (BM; iso- BM).
Current name: ***Anadenanthera peregrina*** (L.) Speg. (Fabaceae: Mimosoideae).
Note: There may once have been a specimen in the Clifford herbarium (BM), but no relevant material can be traced. Such a sheet was indicated as the lectotype by Reis Altschul (in *Contr. Gray Herb.* 193: 46. 1964), who noted its apparent absence in 1957, and by Howard (*Fl. Lesser Antilles* 4: 348. 1988) as "Hort. Cliff. 109" (in error for p. 209). In the absence of any original material, Rico designated a neotype.

Mimosa pernambucana Linnaeus, *Species Plantarum* 1: 519. 1753.
"Habitat in America." RCN: 7670.
Lectotype (Luckow in *Syst. Bot. Monogr.* 38: 113. 1993): [icon] *"Mimosa Americana pigra siliquis longis angustis allium olentibus"* in Plukenet, Phytographia: t. 307, f. 3. 1694; Almag. Bot.: 252. 1696. – Typotype: Herb. Sloane 96: 196 (BM-SL).
Current name: ***Desmanthus pernambucanus*** (L.) Thell. (Fabaceae: Mimosoideae).

Mimosa pigra Linnaeus, *Centuria I Plantarum*: 13. 1755, *nom. cons.*
"Habitat – – –" RCN: 7686.
Conserved type (Verdcourt in *Taxon* 38: 522. 1989): Mozambique. Gaza District, between Chibuto and Canicado by R. Limpopo, *Barbosa & Lemos 7999* (K; iso- COI, LISC, LMJ).
Current name: ***Mimosa pigra*** L. (Fabaceae: Mimosoideae).
Note: Brenan (in Hubbard & Milne-Redhead, *Fl. Trop. E. Africa, Leguminosae* 1: 43. 1953) chose a Commelin plate as lectotype, Barneby (in Tan, *Davis & Hedge Festschr.*: 139. 1989) later restricting this to the leaves, which he identified as of *M. vellosiella* Herter. To avoid the consequent changes, Verdcourt (in *Taxon* 38: 522. 1989) successfully proposed the name for conservation with a

conserved type. Cowan (in *Nuytsia* 11: 17. 1996), however, criticised both Verdcourt's "weedy" choice of type and the conservation of the name.

Mimosa plena Linnaeus, *Species Plantarum* 1: 519. 1753.
"Habitat in Vera Cruce." RCN: 7667.
Lectotype (Kostermans in Dassanayake & Fosberg, *Revised Handb. Fl. Ceylon* 1: 462. 1980): Herb. Linn. No. 1228.12 (LINN).
Current name: ***Neptunia plena*** (L.) Benth. (Fabaceae: Mimosoideae).
Note: Fawcett & Rendle (*Fl. Jamaica* 4: 131. 1920) noted the existence of what is evidently 1228.12 (LINN) but did not indicate it as the type. Although Kostermans did not cite the sheet number, 1228.12 is the only material associated with this name and his statement is therefore accepted as a formal typification.

Mimosa polystachya Linnaeus, *Species Plantarum* 1: 520. 1753.
"Habitat in America calidiore." RCN: 7675.
Lectotype (Howard, *Fl. Lesser Antilles* 4: 356. 1988): [icon] *"Mimosa inermis, foliis bipinnatis, partialibus quatuor jugis"* in Plumier in Burman, Pl. Amer.: 7, t. 12. 1755.
Current name: ***Entada polystachya*** (L.) DC. (Fabaceae: Mimosoideae).

Mimosa pudica Linnaeus, *Species Plantarum* 1: 518. 1753.
"Habitat in Brasilia." RCN: 7664.
Lectotype (Brenan in *Kew Bull.* 10: 185. 1955): Herb. Clifford: 208, *Mimosa* 3, excl. inflorescences (BM-000628752).
Generitype of *Mimosa* Linnaeus (vide Green, *Prop. Brit. Bot.*: 162. 1929).
Current name: ***Mimosa pudica*** L. (Fabaceae: Mimosoideae).
Note: Mimosa sensitiva was treated as the generitype by Britton & Wilson (*Scient. Surv. Porto Rico* 5: 357. 1924; see McNeill & al. in *Taxon* 36: 378. 1987). However, under Art. 10.5, Ex. 7 (a voted example) of the Vienna Code, this is a type choice made under the American Code and is to be replaced under Art. 10.5b by Green's choice (*Prop. Brit. Bot.*: 162. 1929) of *M. pudica* L. Barneby (in *Mem. New York Bot. Gard.* 65: 624. 1991) notes that the type is not identifiable below species level.

Mimosa punctata Linnaeus, *Systema Naturae,* ed. 10, 2: 1311. 1759.
["Habitat in America."] Sp. Pl., ed. 2, 2: 1502 (1763). RCN: 7668.
Lectotype (Wijnands, *Bot. Commelins*: 152. 1983): *Browne*, Herb. Linn. No. 1228.14 (LINN).
Current name: ***Neptunia plena*** (L.) Benth. (Fabaceae: Mimosoideae).
Note: Fawcett & Rendle (*Fl. Jamaica* 4: 131. 1920) noted the existence of what is evidently 1228.14 (LINN) but did not indicate it as the type.

Mimosa purpurea Linnaeus, *Species Plantarum* 1: 517. 1753.
"Habitat in America meridionali." RCN: 7657.
Lectotype (Howard, *Fl. Lesser Antilles* 4: 350. 1988): [icon] *"Mimosa foliis conjugatis, pinnatis"* in Plumier in Burman, Pl. Amer.: 5, t. 10, f. 2. 1755.
Current name: ***Calliandra purpurea*** (L.) Benth. (Fabaceae: Mimosoideae).

Mimosa quadrivalvis Linnaeus, *Species Plantarum* 1: 522. 1753.
"Habitat in Vera Cruce." RCN: 7692.
Lectotype (Barneby in *Mem. New York Bot. Gard.* 65: 295. 1991): [icon] *"Mimosa herbacea procumbens & spinosa caule anguloso, siliquis quadrivalvibus"* in Houstounia Gen. Pl. Amer.: t. 21. 1736 (LINN).
Current name: ***Mimosa quadrivalvis*** L. var. ***quadrivalvis*** (Fabaceae: Mimosoideae).

Mimosa reticulata Linnaeus, *Systema Naturae,* ed. 12, 2: 676; *Mantissa Plantarum*: 129. 1767.

"Habitat ad Cap. b. spei." RCN: 7658.

Type not designated.

Original material: [icon] in Plukenet, Phytographia: t. 123, f. 2. 1692; Almag. Bot.: 3. 1696.

Current name: ***Acacia karroo*** Hayne (Fabaceae: Mimosoideae).

Note: Most recent authors, including Verdoorn (in *Bothalia* 6: 411, f. 2. 1954) and Ross (*l.c.* 10: 386. 1971; 11: 446. 1975), have informally rejected the name, *Acacia karroo* Hayne being taken up in its place. However, no formal rejection proposal has been made.

Mimosa scandens Linnaeus, *Species Plantarum,* ed. 2, 2: 1501. 1763, *nom. illeg.*

"Habitat in Indiis." RCN: 7665.

Lectotype (Panigrahi in *Taxon* 34: 714. 1985): [icon] *"Faba marina"* in Rumphius, Herb. Amboin. 5: 5, t. 4. 1747.

Current name: ***Entada phaseoloides*** (L.) Merr. (Fabaceae: Mimosoideae).

Note: The Rumphius plate cited as a synonym of this name is also the lectotype of *Lens phaseoloides* L. (1754), and *M. scandens* is therefore illegitimate (Art. 52.2); see Smith (*Fl. Vitiensis Nova* 3: 59. 1985) and Panigrahi (in *Taxon* 34: 714. 1985) on this question.

Mimosa scorpioides Linnaeus, *Species Plantarum* 1: 521. 1753.

"Habitat in Aegypto, Arabia." RCN: 7684.

Lectotype (Thulin in Turland & Jarvis in *Taxon* 46: 476. 1997): Herb. Burser XXII: 16 (UPS).

Current name: ***Acacia nilotica*** (L.) Delile (Fabaceae: Mimosoideae).

Note: Ross (in *Bothalia* 11: 446, f. 3. 1975) reproduces the Plukenet plate cited as a synonym by Linnaeus.

Mimosa semispinosa Linnaeus, *Species Plantarum* 1: 522. 1753.

"Habitat in America." RCN: 7691.

Type not designated.

Original material: Herb. Clifford: 208, *Mimosa* 6 (BM).

Current name: ***Acacia macracantha*** Humb. & Bonpl. ex Willd. (Fabaceae: Mimosoideae).

Note: The application of this name is uncertain. Barneby (in *Mem. New York. Bot. Gard.* 65: 777. 1991) treated it as a *species incertae sedis* and did not trace a type. He noted that if the name proved to apply to a true *Mimosa*, the armature and leaf-formula would fit *M. distachya* var. *oligacantha* (DC.) Barneby. A Clifford collection (BM), only rather doubtfully associated with the name, is not a *Mimosa*, but close to *Acacia macracantha* Humb. & Bonpl. ex Willd., a very large and widely distributed complex in the neotropics (Rico, pers. comm.). *Mimosa semispinosa* appears to be a candidate for rejection.

Mimosa senegal Linnaeus, *Species Plantarum* 1: 521. 1753.

"Habitat in Arabia." RCN: 7685.

Neotype (Ross in *Bothalia* 11: 451, f. 1. 1975): Herb. Adanson, No. 16899 (P).

Current name: ***Acacia senegal*** (L.) Willd. (Fabaceae: Mimosoideae).

Note: Ross (in *Bothalia* 11: 451, f. 1. 1975) argued convincingly that Linnaeus, who mentioned both Bernard de Jussieu and Michel Adanson in the protologue, was sent material that had been collected by Adanson, by Jussieu. Comparing the *Hort. Cliff.* (1738) account of the species with that in 1753, it is evident that something changed Linnaeus' concept of the species and this was almost certainly the receipt of the Adanson material. The specimen he received appears no longer to exist, but a corresponding specimen in Paris is almost certainly a duplicate. It is not eligible as

a lectotype, and Ross' treatment of it as a neotype is regarded as correct. The other original elements are identifiable as *Acacia nilotica* (L.) Del. (Rico, pers. comm.).

Mimosa sensitiva Linnaeus, *Species Plantarum* 1: 518. 1753.

"Habitat in Brasilia." RCN: 7663.

Lectotype (Barneby in *Mem. New York Bot. Gard.* 65: 538. 1991): [icon] *"Mimosa spinosa prima, s. Brasiliana latifolia siliquis radiatis"* in Breyn, Exot. Pl. Cent.: 31, t. 16. 1678.

Current name: ***Mimosa sensitiva*** L. var. ***sensitiva*** (Fabaceae: Mimosoideae).

Note: Mimosa sensitiva was treated as the generitype by Britton & Wilson (*Scient. Surv. Porto Rico* 5: 357. 1924; see McNeill & al. in *Taxon* 36: 378. 1987). However, under Art. 10.5, Ex. 7 (a voted example) of the Vienna Code, this is a type choice made under the American Code and is to be replaced under Art. 10.5b by Green's choice (*Prop. Brit. Bot.*: 162. 1929) of *M. pudica* L.

Mimosa tamarindifolia Linnaeus, *Species Plantarum* 1: 523. 1753.

"Habitat in America meridionali." RCN: 7695.

Lectotype (Howard, *Fl. Lesser Antilles* 4: 344. 1988): [icon] *"Mimosa aculeata, foliis bipinnatis, partialibus quinque jugatis"* in Plumier in Burman, Pl. Amer.: 4, t. 7. 1755.

Current name: ***Acacia tamarindifolia*** (L.) Willd. (Fabaceae: Mimosoideae).

Mimosa tenuifolia Linnaeus, *Species Plantarum* 1: 523. 1753.

"Habitat in America calidiore." RCN: 7693.

Type not designated.

Original material: none traced.

Current name: ***Acacia tenuifolia*** (L.) Willd. (Fabaceae: Mimosoideae).

Note: There appear to be no extant original elements, although Linnaeus provided a short description, and referred to a Plumier polynomial. Grimes (in *Brittonia* 44: 266–267. 1992) discussed the typification of the name, concluding that it was based on the Plumier element, but he refrained from typifying it. Linnaeus placed the name in the synonymy of *M. pennata* L. in *Sp. Pl.*, ed. 2, 2: 1507 (1763).

Mimosa tergemina Linnaeus, *Species Plantarum* 1: 517. 1753.

"Habitat in America meridionali." RCN: 7655.

Lectotype (Howard, *Fl. Lesser Antilles* 4: 352. 1988): [icon] *"Mimosa foliis tergeminis"* in Plumier in Burman, Pl. Amer.: 6, t. 10, f. 1. 1755.

Current name: ***Calliandra tergemina*** (L.) Benth. (Fabaceae: Mimosoideae).

Mimosa tortuosa Linnaeus, *Systema Naturae,* ed. 10, 2: 1312. 1759.

["Habitat in Jamaica."] Sp. Pl., ed. 2, 2: 1505 (1763). RCN: 7682.

Lectotype (Fawcett & Rendle, *Fl. Jamaica* 4: 138. 1920): *Browne,* Herb. Linn. No. 1228.27 (LINN).

Current name: ***Acacia tortuosa*** (L.) Willd. (Fabaceae: Mimosoideae).

Mimosa unguis-cati Linnaeus, *Species Plantarum* 1: 517. 1753.

"Habitat in Jamaica, Caribaeis." RCN: 7654.

Lectotype (Rico in Turland & Jarvis in *Taxon* 46: 476. 1997): [icon] *"Acaciae quodammodo accedens, s. Ceratiae & Acaciae media Jamaicensis spinosa bigeminatis foliis, flosculis stamin. atronitente fructu, siliquis parum intortis"* in Plukenet, Phytographia: t. 1, f. 6. 1691; Almag. Bot.: 4, 95. 1696.

Current name: ***Pithecellobium unguis-cati*** (L.) Mart. (Fabaceae: Mimosoideae).

Note: Although Isely (in *Madroño* 21: 287. 1972) noted the existence of material in LINN, he did not designate a type.

M

Mimosa vaga Linnaeus, *Species Plantarum* 1: 519. 1753.
"Habitat in India." RCN: 7673.
Lectotype (Rico in Turland & Jarvis in *Taxon* 46: 476. 1997): [icon] *"Acacia non spinosa Ind. Or. Coluteae foliis, floribus stamineis amplis, siliqua crustacea gemella Placentae in modum colorata"* in Plukenet, Almag. Mant.: 2, t. 331, f. 1. 1700. – Voucher: Herb. Sloane 94: 139 (BM-SL).
Current name: ***Albizia lebbeck*** (L.) Benth. (Fabaceae: Mimosoideae).

Mimosa virgata Linnaeus, *Species Plantarum* 1: 519. 1753.
"Habitat in India." RCN: 7669.
Lectotype (Fawcett & Rendle, *Fl. Jamaica* 4: 132. 1920): Herb. Linn. No. 1228.13 (LINN).
Current name: ***Desmanthus virgatus*** (L.) Willd. (Fabaceae: Mimosoideae).
Note: See comments on the type by Luckow (in *Syst. Bot. Monogr.* 38: 139. 1993).

Mimosa viva Linnaeus, *Species Plantarum* 1: 517. 1753.
"Habitat in Jamaicae pratis." RCN: 7659.
Lectotype (Barneby in *Mem. New York Bot. Gard.* 65: 772. 1991): [icon] *"Mimosa herbacea non spinosa minima, repens"* in Sloane, Voy. Jamaica 2: 58, t. 182, f. 7. 1725. – Typotype: Herb. Sloane 6: 49, right specimen (BM-SL).
Current name: ***Mimosa viva*** L. (Fabaceae: Mimosoideae).
Note: Fawcett & Rendle (*Fl. Jamaica* 4: 133. 1920) treated the corresponding material in Herb. Sloane (6: 49, BM) as the type, but this was not seen by Linnaeus and is not itself original material for the name.

Mimosa zygia Linnaeus, *Flora Jamaicensis*: 22. 1759.
"Habitat [in Jamaica.]"
Lectotype (Rico in Turland & Jarvis in *Taxon* 46: 476. 1997): [icon] *"Zygia arborescens, foliis ovatis paucioribus jugatis, floribus spicillatis"* in Browne, Civ. Nat. Hist. Jamaica: 279, t. 22, f. 3. 1756.
Current name: ***Zygia latifolia*** (L.) Fawc. & Rendle (Fabaceae: Mimosoideae).

Mimulus luteus Linnaeus, *Species Plantarum*, ed. 2, 2: 884. 1763.
"Habitat in Peru." RCN: 4605.
Type not designated.
Original material: [icon] in Feuillée, J. Obs. 2: 745, t.34. 1714.
Current name: ***Mimulus luteus*** L. (Scrophulariaceae).

Mimulus ringens Linnaeus, *Species Plantarum* 2: 634. 1753.
"Habitat in Virginia, Canada." RCN: 4604.
Lectotype (Pennell in *Monogr. Acad. Nat. Sci. Philadelphia* 1: 123. 1935): Herb. Linn. No. 803.1 (LINN).
Generitype of *Mimulus* Linnaeus.
Current name: ***Mimulus ringens*** L. (Scrophulariaceae).

Mimusops elengi Linnaeus, *Species Plantarum* 1: 349. 1753.
["Habitat in India."] Sp. Pl., ed. 2, 1: 497. 1762. RCN: 2675.
Lectotype (Pennington in Jarvis & al., *Regnum Veg.* 127: 67. 1993): Herb. Hermann 3: 23, No. 138 (BM-000621879).
Generitype of *Mimusops* Linnaeus (vide Hitchcock, *Prop. Brit. Bot.*: 149. 1929).
Current name: ***Mimusops elengi*** L. (Sapotaceae).
Note: Friedmann (in Bosser & al., *Fl. Mascareignes* 116: 23. 1981) indicated material in LINN (presumably sheet 492.1) as the holotype, but this material was a later addition to the herbarium and not original material for the name.

Mimusops kauki Linnaeus, *Species Plantarum* 1: 349. 1753.
"Habitat in Zeylona." RCN: 2676.

Lectotype (Trimen, *Handb. Fl. Ceylon* 3: 87. 1895): Herb. Hermann 1: 35, No. 137 (BM-000594466).
Current name: ***Manilkara kauki*** (L.) Dubard (Sapotaceae).

Minuartia campestris Loefling ex Linnaeus, *Species Plantarum* 1: 89. 1753.
"Habitat in Hispaniae collibus planis." RCN: 750.
Neotype (López González in Cafferty & Jarvis in *Taxon* 53: 1052. 2004): Herb. Linn. No. 113.5 (LINN).
Current name: ***Minuartia campestris*** Loefl. ex L. (Caryophyllaceae).
Note: López González (in *Anales Jard. Bot. Madrid* 60: 429–434 (2003 [2002]) provides an extremely detailed account of Löfling's materials and descriptions involved in the treatment of *Minuartia* and *Queria* by Linnaeus.

Minuartia dichotoma Loefling ex Linnaeus, *Species Plantarum* 1: 89. 1753.
"Habitat in Hispania." RCN: 749.
Lectotype (López González in Cafferty & Jarvis in *Taxon* 53: 1052. 2004): Herb. Linn. No. 113.1 (LINN).
Generitype of *Minuartia* Linnaeus.
Current name: ***Minuartia dichotoma*** Loefl. ex L. (Caryophyllaceae).
Note: López González (in *Anales Jard. Bot. Madrid* 60: 429–434 (2003 [2002]) provides an extremely detailed account of Löfling's materials and descriptions involved in the treatment of *Minuartia* and *Queria* by Linnaeus.

Minuartia montana Loefling ex Linnaeus, *Species Plantarum* 1: 90. 1753.
"Habitat in Hispaniae collibus altis." RCN: 751.
Lectotype (Ghafoor in Jafri & El-Gadi, *Fl. Libya* 59: 54. 1978): Herb. Linn. No. 113.9 (LINN).
Current name: ***Minuartia montana*** Loefl. ex L. (Caryophyllaceae).
Note: Although McNeill (in *Notes Roy. Bot. Gard. Edinburgh* 24: 359. 1963) indicated type specimens in LINN, he did not distinguish between sheets 113.4, 113.5 and 113.9, which are evidently not part of a single gathering and so Art. 9.15 does not apply. López González (in *Anales Jard. Bot. Madrid* 60: 429–434 (2003 [2002]) provides an extremely detailed account of Löfling's materials and descriptions involved in the treatment of *Minuartia* and *Queria* by Linnaeus.

Mirabilis dichotoma Linnaeus, *Systema Naturae*, ed. 10, 2: 931. 1759, *nom. illeg.*
["Habitat in Mexico."] Sp. Pl., ed. 2, 2: 252 (1762). RCN: 1399.
Replaced synonym: *Mirabilis odorata* L. (1755).
Lectotype (Le Duc in *Sida* 16: 640. 1995): Herb. Linn. No. 240.1 (LINN).
Current name: ***Mirabilis jalapa*** L. (Nyctaginaceae).
Note: A superfluous name for *M. odorata* L. (1755).

Mirabilis jalapa Linnaeus, *Species Plantarum* 1: 177. 1753.
"Habitat in India utraque." RCN: 1400.
Lectotype (Larsen in Morat, *Fl. Cambodge Laos Viêtnam* 24: 108. 1989): Herb. Linn. No. 240.2 (LINN).
Generitype of *Mirabilis* Linnaeus.
Current name: ***Mirabilis jalapa*** L. (Nyctaginaceae).
Note: Kellogg (in Howard, *Fl. Lesser Antilles* 4: 181. 1988) indicated unseen material in the Clifford herbarium (BM) as "type". However, as there are two sheets associated with this name, which are not part of a single gathering, this is not an effective choice and Art. 9.15 does not apply. Although Le Duc (in Jarvis & al., *Regnum Veg.* 127: 67. 1993) accepted a single Clifford sheet (BM) as lectotype, Larsen had, in the meantime, designated a sheet in LINN as type and this appears to be the earliest explicit choice.

Mirabilis longiflora Linnaeus, *Centuria I Plantarum*: 7, 34. 1755. ["Habitat – – – [in Mexicae frigidis montibus. Monnier."] Sp. Pl., ed. 2, 1: 252 (1762). RCN: 1401.
Type not designated.
Original material: Herb. Linn. No. 240.3 (LINN); [icon] in Hernandez, Rer. Med. Nov. Hisp.: 170. 1651.
Current name: ***Mirabilis longiflora*** L. var. ***longiflora*** (Nyctaginaceae).
Note: On the assumption that this name was first published in *Kongl. Svenska Vetensk. Acad. Handl.* 16: 176, t. 6, f. 1. 1755), Le Duc (in *Sida* 16: 628. 1995) designated as type the figure published there. However, this article by Linnaeus (for the period Jul–Aug–Sep) appears to be pre-dated by an account of the species in *Centuria I Plantarum* (Feb 1755), from which this figure is absent, and cannot therefore be original material for the name.

Mirabilis odorata Linnaeus, *Centuria I Plantarum*: 7, 34. 1755. ["Habitat in America."] Amoen. Acad. 4: 267 (1759). RCN: 1399.
Replaced synonym of: *Mirabilis dichotoma* L. (1759), *nom. illeg.*
Lectotype (Le Duc in *Sida* 16: 640. 1995): Herb. Linn. No. 240.1 (LINN).
Current name: ***Mirabilis jalapa*** L. (Nyctaginaceae).

Mirabilis planta Linnaeus, *Herbarium Amboinense*: 25. 1754, *nom. inval.*
Type not relevant.

Mitchella repens Linnaeus, *Species Plantarum* 1: 111. 1753. "Habitat in Carolina, Terra Mariana, Virginia." RCN: 905.
Lectotype (Reveal & al. in *Huntia* 7: 215. 1987): Herb. Linn. No. 135.1 (LINN).
Generitype of *Mitchella* Linnaeus.
Current name: ***Mitchella repens*** L. (Rubiaceae).

Mitella diphylla Linnaeus, *Species Plantarum* 1: 406. 1753. "Habitat in America septentrionali." RCN: 3179.
Lectotype (Reveal in Jarvis & al., *Regnum Veg.* 127: 67. 1993): Herb. Clifford: 167, *Mitella* 1 (BM-000628480).
Generitype of *Mitella* Linnaeus (vide Hitchcock, *Prop. Brit. Bot.*: 154. 1929).
Current name: ***Mitella diphylla*** L. (Saxifragaceae).

Mitella nuda Linnaeus, *Species Plantarum* 1: 406. 1753. "Habitat in Asia boreali." RCN: 3180.
Type not designated.
Original material: *Amman s.n.*, Herb. Linn. No. 577.2 (LINN).
Current name: ***Mitella nuda*** L. (Saxifragaceae).

Mnium fissum Linnaeus, *Species Plantarum* 2: 1114. 1753, *nom. cons.* "Habitat in Europae riguis." RCN: 8025.
Conserved type (Stotler & Crotz in *Taxon* 39: 290. 1990): [icon] *"Jungermannia terrestris, repens, foliis ex rotunditate acuminatis, bifidis, apertura pene visibili"* in Micheli, Nov. Pl. Gen.: 8, t. 5, f. 14. 1729.
Generitype of *Mnium* Linnaeus, *nom. rej.* (vide Proskauer in *Taxon* 12: 200. 1963).
Current name: ***Calypogeia fissa*** (L.) Raddi (Calypogeiaceae).
Note: Mnium Linnaeus, *nom. rej.* against *Mnium* Hedw., *nom. cons.*

Mnium jungermannia Linnaeus, *Species Plantarum* 2: 1114. 1753. "Habitat in Europae subhumidis." RCN: 8026.
Lectotype (Grolle & al. in *Taxon* 54: 507. 2005): [icon] *"Lichenastrum Alpinum purpureum, foliis auritis & cochleariformibus"* in Dillenius, Hist. Musc.: 479, t. 69, f. 1 H. 1741. – Epitype (Grolle & al. in

Taxon 54: 507, f. 1C. 2005): "1 *Lichenastrum alpinum purpureum, foliis auritis & cochleariformibis* Var. G", Herb. Dillenius (OXF).
Current name: ***Scapania undulata*** (L.) Dumort. (Scapaniaceae).

Mnium serpyllifolium Linnaeus, *Species Plantarum* 2: 1113. 1753. "Habitat in Europa fere ubique." RCN: 8022.
Type not designated.
Original material: none traced.
Note: Although the name does include at least one liverwort element (see Isoviita in *Acta. Bot. Fenn.* 89: 8. 1970), it seems likely that the name applies to a member of the Musci, in which case it would be a pre-Starting Point name, and of no nomenclatural significance.

Mnium setaceum Linnaeus, *Species Plantarum*, ed. 2, 2: 1575. 1763. "Habitat in Europae muris, aggeribus, sepibus." RCN: 8014.
Type not designated.
Original material: [icon] in Dillenius, Hist. Musc.: 381, t. 48, f. 44. 1741.
Note: The application of this name is uncertain, but it seems likely that it applies to a member of the Musci, in which case it would be a pre-Starting Point name, and of no nomenclatural significance.

Mnium trichomanis Linnaeus, *Species Plantarum* 2: 1114. 1753, *nom. utique rej.*
"Habitat in Sueciae, Angliae udis." RCN: 8024.
Lectotype (Isoviita in *Acta Bot. Fenn.* 89: 15. 1970): [icon] *"Mnium Trichomanis facie, foliolis integris"* in Dillenius, Hist. Musc.: 236, t. 31, f. 5. 1741. – Voucher: Herb. Dillenius (OXF).

Moehringia muscosa Linnaeus, *Species Plantarum* 1: 359. 1753. "Habitat in Alpibus Helvetiae, Italiae, Austriae." RCN: 2851.
Lectotype (Hind in Jarvis & al., *Regnum Veg.* 127: 67. 1993): Herb. Linn. No. 509.1 (LINN).
Generitype of *Moehringia* Linnaeus.
Current name: ***Moehringia muscosa*** L. (Caryophyllaceae).

Mollugo oppositifolia Linnaeus, *Species Plantarum* 1: 89. 1753. "Habitat in Zeylona." RCN: 744.
Lectotype (Jeffrey in Hubbard & Milne-Redhead, *Fl. Trop. E. Africa, Aizoaceae*: 13. 1961): Herb. Hermann 1: 20, No. 52 (BM-000621295).
Current name: ***Glinus oppositifolius*** (L.) A. DC. (Molluginaceae).

Mollugo pentaphylla Linnaeus, *Species Plantarum* 1: 89. 1753. "Habitat in Zeylona." RCN: 748.
Lectotype (Tardieu-Blot in Aubréville, *Fl. Cambodge Laos Vietnam* 5: 94. 1967): *Osbeck s.n.*, Herb. Linn. No. 112.8 (LINN).
Current name: ***Mollugo pentaphylla*** L. (Molluginaceae).
Note: See Hansen & Fox Maule (in *Bot. J. Linn. Soc.* 67: 199. 1973) for comments on the Osbeck material.

Mollugo spergula Linnaeus, *Systema Naturae*, ed. 10, 2: 881. 1759. ["Habitat in India."] Sp. Pl., ed. 2, 1: 131 (1762). RCN: 745.
Type not designated.
Original material: Herb. Linn. No. 112.3 (LINN); Herb. Linn. No. 112.2 (LINN).
Current name: ***Glinus oppositifolius*** (L.) A. DC. (Molluginaceae).
Note: Jeffrey (in Hubbard & Milne-Redhead, *Fl. Trop. E. Africa, Aizoaceae*: 15. 1961) indicated type material in LINN, but did not distinguish between sheets 112.2 and 112.3. As they do not appear to be part of a single gathering, Art. 9.15 does not apply and the name remains untypified.

Mollugo stricta Linnaeus, *Species Plantarum*, ed. 2, 1: 131. 1762. "Habitat in Asia." RCN: 745.

Type not designated.
Original material: Herb. Linn. No. 112.1 (LINN).
Current name: ***Mollugo pentaphylla*** L. (Molluginaceae).

Mollugo tetraphylla Linnaeus, *Species Plantarum* 1: 89. 1753.
"Habitat in Italia, Narbonae vineis." RCN: 743.
Basionym of: *Polycarpon tetraphyllum* (L.) L. (1759).
Lectotype (Burtt & Lewis in *Kew Bull.* 7: 339. 1952): Herb. Clifford:
 28, *Mollugo* 2 (BM-000557701).
Current name: ***Polycarpon tetraphyllum*** (L.) L. (Caryophyllaceae).

Mollugo verticillata Linnaeus, *Species Plantarum* 1: 89. 1753.
"Habitat in Africa, Virginia." RCN: 747.

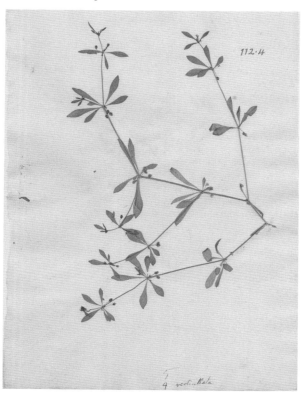

Lectotype (Reveal & al. in *Huntia* 7: 212. 1987): Herb. Linn. No.
 112.4 (LINN).
Generitype of *Mollugo* Linnaeus (vide Hitchcock, *Prop. Brit. Bot.*: 122.
 1929).
Current name: ***Mollugo verticillata*** L. (Molluginaceae).
Note: Fawcett & Rendle (*Fl. Jamaica* 3: 165. 1914) indicated material
 in LINN as type, but as there are three sheets associated with the
 name (and they are evidently not part of a single gathering), this is
 not an effective typification.

Moluccella frutescens Linnaeus, *Species Plantarum* 2: 587. 1753.
"Habitat in Pedemomtio inter Tende & Braille e rupibus. D.
 Sauvages." RCN: 4283.
Lectotype (Seybold in Jarvis & al. in *Taxon* 50: 513. 2001): Herb.
 Linn. No. 741.4 (LINN).
Current name: ***Ballota frutescens*** (L.) J. Woods (Lamiaceae).
Note: Patzak (in *Ann. Naturhist. Mus. Wien* 63: 45. 1959) quotes habitat
 information from Linnaeus' protologue, stating "D. Sauvages,
 Holotypus, non vidi". This is not accepted as a valid typification as
 no specimen or herbarium is indicated, and the information quoted
 appears to have been drawn solely from the protologue.

Moluccella laevis Linnaeus, *Species Plantarum* 2: 587. 1753.
"Habitat in Syria." RCN: 4281.
Lectotype (Hedge in Ali & Nasir, *Fl. Pakistan* 192: 176. 1990): Herb.
 Linn. No. 741.1 (LINN).
Generitype of *Moluccella* Linnaeus (vide Green, *Prop. Brit. Bot.*: 165.
 1929).
Current name: ***Moluccella laevis*** L. (Lamiaceae).

Moluccella spinosa Linnaeus, *Species Plantarum* 2: 587. 1753.
"Habitat in Moluccis." RCN: 4282.
Lectotype (Hedge in Jarvis & al. in *Taxon* 50: 514. 2001): Herb. Linn.
 No. 741.2 (LINN).
Current name: ***Moluccella spinosa*** L. (Lamiaceae).

Momordica balsamina Linnaeus, *Species Plantarum* 2: 1009. 1753.
"Habitat in India." RCN: 7314.
Lectotype (Meeuse in *Bothalia* 8: 49. 1962): Herb. Linn. No. 1150.1
 (LINN), see frontispiece.
Current name: ***Momordica balsamina*** L. (Cucurbitaceae).
Note: Momordica balsamina was treated as the generitype by Britton &
 Millspaugh (*Bahama Fl.*: 425. 1920; see McNeill & al. in *Taxon* 36:
 378. 1987). However, under Art. 10.5, Ex. 7 (a voted example) of
 the Vienna Code, this is a type choice made under the American
 Code and is to be replaced under Art. 10.5b by Green's choice
 (*Prop. Brit. Bot.*: 190. 1929) of *M. charantia* L.
  Jeffrey (in *Kew Bull.* 34: 790. 1980) rejected Meeuse's
 typification, arguing that Linnaeus' diagnosis came from the *Hortus
 Cliffortianus* account and that there was no evidence that 1150.1
 (LINN) was in Linnaeus' possession in 1753. The first point does
 not provide grounds for rejection, and what evidence there is
 suggests that the LINN sheet was within the herbarium in 1753.
 Meeuse's choice is therefore accepted here, rather than Jeffrey's later
 choice of a Clifford sheet.

Momordica charantia Linnaeus, *Species Plantarum* 2: 1009. 1753.
"Habitat in India." RCN: 7315.
Lectotype (Jeffrey in Milne-Redhead & Polhill, *Fl. Trop. E. Africa,
 Cucurbitaceae*: 31. 1967): Herb. Clifford: 451, *Momordica* 2 (BM-
 000647445).
Generitype of *Momordica* Linnaeus (vide Green, *Prop. Brit. Bot.*: 190.
 1929).
Current name: ***Momordica charantia*** L. (Cucurbitaceae).
Note: Momordica balsamina was treated as the generitype by Britton &
 Millspaugh (*Bahama Fl.*: 425. 1920; see McNeill & al. in *Taxon* 36:
 378. 1987). However, under Art. 10.5, Ex. 7 (a voted example) of
 the Vienna Code, this is a type choice made under the American
 Code and is to be replaced under Art. 10.5b by Green's choice
 (*Prop. Brit. Bot.*: 190. 1929) of *M. charantia* L.

Momordica cylindrica Linnaeus, *Species Plantarum* 2: 1009. 1753.
"Habitat in Zeylona, China." RCN: 7318.
Lectotype (Wunderlin in *Ann. Missouri Bot. Gard.* 65: 329. 1978):
 Herb. Linn. No. 1150.9 (LINN).
Current name: ***Luffa cylindrica*** (L.) M. Roem. (Cucurbitaceae).
Note: Jeffrey (in *Kew Bull.* 15: 355. 1962) stated that the type was
 apparently a cultivated plant but that no specimen had been traced.
 Keraudren-Aymonin (in *Adansonia*, sér. 2, 8: 399. 1968) indicated a
 LINN sheet, annotated as "M. luffa" (so presumably 1150.6), as the
 holotype but this is original material for *M. luffa* L. rather than *M.
 cylindrica.* Wunderlin (in *Ann. Missouri Bot. Gard.* 65: 329. 1978)
 indicated 1150.9 (LINN), which he had seen only via a fiche image,
 as the type. This appears to be original material for the name but
 seems to be identifiable as *Cucumis melo* L. Jeffrey (in *Kew Bull.* 34:
 791. 1980) subsequently indicated a Hermann description as the
 lectotype but this is contrary to Art. 8.1. Depending on the identity

of 1150.9 (LINN), and whether it conflicts with the protologue, there may be a need to propose *M. cylindrica* for conservation with a conserved type if it is to continue to be used in its current sense.

Momordica elaterium Linnaeus, *Species Plantarum* 2: 1010. 1753.
"Habitat in Europa australi." RCN: 7321.
Lectotype (Andersen in Rechinger, *Fl. Iranica* 123: 2. 1977): Herb. Linn. No. 1150.10 (LINN).
Current name: ***Ecballium elaterium*** (L.) A. Rich. (Cucurbitaceae).

Momordica indica Linnaeus, *Herbarium Amboinense*: 24. 1754.
RCN: 7315.
Lectotype (Merrill, *Interpret. Rumph. Herb. Amb.*: 33, 495. 1917): [icon] *"Amara Indica"* in Rumphius, Herb. Amboin. 5: 410, t. 151. 1747.
Current name: ***Momordica charantia*** L. (Cucurbitaceae).

Momordica luffa Linnaeus, *Species Plantarum* 2: 1009. 1753.
"Habitat in Zeylona." RCN: 7317.
Lectotype (Jeffrey in *Kew Bull.* 15: 355. 1962): Herb. Clifford: 451, *Momordica* 3 (BM-000647446).
Current name: ***Luffa cylindrica*** (L.) M. Roem. (Cucurbitaceae).
Note: See notes by McVaugh (*Fl. Novo-Galiciana* 3: 587. 2001) on the correct name for this taxon.

Momordica operculata Linnaeus, *Systema Naturae,* ed. 10, 2: 1278. 1759.
["Habitat in America."] Sp. Pl., ed. 2, 2: 1433 (1763). RCN: 7316.
Lectotype (Wijnands, *Bot. Commelins*: 92. 1983): [icon] *"Momordica Americana fructu reticulato sicco"* in Commelin, Hort. Med. Amstelaed. Pl. Rar.: 22, t. 22. 1706.
Current name: ***Luffa operculata*** (L.) Cogn. (Cucurbitaceae).
Note: Although Wunderlin (in *Ann. Missouri Bot. Gard.* 65: 331. 1978) indicated 1150.4 and 1150.5 (LINN) as syntypes, they are evidently not part of a single gathering so Art. 9.15 does not, in any case, apply. Although later authors have indicated one or other as the type, Wijnands' choice of a Commelin plate appears to have priority. Jeffrey (in *Kew Bull.* 47: 742. 1992) has discussed the application of this name.

Momordica pedata Linnaeus, *Species Plantarum* 2: 1009. 1753.
"Habitat in Peru." RCN: 7320.
Lectotype (Jeffrey in *Kew Bull.* 34: 796. 1980): [icon] *"Momordica fructu striato, Laevi, vulgo Caigua"* in Feuillée, J. Obs. 2: 754, t. 41. 1714 (see p. 130).
Current name: ***Cyclanthera pedata*** (L.) Schrad. (Cucurbitaceae).

Momordica trifolia Linnaeus, *Herbarium Amboinense*: 24. 1754.
["Habitat in India."] Sp. Pl., ed. 2, 2: 1434 (1763). RCN: 7319.
Lectotype (Merrill, *Interpret. Rumph. Herb. Amb.*: 33, 494. 1917): [icon] *"Poppya silvestris"* in Rumphius, Herb. Amboin. 5: 414, t. 152, f. 2. 1747.
Current name: ***Momordica trifolia*** L. (Cucurbitaceae).
Note: Jeffrey & de Wilde (in *Taxon* 48: 599. 1999) proposed the name for rejection as its type, a Rumphius plate, is identifiable as the widespread *M. cochinchinensis* (Lour.) Spreng. However, the proposal was later withdrawn by its authors – see Brummitt (in *Taxon* 53: 814. 2004).

Momordica trifoliata Linnaeus, *Species Plantarum*, ed. 2, 2: 1434. 1763, *orth. var.*
RCN: 7319.
Lectotype (Merrill, *Interpret. Rumph. Herb. Amb.*: 33, 494. 1917): [icon] *"Poppya silvestris"* in Rumphius, Herb. Amboin. 5: 414, t. 152, f. 2. 1747.

Current name: ***Momordica trifolia*** L. (Cucurbitaceae).
Note: As noted by Rugayah & de Wilde (in *Blumea* 42: 48. 1997), this is an orthographic variant of *M. trifolia* L.

Monarda ciliata Linnaeus, *Species Plantarum* 1: 23. 1753.
"Habitat in Virginia." RCN: 180.
Lectotype (Reveal in Jarvis & al. in *Taxon* 50: 514. 2001): *Clayton 412* (BM-000051214).
Current name: ***Blephilia ciliata*** (L.) Raf. (Lamiaceae).
Note: Epling (in *J. Bot.* 67: 5. 1929) discussed the original elements for the name, and treated *Clayton 412* (BM) as the "standard specimen" but this is not equivalent to a type statement (see Jarvis & al. in *Taxon* 50: 508. 2001). However, this material does appear to be the obvious choice as type, and has been subsequently designated as such by Reveal.

Monarda clinopodia Linnaeus, *Species Plantarum* 1: 22. 1753.
"Habitat in Virginia." RCN: 178.
Lectotype (Reveal in Jarvis & al. in *Taxon* 50: 514. 2001): Herb. Linn. No. 40.4 (LINN).
Current name: ***Monarda clinopodia*** L. (Lamiaceae).
Note: Epling (in *J. Bot.* 67: 4. 1929), followed by McClintock & Epling (in *Univ. Calif. Publ. Bot.* 20: 173. 1942), discussed the original elements for the name, and treated a sheet in LINN as the "standard specimen" (not the same as the type). Scora (in *Univ. Calif. Publ. Bot.* 41: 41. 1967) also followed Epling but made no distinction as to which of the two sheets at LINN might be intended. As they come from different gatherings, Art. 9.15 does not, in any case, apply. One of the sheets in LINN (40.4 and 40.7 are both annotated by Linnaeus) has been chosen as lectotype by Reveal.

Monarda didyma Linnaeus, *Species Plantarum* 1: 22. 1753.
"Habitat in Pensilvania, Noveboraco." RCN: 177.
Lectotype (Wijnands, *Bot. Commelins*: 117. 1983): Herb. Linn. No. 40.3 (LINN).
Current name: ***Monarda didyma*** L. (Lamiaceae).
Note: Epling (in *J. Bot.* 67: 4. 1929) noted material at LINN but did not designate a type. McClintock & Epling (in *Univ. Calif. Publ. Bot.* 20: 158. 1942) treated material in the Linnaean herbarium as "the standard" (not the same as a type) and Scora (in *Univ. Calif. Publ. Bot.* 41: 31. 1967) suggested that this "may be taken as the type". Wijnands appears to have been the first to make an unequivocal type designation.

Monarda fistulosa Linnaeus, *Species Plantarum* 1: 22. 1753.
"Habitat in Canada." RCN: 176.
Lectotype (Reveal in Jarvis & al. in *Taxon* 50: 513. 2001): Herb. Clifford: 11, *Monarda* 1, sheet 5 (BM-000557572).
Generitype of *Monarda* Linnaeus (vide Hitchcock, *Prop. Brit. Bot.*: 116. 1929).
Current name: ***Monarda fistulosa*** L. (Lamiaceae).
Note: Fernald (in *Rhodora* 3: 14. 1901) discussed Herb. Linn. 40.1 (LINN) in some detail but did not call it the type (in contrast to his comments on *M. mollis* L. on the same page). Epling (in *J. Bot.* 67: 3. 1929) noted material in LINN, as well as in Clifford's herbarium, and treated one of the latter sheets as the "standard specimen" (not the same as the type). McClintock & Epling (in *Univ. Calif. Publ. Bot.* 20: 165. 1942) followed Epling, and Scora (in *Univ. Calif. Publ. Bot.* 41: 34. 1967) stated that the name was probably based on a garden plant in the Linnaean herbarium. Scora's statement is insufficiently precise to be admitted as a typification, particularly as it is unclear which sheet (40.1 or 40.2, both annotated by Linnaeus) was intended. The collections are not part of a single gathering, so Art. 9.15 does not apply. Reveal's type choice is therefore the earliest formal typification.

M

Monarda mollis Linnaeus, *Demonstr. Pl. Horto Upsaliensi*: 2. 1753.
RCN: 176.
Lectotype (Fernald in *Rhodora* 3: 14. 1901): Herb. Linn. No. 40.2 (LINN).
Current name: ***Monarda fistulosa*** L. (Lamiaceae).

Monarda punctata Linnaeus, *Species Plantarum* 1: 22. 1753.
"Habitat in Virginia." RCN: 179.
Lectotype (Reveal in Jarvis & al. in *Taxon* 50: 514. 2001): Herb. Linn. No. 40.6 (LINN).
Current name: ***Monarda punctata*** L. (Lamiaceae).
Note: Epling (in *J. Bot.* 67: 4. 1929), followed by various later authors, noted material in LINN, evidently sheet 40.6, as the "standard specimen" (not the same as the type). However, sheet 40.6 is the only relevant original element at LINN and, since it corresponds with current usage, was designated as lectotype by Reveal.

Moniera trifolia Linnaeus, *Systema Naturae*, ed. 10, 2: 1153. 1759.
["Habitat in Cumana Americae."] Sp. Pl., ed. 2, 2: 986 (1763). RCN: 5116.
Type not designated.
Original material: none traced.
Current name: ***Ertela trifolia*** (L.) Kuntze (Rutaceae).
Note: Generic name spelled "Monniera" in the protologue.

Monotropa hypopitys Linnaeus, *Species Plantarum* 1: 387. 1753.
"Habitat in Sueciae, Germaniae, Angliae, Canadae sylvis." RCN: 3055.
Lectotype (Wallace, *Fl. Neotropica* 66: 20. 1995): Herb. Burser III: 156 (UPS).
Current name: ***Monotropa hypopitys*** L. (Ericaceae).
Note: The epithet was originally spelled "hypopithys" but this has generally been treated as correctable to "hypopitys".

Monotropa uniflora Linnaeus, *Species Plantarum* 1: 387. 1753.
"Habitat in Marilandia, Virginia, Canada." RCN: 3056.
Lectotype (Wallace in *Wasmann J. Biol.* 33: 31. 1975): *Kalm*, Herb. Linn. No. 551.3 (LINN).
Generitype of *Monotropa* Linnaeus (vide Hitchcock, *Prop. Brit. Bot.*: 153. 1929).
Current name: ***Monotropa uniflora*** L. (Ericaceae).
Note: Wallace (1975) evidently regarded material in LINN as the type while Wilbur & Luteyn (in *Ann. Missouri Bot. Gard.* 65: 102. 1978) indicated *Clayton 245* (BM), which they had not seen and believed to be instead at LINN, as type. Reveal & al. (in *Huntia* 7: 228. 1987) provided a detailed review, concluding that the Kalm specimen in LINN should be the type.

Monsonia speciosa Linnaeus, *Systema Naturae*, ed. 12, 2: 508; *Mantissa Plantarum*: 105. 1767.
"Habitat ad Cap. b. spei." RCN: 5725.
Lectotype (Gibby in Jarvis & al., *Regnum Veg.* 127: 67. 1993): Herb. Linn. No. 936.2 (LINN).
Generitype of *Monsonia* Linnaeus.
Current name: ***Monsonia speciosa*** L. (Geraniaceae).
Note: Venter (in *Meded. Landbouwhoogeschool* 79–9: 106. 1979), followed by Albers (in Eggli, *Ill. Handb. Succ. Pl., Dicots*: 244. 2002), wrongly indicated a post-1767 Sparrman collection (936.3 LINN) as holotype. It is not original material for the name and was therefore rejected in favour of Gibby's choice.

Montia fontana Linnaeus, *Species Plantarum* 1: 87. 1753.
"Habitat in Europa ad scaturigines." RCN: 735.

Lectotype (Jonsell & Jarvis in Jarvis & al., *Regnum Veg.* 127: 67. 1993): Herb. Linn. No. 57 (LAPP).
Generitype of *Montia* Linnaeus.
Current name: ***Montia fontana*** L. (Portulacaceae).
Note: Walters (in *Watsonia* 3: 2. 1953), followed by Hedberg (in *Symb. Bot. Upsal.* 15(1): 38. 1957) and Pedersen (in *Bot. Tidsskr.* 63: 369. 1968), referred to the type subspecies as being "the plant of the Linnaean herbarium" but this fails to distinguish between sheets 106.1 and 106.2 (LINN) and is therefore ineffective. The two collections do not appear to be part of a single gathering so Art. 9.15 does not apply. Jonsell & Jarvis designated material from Lapland as the lectotype (see further discussion by them in *Nordic J. Bot.* 14: 155. 1994).

Moraea iridioides Linnaeus, *Systema Naturae*, ed. 12, 2: 78; *Mantissa Plantarum*: 28. 1767.
"Habitat in Oriente: Constantinopoli." RCN: 342.
Lectotype (Goldblatt in *Taxon* 22: 504. 1973): [icon] *"Morea, spatha unifloro, foliis gladiolatis, radice fibrosa"* in Miller, Fig. Pl. Gard. Dict. 2: 159, t. 239, f. 1. 1758.
Current name: ***Dietes iridioides*** (L.) Sweet ex Klatt (Iridaceae).

Moraea juncea Linnaeus, *Species Plantarum*, ed. 2, 1: 59. 1762.
"Habitat in Africa." RCN: 341.
Type not designated.
Original material: [icon] in Miller, Fig. Pl. Gard. Dict. 2: 159, t. 238. 1758.
Note: The application of this name is uncertain and it has been informally rejected by Barnard & Goldblatt (in *Taxon* 24: 125. 1975) and later authors.

Moraea vegeta Linnaeus, *Species Plantarum*, ed. 2, 1: 59. 1762.
"Habitat in Africa." RCN: 340.
Lectotype (Barnard & Goldblatt in *Taxon* 24: 131, f. 1. 1975): [icon] *"Morea, spatha biflora et uniflora, caule planifolio, floribus minoribus et majoribus"* in Miller, Fig. Pl. Gard. Dict. 2: 159, t. 238, f. 1, 2. 1758 (see p. 144).
Current name: ***Moraea vegeta*** L. (Iridaceae).

Morina persica Linnaeus, *Species Plantarum* 1: 28. 1753.
"Habitat in Persia ad Hispaham." RCN: 223.
Lectotype (Cannon & Cannon in *Bull. Brit. Mus. (Nat. Hist.), Bot.* 12: 28. 1984): Herb. Linn. No. 44.1 (LINN).
Generitype of *Morina* Linnaeus.
Current name: ***Morina persica*** L. (Morinaceae).

Morinda citrifolia Linnaeus, *Species Plantarum* 1: 176. 1753.
"Habitat in India." RCN: 1387.
Lectotype (Dwyer in Woodson & Schery in *Ann. Missouri Bot. Gard.* 67: 288. 1980): Herb. Linn. No. 236.1 (LINN).
Current name: ***Morinda citrifolia*** L. (Rubiaceae).

Morinda royoc Linnaeus, *Species Plantarum* 1: 176. 1753.
"Habitat in America calidiore." RCN: 1388.
Lectotype (Lorence in Jarvis & al., *Regnum Veg.* 127: 68. 1993): Herb. Clifford: 73, *Morinda* 1 (BM-000558129).
Generitype of *Morinda* Linnaeus (vide Hitchcock, *Prop. Brit. Bot.*: 132. 1929).
Current name: ***Morinda royoc*** L. (Rubiaceae).

Morinda umbellata Linnaeus, *Species Plantarum* 1: 176. 1753.
"Habitat in India." RCN: 1386.
Lectotype (Smith, *Fl. Vitiensis Nova* 4: 333. 1988): Herb. Hermann 3: 11, No. 81 (BM-000621833).
Current name: ***Morinda umbellata*** L. (Rubiaceae).

Morisonia americana Linnaeus, *Species Plantarum* 1: 503.
1753.
"Habitat in America calidiore." RCN: 5113.
Lectotype (Al-Shehbaz in Howard, *Fl. Lesser Antilles* 4: 308. 1988):
[icon] *"Morisona"* in Plumier, Nov. Pl. Amer.: 36, t. 23. 1703.
Generitype of *Morisonia* Linnaeus.
Current name: ***Morisonia americana*** L. (Capparaceae).

Morisonia flexuosa Linnaeus, *Plantarum Jamaicensium Pugillus*: 14.
1759.
["Habitat in Jamaica."] Sp. Pl., ed. 2, 1: 722 (1762). RCN: 3828.
Basionym of: *Capparis flexuosa* (L.) L. (1762).
Lectotype (Fawcett & Rendle, *Fl. Jamaica* 3: 234. 1914): *Browne*,
Herb. Linn. No. 664.10 (LINN).
Current name: ***Capparis flexuosa*** (L.) L. (Capparaceae).
Note: Rankin & Greuter (in *Willdenowia* 34: 261. 2004) attribute the
type choice to Fawcett & Rendle's earlier account (in *J. Bot.* 52:
142. May 1914), where they use the expression "founded upon".
However, this is not accepted here as effecting typification.

Morus alba Linnaeus, *Species Plantarum* 2: 986. 1753.
"Habitat in China." RCN: 7146.
Lectotype (Browicz in Rechinger, *Fl. Iranica* 153: 3. 1982; Rao &
Jarvis in *Taxon* 35: 705. 1986): Herb. Linn. No. 1112.1, upper left
specimen (LINN).
Current name: ***Morus alba*** L. (Moraceae).
Note: Bhopal & Chaudhri (in *Pakistan Syst.* 1(2): 29. 1977) indicated
unspecified material in LINN as the holotype but did not
distinguish between sheets 1112.1 and 1112.2. As they do not
appear to be part of a single gathering, Art. 9.15 does not apply.
Browicz designated 1112.1 (LINN) as lectotype and this choice was
subsequently restricted to the upper left specimen on the sheet by
Rao & Jarvis.

Morus indica Linnaeus, *Species Plantarum* 2: 986. 1753.
"Habitat in India." RCN: 7150.
Lectotype (Rao & Jarvis in *Taxon* 35: 706. 1986): Herb. Hermann 3:
26, No. 337 (BM-000621897).
Current name: ***Morus alba*** L. var. ***indica*** (L.) Bureau (Moraceae).

Morus nigra Linnaeus, *Species Plantarum* 2: 986. 1753.
"Habitat in Italiae maritimis." RCN: 7147.
Lectotype (Bhopal & Chaudhri in *Pakistan Syst.* 1(2): 29. 1977):
Herb. Linn. No. 1112.3 (LINN), see above, right.
Generitype of *Morus* Linnaeus (vide Green, *Prop. Brit. Bot.*: 188.
1929).
Current name: ***Morus nigra*** L. (Moraceae).

Morus papyrifera Linnaeus, *Species Plantarum* 2: 986. 1753.
"Habitat in Japonia." RCN: 7148.
Lectotype (Florence, *Fl. Polynésie Française* 1: 146. 1997): [icon]
"Morus papyrifera" in Kaempfer, Amoen. Exot. Fasc.: 471, 472.
1712.
Current name: ***Broussonetia papyrifera*** (L.) Vent. (Moraceae).
Note: Browicz (in Rechinger, *Fl. Iranica* 153: 5. 1982) designated
1112.4 (LINN) as the type but this appears to be a Kleynhof
collection, which would not have been acquired by Linnaeus until
long after 1753. It cannot therefore be original material for the
name.

Morus rubra Linnaeus, *Species Plantarum* 2: 986. 1753.
"Habitat in Virginia." RCN: 7149.
Lectotype (designated here by Reveal): *Kalm*, Herb. Linn. No. 1112.6
(LINN).
Current name: ***Morus rubra*** L. (Moraceae).

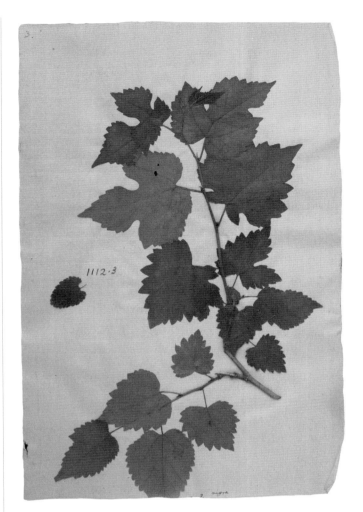

The lectotype of *Morus nigra* L.

Morus tatarica Linnaeus, *Species Plantarum* 2: 986. 1753.
"Habitat in Assoff." RCN: 7151.
Lectotype (Rao & Jarvis in *Taxon* 35: 706. 1986): Herb. Linn. No.
1112.9 (LINN), see p. 28.
Current name: ***Morus alba*** L. (Moraceae).

Morus tinctoria Linnaeus, *Species Plantarum* 2: 986. 1753.
"Habitat in Brasilia, Jamaica." RCN: 7152.
Lectotype (Kaastra in *Acta Bot. Neerl.* 21: 661. 1972): [icon] *"Morus
fructu viridi, ligno sulphureo tinctorio"* in Sloane, Voy. Jamaica 2: 3, t.
158, f. 1. 1725.
Current name: ***Maclura tinctoria*** (L.) Steud. (Moraceae).

Morus zanthoxylon Linnaeus, *Systema Naturae*, ed. 10, 2: 1266.
1759.
RCN: 7152.
Lectotype (Kaastra in *Acta Bot. Neerl.* 21: 661. 1972): [icon]
"Zanthoxylum aculeatum Carpini foliis American. cortice cinereo"
in Plukenet, Phytographia: t. 239, f. 3. 1692; Almag. Bot.:
396. 1696. – Voucher: Herb. Sloane 98: 178; 102: 143
(BM-SL).
Current name: ***Maclura tinctoria*** (L.) Steud. subsp. ***tinctoria***
(Moraceae).

M

Mucor cespitosus Linnaeus, *Species Plantarum* 2: 1186. 1753.
"Habitat in Putrescentibus." RCN: 8536.
Lectotype (Pitt, *Genus* Penicillium: 387. 1979): [icon] *"Aspergillus albus, tenuissimus, graminis dactyloidis facie, seminibus rotundis"* in Micheli, Nov. Pl. Gen.: 213, t. 91, f. 3. 1729.
Current name: ***Penicillium digitatum*** (Pers.: Fr.) Sacc. (Trichocomaceae).

Mucor crustaceus Linnaeus, *Species Plantarum* 2: 1186. 1753.
"Habitat in Cibis corruptis." RCN: 8535.
Type not designated.
Original material: [icon] in Micheli, Nov. Pl. Gen.: 212, t. 91, f. 3. 1729.
Current name: ***Botrytis ramosa*** Pers. (Sclerotiniaceae).
Note: Martin (in *Iowa Stud. Nat. Hist.* 20(8): 29. 1966) treated Micheli's t. 96, f. 2 as the type of *Spumaria* Pers. and, apparently, the type of *M. crustaceus* L. However, this figure was not cited in its protologue so it is not original material for the name. Hawksworth & al. (in *Taxon* 25: 666. 1976) considered the name to be a *nomen dubium* for a *Botrytis*-like fungus, the specific and generic identities of which were uncertain.

Mucor embolus Linnaeus, *Species Plantarum* 2: 1185. 1753.
"Habitat in lignis putridis." RCN: 8528.
Type not designated.
Original material: [icon] in Haller, Enum. Meth. Stirp. Helv. 1: 8, t. 1, f. 1. 1742.
Current name: ***Comatricha nigra*** (Pers.) J. Schröt. (Stemonitaceae).
Note: See discussion by Lister (in *J. Bot.* 51: 161. 1913) and Martin (in *Iowa Stud. Nat. Hist.* 20(8): 24. 1966).

Mucor erysiphe Linnaeus, *Species Plantarum* 2: 1186. 1753.
"Habitat in foliis Humuli, Aceris, Lamii, Galeopsidis, Lithospermi." RCN: 8538.
Type not designated.
Original material: none traced.
Current name: ***Sclerotium erysiphe*** (L.) Pers. (Typhulaceae).

Mucor fulvus Linnaeus, *Species Plantarum* 2: 1185. 1753, *nom. utique rej.*
"Habitat Upsaliae. D. Solander." RCN: 8529.
Type not designated.
Original material: none traced.
Note: Jørgensen & al. (in *Bot. J. Linn. Soc.* 115: 367, 383. 1994) concluded that this is a *nomen non satis nota* and since it is not in current use, they (in *Taxon* 43: 647. 1994) successfully proposed it for rejection.

Mucor furfuraceus Linnaeus, *Species Plantarum* 2: 1185. 1753.
"Habitat in Terra nuda passim in Suecia. Dan. Solander." RCN: 8530.
Neotype (Jørgensen & al. in *Bot. J. Linn. Soc.* 115: 367, 383. 1994): Sweden. Uppland, Vänge parish, Fiby urskog, on upturned roots ('rotvälta'), 4 Aug 1962, *R. Santesson 14432* (UPS).
Current name: ***Chaenotheca furfuracea*** (L.) Tibell (Caliciaceae).

Mucor glaucus Linnaeus, *Species Plantarum* 2: 1186. 1753.
"Habitat in Citris, Melonibus, Pomis aliisque corruptis." RCN: 8533.
Type not designated.
Original material: [icon] in Micheli, Nov. Pl. Gen.: 212, t. 91, f. 1. 1729.
Current name: ***Aspergillus glaucus*** (L.: Fr.) Link (Trichocomaceae).
Note: Pitt & Sampson (in *Regnum Veg.* 128: 19. 1993) designated No. 211383 (IMI) as a neotype but the existence of original material for the Linnaean name appears to preclude the neotypification of the name (Art. 9.11).

Mucor leprosus Linnaeus, *Species Plantarum* 2: 1185. 1753.
"Habitat in cavernulis autumno." RCN: 8532.
Type not designated.
Original material: [icon] in Micheli, Nov. Pl. Gen.: 213, t. 91, f. 5. 1729.
Current name: ***Mucor leprosus*** L. (Mucoraceae).

Mucor lichenoides Linnaeus, *Species Plantarum* 2: 1185. 1753, *nom. rej.*
"Habitat in corticibus Pini." RCN: 8527.
Lectotype (Jørgensen & al. in *Bot. J. Linn. Soc.* 115: 369, 383. 1994): [icon] *"Coralloides fungiforme arboreum nigrum, vix crustosum"* in Dillenius, Hist. Musc.: 78, t. 14, f. 3 B. 1741. – Voucher: Herb. Dillenius (OXF).
Current name: ***Calicium salicinum*** Pers. (Caliciaceae).
Note: Jørgensen & al. (*l.c.*) found that the lectotype belongs to *Calicium salicinum* Pers. and so *C. lichenoides* (L.) Schum. would become the correct name for this taxon. The Linnaean name was successfully proposed for rejection (in *Taxon* 43: 649. 1994).

Mucor mucedo Linnaeus, *Species Plantarum* 2: 1185. 1753.
"Habitat in variis putridis: pane, plantis. &c." RCN: 8531.
Lectotype (Kirk in *Taxon* 35: 373. 1986): [icon] *"Mucedo capitulo diaphano deinde viridi & postremo nigro"* in Malpighi, Anat. Pl. Pars Altera: 64, t. 28, f. 108, A–B, E–G. 1679.
Generitype of *Mucor* Linnaeus: Fr., *nom. rej.* (vide Sumstine in *Mycologia* 2: 127. 1910).
Current name: ***Rhizopus stolonifer*** (Ehrenb.: Fr.) Vuill. (Mucoraceae).
Note: Mucor L.: Fr., *nom. rej.* in favour of *Mucor* Fresen.

Mucor septicus Linnaeus, *Species Plantarum*, ed. 2, 2: 1656. 1763.
"Habitat in Vaporariis defervescentibus visibili incremento; maturus semina explodens." RCN: 8539.
Type not designated.
Original material: [icon] in Marchant in Mém. Acad. Roy. Sci. Paris 1727: 339, t. 14. 1727.
Current name: ***Fuligo septica*** (L.) F.H. Wigg. (Physaraceae).
Note: See discussion by Lister (in *J. Bot.* 51: 161–162. 1913), who also reproduced the protologue.

Mucor sphaerocephalus Linnaeus, *Species Plantarum* 2: 1185. 1753, *nom. utique rej.*
"Habitat in Parietibus, Lapidibus, Lignis." RCN: 8526.
Type not designated.
Original material: [icon] in Haller, Enum. Meth. Stirp. Helv. 1: 9, t. 1, f. 3. 1742.
Note: Jørgensen & al. (in *Bot. J. Linn. Soc.* 115: 369. 1994) concluded that this name is best regarded as a *nomen non satis nota* and successfully proposed it (in *Taxon* 43: 647. 1994) for rejection.

Mucor unctuosus Linnaeus, *Flora Suecica*, ed. 2: 460. 1755.
"Habitat in hortorum terra praegnante ubique, nec non quibusdam in locis ad parietes & pavimenta lignea, quae destruit." RCN: 8538.
Type not designated.
Original material: none traced.
Current name: ***Mucilago*** sp. (Didymiaceae).

Mucor viridescens Linnaeus, *Mantissa Plantarum Altera*: 313. 1771.
"Habitat in Europa: Svecia lignis putridis." RCN: 8537.
Type not designated.
Original material: none traced.
Current name: ***Mucor viridescens*** L. (Mucoraceae).

Munchausia speciosa Linnaeus, *Munchausen, Hausvater* 5(1): 357. 1770.

"Habitat in Java, China." RCN: 5731.

Lectotype (Dar in Nasir & Ali, *Fl. W. Pakistan* 78: 3. 1975): Herb. Linn. No. 939.1 (LINN).

Generitype of *Munchausia* Linnaeus.

Current name: ***Lagerstroemia speciosa*** (L.) Pers. (Lythraceae).

Note: Furtado & Srisuko (in *Gard. Bull. Singapore* 24: 267–268. 1969) commented on the material in LINN but did not formally treat it as the type.

Muntingia bartramia Linnaeus, *Amoenitates Academicae* 4: 124. 1759.

RCN: 3451.

Lectotype (Merrill, *Interpret. Rumph. Herb. Amb.*: 362. 1917): [icon] "*Restiaria alba*" in Rumphius, Herb. Amboin. 3: 187, t. 119. 1743.

Current name: ***Commersonia bartramia*** (L.) Merr. (Sterculiaceae).

Muntingia calabura Linnaeus, *Species Plantarum* 1: 509. 1753.

"Habitat in Jamaica." RCN: 3852.

Lectotype (Dorr in Jarvis & al., *Regnum Veg.* 127: 68. 1993): Herb. Clifford: 202, *Muntingia* 1 (BM-000628726).

Generitype of *Muntingia* Linnaeus.

Current name: ***Muntingia calabura*** L. (Tiliaceae).

Murraya exotica Linnaeus, *Mantissa Plantarum Altera*: 563. 1771.

"Habitat in India orientali." RCN: 3022.

Neotype (Nair in Jarvis & al., *Regnum Veg.* 127: 68. 1993): Herb. Linn. No. 539.1 (LINN).

Generitype of *Murraya* Linnaeus, *nom. & orth. cons.*

Current name: ***Murraya exotica*** L. (Rutaceae).

Note: Murraya Linnaeus, *nom. & orth. cons.* against *Bergera* Linnaeus.

Musa bihai Linnaeus, *Species Plantarum* 2: 1043. 1753.

"Habitat in America calidiore." RCN: 1653.

Basionym of: *Heliconia bihai* (L.) L. (1771).

Neotype (Maas & De Rooij in Stoffers & Lindeman, *Fl. Suriname* 5(1): 399. 1979): Herb. Linn. No. 286.1 (LINN).

Current name: ***Heliconia bihai*** (L.) L. (Musaceae).

Note: Andersson (in *Nordic J. Bot.* 1: 769. 1981) gave an extensive review of the history of this name. The cited Plumier element leads to a generic illustration (t. 3) for *Bihai* which included what Plumier regarded as three different species, so the plate cannot be treated as original material for *M. bihai*. Andersson therefore designated a later Dahlberg collection (286.1 LINN) as a neotype, but Maas & De Rooij had previously treated the same collection as the type (accepted as a neotypification under Art. 9.8).

Musa paradisiaca Linnaeus, *Species Plantarum* 2: 1043. 1753.

"Habitat in India." RCN: 7536.

Lectotype (Argent in Jarvis & al., *Regnum Veg.* 127: 68. 1993): [icon] "*Musa cliffortiana*" in Linnaeus, Musa Cliff.: unnumbered plate. 1736 (see p. 69).

Generitype of *Musa* Linnaeus (vide Adanson, *Fam.* 2: 525, 580. 1763).

Current name: ***Musa × paradisiaca*** L. (Musaceae).

Note: See extensive discussion by Cheeseman (in *Kew Bull.* 3: 146. 1948) who, however, did not explicitly refer to any of the plates as type. Ghazanfar (in Ali & Nasir, *Fl. Pakistan* 144: 2. 1982) indicated 1207.1 (LINN) as type, but this was a post-1753 addition to the herbarium and not original material for the name.

Musa sapientum Linnaeus, *Systema Naturae,* ed. 10, 2: 1303. 1759.

["Habitat in Indiis."] Sp. Pl., ed. 2, 2: 1477 (1763). RCN: 7537.

Lectotype (Cheeseman in *Kew Bull.* 3: 13. 1948): [icon] "*Musae fructu breviore spadix floriger in magnitudine naturali.*" in Trew, Pl. Select.: 4, t. 22. 1752 (see p. 79).

Current name: ***Musa × sapientum*** L. (Musaceae).

Musa troglodytarum Linnaeus, *Species Plantarum,* ed. 2, 2: 1478. 1763.

"Habitat in Moluccis." RCN: 7538.

Lectotype (Merrill, *Interpret. Rumph. Herb. Amb.*: 150. 1917): [icon] "*Musa Uranoscopos*" in Rumphius, Herb. Amboin. 5: 137, t. 61, f. 2. 1747.

Current name: ***Musa troglodytarum*** L. (Musaceae).

Mussaenda frondosa Linnaeus, *Species Plantarum* 1: 177. 1753.

"Habitat in India." RCN: 1395.

Replaced synonym of: *Mussaenda fruticosa* L. (1767), *nom. illeg.*

Lectotype (Jayaweera in *J. Arnold Arbor.* 44: 239, f. 4. 1963): Herb. Hermann 3: 44, No. 84, upper specimen (BM-000621963).

Generitype of *Mussaenda* Linnaeus.

Current name: ***Mussaenda frondosa*** L. (Rubiaceae).

Note: Although originally appearing as "M. fr. [fructu] frondoso", the name is to be cited as "M. frondosa" (Art. 23.7, Ex. 18). Smith (in *J. Arnold Arbor.* 26: 104. 1945) stated that "the actual type is a collection of Hermann from Ceylon" but did not indicate where this might be held (BM, L, etc.). Jayaweera's explicit statement is therefore accepted here as typifying the name.

Mussaenda fruticosa Linnaeus, *Systema Naturae,* ed. 12, 2: 168. 1767, *nom. illeg.*

["Habitat in India."] Sp. Pl. 1: 177 (1753). RCN: 1395.

Replaced synonym: *Mussaenda frondosa* L. (1753).

Lectotype (Jayaweera in *J. Arnold Arbor.* 44: 239, f. 4. 1963): Herb. Hermann 3: 44, No. 84 (BM-000621963).

Current name: ***Mussaenda frondosa*** L. (Rubiaceae).

Myagrum aegyptium Linnaeus, *Species Plantarum* 2: 641. 1753.

"Habitat in Aegypto." RCN: 4662.

Lectotype (Meikle, *Fl. Cyprus* 1: 112. 1977): *Hasselquist*, Herb. Linn. No. 819.16 (LINN).

Current name: ***Didesmus aegyptius*** (L.) Desv. (Brassicaceae).

Myagrum hispanicum Linnaeus, *Species Plantarum* 2: 640. 1753.

"Habitat in Hispania." RCN: 4657.

Type not designated.

Original material: Herb. Linn. No. 819.6 (LINN).

Current name: ***Rapistrum rugosum*** (L.) All. subsp. ***linnaeanum*** (Coss.) Rouy & Foucaud (Brassicaceae).

Myagrum monospermum Linnaeus, *Amoenitates Academicae* 4: 486. 1759, *nom. nud.*

Type not relevant.

Note: Although this name appears in Linnaeus' *Flora Monspeliensis*, it has no validating reference to Magnol's *Bot. Monspeliensis* (see Stearn in Geck & Pressler, *Festschr. Claus Nissen*: 632. 1974).

Myagrum orientale Linnaeus, *Species Plantarum* 2: 640. 1753.

"Habitat in Oriente." RCN: 4655.

Lectotype (Al-Shehbaz & Turland in Cafferty & Jarvis in *Taxon* 51: 535. 2002): Herb. Linn. No. 819.4 (LINN).

Current name: ***Rapistrum rugosum*** (L.) All. subsp. ***orientale*** (L.) Arcang. (Brassicaceae).

Myagrum paniculatum Linnaeus, *Species Plantarum* 2: 641. 1753.

"Habitat in Europa, juxta agros." RCN: 4660.

M

Lectotype (Jonsell & Jarvis in *Nordic J. Bot.* 22: 71. 2002): Herb.
  Clifford: 328, *Myagrum 3* (BM-000646252).
Current name: **Neslia paniculata** (L.) Desv. (Brassicaceae).

Myagrum perenne Linnaeus, *Species Plantarum* 2: 640. 1753.
"Habitat in Alsatia." RCN: 4654.
Lectotype (Hedge in Cafferty & Jarvis in *Taxon* 51: 535. 2002): Herb.
  Linn. No. 819.1 (LINN).
Current name: **Rapistrum perenne** (L.) All. (Brassicaceae).

Myagrum perfoliatum Linnaeus, *Species Plantarum* 2: 640. 1753.
"Habitat inter Galliae segetes." RCN: 4658.
Lectotype (Hedge in Jarvis & al., *Regnum Veg.* 127: 68. 1993): Herb.
  Linn. No. 819.10 (LINN).
Generitype of *Myagrum* Linnaeus (vide Green, *Prop. Brit. Bot.*: 170.
  1929).
Current name: **Myagrum perfoliatum** L. (Brassicaceae).

Myagrum rugosum Linnaeus, *Species Plantarum* 2: 640. 1753.
"Habitat in Europa australi." RCN: 4656.
Lectotype (Hedge in Cafferty & Jarvis in *Taxon* 51: 535. 2002): Herb.
  Linn. No. 819.5 (LINN).
Current name: **Rapistrum rugosum** (L.) All. (Brassicaceae).

Myagrum sativum Linnaeus, *Species Plantarum* 2: 641. 1753.
"Habitat in Europa inter linum." RCN: 4659.
Lectotype (Jonsell & Jarvis in *Nordic J. Bot.* 22: 71. 2002): Herb.
  Clifford: 328, *Myagrum 2* (BM-000646251).
Current name: **Camelina sativa** (L.) Crantz (Brassicaceae).

Myagrum saxatile (Linnaeus) Linnaeus, *Systema Naturae,* ed. 10, 2:
  1126. 1759.
["Habitat in Alpibus Helvetiae, Baldi, Carniolae, Monspelii."] Sp. Pl.,
  ed. 2, 2: 894 (1763). RCN: 4661.
Basionym: *Cochlearia saxatilis* L. (1753).
Lectotype (Kit Tan in Cafferty & Jarvis in *Taxon* 51: 533. 2002):
  Herb. Linn. No. 819.13 (LINN).
Current name: **Kernera saxatilis** (L.) Sweet (Brassicaceae).

Myosotis apula Linnaeus, *Species Plantarum* 1: 131. 1753.
"Habitat in Italia, Hispania, Narbona." RCN: 1067.
Lectotype (Qaiser in Jafri & El-Gadi, *Fl. Libya* 68: 88. 1979): *Löfling
  145*, Herb. Linn. No. 180.11 (LINN).
Current name: **Neatostema apulum** (L.) I.M. Johnst. (Boraginaceae).

Myosotis fruticosa Linnaeus, *Mantissa Plantarum Altera*: 201. 1771.
"Habitat ad Cap. b. spei." RCN: 1064.
Lectotype (Förther in Cafferty & Jarvis in *Taxon* 53: 803. 2004):
  Herb. Linn. No. 180.7 (LINN).
Current name: **Heliotropium linifolium** Lehm. (Boraginaceae).

Myosotis lappula Linnaeus, *Species Plantarum* 1: 131. 1753.
"Habitat in Europae argillosis, nudis, ruderatis." RCN: 1066.
Lectotype (Selvi in Cafferty & Jarvis in *Taxon* 53: 803. 2004): Herb.
  Linn. No. 180.9 (LINN).
Current name: **Lappula squarrosa** Retz. (Boraginaceae).

Myosotis scorpioides Linnaeus, *Species Plantarum* 1: 131. 1753.
"Habitat in Europae α campis aridis & β aquosis scaturiginosis."
  RCN: 1063.
Type not designated.
Original material: *Kalm*, Herb. Linn. No. 180.2 (LINN); *Löfling 141*,
  Herb. Linn. No. 180.1 (LINN); Herb. Linn. No. 180.3 (LINN).
Generitype of *Myosotis* Linnaeus (vide Hitchcock, *Prop. Brit. Bot.*:
  127. 1929).

Current name: **Myosotis scorpioides** L. (Boraginaceae).
Note: Although Wade (in *J. Bot.* 80: 128. 1944) indicated Clifford
  material (BM), identifiable with *M. palustris* (L.) Hill as lectotype,
  there have been difficulties with the application of the name, which
  has been used in the sense of both *M. arvensis* (L.) Hill and *M.
  palustris*, and occasionally discarded as a *nomen ambiguum.* Verberne
  (in *Acta Bot. Neerl.* 8: 330–337. 1959) and Holub (in *Preslia* 38:
  130–136. 1966) have both discussed the matter at length. It may be
  that a formal proposal (for conservation or rejection) will be needed
  to resolve this problem.

Myosotis scorpioides Linnaeus var. **arvensis** Linnaeus, *Species
  Plantarum* 1: 131. 1753.
"Habitat in Europae α campis aridis." RCN: 1063.
Lectotype (Selvi in Cafferty & Jarvis in *Taxon* 53: 803. 2004): Herb.
  Clifford: 45, *Myosotis 1* (BM-000557904).
Current name: **Myosotis arvensis** (L.) Hill (Boraginaceae).

Myosotis scorpioides Linnaeus var. **palustris** Linnaeus, *Species
  Plantarum* 1: 131. 1753.
"Habitat in Europae [...] β aquosis scaturiginosis." RCN: 1063.
Lectotype (Wade in *J. Bot.* 80: 128. 1944 [1942]): Herb. Clifford: 46,
  Myosotis 2 (BM-000557905).
Current name: **Myosotis scorpioides** L. (Boraginaceae).
Note: See extensive discussion by Holub (in *Preslia* 38: 130–136. 1966).

Myosotis virginiana Linnaeus, *Species Plantarum* 1: 131. 1753.
"Habitat in Virginia." RCN: 1065.
Lectotype (Wells in Cafferty & Jarvis in *Taxon* 53: 803. 2004):
  Clayton 111 (BM-000038161).
Current name: **Cynoglossum virginianum** L. (Boraginaceae).

Myosurus minimus Linnaeus, *Species Plantarum* 1: 284. 1753.
"Habitat in Europae collibus apricis aridis." RCN: 2263.
Lectotype (Lourteig in *Darwiniana* 9: 562. 1951): Herb. Linn. No.
  402.1 (LINN).
Generitype of *Myosurus* Linnaeus.
Current name: **Myosurus minimus** L. (Ranunculaceae).

Myrica aethiopica Linnaeus, *Mantissa Plantarum Altera*: 298. 1771,
  nom. illeg.
"Habitat ad Cap. b. spei." RCN: 7412.
Replaced synonym: *Myrica conifera* Burm. f. (1768).
Type not designated.
Current name: **Myrica conifera** Burm. f. (Myricaceae).
Note: A superfluous name for *Myrica conifera* Burm. f. (1768), as
  noted by Killick (in *Bothalia* 10: 7. 1969).

Myrica aspleniifolia Linnaeus, *Species Plantarum* 2: 1024. 1753.
"Habitat in America septentrionali." RCN: 7238.
Basionym of: *Liquidambar aspleniifolia* (L.) L. (1763).
Type not designated.
Original material: [icon] in Plukenet, Phytographia: t. 100, f. 7. 1691;
  Almag. Bot.: 260. 1696 – Voucher: Herb. Sloane 97: 13; 101: 49
  (BM-SL); [icon] in Plukenet, Phytographia: t. 100, f. 6. 1691;
  Almag. Bot.: 260. 1696 – Voucher: Herb. Sloane 97: 13; 101: 49
  (BM-SL).
Current name: **Comptonia peregrina** (L.) J.M. Coult. (Myricaceae).
Note: Specific epithet spelled "asplenifolia" in the protologue.
    See discussion by Fernald (in *Rhodora* 40: 411, pl. 514, f. 1, 2.
  1938) who, however, does not formally choose a type. Reveal & al.
  in *Huntia* 7: 223. 1987) did designate "*Clayton 684*" (BM) as
  lectotype but no such specimen can be traced and this statement
  appears to be an error. The name consequently remains
  untypified.

Myrica cerifera Linnaeus, *Species Plantarum* 2: 1024. 1753.
"Habitat in Carolina, Virginia, Pensylvania." RCN: 7411.
Lectotype (Parra-Osorio in *Caldasia* 23: 136. 2001): *Clayton 692*
(BM). – Epitype (Parra-Osorio in *Caldasia* 23: 137. 2001): U.S.A.
Virginia. New Gloucester. Gloucester County. "Thickets along
stream, sandy and marly soil", *E.J. Palmer 39776*, 11 Apr 1932
(NY; iso- A).
Current name: ***Morella cerifera*** (L.) Small (Myricaceae).

Myrica cordifolia Linnaeus, *Species Plantarum* 2: 1025. 1753.
"Habitat in Aethiopia." RCN: 7414.
Lectotype (Killick in *Bothalia* 10: 14. 1969): Herb. Linn. No. 1169.7
(LINN).
Current name: ***Morella cordifolia*** (L.) Killick (Myricaceae).

Myrica gale Linnaeus, *Species Plantarum* 2: 1024. 1753.
"Habitat in Europae septentrionalis uliginosis." RCN: 7410.
Lectotype (Jonsell & Jarvis in Jarvis & al., *Regnum Veg.* 127: 68.
1993): Herb. Linn. No. 373 (LAPP).
Generitype of *Myrica* Linnaeus (vide Green, *Prop. Brit. Bot.*: 191.
1929).
Current name: ***Myrica gale*** L. (Myricaceae).
Note: Verdcourt & Polhill (in *Taxon* 46: 347. 1997) proposed *M.
cerifera* L. as conserved type of the genus but the proposal was not
recommended by the Committee for Spermatophyta (in *Taxon* 48:
365. 1999).
    Jonsell & Jarvis (in *Nordic J. Bot.* 14: 152. 1994) provide
additional information on their 1993 choice of lectotype.

Myrica quercifolia Linnaeus, *Species Plantarum* 2: 1025. 1753.
"Habitat in Aethiopia." RCN: 7413.
Lectotype (Wijnands, *Bot. Commelins*: 154. 1983): Herb. Clifford:
456, *Myrica* 3 (BM-000647471).
Current name: ***Morella quercifolia*** (L.) Killick (Myricaceae).

Myrica trifoliata Linnaeus, *Plantae Rariores Africanae*. 28. 1760.
["Habitat ad Cap. b. spei."] Sp. Pl., ed. 2, 2: 1453 (1763). RCN:
7415.
Type not designated.
Original material: none traced.
Current name: ***Toddalia trifoliata*** (L.) Druce (Rutaceae).

Myriophyllum spicatum Linnaeus, *Species Plantarum* 2: 992. 1753.
"Habitat in Europae aquis quietis." RCN: 7198.
Lectotype (Ghazanfar in Nasir & Ali, *Fl. W. Pakistan* 113: 4. 1977):
Herb. Linn. No. 1123.1 (LINN).
Generitype of *Myriophyllum* Linnaeus (vide Green, *Prop. Brit. Bot.*:
188. 1929).
Current name: ***Myriophyllum spicatum*** L. (Haloragaceae).
Note: Aiken & McNeill (in *Bot. J. Linn. Soc.* 80: 216–218. 1980)
provided a very thorough investigation of the original materials for
this name, illustrating most of them, and concluded by designating
Herb. Burser VII(1): 79 (UPS) as lectotype. However, they were
evidently unaware of Ghazanfar's earlier choice of material in LINN
as type. Aiken & McNeill identified the material on Ghazanfar's
type sheet as mixed, the two specimens to the left being *M.
exalbescens* Fernald, and only the right specimen being *M. spicatum*.
Restriction of the type to the latter specimen appears to be highly
desirable.

Myriophyllum verticillatum Linnaeus, *Species Plantarum* 2: 992.
1753.
"Habitat in Europae inundatis." RCN: 7199.
Lectotype (Ghazanfar in Nasir & Ali, *Fl. W. Pakistan* 113: 2. 1977):
Herb. Linn. No. 1123.2 (LINN).

Current name: ***Myriophyllum verticillatum*** L. (Haloragaceae).
Note: Aiken & McNeill (in *Bot. J. Linn. Soc.* 80: 219. 1980), evidently
unaware of Ghazanfar's earlier choice of 1123.2 (LINN) as type,
discussed the original material for this name and concluded by
designating part (the specimen to the left) of the material of 1123.3
(LINN) as lectotype. Despite being sterile, the type designated by
Ghazanfar is identifiable as *M. verticillatum*, according to Aiken &
McNeill.

Myrsine africana Linnaeus, *Species Plantarum* 1: 196. 1753.
"Habitat in Aethiopia." RCN: 1590.
Lectotype (Dyer in Dyer & al., *Fl. Southern Africa* 26: 5. 1963): Herb.
Linn. No. 267.1 (LINN).
Generitype of *Myrsine* Linnaeus.
Current name: ***Myrsine africana*** L. (Myrsinaceae).

Myrtus androsaemoides Linnaeus, *Species Plantarum* 1: 472. 1753.
"Habitat in Zeylona." RCN: 3613.
Lectotype (Kostermans in *Quart. J. Taiwan Mus.* 34: 152. 1981):
Herb. Hermann 2: 53, No. 184 (BM).
Current name: ***Syzygium cordifolium*** Walp. subsp. ***spissum*** (Alston)
P.S. Ashton (Myrtaceae).

Myrtus angustifolia Linnaeus, *Systema Naturae*, ed. 12, 2: 340;
Mantissa Plantarum: 74. 1767.
"Habitat ad Cap. b. spei." RCN: 3606.
Type not designated.
Original material: *Schreber*, Herb. Linn. No. 637.7 (LINN); [icon] in
Burman, Rar. Afric. Pl.: 237, t. 83, f. 2. 1739.
Current name: ***Metrosideros angustifolia*** (L.) Sm. (Myrtaceae).

Myrtus biflora Linnaeus, *Systema Naturae*, ed. 10, 2: 1056. 1759.
["Habitat in Jamaica."] Sp. Pl., ed. 2, 1: 674 (1762). RCN: 3605.
Lectotype (Fawcett & Rendle, *Fl. Jamaica* 5: 338. 1926): *Browne*,
Herb. Linn. No. 637.6 (LINN).
Current name: ***Eugenia biflora*** (L.) DC. (Myrtaceae).

Myrtus brasiliana Linnaeus, *Species Plantarum* 1: 471. 1753.
"Habitat in Brasilia. D. Wachend." RCN: 3604.
Lectotype (Wijnands, *Bot. Commelins*: 155. 1983): Herb. Linn. No.
637.5 (LINN), see p. 233.
Current name: ***Eugenia uniflora*** L. (Myrtaceae).

Myrtus caryophyllata Linnaeus, *Species Plantarum* 1: 472. 1753.
"Habitat in Zeylona." RCN: 3614.
Lectotype (Kostermans in *Quart. J. Taiwan Mus.* 34: 133. 1981):
Herb. Hermann 2: 3; 4: 34, No. 183 (BM).
Current name: ***Syzygium caryophyllatum*** (L.) Alston (Myrtaceae).
Note: As the material in Herb. Hermann appears to be part of a single
gathering (Art. 9.15), Kostermans is accepted as having typified the
name.

Myrtus chytraculia Linnaeus, *Systema Naturae*, ed. 10, 2: 1056. 1759.
["Habitat in Jamaica."] Sp. Pl., ed. 2, 1: 675 (1762). RCN: 3610.
Lectotype (designated here by Holst): *Browne*, Herb. Linn. No.
637.12 (LINN).
Current name: ***Calyptranthes chytraculia*** (L.) Sw. (Myrtaceae).

Myrtus communis Linnaeus, *Species Plantarum* 1: 471. 1753.
"Habitat in Europa australi, Asia, Africa." RCN: 3603.
Lectotype (Chamberlain in Jarvis & al., *Regnum Veg.* 127: 68. 1993):
Herb. Clifford: 184, *Myrtus* 1 (BM-000628600).
Generitype of *Myrtus* Linnaeus (vide de Candolle, *Note Myrt.*: 7.
1826).
Current name: ***Myrtus communis*** L. subsp. ***communis*** (Myrtaceae).

M

Note: McVaugh (in Howard, *Fl. Lesser Antilles* 5: 515. 1989) indicated 637.1 (LINN) as a possible type, but his "?" makes this statement contrary to Art. 7.11.

Myrtus communis Linnaeus var. **acutifolia** Linnaeus, *Species Plantarum* 1: 471. 1753.
RCN: 3603.
Replaced synonym of: *Myrtus communis* L. var. *lusitanica* L. (1762), *nom. illeg.*
Type not designated.
Original material: Herb. Burser XXIV: 89 (UPS).
Current name: *Myrtus* **sp.** (Myrtaceae).
Note: The application of this name appears uncertain.

Myrtus communis Linnaeus var. **angustifolia** Linnaeus, *Species Plantarum* 1: 471. 1753.
RCN: 3603.
Type not designated.
Original material: none traced.
Current name: *Myrtus* **sp.** (Myrtaceae).
Note: The application of this name appears uncertain.

Myrtus communis Linnaeus var. **baetica** Linnaeus, *Species Plantarum* 1: 471. 1753.
RCN: 3603.
Type not designated.
Original material: Herb. Clifford: 184, *Myrtus* 1 β (BM); Herb. Burser XXIV: 88 (UPS); [icon] in Clusius, Rar. Pl. Hist. 1: 65. 1601.
Current name: *Myrtus communis* L. var. *baetica* L. (Myrtaceae).
Note: See notes by Andrews (in *Kew Mag.* 9: 32–33. 1992).

Myrtus communis Linnaeus var. **belgica** Linnaeus, *Species Plantarum* 1: 471. 1753.
RCN: 3603.
Type not designated.
Original material: none traced.
Current name: *Myrtus* **sp.** (Myrtaceae).
Note: The application of this name appears uncertain.

Myrtus communis Linnaeus var. **italica** Linnaeus, *Species Plantarum,* ed. 2, 1: 673. 1762.
RCN: 3603.
Type not designated.
Original material: Herb. Burser XXIV: 87 (UPS).
Current name: *Myrtus* **sp.** (Myrtaceae).
Note: The application of this name appears uncertain.

Myrtus communis Linnaeus var. **lusitanica** Linnaeus, *Species Plantarum,* ed. 2, 1: 674. 1762, *nom. illeg.*
RCN: 3603.
Replaced synonym: *Myrtus communis* L. var. *acutifolia* L. (1753).
Type not designated.
Original material: as replaced synonym.
Current name: *Myrtus* **sp.** (Myrtaceae).
Note: An illegitimate replacement name for *M. communis* var. *acutifolia* L. (1753), the validating diagnosis of which is cited in the synonymy of var. *lusitanica*. The application of both names appears uncertain.

Myrtus communis Linnaeus var. **mucronata** Linnaeus, *Species Plantarum* 1: 471. 1753.
RCN: 3603.
Type not designated.
Original material: Herb. Clifford: 184, *Myrtus* 1 (BM).
Current name: *Myrtus* **sp.** (Myrtaceae).
Note: The application of this name appears uncertain.

Myrtus communis Linnaeus var. **romana** Linnaeus, *Species Plantarum* 1: 471. 1753.
RCN: 3603.
Type not designated.
Original material: none traced.
Current name: *Myrtus* **sp.** (Myrtaceae).
Note: The application of this name appears uncertain.

Myrtus communis Linnaeus var. **tarentina** Linnaeus, *Species Plantarum* 1: 471. 1753.
RCN: 3603.
Type not designated.
Original material: Herb. Burser XXIV: 90 (UPS); Herb. Clifford: 184, *Myrtus* 1 γ (BM).
Current name: *Myrtus communis* L. subsp. *tarentina* (L.) Nyman (Myrtaceae).

Myrtus cumini Linnaeus, *Species Plantarum* 1: 471. 1753.
"Habitat in Zeylona." RCN: 3608.
Lectotype (Kostermans in *Quart. J. Taiwan Mus.* 34: 134. 1981; Verdcourt in Beentje, *Fl. Trop. E. Africa, Myrtaceae*: 72. 2001): Herb. Hermann 1: 45, No. 185, right specimen (BM-000621389).
Current name: *Syzygium cumini* (L.) Skeels (Myrtaceae).
Note: The earliest type choice appears to be that of Kostermans who designated material in Herb. Hermann 1: 41 (BM) as the type. Presumably unaware of this, Scott (in Bosser & al., *Fl. Mascareignes* 92: 40. 1990) designated 637.10 (LINN) as type, but Parnell & Chantaranothai (in *Thai Forest Bull., Bot.* 21: 57. 1994) pointed out that this collection is not identifiable as *S. cumini*. Verdcourt subsequently restricted the type choice to one of the two collections on Hermann's sheet.

Myrtus dioica Linnaeus, *Systema Naturae,* ed. 10, 2: 1056. 1759.
["Habitat in America. Miller."] Sp. Pl., ed. 2, 1: 675 (1762). RCN: 3609.
Lectotype (Merrill in *Contr. Gray Herb.* 165: 32. 1947): *Miller*, Herb. Linn. No. 637.11 (LINN).
Current name: *Pimenta dioica* (L.) Merr. (Myrtaceae).

Myrtus leucadendra Linnaeus, *Herbarium Amboinense*: 9. 1754, *typ. cons.*
["Habitat in Amboina."] Sp. Pl., ed. 2, 1: 676 (1762). RCN: 5733.
Basionym of: *Melaleuca leucadendra* (L.) L. (1767).
Lectotype (Blake in *Contr. Queensland Herb.* 1: 17. 1968): [icon] *"Arbor alba"* in Rumphius, Herb. Amboin. 2: 72, t. 16. 1741.
Generitype of *Melaleuca* Linnaeus, *nom. cons.*
Current name: *Melaleuca leucadendra* (L.) L. (Myrtaceae).
Note: Merrill (*Interpret. Rumph. Herb. Amb.*: 33, 402. 1917) indicated Rumphius' plates and descriptions as the type, but did not distinguish between the two plates (2: t. 16 and t. 17).

Myrtus lucida Linnaeus, *Systema Naturae,* ed. 10, 2: 1056. 1759.
["Habitat Surinami. Rolander."] Sp. Pl., ed. 2, 1: 674 (1762). RCN: 3607.
Lectotype (McVaugh in *Publ. Field Mus. Nat. Hist., Bot. Ser.* 13: 662. 1958): Herb. Linn. No. 637.9 (LINN).
Current name: *Myrcia sylvatica* (G. Mey.) DC. (Myrtaceae).

Myrtus pimenta Linnaeus, *Species Plantarum* 1: 472. 1753.
"Habitat in India." RCN: 3615.
Lectotype (Landrum, *Fl. Neotropica* 45: 83. 1986): [icon] *"Myrtus arborea, foliis laurinis, aromatica"* in Sloane, Voy. Jamaica 2: 76, t. 191, f. 1. 1725. – Typotype: Herb. Sloane 6: 78 (BM-SL).
Current name: *Pimenta dioica* (L.) Merr. (Myrtaceae).

Myrtus zeylanica Linnaeus, *Species Plantarum* 1: 472. 1753.
"Habitat in Zeylona." RCN: 3612.
Lectotype (Kostermans in *Quart. J. Taiwan Mus.* 34: 156. 1981):
Herb. Hermann 1: 47; 4: 21, No. 182 (BM).
Current name: ***Syzygium zeylanicum*** (L.) DC. (Myrtaceae).
Note: As the material in Herb. Hermann appears to be part of a single
gathering (Art. 9.15), Kostermans is accepted as having typified the
name.

Myrtus zuzygium Linnaeus, *Systema Naturae,* ed. 10, 2: 1056.
1759.
["Habitat in Jamaica."] Sp. Pl., ed. 2, 1: 675 (1762). RCN: 3611.
Lectotype (designated here by Holst): *Browne*, Herb. Linn. No.
637.13 (LINN).
Current name: ***Calyptranthes zuzygium*** (L.) Sw. (Myrtaceae).

M

N

Najas marina Linnaeus, *Species Plantarum* 2: 1015. 1753.
"Habitat in Europae maribus." RCN: 7354.
Lectotype (Viinikka in *Ann. Bot. Fenn.* 13: 128. 1976): Herb. Linn.
No. 1156.1 (LINN).
Generitype of *Najas* Linnaeus.
Current name: ***Najas marina*** L. (Najadaceae).
Note: Casper (in *Feddes Repert.* 90: 217. 1979) designated a Vaillant
illustration as the lectotype but Viinikka's choice of 1156.1 (LINN)
has priority and, as the annotations on the sheet support the
contention that the sheet was in Linnaeus' possession in 1753, there
seem to be no valid grounds for rejecting this choice.

Nama jamaicensis Linnaeus, *Systema Naturae*, ed. 10, 2: 950. 1759,
typ. cons.
["Habitat in Jamaica."] Sp. Pl., ed. 2, 1: 327 (1762). RCN: 1849.

Lectotype (Howard, *Fl. Lesser Antilles* 6: 187. 1989): [icon] *"Nama
reclinata villosa, foliis ovatis, petiolis marginatis recurrentibus, floribus
solitariis"* in Browne, Civ. Nat. Hist. Jamaica: 185, t. 18, f. 2. 1756.
Generitype of *Nama* Linnaeus (1759), *nom. cons.*
Current name: ***Nama jamaicensis*** L. (Hydrophyllaceae).
Note: Nama Linnaeus (1759), *nom. cons.* against *Nama* Linnaeus
(1753).

Nama zeylanica Linnaeus, *Species Plantarum* 1: 226. 1753.
"Habitat in India." RCN: 1848.
Lectotype (Verdcourt in Polhill, *Fl. Trop. E. Africa, Hydrophyllaceae*: 4.
1989): Herb. Hermann 3: 42, No. 117 (BM-000621954).
Generitype of *Nama* Linnaeus (1753), *nom. rej.*
Current name: ***Hydrolea zeylanica*** (L.) Vahl (Hydrophyllaceae).
Note: Nama Linnaeus (1753), *nom. rej.* in favour of *Nama* Linnaeus
(1759).
    Davenport (in *Rhodora* 90: 198. 1988) indicated 322.1 (LINN)
as lectotype, but it was a later addition to the herbarium and is not
original material for the name.

Napaea dioica Linnaeus, *Species Plantarum* 2: 686. 1753.
"Habitat in Virginia." RCN: 7519.
Replaced synonym of: *Napaea scabra* L. (1771), *nom. illeg.*
Lectotype (Iltis in *Amer. Midl. Naturalist* 70: 94. 1963): Herb. Linn.
No. 1203.2 (LINN).
Generitype of *Napaea* Linnaeus (vide Green, *Prop. Brit. Bot.*: 172.
1929).
Current name: ***Napaea dioica*** L. (Malvaceae).

Napaea hermaphrodita Linnaeus, *Species Plantarum* 2: 686. 1753.
"Habitat in Virginia." RCN: 7518.
Replaced synonym of: *Napaea laevis* L. (1771), *nom. illeg.*
Lectotype (Iltis in *Amer. Midl. Naturalist* 70: 106. 1963): Herb. Linn.
No. 1203.1 (LINN).
Current name: ***Sida hermaphrodita*** (L.) Rusby (Malvaceae).

Napaea laevis Linnaeus, *Mantissa Plantarum Altera*: 435. 1771, *nom.
illeg.*
["Habitat in Virginia."] Sp. Pl. 2: 686 (1753). RCN: 7518.
Replaced synonym: *Napaea hermaphrodita* L. (1753).
Lectotype (Iltis in *Amer. Midl. Naturalist* 70: 106. 1963): Herb. Linn.
No. 1203.1 (LINN).
Current name: ***Sida hermaphrodita*** (L.) Rusby (Malvaceae).
Note: A superfluous name for *N. hermaphrodita* L. (1753).

Napaea scabra Linnaeus, *Mantissa Plantarum Altera*: 435. 1771, *nom.
illeg.*
["Habitat in Virginia."] Sp. Pl. 2: 686 (1753). RCN: 7519.
Replaced synonym: *Napaea dioica* L. (1753).
Lectotype (Iltis in *Amer. Midl. Naturalist* 70: 94. 1963): Herb. Linn.
No. 1203.2 (LINN).
Current name: ***Napaea dioica*** L. (Malvaceae).
Note: A superfluous name for *N. dioica* L. (1753).

Narcissus bicolor Linnaeus, *Species Plantarum*, ed. 2, 1: 415.
1762.
"Habitat in Europa australi." RCN: 2306.
Lectotype (Pugsley in *J. Roy. Hort. Soc.* 58: 85, f. 18. 1933): Herb.
Linn. No. 412.3 (LINN).
Current name: ***Narcissus bicolor*** L. (Liliaceae/Amaryllidaceae).
Note: See also discussion by Barra & López González (in *Anales Jard.
Bot. Madrid* 40: 350. 1984).

Narcissus bulbocodium Linnaeus, *Species Plantarum* 1: 289.
1753.
"Habitat inter Ulyssiponem & Hispalim." RCN: 2314.
Lectotype (Barra & López González in *Anales Jard. Bot. Madrid* 40:
357. 1984): Herb. Linn. No. 412.12 (LINN).
Current name: ***Narcissus bulbocodium*** L. (Liliaceae/Amaryllidaceae).
Note: See Meikle (in *Curtis's Bot. Mag.* 179: t. 650. 1973).

Narcissus calathinus Linnaeus, *Species Plantarum*, ed. 2, 1: 415. 1762.
"Habitat in Europa australi, Oriente." RCN: 2312.
Lectotype (Barra & López González in *Anales Jard. Bot. Madrid* 40: 352. 1984): [icon] *"Narcissus angustifolius flavus magno calice"* in Rudbeck, Campi Elysii 2: 60, f. 5. 1701.
Current name: **Narcissus calathinus** L. (Liliaceae/Amaryllidaceae).

Narcissus jonquilla Linnaeus, *Species Plantarum* 1: 290. 1753.
"Habitat inter Hispalim & Gades inter Guadalopam & Toletum in uliginosis." RCN: 2316.
Lectotype (Barra & López González in *Anales Jard. Bot. Madrid* 40: 358. 1984): Herb. Burser III: 40, left specimen (UPS).
Current name: **Narcissus jonquilla** L. (Liliaceae/Amaryllidaceae).

Narcissus minor Linnaeus, *Species Plantarum*, ed. 2, 1: 415. 1762.
"Habitat in Hispania." RCN: 2307.
Lectotype (Pugsley in *J. Roy. Hort. Soc.* 58: 44, f. 10. 1933): Herb. Linn. No. 412.4 (LINN).
Current name: **Narcissus minor** L. (Liliaceae/Amaryllidaceae).
Note: Barra & López González (in *Anales Jard. Bot. Madrid* 40: 351. 1984) also indicated 412.4 (LINN) as lectotype but later (*l.c.* 52: 171–178. 1995) questioned its identity. Like Pugsley, they published a photograph of the type (their f. 3), but concluded that *N. minor* is the correct name for what has been known as *N. jacetanus* Fern. Casas.

Narcissus moschatus Linnaeus, *Species Plantarum*, ed. 2, 1: 415. 1762.
"Habitat in Hispania." RCN: 2308.
Lectotype (Pugsley in *J. Roy. Hort. Soc.* 58: 77, f. 16. 1933): Herb. Linn. No. 412.5 (LINN).
Current name: **Narcissus moschatus** L. (Liliaceae/Amaryllidaceae).
Note: See also discussion by Barra & López González (in *Anales Jard. Bot. Madrid* 40: 352. 1984).

Narcissus odorus Linnaeus, *Centuria II Plantarum*: 14. 1756.
"Habitat in Stiria." RCN: 2311.
Type not designated.
Original material: Herb. Linn. No. 13.1 (S); Herb. Linn. No. 412.8 (LINN); [icon] in Rudbeck, Campi Elysii 2: 44, f. 3. 1701.
Current name: **Narcissus × odorus** L. (Liliaceae/Amaryllidaceae).

Narcissus orientalis Linnaeus, *Systema Naturae*, ed. 12, 2: 235; *Mantissa Plantarum*: 62. 1767.
"Habitat in Oriente." RCN: 2310.
Lectotype (Barra & López González in *Anales Jard. Bot. Madrid* 40: 359. 1984): [icon] *"Narcissus niveus calice flavo odoris fragrantissimi"* in Rudbeck, Campi Elysii 2: 58, f. 13. 1701.
Current name: **Narcissus orientalis** L. (Liliaceae/Amaryllidaceae).

Narcissus poëticus Linnaeus, *Species Plantarum* 1: 289. 1753.
"Habitat in Gallia Narbonensi, Italia." RCN: 2304.
Lectotype (Barra & López González in *Anales Jard. Bot. Madrid* 40: 348. 1984): Herb. Linn. No. 412.1, left specimen (LINN).
Generitype of *Narcissus* Linnaeus (vide Hitchcock, *Prop. Brit. Bot.*: 144. 1929).
Current name: **Narcissus poëticus** L. (Liliaceae/Amaryllidaceae).

Narcissus pseudonarcissus Linnaeus, *Species Plantarum* 1: 289. 1753.
"Habitat in Angliae, Hispaniae, Italiae nemoribus." RCN: 2305.
Lectotype (Barra & López González in *Anales Jard. Bot. Madrid* 40: 349. 1984): Herb. Burser III: 42 (UPS).
Current name: **Narcissus pseudonarcissus** L. (Liliaceae/Amaryllidaceae).

Note: Specific epithet spelled "Pseudo Narcissus" in the protologue. Pugsley (in *J. Roy. Hort. Soc.* 58: 18–21. 1933) discussed the early treatment of daffodils by pre-Linnaean authors, including (p. 65) some of the elements for this name, but without choosing a type.

Narcissus serotinus Linnaeus, *Species Plantarum* 1: 290. 1753.
"Habitat in Hispania." RCN: 2315.
Lectotype (Barra & López González in *Anales Jard. Bot. Madrid* 40: 358. 1984): *Löfling s.n.*, Herb. Linn. No. 412.14 (LINN).
Current name: **Narcissus serotinus** L. (Liliaceae/Amaryllidaceae).

Narcissus tazetta Linnaeus, *Species Plantarum* 1: 290. 1753.
"Habitat in Galliae Narbonensis, Lusitaniae, Hispaniae maritimis." RCN: 2313.
Type not designated.
Original material: Herb. Burser III: 35 (UPS); [icon] in Clusius, Rar. Pl. Hist. 1: 159, 160. 1601.
Current name: **Narcissus tazetta** L. (Liliaceae/Amaryllidaceae).
Note: Barra & López González (in *Anales Jard. Bot. Madrid* 40: 356. 1984) indicated 412.9 (LINN) as the lectotype, but this collection lacks the relevant *Species Plantarum* number (i.e. "6") and was a post-1753 addition to the herbarium, and is not original material for the name.

Narcissus triandrus Linnaeus, *Species Plantarum*, ed. 2, 1: 416. 1762.
"Habitat in Pyrenaeis." RCN: 2309.
Lectotype (Barra & López González in *Anales Jard. Bot. Madrid* 39: 70, f. 1. 1982): [icon] *"Narcissus juncifolius albo flo. reflexo"* in Clusius, Cur. Post. (App. Alt.): [20]. 1611.
Current name: **Narcissus triandrus** L. (Liliaceae/Amaryllidaceae).
Note: See also Barra & López González (in *Anales Jard. Bot. Madrid* 40: 353. 1984).

Narcissus trilobus Linnaeus, *Species Plantarum*, ed. 2, 1: 417. 1762.
"Habitat in Europa australi." RCN: 2317.
Lectotype (Barra & López González in *Anales Jard. Bot. Madrid* 40: 354. 1984): Herb. Linn. No. 412.7 (LINN).
Current name: **Narcissus jonquilla L. × N. bicolor L.** (Liliaceae/Amaryllidaceae).

Nardus aristata Linnaeus, *Species Plantarum*, ed. 2, 1: 78. 1762, *nom. illeg.*
"Habitat Romae." RCN: 446.
Replaced synonym: *Nardus incurva* Gouan (1762).
Type not designated.
Current name: **Psilurus incurvus** (Gouan) Schinz & Thell. (Poaceae).
Note: Specific epithet spelled "aristatus" in the protologue.
Stace & Jarvis (in *Bot. J. Linn. Soc.* 91: 441. 1985) noted that this is an illegitimate replacement name, published in September 1762, for *Nardus incurva* Gouan (*Hort. Reg. Monsp.*: 33. Apr 1762). Linnaeus cited the latter as a synonym of *N. aristata* (Sep 1762) in the Appendix to *Sp. Pl.*, ed. 2, 2: 1676 (1763).

Nardus articulata Linnaeus, *Species Plantarum* 1: 53. 1753.
"Habitat in Italia, Hispania, G. Narbonensi." RCN: 7594.
Lectotype (Cope in Cafferty & al. in *Taxon* 49: 252. 2000): [icon] *"Gramen Myuros erectum minimum arundinaceum"* in Boccone, Mus. Piante Rar. Sicilia: 70, t. 59. 1697. – Epitype (Cope in Cafferty & al. in *Taxon* 49: 252. 2000): Italy. Veneto, Prov. di Padova: "Abano loco dicto Montiron et Montegrotto...". Flora Italica Exsiccata curantibus Adr. Fiori, 16 Jun 1905, *Beguinot & Pampanini 216* (K; iso- BM, FI).
Current name: **Parapholis incurva** (L.) C.E. Hubb. (Poaceae).

N

Nardus ciliaris Linnaeus, *Species Plantarum* 1: 53. 1753.
"Habitat in India." RCN: 447.
Lectotype (Stearn in *Taxon* 10: 17. 1961): Herb. Linn. No. 73.7 (LINN).
Current name: ***Eremochloa ciliaris*** (L.) Merr. (Poaceae).

Nardus gangitis Linnaeus, *Species Plantarum* 1: 53. 1753, *nom. utique rej.*
"Habitat in G. Narbonensi." RCN: 445.
Type not designated.
Original material: Herb. Linn. No. 73.6 (LINN); [icon] in Morison, Pl. Hist. Univ. 3: 257, s. 8, t. 13, f. penult., ult. 1699; [icon] in Plantin, Pl. Stirp. Icon.: 84. 1581.
Current name: ***Ctenium aromaticum*** (Walter) Alph. Wood (Poaceae).

Nardus stricta Linnaeus, *Species Plantarum* 1: 53. 1753.
"Habitat in Europae asperis, sterilibus, duris." RCN: 444.
Lectotype (Cope in Jarvis & al., *Regnum Veg.* 127: 69. 1993): Herb. Linn. No. 73.5 (LINN).
Generitype of *Nardus* Linnaeus (vide Hitchcock, *Prop. Brit. Bot.*: 119. 1929).
Current name: ***Nardus stricta*** L. (Poaceae).
Note: Although Kerguélen (in *Lejeunia*, n.s., 75: 215. 1975) indicated unspecified material in LINN as type, this is not accepted as an effective typification (Art. 7.11). See Cafferty & al. (in *Taxon* 49: 240. 2000) for a detailed explanation.

Nauclea orientalis (Linnaeus) Linnaeus, *Species Plantarum*, ed. 2, 1: 243. 1762.
"Habitat in India Asiatica." RCN: 1350.
Basionym: *Cephalanthus orientalis* L. (1753).
Lectotype (Merrill in *J. Washington Acad. Sci.* 5: 533. 1915): Herb. Hermann 5: 338, No. 53 [icon] (BM-000621104).
Generitype of *Nauclea* Linnaeus.
Current name: ***Nauclea orientalis*** (L.) L. (Rubiaceae).

Nepenthes distillatoria Linnaeus, *Species Plantarum* 2: 955. 1753.
"Habitat in Zeylona." RCN: 6913.
Lectotype (designated here by Cheek): Herb. Hermann 3: 52, No. 321 (BM).
Generitype of *Nepenthes* Linnaeus.
Current name: ***Nepenthes distillatoria*** L. (Nepenthaceae).

Nepeta cataria Linnaeus, *Species Plantarum* 2: 570. 1753.
"Habitat in Europa." RCN: 4168.
Lectotype (Ubera & Valdés in *Lagascalia* 12: 17. 1983): Herb. Linn. No. 726.1 (LINN).
Generitype of *Nepeta* Linnaeus (vide Green, *Prop. Brit. Bot.*: 164. 1929).
Current name: ***Nepeta cataria*** L. (Lamiaceae).

Nepeta hirsuta Linnaeus, *Species Plantarum* 2: 571. 1753, *nom. utique rej.*
"Habitat in Sicilia." RCN: 4174.
Type not designated.
Original material: Herb. Clifford: 311, *Nepeta* 3 (BM); [icon] in Boccone, Icon. Descr. Rar. Pl. Siciliae: 48, 49, t. 25, f. 2. 1674.
Current name: ***Nepeta scordotis*** L. (Lamiaceae).

Nepeta indica Linnaeus, *Species Plantarum* 2: 571. 1753.
"Habitat in India." RCN: 4180.
Lectotype (Cramer in Dassanayake & Fosberg, *Revised Handb. Fl. Ceylon* 3: 176. 1981): Herb. Linn. No. 726.28 (LINN).
Current name: ***Anisomeles indica*** (L.) Kuntze (Lamiaceae).

Nepeta italica Linnaeus, *Species Plantarum* 2: 571. 1753.
"Habitat in Italia. D. Ratgeb." RCN: 4175.
Lectotype (Budantzev in Jarvis & al. in *Taxon* 50: 515. 2001): Herb. Linn. No. 726.24 (LINN).
Current name: ***Nepeta italica*** L. (Lamiaceae).

Nepeta malabarica Linnaeus, *Mantissa Plantarum Altera*: 566. 1771.
RCN: 4179.
Lectotype (Cramer in Dassanayake & Fosberg, *Revised Handb. Fl. Ceylon* 3: 178. 1981): Herb. Linn. No. 726.26 (LINN).
Current name: ***Anisomeles malabarica*** (L.) Sims (Lamiaceae).

Nepeta multifida Linnaeus, *Species Plantarum* 2: 572. 1753.
"Habitat in Dauria." RCN: 4181.
Lectotype (Hedge in Jarvis & al. in *Taxon* 50: 515. 2001): *Steller?*, Herb. Linn. No. 726.30 (LINN).
Current name: ***Schizonepeta multifida*** (L.) Briq. (Lamiaceae).

Nepeta nepetella Linnaeus, *Systema Naturae*, ed. 10, 2: 1096. 1759.
["Habitat in Europa australi."] Sp. Pl., ed. 2, 2: 797 (1763). RCN: 4172.
Lectotype (Budantzev in Jarvis & al. in *Taxon* 50: 515. 2001): Herb. Linn. No. 726.11 (LINN).
Current name: ***Nepeta nepetella*** L. (Lamiaceae).
Note: Ubera & Valdés (in *Lagascalia* 12: 21. 1983) discussed sheet 726.9 (LINN), noting that at least some of the material (annotated "Roy 20"), had been received from (they believed) Adriaan van Royen. In fact it came from his nephew, David van Royen, as confirmed by a numbered list contained in his letter to Linnaeus dated 16 March 1765. It cannot, therefore, be original material for this 1759 name.

Nepeta nuda Linnaeus, *Species Plantarum* 2: 570. 1753.
"Habitat in Hispania." RCN: 4173.
Lectotype (Ubera & Valdés in *Lagascalia* 12: 47. 1983): Herb. Linn. No. 726.14 (LINN).
Current name: ***Nepeta nuda*** L. (Lamiaceae).

Nepeta pannonica Linnaeus, *Species Plantarum* 2: 570. 1753.
"Habitat in Pannonia." RCN: 4169.
Lectotype (Budantzev in Jarvis & al. in *Taxon* 50: 515. 2001): Herb. Burser XIII: 10 (UPS).
Current name: ***Nepeta nuda*** L. subsp. ***nuda*** (Lamiaceae).

Nepeta pectinata Linnaeus, *Systema Naturae*, ed. 10, 2: 1097. 1759.
["Habitat in Jamaica."] Sp. Pl., ed. 2, 2: 799 (1763). RCN: 4182.
Lectotype (Howard, *Fl. Lesser Antilles* 6: 248. 1989): *Browne*, Herb. Linn. No. 726.31 (LINN).
Current name: ***Hyptis pectinata*** (L.) Poit. (Lamiaceae).

Nepeta scordotis Linnaeus, *Centuria II Plantarum*: 20. 1756.
"Habitat in Creta. Miller." RCN: 4177.
Lectotype (Turland in *Bull. Nat. Hist. Mus. London, Bot.* 25: 152, f. 23. 1995): Herb. Linn. No. 726.23 (LINN).
Current name: ***Nepeta scordotis*** L. (Lamiaceae).
Note: Siddiqi (in Jafri & El Gadi, *Fl. Libya* 118: 96. 1985) stated "Type: Herb. Linn. 726.23/24 (LINN)". However, as these two collections are clearly not part of a single gathering, Art. 9.15 does not apply.

Nepeta sibirica Linnaeus, *Species Plantarum* 2: 572. 1753.
"Habitat in Sibiria." RCN: 4321.

Basionym of: *Dracocephalum sibiricum* (L.) L. (1759).
Lectotype (Hedge in Jarvis & al. in *Taxon* 50: 511. 2001): [icon]
   "Cataria montana, folio Veronicae pratensis" in Buxbaum, Pl. Minus
   Cognit. Cent. 3: 27, t. 50, f. 1. 1729.
Current name: **Nepeta sibirica** L. (Lamiaceae).

Nepeta tuberosa Linnaeus, *Species Plantarum* 2: 571. 1753.
"Habitat in Hispania, Lusitania." RCN: 4176.
Lectotype (Ubera & Valdés in *Lagascalia* 12: 60. 1983): Herb. Linn.
   No. 726.20 (LINN).
Current name: **Nepeta tuberosa** L. (Lamiaceae).

Nepeta ucranica Linnaeus, *Species Plantarum* 2: 570. 1753.
"Habitat in Ucrania." RCN: 4171.
Lectotype (Budantzev in Jarvis & al. in *Taxon* 50: 515. 2001): *Gerber*,
   Herb. Linn. No. 726.8 (LINN).
Current name: **Nepeta ucranica** L. (Lamiaceae).

Nepeta violacea Linnaeus, *Species Plantarum* 2: 570. 1753.
"Habitat in Hispania." RCN: 4170.
Lectotype (Hedge in Jarvis & al. in *Taxon* 50: 515. 2001): Herb. Linn.
   No. 726.6 (LINN).
Current name: **Nepeta nuda** L. (Lamiaceae).

Nepeta virginica Linnaeus, *Species Plantarum* 2: 571. 1753.
"Habitat in Virginia." RCN: 4178.
Type not designated.
Original material: Herb. Linn. No. 726.25 (LINN); [icon] in
   Plukenet, Phytographia: t. 85, f. 2. 1691; Almag. Bot.: 110. 1696 –
   Typotype: Herb. Sloane 95: 181 (BM-SL) – Voucher: Herb. Sloane
   99: 208 (BM-SL); [icon] in Morison, Pl. Hist. Univ. 3: 374, s. 11,
   t. 8, f. 7. 1699.
Current name: **Pycnanthemum sp.** (Lamiaceae).
Note: This name appears to have fallen out of use. The original
   material suggests that *N. virginica* relates to *Pycnanthemum*, and
   may be a candidate for rejection.

Nephelium lappaceum Linnaeus, *Systema Naturae,* ed. 12, 2: 623;
   Mantissa Plantarum: 125. 1767.
"Habitat in India." RCN: 7153.
Neotype (Leenhouts in *Blumea* 31: 398. 1986): Bogor Botanic
   Gardens III. H.10 (L; iso- BO, M, NY, U).
Generitype of *Nephelium* Linnaeus.
Current name: **Nephelium lappaceum** L. (Sapindaceae).
Note: Although there is a sheet (1112a.1) in LINN that carries an
   extensive generic description written by Linnaeus on the verso, all of
   the material that was originally on the recto has been lost.
   Consequently, Leenhouts designated a neotype.

Nerium antidysentericum Linnaeus, *Species Plantarum* 1: 209.
   1753.
"Habitat in India." RCN: 1717.
Lectotype (Trimen, *Handb. Fl. Ceylon* 3: 138. 1895): Herb. Hermann
   4: 76, No. 107 (BM-000594775).
Current name: **Wrightia antidysenterica** (L.) R. Br. (Apocynaceae).

Nerium divaricatum Linnaeus, *Species Plantarum* 1: 209. 1753.
"Habitat in India." RCN: 1716.
Lectotype (Leeuwenberg in *J. Ethnopharmacol.* 10: 11. 1984): Herb.
   Hermann 1: 7, No. 109 (BM-000594438).
Current name: **Tabernaemontana divaricata** (L.) Roem. & Schult.
   (Apocynaceae).

Nerium floridum Linnaeus, *Mantissa Plantarum Altera*: 346. 1771,
   nom. illeg.

["Habitat in India orientali: Suratte, Amboina, Cap. b. spei."] Sp. Pl.,
   ed. 2, 1: 305 (1762). RCN: 1709.
Replaced synonym: *Gardenia jasminoides* J. Ellis (1761); *G. florida* L.
   (1762), *nom. illeg.*
Type not designated.
Current name: **Gardenia jasminoides** J. Ellis (Rubiaceae).
Note: A recombination of *Gardenia florida* L. (1762), itself an
   illegitimate renaming of *G. jasminoides* J. Ellis (1761).

Nerium oleander Linnaeus, *Species Plantarum* 1: 209. 1753.
"Habitat in Creta, Palaestina, Syria, India." RCN: 1715.
Lectotype (Stearn in Davis, *Fl. Turkey* 6: 159. 1978): Herb. Clifford:
   76, *Nerium* 1 β (BM-000558145).
Generitype of *Nerium* Linnaeus (vide Steudel, *Nom.* 1: 553. 1821).
Current name: **Nerium oleander** L. (Apocynaceae).
Note: Pagen (in *Agric. Univ. Wageningen Pap.* 87–2: 7. 1987) illustrates
   the lectotype, as well as (pp. 44–48) illustrations from Dodoëns,
   Hermann, Rheede and Weinmann.

Nerium zeylonicum Linnaeus, *Centuria II Plantarum*: 12. 1756.
"Habitat in India." RCN: 1715b.
Type not designated.
Original material: Herb. Linn. No. 300.2 (LINN); [icon] in Burman,
   Thes. Zeylan.: 23, t. 12, f. 2. 1737.
Current name: **Wrightia antidysenterica** (L.) R. Br. (Apocynaceae).

Neurada procumbens Linnaeus, *Species Plantarum* 1: 441. 1753.
"Habitat in Aegypto, Arabia." RCN: 3417.
Type not designated.
Original material: [icon] in Plukenet, Phytographia: t. 275, f. 6. 1694;
   Almag. Bot.: 97. 1696.
Generitype of *Neurada* Linnaeus.
Current name: **Neurada procumbens** L. (Neuradaceae).
Note: Purohit & Panigrahi (in *J. Econ. Taxon. Bot.* 4: 1036. 1983)
   indicated 606.1 (LINN) as type, but it is a post-1753 addition to
   the herbarium and not original material for the name.

Nicotiana fruticosa Linnaeus, *Systema Naturae,* ed. 10, 2: 932.
   1759.
["Habitat ad Cap. b. spei, China."] Sp. Pl., ed. 2, 1: 258 (1762).
   RCN: 1432.
Lectotype (Setchell in *Univ. Calif. Publ. Bot.* 5: 6. 1912): Herb. Linn.
   No. 245.2 (LINN).
Current name: **Nicotiana tabacum** L. (Solanaceae).

Nicotiana glutinosa Linnaeus, *Species Plantarum* 1: 181. 1753.
"Habitat in Peru. D.B. Jussieu." RCN: 1436.
Lectotype (Goodspeed, *Genus* Nicotiana: 369. 1954): Herb. Linn. No.
   245.5 (LINN).
Current name: **Nicotiana glutinosa** L. (Solanaceae).

Nicotiana paniculata Linnaeus, *Species Plantarum* 1: 180. 1753.
"Habitat in Peru." RCN: 1434.
Lectotype (Goodspeed, *Genus* Nicotiana: 339. 1954): Herb. Linn. No.
   245.4 (LINN).
Current name: **Nicotiana paniculata** L. (Solanaceae).

Nicotiana pusilla Linnaeus, *Systema Naturae,* ed. 10, 2: 933. 1759,
   nom. rej.
["Habitat in Vera cruce."] Sp. Pl., ed. 2, 1: 258 (1762). RCN: 1437.
Lectotype (Knapp & Clarkson in *Taxon* 53: 844. 2004): [icon]
   *"Nicotiana, foliis ovato-lanceolatis obtusis rugosis, calycibus
   brevissimis"* in Miller, Fig. Pl. Gard. Dict. 2: 124, t. 185, f. 2. 1757.
   – Epitype (Knapp & Clarkson in *Taxon* 53: 845. 2004): Mexico. "E
   Vera Cruz Houston" in Herb. Miller (BM).

Current name: ***Nicotiana plumbaginifolia*** Viv. (Solanaceae).
Note: Knapp & al. (in *Taxon* 53: 74. 2004) noted that this is synonymous with the widespread and well-known *N. plumbaginifolia* Viv., and Knapp & Clarkson (in *Taxon* 53: 844. 2004) successfully proposed the rejection of *N. pusilla*.

Nicotiana rustica Linnaeus, *Species Plantarum* 1: 180. 1753.
"Habitat in America, nunc in Europa." RCN: 1433.
Lectotype (Goodspeed, *Genus* Nicotiana: 351. 1954): Herb. Linn. No. 245.3 (LINN).
Current name: ***Nicotiana rustica*** L. (Solanaceae).

Nicotiana tabacum Linnaeus, *Species Plantarum* 1: 180. 1753.
"Habitat in America, nota Europaeis ab 1560." RCN: 1431.
Lectotype (Setchell in *Univ. Calif. Publ. Bot.* 5: 6. 1912): Herb. Linn. No. 245.1 (LINN).
Generitype of *Nicotiana* Linnaeus (vide Hitchcock, *Prop. Brit. Bot.*: 132. 1929).
Current name: ***Nicotiana tabacum*** L. (Solanaceae).

Nicotiana urens Linnaeus, *Systema Naturae*, ed. 10, 2: 932. 1759.
["Habitat in America meridionali."] Sp. Pl., ed. 2, 1: 259 (1762). RCN: 1435.
Type not designated.
Original material: none traced.
Note: The application of this name appears uncertain.

Nigella arvensis Linnaeus, *Species Plantarum* 1: 534. 1753.
"Habitat in Germanniae, Galliae, Italiae agris." RCN: 3969.
Lectotype (Strid in *Opera Bot.* 28: 28. 1970): Herb. Burser VII(1): 118 (UPS).
Generitype of *Nigella* Linnaeus (vide Hutchinson in *Bull. Misc. Inform. Kew* 1923: 87. 1923).
Current name: ***Nigella arvensis*** L. (Ranunculaceae).

Nigella damascena Linnaeus, *Species Plantarum* 1: 534. 1753.
"Habitat inter segetes Europae australis." RCN: 3967.
Lectotype (Zohary in *Pl. Syst. Evol.* 142: 97. 1983): Herb. Linn. No. 700.1 (LINN).
Current name: ***Nigella damascena*** L. (Ranunculaceae).

Nigella hispanica Linnaeus, *Species Plantarum* 1: 534. 1753.
"Habitat in Hispania, Monspelii." RCN: 3970.
Lectotype (Zohary in *Pl. Syst. Evol.* 142: 80. 1983): [icon] *"Nigella Hispanica flore amplo"* in Morison, Pl. Hist. Univ. 3: 516, s. 12, t. 18, f. 9. 1699.
Current name: ***Nigella hispanica*** L. (Ranunculaceae).
Note: López González (in *Anales Jard. Bot. Madrid* 41: 467–468. 1985), in a discussion of Art. 9.3 in the Sydney Code, argued that specimens held precedence over illustrations as types, and that 700.8 (LINN), identifiable as *N. gallica* Jordan, should displace the type chosen by Zohary. This is, however, erroneous.

Nigella orientalis Linnaeus, *Species Plantarum* 1: 534. 1753.
"Habitat circum Alepum." RCN: 3971.
Lectotype (Zohary in *Pl. Syst. Evol.* 142: 99. 1983): Herb. Linn. No. 700.8 (LINN).
Current name: ***Nigella orientalis*** L. (Ranunculaceae).

Nigella sativa Linnaeus, *Species Plantarum* 1: 534. 1753.
"Habitat in Aegypto, Creta." RCN: 3968.
Lectotype (Strid in Jarvis & al. in *Taxon* 54: 469. 2005): Herb. Burser VII(1): 123 (UPS).
Current name: ***Nigella sativa*** L. (Ranunculaceae).
Note: Strid provides a detailed review of earlier attempts at typification of this name.

Nigrina viscosa Linnaeus, *Systema Naturae*, ed. 12, 2: 154; *Mantissa Plantarum*: 42. 1767.
"Habitat ad Cap. b. Spei. Burmannus." RCN: 1204.
Type not designated.
Original material: none traced.
Generitype of *Nigrina* Linnaeus.
Current name: ***Melasma scabrum*** P.J. Bergius (Scrophulariaceae).
Note: According to Wijnands (in *Bot. J. Linn. Soc.* 109: 499. 1992), an unspecified Burman specimen should probably be the type.

Nitraria schoberi Linnaeus, *Systema Naturae*, ed. 10, 2: 1044. 1759.
["Habitat ad Salsas aquas Vrunscinensis Lacus, Astrachanensis, Volgae finitimis."] Sp. Pl., ed. 2, 1: 638 (1762). RCN: 3457.
Lectotype (Ghafoor in Nasir & Ali, *Fl. W. Pakistan* 66: 4. 1974): Herb. Linn. No. 624.1 (LINN).
Generitype of *Nitraria* Linnaeus.
Current name: ***Nitraria schoberi*** L. (Zygophyllaceae).

Nolana prostrata Linnaeus filius, *Dec. Prima Pl. Horti Upsal.*: 15. 1762.
"Habitat – – – –" RCN: 1139.
Lectotype (Mesa, *Fl. Neotropica* 26: 129. 1981): Herb. Linn. No. 194.1 (LINN).
Current name: ***Nolana humifusa*** (Gouan) I.M. Johnst. (Nolanaceae).
Note: Linnaeus includes this name in *Species Plantarum*, ed. 2, 1: 202 (1762), with reference to Linnaeus filius. Johnson (in *Proc. Amer. Acad. Sci.* 71: 51–52. 1936) shows that Gouan's name pre-dates that of L. f.

Nyctanthes angustifolia Linnaeus, *Species Plantarum* 1: 6. 1753.
"Habitat in Malabariae arenosis." RCN: 42.
Lectotype (Majumdar & Bakshi in *Taxon* 28: 354. 1979): [icon] *"Katu-pitsjegam-mulla"* in Rheede, Hort. Malab. 6: 93, t. 53. 1686.
Current name: ***Jasminum angustifolium*** (L.) Willd. (Oleaceae).

Nyctanthes arbor-tristis Linnaeus, *Species Plantarum* 1: 6. 1753.
"Habitat in India." RCN: 38.
Type not designated.
Original material: [icon] in Rheede, Hort. Malab. 1: 35, t. 21. 1678.
Generitype of *Nyctanthes* Linnaeus (vide Hitchcock in *Amer. J. Bot.* 10: 514. 1923).
Current name: ***Nyctanthes arbor-tristis*** L. (Oleaceae).
Note: Moldenke & Moldenke (in Dassanayake & Fosberg, *Revised Handb. Fl. Ceylon* 4: 179. 1993) indicated "Grimm 116" (LINN) as type, but no such specimen (which in any case seems most unlikely to be an original element) has been traced.

Nyctanthes hirsuta Linnaeus, *Species Plantarum* 1: 6. 1753.
"Habitat in India." RCN: 41.
Lectotype (Ridsdale in Manilal, *Bot. Hist. Hort. Malab.*: 132. 1980): [icon] *"Rava-pou"* in Rheede, Hort. Malab. 4: 99, t. 48. 1683.
Current name: ***Nyctanthes hirsuta*** L. (Oleaceae).
Note: Green (in *Kew Bull.* 39: 653. 1984) discussed the name and its typification in some detail, but the type choice is attributable to an earlier account by Ridsdale.

Nyctanthes sambac Linnaeus, *Species Plantarum* 1: 6. 1753.
"Habitat in India." RCN: 39.
Lectotype (Howard, *Fl. Lesser Antilles* 6: 83. 1989): Herb. Clifford: 5, *Nyctanthes* 1 (BM-000557517).
Current name: ***Jasminum sambac*** (L.) Aiton (Oleaceae).
Note: D'Arcy (in *Ann. Missouri Bot. Gard.* 63: 560. 1977) indicated 16.2 (LINN) as the type, but this is a Browne specimen received by Linnaeus only in 1758 and it is not original material for the name.

Nyctanthes undulata Linnaeus, *Species Plantarum* 1: 6. 1753.
"Habitat in Malabaria." RCN: 40.
Lectotype (Green in *Kew Bull.* 58: 296. 2003): [icon] *"Tsjiregam-mulla"* in Rheede, Hort. Malab. 6: 97, t. 55. 1686.
Current name: ***Jasminum sambac*** (L.) Aiton (Oleaceae).

Nymphaea alba Linnaeus, *Species Plantarum* 1: 510. 1753, *typ. cons.*
"Habitat in Europae & America aquis dulcibus." RCN: 3856.

Lectotype (Mitra in Nayar & al. in *Fasc. Fl. India* 20: 16. 1990): Herb. Linn. No. 673.4 (LINN).
Generitype of *Nymphaea* Linnaeus, *nom. cons.*
Current name: ***Nymphaea alba*** L. (Nymphaeaceae).

Note: Mitra's choice of the material in LINN as type is unfortunate because detailed morphological and palynological studies show that it belongs not to *N. alba* but to *N. candida* C. Presl & J. Presl (which Mitra recognised as a species distinct from *N. alba*). The two taxa are usually treated as distinct, though often at subspecific rank. Although Art. 57.1 provides some temporary protection for the name, a conservation proposal appears to be necessary.

Nymphaea lotus Linnaeus, *Species Plantarum* 1: 511. 1753.
"Habitat in calidis Indiae, Africae, Americae." RCN: 3857.
Lectotype (Verdcourt in Polhill, *Fl. Trop. E. Africa, Nymphaeaceae*: 3. 1989): [icon] *"Lotus Aegyptia"* in Alpino, Pl. Exot.: 214, 213. 1627.
Current name: ***Nymphaea lotus*** L. (Nymphaeaceae).
Note: Verdcourt (in *Kew Bull.* 44: 179. 20 Mar 1989) gave a detailed account but the typification dates from his slightly earlier (15 Feb 1989) Flora account.

Nymphaea lutea Linnaeus, *Species Plantarum* 1: 510. 1753.
"Habitat in Europae littora sub dulci aqua." RCN: 3855.
Lectotype (Jonsell & Jarvis in *Nordic J. Bot.* 14: 159. 1994): Herb. Linn. No. 218 (LAPP), see p. 171.
Current name: ***Nuphar lutea*** (L.) Sibth. & Sm. (Nymphaeaceae).
Note: Beal (in *J. Elisha Mitchell Sci. Soc.* 72: 323. 1956) indicated material associated with genus 673 in LINN as the type, but there are three sheets (673.1, 673.2 and 673.3) associated with this name. As they are evidently not part of a single gathering, Art. 9.15 does not apply, and Jonsell & Jarvis' type choice appears to be the earliest.

Nymphaea nelumbo Linnaeus, *Species Plantarum* 1: 511. 1753.
"Habitat in Indiis." RCN: 3858.
Type not designated.
Original material: Herb. Hermann 3: 52, No. 193 (BM); Herb. Hermann 4: 69, No. 193 (BM); Herb. Hermann 5: 286, 287, No. 193 [icon] (BM); [icon] in Rheede, Hort. Malab. 11: 59, 61, t. 30, 31. 1692; [icon] in Plukenet, Phytographia: t. 207, f. 5. 1692; Almag. Bot.: 267. 1696.; [icon] in Plukenet, Phytographia: t. 322, f. 1. 1694; Almag. Bot.: 267. 1696.; [icon] in Hermann, Parad. Bat.: 205. 1698.
Current name: ***Nelumbo nucifera*** Gaertn. (Nelumbonaceae).

Nyssa aquatica Linnaeus, *Species Plantarum* 2: 1058. 1753.
"Habitat in Americae septentrionalis aquosis." RCN: 7703.
Lectotype (Reveal in *Phytologia* 71: 470. 1991): *Clayton s.n.* "Nyssa foeminea pedunculis unifloris" (BM-000042689).
Generitype of *Nyssa* Linnaeus.
Current name: ***Nyssa aquatica*** L. (Nyssaceae).
Note: Detailed reviews of this name and the complexities of its application were published by Eyde (in *Rhodora* 61: 209–218. 1959; *Taxon* 13: 129–131. 1964), but neither he nor Howard & Staples (in *J. Arnold Arbor.* 64: 533. 1983) explicitly chose a type.

N

O

Obolaria virginica Linnaeus, *Species Plantarum* 2: 632. 1753.
"Habitat in Virginia." RCN: 4587.
Lectotype (Gillett in *Rhodora* 61: 61. 1959): *Clayton 286* (BM-000042237).
Generitype of *Obolaria* Linnaeus.
Current name: ***Obolaria virginica*** L. (Gentianaceae).

Ochna jabotapita Linnaeus, *Species Plantarum* 1: 513. 1753.
"Habitat in India, β in Africa, γ in America." RCN: 3865.
Replaced synonym of: *Ochna squarrosa* L. (1762), *nom. illeg.*
Lectotype (Robson in *Taxon* 11: 49. 1962): Herb. Hermann 1: 52, No. 209, left specimen (BM-000621408).
Generitype of *Ochna* Linnaeus.
Current name: ***Ochna jabotapita*** L. (Ochnaceae).
Note: In 1762, Linnaeus restricted the use of this name to the var. γ, thereby excluding the type. This 1762 name is therefore a later homonym, but has been chosen as the lectotype of *Gomphia* Schreb. (see *Taxon* 43: 91. 1994).

Ochna jabotapita Linnaeus, *Species Plantarum*, ed. 2, 1: 732. 1762, *nom. illeg.*
"Habitat in America meridionali." RCN: 3866.
Type not designated.
Original material: none traced.
Current name: ***Ouratea plumieri*** Tiegh. (Ochnaceae).
Note: An illegitimate later homonym of *O. jabotapita* Linnaeus (1753), as Linnaeus excluded the type of that name in the protologue. Bittrich & Amaral (in *Taxon* 43: 91. 1994) stated both that they were designating Plumier (1703: t. 32) as lectotype, and that a Boerhaave copy of it "must be accepted as the lectotype". It is highly likely that the Boerhaave copy corresponds with Plumier (in Burman, *Pl. Amer.*: t. 153. 1758) and not the earlier t. 32. They designated the Boerhaave copy as the lectotype of *Gomphia* Schreber, which falls into the synonymy of *Ouratea* Aubl.

Ochna squarrosa Linnaeus, *Species Plantarum*, ed. 2, 1: 731. 1762, *nom. illeg.*
"Habitat in India, β. in Africa." RCN: 3865.
Replaced synonym: *Ochna jabotapita* L. (1753), non L. (1762).
Lectotype (Robson in *Taxon* 11: 50. 1962): Herb. Hermann 1: 52, No. 209, left specimen (BM-000621408).
Current name: ***Ochna jabotapita*** L. (Ochnaceae).
Note: A superfluous name for *O. jabotapita* L. (1753).

Ocimum album Linnaeus, *Systema Naturae*, ed. 12, 2: 402; *Mantissa Plantarum*: 85. 1767.
"Habitat in India, Java." RCN: 4334.
Lectotype (Cramer in Dassanayake & Fosberg, *Revised Handb. Fl. Ceylon* 3: 116. 1981): Herb. Linn. No. 749.3 (LINN).
Current name: ***Ocimum basilicum*** L. (Lamiaceae).
Note: Generic name spelled "Ocymum" in the protologue.

Ocimum americanum Linnaeus, *Centuria I Plantarum*: 15. 1755.
"Habitat in America. Miller." RCN: 4338.
Lectotype (Morton in *J. Linn. Soc., Bot.* 58: 234. 1962): Herb. Linn. No. 749.9 (LINN). – Epitype (Paton & Putievsky in *Kew Bull.* 51: 513. 1996): India. Kerala, 10 Nov 1972, *Pushpangadan & Sobti 1* (K; iso- Regional Research Lab., Jammu).
Current name: ***Ocimum americanum*** L. (Lamiaceae).
Note: Generic name spelled "Ocymum" in the protologue. See comments by Paton & Putievsky (in *Kew Bull.* 51: 511. 1996) on the difficulty of identifying the type, which led them to designate an epitype.

Ocimum basilicum Linnaeus, *Species Plantarum* 2: 597. 1753.
"Habitat in India, Persia." RCN: 4335.
Lectotype (Morton in *J. Linn. Soc., Bot.* 58: 234. 1962): Herb. Linn. No. 749.5 (LINN).
Generitype of *Ocimum* Linnaeus (vide Green, *Prop. Brit. Bot.*: 166. 1929).
Current name: ***Ocimum basilicum*** L. (Lamiaceae).

Ocimum frutescens Linnaeus, *Species Plantarum* 2: 597. 1753.
"Habitat in India." RCN: 4332.
Replaced synonym of: *Perilla ocymoides* L. (1764), *nom. illeg.*; *Mentha perilloides* L. (1767), *nom. illeg.*
Lectotype (Paton in Jarvis & al., *Regnum Veg.* 127: 74. 1993): [icon] "*Ocymum Zeylanicum perenne, odoratissimum, latifolium*" in Burman, Thes. Zeylan.: 174, t. 80, f. 1. 1737 (see p. 68).
Current name: ***Perilla frutescens*** (L.) Britton (Lamiaceae).
Note: Hedge (in Ali & Nasir, *Fl. Pakistan* 192: 265. 1990) designated Herb. Linn. No. 731.2 (LINN) as type but this is an Arduino collection not received by Linnaeus until 1763 and not original material for the name. See notes on the large number of different taxa included by Linnaeus within this name in Jarvis (in *Webbia* 48: 497. 1994).

Ocimum gratissimum Linnaeus, *Species Plantarum* 2: 1197. 1753.
"Habitat in India." RCN: 4333.
Neotype (Cramer in Dassanayake & Fosberg, *Revised Handb. Fl. Ceylon* 3: 112. 1981): Herb. Linn. No. 749.2 (LINN).
Current name: ***Ocimum gratissimum*** L. (Lamiaceae).
Note: Although Herb. Linn. 749.2 (LINN) is not original material for this name, the absence of any other original material means that Cramer's treatment of it as "type" is to be treated as a correctable error and accepted as a neotypification under Art. 9.8. This predates its explicit treatment as a neotype by Paton (in *Kew Bull.* 47: 411. 1992).

Ocimum menthoides Linnaeus, *Species Plantarum* 2: 598. 1753.
"Habitat in Zeylona." RCN: 4341.
Lectotype (Press & Sivarajan in *Bull. Brit. Mus. (Nat. Hist.), Bot.* 19: 114. 1989): Herb. Hermann 1: 62, No. 229, left specimen (BM-000621440).
Current name: ***Platostoma menthoides*** (L.) A.J. Paton (Lamiaceae).

Ocimum minimum Linnaeus, *Species Plantarum* 2: 597. 1753.
"Habitat in Zeylona." RCN: 4336.
Lectotype (Paton & Putievsky in *Kew Bull.* 51: 514. 1996): Herb. Linn. No. 749.6 (LINN).
Current name: ***Ocimum minimum*** L. (Lamiaceae).

Ocimum monachorum Linnaeus, *Systema Naturae*, ed. 12, 2: 402; *Mantissa Plantarum*: 85. 1767.
"Habitat in – – –" RCN: 4331.
Lectotype (Sudee in Jarvis & al. in *Taxon* 50: 515. 2001): [icon] "*Ocimum caryophyllatum Monachorum sive Acinos Columnae*" in Bauhin & Cherler, Hist. Pl. Univ. 3(2): 260. 1651.
Current name: ***Ocimum tenuiflorum*** L. (Lamiaceae).

Ocimum polystachyon Linnaeus, *Mantissa Plantarum Altera*: 567. 1771.
"Habitat in India." RCN: 4340.
Lectotype (Scott & Harley in Bosser & al., *Fl. Mascareignes* 139: 24. 1994; Paton & Cafferty in *Kew Bull.* 53: 466. 1998): Herb. Linn. No. 749.15, right specimen (LINN).

Current name: ***Basilicum polystachyon*** (L.) Moench (Lamiaceae).
Note: Generic name spelled "Ocymum" in the protologue.
    Scott & Harley appear to have made the earliest choice; this was subsequently restricted to the specimen on the right of the sheet by Paton & Cafferty.

Ocimum prostratum Linnaeus, *Mantissa Plantarum Altera*: 566. 1771.
"Habitat in India orientali." RCN: 4343.
Lectotype (Cramer in Dassanayake & Fosberg, *Revised Handb. Fl. Ceylon* 3: 119. 1981): Herb. Linn. No. 749.19 (LINN).
Current name: ***Platostoma menthoides*** (L.) A.J. Paton (Lamiaceae).
Note: Generic name spelled "Ocymum" in the protologue.

Ocimum sanctum Linnaeus, *Systema Naturae,* ed. 12, 2: 402; *Mantissa Plantarum*: 85. 1767.
"Habitat in India." RCN: 4337.
Lectotype (Cramer in Dassanayake & Fosberg, *Revised Handb. Fl. Ceylon* 3: 116. 1981): Herb. Linn. No. 749.7 (LINN).
Current name: ***Ocimum tenuiflorum*** L. (Lamiaceae).
Note: Generic name spelled "Ocymum" in the protologue.

Ocimum scutellarioides Linnaeus, *Species Plantarum,* ed. 2, 2: 834. 1763.
"Habitat in Amboina." RCN: 4342.
Lectotype (Merrill, *Interpret. Rumph. Herb. Amb.*: 460. 1917): [icon] "*Majana alba et rubra*" in Rumphius, Herb. Amboin. 5: 291, t. 101. 1747.
Current name: ***Plectranthus scutellarioides*** (L.) R. Br. (Lamiaceae).

Ocimum tenuiflorum Linnaeus, *Species Plantarum* 2: 597. 1753.
"Habitat in Malabaria." RCN: 4339.
Lectotype (Cramer in Dassanayake & Fosberg, *Revised Handb. Fl. Ceylon* 3: 119. 1981): Herb. Linn. No. 749.13 (LINN).
Current name: ***Ocimum tenuiflorum*** L. (Lamiaceae).

Ocimum thyrsiflorum Linnaeus, *Systema Naturae,* ed. 12, 2: 402; *Mantissa Plantarum*: 84. 1767.
"Habitat in India, diutius virens." RCN: 4330.
Lectotype (Paton in Jarvis & al. in *Taxon* 50: 515. 2001): Herb. Linn. No. 749.1 (LINN).
Current name: ***Ocimum basilicum*** L. var. ***thyrsiflorum*** (L.) Benth. (Lamiaceae).
Note: Generic name spelled "Ocymum" in the protologue.

Oedera prolifera Linnaeus, *Mantissa Plantarum Altera*: 291. 1771, *nom. illeg.*
"Habitat ad Cap. b. spei arenosis." RCN: 6715.
Replaced synonym: *Buphthalmum capense* L. (1759).
Lectotype (Anderberg in Jarvis & Turland in *Taxon* 47: 355. 1998): Herb. Linn. No. 1047.1 (LINN).
Generitype of *Oedera* Linnaeus, *nom. cons.*
Current name: ***Oedera capensis*** (L.) Druce (Asteraceae).
Note: Oedera Linnaeus, *nom. cons.* against *Oedera* Crantz.
    An illegitimate replacement name in *Oedera* for *Buphthalmum capense* L. (1759).

Oenanthe crocata Linnaeus, *Species Plantarum* 1: 254. 1753.
"Habitat in Europae paludibus." RCN: 2042.
Lectotype (Jury & al. in Jarvis & al. in *Taxon* 55: 213. 2006): Herb. Clifford: 99, *Oenanthe* 3 α (BM-000558320).
Current name: ***Oenanthe crocata*** L. (Apiaceae).

Oenanthe fistulosa Linnaeus, *Species Plantarum* 1: 254. 1753.
"Habitat in Europae fossis, paludibus." RCN: 2041.

Lectotype (Reduron & Jarvis in Jarvis & al., *Regnum Veg.* 127: 70. 1993): Herb. Clifford: 99, *Oenanthe* 1 (BM-000558313).
Generitype of *Oenanthe* Linnaeus (vide Hitchcock, *Prop. Brit. Bot.*: 140. 1929).
Current name: ***Oenanthe fistulosa*** L. (Apiaceae).
Note: Rechinger (*Fl. Iranica* 162: 368. 1987) indicated material in LINN as type without specifying a sheet within the genus. The only one that can be associated with the name is sheet 359.1 (LINN), but this was a later addition to the herbarium and is not original material for the name.

Oenanthe globulosa Linnaeus, *Species Plantarum* 1: 255. 1753.
"Habitat in Lusitania." RCN: 2044.
Lectotype (Jury & al. in Jarvis & al. in *Taxon* 55: 213. 2006): Herb. Clifford: 99, *Oenanthe* 5 (BM-000558322).
Current name: ***Oenanthe globulosa*** L. (Apiaceae).

Oenanthe pimpinelloides Linnaeus, *Species Plantarum* 1: 255. 1753.
"Habitat Monspelii & in Europa australi." RCN: 2045.
Lectotype (Hedge & Lamond in Davis, *Fl. Turkey* 4: 374. 1972): Herb. Linn. No. 359.4 (LINN).
Current name: ***Oenanthe pimpinelloides*** L. (Apiaceae).

Oenanthe prolifera Linnaeus, *Species Plantarum* 1: 254. 1753.
"Habitat in Sicilia, Apulia." RCN: 2043.
Lectotype (Jury & Southam in Jarvis & al. in *Taxon* 55: 213. 2006): Herb. Clifford: 99, *Oenanthe* 4 (BM-000558321).
Current name: ***Oenanthe prolifera*** L. (Apiaceae).

Oenothera biennis Linnaeus, *Species Plantarum* 1: 346. 1753.
"Habitat in Virginia, unde 1641, nunc vulgaris Europae." RCN: 2652.
Lectotype (Gates in *Amer. Naturalist* 45: 587. 1911): Herb. Linn. No. 484.1 (LINN).
Generitype of *Oenothera* Linnaeus (vide Hitchcock, *Prop. Brit. Bot.*: 148. 1929).
Current name: ***Oenothera biennis*** L. (Onagraceae).

Oenothera fruticosa Linnaeus, *Species Plantarum* 1: 346. 1753.
"Habitat in Virginia." RCN: 2660.
Lectotype (Pennell in *Bull. Torrey Bot. Club* 46: 367. 1919): *Clayton* 36 (BM-000032600).
Current name: ***Oenothera fruticosa*** L. (Onagraceae).

Oenothera hirta Linnaeus, *Systema Naturae,* ed. 10, 2: 998. 1759.
["Habitat in America calidiore."] Sp. Pl., ed. 2, 1: 491 (1762). RCN: 2658.
Type not designated.
Original material: [icon] in Plumier in Burman, Pl. Amer.: 167, t. 174, f. 2. 1758.
Current name: ***Ludwigia peruviana*** (L.) H. Hara (Onagraceae).

Oenothera longiflora Linnaeus, *Mantissa Plantarum Altera*: 227. 1771.
"Habitat in Agro Bonariensi." RCN: 2655.
Lectotype (Dietrich in *Ann. Missouri Bot. Gard.* 64: 509. 1978 [1977]): Herb. Linn. No. 484.4 (LINN).
Current name: ***Oenothera longiflora*** L. (Onagraceae).

Oenothera mollissima Linnaeus, *Species Plantarum* 1: 346. 1753.
"Habitat in agro Bonariensi." RCN: 2657.
Lectotype (Dietrich in *Ann. Missouri Bot. Gard.* 64: 532. 1978 [1977]): Herb. Clifford: 144, *Oenothera* 2 (BM-000558613).
Current name: ***Oenothera mollissima*** L. (Onagraceae).
Note: See discussion by Munz (in *Amer. J. Bot.* 22: 659. 1935).

Oenothera muricata Linnaeus, *Systema Naturae,* ed. 12, 2: 263. 1767.
"Habitat in Canada." RCN: 2654.
Lectotype (Fernald in *Rhodora* 51: 65. 1949): Herb. Linn. No. 484.3 (LINN).
Current name: ***Oenothera biennis*** L. (Onagraceae).

Oenothera parviflora Linnaeus, *Systema Naturae,* ed. 10, 2: 998. 1759.
["Habitat in America septentrionali."] Sp. Pl., ed. 2, 1: 492 (1762). RCN: 2653.
Lectotype (Raven & al. in *Syst. Bot.* 4: 249. 1979): Herb. Linn. No. 484.2 (LINN).
Current name: ***Oenothera parviflora*** L. (Onagraceae).

Oenothera perennis Linnaeus, *Systema Naturae,* ed. 10, 2: 998. 1759.
["Habitat in America meridionali."] Sp. Pl., ed. 2, 1: 493 (1762). RCN: 2661.
Replaced synonym of: *Oenothera pumila* L. (1762), *nom. illeg.*
Lectotype (Straley in *Ann. Missouri Bot. Gard.* 64: 415. 1978 [1977]): [icon] *"Oenothera, foliis radicalibus ovatis caulinis lanceolatis obtusis, capsulis ovatis sulcatis"* in Miller, Fig. Pl. Gard. Dict. 2: 125, t. 188. 1757.
Current name: ***Oenothera perennis*** L. (Onagraceae).
Note: See notes by Reveal & al. (in *Huntia* 7: 228. 1987).

Oenothera pumila Linnaeus, *Species Plantarum,* ed. 2, 1: 493. 1762, *nom. illeg.*
"Habitat in America septentrionali." RCN: 2661.
Replaced synonym: *Oenothera perennis* L. (1759).
Lectotype (Straley in *Ann. Missouri Bot. Gard.* 64: 415. 1978 [1977]): [icon] *"Oenothera, foliis radicalibus ovatis caulinis lanceolatis obtusis, capsulis ovatis sulcatis"* in Miller, Fig. Pl. Gard. Dict. 2: 125, t. 188. 1757.
Current name: ***Oenothera perennis*** L. (Onagraceae).
Note: An illegitimate replacement name for *O. perennis* L. (1759).

Oenothera sinuata Linnaeus, *Mantissa Plantarum Altera*: 228. 1771.
"Habitat in Virginia." RCN: 2659.
Type not designated.
Original material: Herb. Linn. No. 484.6 (LINN); [icon] in Plukenet, Phytographia: t. 203, f. 3. 1692; Almag. Bot.: 235. 1696.
Current name: ***Oenothera laciniata*** Hill (Onagraceae).

Olax zeylanica Linnaeus, *Species Plantarum* 1: 34. 1753.
"Habitat in Zeylona." RCN: 270.
Lectotype (Sleumer, *Fl. Neotropica* 22: 156. 1980): Herb. Hermann 1: 76, No. 34 (BM-000621487; iso- L).
Generitype of *Olax* Linnaeus.
Current name: ***Olax zeylanica*** L. (Olacaceae).

Oldenlandia biflora Linnaeus, *Species Plantarum* 1: 119. 1753.
"Habitat in India." RCN: 981.
Lectotype (Trimen, *Handb. Fl. Ceylon* 2: 317. 1894; Biju & al. in *Rheedea* 2: 11, f. 1A. 1992): Herb. Hermann 3: 19, No. 68 (BM-000594661).
Current name: ***Hedyotis biflora*** (L.) Lam. (Rubiaceae).
Note: Biju & al. provided a detailed consideration of the original elements, together with an image (f. 1A) of the type. The Hermann collections consist of two specimens on a single page, but Biju & al. illustrate only the smaller of the two, referring to it as "type". This is accepted as a restriction of Trimen's original designation (Art. 9.15).

Oldenlandia corymbosa Linnaeus, *Species Plantarum* 1: 119. 1753.
"Habitat in America meridionali." RCN: 983.

Lectotype (Verdcourt in Polhill, *Fl. Trop. E. Africa, Rubiaceae* 1: 308. 1976): [icon] *"Oldenlandia"* in Plumier, Nov. Pl. Amer.: 42, t. 36. 1703.
Generitype of *Oldenlandia* Linnaeus (vide Hitchcock, *Prop. Brit. Bot.*: 125. 1929).
Current name: ***Oldenlandia corymbosa*** L. (Rubiaceae).
Note: Verdcourt's choice of type appears to be the earliest though some later authors (e.g. Nazimuddin & Qaiserin (in Nasir & Ali, *Fl. Pakistan* 190: 15. 1989) have erroneously treated the post-1753 Herb. Linn. 155.9 (LINN) as "type".

Oldenlandia paniculata Linnaeus, *Species Plantarum*, ed. 2, 2: 1667. 1763.
"Habitat in India orientali." RCN: 984.
Lectotype (Merrill in *J. Arnold Arbor.* 19: 368. 1938): Herb. Linn. No. 155.10 (LINN).
Current name: ***Hedyotis racemosa*** Lam. (Rubiaceae).
Note: Trimen (*Handb, Fl. Ceylon* 2: 317. 1894) says that this is "entirely based on a figure of Burman". However, as pointed out by Merrill (*l.c.*), and Biju & al. (in *Rheedea* 2: 12. 1992), this illustration is not part of the protologue. Merrill is here accepted as having made an effective choice of type; see Biju & al., f. 1B for an illustration of the type specimen.

Oldenlandia repens Linnaeus, *Systema Naturae,* ed. 12, 2: 126; *Mantissa Plantarum*: 40. 1767.
"Habitat in India." RCN: 979.
Lectotype (Verdcourt in *Kew Bull.* 37: 545. 1983): Herb. Linn. No. 155.2 (LINN).
Current name: ***Dentella repens*** (L.) J.R. Forst. & G. Forst. (Rubiaceae).

Oldenlandia stricta Linnaeus, *Mantissa Plantarum Altera*: 200. 1771.
"Habitat in Malabaria. D. Koenig." RCN: 985.
Lectotype (Deb & Dutta in *Taxon* 32: 285. 1983): Herb. Linn. No. 155.11 (LINN).
Current name: ***Hedyotis graminifolia*** L. f. (Rubiaceae).

Oldenlandia umbellata Linnaeus, *Species Plantarum* 1: 119. 1753.
"Habitat in India." RCN: 982.
Lectotype (Sivarajan & al. in *Kew Bull.* 48: 393. 1993): Herb. Hermann 2: 35, No. 67 (BM-000621636).
Current name: ***Hedyotis brevicalyx*** Sivar. & al. (Rubiaceae).

Oldenlandia uniflora Linnaeus, *Species Plantarum* 1: 119. 1753.
"Habitat in Virginia." RCN: 980.
Lectotype (designated here by Terrell & Robinson): *Clayton 587,* Herb. Linn. No. 155.3 (LINN; iso- BM).
Current name: ***Oldenlandia uniflora*** L. (Rubiaceae).
Note: Terrell & Robinson (in *Sida* 22: 317. 2006) indicated *Clayton 587*, Herb. Linn. No. 155.3 (LINN) as the type. However, this choice was published after 1 Jan 2001 and so the omission of the phrase "designated here" or an equivalent (Art. 7.11) means that the choice is not effective. The name is now formally typified here.

Oldenlandia verticillata Linnaeus, *Systema Naturae,* ed. 12, 2: 126; *Mantissa Plantarum*: 40. 1767.
"Habitat in Amboinae, Javae collibus apricis." RCN: 978.
Lectotype (Fosberg & Sachet in *Allertonia* 6: 210, 242. 1991): Herb. Linn. No. 155.1 (LINN).
Current name: ***Hedyotis verticillata*** (L.) Lam. (Rubiaceae).

Olea americana Linnaeus, *Systema Naturae,* ed. 12, 2: 56; *Mantissa Plantarum*: 24. 1767.
"Habitat in Carolina." RCN: 55.

Lectotype (Green in *Notes Roy. Bot. Gard. Edinburgh* 22: 462. 1958):
Herb. Linn. No. 20.6 (LINN).
Current name: ***Osmanthus americanus*** (L.) A. Gray (Oleaceae).

Olea capensis Linnaeus, *Species Plantarum* 1: 8. 1753.
"Habitat ad Cap. b. spei." RCN: 54.
Lectotype (Verdoorn in *Bothalia* 6: 582, pl. 16. 1956): Herb. Linn.
No. 20.4 (LINN).
Current name: ***Olea capensis*** L. (Oleaceae).

Olea europaea Linnaeus, *Species Plantarum* 1: 8. 1753.
"Habitat in Europa australi." RCN: 53.
Lectotype (Green & Wickens in Kit Tan, *Davis & Hedge Festschr.*: 294.
1989): Herb. Clifford: 4, *Olea* 1 α (BM-000557513).
Generitype of *Olea* Linnaeus (vide Hitchcock, *Prop. Brit. Bot.*: 115.
1929).
Current name: ***Olea europaea*** L. (Oleaceae).

Olyra latifolia Linnaeus, *Systema Naturae*, ed. 10, 2: 1261. 1759.
["Habitat in Jamaica."] Sp. Pl., ed. 2, 2: 1379. 1763. RCN: 7053.
Lectotype (Jarvis & al., *Regnum Veg.* 127: 70. 1993): [icon] *"Gramen
paniceum majus, spica simplici laevi, granis petiolis insidentibus"* in
Sloane, Voy. Jamaica 1: 107, t. 64, f. 2. 1707. – Typotype: Herb.
Sloane 2: 7 (BM-SL).
Generitype of *Olyra* Linnaeus.
Current name: ***Olyra latifolia*** L. (Poaceae).

Note: Hitchcock (in *Contr. U. S. Natl. Herb.* 12: 124. 1908) indicated
Sloane's specimen (HS 2: 7, BM-SL) as the type. Despite its close
association with the published illustration, Linnaeus did not see the
material and it is not original material for the name. Subsequently,
Hitchcock (in *Contr. U. S. Natl. Herb.* 17: 269. 1913) referred to
"the type specimen collected by Browne" but without indicating
where it was located. Formal typification on Sloane's illustration was
effected in Jarvis & al.

Omphalea diandra Linnaeus, *Systema Naturae*, ed. 10, 2: 1264. 1759.
["Habitat in Jamaica."] Sp. Pl., ed. 2, 2: 1377 (1763). RCN: 7100.
Type not designated.
Original material: none traced.
Current name: ***Omphalea diandra*** L. (Euphorbiaceae).
Note: Although Webster & Huft (in *Ann. Missouri Bot. Gard.* 75:
1110. 1988) indicated Browne material which they presumed to be
in LINN as the type, there is no relevant material preserved there.

Omphalea triandra Linnaeus, *Systema Naturae*, ed. 10, 2: 1264.
1759, *typ. cons.*
["Habitat in Jamaica."] Sp. Pl., ed. 2, 2: 1377 (1763). RCN: 7101.
Type not designated.
Original material: Herb. Linn. No. 1102.1 (LINN); [icon] in Browne,
Civ. Nat. Hist. Jamaica: 335, t. 22, f. 4. 1756.
Generitype of *Omphalea* Linnaeus, *nom. cons.*
Current name: ***Omphalea triandra*** L. (Euphorbiaceae).
Note: Omphalea Linnaeus, *nom. cons.* against *Omphalandria* P. Browne.
Omphalea triandra presents particular difficulties because the
original material, a Patrick Browne specimen (1102.1 LINN) and
Browne's cited illustration (t. 22, f. 4) are identifiable as *Pouteria
multiflora* (A. DC.) Eyma (Sapotaceae). Gillespie (in Jarvis & al.,
Regnum Veg. 127: 70. 1993) designated a Swartz collection in Herb.
Thunberg (No. 22721, UPS) as a neotype. As explained by Jarvis &
al., *l.c.*: 6. 1993), with the non adoption of the NCU proposals
with which their Linnaean Generic List was linked, this
neotypification is untenable because original material is in existence.
It appears that a conservation proposal is necessary if *Omphalea*
(Euphorbiaceae, and itself conserved) is not to become the correct
name for *Pouteria* (Sapotaceae).

Onoclea polypodioides Linnaeus, *Mantissa Plantarum Altera*: 306.
1771.
"Habitat ad Cap. b. spei in fissuris rupium summarum montis
Tabularis. Koenig 44." RCN: 7739.
Type not designated.
Original material: *Sparrman 31*, Herb. Linn. No. 1242.3 (LINN).
Current name: ***Gleichenia polypodioides*** (L.) Sm. (Gleicheniaceae).

Onoclea sensibilis Linnaeus, *Species Plantarum* 2: 1062. 1753.
"Habitat in Virginia." RCN: 7738.
Type not designated.
Original material: Herb. Clifford: 472, *Osmunda* 5 (BM); [icon] in
Morison, Pl. Hist. Univ. 3: 563, s. 14, t. 2, f. 10. 1699; [icon] in
Mentzel, Ind. Nom. Pl. Univ.: t. 10. 1682; [icon] in Plukenet,
Amalth. Bot.: t. 404, f. 2. 1705; Almag. Mant. 80. 1700 – Voucher:
Herb. Sloane 92: 67 (BM-SL).
Generitype of *Onoclea* Linnaeus.
Current name: ***Onoclea sensibilis*** L. (Onocleaceae).
Note: Although both Copeland (in *Univ. Calif. Publ. Bot.* 16: 55.
1929) and Reveal & al. (in *Huntia* 7: 223. 1987) designated Herb.
Linn. 1242.1 (LINN) as lectotype (also accepted in Jarvis & al.
(*Regnum Veg.* 127: 71. 1993)), the material appears to be a post-
1753 addition to the collection and not original material for the
name. As original material exists, this choice cannot be interpreted
as a neotypification.

Ononis alopecuroides Linnaeus, *Species Plantarum* 2: 717. 1753.
"Habitat in Sicilia, Lusitania, Hispania." RCN: 5270.
Lectotype (Förther in Turland & Jarvis in *Taxon* 46: 476. 1997):
  Herb. Clifford: 358, *Ononis* 4 α (BM-000646582).
Current name: ***Ononis alopecuroides*** L. subsp. ***alopecuroides***
  (Fabaceae: Faboideae).

Ononis antiquorum Linnaeus, *Species Plantarum*, ed. 2, 2: 1006.
  1763.
"Habitat in Europa australi." RCN: 5264.
Lectotype (Ali in Nasir & Ali, *Fl. W. Pakistan* 100: 283. 1977): Herb.
  Linn. No. 896.1 (LINN).
Current name: ***Ononis spinosa*** L. subsp. ***antiquorum*** (L.) Arcang.
  (Fabaceae: Faboideae).

Ononis arvensis Linnaeus, *Systema Naturae*, ed. 10, 2: 1159. 1759.
  RCN: 5265.
Neotype (Förther in Turland & Jarvis in *Taxon* 46: 477. 1997):
  Germany. München: cultivated in the Botanic Garden, *Lippert
  21111* (M).
Current name: ***Ononis spinosa*** L. subsp. ***arvensis*** (L.) Greuter &
  Burdet (Fabaceae: Faboideae).
Note: The specimen Herb. Linn. No. 896.2 (LINN) (which
  taxonomically is not *Ononis arvensis* as currently understood),
  although annotated with "arvensis" (as well as "spinosa") by
  Linnaeus, has spiny stems and thereby is fundamentally at odds
  with Linnaeus' *nomen specificum legitimum* which states "ramis
  inermibus". This specimen could not possibly have been that upon
  which the validating diagnosis was based and is therefore not
  original material for *O. arvensis*. There is no other potential original
  material and, for this reason, Förther designated a neotype.

Ononis capensis Linnaeus, *Plantae Rariores Africanae*: 16. 1760.
  ["Habitat ad Cap. b. spei."] Sp. Pl., ed. 2, 2: 1011 (1763). RCN: 5276.
Type not designated.
Original material: none traced.
Note: The application of this name is uncertain, and there appear to be
  no extant original elements. The name has been referred to the
  genus *Lotononis* but it is not mentioned by Van Wyk (in *Contr.
  Bolus Herb.* 14: 1–292. 1991).

Ononis cenisia Linnaeus, *Mantissa Plantarum Altera*: 267. 1771.
"Habitat ad pedem montis Cenisii. Latourette." RCN: 5279.
Lectotype (Förther in Turland & Jarvis in *Taxon* 46: 477. 1997):
  Capeller, Herb. Linn. No. 896.16 (LINN).
Current name: ***Ononis cristata*** Mill. (Fabaceae: Faboideae).

Ononis cernua Linnaeus, *Plantae Rariores Africanae*: 16. 1760.
  ["Habitat ad Cap. b. spei."] Sp. Pl., ed. 2, 2: 1011 (1763). RCN:
  5273.
Lectotype (Schrire in Turland & Jarvis in *Taxon* 46: 477. 1997): [icon]
  "*Lotus Africana annua hirsuta, floribus luteis*" in Commelin, Hort.
  Med. Amstelod. Pl. Rar. 2: 163, t. 82. 1701. – Epitype (Schrire in
  Turland & Jarvis in *Taxon* 46: 477. 1997): South Africa. Cape,
  3218 Clanwilliam BD, Trawal near Clanwilliam-Klawer rd, 23 Jul
  1981, *P. Goldblatt 6051* (K; iso- MO, NBG?).
Current name: ***Melolobium aethiopicum*** (L.) Druce (Fabaceae:
  Faboideae).

Ononis cherleri Linnaeus, *Systema Naturae*, ed. 10, 2: 1160. 1759.
  ["Habitat in G. Narbonensi, Hispania, Italia."] Sp. Pl., ed. 2, 2: 1007
  (1763). RCN: 5268.
Type not designated.
Original material: Herb. Linn. No. 298.19? (S); Herb. Linn. No. 55
  (SBT); Herb. Linn. No. 896.17 (LINN).

Current name: ***Ononis* sp.** (Fabaceae: Faboideae).
Note: The application of this name is uncertain. Devesa & López (in
  Anales Jard. Bot. Madrid 55: 251. 1997) indicated Herb. Linn.
  896.6 (LINN) as original material for *O. pusilla* L., and treated *O.
  cherleri* (1763: 1007, non 1759) as homotypic with it, and hence
  illegitimate.

Ononis crispa Linnaeus, *Species Plantarum*, ed. 2, 2: 1010. 1763.
"Habitat in Hispaniae monte Mariola prope Valentiam." RCN:
  5286.
Type not designated.
Original material: Herb. Linn. No. 896.23 (LINN); Herb. Linn. No.
  896.25 (LINN); [icon] in Magnol, Hort. Reg. Monspel.: 17,
  unnumbered plate. 1697.
Current name: ***Ononis crispa*** L. (Fabaceae: Faboideae).
Note: See extensive discussion by Devesa & López González (in *Anales
  Jard. Bot. Madrid* 55: 253–254. 1997) who note that 896.25
  (LINN) matches Linnaeus' description, but is sterile and difficult to
  identify. The cited illustration from Magnol is identifiable as *O.
  aragonensis* Asso.

Ononis filiformis (P.J. Bergius) Linnaeus, *Mantissa Plantarum Altera*:
  266. 1771.
"Habitat ad Cap. b. spei." RCN: 5275.
Basionym: *Lotus filiformis* P.J. Bergius (1767).
Type not designated.
Current name: ***Indigofera sarmentosa*** L. f. (Fabaceae: Faboideae).

Ononis fruticosa Linnaeus, *Species Plantarum* 2: 718. 1753.
"Habitat in montibus Delphinatus." RCN: 5287.
Lectotype (Förther in Turland & Jarvis in *Taxon* 46: 477. 1997):
  Herb. Clifford: 358, *Ononis* 2 (BM).
Current name: ***Ononis fruticosa*** L. (Fabaceae: Faboideae).

Ononis mauritanica (Linnaeus) Linnaeus, *Mantissa Plantarum Altera*:
  267. 1771.
  ["Habitat ad Cap. b. spei."] Sp. Pl., ed. 2, 2: 1091 (1763). RCN:
  5289.
Basionym: *Lotus mauritanicus* L. (1759).
Lectotype (Schrire in Turland & Jarvis in *Taxon* 46: 475. 1997): Herb.
  Linn. No. 931.34 (LINN).
Current name: ***Indigofera mauritanica*** (L.) Thunb. (Fabaceae:
  Faboideae).

Ononis minutissima Linnaeus, *Species Plantarum* 2: 717. 1753.
"Habitat in Italia, Monspelii." RCN: 5267.
Lectotype (Förther in Turland & Jarvis in *Taxon* 46: 477. 1997):
  Herb. Burser XXI: 84 (UPS).
Current name: ***Ononis minutissima*** L. (Fabaceae: Faboideae).

Ononis mitissima Linnaeus, *Species Plantarum* 2: 717. 1753.
"Habitat in Barbados, Lusitania." RCN: 5269.
Lectotype (Devesa in *Mem. Soc. Brot.* 28: 21. 1988): Herb. Linn. No.
  896.7 (LINN).
Current name: ***Ononis mitissima*** L. (Fabaceae: Faboideae).
Note: Devesa's type choice pre-dates that made independently by
  Förther (in *Taxon* 46: 477. 1997).

Ononis natrix Linnaeus, *Species Plantarum* 2: 717. 1753.
"Habitat in G. Narbonensi, Hispania, inter segetes." RCN: 5284.
Lectotype (Förther & Podlech in *Mitt. Bot. Staatssamml. München* 30:
  263. 1991; Devesa & López González in *Anales Jard. Bot. Madrid*
  55: 251. 1997): Herb. Linn. No. 896.22, lower right specimen
  (LINN).
Current name: ***Ononis natrix*** L. subsp. ***natrix*** (Fabaceae: Faboideae).

Note: Förther & Podlech (1991) designated 896.22 (LINN) as lectotype. This choice was later restricted to the lower, right specimen by Devesa & López González (1997).

Ononis ornithopodioides Linnaeus, *Species Plantarum* 2: 718. 1753.
"Habitat in Sicilia ad Capo passaro." RCN: 5282.
Lectotype (Jafri in Jafri & El-Gadi, *Fl. Libya* 86: 160. 1980): Herb. Linn. No. 896.20 (LINN).
Current name: ***Ononis ornithopodioides*** L. (Fabaceae: Faboideae).

Ononis pinguis Linnaeus, *Species Plantarum*, ed. 2, 2: 1009. 1763.
"Habitat in Europa australi." RCN: 5283.
Lectotype (Förther & Podlech in *Mitt. Bot. Staatssamml. München* 30: 263. 1992): *Magnol*, Herb. Linn. No. 896.21 (LINN).
Current name: ***Ononis natrix*** L. subsp. ***natrix*** (Fabaceae: Faboideae).

Ononis prostrata (Linnaeus) Linnaeus, *Mantissa Plantarum Altera*: 266. 1771.
["Habitat ad Cap. b. spei."] Sp. Pl., ed. 2, 2: 1090 (1763). RCN: 5277.
Basionym: *Lotus prostratus* L. (1759).
Lectotype (Van Wyk in *Contr. Bolus Herb.* 14: 232. 1991): Herb. Linn. No. 931.35 (LINN).
Current name: ***Lotononis prostrata*** (L.) Benth. (Fabaceae: Faboideae).

Ononis pubescens Linnaeus, *Mantissa Plantarum Altera*: 267. 1771.
"Habitat in Europa australi." RCN: 5272.
Lectotype (Förther in Turland & Jarvis in *Taxon* 46: 477. 1997): *Gouan, s.n.?*, Herb. Linn. No. 896.10 (LINN).
Current name: ***Ononis pubescens*** L. (Fabaceae: Faboideae).

Ononis pusilla Linnaeus, *Systema Naturae*, ed. 10, 2: 1159. 1759.
RCN: 5268.
Lectotype (Devesa in *Mem. Soc. Brot.* 28: 18. 1988): *Scopoli s.n.*, Herb. Linn. No. 896.6 (LINN), see p. 228.
Current name: ***Ononis pusilla*** L. (Fabaceae: Faboideae).
Note: Devesa & López González (in *Anales Jard. Bot. Madrid* 55: 251. 1997) indicated 896.6 (LINN) as original material but did not typify the name.

Ononis reclinata Linnaeus, *Species Plantarum*, ed. 2, 2: 1011. 1763.
"Habitat in Delphinatu, Hispania, Italia." RCN: 5278.
Lectotype (Förther in Turland & Jarvis in *Taxon* 46: 477. 1997): [icon] *"Anonis non spinosa purpurascens, minor, Italica"* in Barrelier, Pl. Galliam: 74, t. 354. 1714.
Current name: ***Ononis reclinata*** L. (Fabaceae: Faboideae).

Ononis repens Linnaeus, *Species Plantarum* 2: 717. 1753.
"Habitat in Angliae littoribus maris." RCN: 5266.
Lectotype (Förther in Turland & Jarvis in *Taxon* 46: 477. 1997): [icon] *"Anonis maritima procumbens, foliis hirsutie pubescentibus Pluk."* in Dillenius, Hort. Eltham. 1: 29, t. 25, f. 28. 1732.
Current name: ***Ononis repens*** L. (Fabaceae: Faboideae).

Ononis rotundifolia Linnaeus, *Species Plantarum* 2: 719. 1753.
"Habitat in Alpibus Helveticis." RCN: 5288.
Lectotype (Förther in Turland & Jarvis in *Taxon* 46: 477. 1997): Herb. Clifford: 358, *Ononis* 1 (BM-000646573).
Current name: ***Ononis rotundifolia*** L. (Fabaceae: Faboideae).

Ononis spinosa Linnaeus, *Species Plantarum* 2: 716. 1753, *nom. cons.*
"Habitat in aridis Europae." RCN: 5265.
Conserved type (Jarvis & al. in Brummitt in *Taxon* 38: 299. 1989): Herb. Burser XXI: 79 (UPS).

Generitype of *Ononis* Linnaeus (vide Green, *Prop. Brit. Bot.*: 174. 1929).
Current name: ***Ononis spinosa*** L. (Fabaceae: Faboideae).
Note: Jarvis & al. (in *Taxon* 32: 314. 1983) proposed the rejection of this name, initially recommended by the Committee for Spermatophyta (in *Taxon* 34: 662. 1985). However, following the modification of Art. 69 at the Berlin Congress to allow the conservation of species names, this case was reconsidered and the name instead recommended for conservation by the Committee for Spermatophyta (in *Taxon* 38: 299. 1989), with Herb. Burser XXI: 79 (UPS) as the conserved type.

Ononis spinosa Linnaeus var. **mitis** Linnaeus, *Species Plantarum*, ed. 2, 2: 1006. 1763.
RCN: 5265.
Lectotype (Förther in Turland & Jarvis in *Taxon* 46: 478. 1997): Herb. Clifford: 359, *Ononis* 5 (BM-000646583).
Current name: ***Ononis repens*** L. (Fabaceae: Faboideae).

Ononis tridentata Linnaeus, *Species Plantarum* 2: 718. 1753.
"Habitat in Hispania." RCN: 5285.
Lectotype (Förther in Turland & Jarvis in *Taxon* 46: 478. 1997): [icon] *"Anonis Hispanica frutescens folio tridentato carnoso"* in Magnol, Hort. Reg. Monspel.: 16, unnumbered plate. 1697. – Epitype (Förther in Turland & Jarvis in *Taxon* 46: 478. 1997): Spain. Granada, in salsis et collibus argillosis La Mala prope Granatam, Jul 1837, *E. Boissier s.n.* (M).
Current name: ***Ononis tridentata*** L. (Fabaceae: Faboideae).

Ononis trifoliata Linnaeus, *Systema Naturae*, ed. 12, 2: 479. 1767, *nom. illeg.*
["Habitat in Aethiopia."] Sp. Pl. 2: 770 (1753). RCN: 5621.
Replaced synonym: *Trifolium fruticans* L. (1753).
Lectotype (Stirton in *S. African J. Bot.* 52: 3. 1986): Herb. Clifford: 373, *Trifolium* 5 (BM-000646736).
Current name: ***Otholobium fruticans*** (L.) C.H. Stirt. (Fabaceae: Faboideae).
Note: An illegitimate renaming of *Trifolium fruticans* L. (1753).

Ononis umbellata Linnaeus, *Mantissa Plantarum Altera*: 266. 1771.
"Habitat ad Cap. b. spei." RCN: 5274.
Lectotype (Van Wyk in *Contr. Bolus Herb.* 14: 247. 1991): Herb. Linn. No. 896.12 (LINN).
Current name: ***Lotononis umbellata*** (L.) Benth. (Fabaceae: Faboideae).

Ononis variegata Linnaeus, *Species Plantarum* 2: 717. 1753.
"Habitat in Europae australis maritimis." RCN: 5271.
Lectotype (Förther in Turland & Jarvis in *Taxon* 46: 478. 1997): Herb. A. van Royen No. 908.120–1904 (L).
Current name: ***Ononis variegata*** L. (Fabaceae: Faboideae).
Note: Several authors (e.g. Jafri in Jafri & El-Gadi, *Fl. Libya* 86: 167. 1980; Devesa in *Mem. Soc. Brot.* 28: 19. 1988) have treated Herb. Linn. 896.9 (LINN) as the type, but this collection lacks a *Species Plantarum* number (i.e. "6"), is a post-1753 addition to the herbarium, and is not original material for the name.

Ononis villosa Linnaeus, *Systema Naturae*, ed. 10, 2: 1160. 1759.
RCN: 5281.
Neotype (Förther in Turland & Jarvis in *Taxon* 46: 478. 1997): Spain. Cádiz, in arenis et sylvaticis circa San Roque, Jun 1837, *Boissier s.n.* (M).
Current name: ***Ononis viscosa*** L. (Fabaceae: Faboideae).

Ononis viscosa Linnaeus, *Species Plantarum* 2: 718. 1753.
"Habitat Monspelii." RCN: 5281.
Lectotype (Förther in Turland & Jarvis in *Taxon* 46: 478. 1997):
[icon] *"Anonis lutea non viscosa latifolia minor flore pallido"* in
Barrelier, Pl. Galliam: 75, t. 1239. 1714. – Epitype (Förther in
Turland & Jarvis in *Taxon* 46: 478. 1997): France. Var, La Seyne,
June 1890, *P. Robin s.n.* (M; iso- BM).
Current name: ***Ononis viscosa*** L. (Fabaceae: Faboideae).
Note: Townsend (in *Kew Bull.* 21: 437. 1967) discussed Herb. Linn.
896.19 (LINN), concluding that it could not be the type but he did
not typify the name.

Onopordum acanthium Linnaeus, *Species Plantarum* 2: 827. 1753.
"Habitat in Europae ruderatis, cultis." RCN: 5984.
Lectotype (Danin in Davis, *Fl. Turkey* 5: 368. 1975): Herb. Burser
XXI: 44 (UPS).
Generitype of *Onopordum* Linnaeus (vide Green, *Prop. Brit. Bot.*: 179.
1929).
Current name: ***Onopordum acanthium*** L. (Asteraceae).

Onopordum acaulon Linnaeus, *Species Plantarum,* ed. 2, 2: 1159.
1763.
"Habitat – – – –" RCN: 5987.
Neotype (López González in Jarvis & Turland in *Taxon* 47: 364.
1998): Herb. Jussieu No. 8174 (P-JUS).
Current name: ***Onopordum acaulon*** L. (Asteraceae).

Onopordum arabicum Linnaeus, *Species Plantarum* 2: 827. 1753.
"Habitat in Lusitania, G. Narbonensi." RCN: 5986.
Lectotype (López González in Jarvis & Turland in *Taxon* 47: 364.
1998): [icon] *"Carduus tomentosus Acanthium dictus Arabicus"* in
Plukenet, Phytographia: t. 154, f. 5. 1692; Almag. Bot.: 85. 1696.
Current name: ***Onopordum illyricum*** L. (Asteraceae).
Note: As noted by authors such as Dress (in *Baileya* 14: 86. 1966) and
González Sierra & al. (in *Candollea* 47: 190. 1992), this name
included elements of both *O. nervosum* Boiss. and *O. illyricum* L.
(1753). López González's typification makes *O. arabicum* a
synonym of the latter.

Onopordum illyricum Linnaeus, *Species Plantarum* 2: 827. 1753.
"Habitat in Europa australi." RCN: 5985.
Lectotype (Danin in Davis, *Fl. Turkey* 5: 361. 1975): [icon]
"Acanthium Illyricum" in Plantin, Pl. Stirp. Icon. 2: 1. 1581.
Current name: ***Onopordum illyricum*** L. (Asteraceae).

Onosma echioides (Linnaeus) Linnaeus, *Species Plantarum,* ed. 2, 1:
196. 1762.
"Habitat in Austriae, Pannoniae, Helvetiae, Galliae, Italiae rupibus."
RCN: 1105.
Basionym: *Cerinthe echioides* L. (1753).
Lectotype (Lacaita, *Nuovo Giorn. Bot. Ital.,* n.s., 31: 24. 1924): [icon]
"Anchusa echioides lutea, cerinthoides mont." in Colonna, Ekphr.:
182, 183. 1606.
Generitype of *Onosma* Linnaeus (vide Johnston in *J. Arnold Arbor.* 35:
73. 1954).
Current name: ***Onosma echioides*** (L.) L. (Boraginaceae).
Note: See Stearn (in *Ann. Mus. Goulandris* 9: 235–238. 1994) on the
gender of *Onosma.*

Onosma orientalis (Linnaeus) Linnaeus, *Species Plantarum,* ed. 2, 1:
196. 1762.
"Habitat in Oriente." RCN: 1104.
Basionym: *Cerinthe orientalis* L. (1755).
Lectotype (Edmondson in Cafferty & Jarvis in *Taxon* 53: 801. 2004):
Herb. Hasselquist No. 137 (UPS).
Current name: ***Onosma orientalis*** (L.) L. (Boraginaceae).

Onosma simplicissima Linnaeus, *Species Plantarum,* ed. 2, 1: 196.
1762.
"Habitat in Sibiria. Gmelin." RCN: 1103.
Lectotype (Turland in *Bull. Nat. Hist. Mus. London, Bot.* 25: 144, f.
16. 1995): *Gerber,* Herb. Linn. No. 187.1 (LINN).
Current name: ***Onosma simplicissima*** L. (Boraginaceae).

Ophioglossum flexuosum Linnaeus, *Species Plantarum* 2: 1063.
1753.
"Habitat in India." RCN: 7746.
Lectotype (Alston & Holttum in *Reinwardtia* 5: 15. 1959): Herb.
Hermann 1: 32, No. 375 (BM-000621342).
Current name: ***Lygodium flexuosum*** (L.) Sw. (Schizaeaceae).

Ophioglossum lusitanicum Linnaeus, *Species Plantarum* 2: 1063.
1753.
"Habitat in Lusitania." RCN: 7741.
Type not designated.
Original material: [icon] in Barrelier, Pl. Galliam: 117, t. 252, f. 2.
1714.
Current name: ***Ophioglossum lusitanicum*** L. (Ophioglossaceae).

Ophioglossum palmatum Linnaeus, *Species Plantarum* 2: 1063.
1753.
"Habitat in America meridionali." RCN: 7744.
Lectotype (Proctor in Howard, *Fl. Lesser Antilles* 2: 45. 1977): [icon]
"Ophioglossum palmatum" in Plumier, Traité Foug. Amér.: 139, t.
163. 1705.
Current name: ***Ophioglossum palmatum*** L. (Ophioglossaceae).

Ophioglossum pendulum Linnaeus, *Herbarium Amboinense*: 27.
1754.
["Habitat in Indiae arboribus parasiticum, pendulum."] Sp. Pl., ed. 2,
2: 1518 (1763). RCN: 7742.
Lectotype (Green in *Kew Bull.* 43: 656. 1988): [icon] *"Scolopendria
major"* in Rumphius, Herb. Amboin. 6: 84, t. 37, f. 3. 1750.
Current name: ***Ophioglossum pendulum*** L. (Ophioglossaceae).

Ophioglossum reticulatum Linnaeus, *Species Plantarum* 2: 1063.
1753.
"Habitat in America meridionali." RCN: 7743.
Lectotype (Tardieu-Blot in Aubréville, *Fl. Gabon* 8: 30. 1964): [icon]
"Ophioglossum cordatum et reticulatum" in Plumier, Traité Foug.
Amér.: 141, t. 164. 1705.
Current name: ***Ophioglossum reticulatum*** L. (Ophioglossaceae).

Ophioglossum sarmentosum Linnaeus, *Flora Jamaicensis*: 22. 1759.
"Habitat [in Jamaica.]"
Type not designated.
Original material: none traced.
Note: The application of this name is uncertain.

Ophioglossum scandens Linnaeus, *Species Plantarum* 2: 1063. 1753.
"Habitat in India." RCN: 7745.
Lectotype (Adams & Alston in *Bull. Brit. Mus. (Nat. Hist.), Bot.* 1:
152. 1955): Herb. Hermann 1: 32, No. 374 (BM-000621341).
Current name: ***Lygodium flexuosum*** (L.) Sw. (Schizaeaceae).

Ophioglossum vulgatum Linnaeus, *Species Plantarum* 2: 1062. 1753.
"Habitat in Europae pratis sylvaticis." RCN: 7740.
Lectotype (Bobrov in *Novosti Sist. Vyssh. Rast.* 21: 6. 1984): Herb.
Linn. No. 1243.1 (LINN).
Generitype of *Ophioglossum* Linnaeus (vide Smith, *Hist. Fil.*: 367.
1875).
Current name: ***Ophioglossum vulgatum*** L. (Ophioglossaceae).

Note: Pichi Sermolli (in *Webbia* 26: 492. 1972) provided an extensive discussion of the typification of *Ophioglossum*.

Jonsell & Jarvis (in Jarvis & al., *Regnum Veg.* 127: 71. 1993; in *Nordic J. Bot.* 14: 148. 1994) designated a Clifford sheet as lectotype, unaware of Bobrov's earlier type choice.

Ophiorrhiza mitreola Linnaeus, *Species Plantarum* 1: 150. 1753.
"Habitat in America meridionali." RCN: 1189.
Lectotype (Tirel-Roudet in Aubréville & Leroy, *Fl. Cambodge Laos Vietnam* 13: 76. 1972): *Clayton 178* (BM-000051161).
Generitype of *Mitreola* Linnaeus, *Opera Varia*: 214 (1758).
Current name: **Mitreola petiolata** (J.G. Gmel.) Torr. & A. Gray (Loganiaceae).

Ophiorrhiza mungos Linnaeus, *Species Plantarum* 1: 150. 1753.
"Habitat in India orientali." RCN: 1188.
Lectotype (Verdcourt in Jarvis & al., *Regnum Veg.* 127: 71. 1993): Herb. Hermann 3: 50, No. 402 (BM-000594692).
Generitype of *Ophiorrhiza* Linnaeus (vide Hitchcock, *Prop. Brit. Bot.*: 129. 1929).
Current name: **Ophiorrhiza mungos** L. (Rubiaceae).

Ophioxylon serpentinum Linnaeus, *Species Plantarum* 2: 1043. 1753.
"Habitat in Zeylona." RCN: 7631.
Lectotype (Monachino in *Econ. Bot.* 8: 353. 1954; Leeuwenberg in Jarvis & al., *Regnum Veg.* 127: 71. 1993): Herb. Hermann 4: 77, No. 398, upper specimen (BM-000628401).
Generitype of *Ophioxylon* Linnaeus.
Current name: **Rauvolfia serpentina** (L.) Benth. ex Kurz (Apocynaceae).
Note: Monachino's type statement did not distinguish between material in volumes 1 and 4 of the Hermann herbarium, but as the specimens appear to have been part of a single gathering, Art. 9.15 applies, and Monachino is accepted as having typified the name, with subsequent restriction to one of the specimens being made by Leeuwenberg.

Ophira stricta Linnaeus, *Mantissa Plantarum Altera*: 229. 1771.
"Habitat in Africa. D. Burmannus." RCN: 2816.
Type not designated.
Original material: Herb. Linn. No. 499.1? (LINN).
Generitype of *Ophira* Linnaeus.
Current name: **Grubbia rosmarinifolia** P.J. Bergius (Grubbiaceae).

Ophrys alpina Linnaeus, *Species Plantarum* 2: 948. 1753.
"Habitat in Alpibus Lapponiae, Helvetiae." RCN: 6852.
Lectotype (Baumann & al. in *Mitteilungsbl. Arbeitskr. Heim. Orchid. Baden-Württemberg* 21: 445, Abb. 6. 1989): Herb. Linn. No. 1056.23, middle specimen (LINN).
Current name: **Chamorchis alpina** (L.) Rich. (Orchidaceae).
Note: Baumann & al. assume, on the basis of Linnaeus' later *Flora Suecica* (1755: 317) account, that the type collection was made in Lapland by Hollsten, although there are no annotations on the sheet itself to indicate this.

Ophrys anthropophora Linnaeus, *Species Plantarum* 2: 948. 1753.
"Habitat in Italia, Lusitania, Gallia." RCN: 6854.
Lectotype (Baumann & al. in *Mitteilungsbl. Arbeitskr. Heim. Orchid. Baden-Württemberg* 21: 437, Abb. 1. 1989): [icon] *"Orchis"* in Vaillant, Bot. Paris.: 147, t. 31, f. 19, 20. 1727.
Current name: **Orchis anthropophora** (L.) All. (Orchidaceae).

Ophrys arachnites (Linnaeus) Linnaeus, *Flora Anglica*: 23. 1754, *nom. inval.*

Type not relevant.
Current name: **Ophrys arachnites** (L.) Mill. (Orchidaceae).
Note: Britten (in *J. Bot.* 47, Suppl. 1909; 50: 312–314. 1912) argued that this apparent novelty results from a typographic error for the previously published *O. insectifera* var. *arachnites* L. (1753). Stearn (*Introd. Ray's Syn. Meth. Stirp. Brit.* (Ray Soc. ed.): 42–68. 1973) evidently agreed as he did not list the name as new. However, Rothmaler (in *Repert. Spec. Nov. Regni Veg.* 49: 280. 1941) did accept *O. arachnites* as a new combination. He has been followed by Greuter (in *Candollea* 44: 566. 1989) who, however, treated the name as a *nomen dubium et confusum*.

Ophrys atrata Linnaeus, *Systema Naturae,* ed. 12, 2: 593; *Mantissa Plantarum*: 121. 1767.
"Habitat ad Cap. b. spei. Schreber." RCN: 6856.
Lectotype (Linder in Cafferty & Jarvis in *Taxon* 48: 48. 1999): *Schreber*, Herb. Linn. No. 1056.31 (LINN), see p. 227.
Current name: **Ceratandra atrata** (L.) T. Durand & Schinz (Orchidaceae).

Ophrys caffra Linnaeus, *Plantae Rariores Africanae*: 28. 1760.
["Habitat ad Cap. b. spei."] Sp. Pl. ed. 2, 2: 1344 (1763). RCN: 6859.
Lectotype (Steiner in Cafferty & Jarvis in *Taxon* 48: 48. 1999): Herb. Linn. No. 1056.39 (LINN).
Current name: **Pterygodium caffrum** (L.) Sw. (Orchidaceae).

Ophrys camtschatea Linnaeus, *Species Plantarum* 2: 948. 1753.
"Habitat in Sibiria." RCN: 6853.
Lectotype (Cribb & Wood in Cafferty & Jarvis in *Taxon* 48: 48. 1999): *Steller*, Herb. Linn. No. 1056.24 (LINN).
Current name: **Neottia camtschatea** (L.) Rchb. f. (Orchidaceae).

Ophrys catholica Linnaeus, *Plantae Rariores Africanae*: 27. 1760.
["Habitat ad Cap. b. spei."] Sp. Pl., ed. 2, 2: 1344 (1763). RCN: 6857.
Lectotype (Steiner in Cafferty & Jarvis in *Taxon* 48: 48. 1999): [icon] *"Orchidi affinis, flore luteo"* in Buxbaum, Pl. Minus Cognit. Cent. 3: 13, t. 21. 1729. – Epitype (Steiner in Cafferty & Jarvis in *Taxon* 48: 48. 1999): South Africa. Signal Hill, above Cape Town, ca. 50m S of main parking area on top along path to Lion's Head, ca. 340m, 17 Sep 1997, *Steiner 3246* (NBG; iso- B, BM, E, K, MO, NSW, etc.).
Current name: **Pterygodium catholicum** (L.) Sw. (Orchidaceae).

Ophrys cernua Linnaeus, *Species Plantarum* 2: 946. 1753.
"Habitat in Virginia, Canada." RCN: 6844.
Lectotype (Sheviak in Cafferty & Jarvis in *Taxon* 48: 48. 1999): *Kalm*, Herb. Linn. No. 1056.9 (LINN).
Current name: **Spiranthes cernua** (L.) Rich. (Orchidaceae).

Ophrys circumflexa Linnaeus, *Plantae Rariores Africanae*: 27. 1760.
["Habitat ad Cap. b. Spei."] Sp. Pl., ed. 2, 2: 1344 (1763). RCN: 6858.
Lectotype (Manning in Cafferty & Jarvis in *Taxon* 48: 48. 1999): *"Orchis angustifolio fl...muscam referente. Herb. Old."*, Herb. Burman (G).
Current name: **Disperis circumflexa** (L.) T. Durand & Schinz (Orchidaceae).

Ophrys corallorhiza Linnaeus, *Species Plantarum* 2: 945. 1753.
"Habitat in Europae borealis desertis." RCN: 6832.
Lectotype (Baumann & al. in *Mitteilungsbl. Arbeitskr. Heim. Orchid. Baden-Württemberg* 21: 449, Abb. 8. 1989): Herb. Linn. No. 1056.5, middle specimen (LINN).

Current name: ***Corallorhiza trifida*** Châtel. (Orchidaceae).
Note: As noted by Baumann & al., the type is a Lapland collection made by Linnaeus in 1732.

Ophrys cordata Linnaeus, *Species Plantarum* 2: 946. 1753.
"Habitat in Europae frigidae sylvis humentibus." RCN: 6846.
Lectotype (Baumann & al. in *Mitteilungsbl. Arbeitskr. Heim. Orchid. Baden-Württemberg* 21: 497, Abb. 25. 1989): Herb. Linn. No. 1056.11 (LINN).
Current name: ***Listera cordata*** (L.) R. Br. (Orchidaceae).
Note: Linnaeus knew this species from several different parts of Sweden. Baumann & al. assume the type to have been collected by Linnaeus in Småland in 1741, although the material bears no annotation that might confirm this.

Ophrys insectifera Linnaeus, *Species Plantarum* 2: 948. 1753.
"Habitat in Europa temperatiori." RCN: 6855.
Lectotype (Baumann & al. in *Mitteilungsbl. Arbeitskr. Heim. Orchid. Baden-Württemberg* 21: 512, Abb. 32. 1989): Herb. Linn. No. 1056.20 (LINN).
Generitype of *Ophrys* Linnaeus (vide Green, *Prop. Brit. Bot.*: 185. 1929).
Current name: ***Ophrys insectifera*** L. (Orchidaceae).
Note: Ophrys insectifera, with the type designated by Baumann & al., was proposed as conserved type of the genus by Jarvis (in *Taxon* 41: 566. 1992). However, the proposal was eventually ruled unnecessary by the General Committee (see Barrie, *l.c.* 55: 795–796. 2006 for a review of the history of this and related proposals).
    Linnaeus knew this species from several different parts of Sweden. Baumann & al. assume the type to have been collected by Linnaeus in Öland in 1741, although the material bears no annotation that might confirm this.

Ophrys insectifera Linnaeus var. **arachnites** Linnaeus, *Species Plantarum* 2: 949. 1753.
RCN: 6855.
Lectotype (Baumann & al. in *Mitteilungsbl. Arbeitskr. Heim. Orchid. Baden-Württemberg* 21: 509, Abb. 31. 1989): [icon] *"Orchis andrachnitis"* in Plantin, Pl. Stirp. Icon.: 185. 1581.
Current name: ***Ophrys apifera*** Huds. (Orchidaceae).
Note: The varietal epithet was originally spelled "adrachnites" in the protologue but was subsequently corrected by Linnaeus. Rothmaler (in *Repert. Spec. Nov. Regni Veg.* 49: 280. 1940) treated this as the basionym of *O. arachnites* (L.) L. (1754), followed by Greuter (in *Candollea* 44: 566. 1989). However, Britten (in *J. Bot.* 47, Suppl. 1909; 50: 312–314. 1912) argued that *"O. arachnites"* resulted from a typographic error. Stearn (*Introd. Ray's Syn. Meth. Stirp. Brit.* (Ray Soc. ed.): 42–68. 1973) evidently agreed as he did not list the name as new.

Ophrys insectifera Linnaeus var. **myodes** Linnaeus, *Species Plantarum* 2: 948. 1753.
RCN: 6855.
Lectotype (Baumann & al. in *Mitteilungsbl. Arbeitskr. Heim. Orchid. Baden-Württemberg* 21: 513, Abb. 32. 1989): Herb. Linn. No. 1056.20 (LINN).
Current name: ***Ophrys insectifera*** L. var. ***insectifera*** (Orchidaceae).

Ophrys liliifolia Linnaeus, *Species Plantarum* 2: 946. 1753.
"Habitat in Virginiae, Canadae, Sueciae paludibus." RCN: 6847.
Lectotype (Fernald in *Rhodora* 49: 137. 1947): *Clayton 658* (BM-000051727).
Current name: ***Liparis liliifolia*** (L.) Rich. ex Lindl. (Orchidaceae).
Note: Specific epithet spelled "lilifolia" in the protologue.

Ophrys linifolia Linnaeus, *Systema Naturae*, ed. 12, 2: 592. 1767, *orth. var.*
["Habitat in Virginiae, Canadae, Sueciae paludibus."] Sp. Pl. 2: 946 (1753). RCN: 6847.
Lectotype (Fernald in *Rhodora* 49: 137. 1947): *Clayton 658* (BM).
Current name: ***Liparis liliifolia*** (L.) Rich. ex Lindl. (Orchidaceae).
Note: Ophrys linifolia is evidently a misprint for *Ophrys liliifolia* L. (1753).

Ophrys loeselii Linnaeus, *Species Plantarum* 2: 947. 1753.
"Habitat in Sueciae, Borussiae paludibus." RCN: 6848.
Lectotype (Baumann & al. in *Mitteilungsbl. Arbeitskr. Heim. Orchid. Baden-Württemberg* 21: 495, Abb. 24. 1989): *Bergius*, Herb. Linn. No. 1056.14 (LINN).
Current name: ***Liparis loeselii*** (L.) Rich. (Orchidaceae).

Ophrys monophyllos Linnaeus, *Species Plantarum* 2: 947. 1753.
"Habitat in Borussiae, Medelpadiae paludibus sylvaticis." RCN: 6850.
Lectotype (Baumann & al. in *Mitteilungsbl. Arbeitskr. Heim. Orchid. Baden-Württemberg* 21: 501, Abb. 27. 1989): Herb. Linn. No. 1056.17, left specimen (LINN).
Current name: ***Malaxis monophyllos*** (L.) Sw. (Orchidaceae).
Note: Baumann & al. deduce, on the basis of Linnaeus' later *Flora Suecica* (1755: 316) account ("Habitat in Alnoen Medelpadiae D.D. Gisler"), that the type collection was made by Nils Gissler in Medelpad.

Ophrys monorchis Linnaeus, *Species Plantarum* 2: 947. 1753.
"Habitat in Europae pratis uliginosis." RCN: 6851.
Lectotype (Baumann & al. in *Mitteilungsbl. Arbeitskr. Heim. Orchid. Baden-Württemberg* 21: 489, Abb. 21. 1989): Herb. Linn. No. 1056.22, middle specimen (LINN).
Generitype of *Herminium* Linnaeus.
Current name: ***Herminium monorchis*** (L.) R. Br. (Orchidaceae).
Note: Epithet spelled "monochris" in the protologue.
    Ophrys monorchis is the basionym of *Herminium monorchis* (L.) R. Br., the type of *Herminium*. Linnaeus knew this species from several different parts of Sweden. Baumann & al. assume the type (which Linnaeus associates with his *Flora Suecica* account of 1745) to have been collected by Linnaeus in Skåne in 1741, although the material bears no annotation that might confirm this.

Ophrys nidus-avis Linnaeus, *Species Plantarum* 2: 945. 1753.
"Habitat in Sueciae, Germaniae, Galliae nemoribus." RCN: 6841.
Lectotype (Baumann & al. in *Mitteilungsbl. Arbeitskr. Heim. Orchid. Baden-Württemberg* 21: 504, Abb. 28. 1989): [icon] *"Nidus avis, ex speciebus Satyrii abortivi"* in Plantin, Pl. Stirp. Icon.: 195. 1581.
Current name: ***Neottia nidus-avis*** (L.) Rich. (Orchidaceae).

Ophrys ovata Linnaeus, *Species Plantarum* 2: 946. 1753.
"Habitat in Europae subhumidis pratis." RCN: 6845.
Lectotype (Renz in Nasir & Ali, *Fl. Pakistan* 164: 8. 1984): Herb. Linn. No. 1056.10 (LINN).
Current name: ***Listera ovata*** (L.) R. Br. (Orchidaceae).
Note: Baumann & al. (in *Mitteilungsbl. Arbeitskr. Heim. Orchid. Baden-Württemberg* 21: 499, Abb. 26. 1989) provided a detailed discussion of the name, designating a Fuchs plate as lectotype but overlooked the earlier type choice by Renz.

Ophrys paludosa Linnaeus, *Species Plantarum* 2: 947. 1753.
"Habitat in Sueciae paludibus turfosis." RCN: 6849.
Lectotype (Baumann & al. in *Mitteilungsbl. Arbeitskr. Heim. Orchid. Baden-Württemberg* 21: 487, Abb. 20. 1989): Herb. Linn. No. 1056.16, middle specimen (LINN).
Current name: ***Hammarbya paludosa*** (L.) Kuntze (Orchidaceae).

Note: Baumann & al. assume, on the basis of Linnaeus' later *Flora Suecica* (1755: 316) account, that the type collection was made near Uppsala by Linnaeus and Bergius, although there are no annotations on the sheet itself to indicate this.

Ophrys spiralis Linnaeus, *Species Plantarum* 2: 945. 1753.
"Habitat in Italiae, Galliae, Angliae graminosis." RCN: 6843.
Lectotype (Baumann & al. in *Mitteilungsbl. Arbeitskr. Heim. Orchid. Baden-Württemberg* 21: 562, Abb. 49. 1989): [icon] *"Satyrion odoriferum"* in Brunfels, Herbarum Vivae Eicones 1: 105. 1530.
Current name: ***Spiranthes spiralis*** (L.) Chevall. (Orchidaceae).

Orchis abortiva Linnaeus, *Species Plantarum* 2: 943. 1753.
"Habitat in Gallia, Helvetia, Anglia, Italia." RCN: 6830.
Lectotype (Al-Eisawi in *Kew Bull.* 41: 361. 1986; Baumann & al. in *Mitteilungsbl. Arbeitskr. Heim. Orchid. Baden-Württemberg* 21: 493, Abb. 23. 1989): Herb. Linn. No. 1054.43, middle specimen (LINN).
Current name: ***Limodorum abortivum*** (L.) Sw. (Orchidaceae).
Note: Al-Eisawi indicated material in LINN as type, sheet 1054.43 being the only one associated with this name. Baumann & al. restricted the type to the middle specimen on the type sheet, and assume that it was collected in Fontainebleau by Linnaeus in 1738, but there are no annotations on the sheet itself to indicate this. At least one of the other specimens on the sheet came from Magnol (from Provence).

Orchis bicornis Linnaeus, *Plantae Rariores Africanae*: 26. 1760. ["Habitat ad Cap. b. spei."] Sp. Pl., ed. 2, 2: 1330 (1763). RCN: 6799.
Lectotype (Hall in *Contr. Bolus Herb.* 10: 36. 1982): [icon] *"Orchis lutea, caule geniculato"* in Buxbaum, Pl. Minus Cognit. Cent. 3: 6, t. 8. 1729 (see p. 115).
Current name: ***Satyrium bicorne*** (L.) Thunb. (Orchidaceae).

Orchis biflora Linnaeus, *Species Plantarum*, ed. 2, 2: 1330. 1763.
"Habitat ad Cap. b. Spei." RCN: 6800.
Replaced synonym: *Satyrium cornutum* L. (1760).
Lectotype (Linder in *J. S. African Bot.* 47: 359, f. 9.1, 9.2. 1981): Herb. Burman (G).
Current name: ***Schizodium cornutum*** (L.) Schltr. (Orchidaceae).
Note: A *nomen novum* in *Orchis* for *Satyrium cornutum* L. (1760), non *Orchis cornuta* L. (1760). Garay (in *Harvard Pap. Bot.* 2: 49. 1997) wrongly treated *O. biflora* as illegitimate.

Orchis bifolia Linnaeus, *Species Plantarum* 2: 939. 1753.
"Habitat in Europae pascuis asperis." RCN: 6806.
Lectotype (Løjtnant in *Feddes Repert.* 89: 14. 1978): Herb. Linn. No. 1054.15 (LINN).
Current name: ***Platanthera bifolia*** (L.) Rich. (Orchidaceae).
Note: Baumann & al. (in *Mitteilungsbl. Arbeitskr. Heim. Orchid. Baden-Württemberg* 21: 540, Abb. 43. 1989) rejected the earlier typification by Løjtnant because they believed the type to be a post-1753 addition to the herbarium, and designated a Mattioli illustration in its place. However, the sheet treated as the type by Løjtnant was annotated by Linnaeus with "bifolia" and "3", the number corresponding with the account of this species (i.e. *Orchis* no. 3) in *Species Plantarum*, and there is nothing to suggest that it was not in Linnaeus' possession by 1753. The annotation "Sw. 9" is a much later addition by James Edward Smith. Consequently, Løjtnant's typification, which has priority over that of Baumann & al., is accepted here.

Orchis burmanniana Linnaeus, *Plantae Rariores Africanae*: 26. 1760. ["Habitat ad Cap. b. spei."] Sp. Pl. ed. 2, 2: 1334 (1763). RCN: 6818.

Lectotype (Linder in Cafferty & Jarvis in *Taxon* 48: 48. 1999): *"Orchis pectinata Burmanniana"*, Herb. Burman (G).
Current name: ***Bartholina burmanniana*** (L.) Ker-Gawl. (Orchidaceae).

Orchis ciliaris Linnaeus, *Species Plantarum* 2: 939. 1753.
"Habitat in Virginia, Canada." RCN: 6804.

Lectotype (Reveal & al. in *Huntia* 7: 229. 1987): Herb. Linn. No. 1054.13 (LINN).
Current name: ***Platanthera ciliaris*** (L.) Lindl. (Orchidaceae).

Orchis conopsea Linnaeus, *Species Plantarum* 2: 942. 1753.
"Habitat in Europae pratis montosis." RCN: 6825.
Lectotype (Baumann & al. in *Mitteilungsbl. Arbeitskr. Heim. Orchid. Baden-Württemberg* 21: 482, Abb. 18. 1989): [icon] *"Satyrium basilicum mas"* in Fuchs, Hist. Stirp.: 711, 712. 1542.
Current name: ***Gymnadenia conopsea*** (L.) R. Br. (Orchidaceae).

Orchis coriophora Linnaeus, *Species Plantarum* 2: 940. 1753.
"Habitat in Europae australioris pascuis." RCN: 6811.
Lectotype (Baumann & al. in *Mitteilungsbl. Arbeitskr. Heim. Orchid. Baden-Württemberg* 21: 514, Abb. 33. 1989): [icon] *"Tragorchis minor & verior, sive Coriosmites, vel Coriophora, flore instar cimicium"* in Plantin, Pl. Stirp. Icon.: 177. 1581.
Current name: ***Orchis coriophora*** L. (Orchidaceae).

O

Note: Enayet Hossain & El-Gadi (in Jafri & El-Gadi, *Fl. Libya* 119: 25. 1985) indicated 1054.18 (LINN) as type. However, the material lacks a *Species Plantarum* number (i.e. "6") and was a post-1753 addition to the collection, and is not original material for the name.

Orchis cornuta Linnaeus, *Plantae Rariores Africanae*: 27. 1760. ["Habitat ad Cap. b. spei."] Sp. Pl. ed. 2, 2: 1330 (1763). RCN: 6801.
Lectotype (Linder in *J. S. African Bot.* 47: 359, f. 9.1, 9.2. 1981): Herb. Burman (G).
Current name: ***Disa cornuta*** (L.) Sw. (Orchidaceae).

Orchis cubitalis Linnaeus, *Species Plantarum* 2: 940. 1753.
"Habitat in Zeylona." RCN: 6812.
Lectotype (Cribb in Cafferty & Jarvis in *Taxon* 48: 48. 1999): Herb. Hermann 2: 35, No. 320 (BM-000621637).
Current name: ***Peristylis cubitalis*** (L.) Kraenzl. (Orchidaceae).

Orchis cucullata Linnaeus, *Species Plantarum* 2: 939. 1753.
"Habitat in Sibiria." RCN: 6808.
Lectotype (Baumann & al. in *Mitteilungsbl. Arbeitskr. Heim. Orchid. Baden-Württemberg* 21: 506, Abb. 29. 1989): [icon] *"Orchis radice rotunda, cucullo tridentato"* in Gmelin, Fl. Sibirica 1: 16, t. 3, f. 2*. 1747.
Current name: ***Neottianthe cucullata*** (L.) Schltr. (Orchidaceae).

Orchis flava Linnaeus, *Species Plantarum* 2: 942. 1753.
"Habitat in Virginia." RCN: 6826.
Lectotype (Sheviak in Cafferty & Jarvis in *Taxon* 48: 48. 1999): *Clayton 639* (BM-000051710).
Current name: ***Platanthera flava*** (L.) Lindl. var. ***flava*** (Orchidaceae).

Orchis flexuosa Linnaeus, *Plantae Rariores Africanae*: 26. 1760. ["Habitat ad Cap. b. spei."] Sp. Pl., ed. 2, 2: 1331 (1763). RCN: 6807.
Lectotype (Linder in *J. S. African Bot.* 47: 343. 1981): *Oldenland*, Herb. Burman (G).
Current name: ***Schizodium flexuosum*** (L.) Lindl. (Orchidaceae).

Orchis fuscescens Linnaeus, *Species Plantarum* 2: 943. 1753.
"Habitat in Sibiria." RCN: 6827.
Lectotype (Cribb & Wood in Cafferty & Jarvis in *Taxon* 48: 48. 1999): [icon] *"Orchis radicibus multis, labello basi alato, calcare germinis longitudine"* in Gmelin, Fl. Sibirica 1: 20, t. 4, f. 2. 1747. – Epitype (Cribb & Wood in Cafferty & Jarvis in *Taxon* 48: 48. 1999): China. Flora Manshuriae, Prov. Kininensis, 12 Jun 1897 *Komarov 445* (BM-000034213).
Current name: ***Tulotis fuscescens*** (L.) Czerep. (Orchidaceae).

Orchis globosa Linnaeus, *Systema Naturae*, ed. 10, 2: 1242. 1759. ["Habitat in Helvetica."] Sp. Pl., ed. 2, 2: 1332 (1763). RCN: 6809.
Lectotype (Baumann & al. in *Mitteilungsbl. Arbeitskr. Heim. Orchid. Baden-Württemberg* 21: 564, Abb. 50. 1989): Herb. Linn. No. 1054.16 (LINN).
Current name: ***Orchis globosa*** L. (Orchidaceae).

Orchis habenaria Linnaeus, *Systema Naturae*, ed. 10, 2: 1242. 1759. ["Habitat in Jamaica."] Sp. Pl., ed. 2, 2: 1331 (1763). RCN: 6805.
Lectotype (Cribb in Cafferty & Jarvis in *Taxon* 48: 48. 1999): Herb. Linn. No. 1054.14 (LINN).
Current name: ***Habenaria quinqueseta*** (Michx.) Sw. var. ***macroceratitis*** (Willd.) Luer (Orchidaceae).

Orchis hyperborea Linnaeus, *Systema Naturae*, ed. 12, 2: 591; *Mantissa Plantarum*: 121. 1767.

"Habitat in Islandia. König." RCN: 6829.
Lectotype (Ames, *Orchidaceae* 4: 81. 1910): Herb. Linn. No. 1054.42 (LINN).
Current name: ***Orchis hyperborea*** L. (Orchidaceae).
Note: Baumann & al. (in *Mitteilungsbl. Arbeitskr. Heim. Orchid. Baden-Württemberg* 21: 542. 1989) discuss the typification, figuring the type as Abb. 44. Sheviak (in *Lindleyana* 14: 200. 1999) reassessed the identity of the type, as well as providing a floral dissection (f. 5) of it.

Orchis incarnata Linnaeus, *Flora Suecica*, ed. 2: 312. 1755.
"Habitat [in Suecia] in Pratis rarius." RCN: 6821.
Lectotype (Vermeulen, *Stud. Dactylorchids*: 89. 1947): Herb. Linn. No. 1054.33 (LINN).
Current name: ***Dactylorhiza incarnata*** (L.) Soó (Orchidaceae).
Note: See reviews by Baumann & al. (in *Mitteilungsbl. Arbeitskr. Heim. Orchid. Baden-Württemberg* 21: 458, Abb. 10. 1989) and Pedersen (in *Taxon* 49: 541. 2000), both of whom follow Vermeulen's choice of type.

Orchis latifolia Linnaeus, *Species Plantarum* 2: 941. 1753, *nom. rej.*
"Habitat in Europae pratis." RCN: 6820.
Lectotype (Pugsley in *J. Linn. Soc., Bot.* 49: 563, pl. 31. 1935): Herb. Linn. No. 1054.32 (LINN).
Current name: ***Dactylorhiza sambucina*** (L.) Soó (Orchidaceae).

Orchis maculata Linnaeus, *Species Plantarum* 2: 942. 1753.
"Habitat in Europae pratis succulentis." RCN: 6823.
Lectotype (Vermeulen, *Stud. Dactylorchids*: 128. 1947): Herb. Linn. No. 1054.36 (LINN).
Current name: ***Dactylorhiza maculata*** (L.) Soó (Orchidaceae).
Note: See also Baumann & al. (in *Mitteilungsbl. Arbeitskr. Heim. Orchid. Baden-Württemberg* 21: 465, Abb. 12. 1989), who follow Vermeulen's choice of type.

Orchis mascula (Linnaeus) Linnaeus, *Flora Suecica*, ed. 2: 310. 1755.
Basionym: *Orchis morio* var. *mascula* L. (1753).
Lectotype (Baumann & al. in *Mitteilungsbl. Arbeitskr. Heim. Orchid. Baden-Württemberg* 21: 530, Abb. 38. 1989): [icon] *"Testiculi species IIII"* in Mattioli, Pl. Epit.: 624. 1586.
Current name: ***Orchis mascula*** (L.) L. (Orchidaceae).
Note: Baumann & al. (in *Mitteilungsbl. Arbeitskr. Heim. Orchid. Baden-Württemberg* 21: 518, Abb. 34. 1989) wrongly treated this as a new name, rather than a new combination based on *O. morio* var. *mascula* L. (1753), and designated 1054.19 (LINN) as lectotype. However, *O. mascula* is homotypic with *O. morio* var. *mascula*, which is typified by a Mattioli plate.

Orchis militaris Linnaeus, *Species Plantarum* 2: 941. 1753.
"Habitat in Europae temperatae pratis." RCN: 6816.
Lectotype (Baumann & al. in *Mitteilungsbl. Arbeitskr. Heim. Orchid. Baden-Württemberg* 21: 521, Abb. 35. 1989): [icon] *"Orchis mas latifolia"* in Fuchs, Hist. Stirp.: 558, 554. 1542.
Generitype of *Orchis* Linnaeus (vide Green, *Prop. Brit. Bot.*: 184. 1929).
Current name: ***Orchis militaris*** L. (Orchidaceae).

Orchis morio Linnaeus, *Species Plantarum* 2: 940. 1753.
"Habitat in Europae nemoribus." RCN: 6813.
Lectotype (Baumann & al. in *Mitteilungsbl. Arbeitskr. Heim. Orchid. Baden-Württemberg* 21: 523, Abb. 36. 1989): [icon] *"Triorchis serapias mas"* in Fuchs, Hist. Stirp.: 561, 559. 1542 (see p. 131).
Current name: ***Anacamptis morio*** (L.) R.M. Bateman & al. (Orchidaceae).

Orchis morio Linnaeus var. **angustifolia** Linnaeus, *Species Plantarum* 2: 940. 1753.
RCN: 6813.
Lectotype (Cribb & Wood in Cafferty & Jarvis in *Taxon* 48: 48. 1999): [icon] *"Orchis morio, foemina, procerior, majore flore"* in Vaillant, Bot. Paris.: 150, t. 31, f. 33, 34. 1727.
Current name: *Anacamptis laxiflora* (Lam.) R.M. Bateman & al. (Orchidaceae).

Orchis morio Linnaeus var. **mascula** Linnaeus, *Species Plantarum* 2: 941. 1753.
RCN: 6813.
Basionym of: *Orchis mascula* (L.) L. (1755).
Lectotype (Baumann & al. in *Mitteilungsbl. Arbeitskr. Heim. Orchid. Baden-Württemberg* 21: 530, Abb. 38. 1989): [icon] *"Testiculi species IIII"* in Mattioli, Pl. Epit.: 624. 1586.
Current name: *Orchis mascula* (L.) L. (Orchidaceae).
Note: Varietal epithet spelled "masculus" in the protologue.

Orchis odoratissima Linnaeus, *Systema Naturae*, ed. 10, 2: 1243. 1759.
["Habitat in Italia, Gallia, Germania, rarissima in Svecia."] Sp. Pl., ed. 2, 2: 1335 (1763). RCN: 6824.
Lectotype (Cribb & Wood in Cafferty & Jarvis in *Taxon* 48: 48. 1999): Herb. Linn. No. 1054.37 (LINN).
Current name: *Gymnadenia odoratissima* (L.) Rich. (Orchidaceae).

Orchis pallens Linnaeus, *Mantissa Plantarum Altera*: 292. 1771.
"Habitat in Europae sylvosis." RCN: 6819.
Lectotype (Baumann & al. in *Mitteilungsbl. Arbeitskr. Heim. Orchid. Baden-Württemberg* 21: 532, Abb. 39. 1989): [icon] *"Orchis radicibus subrotundis, petalis galeae lineatis, labello quadrifido integerrimo"* in Haller, Hist. Stirp. Helv. 2: 143, t. 30. 1768.
Current name: *Orchis pallens* L. (Orchidaceae).

Orchis papilionacea Linnaeus, *Systema Naturae*, ed. 10, 2: 1242. 1759.
["Habitat in Hispania. Alstroemer."] Sp. Pl., ed. 2, 2: 1331 (1763). RCN: 6817.
Lectotype (Baumann & al. in *Mitteilungsbl. Arbeitskr. Heim. Orchid. Baden-Württemberg* 21: 533, Abb. 40. 1989): Herb. Linn. No. 1054.30, right specimen (LINN).
Current name: *Anacamptis papilionacea* (L.) R.M. Bateman & al. (Orchidaceae).
Note: Enayet Hossain & El-Gadi (in Jafri & El-Gadi, *Fl. Libya* 119: 27. 1985) indicated 1054.29 and 1054.30 (LINN) as "type". However, as they are evidently not part of a single gathering, Art. 9.15 does not apply.

Orchis psycodes Linnaeus, *Species Plantarum* 2: 943. 1753.
"Habitat in Canada." RCN: 6831.
Lectotype (Stoutamire in *Brittonia* 26: 54. 1974): *Kalm*, Herb. Linn. No. 1054.51 (LINN).
Current name: *Platanthera psycodes* (L.) Lindl. (Orchidaceae).

Orchis pyramidalis Linnaeus, *Species Plantarum* 2: 940. 1753.
"Habitat in Helvetiae, Belgii, Angliae, Galliae arenosis, cretaceis." RCN: 6810.
Lectotype (Al-Eisawi in *Kew Bull.* 41: 389. 1986): Herb. Linn. No. 1054.17 (LINN).
Current name: *Anacamptis pyramidalis* (L.) Rich. (Orchidaceae).
Note: Al-Eisawi's indication of type material in LINN can refer only to one collection (1054.17) and his choice therefore has priority over that of Baumann & al. (in *Mitteilungsbl. Arbeitskr. Heim. Orchid. Baden-Württemberg* 21: 439, Abb. 2. 1989), who chose a Ray figure instead.

Orchis pyramidata Linnaeus, *Amoenitates Academicae* 4: 492. 1759, *orth. var.*
RCN: 6810.
Lectotype (Al-Eisawi in *Kew Bull.* 41: 389. 1986): Herb. Linn. No. 1054.17 (LINN).
Current name: *Anacamptis pyramidalis* (L.) Rich. (Orchidaceae).
Note: As noted by Stearn (in Geck & Pressler, *Festschr. Claus Nissen*: 632. 1974), this is an orthographic error for *O. pyramidalis* L. (1753).

Orchis sambucina Linnaeus, *Flora Suecica,* ed. 2: 312. 1755.
"Habitat Holmiae ad praedium Mart. Triewald Mariaeberg, in planitie montium humentium; eandem aliis in locis juxta Holmiam lectam misit Eric. Tuwen." RCN: 6822.
Lectotype (Baumann & al. in *Mitteilungsbl. Arbeitskr. Heim. Orchid. Baden-Württemberg* 21: 468, Abb. 13. 1989): Herb. Linn. No. 1054.34 (LINN).
Current name: *Dactylorhiza sambucina* (L.) Soó (Orchidaceae).
Note: Baumann & al. assume that the type collection was made near Stockholm by Tuwen, although there are no annotations on the sheet itself to confirm this.

Orchis sancta Linnaeus, *Systema Naturae,* ed. 10, 2: 1242. 1759.
["Habitat in Palaestina."] Sp. Pl., ed. 2, 2: 1330 (1763). RCN: 6802.
Lectotype (Al-Eisawi in *Kew Bull.* 41: 371. 1986): *Hasselquist*, Herb. Linn. No. 1054.12 (LINN).
Current name: *Anacamptis sancta* (L.) R.M. Bateman & al. (Orchidaceae).
Note: This name appears first in *Fl. Palaestina*: 29 (1756). However, there it is a *nomen nudum* as the validating diagnosis merely states "Orchis sancta, radix desuit in speciminibus" (the root lacking in the specimens). The name dates from 1759, rather than 1763 as suggested by Wood (in *Kew Mag.* 10: 11. 1993). The type is figured by Baumann & al. (in *Mitteilungsbl. Arbeitskr. Heim. Orchid. Baden-Württemberg* 21: 647, Abb. 41. 1989).

Orchis satyrioides Linnaeus, *Amoenitates Academicae* 6: 109. 1763, *nom. illeg.*
RCN: 6800.
Replaced synonym: *Satyrium cornutum* L. (1760).
Lectotype (Linder in *J. S. African Bot.* 47: 359, f. 9.1, 9.2. 1981): Herb. Burman (G).
Current name: *Schizodium cornutum* (L.) Schltr. (Orchidaceae).
Note: Linnaeus (*Sp. Pl.*, ed. 2, 2: 1330. Jul 1763) transferred *Satyrium cornutum* L. (1760) to *Orchis*, coining the name *O. biflora* L. because of the existence of *O. cornuta* L. (1760). However, three months later (Oct 1763), Linnaeus published yet another name, *O. satyrioides*, as a replacement for *S. cornutum*, and *O. satyrioides* is therefore illegitimate.

Orchis spectabilis Linnaeus, *Species Plantarum* 2: 943. 1753.
"Habitat in Virginia. D. Gronovius." RCN: 6832.
Lectotype (Sheviak in Cafferty & Jarvis in *Taxon* 48: 49. 1999): *Clayton s.n.*, Herb. Linn. No. 1054.44 (LINN).
Current name: *Galearis spectabilis* (L.) Raf. (Orchidaceae).

Orchis strateumatica Linnaeus, *Species Plantarum* 2: 943. 1753.
"Habitat in Zeylona." RCN: 6828.
Lectotype (Cribb in Cafferty & Jarvis in *Taxon* 48: 49. 1999): Herb. Hermann 2: 35, No. 319 (BM-000621635).
Current name: *Zeuxine strateumatica* (L.) Schltr. (Orchidaceae).

Orchis susannae Linnaeus, *Species Plantarum* 2: 939. 1753.
"Habitat in Amboina." RCN: 6803.

Lectotype (Cribb in Cafferty & Jarvis in *Taxon* 48: 49. 1999): [icon] *"Orchis Amboinensis"* in Hermann, Parad. Bat.: 209. 1698.
Current name: ***Pecteilis susannae*** (L.) Raf. (Orchidaceae).

Orchis ustulata Linnaeus, *Species Plantarum* 2: 941. 1753.
"Habitat in Europae temperatae pratis." RCN: 6815.
Lectotype (Baumann & al. in *Mitteilungsbl. Arbeitskr. Heim. Orchid. Baden-Württemberg* 21: 537, Abb. 42. 1989): Herb. Linn. No. 1054.21, left specimen (LINN).
Current name: ***Neotinea ustulata*** (L.) R.M. Bateman & al. (Orchidaceae).
Note: Linnaeus knew this species from several parts of Sweden. Baumann & al. assume the type to have been collected by Linnaeus in Skåne in 1751, although the material bears no annotation that might confirm this.

Origanum aegyptiacum Linnaeus, *Species Plantarum* 2: 588. 1753.
"Habitat in Aegypto." RCN: 4287.
Lectotype (Hedge in Jarvis & al. in *Taxon* 50: 515. 2001): [icon] *"Origano cognata Zatarhendi"* in Morison, Pl. Hist. Univ. 3: 360, s. 11, t. 3, f. 17. 1699.
Current name: ***Origanum syriacum*** L. (Lamiaceae).
Note: Ietswaart (in *Leiden Bot. Ser.* 4: 145. 1980) regarded the name as of uncertain application. However, Hedge's typification makes it a synonym of *O. syriacum* L.

Origanum creticum Linnaeus, *Species Plantarum* 2: 589. 1753.
"Habitat in Europa australi." RCN: 4290.
Lectotype (Paton in Jarvis & al. in *Taxon* 50: 515. 2001): Herb. Linn. No. 743.4 (LINN).
Current name: ***Origanum vulgare*** L. subsp. ***vulgare*** (Lamiaceae).
Note: Ietswaart (in *Leiden Bot. Ser.* 4: 107. 1980) wrongly indicated 743.3 (LINN) as the holotype which he also simultaneously indicated as the type of *O. sipyleum* L. This collection is not original material for *O. creticum*.

Origanum dictamnus Linnaeus, *Species Plantarum* 2: 589. 1753.
"Habitat in Cretae monte Ida." RCN: 4288.
Lectotype (Ietswaart in *Leiden Bot. Ser.* 4: 42. 1980): Herb. Linn. No. 743.2 (LINN).
Current name: ***Origanum dictamnus*** L. (Lamiaceae).

Origanum heracleoticum Linnaeus, *Species Plantarum* 2: 589. 1753.
"Habitat in Europa australi, Graecia." RCN: 4292.
Lectotype (Ietswaart in *Leiden Bot. Ser.* 4: 116. 1980): Herb. Linn. No. 743.8 (LINN).
Current name: ***Origanum dictamnus*** L. subsp. ***viride*** (Boiss.) Hayek (Lamiaceae).

Origanum majorana Linnaeus, *Species Plantarum* 2: 590. 1753.
"Habitat – – – –" RCN: 4297.
Lectotype (Paton in Jarvis & al. in *Taxon* 50: 516. 2001): Herb. Clifford: 304, *Origanum* 3, sheet A (BM-000628967).
Current name: ***Origanum majorana*** L. (Lamiaceae).
Note: Ietswaart (in *Leiden Bot. Ser.* 4: 83. 1980) stated, "Type: Linnaeus s.n. (holo BM)", possibly in reference to Clifford material, as did Hedge (in Ali & Nasir, *Fl. Pakistan* 192: 247. 1990). However, these statements are insufficiently precise to constitute formal typification. Siddiqi (in Jafri & El-Gadi, *Fl. Libya* 118: 99. 1985) stated "Type: Herb. Linn. 743.13 (LINN)", but this specimen lacks the relevant *Species Plantarum* number (i.e. "10") and is not considered original material. A Clifford sheet was designated as lectotype by Paton.

Origanum maru Linnaeus, *Species Plantarum*, ed. 2, 2: 825. 1763.
"Habitat in Creta." RCN: 4296.
Lectotype (Harley in *Watsonia* 14: 86. 1982): Herb. Linn. No. 743.12 (LINN).
Current name: ***Origanum syriacum*** L. (Lamiaceae).
Note: As pointed out by Harley (in *Watsonia* 14: 86. 1982), Ietswaart (in *Leiden Bot. Ser.* 4: 88. 1980) designated 743.12 (LINN) as the type of both *O. syriacum* and *O. maru* L. In clarifying this situation, Harley stated that the sheet in question "is unquestionably the type of *O. maru*", thereby typifying the name himself.

Origanum onites Linnaeus, *Species Plantarum* 2: 590. 1753.
"Habitat Syracusae." RCN: 4294.
Lectotype (Ietswaart in *Leiden Bot. Ser.* 4: 85. 1980): Herb. Linn. No. 743.11 (LINN).
Current name: ***Origanum onites*** L. (Lamiaceae).

Origanum sipyleum Linnaeus, *Species Plantarum* 2: 589. 1753.
"Habitat in Phrygiae monte Sipylo." RCN: 4289.
Lectotype (Ietswaart in *Leiden Bot. Ser.* 4: 55. 1980): Herb. Linn. No. 743.3 (LINN).
Current name: ***Origanum sipyleum*** L. (Lamiaceae).

Origanum smyrnaeum Linnaeus, *Species Plantarum* 2: 589. 1753.
"Habitat in Creta & Smyrnae in monte cui arx inaedificata." RCN: 4291.
Lectotype (Paton in Jarvis & al. in *Taxon* 50: 516. 2001): Herb. Clifford: 304, *Origanum* 4 (BM-000628969).
Current name: ***Origanum onites*** L. (Lamiaceae).
Note: Ietswaart (in *Leiden Bot. Ser.* 4: 85. 1980) stated, "Type: Linnaeus s.n. (holo BM)", possibly in reference to Clifford material, but this is insufficiently precise to constitute formal typification.

Origanum syriacum Linnaeus, *Species Plantarum* 2: 590. 1753.
"Habitat – – – –" RCN: 4295.
Lectotype (Paton in Jarvis & al. in *Taxon* 50: 516. 2001): [icon] *"Marum syriacum"* in Plantin, Pl. Stirp. Icon.: 499. 1581.
Current name: ***Origanum syriacum*** L. (Lamiaceae).
Note: As pointed out by Harley (in *Watsonia* 14: 86. 1982), Ietswaart (in *Leiden Bot. Ser.* 4: 87. 1980) designated 743.12 (LINN) as the type of both *O. syriacum* and *O. maru* L. Harley stated "while the sheet indicated is unquestionably the type of *O. maru*, it can hardly be the type of *O. syriacum*, which apparently does not occur among the sheets in Linnaeus' herbarium in London, and must be looked for elsewhere". Meikle (*Fl. Cyprus* 2: 1267. 1985) stated "TYPE: Probably the illustration in Lobel...t. 499 (1591)", i.e. the Plantin illustration, but his use of the word "probably" contradicts Art. 7.11 of the Code.

Origanum vulgare Linnaeus, *Species Plantarum* 2: 590. 1753.
"Habitat in Europae, Canadae rupestribus." RCN: 4293.
Lectotype (Ietswaart in *Leiden Bot. Ser.* 4: 106. 1980): *Kalm*, Herb. Linn. No. 743.9 (LINN).
Generitype of *Origanum* Linnaeus (vide Green, *Prop. Brit. Bot.*: 165. 1929).
Current name: ***Origanum vulgare*** L. (Lamiaceae).

Ornithogalum arabicum Linnaeus, *Species Plantarum* 1: 307. 1753.
"Habitat juxta Alexandriam Aegypti." RCN: 2423.
Lectotype (Stearn in *Ann. Mus. Goulandris* 6: 153. 1983): Herb. A. van Royen No. 913.63–565 (L).
Current name: ***Ornithogalum arabicum*** L. (Liliaceae/Hyacinthaceae).

Ornithogalum bivalve Linnaeus, *Species Plantarum* 1: 306. 1753.
"Habitat in Virginia." RCN: 2417.
Type not designated.
Original material: none traced.
Current name: ***Nothoscordum bivalve*** (L.) Britton (Liliaceae/Alliaceae).
Note: See discussion by Stearn (in *Ann. Mus. Goulandris* 6: 150. 1983).

Ornithogalum canadense Linnaeus, *Species Plantarum* 1: 308. 1753.
"Habitat in Africa." RCN: 2408.
Replaced synonym of: *Albuca major* L. (1762), *nom. illeg.*
Lectotype (Müller-Doblies in Jarvis & al., *Regnum Veg.* 127: 16. 1993): Herb. Linn. No. 140.5 (S).
Current name: ***Albuca canadensis*** (L.) F.M. Leight. (Liliaceae/Hyacinthaceae).
Note: Stearn (in *Ann. Mus. Goulandris* 6: 158, f. 10. 1983) indicated as "suggested lectotype" for *Ornithogalum canadense* L. (the basis of *A. major*) a Cornut plate, but as he also added "but Linn. Herb. 426.1...possible", this cannot be accepted as an unequivocal choice of type. The name was formally typified by U. Müller-Doblies in 1993 but subsequently (see *Feddes Repert.* 105: 367. 1994; 117: 116. 2006) informally rejected as a *nomen confusum* (as the basionym of *Albuca canadensis*) in favour of *A. maxima* Burm. f. (1768). However, no formal proposal for the rejection of the name appears to have been made.

Ornithogalum capense Linnaeus, *Species Plantarum* 1: 308. 1753.
"Habitat ad Cap. b. spei." RCN: 2426.
Lectotype (Stearn in *Ann. Mus. Goulandris* 6: 157, f. 8. 1983): [icon] "*Ornithogalum Afric. plantaginis roseae folio, radice tuberosa*" in Commelin, Hort. Med. Amstelod. Pl. Rar. 2: 175, t. 88. 1701.
Current name: ***Eriospermum capense*** (L.) T.M. Salter (Liliaceae/Eriospermaceae).

Ornithogalum comosum Linnaeus, *Centuria II Plantarum*: 15. 1756.
["Habitat – – – – –"] Sp. Pl., ed. 2, 1: 440 (1762). RCN: 2421.
Lectotype (Stearn in *Ann. Mus. Goulandris* 6: 164, f. 12, 13. 1983): [icon] "*Ornithogalum spicatum seu comosum flore lacteo*" in Rudbeck, Campi Elysii 2: 135, f. 5. 1701.
Current name: ***Ornithogalum comosum*** L. (Liliaceae/Hyacinthaceae).

Ornithogalum hirsutum Linnaeus, *Species Plantarum* 1: 306. 1753.
"Habitat in Virginia, Canada." RCN: 2410.
Replaced synonym of: *Hypoxis sessilis* L. (1759), *nom. illeg.*
Lectotype (Stearn in *Ann. Mus. Goulandris* 6: 148. 1983): *Kalm*, Herb. Linn. No. 427.1 (LINN; iso- UPS).
Current name: ***Hypoxis hirsuta*** (L.) Coville (Liliaceae/Hypoxidaceae).

Ornithogalum latifolium Linnaeus, *Species Plantarum* 1: 307. 1753.
"Habitat in Arabia, Aegypto." RCN: 2420.
Lectotype (Stearn in *Ann. Mus. Goulandris* 6: 151, f. 4. 1983): Herb. Linn. No. 428.8 (LINN).
Current name: ***Ornithogalum latifolium*** L. (Liliaceae/Hyacinthaceae).

Ornithogalum luteum Linnaeus, *Species Plantarum* 1: 306. 1753.
"Habitat in Europae cultis macellis." RCN: 2415.
Lectotype (Stearn in *Ann. Mus. Goulandris* 6: 147, f. 1. 1983): Herb. Linn. No. 428.3 (LINN).
Current name: ***Gagea lutea*** (L.) Ker-Gawl. (Liliaceae).

Ornithogalum minimum Linnaeus, *Species Plantarum* 1: 306. 1753.
"Habitat in Europae cultis oleraceis." RCN: 2416.
Lectotype (Stearn in *Ann. Mus. Goulandris* 6: 148. 1983): Herb. Linn. No. 428.4 (LINN).
Current name: ***Gagea minima*** (L.) Ker-Gawl. (Liliaceae).

Ornithogalum minus Linnaeus, *Mantissa Plantarum Altera*: 364. 1771.
RCN: 2416.
Type not designated.
Original material: none traced.
Current name: ***Ornithogalum umbellatum*** L. (Liliaceae/Hyacinthaceae).
Note: See comments by Stearn (in *Ann. Mus. Goulandris* 6: 168. 1983). Van Raamsdonk (in *Proc. Kon. Ned. Akad. Wetensch. C*, 85: 565. 1982) wrongly treated this as a *nomen nudum* for, though very brief, Linnaeus' "simillimum praecedenti...sed huic petala acutiora" does provide a diagnosis.

Ornithogalum narbonense Linnaeus, *Centuria II Plantarum*: 15. 1756.
"Habitat in Galliae australis, Italiae agris." RCN: 2419.
Lectotype (Stearn in *Ann. Mus. Goulandris* 6: 164, f. 14. 1983): Herb. Linn. No. 428.7 (LINN).
Current name: ***Ornithogalum narbonense*** L. (Liliaceae/Hyacinthaceae).

Ornithogalum nutans Linnaeus, *Species Plantarum* 1: 308. 1753.
"Habitat in Italia Neapoli." RCN: 2425.
Lectotype (Stearn in *Ann. Mus. Goulandris* 6: 156. 1983): Herb. Linn. No. 428.15 (LINN).
Current name: ***Ornithogalum nutans*** L. (Liliaceae/Hyacinthaceae).

Ornithogalum pyramidale Linnaeus, *Species Plantarum* 1: 307. 1753.
"Habitat in collibus Lusitaniae." RCN: 2422.
Lectotype (Stearn in *Ann. Mus. Goulandris* 6: 151, f. 5. 1983): Herb. A. van Royen No. 913.18–72 (L).
Current name: ***Ornithogalum pyramidale*** L. (Liliaceae/Hyacinthaceae).

Ornithogalum pyrenaicum Linnaeus, *Species Plantarum* 1: 306. 1753.
"Habitat in Alpibus Helveticis, Genevensibus, Pyrenaicis." RCN: 2418.
Lectotype (El-Gadi in Jafri & El-Gadi, *Fl. Libya* 57: 50. 1978): Herb. Linn. No. 428.5 (LINN).
Current name: ***Ornithogalum pyrenaicum*** L. (Liliaceae/Hyacinthaceae).
Note: See additional comments by Stearn (in *Ann. Mus. Goulandris* 6: 150. 1983).

Ornithogalum umbellatum Linnaeus, *Species Plantarum* 1: 307. 1753.
"Habitat in Germannia, Gallia." RCN: 2424.
Lectotype (Stearn in *Ann. Mus. Goulandris* 6: 153, f. 6. 1983): [icon] "*Heliocharmos*" in Reneaulme, Specim. Hist. Pl.: 88, 87. 1611 (see p. 152).
Generitype of *Ornithogalum* Linnaeus.
Current name: ***Ornithogalum umbellatum*** L. (Liliaceae/Hyacinthaceae).
Note: Ornithogalum umbellatum, with the type designated by Stearn, was proposed as conserved type of the genus by Jarvis (in *Taxon* 41: 566. 1992). However, the proposal was eventually ruled unnecessary by the General Committee (see Barrie, *l.c.* 55: 795–796. 2006 for a review of the history of this and related proposals).
El-Gadi (in Jafri & El-Gadi, *Fl. Libya* 57: 48. 1978) indicated "Herb. Linn. 228.9 (LINN)", a non-existent specimen, as type. Raamsdonk (in *Proc. Kon. Ned. Akad. Wetensch. C*, 85: 565. 1982) treated 428.13 (LINN) as the type. However, as it apparently came from Hasselquist (and hence not from Germany or France), it conflicts with the protologue, and Stearn's subsequent choice is accepted here.

Ornithogalum uniflorum Linnaeus, *Systema Naturae,* ed. 12, 2: 242; *Mantissa Plantarum*: 62. 1767.
"Habitat in Sibiriae montis Sini Sopka summo apice. Eric Laxman." RCN: 2414.
Neotype (Levichev in *Bot. Zhurn.* 82(12): 89. 1997): Russia. "Prato altaica", *Laxman* (LE).
Current name: ***Tulipa uniflora*** (L.) Besser ex Baker (Liliaceae).

Ornithopus compressus Linnaeus, *Species Plantarum* 2: 744. 1753.
"Habitat in Italia, Siclia [sic]" RCN: 5476.
Lectotype (Lassen in Turland & Jarvis in *Taxon* 46: 478. 1997): *Magnol*, Herb. Linn. No. 918.3 (LINN).
Current name: ***Ornithopus compressus*** L. (Fabaceae: Faboideae).

Ornithopus perpusillus Linnaeus, *Species Plantarum* 2: 743. 1753.
"Habitat in Angliae, Belgii, Galliae, Hispaniae arenosis." RCN: 5475.
Lectotype (Chamberlain in Jarvis & al., *Regnum Veg.* 127: 71. 1993): Herb. Burser XIX: 130 (UPS).
Generitype of *Ornithopus* Linnaeus (vide Green, *Prop. Brit. Bot.*: 175. 1929).
Current name: ***Ornithopus perpusillus*** L. (Fabaceae: Faboideae).

Ornithopus pusillus Linnaeus, *Flora Anglica*: 21. 1754, *orth. var.*
["Habitat in Angliae, Belgii, Galliae, Hispaniae arenosis."] Sp. Pl. 2: 743 (1753).
Lectotype (Chamberlain in Jarvis & al., *Regnum Veg.* 127: 71. 1993): Herb. Burser XIX: 130 (UPS).
Current name: ***Ornithopus perpusillus*** L. (Fabaceae: Faboideae).
Note: Evidently an orthographic variant of *Ornithopus perpusillus* L. (1753), and treated as such by Stearn (*Introd. Ray's Syn. Meth. Stirp. Brit.* (Ray Soc. ed.): 68. 1973).

Ornithopus scorpioides Linnaeus, *Species Plantarum* 2: 744. 1753.
"Habitat in G. Narbonensi, Hispania, Italia inter segetes." RCN: 5477.
Lectotype (Jafri in Jafri & El-Gadi, *Fl. Libya* 86: 125. 1980): Herb. Linn. No. 918.4 (LINN).
Current name: ***Coronilla scorpioides*** (L.) W.D.J. Koch (Fabaceae: Faboideae).

Ornithopus tetraphyllus Linnaeus, *Systema Naturae,* ed. 10, 2: 1168. 1759.
["Habitat in Jamaica."] Sp. Pl., ed. 2, 2: 1049 (1763). RCN: 5478.
Lectotype (Verdcourt & Adams in Turland & Jarvis in *Taxon* 46: 478. 1997): [icon] *"Quadrifolium erectum flore luteo"* in Sloane, Voy. Jamaica 1: 186, t. 116, f. 3. 1707. – Typotype: Herb. Sloane 3: 92 (BM-SL).
Current name: ***Zornia myriadena*** Benth. (Fabaceae: Faboideae).

Orobanche aeginetia Linnaeus, *Species Plantarum,* ed. 2, 2: 883. 1763, *nom. illeg.*
"Habitat in Malabaria." RCN: 4595.
Replaced synonym: *Aeginetia indica* L. (1753).
Lectotype (Parnell in *Thai Forest Bull., Bot.* 29: 73. 2001): [icon] *"Tsjem-cumulu"* in Rheede, Hort. Malab. 11: 97, t. 47. 1692.
Current name: ***Aeginetia indica*** L. (Orobanchaceae).
Note: A superfluous name for *Aeginetia indica* L. (1753).

Orobanche americana Linnaeus, *Systema Naturae,* ed. 12, 2: 422; *Mantissa Plantarum*: 88. 1767.
"Habitat in Carolina." RCN: 4590.
Lectotype (Haynes in *Sida* 4: 254, f. 6. 1971): Herb. Linn. No. 798.5 (LINN).
Current name: ***Conopholis americana*** (L.) Wallr. (Orobanchaceae).

Orobanche laevis Linnaeus, *Species Plantarum* 2: 632. 1753, *nom. utique rej.*
"Habitat Monspelii." RCN: 4591.
Type not designated.
Original material: Herb. Linn. No. 798.1? (LINN); Herb. Linn. No. 260.19? (S); [icon] in Morison, Pl. Hist. Univ. 3: 502, s. 12, t. 16, f. 2. 1699; [icon] in Bauhin & Cherler, Hist. Pl. Univ. 2: 782. 1651.

Orobanche major Linnaeus, *Species Plantarum* 2: 632. 1753, *nom. utique rej.*
"Habitat in Europae agris, pratis siccis." RCN: 4589.
Lectotype (Turland & Rumsey in *Taxon* 46: 787. 1997): Herb. Clifford: 321, *Orobanche* 1, sheet A (BM-000646202).
Generitype of *Orobanche* Linnaeus (vide Green, *Prop. Brit. Bot.*: 169. 1929).
Current name: ***Orobanche caryophyllacea*** Sm. (Orobanchaceae).

Orobanche ramosa Linnaeus, *Species Plantarum* 2: 633. 1753.
"Habitat in Europae siccis." RCN: 4592.
Lectotype (Foley in *Anales Jard. Bot. Madrid* 58: 231. 2001): Herb. Clifford: 321, *Orobanche* 2 (BM-000646204).
Current name: ***Orobanche ramosa*** L. (Orobanchaceae).
Note: Graham (in Turrill & Milne-Redhead, *Fl. Trop. E. Africa, Orobanchaceae*: 3. 1957) indicated unspecified material at LINN as the lectotype. However, this does not distinguish between sheets 798.8 and 798.9 (which are evidently not part of a single gathering so Art. 9.15 does not apply).

Orobanche uniflora Linnaeus, *Species Plantarum* 2: 633. 1753.
"Habitat in Virginia." RCN: 4594.
Lectotype (Reveal & al. in *Huntia* 7: 224. 1987): *Clayton 387* ["83"] (BM-000051200).
Current name: ***Orobanche uniflora*** L. (Orobanchaceae).
Note: Reveal & al. indicated "Clayton 83", a collection associated with *Asclepias decumbens* L., as the lectotype of *O. uniflora*. However, it is clear that this is simply an error for "Clayton 387" as all other synonyms cited by Reveal & al. are associated with the latter collection.

Orobanche virginiana Linnaeus, *Species Plantarum* 2: 633. 1753.
"Habitat in Virginia." RCN: 4593.
Lectotype (Gillett in *Rhodora* 61: 61. 1959): *Clayton 604* (BM-000051684).
Current name: ***Epifagus virginiana*** (L.) W.P.C. Barton (Orobanchaceae).

Orobus angustifolius Linnaeus, *Species Plantarum* 2: 729. 1753.
"Habitat in Sibiria." RCN: 5382.
Type not designated.
Original material: Herb. Linn. No. 904.5 (LINN).
Current name: ***Lathyrus pallescens*** (M. Bieb.) K. Koch (Fabaceae: Faboideae).

Orobus hirsutus Linnaeus, *Species Plantarum* 2: 728. 1753.
"Habitat in Thracia." RCN: 5377.
Lectotype (Lassen in Turland & Jarvis in *Taxon* 46: 478. 1997): Herb. Clifford: 366, *Orobus* 4 (BM-000646660).
Current name: ***Lathyrus laxiflorus*** (Desf.) Kuntze (Fabaceae: Faboideae).

Orobus lathyroides Linnaeus, *Species Plantarum* 2: 728. 1753.
"Habitat in Sibiria." RCN: 5376.
Lectotype (Lassen in Turland & Jarvis in *Taxon* 46: 478. 1997): Herb. Linn. No. 904.1 (LINN).
Current name: ***Vicia unijuga*** A. Braun (Fabaceae: Faboideae).

Orobus luteus Linnaeus, *Species Plantarum* 2: 728. 1753.
"Habitat in Sibiria." RCN: 5378.
Type not designated.
Original material: Herb. Linn. No. 904.2 (LINN).
Current name: ***Lathyrus ochraceus*** Kitt. (Fabaceae: Faboideae).
Note: Bässler (in *Feddes Repert.* 84: 354. 1973) describes Linnaeus'
changing concept of the species, from Siberian in 1753, taking in
European forms in 1763, and relegating the Siberian plant to an
unnamed variety in 1771. He treats the Linnaean name as a
synonym of *L. gmelinii* Fritsch.

Orobus niger Linnaeus, *Species Plantarum* 2: 729. 1753.
"Habitat in Europae borealis montosis." RCN: 5383.
Lectotype (Jonsell & Jarvis in *Nordic J. Bot.* 22: 78. 2002): Herb.
Clifford: 366, *Orobus* 1 (BM).
Current name: ***Lathyrus niger*** (L.) Bernh. (Fabaceae: Faboideae).

Orobus pyrenaicus Linnaeus, *Species Plantarum* 2: 729. 1753.
"Habitat in Pyrenaeis." RCN: 5384.
Lectotype (Lassen in Turland & Jarvis in *Taxon* 46: 478. 1997): [icon]
"Orobus Pyraenaicus, latifolius, nervosus" in Plukenet, Phytographia:
t. 210, f. 2. 1692; Almag. Bot.: 274. 1696. – Typotype: Herb.
Sloane 97: 44 (BM-SL).
Current name: ***Lathyrus linifolius*** (Reichard) Bässler (Fabaceae:
Faboideae).
Note: Britten (in *J. Bot.* 39: 100. 1901) noted the absence of a type
collection in LINN but did not designate a type.

Orobus sylvaticus Linnaeus, *Flora Anglica*: 21. 1754.
["Habitat in Anglia, Gallia."] Sp. Pl., ed. 2, 2: 1029 (1763). RCN:
5381.
Lectotype (Lassen in Turland & Jarvis in *Taxon* 46: 478. 1997): [icon]
"Orobus sylvaticus nostras" in Chomel in Mém. Acad. Roy. Sci. Paris
1706: 87, t. 8. 1706.
Current name: ***Vicia orobus*** DC. (Fabaceae: Faboideae).

Orobus tuberosus Linnaeus, *Species Plantarum* 2: 728. 1753.
"Habitat in Europae borealis pratis & sylvis." RCN: 5380.
Lectotype (Goyder in Jarvis & al., *Regnum Veg.* 127: 71. 1993): Herb.
Clifford: 360, *Orobus* 3 (BM-000646657).
Generitype of *Orobus* Linnaeus (vide Green, *Prop. Brit. Bot.*: 175.
1929).
Current name: ***Lathyrus linifolius*** (Reichard) Bässler (Fabaceae:
Faboideae).

Orobus vernus Linnaeus, *Species Plantarum* 2: 728. 1753.
"Habitat in Europae borealis nemoribus." RCN: 5379.
Lectotype (Jonsell & Jarvis in *Nordic J. Bot.* 22: 78. 2002): Herb.
Clifford: 366, *Orobus* 2, sheet A (BM-000646655).
Current name: ***Lathyrus vernus*** (L.) Bernh. subsp. ***vernus*** (Fabaceae:
Faboideae).

Orontium aquaticum Linnaeus, *Species Plantarum* 1: 324. 1753.
"Habitat in Virginiae, Canadae paludibus, scaturiginibus." RCN:
2527.
Lectotype (Reveal in Jarvis & al., *Regnum Veg.* 127: 72. 1993): Herb.
Linn. No. 448.1 (LINN).
Generitype of *Orontium* Linnaeus.
Current name: ***Orontium aquaticum*** L. (Araceae).

Ortegia dichotoma Linnaeus, *Mantissa Plantarum Altera*: 174. 1771.
"Habitat in Javanium in saxosis." RCN: 280.
Lectotype (Amich in Cafferty & Jarvis in *Taxon* 53: 1052. 2004):
[icon] *"Ortegia dichotoma, axillis ramorum unifloris"* in Allioni,
Stirp. Descr. Misc. Taurinensia: 176, t. 4, f. 1. 1766.
Current name: ***Ortegia hispanica*** L. (Caryophyllaceae).

Ortegia hispanica Linnaeus, *Species Plantarum* 1: 560. 1753.
"Habitat in Castilia Minuart. Baetica Velez, Salamantica." RCN:
279.
Lectotype (López González in Jarvis & al., *Regnum Veg.* 127: 72.
1993): *Löfling s.n.*, Herb. Linn. No. 53.1 (LINN).
Generitype of *Ortegia* Linnaeus.
Current name: ***Ortegia hispanica*** L. (Caryophyllaceae).
Note: See López González (in *Anales Jard. Bot. Madrid* 56: 369–370.
1998), who argues that the correct generic form is, as used by
Linnaeus in 1753, "Ortega".

Orvala garganica Linnaeus, *Species Plantarum* 2: 578. 1753.
"Habitat in valle Garganica montis Apuliae." RCN: 4217.
Lectotype (Mennema in *Leiden Bot. Ser.* 11: 132. 1989): [icon] *"Papia
Garganica, foliis Urticae, altius & eleganter incisis, flore purpureo"* in
Micheli, Nov. Pl. Gen.: 20, t. 17. 1729.
Generitype of *Orvala* Linnaeus.
Current name: ***Lamium orvala*** L. (Lamiaceae).

Oryza sativa Linnaeus, *Species Plantarum* 1: 333. 1753.
"Habitat forte in Aethiopia, colitur in Indiae paludosis." RCN: 2574.
Lectotype (Meikle, *Fl. Cyprus* 2: 1716. 1985): Herb. Linn. No. 460.1
(LINN).
Generitype of *Oryza* Linnaeus.
Current name: ***Oryza sativa*** L. (Poaceae).
Note: Although Kerguélen (in *Lejeunia, n.s.,* 75: 217. 1975) indicated
unspecified material in LINN as type, this is not accepted as an
effective typification (Art. 7.11). See Cafferty & al. (in *Taxon* 49:
240. 2000) for a detailed explanation.

Osbeckia chinensis Linnaeus, *Species Plantarum* 1: 345. 1753.
"Habitat in India." RCN: 2648.
Lectotype (Hansen in *Taxon* 21: 656. 1972): Herb. Linn. No. 482.1
(LINN).
Generitype of *Osbeckia* Linnaeus.
Current name: ***Osbeckia chinensis*** L. (Melastomataceae).

Osmites asteriscoides Linnaeus, *Systema Naturae,* ed. 12, 2: 571.
1767, *nom. illeg.*
RCN: 6570.
Type not designated.
Original material: none traced.
Current name: ***Osmitopsis asteriscoides*** (L. ex P.J. Bergius) Less.
(Asteraceae).
Note: Although this binomial appeared first in Linnaeus' *Pl. Rar. Afr.*:
24 (1760), *Osmites* L. was not published until 1764, and the
binomial was consequently not validated until 1767 when Bergius
(in *Descr. Pl. Cap. Bon. Spei*: 305. Sep 1767) published it,
attributing it to Linnaeus. Bremer (in *Bot. Not.* 125: 40. 1972)
treated Bergius' name, typified by a collection in Bergius' herbarium
(SBT), as heterotypic with respect to Linnaeus' slightly later use of
the name (in *Syst. Nat.,* ed. 12, 2: 571. Oct 1767). This
interpretation leaves Linnaeus' 1767 name as a later homonym of
that of Bergius, and hence illegitimate.

Osmites bellidiastrum Linnaeus, *Plantae Rariores Africanae*: 24.
1760, *nom. inval.*
["Habitat in Aethiopia."] Sp. Pl., ed. 2, 2: 1285. 1763. RCN: 6568.
Replaced synonym: *Anthemis fruticosa* L. (1756); *A. bellidiastrum* L.
(1759), *nom. illeg.*
Type not relevant.
Generitype of *Osmites* Linnaeus, *nom. rej.* (vide Bremer in *Taxon* 28:
412. 1979).
Current name: ***Relhania fruticosa*** (L.) K. Bremer (Asteraceae).
Note: Osmites Linnaeus, *nom. rej.* in favour of *Relhania* L'Héritier.

As *Osmites* L. was not published until 1764, *O. bellidiastrum* is an invalid name (and would in any case be an illegitimate name for *Anthemis fruticosa* L. (1756)).

Osmites camphorina Linnaeus, *Systema Naturae,* ed. 12, 2: 571. 1767.
RCN: 6569.
Neotype (Bremer in Jarvis & Turland in *Taxon* 47: 364. 1998): Herb. Linn. No. 1029.5 (LINN).
Current name: ***Osmitopsis asteriscoides*** (L. ex Bergius) Less. (Asteraceae).
Note: Although this binomial appeared first in Linnaeus' *Pl. Rar. Afr.*: 24 (1760), *Osmites* L. was not published until 1764, and *O. camphorina* was consequently not validated until 1767, as noted by Bremer (in *Bot. Not.* 125: 40. 1972).

Osmites camphorina Linnaeus, *Mantissa Plantarum Altera*: 477. 1771, *nom. illeg.*
RCN: 6569.
Lectotype (Bremer in *Bot. Not.* 125: 33. 1972): Herb. Linn. No. 1029.2 (LINN).
Current name: ***Osmitopsis dentata*** (Thunb.) K. Bremer (Asteraceae).
Note: Bremer (in *Bot. Not.* 125: 33. 1972) treated this as distinct from *O. camphorina* L. (1767), and based on a different type. *Osmites camphorina* L. (1771) is therefore a later homonym, and illegitimate.

Osmites camphorina Linnaeus var. **leucantha** (Linnaeus) Linnaeus, *Mantissa Plantarum Altera*: 477. 1771.
["Habitat ad Cap. b. Spei."] Sp. Pl. ed. 2, 2: 1261 (1763). RCN: 6569.
Basionym: *Anthemis leucantha* L. (1760).
Lectotype (Bremer in *Bot. Not.* 125: 30. 1972): Herb. Linn. No. 1029.3 (LINN).
Current name: ***Osmitopsis afra*** (L.) K. Bremer (Asteraceae).

Osmunda adiantifolia Linnaeus, *Species Plantarum* 2: 1065. 1753.
"Habitat in Dominicae, Jamaicae rupibus." RCN: 7753.
Lectotype (Duek in *Feddes Repert.* 87: 348. 1976): [icon] *"Osmunda filiculae folio major"* in Plumier, Traité Foug. Amér.: 135, t. 158. 1705.
Current name: ***Anemia adiantifolia*** (L.) Sw. (Schizaeaceae).

Osmunda bipinnata Linnaeus, *Species Plantarum* 2: 1065. 1753.
"Habitat in America meridionali." RCN: 7756.
Lectotype (Proctor, *Ferns Jamaica*: 66. 1985): [icon] *"Osmunda latis Crenis incisa"* in Plumier, Traité Foug. Amér.: 133, t. 155. 1705.
Current name: ***Osmunda cinnamomea*** L. (Osmundaceae).

Osmunda capensis Linnaeus, *Mantissa Plantarum Altera*: 306. 1771.
"Habitat inter montes Cap. b. spei, inter montem tabularem et Diaboli, ad rivulum. Koenig." RCN: 7760.
Lectotype (Schelpe in *J. Linn. Soc., Bot.* 53: 487. 1952): *König s.n.*, Herb. Linn. No. 1244.11 (LINN), see p. 217.
Current name: ***Blechnum capense*** Burm. f. (Blechnaceae).

Osmunda cervina Linnaeus, *Species Plantarum* 2: 1065. 1753.
"Habitat in America meridionali." RCN: 7755.
Lectotype (Proctor in Howard, *Fl. Lesser Antilles* 2: 223. 1977): [icon] *"Osmunda Linguae Cervinae folio"* in Plumier, Traité Foug. Amér.: 132, t. 154. 1705.
Current name: ***Polybotrya cervina*** (L.) Kaulf. (Dryopteridaceae).

Osmunda cinnamomea Linnaeus, *Species Plantarum* 2: 1066. 1753.
"Habitat in Marilandia." RCN: 7761.

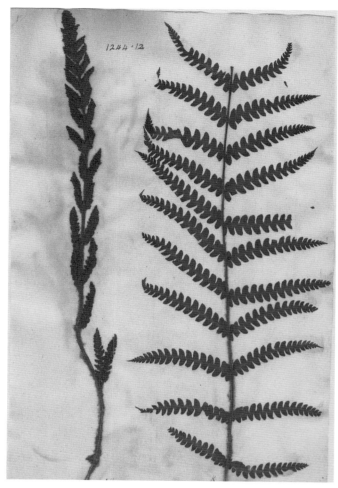

Lectotype (Duek in *Feddes Repert.* 87: 329. 1976): *Kalm*, Herb. Linn. No. 1244.12 (LINN).
Current name: ***Osmunda cinnamomea*** L. (Osmundaceae).
Note: See discussion by Reveal & al. (in *Huntia* 7: 229. 1987).

Osmunda claytoniana Linnaeus, *Species Plantarum* 2: 1066. 1753.
"Habitat in Virginia." RCN: 7759.
Lectotype (Reveal & al. in *Huntia* 7: 229. 1987): *Clayton s.n.*, Herb. Linn. No. 1244.10 (LINN; iso- BM).
Current name: ***Osmunda claytoniana*** L. (Osmundaceae).

Osmunda crispa Linnaeus, *Species Plantarum* 2: 1067. 1753.
"Habitat in Anglia, Helvetia." RCN: 7764.
Lectotype (Jonsell & Jarvis in *Nordic J. Bot.* 14: 148. 1994): [icon] *"Adianth. album floridum s. Filicula petraea crispa"* in Plukenet, Phytographia: t. 3, f. 2. 1691; Almag. Bot.: 9. 1696. – Typotype: Herb. Sloane 85: 128 (BM-SL).
Current name: ***Cryptogramma crispa*** (L.) R. Br. ex Hook. (Pteridaceae).

Osmunda filiculifolia Linnaeus, *Species Plantarum* 2: 1065. 1753.
"Habitat in America meridionali." RCN: 7757.
Type not designated.
Original material: Herb. Linn. No. 1244.7 (LINN); [icon] in Plumier, Traité Foug. Amér.: 138, t. 161. 1758; [icon] in Petiver, Pterigraphia Amer.: 170, t. 9, f. 3. 1712.
Current name: ***Polybotrya osmundacea*** Willd. (Dryopteridaceae).
Note: Specific epithet spelled "filiculaefolia" in the protologue.

Osmunda hirsuta Linnaeus, *Species Plantarum* 2: 1064. 1753.
"Habitat in Americae meridionalis rupibus." RCN: 7752.
Lectotype (Duek in *Feddes Repert.* 87: 342. 1976): [icon] *"Osmunda molliter hirsuta, et profunde Laciniata"* in Plumier, Traité Foug. Amér.: 139, t. 162. 1705.
Current name: ***Anemia hirsuta*** (L.) Sw. (Schizaeaceae).

Osmunda hirta Linnaeus, *Species Plantarum* 2: 1064. 1753.
"Habitat in Martinica." RCN: 7751.
Lectotype (Proctor in Howard, *Fl. Lesser Antilles* 2: 53. 1977): [icon] *"Lonchitis hirsuta florida"* in Plumier, Descr. Pl. Amér.: 18, t. 26. 1693.
Current name: ***Anemia hirta*** (L.) Sw. (Schizaeaceae).

Osmunda lunaria Linnaeus, *Species Plantarum* 2: 1064. 1753.
"Habitat in Europa." RCN: 7748.
Lectotype (Bobrov in *Novosti Sist. Vyssh. Rast.* 21: 6. 1984): Herb. Clifford: 472, *Osmunda* 1 (BM-000647551).
Current name: ***Botrychium lunaria*** (L.) Sw. (Ophioglossaceae).
Note: See discussion by Jonsell & Jarvis (in *Nordic J. Bot.* 14: 148. 1994), who independently chose as lectotype the same Clifford material as Bobrov.

Osmunda phyllitidis Linnaeus, *Species Plantarum* 2: 1064. 1753.
"Habitat in America meridionali." RCN: 7750.
Lectotype (Proctor, *Ferns Jamaica*: 77. 1985): [icon] *"Osmunda lanceolata et subtiliter serrata"* in Plumier, Traité Foug. Amér.: 133, t. 156. 1705.
Current name: ***Anemia phyllitidis*** (L.) Sw. (Schizaeaceae).
Note: Duek (in *Feddes Repert.* 87: 341. 1976) wrongly indicated Plumier's t. 155 as the type but this plate is not original material for this name.

Osmunda regalis Linnaeus, *Species Plantarum* 2: 1065. 1753.
"Habitat in Europa, Virginia ad fluvios." RCN: 7758.
Lectotype (Jonsell & Jarvis in Jarvis & al., *Regnum Veg.* 127: 72. 1993): Herb. Burser XX: 26 (UPS).
Generitype of *Osmunda* Linnaeus (vide Leman, *Dict. Sci. Nat.* 37: 9. 1825; Smith, *Hist. Fil.*: 359. 1875).
Current name: ***Osmunda regalis*** L. (Osmundaceae).
Note: Schelpe & Anthony (in Leistner, *Fl. Southern Africa, Pteridophyta*: 43. 1986) indicated a Rolander specimen from Småland as lectotype. As pointed out by Jonsell & Jarvis (in *Nordic J. Bot.* 14: 148. 1994), it is a post-1753 specimen and ineligible as lectotype.

Osmunda spicant Linnaeus, *Species Plantarum* 2: 1066. 1753.
"Habitat in Europa." RCN: 7763.
Lectotype (Jonsell & Jarvis in *Nordic J. Bot.* 14: 150. 1994): Herb. Linn. No. 1244.14 (LINN).
Current name: ***Blechnum spicant*** (L.) Roth (Blechnaceae).

Osmunda struthiopteris Linnaeus, *Species Plantarum* 2: 1066. 1753.
"Habitat in Suecia, Helvetia, Russia, Norvegia." RCN: 7762.
Lectotype (Jonsell & Jarvis in *Nordic J. Bot.* 14: 149. 1994): Herb. Burser XX: 29 (UPS).
Current name: ***Matteuccia struthiopteris*** (L.) Tod. (Dryopteridaceae).
Note: Both Copeland (in *Univ. Calif. Publ. Bot.* 16: 54. 1929) and Bobrov (in *Novosti Sist. Vyssh. Rast.* 21: 7. 1984) indicated 1244.13 (LINN) as type, but this is an Arduino collection, not received by Linnaeus until long after 1753 and consequently not original material for the name.

Osmunda verticillata Linnaeus, *Species Plantarum* 2: 1065. 1753.
"Habitat in America meridionali." RCN: 7754.
Lectotype (Lellinger & Proctor in *Taxon* 32: 570. 1983): [icon] *"Osmunda verticillata"* in Plumier, Traité Foug. Amér.: 137, t. 160. 1705.
Current name: ***Pteris verticillata*** (L.) Lellinger & Proctor (Pteridaceae).

Osmunda virginiana Linnaeus, *Species Plantarum* 2: 1064. 1753.
"Habitat in America." RCN: 7749.
Lectotype (Proctor, *Ferns Jamaica*: 51. 1985): *Kalm*, Herb. Linn. No. 1244.3 (LINN).
Current name: ***Botrychium virginianum*** (L.) Sw. (Ophioglossaceae).

Osmunda zeylanica Linnaeus, *Species Plantarum* 2: 1063. 1753.
"Habitat in Zeylona." RCN: 7747.
Type not designated.
Original material: Herb. Hermann 5: 272, No. 373 [icon] (BM).
Current name: ***Helminthostachys zeylanica*** (L.) Hook. (Ophioglossaceae).
Note: Van Ooststroom (in *Blumea*, Suppl. 1: 195. 1937) regarded a Hermann specimen in L as the type. However, it was almost certainly never seen by Linnaeus, a supposition borne out by Linnaeus' statement (*Fl. Zeylanica*: 178. 1748) "Inter pictas Hermanni plantas est" implying he had seen only the drawing in the Hermann collection (now in BM) rather than a Hermann specimen.

Osteospermum corymbosum Linnaeus, *Mantissa Plantarum Altera*: 290. 1771.
"Habitat ad Cap. b. spei montosis lapidosis." RCN: 6687.
Lectotype (Norlindh, *Stud. Calenduleae* 1: 166. 1943): *Tulbagh 40*, Herb. Linn. No. 1037.15 (LINN).
Current name: ***Osteospermum corymbosum*** L. (Asteraceae).

Osteospermum ilicifolium Linnaeus, *Systema Naturae*, ed. 10, 2: 1234. 1759.
["Habitat ad Cap. b. spei."] Sp. Pl., ed. 2, 2: 1308 (1763). RCN: 6684.
Lectotype (Norlindh, *Stud. Calenduleae* 1: 364. 1943): Herb. Linn. No. 1037.9 (LINN).
Current name: ***Gibbaria ilicifolia*** (L.) Norl. (Asteraceae).

Osteospermum imbricatum Linnaeus, *Mantissa Plantarum Altera*: 290. 1771.
"Habitat ad Cap. b. spei." RCN: 6688.
Lectotype (Norlindh, *Stud. Calenduleae* 1: 152. 1943): *Tulbagh 144*, Herb. Linn. No. 1037.16 (LINN).
Current name: ***Osteospermum imbricatum*** L. (Asteraceae).

Osteospermum moniliferum Linnaeus, *Species Plantarum* 2: 923. 1753.
"Habitat in Aethiopia." RCN: 6683.
Lectotype (Norlindh, *Stud. Calenduleae* 1: 375. 1943): [icon] *"Chrysanthemoides African. populi albae foliis Tourn."* in Dillenius, Hort. Eltham. 1: 80, t. 68, f. 79. 1732.
Current name: ***Chrysanthemoides monilifera*** (L.) Norl. (Asteraceae).

Osteospermum pisiferum Linnaeus, *Systema Naturae*, ed. 10, 2: 1234. 1759.
["Habitat ad Cap. b. spei."] Sp. Pl., ed. 2, 2: 1308 (1763). RCN: 6682.
Lectotype (Norlindh, *Stud. Calenduleae* 1: 384. 1943): [icon] *"Osteospermum, foliis lanceolatis acute dentatis, caule fruticoso"* in Miller, Fig. Pl. Gard. Dict. 2: 129, t. 194, f. 1. 1757.

Current name: ***Chrysanthemoides monilifera*** (L.) Norl. subsp. ***pisifera*** (L.) Norl. (Asteraceae).

Osteospermum polygaloides Linnaeus, *Species Plantarum* 2: 924. 1753.

"Habitat in Aethiopia." RCN: 6689.

Lectotype (Merrill in *J. Arnold Arbor.* 19: 374. 1938): [icon] *"Chrysanthemum fruticosum Polygoni foliis Africanum, cauliculis scabris, flore minore"* in Plukenet, Amalth. Bot.: t. 382, f. 2. 1705; Almag. Mant.: 47. 1700. – Typotype: Herb. Sloane 102: 165 (BM-SL).

Current name: ***Osteospermum polygaloides*** L. (Asteraceae).

Note: Norlindh (*Stud. Calendulae* 1: 145. 1943) treated material in LINN as the type but this choice is pre-dated by that of Merrill, and the material in LINN associated with this name in any case appears to have reached Linnaeus after 1753.

Osteospermum spinosum Linnaeus, *Species Plantarum* 2: 923. 1753, *typ. cons.*

"Habitat in Aethiopia." RCN: 6681.

Conserved type (Norlindh, *Stud. Calenduleae* 1: 219. 1943): Herb. Linn. No. 1037.1 (LINN).

Generitype of *Osteospermum* Linnaeus, *nom. cons.*

Current name: ***Osteospermum spinosum*** L. (Asteraceae).

Note: Osteospermum spinosum, with the type designated by Norlindh, was proposed as conserved type of the genus by Jarvis (in *Taxon* 41: 567. 1992). This was eventually approved by the General Committee (see review of the history of this proposal by Barrie, *l.c.* 55: 795–796. 2006).

Osteospermum unceum Linnaeus, *Mantissa Plantarum Altera*: 290. 1771, *orth. var.*

"Habitat ad Cap. b. spei montibus." RCN: 6686.

Type not designated.

Current name: ***Osteospermum junceum*** P.J. Bergius (Asteraceae).

Note: The new epithet "unceum" appears to be the result of a simple error, with the "j" of "junceum", an epithet coined by Bergius in 1767, having been accidentally omitted.

Osteospermum uvedalia Linnaeus, *Species Plantarum* 2: 923. 1753.

"Habitat in Virginia." RCN: 6654.

Basionym of: *Polymnia uvedalia* (L.) L. (1763).

Lectotype (Wells in *Brittonia* 17: 152. 1965): Herb. Linn. No. 1033.3 (LINN).

Current name: ***Polymnia uvedalia*** (L.) L. (Asteraceae).

Osyris alba Linnaeus, *Species Plantarum* 2: 1022. 1753.

"Habitat in Italia, Hispania, Monspelii." RCN: 7390.

Lectotype (Miller in Jarvis & al., *Regnum Veg.* 127: 72. 1993): Herb. Linn. No. 1116.1 (LINN).

Generitype of *Osyris* Linnaeus.

Current name: ***Osyris alba*** L. (Santalaceae).

Note: Although Stauffer (in *Mitt. Bot. Mus. Univ. Zürich* 217: 314. 1961) indicated that the type was in LINN, he did not distinguish between the two collections there (which are not part of a single gathering so Art. 9.15 does not apply).

Othonna abrotanifolia Linnaeus, *Species Plantarum* 2: 926. 1753.

"Habitat in Aethiopia." RCN: 6693.

Lectotype (designated here by Nordenstam): [icon] *"Jacobaea Africana frutescens foliis Abrotani seu Crithmi"* in Volckamer, Fl. Noriberg.: 225, unnumbered plate. 1700.

Current name: ***Euryops abrotanifolius*** (L.) DC. (Asteraceae).

Note: Although Nordenstam (in *Opera Bot.* 20: 272. 1968) designated 1038.5 (LINN) as lectotype, this collection lacks the *Species*

Plantarum number (i.e "11"), is a post-1753 addition to the collection, and is not original material for the name. The cited Volckamer figure is here designated as lectotype in its place.

Othonna arborescens Linnaeus, *Species Plantarum*, ed. 2, 2: 1310. 1763.

"Habitat in Aethiopia." RCN: 6700.

Lectotype (designated here by Nordenstam): [icon] *"Doria Africana arborescens, floribus singularibus"* in Dillenius, Hort. Eltham. 1: 123, t. 103, f. 123. 1732.

Current name: ***Othonna arborescens*** L. (Asteraceae).

Othonna bulbosa Linnaeus, *Species Plantarum* 2: 924. 1753.

"Habitat in Aethiopia." RCN: 6690.

Lectotype (designated here by Nordenstam): [icon] *"Jacobaeae affinis planta tuberosa, capitis bonae spei"* in Breyn, Exot. Pl. Cent.: 138, t. 66. 1678.

Current name: ***Othonna bulbosa*** L. (Asteraceae).

Note: Levyns (in *J. S. African Bot.* 7: 143. 1941) interpreted the name through the Breyn reference, though without explicitly referring to it as the type.

Othonna cheirifolia Linnaeus, *Species Plantarum* 2: 926. 1753.

"Habitat in Aethiopia." RCN: 6696.

Type not designated.

Original material: Herb. Linn. No. 1038.14 (LINN); [icon] in Commelin, Hort. Med. Amsteld. Pl. Rar. 2: 147, t. 74. 1701.

Current name: ***Othonna cheirifolia*** L. (Asteraceae).

Note: Wijnands (*Bot. Commelins*: 79. 1983) suggested that 1038.14 (LINN) should be taken into consideration for the typification of this name but made no formal choice himself.

Othonna cineraria Linnaeus, *Species Plantarum* 2: 925. 1753.

"Habitat in Canada." RCN: 6369.

Replaced synonym of: *Cineraria canadensis* L. (1763).

Lectotype (Reveal in Jarvis & Turland in *Taxon* 47: 365. 1998): Herb. Linn. No. 1000.25 (LINN).

Current name: ***Jacobaea maritima*** (L.) Pelser & Meijden subsp. ***maritima*** (Asteraceae).

Othonna coronopifolia Linnaeus, *Species Plantarum* 2: 926. 1753.

"Habitat in Aethiopia." RCN: 6694.

Lectotype (Wijnands, *Bot. Commelins*: 79. 1983): Herb. Linn. No. 1038.12 (LINN).

Generitype of *Othonna* Linnaeus (vide Green, *Prop. Brit. Bot.*: 184. 1929).

Current name: ***Othonna coronopifolia*** L. (Asteraceae).

Othonna crassifolia Linnaeus, *Systema Naturae*, ed. 12, 2: 579; *Mantissa Plantarum*: 118. 1767.

"Habitat ad Cap. b. spei." RCN: 6696.

Type not designated.

Original material: [icon] in Commelin, Hort. Med. Amsteld. Pl. Rar. 2: 147, t. 74. 1701; [icon] in Miller, Fig. Pl. Gard. Dict. 2: 164, t. 245, f. 2. 1758.

Current name: ***Othonna othonnites*** (L.) Druce (Asteraceae).

Note: Wijnands (*Bot. Commelins*: vii, 80. 1983) noted the links between this name, *O. cheirifolia* L. (1753), *Cineraria othonnites* L. (1763) and *O. frutescens* L. provided by a cited Commelin plate.

Othonna cymbalarifolia Linnaeus, *Plantae Rariores Africanae*: 24. 1760.

["Habitat ad Cap. b. spei. Burmannus."] Sp. Pl., ed. 2, 2: 1242 (1763). RCN: 6361.

Basionym of: *Cineraria cymbalarifolia* (L.) L. (1763).

Type not designated.
Original material: *Oldenland*, Herb. Burman, 3 sheets (G).
Current name: **Senecio cymbalarifolius** (L.) Less. (Asteraceae).

Othonna dentata Linnaeus, *Species Plantarum* 2: 926. 1753.
"Habitat in Aethiopia." RCN: 6690.
Lectotype (designated here by Nordenstam): [icon] *"Solidago foliis oblongis, dentatis, glabris, floribus magnis, umbellatis"* in Burman, Rar. Afric. Pl.: 164, t. 59. 1739.
Current name: **Othonna dentata** L. (Asteraceae).

Othonna frutescens Linnaeus, *Mantissa Plantarum Altera*: 288. 1771, *nom. illeg.*
"Habitat ad Cap. b. spei. H.U." RCN: 6699.
Replaced synonym: *Cineraria othonnites* L. (1763).
Type not designated.
Original material: as replaced synonym.
Current name: **Othonna othonnites** (L.) Druce (Asteraceae).
Note: Wijnands (*Bot. Commelins*: vii, 80. 1983) noted the links between this name, *O. cheirifolia* L. (1753), *Cineraria othonnites* L. (1763) and *O. crassifolia* L. (1767) provided by a cited Commelin plate.

Othonna geifolia Linnaeus, *Species Plantarum* 2: 924. 1753.
"Habitat in Aethiopia." RCN: 6360.
Basionym of: *Cineraria geifolia* (L.) L. (1763).
Lectotype (Wijnands, *Bot. Commelins*: 73. 1983): Herb. Clifford: 410, *Solidago* 7 (BM-000647123).
Current name: **Cineraria geifolia** (L.) L. (Asteraceae).

Othonna helenitis Linnaeus, *Species Plantarum* 2: 925. 1753.
"Habitat in Sibiria. D. Gmelin. Gallia." RCN: 6366.
Basionym of: *Cineraria alpina* (L.) L. var. *helenitis* (L.) L. (1763).
Type not designated.
Original material: [icon] in Plantin, Pl. Stirp. Icon.: 347. 1581.
Current name: **Tephroseris helenitis** (L.) B. Nord. (Asteraceae).
Note: Holub (in *Folia Geobot. Phytotax.* 8: 163. 1973; *Preslia* 49: 320. 1977) stated that this name should apply to a Siberian, rather than a western European, species but did not designate a type.

Othonna integrifolia Linnaeus, *Species Plantarum* 2: 925. 1753.
"Habitat in Alpibus Pyrenaicis, Helveticis, Austriacis, Sibiricis." RCN: 6366.
Basionym of: *Cineraria alpina* (L.) L. var. *integrifolia* (L.) L. (1763).
Type not designated.
Original material: Herb. Burser VI: 122 (UPS); [icon] in Gmelin, Fl. Sibirica 2: 154, t. 71. 1752; [icon] in Morison, Pl. Hist. Univ. 3: 111, s. 7, t. 12, f. 28. 1699; [icon] in Clusius, Rar. Pl. Hist. 2: 22. 1601.
Current name: **Tephroseris integrifolia** (L.) Holub subsp. **integrifolia** (Asteraceae).

Othonna linifolia Linnaeus, *Plantae Rariores Africanae*: 25. 1760. ["Habitat ad Cap. b. spei."] Sp. Pl., ed. 2, 2: 1244 (1763). RCN: 6370.
Basionym of: *Cineraria linifolia* (L.) L. (1763).
Type not designated.
Original material: *Oldenland*, Herb. Burman? (G).
Current name: **Euryops linifolius** (L.) DC. (Asteraceae).
Note: Nordenstam (in *Opera Bot.* 20: 92. 1968) did not trace an original collection but states "a probable isotype is H.S. 156 f. 30 in the Sloane Herbarium (BM)". Although the latter material would not have been seen by Linnaeus, it might well prove to be a duplicate of material at one time in Herb. Delessert (G).

Othonna maritima Linnaeus, *Species Plantarum* 2: 925. 1753.
"Habitat ad Maris inferi littora." RCN: 6368.
Basionym of: *Cineraria maritima* (L.) L. (1763).
Lectotype (Peruzzi & al. in *Taxon* 55: 1003, f. 2A. 2006): Herb. Clifford: 410, *Solidago* 11 (BM-000647125).
Current name: **Jacobaea maritima** (L.) Pelser & Meijden subsp. **maritima** (Asteraceae).

Othonna palustris Linnaeus, *Species Plantarum* 2: 924. 1753.
"Habitat in Europae paludibus maritimis." RCN: 6365.
Basionym of: *Cineraria palustris* (L.) L. (1763).
Lectotype (Jeffrey & Chen in *Kew Bull.* 39: 284. 1984): Herb. Linn. No. 1000.13 (LINN).
Current name: **Tephroseris palustris** (L.) Fourr. (Asteraceae).

Othonna parviflora Linnaeus, *Mantissa Plantarum Altera*: 289. 1771, *nom. illeg.*
"Habitat ad Cap. b. spei locis aquosis, florens Majo." RCN: 6697.
Replaced synonym: *Senecio rigens* L. (1763).
Lectotype (Wijnands, *Bot. Commelins*: 84. 1983): [icon] *"Jacobaea Africana frutescens folio longo et glauco"* in Commelin, Hort. Med. Amstelod. Pl. Rar. 2: 143, t. 72. 1701.
Current name: **Senecio rigens** L. (Asteraceae).
Note: Linnaeus' protologue for this name included both *Senecio rigens* L. (1763) and *O. parviflora* P.J. Bergius (1767), which Levyns (in *J. S. African Bot.* 7: 143. 1941) believed to represent different taxa. Wijnands (*Bot. Commelins*: 83–84. 1983) has confirmed this through typification, *O. parviflora* L. being homotypic, and synonymous, with *S. rigens* (which is the correct name for the species). Wijnands typified *O. parviflora* P.J. Bergius in the sense of what had been called *O. amplexicaulis* Thunb. (1800). *Othonna parviflora* L. is a later homonym of *O. parviflora* P.J. Bergius, and illegitimate.

Othonna pectinata Linnaeus, *Species Plantarum* 2: 926. 1753.
"Habitat in Aethiopia." RCN: 6692.
Lectotype (Nordenstam in *Opera Bot.* 20: 220. 1968): Herb. Clifford: 419, *Othonna* 1 (BM-000647238).
Current name: **Euryops pectinatus** (L.) Cass. (Asteraceae).

Othonna rigens Linnaeus, *Plantae Rariores Africanae*: 24. 1760. ["Habitat ad Cap. b. spei."] Sp. Pl., ed. 2, 2: 1284 (1763). RCN: 6572.
Basionym of: *Gorteria rigens* (L.) L. (1763).
Lectotype (Roessler in *Mitt. Bot. Staatssamml. München* 3: 371. 1959): *Schreber*, Herb. Linn. No. 1027.3 (LINN).
Current name: **Gazania rigens** (L.) Gaertn. (Asteraceae).
Note: Wijnands (*Bot. Commelins*: 84. 1981) argued that the typification by Roessler should be rejected because the thesis in which the Linnaean name was published was based largely on specimens lent to Linnaeus by Burman. While this is, in general, true, 1027.3 (LINN) is annotated as *Othonna rigens* by Linnaeus, and appears to be original material for both this name and *Gorteria rigens* (L.) L. (1763). Consequently, Roessler's typification is accepted here.

Othonna sibirica Linnaeus, *Species Plantarum* 2: 924. 1753.
"Habitat in Sibiria." RCN: 6362.
Basionym of: *Cineraria sibirica* (L.) L. (1763).
Lectotype (Nordenstam & Illarionova in *Taxon* 54: 141, f. 2. 2005): Herb. Linn. No. 348.13 (S).
Current name: **Ligularia sibirica** (L.) Cass. (Asteraceae).

Othonna sonchifolia Linnaeus, *Species Plantarum* 2: 924. 1753.
"Habitat in Aethiopia." RCN: 6364.

Basionym of: *Cineraria sonchifolia* (L.) L. (1763).
Type not designated.
Original material: [icon] in Breyn, Prodr. Fasc. Rar. Pl.: 31, t. 21, f. 1. 1739.
Current name: ***Cineraria sonchifolia*** (L.) L. (Asteraceae).

Othonna tagetes Linnaeus, *Systema Naturae*, ed. 10, 2: 1234. 1759.
["Habitat ad Cap. b. spei."] Sp. Pl., ed. 2, 2: 1309 (1763). RCN: 6691.
Lectotype (designated here by Nordenstam): Herb. Linn. No. 1038.1 (LINN).
Current name: ***Steirodiscus tagetes*** (L.) Schltr. (Asteraceae).

Othonna tenuissima Linnaeus, *Systema Naturae*, ed. 12, 2: 579; *Mantissa Plantarum*: 118. 1767.
"Habitat ad Cap. b. spei." RCN: 6698.
Lectotype (designated here by Nordenstam): [icon] *"Tithymalus dendroides Linariae foliis"* in Plukenet, Phytographia: t. 319, f. 5. 1694; Almag. Bot.: 369. 1696. – Epitype (designated here by Nordenstam): Herb. Linn. No. 1038.17 (LINN).
Current name: ***Euryops tenuissimus*** (L.) DC. (Asteraceae).
Note: In the absence of any relevant material in LINN, Nordenstam (in *Opera Bot.* 20: 74. 1968) designated 1038.17 (LINN) as a neotype. However, original material (a cited Plukenet illustration) exists which precludes the possibility of neotypification. Plukenet's figure (which depicts a sterile branch) is designated here as the lectotype, with 1038.7 (LINN) as its epitype.

Ovieda mitis Linnaeus, *Species Plantarum*, ed. 2, 2: 889. 1763.
"Habitat in Java." RCN: 4629.
Lectotype (Rueda in *Ann. Missouri Bot. Gard.* 80: 875. 1993): Herb. Linn. No. 807.1 (LINN).
Current name: ***Clerodendrum indicum*** (L.) Kuntze (Verbenaceae).

Ovieda spinosa Linnaeus, *Species Plantarum* 2: 637. 1753.
"Habitat in America meridionali." RCN: 4628.
Type not designated.
Original material: [icon] in Plumier, Nov. Pl. Amer.: 11, t. 24. 1703.
Generitype of *Ovieda* Linnaeus.
Current name: ***Clerodendrum spinosum*** (L.) Spreng. (Verbenaceae).

Oxalis acetosella Linnaeus, *Species Plantarum* 1: 433. 1753.
"Habitat in Europae borealis sylvis." RCN: 3369.
Lectotype (Nasir in Nasir & Ali, *Fl. W. Pakistan* 4: 2. 1971): Herb. Linn. No. 600.7 (LINN).
Generitype of *Oxalis* Linnaeus (vide Green, *Prop. Brit. Bot.*: 156. 1929).
Current name: ***Oxalis acetosella*** L. (Oxalidaceae).

Oxalis barrelieri Linnaeus, *Species Plantarum*, ed. 2, 1: 624. 1762.
"Habitat in America." RCN: 3389.
Lectotype (Lourteig in *Phytologia* 29: 456. 1975): [icon] *"Trifolium acetosum Americanum rubro flore"* in Barrelier, Pl. Galliam: 8, t. 1139. 1714.
Current name: ***Oxalis barrelieri*** L. (Oxalidaceae).

Oxalis corniculata Linnaeus, *Species Plantarum* 1: 435. 1753.
"Habitat in Italia, Sicilia." RCN: 3380.
Lectotype (Watson in *Bot. J. Linn. Soc.* 101: 357, f. 7. 1989): Herb. Burser XVIII(2): 60 (UPS).
Current name: ***Oxalis corniculata*** L. (Oxalidaceae).
Note: An exhaustive review of the complexities surrounding this name has been provided by Watson (in *Bot. J. Linn. Soc.* 101: 347–357. 1989). He rejected Eiten's type choice (in *Taxon* 4: 101. 1955) of a collection made in Palestine by Hasselquist (630.31, LINN) on the

grounds of geographical conflict with the protologue, designating a Burser collection in its place.

Oxalis flava Linnaeus, *Species Plantarum* 1: 433. 1753.
"Habitat in Aethiopia." RCN: 3372.
Type not designated.
Original material: [icon] in Burman, Rar. Afric. Pl.: 68, 69, 75, t. 27, f. 4, 5, t. 30, f. 1. 1738.
Current name: ***Oxalis flava*** L. (Oxalidaceae).

Oxalis frutescens Linnaeus, *Species Plantarum* 1: 435. 1753.
"Habitat in America meridionali." RCN: 3382.
Lectotype (Lourteig in *Phytologia* 29: 461. 1975): [icon] *"Oxalis caule fruticoso, foliis ternatis"* in Plumier in Burman, Pl. Amer.: 207, t. 213, f. 1. 1759.
Current name: ***Oxalis frutescens*** L. (Oxalidaceae).

Oxalis hirta Linnaeus, *Species Plantarum* 1: 434. 1753.
"Habitat in Aethiopia." RCN: 3379.
Type not designated.
Original material: Herb. A. van Royen No. 903.281–133? (L); [icon] in Plukenet, Amalth. Bot.: 164, t. 434, f. 7. 1705 – Typotype: Herb. Sloane 92: 101 (BM-SL); [icon] in Burman, Rar. Afric. Pl.: 70, t. 28, f. 1. 1738; [icon] in Burman, Rar. Afric. Pl.: 71, t. 28, f. 2. 1738.
Current name: ***Oxalis hirta*** L. (Oxalidaceae).

Oxalis incarnata Linnaeus, *Species Plantarum* 1: 433. 1753.
"Habitat in Aethiopia." RCN: 3377.
Lectotype (Wijnands, *Bot. Commelins*: 159. 1983): [icon] *"Oxys bulbosa Aethiopica minor folio cordato"* in Commelin, Hort. Med. Amstelod. Pl. Rar. 1: 43, t. 22. 1697.
Current name: ***Oxalis incarnata*** L. (Oxalidaceae).

Oxalis longiflora Linnaeus, *Species Plantarum* 1: 433. 1753.
"Habitat in Virginia." RCN: 3371.
Lectotype (designated here by Reveal): Herb. Linn. No. 600.11 (LINN).
Current name: ***Oxalis acetosella*** L. (Oxalidaceae).

Oxalis monophylla Linnaeus, *Mantissa Plantarum Altera*: 241. 1771.
"Habitat in Cap. b. spei." RCN: 3368.
Type not designated.
Original material: Herb. Linn. No. 600.1? (LINN); Herb. Linn. No. 600.2 (LINN).
Current name: ***Oxalis monophylla*** L. (Oxalidaceae).

Oxalis pes-caprae Linnaeus, *Species Plantarum* 1: 434. 1753.
"Habitat in Aethiopia." RCN: 3374.
Lectotype (Salter in *J. S. African Bot.* 5: 48. 1939): [icon] *"Oxalis bulbosa, pentaphylla, & hexaphylla, floribus magnis, luteis, copiosis"* in Burman, Rar. Afric. Pl.: 80, t. 29. 1738 (see p. 38).
Current name: ***Oxalis pes-caprae*** L. (Oxalidaceae).

Oxalis purpurea Linnaeus, *Species Plantarum* 1: 433. 1753.
"Habitat in Aethiopia." RCN: 3370.
Lectotype (Wijnands, *Bot. Commelins*: 160. 1983): Herb. Clifford: 175, *Oxalis* 2 (BM-000628563).
Current name: ***Oxalis purpurea*** L. (Oxalidaceae).
Note: See Salter (in *J. S. African Bot.* 5: 48–51. 1939) for a discussion on the application of this name.

Oxalis sensitiva Linnaeus, *Species Plantarum* 1: 434. 1753.
"Habitat in India." RCN: 3375.

Type not designated.

Original material: Herb. Hermann 1: 28, No. 180 (BM); Herb. Hermann 3: 54, No. 180 (BM); [icon] in Rheede, Hort. Malab. 9: 33, t. 19. 1689; [icon] in Zanoni, Istoria Bot.: 199, t. 61. 1675; [icon] in Garcin in Philos. Trans. 36(415): 378, t. 2. 1731.

Current name: ***Biophytum sensitivum*** (L.) DC. (Oxalidaceae).

Note: See the extensive treatment by Veldkamp (in *Taxon* 38: 110–116. 1989). He concludes that none of the varied and various elements within Linnaeus' very broad species concept can be chosen as a lectotype, and instead chooses 600.38 LINN as a neotype. However, with the existence of original material, this choice is contrary to Art. 9.11.

Oxalis sessilifolia Linnaeus, *Mantissa Plantarum Altera*: 241. 1771.

"Habitat ad Cap. b. spei." RCN: 3378.

Type not designated.

Original material: [icon] in Burman, Rar. Afric. Pl.: 70, t. 28, f. 1. 1738; [icon] in Plukenet, Amalth. Bot.: 164, t. 434, f. 7. 1705 – Typotype: Herb. Sloane 92: 101 (BM-SL).

Note: The application of this name appears uncertain.

Oxalis stricta Linnaeus, *Species Plantarum* 1: 435. 1753.

"Habitat in Virginia." RCN: 3381.

Lectotype (Eiten in *Taxon* 4: 103. 1955): [icon] *"Oxys s. trifolium luteum corniculatum, virginianum rectum majus"* in Morison, Pl. Hist. Univ. 2: 184, s. 2, t. 17, f. 3. 1680.

Current name: ***Oxalis stricta*** L. (Oxalidaceae).

Note: Watson (in *Bot. J. Linn. Soc.* 101: 358–361. 1989) gives a detailed review, and reproduces the type illustration (as f. 3).

Oxalis versicolor Linnaeus, *Species Plantarum* 1: 434. 1753.

"Habitat in Aethiopia." RCN: 3376.

Type not designated.

Original material: [icon] in Burman, Rar. Afric. Pl.: 65, t. 27, f. 1. 1738; [icon] in Burman, Rar. Afric. Pl.: 66, t. 27, f. 2. 1738; [icon] in Plukenet, Amalth. Bot.: 164, t. 434, f. 6. 1705.

Current name: ***Oxalis versicolor*** L. (Oxalidaceae).

Oxalis violacea Linnaeus, *Species Plantarum* 1: 434. 1753.

"Habitat in Virginia, Canada." RCN: 3373.

Lectotype (designated here by Reveal): *Kalm*, Herb. Linn. No. 600.12 (LINN).

Current name: ***Oxalis violacea*** L. (Oxalidaceae).

P

Paederia foetida Linnaeus, *Systema Naturae*, ed. 12, 2: 189; *Mantissa Plantarum*: 52. 1767.
"Habitat in India." RCN: 1703.
Lectotype (Puff in *Opera Bot. Belg.* 3: 211. 1991): Herb. Linn. No. 294.1 (LINN).
Generitype of *Paederia* Linnaeus, *nom. cons.*
Current name: ***Paederia foetida*** L. (Rubiaceae).
Note: Paederia Linnaeus, *nom. cons.* against *Daun-contu* Adans. and *Hondbessen* Adans.
  Merrill (*Interpret. Rumph. Herb. Amb.*: 489. 1917) stated that the type is a specimen (but without specifying what that might be). Deb & Roy (in *J. Econ. Taxon. Bot.* 4: 748. 1983) indicated 580.12 LINN (which does not exist) as "type". Puffs therefore appears to be the first explicit type choice.

Paederota ageria Linnaeus, *Mantissa Plantarum Altera*: 171. 1771, *nom. illeg.*
RCN: 105.
Replaced synonym: *Paederota lutea* Scop. (1769).
Type not designated.
Current name: ***Paederota lutea*** Scop. (Scrophulariaceae).
Note: An illegitimate replacement name for *Paederota lutea* Scop. (1769).

Paederota bonae-spei (Linnaeus) Linnaeus, *Species Plantarum*, ed. 2, 1: 20. 1762.
"Habitat ad Cap. bon. spei." RCN: 104.
Basionym: *Hemimeris bonae-spei* L. (1760).
Type not designated.
Original material: as basionym.
Current name: ***Diascia capensis*** (L.) Britten (Scrophulariaceae).

Paederota bonarota (Linnaeus) Linnaeus, *Species Plantarum*, ed. 2, 1: 20. 1762.
"Habitat in Alpibus Italicis, Austriacis." RCN: 106.
Basionym: *Veronica bonarota* L. (1753).
Lectotype (Sutton in Jarvis & al., *Regnum Veg.* 127: 72. 1993): Herb. Burser XIV(1): 46 (UPS).
Generitype of *Paederota* Linnaeus (vide Steudel, *Nom.* 1: 581. 1821).
Current name: ***Paederota bonarota*** (L.) L. (Scrophulariaceae).

Paeonia anomala Linnaeus, *Mantissa Plantarum Altera*: 247. 1771.
"Habitat in omnia Sibiria." RCN: 3940.
Lectotype (Schmitt in *Candollea* 58: 187. 2003): Herb. Linn. No. 692.3 (LINN).
Current name: ***Paeonia anomala*** L. (Paeoniaceae).
Note: See also Hong & Pan (in *Ann. Missouri Bot. Gard.* 91: 89. 2004) who reproduce the type (their f. 1A).

Paeonia officinalis Linnaeus, *Species Plantarum* 1: 530. 1753.
"Habitat in Nemoribus montium Idae, Helvetiae." RCN: 3939.
Lectotype (Schmitt in *Candollea* 58: 183. 2003): Herb. Linn. No. 692.1 (LINN).
Generitype of *Paeonia* Linnaeus.
Current name: ***Paeonia officinalis*** L. (Paeoniaceae).
Note: Stern (*Study Genus* Paeonia: 126. 1946) suggested that the indirectly cited ("these quotations") Mattioli plates (for this and *P. officinalis* var. *mascula*) "appear to fix the type of the 2 peonies Linnaeus had in mind". Stern figured a plate on p. 121, as well as others from Mattioli and Fuchs. As the Mattioli plates are not directly cited by Linnaeus, they are not original material for the name. Stearn & Davis (*Peonies of Greece*: 78. 1984) also reproduced all the early cited illustrations.

Paeonia officinalis Linnaeus var. **feminea** Linnaeus, *Species Plantarum* 1: 530. 1753.
RCN: 3939.
Lectotype (Schmitt in *Candollea* 58: 183. 2003): Herb. Clifford: 211, *Paeonia* 1, sheet C (BM-000628769). – Epitype (Schmitt in *Candollea* 58: 183. 2003): Switzerland. In pascuis M. Generosi, Herb. Haller 30: 122, lower specimen (P).
Current name: ***Paeonia officinalis*** L. (Paeoniaceae).

Paeonia officinalis Linnaeus var. **mascula** Linnaeus, *Species Plantarum* 1: 530. 1753.
RCN: 3939.
Lectotype (Schmitt in *Candollea* 58: 184. 2003): Herb. Clifford: 211, *Paeonia* 1, sheet A (BM-000628767). – Epitype (Schmitt in *Candollea* 58: 184. 2003): France. Savigny lès Beaune (Côte d'Or) bois, taillis pierreux calcaire, vers la partie supérieure de la Combe Vauteloy, 400m, 24 mai 1911, Legi Ldevergnes (P).
Current name: ***Paeonia mascula*** (L.) Mill. (Paeoniaceae).
Note: Meikle (*Fl. Cyprus* 1: 69. 1977) indicated *P. mas.* Lobel, *Pl. Stirp.* t. 832 (1581) as "probably" the type but his uncertainty means that this cannot be accepted as a formal typification.

Paeonia tenuifolia Linnaeus, *Systema Naturae*, ed. 10, 2: 1079. 1759.
["Habitat in Ucrania. Gorter."] Sp. Pl., ed. 2, 1: 747 (1762). RCN: 3941.

Lectotype (Schmitt in *Candollea* 58: 187. 2003): Herb. Linn. No. 692.4 (LINN), see opposite, below.
Current name: ***Paeonia tenuifolia*** L. (Paeoniaceae).

Panax fruticosus Linnaeus, *Species Plantarum,* ed. 2, 2: 1513. 1763. "Habitat in Ternateis." RCN: 7713.
Lectotype (Grushvitzky & al. in *Novosti Sist. Vyssh. Rast.* 22: 182. 1985): Herb. Linn. No. 1237.5 (LINN).
Current name: ***Polyscias fruticosa*** (L.) Harms (Araliaceae).
Note: Specific epithet spelled "fruticosum" in the protologue.

Panax quinquefolius Linnaeus, *Species Plantarum* 2: 1058. 1753. "Habitat in Canada, Pensylvania, Virginia." RCN: 7711.
Lectotype (Reveal in *Phytologia* 71: 473. 1991): *Kalm*, Herb. Linn. No. 1237.1 (LINN; iso- BM).
Generitype of *Panax* Linnaeus (vide Green, *Prop. Brit. Bot.*: 194. 1929).
Current name: ***Panax quinquefolius*** L. (Araliaceae).
Note: Specific epithet spelled "quinquefolium" in the protologue.

Panax trifolius Linnaeus, *Species Plantarum* 2: 1059. 1753. "Habitat in Virginia." RCN: 7712.
Lectotype (Reveal & al. in *Huntia* 7: 228. 1987): *Clayton 329*, Herb. Linn. No. 1237.4 (LINN).
Current name: ***Panax trifolius*** L. (Araliaceae).
Note: Specific epithet spelled "trifolium" in the protologue.

Pancratium amboinense Linnaeus, *Species Plantarum* 1: 291. 1753. "Habitat in Ambonia." RCN: 2324.
Lectotype (Wijnands, *Bot. Commelins*: 41. 1983): [icon] *"Narcissus Amboinensis folio latissimo rotundo, floribus niveis inodoris"* in Commelin, Hort. Med. Amsteled. Pl. Rar. 1: 77, t. 39. 1697.
Current name: ***Proiphys amboinensis*** (L.) Herb. (Liliaceae/Amaryllidaceae).

Pancratium caribaeum Linnaeus, *Species Plantarum* 1: 291. 1753. "Habitat in Jamaica, Caribaeis." RCN: 2320.
Lectotype (Howard in *J. Arnold Arbor.* 60: 295. 1979): [icon] *"Narcissus Americanus flore multiplici albo hexagono odorato"* in Commelin, Hort. Med. Amsteled. Pl. Rar. 2: 173, t. 87. 1701.
Current name: ***Hymenocallis caribaea*** (L.) Herb. (Liliaceae/Amaryllidaceae).
Note: See discussion of the original elements by Sealy (in *Kew Bull.* 9: 220. 1954), who uses the name in the sense of Commelin's plant, but does not formally call the latter the type.

Pancratium carolinianum Linnaeus, *Species Plantarum* 1: 291. 1753. "Habitat in Jamaica, Carolina." RCN: 2322.
Lectotype (Dandy, *Sloane Herbarium*: 112. 1958): [icon] *"Lilio-Narcissus Polianthus, flore albo"* in Catesby, Nat. Hist. Carolina 2, App.: 5, t. 5. 1747.
Current name: ***Pancratium maritimum*** L. (Liliaceae/Amaryllidaceae).
Note: The taxonomic identity of the type has provoked differences of opinion, with many authors (e.g. Howard & Staples in *J. Arnold Arbor.* 64: 513. 1983) treating it as *Hymenocallis caroliniana* (L.) Herb. but others (e.g. Smith & Garland in *Taxon* 52: 814. 2003) arguing that it is a depiction of *Pancratium maritimum*.

Pancratium illyricum Linnaeus, *Species Plantarum* 1: 291. 1753. "Habitat in Illyria?" RCN: 2323.
Type not designated.
Original material: Herb. A. van Royen No. 897.326–441 (L); *Hasselquist*, Herb. Linn. No. 413.4 (LINN); [icon] in Seba, Locupl. Rer. Nat. Thes. 1: 17, t. 8, f. 1. 1734; [icon] in Besler, Hort. Eystett. vern.: ord. 3, fol. 16, f. 1. 1613.
Current name: ***Pancratium illyricum*** L. (Liliaceae/Amaryllidaceae).

Pancratium maritimum Linnaeus, *Species Plantarum* 1: 291. 1753. "Habitat in Hispaniae maritimis circa Valentiam & infra Monspelium." RCN: 2321.
Lectotype (Wijnands in Jarvis & al., *Regnum Veg.* 127: 73. 1993): [icon] *"Narcissus maritimus"* in Morison, Pl. Hist. Univ. 2: 365, s. 4, t. 10, f. 28. 1680.
Generitype of *Pancratium* Linnaeus.
Current name: ***Pancratium maritimum*** L. (Liliaceae/Amaryllidaceae).
Note: Although Mill (in Davis, *Fl. Turkey* 8: 381. 1984) suggested that 413.3 (LINN) may be the basis of this name, the specimen is an Alströmer collection not received by Linnaeus until 1761. The lectotype figure was apparently itself based on "Narc. pancratium marinum flo. alb." Sweerts (*Florilegium*: t. 27. 1612).

Pancratium mexicanum Linnaeus, *Species Plantarum* 1: 290. 1753. "Habitat in Mexico." RCN: 2319.
Lectotype (Sealy in *Kew Bull.* 9: 217. 1954): [icon] *"Pancratium Mexicanum, flore gemello candido"* in Dillenius, Hort. Eltham. 2: 299, t. 222, f. 289. 1732.
Current name: ***Hymenocallis dillenii*** M. Roem. (Liliaceae/Amaryllidaceae).

Pancratium narbonense Linnaeus, *Herbarium Amboinense*: 28. 1754. RCN: 2324.
Lectotype (Merrill, *Interpret. Rumph. Herb. Amb.*: 33, 142. 1917): [icon] *"Cepa silvestris"* in Rumphius, Herb. Amboin. 6: 160, t. 70, f. 1. 1750.
Current name: ***Proiphys amboinense*** (L.) Herb. (Liliaceae/Amaryllidaceae).

Pancratium zeylanicum Linnaeus, *Species Plantarum* 1: 290. 1753. "Habitat in India." RCN: 2318.
Lectotype (Wijnands, *Bot. Commelins*: 40. 1983): Herb. Hermann 5: 2, No. 126 [icon] (BM-000594787).
Current name: ***Pancratium zeylanicum*** L. (Liliaceae/Amaryllidaceae).

Panicum alopecuroides Linnaeus, *Species Plantarum* 1: 55. 1753. "Habitat in China." RCN: 472.
Replaced synonym of: *Alopecurus indicus* L. (1774), *nom. illeg.*
Lectotype (Veldkamp in Cafferty & al. in *Taxon* 49: 253. 2000): Herb. Linn. No. 80.1 (LINN).
Current name: ***Pennisetum alopecuroides*** (L.) Spreng. (Poaceae).
Note: Chase (in *Amer. J. Bot.* 8: 48. 1921) discussed the application of the name, suggesting that it "should be restricted...leaving the Chinese specimen as the type (= *Pennisetum alopecuroides* (L.) Spreng.) but not as Sprengel applied the name". However, her use of the uncertain term "should", and uncertainty about which of the specimens at LINN she may have intended (80.1 and 80.2 are candidates), means this cannot be accepted as a typification.

Panicum americanum Linnaeus, *Species Plantarum* 1: 56. 1753. "Habitat in America." RCN: 7564.
Lectotype (Clayton & Renvoize in Polhill, *Fl. Trop. E. Africa, Gramineae* 3: 672. 1982): [icon] *"Panicum Americanum"* in Clusius, Rar. Pl. Hist. 2: 215. 1601.
Current name: ***Pennisetum glaucum*** (L.) R. Br. (Poaceae).
Note: Terrell (in *Taxon* 25: 297–304. 1976) provides a discussion.

Panicum arborescens Linnaeus, *Species Plantarum* 1: 59. 1753. "Habitat in India." RCN: 502.
Lectotype (Renvoize in Cafferty & al. in *Taxon* 49: 253. 2000): Herb. Hermann 1: 30, No. 43 (BM-000621336).
Current name: ***Panicum brevifolium*** L. (Poaceae).

P

Panicum brevifolium Linnaeus, *Species Plantarum* 1: 59. 1753.
"Habitat in India." RCN: 506.
Lectotype (Clayton & Renvoize in Polhill, *Fl. Trop. E. Africa, Gramineae* 3: 496. 1982): Herb. Linn. No. 80.64 (LINN).
Current name: ***Panicum brevifolium*** L. (Poaceae).

Panicum brizoides Linnaeus, *Mantissa Plantarum Altera*: 184. 1771, *nom. illeg.*
"Habitat in India. Koenig." RCN: 482.
Replaced synonym: *Panicum punctatum* Burm. f. (1768).
Type not designated.
Current name: ***Setaria punctata*** (Burm. f.) Veldkamp (Poaceae).
Note: As noted by Veldkamp (in *Blumea* 39: 381–382. 1994), this is an illegitimate renaming of *P. punctatum* Burm. f. (1768), and therefore homotypic with it. Earlier treatments, where this had not been recognised and the Linnaean name treated as legitimate, had placed *P. brizoides* as a synonym of *Echinochloa colona* (L.) Link.

Panicum capillare Linnaeus, *Species Plantarum* 1: 58. 1753.
"Habitat in Virginia, Jamaica." RCN: 498.
Lectotype (Hitchcock in *Contr. U. S. Natl. Herb.* 12: 118. 1908): *Clayton 454* (BM-000042600; iso- US, fragm., No. 80553).
Current name: ***Panicum capillare*** L. (Poaceae).

Panicum clandestinum Linnaeus, *Species Plantarum* 1: 58. 1753.
"Habitat in Jamaica, Pensylvania. Kalm." RCN: 501.
Lectotype (Hitchcock in *Contr. U. S. Natl. Herb.* 12: 118. 1908): *Kalm*, Herb. Linn. No. 80.57 (LINN; iso- UPS).
Current name: ***Dichanthelium clandestinum*** (L.) Gould (Poaceae).
Note: Baum (in *Canad. J. Bot.* 45: 1847. 1967) noted a duplicate of the Kalm type collection in UPS.

Panicum colonum Linnaeus, *Systema Naturae*, ed. 10, 2: 870. 1759.
["Habitat in Indiae cultis."] Sp. Pl., ed. 2, 1: 84 (1753). RCN: 481.
Lectotype (Hitchcock in *Contr. U. S. Natl. Herb.* 12: 119. 1908): *Browne*, Herb. Linn. No. 80.23 (LINN).
Current name: ***Echinochloa colonum*** (L.) Link (Poaceae).
Note: Nicolson (in *Taxon* 35: 324. 1986) discusses the gender of the epithet "colonum" as, in some detail, does Ward (in *Sida* 21: 2171–2183. 2005). The latter concludes that the correct form in *Echinochloa* is "*colonum*" rather than "*colona*".

Panicum coloratum Linnaeus, *Systema Naturae*, ed. 12, 2: 88; *Mantissa Plantarum*: 30. 1767.
"Habitat in Cairi. Forskohl." RCN: 495.
Lectotype (Zuloaga in Görts-van Rijn, *Fl. Guianas,* ser. A, 8: 384. 1990): Herb. Linn. No. 80.46 (LINN).
Current name: ***Panicum coloratum*** L. (Poaceae).
Note: Clayton & Renvoize (in Polhill, *Fl. Trop. E. Africa, Gramineae* 3: 485. 1982) indicated material at LINN as type but did not distinguish between sheets 80.45 and 80.46. As these do not appear to be part of a single gathering, Art. 9.15 does not apply.

Panicum compositum Linnaeus, *Species Plantarum* 1: 57. 1753.
"Habitat in Zeylona." RCN: 492.
Lectotype (Davey & Clayton in *Kew Bull.* 33: 156. 1978): Herb. Hermann 3: 45, No. 42 (BM-000621970).
Current name: ***Oplismenus compositus*** (L.) P. Beauv. (Poaceae).

Panicum conglomeratum Linnaeus, *Mantissa Plantarum Altera*: 324. 1771.
["Habitat in India."] Sp. Pl. 1: 63 (1753). RCN: 485.
Replaced synonym: *Aira indica* L. (1753).

Neotype (Renvoize in Cafferty & al. in *Taxon* 49: 244. 2000): Sri Lanka. Sabaragamuwa Province, Ratnagsura District, 22 Oct 1974, *Davidse 7871* (K; iso- MO).
Current name: ***Sacciolepis indica*** (L.) Chase (Poaceae).
Note: Evidently a *nomen novum* for *Aira indica* L. (1753), the epithet being pre-occupied in *Panicum* by *P. indicum* Mill. (1768), and *P. indicum* (L.) L. (1771) is illegitimate as a consequence.

Panicum crus-corvi Linnaeus, *Systema Naturae,* ed. 10, 2: 870. 1759.
["Habitat in Indiis."] Sp. Pl., ed. 2, 1: 84 (1753). RCN: 479.
Type not designated.
Original material: none traced.
Current name: ***Echinochloa crus-corvi*** (L.) P. Beauv. (Poaceae).
Note: The identity of this name is uncertain. Carretero (in *Anales Jard. Bot. Madrid* 38: 98. 1981) interpreted it as a synonym of *P. crus-gallii* L. (syn. *Echinochloa crus-gallii* (L.) P. Beauv.) on the basis of 80.17 (LINN), though without explicitly treating the latter as the type. However, this specimen is unannotated by Linnaeus and is not original material for the name. This name may well be a candidate for rejection.

Panicum crus-galli Linnaeus, *Species Plantarum* 1: 56. 1753.
"Habitat in Europae, Virginiae cultis." RCN: 480.
Lectotype (Hitchcock in *Contr. U. S. Natl. Herb.* 12: 117. 1908): *Kalm*, Herb. Linn. No. 80.18 (LINN).
Current name: ***Echinochloa crus-galli*** (L.) P. Beauv. (Poaceae).
Note: Specific epithet spelled "Crusgalli" in the protologue. Hitchcock (in *Contr. U. S. Natl. Herb.* 22: 140. 1920) reconsidered his earlier (1908) type choice, excluding the American plant in favour of a European concept for the species and Wiegand (in *Rhodora* 23: 55. 1921) concurred with Hitchcock's reinterpretation. Baum (in *Canad. J. Bot.* 45: 1846. 1967) also disagreed with the choice of a Kalm collection as type, though on the spurious grounds that Kalm's name was not explicitly cited in the protologue. However, the Kalm collection is clearly original material for this name, and Hitchcock's 1908 type choice has priority.

Panicum curvatum Linnaeus, *Systema Naturae,* ed. 12, 2: 732. 1767. RCN: 503.
Lectotype (Simon in *Kew Bull.* 27: 390. 1972): Herb. Linn. No. 80.60 (LINN).
Current name: ***Sacciolepis curvata*** (L.) Chase (Poaceae).

Panicum cynosuroides Linnaeus, *Systema Naturae,* ed. 10, 2: 870. 1759.
RCN: 473.
Type not designated.
Original material: none traced.
Note: The application of this name is uncertain and it has been suggested by some authors, e.g. Chase (in *Amer. J. Bot.* 8: 44, 48. 1921) that it should be rejected, though no formal proposal has been made.

Panicum dactylon Linnaeus, *Species Plantarum* 1: 58. 1753.
"Habitat in Europa australi." RCN: 488.
Lectotype (Clayton & Harlan in *Kew Bull.* 24: 186. 1970): Herb. Linn. No. 80.35 (LINN).
Current name: ***Cynodon dactylon*** (L.) Pers. (Poaceae).

Panicum dichotomum Linnaeus, *Species Plantarum* 1: 58. 1753.
"Habitat in Virginia." RCN: 493.
Lectotype (Hitchcock in *Contr. U. S. Natl. Herb.* 12: 117. 1908): *Clayton 458*, left specimen (BM-000042601; iso- US, fragm.).
Current name: ***Dichanthelium dichotomum*** (L.) Gould (Poaceae).

Panicum dimidiatum Linnaeus, *Species Plantarum* 1: 57. 1753.
"Habitat in India." RCN: 483.
Lectotype (Renvoize in Cafferty & al. in *Taxon* 49: 253. 2000): Herb.
  Linn. No. 80.25 (LINN).
Current name: **Stenotaphrum dimidiatum** (L.) Brongn. (Poaceae).
Note: Sauer (in *Brittonia* 24: 207. 1972) restricted the use of the name
  to two specimens at LINN but did not formally typify the name.
  Clayton & Renvoize (in Polhill, *Fl. Trop. E. Africa, Gramineae* 3:
  549. 1982) indicated unspecified material at LINN as the type, but
  Renvoize later restricted this to sheet 80.25 as lectotype.

Panicum dissectum Linnaeus, *Species Plantarum* 1: 57. 1753.
"Habitat in Indiis." RCN: 467.
Basionym of: *Paspalum dissectum* (L.) L. (1762); *P. dimidiatum* L.
  (1759), *nom. illeg.*
Lectotype (Hitchcock in *Contr. U. S. Natl. Herb.* 12: 116. 1908):
  Kalm, Herb. Linn. No. 79.1 (LINN; iso- US).
Current name: **Paspalum dissectum** (L.) L. (Poaceae).
Note: Baum (in *Canad. J. Bot.* 45: 1845. 1967) incorrectly interpreted
  Hitchcock's choice of lectotype as 80.25 (LINN), and proposed a
  Plukenet description and illustration as lectotype in its place.
  However, Hitchcock's type choice of 79.1 (LINN) is original
  material for the name and therefore has priority.

Panicum distachyon Linnaeus, *Mantissa Plantarum Altera*: 183.
  1771.
"Habitat in India orientali. Koenig." RCN: 491.
Lectotype (Henrard, *Monogr.* Digitaria: 191. 1950): Herb. Linn. No.
  80.41 (LINN; iso- L).
Current name: **Urochloa distachya** (L.) T.Q. Nguyen (Poaceae).

Panicum divaricatum Linnaeus, *Systema Naturae,* ed. 10, 2: 871.
  1759.
["Habitat in Jamaica."] Sp. Pl., ed. 2, 1: 86 (1753). RCN: 507.
Lectotype (Hitchcock & Chase in *Contr. U. S. Natl. Herb.* 22: 20.
  1920): *Browne*, Herb. Linn. No. 80.65 (LINN).
Current name: **Lasiacis divaricata** (L.) Hitchc. (Poaceae).

Panicum filiforme Linnaeus, *Species Plantarum* 1: 57. 1753.
"Habitat in America septentrionali. Kalm." RCN: 489.
Lectotype (Hitchcock in *Contr. U. S. Natl. Herb.* 12: 117. 1908):
  Kalm, Herb. Linn. No. 80.38 (LINN).
Current name: **Digitaria filiformis** (L.) Koeler (Poaceae).

Panicum glaucum Linnaeus, *Species Plantarum* 1: 56. 1753.
"Habitat in Indiis." RCN: 476.
Lectotype (Rauschert in *Feddes Repert.* 83: 662. 1973): Herb.
  Hermann 3: 17, No. 44 (BM-000621854).
Current name: **Pennisetum glaucum** (L.) R. Br. (Poaceae).
Note: Chase (in *Contr. U. S. Natl. Herb.* 22: 216. 1920) used the name
  in the sense of pearl millet but did not explicitly designate a type.
  There is also discussion of the name and its usage by Stapf (in *Kew
  Bull.* 1928: 147–149. 1928) and Terrell (in *Taxon* 25: 297–304.
  1976). Rauschert, however, appears to have been the first to make
  an unequivocal choice of type.

Panicum grossarium Linnaeus, *Systema Naturae,* ed. 10, 2: 871.
  1759.
["Habitat in Jamaica."] Sp. Pl., ed. 2, 1: 86 (1762). RCN: 499.
Lectotype (Hitchcock & Chase in *Contr. U. S. Natl. Herb.* 15: 36.
  1910; Veldkamp in *Blumea* 41: 427. 1996): *Browne*, Herb. Linn.
  No. 80.52, upper specimen (LINN).
Current name: **Urochloa reptans** (L.) Stapf (Poaceae).
Note: Veldkamp (in *Blumea* 41: 429. 1996) followed Hitchcock (in
  Contr. U. S. Natl. Herb. 12: 119. 1908) in regarding this and *P.*

reptans L. (1759) as homotypic. However, the first clear type choice
  dates from Hitchcock & Chase (in *Contr. U. S. Natl. Herb.* 15: 36.
  1910), later restricted to the upper specimen on the sheet by
  Veldkamp.

Panicum hirtellum Linnaeus, *Systema Naturae,* ed. 10, 2: 870. 1759.
["Habitat in Indiis, etiam ibi colitur."] Sp. Pl., ed. 2, 1: 83 (1762).
  RCN: 484.
Lectotype (Hitchcock in *Contr. U. S. Natl. Herb.* 12: 119. 1908):
  Browne, Herb. Linn. No. 80.28 (LINN).
Current name: **Oplismenus hirtellus** (L.) P. Beauv. (Poaceae).

Panicum indicum (Linnaeus) Linnaeus, *Mantissa Plantarum Altera*:
  184. 1771, *nom. illeg.*
"Habitat ad villas et plateas Indiae orientalis. Koenig." RCN: 485.
Basionym: *Aira indica* L. (1753).
Neotype (Renvoize in Cafferty & al. in *Taxon* 49: 244. 2000): Sri
  Lanka. Sabaragamuwa Province, Ratnagsura District, 22 Oct 1974,
  Davidse 7871 (K; iso- MO).
Current name: **Sacciolepis indica** (L.) Chase (Poaceae).
Note: A later homonym of *P. indicum* Mill. (1768) and hence
  illegitimate. See also *P. conglomeratum* L. (1771).

Panicum italicum Linnaeus, *Species Plantarum* 1: 56. 1753.
"Habitat in Indiis." RCN: 478.
Lectotype (Veldkamp in Cafferty & al. in *Taxon* 49: 253. 2000): Herb.
  A. van Royen No. 912.356–242 (L).
Current name: **Setaria italica** (L.) P. Beauv. (Poaceae).
Note: Although Kerguélen (in *Lejeunia*, n.s., 75: 259. 1975) stated
  "Type: ...LINN", this is not accepted as a formal typification, for the
  reasons explained by Cafferty & al. (in *Taxon* 49: 240. 2000). Meikle
  (*Fl. Cyprus* 2: 1860. 1985), Sherif & Siddiqi (in El-Gadi, *Fl. Libya*
  145: 298. 1988), Pensiero & Judziewicz (in Görts-van Rijn, *Fl.
  Guianas*, ser. A, 8: 585. 1990) and Veldkamp (in *Blumea* 39: 377.
  1994) have all indicated material at LINN as type, but sheet 80.14 is
  a post-1753 addition to the herbarium, and therefore ineligible as
  original material. In the absence of other relevant material at LINN,
  Veldkamp designated a van Royen collection as lectotype.

Panicum latifolium Linnaeus, *Species Plantarum* 1: 58. 1753.
"Habitat in America." RCN: 500.
Lectotype (Hitchcock in *Contr. U. S. Natl. Herb.* 12: 118. 1908):
  Kalm, Herb. Linn. No. 80.54, left specimen (LINN; iso- US,
  fragm.).
Current name: **Dichanthelium latifolium** (L.) Harvill (Poaceae).
Note: Baum (in *Canad. J. Bot.* 45: 1847. 1967) rejected Hitchcock's
  choice of a Kalm collection as type on the spurious grounds that
  Kalm's name was not explicitly cited in the protologue. However,
  the Kalm collection is clearly original material for this name, and
  Hitchcock's 1908 type choice has priority.

Panicum lineare Linnaeus, *Species Plantarum,* ed. 2, 1: 85. 1762.
"Habitat in Indiis." RCN: 490.
Type not designated.
Original material: none traced.
Note: This name has variously been identified with the genera *Cynodon*
  and *Digitaria* but, in the absence of original material, its application
  remains uncertain. It may prove to be a candidate for rejection.

Panicum miliaceum Linnaeus, *Species Plantarum* 1: 58. 1753.
"Habitat in India." RCN: 497.
Lectotype (Sherif & Siddiqi in El-Gadi, *Fl. Libya* 145: 282. 1988):
  Herb. Linn. No. 80.49 (LINN).
Generitype of *Panicum* Linnaeus (vide Hitchcock, *Prop. Brit. Bot.*:
  119. 1929).

P

Current name: ***Panicum miliaceum*** L. (Poaceae).
Note: Although Kerguélen (in *Lejeunia*, n.s., 75: 220. 1975) indicated unspecified material in LINN as type, this is not accepted as an effective typification (Art. 7.11). See Cafferty & al. (in *Taxon* 49: 240. 2000) for a detailed explanation.

Panicum patens Linnaeus, *Species Plantarum* 1: 58. 1753.
"Habitat in India; similis e Lusitania." RCN: 505.
Lectotype (Mitra & Jain in Manilal, *Bot. Hist. Hort. Malab.*: 151. 1980): Herb. Linn. No. 80.63 (LINN).
Current name: ***Cyrtococcum patens*** (L.) A. Camus (Poaceae).

Panicum polystachion Linnaeus, *Systema Naturae*, ed. 10, 2: 870. 1759.
["Habitat in India."] Sp. Pl., ed. 2, 1: 82 (1762). RCN: 474.
Lectotype (van der Zon in *Wageningen Agric. Univ. Pap.* 92–1: 335. 1992): Herb. Linn. No. 80.4 (LINN).
Current name: ***Pennisetum polystachion*** (L.) Schult. (Poaceae).
Note: There appear to be difficulties with this name. It has traditionally been applied, as *Pennisetum polystachion* (L.) Schult., to a widespread weedy species of which several specimens are present in LINN. However, Merrill (*Interpret. Rumph. Herb. Amb.*: 91. 1917) clearly accepts the Rumphius plate as the type of this name (which he treats as a synonym of *Setaria flava* (Nees) Kunth, an entirely different species). A number of authors have indicated material in LINN as the type but most failed to distinguish between sheets 80.4, 80.5 and 80.6. Van der Zon (in *Wageningen Agric. Univ. Pap.* 92–1: 335. 1992) treated 80.4 as the type but his choice is clearly pre-dated by that of Merrill. As the Linnaean epithet is pre-occupied in *Setaria* by *S. polystachion* Schrad. ex Schult. (1824), Merrill's typification does not result in the displacement of any name in use in that genus. However, if the traditional usage of the Linnaean name as a species of *Pennisetum* is to be maintained, it appears that a conservation proposal will be necessary.

Panicum ramosum Linnaeus, *Systema Naturae*, ed. 12, 2: 88; *Mantissa Plantarum*: 29. 1767.
"Habitat in Indiis." RCN: 494.
Lectotype (Cope in Nasir & Ali, *Fl. Pakistan* 143: 207. 1982): Herb. Linn. No. 80.44 (LINN).
Current name: ***Brachiaria ramosa*** (L.) Stapf (Poaceae).
Note: The typification of this name is attributable to Cope (June 1982), who published it some months ahead of Clayton & Renvoize (in Polhill, *Fl. Trop. E. Africa, Gramineae* 3: 599. 5 November 1982).

Panicum repens Linnaeus, *Species Plantarum*, ed. 2, 1: 87. 1762.
"Habitat in Hispania? inde missum a Claud. Alstroemer." RCN: 496.
Lectotype (Hitchcock & Chase in *Contr. U. S. Natl. Herb.* 15: 85. 1910): *Alströmer 2a*, Herb. Linn. No. 80.47 (LINN).
Current name: ***Panicum repens*** L. (Poaceae).

Panicum reptans Linnaeus, *Systema Naturae*, ed. 10, 2: 870. 1759. RCN: 486.
Lectotype (Hitchcock & Chase in *Contr. U. S. Natl. Herb.* 15: 36. 1910; Veldkamp in *Blumea* 41: 427. 1996): *Browne*, Herb. Linn. No. 80.52, upper specimen (LINN).
Current name: ***Brachiaria reptans*** (L.) C.A. Gardner & C.E. Hubb. (Poaceae).
Note: Veldkamp (in *Blumea* 41: 429. 1996) followed Hitchcock (in *Contr. U. S. Natl. Herb.* 12: 119. 1908) in regarding this and *P. reptans* L. (1759) as homotypic. However, the first clear type choice dates from Hitchcock & Chase (in *Contr. U. S. Natl. Herb.* 15: 36. 1910), later restricted to the upper specimen on the sheet by Veldkamp.

Panicum sanguinale Linnaeus, *Species Plantarum* 1: 57. 1753.
"Habitat in America, Europa australi." RCN: 487.
Lectotype (Henrard, *Monogr. Digitaria*: 649. 1950): Herb. Linn. No. 80.31 (LINN).
Current name: ***Digitaria sanguinalis*** (L.) Scop. (Poaceae).

Panicum verticillatum Linnaeus, *Species Plantarum*, ed. 2, 1: 82. 1762.
"Habitat in Europa australi & Oriente." RCN: 475.
Lectotype (Sherif & Siddiqi in El-Gadi, *Fl. Libya* 145: 296. 1988): Herb. Linn. No. 80.7 (LINN).
Current name: ***Setaria verticillata*** (L.) P. Beauv. (Poaceae).
Note: Although Kerguélen (in *Lejeunia*, n.s., 75: 260. 1975) stated "Type: ...LINN", this is not accepted as a formal typification, for the reasons explained by Cafferty & al. (in *Taxon* 49: 240. 2000). Cope (in Nasir & Ali, *Fl. Pakistan* 143: 207. 1982) stated that the type was based on a Scheuchzer account but as this is not accompanied by an illustration, it cannot be a type. Meikle (*Fl. Cyprus* 2: 1861. 1985) indicated unspecified material in LINN as type but failed to distinguish between sheets 80.7 and 80.13. As they are evidently not part of a single gathering, Art. 9.15 does not apply. Sherif & Siddiqi's type choice therefore appears to be the earliest.

Panicum virgatum Linnaeus, *Species Plantarum* 1: 59. 1753.
"Habitat in Virginia." RCN: 504.
Lectotype (Hitchcock in *Contr. U. S. Natl. Herb.* 12: 118. 1908): *Clayton 578*, Herb. Linn. No. 80.61 (LINN; iso- US, fragm.).
Current name: ***Panicum virgatum*** L. (Poaceae).

Panicum viride Linnaeus, *Systema Naturae*, ed. 10, 2: 870. 1759.
["Habitat in Europa australi."] Sp. Pl., ed. 2, 1: 83 (1762). RCN: 477.
Lectotype (Meikle, *Fl. Cyprus* 2: 1861. 1985): *Browne*, Herb. Linn. No. 80.12 (LINN).
Current name: ***Setaria viridis*** (L.) P. Beauv. (Poaceae).
Note: Although Kerguélen (in *Lejeunia*, n.s., 75: 260. 1975) stated "Type: ...LINN", this is not accepted as a formal typification, for the reasons explained by Cafferty & al. (in *Taxon* 49: 240. 2000).

Panicum vulpinum Linnaeus, *Amoenitates Academicae* 4: 134. 1759.
Lectotype (Merrill, *Interpret. Rumph. Herb. Amb.*: 91. 1917): [icon] "*Gramen caricosum*" in Rumphius, Herb. Amboin. 6: 17, t. 7, f. 2 B. 1750. – Epitype (Veldkamp in Cafferty & al. in *Taxon* 49: 253. 2000): Indonesia. Amboina, Jul–Nov 1913, Robinson, Pl. Rumphianae Amboinensis No. 41 (L; iso- BM).
Current name: ***Setaria parviflora*** (Poir.) Kerguélen (Poaceae).

Papaver alpinum Linnaeus, *Species Plantarum* 1: 507. 1753.
"Habitat in Helvetia, Sneeburg Austriae." RCN: 3841.
Lectotype (Markgraf in *Taxon* 12: 145. 1963): Herb. Burser IX: 58 (UPS; iso- BAU?).
Current name: ***Papaver alpinum*** L. (Papaveraceae).

Papaver argemone Linnaeus, *Species Plantarum* 1: 506. 1753.
"Habitat in Europae campis arenosis." RCN: 3840.
Lectotype (Jonsell & Jarvis in *Nordic J. Bot.* 14: 162. 1994): Herb. Linn. No. 669.2 (LINN).
Current name: ***Papaver argemone*** L. subsp. ***argemone*** (Papaveraceae).

Papaver cambricum Linnaeus, *Species Plantarum* 1: 508. 1753.
"Habitat in Cambriae septentrionalis nemorosis." RCN: 3846.
Type not designated.

Original material: Herb. Clifford: 201, *Papaver* 4 (BM); Herb. Linn. No. 669.9 (LINN); Herb. Burser IX: 45, syntype (UPS); [icon] in Dillenius, Hort. Eltham. 2: 300, t. 223, f. 290. 1732; [icon] in Morison, Pl. Hist. Univ. 2: 279, s. 3, t. 14, f. 12. 1680.
Current name: ***Meconopsis cambrica*** (L.) Vig. (Papaveraceae).

Papaver dubium Linnaeus, *Species Plantarum* 2: 1196. 1753.
"Habitat inter Sueciae, Angliae segetes." RCN: 3844.
Lectotype (Jafri & Qaiser in Nasir & Ali, *Fl. W. Pakistan* 61: 15. 1974): Herb. Linn. No. 669.7 (LINN).
Current name: ***Papaver dubium*** L. subsp. ***dubium*** (Papaveraceae).

Papaver hybridum Linnaeus, *Species Plantarum* 1: 506. 1753.
"Habitat in Europa australiore." RCN: 3839.
Type not designated.
Original material: Herb. Burser IX: 56 (UPS); [icon] in Morison, Pl. Hist. Univ. 2: 278, s. 3, t. 14, f. 9. 1680; [icon] in Plantin, Pl. Stirp. Icon.: 276. 1581.
Current name: ***Papaver hybridum*** L. (Papaveraceae).
Note: Jafri & Qaiser (in Nasir & Ali, *Fl. W. Pakistan* 61: 10. 1974) indicated 669.1 (LINN) as the type but this collection lacks the relevant *Species Plantarum* number (i.e. "1") and was a post-1753 addition to the herbarium, and is not original material for the name.

Papaver medium Linnaeus, *Flora Anglica*: 17. 1754.
"Habitat [in Anglia.]"
Type not designated.
Original material: [icon] in Morison, Pl. Hist. Univ. 2: 279, s. 3, t. 14, f. 11. 1680.
Current name: ***Papaver dubium*** L. (Papaveraceae).
Note: See notes by Stearn (*Introd. Ray's Syn. Meth. Stirp. Brit.* (Ray Soc. ed.): 67. 1973).

Papaver nudicaule Linnaeus, *Species Plantarum* 1: 507. 1753.
"Habitat in Sibiria." RCN: 3842.
Lectotype (Hanelt in *Kulturpflanze* 18: 80, Abb. 2. 1970): [icon] "*Papaver erraticum nudicaule, flore flavo, odorato*" in Dillenius, Hort. Eltham. 2: 302, t. 224, f. 291. 1732.
Current name: ***Papaver nudicaule*** L. (Papaveraceae).

Papaver orientale Linnaeus, *Species Plantarum* 1: 508. 1753.
"Habitat in Oriente." RCN: 3847.
Lectotype (Goldblatt in *Ann. Missouri Bot. Gard.* 61: 288. 1974): Herb. Linn. No. 669.10 (LINN) see above, right.
Current name: ***Papaver orientale*** L. (Papaveraceae).
Note: Wijnands (*Bot. Commelins*: 160. 1983) incorrectly attributed typification using a Tournefort collection to Cullen (in Davis, *Fl. Turkey* 1: 221. 1965), where it is unclear if a specimen is intended. A Tournefort collection would in any case not have been studied by Linnaeus and would not be original material for the name.

Papaver rhoeas Linnaeus, *Species Plantarum* 1: 507. 1753.
"Habitat in Europae arvis, agris." RCN: 3843.
Lectotype (Jonsell & Jarvis in *Nordic J. Bot.* 14: 162. 1994): Herb. Linn. No. 669.6 (LINN).
Current name: ***Papaver rhoeas*** L. (Papaveraceae).

Papaver somniferum Linnaeus, *Species Plantarum* 1: 508. 1753.
"Habitat in Europae australioris ruderatis." RCN: 3845.
Lectotype (Jafri & Qaiser in Nasir & Ali, *Fl. W. Pakistan* 61: 20. 1974): Herb. Linn. No. 669.8 (LINN).
Generitype of *Papaver* Linnaeus (vide Green, *Prop. Brit. Bot.*: 160. 1929).
Current name: ***Papaver somniferum*** L. (Papaveraceae).

The lectotype of *Papaver orientale* L.

Parietaria cretica Linnaeus, *Species Plantarum* 2: 1052. 1753.
"Habitat in Creta." RCN: 7609.
Neotype (Townsend in Davis, *Fl. Turkey* 7: 638. 1982): Herb. Tournefort, "Parietaria cretica minor, capsulis seminum alatis, Tournefort" (P-TOURN).
Current name: ***Parietaria cretica*** L. (Urticaceae).
Note: In the absence of any original material, Townsend's treatment of a Tournefort collection as the holotype is corrected to a neotype in accordance with Art. 9.8.

Parietaria indica Linnaeus, *Systema Naturae*, ed. 12, 2: 672; *Mantissa Plantarum*: 128. 1767.
"Habitat in India." RCN: 7605.
Lectotype (Wilmot-Dear & Friis in *Opera Bot.* 129: 93. 1996): Herb. Linn. No. 1220.1 (LINN).
Current name: ***Pouzolzia zeylanica*** (L.) Benn. subsp. ***zeylanica*** (Urticaceae).

Parietaria judaica Linnaeus, *Flora Palaestina*: 32. 1756.
"Habitat [in Palaestina.]" RCN: 7607.
Lectotype (Townsend in *Watsonia* 6: 366. 1968): *Hasselquist*, Herb. Linn. No. 1220.3 (LINN; iso- UPS-HASSELQ 790, 791).
Current name: ***Parietaria judaica*** L. (Urticaceae).

P

Parietaria lusitanica Linnaeus, *Species Plantarum* 2: 1052. 1753.
"Habitat in Lusitanica, Hispania." RCN: 7608.
Lectotype (Monro in Monro & Spencer in *Taxon* 54: 796. 2005):
[icon] *"Parietaria Alsines folio, Sicula"* in Boccone, Icon. Descr. Rar.
Pl. Siciliae: 47, t. 24 B. 1674. – Epitype (Monro in Monro &
Spencer in *Taxon* 54: 796. 2005): Italy. Flora aetnensis. In saxosis
vulcanicis prope Catanum, 21–26 Mar 1874, *Strobl s.n.* (BM).
Current name: ***Parietaria lusitanica*** L. (Urticaceae).

Parietaria microphylla Linnaeus, *Systema Naturae*, ed. 10, 2: 1308.
1759.
["Habitat in Jamaica."] Sp. Pl., ed. 2, 2: 1492 (1763). RCN: 7611.
Lectotype (de Rooij in Lanjouw & Stoffers, *Fl. Suriname* 5(1): 314.
1975): Herb. Linn. No. 1220.8 (LINN).
Current name: ***Pilea microphylla*** (L.) Liebm. (Urticaceae).
Note: Although Fawcett & Rendle (*Fl. Jamaica* 3: 63. 1914) indicated
material in BM as type, they did not specify what this was (though
probably material in Herb. Sloane, unseen by Linnaeus and not
original material for the name).

Parietaria officinalis Linnaeus, *Species Plantarum* 2: 1052. 1753.
"Habitat in Europae temperatioris ruderatis." RCN: 7606.
Lectotype (Paclt in *Phyton (Horn)* 4: 48, f. 1 (left). 1952): Herb.
Clifford: 469, *Parietaria* 1, sheet A (BM-000647535).
Generitype of *Parietaria* Linnaeus (vide Green, *Prop. Brit. Bot.*: 193.
1929).
Current name: ***Parietaria officinalis*** L. (Urticaceae).
Note: Townsend (in *Watsonia* 6: 365–370. 1968) rejected Paclt's
designation in favour of 1220.2 (LINN), arguing that Linnaeus did
not have Clifford's herbarium available to him when writing *Species
Plantarum* and that the description was arguably based on the
LINN sheet. However, the Clifford material is clearly original
material for the name, despite the probable role of the LINN
specimen; Paclt's choice has priority and is accepted here with his
use of "holotype" treated as a correctable error under Art. 9.8.

Parietaria officinarum Linnaeus, *Flora Anglica*: 25. 1754, *orth. var.*
"Habitat [in Anglia.]"
Lectotype (Paclt in *Phyton (Horn)* 4: 48, f. 1 (left). 1952): Herb.
Clifford: 469, *Parietaria* 1, sheet A (BM).
Current name: ***Parietaria officinalis*** L. (Urticaceae).
Note: As noted by Stearn (*Introd. Ray's Syn. Meth. Stirp. Brit.* (Ray Soc.
ed.): 68. 1973), this is an orthographic variant of *P. officinalis* L.
(1753).

Parietaria zeylanica Linnaeus, *Species Plantarum* 2: 1052. 1753.
"Habitat in Zeylona." RCN: 7135.
Replaced synonym of: *Urtica alienata* L. (1767), *nom. illeg.*
Lectotype (Wadhwa in Dassanayake & Clayton, *Revised Handb. Fl.
Ceylon* 13: 269. 1999): Herb. Hermann 3: 5, No. 371 (BM-
000621805).
Current name: ***Pouzolzia zeylanica*** (L.) Benn. (Urticaceae).
Note: Bhopal & Chaudhri (in *Pakistan Syst.* 1(2): 48. 1977) indicated
unspecified material in LINN as the holotype but there is no
material there that can be associated with this name.

Paris quadrifolia Linnaeus, *Species Plantarum* 1: 367. 1753.
"Habitat in Europae nemoribus." RCN: 2906.
Lectotype (Mathew in Jarvis & al., *Regnum Veg.* 127: 73. 1993): Herb.
Burser IX: 9 (UPS).
Generitype of *Paris* Linnaeus.
Current name: ***Paris quadrifolia*** L. (Liliaceae/Trilliaceae).

Parkinsonia aculeata Linnaeus, *Species Plantarum* 1: 375. 1753.
"Habitat in America calidiore." RCN: 2956.

Lectotype (Stearn, *Introd. Linnaeus' Sp. Pl.* (Ray Soc. ed.): 47. 1957):
[icon] *"Parkinsonia"* in Linnaeus, Hort. Cliff.: 157, t. 13. 1738.
Generitype of *Parkinsonia* Linnaeus.
Current name: ***Parkinsonia aculeata*** L. (Fabaceae: Caesalpinioideae).

Parnassia palustris Linnaeus, *Species Plantarum* 1: 273. 1753.
"Habitat in Europae uliginosis." RCN: 2174.
Lectotype (Hultgård in *Symb. Bot. Upsal.* 28(1): 111. 1987): Herb.
Burser XVII: 91 (UPS).
Generitype of *Parnassia* Linnaeus.
Current name: ***Parnassia palustris*** L. (Parnassiaceae).

Parthenium hysterophorus Linnaeus, *Species Plantarum* 2: 988.
1753.
"Habitat in Jamaicae glareosis." RCN: 7161.
Lectotype (Stuessy in Woodson & Schery in *Ann. Missouri Bot. Gard.*
62: 1094. 1975): Herb. Linn. No. 1115.1 (LINN).
Generitype of *Parthenium* Linnaeus (vide Green, *Prop. Brit. Bot.*: 188.
1929).
Current name: ***Parthenium hysterophorus*** L. (Asteraceae).
Note: Although Stuessy incorrectly described the Linnaean sheet as the
holotype, this is treated as correctable under Art. 9.8.

Parthenium integrifolium Linnaeus, *Species Plantarum* 2: 988.
1753.
"Habitat in Virginia." RCN: 7162.
Lectotype (Mears in *Phytologia* 31: 465. 1975): Herb. Linn. No.
1115.2 (LINN).
Current name: ***Parthenium integrifolium*** L. (Asteraceae).
Note: Mears stated "HOLOTYPE: Maryland (or Virginia), Clayton
(LINN!)". Although there is no evidence that the material in LINN
came from Clayton, Mears' indication of LINN is clear, and there is
only one sheet there associated with this name.

Paspalum dimidiatum Linnaeus, *Systema Naturae*, ed. 10, 2: 855.
1759, *nom. illeg.*
["Habitat in Indiis."] Sp. Pl. 1: 53 (1753). RCN: 467.
Replaced synonym: *Panicum dissectum* L. (1753).
Lectotype (Hitchcock in *Contr. U. S. Natl. Herb.* 12: 116. 1908):
Kalm, Herb. Linn. No. 79.1 (LINN).
Generitype of *Paspalum* Linnaeus (vide Nash, *N. Amer. Fl.* 17: 165.
1912).
Current name: ***Paspalum dissectum*** (L.) L. (Poaceae).
Note: An illegitimate name for *Panicum dissectum* L. (1753).

Paspalum dissectum (Linnaeus) Linnaeus, *Species Plantarum*, ed. 2, 1:
81. 1762.
"Habitat in America calidiore." RCN: 467.
Basionym: *Panicum dissectum* L. (1753).
Lectotype (Hitchcock in *Contr. U. S. Natl. Herb.* 12: 116. 1908):
Kalm, Herb. Linn. No. 79.1 (LINN).
Current name: ***Paspalum dissectum*** (L.) L. (Poaceae).

Paspalum distichum Linnaeus, *Systema Naturae*, ed. 10, 2: 855.
1759.
["Habitat in Jamaica."] Sp. Pl., ed. 2, 1: 82 (1762). RCN: 471.
Lectotype (Guédès in *Taxon* 25: 513. 1976): Herb. Linn. No. 79.9,
second specimen from the left (LINN).
Current name: ***Paspalum distichum*** L. (Poaceae).
Note: Renvoize & Clayton (in *Taxon* 29: 339–340. 1980) proposed
the name for rejection as a *nomen confusum*. However, the
Committee for Spermatophyta (in *Taxon* 32: 281. 1983) declined
to support rejection, and the name is therefore in use in the sense of
the typification made by Guédès. De Koning & Sosef (in *Blumea*
30: 296. 1985) provide a summary.

Paspalum paniculatum Linnaeus, *Systema Naturae*, ed. 10, 2: 855. 1759.
["Habitat in Jamaica."] Sp. Pl., ed. 2, 1: 81 (1762). RCN: 470.
Lectotype (Chase in *Contr. U. S. Natl. Herb.* 28: 122. 1929): Herb. Linn. No. 79.7 (LINN).
Current name: ***Paspalum paniculatum*** L. (Poaceae).

Paspalum scrobiculatum Linnaeus, *Systema Naturae*, ed. 12, 2: 86; *Mantissa Plantarum*: 29. 1767.
"Habitat in India orientali." RCN: 468.
Lectotype (Clayton in *Kew Bull.* 30: 101. 1975): Herb. Linn. No. 79.4 (LINN).
Current name: ***Paspalum scrobiculatum*** L. (Poaceae).

Paspalum virgatum Linnaeus, *Systema Naturae*, ed. 10, 2: 855. 1759.
["Habitat in Jamaica."] Sp. Pl., ed. 2, 1: 81 (1762). RCN: 469.
Lectotype (Hitchcock in *Contr. U. S. Natl. Herb.* 12: 116. 1908): *Browne*, Herb. Linn. No. 79.6 (LINN).
Current name: ***Paspalum virgatum*** L. (Poaceae).
Note: Baum (in *Canad. J. Bot.* 45: 1846. 1967) disagreed with Hitchcock's choice of a Browne collection as type, arguing that Linnaeus' name was instead based on a cited Sloane illustration. However, the Browne collection is clearly original material for this name, and Hitchcock's 1908 type choice has priority.

Passerina capitata Linnaeus, *Plantae Rariores Africanae*: 11. 1760.
["Habitat ad Cap. b. spei."] Sp. Pl., ed. 2, 1: 514 (1762). RCN: 2842.
Lectotype (Beyers in *Strelitzia* 11: 66. 2001): [icon] *"Thymelaea foliis linearibus alternis, floribus ex uno petiolo copiosis"* in Burman, Rar. Afric. Pl.: 133, t. 48, f. 3. 1739.
Current name: ***Lachnaea capitata*** (L.) Crantz (Thymelaeaceae).

Passerina ciliata Linnaeus, *Species Plantarum* 1: 559. 1753.
"Habitat in Aethiopia, Hispania." RCN: 2843.
Lectotype (Rogers in Rogers & Spencer in *Taxon* 55: 486. 2006): Herb. Clifford: 146, *Passerina* 2, specimen on left of sheet (BM).
Current name: ***Struthiola ciliata*** (L.) Lam. (Thymelaeaceae).

Passerina dodecandra Linnaeus, *Centuria I Plantarum*: 10. 1755.
"Habitat in Aethiopia. D. Gronovius." RCN: 1002.
Replaced synonym of: *Struthiola erecta* L. (1767), *nom. illeg.*
Neotype (Rogers in Rogers & Spencer in *Taxon* 55: 487. 2006): South Africa. Western Cape Province, Caledon District, Cape Hangklip, near the hotel, 50m, 1 Oct 1956, *R. Dahlgren & B. Peterson 526* (MO-5033766).
Current name: ***Struthiola dodecandra*** (L.) Druce (Thymelaeaceae).

Passerina ericoides Linnaeus, *Systema Naturae*, ed. 12, 2: 733. 1767.
"Habitat ad Cap. b. spei." RCN: 2841.
Lectotype (Thoday in *Bull. Misc. Inform. Kew* 1924: 388. 1924): Herb. Linn. No. 504.5 (LINN).
Current name: ***Passerina ericoides*** L. (Thymelaeaceae).

Passerina filiformis Linnaeus, *Species Plantarum* 1: 559. 1753.
"Habitat in Aethiopia." RCN: 2839.
Lectotype (Stearn, *Introd. Linnaeus' Sp. Pl.* (Ray Soc. ed.): 47. 1957): [icon] *"Passerina foliis linearibus"* in Linnaeus, Hort. Cliff.: 146, t. 11. 1738. – Voucher: Herb. Clifford: 146, *Passerina* 1 (BM).
Generitype of *Passerina* Linnaeus (vide Meyer in *Bull. Cl. Phys.-Math. Acad. Imp. Sci. St.-Pétersbourg* 1: 357. 1843).
Current name: ***Passerina filiformis*** L. (Thymelaeaceae).
Note: Thoday (in *Bull. Misc. Inform. Kew* 1924: 148. 1924) apparently regarded 504.1 (LINN) as the type, one of the two sheets bearing Dutch paper urns which he therefore assumed to be from Clifford's herbarium, and hence either in Linnaeus' possession in 1753, or

seen by him previously. However, the urn of 504.1 is not of a type commonly seen in Clifford's herbarium and, together with the absence of the *Species Plantarum* number (i.e. "1"), suggests this was not in his hands in 1753. Stearn subsequently came to the conclusion that the name should be typified by the Clifford plate, which is accepted here. Bredenkamp & Van Wyk (in *Bothalia* 32: 29. 2002; 33: 85. 2003) apparently overlooked this earlier choice, designating 504.1 (LINN) as lectotype. They suggest (*l.c.*, 32: 31) that the Clifford illustration is identifiable as *P. filiformis* subsp. *glutinosa* (Thoday) Bredenk. & A.E. van Wyk, which will cause disruption at subspecific rank if Stearn's type choice is upheld.

Passerina hirsuta Linnaeus, *Species Plantarum* 1: 559. 1753.
"Habitat in Hispania." RCN: 2840.
Lectotype (Rogers in Rogers & Spencer in *Taxon* 55: 487. 2006): Herb. Burser XXIV: 44 (UPS).
Current name: ***Thymelaea hirsuta*** (L.) Endl. (Thymelaeaceae).

Passerina laevigata Linnaeus, *Centuria II Plantarum*: 15. 1756.
"Habitat in Aethiopia." RCN: 2836.
Lectotype (Rogers in Rogers & Spencer in *Taxon* 55: 487. 2006): Herb. Linn. No. 502.9 (LINN).
Current name: ***Gnidia oppositifolia*** L. (Thymelaeaceae).

Passerina sericea Linnaeus, *Centuria II Plantarum*: 15. 1756.
"Habitat in Aethiopia. Burmannus." RCN: 2835.
Basionym of: *Gnidia sericea* (L.) L. (1767).
Lectotype (Rogers in Rogers & Spencer in *Taxon* 55: 487. 2006): *"Passerina (sericea) foliis ovatis tomentosis, caule hirsuto, floribus coronatis..."*, Herb. Burman (G).
Current name: ***Gnidia sericea*** (L.) L. (Thymelaeaceae).

Passerina uniflora Linnaeus, *Species Plantarum* 1: 560. 1753.
"Habitat in Aethiopia." RCN: 2844.
Lectotype (Beyers in *Strelitzia* 11: 43. 2001): [icon] *"Thymelaea ramosa, linearibus foliis angustis, flore solitario"* in Burman, Rar. Afric. Pl.: 131, t. 48, f. 1. 1739.
Current name: ***Lachnaea uniflora*** (L.) Crantz (Thymelaeaceae).

Passiflora caerulea Linnaeus, *Species Plantarum* 2: 959. 1753.
"Habitat in Brasilia." RCN: 6941.
Lectotype (Killip in *Publ. Field Mus. Nat. Hist., Bot. Ser.* 19: 424. 1938): Herb. Linn. No. 1070.26 (LINN), see p. 45.
Current name: ***Passiflora caerulea*** L. (Passifloraceae).

Passiflora capsularis Linnaeus, *Species Plantarum* 2: 957. 1753.
"Habitat in Gallia aequinoctiali." RCN: 6931.
Type not designated.
Original material: [icon] in Plumier in Burman, Pl. Amer.: 129, t. 138, f. 2. 1757; [icon] in Barrelier, Pl. Galliam: title page, f. 1. 1714.
Current name: ***Passiflora capsularis*** L. (Passifloraceae).
Note: Killip (in *Publ. Field Mus. Nat. Hist., Bot. Ser.* 19: 217. 1938) noted that this was based on a cited Plumier reference (which it is, in part) while Deginani (in *Darwiniana* 39: 66. 2001) indicated unspecified, unseen material in LINN as the holotype. However, there is no material associated with this name now in LINN.

Passiflora cupraea Linnaeus, *Species Plantarum* 2: 955. 1753.
"Habitat in Providentia, Bahama." RCN: 6920.
Type not designated.
Original material: [icon] in Dillenius, Hort. Eltham. 1: 165, t. 138, f. 165. 1732; [icon] in Linnaeus, Amoen. Acad. 1: 219, t. 10, f. 3. 1749; [icon] in Catesby, Nat. Hist. Carolina 2: 93, t. 93. 1743 (see p. 117); [icon] in Martyn, Hist. Pl. Rar.: 37, t. 37. 1728.

P

Current name: ***Passiflora cupraea*** L. (Passifloraceae).
Note: Although Howard & Staples (in *J. Arnold Arbor.* 64: 534. 1983) attributed the typification of this name to Ewan, this is erroneous.

Passiflora digitata Linnaeus, *Species Plantarum*, ed. 2, 2: 1360. 1763, *nom. illeg.*
"Habitat in Martinica." RCN: 6942.
Replaced synonym: *Passiflora serratodigitata* L. (1753).
Type not designated.
Original material: as replaced synonym.
Current name: ***Passiflora serratodigitata*** L. (Passifloraceae).
Note: A superfluous name for *P. serratodigitata* L. (1753).

Passiflora divaricata Linnaeus, *Mantissa Plantarum Altera*: 491. 1771.
RCN: 6926.
Type not designated.
Original material: none traced.
Current name: ***Passiflora perfoliata*** L. (Passifloraceae).

Passiflora foetida Linnaeus, *Species Plantarum* 2: 959. 1753.
"Habitat in Dominica, Martinicana, Curassao." RCN: 6939.
Lectotype (Killip in *Publ. Field Mus. Nat. Hist., Bot. Ser.* 19: 481. 1938): Herb. Linn. No. 1070.24 (LINN).
Current name: ***Passiflora foetida*** L. (Passifloraceae).

Passiflora hirsuta Linnaeus, *Species Plantarum* 2: 958. 1753.
"Habitat in Dominica, Curassao." RCN: 6938.
Type not designated.
Original material: [icon] in Hermann, Parad. Bat.: 176. 1698; [icon] in Linnaeus, Amoen. Acad. 1: 227, t. 10, f. 16. 1749; [icon] in Plumier, Descr. Pl. Amér.: 73, t. 88. 1693; [icon] in Plukenet, Phytographia: t. 212, f. 1. 1692; Almag. Bot.: 282. 1696.
Current name: ***Passiflora suberosa*** L. (Passifloraceae).

Passiflora holosericea Linnaeus, *Species Plantarum* 2: 958. 1753.
"Habitat in Vera Cruce." RCN: 6937.
Type not designated.
Original material: [icon] in Linnaeus, Amoen. Acad. 1: 226, t. 10, f. 15. 1749; [icon] in Martyn, Hist. Pl. Rar.: 51, t. 51. 1728.
Current name: ***Passiflora holosericea*** L. (Passifloraceae).
Note: See comments by Killip (in *Publ. Field Mus. Nat. Hist., Bot. Ser.* 19: 101. 1938) who, however, did not formally typify the name.

Passiflora incarnata Linnaeus, *Species Plantarum* 2: 959. 1753, *typ. cons.*
"Habitat in Virginia, Brasilia, Peru." RCN: 6940.
Conserved type (Killip in *Publ. Field Mus. Nat. Hist., Bot. Ser.* 19: 390. 1938): Herb. Linn. No. 1070.25 (LINN).
Generitype of *Passiflora* Linnaeus, *nom. cons.*
Current name: ***Passiflora incarnata*** L. (Passifloraceae).
Note: Passiflora incarnata, with the type designated by Killip, was proposed as conserved type of the genus by Jarvis (in *Taxon* 41: 567. 1992). This was eventually approved by the General Committee (see review of the history of this proposal by Barrie, *l.c.* 55: 795–796. 2006).

Passiflora laurifolia Linnaeus, *Species Plantarum* 2: 956. 1753.
"Habitat in Surinamo." RCN: 6924.
Lectotype (Cusset in Aubréville, *Fl. Cambodge Laos Vietnam* 5: 119. 1967): [icon] *"Marquiaas"* in Merian, Metamorph. Insect. Surinam.: 21, t. 21. 1705 (see p. 7).
Current name: ***Passiflora laurifolia*** L. (Passifloraceae).

Passiflora lutea Linnaeus, *Species Plantarum* 2: 958. 1753.
"Habitat in Virginiae, Jamaicae glareosis, saxosis." RCN: 6934.
Lectotype (Killip in *Publ. Field Mus. Nat. Hist., Bot. Ser.* 19: 136. 1938): Herb. Linn. No. 1070.19 (LINN).
Current name: ***Passiflora lutea*** L. (Passifloraceae).

Passiflora maliformis Linnaeus, *Species Plantarum* 2: 956. 1753.
"Habitat in Dominica & de la Tortue." RCN: 6922.
Type not designated.
Original material: [icon] in Linnaeus, Amoen. Acad. 1: 220, t. 10, f. 5. 1749; [icon] in Plumier, Descr. Pl. Amér.: 67, t. 82. 1693.
Current name: ***Passiflora maliformis*** L. (Passifloraceae).

Passiflora minima Linnaeus, *Species Plantarum* 2: 959. 1753.
"Habitat in Curassao." RCN: 6935.
Lectotype (Killip in *Publ. Field Mus. Nat. Hist., Bot. Ser.* 19: 93. 1938): Herb. Linn. No. 1070.20 (LINN).
Current name: ***Passiflora suberosa*** L. (Passifloraceae).

Passiflora multiflora Linnaeus, *Species Plantarum* 2: 956. 1753.
"Habitat in Dominica." RCN: 6925.
Type not designated.
Original material: [icon] in Linnaeus, Amoen. Acad. 1: 221, t. 10, f. 7. 1749; [icon] in Plumier, Descr. Pl. Amér.: 75, t. 90. 1693.
Current name: ***Passiflora multiflora*** L. (Passifloraceae).

Passiflora murucuja Linnaeus, *Species Plantarum* 2: 957. 1753.
"Habitat in Dominica." RCN: 6929.
Type not designated.
Original material: [icon] in Linnaeus, Amoen. Acad. 1: 223, t. 10, f. 10. 1749; [icon] in Plumier, Descr. Pl. Amér.: 72, t. 87. 1693.
Current name: ***Passiflora murucuja*** L. (Passifloraceae).
Note: Killip (in *Publ. Field Mus. Nat. Hist., Bot. Ser.* 19: 241. 1938) indicated 1070.11 (LINN) as the type, but this collection lacks the relevant *Species Plantarum* number (i.e. "10") and was a post-1753 addition to the herbarium, and is not original material for the name.

Passiflora normalis Linnaeus, *Systema Naturae,* ed. 10, 2: 1248. 1759.
["Habitat in America meridionali."] Sp. Pl., ed. 2, 2: 1357 (1763). RCN: 6928.
Lectotype (Fawcett & Rendle, *Fl. Jamaica* 5: 242. 1926): Herb. Linn. No. 1070.10 (LINN).
Current name: ***Passiflora perfoliata*** L. var. ***normalis*** (L.) Fawc. & Rendle (Passifloraceae).

Passiflora pallida Linnaeus, *Species Plantarum* 2: 955. 1753.
"Habitat in Dominica, Brasilia." RCN: 6919.
Type not designated.
Original material: [icon] in Morison, Pl. Hist. Univ. 2: 7, s. 1, t. 2, f. 4. 1680; [icon] in Linnaeus, Amoen. Acad. 1: 218, t. 10, f. 2. 1749; [icon] in Plumier, Descr. Pl. Amér.: 74, t. 89. 1693.
Current name: ***Passiflora suberosa*** L. (Passifloraceae).
Note: Holm-Nielsen & al. (in Harling & Andersson, *Fl. Ecuador* 31: 26. 1988) indicated unspecified (but presumably sheet 1070.2) material in LINN as lectotype. However, this collection lacks the relevant *Species Plantarum* number (i.e. "2") and was a post-1753 addition to the herbarium, and is not original material for the name.

Passiflora pedata Linnaeus, *Species Plantarum* 2: 960. 1753.
"Habitat in Dominica." RCN: 6943.
Type not designated.
Original material: [icon] in Linnaeus, Amoen. Acad. 1: 233, t. 10, f. 22. 1749; [icon] in Plumier, Descr. Pl. Amér.: 66, t. 81. 1693.
Current name: ***Passiflora pedata*** L. (Passifloraceae).

Passiflora perfoliata Linnaeus, *Species Plantarum* 2: 956. 1753.
"Habitat in Jamaicae sylvis saxosis." RCN: 6926.
Type not designated.
Original material: [icon] in Linnaeus, Amoen. Acad. 1: 222, t. 10, f. 8.
   1749; [icon] in Sloane, Voy. Jamaica 1: 230, t. 142, f. 3, 4. 1707.
Current name: ***Passiflora perfoliata*** L. (Passifloraceae).
Note: Killip (in *Publ. Field Mus. Nat. Hist., Bot. Ser.* 19: 243. 1938)
   indicated 1070.7 (LINN) as the type, but as this material was
   collected by Patrick Browne and was not received by Linnaeus until
   1758, it cannot be original material for the name.

Passiflora punctata Linnaeus, *Species Plantarum* 2: 957. 1753.
"Habitat in Peru." RCN: 6933.
Type not designated.
Original material: [icon] in Feuillée, J. Obs. 2: 718, t. 11. 1714; [icon]
   in Linnaeus, Amoen. Acad. 1: 224, t. 10, f. 12. 1749.
Current name: ***Passiflora punctata*** L. (Passifloraceae).
Note: Killip (in *Publ. Field Mus. Nat. Hist., Bot. Ser.* 19: 184. 1938)
   indicated that this name was "probably" based on Feuillée's account,
   and Holm-Nielsen & al. (in Harling & Andersson, *Fl. Ecuador* 31:
   43. 1988) indicated unspecified (but presumably sheet 1070.15)
   material in LINN as lectotype. However, this collection lacks the
   relevant *Species Plantarum* number (i.e. "14") and was a post-1753
   addition to the herbarium, and is not original material for the
   name.

Passiflora quadrangularis Linnaeus, *Systema Naturae*, ed. 10, 2:
   1248. 1759.
["Habitat in Jamaica."] Sp. Pl., ed. 2, 2: 1356 (1763). RCN: 6923.
Lectotype (Cervi in *Fontqueria* 45: 15. 1997): *Browne*, Herb. Linn.
   No. 373.15 (S).
Current name: ***Passiflora quadrangularis*** L. (Passifloraceae).
Note: Killip (in *Publ. Field Mus. Nat. Hist., Bot. Ser.* 19: 337. 1938)
   indicated a Browne specimen in LINN as type but the only material
   there associated with this name came later from Surinam, via
   Dahlberg, and is not original material for the name. Noting the
   absence of Browne material in LINN, de Wilde (in Polhill, *Fl. Trop.
   E. Africa, Passifloraceae*: 15. 1975) suggested that a holotype might
   possibly be sought in S, while Bornstein (in Howard, *Fl. Lesser
   Antilles* 5: 380. 1989) indicated Browne's cited description as the
   type. However, the latter is contrary to Art. 8.1.

Passiflora rotundifolia Linnaeus, *Species Plantarum* 2: 957. 1753.
"Habitat in America australiori." RCN: 6932.
Type not designated.
Original material: [icon] in Plumier in Burman, Pl. Amer.: 128, t.
   138, f. 1. 1757; [icon] in Barrelier, Pl. Galliam: title page, f. 2.
   1714.
Current name: ***Passiflora rotundifolia*** L. (Passifloraceae).

Passiflora rubra Linnaeus, *Species Plantarum* 2: 956. 1753.
"Habitat in Jamaica, Dominica, Martinica, Cayenne." RCN: 6927.
Type not designated.
Original material: [icon] in Plumier, Descr. Pl. Amér.: 68, t. 83. 1693.
Current name: ***Passiflora rubra*** L. (Passifloraceae).
Note: Killip (in *Publ. Field Mus. Nat. Hist., Bot. Ser.* 19: 219. 1938)
   indicated 1070.8 (LINN) as the type, but as this material was
   collected by Patrick Browne and was not received by Linnaeus until
   1758, it cannot be original material for the name.

Passiflora serrata Linnaeus, *Systema Naturae*, ed. 10, 2: 1248. 1759,
   nom. illeg.
["Habitat in Martinica."] Sp. Pl. 2: 960 (1753). RCN: 6942.
Replaced synonym: *Passiflora serratodigitata* L. (1753).
Type not designated.

Original material: as replaced synonym.
Current name: ***Passiflora serratodigitata*** L. (Passifloraceae).
Note: A superfluous name for *P. serratodigitata* L. (1753).

Passiflora serratifolia Linnaeus, *Species Plantarum* 2: 955. 1753.
"Habitat Surinami." RCN: 6918.
Type not designated.
Original material: Herb. Clifford: 431, *Passiflora* 1 (BM); [icon] in
   Martyn, Hist. Pl. Rar.: 36, t. 36. 1728; [icon] in Linnaeus, Amoen.
   Acad. 1: 217, t. 10, f. 1. 1749.
Current name: ***Passiflora serratifolia*** L. (Passifloraceae).
Note: Killip (in *Publ. Field Mus. Nat. Hist., Bot. Ser.* 19: 380. 1938)
   treated a Houstoun collection from Veracruz (BM) as the type,
   presumably by association with the cited account by Martyn, who
   described a plant raised by Miller at Chelsea from seeds sent to the
   latter by Houstoun. However, this material would not have been
   seen by Linnaeus and is not original material for the name.

Passiflora serratodigitata Linnaeus, *Species Plantarum* 2: 960. 1753.
"Habitat in Martinica." RCN: 6942.
Replaced synonym of: *Passiflora serrata* L. (1759), *nom. illeg.*; *Passiflora
   digitata* L. (1763), *nom. illeg.*
Type not designated.
Original material: [icon] in Plumier, Descr. Pl. Amér.: 62, t. 79. 1693;
   [icon] in Linnaeus, Amoen. Acad. 1: 232, t. 10, f. 21. 1749.
Current name: ***Passiflora serratodigitata*** L. (Passifloraceae).
Note: Feuillet & Cremers (*Proc. Kon. Ned. Akad. Wetensch. C*, 87: 385.
   1984) indicated Linnaeus' diagnosis as the type but this is contrary
   to Art. 8.1. Cervi (in *Fontqueria* 45: 20. 1997) stated "TYPUS:
   "Martinica" (P)", but this statement appears to have been derived
   purely from bibliographic sources and does not indicate any
   particular collection.

Passiflora suberosa Linnaeus, *Species Plantarum* 2: 958. 1753.
"Habitat in Dominica, Antillis." RCN: 6936.
Lectotype (Wijnands, *Bot. Commelins*: 171. 1983): Herb. Linn. No.
   1070.21 (LINN).
Current name: ***Passiflora suberosa*** L. (Passifloraceae).
Note: De Wilde (in Ross, *Fl. Southern Africa* 22: 126. 1976) indicated
   unspecified material in LINN as type but did not distinguish
   between sheets 1070.21 and 1070.22 (which are not part of a single
   gathering so Art. 9.15 does not apply).

Passiflora tiliifolia Linnaeus, *Species Plantarum* 2: 956. 1753.
"Habitat in Peru, Lima." RCN: 6921.
Type not designated.
Original material: [icon] in Linnaeus, Amoen. Acad. 1: 219, t. 10, f. 4.
   1749; [icon] in Feuillée, J. Obs. 2: 720, t. 12. 1714.
Current name: ***Passiflora tiliifolia*** L. (Passifloraceae).
Note: Specific epithet spelled "tiliaefolia" in the protologue.
      Killip (in *Publ. Field Mus. Nat. Hist., Bot. Ser.* 19: 351. 1938)
   suggested that Linnaeus knew this only from Feuillée's account, but
   did not designate a type.

Passiflora vesicaria Linnaeus, *Flora Jamaicensis*: 20. 1759.
"Habitat [in Jamaica.]"
Type not designated.
Original material: *Browne*, Herb. Linn. No. 375.1 (S).
Current name: ***Passiflora foetida*** L. (Passifloraceae).

Passiflora vespertilio Linnaeus, *Species Plantarum* 2: 957. 1753.
"Habitat in America." RCN: 6930.
Type not designated.
Original material: Herb. Linn. No. 1070.12 (LINN); Herb. Linn. No.
   374.1 (S); Herb. Clifford: 431, *Passiflora* 2 (BM); [icon] in

P

Linnaeus, Amoen. Acad. 1: 223, t. 10, f. 11. 1749; [icon] in Dillenius, Hort. Eltham. 1: 164, t. 137, f. 164. 1732.
Current name: ***Passiflora vespertilio*** L. (Passifloraceae).
Note: Killip (in *Publ. Field Mus. Nat. Hist., Bot. Ser.* 19: 158. 1938) appears to have interpreted this name via a Martyn reference which was not cited in the Linnaean protologue. Holm-Nielsen & al. (in Harling & Andersson, *Fl. Ecuador* 31: 44. 1988) indicated unspecified material in LINN as type, but failed to distinguish between sheets 1070.12 and 1070.13 (which are not part of a single gathering so Art. 9.15 does not apply).

Pastinaca lucida Linnaeus, *Systema Naturae,* ed. 12, 2: 216; *Mantissa Plantarum*: 58. 1767.
"Habitat in Europa australi." RCN: 2090.
Lectotype (Rosselló & Sáez in *Collect. Bot. (Barcelona)* 25: 15. 2000): Herb. Linn. No. 369.1 (LINN).
Current name: ***Pastinaca lucida*** L. (Apiaceae).

Pastinaca opopanax Linnaeus, *Species Plantarum* 1: 262. 1753.
"Habitat in Italia, Sicilia." RCN: 2092.
Lectotype (Reduron & Jarvis in Jarvis & al. in *Taxon* 55: 213, 560. 2006): Herb. Clifford: 105, *Pastinaca* 2, sheet A (BM-000558369).
Current name: ***Opopanax chironium*** W.D.J. Koch (Apiaceae).
Note: Reduron & Jarvis (in Jarvis & al. in *Taxon* 55: 213. 2006) designated Clifford material (BM) as the type, but failed to distinguish between three relevant sheets (which are evidently not part of a single gathering so Art. 9.15 does not apply). However, this omission was corrected (in *Taxon* 55: 560. 2006), from where the typification dates.

Pastinaca sativa Linnaeus, *Species Plantarum* 1: 262. 1753.
"Habitat in Europae australioris ruderatis & pascuis." RCN: 2091.
Lectotype (Sell in Jarvis & al., *Regnum Veg.* 127: 73. 1993): Herb. Clifford: 105, *Pastinaca* 1A (BM-000558367).
Generitype of *Pastinaca* Linnaeus (vide Hitchcock, *Prop. Brit. Bot.*: 141. 1929).
Current name: ***Pastinaca sativa*** L. (Apiaceae).

Patagonula americana Linnaeus, *Species Plantarum* 1: 149. 1753.
"Habitat in Patagonia Americes australi." RCN: 1527.
Lectotype (Miller in Jarvis & al., *Regnum Veg.* 127: 73. 1993): [icon] "*Patagonica foliis partim serratis, partim integris*" in Dillenius, Hort. Eltham. 2: 304, t. 226, f. 293. 1732.
Generitype of *Patagonula* Linnaeus.
Current name: ***Patagonula americana*** L. (Boraginaceae).

Paullinia asiatica Linnaeus, *Species Plantarum* 1: 365. 1753.
"Habitat in India." RCN: 2886.
Conserved type (Barrie & Nair in *Taxon* 40: 646. 1991): Herb. Hermann 3: 45. No. 143 (BM-000621969).
Current name: ***Toddalia asiatica*** (L.) Lam. (Rutaceae).

Paullinia curassavica Linnaeus, *Species Plantarum* 1: 366. 1753.
"Habitat in Curassao." RCN: 2893.
Type not designated.
Original material: Herb. Clifford: 152, *Paullinia* 5 (BM); Herb. Linn. No. 512.6 (LINN); [icon] in Plukenet, Phytographia: t. 168, f. 6. 1692; Almag. Bot.: 120. 1696; [icon] in Plumier in Burman, Pl. Amer.: 102, t. 111, f. 1. 1757.
Current name: ***Serjania curassavica*** (L.) Radlk. (Sapindaceae).

Paullinia cururu Linnaeus, *Species Plantarum* 1: 365. 1753.
"Habitat in America calidiore." RCN: 2889.
Type not designated.
Original material: [icon] in Plumier in Burman, Pl. Amer.: 102, t. 111, f. 2. 1757.
Current name: ***Paullinia cururu*** L. (Sapindaceae).
Note: Howard (in *Fl. Lesser Antilles* 5: 148. 1989) indicated the Clifford element as type, but there is no material in the Clifford herbarium (BM) associated with this name.

Paullinia mexicana Linnaeus, *Species Plantarum* 1: 366. 1753.
"Habitat in America calidiore." RCN: 2890.
Type not designated.
Original material: Herb. Clifford: 152, *Paullinia* 4 (BM); Herb. Linn. No. 512.3 (LINN); [icon] in Plumier in Burman, Pl. Amer.: 103, t. 113, f. 1. 1757; [icon] in Hernandez, Rer. Med. Nov. Hisp.: 289. 1651.
Current name: ***Serjania mexicana*** (L.) Willd. (Sapindaceae).
Note: Croat (in *Ann. Missouri Bot. Gard.* 63: 519. 1977) indicated either 512.3 or 512.4 (LINN) as type.

Paullinia pinnata Linnaeus, *Species Plantarum* 1: 365. 1753.
"Habitat in Brasilia, Jamaica, Domingo." RCN: 2897.
Lectotype (Davies in *Kew Bull.* 32: 430. 1978): [icon] "*Clematis pentaphylla, pediculis alatis, fructu racemoso, tricocco & coccineo*" in Plumier, Descr. Pl. Amér.: 76, t. 91. 1693.
Generitype of *Paullinia* Linnaeus (vide Hitchcock, *Prop. Brit. Bot.*: 151. 1929).
Current name: ***Paullinia pinnata*** L. (Sapindaceae).

Paullinia polyphylla Linnaeus, *Species Plantarum* 1: 366. 1753.
"Habitat in America calidiore." RCN: 2895.
Type not designated.
Original material: Herb. Clifford: 153, *Paullinia* 6 (BM); Herb. Linn. No. 512.7 (LINN); [icon] in Plumier in Burman, Pl. Amer.: 103, t. 112. 1757; [icon] in Plukenet, Phytographia: t. 168, f. 5. 1692; Almag. Bot.: 120. 1696.
Current name: ***Serjania polyphylla*** (L.) Radlk. (Sapindaceae).

Paullinia seriana Linnaeus, *Species Plantarum* 1: 365. 1753.
"Habitat in America calidiore." RCN: 2887.
Type not designated.
Original material: Herb. Clifford: 152, *Paullinia* 2 (BM); [icon] in Plumier in Burman, Pl. Amer.: 104, t. 113, f. 2. 1757.
Current name: ***Serjania sp.*** (Sapindaceae).
Note: The application of this name appears to be uncertain.

Pavetta indica Linnaeus, *Species Plantarum* 1: 110. 1753.
"Habitat in India." RCN: 901.
Lectotype (Nicolson & al., *Interpret. Van Rheede's Hort. Malab.*: 228. 1988): Herb. Hermann 1: 11, No. 56 (BM-000594442).
Generitype of *Pavetta* Linnaeus.
Current name: ***Pavetta indica*** L. (Rubiaceae).
Note: Van Oostroom (in *Blumea*, Suppl. 1: 194, f. 1. 1937) illustrates the type.

Pectis ciliaris Linnaeus, *Systema Naturae,* ed. 10, 2: 1221. 1759.
["Habitat in America."] Sp. Pl., ed. 2, 2: 1250 (1763). RCN: 6425.
Lectotype (Keil in *Taxon* 34: 284. 1985): *Browne*, Herb. Linn. No. 1011.1 (LINN).
Current name: ***Pectis ciliaris*** L. (Asteraceae).
Note: Although *P. ciliaris* was designated as generitype by Britton & Brown (*Ill. Fl. N. U. S.*, ed. 2, 3: 514. 1913), Keil (in *Taxon* 34: 283. 1985) argued that this choice conflicts with the generic description, and that *P. linifolia* is the generitype.

Pectis linifolia Linnaeus, *Systema Naturae,* ed. 10, 2: 1221. 1759.
["Habitat in America."] Sp. Pl., ed. 2, 2: 1250. 1763. RCN: 6427.

Lectotype (Keil in *Rhodora* 80: 139. 1978): *Browne*, Herb. Linn. No. 1011.2 (LINN).
Generitype of *Pectis* Linnaeus (vide Britton & Millspaugh, *Bahama Fl.*: 456. 1920).
Current name: ***Pectis linifolia*** L. (Asteraceae).
Note: Although *P. ciliaris* was designated as generitype by Britton & Brown (*Ill. Fl. N. U. S.*, ed. 2, 3: 514. 1913), Keil (in *Taxon* 34: 283. 1985) argued that this choice conflicts with the generic description, and that *P. linifolia* is the generitype. *Verbesina linifolia* L. (1759) was published simultaneously and evidently applies to the same taxon.

Pectis minuta Linnaeus, *Species Plantarum,* ed. 2, 2: 1250. 1763.
"Habitat in Creta & Oriente." RCN: 6416.
Basionym of: *Bellium minutum* (L.) L. (1771).
Lectotype (Turland in Jarvis & Turland in *Taxon* 47: 365. 1998): Herb. Linn. No. 1007.2 (LINN).
Current name: ***Bellium minutum*** (L.) L. (Asteraceae).

Pedalium murex Linnaeus, *Systema Naturae,* ed. 10, 2: 1123. 1759.
["Habitat in Malabaria, Zeylona. Dav. Royen."] Sp. Pl., ed. 2, 2; 892 (1763). RCN: 4651.
Lectotype (Bruce in Turrill & Milne-Redhead, *Fl. Trop. E. Africa, Pedaliaceae*: 6. 1953): Herb. Linn. No. 817.1 (LINN).
Generitype of *Pedalium* Linnaeus.
Current name: ***Pedalium murex*** L. (Pedaliaceae).

Pedicularis canadensis Linnaeus, *Systema Naturae,* ed. 12, 2: 408; *Mantissa Plantarum*: 86. 1767.
"Habitat in America septentrionali. Kalm." RCN: 4411.
Lectotype (Pennell in *Monogr. Acad. Nat. Sci. Philadelphia* 1: 498. 1935): *Kalm*, Herb. Linn. No. 763.17 (LINN).
Current name: ***Pedicularis canadensis*** L. (Scrophulariaceae).

Pedicularis comosa Linnaeus, *Species Plantarum* 2: 609. 1753.
"Habitat in Helveticis." RCN: 4409.
Type not designated.
Original material: Herb. Burser VIII: 87 (UPS); [icon] in Haller, Iter Helveticum 2: 623, t. 17. 1740.
Current name: ***Pedicularis comosa*** L. (Scrophulariaceae).

Pedicularis flammea Linnaeus, *Species Plantarum* 2: 609. 1753.
"Habitat in Alpibus Lapponiae, Helvetiae." RCN: 4405.
Type not designated.
Original material: Herb. Linn. No. 763.21 (LINN); [icon] in Linnaeus, Fl. Lapponica: 202, t. 4, f. 2. 1737.
Current name: ***Pedicularis flammea*** L. (Scrophulariaceae).

Pedicularis foliosa Linnaeus, *Systema Naturae,* ed. 12, 2: 407; *Mantissa Plantarum*: 86. 1767.
"Habitat in Alpibus Helvetiae, Austriae." RCN: 4410.
Lectotype (Fischer in *Feddes Repert.* 108: 113. 1997): Herb. Linn. No. 763.16 (LINN).
Current name: ***Pedicularis foliosa*** L. (Scrophulariaceae).

Pedicularis hirsuta Linnaeus, *Species Plantarum* 2: 609. 1753.
"Habitat in Lapponiae Alpibus." RCN: 4406.
Type not designated.
Original material: Herb. Linn. No. 763.23 (LINN); Herb. Linn. No. 763.24 (LINN); Herb. Schreber (M); Herb. Linn. No. 763.22 (LINN); [icon] in Linnaeus, Fl. Lapponica: 203, t. 4, f. 3. 1737.
Current name: ***Pedicularis hirsuta*** L. (Scrophulariaceae).

Pedicularis incarnata Linnaeus, *Species Plantarum* 2: 609. 1753.
"Habitat in Sibiria." RCN: 4407.
Type not designated.
Original material: *Gmelin*, Herb. Linn. No. 763.18 (LINN).
Current name: ***Pedicularis incarnata*** L. (Scrophulariaceae).

Pedicularis lapponica Linnaeus, *Species Plantarum* 2: 609. 1753.
"Habitat in Alpibus Lapponicis frequens." RCN: 4408.
Type not designated.
Original material: Herb. Linn. in Herb. Burman (G); Herb. Linn. No. 763.10 (LINN); Herb. Clifford: 326, *Pedicularis* 2 (BM); [icon] in Linnaeus, Fl. Lapponica: 197, t. 4, f. 1. 1737.
Current name: ***Pedicularis lapponica*** L. (Scrophulariaceae).

Pedicularis palustris Linnaeus, *Species Plantarum* 2: 607. 1753.
"Habitat in Europae septentrionalis paludibus." RCN: 4397.
Lectotype (Fischer in *Feddes Repert.* 108: 113. 1997): Herb. Linn. No. 763.1 (LINN).
Generitype of *Pedicularis* Linnaeus (vide Green, *Prop. Brit. Bot.*: 167. 1929).
Current name: ***Pedicularis palustris*** L. (Scrophulariaceae).
Note: Pedicularis sylvatica was treated as the generitype by Britton & Brown (*Ill. Fl. N. U. S.*, ed. 2, 3: 220. 1913; see McNeill & al. in *Taxon* 36: 380. 1987). However, under Art. 10.5, Ex. 7 (a voted example) of the Vienna Code, this is a type choice made under the American Code and is to be replaced under Art. 10.5b by Green's choice (*Prop. Brit. Bot.*: 167. 1929) of *P. palustris* L.

Pedicularis recutita Linnaeus, *Species Plantarum* 2: 608. 1753.
"Habitat in Helvetiae summis Alpibus." RCN: 4403.

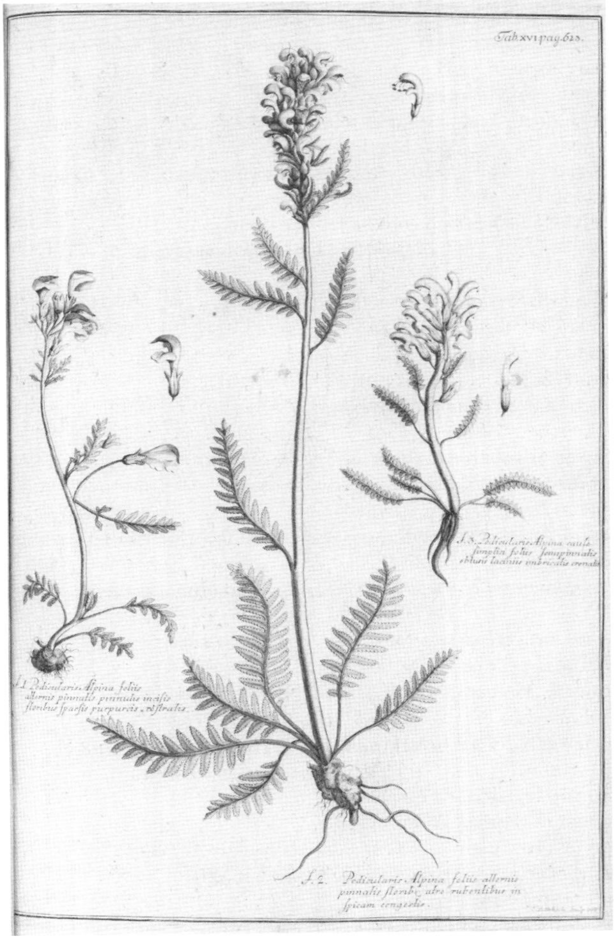

Lectotype (Fischer in *Feddes Repert.* 108: 113. 1997): [icon] *"Pedicularis Alpina foliis alternis pinnatis florib. atro rubentibus in spicam congestis"* in Haller, Enum. Meth. Stirp. Helv. 2: 623, t. 16, f. 2. 1742.
Current name: ***Pedicularis recutita*** L. (Scrophulariaceae).

Pedicularis resupinata Linnaeus, *Species Plantarum* 2: 608. 1753.
"Habitat in Sibiria D. Gmelin. D. Demidoff." RCN: 4402.
Type not designated.
Original material: Herb. Linn. No. 763.7 (LINN).
Current name: ***Pedicularis resupinata*** L. (Scrophulariaceae).

Pedicularis rostrata Linnaeus, *Species Plantarum* 2: 607. 1753.
"Habitat in Alpibus Helvetiae, Austriae." RCN: 4399.
Type not designated.
Original material: Herb. Burser VIII: 89 (UPS); [icon] in Clusius, Rar. Pl. Hist. 2: 210. 1601.
Current name: ***Pedicularis* sp.** (Scrophulariaceae).
Note: The application of this name is uncertain.

Pedicularis sceptrum-carolinum Linnaeus, *Species Plantarum* 2: 608. 1753.
"Habitat in Sueciae, Borussiae, Rutheni spongiosis, sylvaticis, riguis." RCN: 4400.
Lectotype (Fischer in *Feddes Repert.* 108: 113. 1997): Herb. Linn. No. 763.6 (LINN).
Current name: ***Pedicularis sceptrum-carolinum*** L. (Scrophulariaceae).

Pedicularis sylvatica Linnaeus, *Species Plantarum* 2: 607. 1753.
"Habitat in Europae sylvis paludosis." RCN: 4398.
Lectotype (Sutton in Jarvis & al., *Regnum Veg.* 127: 74. 1993): Herb. Linn. No. 763.2 (LINN).
Current name: ***Pedicularis sylvatica*** L. (Scrophulariaceae).
Note: Pedicularis sylvatica was treated as the generitype by Britton & Brown (*Ill. Fl. N. U. S.*, ed. 2, 3: 220. 1913; see McNeill & al. in *Taxon* 36: 380. 1987). However, under Art. 10.5, Ex. 7 (a voted example) of the Vienna Code, this is a type choice made under the American Code and is to be replaced under Art. 10.5b by Green's choice (*Prop. Brit. Bot.*: 167. 1929) of *P. palustris* L.

Pedicularis tristis Linnaeus, *Species Plantarum* 2: 608. 1753.
"Habitat in Sibiria." RCN: 4404.
Type not designated.
Original material: Herb. Linn. No. 763.9 (LINN).
Current name: ***Pedicularis tristis*** L. (Scrophulariaceae).

Pedicularis tuberosa Linnaeus, *Species Plantarum* 2: 610. 1753.
"Habitat in America calidiore." RCN: 4412.
Type not designated.
Original material: Herb. Linn. No. 763.28 (LINN); *Scopoli s.n.*, Herb. Linn. No. 763.27 (LINN).
Current name: ***Pedicularis tuberosa*** L. (Scrophulariaceae).

Pedicularis verticillata Linnaeus, *Species Plantarum* 2: 608. 1753.
"Habitat in Sibiria, Helvetia, Austria." RCN: 4401.
Lectotype (Fischer in *Feddes Repert.* 108: 113. 1997): Herb. Linn. No. 763.20 (LINN).
Current name: ***Pedicularis verticillata*** L. (Scrophulariaceae).

Peganum dauricum Linnaeus, *Species Plantarum* 1: 445. 1753.
"Habitat in Sibiria." RCN: 3455.
Neotype (Townsend in *Hooker's Icon. Pl.* 40(1–3): 37. 1986): [icon] *"Ruta foliis simplicibus alternis"* in Gmelin, Fl. Sibirica 4: 176, t. 68, f. 1. 1769.
Current name: ***Haplophyllum dauricum*** (L.) G. Don (Rutaceae).

Note: Townsend treated an uncited Gmelin plate as an "isolectotype" as he had failed to locate any Gmelin material. In the absence of any original material, Townsend's choice is treated as a neotypification under Art. 9.8.

Peganum harmala Linnaeus, *Species Plantarum* 1: 444. 1753.
"Habitat in arena Madritii, Alexandriae, Cappadociae, Galatia." RCN: 3454.
Lectotype (El Hadidi in Jarvis & al., *Regnum Veg.* 127: 74. 1993): Herb. Clifford: 206, *Peganum* 1 (BM-000628746).
Generitype of *Peganum* Linnaeus.
Current name: ***Peganum harmala*** L. (Zygophyllaceae).
Note: Burtt (in *Kew Bull.* 9: 409. 1954) indicated material at LINN as type but did not distinguish between sheets 621.1 and 621.2. As they do not appear to be part of a single gathering, Art. 9.15 does not apply, and El Hadidi's choice of the Clifford sheet as type is accepted here.

Penaea fucata Linnaeus, *Mantissa Plantarum Altera*: 199. 1771, *nom. illeg.*
"Habitat in Capitis b. spei. montibus." RCN: 914.
Replaced synonym: *Penaea sarcocolla* L. (1753).
Type not designated.
Original material: as replaced synonym.
Current name: ***Saltera sarcocolla*** (L.) Bullock (Penaeaceae).
Note: A superfluous name for *P. sarcocolla* L. (1753), and hence homotypic with it. Although Dahlgren (in *Opera Bot.* 18: 6, 28. 1968) indicated material in the Bergius herbarium (SBT) as the type, he designated a different type (which unfortunately appears not to be original material for the name) for *P. sarcocolla*.

Penaea marginata Linnaeus, *Mantissa Plantarum Altera*: 199. 1771.
"Habitat juxta Capitis b. spei fluvios." RCN: 913.
Lectotype (Dahlgren & Rao in *Bot. Not.* 122: 208. 1969): Herb. Linn. No. 140.4 (LINN).
Current name: ***Geissoloma marginatum*** (L.) A. Juss. (Geissolomataceae).

Penaea mucronata Linnaeus, *Species Plantarum* 1: 111. 1753.
"Habitat in Aethiopia." RCN: 912.
Lectotype (Dahlgren in *Opera Bot.* 29: 21. 1971): Herb. Clifford: 37, *Penaea* 1 (BM-000557817).
Generitype of *Penaea* Linnaeus (vide Kunth in *Linnaea* 5: 677. 1830).
Current name: ***Penaea mucronata*** L. (Penaeaceae).

Penaea sarcocolla Linnaeus, *Species Plantarum* 1: 111. 1753.
"Habitat in Aethiopia." RCN: 911.
Replaced synonym of: *Penaea fucata* L. (1771), *nom. illeg.*
Type not designated.
Original material: none traced.
Current name: ***Saltera sarcocolla*** (L.) Bullock (Penaeaceae).
Note: Although Dahlgren (in *Opera Bot.* 18: 52. 1968) indicated material in the Wahlbom herbarium in UPS as the lectotype, this collection lacks the relevant *Species Plantarum* number (i.e. "1") and was a post-1753 addition to the herbarium, and is not original material for the name. He also incorrectly indicated a different type, from the Bergius herbarium (SBT), for the superfluous *P. fucata* L. (1771) which is necessarily homotypic with *P. sarcocolla*.

Penaea squamosa Linnaeus, *Species Plantarum* 1: 112. 1753.
"Habitat in Aethiopia." RCN: 915.
Type not designated.
Original material: none traced.
Note: The application of this name is uncertain. See Salter (in *J. S. African Bot.* 6: 41. 1940) and Dahlgren (in *Opera Bot.* 18: 6, 53. 1968) who regards this as a *nomen dubium et ambiguum*.

Penstemon chelonoides Linnaeus, *Plantae Surinamenses*: 6. 1775.
"Habitat [in Surinamo.]" RCN: 1191.
Type not designated.
Original material: none traced.
Note: The application of this name is uncertain.

Pentapetes acerifolia Linnaeus, *Species Plantarum* 2: 698. 1753.
"Habitat in India." RCN: 5002.
Type not designated.
Original material: [icon] in Amman in Comment. Acad. Sci. Imp.
Petrop. 8: 216, t. 16, 17. 1736.
Note: The application of this name appears uncertain.

Pentapetes phoenicea Linnaeus, *Species Plantarum* 2: 698. 1753.
"Habitat in India." RCN: 5000.
Lectotype (Wijnands, *Bot. Commelins*: 195. 1983): Herb. Linn. No.
860.1 (LINN).
Generitype of *Pentapetes* Linnaeus (vide Green, *Prop. Brit. Bot.*: 173.
1929).
Current name: ***Pentapetes phoenicea*** L. (Sterculiaceae).

Pentapetes suberifolia Linnaeus, *Species Plantarum* 2: 698. 1753.
"Habitat in India." RCN: 5001.
Lectotype (Verdcourt in Dassanayake & al., *Revised Handb. Fl.
Ceylon* 9: 423. 1995): Herb. Hermann 1: 10, No. 250 (BM-
000594441).
Current name: ***Pterospermum suberifolium*** (L.) Willd.
(Sterculiaceae).

Penthorum sedoides Linnaeus, *Species Plantarum* 1: 432. 1753.
"Habitat in Virginia." RCN: 3364.
Lectotype (designated here by Reveal): Herb. Linn. No. 596.1
(LINN).
Generitype of *Penthorum* Linnaeus.
Current name: ***Penthorum sedoides*** L. (Penthoraceae).

Peplis portula Linnaeus, *Species Plantarum* 1: 332. 1753.
"Habitat in Europae inundatis." RCN: 2572.
Lectotype (Chamberlain in Jarvis & al., *Regnum Veg.* 127: 74. 1993):
Herb. Linn. No. 128 ["38"] (LAPP).
Generitype of *Peplis* Linnaeus.
Current name: ***Lythrum portula*** (L.) D.A. Webb (Lythraceae).

Peplis tetrandra Linnaeus, *Amoenitates Academicae* 5: 378, 413. 1760.
RCN: 2573.
Type not designated.
Original material: Herb. Linn. No. 458.3 (LINN).
Current name: ***Lucya tetrandra*** (L.) K. Schum. (Lythraceae).
Note: This name did not appear in either *Syst. Nat.*, ed. 10, 2
(May–Jun 1759), *Fl. Jamaicensis* (Nov 1759) or *Pugill. Jam. Pl.*
(Dec 1759). However, it was an addition to both of the latter
dissertations in their reprinted editions in the *Amoenitates
Academicae* in 1760. In *Amoen. Acad.* 5: 378 (*Fl. Jamaicensis*) there
is a cross-reference to the account in the reprint of *Pugill. Jam. Pl.*
(in *Amoen. Acad.* 5: 413), where there is a description.
Consequently, Howard (in *J. Arnold Arbor.* 54: 460. 1973) was
incorrect to give the date of the name as 1759, nor can the Browne
description (there is no figure) be the holotype.

Perdicium brasiliense Linnaeus, *Systema Naturae*, ed. 12, 2: 559;
Mantissa Plantarum: 115. 1767.
"Habitat in Brasilia. Arduini." RCN: 6411.
Lectotype (Katinas in Jarvis & Turland in *Taxon* 47: 365. 1998):
Arduino 17, Herb. Linn. No. 1003.4 (LINN).
Current name: ***Holocheilus brasiliensis*** (L.) Cabrera (Asteraceae).

Perdicium capense Linnaeus, *Plantae Rariores Africanae*: 22. 1760.
["Habitat ad Cap. b. spei."] Sp. Pl., ed. 2, 2: 1248 (1763). RCN:
6409.
Replaced synonym of: *Perdicium semiflosculare* L. (1763), *nom. illeg.*
Lectotype (Hansen in *Nordic J. Bot.* 5: 544. 1985): *Oldenland*, Herb.
Burman (G).
Generitype of *Perdicium* Linnaeus.
Current name: ***Perdicium capense*** L. (Asteraceae).

Perdicium radiale Linnaeus, *Species Plantarum*, ed. 2, 2: 1248. 1763,
nom. illeg.
"Habitat in Jamaica." RCN: 6410.
Replaced synonym: *Inula trixis* L. (1759).
Lectotype (Anderson in *Brittonia* 23: 349. 1971): *Browne*, Herb. Linn.
No. 1003.3 (LINN).
Current name: ***Trixis inula*** Crantz (Asteraceae).
Note: An illegitimate replacement name in *Perdicium* for *Inula trixis* L.
(1759).

Perdicium semiflosculare Linnaeus, *Species Plantarum*, ed. 2, 2:
1248. 1763, *nom. illeg.*
"Habitat ad Cap. b. spei." RCN: 6409.
Replaced synonym: *Perdicium capense* L. (1760).
Lectotype (Hansen in *Nordic J. Bot.* 5: 544. 1985): *Oldenland*, Herb.
Burman (G).
Current name: ***Perdicium capense*** L. (Asteraceae).
Note: An illegitimate replacement name for *Perdicium capense* L.
(1760), as noted by Nordenstam (in *Bot. Not.* 114: 279.
1961).

Pergularia glabra Linnaeus, *Systema Naturae*, ed. 12, 2: 191; *Mantissa
Plantarum*: 53. 1767.
"Habitat in India." RCN: 1747.
Lectotype (Rudjiman in *Meded. Landbouwhoogeschool* 82–11: 5.
1982): Herb. Linn. No. 306.1 (LINN).
Current name: ***Vallaris glabra*** (L.) Kuntze (Apocynaceae).

Pergularia tomentosa Linnaeus, *Systema Naturae*, ed. 12, 2: 191;
Mantissa Plantarum: 53. 1767.
"Habitat in Arabia. Forskåhl." RCN: 1748.
Lectotype (Goyder in *Kew Bull.* 61: 248. 2006): *Forsskål 972* (C).
Generitype of *Pergularia* Linnaeus (vide Brown in *Bull. Misc. Inform.
Kew* 1907: 324–325. 1907).
Current name: ***Pergularia tomentosa*** L. (Asclepiadaceae).
Note: Brown (in *Bull. Misc. Inform. Kew* 1907: 323–325. 1907) argued
that Linnaeus' generic description could not include either of the
species included within the genus in 1767. The protologue of *P.
tomentosa* indicates that the plant came originally from "Arabia", via
Forsskål, and was cultivated in Uppsala. However, sheet 306.2
(LINN) is from China, and Brown argues that it cannot be
accepted as the basis of *P. tomentosa*. Swarapanandan (in *Taxon* 32:
468–469. 1983) provided a review of the confusion in the generic
concept, but neither he nor Brown (his "I suspect that [308.6
LINN] may be the very specimen on which Linnaeus
based...*Pergularia*" is inadequate) provided a formal typification for
P. tomentosa. This was subsequently done by Liede (in *Asklepios* 51:
65. 1990) who designated *Forsskål 269* (C) as a neotype. However,
it is from Egypt, and Goyder (in *Kew Bull.* 61: 248–249. 2006)
therefore rejected it in favour of *Forsskål 972* from Arabia, which he
treats as the lectotype.

Perilla ocymoides Linnaeus, *Genera Plantarum*, ed. 6: 578. 1764,
nom. illeg.
"Habitat in India. Arduini." RCN: 4215.
Replaced synonym: *Ocimum frutescens* L. (1753).

Lectotype (Paton in Jarvis & al., *Regnum Veg.* 127: 74. 1993): [icon]
"*Ocymum Zeylanicum perenne, odoratissimum, latifolium*" in
Burman, Thes. Zeylan.: 174, t. 80, f. 1. 1737 (see p. 68).
Generitype of *Perilla* Linnaeus.
Current name: **Perilla frutescens** (L.) Britton (Lamiaceae).
Note: An illegitimate replacement name for *Ocimum frutescens* L.
(1753) and hence homotypic with it. Hedge (in Ali & Nasir, *Fl.
Pakistan* 192: 265. 1990) designated 731.2 (LINN) as the type of
O. frutescens but this is an Arduino collection not received by
Linnaeus until 1763 and not original material for the name. See
notes by Jarvis (in *Webbia* 48: 497. 1994) on the large number of
different taxa included within this name by Linnaeus.

Periploca africana Linnaeus, *Species Plantarum* 1: 211. 1753.
"Habitat in Africa." RCN: 1752.
Lectotype (Wijnands, *Bot. Commelins*: 49. 1983): Herb. Clifford: 79,
Cynanchum 1 (BM-000558170).
Current name: **Cynanchum africanum** (L.) Hoffmanns.
(Asclepiadaceae).

Periploca graeca Linnaeus, *Species Plantarum* 1: 211. 1753.
"Habitat in Syria." RCN: 1749.
Lectotype (Goyder in Jarvis & al., *Regnum Veg.* 127: 74. 1993): Herb.
Clifford: 78, *Periploca* 1 (BM-000558169).
Generitype of *Periploca* Linnaeus (vide Hitchcock, *Prop. Brit. Bot.*:
136. 1929).
Current name: **Periploca graeca** L. (Asclepiadaceae).

Periploca indica Linnaeus, *Species Plantarum* 1: 211. 1753.
"Habitat in Zeylona." RCN: 1751.
Lectotype (Huber in Abeywickrama, *Revised Handb. Fl. Ceylon* 1(1):
30. 1973): Herb. Hermann 3: 51, No. 113 (BM-000621992).
Current name: **Hemidesmus indicus** (L.) Sm. (Asclepiadaceae).

Periploca secamone Linnaeus, *Mantissa Plantarum Altera*: 216. 1771.
"Habitat in Aegypto." RCN: 1750.
Lectotype (Goyder & Singh in *Taxon* 40: 630. 1991): Herb. Linn. No.
307.2 (LINN).
Current name: **Secamone alpini** Schult. (Asclepiadaceae).

Periploca tenuifolia Linnaeus, *Species Plantarum* 1: 212. 1753.
"Habitat in Cap. b. spei dunis." RCN: 1746.
Basionym of: *Ceropegia tenuifolia* (L.) L. (1771).
Lectotype (Wanntorp in *Opera Bot.* 98: 50, f. 34. 1988): [icon]
"*Cynanchum radice glandulosa, foliis angustis, sinuatis, floribus
urceolatis, miniatis*" in Burman, Rar. Afric. Pl.: 36, t. 15. 1738.
Current name: **Microloma tenuifolia** (L.) K. Schum.
(Asclepiadaceae).

Petesia lygistum Linnaeus, *Systema Naturae*, ed. 10, 2: 894. 1759.
["Habitat in Jamaica."] Sp. Pl., ed. 2, 1: 160 (1762). RCN: 903.
Type not designated.
Original material: *Browne*, Herb. Linn. No. 134.2 (LINN); [icon] in
Browne, Civ. Nat. Hist. Jamaica: 142, t. 3, f. 2. 1756.
Current name: **Manettia lygistum** (L.) Sw. (Rubiaceae).

Petesia stipularis Linnaeus, *Systema Naturae*, ed. 10, 2: 894. 1759.
["Habitat in Iamaica."] Sp. Pl., ed. 2, 1: 160 (1762). RCN: 902.
Type not designated.
Original material: *Browne*, Herb. Linn. No. 134.1 (LINN); [icon] in
Browne, Civ. Nat. Hist. Jamaica: 143, t. 2, f. 2. 1756.
Current name: **Petesia stipularis** L. (Rubiaceae).

Petiveria alliacea Linnaeus, *Species Plantarum* 1: 342. 1753.
"Habitat in Jamaicae nemorosis." RCN: 2626.

Lectotype (Barrie in Jarvis & al., *Regnum Veg.* 127: 74. 1993): Herb.
Clifford: 141, *Petiveria* 1 (BM-000558594).
Generitype of *Petiveria* Linnaeus.
Current name: **Petiveria alliacea** L. (Phytolaccaceae).
Note: Fawcett & Rendle (*Fl. Jamaica* 3: 158. 1914) stated "type in
Herb. Linn.", evidently intending sheet 472.1 (LINN), and this
choice has been followed by authors such as Nowicke (in *Ann.
Missouri Bot. Gard.* 55: 344. 1969) and Ghosh & Sikdar (in *J. Econ.
Taxon. Bot.* 4: 155. 1983). However, the sheet lacks a *Species
Plantarum* number (i.e. "1"), written by Linnaeus, and is a post-
1753 addition to the collection and so not original material for the
name. Barrie's 1993 choice is therefore accepted here.

Petiveria octandra Linnaeus, *Species Plantarum,* ed. 2, 1: 486. 1762.
"Habitat in America meridionali. Jacquin." RCN: 2627.
Lectotype (Kellogg in Howard, *Fl. Lesser Antilles* 4: 189. 1988): Herb.
Linn. No. 472.2 (LINN).
Current name: **Petiveria alliacea** L. (Phytolaccaceae).

Petrea volubilis Linnaeus, *Species Plantarum* 2: 626. 1753.
"Habitat in America." RCN: 4534.
Lectotype (Moldenke in *Repert. Spec. Nov. Regni Veg.* 43: 35. 1938):
Herb. Clifford: 319, *Petrea* 1 (BM-000646189).
Generitype of *Petrea* Linnaeus.
Current name: **Petrea volubilis** L. (Verbenaceae).
Note: Although some later authors (e.g. Jafri in Nasir & Ali, *Fl. W.
Pakistan* 77: 16. 1974) have treated 781.1 (LINN) as the type,
Moldenke's 1938 choice clearly has priority.

Peucedanum alpestre Linnaeus, *Species Plantarum* 1: 246. 1753.
"Habitat – – – –" RCN: 1974.
Lectotype (Reduron in Jarvis & al. in *Taxon* 55: 213. 2006): Herb.
Linn. No. 346.4 (LINN).
Current name: **Silaum silaus** (L.) Schinz & Thell. (Apiaceae).

Peucedanum alsaticum Linnaeus, *Species Plantarum,* ed. 2, 1: 354.
1762.
"Habitat in Alsatiae, Palatinatus dumetis humidiusculis." RCN: 1977.
Lectotype (Reduron & al. in *J. Bot. Soc. Bot. France* 1: 97. 1997):
[icon] "*Daucus alsaticus*" in Bauhin, Prodr. Theatri Bot.: 77. 1620. –
Epitype (Reduron in Jarvis & al. in *Taxon* 55: 213. 2006): France.
"Haut-Rhin Westhalten colline du Lutzelberg", 250m, 21 Aug
1979, Herb. Reduron 19790821–01 (STR).
Current name: **Peucedanum alsaticum** L. (Apiaceae).

Peucedanum nodosum Linnaeus, *Species Plantarum* 1: 246. 1753,
nom. cons.
"Habitat in Creta." RCN: 1978.
Conserved type (Turland & Cafferty in *Taxon* 48: 595. 1999): Greece.
Crete, "In pratis supra Kastelli Pedhiada", 2 Jul 1899, *Baldacci 317*
(BM).
Current name: **Ferulago nodosa** (L.) Boiss. (Apiaceae).

Peucedanum officinale Linnaeus, *Species Plantarum* 1: 245. 1753.
"Habitat in Europae australioris pratis pinguibus." RCN: 1973.
Lectotype (Frey in *Candollea* 44: 271. 1989): Herb. Linn. No. 346.1
(LINN). – Epitype (Reduron & Jacquemoud in Jarvis & al. in
Taxon 55: 213. 2006): France. Grammont près de Montpellier, Sep
1846, legit *Aug. de St Hilaire s.n.*, Herb. Planchon ex Herb. Alioth
(G).
Generitype of *Peucedanum* Linnaeus (vide Hitchcock, *Prop. Brit. Bot.*:
139. 1929).
Current name: **Peucedanum officinale** L. (Apiaceae).
Note: Reduron & Jarvis (in Jarvis & al., *Regnum Veg.* 127: 75. 1993)
designated Herb. Clifford: 93, *Peucedanum* No. 1β, fol. 2 (BM) as

the lectotype. However, their choice is pre-dated by that of Frey, who designated a sterile specimen in LINN as type. Reduron & Jacquemoud subsequently designated an epitype to allow the name to be applied precisely.

Peucedanum silaus Linnaeus, *Species Plantarum* 1: 246. 1753.
"Habitat in Helvetia, Narbona." RCN: 1976.
Lectotype (Reduron in Jonsell & Jarvis in *Nordic J. Bot.* 22: 84. 2002): Herb. Burser VIII: 73 (UPS).
Current name: ***Silaum silaus*** (L.) Schinz & Thell. (Apiaceae).

Peziza acetabulum Linnaeus, *Species Plantarum* 2: 1181. 1753.
"Habitat in Europa australi." RCN: 8497.
Type not designated.
Original material: [icon] in Buxbaum in Comment. Acad. Sci. Imp. Petrop. 4: 282, t. 29, f. 1, 2. 1729; [icon] in Vaillant, Bot. Paris.: 57, t. 13, f. 1. 1727; [icon] in Micheli, Nov. Pl. Gen.: 207, t. 86, f. 1. 1729.
Current name: ***Helvella acetabulum*** (L.: Fr.) Quél. (Helvellaceae).

Peziza auricula (Linnaeus) Linnaeus, *Systema Naturae*, ed. 12, 2: 725. 1767.
["Habitat in Arbores putridas."] Sp. Pl. 2: 1157 (1753). RCN: 8502.
Basionym: *Tremella auricula* L. (1753).
Type not designated.
Original material: as basionym.
Current name: ***Auricularia auricula-judae*** (Fr.: Fr.) J. Schröt. (Auriculariaceae).

Peziza cochleata Linnaeus, *Species Plantarum* 2: 1181. 1753.
"Habitat in umbrosis." RCN: 8501.
Type not designated.
Original material: [icon] in Vaillant, Bot. Paris.: 57, t. 11, f. 8. 1727.
Current name: ***Otidea cochleata*** (Huds.: Fr.) Fuckel (Pyronemataceae).
Note: See comments by Nannfeldt (in *Ann. Bot. Fenn.* 3: 312. 1966).

Peziza cornucopioides Linnaeus, *Species Plantarum* 2: 1181. 1753.
"Habitat in Gallia." RCN: 8496.
Type not designated.
Original material: [icon] in Vaillant, Bot. Paris.: 57, t. 13, f. 2, 3. 1727.
Current name: ***Craterellus cornucopioides*** (L.: Fr.) Pers. (Cantharellaceae).

Peziza cupularis Linnaeus, *Species Plantarum* 2: 1181. 1753.
"Habitat in Gallia." RCN: 8499.
Type not designated.
Original material: [icon] in Vaillant, Bot. Paris.: 57, t. 11, f. 1, 2, 3. 1727.
Current name: ***Tarzetta cupularis*** (L.: Fr.) Svrček (Pyronemataceae).
Note: See comments by Dennis (in *Kew Bull.* 37: 645. 1983).

Peziza cyathoides Linnaeus, *Species Plantarum* 2: 1181. 1753.
"Habitat in Terra." RCN: 8498.
Type not designated.
Original material: [icon] in Ray, Syn. Meth. Stirp. Brit., ed. 3: 479, t. 24, f. 4. 1724.
Current name: ***Sarcoscypha coccinea*** (Jacq.: Fr.) Sacc. (Sarcoscyphaceae).

Peziza lentifera Linnaeus, *Species Plantarum* 2: 1180. 1753.
"Habitat in Agris, Lignis, Sepimentis." RCN: 8494.
Type not designated.
Original material: [icon] in Plukenet, Phytographia: t. 184, f. 9. 1692;

Almag. Bot.: 163. 1696; [icon] in Loesel, Fl. Prussica: 98, t. 16. 1703; [icon] in Mentzel, Ind. Nom. Pl. Univ.: t. 6. 1682; [icon] in Vaillant, Bot. Paris.: 56, t. 11, f. 6, 7. 1727; [icon] in Micheli, Nov. Pl. Gen.: 222, t. 102, f. 1. 1729.
Current name: ***Peziza lentifera*** L. (Pezizaceae).

Peziza punctata Linnaeus, *Species Plantarum* 2: 1180. 1753.
"Habitat in Stercore equino." RCN: 8495.
Type not designated.
Original material: [icon] in Boccone, Mus. Piante Rar. Sicilia: 149, t. 107. 1697.
Current name: ***Poronia punctata*** (L.: Fr.) Fr. (Xylariaceae).

Peziza scutellata Linnaeus, *Species Plantarum* 2: 1181. 1753.
"Habitat in Parietibus putridis." RCN: 8500.
Type not designated.
Original material: [icon] in Ray, Syn. Meth. Stirp. Brit., ed. 3: 18, t. 24, f. 3. 1724; [icon] in Vaillant, Bot. Paris.: 57, t. 13, f. 13, 14. 1727.
Current name: ***Scutellinia scutellata*** (L.: Fr.) Lambotte (Pyronemataceae).
Note: Schumacher (in *Opera Bot.* 101: 68. 1990) indicated a Lundell collection (S) as a neotype but original material is in existence which, under Art. 9.11, precludes the selection of a neotype.

Phaca alpina Linnaeus, *Species Plantarum* 2: 755. 1753.
"Habitat in Lapponia, Sibiria." RCN: 5570.
Lectotype (Greuter in *Candollea* 23: 265. 1968): Herb. Linn. No. 925.3 (LINN).
Generitype of *Phaca* Linnaeus (vide Green, *Prop. Brit. Bot.*: 176. 1929).
Current name: ***Astragalus penduliflorus*** Lam. (Fabaceae: Faboideae).
Note: Phaca baetica was treated as the generitype by Britton & Brown (*Ill. Fl. N. U. S.*, ed. 2, 2: 385. 1913; see McNeill & al. in *Taxon* 36: 380. 1987). However, under Art. 10.5, Ex. 7 (a voted example) of the Vienna Code, this is a type choice made under the American Code and is to be replaced under Art. 10.5b by Green's choice (*Prop. Brit. Bot.*: 176. 1929) of *P. alpina* L.
There is some doubt whether, taxonomically, the Siberian and European plants included by Linnaeus are conspecific. If treated as conspecific, the correct name is *A. penduliflorus* Lam., "alpina" being pre-occupied in *Astragalus* by *A. alpinus* L. (1753).

Phaca australis Linnaeus, *Systema Naturae*, ed. 12, 2: 497; *Mantissa Plantarum*: 103. 1767.
"Habitat in Alpibus Helvetiae, Italiae, Galloprovinciae." RCN: 5571.
Lectotype (Podlech in Turland & Jarvis in *Taxon* 46: 479. 1997): [icon] *"Astragaloides Alpina, supina, glabra, foliis acutioribus"* in Tilli, Cat. Pl. Hort. Pisani: 19, t. 14, f. 1. 1723. – Epitype (Podlech in Turland & Jarvis in *Taxon* 46: 479. 1997): France. Vaucluse, Mont Ventoux, 7 Jul 1877, *E. Reverchon s.n.* (BM).
Current name: ***Astragalus australis*** (L.) Lam. (Fabaceae: Faboideae).

Phaca baetica Linnaeus, *Species Plantarum* 2: 755. 1753.
"Habitat in Hispania, Lusitania." RCN: 5569.
Lectotype (Podlech in Jarvis & al., *Regnum Veg.* 127: 75. 1993): [icon] *"Astragalus Baeticus"* in Clusius, Rar. Pl. Hist. 2: 233, 234. 1601.
Current name: ***Phaca baetica*** L. (Fabaceae: Faboideae).
Note: Phaca baetica was treated as the generitype by Britton & Brown (*Ill. Fl. N. U. S.*, ed. 2, 2: 385. 1913; see McNeill & al. in *Taxon* 36: 380. 1987). However, under Art. 10.5, Ex. 7 (a voted example) of the Vienna Code, this is a type choice made under the American Code and is to be replaced under Art. 10.5b by Green's choice (*Prop. Brit. Bot.*: 176. 1929) of *P. alpina* L.

P

Phaca frigida Linnaeus, *Systema Naturae,* ed. 10, 2: 1173. 1759.
["Habitat in Alpinis Italiae, Sibiriae, Lapponiae umbrosis."] Sp. Pl.,
   ed. 2, 2: 1064 (1763). RCN: 5570.
Neotype (Podlech in Turland & Jarvis in *Taxon* 46: 479. 1997):
   France. Haute-Savoie: in petrosis montis "Vergy" prope "Brizon",
   2,300m, Jul 1898, *J. Thimothée s.n.* [Herbarium Normale, editum
   ab I. Dörfler, No. 4240] (M; iso- BM).
Current name: ***Astragalus frigidus*** (L.) A. Gray (Fabaceae: Faboideae).
Note: Although Greuter (in *Candollea* 23: 265. 1968) stated that 925.5
   and 925.6 (LINN) typify this name, these collections do not appear
   to be original material, and are not part of a single gathering (Art.
   9.15). In the absence of any original material, Podlech designated a
   neotype.

Phaca sibirica Linnaeus, *Species Plantarum* 2: 755. 1753.
"Habitat in Alpibus Sibiricis." RCN: 5574.
Type not designated.
Original material: [icon] in Amman, Stirp. Rar. Ruth.: 111, t. 19, f. 1.
   1739; [icon] in Amman, Stirp. Rar. Ruth.: 113, t. 19, f. 2. 1739.
Current name: ***Oxytropis lanata*** DC. (Fabaceae: Faboideae).
Note: The application of this name is uncertain.

Phaca sulcata (Linnaeus) Linnaeus, *Systema Naturae,* ed. 10, 2: 1173.
   1759.
["Habitat in Sibiria."] Sp. Pl. 2: 756 (1753). RCN: 5579.
Basionym: *Astragalus sulcatus* L. (1753).
Lectotype (Podlech in Turland & Jarvis in *Taxon* 46: 465. 1997):
   Herb. Linn. No. 926.5, right specimen (LINN).
Current name: ***Astragalus sulcatus*** L. (Fabaceae: Faboideae).

Phaca trifoliata Linnaeus, *Mantissa Plantarum Altera*: 270. 1771,
   nom. utique rej.
"Habitat in China." RCN: 5572.
Type not designated.
Original material: Herb. Linn. No. 925.9 (LINN).
Current name: ***Pycnospora lutescens*** (Poir.) Schindl. (Fabaceae:
   Faboideae).

Phalaris aquatica Linnaeus, *Centuria I Plantarum*: 4. 1755.
"Habitat in Aegypto & ad Tyberin." RCN: 459.
Lectotype (Anderson in *Iowa State J. Sci.* 36: 43. 1961): *Hasselquist,*
   Herb. Linn. No. 78.4 (LINN).
Current name: ***Phalaris aquatica*** L. (Poaceae).
Note: See Baldini & Jarvis (in *Taxon* 40: 475–477. 1991) for an
   extensive review.

Phalaris arundinacea Linnaeus, *Species Plantarum* 1: 55. 1753.
"Habitat in Europae subhumidis ad ripas lacuum." RCN: 463.
Lectotype (Anderson in *Iowa State J. Sci.* 36: 37. 1961): Herb. Linn.
   No. 78.7 (LINN).
Current name: ***Phalaris arundinacea*** L. (Poaceae).
Note: See extensive review by Baldini & Jarvis (in *Taxon* 40: 480.
   1991).

Phalaris arundinacea Linnaeus var. **picta** Linnaeus, *Species Plantarum*
   1: 55. 1753.
RCN: 463.
Lectotype (Baldini & Jarvis in *Taxon* 40: 480. 1991): Herb. Burser I:
   22 (UPS).
Current name: ***Phalaris arundinacea*** L. var. ***picta*** L. (Poaceae).

Phalaris bulbosa Linnaeus, *Centuria I Plantarum*: 4. 1755.
"Habitat in Oriente." RCN: 457.
Lectotype (Anderson in *Iowa State J. Sci.* 36: 49. 1961): *Hasselquist,*
   Herb. Linn. No. 78.2 (LINN).

Current name: ***Phleum subulatum*** (Savi) Asch. & Graebn. (Poaceae).
Note: See extensive review by Baldini & Jarvis in *Taxon* 40: 478.
   1991).

Phalaris canariensis Linnaeus, *Species Plantarum* 1: 54. 1753.
"Habitat in Europa australi, Canariis." RCN: 456.
Lectotype (Baldini & Jarvis in *Taxon* 40: 482. 1991): Herb. Clifford:
   23, *Phalaris* 1 (BM-000557659).
Generitype of *Phalaris* Linnaeus (vide Host, *Icon. Descript. Gram.
   Austr.* 3: 5. 1805; Hitchcock in *U.S. Dept. Agric. Bull.* 772: 202.
   1920).
Current name: ***Phalaris canariensis*** L. (Poaceae).
Note: Phalaris canariensis, with the type designated by Baldini & Jarvis,
   was proposed as conserved type of the genus by Jarvis (in *Taxon* 41:
   567. 1992). However, the proposal was eventually ruled
   unnecessary by the General Committee (see Barrie, *l.c.* 55:
   795–796. 2006 for a review of the history of this and related
   proposals).

Phalaris eruciformis Linnaeus, *Species Plantarum* 1: 55. 1753.
"Habitat in Sibiria, Russia, Europa australi." RCN: 464.
Lectotype (Feráková in Cafferty & al. in *Taxon* 49: 253. 2000):
   Gmelin s.n., Herb. Linn. No. 78.9, right specimen (LINN).
Current name: ***Beckmannia eruciformis*** (L.) Host (Poaceae).
Note: Specific epithet spelled "erucaeformis" in the protologue.

Phalaris nodosa Linnaeus, *Systema Vegetabilium,* ed. 13: 88. 1774,
   nom. illeg.
["Habitat in Europae australi."] Mant. Pl. Alt.: 557 (1771). RCN:
   458.
Replaced synonym: *Phalaris tuberosa* L. (1771).
Lectotype (Anderson in *Iowa State J. Sci.* 36: 43. 1961): Herb. Linn.
   No. 78.3 (LINN).
Current name: ***Phalaris aquatica*** L. (Poaceae).
Note: An illegitimate replacement name for *P. tuberosa* L. (1771), as
   noted by Bor (in Rechinger, *Fl. Iranica* 70: 348. 1970).

Phalaris oryzoides Linnaeus, *Species Plantarum* 1: 55. 1753.
"Habitat in Virginiae paludibus nemorosis." RCN: 466.
Lectotype (Hitchcock in *Contr. U. S. Natl. Herb.* 12: 115. 1908):
   Herb. Linn. No. 78.10 (LINN).
Current name: ***Leersia oryzoides*** (L.) Sw. (Poaceae).

Phalaris paradoxa Linnaeus, *Species Plantarum,* ed. 2, 2: 1665. 1763.
"Habitat in Oriente. P. Forskåhl." RCN: 462.
Lectotype (Anderson in *Iowa State J. Sci.* 36: 22. 1961): Herb. Linn.
   No. 78.6 (LINN).
Current name: ***Phalaris paradoxa*** L. (Poaceae).
Note: See extensive review by Baldini & Jarvis (in *Taxon* 40: 482.
   1991).

Phalaris phleoides Linnaeus, *Species Plantarum* 1: 55. 1753.
"Habitat in Europae versuris." RCN: 460.
Lectotype (Doğan in *Karaca Arbor. Mag.* 1: 62. 1991): Herb. Linn.
   No. 78.5 (LINN).
Current name: ***Phleum phleoides*** (L.) H. Karst. (Poaceae).

Phalaris tuberosa Linnaeus, *Mantissa Plantarum Altera*: 557. 1771.
"Habitat in Europa australi." RCN: 458.
Replaced synonym of: *Phalaris nodosa* L. (1774), *nom. illeg.*
Lectotype (Anderson in *Iowa State J. Sci.* 36: 43. 1961): Herb. Linn.
   No. 78.3 (LINN).
Current name: ***Phalaris aquatica*** L. (Poaceae).
Note: See extensive review by Baldini & Jarvis (in *Taxon* 40: 477.
   1991).

Phalaris utriculata Linnaeus, *Systema Naturae,* ed. 10, 2: 869. 1759. ["Habitat in Italia."] Sp. Pl., ed. 2, 1: 80 (1762). RCN: 461.
Lectotype (Cope in Cafferty & al. in *Taxon* 49: 253. 2000): [icon] *"Gramen pratense spica purpurea, ex utriculo prodeunte"* in Bauhin, Theatri Bot.: 44. 1658. – Epitype (Cope in Cafferty & al. in *Taxon* 49: 253. 2000): France. Prairies des bords de la Saône, à Pontanevaux pres Mâcon (Saône-et-Loire), May 1879, *F. Lacroix s.n.* (K).
Current name: ***Alopecurus rendlei*** Eig (Poaceae).
Note: Although Kerguélen (in *Lejeunia,* n.s., 75: 79. 1975) stated "Type: ...LINN", this is not accepted as a formal typification, for the reasons explained by Cafferty & al. (in *Taxon* 49: 240. 2000).

Phalaris zizanioides Linnaeus, *Mantissa Plantarum Altera*: 183. 1771. "Habitat in India orientali. Koenig." RCN: 465.
Lectotype (van der Zon in *Wageningen Agric. Univ. Pap.* 92–1: 409. 1992): Herb. Linn. No. 78.12 (LINN).
Current name: ***Vetiveria zizanioides*** (L.) Nash (Poaceae).

Phallus esculentus Linnaeus, *Species Plantarum* 2: 1178. 1753. "Habitat in Sylvis antiquis." RCN: 8486.
Type not designated.
Original material: [icon] in Tournefort, Inst. Rei Herb.: 561, t. 329, f. A. 1700; [icon] in Micheli, Nov. Pl. Gen.: 203, t. 85, f. 1 & 2. 1729.
Current name: ***Morchella esculenta*** (L.: Fr.) Pers. (Morchellaceae).

Phallus impudicus Linnaeus, *Species Plantarum* 2: 1179. 1753. "Habitat in Sylvis." RCN: 8487.

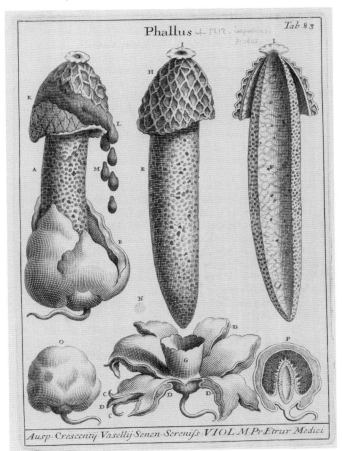

Phallus + 1212. impudicus, Tab 83

Ausp. Crescentij Vasellij Senen· Sereniss. VIOL M Pr Etrur Medici

Lectotype (Greuter & Kuyper in Jarvis & al., *Regnum Veg.* 127: 75. 1993): [icon] *"Phallus vulgaris, totus albus, volva rotundo, pileolo cellulato, ac summa parte umbilico pervio, ornato"* in Micheli, Nov. Pl. Gen.: 201, t. 83. 1729.
Generitype of *Phallus* Linnaeus: Persoon.
Current name: ***Phallus impudicus*** L.: Pers. (Phallaceae).

Pharnaceum cerviana Linnaeus, *Species Plantarum* 1: 272. 1753. "Habitat Rostockii, in Russia, Hispania." RCN: 2160.
Lectotype (Adamson in *J. S. African Bot.* 24: 14. 1958): Herb. Linn. No. 387.1 (LINN).
Current name: ***Mollugo cerviana*** (L.) Ser. (Molluginaceae).

Pharnaceum cordifolium Linnaeus, *Plantae Rariores Africanae*: 9. 1760. ["Habitat ad Cap. b. spei."] Sp. Pl., ed. 2, : 289 (1762). RCN: 2165.
Lectotype (Adamson in *J. S. African Bot.* 24: 44. 1958): Herb. Linn. No. 387.6 (LINN).
Current name: ***Pharnaceum cordifolium*** L. (Molluginaceae).

Pharnaceum depressum Linnaeus, *Mantissa Plantarum Altera*: 562. 1771. "Habitat in India orientali." RCN: 2162.
Lectotype (Turrill in Turrill & Milne-Redhead, *Fl. Trop. E. Africa, Caryophyllaceae*: 5. 1956): Herb. Linn. No. 387.4 (LINN).
Current name: ***Polycarpon prostratum*** (Forssk.) Asch. & Schweinf. (Caryophyllaceae).

Pharnaceum distichum Linnaeus, *Mantissa Plantarum Altera*: 221. 1771. "Habitat in India orientali." RCN: 2164.
Type not designated.
Original material: [icon] in Plukenet, Phytographia: t. 130, f. 6. 1692; Almag. Bot.: 22. 1696; [icon] in Plukenet, Almag. Mant.: 9, t. 332, f. 4. 1700 – Voucher: Herb. Sloane 99: 48 (BM-SL).
Current name: ***Mollugo disticha*** (L.) Ser. (Molluginaceae).

Pharnaceum incanum Linnaeus, *Species Plantarum* 1: 272. 1753. "Habitat in Africa." RCN: 2163.
Type not designated.
Original material: Herb. Clifford: 492, *Pharnaceum* 1 (BM); Herb. A. van Royen No. 903.245–582 (L); [icon] in Plukenet, Phytographia: t. 304, f. 4. 1694; Almag. Bot.: 23. 1696 – Typotype: Herb. Sloane 100: 192 (BM-SL).
Generitype of *Pharnaceum* Linnaeus (vide Hitchcock, *Prop. Brit. Bot.*: 143. 1929).
Current name: ***Pharnaceum incanum*** L. (Molluginaceae).
Note: Adamson (in *S. African J. Bot.* 24: 28. 1958) indicated 287.5 (LINN) as type, but the material came from Tulbagh and was not received by Linnaeus until ca. 1769. It cannot, therefore, be original material for the name.

Pharnaceum mollugo Linnaeus, *Systema Naturae,* ed. 10, 2: 966. 1759. ["Habitat in Aethiopia."] Sp. Pl., ed. 2, 1: 389 (1762). RCN: 2161.
Type not designated.
Original material: Herb. Clifford: 28, *Mollugo* 1 (BM); [icon] in Hermann, Hort. Lugd.-Bat. Cat.: 19, 21. 1687; [icon] in Ehret, Pl. Papil. Rar.: t. 6, f. 3. 1748.
Current name: ***Glinus oppositifolius*** (L.) A. DC. (Molluginaceae).
Note: A name at species rank for *Mollugo verticillata* var. β L. (1753) and not, as suggested by Jeffrey (in Hubbard & Milne-Redhead, *Fl. Trop. E. Africa, Aizoaceae*: 15. 1961), first published in 1771 where it could appear to be a superfluous name for *Mollugo spergula* L. (1759). Consequently, *P. mollugo* is not homotypic with the latter, as indicated by Jeffrey.

Pharus latifolius Linnaeus, *Systema Naturae*, ed. 10, 2: 1269. 1759.
["Habitat in Jamaica."] Sp. Pl., ed. 2, 2: 1498 (1763). RCN: 7194.
Lectotype (Hitchcock in *Contr. U. S. Natl. Herb.* 12: 125. 1908):
Browne, Herb. Linn. No. 1120.1 (LINN).
Current name: ***Pharus latifolius*** L. (Poaceae).
Note: Pharus latifolius was published in May–June 1759 and therefore
pre-dates *P. resupinatus* L. (Dec 1759). The latter appears to have
been coined in error, for although Linnaeus included it in the
reprint of *Fl. Jamaicensis* (in *Amoen. Acad.* 5: 382. 1759), he
subsequently omitted it from *Sp. Pl.*, ed. 2, 2: 1408 (1763),
referring only to *P. latifolius*. However, as *P. resupinatus* was not
based on exactly the same elements as *P. latifolius*, it is a heterotypic
synonym of the earlier name, rather than illegitimate and
homotypic with it.

Pharus resupinatus Linnaeus, *Flora Jamaicensis*: 21. 1759.
"Habitat [in Jamaica.]"
Type not designated.
Original material: [icon] in Browne, Civ. Nat. Hist. Jamaica: 344, t.
38, f. 3. 1756.
Current name: ***Pharus latifolius*** L. (Poaceae).
Note: Pharus latifolius was published in May–June 1759 and therefore
pre-dates *P. resupinatus* L. (Dec 1759). The latter appears to have
been coined in error, for although Linnaeus included it in the
reprint of *Fl. Jamaicensis* (in *Amoen. Acad.* 5: 382. 1759), he
subsequently omitted it from *Sp. Pl.*, ed. 2, 2: 1408 (1763),
referring only to *P. latifolius*. However, as *P. resupinatus* was not
based on exactly the same elements as *P. latifolius*, it is a heterotypic
synonym of the earlier name, rather than illegitimate and
homotypic with it.

Phaseolus alatus Linnaeus, *Species Plantarum* 2: 725. 1753.
"Habitat – – – –" RCN: 5321.
Type not designated.
Original material: [icon] in Dillenius, Hort. Eltham. 2: 314, t. 235, f.
303. 1732.
Current name: ***Vigna* sp.** (Fabaceae: Faboideae).
Note: The application of this name is uncertain.

Phaseolus caracalla Linnaeus, *Species Plantarum* 2: 725. 1753.
"Habitat in India." RCN: 5322.
Lectotype (Verdcourt in Turland & Jarvis in *Taxon* 46: 479. 1997):
[icon] *"Phaseolus Indicus cochleato flore"* in Trionfetti, Obs. Ortu
Veg. Pl.: 93, unnumbered plate. 1685 (see p. 164). – Epitype
(Verdcourt in Turland & Jarvis in *Taxon* 46: 479. 1997): Brasil. S.
of Rio Ivaí, N. of Boa Esperança, ca. 30km E of Cianorte, 29 Mar
1966, *Lindeman & de Haas 823* (K).
Current name: ***Vigna caracalla*** (L.) Verdc. (Fabaceae: Faboideae).

Phaseolus coccineus Linnaeus, *Species Plantarum* 2: 724. 1753.
"Habitat – – – –" RCN: 5314.
Basionym of: *Phaseolus vulgaris* L. var. *coccineus* (L.) L. (1763).
Lectotype (Westphal, *Pulses Ethiopia, Taxon. Agric. Signif.*: 139. 1974):
Herb. Linn. No. 899.2 (LINN).
Current name: ***Phaseolus coccineus*** L. (Fabaceae: Faboideae).

Phaseolus cylindricus Linnaeus, *Amoenitates Academicae* 4: 132.
1759.
Lectotype (Merrill, *Interpret. Rumph. Herb. Amb.*: 284. 1917): [icon]
"Phaseolus minor" in Rumphius, Herb. Amboin. 5: 383, t. 139, f. 1.
1747.
Current name: ***Vigna unguiculata*** (L.) Walp. subsp. ***cylindrica*** (L.)
Van Eselt. (Fabaceae: Faboideae).
Note: In the dissertation *Herb. Amboin.*: 23 (1754), Linnaeus gave the
name "Phaseolus cylindraceus" in an entry corresponding with

Rumphius' t. 140 (vol. 4). However, this name appears in the left-
hand column, rather than the right where new Linnaean binomials
appear, and the name is invalid (Art. 34.1, Ex. 2(a)). However, it
appears as *P. cylindricus* in the right-hand column in the reprint of
the dissertation in *Amoen. Acad.* 4 (1759), where it is validly
published.

Phaseolus farinosus Linnaeus, *Species Plantarum* 2: 724. 1753.
"Habitat in India." RCN: 5317.
Lectotype (Verdcourt in *Taxon* 46: 358. 1997): [icon] *"Phaseolus
peregrinus, flore roseo, semine tomentoso"* in Nissole in Mém. Acad.
Roy. Sci. Paris 1730: 577, t. 24. 1730.
Current name: ***Strophostyles helvola*** (L.) Elliott (Fabaceae:
Faboideae).

Phaseolus helvolus Linnaeus, *Species Plantarum* 2: 724. 1753, *nom.
& orth. cons.*
"Habitat in Carolina." RCN: 5319.
Conserved type (Delgado Salinas & Lavin in *Taxon* 53: 839. 2004):
U.S.A. South Carolina, Georgetown County, edge of marsh on
ocean side of Beach Rd., about 1 mile N of its terminus on South
Island, 22 Aug 1991, *J.B. Nelson 11140* (USC; iso- MEXU).
Current name: ***Strophostyles helvola*** (L.) Elliott (Fabaceae:
Faboideae).
Note: Verdcourt (in *Taxon* 46: 357. 1997) proposed a conserved type
for the name, duly recommended by the Committee for
Spermatophyta (in *Taxon* 48: 369. 1999), as was the conservation of
the spelling "helvolus". However, Delgado Salinas & Lavin (in
Taxon 53: 839. 2004) subsequently found that the conserved type
(U.S.A. North Carolina, Biltmore, sandy flats, 19 Aug 1896;
Biltmore herb. No. 1302, US No. 966089) was identifiable as
Strophostyles umbellata (Muhl. ex Willd.) Britton. They successfully
proposed the replacement of Verdcourt's type with another
conserved type corresponding with current usage of *S. helvola*.

Phaseolus inamoenus Linnaeus, *Species Plantarum* 2: 724. 1753.
"Habitat in Africa." RCN: 5316.
Neotype (Westphal, *Pulses Ethiopia, Taxon. Agric. Signif.*: 148. 1974):
Cultivated material "grown from seeds collected in Ethiopia",
Westphal 8652 (WAG; iso- K, P).
Current name: ***Phaseolus lunatus*** L. (Fabaceae: Faboideae).

Phaseolus lathyroides Linnaeus, *Species Plantarum*, ed. 2, 2: 1018.
1763.
"Habitat in Jamaica." RCN: 5327.
Lectotype (Howard, *Fl. Lesser Antilles* 4: 506. 1988): [icon]
"Phaseolus erectus lathyroides, flore amplo, coccineo" in Sloane, Voy.
Jamaica 1: 183, t. 116, f. 1. 1707. – Typotype: Herb. Sloane 3: 83
(BM-SL).
Current name: ***Macroptilium lathyroides*** (L.) Urb. var. ***lathyroides***
(Fabaceae: Faboideae).

Phaseolus lunatus Linnaeus, *Species Plantarum* 2: 724. 1753.
"Habitat in Benghala." RCN: 5315.
Neotype (Westphal, *Pulses Ethiopia, Taxon. Agric. Signif.*: 146. 1974):
Cultivated material "grown from seeds collected in Ethiopia",
Westphal 8622 (WAG; iso- K, P).
Current name: ***Phaseolus lunatus*** L. var. ***lunatus*** (Fabaceae:
Faboideae).
Note: A number of authors, following Verdcourt (in Milne-Redhead &
Polhill, *Fl. Trop. East Africa, Leguminosae* 4: 615. 1971) have treated
a description by Bergen (*Cat. Stirp. Hort. Med. Acad. Viandr.*: 99.
1744) as the type. However, it is not accompanied by an illustration
and, in the absence of any original material, Westphal designated a
neotype.

Phaseolus max Linnaeus, *Species Plantarum* 2: 725. 1753.
"Habitat in India." RCN: 5325.
Lectotype (Nguyên Van Thuân in Aubréville & Leroy, *Fl. Cambodge Laos Viêt-Nam* 17: 58. 1979): Herb. Linn. No. 899.9 (LINN).
Current name: *Glycine max* (L.) Merr. (Fabaceae: Faboideae).

Phaseolus mungo Linnaeus, *Systema Naturae*, ed. 12, 2: 482; *Mantissa Plantarum*: 101. 1767.
"Habitat in India orientali." RCN: 5326.
Type not designated.
Original material: none traced.
Current name: *Vigna mungo* (L.) Hepper (Fabaceae: Faboideae).
Note: There appear to be no extant original elements and the name needs a neotype. Nguyên Van Thuân (in Aubréville & Leroy, *Fl. Cambodge Laos Viêt-Nam* 17: 143. 1979) indicates what appears to be a Plukenet plate ("tab. 290") as type. However, "290" is the page number in Plukenet's *Almag. Bot.* (1696), where there is only a description, and no plate.

Phaseolus nanus Linnaeus, *Centuria I Plantarum*: 23. 1755.
"Habitat in India." RCN: 5323.
Lectotype (Pasquet in Turland & Jarvis in *Taxon* 46: 479. 1997): Herb. Burser XIX: 54 (UPS).
Current name: *Vigna unguiculata* (L.) Walp. (Fabaceae: Faboideae).

Phaseolus radiatus Linnaeus, *Species Plantarum* 2: 725. 1753.
"Habitat in China, Zeylona." RCN: 5324.
Lectotype (Verdcourt in Milne-Redhead & Polhill, *Fl. Trop. E. Africa, Leguminosae* 4: 655. 1971): [icon] *"Phaseolus Zeylanicus siliquis radiat. digestis"* in Dillenius, Hort. Eltham. 2: 315, t. 235, f. 304. 1732.
Current name: *Vigna radiata* (L.) R. Wilczek var. *radiata* (Fabaceae: Faboideae).
Note: Hara (in *J. Jap. Bot.* 30: 138. 1955) indicated 899.8 (LINN) as the holotype, a specimen which lacks the *Species Plantarum* number (i.e. "10") and was a post-1753 addition to the collection. It is not original material for the name.

Phaseolus semierectus Linnaeus, *Systema Naturae*, ed. 12, 2: 481; *Mantissa Plantarum*: 100. 1767.
"Habitat in America calidiore." RCN: 5320.
Lectotype (Nguyên Van Thuân in Aubréville & Leroy, *Fl. Cambodge Laos Viêt-Nam* 17: 202. 1979): Herb. Linn. No. 899.3 (LINN).
Current name: *Macroptilium lathyroides* (L.) Urb. var. *semierectum* (L.) Urb. (Fabaceae: Faboideae).

Phaseolus sphaerospermus Linnaeus, *Species Plantarum*, ed. 2, 2: 1018. 1763.
"Habitat in Indiis." RCN: 5328.
Type not designated.
Original material: none traced.
Current name: *Vigna unguiculata* (L.) Walp. subsp. *unguiculata* (Fabaceae: Faboideae).

Phaseolus unguiculatus Linnaeus, *Herbarium Amboinense*: 23. 1754.
"Habitat [in Amboina.]"
Lectotype (Verdcourt in Turland & Jarvis in *Taxon* 46: 479. 1997): [icon] *"Cacara nigra"* in Rumphius, Herb. Amboin. 5: 381, t. 138. 1747. – Epitype (Verdcourt in Turland & Jarvis in *Taxon* 46: 479. 1997): U.S.A. Mississippi, Biloxi, 23 Nov 1910, Tracy, S.P.I. No. 25755 "Stizolobium aterrimum" (K; iso- US?).
Current name: *Mucuna pruriens* (L.) DC. var. *utilis* (Wight) Burck (Fabaceae: Faboideae).

Phaseolus vexillatus Linnaeus, *Species Plantarum* 2: 724. 1753.
"Habitat in Havana." RCN: 5318.
Lectotype (Verdcourt in Milne-Redhead & Polhill, *Fl. Trop. E. Africa, Leguminosae* 4: 653. 1971): [icon] *"Phaseolus flore odorato, vexillo amplo patulo"* in Dillenius, Hort. Eltham. 2: 313, t. 234, f. 302. 1732.
Current name: *Vigna vexillata* (L.) A. Rich. (Fabaceae: Faboideae).

Phaseolus vulgaris Linnaeus, *Species Plantarum* 2: 723. 1753.
"Habitat in India." RCN: 5314.
Lectotype (Verdcourt in Milne-Redhead & Polhill, *Fl. Trop. E. Africa, Leguminosae* 4: 614. 1971): Herb. Linn. No. 899.1 (LINN).
Generitype of *Phaseolus* Linnaeus (vide Green, *Prop. Brit. Bot.*: 175. 1929).
Current name: *Phaseolus vulgaris* L. (Fabaceae: Faboideae).

Phaseolus vulgaris Linnaeus var. **coccineus** (Linnaeus) Linnaeus, *Species Plantarum*, ed. 2, 2: 1016. 1763.
["Habitat – – – –"] Sp. Pl. 2: 724 (1753). RCN: 5314.
Basionym: *Phaseolus coccineus* L. (1753).
Lectotype (Westphal, *Pulses Ethiopia, Taxon. Agric. Signif.*: 139. 1974): Herb. Linn. No. 899.2 (LINN).
Current name: *Phaseolus coccineus* L. (Fabaceae: Faboideae).

Phellandrium aquaticum Linnaeus, *Species Plantarum* 1: 255. 1753.
"Habitat in Europae fossis." RCN: 2046.
Lectotype (Reduron & Jarvis in Jarvis & al., *Regnum Veg.* 127: 75. 1993): Herb. Clifford: 100, *Phellandrium* 1 (BM-000558326).
Generitype of *Phellandrium* Linnaeus (vide Wolf, *Gen. Sp.*: 77. 1781; Hitchcock, *Prop. Brit. Bot.*: 140. 1929).
Current name: *Oenanthe aquatica* (L.) Poir. (Apiaceae).

Phellandrium mutellina Linnaeus, *Species Plantarum* 1: 255. 1753.
"Habitat in Helvetica." RCN: 2047.
Lectotype (Reduron & al. in *J. Bot. Soc. Bot. France* 1: 100. 1997): Herb. Burser VII(2): 6 (UPS).
Current name: *Ligusticum mutellina* (L.) Crantz (Apiaceae).
Note: Leute (in *Ann. Naturhist. Mus. Wien* 74: 468. 1970) indicated unspecified material in LINN as "Holo-Typus". However, 360.2 is a post-1753 addition from Scopoli, and 360.3 came from Gmelin, certainly not from Switzerland as stated by Linnaeus. Neither is original material for the name.

Philadelphus coronarius Linnaeus, *Species Plantarum* 1: 470. 1753.
"Habitat – – – –" RCN: 3592.
Lectotype (Hu in *J. Arnold Arbor.* 36: 99. 1955): Herb. Linn. No. 634.1 (LINN).
Generitype of *Philadelphus* Linnaeus (vide Green, *Prop. Brit. Bot.*: 158. 1929).
Current name: *Philadelphus coronarius* L. (Hydrangeaceae).

Philadelphus inodorus Linnaeus, *Species Plantarum* 1: 470. 1753.
"Habitat in Carolina." RCN: 3593.
Lectotype (Dandy, *Sloane Herbarium*: 112. 1958): [icon] *"Philadelphus flore albo majore inodoro"* in Catesby, Nat. Hist. Carolina 2: 84, t. 84. 1743. – Voucher: Herb. Sloane 212: 16 (BM-SL).
Current name: *Philadelphus inodorus* L. (Hydrangeaceae).

Phillyrea angustifolia Linnaeus, *Species Plantarum* 1: 7. 1753.
"Habitat in Europae australioris collibus." RCN: 50.
Type not designated.
Original material: Herb. Clifford: 4, *Phillyrea* 2 (BM); Herb. Burser XXIV: 130 (UPS); Herb. Linn. No. 4.1 (S); Herb. Linn. No. 19.3 (LINN); Herb. Burser XXIV: 127 (UPS).
Current name: *Phillyrea angustifolia* L. (Oleaceae).

Phillyrea latifolia Linnaeus, *Species Plantarum* 1: 8. 1753.
"Habitat in Europa australi." RCN: 52.
Lectotype (Green in Jarvis & al., *Regnum Veg.* 127: 75. 1993): Herb.
Linn. No. 19.4, upper specimen (LINN).
Generitype of *Phillyrea* Linnaeus (vide Hitchcock in *Amer. J. Bot.* 10:
514. 1923).
Current name: ***Phillyrea latifolia*** L. (Oleaceae).

Phillyrea ligustrifolia Linnaeus, *Amoenitates Academicae* 4: 476.
1759.
Type not designated.
Original material: none traced.
Current name: ***Phillyrea latifolia*** L. (Oleaceae).
Note: For a discussion of this name, see Stearn (in Geck & Pressler,
Festschr. Claus Nissen: 640. 1974).

Phillyrea media Linnaeus, *Systema Naturae,* ed. 10, 2: 847. 1759.
["Habitat in Europae australioris collibus."] Sp. Pl., ed. 2, 1: 10
(1762). RCN: 50.
Type not designated.
Original material: Herb. Linn. No. 19.2 (LINN); Herb. Linn. No.
19.1 (LINN).
Current name: ***Phillyrea latifolia*** L. (Oleaceae).

Phleum alpinum Linnaeus, *Species Plantarum* 1: 59. 1753.
"Habitat in Alpibus." RCN: 510.
Lectotype (Bowden in *Canad. J. Bot.* 43: 286. 1965): Herb. Linn. No.
81.4 (LINN).
Current name: ***Phleum alpinum*** L. (Poaceae).
Note: Humphries (in *Bot. J. Linn. Soc.* 76: 338. 1978) designated a
Lapland specimen, collected by Linnaeus and now in the Institut de
France, as the lectotype. However, the earlier choice by Bowden of a
collection in LINN has priority.

Phleum arenarium Linnaeus, *Species Plantarum* 1: 60. 1753.
"Habitat in Europae locis arenosis." RCN: 511.
Lectotype (Doğan in Cafferty & al. in *Taxon* 49: 254. 2000): Herb.
Linn. No. 81.6 (LINN).
Current name: ***Phleum arenarium*** L. (Poaceae).
Note: Although Kerguélen (in *Lejeunia*, n.s., 75: 229. 1975) stated
"Type: ...LINN", this is not accepted as a formal typification, for
the reasons explained by Cafferty & al. (in *Taxon* 49: 240. 2000).

Phleum nodosum Linnaeus, *Systema Naturae,* ed. 10, 2: 871. 1759.
["Habitat in Gallia, Helvetia, Italia."] Sp. Pl., ed. 2, 1: 88 (1762).
RCN: 509.
Lectotype (Doğan in Cafferty & al. in *Taxon* 49: 254. 2000): *Séguier,*
Herb. Linn. No. 81.2 (LINN).
Current name: ***Phleum nodosum*** L. (Poaceae).
Note: Although often treated as a variety of *P. pratense* L., *P. nodosum*
has also been taken up at species rank in the sense of *P. bertolonii*
DC., over which the Linnaean name has priority. However, recent
accounts have tended either to use *P. bertolonii* at species rank, or *P.
pratensis* subsp. *bertolonii* (DC.) Bornm. at subspecific rank. Doğan,
in typifying the name, favoured recognition at species rank with *P.
bertolonii* falling into the synonymy of *P. nodosum*. However, if
treated at the subspecies level, the correct name appears to be *P.
pratensis* subsp. *nodosum* (L.) Dumort.

Phleum pratense Linnaeus, *Species Plantarum* 1: 59. 1753.
"Habitat in Europae versuris & pratis." RCN: 508.
Lectotype (Humphries in Jarvis & al., *Regnum Veg.* 127: 75. 1993):
Herb. Linn. No. 26 (LAPP).
Generitype of *Phleum* Linnaeus (vide Hitchcock, *Prop. Brit. Bot.*: 119.
1929).

Current name: ***Phleum pratense*** L. (Poaceae).
Note: Although Kerguélen (in *Lejeunia*, n.s., 75: 232. 1975) stated
"Type: ...LINN", this is not accepted as a formal typification, for
the reasons explained by Cafferty & al. (in *Taxon* 49: 240. 2000).
Doğan (in *Karaca Arbor. Mag.* 1: 56. 1991) indicated 81.1 (LINN)
as the type, but this sheet lacks the *Species Plantarum* number (i.e.
"1") and is a post-1753 addition to the collection. It is not
original material for the name and Humphries' later choice is
accepted here.

Phleum schoenoides Linnaeus, *Species Plantarum* 1: 60. 1753.
"Habitat in Italia, Smyrna, inque Hispania. Loefling." RCN: 512.
Lectotype (Clayton in Polhill, *Fl. Trop. E. Africa, Gramineae* 2: 353.
1974): Herb. Linn. No. 81.7 (LINN).
Current name: ***Crypsis schoenoides*** (L.) Lam. (Poaceae).

Phlomis fruticosa Linnaeus, *Species Plantarum* 2: 584. 1753.
"Habitat in Sicilia, Hispania." RCN: 4267.
Lectotype (Press in Jarvis & al., *Regnum Veg.* 127: 75. 1993): Herb.
Clifford: 315, *Phlomis* 3, sheet 2 (BM-000646141).
Generitype of *Phlomis* Linnaeus (vide Green, *Prop. Brit. Bot.*: 165.
1929).
Current name: ***Phlomis fruticosa*** L. (Lamiaceae).

Phlomis herba-venti Linnaeus, *Species Plantarum* 2: 586. 1753.
"Habitat in Persia, Tataria, Narbona ad aggeres." RCN: 4274.
Lectotype (Alziar & Cafferty in *Biocosme Mésogéen* 14: 120. 1998):
Herb. Burser XIII: 34 (UPS).
Current name: ***Phlomis herba-venti*** L. (Lamiaceae).

Phlomis indica Linnaeus, *Species Plantarum* 2: 586. 1753.
"Habitat in India." RCN: 4277.
Neotype (Paton in Jarvis & al. in *Taxon* 50: 516. 2001): India. Nilgiri
Hills, Pykura, 1878, *G. King s.n.* (K).
Current name: ***Leucas zeylanica*** (L.) R. Br. (Lamiaceae).
Note: This name has been out of use for many years. From Linnaeus'
lengthy description, he evidently had material available to him but
this is now lost. It seems very likely that this name referred to the
same species which Linnaeus described as *P. zeylanica* in 1753, and a
neotype was chosen by Paton to formalise this, with *P. indica* falling
into the synonymy of *L. zeylanica*.

Phlomis italica Linnaeus, *Systema Naturae,* ed. 10, 2: 1102. 1759.
RCN: 4269.
Neotype (Alziar & Cafferty in *Biocosme Mésogéen* 14: 120, f. 1. 1998):
Spain. Pl. d'espagne Baleares 1869. 2786. *E. Bourgeau, Sheet A-
2193* (NICE; iso- BM).
Current name: ***Phlomis italica*** L. (Lamiaceae).

Phlomis laciniata Linnaeus, *Species Plantarum* 2: 585. 1753.
"Habitat in Oriente." RCN: 4272.
Lectotype (Hedge in *Notes Roy. Bot. Gard. Edinburgh* 27: 161. 1967):
Herb. Linn. No. 740.8 (LINN).
Current name: ***Eremostachys laciniata*** (L.) Bunge (Lamiaceae).
Note: Hedge stated "Type: Tournefort (LINN-photo!)". Although its
provenance is uncertain, there is only one sheet in LINN that could
possibly have been intended, so Hedge's statement is accepted as a
formal typification.

Phlomis leonotis Linnaeus, *Systema Naturae,* ed. 12, 2: 398; *Mantissa
Plantarum*: 83. 1767.
"Habitat ad Cap. b. Spei." RCN: 4280.
Lectotype (Iwarsson in Leistner, *Fl. Southern Africa* 28(4): 34. 1985):
Herb. Linn. No. 740.21 (LINN).
Current name: ***Leonotis ocymifolia*** (Burm. f.) Iwarsson (Lamiaceae).

Phlomis leonurus Linnaeus, *Species Plantarum* 2: 587. 1753.
"Habitat ad Cap. b. Spei." RCN: 4279.
Lectotype (Wijnands, *Bot. Commelins*: 116. 1983): Herb. Linn. No. 740.19 (LINN).
Current name: **Leonotis leonurus** (L.) R. Br. (Lamiaceae).

Phlomis lychnitis Linnaeus, *Species Plantarum* 2: 585. 1753.
"Habitat in Europa australi. D. Sauvages." RCN: 4271.
Lectotype (Alziar & Cafferty in *Biocosme Mésogéen* 14: 123. 1998): Herb. Burser XIII: 132 (UPS).
Current name: **Phlomis lychnitis** L. (Lamiaceae).
Note: Mateu (in *Acta Bot. Malac.* 11: 188. 1986) indicated 740.7 LINN, a Löfling collection from Spain, as the type. However, Alziar & Cafferty, citing doubts as to its date of receipt and the absence of any reference to Spain in the protologue, declined to accept it as original material and designated Burser material as the lectotype.

Phlomis nepetifolia Linnaeus, *Species Plantarum* 2: 586. 1753.
"Habitat Surinami?" RCN: 4278.
Lectotype (Iwarsson in Leistner, *Fl. Southern Africa* 28(4): 37. 1985): [icon] *"Cardiaca Americana annua Nepetae folio, floribus brevibus phoeniceis villosis"* in Hermann, Hort. Lugd.-Bat. Cat.: 115, 117. 1687.
Current name: **Leonotis nepetifolia** (L.) R. Br. (Lamiaceae).
Note: Specific epithet spelled "nepetaefolia" in the protologue.

Phlomis nissolii Linnaeus, *Species Plantarum* 2: 585. 1753.
"Habitat in Oriente." RCN: 4270.
Neotype (Alziar & Cafferty in *Biocosme Mésogéen* 14: 124, f. 2. 1998): Turkey. Anatolie, Antalya, Akseki, Manavgat-Akseki, 4 Jul 1964, *A. Huber-Morath 16916* (G).
Current name: **Phlomis nissolii** L. (Lamiaceae).

Phlomis purpurea Linnaeus, *Species Plantarum* 2: 585. 1753.
"Habitat in Lusitania." RCN: 4268.
Lectotype (Alziar & Cafferty in *Biocosme Mésogéen* 14: 125. 1998): [icon] *"Salvia fruiticosa Cisti folio haud incano, floribus purpureis"* in Plukenet, Phytographia: t. 57, f. 6. 1691; Almag. Bot.: 329. 1696. – Typotype: Herb. Sloane 83: 105 (BM-SL). – Epitype (Alziar & Cafferty in *Biocosme Mésogéen* 14: 125. 1998): Spain. Almeria, Sierra de Gador, Fuente Victoria, Cerro Alto, 18 Jun 1988, *B. Valdes et al., Optima – Iter Medit. No. 635.* Herbiers du Jardin Botanique de la Ville de Nice (JBVN No. A-3301; iso- B, FI, G, LAU, PAL, RNG, SEV).
Current name: **Phlomis purpurea** L. (Lamiaceae).
Note: Mateu (in *Acta Bot. Malac.* 11: 195. 1986) indicated 740.5 LINN as type, but this sheet is unannotated by Linnaeus, and also comes from much further east than Iberia; it is not original material for the name.

Phlomis samia Linnaeus, *Species Plantarum* 2: 585. 1753.
"Habitat in Samo." RCN: 4273.
Lectotype (Turland in Jarvis & al. in *Taxon* 50: 516. 2001): Herb. Clifford: 315, *Phlomis* 1 (BM-000646138).
Current name: **Phlomis samia** L. (Lamiaceae).

Phlomis tuberosa Linnaeus, *Species Plantarum* 2: 586. 1753.
"Habitat in Sibiriae campestribus." RCN: 4275.
Lectotype (Alziar & Cafferty in *Biocosme Mésogéen* 14: 125. 1998): Herb. Linn. No. 740.13 (LINN).
Current name: **Phlomis tuberosa** L. (Lamiaceae).

Phlomis zeylanica Linnaeus, *Species Plantarum* 2: 586. 1753.
"Habitat in India." RCN: 4276.
Lectotype (Hedge in Jarvis & al. in *Taxon* 50: 516. 2001): Herb. Hermann 1: 1, No. 227 (BM-000621228).

Current name: **Leucas zeylanica** (L.) R. Br. (Lamiaceae).
Note: Cramer (in *Revised Handb. Fl. Ceylon 3*: 183. 1981) indicated as "type" a specimen (sheet 740.14) in LINN, but this is a post-1753 addition to the collection and is not considered original material for the name. Barker (*Fl. Australia* 50: 369. 1993) indicated various Hermann specimens as possible syntypes, and one of these was designated as lectotype by Hedge.

Phlox carolina Linnaeus, *Species Plantarum*, ed. 2, 1: 216. 1762.
"Habitat in Carolina." RCN: 1208.
Lectotype (Wherry, *Genus* Phlox: 104. 1955): Herb. Linn. No. 217.7 (LINN).
Current name: **Phlox carolina** L. (Polemoniaceae).

Phlox divaricata Linnaeus, *Species Plantarum* 1: 152. 1753.
"Habitat in Virginia." RCN: 1210.
Lectotype (Wherry, *Genus* Phlox: 39. 1955): Herb. Linn. No. 217.9 (LINN).
Current name: **Phlox divaricata** L. (Polemoniaceae).

Phlox glaberrima Linnaeus, *Species Plantarum* 1: 152. 1753.
"Habitat in Virginia." RCN: 1209.
Lectotype (Reveal in *Phytologia* 71: 477. 1991): Herb. Linn. No. 217.8 (LINN).
Generitype of *Phlox* Linnaeus (vide Hitchcock, *Prop. Brit. Bot.*: 130. 1929).
Current name: **Phlox glaberrima** L. (Polemoniaceae).

Phlox maculata Linnaeus, *Species Plantarum* 1: 152. 1753.
"Habitat in Virginia. Kalm." RCN: 1206.
Lectotype (Wherry, *Genus* Phlox: 113. 1955): *Kalm*, Herb. Linn. No. 217.3 (LINN).
Current name: **Phlox maculata** L. (Polemoniaceae).
Note: See discussion by Reveal & al. (in *Huntia* 7: 227. 1987).

Phlox ovata Linnaeus, *Species Plantarum* 1: 152. 1753.
"Habitat in Virginia." RCN: 1211.
Lectotype (Wilbur in *Taxon* 36: 131. 1987): Herb. Linn. No. 217.10 (LINN), see p. 200.
Current name: **Phlox ovata** L. (Polemoniaceae).
Note: Wherry (*Genus* Phlox: 100. 1955) treated the Plukenet element as the type, but the voucher collection was subsequently shown to belong to *Ruellia caroliniensis* (Walt.) Steud. (Acanthaceae). Wilbur (in *Taxon* 36: 131. 1987) rejected this choice on the grounds that the plate conflicted with the generic description, and chose 217.10 (LINN) as lectotype in its place. Reveal, however, believed Wherry's choice to be valid and proposed (in *Taxon* 38: 515. 1989) *P. ovata* for conservation with a conserved type. After a further response from Wilbur (*l.c.* 39: 297–298. 1990), the Committee for Spermatophyta ruled (*l.c.* 42: 694. 1993) that Wherry's choice should be superseded, that Wilbur's choice was valid, and that the proposal was therefore unnecessary, and not recommended.

Phlox paniculata Linnaeus, *Species Plantarum* 1: 151. 1753.
"Habitat in America septentrionali. Collinson." RCN: 1205.
Lectotype (Wherry, *Genus* Phlox: 120. 1955): Herb. Linn. No. 217.1 (LINN).
Current name: **Phlox paniculata** L. (Polemoniaceae).

Phlox pilosa Linnaeus, *Species Plantarum* 1: 152. 1753.
"Habitat in Virginia." RCN: 1207.
Lectotype (Wherry, *Genus* Phlox: 48. 1955): [icon] *"Lychinidaea umbellifera Blattariae accedens Virginiana major, repens, Pseudo-melanthii foliis pilosis, flore albo, pentapetaloide, fistuloso"* in Plukenet, Phytographia: t. 98, f. 1. 1691; Almag. Bot.: 233. 1696. – Voucher: Herb. Sloane 90: 59 (BM-SL).

Current name: ***Phlox pilosa*** L. (Polemoniaceae).
Note: See also discussion by Reveal & al. (in *Huntia* 7: 227. 1987).

Phlox setacea Linnaeus, *Species Plantarum* 1: 153. 1753.
"Habitat in Virginia." RCN: 1214.
Lectotype (Reveal & al. in *Taxon* 31: 735. 1982): [icon] *"Lychnidaea Blattariae accedens Virginiana Camphoratae congeneris glabris foliis, flore ad summitatem ramulorum singulari"* in Plukenet, Phytographia: t. 98, f. 3. 1691; Almag. Bot.: 233. 1696. – Typotype: Herb. Sloane 90: 59 (BM-SL).
Current name: ***Phlox subulata*** L. var. ***setacea*** (L.) Brand (Polemoniaceae).

Phlox sibirica Linnaeus, *Species Plantarum* 1: 153. 1753.
"Habitat in Asia boreali." RCN: 1213.
Lectotype (Wherry, *Genus Phlox*: 126. 1955): Herb. Linn. No. 217.13 (LINN; iso- MW No. 466).
Current name: ***Phlox sibirica*** L. (Polemoniaceae).
Note: See comments by Jarvis & al. (in *Taxon* 50: 1133, f. 3. 2002) on the Demidoff material in MW, and its relationship to the sheet in LINN.

Phlox subulata Linnaeus, *Species Plantarum* 1: 152. 1753.
"Habitat in Virginia." RCN: 1212.
Lectotype (Wherry, *Genus Phlox*: 22. 1955): *Kalm*, Herb. Linn. No. 217.12 (LINN).
Current name: ***Phlox subulata*** L. (Polemoniaceae).
Note: Specific epithet misprinted as "ulata" in the protologue. Printed correctly, with the same phrase name and species number, in *Systema Naturae*, ed. 10, 2: 921 (1759).

Phoenix dactylifera Linnaeus, *Species Plantarum* 2: 1188. 1753.
"Habitat in India." RCN: 8546.
Lectotype (Moore & Dransfield in *Taxon* 28: 64, f. 6. 1979; Greuter & Jarvis in Jarvis & al., *Regnum Veg.* 127: 75. 1993): [icon] *"Palma hortensis"* in Kaempfer, Amoen. Exot. Fasc.: 668, 697, t. 2, f. 11. 1712.
Generitype of *Phoenix* Linnaeus.
Current name: ***Phoenix dactylifera*** L. (Arecaceae).
Note: Moore & Dransfield (in *Taxon* 28: 64–67. 1979) gave a detailed account of the typification of this name, also reproducing Kaempfer's plates (t. 1, 2). As these comprise a large number of elements, Greuter & Jarvis restricted this choice to an infructescence.

Phryma leptostachya Linnaeus, *Species Plantarum* 2: 601. 1753.
"Habitat in America septentrionali." RCN: 4367.
Lectotype (Qaiser in Nasir & Ali, *Fl. W. Pakistan* 46: 3. 1973): *Kalm*, Herb. Linn. No. 755.1 (LINN).
Generitype of *Phryma* Linnaeus.
Current name: ***Phryma leptostachya*** L. (Phrymaceae).
Note: See discussion by Reveal & al. (in *Huntia* 7: 237. 1987), who independently chose the same type as Qaiser.

Phylica bicolora Linnaeus, *Mantissa Plantarum Altera*: 208. 1771.
"Habitat ad Cap. b. spei, in campis arenosis." RCN: 1575.
Type not designated.
Original material: *Tulbagh 104*, Herb. Linn. No. 263.4 (LINN).
Current name: ***Phylica strigosa*** P.J. Bergius (Rhamnaceae).

Phylica buxifolia Linnaeus, *Species Plantarum* 1: 195. 1753.
"Habitat in Aethiopia." RCN: 1581.
Lectotype (Wijnands, *Bot. Commelins*: 181. 1983): Herb. Linn. No. 263.10 (LINN).
Current name: ***Phylica buxifolia*** L. (Rhamnaceae).

Phylica cordata Linnaeus, *Species Plantarum*, ed. 2, 1: 283. 1762.
"Habitat ad Cap. b. Spei." RCN: 1580.
Lectotype (Wijnands, *Bot. Commelins*: 181. 1983): [icon] *"Alaternoides Afric. chamaemespili folio"* in Commelin, Praeludia Bot.: 62, t. 12. 1703.
Current name: ***Phylica buxifolia*** L. (Rhamnaceae).

Phylica dioica Linnaeus, *Systema Naturae*, ed. 10, 2: 938. 1759.
["Habitat ad Cap. b. spei."] Sp. Pl., ed. 2, 1: 283 (1762). RCN: 1579.
Type not designated.
Original material: Herb. Burman (G); Herb. Linn. No. 263.8 (LINN).
Current name: ***Phylica dioica*** L. (Rhamnaceae).

Phylica ericoides Linnaeus, *Species Plantarum* 1: 195. 1753.
"Habitat in Aethiopia." RCN: 1574.
Lectotype (Wijnands, *Bot. Commelins*: 182. 1983): Herb. Linn. No. 263.1 (LINN).
Generitype of *Phylica* Linnaeus (vide Hitchcock, *Prop. Brit. Bot.*: 134. 1929).
Current name: ***Phylica ericoides*** L. (Rhamnaceae).

Phylica plumosa Linnaeus, *Species Plantarum* 1: 195. 1753.
"Habitat in Aethiopia." RCN: 1576.
Lectotype (Wijnands, *Bot. Commelins*: 182. 1983): Herb. Linn. No. 263.5, central specimen (LINN).
Current name: ***Phylica plumosa*** L. (Rhamnaceae).

Phylica racemosa Linnaeus, *Mantissa Plantarum Altera*: 209. 1771.
"Habitat juxta Cap. b. spei. Fossas." RCN: 1582.
Type not designated.
Original material: *Tulbagh 131*, Herb. Linn. No. 263.12 (LINN).
Current name: ***Pseudobaeckia racemosa*** (L.) Nied. (Bruniaceae).

Phylica radiata Linnaeus, *Centuria I Plantarum*: 8. 1755.
"Habitat ad Caput Bonae Spei." RCN: 1618.
Type not designated.
Original material: Herb. Linn. No. 217.8 (LINN); [icon] in Breyn, Exot. Pl. Cent.: 165, t. 82. 1678.
Current name: ***Staavia radiata*** (L.) Dahl (Bruniaceae).

Phylica stipularis Linnaeus, *Mantissa Plantarum Altera*: 208. 1771.
"Habitat ad Cap. b. spei arenosa." RCN: 1578.
Lectotype (Cafferty & Beyers in *Taxon* 48: 172. 1999): *Tulbagh 24*, Herb. Linn. No. 263.7 (LINN).
Current name: ***Phylica stipularis*** L. (Rhamnaceae).
Note: The name was threatened by *Lachnaea conglomerata* L. (1753), which was successfully proposed for rejection by Cafferty & Beyers (in *Taxon* 48: 171. 1999).

Phyllanthus bacciformis Linnaeus, *Mantissa Plantarum Altera*: 294. 1771.
"Habitat in Tranquebaria. Koenig." RCN: 7112.
Lectotype (Scott in Bosser & al., *Fl. Mascareignes* 160: 37. 1982): *König s.n.*, Herb. Linn. No. 1105.6 (LINN).
Current name: ***Sauropus bacciformis*** (L.) Airy Shaw (Euphorbiaceae).

Phyllanthus emblica Linnaeus, *Species Plantarum* 2: 982. 1753.
"Habitat in India." RCN: 7114.
Type not designated.
Original material: Herb. Hermann 5: 85, No. 333 [icon] (BM); Herb. Burser XXIII: 47 (UPS); [icon] in Zanoni, Istoria Bot.: 154, t. 61. 1675; [icon] in Rheede, Hort. Malab. 1: 69, t. 38. 1678.
Current name: ***Phyllanthus emblica*** L. (Euphorbiaceae).

Note: Radcliffe-Smith (in *Kew Bull.* 41: 35. 1986) indicated 1105.11 (LINN) as holotype, but this collection lacks the relevant *Species Plantarum* number (i.e. "6") and was a post-1753 addition to the herbarium, and is not original material for the name.

Phyllanthus epiphyllanthus Linnaeus, *Species Plantarum* 2: 981. 1753.
"Habitat in America calidiore, Surinamo, Jamaica, Carolina, Porto Rico." RCN: 2152.
Replaced synonym of: *Xylophylla latifolia* L. (1771), *nom. illeg.*
Lectotype (Webster in *J. Arnold Arbor.* 37: 2. 1956): Herb. Clifford: 439, *Phyllanthus* 1 (BM-000647366).
Current name: ***Phyllanthus epiphyllanthus*** L. (Euphorbiaceae).
Note: Merrill (*Interpret. Rumph. Herb. Amb.*: 208. 1917) indicated a Rumphius element as the type but, although it appears in a 1759 account of the species, it is not cited in the protologue and is therefore not original material for the name.

Phyllanthus grandifolius Linnaeus, *Species Plantarum* 2: 981. 1753.
"Habitat in America." RCN: 7109.
Lectotype (Webster in *J. Arnold Arbor.* 37: 10. 1956): Herb. Clifford: 440, *Phyllanthus* 3 (BM).
Current name: ***Phyllanthus grandifolius*** L. (Euphorbiaceae).

Phyllanthus maderaspatensis Linnaeus, *Species Plantarum* 2: 982. 1753.
"Habitat in India." RCN: 7113.
Neotype (Radcliffe-Smith in *Kew Bull.* 40: 658. 1985): India. Madras, Herb. Heyne in Wall. Num. List No. 7906Fa (K-WAL).
Current name: ***Phyllanthus maderaspatensis*** L. (Euphorbiaceae).
Note: Coode (in Bosser & al., *Fl. Mascareignes* 160: 26. 1982) indicated 1105.12 (LINN) as the type, but this is a König collection received by Linnaeus long after 1753 and is not original material for the name.

Phyllanthus niruri Linnaeus, *Species Plantarum* 2: 981. 1753.
"Habitat in Indiis." RCN: 7110.
Lectotype (Webster in *J. Arnold Arbor.* 37: 13. 1956): Herb. Clifford: 440, *Phyllanthus* 2 (BM-000647367).
Generitype of *Phyllanthus* Linnaeus (vide Green, *Prop. Brit. Bot.*: 188. 1929).
Current name: ***Phyllanthus niruri*** L. (Euphorbiaceae).
Note: Fawcett & Rendle (*Fl. Jamaica* 4: 256. 1920) indicated type material in LINN, but did not distinguish between sheets 1105.2 and 1105.3. The sheets are not from a single gathering so Art. 9.15 does not apply. Webster (pp. 4–7) provides a detailed review of the elements associated with this name.

Phyllanthus urinaria Linnaeus, *Species Plantarum* 2: 982. 1753.
"Habitat in India." RCN: 7111.
Lectotype (Fawcett & Rendle, *Fl. Jamaica* 4: 255. 1920): Herb. Hermann 1: 15; 2: 7; 3: 55; 4: 41, No. 332 (BM).
Current name: ***Phyllanthus urinaria*** L. (Euphorbiaceae).
Note: Fawcett & Rendle indicated type material in the Hermann herbarium (BM). Although there is material in a number of its volumes, they appear to be part of a single gathering, and this type choice is therefore accepted (Art. 9.15). No effective restriction appears to have been published. See Webster (in *J. Arnold Arbor.* 37: 7. 1956).

Phyllis indica Linnaeus, *Species Plantarum* 1: 232. 1753.
"Habitat in India." RCN: 1890.
Type not designated.
Original material: none traced.
Note: The application of this name is uncertain.

Phyllis nobla Linnaeus, *Species Plantarum* 1: 232. 1753.
"Habitat in Canariis." RCN: 1889.
Lectotype (Verdcourt in Jarvis & al., *Regnum Veg.* 127: 76. 1993): [icon] "*Valerianella Canariensis frutescens, Simpla nobla dicta*" in Dillenius, Hort. Eltham. 2: 405, t. 299, f. 386. 1732.
Generitype of *Phyllis* Linnaeus (vide Hitchcock, *Prop. Brit. Bot.*: 138. 1929).
Current name: ***Phyllis nobla*** L. (Rubiaceae).

Physalis alkekengi Linnaeus, *Species Plantarum* 1: 183. 1753.
"Habitat in Italia." RCN: 1450.
Lectotype (Schönbeck-Temesy in Rechinger, *Fl. Iranica* 100: 24. 1972): Herb. Linn. No. 247.5 (LINN).
Generitype of *Physalis* Linnaeus (vide Hitchcock, *Prop. Brit. Bot.*: 132. 1929).
Current name: ***Physalis alkekengi*** L. (Solanaceae).

Physalis angulata Linnaeus, *Species Plantarum* 1: 183. 1753.
"Habitat in India utraque." RCN: 1452.
Lectotype (D'Arcy in Woodson & Schery in *Ann. Missouri Bot. Gard.* 60: 662. 1974): Herb. Linn. No. 247.9 (LINN).
Current name: ***Physalis angulata*** L. (Solanaceae).

Physalis arborescens Linnaeus, *Species Plantarum*, ed. 2, 1: 261. 1762, *nom. illeg.*
"Habitat in Campechia." RCN: 1446.
Replaced synonym: *Physalis campechiana* L. (1759).
Type not designated.
Original material: as replaced synonym.
Current name: ***Physalis campechiana*** L. (Solanaceae).
Note: This appears to be an illegitimate renaming of *P. campechiana* L. (1759). Nee (in Gómez-Pompa, *Fl. Veracruz* 49: 142. 1986) used *P. arborescens*, treating Houstoun material (BM) as "type". However, this is very unlikely to be original material for the name, and a Miller plate is cited by Linnaeus in the synonymy of *P. campechiana*, so the Houstoun material cannot be treated as a neotype.

Physalis campechiana Linnaeus, *Systema Naturae*, ed. 10, 2: 933. 1759.
["Habitat in Campechia."] Sp. Pl., ed. 2, 1: 261 (1762). RCN: 1446.
Replaced synonym of: *Physalis arborescens* L. (1762), *nom. illeg.*
Type not designated.
Original material: [icon] in Miller, Fig. Pl. Gard. Dict. 2: 138, t. 206, f. 2. 1758.
Current name: ***Physalis campechiana*** L. (Solanaceae).
Note: Specific epithet spelled "campech." in the protologue.

Physalis curassavica Linnaeus, *Species Plantarum* 1: 182. 1753.
"Habitat in Curassao." RCN: 1447.
Type not designated.
Original material: Herb. Clifford: 62, *Physalis* 3 (BM); [icon] in Plukenet, Phytographia: t. 111, f. 5. 1691; Almag. Bot.: 352. 1696.
Current name: ***Physalis viscosa*** L. (Solanaceae).

Physalis flexuosa Linnaeus, *Species Plantarum* 1: 182. 1753.
"Habitat in India." RCN: 1445.
Lectotype (Deb in *J. Econ. Taxon. Bot.* 1: 52. 1980): Herb. Linn. No. 247.2 (LINN).
Current name: ***Withania somnifera*** (L.) Dunal (Solanaceae).

Physalis minima Linnaeus, *Species Plantarum* 1: 183. 1753.
"Habitat in Indiae aridis sordidis." RCN: 1454.
Lectotype (designated here by Edmonds): Herb. Clifford: 62, *Physalis* 6 (BM).
Current name: ***Physalis angulata*** L. (Solanaceae).

P

Note: Heine (in Aubréville & Leroy, *Fl. Nouvelle-Calédonie* 7: 132. 1975) wrongly indicated Hermann material (BM) as lectotype but, in the absence of a reference in the protologue to Linnaeus' *Flora Zeylanica*, this cannot be original material for this name. Heine took up *P. minima* in the sense of *P. lagascae* Roem. & Schult. and was followed by a number of later authors. However, others have treated it as a synonym of *P. angulata* L. (see Nicolson & al. in *Regnum Veg* 119: 248. 1988), and this is confirmed by Edmonds' formal typification.

Physalis pensylvanica Linnaeus, *Species Plantarum*, ed. 2, 2: 1670. 1763.
"Habitat in Virginia." RCN: 1449.
Type not designated.
Original material: Herb. Linn. No. 247.4 (LINN).
Current name: ***Physalis viscosa*** L. (Solanaceae).

Physalis peruviana Linnaeus, *Species Plantarum*, ed. 2, 2: 1670. 1763.
"Habitat Limae. Alstroemer." RCN: 1451.
Lectotype (Heine in Aubréville & Leroy, *Fl. Nouvelle-Calédonie* 7: 132. 1975): Herb. Linn. No. 247.7 (LINN).
Current name: ***Physalis peruviana*** L. (Solanaceae).

Physalis pruinosa Linnaeus, *Species Plantarum* 1: 184. 1753.
"Habitat in America." RCN: 1455.
Lectotype (Waterfall in *Rhodora* 60: 167. 1958): Herb. Linn. No. 247.13 (LINN).
Current name: ***Physalis pruinosa*** L. (Solanaceae).
Note: Although the reference by Waterfall (in *Rhodora* 60: 167. 1958) to a photo ("A") of the type may appear vague, on p. 165 it is made clear that this is one of the "photographs of specimens in the Linnaean Herbarium, London". See also Martínez (in *Taxon* 42: 103. 1993).

Physalis pubescens Linnaeus, *Species Plantarum* 1: 183. 1753.
"Habitat in India utraque." RCN: 1453.
Lectotype (Waterfall in *Rhodora* 60: 165. 1958): Herb. Linn. No. 247.11 (LINN).
Current name: ***Physalis pubescens*** L. (Solanaceae).

Physalis somnifera Linnaeus, *Species Plantarum* 1: 182. 1753.
"Habitat in Mexico, Creta, Hispania." RCN: 1444.
Lectotype (Schönbeck-Temesy in Rechinger, *Fl. Iranica* 100: 27. 1972): Herb. Linn. No. 247.1 (LINN).
Current name: ***Withania somnifera*** (L.) Dunal (Solanaceae).

Physalis viscosa Linnaeus, *Species Plantarum* 1: 183. 1753.
"Habitat in Virginia, Bonaria." RCN: 1448.
Lectotype (Symon in *J. Adelaide Bot. Gard.* 3: 158. 1981): Herb. Linn. No. 247.3 (LINN).
Current name: ***Physalis viscosa*** L. (Solanaceae).

Phyteuma comosum Linnaeus, *Species Plantarum* 1: 171. 1753.
"Habitat in Baldi & Tyrolensibus montibus." RCN: 1344.
Type not designated.
Original material: Herb. Burser IV: 20 (UPS); [icon] in Bauhin, Prodr. Theatri Bot.: 33. 1620; [icon] in Clusius, Rar. Pl. Hist. 2: 333. 1601; [icon] in Plukenet, Phytographia: t. 152, f. 6. 1692; Almag. Bot.: 77. 1696 – Voucher: Herb. Sloane 95: 132 (BM-SL).
Current name: ***Physoplexis comosa*** (L.) Schur (Campanulaceae).
Note: Specific epithet spelled "comosa" in the protologue.

Phyteuma hemisphaericum Linnaeus, *Species Plantarum* 1: 170. 1753.
"Habitat in alpibus Helvetiae, Italiae, Pyrenaeis." RCN: 1343.

Lectotype (designated here by Pistarino & Jarvis): Herb. Linn. No. 223.4 (LINN).
Current name: ***Phyteuma hemisphaericum*** L. (Campanulaceae).
Note: Specific epithet spelled "hemisphaerica" in the protologue.

Phyteuma orbiculare Linnaeus, *Species Plantarum* 1: 170. 1753.
"Habitat in alpibus Italiae, Helvetiae, Veronae, Sussexiae." RCN: 1345.
Lectotype (designated here by Pistarino & Jarvis): Herb. Linn. No. 82.15 (S).
Current name: ***Phyteuma orbiculare*** L. (Campanulaceae).
Note: Specific epithet spelled "orbicularis" in the protologue.

Phyteuma pauciflorum Linnaeus, *Species Plantarum* 1: 170. 1753, *nom. rej.*
"Habitat in alpibus Helveticis Styriacis." RCN: 1342.
Lectotype (Cafferty & Sales in *Taxon* 48: 601. 1999): [icon] *"Rapunculus alpinus parvus comosus"* in Bauhin & Cherler, Hist. Pl. Univ. 2: 811. 1651.
Current name: ***Phyteuma globulariifolium*** Sternb. & Hoppe (Campanulaceae).
Note: Specific epithet spelled "pauciflora" in the protologue.

Phyteuma pinnatum Linnaeus, *Species Plantarum* 1: 171. 1753.
"Habitat in Creta." RCN: 1347.
Lectotype (Turland in *Willdenowia* 36: 306, f. 2. 2006): [icon] *"Pietra marola sive Lactuca Petraea"* in Bauhin & Cherler, Hist. Pl. Univ. 2: 812. 1651.
Current name: ***Petromarula pinnata*** (L.) A. DC. (Campanulaceae).
Note: Specific epithet spelled "pinnata" in the protologue.

Phyteuma spicatum Linnaeus, *Species Plantarum* 1: 171. 1753.
"Habitat in Alpestribus Helvetiae, Baldi, Angliae, Galliae." RCN: 1346.
Lectotype (Ayers in Jarvis & al., *Regnum Veg.* 127: 76. 1993): Herb. Linn. No. 223.8 (LINN).
Generitype of *Phyteuma* Linnaeus (vide Hitchcock, *Prop. Brit. Bot.*: 131. 1929).
Current name: ***Phyteuma spicatum*** L. (Campanulaceae).
Note: Specific epithet spelled "spicata" in the protologue.

Phytolacca americana Linnaeus, *Species Plantarum* 1: 441. 1753.
"Habitat in Virginia, Mexico." RCN: 3419.
Lectotype (Larsen in Morat, *Fl. Cambodge Laos Viêtnam* 24: 118. 1989): Herb. Linn. No. 607.3 (LINN).
Generitype of *Phytolacca* Linnaeus (vide Green, *Prop. Brit. Bot.*: 157. 1929).
Current name: ***Phytolacca americana*** L. (Phytolaccaceae).
Note: Although Nowicke (in *Ann. Missouri Bot. Gard.* 55: 318. 1969) typified *P. decandra* L. (1762), a synonym of *P. americana*, she gave no indication that she was treating the two names as homotypic, so she cannot be accepted as having typified *P. americana*. The first typification appears to be that of Larsen, which is accepted here. Reveal (in Jarvis & al., *Regnum Veg.* 127: 76. 1993) was unaware of Larsen's choice in designating a Clifford sheet (BM) as lectotype.

Phytolacca asiatica Linnaeus, *Species Plantarum* 1: 441. 1753.
"Habitat in Malabaria." RCN: 3422.
Lectotype (Ridsdale in Manilal, *Bot. Hist. Hort. Malab.*: 189. 1980): [icon] *"Nalugu"* in Rheede, Hort. Malab. 2: 43, t. 26. 1679.
Current name: ***Leea asiatica*** (L.) Ridsdale (Leeaceae).

Phytolacca decandra Linnaeus, *Species Plantarum*, ed. 2, 1: 631. 1762.
"Habitat in Virginia." RCN: 3419.

Lectotype (Nowicke in *Ann. Missouri Bot. Gard.* 55: 318. 1969): Herb. Linn. No. 607.3 (LINN).
Current name: ***Phytolacca americana*** L. (Phytolaccaceae).

Phytolacca dioica Linnaeus, *Species Plantarum,* ed. 2, 1: 632. 1762.
"Habitat in – – – – Alstroemer ex horto Madritensi." RCN: 3421.
Lectotype (Nowicke in *Ann. Missouri Bot. Gard.* 55: 311. 1969): *Alströmer 129a*, Herb. Linn. No. 607.5 (LINN).
Current name: ***Phytolacca dioica*** L. (Phytolaccaceae).

Phytolacca icosandra Linnaeus, *Systema Naturae,* ed. 10, 2: 1040. 1759.
["Habitat in Malabaria."] Sp. Pl., ed. 2, 1: 631 (1762). RCN: 3420.
Lectotype (Nowicke in *Ann. Missouri Bot. Gard.* 55: 312. 1969): Herb. Linn. No. 607.4 (LINN).
Current name: ***Phytolacca icosandra*** L. (Phytolaccaceae).

Phytolacca octandra Linnaeus, *Species Plantarum,* ed. 2, 1: 631. 1762.
"Habitat in Mexico." RCN: 3418.
Lectotype (Nowicke in *Ann. Missouri Bot. Gard.* 55: 313. 1969): Herb. Linn. No. 607.1 (LINN).
Current name: ***Phytolacca octandra*** L. (Phytolaccaceae).

Picris asplenioides Linnaeus, *Species Plantarum* 2: 793. 1753.
"Habitat in Aegypto." RCN: 5804.
Neotype (Lack in *Taxon* 24: 115, f. 1, 2. 1975): *Lippi* in Herb. Vaillant (P).
Current name: ***Picris asplenioides*** L. (Asteraceae).

Picris echioides Linnaeus, *Species Plantarum* 2: 792. 1753.
"Habitat in Angliae, Galliae sylvis caeduis, aggeribus." RCN: 5802.
Lectotype (Lack in *Taxon* 24: 113. 1975): Herb. Linn. No. 948.1 (LINN).
Current name: ***Helminthotheca echioides*** (L.) Holub (Asteraceae).

Picris hieracioides Linnaeus, *Species Plantarum* 2: 792. 1753.
"Habitat in Germaniae, Angliae, Belgii, Galliae versuris agrorum." RCN: 5803.
Lectotype (Lack in *Taxon* 24: 113. 1975): Herb. Clifford: 387, *Picris* 2 (BM-000646868).
Generitype of *Picris* Linnaeus (vide Steudel, *Nom.,* ed. 2, 2: 333. 1841).
Current name: ***Picris hieracioides*** L. (Asteraceae).
Note: *Picris hieracioides*, with the type designated by Lack, was proposed as conserved type of the genus by Jarvis (in *Taxon* 41: 567. 1992). However, the proposal was eventually ruled unnecessary by the General Committee (see Barrie, *l.c.* 55: 795–796. 2006 for a review of the history of this and related proposals).

Picris pyrenaica Linnaeus, *Species Plantarum* 2: 792. 1753.
"Habitat in Pyrenaeis." RCN: 5870.
Replaced synonym of: *Hieracium pyrenaicum* var. *pilosum* L. (1767).
Lectotype (Lack in *Taxon* 24: 113. 1975): [icon] *"Hieracium Blattariae folio"* in Hermann, Parad. Bat.: 184. 1698.
Current name: ***Crepis* sp.** (Asteraceae).
Note: Lack says this name relates to a species of *Crepis*, but notes that it cannot be taken up there as the epithet is pre-occupied by *C. pyrenaica* (L.) Greuter, based on *Hieracium pyrenaicum* L. (1753).

Pilularia globulifera Linnaeus, *Species Plantarum* 2: 1100. 1753.
"Habitat in Europae inundatis." RCN: 7958.
Lectotype (Bobrov in *Novosti Sist. Vyssh. Rast.* 21: 20. 1984): Herb. Linn. No. 1255.1 (LINN).
Generitype of *Pilularia* Linnaeus.

Current name: ***Pilularia globulifera*** L. (Marsileaceae).
Note: Further information on the original elements for this name is provided by Jonsell & Jarvis (in *Nordic J. Bot.* 14: 150. 1994) who, however, overlooked Bobrov's earlier choice.

Pimpinella anisum Linnaeus, *Species Plantarum* 1: 264. 1753.
"Habitat in Aegypto." RCN: 2106.
Lectotype (Yurtseva in *Byull. Moskovsk. Obshch. Isp. Prir., Otd. Biol.* 100(3): 66. 1995): Herb. Linn. No. 373.10 (LINN).
Current name: ***Pimpinella anisum*** L. (Apiaceae).

Pimpinella dichotoma Linnaeus, *Systema Naturae,* ed. 12, 2: 217; *Mantissa Plantarum*: 58. 1767.
"Habitat in Hispania." RCN: 2107.
Neotype (López González in Jarvis & al. in *Taxon* 55: 214. 2006): Herb. Linn. No. 373.11 (LINN).
Current name: ***Stoibrax dichotomum*** (L.) Raf. (Apiaceae).

Pimpinella dioica Linnaeus, *Systema Vegetabilium,* ed. 13: 241. 1774, *nom. illeg.*
["Habitat in Austria, Galloprovincia."] Sp. Pl., ed. 2, 1: 373 (1762). RCN: 2108.
Replaced synonym: *Seseli pumilum* L. (1759).
Lectotype (Reduron in Jarvis & al. in *Taxon* 55: 214. 2006): Herb. Linn. No. 367.22 (LINN).
Current name: ***Trinia glauca*** (L.) Dumort. (Apiaceae).
Note: A later, illegitimate replacement name for *Seseli pumilum* L. (1759), which had already been transferred to *Pimpinella*, as *P. pumila* (L.) Jacq. (1762). Linnaeus' phrase name of 1759 is entirely different from that given in *Mant. Pl. Alt.* (1771).

Pimpinella glauca Linnaeus, *Species Plantarum* 1: 264. 1753.
"Habitat in Helvetia, Gallia." RCN: 2104.
Lectotype (Reduron & Jarvis in Jarvis & al. in *Taxon* 55: 214. 2006): Herb. Linn. No. 373.8 (LINN).
Current name: ***Trinia glauca*** (L.) Dumort. (Apiaceae).

Pimpinella magna Linnaeus, *Mantissa Plantarum Altera*: 219. 1771, *nom. illeg.*
"Habitat in Europa australiore." RCN: 2103.
Replaced synonym: *Pimpinella major* Huds. (1762).
Type not designated.
Current name: ***Pimpinella major*** (L.) Huds. (Apiaceae).
Note: An illegitimate replacement name for *Pimpinella major* Huds. (1762).

Pimpinella peregrina Linnaeus, *Species Plantarum* 1: 264. 1753.
"Habitat in Italiae pascuis sterilibus." RCN: 2105.
Lectotype (Abebe in *Bot. J. Linn. Soc.* 110: 367. 1993): Herb. Linn. No. 373.9 (LINN).
Current name: ***Pimpinella peregrina*** L. (Apiaceae).

Pimpinella saxifraga Linnaeus, *Species Plantarum* 1: 263. 1753.
"Habitat in Europae pascuis siccis." RCN: 2102.
Lectotype (Reduron & Jarvis in Jarvis & al., *Regnum Veg.* 127: 76. 1993): Herb. Linn. No. 373.1 (LINN).
Generitype of *Pimpinella* Linnaeus (vide Rafinesque, *Good Book*: 52. 1840).
Current name: ***Pimpinella saxifraga*** L. (Apiaceae).
Note: Although Weide (in *Feddes Repert.* 64: 251. 1962) indicated unspecified material in BM (presumably in the Clifford herbarium) as "Standard", this does not effect typification.

Pimpinella saxifraga Linnaeus var. **hircina** Linnaeus, *Species Plantarum,* ed. 2, 1: 378. 1762.

RCN: 2102, 2103.
Type not designated.
Original material: Herb. Burser VIII: 51 (UPS).
Current name: *Pimpinella* **sp.** (Apiaceae).

Pimpinella saxifraga Linnaeus var. **major** Linnaeus, *Species Plantarum* 1: 264. 1753.
RCN: 2102, 2103.

Lectotype (Reduron in Jonsell & Jarvis in *Nordic J. Bot.* 22: 84. 2002): Herb. Linn. No. 373.14 (LINN).
Current name: *Pimpinella major* (L.) Huds. (Apiaceae).

Pinguicula alpina Linnaeus, *Species Plantarum* 1: 17. 1753.
"Habitat in Alpibus Lapponicis." RCN: 142.
Lectotype (Blanca & Jarvis in *Folia Geobot.* 34: 351. 1999): [icon] *"Pinguicula nectario conico petalo breviore"* in Linnaeus, Fl. Lapponica: 11, t. 12, f. 3. 1737 (see p. 85).
Current name: *Pinguicula alpina* L. (Lentibulariaceae).
Note: Casper (in *Biblioth. Bot.* 127/128: 122. 1966) indicated 33.2 (LINN, though cited as if at K) as the holotype, but the annotations on the sheet are not by Linnaeus and it cannot be original material for the name. Blanca & Jarvis' type choice is accepted here; the type illustration is reproduced (Abb. 1, f. 5) by Casper (*l.c.*: 6. 1966).

Pinguicula lusitanica Linnaeus, *Species Plantarum* 1: 17. 1753.
"Habitat in Lusitania." RCN: 140.

Neotype (Blanca & Jarvis in *Folia Geobot.* 34: 353. 1999): Portugal. Arredores do Porto pr. S. Gens, Sta Cruz do Bispo, circa Porto (May 1883, *E. Johnston* – Fl. Lusitanica exs. No. 2662, Herb. A.A. de Carvalho Monteiro) (BM).
Current name: *Pinguicula lusitanica* L. (Lentibulariaceae).

Pinguicula villosa Linnaeus, *Species Plantarum* 1: 17. 1753.
"Habitat in Lapponia, Sibiria." RCN: 143.
Lectotype (Casper in *Biblioth. Bot.* 127/128: 180. 1966): Herb. Linn. No. 33.3 (LINN).
Current name: *Pinguicula villosa* L. (Lentibulariaceae).
Note: Although Casper (in *Biblioth. Bot.* 127/128: 180. 1966), in indicating 33.3 (LINN) as the holotype, cited the sheet as if it was at K, his explicit use of the sheet number makes his intention clear and his choice is accepted here.

Pinguicula vulgaris Linnaeus, *Species Plantarum* 1: 17. 1753.
"Habitat in Europae uliginosis." RCN: 141.
Lectotype (Casper in *Biblioth. Bot.* 127/128: 171. 1966): Herb. Linn. No. 33.1 (LINN).
Generitype of *Pinguicula* Linnaeus (vide Hitchcock, *Prop. Brit. Bot.*: 116. 1929).
Current name: *Pinguicula vulgaris* L. (Lentibulariaceae).
Note: Although Casper (in *Biblioth. Bot.* 127/128: 171. 1966), in indicating 33.1 (LINN) as the holotype, cited the sheet as if it was at K, his explicit use of the sheet number makes his intention clear and his choice is accepted here. Cheek (in Jarvis & al., *Regnum Veg.* 127: 76. 1993) independently made the same type choice.

Pinus abies Linnaeus, *Species Plantarum* 2: 1002. 1753.
"Habitat in Europae, Asiae borealibus humidiusculis." RCN: 7250.
Lectotype (Farjon & Jarvis in Greuter, *Regnum Veg.* 128: 122. 1993): [icon] *"Picea"* in Camerarius, Pl. Epit.: 47. 1586.
Current name: *Picea abies* (L.) H. Karst. (Pinaceae).

Pinus balsamea Linnaeus, *Species Plantarum* 2: 1002. 1753.
"Habitat in Virginia, Canada." RCN: 7248.
Lectotype (Farjon & Jarvis in Greuter, *Regnum Veg.* 128: 110. 1993): Herb. Linn. No. 1135.14 (LINN).
Current name: *Abies balsamea* (L.) Mill. (Pinaceae).
Note: Farwell (in *Bull. Torrey Bot. Club* 41: 626. 1914) noted that Linnaeus' concept included more than one species, but did not typify the name.

Pinus canadensis Linnaeus, *Species Plantarum*, ed. 2, 2: 1421. 1763.
"Habitat in America septentrionali." RCN: 7249.
Lectotype (Fernald & Weatherby in *Rhodora* 34: 188. 1932): *Clayton 547* (BM-000051613).
Current name: *Tsuga canadensis* (L.) Carrière (Pinaceae).

Pinus cedrus Linnaeus, *Species Plantarum* 2: 1001. 1753.
"Habitat in Syriae, Libani, Amani, Tauri montibus." RCN: 7245.
Lectotype (Farjon & Jarvis in Greuter, *Regnum Veg.* 128: 118. 1993): [icon] *"Cedrus"* in Belon, Plur. Rer. Obs.: 162. 1605.
Current name: *Cedrus libani* A. Rich. (Pinaceae).

Pinus cembra Linnaeus, *Species Plantarum* 2: 1000. 1753.
"Habitat in Alpibus Sibiriae, Tatariae, Helvetiae, Vallesiae, Baldi, Allobrogum, Tirolensium, Tridentinorum." RCN: 7243.
Lectotype (Farjon & Jarvis in Greuter, *Regnum Veg.* 128: 130. 1993): [icon] *"Larix semper virens, foliis quinis, nucleis edulibus"* in Breyn in Acad. Caes.-Leop. Carol. Nat. Cur. Ephem. 7: 8, t. 1. 1719.
Current name: *Pinus cembra* L. (Pinaceae).

Pinus larix Linnaeus, *Species Plantarum* 2: 1001. 1753.
"Habitat in Alpibus Helveticis, Vallesiacis, Stiriacis, Corinthiacis,
    Tridentinis, Sibiriae." RCN: 7246.
Lectotype (Farjon & Jarvis in Greuter, *Regnum Veg.* 128: 119. 1993):
    [icon] *"Larix folio deciduo Conifera"* in Miller, Cat. Pl.: 43, t. 11.
    1730 (see p. 15).
Current name: ***Larix decidua*** Mill. (Pinaceae).

Pinus orientalis Linnaeus, *Species Plantarum*, ed. 2, 2: 1421. 1763.
"Habitat in Oriente." RCN: 7251.
Neotype (designated here by Farjon): Turkey. Prov. Trabzon
    ("Trébizonde"), 1866, *B. Balansa s.n.* (K).
Current name: ***Picea orientalis*** (L.) Peterm. (Pinaceae).

Pinus picea Linnaeus, *Species Plantarum* 2: 1001. 1753.
"Habitat in Alpibus Helvetiae, Sueviae [sic], Bavariae, Scothiae."
    RCN: 7247.
Lectotype (Farjon & Jarvis in Greuter, *Regnum Veg.* 128: 110. 1993):
    Herb. Clifford: 449, *Abies* 2 (BM-000647435).
Current name: ***Abies alba*** Mill. (Pinaceae).

Pinus pinea Linnaeus, *Species Plantarum* 2: 1000. 1753.
"Habitat in Italia." RCN: 7241.
Lectotype (Farjon & Jarvis in Greuter, *Regnum Veg.* 128: 138. 1993):
    [icon] *"Pinus ossiculis duris, foliis longis"* in Bauhin & Cherler, Hist.
    Pl. Univ. 1(2): 248. 1650.
Current name: ***Pinus pinea*** L. (Pinaceae).

Pinus strobus Linnaeus, *Species Plantarum* 2: 1001. 1753.
"Habitat in Virginia, Canada." RCN: 7244.
Lectotype (Farjon & Jarvis in Greuter, *Regnum Veg.* 128: 140. 1993):
    Kalm, Herb. Linn. No. 1135.10 (LINN).
Current name: ***Pinus strobus*** L. (Pinaceae).

Pinus sylvestris Linnaeus, *Species Plantarum* 2: 1000. 1753.
"Habitat in Europae borealis sylvis glareosis." RCN: 7240.
Lectotype (Farjon & Jarvis in Jarvis & al., *Regnum Veg.* 127: 76.
    1993): [icon] *"Pinus sylvestris"* in Daléchamps, Hist. General. Pl. 1:
    45. 1587.
Generitype of *Pinus* Linnaeus (vide Green, *Prop. Brit. Bot.*: 189. 1929).
Current name: ***Pinus sylvestris*** L. (Pinaceae).

Pinus taeda Linnaeus, *Species Plantarum* 2: 1000. 1753.
"Habitat in Virginiae, Canadae paludosis." RCN: 7242.
Lectotype (Farjon & Jarvis in Greuter, *Regnum Veg.* 128: 141. 1993):
    Clayton 496 (BM-000042621).
Current name: ***Pinus taeda*** L. (Pinaceae).

Piper acuminatum Linnaeus, *Species Plantarum* 1: 30. 1753.
"Habitat in America calidiore." RCN: 240.
Lectotype (Stearn in *Taxon* 10: 17. 1961): [icon] *"Saururus alius
    humilis, folio carnoso, et acuminato"* in Plumier, Descr. Pl. Amér.: 54,
    t. 71. 1693.
Current name: ***Peperomia nigropunctata*** Miq. (Piperaceae).

Piper aduncum Linnaeus, *Species Plantarum* 1: 29. 1753.
"Habitat in Jamaica." RCN: 238.
Lectotype (Saralegui Boza in Greuter & Rankin, *Fl. Republ. Cuba*, ser.
    A, 9(3): 81. 2004): [icon] *"Saururus arborescens, fructu adunco"* in
    Plumier, Descr. Pl. Amér.: 58, t. 77. 1693.
Current name: ***Piper aduncum*** L. (Piperaceae).
Note: Tebbs (in *Bull. Nat. Hist. Mus. London, Bot.* 23: 19. 1993)
    indicated Houstoun material (presumably in Herb. Sloane, BM) as
    "?lectotype" but this was not seen by Linnaeus and is not original
    material for the name.

Piper amalago Linnaeus, *Species Plantarum* 1: 29. 1753.
"Habitat in Jamaica." RCN: 235.
Lectotype (Howard in *J. Arnold Arbor.* 54: 400. 1973): [icon] *"Piper
    longum arboreum altius, folio nervoso minore, spica graciliori et
    breviori"* in Sloane, Voy. Jamaica 1: 134, t. 87, f. 1. 1707. –
    Typotype: Herb. Sloane 2: 80 (BM-SL).
Current name: ***Piper amalago*** L. (Piperaceae).

Piper betle Linnaeus, *Species Plantarum* 1: 28. 1753.
"Habitat in India." RCN: 231.
Lectotype (Huber in Dassanayake & Fosberg, *Revised Handb. Fl.
    Ceylon* 6: 287. 1987): Herb. Hermann 3: 32; 4: 9, No. 27 (BM).
Current name: ***Piper betle*** L. (Piperaceae).
Note: Fosberg & Sachet (in *Smithsonian Contr. Bot.* 24: 17. 1975) were
    cited by Smith (*Fl. Vitiensis Nova* 2: 60. 1981) as indicating a
    Hermann collection as the type but they only referred to unseen
    and unspecified material. Although Huber indicated type material
    in more than one volume of the Hermann herbarium, it appears to
    have been part of a single gathering. Consequently, his is accepted
    as the first typification (Art. 9.15).

Piper decumanum Linnaeus, *Herbarium Amboinense*: 19. 1754.
["Habitat in Indiis."] Sp. Pl., ed. 2, 1: 41 (1762). RCN: 236.
Lectotype (Merrill, *Interpret. Rumph. Herb. Amb.*: 33, 181. 1917):
    [icon] *"Sirum decumanum"* in Rumphius, Herb. Amboin. 5: 45, t.
    27. 1747.
Current name: ***Piper decumanum*** L. (Piperaceae).

Piper distachyon Linnaeus, *Species Plantarum* 1: 30. 1753.
"Habitat in Americes Gallia aequinoctiali." RCN: 245.
Lectotype (Saralegui Boza in Greuter & Rankin, *Fl. Republ. Cuba*, ser.
    A, 9(3): 29. 2004): [icon] *"Saururus hederaceus, cauliculis maculosis
    minor"* in Plumier, Descr. Pl. Amér.: 51, t. 67. 1693.
Current name: ***Piper distachya*** (L.) A. Dietr. (Piperaceae).

Piper longum Linnaeus, *Species Plantarum* 1: 29. 1753.
"Habitat in India." RCN: 234.
Lectotype (Huber in Dassanayake & Fosberg, *Revised Handb. Fl.
    Ceylon* 6: 288. 1987): Herb. Hermann 4: 13, No. 30 (BM).
Current name: ***Piper longum*** L. (Piperaceae).
Note: Huber refers to the type as located in vol. 4: 48 of the Hermann
    herbarium but as the only material is in vol. 4: 13, it seems clear
    that this was an error, treated here as correctable.

Piper maculosum Linnaeus, *Species Plantarum* 1: 30. 1753.
"Habitat in Domingo." RCN: 243.
Lectotype (Saralegui Boza in Greuter & Rankin, *Fl. Republ. Cuba*, ser.
    A, 9(3): 27. 2004): [icon] *"Saururus hederaceus, cauliculis maculosis
    major"* in Plumier, Descr. Pl. Amér.: 50, t. 66. 1693.
Current name: ***Peperomia maculosa*** (L.) Hook. (Piperaceae).

Piper malamiris Linnaeus, *Species Plantarum* 1: 29. 1753.
"Habitat in India utraque." RCN: 232.
Type not designated.
Original material: Herb. Hermann 2: 23, No. 28 (BM); Herb.
    Hermann 2: 51, No. 28 (BM); [icon] in Rheede, Hort. Malab. 7:
    31, t. 16. 1688; [icon] in Plukenet, Phytographia: t. 215, f. 2. 1692;
    Almag. Bot.: 297. 1696.
Current name: ***Piper betle*** L. (Piperaceae).
Note: Huber (in Dassanayake & Fosberg, *Revised Handb. Fl. Ceylon* 6:
    282. 1987) agreed the identity of the Hermann material (BM) but,
    claiming wrongly that there is no evidence linking the specimens
    with this name, he discarded it in favour of *P. sylvestre* Lam.

Piper nigrum Linnaeus, *Species Plantarum* 1: 28. 1753.
"Habitat in India." RCN: 230.

P

Lectotype (Huber in Dassanayake & Fosberg, *Revised Handb. Fl. Ceylon* 6: 283. 1987): Herb. Hermann 3: 21; 4: 11, No. 26 (BM).

Generitype of *Piper* Linnaeus (vide Hitchcock in *Amer. J. Bot.* 10: 513. 1923).

Current name: ***Piper nigrum*** L. (Piperaceae).

Note: Huber's type choice is of material from a single gathering, but distributed between two of Hermann's bound volumes, so the typification is valid under Art. 9.15.

Piper obtusifolium Linnaeus, *Species Plantarum* 1: 30. 1753.
"Habitat in America calidiore." RCN: 241.
Lectotype (Howard in *J. Arnold Arbor.* 54: 392. 1973): [icon] *"Saururus humilis folio carnoso subrotundo"* in Plumier, Descr. Pl. Amér.: 53, t. 70. 1693.
Current name: ***Peperomia obtusifolia*** (L.) A. Dietr. (Piperaceae).

Piper pellucidum Linnaeus, *Species Plantarum* 1: 30. 1753.
"Habitat in America." RCN: 239.
Lectotype (Stearn, *Introd. Linnaeus' Sp. Pl.* (Ray Soc. ed.): 47. 1957): [icon] *"Piper foliis cordatis, caule procumbente"* in Linnaeus, Hort. Cliff.: 6, t. 4. 1738.
Current name: ***Peperomia pellucida*** (L.) Kunth (Piperaceae).

Piper peltatum Linnaeus, *Species Plantarum* 1: 30. 1753.
"Habitat in America calidiore." RCN: 244.
Lectotype (Howard in *J. Arnold Arbor.* 54: 381. 1973): [icon] *"Saururus arborescens foliis amplis rotundis et umbilicatis"* in Plumier, Descr. Pl. Amér.: 56, t. 74. 1693.
Current name: ***Piper peltatum*** L. (Piperaceae).

Piper quadrifolium Linnaeus, *Species Plantarum*, ed. 2, 1: 43. 1762.
"Habitat in America meridionali." RCN: 248.
Lectotype (Saralegui Boza in Greuter & Rankin, *Fl. Republ. Cuba*, ser. A, 9(3): 18. 2004): [icon] *"Piper foliis quaternis"* in Plumier in Burman, Pl. Amer.: 238, t. 242, f. 3. 1760.
Current name: ***Peperomia quadrifolia*** (L.) Kunth (Piperaceae).

Piper reticulatum Linnaeus, *Species Plantarum* 1: 29. 1753.
"Habitat in Martinica, Brasilia." RCN: 237.
Lectotype (Howard, *Fl. Lesser Antilles* 4: 29. 1988): [icon] *"Saururus Botryitis major, arborescens, foliis plantagineis"* in Plumier, Descr. Pl. Amér.: 57, t. 75. 1693.
Current name: ***Piper reticulatum*** L. (Piperaceae).

Piper rotundifolium Linnaeus, *Species Plantarum* 1: 30. 1753.
"Habitat in America calidiore." RCN: 242.
Lectotype (Howard in *J. Arnold Arbor.* 54: 394. 1973): [icon] *"Saururus repens, folio orbiculari, nummulariae facie"* in Plumier, Descr. Pl. Amér.: 52, t. 69. 1693.
Current name: ***Peperomia rotundifolia*** (L.) Kunth (Piperaceae).

Piper siriboa Linnaeus, *Species Plantarum* 1: 29. 1753.
"Habitat in India." RCN: 233.
Type not designated.
Original material: Herb. Hermann 3: 17, No. 29 (BM); [icon] in Piso, Ind. Nat. Med.: 91. 1658.
Current name: ***Piper siriboa*** L. (Piperaceae).
Note: Huber (in Dassanayake & Fosberg, *Revised Handb. Fl. Ceylon* 6: 285. 1987) wrongly indicates a Rumphius plate, not included in Linnaeus' protologue, as the type. It is not original material for the name.

Piper trifoliatum Linnaeus, *Flora Jamaicensis*: 12. 1759, *orth. var.*
"Habitat [in Jamaica.]"

Lectotype (Howard in *J. Arnold Arbor.* 54: 395. 1973): [icon] *"Saururus hederaceus, triphyllus folio rotundo"* in Plumier, Descr. Pl. Amér.: 52, t. 68. 1693.
Current name: ***Peperomia trifolia*** (L.) A. Dietr. (Piperaceae).
Note: This is an orthographic variant of *P. trifolium* L. (1753).

Piper trifolium Linnaeus, *Species Plantarum* 1: 30. 1753.
"Habitat in Americes Gallia aequinoctiali." RCN: 247.
Lectotype (Howard in *J. Arnold Arbor.* 54: 395. 1973): [icon] *"Saururus hederaceus, triphyllus folio rotundo"* in Plumier, Descr. Pl. Amér.: 52, t. 68. 1693.
Current name: ***Peperomia trifolia*** (L.) A. Dietr. (Piperaceae).

Piper umbellatum Linnaeus, *Species Plantarum* 1: 30. 1753.
"Habitat in Domingo." RCN: 246.
Lectotype (Huber in Dassanayake & Fosberg, *Revised Handb. Fl. Ceylon* 6: 289. 1987): [icon] *"Saururus arborescens, foliis amplis, cordatis non umbilicatis"* in Plumier, Descr. Pl. Amér.: 55, t. 73. 1693.
Current name: ***Piper umbellatum*** L. (Piperaceae).

Piper verticillatum Linnaeus, *Systema Naturae,* ed. 10, 2: 856. 1759.
["Habitat in Jamaica."] Sp. Pl., ed. 2, 1: 43 (1762). RCN: 249.
Lectotype (Fawcett & Rendle, *Fl. Jamaica* 3: 16. 1914): *Browne*, Herb. Linn. No. 47.12 (LINN).
Current name: ***Peperomia verticillata*** (L.) A. Dietr. (Piperaceae).

Piscidia erythrina Linnaeus, *Systema Naturae,* ed. 10, 2: 1155. 1759, *nom. illeg.*
["Habitat in America calidiore."] Sp. Pl. 2: 707. 1753. RCN: 5179.
Replaced synonym: *Erythrina piscipula* L. (1753).
Lectotype (Rudd in *Phytologia* 18: 486. 1969): [icon] *"Coral arbor polyphylla non spinosa, fraxini folio, siliqua alis foliaceis extantibus, rotae molendinariae fluviatilis, vel seminum laserpitii instar, aucta"* in Sloane, Voy. Jamaica 2: 39, t. 176, f. 4, 5. 1725. – Typotype: Herb. Sloane 6: 18 (BM-SL).
Generitype of *Piscidia* Linnaeus, *nom. cons.*
Current name: ***Piscidia piscipula*** (L.) Sarg. (Fabaceae: Faboideae).
Note: Piscidia Linnaeus, *nom. cons.* against *Ichthyomethia* P. Browne.

Pisonia aculeata Linnaeus, *Species Plantarum* 2: 1026. 1753.
"Habitat in America meridionali." RCN: 7709.
Lectotype (Smith, *Fl. Vitiensis Nova* 2: 269. 1981): [icon] *"Pisonia"* in Plumier, Nov. Pl. Amer.: 7, t. 11. 1703.
Generitype of *Pisonia* Linnaeus (vide Green, *Prop. Brit. Bot.*: 191. 1929).
Current name: ***Pisonia aculeata*** L. (Nyctaginaceae).
Note: Stemmerik (in *Blumea* 12: 284. 1964) stated that the name was "based on" a Plumier plate (t. 11) and Smith (*Fl. Vitiensis Nova* 2: 269. 1981) accepted this element as the lectotype, attributing the choice to Stemmerik. This typification is accepted as dating from 1981. Díaz (in *Rev. Jard. Bot. Nac. Univ. Habana* 9: 9–13. 1988) reviewed the original elements in detail, reproducing most of the relevant original text and illustrations (f. 1–5), although her conclusion that the later Plumier plate (in Burman, *Pl. Amer.*: t. 227, f. 1. 1760) should be the type is pre-dated by Smith's choice.

Pisonia inermis Linnaeus, *Systema Naturae,* ed. 10, 2: 1314. 1759, *nom. illeg.*
RCN: 7710.
Replaced synonym: *Pisonia mitis* L. (1753).
Type not designated.
Original material: as replaced synonym.
Current name: ***Pisonia mitis*** L. (Nyctaginaceae).

Note: Evidently an illegitimate renaming of *P. mitis* L. (1753). The diagnosis of *P. inermis* is "P. caule inermi", compared with "P. inermis" for *P. mitis* in both *Sp. Pl.* 2: 1026. 1753, and in *Sp. Pl.*, ed. 2, 2: 1511. 1763.

Pisonia mitis Linnaeus, *Species Plantarum* 2: 1026. 1753.
"Habitat in India." RCN: 7710.
Type not designated.
Original material: [icon] in Rheede, Hort. Malab. 7: 33, t. 17. 1688.
Current name: ***Pisonia mitis*** L. (Nyctaginaceae).
Note: Stemmerik (in *Blumea* 12: 284. 1964) regarded material in LE, linked to Linnaeus' reference to Amman, as the type. However, this material would not have been seen by Linnaeus and is not original material for the name.

Pistacia lentiscus Linnaeus, *Species Plantarum* 2: 1026. 1753.
"Habitat in Hispania, Lusitania, Italia." RCN: 7420.
Lectotype (Siddiqi in Jafri & El-Gadi, *Fl. Libya* 52: 3. 1978): Herb. Linn. No. 1170.8 (LINN).
Current name: ***Pistacia lentiscus*** L. (Anacardiaceae).

Pistacia narbonensis Linnaeus, *Species Plantarum* 2: 1025. 1753.
"Habitat Monspelii." RCN: 7417.
Type not designated.
Original material: Herb. Linn. No. 1170.2 (LINN); [icon] in Bauhin & Cherler, Hist. Pl. Univ. 1(1): 278. 1650; [icon] in Lobel, Stirp. Adversaria: 412. 1570.
Note: The application of this name appears uncertain.

Pistacia simaruba Linnaeus, *Species Plantarum* 2: 1026. 1753.
"Habitat in Jamaica, Carolina." RCN: 2554.
Replaced synonym of: *Bursera gummifera* L. (1762), *nom. illeg.*
Lectotype (Wijnands, *Bot. Commelins*: 55. 1983): [icon] "Terebinthus major, betulae cortice, fructu triangulari" in Sloane, Voy. Jamaica 2: 89, t. 199, f. 1, 2. 1725. – Typotype: Herb. Sloane 6: 104, 105 (BM-SL).
Current name: ***Bursera simaruba*** (L.) Sarg. (Burseraceae).
Note: Fawcett & Rendle (*Fl. Jamaica* 4: 206. 1920) indicated material in Herb. Sloane (BM-SL) as type but as this was not seen by Linnaeus, it is not original material for the name.

Pistacia terebinthus Linnaeus, *Species Plantarum* 2: 1025. 1753.
"Habitat in Europa australi, Africa boreali, India." RCN: 7419.
Type not designated.
Original material: Herb. Clifford: 456, *Pistacia* 2, 2 sheets (BM); Herb. Burser XXII: 58 (UPS); Herb. Linn. No. 1170.4 (LINN); [icon] in Dodoëns, Stirp. Hist. Pempt., ed. 2: 870. 1616; [icon] in Clusius, Rar. Pl. Hist. 1: 15. 1601.
Current name: ***Pistacia terebinthus*** L. (Anacardiaceae).

Pistacia trifolia Linnaeus, *Species Plantarum* 2: 1025. 1753.
"Habitat in Sicilia." RCN: 7416.
Type not designated.
Original material: Herb. Clifford: 456, *Pistacia* 1 (BM); [icon] in Boccone, Mus. Piante Rar. Sicilia: 139, t. 93. 1697.
Current name: ***Pistacia vera*** L. (Anacardiaceae).

Pistacia vera Linnaeus, *Species Plantarum* 2: 1025. 1753.
"Habitat in Persia, Arabia, Syria, India." RCN: 7418.
Type not designated.
Original material: Herb. Linn. No. 1170.3 (LINN); Herb. Burser XXII: 60 (UPS); [icon] in Lobel, Stirp. Adversaria: 413. 1570; [icon] in Bauhin & Cherler, Hist. Pl. Univ. 1(1): 275. 1650.
Generitype of *Pistacia* Linnaeus (vide Green, *Prop. Brit. Bot.*: 191. 1929).
Current name: ***Pistacia vera*** L. (Anacardiaceae).

Pistia stratiotes Linnaeus, *Species Plantarum* 2: 963. 1753.
"Habitat in Asiae, Africae, Americae meridionalibus, natans." RCN: 6967.
Lectotype (Suresh & al. in *Taxon* 32: 127. 1983): [icon] "Kodda-pail" in Rheede, Hort. Malab. 11: 63, t. 32. 1692.
Generitype of *Pistia* Linnaeus.
Current name: ***Pistia stratiotes*** L. (Araceae).
Note: Bogner (in Leroy, *Fl. Madagascar* 31: 67. 1975) indicated 1072.1 (LINN) as type, but this choice was rejected by Suresh & al. (in *Taxon* 32: 127–128. 1983) on the grounds of conflict with the protologue. The material also appears to be a post-1753 addition to the herbarium, and not original material for the name.

Pisum arvense Linnaeus, *Species Plantarum* 2: 727. 1753.
"Habitat inter Europae segetes." RCN: 5373.
Lectotype (Jonsell & Jarvis in *Nordic J. Bot.* 22: 78. 2002): [icon] "Pisum pulchrum folio anguloso" in Morison, Pl. Hist. Univ. 2: 47, s. 2, t. 1, f. 4. 1680.
Current name: ***Pisum sativum*** L. (Fabaceae: Faboideae).
Note: Westphal (*Pulses Ethiopia, Taxon. Agric. Signif.*: 188. 1974) discussed this name and the cited synonyms but did not designate a type. Nguyên Van Thuân (in Morat, *Fl. Cambodge Laos Viêtnam* 23: 182. 1987) wrongly indicated 903.1 (LINN) as type – it is not original material for this name (and is, in fact, the lectotype of *P. sativum*).

Pisum maritimum Linnaeus, *Species Plantarum* 2: 727. 1753.
"Habitat in Europae borealis littoribus maris arenosis." RCN: 5374.
Lectotype (Jonsell & Jarvis in *Nordic J. Bot.* 22: 78. 2002): Herb. Linn. No. 903.2 (LINN).
Current name: ***Lathyrus japonicus*** Willd. subsp. ***maritimus*** (L.) P.W. Ball (Fabaceae: Faboideae).
Note: Fernald (in *Rhodora* 34: 187. 1932) noted that two infraspecific taxa were involved within Linnaeus' concept of the species, but chose no type, and neither did Ball (in *Feddes Repert.* 79: 46. 1968).

Pisum ochrus Linnaeus, *Species Plantarum* 2: 727. 1753.
"Habitat in Cretae, Italiae." RCN: 5375.
Lectotype (Jafri in Jafri & El-Gadi, *Fl. Libya* 86: 288. 1980): Herb. Linn. No. 903.3 (LINN), see p. 748.
Current name: ***Lathyrus ochrus*** (L.) DC. (Fabaceae: Faboideae).

Pisum sativum Linnaeus, *Species Plantarum* 2: 727. 1753.
"Habitat in Europae agris." RCN: 5372.
Lectotype (Westphal, *Pulses Ethiopia, Taxon. Agric. Signif.*: 186. 1974): Herb. Linn. No. 903.1 (LINN).
Generitype of *Pisum* Linnaeus (vide Green, *Prop. Brit. Bot.*: 175. 1929).
Current name: ***Pisum sativum*** L. (Fabaceae: Faboideae).

Pisum sativum Linnaeus var. **quadratum** Linnaeus, *Species Plantarum* 2: 727. 1753.
RCN: 5372.
Type not designated.
Original material: Herb. Burser XIX: 57 (UPS).
Current name: ***Pisum sp.*** (Fabaceae: Faboideae).
Note: The application of this name is uncertain.

Pisum sativum Linnaeus var. **umbellatum** Linnaeus, *Species Plantarum* 2: 727. 1753.
RCN: 5372.
Type not designated.
Original material: Herb. Burser XIX: 58 (UPS).
Current name: ***Pisum sp.*** (Fabaceae: Faboideae).
Note: The application of this name is uncertain.

P

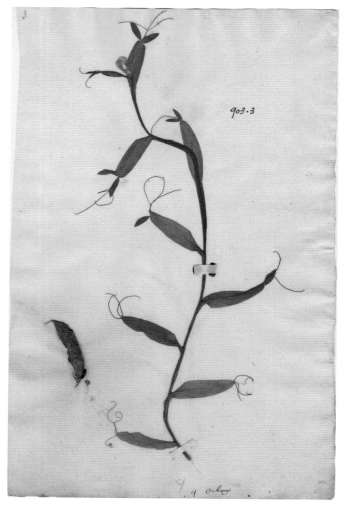

The lectotype of *Pisum ochrus* L.

Plantago afra Linnaeus, *Species Plantarum*, ed. 2, 1: 168. 1762.
"Habitat in Sicilia, Barbaria." RCN: 944.
Type not designated.
Original material: Herb. Linn. No. 144.31 (LINN); [icon] in
   Morison, Pl. Hist. Univ. 3: 262, s. 8, t. 17, f. 4. 1699; [icon] in
   Boccone, Icon. Descr. Rar. Pl. Siciliae: 8, 7, t. 4, f. A. 1674.
Current name: ***Plantago afra*** L. (Plantaginaceae).
Note: Verdcourt (in *Fl. Trop. E. Africa, Plantaginaceae*: 6. 1971)
   indicated the cited Morison illustration as a syntype, and suggested
   that Linnaeus' reference to North Africa and his description are
   probably derived from Brander's specimen from Algiers (144.31,
   LINN). As a syntype (which is not, by definition, the sole type of a
   name, unlike a holotype, lectotype or neotype), Verdcourt's
   statement is not accepted as correctable to lectotype under Art. 9.8.

Plantago albicans Linnaeus, *Species Plantarum* 1: 114. 1753.
"Habitat in Hispaniae & Narbonae aridis." RCN: 932.
Lectotype (Peruzzi & al. in *Taxon* 53: 541. 2004): Herb. Linn. No.
   144.15 (LINN).
Current name: ***Plantago albicans*** L. (Plantaginaceae).

Plantago alpina Linnaeus, *Species Plantarum* 1: 114. 1753.
"Habitat in Helvetiae alpibus." RCN: 933.

Type not designated.
Original material: Herb. Linn. No. 59.13? (S).
Current name: ***Plantago alpina*** L. (Plantaginaceae).

Plantago altissima Linnaeus, *Species Plantarum*, ed. 2, 1: 164. 1762.
"Habitat in Italia." RCN: 927.
Type not designated.
Original material: Herb. Linn. No. 144.10 (LINN).
Current name: ***Plantago altissima*** L. (Plantaginaceae).

Plantago asiatica Linnaeus, *Species Plantarum* 1: 113. 1753.
"Habitat in China, Sibiria." RCN: 924.
Type not designated.
Original material: Herb. Linn. No. 144.3 (LINN); Herb. Linn. No.
   144.4 (LINN).
Current name: ***Plantago asiatica*** L. (Plantaginaceae).

Plantago coronopus Linnaeus, *Species Plantarum* 1: 115. 1753.
"Habitat in Europae, glareosis." RCN: 939.
Lectotype (Glen in *Bothalia* 28: 153. 1998): Herb. Burser X: 89
   (UPS).
Current name: ***Plantago coronopus*** L. (Plantaginaceae).
Note: Patzak & Rechinger (in Rechinger, *Fl. Iranica* 15: 5. 1965)
   indicated unspecified material in LINN as the type. However, the
   only material linked with this name is sheet 144.24, but this
   collection lacks the relevant *Species Plantarum* number (i.e. "12")
   and was a post-1753 addition to the herbarium, and is not original
   material for the name.

Plantago cretica Linnaeus, *Species Plantarum* 1: 114. 1753.
"Habitat in Creta." RCN: 934.
Lectotype (designated here by Turland): Herb. Clifford: 36, *Plantago* 5
   (BM-000557807).
Current name: ***Plantago cretica*** L. (Plantaginaceae).

Plantago cynops Linnaeus, *Species Plantarum* 1: 116. 1753, *nom.
   utique rej. prop.*
"Habitat in India." RCN: 943.
Type not designated.
Original material: Herb. Linn. No. 144.30 (LINN).
Current name: ***Plantago afra*** L. (Plantaginaceae).
Note: Widely treated as a *nomen ambiguum*, and informally rejected by
   authors such as Greuter (in *Boissiera* 13: 122. 1967), Verdcourt (in
   Kew Bull. 23: 509. 1969) and Rahn (in *Bot. J. Linn. Soc.* 120: 183.
   1996), Applequist (in *Taxon* 55: 235. 2006) formally proposed the
   rejection of this name.

Plantago indica Linnaeus, *Systema Naturae*, ed. 10, 2: 896. 1759,
   nom. illeg.
["Habitat in Europae australis sepibus."] Sp. Pl. 1: 115 (1753). RCN:
   942.
Replaced synonym: *Plantago psyllium* L. (1753).
Type not designated.
Original material: as replaced synonym.
Current name: ***Plantago arenaria*** Waldst. & Kit. (Plantaginaceae).
Note: Apparently a *nomen novum* for *P. psyllium* L. (1753) and hence
   illegitimate, as noted by Rauschert (in *Feddes Repert.* 88: 313.
   1977).

Plantago lagopus Linnaeus, *Species Plantarum* 1: 114. 1753.
"Habitat in G. Narbonensi, Hispania, Lusitania." RCN: 930.
Type not designated.
Original material: Herb. Linn. No. 144.12 (LINN); Herb. Burser X:
   76 (UPS); [icon] in Morison, Pl. Hist. Univ. 3: 259, s. 8, t. 16, f.
   13. 1699.

Current name: **Plantago lagopus** L. (Plantaginaceae).
Note: Patzak & Rechinger (in Rechinger, *Fl. Iranica* 15: 13. 1965) indicated unspecified material in LINN as the type, but did not distinguish between sheets 144.12 and 144.14 (which are evidently not part of a single gathering so Art. 9.15 does not apply).

Plantago lanceolata Linnaeus, *Species Plantarum* 1: 113. 1753.
"Habitat in Europae campis sterilibus." RCN: 928.
Lectotype (Verdcourt in Milne-Redhead & Polhill, *Fl. Trop. E. Africa, Plantaginaceae*: 6. 1971): Herb. Clifford: 6, *Plantago* 3, sheet A (BM-000557805).
Current name: **Plantago lanceolata** L. (Plantaginaceae).
Note: Although Patzak & Rechinger (in Rechinger, *Fl. Iranica* 15: 12. 1965) indicated unspecified material in LINN as the type, it is not clear which material they intended as none is annotated with the relevant epithet.

Plantago latifolia Linnaeus, *Flora Jamaicensis*: 13. 1759.
"Habitat [in Jamaica.]"
Type not designated.
Original material: none traced.
Note: The application of this name is uncertain.

Plantago loeflingii Linnaeus, *Species Plantarum* 1: 115. 1753.
"Habitat in Hispaniae collibus agrorumque marginibus." RCN: 940.
Lectotype (Patzak & Rechinger in Rechinger, *Fl. Iranica* 15: 16. 1965): *Löfling s.n.*, Herb. Linn. No. 144.25 (LINN).
Current name: **Plantago loeflingii** L. (Plantaginaceae).

Plantago lusitanica Linnaeus, *Species Plantarum*, ed. 2, 2: 1667. 1763.
"Habitat in Hispania. Cl. Alstroemer." RCN: 931.
Type not designated.
Original material: Herb. Linn. No. 144.13 (LINN); [icon] in Barrelier, Pl. Galliam: 14, t. 745. 1714.
Current name: **Plantago lagopus** L. var. **cylindrica** Boiss. (Plantaginaceae).

Plantago major Linnaeus, *Species Plantarum* 1: 112. 1753.
"Habitat in Europa ad vias." RCN: 923.
Lectotype (Verdcourt in Milne-Redhead & Polhill, *Fl. Trop. E. Africa, Plantaginaceae*: 2. 1971): Herb. Linn. No. 144.1 (LINN).
Generitype of *Plantago* Linnaeus.
Current name: **Plantago major** L. subsp. **major** (Plantaginaceae).
Note: Patzak & Rechinger (in Rechinger, *Fl. Iranica* 15: 3. 1965) indicated material at LINN as type, but did not distinguish between sheets 144.1 and 144.2. As these do not form part of a single gathering, Art. 9.15 does not apply.

Plantago maritima Linnaeus, *Species Plantarum* 1: 114. 1753.
"Habitat in littoribus marimis Europae borealis." RCN: 935.
Lectotype (Patzak & Rechinger in Rechinger, *Fl. Iranica* 15: 6. 1965): Herb. Linn. No. 114.17 (LINN).
Current name: **Plantago maritima** L. (Plantaginaceae).

Plantago media Linnaeus, *Species Plantarum* 1: 113. 1753.
"Habitat in Europae pascuis sterilibus apricis argillosis." RCN: 925.
Lectotype (Patzak & Rechinger in Rechinger, *Fl. Iranica* 15: 7. 1965): Herb. Linn. No. 144.5 (LINN).
Current name: **Plantago media** L. (Plantaginaceae).

Plantago psyllium Linnaeus, *Species Plantarum* 1: 115. 1753, *nom. utique rej. prop.*
"Habitat in Europae australis sepibus." RCN: 941.

Replaced synonym of: *Plantago indica* L. (1759), *nom. illeg.*
Type not designated.
Original material: Herb. Linn. No. 144.26 (LINN); Herb. Burser X: 97 (UPS); Herb. Linn. No. 144.27 (LINN); Herb. Clifford: 37, *Plantago* 8 (BM).
Current name: **Plantago arenaria** Waldst. & Kit. (Plantaginaceae).
Note: Having long been informally treated as a *nomen ambiguum*, Applequist (in *Taxon* 55: 235. 2006) formally proposed the rejection of this name.

Plantago recurvata Linnaeus, *Mantissa Plantarum Altera*: 198. 1771.
"Habitat in Europa australi." RCN: 937.
Type not designated.
Original material: none traced.
Current name: **Plantago holosteum** Scop. (Plantaginaceae).

Plantago serraria Linnaeus, *Systema Naturae*, ed. 10, 2: 896. 1759.
["Habitat in Apulia, Mauritania. Brander."] Sp. Pl., ed. 2, 1: 166 (1762). RCN: 938.
Type not designated.
Original material: *Brander*, Herb. Linn. No. 144.23 (LINN).
Current name: **Plantago serraria** L. (Plantaginaceae).

Plantago strictissima Linnaeus, *Amoenitates Academicae* 4: 478. 1759.
"Habitat [Monspelii.]"
Type not designated.
Original material: none traced.
Current name: **Plantago maritima** L. (Plantaginaceae).
Note: See discussion of this name by Stearn (in Geck & Pressler, *Festschr. Claus Nissen*: 640–641. 1974).

Plantago subulata Linnaeus, *Species Plantarum* 1: 115. 1753.
"Habitat in maritimis Mediterranei arenosis." RCN: 936.
Type not designated.
Original material: Herb. Linn. No. 144.21 (LINN); Herb. Burser X: 86 (UPS); Herb. Linn. No. 59.15 (S); Herb. Linn. No. 144.22 (LINN); [icon] in Plantin, Pl. Stirp. Icon.: 439. 1581.
Current name: **Plantago subulata** L. (Plantaginaceae).

Plantago uniflora Linnaeus, *Species Plantarum* 1: 115. 1753.
"Habitat ad Europae littora lacuum." RCN: 7118.
Replaced synonym of: *Littorella lacustris* L. (1771), *nom. illeg.*
Type not designated.
Original material: [icon] in Jussieu in Mém. Acad. Roy. Sci. Paris 1742: 131, t. 7. 1742; [icon] in Morison, Pl. Hist. Univ. 3: 233, s. 8, t. 9, f. 30. 1699; [icon] in Plukenet, Phytographia: t. 35, f. 2. 1691; Almag. Bot.: 180. 1696.
Current name: **Plantago uniflora** L. (Plantaginaceae).

Plantago virginica Linnaeus, *Species Plantarum* 1: 113. 1753.
"Habitat in Virginia." RCN: 926.
Lectotype (Glen in *Bothalia* 28: 154. 1998): *Kalm*, Herb. Linn. No. 144.8 (LINN).
Current name: **Plantago virginica** L. (Plantaginaceae).

Platanus occidentalis Linnaeus, *Species Plantarum* 2: 999. 1753.
"Habitat in America septentrionali." RCN: 7236.
Type not designated.
Original material: Herb. Linn. No. 1133.5 (LINN); Herb. Clifford: 447, *Platanus* 2 (BM); Herb. Linn. No. 388.17 (S); [icon] in Catesby, Nat. Hist. Carolina 1: 56, t. 56. 1730 – Voucher: Herb. Sloane 212: 68 (BM-SL); [icon] in Parkinson, Theatr. Bot.: 1427. 1640.

P

Current name: ***Platanus occidentalis*** L. (Platanaceae).
Note: Nixon & Poole (in *Lundellia* 6: 133. 2003) wrongly indicated 1133.5 (LINN) as the holotype. As this statement was published after 1 Jan 2001, "holotype" cannot be modified to lectotype because the omission of the phrase "designated here" or an equivalent (Art. 7.11) means that this choice cannot be effective.

Platanus orientalis Linnaeus, *Species Plantarum* 2: 999. 1753.
"Habitat in Asia, Tauro, Macedonia, Atho, Lemno, Creta, locis riguis." RCN: 7235.
Lectotype (Barrie & Nixon in Jarvis & al., *Regnum Veg.* 127: 77. 1993): Herb. Clifford: 447, *Platanus* 1 (BM-000647415).
Generitype of *Platanus* Linnaeus (vide Green, *Prop. Brit. Bot.*: 189. 1929).
Current name: ***Platanus orientalis*** L. (Platanaceae).

Plectronia ventosa Linnaeus, *Systema Naturae*, ed. 12, 2: 183; *Mantissa Plantarum*: 52. 1767.
"Habitat ad Cap. b. spei." RCN: 1626.
Lectotype (Ross in *Bothalia* 11: 491. 1975): Herb. Linn. No. 277.2 (LINN).
Generitype of *Plectronia* Linnaeus, *nom. rej.*
Current name: ***Olinia ventosa*** (L.) Cufod. (Oliniaceae).
Note: Plectronia Linnaeus, *nom. rej.* in favour of *Olinia* Thunb. The name was evidently based on a mixture including *Canthium inerme* (L.) Lam. (Rubiaceae) (as to the fruit characters and the Burman synonym). The rest of the generic description (*Mant. Pl.*: 6) was drawn from specimens in LINN, as noted by Bullock (in *Kew Bull.* 1932: 354. 1932). Sheet 277.2 (LINN) is accepted as the lectotype, with *Olinia ventosa* (L.) Cufod. as the correct name for the taxon, as treated by Sebola & Balkwill (in *S. African J. Bot.* 65: 100. 1999).

Plinia crocea Linnaeus, *Mantissa Plantarum Altera*: 244. 1771, *nom. illeg.*
["Habitat in America."] Sp. Pl. 1: 516 (1753). RCN: 3636.
Replaced synonym: *Plinia pinnata* L. (1753).
Lectotype (McVaugh in *Taxon* 17: 388. 1968): [icon] *"Plinia"* in Plumier, Nov. Pl. Amer.: 9, t. 11. 1703.
Current name: ***Plinia pinnata*** L. (Myrtaceae).
Note: A superfluous name for *P. pinnata* L. (1753) and hence illegitimate.

Plinia petiolata Linnaeus, *Plantae Surinamenses*: 10. 1775.
"Habitat [in Surinamo.]" RCN: 3638.
Type not designated.
Original material: none traced.
Current name: ***Eugenia uniflora*** L. (Myrtaceae).

Plinia pinnata Linnaeus, *Species Plantarum* 1: 516. 1753.
"Habitat in America." RCN: 3636.
Replaced synonym of: *Plinia crocea* L. (1771), *nom. illeg.*
Lectotype (McVaugh in *Taxon* 17: 388. 1968): [icon] *"Plinia"* in Plumier, Nov. Pl. Amer.: 9, t. 11. 1703.
Generitype of *Plinia* Linnaeus.
Current name: ***Plinia pinnata*** L. (Myrtaceae).

Plinia rubra Linnaeus, *Mantissa Plantarum Altera*: 243. 1771.
"Habitat in Brasilia, Surinamo. Allemand." RCN: 3637.
Type not designated.
Original material: [icon] in Piso, Med. Brasil.: 121. 1648.
Current name: ***Eugenia uniflora*** L. (Myrtaceae).

Plinia tetrapetala Linnaeus, *Mantissa Plantarum Altera*: 402. 1771. RCN: 3637.
Type not designated.

Original material: none traced.
Current name: ***Eugenia uniflora*** L. (Myrtaceae).

Plukenetia volubilis Linnaeus, *Species Plantarum* 2: 1192. 1753.
"Habitat in Indiis." RCN: 7260.

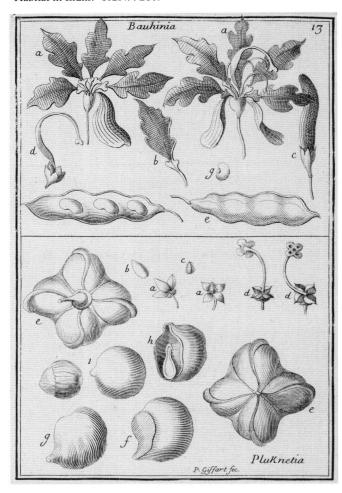

Lectotype (Howard, *Fl. Lesser Antilles* 5: 82. 1989): [icon] *"Pluknetia"* in Plumier, Nov. Pl. Amer.: 47, t. 13. 1703.
Generitype of *Plukenetia* Linnaeus.
Current name: ***Plukenetia volubilis*** L. (Euphorbiaceae).

Plumbago americana Linnaeus, *Flora Jamaicensis*: 14. 1759.
"Habitat [in Jamaica.]"
Type not designated.
Original material: none traced.
Note: The application of this name is uncertain.

Plumbago europaea Linnaeus, *Species Plantarum* 1: 151. 1753.
"Habitat in Europa australi." RCN: 1200.
Lectotype (Edmondson in Jarvis & al., *Regnum Veg.* 127: 77. 1993): Herb. Linn. No. 216.1 (LINN).
Generitype of *Plumbago* Linnaeus (vide Hitchcock, *Prop. Brit. Bot.*: 129. 1929).
Current name: ***Plumbago europaea*** L. (Plumbaginaceae).

Plumbago indica Linnaeus, *Herbarium Amboinense*: 24. 1754.
["Habitat in India."] Sp. Pl., ed. 2, 1: 215 (1762). RCN: 1202.
Replaced synonym of: *Plumbago rosea* L. (1762), *nom. illeg.*

Lectotype (Merrill, *Interpret. Rumph. Herb. Amb.*: 33, 414. 1917): [icon] *"Radix Vesicatoria"* in Rumphius, Herb. Amboin. 5: 453, t. 168. 1747.
Current name: ***Plumbago indica*** L. (Plumbaginaceae).

Plumbago rosea Linnaeus, *Species Plantarum,* ed. 2, 1: 215. 1762, *nom. illeg.*
"Habitat in India." RCN: 1202.
Replaced synonym: *Plumbago indica* L. (1754).
Lectotype (Merrill, *Interpret. Rumph. Herb. Amb.*: 33. 1917): [icon] *"Radix Vesicatoria"* in Rumphius, Herb. Amboin. 5: 453, t. 168. 1747.
Current name: ***Plumbago indica*** L. (Plumbaginaceae).
Note: A superfluous name for *P. indica* L. (1754).

Plumbago scandens Linnaeus, *Species Plantarum,* ed. 2, 1: 215. 1762.
"Habitat in America calidiore." RCN: 1203.
Lectotype (Howard, *Fl. Lesser Antilles* 6: 54. 1989): [icon] *"Dentellaria lychnioides sylvatica scandens flore albo"* in Sloane, Voy. Jamaica 1: 211, t. 133, f. 1. 1707. – Typotype: Herb. Sloane 4: 29 (BM-SL).
Current name: ***Plumbago scandens*** L. (Plumbaginaceae).

Plumbago zeylanica Linnaeus, *Species Plantarum* 1: 151. 1753.
"Habitat in India utraque." RCN: 1201.
Lectotype (Dyer in Dyer & al., *Fl. Southern Africa* 26: 17. 1963): Herb. Linn. No. 216.2 (LINN).
Current name: ***Plumbago zeylanica*** L. (Plumbaginaceae).

Plumeria alba Linnaeus, *Species Plantarum* 1: 210. 1753.
"Habitat in Jamaica." RCN: 1732.
Type not designated.
Original material: [icon] in Commelin, Hort. Med. Amstelod. Pl. Rar. 2: 47, t. 24. 1701.
Current name: ***Plumeria alba*** L. (Apocynaceae).
Note: Wijnands (*Bot. Commelins*: 44. 1983) discussed the name in detail and concluded that it should be lectotypified by a Plumier plate that did not feature in the protologue. This cannot be accepted as a neotypification because original material is in existence, though apparently identifiable as *P. rubra.*

Plumeria obtusa Linnaeus, *Species Plantarum* 1: 210. 1753.
"Habitat in America calidiore." RCN: 1733.
Lectotype (Dandy, *Sloane Herbarium*: 112. 1958): [icon] *"Plumeria flore niveo, foliis brevioribus obtusis"* in Catesby, Nat. Hist. Carolina 2: 93, t. 93. 1743 (see p. 117).
Current name: ***Plumeria obtusa*** L. (Apocynaceae).

Plumeria rubra Linnaeus, *Species Plantarum* 1: 209. 1753.
"Habitat in Jamaica, Surinamo." RCN: 1731.
Lectotype (Wijnands, *Bot. Commelins*: 44. 1983): [icon] *"Nerium arboreum, folio maximo obtusiore, flore incarnato"* in Sloane, Voy. Jamaica 2: 61, t. 185. 1725. – Typotype: Herb. Sloane 6: 56 (BM-SL).
Generitype of *Plumeria* Linnaeus (vide Hitchcock, *Prop. Brit. Bot.*: 136. 1929).
Current name: ***Plumeria rubra*** L. (Apocynaceae).

Poa alpina Linnaeus, *Species Plantarum* 1: 67. 1753.
"Habitat in alpibus Lapponicis, Helveticis." RCN: 568.
Lectotype (Soreng in Cafferty & al. in *Taxon* 49: 254. 2000): Herb. Linn. No. 87.2 (LINN).
Current name: ***Poa alpina*** L. (Poaceae).
Note: Although Kerguélen (in *Lejeunia*, n.s., 75: 235. 1975) stated "Type: ...LINN", this is not accepted as a formal typification, for the reasons explained by Cafferty & al. (in *Taxon* 49: 240. 2000).

Poa alpina Linnaeus var. **vivipara** Linnaeus, *Species Plantarum* 1: 67. 1753.
RCN: 568.
Lectotype (Soreng in Cafferty & al. in *Taxon* 49: 254. 2000): Herb. Linn. No. 87.4, three left culms (LINN).
Current name: ***Poa alpina*** L. (Poaceae).

Poa amabilis Linnaeus, *Species Plantarum* 1: 68. 1753.
"Habitat in India." RCN: 576.
Lectotype (Veldkamp in Cafferty & al. in *Taxon* 49: 254. 2000): Herb. Hermann 2: 59, No. 46 (BM-000621703).
Current name: ***Eragrostis amabilis*** (L.) Wight & Arn. ex Nees (Poaceae).
Note: Henrard (in *Blumea* 3: 423. 1940) indicated unspecified material at LINN as type, but there is no relevant original material extant there, 87.22 (LINN) being annotated only by J.E. Smith. Clayton (in Polhill, *Fl. Trop. E. Africa, Gramineae* 2: 212. 1974) indicated both the cited Hermann and Plukenet elements as syntypes.

Poa amboinica Linnaeus, *Mantissa Plantarum Altera*: 557. 1771.
"Habitat in India." RCN: 584.
Lectotype (Airy Shaw in *Kew Bull.* 2: 36. 1947): [icon] *"Phoenix Amboinica montana"* in Rumphius, Herb. Amboin. 6: 19, t. 7, f. 3. 1750.
Note: The application of this name is unclear. Veldkamp (in *Blumea* 37: 233–237. 1992) gave an extensive review, concluding that the name is best treated as a *nomen incertae sedis*, and informally rejected it as such.

Poa angustifolia Linnaeus, *Species Plantarum* 1: 67. 1753.
"Habitat in Europa ad agrorum versuras." RCN: 570.
Lectotype (Soreng in Cafferty & al. in *Taxon* 49: 254. 2000): Herb. Linn. No. 87.12, excl. second culm from left (LINN).
Current name: ***Poa angustifolia*** L. (Poaceae).
Note: Although Kerguélen (in *Lejeunia*, n.s., 75: 235. 1975) stated "Type: ...LINN", this is not accepted as a formal typification, for the reasons explained by Cafferty & al. (in *Taxon* 49: 240. 2000). Meikle (*Fl. Cyprus* 2: 1744. 1985) indicated unspecified material at LINN as type, but did not distinguish between several possible specimens, which are evidently not part of a single gathering so Art. 9.15 does not apply.

Poa annua Linnaeus, *Species Plantarum* 1: 68. 1753.
"Habitat in Europa ad vias." RCN: 572.
Lectotype (Soreng in Cafferty & al. in *Taxon* 49: 254. 2000): Herb. Linn. No. 87.17, right specimen (LINN).
Current name: ***Poa annua*** L. (Poaceae).
Note: Clayton (in Milne-Redhead & Polhill, *Fl. Trop. E. Africa, Gramineae* 1: 49. 1970) and a number of later authors indicated unspecified material at LINN as "Type" but failed to distinguish between several possible specimens, evidently not from a single gathering, there. Veldkamp (in *Blumea* 38: 421. 1994) indicated, with uncertainty ("?"), the right-hand specimen on Herb. Linn. 87.17 (LINN) as the holotype but, in order to eliminate any uncertainty, Soreng formalised this choice.

Poa aquatica Linnaeus, *Species Plantarum* 1: 67. 1753.
"Habitat in Europa ad ripas piscinarum, fluviorum." RCN: 567.
Lectotype (Cope in Cafferty & al. in *Taxon* 49: 255. 2000): Herb. Linn. No. 87.1 (LINN).
Current name: ***Glyceria maxima*** (Hartm.) Holmb. (Poaceae).
Note: Although Kerguélen (in *Lejeunia*, n.s., 75: 185. 1975) stated "Type: ...LINN", this is not accepted as a formal typification, for the reasons explained by Cafferty & al. (in *Taxon* 49: 240. 2000). The epithet "aquatica" is pre-occupied in *Glyceria* by *G. aquatica*

(L.) J. Presl & C. Presl (1819), based on *Aira aquatica* L. (1753). *Glyceria aquatica* (L.) Wahlenb. (1820), based on *Poa aquatica* L., is therefore a later homonym, and illegitimate.

Poa bulbosa Linnaeus, *Species Plantarum* 1: 70. 1753.
"Habitat in Gallia...Loefl." RCN: 586.
Lectotype (Meikle, *Fl. Cyprus* 2: 1742. 1985; Soreng in Cafferty & al. in *Taxon* 49: 255. 2000): Herb. Linn. No. 87.57 (LINN).
Current name: *Poa bulbosa* L. (Poaceae).
Note: Although Kerguélen (in *Lejeunia*, n.s., 75: 237. 1975) stated "Type: ...LINN", this is not accepted as a formal typification, for the reasons explained by Cafferty & al. (in *Taxon* 49: 240. 2000). Meikle (*Fl. Cyprus* 2: 1742. 1985) and later authors indicated material at LINN as type, but did not distinguish between three possible sheets. However, as all of these (sheets 87.57, 87.58 and 87.59) came from Hasselquist, they probably constitute a single gathering in the sense of Art. 9.15. This choice was subsequently restricted to one of the sheets by Soreng.

Poa capillaris Linnaeus, *Species Plantarum* 1: 68. 1753.
"Habitat in Virginia, Canada. D. Kalm." RCN: 578.
Lectotype (Hitchcock in *Contr. U. S. Natl. Herb.* 12: 121. 1908): *Kalm*, Herb. Linn. No. 87.27 (LINN).
Current name: *Eragrostis capillaris* (L.) Nees (Poaceae).

Poa chinensis Linnaeus, *Species Plantarum* 1: 69. 1753.
"Habitat in India. Osbeck." RCN: 580.
Lectotype (Phillips in Polhill, *Fl. Trop. E. Africa, Gramineae* 2: 279. 1974): *Osbeck s.n.*, Herb. Linn. No. 87.32 (LINN).
Current name: *Leptochloa chinensis* (L.) Nees (Poaceae).

Poa ciliaris Linnaeus, *Systema Naturae*, ed. 10, 2: 875. 1759.
["Habitat in Jamaica."] Sp. Pl., ed. 2, 1: 102 (1762). RCN: 590.
Lectotype (Hitchcock in *Contr. U. S. Natl. Herb.* 12: 121. 1908): *Browne*, Herb. Linn. No. 87.66 (LINN).
Current name: *Eragrostis ciliaris* (L.) R. Br. (Poaceae).

Poa compressa Linnaeus, *Species Plantarum* 1: 69. 1753.
"Habitat in Europae & Americae septentrionalis siccis. muris, tectis." RCN: 583.
Lectotype (Soreng in Cafferty & al. in *Taxon* 49: 255. 2000): Herb. Linn. No. 87.41 (LINN).
Current name: *Poa compressa* L. (Poaceae).
Note: Although Kerguélen (in *Lejeunia*, n.s., 75: 238. 1975) stated "Type: ...LINN", this is not accepted as a formal typification, for the reasons explained by Cafferty & al. (in *Taxon* 49: 240. 2000). Meikle (*Fl. Cyprus* 2: 1745. 1985) indicated unspecified material in LINN as type, but did not distinguish between sheets 87.41–87.45 (which are not part of a single gathering so Art. 9.15 does not apply).

Poa cristata (Linnaeus) Linnaeus, *Systema Naturae*, ed. 12, 2: 94. 1767.
["Habitat in Angliae, Galliae, Helvetiae siccioribus."] Sp. Pl. 1: 63 (1753). RCN: 589.
Basionym: *Aira cristata* L. (1753).
Lectotype (Humphries in Cafferty & al. in *Taxon* 49: 244. 2000): Herb. A. van Royen No. 913.62–99 (L). – Epitype (Humphries in Cafferty & al. in *Taxon* 49: 244. 2000): France. Jura, Bas-Bugey, Montagny de Ste Claire sur Brioguier, 400–500m, 3 Jun 1929, *Briquet 6737* (BM; iso- G).
Current name: *Koeleria macrantha* (Ledeb.) Schult. (Poaceae).

Poa distans Linnaeus, *Systema Naturae*, ed. 12, 2: 94; *Mantissa Plantarum*: 32. 1767.

"Habitat in Austria. D. Jacquin." RCN: 588.
Lectotype (Cope in Cafferty & al. in *Taxon* 49: 255. 2000): Austria. "Poa distans. triandra digyn. Crescit in fossis aquosis et locis humidis per Austriam". Herb. Jacquin fil. (W).
Current name: *Puccinellia distans* (Jacq.) Parl. (Poaceae).
Note: Poa distans has been widely, but incorrectly, treated as a Linnaean name dating from 1767, and the basionym of *Puccinellia distans* (L.) Parl., hence its inclusion here. While Linnaeus did refer to Jacquin ("Habitat in Austria. D. Jacquin"), he gave no reference to any earlier publication. However, as noted by Walter Gutermann (pers. comm.), *P. distans* was, in fact, published by Jacquin in 1764.

Poa eragrostis Linnaeus, *Species Plantarum* 1: 68. 1753.
"Habitat in Italia supra muros. D. Baeck." RCN: 577.
Lectotype (Clayton in Polhill, *Fl. Trop. E. Africa, Gramineae* 2: 234. 1974): *Baeck 7*, Herb. Linn. No. 87.23 (LINN).
Current name: *Eragrostis minor* Host (Poaceae).

Poa flava Linnaeus, *Species Plantarum* 1: 68. 1753.
"Habitat in Virginia." RCN: 573.
Lectotype (Hitchcock in *Bot. Gaz.* 38: 297. 1904): *Clayton 273* (BM-000042229).
Current name: *Tridens flava* (L.) Hitchc. (Poaceae).

Poa malabarica Linnaeus, *Species Plantarum* 1: 69. 1753, *nom. rej.*
"Habitat in India arenosis." RCN: 579.
Lectotype (Merrill in *Bull. Torrey Bot. Club* 60: 635. 1933): [icon] *"Tsjama-pullu"* in Rheede, Hort. Malab. 12: 83, t. 45. 1693.
Current name: *Leptochloa fusca* (L.) Kunth (Poaceae).

Poa nemoralis Linnaeus, *Species Plantarum* 1: 69. 1753.
"Habitat in Europa ad radices montium umbrosas." RCN: 585.
Lectotype (Soreng in Cafferty & al. in *Taxon* 49: 255. 2000): [icon] *"Gramen paniculatum angusti-folium Alpin. Locustis rarioribus et angustioribus non aristatis"* in Scheuchzer, Agrostographia Helv. Prodr.: 18, t. 2. 1708. – Epitype (Soreng & Edmondson in Cafferty & al. in *Taxon* 49: 255. 2000): Sweden. Uppland: Danmark Parish, Linnés Hammarby, 14 Jun 1933, *Hylander s.n.* (BM-000641656).
Current name: *Poa nemoralis* L. (Poaceae).
Note: Although Kerguélen (in *Lejeunia*, n.s., 75: 242. 1975) stated "Type: ...LINN", this is not accepted as a formal typification, for the reasons explained by Cafferty & al. (in *Taxon* 49: 240. 2000).

Poa palustris Linnaeus, *Systema Naturae*, ed. 10, 2: 874. 1759.
["Habitat in Helvetiae, Italiae paludibus."] Sp. Pl., ed. 2, 1: 99 (1762). RCN: 575.
Lectotype (Soreng in Cafferty & al. in *Taxon* 49: 256. 2000): Herb. Linn. No. 87.21 (LINN).
Current name: *Poa palustris* L. (Poaceae).
Note: Although Hitchcock (in *Bot. Gaz.* 38: 298. 1904) stated that the name was "founded on" the cited Morison plate (which he identified as *Phalaris arundinacea* L.), this wording is not accepted as effecting a formal choice of type. Similarly, the comments of Kerguélen (in *Lejeunia*, n.s., 75: 242. 1975) are not accepted as a formal typification, for the reasons explained by Cafferty & al. (in *Taxon* 49: 240. 2000). The plate cited by Linnaeus is Morison's s. 8, t. 6, f. 27, which not only conflicts somewhat with the diagnosis in having a dense rather than a diffuse panicle, but is also identified (by Soreng) as a species of *Agrostis*, possibly from Jamaica where *Poa palustris* does not occur. Linnaeus described his plant from central Europe. Sheet 87.21 (LINN), which corresponds with usage of the name, was therefore chosen as the lectotype by Soreng.

Poa pilosa Linnaeus, *Species Plantarum* 1: 68. 1753.
"Habitat in Italia." RCN: 574.

Lectotype (Du Puy & al. in George & al., *Fl. Australia* 50: 472. 1992): [icon] *"Gramen paniculis elegantissimis, majus, locustis purpureo-spadiceis, minoribus"* in Scheuchzer, Agrostographia: 193, t. 4, f. 3. 1719. – Epitype (Scholz in Cafferty & al. in *Taxon* 49: 256. 2000): Italy. an Wegen zwischen den Reisfeldern von Oldenico unweit Vercelli in Oberitalien, 9–10 Aug 1902, A. Kneucker, Gram. Exsicc. XII, No. 344 (B).

Current name: ***Eragrostis pilosa*** (L.) P. Beauv. (Poaceae).

Note: The plate designated as lectotype by Du Puy & al. was subsequently supported by an epitype chosen by Scholz, who also reviewed the typification of the name.

Poa pratensis Linnaeus, *Species Plantarum* 1: 67. 1753, *nom. cons.*
"Habitat in Europae pratis fertilissimis." RCN: 571.

Conserved type (Soreng & Barrie in *Taxon* 48: 157. 1999): Russia. Prov. Sanct-Petersburg, 5km australi-occidentem versus a st. viae ferr. Mga, pratulum ad ripam dextram fl. Mga, 26 Jun 1997, *Tzvelev N-257* (BM-000576302; iso- B, C, CAN, CONC, H, K, KW, L, etc.).

Generitype of *Poa* Linnaeus (vide Hitchcock, *Prop. Brit. Bot.*: 120. 1929).

Current name: ***Poa pratensis*** L. (Poaceae).

Poa rigida Linnaeus, *Flora Anglica*: 10. 1754.
"Habitat [in Anglia.]" RCN: 582.

Lectotype (Stace in Cafferty & al. in *Taxon* 49: 256. 2000): [icon] *"Gramen panicula multiplici"* in Bauhin, Prodr. Theatri Bot.: 6. 1620.

Current name: ***Catapodium rigidum*** (L.) C.E. Hubb. (Poaceae).

Note: Stace & Jarvis (in *Bot. J. Linn. Soc.* 91: 439. 1985) designated 87.37 (LINN) as lectotype, but they treated the name as if first described in *Centuria I Plantarum* (1755: 5), when in fact it first appeared in *Flora Anglica* (1754: 10) where it is validated solely by a reference to a work by Ray. Under Art. 7.7, the name must therefore be typified in the context of Ray, and so the material in Linnaeus' herbarium is ineligible.

Poa setacea Linnaeus, *Amoenitates Academicae* 4: 477. 1759, *nom. nud.*
Type not relevant.

Note: A *nomen nudum*, as noted by Stearn (in Geck & Pressler, *Festschr. Claus Nissen*: 632. 1974).

Poa spicata Linnaeus, *Systema Naturae*, ed. 12, 2: 94; *Mantissa Plantarum*: 32. 1767.
"Habitat in Lusitania. Vandelli." RCN: 587.
Type not designated.
Original material: none traced.

Note: The application of this name is unclear.

Poa tenella Linnaeus, *Species Plantarum* 1: 69. 1753.
"Habitat in India." RCN: 581.

Lectotype (Mitra & Jain in Manilal, *Bot. Hist. Hort. Malab.*: 151. 1980): Herb. Linn. No. 87.33 (LINN).

Current name: ***Eragrostis amabilis*** (L.) Wight & Arn. ex Nees (Poaceae).

Note: Clayton (in Polhill, *Fl. Trop. E. Africa, Gramineae* 2: 206. 1974) indicated unspecified material in LINN as type but did not distinguish between sheets 87.33 and 87.34 (which are not part of a single gathering so Art. 9.15 does not apply).

Poa trivialis Linnaeus, *Species Plantarum* 1: 67. 1753.
"Habitat in Europae pascuis." RCN: 569.

Neotype (Soreng in Cafferty & al. in *Taxon* 49: 256. 2000): *Hudson 16*, Herb. Linn. No. 87.9 (LINN).

Current name: ***Poa trivialis*** L. (Poaceae).

Note: In the absence of original material for the name, a neotype was designated by Soreng (who also discussed other elements linked to the name).

Podophyllum diphyllum Linnaeus, *Species Plantarum* 1: 505. 1753.
"Habitat in Virginia. Collinson." RCN: 3834.

Lectotype (designated here by Reveal): *Bartram?*, Herb. Linn. No. 667.2 (LINN).

Current name: ***Jeffersonia diphylla*** (L.) Pers. (Berberidaceae).

Note: Stearn (*Genus* Epimedium: 222. 2002) indicated 667.1 (LINN) as type but this is associated with *P. peltatum* L., not *P. diphyllum*, and is not original material for the latter.

Podophyllum peltatum Linnaeus, *Species Plantarum* 1: 505. 1753.
"Habitat in America septentrionali." RCN: 3833.

Lectotype (Reveal in Jarvis & al., *Regnum Veg.* 127: 77. 1993): Herb. Linn. No. 667.1 (LINN).

Generitype of *Podophyllum* Linnaeus (vide Green, *Prop. Brit. Bot.*: 160. 1929).

Current name: ***Podophyllum peltatum*** L. (Berberidaceae).

Poinciana bijuga Linnaeus, *Species Plantarum*, ed. 2, 1: 544. 1762, *nom. illeg.*
"Habitat in Indiis." RCN: 2990.
Replaced synonym: *Poinciana bijugata* Jacq. (1760).
Type not designated.

Current name: ***Caesalpinia vesicaria*** L. (Fabaceae: Caesalpinioideae).

Note: This is evidently an illegitimate renaming of *Poinciana bijugata* Jacq. (1760), or possibly an orthographic variant of it. In either case, the name is homotypic with that of Jacquin.

Poinciana elata Linnaeus, *Centuria II Plantarum*: 16. 1756.
"Habitat in India." RCN: 2989.

Lectotype (Schrire in Turland & Jarvis in *Taxon* 46: 479. 1997): Herb. Linn. No. 529.3 (LINN).

Current name: ***Delonix elata*** (L.) Gamble (Fabaceae: Caesalpinioideae).

Note: Brenan (in Milne-Redhead & Polhill, *Fl. Trop. E. Africa, Leguminosae* 2: 23. 1967) indicated 529.3 and 529.4 (LINN) as syntypes. However, they are neither syntypes, nor apparently part of a single gathering so Art. 9.15 does not apply.

Poinciana pulcherrima Linnaeus, *Species Plantarum* 1: 380. 1753.
"Habitat in Indiis." RCN: 2988.

Lectotype (Roti-Michelozzi in *Webbia* 13: 214. 1957): [icon] *"Crista Pavonis"* in Breyn, Exot. Pl. Cent.: 61, t. 22. 1678 (see p. 110).

Generitype of *Poinciana* Linnaeus.

Current name: ***Caesalpinia pulcherrima*** (L.) Sw. (Fabaceae: Caesalpinioideae).

Note: Fawcett & Rendle (*Fl. Jamaica* 4: 95. 1920) indicated material in LINN as type but did not distinguish between sheets 529.1 and 529.2. As these were not part of a single gathering, Art. 9.15 does not apply.

Polemonium caeruleum Linnaeus, *Species Plantarum* 1: 162. 1753.
"Habitat in Europae, Asiae, Americae septentrionalibus." RCN: 1292.

Lectotype (Grohmann in Nasir & Ali, *Fl. W. Pakistan* 8: 1. 1971): Herb. Linn. No. 220.1 (LINN).

Generitype of *Polemonium* Linnaeus (vide Hitchcock, *Prop. Brit. Bot.*: 130. 1929).

Current name: ***Polemonium caeruleum*** L. (Polemoniaceae).

Polemonium dubium Linnaeus, *Species Plantarum* 1: 163. 1753.
"Habitat in Virginia." RCN: 1294.

Lectotype (designated here by Reveal): *Clayton 556*, Herb. Linn. No. 220.4 (LINN; iso- BM-000051652).

Current name: ***Phacelia dubia*** (L.) Trel. (Hydrophyllaceae).

Note: Although Fernald (in *Rhodora* 46: 54. 1944) noted that he had seen a photograph of the type, he did not specify which collection he considered this to be.

Polemonium nyctelea (Linnaeus) Linnaeus, *Species Plantarum*, ed. 2, 1: 231. 1762.

"Habitat in Virginia." RCN: 1169.

Basionym: *Ipomoea nyctelea* L. (1753).

Lectotype (Reveal in Jarvis & al., *Regnum Veg.* 127: 45. 1993): Herb. Linn. No. 206.1 (LINN).

Current name: ***Ellisia nyctelea*** (L.) L. (Hydrophyllaceae).

Polemonium reptans Linnaeus, *Systema Naturae*, ed. 10, 2: 925. 1759.

["Habitat in Virginia."] Sp. Pl., ed. 2, 1: 230 (1762). RCN: 1293.

Lectotype (designated here by Reveal): Herb. Linn. No. 220.3 (LINN).

Current name: ***Polemonium reptans*** L. (Polemoniaceae).

Polemonium rubrum Linnaeus, *Species Plantarum* 1: 163. 1753.

"Habitat in Carolinae citerioris arenosis. B. Jussieu." RCN: 1272.

Basionym of: *Ipomoea rubra* (L.) L. (1767).

Lectotype (designated here by Reveal): [icon] *"Quamoclit pennatum, erectum, floribus in thyrsum digestis"* in Dillenius, Hort. Eltham. 2: 321, t. 241, f. 312. 1732.

Current name: ***Ipomopsis rubra*** (L.) Wherry (Polemoniaceae).

Polianthes tuberosa Linnaeus, *Species Plantarum* 1: 316. 1753.

"Habitat in India." RCN: 2486.

Lectotype (Verhoek in Jarvis & al., *Regnum Veg.* 127: 78. 1993): Herb. Hermann 3: 34, No. 125 (BM-000594676).

Generitype of *Polianthes* Linnaeus.

Current name: ***Polianthes tuberosa*** L. (Agavaceae).

Note: Enayet Hossain & El-Gadi (in Jafri & El-Gadi, *Fl. Libya* 121: 18. 1986) indicated 437.1 (LINN) as type but this lacks a *Species Plantarum* number (i.e. "1") and is a post-1753 addition to the collection and not original material. Several authors have discussed the early literature surrounding this name including Trueblood (in *Econ. Bot.* 27: 165. 1973), and Ullrich (in *Herbertia* 49: 50–57. 1994), who lists many early illustrations, including a Clusius plate cited by Linnaeus, which is also reproduced by Ramón-Laca (in *Anales Jard. Bot. Madrid* 57: 100. 1999).

Polycarpon tetraphyllum (Linnaeus) Linnaeus, *Systema Naturae*, ed. 10, 2: 881. 1759.

["Habitat in Italia, Narbonae vineis."] Sp. Pl. 1: 89. 1753. RCN: 743.

Basionym: *Mollugo tetraphylla* L. (1753).

Lectotype (Burtt & Lewis in *Kew Bull.* 7: 339. 1952): Herb. Clifford: 28, *Mollugo* 2 (BM-000557701).

Generitype of *Polycarpon* Linnaeus.

Current name: ***Polycarpon tetraphyllum*** (L.) L. (Caryophyllaceae).

Polycnemum arvense Linnaeus, *Species Plantarum* 1: 35. 1753.

"Habitat in Galliae, Italiae, Germaniae arvis." RCN: 282.

Lectotype (Hedge in Jarvis & al., *Regnum Veg.* 127: 78. 1993): Herb. Linn. No. 55.2 (LINN).

Generitype of *Polycnemum* Linnaeus.

Current name: ***Polycnemum arvense*** L. (Chenopodiaceae).

Polygala acutifolia Linnaeus, *Systema Naturae*, ed. 10, 2: 1154. 1759. RCN: 5137.

Type not designated.

Original material: none traced.

Note: The application of this name is uncertain.

Polygala alopecuroides Linnaeus, *Mantissa Plantarum Altera*: 260. 1771.

"Habitat ad Cap. b. spei montibus." RCN: 5152.

Lectotype (Levyns in *J. S. African Bot., Suppl.* 2: 190. 1954): Herb. Linn. No. 882.30 (LINN).

Current name: ***Muraltia alopecuroides*** (L.) DC. (Polygalaceae).

Polygala amara Linnaeus, *Systema Naturae*, ed. 10, 2: 1154. 1759.

["Habitat in Galliae, Austriae subalpinis montosis."] Sp. Pl., ed. 2, 2: 987 (1763). RCN: 5135.

Neotype (Heubl in *Mitt. Bot. Staatssamml. München* 20: 269. 1984): Austria. Niederösterreich, Brühl b. Wien, Herb. Jacquin, *Hayne s.n.* (W).

Current name: ***Polygala amara*** L. (Polygalaceae).

Polygala aspalatha Linnaeus, *Systema Naturae*, ed. 12, 2: 470; *Mantissa Plantarum*: 99. 1767.

"Habitat in Brasilia. Arduini." RCN: 5132.

Type not designated.

Original material: *Arduino 13*, Herb. Linn. No. 882.2 (LINN).

Current name: ***Polygala aspalatha*** L. (Polygalaceae).

Polygala bracteolata Linnaeus, *Species Plantarum* 2: 702. 1753.

"Habitat in Aethiopia." RCN: 5141.

Type not designated.

Original material: Herb. Clifford: 353, *Polygala* 2 (BM); Herb. Linn. No. 98 (SBT); [icon] in Plukenet, Phytographia: t. 53, f. 2. 1691; Almag. Bot.: 300. 1696; [icon] in Burman, Rar. Afric. Pl.: 202, t. 73, f. 2. 1739; [icon] in Burman, Rar. Afric. Pl.: 203, t. 73, f. 3. 1739.

Current name: ***Polygala bracteolata*** L. (Polygalaceae).

Note: Levyns (in *J. S. African Bot.* 21: 24. 1955) and Paiva (in *Fontqueria* 50: 273. 1998) wrongly indicated material (presumably sheet 882.12) in LINN as the type. However, this collection lacks the relevant *Species Plantarum* number (i.e. "5") and was a post-1753 addition to the herbarium, and is not original material for the name.

Polygala brasiliensis Linnaeus, *Systema Naturae*, ed. 12, 2: 470; *Mantissa Plantarum*: 99. 1767.

"Habitat in Brasilia." RCN: 5133.

Lectotype (Marques in *Rodriguésia* 48: 288. 1979): *Arduino 16*, Herb. Linn. No. 882.3 (LINN).

Current name: ***Polygala brasiliensis*** L. (Polygalaceae).

Polygala chamaebuxus Linnaeus, *Species Plantarum* 2: 704. 1753.

"Habitat in Austriae, Helvetiae, Alsatiae montanis." RCN: 5151.

Type not designated.

Original material: Herb. Linn. No. 882.28 (LINN); Herb. Burser XXIV: 100 (UPS); [icon] in Clusius, Rar. Pl. Hist. 1: 105. 1601.

Current name: ***Polygala chamaebuxus*** L. (Polygalaceae).

Polygala chinensis Linnaeus, *Species Plantarum* 2: 704. 1753.

"Habitat in India." RCN: 5150.

Lectotype (Fawcett & Rendle, *Fl. Jamaica* 4: 244. 1920): Herb. Linn. No. 882.26 (LINN), see opposite.

Current name: ***Polygala chinensis*** L. (Polygalaceae).

Note: See discussion by Burtt (in *Notes Roy. Bot. Gard. Edinburgh* 32: 403–404. 1973) who proposed (though not formally) the rejection of the name. However, it appears to have continued in use.

Polygala ciliata Linnaeus, *Species Plantarum* 2: 705. 1753.

"Habitat in India." RCN: 5160.

Lectotype (Sumithra'arachchi in Dassanayake & Fosberg, *Revised Handb. Fl. Ceylon* 6: 316. 1987): Herb. Hermann 2: 61, No. 268 (BM-000621714).

Current name: ***Salomonia ciliata*** (L.) DC. (Polygalaceae).

The lectotype of *Polygala chinensis* L.

Polygala cruciata Linnaeus, *Species Plantarum* 2: 706. 1753.
"Habitat in Virginia." RCN: 5163.
Lectotype (designated here by Reveal): *Clayton 157* (BM-000038187).
Current name: ***Polygala cruciata*** L. (Polygalaceae).
Note: Although Fernald & Schubert (in *Rhodora* 50: 164. 1948) discussed the identity of *Clayton 157* (BM), they did not typify the name.

Polygala diversifolia Linnaeus, *Species Plantarum* 2: 703. 1753.
"Habitat in America calidiore." RCN: 5148.
Lectotype (Blake in *Contr. Gray Herb.* 47: 1, 15. 1916): Herb. Clifford: 353, *Polygala* 4 (BM-000646531).
Current name: ***Securidaca diversifolia*** (L.) Blake (Polygalaceae).

Polygala glaucoides Linnaeus, *Species Plantarum* 2: 705. 1753.
"Habitat in Zeylona." RCN: 5159.
Lectotype (Sumithra'arachchi in Dassanayake & Fosberg, *Revised Handb. Fl. Ceylon* 6: 313. 1987): Herb. Hermann 3: 24, No. 270 (BM-000621889).
Current name: ***Polygala glaucoides*** L. (Polygalaceae).

Polygala heisteria Linnaeus, *Species Plantarum* 2: 704. 1753.
"Habitat in Aethiopia." RCN: 5153.
Replaced synonym of: *Heisteria pungens* P.J. Bergius (1767).

Lectotype (Wijnands in Jarvis & al., *Regnum Veg.* 127: 52. 1993): Herb. Clifford: 352, *Heisteria* 1 (BM-000646524).
Current name: ***Muraltia heisteria*** (L.) DC. (Polygalaceae).
Note: Polygala heisteria is homotypic with *Heisteria pungens* P.J. Bergius (1767), the generitype of *Heisteria* Linnaeus (1758), *nom. rej.* in favour of *Heisteria* Jacq. (1760) (Olacaceae), *nom. cons.* Levyns (in *J. S. African Bot., Suppl.* 2: 216. 1954) indicated 882.33 (LINN) as lectotype, but this collection lacks the relevant *Species Plantarum* number (i.e. "13") and was a post-1753 addition to the herbarium, and is not original material for the name.

Polygala incarnata Linnaeus, *Species Plantarum* 2: 701. 1753.
"Habitat in Virginia, Canada." RCN: 5131.
Lectotype (Reveal & al. in *Huntia* 7: 232. 1987): *Kalm*, Herb. Linn. No. 882.1 (LINN).
Current name: ***Polygala incarnata*** L. (Polygalaceae).

Polygala ipulacea Linnaeus, *Mantissa Plantarum Altera*: 260. 1771, *orth. var.*
"Habitat ad Cap. b. spei."
Lectotype (Levyns in *J. S. African Bot., Suppl.* 2: 105, frontis. 1954): *Polygala floribus imberbibus caules fruticoso foliis lanceolatis linearibus acutis stipulatis*, Herb. Burman (G).
Current name: ***Muraltia stipulacea*** (Burm. f.) DC. (Polygalaceae).
Note: Evidently an orthographic error for *P. stipulacea* Burm. f. (1768), cited by Linnaeus in synonymy. Another valid binomial cited in synonymy by Linnaeus, *Heisteria mitior* P.J. Bergius (1767), is not mentioned by Burman.

Polygala lutea Linnaeus, *Species Plantarum* 2: 705. 1753.
"Habitat in Virginia." RCN: 5156.
Lectotype (Smith & Ward in *Sida* 6: 302. 1976): *Kalm*, Herb. Linn. No. 882.39 (LINN).
Current name: ***Polygala lutea*** L. (Polygalaceae).
Note: See also discussion by Reveal & al. (in *Huntia* 7: 232. 1987).

Polygala microphylla Linnaeus, *Species Plantarum*, ed. 2, 2: 989. 1763.
"Habitat in Lusitania, Hispania. Alstroemer." RCN: 5149.
Type not designated.
Original material: *Alströmer 158*, Herb. Linn. No. 882.21 (LINN).
Current name: ***Polygala microphylla*** L. (Polygalaceae).

Polygala monspeliaca Linnaeus, *Species Plantarum* 2: 702. 1753.
"Habitat Monspelii in collibus sterilibus." RCN: 5138.
Lectotype (Paiva in *Fontqueria* 50: 286. 1998): *Magnol*, Herb. Linn. No. 882.7 (LINN).
Current name: ***Polygala monspeliaca*** L. (Polygalaceae).

Polygala myrtifolia Linnaeus, *Species Plantarum* 2: 703. 1753.
"Habitat in Aethiopia." RCN: 5143.
Type not designated.
Original material: Herb. Clifford: 353, *Polygala* 3 (BM); Herb. Linn. No. 292.1 (S); [icon] in Plukenet, Amalth. Bot.: 153, t. 437, f. 4. 1705; Almag. Mant.: 153. 1700 – Voucher: Herb. Sloane 94: 52 (BM-SL); [icon] in Commelin, Hort. Med. Amstelod. Pl. Rar. 1: 87, t. 46. 1697; [icon] in Burman, Rar. Afric. Pl.: 200, t. 73, f. 1. 1739.
Current name: ***Polygala myrtifolia*** L. (Polygalaceae).
Note: Levyns (in *J. S. African Bot.* 21: 19. 1955) indicated 882.14 (LINN) as type, but this collection lacks the relevant *Species Plantarum* number (i.e. "7") and was a post-1753 addition to the herbarium, and is not original material for the name. Although Wijnands (*Bot. Commelins*: 174. 1983) suggested that Herb. Linn. 292.1 (S) would "probably" be a better choice of type, this has not been formally designated.

P

Polygala oppositifolia Linnaeus, *Mantissa Plantarum Altera*: 259. 1771, *nom. illeg.*
"Habitat ad Cap. b. spei, in montosis, Augusto florens." RCN: 5144.
Replaced synonym: *Polygala fruticosa* P.J. Bergius (1767).
Type not designated.
Current name: ***Polygala fruticosa*** P.J. Bergius (Polygalaceae).
Note: An illegitimate replacement name for *Polygala fruticosa* P.J. Bergius (1767).

Polygala paniculata Linnaeus, *Systema Naturae*, ed. 10, 2: 1154. 1759.
["Habitat in Jamaica."] Sp. Pl., ed. 2, 2: 987 (1763). RCN: 5139.
Lectotype (Fawcett & Rendle, *Fl. Jamaica* 4: 242. 1920): *Browne*, Herb. Linn. No. 882.9 (LINN).
Current name: ***Polygala paniculata*** L. (Polygalaceae).

Polygala penaea Linnaeus, *Species Plantarum* 2: 703. 1753.
"Habitat in America meridionali." RCN: 5147.
Type not designated.
Original material: [icon] in Plumier in Burman, Pl. Amer.: 208, t. 214, f. 1. 1759.
Current name: ***Badiera penaea*** (L.) DC. (Polygalaceae).
Note: Gillis (in *Phytologia* 32: 37. 1975) stated "Type: LINN, not seen" but there is no material in LINN annotated to suggest a link with this name.

Polygala sanguinea Linnaeus, *Species Plantarum* 2: 705. 1753.
"Habitat in Virginia. Kalm." RCN: 5161.
Lectotype (designated here by Reveal): *Kalm*, Herb. Linn. No. 882.44 (LINN).
Current name: ***Polygala sanguinea*** L. (Polygalaceae).

Polygala scabra Linnaeus, *Species Plantarum* 2: 703. 1753.
"Habitat in Aethiopia." RCN: 5141.
Type not designated.
Original material: [icon] in Plukenet, Amalth. Bot.: t. 440, f. 6. 1705; Almag. Mant.: 153. 1700; [icon] in Burman, Rar. Afric. Pl.: 204, t. 73, f. 4. 1739.
Current name: ***Polygala scabra*** L. (Polygalaceae).
Note: Paiva (in *Fontqueria* 50: 268. 1998) wrongly indicated unspecified material in G as the holotype (presumably Burman material linked to the cited figure).

Polygala senega Linnaeus, *Species Plantarum* 2: 704. 1753.
"Habitat in Virginia, Pensylvania, Marilandia." RCN: 5155.
Lectotype (Reveal & al. in *Huntia* 7: 231. 1987): Herb. Linn. No. 882.38 (LINN).
Current name: ***Polygala senega*** L. (Polygalaceae).

Polygala sibirica Linnaeus, *Species Plantarum* 2: 702. 1753.
"Habitat in Sibiria. D. Gmelin." RCN: 5140.
Type not designated.
Original material: *Gmelin*, Herb. Linn. No. 882.11 (LINN).
Current name: ***Polygala sibirica*** L. (Polygalaceae).

Polygala spinosa Linnaeus, *Species Plantarum* 2: 704. 1753.
"Habitat in Aethiopia." RCN: 5145.
Neotype (Johnson & Weitz in *S. African J. Bot.* 57: 230. 1991): Herb. Burman (G).
Current name: ***Muraltia spinosa*** (L.) F. Forrest & J.C. Manning (Polygalaceae).

Polygala theezans Linnaeus, *Mantissa Plantarum Altera*: 260. 1771, *nom. illeg.*
"Habitat in Japonia, Java." RCN: 5146.

Replaced synonym: *Polygala thea* Burm. f. (1768).
Type not designated.
Note: An illegitimate replacement name for *Polygala thea* Burm. f. (1768). The application of Burman's name appears to be uncertain.

Polygala trichosperma Linnaeus, *Systema Naturae*, ed. 12, 3: 232. 1768.
"Habitat in Indiis." RCN: 5134a.
Type not designated.
Original material: Herb. Linn. No. 882.4 (LINN).
Current name: ***Polygala trichosperma*** L. (Polygalaceae).

Polygala triflora Linnaeus, *Species Plantarum* 2: 705. 1753.
"Habitat in Zeylona." RCN: 5158.
Lectotype (Sumithra'arachchi in Dassanayake & Fosberg, *Revised Handb. Fl. Ceylon* 6: 310. 1987): Herb. Hermann 3: 10, No. 269 (BM-000594652).
Current name: ***Polygala triflora*** L. (Polygalaceae).

Polygala umbellata Linnaeus, *Mantissa Plantarum Altera*: 259. 1771.
"Habitat ad Cap. b. spei montibus." RCN: 5142.
Lectotype (Levyns in *J. S. African Bot.* 21: 30. 1955): *Tulbagh 163*, Herb. Linn. No. 882.13 (LINN).
Current name: ***Polygala umbellata*** L. (Polygalaceae).

Polygala verticillata Linnaeus, *Species Plantarum* 2: 706. 1753.
"Habitat in Virginia." RCN: 5162.
Lectotype (Fernald in *Rhodora* 40: 335, pl. 501, f. 1. 1938): *Kalm*, Herb. Linn. No. 882.45 (LINN).
Current name: ***Polygala verticillata*** L. (Polygalaceae).
Note: Pennell (in *Bartonia* 13: 10. 1931) wrongly indicated Krieg material (BM-SL) as type and this choice was rejected by Fernald in favour of a Kalm collection in LINN. Reveal & al. (in *Huntia* 7: 231. 1987) give an extensive review.

Polygala viridescens Linnaeus, *Species Plantarum* 2: 705. 1753.
"Habitat in Virginia." RCN: 5157.
Lectotype (designated here by Reveal): *Kalm*, Herb. Linn. No. 882.41 (LINN).
Current name: ***Polygala sanguinea*** L. (Polygalaceae).

Polygala vulgaris Linnaeus, *Species Plantarum* 2: 702. 1753.
"Habitat in Europae pratis, & pascuis siccis." RCN: 5136.
Lectotype (Heubl in *Mitt. Bot. Staatssamml. München* 20: 348. 1984): Herb. Linn. No. 882.6 (LINN).
Generitype of *Polygala* Linnaeus (vide Green, *Prop. Brit. Bot.*: 173. 1929).
Current name: ***Polygala vulgaris*** L. (Polygalaceae).
Note: Heubl designated 882.6 (LINN) as lectotype, which subsequent study has shown to be identifiable as *P. comosa* Schkuhr. The nomenclatural consequences of this are marked, with *P. vulgaris* becoming the correct name for what has been called *P. comosa*, and the next available name, apparently *P. podolica* DC., having to be taken up for the species formerly known as *P. comosa*. *Polygala vulgaris* therefore appears to be a candidate for conservation with a conserved type and, under Art. 57, this name "is not to be used in a sense that conflicts with current usage unless and until a proposal to deal with it under Art. 14.1 or 56.1 has been submitted and rejected". The name should therefore continue to be used in its traditional sense in the meantime. See brief review by Jonsell & Jarvis (in *Nordic J. Bot.* 22: 80. 2002).

Polygonum amphibium Linnaeus, *Species Plantarum* 1: 361. 1753.
"Habitat in Europa." RCN: 2857.
Lectotype (Bhopal & Chaudhri in *Pakistan Syst.* 1(2): 76. 1977;

Ekman & Knutsson in *Nordic J. Bot.* 14: 23. 1994): *Gmelin s.n.*, Herb. Linn. No. 510.7, left specimen (LINN).

Current name: ***Persicaria amphibia*** (L.) Gray (Polygonaceae).

Note: Bhopal & Chaudhri first designated 510.7 (LINN) as type but this choice was subsequently restricted to the specimen on the left by Ekman & Knutsson.

Polygonum arifolium Linnaeus, *Species Plantarum* 1: 364. 1753.

"Habitat in Virginia, Florida." RCN: 2872.

Lectotype (Reveal in *Bot. J. Linn. Soc.* 92: 168. 1986): Herb. Linn. No. 510.34 (LINN).

Current name: ***Polygonum arifolium*** L. (Polygonaceae).

Polygonum articulatum Linnaeus, *Species Plantarum* 1: 363. 1753.

"Habitat in Canada. Kalm." RCN: 2867.

Lectotype (Horton in *Brittonia* 15: 199. 1963): *Kalm*, Herb. Linn. No. 510.28 (LINN).

Current name: ***Polygonella articulata*** (L.) Meisn. (Polygonaceae).

Polygonum aviculare Linnaeus, *Species Plantarum* 1: 362. 1753, *typ. cons.*

"Habitat in Europae cultis ruderatis." RCN: 2865.

Lectotype (Styles in *Bull. Soc. Roy. Bot. Belgique* 91: 294. 1959): Herb. Linn. No. 510.23 (LINN).

Generitype of *Polygonum*, Linnaeus, *nom. cons.*

Current name: ***Polygonum aviculare*** L. (Polygonaceae).

Note: Confusion over the application of *P. aviculare* led McNeill (in *Taxon* 30: 638. 1981) to propose the rejection of the name under the then Art. 69. However, the Committee for Spermatophyta (in *Taxon* 33: 299. 1984) did not recommend rejection.

Polygonum barbatum Linnaeus, *Species Plantarum* 1: 362. 1753, *nom. cons.*

"Habitat in China." RCN: 2861.

Conserved type (Wilson in *Taxon* 47: 461. 1998): China. Canton, Sep. 1885, *T. Sampson 541* (BM).

Current name: ***Persicaria barbata*** (L.) H. Hara (Polygonaceae).

Polygonum bistorta Linnaeus, *Species Plantarum* 1: 360. 1753.

"Habitat in montibus Helvetiae, Austriae, Galliae." RCN: 2853.

Lectotype (Jonsell & Jarvis in *Nordic J. Bot.* 14: 153. 1994): Herb. Linn. No. 510.3 (LINN).

Current name: ***Persicaria bistorta*** (L.) Samp. (Polygonaceae).

Polygonum chinense Linnaeus, *Species Plantarum* 1: 363. 1753.

"Habitat in India, China." RCN: 2870.

Lectotype (Scott in Bosser & al., *Fl. Mascareignes* 146: 10. 1994): Herb. Linn. No. 510.30 (LINN).

Current name: ***Polygonum chinense*** L. (Polygonaceae).

Polygonum convolvulus Linnaeus, *Species Plantarum* 1: 364. 1753.

"Habitat in Europae agris." RCN: 2876.

Lectotype (Bhopal & Chaudhri in *Pakistan Syst.* 1(2): 70. 1977): Herb. Linn. No. 510.38 (LINN).

Current name: ***Fallopia convolvulus*** (L.) Á. Löve (Polygonaceae).

Note: Elkington's type choice (in *Nordic J. Bot.* 14: 153. 1994) is pre-dated by that of Bhopal & Chaudhri.

Polygonum divaricatum Linnaeus, *Species Plantarum* 1: 363. 1753.

"Habitat in Sibiria, Corsica." RCN: 2868.

Type not designated.

Original material: Herb. Linn. No. 510.29 (LINN); Herb. Linn. No. 159.7 (S); [icon] in Buxbaum, Pl. Minus Cognit. Cent. 2: 31, t. 31. 1728; [icon] in Boccone, Mus. Piante Rar. Sicilia: 108, t. 83. 1697.

Current name: ***Polygonum divaricatum*** L. (Polygonaceae).

Polygonum dumetorum Linnaeus, *Species Plantarum*, ed. 2, 1: 522. 1762.

"Habitat in Europae australioris sylvis umbrosis." RCN: 2877.

Lectotype (Bhopal & Chaudhri in *Pakistan Syst.* 1(2): 70. 1977): Herb. Linn. No. 510.40 (LINN).

Current name: ***Fallopia dumetorum*** (L.) Holub (Polygonaceae).

Note: Elkington's type choice (in *Nordic J. Bot.* 14: 153. 1994) is pre-dated by that of Bhopal & Chaudhri.

Polygonum erectum Linnaeus, *Species Plantarum* 1: 363. 1753.

"Habitat in Philadelphia, enata ex seminibus D. Kalmii." RCN: 2866.

Neotype (designated here by McNeill & Katz-Downie): Herb. Linn. No. 510.26 (LINN).

Current name: ***Polygonum erectum*** L. (Polygonaceae).

Polygonum fagopyrum Linnaeus, *Species Plantarum* 1: 364. 1753.

"Habitat in Asia." RCN: 2875.

Lectotype (Graham in Turrill & Milne-Redhead, *Fl. Trop. E. Africa, Polygonaceae*: 26. 1958): Herb. Linn. No. 510.37 (LINN).

Generitype of *Helxine* Linnaeus (vide Reveal in Jarvis & al., *Regnum Veg.* 127: 53. 1993).

Current name: ***Fagopyrum esculentum*** Moench (Polygonaceae).

Note: Polygonum fagopyrum L. is the basionym of *Fagopyrum esculentum* Moench, the conserved type of *Fagopyrum* Mill.

Polygonum frutescens Linnaeus, *Species Plantarum* 1: 359. 1753.

"Habitat in Sibiria, Dauria." RCN: 2852.

Type not designated.

Original material: Herb. Linn. No. 510.1 (LINN).

Current name: ***Atraphaxis frutescens*** (L.) K. Koch (Polygonaceae).

Polygonum hydropiper Linnaeus, *Species Plantarum* 1: 361. 1753.

"Habitat in Europae subhumidis." RCN: 2859.

Lectotype (Bhopal & Chaudhri in *Pakistan Syst.* 1(2): 76. 1977): Herb. Linn. No. 510.9 (LINN).

Current name: ***Persicaria hydropiper*** (L.) Spach (Polygonaceae).

Note: Ekman & Knutsson (in *Nordic J. Bot.* 14: 24. 1994) assessed the identities of the original material for this name and designated Herb. Clifford: 42, *Persicaria* 4 (BM) as lectotype, a choice that maintained the traditional usage of the name. They noted that 510.9 (LINN), part of the original material, was identifiable as *Persicaria minor* (Huds.) Opiz, but were unaware that Bhopal & Chaudhri had already designated this collection as the type. If this identification is confirmed, *P. hydropiper* would seem likely to be a candidate for conservation.

Polygonum lapathifolium Linnaeus, *Species Plantarum* 1: 360. 1753.

"Habitat in Gallia." RCN: 2856.

Lectotype (Timson in *Watsonia* 5: 394. 1963): Herb. Clifford: 42, *Persicaria* 2 (BM-000557852).

Current name: ***Persicaria lapathifolia*** (L.) Gray (Polygonaceae).

Note: See treatment by Wisskirchen (in *Flor. Rundbr.* 29: 1–25. 1995), in which the type sheet is illustrated.

Polygonum maritimum Linnaeus, *Species Plantarum* 1: 361. 1753.

"Habitat Monspelii, in Italia, Virginia." RCN: 2864.

Lectotype (Styles in *Watsonia* 5: 212. 1962): *Löfling s.n.*, Herb. Linn. No. 510.22 (LINN).

Current name: ***Polygonum maritimum*** L. (Polygonaceae).

Note: Raffaelli (in *Taxon* 32: 115. 1983), believing incorrectly that Linnaeus received no specimens from Löfling until after 1753, rejected Styles' choice of type in favour of a collection in Herb. Burser XVI: 35 (UPS). However, Löfling's material almost certainly reached Linnaeus in late April 1752 (López González, pers. comm.) and so is original material for the name.

P

Polygonum ocreatum Linnaeus, *Species Plantarum* 1: 361. 1753.
"Habitat in Sibiria. D. Gmelin." RCN: 2858.
Type not designated.
Original material: *Gmelin*, Herb. Linn. No. 510.8 (LINN).
Current name: ***Polygonum ocreatum*** L. (Polygonaceae).

Polygonum orientale Linnaeus, *Species Plantarum* 1: 362. 1753.
"Habitat in Oriente, India." RCN: 2862.
Lectotype (Wijnands, *Bot. Commelins*: 175. 1983): Herb. Linn. No. 510.16 (LINN).
Current name: ***Polygonum orientale*** L. (Polygonaceae).

Polygonum pensylvanicum Linnaeus, *Species Plantarum* 1: 362. 1753.
"Habitat in Pensylvania. Kalm." RCN: 2863.
Lectotype (designated here by Reveal): *Kalm*, Herb. Linn. No. 510.20 (LINN).
Current name: ***Persicaria pensylvanica*** (L.) M. Gómez (Polygonaceae).

Polygonum perfoliatum Linnaeus, *Systema Naturae*, ed. 10, 2: 1006. 1759.
["Habitat in India. Burmannus."] Sp. Pl., ed. 2, 1: 521 (1762). RCN: 2873.
Lectotype (Park in *Brittonia* 38: 396. 1986): *J. Burman s.n.*, Herb. Linn. No. 510.35 (LINN).
Current name: ***Polygonum perfoliatum*** L. (Polygonaceae).

Polygonum persicaria Linnaeus, *Species Plantarum* 1: 361. 1753.
"Habitat in Europae cultis." RCN: 2860.
Lectotype (Ekman & Knutsson in *Nordic J. Bot.* 14: 24. 1994): Herb. Burser IV: 101, left specimen (UPS).
Current name: ***Persicaria maculosa*** Gray (Polygonaceae).
Note: Bhopal & Chaudhri (in *Pakistan Syst.* 1(2): 76. 1977) indicated 510.12 (LINN) as the type, but this is a Hudson collection received by Linnaeus after 1753, so it cannot be original material for the name.

Polygonum sagittatum Linnaeus, *Species Plantarum* 1: 363. 1753.
"Habitat in Virginiae, Marilandiae madidis." RCN: 2871.
Lectotype (Stearn, *Introd. Linnaeus' Sp. Pl.* (Ray Soc. ed.): 47. 1957): [icon] *"Helxine caule erecto, aculeis reflexis exasperato"* in Linnaeus, Hort. Cliff.: 151, t. 12. 1738.
Current name: ***Persicaria sagittata*** (L.) H. Gross (Polygonaceae).
Note: Reveal (in *Bot. J. Linn. Soc.* 92: 169. 1986) indicated a Clifford sheet (BM) as lectotype, but this choice is pre-dated by that of Stearn.

Polygonum scandens Linnaeus, *Species Plantarum* 1: 364. 1753.
"Habitat in America." RCN: 2878.
Lectotype (Fawcett & Rendle, *Fl. Jamaica* 3: 174. 1914): Herb. Linn. No. 510.42 (LINN).
Current name: ***Polygonum scandens*** L. (Polygonaceae).

Polygonum serratum Linnaeus, *Species Plantarum* 1: 360. 1753.
"Habitat in Mauritania." RCN: 2869.
Type not designated.
Original material: none traced.
Current name: ***Polygonum serratum*** L. (Polygonaceae).

Polygonum tataricum Linnaeus, *Species Plantarum* 1: 364. 1753.
"Habitat in Tataria." RCN: 2874.
Lectotype (Bhopal & Chaudhri in *Pakistan Syst.* 1(2): 89. 1977): Herb. Linn. No. 510.36 (LINN).
Current name: ***Fagopyrum tataricum*** (L.) Gaertn. (Polygonaceae).

Polygonum uvifera Linnaeus, *Species Plantarum* 1: 365. 1753.
"Habitat in Caribearum littoribus maritimis." RCN: 2879.
Basionym of: *Coccoloba uvifera* (L.) L. (1759).
Lectotype (Brandbyge in Harling & Andersson, *Fl. Ecuador* 38: 39. 1989): Herb. Linn. No. 511.1 (LINN).
Current name: ***Coccoloba uvifera*** (L.) L. (Polygonaceae).

Polygonum virginianum Linnaeus, *Species Plantarum* 1: 360. 1753.
"Habitat in Virginia." RCN: 2855.
Lectotype (designated here by Reveal): Herb. Linn. No. 510.5 (LINN).
Current name: ***Persicaria virginiana*** (L.) Gaertn. (Polygonaceae).

Polygonum viviparum Linnaeus, *Species Plantarum* 1: 360. 1753.
"Habitat in Europae subalpinis pascuis duris." RCN: 2854.
Lectotype (Jonsell & Jarvis in *Nordic J. Bot.* 14: 154. 1994): Herb. Linn. No. 510.4 (LINN).
Current name: ***Persicaria vivipara*** (L.) Ronse Decr. (Polygonaceae).

Polymnia canadensis Linnaeus, *Species Plantarum* 2: 926. 1753.
"Habitat in Canada. Kalm." RCN: 6653.
Lectotype (Reveal in Jarvis & al., *Regnum Veg.* 127: 78. 1993): Herb. Linn. No. 1033.1 (LINN).
Generitype of *Polymnia* Linnaeus.
Current name: ***Polymnia canadensis*** L. (Asteraceae).
Note: Wells (in *Brittonia* 17: 149. 1965) quoted the protologue and suggested that a type was "probably" in LINN, but this is insufficiently precise to be accepted as a formal typification.

Polymnia tetragonotheca Linnaeus, *Systema Naturae*, ed. 12, 2: 576. 1767, *nom. illeg.*
["Habitat in Virginia."] Sp. Pl. 2: 903 (1753). RCN: 6655.
Replaced synonym: *Tetragonotheca helianthoides* L. (1753).
Lectotype (Reveal in Jarvis & al., *Regnum Veg.* 127: 93. 1993): *Clayton 97* (BM-000051150).
Current name: ***Tetragonotheca helianthoides*** L. (Asteraceae).
Note: An illegitimate replacement name in *Polymnia* for *Tetragonotheca helianthoides* L. (1753).

Polymnia uvedalia (Linnaeus) Linnaeus, *Species Plantarum*, ed. 2, 2: 1303. 1763.
"Habitat in Virginia." RCN: 6654.
Basionym: *Osteospermum uvedalia* L. (1753).
Lectotype (Wells in *Brittonia* 17: 152. 1965): Herb. Linn. No. 1033.3 (LINN).
Current name: ***Polymnia uvedalia*** (L.) L. (Asteraceae).

Polymnia wedelia Linnaeus, *Systema Naturae*, ed. 12, 2: 576; *Mantissa Plantarum*: 118. 1767, *nom. illeg.*
"Habitat in Carthagenae sylvis." RCN: 6656.
Replaced synonym: *Wedelia frutescens* Jacq. (1760).
Type not designated.
Current name: ***Wedelia frutescens*** Jacq. (Asteraceae).
Note: An illegitimate new name in *Polymnia* for *Wedelia frutescens* Jacq. (1760).

Polypodium aculeatum Linnaeus, *Species Plantarum* 2: 1090. 1753.
"Habitat in Europa." RCN: 7898.
Lectotype (Alston in *J. Bot.* 78: 164. 1940): Herb. A. van Royen No. 908.311–72 (L).
Current name: ***Polystichum aculeatum*** (L.) Schott (Dryopteridaceae).

Polypodium alatum Linnaeus, *Species Plantarum* 2: 1086. 1753.
"Habitat in America." RCN: 7873.

Lectotype (Sánchez & al. in Greuter & Rankin, *Fl. Republ. Cuba*, ser. A, 11(13): 66. 2006): [icon] *"Polypodium serratum majus costa alata"* in Petiver, Pteri-graphia Amer.: 37, t. 7, f. 13. 1712.
Current name: ***Thelypteris alata*** (L.) C.F. Reed (Thelypteridaceae).

Polypodium arboreum Linnaeus, *Species Plantarum* 2: 1092. 1753.
"Habitat in America meridionali." RCN: 7910.
Lectotype (Caluff & Shelton Serrano in Rankin & Greuter, *Fl. Republ. Cuba*, ser. A, 8(2): 51. 2003): [icon] *"Filix arborescens pinnulis dentatis"* in Plumier, Descr. Pl. Amér.: 1, t. 2. 1693.
Current name: ***Cyathea arborea*** (L.) Sm. (Cyatheaceae).
Note: Copeland (in *Univ. Calif. Publ. Bot.* 16: 54. 1929) stated that the type is in LINN, but the only sheet there associated with this name appears to be 1251.60, unannotated by Linnaeus and not original material for the name. Tryon (in *Contr. Gray Herb.* 206: 50. 1976) indicated both Plumier's *Traité Foug. Amér.*: t. 1 (1705) and his *Descr. Pl. Amér.* t. 1 and t. 2 (1693) as holotype, and Caluff & Shelton Serrano subsequently restricted this to t. 2 (1693).

Polypodium asperum Linnaeus, *Species Plantarum* 2: 1093. 1753.
"Habitat in America." RCN: 7914.
Lectotype (Proctor, *Ferns Jamaica*: 143. 1985): [icon] *"Filix arborescens, caudice & caule spinosis"* in Petiver, Pteri-graphia Amer.: 47, t. 4, f. 7. 1712.
Current name: ***Trichipteris aspera*** (L.) Tryon (Cyatheaceae).

Polypodium aspleniifolium Linnaeus, *Species Plantarum* 2: 1084. 1753.
"Habitat in America meridionali." RCN: 7863.
Lectotype (Proctor in *Brit. Fern Gaz.* 9: 76. 1962): [icon] *"Polypodium Asplenii folio villoso"* in Petiver, Pteri-graphia Amer.: 26, t. 7, f. 16. 1712.
Current name: ***Grammitis aspleniifolia*** (L.) Proctor (Grammitidaceae).
Note: Specific epithet spelled "asplenifolia" in the protologue.

Polypodium aureum Linnaeus, *Species Plantarum* 2: 1087. 1753.
"Habitat in America ad caudices vetustarum arborum." RCN: 7875.
Lectotype (Proctor in Howard, *Fl. Lesser Antilles* 2: 334. 1977): Herb. Linn. No. 1251.10 (LINN).
Current name: ***Polypodium aureum*** L. (Polypodiaceae).

Polypodium auriculatum Linnaeus, *Species Plantarum* 2: 1088. 1753, *nom. utique rej.*
"Habitat in India." RCN: 7881.
Lectotype (Trimen in *J. Linn. Soc., Bot.* 24: 152. 1887): Herb. Hermann 1: 39, No. 383 (BM-000621367).
Current name: ***Nephrolepis biserrata*** (Sw.) Schott (Nephrolepidaceae).

Polypodium barometz Linnaeus, *Species Plantarum* 2: 1092. 1753.
"Habitat in China, unde habui cum radice." RCN: 7909.
Type not designated.
Original material: none traced.
Current name: ***Cibotium barometz*** (L.) J. Sm. (Cyatheaceae).
Note: See discussion by Holttum (in van Steenis, *Fl. Malesiana*, ser. II, 1: 166. 1963).

Polypodium bulbiferum Linnaeus, *Species Plantarum* 2: 1091. 1753.
"Habitat in Canada." RCN: 7903.
Type not designated.
Original material: Herb. Linn. No. 1251.50 (LINN); [icon] in Morison, Pl. Hist. Univ. 3: 579, s. 14, t. 3, f. 10. 1699; [icon] in Cornut, Canad. Pl. Hist.: 5, 4. 1635.
Current name: ***Cystopteris bulbifera*** (L.) Bernh. (Dryopteridaceae).

Polypodium caffrorum Linnaeus, *Mantissa Plantarum Altera*: 307. 1771.
"Habitat ad Cap. b. spei. Koenig." RCN: 7905.
Lectotype (Schelpe & Anthony in Leistner, *Fl. Southern Africa, Pteridophyta*: 53. 1986): *König s.n.*, Herb. Linn. No. 1251.67 (LINN).
Current name: ***Mohria caffrorum*** (L.) Desv. (Schizaeaceae).

Polypodium cambricum Linnaeus, *Species Plantarum* 2: 1086. 1753.
"Habitat in Anglia." RCN: 7874.
Lectotype (Nardi in *Webbia* 33: 426. 1979): Herb. Linn. No. 1251.9 (LINN).
Current name: ***Polypodium cambricum*** L. (Polypodiaceae).
Note: Shivas (in *Bot. J. Linn. Soc.* 58: 28. 1961) rejected the name as based on a monstrosity but, since the Leningrad Code (1975), names based on such specimens are valid, and later authors have again taken up *P. cambricum*. See review by Pichi Sermolli (in *Webbia* 40: 49–50. 1986).

Polypodium cicutarium Linnaeus, *Systema Naturae*, ed. 10, 2: 1326. 1759.
["Habitat in Virginia, Jamaica."] Sp. Pl., ed. 2, 2: 1550 (1763). RCN: 7887.
Lectotype (Proctor, *Ferns Jamaica*: 430. 1985): [icon] *"Filix Jamaicensis, s. Polypodium Cicutariae latifoliae foetidis. foliis quodammodo conveniens, pinnulis amplis mucronatis, circa margines serris latiusculis profunde sinuosis"* in Plukenet, Phytographia: t. 289, f. 4. 1694; Almag. Bot.: 153. 1696.
Current name: ***Tectaria cicutaria*** (L.) Copel. (Dryopteridaceae).

Polypodium comosum Linnaeus, *Species Plantarum* 2: 1084. 1753.
"Habitat in America meridionali." RCN: 7858.
Lectotype (Lellinger & Proctor in *Taxon* 32: 569. 1983): [icon] *"Lingua Cervina multifido cacumine laciniata"* in Plumier, Traité Foug. Amér.: 115, t. 131. 1705.
Current name: ***Polypodium phyllitidis*** L. (Polypodiaceae).

Polypodium cordifolium Linnaeus, *Species Plantarum* 2: 1089. 1753, *nom. cons.*
"Habitat in America." RCN: 7853.
Conserved type (Verdcourt in *Taxon* 45: 539. 1996): Hispaniola. Dominican Republic, Azua, San José de Ocoa, slope of Loma de Rancho, 23 Feb 1929, *Ekman H 11627* (K; iso- B, LD, S, UPS).
Current name: ***Nephrolepis cordifolia*** (L.) C. Presl (Nephrolepidaceae).

Polypodium crassifolium Linnaeus, *Species Plantarum* 2: 1083. 1753.
"Habitat in America meridionali." RCN: 7856.
Lectotype (Lellinger in *Amer. Fern J.* 62: 106. 1972): [icon] *"Phyllitis maculata, breviori & crassiori folio"* in Petiver, Pteri-graphia Amer.: 2, t. 6, f. 1. 1712.
Current name: ***Polypodium crassifolium*** L. (Polypodiaceae).

Polypodium crispatum Linnaeus, *Species Plantarum* 2: 1084. 1753.
"Habitat in America meridionali." RCN: 7861.
Lectotype (Bishop & Smith in *Syst. Bot.* 17: 360. 1992): [icon] *"Polypodium Asplenii folio crispo, pendulum"* in Petiver, Pteri-graphia Amer.: 25, t. 13, f. 12. 1712 (see p. 147).
Note: The type illustration is unidentifiable, and the name has been informally rejected by Bishop & Smith and others.

Polypodium cristatum Linnaeus, *Species Plantarum* 2: 1090. 1753.
"Habitat in Europa septentrionali." RCN: 7894.
Lectotype (Bobrov in *Novosti Sist. Vyssh. Rast.* 21: 11. 1984): Herb. Linn. No. 1251.36 (LINN).
Current name: ***Dryopteris cristata*** (L.) A. Gray (Dryopteridaceae).

P

Polypodium decussatum Linnaeus, *Species Plantarum* 2: 1093. 1753.
"Habitat in India." RCN: 7917.
Lectotype (Proctor in Howard, *Fl. Lesser Antilles* 2: 288. 1977): [icon] *"Filix Taxi foliis major"* in Petiver, Pteri-graphia Amer.: 61, t. 2, f. 5. 1712.
Current name: ***Thelypteris decussata*** (L.) Proctor (Thelypteridaceae).

Polypodium dissimile Linnaeus, *Systema Naturae*, ed. 10, 2: 1325. 1759.
["Habitat in America."] Sp. Pl., ed. 2, 2: 1549 (1763). RCN: 7885.
Lectotype (Proctor in Howard, *Fl. Lesser Antilles* 2: 329. 1977): Herb. Linn. No. 1251.24 (LINN).
Current name: ***Serpocaulon dissimile*** (L.) A.R. Sm. (Polypodiaceae).

Polypodium dryopteris Linnaeus, *Species Plantarum* 2: 1093. 1753.
"Habitat in Europae nemoribus." RCN: 7918.
Lectotype (McNeill & Pryer in *Taxon* 34: 142, f. 1. 1985): Herb. Burser XX: 32 (UPS).
Current name: ***Gymnocarpium dryopteris*** (L.) Newman (Polypodiaceae).
Note: Although Bobrov (in *Novosti Sist. Vyssh. Rast.* 21: 12. 1984) indicated unspecified material in UPS as type, this is insufficiently precise to be accepted as a typification.

Polypodium exaltatum Linnaeus, *Systema Naturae,* ed. 10, 2: 1326. 1759.
["Habitat in America."] Sp. Pl., ed. 2, 2: 1549 (1763). RCN: 7880.
Lectotype (Alston in *Philipp. J. Sci.* 50: 182. 1933): [icon] *"Lonchitis altissima, pinnulis utrinque, seu ex utroque latere auriculatis"* in Sloane, Voy. Jamaica 1: 77, t. 31. 1707. – Typotype: Herb. Sloane 1: 52 (BM-SL).
Current name: ***Nephrolepis exaltata*** (L.) Schott (Nephrolepidaceae).

Polypodium filix-femina Linnaeus, *Species Plantarum* 2: 1090. 1753.
"Habitat in Europae frigidioris subhumidis." RCN: 7896.
Lectotype (Jonsell & Jarvis in *Nordic J. Bot.* 14: 149. 1994): [icon] *"Filix mas non ramosa, pinnulis angustis, rarioribus, profunde dentatis"* in Plukenet, Phytographia: t. 180, f. 4. 1692; Almag. Bot.: 151. 1696. – Typotype: Herb. Sloane 85: 127 (BM-SL).
Current name: ***Athyrium filix-femina*** (L.) Roth (Dryopteridaceae).
Note: In accordance with Art. 23.8, Ex. 19 of the Code, *P. filix-femina* is to continue to be treated as *P. filix-femina*. Although Bobrov (in *Novosti Sist. Vyssh. Rast.* 21: 8. 1984) indicated 1251.39 (LINN) as the type, this collection lacks the relevant *Species Plantarum* number (i.e. "38") and was a post-1753 addition to the herbarium, and is not original material for the name.

Polypodium filix-fragile Linnaeus, *Species Plantarum* 2: 1091. 1753.
"Habitat in collibus Europae frigidioris." RCN: 7904.
Lectotype (Copeland in *Univ. Calif. Publ. Bot.* 16: 56. 1929): *Amman 52*, Herb. Linn. No. 1251.51 (LINN).
Current name: ***Cystopteris fragilis*** (L.) Bernh. (Dryopteridaceae).
Note: In accordance with Art. 23.8, Ex. 19 of the Code, *P. filix-fragile* is to be treated as *P. fragile*. Proctor (*Ferns Jamaica*: 410. 1985) erroneously believed Copeland's type (as "1251.44") to have been a post-1753 addition to the collection and designated a cited Plukenet plate as type in its place. However, the type carries both the epithet and "44" written by Linnaeus, along with an Amman label suggesting it was in Linnaeus' possession long before 1753.

Polypodium filix-mas Linnaeus, *Species Plantarum* 2: 1090. 1753.
"Habitat in Europae sylvis." RCN: 7895.
Lectotype (Jonsell & Jarvis in *Nordic J. Bot.* 14: 149. 1994): Herb. Clifford: 475, *Polypodium* 10 (BM-000647599).
Current name: ***Dryopteris filix-mas*** (L.) Schott (Dryopteridaceae).

Note: In accordance with Art. 23.8, Ex. 19 of the Code, *P. filix-mas* is to continue to be treated as *P. filix-mas*. Bobrov (in *Novosti Sist. Vyssh. Rast.* 21: 11. 1984) indicated 1251.13 (LINN) as the type, but this collection is associated with *P. trifoliatum* L. and is not original material for *P. filix-mas*.

Polypodium fontanum Linnaeus, *Species Plantarum* 2: 1089. 1753.
"Habitat in Sibiria, Galloprovincia." RCN: 7888.
Lectotype (Taylor in *J. Bot.* 76: 279. 1938): Herb. Burser XX: 38 (UPS).
Current name: ***Asplenium fontanum*** (L.) Bernh. (Aspleniaceae).
Note: Although Taylor's type choice has priority, some authors have treated 1251.27 (LINN) as the type, taking up *Woodsia fontana* (L.) Fuchs for the species more generally known as *W. glabella* R. Br. as a consequence. See review by Pichi Sermolli (in *Webbia* 40: 93–94. 1986).

Polypodium fragile Linnaeus, *Flora Anglica*: 25. 1754.
["Habitat in collibus Europae frigidioris."] Sp. Pl., ed. 2, 2: 1553 (1763). RCN: 7904.
Lectotype (Copeland in *Univ. Calif. Publ. Bot.* 16: 56. 1929): *Amman 52*, Herb. Linn. No. 1251.51 (LINN).
Current name: ***Cystopteris fragilis*** (L.) Bernh. (Dryopteridaceae).
Note: In accordance with Art. 23.8, Ex. 19 of the Code, *P. filix-fragile* L. (1753) is to be treated as *P. fragile*.

Polypodium fragrans Linnaeus, *Species Plantarum* 2: 1089. 1753.
"Habitat in Sibiria." RCN: 7891.
Lectotype (Bobrov in *Novosti Sist. Vyssh. Rast.* 21: 9. 1984): *Amman 49*, Herb. Linn. No. 1251.32 (LINN).
Current name: ***Dryopteris fragrans*** (L.) Schott (Polypodiaceae).

Polypodium fragrans Linnaeus, *Mantissa Plantarum Altera*: 307. 1771, *nom. illeg.*
"Habitat in Gallia australi Baro Capucinus; ad muros Funschal. Koenig." RCN: 7906.
Lectotype (Panigrahi & Basu in *Taxon* 31: 103. 1982): *König s.n.*, Herb. Linn. No. 1251.33 (LINN).
Current name: ***Cheilanthes fragrans*** (L. f.) Sw. (Pteridaceae).
Note: A later homonym of *P. fragrans* L. (1753) and therefore illegitimate. See extensive discussion by Nardi & Reichstein (in *Webbia* 39: 136. 1986), who concluded that the original elements were conspecific and diploid in nature.

Polypodium heterophyllum Linnaeus, *Species Plantarum* 2: 1083. 1753.
"Habitat in America meridionali." RCN: 7855.
Lectotype (Proctor in Howard, *Fl. Lesser Antilles* 2: 337. 1977): [icon] *"Lingua Cervina heterophylla, scandens et repens"* in Plumier, Traité Foug. Amér.: 105, t. 120. 1705.
Current name: ***Polypodium heterophyllum*** L. (Polypodiaceae).

Polypodium horridum Linnaeus, *Species Plantarum* 2: 1092. 1753.
"Habitat in America meridionali." RCN: 7912.
Lectotype (Stolze in *Fieldiana, Bot.* 37: 42. 1974): [icon] *"Filix latifolia ramosa cauliculis nigris et spinosis"* in Plumier, Descr. Pl. Amér.: 3, t. 4. 1693.
Current name: ***Cyathea horrida*** (L.) Sm. (Cyatheaceae).
Note: Although Maxon (in *Contr. U. S. Natl. Herb.* 16: 44. 1912) stated that Plumier's *Traité Foug. Amér.* t. 8 (1705) is the type, it was not actually cited in the protologue and is therefore not original material for the name.

Polypodium lanceolatum Linnaeus, *Species Plantarum* 2: 1082. 1753.
"Habitat in America meridionali." RCN: 7852.

Lectotype (Hedberg in *Symb. Bot. Upsal.* 15(1): 31. 1957): [icon]
"*Phyllitis maculata, folio longo angustifolia maculis majoribus*" in
Petiver, Pteri-graphia Amer.: 8, t. 6, f. 2. 1712.
Current name: **Pleopeltis macrocarpa** (Willd.) Kaulf.
(Polypodiaceae).
Note: See comments by Weatherby (in *Contr. Gray Herb.* 65: 3. 1922),
who did not, however, explicitly refer to the Petiver plate as the
type.

Polypodium leptophyllum Linnaeus, *Species Plantarum* 2: 1092.
1753.
"Habitat in Hispania, Lusitania, Galloprovincia." RCN: 7908.
Lectotype (Morton in *Amer. Fern J.* 60: 103. 1970): Herb. Linn. No.
1251.56 (LINN).
Current name: **Anogramma leptophylla** (L.) Link (Pteridaceae).
Note: Pichi Sermolli (in *Webbia* 21: 497. 1966) provided an extensive
discussion of the original elements for this name but opted to
interpret it via Magnol's synonym, and designated a Tournefort
specimen, not seen by Linnaeus, as the lectotype. With the existence
of original material, the latter cannot be accepted as a neotype, and
Morton's subsequent choice of type stands.

Polypodium lonchitis Linnaeus, *Species Plantarum* 2: 1088. 1753.
"Habitat in Alpinis Helvetiae, Baldi, Arvoniae, Monspelii, Virginiae."
RCN: 7879.
Lectotype (Jonsell & Jarvis in *Nordic J. Bot.* 14: 149. 1994): Herb.
Clifford: 475, *Polypodium* 5 (BM-000647595).
Current name: **Polystichum lonchitis** (L.) Roth (Dryopteridaceae).
Note: Although Bobrov (in *Novosti Sist. Vyssh. Rast.* 21: 11. 1984)
indicated 1251.14 (LINN) as the type, this collection lacks the
relevant *Species Plantarum* number (i.e. "26") and was a post-1753
addition to the herbarium, and is not original material for the
name.

Polypodium loriceum Linnaeus, *Species Plantarum* 2: 1086. 1753.
"Habitat in America." RCN: 7872.
Lectotype (Proctor in Howard, *Fl. Lesser Antilles* 2: 331. 1977): [icon]
"*Polypodium longifolium, radice dulci*" in Petiver, Pteri-graphia
Amer.: 27, t. 7, f. 10. 1712.
Current name: **Serpocaulon loriceum** (L.) A.R. Sm. (Polypodiaceae).

Polypodium lusitanicum Linnaeus, *Species Plantarum* 2: 1094. 1753.
"Habitat in Lusitania." RCN: 7920.
Type not designated.
Original material: [icon] in Magnol, Hort. Reg. Monspel.: 79,
unnumbered plate. 1697.
Current name: **Davallia canariensis** (L.) Sm. (Davalliaceae).

Polypodium lycopodioides Linnaeus, *Species Plantarum* 2: 1082.
1753.
"Habitat in America: Martinica, Domingo, Jamaica." RCN: 7853.
Lectotype (Proctor in Howard, *Fl. Lesser Antilles* 2: 338. 1977): Herb.
Linn. No. 1251.2 (LINN).
Current name: **Polypodium lycopodioides** L. (Polypodiaceae).

Polypodium marginale Linnaeus, *Species Plantarum* 2: 1091. 1753.
"Habitat in Canada. Kalm." RCN: 7902.
Lectotype (designated here by Reveal): *Kalm?*, Herb. Linn. No.
1251.49 (LINN).
Current name: **Dryopteris marginalis** (L.) A. Gray
(Dryopteridaceae).

Polypodium muricatum Linnaeus, *Species Plantarum* 2: 1093.
1753.
"Habitat in America." RCN: 7915.

Lectotype (Proctor, *Ferns Jamaica*: 460. 1985): [icon] "*Filix pinnis
aculeatis*" in Petiver, Pteri-graphia Amer.: 53, t. 1, f. 6. 1712.
Current name: **Polystichum muricatum** (L.) Fée (Dryopteridaceae).

Polypodium noveboracense Linnaeus, *Species Plantarum* 2: 1091.
1753.
"Habitat in Canada. Kalm." RCN: 7900.
Lectotype (designated here by Reveal): *Kalm*, Herb. Linn. No.
1251.47 (LINN).
Current name: **Thelypteris noveboracensis** (L.) Nieuwl.
(Thelypteridaceae).

Polypodium otites Linnaeus, *Species Plantarum* 2: 1085. 1753.
"Habitat in America." RCN: 7867.
Lectotype (Proctor, *Ferns Jamaica*: 521. 1985): [icon] "*Polypodium
Lonchitidis folio undulato minus*" in Petiver, Pteri-graphia Amer.: 32,
t. 1, f. 16. 1712.
Current name: **Polypodium otites** L. (Polypodiaceae).

Polypodium parasiticum Linnaeus, *Species Plantarum* 2: 1090. 1753.
"Habitat in India supra arbores." RCN: 7892.
Lectotype (Holttum in *J. S. African Bot.* 40: 141. 1974): *Osbeck s.n.*,
Herb. Swartz (S-PA).
Current name: **Christella parasitica** (L.) H. Lév. (Thelypteridaceae).
Note: See Hansen & Fox Maule (in *Bot. J. Linn. Soc.* 67: 207. 1973)
for comments on Osbeck material.

Polypodium pectinatum Linnaeus, *Species Plantarum* 2: 1085. 1753.
"Habitat in Jamaica." RCN: 7868.
Lectotype (Evans in *Ann. Missouri Bot. Gard.* 55: 246. 1969): [icon]
"*Polypodium nigrum, tenuius sectum*" in Plumier, Descr. Pl. Amér.:
26, t. 37. 1693.
Current name: **Pecluma pectinata** (L.) M.G. Price (Polypodiaceae).

Polypodium phegopteris Linnaeus, *Species Plantarum* 2: 1089. 1753.
"Habitat in Europae fagetis & in Virginia." RCN: 7889.
Lectotype (Jonsell & Jarvis in *Nordic J. Bot.* 14: 148. 1994): Herb.
Clifford: 475, *Polypodium* 8 (BM-000647597).
Current name: **Phegopteris connectilis** (Michx.) Watt
(Thelypteridaceae).
Note: Although Holttum (in *Blumea* 17: 11. 1969) indicated material
in LINN as the type, he did not distinguish between sheets
1251.28, 1251.29 and 1251.30. As these are evidently not part of a
single gathering, Art. 9.15 does not apply.

Polypodium phyllitidis Linnaeus, *Species Plantarum* 2: 1083. 1753.
"Habitat in America meridionali." RCN: 7857.
Lectotype (Proctor in Howard, *Fl. Lesser Antilles* 2: 341. 1977): [icon]
"*Polypodium foliis Linguae Cervinae majus*" in Plumier, Descr. Pl.
Amér.: 26, t. 38. 1693. – Typotype: Herb. Surian 273 (P); Herb.
Jussieu 1071D (P).
Current name: **Polypodium phyllitidis** L. (Polypodiaceae).

Polypodium phymatodes Linnaeus, *Mantissa Plantarum Altera*: 306.
1771, *nom. illeg.*
"Habitat in India orientali." RCN: 7860.
Replaced synonym: *Polypodium scolopendria* Burm. f. (1768).
Type not designated.
Current name: **Microsorum scolopendria** (Burm. f.) Copel.
(Polypodiaceae).
Note: A superfluous name for *Polypodium scolopendria* Burm. f. (1768),
with which *P. phymatodes* is therefore homotypic. Roux (in *Bothalia*
29: 106. 1999) treated 1251.6 (LINN) as the holotype of *P.
phymatodes*, but as there is no indication that it came from Burman,
it seems most unlikely that it can be original material for

P. scolopendria. Verdcourt (in Beentje, *Fl. Trop. E. Africa, Polypodiaceae*: 24. 2001) indicated *Pryon s.n.* (G) as lectotype but this was published after 1 Jan 2001 and so the omission of the phrase "designated here" or an equivalent (Art. 7.11) means that the choice is not effective.

Polypodium piloselloides Linnaeus, *Species Plantarum* 2: 1083. 1753.
"Habitat in America meridionali." RCN: 7854.
Lectotype (Proctor in Howard, *Fl. Lesser Antilles* 2: 336. 1977): Herb. Linn. No. 1251.3 (LINN).
Current name: ***Polypodium piloselloides*** L. (Polypodiaceae).

Polypodium pubescens Linnaeus, *Systema Naturae*, ed. 10, 2: 1327. 1759.
["Habitat in Jamaica."] Sp. Pl., ed. 2, 2: 1552 (1763). RCN: 7901.
Lectotype (Proctor in *Amer. Fern J.* 72: 109. 1982): Herb. Linn. No. 1251.48 (LINN).
Current name: ***Arachniodes pubescens*** (L.) Proctor (Dryopteridaceae).

Polypodium pyramidale Linnaeus, *Species Plantarum* 2: 1093. 1753.
"Habitat in America." RCN: 7913.
Lectotype (Proctor in Howard, *Fl. Lesser Antilles* 2: 188. 1977): [icon] *"Filix ramosa piramidalis, pinnis parvis"* in Petiver, Pteri-graphia Amer.: 40, t. 4, f. 12. 1712.
Current name: ***Adiantum pyramidale*** (L.) Willd. (Pteridaceae).

Polypodium quercifolium Linnaeus, *Species Plantarum* 2: 1087. 1753.
"Habitat in India." RCN: 7876.
Lectotype (Sledge in *Bull. Brit. Mus. (Nat. Hist.), Bot.* 2: 144. 1960): Herb. Hermann 1: 39, No. 382 (BM-000621366).
Current name: ***Drynaria quercifolia*** (L.) J. Sm. (Polypodiaceae).

Polypodium regium Linnaeus, *Species Plantarum* 2: 1091. 1753.
"Habitat in Gallia." RCN: 7907.
Type not designated.
Original material: Herb. Clifford: 475, *Polypodium* 9 (BM); *Magnol,* Herb. Linn. No. 1251.52 (LINN); [icon] in Vaillant, Bot. Paris.: 52, t. 9, f. 1. 1727.
Current name: ***Cystopteris fragilis*** (L.) Bernh. (Polypodiaceae).
Note: See discussion by Fuchs-Eckhart (in *Feddes Repert.* 90: 531. 1979).

Polypodium reticulatum Linnaeus, *Systema Naturae*, ed. 10, 2: 1325. 1759.
["Habitat in America."] Sp. Pl., ed. 2, 2: 1549 (1763). RCN: 7886.
Lectotype (Underwood in *Bull. Torrey Bot. Club* 33: 198. 1906): [icon] *"Filix latifolia, non ramosa nigris tuberculis pulverulenta"* in Plumier, Descr. Pl. Amér.: 6, t. 9. 1693.
Current name: ***Thelypteris reticulata*** (L.) Proctor (Thelypteridaceae).
Note: Proctor (in Howard, *Fl. Lesser Antilles* 2: 309. 1977) designated 1251.25 (LINN) as type, but his choice is pre-dated by that of Underwood. Jarvis (in *Symb. Bot. Upsal.* 33(3): 28, f. 3. 2005) reproduces an image of Underwood's lectotype.

Polypodium retroflexum Linnaeus, *Species Plantarum* 2: 1089. 1753.
"Habitat in America." RCN: 7890.
Lectotype (Proctor & Lourteig in *Bradea* 5: 385. 1990): [icon] *"Filicula alis inferioribus pendulis"* in Petiver, Pteri-graphia Amer.: 72, t. 1, f. 9. 1712.
Current name: ***Thelypteris retroflexa*** (L.) Proctor & Lourteig (Thelypteridaceae).

Polypodium rhaeticum Linnaeus, *Species Plantarum* 2: 1091. 1753.
"Habitat in Gallia, Helvetia." RCN: 7899.
Type not designated.
Original material: *Magnol?,* Herb. Linn. No. 1251.46 (LINN); [icon] in Bauhin & Cherler, Hist. Pl. Univ. 3(2): 740. 1651.
Current name: ***Athyrium filix-femina*** (L.) Roth (Dryopteridaceae).
Note: See discussion by Fuchs (in *Candollea* 29: 183. 1974) who did not designate a type, but illustrated 1251.46 (LINN) as his plate Ia.

Polypodium scolopendrioides Linnaeus, *Species Plantarum* 2: 1085. 1753.
"Habitat in Jamaica." RCN: 7864.
Lectotype (Christensen, *Kongel. Danske Vidensk. Selsk. Skr. Naturvidensk. Math. Afd.,* ser. 7, 10: 212. 1913): [icon] *"Polypodium incisuris asplenii"* in Plumier, Traité Foug. Amér.: 70, t. 91. 1705.
Current name: ***Thelypteris scolopendrioides*** (L.) Proctor (Thelypteridaceae).

Polypodium simile Linnaeus, *Systema Naturae*, ed. 10, 2: 1325. 1759.
["Habitat in America."] Sp. Pl., ed. 2, 2: 1549 (1763). RCN: 7884.
Type not designated.
Original material: Herb. Linn. No. 1251.23 (LINN); [icon] in Sloane, Voy. Jamaica 1: 77, t. 32. 1707 – Voucher: Herb. Sloane 1: 51 (BM-SL).
Current name: ***Polypodium simile*** L. (Polypodiaceae).
Note: Proctor (in *Bull. Inst. Jamaica, Sci. Ser.* 5: 50. 1953) treated a Sloane collection as the type, but this was not seen by Linnaeus and is not original material for the name.

Polypodium speluncae Linnaeus, *Species Plantarum* 2: 1093. 1753.
"Habitat in Indiis." RCN: 7919.
Lectotype (Sledge in *Bot. J. Linn. Soc.* 84: 25. 1982): Herb. Hermann 3: 41, No. 384 (BM-000621951).
Current name: ***Microlepia speluncae*** (L.) T. Moore (Dennstaedtiaceae).

Polypodium spinosum Linnaeus, *Species Plantarum* 2: 1092. 1753.
"Habitat in America meridionali." RCN: 7911.
Type not designated.
Original material: Herb. Linn. No. 1251.57 (LINN); [icon] in Plumier, Traité Foug. Amér.: 4, t. 3. 1705; [icon] in Petiver, Pteri-graphia Amer.: 42, t. 4, f. 1. 1712; [icon] in Plumier, Descr. Pl. Amér.: 3, t. 3. 1693.
Current name: ***Pteris spinosa*** (L.) Desv. (Pteridaceae).

Polypodium squamatum Linnaeus, *Species Plantarum* 2: 1086. 1753.
"Habitat – – – – – – – –" RCN: 7871.
Lectotype (Proctor, *Ferns Jamaica*: 529. 1985): [icon] *"Polypodium longifolium, squamulis argenteis"* in Petiver, Pteri-graphia Amer.: 29, t. 7, f. 11. 1712.
Current name: ***Polypodium squamatum*** L. (Polypodiaceae).

Polypodium struthionis Linnaeus, *Species Plantarum* 2: 1086. 1753.
"Habitat in America." RCN: 7870.
Type not designated.
Original material: [icon] in Petiver, Pteri-graphia Amer.: 30, t. 3, f. 8. 1712; [icon] in Plumier, Traité Foug. Amér.: 60, t. 78. 1705.
Current name: ***Polypodium struthionis*** L. (Polypodiaceae).

Polypodium suspensum Linnaeus, *Species Plantarum* 2: 1084. 1753.
"Habitat in America meridionali." RCN: 7862.
Lectotype (Proctor in *Brit. Fern Gaz.* 9: 77. 1962): [icon] *"Polypodium pendulum et glabrum"* in Plumier, Traité Foug. Amér.: 67, t. 87. 1705.
Current name: ***Grammitis suspensa*** (L.) Proctor (Grammitidaceae).

Polypodium taxifolium Linnaeus, *Species Plantarum* 2: 1086. 1753.
"Habitat in America meridionali." RCN: 7869.
Lectotype (Morton in *Contr. U. S. Natl. Herb.* 38: 109. 1967): [icon]
"*Polypodium tenue et pendulum*" in Plumier, Traité Foug. Amér.: 69,
t. 89. 1705.
Current name: **Grammitis taxifolia** (L.) Proctor (Grammitidaceae).

Polypodium thelypteris (Linnaeus) Linnaeus, *Systema Vegetabilium*,
ed. 13: 788. 1774.
["Habitat in Europae septentrionalis paludibus."] Sp. Pl. 2: 1071
(1753). RCN: 7897.
Basionym: *Acrostichum thelypteris* L. (1753).
Type not designated.
Original material: as basionym.
Current name: **Thelypteris palustris** Schott (Thelypteridaceae).

Polypodium tornatile Linnaeus, *Flora Jamaicensis*: 23. 1759.
"Habitat [in Jamaica.]"
Type not designated.
Original material: Herb. Linn. No. 1251.63 (LINN).
Note: The application of this name is uncertain.

Polypodium triangulum Linnaeus, *Species Plantarum* 2: 1088. 1753.
"Habitat in America." RCN: 7882.
Lectotype (Morton in *Bot. J. Linn. Soc.* 60: 67. 1967): [icon]
"*Trichomanes folio triangulo dentato*" in Petiver, Pteri-graphia Amer.:
76, t. 1, f. 10. 1712.
Current name: **Polystichum triangulum** (L.) Fée (Dryopteridaceae).
Note: Morton treated the cited Petiver illustration as the type though
noting that it had been redrawn from a Plumier plate, via which
Morton interpreted it. However, the Plumier plate was not cited in
the protologue of this name.

Polypodium trifoliatum Linnaeus, *Species Plantarum* 2: 1087. 1753.
"Habitat in Caribaeis insulis." RCN: 7877.
Lectotype (Proctor in Howard, *Fl. Lesser Antilles* 2: 237. 1977): [icon]
"*Hemionitis maxima trifolia*" in Plumier, Traité Foug. Amér.: 127, t.
148. 1705.
Current name: **Tectaria trifoliata** (L.) Sw. (Dryopteridaceae).

Polypodium trifurcatum Linnaeus, *Species Plantarum* 2: 1084. 1753.
"Habitat in America meridionali." RCN: 7859.
Lectotype (Morton in *Contr. U. S. Natl. Herb.* 38: 100. 1967): [icon]
"*Lingua Cervina sinuosa in summitate trisulca*" in Plumier, Traité
Foug. Amér.: 120, t. 138. 1705.
Current name: **Grammitis trifurcata** (L.) Copel. (Grammitidaceae).

Polypodium unitum Linnaeus, *Systema Naturae,* ed. 10, 2: 1326.
1759.
["Habitat in Indiis."] Sp. Pl., ed. 2, 2: 1548 (1763). RCN: 7878.
Lectotype (Holttum in *J. S. African Bot.* 40: 165. 1974): Herb. Linn.
No. 1251.21 (LINN).
Current name: **Sphaerostephanos unitus** (L.) Holttum
(Thelypteridaceae).

Polypodium varium Linnaeus, *Species Plantarum* 2: 1090. 1753.
"Habitat in China. Osbeck." RCN: 7893.
Type not designated.
Original material: none traced.
Current name: **Dryopteris varia** (L.) Kuntze (Dryopteridaceae).
Note: See Hansen & Fox Maule (in *Bot. J. Linn. Soc.* 67: 207. 1973)
for comments on Osbeck material.

Polypodium villosum Linnaeus, *Species Plantarum* 2: 1093. 1753.
"Habitat in America." RCN: 7916.

Lectotype (Proctor in Howard, *Fl. Lesser Antilles* 2: 245. 1977): [icon]
"*Filix ramosa, villosa major, crenis rotundis dentata*" in Plumier,
Descr. Pl. Amér.: 15, t. 23. 1693.
Current name: **Ctenitis villosa** (L.) Copel. (Dryopteridaceae).

Polypodium virginianum Linnaeus, *Species Plantarum* 2: 1085.
1753.
"Habitat in Virginia." RCN: 7866.
Lectotype (Cranfill & Britton in *Taxon* 32: 558, f. 1. 1983): [icon]
"*Polypodium minus Virgin. foliis obtusioribus*" in Morison, Pl. Hist.
Univ. 3: 563, s. 14, t. 2, f. 3. 1699.
Current name: **Polypodium virginianum** L. (Polypodiaceae).

Polypodium vulgare Linnaeus, *Species Plantarum* 2: 1085. 1753.
"Habitat in Europae rimis rupium." RCN: 7865.
Lectotype (Jonsell & Jarvis in Jarvis & al., *Regnum Veg.* 127: 78.
1993): Herb. Burser XX: 44 (UPS).
Generitype of *Polypodium* Linnaeus (vide Cavanilles in *Anales Hist.
Nat.* 1(2): 115. 1799).
Current name: **Polypodium vulgare** L. (Polypodiaceae).
Note: Shivas (in *Bot. J. Linn. Soc.* 58: 27. 1961) discussed various
original elements (illustrating a Clifford sheet as pl. 1), but did not
designate a lectotype (although noting that the Burser specimen
would "not be inappropriate for the purpose"). He applied the
name to the tetraploid cytotype. Jonsell & Jarvis (in *Nordic J. Bot.*
14: 150. 1994) discussed the reasons for their 1993 type choice.

Polypremum procumbens Linnaeus, *Species Plantarum* 1: 111.
1753.
"Habitat in Carolina, Virginia." RCN: 910.
Lectotype (Reveal & al. in *Huntia* 7: 237. 1987): *Clayton 768*, Herb.
Linn. No. 139.1 (LINN; iso- BM).
Generitype of *Polypremum* Linnaeus.
Current name: **Polypremum procumbens** L.
(Loganiaceae/Buddlejaceae).

Pontederia cordata Linnaeus, *Species Plantarum* 1: 288. 1753.
"Habitat in Virginia aquosis." RCN: 2293.
Lectotype (Lowden in *Rhodora* 75: 452. 1973): *Kalm*, Herb. Linn. No.
407.4 (LINN).
Generitype of *Pontederia* Linnaeus (vide Hitchcock, *Prop. Brit. Bot.*:
144. 1929).
Current name: **Pontederia cordata** L. (Pontederiaceae).
Note: Fernald (in *Rhodora* 27: 76. 1927) discussed the generic
typification at length.
  Lowden (in *Rhodora* 75: 452. 1973), believing the type (from
Gronovius) to be missing, designated Kalm's collection (407.4
LINN) as a neotype. As this material was original material for the
name, and hence eligible as a lectotype, Lowden is accepted as
having typified the name (in accordance with Art. 9.8).
Obermeyer (in Leistner, *Fl. Southern Afr.* 4(2): 66. 1985) and
Reveal (in *Huntia* 7: 231. 1987) independently opted for the same
choice of type.

Pontederia hastata Linnaeus, *Species Plantarum* 1: 288. 1753.
"Habitat in India." RCN: 2294.
Lectotype (Horn & Haynes in *Taxon* 36: 622. 1987): Herb. Hermann
2: 52, No. 129 (BM-000621681).
Current name: **Monochoria hastata** (L.) Solms (Pontederiaceae).

Pontederia ovata Linnaeus, *Species Plantarum* 1: 288. 1753.
"Habitat in Malabariae aquosis." RCN: 2291.
Lectotype (Suresh & Nicolson in *Taxon* 35: 355. 1986): [icon] "*Naru
kila*" in Rheede, Hort. Malab. 11: 67, t. 34. 1692.
Current name: **Phrynium pubinerve** Blume (Marantaceae).

P

Note: See also discussion by Horn & Haynes (in *Taxon* 36: 621. 1987), and Turner (in *Gard. Bull. Singapore* 46: 127–129. 1994), who notes that the correct name for this taxon is not *Phrynium rheedei* Suresh & Nicolson but *Phrynium pubinerve* Blume.

Pontederia rotundifolia Linnaeus, *Plantae Surinamenses*: 7. 1775. "Habitat [in Surinamo.]" RCN: 2294.
Lectotype (Lowden in *Rhodora* 75: 473. 1973): *Dahlberg 137*, Herb. Linn. No. 407.2 (LINN).
Current name: **Pontederia rotundifolia** L. (Pontederiaceae).
Note: See discussion by Horn & Haynes (in *Taxon* 36: 623. 1987), who concur with Lowden's type choice.

Populus alba Linnaeus, *Species Plantarum* 2: 1034. 1753. "Habitat in Europa temperatiori." RCN: 7462.
Lectotype (Jonsell in Jarvis & al., *Regnum Veg.* 127: 78. 1993): Herb. Burser XXIII: 19 (UPS).
Generitype of *Populus* Linnaeus (vide Green, *Prop. Brit. Bot.*: 192. 1929).
Current name: **Populus alba** L. (Salicaceae).
Note: Siddiqi (in Jafri & El-Gadi, *Fl. Libya* 142: 10. 1987) indicated 1185.1 (LINN) as type, but this appears to be a Gerber collection from the River Don region, and therefore conflicts with the geographical part of Linnaeus' protologue. For this reason, Jonsell designated a Burser collection as lectotype.

Populus balsamifera Linnaeus, *Species Plantarum* 2: 1034. 1753. "Habitat in America septentrionali." RCN: 7465.
Lectotype (Rouleau in *Rhodora* 48: 105. 1946): Herb. Linn. No. 1185.6 (LINN).
Current name: **Populus balsamifera** L. (Salicaceae).
Note: Although some earlier authors (e.g. Farwell in *Rhodora* 21: 101. 1919) rejected this as a *nomen ambiguum*, Rouleau (*l.c.* 48: 103–110. 1946) studied the case in some detail and concluded that the name should continue to be used for the Northern Balsam Poplar.

Populus heterophylla Linnaeus, *Species Plantarum* 2: 1034. 1753. "Habitat in Virginia." RCN: 7467.
Lectotype (designated here by Belyaeva): Herb. Linn. No. 1185.8 (LINN).
Current name: **Populus heterophylla** L. (Salicaceae).

Populus nigra Linnaeus, *Species Plantarum* 2: 1034. 1753. "Habitat in Europae temperatiore." RCN: 7464.
Lectotype (Bhopal & Chaudhri in *Pakistan Syst.* 1(2): 12. 1977): Herb. Linn. No. 1185.5 (LINN).
Current name: **Populus nigra** L. (Salicaceae).

Populus tremula Linnaeus, *Species Plantarum* 2: 1034. 1753. "Habitat in Europae frigidioribus." RCN: 7463.
Lectotype (Jonsell & Jarvis in *Nordic J. Bot.* 14: 150. 1994): Herb. Clifford: 460, *Populus* 2 (BM-000647500).
Current name: **Populus tremula** L. (Salicaceae).

Porella pinnata Linnaeus, *Species Plantarum* 2: 1106. 1753. "Habitat in Pensylvania." RCN: 7985.
Lectotype (Howe in Jarvis & al., *Regnum Veg.* 127: 78. 1993): [icon] *"Porella pinnis obtusis"* in Dillenius, Hist. Musc.: 459, t. 68, f. "Porella". 1741. – Voucher: Herb. Dillenius (OXF).
Generitype of *Porella* Linnaeus.
Current name: **Porella pinnata** L. (Porellaceae).
Note: After an extensive discussion, Howe (in *Bull. Torrey Bot. Club* 24: 518. 1897) treated the Dillenian material (OXF) associated with the cited Dillenius figure as the type of this name, followed in this by

others such as Evans (in *Rhodora* 18: 82. 1916) and Grolle (in *Feddes Repert.* 87: 221. 1976). However, Linnaeus did not study Dillenius' material and would have based his own account on Dillenius' published description and illustration (Linnaeus wrote "Hanc neque ego vidi"). For this reason, Jarvis & al. designated the published illustration as the type, with the material as the typotype (while attributing the choice to Howe).

Portlandia grandiflora Linnaeus, *Systema Naturae*, ed. 10, 2: 928. 1759.
["Habitat in Jamaica."] Sp. Pl., ed. 2, 1: 244 (1762). RCN: 1357.

Lectotype (Aiello in *J. Arnold Arbor.* 60: 100. 1979): [icon] *"Portlandia foliis majoribus nitidis ovatis oppositis, floribus amplissimis"* in Browne, Civ. Nat. Hist. Jamaica: 164, t. 11. 1756.
Current name: **Portlandia grandiflora** L. (Rubiaceae).

Portulaca anacampseros Linnaeus, *Species Plantarum* 1: 445. 1753. "Habitat ad Cap. b. spei." RCN: 3463.
Lectotype (Wijnands, *Bot. Commelins*: 175. 1983): [icon] *"Telephiastrum folio globoso"* in Dillenius, Hort. Eltham. 2: 375, t. 281, f. 363. 1732.
Current name: **Anacampseros telephiastrum** DC. (Portulacaceae).
Note: Anacampseros Linnaeus, *nom. cons.* against *Anacampseros* Miller.

Portulaca fruticosa Linnaeus, *Systema Naturae,* ed. 10, 2: 1045. 1759. RCN: 3464a.
Lectotype (Wijnands, *Bot. Commelins*: 176. 1983): [icon] *"Portulaca foliis obovatis"* in Plumier in Burman, Pl. Amer.: 142, t. 150, f. 2. 1757.
Current name: ***Talinum fruticosum*** (L.) Juss. (Portulacaceae).
Note: This name has sometimes been treated as ambiguous (e.g. by Howard in *J. Arnold Arbor.* 54: 462. 1973), but now appears to be consistently in use in *Talinum*.

Portulaca halimoides Linnaeus, *Species Plantarum,* ed. 2, 1: 639. 1762.
"Habitat in Jamaica." RCN: 3461.
Lectotype (Howard, *Fl. Lesser Antilles* 4: 202. 1988): [icon] *"Portulaca erecta sedi minoris facie capitulo tomentoso"* in Sloane, Voy. Jamaica 1: 205, t. 129, f. 3. 1707. – Typotype: Herb. Sloane 4: 10 (BM-SL).
Current name: ***Portulaca halimoides*** L. (Portulacaceae).

Portulaca oleracea Linnaeus, *Species Plantarum* 1: 445. 1753.
"Habitat in Europa australi, India, Ins. Ascensionis, America." RCN: 3458.
Lectotype (Geesink in *Blumea* 17: 292. 1969): *Löfling s.n.,* Herb. Linn. No. 625.1 (LINN).
Generitype of *Portulaca* Linnaeus (vide Green, *Prop. Brit. Bot.*: 157. 1929).
Current name: ***Portulaca oleracea*** L. subsp. ***oleracea*** (Portulacaceae).
Note: Geesink stated "T[ype]: LINN (photograph seen)" and as the only sheet he could have intended is 625.1 (LINN), and it is original material for the name, this choice is accepted here. Danin & al. (in *Israel J. Bot.* 27: 196. 1978), however, stated "the lectotype should be chosen from the Hortus Siccus Cliffortianus material in the British Museum (Natural History!)", and applied their infraspecific nomenclature accordingly. They identified (*l.c.*: 198) the LINN material (accepted here as the type) with subsp. *stellata* Danin & Baker. Most recent authors appear to accept Geesink's choice of type but have adopted a broad species concept.

Portulaca panicula Linnaeus, *Mantissa Plantarum Altera*: 391. 1771. RCN: 3464b.
Type not designated.
Original material: none traced.
Note: The application of this name appears uncertain.

Portulaca patens Linnaeus, *Mantissa Plantarum Altera*: 242. 1771, *nom. illeg.*
"Habitat in America." RCN: 3465.
Replaced synonym: *Portulaca paniculata* Jacq. (1760).
Type not designated.
Current name: ***Talinum paniculatum*** (Jacq.) Gaertn. (Portulacaceae).
Note: A superfluous name for *P. paniculata* Jacq. (1760).

Portulaca pilosa Linnaeus, *Species Plantarum* 1: 445. 1753.
"Habitat in America meridionali." RCN: 3459.
Lectotype (Geesink in *Blumea* 17: 294. 1969): Herb. Linn. No. 625.2 (LINN).
Current name: ***Portulaca pilosa*** L. (Portulacaceae).
Note: See discussion, and illustrations of the lectotype (f. 4) and the Commelin (f. 1) and Hermann (f. 2) illustrations by Matthews & al. (in *Sida* 15: 78. 1992).

Portulaca portulacastrum Linnaeus, *Species Plantarum* 1: 446. 1753.
"Habitat in Curassao." RCN: 3652.
Basionym of: *Sesuvium portulacastrum* (L.) L. (1759).
Lectotype (Wijnands, *Bot. Commelins*: 175. 1983): [icon] *"Portulaca Corassavica Angusto longo lucidoque folio"* in Hermann, Parad. Bat.: 212. 1698.

Current name: ***Sesuvium portulacastrum*** (L.) L. (Aizoaceae).
Note: Jeffrey (in Hubbard & Milne-Redhead, *Fl. Trop. E. Africa, Aizoaceae*: 20. 1961) indicated an unspecified Hermann specimen in Herb. Sloane (BM-SL) as "typotype". This would not have been seen by Linnaeus and is not original material for the name. Jeffrey was followed by many later authors, but Wijnands appears to have been the first to designate clearly, as lectotype, the Hermann plate cited in Linnaeus' protologue.

Portulaca quadrifida Linnaeus, *Systema Naturae,* ed. 12, 2: 328; *Mantissa Plantarum*: 73. 1767.
"Habitat in Aegypto." RCN: 3460.
Lectotype (designated here by Phillips): [icon] *"Portulaca Corassavica lanuginosa procumbens"* in Hermann, Parad. Bat.: 215. 1698.
Current name: ***Portulaca quadrifida*** L. (Portulacaceae).
Note: Geesink (in *Blumea* 17: 290. 1969) indicated material in LINN as the type but there are no annotations linking any of the material there with this name. Phillips (in Beentje, *Fl. Trop. E. Africa, Portulacaceae*: 8. 2002) indicated the cited Hermann figure as type but this choice was published after 1 Jan 2001 and so the omission of the phrase "designated here" or an equivalent (Art. 7.11) means that this choice is not effective. However, it is validated here.

Portulaca racemosa Linnaeus, *Species Plantarum,* ed. 2, 1: 640. 1762, *nom. illeg.*
"Habitat in America ad maris littora." RCN: 3462.
Replaced synonym: *Portulaca triangularis* Jacq. (1760).
Type not designated.
Current name: ***Talinum fruticosum*** (L.) Juss. (Portulacaceae).
Note: A superfluous name for *P. triangularis* Jacq. (1760).

Potamogeton compressus Linnaeus, *Species Plantarum* 1: 127. 1753.
"Habitat in Europae fossis paludosis." RCN: 1040.
Lectotype (Dandy ex Haynes in *Taxon* 35: 569. 1986): Herb. Clifford: 40, *Potamogeton* 3 (BM-000557843).
Current name: ***Potamogeton compressus*** L. (Potamogetonaceae).
Note: Specific epithet spelled "compressum" in the protologue.

Potamogeton crispus Linnaeus, *Species Plantarum* 1: 126. 1753.
"Habitat in Europae fossis & rivulis." RCN: 1038.
Lectotype (Obermeyer in Codd & al., *Fl. Southern Africa* 1: 66. 1966): Herb. Linn. No. 175.6 (LINN).
Current name: ***Potamogeton crispus*** L. (Potamogetonaceae).
Note: Specific epithet spelled "crispum" in the protologue.

Potamogeton densus Linnaeus, *Species Plantarum* 1: 126. 1753.
"Habitat in Gallia." RCN: 1036.
Lectotype (Haynes in *Taxon* 35: 566. 1986): *Séguier,* Herb. Linn. No. 175.4 (LINN).
Current name: ***Potamogeton densus*** L. (Potamogetonaceae).
Note: Specific epithet spelled "densum" in the protologue.

Potamogeton gramineus Linnaeus, *Species Plantarum* 1: 127. 1753.
"Habitat in Europae fossis & paludibus." RCN: 1043.
Lectotype (Haynes in *Taxon* 35: 570. 1986): Herb. Linn. No. 70 (LAPP).
Current name: ***Potamogeton gramineus*** L. (Potamogetonaceae).
Note: Specific epithet spelled "gramineum" in the protologue.

Potamogeton lucens Linnaeus, *Species Plantarum* 1: 126. 1753.
"Habitat in Europae lacubus, stagnis, fluviis argillosis." RCN: 1037.
Lectotype (Haynes in *Taxon* 35: 567. 1986): Herb. Linn. No. 175.5 (LINN).
Current name: ***Potamogeton lucens*** L. (Potamogetonaceae).

P

Potamogeton marinus Linnaeus, *Species Plantarum* 1: 127. 1753.
"Habitat in Europa ad maris littora." RCN: 1044.
Lectotype (Haynes in *Taxon* 35: 571. 1986): Herb. Linn. No. 175.13 (LINN).
Current name: ***Potamogeton pectinatus*** L. (Potamogetonaceae).
Note: Specific epithet spelled "marinum" in the protologue.

Potamogeton natans Linnaeus, *Species Plantarum* 1: 126. 1753.
"Habitat in Europae lacubus & fluviis." RCN: 1034.
Lectotype (Dandy in Rechinger, *Fl. Iranica* 78: 3. 1971): Herb. Linn. No. 175.1 (LINN).
Generitype of *Potamogeton* Linnaeus (vide Hitchcock, *Prop. Brit. Bot.*: 127. 1929).
Current name: ***Potamogeton natans*** L. (Potamogetonaceae).
Note: Haynes (in *Taxon* 35: 564. 1986) provided a detailed study of Linnaeus' sources and, concluding that 175.1 (LINN) came from Gmelin (and must therefore have come from Asia), rejected Dandy's choice of it as type on the grounds of conflict with "Habitat in Europa" in favour of a Clifford sheet (BM). Gmelin is not explicitly mentioned in the protologue. However, based in St Petersburg, he sent Linnaeus specimens from places other than Siberia and the Russian Far East, and without further evidence, the grounds for rejecting Dandy's type choice are weak. Sheet 175.1 (LINN) is therefore accepted as the lectotype. Both type choices, Dandy's and Haynes', correspond with usage so there are no nomenclatural implications.

Potamogeton pectinatus Linnaeus, *Species Plantarum* 1: 127. 1753.
"Habitat in Europae fossis & paludibus." RCN: 1041.
Lectotype (Haynes in *Taxon* 35: 569. 1986): Herb. Burser X: 124 (UPS).
Current name: ***Potamogeton pectinatus*** L. (Potamogetonaceae).
Note: Specific epithet spelled "pectinatum" in the protologue.

Potamogeton perfoliatus Linnaeus, *Species Plantarum* 1: 126. 1753.
"Habitat in Europae lacubus fluviisque argillosis." RCN: 1035.
Lectotype (Haynes in *Sida* 11: 178. 1985): Herb. Linn. No. 69 (LAPP).
Current name: ***Potamogeton perfoliatus*** L. (Potamogetonaceae).
Note: Specific epithet spelled "perfoliatum" in the protologue.

Potamogeton pusillus Linnaeus, *Species Plantarum* 1: 127. 1753.
"Habitat in Europae paludibus." RCN: 1045.
Lectotype (Dandy & Taylor in *J. Bot.* 76: 92. 1938): Herb. Linn. No. 175.15, left specimen (LINN).
Current name: ***Potamogeton pusillus*** L. (Potamogetonaceae).
Note: Specific epithet spelled "pusillum" in the protologue.

Potamogeton serratus Linnaeus, *Species Plantarum* 1: 126. 1753.
"Habitat in Europae rivulis." RCN: 1039.
Neotype (Haynes in *Taxon* 35: 568. 1986): Herb. Linn. No. 66.1 (S).
Current name: ***Potamogeton densus*** L. (Potamogetonaceae).
Note: Specific epithet spelled "serratum" in the protologue.

Potamogeton setaceus Linnaeus, *Species Plantarum* 1: 127. 1753.
"Habitat in Europae fossis paludosis." RCN: 1042.
Lectotype (Haynes in *Taxon* 35: 570. 1986): Herb. A. van Royen No. 906.269–146 (L).
Current name: ***Potamogeton densus*** L. (Potamogetonaceae).
Note: Specific epithet spelled "setaceum" in the protologue.

Potentilla acaulis Linnaeus, *Species Plantarum* 1: 500. 1753.
"Habitat in Sibiria." RCN: 3801.
Replaced synonym of: *Potentilla subacaulis* L. (1759), *nom. illeg.*
Type not designated.

Original material: Herb. Linn. No. 655.46 (LINN); Herb. Linn. No. 655.47 (LINN).
Current name: ***Potentilla acaulis*** L. (Rosaceae).
Note: Although Stearn (*Introd. Linnaeus' Sp. Pl.* (Ray Soc. ed.): 127. 1957) says this is "to be typified by [a] specimen...from Gmelin in the Linnaean herbarium", it is unclear which collection was intended. Both 655.46 and 655.47 (LINN) carry "22" (the number of this species account in *Species Plantarum*), but neither is indicated directly as coming from Gmelin, and the collections are not clearly part of a single gathering. The name, which is currently untypified, is in use for an Asiatic taxon (see Soják in *Preslia* 65: 129. 1993) in a taxonomically complex group of species.

Potentilla alba Linnaeus, *Species Plantarum* 1: 498. 1753.
"Habitat in alpibus Stiriae, Austriae, Panoniae." RCN: 3792.
Lectotype (Rico & Guillén in Cafferty & Jarvis in *Taxon* 51: 542. 2002): Herb. Linn. No. 655.27 (LINN).
Current name: ***Potentilla alba*** L. (Rosaceae).

Potentilla anserina Linnaeus, *Species Plantarum* 1: 495. 1753.
"Habitat in Europae pascuis; in argillosis argentea." RCN: 3774.
Lectotype (Rousi in *Ann. Bot. Fenn.* 2: 101. 1965): Herb. Clifford: 193, *Potentilla* 1 (BM-000628646).
Current name: ***Potentilla anserina*** L. (Rosaceae).

Potentilla argentea Linnaeus, *Species Plantarum* 1: 497. 1753.
"Habitat in Europae ruderatis." RCN: 3784.
Lectotype (Jonsell & Jarvis in *Nordic J. Bot.* 22: 75. 2002): Herb. Burser XVIII(2): 3 (UPS).
Current name: ***Potentilla argentea*** L. (Rosaceae).

Potentilla aurea Linnaeus, *Centuria II Plantarum*: 18. 1756.
"Habitat in alpibus Helvetiae." RCN: 3790.
Lectotype (Rico & Martínez Ortega in Cafferty & Jarvis in *Taxon* 51: 542. 2002): Herb. Burser XVIII(1): 98 (UPS).
Current name: ***Potentilla aurea*** L. (Rosaceae).

Potentilla bifurca Linnaeus, *Species Plantarum* 1: 497. 1753.
"Habitat in Sibiria." RCN: 3779.
Lectotype (Soják in *Candollea* 43: 438. 1988): Herb. Linn. No. 655.10, left specimen (LINN).
Current name: ***Potentilla bifurca*** L. (Rosaceae).

Potentilla canadensis Linnaeus, *Species Plantarum* 1: 498. 1753.
"Habitat in Canada. Kalm." RCN: 3791.
Lectotype (Britton in *Bull. Torrey Bot. Club* 18: 366. 1891): *Kalm*, Herb. Linn. No. 655.26 (LINN; iso- UPS).
Current name: ***Potentilla canadensis*** L. (Rosaceae).
Note: Fernald (in *Rhodora* 33: 181, pl. 214, f. 1. 1931) provides a photograph of the type specimen.

Potentilla caulescens Linnaeus, *Centuria II Plantarum*: 19. 1756.
"Habitat in Alpibus Helvetiae, Austriae, Stiriae, Tyroli, Horti Dei." RCN: 3793.
Lectotype (Rico & Guillén in Cafferty & Jarvis in *Taxon* 51: 542. 2002): Herb. Linn. No. 655.29 (LINN).
Current name: ***Potentilla caulescens*** L. (Rosaceae).

Potentilla fragarioides Linnaeus, *Species Plantarum* 1: 496. 1753.
"Habitat in Sibiria." RCN: 3777.
Lectotype (Stearn, *Introd. Linnaeus' Sp. Pl.* (Ray Soc. ed.): 127. 1957): *Gmelin s.n.*, Herb. Linn. No. 655.7 (LINN).
Current name: ***Potentilla fragarioides*** L. (Rosaceae).

Potentilla fruticosa Linnaeus, *Species Plantarum* 1: 495. 1753.
"Habitat in Eboraco, Anglia, Oelandia australi, Sibiria." RCN: 3773.

Lectotype (Elkington in *New Phytol.* 68: 156. 1969): Herb. Clifford: 193, *Potentilla* 3 (BM-000628648).
Current name: ***Potentilla fruticosa*** L. (Rosaceae).

Potentilla grandiflora Linnaeus, *Species Plantarum* 1: 499. 1753.
"Habitat in Helvetia, Sibiria." RCN: 3800.
Lectotype (Rico & Martínez Ortega in Cafferty & Jarvis in *Taxon* 51: 542. 2002): Herb. Linn. No. 655.45 (LINN).
Current name: ***Potentilla grandiflora*** L. (Rosaceae).

Potentilla heptaphylla Linnaeus, *Centuria I Plantarum*: 13. 1755.
"Habitat in Helvetia." RCN: 3788.
Replaced synonym of: *Potentilla opaca* L. (1759), *nom. illeg.*
Type not designated.
Original material: Herb. Burser XVIII(2): 2 (UPS).
Current name: ***Potentilla heptaphylla*** L. (Rosaceae).
Note: Material in the Burser herbarium appears to be the sole original element, and is a specimen of *P. supina* L. (1753). *Potentilla heptaphylla* appears to be a candidate for conservation with a conserved type.

Potentilla hirta Linnaeus, *Species Plantarum* 1: 497. 1753.
"Habitat Monspelii D. Sauvages; inque Pyrenaeis." RCN: 3786.
Lectotype (Rico & Martínez Ortega in Cafferty & Jarvis in *Taxon* 51: 542. 2002): Herb. Linn. No. 655.19 (LINN).
Current name: ***Potentilla hirta*** L. (Rosaceae).

Potentilla intermedia Linnaeus, *Systema Naturae,* ed. 12, 2: 351; *Mantissa Plantarum*: 76. 1767.
"Habitat in Helvetia." RCN: 3785.
Lectotype (Jonsell & Jarvis in *Nordic J. Bot.* 22: 75. 2002): Herb. Linn. No. 655.17 (LINN).
Current name: ***Potentilla intermedia*** L. (Rosaceae).

Potentilla monspeliensis Linnaeus, *Species Plantarum* 1: 499. 1753.
"Habitat Monspelii." RCN: 3797.
Lectotype (Rico & Martínez Ortega in Cafferty & Jarvis in *Taxon* 51: 542. 2002): Herb. Linn. No. 655.40 (LINN).
Current name: ***Potentilla norvegica*** L. (Rosaceae).

Potentilla multifida Linnaeus, *Species Plantarum* 1: 496. 1753.
"Habitat in Sibiria, Tataria, Cappadocia." RCN: 3776.
Lectotype (Soják in *Candollea* 43: 441. 1988): Herb. Linn. No. 655.6 (LINN).
Current name: ***Potentilla multifida*** L. (Rosaceae).

Potentilla nitida Linnaeus, *Centuria II Plantarum*: 18. 1756.
"Habitat in Baldo. Seguier." RCN: 3794.
Lectotype (Rico & Guillén in Cafferty & Jarvis in *Taxon* 51: 542. 2002): *Séguier*, Herb. Linn. No. 655.36 (LINN).
Current name: ***Potentilla nitida*** L. (Rosaceae).

Potentilla nivea Linnaeus, *Species Plantarum* 1: 499. 1753, *nom. cons.*
"Habitat in Alpibus Lapponiae, Sibiriae." RCN: 3799.
Conserved type (Eriksen & al. in *Taxon* 48: 165. 1999): Sweden. Torne Lappmark, Abisko area, Latnjajaure, *Eriksen 620* (GB; iso-ALA, BM, C, H, LE, O, S, UPS).
Current name: ***Potentilla nivea*** L. (Rosaceae).

Potentilla norvegica Linnaeus, *Species Plantarum* 1: 499. 1753.
"Habitat in Norvegiae, Sueciae, Borussiae, Canadae agris." RCN: 3798.
Lectotype (Jonsell & Jarvis in *Nordic J. Bot.* 22: 75. 2002): Herb. Linn. No. 655.41 (LINN).
Current name: ***Potentilla norvegica*** L. (Rosaceae).

Potentilla opaca Linnaeus, *Systema Naturae,* ed. 10, 2: 1064. 1759, *nom. illeg.*
["Habitat in Helvetia."] Cent. I Pl.: 13 (1755). RCN: 3788.
Replaced synonym: *Potentilla heptaphylla* L. (1755).
Type not designated.
Original material: as replaced synonym.
Current name: ***Potentilla heptaphylla*** L. (Rosaceae).
Note: As noted by Nordenstam (in *Bot. Not.* 114: 277. 1961), *P. opaca* replaced *P. heptaphylla* L. (1755) in the reprint of the dissertation *Cent. I Pl.* in *Amoen. Acad.* 4: 274. 1759). *Potentilla opaca* was, in fact, first published earlier (May–Jun) in 1759 in *Syst. Nat.,* ed. 10, 2: 1064, but it is in any case a replacement name for *P. heptaphylla,* and is illegitimate.

Potentilla pensylvanica Linnaeus, *Systema Naturae,* ed. 12, 2: 350; *Mantissa Plantarum*: 76. 1767.
"Habitat in Canada." RCN: 3781.
Lectotype (Fernald in *Rhodora* 37: 288. 1935): *Arduino 13*, Herb. Linn. No. 655.12 (LINN).
Current name: ***Potentilla pensylvanica*** L. (Rosaceae).
Note: Soják (in *Preslia* 59: 290, 298. 1987; *Candollea* 60: 66. 2005) provides further discussion on the material in LINN associated with this name.

Potentilla pimpinelloides Linnaeus, *Species Plantarum* 1: 497. 1753.
"Habitat in Armeniae saxosis." RCN: 3780.
Lectotype (Rico & Martínez Ortega in Cafferty & Jarvis in *Taxon* 51: 542. 2002): Herb. Linn. No. 655.11 (LINN).
Current name: ***Potentilla pimpinelloides*** L. (Rosaceae).

Potentilla recta Linnaeus, *Species Plantarum* 1: 497. 1753.
"Habitat in Italia, Narbona, ad agrorum margines." RCN: 3783.
Type not designated.
Original material: Herb. Burser XVIII(2):10 (UPS); [icon] in Dodoëns, Stirp. Hist. Pempt., ed. 2: 116. 1616.
Current name: ***Potentilla recta*** L. (Rosaceae).
Note: Although Dikshit & Panigrahi (*Fam. Rosaceae India* 4: 212. 1998) indicated 655.15 (LINN) as type, this collection lacks a *Species Plantarum* number (i.e. "10"), is a post-1753 addition to the collection, and is not original material for the name.

Potentilla repens Linnaeus, *Amoenitates Academicae* 4: 484. 1759.
Neotype (Rico & Muñoz Garmendia in Cafferty & Jarvis in *Taxon* 51: 542. 2002): France. Bouches du Rhone, Camargue, Tour du Valat, near Le Sambuc, 1 Sep 1967, *Kendrick & Moyes 63* (BM-000576295).
Current name: ***Potentilla reptans*** L. (Rosaceae).
Note: Stearn (in Geck & Pressler, *Festschr. Claus Nissen*: 641. 1974) considered this to be a synonym of *P. reptans* L. (1753). In the absence of any original material, Rico & Muñoz Garmendia designated a neotype which formalised this synonymy.

Potentilla reptans Linnaeus, *Species Plantarum* 1: 499. 1753.
"Habitat in Europae apricis argillosis." RCN: 3796.
Lectotype (Jafri in Ali & Jafri, *Fl. Libya* 11: 20. 1977): Herb. Linn. No. 655.38 (LINN).
Generitype of *Potentilla* Linnaeus (vide Green, *Prop. Brit. Bot.*: 159. 1929).
Current name: ***Potentilla reptans*** L. (Rosaceae).

Potentilla rupestris Linnaeus, *Species Plantarum* 1: 496. 1753.
"Habitat ad latera montium Westrogothiae, Sibiria, Germaniae." RCN: 3778.
Lectotype (Jonsell & Jarvis in *Nordic J. Bot.* 22: 75. 2002): Herb. Clifford: 193, *Potentilla* 4 (BM-000628649).
Current name: ***Potentilla rupestris*** L. (Rosaceae).

P

Potentilla sericea Linnaeus, *Species Plantarum* 1: 495. 1753.
"Habitat in Sibiria." RCN: 3775.
Lectotype (Stearn, *Introd. Linnaeus' Sp. Pl.* (Ray Soc. ed.): 127. 1957):
Gmelin s.n., Herb. Linn. No. 655.5 (LINN).
Current name: ***Potentilla sericea*** L. (Rosaceae).

Potentilla stipularis Linnaeus, *Species Plantarum* 1: 498. 1753.
"Habitat in Sibiria." RCN: 3787.
Lectotype (Stearn, *Introd. Linnaeus' Sp. Pl.* (Ray Soc. ed.): 127. 1957):
Gmelin s.n., Herb. Linn. No. 655.20 (LINN).
Current name: ***Potentilla stipularis*** L. (Rosaceae).

Potentilla subacaulis Linnaeus, *Systema Naturae*, ed. 10, 2: 1065.
1759, *nom. illeg.*
["Habitat in Sibiria."] Sp. Pl. 1: 500 (1753). RCN: 3801.
Replaced synonym: *Potentilla acaulis* L. (1753).
Type not designated.
Original material: as replaced synonym.
Current name: ***Potentilla acaulis*** L. (Rosaceae).
Note: An illegitimate replacement name for *P. acaulis* L. (1753).

Potentilla supina Linnaeus, *Species Plantarum* 1: 497. 1753.
"Habitat ad Moguntiam & in Sibiria." RCN: 3782.
Lectotype (Vidal in Aubréville, *Fl. Cambodge Laos Vietnam* 5: 122.
1967): Herb. Linn. No. 655.14 (LINN).
Current name: ***Potentilla supina*** L. (Rosaceae).

Potentilla valderia Linnaeus, *Systema Naturae*, ed. 10, 2: 1064. 1759.
["Habitat in Alpibus Valderianis & Vinadensibus."] Sp. Pl., ed. 2, 1:
714 (1762). RCN: 3795.
Lectotype (Rico & al. in Cafferty & Jarvis in *Taxon* 51: 542. 2002):
Allioni, Herb. Linn. No. 655.37 (LINN).
Current name: ***Potentilla valderia*** L. (Rosaceae).

Potentilla verna Linnaeus, *Species Plantarum* 1: 498. 1753.
"Habitat in Europae pascuis siccis, frigidioribus." RCN: 3789.
Lectotype (Rico & Martínez Ortega in Cafferty & Jarvis in *Taxon* 51:
542. 2002): Herb. Burser XVIII(2): 1 (UPS).
Current name: ***Potentilla grandiflora*** L. (Rosaceae).

Poterium hybridum Linnaeus, *Species Plantarum* 2: 994. 1753.
"Habitat Monspelii." RCN: 7208.
Lectotype (Nordborg in *Opera Bot.* 11: 67. 1966): Herb. Linn. No.
1127.2 (LINN).
Current name: ***Sanguisorba hybrida*** (L.) Nordborg (Rosaceae).

Poterium sanguisorba Linnaeus, *Species Plantarum* 2: 994. 1753.
"Habitat in Creta, Libano." RCN: 7207.
Lectotype (Purohit & Panigrahi, *Fam. Rosaceae India* 1: 255. 1991):
Löfling 673, Herb. Linn. No. 1127.1 (LINN). – Epitype (Nordborg
in *Opera Bot.* 16: 98. 1967): Spain. Jaén, Sierra de Cazorla, 1,300m,
20 May 1964, *Nordborg 8040* (LD).
Generitype of *Poterium* Linnaeus (vide Green, *Prop. Brit. Bot.*: 189.
1929).
Current name: ***Sanguisorba minor*** Scop. (Rosaceae).
Note: Nordborg (in *Opera Bot.* 16: 98. 1967) chose a neotype for this
name because 1127.1 (LINN), although original material, was
unidentifiable as to subspecies. A neotype cannot be maintained
when original material exists (Art. 9.17) so, despite the deficiencies
of the material, Purohit & Panigrahi's lectotype choice has priority.
However, under Art. 9.8, Nordborg's neotype choice can be
accepted as an epitype.

Poterium spinosum Linnaeus, *Species Plantarum* 2: 994. 1753.
"Habitat in Creta, Libano." RCN: 7209.

Lectotype (Nordborg in *Opera Bot.* 11: 75. 1966): Herb. Linn. No.
1127.3 (LINN).
Current name: ***Sarcopoterium spinosum*** (L.) Spach (Rosaceae).

Pothos cordatus Linnaeus, *Species Plantarum*, ed. 2, 2: 1373. 1763.
"Habitat in America." RCN: 7022.
Lectotype (Howard in *J. Arnold Arbor.* 60: 277. 1979): [icon]
"*Dracontium foliis cordatis, longitudinaliter nervosis*" in Plumier in
Burman, Pl. Amer.: 26, t. 38. 1756.
Current name: ***Anthurium cordatum*** (L.) Schott (Araceae).
Note: Specific epithet spelled "cordata" in the protologue.

Pothos crenatus Linnaeus, *Species Plantarum*, ed. 2, 2: 1373. 1763.
"Habitat in insula S. Thomae." RCN: 7021.
Lectotype (Mayo in *Kew Bull.* 36: 705. 1982): [icon] "*Dracontium
acaule, foliis lanceolatis, serratis*" in Plumier in Burman, Pl. Amer.:
27, t. 39. 1756.
Current name: ***Anthurium crenatum*** (L.) Kunth (Araceae).
Note: Specific epithet spelled "crenata" in the protologue.
Lourteig (in *Bradea* 5: 339. 1990) wrongly treated this as
illegitimate, on the grounds that its type (Burman's plate) was
originally based on the Plumier plate that is the type of *P. acaulis*
Jacq. (1760). However, the protologue of Linnaeus' name did not
include *P. acaulis* so, as names cannot be made illegitimate through
typification, *P. crenatus* is legitimate.

Pothos lanceolatus Linnaeus, *Species Plantarum*, ed. 2, 2: 1373. 1763.
"Habitat in America." RCN: 7020.
Lectotype (Howard in *J. Arnold Arbor.* 60: 275, 280. 1979): [icon]
"*Arum foliis rigidis, angustis et acuminatis*" in Plumier, Descr. Pl.
Amér.: 47, t. 62. 1693.
Current name: ***Anthurium acaule*** (Jacq.) Schott (Araceae).
Note: Specific epithet spelled "lanceolata" in the protologue.

Pothos latifolius Linnaeus, *Herbarium Amboinense*: 25. 1754.
"Habitat [in Amboina.]" RCN: 7019.
Lectotype (Merrill, *Interpret. Rumph. Herb. Amb.*: 33, 125. 1917;
Boyce & Hay in *Telopea* 9: 562. 2001): [icon] "*Adpendix arborum*"
in Rumphius, Herb. Amboin. 5: 483, t. 181, f. 1. 1747.
Current name: ***Piper* sp.** (Piperaceae).
Note: Boyce & Hay disagree with Merrill's interpretation of the cited
Rumphius plate, excluding t. 181, f. 2 (which is a *Pothos*), and
follow Roxburgh in restricting the Linnaean name to t. 181, f. 1,
which they identify as a species of *Piper* (Piperaceae). Although they
wrongly accept Roxburgh's implicit typification, their statement that
it is "here confirmed" is accepted as a formal typification (Art. 7.11).

Pothos palmatus Linnaeus, *Species Plantarum*, ed. 2, 2: 1374. 1763.
"Habitat in America." RCN: 7024.
Type not designated.
Original material: [icon] in Plumier, Descr. Pl. Amér.: 49, t. 64, 65.
1693.
Current name: ***Anthurium palmatum*** (L.) G. Don (Araceae).
Note: Specific epithet spelled "palmata" in the protologue.

Pothos pinnatus Linnaeus, *Species Plantarum*, ed. 2, 2: 1374. 1763.
"Habitat in India." RCN: 7023.
Lectotype (Merrill, *Interpret. Rumph. Herb. Amb.*: 127. 1917): [icon]
"*Adpendix laciniata*" in Rumphius, Herb. Amboin. 5: 489, t. 183, f.
2. 1747.
Current name: ***Epipremnum pinnatum*** (L.) Engl. (Araceae).
Note: Specific epithet spelled "pinnata" in the protologue.

Pothos scandens Linnaeus, *Species Plantarum* 2: 968. 1753.
"Habitat in Zeylona." RCN: 7017.

Lectotype (Bogner in Leroy, *Fl. Madagascar* 31: 12. 1975; Suresh & al. in *Taxon* 32: 127. 1983): Herb. Hermann 4: 39, No. 329 (BM-000628180).
Generitype of *Pothos* Linnaeus.
Current name: ***Pothos scandens*** L. (Araceae).
Note: Bogner indicated Herb. Hermann material (BM) as type. Although there is material in two volumes, it appears to have been part of a single gathering so his is accepted as the first typification (Art. 9.15), with the choice subsequently restricted by Suresh & al.

Prasium majus Linnaeus, *Species Plantarum* 2: 601. 1753.
"Habitat in Sicilia, Romae & in agro Tingitano." RCN: 4365.
Lectotype (Press in Jarvis & al., *Regnum Veg.* 127: 79. 1993): Herb. Clifford: 309, *Prasium* 1 (BM-000646040).
Generitype of *Prasium* Linnaeus (vide Green, *Prop. Brit. Bot.*: 166. 1929).
Current name: ***Prasium majus*** L. (Lamiaceae).

Prasium minus Linnaeus, *Species Plantarum* 2: 601. 1753.
"Habitat in Sicilia." RCN: 4366.
Lectotype (Hedge in Jarvis & al. in *Taxon* 50: 517. 2001): Herb. Clifford: 309, *Prasium* 2 (BM-000646041).
Current name: ***Prasium majus*** L. (Lamiaceae).

Premna integrifolia Linnaeus, *Mantissa Plantarum Altera*: 252. 1771, *nom. illeg.*
"Habitat in India orientali." RCN: 4535.
Replaced synonym: *Cornutia corymbosa* Burm. f. (1768).
Type not designated.
Current name: ***Premna corymbosa*** (Burm. f.) Rottler & Willd. (Lamiaceae).
Note: An illegitimate replacement name for *Cornutia corymbosa* Burm. f. (1768).

Premna serratifolia Linnaeus, *Mantissa Plantarum Altera*: 253. 1771, *typ. cons.*
"Habitat in India orientali." RCN: 4536.
Lectotype (Munir in *J. Adelaide Bot. Gard.* 7: 13. 1984): Herb. Linn. No. 782.4 (LINN).
Generitype of *Premna* Linnaeus, *nom. cons.*
Current name: ***Premna serratifolia*** L. (Lamiaceae).
Note: Premna Linnaeus, *nom. cons.* against *Appella* Adans. Merrill (in *Philipp. Isl. Bur. Sci. Publ.* 9: 450. 1917) and Fosberg (in *Taxon* 2: 89. 1952) treated this as a superfluous name for *Cornutia corymbosa* Burm. f. (1768) but this is erroneous. Moldenke & Moldenke (in Dassanayake & Fosberg, *Revised Handb. Fl. Ceylon* 4: 343. 1983) indicated unspecified material at LINN as type, but did not distinguish between three sheets there. Munir's 1984 type choice is therefore accepted here.

Prenanthes alba Linnaeus, *Species Plantarum* 2: 798. 1753.
"Habitat in Carolina, Virginia, Pensylvania." RCN: 5835.
Lectotype (Reveal in Jarvis & Turland in *Taxon* 47: 365. 1998): *Kalm*, Herb. Linn. No. 952.7 (LINN).
Current name: ***Prenanthes alba*** L. (Asteraceae).

Prenanthes altissima Linnaeus, *Species Plantarum* 2: 797. 1753.
"Habitat in Virginia, Canada." RCN: 5832.
Lectotype (Fusiak & Schilling in *Bull. Torrey Bot. Club* 111: 345. 1984): [icon] "*Sonchus elatus s. dendroides Virginianus, Ari in modum auriculatis foliis, ramosissimus, floribus luteis parvis pentapetalis*" in Plukenet, Phytographia: t. 317, f. 2. 1694; Almag. Bot.: 355. 1696. – Typotype: Herb. Sloane 102: 30 (BM-SL).
Current name: ***Prenanthes altissima*** L. (Asteraceae).

Prenanthes japonica Linnaeus, *Systema Naturae,* ed. 12, 2: 521; *Mantissa Plantarum*: 107. 1767.
"Habitat in Japonia. Kleynhoff." RCN: 5834.
Lectotype (Grierson in Dassanayake & Fosberg, *Revised Handb. Fl. Ceylon* 1: 268. 1980): *Kleynhoff*, Herb. Linn. No. 952.6 (LINN).
Current name: ***Youngia japonica*** (L.) DC. (Asteraceae).

Prenanthes muralis Linnaeus, *Species Plantarum* 2: 797. 1753.
"Habitat in Europae nemoribus umbrosis." RCN: 5831.
Type not designated.
Original material: Herb. Linn. No. 952.4 (LINN); Herb. Burser VI: 19 (UPS); Herb. Clifford: 383, *Prenanthes* 1 (BM); [icon] in Clusius, Rar. Pl. Hist. 2: 146. 1601.
Current name: ***Lactuca muralis*** (L.) Gaertn. (Asteraceae).

Prenanthes purpurea Linnaeus, *Species Plantarum* 2: 797. 1753.
"Habitat in Germaniae, Helvetiae, Italiae nemoribus montanis." RCN: 5830.
Lectotype (Jeffrey in Jarvis & al., *Regnum Veg.* 127: 79. 1993): Herb. Clifford: 383, *Prenanthes* 2 (BM-000646836).
Generitype of *Prenanthes* Linnaeus (vide Cassini, *Dict. Sci. Nat.*: 34: 98. 1825).
Current name: ***Prenanthes purpurea*** L. (Asteraceae).

Prenanthes repens Linnaeus, *Species Plantarum* 2: 798, Err. 1753.
"Habitat in Sibiria." RCN: 5836.
Type not designated.
Original material: *Steller*, Herb. Linn. No. 952.9 (LINN); [icon] in Linnaeus, Amoen. Acad. 2: 360, t. 4, f. 23. 1751.
Current name: ***Lactuca repens*** (L.) Benth. ex Maxim. (Asteraceae).
Note: The specific epithet is given as "altissima" in the protologue on p. 798 (duplicating that in *P. altissima* L. on p. 797), but is corrected to "repens" in the Errata.
    Merrill (in *J. Arnold Arbor.* 21: 389. 1940) stated that this is based wholly on the Kamchatka plant described and figured by Linnaeus (in *Amoen. Acad.* 2: 360, t. 4, f. 23. 1751). There is, however, also a Kamchatka specimen in existence (952.9 LINN).

Prenanthes tenuifolia Linnaeus, *Species Plantarum* 2: 797. 1753.
"Habitat in Alpibus Europae australis." RCN: 5828.
Type not designated.
Original material: none traced.
Current name: ***Prenanthes purpurea*** L. (Asteraceae).

Prenanthes viminea Linnaeus, *Species Plantarum* 2: 797. 1753.
"Habitat in Gallia, Lusitania." RCN: 5829.
Lectotype (van Raamsdonk in Wisskirchen in *Feddes Repert.* 108: 105. 1997): Herb. A. van Royen No. 900.344–290 (L).
Current name: ***Lactuca viminea*** (L.) J. Presl & C. Presl (Asteraceae).

Primula acaulis (Linnaeus) Linnaeus, *Flora Anglica*: 12. 1754, *nom. inval.*
Type not relevant.
Current name: ***Primula vulgaris*** Huds. (Primulaceae).
Note: Greuter (in *Candollea* 44: 566. 1989) argued that this is a new combination made by Linnaeus in 1754, and therefore pre-dating the usual name for the primrose, *P. vulgaris* Huds. However, Brummitt & Meikle (in *Watsonia* 19: 181–183. 1993) argued that there are typographical variants of the thesis which make it unreasonable to interpret this as a new combination.

Primula auricula Linnaeus, *Species Plantarum* 1: 143. 1753.
"Habitat in alpibus Helveticis, Styriacis." RCN: 1152.
Lectotype (Halda, *Genus* Primula: 14. 1992): Herb. Linn. No. 198.10 (LINN).

P

Current name: ***Primula auricula*** L. (Primulaceae).
Note: Zhang & Kadereit (in *Taxon* 54: 777. 2005) discuss the
typification of this name, and follow Halda's type choice. As they
recognise two distinct species within what has been treated as *P.*
auricula, they use *P. lutea* Vill. for populations in the northern part
of the range, with *P. auricula* retained for those from further south.

Primula cortusoides Linnaeus, *Species Plantarum* 1: 144. 1753.
"Habitat in Sibiria. D. Gmelin." RCN: 1155.
Lectotype (Halda, *Genus* Primula: 74. 1992): *Amman s.n.*, Herb. Linn.
No. 198.18 (LINN).
Current name: ***Primula cortusoides*** L. (Primulaceae).

Primula elatior (Linnaeus) Linnaeus, *Flora Anglica*: 12. 1754, nom.
inval.
Type not relevant.
Current name: ***Primula elatior*** (L.) Hill (Primulaceae).
Note: Greuter (in *Candollea* 44: 566. 1989) argues that this is a new
combination for *P. veris* var. *elatior* L. 1753, made in 1754, and the
correct name for what has been called *P. elatior* (L.) Hill. However,
this is disputed by Brummitt & Meikle (in *Watsonia* 19: 181–183.
1993), who point out typographical inconsistencies between
different copies of the thesis, and they argue that no new
combination is made until 1765.

Primula farinosa Linnaeus, *Species Plantarum* 1: 143. 1753.
"Habitat in Alpinis frigidisque Europae pratis uliginosis." RCN: 1151.
Lectotype (Halda, *Genus* Primula: 244. 1992): Herb. Linn. No. 198.7
(LINN).
Current name: ***Primula farinosa*** L. (Primulaceae).

Primula integrifolia Linnaeus, *Species Plantarum* 1: 144. 1753.
"Habitat in alpibus Helveticis, Styriacis, Pyrenaicis." RCN: 1154.
Lectotype (Zhang & Kadereit in *Taxon* 54: 785. 2005): Herb. Linn.
No. 198.17 (LINN).
Current name: ***Primula integrifolia*** L. (Primulaceae).

Primula minima Linnaeus, *Species Plantarum* 1: 143. 1753.
"Habitat in Sneberg, Tauro, Judenberg inque altissimo monte prope
salinas Austriae superioris, qua tenditur in Styriam." RCN: 1153.
Lectotype (Zhang & Kadereit in *Taxon* 54: 783. 2005): [icon]
"Auricula ursi VIII. minima" in Clusius, Rar. Pl. Hist. 1: 305. 1601.
Current name: ***Primula minima*** L. (Primulaceae).

Primula veris Linnaeus, *Species Plantarum* 1: 142. 1753.
"Habitat in Europae pratis." RCN: 1150.
Lectotype (Richards in Jarvis & al., *Regnum Veg.* 127: 79. 1993):
Herb. Burser XIII: 137 (UPS).
Generitype of *Primula* Linnaeus (vide Hitchcock, *Prop. Brit. Bot.*: 128.
1929).
Current name: ***Primula veris*** L. (Primulaceae).
Note: The original elements for this name represent a number of
different taxonomic entities and Richards therefore designated
Herb. Burser XIII: 137 (UPS) as lectotype, since it corresponded
with var. *veris* of usage. However, he was unaware of an earlier type
designation, made by Halda (*Genus* Primula: 49. 1992) tying the
name to Herb. Linn. 198.1 (LINN). In the opinion of Richards,
this specimen is identifiable as subsp. *canescens* (Opiz) Hayek ex
Hegi, sometimes recognised at species level as *P. canescens* Opiz.
Confirmation of this identification and acceptance of Halda's type
choice would cause *P. veris* to become the correct name for what has
been called *P. canescens*, and require a new name to be found for the
latter. It seems that a conservation proposal may be necessary, but in
the meantime, *P. veris* is not to be used in a sense that conflicts with
current usage (Art. 57).

Primula veris Linnaeus var. **acaulis** Linnaeus, *Species Plantarum* 1:
143. 1753.
RCN: 1150.
Type not designated.
Original material: Herb. Burser XIII: 139 (UPS).
Current name: ***Primula vulgaris*** Huds. (Primulaceae).
Note: Greuter (in *Candollea* 44: 566. 1989) argues that Linnaeus made
a new combination based on this (i.e. *P. acaulis* (L.) L.) in *Fl.*
Anglica: 12. 1754. This would have priority over *P. vulgaris*
Hudson, long used for the primrose. However, Brummitt & Meikle
(in *Watsonia* 19: 181–184. 1993) have argued that Greuter's
interpretation is erroneous, based on the variable typography that
the theses display.

Primula veris Linnaeus var. **elatior** Linnaeus, *Species Plantarum* 1:
143. 1753.
RCN: 1150.
Type not designated.
Original material: Herb. Burser XIII: 138 (UPS); [icon] in Clusius,
Rar. Pl. Hist. 1: 301. 1601.
Current name: ***Primula elatior*** (L.) Hill (Primulaceae).
Note: Greuter (in *Candollea* 44: 1989) argues that this is the basionym
of a new combination, *P. elatior* (L.) L., *Fl. Anglica* (1754), which is
the correct form of the more usual *P. elatior* (L.) Hill (1765), for the
oxlip. However, this is disputed by Brummitt & Meikle (in
Watsonia 19: 183–184. 1993), who argued that there is variability
in the typography of different versions of the thesis. They argue that
the correct name remains *P. elatior* (L.) Hill.

Primula veris Linnaeus var. **officinalis** Linnaeus, *Species Plantarum* 1:
142. 1753.
RCN: 1150.
Type not designated.
Original material: Herb. Clifford: 51, *Primula* 3, 8 sheets (BM); Herb.
Burser XIII: 137 (UPS).
Current name: ***Primula veris*** L. (Primulaceae).

Primula vitaliana Linnaeus, *Species Plantarum* 1: 143. 1753.
"Habitat in alpibus Pyrenaeis & Italicis." RCN: 1143.
Basionym of: *Aretia vitaliana* (L.) L. (1774).
Lectotype (Kress in Hegi, *Ill. Fl. Mitt.-Eur.,* ed. 2., 5(3): 2248d.
1966): Herb. Burser XIII: 154 (UPS).
Current name: ***Androsace vitaliana*** (L.) Lapeyr. (Primulaceae).
Note: Schwartz (in *Feddes Repert.* 67: 23. 1963) designated material in
LINN (presumably 198.15) as the type, but this was received from
Arduino and was not in Linnaeus' possession until after 1753. This
was noted by Kress, who rejected this type choice in favour of Herb.
Burser XIII: 154 (UPS). Ferguson (in *Taxon* 18: 302. 1969)
designated the cited plate from Donati as lectotype but Kress'
choice has priority.

Prinos glaber Linnaeus, *Species Plantarum* 1: 330. 1753.
"Habitat in Canada." RCN: 2553.
Lectotype (designated here by Reveal): *Kalm*, Herb. Linn. No. 452.3
(LINN).
Current name: ***Ilex glabra*** (L.) A. Gray (Aquifoliaceae).

Prinos verticillatus Linnaeus, *Species Plantarum* 1: 330. 1753.
"Habitat in Virginia." RCN: 2552.
Lectotype (Reveal in Jarvis & al., *Regnum Veg.* 127: 79. 1993): *Kalm,*
Herb. Linn. No. 452.1 (LINN; iso- UPS).
Generitype of *Prinos* Linnaeus (vide Rafinesque, *Sylva Tell.*: 52.
1838).
Current name: ***Ilex verticillata*** (L.) A. Gray (Aquifoliaceae).

Prockia crucis Linnaeus, *Systema Naturae,* ed. 10, 2: 1074. 1759. ["Habitat in Ins. S. Crucis."] Sp. Pl., ed. 2, 1: 745 (1762). RCN: 3928.
Lectotype (Sleumer, *Fl. Neotropica* 22: 70. 1980): Herb. Linn. No. 690.1 (LINN).
Generitype of *Prockia* Linnaeus.
Current name: ***Prockia crucis*** L. (Flacourtiaceae).

Proserpinaca palustris Linnaeus, *Species Plantarum* 1: 88. 1753.
"Habitat in Virginiae paludibus." RCN: 736.
Lectotype (Fernald & Griscom in *Rhodora* 37: 177. 1935; Reveal in Jarvis & al., *Regnum Veg.* 127: 79. 1993): Herb. Linn. No. 107.1, right specimen (LINN).
Generitype of *Proserpinaca* Linnaeus.
Current name: ***Proserpinaca palustris*** L. (Haloragaceae).
Note: Fernald & Griscom (1935) designated 107.1 (LINN) as the type; Reveal subsequently restricted this to one of the specimens as the sheet bears a mixture of taxa.

Prosopis spicigera Linnaeus, *Systema Naturae,* ed. 12, 2: 293; *Mantissa Plantarum*: 68. 1767.
"Habitat in India." RCN: 3020.
Neotype (Lewis in Jarvis & al., *Regnum Veg.* 127: 79. 1993): *Wight 877* (K).
Generitype of *Prosopis* Linnaeus.
Current name: ***Prosopis cineraria*** (L.) Druce (Fabaceae: Mimosoideae).

Protea argentea Linnaeus, *Species Plantarum* 1: 94. 1753.
"Habitat ad Cap. b. spei." RCN: 777.
Lectotype (Williams in *Contr. Bolus Herb.* 3: 134. 1972): Herb. Clifford: 29, *Protea* 1 (BM-000557732).
Generitype of *Protea* Linnaeus (1753), *nom. rej.* (vide Hitchcock, *Prop. Brit. Bot.*: 113. 1929).
Current name: ***Leucadendron argenteum*** (L.) R. Br. (Proteaceae).
Note: Protea Linnaeus (1753), *nom. rej.* in favour of *Protea* Linnaeus (1771).

Protea conifera Linnaeus, *Species Plantarum,* ed. 2, 1: 138. 1762.
"Habitat ad Cap. b. spei." RCN: 774.
Lectotype (Williams in *Contr. Bolus Herb.* 3: 326. 1972): Herb. Linn. No. 116.21 (ex Herb. Clifford) (LINN; iso- BM (2 sheets)).
Current name: ***Leucadendron coniferum*** (L.) Druce (Proteaceae).

Protea cucullata (Linnaeus) Linnaeus, *Mantissa Plantarum Altera*: 189. 1771.
["Habitat ad Cap. b. spei locis uliginosis."] Sp. Pl. 1: 93 (1753). RCN: 764.
Basionym: *Leucadendron cucullatum* L. (1753).
Lectotype (Rourke in *J. S. African Bot.* 50: 182. 1984): [icon] *"Hypophyllocarpodendron; foliis inferioribus apice trifido, rubro, superioribus penitus rubris, glabris"* in Boerhaave, Index Alter Pl. Hort. Lugdb.-Bat. 2: 206. 1720.
Current name: ***Mimetes cucullatus*** (L.) R. Br. (Proteaceae).

Protea cyanoides (Linnaeus) Linnaeus, *Mantissa Plantarum Altera*: 188. 1771.
["Habitat ad Cap. b. spei."] Sp. Pl. 1: 93 (1753). RCN: 761.
Basionym: *Leucadendron cyanoides* L. (1753).
Type not designated.
Original material: as basionym.
Current name: ***Serruria cyanoides*** (L.) R. Br. (Proteaceae).

Protea cynaroides (Linnaeus) Linnaeus, *Mantissa Plantarum Altera*: 190. 1771, *typ. cons.*

"Habitat ad Cap. b. spei." RCN: 767.
Basionym: *Leucadendron cynaroides* L. (1753), *typ. cons.*
Type not designated.
Original material: as basionym.
Generitype of *Protea* Linnaeus (1771), *nom. cons.*
Current name: ***Protea cynaroides*** (L.) L. (Proteaceae).
Note: Protea Linnaeus (1771), *nom. cons.* against *Protea* Linnaeus (1753) and *Lepidocarpus* Adans. (1763).

Protea divaricata (P.J. Bergius) Linnaeus, *Mantissa Plantarum Altera*: 194. 1771.
"Habitat ad Cap. b. spei." RCN: 779.
Basionym: *Leucadendron divaricatum* P.J. Bergius (1767).
Lectotype (Rourke in *J. S. African Bot.* 42: 193. 1976): *Grubb,* Herb. Bergius (SBT).
Current name: ***Diastella divaricata*** (P.J. Bergius) Rourke (Proteaceae).

Protea fusca Linnaeus, *Species Plantarum* 1: 95. 1753.
"Habitat in Aethiopia." RCN: 778.
Type not designated.
Original material: [icon] in Boerhaave, Index Alter Pl. Hort. Lugdb.-Bat. 2: 202. 1720; [icon] in Plukenet, Almag. Mant.: 47, t. 343, f. 9. 1700.
Current name: ***Leucadendron levisanus*** (L.) P.J. Bergius (Proteaceae).

Protea glomerata Linnaeus, *Mantissa Plantarum Altera*: 187. 1771.
"Habitat ad Cap. b. spei." RCN: 759.
Type not designated.
Original material: Herb. Linn. No. 116.8 (LINN); Herb. Linn. No. 116.7 (LINN).
Current name: ***Serruria glomerata*** (L.) R. Br. (Proteaceae).

Protea hirta (Linnaeus) Linnaeus, *Mantissa Plantarum Altera*: 188. 1771.
["Habitat ad Cap. b. spei."] Sp. Pl., ed. 2, 1: 136 (1762). RCN: 763.
Basionym: *Leucadendron hirtum* L. (1760).
Lectotype (Rourke in *J. S. African Bot.* 50: 218. 1984): Herb. Linn. No. 116.36 (LINN).
Current name: ***Mimetes hirta*** (L.) Knight (Proteaceae).

Protea hypophyllocarpodendron (Linnaeus) Linnaeus, *Mantissa Plantarum Altera*: 191. 1771.
"Habitat ad Cap. b. spei in campis arenosis." RCN: 771.
Basionym: *Leucadendron hypophyllocarpodendron* L. (1753).
Lectotype (Rourke in *J. S. African Bot., Suppl.* 8: 104. 1972): [icon] *"Conocarpodendron; folio rigido, angusto, apice tridentato rubro; flore aureo"* in Boerhaave, Index Alter Pl. Hort. Lugdb.-Bat. 2: 198. 1720.
Current name: ***Leucospermum hypophyllocarpodendron*** (L.) Druce (Proteaceae).

Protea lepidocarpodendron (Linnaeus) Linnaeus, *Mantissa Plantarum Altera*: 190. 1771.
"Habitat ad Cap. b. spei." RCN: 768.
Basionym: *Leucadendron lepidocarpodendron* L. (1753).
Type not designated.
Original material: as basionym.
Current name: ***Protea lepidocarpodendron*** (L.) L. (Proteaceae).

Protea levisanus (Linnaeus) Linnaeus, *Systema Naturae,* ed. 12, 2: 111. 1767.
["Habitat in Aethiopia."] Sp. Pl. 1: 199 (1753). RCN: 778.
Basionym: *Brunia levisanus* L. (1753).
Lectotype (Williams in *Contr. Bolus Herb.* 3: 59. 1972): [icon] *"Brunia*

P

foliis oblongis, incanis, florum capitulo ramulum terminante" in
Burman, Rar. Afric. Pl.: 267, t. 100, f. 2. 1739.
Current name: ***Leucadendron levisanus*** (L.) P.J. Bergius (Proteaceae).

Protea pallens Linnaeus, *Mantissa Plantarum Altera*: 193. 1771.
"Habitat in Capitis b. spei. arenosis." RCN: 775.
Lectotype (Williams in *Contr. Bolus Herb.* 3: 272. 1972): *Tulbagh 28*,
Herb. Linn. No. 116.23 (LINN).
Current name: ***Leucadendron salignum*** P.J. Bergius (Proteaceae).

Protea parviflora Linnaeus, *Mantissa Plantarum Altera*: 195. 1771.
"Habitat ad Cap. b. spei." RCN: 780.
Lectotype (Williams in *Contr. Bolus Herb.* 3: 129. 1972): *Tulbagh 157*,
Herb. Linn. No. 116.19 (LINN).
Current name: ***Leucadendron rubrum*** Burm. f. (Proteaceae).

Protea pinifolia (Linnaeus) Linnaeus, *Mantissa Plantarum Altera*:
187. 1771.
["Habitat ad Cap. b. spei. D. Royen."] Mant. Pl.: 36 (1767). RCN:
756.
Basionym: *Leucadendron pinifolium* L. (1767).
Lectotype (Rourke in *S. African J. Bot.* 53: 479. 1987): [icon] *"Pini
foliis planta Africana, Cyperi capitulis Herm."* in Burman, Rar. Afric.
Pl.: 193, t. 70, f. 3. 1739.
Current name: ***Aulax cancellata*** (L.) Druce (Proteaceae).

Protea pubera Linnaeus, *Mantissa Plantarum Altera*: 192. 1771, *nom.
illeg.*
"Habitat in Capitis b. spei arena rubra." RCN: 772.
Replaced synonym: *Leucadendron oleifolium* P.J. Bergius (1767).
Lectotype (Rourke in *J. S. African Bot., Suppl.* 8: 157. 1972): *Grubb*,
Herb. Bergius (SBT).
Current name: ***Leucospermum oleifolium*** (P.J. Bergius) R. Br.
(Proteaceae).
Note: A superfluous new name in *Protea* for *Leucadendron oleifolium*
P.J. Bergius (1767).

Protea purpurea Linnaeus, *Mantissa Plantarum Altera*: 195. 1771,
nom. illeg.
"Habitat ad Caput b. spei." RCN: 780.
Replaced synonym: *Leucadendron proteoides* L. (1753).
Neotype (Rourke in *J. S. African Bot.* 42: 203. 1976): Herb. Linn. No.
116.16 (LINN).
Current name: ***Diastella proteoides*** (L.) Druce (Proteaceae).
Note: An illegitimate replacement name in *Protea* for *Leucadendron
proteoides* L. (1753).

Protea racemosa (Linnaeus) Linnaeus, *Mantissa Plantarum Altera*:
187. 1771.
["Habitat in Aethiopia."] Sp. Pl. 1: 91 (1753). RCN: 757.
Basionym: *Leucadendron racemosum* L. (1753).
Neotype (Rourke in *J. S. African Bot., Suppl.* 7: 117, pl. 10. 1969):
Grubb, Herb. Bergius (SBT).
Current name: ***Spatalla racemosa*** (L.) Druce (Proteaceae).

Protea repens (Linnaeus) Linnaeus, *Mantissa Plantarum Altera*: 189.
1771.
"Habitat ad Cap. b. spei." RCN: 766.
Basionym: *Leucadendron repens* L. (1753).
Lectotype (Rycroft in *J. S. African Bot.* 27: 191. 1961): [icon]
*"Lepidocarpodendron; foliis angustis, brevioribus, salignis; calicis
squamis elegantissime ex roseo, aureo, albo, atro-rubro variegatis;
florum plumis albis"* in Boerhaave, Index Alter Pl. Hort. Lugdb.-Bat.
2: 187. 1720.
Current name: ***Protea repens*** (L.) L. (Proteaceae).

Protea rosacea Linnaeus, *Mantissa Plantarum Altera*: 189. 1771, *nom.
illeg.*
"Habitat ad Cap. b. spei." RCN: 765.
Replaced synonym: *Leucadendron nanum* P.J. Bergius (1767).
Type not designated.
Current name: ***Protea nana*** (P.J. Bergius) Thunb. (Proteaceae).
Note: A superfluous name in *Protea* for *Leucadendron nanum* P.J.
Bergius (1767).

Protea saligna (P.J. Bergius) Linnaeus, *Mantissa Plantarum Altera*:
194. 1771.
"Habitat ad Cap. b. spei." RCN: 776.
Basionym: *Leucadendron salignum* P.J. Bergius (1767).
Lectotype (Williams in *Contr. Bolus Herb.* 3: 298. 1972): Herb. P.J.
Bergius, "Leucadendron salignum mihi" (SBT).
Current name: ***Leucadendron salignum*** P.J. Bergius (Proteaceae).

Protea serraria (Linnaeus) Linnaeus, *Mantissa Plantarum Altera*: 188.
1771.
"Habitat ad Cap. b. spei." RCN: 760.
Basionym: *Leucadendron serraria* L. (1753).
Type not designated.
Original material: as basionym.
Current name: ***Serruria fasciflora*** Knight (Proteaceae).

Protea speciosa (Linnaeus) Linnaeus, *Mantissa Plantarum Altera*: 191.
1771.
["Habitat ad Cap. b. spei."] Mant. Pl.: 36 (1767). RCN: 769.
Basionym: *Leucadendron speciosum* L. (1767).
Type not designated.
Original material: as basionym.
Current name: ***Protea speciosa*** (L.) L. (Proteaceae).

Protea sphaerocephala (P.J. Bergius) Linnaeus, *Mantissa Plantarum
Altera*: 188. 1771.
RCN: 762.
Basionym: *Leucadendron sphaerocephalum* P.J. Bergius (1767).
Type not designated.
Note: The application of this name appears uncertain.

Protea spicata (P.J. Bergius) Linnaeus, *Mantissa Plantarum Altera*:
187. 1771.
RCN: 758.
Basionym: *Leucadendron spicatum* P.J. Bergius (1767).
Type not designated.
Current name: ***Paranomus spicatus*** (P.J. Bergius) Kuntze
(Proteaceae).

Protea strobilina Linnaeus, *Mantissa Plantarum Altera*: 192. 1771.
"Habitat ad Cap. b. spei." RCN: 733.
Lectotype (Williams in *Contr. Bolus Herb.* 3: 338. 1972): Herb. Linn.
No. 116.28 (LINN), see opposite, above left.
Current name: ***Leucadendron strobilinum*** (L.) Druce (Proteaceae).

Protea totta Linnaeus, *Mantissa Plantarum Altera*: 191. 1771.
"Habitat in Cap. b. spei. montibus arena nigra." RCN: 770.
Lectotype (Rourke in *J. S. African Bot., Suppl.* 8: 71. 1972): *Tulbagh
45*, Herb. Linn. No. 116.35 (LINN).
Current name: ***Leucospermum tottum*** (L.) R. Br. (Proteaceae).

Prunella hyssopifolia Linnaeus, *Species Plantarum* 2: 600. 1753.
"Habitat Monspelii." RCN: 4363.
Lectotype (Paton in Jarvis & al. in *Taxon* 50: 517. 2001): Herb. Burser
XIV(2): 60 (UPS).
Current name: ***Prunella hyssopifolia*** L. (Lamiaceae).

Lectotype (Tryon in *Contr. Gray Herb.* 143: 37. 1942): Herb. Linn. No. 1246.11 (LINN).
Current name: ***Doryopteris pedata*** (L.) Fée (Pteridaceae).

Pteris piloselloides Linnaeus, *Species Plantarum,* ed. 2, 2: 1530. 1763.
"Habitat in India orientali." RCN: 7795.
Neotype (Ravensburg & Hennipman in *Leiden Bot. Ser.* 9: 303. 1986): *Pteris piloselloides,* ex Java 1759, Herb. Burman (G).
Current name: ***Pyrrosia piloselloides*** (L.) M.G. Price (Polypodiaceae).

Pteris quadrifoliata Linnaeus, *Systema Naturae,* ed. 10, 2: 1321. 1759.
["Habitat in America meridionali."] Sp. Pl., ed. 2, 2: 1531 (1763). RCN: 7800.
Type not designated.
Original material: [icon] in Plukenet, Amalth. Bot.: 95, t. 401, f. 5. 1705.
Current name: ***Marsilea quadrifolia*** L. (Marsileaceae).

Pteris rufa Linnaeus, *Species Plantarum* 2: 1074. 1753.
"Habitat in America septentrionaliore." RCN: 7777.
Lectotype (Proctor, *Ferns Jamaica*: 212. 1985): [icon] *"Filix minor ruffa lanugine tota obducta, in pinnas tantum divisa, raras, non crenatas subrotundas"* in Sloane, Voy. Jamaica 1: 87, t. 45, f. 1. 1707. – Typotype: Herb. Sloane 1: 96 (BM-SL).
Current name: ***Hemionitis rufa*** (L.) Sw. (Pteridaceae).
Note: Specific epithet spelled "ruffa" in the protologue.
   Although *Acrostichum rufum* L. (1759) has been treated as a new combination based on *Pteris rufa* by some authors, this is unjustified as there is no direct reference to the earlier name in the protologue of *A. rufum,* and *P. rufa* also appears in the same work (1759), as noted by Tryon & Stolze (in *Fieldiana, Bot.* 22: 47. 1989). Linnaeus did, however, treat the two names as synonymous in 1763.

Pteris semipinnata Linnaeus, *Species Plantarum* 2: 1076. 1753.
"Habitat in China. Osbeck." RCN: 7814.
Type not designated.
Original material: *Osbeck 3,* Herb. Linn. No. 1246.21 (LINN).
Current name: ***Pteris semipinnata*** L. (Pteridaceae).
Note: See Hansen & Fox Maule (in *Bot. J. Linn. Soc.* 67: 207. 1973) for comments on Osbeck material.

Pteris stipularis Linnaeus, *Species Plantarum* 2: 1074. 1753.
"Habitat in America meridionali." RCN: 7805.
Lectotype (Proctor & Lourteig in *Bradea* 5: 385. 1990): [icon] *"Filix altera, longissimis, angustis, et ad basim foliosis foliis"* in Plumier, Descr. Pl. Amér.: 12, t. 19. 1693 (see above, right).
Current name: ***Pteris longifolia*** L. forma ***stipularis*** (L.) Proctor & Lourteig (Pteridaceae).

Pteris trichomanoides Linnaeus, *Species Plantarum* 2: 1074. 1753.
"Habitat in Jamaicae, Dominicae rupibus." RCN: 7806.
Lectotype (Tryon in *Contr. Gray Herb.* 179: 51. 1956): Herb. Linn. No. 1246.6 (LINN).
Current name: ***Notholaena trichomanoides*** (L.) Desv. (Pteridaceae).

Pteris tricuspidata Linnaeus, *Species Plantarum* 2: 1073. 1753.
"Habitat in Domingo." RCN: 7798.
Type not designated.
Original material: [icon] in Petiver, Pteri-Graphia Amer.: 124, t. 10, f. 6. 1712; [icon] in Plumier, Traité Foug. Amér.: 121, t. 140. 1705.
Current name: ***Dicranoglossum furcatum*** (L.) J. Sm. (Vittariaceae).

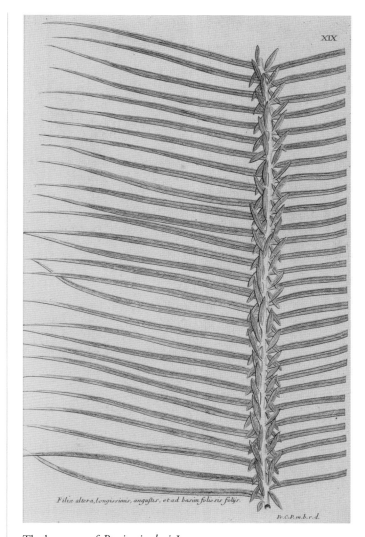

Filix altera, longissimis, angustis, et ad basim foliosis foliis.

The lectotype of *Pteris stipularis* L.

Pteris vittata Linnaeus, *Species Plantarum* 2: 1074. 1753.
"Habitat in China. Osbeck." RCN: 7804.
Lectotype (Tryon in *Contr. Gray Herb.* 194: 191. 1964): Herb. Linn. No. 1246.3 (LINN).
Current name: ***Pteris vittata*** L. (Pteridaceae).
Note: See Hansen & Fox Maule (in *Bot. J. Linn. Soc.* 67: 207. 1973) for comments on Osbeck material.

Pterocarpus draco Linnaeus, *Species Plantarum,* ed. 2, 2: 1662. 1763, *nom. illeg.*
"Habitat in India." RCN: 5169.
Replaced synonym: *Pterocarpus officinalis* Jacq. (1763).
Type not designated.
Current name: ***Pterocarpus officinalis*** Jacq. (Fabaceae: Faboideae).
Note: An illegitimate replacement name for the earlier *Pterocarpus officinalis* Jacq. (5 Jan 1763). Airy Shaw (in *Kew Bull.* 1937: 63. 1937) wrongly treated the Commelin plate, cited by Linnaeus but not by Jacquin, as the type.

Pterocarpus ecastaphyllum (Linnaeus) Linnaeus, *Systema Vegetabilium,* ed. 13: 533. 1774.

["Habitat in America meridionali."] Sp. Pl., ed. 2, 2: 1052 (1763). RCN: 5172.
Basionym: *Hedysarum ecastaphyllum* L. (1759).
Lectotype (Fawcett & Rendle, *Fl. Jamaica* 4: 78. 1920): *Browne*, Herb. Linn. No. 887.4 (LINN).
Current name: ***Dalbergia ecastaphyllum*** (L.) Taub. (Fabaceae: Faboideae).

Pterocarpus lunatus Linnaeus, *Plantae Surinamenses*: 13. 1775.
"Habitat [in Surinamo.]" RCN: 5171.
Type not designated.
Original material: Herb. Linn. No. 887.1 (LINN).
Current name: ***Machaerium lunatum*** (L.) Ducke (Fabaceae: Faboideae).

Pterocarpus ovalis Linnaeus, *Plantae Surinamenses*: 12. 1775.
"Habitat [in Surinamo.]" RCN: 5170.
Type not designated.
Original material: Herb. Linn. No. 886.4 (LINN).
Current name: ***Dalbergia* sp.** (Fabaceae: Faboideae).
Note: The application of this name appears uncertain.

Pteronia camphorata (Linnaeus) Linnaeus, *Species Plantarum,* ed. 2, 2: 1176. 1763.
"Habitat in Aethiopia." RCN: 6076.
Basionym: *Pterophora camphorata* L. (1760).
Lectotype (Lowrey in Jarvis & Turland in *Taxon* 47: 365. 1998): Herb. Linn. No. 980.2 (LINN).
Generitype of *Pteronia* Linnaeus, *nom. cons.*
Current name: ***Pteronia camphorata*** (L.) L. (Asteraceae).
Note: Pteronia Linnaeus (1763), *nom. cons.* against *Pterophorus* Boehm. (Oct 1760) and *Pterophora* Linnaeus (Dec 1760).
Hutchinson & Phillips (in *Ann. S. African Mus.* 9: 278. 1917) said that the genus is "founded by Linnaeus...on a figure published by Plukenet" which is "an excellent representation of *P. camphorata* L. the type of the genus". However, the statement is not accepted here as effecting typification of the name.

Pteronia oppositifolia Linnaeus, *Systema Naturae,* ed. 12, 2: 538. 1767. RCN: 6077.
Lectotype (Lowrey in Jarvis & Turland in *Taxon* 47: 365. 1998): Herb. Linn. No. 980.3 (LINN).
Current name: ***Pteronia oppositifolia*** L. (Asteraceae).

Pterophora camphorata Linnaeus, *Plantae Rariores Africanae*: 17. 1760.
["Habitat in Aethiopia."] Sp. Pl., ed. 2, 2: 1176 (1763). RCN: 6076.
Basionym of: *Pteronia camphorata* (L.) L. (1763).
Lectotype (Lowrey in Jarvis & Turland in *Taxon* 47: 365. 1998): Herb. Linn. No. 980.2 (LINN).
Generitype of *Pterophora* Linnaeus, *nom. rej.*
Current name: ***Pteronia camphorata*** (L.) L. (Asteraceae).
Note: Pterophora Linnaeus (Dec 1760), *nom. rej.*, in favour of *Pteronia* Linnaeus (1763), *nom. cons.*

Pulmonaria angustifolia Linnaeus, *Species Plantarum* 1: 135. 1753.
"Habitat in Pannonia, Helvetia, Suecia." RCN: 1091.
Lectotype (Selvi in Cafferty & Jarvis in *Taxon* 53: 803. 2004): Herb. Linn. No. 184.1 (LINN).
Current name: ***Pulmonaria angustifolia*** L. (Boraginaceae).

Pulmonaria hirta Linnaeus, *Species Plantarum,* ed. 2, 2: 1667. 1763.
"Habitat in Hetruriae montibus." RCN: 1429.
Lectotype (Selvi & Cristofolini in Cafferty & Jarvis in *Taxon* 53: 803. 2004): [icon] *"Pulmonaria Fragariae odore"* in Boccone, Mus. Piante

Rar. Sicilia: 148, t. 105. 1697. – Epitype (Selvi in Cafferty & Jarvis in *Taxon* 53: 803. 2004): Italy. Tuscany, Prov. Arezzo: montane *Abies-Fagus* woods close around the walls of Eremo di Camaldoli, 1,100m, 26 Mar 2002; 31 May 2002, *Selvi & Cristofolini s.n.* (FI; iso- BM).
Current name: ***Pulmonaria hirta*** L. (Boraginaceae).

Pulmonaria maritima Linnaeus, *Species Plantarum* 1: 136. 1753.
"Habitat in Angliae littoribus siliceis." RCN: 1096.
Lectotype (Selvi in Cafferty & Jarvis in *Taxon* 53: 803. 2004): Herb. Clifford: 48, *Cerinthe* 3 (BM-000557936).
Current name: ***Mertensia maritima*** (L.) Gray (Boraginaceae).

Pulmonaria officinalis Linnaeus, *Species Plantarum* 1: 135. 1753.
"Habitat in Europae nemoribus." RCN: 1092.
Lectotype (Selvi in Cafferty & Jarvis in *Taxon* 53: 804. 2004): Herb. Burser XIV(2): 51, left specimen (UPS).
Generitype of *Pulmonaria* Linnaeus (vide Hitchcock, *Prop. Brit. Bot.*: 127. 1929).
Current name: ***Pulmonaria officinalis*** L. (Boraginaceae).

Pulmonaria sibirica Linnaeus, *Species Plantarum* 1: 135. 1753.
"Habitat in Sibiria." RCN: 1095.
Lectotype (Selvi in Cafferty & Jarvis in *Taxon* 53: 804. 2004): Herb. Linn. No. 184.6 (LINN).
Current name: ***Mertensia sibirica*** (L.) G. Don (Boraginaceae).

Pulmonaria suffruticosa Linnaeus, *Species Plantarum,* ed. 2, 2: 1667. 1763.
"Habitat in Alpibus Italiae. Seguier, Arduini." RCN: 1093.
Lectotype (Bechi & al. in *Atti Soc. Tosc. Sci. Nat. Mem.,* ser. B, 98: 208. 1992 [1991]): *Séguier*, Herb. Linn. No. 184.3 (LINN).
Current name: ***Moltkia suffruticosa*** (L.) Brand (Boraginaceae).

Pulmonaria virginica Linnaeus, *Species Plantarum* 1: 135. 1753.
"Habitat in Virginia." RCN: 1094.
Lectotype (Williams in *Ann. Missouri Bot. Gard.* 24: 74. 1937): *Kalm*, Herb. Linn. No. 184.5 (LINN).
Current name: ***Mertensia virginica*** (L.) Pers. ex Link (Boraginaceae).
Note: For a review of the history of the competing use of *M. virginica* (L.) Pers. ex Link and *M. pulmonarioides* Roth, see Pringle (in *Sida* 21: 771–775. 2004).

Punica granatum Linnaeus, *Species Plantarum* 1: 472. 1753.
"Habitat in Hispania, Italia, Mauritania solo cretaceo." RCN: 3616.
Lectotype (Graham in Jarvis & al., *Regnum Veg.* 127: 80. 1993): Herb. Clifford: 184, *Punica* 1 (BM-000628599).
Generitype of *Punica* Linnaeus.
Current name: ***Punica granatum*** L. (Punicaceae).
Note: Vu Van Cuong (in Aubréville, *Fl. Cambodge Laos Vietnam* 4: 191. 1965) and Siddiqi (in Jafri & El-Gadi, *Fl. Libya* 76: 2. 1980) indicated material at LINN as type but failed to distinguish between 638.1 and 638.2. As they do not appear to be part of the same gathering, Art. 9.15 does not apply.

Punica nana Linnaeus, *Species Plantarum,* ed. 2, 1: 676. 1762.
"Habitat in Antillis." RCN: 3617.
Type not designated.
Original material: none traced.
Current name: ***Punica granatum*** L. (Punicaceae).

Pyrola maculata Linnaeus, *Species Plantarum* 1: 396. 1753.
"Habitat in Americae septentrionalis sylvis." RCN: 3117.
Lectotype (Reveal & al. in *Huntia* 7: 232. 1987): *Clayton 88* (BM-000051146).

Current name: ***Chimaphila maculata*** (L.) Pursh (Ericaceae/Pyrolaceae).
Note: See discussion by Dorr & Barrie (in *Brittonia* 45: 177–178. 1993).

Pyrola minor Linnaeus, *Species Plantarum* 1: 396. 1753.
"Habitat in Europa frigidiore." RCN: 3114.
Lectotype (Dorr & Barrie in *Brittonia* 45: 178. 1993): Herb. Linn. No. 568.3 (LINN).
Current name: ***Pyrola minor*** L. (Ericaceae/Pyrolaceae).
Note: Stearn (in *Biol. J. Linn. Soc.* 5: 12. 1973), in an account of Linnaeus' Öland and Gotland journey of 1741, treated Färö in Gotland as the restricted type locality, and noted the existence of 568.3 (LINN). In his paper, he attributed restricted type localities irrespective of whether any material existed in LINN and, where specimens do exist, he does not refer to any of them as type specimens. The collection subsequently designated as the type shows no annotation associating it with Gotland.

Pyrola rotundifolia Linnaeus, *Species Plantarum* 1: 396. 1753.
"Habitat in Europae septentrionaliore, Virginia, Brasilia." RCN: 3113.
Lectotype (Krísa in *Bot. Not.* 117: 403. 1964): Herb. Linn. No. 568.1 (LINN).
Generitype of *Pyrola* Linnaeus (vide Hitchcock, *Prop. Brit. Bot.*: 154. 1929).
Current name: ***Pyrola rotundifolia*** L. (Ericaceae/Pyrolaceae).
Note: See also Dorr & Barrie (in *Brittonia* 45: 178. 1993).

Pyrola secunda Linnaeus, *Species Plantarum* 1: 396. 1753.
"Habitat in Europae borealis sylvis." RCN: 3115.
Lectotype (Dorr & Barrie in *Brittonia* 45: 178. 1993): Herb. Linn. No. 568.5 (LINN).
Current name: ***Orthilia secunda*** (L.) House (Ericaceae/Pyrolaceae).
Note: Basu (in *J. Econ. Taxon. Bot.* 14: 464. 1990) indicated unspecified material in LINN as the holotype but this does not distinguish between sheets 568.5 and 568.6. As they do not appear to be part of a single gathering, Art. 9.15 does not apply, and Dorr & Barrie's type choice is accepted.

Pyrola umbellata Linnaeus, *Species Plantarum* 1: 396. 1753.
"Habitat in Europae, Asiae & Americae septentrionalis sylvis." RCN: 3116.
Lectotype (Dorr & Barrie in *Brittonia* 45: 179. 1993): Herb. Burser X: 108 (UPS).
Current name: ***Chimaphila umbellata*** (L.) Nutt. (Ericaceae/Pyrolaceae).

Pyrola uniflora Linnaeus, *Species Plantarum* 1: 397. 1753.
"Habitat in Europae borealis sylvis." RCN: 3118.
Lectotype (Basu in *J. Econ. Taxon. Bot.* 14: 463. 1990): Herb. Linn. No. 568.10 (LINN).
Current name: ***Moneses uniflora*** (L.) A. Gray (Ericaceae/Pyrolaceae).
Note: Basu (in *J. Econ. Taxon. Bot.* 14: 463. 1990) indicated unspecified material in LINN as the holotype. As there is only a single sheet associated with this name, Biju's statement is accepted as a formal typification (with holotype modified to lectotype under Art. 9.8). Dorr & Barrie (in *Brittonia* 45: 179. 1993), unaware of Basu's choice, reached the same conclusion, and provide some discussion about the name.

Pyrus baccata Linnaeus, *Systema Naturae*, ed. 12, 2: 344; *Mantissa Plantarum*: 75. 1767.
"Habitat in Sibiria, Dauria ad Schilkam fluvium." RCN: 3663.
Lectotype (Ponomarenko in *Trudy Prikl. Bot.* 62(3): 31, t. 2. 1978): Herb. Linn. No. 647.4 (LINN).
Current name: ***Malus baccata*** (L.) Borkh. (Rosaceae).

Pyrus communis Linnaeus, *Species Plantarum* 1: 479. 1753.
"Habitat in Europa." RCN: 3660.
Lectotype (Amaral Franco & Rocha Afonso in *Rev. Fac. Ci. Univ. Lisboa, Sér. 2, C, Ci. Nat.* 13: 177. 1965): Herb. Linn. No. 647.1 (LINN).
Generitype of *Pyrus* Linnaeus (vide Green, *Prop. Brit. Bot.*: 158. 1929).
Current name: ***Pyrus communis*** L. (Rosaceae).
Note: Ghora & Panigrahi (*Fam. Rosaceae India* 2: 395, pl. 75. 1995) illustrate the type.

Pyrus communis Linnaeus var. **pompejana** Linnaeus, *Species Plantarum* 1: 479. 1753.
"Habitat in Europa." RCN: 3660.
Type not designated.
Original material: none traced.
Note: The application of this name is uncertain.

Pyrus communis Linnaeus var. **pyraster** Linnaeus, *Species Plantarum* 1: 479. 1753.
RCN: 3660.
Type not designated.
Original material: Herb. Burser XXIII: 37? (UPS).
Current name: ***Pyrus pyraster*** (L.) Burgsd. (Rosaceae).

Pyrus communis Linnaeus var. **salerna** Linnaeus, *Species Plantarum* 1: 479. 1753.
RCN: 3660.
Type not designated.
Original material: none traced.
Note: The application of this name is uncertain.

Pyrus communis Linnaeus var. **savonia** Linnaeus, *Species Plantarum* 1: 479. 1753.
RCN: 3660.
Type not designated.
Original material: none traced.
Note: The application of this name is uncertain.

Pyrus communis Linnaeus var. **volema** Linnaeus, *Species Plantarum* 1: 479. 1753.
RCN: 3660.
Lectotype (Aldasoro & Aedo in Cafferty & Jarvis in *Taxon* 51: 543. 2002): [icon] *"Pira dorsalia eademque Libralia dicta"* in Bauhin & Cherler, Hist. Pl. Univ. 1(1): 53. 1650.
Current name: ***Pyrus communis*** L. (Rosaceae).

Pyrus coronaria Linnaeus, *Species Plantarum* 1: 480. 1753.
"Habitat in Virginia." RCN: 3664.
Lectotype (Aldasoro & Aedo in Cafferty & Jarvis in *Taxon* 51: 543. 2002): Herb. Linn. No. 647.5 (LINN).
Current name: ***Malus coronaria*** (L.) Mill. (Rosaceae).

Pyrus cydonia Linnaeus, *Species Plantarum* 1: 480. 1753.
"Habitat ad ripas petrosas Danubii." RCN: 3665.
Lectotype (Aldasoro & Aedo in Cafferty & Jarvis in *Taxon* 51: 543. 2002): Herb. Burser XXIII: 32 (UPS).
Current name: ***Cydonia oblonga*** Mill. (Rosaceae).

Pyrus malus Linnaeus, *Species Plantarum* 1: 479. 1753.
"Habitat in Europa." RCN: 3662.
Lectotype (Ghora & Panigrahi, *Fam. Rosaceae India* 2: 375, pl. 72A. 1995): Herb. Linn. No. 647.3 (LINN).
Current name: ***Malus pumila*** Mill. (Rosaceae).
Note: See discussion by Mabberley & al. (in *Telopea* 9: 422–423. 2001), who follow Ghora & Panigrahi's choice.

Pyrus malus Linnaeus var. **cavillea** Linnaeus, *Species Plantarum*, ed. 2, 1: 686. 1762.
RCN: 3662.
Neotype (Mabberley & al. in *Telopea* 9: 423. 2001): Cultivated. National Fruit Collections [Accession 1949011 ex W. Barnes, Bexhill, Oct 1949], Brogdale, Faversham, Kent, 20 May 1999 (fl.), *E-J. Lamont 1309 p.p.* (NSW; iso- BM, FHO). – Epitype (Mabberley & al. in *Telopea* 9: 423. 2001): Cultivated. National Fruit Collections [Accession 1949011 ex W. Barnes, Bexhill, Oct 1949], Brogdale, Faversham, Kent, 5 Aug 1999 (lvs), *E-J. Lamont 1309 p.p.* (NSW; iso- BM, FHO).
Current name: ***Malus pumila*** Mill. **'Calville Rouge d'Automne'** (Rosaceae).

Pyrus malus Linnaeus var. **cestiana** Linnaeus, *Species Plantarum* 1: 479. 1753.
RCN: 3662.
Neotype (Mabberley & al. in *Telopea* 9: 423. 2001): Cultivated. Badger's Keep Nursery, Chewton, Victoria, Australia, 31 Mar 1999 (fr.), *D.J. Mabberley, K. Robertson & C. Winmill 2474* (NSW; iso- BM, FHO, L, MEL).
Current name: ***Malus pumila*** Mill. **'Court-Pendu Plat'** (Rosaceae).

Pyrus malus Linnaeus var. **epirotica** Linnaeus, *Species Plantarum* 1: 480. 1753.
RCN: 3662.
Neotype (Mabberley & al. in *Telopea* 9: 423. 2001): [icon] *"Api"* in Hogg, Herefordshire Pomona: t. 74, f. 2. 1884 (see pp. 22, 23).
Current name: ***Malus pumila*** Mill. **'Pomme d'Api'** (Rosaceae).

Pyrus malus Linnaeus var. **paradisiaca** Linnaeus, *Species Plantarum* 1: 479. 1753.
RCN: 3662.
Neotype (Mabberley & al. in *Telopea* 9: 424. 2001): Cultivated. ('Malus M8 rootstock'), HRI East Malling, Kent, England, 25 Apr 2000 (fl.), *A. King, s.n.* (NSW; iso- BM, FHO).
Current name: ***Malus pumila*** Mill. **'Malling VIII' ('M8')** (Rosaceae).

Pyrus malus Linnaeus var. **prasomila** Linnaeus, *Species Plantarum* 1: 479. 1753.
RCN: 3662.
Neotype (Mabberley & al. in *Telopea* 9: 424. 2001): Cultivated. National Fruit Collection, Brogdale, Kent [Accession 1947288 ex A. Viennois, Odenas, Rhône, Mar 1947], 20 May 1999 (fl.), *E.-J. Lamont 1308 p.p.* (NSW; iso- BM, FHO). – Epitype (Mabberley & al. in *Telopea* 9: 424. 2001): Cultivated. National Fruit Collection, Brogdale, Kent [Accession 1947288 ex A. Viennois, Odenas, Rhône, Mar 1947], 5 Aug 1999 (lvs), *E.-J. Lamont 1308 p.p.* (NSW; iso- BM, FHO).
Current name: ***Malus pumila*** Mill. **'Reinette Franche'** (Rosaceae).

Pyrus malus Linnaeus var. **rubelliana** Linnaeus, *Species Plantarum* 1: 479. 1753.
RCN: 3662.
Type not designated.
Original material: none traced.
Current name: ***Malus pumila*** Mill. **cv.** (Rosaceae).
Note: See extensive discussion by Mabberley & al. (in *Telopea* 9: 425. 2001).

Pyrus malus Linnaeus var. **sylvestris** Linnaeus, *Species Plantarum* 1: 479. 1753.
RCN: 3662.
Neotype (Langenfelds, *Apple-trees*: 186. 1991): Latvia. Dist. Madonensis, prope villula Grasi, *Langenfelds 105* (RIG).
Current name: ***Malus sylvestris*** (L.) Mill. (Rosaceae).
Note: See discussion by Mabberley & al. (in *Telopea* 9: 425–426. 2001).

Pyrus pollveria Linnaeus, *Mantissa Plantarum Altera*: 244. 1771.
"Habitat in Germania. Ott. Munchhausen. L.B." RCN: 3661.
Lectotype (Aldasoro & Aedo in Cafferty & Jarvis in *Taxon* 51: 543. 2002): [icon] *"Pirus polwilleriana"* in Bauhin & Cherler, Hist. Pl. Univ. 1(1): 59. 1650. – Epitype (Aldasoro & Aedo in Cafferty & Jarvis in *Taxon* 51: 543. 2002): Cultivated. Jardin des Plantes, Paris, 4–8 Apr 1815, Herb. J. Gay (K).
Current name: × ***Sorbopyrus auricularis*** (Knoop) C.K. Schneid. (Rosaceae).

Q

Quassia amara Linnaeus, *Species Plantarum*, ed. 2, 1: 553. 1762.
"Habitat in Surinamo C. Dahlberg." RCN: 3042.
Type not designated.
Original material: Herb. Linn. No. 545.1 (LINN).
Generitype of *Quassia* Linnaeus.
Current name: ***Quassia amara*** L. (Simaroubaceae).

Quercus aegilops Linnaeus, *Species Plantarum* 2: 996. 1753, *nom. utique rej.*
"Habitat in Hispania." RCN: 7221.
Lectotype (Menitsky in *Novosti Sist. Vyssh. Rast.* 9: 126. 1972): [icon] *"Cerri glans, Aegilops aspris"* in Bauhin & Cherler, Hist. Pl. Univ. 1(2): 77. 1650.
Current name: ***Quercus ithaburensis*** Decne. subsp. ***macrolepis*** (Kotschy) Hedge & Yalt. (Fagaceae).

Quercus alba Linnaeus, *Species Plantarum* 2: 996. 1753.
"Habitat in Virginia." RCN: 7218.
Lectotype (designated here by Nixon & Barrie): *Kalm*, Herb. Linn. No. 1128.26 (LINN).
Current name: ***Quercus alba*** L. (Fagaceae).

Quercus cerris Linnaeus, *Species Plantarum* 2: 997. 1753.
"Habitat in Hispania." RCN: 7222.
Type not designated.
Original material: Herb. Burser XXII: 96 (UPS); [icon] in Bauhin & Cherler, Hist. Pl. Univ. 1(2): 74. 1650.
Current name: ***Quercus cerris*** L. (Fagaceae).
Note: Several authors, including Brullo & al. (in *Webbia* 54: 13. 1999), have treated 1128.33 (LINN) as the type but it was sent by Scopoli, and not received by Linnaeus until 1762 so it is not original material for the name.

Quercus coccifera Linnaeus, *Species Plantarum* 2: 995. 1753.
"Habitat in G. Narbonensi, Hispania." RCN: 7214.
Type not designated.
Original material: *Magnol*, Herb. Linn. No. 1128.13 (LINN); Herb. A. van Royen No. 901.310–86 (L); Herb. A. van Royen No. 912.356–37 (L); Herb. Burser XXII: 113 (UPS); [icon] in Mattioli, Pl. Epit.: 774. 1586.
Current name: ***Quercus coccifera*** L. (Fagaceae).
Note: Jafri (in Jafri & El-Gadi, Fl. Libya 27: 2. 1977) indicated both 1128.13 and 1128.14 (LINN) as the type, but as they are evidently not part of a single gathering, Art. 9.15 does not apply.

Quercus esculus Linnaeus, *Species Plantarum* 2: 996. 1753, *nom. utique rej.*
"Habitat in Europa australi." RCN: 7219.
Lectotype (Govaerts in *Taxon* 44: 631. 1995): Herb. Linn. No. 1128.28 (LINN).
Current name: ***Quercus petraea*** (Matt.) Liebl. (Fagaceae).

Quercus gramuntia Linnaeus, *Species Plantarum* 2: 995. 1753.
"Habitat Monspelii." RCN: 7212.
Type not designated.
Original material: *Magnol*, Herb. Linn. No. 1128.7 (LINN).
Current name: ***Quercus ilex*** L. (Fagaceae).

Quercus ilex Linnaeus, *Species Plantarum* 2: 995. 1753.
"Habitat in Europa australi." RCN: 7212.
Type not designated.
Original material: Herb. Clifford: 448, *Quercus* 2 (BM); [icon] in Bauhin & Cherler, Hist. Pl. Univ. 1(2): 95. 1650.

Current name: ***Quercus ilex*** L. (Fagaceae).
Note: Jafri (in Jafri & El-Gadi, Fl. Libya 27: 4. 1977) indicated 1128.4 (LINN) as type but this collection lacks the relevant *Species Plantarum* number (i.e. "3") and was a post-1753 addition to the herbarium, and is not original material for the name. Menitsky (*Oaks Asia*: 111. 2005) indicated 1128.6 (LINN) as type but this came from Browne and, received only in 1758, cannot be original material either.

Quercus molucca Linnaeus, *Species Plantarum* 2: 1199. 1753.
"Habitat in Moluccis." RCN: 7211.
Type not designated.
Original material: [icon] in Rumphius, Herb. Amboin. 3: 85, t. 56. 1743.
Current name: ***Lithocarpus moluccus*** (L.) Soepadmo (Fagaceae).
Note: Merrill (*Interpret. Rumph. Herb. Amb.*: 31, 186. 1917) indicates both that Linnaeus' name is wholly based on the cited Rumphius element, and also that it is to be typified by material from the Sula Islands. See also Soepadmo (in *Reinwardtia* 8: 290. 1970), who stated that as the original specimen was lost and the original description and figure are not recognisable, the name should be treated as doubtful.

Quercus nigra Linnaeus, *Species Plantarum* 2: 995. 1753.
"Habitat in America septentrionalis." RCN: 7216.
Lectotype (Dandy, *Sloane Herbarium*: 112. 1958): [icon] *"Quercus (forte) Marilandica, folio trifido ad sassafras accedente"* in Catesby, Nat. Hist. Carolina 1: 19, t. 19. 1730.
Current name: ***Quercus nigra*** L. (Fagaceae).
Note: See discussion by Reveal & al. (in *Huntia* 7: 233. 1987).

Quercus phellos Linnaeus, *Species Plantarum* 2: 994. 1753.
"Habitat in America septentrionali." RCN: 7210.
Lectotype (Reveal & al. in *Huntia* 7: 233. 1987): *Clayton 780* ["906"] (BM-000051783; iso- LINN 1128.3).
Current name: ***Quercus phellos*** L. (Fagaceae).
Note: Dandy (*Sloane Herbarium*: 112. 1958) designated two Catesby plates as the type for this name, and as they were sufficiently different to be treated as distinct, though unnamed, varieties by Linnaeus, they are evidently not part of a single gathering (Art. 9.15). The type is therefore that designated by Reveal & al. See also Howard & Staples (in *J. Arnold Arbor.* 64: 525. 1983).

Quercus prinus Linnaeus, *Species Plantarum* 2: 995. 1753, *nom. rej. prop.*
"Habitat in America boreali." RCN: 7215.
Type not designated.
Original material: Herb. Clifford: 448, *Quercus* 3 (BM); Herb. Linn. No. 1128.15 (LINN); [icon] in Catesby, Nat. Hist. Carolina 1: 18, t. 18. 1730 – Voucher: Herb. Sloane 212: 5; 232: 14 (BM-SL); [icon] in Plukenet, Phytographia: t. 54, f. 3. 1691; Almag. Bot.: 309. 1696.
Current name: ***Quercus prinus*** L. (Fagaceae).
Note: This name has been applied to the two species more recently known as *Q. montana* Willd. and *Q. michauxii* Nutt., and Whittemore & Nixon (in *Taxon* 54: 213. 2005) therefore proposed *Q. prinus* for rejection.

Quercus robur Linnaeus, *Species Plantarum* 2: 996. 1753.
"Habitat in Europa." RCN: 1220.
Lectotype (Jonsell & Jarvis in Jarvis & al., *Regnum Veg.* 127: 80. 1993): Herb. Burser XXII: 93 (UPS).

Generitype of *Quercus* Linnaeus (vide Green, *Prop. Brit. Bot.*: 189. 1929).

Current name: ***Quercus robur*** L. (Fagaceae).

Note: Jonsell & Jarvis (in *Nordic J. Bot.* 14: 153. 1994) discuss the reasons for their 1993 choice of type. Brullo & al. (in *Webbia* 54: 55. 1999) accepted 1128.30 (LINN) as type, wrongly attributing the choice to Hedge & Yaltirik in Davis, *Fl. Turkey* 7: 663 (1982). This is in any case a Kalm collection from North America (not Europe as indicated in the protologue), and is identifiable as *Q. alba* L. It is not accepted as original material, and the choice of the Burser material as type in any case has priority.

Quercus rubra Linnaeus, *Species Plantarum* 2: 996. 1753.

"Habitat in Virginia, Carolina." RCN: 7217.

Lectotype (designated here by Nixon & Barrie): [icon] *"Quercus esculi divisura, foliis ampleoribus aculeatis, an Quercus alba Virginiana Park."* in Plukenet, Phytographia: t. 54, f. 4. 1691; Almag. Bot.: 309. 1696.

Current name: ***Quercus rubra*** L. (Fagaceae).

Note: Linnaeus included several different taxa within his concept of *Q. rubra*. Although most early authors applied it to the northern red oak, Sargent (in *Rhodora* 17: 39. 1915; *l.c.* 18: 45. 1916) argued that the name should be used for the species widely known as *Q. falcata* Michx. Others (e.g. Svenson, *l.c.* 41: 521. 1941; 47: 298, 366. 1945; and Fernald (in *J. Arnold Arbor.* 27: 391. 1946) disagreed but as a result of this divergence, some (e.g. Rehder in *J. Arnold. Arbor.* 19: 283. 1938) have treated the the name as a *nomen ambiguum*. However, as the name continues to be in use, the name is formally typified here in its traditional sense, that of the northern red oak.

Quercus smilax Linnaeus, *Species Plantarum* 2: 994. 1753.

"Habitat in Hispania & adjacentibus." RCN: 7212.

Type not designated.

Original material: Herb. Linn. No. 1128.4? (LINN); Herb. A. van Royen No. 901.310–351 (L); [icon] in Bauhin & Cherler, Hist. Pl. Univ. 1(2): 101. 1650.

Current name: ***Quercus ilex*** L. (Fagaceae).

Quercus suber Linnaeus, *Species Plantarum* 2: 995. 1753.

"Habitat in Europa australi." RCN: 7213.

Type not designated.

Original material: *Löfling 675*, Herb. Linn. No. 1128.11 (LINN); Herb. Clifford: 448, *Quercus* 1 (BM); Herb. Burser XXII: 104 (UPS); *Löfling 677*, Herb. Linn. No. 78? (SBT).

Current name: ***Quercus suber*** L. (Fagaceae).

Queria canadensis Linnaeus, *Species Plantarum* 1: 90. 1753.

"Habitat in Canada, Virginia." RCN: 753.

Lectotype (Chaudhri, *Rev. Paronychiinae*: 120. 1968): Herb. Linn. No. 114.2 (LINN).

Current name: ***Paronychia canadensis*** (L.) Alph. Wood (Caryophyllaceae).

Queria hispanica Loefling ex Linnaeus, *Species Plantarum* 1: 90. 1753.

"Habitat in Hispania." RCN: 752.

Neotype (López González in Jarvis & al., *Regnum Veg.* 127: 80. 1993): Herb. Linn. No. 114.1 (LINN).

Generitype of *Queria* Linnaeus (vide Hitchcock in *Amer. J. Bot.* 10: 514. 1923).

Current name: ***Minuartia hamata*** (Hausskn. & Bornm.) Mattf. (Caryophyllaceae).

Note: López González (in *Anales Jard. Bot. Madrid* 60: 429–434 (2003–2004 "2002") provides an extremely detailed account of Löfling's materials and descriptions involved in the treatment of *Minuartia* and *Queria* by Linnaeus.

Quisqualis indica Linnaeus, *Species Plantarum*, ed. 2, 1: 556. 1762.

"Habitat in India." RCN: 3065.

Lectotype (Merrill, *Interpret. Rumph. Herb. Amb.*: 390. 1917): [icon] *"Quis qualis"* in Rumphius, Herb. Amboin. 5: 71, t. 38. 1747.

Generitype of *Quisqualis* Linnaeus.

Current name: ***Combretum indicum*** (L.) Jongkind (Combretaceae).

Note: Merrill's type choice appears to be the earliest, and has been followed by e.g. Smith (*Fl. Vitiensis Nova* 3: 417. 1985). However, alternative choices have been made by Exell (in *J. Bot.* 69: 124. 1931), who indicated 553.1 (LINN) as type, and Lecompte (in Aubréville, *Fl. Cambodge Laos Vietnam* 10: 28. 1969), who regarded a Clifford sheet as lectotype.

R

Rajania cordata Linnaeus, *Species Plantarum* 2: 1032. 1753.
"Habitat in America meridionali." RCN: 7451.
Type not designated.
Original material: [icon] in Plumier in Burman, Pl. Amer.: 148, t. 155, f. 1. 1758.
Current name: ***Rajania cordata*** L. (Dioscoreaceae).

Rajania hastata Linnaeus, *Species Plantarum* 2: 1032. 1753.
"Habitat in Domingo." RCN: 7450.
Type not designated.
Original material: Herb. Clifford: 458, *Rajania* 1 (BM); [icon] in Plumier, Descr. Pl. Amér.: 84, t. 98. 1693.
Generitype of *Rajania* Linnaeus (vide Green, *Prop. Brit. Bot.*: 192. 1929).
Current name: ***Rajania hastata*** L. (Dioscoreaceae).

Rajania quinquefolia Linnaeus, *Species Plantarum* 2: 1032. 1753.
"Habitat in America." RCN: 7452.
Type not designated.
Original material: [icon] in Plumier in Burman, Pl. Amer.: 149, t. 155, f. 2. 1758.
Current name: ***Rajania quinquefolia*** L. (Dioscoreaceae).

Randia aculeata Linnaeus, *Species Plantarum* 2: 1192. 1753.
"Habitat – – – –" RCN: 1193.
Neotype (Steyermark in *Mem. New York Bot. Gard.* 23: 340. 1972): Herb. Linn. No. 214.1 (LINN).
Current name: ***Randia aculeata*** L. (Rubiaceae).
Note: In the absence of any original material, Steyermark's type statement is accepted as a neotypification (Art. 9.8).

Randia mitis Linnaeus, *Species Plantarum* 2: 1192. 1753.
"Habitat in Jamaica." RCN: 1192.
Lectotype (Lorence in Jarvis & al., *Regnum Veg.* 127: 80. 1993): [icon] *"Lycium majus Americanum, Jasmini flore, foliis subrotundis lucidis"* in Plukenet, Phytographia: t. 97, f. 6. 1691; Almag. Bot.: 234. 1696.
Generitype of *Randia* Linnaeus (vide Hitchcock, *Prop. Brit. Bot.*: 129. 1929).
Current name: ***Randia aculeata*** L. (Rubiaceae).

Ranunculus abortivus Linnaeus, *Species Plantarum* 1: 551. 1753.
"Habitat in Virginia, Canada." RCN: 4074.
Lectotype (Benson in *Amer. Midl. Naturalist* 52: 356. 1954): *Kalm*, Herb. Linn. No. 715.23 (LINN).
Current name: ***Ranunculus abortivus*** L. (Ranunculaceae).

Ranunculus aconitifolius Linnaeus, *Species Plantarum* 1: 551. 1753.
"Habitat in Alpibus Helveticis, Austriacis." RCN: 4076.
Lectotype (Baldini in Jarvis & al. in *Taxon* 54: 469. 2005): Herb. Clifford: 229, *Ranunculus* 9 (BM). – Epitype (Baldini in Jarvis & al. in *Taxon* 54: 469. 2005): Switzerland. Below the Col de Jaman: Vaud, 24 Jun 1896, *R. P. Murray s.n.* (BM).
Current name: ***Ranunculus aconitifolius*** L. (Ranunculaceae).

Ranunculus acris Linnaeus, *Species Plantarum* 1: 554. 1753.
"Habitat in Europae pratis, pascuis." RCN: 4089.
Lectotype (Benson in *Amer. Midl. Naturalist* 52: 337. 1954): Herb. Clifford: 231, *Ranunculus* 18 (BM-000628911).
Generitype of *Ranunculus* Linnaeus.
Current name: ***Ranunculus acris*** L. (Ranunculaceae).
Note: Ranunculus auricomus L. was treated as the generitype by Britton

& Brown (*Ill. Fl. N. U. S.*, ed. 2, 2: 104. 1913; see McNeill & al. (in *Taxon* 36: 381. 1987). However, under Art. 10.5, Ex. 7 (a voted example) of the Vienna Code, this is a type choice made under the American Code and is to be replaced under Art. 10.5b by Green's choice (*Prop. Brit. Bot.*: 163. 1929) of *R. acris* L.

Ranunculus alpestris Linnaeus, *Species Plantarum* 1: 553. 1753.
"Habitat in Alpibus Austriacis, Helveticis." RCN: 4083.
Lectotype (Baldini in Jarvis & al. in *Taxon* 54: 470. 2005): Herb. Burser IX: 132 (UPS).
Current name: ***Ranunculus alpestris*** L. (Ranunculaceae).

Ranunculus amplexicaulis Linnaeus, *Species Plantarum* 1: 549. 1753.
"Habitat in Pyrenaeis, Apenninis." RCN: 4067.
Lectotype (Baldini in Jarvis & al. in *Taxon* 54: 470. 2005): Herb. Burser IX: 125 (UPS).
Current name: ***Ranunculus amplexicaulis*** L. (Ranunculaceae).

Ranunculus aquatilis Linnaeus, *Species Plantarum* 1: 556. 1753.
"Habitat in Europae aquis undosis, fossis, rivulis." RCN: 4100.
Lectotype (Cook in *Mitt. Bot. Staatssamml. München* 6: 123. 1966): Herb. Linn. No. 715.75 (LINN).
Current name: ***Ranunculus aquatilis*** L. (Ranunculaceae).
Note: Misled by Jackson's erroneous assertion that 715.75 (LINN) was unavailable to Linnaeus until 1767, Cook designated it as neotype. However, as it is original material, his choice is accepted as being correctable to a lectotype (Art. 9.8).

Ranunculus arvensis Linnaeus, *Species Plantarum* 1: 555. 1753.
"Habitat in Europae australioris agris." RCN: 4093.
Lectotype (Benson in *Amer. Midl. Naturalist* 52: 349. 1954): Herb. Linn. No. 715.65 (LINN).
Current name: ***Ranunculus arvensis*** L. (Ranunculaceae).

Ranunculus asiaticus Linnaeus, *Species Plantarum* 1: 552. 1753.
"Habitat in Asia vel Mauritania." RCN: 4079.
Lectotype (Turland in Jarvis & al. in *Taxon* 54: 470. 2005): Herb. Linn. No. 715.34 (LINN).
Current name: ***Ranunculus asiaticus*** L. (Ranunculaceae).
Note: Meikle (in *Curtis's Bot. Mag.* 181: 159–162. 1977) discussed the history of this name but did not indicate any type material. However, he (*Fl. Cyprus* 1: 50. 1977) separately indicated type material at LINN without specifying a sheet number, but adding that it is "a double-flowered garden form, probably with red flowers". As there are two sheets at LINN, a formal choice of lectotype was made by Turland to remove any uncertainty as to the intended type.

Ranunculus auricomus Linnaeus, *Species Plantarum* 1: 551. 1753.
"Habitat in Europae pascuis humidiusculis." RCN: 4073.
Lectotype (Benson in *Amer. Midl. Naturalist* 52: 354. 1954): Herb. Clifford: 229, *Ranunculus* 8 (BM-000628885).
Current name: ***Ranunculus auricomus*** L. (Ranunculaceae).
Note: Ranunculus auricomus was treated as the generitype by Britton & Brown (*Ill. Fl. N. U. S.*, ed. 2, 2: 104. 191); see McNeill & al. (in *Taxon* 36: 381. 1987). However, under Art. 10.5, Ex. 7 (a voted example) of the Vienna Code, this is a type choice made under the American Code and is to be replaced under Art. 10.5b by Green's choice (*Prop. Brit. Bot.*: 163. 1929) of *R. acris* L.
Jasiewicz (in *Fragm. Fl. Geobot.* 2: 70. 1956), aware that 715.21 and 715.22 (LINN) represented more than one taxon (illustrated as t. 4, f. 1, 2), rejected the name as a *nomen ambiguum*. Kvist (in *Ann.*

Bot. Fenn. 24: 73–77. 1987) also discussed and illustrated (as f. 2 and 4) these specimens and concluded that 715.22 (LINN) should be the lectotype. These authors were apparently unaware of Benson's earlier choice, as noted by Ericsson (in *Ann. Bot. Fenn.* 29: 134. 1992), who also discusses the possible identity of the type.

Ranunculus bulbosus Linnaeus, *Species Plantarum* 1: 554. 1753.
"Habitat in Europae pratis, pascuis." RCN: 4086.
Lectotype (Sell in Jarvis & al. in *Taxon* 54: 470. 2005): Herb. Linn. No. 227.20 (S).
Current name: *Ranunculus bulbosus* L. (Ranunculaceae).
Note: Sell provided a detailed review of earlier attempts at typification and justified his rejection of Benson's type choice in favour of his own.

Ranunculus bullatus Linnaeus, *Species Plantarum* 1: 550. 1753.
"Habitat in Lusitania, Creta." RCN: 4068.
Lectotype (Baldini & Jarvis in *Bull. Nat. Hist. Mus. London, Bot.* 32: 8, f. 2. 2002): [icon] *"Ranuncul. grumosa radice I"* in Clusius, Rar. Pl. Hist. 1: 237, 238. 1601. – Epitype (Baldini & Jarvis in *Bull. Nat. Hist. Mus. London, Bot.* 32: 8. 2002): Portugal. Flora Lusitanica. Prov. Estremadura, ad pagum, 1848. leg. *Dr. Welwitsch 198* (BM).
Current name: *Ranunculus bullatus* L. (Ranunculaceae).

Ranunculus cassubicus Linnaeus, *Species Plantarum* 1: 551. 1753.
"Habitat in Cassubia, Sibiria." RCN: 4072.
Lectotype (Kvist in *Ann. Bot. Fenn.* 24: 73, f. 1. 1987): *Gerber?*, Herb. Linn. No. 715.20 (LINN).
Current name: *Ranunculus cassubicus* L. (Ranunculaceae).
Note: Borchers-Kolb (in *Mitt. Bot. Staatssamml. München* 21: 64. 1985) stated "Typus: "Habitat in Cassubia, Sibiria". (L.)" but this cannot be accepted as an explicit typification (with Leiden cited, possibly in error for LINN).

Ranunculus chaerophyllos Linnaeus, *Species Plantarum* 1: 555. 1753.
"Habitat in Gallia, Italia." RCN: 4091.
Type not designated.
Original material: Herb. Linn. No. 715.64 (LINN); [icon] in Colonna, Ekphr.: 312, 311. 1606.
Current name: *Ranunculus sp.* (Ranunculaceae).
Note: The application of this name is uncertain.

Ranunculus creticus Linnaeus, *Species Plantarum* 1: 550. 1753.
"Habitat in Creta." RCN: 4071.
Lectotype (Turland in Jarvis & al. in *Taxon* 54: 470. 2005): Herb. Burser IX: 117 (UPS).
Current name: *Ranunculus creticus* L. (Ranunculaceae).

Ranunculus falcatus Linnaeus, *Species Plantarum* 1: 556. 1753.
"Habitat inter segetes Europae australis." RCN: 4098.
Lectotype (Benson in *Amer. Midl. Naturalist* 52: 364. 1954): Herb. Linn. No. 715.71 (LINN).
Current name: *Ceratocephala falcata* (L.) Pers. (Ranunculaceae).

Ranunculus ficaria Linnaeus, *Species Plantarum* 1: 550. 1753.
"Habitat in Europae ruderatis, umbrosis, spongiosis." RCN: 4069.
Lectotype (Benson in *Amer. Midl. Naturalist* 52: 369. 1954): Herb. Linn. No. 715.12 (LINN).
Current name: *Ranunculus ficaria* L. (Ranunculaceae).
Note: Laegaard (in *Nordic J. Bot.* 20: 525. 2001) reviewed the history of this name, accepted Benson's typification (rather than the later one made by Sell in *Watsonia* 20: 42–43. 1994), and validated subsp. *fertilis* Clapham for the diploid variant.

Ranunculus flammula Linnaeus, *Species Plantarum* 1: 548. 1753.
"Habitat in Europae pascuis udis." RCN: 4060.
Lectotype (Benson in *Amer. Midl. Naturalist* 52: 359. 1954): Herb. Linn. No. 715.1 (LINN).
Current name: *Ranunculus flammula* L. (Ranunculaceae).

Ranunculus glacialis Linnaeus, *Species Plantarum* 1: 553. 1753.
"Habitat in Alpibus Lapponiae, Helvetiae." RCN: 4081.
Lectotype (Benson in *Amer. Midl. Naturalist* 52: 364. 1954): Herb. Linn. No. 715.37 (LINN).
Current name: *Ranunculus glacialis* L. (Ranunculaceae).

Ranunculus gramineus Linnaeus, *Species Plantarum* 1: 549. 1753.
"Habitat in Pyrenaeis & Galliae pratis aridis." RCN: 4064.
Lectotype (Baldini in Jarvis & al. in *Taxon* 54: 470. 2005): Herb. Clifford: 288, *Ranunculus* 1 (BM-000628877).
Current name: *Ranunculus gramineus* L. (Ranunculaceae).

Ranunculus grandiflorus Linnaeus, *Species Plantarum* 1: 555. 1753.
"Habitat in Oriente." RCN: 4097.
Neotype (Davis, *Fl. Turkey* 1: 168. 1965): Herb. Tournefort, "Ranunculus cappadocicus aconitifolio flore luteo maximo" (P-TOURN).
Current name: *Ranunculus grandiflorus* L. (Ranunculaceae).
Note: Davis (in *Notes Roy. Bot. Gard. Edinburgh* 23: 113. 1960) discussed the absence of material and treated the name as a *nomen ambiguum* but later (1965) used the name, treating a Tournefort collection at P as the type. In this, he was followed by Jelenevsky & Derviz-Sokolova (in *Novosti Sist. Vyssh. Rast.* 16: 117. 1979) and others. As there are no original elements for the name, this is accepted as a formal neotypification (for Linnaeus did not make a study of Tournefort's herbarium).

Ranunculus hederaceus Linnaeus, *Species Plantarum* 1: 556. 1753.
"Habitat in aquis vadosis Angliae, Belgii." RCN: 4099.
Lectotype (Benson in *Amer. Midl. Naturalist* 52: 364. 1954): *Löfling 436 γ*, Herb. Linn. No. 715.74 (LINN).
Current name: *Ranunculus hederaceus* L. (Ranunculaceae).

Ranunculus illyricus Linnaeus, *Species Plantarum* 1: 552. 1753.
"Habitat in Oelandia, Hungaria, Narbona, Italia." RCN: 4078.
Lectotype (Jonsell & Jarvis in *Nordic J. Bot.* 14: 161. 1994): Herb. Linn. No. 715.31 (LINN), see opposite, upper left.
Current name: *Ranunculus illyricus* L. (Ranunculaceae).

Ranunculus lanuginosus Linnaeus, *Species Plantarum* 1: 554. 1753.
"Habitat Monspelii." RCN: 4090.
Lectotype (La Valva & Caputo in *Delpinoa*, n.s., 27–28: 42. 1988): Herb. Burser IX: 141 (UPS).
Current name: *Ranunculus lanuginosus* L. (Ranunculaceae).
Note: Lacaita (in *Bull. Orto Bot. Napoli* 3: 257–258. 1913) and others such as Jelenevsky & Derviz-Sokolova (in *Novosti Sist. Vyssh. Rast.* 16: 117. 1979) treated 715.59 (LINN) as the type. However, this was a post-1753 addition to the collection, and La Valva & Caputo (who illustrated the Linnaean material as their Tav. I) therefore rejected this choice, designating Herb. Burser IX: 141 (UPS) as lectotype in its place.

Ranunculus lapponicus Linnaeus, *Species Plantarum* 1: 553. 1753.
"Habitat in Alpibus Lapponicis." RCN: 4084.
Lectotype (Benson in *Amer. Midl. Naturalist* 52: 369. 1954): Herb. Linn. No. 715.43 (LINN).
Current name: *Ranunculus lapponicus* L. (Ranunculaceae).

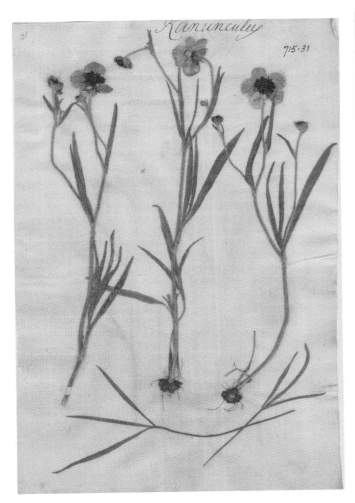

The lectotype of *Ranunculus illyricus* L.

Ranunculus lingua Linnaeus, *Species Plantarum* 1: 549. 1753.
"Habitat in Europae borealioris fossis, aquis limosis." RCN: 4062.
Lectotype (Iranshahr & al. in Rechinger, *Fl. Iranica* 171: 169. 1992): Herb. Linn. No. 715.3 (LINN).
Current name: ***Ranunculus lingua*** L. (Ranunculaceae).

Ranunculus monspeliacus Linnaeus, *Species Plantarum* 1: 553. 1753.
"Habitat Monspelii." RCN: 4085.
Neotype (Baldini in Jarvis & al. in *Taxon* 54: 470. 2005): France. Narbonne (Aude), Jun 1874, ex Herb. R.P. Murray, *Boutigny s.n.* (BM).
Current name: ***Ranunculus monspeliacus*** L. (Ranunculaceae).

Ranunculus muricatus Linnaeus, *Species Plantarum* 1: 555. 1753.
"Habitat in Europae australis fossis & humentibus." RCN: 4094.
Lectotype (Lourteig in *Darwiniana* 9: 487. 1951): Herb. Linn. No. 715.66 (LINN).
Current name: ***Ranunculus muricatus*** L. (Ranunculaceae).

Ranunculus nivalis Linnaeus, *Species Plantarum* 1: 553. 1753.
"Habitat in Alpibus Lapponiae, Helvetiae." RCN: 4082.
Lectotype (Benson in *Amer. Midl. Naturalist* 52: 350. 1954): Herb. Linn. No. 715.38 (LINN).
Current name: ***Ranunculus nivalis*** L. (Ranunculaceae).

Ranunculus nodiflorus Linnaeus, *Species Plantarum* 1: 549. 1753.
"Habitat Parisiis & in Siciliae locis paludosis." RCN: 4063.
Lectotype (Baldini in Jarvis & al. in *Taxon* 54: 470. 2005): Herb. Clifford: 228, *Ranunculus* 4 (BM-000628880).
Current name: ***Ranunculus nodiflorus*** L. (Ranunculaceae).

Ranunculus orientalis Linnaeus, *Species Plantarum* 1: 555. 1753.
"Habitat in Oriente." RCN: 4096.
Lectotype (Davis in *Notes Roy. Bot. Gard. Edinburgh* 23: 149. 1960): *Hasselquist*, Herb. Linn. No. 715.70 (LINN).
Current name: ***Ranunculus orientalis*** L. (Ranunculaceae).

Ranunculus parnassifolius Linnaeus, *Species Plantarum* 1: 549. 1753.
"Habitat in Europa australi." RCN: 4066.
Lectotype (Küpfer in *Boissiera* 23: 181. 1974): Herb. Linn. No. 715.8 (LINN).
Current name: ***Ranunculus parnassifolius*** L. (Ranunculaceae).

Ranunculus parviflorus Linnaeus, *Systema Naturae,* ed. 10, 2: 1087. 1759.
["Habitat in Europa australi."] Sp. Pl., ed. 2, 1: 781 (1762). RCN: 4095.
Lectotype (Benson in *Amer. Midl. Naturalist* 52: 348. 1954): Herb. Linn. No. 715.67 (LINN).
Current name: ***Ranunculus parviflorus*** L. (Ranunculaceae).

Ranunculus parvulus Linnaeus, *Systema Naturae,* ed. 12, 2: 380; *Mantissa Plantarum*: 79. 1767.
"Habitat Monspelii inque Italia." RCN: 092.
Replaced synonym: *Ranunculus parviflorus* Gouan (1765), *nom. illeg.,* non L. (1759).
Type not designated.
Current name: ***Ranunculus sardous*** Crantz (Ranunculaceae).
Note: Evidently a *nomen novum* for *R. parviflorus* Gouan (in *Flora Monspeliaca*: 270. 1765), non L., *Syst. Nat.,* ed. 10, 2: 1087 (1759). Linnaeus cited Gouan explicitly in the synonymy of *R. parvulus.*

Ranunculus platanifolius Linnaeus, *Systema Naturae,* ed. 12, 2: 379; *Mantissa Plantarum*: 79. 1767.
"Habitat in Germaniae & Italiae alpinis." RCN: 4077.
Lectotype (Huber in Jonsell & Jarvis in *Nordic J. Bot.* 14: 161. 1994): Herb. Linn. No. 715.29 (LINN).
Current name: ***Ranunculus platanifolius*** L. (Ranunculaceae).

Ranunculus polyanthemos Linnaeus, *Species Plantarum* 1: 554. 1753.
"Habitat in Europae borealis graminosis." RCN: 4088.
Lectotype (Iranshahr & al. in Rechinger, *Fl. Iranica* 171: 182. 1992): Herb. Linn. No. 715.54 (LINN).
Current name: ***Ranunculus polyanthemos*** L. (Ranunculaceae).

Ranunculus pyrenaeus Linnaeus, *Mantissa Plantarum Altera*: 248. 1771.
"Habitat in Pyrenaeis. Gouan." RCN: 4065.
Lectotype (Küpfer in *Boissiera* 23: 157. 1974): *Gouan s.n.,* Herb. Linn. No. 715.7 (LINN).
Current name: ***Ranunculus pyrenaeus*** L. (Ranunculaceae).

Ranunculus repens Linnaeus, *Species Plantarum* 1: 554. 1753.
"Habitat in Europae cultis." RCN: 4087.
Lectotype (Benson in *Amer. Midl. Naturalist* 52: 336. 1954): Herb. Linn. No. 715.52 (LINN).
Current name: ***Ranunculus repens*** L. (Ranunculaceae).
Note: Lourteig (in *Darwiniana* 9: 491. 1951) indicated both 715.52 and 751.53 (LINN) as types, but as they do not appear to be part of a single gathering, Art. 9.15 does not apply.

Ranunculus reptans Linnaeus, *Species Plantarum* 1: 549. 1753.
"Habitat in Suecia, Russia ad ripas lacuum antecedenti valde affinis & forte varietas." RCN: 4061.
Lectotype (Jonsell & Jarvis in *Nordic J. Bot.* 14: 161. 1994): Herb. Linn. No. 236 (LAPP).
Current name: ***Ranunculus reptans*** L. (Ranunculaceae).

Ranunculus rutifolius Linnaeus, *Species Plantarum* 1: 552. 1753.
"Habitat in Alpibus Austriae, Delphinatus." RCN: 4080.
Type not designated.
Original material: Herb. Burser IX: 131 (UPS); Herb. Clifford: 230, *Ranunculus* 14, 2 sheets (BM); [icon] in Morison, Pl. Hist. Univ. 2: 448, s. 4, t. 31, f. 54. 1680; [icon] in Clusius, Rar. Pl. Hist. 1: 232. 1601.
Current name: ***Callianthemum coriandrifolium*** Rchb. (Ranunculaceae).
Note: Specific epithet spelled "rutaefolius" in the protologue.
    This name has been treated as ambiguous by a number of authors, e.g. Zimmermann (in *Feddes Repert.* 73: 3. 1966), and does not appear to be in current use. However, no formal rejection proposal appears to have been made.

Ranunculus sceleratus Linnaeus, *Species Plantarum* 1: 551. 1753.
"Habitat ad Europae fossas & paludes." RCN: 4075.
Lectotype (Benson in *Amer. Midl. Naturalist* 52: 361. 1954): Herb. Clifford: 230, *Ranunculus* 12 (BM-000628891).
Current name: ***Ranunculus sceleratus*** L. (Ranunculaceae).

Ranunculus thora Linnaeus, *Species Plantarum* 1: 550. 1753.
"Habitat in Alpibus Helveticis, Pyrenaicis." RCN: 4070.
Lectotype (Baldini in Jarvis & al. in *Taxon* 54: 470. 2005): Séguier, Herb. Linn. No. 715.16 (LINN).
Current name: ***Ranunculus thora*** L. (Ranunculaceae).

Raphanus raphanistrum Linnaeus, *Species Plantarum* 2: 669. 1753.
"Habitat inter segetes Europae." RCN: 4875.
Lectotype (Jonsell & Jarvis in *Nordic J. Bot.* 22: 71. 2002): Herb. Clifford: 340, *Raphanus* 2 (BM-000646374).
Current name: ***Raphanus raphanistrum*** L. (Brassicaceae).
Note: Jafri (in Nasir & Ali, *Fl. W. Pakistan* 55: 34. 1973) and later authors have treated 846.4 (LINN) as the type, but this collection was sent to Linnaeus by Brander and did not reach him until after 1753. It cannot, therefore, be original material for the name.

Raphanus sativus Linnaeus, *Species Plantarum* 2: 669. 1753.
"Habitat – – – –" RCN: 4873.
Lectotype (Jonsell in Humbert, *Fl. Madagascar* 84: 8. 1982): Herb. Linn. No. 846.1 (LINN). – Epitype (Pistrick & Jarvis in *Feddes Repert.* 98: 477. 1987): Herb. Burser IV: 52 (UPS).
Generitype of *Raphanus* Linnaeus (vide Green, *Prop. Brit. Bot.*: 172. 1929).
Current name: ***Raphanus sativus*** L. (Brassicaceae).
Note: Jonsell (in Humbert, *Fl. Madagascar* 84: 8. 1982) typified the name with 846.1 (LINN). However, the absence of a root (necessary to apply infraspecific nomenclature) caused Pistrick & Jarvis (in *Feddes Repert.* 98: 477. 1987) to reject Jonsell's choice in favour of a more complete collection in Herb. Burser (UPS). Under Art. 9.17, however, Jonsell's choice of lectotype must stand but Pistrick & Jarvis' choice of the Burser material as lectotype, is correctable to an epitype (Art. 9.8).

Raphanus sibiricus Linnaeus, *Species Plantarum* 2: 669. 1753.
"Habitat in Sibiria." RCN: 4876.

Lectotype (Ebel in Cafferty & Jarvis in *Taxon* 51: 535. 2002): Herb. Linn. No. 846.6 (LINN).
Current name: ***Chorispora sibirica*** (L.) DC. (Brassicaceae).

Rauvolfia canescens Linnaeus, *Species Plantarum*, ed. 2, 1: 303. 1762.
"Habitat in Jamaica." RCN: 1701.
Type not designated.
Original material: *Browne*, Herb. Linn. No. 293.4 (LINN).
Current name: ***Rauvolfia tetraphylla*** L. (Apocynaceae).
Note: Rendle (in *Proc. Linn. Soc. London* 149: 108. 1937) says the name is "founded on" Browne specimens in LINN, which he illustrates as his pl. 3 (= 293.4 LINN). However, "founded on" is not accepted as an equivalent of "type".

Rauvolfia subpubescens Linnaeus, *Mantissa Plantarum Altera*: 345. 1771, *nom. illeg.*
RCN: 1701.
Replaced synonym: *Rauvolfia hirsuta* Jacq. (1760).
Type not designated.
Current name: ***Rauvolfia tetraphylla*** L. (Apocynaceae).
Note: An illegitimate replacement name for *R. hirsuta* Jacq. (1760).

Rauvolfia tetraphylla Linnaeus, *Species Plantarum* 1: 208. 1753.
"Habitat in America calidiore." RCN: 1700.
Lectotype (Stearn, *Introd. Linnaeus' Sp. Pl.* (Ray Soc. ed.): 47. 1957): [icon] *"Rauvolfia"* in Linnaeus, Hort. Cliff.: 75, t. 9. 1738. – Voucher: Herb. Clifford: 75, *Rauvolfia* 1 (BM).
Generitype of *Rauvolfia* Linnaeus.
Current name: ***Rauvolfia tetraphylla*** L. (Apocynaceae).
Note: See extensive discussion by Rendle (in *Proc. Linn. Soc. London* 149: 108. 1937), Rao (in *Ann. Missouri Bot. Gard.* 43: 255, 285. 1956) and Fuchs (in *Taxon* 9: 37–40. 1960). Leeuwenberg (in Jarvis & al., *Regnum Veg.* 127: 81. 1993) designated a Clifford sheet as lectotype but this choice is pre-dated by that of Stearn.

Reaumuria vermiculata Linnaeus, *Systema Naturae*, ed. 10, 2: 1080. 1759.
["Habitat in Aegypti, Syriae, Siciliae littoribus. D. Roque."] Sp. Pl., ed. 2, 1: 754 (1762). RCN: 3972.
Lectotype (Zohary & Danin in *Israel J. Bot.* 19: 306. 1970): *Hasselquist*, Herb. Linn. No. 701.1 (LINN).
Generitype of *Reaumuria* Linnaeus.
Current name: ***Reaumuria vermiculata*** L. (Tamaricaceae).

Renealmia disticha Linnaeus, *Systema Naturae*, ed. 10, 2: 974. 1759.
RCN: 2279.
Lectotype (Smith in *Contr. Gray Herb.* 114: 10. 1936): [icon] *"Viscum cariophilloides minus foliorum imis viridibus apicibus subrubicundis flore tripetalo purpureo semine filamentoso"* in Sloane, Voy. Jamaica 1: 190, t. 122, f. 1. 1707.
Current name: ***Tillandsia tenuifolia*** L. (Bromeliaceae).

Renealmia monostachia Linnaeus, *Species Plantarum* 1: 287. 1753.
"Habitat in America meridionali." RCN: 2278.
Basionym of: *Tillandsia monostachia* (L.) L. (1762).
Type not designated.
Original material: Herb. Linn. No. 403.2 (LINN); [icon] in Plumier in Burman, Pl. Amer.: 233, t. 238, f. 1. 1760.
Current name: ***Guzmania monostachia*** (L.) Mez (Bromeliaceae).
Note: Smith & Downs (in *Fl. Neotropica* 14: 1338. 1977) indicated an unpublished Plumier plate in Paris as type, but this was not studied by Linnaeus and is not original material for the name.

Renealmia paniculata Linnaeus, *Species Plantarum* 1: 286. 1753.
"Habitat in America meridionali." RCN: 2276.

Basionym of: *Tillandsia paniculata* (L.) L. (1762).

Lectotype (Smith & Downs, *Fl. Neotropica* 14: 1018. 1977): [icon] *"Renalmia foliis brevissimis"* in Plumier in Burman, Pl. Amer.: 233, t. 237. 1760.

Generitype of *Renealmia* Linnaeus, *nom. rej.*

Current name: ***Tillandsia paniculata*** (L.) L. (Bromeliaceae).

Note: Renealmia Linnaeus, *nom. rej.* in favour of *Renealmia* Linnaeus filius.

Renealmia polystachia Linnaeus, *Species Plantarum* 1: 286. 1753.

"Habitat in America calidiore." RCN: 2277.

Basionym of: *Tillandsia polystachia* (L.) L. (1762).

Neotype (Smith & Downs, *Fl. Neotropica* 14: 924. 1977): *Plumier, s.n.* (P).

Current name: ***Tillandsia polystachia*** (L.) L. (Bromeliaceae).

Note: Smith & Downs designated a Plumier specimen (P) as the type. It would not, however, have been studied by Linnaeus and is not original material for the name. Although one illustration, Catesby's 2: t. 89, is mentioned in the protologue, it is accompanied by "?", indicating Linnaeus' doubts as to whether it belonged with this name. These seem to have been well-founded as the plate is identifiable as *Tillandsia balbisiana* (Schultes) Roemer & Schultes (see Howard & Staples in *J. Arnold Arbor.* 64: 514. 1983). In the absence of original material, Smith & Downs' choice is treated as a neotypification under Art. 9.8.

Renealmia recurvata Linnaeus, *Species Plantarum* 1: 287. 1753.

"Habitat in Jamaicae arboribus." RCN: 2280.

Basionym of: *Tillandsia recurvata* (L.) L. (1762).

Type not designated.

Original material: Herb. Linn. No. 403.8 (LINN); [icon] in Sloane, Voy. Jamaica 1: 190, t. 121, f. 1. 1707 – Typotype: Herb. Sloane 3: 103 (BM) – Voucher: Herb. Sloane 3: 102 (BM).

Current name: ***Tillandsia recurvata*** (L.) L. (Bromeliaceae).

Note: Smith (in *Proc. Amer. Acad. Arts* 70: 208, 219. 1935), and followed by many later authors, treated material in the Sloane herbarium (BM-SL) as the type but this was not studied by Linnaeus and is not original material for the name.

Renealmia usneoides Linnaeus, *Species Plantarum* 1: 287. 1753.

"Habitat in Virginiae, Jamaicae, Brasiliae arboribus." RCN: 2281.

Basionym of: *Tillandsia usneoides* (L.) L. (1762).

Lectotype (Gouda in Görts-van Rijn, *Fl. Guianas*, ser. A, 3: 68. 1987): Herb. Clifford: 129, *Renealmia* 1 (BM-000558543).

Current name: ***Tillandsia usneoides*** (L.) L. (Bromeliaceae).

Note: Although Smith & Downs (in *Fl. Neotropica* 14: 900. 1977) treated material in the Sloane herbarium (BM-SL) as the type, this was not studied by Linnaeus and is not original material for the name.

Reseda alba Linnaeus, *Species Plantarum* 1: 449. 1753.

"Habitat Monspelii." RCN: 3487.

Lectotype (Jafri in Jafri & El-Gadi, *Fl. Libya* 34: 23. 1977): Herb. Linn. No. 629.14 (LINN).

Current name: ***Reseda alba*** L. (Resedaceae).

Reseda canescens Linnaeus, *Species Plantarum* 1: 448. 1753.

"Habitat in Salmantica." RCN: 3482.

Lectotype (Heywood in *Feddes Repert.* 69: 42. 1964): [icon] *"Sesamoides parvum Salmantic."* in Clusius, Rar. Pl. Hist. 1: 296, 295. 1601.

Current name: ***Sesamoides clusii*** (Spreng.) Greuter & Burdet (Resedaceae).

Note: This has been treated as a *nomen ambiguum* by some authors (e.g. López González in *Anales Jard. Bot. Madrid* 42: 320. 1986; 45:

368. 1988; 48: 97–98. 1990), and placed as a possible synonym of *Sesamoides clusii* (Spreng.) Greuter & Burdet. However, no formal rejection proposal appears to have been made.

Reseda canescens Linnaeus, *Systema Naturae,* ed. 12, 2: 330. 1767, *nom. illeg.*

RCN: 3482.

Lectotype (Abdallah in *Meded. Landbouwhoogeschool* 67–8: 44. 1967): Herb. Linn. No. 629.3 (LINN).

Current name: ***Caylusea hexagyna*** (Forssk.) M.L. Green (Resedaceae).

Note: Abdallah (in *Meded. Landbouwhoogeschool* 67–8: 44. 1967) treats this as heterotypic with regard to *R. canescens* L. (1753), and hence illegitimate.

Reseda fruticulosa Linnaeus, *Systema Naturae,* ed. 10, 2: 1046. 1759.

["Habitat in Hispania."] Sp. Pl., ed. 2, 1: 645 (1762). RCN: 3486.

Replaced synonym of: *Reseda suffruticulosa* L. (1762), *nom. illeg.*

Lectotype (Yeo in *Feddes Repert.* 69: 153. 1964): Herb. Linn. No. 629.12 (LINN).

Current name: ***Reseda alba*** L. (Resedaceae).

Reseda glauca Linnaeus, *Species Plantarum* 1: 449. 1753.

"Habitat in Pyrenaeis." RCN: 3483.

Lectotype (Abdallah & de Wit in *Meded. Landbouwhoogeschool* 78–14: 216. 1978): *Löfling 396*, Herb. Linn. No. 629.4, right specimen (LINN).

Current name: ***Reseda glauca*** L. (Resedaceae).

Reseda lutea Linnaeus, *Species Plantarum* 1: 449. 1753.

"Habitat in Europae australioris montibus cretaceis." RCN: 3489.

Lectotype (Leistner in Codd & al., *Fl. Southern Africa* 13: 178. 1970): Herb. Linn. No. 629.18 (LINN).

Generitype of *Reseda* Linnaeus (vide Green, *Prop. Brit. Bot.*: 157. 1929).

Current name: ***Reseda lutea*** L. (Resedaceae).

Reseda luteola Linnaeus, *Species Plantarum* 1: 448. 1753.

"Habitat in Europa ad vias & pagos." RCN: 3481.

Lectotype (Jafri in Jafri & El-Gadi, *Fl. Libya* 34: 12. 1977): Herb. Linn. No. 629.1 (LINN), see p. 790.

Current name: ***Reseda luteola*** L. (Resedaceae).

Reseda mediterranea Linnaeus, *Mantissa Plantarum Altera*: 564. 1771.

"Habitat in Palaestina." RCN: 3491.

Neotype (Abdallah & de Wit in *Meded. Landbouwhoogeschool* 78–14: 245. 1978): Herb. Linn. No. 629.26 (LINN).

Current name: ***Reseda lutea*** L. (Resedaceae).

Note: Abdallah & de Wit reviewed the usage of *R. mediterranea,* concluding that it is synonymous with *R. lutea* L. (1753). Although 629.25 (LINN) is annotated with "mediterranea", they apparently concluded that it was not original material for the name (presumably because, as a species of *Caylusia*, it conflicts with Linnaeus' very detailed description), and designated a neotype.

Reseda odorata Linnaeus, *Amoenitates Academicae* 3: 51. 1756.

["Habitat in Aegypto."] Sp. Pl., ed. 2, 1: 646 (1762). RCN: 3492.

Lectotype (Nasir in Nasir & Ali, *Fl. W. Pakistan* 90: 7. 1975): Herb. Linn. No. 629.28 (LINN).

Current name: ***Reseda odorata*** L. (Resedaceae).

Note: See discussion by Abdallah & de Wit (in *Meded. Landbouwhoogeschool* 78–14: 289. 1978).

R

The lectotype of *Reseda luteola* L.

Reseda phyteuma Linnaeus, *Species Plantarum* 1: 449. 1753.
"Habitat in Gallia, Italia." RCN: 3490.
Lectotype (Jafri in Jafri & El-Gadi, *Fl. Libya* 34: 14. 1977): Herb. Linn. No. 629.21 (LINN).
Current name: ***Reseda phyteuma*** L. (Resedaceae).
Note: See discussion by Abdallah & de Wit (in *Meded. Landbouwhoogeschool* 78–14: 303. 1978).

Reseda purpurascens Linnaeus, *Species Plantarum* 1: 449. 1753.
"Habitat in collibus Salamanticis, Monspelii." RCN: 3484.
Lectotype (Abdallah & de Wit in *Meded. Landbouwhoogeschool* 78–14: 365. 1978): *Löfling 398*, Herb. Linn. No. 629.7 (LINN).
Current name: ***Sesamoides canescens*** (L.) Kuntze (Resedaceae).

Reseda sesamoides Linnaeus, *Species Plantarum* 1: 449. 1753.
"Habitat Monspelii in Horto Dei." RCN: 3485.
Lectotype (Heywood in *Feddes Repert.* 69: 41. 1964): Herb. Linn. No. 629.9 (LINN).
Current name: ***Sesamoides pygmaea*** (Scheele) Kuntze (Resedaceae).
Note: See discussion by Abdallah & de Wit (in *Meded. Landbouwhoogeschool* 78–14: 362. 1978).

Reseda suffruticulosa Linnaeus, *Species Plantarum*, ed. 2, 1: 645. 1762, *nom. illeg.*
"Habitat in Hispania." RCN: 3486.
Replaced synonym: *Reseda fruticulosa* L. (1759).
Lectotype (Yeo in *Feddes Repert.* 69: 153. 1964): Herb. Linn. No. 629.12 (LINN).
Current name: ***Reseda alba*** L. (Resedaceae).
Note: A superfluous name for *Reseda fruticulosa* L. (1759).

Reseda undata Linnaeus, *Systema Naturae*, ed. 10, 2: 1046. 1759.
["Habitat in Hispania."] Sp. Pl., ed. 2, 1: 644 (1762). RCN: 3488.
Lectotype (Yeo in *Feddes Repert.* 69: 152. 1964): *Löfling 375a*, Herb. Linn. No. 629.16 (LINN).
Current name: ***Reseda undata*** L. (Resedaceae).

Restio dichotomus Linnaeus, *Systema Naturae*, ed. 12, 2: 735. 1767, *nom. illeg.*
["Habitat ad Caput Bonae Spei."] Cent. I Pl.: 4 (1755). RCN: 7392.
Replaced synonym: *Schoenus capensis* L. (1755).
Lectotype (Linder in *Bothalia* 15: 402. 1985): Herb. Linn. No. 1164.3 (LINN).
Generitype of *Restio* Linnaeus, *nom. rej.*
Current name: ***Ischyrolepis capensis*** (L.) H.P. Linder (Restionaceae).
Note: Restio Linnaeus, *nom. rej.* in favour of *Restio* Rottböll. *Restio dichotomus* is a superfluous name for *Schoenus capensis* L.

Restio elegia Linnaeus, *Systema Vegetabilium*, ed. 13: 738. 1774, *nom. illeg.*
["Habitat ad Cap. b. spei. Koenig."] Mant. Pl. Alt.: 297 (1771). RCN: 7396.
Replaced synonym: *Elegia juncea* L. (1771).
Neotype (Linder in *Bothalia* 15: 424. 1985): Herb. Linn. No. 1164a.4 (LINN).
Current name: ***Elegia juncea*** L. (Restionaceae).

Restio simplex Linnaeus, *Systema Vegetabilium*, ed. 13: 738. 1774. RCN: 7395.
Type not designated.
Original material: none traced.
Current name: ***Leptocarpus simplex*** (L.) R. Br. (Restionaceae).

Rhacoma crossopetalum Linnaeus, *Systema Naturae*, ed. 10, 2: 896. 1759.
["Habitat in Jamaica."] Sp. Pl., ed. 2, 1: 169 (1762). RCN: 947.
Lectotype (Fawcett & Rendle, *Fl. Jamaica* 5: 29. 1926): *Browne*, Herb. Linn. No. 146.1 (LINN).
Generitype of *Rhacoma* Linnaeus, *nom. illeg.*
Current name: ***Crossopetalum rhacoma*** Crantz (Celastraceae).
Note: Rhacoma Linnaeus (1759), *nom. illeg.* = *Crossopetalum* P. Browne (1756).

Rhamnus alaternus Linnaeus, *Species Plantarum* 1: 193. 1753.
"Habitat in Europa australi." RCN: 1565.
Lectotype (Jafri in Jafri & El-Gadi, *Fl. Libya* 30: 9. 1977): Herb. Linn. No. 262.24 (LINN).
Current name: ***Rhamnus alaternus*** L. (Rhamnaceae).

Rhamnus alpina Linnaeus, *Species Plantarum* 1: 193. 1753.
"Habitat in alpibus Helveticis." RCN: 1561.
Lectotype (Baldini in *Taxon* 51: 378. 2002): Herb. Burser XXIII: 14 (UPS).
Current name: ***Rhamnus alpina*** L. (Rhamnaceae).
Note: Specific epithet spelled "alpinus" in the protologue.

Rhamnus cathartica Linnaeus, *Species Plantarum* 1: 193. 1753.
"Habitat in Europae australioris sepibus." RCN: 1549.
Lectotype (Schirarend in Jarvis & al., *Regnum Veg.* 127: 81. 1993):
 Herb. Linn. No. 262.1 (LINN).
Generitype of *Rhamnus* Linnaeus (vide Hitchcock, *Prop. Brit. Bot.*:
 133. 1929).
Current name: ***Rhamnus cathartica*** L. (Rhamnaceae).
Note: Specific epithet spelled "catharticus" in the protologue.

Rhamnus frangula Linnaeus, *Species Plantarum* 1: 193. 1753.
"Habitat in Europae borealis nemorosis humidiusculis." RCN: 1563.
Lectotype (Jonsell & Jarvis in *Nordic J. Bot.* 22: 80. 2002): Herb.
 Clifford: 70, *Rhamnus* 5 (BM-000558106).
Current name: ***Frangula alnus*** Mill. (Rhamnaceae).

Rhamnus frangula Linnaeus var. **laevifolia** Linnaeus, *Species
 Plantarum* 1: 193. 1753.
RCN: 1563.
Type not designated.
Original material: none traced.
Current name: ***Frangula alnus*** Mill. (Rhamnaceae).
Note: Varietal epithet spelled "laevifolius" in the protologue.

Rhamnus infectoria Linnaeus, *Systema Naturae,* ed. 12, 2: 178;
 Mantissa Plantarum: 49. 1767.
"Habitat in Hispania, Gallia, Italia." RCN: 1550.
Type not designated.
Original material: *Scopoli 45,* Herb. Linn. No. 262.2? (LINN); Herb.
 Burser XXV: 9 (UPS); [icon] in Clusius, Rar. Pl. Hist. 1: 111.
 1601; [icon] in Bauhin & Cherler, Hist. Pl. Univ. 1(2): 58. 1650.
Current name: ***Rhamnus saxatilis*** Jacq. subsp. ***infectoria*** (L.) P.
 Fourn. (Rhamnaceae).
Note: Specific epithet spelled "infectorius" in the protologue.

Rhamnus jujuba Linnaeus, *Species Plantarum* 1: 194. 1753.
"Habitat in India." RCN: 1570.
Lectotype (Johnston in Milne-Redhead & Polhill, *Fl. Trop. E. Africa,
 Rhamnaceae:* 29. 1972; Wadhwa in Dassanayake & Clayton,
 Revised Handb. Fl. Ceylon 10: 369. Herb. Hermann 3: 14, No. 89
 (BM-000594656).
Current name: ***Ziziphus mauritiana*** Lam. (Rhamnaceae).
Note: Johnston (1972) indicated Herb. Hermann material (BM) as
 type. Although there is material in more than one volume, it
 appears to have been part of a single gathering. Consequently, this is
 accepted as the first typification (Art. 9.15), with the choice
 subsequently restricted by Wadhwa.

Rhamnus lineata Linnaeus, *Centuria II Plantarum*: 11. 1756.
"Habitat in Zeylona, China. Osbeck." RCN: 1564.
Type not designated.
Original material: Herb. Linn. No. 262.23? (LINN).
Current name: ***Berchemia lineata*** (L.) DC. (Rhamnaceae).

Rhamnus lotus Linnaeus, *Species Plantarum* 1: 194. 1753.
"Habitat in Regno Tunetano." RCN: 1567.
Type not designated.
Original material: Herb. Linn. No. 262.27 (LINN); [icon] in Shaw,
 Cat. Pl. Afr. As.: 47, f. 631. 1738.
Current name: ***Ziziphus lotus*** (L.) Lam. (Rhamnaceae).

Rhamnus lycioides Linnaeus, *Species Plantarum,* ed. 2, 1: 279. 1762.
"Habitat in Hispania." RCN: 1551.
Lectotype (Jafri in Jafri & El-Gadi, *Fl. Libya* 30: 10. 1977): Herb.
 Linn. No. 262.3 (LINN).
Current name: ***Rhamnus lycioides*** L. (Rhamnaceae).

Rhamnus micrantha Linnaeus, *Systema Naturae,* ed. 10, 2: 937.
 1759.
["Habitat in America."] Sp. Pl., ed. 2, 1: 280 (1762). RCN: 1558.
Lectotype (Wijnands, *Bot. Commelins*: 199. 1983): [icon] *"Rhamnus
 foliis ovatis glabris fructibus bilocularibus subcaliptratis"* in Browne,
 Civ. Nat. Hist. Jamaica: 172, t. 12, f. 1. 1756.
Current name: ***Trema micrantha*** (L.) Blume (Ulmaceae).
Note: Specific epithet spelled "micranthus" in the protologue.

Rhamnus minor Linnaeus, *Plantae Tinctoriae*: 14. 1759.
Type not designated.
Original material: Herb. Burser XXV: 8? (UPS).
Current name: ***Rhamnus*** sp. (Rhamnaceae).
Note: The precise synonymy of this name is uncertain.

Rhamnus napeca Linnaeus, *Species Plantarum* 1: 194. 1753.
"Habitat in Zeylona." RCN: 1569.
Lectotype (Wadhwa in Dassanayake & Clayton, *Revised Handb. Fl.
 Ceylon* 10: 365. 1996): Herb. Hermann 3: 43, No. 87 (BM-
 000594685).
Current name: ***Ziziphus napeca*** (L.) Willd. (Rhamnaceae).

Rhamnus oenopolia Linnaeus, *Species Plantarum* 1: 194. 1753.
"Habitat in Zeylona." RCN: 1571.
Lectotype (Forster in *Austrobaileya* 3: 563. 1991): [icon] *"Jujuba
 aculeata, nervosis foliis, infra sericeis, flavis"* in Burman, Thes.
 Zeylan.: 131, t. 61. 1737.
Current name: ***Ziziphus oenopolia*** (L.) Mill. (Rhamnaceae).

Rhamnus oleoides Linnaeus, *Species Plantarum,* ed. 2, 1: 279. 1762.
"Habitat in Hispania. C. Alstromer." RCN: 1552.
Lectotype (Jafri in Jafri & El-Gadi, *Fl. Libya* 30: 10. 1977): *Alströmer
 35,* Herb. Linn. No. 262.4 (LINN).
Current name: ***Rhamnus lycioides*** L. subsp. ***oleoides*** (L.) Jahand. &
 Maire (Rhamnaceae).

Rhamnus paliurus Linnaeus, *Species Plantarum* 1: 194. 1753.
"Habitat in Europa australi." RCN: 1566.
Lectotype (Jafri in Jafri & El-Gadi, *Fl. Libya* 30: 2. 1977): Herb. Linn.
 No. 262.25 (LINN).
Current name: ***Paliurus spina-christi*** Mill. (Rhamnaceae).

Rhamnus sarcomphalus Linnaeus, *Systema Naturae,* ed. 10, 2: 937.
 1759.
["Habitat in America."] Sp. Pl., ed. 2, 1: 280 (1762). RCN: 1557.
Type not designated.
Original material: *Browne 179,* Herb. Linn. No. 262.11 (LINN).
Current name: ***Ziziphus sarcomphalus*** (L.) M.C. Johnst.
 (Rhamnaceae).

Rhamnus spina-christi Linnaeus, *Species Plantarum* 1: 195. 1753.
"Habitat in Aethiopia, Palaestina." RCN: 1573.
Lectotype (Johnston in Milne-Redhead & Polhill, *Fl. Trop. E. Africa,
 Rhamnaceae*: 30. 1972): *Hasselquist,* Herb. Linn. No. 262.36
 (LINN).
Current name: ***Ziziphus spina-christi*** (L.) Desf. (Rhamnaceae).
Note: Johnston indicated a Hasselquist specimen in LINN as holotype,
 but gave the sheet number as 262.38. As this relates to a Browne
 collection associated with *R. zizyphus* L., it seems clear that this is
 simply an error for 262.36.

Rhamnus theezans Linnaeus, *Mantissa Plantarum Altera*: 207. 1771,
 nom. illeg.
"Habitat in China." RCN: 1554.
Replaced synonym: *Rhamnus thea* Osbeck (1757).

R

Type not designated.
Current name: ***Sageretia thea*** (Osbeck) M.C. Johnst. (Rhamnaceae).
Note: A superfluous name for *R. thea* Osbeck (1757).

Rhamnus zizyphus Linnaeus, *Species Plantarum* 1: 194. 1753.
"Habitat in Europa australi." RCN: 1572.
Lectotype (Kirkbride & al. in *Taxon* 55: 1050. 2006): Herb. Burser
   XXIII: 50 (UPS)
Current name: ***Ziziphus jujuba*** Mill. (Rhamnaceae).
Note: Kirkbride & al. typified this name as part of a proposal to
   conserve *Ziziphus jujuba* Mill. against *Ziziphus zizyphus* (L.) H.
   Karst., the latter otherwise being the little used, but correct, name
   for this taxon.

Rheedia lateriflora Linnaeus, *Species Plantarum* 2: 1193. 1753.
"Habitat in America." RCN: 3816.
Lectotype (Howard, *Fl. Lesser Antilles* 5: 327. 1989): [icon]
   "Vanrheedia" in Plumier, Nov. Pl. Amer.: 45, t. 18. 1703.
Generitype of *Rheedia* Linnaeus.
Current name: ***Garcinia humilis*** (Vahl) C.D. Adams (Clusiaceae).
Note: D'Arcy (in *Ann. Missouri Bot. Gard.* 67: 1014. 1981) treated
   unseen Plumier material, which he supposed to be in P, as type.
   Even if it exists, it would not have been seen by Linnaeus and would
   not have been original material for the name. Howard's type choice
   is therefore accepted here.

Rheum compactum Linnaeus, *Species Plantarum*, ed. 2, 1: 531. 1762.
"Habitat in Tataria, China." RCN: 2929.
Type not designated.
Original material: [icon] in Miller, Fig. Pl. Gard. Dict. 2: 145, t. 218.
   1758.
Current name: ***Rheum compactum*** L. (Polygonaceae).

Rheum palmatum Linnaeus, *Systema Naturae*, ed. 10, 2: 1010. 1759.
["Habitat in China ad murum. a. Dav. Gortero."] Sp. Pl., ed. 2, 1:
   531 (1762). RCN: 2928.
Type not designated.
Original material: Herb. Linn. No. 520.3 (LINN).
Current name: ***Rheum palmatum*** L. (Polygonaceae).

Rheum rhabarbarum Linnaeus, *Species Plantarum* 1: 372. 1753.
"Habitat in China ad murum & in Sibiria." RCN: 2927.
Lectotype (Jonsell & Jarvis in *Nordic J. Bot.* 14: 154. 1994): Herb.
   Linn. No. 520.2 (LINN).
Current name: ***Rheum rhabarbarum*** L. (Polygonaceae).

Rheum rhaponticum Linnaeus, *Species Plantarum* 1: 371. 1753.
"Habitat in Thracia, Scythia." RCN: 2926.
Lectotype (Libert & Englund in *Willdenowia* 19: 92. 1989): Herb.
   Linn. No. 520.1 (LINN).
Generitype of *Rheum* Linnaeus (vide Hitchcock, *Prop. Brit. Bot.*: 151.
   1929).
Current name: ***Rheum rhaponticum*** L. (Polygonaceae).
Note: Turrill (in *Izv. Bulg. Bot. Druz.* 7: 23–25. 1936) discussed the
   history of this name and provided detailed descriptions of the
   material on sheets 520.1 and 520.2 (LINN). He identified
   Bulgarian material as conspecific with that on 520.1, adding that *R.
   rhapontium* L. is the correct name for this taxon. However, his
   statement is insufficiently explicit to effect formal typification.

Rheum ribes Linnaeus, *Species Plantarum* 1: 372. 1753.
"Habitat in Persia, Libano, Carmelo." RCN: 2930.
Type not designated.
Original material: [icon] in Rauwolf, Aigent. Beschr. Morgenl.: 266,
   282, t. 266.282. 1583; [icon] in Pococke, Descr. East 2: 189, t. 84.

1745; [icon] in Breyn in Acad. Caes.-Leop. Carol. Nat. Cur.
   Ephem. 7: 10, t. 2. 1719; [icon] in Dillenius, Hort. Eltham. 1: 191,
   t. 158, f. 192. 1732.
Current name: ***Rheum ribes*** L. (Polygonaceae).

Rheum undulatum Linnaeus, *Species Plantarum*, ed. 2, 1: 531. 1762.
"Habitat in China, Sibiria." RCN: 2927.
Type not designated.
Original material: [icon] in Linnaeus, Amoen. Acad. 3: 212, t. 4.
   1751; [icon] in Amman, Stirp. Rar. Ruth.: 9. 1739.
Current name: ***Rheum undulatum*** L. (Polygonaceae).

Rhexia acisanthera Linnaeus, *Systema Naturae*, ed. 10, 2: 998.
   1759.
["Habitat in Jamaica."] Sp. Pl., ed. 2, 1: 491 (1762). RCN: 2651.
Lectotype (designated here by Cellinese): *Browne*, Herb. Linn. No.
   483.2 (LINN).
Current name: ***Acisanthera quadrata*** Pers. (Melastomataceae).

Rhexia mariana Linnaeus, *Species Plantarum* 1: 346. 1753.
"Habitat in Marilandia." RCN: 2650.
Lectotype (James in *Brittonia* 8: 224. 1956): [icon] *"Lysimachia non
   papposa Terrae Marianae, leptoneurophyllos, flore tetrapetalo rubello,
   folio & caule hirsutie ferruginea hispidis"* in Plukenet, Amalth. Bot.:
   t. 428, f. 1. 1705; Almag. Mant.: 123. 1700. – Typotype: Herb.
   Sloane 92: 90 (BM-SL).
Current name: ***Rhexia mariana*** L. (Melastomataceae).
Note: A detailed discussion is provided by Reveal & al. (in *Huntia* 7:
   227. 1987).

Rhexia virginica Linnaeus, *Species Plantarum* 1: 346. 1753.
"Habitat in Virginia." RCN: 2649.
Lectotype (James in *Brittonia* 8: 226. 1956): *Clayton 227* (BM-
   000042221).
Generitype of *Rhexia* Linnaeus (vide Hitchcock, *Prop. Brit. Bot.*: 149.
   1929).
Current name: ***Rhexia virginica*** L. (Melastomataceae).
Note: Although Griscom (in *Rhodora* 37: 171. 1935) claimed to have
   studied the type, he gave no indication of which element this might
   be. James' choice is accepted here.

Rhinanthus capensis Linnaeus, *Systema Naturae*, ed. 12, 2: 405.
   1767, *nom. illeg.*
["Habitat in Aethiopia."] Sp. Pl., ed. 2, 2: 879 (1763). RCN: 4376.
Replaced synonym: *Buchnera africana* L. (1760).
Type not designated.
Original material: as replaced synonym.
Note: An illegitimate renaming of *Buchnera africana* L. (1760). The
   application of this name, however, appears uncertain.

Rhinanthus crista-galli Linnaeus, *Species Plantarum* 2: 603. 1753.
"Habitat in Europae pratis." RCN: 4374.
Lectotype (Pennell in *Monogr. Acad. Nat. Sci. Philadelphia* 1: 491.
   1935): Herb. Linn. No. 758.2 (LINN).
Generitype of *Rhinanthus* Linnaeus (vide Green, *Prop. Brit. Bot.*: 166.
   1929).
Current name: ***Rhinanthus crista-galli*** L. (Scrophulariaceae).
Note: This name has been treated as a *nomen ambiguum* by many
   authors (see Sell in *Watsonia* 6: 301. 1967; Bullock in *Kew Bull.* 23:
   265. 1969 etc.), with *R. minor* L. (1756) often taken up in its place.
   However, to date, *R. crista-galli* has not been formally proposed for
   rejection.

Rhinanthus elephas Linnaeus, *Species Plantarum* 2: 603. 1753.
"Habitat in umbrosis Italiae." RCN: 4373.

Lectotype (Burbidge & Richardson in *Notes Roy. Bot. Gard. Edinburgh* 30: 105. 1970): Herb. Linn. No. 758.1 (LINN).
Current name: ***Rhynchocorys elephas*** (L.) Griseb. (Scrophulariaceae).

Rhinanthus indicus Linnaeus, *Species Plantarum* 2: 603. 1753.
"Habitat in Zeylona." RCN: 4377.
Lectotype (Cramer in Dassanayake & Fosberg, *Revised Handb. Fl. Ceylon* 3: 396. 1981): Herb. Hermann 2: 22, No. 238 (BM-000621584).
Current name: ***Centranthera indica*** (L.) Gamble (Scrophulariaceae).
Note: Specific epithet spelled "indica" in the protologue.
    Although Cramer indicated the type in the Hermann herbarium (BM) as "Mus. No. 20", the only material that could have been intended is that in vol. 2: 22, comprising two closely associated specimens and this material is therefore accepted as the type.

Rhinanthus major Linnaeus, *Amoenitates Academicae* 3: 53. 1756.
RCN: 4374.
Type not designated.
Original material: none traced.
Current name: ***Rhinanthus alectorolophus*** (Scop.) Pollich (Scrophulariaceae).
Note: This has been treated as a *nomen ambiguum* by many authors but no formal rejection proposal has been made.

Rhinanthus minor Linnaeus, *Amoenitates Academicae* 3: 54. 1756.
RCN: 4374.
Type not designated.
Original material: none traced.
Current name: ***Rhinanthus minor*** L. (Scrophulariaceae).

Rhinanthus orientalis Linnaeus, *Species Plantarum* 2: 603. 1753.
"Habitat in Oriente." RCN: 4372.
Type not designated.
Original material: [icon] in Tournefort, Rel. Voy. Levant (Paris ed.) 2: 299. 1717.
Current name: ***Rhynchocorys orientalis*** (L.) Benth. (Scrophulariaceae).

Rhinanthus trixago (Linnaeus) Linnaeus, *Systema Naturae,* ed. 10, 2: 1107. 1759.
["Habitat in Italiae maritimis, humentibus."] Sp. Pl. 2: 602 (1753). RCN: 4375.
Basionym: *Bartsia trixago* L. (1753).
Lectotype (Molau in *Opera Bot.* 102: 27. 1990): Herb. Burser XIV(1): 36 (UPS).
Current name: ***Bartsia trixago*** L. (Scrophulariaceae).

Rhinanthus virginicus Linnaeus, *Species Plantarum* 2: 603. 1753.
"Habitat in Virginica." RCN: 4378.
Lectotype (Pennell in *Torreya* 19: 207. 1919): *Clayton 488* (BM-000042611).
Current name: ***Aureolaria virginica*** (L.) Pennell (Scrophulariaceae).
Note: Specific epithet spelled "virginica" in the protologue.

Rhizophora candel Linnaeus, *Species Plantarum* 1: 443. 1753.
"Habitat in Indiae salsis". RCN: 3431.
Lectotype (Vu Van Cuong in Aubréville, *Fl. Cambodge Laos Vietnam* 4: 168. 1965): [icon] *"Tsjerou-kandel"* in Rheede, Hort. Malab. 6: 63, t. 35. 1686.
Current name: ***Kandelia candel*** (L.) Druce (Rhizophoraceae).

Rhizophora caseolaris Linnaeus, *Herbarium Amboinense*: 13. 1754.
["Habitat in Moluccis."] Sp. Pl., ed. 2, 1: 635 (1762). RCN: 3435.

Lectotype (Vu Van Cuong, *Fl. Cambodge Laos Vietnam* 4: 191. 1965): [icon] *"Mangium Caseolare rubrum"* in Rumphius, Herb. Amboin. 3: 113, t. 74. 1743.
Current name: ***Sonneratia caseolaris*** (L.) Engl. (Rhizophoraceae).
Note: Believing the name to be typified by a Rumphius plate identifiable as *S. alba* J.E. Sm., Hoogland (in *Taxon* 37: 980. 1988) proposed the name for conservation with a conserved type. However, the Committee for Spermatophyta (in *Taxon* 42: 689. 1993) ruled that the name had not been typified previously, and so the proposal was unnecessary as Hoogland had made the first lectotype choice. In fact, the same type choice had been made earlier by Vu Van Cuong (1965).

Rhizophora conjugata Linnaeus, *Species Plantarum* 1: 443. 1753.
"Habitat in India." RCN: 3429.
Lectotype (Lewis in Turrill & Milne-Redhead, *Fl. Trop. E. Africa, Rhizophoraceae*: 6. 1956): Herb. Hermann 5: 279, No. 181 [icon] (BM).
Current name: ***Bruguiera gymnorhiza*** (L.) Sav. (Rhizophoraceae).

Rhizophora corniculata Linnaeus, *Herbarium Amboinense*: 13. 1754.
["Habitat in Moluccis."] Sp. Pl., ed. 2, 1: 635 (1762). RCN: 3432.
Lectotype (Merrill, *Interpret. Rumph. Herb. Amb.*: 33, 413. 1917): [icon] *"Mangium fruticans corniculatum"* in Rumphius, Herb. Amboin. 3: 117, t. 77. 1743.
Current name: ***Aegiceras corniculatum*** (L.) Blanco (Myrsinaceae).

Rhizophora cylindrica Linnaeus, *Species Plantarum* 1: 443. 1753.
"Habitat in uliginosis Malabariae." RCN: 3434.
Lectotype (Merrill, *Interpret. Rumph. Herb. Amb.*: 389. 1917): [icon] *"Karii-kandel"* in Rheede, Hort. Malab. 6: 59, t. 33. 1686.
Current name: ***Bruguiera cylindrica*** (L.) Blume (Rhizophoraceae).

Rhizophora gymnorhiza Linnaeus, *Species Plantarum* 1: 443. 1753.
"Habitat in Indiae ripis salsis." RCN: 3430.
Lectotype (Lewis in Turrill & Milne-Redhead, *Fl. Trop. E. Africa, Rhizophoraceae*: 6. 1956): [icon] *"Kandel"* in Rheede, Hort. Malab. 6: 57, t. 31. 1686.
Current name: ***Bruguiera gymnorhiza*** (L.) Sav. (Rhizophoraceae).

Rhizophora mangle Linnaeus, *Species Plantarum* 1: 443. 1753.
"Habitat in paludibus Caribaearum, Malabariae." RCN: 3433.
Type not designated.
Original material: [icon] in Rheede, Hort. Malab. 6: 91, t. 34. 1686; [icon] in Plumier, Nov. Pl. Amer.: 13, t. 15. 1703.
Generitype of *Rhizophora* Linnaeus (vide Green, *Prop. Brit. Bot.*: 157. 1929).
Current name: ***Rhizophora mangle*** L. (Rhizophoraceae).
Note: Fawcett & Rendle (*Fl. Jamaica* 5: 300. 1926) noted the presence of material in LINN but did not refer to it as the type, despite the attribution of Nicolson & al. (in *Regnum Veg.* 119: 217. 1988) of a typification to these authors. Keay (in *Kew Bull.* 8: 123. 1953) designated material in Herb. Sloane (BM-SL) as lectotype, but as it was neither seen by Linnaeus, nor was it even the basis for a Sloane illustration, it is not original material for the name.

Rhodiola rosea Linnaeus, *Species Plantarum* 2: 1035. 1753.
"Habitat in Alpibus Lapponiae, Austriae, Helvetiae, Britanniae." RCN: 7468.
Lectotype (Ohba in Jarvis & al., *Regnum Veg.* 127: 81. 1993): Herb. Linn. No. 1186.1 (LINN).
Generitype of *Rhodiola* Linnaeus.
Current name: ***Rhodiola rosea*** L. (Crassulaceae).
Note: Although Clausen (*Sedum N. Amer.*: 532. 1975) referred to the type sheet as at LINN, this was based on an illustration of

specimens by Fröderström (in *Acta Horti Gothob.* 5, App.: Plate XI. 1930) which was, in fact, a composite of the material on sheets 1186.1, 1186.2 and 1186.3. As these specimens are not part of a single gathering, Art. 9.15 does not apply and Ohba's choice is accepted here.

Rhododendron chamaecistus Linnaeus, *Species Plantarum* 1: 392. 1753.
"Habitat in Baldo & prope Salisburgum." RCN: 3090.
Lectotype (Chamberlain in Cafferty & Jarvis in *Taxon* 51: 753. 2003 [2002]): Herb. Burser XXIV: 71 (UPS).
Current name: ***Rhodothamnus chamaecistus*** (L.) Rchb. (Ericaceae).

Rhododendron dauricum Linnaeus, *Species Plantarum* 1: 392. 1753.
"Habitat in Dauria." RCN: 3088.
Lectotype (Chamberlain in Cafferty & Jarvis in *Taxon* 51: 753. 2003 [2002]): [icon] *"Chamaerhododendros folio glabro, majusculo, amplo, flore roseo"* in Amman, Stirp. Rar. Ruth.: 181, t. 27. 1739.
Current name: ***Rhododendron dauricum*** L. (Ericaceae).

Rhododendron ferrugineum Linnaeus, *Species Plantarum* 1: 392. 1753.
"Habitat in Alpibus Helveticis, Allobrogicis, Pyrenaeis." RCN: 3087.
Lectotype (Chamberlain in Jarvis & al., *Regnum Veg.* 127: 81. 1993): Herb. Linn. No. 562.1 (LINN).
Generitype of *Rhododendron* Linnaeus (vide Hitchcock, *Prop. Brit. Bot.*: 153. 1929).
Current name: ***Rhododendron ferrugineum*** L. (Ericaceae).

Rhododendron hirsutum Linnaeus, *Species Plantarum* 1: 392. 1753.
"Habitat in Alpibus Helveticis, Austriacis, Styriacis." RCN: 3089.
Lectotype (Chamberlain in Cafferty & Jarvis in *Taxon* 51: 753. 2003 [2002]): [icon] *"Ledum Alpinum"* in Clusius, Rar. Pl. Hist. 1: 81, 82. 1601.
Current name: ***Rhododendron hirsutum*** L. (Ericaceae).

Rhododendron maximum Linnaeus, *Species Plantarum* 1: 392. 1753.
"Habitat in Virginia. Collinson." RCN: 3092.
Lectotype (Chamberlain in Cafferty & Jarvis in *Taxon* 51: 753. 2003 [2002]): [icon] *"Chamaerhododendros lauri-folio semper virens, floribus bullatis corymbosis"* in Catesby, Nat. Hist. Carolina 2, App.: 17, t. 17. 1747.
Current name: ***Rhododendron maximum*** L. (Ericaceae).
Note: Chamberlain (in *Notes Roy. Bot. Gard. Edinburgh* 39: 316. 1982) indicated unseen Collinson material as the type (based on Linnaeus' "Habitat in Virginia. Collinson."), but as it was not possible to trace any such material, he subsequently designated Catesby's illustration as the lectotype.

Rhododendron ponticum Linnaeus, *Species Plantarum*, ed. 2, 1: 562. 1762.
"Habitat in Oriente, Gibraltariae subhumidis umbrosis. Alstroemer." RCN: 3091.
Type not designated.
Original material: *Alström 95*, Herb. Linn. No. 562.5 (LINN).
Current name: ***Rhododendron ponticum*** L. (Ericaceae).
Note: This name was based on a description from Tournefort and material (Herb. Linn. No. 562.5) collected by Alströmer at Gibraltar – see López González (in *Anales Jard. Bot. Madrid* 52: 224. 1995). These elements are taxonomically distinct, and with usage of the name being in the sense of Tournefort's plant (for which no original element exists), the name may require proposing for conservation with a conserved type.

Rhodora canadensis Linnaeus, *Species Plantarum*, ed. 2, 1: 561. 1762.
"Habitat in Canada." RCN: 3086.
Holotype (Jarvis & al. in Jarvis & al., *Regnum Veg.* 127: 81. 1993): [icon] *"Chamaerhododendros"* in Duhamel, Semis Plantat. Arbr. (Add.): 10, unnumbered plate, f. 2. 1760 (see p. 127).
Generitype of *Rhodora* Linnaeus.
Current name: ***Rhododendron canadensis*** (L.) Torr. (Ericaceae).

Rhus angustifolia Linnaeus, *Species Plantarum* 1: 267. 1753.
"Habitat in Aethiopia." RCN: 2125.
Lectotype (Moffett in Leistner, *Fl. Southern Africa* 19(3:1): 100. 1993): Herb. Linn. No. 378.21 (LINN).
Current name: ***Rhus angustifolia*** L. (Anacardiaceae).
Note: Specific epithet spelled "angustifolium" in the protologue.

Rhus cobbe Linnaeus, *Species Plantarum* 1: 267. 1753.
"Habitat in Zeylona." RCN: 2123.
Lectotype (Leenhouts in Adema & al., *Fl. Malesiana*, ser. I, 11: 460. 1994): Herb. Hermann 2: 46, No. 441 (BM-000594608).
Current name: ***Allophylus cobbe*** (L.) Raeusch. (Sapindaceae).

Rhus cominia Linnaeus, *Plantarum Jamaicensium Pugillus*: 10. 1759. ["Habitat in Indiis."] Sp. Pl., ed. 2, 1: 382 (1762). RCN: 2122.
Lectotype (Fawcett & Rendle, *Fl. Jamaica* 5: 50. 1926): Herb. Linn. No. 378.19 (LINN).
Current name: ***Allophylus cominia*** (L.) Sw. (Sapindaceae).

Rhus copallina Linnaeus, *Species Plantarum* 1: 266. 1753.
"Habitat in America septentrionali." RCN: 2118.
Lectotype (Fernald & Griscom in *Rhodora* 37: 168. 1935): *Clayton 728* (BM-000051815).
Current name: ***Rhus copallina*** L. (Anacardiaceae).
Note: Specific epithet spelled "copallinum" in the protologue.

Rhus coriaria Linnaeus, *Species Plantarum* 1: 265. 1753.
"Habitat in Europa australis." RCN: 2112.
Lectotype (Barrie in Jarvis & al., *Regnum Veg.* 127: 82. 1993): Herb. Burser XXII: 76 (UPS).
Generitype of *Rhus* Linnaeus (vide Hitchcock, *Prop. Brit. Bot.*: 142. 1929).
Current name: ***Rhus coriaria*** L. (Anacardiaceae).

Rhus cotinus Linnaeus, *Species Plantarum* 1: 267. 1753.
"Habitat in Lombardia Italiae & ad radices Apenninorum." RCN: 2128.
Type not designated.
Original material: Herb. Clifford: 111, *Cotinus* 1, 3 sheets (BM); [icon] in Dodoëns, Stirp. Hist. Pempt., ed. 2: 779, 780. 1616.
Current name: ***Cotinus coggygria*** Scop. (Anacardiaceae).

Rhus glabra Linnaeus, *Species Plantarum* 1: 265. 1753.
"Habitat in America septentrionali." RCN: 2115.
Lectotype (designated here by Reveal): Herb. Burser XXII: 77 (UPS).
Current name: ***Rhus glabra*** L. (Anacardiaceae).

Rhus javanica Linnaeus, *Species Plantarum* 1: 265. 1753.
"Habitat in Java. Osbeck." RCN: 2114.
Lectotype (Basak in Jain & al. in *Fasc. Fl. India* 4: 8. 1980): *Osbeck 14*, Herb. Linn. No. 378.4 (LINN), see opposite, above left.
Current name: ***Brucea javanica*** (L.) Merr. (Simaroubaceae).
Note: See Hansen & Fox Maule (in *Bot. J. Linn. Soc.* 67: 205. 1973) for comments on Osbeck material.

Rhus laevigata Linnaeus, *Species Plantarum*, ed. 2, 2: 1672. 1763.
"Habitat ad Cap. b. spei. Arduini." RCN: 2126.

The lectotype of *Rhus javanica* L.

Lectotype (Schonland in *Bothalia* 3: 18. 1930): *Turra*, Herb. Linn. No. 378.23 (LINN).
Current name: ***Rhus laevigata*** L. (Anacardiaceae).
Note: Specific epithet spelled "laevigatum" in the protologue.
 See discussion of this name by Fernandes (in *Bol. Soc. Brot.*, sér. 2, 41: 129. 1967).

Rhus lucida Linnaeus, *Species Plantarum* 1: 267. 1753.
"Habitat ad Cap. b. spei." RCN: 2127.
Lectotype (Moffett in Leistner, *Fl. Southern Africa* 19(3:1): 79. 1993): Herb. Clifford: 111, *Rhus* 6 α (BM-000558433).
Current name: ***Rhus lucida*** L. (Anacardiaceae).
Note: Specific epithet spelled "lucidum" in the protologue.
 Fernandes (in *Bol. Soc. Brot.*, sér. 2, 41: 13. 1967) indicated a lectotype in Herb. Clifford (BM), but did not distinguish between several specimens there associated with this name. As they are evidently not part of a single gathering, Art. 9.15 does not apply. Wijnands (*Bot. Commelins*: 41. 1983) stated that one of the Clifford specimens is labelled as lectotype but, though one is determined by him, it merely states that it is the specimen closest to 378.29 (LINN).

Rhus metopium Linnaeus, *Systema Naturae,* ed. 10, 2: 964. 1759.
["Habitat in America."] Sp. Pl., ed. 2, 1: 381 (1762). RCN: 2119.
Lectotype (Fawcett & Rendle, *Fl. Jamaica* 5: 9. 1926): *Browne*, Herb. Linn. No. 378.12 (LINN).
Current name: ***Metopium brownii*** (Jacq.) Urb. (Anacardiaceae).

Rhus radicans Linnaeus, *Species Plantarum* 1: 266. 1753.
"Habitat in Virginia, Canada." RCN: 2120.
Lectotype (Fernald in *Rhodora* 43: 589, pl. 683, f. 1. 1941): *Kalm*, Herb. Linn. No. 378.14 (LINN).
Current name: ***Toxicodendron radicans*** (L.) Kuntze (Anacardiaceae).
Note: See discussion by Gillis (in *Rhodora* 73: 190, f. 32. 1971).

Rhus succedanea Linnaeus, *Mantissa Plantarum Altera*: 221. 1771.
"Habitat in Japonia, China." RCN: 2117.
Type not designated.
Original material: [icon] in Kaempfer, Amoen. Exot. Fasc.: 794, 795. 1712.
Current name: ***Rhus succedanea*** L. (Anacardiaceae).

Rhus tomentosa Linnaeus, *Species Plantarum* 1: 266. 1753.
"Habitat ad Cap. b. spei." RCN: 2124.
Lectotype (Wijnands, *Bot. Commelins*: 42. 1983): Herb. Linn. No. 378.20 (LINN).
Current name: ***Rhus tomentosa*** L. (Anacardiaceae).
Note: Specific epithet spelled "tomentosum" in the protologue.

Rhus toxicodendron Linnaeus, *Species Plantarum* 1: 266. 1753.
"Habitat in Virginia, Canada." RCN: 2121.
Lectotype (Fernald in *Rhodora* 43: 589, pl. 685, f. 1, 2. 1941): Herb. Linn. No. 378.16, left specimen (LINN).
Current name: ***Toxicodendron pubescens*** Mill. (Anacardiaceae).
Note: See discussion by Gillis (in *Rhodora* 73: 402, f. 52. 1971).

Rhus typhina Linnaeus, *Centuria II Plantarum*: 14. 1756.
"Habitat in Virginia." RCN: 2113.
Lectotype (Reveal in *Taxon* 40: 489. 1991): Herb. Linn. No. 378.2 (LINN).
Current name: ***Rhus typhina*** L. (Anacardiaceae).
Note: Specific epithet spelled "typhinum" in the protologue.

Rhus vernix Linnaeus, *Species Plantarum* 1: 265. 1753.
"Habitat in America septentrionali, Iaponia." RCN: 2116.
Lectotype (designated here by Reveal): *Kalm*, Herb. Linn. No. 378.8 (LINN).
Current name: ***Toxicodendron vernix*** (L.) Kuntze (Anacardiaceae).

Ribes alpinum Linnaeus, *Species Plantarum* 1: 200. 1753.
"Habitat in Sueciae, Helvetiae, Angliae sepibus siccis." RCN: 1628.
Lectotype (Imkhanitskaya in *Bot. Zhurn.* 84(1): 120. 1999): Herb. Linn. No. 278.3 (LINN).
Current name: ***Ribes alpinum*** L. (Grossulariaceae).

Ribes cynosbati Linnaeus, *Species Plantarum* 1: 202. 1753.
"Habitat in Canada. Kalm." RCN: 1634.
Lectotype (Sinnott in *Rhodora* 87: 220. 1985): *Kalm*, Herb. Linn. No. 278.9 (LINN).
Current name: ***Ribes cynosbati*** L. (Grossulariaceae).

Ribes grossularia Linnaeus, *Species Plantarum* 1: 201. 1753.
"Habitat in Europa." RCN: 1631.
Type not designated.
Original material: Herb. Linn. No. 278.6 (LINN).
Current name: ***Ribes uva-crispa*** L. (Grossulariaceae).

Ribes nigrum Linnaeus, *Species Plantarum* 1: 201. 1753.
"Habitat in Suecia, Helvetia, Pensylvania." RCN: 1629.
Lectotype (Jonsell & Jarvis in *Nordic J. Bot.* 22: 73. 2002): Herb.
   Linn. No. 278.4 (LINN).
Current name: ***Ribes nigrum*** L. (Grossulariaceae).

Ribes oxyacanthoides Linnaeus, *Species Plantarum* 1: 201. 1753.
"Habitat in Canada." RCN: 1632.
Lectotype (Sinnott in *Rhodora* 87: 228. 1985): [icon] *"Grossularia
   Oxyacanthae foliis amplioribus &c. Pluk."* in Dillenius, Hort.
   Elth. 1: 166, t. 139, f. 166. 1732.
Current name: ***Ribes oxyacanthoides*** L. (Grossulariaceae).

Ribes reclinatum Linnaeus, *Species Plantarum* 1: 201. 1753.
"Habitat in Germania, Helvetia." RCN: 1630.
Lectotype (Imkhanitskaya in *Bot. Zhurn.* 84(1): 123. 1999): Herb.
   Linn. No. 278.5 (LINN).
Current name: ***Ribes uva-crispa*** L. subsp. ***reclinatum*** (L.) Rchb.
   (Grossulariaceae).

Ribes rubrum Linnaeus, *Species Plantarum* 1: 200. 1753.
"Habitat in Sueciae borealis." RCN: 1627.
Lectotype (Weber in Jarvis & al., *Regnum Veg.* 127: 82. 1993): Herb.
   Clifford: 82, *Ribes* 2 β (BM-000558193).
Generitype of *Ribes* Linnaeus (vide Hitchcock, *Prop. Brit. Bot.*: 134.
   1929).
Current name: ***Ribes rubrum*** L. (Grossulariaceae).
Note: Wilmott (in *J. Bot.* 56: 23. 1918) and Webb (in *Feddes Repert.*
   64: 26. 1961) discussed the identity of some elements but did not
   designate a type. Weber (in *Flor. Rundbr.* 27: 1–6. 1993) gives a
   more detailed justification of his typification, including an
   illustration of the type (Abb. 1).

Ribes uva-crispa Linnaeus, *Species Plantarum* 1: 201. 1753.
"Habitat in Europa boreali." RCN: 1633.
Lectotype (Jonsell & Jarvis in *Nordic J. Bot.* 22: 73. 2002): Herb.
   Burser XXIV: 10 (UPS).
Current name: ***Ribes uva-crispa*** L. (Grossulariaceae).

Riccia crystallina Linnaeus, *Species Plantarum* 2: 1138. 1753.
"Habitat in Europae locis subhumidis." RCN: 8148.
Lectotype (Perold in *Bothalia* 22: 187, f. 4B. 1992): [icon] *"Riccia
   minor, latifolia, pinguis, aspergine chrystallina perfusa"* in Micheli,
   Nov. Pl. Gen.: 107, t. 57, f. 3. 1729. – Typotype: Herb. Micheli,
   vol. IV: Riccia Ordo 2. n: 1 (FI).
Current name: ***Riccia crystallina*** L. (Ricciaceae).

Riccia fluitans Linnaeus, *Species Plantarum* 2: 1139. 1753.
"Habitat in Europae fossis, piscinis, ad ripas supra aquam extensa."
   RCN: 8151.
Type not designated.
Original material: Herb. Linn. No. 1271.3 (LINN); [icon] in Vaillant,
   Bot. Paris.: 56, t. 10, t. 3. 1727; [icon] in Dillenius, Hist. Musc.:
   514, t. 74, f. 47. 1741.
Current name: ***Riccia fluitans*** L. (Ricciaceae).
Note: See notes by Isoviita (in *Acta Bot. Fenn.* 89: 8. 1970) and Grolle
   (in *Feddes Repert.* 87: 227. 1976).

Riccia glauca Linnaeus, *Species Plantarum* 2: 1139. 1753, *typ. cons.*
"Habitat in Anglia, Italia, Gallia." RCN: 8150.
Lectotype (Isoviita & Grolle in *Taxon* 41: 568. 1992): [icon] *"Lichen
   minimus, foliis venosis bifariam vel trifariam se dividendo
   progredientibus"* in Dillenius, Hist. Musc.: 533, t. 78, f. 10. 1741. –
   Voucher: Herb. Dillenius (OXF; iso- H-SOL).
Generitype of *Riccia* Linnaeus, *nom. cons.*
Current name: ***Riccia glauca*** L. (Ricciaceae).

Riccia minima Linnaeus, *Species Plantarum* 2: 1139. 1753, *nom. rej.*
"Habitat in Europae inundatis." RCN: 8149.
Type not designated.
Original material: Herb. Burser XX: 70 (UPS); [icon] in Micheli, Nov.
   Pl. Gen.: 107, t. 57, f. 6. 1729; [icon] in Dillenius, Hist. Musc.:
   534, t. 78, f. 11. 1741.
Current name: ***Riccia sorocarpa*** Bisch. (Ricciaceae).

Riccia natans Linnaeus, *Systema Naturae*, ed. 10, 2: 1339. 1759.
RCN: 8152.
Type not designated.
Original material: [icon] in Dillenius, Hist. Musc.: 536, t. 78, f. 18.
   1741.
Current name: ***Ricciocarpos natans*** (L.) Corda (Ricciaceae).
Note: See comments by Isoviita (in *Acta Bot. Fenn.* 89: 23. 1970), and
   Grolle (in *Feddes Repert.* 87: 229. 1976), who indicated a Buddle
   collection in OXF as the holotype (iso- H-SOL). However, this
   material was not studied by Linnaeus and is not original material
   for the name.

Richardia scabra Linnaeus, *Species Plantarum* 1: 330. 1753.
"Habitat in Vera Cruce." RCN: 2548.
Lectotype (Lewis & Oliver in *Brittonia* 26: 282. 1974): Herb. Linn.
   No. 451.1 (LINN; iso- BM?).
Generitype of *Richardia* Linnaeus.
Current name: ***Richardia scabra*** L. (Rubiaceae).

Ricinus communis Linnaeus, *Species Plantarum* 2: 1007. 1753.
"Habitat in India utraque, Africa, Europa australi." RCN: 7298.
Lectotype (Seegeler, *Oil Pl. Ethiopia*: 212. 1983): Herb. Clifford: 450,
   Ricinus 1 (BM-000647441).
Generitype of *Ricinus* Linnaeus.
Current name: ***Ricinus communis*** L. (Euphorbiaceae).
Note: Fawcett & Rendle (*Fl. Jamaica* 4: 307. 1920) indicated 1142.1
   (LINN) as type but this was a post-1753 addition to the collection,
   from Brander, and not original material for the name.

Ricinus mappa Linnaeus, *Herbarium Amboinense*: 14. 1754.
["Habitat in Ternateis & Moluccis."] Sp. Pl., ed. 2, 2: 1430 (1763).
   RCN: 7300.
Lectotype (Merrill, *Interpret. Rumph. Herb. Amb.*: 29, 33, 319. 1917):
   [icon] *"Folium Mappae"* in Rumphius, Herb. Amboin. 3: 172, t.
   108. 1743.
Current name: ***Macaranga mappa*** (L.) Müll. Arg. (Euphorbiaceae).

Ricinus tanarius Linnaeus, *Herbarium Amboinense*: 14. 1754.
["Habitat in India."] Sp. Pl., ed. 2, 2: 1430 (1763). RCN: 7299.
Lectotype (Merrill, *Interpret. Rumph. Herb. Amb.*: 33, 320. 1917):
   [icon] *"Tanarius minor"* in Rumphius, Herb. Amboin. 3: 190, t.
   121. 1743.
Current name: ***Macaranga tanarius*** (L.) Müll. Arg.
   (Euphorbiaceae).

Ricotia aegyptiaca Linnaeus, *Species Plantarum*, ed. 2, 2: 912. 1763,
   nom. illeg.
"Habitat in Aegypto." RCN: 4758.
Replaced synonym: *Cardamine lunaria* L. (1753).
Lectotype (Burtt in Jarvis & al., *Regnum Veg.* 127: 82. 1993): Herb.
   Linn. No. 833.1, excl. fruiting material (LINN).
Generitype of *Ricotia*, Linnaeus, *nom. cons.*
Current name: ***Ricotia lunaria*** (L.) DC. (Brassicaceae).
Note: Ricotia Linnaeus, *nom. cons.* against *Scopolia* Adans., *nom. rej.*
   Ricotia aegyptiaca is an illegitimate renaming of *Cardamine
   lunaria* L. (1753), a name discussed by Marhold (in *Bot. J. Linn.
   Soc.* 121: 121. 1996).

Rivina humilis Linnaeus, *Species Plantarum* 1: 121. 1753.
"Habitat in Caribaeis, Jamaica, Barbados." RCN: 1006.
Lectotype (Wijnands, *Bot. Commelins*: 172. 1983): Herb. Clifford: 35, *Rivina* 1 (BM-000557794).
Generitype of *Rivina* Linnaeus.
Current name: ***Rivina humilis*** L. (Phytolaccaceae).
Note: Fawcett & Rendle (*Fl. Jamaica* 3: 156. 1914), followed by a number of later authors, indicated 163.1 (LINN) as type, but this sheet lacks Linnaeus' *Species Plantarum* number ("1") and appears to be a post-1753 addition to the collection, and not original material for the name. Smith (*Fl. Vitiensis Nova* 2: 262. 1981) suggested that Clifford material might make a suitable lectotype, subsequently formalised by Wijnands.

Rivina humilis Linnaeus var. **canescens** Linnaeus, *Species Plantarum* 1: 122. 1753.
RCN: 1006.
Lectotype (Wijnands, *Bot. Commelins*: 172. 1983): [icon] *"Amaranthus baccifer, Circeae foliis"* in Commelin, Hort. Med. Amstelod. Pl. Rar. 1: 127, t. 66. 1697.
Current name: ***Rivina humilis*** L. (Phytolaccaceae).

Rivina humilis Linnaeus var. **glabra** Linnaeus, *Species Plantarum* 1: 122. 1753.
RCN: 1007.
Neotype (Greuter in Greuter & al., *Fl. Republ. Cuba*, ser. A, 6(3): 13. 2002): Herb. Linn. No. 163.2 (LINN).
Current name: ***Rivina humilis*** L. (Phytolaccaceae).

Rivina humilis Linnaeus var. **scandens** Linnaeus, *Species Plantarum* 1: 122. 1753.
RCN: 1008.
Neotype (Greuter in Greuter & al., *Fl. Republ. Cuba*, ser. A, 6(3): 18. 2002): [icon] *"Rivina"* in Plumier, Nov. Pl. Amer.: t. 39, f. [3] a–g. 1703.
Current name: ***Trichostigma octandrum*** (L.) H. Walter (Phytolaccaceae).
Note: Although Kellogg (in Howard, *Fl. Lesser Antilles* 4: 193. 1988) stated "Type: Plumier", the precise element intended is unclear. Linnaeus' variety has Plumier's "Rivina scandens racemosa, amplis solani foliis, baccis violaceis" as its diagnosis, but the illustration (t. 39) accompanying this 1703 work is for the genus as a whole, including both this and "Rivina humilis racemosa, baccis puniceis", so it cannot be assumed to depict only one of them, and cannot be regarded as original material for either. However, in the absence of original material for the name, Greuter's treatment of the plate as the lectotype is accepted as a neotypification.

Rivina laevis Linnaeus, *Systema Naturae*, ed. 12, 2: 128; *Mantissa Plantarum*: 41. 1767.
"Habitat in America." RCN: 1007.
Lectotype (Kellogg in Howard, *Fl. Lesser Antilles* 4: 193. 1988): Herb. Linn. No. 163.2 (LINN).
Current name: ***Rivina humilis*** L. (Phytolaccaceae).

Rivina octandra Linnaeus, *Centuria II Plantarum*: 9. 1756.
"Habitat in America meridionali. Miller." RCN: 1008.
Lectotype (Fawcett & Rendle, *Fl. Jamaica* 3: 156. 1914): *Miller*, Herb. Linn. No. 163.3 (LINN).
Current name: ***Trichostigma octandrum*** (L.) H. Walter (Phytolaccaceae).

Rivina paniculata Linnaeus, *Centuria II Plantarum*: 9. 1756.
"Habitat in America meridionali. Miller." RCN: 1009.
Type not designated.

Original material: none traced.
Current name: ***Salvadora persica*** L. (Salvadoraceae).

Robinia acacia Linnaeus, *Systema Naturae*, ed. 10, 2: 1161. 1759, *nom. illeg.*
["Habitat in Virginia."] Sp. Pl. 2: 722 (1753). RCN: 5449.
Replaced synonym: *Robinia pseudoacacia* L. (1753).
Lectotype (Barrie in Jarvis & al., *Regnum Veg.* 127: 82. 1993): Herb. Clifford: 354, *Robinia* 1, sheet B (BM-000646538).
Current name: ***Robinia pseudoacacia*** L. (Fabaceae: Faboideae).
Note: Evidently an illegitimate replacement name for *Robinia pseudoacacia* L. (1753). Linnaeus' polynomial and species number ("1") are the same in both works.

Robinia caragana Linnaeus, *Species Plantarum* 2: 722. 1753.
"Habitat in Sibiria." RCN: 5453.
Lectotype (Yakovlev & Sviazeva in *Bot. Zhurn.* 70: 909, 913. 1985): *Gerber*, Herb. Linn. No. 913.5 (LINN).
Current name: ***Caragana arborescens*** Lam. (Fabaceae: Faboideae).
Note: Sanchir (in *Acta Sci. Nat. Univ. Neimongol* 30: 502. 1999) discussed the possible provenance of the type collection.

Robinia frutescens Linnaeus, *Species Plantarum*, ed. 2, 2: 1044. 1763, *nom. illeg.*
"Habitat in Sibiria, Tataria." RCN: 5455.
Replaced synonym: *Robinia frutex* L. (1753).
Type not designated.
Original material: as replaced synonym.
Current name: ***Caragana frutex*** (L.) K. Koch (Fabaceae: Faboideae).
Note: This is evidently an illegitimate renaming of *R. frutex* L. (1753).

Robinia frutex Linnaeus, *Species Plantarum* 2: 723. 1753.
"Habitat in Sibiria, Tataria." RCN: 5455.
Replaced synonym of: *Robinia frutescens* L. (1763), *nom. illeg.*
Type not designated.
Original material: *Gerber*, Herb. Linn. No. 913.6 (LINN).
Current name: ***Caragana frutex*** (L.) K. Koch (Fabaceae: Faboideae).

Robinia grandiflora Linnaeus, *Species Plantarum* 2: 722. 1753.
"Habitat in India." RCN: 5486.
Basionym of: *Aeschynomene grandiflora* (L.) L. (1763).
Lectotype (Ali in Nasir & Ali, *Fl. W. Pakistan* 100: 87. 1977): Herb. Linn. No. 922.1 (LINN).
Current name: ***Sesbania grandiflora*** (L.) Pers. (Fabaceae: Faboideae).
Note: Although Fawcett & Rendle (*Fl. Jamaica* 4: 24. 1920) indicated material in LINN as type, they did not distinguish between sheets 922.1 and 922.2 (which are evidently not part of a single gathering so Art. 9.15 does not apply). Ali appears to have been the first to make an unequivocal choice.

Robinia hispida Linnaeus, *Systema Naturae*, ed. 12, 2: 490; *Mantissa Plantarum*: 101. 1767, *nom. illeg.*
"Habitat in Carolina, Carthagena." RCN: 5451.
Replaced synonym: *Robinia sepium* Jacq. (1760).
Type not designated.
Current name: ***Gliricidia sepium*** (Jacq.) Steud. (Fabaceae: Faboideae).
Note: An illegitimate replacement name for *Robinia sepium* Jacq. (1760), with which *R. hispida* is therefore homotypic. Clausen (in *Gentes Herb.* 4: 287. 1940) was therefore incorrect to treat 913.2 (LINN) as the type (illustrating it as t. 185). Lavin & Sousa S. (in *Syst. Bot. Monogr.* 45: 93, 106. 1995) recognise both *Gliricidia sepium* (Jacq.) Steud. and *R. hispida* L. as separate species.

Robinia mitis Linnaeus, *Species Plantarum*, ed. 2, 2: 1044. 1763, *nom. illeg.*

"Habitat in India." RCN: 5452.

Replaced synonym: *Cytisus pinnatus* L. (1753).

Lectotype (Smith, *Fl. Vitiensis Nova* 3: 170. 1985): [icon] *"Phaseolo affinis Arbor Indica Coral dicta polyphyllos non spinosa, foliis mollibus subhirsutis"* in Plukenet, Phytographia: t. 104, f. 3. 1691; Almag. Bot.: 293. 1696.

Current name: **Millettia pinnata** (L.) Panigrahi (Fabaceae: Faboideae).

Note: Merrill (in *Philipp. J. Sci., C,* 5: 101. 1910) took up this name in place of *Cytisus pinnatus* L. (1753) and interpreted *R. mitis* via Herb. Linn. No. 913.3 (LINN). *Robinia mitis* is, however, an illegitimate renaming of *C. pinnatus* and consequently the two names are homotypic. Although annotated with "mitis" by Linnaeus, sheet 913.3 (LINN) is not original material for *C. pinnatus*. Smith appears to have been the first to make a formal choice of type for *C. pinnatus* (and hence *R. mitis*).

Robinia pseudoacacia Linnaeus, *Species Plantarum* 2: 722. 1753.

"Habitat in Virginia." RCN: 5449.

Replaced synonym of: *Robinia acacia* L. (1759), *nom. illeg.*

Lectotype (Barrie in Jarvis & al., *Regnum Veg.* 127: 82. 1993): Herb. Clifford: 354, *Robinia* 1, sheet B (BM-000646538).

Generitype of *Robinia* Linnaeus (vide Green, *Prop. Brit. Bot.*: 174. 1929).

Current name: **Robinia pseudoacacia** L. (Fabaceae: Faboideae).

Note: Polhill (in Bosser & al., *Fl. Mascareignes* 80: 80. 1990) indicated 913.1 (LINN) as type, but this sheet lacks the *Species Plantarum* number (i.e. "1") and is a post-1753 addition to the herbarium, and not original material for the name. Brummitt & Taylor (in *Taxon* 39: 303. 1990) discussed the orthography of the specific epithet, concluding that "pseudoacacia" is correct.

Robinia pygmaea Linnaeus, *Species Plantarum* 2: 723. 1753.

"Habitat in Sibiria." RCN: 5456.

Type not designated.

Original material: *Gerber?*, Herb. Linn. No. 913.7 (LINN); [icon] in Amman, Stirp. Rar. Ruth.: 204, t. 35. 1739.

Current name: **Caragana pygmaea** (L.) DC. (Fabaceae: Faboideae).

Robinia spinosa Linnaeus, *Mantissa Plantarum Altera*: 269. 1771.

"Habitat in Sibiriae montibus arenosis siccissimis Salengiae et Kiaechae." RCN: 5454.

Type not designated.

Original material: none traced.

Current name: **Caragana spinosa** (L.) Hornem. (Fabaceae: Faboideae).

Roella ciliata Linnaeus, *Species Plantarum* 1: 170. 1753.

"Habitat in Mauritania, Aethiopia." RCN: 1340.

Lectotype (Stearn, *Introd. Linnaeus' Sp. Pl.* (Ray Soc. ed.): 47. 1957): [icon] *"Roellia"* in Linnaeus, Hort. Cliff.: 492, t. 35. 1738.

Generitype of *Roella* Linnaeus (vide Hitchcock, *Prop. Brit. Bot.*: 131. 1929).

Current name: **Roella ciliata** L. (Campanulaceae).

Note: Adamson (in *J. S. African Bot.* 17: 132. 1951) indicated material in LINN as type but sheet 222.1 (LINN) lacks the *Species Plantarum* number (i.e. "21"), and is a post-1753 addition to the herbarium, and is not original material for the name.

Roella reticulata Linnaeus, *Species Plantarum* 1: 170. 1753.

"Habitat ad Caput b. spei." RCN: 1341.

Lectotype (Adamson in *J. S. African Bot.* 12: 108. 1946): [icon] *"Campanula Cap. B.S. foliis reticulatis spinosis"* in Petiver, Mus. Petiv. Cent. Prima: 21, f. 157. 1695–1703.

Current name: **Cullumia reticulata** (L.) Greuter & al. (Asteraceae).

Note: Adamson concluded that this name was typified by Petiver's cited plate, identifiable as *Cullumia ciliaris* (L.) R. Br. However, Adamson appeared to overlook that the basionym of the latter is *Atractylis ciliaris* L. (1759), over which *R. reticulata* would therefore have priority. Greuter & al. (in *Taxon* 54: 155. 2005) have subsequently discussed this difficulty and made the necessary combination.

Rondeletia americana Linnaeus, *Species Plantarum* 1: 172. 1753.

"Habitat in America." RCN: 1351.

Lectotype (Howard, *Fl. Lesser Antilles* 6: 455. 1989): [icon] *"Rondeletia foliis sessilibus"* in Plumier in Burman, Pl. Amer.: 237, t. 242, f. 1. 1760.

Generitype of *Rondeletia* Linnaeus (vide Hitchcock, *Prop. Brit. Bot.*: 131. 1929).

Current name: **Rondeletia americana** L. (Rubiaceae).

Rondeletia asiatica Linnaeus, *Species Plantarum* 1: 172. 1753.

"Habitat in Malabaria, Zeylona." RCN: 1352.

Lectotype (Ridsdale in Dassanayake & Clayton, *Revised Handb. Fl. Ceylon* 12: 205. 1998): [icon] *"Cupi"* in Rheede, Hort. Malab. 2: 37, t. 23. 1679.

Generitype of *Chomelia*, Linnaeus, *nom. rej.* (vide Dandy in *Taxon* 18: 470. 14 Aug 1969).

Current name: **Tarenna asiatica** (L.) Kunze ex K. Schum. (Rubiaceae).

Note: Chomelia Linnaeus, *nom. rej.* in favour of *Chomelia* Jacq.

Rondeletia repens Linnaeus, *Systema Naturae*, ed. 10, 2: 928. 1759. RCN: 1364.

Type not designated.

Original material: [icon] in Rheede, Hort. Malab. 10: 41, t. 21. 1690.

Current name: **Geophila repens** (L.) I.M. Johnst. (Rubiaceae).

Roridula dentata Linnaeus, *Genera Plantarum*, ed. 6: 577. 1764.

"Habitat ad Cap. b. Spei." RCN: 1648.

Lectotype (Barrie in Jarvis & al., *Regnum Veg.* 127: 82. 1993): Herb. Linn. No. 284.1 (LINN).

Generitype of *Roridula* Linnaeus.

Current name: **Roridula dentata** L. (Roridulaceae).

Rosa alba Linnaeus, *Species Plantarum* 1: 492. 1753.

"Habitat in Europa." RCN: 3747.

Lectotype (Maskew & Primavesi in Cafferty & Jarvis in *Taxon* 51: 543. 2002): Herb. Linn. No. 652.44 (LINN).

Current name: **Rosa × alba** L. (Rosaceae).

Note: Maskew & Primavesi (in *Watsonia* 25: 412. 2005) discuss the identity of the original elements for the name and the possible parentage of the hybrid to which it applies.

Rosa alpina Linnaeus, *Species Plantarum*, ed. 2, 1: 703. 1762.

"Habitat in alpibus Helvetiae." RCN: 4743.

Lectotype (Nepi in Cafferty & Jarvis in *Taxon* 51: 543. 2002): Scopoli 78, Herb. Linn. No. 652.28 (LINN).

Current name: **Rosa pendulina** L. (Rosaceae).

Rosa canina Linnaeus, *Species Plantarum* 1: 491. 1753.

"Habitat in Europa." RCN: 3744.

Lectotype (Zieliński in Rechinger, *Fl. Iranica* 152: 22. 1982): Herb. Linn. No. 652.31 (LINN).

Current name: **Rosa canina** L. (Rosaceae).

Note: Zieliński made a clear choice of type and he has been followed by most, if not all later authors (see Heath in *Taxon* 40: 95. 1991; *Calyx* 2: 129. 1992; but see also rebuttal by Jarvis in *Taxon* 41: 63. 1992).

Rosa carolina Linnaeus, *Species Plantarum* 1: 492. 1753.
"Habitat in Carolina." RCN: 3737.
Lectotype (Heath in *Calyx* 2: 51, 80. 1992): [icon] *"Rosa Carolina fragrans, foliis mediotenus serratis"* in Dillenius, Hort. Eltham. 2: 325, t. 245, f. 316. 1732.
Current name: ***Rosa carolina*** L. (Rosaceae).

Rosa centifolia Linnaeus, *Species Plantarum* 1: 491. 1753.
"Habitat in Europa." RCN: 3741.
Lectotype (Nepi in Cafferty & Jarvis in *Taxon* 51: 543. 2002): Herb. Linn. No. 652.18 (LINN).
Current name: ***Rosa × centifolia*** L. (Rosaceae).
Note: Heath (in *Calyx* 1: 169–170. 1992; 2: 125. 1992) discussed the name, and its status as generitype, but did not typify it. Ghora & Panigrahi (*Fam. Rosaceae India* 2: 323, pl. 62. 1995) illustrated 652.18 (LINN).

Rosa cinnamomea Linnaeus, *Species Plantarum* 1: 491. 1753, *typ. cons.*
"Habitat in Helvetia." RCN: 3733.
Conserved type (Rowley in Jarvis in *Taxon* 41: 568. 1992): Herb. Linn. No. 652.8 (LINN).
Generitype of *Rosa* Linnaeus, *nom. cons.*
Current name: ***Rosa cinnamomea*** L. (Rosaceae).
Note: Rosa cinnamomea, with the type designated by Rowley, was proposed as conserved type of the genus by Jarvis (in *Taxon* 41: 568. 1992). This was eventually approved by the General Committee (see review of the history of this proposal by Barrie, *l.c.* 55: 795–796. 2006).

Rosa eglanteria Linnaeus, *Species Plantarum* 1: 491. 1753, *nom. utique rej.*
"Habitat in Helvetia, anglia [sic]." RCN: 3731.
Lectotype (Heath in *Calyx* 1: 153. 1992): [icon] *"Rosa Eglenteria"* in Tabernaemontanus, Eicones Pl.: 1087. 1590.
Current name: ***Rosa rubiginosa*** L. (Rosaceae).
Note: See an extremely detailed discussion by Reichert (in *Gleditschia* 24: 18–22. 1997), who also illustrates the type (p. 21). The name has subsequently been formally rejected.

Rosa gallica Linnaeus, *Species Plantarum* 1: 492. 1753.
"Habitat in Gallia." RCN: 3742.
Lectotype (Jafri in Jafri & El-Gadi, *Fl. Libya* 31: 26. 1977): Herb. Linn. No. 652.26 (LINN).
Current name: ***Rosa gallica*** L. (Rosaceae).
Note: Jafri's type choice is clear, though there has been some subsequent discussion as to its appropriateness (see Heath in *Calyx* 4: 60–61. 1994; Reichert in *Gleditschia* 24: 13, 15–16. 1997). Ghora & Panigrahi (*Fam. Rosaceae India* 2: 316–322. 1995) illustrate the type (as pl. 60A).

Rosa gallica Linnaeus var. **versicolor** Linnaeus, *Species Plantarum*, ed. 2, 1: 704. 1762.
RCN: 3742.
Lectotype (Heath in *Calyx* 4: 59. 1994): [icon] *"Rosa praenestina, variegata plena"* in Miller, Fig. Pl. Gard. Dict. 2: 148, t. 221, f. 2. 1758.
Current name: ***Rosa damascena*** Mill. (Rosaceae).

Rosa indica Linnaeus, *Species Plantarum* 1: 492. 1753.
"Habitat in China." RCN: 3745.
Lectotype (Heath in *Calyx* 2: 51. 1992): [icon] *"Rosa Chusan, glabra, Juniperi fructu"* in Petiver, Gazophyl. Nat.: 56, t. 35, f. 11. 1702–1709.
Current name: ***Rosa cymosa*** Tratt. (Rosaceae).

Note: This name has been widely treated as a *nomen ambiguum*. However, no proposal has been made for its formal rejection.

Rosa millesia Linnaeus, *Amoenitates Academicae* 4: 484. 1759.
Type not designated.
Original material: none traced.
Current name: ***Rosa gallica*** L. (Rosaceae).
Note: Stearn (in Geck & Pressler, *Festschr. Claus Nissen*: 641. 1974) discussed this name, concluding that it probably relates to a form of *R. gallica* L.

Rosa moschata Linnaeus, *Amoenitates Academicae* 4: 484. 1759, *nom. nud.*
Type not relevant.
Note: As noted by Stearn (in Geck & Pressler, *Festschr. Claus Nissen*: 632. 1974), this is a *nomen nudum*.

Rosa pendulina Linnaeus, *Species Plantarum* 1: 492. 1753.
"Habitat in Europa." RCN: 3746.
Lectotype (Heath in *Calyx* 1: 165. 1992): [icon] *"Rosa Sanguisorbae majoris folio, fructu longo pendulo ex N. A."* in Dillenius, Hort. Eltham. 2: 325, t. 245, f. 317. 1732.
Current name: ***Rosa pendulina*** L. (Rosaceae).

Rosa pimpinellifolia Linnaeus, *Systema Naturae*, ed. 10, 2: 1062. 1759.
["Habitat forte in Europa."] Sp. Pl., ed. 2, 1: 703 (1762). RCN: 3735.
Lectotype (Zieliński in Rechinger, *Fl. Iranica* 152: 11. 1982): Herb. Linn. No. 652.12 (LINN).
Current name: ***Rosa spinosissima*** L. var. ***pimpinellifolia*** (L.) Hook. f. (Rosaceae).
Note: Zieliński's type choice is clear and has priority but Heath (in *Calyx* 2: 51; 81. 1992) incorrectly treated a cited Dillenian figure as the holotype.

Rosa rubiginosa Linnaeus, *Mantissa Plantarum Altera*: 564. 1771.
"Habitat in Europa australi. Mygind." RCN: 3732.
Lectotype (Ghora & Panigrahi, *Fam. Rosaceae India* 2: 240. 1995): *Mygind 8*, Herb. Linn. No. 652.6 (LINN), see p. 223.
Current name: ***Rosa rubiginosa*** L. (Rosaceae).
Note: Turland (in *Taxon* 45: 565. 1996) independently made the same choice of type as Ghora & Panigrahi. See an extremely detailed discussion by Reichert (in *Gleditschia* 24: 18–22. 1997).

Rosa sempervirens Linnaeus, *Species Plantarum* 1: 492. 1753.
"Habitat in Germania." RCN: 3740.
Lectotype (Heath in *Calyx* 2: 51. 1992): [icon] *"Rosa sempervirens Jungerm. Clus."* in Dillenius, Hort. Eltham. 2: 326, t. 246, f. 318. 1732.
Current name: ***Rosa sempervirens*** L. (Rosaceae).
Note: Stearn (in de la Roche & al., *Comment. Les Roses*: 344. 1978) suggested that the lectotype "could be" the cited Dillenius plate, and this was later formalised by Heath.

Rosa sinica Linnaeus, *Systema Vegetabilium*, ed. 13: 394. 1774.
RCN: 3739.
Lectotype (Heath in *Calyx* 3: 1. 1993): Herb. Linn. No. 652.37 (LINN).
Current name: ***Rosa × sinica*** L. (Rosaceae).

Rosa spinosissima Linnaeus, *Species Plantarum* 1: 491. 1753.
"Habitat in Europa." RCN: 3736.
Lectotype (Turland in Cafferty & Jarvis in *Taxon* 51: 543. 2002): Herb. Burser XXV: 31 (UPS).
Current name: ***Rosa spinosissima*** L. var. ***spinosissima*** (Rosaceae).

R

Rosa villosa Linnaeus, *Species Plantarum* 1: 491. 1753.
"Habitat in Europa australi." RCN: 3738.
Lectotype (Nepi & al. in Jonsell & Jarvis in *Nordic J. Bot.* 22: 76. 2002): Herb. Burser XXV: 33 (UPS).
Current name: ***Rosa villosa*** L. (Rosaceae).

Rosmarinus officinalis Linnaeus, *Species Plantarum* 1: 23. 1753.
"Habitat in Hispania, G. narbonensi, Galilaea." RCN: 181.
Lectotype (Hedge in Jarvis & al., *Regnum Veg.* 127: 82. 1993): Herb. Clifford: 14, *Rosmarinus* 1 α, sheet 5 (BM-000557615).
Generitype of *Rosmarinus* Linnaeus.
Current name: ***Rosmarinus officinalis*** L. (Lamiaceae).
Note: Siddiqi (in Jafri & El-Gadi, *Fl. Libya* 118: 30. 1985) and Hedge (in Ali & Nasir, *Fl. Pakistan* 192: 26. 1990) treated 41.2 and 41.1 (LINN) respectively as the type. However, neither sheet appears to have been present in the herbarium in 1753, and Hedge subsequently designated Clifford material as the lectotype.

Rotala verticillaris Linnaeus, *Mantissa Plantarum Altera*: 175. 1771.
"Habitat in India orientali." RCN: 278.
Lectotype (Cook in *Boissiera* 29: 23. 1979): Herb. Linn. No. 52.1 (LINN).
Generitype of *Rotala* Linnaeus.
Current name: ***Rotala verticillaris*** L. (Lythraceae).

Royena glabra Linnaeus, *Species Plantarum* 1: 397. 1753.
"Habitat ad Cap. b. Spei." RCN: 3130.
Type not designated.
Original material: Herb. A. van Royen No. 941.6–396 [icon] (L); Herb. Clifford: 149, *Royena* 2 (BM); [icon] in Commelin, Hort. Med. Amstelod. Pl. Rar. 1: 125, t. 65. 1697; [icon] in Plukenet, Phytographia: t. 321, f. 4. 1694; Almag. Bot.: 391. 1696.
Current name: ***Diospyros glabra*** (L.) De Winter (Ebenaceae).
Note: De Winter (in Dyer et al., *Fl. Southern Africa* 26: 63. 1963) indicated 570.3 (LINN) as lectotype, but this collection lacks the relevant *Species Plantarum* number (i.e. "2") and was a post-1753 addition to the herbarium, and is not original material for the name. This was noted by Wijnands (*Bot. Commelins*: 94. 1983), who also suggested that there was a good specimen in the Clifford herbarium, but did not designate it as the type.

Royena hirsuta Linnaeus, *Species Plantarum* 1: 397. 1753.
"Habitat ad Cap. b. Spei." RCN: 3131.
Neotype (de Winter in Dyer & al., *Fl. Southern Africa* 26: 64. 1963): *Thunberg 383*, Herb. Linn. No. 570.7 (LINN).
Current name: ***Diospyros austroafricana*** De Winter (Ebenaceae).
Note: De Winter treated 570.7 (LINN) as the type of this name. While it was clearly not available to Linnaeus in 1753, there is no original material in existence so de Winter's choice is treated as a neotypification (Art. 9.8).

Royena lucida Linnaeus, *Species Plantarum* 1: 397. 1753.
"Habitat in Cap. b. Spei." RCN: 3128.
Lectotype (de Winter in Dyer & al., *Fl. Southern Africa* 26: 69. 1963): Herb. Linn. No. 570.1 (LINN).
Generitype of *Royena* Linnaeus (vide Hitchcock, *Prop. Brit. Bot.*: 154. 1929).
Current name: ***Diospyros whyteana*** (Hiern) F. White (Ebenaceae).
Note: There are no grounds for the rejection of de Winter's type choice by Wijnands (*Bot. Commelins*: 94. 1983) because the designated type was original material for the name.

Royena villosa Linnaeus, *Systema Naturae*, ed. 12, 2: 302. 1767.
"Habitat ad Cap. b. spei. Dav. Royen." RCN: 3129.

Lectotype (de Winter in Dyer & al., *Fl. Southern Africa* 26: 79. 1963): Herb. Linn. No. 570.2 (LINN).
Current name: ***Diospyros villosa*** (L.) De Winter (Ebenaceae).

Rubia angustifolia Linnaeus, *Systema Naturae*, ed. 12, 2: 119; *Mantissa Plantarum*: 39. 1767.
"Habitat in Minorca. Richard." RCN: 893.
Neotype (Cardona & Sierra-Ràfols in *Anales Jard. Bot. Madrid* 37: 561. 1981): *Willkomm*, Herb. Balear. No. 329 (COI).
Current name: ***Rubia angustifolia*** L. (Rubiaceae).
Note: Cardona & Sierra-Ràfols typify the name in the sense of *R. peregrina* var. *balearica* Willk., a taxon absent from Menorca. López González (in *Anales Jard. Bot. Madrid* 53: 133–135. 1995) therefore rejects their neotypification, arguing that the name must apply to *R. peregrina* var. *longifolia* (Poir.) Gren. López González does not propose a new neotype but appears to conclude that the name must now be regarded as ambiguous, and takes up *R. balearica* (Willk.) G. López for the Menorcan plant (syn. *R. angustifolia* auct. non L.). See review by Rosselló & Sáez (in *Anales Jard. Bot. Madrid* 55: 479–480. 1997; *Collect. Bot. (Barcelona)* 25: 159. 2000).

Rubia cordifolia Linnaeus, *Systema Naturae*, ed. 12, 3: 229. 1768.
"Habitat in Maiorca. Gerard." RCN: 894.
Type not designated.
Original material: Herb. Linn. No. 131.7 (LINN).
Current name: ***Rubia cordifolia*** L. (Rubiaceae).
Note: There have been difficulties in interpreting this name, partly because Linnaeus originally described it as coming from Majorca, and later (in *Mant. Pl. Alt.*: 197. 1771) modified this to "Sibiria, China") – see Hara & Kurosawa (in *Sci. Rep. Tôhoku Univ., Ser. 4, Biol.* 29: 258. 1963) and Verdcourt (in *Kew Bull.* 30: 322. 1975). Although Ehrendorfer & Schönbeck-Temesy (in Rechinger, *Fl. Iranica* 176: 52. 2005) indicated 131.7 (LINN) as type, they did not state "designated here" or an equivalent as required by Art. 7.11.

Rubia lucida Linnaeus, *Systema Naturae*, ed. 12, 2: 732. 1767.
"Habitat in Majorca. D. Richard." RCN: 892.
Lectotype (Natali & Jeanmonod in Jeanmonod, *Compl. Prodr. Fl. Corse, Rubiaceae*: 167. 2000): Herb. Linn. No. 131.5 (LINN).
Current name: ***Rubia peregrina*** L. subsp. ***longifolia*** (Poir.) O. Bolòs (Rubiaceae).

Rubia peregrina Linnaeus, *Species Plantarum* 1: 109. 1753.
"Habitat – – – –" RCN: 891.
Lectotype (Natali & Jeanmonod in Jeanmonod, *Compl. Prodr. Fl. Corse, Rubiaceae*: 162. 2000): Herb. A. van Royen No. 908.221–523 (L).
Current name: ***Rubia peregrina*** L. (Rubiaceae).

Rubia tinctorum Linnaeus, *Species Plantarum* 1: 109. 1753.
"Habitat Monspelii & ad Danubium." RCN: 890.
Lectotype (Natali in Jarvis & al., *Regnum Veg.* 127: 83. 1993): Herb. Clifford: 35, *Rubia* 1 β (BM-000557792).
Generitype of *Rubia* Linnaeus (vide Hitchcock, *Prop. Brit. Bot.*: 124. 1929).
Current name: ***Rubia tinctorum*** L. (Rubiaceae).
Note: Nazimuddin & Qaiser (in Nasir & Ali, *Fl. Pakistan* 190: 46. 1989) indicated unspecified material in LINN as type. They did not distinguish between sheets 131.1 and 131.2 (LINN) but, as they are not part of the same gathering, Art. 9.15 does not apply.

Rubus arcticus Linnaeus, *Species Plantarum* 1: 494. 1753.
"Habitat in Bothnia Sueciae, Sibiria, Canada." RCN: 3766.
Lectotype (Chater & al. in Edees & Newton, *Brambles Brit. Isles*: 17. 1988): Herb. Linn. No. 653.18 (LINN).
Current name: ***Rubus arcticus*** L. (Rosaceae).

Rubus caesius Linnaeus, *Species Plantarum* 1: 493. 1753.
"Habitat in Europae dumetis." RCN: 3759.
Lectotype (van de Beek in *Meded. Bot. Mus. Herb. Rijks Univ. Utrecht* 415: 111. 1974): Herb. Linn. No. 653.7 (LINN).
Current name: ***Rubus caesius*** L. (Rosaceae).

Rubus canadensis Linnaeus, *Species Plantarum* 1: 494. 1753.
"Habitat in Canada. Kalm." RCN: 3761.
Lectotype (Bailey in *Gentes Herb.* 1: 182, f. 82. 1923): *Kalm*, Herb. Linn. No. 653.10 (LINN).
Current name: ***Rubus canadensis*** L. (Rosaceae).
Note: Bailey (in *Gentes Herb.* 5: 472–476. 1944) provided a later, extensive review.

Rubus chamaemorus Linnaeus, *Species Plantarum* 1: 494. 1753.
"Habitat in Sueciae paludibus uliginosis, turfosis frequens." RCN: 3767.
Lectotype (Chater & al. in Edees & Newton, *Brambles Brit. Isles*: 16. 1988): Herb. Linn. No. 653.21 (LINN).
Current name: ***Rubus chamaemorus*** L. (Rosaceae).

Rubus dalibarda Linnaeus, *Species Plantarum*, ed. 2, 1: 708. 1762, *nom. illeg.*
["Habitat in Canada. Kalm."] Sp. Pl. 1: 491 (1753). RCN: 3768.
Replaced synonym: *Dalibarda repens* L. (1753).
Lectotype (Reveal in Jarvis & al., *Regnum Veg.* 127: 41. 1993): *Kalm*, Herb. Linn. No. 653.24 (LINN).
Current name: ***Dalibarda repens*** L. (Rosaceae).
Note: An illegitimate replacement name for *Dalibarda repens* L. (1753).

Rubus fruticosus Linnaeus, *Species Plantarum* 1: 493. 1753, *typ. cons.*
"Habitat in sepibus praesertim maritimis Europae." RCN: 3760.
Conserved type (van de Beek in *Meded. Bot. Mus. Herb. Rijks Univ. Utrecht* 415: 59. 1974; Weber in *Bot. Jahrb. Syst.* 106: 293, f. 1. 1986): Herb. Linn. No. 653.9, inflorescence only (LINN).
Generitype of *Rubus* Linnaeus, *nom. cons.*
Current name: ***Rubus fruticosus*** L. (Rosaceae).
Note: Rubus fruticosus, with the type designated by Weber, was proposed as conserved type of the genus by Jarvis (in *Taxon* 41: 573. 1992). This was eventually approved by the General Committee (see review of the history of this proposal by Barrie, *l.c.* 55: 795–796. 2006).
  Rubus fruticosus has long been treated as an ambiguous name, and its type is identifiable with *R. plicatus* Weihe & Nees. Weber has provided a review, and restricted van de Beek's (1974) type choice to the inflorescence only.

Rubus hispidus Linnaeus, *Species Plantarum* 1: 493. 1753.
"Habitat in Canada. Kalm." RCN: 3756.
Lectotype (Bailey in *Gentes Herb.* 1: 249. 1925): *Kalm*, Herb. Linn. No. 653.4 (LINN).
Current name: ***Rubus hispidus*** L. (Rosaceae).

Rubus idaeus Linnaeus, *Species Plantarum* 1: 492. 1753.
"Habitat in Europae lapidosis." RCN: 3754.
Lectotype (Chater & al. in Edees & Newton, *Brambles Brit. Isles*: 18. 1988): Herb. Linn. No. 653.1 (LINN).
Current name: ***Rubus idaeus*** L. (Rosaceae).

Rubus jamaicensis Linnaeus, *Systema Naturae*, ed. 12, 2: 349; *Mantissa Plantarum*: 75. 1767.
"Habitat in Jamaica proximisque." RCN: 3758.
Lectotype (Adams in Cafferty & Jarvis in *Taxon* 51: 543. 2002): [icon] *"Rubus foliis longioribus, subtus molli lanugine obductis & incanis,*

flore & fructu minoribus" in Sloane, Voy. Jamaica 2: 109, t. 213, f. 1. 1725. – Typotype: Herb. Sloane 7: 51 (BM-SL).
Current name: ***Rubus jamaicensis*** L. (Rosaceae).

Rubus japonicus Linnaeus, *Mantissa Plantarum Altera*: 245. 1771.
"Habitat in Japonia." RCN: 3764.
Lectotype (Cullen in Cafferty & Jarvis in *Taxon* 51: 543. 2002): Herb. Linn. No. 653.15 (LINN).
Current name: ***Kerria japonica*** (L.) DC. (Rosaceae).

Rubus moluccanus Linnaeus, *Species Plantarum* 2: 1197. 1753.
"Habitat in Amboina." RCN: 3763.
Lectotype (Merrill, *Interpret. Rumph. Herb. Amb.*: 31, 245–246. 1917): [icon] *"Rubus Moluccus latifolius"* in Rumphius, Herb. Amboin. 5: 88, t. 47, f. 2. 1747.
Current name: ***Rubus moluccanus*** L. (Rosaceae).

Rubus occidentalis Linnaeus, *Species Plantarum* 1: 493. 1753.
"Habitat in Canada. Kalm." RCN: 3755.
Lectotype (Widrlechner in *Castanea* 63: 423. 1998): *Kalm*, Herb. Linn. No. 653.2 (LINN).
Current name: ***Rubus occidentalis*** L. (Rosaceae).
Note: Although Bailey (in *Gentes Herb.* 1: 147. 1923; 5: 883. 1945) noted the existence of 653.2 and 652.3 (LINN), and interpreted the name from the former and the description, he did not explicitly call it the type.

Rubus odoratus Linnaeus, *Species Plantarum* 1: 494. 1753.
"Habitat in Canada." RCN: 3762.
Lectotype (Widrlechner in *Castanea* 63: 420. 1998): Herb. Linn. No. 653.13 (LINN).
Current name: ***Rubus odoratus*** L. (Rosaceae).

Rubus parvifolius Linnaeus, *Species Plantarum* 2: 1197. 1753.
"Habitat in India. Osbeck." RCN: 3757.
Lectotype (Zandee & Kalkman in *Blumea* 27: 90. 1981): Herb. Linn. No. 653.5 (LINN).
Current name: ***Rubus parvifolius*** L. (Rosaceae).

Rubus saxatilis Linnaeus, *Species Plantarum* 1: 494. 1753.
"Habitat in Europae collibus lapidosis." RCN: 3765.
Lectotype (Chater & al. in Edees & Newton, *Brambles Brit. Isles*: 17. 1988): Herb. Linn. No. 653.16 (LINN).
Current name: ***Rubus saxatilis*** L. (Rosaceae).

Rudbeckia angustifolia (Linnaeus) Linnaeus, *Species Plantarum*, ed. 2, 2: 1281. 1763.
"Habitat in Virginia." RCN: 6555.
Basionym: *Coreopsis angustifolia* L. (1753).
Lectotype (Reveal in Jarvis & Turland in *Taxon* 47: 359. 1998): *Clayton 667* (BM-000051730).
Current name: ***Helianthus angustifolia*** L. (Asteraceae).
Note: As noted by Reveal, Fernald (in *Rhodora* 49: 190, pl. 1084, f. 1. 1947) treated *Clayton 667* as the type of *Helianthus angustifolius* L. (1753), a name for which it is not original material.

Rudbeckia hirta Linnaeus, *Species Plantarum* 2: 907. 1753.
"Habitat in Virginia, Canada." RCN: 6552.
Lectotype (Fernald & Schubert in *Rhodora* 50: 173, pl. 1102. 1948): Herb. Linn. No. 1025.4 (LINN).
Current name: ***Rudbeckia hirta*** L. (Asteraceae).
Note: Rudbeckia hirta L. was treated as the generitype by Britton & Brown (*Ill. Fl. N. U. S.*, ed. 2, 3: 469. 1913; see McNeill & al. in *Taxon* 36: 382. 1987). However, under Art. 10.5, Ex. 7 (a voted

R

example) of the Vienna Code, this is a type choice made under the American Code and is to be replaced under Art. 10.5b by Green's choice (*Prop. Brit. Bot.*: 183. 1929) of *R. laciniata* L.

Rudbeckia laciniata Linnaeus, *Species Plantarum* 2: 906. 1753.
"Habitat in Virginia, Canada." RCN: 6550.
Type not designated.
Original material: [icon] in Cornut, Canad. Pl. Hist.: 178, 179. 1635; [icon] in Morison, Pl. Hist. Univ. 3: 22, s. 6, t. 6, f. 53, 54. 1699.
Generitype of *Rudbeckia* Linnaeus (vide Green, *Prop. Brit. Bot.*: 183. 1929).
Current name: ***Rudbeckia laciniata*** L. (Asteraceae).
Note: Rudbeckia hirta L. was treated as the generitype by Britton & Brown (*Ill. Fl. N. U. S.*, ed. 2, 3: 469. 1913; see McNeill & al. in *Taxon* 36: 382. 1987). However, under Art. 10.5, Ex. 7 (a voted example) of the Vienna Code, this is a type choice made under the American Code and is to be replaced under Art. 10.5b by Green's choice (*Prop. Brit. Bot.*: 183. 1929) of *R. laciniata* L.
    Fernald & Schubert (in *Rhodora* 50: 171. 1948) referred to a "photograph of the TYPE" but did not indicate which of the possible collections in London (Clifford, Clayton or LINN) it might be. Jarvis & al. (*Regnum Veg.* 127: 83. 1993) erroneously attributed typification to Fernald & Schubert.

Rudbeckia oppositifolia Linnaeus, *Species Plantarum* 2: 907. 1753.
"Habitat in Virginia." RCN: 6554.
Lectotype (Reveal in *Taxon* 32: 653. 1983): *Clayton 609* (BM-000051688).
Current name: ***Heliopsis helianthoides*** (L.) Sweet (Asteraceae).

Rudbeckia purpurea Linnaeus, *Species Plantarum* 2: 907. 1753, *nom. cons.*
"Habitat in Virginia, Carolina." RCN: 6553.
Conserved type (Binns & al. in *Taxon* 50: 1199. 2002 [2001]): U.S.A. Arkansas, "Echinacea serotina Arkansa", *Nuttall, s.n.* (BM-000541360).
Current name: ***Echinacea purpurea*** (L.) Moench (Asteraceae).

Rudbeckia triloba Linnaeus, *Species Plantarum* 2: 907. 1753.
"Habitat in Virginia." RCN: 6551.
Type not designated.
Original material: Herb. Linn. No. 74 (SBT); *Clayton 657* (BM); [icon] in Plukenet, Phytographia: t. 22, f. 2. 1691; Almag. Bot.: 100. 1696.
Current name: ***Rudbeckia triloba*** L. var. ***triloba*** (Asteraceae).

Ruellia antipoda Linnaeus, *Species Plantarum* 2: 635. 1753.
"Habitat in Indiis." RCN: 4617.
Lectotype (Philcox in *Kew Bull.* 17: 482. 1964): Herb. Hermann 2: 9, No. 235, upper specimen (BM-000621524).
Current name: ***Lindernia antipoda*** (L.) Alston (Scrophulariaceae).

Ruellia biflora Linnaeus, *Species Plantarum* 2: 635. 1753.
"Habitat in Carolina." RCN: 4613.
Type not designated.
Original material: Herb. Linn. No. 804.10? (LINN).
Current name: ***Calophanes* sp.** (Acanthaceae).
Note: The application of this name appears to be uncertain.

Ruellia blechum Linnaeus, *Systema Naturae*, ed. 10, 2: 1120. 1759.
["Habitat in America meridionali."] Sp. Pl., ed. 2, 2: 885 (1763). RCN: 4606.
Lectotype (Wasshausen in Jansen-Jacobs, *Fl. Guianas*, ser. A, 23: 20. 2006): [icon] *"Prunella elatior flore albo"* in Sloane, Voy. Jamaica 1: 173, t. 109, f. 1. 1707. – Voucher: Herb. Sloane 3: 56 (BM-SL).

Current name: ***Blechum pyramidatum*** (Lam.) Urb. (Acanthaceae).
Note: Daniel (in *Proc. Calif. Acad. Sci.* 48: 255. 1995) discussed the typification of this name, concluding that only one or the other of the cited Sloane and Plumier illustrations would be a logical choice as lectotype.

Ruellia ciliaris Linnaeus, *Systema Naturae,* ed. 12, 2: 424; *Mantissa Plantarum*: 89. 1767.
"Habitat in India." RCN: 4612.
Neotype (Vollesen, *Blepharis*: 96. 2000): *Garcin s.n.* (G).
Current name: ***Blepharis ciliaris*** (L.) B.L. Burtt (Acanthaceae).
Note: Vollesen (*Blepharis*: 96. 2000) indicates Garcin material in G (unseen by him) as the type. Such material may well not have been seen by Linnaeus so should probably be treated as a neotype.

Ruellia clandestina Linnaeus, *Species Plantarum* 2: 634. 1753.
"Habitat in Barbados." RCN: 4608.
Type not designated.
Original material: Herb. Linn. No. 804.4 (LINN); Herb. Clifford: 318, *Ruellia* 2 (BM); [icon] in Dillenius, Hort. Eltham. 2: 328, t. 248, f. 320. 1732.
Current name: ***Ruellia tuberosa*** L. (Acanthaceae).

Ruellia crispa Linnaeus, *Species Plantarum* 2: 635. 1753.
"Habitat in India. Osbeck." RCN: 4614.
Type not designated.
Original material: *Osbeck 116*, Herb. Linn. No. 804.11 (LINN); [icon] in Petiver, Gazophyl. Nat.: 7, t. 72, f. 2. 1709.
Current name: ***Hemigraphis crispa*** (L.) T. Anderson (Acanthaceae).
Note: See comments on 804.11 (LINN) by Hansen & Fox Maule (in *Bot. J. Linn. Soc.* 67: 205. 1973).

Ruellia paniculata Linnaeus, *Species Plantarum* 2: 635. 1753.
"Habitat in Jamaica." RCN: 4609.
Type not designated.
Original material: Herb. Clifford: 318, *Ruellia* 3 (BM); [icon] in Sloane, Voy. Jamaica 1: 158, t. 100, f. 2. 1707 – Voucher: Herb. Sloane 3: 25 (BM-SL).
Current name: ***Ruellia paniculata*** L. (Acanthaceae).

Ruellia repanda Linnaeus, *Species Plantarum*, ed. 2, 2: 886. 1763.
"Habitat in Java." RCN: 4615.
Type not designated.
Original material: Herb. Linn. No. 804.12 (LINN); [icon] in Rumphius, Herb. Amboin. 6: 30, t. 13, f. B. 1750.
Current name: ***Ruellia repanda*** L. (Acanthaceae).

Ruellia repens Linnaeus, *Systema Naturae,* ed. 12, 2: 424; *Mantissa Plantarum*: 89. 1767.
"Habitat in India." RCN: 4618.
Lectotype (Hochreutiner in *Candollea* 5: 230. 1936): Herb. Linn. No. 804.18 (LINN).
Current name: ***Ruellia repens*** L. (Acanthaceae).

Ruellia ringens Linnaeus, *Species Plantarum* 2: 635. 1753.
"Habitat in India." RCN: 4616.
Lectotype (Hansen in Nicolson & al., *Interpret. Van Rheede's Hort. Malab.*: 40. 1988): Herb. Linn. No. 804.13 (LINN).
Current name: ***Hygrophila ringens*** (L.) R. Br. ex Steud. (Acanthaceae).

Ruellia strepens Linnaeus, *Species Plantarum* 2: 634. 1753.
"Habitat in Virginia, Carolina." RCN: 4607.
Type not designated.
Original material: Herb. Clifford: 318, *Ruellia* 1, 2 sheets (BM);

Clayton 85 (BM); Herb. Linn. No. 804.3 (LINN); [icon] in Dillenius, Hort. Eltham. 2: 330, t. 249, f. 321. 1732.
Current name: ***Ruellia strepens*** L. (Acanthaceae).
Note: See comments by Fernald (in *Rhodora* 47: 19, pl. 863. 1945).

Ruellia tentaculata Linnaeus, *Centuria II Plantarum*: 22. 1756.
"Habitat in India." RCN: 4611.
Type not designated.
Original material: Herb. Linn. No. 262.5 (S); Herb. Linn. No. 804.9 (LINN); [icon] in Plukenet, Phytographia: t. 279, f. 7. 1694; Almag. Bot.: 142. 1696.
Current name: ***Haplanthus tentaculatis*** (L.) Nees (Acanthaceae).

Ruellia tuberosa Linnaeus, *Species Plantarum* 2: 635. 1753.
"Habitat in Jamaica." RCN: 4610.
Lectotype (Howard, *Fl. Lesser Antilles* 6: 380. 1989): Herb. Linn. No. 804.8 (LINN).
Generitype of *Ruellia* Linnaeus (vide Green, *Prop. Brit. Bot.*: 169. 1929).
Current name: ***Ruellia tuberosa*** L. (Acanthaceae).

Rumex acetosa Linnaeus, *Species Plantarum* 1: 337. 1753, *nom. cons.*
"Habitat in Europae pascuis. δ in Alpibus." RCN: 2602.
Conserved type (Jonsell & Nilsson in *Taxon* 45: 131. 1996): Sweden. Södermanland, Salem, Wiksberg, *Jonsell 7110* (UPS; iso- BM, C, H, K, LD, O, S).
Current name: ***Rumex acetosa*** L. (Polygonaceae).

Rumex acetosella Linnaeus, *Species Plantarum* 1: 338. 1753.
"Habitat in Europae pascuis & arvis arenosis." RCN: 2603.
Lectotype (Löve in *Bot. Helv.* 93: 164. 1983): Herb. Linn. No. 464.41 (LINN).
Current name: ***Rumex acetosella*** L. subsp. ***acetosella*** (Polygonaceae).
Note: Löve indicates the type as "LINN. "22".", but on p. 161 mentions that the type sheet bears two specimens. This clearly refers to sheet 464.41, and not to sheet 464.38 (which bears three specimens), subsequently treated as the type by den Nijs (in *Feddes Repert.* 95: 51–52. 1984). See discussion of this by Wilson (in *Telopea* 7: 85. 1996).

Rumex aculeatus Linnaeus, *Systema Naturae*, ed. 10, 2: 991. 1759.
["Habitat in Creta, Hispania."] Sp. Pl., ed. 2, 1: 482 (1762). RCN: 2604.
Type not designated.
Original material: Herb. Linn. No. 464.39 (LINN); Herb. Linn. No. 464.40 (LINN).
Current name: ***Rumex bucephalophorus*** L. (Polygonaceae).
Note: Specific epithet spelled "aculeata" in the protologue.
   López González (in *Anales Jard. Bot. Madrid* 44: 589. 1987) treated this name as a synonym of *R. bucephalophorus*, noting that typification using either 464.39 or 464.40 (LINN) would maintain this position.

Rumex acutus Linnaeus, *Species Plantarum* 1: 335. 1753.
"Habitat in Europae succulentis." RCN: 2587.
Lectotype (López González in *Anales Jard. Bot. Madrid* 44: 588. 1987): Herb. Linn. No. 150.5 (S).
Current name: ***Rumex acutus*** L. (Polygonaceae).

Rumex aegyptiacus Linnaeus, *Species Plantarum* 1: 335. 1753.
"Habitat in Aegypto." RCN: 2583.
Type not designated.
Original material: Herb. Linn. No. 149.17 (S); [icon] in Dillenius, Hort. Eltham. 1: 191, t. 158, f. 191. 1732; [icon] in Tilli, Cat. Pl. Hort. Pisani: 93, t. 37, f. 1. 1723.

Current name: ***Rumex aegyptiacus*** L. (Polygonaceae).
Note: El Hadidi & al. (in *Taeckholmia* 10: 57. 1987) indicated 464.11 (LINN) as type, but this collection lacks the relevant *Species Plantarum* number (i.e. "6") and was a post-1753 addition to the herbarium, and is not original material for the name.

Rumex alpinus Linnaeus, *Species Plantarum* 1: 334. 1753, *nom. cons.*
"Habitat in Helvetia, Monspelii." RCN: 2598.
Conserved type (Cafferty & Snogerup in *Taxon* 49: 571. 2000): Herb. Linn. No. 464.35 (LINN).
Current name: ***Rumex alpinus*** L. (Polygonaceae).

Rumex aquaticus Linnaeus, *Species Plantarum* 1: 336. 1753.
"Habitat in Europa ad ripas fluviorum & paludum." RCN: 2591.
Lectotype (Jonsell & Jarvis in *Nordic J. Bot.* 14: 154. 1994): Herb. Linn. No. 464.23 (LINN).
Current name: ***Rumex aquaticus*** L. (Polygonaceae).

Rumex britannica Linnaeus, *Species Plantarum* 1: 334. 1753.
"Habitat in Virginia." RCN: 2580.
Type not designated.
Original material: Herb. Clayton s.n.? (BM).
Current name: ***Rumex britannica*** L. (Polygonaceae).
Note: See Fernald (in *Rhodora* 47: 134, pl. 883. 1945), who regards this as a *nomen confusum*.

Rumex bucephalophorus Linnaeus, *Species Plantarum* 1: 336. 1753.
"Habitat in Italia." RCN: 2590.
Lectotype (Siddiqi & El-Taife in Jafri & El-Gadi, *Fl. Libya* 106: 12. 1983): Herb. Linn. No. 464.21 (LINN).
Current name: ***Rumex bucephalophorus*** L. (Polygonaceae).

Rumex crispus Linnaeus, *Species Plantarum* 1: 335. 1753.
"Habitat in Europae succulentis." RCN: 2581.
Lectotype (Siddiqi & El-Taife in Jafri & El-Gadi, *Fl. Libya* 106: 14. 1983): Herb. Linn. No. 464.7 (LINN).
Current name: ***Rumex crispus*** L. (Polygonaceae).
Note: Kanodia (in *Bull. Bot. Surv. India* 5: 377. 1963) indicated that he had looked at material in LINN but nowhere described it as the type.

Rumex dentatus Linnaeus, *Mantissa Plantarum Altera*: 226. 1771.
"Habitat in Aegypto." RCN: 2584.
Lectotype (Graham in Turrill & Milne-Redhead, *Fl. Trop. E. Africa, Polygonaceae*: 9. 1958): Herb. Linn. No. 464.12 (LINN).
Current name: ***Rumex dentatus*** L. (Polygonaceae).

Rumex digynus Linnaeus, *Species Plantarum* 1: 337. 1753.
"Habitat in Alpibus Lapponicis, Helveticis, Wallicis." RCN: 2597.
Lectotype (Bhopal & Chaudhri in *Pakistan Syst.* 1(2): 89. 1977): Herb. Linn. No. 464.32 (LINN).
Current name: ***Oxyria digyna*** (L.) Hill (Polygonaceae).
Note: Jonsell & Jarvis (in *Nordic J. Bot.* 14: 154. 1994) designated Herb. Linn. No. 132 (LAPP) as lectotype but this choice is pre-dated by that of Bhopal & Chaudhri.

Rumex divaricatus Linnaeus, *Species Plantarum,* ed. 2, 1: 478. 1762.
"Habitat in Italia." RCN: 2586.
Type not designated.
Original material: [icon] in Tilli, Cat. Pl. Hort. Pisani: 93, t. 37, f. 2. 1723.
Current name: ***Rumex pulcher*** L. subsp. ***divaricatus*** (L.) Murb. (Polygonaceae).

R

Rumex lunaria Linnaeus, *Species Plantarum* 1: 336. 1753.
"Habitat in Canariis." RCN: 2592.
Type not designated.
Original material: Herb. Linn. No. 464.24 (LINN); Herb. Clifford:
139, *Rumex* 8 (BM); [icon] in Plukenet, Phytographia: t. 252, f. 3.
1694; Almag. Bot.: 8. 1696; [icon] in Bauhin & Cherler, Hist. Pl.
Univ. 2: 994. 1651.
Current name: ***Rumex lunaria*** L. (Polygonaceae).
Note: Siddiqi & El Taife (in Jafri & El-Gadi, *Fl. Libya* 106: 12. 1983)
indicated as type 464.25 (LINN). However, this is an Alström̈er
collection that did not reach Linnaeus until 1762 so it cannot be
original material for the name.

Rumex luxurians Linnaeus, *Systema Naturae*, ed. 12, 2: 255; *Mantissa
Plantarum*: 64. 1767.
"Habitat in Alpibus Bononiensibus." RCN: 2605.
Type not designated.
Original material: *Bladh*, Herb. Linn. No. 464.45 (LINN); [icon] in
Boccone, Mus. Piante Rar. Sicilia: 165, t. 126. 1697.
Current name: ***Rumex luxurians*** L. (Polygonaceae).
Note: Roberty & Vautier (in *Boissiera* 10: 61. 1964) describe this as a
nomen incertae sedis.

Rumex maritimus Linnaeus, *Species Plantarum* 1: 335. 1753.
"Habitat in Europae litoribus maritimis." RCN: 2585.
Lectotype (Jonsell & Jarvis in *Nordic J. Bot.* 14: 154. 1994): Herb.
Linn. No. 150.3 (S).
Current name: ***Rumex maritimus*** L. (Polygonaceae).

Rumex multifidus Linnaeus, *Species Plantarum*, ed. 2, 1: 482. 1762.
"Habitat in Alpibus Calabriae, Hetruriae, Orientis." RCN: 2601.
Lectotype (Löve in *Bot. Helv.* 93: 165. 1983): [icon] *"Acetosa minor
lobis multifidis"* in Boccone, Mus. Piante Rar. Sicilia: 164, t. 126.
1697.
Current name: ***Rumex acetosella*** L. subsp. ***multifidus*** (L.) Schübl. &
G. Martens (Polygonaceae).

Rumex obtusifolius Linnaeus, *Species Plantarum* 1: 335. 1753.
"Habitat in Germania, Helvetia, Gallia, Anglia." RCN: 2588.
Lectotype (Jonsell & Jarvis in *Nordic J. Bot.* 14: 154. 1994): Herb.
Linn. No. 464.17 (LINN).
Current name: ***Rumex obtusifolius*** L. subsp. ***obtusifolius***
(Polygonaceae).

Rumex patientia Linnaeus, *Species Plantarum* 1: 333. 1753.
"Habitat in Italia." RCN: 2577.
Type not designated.
Original material: [icon] in Dodoëns, Stirp. Hist. Pempt., ed. 2: 647,
648. 1616.
Generitype of *Rumex* Linnaeus (vide Hitchcock, *Prop. Brit. Bot.*: 148.
1929).
Current name: ***Rumex patientia*** L. (Polygonaceae).
Note: López González (in *Anales Jard. Bot. Madrid* 44: 586. 1987)
noted that 464.1 (LINN), treated as the type by Bhopal &
Chaudhri (in *Pakistan Syst.* 1(2): 94. 1977), conflicts with Linnaeus'
protologue and lacks the relevant *Species Plantarum* number (i.e.
"1"), making it a post-1753 addition to the herbarium, and not
original material for the name.

Rumex persicarioides Linnaeus, *Species Plantarum* 1: 335. 1753.
"Habitat in Virginia." RCN: 2582.
Lectotype (St John in *Rhodora* 17: 74. 1915): *Kalm*, Herb. Linn. No.
464.9 (LINN).
Current name: ***Rumex maritimus*** L. var. ***persicarioides*** (L.) R.S.
Mitch. (Polygonaceae).

Rumex pulcher Linnaeus, *Species Plantarum* 1: 336. 1753.
"Habitat in Gallia, Italia, Veronae." RCN: 2589.
Lectotype (Siddiqi & El-Taife in Jafri & El-Gadi, *Fl. Libya* 106: 14.
1983): Herb. Linn. No. 464.19 (LINN).
Current name: ***Rumex pulcher*** L. subsp. ***pulcher*** (Polygonaceae).

Rumex roseus Linnaeus, *Species Plantarum* 1: 337. 1753.
"Habitat in Aegypto." RCN: 2594.
Type not designated.
Original material: *Hasselquist*, Herb. Linn. No. 464.27 (LINN); [icon]
in Shaw, Cat. Pl. Afr. As.: 37, f. 5. 1738.
Current name: *Rumex roseus* L. (Polygonaceae).
Note: See discussion by López González (in *Anales Jard. Bot. Madrid*
44: 581. 1987).

Rumex sanguineus Linnaeus, *Species Plantarum* 1: 334. 1753.
"Habitat in Virginia." RCN: 2578.
Lectotype (Jonsell & Jarvis in *Nordic J. Bot.* 14: 154. 1994): Herb.
Linn. No. 464.2 (LINN).
Current name: ***Rumex sanguineus*** L. (Polygonaceae).

Rumex scutatus Linnaeus, *Species Plantarum* 1: 337. 1753.
"Habitat in Helvetia, Galloprovincia; inter acervos lapidum." RCN:
2596.
Lectotype (Jonsell & Jarvis in *Nordic J. Bot.* 14: 154. 1994): Herb.
Linn. No. 464.30 (LINN).
Current name: ***Rumex scutatus*** L. (Polygonaceae).

Rumex sinuatus Linnaeus, *Amoenitates Academicae* 4: 481. 1759.
Type not designated.
Original material: none traced.
Current name: ***Rumex roseus*** L. (Polygonaceae).
Note: López González (in *Anales Jard. Bot. Madrid* 44: 581. 1987)
treats this as a synonym of *R. roseus* L.

Rumex spinosus Linnaeus, *Species Plantarum* 1: 337. 1753.
"Habitat in Creta." RCN: 2599.
Lectotype (Graham in Turrill & Milne-Redhead, *Fl. Trop. E. Africa,
Polygonaceae*: 3. 1958): Herb. Linn. No. 464.36 (LINN).
Current name: ***Emex spinosa*** (L.) Campd. (Polygonaceae).

Rumex tingitanus Linnaeus, *Systema Naturae*, ed. 10, 2: 991. 1759.
["Habitat in Barbaria, Hispania. Alstroemer."] Sp. Pl., ed. 2, 1: 479
(1762). RCN: 2595.
Lectotype (Siddiqi & El-Taife in Jafri & El-Gadi, *Fl. Libya* 106: 21.
1983): *Löfling 276a*, Herb. Linn. No. 464.28 (LINN).
Current name: ***Rumex tingitanus*** L. (Polygonaceae).

Rumex tuberosus Linnaeus, *Species Plantarum*, ed. 2, 1: 481. 1762.
"Habitat in Italia." RCN: 2600.
Lectotype (Snogerup & Snogerup in Strid & Kit Tan, *Fl. Hellenica* 1:
94. 1997): *Séguier*, Herb. Linn. No. 464.37 (LINN).
Current name: ***Rumex tuberosus*** L. subsp. ***tuberosus*** (Polygonaceae).

Rumex verticillatus Linnaeus, *Species Plantarum* 1: 334. 1753.
"Habitat in Virginia." RCN: 2579.
Type not designated.
Original material: Herb. Linn. No. 464.5 (LINN).
Current name: ***Rumex verticillatus*** L. (Polygonaceae).

Rumex vesicarius Linnaeus, *Species Plantarum* 1: 336. 1753.
"Habitat in Africa." RCN: 2593.
Lectotype (Bhopal & Chaudhri in *Pakistan Syst.* 1(2): 94. 1977):
Herb. Linn. No. 464.26 (LINN).
Current name: ***Rumex vesicarius*** L. (Polygonaceae).

Rumphia amboinensis Linnaeus, *Species Plantarum* 2: 1193. 1753.
"Habitat in India." RCN: 272.
Lectotype (Nicolson & al., *Interpret. Van Rheede's Hort. Malab.*: 8, f. 1. 1988): [icon] *"Tsjem-tani"* in Rheede, Hort. Malab. 4: 25, t. 11. 1683.
Generitype of *Rumphia* Linnaeus.
Current name: ***Rumphia amboinensis*** L. (Anacardiaceae).
Note: The identity of the type illustration is uncertain; Nicolson & al. (*loc. cit.*: 319) treat both the generic and specific names as *nomina dubia*.

Ruppia maritima Linnaeus, *Species Plantarum* 1: 127. 1753.
"Habitat in Europae maritimis." RCN: 1046.
Lectotype (Setchell in *Proc. Calif. Acad. Sci.,* ser. 4, 25: 470. 1946): [icon] *"Buccaferrea maritima, foliis minus acutis"* in Micheli, Nov. Pl. Gen.: 72, t. 35. 1729.
Generitype of *Ruppia* Linnaeus.
Current name: ***Ruppia maritima*** L. (Ruppiaceae).
Note: Setchell illustrates (pl. 47, 48) two sheets in LINN, one of which (sheet 176.1) has been accepted as the type by some later authors (e.g. Obermeyer in Leistner, *Fl. Southern Africa* 1: 71. 1966). However, Setchell's choice has priority.

Ruscus aculeatus Linnaeus, *Species Plantarum* 2: 1041. 1753.
"Habitat in Galliae, Italiae nemorosis asperis." RCN: 7524.
Lectotype (Yeo & Mathew in Jarvis & al., *Regnum Veg.* 127: 83. 1993): Herb. Burser XXIV: 91 (UPS).
Generitype of *Ruscus* Linnaeus (vide Green, *Prop. Brit. Bot.*: 192. 1929).
Current name: ***Ruscus aculeatus*** L. (Liliaceae/Ruscaceae).

Ruscus androgynus Linnaeus, *Species Plantarum* 2: 1041. 1753.
"Habitat in Canariis." RCN: 7527.
Type not designated.
Original material: Herb. Clifford: 466, *Ruscus* 4 (BM); [icon] in Dillenius, Hort. Eltham. 2: 332, t. 250, f. 322. 1732.
Current name: ***Semele androgyna*** (L.) Kunth (Liliaceae/Ruscaceae).

Ruscus hypoglossum Linnaeus, *Species Plantarum* 2: 1041. 1753.
"Habitat in Hungariae, Liguriae, Italiae montibus umbrosis." RCN: 7526.
Type not designated.
Original material: Herb. Clifford: 465, *Ruscus* 3, 2 sheets (BM); [icon] in Colonna, Ekphr.: 166, 165. 1606.
Current name: ***Ruscus hypoglossum*** L. (Liliaceae/Ruscaceae).
Note: Yeo (in *Notes Roy. Bot. Gard. Edinburgh* 28: 252. 1968) indicated Clifford material as the lectotype but did not distinguish between two sheets there associated with this name. As they are evidently not part of a single gathering, Art. 9.15 does not apply.

Ruscus hypophyllum Linnaeus, *Species Plantarum* 2: 1041. 1753.
"Habitat in Italia ad latera collium." RCN: 7525.
Lectotype (Yeo in *Notes Roy. Bot. Gard. Edinburgh* 28: 256. 1968): Herb. Clifford: 465, *Ruscus* 2 (BM-000647524).
Current name: ***Ruscus hypophyllum*** L. (Liliaceae/Ruscaceae).

Ruscus racemosus Linnaeus, *Species Plantarum* 2: 1041. 1753.
"Habitat – – – –" RCN: 7528.
Type not designated.
Original material: Herb. Clifford: 466, *Ruscus* 5 (BM); [icon] in Hermann, Hort. Lugd.-Bat. Cat.: 360, 681. 1687.
Current name: ***Danaë racemosa*** (L.) Moench (Liliaceae/Ruscaceae).

Ruta chalepensis Linnaeus, *Systema Naturae,* ed. 12, 2: 293; *Mantissa Plantarum*: 69. 1767.
"Habitat in Africa." RCN: 3015.
Lectotype (Meikle, *Fl. Cyprus* 1: 349. 1977): Herb. Linn. No. 537.4 (LINN).
Current name: ***Ruta chalepensis*** L. (Rutaceae).
Note: Although the precise date of publication of Meikle's typification is uncertain, it is clearly earlier than that of Jafri (in Jafri & El-Gadi, *Fl. Libya* 50: 2. 30 Dec 1977).

Ruta graveolens Linnaeus, *Species Plantarum* 1: 383. 1753.
"Habitat in Europae australis, Alexandriae, Mauritaniae sterilibus." RCN: 3014.
Lectotype (Nair in Jarvis & al., *Regnum Veg.* 127: 83. 1993): Herb. Linn. No. 537.1 (LINN).
Generitype of *Ruta* Linnaeus (vide Hitchcock, *Prop. Brit. Bot.*: 152. 1929).
Current name: ***Ruta graveolens*** L. (Rutaceae).

Ruta graveolens Linnaeus var. **montana** Linnaeus, *Species Plantarum* 1: 383. 1753.
RCN: 3014.
Basionym of: *Ruta montana* (L.) L. (1753).
Type not designated.
Original material: Herb. Burser XIX: 37 (UPS); Herb. Linn. No. 537.3 (LINN); [icon] in Clusius, Rar. Pl. Hist. 2: 136. 1601; [icon] in Mattioli, Pl. Epit.: 495. 1586.
Current name: ***Ruta montana*** (L.) L. (Rutaceae).

Ruta linifolia Linnaeus, *Species Plantarum* 1: 384. 1753.
"Habitat in Hispania; β in Rodastro; γ in Media." RCN: 3017.
Lectotype (Townsend in *Hooker's Icon. Pl.* 40(1–3): 281. 1986): *Löfling 276* α, Herb. Linn. No. 537.5 (LINN).
Current name: ***Haplophyllum linifolium*** (L.) G. Don (Rutaceae).

Ruta montana (Linnaeus) Linnaeus, *Amoenitates Academicae* 3: 52. 1756.
RCN: 3014.
Basionym: *Ruta graveolens* L. var. *montana* L. (1753).
Type not designated.
Original material: as basionym.
Current name: ***Ruta montana*** (L.) L. (Rutaceae).

Ruta patavina Linnaeus, *Species Plantarum* 1: 384. 1753.
"Habitat prope Patavium." RCN: 3016.
Lectotype (Townsend in *Hooker's Icon. Pl.* 40(1–3): 269. 1986): [icon] *"Pseudo-Ruta Patavina, trifolia, floribus luteis, umbellatis"* in Micheli, Nov. Pl. Gen.: 22, t. 19. 1729.
Current name: ***Haplophyllum patavinum*** (L.) G. Don (Rutaceae).

R

S

Saccharum officinarum Linnaeus, *Species Plantarum* 1: 54. 1753.

"Habitat in Indiae utriusque locis inundatis." RCN: 453.

Lectotype (Reveal & al. in *Taxon* 38: 96. 1989): [icon] *"Arundo saccharifera C. B."* in Sloane, Voy. Jamaica 1: 108, t. 66. 1707. – Typotype: Herb. Sloane 2: 14 (BM-SL).

Generitype of *Saccharum* Linnaeus (vide Hitchcock, *Prop. Brit. Bot.*: 119. 1929).

Current name: ***Saccharum officinarum*** L. (Poaceae).

Note: As has been noted by Barrie & al. (in *Taxon* 41: 511. 1992), the typification made by Reveal & al. is pre-dated by the competing choice of Sherif & Siddiqi (in El-Gadi, *Fl. Libya* 145: 328. 1988), who chose 77.2 (LINN), a specimen of *Miscanthus floridulus* (Labill.) Warb. ex Schum. & Lander. It appears that a conservation proposal may be necessary but in the meantime, Art. 57.1 applies, and no change in the application of the name should occur.

Saccharum ravennae (Linnaeus) Linnaeus, *Systema Vegetabilium,* ed. 13: 88. 1774.

["Habitat in Italia."] Sp. Pl., ed. 2, 2: 1481 (1763). RCN: 454.

Basionym: *Andropogon ravennae* L. (1763).

Lectotype (Cope in Cafferty & al. in *Taxon* 49: 246. 2000): Herb. Linn. No. 77.4 (LINN).

Current name: ***Saccharum ravennae*** (L.) L. (Poaceae).

Note: Although Kerguélen (in *Lejeunia,* n.s., 75: 145. 1975) stated "Type: ...LINN", this is not accepted as a formal typification, for the reasons explained by Cafferty & al. (in *Taxon* 49: 240. 2000). Sherif & Siddiqi (in El-Gadi, *Fl. Libya* 145: 325. 1988) indicated Herb. Linn. 77.4 (LINN) and Zanoni, *Istoria Botanica*: t. 24 (1675) as "type", but this is not a single gathering (Art. 9.15) so no effective choice was made.

Saccharum spicatum Linnaeus, *Species Plantarum* 1: 54. 1753.

"Habitat in Indiae petrosis." RCN: 455.

Lectotype (Clayton in Polhill, *Fl. Trop. E. Africa, Gramineae* 2: 395. 1974): [icon] *"Tsjeria-kuren-pullu"* in Rheede, Hort. Malab. 12: 117, t. 62. 1693.

Current name: ***Perotis indica*** (L.) Kuntze (Poaceae).

Note: Veldkamp & van Steenbergen (in *Austrobaileya* 3: 610. 1992) treated 77.5 (LINN) as the type but their choice is pre-dated by that of Clayton.

Saccharum spontaneum Linnaeus, *Mantissa Plantarum Altera*: 183. 1771.

"Habitat in Malabariae aquosis. Koenig." RCN: 452.

Lectotype (Cope in Nasir & Ali, *Fl. Pakistan* 143: 263. 1982): Herb. Linn. No. 77.1 (LINN).

Current name: ***Saccharum spontaneum*** L. (Poaceae).

Note: Although the same type choice was made by both Cope and Clayton & Renvoize (in Polhill, *Fl. Trop. E. Africa, Gramineae* 3: 704) in 1982, that of Cope was published earlier.

Sagina erecta Linnaeus, *Species Plantarum* 1: 128. 1753.

"Habitat in Galliae, Angliae, Germaniae, sterilibus glareosis." RCN: 1049.

Lectotype (Strid in Cafferty & Jarvis in *Taxon* 53: 1053. 2004): Herb. Linn. No. 177.3 (LINN).

Current name: ***Moenchia erecta*** (L.) G. Gaertn. & al. (Caryophyllaceae).

Note: Williams (in *J. Bot.* 39: 365–369. 1901) provides a detailed historical review, noting the literature cited by Linnaeus.

Sagina procumbens Linnaeus, *Species Plantarum* 1: 128. 1753.

"Habitat in Europae pascuis sterilibus uliginosis aridis." RCN: 1047.

Lectotype (Jonsell & Jarvis in Jarvis & al., *Regnum Veg.* 127: 83. 1993): [icon] *"Alsine pusilla graminea, flore tetrapetalo"* in Séguier, Pl. Veron. 1: 421, 417, t. 5, f. 3. 1745.

Generitype of *Sagina* Linnaeus (vide Hitchcock, *Prop. Brit. Bot.*: 127. 1929).

Current name: ***Sagina procumbens*** L. (Caryophyllaceae).

Note: Jonsell & Jarvis (in *Nordic J. Bot.* 14: 158. 1994) provided an explanation of their formal 1993 typification.

Sagina virginica Linnaeus, *Species Plantarum* 1: 128. 1753.

"Habitat in Virginia inter muscos ad margines fontium. D. Gronovius." RCN: 1050.

Lectotype (Gillett in *Rhodora* 61: 44, 49. 1959): *Clayton* 649 (BM-000051719).

Current name: ***Bartonia virginica*** (L.) Britton & al. (Gentianaceae).

Sagittaria lancifolia Linnaeus, *Systema Naturae,* ed. 10, 2: 1270. 1759.

["Habitat in America."] Sp. Pl., ed. 2, 2: 1411 (1763). RCN: 7202.

Lectotype (Haynes & Holm-Nielsen, *Fl. Neotropica* 64: 89. 1994): *Browne,* Herb. Linn. No. 1124.6 (LINN).

Current name: ***Sagittaria lancifolia*** L. (Alismataceae).

Note: Although Bogin (in *Mem. New York Bot. Gard.* 9: 214. 1955) discussed the original material for this name, no type was designated.

Sagittaria obtusifolia Linnaeus, *Species Plantarum* 2: 993. 1753.
"Habitat in Asia." RCN: 7201.
Lectotype (Carter in Hubbard & Milne-Redhead, *Fl. Trop. E. Africa, Alismataceae*: 9. 1960): [icon] *"Sagittariae foliis planta glomerato fructu, monopyrene, Coriandri fere figura"* in Plukenet, Phytographia: t. 220, f. 7. 1692; Almag. Bot.: 326. 1696. – Typotype: Herb. Sloane 97: 181 (BM-SL).
Current name: ***Limnophytum obtusifolium*** (L.) Miq. (Alismataceae).

Sagittaria pugioniformis Linnaeus, *Plantae Surinamenses*: 15. 1775.
"Habitat [in Surinamo.]" RCN: 7204.
Lectotype (Haynes & Holm-Nielsen, *Fl. Neotropica* 64: 90. 1994): Herb. Linn. No. 1124.7 (LINN).
Current name: ***Sagittaria lancifolia*** L. (Alismataceae).
Note: Although Bogin (in *Mem. New York Bot. Gard.* 9: 191. 1955) referred to "the Linnaean type specimen", he did not indicate what he believed it to be.

Sagittaria sagittifolia Linnaeus, *Species Plantarum* 2: 993. 1753.
"Habitat in Europae, Americae fluviis lacubus argillosis." RCN: 7200.
Type not designated.
Original material: Herb. Linn. No. 344 (LAPP); Herb. Burser X: 135 (UPS); Herb. Burser X: 134 (UPS); Herb. Burser X: 133 (UPS); *Clayton 278* (BM); Herb. Linn. No. 1124.1 (LINN); [icon] in Loesel, Fl. Prussica: 234, t. 74. 1703; [icon] in Dodoëns, Stirp. Hist. Pempt., ed. 2: 587, 588. 1616; [icon] in Bauhin, Prodr. Theatri Bot.: 4. 1620.
Generitype of *Sagittaria* Linnaeus (vide Green, *Prop. Brit. Bot.*: 188. 1929).
Current name: ***Sagittaria sagittifolia*** L. (Alismataceae).
Note: Bogin (in *Mem. New York Bot. Gard.* 9: 229. 1955) noted the existence of a number of sheets at LINN but did not designate a type.

Sagittaria trifolia Linnaeus, *Species Plantarum* 2: 993. 1753.
"Habitat in China." RCN: 7203.
Lectotype (Dandy in Rechinger, *Fl. Iranica* 78: 2. 1971): [icon] *"Sagittaria Chinensis foliis ternis longissimis"* in Petiver, Gazophyl. Nat.: 29, t. 19, f. 5. 1702–1709.
Current name: ***Sagittaria trifolia*** L. (Alismataceae).

Salacia chinensis Linnaeus, *Mantissa Plantarum Altera*: 293. 1771.
"Habitat in China." RCN: 6911.
Lectotype (Ding Hou in *Blumea* 12: 34. 1963): Herb. Linn. No. 1066.1 (LINN).
Generitype of *Salacia* Linnaeus, *nom. cons.*
Current name: ***Salacia chinensis*** L. (Celastraceae).
Note: Salacia Linnaeus, *nom. cons.* against *Courondi* Adans.

Salicornia arabica Linnaeus, *Species Plantarum* 1: 3. 1753.
"Habitat in Arabia." RCN: 27.
Type not designated.
Original material: Herb. Burser XVI(2): 22 (UPS); [icon] in Morison, Pl. Hist. Univ. 2: 610, s. 5, t. 33, f. 7. 1680.
Current name: ***Kalidium caspicum*** (L.) Ung.-Sternb. (Chenopodiaceae).
Note: Moss (in *J. Bot.* 49: 178. 1911) interpreted this name via 10.6 (LINN), which lacks a *Species Plantarum* number (i.e. "2") and is a post-1753 addition to the herbarium and not original material for this name.

Salicornia caspica Linnaeus, *Species Plantarum* 1: 4. 1753.
"Habitat in squalidis maris Caspii & Mediae." RCN: 28.
Type not designated.
Original material: Herb. Linn. No. 10.7 (LINN); [icon] in Buxbaum, Pl. Minus Cognit. Cent. 1: 7, t. 11, f. 1. 1728.
Current name: ***Kalidium caspicum*** (L.) Ung.-Sternb. (Chenopodiaceae).
Note: Hedge (in Rechinger, *Fl. Iranica* 172: 122. 1997) indicated 10.8 (LINN) as (doubtfully) the type, and there are also doubts as to whether it was in the collection in 1753.

Salicornia europaea Linnaeus, *Species Plantarum* 1: 3. 1753.
"Habitat in Europae litoribus maritimis." RCN: 24.
Lectotype (Jafri & Rateeb in Jafri & El-Gadi, *Fl. Libya* 58: 57. 1978): Herb. Linn. No. 10.1 (LINN).
Generitype of *Salicornia* Linnaeus (vide Hitchcock, *Prop. Brit. Bot.*: 115. 1929).
Current name: ***Salicornia europaea*** L. (Chenopodiaceae).
Note: Ball (in *Feddes Repert.* 69: 6. 1964) noted 10.1 (LINN) from Gotland, and therefore concluded it to be the diploid cytotype (as this is the form that occurs there). However, he did not explicitly typify the name; Jafri & Rateeb appear to have been the first to do this. Piirainen (in *Ann. Bot. Fenn.* 28: 82. 1991) also reached the same conclusion as to the type.

Salicornia europaea Linnaeus var. **fruticosa** Linnaeus, *Species Plantarum* 1: 3. 1753.
"Habitat in Europae litoribus maritimis." RCN: 25.
Basionym of: *Salicornia fruticosa* (L.) L. (1762).
Lectotype (designated here by Ball): Herb. Burser XVI(2): 22, right specimen (UPS).
Current name: ***Sarcocornia fruticosa*** (L.) A.J. Scott (Chenopodiaceae).
Note: Castroviejo & Coello (in *Anales Jard. Bot. Madrid* 37: 49. 1980) indicated 10.4 (LINN) as type but this lacks the *Species Plantarum* number (i.e. "1"), is a post-1753 addition to the herbarium, and is not original material for the name.

Salicornia europaea Linnaeus var. **herbacea** Linnaeus, *Species Plantarum* 1: 3. 1753.
"Habitat in Europae litoribus maritimis." RCN: 24.
Basionym of: *Salicornia herbacea* (L.) L. (1762).
Lectotype (Piirainen in *Ann. Bot. Fenn.* 28: 82. 1991): Herb. Linn. No. 10.1 (LINN).
Current name: ***Salicornia europaea*** L. (Chenopodiaceae).
Note: López González (in *Anales Jard. Bot. Madrid* 55: 469. 1997) believed this name to be invalid but Art. 26.2 Ex. 3 indicates that this is a valid name.

Salicornia fruticosa (Linnaeus) Linnaeus, *Species Plantarum*, ed. 2, 1: 5. 1762.
"Habitat in Europae maritimis." RCN: 25.
Basionym: *Salicornia europaea* L. var. *fruticosa* L. (1753).
Lectotype (designated here by Ball): Herb. Burser XVI(2): 22, right specimen (UPS).
Current name: ***Sarcocornia fruticosa*** (L.) A.J. Scott (Chenopodiaceae).

Salicornia herbacea (Linnaeus) Linnaeus, *Species Plantarum*, ed. 2, 1: 5. 1762.
"Habitat in Europae litoribus maritimis." RCN: 24.
Basionym: *Salicornia europaea* L. var. *herbacea* L. (1753).
Lectotype (Piirainen in *Ann. Bot. Fenn.* 28: 82. 1991): Herb. Linn. No. 10.1 (LINN).
Current name: ***Salicornia europaea*** L. (Chenopodiaceae).

S

Note: An illegitimate replacement name for *S. europaea*, as noted by Ball (in *Feddes Repert.* 69: 5. 1964) and López González (in *Anales Jard. Bot. Madrid* 55: 469. 1997).

Salicornia herbacea (Linnaeus) Linnaeus var. **virginica** (Linnaeus) Linnaeus, *Species Plantarum*, ed. 2, 1: 5. 1762.
["Habitat in Virginia, & ad Salinas Saxoniae."] Sp. Pl. 1: 4 (1753). RCN: 26.
Basionym: *Salicornia virginica* L. (1753).
Lectotype (Fernald & Schubert in *Rhodora* 50: 163. 1948): *Clayton 572/667* (BM-000051639).
Current name: **Salicornia virginica** L. (Chenopodiaceae).

Salicornia virginica Linnaeus, *Species Plantarum* 1: 4. 1753.
"Habitat in Virginia, & ad Salinas Saxoniae." RCN: 26.
Basionym of: *Salicornia herbacea* (L.) L. var. *virginica* (L.) L. (1762).
Lectotype (Fernald & Schubert in *Rhodora* 50: 163. 1948): *Clayton 572/667* (BM-000051639).
Current name: **Salicornia virginica** L. (Chenopodiaceae).

Salix aegyptiaca Linnaeus, *Centuria I Plantarum*: 33. 1755.
"Habitat in Aegypto. D. Hasselquist." RCN: 7364.
Lectotype (Neumann & Skvortsov in Rechinger, *Fl. Iranica* 65: 31. 1969): Herb. Hasselquist, No. 44 (UPS; iso- LINN 158.91).
Current name: **Salix aegyptiaca** L. (Salicaceae).

Salix alba Linnaeus, *Species Plantarum* 2: 1021. 1753, *typ. cons.*
"Habitat ad pagos & urbes Europae." RCN: 7387.
Conserved type (Groendijk-Wilders & al. in *Taxon* 37: 166, f. 1. 1988): Herb. Burser XXIV: 104 (UPS).
Generitype of *Salix* Linnaeus, *nom. cons.*
Current name: **Salix alba** L. subsp. **alba** (Salicaceae).
Note: Salix alba, with the type designated by Groendijk-Wilders & al., was proposed as conserved type of the genus by Jarvis (in *Taxon* 41: 573. 1992). This was eventually approved by the General Committee (see review of the history of this proposal by Barrie, *l.c.* 55: 795–796. 2006).

Salix amygdalina Linnaeus, *Species Plantarum* 2: 1016. 1753.
"Habitat in Europae sylvis." RCN: 7362.
Neotype (designated here by Belyaeva): *Salix amygdalina* L., Carlstad, *A. Axel W. Lund* (S-4884).
Current name: **Salix triandra** L. (Salicaceae).

Salix amygdaloides Linnaeus, *Flora Anglica*: 24. 1754, *orth. var.*
"Habitat [in Anglia.]". RCN: 7362.
Neotype (designated here by Belyaeva): *Salix amygdalina* L., Carlstad, *A. Axel W. Lund* (S-4884).
Current name: **Salix triandra** L. (Salicaceae).
Note: An orthographic variant of *Salix amygdalina* L. (1753), as noted by Stearn (*Introd. Ray's Syn. Meth. Stirp. Brit.* (Ray Soc. ed.): 68. 1973).

Salix arbuscula Linnaeus, *Species Plantarum* 2: 1018. 1753.
"Habitat in Lapponiae campis arenosis." RCN: 7370.
Lectotype (Jonsell & Jarvis in *Nordic J. Bot.* 14: 150. 1994): Herb. Linn. No. 1158.27 (LINN).
Current name: **Salix arbuscula** L. (Salicaceae).

Salix arenaria Linnaeus, *Species Plantarum* 2: 1019. 1753.
"Habitat in Europae paludibus." RCN: 7379.
Lectotype (designated here by Belyaeva): [icon] *"Salix integris utrinque hirsutis lanceolatis"* in Haller, Enum. Meth. Stirp. Helv. 1: 155, t. 5. 1742. – Epitype (designated here by Belyaeva): Herb. Burser XXIV: post 116 (UPS).

Current name: **Salix repens** L. var. **argentea** (Sm.) Ser. (Salicaceae).
Note: This name presents some difficulties as none of the original elements appears to correspond with current usage of the name.

Salix aurita Linnaeus, *Species Plantarum* 2: 1019. 1753.
"Habitat in Europae borealis sylvis." RCN: 7376.
Lectotype (Jonsell & Jarvis in *Nordic J. Bot.* 14: 151. 1994): Herb. Linn. No. 1158.92 (LINN).
Current name: **Salix aurita** L. (Salicaceae).

Salix babylonica Linnaeus, *Species Plantarum* 2: 1017. 1753.
"Habitat in Oriente." RCN: 7366.
Lectotype (Jordaan in *Bothalia* 35: 17. 2005): Herb. Linn. No. 1158.20 (LINN).
Current name: **Salix babylonica** L. (Salicaceae).
Note: Siddiqi (in Jafri & El-Gadi, *Fl. Libya* 142: 6. 1987) indicated 1158.22 (LINN) as the type, as did Ali (in Ali & Qaiser, *Fl. Pakistan* 203: 34. 2001) for 1158.21 (LINN), but both collections lack the *Species Plantarum* number (i.e. "9") and were post-1753 additions to the herbarium and are not original material for the name.

Salix caprea Linnaeus, *Species Plantarum* 2: 1020. 1753.
"Habitat in Europae siccis." RCN: 7384.
Lectotype (Jonsell & Jarvis in *Nordic J. Bot.* 14: 151. 1994): *Dillenius*, Herb. Linn. No. 1158.88 (LINN).
Current name: **Salix caprea** L. (Salicaceae).

Salix cinerea Linnaeus, *Species Plantarum* 2: 1021. 1753.
"Habitat in Europae nemoribus paludosis subhumidis." RCN: 7386.
Lectotype (Jonsell & Jarvis in *Nordic J. Bot.* 14: 151. 1994): Herb. Linn. No. 1158.93 (LINN).
Current name: **Salix cinerea** L. (Salicaceae).

Salix depressa Linnaeus, *Flora Suecica*, ed. 2: 352. 1755.
"Habitat in Alpibus Lapponis." RCN: 7377.
Lectotype (designated here by Belyaeva): [icon] *"Salix foliis integris subtus villosis ovato-lanceolatis utrimque acutis"* in Linnaeus, Fl. Lapponica: 289, t. 8, f. n. 1737. – Epitype (designated here by Belyaeva): Lappland. Vassijaure. *Salix lanata* L., female, 28 Jul 1906, *Björn Floderus* (S).
Current name: **Salix lanata** L. (Salicaceae).

Salix fragilis Linnaeus, *Species Plantarum* 2: 1017. 1753.
"Habitat in Europae borealibus." RCN: 7365.
Proposed conserved type (Christensen & Jonsell in *Taxon* 54: 555. 2005): Transcaucasia [Turkey], Karsskaya obl., Promezhutochoj, bereg r. Kjaklik, 11 May 1914, *Turkevich*, Iter Transcauc. No. 245 (LE).
Current name: **Salix fragilis** L. (Salicaceae).
Note: Although the usage of this name has not always been clear, none of the original elements corresponds with recent usage. Christensen & Jonsell (in *Taxon* 54: 555. 2005) have therefore proposed the conservation of the name with a conserved type. Jordaan (in *Bothalia* 35: 17. 2005) proposed 1158.19 (LINN) as lectotype but this does not appear to be original material for the name, and is apparently identifiable as *S. alba* L.

Salix fusca Linnaeus, *Species Plantarum* 2: 1020. 1753.
"Habitat in Europae pascuis humidis." RCN: 7382.
Lectotype (designated here by Belyaeva): Herb. Linn. No. 1158.74 (LINN).
Current name: **Salix repens** L. (Salicaceae).

Salix glauca Linnaeus, *Species Plantarum* 2: 1019. 1753.
"Habitat in Alpibus Lapponicis & Pyrenaicis. Sauv." RCN: 7375.

Lectotype (Jonsell & Jarvis in *Nordic J. Bot.* 14: 151. 1994): [icon]
"Salix foliis integris, subtus tenuissime villosis ovatis" in Linnaeus, Fl.
Lapponica: 290, t. 7, f. 5. 1737.
Current name: ***Salix glauca*** L. (Salicaceae).

Salix hastata Linnaeus, *Species Plantarum* 2: 1017. 1753.
"Habitat in Lapponia, Helvetia." RCN: 7363.
Lectotype (Jonsell & Jarvis in *Nordic J. Bot.* 14: 151. 1994): [icon]
"Salix foliis serratis glabris subovatis sessilibus appendiculatis" in
Linnaeus, Fl. Lapponica: 285, t. 8, f. g. 1737.
Current name: ***Salix hastata*** L. (Salicaceae).

Salix helix Linnaeus, *Species Plantarum* 2: 1017. 1753.
"Habitat in Europae australiori ad sepes, locis aquosis." RCN: 7368.
Lectotype (designated here by Belyaeva): [icon] *"Salix Helice
Theophrasti"* in Daléchamps, Hist. General. Pl. 1: 277. 1587.
Current name: ***Salix purpurea*** L. (Salicaceae).

Salix herbacea Linnaeus, *Species Plantarum* 2: 1018. 1753.
"Habitat in Alpibus lapponiae, Helvetiae." RCN: 7371.
Lectotype (Jonsell & Jarvis in *Nordic J. Bot.* 14: 151. 1994): Herb.
Linn. No. 1158.40, central specimen (LINN).
Current name: ***Salix herbacea*** L. (Salicaceae).

Salix hermaphroditica Linnaeus, *Species Plantarum* 2: 1015. 1753.
"Habitat Upsaliae." RCN: 7357.
Lectotype (designated here by Belyaeva): Herb. Linn. No. 1158.1
(LINN).
Current name: ***Salix fragilis*** L. × ***S. pentandra*** L. (Salicaceae).

Salix incubacea Linnaeus, *Species Plantarum* 2: 1020. 1753.
"Habitat in Europae pascuis duriusculis, uliginosis." RCN: 7380.
Lectotype (designated here by Belyaeva): Herb. Linn. No. 1158.69
(LINN).
Current name: ***Salix repens*** L. (Salicaceae).

Salix lanata Linnaeus, *Species Plantarum* 2: 1019. 1753.
"Habitat in Alpibus Lapponicis." RCN: 7377.
Lectotype (Jonsell & Jarvis in *Nordic J. Bot.* 14: 151. 1994): Herb.
Linn. No. 1158.54 (LINN).
Current name: ***Salix lanata*** L. (Salicaceae).

Salix lapponum Linnaeus, *Species Plantarum* 2: 1019. 1753.
"Habitat in Alpibus Lapponiae ubique, Helvetiae." RCN: 7378.
Lectotype (Jonsell & Jarvis in *Nordic J. Bot.* 14: 151. 1994): Herb.
Linn. No. 1158.57, upper female specimen (LINN).
Current name: ***Salix lapponum*** L. (Salicaceae).

Salix myrsinites Linnaeus, *Species Plantarum* 2: 1018. 1753.
"Habitat in Alpibus Lapponiae, Helvetiae, Italiae." RCN: 7369.
Lectotype (Jonsell & Jarvis in *Nordic J. Bot.* 14: 151. 1994): Herb.
Linn. No. 1158.30 (LINN).
Current name: ***Salix myrsinites*** L. (Salicaceae).

Salix myrtilloides Linnaeus, *Species Plantarum* 2: 1019. 1753.
"Habitat in Suecia septentrionali." RCN: 7374.
Lectotype (Jonsell & Jarvis in *Nordic J. Bot.* 14: 151. 1994): Herb.
Linn. No. 1158.49 (LINN).
Current name: ***Salix myrtilloides*** L. (Salicaceae).

Salix pentandra Linnaeus, *Species Plantarum* 2: 1016. 1753.
"Habitat in Europae paludibus montosis duris." RCN: 7359.
Lectotype (Jonsell & Jarvis in *Nordic J. Bot.* 14: 152. 1994): *Amman
8*, Herb. Linn. No. 1158.5 (LINN).
Current name: ***Salix pentandra*** L. (Salicaceae).

Salix phylicifolia Linnaeus, *Species Plantarum* 2: 1016. 1753.
"Habitat in Sueciae borealibus." RCN: 7360.
Lectotype (Jonsell & Jarvis in *Nordic J. Bot.* 14: 152. 1994): Herb.
Linn. No. 1158.9 (LINN).
Current name: ***Salix phylicifolia*** L. (Salicaceae).

Salix purpurea Linnaeus, *Species Plantarum* 2: 1017. 1753.
"Habitat in Europae australioribus." RCN: 7367.
Neotype (Jonsell & Jarvis in *Nordic J. Bot.* 14: 152. 1994): Sweden.
Scania, Solberga, Torsjö, *Karlsson 93149* (LD; iso- BM, C, H, O, S,
UPS).
Current name: ***Salix purpurea*** L. (Salicaceae).

Salix repens Linnaeus, *Species Plantarum* 2: 1020. 1753.
"Habitat inter montes Sueciae, locis humidis." RCN: 7381.
Lectotype (Jonsell & Jarvis in *Nordic J. Bot.* 14: 152. 1994): Herb.
Linn. No. 1158.71 (LINN).
Current name: ***Salix repens*** L. (Salicaceae).

Salix reticulata Linnaeus, *Species Plantarum* 2: 1018. 1753.
"Habitat in Alpibus Lapponiae, Helvetiae." RCN: 7373.
Lectotype (Jonsell & Jarvis in *Nordic J. Bot.* 14: 152. 1994): Herb.
Linn. No. 1158.45 (LINN).
Current name: ***Salix reticulata*** L. (Salicaceae).

Salix retusa Linnaeus, *Systema Naturae*, ed. 10, 2: 1287. 1759.
["Habitat in Alpibus Helvetiae, Austriae, Italiae."] Sp. Pl., ed. 2, 2:
1445 (1763). RCN: 7372.
Lectotype (designated here by Belyaeva): *Séguier*, Herb. Linn. No.
1158.43 (LINN).
Current name: ***Salix retusa*** L. (Salicaceae).

Salix rosmarinifolia Linnaeus, *Species Plantarum* 2: 1020. 1753.
"Habitat in Europae campis depressis." RCN: 7383.
Lectotype (Jonsell & Jarvis in *Nordic J. Bot.* 14: 152. 1994): Herb.
Linn. No. 1158.80 (LINN).
Current name: ***Salix repens*** L. subsp. ***rosmarinifolia*** (L.) Andersson
(Salicaceae).

Salix triandra Linnaeus, *Species Plantarum* 2: 1016. 1753.
"Habitat in Helvetia, Sibiria." RCN: 7358.
Lectotype (Jonsell & Jarvis in *Nordic J. Bot.* 14: 152. 1994): *Amman
9*, Herb. Linn. No. 1158.4 (LINN).
Current name: ***Salix triandra*** L. (Salicaceae).

Salix viminalis Linnaeus, *Species Plantarum* 2: 1021. 1753.
"Habitat in Europa ad pagos." RCN: 7385.
Lectotype (Larsson in *Nordic J. Bot.* 15: 343. 1996 [1995]): Herb.
Linn. No. 1158.82 (LINN).
Current name: ***Salix viminalis*** L. (Salicaceae).

Salix vitellina Linnaeus, *Species Plantarum* 2: 1016. 1753.
"Habitat in Europa temperatiore." RCN: 7361.
Lectotype (designated here by Belyaeva): Herb. Linn. No. 1158.13,
female specimen (LINN).
Current name: ***Salix alba*** L. var. ***vitellina*** (L.) Stokes (Salicaceae).

Salsola altissima (Linnaeus) Linnaeus, *Species Plantarum*, ed. 2, 1:
324. 1762.
"Habitat in Salinas Italiae, Saxoniae, Astracani." RCN: 1824.
Basionym: *Chenopodium altissimum* L. (1753).
Lectotype (designated here by Freitag): Herb. Linn. No. 315.10, right
specimen (LINN).
Current name: ***Salsola altissima*** (L.) L. (Chenopodiaceae).

S

Salsola fruticosa (Linnaeus) Linnaeus, *Species Plantarum,* ed. 2, 1: 324. 1762.
"Habitat in maritimis Galliae, Hispaniae, Persiae." RCN: 1830.
Basionym: *Chenopodium fruticosum* L. (1753).
Lectotype (Heath in *Calyx* 2: 78. 1992): [icon] *"Sedum minus arborescens"* in Munting, Naauwk. Beschryv. Aardgew.: 469, t. 469. 1696.
Current name: ***Suaeda vera*** Forssk. ex J.F. Gmel. (Chenopodiaceae).

Salsola hirsuta (Linnaeus) Linnaeus, *Species Plantarum,* ed. 2, 1: 323. 1762.
"Habitat in Daniae, Monspelii maritimis." RCN: 1826.
Basionym: *Chenopodium hirsutum* L. (1753).
Lectotype (Jonsell & Jarvis in *Nordic J. Bot.* 14: 155. 1994): Herb. Burser XVI(2): 19 (UPS).
Current name: ***Bassia hirsuta*** (L.) Asch. (Chenopodiaceae).

Salsola kali Linnaeus, *Species Plantarum* 1: 222. 1753.
"Habitat in Europae litoribus maris." RCN: 1819.
Lectotype (Jonsell & Jarvis in *Nordic J. Bot.* 14: 155. 1994; Rilke in *Biblioth. Bot.* 149: 141. 1999): Herb. Burser XVI(2): 24, right specimen (UPS). – Epitype (Rilke in *Biblioth. Bot.* 149: 141. 1999): Herb. Clifford: 86, *Salsola* 2 (BM).
Current name: ***Salsola kali*** L. (Chenopodiaceae).
Note: Jonsell & Jarvis (in *Nordic J. Bot.* 14: 155. 1994) designated the Burser material as lectotype. However, Freitag (*in litt.*) has pointed out that this is a mixed sheet of *S. tragus* (left) and *S. kali* (right) and Rilke (in *Biblioth. Bot.* 149: 141. 1999) restricts this choice to the right-hand specimen, and also designates an epitype.

Salsola muricata Linnaeus, *Systema Naturae,* ed. 12, 2: 196; *Mantissa Plantarum*: 54. 1767.
"Habitat in Europa australi, Aegypto." RCN: 1831.
Lectotype (Jafri & Rateeb in Jafri & El-Gadi, *Fl. Libya* 58: 23. 1978): Herb. Linn. No. 315.22 (LINN).
Current name: ***Bassia muricata*** (L.) Asch. (Chenopodiaceae).

Salsola polyclonos Linnaeus, *Systema Naturae,* ed. 12, 2: 196; *Mantissa Plantarum*: 54. 1767.
"Habitat in Siciliae, Hispaniae maritimis." RCN: 1827.
Lectotype (Castroviejo & al. in *Anales Jard. Bot. Madrid* 43: 478. 1987): *Alströmer s.n.*, Herb. Linn. No. 315.18 (LINN).
Current name: ***Halogeton sativus*** (L.) Moq. (Chenopodiaceae).

Salsola prostrata Linnaeus, *Species Plantarum* 1: 222. 1753.
"Habitat in Asia boreali, Virginia." RCN: 1828.
Lectotype (Kit Tan in Strid & Kit Tan, *Fl. Hellenica* 1: 128. 1997): *Steller*, Herb. Linn. No. 315.15 (LINN).
Current name: ***Kochia prostrata*** (L.) Schrad. (Chenopodiaceae).

Salsola rosacea Linnaeus, *Species Plantarum* 1: 222. 1753, *nom. cons.*
"Habitat ad Asiae septentrionalis salinas." RCN: 1821.
Conserved type (Rilke in *Taxon* 47: 165. 1998): Kazakstan. Taldy-Kurgan Distr, 9 Sep 1992, *Freitag & Rilke 26208a* (LE; iso- AA, B, C, K, KAS).
Current name: ***Salsola rosacea*** L. (Chenopodiaceae).

Salsola salsa (Linnaeus) Linnaeus, *Species Plantarum,* ed. 2, 1: 324. 1762.
"Habitat ad Astracanum." RCN: 1825.
Basionym: *Chenopodium salsum* L. (1753).
Lectotype (Freitag & Lomonosova in *Willdenowia* 36: 25. 2006): Herb. Linn. No. 315.12 (LINN). – Epitype (Freitag & Lomonosova in *Willdenowia* 36: 25, f. 3, 4. 2006): Russia.

Astrakhan prov., northern part of Astrakhan city, near bus station Novostroi, 7 Oct 2004, *M. Lomonosova 716* (NS; iso- AA, ALTB, B, C etc.).
Current name: ***Suaeda salsa*** (L.) Pall. (Chenopodiaceae).

Salsola sativa Linnaeus, *Species Plantarum,* ed. 2, 1: 323. 1762.
"Habitat in Hispaniae australis maritimis." RCN: 1823.
Type not designated.
Original material: Herb. Linn. No. 315.9 (LINN); Herb. Linn. No. 315.32? (LINN); Herb. Linn. No. 315.18? (LINN).
Current name: ***Halogeton sativus*** (L.) Moq. (Chenopodiaceae).
Note: Blackwell & al. (in *Sida* 8: 161. 1979) referred to a specimen in LINN as the "type specimen" but did not distinguish between sheets 315.9, 315.18 and 315.32 (which are not part of a single gathering so Art. 9.15 does not apply). Castroviejo & al. (in *Anales Jard. Bot. Madrid* 43: 477. 1987) discussed these specimens in some detail and concluded that *S. sativa* was a new species based in part on *S. souda* Loefl. (1758), which Linnaeus cited in the protologue of *S. sativa*. Castroviejo & al. argue that *S. souda* is merely an orthographic variant of *S. soda* L. (1753) but that in 1762, Linnaeus recognised that Löfling's plant was distinct from *S. soda* and gave it the name *S. sativa*. In the absence of *Löfling 123*, they typified the name using Löfling's description, though this is now contrary to Art. 9, a type being either a specimen or an illustration.

Salsola sedoides Linnaeus, *Amoenitates Academicae* 4: 98. 1759.
"Habitat [in Anglia.]"
Type not designated.
Original material: none traced.
Current name: ***Suaeda maritima*** (L.) Dumort. (Chenopodiaceae).
Note: See Stearn (*Introd. Ray's Syn. Meth. Stirp. Brit.* (Ray Soc. ed.): 67. 1973), who treated this as synonymous with *Chenopodium maritimum* L.

Salsola soda Linnaeus, *Species Plantarum* 1: 223. 1753.
"Habitat in Europae australis salsis." RCN: 1822.
Lectotype (Hedge in Jarvis & al., *Regnum Veg.* 127: 84. 1993): *Löfling s.n.*, Herb. Linn. No. 315.7 (LINN).
Generitype of *Salsola* Linnaeus (vide Hitchcock, *Prop. Brit. Bot.*: 137. 1929).
Current name: ***Salsola soda*** L. (Chenopodiaceae).

Salsola tragus Linnaeus, *Centuria II Plantarum*: 13. 1756.
"Habitat in Europa australi. Sauvage." RCN: 1820.
Lectotype (Degen, *Fl. Velebitica* 2: 46. 1937): Herb. Linn. No. 315.3 (LINN). – Epitype (Rilke in *Biblioth. Bot.* 149: 111. 1999): Herb. Burser XVI(2): 24, left specimen (UPS).
Current name: ***Salsola tragus*** L. (Chenopodiaceae).

Salsola vermiculata Linnaeus, *Species Plantarum* 1: 223. 1753.
"Habitat in Hispania." RCN: 1829.
Lectotype (Jafri & Rateeb in Jafri & El-Gadi, *Fl. Libya* 58: 85. 1978): Herb. Linn. No. 315.19 (LINN).
Current name: ***Salsola vermiculata*** L. (Chenopodiaceae).
Note: Botschantzev (in *Novosti Sist. Vyssh. Rast.* 12: 176. 1975) indicated 315.20 (LINN) as the type. This sheet is annotated "vermiculata L[oefling] 200" by Linnaeus, and lacks the *Species Plantarum* number (i.e. "4") that would ordinarily indicate a collection in Linnaeus' possession in 1753. Linnaeus' statement "Habitat in Hispania" was probably derived from the cited synonyms rather than this specimen, so the latter is not regarded as relevant original material. Jafri & Rateeb designated 315.19 (LINN) as type which, as it appears to be original material, is accepted here.

Salvadora persica Linnaeus, *Species Plantarum* 1: 122. 1753.
"Habitat ad Sinum Persicum." RCN: 1010.
Lectotype (Riedl in *Bol. Soc. Brot., sér. 2*, 53: 217, f. 2. 1980): *"Galenia forte Linnaei"*, Herb. Burman (G).
Generitype of *Salvadora* Linnaeus.
Current name: ***Salvadora persica*** L. (Salvadoraceae).
Note: Verdcourt (in *Kew Bull.* 14: 150. 1964) provided an extensive discussion and reluctantly designated 164.1 (LINN), a post-1753 addition to the herbarium, as lectotype. It was not original material for the name, and Riedl subsequently designated Garcin material (G) as lectotype.

Salvia acetabulosa Linnaeus, *Systema Naturae*, ed. 12, 2: 66; *Mantissa Plantarum*: 25. 1767.
"Habitat in Oriente." RCN: 212.
Lectotype (Hedge in *Notes Roy. Bot. Gard. Edinburgh* 22: 427. 1958): *J. Burman s.n.*, Herb. Linn. No. 42.42 (LINN).
Current name: ***Salvia africana*** L. (Lamiaceae).

Salvia aegyptiaca Linnaeus, *Species Plantarum* 1: 23. 1753.
"Habitat in Aegypto." RCN: 182.
Lectotype (Hedge in *Notes Roy. Bot. Gard. Edinburgh* 33: 37. 1974): Herb. Clifford: 13, *Salvia* 17 (BM-000557609).
Current name: ***Salvia aegyptiaca*** L. (Lamiaceae).

Salvia aegyptiaca Linnaeus, *Systema Naturae*, ed. 12, 2: 66; *Mantissa Plantarum*: 26. 1767, *nom. illeg.*
"Habitat in Aegypto. Forskåhl." RCN: 213.
Replaced synonym of: *Salvia spinosa* L. (1771).
Lectotype (Hedge in *Notes Roy. Bot. Gard. Edinburgh* 33: 89. 1974): Herb. Linn. No. 42.44 (LINN).
Current name: ***Salvia spinosa*** L. (Lamiaceae).
Note: Salvia aegyptiaca L. (1767) is a later homonym (and therefore illegitimate) of *S. aegyptiaca* L. (1753), the latter also appearing in *Syst. Nat.*, ed. 12, 2 : 64 (1767). *Salvia spinosa* was published as a *nomen novum* for *S. aegyptiaca* L. (1767, non 1753).

Salvia aethiopis Linnaeus, *Species Plantarum* 1: 27. 1753.
"Habitat in Illyria, Graecia, Africa." RCN: 216.
Lectotype (Hedge in Rechinger, *Fl. Iranica* 150: 451. 1982): Herb. Linn. No. 42.48 (LINN).
Current name: ***Salvia aethiopis*** L. (Lamiaceae).

Salvia africana Linnaeus, *Species Plantarum*, ed. 2, 1: 38. 1762.
"Habitat ad Cap. b. spei, locis argillosis." RCN: 208.
Lectotype (Hedge in *Notes Roy. Bot. Gard. Edinburgh* 22: 427. 1958): Herb. Clifford: 13, *Salvia* 13 (BM-000557605).
Current name: ***Salvia africana*** L. (Lamiaceae).
Note: A replacement for the invalid *"Salvia africana caerulea"* L. (1753) – see Art. 23.6(c) Ex. 15.

Salvia africana caerulea Linnaeus, *Species Plantarum* 1: 26. 1753, *nom. inval.*
"Habitat ad Cap. b. spei, locis argillosis." RCN: 208.
Type not relevant.
Current name: ***Salvia africana*** L. (Lamiaceae).
Note: "Salvia africana caerulea" L. (1753) is a generic name followed by two adjectival words in the nominative case and is not a valid species name (Art. 23.6(c) Ex. 15).

Salvia africana lutea Linnaeus, *Species Plantarum* 1: 26. 1753, *nom. inval.*
"Habitat ad Cap. b. spei, juxta rivulos." RCN: 209.
Type not relevant.
Current name: ***Salvia aurea*** L. (Lamiaceae).

Note: "Salvia africana lutea" L. (1753) is a generic name followed by two adjectival words in the nominative case and is not a valid species name (Art. 23.6(c) Ex. 15).

Salvia agrestis Linnaeus, *Demonstr. Pl. Horto Upsaliensi*: 2. 1753.
"Habitat in Germaniae pratis." RCN: 196.
Lectotype (Del Carratore & al. in *Pl. Biosystems* 132: 171. 1998): Herb. Linn. No. 42.18 (LINN).
Current name: ***Salvia pratensis*** L. (Lamiaceae).

Salvia argentea Linnaeus, *Species Plantarum*, ed. 2, 1: 38. 1762.
"Habitat in Creta." RCN: 218.
Lectotype (Rosúa & Blanca in *Taxon* 35: 719. 1986): Herb. Linn. No. 42.53 (LINN).
Current name: ***Salvia argentea*** L. (Lamiaceae).

Salvia aurea Linnaeus, *Species Plantarum*, ed. 2, 1: 38. 1762.
"Habitat ad Cap. b. spei juxta rivulos." RCN: 209.
Lectotype (Hedge in *Notes Roy. Bot. Gard. Edinburgh* 33: 44. 1974): Herb. Linn. No. 42.38 (LINN).
Current name: ***Salvia aurea*** L. (Lamiaceae).
Note: A replacement for the invalid *"Salvia africana aurea"* L. (1753) – see Art. 23.6(c) Ex. 15.

Salvia canariensis Linnaeus, *Species Plantarum* 1: 26. 1753.
"Habitat in Canariis." RCN: 207.
Lectotype (Hedge in *Notes Roy. Bot. Gard. Edinburgh* 33: 49. 1974): Herb. Clifford: 13, *Salvia* 12 (BM-000557604).
Current name: ***Salvia canariensis*** L. (Lamiaceae).

Salvia ceratophylla Linnaeus, *Species Plantarum* 1: 27. 1753.
"Habitat in Persia." RCN: 215.
Lectotype (Hedge in Rechinger, *Fl. Iranica* 150: 452. 1982): Herb. Linn. No. 42.47 (LINN).
Current name: ***Salvia ceratophylla*** L. (Lamiaceae).

Salvia clandestina Linnaeus, *Species Plantarum*, ed. 2, 1: 36. 1762.
"Habitat in Italia." RCN: 200.
Lectotype (Del Carratore & al. in *Pl. Biosystems* 132: 174, f. 4. 1998): [icon] *"Horminum syl. inciso folio, caesio flore, Ital."* in Barrelier, Pl. Galliam: 24, t. 220. 1714.
Current name: ***Salvia clandestina*** L. (Lamiaceae).
Note: Codd (in Leistner, *Fl. Southern Africa* 28(4): 97. 1985) indicated material at LINN (conceivably only 42.23) as holotype. However, this material conflicts with the protologue in several ways and also is identifiable as *S. lanigera* Poiret. Del Carratore & al. therefore rejected this type choice in favour of the Barrelier plate. They also recognise *S. clandestina* as a species distinct from *S. verbenaca* L., in contrast to many other authors.

Salvia colorata Linnaeus, *Systema Naturae*, ed. 12, 2: 66. 1767.
RCN: 210.
Lectotype (Codd in Leistner, *Fl. Southern Africa* 28(4): 83. 1985): Herb. Linn. No. 42.39 (LINN).
Current name: ***Salvia aurea*** L. (Lamiaceae).

Salvia cretica Linnaeus, *Species Plantarum* 1: 23. 1753.
"Habitat in Creta." RCN: 183.
Neotype (Paton in Jarvis & al. in *Taxon* 50: 517. 2001): Cultivated. Royal Botanic Gardens, Kew, 6 Jul 1880, *Nicholson 1586* (K).
Current name: ***Salvia officinalis*** L. (Lamiaceae).
Note: This name has not been in use for many years, and has been variously associated with *S. lavandulifolia* Vahl, *S. officinalis* L. and *S. aucheri* Benth. There are no extant original elements for the name, and the neotype chosen by Paton results in *S. cretica* becoming a synonym of *S. officinalis*.

S

Salvia disermas Linnaeus, *Species Plantarum*, ed. 2, 1: 36. 1762.
"Habitat in Syria." RCN: 202.
Lectotype (Hedge in *Notes Roy. Bot. Gard. Edinburgh* 33: 107. 1974):
   Herb. Linn. No. 42.26 (LINN).
Current name: ***Salvia disermas*** L. (Lamiaceae).

Salvia dominica Linnaeus, *Species Plantarum* 1: 25. 1753.
"Habitat in Domingo." RCN: 198.
Lectotype (Hedge in *Notes Roy. Bot. Gard. Edinburgh* 23: 55. 1959):
   Herb. Linn. No. 42.19 (LINN).
Current name: ***Salvia dominica*** L. (Lamiaceae).

Salvia forskahlei Linnaeus, *Systema Naturae,* ed. 12, 2: 67; *Mantissa
   Plantarum*: 26. 1767.
"Habitat in Oriente. Forskåhl." RCN: 220.
Lectotype (Hedge in *Notes Roy. Bot. Gard. Edinburgh* 23: 53. 1959):
   Herb. Linn. No. 42.56 (LINN).
Current name: ***Salvia forskahlei*** L. (Lamiaceae).

Salvia glutinosa Linnaeus, *Species Plantarum* 1: 26. 1753.
"Habitat in Europae lutosis." RCN: 206.
Lectotype (Hedge in Jarvis & al. in *Taxon* 50: 517. 2001): Herb. Linn.
   No. 19: *Salvia glutinosa* (H).
Current name: ***Salvia glutinosa*** L. (Lamiaceae).
Note: Hedge (in *Notes Roy. Bot. Gard. Edinburgh* 23: 206. 1961; in
   Rechinger, *Fl. Iranica* 150: 467. 1982) indicated sheet 42.34
   (LINN) as type, but this is a post-1753 addition to the herbarium. A
   sheet from the Linnaean herbarium in Helsinki, described and
   illustrated by Kukkonen & Viljamaa (in *Ann. Bot. Fennici* 10: 313, f.
   1. 1973), was therefore designated by Hedge as lectotype in its place.

Salvia haematodes Linnaeus, *Species Plantarum* 1: 24. 1753.
"Habitat in Italia." RCN: 195.
Lectotype (Del Carratore & al. in *Pl. Biosystems* 132: 172, f. 2. 1998):
   [icon] *"Horminum sanguineum Asphodeli radice"* in Trionfetti, Obs.
   Ortu Veg. Pl.: 69, unnumbered plate. 1685 (see right).
Current name: ***Salvia pratensis*** L. subsp. ***haematodes*** (L.) Briq.
   (Lamiaceae).

Salvia hispanica Linnaeus, *Species Plantarum* 1: 25. 1753.
"Habitat in Italia. D. Rathgeb; in Hispania. Loefling." RCN: 204.
Lectotype (Wood & Harley in *Kew Bull.* 44: 225. 1989): [icon]
   "Sclarea hispanica" in Tabernaemontanus, New Vollk. Kräuterb.:
   764. 1664.
Current name: ***Salvia hispanica*** L. (Lamiaceae).
Note: Epling (in *J. Bot.* 67: 5. 1929) treated a Linnaean sheet as the
   standard (but not the same as a type). Wood & Harley's appears to
   be the earliest formal choice of type.

Salvia horminum Linnaeus, *Species Plantarum* 1: 24. 1753.
"Habitat in Graecia, Apulia." RCN: 190.
Lectotype (Hedge in Jarvis & al. in *Taxon* 50: 517. 2001): Herb.
   Clifford: 12, *Salvia* 3 (BM-000557585).
Current name: ***Salvia viridis*** L. (Lamiaceae).
Note: Although Heath (in *Calyx* 5: 152. 1997) says this is partly based
   on a Bauhin & Cherler element, this statement does not constitute
   typification.

Salvia indica Linnaeus, *Species Plantarum* 1: 26. 1753.
"Habitat in India." RCN: 197.
Neotype (Hedge in Jarvis & al. in *Taxon* 50: 517. 2001): Herb.
   Tournefort No. 1079 (P-TOURN).
Current name: ***Salvia indica*** L. (Lamiaceae).
Note: Hedge (in Davis, *Fl. Turkey* 7: 451. 1982; in Rechinger, *Fl.
   Iranica* 150: 466. 1982) noted the absence of material in LINN and

The lectotype of *Salvia haematodes* L.

suggested that a Tournefort collection "could possibly be selected as
type". He subsequently (2001) formalised this suggestion by
designating it as a neotype.

Salvia lyrata Linnaeus, *Species Plantarum* 1: 23. 1753.
"Habitat in Virginia." RCN: 184.
Lectotype (Reveal & al. in *Huntia* 7: 236. 1987): *Kalm*, Herb. Linn.
   No. 42.2 (LINN).
Current name: ***Salvia lyrata*** L. (Lamiaceae).
Note: Although Epling (in *J. Bot.* 67: 6. 1929) noted the existence of
   Kalm's sheet in LINN, and treated a Clayton sheet as the standard
   (not the same as the type), Reveal & al. appear to have been the first
   to make a formal typification.

Salvia mexicana Linnaeus, *Species Plantarum* 1: 25. 1753.
"Habitat in Mexicae humentibus." RCN: 203.
Lectotype (Hedge in Jarvis & al. in *Taxon* 50: 518. 2001): [icon]
   "Sclarea Mexicana altissima, facie Heliotropii" in Dillenius, Hort.
   Eltham. 2: 339, t. 254, f. 330. 1732.
Current name: ***Salvia mexicana*** L. (Lamiaceae).
Note: Epling (in *J. Bot.* 67: 5. 1929) treated Dillenius' plate as the
   standard (as distinct from the type) but he later (*Repert. Spec. Nov.
   Regni Veg. Beih.* 110: 268. 1939) says "per icon et descriptionem
   Dillenii constituta est; typum in herb. Dillenio in horto Elthamensi

cultum vidi". He adds that Linnaeus' name "was based upon Dillenius's plant which is the large flowered form and a well-preserved specimen. *S. mexicana* in the Linnean Herbarium [42.28 (LINN)] is a sterile twig". As Dillenius' specimen is not technically eligible as lectotype, because it was not seen by Linnaeus, Dillenius' illustration was designated as lectotype by Hedge.

Salvia nemorosa Linnaeus, *Species Plantarum*, ed. 2, 1: 35. 1762.
"Habitat in Austria, Tataria." RCN: 193.
Lectotype (Hedge in *Notes Roy. Bot. Gard. Edinburgh* 23: 565. 1961): *Gerber*, Herb. Linn. No. 42.14 (LINN).
Current name: *Salvia nemorosa* L. (Lamiaceae).
Note: López González (in *Anales Jard. Bot. Madrid* 37: 207. 1980), presumably in ignorance of Hedge's typifications, argued that this and *S. sylvestris* L. (1753) are homotypic, based on 42.14 (LINN). However, Hedge's type choices for these names have priority.

Salvia nutans Linnaeus, *Species Plantarum* 1: 27. 1753.
"Habitat in Imperio Rutheno." RCN: 221.
Lectotype (Stearn in *Taxon* 10: 17. 1961): Herb. Linn. No. 42.57 (LINN).
Current name: *Salvia nutans* L. (Lamiaceae).

Salvia officinalis Linnaeus, *Species Plantarum* 1: 23. 1753.
"Habitat in Europa australi." RCN: 185.
Lectotype (Rosúa & Jarvis in *Taxon* 36: 635. 1987): Herb. Clifford: 12, *Salvia* 2 (BM-000557576).
Generitype of *Salvia* Linnaeus (vide Hitchcock, *Prop. Brit. Bot.*: 117. 1929).
Current name: *Salvia officinalis* L. (Lamiaceae).
Note: A number of authors (e.g. Valdés-Bermejo & López González in *Anales Inst. Bot. Cavanilles* 34: 165. 1977; Rosúa & Blanca in *Acta Bot. Malac.* 11: 266. 1986) have treated 42.3 (LINN) as the type. However, the sheet lacks the *Species Plantarum* number (i.e. "4") and is a post-1753 addition to the herbarium. It was therefore rejected as the type by Rosúa & Jarvis in favour of the Clifford material.

Salvia paniculata Linnaeus, *Systema Naturae*, ed. 12, 2: 66; *Mantissa Plantarum*: 25. 1767.
"Habitat in Africa. D. Royen." RCN: 211.
Lectotype (Codd in Leistner, *Fl. Southern Africa* 28(4): 87. 1985): Herb. Linn. No. 42.40 (LINN).
Current name: *Salvia chamelaeagnea* P.J. Bergius (Lamiaceae).

Salvia pinnata Linnaeus, *Species Plantarum* 1: 27. 1753.
"Habitat in Oriente & Arabia." RCN: 217.
Lectotype (Hedge in Jarvis & al. in *Taxon* 50: 518. 2001): Herb. Clifford: 13, *Salvia* 16 (BM-000557608).
Current name: *Salvia pinnata* L. (Lamiaceae).
Note: Hedge (in Meikle, *Fl. Cyprus*: 1291. 1985) treated 42.52 (LINN) as the type, but this is rejected as a post-1753 addition to the herbarium. However, there is good material in the Clifford herbarium which Hedge subsequently designated as the lectotype.

Salvia pomifera Linnaeus, *Species Plantarum* 1: 24. 1753.
"Habitat in Creta." RCN: 186.
Lectotype (Hedge in Jarvis & al. in *Taxon* 50: 518. 2001): [icon] *"Salvia Cretica, frutescens, pomifera, foliis longioribus, incanis et crispis"* in Tournefort, Rel. Voy. Levant (Paris ed.) 1: 77. 1717. – Epitype (Hedge in Jarvis & al. in *Taxon* 50: 518. 2001): Greece. Crete, Agios Vasilios/Amari, 2.5km SE of Spili, gorge 1.25km N of Kissos, 700m, 28 Jun 1994, *Turland 783* (BM-000098211; iso-UPA).
Current name: *Salvia pomifera* L. (Lamiaceae).

Salvia pratensis Linnaeus, *Species Plantarum* 1: 25. 1753.
"Habitat in Europae pratis." RCN: 196.
Lectotype (Del Carratore & al. in *Pl. Biosystems* 132: 170, f. 1. 1998): Herb. Burser XIII: 111 (UPS).
Current name: *Salvia pratensis* L. (Lamiaceae).

Salvia pyrenaica Linnaeus, *Species Plantarum* 1: 25. 1753.
"Habitat in Pyrenaeis." RCN: 201.
Lectotype (Hedge in Jarvis & al. in *Taxon* 50: 518. 2001): [icon] *"Horminum Anguriae folio"* in Hermann, Parad. Bat.: 187. 1698.
Current name: *Salvia verbenaca* L. (Lamiaceae).

Salvia sclarea Linnaeus, *Species Plantarum* 1: 27. 1753.
"Habitat in Syria, Italia." RCN: 214.
Lectotype (Rosúa & Blanca in *Taxon* 35: 719. 1986): Herb. Burser XIII: 108 (UPS).
Current name: *Salvia sclarea* L. (Lamiaceae).
Note: Hedge (in Rechinger, *Fl. Iranica* 150: 452. 1982) indicated the inadequate 42.45 (LINN) as the type, but Rosúa & Blanca argued that this collection conflicted with Linnaeus' protologue (and was also identifiable as *S. argentea* L. 1762). They therefore designated Burser material, from Italy, as the lectotype.

Salvia serotina Linnaeus, *Systema Naturae,* ed. 12, 2: 65; *Mantissa Plantarum*: 25. 1767.
"Habitat in Chio? Arduini." RCN: 188.
Lectotype (Hedge in Jarvis & al. in *Taxon* 50: 519. 2001): Herb. Linn. No. 42.9 (LINN).
Current name: *Salvia serotina* L. (Lamiaceae).
Note: Epling (in *J. Bot.* 67: 5. 1929) treated 42.9 (LINN) as "the probable historical type" but he later (in *Repert. Spec. Nov. Regni Veg. Beih.* 110: 77. 1939) concluded that the name had been based on material originally sent to Linnaeus by Arduino but subsequently lost, and discounted 42.9 (LINN) as type. Howard (in *Fl. Lesser Antilles* 6: 262. 1989) indicated de Jussieu material (P 5253) as type but this would necessarily be a neotype, which cannot be accepted in the presence of original material (42.9 LINN; Arduino's cited t. 2, 1759) for the name. The extant specimen was therefore chosen as the lectotype by Hedge.

Salvia spinosa Linnaeus, *Mantissa Plantarum Altera*: 511. 1771.
"Habitat in Aegypto. Forskåhl." RCN: 213.
Replaced synonym: *Salvia aegyptiaca* L. (1767), *nom. illeg.*, non L. (1753).
Lectotype (Hedge in *Notes Roy. Bot. Gard. Edinburgh* 33: 89. 1974): Herb. Linn. No. 42.44 (LINN).
Current name: *Salvia spinosa* L. (Lamiaceae).
Note: Salvia aegyptiaca L. (1767) is a later homonym of *S. aegyptiaca* L. (1753), and therefore illegitimate, the latter name also appearing in *Syst. Nat.*, ed. 12, 2 : 64 (1767). *Salvia spinosa* was published as a *nomen novum* for *S. aegyptiaca* (1767, non 1753).

Salvia sylvestris Linnaeus, *Species Plantarum* 1: 24. 1753.
"Habitat in Austriae inferioris, Bohemiae agrorum, marginibus, vineis." RCN: 192.
Lectotype (Hedge in *Notes Roy. Bot. Gard. Edinburgh* 23: 564. 1961): Herb. Burser XIII: 117 (UPS).
Current name: *Salvia sylvestris* L. (Lamiaceae).
Note: López González (in *Anales Jard. Bot. Madrid* 37: 207. 1980), presumably in ignorance of Hedge's typifications, argued that this and *S. nemorosa* L. (1762) are homotypic, based on 42.14 (LINN). However, Hedge's type choices for these names have priority.

Salvia syriaca Linnaeus, *Systema Naturae*, ed. 10, 2: 854. 1759.
["Habitat in Oriente, Palaestina. Hasselquist."] Sp. Pl. ed. 2, 1: 37 (1762). RCN: 194.

S

Lectotype (Hedge in Rechinger, *Fl. Iranica* 150: 435. 1982):
Hasselquist, Herb. Linn. No. 42.15 (LINN; iso- UPS-HASSELQ
471, 472).
Current name: **Salvia syriaca** L. (Lamiaceae).

Salvia urticifolia Linnaeus, *Species Plantarum* 1: 24. 1753.
"Habitat in Virginia." RCN: 187.
Lectotype (Epling in *Repert. Spec. Nov. Regni Veg. Beih.* 110: 58.
1939): *Clayton 292* (BM-000042241).
Current name: **Salvia urticifolia** L. (Lamiaceae).
Note: Epling (in *J. Bot.* 67: 6. 1929) noted the existence of a sheet in
LINN, and treated a Clayton sheet as the standard (not the same as
a type). However, he subsequently designated *Clayton 292* as the
type.

Salvia verbenaca Linnaeus, *Species Plantarum* 1: 25. 1753.
"Habitat in Europae pascuis." RCN: 199.
Lectotype (Del Carratore & al. in *Pl. Biosystems* 132: 173, f. 3. 1998):
[icon] *"Horminum syl. minus inciso folio fl. azureo"* in Barrelier, Pl.
Galliam: 24, t. 208. 1714.
Current name: **Salvia verbenaca** L. (Lamiaceae).
Note: Hedge (in *Notes Roy. Bot. Gard. Edinburgh* 33: 96. 1974),
followed by later authors, indicated the post-1753 42.20 (LINN) as
"type", but this collection lacks the *Species Plantarum* number (i.e.
"13"), is a post-1753 addition to the collection, and not original
material for the name. Del Carratore & al. therefore designated a
Barrelier plate as lectotype.

Salvia verticillata Linnaeus, *Species Plantarum* 1: 26. 1753.
"Habitat in Austriae, Misniae cultis & ruderatis." RCN: 205.
Lectotype (Hedge in Rechinger, *Fl. Iranica* 150: 473. 1982): Herb.
Linn. No. 42.30 (LINN).
Current name: **Salvia verticillata** L. (Lamiaceae).

Salvia viridis Linnaeus, *Species Plantarum* 1: 24. 1753.
"Habitat – – – –" RCN: 189.
Lectotype (Hedge in *Notes Roy. Bot. Gard. Edinburgh* 33: 94. 1974):
Herb. Linn. No. 42.11 (LINN).
Current name: **Salvia viridis** L. (Lamiaceae).

Samara laeta Linnaeus, *Mantissa Plantarum Altera*: 199. 1771, *nom.
illeg.*
"Habitat in India orientali." RCN: 966.
Replaced synonym: *Memecylon umbellatum* Burm. f. (1768).
Type not designated.
Generitype of *Samara* Linnaeus.
Current name: **Embelia laeta** (L.) Mez (Myrsinaceae).
Note: An illegitimate replacement name for *Memecylon umbellatum*
Burm. f. (1768) ["Menecyclon"]. However, *Embelia laeta* (L.)
Mez is a name in use (e.g. by Pipoly & Chen in *Novon* 5: 358.
1995) so there may be a case for the conservation of the Linnaean
name.

Sambucus canadensis Linnaeus, *Species Plantarum* 1: 269. 1753.
"Habitat in Canada. D. Kalm." RCN: 2143.
Lectotype (Bolli in *Diss. Bot.* 223: 168. 1994): Herb. Linn. No. 381.2
(LINN).
Current name: **Sambucus canadensis** L. (Caprifoliaceae).

Sambucus ebulus Linnaeus, *Species Plantarum* 1: 269. 1753.
"Habitat in Europa." RCN: 2142.
Lectotype (Bolli in *Diss. Bot.* 223: 140. 1994): Herb. Linn. No. 381.1
(LINN).
Current name: **Sambucus ebulus** L. (Caprifoliaceae).

Sambucus nigra Linnaeus, *Species Plantarum* 1: 269. 1753.
"Habitat in Germania." RCN: 2144.
Lectotype (Press in Jarvis & al., *Regnum Veg.* 127: 84. 1993): Herb.
Burser XXIV: 17 (UPS).
Generitype of *Sambucus* Linnaeus (vide Hitchcock, *Prop. Brit. Bot.*:
142. 1929).
Current name: **Sambucus nigra** L. (Caprifoliaceae).
Note: Bolli in *Diss. Bot.* 223: 161. 1994) indicated a sheet in LINN as
lectotype but this post-dates Press' choice.

Sambucus nigra Linnaeus var. **laciniata** Linnaeus, *Species Plantarum*
1: 270. 1753.
RCN: 2144.
Type not designated.
Original material: Herb. Burser XXIV: 20 (UPS); [icon] in Dodoëns,
Stirp. Hist. Pempt., ed. 2: 844, 845. 1616.
Current name: **Sambucus nigra** L. (Caprifoliaceae).
Note: Greuter (in *Candollea* 44 : 566. 1989) argues that Linnaeus
provided a new combination for this variety at the rank of species in
Fl. Anglica: 14 (1754). However the epithet is indented beneath
"nigra", elsewhere accepted by Greuter as acceptance of varietal rank.

Sambucus racemosa Linnaeus, *Species Plantarum* 1: 270. 1753.
"Habitat in Europae australis montosis." RCN: 2145.
Lectotype (Samutina in *Novosti Sist. Vyssh. Rast.* 23: 165. 1986): Herb.
Linn. No. 381.5 (LINN).
Current name: **Sambucus racemosa** L. (Caprifoliaceae).

Samolus valerandi Linnaeus, *Species Plantarum* 1: 171. 1753.
"Habitat in maritimis Europae, Asiae & Americae borealis." RCN:
1349.
Lectotype (Ali in Ali & Jafri, *Fl. Libya* 1: 4. 1976): Herb. Clifford: 51,
Samolus 1 (BM-000557957).
Generitype of *Samolus* Linnaeus.
Current name: **Samolus valerandi** L. (Primulaceae).
Note: Although Taylor (in Hubbard & Milne-Redhead, *Fl. Trop. E.
Africa, Primulaceae*: 19. 1958) indicated Clifford material (BM) as a
syntype (which is not, by definition, the sole type of a name, unlike
a holotype, lectotype or neotype), this statement is not accepted as
correctable to lectotype under Art. 9.8. Dyer (in Dyer & al., *Fl.
Southern Africa* 26: 10. 1963) indicated 225.1 (LINN) as type, but
this collection lacks the relevant *Species Plantarum* number (i.e. "1")
and was a post-1753 addition to the herbarium, and is not original
material for the name. Bizzarri (in *Webbia* 24: 687–688. 1970)
discussed the typification of the name in some detail but did not
designate a type.

Samolus valerandi Linnaeus var. **africanus** Linnaeus, *Species
Plantarum* 1: 172. 1753.
RCN: 1349.
Type not designated.
Original material: [icon] in Walther, Design. Pl.: 162, t. 23. 1735.
Current name: **Samolus valerandi** L. var. **africanus** L. (Primulaceae).
Note: Dyer (in Dyer & al., *Fl. Southern Africa* 26: 11. 1963) suggested
that this name probably relates to a North African taxon and may
be equivalent to *S. africanus* Burm. f.

Samyda guidonia Linnaeus, *Species Plantarum* 1: 443. 1753.
"Habitat in America calidiore." RCN: 3120.
Lectotype (Pennington, *Fl. Neotropica* 28: 265. 1981): [icon] *"Samyda
foliis ovatis acuminatis"* in Plumier in Burman, Pl. Amer.: 139, t.
147, f. 2. 1757.
Generitype of *Samyda* Linnaeus, *nom. rej.*
Current name: **Guarea guidonia** (L.) Sleumer (Meliaceae).
Note: Samyda Linnaeus, *nom. rej.* in favour of *Samyda* Jacq.

Samyda nitida Linnaeus, *Systema Naturae,* ed. 10, 2: 1025. 1759. ["Habitat in America."] Sp. Pl., ed. 2, 1: 557 (1762). RCN: 3122.
Lectotype (Sleumer, *Fl. Neotropica* 22: 297. 1980): [icon] *"Samyda fruticosa foliis nitidis cordatis, levissime crenatis; rudimentis mollibus rubentibus; racemis tenuioribus alaribus"* in Browne, Civ. Nat. Hist. Jamaica: 217, t. 23, f. 3. 1756.
Current name: ***Casearia nitida*** (L.) Jacq. (Flacourtiaceae).

Samyda parviflora Linnaeus, *Systema Naturae,* ed. 10, 2: 1025. 1759. ["Habitat in America."] Sp. Pl., ed. 2, 1: 557 (1762). RCN: 3121.
Lectotype (Sleumer, *Fl. Neotropica* 22: 391. 1980): *Browne,* Herb. Linn. No. 558.1 (LINN).
Current name: ***Casearia sylvestris*** Sw. (Flacourtiaceae).

Samyda pubescens Linnaeus, *Species Plantarum,* ed. 2, 1: 557. 1762. "Habitat in America." RCN: 3124.
Lectotype (Kiger ex Sleumer, *Fl. Neotropica* 22: 336. 1980): Herb. Linn. No. 558.2 (LINN).
Current name: ***Casearia guianensis*** (Aubl.) Urb. (Flacourtiaceae).

Samyda serrulata Linnaeus, *Species Plantarum,* ed. 2, 1: 557. 1762, *nom. illeg.*
"Habitat in America." RCN: 3125.
Replaced synonym: *Samyda dodecandra* Jacq. (1760).
Lectotype (Sleumer in *Taxon* 5: 194. 1956): [icon] *"Samyda foliis serratis, oblongis"* in Plumier in Burman, Pl. Amer.: 137, t. 146, f. 2. 1757.
Current name: ***Samyda dodecandra*** Jacq. (Flacourtiaceae).
Note: A superfluous name for *S. dodecandra* Jacq. (1760).

Samyda spinosa Linnaeus, *Species Plantarum,* ed. 2, 1: 557. 1762, *nom. illeg.*
"Habitat in America." RCN: 3123.
Replaced synonym: *Casearia aculeata* Jacq. (1760).
Lectotype (Sleumer, *Fl. Neotropica* 22: 328. 1980): [icon] *"Samyda spinosa, foliis ovatis, denticulatis"* in Plumier in Burman, Pl. Amer.: 138, t. 147, f. 1. 1757.
Current name: ***Casearia aculeata*** Jacq. (Flacourtiaceae).
Note: A superfluous name for *Casearia aculeata* Jacq. (1760).

Sanguinaria canadensis Linnaeus, *Species Plantarum* 1: 505. 1753. "Habitat in America septentrionali." RCN: 3832.
Lectotype (Reveal in Jarvis & al., *Regnum Veg.* 127: 84. 1993): *Kalm,* Herb. Linn. No. 666.1 (LINN).
Generitype of *Sanguinaria* Linnaeus.
Current name: ***Sanguinaria canadensis*** L. (Papaveraceae).

Sanguisorba canadensis Linnaeus, *Species Plantarum* 1: 117. 1753. "Habitat in Canada." RCN: 951.
Lectotype (Nordborg in *Opera Bot.* 11: 52. 1966): *Kalm,* Herb. Linn. No. 148.3 (LINN).
Current name: ***Sanguisorba canadensis*** L. (Rosaceae).

Sanguisorba media Linnaeus, *Species Plantarum,* ed. 2, 1: 169. 1762.
"Habitat in Canada." RCN: 950.
Lectotype (Robertson in Cafferty & Jarvis in *Taxon* 51: 544. 2002): [icon] *"Pimpinella minore di Canada"* in Zanoni, Istoria Bot.: 163, t. 65. 1675. – Epitype (Robertson in Cafferty & Jarvis in *Taxon* 51: 544. 2002): Canada. Yukon, West Dawson, 18 Aug 1902, Geog. Survey Can. No. 58, 463, *Macoun s.n.* (CAN-76417).
Current name: ***Sanguisorba officinalis*** L. (Rosaceae).

Sanguisorba officinalis Linnaeus, *Species Plantarum* 1: 116. 1753. "Habitat in Europae pratis siccioribus." RCN: 949.

Lectotype (Jonsell & Jarvis in *Nordic J. Bot.* 22: 76. 2002): Herb. Linn. No. 61.7 (S).
Generitype of *Sanguisorba* Linnaeus (vide Hitchcock, *Prop. Brit. Bot.*: 125. 1929).
Current name: ***Sanguisorba officinalis*** L. (Rosaceae).
Note: Nordborg (in *Opera Bot.* 11(2): 46. 1966) designated 148.2 (LINN), material associated with *S. media* by Linnaeus, as lectotype. It is not, however, original material for *S. officinalis.*

Sanicula canadensis Linnaeus, *Species Plantarum* 1: 235. 1753. "Habitat in Virginia." RCN: 1906.
Lectotype (Reveal in *Bot. J. Linn. Soc.* 92: 171. 1986): *Clayton s.n.* (BM-000553910).
Current name: ***Sanicula canadensis*** L. (Apiaceae).
Note: See reviews by Reveal & al. (in *Bot. J. Linn. Soc.* 92: 169–172. 1986; *Huntia* 7: 234. 1987).

Sanicula europaea Linnaeus, *Species Plantarum* 1: 235. 1753. "Habitat in Europae sylvis montosis." RCN: 1905.

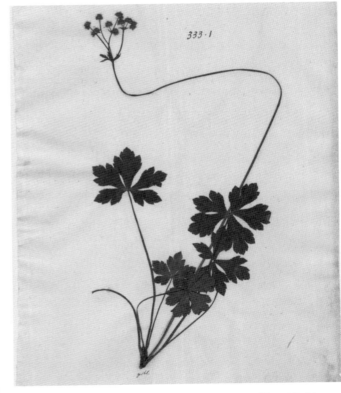

Lectotype (Reduron & Jarvis in Jarvis & al., *Regnum Veg.* 127: 84. 1993): Herb. Linn. No. 333.1 (LINN), see also p. 74.
Generitype of *Sanicula* Linnaeus (vide Hitchcock, *Prop. Brit. Bot.*: 138. 1929).
Current name: ***Sanicula europaea*** L. (Apiaceae).

Sanicula marilandica Linnaeus, *Species Plantarum* 1: 235. 1753. "Habitat in Marilandia, Virginia." RCN: 1907.
Lectotype (Shan & Constance in *Univ. Calif. Publ. Bot.* 25: 30. 1951): *Clayton 28,* long-styled specimen (BM-000051129).
Current name: ***Sanicula marilandica*** L. (Apiaceae).
Note: See Reveal (in *Bot. J. Linn. Soc.* 92: 169–172. 1986) for a review.

Santalum album Linnaeus, *Species Plantarum* 1: 349. 1753. "Habitat in India." RCN: 1000.

S

Lectotype (Macklin & Parnell in *Thai Forest Bull., Bot.* 30: 100. 2002): [icon] "*Santalum verum, ligno citrino & albo, foliis Laurinis*" in Breyn, Prodr. Fasc. Rar. Pl.: 19, t. 5, f. 1. 1739. – Epitype (Macklin & Parnell in *Thai Forest Bull., Bot.* 30: 100. 2002): Timor 5km from Soe, *Kartawinata 1758* (BO).
Generitype of *Santalum* Linnaeus.
Current name: ***Santalum album*** L. (Santalaceae).
Note: Sa'ad (in *Taeckholmia, Add. Ser.* 2: 16. 1983) indicated 161.1 (LINN) as type, but this sheet lacks a *Species Plantarum* number (i.e. "1") and is not original material for the name.

Santolina alpina Linnaeus, *Species Plantarum*, ed. 2, 2: 1180. 1763.
"Habitat in monte Moronis Italiae." RCN: 6102.
Lectotype (Fernandes in *Anales Inst. Bot. Cavanilles* 32: 1442. 1975): Herb. Linn. No. 985.3 (LINN).
Current name: ***Anthemis cretica*** L. subsp. ***alpina*** (L.) R.R. Fern. (Asteraceae).
Note: Humphries (in *Taxon* 47: 365. 1998) independently made the same type choice as Fernandes.

Santolina amellus Linnaeus, *Systema Naturae,* ed. 10, 2: 1207. 1759.
["Habitat in Jamaica."] Sp. Pl. ed. 2, 2: 1179 (1763). RCN: 6098.
Basionym of: *Calea amellus* (L.) L. (1763).
Lectotype (Wussow & al. in *Syst. Bot.* 10: 263. 1985): *Browne*, Herb. Linn. No. 984.3 (LINN).
Current name: ***Salmea scandens*** (L.) DC. var. ***amellus*** (L.) Kuntze (Asteraceae).

Santolina annua Linnaeus, *Species Plantarum* 2: 842. 1753.
"Habitat in Africa." RCN: 6110.
Basionym of: *Athanasia annua* (L.) L. (1763).
Lectotype (Humphries in Jarvis & Turland in *Taxon* 47: 365. 1998): *Magnol*, Herb. Linn. No. 986.12 (LINN).
Current name: ***Lonas annua*** (L.) Vines & Druce (Asteraceae).

Santolina anthemoides Linnaeus, *Species Plantarum*, ed. 2, 2: 1180. 1763.
"Habitat in Hispania, Italia. Cl. Alstroemer." RCN: 6103.
Lectotype (Humphries in Jarvis & Turland in *Taxon* 47: 365. 1998): *Alströmer s.n.*, Herb. Linn. No. 985.4 (LINN).
Current name: ***Anacyclus valentinus*** L. (Asteraceae).

Santolina capitata Linnaeus, *Plantae Rariores Africanae*: 18. 1760.
["Habitat in Aethiopia."] Sp. Pl., ed. 2, 2: 1181 (1763). RCN: 6106.
Basionym of: *Athanasia capitata* (L.) L. (1763).
Lectotype (Wijnands, *Bot. Commelins*: 69. 1983): Herb. Burman (G).
Current name: ***Athanasia capitata*** (L.) L. (Asteraceae).

Santolina chamaecyparissus Linnaeus, *Species Plantarum* 2: 842. 1753.
"Habitat in Europa australi." RCN: 6100.
Lectotype (Arrigoni in *Webbia* 34: 260. 1979): Herb. Linn. No. 985.1 (LINN).
Generitype of *Santolina* Linnaeus (vide Green, *Prop. Brit. Bot.*: 180. 1929).
Current name: ***Santolina chamaecyparissus*** L. (Asteraceae).
Note: Although Marchi & D'Amato (in *Inform. Bot. Ital.* 5: 93. 1973) suggested that the type should be chosen from among three Clifford sheets (BM) (there are, in fact, four), this was not a formal typification. Although Humphries (in Jarvis & al., *Regnum Veg.* 127: 84. 1993) designated one of the Clifford sheets as type, his choice is pre-dated by that of Arrigoni, who chose material in LINN.

Santolina crenata Linnaeus, *Species Plantarum* 2: 842. 1753.
"Habitat in Aethiopia." RCN: 6105.
Basionym of: *Athanasia crenata* (L.) L. (1763).

Lectotype (Wijnands in *Taxon* 32: 302, f. 1. 1983): Herb. Clifford: 398, *Santolina* 6 (BM-000646973).
Current name: ***Athanasia crenata*** (L.) L. (Asteraceae).

Santolina crithmifolia Linnaeus, *Species Plantarum* 2: 843. 1753.
"Habitat in Aethiopia." RCN: 6113.
Basionym of: *Athanasia crithmifolia* (L.) L. (1763).
Lectotype (Bremer & Wijnands in *Taxon* 31: 544. 1982): Herb. Linn. No. 986.16 (LINN).
Current name: ***Athanasia crithmifolia*** (L.) L. (Asteraceae).

Santolina cyparissus Linnaeus, *Amoenitates Academicae* 4: 490. 1759, *orth. var.*
RCN: 6100.
Lectotype (Arrigoni in *Webbia* 34: 260. 1979): Herb. Linn. No. 985.1 (LINN).
Current name: ***Santolina chamaecyparissus*** L. (Asteraceae).
Note: An orthographic variant of *S. chamaecyparissus* L. (1753).

Santolina dentata Linnaeus, *Species Plantarum* 2: 843. 1753.
"Habitat in Aethiopia." RCN: 6111.
Basionym of: *Athanasia dentata* (L.) L. (1763).
Lectotype (Wijnands, *Bot. Commelins*: 69. 1983): Herb. Clifford: 398, *Santolina* 5 (BM-000646972).
Current name: ***Athanasia dentata*** (L.) L. (Asteraceae).

Santolina jamaicensis Linnaeus, *Systema Naturae,* ed. 10, 2: 1207. 1759.
["Habitat in Jamaica."] Sp. Pl. ed. 2, 2: 1179 (1763). RCN: 6096.
Basionym of: *Calea jamaicensis* (L.) L. (1763).
Lectotype (Moore in Fawcett & Rendle, *Fl. Jamaica* 7: 260. 1936): *Browne*, Herb. Linn. No. 984.1 (LINN).
Current name: ***Calea jamaicensis*** (L.) L. (Asteraceae).

Santolina laevigata Linnaeus, *Plantae Rariores Africanae*: 18. 1760.
["Habitat ad Cap. b. spei."] Sp. pl. ed. 2, 2: 1181 (1763). RCN: 6111.
Basionym of: *Athanasia laevigata* (L.) L. (1763).
Lectotype (Källersjö in Jarvis & Turland in *Taxon* 47: 365. 1998): "*Helychrys. afric. ericoides umbellatum Breyn. in Herm. cat. p. 7*", Herb. Burman (G).
Current name: ***Athanasia dentata*** (L.) L. (Asteraceae).

Santolina oppositifolia Linnaeus, *Systema Naturae,* ed. 10, 2: 1207. 1759.
RCN: 6097.
Basionym of: *Calea oppositifolia* (L.) L. (1763).
Lectotype (King & Robinson in Woodson & Schery in *Ann. Missouri Bot. Gard.* 62: 958. 1975): *Browne*, Herb. Linn. No. 984.2 (LINN).
Current name: ***Isocarpha oppositifolia*** (L.) Cass. (Asteraceae).

Santolina pubescens Linnaeus, *Centuria II Plantarum*: 31. 1756.
"Habitat in Aethiopia. Burmannus." RCN: 6109.
Basionym of: *Athanasia pubescens* (L.) L. (1763).
Lectotype (Wijnands, *Bot. Commelins*: 70. 1983): "*Afr. austr...Athanasia pubescens*", Herb. Burman (G).
Current name: ***Athanasia pubescens*** (L.) L. (Asteraceae).

Santolina rosmarinifolia Linnaeus, *Species Plantarum* 2: 842. 1753.
"Habitat in Hispania." RCN: 6101.
Lectotype (Humphries in Jarvis & Turland in *Taxon* 47: 365. 1998): Herb. Linn. No. 985.2 (LINN).
Current name: ***Santolina rosmarinifolia*** L. (Asteraceae).

Santolina squarrosa Linnaeus, *Centuria II Plantarum*: 30. 1756.
"Habitat in Aethiopia. Burmannus." RCN: 6104.

Basionym of: *Athanasia squarrosa* (L.) L. (1763).
Lectotype (Bremer in *Opera Bot.* 40: 42. 1976): Herb. Linn. No. 986.1 (LINN).
Current name: ***Oedera squarrosa*** (L.) Anderb. & K. Bremer (Asteraceae).

Santolina trifurcata Linnaeus, *Species Plantarum* 2: 843. 1753.
"Habitat in Aethiopia." RCN: 6112.
Basionym of: *Athanasia trifurcata* (L.) L. (1763).
Lectotype (Wijnands, *Bot. Commelins*: 70. 1983): Herb. Linn. No. 986.13 (LINN).
Current name: ***Athanasia trifurcata*** (L.) L. (Asteraceae).

Sapindus chinensis Linnaeus, *Systema Vegetabilium*, ed. 13: 315. 1774.
RCN: 2905.
Type not designated.
Original material: Herb. Linn. No. 514.5 (LINN).
Note: The application of this name appears to be uncertain.

Sapindus melicoccus Linnaeus, *Flora Jamaicensis*: 15. 1759.
"Habitat [in Jamaica.]"
Lectotype (Wijnands, *Bot. Commelins*: 186. 1983): Herb. Linn. No. 488.1 (LINN).
Current name: ***Melicoccus bijugatus*** Jacq. (Sapindaceae).

Sapindus saponaria Linnaeus, *Species Plantarum* 1: 367. 1753.
"Habitat in Brasilia, Jamaica." RCN: 2902.
Lectotype (Pennington in Jarvis & al., *Regnum Veg.* 127: 84. 1993): [icon] *"Prunif. s. Nuci-prunifera fructu saponario, orbiculato, monococco nigro, Americana"* in Plukenet, Phytographia: t. 217, f. 7. 1692; Almag. Bot.: 265. 1696. – Typotype: Herb. Sloane 97: 127; 101: 122 (BM-SL).
Generitype of *Sapindus* Linnaeus (vide Hitchcock, *Prop. Brit. Bot.*: 151. 1929).
Current name: ***Sapindus saponaria*** L. (Sapindaceae).
Note: Verdcourt (in *Taxon* 46: 360. 1997) proposed the conservation of the gender of the generic name as masculine. This was recommended by the Committee for Spermatophyta (in *Taxon* 48: 369. 1999).
  Croat (in *Ann. Missouri Bot. Gard.* 63: 504. 1977) indicated either 514.1 or 514.2 (LINN) as type but, as noted by Wijnands (*Bot. Commelins*: 185. 1983), neither is original material for the name. Although Wijnands suggested that Clifford material (BM) might be an appropriate choice as type, he did not do this formally and Pennington's choice therefore has priority.

Sapindus spinosus Linnaeus, *Species Plantarum*, ed. 2, 1: 526. 1762.
"Habitat in Jamaica." RCN: 2903.
Type not designated.
Original material: [icon] in Browne, Civ. Nat. Hist. Jamaica: 207, t. 20, f. 2. 1756.
Current name: ***Zanthoxylum spinosum*** (L.) Sw. (Rutaceae).

Sapindus trifoliatus Linnaeus, *Species Plantarum* 1: 367. 1753.
"Habitat in Malabaria." RCN: 2904.
Lectotype (Mujamdar & Bakshi in *Taxon* 28: 354. 1979): [icon] *"Poerinsii"* in Rheede, Hort. Malab. 4: 43, t. 19. 1683.
Current name: ***Sapindus trifoliatus*** L. (Sapindaceae).

Saponaria cretica Linnaeus, *Species Plantarum*, ed. 2, 1: 584. 1762.
"Habitat in Cretae aridis." RCN: 3197.
Lectotype (Davis in *Notes Roy. Bot. Gard. Edinburgh* 22: 164. 1957): Herb. Linn. No. 580.4 (LINN).
Current name: ***Petrorhagia cretica*** (L.) P.W. Ball & Heywood (Caryophyllaceae).

Saponaria lutea Linnaeus, *Species Plantarum*, ed. 2, 1: 585. 1762.
"Habitat in Alpibus Exilliarum, Fenestrellarum, Canisio." RCN: 3202.
Lectotype (Phitos in Cafferty & Jarvis in *Taxon* 53: 1053. 2004): [icon] *"Lychnis floribus umbellatis ochroleucis, petalis ovatis, filamentis nigris"* in Allioni, Rar. Pedem. Stirp.: 29, t. 5, f. 2. 1755.
Current name: ***Saponaria lutea*** L. (Caryophyllaceae).

Saponaria ocymoides Linnaeus, *Species Plantarum* 1: 409. 1753.
"Habitat in Helvetia & Monspelii locis petrosis." RCN: 3200.
Lectotype (Phitos in Cafferty & Jarvis in *Taxon* 53: 1053. 2004): Herb. Linn. No. 580.8 (LINN).
Current name: ***Saponaria ocymoides*** L. (Caryophyllaceae).

Saponaria officinalis Linnaeus, *Species Plantarum* 1: 408. 1753.
"Habitat in Europa media." RCN: 3195.
Lectotype (Schultz in *Bot. Zhurn.* 69: 1479. 1984): Herb. Linn. No. 580.1 (LINN).
Generitype of *Saponaria* Linnaeus (vide Hitchcock, *Prop. Brit. Bot.*: 155. 1929).
Current name: ***Saponaria officinalis*** L. (Caryophyllaceae).
Note: Ghazanfar & Nasir (in Nasir & Ali, *Fl. Pakistan* 175: 102. 1986) designated Clifford material (BM) as type, but Schultz's choice predates this.

Saponaria officinalis Linnaeus var. **hybrida** Linnaeus, *Species Plantarum* 1: 408. 1753.
RCN: 3195.
Type not designated.
Original material: [icon] in Bauhin & Cherler, Hist. Pl. Univ. 3(2): 521. 1651; [icon] in Morison, Pl. Hist. Univ. 2: 548, s. 5, t. 22, f. 53. 1680.
Current name: ***Saponaria officinalis*** L. (Caryophyllaceae).

Saponaria orientalis Linnaeus, *Species Plantarum* 1: 409. 1753.
"Habitat in Oriente." RCN: 3201.
Lectotype (Schultz in *Bot. Zhurn.* 69: 1480. 1984): Herb. Linn. No. 580.10 (LINN).
Current name: ***Saponaria orientalis*** L. (Caryophyllaceae).

Saponaria porrigens (Linnaeus) Linnaeus, *Mantissa Plantarum Altera*: 239. 1771.
"Habitat in Oriente." RCN: 3198.
Basionym: *Silene porrigens* L. (1768).
Lectotype (Burtt & Lewis in *Kew Bull.* 7: 333. 1952): Herb. Linn. No. 580.5 (LINN).
Current name: ***Gypsophila porrigens*** (L.) Boiss. (Caryophyllaceae).

Saponaria vaccaria Linnaeus, *Species Plantarum* 1: 409. 1753.
"Habitat inter segetes Galliae, Germaniae." RCN: 3196.
Lectotype (Burtt & Lewis in *Kew Bull.* 7: 342. 1952): Herb. Clifford: 166, *Saponaria* 2 (BM-000628472).
Current name: ***Vaccaria hispanica*** (Mill.) Rauschert var. ***vaccaria*** (L.) Greuter (Caryophyllaceae).

Saraca indica Linnaeus, *Systema Naturae*, ed. 12, 2: 469; *Mantissa Plantarum*: 98. 1767.
"Habitat in India. Kleynhoff." RCN: 5117.
Lectotype (Vidal in Aubréville & Leroy, *Fl. Cambodge Laos Viêt-Nam* 18: 137. 1980): *Kleynhoff*, Herb. Burman (G).
Generitype of *Saraca* Linnaeus.
Current name: ***Saraca indica*** L. (Fabaceae: Caesalpinioideae).

Sarothra gentianoides Linnaeus, *Species Plantarum* 1: 272. 1753.
"Habitat in Virginiae, Pensylvaniae apricis glareosis." RCN: 2173.
Lectotype (Rodríguez Jiménez in *Mem. Soc. Ci. Nat. "La Salle"* 33: 112. 1973): *Kalm*, Herb. Linn. No. 391.1 (LINN).

S

Generitype of *Sarothra* Linnaeus.
Current name: **Hypericum gentianoides** (L.) Britton & al.
(Clusiaceae).
Note: Gillett & Robson (*St John's Worts Canada*: 11. 1981) designated
Clayton 110 (BM) as type but this choice was criticised as contrary
to the protologue by Reveal & al. (in *Huntia* 7: 217. 1987), and in
any case post-dates Rodríguez Jiménez's type choice of a Kalm
collection. Robson (in *Bull. Brit. Mus. (Nat. Hist.), Bot.* 20: 45.
1990) subsequently concurred with this earlier choice.

Sarracenia flava Linnaeus, *Species Plantarum* 1: 510. 1753.
"Habitat in Americae septentrionalis udis." RCN: 3854.
Lectotype (McDaniel in *Bull. Tall Timbers Res. Sta.* 9: 15. 1971):
[icon] *"Sarracena, foliis longioribus & angustioribus"* in Catesby, Nat.
Hist. Carolina 2: 69, t. 69. 1738 (see p. 116).
Current name: **Sarracenia flava** L. (Sarraceniaceae).

Sarracenia purpurea Linnaeus, *Species Plantarum* 1: 510. 1753, *nom.
cons.*
"Habitat in Americae septentrionalis udis." RCN: 3853.
Conserved type (Cheek & al. in *Taxon* 46: 781. 1997): Canada.
Quebec, Amos, East Abitibi County: about 4 miles west around L.
Beauchamp, 7 Jan 1952, *Baldwin & Breitung 2910* (K; iso- CAN,
GH, MT, O, WLU).
Generitype of *Sarracenia* Linnaeus (vide Green, *Prop. Brit. Bot.*: 160.
1929).
Current name: **Sarracenia purpurea** L. (Sarraceniaceae).

Satureja capitata Linnaeus, *Species Plantarum* 2: 568. 1753.
"Habitat in Creta, Baetica, Hispali, Graecia." RCN: 4160.
Lectotype (Siddiqi in Jafri & El-Gadi, *Fl. Libya* 118: 90. 1985):
Löfling s.n., Herb. Linn. No. 723.11 (LINN).
Current name: **Coridothymus capitatus** (L.) Rchb. f. (Lamiaceae).

Satureja graeca Linnaeus, *Species Plantarum* 2: 568. 1753.
"Habitat ad Archipelagum." RCN: 4157.
Lectotype (Morales in *Anales Jard. Bot. Madrid* 48: 143. 1991): Herb.
Linn. No. 723.4 (LINN).
Current name: **Micromeria graeca** (L.) Benth. ex Rchb. (Lamiaceae).
Note: Although Siddiqi (in Jafri & El-Gadi, *Fl. Libya* 118: 110. 1985)
indicated 723.3 (LINN) as type, this collection is unannotated by
Linnaeus and is not original material for the name.

Satureja hortensis Linnaeus, *Species Plantarum* 2: 568. 1753.
"Habitat in G. Narbonensi & Italia." RCN: 4159.
Lectotype (López González in *Anales Jard. Bot. Madrid* 38: 385.
1982): Herb. Linn. No. 723.9 (LINN).
Generitype of *Satureja* Linnaeus (vide Green, *Prop. Brit. Bot.*: 164.
1929).
Current name: **Satureja hortensis** L. (Lamiaceae).
Note: Hedge & Lamond (in *Notes Roy. Bot. Gard. Edinburgh* 28: 134.
1968) indicated unspecified material in LINN as type, but this
failed to distinguish between sheets 723.9 and 723.10. As these are
not part of a single gathering, Art. 9.15 does not apply.

Satureja juliana Linnaeus, *Species Plantarum* 2: 567. 1753.
"Habitat in Hetruria, in Tyrrheni maris asperis, Florentiae." RCN:
4155.
Lectotype (Siddiqi in Jafri & El-Gadi, *Fl. Libya* 118: 108. 1985):
Herb. Linn. No. 723.1 (LINN).
Current name: **Micromeria juliana** (L.) Benth. ex Rchb. (Lamiaceae).

Satureja mastichina Linnaeus, *Species Plantarum* 2: 567. 1753.
"Habitat in Hispaniae petrosis." RCN: 4306.
Basionym of: *Thymus mastichina* (L.) L. (1763).

Lectotype (Morales in *Ruizia* 3: 151. 1986): Herb. Linn. No. 744.19,
right specimen (LINN).
Current name: **Thymus mastichina** (L.) L. (Lamiaceae).

Satureja montana Linnaeus, *Species Plantarum* 2: 568. 1753.
"Habitat in Hetruria, Narbona." RCN: 4158.
Lectotype (López González in *Anales Jard. Bot. Madrid* 38: 388.
1982): Herb. Linn. No. 723.6 (LINN).
Current name: **Satureja montana** L. (Lamiaceae).

Satureja origanoides Linnaeus, *Species Plantarum* 2: 568. 1753.
"Habitat in Virginia." RCN: 169.
Replaced synonym of: *Cunila mariana* L. (1762), *nom. illeg.*
Lectotype (Reveal & al. in *Huntia* 7: 215. 1987): *Kalm*, Herb. Linn.
No. 38.1 (LINN).
Current name: **Cunila origanoides** (L.) Britton (Lamiaceae).
Note: Although Epling (in *J. Bot.* 67: 7. 1929) noted a Kalm sheet in
LINN, and Clayton material as a standard specimen, this is not
equivalent to a type statement (see Jarvis & al. in *Taxon* 50: 508.
2001).

Satureja spinosa Linnaeus, *Centuria II Plantarum*: 19. 1756.
"Habitat in Creta." RCN: 4161.
Neotype (Turland in Jarvis & al. in *Taxon* 50: 519. 2001): Greece.
Kriti: Lasithi: 3km S of Agios Georgios, small plain between Lasithi
plain and Mt Dikti, 22 Jun 1994, *Turland 749* (BM-000098421;
iso- UPA).
Current name: **Satureja spinosa** L. (Lamiaceae).

Satureja thymbra Linnaeus, *Species Plantarum* 2: 567. 1753.
"Habitat in Creta." RCN: 4156.
Lectotype (Siddiqi in Jafri & El-Gadi, *Fl. Libya* 118: 102. 1985):
Herb. Linn. No. 723.2 (LINN).
Current name: **Satureja thymbra** L. (Lamiaceae).

Satureja viminea Linnaeus, *Systema Naturae*, ed. 10, 2: 1096. 1759.
["Habitat in Jamaica."] Sp. Pl., ed. 2, 2: 795 (1763). RCN: 4162.
Lectotype (Harley & Granda in *Kew Bull.* 55: 926. 2000; Morales in
Jarvis & al. in *Taxon* 50: 519. 2001): *Browne*, Herb. Linn. No.
723.12, left specimen (LINN).
Current name: **Clinopodium vimineum** (L.) Kuntze (Lamiaceae).
Note: Epling (in *J. Bot.* 67: 7. 1929) noted the Browne specimen in
LINN but did not treat it as the type. The type choice made by
Harley & Granda (2000) was restricted to the left-hand specimen
on the sheet by Morales (2001).

Satureja virginiana Linnaeus, *Species Plantarum* 2: 567. 1753.
"Habitat in Virginia." RCN: 4154.
Replaced synonym of: *Thymus virginicus* L. (1774), *nom. illeg.*
Type not designated.
Original material: Herb. Clifford: 305, *Clinopodium* 3 (BM); *Clayton
141* (BM); Herb. Linn. No. 744.21 (LINN); [icon] in Hermann,
Parad. Bat.: 218. 1698; [icon] in Boccone, Mus. Piante Rar. Sicilia:
161, t. 115. 1697; [icon] in Morison, Pl. Hist. Univ. 3: 371, s. 11,
t. 7, f. 8. 1699; [icon] in Plukenet, Phytographia: t. 54, f. 2. 1691;
Almag. Bot.: 110. 1696.
Current name: **Pycnanthemum virginianum** (L.) B.L. Rob. &
Fernald (Lamiaceae).
Note: Epling (in *J. Bot.* 67: 7. 1929) reviewed the original elements for
the name and described as "standard" the Clifford sheet. This and
most other elements are identifiable with the species sometimes
known as *Pycnanthemum linifolium* Pursh. However, 744.21
(LINN) is identifiable as the closely related *P. lanceolatum* Pursh,
and Grant & Epling (in *Univ. Calif. Publ. Bot.* 20: 221. 1943)
reversed the usage adopted by Epling, interpreting the Linnaean

name instead via 744.21 (LINN) in the sense of *P. lanceolatum*. However, they did not designate a type. The name appears to remain untypified.

Satyrium albidum Linnaeus, *Species Plantarum* 2: 944. 1753.
"Habitat in Scaniae, Germaniae, Helvetiae, Averniae pratis sylvaticis." RCN: 6836.
Lectotype (Baumann & al. in *Mitteilungsbl. Arbeitskr. Heim. Orchid. Baden-Württemberg* 21: 544, Abb. 45. 1989): [icon] *"Pseudo-orchis Alpina, flore herbaceo"* in Micheli, Nov. Pl. Gen.: 30, t. 26, f. A, B, C. 1729.
Current name: **Pseudorchis albida** (L.) Á. Löve & D. Löve (Orchidaceae).

Satyrium capense Linnaeus, *Plantae Rariores Africanae*: 27. 1760.
["Habitat ad Cap. b. spei."] Sp. Pl., ed. 2, 2: 1339 (1763). RCN: 6840.
Type not designated.
Original material: none traced.
Current name: **Eulophia sp.** (Orchidaceae).
Note: An unidentifiable, ambiguous name (see Cribb in Cafferty & Jarvis, *Taxon* 48: 49. 1999).

Satyrium cornutum Linnaeus, *Plantae Rariores Africanae*: 27. 1760.
["Habitat ad Cap. b. Spei."] Sp. Pl., ed. 2, 2: 1330 (1763). RCN: 6800.
Replaced synonym of: *Orchis biflora* L. (1763); *Orchis satyrioides* L. (1763), *nom. illeg.*
Lectotype (Linder in *J. S. African Bot.* 47: 359, f. 9.1, 9.2. 1981): Herb. Burman (G).
Current name: **Schizodium cornutum** (L.) Schltr. (Orchidaceae).

Satyrium epipogium Linnaeus, *Species Plantarum* 2: 945. 1753.
"Habitat in Sibiriae montibus arenosis." RCN: 6837.
Lectotype (Renz & Taubenheim in Davis, *Fl. Turkey* 8: 470. 1984): [icon] *"Epipogum"* in Gmelin, Fl. Sibirica 1: 12, t. 2, f. 2. 1747.
Current name: **Epipogium aphyllum** Sw. (Orchidaceae).
Note: Baumann & al. (in *Mitteilungsbl. Arbeitskr. Heim. Orchid. Baden-Württemberg* 21: 597, Abb. 16. 1989) reproduce the type plate.

Satyrium hircinum Linnaeus, *Species Plantarum* 2: 944. 1753.
"Habitat in Galliae, Cantii campestris." RCN: 6833.
Lectotype (Baumann & al. in *Mitteilungsbl. Arbeitskr. Heim. Orchid. Baden-Württemberg* 21: 491, Abb. 22. 1989): [icon] *"Orchis barbata foetida"* in Vaillant, Bot. Paris.: 149, t. 30, f. 6. 1727.
Current name: **Himantoglossum hircinum** (L.) Spreng. (Orchidaceae).

Satyrium latifolium Linnaeus, *Flora Jamaicensis*: 20. 1759.
"Habitat [in Jamaica.]"
Lectotype (Garay & Sweet in Howard, *Fl. Lesser Antilles, Orchidaceae*: 83. 1974): Herb. Linn. No. 1055.6 (LINN).
Current name: **Erythrodes hirtella** (Sw.) Fawc. & Rendle (Orchidaceae).

Satyrium nigrum Linnaeus, *Species Plantarum* 2: 944. 1753.
"Habitat in Alpibus Helveticis, Lapponicis." RCN: 6835.
Lectotype (Baumann & al. in *Mitteilungsbl. Arbeitskr. Heim. Orchid. Baden-Württemberg* 21: 507, Abb. 30. 1989): Sweden. Jämtland, *Hagström*, Herb. Linn. No. 1055.4, "planta dextra" (LINN).
Current name: **Nigritella nigra** (L.) Rchb. (Orchidaceae).

Satyrium plantagineum Linnaeus, *Systema Naturae*, ed. 10, 2: 1244. 1759.

["Habitat in America."] Sp. Pl., ed. 2, 2: 1339 (1763). RCN: 6838.
Lectotype (Cribb in Cafferty & Jarvis in *Taxon* 48: 49. 1999): [icon] *"Orchis elatior latifolia, asphodeli radice, spica strigosa"* in Sloane, Voy. Jamaica 1: 250, t. 147, f. 2. 1707. – Typotype: Herb. Sloane 4: 116 (BM-SL). – Voucher: Herb. Sloane 4: 115 (BM-SL).
Current name: **Erythrodes plantaginea** (L.) Fawc. & Rendle (Orchidaceae).

Satyrium repens Linnaeus, *Species Plantarum* 2: 945. 1753.
"Habitat in Sueciae, Angliae, Sibiriae, Helvetiae sylvis." RCN: 6839.
Lectotype (Baumann & al. in *Mitteilungsbl. Arbeitskr. Heim. Orchid. Baden-Württemberg* 21: 479, Abb. 17. 1989): [icon] *"Orchis radice repente"* in Camerarius, Hort. Med. Phil.: 111, t. 35. 1588.
Current name: **Goodyera repens** (L.) R. Br. (Orchidaceae).
Note: Although Renz (in Nasir & Ali, *Fl. Pakistan* 164: 20. 1984) indicated 1055.7 (LINN) as type, it lacks a *Species Plantarum* number (i.e. "6"), is a post-1753 addition to the herbarium, and is not original material for the name.

Satyrium viride Linnaeus, *Species Plantarum* 2: 944. 1753.
"Habitat in Europae frigidioris asperis." RCN: 6834.
Lectotype (Renz in Nasir & Ali, *Fl. Pakistan* 164: 32. 1984): Herb. Linn. No. 1055.3 (LINN).
Generitype of *Satyrium* Linnaeus, *nom. rej.* (vide Green, *Prop. Brit. Bot.*: 185. 1929).
Current name: **Dactylorhiza viride** (L.) R.M. Bateman & al. (Orchidaceae).
Note: Satyrium Linnaeus, *nom. rej.* vs. *Satyrium* Swartz. Baumann & al. (in *Mitteilungsbl. Arbeitskr. Heim. Orchid. Baden-Württemberg* 21: 447, Abb. 7. 1989) designated a Loesel illustration as type but this choice is pre-dated by that of Renz.

Saururus cernuus Linnaeus, *Species Plantarum* 1: 341. 1753.
"Habitat in Marilandia, Virginia." RCN: 2641.
Lectotype (Reveal & al. in *Huntia* 7: 234. 1987): Herb. Linn. No. 478.1 (LINN).
Generitype of *Saururus* Linnaeus.
Current name: **Saururus cernuus** L. (Saururaceae).

Saururus natans Linnaeus, *Mantissa Plantarum Altera*: 227. 1771.
"Habitat in Indiae orientalis aquis. Koenig." RCN: 2632.
Lectotype (van Bruggen in *Blumea* 18: 478. 1970): *König s.n.*, Herb. Linn. No. 479.1 (LINN; iso- UPS).
Current name: **Aponogeton natans** (L.) Engl. & K. Krause (Aponogetonaceae).

Sauvagesia erecta Linnaeus, *Species Plantarum* 1: 203. 1753.
"Habitat in Domingo." RCN: 1649.
Lectotype (Whiteford in Jarvis & al., *Regnum Veg.* 127: 85. 1993): Herb. Linn. No. 283.2 (LINN).
Generitype of *Sauvagesia* Linnaeus.
Current name: **Sauvagesia erecta** L. (Ochnaceae).
Note: Sastre (in *Adansonia*, sér. 2, 8: 122. 1968) indicated Plumier material, from Martinique, as the type and (in *Caldasia* 11(51): 5, 27. 1971), suggested the name was based on a Surian collection drawn by Plumier. However, Linnaeus made no reference to Plumier in either his specific or generic protologues so this material cannot be accepted as original material for the name. Bornstein (in Howard, *Fl. Lesser Antilles* 5: 300. 1989) stated that 283.1 and 283.2 (LINN) were possible types. It is difficult to be certain if these were part of a single collection but Whiteford subsequently designated 283.2 (LINN) as lectotype.

Saxifraga adscendens Linnaeus, *Species Plantarum* 1: 405. 1753.
"Habitat in Pyrenaeis, Baldo, Tauro Rastadiensi." RCN: 3171.

Lectotype (Aldén & Strid in Strid, *Mountain Fl. Greece* 1: 367. 1986):
Herb. Burser XVI(1): 89 (UPS).
Current name: ***Saxifraga adscendens*** L. (Saxifragaceae).
Note: See additional notes by Webb (in *Bot. J. Linn. Soc.* 95: 265.
1987).

Saxifraga aizoides Linnaeus, *Species Plantarum* 1: 403. 1753.
"Habitat in Alpibus Lapponicis, Styriacis, Westmorlandicis, Baldis."
RCN: 3159.
Lectotype (Webb in *Bot. J. Linn. Soc.* 95: 264. 1987): Herb. Burser
XVI(1): 74 (UPS).
Current name: ***Saxifraga aizoides*** L. (Saxifragaceae).

Saxifraga ajugifolia Linnaeus, *Centuria I Plantarum*: 11. 1755.
"Habitat in Gallo-provinciae montibus." RCN: 3167.
Lectotype (Webb in *Bot. J. Linn. Soc.* 95: 266. 1987): Herb. Linn. No.
575.47 (LINN).
Current name: ***Saxifraga prostii*** Sternb. (Saxifragaceae).
Note: Specific epithet spelled "ajugaefolia" in the protologue.
Webb (in *Feddes Repert.* 68: 204. 1963) rejected the name as a
nomen ambiguum and, in later typifying it, recommended that a
formal proposal for its rejection would be "most desirable".
However, no such proposal has been made. If so rejected, the
correct name would be *S. prostii* Sternb.

Saxifraga androsacea Linnaeus, *Species Plantarum* 1: 399. 1753.
"Habitat in Sibiria, Helvetia." RCN: 3142.
Lectotype (Webb in *Bot. J. Linn. Soc.* 95: 261. 1987): [icon] *"Sedum
alpinum III. Sassifragia III"* in Colonna, Ekphr., ed. 2: 66, 67 [last
fig.]. 1616.
Current name: ***Saxifraga androsacea*** L. (Saxifragaceae).

Saxifraga aspera Linnaeus, *Species Plantarum* 1: 402. 1753.
"Habitat in Alpibus Helveticis." RCN: 3157.
Lectotype (Webb in *Bot. J. Linn. Soc.* 95: 264. 1987): Herb. Burser
XVI(1): 79 (UPS).
Current name: ***Saxifraga aspera*** L. (Saxifragaceae).

Saxifraga autumnalis Linnaeus, *Species Plantarum* 1: 402. 1753.
"Habitat in humentibus Borussiae, Angliae, Helvetiae." RCN: 3160.
Lectotype (Webb in *Bot. J. Linn. Soc.* 95: 264. 1987): [icon]
"Saxifraga angustifolia autumnalis, flore luteo guttato" in Breyn, Exot.
Pl. Cent.: 104, t. 48 [right half]. 1678.
Current name: ***Saxifraga hirculus*** L. (Saxifragaceae).

Saxifraga bronchialis Linnaeus, *Species Plantarum* 1: 400. 1753.
"Habitat in Sibiria." RCN: 3147.
Lectotype (Webb in *Bot. J. Linn. Soc.* 95: 262. 1987): Herb. Linn. No.
575.37 (LINN).
Current name: ***Saxifraga bronchialis*** L. (Saxifragaceae).
Note: Webb argued that the only possible original element is 575.37
(LINN), annotated as "15 aspera" by Linnaeus, but from Siberia,
where *S. aspera* does not occur (and for which Linnaeus indicated a
European origin), suggesting that Linnaeus probably omitted to
change his annotation when he decided to recognise this as a
separate species. Holmgren & Holmgren (*Intermountain Fl.* 3A: 56.
1997) accepted this, noting that Webb's choice supersedes the
neotype choice made by Siplivinsky (in *Novosti Sist. Vyssh. Rast.* 8:
149. 1971).

Saxifraga bryoides Linnaeus, *Species Plantarum* 1: 400. 1753.
"Habitat in Alpibus Helveticis, Pyrenaicis." RCN: 3146.
Lectotype (Webb in *Bot. J. Linn. Soc.* 95: 261. 1987): Herb. Linn. No.
575.11 (LINN).
Current name: ***Saxifraga bryoides*** L. (Saxifragaceae).

Saxifraga bulbifera Linnaeus, *Species Plantarum* 1: 403. 1753.
"Habitat in Italia, pratis saxosis umbrosis." RCN: 3163.
Lectotype (Siplivinsky in *Novosti Sist. Vyssh. Rast.* 14: 108. 1977):
[icon] *"Saxifragia bulbosa altera bulbifera montana"* in Colonna,
Ekphr.: 318, 317. 1606.
Current name: ***Saxifraga bulbifera*** L. (Saxifragaceae).
Note: Webb (in *Bot. J. Linn. Soc.* 95: 264. 1987), evidently unaware of
Siplivinsky's earlier choice, independently designated the same type.

Saxifraga burseriana Linnaeus, *Species Plantarum* 1: 400. 1753.
"Habitat in Tauro, Rastadiensi." RCN: 3144.
Lectotype (Stearn, *Introd. Linnaeus' Sp. Pl.* (Ray Soc. ed.): 127. 1957):
Herb. Burser XVI(1): 68 (UPS).
Current name: ***Saxifraga burseriana*** L. (Saxifragaceae).
Note: See additional notes by Webb (in *Bot. J. Linn. Soc.* 95: 261.
1987).

Saxifraga caesia Linnaeus, *Species Plantarum* 1: 399. 1753.
"Habitat in Alpibus Helveticis, Austriacis, Pyrenacis, Baldo." RCN:
3143.
Lectotype (Webb in *Bot. J. Linn. Soc.* 95: 261. 1987): Herb. Burser
XVI(1): 70 (UPS).
Current name: ***Saxifraga caesia*** L. (Saxifragaceae).

Saxifraga cernua Linnaeus, *Species Plantarum* 1: 403. 1753.
"Habitat in Alpibus Lapponicis frequens." RCN: 3164.
Lectotype (Siplivinsky in *Novosti Sist. Vyssh. Rast.* 14: 108. 1977):
Herb. Linn. No. 575.44 (LINN).
Current name: ***Saxifraga cernua*** L. (Saxifragaceae).
Note: Webb (in *Bot. J. Linn. Soc.* 95: 264. 1987), evidently unaware of
Siplivinsky's earlier choice, independently designated the same type.

Saxifraga cespitosa Linnaeus, *Species Plantarum* 1: 404. 1753.
"Habitat in Alpibus Lapponicis, Helveticis, Tridentinis, Monspelii."
RCN: 3172.
Lectotype (Webb, *Proc. Roy. Irish Academy* 53B: 222. 1950): Herb.
Linn. No. 575.57 (LINN).
Current name: ***Saxifraga cespitosa*** L. (Saxifragaceae).
Note: See additional notes by Webb (in *Bot. J. Linn. Soc.* 95: 265.
1987).

Saxifraga cotyledon Linnaeus, *Species Plantarum* 1: 398. 1753.
"Habitat in Alpibus Europae." RCN: 3139.
Lectotype (Webb in *Bot. J. Linn. Soc.* 95: 260. 1987): Herb. Linn. No.
575.1, left specimen (LINN).
Current name: ***Saxifraga cotyledon*** L. (Saxifragaceae).

Saxifraga crassifolia Linnaeus, *Species Plantarum* 1: 401. 1753.
"Habitat in Alpibus Sibiriae." RCN: 3149.
Lectotype (Yeo in *Kew Bull.* 20: 118. 1966): Herb. Linn. No. 575.16
(LINN).
Current name: ***Bergenia crassifolia*** (L.) Fritsch (Saxifragaceae).
Note: See additional notes by Webb (in *Bot. J. Linn. Soc.* 95: 262.
1987).

Saxifraga cuneifolia Linnaeus, *Systema Naturae,* ed. 10, 2: 1026.
1759.
["Habitat in Alpibus Stiriae, Gotthardo. Gerard."] Sp. Pl., ed. 2, 1:
574 (1762). RCN: 3154.
Lectotype (Webb in *Bot. J. Linn. Soc.* 95: 266. 1987): *Gérard 67,*
Herb. Linn. No. 575.28 (LINN), see p. 205.
Current name: ***Saxifraga cuneifolia*** L. (Saxifragaceae).

Saxifraga cymbalaria Linnaeus, *Species Plantarum* 1: 405. 1753.
"Habitat in Oriente." RCN: 3174.

Lectotype (Siplivinsky in *Novosti Sist. Vyssh. Rast.* 14: 113. 1977): [icon] *"Saxifraga exigua, foliis Cymbalariae"* in Buxbaum, Pl. Minus Cognit. Cent. 2: 40, t. 45, f. 2. 1728.
Current name: **Saxifraga cymbalaria** L. (Saxifragaceae).
Note: Webb (in *Bot. J. Linn. Soc.* 95: 265. 1987), evidently unaware of Siplivinsky's earlier choice, independently designated the same type.

Saxifraga geranioides Linnaeus, *Centuria I Plantarum*: 10. 1755.
"Habitat in Pyrenaeis. Burs. XVI. 86." RCN: 3166.
Lectotype (Webb in *Bot. J. Linn. Soc.* 95: 266. 1987): Herb. Burser XVI(1): 86 (UPS).
Current name: **Saxifraga geranioides** L. (Saxifragaceae).

Saxifraga geum Linnaeus, *Species Plantarum* 1: 401. 1753.
"Habitat in Alpibus Helveticis, Pyrenaicis." RCN: 3155.
Lectotype (Pugsley in *J. Linn. Soc., Bot.* 50: 270, pl. 6. 1936): Herb. Linn. No. 575.29 (LINN).
Current name: **Saxifraga × geum** L. (Saxifragaceae).
Note: See additional notes by Webb (in *Bot. J. Linn. Soc.* 95: 263. 1987).

Saxifraga granulata Linnaeus, *Species Plantarum* 1: 403. 1753.
"Habitat in Europae apricis." RCN: 3162.
Lectotype (Siplivinsky in *Novosti Sist. Vyssh. Rast.* 14: 108. 1977): Herb. Linn. No. 575.43 (LINN).
Generitype of *Saxifraga* Linnaeus (vide Hitchcock, *Prop. Brit. Bot.*: 154. 1929).
Current name: **Saxifraga granulata** L. (Saxifragaceae).
Note: Webb (in *Bot. J. Linn. Soc.* 95: 264. 1987), evidently unaware of Siplivinsky's earlier choice, independently designated the same collection as type.

Saxifraga groenlandica Linnaeus, *Species Plantarum* 1: 404. 1753.
"Habitat in Groenlandia, forte etiam in Pyrenaeis & Helveticis Alpibus." RCN: 3173.
Lectotype (Webb in *Bot. J. Linn. Soc.* 95: 264. 1987): [icon] *"Saxifraga tridact. Groenl. caulic. valde foliosis"* in Dillenius, Hort. Eltham. 2: 337, t. 253, f. 329. 1732.
Current name: **Saxifraga cespitosa** L. (Saxifragaceae).
Note: Sometimes informally rejected as a *nomen ambiguum* by earlier authors (see Webb in *Proc. Roy. Irish Acad.* 53B: 222. 1950), Webb's typification allows *S. groenlandica* to fall into the synonymy of *S. cespitosa* L.

Saxifraga hederacea Linnaeus, *Species Plantarum* 1: 405. 1753.
"Habitat in Creta." RCN: 3175.
Neotype (Webb in *Bot. J. Linn. Soc.* 95: 265. 1987): Herb. Tournefort No. 2129 (P-TOURN).
Current name: **Saxifraga hederacea** L. (Saxifragaceae).

Saxifraga hirculus Linnaeus, *Species Plantarum* 1: 402. 1753.
"Habitat in Suecia, Helvetia, Lapponia, Sibiria." RCN: 3158.
Lectotype (Siplivinsky in *Novosti Sist. Vyssh. Rast.* 14: 99. 1977): Herb. Linn. No. 575.38 (LINN).
Current name: **Saxifraga hirculus** L. (Saxifragaceae).
Note: Webb (in *Bot. J. Linn. Soc.* 95: 264. 1987), evidently unaware of Siplivinsky's earlier choice, independently designated the same collection as type.

Saxifraga hirsuta Linnaeus, *Systema Naturae,* ed. 10, 2: 1026. 1759.
["Habitat in Alpibus Pyrenaeis, Sibiricis."] Sp. Pl. 1: 401 (1753). RCN: 3153a.
Replaced synonym: *Saxifraga rotundifolia* L. (1753: 401, No. 12, non 1753: 403, No. 19).

Lectotype (Webb in *Bot. J. Linn. Soc.* 95: 266. 1987): [icon] *"Geum folio circinato acute crenato, pistillo floris rubro"* in Magnol, Hort. Reg. Monspel.: 87, unnumbered plate. 1697.
Current name: **Saxifraga hirsuta** L. (Saxifragaceae).
Note: A *nomen novum* for *S. rotundifolia* L. (1753: 401, No. 12), non *S. rotundifolia* L. (1753: 403, No. 19).

Saxifraga hypnoides Linnaeus, *Species Plantarum* 1: 405. 1753.
"Habitat in Alpibus Helveticis, Austriacis, Pyrenaicis, Westmorlandicis." RCN: 3176.
Lectotype (Webb in *Proc. Roy. Irish Acad.* 53B: 223. 1950): Herb. Linn. No. 575.62 (LINN).
Current name: **Saxifraga hypnoides** L. (Saxifragaceae).
Note: See additional comments by García Adá & al. (in *Candollea* 51: 375. 1996).

Saxifraga mutata Linnaeus, *Species Plantarum,* ed. 2, 1: 570. 1762.
"Habitat in Alpibus Helvetiae, Italiae." RCN: 3140.
Lectotype (Webb in *Bot. J. Linn. Soc.* 95: 267. 1987): Herb. Burser XVI(1): 98 (UPS).
Current name: **Saxifraga mutata** L. (Saxifragaceae).

Saxifraga nivalis Linnaeus, *Species Plantarum* 1: 401. 1753.
"Habitat in summis Alpibus Spitzbergensibus, Lapponicis, Arvonicis, Virginia, Canada." RCN: 3150.
Lectotype (Jonsell & Jarvis in *Nordic J. Bot.* 22: 72. 2002): Herb. Linn. No. 575.19, furthest right specimen; Lapland Herb. No. 176 β (LINN).
Current name: **Saxifraga nivalis** L. (Saxifragaceae).

Saxifraga oppositifolia Linnaeus, *Species Plantarum* 1: 402. 1753.
"Habitat in rupibus Alpium Spitzbergensium, Lapponicarum, Pyrenaicarum, Helveticarum." RCN: 3156.
Lectotype (Webb in *Bot. J. Linn. Soc.* 95: 263. 1987): Herb. Linn. No. 575.32, upper specimen (LINN).
Current name: **Saxifraga oppositifolia** L. (Saxifragaceae).
Note: Siplivinsky (in *Novosti Sist. Vyssh. Rast.* 9: 188. 1972) indicated unspecified material in LINN as "typus". However, this did not distinguish between sheets 575.32–575.35, and as they are not part of a single gathering, Art. 9.15 does not apply.

Saxifraga pensylvanica Linnaeus, *Species Plantarum* 1: 399. 1753.
"Habitat in Virginia, Pensylvania, Canada." RCN: 3141.
Lectotype (Webb in *Bot. J. Linn. Soc.* 95: 260. 1987): *Kalm,* Herb. Linn. No. 575.4 (LINN).
Current name: **Saxifraga pensylvanica** L. (Saxifragaceae).

Saxifraga petraea Linnaeus, *Systema Naturae,* ed. 10, 2: 1027. 1759.
["Habitat in Alpibus Norvegicis, Pyrenaeis, Baldi."] Sp. Pl., ed. 2, 1: 578 (1762). RCN: 3170.
Replaced synonym: *Saxifraga tridactylites* L. var. *alpina* L. (1753).
Lectotype (Webb in *Bot. J. Linn. Soc.* 95: 266. 1987): [icon] *"Saxifraga alba petraea"* in Clusius, Rar. Pl. Hist. 2: 337. 1601.
Current name: **Saxifraga tridactylites** L. var. **alpina** L. (Saxifragaceae).

Saxifraga punctata Linnaeus, *Species Plantarum* 1: 401. 1753.
"Habitat in Sibiria." RCN: 3151.
Lectotype (Pugsley in *J. Linn. Soc., Bot.* 50: 272, pl. 7. 1936): Herb. Linn. No. 575.24 (LINN).
Current name: **Saxifraga punctata** L. (Saxifragaceae).
Note: Webb (in *Feddes Repert.* 69: 153. 1964) treated this as a *nomen ambiguum* and later (in *Bot. J. Linn. Soc.* 95: 263. 1987) stated that he intended to propose the name for rejection. However, no formal proposal appears to have been made.

S

Saxifraga rivularis Linnaeus, *Species Plantarum* 1: 404. 1753.
"Habitat ad Alpium Lapponicarum latera & rivulos." RCN: 3165.
Lectotype (Jonsell & Jarvis in *Nordic J. Bot.* 22: 73. 2002): [icon]
   "Saxifraga foliis radicalibus quinquelobis, florali ovato" in Linnaeus,
   Fl. Lapponica: 136, t. 2, f. 7. 1737.
Current name: ***Saxifraga rivularis*** L. (Saxifragaceae).

Saxifraga rotundifolia Linnaeus, *Species Plantarum* 1: 401. 1753.
"Habitat in Alpibus Pyrenaeis, Sibiricis." RCN: 3153.
Replaced synonym of: *Saxifraga hirsuta* L. (1759).
Lectotype (Webb in *Bot. J. Linn. Soc.* 95: 266. 1987): [icon] *"Geum
   folio circinato acute crenato, pistillo floris rubro"* in Magnol, Hort.
   Reg. Monspel.: 87, unnumbered plate. 1697.
Current name: ***Saxifraga hirsuta*** L. (Saxifragaceae).
Note: Two *Saxifraga* species were given this epithet by Linnaeus, this
   one (p. 401, non 403) being subsequently renamed by Linnaeus as
   S. hirsuta (1759).

Saxifraga rotundifolia Linnaeus, *Species Plantarum* 1: 403. 1753.
"Habitat in Alpibus Helveticis, Austriacis." RCN: 3161.

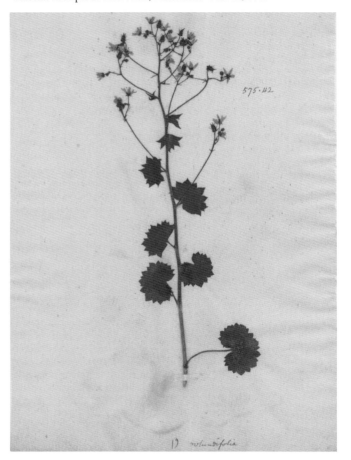

Lectotype (Webb in *Bot. J. Linn. Soc.* 95: 264. 1987): Herb. Linn. No.
   575.42 (LINN).
Current name: ***Saxifraga rotundifolia*** L. (Saxifragaceae).
Note: Two *Saxifraga* species were given this epithet by Linnaeus, the
   other one (p. 401, non 403) being subsequently renamed by
   Linnaeus as *S. hirsuta* (1759).

Saxifraga sedoides Linnaeus, *Species Plantarum* 1: 404. 1753.
"Habitat in Alpibus Tridentinis, Sibiricis." RCN: 3145.

Type not designated.
Original material: [icon] in Séguier, Pl. Veron.: 450, t. 9, f. 3. 1745.
Current name: ***Saxifraga sedoides*** L. (Saxifragaceae).
Note: Webb in (*Bot. J. Linn. Soc.* 95: 265. 1987) designated 174.15 (S)
   as lectotype, but this collection lacks the relevant *Species Plantarum*
   number (i.e. "26") and was a post-1753 addition to the herbarium,
   and is not original material for the name.

Saxifraga sibirica Linnaeus, *Species Plantarum,* ed. 2, 1: 577. 1762.
"Habitat in Sibiria." RCN: 3168.
Lectotype (Ghazanfar in Nasir & Ali, *Fl. W. Pakistan* 108: 12. 1977):
   Herb. Linn. No. 575.49 (LINN).
Current name: ***Saxifraga sibirica*** L. (Saxifragaceae).
Note: See additional notes by Webb (in *Bot. J. Linn. Soc.* 95: 266.
   1987).

Saxifraga stellaris Linnaeus, *Species Plantarum* 1: 400. 1753.
"Habitat in Alpibus Spitsbergensibus, Laponicis, Helveticis, Styriacis,
   Westmorlandicis." RCN: 3148.
Lectotype (Siplivinsky in *Novosti Sist. Vyssh. Rast.* 13: 142. 1976):
   Herb. Linn. No. 575.12 (LINN).
Current name: ***Saxifraga stellaris*** L. (Saxifragaceae).
Note: Webb (in *Bot. J. Linn. Soc.* 95: 262. 1987) unaware of
   Siplivinsky's typification, independently chose the same lectotype.

Saxifraga tridactylites Linnaeus, *Species Plantarum* 1: 404. 1753.
"Habitat α in Europae arenosis, β in Alpibus Lapponicis, Pyrenaeis."
   RCN: 3169.
Lectotype (Webb in *Bot. J. Linn. Soc.* 95: 265. 1987): Herb. Linn. No.
   174.11 (S).
Current name: ***Saxifraga tridactylites*** L. (Saxifragaceae).
Note: Ali (in Ali & Jafri, *Fl. Libya* 5: 4. 1976) indicated 575.50
   (LINN) as type, but this choice (which carries a symbol for the
   western edge of Asia) was rejected by Webb as being in conflict with
   the geographical statement in the protologue.

Saxifraga tridactylites Linnaeus var. **alpina** Linnaeus, *Species
   Plantarum* 1: 404. 1753.
"Habitat β in Alpibus Lapponicis, Pyrenaeis." RCN: 3170.
Replaced synonym of: *Saxifraga petraea* L. (1759).
Lectotype (Webb in *Bot. J. Linn. Soc.* 95: 266. 1987): [icon]
   "Saxifraga alba petraea" in Clusius, Rar. Pl. Hist. 2: 337. 1601.
Current name: ***Saxifraga tridactylites*** L. var. ***alpina*** L.
   (Saxifragaceae).

Saxifraga tridactylites Linnaeus var. **tectorum** Linnaeus, *Species
   Plantarum* 1: 404. 1753.
"Habitat α in Europae arenosis." RCN: 3169.
Type not designated.
Original material: Herb. Burser XVI(1): 91 (UPS); [icon] in Dodoëns,
   Stirp. Hist. Pempt., ed. 2: 113, 112. 1616.
Current name: ***Saxifraga tridactylites*** L. (Saxifragaceae).
Note: See comments by Webb (in *Bot. J. Linn. Soc.* 95: 265. 1987).

Saxifraga umbrosa Linnaeus, *Species Plantarum,* ed. 2, 1: 574.
   1762.
"Habitat in Montibus apud Cantabros." RCN: 3152.
Lectotype (Webb in *Bot. J. Linn. Soc.* 95: 267. 1987): [icon] *"Geum
   folio subrotundo minori pistillo floris rubro"* in Magnol, Hort. Reg.
   Monspel.: 88, unnumbered plate. 1697 (see p. 140).
Current name: ***Saxifraga umbrosa*** L. (Saxifragaceae).

Scabiosa africana Linnaeus, *Species Plantarum* 1: 100. 1753.
"Habitat in Africa." RCN: 817.
Type not designated.

Original material: Herb. Clifford: 31, *Scabiosa* 6 (BM); Herb. Linn. No. 52.19 (S); Herb. Linn. No. 120.31 (LINN); [icon] in Hermann, Parad. Bat.: 219. 1698; [icon] in Breyn, Prodr. Fasc. Rar. Pl.: 33, t. 26. 1739.
Current name: ***Scabiosa africana*** L. (Dipsacaceae).

Scabiosa alpina Linnaeus, *Species Plantarum* 1: 98. 1753.
"Habitat in alpibus Helveticis, Italicis." RCN: 797.
Type not designated.
Original material: Herb. Linn. No. 120.1 (LINN); Herb. Burser XV(2): 12 (UPS); Herb. Clifford: 30, *Scabiosa* 3 (BM); [icon] in Besler, Hort. Eystett. aest.: ord. 9, fol. 8, f. 1. 1613.
Current name: ***Cephalaria alpina*** (L.) Roem. & Schult. (Dipsacaceae).

Scabiosa amplexicaulis Linnaeus, *Mantissa Plantarum Altera*: 195. 1771.
"Habitat – – –" RCN: 804.
Type not designated.
Original material: Herb. Linn. No. 120.10 (LINN); Herb. Burser XV(2): 20? (UPS).
Note: The application of this name appears uncertain.

Scabiosa argentea Linnaeus, *Species Plantarum* 1: 100. 1753.
"Habitat in Oriente." RCN: 815.
Neotype (Lack in Rechinger, *Fl. Iranica* 168: 41. 1991): Herb. Linn. No. 120.27 (LINN).
Current name: ***Lomelosia argentea*** (L.) Greuter & Burdet (Dipsacaceae).
Note: As there appears to be no original material in existence, Lack's treatment of the post-1753 120.27 (LINN) as "typus" is accepted as a neotypification under Art. 9.8.

Scabiosa arvensis Linnaeus, *Species Plantarum* 1: 99. 1753.
"Habitat in Europa solo glareoso, juxta segetes inque pratis." RCN: 806.
Type not designated.
Original material: Herb. Clifford: 31, *Scabiosa* 5 ∈ (BM); Herb. Clifford: 31, *Scabiosa* 5, 2 sheets (BM); Herb. Burser XV(2): 5? (UPS); Herb. Linn. No. 120.13 (LINN); Herb. Linn. No. 52.1 (S); [icon] in Bauhin & Cherler, Hist. Pl. Univ. 3(1): 2. 1651; [icon] in Tabernaemontanus, New Vollk. Kräuterb.: 442. 1664.
Current name: ***Knautia arvensis*** (L.) Duby (Dipsacaceae).

Scabiosa atropurpurea Linnaeus, *Species Plantarum* 1: 100. 1753.
"Habitat in India?" RCN: 814.
Lectotype (Alavi in Jafri & El-Gadi, *Fl. Libya* 56: 10. 1978): Herb. Linn. No. 120.25 (LINN).
Current name: ***Scabiosa atropurpurea*** L. (Dipsacaceae).

Scabiosa columbaria Linnaeus, *Species Plantarum* 1: 99. 1753.
"Habitat in Europae montosis, siccioribus." RCN: 809.
Lectotype (Napper in Milne-Redhead & Polhill, *Fl. Trop. E. Africa, Dipsacaceae*: 7. 1968): Herb. Linn. No. 120.17 (LINN).
Generitype of *Scabiosa* Linnaeus (vide Hitchcock, *Prop. Brit. Bot.*: 123. 1929).
Current name: ***Scabiosa columbaria*** L. (Dipsacaceae).
Note: Scabiosa columbaria, with the type designated by Napper, was proposed as conserved type of the genus by Jarvis (in *Taxon* 41: 569. 1992). However, the proposal was eventually ruled unnecessary by the General Committee (see Barrie, *l.c.* 55: 795–796. 2006 for a review of the history of this and related proposals).

Scabiosa cretica Linnaeus, *Species Plantarum* 1: 100. 1753.
"Habitat in Creta & adjacentibus." RCN: 819.

Lectotype (Davis in *Notes Roy. Bot. Gard. Edinburgh* 21: 122. 1953): Herb. Clifford: 31, *Scabiosa* 10 (BM-000557761).
Current name: ***Scabiosa cretica*** L. (Dipsacaceae).

Scabiosa graminifolia Linnaeus, *Centuria I Plantarum*: 6. 1755.
"Habitat in alpibus Helveticis." RCN: 820.
Lectotype (Devesa in *Lagascalia* 12: 187. 1984): Herb. Linn. No. 120.35 (LINN).
Current name: ***Scabiosa graminifolia*** L. (Dipsacaceae).

Scabiosa gramuntia Linnaeus, *Amoenitates Academicae* 4: 477. 1759, *nom. illeg.*
["Habitat Monspelii."] Sp. Pl. 1: 99 (1753). RCN: 808.
Replaced synonym: *Scabiosa triandra* L. (1753).
Type not designated.
Original material: as replaced synonym.
Current name: ***Scabiosa triandra*** L. (Dipsacaceae).
Note: A superfluous name for *Scabiosa triandra* L. (1753). Devesa (in *Lagascalia* 12: 162. 1984) wrongly indicated 120.17 (LINN), associated with *S. columbaria* L. rather than *S. triandra*, as the type of *S. gramuntia*.

Scabiosa indurata Linnaeus, *Mantissa Plantarum Altera*: 196. 1771.
"Habitat in Africa." RCN: 816.
Type not designated.
Original material: Herb. Linn. No. 120.29 (LINN); Herb. Linn. No. 120.30 (LINN).
Current name: ***Scabiosa africana*** L. (Dipsacaceae).

Scabiosa integrifolia Linnaeus, *Species Plantarum* 1: 99. 1753.
"Habitat monspelii." RCN: 803.
Type not designated.
Original material: none traced.
Current name: ***Knautia integrifolia*** (L.) Bertol. (Dipsacaceae).

Scabiosa isetensis Linnaeus, *Systema Naturae,* ed. 12, 2: 114; *Mantissa Plantarum*: 37. 1767.
"Habitat in Sibiriae Isetensis rupibus." RCN: 822.
Type not designated.
Original material: Herb. Linn. No. 120.37 (LINN); [icon] in Gmelin, Fl. Sibirica 2: 214, t. 88, f. 1. 1752.
Current name: ***Scabiosa isetensis*** L. (Dipsacaceae).

Scabiosa leucantha Linnaeus, *Species Plantarum* 1: 98. 1753.
"Habitat in collibus Narbonae." RCN: 801.
Type not designated.
Original material: Herb. Burser XV(2): 11 (UPS); Herb. Clifford: 30, *Scabiosa* 4 β (BM); Herb. Clifford: 30, *Scabiosa* 4 α (BM); Herb. Clifford: 30, *Scabiosa* 4 (BM).
Current name: ***Cephalaria leucantha*** (L.) Roem. & Schult. (Dipsacaceae).

Scabiosa leucantha Linnaeus var. **spuria** Linnaeus, *Species Plantarum* 1: 98. 1753.
"Habitat in collibus Africae." RCN: 798.
Lectotype (Wijnands, *Bot. Commelins*: 93. 1983): [icon] "*Scabiosa Afric. frutesc. fol. rigidis splendentibus et serratis flore albicanti*" in Commelin, Hort. Med. Amstelod. Pl. Rar. 2: 185, t. 93. 1701.
Current name: ***Cephalaria rigida*** (L.) Roem. & Schult. (Dipsacaceae).

Scabiosa leucanthema Linnaeus, *Amoenitates Academicae* 4: 477. 1759, *orth. var.*
RCN: 801.
Type not designated.

S

Original material: as *Scabiosa leucantha*.
Current name: ***Cephalaria leucantha*** (L.) Roem. & Schult. (Dipsacaceae).
Note: As noted by Stearn (in Geck & Pressler, *Festschr. Claus Nissen*: 631. 1974), this is an orthographic variant of *S. leucantha* L. (1753).

Scabiosa marina Linnaeus, *Mantissa Plantarum Altera*: 329. 1771, *orth. var.*
["Habitat Monspelii."] Cent. II Pl.: 8 (1756). RCN: 811.
Lectotype (Devesa in *Lagascalia* 12: 174. 1984): Herb. Linn. No. 120.21 (LINN).
Current name: ***Scabiosa atropurpurea*** L. subsp. ***maritima*** (L.) Arcang. (Dipsacaceae).
Note: This appears to be an error for *S. maritima* L. (1756), from which the 1771 account excludes a Boccone reference previously included in the synonymy of *S. maritima*.

Scabiosa maritima Linnaeus, *Centuria II Plantarum*: 8. 1756.
"Habitat Monspelii." RCN: 811.
Lectotype (Devesa in *Lagascalia* 12: 174. 1984): Herb. Linn. No. 120.21 (LINN).
Current name: ***Scabiosa atropurpurea*** L. subsp. ***maritima*** (L.) Arcang. (Dipsacaceae).

Scabiosa ochroleuca Linnaeus, *Species Plantarum* 1: 101. 1753.
"Habitat in Germaniae pratis siccis." RCN: 824.
Type not designated.
Original material: Herb. Burser XV(2): 10 (UPS); [icon] in Morison, Pl. Hist. Univ. 3: 48, s. 6, t. 13, f. 23. 1699; [icon] in Clusius, Rar. Pl. Hist. 2: 3. 1601.
Current name: ***Scabiosa columbaria*** L. subsp. ***ochroleuca*** (L.) Čelak. (Dipsacaceae).
Note: Devesa (in *Lagascalia* 12: 165. 1984) wrongly indicated 120.28 (LINN) as lectotype but this collection lacks the relevant *Species Plantarum* number (i.e. "17") and was a post-1753 addition to the herbarium, and is not original material for the name.

Scabiosa palaestina Linnaeus, *Systema Naturae*, ed. 12, 2: 114; *Mantissa Plantarum*: 37. 1767.
"Habitat in Palaestina. Hasselquist." RCN: 821.
Type not designated.
Original material: Herb. Linn. No. 120.36 (LINN); Herb. Linn. No. 53.1 (S); Herb. Hasselquist No. 102 (UPS).
Current name: ***Lomelosia palaestina*** (L.) Raf. (Dipsacaceae).

Scabiosa papposa Linnaeus, *Species Plantarum* 1: 101. 1753, *nom. utique rej.*
"Habitat in Creta." RCN: 825.
Neotype (Meikle in *Taxon* 31: 542. 1982): Herb. A. van Royen No. 902.125–731 (L).
Current name: ***Pterocephalus plumosus*** (L.) Coult. (Dipsacaceae).

Scabiosa prolifera Linnaeus, *Systema Naturae*, ed. 10, 2: 889. 1759.
["Habitat in India."] Sp. Pl., ed. 2, 1: 144 (1762). RCN: 813.
Type not designated.
Original material: Herb. Linn. No. 120.24 (LINN); [icon] in Hermann, Parad. Bat.: 125. 1698.
Current name: ***Lomelosia prolifera*** (L.) Greuter & Burdet (Dipsacaceae).

Scabiosa pterocephala Linnaeus, *Species Plantarum* 1: 100. 1753.
"Habitat in Graecia?" RCN: 826.
Type not designated.
Original material: none traced.
Current name: ***Pterocephalus perennis*** Coult. (Dipsacaceae).

Scabiosa rigida Linnaeus, *Plantae Rariores Africanae*: 8. 1760.
["Habitat in Aethiopia."] Sp. Pl., ed. 2, 1: 142 (1762). RCN: 798.
Lectotype (Wijnands, *Bot. Commelins*: 94. 1983): Herb. Burman (specimen "with an annotation on the differential characters between *S. rigida* and *C. leucantha*, also found in Linnaeus' protologue") (G).
Current name: ***Cephalaria rigida*** (L.) Roem. & Schult. (Dipsacaceae).

Scabiosa sicula Linnaeus, *Mantissa Plantarum Altera*: 196. 1771.
"Habitat in Sicilia." RCN: 810.
Lectotype (Devesa in *Lagascalia* 12: 193. 1984): Herb. Linn. No. 120.20 (LINN).
Current name: ***Lomelosia divaricata*** (Jacq.) Greuter & Burdet (Dipsacaceae).

Scabiosa stellata Linnaeus, *Species Plantarum* 1: 100. 1753.
"Habitat in Hispania, praesertim in agro Granatensi ad versuras." RCN: 812.
Lectotype (Devesa in *Lagascalia* 12: 196. 1984): *Löfling 111*, Herb. Linn. No. 120.23 (LINN).
Current name: ***Scabiosa stellata*** L. (Dipsacaceae).

Scabiosa succisa Linnaeus, *Species Plantarum* 1: 98. 1753.
"Habitat in Europae pascuis humidiusculis." RCN: 802.
Type not designated.
Original material: Herb. Burser XV(2): 2 (UPS); Herb. Linn. No. 120.4 (LINN); Herb. Clifford: 30, *Scabiosa* 2, 3 sheets (BM); [icon] in Mattioli, Pl. Epit.: 397. 1586.
Current name: ***Succisa pratensis*** Moench (Dipsacaceae).

Scabiosa sylvatica Linnaeus, *Species Plantarum*, ed. 2, 1: 142. 1762.
"Habitat in Austriae, Helvetiae, Monspelii sylvaticis." RCN: 807.
Lectotype (Gutermann & al. in *Österr. Bot. Zeitschr.* 122: 262. 1973): Herb. Linn. No. 120.14 (LINN).
Current name: ***Knautia drymeia*** Heuff. (Dipsacaceae).
Note: Gutermann & al., in typifying the name, concluded that as their chosen type was identifiable as *K. drymeia* Heuff. (1856), *S. sylvatica* should be rejected as a *nomen ambiguum*. However, no formal proposal for its rejection appears to have been made.

Scabiosa syriaca Linnaeus, *Species Plantarum* 1: 98. 1753.
"Habitat in Syria." RCN: 800.
Lectotype (Lack in Rechinger, *Fl. Iranica* 168: 12. 1991): *Hasselquist*, Herb. Linn. No. 120.5 (LINN).
Current name: ***Cephalaria syriaca*** (L.) Roem. & Schult. (Dipsacaceae).

Scabiosa tatarica Linnaeus, *Species Plantarum* 1: 99. 1753.
"Habitat in Tataria." RCN: 805.
Type not designated.
Original material: Herb. Linn. No. 120.12 (LINN); [icon] in Linnaeus in Acta Soc. Regiae Sci. Upsal. 1744–50: 11, t. 1. 1751 (see p. 89).
Current name: ***Cephalaria tatarica*** (L.) Schrad. (Dipsacaceae).

Scabiosa transsylvanica Linnaeus, *Species Plantarum* 1: 98. 1753.
"Habitat in Transylvania." RCN: 799.
Type not designated.
Original material: Herb. Linn. No. 120.4 (LINN); Herb. Linn. No. 51.16 (S); [icon] in Hermann, Hort. Lugd.-Bat. Cat.: 539, 541. 1687; [icon] in Morison, Pl. Hist. Univ. 3: 46, s. 6, t. 13, f. 13. 1699.
Current name: ***Cephalaria transsylvanica*** (L.) Roem. & Schult. (Dipsacaceae).

Scabiosa triandra Linnaeus, *Species Plantarum* 1: 99. 1753.
"Habitat Monspelii." RCN: 808.
Replaced synonym of: *Scabiosa gramuntia* L. (1759), *nom. illeg.*
Type not designated.
Original material: Herb. Linn. No. 120.16? (LINN).
Current name: ***Scabiosa triandra*** L. (Dipsacaceae).

Scabiosa ucranica Linnaeus, *Systema Naturae*, ed. 10, 2: 889. 1759.
["Habitat in Ucranica. P. Forskåhl."] Sp. Pl., ed. 2, 1: 144 (1762).
  RCN: 823.
Type not designated.
Original material: Herb. Linn. No. 120.40 (LINN).
Current name: ***Lomelosia argentea*** (L.) Greuter & Burdet
  (Dipsacaceae).

Scabrita scabra Linnaeus, *Systema Naturae,* ed. 12, 2: 115. 1767.
RCN: 836.
Type not designated.
Original material: Herb. Linn. No. 124.1? (LINN).
Current name: ***Nyctanthes arbor-tristis*** L. (Oleaceae).

Scabrita triflora Linnaeus, *Mantissa Plantarum*: 37. 1767.
"Habitat in India." RCN: 836.
Type not designated.
Original material: Herb. Linn. No. 124.1? (LINN).
Generitype of *Scabrita* Linnaeus.
Current name: ***Nyctanthes arbor-tristis*** L. (Oleaceae).
Note: Scabrita L. was monospecific when published simultaneously in
  Syst. Nat., ed. 12 and *Mant. Pl. Scabrita triflora* was the binomial
  given in *Mant. Pl.,* but it appeared as *S. scabra* in *Syst. Nat.,*
  presumably in error.

Scaevola lobelia Linnaeus, *Systema Vegetabilium,* ed. 13: 178. 1774,
  nom. illeg.
"Habitat in Indiis." RCN: 1359.
Replaced synonym: *Lobelia plumieri* L. (1753).
Lectotype (Davies in Polhill, *Fl. Trop. E. Africa, Goodeniaceae*: 3.
  1978): [icon] *"Lobelia frutescens, Portulacae folio"* in Catesby, Nat.
  Hist. Carolina 1: 79, t. 79. 1731.
Generitype of *Scaevola* Linnaeus, *nom. cons.*
Current name: ***Scaevola plumieri*** (L.) Vahl (Goodeniaceae).
Note: A superfluous name for *Lobelia plumieri* L. (1753).

Scandix anthriscus Linnaeus, *Species Plantarum* 1: 257. 1753.
"Habitat in Europae aggeribus terrenis." RCN: 2058.
Lectotype (Spalik & Jarvis in *Taxon* 38: 288, f. 1. 1989): Herb. Linn.
  No. 364.5 (LINN).
Current name: ***Anthriscus caucalis*** M. Bieb. (Apiaceae).
Note: See also detailed comments by Reduron & Spalik (in *Acta Bot.
  Gallica* 142: 58. 1995).

Scandix australis Linnaeus, *Species Plantarum* 1: 257. 1753.
"Habitat in G. Narbonensi, Italia, Creta." RCN: 2059.
Lectotype (Reduron & Jarvis in Jarvis & al. in *Taxon* 55: 214. 2006):
  Herb. Burser VII(2): 49 (UPS).
Current name: ***Scandix australis*** L. (Apiaceae).

Scandix cerefolium Linnaeus, *Species Plantarum* 1: 257. 1753.
"Habitat in apris & arvis Europae australioris." RCN: 2057.
Lectotype (Jafri in Jafri & El-Gadi, *Fl. Libya* 117: 16. 1985): Herb.
  Linn. No. 364.4 (LINN).
Current name: ***Anthriscus cerefolium*** (L.) Hoffm. (Apiaceae).
Note: See detailed reviews by Spalik & Jarvis (in *Taxon* 38: 290, f. 2.
  1989) and Reduron & Spalik (in *Acta Bot. Gallica* 142: 63–64.
  1995).

Scandix grandiflora Linnaeus, *Species Plantarum* 1: 257. 1753.
"Habitat in Oriente." RCN: 2063.
Neotype (Reduron in Jarvis & al. in *Taxon* 55: 214. 2006): Herb.
  Tournefort No. 2930, "Scandix Smyrnea, flore maximo" (P-
  TOURN).
Current name: ***Scandix australis*** L. subsp. ***grandiflora*** (L.) Thell.
  (Apiaceae).

Scandix infesta Linnaeus, *Systema Naturae,* ed. 12, 2: 732. 1767.
"Habitat in . . . D. Zoega." RCN: 2062.
Lectotype (Townsend in Polhill, *Fl. Trop. E. Africa, Umbelliferae*: 27.
  1989): Herb. Linn. No. 364.10 (LINN).
Current name: ***Torilis arvensis*** (Huds.) Link (Apiaceae).

Scandix nodosa Linnaeus, *Species Plantarum* 1: 257. 1753.
"Habitat in Sicilia." RCN: 2060.
Lectotype (Hedge & Lamond in Rechinger, *Fl. Iranica* 162: 101.
  1987): Herb. Linn. No. 364.6 (LINN).
Current name: ***Myrrhoides nodosa*** (L.) Cannon (Apiaceae).

Scandix odorata Linnaeus, *Species Plantarum* 1: 256. 1753.
"Habitat in alpibus Alvarniae." RCN: 2055.
Lectotype (Reduron in Jonsell & Jarvis in *Nordic J. Bot.* 22: 85. 2002):
  Herb. Linn. No. 364.1 (LINN).
Current name: ***Myrrhis odorata*** (L.) Scop. (Apiaceae).

Scandix pecten-veneris Linnaeus, *Species Plantarum* 1: 256. 1753.
"Habitat inter Germaniae & Europae australioris segetes." RCN:
  2056.
Lectotype (Jafri in Jafri & El-Gadi, *Fl. Libya* 117: 20. 1985): Herb.
  Linn. No. 364.2 (LINN).
Generitype of *Scandix* Linnaeus (vide Rafinesque, *Good Book*: 53.
  1840).
Current name: ***Scandix pecten-veneris*** L. (Apiaceae).

Scandix procumbens Linnaeus, *Species Plantarum* 1: 257. 1753.
"Habitat in Virginia." RCN: 2064.
Lectotype (Naczi in Jarvis & al. in *Taxon* 55: 214. 2006): [icon]
  "Cerefolium Virgin. minus Fumariae foliis" in Morison, Pl. Hist.
  Univ. 3: 303, s. 9, t. 11, f. 3. 1699. – Epitype (Naczi in Jarvis & al.
  in *Taxon* 55: 214. 2006): U.S.A. Virginia, Halifax County: 1mi
  (1.6km) S of Brookneal, floodplain along S side of Roanoke River,
  30 Apr 1992, *Naczi 10816* (DOV; iso- BM, MICH, MO, NY, PH,
  US, etc.).
Current name: ***Chaerophyllum procumbens*** (L.) Crantz (Apiaceae).

Scandix trichosperma Linnaeus, *Systema Naturae,* ed. 12, 2: 214;
  Mantissa Plantarum: 57. 1767.
"Habitat in Aegypto. D. Ant. Turra." RCN: 2061.
Lectotype (Jury & Southam in Jarvis & al. in *Taxon* 55: 214. 2006):
  Herb. Linn. No. 364.8 (LINN).
Current name: ***Chaetosciadium trichospermum*** (L.) Boiss.
  (Apiaceae).

Scheuchzeria palustris Linnaeus, *Species Plantarum* 1: 338. 1753.
"Habitat in Lapponiae, Helvetiae, Borussiae, Sueciae paludosis."
  RCN: 2607.
Lectotype (Barrie in Jarvis & al., *Regnum Veg.* 127: 85. 1993): Herb.
  Linn. No. 465.1 (LINN).
Generitype of *Scheuchzeria* Linnaeus.
Current name: ***Scheuchzeria palustris*** L. (Scheuchzeriaceae).

Schinus areira Linnaeus, *Species Plantarum* 1: 389. 1753.
"Habitat in Brasilia, Peru." RCN: 7479.
Type not designated.

S

Original material: [icon] in Feuillée, J. Obs. 3: 43, t. 30. 1725; [icon] in Marggraf, Hist. Rer. Nat. Bras.: 90. 1648.
Current name: ***Schinus molle*** L. (Anacardiaceae).

Schinus fagara Linnaeus, *Species Plantarum* 1: 389. 1753.
"Habitat in Jamaicae campestribus." RCN: 967.
Lectotype (Porter in *Brittonia* 28: 445. 1977): [icon] *"Lauro affinis Jasmini folio alato, costa media membranulis utrinque extantibus alata, ligni duritie ferro vix cedens"* in Sloane, Voy. Jamaica 2: 25, t. 162, f. 1. 1725. – Typotype: Herb. Sloane 5: 87 (BM-SL).
Current name: ***Zanthoxylum fagara*** (L.) Sarg. (Rutaceae).
Note: Fawcett & Rendle (*Fl. Jamaica* 4: 175. 1920) indicated material in Herb. Sloane as the type, but this was not seen by Linnaeus and is not original material for the name.

Schinus limonia Linnaeus, *Species Plantarum* 1: 389. 1753.
"Habitat in India utraque." RCN: 3054.
Replaced synonym of: *Limonia acidissima* L. (1762).
Lectotype (Tanaka in *Meded. Rijks-Herb.* 69: 8. 1931): Herb. Hermann 1: 76, No. 175 (BM-000594508).
Current name: ***Limonia acidissima*** L. (Rutaceae).

Schinus melicoccus Linnaeus, *Amoenitates Academicae* 5: 379. 1760.
"Habitat [in Jamaica.]"
Type not designated.
Original material: none traced.
Note: The application of this name is uncertain.

Schinus molle Linnaeus, *Species Plantarum* 1: 388. 1753.
"Habitat in Peru." RCN: 5478.
Lectotype (Nasir in Nasir & Ali, *Fl. Pakistan* 152: 20. 1983): Herb. Linn. No. 1193.1 (LINN).
Generitype of *Schinus* Linnaeus (vide Hitchcock, *Prop. Brit. Bot.*: 153. 1929).
Current name: ***Schinus molle*** L. (Anacardiaceae).

Schinus myricoides Linnaeus, *Species Plantarum* 1: 388. 1753.
"Habitat in Aethiopia." RCN: 1851.
Replaced synonym of: *Schrebera schinoides* L. (1763), *nom. illeg.*
Type not designated.
Original material: none traced.
Note: Meeuse (in *Bothalia* 6: 652–653. 1957) stated that *Schrebera schinoides* (homotypic with *Schinus myricoides*) probably relates in part to *Cuscuta africana* Willd. and in part to its host *Myrica conifera* Burm. Although *Schrebera schinoides* is illegitimate, *Schinus myricoides* is not, and could threaten the current names of either of the taxa to which it is supposed to belong. It may therefore be a candidate for rejection.

Schinus tragodes Linnaeus, *Species Plantarum* 1: 389. 1753.
"Habitat in America." RCN: 969.
Type not designated.
Original material: Herb. Clifford: 489, *Oidea (Schinoides)* 11 (BM); [icon] in Plukenet, Phytographia: t. 107, f. 4. 1691; Almag. Bot.: 319. 1696 – Typotype: Herb. Sloane 97: 152 (BM-SL).
Current name: ***Zanthoxylum tragodes*** (L.) DC. (Rutaceae).

Schmidelia racemosa Linnaeus, *Systema Naturae,* ed. 12, 2: 274; *Mantissa Plantarum*: 67. 1767.
"Habitat in India orientali sub Klinting birae." RCN: 2848.
Neotype (Adema in Jarvis & al., *Regnum Veg.* 127: 86. 1993): *Kleynhoff*, sheet No. 908.269–889 (L).
Generitype of *Schmidelia* Linnaeus, *nom. illeg.*, non Boehm.
Current name: ***Allophylus cobbe*** (L.) Raeusch. (Sapindaceae).
Note: Schmidelia Linnaeus (1767) is a later homonym of *Schmidelia* Boehm. (1760) and therefore illegitimate.

Schoenus aculeatus Linnaeus, *Species Plantarum* 1: 42. 1753.
"Habitat in Italia, Narbona, Lusitania, Archipelagi insulis." RCN: 360.
Lectotype (Meikle, *Fl. Cyprus* 2: 1848. 1985): *Löfling s.n.*, Herb. Linn. No. 68.3 (LINN).
Current name: ***Crypsis aculeata*** (L.) Aiton (Poaceae).
Note: Although Kerguélen (in *Lejeunia*, n.s., 75: 122. 1975) stated "Type: ...LINN", this is not accepted as a formal typification, for the reasons explained by Cafferty & al. (in *Taxon* 49: 240. 2000).

Schoenus albus Linnaeus, *Species Plantarum* 1: 44. 1753.
"Habitat in Europae borealis paludibus siccatis." RCN: 373.
Lectotype (Simpson in Cafferty & Jarvis in *Taxon* 53: 179. 2004): Herb. Linn. No. 68.17 (LINN).
Current name: ***Rhynchospora alba*** (L.) Vahl (Cyperaceae).

Schoenus bulbosus Linnaeus, *Mantissa Plantarum Altera*: 178. 1771.
"Habitat ad Cap. b. spei." RCN: 369.
Lectotype (Archer in Cafferty & Jarvis in *Taxon* 53: 179. 2004): Herb. Linn. No. 68.14 (LINN).
Current name: ***Ficinia bulbosa*** (L.) Nees (Cyperaceae).

Schoenus capensis Linnaeus, *Centuria I Plantarum*: 4. 1755.
"Habitat ad Caput Bonae Spei." RCN: 7392.
Lectotype (Linder in *Bothalia* 15: 402. 1985): Herb. Linn. No. 1164.3 (LINN).
Current name: ***Ischyrolepis capensis*** (L.) H.P. Linder (Restionaceae).

Schoenus coloratus Linnaeus, *Species Plantarum* 1: 43. 1753.
"Habitat in Jamaica, Bahama." RCN: 368.
Lectotype (Thomas in *Mem. New York Bot. Gard.* 37: 83. 1984): [icon] *"Gramen cyperoides spica compacta alba, foliis ad spicam partim albis partim viridibus"* in Sloane, Voy. Jamaica 1: 119, t. 78, f. 1. 1707. – Typotype: Herb. Sloane 2: 56 (BM-SL).
Current name: ***Rhynchospora colorata*** (L.) H. Pfeiff. (Cyperaceae).

Schoenus compar Linnaeus, *Mantissa Plantarum Altera*: 177. 1771.
"Habitat ad Cap. b. spei. D. König." RCN: 365.
Lectotype (Archer in Cafferty & Jarvis in *Taxon* 53: 179. 2004): Herb. Linn. No. 68.11 (LINN).
Current name: ***Tetraria compar*** (L.) T. Lestib. (Cyperaceae).

Schoenus compressus Linnaeus, *Species Plantarum* 1: 43. 1753.
"Habitat in Anglia, Helvetia, Italia." RCN: 370.
Lectotype (Kukkonen in Cafferty & Jarvis in *Taxon* 53: 179. 2004): [icon] *"Gramen cyperoides spica simplici compressa disticha"* in Plukenet, Phytographia: t. 34, f. 9. 1691; Almag. Bot.: 178. 1696. – Voucher: Herb. Sloane 96: 80 (BM-SL).
Current name: ***Blysmus compressus*** (L.) Panz. ex Link (Cyperaceae).

Schoenus ferrugineus Linnaeus, *Species Plantarum* 1: 43. 1753.
"Habitat in Gotlandiae, Angliae paludibus." RCN: 363.
Lectotype (Simpson in Cafferty & Jarvis in *Taxon* 53: 179. 2004): Herb. Linn. No. 68.7 (LINN).
Current name: ***Schoenus ferrugineus*** L. (Cyperaceae).

Schoenus fuscus Linnaeus, *Species Plantarum,* ed. 2, 2: 1664. 1763.
"Habitat in Sveciae, Angliae, Italiae palustribus caespitosis." RCN: 364.
Lectotype (Simpson in Cafferty & Jarvis in *Taxon* 53: 179. 2004): Herb. Linn. No. 68.10 (LINN).
Current name: ***Rhynchospora fusca*** (L.) W.T. Aiton (Cyperaceae).

Schoenus glomeratus Linnaeus, *Species Plantarum* 1: 44. 1753.
"Habitat in Virginia." RCN: 371.

Lectotype (Reznicek in Cafferty & Jarvis in *Taxon* 53: 179. 2004): *Kalm*, Herb. Linn. No. 68.15 (LINN).
Current name: ***Rhynchospora glomerata*** (L.) Vahl var. ***glomerata*** (Cyperaceae).

Schoenus lithospermus (Linnaeus) Linnaeus, *Systema Naturae*, ed. 10, 2: 865. 1759.
["Habitat in India."] Sp. Pl. 1: 51 (1753). RCN: 7095.
Basionym: *Scirpus lithospermus* L. (1753).
Lectotype (Camelbeke & Goetghebeur in *Taxon* 49: 295. 2000): [icon] *"Kaden-pullu"* in Rheede, Hort. Malab. 12: 89, t. 48. 1693.
Current name: ***Scleria lithosperma*** (L.) Sw. (Cyperaceae).

Schoenus mariscus Linnaeus, *Species Plantarum* 1: 42. 1753.
"Habitat in Europae paludibus." RCN: 359.
Lectotype (Kukkonen in Cafferty & Jarvis in *Taxon* 53: 179. 2004): Herb. Linn. No. 68.1 (LINN).
Current name: ***Cladium mariscus*** (L.) Pohl (Cyperaceae).
Note: Stearn (in *Biol. J. Linn. Soc.* 5: 12. 1973), in an account of Linnaeus' Öland and Gotland journey of 1741, treated Lummelund in Gotland as the restricted type locality. In his paper, he attributed restricted type localities irrespective of whether any material existed in LINN and, where specimens do exist, he does not refer to any of them as type specimens. None is mentioned in this case. The collection subsequently designated as the type shows no annotation associating it with Gotland.

Schoenus mucronatus Linnaeus, *Species Plantarum* 1: 42. 1753.
"Habitat in Galliae, Narbonae, Tyrrheni, Smyrnae maritimis." RCN: 361.
Lectotype (Simpson in Cafferty & Jarvis in *Taxon* 53: 180. 2004): Herb. Linn. No. 19.1 (S). – Epitype (Simpson in Cafferty & Jarvis in *Taxon* 53: 180. 2004): Italy. Liguria, In arenosis maritimis prope "Bordighera", May 1895, *Bicknell s.n.*, Herbarium Normale, ed. I. Dörfler. (BM).
Current name: ***Cyperus capitatus*** Vand. (Cyperaceae).

Schoenus nigricans Linnaeus, *Species Plantarum* 1: 43. 1753.
"Habitat in Europae paludibus aestate, exsiccatis." RCN: 362.
Lectotype (Simpson in Jarvis & al., *Regnum Veg.* 127: 86. 1993): Herb. Linn. No. 68.5 (LINN).
Generitype of *Schoenus* Linnaeus (vide Hitchcock in *Amer. J. Bot.* 10: 514. 1923).
Current name: ***Schoenus nigricans*** L. (Cyperaceae).
Note: Stearn (in *Biol. J. Linn. Soc.* 5: 12. 1973), in an account of Linnaeus' Öland and Gotland journey of 1741, treated Gamelgarn in Gotland as the restricted type locality, and noted the existence of 68.6 (LINN), annotated by Linnaeus as from Gotland. In his paper, he attributed restricted type localities irrespective of whether any material existed in LINN and, where specimens do exist, he does not refer to any of them as type specimens. Simpson's subsequent formal typification is accepted here.

Schoenus niveus Linnaeus, *Systema Vegetabilium*, ed. 13: 81. 1774.
["Habitat in Virginia, India."] Sp. Pl. 1: 52 (1753). RCN: 367.
Replaced synonym: *Scirpus glomeratus* L. (1753).
Type not designated.
Original material: as replaced synonym.
Note: A *nomen novum* in *Schoenus* for *Scirpus glomeratus* Linnaeus (1753), the epithet being pre-occupied by *Schoenus glomeratus* L. (1753). Linnaeus erroneously cited the basionym as "Schoenus glomeratus. *Spec. plant.* (edit. 1.) 52.". However, the page number is correct for *Scirpus glomeratus*, and the same name is included on p. 82 of *Systema Vegetabilium*, ed. 13 (species No. 11). The application of this name is uncertain.

Schoenus secans Linnaeus, *Systema Naturae,* ed. 10, 2: 865. 1759.
RCN: 7095.
Lectotype (Koyama in Howard, *Fl. Lesser Antilles* 3: 309. 1979): [icon] *"Gramen cyperoides sylvaticum maximum geniculatum asperius, semine milii solis"* in Sloane, Voy. Jamaica 1: 118, t. 77, f. 1. 1707. – Typotype: Herb. Sloane 2: 54 (BM-SL).
Current name: ***Scleria secans*** (L.) Urb. (Cyperaceae).

Schoenus spathaceus Linnaeus, *Species Plantarum*, ed. 2, 1: 63. 1762, *nom. illeg.*
"Habitat in Virginia, Cap. b. spei." RCN: 400.
Replaced synonym: *Cyperus arundinaceus* L. (1753).
Replaced synonym of: *Cyperus spathaceus* L. (1767), *nom. illeg.*
Lectotype (Kukkonen in *Ann. Bot. Fenn.* 27: 65. 1990): Herb. Linn. No. 70.39 (LINN; iso- BM).
Current name: ***Dulichium arundinaceum*** (L.) Britton (Cyperaceae).
Note: Linnaeus erroneously cites "Cyperus ferrugineus. *Sp. pl.* 44." in synonymy in the protologue. However, there is no *C. ferrugineus* on p. 44 of *Species Plantarum*, or indeed anywhere else in that work. The similarities of the phrase names, inclusion of the same three pre-1753 synonyms, and the same habitat statement show that *C. arundinaceus* is the name Linnaeus was intending.

Schoenus thermalis Linnaeus, *Mantissa Plantarum Altera*: 179. 1771.
"Habitat ad aquas calidas Capitis b. spei, juxta montes nigros." RCN: 372.
Neotype (Archer in Cafferty & Jarvis in *Taxon* 53: 180. 2004): South Africa. Western Cape, Caledon district, Kogelberg Research Site, 7 Sep 1976, *Durand 149* (PRE; iso- NBG).
Current name: ***Tetraria thermalis*** (L.) C.B. Clarke (Cyperaceae).

Schoenus ustulatus Linnaeus, *Mantissa Plantarum Altera*: 178. 1771.
"Habitat in Cap b. spei." RCN: 366.
Neotype (Archer in Cafferty & Jarvis in *Taxon* 53: 180. 2004): South Africa. Ceres district, 1.4km along road to Witsenberg Valley from top of Gydo Pass, 20 Sep 1991, *Reid 1381* (PRE; iso- NBG).
Current name: ***Tetraria ustulata*** (L.) C.B. Clarke (Cyperaceae).

Schrebera schinoides Linnaeus, *Species Plantarum*, ed. 2, 2: 1662. 1763, *nom. illeg.*
RCN: 1851.
Replaced synonym: *Schinus myricoides* L. (1753).
Type not designated.
Original material: as replaced synonym.
Generitype of *Schrebera* Linnaeus, *nom. rej.*
Note: *Schrebera* Linnaeus, *nom. rej.* in favour of *Schrebera* Roxb. Meeuse (in *Bothalia* 6: 652–653. 1957) says that this probably relates in part to *Cuscuta africana* Willd. and in part to its host *Myrica conifera* Burm. Although *S. schinoides* is illegitimate, *Schinus myricoides* is not, and could threaten the current names of either of the taxa to which it is supposed to belong. It may therefore be a candidate for rejection.

Schwalbea americana Linnaeus, *Species Plantarum* 2: 606. 1753.
"Habitat in America septentrionali." RCN: 4395.
Lectotype (Pennell in *Torreya* 19: 235. 1920): *Clayton 33* (BM-000032598).
Generitype of *Schwalbea* Linnaeus.
Current name: ***Schwalbea americana*** L. (Scrophulariaceae).
Note: See extensive discussion by Reveal & al. (in *Huntia* 7: 222. 1987).

Schwenckia americana Linnaeus, *Genera Plantarum,* ed. 6: 577. 1764.
"Habitat in Barbyce." RCN: 137.

S

Lectotype (Knapp in Jarvis & al., *Regnum Veg.* 127: 86. 1993): Herb. Linn. No. 31.1 (LINN).
Generitype of *Schwenckia* Linnaeus.
Current name: ***Schwenckia americana*** L. (Solanaceae).

Scilla amoena Linnaeus, *Species Plantarum* 1: 309. 1753.
"Habitat forte Bizantii, unde venit in Europam 1590." RCN: 2431.
Lectotype (van Raamsdonk in Wisskirchen in *Feddes Repert.* 108: 106. 1997): Herb. Linn. No. 429.4 (LINN).
Current name: ***Scilla amoena*** L. (Liliaceae/Hyacinthaceae).

Scilla autumnalis Linnaeus, *Species Plantarum* 1: 309. 1753.
"Habitat in Hispania, Gallia, Verona solo glareoso." RCN: 2435.
Type not designated.
Original material: Herb. Linn. No. 429.9? (LINN); Herb. Burser III: 28 (UPS); [icon] in Clusius, Rar. Pl. Hist. 1: 185. 1601.
Current name: ***Scilla autumnalis*** L. (Liliaceae/Hyacinthaceae).
Note: El-Gadi (in Jafri & El-Gadi, *Fl. Libya* 57: 40. 1978) indicated 429.11 (LINN) as type but it is a Brander collection, not received by Linnaeus until 1756 and so not original material for the name.

Scilla bifolia Linnaeus, *Species Plantarum* 1: 309. 1753.
"Habitat in Gallia, Germania." RCN: 2432.
Lectotype (van Raamsdonk in Wisskirchen in *Feddes Repert.* 108: 106. 1997): Herb. Burser III: 23 (UPS).
Generitype of *Scilla* Linnaeus (vide Hitchcock, *Prop. Brit. Bot.*: 146. 1929).
Current name: ***Scilla bifolia*** L. (Liliaceae/Hyacinthaceae).
Note: Speta (in *Naturk. Jahrb. Stadt Linz* 25: 41. 1980) designated 429.5 (LINN) as the type. However, this sheet came from Hasselquist, from the "Middle East" conflicting with Linnaeus' "Hab. in Gallia, Germania". Van Raamsdonk therefore rejected this choice in favour of the Burser sheet, formalising the suggestion made by Andersson (in Strid & Kit Tan, *Mountain Fl. Greece* 2: 694. 1991).

Scilla hyacinthoides Linnaeus, *Systema Naturae*, ed. 12, 2: 243. 1767. RCN: 2434.
Lectotype (Speta in *Naturk. Jahrb. Stadt Linz* 25: 182. 1980): *Gouan s.n.*, Herb. Linn. No. 429.10 (LINN).
Current name: ***Scilla hyacinthoides*** L. (Liliaceae/Hyacinthaceae).

Scilla italica Linnaeus, *Species Plantarum* 1: 308. 1753.
"Habitat – – – –" RCN: 2429.
Lectotype (van Raamsdonk in Wisskirchen in *Feddes Repert.* 108: 105. 1997): Herb. Linn. No. 429.1 (LINN).
Current name: ***Hyacinthoides italica*** (L.) Rothm. (Liliaceae/Hyacinthaceae).

Scilla liliohyacinthus Linnaeus, *Species Plantarum* 1: 308. 1753.
"Habitat in Biscaria, Aquitania, Hispania, Pyrenaeis." RCN: 2428.
Type not designated.
Original material: Herb. A. van Royen No. 913.62–340 (L).
Current name: ***Scilla liliohyacinthus*** L. (Liliaceae/Hyacinthaceae).
Note: Specific epithet spelled "Lilia Hyacinthus" in the protologue.

Scilla lusitanica Linnaeus, *Systema Naturae,* ed. 12, 2: 243. 1767.
"Habitat in Lusitania." RCN: 2433.
Type not designated.
Original material: Herb. Linn. No. 429.8 (LINN); Herb. Linn. No. 429.9 (LINN); [icon] in Rudbeck, Campi Elysii 2: 34, t. 4. 1701.
Current name: ***Scilla lusitanica*** L. (Liliaceae/Hyacinthaceae).
Note: See Speta (in *Naturk. Jahrb. Stadt Linz* 25: 179. 1980), who states that of the two sheets in LINN relating to this name, one is identifiable as *S. numidica* Poir., and the other as *S. bifolia* L.

Scilla maritima Linnaeus, *Species Plantarum* 1: 308. 1753.
"Habitat ad Hispaniae, Siciliae, Syriae littoria arenosa." RCN: 2427.
Type not designated.
Original material: Herb. Burser III: 89 (UPS); Herb. A. van Royen No. 913.62–327 (L); [icon] in Clusius, Rar. Pl. Hist. 1: 171. 1601.
Current name: ***Drimia maritima*** (L.) Stearn (Liliaceae/Hyacinthaceae).

Scilla peruviana Linnaeus, *Species Plantarum* 1: 309. 1753.
"Habitat in Lusitania." RCN: 2430.
Lectotype (El-Gadi in Jafri & El-Gadi, *Fl. Libya* 57: 31. 1978): Herb. Linn. No. 429.3 (LINN).
Current name: ***Scilla peruviana*** L. (Liliaceae/Hyacinthaceae).

Scilla unifolia Linnaeus, *Species Plantarum* 1: 309. 1753.
"Habitat in Lusitania." RCN: 2436.
Lectotype (Stearn in *Ann. Mus. Goulandris* 6: 161. 1983): [icon] *"Bulbus monophyllos flore albo"* in Bauhin & Cherler, Hist. Pl. Univ. 2: 622. 1651.
Current name: ***Ornithogalum broteroi*** M. Laínz (Liliaceae/Hyacinthaceae).
Note: Martínez-Azorin & al. (in *Taxon* 55: 1014–1018. 2006) discuss the typification of this and related names.

Scirpus acicularis Linnaeus, *Species Plantarum* 1: 48. 1753.
"Habitat in Europa sub aquis purioribus." RCN: 409.
Lectotype (Egorova in *Novosti Sist. Vyssh. Rast.* 17: 69. 1980): Herb. Linn. No. 71.13 (UPS). – Epitype (Kukkonen in *Taxon* 53: 180. 2004): Herb. Celsius 5: 677 (UPS).
Current name: ***Eleocharis acicularis*** (L.) Roem. & Schult. (Cyperaceae).
Note: The material designated as lectotype by Egorova is sterile, so a fertile sheet from the Celsius herbarium, also studied by Linnaeus, was designated as an epitype by Kukkonen.

Scirpus antarcticus Linnaeus, *Mantissa Plantarum Altera*: 181. 1771.
"Habitat ad Cap. b. spei. Burmannus." RCN: 437.
Lectotype (Blake in *Contr. Queensland Herb.* 8: 17. 1969): *J. Burman s.n.*, Herb. Linn. No. 71.54 (LINN).
Current name: ***Scirpus antarcticus*** L. (Cyperaceae).

Scirpus articulatus Linnaeus, *Species Plantarum* 1: 47. 1753.
"Habitat in Malabariae aquosis arenosis." RCN: 404.
Lectotype (Simpson in Cafferty & Jarvis in *Taxon* 53: 180. 2004): [icon] *"Tsjeli"* in Rheede, Hort. Malab. 12: 135, t. 71. 1693. – Epitype (Simpson in Cafferty & Jarvis in *Taxon* 53: 180. 2004): India. Kerala, Ramnanatukarat, 50m, 16 Jan 1977, *Suresh 22191* (BM-000576301; iso- CALI).
Current name: ***Schoenoplectus articulatus*** (L.) Palla (Cyperaceae).

Scirpus australis Linnaeus, *Systema Vegetabilium*, ed. 13: 85. 1774. RCN: 413.
Lectotype (Kukkonen in Rechinger, *Fl. Iranica* 173: 40. 1998): Herb. Linn. No. 71.20 (LINN).
Current name: ***Scirpoides holoschoenus*** (L.) Soják subsp. ***australis*** (L.) Soják (Cyperaceae).

Scirpus autumnalis Linnaeus, *Mantissa Plantarum Altera*: 180. 1771.
"Habitat in Virginia." RCN: 417.
Lectotype (Blake in *Rhodora* 20: 24. 1918): *Clayton 772* (BM-000553915; iso- LINN 71.24).
Current name: ***Fimbristylis autumnalis*** (L.) Roem. & Schult. (Cyperaceae).

Scirpus capillaris Linnaeus, *Species Plantarum* 1: 49. 1753.
"Habitat in Virginia, Aethiopia, Zeylona." RCN: 418.

Lectotype (Fernald in *Rhodora* 40: 395, pl. 510. 1938): Herb. Linn. No. 71.25 (LINN).

Current name: ***Bulbostylis capillaris*** (L.) C.B. Clarke (Cyperaceae).

Scirpus capitatus Linnaeus, *Species Plantarum* 1: 48. 1753.

"Habitat in Virginia." RCN: 408.

Lectotype (Blake in *Rhodora* 20: 23. 1918): *Clayton 380* (BM-000051193).

Current name: ***Eleocharis capitatus*** (L.) R. Br. (Cyperaceae).

Note: Blake (1918) treated the Clayton material as the type but this choice provoked extensive discussion by Fernald (in *Rhodora* 23: 106. 1921), Mackenzie (*l.c.* 30: 237. 1928), Farwell (*l.c.* 32: 181. 1930), Blake (*l.c.* 32: 182. 1930) again, Svenson (*l.c.* 34: 195. 1932; 41: 50. 1939) and Furtado (in *Gard. Bull. Straits Settlem.* 9: 243. 1937). However, Blake's original choice has priority.

Scirpus cephalotes Linnaeus, *Species Plantarum,* ed. 2, 1: 76. 1762.

"Habitat in India." RCN: 438.

Lectotype (Clarke in *J. Linn. Soc., Bot.* 30: 314. 1894): Herb. Linn. No. 71.56 (LINN).

Current name: ***Rhynchospora cephalotes*** (L.) Vahl (Cyperaceae).

Scirpus cespitosus Linnaeus, *Species Plantarum* 1: 48. 1753.

"Habitat in Europae paludibus cespitosis sylvaticis." RCN: 407.

Lectotype (Swan in Cafferty & Jarvis in *Taxon* 53: 180. 2004): Herb. Linn. No. 20 (LAPP).

Current name: ***Trichophorum cespitosum*** (L.) Hartm. subsp. ***cespitosum*** (Cyperaceae).

Scirpus ciliaris Linnaeus, *Mantissa Plantarum Altera*: 182. 1771.

"Habitat in India orientali. Koenig." RCN: 435.

Lectotype (Clarke in *J. Linn. Soc., Bot.* 30: 314. 1894): Herb. Linn. No. 71.51 (LINN).

Current name: ***Fuirena ciliaris*** (L.) Roxb. var. ***ciliaris*** (Cyperaceae).

Scirpus corymbosus Linnaeus, *Centuria II Plantarum*: 7. 1756.

"Habitat in India." RCN: 431.

Lectotype (Gordon-Gray in *Strelitzia* 2: 150. 1995): Herb. Linn. No. 71.48 (LINN).

Current name: ***Rhynchospora corymbosa*** (L.) Britton (Cyperaceae).

Scirpus cyperoides Linnaeus, *Mantissa Plantarum Altera*: 181. 1771.

"Habitat in India orientali. Koenig." RCN: 427.

Lectotype (Gordon-Gray in *Strelitzia* 2: 136. 1995): Herb. Linn. No. 71.42 (LINN).

Current name: ***Mariscus sumatrensis*** (Retz.) J. Raynal (Cyperaceae).

Scirpus dichotomus Linnaeus, *Species Plantarum* 1: 50. 1753.

"Habitat in India." RCN: 421.

Lectotype (Koyama in Smith, *Fl. Vitiensis Nova* 1: 244. 1979): Herb. Hermann 2: 63, No. 40 (BM-000621720).

Current name: ***Fimbristylis dichotoma*** (L.) Vahl (Cyperaceae).

Scirpus echinatus Linnaeus, *Species Plantarum* 1: 50. 1753.

"Habitat in India utraque." RCN: 422.

Lectotype (Carter & Kral in *Taxon* 39: 324. 1990): Herb. Linn. No. 71.35 (LINN).

Current name: ***Cyperus echinatus*** (L.) Alph. Wood (Cyperaceae).

Scirpus ferrugineus Linnaeus, *Species Plantarum* 1: 50. 1753.

"Habitat in Jamaicae paludibus maritimis." RCN: 424.

Lectotype (Adams in Cafferty & Jarvis in *Taxon* 53: 180. 2004): Herb. A. van Royen No. 902.77–420 (L).

Current name: ***Fimbristylis ferruginea*** (L.) Vahl (Cyperaceae).

Scirpus fluitans Linnaeus, *Species Plantarum* 1: 48. 1753.

"Habitat in Angliae, Galliae udis." RCN: 410.

Lectotype (Simpson & al. in *Kew Bull.* 56: 1011. 2001): [icon] *"Gramen junceum clavatum repens foliis et capitulis Psyllii"* in Morison, Pl. Hist. Univ. 3: 230, s. 8, t. 10, f. 31. 1699.

Current name: ***Isolepis fluitans*** (L.) R. Br. (Cyperaceae).

Scirpus geniculatus Linnaeus, *Species Plantarum* 1: 48. 1753.

"Habitat in Jamaica." RCN: 406.

Lectotype (Furtado in *Gard. Bull. Straits Settlem.* 9: 299. 1937): Herb. Clifford: 21, *Scirpus* 1 (BM-000557653).

Current name: ***Eleocharis geniculata*** (L.) Roem. & Schult. (Cyperaceae).

Scirpus glomeratus Linnaeus, *Species Plantarum* 1: 52. 1753.

"Habitat in Virginia, India." RCN: 367.

Replaced synonym of: *Schoenus niveus* L. (1774).

Type not designated.

Original material: Herb. Linn. No. 68.9 (LINN); *Clayton 570* (BM); [icon] in Rheede, Hort. Malab. 12: 99, t. 53. 1693.

Note: The application of this name is uncertain. Its original material represents a number of taxa, and it may be a candidate for rejection.

Scirpus holoschoenus Linnaeus, *Species Plantarum* 1: 49. 1753.

"Habitat in Europa australi." RCN: 412.

Lectotype (Pignotti in *Webbia* 58: 315. 2003): Herb. Linn. No. 71.17 (LINN).

Current name: ***Scirpoides holoschoenus*** (L.) Soják (Cyperaceae).

Note: Simpson (in *Taxon* 53: 180. 2004) independently made the same choice of type as Pignotti, whose typification was published a few months earlier.

Scirpus hottentotus Linnaeus, *Mantissa Plantarum Altera*: 182. 1771.

"Habitat ad Cap. b. spei, locis paludosis ad rivulos. Koenig." RCN: 436.

Lectotype (Clarke in *J. Linn. Soc., Bot.* 30: 314. 1894): *König s.n.*, Herb. Linn. No. 71.52 (LINN).

Current name: ***Fuirena hirsuta*** (P.J. Bergius) P.L. Forbes (Cyperaceae).

Scirpus intricatus Linnaeus, *Mantissa Plantarum Altera*: 182. 1771.

"Habitat in India orientali et Cap. b. spei." RCN: 433.

Lectotype (Clarke in *J. Linn. Soc., Bot.* 30: 313. 1894): Herb. Linn. No. 71.50 (LINN).

Current name: ***Mariscus squarrosus*** (L.) C.B. Clarke (Cyperaceae).

Scirpus lacustris Linnaeus, *Species Plantarum* 1: 48. 1753.

"Habitat in Europae aquis puris stagnantibus & fluviatilibus." RCN: 411.

Lectotype (Kukkonen & Simpson in Cafferty & Jarvis in *Taxon* 53: 180. 2004): Herb. Linn. No. 71.15 (LINN).

Current name: ***Schoenoplectus lacustris*** (L.) Palla (Cyperaceae).

Scirpus lithospermus Linnaeus, *Species Plantarum* 1: 51. 1753.

"Habitat in India." RCN: 7095.

Basionym of: *Schoenus lithospermus* (L.) L. (1759); *Carex lithosperma* (L.) L. (1767).

Lectotype (Camelbeke & Goetghebeur in *Taxon* 49: 295. 2000): [icon] *"Kaden-pullu"* in Rheede, Hort. Malab. 12: 89, t. 48. 1693.

Current name: ***Scleria lithosperma*** (L.) Sw. (Cyperaceae).

Scirpus luzulae Linnaeus, *Systema Naturae*, ed. 10, 2: 868. 1759.

["Habitat in India."] Sp. Pl., ed. 2, 1: 75 (1762). RCN: 429.

Lectotype (Denton in *Contr. Univ. Michigan Herb.* 11: 228. 1978): Herb. Linn. No. 71.45 (LINN).

Current name: ***Cyperus luzulae*** (L.) Retz. (Cyperaceae).

S

Scirpus maritimus Linnaeus, *Species Plantarum* 1: 51. 1753.
"Habitat in Europae, litoribus maritimis." RCN: 428.
Lectotype (Galen Smith & Kukkonen in *Taxon* 48: 356. 1999): Herb.
   Celsius 2: 212 (UPS). – Epitype (Galen Smith & Kukkonen in
   Taxon 48: 356. 1999): Sweden. E. Roslagen, par. Börstill, 2km W
   Kallö, near Husbacka, 14 Oct 1995, *Nilsson 9515* (UPS; iso- BM,
   H, MO, NU, NY).
Current name: ***Bolboschoenus maritimus*** (L.) Palla (Cyperaceae).
Note: Koyama (in *Canad. J. Bot.* 40: 933. 1962), probably preceded by
   Beetle (in *Amer. J. Bot.* 29: 85. 1942 – "Type in the Linnaean
   Herbarium"), designated the North American *Clayton 570* (71.43
   LINN) as lectotype, which is a specimen of *S. robustus* Pursh. Galen
   Smith & Kukkonen (in *Taxon* 48: 355. 1999) rejected this choice of
   type on the grounds that Linnaeus was describing a European
   taxon, not a North American one. A photograph of an iso-epitype
   is reproduced by Marhold & al. (in *Willdenowia* 36: 105, f. 1.
   2006).

Scirpus michelianus Linnaeus, *Species Plantarum* 1: 52. 1753.
"Habitat in Italia rarius." RCN: 434.
Lectotype (Simpson in Cafferty & Jarvis in *Taxon* 53: 180. 2004):
   [icon] *"Cyperus italicus, omnium minimus, locustis in capi. subro.
   collectis D. Micheli"* in Tilli, Cat. Pl. Hort. Pisani: 51, t. 20, f. 5.
   1723. – Epitype (Simpson in Cafferty & Jarvis in *Taxon* 53: 180.
   2004): Italy. Lombardia, Prov. di Mantova: juxta Padum (Po) ad
   Ponte di Borgoforte, 17m, 19 Sep 1904, *A. Fiori, s.n.* Fl. Italica
   Exsicc., cur. Fiori, Béguinot & Pampanini No. 745 (BM).
Current name: ***Cyperus michelianus*** (L.) Link (Cyperaceae).

Scirpus miliaceus Linnaeus, *Systema Naturae*, ed. 10, 2: 868. 1759,
   nom. rej.
["Habitat in India."] Sp. Pl., ed. 2, 1: 75 (1762). RCN: 426.
Lectotype (Blake in *J. Arnold Arbor.* 35: 216–219. 1954): Herb. Linn.
   No. 71.40 (LINN).
Current name: ***Fimbristylis quinquangularis*** (Vahl) Kunth
   (Cyperaceae).

Scirpus mucronatus Linnaeus, *Species Plantarum* 1: 50. 1753.
"Habitat in Angliae, Italiae, Helvetiae, Virginiae stagnis maritimis."
   RCN: 361.
Lectotype (Kukkonen in Cafferty & Jarvis in *Taxon* 53: 181. 2004):
   Rathgeb?, Herb. Linn. No. 71.31 (LINN).
Current name: ***Schoenoplectus mucronatus*** (L.) Palla (Cyperaceae).

Scirpus mutatus Linnaeus, *Systema Naturae*, ed. 10, 2: 867.
   1759.
["Habitat in Jamaica."] Sp. Pl., ed. 2, 1: 70 (1762). RCN: 403.
Lectotype (Browning & al. in *S. African J. Bot.* 63: 177. 1997):
   Browne, Herb. Linn. No. 71.2 (LINN).
Current name: ***Eleocharis mutata*** (L.) R. Br. (Cyperaceae).

Scirpus palustris Linnaeus, *Species Plantarum* 1: 47. 1753.
"Habitat in Europae fossis & inundatis." RCN: 405.
Lectotype (Strandhede in *Bot. Not.* 113: 168. 1960): *Löfling 36*, Herb.
   Linn. s.n. (S).
Current name: ***Eleocharis palustris*** (L.) Roem. & Schult.
   (Cyperaceae).

Scirpus retrofractus Linnaeus, *Species Plantarum* 1: 50. 1753.
"Habitat in Virginia." RCN: 423.
Lectotype (Fernald in *Rhodora* 47: 111, pl. 878. 1945): Herb. Linn.
   No. 71.36 (LINN).
Current name: ***Cyperus retrofractus*** (L.) Torr. (Cyperaceae).
Note: Carter & Jarvis (in *Rhodora* 88: 451–456. 1986) provide a
   review.

Scirpus romanus Linnaeus, *Species Plantarum* 1: 49. 1753.
"Habitat in Galloprovincia & Romae." RCN: 414.
Lectotype (Pignotti in *Webbia* 58: 315. 2003): *Rathgeb?*, Herb. Linn.
   No. 71.19 (LINN), see p. 225.
Current name: ***Scirpoides holoschoenus*** (L.) Soják (Cyperaceae).
Note: Simpson (in *Taxon* 53: 181. 2004) independently made the same
   choice of type as Pignotti, whose typification was published a few
   months earlier.

Scirpus setaceus Linnaeus, *Species Plantarum* 1: 49. 1753.
"Habitat in Europae litoribus maritimis." RCN: 415.
Lectotype (Simpson & al. in *Kew Bull.* 56: 1011. 2001): Herb. A. van
   Royen No. 902.88–689 (L).
Current name: ***Isolepis setacea*** (L.) R. Br. (Cyperaceae).

Scirpus spadiceus Linnaeus, *Species Plantarum* 1: 51. 1753.
"Habitat in Jamaicae fluviis." RCN: 425.
Lectotype (McVaugh, *Fl. Novo-Galiciana* 13: 380. 1993): [icon]
   *"Gramen cyperoides majus aquaticum, paniculis plurimis junceis
   sparsis, spicis ex oblongo rotundis spadiceis"* in Sloane, Voy. Jamaica 1:
   118, t. 76, f. 2. 1707. – Typotype: Herb. Sloane 2: 53 (BM-SL).
Current name: ***Fimbristylis spadicea*** (L.) Vahl (Cyperaceae).

Scirpus squarrosus Linnaeus, *Mantissa Plantarum Altera*: 181. 1771.
"Habitat in India orientali. Koenig." RCN: 432.
Lectotype (Raynal in *Adansonia*, n.s., 8: 86. 1968): Herb. Linn. No.
   71.49 (LINN).
Current name: ***Rikliella squarrosa*** (L.) J. Raynal (Cyperaceae).

Scirpus supinus Linnaeus, *Species Plantarum* 1: 49. 1753.
"Habitat Parisiis." RCN: 416.
Neotype (Raynal in *Adansonia*, n.s., 16: 145. 1976): Herb. Tournefort
   No. 5117 (P-TOURN).
Current name: ***Schoenoplectus supinus*** (L.) Palla (Cyperaceae).
Note: In the absence of original material, Raynal's choice of a
   Tournefort collection as lectotype is treated as a neotype under Art.
   9.8.

Scirpus sylvaticus Linnaeus, *Species Plantarum* 1: 51. 1753, *typ. cons.*
"Habitat in Europae sylvis." RCN: 430.
Lectotype (Kukkonen in Jarvis & al., *Regnum Veg.* 127: 86. 1993):
   Herb. Linn. No. 71.47 (LINN).
Generitype of *Scirpus* Linnaeus, *nom. cons.*
Current name: ***Scirpus sylvaticus*** L. (Cyperaceae).

Scirpus trigynus Linnaeus, *Mantissa Plantarum Altera*: 180. 1771.
"Habitat in India orientali. Koenig." RCN: 402.
Lectotype (Simpson in Cafferty & Jarvis in *Taxon* 53: 181. 2004):
   König s.n., Herb. Linn. No. 71.1 (LINN).
Current name: ***Scirpus trigynus*** L. (Cyperaceae).

Scirpus triqueter Linnaeus, *Systema Naturae*, ed. 12, 2: 83; *Mantissa
   Plantarum*: 29. 1767.
"Habitat in Europa australi." RCN: 419.
Lectotype (Simpson in Cafferty & Jarvis in *Taxon* 53: 181. 2004):
   Herb. Linn. No. 71.29 (LINN). – Epitype (Simpson in Cafferty &
   Jarvis in *Taxon* 53: 181. 2004): France. Avignon, Bagatelle, bords
   du Rhône, Jul 1822, *Palun s.n.* (MPU).
Current name: ***Schoenoplectus triqueter*** L. (Cyperaceae).

Scleranthus annuus Linnaeus, *Species Plantarum* 1: 406. 1753.
"Habitat in Europae arvis, arenosis." RCN: 3181.
Lectotype (Jonsell & Jarvis in Jarvis & al., *Regnum Veg.* 127: 86.
   1993): Herb. Linn. No. 578.1 (LINN).
Generitype of *Scleranthus* Linnaeus (vide Hitchcock, *Prop. Brit. Bot.*:
   154. 1929).

Current name: **Scleranthus annuus** L. (Caryophyllaceae).
Note: Jonsell & Jarvis (in *Nordic J. Bot.* 14: 158. 1994) give a more
detailed account of the reasons for their 1993 type choice.

Scleranthus perennis Linnaeus, *Species Plantarum* 1: 406. 1753.
"Habitat in Europae campis apricis arenosis." RCN: 3182.

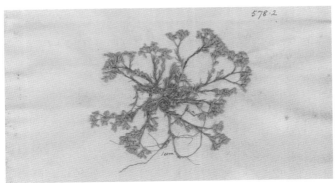

Lectotype (Jonsell & Jarvis in *Nordic J. Bot.* 14: 158. 1994): Herb.
Linn. No. 578.2 (LINN).
Current name: **Scleranthus perennis** L. (Caryophyllaceae).

Scleranthus polycarpos Linnaeus, *Centuria II Plantarum*: 16. 1756.
"Habitat Monspelii & in Italia. Sauvages." RCN: 3183.
Lectotype (Jonsell & Jarvis in *Nordic J. Bot.* 14: 158. 1994): Herb.
Linn. No. 578.3 (LINN).
Current name: **Scleranthus polycarpos** L. (Caryophyllaceae).

Scolymus hispanicus Linnaeus, *Species Plantarum* 2: 813. 1753.
"Habitat in Italia, Sicilia, G. Narbonense." RCN: 5925.
Lectotype (Vázquez in *Anales Jard. Bot. Madrid* 58: 86. 2000): *Löfling
s.n.*, Herb. Linn. No. 963.2 (LINN).
Current name: **Scolymus hispanicus** L. (Asteraceae).

Scolymus maculatus Linnaeus, *Species Plantarum* 2: 813. 1753.
"Habitat in G. Narbonensi, Italia." RCN: 5924.
Lectotype (Jeffrey in Jarvis & al., *Regnum Veg.* 127: 86. 1993): Herb.
Linn. No. 963.1 (LINN).
Generitype of *Scolymus* Linnaeus (vide Green, *Prop. Brit. Bot.*: 178.
1929).
Current name: **Scolymus maculatus** L. (Asteraceae).

Scoparia dulcis Linnaeus, *Species Plantarum* 1: 116. 1753.
"Habitat in Jamaica, Curassao." RCN: 946.
Lectotype (Sutton in Jarvis & al., *Regnum Veg.* 127: 86. 1993): Herb.
A. van Royen No. 921.348–49 (L).
Generitype of *Scoparia* Linnaeus.
Current name: **Scoparia dulcis** L. (Scrophulariaceae).
Note: D'Arcy (in *Ann. Missouri Bot. Gard.* 66: 249. 1979) indicated
unseen and unspecified Sloane material as type, but this would not
have been seen by Linnaeus and is not original material for the
name. Cramer (in Dassanayake & Fosberg, *Revised Handb. Fl.
Ceylon* 3: 439. 1981) indicated Clifford material (evidently unseen)
as type, and has been followed by a number of later authors.
However, no Clifford material associated with this name can be
traced in the Clifford herbarium (BM). Sutton's type choice is
therefore accepted here.

Scorpiurus muricatus Linnaeus, *Species Plantarum* 2: 745. 1753.
"Habitat in Europa australi." RCN: 5483.
Lectotype (Domínguez & Galiano in *Lagascalia* 4: 268. 1974): Herb.
Linn. No. 920.2 (LINN).

Current name: **Scorpiurus muricatus** L. var. **muricatus** (Fabaceae:
Faboideae).
Note: Specific epithet spelled "muricata" in the protologue.

Scorpiurus subvillosus Linnaeus, *Species Plantarum* 2: 745. 1753.
"Habitat in Europa australi." RCN: 5485.
Lectotype (Domínguez & Galiano in *Lagascalia* 4: 264. 1974): Herb.
Linn. No. 920.4 (LINN).
Current name: **Scorpiurus muricatus** L. var. **subvillosus** (L.) Lam.
(Fabaceae: Faboideae).
Note: Specific epithet spelled "subvillosa" in the protologue.

Scorpiurus sulcatus Linnaeus, *Species Plantarum* 2: 745. 1753.
"Habitat in Europa australi." RCN: 5484.
Lectotype (Domínguez & Galiano in *Lagascalia* 4: 272. 1974): Herb.
Linn. No. 920.3 (LINN).
Generitype of *Scorpiurus* Linnaeus (vide Green, *Prop. Brit. Bot.*: 176.
1929).
Current name: **Scorpiurus muricatus** L. var. **sulcatus** (L.) Lam.
(Fabaceae: Faboideae).
Note: Specific epithet spelled "sulcata" in the protologue.

Scorpiurus vermiculatus Linnaeus, *Species Plantarum* 2: 744. 1753.
"Habitat in Europa australi." RCN: 5482.
Lectotype (Domínguez & Galiano in *Lagascalia* 4: 264. 1974): Herb.
Linn. No. 920.1 (LINN).
Current name: **Scorpiurus vermiculatus** L. (Fabaceae: Faboideae).
Note: Specific epithet spelled "vermiculata" in the protologue.

Scorzonera angustifolia Linnaeus, *Species Plantarum* 2: 791. 1753.
"Habitat in Hispania. Loefling." RCN: 5795.
Lectotype (Díaz de la Guardia & Blanca in *Anales Jard. Bot. Madrid*
42: 114. 1985): *Löfling 596*, Herb. Linn. No. 947.6 (LINN).
Current name: **Scorzonera angustifolia** L. (Asteraceae).

Scorzonera graminifolia Linnaeus, *Species Plantarum* 2: 791. 1753.
"Habitat in Lusitania, Sibiria." RCN: 5793.
Lectotype (Díaz de la Guardia & Blanca in *Anales Jard. Bot. Madrid*
43: 115. 1987): Herb. Linn. No. 947.4 (LINN).
Current name: **Scorzonera graminifolia** L. (Asteraceae).

Scorzonera hirsuta Linnaeus, *Mantissa Plantarum Altera*: 278.
1771.
"Habitat in Apulia. H. U." RCN: 5796.
Lectotype (Díaz de la Guardia & Blanca in *Taxon* 46: 759. 1997):
[icon] *"Tragopogon Apulum humile hirsutum luteum"* in Colonna,
Ekphr.: 234, 233. 1606.
Current name: **Scorzonera hirsuta** L. (Asteraceae).
Note: Although the protologues of both this and *Tragopogon hirsutus*
Gouan (1764) are not identical, and despite Linnaeus making no
reference to Gouan's publication, Art. 33.3 allows *S. hirsuta* to be
interpreted as a new combination based on Gouan's name. If this
interpretation is adopted, *S. hirsuta* (Gouan) L. is apparently
untypified.

Scorzonera hispanica Linnaeus, *Species Plantarum* 2: 791. 1753.
"Habitat in Hispania, Sibiria." RCN: 5792.
Lectotype (Díaz de la Guardia & Blanca in *Anales Jard. Bot. Madrid*
43: 302. 1987): Herb. Linn. No. 947.3 (LINN).
Current name: **Scorzonera hispanica** L. (Asteraceae).

Scorzonera humilis Linnaeus, *Species Plantarum* 2: 790. 1753.
"Habitat in Europae septentrionalioris pratis apricis." RCN: 5791.
Lectotype (Díaz de la Guardia & Blanca in *Anales Jard. Bot. Madrid*
43: 291. 1987): *Steller?*, Herb. Linn. No. 947.2 (LINN).

S

Generitype of *Scorzonera* Linnaeus (vide Green, *Prop. Brit. Bot.*: 177. 1929).
Current name: ***Scorzonera humilis*** L. (Asteraceae).

Scorzonera laciniata Linnaeus, *Species Plantarum* 2: 791. 1753.
"Habitat in Germania, Gallia." RCN: 5799.
Lectotype (Alavi in Jafri & El-Gadi, *Fl. Libya* 107: 363. 1983): Herb. Linn. No. 947.8 (LINN).
Current name: ***Podospermum laciniatum*** (L.) DC. (Asteraceae).

Scorzonera orientalis Linnaeus, *Systema Naturae*, ed. 10, 2: 1191. 1759.
["Habitat in Oriente. Hasselquist."] Sp. Pl., ed. 2, 2: 1113 (1763). RCN: 5798.
Lectotype (Jeffrey in *Kew Bull.* 18: 477. 1966): Herb. Hasselquist, No. 672 (UPS).
Current name: ***Reichardia tingitana*** (L.) Roth (Asteraceae).

Scorzonera picroides Linnaeus, *Species Plantarum* 2: 792. 1753.
"Habitat – – – –" RCN: 5801.
Lectotype (Gallego & al. in *Lagascalia* 9: 194. 1980): Herb. Linn. No. 947.11 (LINN).
Current name: ***Reichardia picroides*** (L.) Roth (Asteraceae).

Scorzonera purpurea Linnaeus, *Species Plantarum* 2: 791. 1753.
"Habitat in Marchia Brandeburgica, Sibiria." RCN: 5794.
Lectotype (Díaz de la Guardia & Blanca in *Taxon* 46: 759. 1997): [icon] *"Scorzonera caule ramoso, tereti, foliis linearibus acuminatis, calicibus obtusiusculis"* in Gmelin, Fl. Sibirica 2: 7, t. 2. 1752.
Current name: ***Podospermum purpureum*** (L.) Gemeinholzer & Greuter (Asteraceae).

Scorzonera resedifolia Linnaeus, *Species Plantarum* 2: 1198. 1753.
"Habitat in Hispania. Loefling." RCN: 5797.
Lectotype (López González in *Anales Jard. Bot. Madrid* 36: 136. 1980): *Löfling 595*, Herb. Linn. No. 947.7 (LINN).
Current name: ***Podospermum laciniatum*** (L.) DC. subsp. ***decumbens*** (Guss.) Gemeinholzer & Greuter (Asteraceae).
Note: Kilian (in *Taxon* 43: 299. 1994) proposed a conserved type for the name. However, the Committee for Spermatophyta (in *Taxon* 45: 676. 1996) declined to support the proposal.

Scorzonera tingitana Linnaeus, *Species Plantarum* 2: 791. 1753.
"Habitat in Tingide." RCN: 5800.
Lectotype (Jeffrey in *Kew Bull.* 18: 477. 1966): Herb. Linn. No. 947.10 (LINN).
Current name: ***Reichardia tingitana*** (L.) Roth (Asteraceae).
Note: Gallego & al. (in *Lagascalia* 9: 178. 1980) provide a detailed description of the type.

Scorzonera tomentosa Linnaeus, *Species Plantarum*, ed. 2, 2: 1112. 1763.
"Habitat in Oriente. Burmannus." RCN: 5790.
Lectotype (Díaz de la Guardia & Blanca in *Taxon* 46: 761. 1997): Herb. Linn. No. 947.1 (LINN).
Current name: ***Scorzonera tomentosa*** L. (Asteraceae).

Scrophularia aquatica Linnaeus, *Species Plantarum* 2: 620. 1753, *nom. utique rej.*
"Habitat in Angliae, Helvetiae, Galliae humidis." RCN: 4482.
Lectotype (Dandy in *Watsonia* 7: 164. 1969): Herb. Linn. No. 773.3 (LINN).
Current name: ***Scrophularia umbrosa*** Dumort. (Scrophulariaceae).

Scrophularia auriculata Linnaeus, *Species Plantarum* 2: 620. 1753, *nom. cons.*

"Habitat in Hispania." RCN: 4483.
Conserved type (Ortega & Devesa in *Ruizia* 11: 51. 1993): *Löfling 461*, Herb. Linn. No. 256.12, right specimen (S).
Current name: ***Scrophularia auriculata*** L. (Scrophulariaceae).

Scrophularia betonicifolia Linnaeus, *Systema Naturae*, ed. 12, 2: 413; *Mantissa Plantarum*: 87. 1767.
"Habitat in Lusitania." RCN: 4485.
Lectotype (Dalgaard in *Opera Bot.* 51: 18. 1979): Herb. Linn. No. 773.9 (LINN).
Current name: ***Scrophularia scorodonia*** L. var. ***scorodonia*** (Scrophulariaceae).

Scrophularia canina Linnaeus, *Species Plantarum* 2: 621. 1753.
"Habitat in Helvetia, Narbona, Italia." RCN: 4491.
Lectotype (Ortega & Devesa in *Ruizia* 11: 125. 1993): Herb. Clifford: 322, Scrophularia 5, right specimen (BM-000646214).
Current name: ***Scrophularia canina*** L. (Scrophulariaceae).

Scrophularia chinensis Linnaeus, *Mantissa Plantarum Altera*: 250. 1771.
"Habitat in China." RCN: 4495.
Lectotype (Cramer in Dassanayake & Fosberg, *Revised Handb. Fl. Ceylon* 3: 390. 1981): Herb. Linn. No. 773.20 (LINN).
Current name: ***Verbascum chinense*** (L.) Santapau (Scrophulariaceae).

Scrophularia coccinea Linnaeus, *Species Plantarum* 2: 621. 1753.
"Habitat in Vera Cruce." RCN: 4493.
Neotype (Carlson in *Fieldiana, Bot.* 29: 251. 1957): Mexico. San Luis Potosí: near Tancanhuitz, *E. Seler 705* (GH).
Current name: ***Russelia coccinea*** (L.) Wettst. (Scrophulariaceae).

Scrophularia frutescens Linnaeus, *Species Plantarum* 2: 621. 1753.
"Habitat in Lusitania." RCN: 4487.
Neotype (Ortega & Devesa in *Ruizia* 11: 138. 1993): UNEX 6183, central specimen (UNEX).
Current name: ***Scrophularia frutescens*** L. (Scrophulariaceae).

Scrophularia lucida Linnaeus, *Systema Naturae*, ed. 10, 2: 1114. 1759.
["Habitat in Oriente, Creta, Neapoli, in ipsis muris Hydrunti."] Sp. Pl., ed. 2, 2: 866 (1763). RCN: 4492.
Type not designated.
Original material: none traced.
Current name: ***Scrophularia lucida*** L. (Scrophulariaceae).

Scrophularia marilandica Linnaeus, *Species Plantarum* 2: 619. 1753.
"Habitat in Virginia." RCN: 4480.
Lectotype (Reveal & al. in *Huntia* 7: 235. 1987): *Clayton 220* (BM-000042216).
Current name: ***Scrophularia marilandica*** L. (Scrophulariaceae).
Note: Reveal & al. (in *Huntia* 7: 235. 1987) provide a review.

Scrophularia nodosa Linnaeus, *Species Plantarum* 2: 619. 1753.
"Habitat in Europae succulentis." RCN: 4481.
Lectotype (Sutton in Jarvis & al., *Regnum Veg.* 127: 86. 1993): Herb. Clifford: 322, Scrophularia 1 (BM-000646206).
Generitype of *Scrophularia* Linnaeus (vide Green, *Prop. Brit. Bot.*: 168. 1929).
Current name: ***Scrophularia nodosa*** L. (Scrophulariaceae).
Note: Grau (in Rechinger, *Fl. Iranica* 147: 235. 1981) indicated 773.2 (LINN) as type, but the sheet lacks a *Species Plantarum* number (i.e. "2"), and is a post-1753 addition to the collection, and not original material for the name. Sutton's type choice is therefore accepted here.

Scrophularia orientalis Linnaeus, *Species Plantarum* 2: 620. 1753.
"Habitat in Oriente." RCN: 4486.
Type not designated.
Original material: Herb. Linn. No. 773.11 (LINN).
Current name: *Scrophularia orientalis* L. (Scrophulariaceae).
Note: Grau (in Rechinger, *Fl. Iranica* 147: 228. 1981) indicated unspecified material in L as the holotype. However, there do not appear to be any relevant (presumably van Royen) collections extant there.

Scrophularia peregrina Linnaeus, *Species Plantarum* 2: 621. 1753.
"Habitat in Italia." RCN: 4494.
Lectotype (Ortega & Devesa in *Ruizia* 11: 112. 1993): Herb. Clifford: 322, *Scrophularia* 4, right specimen (BM-000646213).
Current name: *Scrophularia peregrina* L. (Scrophulariaceae).

Scrophularia sambucifolia Linnaeus, *Species Plantarum* 2: 620. 1753.
"Habitat in Hispania, Lusitania." RCN: 4490.
Lectotype (Ortega & Devesa in *Ruizia* 11: 96. 1993): Herb. Burser XIII: 92 (UPS).
Current name: *Scrophularia sambucifolia* L. (Scrophulariaceae).

Scrophularia scorodonia Linnaeus, *Species Plantarum* 2: 620. 1753.
"Habitat in Lusitania & Jersea insula Angliae." RCN: 4484.
Type not designated.
Original material: [icon] in Plukenet, Phytographia: t. 59, f. 5. 1691; Almag. Bot.: 338. 1696 – Voucher: Herb. Sloane 98: 19 (BM-SL).
Current name: *Scrophularia scorodonia* L. (Scrophulariaceae).
Note: Ortega & Devesa (in *Ruizia* 11: 75. 1993) rejected Dalgaard's choice (in *Opera Bot.* 51: 18. 1979) of 773.5 (LINN) as type (it is in any case a post-1753 addition) because they say the name was based on van Royen material. However, concluding, on Veldkamp's advice, that there was no original van Royen material extant, they chose a neotype from Boerhaave's herbarium (No. 908.232–872, L). However, as there is a Plukenet plate cited in the protologue, their choice is contrary to Art. 9.6.

Scrophularia trifoliata Linnaeus, *Systema Naturae*, ed. 10, 2: 1114. 1759.
["Habitat in Africa, Corsica."] Sp. Pl., ed. 2, 2: 865 (1763). RCN: 4489.
Type not designated.
Original material: Herb. Linn. No. 773.14 (LINN); [icon] in Plukenet, Phytographia: t. 313, f. 6. 1694; Almag. Bot.: 338. 1696.
Current name: *Scrophularia trifoliata* L. (Scrophulariaceae).

Scrophularia vernalis Linnaeus, *Species Plantarum* 2: 620. 1753.
"Habitat in Italia, Helvetia." RCN: 4488.
Lectotype (Ortega & Devesa in *Ruizia* 11: 120. 1993): Herb. Clifford: 322, *Scrophularia* 2, sheet C (BM-000646209).
Current name: *Scrophularia vernalis* L. (Scrophulariaceae).

Scurrula parasitica Linnaeus, *Species Plantarum* 1: 110. 1753.
"Habitat in China." RCN: 2558.
Replaced synonym of: *Loranthus scurrula* L. (1762), nom. illeg.
Lectotype (Barlow in Kalkman & al., *Fl. Malesiana*, ser. I, 13: 387. 1997): Herb. Linn. No. 455.1 (LINN).
Generitype of *Scurrula* Linnaeus, nom. rej.
Current name: *Scurrula parasitica* L. (Loranthaceae).
Note: *Scurrula* Linnaeus, nom. rej. in favour of *Loranthus* Jacq.

Scutellaria albida Linnaeus, *Mantissa Plantarum Altera*: 248. 1771.
"Habitat in Oriente." RCN: 4347.
Lectotype (Bothmer in *Nordic J. Bot.* 5: 436. 1985): Herb. Linn. No. 751.2 (LINN).
Current name: *Scutellaria albida* L. (Lamiaceae).

Scutellaria alpina Linnaeus, *Species Plantarum* 2: 599. 1753.
"Habitat in Alpibus Helvetiae." RCN: 4349.
Lectotype (Edmondson in Jarvis & al. in *Taxon* 50: 519. 2001): Herb. Burser XIV(1): 35 (UPS).
Current name: *Scutellaria alpina* L. (Lamiaceae).

Scutellaria altissima Linnaeus, *Species Plantarum* 2: 600. 1753.
"Habitat in Oriente." RCN: 4359.
Neotype (Edmondson in Davis, *Fl. Turkey* 7: 81. 1982): Herb. Tournefort No. 1139 (P-TOURN; iso- BM).
Current name: *Scutellaria altissima* L. (Lamiaceae).

Scutellaria cretica Linnaeus, *Species Plantarum* 2: 600. 1753.
"Habitat in Creta." RCN: 4360.
Lectotype (Turland in Jarvis & al. in *Taxon* 50: 519. 2001): Herb. Linn. No. 751.16 (LINN).
Current name: *Teucrium lamiifolium* D'Urv. subsp. *lamiifolium* (Lamiaceae).
Note: The epithet "creticum" is pre-occupied in *Teucrium* by *T. creticum* L. (1753).

Scutellaria galericulata Linnaeus, *Species Plantarum* 2: 599. 1753.
"Habitat in Europae littoribus." RCN: 4351.
Lectotype (Paton in *Kew Bull.* 45: 424. 1990): Herb. Linn. No. 751.6 (LINN).
Generitype of *Scutellaria* Linnaeus.
Current name: *Scutellaria galericulata* L. (Lamiaceae).
Note: *Scutellaria galericulata*, with the type designated by Paton, was proposed as conserved type of the genus by Jarvis (in *Taxon* 41: 569. 1992). However, the proposal was eventually ruled unnecessary by the General Committee (see Barrie, *l.c.* 55: 795–796. 2006 for a review of the history of this and related proposals).

Scutellaria hastifolia Linnaeus, *Species Plantarum* 2: 599. 1753.
"Habitat ad littora Sueciae rarius." RCN: 4352.
Lectotype (Paton in Jarvis & al. in *Taxon* 50: 519. 2001): [icon] "Scutellaria fol. non serrato" in Rivinus, Ordo Pl. Fl. Monopetal.: 15, t. 77. 1690.
Current name: *Scutellaria hastifolia* L. (Lamiaceae).
Note: Stearn (in *Biol. J. Linn. Soc.* 5: 12. 1973), in an account of Linnaeus' Öland and Gotland journey of 1741, treated Bunge in Gotland as the restricted type locality but did not refer to any material. In his paper, he attributed restricted type localities irrespective of whether any material existed in LINN and, where specimens do exist, he does not refer to any of them as type specimens.

Scutellaria hyssopifolia Linnaeus, *Species Plantarum* 2: 599. 1753.
"Habitat in Virginia." RCN: 4356.
Lectotype (Epling in *Univ. Calif. Publ. Bot.* 20: 90. 1942): *Clayton 261* (BM-000038156).
Current name: *Scutellaria hyssopifolia* L. (Lamiaceae).
Note: Although Epling (in *J. Bot.* 67: 11. 1929) treated Kalm material (751.12 LINN) as the standard specimen, this is not equivalent to a type statement (see Jarvis & al. in *Taxon* 50: 508. 2001). Epling subsequently designated a Clayton collection as the type. Reveal (in *Bot. J. Linn. Soc.* 92: 172–175. 1986) and Reveal & al. (in *Huntia* 7: 216. 1987) provide a detailed review but claim that the name was first typified by Smith (in *Rees' Cyclop.*: unpaged. 1815). However, Smith's statements appear to fall short of formal, modern typification and Epling's choice is accepted here.

Scutellaria indica Linnaeus, *Species Plantarum* 2: 600. 1753.
"Habitat in China." RCN: 4358.

Lectotype (Paton in Jarvis & al. in *Taxon* 50: 519. 2001): Herb. Linn. No. 751.15 (LINN).
Current name: ***Scutellaria indica*** L. (Lamiaceae).

Scutellaria integrifolia Linnaeus, *Species Plantarum* 2: 599. 1753.
"Habitat in Virginia, Canada." RCN: 4354.
Lectotype (Epling in *Univ. Calif. Publ. Bot.* 20: 90. 1942): *Clayton 205* (BM-000038158).
Current name: ***Scutellaria integrifolia*** L. (Lamiaceae).
Note: Reveal (in *Taxon* 38: 517. 1989), believing Smith, in 1815, to have typified the name on material in LINN belonging to a different taxon, proposed the name for conservation with a conserved type (*Clayton 205*, BM). However, the Committee for Spermatophyta (in *Taxon* 42: 695. 1993) ruled that Smith had made no formal type choice. Consequently, Epling's (1942) type choice of the same Clayton material is the earliest, and the conservation proposal was ruled unnecessary.

Scutellaria lateriflora Linnaeus, *Species Plantarum* 2: 598. 1753.
"Habitat in Canada, Virginia." RCN: 4350.
Lectotype (Epling in *Univ. Calif. Publ. Bot.* 20: 41. 1942): *Clayton 280* (BM-000042234).
Current name: ***Scutellaria lateriflora*** L. (Lamiaceae).
Note: Although Epling (in *J. Bot.* 67: 11. 1929) noted material in LINN, and treated a Clayton collection as the standard specimen, this is not equivalent to a type statement (see Jarvis & al. in *Taxon* 50: 508. 2001). Epling subsequently designated the Clayton collection as the type.

Scutellaria lupulina Linnaeus, *Species Plantarum*, ed. 2, 2: 835. 1763, *nom. illeg.*
"Habitat in Sibiria, Tataria." RCN: 4349.
Replaced synonym: *Scutellaria supina* L. (1753).
Lectotype (Edmondson in Jarvis & al. in *Taxon* 50: 519. 2001): Herb. Linn. No. 751.4 (LINN).
Current name: ***Scutellaria alpina*** L. subsp. ***supina*** (L.) I. Richardson (Lamiaceae).

Scutellaria orientalis Linnaeus, *Species Plantarum* 2: 598. 1753.
"Habitat in Armeria [sphalm. America] circa Tephlin." RCN: 4346.
Lectotype (Edmondson in Davis, *Fl. Turkey* 7: 91. 1982): Herb. Linn. No. 751.1 (LINN).
Current name: ***Scutellaria orientalis*** L. (Lamiaceae).

Scutellaria peregrina Linnaeus, *Species Plantarum* 2: 599. 1753.
"Habitat in nemoribus Florentiae, Liburni." RCN: 4357.
Lectotype (Siddiqi in Jafri & El-Gadi, *Fl. Libya* 118: 65. 1985): Herb. Linn. No. 751.13 (LINN).
Current name: ***Scutellaria peregrina*** L. (Lamiaceae).
Note: Although treated as a *nomen ambiguum* by Caruel (in Parlatore, *Fl. Ital.* 6: 332. 1889), Rechinger (in *Bot. Archiv.* 43: 21–22. 1941) and Greuter (in *Boissiera* 13: 114. 1967), the name has subsequently been typified and is in use.

Scutellaria supina Linnaeus, *Species Plantarum* 2: 598. 1753.
"Habitat in Sibiria, Tataria." RCN: 4349.
Replaced synonym of: *Scutellaria lupulina* L. (1763), *nom. illeg.*
Lectotype (Edmondson in Jarvis & al. in *Taxon* 50: 519. 2001): Herb. Linn. No. 751.4 (LINN).
Current name: ***Scutellaria alpina*** L. subsp. ***supina*** (L.) I. Richardson (Lamiaceae).

Secale cereale Linnaeus, *Species Plantarum* 1: 84. 1753.
"Habitat – – – –" RCN: 706.

Lectotype (Bowden in *Canad. J. Bot.* 40: 1704. 1962): Herb. Linn. No. 102.1 (LINN).
Generitype of *Secale* Linnaeus (vide Hitchcock in *U. S. D. A. Bull.* 772: 91. 1920).
Current name: ***Secale cereale*** L. (Poaceae).

Secale cereale Linnaeus var. **hybernum** Linnaeus, *Species Plantarum* 1: 84. 1753.
RCN: 706.
Lectotype (Bowden in *Canad. J. Bot.* 40: 1704. 1962): Herb. Linn. No. 102.1 (LINN).
Current name: ***Secale cereale*** L. (Poaceae).

Secale cereale Linnaeus var. **vernum** Linnaeus, *Species Plantarum* 1: 84. 1753.
RCN: 706.
Neotype (Cope in Cafferty & al. in *Taxon* 49: 257. 2000): Italy. Florence, "Straw from which the hats are made", 1830, *Herb. Shuttleworth s.n.* (BM-000576273).
Current name: ***Secale cereale*** L. (Poaceae).

Secale creticum Linnaeus, *Species Plantarum* 1: 84. 1753, *nom. utique rej.*
"Habitat in Creta." RCN: 709.
Type not designated.
Original material: [icon] in Scheuchzer, Agrostographia: 22, t. 1, f. 5. 1719.
Current name: ***Hordeum vulgare*** L. subsp. ***agriocrithon*** Á. Löve & D. Löve emend. H. Scholz (Poaceae).

Secale orientale Linnaeus, *Species Plantarum* 1: 84. 1753.
"Habitat ad Archipelagum." RCN: 708.
Neotype (Frederiksen in *Nordic J. Bot.* 11: 277. 1991): Herb. Tournefort No. 4939 (P-TOURN).
Current name: ***Eremopyrum orientale*** (L.) Jaub. & Spach (Poaceae).

Secale villosum Linnaeus, *Species Plantarum* 1: 84. 1753.
"Habitat in Europa australi, & in oriente." RCN: 707.
Lectotype (Turland in Cafferty & al. in *Taxon* 49: 257. 2000): [icon] *"Gramen Creticum spicatum, secalinum, glumis ciliaribus"* in Buxbaum, Pl. Minus Cognit. Cent. 5: 21, t. 41. 1740. – Epitype (Turland in Cafferty & al. in *Taxon* 49: 257. 2000): Greece. Crete, Ep. Agios vasilios: between Plakias & Lefkogia, 50m, 12 Apr 1990, *Turland 157* (BM-000576283).
Current name: ***Dasypyrum villosum*** (L.) P. Candargy (Poaceae).
Note: Frederiksen (in *Nordic J. Bot.* 11: 139. 1991) designated Herb. Tournefort No. 4943 (P) as a neotype for this name, wrongly excluding as ineligible for lectotypification cited plates from Parkinson and Buxbaum. Turland therefore rejected Frederiksen's neotypification, designating a lectotype along with a supporting epitype.

Securidaca volubilis Linnaeus, *Species Plantarum* 2: 707. 1753.
"Habitat in America meridionali." RCN: 5165.
Type not designated.
Original material: Herb. Linn. No. 883.3 (LINN); [icon] in Plumier in Burman, Pl. Amer.: 244, t. 246, f. 1. 1760.
Generitype of *Securidaca* Linnaeus (1753), *nom. rej.*
Current name: ***Dalbergia monetaria*** L. f. (Fabaceae: Faboideae).
Note: Securidaca Linnaeus (1753, Fabaceae), *nom. rej.* in favour of *Securidaca* Linnaeus (1759, Polygalaceae), *nom. cons.*
See Oort (in *Rec. Trav. Bot. Néerl.* 36: 678–680. 1939) for an outline of the confusion caused by Linnaeus' change of generic concept.

Carvalho (in *Brittonia* 49: 107. 1997) has treated an original Plumier drawing of "Sparteum scandens, citri foliis, floribus albis ad nodos confertim nascentibus" (Cat. Pl. Amer.: 19. 1703), a copy of which he saw at Kew, as type. However, Linnaeus did not study Plumier's original drawings, usually relying on the line drawings that were subsequently published by Burman. Presumably the illustration intended by Carvalho is that later published as Plumier's t. 246, f. 1 (1760). However, Carvalho is not explicit about this and the name is therefore still untypified at present.

Securidaca volubilis Linnaeus, *Systema Naturae,* ed. 10, 2: 1155. 1759, *nom. illeg.*
RCN: 5165.
Neotype (Adams in Jarvis & al., *Regnum Veg.* 127: 87. 1993): Jamaica. Red Hill, St Andrew, 1,000ft, 26 Dec 1914, *W. Harris 11838* (BM-000566451).
Generitype of *Securidaca* Linnaeus 1759, *nom. cons.*
Current name: **Securidaca brownei** Griseb. (Polygalaceae).
Note: Securidaca Linnaeus (1759, Polygalaceae), *nom. cons.* against *Securidaca* Linnaeus (1753, Fabaceae), *nom. rej.*
   Securidaca volubilis L. (1759) is a later homonym of *S. volubilis* L. (1753), and hence illegitimate. See Oort (in *Rec. Trav. Bot. Néerl.* 36: 678–680. 1939) for a discussion of the complexities of this case. Oort regarded three sheets of material at LINN (883.1–883.3) as comprising the type material and, though apparently restricting this to the two sheets (883.1, 883.2) representing a member of the Polygalaceae, rather than the one (883.3) of the Leguminosae, this is not an effective typification. Neither 883.1 nor 883.2 is original material for the name. In the absence of any original material, Adams designated a more recent neotype.

Sedum acre Linnaeus, *Species Plantarum* 1: 432. 1753.
"Habitat in Europae campis siccissimis sterilissimis." RCN: 3357.
Lectotype ('t Hart in Jarvis in *Taxon* 41: 569. 1992): Herb. Clifford: 177, *Sedum* 5 (BM-000628577).
Generitype of *Sedum* Linnaeus.
Current name: **Sedum acre** L. (Crassulaceae).
Note: Sedum acre, with the type designated by 't Hart, was proposed as conserved type of the genus by Jarvis (in *Taxon* 41: 569. 1992). However, the proposal was eventually ruled unnecessary by the General Committee (see Barrie, *l.c.* 55: 795–796. 2006 for a review of the history of this and related proposals).
   Clausen, *Sedum N. America*: 550 (1975) incorrectly treated Herb. Linn. 192.1 (S) as the type (material illustrated by Fröderström in *Acta Horti Gothob.* 7, Suppl.: 64, pl. XXXIX, f. 1. 1931), but this sheet is annotated only by Linnaeus filius and is not original material for the name. 't Hart & Jarvis (in *Taxon* 42: 400. 1993) explained the reasons for 't Hart's 1992 type choice.

Sedum aizoon Linnaeus, *Species Plantarum* 1: 430. 1753.
"Habitat in Sibiria." RCN: 3347.
Lectotype (designated here by Ohba): Herb. Linn. No. 595.1 (LINN).
Current name: **Phedimus aizoon** (L.) 't Hart & Eggli (Crassulaceae).
Note: See discussion by Fröderström (in *Acta Horti Gothob.* 7, Suppl.: 109, pl. XLIII, XLIV. 1931). Although 't Hart & Bleij (in Eggli, *Ill. Handb. Succ. Pl., Crassulaceae*: 197. 2003) indicated material in LINN as the type, this choice was published after 1 Jan 2001 and so the omission of the phrase "designated here" or an equivalent (Art. 7.11) means that it is not effective.

Sedum album Linnaeus, *Species Plantarum* 1: 432. 1753.
"Habitat in Europae petris." RCN: 3356.
Lectotype (Chamberlain in Davis, *Fl. Turkey* 4: 233. 1972): Herb. Clifford: 177, *Sedum* 6 (BM-000628578).
Current name: **Sedum album** L. (Crassulaceae).

Note: See Fröderström (in *Acta Horti Gothob.* 7, Suppl.: pl. XLII, f. 1–3. 1931). 't Hart & Jarvis (in *Taxon* 42: 401. 1993) provided a detailed discussion of the typification of this name, concluding that Clifford material should be the lectotype. However, the typification itself is correctly attributable to Chamberlain.

Sedum anacampseros Linnaeus, *Species Plantarum* 1: 430. 1753.
"Habitat – – – – –" RCN: 3346.
Type not designated.
Original material: [icon] in Bauhin & Cherler, Hist. Pl. Univ. 3(2): 682. 1651; [icon] in Clusius, Rar. Pl. Hist. 2: 66, 67. 1601.
Current name: **Hylotelephium anacampseros** (L.) H. Ohba (Crassulaceae).

Sedum annuum Linnaeus, *Species Plantarum* 1: 432. 1753.
"Habitat in Europae boreali." RCN: 3359.
Lectotype ('t Hart & Jarvis in *Taxon* 42: 401. 1993): Herb. Linn. No. 595.9 (LINN).
Current name: **Sedum annuum** L. (Crassulaceae).
Note: See Fröderström (in *Acta Horti Gothob.* 7, Suppl.: pl. XXXIII, f. 1. 1931).

Sedum atratum Linnaeus, *Species Plantarum,* ed. 2, 2: 1673. 1763.
"Habitat in Italiae alpibus. Allioni." RCN: 3361.
Lectotype ('t Hart & Jarvis in *Taxon* 42: 402. 1993): *Allioni*, Herb. Linn. No. 595.10 (LINN).
Current name: **Sedum atratum** L. (Crassulaceae).
Note: See Fröderström (in *Acta Horti Gothob.* 7, Suppl.: 124, pl. XLIX, f. 2. 1931).

Sedum caeruleum Linnaeus, *Mantissa Plantarum Altera*: 241. 1771.
"Habitat ad Cap. b. spei." RCN: 3363.
Lectotype ('t Hart & Jarvis in *Taxon* 42: 402. 1993): Herb. Linn. No. 595.3 (LINN).
Current name: **Sedum caeruleum** L. (Crassulaceae).

Sedum cepaea Linnaeus, *Species Plantarum* 1: 431. 1753.
"Habitat Monspelii, Genevae." RCN: 3350.
Lectotype ('t Hart & Jarvis in *Taxon* 42: 403. 1993): Herb. Clifford: 176, *Sedum* 3 (BM-000628575).
Current name: **Sedum cepaea** L. (Crassulaceae).
Note: See Fröderström (in *Acta Horti Gothob.* 7, Suppl.: 125, pl. LII, f. 1. 1931). 't Hart & Jarvis unfortunately erred in giving "Sedum 5", rather than the correct "Sedum 3" as the type, but as it is clearly the latter that is linked with the binomial, this is treated as a correctable error.

Sedum dasyphyllum Linnaeus, *Species Plantarum* 1: 431. 1753.
"Habitat in Helvetia, Lusitania, Hispania." RCN: 3352.
Lectotype ('t Hart & Jarvis in *Taxon* 42: 403. 1993): Herb. Burser XVI(1): 60 (UPS).
Current name: **Sedum dasyphyllum** L. (Crassulaceae).
Note: See comments by Castroviejo & Velayos (in *Anales Jard. Bot. Madrid* 53: 275. 1995) on the interpretation of indumentum form of the type.

Sedum hispanicum Linnaeus, *Centuria I Plantarum*: 12. 1755.
"Habitat in Hispania." RCN: 3355.
Lectotype ('t Hart & Jarvis in *Taxon* 42: 403. 1993): [icon] *"Sedum Hisp. folio glauco acuto, flore albido Boerh."* in Dillenius, Hort. Eltham. 2: 342, t. 256, f. 332. 1732.
Current name: **Sedum hispanicum** L. (Crassulaceae).

Sedum hybridum Linnaeus, *Species Plantarum* 1: 431. 1753.
"Habitat in Tataria ad radices montium uralensium." RCN: 3348.

S

Type not designated.

Original material: none traced.

Current name: ***Phedimus hybridus*** (L.) 't Hart (Crassulaceae).

Note: There appear to be no extant original elements, and a neotype is needed. See Fröderström (in *Acta Horti Gothob.* 7, Suppl.: 110, pl. XLIX. 1931).

Sedum libanoticum Linnaeus, *Systema Naturae,* ed. 10, 2: 1037. 1759.

["Habitat in Palaestina. Hasselquist."] Sp. Pl., ed. 2, 1: 617 (1762). RCN: 3351.

Lectotype (Eggli in *Bradleya* 6, Suppl.: 103. 1988): *Hasselquist*, Herb. Linn. No. 595.4 (LINN; iso- UPS-HASSELQ 370).

Current name: ***Rosularia serrata*** (L.) A. Berger (Crassulaceae).

Note: See Fröderström (in *Acta Horti Gothob.* 7, Suppl.: 125, pl. LVII, f. 1. 1932).

Sedum mixtum Linnaeus, *Systema Naturae,* ed. 10, 2: 1037. 1759.

RCN: 3362.

Type not designated.

Original material: none traced.

Current name: ***Sedum sp.*** (Crassulaceae).

Note: The application of this name appears to be uncertain.

Sedum reflexum Linnaeus, *Flora Suecica,* ed. 2: 463. 1755.

"Habitat in Gotlandia. DD. Bergius." RCN: 3353.

Lectotype ('t Hart & Jarvis in *Taxon* 42: 404. 1993): Herb. Linn. No. 595.5 (LINN).

Current name: ***Sedum rupestre*** L. subsp. ***rupestre*** (Crassulaceae).

Sedum rubens Linnaeus, *Species Plantarum* 1: 432. 1753.

"Habitat in Gallia, Italia." RCN: 2254.

Basionym of: *Crassula rubens* (L.) L. (1759).

Lectotype ('t Hart & Jarvis in *Taxon* 42: 405. 1993): Herb. Burser XVI(1): 62 (UPS).

Current name: ***Sedum rubens*** L. (Crassulaceae).

Sedum rupestre Linnaeus, *Species Plantarum* 1: 431. 1753.

"Habitat ad radices montium Europae." RCN: 3354.

Lectotype (Heath in *Calyx* 2: 82. 1992): [icon] *"Sedum rupestre repens, foliis compressis"* in Dillenius, Hort. Eltham. 2: 343, t. 256, f. 333. 1732.

Current name: ***Sedum rupestre*** L. (Crassulaceae).

Note: 't Hart & Jarvis (in *Taxon* 42: 407, f. 1. 1993) designated Herb. Clifford: 176, *Sedum* 4 (BM) as lectotype, a choice that would have maintained traditional usage of the name. However, unknown to them, Heath had made an earlier (1992) choice of the Dillenian plate as lectotype. Unfortunately, this clearly depicts a plant of *S. forsterianum* Sm., a fact either unknown to, or not mentioned by, Heath (in *Calyx* 2: 82. 1992; 5: 52. 1995). *Sedum rupestre* does not appear to have been taken up in its new sense, nor has a proposal for its conservation yet been made.

Sedum sexangulare Linnaeus, *Species Plantarum* 1: 432. 1753.

"Habitat in Europae borealis campis apricis siccis." RCN: 3358.

Neotype ('t Hart & Jarvis in *Taxon* 42: 407. 1993): Herb. Linn. No. 192.3 (S).

Current name: ***Sedum sexangulare*** L. (Crassulaceae).

Sedum stellatum Linnaeus, *Species Plantarum* 1: 431. 1753.

"Habitat in Italia, Grecia, Helvetia." RCN: 3349.

Lectotype ('t Hart & Jarvis in *Taxon* 42: 408. 1993): Herb. Clifford: 176, *Sedum* 2 (BM-000628574).

Current name: ***Phedimus stellatus*** (L.) Raf. (Crassulaceae).

Sedum telephium Linnaeus, *Species Plantarum* 1: 430. 1753.

"Habitat in Europae siccissimis." RCN: 3345.

Lectotype (Webb in *Feddes Repert.* 64: 19. 1961): [icon] *"Telephium album"* in Fuchs, Hist. Stirp.: 799, 800. 1542.

Current name: ***Hylotelephium telephium*** (L.) H. Ohba (Crassulaceae).

Note: Fröderström (in *Acta Horti Gothob.* 5, App.: 55–56. 1930) discussed the varied application of the autonym, himself favouring the white-flowered Scandinavian form as the typical variety. This was formalised by Webb's type choice but other authors have sometimes treated this form as taxonomically distinct from *H. telephium sensu stricto*.

Sedum telephium Linnaeus var. **album** Linnaeus, *Species Plantarum* 1: 430. 1753.

"Habitat in Europae siccissimis." RCN: 3345.

Lectotype (Webb in *Feddes Repert.* 64: 19. 1961): [icon] *"Telephium album"* in Fuchs, Hist. Stirp.: 799, 800. 1542.

Current name: ***Hylotelephium telephium*** (L.) H. Ohba (Crassulaceae).

Sedum telephium Linnaeus var. **maximum** Linnaeus, *Species Plantarum* 1: 430. 1753.

"Habitat in Europae siccissimis." RCN: 3345.

Lectotype (Ohba in Jonsell & Jarvis in *Nordic J. Bot.* 22: 72. 2002): Herb. Clifford: 176, *Sedum* 1 γ (BM-000628573).

Current name: ***Hylotelephium maximum*** (L.) Holub (Crassulaceae).

Sedum telephium Linnaeus var. **purpureum** Linnaeus, *Species Plantarum* 1: 430. 1753.

"Habitat in Europae siccissimis." RCN: 3345.

Type not designated.

Original material: Herb. Clifford: 176, *Sedum* 1 α (BM).

Current name: ***Hylotelephium telephium*** (L.) H. Ohba (Crassulaceae).

Note: Clausen (Sedum *N. America*: 541. 1975) incorrectly treated a Bauhin polynomial as the type.

Sedum verticillatum Linnaeus, *Species Plantarum* 1: 430. 1753.

"Habitat in Europa maxime australi, & Sibiria." RCN: 3344.

Lectotype (designated here by Ohba): [icon] *"Sedum foliis quaternis"* in Linnaeus, Amoen. Acad. 2: 352, t. 4, f. 14. 1751.

Current name: ***Hylotelephium verticillatum*** (L.) H. Ohba (Crassulaceae).

Note: Although Ohba (in Eggli, *Ill. Handb. Succ. Pl., Crassulaceae*: 141. 2003) indicated an illustration published by Linnaeus as the type, this choice was published after 1 Jan 2001 and so the omission of the phrase "designated here" or an equivalent (Art. 7.11) means that it is not effective.

Sedum villosum Linnaeus, *Species Plantarum* 1: 432. 1753.

RCN: 3360.

Lectotype ('t Hart & Jarvis in *Taxon* 42: 408. 1993): Herb. Burser XVI(1): 92 (UPS).

Current name: ***Sedum villosum*** L. (Crassulaceae).

Seguieria americana Linnaeus, *Systema Naturae,* ed. 10, 2: 1074. 1759.

["Habitat in Americae meridionalis umbrosis."] Sp. Pl., ed. 2, 1: 747 (1762). RCN: 3938.

Neotype (Rohwer in *Mitt. Bot. Staatssamml. München* 18: 237. 1982): British Guiana. Rupununi District, south of Lethem, Takutu River, *H. S. Irwin 797* (US).

Current name: ***Seguieria americana*** L. (Phytolaccaceae).

Note: In the absence of original material, Nowicke (in *Ann. Missouri Bot. Gard.* 55: 331. 1968) designated a neotype, but her choice was subsequently rejected by Rohwer on the grounds of its conflict with the protologue, and another neotype designated in its place.

Selago coccinea Linnaeus, *Plantae Rariores Africanae*: 12. 1760.
["Habitat ad Cap. b. spei."] Sp. Pl., ed. 2, 2: 877 (1763). RCN: 4557.
Type not designated.
Original material: *"Selago spuria dubia"*, Herb. Burman (G); *"Selago coccinea"*, Herb. Burman (G).
Current name: ***Pseudoselago rapunculoides*** (L.) Hilliard (Scrophulariaceae).
Note: The epithet appears originally as "cocinea" in 1760, corrected in later works.

Selago corymbosa Linnaeus, *Species Plantarum* 2: 629. 1753.
"Habitat in Aethiopia." RCN: 4552.
Lectotype (Wijnands, *Bot. Commelins*: 191. 1983): Herb. Linn. No. 786.1 (LINN).
Generitype of *Selago* Linnaeus (vide Green, *Prop. Brit. Bot.*: 168. 1929).
Current name: ***Selago corymbosa*** L. (Scrophulariaceae).

Selago dubia Linnaeus, *Species Plantarum* 2: 629. 1753.
"Habitat in Aethiopia." RCN: 63.
Replaced synonym of: *Eranthemum angustum* L. (1771), *nom. illeg.*
Lectotype (Wijnands, *Bot. Commelins*: 192. 1983): [icon] *"Thymaelea foliis angustissimis linearibus, flosculis spicatis"* in Burman, Rar. Afric. Pl.: 130, t. 47, f. 3. 1739.
Current name: ***Microdon dubius*** (L.) Hilliard (Globulariaceae).

Selago ericoides Linnaeus, *Systema Naturae,* ed. 12, 2: 419; *Mantissa Plantarum*: 87. 1767.
"Habitat ad Cap. b. spei." RCN: 7707.
Basionym of: *Stilbe ericoides* (L.) L. (1771).
Type not designated.
Original material: Herb. Linn. No. 410.15? (S).
Current name: ***Stilbe ericoides*** (L.) L. (Stilbaceae).

Selago fasciculata Linnaeus, *Mantissa Plantarum Altera*: 250. 1771.
"Habitat in Cap. b. spei montibus." RCN: 4556.
Type not designated.
Original material: *Thunberg 437 & 492*, Herb. Linn. No. 786.11? (LINN); *Tulbagh 186*, Herb. Linn. No. 786.12 (LINN).
Current name: ***Pseudoselago serrata*** (P.J. Bergius) Hilliard (Scrophulariaceae).
Note: Hilliard (in *Edinburgh J. Bot.* 52: 254. 1995) mentioned material at LINN but did not typify the name, incorrectly suggesting that the Tulbagh material (786.12 LINN) was received after publication of the name (1771, not 1767 as she suggests).

Selago fruticosa Linnaeus, *Systema Naturae,* ed. 12, 2: 419; *Mantissa Plantarum*: 87. 1767.
"Habitat ad Cap. b. spei." RCN: 4560.
Lectotype (Hilliard, *Tribe Selagineae*: 73. 1999): Herb. Linn. No. 786.13 (LINN).
Current name: ***Selago fruticosa*** L. (Scrophulariaceae).

Selago lychnidea Linnaeus, *Plantae Rariores Africanae*: 12. 1760.
["Habitat ad Cap. b. spei."] Sp. Pl., ed. 2, 2: 877 (1763). RCN: 4559.
Lectotype (Hilliard, *Manuleae, Tribe Scrophulariaceae*: 214. 1994): [icon] *"Lychnidea villosa, foliis oblongis, dentatis, floribus spicatis"* in Burman, Rar. Afric. Pl.: 138, t. 49, f. 4. 1739.
Current name: ***Lyperia lychnidea*** (L.) Druce (Scrophulariaceae).

Selago pinastra Linnaeus, *Species Plantarum,* ed. 2, 2: 876. 1763.
"Habitat ad Cap. b. spei." RCN: 7706.
Basionym of: *Stilbe pinastra* (L.) L. (1771).
Type not designated.
Original material: Herb. Linn. No. 1234.1 (LINN); "Selago prunastri", Herb. Linn. (UPS); [icon] in Commelin, Hort. Med. Amstelod. Pl. Rar. 2: 219, t. 110. 1701.
Current name: ***Stilbe pinastra*** (L.) L. (Stilbaceae).
Note: Selago pinastra L. (1763) appears to be merely a correction of the specific epithet in *Selago prunastri* L. (1759). Although Wijnands (*Bot. Commelins*: 191. 1983) indicated that 1234.1 (LINN) should "probably" be the type, his uncertainty prevents this from acceptance as a formal typification.

Selago polystachya Linnaeus, *Mantissa Plantarum Altera*: 250. 1771.
"Habitat in Cap. b. spei campis arenosis." RCN: 4553.
Lectotype (Hilliard, *Tribe Selagineae*: 118. 1999): Herb. Linn. No. 786.5 (LINN).
Current name: ***Selago polystachya*** L. (Scrophulariaceae).
Note: The uncertainty expressed by Wijnands (*Bot. Commelins*: 191, 192. 1981) as to whether 786.5 (LINN) is either "probably" (p. 191) or "can be" (p. 192) the type means that Hilliard's later, but unequivocal, choice is accepted here.

Selago prunastri Linnaeus, *Systema Naturae,* ed. 10, 2: 1117. 1759, *orth. var.*
["Habitat ad Cap. b. spei."] Sp. Pl., ed. 2, 2: 876 (1763). RCN: 7706.
Type not designated.
Original material: as *S. pinastra.*
Current name: ***Stilbe pinastra*** (L.) L. (Stilbaceae).
Note: Selago pinastra L. (1763) appears to be merely a correction of the epithet "prunastri".

Selago rapunculoides Linnaeus, *Centuria II Plantarum*: 22. 1756.
"Habitat in Aethiopia. Burmannus." RCN: 4554.
Lectotype (Hilliard in *Edinburgh J. Bot.* 52: 303, f. 16A. 1995): [icon] *"Rapunculus, foliis angustissimis, dentatis, floribus umbellatis"* in Burman, Rar. Afric. Pl.: 113, t. 42, f. 1. 1739.
Current name: ***Pseudoselago rapunculoides*** (L.) Hilliard (Scrophulariaceae).

Selago spuria Linnaeus, *Species Plantarum* 2: 629. 1753.
"Habitat in Aethiopia." RCN: 4555.
Lectotype (Hilliard in *Edinburgh J. Bot.* 52: 284, f. 16. 1995): [icon] *"Melampyrum Africanum, spicatum, foliis angustissimis, dentatis"* in Burman, Rar. Afric. Pl.: 115, t. 42, f. 3. 1739. – Typotype: Herb. Burman (G).
Current name: ***Pseudoselago spuria*** (L.) Hilliard (Scrophulariaceae).

Selago tomentosa Linnaeus, *Plantae Rariores Africanae*: 13. 1760.
["Habitat ad Cap. b. spei. David Royen & J. Burmannus."] Sp. Pl., ed. 2, 2: 877 (1763). RCN: 4562.
Basionym of: *Manulea tomentosa* (L.) L. (1774).
Type not designated.
Original material: Herb. Linn. No. 787.4 (LINN); Herb. Linn. No. 787.6 (LINN); Herb. Linn. No. 259.10 (S); Herb. Burman (G); [icon] in Plukenet, Phytographia: t. 319, f. 2. 1694; Almag. Bot.: 367. 1696 – Voucher: Herb. Sloane 102: 72 (BM-SL).
Current name: ***Manulea tomentosa*** (L.) L. (Scrophulariaceae).
Note: Hilliard (*Manuleae, Tribe Scrophulariaceae*: 333. 1994) indicated what is evidently the voucher (Herb. Sloane 102: 72, top right specimen, BM-SL) of the cited Plukenet plate as "type". However, this is not original material for the name as it was never seen by Linnaeus, and as other original material exists, the statement cannot be treated as a neotypification under Art. 9.8.

S

Selinum carvifolia (Linnaeus) Linnaeus, *Species Plantarum*, ed. 2, 1: 350. 1762, *typ. cons.*
"Habitat in Sibiriae campis a Jacco ad Obium, in Germania." RCN: 1960.
Basionym: *Seseli carvifolia* L. (1753).
Lectotype (Reduron & Jarvis in Jarvis & al., *Regnum Veg.* 127: 87. 1993): [icon] *"Angelica tenuifolia"* in Rivinus, Ordo Pl. Fl. Pentapetal.: t. 18. 1699.
Generitype of *Selinum* Linnaeus (1762), *nom. cons.*
Current name: ***Selinum carvifolia*** (L.) L. (Apiaceae).
Note: *Selinum* Linnaeus (1762), *nom. cons.* against *Selinum* Linnaeus (1753), *nom. rej.*

Selinum cervaria Linnaeus, *Species Plantarum* 2: 1194. 1753.
"Habitat in Helvetiae, Sabaudiae, Genevae, Alsatiae, Galloprovinciae montibus." RCN: 1964.
Basionym of: *Athamanta cervaria* (L.) L. (1759).
Lectotype (Jarvis & Knees in *Taxon* 37: 476. 1988): Herb. Burser VII(2): 30 (UPS).
Current name: ***Peucedanum cervaria*** (L.) Lapeyr. (Apiaceae).

Selinum monnieri Linnaeus, *Centuria I Plantarum*: 9. 1755.
"Habitat in Gallia australi." RCN: 1962.
Type not designated.
Original material: Herb. Linn. No. 344.15 (LINN); Herb. Linn. No. 344.14 (LINN); Herb. Linn. No. 119.11 (S).
Current name: ***Cnidium monnieri*** (L.) Cusson (Apiaceae).

Selinum palustre Linnaeus, *Species Plantarum* 1: 244. 1753.
"Habitat in Europae septentrionalis paludibus." RCN: 1959.
Lectotype (Reduron & al. in *J. Bot. Soc. Bot. France* 1: 96. 1997): [icon] *"Seseli palustre lactescens"* in Bauhin, Prodr. Theatri Bot.: 85. 1620. – Epitype (Reduron & Jarvis in Jarvis & al. in *Taxon* 55: 214. 2006): Germany. "Im Bruche zu Hüls bei Crefeld", Jul–Aug 1866, Wirtg. Herb. Plant. Crit. Etc. Flor. Rhen., Ed. 2, Fasc. 8: 400, *G. Becker s.n.* (BM).
Current name: ***Peucedanum palustre*** (L.) Moench (Apiaceae).

Selinum sylvestre Linnaeus, *Species Plantarum* 1: 244. 1753.
"Habitat in Harcynia, Gallia." RCN: 1958.
Lectotype (Reduron & Jarvis in Jarvis & al., *Regnum Veg.* 127: 87. 1993): Herb. Burser VII(2): 67 (UPS).
Generitype of *Selinum* Linnaeus (1753), *nom. rej.*
Current name: ***Peucedanum palustre*** (L.) Moench (Apiaceae).
Note: *Selinum* Linnaeus (1753), *nom. rej.* in favour of *Selinum* Linnaeus (1762), *nom. cons.* See detailed discussion of the typification of this binomial by Reduron & al. (in *J. Bot. Soc. Bot. France* 1: 95–96. 1997).

Sempervivum arachnoideum Linnaeus, *Species Plantarum* 1: 465. 1753.
"Habitat in Alpibus Italiae, Helvetiae." RCN: 3563.
Lectotype (Letz & Marhold in *Taxon* 45: 113. 1996): Herb. Clifford: 180, *Sempervivum* 5 (BM). – Epitype (Letz & Marhold in *Taxon* 45: 113. 1996): Austria. Nord-Tirol, 18 August 1902, *Handel-Mazzetti s.n.* [as *S. doellianum*] (WU).
Current name: ***Sempervivum arachnoideum*** L. (Crassulaceae).

Sempervivum arboreum Linnaeus, *Species Plantarum* 1: 464. 1753.
"Habitat in Lusitania, Creta, Corcyra, Zacintho." RCN: 3559.
Lectotype (Liu in *Special Publ. Natl. Mus. Nat. Sci. Taiwan* 3: 65. 1989): Herb. Burser XVI(1): 52 (UPS).
Current name: ***Aeonium arboreum*** (L.) Webb & Berthel. (Crassulaceae).

Sempervivum canariense Linnaeus, *Species Plantarum* 1: 464. 1753.
"Habitat in Canariis." RCN: 3560.
Lectotype (Wijnands, *Bot. Commelins*: 89. 1983): [icon] *"Sedum canarinum foliis omnium maximis"* in Commelin, Hort. Med. Amstelod. Pl. Rar. 2: 189, t. 95. 1701.
Current name: ***Aeonium canariense*** (L.) Webb & Berthel. (Crassulaceae).

Sempervivum globiferum Linnaeus, *Species Plantarum* 1: 464. 1753.
"Habitat in Rutheno. D. Gmelin." RCN: 3562.
Lectotype (Letz & Marhold in *Taxon* 45: 111. 1996): *Gerber*, Herb. Linn. No. 632.1 (LINN).
Current name: ***Jovibarba globifera*** (L.) J. Parn. subsp. ***globifera*** (Crassulaceae).
Note: Muirhead (in *Notes Roy. Bot. Gard. Edinburgh* 26: 280. 1965) informally proposed that the name should be rejected on account of its usage for a large number of different species, and uncertainty as to its correct application. Tjaden (in *Bull. Afr. Succ. Pl. Soc.* 4: 40–43, 85–88, 124–125, 167–170. 1969; 5: 192–193. 1970) agreed but did not formally typify the name. Parnell & Faverger (in *Bot. J. Linn. Soc.* 103: 218. 1990) took the name up (in *Jovibarba*) in the sense of *S. soboliferum* J. Sims but the name was only formally typified by Letz & Marhold in 1996.

Sempervivum hirtum Linnaeus, *Centuria I Plantarum*: 12. 1755.
"Habitat in Taur[er]o Rastadiensi." RCN: 3564.
Lectotype (Letz & Marhold in *Taxon* 45: 112. 1996): Herb. Burser XVI(1): 54 (UPS).
Current name: ***Jovibarba globifera*** (L.) J. Parn. subsp. ***hirta*** (L.) J. Parn. (Crassulaceae).

Sempervivum montanum Linnaeus, *Species Plantarum* 1: 465. 1753.
"Habitat in rupibus Helvetiae." RCN: 3565.
Lectotype (Letz & Marhold in *Taxon* 45: 114. 1996): Herb. Burser XVI(1): 55 (UPS). – Epitype (Letz & Marhold in *Taxon* 45: 114. 1996): Switzerland. Engadin, Piz Padella, 8 Aug 1906, *Handel-Mazzetti s.n.* (WU).
Current name: ***Sempervivum montanum*** L. (Crassulaceae).

Sempervivum tectorum Linnaeus, *Species Plantarum* 1: 464. 1753.
"Habitat in Europae tectis & collibus." RCN: 3561.
Lectotype (Parnell in Jarvis & al., *Regnum Veg.* 127: 87. 1993): Herb. Clifford: 179, *Sempervivum* 3 (BM-000628594).
Generitype of *Sempervivum* Linnaeus (vide Green, *Prop. Brit. Bot.*: 158. 1929).
Current name: ***Sempervivum tectorum*** L. (Crassulaceae).

Senecio abrotanifolius Linnaeus, *Species Plantarum* 2: 869. 1753.
"Habitat in Alpibus Stiriacis, Pyrenaicis." RCN: 6292.
Lectotype (Kadereit in Jarvis & Turland in *Taxon* 47: 365. 1998): Herb. Burser VII(1): 22 (UPS).
Current name: ***Jacobaea abrotanifolia*** (L.) Moench (Asteraceae).

Senecio aegyptius Linnaeus, *Species Plantarum* 2: 867. 1753.
"Habitat in Aegypto." RCN: 6278.
Lectotype (Alexander in *Notes Roy. Bot. Gard. Edinburgh* 37: 419. 1979): Herb. Linn. No. 996.13 (LINN).
Current name: ***Senecio aegyptius*** L. (Asteraceae).

Senecio arabicus Linnaeus, *Systema Naturae*, ed. 12, 2: 551; *Mantissa Plantarum*: 114. 1767.
"Habitat in Aegypto." RCN: 6276.
Lectotype (Alexander & Mill in Jarvis & Turland in *Taxon* 47: 365. 1998): Herb. Linn. No. 996.8 (LINN).
Current name: ***Senecio aegyptius*** L. var. ***discoideus*** Boiss. (Asteraceae).

Senecio aureus Linnaeus, *Species Plantarum* 2: 870. 1753.
"Habitat in Virginia, Canada." RCN: 6295.

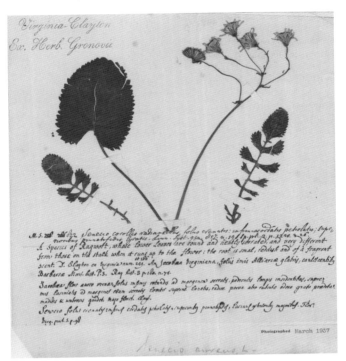

Lectotype (Fernald in *Rhodora* 45: 495, pl. 800, f. 1. 1943): *Clayton 249/286* (BM-000051179).
Current name: **Senecio aureus** L. (Asteraceae).

Senecio byzantinus Linnaeus, *Species Plantarum* 2: 871. 1753.
"Habitat Byzantinii." RCN: 6304.
Type not designated.
Original material: Herb. Linn. No. 348.11? (S); Herb. Linn. No. 348.7 (S).
Current name: **Senecio paludosus** L. (Asteraceae).

Senecio canadensis Linnaeus, *Species Plantarum* 2: 869. 1753.
"Habitat in Canada. Kalm." RCN: 6293.
Type not designated.
Original material: none traced.
Note: The application of this name is uncertain. Gray (in *J. Bot.* 19: 326. 1881) noted that Schultz Bipontinus (in *J. Bot.* 4: 233. 869. 1866) thought this to be the European *S. artemesiifolius* Pers., based on the identity of 996.43 (LINN). However, there are doubts as to whether this collection is original material for the name.

Senecio divaricatus Linnaeus, *Species Plantarum* 2: 866. 1753.
"Habitat in China. Osbeck." RCN: 6273.
Lectotype (Davies in *Kew Bull.* 33: 635. 1979): Herb. Linn. No. 996.5 (LINN).
Current name: **Gynura divaricata** (L.) DC. (Asteraceae).

Senecio doria Linnaeus, *Systema Naturae*, ed. 10, 2: 1215. 1759.
["Habitat in Oriente, Austriae sylvis, Monspelii ad Ladi ripas."] Sp. Pl., ed. 2, 2: 1221 (1763). RCN: 6301.
Type not designated.
Original material: Herb. Linn. No. 996.61 (LINN); *Gerber*, Herb. Linn. No. 996.62 (LINN).
Current name: **Senecio doria** L. (Asteraceae).

Senecio doronicum (Linnaeus) Linnaeus, *Systema Naturae*, ed. 10, 2: 1215. 1759.
["Habitat in Alpibus Helvetiae, Austriae, Italiae, Monspelii."] Sp. Pl. 2: 880 (1753). RCN: 6302.
Basionym: *Solidago doronicum* L. (1753).
Lectotype (Kadereit in Jarvis & Turland in *Taxon* 47: 367. 1998): Herb. Linn. No. 996.63 (LINN).
Current name: **Senecio doronicum** (L.) L. (Asteraceae).

Senecio elegans Linnaeus, *Species Plantarum* 2: 869. 1753.
"Habitat in Aethiopia." RCN: 6288.
Lectotype (Kippist in Harvey & Sonder, *Fl. Cap.* 3: 361. 1865): Herb. Linn. No. 996.31 (LINN).
Current name: **Senecio elegans** L. (Asteraceae).
Note: Although an unusually early typification, Kippist clearly referred to one of the Linnaean sheets as "the type specimen" and this appears to be a valid choice, pre-dating that of Belcher (in *Fl. Australia* 50: 617. 1994) who chose a Clifford sheet (BM).

Senecio erucifolius Linnaeus, *Species Plantarum* 2: 869, Err. 1753.
"Habitat in aggeribus Europae temperatae." RCN: 6290.
Lectotype (Kadereit in Jarvis & Turland in *Taxon* 47: 366. 1998): [icon] *"Jacobaea incana repens herba"* in Barrelier, Pl. Galliam: 96, t. 153. 1714. – Epitype (Kadereit in Jarvis & Turland in *Taxon* 47: 366. 1998): France. Vendée, Vignes de Ste Cécile, 1872. *E.J.A. Gadeceau 1103* (BM-000576319).
Current name: **Jacobaea erucifolia** (L.) G. Gaertn. & al. (Asteraceae).
Note: The specific epithet was omitted from the main part of the protologue (p. 869) but was added in the Errata (as "erucifolia").

Senecio glaucus Linnaeus, *Species Plantarum* 2: 868. 1753.
"Habitat in Aegypto." RCN: 6284.
Lectotype (Nordenstam in Rechinger, *Fl. Iranica* 164: 86. 1989): Herb. Linn. No. 996.24 (LINN).
Current name: **Senecio glaucus** L. (Asteraceae).

Senecio halimifolius Linnaeus, *Species Plantarum* 2: 871. 1753.
"Habitat in Aethiopia." RCN: 6305.
Type not designated.
Original material: Herb. Linn. No. 996.67 (LINN); [icon] in Dillenius, Hort. Eltham. 1: 124, t. 104, f. 124. 1732.
Current name: **Senecio halimifolius** L. (Asteraceae).

Senecio hastatus Linnaeus, *Species Plantarum* 2: 868. 1753.
"Habitat in Africa." RCN: 6286.
Lectotype (Hilliard & Burtt in *Notes Roy. Bot. Gard. Edinburgh* 33: 378. 1973): Herb. A. van Royen No. 900.57–332 (L).
Current name: **Senecio hastatus** L. (Asteraceae).

Senecio hieraciifolius Linnaeus, *Species Plantarum* 2: 866. 1753.
"Habitat in America septentrionali." RCN: 6269.
Lectotype (Belcher in *Ann. Missouri Bot. Gard.* 43: 14. 1956): Herb. Linn. No. 996.1 (LINN).
Current name: **Erechtites hieraciifolia** (L.) Raf. ex DC. (Asteraceae).
Note: Specific epithet spelled "hieracifolius" in the protologue.

Senecio ilicifolius Linnaeus, *Species Plantarum* 2: 871. 1753.
"Habitat in Aethiopia." RCN: 6306.
Lectotype (Wijnands, *Bot. Commelins*: 82. 1983): Herb. Clifford: 406, *Senecio* 7 (BM-000647059).
Current name: **Senecio ilicifolius** L. (Asteraceae).

Senecio incanus Linnaeus, *Species Plantarum* 2: 869. 1753.
"Habitat in Alpibus Helvetiae, Austriae, Pyrenaeorum." RCN: 6291.

S

Lectotype (Kadereit in Jarvis & Turland in *Taxon* 47: 366. 1998): Herb. Burser VII(1): 21 (UPS).
Current name: ***Jacobaea incana*** (L.) Veldkamp (Asteraceae).

Senecio jacobaea Linnaeus, *Species Plantarum* 2: 870. 1753.
"Habitat in Europae pascuis." RCN: 6294.
Lectotype (Kadereit & Sell in *Watsonia* 16: 22. 1986): Herb. Linn. No. 996.44 (LINN).
Current name: ***Jacobaea vulgaris*** Gaertn. (Asteraceae).
Note: Jeffrey & Chen Yi-Ling (in *Kew Bull.* 39: 414. 1984) designated the *Hortus Cliffortianus* polynomial as "lectotype". However, descriptions cannot serve as types (Art. 9).

Senecio lanatus Linnaeus, *Systema Naturae*, ed. 10, 2: 1216. 1759.
RCN: 6308.
Type not designated.
Original material: none traced.
Current name: ***Senecio sp.*** (Asteraceae).
Note: The application of this name is uncertain.

Senecio linifolius Linnaeus, *Systema Naturae*, ed. 10, 2: 1215. 1759.
["Habitat ad Cap. b. spei. Burmannus."] Sp. Pl., ed. 2, 2: 1222 (1763). RCN: 6303.
Replaced synonym of: *Senecio longifolius* L. (1763), *nom. illeg.*
Lectotype (Wijnands, *Bot. Commelins*: 82. 1983): Herb. Burman (G).
Current name: ***Senecio linifolius*** L. (Asteraceae).
Note: Senecio linifolius L. (1759) [as "linifolia"] is distinct from *Senecio linifolius* (L.) L. (1763), *nom. illeg.* (= *Solidago linifolia* L. (1753)).

Senecio linifolius (Linnaeus) Linnaeus, *Species Plantarum*, ed. 2, 2: 1220. 1763, *nom. illeg.*
"Habitat in Hispania, Italia." RCN: 6297.
Basionym: *Solidago linifolia* L. (1753).
Lectotype (Wijnands, *Bot. Commelins*: 83. 1983): [icon] *"Jacobaea, linifolio, Hispanica et Ital."* in Boccone, Mus. Piante Rar. Sicilia: 60, t. 49. 1697.
Current name: ***Senecio nevadensis*** Boiss. & Reut. subsp. **malacitanus** (Huter) Greuter (Asteraceae).
Note: Senecio linifolius (L.) L. (1763), *nom. illeg.* is a new combination based on *Solidago linifolia* L. (1753), and a later homonym of *Senecio linifolius* L. (1759). López González (in *Anales Jard. Bot. Madrid* 44: 546. 1987), identified *Senecio malacitanus* Huter (1905) as the correct name in *Senecio* for this species, pre-dating two *nomina nova* that had been proposed (*Senecio linifoliaster* G. López and *Senecio lythroides* Wijnands).

Senecio lividus Linnaeus, *Species Plantarum* 2: 867. 1753.
"Habitat in Hispania." RCN: 6279.
Lectotype (Alexander & Mill in Jarvis & Turland in *Taxon* 47: 366. 1998): Herb. Linn. No. 996.14 (LINN).
Current name: ***Senecio lividus*** L. (Asteraceae).
Note: Although Alexander (in *Notes Roy. Bot. Gard. Edinburgh* 37: 418. 1979) noted the existence of 996.14 (LINN), he did not designate it as type.

Senecio longifolius Linnaeus, *Species Plantarum*, ed. 2, 2: 1222. 1763, *nom. illeg.*
"Habitat ad Cap. b. spei. Burmannus." RCN: 6303.
Replaced synonym: *Senecio linifolius* L. (1759) non (L.) L. (1763).
Lectotype (Wijnands, *Bot. Commelins*: 82. 1983): Herb. Burman (G).
Current name: ***Senecio linifolius*** L. (Asteraceae).
Note: This appears to be an illegitimate replacement name for *Senecio linifolius* L. (1759), the change being made in 1763 to avoid homonymy with *Senecio linifolius* (L.) L. (1763), which was based on *Solidago linifolia* L. (1753). *Senecio linifolius* (L.) L. (1763) is a

heterotypic, later homonym of *Senecio linifolius* L. (1759), and therefore illegitimate.

Senecio montanus Linnaeus, *Flora Anglica*: 22. 1754.
Type not designated.
Original material: none traced.
Current name: ***Senecio sylvaticus*** L. (Asteraceae).
Note: Stearn (*Ray, Dill. Linn. Syn. Meth. Stirp. Brit.*: 67. 1973) treats this as a synonym of *S. sylvaticus* L. (1753).

Senecio nebrodensis Linnaeus, *Species Plantarum*, ed. 2, 2: 1217. 1763.
"Habitat in Sicilia, Hispania, Pyrenaeis. Alstroemer." RCN: 6283.
Lectotype (Alexander in *Notes Roy. Bot. Gard. Edinburgh* 37: 394, 396. 1979): Herb. Linn. No. 996.23 (LINN).
Current name: ***Senecio duriaei*** J. Gay (Asteraceae).
Note: This name has often been treated as a *nomen confusum* and informally rejected in favour of *S. duriaei* J. Gay. However, no formal proposal for its rejection has been made.

Senecio nemorensis Linnaeus, *Species Plantarum* 2: 870. 1753.
"Habitat in Germaniae, Sibiriae nemoribus." RCN: 6299.
Lectotype (Jeffrey & Chen in *Kew Bull.* 39: 362. 1984): Herb. Linn. No. 996.59 (LINN).
Current name: ***Senecio nemorensis*** L. (Asteraceae).

Senecio paludosus Linnaeus, *Species Plantarum* 2: 870. 1753.
"Habitat in Europae paludibus maritimis." RCN: 6298.
Lectotype (Kadereit in Jarvis & Turland in *Taxon* 47: 366. 1998): Herb. Linn. No. 996.57 (LINN).
Current name: ***Jacobaea paludosa*** (L.) G. Gaertn. & al. (Asteraceae).

Senecio palustris Linnaeus, *Flora Anglica*: 22. 1754, *orth. var.*
RCN: 6298.
Lectotype (Kadereit in Jarvis & Turland in *Taxon* 47: 366. 1998): Herb. Linn. No. 996.57 (LINN).
Current name: ***Senecio paludosus*** L. (Asteraceae).
Note: Evidently an orthographic variant of *S. paludosus* L. (1753), "palustris" being corrected by Linnaeus in the revised version of the thesis (published in *Amoen. Acad.* 4: 106. 1759).

Senecio persicifolius Linnaeus, *Plantae Rariores Africanae*: 20. 1760.
["Habitat ad Cap. b. spei."] Sp. Pl., ed. 2, 2: 1215 (1763). RCN: 6271.
Type not designated.
Original material: Herb. Burman (2 sheets) (G).
Current name: ***Senecio persicifolius*** L. (Asteraceae).

Senecio populifolius Linnaeus, *Species Plantarum*, ed. 2, 2: 1224. 1763.
"Habitat ad Cap. b. spei. Burmannus." RCN: 6308.
Type not designated.
Original material: Herb. Linn. No. 996.76 (LINN).
Current name: ***Senecio halimifolius*** L. (Asteraceae).

Senecio pseudochina Linnaeus, *Species Plantarum* 2: 867. 1753.
"Habitat in India." RCN: 6274.
Type not designated.
Original material: Herb. A. van Royen No. 900.288–368 (L); [icon] in Dillenius, Hort. Eltham. 2: 345, t. 258, f. 335. 1732.
Current name: ***Gynura pseudochina*** (L.) DC. (Asteraceae).
Note: Although a few authors have commented on the original material for the name, none seems to have made a formal typification. Davies (in *Kew Bull.* 33: 638. 1979; 35: 364. 1980) indicated both "Royen 164 (L)" and the cited Dillenius plate (t.

258, f. 335) as syntypes (followed by Jeffrey in *Kew Bull.* 41: 930. 1986). Davies (in *Kew Bull.* 35: 733. 1981) also stated that the name was "based on Senecio madraspatanus rapifolio Dill." but none of these statements effects a formal typification.

Senecio pubigerus Linnaeus, *Plantae Rariores Africanae*: 21. 1760. ["Habitat ad Cap. b. spei."] Sp. Pl., ed. 2, 2: 1218 (1763). RCN: 6287.
Type not designated.
Original material: Herb. Linn. No. 996.28 (LINN); [icon] in Breyn, Exot. Pl. Cent.: 137, t. 65. 1678.
Current name: ***Senecio pubigerus*** L. (Asteraceae).

Senecio purpureus Linnaeus, *Systema Naturae*, ed. 10, 2: 1214. 1759. ["Habitat in Aethiopia."] Sp. Pl., ed. 2, 2: 1216 (1763). RCN: 6270.
Lectotype (Hilliard, *Compositae Natal*: 419. 1977): [icon] "*Senecio viscosus Aethiopicus, flore purpureo*" in Breyn, Exot. Pl. Cent.: 139, t. 67. 1678.
Current name: ***Senecio purpureus*** L. (Asteraceae).

Senecio rigens Linnaeus, *Species Plantarum*, ed. 2, 2: 1224. 1763. "Habitat ad Cap. b. spei." RCN: 6697.
Replaced synonym of: *Othonna parviflora* L. (1771), *nom. illeg.*, non P.J. Bergius (1767).
Lectotype (Wijnands, *Bot. Commelins*: 84. 1983): [icon] "*Jacobaea Africana frutescens folio longo et glauco*" in Commelin, Hort. Med. Amstelod. Pl. Rar. 2: 143, t. 72. 1701.
Current name: ***Senecio rigens*** L. (Asteraceae).

Senecio rigidus Linnaeus, *Species Plantarum* 2: 872. 1753. "Habitat in Aethiopia." RCN: 6307.
Lectotype (Wijnands, *Bot. Commelins*: 85. 1983): Herb. Clifford: 406, *Senecio* 6 (BM-000647058).
Current name: ***Senecio rigidus*** L. (Asteraceae).

Senecio sarracenicus Linnaeus, *Species Plantarum* 2: 871. 1753. "Habitat in Helvetiae montanis, nemorosis." RCN: 6300.
Lectotype (Lacaita in *Bull. Orto Bot. Regia Univ. Napoli* 3: 284. 1913): Herb. Clifford: 410, *Solidago* 4 (BM-000647118).
Current name: ***Senecio sarracenicus*** L. (Asteraceae).
Note: Jeffrey & Chen Yi-Ling (in *Kew Bull.* 39: 362. 1984) and Herborg (in *Diss. Bot.* 107: 184. 1987) indicated 996.60 (LINN) as type, but this choice is pre-dated by that of Lacaita. Herborg recognises *S. sarracenicus* as a species distinct from *S. nemorensis* L. (into which Jeffrey & Chen place *S. sarracenicus* as a synonym).

Senecio squalidus Linnaeus, *Species Plantarum* 2: 869. 1753. "Habitat in Europa australi." RCN: 6289.
Lectotype (Alexander & Mill in Jarvis & Turland in *Taxon* 47: 366. 1998): Herb. Linn. No. 996.33 (LINN).
Current name: ***Senecio squalidus*** L. (Asteraceae).
Note: Although Alexander (in *Notes Roy. Bot. Gard. Edinburgh* 37: 396. 1979) noted the existence of 996.33 (LINN), he did not designate it as type.
   Abbott & al. (in *Watsonia* 23: 123–137. 2000) provide evidence for the hybrid origin of this taxon.

Senecio sylvaticus Linnaeus, *Species Plantarum* 2: 868. 1753. "Habitat in Europae borealis sylvis ceduis." RCN: 6282.
Lectotype (Kadereit in Jarvis & Turland in *Taxon* 47: 366. 1998): Herb. Linn. No. 996.21 (LINN).
Current name: ***Senecio sylvaticus*** L. (Asteraceae).
Note: Although Alexander (in *Notes Roy. Bot. Gard. Edinburgh* 37: 418. 1979) noted the existence of 996.21 (LINN), he did not designate it as type.

Senecio triflorus Linnaeus, *Species Plantarum* 2: 867. 1753. "Habitat in Aegypto." RCN: 6277.
Lectotype (Alexander & Mill in Jarvis & Turland in *Taxon* 47: 366. 1998): Herb. Linn. No. 996.12 (LINN).
Current name: ***Senecio aegyptius*** L. var. ***aegyptius*** (Asteraceae).

Senecio trilobus Linnaeus, *Species Plantarum* 2: 868. 1753. "Habitat in Hispania." RCN: 6280.
Neotype (Alexander & Mill in Jarvis & Turland in *Taxon* 47: 366. 1998): Herb. Linn. No. 346.17 (S), see p. 175, above.
Current name: ***Senecio trilobus*** L. (Asteraceae).
Note: Alexander (in *Notes Roy. Bot. Gard. Edinburgh* 37: 421. 1979) discussed the elements associated with this name, and referred to Herb. Linn. No. 346.17 (S; as "364.17"), from Montin's herbarium, as a "provisional lectotype". This sheet carries nothing written by Linnaeus, and the main annotations appear to have been added after 1767. As no alternative original elements for the name appear to exist, that specimen was subsequently designated as neotype.

Senecio umbellatus Linnaeus, *Plantae Rariores Africanae*: 21. 1760. ["Habitat ad Cap. b. spei."] Sp. Pl., ed. 2, 2: 1220 (1763). RCN: 6296.
Type not designated.
Original material: *Oldenland*, Herb. Burman (G), see p. 11.
Current name: ***Senecio umbellatus*** L. (Asteraceae).

Senecio varicosus Linnaeus filius, *Dec. Prima Pl. Horti Upsal.*: 9. 1762. "Habitat in Aegypto, unde semina praeterlapsa aestate missa fuere a D. D. Roquè." RCN: 6285.
Lectotype (Nordenstam in *Taxon* 54: 551. 2005): Herb. Linn. No. 996.25 (LINN).
Current name: ***Senecio varicosus*** L. f. (Asteraceae).
Note: The application of this name has been uncertain but Nordenstam (in *Taxon* 54: 552. 2005) argues that it applies correctly to the species known as *S. rodriguezii* Willk. ex J.J. Rodr. (1874). This species is sometimes treated as a synonym of the variable *S. leucanthemifolius* Poir. (1789) and in order to avoid displacement of the latter name (for those who favour a broad species concept), Nordenstam has proposed *S. leucanthemifolius* for conservation against *S. varicosus*.

Senecio virgatus Linnaeus, *Plantae Rariores Africanae*: 20. 1760. ["Habitat ad Cap. b. spei."] Sp. Pl., ed. 2, 2: 1215 (1763). RCN: 6272.
Type not designated.
Original material: Herb. Linn. No. 996.4 (LINN); Herb. Burman (G).
Current name: ***Senecio virgatus*** L. (Asteraceae).

Senecio viscosus Linnaeus, *Species Plantarum* 2: 868. 1753. "Habitat in Europae pagis, urbibus." RCN: 6281.
Lectotype (Kadereit in Jarvis & Turland in *Taxon* 47: 366. 1998): Herb. Linn. No. 996.19 (LINN).
Current name: ***Senecio viscosus*** L. (Asteraceae).
Note: Although Alexander (in *Notes Roy. Bot. Gard. Edinburgh* 37: 418. 1979) noted the existence of 996.19 (LINN), he did not designate it as type.

Senecio vulgaris Linnaeus, *Species Plantarum* 2: 867. 1753. "Habitat in Europae cultis, ruderatis, succulentis." RCN: 6275.
Lectotype (Jeffrey in Jarvis & al., *Regnum Veg.* 127: 87. 1993): Herb. Clifford: 406, *Senecio* 1, sheet A (BM-000647048).
Generitype of *Senecio* Linnaeus (vide Green, *Prop. Brit. Bot.*: 181. 1929).

S

Current name: ***Senecio vulgaris*** L. (Asteraceae).

Note: Alexander (in *Notes Roy. Bot. Gard. Edinburgh* 37: 408. 1979) noted the existence of 996.7 (LINN) but did not indicate it as type. Jeffrey & Chen Yi-Ling (in *Kew Bull.* 39: 428. 1984) and Jeffrey (in *Kew Bull.* 41: 904. 1986) treated the *Hortus Cliffortianus* polynomial as the type, and Nordenstam (in Rechinger, *Fl. Iranica* 164: 83. 1989) indicated Clifford material as the type. However, his statement did not distinguish between the two collections there associated with this name. As they are evidently not part of a single gathering, Art. 9.15 does not apply. Consequently, Jeffrey's 1992 type choice is accepted.

Septas capensis Linnaeus, *Plantae Rariores Africanae*: 10. 1760. ["Habitat ad Cap. b. spei. Dav. v. Royen."] Sp. Pl., ed. 2, 1: 489. 1762. RCN: 2643.

Lectotype (Tölken in *Contr. Bolus Herb.* 8: 228. 1977): Herb. Linn. No. 480.2 (LINN).

Generitype of *Septas* Linnaeus.

Current name: ***Crassula capensis*** (L.) Baill. (Crassulaceae).

Note: Schonland (in *Trans. Roy. Soc. S. Africa* 17: 205. 1929) appears to treat material in Herb. Thunberg (UPS) as the type but this is not original material for the name.

Serapias capensis Linnaeus, *Mantissa Plantarum Altera*: 293. 1771. "Habitat ad Cap. b. spei." RCN: 6868.

Lectotype (Summerhayes & Hall in *Taxon* 11: 202. 1962): Herb. Linn. No. 1057.9 (LINN).

Current name: ***Acrolophia barbata*** (Thunb.) Pfitzer (Orchidaceae).

Serapias cordigera Linnaeus, *Species Plantarum*, ed. 2, 2: 1345. 1763. "Habitat in Hispania, Italia, Oriente." RCN: 6867.

Lectotype (Enayet Hossain & El-Gadi in Jafri & El-Gadi, *Fl. Libya* 119: 35. 1985): *Alströmer 215*, Herb. Linn. No. 1057.8 (LINN).

Current name: ***Serapias cordigera*** L. (Orchidaceae).

Note: Baumann & al. (in *Mitteilungsbl. Arbeitskr. Heim. Orchid. Baden-Württemberg* 21: 656, Abb. 46. 1989) illustrate the type.

Serapias grandiflora Linnaeus, *Systema Naturae*, ed. 12, 2: 594. 1767, *nom. illeg.*

RCN: 6862.

Replaced synonym: *Serapias helleborine* var. *longifolia* L. (1753).

Neotype (Renz in Nasir & Ali, *Fl. Pakistan* 164: 12. 1984): Herb. Linn. No. 1057.4 (LINN).

Current name: ***Cephalanthera longifolia*** (L.) Fritsch (Orchidaceae).

Note: This name is based on *S. longifolia* (L.) Huds. (1762), itself based on *S. helleborine* var. *longifolia* L. (1753). Hudson's name has priority at specific rank over *S. grandiflora* L., which is illegitimate.

Serapias helleborine Linnaeus, *Species Plantarum* 2: 949. 1753. "Habitat in Europae asperis." RCN: 6864.

Lectotype (Cribb & Wood in Cafferty & Jarvis in *Taxon* 48: 49. 1999): Herb. Burser X: 40 (UPS).

Current name: ***Epipactis helleborine*** (L.) Crantz (Orchidaceae).

Serapias helleborine Linnaeus var. **latifolia** Linnaeus, *Species Plantarum* 2: 949. 1753.

RCN: 6864.

Lectotype (Cribb & Wood in Cafferty & Jarvis in *Taxon* 48: 49. 1999): Herb. Burser X: 39 (UPS).

Current name: ***Epipactis helleborine*** (L.) Crantz (Orchidaceae).

Serapias helleborine Linnaeus var. **longifolia** Linnaeus, *Species Plantarum* 2: 950. 1753.

RCN: 6864.

Replaced synonym of: *Serapias grandiflora* L. (1767), *nom. illeg.*

Neotype (Renz in Nasir & Ali, *Fl. Pakistan* 164: 12. 1984): Herb. Linn. No. 1057.4 (LINN).

Current name: ***Cephalanthera longifolia*** (L.) Fritsch (Orchidaceae).

Note: In the absence of any original material for the name, Renz's designation of 1057.4 (LINN) as "type" can be accepted as a neotypification under Art. 9.8. It pre-dates a different choice as neotype (an Oeder illustration) made by Baumann & al. (in *Mitteilungsbl. Arbeitskr. Heim. Orchid. Baden-Württemberg* 21: 443, Abb. 4. 1989).

Serapias helleborine Linnaeus var. **palustris** Linnaeus, *Species Plantarum* 2: 950. 1753.

RCN: 6864.

Basionym of: *Serapias palustris* (L.) L. (1759).

Lectotype (Baumann & al. in *Mitteilungsbl. Arbeitskr. Heim. Orchid. Baden-Württemberg* 21: 474. 1989): [icon] *"Helleborine angustifolia palustris sive pratensis"* in Morison, Pl. Hist. Univ. 3: 487, s. 12, t. 11, f. 7. 1699.

Current name: ***Epipactis palustris*** (L.) Crantz (Orchidaceae).

Note: See discussion by Cafferty & Jarvis (in *Taxon* 48: 50. 1999), who treat Baumann & al.'s type choice of a Dodoëns plate as a correctable error of citation for Morison's copy of that plate.

Serapias lingua Linnaeus, *Species Plantarum* 2: 950. 1753, *typ. cons.* "Habitat in Italia, Lusitania." RCN: 6866.

Lectotype (Baumann & al. in *Mitteilungsbl. Arbeitskr. Heim. Orchid. Baden-Württemberg* 21: 558, Abb. 47. 1989): [icon] *"Orchis macrophylla"* in Colonna, Ekphr.: 321, 322. 1606.

Generitype of *Serapias* Linnaeus, *nom. cons.*

Current name: ***Serapias lingua*** L. (Orchidaceae).

Note: Wood (in *Kew Mag.* 3: 25. 1986) indicated 1057.7 (LINN) as the holotype, but this is an Alströmer collection, not received by Linnaeus until after 1753 and hence not original material for the name.

Serapias palustris (Linnaeus) Linnaeus, *Amoenitates Academicae* 4: 107. 1759.

RCN: 6864.

Basionym: *Serapias helleborine* var. *palustris* L. (1753).

Lectotype (Baumann & al. in *Mitteilungsbl. Arbeitskr. Heim. Orchid. Baden-Württemberg* 21: 474. 1989): [icon] *"Helleborine angustifolia palustris sive pratensis"* in Morison, Pl. Hist. Univ. 3: 487, s. 12, t. 11, f. 7. 1699.

Current name: ***Epipactis palustris*** (L.) Crantz (Orchidaceae).

Note: See discussion by Cafferty & Jarvis (in *Taxon* 48: 50. 1999), who treat Baumann & al.'s type choice of a Dodoëns plate as a correctable error of citation for Morison's copy of that plate.

Serapias rubra Linnaeus, *Systema Naturae*, ed. 12, 2: 594. 1767. RCN: 6863.

Lectotype (Baumann & al. in *Mitteilungsbl. Arbeitskr. Heim. Orchid. Baden-Württemberg* 21: 444, Abb. 5. 1989): Herb. Linn. No. 1057.5 (LINN), see opposite, above left.

Current name: ***Cephalanthera rubra*** (L.) Rich. (Orchidaceae).

Seriola aethnensis Linnaeus, *Species Plantarum*, ed. 2, 2: 1139. 1763. "Habitat in Italia." RCN: 5907.

Lectotype (Turland in Jarvis & Turland in *Taxon* 47: 366. 1998): Herb. Linn. No. 958.1 (LINN).

Current name: ***Hypochaeris achyrophorus*** L. (Asteraceae).

Seriola cretensis Linnaeus, *Species Plantarum*, ed. 2, 2: 1139. 1763. "Habitat in Creta." RCN: 5908.

Neotype (Turland in Jarvis & Turland in *Taxon* 47: 366. 1998): Greece. Kriti: "Sfakia, abandoned village of Mouri", 860–1,100m, 7 Jun 1994, *Bergmeier & Matthäs 3998* (C).

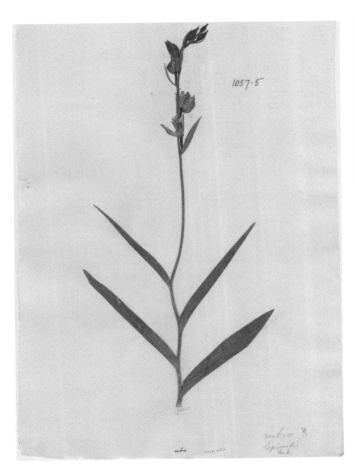

The lectotype of *Serapias rubra* L.

Current name: ***Hypochaeris cretensis*** (L.) Bory & Chaub. (Asteraceae).

Seriola laevigata Linnaeus, *Species Plantarum*, ed. 2, 2: 1139. 1763.
"Habitat in Creta." RCN: 5906.
Neotype (Turland in Jarvis & Turland in *Taxon* 47: 366. 1998): Italy. Calabria, "ca. 40km N of Catanzaro, road from Taverna Villaggio Mancuso to Butoro", 16 Jun 1979, *Davis, Sutton & Sutton sub Davis 65251* (BM-000576303).
Generitype of *Seriola* Linnaeus (vide Steudel, *Nom.*, ed. 2, 2: 568. 1841).
Current name: ***Hypochaeris laevigata*** (L.) Ces. & al. (Asteraceae).

Seriola urens (Linnaeus) Linnaeus, *Species Plantarum*, ed. 2, 2: 1139. 1763.
"Habitat in Sicilia." RCN: 5909.
Basionym: *Hypochaeris urens* L. (1753).
Neotype (Turland in Jarvis & Turland in *Taxon* 47: 363. 1998): Italy. Sicilia: Palermo, S. Martino, in pascuis apricis submontosis, *Todaro 1257* [Todaro, Flora Sicula Exsiccata] (BM-000576306).
Current name: ***Hypochaeris cretensis*** (L.) Bory & Chaub. (Asteraceae).

Seriphium ambiguum (Linnaeus) Linnaeus, *Systema Vegetabilium*, ed. 13: 665. 1774.
RCN: 6732.
Basionym: *Artemisia ambigua* L. (1763).

Lectotype (Hilliard & Burtt in *Notes Roy. Bot. Gard. Edinburgh* 31: 23. 1971): Herb. Linn. No. 988.55 (LINN).
Current name: ***Ifloga ambigua*** (L.) Druce (Asteraceae).

Seriphium cinereum Linnaeus, *Species Plantarum* 2: 928. 1753.
"Habitat in Aethiopia." RCN: 6729.
Lectotype (Koekemoer in Jarvis & Turland in *Taxon* 47: 366. 1998): Herb. Linn. No. 1049.3 (LINN).
Generitype of *Seriphium* Linnaeus (vide Green, *Prop. Brit. Bot.*: 184. 1929).
Current name: ***Stoebe cinerea*** (L.) Thunb. (Asteraceae).

Seriphium corymbiferum Linnaeus, *Systema Naturae*, ed. 12, 2: 582; *Mantissa Plantarum*: 119. 1767.
"Habitat ad Cap. b. spei." RCN: 6728.
Type not designated.
Original material: "Seriphium corymbiferum", Herb. Linn. (UPS).
Current name: ***Helichrysum niveum*** (L.) Less. (Asteraceae).

Seriphium fuscum Linnaeus, *Species Plantarum* 2: 928. 1753.
"Habitat in Aethiopia." RCN: 6731.
Lectotype (Koekemoer in Jarvis & Turland in *Taxon* 47: 367. 1998): [icon] *"Eupatorium ericoides Capitis Bonae Spei"* in Breyn, Exot. Pl. Cent.: 140, t. 69. 1678.
Current name: ***Stoebe fusca*** (L.) Thunb. (Asteraceae).

Seriphium gnaphaloides Linnaeus, *Centuria I Plantarum*: 30. 1755.
"Habitat in Aethiopia. D. Royen." RCN: 6731.
Type not designated.
Original material: none traced.
Current name: ***Elytropappus gnaphaloides*** (L.) Levyns (Asteraceae).

Seriphium plumosum Linnaeus, *Species Plantarum* 2: 928. 1753.
"Habitat in Aethiopia." RCN: 6730.
Lectotype (Wijnands, *Bot. Commelins*: 74, 75. 1983): Herb. Linn. No. 1049.4 (LINN).
Current name: ***Stoebe plumosa*** (L.) Thunb. (Asteraceae).

Serpicula repens Linnaeus, *Systema Naturae*, ed. 12, 2: 620; *Mantissa Plantarum*: 124. 1767.
"Habitat ad Cap. b. spei." RCN: 7117.
Type not designated.
Original material: Herb. Linn. No. 1106.2 (LINN).
Generitype of *Serpicula* Linnaeus.
Current name: ***Laurembergia repens*** P.J. Bergius (Haloragaceae).

Serratula alpina Linnaeus, *Species Plantarum* 2: 816. 1753.
"Habitat in Alpibus Lapponiae, Austriae, Helvetiae, Arvoniae, Sibiriae." RCN: 5931.
Type not designated.
Original material: Herb. Linn. No. 965.5 (LINN); Herb. Linn. No. 370.11 (S); Herb. Linn. No. 291 (LAPP); [icon] in Gmelin, Fl. Sibirica 2: 67, t. 26. 1752; [icon] in Plukenet, Phytographia: t. 154, f. 3. 1692; Almag. Bot.: 83. 1696 – Voucher: Herb. Sloane 95: 143 (BM-SL).
Current name: ***Saussurea alpina*** (L.) DC. (Asteraceae).
Note: Although Lipshits (*Rod Saussurea*: 225. 1979) indicated unspecified and unseen material in LINN as "typus", this statement does not distinguish between sheets 965.5 and 965.6 (which are not part of a single gathering, so Art. 9.15 does not apply).

Serratula alpina Linnaeus var. **angustifolia** Linnaeus, *Species Plantarum* 2: 817. 1753.
RCN: 5931.
Type not designated.

S

Original material: [icon] in Gmelin, Fl. Sibirica 2: 78, t. 33. 1752.
Current name: *Saussurea angustifolia* (L.) DC. (Asteraceae).

Serratula alpina Linnaeus var. **cynoglossifolia** Linnaeus, *Species Plantarum* 2: 817. 1753.
RCN: 5931.
Type not designated.
Original material: [icon] in Dillenius, Hort. Eltham. 1: 82, t. 70, f. 81. 1732; [icon] in Gmelin, Fl. Sibirica 2: 76, t. 32. 1752.
Current name: *Saussurea parviflora* (Poir.) DC. (Asteraceae).

Serratula alpina Linnaeus var. **lapatifolia** Linnaeus, *Species Plantarum* 2: 817. 1753.
RCN: 5931.
Type not designated.
Original material: Herb. Burser XXI: 14 (UPS); [icon] in Morison, Pl. Hist. Univ. 3: 148, s. 7, t. 29, f. 1. 1699; [icon] in Clusius, Rar. Pl. Hist. 2: 150, 151. 1601; [icon] in Haller, Enum. Meth. Stirp. Helv. 2: 683, t. 22. 1742.
Current name: *Saussurea discolor* (Willd.) DC. (Asteraceae).

Serratula amara Linnaeus, *Species Plantarum* 2: 819. 1753.
"Habitat in Sibiria." RCN: 5940.
Type not designated.
Original material: *Gmelin*, Herb. Linn. No. 965.16 (LINN); [icon] in Gmelin, Fl. Sibirica 2: 72, t. 29. 1752.
Current name: *Saussurea amara* (L.) DC. (Asteraceae).
Note: Lipshits (*Rod Saussurea*: 68. 1979) notes that a Gmelin specimen (in LE) is identifiable as *Saussurea amara* but does not treat it as the type.

Serratula arvensis Linnaeus, *Species Plantarum* 2: 820. 1753.
"Habitat in Europae cultis agris." RCN: 5943.
Lectotype (Moore & Frankton, *Thistles Canada*: 24. 1974): Herb. Linn. No. 965.19 (LINN).
Current name: *Cirsium arvense* (L.) Scop. (Asteraceae).

Serratula babylonica Linnaeus, *Systema Naturae*, ed. 10, 2: 1199. 1759.
["Habitat in Oriente."] Sp. Pl., ed. 2, 2: 1149 (1763). RCN: 6611.
Basionym of: *Centaurea babylonica* (L.) L. (1771).
Type not designated.
Original material: none traced.
Current name: *Centaurea babylonica* (L.) L. (Asteraceae).

Serratula centauroides Linnaeus, *Species Plantarum* 2: 820. 1753.
"Habitat in Sibiria." RCN: 5941.
Type not designated.
Original material: Herb. Linn. No. 965.17 (LINN); [icon] in Gmelin, Fl. Sibirica 2: 80, t. 35. 1752.
Current name: *Klasea centauroides* (L.) Cass. ex Kitag. (Asteraceae).

Serratula chamaepeuce Linnaeus, *Species Plantarum* 2: 819. 1753.
"Habitat in Creta." RCN: 6082.
Basionym of: *Staehelina chamaepeuce* (L.) L. (1767).
Lectotype (Greuter in *Boissiera* 22: 105. 1973): [icon] *"Chamaepeuce"* in Alpino, Pl. Exot.: 77, 76. 1627 (see p. 105). – Epitype (Greuter in *Boissiera* 22: 105. 1972): Greece. Crete, Distr. Hagios Vasilis. "An Felsen ober Spili, 16.IV" Dörfler, Iter Creticum 1904, n. 1014 (G; iso- B, GB, Gr, M, PI, PR etc.).
Current name: *Ptilostemon chamaepeuce* (L.) Less. (Asteraceae).
Note: Greuter also designated a "standard specimen" in conjunction with the Alpino plate – similar to the epitype (Art. 9.7) of subsequent Codes. He publishes a photograph of the capitula of this material in his plate Ia.

Serratula coronata Linnaeus, *Species Plantarum*, ed. 2, 2: 1144. 1763.
"Habitat in Sibiria, Italia." RCN: 5930.
Replaced synonym: *Serratula tinctoria* var. *praealta* L. (1753).
Type not designated.
Original material: as replaced synonym.
Current name: *Serratula coronata* L. (Asteraceae).
Note: A *nomen novum* at specific rank for *Serratula tintoria* var. *praealta* L. (1753).

Serratula glauca Linnaeus, *Species Plantarum* 2: 818. 1753.
"Habitat in Marilandia, Virginia, Carolina." RCN: 5936.
Lectotype (Reveal & al. in *Huntia* 7: 217. 1987): *Clayton 175*, lower specimen (BM-000576252).
Current name: *Vernonia glauca* (L.) Willd. (Asteraceae).

Serratula lanceolatus Linnaeus, *Amoenitates Academicae* 4: 490. 1759, *nom. inval.*
Type not relevant.
Note: It seems clear that this name was created through a typographical error in the thesis, *Flora Monspeliensis*. In the column containing generic names, *Carduus* was wrongly placed one line too low, resulting in *C. lanceolatus* L. (1753) appearing as "Serratula lanceolatus". The latter name does not appear in later treatments by Linnaeus and is to be treated as an error, as noted by Stearn (in Geck & Pressler, *Festschr. Claus Nissen*: 631. 1974).

Serratula multiflora Linnaeus, *Species Plantarum* 2: 817. 1753.
"Habitat in Sibiria. D. Gmelin." RCN: 5933.
Lectotype (Tscherneva in *Bot. Zhurn.* 79(5): 123. 1994): *Gerber*, Herb. Linn. No. 965.10 (LINN).
Current name: *Jurinea multiflora* (L.) B. Fedtsch. (Asteraceae).

Serratula noveboracensis Linnaeus, *Species Plantarum* 2: 818. 1753.
"Habitat in Noveboraco, Virginia, Carolina, Canada, Kamtschatca." RCN: 5934.
Lectotype (Reveal & Turland in Jarvis & Turland in *Taxon* 47: 367. 1998): Herb. Clifford: 392, *Serratula* 3, sheet A (BM-000646912).
Current name: *Vernonia noveboracensis* (L.) Michx. (Asteraceae).

Serratula praealta Linnaeus, *Species Plantarum* 2: 818. 1753.
"Habitat in Carolina, Virginia, Pensylvania." RCN: 5935.
Lectotype (Reveal & Turland in Jarvis & Turland in *Taxon* 47: 367. 1998): *Kalm*, Herb. Linn. No. 965.12 (LINN).
Current name: *Vernonia noveboracensis* (L.) Michx. (Asteraceae).

Serratula salicifolia Linnaeus, *Species Plantarum* 2: 817. 1753.
"Habitat in Sibiriae apricis, siccis." RCN: 5932.
Type not designated.
Original material: *Gmelin*, Herb. Linn. No. 965.8 (LINN); [icon] in Gmelin, Fl. Sibirica 2: 69, t. 27. 1752.
Current name: *Saussurea salicifolia* (L.) DC. (Asteraceae).

Serratula scariosa Linnaeus, *Species Plantarum* 2: 818. 1753.
"Habitat in Virginia." RCN: 5938.
Lectotype (Gaiser in *Rhodora* 48: 294. 1946): Herb. Linn. No. 965.14 (LINN).
Current name: *Liatris scariosa* (L.) Willd. var. *scariosa* (Asteraceae).

Serratula spicata Linnaeus, *Species Plantarum* 2: 819. 1753.
"Habitat in America septentrionali." RCN: 5939.
Lectotype (Gaiser in *Rhodora* 48: 221. 1946): *Kalm*, Herb. Linn. No. 965.15 (LINN).
Current name: *Liatris spicata* (L.) Willd. var. *spicata* (Asteraceae).

Serratula squarrosa Linnaeus, *Species Plantarum* 2: 818. 1753.
"Habitat in Virginia." RCN: 5937.
Lectotype (Gaiser in *Rhodora* 48: 403. 1946): Herb. Linn. No. 965.13 (LINN).
Current name: *Liatris squarrosa* (L.) Michx. var. *squarrosa* (Asteraceae).

Serratula tinctoria Linnaeus, *Species Plantarum* 2: 816. 1753.
"Habitat in Europae borealioris pratis." RCN: 5929.
Lectotype (Cantó in *Lazaroa* 6: 16. 1985 [1984]): Herb. Clifford: 391, *Serratula* 1 (BM-000646910).
Generitype of *Serratula* Linnaeus (vide Green, *Prop. Brit. Bot.*: 179. 1929).
Current name: *Serratula tinctoria* L. (Asteraceae).

Serratula tinctoria Linnaeus var. **praealta** Linnaeus, *Species Plantarum* 2: 816. 1753.
"Habitat in Italia, Sibiria." RCN: 5930.
Replaced synonym of: *Serratula coronata* L. (1763).
Type not designated.
Original material: Herb. Linn. No. 965.3 (LINN); [icon] in Boccone, Mus. Piante Rar. Sicilia: 45, t. 37. 1697; [icon] in Gmelin, Fl. Sibirica 2: 49, t. 20. 1752.
Current name: *Serratula coronata* L. (Asteraceae).

Sesamum indicum Linnaeus, *Species Plantarum* 2: 634. 1753, *nom. cons.*
"Habitat in India." RCN: 4603.
Lectotype (Abedin in Nasir & Ali, *Fl. W. Pakistan* 33: 4. 1973): Herb. Linn. No. 802.3 (LINN).
Current name: *Sesamum indicum* L. (Pedaliaceae).
Note: Sesamum indicum is conserved against *S. orientale* L. (1753).

Sesamum orientale Linnaeus, *Species Plantarum* 2: 634. 1753, *nom. rej.*
"Habitat in Zeylona, Malabaria." RCN: 4602.
Lectotype (Bruce in Turrill & Milne-Redhead, *Fl. Trop. E. Africa, Pedaliaceae*: 19. 1953): Herb. Clifford: 318, *Sesamum* 1 (BM-000646183).
Generitype of *Sesamum* Linnaeus (vide Green, *Prop. Brit. Bot.*: 169. 1929).
Current name: *Sesamum indicum* L. (Pedaliaceae).
Note: Sesamum indicum L. (1753) is conserved against *S. orientale* L.

Seseli ammoides Linnaeus, *Species Plantarum* 1: 260. 1753.
"Habitat in Lusitania." RCN: 2078.
Neotype (Reduron in Jarvis & al. in *Taxon* 55: 214. 2006): Herb. Linn. No. 367.12 (LINN).
Current name: *Ammoides pusilla* (Brot.) Breistr. (Apiaceae).

Seseli annuum Linnaeus, *Species Plantarum* 1: 260. 1753.
"Habitat in Pannonia, Gallia." RCN: 2077.
Lectotype (Reduron in Jarvis & al. in *Taxon* 55: 214. 2006): Herb. Burser VIII: 33 (UPS).
Current name: *Seseli annuum* L. (Apiaceae).

Seseli carvifolia Linnaeus, *Species Plantarum* 1: 260. 1753.
"Habitat in Helvetia, Germania, Anglia." RCN: 1960.
Basionym of: *Selinum carvifolia* (L.) L. (1762).
Conserved type (Reduron & Jarvis in Jarvis & al., *Regnum Veg.* 127: 87. 1993): [icon] *"Angelica tenuifolia"* in Rivinus, Ordo Pl. Fl. Pentapetal.: t. 18. 1699.
Current name: *Selinum carvifolia* (L.) L. (Apiaceae).

Seseli elatum Linnaeus, *Species Plantarum*, ed. 2, 1: 375. 1762, *nom. illeg.*

"Habitat in Austria, Gallia." RCN: 2084.
Basionym: *Seseli longifolium* L. (1759).
Neotype (Reduron & Schäfer in Jarvis & al. in *Taxon* 55: 214. 2006): *"Seseli elatum* L. Fontfroide 1 IX 1914 bord pierreux des bois" (ex herb. Squivet de Carondelet) (MPU).
Current name: *Seseli longifolium* L. (Apiaceae).
Note: An illegitimate renaming of *S. longifolium* L. (1759).

Seseli glaucum Linnaeus, *Species Plantarum* 1: 260. 1753.
"Habitat in Gallia." RCN: 2076.
Lectotype (Reduron & Jarvis in Reduron in *Bull. Soc. Échange Pl. Vasc. Eur. Occid. Bassin Médit.* 24: 80. 1993): [icon] *"Daucus glauco folio, similis Foeniculo tortuoso"* in Bauhin & Cherler, Hist. Pl. Univ. 3(2): 16. 1651.
Current name: *Seseli montanum* L. (Apiaceae).

Seseli longifolium Linnaeus, *Amoenitates Academicae* 4: 480. 1759.
["Habitat in Austria, Gallia."] Sp. Pl., ed. 2, 1: 375. 1762.
Neotype (Reduron & Schäfer in Jarvis & al. in *Taxon* 55: 214. 2006): *"Seseli elatum* L. Fontfroide 1 IX 1914 bord pierreux des bois" (ex herb. Squivet de Carondelet) (MPU).
Current name: *Seseli longifolium* L. (Apiaceae).

Seseli montanum Linnaeus, *Species Plantarum* 1: 260. 1753.
"Habitat in Galliae, Italiae collibus." RCN: 2075.
Lectotype (Reduron & Jarvis in Reduron in *Bull. Soc. Échange Pl. Vasc. Eur. Occid. Bassin Médit.* 24: 78, f. 1. 1993): Herb. Clifford: 102, *Seseli* 1 (BM-000558349).
Current name: *Seseli montanum* L. (Apiaceae).

Seseli pimpinelloides Linnaeus, *Species Plantarum* 1: 259. 1753.
"Habitat in Europa australiore." RCN: 2074.
Type not designated.
Original material: Herb. Linn. No. 367.1 (LINN).
Note: The application of this name is uncertain. It does not appear to be in use and as it may threaten *Holandrea schottii* (Besser ex DC.) Reduron & al., it could be a candidate for rejection.

Seseli pumilum Linnaeus, *Systema Naturae*, ed. 10, 2: 962. 1759.
["Habitat in Austria, Galloprovincia."] Sp. Pl., ed. 2, 1: 373 (1762). RCN: 2108.
Replaced synonym of: *Pimpinella dioica* L. (1774), *nom. illeg.*
Lectotype (Reduron in Jarvis & al. in *Taxon* 55: 214. 2006): Herb. Linn. No. 367.22 (LINN).
Current name: *Trinia glauca* (L.) Dumort. (Apiaceae).

Seseli pyrenaeum Linnaeus, *Species Plantarum* 1: 261. 1753.
"Habitat in Pyrenaeis." RCN: 2082.
Lectotype (Reduron & Jarvis in *J. Bot. Soc. Bot. France* 1: 99. 1997): Herb. Burser VIII: 36 (UPS).
Current name: *Selinum pyrenaeum* (L.) Gouan (Apiaceae).

Seseli saxifragum Linnaeus, *Species Plantarum* 1: 261. 1753.
"Habitat in Lacum Genevensem." RCN: 2083.
Conserved type (Gutermann in *Taxon* 25: 198. 1976): Herb. Burser VIII: 51 (UPS).
Current name: *Ptychotis saxifraga* (L.) Loret & Barrandon (Apiaceae).

Seseli tortuosum Linnaeus, *Species Plantarum* 1: 260. 1753.
"Habitat in Europa australi." RCN: 2079.
Lectotype (Reduron & Jarvis in Jarvis & al., *Regnum Veg.* 127: 88. 1993): Herb. Clifford: 99, *Oenanthe* 6 (BM-000558323).
Generitype of *Seseli* Linnaeus (vide Hitchcock, *Prop. Brit. Bot.*: 141. 1929).

S

Current name: ***Seseli tortuosum*** L. (Apiaceae).
Note: Pardó (in *Lazaroa* 3: 178. 1981), followed by a number of later authors, indicated 367.14 (LINN) as type but this is a Kähler collection, not received by Linnaeus until after 1753, which cannot therefore be original material for the name.

Seseli turbith Linnaeus, *Centuria II Plantarum*: 14. 1756.
"Habitat in Europa australi." RCN: 2080.
Lectotype (Jarvis & Knees in *Taxon* 37: 476. 1988): Herb. Linn. No. 367.18 (LINN).
Current name: ***Athamanta turbith*** (L.) Brot. (Apiaceae).

Sesuvium portulacastrum (Linnaeus) Linnaeus, *Systema Naturae*, ed. 10, 2: 1058. 1759.
["Habitat in Curassao."] Sp. Pl. 1: 446. 1753. RCN: 3652.
Basionym: *Portulaca portulacastrum* L. (1753).
Lectotype (Wijnands, *Bot. Commelins*: 175. 1983): [icon] *"Portulaca Corassavica Angusto longo lucidoque folio"* in Hermann, Parad. Bat.: 212. 1698.
Generitype of *Sesuvium* Linnaeus.
Current name: ***Sesuvium portulacastrum*** (L.) L. (Aizoaceae).

Sherardia arvensis Linnaeus, *Species Plantarum* 1: 102. 1753.
"Habitat in arvis Scaniae, Germaniae, Angliae." RCN: 844.
Lectotype (Natali in Jarvis & al., *Regnum Veg.* 127: 88. 1993): *Sherard*, Herb. Clifford: 33, *Sherardia* 1 (BM-000557768).
Generitype of *Sherardia* Linnaeus (vide de Candolle, *Prodr.* 4: 581. 1830).
Current name: ***Sherardia arvensis*** L. (Rubiaceae).

Sherardia fruticosa Linnaeus, *Species Plantarum* 1: 103. 1753.
"Habitat in insula Adscensionis. Osbeck." RCN: 846.
Type not designated.
Original material: Herb. Linn. No. 126.3 (LINN).
Current name: ***Sherardia fruticosa*** L. (Rubiaceae).

Sherardia muralis Linnaeus, *Species Plantarum* 1: 103. 1753.
"Habitat in Italia." RCN: 845.
Lectotype (Natali & Jeanmonod in Jeanmonod, *Compl. Prodr. Fl. Corse, Rubiaceae*: 105. 2000): Herb. Linn. No. 126.2 (LINN).
Current name: ***Galium murale*** (L.) All. (Rubiaceae).

Sibbaldia erecta Linnaeus, *Species Plantarum* 1: 284. 1753.
"Habitat in Sibiria. D. Gmelin." RCN: 2262.
Lectotype (Pyak & Ebel in Cafferty & Jarvis in *Taxon* 51: 544. 2002): *Amman s.n.*, Herb. Linn. No. 401.2 (LINN).
Current name: ***Chamaerhodos erecta*** (L.) Bunge (Rosaceae).

Sibbaldia procumbens Linnaeus, *Species Plantarum* 1: 284. 1753.
"Habitat in Alpibus Lapponiae, Helvetiae, Scothiae." RCN: 2261.
Lectotype (Barrie in Jarvis & al., *Regnum Veg.* 127: 88. 1993): *Amman s.n.*, Herb. Linn. No. 401.1 (LINN).
Generitype of *Sibbaldia* Linnaeus (vide Hitchcock, *Prop. Brit. Bot.*: 144. 1929).
Current name: ***Sibbaldia procumbens*** L. (Rosaceae).

Sibthorpia africana Linnaeus, *Species Plantarum* 2: 631. 1753.
"Habitat in Africa." RCN: 2637.
Type not designated.
Original material: [icon] in Shaw, Cat. Pl. Afr. As.: 39, f. 149. 1738.
Current name: ***Sibthorpia africana*** L. (Scrophulariaceae).
Note: Hedberg (in *Bot. Not.* 108: 174. 1955) indicated "Shaw's afric. 149" ex herb, Goodenough (K) as the holotype, but this material was never seen by Linnaeus and is not original material for the name.

Sibthorpia europaea Linnaeus, *Species Plantarum* 2: 631. 1753.
"Habitat in Cornubiae, Devioniae, Lusitaniae udis aggeribus." RCN: 4582.
Lectotype (Hampshire in Jarvis & al., *Regnum Veg.* 127: 88. 1993): [icon] *"Alsine spuria pusilla repens foliis Saxifragae aureae"* in Plukenet, Phytographia: t. 7, f. 6. 1691; Almag. Bot.: 23. 1696.
Generitype of *Sibthorpia* Linnaeus (vide Green, *Prop. Brit. Bot.*: 169. 1929).
Current name: ***Sibthorpia europaea*** L. (Scrophulariaceae).
Note: Hedberg (in *Bot. Not.* 108: 168. 1955), followed by a number of later authors, indicated 793.1 (LINN) as type but it is unannotated by Linnaeus and is not original material for the name.

Sibthorpia peregrina Linnaeus, *Species Plantarum* 2: 631. 1753.
"Habitat – – – –" RCN: 2637.
Replaced synonym of: *Disandra prostrata* L. (1774), *nom. illeg.*
Lectotype (Hampshire in Jarvis & al., *Regnum Veg.* 127: 43. 1993): [icon] *"Planta"* in Plukenet, Phytographia: t. 257, f. 5. 1694.
Current name: ***Sibthorpia peregrina*** L. (Scrophulariaceae).
Note: Hedberg (in *Bot. Not.* 108: 175. 1955) indicated 475.1 (LINN) as lectotype, but it is annotated only with "Giseke" and associated in the herbarium with the illegitimate *Disandra prostrata* L. (1774). It is not original material for *S. peregrina*.

Sicyos angulata Linnaeus, *Species Plantarum* 2: 1013. 1753.
"Habitat in Canada, Mexico." RCN: 7337.
Lectotype (Jeffrey, *Cucurbitaceae Eastern Asia*: 88. 1980): Herb. Clifford: 452, *Sicyos* 1 (BM-000647449).
Generitype of *Sicyos* Linnaeus (vide Green, *Prop. Brit. Bot.*: 190. 1929).
Current name: ***Sicyos angulata*** L. (Cucurbitaceae).

Sicyos laciniata Linnaeus, *Species Plantarum* 2: 1013. 1753.
"Habitat in America calidiori." RCN: 7348.
Basionym of: *Cissus laciniata* (L.) L. (1759).
Lectotype (Lombardi in *Taxon* 46: 430. 1997): [icon] *"Sicyos foliis laciniatis"* in Plumier in Burman, Pl. Amer.: 239, t. 243, f. 1. 1760.
Current name: ***Sicyos laciniata*** L. (Cucurbitaceae).

Sicyos trifoliata Linnaeus, *Species Plantarum* 2: 1013. 1753.
"Habitat in Jamaica." RCN: 956.
Basionym of: *Cissus trifoliata* (L.) L. (1759), non L. (1762).
Lectotype (Lombardi in *Taxon* 44: 203. 1995): [icon] *"Bryonia alba triphylla geniculata, foliis crassis acidis"* in Sloane, Voy. Jamaica 1: 233, t. 142, f. 5, 6. 1707. – Typotype: Herb. Sloane 4: 87, 88 (BM-SL).
Current name: ***Cissus trifoliata*** (L.) L. (Vitaceae).

Sida abutilon Linnaeus, *Species Plantarum* 2: 685. 1753.
"Habitat in Indiis." RCN: 5024.
Lectotype (Borssum Waalkes in *Blumea* 14: 167. 1966): Herb. Clifford: 346, *Sida* 4 (BM-000646455).
Current name: ***Abutilon theophrasti*** Medik. (Malvaceae).

Sida alba Linnaeus, *Flora Jamaicensis*: 18. 1759, *nom. nud.*
"Habitat [in Jamaica.]"
Type not relevant.

Sida alba Linnaeus, *Species Plantarum*, ed. 2, 2: 960. 1763.
"Habitat in India." RCN: 5009.
Lectotype (Abedin in Nasir & Ali, *Fl. W. Pakistan* 125: 130. 1979): Herb. Linn. No. 866.2 (LINN).
Current name: ***Sida spinosa*** L. (Malvaceae).
Note: See discussion by Sivarajan & Pradeep (in *Sida* 16: 65. 1995) on the synonymy of this name.

Sida alnifolia Linnaeus, *Species Plantarum* 2: 684. 1753.
"Habitat in India." RCN: 5011.
Lectotype (Borssum Waalkes in *Blumea* 14: 198. 1966): Herb.
   Hermann 3: 4, No. 253 (BM-000594646).
Current name: **Sida alnifolia** L. (Malvaceae).
Note: Sida alnifolia was treated as the generitype by Britton & Brown
   (*Ill. Fl. N. U. S.*, ed. 2, 2: 520. 1913; see McNeill & al. in *Taxon* 36:
   384. 1987). However, under Art. 10.5, Ex. 7 (a voted example) of
   the Vienna Code, this is a type choice made under the American
   Code and is to be replaced under Art. 10.5b by Green's choice
   (*Prop. Brit. Bot.*: 172. 1929) of *S. rhombifolia* L.
      See discussion on the application of *S. alnifolia* by Sivarajan &
   Pradeep (in *Sida* 16: 65. 1995).

Sida americana Linnaeus, *Species Plantarum*, ed. 2, 2: 963. 1763.
"Habitat in Jamaica." RCN: 5023.
Type not designated.
Original material: *Browne*, Herb. Linn. No. 866.25 (LINN); [icon] in
   Plumier in Burman, Pl. Amer.: 1, t. 2. 1755.
Current name: **Abutilon abutiloides** (Jacq.) Garcke ex Hochr.
   (Malvaceae).

Sida amplissima Linnaeus, *Species Plantarum* 2: 685. 1753.
"Habitat in America calidiore." RCN: 5020.
Lectotype (Krapovickas in *Bonplandia* 9: 90, f. 1. 1996): [icon] *"Sida
   foliis subrotundo-cordatis"* in Plumier in Burman, Pl. Amer.: 2, t. 3.
   1755.
Current name: **Wissadula amplissima** (L.) R.E. Fr. (Malvaceae).

Sida asiatica Linnaeus, *Centuria II Plantarum*: 26. 1756.
"Habitat in India." RCN: 5025.
Lectotype (Verdcourt in *Taxon* 51: 860. 2003 [2002]): Herb.
   Hermann 5: 77, No. 520 [icon] (BM).
Current name: **Abutilon indicum** (L.) Sweet (Malvaceae).

Sida capitata Linnaeus, *Species Plantarum* 2: 685. 1753.
"Habitat in Carabaeis, locis paludosis." RCN: 5029.
Basionym of: *Malachra capitata* (L.) L. (1767).
Lectotype (Fawcett & Rendle, *Fl. Jamaica* 5: 124. 1926): Herb. Linn.
   No. 867.1 (LINN).
Current name: **Malachra capitata** (L.) L. (Malvaceae).

Sida ciliaris Linnaeus, *Systema Naturae*, ed. 10, 2: 1145. 1759.
["Habitat in Jamaica."] Sp. Pl., ed. 2, 2: 961 (1763). RCN: 5012.
Lectotype (Clement in *Contr. Gray Herb.* 180: 24. 1957): *Browne*,
   Herb. Linn. No. 866.8 (LINN).
Current name: **Sida ciliaris** L. (Malvaceae).

Sida cordifolia Linnaeus, *Species Plantarum* 2: 684. 1753.
"Habitat in India." RCN: 5017.
Lectotype (Borssum Waalkes in *Blumea* 14: 200. 1966): Herb. Linn.
   No. 866.12 (LINN).
Current name: **Sida cordifolia** L. (Malvaceae).
Note: Rodrigo (in *Rev. Mus. La Plata, Bot.* 6: t. 31. 1944) refers to
   866.13 (LINN) as the type. However, this sheet lacks the
   relevant *Species Plantarum* number (i.e. "4") and was a post-1753
   addition to the herbarium and is not original material for the
   name.

Sida crispa Linnaeus, *Species Plantarum* 2: 685. 1753.
"Habitat in Carolina, Providentia, Panama." RCN: 5027.
Lectotype (Borssum Waalkes in *Blumea* 14: 161. 1966): [icon]
   "Abutilon vesicarium crispum, floribus melinis parvis" in Dillenius,
   Hort. Eltham. 1: 6, t. 5, f. 5. 1732.
Current name: **Herissantia crispa** (L.) Brizicky (Malvaceae).

Sida cristata Linnaeus, *Species Plantarum* 2: 685. 1753.
"Habitat in Mexico." RCN: 5028.
Lectotype (Fryxell in *Aliso* 11: 495. 1987): Herb. Linn. No. 866.31
   (LINN).
Current name: **Anoda cristata** (L.) Schltdl. (Malvaceae).

Sida indica Linnaeus, *Centuria II Plantarum*: 26. 1756.
"Habitat in India." RCN: 5026.
Lectotype (Borssum Waalkes in *Blumea* 14: 173. 1966): Herb. Linn.
   No. 866.29 (LINN).
Current name: **Abutilon indicum** (L.) Sweet (Malvaceae).

Sida jamaicensis Linnaeus, *Systema Naturae*, ed. 10, 2: 1145. 1759.
["Habitat in Jamaica."] Sp. Pl., ed. 2, 2: 962 (1763). RCN: 5015.
Lectotype (Fryxell in *Sida* 11: 75. 1985): *Browne*, Herb. Linn. No.
   866.10 (LINN).
Current name: **Sida jamaicensis** L. (Malvaceae).

Sida occidentalis Linnaeus, *Centuria II Plantarum*: 26. 1756.
"Habitat in America." RCN: 5022.
Lectotype (Fryxell in *Syst. Bot. Monogr.* 25: 157. 1988): [icon]
   "Abutilon vesicarium, flore & fructu majore, non crispo" in Dillenius,
   Hort. Eltham. 1: 7, t. 6, f. 6. 1732.
Current name: **Gaya occidentalis** (L.) Sweet (Malvaceae).

Sida paniculata Linnaeus, *Systema Naturae*, ed. 10, 2: 1145. 1759.
["Habitat in Jamaica."] Sp. Pl., ed. 2, 2: 962 (1763). RCN: 5019.
Lectotype (Fryxell in *Brittonia* 30: 453. 1978): *Browne*, Herb. Linn.
   No. 866.17 (LINN).
Current name: **Sidastrum paniculatum** (L.) Fryxell (Malvaceae).

Sida periplocifolia Linnaeus, *Species Plantarum* 2: 684. 1753.
"Habitat in Zeylona." RCN: 5020.
Lectotype (Fries in *Kongl. Svenska Vetensk. Acad. Handl.* 43(4): 37.
   1908): Herb. Hermann 3: 11, No. 251 (BM-000594653).
Current name: **Wissadula periplocifolia** (L.) Thwaites (Malvaceae).

Sida radiata Linnaeus, *Species Plantarum*, ed. 2, 2: 965. 1763.
"Habitat in America." RCN: 5030.
Basionym of: *Malachra radiata* (L.) L. (1767).
Lectotype (Fryxell in *Syst. Bot. Monogr.* 25: 269. 1988): [icon] *"Sida
   foliis palmatis, caule hispido"* in Plumier in Burman, Pl. Amer.: 10, t.
   19. 1755.
Current name: **Malachra radiata** (L.) L. (Malvaceae).

Sida retusa Linnaeus, *Species Plantarum*, ed. 2, 2: 961. 1763.
"Habitat in India." RCN: 5013.
Lectotype (Borssum Waalkes in *Blumea* 14: 198. 1966): Herb. Linn.
   No. 866.7 (LINN).
Current name: **Sida alnifolia** L. (Malvaceae).
Note: Borssum Waalkes incorrectly indicated 866.7 (LINN) as the
   holotype (illustrations were also cited in the protologue), but this
   error is correctable under Art. 9.8, with this case listed (see Ex. 6) as
   an example where the choice is to be accepted as a lectotype.

Sida rhombifolia Linnaeus, *Species Plantarum* 2: 684. 1753.
"Habitat in India utraque." RCN: 5010.
Lectotype (Rodrigo in *Revista Mus. La Plata, Secc. Bot., n.s.,* 6(24): pl.
   28. 1944): Herb. Linn. No. 866.3 (LINN).
Generitype of *Sida* Linnaeus (vide Green, *Prop. Brit. Bot.*: 172. 1929).
Current name: **Sida rhombifolia** L. (Malvaceae).
Note: Sida alnifolia L. was treated as the generitype by Britton &
   Brown (*Ill. Fl. N. U. S.*, ed. 2, 2: 520. 1913; see McNeill & al. in
   Taxon 36: 384. 1987). However, under Art. 10.5, Ex. 7 (a voted
   example) of the Vienna Code, this is a type choice made under the

American Code and is to be replaced under Art. 10.5b by Green's choice (*Prop. Brit. Bot.*: 172. 1929) of *S. rhombifolia*.

See extensive discussion by Sivarajan & Pradeep (in *Sida* 16: 65. 1995), and the results of a detailed examination of Rodrigo's type by Verdcourt (in *Kew Bull.* 59: 233–234. 2004).

Sida spinosa Linnaeus, *Species Plantarum* 2: 683. 1753.
"Habitat in India utraque." RCN: 5008.
Lectotype (Fawcett & Rendle, *Fl. Jamaica* 5: 111. 1926): Herb. Linn. No. 866.1 (LINN).
Current name: ***Sida spinosa*** L. (Malvaceae).
Note: The type has been figured by Rodrigo (in *Revista Mus. La Plata, Secc. Bot.*, n.s., 6(24): pl. 13. 1944) and Ughborogho (in *Bol. Soc. Brot.*, sér. 2, 54: 15, f. 5a. 1982).

Sida triquetra Linnaeus, *Species Plantarum*, ed. 2, 2: 962. 1763, *nom. illeg.*
"Habitat in America calidiore. D. Jacquin." RCN: 5014.
Replaced synonym: *Sida trisulcata* Jacq. (1760).
Type not designated.
Current name: ***Abutilon trisulcatum*** (Jacq.) Urb. (Malvaceae).
Note: A superfluous name for *S. trisulcata* Jacq. (1760).

Sida umbellata Linnaeus, *Systema Naturae*, ed. 10, 2: 1145. 1759.
["Habitat in Jamaica."] Sp. Pl., ed. 2, 2: 962 (1763). RCN: 5018.
Lectotype (Fryxell in *Syst. Bot. Monogr.* 25: 65. 1988): *Browne*, Herb. Linn. No. 866.16 (LINN).
Current name: ***Pseudabutilon umbellatum*** (L.) Fryxell (Malvaceae).

Sida urens Linnaeus, *Systema Naturae*, ed. 10, 2: 1145. 1759.
["Habitat in Jamaica."] Sp. Pl., ed. 2, 2: 963 (1763). RCN: 5021.
Lectotype (Rodrigo in *Revista Mus. La Plata, Secc. Bot.*, n.s., 6(24): pl. 14. 1944): *Browne*, Herb. Linn. No. 866.20 (LINN).
Current name: ***Sida urens*** L. (Malvaceae).

Sida viscosa Linnaeus, *Systema Naturae*, ed. 10, 2: 1145. 1759.
["Habitat in Jamaica."] Sp. Pl., ed. 2, 2: 963 (1763). RCN: 5016.
Lectotype (Fryxell in *Syst. Bot. Monogr.* 25: 117. 1988): [icon] *"Alcea populifolio, villoso, leviter serrato"* in Sloane, Voy. Jamaica 1: 222, t. 139, f. 4. 1707.
Current name: ***Bastardia viscosa*** (L.) Kunth (Malvaceae).

Sideritis canariensis Linnaeus, *Species Plantarum* 2: 574. 1753.
"Habitat in Canariis." RCN: 4187.
Lectotype (Heuer-Mendoza in *Ber. Schweiz. Bot. Ges.* 84: 278. 1975): Herb. Linn. No. 729.1 (LINN).
Current name: ***Sideritis canariensis*** L. (Lamiaceae).

Sideritis cretica Linnaeus, *Species Plantarum* 2: 574. 1753.
"Habitat in Creta." RCN: 4188.
Lectotype (Heuer-Mendoza in *Ber. Schweiz. Bot. Ges.* 84: 279. 1975): Herb. Linn. No. 729.2 (LINN), see above, right.
Current name: ***Sideritis cretica*** L. (Lamiaceae).

Sideritis hirsuta Linnaeus, *Species Plantarum* 2: 575. 1753.
"Habitat in G. Narbonensi." RCN: 4196.
Lectotype (Rivera Nuñez & Obón de Castro in Jarvis & al., *Regnum Veg.* 127: 88. 1993): Herb. Linn. No. 729.15 (LINN).
Current name: ***Sideritis hirsuta*** L. (Lamiaceae).
Note: Sideritis hirsuta was treated as the generitype by Britton & Brown (*Ill. Fl. N. U. S.*, ed. 2, 3: 111. 1913; see McNeill & al. in *Taxon* 36: 385. 1987). However, under Art. 10.5, Ex. 7 (a voted example) of the Vienna Code, this is a type choice made under the American Code and is to be replaced under Art. 10.5b by Green's choice (*Prop. Brit. Bot.*: 164. 1929) of *S. hyssopifolia* L.

The lectotype of *Sideritis cretica* L.

A discussion of the type elements was provided by Rivera Nuñez & al. (in *Bot. J. Linn. Soc.* 103: 336. 1990).

Sideritis hyssopifolia Linnaeus, *Species Plantarum* 2: 575. 1753.
"Habitat in Hetruria, Pyrenaeis, Thuiri." RCN: 4194.
Lectotype (Obón de Castro & Rivera Nuñez in *Phanerog. Monogr.* 21: 221. 1994): Herb. Clifford: 313, *Sideritis* 3 (BM-000646111).
Generitype of *Sideritis* Linnaeus (vide Green, *Prop. Brit. Bot.*: 164. 1929).
Current name: ***Sideritis hyssopifolia*** L. (Lamiaceae).
Note: Sideritis hirsuta L. was treated as the generitype by Britton & Brown (*Ill. Fl. N. U. S.*, ed. 2, 3: 111. 1913; see McNeill & al. in *Taxon* 36: 385. 1987). However, under Art. 10.5, Ex. 7 (a voted example) of the Vienna Code, this is a type choice made under the American Code and is to be replaced under Art. 10.5b by Green's choice (*Prop. Brit. Bot.*: 164. 1929) of *S. hyssopifolia* L.

Sideritis incana Linnaeus, *Species Plantarum*, ed. 2, 2: 802. 1763.
"Habitat in Hispania. Loefling, Alstroemer." RCN: 4193.
Lectotype (Peris & al. in *Bot. J. Linn. Soc.* 103: 7. 1990): *Löfling 424a*, Herb. Linn. No. 729.9 (LINN).
Current name: ***Sideritis incana*** L. (Lamiaceae).

Sideritis lanata Linnaeus, *Flora Palaestina*: 22. 1756.
"Habitat Palaestinae." RCN: 4197.
Lectotype (Rivera Nuñez & Obón de Castro in Jarvis & al. in *Taxon* 50: 519. 2001): *Hasselquist*, Herb. Linn. No. 729.17 (LINN; iso-UPS-HASSELQ 478).
Current name: ***Sideritis lanata*** L. (Lamiaceae).

Sideritis montana Linnaeus, *Species Plantarum* 2: 575. 1753.
"Habitat in Italia." RCN: 4191.
Lectotype (Siddiqi in Jafri & El-Gadi, *Fl. Libya* 118: 61. 1985): Herb. Linn. No. 729.6 (LINN).
Current name: ***Sideritis montana*** L. (Lamiaceae).

Sideritis ocymastrum Linnaeus, *Systema Naturae*, ed. 10, 2: 1098. 1759.
["Habitat in Hispania."] Sp. Pl. 2: 580 (1753). RCN: 4244.
Replaced synonym: *Galeopsis hirsuta* L. (1753).
Lectotype (Turland in Jarvis & al. in *Taxon* 50: 511. 2001): Herb. Linn. No. 736.16 (LINN).
Current name: ***Stachys ocymastrum*** (L.) Briq. (Lamiaceae).
Note: A *nomen novum* for *Galeopsis hirsuta* L. (1753), the epithet being pre-occupied in *Sideritis* by *S. hirsuta* L. (1753). Linnaeus illegitimately renamed the species as *Stachys hirta* in *Sp. Pl.*, ed. 2, 2: 813 (1763).

Sideritis perfoliata Linnaeus, *Species Plantarum* 2: 575. 1753.
"Habitat in Oriente?" RCN: 4190.
Lectotype (Rivera Nuñez & Obón de Castro in Jarvis & al. in *Taxon* 50: 519. 2001): Herb. Linn. No. 729.5 (LINN).
Current name: ***Sideritis perfoliata*** L. (Lamiaceae).

Sideritis romana Linnaeus, *Species Plantarum* 2: 575. 1753.
"Habitat in agris Europae australis." RCN: 4192.
Lectotype (Rivera Nuñez & Obón de Castro in Jarvis & al. in *Taxon* 50: 519. 2001): Herb. Clifford: 313, *Cunila* 1 (BM-000646113).
Current name: ***Sideritis romana*** L. (Lamiaceae).
Note: Socorro & al. (in *Lagascalia* 14: 98. 1986) indicated Herb. Linn. 729.6 (LINN) as the type, but this material is associated with *S. montana* L. (for which it is the type), and it is not original material for *S. romana*.

Sideritis scordioides Linnaeus, *Systema Naturae*, ed. 10, 2: 1098. 1759.
["Habitat Monspelii. D. Sauvages."] Sp. Pl., ed. 2, 2: 803 (1763). RCN: 4195.
Lectotype (Obón de Castro & Rivera Nuñez in *Phanerog. Monogr.* 21: 223. 1994): Herb. Linn. No. 729.12, left specimen (LINN).
Current name: ***Sideritis hyssopifolia*** L. (Lamiaceae).

Sideritis syriaca Linnaeus, *Species Plantarum* 2: 574. 1753.
"Habitat in Creta." RCN: 4189.
Lectotype (Rivera Nuñez & Obón de Castro in Jarvis & al. in *Taxon* 50: 520. 2001): Herb. Burser XIII: 97 (UPS).
Current name: ***Sideritis syriaca*** L. (Lamiaceae).

Sideroxylon decandrum Linnaeus, *Systema Naturae*, ed. 12, 2: 178; *Mantissa Plantarum*: 48. 1767.
"Habitat in America septentrionali." RCN: 1548b.
Type not designated.
Original material: *Kalm*, Herb. Linn. No. 261.9 (LINN).
Current name: ***Sideroxylon lycioides*** L. (Sapotaceae).

Sideroxylon inerme Linnaeus, *Species Plantarum* 1: 192. 1753.
"Habitat in Aethiopia." RCN: 1543.
Lectotype (Meeuse in *Bothalia* 7: 325. 1960): Herb. Linn. No. 261.1 (LINN).

Generitype of *Sideroxylon* Linnaeus (vide Baillon, *Bull. Mens. Soc. Linn. Paris* 114: 908. 1891).
Current name: ***Sideroxylon inerme*** L. (Sapotaceae).

Sideroxylon lycioides Linnaeus, *Species Plantarum*, ed. 2, 1: 279. 1762.
"Habitat in Canada." RCN: 1546.
Type not designated.
Original material: Herb. Linn. No. 94.19 (S); Herb. Linn. No. 261.6 (LINN); [icon] in Duhamel, Traité Arbr. Arbust. 2: 260, t. 68. 1755.
Current name: ***Sideroxylon lycioides*** L. (Sapotaceae).
Note: Pennington (*Fl. Neotropica* 52: 170. 1990) indicated unspecified material in LINN as the holotype but did not distinguish between sheets 261.6 and 261.7. As they are evidently not part of a single gathering, Art. 9.15 does not apply and the name remains untypified.

Sideroxylon melanophleos Linnaeus, *Systema Naturae*, ed. 12, 2: 178; *Mantissa Plantarum*: 48. 1767.
"Habitat ad Cap. b. spei. David v. Royen." RCN: 1544.
Lectotype (Dyer in Dyer & al., *Fl. Southern Africa* 26: 8. 1963): Herb. Linn. No. 261.3 (LINN).
Current name: ***Rapanea melanophleos*** (L.) Mez (Sapotaceae).

Sideroxylon mite Linnaeus, *Systema Naturae*, ed. 12, 2: 178. 1767. RCN: 1542.
Neotype (Verdcourt in *Kew Bull.* 21: 243. 1967): Herb. Linn. No. 261.2 (LINN).
Current name: ***Ilex mitis*** (L.) Radlk. (Aquifoliaceae).

Sideroxylon spinosum Linnaeus, *Species Plantarum* 1: 193. 1753.
"Habitat in Malabaria." RCN: 1547.
Lectotype (Wijnands, *Bot. Commelins*: 186. 1983): Herb. Clifford: 69, *Sideroxylon* 2 (BM-000558091).
Current name: ***Argania spinosa*** (L.) Skeels (Sapotaceae).

Sideroxylon tenax Linnaeus, *Systema Naturae*, ed. 12, 2: 178; *Mantissa Plantarum*: 48. 1767.
"Habitat in Carolinae siccioribus. D. Garden." RCN: 1545.
Lectotype (Pennington, *Fl. Neotropica* 52: 169. 1990): Herb. Linn. No. 261.5 (LINN).
Current name: ***Sideroxylon tenax*** L. (Sapotaceae).

Sigesbeckia occidentalis Linnaeus, *Species Plantarum* 2: 900. 1753.
"Habitat in Virginia." RCN: 6517.
Lectotype (Reveal & al. in *Huntia* 7: 218. 1987): *Clayton 511*, Herb. Linn. No. 1018.2 (LINN; iso- BM).
Current name: ***Verbesina occidentalis*** (L.) Walter (Asteraceae).

Sigesbeckia orientalis Linnaeus, *Species Plantarum* 2: 900. 1753.
"Habitat in China, Media ad pagos." RCN: 6516.
Lectotype (Stearn, *Introd. Linnaeus' Sp. Pl.* (Ray Soc. ed.): 47. 1957): [icon] *"Sigesbeckia"* in Linnaeus, Hort. Cliff.: 412, t. 23. 1738.
Generitype of *Sigesbeckia* Linnaeus (vide Steudel, *Nom.* 1: 777. 1821).
Current name: ***Sigesbeckia orientalis*** L. (Asteraceae).
Note: McVaugh & Anderson (in *Contr. Univ. Mich. Herb.* 9: 488. 1972) indicated 1018.1 LINN as type, but this choice is pre-dated by that of Stearn.

Silene acaulis (Linnaeus) Linnaeus, *Species Plantarum*, ed. 2, 1: 603. 1762.
"Habitat in Alpibus Lapponicis, Austriacis, Helveticis, Pyrenaeis." RCN: 3272.
Basionym: *Cucubalus acaulis* L. (1753).

S

Lectotype (Talavera & Muñoz Garmendia in *Anales Jard. Bot. Madrid* 45: 445. 1989): Herb. Linn. No. 583.61, upper specimen (LINN).
Current name: ***Silene acaulis*** (L.) Jacq. subsp. ***acaulis*** (Caryophyllaceae).

Silene amoena Linnaeus, *Species Plantarum* 1: 417. 1753.
"Habitat in Tataria." RCN: 3246.
Lectotype (Lazkov in *Byull. Moskovsk. Obshch. Isp. Prir., Otd. Biol.* 104(2): 39. 1999): Herb. Linn. No. 583.19 (LINN).
Current name: ***Silene amoena*** L. (Caryophyllaceae).

Silene anglica Linnaeus, *Species Plantarum* 1: 416. 1753, *nom. rej.*
"Habitat in Anglia, Gallia." RCN: 3238.
Lectotype (Talavera & Muñoz Garmendia in *Anales Jard. Bot. Madrid* 45: 408. 1989): Herb. Linn. No. 583.1 (LINN).
Generitype of *Silene* Linnaeus, *nom. cons.* (vide Green, *Prop. Brit. Bot.*: 155. 1929).
Current name: ***Silene gallica*** L. (Caryophyllaceae).
Note: Silene Linnaeus, *nom. cons.* against *Lychnis* Linnaeus. *Silene gallica* L. is conserved against *S. anglica.*

Silene antirrhina Linnaeus, *Species Plantarum* 1: 419. 1753.
"Habitat in Virginia, Carolina." RCN: 3260.
Lectotype (Rabeler in Cafferty & Jarvis in *Taxon* 53: 1053. 2004): Herb. Linn. No. 583.42 (LINN).
Current name: ***Silene antirrhina*** L. (Caryophyllaceae).

Silene armeria Linnaeus, *Species Plantarum* 1: 420. 1753.
"Habitat in Anglia, Gallia." RCN: 3267.
Lectotype (Talavera & Muñoz Garmendia in *Anales Jard. Bot. Madrid* 45: 435. 1989): Herb. Linn. No. 583.49 (LINN).
Current name: ***Silene armeria*** L. (Caryophyllaceae).

Silene behen Linnaeus, *Species Plantarum* 1: 418. 1753.
"Habitat in Creta." RCN: 3255.
Lectotype (Talavera & Muñoz Garmendia in *Anales Jard. Bot. Madrid* 45: 439. 1989): Herb. Linn. No. 583.32 (LINN).
Current name: ***Silene behen*** L. (Caryophyllaceae).
Note: Ghafoor (in Jafri & El-Gadi, *Fl. Libya* 59: 65. 1978) indicated "582.3" LINN as type. Presumably an error for either sheet 582.31 or 582.32, his statement nevertheless fails to distinguish between these two collections.

Silene bupleuroides Linnaeus, *Species Plantarum* 1: 421. 1753.
"Habitat in Persia." RCN: 3249.
Lectotype (Melzheimer in Rechinger, *Fl. Iranica* 163: 399. 1988): Herb. Linn. No. 583.25 (LINN; iso- BM?).
Current name: ***Silene bupleuroides*** L. (Caryophyllaceae).
Note: Chowdhuri (in *Notes Roy. Bot. Gard. Edinburgh* 22: 255. 1957) indicated Clifford material at BM as type but did not distinguish between two relevant sheets there. They are evidently not part of a single gathering so Art. 9.15 does not apply. Although Greuter (in Strid & Kit Tan, *Fl. Hellenica* 1: 264. 1997) indicated one of the two sheets as lectotype, Melzheimer (in Rechinger, *Fl. Iranica* 163: 399. 1988) had in the meantime designated material in LINN as the lectotype, and this choice has priority.

Silene cerastoides Linnaeus, *Species Plantarum* 1: 417. 1753.
"Habitat in Europa australi." RCN: 3243.
Lectotype (Talavera & Muñoz Garmendia in *Anales Jard. Bot. Madrid* 45: 408. 1989): Herb. Linn. No. 583.14 (LINN).
Current name: ***Silene gallica*** L. (Caryophyllaceae).
Note: Greuter (in *Taxon* 44: 102. 1995) proposed the rejection of the name to prevent its possible replacement of *S. gallica* L. However, the Committee for Spermatophyta (in *Taxon* 46: 324. 1997) declined to approve its rejection against *S. gallica* as the application of *S.*

cerastoides was felt to be still unclear. Ghafoor (in Jafri & El-Gadi, *Fl. Libya* 59: 69. 1978) indicated 583.13 (LINN) as type, but this collection lacks a relevant *Species Plantarum* number (i.e. "6"), is a later addition to the collection and is not original material for the name.

Silene conica Linnaeus, *Species Plantarum* 1: 418. 1753.
"Habitat in Hispania, Galloprovincia." RCN: 3254.
Lectotype (Melzheimer in Rechinger, *Fl. Iranica* 163: 483. 1988): Herb. Linn. No. 583.30 (LINN).
Current name: ***Silene conica*** L. (Caryophyllaceae).
Note: Talavera & Muñoz Garmendia (in *Anales Jard. Bot. Madrid* 45: 457. 1989) indicated Burser material (UPS) as the lectotype but their choice is pre-dated by that of Melzheimer.

Silene conoidea Linnaeus, *Species Plantarum* 1: 418. 1753.
"Habitat inter segetes Hispaniae." RCN: 3253.
Lectotype (Burtt & Lewis in *Kew Bull.* 7: 343. 1952): Herb. Linn. No. 583.29 (LINN).
Current name: ***Silene conoidea*** L. (Caryophyllaceae).

Silene crassifolia Linnaeus, *Species Plantarum*, ed. 2, 1: 597. 1762.
"Habitat ad Cap. b. spei." RCN: 3251.
Neotype (Cupido in Cafferty & Jarvis in *Taxon* 53: 1053. 2004): South Africa. Western Cape, Strandfontein, sand dunes, 21 Dec 1941, *Compton 12781* (NBG).
Current name: ***Silene crassifolia*** L. (Caryophyllaceae).

Silene cretica Linnaeus, *Species Plantarum* 1: 420. 1753.
"Habitat in Creta." RCN: 3264.
Lectotype (Talavera & Muñoz Garmendia in *Anales Jard. Bot. Madrid* 45: 439. 1989): Herb. Linn. No. 583.46 (LINN).
Current name: ***Silene cretica*** L. (Caryophyllaceae).

Silene fruticosa Linnaeus, *Species Plantarum* 1: 417. 1753.
"Habitat in Sicilia." RCN: 3248.
Lectotype (Ghafoor in Jafri & El-Gadi, *Fl. Libya* 59: 84. 1978): Herb. Linn. No. 583.24 (LINN).
Current name: ***Silene fruticosa*** L. (Caryophyllaceae).
Note: The Boccone plate, cited in synonymy by Linnaeus, is reproduced by Lack (in *Ann. Naturhist. Mus. Wien* 104 B: 454, Abb. 7. 2003), along with voucher material from the Austrian National Library in Vienna (Abb. 8).

Silene gallica Linnaeus, *Species Plantarum* 1: 417. 1753, *nom. cons.*
"Habitat in Gallia." RCN: 3242.
Lectotype (Greuter in *Taxon* 44: 102. 1995): Herb. Linn. No. 583.11 (LINN).
Current name: ***Silene gallica*** L. (Caryophyllaceae).
Note: Silene gallica is conserved against *S. anglica* L. (1753), *S. lusitanica* L. (1753) and *S. quinquevulnera* L. (1753).

Silene gigantea Linnaeus, *Species Plantarum* 1: 418; *Species Plantarum* 2: 1231. 1753, *nom. inval.*
"Habitat in Lusitania." RCN: 3250.
Type not relevant.
Current name: ***Silene gigantea*** (L.) L. (Caryophyllaceae).
Note: Linnaeus transferred this taxon to *Cucubalus*, as *C. giganteus* L., in the Errata of *Sp. Pl.* 2: 1231 (1753); see Greuter (in *Boissiera* 13: 137. 1967).

Silene gigantea (Linnaeus) Linnaeus, *Systema Naturae*, ed. 10, 2: 1031. 1759.
["Habitat in Lusitania."] Sp. Pl. 1: 418; 2: Errata (1753). RCN: 3250.
Basionym: *Cucubalus giganteus* L. (1753).

Lectotype (Greuter in *Willdenowia* 25: 113. 1995): Herb. Linn. No. 583.26 (LINN).
Current name: **Silene gigantea** (L.) L. (Caryophyllaceae).

Silene inaperta Linnaeus, *Species Plantarum* 1: 419. 1753.
"Habitat in Europa australi." RCN: 3262.
Lectotype (Talavera & Muñoz Garmendia in *Anales Jard. Bot. Madrid* 45: 437. 1989): [icon] *"Viscago laevis, inaperto flore"* in Dillenius, Hort. Eltham. 2: 424, t. 315, f. 407. 1732.
Current name: **Silene inaperta** L. (Caryophyllaceae).

Silene lusitanica Linnaeus, *Species Plantarum* 1: 416. 1753, *nom. rej.*
"Habitat in Lusitania." RCN: 3239.
Lectotype (Talavera & Muñoz Garmendia in *Anales Jard. Bot. Madrid* 45: 408. 1989): Herb. Linn. No. 583.6 (LINN).
Current name: **Silene gallica** L. (Caryophyllaceae).
Note: Silene lusitanica is rejected against *S. gallica* L. (1753).

Silene muscipula Linnaeus, *Species Plantarum* 1: 420. 1753.
"Habitat in Hispania, G. Narbonensi." RCN: 3265.
Lectotype (Talavera & Muñoz Garmendia in *Anales Jard. Bot. Madrid* 45: 439. 1989): [icon] *"Lychnis silvestr. III"* in Clusius, Rar. Pl. Hist. 1: 288, 289. 1601.
Current name: **Silene muscipula** L. (Caryophyllaceae).

Silene mutabilis Linnaeus, *Centuria II Plantarum*: 16. 1756.
"Habitat in Italia." RCN: 3244.
Type not designated.
Original material: Herb. Linn. No. 583.16 (LINN).
Current name: **Silene nocturna** L. (Caryophyllaceae).

Silene noctiflora Linnaeus, *Species Plantarum* 1: 419. 1753.
"Habitat in Suecia, Germania." RCN: 3258.
Lectotype (Jonsell & Jarvis in *Nordic J. Bot.* 14: 159. 1994): Herb. Linn. No. 183.17 (S).
Current name: **Silene noctiflora** L. (Caryophyllaceae).
Note: Melzheimer (in Rechinger, *Fl. Iranica* 163: 474. 1988) indicated unspecified material in LINN as the type. However, the only material associated with this name, 583.36 (LINN), lacks a *Species Plantarum* number (i.e. "15"), is a post-1753 addition to the herbarium, and is not original material for the name.

Silene nocturna Linnaeus, *Species Plantarum* 1: 416. 1753.
"Habitat in Italia, Pensylvania." RCN: 3241.
Lectotype (Ghafoor in Jafri & El-Gadi, *Fl. Libya* 59: 91. 1978): Herb. Linn. No. 583.8 (LINN).
Current name: **Silene nocturna** L. (Caryophyllaceae).

Silene nutans Linnaeus, *Species Plantarum* 1: 417. 1753.
"Habitat in Europae borealis pratis aridis." RCN: 3245.
Lectotype (Hepper in *Watsonia* 2: 81. 1951; Jeanmonod & Bocquet in *Candollea* 38: 287. 1983): Herb. Linn. No. 583.18, middle specimen (LINN).
Current name: **Silene nutans** L. (Caryophyllaceae).
Note: The sheet designated as the type by Hepper bears three specimens, to the middle of which Jeanmonod & Bocquet restricted the type choice. The same authors (in *Candollea* 38: 394, f. 4. 1983) also illustrate the type.

Silene paradoxa Linnaeus, *Species Plantarum,* ed. 2, 2: 1673. 1763.
"Habitat in Italia." RCN: 3247.
Lectotype (Jeanmonod in *Candollea* 40: 22, f. 4A. 1985): Herb. Linn. No. 583.22 (LINN).
Current name: **Silene paradoxa** L. (Caryophyllaceae).

Silene pendula Linnaeus, *Species Plantarum* 1: 418. 1753.
"Habitat in Creta & Sicilia." RCN: 3257.
Lectotype (Talavera in *Lagascalia* 8: 162. 1979): Herb. Linn. No. 583.35 (LINN).
Current name: **Silene pendula** L. (Caryophyllaceae).

Silene polyphylla Linnaeus, *Species Plantarum* 1: 420. 1753, *nom. utique rej.*
"Habitat in Pannonia, Austria, Bohemia." RCN: 3266.
Type not designated.
Original material: [icon] in Clusius, Rar. Pl. Hist. 1: 290. 1601.
Current name: **Silene portensis** L. (Caryophyllaceae).

Silene porrigens Linnaeus, *Systema Naturae,* ed. 12, 3: 230. 1768.
"Habitat in Oriente. Gouan." RCN: 3198.
Basionym of: *Saponaria porrigens* (L.) L. (1771).
Lectotype (Burtt & Lewis in *Kew Bull.* 7: 333. 1952): Herb. Linn. No. 580.5 (LINN).
Current name: **Gypsophila porrigens** (L.) Boiss. (Caryophyllaceae).

Silene portensis Linnaeus, *Species Plantarum* 1: 420, Err. 1753, *nom. inval.*
"Habitat in Lusitania. Loefl." RCN: 3263.
Type not relevant.

S

Note: In the Errata to *Species Plantarum*, Linnaeus included *S. portensis* in the synonymy of *S. inaperta* L., so *S. portensis* is invalid in 1753. However, the binomial was validly published in 1762.

Silene portensis Linnaeus, *Species Plantarum*, ed. 2, 1: 600. 1762.
"Habitat in Lusitania." RCN: 3263.
Neotype (Cafferty & al. in *Taxon* 50: 924. 2001): Portugal. "Porto; auf sandigen Hügeln. 6.91" (Baenitz Herbarium Euroapeum No. 7257), *Buchtien, s.n.* (UPS).
Current name: **Silene portensis** L. (Caryophyllaceae).

Silene quadrifida (Linnaeus) Linnaeus, *Systema Naturae*, ed. 10, 2: 1032. 1759.
["Habitat in Styriae monte ad oppidum Eisenertz."] Sp. Pl. 1: 415 (1753). RCN: 3268.
Basionym: *Cucubalus quadrifidus* L. (1753).
Lectotype (Melzheimer & Polatschek in *Phyton (Horn)* 31: 285. 1992): [icon] *"Caryophyllus minimus humilis alter exoticus flore candido amoeno"* in Plantin, Pl. Stirp. Icon.: 445. 1581.
Current name: **Silene quadrifida** (L.) L. (Caryophyllaceae).

Silene quinquevulnera Linnaeus, *Species Plantarum* 1: 416. 1753, *nom. rej.*
"Habitat in Hispania, Lusatia, Italia, Gallia." RCN: 3240.
Lectotype (Talavera & Muñoz Garmendia in *Anales Jard. Bot. Madrid* 45: 409. 1989): Herb. Burser XI: 72 (UPS).
Current name: **Silene gallica** L. (Caryophyllaceae).

Silene rigidula Linnaeus, *Centuria II Plantarum*: 16. 1756.
RCN: 3243.
Lectotype (Talavera & Muñoz Garmendia in *Anales Jard. Bot. Madrid* 45: 408. 1989): Herb. Linn. No. 583.13 (LINN).
Current name: **Silene gallica** L. (Caryophyllaceae).

Silene rubella Linnaeus, *Species Plantarum* 1: 419. 1753, *nom. utique rej.*
"Habitat in Lusitania." RCN: 3261.
Lectotype (Oxelman & Lidén in *Taxon* 36: 477. 1987): Herb. Linn. No. 583.43 (LINN).
Current name: **Silene diversifolia** Otth (Caryophyllaceae).

Silene rupestris Linnaeus, *Species Plantarum* 1: 421. 1753.
"Habitat in montibus aridis Sueciae, Helvetiae." RCN: 3269.
Lectotype (Talavera & Muñoz Garmendia in *Anales Jard. Bot. Madrid* 45: 445. 1989): Herb. Linn. No. 583.50 (LINN).
Current name: **Silene rupestris** L. (Caryophyllaceae).

Silene saxifraga Linnaeus, *Species Plantarum* 1: 421. 1753.
"Habitat in montibus cretaceis Galliae, Italiae." RCN: 3270.
Lectotype (Talavera & Muñoz Garmendia in *Anales Jard. Bot. Madrid* 45: 443. 1989): Herb. Burser XI: 128 (UPS).
Current name: **Silene saxifraga** L. (Caryophyllaceae).

Silene stricta Linnaeus, *Centuria II Plantarum*: 17. 1756.
"Habitat in Tolosae Burserus, in Hispania. Loefling." RCN: 3256.
Lectotype (Talavera & Muñoz Garmendia in *Anales Jard. Bot. Madrid* 45: 439. 1989): *Löfling 318*, Herb. Linn. No. 583.33 (LINN).
Current name: **Silene stricta** L. (Caryophyllaceae).

Silene vallesia Linnaeus, *Systema Naturae*, ed. 10, 2: 1032. 1759.
["Habitat in Alpibus Vallesiacis, Valdensibus. Allioni."] Sp. Pl., ed. 2, 1: 603 (1762). RCN: 3271.
Lectotype (Cecchi in Ferrarini & Cecchi in *Webbia* 56: 245. 2001): Herb. Linn. No. 185.1 (S).
Current name: **Silene vallesia** L. subsp. **vallesia** (Caryophyllaceae).

Note: Cecchi, in her formal type designation, gives LINN as the location of the type. However, as she also listed three numbered sheets with their correct herbaria in her discussion, this is treated as a correctable error.

Silene virginica Linnaeus, *Species Plantarum* 1: 419. 1753.
"Habitat in Virginia." RCN: 3259.
Lectotype (Rabeler in Cafferty & Jarvis in *Taxon* 53: 1053. 2004): *Clayton 423* (BM-000051556).
Current name: **Silene virginica** L. (Caryophyllaceae).
Note: Although Howard & Staples (in *J. Arnold Arbor.* 64: 521. 1983) noted the existence of material in LINN, they did not indicate any of it as the type.

Silene viridiflora Linnaeus, *Species Plantarum*, ed. 2, 1: 597. 1762.
"Habitat in Lusitania." RCN: 3252.
Lectotype (Greuter in Strid & Kit Tan, *Fl. Hellenica* 1: 251. 1997): Herb. Clifford: 171, *Silene 2* (BM-000628521).
Current name: **Silene viridiflora** L. (Caryophyllaceae).
Note: Jeanmonod (in *Candollea* 40: 16. 1985) indicated Herb. Linn. 183.3 (S) as the holotype but the sheet is unannotated by Linnaeus and is not original material for the name.

Silphium asteriscus Linnaeus, *Species Plantarum* 2: 920. 1753.
"Habitat in Virginia, Carolina." RCN: 6649.

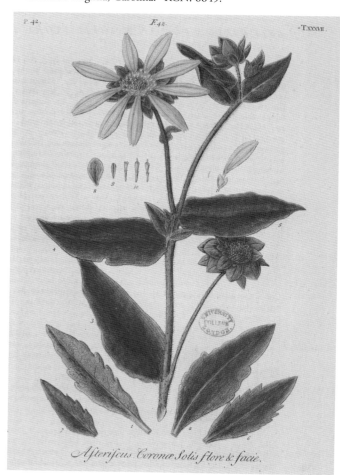

Asteriscus Coronae Solis flore & facie.

Lectotype (Perry in *Rhodora* 39: 292. 1937): [icon] *"Asteriscus Coronae Solis flore & facie"* in Dillenius, Hort. Eltham. 1: 42, t. 37, f. 42. 1732. – Typotype: Herb. Sherard No. 1977 (OXF).

Generitype of *Silphium* Linnaeus (vide Green, *Prop. Brit. Bot.*: 183. 1929).
Current name: ***Silphium asteriscus*** L. var. ***asteriscus*** (Asteraceae).

Silphium connatum Linnaeus, *Mantissa Plantarum Altera*: 574. 1771.
"Habitat in America." RCN: 6648.
Neotype (Reveal in Jarvis & Turland in *Taxon* 47: 367. 1998): Herb. Linn. No. 1032.5 (LINN).
Current name: ***Silphium perfoliatum*** L. var. ***connatum*** (L.) Cronquist (Asteraceae).

Silphium helianthoides Linnaeus, *Species Plantarum* 2: 920. 1753.
"Habitat in Virginia." RCN: 6650.
Lectotype (Reveal in *Taxon* 32: 653. 1983): *Clayton 610* (BM-000051689).
Current name: ***Heliopsis helianthoides*** (L.) Sweet (Asteraceae).

Silphium laciniatum Linnaeus, *Species Plantarum* 2: 919. 1753.
"Habitat in America septentrionali, Misissipi. Collinson." RCN: 6646.
Lectotype (Reveal in Jarvis & Turland in *Taxon* 47: 367. 1998): Herb. Linn. No. 1032.2 (LINN).
Current name: ***Silphium laciniatum*** L. var. ***laciniatum*** (Asteraceae).

Silphium perfoliatum Linnaeus, *Systema Naturae*, ed. 10, 2: 1232. 1759.
["Habitat in Misisippi."] Sp. Pl., ed. 2, 2: 1302 (1763). RCN: 6647.
Lectotype (Reveal in Jarvis & Turland in *Taxon* 47: 367. 1998): Herb. Linn. No. 1032.3 (LINN).
Current name: ***Silphium perfoliatum*** L. var. ***perfoliatum*** (Asteraceae).

Silphium solidaginoides Linnaeus, *Species Plantarum* 2: 920. 1753.
"Habitat in Virginia. D. Gronovius." RCN: 6650.
Lectotype (Reveal in *Taxon* 32: 653. 1983): Herb. Linn. No. 1032.7 (LINN).
Current name: ***Heliopsis helianthoides*** (L.) Sweet (Asteraceae).

Silphium trifoliatum Linnaeus, *Species Plantarum* 2: 920. 1753.
"Habitat in Virginia." RCN: 6651.
Lectotype (Reveal in Jarvis & Turland in *Taxon* 47: 367. 1998): Herb. Linn. No. 1032.8 (LINN).
Current name: ***Silphium trifoliatum*** L. var. ***trifoliatum*** (Asteraceae).

Silphium trilobatum Linnaeus, *Systema Naturae*, ed. 10, 2: 1233. 1759.
["Habitat in America."] Sp. Pl., ed. 2, 2: 1303 (1763). RCN: 6652.
Lectotype (Howard, *Fl. Lesser Antilles* 6: 616. 1989): [icon] *"Buphthalmum caule repente"* in Plumier in Burman, Pl. Amer.: 97, t. 107, f. 2. 1757.
Current name: ***Sphagneticola trilobata*** (L.) Pruski (Asteraceae).
Note: Moore (in Fawcett & Rendle, *Fl. Jamaica* 7: 227. 1936) noted the existence of 1032.9 (LINN) but did not indicate it as type. Similarly, although D'Arcy (in *Ann. Missouri Bot. Gard.* 62: 1168. 1975) suggested the name was based on a Plumier plate, he did not designate it as type, and Howard appears to have been the first to formalise a choice.

Sinapis alba Linnaeus, *Species Plantarum* 2: 668. 1753.
"Habitat in agris Belgii, Angliae, Galliae." RCN: 4863.
Lectotype (Jafri in Nasir & Ali, *Fl. W. Pakistan* 55: 29. 1973): Herb. Linn. No. 845.4 (LINN).
Generitype of *Sinapis* Linnaeus (vide Green, *Prop. Brit. Bot.*: 172. 1929).
Current name: ***Sinapis alba*** L. (Brassicaceae).

Note: Baillargeon (in *Taxon* 37: 969. 1988), believing *S. nigra* L. to be the generitype, proposed *Sinapis* for conservation with *S. alba* as its conserved type. However, the Committee for Spermatophyta (in *Taxon* 42: 688. 1993) declined to support the proposal, ruling it unnecessary.

Sinapis arvensis Linnaeus, *Species Plantarum* 2: 668. 1753.
"Habitat in agris Europae." RCN: 4860.
Lectotype (Jafri in Nasir & Ali, *Fl. W. Pakistan* 55: 29. 1973): Herb. Linn. No. 845.2 (LINN).
Current name: ***Sinapis arvensis*** L. (Brassicaceae).

Sinapis brassicata Linnaeus, *Systema Naturae*, ed. 12, 3: 231. 1768.
"Habitat in China." RCN: 4862.
Neotype (Al-Shehbaz in Cafferty & Jarvis in *Taxon* 51: 535. 2002): China. Kwangtung Province, Honam, 22 Feb 1922, *Kang Peng s.n.* (BM-000576292; iso- IBSC).
Current name: ***Brassica oleracea*** L. (Brassicaceae).
Note: Bailey (in *Gentes Herb.* 1: 101. 1922), in the absence of any herbarium material or cited illustrations, treated this as a *nomen dubium*. The neotype designated by Al-Shehbaz reduces the name to a synonym of *B. oleracea*.

Sinapis chinensis Linnaeus, *Systema Naturae*, ed. 12, 2: 445; *Mantissa Plantarum*: 95. 1767.
"Habitat in China? Arduini." RCN: 4867.
Lectotype (Al-Shehbaz in Cafferty & Jarvis in *Taxon* 51: 535. 2002): *Arduino s.n.*, Herb. Linn. No. 845.9 (LINN).
Current name: ***Brassica tournefortii*** Gouan (Brassicaceae).
Note: Bailey (in *Gentes Herb.* 1: 93. 1922) suggested that Linnaeus had based this on an Arduino description, and noted the existence of an Arduino collection in LINN but did not designate a type. Although Burtt & Lewis (in *Kew Bull.* 4: 285. 1949) referred to material in LINN as "the type specimen", they did not distinguish between sheets 845.9 and 845.10 (which are evidently not part of the same gathering so Art. 9.15 does not apply).

Sinapis erucoides Linnaeus, *Centuria II Plantarum*: 24. 1756.
"Habitat in Italia, Hispania ad vias, vineas." RCN: 4869.
Lectotype (Martínez-Laborde in Cafferty & Jarvis in *Taxon* 51: 535. 2002): Herb. Linn. No. 845.14 (LINN).
Current name: ***Diplotaxis erucoides*** (L.) DC. (Brassicaceae).

Sinapis hispanica Linnaeus, *Species Plantarum* 2: 669. 1753.
"Habitat in Hispania." RCN: 4870.
Lectotype (Burtt & Lewis in *Kew Bull.* 4: 288. 1949): Herb. Clifford: 338, *Sinapis* 4 (BM-000646361).
Current name: ***Erucaria hispanica*** (L.) Druce (Brassicaceae).

Sinapis incana Linnaeus, *Centuria I Plantarum*: 19. 1755.
"Habitat in Gallia, Lusitania, Hispania." RCN: 4871.
Lectotype (Gómez-Campo in Cafferty & Jarvis in *Taxon* 51: 535. 2002): [icon] *"Erysimum brevissimis siliquis subincanum"* in Hermann, Parad. Bat.: 155. 1698.
Current name: ***Hirschfeldia incana*** (L.) Lagr.-Foss. (Brassicaceae).
Note: Jafri (in *Fl. Libya* 23: 27. 1977) designated Herb. Linn. No. 845.16 (LINN) as type, evidently unaware that the material is identifiable as *Brassica nigra* (L.) Koch. The other original element, however, the cited Hermann plate, does correspond with current usage. Although there are few characters in the protologue that allow the two taxa to be distinguished, Linnaeus (1755: 20) did refer to "Folia canescentia", a character pointing strongly to *H. incana* but not to *B. nigra*. Gómez-Campo therefore rejected Jafri's typification in favour of the Hermann plate, in accordance with Art. 9.17(b), in order to preserve nomenclatural stability.

S

Sinapis juncea Linnaeus, *Species Plantarum* 2: 668. 1753.
"Habitat in Asia." RCN: 4868.
Lectotype (Bailey in *Gentes Herb.* 1: 95. 1922): Herb. Linn. No. 845.11 (LINN).
Current name: ***Brassica juncea*** (L.) Czern. (Brassicaceae).

Sinapis laevigata Linnaeus, *Centuria I Plantarum*: 20. 1755.
"Habitat in Lusitania, Hispania." RCN: 4872.
Type not designated.
Original material: Herb. Linn. No. 845.17 (LINN); [icon] in Hermann, Parad. Bat.: 155. 1698.
Current name: ***Erucastrum virgatum*** C. Presl (Brassicaceae).
Note: This name has been informally rejected as a *nomen ambiguum* by the majority of recent authors.

Sinapis nigra Linnaeus, *Species Plantarum* 2: 668. 1753.
"Habitat in aggeribus ruderatis Europae septentrionalioris." RCN: 4864.
Lectotype (Jonsell & Jarvis in *Nordic J. Bot.* 22: 71. 2002): Herb. Clifford: 338, *Sinapis* 2 (BM-000646359).
Current name: ***Brassica nigra*** (L.) W.D.J. Koch (Brassicaceae).

Sinapis orientalis Linnaeus, *Centuria I Plantarum*: 19. 1755.
"Habitat in Oriente." RCN: 4861.
Lectotype (Hedge in Cafferty & Jarvis in *Taxon* 51: 535. 2002): Herb. Linn. No. 845.3 (LINN).
Current name: ***Sinapis arvensis*** L. var. ***orientalis*** (L.) W.D.J. Koch & Ziz (Brassicaceae).

Sinapis pubescens Linnaeus, *Systema Naturae,* ed. 12, 2: 445; *Mantissa Plantarum*: 95. 1767.
"Habitat in Siciliae monte Bussambarensi. Arduin." RCN: 4866.
Lectotype (Jafri in Ali & Jafri, *Fl. Libya* 23: 24. 1977): *Arduino 50,* Herb. Linn. No. 845.7 (LINN).
Current name: ***Sinapis pubescens*** L. (Brassicaceae).

Sinapis pyrenaica Linnaeus, *Species Plantarum,* ed. 2, 2: 934. 1763.
"Habitat in Pyrenaeis. D. Monnier." RCN: 4865.
Lectotype (Pujadas Salvà in Cafferty & Jarvis in *Taxon* 51: 535. 2002): Herb. Linn. No. 845.5 (LINN).
Current name: ***Sisymbrium austriacum*** Jacq. subsp. ***chrysanthemum*** (Jord.) Rouy & Foucaud (Brassicaceae).
Note: The epithet "pyrenaica" is pre-occupied in *Sisymbrium* by *Sisymbrium pyrenaica* Loefl. (1758), preventing the transfer of *Sinapis pyrenaica* to that genus.

Siphonanthus indicus Linnaeus, *Species Plantarum* 1: 109. 1753.
"Habitat in India." RCN: 895.
Lectotype (Moldenke & Moldenke in Dassanayake & Fosberg, *Revised Handb. Fl. Ceylon* 4: 427. 1983): [icon] *"Siphonanthemum salicis folio, flore flavescente"* in Amman in Comment. Acad. Sci. Imp. Petrop. 8: 214, t. 15. 1741.
Generitype of *Siphonanthus* Linnaeus.
Current name: ***Clerodendrum indicum*** (L.) Kuntze (Verbenaceae).

Sirium myrtifolium Linnaeus, *Mantissa Plantarum Altera*: 200. 1771.
"Habitat in India orientali." RCN: 974.
Lectotype (Scott in Bosser & al., *Fl. Mascareignes* 159: 1. 1982): Herb. Linn. No. 138.1 (LINN).
Generitype of *Sirium* Linnaeus.
Current name: ***Santalum album*** L. (Santalaceae).

Sison ammi Linnaeus, *Species Plantarum* 1: 252. 1753.
"Habitat in Apulia, Aegypto." RCN: 2033.

Lectotype (Jansen, *Spices, Condiments Med. Pl. Ethiopia*: 114. 1981): Herb. Linn. No. 356.5 (LINN).
Current name: ***Trachyspermum ammi*** (L.) Sprague (Apiaceae).
Note: Sprague (in *J. Bot.* 60: 212. 1922) noted type material in both LINN and BM, but did not distinguish between the collections (which are not part of a single gathering so Art. 9.15 does not apply).

Sison amomum Linnaeus, *Species Plantarum* 1: 252. 1753.
"Habitat in Angliae humectis lutosis." RCN: 2030.
Lectotype (Reduron & Jarvis in Jarvis & al., *Regnum Veg.* 127: 89. 1993): Herb. Clifford: 98, *Sison* 1 (BM-000558310).
Generitype of *Sison* Linnaeus (vide Hitchcock, *Prop. Brit. Bot.*: 140. 1929).
Current name: ***Sison amomum*** L. (Apiaceae).

Sison aromaticum Linnaeus, *Amoenitates Academicae* 4: 480. 1759, *orth. var.*
RCN: 2030.
Lectotype (Reduron & Jarvis in Jarvis & al., *Regnum Veg.* 127: 89. 1993): Herb. Clifford: 98, *Sison* 1 (BM-000558310).
Current name: ***Sison amomum*** L. (Apiaceae).
Note: Stearn (in Geck & Pressler, *Festschr. Claus Nissen*: 632. 1974) treats this as an orthographic error for *S. amomum* L. (1753), and is followed here.

Sison canadense Linnaeus, *Species Plantarum* 1: 252. 1753.
"Habitat in America septentrionali." RCN: 2032.
Lectotype (Reveal in Jarvis & al. in *Taxon* 55: 214. 2006): Herb. Clifford: 99, *Sison* 2 (BM-000558312).
Current name: ***Cryptotaenia canadensis*** (L.) DC. (Apiaceae).

Sison inundatum Linnaeus, *Species Plantarum* 1: 253. 1753.
"Habitat in Europae inundatis." RCN: 2034.
Lectotype (Reduron in Jonsell & Jarvis in *Nordic J. Bot.* 22: 85. 2002): Herb. Linn. No. 356.7, right specimen (LINN).
Current name: ***Apium inundatum*** (L.) Rchb. f. (Apiaceae).

Sison segetum Linnaeus, *Species Plantarum* 1: 252. 1753.
"Habitat in Angliae agris inter segetes." RCN: 2031.
Lectotype (Reduron & al. in Jarvis & al. in *Taxon* 55: 214. 2006): [icon] *"Sium terrestre seu segetale Nobis"* in Morison, Pl. Hist. Univ. 3: 283, s. 9, t. 5, f. 6. 1699. – Epitype (Jury & Southam in Jarvis & al. in *Taxon* 55: 215. 2006): "37 Sison segetum L. Hall. N. 779. Cl. Lachenal invenit et mihi semen communicavit", Herb. J.J. Roemer in Herb. R.J. Shuttleworth, Recd 1877 (BM).
Current name: ***Petroselinum segetum*** (L.) W.D.J. Koch (Apiaceae).

Sison verticillatum Linnaeus, *Species Plantarum* 1: 253. 1753.
"Habitat in Gallia, Pyrenaeis." RCN: 2035.
Lectotype (Reduron & Jarvis in Jarvis & al. in *Taxon* 55: 215. 2006): Herb. Burser VII(2): 35 (UPS).
Current name: ***Carum verticillatum*** (L.) W.D.J. Koch (Apiaceae).

Sisymbrium altissimum Linnaeus, *Species Plantarum* 2: 659. 1753.
"Habitat in Italia, Gallia, Sibiria." RCN: 4795.
Type not designated.
Original material: Herb. Linn. No. 836.33 (LINN); [icon] in Colonna, Ekphr. 1: 266, t. 268. 1606; [icon] in Walther, Design. Pl.: 135 [55], t. 22. 1735.
Generitype of *Sisymbrium* Linnaeus (vide Payson in *Publ. Sci. Univ. Wyoming, Bot.* 1: 6. 1922).
Current name: ***Sisymbrium altissimum*** L. (Brassicaceae).
Note: Sisymbrium altissimum, with 836.32 (LINN) as the type, was proposed as conserved type of the genus by Jarvis (in *Taxon* 41: 570.

1992). However, the proposal was eventually ruled unnecessary by the General Committee (see Barrie, *l.c.* 55: 795–796. 2006 for a review of the history of this and related proposals).

The collection proposed as the conserved type of *S. altissimum* (and previously treated as the lectotype by authors such as Jafri in Nasir & Ali, *Fl. W. Pakistan* 55: 253. 1973) is unannotated by Linnaeus and is not original material for the name. As original material is in existence, this choice cannot be treated as a neotypification under Art. 9.8, and the name is therefore untypified.

See an extensive review of the generic typification by Mackenzie in *Rhodora* 27: 28–32 (1927).

Sisymbrium amphibium Linnaeus, *Species Plantarum* 2: 657. 1753.
"Habitat in Europae septentrionalioris aquosis." RCN: 4781.
Lectotype (Jonsell in *Symb. Bot. Upsal.* 19(2): 148. 1968): Herb. Clifford: 337, *Sisymbrium* 3 (BM-000646340).
Current name: ***Rorippa amphibia*** (L.) Besser (Brassicaceae).

Sisymbrium amphibium Linnaeus var. **aquaticum** Linnaeus, *Species Plantarum* 2: 657. 1753.
RCN: 4781.
Lectotype (Jonsell in *Symb. Bot. Upsal.* 19(2): 148. 1968): Herb. Clifford: 337, *Sisymbrium* 3 (BM-000646340).
Current name: ***Rorippa amphibia*** (L.) Besser (Brassicaceae).

Sisymbrium amphibium Linnaeus var. **palustre** Linnaeus, *Species Plantarum* 2: 657. 1753.
RCN: 4781.
Lectotype (Jonsell in *Symb. Bot. Upsal.* 19(2): 149. 1968): Herb. Linn. No. 262 (LAPP).
Current name: ***Rorippa palustris*** (L.) Besser (Brassicaceae).

Sisymbrium amphibium Linnaeus var. **terrestre** Linnaeus, *Species Plantarum* 2: 657. 1753.
RCN: 4781.
Type not designated.
Original material: none traced.
Current name: ***Rorippa* sp.** (Brassicaceae).
Note: Jonsell (in *Symb. Bot. Upsal.* 19(2): 147. 1968) suggested that, from the descriptions of the cited synonyms (from Vaillant and Haller), this name is probably applicable to hybrids involving *Rorippa amphibia* (L.) Besser.

Sisymbrium arenosum Linnaeus, *Species Plantarum* 2: 658. 1753.
"Habitat in Germania, Helvetia." RCN: 4790.
Lectotype (O'Kane & Al-Shehbaz in *Novon* 7: 325. 1997): Herb. Linn. No. 836.22 (LINN).
Current name: ***Arabis arenosa*** (L.) Scop. (Brassicaceae).

Sisymbrium asperum Linnaeus, *Species Plantarum* 2: 659. 1753.
"Habitat Monspelii." RCN: 4793.
Lectotype (Martínez-Laborde in Cafferty & Jarvis in *Taxon* 51: 535. 2002): [icon] *"Sinapi monspessulanum siliqua aspera hirsuta"* in Bauhin & Cherler, Hist. Pl. Univ. 2: 858. 1651 (see p. 108). – Epitype (Martínez-Laborde in Cafferty & Jarvis in *Taxon* 51: 535. 2002): France. Aveyron, Montpellier, 25 Jun 1910, *Bec s.n.* (BM-000576293).
Current name: ***Sisymbrella aspera*** (L.) Spach (Brassicaceae).

Sisymbrium barbareae Linnaeus, *Species Plantarum*, ed. 2, 2: 921. 1763.
"Habitat in Oriente. Burmannus." RCN: 4799.
Lectotype (Al-Shehbaz & Turland in Cafferty & Jarvis in *Taxon* 51: 535. 2002): Herb. Linn. No. 836.44 (LINN). – Epitype (Al-

Shehbaz in Cafferty & Jarvis in *Taxon* 51: 535. 2002): Iran. Kerman Prov., montis Kuh Lalesar, 2 Jul 1892, *Bornmüller 2066* (BM-000576291; iso- JE).
Current name: ***Barbarea plantaginea*** DC. (Brassicaceae).

Sisymbrium barrelieri Linnaeus, *Species Plantarum*, ed. 2, 2: 919. 1763.
"Habitat in Hispania, Italia. Loefling." RCN: 4789.
Lectotype (López González in Cafferty & Jarvis in *Taxon* 51: 536. 2002): *Löfling s.n.*, Herb. Linn. No. 836.25, right specimen (LINN).
Current name: ***Brassica barrelieri*** (L.) Janka (Brassicaceae).

Sisymbrium bursifolium Linnaeus, *Centuria II Plantarum*: 24. 1756.
"Habitat in Italiae montibus subhumidis. Miller." RCN: 4785.
Type not designated.
Original material: Herb. Linn. No. 836.16 (LINN); Herb. Linn. No. 836.15 (LINN); Herb. Linn. No. 272.7? (S).
Current name: ***Sisymbrella dentata*** (L.) O.E. Schulz (Brassicaceae).

Sisymbrium catholicum Linnaeus, *Systema Naturae*, ed. 12, 2: 440; *Mantissa Plantarum*: 93. 1767. RCN: 4800.
"Habitat in Hispania, Lusitania." RCN: 4800.
Lectotype (Martínez-Laborde in Cafferty & Jarvis in *Taxon* 51: 536. 2002): Herb. Linn. No. 836.48 (LINN).
Current name: ***Diplotaxis catholica*** (L.) DC. (Brassicaceae).

Sisymbrium indicum Linnaeus, *Species Plantarum*, ed. 2, 2: 917. 1763.
"Habitat in India orientali." RCN: 4803.
Lectotype (Hara in *J. Jap. Bot.* 30: 194. 1955): Herb. Linn. No. 836.52 (LINN).
Current name: ***Rorippa indica*** (L.) Hiern (Brassicaceae).
Note: See notes by Jonsell (in *Svensk Bot. Tidskr.* 68: 386. 1974) who reached the same conclusion as Hara regarding the type.

Sisymbrium integrifolium Linnaeus, *Species Plantarum* 2: 660. 1753.
"Habitat in Sibiria." RCN: 4802.
Lectotype (Ebel in Cafferty & Jarvis in *Taxon* 51: 536. 2002): Herb. Linn. No. 836.51 (LINN).
Current name: ***Dontostemon integrifolius*** (L.) Ledeb. (Brassicaceae).

Sisymbrium irio Linnaeus, *Species Plantarum* 2: 659. 1753.
"Habitat in Europae cultis." RCN: 4796.
Lectotype (Jonsell & Jarvis in *Nordic J. Bot.* 22: 71. 2002): *Löfling 496*, Herb. Linn. No. 836.35 (LINN).
Current name: ***Sisymbrium irio*** L. (Brassicaceae).
Note: Several authors from Franchetti (in *Webbia* 14: 194. 1958) onwards indicated unspecified material in LINN as type but failed to distinguish between several possible collections there. They are evidently not part of a single gathering so Art. 9.15 does not apply.

Sisymbrium loeselii Linnaeus, *Centuria I Plantarum*: 18. 1755.
"Habitat in Borussia, Gedani, in montanis aequicolor." RCN: 4797.
Lectotype (Jafri in Nasir & Ali, *Fl. W. Pakistan* 55: 251. 1973): Herb. Linn. No. 836.40 (LINN).
Current name: ***Sisymbrium loeselii*** L. (Brassicaceae).

Sisymbrium monense Linnaeus, *Species Plantarum* 2: 658. 1753.
"Habitat in Mona, insula Angliae." RCN: 4787.
Lectotype (Leadlay & Heywood in *Bot. J. Linn. Soc.* 102: 364. 1990): [icon] *"Eruca Monensis laciniata, flore luteo majore"* in Dillenius, Hort. Eltham. 1: 135, t. 111, f. 135. 1732.
Current name: ***Coincya monensis*** (L.) Greuter & Burdet (Brassicaceae).

S

Sisymbrium murale Linnaeus, *Species Plantarum* 2: 658. 1753.
"Habitat in Gallia, Sicilia." RCN: 4786.

Lectotype (Jafri in Ali & Jafri, *Fl. Libya* 23: 37. 1977): Herb. Linn.
No. 836.18 (LINN).
Current name: ***Diplotaxis muralis*** (L.) DC. (Brassicaceae).

Sisymbrium nasturtium-aquaticum Linnaeus, *Species Plantarum* 2:
657. 1753.
"Habitat in Europa & America septentrionali ad fontes." RCN: 4777.
Lectotype (Jonsell in *Svensk Bot. Tidskr.* 67: 293. 1973): Herb. Linn.
No. 836.1 (LINN).
Current name: ***Rorippa nasturtium-aquaticum*** (L.) Hayek
(Brassicaceae).
Note: Although Fawcett & Rendle (*Fl. Jamaica* 3: 237. 1914) indicated
material in LINN as the type, they did not distinguish between
sheets 836.1 and 836.2 (which are evidently not part of a single
gathering so Art. 9.15 does not apply).

Sisymbrium orientale Linnaeus, *Centuria II Plantarum*: 24. 1756.
"Habitat in oriente. Miller." RCN: 4798.
Lectotype (Jonsell in Polhill, *Fl. Trop. E. Africa, Cruciferae*: 64. 1982):
Herb. Linn. No. 836.43 (LINN).
Current name: ***Sisymbrium orientale*** L. (Brassicaceae).

Sisymbrium parra Linnaeus, *Mantissa Plantarum Altera*: 255. 1771.
"Habitat in Parra. D. Vandelli." RCN: 4792.
Neotype (Gómez-Campo in Cafferty & Jarvis in *Taxon* 51: 536.
2002): Spain. Madrid, "Entre Puerta de Hierro y El Pardo", Apr
1917, *C. Vicioso* [Madrid 46637(2)] (MA; iso- MA).
Current name: ***Brassica barrelieri*** (L.) Janka (Brassicaceae).

Sisymbrium polyceratium Linnaeus, *Species Plantarum* 2: 658. 1753.
"Habitat in Helvetiae, Italiae ruderatis." RCN: 4784.
Lectotype (Jafri in Ali & Jafri, *Fl. Libya* 23: 180. 1977): Herb. Linn.
No. 836.13 (LINN).
Current name: ***Sisymbrium polyceratium*** L. (Brassicaceae).

Sisymbrium pyrenaicum Linnaeus, *Systema Naturae,* ed. 10, 2: 1132.
1759, *nom. illeg.*
["Habitat in Pyrenaeis, Helveticis alpibus."] Sp. Pl., ed. 2, 2: 916
(1763). RCN: 4779.
Lectotype (López González in *Anales Jard. Bot. Madrid* 52: 102.
1994): Herb. Linn. No. 836.4 (LINN).
Current name: ***Rorippa islandica*** (Gunnerus) Borbás (Brassicaceae).
Note: See extensive discussion on the correct name for this taxon by
López González (in *Anales Jard. Bot. Madrid* 52: 102. 1994). He
indicates 836.4 (LINN) as the lectotype, allegedly following Ball (in
Feddes Repert. 64: 14. 1962), and reproduces the Morison figure (as
his f. 1 on p. 98). Although Ball discussed the identity of this sheet
and the Allioni figure (probably *Rorippa pyrenaica* (All.) Rchb.), he
did not choose a type, concluding "As the name is illegitimate, the
confusion and doubt as to the identity of this species does not have
any serious nomenclatural consequences". It is illegitimate because
it is a later homonym of *S. pyrenaicum* Loefl. (1758).

Sisymbrium sophia Linnaeus, *Species Plantarum* 2: 659. 1753.
"Habitat in Europae maceriis, muris, tectis." RCN: 4794.
Lectotype (Jafri in Nasir & Ali, *Fl. W. Pakistan* 55: 281. 1973): Herb.
Linn. No. 836.31 (LINN).
Current name: ***Descurainia sophia*** (L.) Webb ex Prantl (Brassicaceae).

Sisymbrium strictissimum Linnaeus, *Species Plantarum* 2: 660. 1753.
"Habitat in Helvetiae montibus." RCN: 4801.
Lectotype (Jonsell in Cafferty & Jarvis in *Taxon* 51: 536. 2002): Herb.
Linn. No. 836.49 (LINN).
Current name: ***Sisymbrium strictissimum*** L. (Brassicaceae).

Sisymbrium supinum Linnaeus, *Species Plantarum* 2: 657. 1753.
"Habitat in Parsiis (sic) ad agrorum margines, inque Hispania." RCN:
4783.
Lectotype (Jonsell & Jarvis in *Nordic J. Bot.* 22: 72. 2002): Herb.
Linn. No. 836.12 (LINN).
Current name: ***Erucastrum supinum*** (L.) Al-Shehbaz & Warwick
(Brassicaceae).

Sisymbrium sylvestre Linnaeus, *Species Plantarum* 2: 657. 1753.
"Habitat in Helvetiae, Germaniae, Galliae ruderatis." RCN: 4780.
Lectotype (Jonsell in *Symb. Bot. Upsal.* 19(2): 160. 1968): Herb.
Clifford: 336, *Sisymbrium* 2 (BM-000646339).
Current name: ***Rorippa sylvestris*** (L.) Besser (Brassicaceae).

Sisymbrium tanacetifolium Linnaeus, *Species Plantarum* 2: 659.
1753.
"Habitat in Sabaudia?" RCN: 4778.
Lectotype (Ball in Cafferty & Jarvis in *Taxon* 51: 536. 2002): Herb. A.
van Royen No. 901.256–631 (L).
Current name: ***Hugueninia tanacetifolia*** (L.) Rchb. (Brassicaceae).

Sisymbrium tenuifolium Linnaeus, *Centuria I Plantarum*: 18. 1755.
"Habitat in Gallia, Italia, Helvetia." RCN: 4782.
Lectotype (Hedge in Cafferty & Jarvis in *Taxon* 51: 536. 2002): [icon]
"Eruca tenuifolia perennis flore luteo" in Bauhin & Cherler, Hist. Pl.
Univ. 2: 861. 1651. – Epitype (Hedge in Cafferty & Jarvis in *Taxon*
51: 536. 2002): France. Camargue. Tour du Valat, SE of Mas; 11
Jun 1968, *Kendrick & Moyes 230* (BM-000576296).
Current name: ***Diplotaxis tenuifolia*** (L.) DC. (Brassicaceae).

Sisymbrium valentinum Linnaeus, *Species Plantarum,* ed. 2, 2: 920. 1763.
"Habitat in Regno Valentino, Madriti. Loefling." RCN: 4791.
Lectotype (García Adá & al. in *Candollea* 51: 374. 1996): *Löfling 474,* Herb. Linn. No. 836.27 (LINN).
Current name: ***Biscutella valentina*** (L.) Heywood (Brassicaceae).
Note: See extensive discussion by García Adá & al. (in *Candollea* 51: 374–375. 1996). They conclude that the name must be typified by the Löfling material, which does not correspond with usage of the name, and suggest that the name should be proposed for rejection. López (in *Taxon* 48: 161. 1999) formally proposed the rejection of the name. *Biscutella stenophylla* Dufour would have become the correct name for this taxon had rejection been approved. Mateo & Crespo (in *Bot. J. Linn. Soc.* 132: 14–19. 2000) also discussed the identity of the original elements but disagreed over the desirability of rejecting the name. The Committee for Spermatophyta (in *Taxon* 49: 802. 2000), however, did not recommend rejection.

Sisymbrium vimineum Linnaeus, *Species Plantarum* 2: 658. 1753.
"Habitat in Parisiis & ad Tyberis margines, inque Moravia." RCN: 4788.
Lectotype (Hedge in Cafferty & Jarvis in *Taxon* 51: 536. 2002): Herb. Linn. No. 836.21 (LINN).
Current name: ***Diplotaxis viminea*** (L.) DC. (Brassicaceae).

Sisyrinchium bermudiana Linnaeus, *Species Plantarum* 2: 954. 1753.
"Habitat α in Virginia, β in Bermudis." RCN: 6908.
Lectotype (Boivin in *Phytologia* 42: 24. 1979): *Kalm,* Herb. Linn. No. 1064.1 (LINN).
Generitype of *Sisyrinchium* Linnaeus.
Current name: ***Sisyrinchium bermudiana*** L. (Iridaceae).
Note: Sisyrinchium bermudiana was based on a number of disparate elements and has been treated in a variety of ways. Bicknell (in *Bull. Torrey Bot. Club* 23: 131. 1896) rejected the name because of its "indiscriminate use" for a number of taxa, and several authors, including Parent (in *Lejeunia*, n.s., 99: 6–13. 1980), have rejected the name (though not formally) as a *nomen ambiguum.* Others, however, have continued to use the name, though in different senses. Farwell (in *Mem. Torrey Bot. Club* 17: 82–83. 1918) and Boivin (in *Phytologia* 42: 24. 1979) have applied the name to the Virginian plant (also known as *S. mucronatum* Michaux). By contrast, Hemsley (in *J. Bot.* 22: 108–110. 1884) and Ward (in *Taxon* 17: 270–273. 1968), who provides an extensive review of the problem, have applied it to the Bermudan plant.
　There have been several attempts to resolve matters through typification. Guédès (in *Taxon* 18: 542. 1969) designated Miller material (BM) of the Bermudan taxon as a neotype for *S. bermudiana,* but this is contrary to Art. 9.11 because original material is in existence. Boivin (in *Phytologia* 42: 24. 1979) designated Kalm material (1064.1, LINN) of the Virginian taxon as type. More recently, Barrie & Reveal in Jarvis & al., *Regnum Veg.* 127: 89 (1993) designated as lectotype van Royen material (No. 904.139–289, L) belonging to the Bermudan taxon. The possibility that the Linnaean Generic List might be available for adoption under the Names in Current Use (NCU) proposals then under discussion led Barrie & Reveal to typify the name in a way that they believed best reflected current usage. However, with the defeat of the NCU proposals, Boivin's type choice clearly has priority and the name should be used in the sense of Kalm's type. It may be that a proposal for either conservation or rejection of *S. bermudiana* would now be helpful in resolving the problems still associated with this name.

Sisyrinchium palmifolium Linnaeus, *Systema Naturae,* ed. 12, 2: 597; *Mantissa Plantarum*: 122. 1767.

"Habitat in Brasilia. D. Arduini." RCN: 6909.
Type not designated.
Original material: *Arduino 21,* Herb. Linn. No. 1064.3 (LINN); Herb. Linn. No. 1064.4 (LINN); [icon] in Plumier in Burman, Pl. Amer.: 35, t. 46, f. 2. 1756.
Current name: ***Sisyrinchium palmifolium*** L. (Iridaceae).
Note: Heaton & Mathew (in *Curtis's Bot. Mag.* 15: 106. 1998) excluded Linnaeus' synonym (a cited Plumier plate) and stated "Type: …(LINN)". However, they did not distinguish between sheets 1064.3 and 1064.4 there (which are evidently not part of a single gathering so Art. 9.15 does not apply).

Sium angustifolium Linnaeus, *Species Plantarum,* ed. 2, 2: 1672. 1763, *nom. illeg.*
"Habitat in Europae australis aquosis, nec extra aquas adscendit." RCN: 2022.
Replaced synonym: *Sium erectum* Huds. (1762).
Type not designated.
Current name: ***Berula erecta*** (Huds.) Coville (Apiaceae).
Note: An illegitimate replacement name for *Sium erectum* Huds. (1762)

Sium falcaria Linnaeus, *Species Plantarum* 1: 252. 1753.
"Habitat in Flandria, Helvetia, Bohemia, Alsatia, Gallia." RCN: 2027.
Lectotype (Rechinger, *Fl. Iranica* 162: 306. 1987): Herb. Clifford: 98, *Sium* 5 (BM-000558309).
Current name: ***Falcaria vulgaris*** Bernh. (Apiaceae).

Sium graecum Linnaeus, *Species Plantarum* 1: 252. 1753.
"Habitat in Graecia." RCN: 2028.
Lectotype (Jury & Southam in Jarvis & al. in *Taxon* 55: 215. 2006): Herb. Clifford: 98, *Sium* 4 (BM-000558308).
Current name: ***Bonannia graeca*** (L.) Halácsy (Apiaceae).

Sium latifolium Linnaeus, *Species Plantarum* 1: 251. 1753.
"Habitat in Europae rivulis & ad ripas paludosas." RCN: 2021.
Lectotype (Reduron & Jarvis in Jarvis & al., *Regnum Veg.* 127: 88. 1993): Herb. Clifford: 98, *Sium* 1 (BM-000558303).
Generitype of *Sium* Linnaeus (vide Hitchcock, *Prop. Brit. Bot.*: 140. 1929).
Current name: ***Sium latifolium*** L. (Apiaceae).

Sium ninsi Linnaeus, *Species Plantarum* 1: 251. 1753.
"Habitat in China." RCN: 2025.
Lectotype (Watson in Jarvis & al. in *Taxon* 55: 215. 2006): [icon] *"Sisarum montanum coraeense, radice non tuberosa"* in Kaempfer, Amoen. Exot. Fasc.: 818, 819. 1712. – Voucher: Herb. Sloane 211: 36.2 (BM-SL).
Current name: ***Sium sisarum*** L. (Apiaceae).

Sium nodiflorum Linnaeus, *Species Plantarum* 1: 251. 1753.
"Habitat in Europa ad ripas fluviorum." RCN: 2023.
Lectotype (Jafri in Jafri & El-Gadi, *Fl. Libya* 117: 78. 1985): Herb. Clifford: 98, *Sium* 3 (BM-000558307).
Current name: ***Apium nodiflorum*** (L.) Lag. (Apiaceae).

Sium rigidius Linnaeus, *Species Plantarum* 1: 251. 1753.
"Habitat in Virginia." RCN: 2026.
Lectotype (Reveal in Jarvis & al. in *Taxon* 55: 215. 2006): *Clayton 279* (BM-000042233).
Current name: ***Oxypolis rigidior*** (L.) Raf. (Apiaceae).

Sium siculum Linnaeus, *Species Plantarum* 1: 252. 1753.
"Habitat in Sicilia." RCN: 2029.

Lectotype (Jury & al. in Jarvis & al. in *Taxon* 55: 215. 2006): [icon] *"Dauco con foglia di Pastinaca Siciliano"* in Zanoni, Istoria Bot.: 78, t. 30. 1675. – Epitype (Jury & al. in Jarvis & al. in *Taxon* 55: 215. 2006): Italy. Sicily: Siracusa, 12 May 1979, *Davis, P. & Sutton, D. & S. 62943* (BM).
Current name: ***Kundmannia sicula*** (L.) DC. (Apiaceae).

Sium sisarum Linnaeus, *Species Plantarum* 1: 251. 1753.
"Habitat in China?" RCN: 2024.
Lectotype (Reduron & Jarvis in Jarvis & al. in *Taxon* 55: 215. 2006): Herb. Clifford: 98, *Sium* 2, sheet A (BM-000558305).
Current name: ***Sium sisarum*** L. (Apiaceae).

Sloanea dentata Linnaeus, *Species Plantarum* 1: 512. 1753.
"Habitat in America meridionali." RCN: 3860.
Lectotype (Bornstein in Howard, *Fl. Lesser Antilles* 5: 181. 1989): [icon] *"Sloana"* in Plumier, Nov. Pl. Amer.: 48, t. 15. 1703.
Generitype of *Sloanea* Linnaeus (vide Green, *Prop. Brit. Bot.*: 161. 1929).
Current name: ***Sloanea dentata*** L. (Elaeocarpaceae).
Note: Smith (in *Contr. Gray Herb.* 175: 65. 1954) stated "based on a Plumier plate and description", but this is insufficiently explicit to be accepted as a formal typification. Bornstein (in Howard, *Fl. Lesser Antilles* 5: 181. 1989), however, treated the plate as the type (while attributing the choice to Smith), so the typification dates from 1989.

Sloanea emarginata Linnaeus, *Species Plantarum* 1: 512. 1753.
"Habitat in Carolina." RCN: 3861.
Replaced synonym of: *Achras sapota* L. (1762), *nom. illeg.*
Lectotype (Dandy, *Sloane Herbarium*: 112. 1958): [icon] *"Anona foliis Laurinis, in summitate incisis; fructu compresso scabro fusco, in medio acumine longo"* in Catesby, Nat. Hist. Carolina 2: 87, t. 87. 1743. – Typotype: Herb. Sloane 232: 15 (BM-SL).
Current name: ***Manilkara bahamensis*** (Baker) H.J. Lam & A. Meeuse (Sapotaceae).

Smilax aspera Linnaeus, *Species Plantarum* 2: 1028. 1753.
"Habitat in Hispaniae, Italiae, Siciliae sepibus." RCN: 7437.
Lectotype (Cowley in Jarvis & al., *Regnum Veg.* 127: 89. 1993): Herb. Clifford: 458, *Smilax* 1, sheet A (BM-000647490).
Generitype of *Smilax* Linnaeus (vide Green, *Prop. Brit. Bot.*: 191. 1929).
Current name: ***Smilax aspera*** L. (Smilacaceae).
Note: El-Gadi (in Jafri & El-Gadi, *Fl. Libya* 57: 77. 1978) indicated 1182.1 (LINN) as type, but this is a Kähler collection, not received by Linnaeus until 1757 and not, therefore, original material for the name. Cowley (in Polhill, *Fl. Trop. E. Africa, Smilacaceae*: 2. 1989) indicated Clifford material as the type but did not distinguish between the two sheets preserved there; she made a definitive choice in 1993.

Smilax bona-nox Linnaeus, *Species Plantarum* 2: 1030. 1753.
"Habitat in Carolina." RCN: 7446.
Lectotype (designated here by Reveal): [icon] *"Smilax foliis latis in margine spinosis Caroliniana, stipite leni quadrato, et Smilax Caroliniana, stipite quadrato leni, foliis angustis asperis auriculis ad basim angulosis"* in Plukenet, Phytographia: t. 111, f. 1, 3. 1691; Almag. Bot.: 348. 1696. – Voucher: Herb. Sloane 98: 49 (BM-SL).
Current name: ***Smilax bona-nox*** L. (Smilacaceae).
Note: Huft (in Davidse & al., *Fl. Mesoamericana* 6: 23. 1994) indicated *Beyrich s.n.* as the type. It is, however, not original material for the name.

Smilax caduca Linnaeus, *Species Plantarum* 2: 1030. 1753.
"Habitat in Canada. Kalm." RCN: 7445.

Lectotype (designated here by Reveal): *Kalm*, Herb. Linn. No. 1182.11 (LINN).
Current name: ***Smilax caduca*** L. (Smilacaceae).

Smilax china Linnaeus, *Species Plantarum* 2: 1029. 1753.
"Habitat in China, Japonia." RCN: 7441.
Type not designated.
Original material: Herb. Linn. No. 1182.6 (LINN); [icon] in Plukenet, Amalth. Bot.: 101, t. 408, f. 1. 1705; [icon] in Kaempfer, Amoen. Exot. Fasc.: 781, 782. 1712.
Current name: ***Smilax china*** L. (Smilacaceae).
Note: Koyama (in Leroy, *Fl. Cambodge Laos Viêt-Nam* 20: 78. 1983) treated both 1182.6 and 1182.7 (LINN) as the type, but as they are evidently not part of a single gathering, Art. 9.15 does not apply.

Smilax excelsa Linnaeus, *Species Plantarum* 2: 1029. 1753.
"Habitat in Oriente, Syria." RCN: 7438.
Type not designated.
Original material: Herb. Linn. No. 1182.3 (LINN); *Gerber*, Herb. Linn. No. 1182.4 (LINN); Herb. Linn. No. 1182.2 (LINN); [icon] in Alpino, De Plantis Aegypti: 140, 141. 1640; [icon] in Buxbaum, Pl. Minus Cognit. Cent. 1: 18, t. 27. 1728.
Current name: ***Smilax excelsa*** L. (Smilacaceae).

Smilax herbacea Linnaeus, *Species Plantarum* 2: 1030. 1753.
"Habitat in Virginia, Marilandia." RCN: 7447.
Lectotype (Pennell in *Bull. Torrey Bot. Club* 43: 413. 1916): *Clayton 541*, Herb. Linn. No. 1182.12 (LINN; iso- BM).
Current name: ***Smilax herbacea*** L. (Smilacaceae).

Smilax lanceolata Linnaeus, *Species Plantarum* 2: 1031. 1753.
"Habitat in Virginia." RCN: 7448.
Type not designated.
Original material: [icon] in Plukenet, Phytographia: t. 110, f. 4. 1691; Almag. Bot.: 349. 1696.
Current name: ***Smilax lanceolata*** L. (Smilacaceae).
Note: See discussion of this name by Fernald (in *Rhodora* 46: 39–42. 1944) and Wilbur (in *Sida* 14: 42. 1990).

Smilax laurifolia Linnaeus, *Species Plantarum* 2: 1030. 1753.
"Habitat in Virginia, Carolina." RCN: 7443.
Lectotype (designated here by Reveal): *Clayton 617*, Herb. Linn. No. 1182.9 (LINN).
Current name: ***Smilax laurifolia*** L. (Smilacaceae).
Note: See discussion by Fernald (in *Rhodora* 46: 41. 1944).

Smilax pseudochina Linnaeus, *Species Plantarum* 2: 1031. 1753.
"Habitat in Virginia, Jamaica." RCN: 7449.
Lectotype (Fernald in *Rhodora* 46: 33, pl. 812, f. 2. 1944): *Kalm*, Herb. Linn. No. 1182.14 (LINN).
Current name: ***Smilax pseudochina*** L. (Smilacaceae).
Note: Specific epithet spelled "Pseudo China" in the protologue.

Smilax rotundifolia Linnaeus, *Species Plantarum* 2: 1030. 1753.
"Habitat in Canada. Kalm." RCN: 7442.
Lectotype (Reveal & al. in *Huntia* 7: 236. 1987): *Kalm*, Herb. Linn. No. 1182.8 (LINN; iso- BM).
Current name: ***Smilax rotundifolia*** L. (Smilacaceae).

Smilax sarsaparilla Linnaeus, *Species Plantarum* 2: 1029. 1753.
"Habitat in Peru, Brasilia, Mexico, Virginia." RCN: 7440.
Type not designated.
Original material: Herb. Clifford: 459, *Smilax* 4 (BM); Herb. Linn. No. 1182.5 (LINN); *Clayton 81* (BM); Herb. Burser XVII: 20

(UPS); [icon] in Plukenet, Phytographia: t. 111, f. 2. 1691; Almag. Bot.: 348. 1696 – Voucher: Herb. Sloane 102: 17 (BM-SL).

Note: The application of this name appears uncertain.

Smilax tamnoides Linnaeus, *Species Plantarum* 2: 1030. 1753.
"Habitat in Carolina, Virginia, Pensylvania." RCN: 7444.
Lectotype (Fernald in *Rhodora* 46: 38. 1944): [icon] *"Smilax Bryoniae nigrae foliis caule spinosa, baccis nigris"* in Catesby, Nat. Hist. Carolina 1: 52, t. 52. 1730.
Current name: ***Smilax tamnoides*** L. (Smilacaceae).
Note: There has been much disagreement as to the identity of the type. Fernald identified it as *S. tamnoides*, but Clausen (in *Rhodora* 53: 109–111. 1951) concluded that it was a composite of several taxa, and that the name should therefore be discarded as ambiguous. Wilbur (in *Sida* 14: 38. 1990) supported this view, treating the woody species as *S. hispida* Muhl. ex. Torr. Subsequently, Wilbur (in *Rhodora* 105: 250–259. 2003) has provided an extensive review. He concludes that the bristly greenbriar is correctly known as *S. hispida* Raf. However, no formal proposal for the rejection of *S. tamnoides* seems to have been made.

Smilax zeylanica Linnaeus, *Species Plantarum* 2: 1029. 1753.
"Habitat in Zeylona." RCN: 7439.
Lectotype (Dassanayake in Dassanayake & Clayton, *Revised Handb. Fl. Ceylon* 14: 274. 2000): Herb. Hermann 2: 82; 4: 30, No. 364 (BM).
Current name: ***Smilax zeylanica*** L. (Smilacaceae).
Note: Although Dassanayake did not distinguish between the specimens in two separate volumes of Herb. Hermann, it is likely they are part of a single gathering, and his typification is accepted (Art. 9.15).

Smyrnium aegyptiacum Linnaeus, *Centuria I Plantarum*: 10. 1755.
"Habitat in Aegypto. D. Hasselquist." RCN: 2094.
Type not designated.
Original material: Herb. Linn. No. 370.2 (LINN).
Current name: ***Smyrnium connatum*** Boiss. & Kotschy (Apiaceae).

Smyrnium aureum Linnaeus, *Species Plantarum* 1: 262. 1753.
"Habitat in America boreali." RCN: 2096.
Lectotype (Reveal & al. in *Huntia* 7: 236. 1987): Herb. Linn. No. 370.5 (LINN).
Current name: ***Zizia aurea*** (L.) W.D.J. Koch (Apiaceae).

Smyrnium integerrimum Linnaeus, *Species Plantarum* 1: 263. 1753.
"Habitat in Virginia." RCN: 2097.
Lectotype (Reveal in Jarvis & al. in *Taxon* 55: 215. 2006): *Clayton 549*, Herb. Linn. No. 370.7 (LINN; iso- BM).
Current name: ***Taenidia integerrima*** (L.) Drude (Apiaceae).

Smyrnium olusatrum Linnaeus, *Species Plantarum* 1: 262. 1753.
"Habitat in Scotia, Wallia, Gallia." RCN: 2095.
Lectotype (Jafri in Jafri & El-Gadi, *Fl. Libya* 117: 32. 1985): Herb. Clifford: 105, *Smyrnium* 2 (BM-000558366).
Generitype of *Smyrnium* Linnaeus (vide Hitchcock, *Prop. Brit. Bot.*: 141. 1929).
Current name: ***Smyrnium olusatrum*** L. (Apiaceae).

Smyrnium perfoliatum Linnaeus, *Species Plantarum* 1: 262. 1753.
"Habitat in Italia, Creta." RCN: 2093.
Lectotype (Turland & Reduron in Jarvis & al. in *Taxon* 55: 215. 2006): Herb. Linn. No. 370.1 (LINN).
Current name: ***Smyrnium perfoliatum*** L. (Apiaceae).

Solandra capensis Linnaeus, *Systema Naturae*, ed. 10, 2: 1269. 1759.
["Habitat ad Cap. b. spei. D. C. Solander."] Sp. Pl., ed. 2, 2: 1408. 1763. RCN: 7648.
Neotype (Schubert & Van Wyk in Woodson & Schery in *Nordic J. Bot.* 17: 308. 1997): Herb. Linn. No. 332a.1 (LINN).
Generitype of *Solandra* Linnaeus, *nom. rej.*
Current name: ***Centella capensis*** (L.) Domin (Apiaceae).
Note: Solandra Linnaeus, *nom. rej.* in favour of *Solandra* Swartz.

Solanum aethiopicum Linnaeus, *Centuria II Plantarum*: 10. 1756.
"Habitat in Aethiopia. Burserus." RCN: 1474.
Lectotype (Hepper & Jaeger in *Kew Bull.* 40: 391. 1985): Herb. Burser IX: 17 (UPS).
Current name: ***Solanum aethiopicum*** L. (Solanaceae).

Solanum bahamense Linnaeus, *Species Plantarum* 1: 188. 1753.
"Habitat in Americae insula Providentia." RCN: 1488.
Lectotype (Knapp & Jarvis in *Bot. J. Linn. Soc.* 104: 328, f. 1. 1990): Herb. Linn. No. 248.42 (LINN).
Current name: ***Solanum bahamense*** L. (Solanaceae).

Solanum bonariense Linnaeus, *Species Plantarum* 1: 185. 1753.
"Habitat in agro Bonariensi." RCN: 1465.
Lectotype (Hepper & Jaeger in *Kew Bull.* 40: 391. 1985): [icon] *"Solanum Bonariense arborescens, Papas floribus"* in Dillenius, Hort. Eltham. 2: 364, t. 272, f. 351. 1732. – Typotype: Herb. Dillenius (OXF).
Current name: ***Solanum bonariense*** L. (Solanaceae).
Note: See discussion by Knapp & Jarvis (in *Bot. J. Linn. Soc.* 104: 28, f. 2, 3. 1990).

Solanum campechiense Linnaeus, *Species Plantarum* 1: 187. 1753.
"Habitat in America ad sinum Campechiense." RCN: 1478.
Lectotype (Knapp & Jarvis in *Bot. J. Linn. Soc.* 104: 333, f. 6. 1990): [icon] *"Solanum Campechiense, calycibus echinatis"* in Dillenius, Hort. Eltham. 2: 361, t. 268, f. 347. 1732.
Current name: ***Solanum campechiense*** L. (Solanaceae).

Solanum campechiense Linnaeus var. **fuscatum** (Linnaeus) Linnaeus, *Mantissa Plantarum Altera*: 340. 1771.
["Habitat in America."] Sp. Pl., ed. 2, 1: 268 (1762). RCN: 1483.
Basionym: *Solanum fuscatum* L. (1762).
Type not designated.
Original material: as basionym.
Note: See discussion by Knapp & Jarvis (in *Bot. J. Linn. Soc.* 104: 334. 1990), who treat this, and its basionym *S. fuscatum*, as *nomina non satis nota*.

Solanum capense Linnaeus, *Systema Naturae*, ed. 10, 2: 935. 1759.
RCN: 1491.
Type not designated.
Original material: *Miller*, Herb. Linn. No. 248.46 (LINN).
Current name: ***Solanum capense*** L. (Solanaceae).

Solanum carolinense Linnaeus, *Species Plantarum* 1: 187. 1753.
"Habitat in Carolina." RCN: 1484.
Lectotype (Knapp & Jarvis in *Bot. J. Linn. Soc.* 104: 321, f. 4. 1990): Herb. Linn. No. 248.37 (LINN).
Current name: ***Solanum carolinense*** L. (Solanaceae).

Solanum diphyllum Linnaeus, *Species Plantarum* 1: 184. 1753.
"Habitat in America?". RCN: 1458.
Lectotype (Knapp & Jarvis in *Bot. J. Linn. Soc.* 104: 305, f. 8. 1990): Herb. Linn. No. 248.5 (LINN), see p. 199.
Current name: ***Solanum diphyllum*** L. (Solanaceae).

S

Note: D'Arcy (in *Ann. Missouri Bot. Gard.* 61: 845. 1974) expressed doubt as to whether 248.5 (LINN) was the type, but this was made explicit by Knapp & Jarvis.

Solanum dulcamara Linnaeus, *Species Plantarum* 1: 185. 1753.
"Habitat in Europae sepibus humentibus." RCN: 1459.
Lectotype (Deb in *J. Econ. Taxon. Bot.* 1: 46. 1980): Herb. Linn. No. 248.7 (LINN).
Current name: **Solanum dulcamara** L. (Solanaceae).
Note: See detailed discussion, and an illustration of the lectotype, by Knapp & Jarvis (in *Bot. J. Linn. Soc.* 104: 337, f. 9. 1990) who chose the same type, unaware of Deb's earlier formal choice.

Solanum ferox Linnaeus, *Species Plantarum*, ed. 2, 1: 267. 1762.
"Habitat in Malabaria." RCN: 1477.
Type not designated.
Original material: none traced.
Current name: **Solanum ferox** L. (Solanaceae).
Note: Symon (in *J. Adelaide Bot. Gard.* 4: 106. 1981) indicates type material in LINN (which had been seen on a microfiche in AD). However, there seems to be no material at LINN annotated in a way that can associate it with this name and it is therefore not clear what material Symon intended. However, Whalen & al. (in *Gentes Herb.* 12: 100. 1981) say that Linnaeus' calyx description rules out the traditional application of *S. ferox*, and take up *S. lasiocarpon* Dunal for that taxon. They say that *S. involucratum* Blume is a much more likely identity for Linnaeus' plant. There appear to be no original elements, and a neotype may be needed, although there may also be a case for proposing the rejection of the name altogether.

Solanum fuscatum Linnaeus, *Species Plantarum*, ed. 2, 1: 268. 1762.
"Habitat in America." RCN: 1483.
Basionym of: *Solanum campechiense* L. var. *fuscatum* (L.) L. (1771).
Type not designated.
Original material: none traced.
Note: See discussion by Knapp & Jarvis (in *Bot. J. Linn. Soc.* 104: 334. 1990), who treat this as a *nom. non satis notum*.

Solanum guineense Linnaeus, *Species Plantarum* 1: 184. 1753.
"Habitat in Guinea." RCN: 1441.
Replaced synonym of: *Atropa solanacea* L. (1771), *nom. illeg.*
Lectotype (Wijnands, *Bot. Commelins*: 193. 1983): Herb. Linn. No. 246.4 (LINN).
Current name: **Solanum guineense** L. (Solanaceae).
Note: Heine (in *Kew Bull.* 14: 245. 1960) discussed the various protologue elements but did not designate a type.

Solanum igneum Linnaeus, *Species Plantarum*, ed. 2, 1: 270. 1762.
"Habitat in America." RCN: 1489.
Lectotype (Howard, *Fl. Lesser Antilles* 6: 293. 1989): [icon] *"Solanum spiniferum frutescens spinis igneis Americanum"* in Plukenet, *Phytographia*: t. 225, f. 5. 1692; *Almag. Bot.*: 350. 1696. – Voucher: Herb. Sloane 98: 61; 102: 26 (BM-SL).
Current name: **Solanum bahamense** L. (Solanaceae).
Note: See detailed discussion by Knapp & Jarvis (in *Bot. J. Linn. Soc.* 104: 339, f. 10. 1991) who, unaware of Howard's earlier choice, designated 248.43 (LINN) as lectotype.

Solanum incanum Linnaeus, *Species Plantarum* 1: 188. 1753.
"Habitat – – – –" RCN: 1486.
Replaced synonym of: *Solanum sanctum* L. (1762), *nom. illeg.*
Neotype (Hepper & Jaeger in *Kew Bull.* 40: 388. 1985): Herb. Burser IX: 20 (UPS).
Current name: **Solanum incanum** L. (Solanaceae).

Solanum indicum Linnaeus, *Species Plantarum* 1: 187. 1753, *nom. utique rej.*
"Habitat in India utraque." RCN: 1482.
Lectotype (Hepper in Hawkes in *Bot. J. Linn. Soc.* 76: 288, f. 1A. 1978): Herb. Hermann 3: 16, No. 94 (BM-000594658).
Current name: **Solanum violaceum** Ortega (Solanaceae).

Solanum insanum Linnaeus, *Systema Naturae*, ed. 12, 2: 173; *Mantissa Plantarum*: 46. 1767.
"Habitat in Indiis." RCN: 1476.
Lectotype (Hepper & Jaeger in *Kew Bull.* 40: 388. 1985): Herb. Linn. No. 248.29 (LINN).
Current name: **Solanum melongena** L. (Solanaceae).

Solanum lycioides Linnaeus, *Systema Naturae*, ed. 12, 2: 174; *Mantissa Plantarum*: 46. 1767.
"Habitat in Peru?" RCN: 1492.
Lectotype (Knapp & Jarvis in *Bot. J. Linn. Soc.* 104: 342, f. 11. 1990): Herb. Linn. No. 248.48 (LINN).
Current name: **Lycianthes lycioides** (L.) Hassl. (Solanaceae).

Solanum lycopersicum Linnaeus, *Species Plantarum* 1: 185. 1753.
"Habitat in America calidiore." RCN: 1468.
Lectotype (Deb in *J. Econ. Taxon. Bot.* 1: 41. 1980): Herb. Linn. No. 248.16 (LINN).
Current name: **Solanum lycopersicum** L. (Solanaceae).
Note: See review by Knapp & Jarvis (in *Bot. J. Linn. Soc.* 104: 342, f. 12. 1990).

Solanum macrocarpon Linnaeus, *Mantissa Plantarum Altera*: 205. 1771.
"Habitat in Peru." RCN: 1466.
Lectotype (Hepper & Jaeger in *Kew Bull.* 40: 391. 1985): Herb. Linn. No. 248.11 (LINN).
Current name: **Solanum macrocarpon** L. (Solanaceae).

Solanum mammosum Linnaeus, *Species Plantarum* 1: 187. 1753.
"Habitat in Virginia, Barbados." RCN: 1479.
Lectotype (Knapp & Jarvis in *Bot. J. Linn. Soc.* 104: 344, f. 13. 1990): [icon] *"Solanum Barbadense spinosum, foliis villosis, fructu aureo rotundiore, Pyri parvi inversi forma et magnitudine"* in Plukenet, *Phytographia*: t. 226, f. 1. 1692; *Almag. Bot.*: 350. 1696. – Typotype: Herb. Sloane 98: 59 (BM-SL).
Current name: **Solanum mammosum** L. (Solanaceae).
Note: As noted by Knapp & Jarvis, 248.32 (LINN) is a post-1753 Browne collection and not original material for the name, so its treatment as the type by Symon (in *J. Adelaide Bot. Gard.* 4: 103. 1981) and others is erroneous.

Solanum melongena Linnaeus, *Species Plantarum* 1: 186. 1753.
"Habitat in Asia, Africa, America." RCN: 1475.
Lectotype (Schönbeck-Temesy in Rechinger, *Fl. Iranica* 100: 70. 1972): Herb. Linn. No. 248.28 (LINN).
Current name: **Solanum melongena** L. (Solanaceae).

Solanum montanum Linnaeus, *Species Plantarum* 1: 186. 1753.
"Habitat in Peru." RCN: 1471.
Lectotype (Knapp & Jarvis in *Bot. J. Linn. Soc.* 104: 344, f. 14. 1990): [icon] *"Solanum tuberosum minus, Atriplicis folio, vulgo Papa montana"* in Feuillée, *J. Obs.* 3: 62, t. 45. 1725.
Current name: **Solanum montanum** L. (Solanaceae).

Solanum nigrum Linnaeus, *Species Plantarum* 1: 186. 1753.
"Habitat in Orbis totius cultis." RCN: 1473.
Lectotype (Henderson in *Contr. Queensland Herb.* 16: 19. 1974): Herb. Linn. No. 248.18 (LINN).

Generitype of *Solanum* Linnaeus (vide Börner, *Bot.-Syst. Not.*: 282. 1912; *Abh. Naturwiss. Ver. Bremen* 21: 282. 1913).
Current name: ***Solanum nigrum*** L. subsp. ***nigrum*** (Solanaceae).
Note: Although Baylis (in *Trans. Roy. Soc. New Zealand* 85: 380. 1958) stated that the nomenclatural type had been examined, he did not indicate what it was. D'Arcy's choice of 248.18 (LINN) as type (in *Ann. Missouri Bot. Gard.* 61: 855. 24 Dec 1974) is pre-dated by that of Henderson using the same collection (in *Contr. Queensland Herb.* 16: 19. 2 Apr 1974).

Solanum nigrum Linnaeus var. **guineense** Linnaeus, *Species Plantarum* 1: 186. 1753.
RCN: 1473.
Lectotype (Edmonds in *Bot. J. Linn. Soc.* 78: 224. 1979): [icon] *"Solanum Guin., fructu magno instar Cerasi nigerr. umbellato Boerh."* in Dillenius, Hort. Eltham. 2: 366, t. 274, f. 354. 1732.
Current name: ***Solanum scabrum*** Mill. (Solanaceae).

Solanum nigrum Linnaeus var. **judaicum** Linnaeus, *Species Plantarum* 1: 186. 1753.
RCN: 1473.
Type not designated.
Original material: none traced.
Current name: ***Solanum*** **sp.** (Solanaceae).
Note: The application of this varietal name appears to be uncertain.

Solanum nigrum Linnaeus var. **patulum** Linnaeus, *Species Plantarum* 1: 186. 1753.
RCN: 1473.
Type not designated.
Original material: [icon] in Dillenius, Hort. Eltham. 2: 367, t. 275, f. 355. 1732.
Current name: ***Solanum*** **sp.** (Solanaceae).
Note: The application of this varietal name appears to be uncertain.

Solanum nigrum Linnaeus var. **villosum** Linnaeus, *Species Plantarum* 1: 186. 1753.
RCN: 1473.
Lectotype (Henderson in *Contr. Queensland Herb.* 16: 56. 1974): [icon] *"Solanum annuum hirsutius, baccis luteis Bob."* in Dillenius, Hort. Eltham. 2: 366, t. 274, f. 353. 1732.
Current name: ***Solanum villosum*** Mill. (Solanaceae).
Note: See also Edmonds (in *Bot. J. Linn. Soc.* 78: 214. 1979).

Solanum nigrum Linnaeus var. **virginicum** Linnaeus, *Species Plantarum* 1: 186. 1753.
RCN: 1473.
Lectotype (designated here by Edmonds): [icon] *"Solanum nigrum vulgari simile, caulibus exasperatis"* in Dillenius, Hort. Eltham. 2: 368, t. 275, f. 356. 1732.
Current name: ***Solanum nigrum*** L. var. ***virginicum*** L. (Solanaceae).
Note: While several authors (e.g. Henderson in *Contr. Queensland Herb.* 16: 35. 1974) have suggested that the name is based on the cited Dillenius element, no explicit typification appears to have been made until now.

Solanum nigrum Linnaeus var. **vulgare** Linnaeus, *Species Plantarum* 1: 186. 1753.
RCN: 1473.
Type not designated.
Original material: Herb. Clifford: 60, *Solanum* 3 α? (BM).
Current name: ***Solanum nigrum*** L. var. ***vulgare*** L. (Solanaceae).

Solanum nigrum Linnaeus var. **vulgatum** Linnaeus, *Species Plantarum*, ed. 2, 1: 266. 1762, *orth. var.*

RCN: 1473.
Type not designated.
Original material: as *Solanum nigrum* var. *vulgare.*
Current name: ***Solanum nigrum*** L. var. ***vulgare*** L. (Solanaceae).
Note: Evidently an orthographic variant of *S. nigrum* var. *vulgare* L. (1753).

Solanum paniculatum Linnaeus, *Species Plantarum*, ed. 2, 1: 267. 1762.
"Habitat in Brasilia." RCN: 1480.
Lectotype (Knapp & Jarvis in *Bot. J. Linn. Soc.* 104: 347, f. 15, 16. 1990): [icon] *"Iurepeba"* in Piso, Ind. Nat. Med.: 181, 181 [left fig.]. 1658. – Typotype: Herb. Marggraf, No. 16 (C).
Current name: ***Solanum paniculatum*** L. (Solanaceae).

Solanum peruvianum Linnaeus, *Species Plantarum* 1: 186. 1753.
"Habitat in Peru. D. Jussieu." RCN: 1470.
Lectotype (Knapp & Jarvis in *Bot. J. Linn. Soc.* 104: 348, f. 17. 1990): Herb. Linn. No. 248.17 (LINN).
Current name: ***Solanum peruvianum*** L. (Solanaceae).

Solanum pimpinellifolium Linnaeus, *Centuria I Plantarum*: 8. 1755.
"Habitat in Peru." RCN: 1468.
Lectotype (Knapp & Jarvis in *Bot. J. Linn. Soc.* 104: 350, f. 19. 1990): Herb. Linn. No. 248.15 (LINN).
Current name: ***Solanum pimpinellifolium*** L. (Solanaceae).

Solanum pseudocapsicum Linnaeus, *Species Plantarum* 1: 184. 1753.
"Habitat in Madera." RCN: 1457.
Lectotype (Schönbeck-Temesy in Rechinger, *Fl. Iranica* 100: 6. 1972): Herb. Linn. No. 248.4 (LINN).
Current name: ***Solanum pseudocapsicum*** L. (Solanaceae).
Note: See extensive discussion by Knapp & Jarvis (in *Bot. J. Linn. Soc.* 104: 351, f. 20. 1990).

Solanum pulverulentum Linnaeus, *Systema Naturae*, ed. 10, 2: 935. 1759, *nom. illeg.*
["Habitat in America septentrionali."] Sp. Pl. 1: 188 (1753). RCN: 1487.
Replaced synonym: *Solanum tomentosum* L. (1753).
Lectotype (Knapp & Jarvis in *Bot. J. Linn. Soc.* 104: 358, f. 24. 1990): Herb. Clifford: 61, *Solanum* 13 (BM-000558038).
Current name: ***Solanum tomentosum*** L. (Solanaceae).
Note: An illegitimate replacement name for *S. tomentosum* L. (1753), as noted by Knapp & Jarvis (in *Bot. J. Linn. Soc.* 104: 352. 1990).

Solanum quercifolium Linnaeus, *Species Plantarum* 1: 185. 1753, *nom. utique rej.*
"Habitat in Peru. D. Jussieu." RCN: 1460.
Lectotype (Knapp & Jarvis in *Bot. J. Linn. Soc.* 104: 354, f. 21. 1990): Herb. Linn. No. 248.8 (LINN).
Current name: ***Solanum septemlobum*** Bunge (Solanaceae).

Solanum radicans Linnaeus filius, *Decas Prima Plantarum Horti Upsaliensis*: 19. 1762.
"Habitat in Peru." RCN: 1462.
Lectotype (designated here by Knapp): Herb. Linn. No. 248.9 (LINN).
Current name: ***Solanum radicans*** L. f. (Solanaceae).
Note: Linnaeus includes this name in *Sp. Pl.*, ed. 2, 1: 264 (1762) [Sep], with reference to Linnaeus filius [Apr-Jul].

Solanum rubrum Linnaeus, *Systema Naturae*, ed. 12, 2: 173. 1767.
RCN: 1472.
Type not designated.

Original material: none traced.

Note: The application of this name is uncertain and it has been treated by some authors, e.g. Edmonds (in *Bot. J. Linn. Soc.* 78: 219. 1979) as a *nomen dubium*.

Solanum sanctum Linnaeus, *Species Plantarum,* ed. 2, 1: 269. 1762, *nom. illeg.*
"Habitat in Palaestina." RCN: 1486.
Replaced synonym: *Solanum incanum* L. (1753).
Neotype (Hepper & Jaeger in *Kew Bull.* 40: 388. 1985): Herb. Burser IX: 20 (UPS).
Current name: **Solanum incanum** L. (Solanaceae).
Note: An illegitimate replacement name for *S. incanum* L. (1753).

Solanum scandens Linnaeus, *Plantae Surinamenses*: 6. 1775, *nom. illeg.*
"Habitat [in Surinamo.]" RCN: 1461.
Lectotype (Knapp & Jarvis in *Bot. J. Linn. Soc.* 104: 356, f. 23. 1990): Herb. Linn. No. 248.24 (LINN).
Current name: **Solanum pensile** Sendtner (Solanaceae).
Note: A later homonym of *S. scandens* Mill. (1768) and therefore illegitimate.

Solanum sodomeum Linnaeus, *Species Plantarum* 1: 187. 1753, *nom. utique rej.*
"Habitat in Africa." RCN: 1485.
Lectotype (Siddiqi in Jafri & El-Gadi, *Fl. Libya* 62: 10. 1978): Herb. Linn. No. 248.34 (LINN).
Current name: **Solanum violaceum** Ortega (Solanaceae).

Solanum tomentosum Linnaeus, *Species Plantarum* 1: 188. 1753.
"Habitat in America septentrionali." RCN: 1487.
Replaced synonym of: *Solanum pulverulentum* L. (1759), *nom. illeg.*
Lectotype (Knapp & Jarvis in *Bot. J. Linn. Soc.* 104: 358, f. 24. 1990): Herb. Clifford: 61, *Solanum* 13 (BM-000558038).
Current name: **Solanum tomentosum** L. (Solanaceae).

Solanum trilobatum Linnaeus, *Species Plantarum* 1: 188. 1753.
"Habitat in India." RCN: 1490.
Lectotype (Deb in *J. Econ. Taxon. Bot.* 1: 51. 1980): Herb. Linn. No. 248.44 (LINN).
Current name: **Solanum trilobatum** L. (Solanaceae).

Solanum tuberosum Linnaeus, *Species Plantarum* 1: 185. 1753.
"Habitat in Peru." RCN: 1467.
Lectotype (Hawkes in *Proc. Linn. Soc. London* 166: 106. 1956): Herb. Linn. No. 248.12 (LINN).
Current name: **Solanum tuberosum** L. (Solanaceae).
Note: See review by Knapp & Jarvis (in *Bot. J. Linn. Soc.* 104: 358, f. 25. 1990).

Solanum verbascifolium Linnaeus, *Species Plantarum* 1: 184. 1753, *nom. utique rej.*
"Habitat in America." RCN: 1456.
Lectotype (Roe in *Taxon* 17: 176. 1968): Herb. Linn. No. 248.1 (LINN), see above, right.
Current name: **Solanum donianum** Walp. (Solanaceae).

Solanum virginianum Linnaeus, *Species Plantarum* 1: 187. 1753.
"Habitat in America." RCN: 1487.
Lectotype (Hepper & Jaeger in *Kew Bull.* 41: 434. 1986): [icon] *"Solanum American. laciniatum spinosissimum"* in Dillenius, Hort. Eltham. 2: 360, t. 267, f. 346. 1732. – Typotype: Herb. Sherard No. 456 (OXF).
Current name: **Solanum virginianum** L. (Solanaceae).

The lectotype of *Solanum verbascifolium* L.

Note: See discussion by Knapp & Jarvis (in *Bot. J. Linn. Soc.* 104: 363, f. 27, 28. 1990).

Solanum virginicum Linnaeus, *Mantissa Plantarum Altera*: 340. 1771, *orth. var.*
["Habitat in America."] Sp. Pl. 1: 187 (1753). RCN: 1481.
Lectotype (Hepper & Jaeger in *Kew Bull.* 41: 434. 1986): [icon] *"Solanum American. laciniatum spinosissimum"* in Dillenius, Hort. Eltham. 2: 360, t. 267, f. 346. 1732. – Typotype: Herb. Sherard No. 456 (OXF).
Current name: **Solanum virginianum** L. (Solanaceae).
Note: An orthographic error for *S. virginianum* L. (1753); see Knapp & Jarvis (in *Bot. J. Linn. Soc.* 104: 364. 1990).

Soldanella alpina Linnaeus, *Species Plantarum* 1: 144. 1753.
"Habitat in alpibus Helvetiae, Austriae, Pyrenaeorum." RCN: 1158.
Lectotype (Zhang & Kadereit in *Taxon* 53: 742. 2004): Herb. Clifford: 49, *Soldanella* 1 (BM-000557943).
Generitype of *Soldanella* Linnaeus.
Current name: **Soldanella alpina** L. (Primulaceae).
Note: Meyer (in *Haussknechtia* 2: 26. 1985) designated "Soldanella alpina minor" Clusius, *Rar. Pl. Hist.*: 309 (1601) as lectotype but as it is not cited in the protologue, it cannot be an original element for the name.

Solidago alpina Linnaeus, *Species Plantarum* 2: 880. 1753.
"Habitat in Alpibus Helvetiae, Austriae, Tyroli." RCN: 6366.
Basionym of: *Cineraria alpina* (L.) L. (1763).
Lectotype (Kadereit in Jarvis & Turland in *Taxon* 47: 367. 1998):
[icon] *"Jacobaea alpina foliis rotundis serratis"* in Bauhin, Prodr.
Theatri Bot.: 70, 69. 1620.
Current name: *Jacobaea alpina* (L.) Moench (Asteraceae).

Solidago altissima Linnaeus, *Species Plantarum* 2: 878. 1753.
"Habitat in America septentrionali." RCN: 6348.
Lectotype (Reveal & al. in *Huntia* 7: 238. 1987): [icon] *"Virga aurea
Marilandica, spicis florum racemosis, foliis integris, scabris"* in Martyn,
Hist. Pl. Rar.: 13, t. 13. 1728.
Current name: *Solidago canadensis* L. var. *scabra* Torr. & A. Gray
(Asteraceae).
Note: Gray (in *Proc. Amer. Acad. Arts* 17: 177. 1882), in a study of the
Solidago material in the Linnaean herbarium, concluded that the
specimens associated with this name "are confounded" and that the
cited Martyn plate is "the true original of the Linnaean species".
Gray's conclusion was accepted and followed by Fernald (in *Rhodora*
11: 91. 1908), and formalised by Reveal & al. (in *Huntia* 7: 238.
1987), and accepted here. Mackenzie (in *Rhodora* 29: 73. 1927)
claimed that Linnaeus' original concept (based on what was in
cultivation in Uppsala) was of *S. rugosa* Mill. and proposed that
usage of *S. canadensis* should revert to that. However, Mackenzie
did not typify the name to effect this change. Taylor & Taylor (in
Sida 10: 231. 1984) indicated unspecified material in LINN as
"type" but did not distinguish between the several sheets noted by
Gray. These collections are not part of a single gathering so Art.
9.15 does not apply.

Solidago bicolor Linnaeus, *Systema Naturae*, ed. 12, 2: 556; *Mantissa
Plantarum*: 114. 1767.
"Habitat in America septentrionali. Dav. Royen." RCN: 6350.
Lectotype (designated here by Semple): *D. van Royen 79*, Herb. Linn.
No. 998.8 (LINN).
Current name: *Solidago bicolor* L. (Asteraceae).
Note: Gray (in *Proc. Amer. Acad. Arts* 17: 178. 1882), in a study of the
Solidago material in the Linnaean herbarium, noted the sheet
subsequently numbered 998.8 (LINN), and excluded two others
(998.9; 998.10), but did not refer to it as the type.

Solidago caesia Linnaeus, *Species Plantarum* 2: 879. 1753.
"Habitat in America septentrionali." RCN: 6352.
Lectotype (Uttal in *Sida* 10: 324. 1984): [icon] *"Virga aurea
Marilandica, caesia glabra"* in Dillenius, Hort. Eltham. 2: 414, t.
307, f. 395. 1732. – Typotype: Herb. Dillenius No. 1848 (OXF).
Current name: *Solidago caesia* L. var. *caesia* (Asteraceae).
Note: Gray (in *Proc. Amer. Acad. Arts* 17: 178. 1882), in a study of the
Solidago material in the Linnaean herbarium, believed there to be
no relevant specimens of *S. caesia*, concluding that the name is
"founded on" the cited Dillenian illustration and associated material
in OXF. Taylor & Taylor (in *Sida* 10: 228. 1984) indicated both this
plate and 998.14 (LINN) as "type", and Uttal (in *Sida* 10: 324.
1984) appears to have been the first to formalise a choice. Reveal &
al. (in *Huntia* 7: 238. 1987) provide a concise summary.

Solidago canadensis Linnaeus, *Species Plantarum* 2: 878. 1753.
"Habitat in Virginia, Canada." RCN: 6347.
Lectotype (Reveal & al. in *Huntia* 7: 238. 1987): Herb. Linn. No.
998.2 (LINN).
Current name: *Solidago canadensis* L. var. *canadensis* (Asteraceae).
Note: Gray (in *Proc. Amer. Acad. Arts* 17: 177. 1882), in a study of the
Solidago material in the Linnaean herbarium, noted the existence of
two sheets, one of which (998.2 LINN) was identifiable as *S.*

canadensis, and the other (998.3 LINN) as *S. rugosa* Mill. Gray
added that the cited Plukenet element should be excluded from the
species (a view with which Mackenzie (in *Rhodora* 29: 74. 1927)
disagreed) but did not explicitly indicate a type. Taylor & Taylor (in
Sida 10: 230. 1984) indicated unspecified material in LINN as type
(i.e. not distinguishing between 998.2 and 998.3), and Reveal & al.
(in *Huntia* 7: 238. 1987) followed Gray's conclusion and formally
designated 998.2 (LINN) as lectotype.

Solidago doronicum Linnaeus, *Species Plantarum* 2: 880. 1753.
"Habitat in Alpibus Helvetiae, Austriae, Italiae, Monspelii." RCN:
6302.
Basionym of: *Senecio doronicum* (L.) L. (1759).
Lectotype (Kadereit in Jarvis & Turland in *Taxon* 47: 367. 1998):
Herb. Linn. No. 996.63 (LINN).
Current name: *Senecio doronicum* (L.) L. (Asteraceae).

Solidago flexicaulis Linnaeus, *Species Plantarum* 2: 879. 1753.
"Habitat in Canada." RCN: 6354.
Lectotype (Semple in Jarvis & Turland in *Taxon* 47: 367. 1998): [icon]
"Virga aurea montana Scrophulariae folio" in Plukenet,
Phytographia: t. 235, f. 3. 1692; Almag. Bot.: 390. 1696. –
Voucher: Herb. Sloane 98: 154; 102: 122 (BM-SL).
Current name: *Solidago flexicaulis* L. (Asteraceae).
Note: Gray (in *Proc. Amer. Acad. Arts* 17: 178. 1882) discussed the
identity of various of the original elements, noting that 998.14
(LINN) is identifiable as *S. caesia* L., but did not designate a type.
Other authors such as Mackenzie (in *Rhodora* 30: 223. 1928) and
Taylor & Taylor (in *Sida* 10: 181. 1983) also discussed this material,
but the earliest formal type choice appears to be that of Semple.

Solidago lanceolata Linnaeus, *Systema Naturae*, ed. 12, 2: 556;
Mantissa Plantarum: 114. 1767.
"Habitat in America septentrionali?" RCN: 6351.
Lectotype (Semple in Jarvis & Turland in *Taxon* 47: 367. 1998): *D.
van Royen 80*, Herb. Linn. No. 998.11 (LINN).
Current name: *Euthamia graminifolia* (L.) Nutt. (Asteraceae).
Note: Gray (in *Proc. Amer. Acad. Arts* 17: 178. 1882) discussed
material in LINN but did not designate a type.

Solidago lateriflora Linnaeus, *Species Plantarum* 2: 879. 1753.
"Habitat in America septentrionali. Kalm." RCN: 6349.
Type not designated.
Original material: Herb. Linn. No. 998.6? (LINN); Herb. Linn. No.
998.7? (LINN).
Current name: *Aster lateriflorus* (L.) Britton var. *lateriflorus*
(Asteraceae).
Note: Gray (in *Proc. Amer. Acad. Arts* 17: 178. 1882) discussed the
identity of 998.9 (LINN), which is *Aster diffusus* Ait., but did not
designate a type. Wiegand (in *Rhodora* 30: 177. 1928) noted merely
that this was based on a Kalm specimen (apparently from the
protologue), and Hoffmann (in *Feddes Repert.* 107: 183. 1996)
indicated 998.6 and 998.7 (LINN) as possible type elements.
However, the name currently appears to be untypified.

Solidago latifolia Linnaeus, *Species Plantarum* 2: 879. 1753.
"Habitat in Canada." RCN: 6355.
Lectotype (Semple in Jarvis & Turland in *Taxon* 47: 367. 1998): [icon]
"Virga aurea latissimo folio Canadensis glabra" in Plukenet,
Phytographia: t. 235, f. 4. 1692; Almag. Bot.: 389. 1696. –
Typotype: Herb. Sloane 98: 153 (BM-SL).
Current name: *Solidago flexicaulis* L. (Asteraceae).
Note: Gray (in *Proc. Amer. Acad. Arts* 17: 178. 1882) discussed the
identity of 998.7 (LINN) "which appears to be the original of the
species", and other elements, but did not designate a type.

S

Solidago linifolia Linnaeus, *Species Plantarum* 2: 881. 1753.
"Habitat in Hispania, Italia." RCN: 6297.
Basionym of: *Senecio linifolius* (L.) L. (1763), *nom. illeg.*
Lectotype (Wijnands, *Bot. Commelins*: 83. 1983): [icon] *"Jacobaea, linifolio, Hispanica et Ital."* in Boccone, Mus. Piante Rar. Sicilia: 60, t. 49. 1697.
Current name: ***Senecio nevadensis*** Boiss. & Reut. subsp. ***malacitanus*** (Huter) Greuter (Asteraceae).
Note: See López González (in *Anales Jard. Bot. Madrid* 44: 546. 1987), who demonstrates that *Senecio malacitanus* Huter is the earliest name for this taxon.

Solidago mexicana Linnaeus, *Species Plantarum* 2: 879. 1753.
"Habitat in Mexico?" RCN: 6353.
Lectotype (Taylor & Taylor in *Sida* 10: 243. 1984): Herb. Linn. No. 998.13 (LINN).
Current name: ***Solidago sempervirens*** L. var. ***mexicana*** (L.) Fernald (Asteraceae).
Note: Gray (in *Proc. Amer. Acad. Arts* 17: 178. 1882) noted the identity of the cited Tournefort element, but did not designate a type. McVaugh (in *Contr. Univ. Michigan Herb.* 9: 366. 1972) discussed 998.13 (LINN) and noted that it resembled *S. sempervirens* but did not indicate it as type. Although Taylor & Taylor did not provide a sheet number for their type choice, there is only one sheet associated with this name in LINN.

Solidago minuta Linnaeus, *Species Plantarum*, ed. 2, 2: 1235. 1763.
"Habitat in Pyrenaeis." RCN: 6357.
Lectotype (Garbari & Cecchi in Jarvis & Turland in *Taxon* 47: 367. 1998): [icon] *"Virga Aurea Omnium minima Floribus maximis"* in Hermann, Parad. Bat.: 245. 1698.
Current name: ***Solidago virgaurea*** L. subsp. ***minuta*** (L.) Arcang. (Asteraceae).

Solidago montana Linnaeus, *Species Plantarum* 2: 881. 1753.
"Habitat Monspelii." RCN: 6039.
Type not designated.
Original material: [icon] in Chomel in Mém. Acad. Roy. Sci. Paris 1705: 387, t. 8. 1705.
Current name: ***Senecio sarracenicus*** L. (Asteraceae).

Solidago noveboracensis Linnaeus, *Species Plantarum* 2: 880. 1753.
"Habitat in America septentrionali." RCN: 6359.
Type not designated.
Original material: Herb. Linn. No. 998.22 (LINN).
Current name: ***Aster* sp.** (Asteraceae).
Note: Although Gray (in *Proc. Amer. Acad. Arts* 17: 179. 1882) noted the identity of 998.22 (LINN) as *Aster tataricus* L. f., he did not designate a type.

Solidago rigida Linnaeus, *Species Plantarum* 2: 880. 1753.
"Habitat in Pensylvania." RCN: 6358.
Lectotype (Taylor & Taylor in *Sida* 10: 239. 1984): Herb. Linn. No. 998.20 (LINN).
Current name: ***Solidago rigida*** L. subsp. ***rigida*** (Asteraceae).
Note: Although Gray (in *Proc. Amer. Acad. Arts* 17: 179. 1882) noted the identity of 998.20 (LINN), and the cited Hermann figure, he did not designate a type. Mackenzie (in *Rhodora* 28: 29–31. 1926; 29: 30–31. 1927) also noted the existence of the LINN material but argued that it played no part in establishing the name, which he regarded as based on the Hermann plate t. 243 (representing *S. patula* Muhl.). Weatherby (in *Rhodora* 28: 138. 1926) disagreed strongly with him, and also over the identity of the plate. Taylor & Taylor appear to have been the first to make a formal type choice.

Solidago sempervirens Linnaeus, *Species Plantarum* 2: 878. 1753.
"Habitat in Noveboraco, Canada." RCN: 6346.
Lectotype (Taylor & Taylor in *Sida* 10: 243. 1984): Herb. Linn. No. 998.1 (LINN).
Current name: ***Solidago sempervirens*** L. (Asteraceae).
Note: Although Gray (in *Proc. Amer. Acad. Arts* 17: 177. 1882) noted the identity of 998.1 (LINN) and the cited Plukenet figure, he did not designate a type.

Solidago virgaurea Linnaeus, *Species Plantarum* 2: 880. 1753.
"Habitat in Europae pascuis siccis." RCN: 6356.
Lectotype (Garbari & Cecchi in Jarvis & Turland in *Taxon* 47: 368. 1998): Herb. Linn. No. 998.15 (LINN).
Generitype of *Solidago* Linnaeus (vide Green, *Prop. Brit. Bot.*: 181. 1929).
Current name: ***Solidago virgaurea*** L. (Asteraceae).
Note: Nesom (in *Phytologia* 75: 16. 1993) provided some notes on the material in LINN but did not designate a type.

Sonchus alpinus Linnaeus, *Species Plantarum* 2: 794. 1753.
"Habitat ad latera Alpium Lapponiae, Helvetiae, Austriae." RCN: 5811.
Lectotype (Wegmüller in Jarvis & Turland in *Taxon* 47: 368. 1998): Herb. Burser VI: 23 (UPS).
Current name: ***Cicerbita alpina*** (L.) Wallr. (Asteraceae).

Sonchus arvensis Linnaeus, *Species Plantarum* 2: 793. 1753.
"Habitat in Europae agris argillosis." RCN: 5807.
Lectotype (Boulos in *Bot. Not.* 114: 59, f. 1. 1961): Herb. Linn. No. 949.5 (LINN).
Current name: ***Sonchus arvensis*** L. (Asteraceae).

Sonchus canadensis Linnaeus, *Species Plantarum* 2: 793. 1753.
"Habitat in Canada. Kalm." RCN: 5816.
Lectotype (Reveal & Turland in Jarvis & Turland in *Taxon* 47: 368. 1998): *Kalm*, Herb. Linn. No. 949.18 (LINN).
Current name: ***Cicerbita alpina*** (L.) Wallr. (Asteraceae).

Sonchus floridanus Linnaeus, *Species Plantarum* 2: 794. 1753.
"Habitat in Virginia, Canada." RCN: 5812.
Lectotype (designated here by Reveal): Herb. Linn. No. 949.13 (LINN).
Current name: ***Lactuca floridana*** (L.) Gaertn. var. ***floridana*** (Asteraceae).

Sonchus maritimus Linnaeus, *Systema Naturae*, ed. 10, 2: 1192. 1759.
["Habitat in Europa australi."] Sp. Pl., ed. 2, 2: 1116 (1763). RCN: 5805.
Lectotype (Boulos in *Bot. Not.* 126: 174. 1973): *Kähler*, Herb. Linn. No. 949.1 (LINN), see p. 214.
Current name: ***Sonchus maritimus*** L. (Asteraceae).

Sonchus oleraceus Linnaeus, *Species Plantarum* 2: 794. 1753.
"Habitat in Europae cultis." RCN: 5808.
Lectotype (Boulos in *Bot. Not.* 126: 155. 1973): Herb. Linn. No. 949.6 (LINN).
Generitype of *Sonchus* Linnaeus (vide Green, *Prop. Brit. Bot.*: 177. 1929).
Current name: ***Sonchus oleraceus*** L. (Asteraceae).

Sonchus oleraceus Linnaeus var. **asper** Linnaeus, *Species Plantarum* 2: 794. 1753.
RCN: 5808.

Lectotype (Boulos in Jarvis & Turland in *Taxon* 47: 368. 1998): Herb. Burser VI: 14 (UPS).
Current name: ***Sonchus asper*** (L.) Hill subsp. ***asper*** (Asteraceae).
Note: Boulos (in *Bot. Not.* 126: 164. 1973) and a number of later authors all treated Herb. Linn. No. 949.8 (LINN) as the type, but this sheet is unannotated as to species by Linnaeus and is not original material for the name. Boulos therefore superseded this choice with a new typification in 1998.

Sonchus oleraceus Linnaeus var. **laevis** Linnaeus, *Species Plantarum* 2: 794. 1753.
RCN: 5808.
Lectotype (Boulos in Jarvis & Turland in *Taxon* 47: 368. 1998): Herb. Burser VI: 16 (UPS).
Current name: ***Sonchus oleraceus*** L. (Asteraceae).

Sonchus palustris Linnaeus, *Species Plantarum* 2: 793. 1753.
"Habitat in Belgii, Angliae, Galliae, Hungariae pratis paludosis." RCN: 5806.
Lectotype (Boulos in *Bot. Not.* 126: 177. 1973): Herb. Linn. No. 949.4 (LINN).
Current name: ***Sonchus palustris*** L. (Asteraceae).

Sonchus plumieri Linnaeus, *Systema Naturae*, ed. 10, 2: 1192. 1759.
["Habitat in Pyrenaeis: Monte Aureo prope Carthusiam majorem. Monnier."] Sp. Pl., ed. 2, 2: 1117 (1763). RCN: 5810.
Lectotype (Wegmüller in Jarvis & Turland in *Taxon* 47: 368. 1998): Herb. Linn. No. 949.10 (LINN).
Current name: ***Lactuca plumieri*** (L.) Gren. & Godr. (Asteraceae).
Note: Wegmüller (in *Bot. Jahrb. Syst.* 116: 189. 1994) incorrectly typified the name using an illustration from Kirschleger (who had recombined the Linnaean name in *Cicerbita*), rather than an element from the Linnaean protologue. He superseded this earlier choice with a new typification in 1998.

Sonchus sibiricus Linnaeus, *Species Plantarum* 2: 795. 1753.
"Habitat in Sibiria, Suecia septentrionali, Finlandia." RCN: 5813.
Type not designated.
Original material: Herb. Linn. No. 949.14 (LINN); [icon] in Gmelin, Fl. Sibirica 2: 11, t. 3. 1752.
Current name: ***Lactuca sibirica*** (L.) Benth. ex Maxim. (Asteraceae).

Sonchus tataricus Linnaeus, *Mantissa Plantarum Altera*: 572. 1771.
"Habitat in Tataria, Sibiria." RCN: 5814.
Lectotype (van Raamsdonk in Wisskirchen in *Feddes Repert.* 108: 105. 1997): [icon] *"Sonchus foliis lanceolatis, sessilibus, plerumque denticulatis, floribus corymbosis, caulibus glabris"* in Gmelin, Fl. Sibirica 2: 11, t. 3. 1752.
Current name: ***Lactuca tatarica*** (L.) C.A. Mey. (Asteraceae).

Sonchus tenerrimus Linnaeus, *Species Plantarum* 2: 794. 1753.
"Habitat Monspelii, Florentiae." RCN: 5809.
Lectotype (Boulos in *Bot. Not.* 126: 158. 1973): Herb. Linn. No. 949.9 (LINN).
Current name: ***Sonchus tenerrimus*** L. (Asteraceae).

Sonchus tuberosus Linnaeus, *Systema Vegetabilium*, ed. 13: 594. 1774.
["Habitat in Tataria."] Linnaeus filius, Suppl. Pl.: 346 (1782). RCN: 5815.
Type not designated.
Original material: none traced.
Current name: ***Lactuca sp.*** (Asteraceae).

Sophia carolina Linnaeus, *Plantae Surinamenses*: 11. 1775.
"Habitat [in Surinamo.]" RCN: 5115.

Lectotype (Barrie in Jarvis & al., *Regnum Veg.* 127: 89. 1993): Herb. Linn. No. 865.1 (LINN).
Generitype of *Sophia* Linnaeus.
Current name: ***Pachira aquatica*** Aubl. (Bombacaceae).
Note: Sophia Adanson (1763, Brassicaceae) is an earlier homonym of *Sophia* Linnaeus (1775, Bombacaceae) but is a rejected name.

Sophora alba (Linnaeus) Linnaeus, *Systema Naturae*, ed. 12, 2: 287. 1767.
["Habitat in Carolina."] Sp. Pl. 2: 716 (1753). RCN: 2941.
Basionym: *Crotalaria alba* L. (1753).
Lectotype (Barrie in Turland & Jarvis in *Taxon* 46: 467. 1997): Herb. A. van Royen No. 908.112–704 (L).
Current name: ***Baptisia alba*** (L.) Vent. (Fabaceae: Faboideae).

Sophora alopecuroides Linnaeus, *Species Plantarum* 1: 373. 1753.
"Habitat in Oriente." RCN: 2932.
Lectotype (Ma in Turland & Jarvis in *Taxon* 46: 480. 1997): Herb. Clifford: 156, *Sophora* 1 (BM-000558711).
Current name: ***Sophora alopecuroides*** L. (Fabaceae: Faboideae).

Sophora australis Linnaeus, *Systema Naturae*, ed. 12, 2: 287. 1767.
"Habitat in C. B. S." RCN: 2939.
Type not designated.
Original material: Herb. Linn. No. 522.15 (LINN); Herb. Linn. No. 522.14? (LINN).
Current name: ***Baptisia australis*** (L.) R. Br. (Fabaceae: Faboideae).
Note: Isely (in *Mem. New York Bot. Gard.* 25: 220. 1981) notes that Linnaeus changed the stated provenance, from South Africa (in 1767) to Carolina (in 1771), with specimens in LINN associated with each. However, the name does not appear to have been typified.

Sophora biflora Linnaeus, *Systema Naturae*, ed. 10, 2: 1015. 1759.
["Habitat in Aethiopia."] Sp. Pl., ed. 2, 1: 534 (1762). RCN: 2943.
Lectotype (Schelpe in *Veld Fl.* 4: 28. 1974): Herb. Linn. No. 163.3 (S).
Current name: ***Podalyria biflora*** (L.) Lam. (Fabaceae: Faboideae).

Sophora capensis Linnaeus, *Systema Naturae*, ed. 12, 2: 287; *Mantissa Plantarum*: 67. 1767.
"Habitat ad Cap. b. spei." RCN: 2935.
Lectotype (Van Wyk in *S. African J. Bot.* 52: 350. 1986): Herb. Linn. No. 522.8 (LINN).
Current name: ***Virgilia oroboides*** (P.J. Bergius) T.M. Salter (Fabaceae: Faboideae).

Sophora genistoides Linnaeus, *Species Plantarum* 1: 373. 1753.
"Habitat ad Cap. b. Spei." RCN: 2938.
Lectotype (Schutte in *Edinburgh J. Bot.* 54: 159. 1997): Herb. Linn. No. 522.11 (LINN).
Current name: ***Cyclopia genistoides*** (L.) R. Br. (Fabaceae: Faboideae).

Sophora heptaphylla Linnaeus, *Species Plantarum* 1: 373. 1753.
"Habitat in India." RCN: 2937.
Lectotype (Polhill in *Kew Bull.* 25: 268. 1971; Rudd in Dassanayake & Fosberg, *Revised Handb. Fl. Ceylon* 7: 235. 1991): Herb. Hermann 2: 8, No. 164 (BM-000594571).
Current name: ***Aganope heptaphylla*** (L.) Polhill (Fabaceae: Faboideae).
Note: Polhill (in *Kew Bull.* 25: 268. 1971), possibly following Merrill (*Interpret. Rumph. Herb. Amb.*: 273. 1917) who stated "the type is Fl. Zeyl. 104, and Hermann's specimen on which it is based is Derris sinuata", indicated a specimen in Herb. Hermann that he had not seen, as the holotype. There is material in vol. 2: 8 and 2:

S

80, almost certainly from a single gathering. Polhill is accepted as having typified the name first, with Rudd subsequently restricting the choice to the material on p. 8.

Sophora japonica Linnaeus, *Systema Naturae*, ed. 12, 2: 287; *Mantissa Plantarum*: 68. 1767.
"Habitat in Japonia. Kleinhoff." RCN: 2936.
Type not designated.
Original material: Herb. Linn. No. 522.10 (LINN); Herb. Linn. No. 522.9 (LINN).
Current name: *Sophora japonica* L. (Fabaceae: Faboideae).
Note: This name does not appear to have been typified, although several authors (e.g. Sousa & Rudd in *Ann. Missouri Bot. Gard.* 80: 273. 1993) indicate (presumably from the protologue) unspecified Kleynhoff material as type. Isely (in *Mem. New York Bot. Gard.* 25: 251. 1981) dismissed material in LINN from consideration in typification, and Sousa & Rudd also note that 522.9 (LINN) is not identifiable with the current usage of the name.

Sophora lupinoides Linnaeus, *Species Plantarum* 1: 374. 1753.
"Habitat in Camtschatca. G. Demidoff." RCN: 2943.
Proposed conserved type (Zhu & Kirkbride in *Taxon* 55: 1047. 2006): Kamchatka, *Pallas s.n.* (BM).
Current name: *Thermopsis lupinoides* (L.) Link (Fabaceae: Faboideae).
Note: The lectotype of *Thermopsis lupinoides* (L.) Link (*Steller*, Herb. Linn. No. 522.19 (LINN), designated by Kit Tan in Turland & Jarvis in *Taxon* 46: 480. 1997) has been found to be identifiable as the Siberian/Chinese species long known as *T. lanceolata* R. Br., and not the species from Kamchatka to which it has generally been applied. Zhu & Kirkbride have therefore proposed the Linnaean name for conservation with a conserved type.

Sophora occidentalis Linnaeus, *Systema Naturae*, ed. 10, 2: 1015. 1759.
["Habitat in America."] Sp. Pl., ed. 2, 1: 533 (1762). RCN: 2934.
Lectotype (Dillon in Woodson & Schery in *Ann. Missouri Bot. Gard.* 67: 766. 1980): *Browne*, Herb. Linn. No. 522.6 (LINN).
Current name: *Sophora tomentosa* L. var. *occidentalis* (L.) Isely (Fabaceae: Faboideae).

Sophora tinctoria Linnaeus, *Species Plantarum* 1: 373. 1753.
"Habitat in Barbados, Virginia." RCN: 2940.
Lectotype (Fernald in *Rhodora* 39: 414. 1937): *Kalm*, Herb. Linn. No. 522.16 (LINN; iso- UPS).
Current name: *Baptisia tinctoria* (L.) Vent. (Fabaceae: Faboideae).

Sophora tomentosa Linnaeus, *Species Plantarum* 1: 373. 1753.
"Habitat in Zeylona." RCN: 2933.
Lectotype (Rudd in Dassanayake & Fosberg, *Revised Handb. Fl. Ceylon* 1: 439. 1980): Herb. Hermann 3: 13, No. 163 (BM-000594655).
Generitype of *Sophora* Linnaeus.
Current name: *Sophora tomentosa* L. var. *tomentosa* (Fabaceae: Faboideae).
Note: Sophora tomentosa, with the type designated by Rudd, was proposed as conserved type of the genus by Jarvis (in *Taxon* 41: 570. 1992). However, the proposal was eventually ruled unnecessary by the General Committee (see Barrie, *l.c.* 55: 795–796. 2006 for a review of the history of this and related proposals).

Sorbus aucuparia Linnaeus, *Species Plantarum* 1: 477. 1753.
"Habitat in Europae frigidioribus." RCN: 3649.
Lectotype (Düll in Jarvis & al., *Regnum Veg.* 127: 89. 1993): Herb. Clifford: 188, *Sorbus* 1 α, sheet A (BM-000628622).

Current name: *Sorbus aucuparia* L. (Rosaceae).
Note: Sorbus aucuparia was treated as the generitype by Rehder (*Bibliogr. Cult. Trees Shrubs*: 252. 1949) but this choice is pre-dated by that of Green (*Prop. Brit. Bot.*: 158. 1929) who chose *S. domestica* L.

Sorbus domestica Linnaeus, *Species Plantarum* 1: 477. 1753.
"Habitat in Europae calidioribus." RCN: 3651.
Lectotype (Aldasoro & Aedo in Cafferty & Jarvis in *Taxon* 51: 544. 2002): Herb. Burser XXII: 82 (UPS).
Generitype of *Sorbus* Linnaeus (vide Green, *Prop. Brit. Bot.*: 158. 1929).
Current name: *Sorbus domestica* L. (Rosaceae).
Note: Sorbus aucuparia was treated as the generitype by Rehder (*Bibliogr. Cult. Trees Shrubs*: 252. 1949), but this choice is pre-dated by that of Green (*Prop. Brit. Bot.*: 158. 1929), who chose *S. domestica* L.
   Knees (in *Plantsman* 7: 65–67. 1985) discussed the original elements for the name but did not designate a type.

Sorbus hybrida Linnaeus, *Species Plantarum*, ed. 2, 1: 684. 1762.
"Habitat in Gotlandia." RCN: 3650.
Lectotype (Jonsell & Jarvis in *Nordic J. Bot.* 22: 76. 2002): Herb. Linn. No. 644.4 (LINN).
Current name: *Sorbus × hybrida* L. (Rosaceae).
Note: Hensen (in *Belmontia Hort.* 5(22): 190. 1961) appears to regard *Crataegus hybrida* L. (1761) as a valid name, and the basionym of "*Sorbus hybrida* (L.) L.". However, Sell (in *Watsonia* 17: 386. 1989) regards *C. hybrida* as a *nomen nudum*, and *S. hybrida* as a new name dating from 1762.

Sparganium erectum Linnaeus, *Species Plantarum* 2: 971. 1753.
"Habitat in Zonae frigidae septentrionalis aquosis." RCN: 7047.
Type not designated.
Original material: Herb. Linn. No. 1095.3 (LINN); Herb. Clifford: 439, *Sparganium* 1 α, 2 sheets (BM); Herb. Linn. No. 345 (LAPP); [icon] in Dodoëns, Stirp. Hist. Pempt., ed. 2: 601. 1616.
Generitype of *Sparganium* Linnaeus (vide Green, *Prop. Brit. Bot.*: 187. 1929).
Current name: *Sparganium erectum* L. (Sparganiaceae).
Note: Although some authors (e.g. Hylander in *Uppsala Univ. Årsskr.* 7: 64. 1945) have rejected the name as a *nomen ambiguum*, others have continued to use it. Cook (in *Bot. Jahrb. Syst.* 107: 271. 1985) and Cook & Nicholls (in *Bot. Helvetica* 97: 19. 1987) accepted as type a Lobel plate that was not cited in the protologue and so cannot be an original element. At least some of the original material in the LINN and Clifford herbaria is identifiable as *S. emersum* Rehmann, although other possibilities for lectotypification may exist.

Sparganium natans Linnaeus, *Species Plantarum* 2: 971. 1753.
"Habitat in Europae borealis lacubus, paludibus." RCN: 7048.
Lectotype (Cook in *Bot. Jahrb. Syst.* 107: 272. 1985): *Amman 31*, Herb. Linn. No. 1095.2 (LINN).
Current name: *Sparganium natans* L. (Sparganiaceae).
Note: This name had been rejected as a *nomen ambiguum* by a number of authors (see Cook in *Watsonia* 5: 7. 1961 for a summary). However, Cook took up the Linnaean name in typifying it in 1985 (see also Cook & Nicholls in *Bot. Helvetica* 96: 234. 1986).

Spartium angulatum Linnaeus, *Species Plantarum* 2: 709. 1753.
"Habitat in Oriente." RCN: 5194.
Neotype (Gibbs in Turland & Jarvis in *Taxon* 46: 480. 1997): Turkey. Balikesir, Seitinly, in dumetis, 12 Jul 1883, *Sintenis 673* [flowering specimen] (E).
Current name: *Gonocytisus angulatus* (L.) Spach (Fabaceae: Faboideae).

Spartium capense Linnaeus, *Plantae Rariores Africanae*: 14. 1760, *nom. cons.*

["Habitat ad Cap. b. spei."] Sp. Pl., ed. 2, 2: 995 (1763). RCN: 5433.

Replaced synonym of: *Liparia opposita* L. (1771), *nom. illeg.*

Conserved type (Campbell & al. in *Taxon* 48: 833. 1999): South Africa. Western Cape Province, Cape of Good Hope Nature Reserve, *Campbell & Van Wyk 151* (NBG; iso- K, MO, PRE).

Current name: ***Rafnia capensis*** (L.) Schinz (Fabaceae: Faboideae).

Note: Generic name spelled "Spatium" in the protologue.

Spartium complicatum Linnaeus, *Species Plantarum* 2: 709. 1753.

"Habitat in Hispania, Gallia australiore." RCN: 5196.

Lectotype (Gibbs in *Bol. Soc. Brot.*, sér. 2, 41: 87, 98. 1967): *Sauvages*, Herb. Linn. No. 891.8 (LINN).

Current name: ***Adenocarpus complicatus*** (L.) J. Gay (Fabaceae: Faboideae).

Note: The type designated by Gibbs did not correspond with the usage of *A. complicatus sensu stricto* pre-1967, and Castroviejo (in *Anales Jard. Bot. Madrid* 39: 159. 1982) discusses the nomenclatural consequences of this.

Spartium contaminatum Linnaeus, *Mantissa Plantarum Altera*: 268. 1771.

"Habitat ad Cap. b. spei arenosis." RCN: 5187.

Lectotype (Dahlgren in *Bot. Not.* 117: 193. 1964): *Tulbagh 203*, Herb. Linn. No. 891.1 (LINN).

Current name: ***Lebeckia contaminata*** (L.) Thunb. (Fabaceae: Faboideae).

Spartium junceum Linnaeus, *Species Plantarum* 2: 708. 1753.

"Habitat in G. Narbonensi, Italia, Sicilia, Turcia." RCN: 5189.

Lectotype (Elkington in Jarvis & al., *Regnum Veg.* 127: 90. 1993): Herb. Clifford: 356, *Spartium* 1, sheet 1 (BM-000646559; iso- BM).

Generitype of *Spartium* Linnaeus (vide Green, *Prop. Brit. Bot.*: 174. 1929).

Current name: ***Spartium junceum*** L. (Fabaceae: Faboideae).

Note: Jafri (in Jafri & El-Gadi, *Fl. Libya* 86: 27. 1980) indicated 891.5 (LINN) as type, but this sheet lacks the *Species Plantarum* number (i.e. "1") and is a post-1753 addition to the collection. It is not original material for the name. Rechinger & Ali (in Rechinger, *Fl. Iranica* 157: 27. 1984) indicated unspecified Clifford material as type. Elkington's choice provides the first unequivocal typification.

Spartium monospermum Linnaeus, *Species Plantarum* 2: 708. 1753.

"Habitat in Hispania sterilioribus." RCN: 5190.

Lectotype (Polhill in Turland & Jarvis in *Taxon* 46: 480. 1997): Herb. Linn. No. 891.6 (LINN).

Current name: ***Retama monosperma*** (L.) Boiss. (Fabaceae: Faboideae).

Spartium patens Linnaeus, *Systema Vegetabilium*, ed. 13: 535. 1774. RCN: 5195.

Neotype (Cristofolini in Turland & Jarvis in *Taxon* 46: 480. 1997): Spain. Cádiz, prope Los Barrios, 1 Feb 1980, *Fernandez Casas 2942* [Soc. Exch. Pl. Vasc. Eur. Bassin Medit. Fasc. 19, No. 10335] (FI).

Current name: ***Cytisus arboreus*** (Desf.) DC. subsp. ***baeticus*** (Webb) Maire (Fabaceae: Faboideae).

Note: Talavera & Salgueiro (in *Anales Jard. Bot. Madrid* 57: 213. 1999) wrongly regard this and *Cytisus patens* L. (1774) as homotypic.

Spartium purgans (Linnaeus) Linnaeus, *Systema Naturae,* ed. 12, 2: 474. 1767.

["Habitat Monspelii."] Sp. Pl., ed. 2, 2: 999 (1763). RCN: 5192.

Basionym: *Genista purgans* L. (1759).

Lectotype (López González & Jarvis in *Anales Jard. Bot. Madrid* 40: 342. 1984): *Löfling 231b*, Herb. Linn. No. 892.20 (LINN).

Current name: ***Genista scorpius*** (L.) DC. (Fabaceae: Faboideae).

Spartium radiatum Linnaeus, *Species Plantarum* 2: 708. 1753.

"Habitat in Italia." RCN: 5198.

Lectotype (Gibbs in *Notes Roy. Bot. Gard. Edinburgh* 27: 80. 1966): Herb. Linn. No. 891.14 (LINN).

Current name: ***Genista radiata*** (L.) Scop. (Fabaceae: Faboideae).

Spartium scoparium Linnaeus, *Species Plantarum* 2: 709. 1753.

"Habitat in Europae australioris arenosis." RCN: 5197.

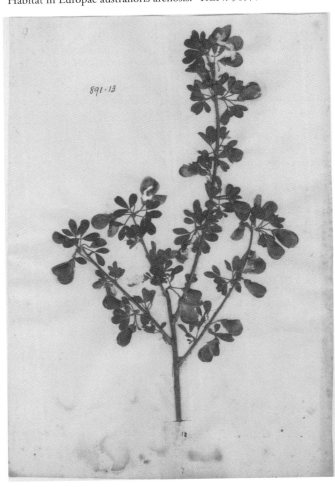

Lectotype (Cristofolini in Turland & Jarvis in *Taxon* 46: 480. 1997): Herb. Linn. No. 891.13 (LINN).

Current name: ***Cytisus scoparius*** (L.) Link subsp. ***scoparius*** (Fabaceae: Faboideae).

Spartium scoparium Linnaeus, *Plantae Rariores Africanae*: 13. 1760, *nom. illeg.*

["Habitat ad Cap. b. spei."] Sp. Pl., ed. 2, 2: 995 (1763). RCN: 5188.

Replaced synonym of: *Spartium sepiarium* L. (1763).

Type not designated.

Original material: Herb. Burman, 7 sheets (G).

Current name: ***Lebeckia sepiaria*** (L.) Thunb. (Fabaceae: Faboideae).

Note: A later homonym of *Spartium scoparium* L. (1753) and hence illegitimate.

S

Spartium scorpius Linnaeus, *Species Plantarum* 2: 708. 1753.
"Habitat in Hispania, G. Narbonensi." RCN: 5193.
Lectotype (Gibbs in Turland & Jarvis in *Taxon* 46: 480. 1997): Herb.
  Burser XXII: 23 (UPS).
Current name: ***Genista scorpius*** (L.) DC. subsp. ***scorpius*** (Fabaceae:
  Faboideae).

Spartium sepiarium Linnaeus, *Species Plantarum*, ed. 2, 2: 995. 1763.
"Habitat ad Cap. b. spei." RCN: 5188.
Replaced synonym: *Spartium scoparium* L. (1760), *nom. illeg.*, non L.
  (1753).
Type not designated.
Original material: as replaced synonym.
Current name: ***Lebeckia sepiaria*** (L.) Thunb. (Fabaceae: Faboideae).
Note: Le Roux & Van Wyk (in *S. African J. Bot.* 73: 128. 2007)
  incorrectly treat this name as dating from 1753, and indicate 891.4
  (LINN), a later addition to the herbarium from Thunberg, as the
  lectotype. As a *nomen novum* for *Spartium scoparium* L. (1760),
  nom. illeg., non L. (1753), *S. sepiarium* will be homotypic with *S.
  scoparium* L. (1760), for which the Thunberg specimen is not
  original material and so cannot be its type.

Spartium sphaerocarpum Linnaeus, *Mantissa Plantarum Altera*: 571.
  1771.
"Habitat in Europa australi." RCN: 5191.
Lectotype (Polhill in Turland & Jarvis in *Taxon* 46: 480. 1997):
  [icon] *"Hyposphairolobion"* in Reneaulme, Specim. Hist. Pl.: 35, 33.
  1611.
Current name: ***Retama sphaerocarpa*** (L.) Boiss. (Fabaceae:
  Faboideae).

Spartium spinosum Linnaeus, *Species Plantarum* 2: 709. 1753.
"Habitat in Europae australis asperis maritimis." RCN: 5199.
Lectotype (Gibbs in Turland & Jarvis in *Taxon* 46: 481. 1997): Herb.
  Clifford: 356, *Spartium* 4 (BM-000646563).
Current name: ***Calicotome spinosa*** (L.) Link (Fabaceae: Faboideae).

Spathalea sorbifolia Linnaeus, *Amoenitates Academicae* 5: 377. 1760,
  nom. inval.
Type not relevant.
Current name: ***Spathelia simplex*** L. (Rutaceae).
Note: See comments under *Spathelia simplex*.

Spathelia simplex Linnaeus, *Species Plantarum*, ed. 2, 1: 386. 1762.
"Habitat in Jamaica." RCN: 2146.
Lectotype (Porter in Jarvis & al., *Regnum Veg.* 127: 90. 1993): [icon]
  *"Aceri aut paliuro affinis arbor, caudice non ramoso foliis sorbi
  sylvestris, floribus pentapetalis racemosis speciosis purpureis, fructu sicco
  tribus membranulis extantibus alato"* in Sloane, Voy. Jamaica 2: 28, t.
  171. 1725.
Generitype of *Spathelia* Linnaeus, *nom. cons.*
Current name: ***Spathelia simplex*** L. (Rutaceae).
Note: Spathalea Linnaeus (1760) was published without a description
  and is therefore not validly published under Art. 42.1. The name
  was validated in 1762, as *Spathelia*, and is a conserved name.
    Although some authors (e.g. Fawcett & Rendle, *Fl. Jamaica* 4:
  193. 1920) have taken up *Spathalea sorbifolia*, this is incorrect.

Spergula arvensis Linnaeus, *Species Plantarum* 1: 440. 1753.
"Habitat in Europae agris." RCN: 3411.
Lectotype (Turrill in Turrill & Milne-Redhead, *Fl. Trop. E. Africa,
  Caryophyllaceae*: 11. 1956): Herb. Linn. No. 604.1 (LINN).
Generitype of *Spergula* Linnaeus (vide Green, *Prop. Brit. Bot.*: 156.
  1929).
Current name: ***Spergula arvensis*** L. (Caryophyllaceae).

Spergula laricina Linnaeus, *Species Plantarum* 1: 441. 1753.
"Habitat in Sibiria. D. Gmelin." RCN: 3414.
Lectotype (Lazkov in Cafferty & Jarvis in *Taxon* 53: 1053. 2004):
  Gmelin s.n., Herb. Linn. No. 604.5 (LINN).
Current name: ***Minuartia laricina*** (L.) Mattf. (Caryophyllaceae).

Spergula nodosa Linnaeus, *Species Plantarum* 1: 440. 1753.
"Habitat in Europae frigidioris campis subhumidis." RCN: 3413.
Lectotype (Crow in *Rhodora* 80: 25. 1978): Herb. Linn. No. 604.4
  (LINN).
Current name: ***Sagina nodosa*** (L.) Fenzl (Caryophyllaceae).

Spergula pentandra Linnaeus, *Species Plantarum* 1: 440. 1753.
"Habitat in Germania, Gallia, Anglia, Hispania." RCN: 3412.
Lectotype (Snogerup & Snogerup in Strid & Kit Tan, *Fl. Hellenica* 1:
  234. 1997): Herb. Linn. No. 604.2 (LINN).
Current name: ***Spergula pentandra*** L. (Caryophyllaceae).

Spergula saginoides Linnaeus, *Species Plantarum* 1: 441. 1753.
"Habitat in Gallia, Sibiria ex D. Gmelin." RCN: 3415.
Lectotype (Crow in *Rhodora* 80: 34. 1978): *Gmelin s.n.*, Herb. Linn.
  No. 604.6 (LINN).
Current name: ***Sagina saginoides*** (L.) H. Karst. (Caryophyllaceae).

Spermacoce corymbosa Linnaeus, *Species Plantarum*, ed. 2, 1: 149.
  1762.
"Habitat in India." RCN: 841.
Type not designated.
Original material: none traced.
Current name: ***Spermacoce corymbosa*** L. (Rubiaceae).

Spermacoce hirta Linnaeus, *Species Plantarum*, ed. 2, 1: 148. 1762.
"Habitat in Jamaica." RCN: 839.
Lectotype (Verdcourt in *Kew Bull.* 30: 318. 1975): Herb. Linn. No.
  125.8 (LINN).
Current name: ***Mitracarpus hirtus*** (L.) DC. (Rubiaceae).
Note: See discussion by Verdcourt, and Nicolson (in *Taxon* 26: 572.
  1977) and Howard (*Fl. Lesser Antilles* 6: 434. 1989).

Spermacoce hispida Linnaeus, *Species Plantarum* 1: 102. 1753.
"Habitat in Zeylona." RCN: 840.
Lectotype (Verdcourt in *Kew Bull.* 30: 307. 1975): Herb. Hermann 1:
  15, No. 62 (BM).
Current name: ***Borreria articularis*** (L. f.) F.N. Williams var. ***hispida***
  (L.) Sivar. & Manilal (Rubiaceae).

Spermacoce procumbens Linnaeus, *Systema Naturae*, ed. 12, 2: 115.
  1767.
RCN: 841.
Type not designated.
Original material: Herb. Linn. No. 125.9 (LINN).
Current name: ***Spermacoce procumbens*** L. (Rubiaceae).

Spermacoce strigosa Linnaeus, *Systema Naturae*, ed. 10, 2: 890. 1759.
RCN: 843.
Type not designated.
Original material: Herb. Linn. No. 125.12 (LINN).
Current name: ***Spermacoce strigosa*** L. (Rubiaceae).

Spermacoce suffruticosa Linnaeus, *Systema Naturae*, ed. 10, 2: 890.
  1759.
RCN: 842.
Type not designated.
Original material: none traced.
Current name: ***Spermacoce suffruticosa*** L. (Rubiaceae).

Spermacoce tenuior Linnaeus, *Species Plantarum* 1: 102. 1753.
"Habitat in Carolina." RCN: 837.
Lectotype (Rendle in *J. Bot.* 72: 333. 1934): [icon] *"Spermacoce verticillis tenuioribus"* in Dillenius, Hort. Eltham. 2: 370, t. 277, f. 359. 1732. – Typotype: *Vaillant*, Herb. Sherard (OXF).
Generitype of *Spermacoce* Linnaeus (vide Hitchcock, *Prop. Brit. Bot.*: 123. 1929).
Current name: ***Spermacoce tenuior*** L. (Rubiaceae).

Spermacoce verticillata Linnaeus, *Species Plantarum* 1: 102. 1753.
"Habitat in Jamaica, Africa." RCN: 838.
Lectotype (Rendle in *J. Bot.* 72: 331. 1934): [icon] *"Spermacoce verticillis globosis"* in Dillenius, Hort. Eltham. 2: 369, t. 277, f. 358. 1732.
Current name: ***Spermacoce verticillata*** L. (Rubiaceae).

Sphaeranthus africanus Linnaeus, *Species Plantarum*, ed. 2, 2: 1314. 1763.
"Habitat in Africa, Asia." RCN: 6717.
Type not designated.
Original material: Herb. Linn. No. 1044.4? (LINN); [icon] in Vaillant in Mém. Acad. Roy. Sci. Paris 1719: 290, t. 20, f. 12. 1719; [icon] in Plukenet, Phytographia: t. 108, f. 7. 1691; Almag. Bot.: 335. 1696 – Typotype: Herb. Sloane 98: 17 (BM-SL) – Voucher: Herb. Sloane 101: 189 (BM-SL).
Current name: ***Sphaeranthus africanus*** L. (Asteraceae).

Sphaeranthus chinensis Linnaeus, *Systema Naturae*, ed. 12, 2: 581; *Mantissa Plantarum*: 119. 1767.
"Habitat in India." RCN: 6718.
Type not designated.
Original material: Herb. Linn. No. 1044.4 (LINN).
Note: The application of this name appears uncertain.

Sphaeranthus indicus Linnaeus, *Species Plantarum* 2: 927. 1753.
"Habitat in India." RCN: 6716.
Lectotype (Anderberg in Jarvis & al., *Regnum Veg.* 127: 90. 1993): [icon] *"Sphaeranthos purpurea, alata, serrata"* in Burman, Thes. Zeylan.: 220, t. 94, f. 3. 1737.
Generitype of *Sphaeranthus* Linnaeus.
Current name: ***Sphaeranthus indicus*** L. (Asteraceae).
Note: Grierson (in *Ceylon J. Sci., Biol. Sci.* 11: 17–18. 1974), in a detailed study, rejected Herb. Hermann 2: 15, No. 312 (BM) as a possible lectotype as it conflicts with Linnaeus' diagnosis, and appeared to argue in favour of 1044.1 (LINN) as the type. Unfortunately, the LINN sheet lacks a *Species Plantarum* number (i.e. "1") and is evidently a post-1753 addition to the herbarium and not original material for the name. Oddly, Grierson later (in Dassanayake & Fosberg, *Revised Handb. Fl. Ceylon* 1: 81. 1980) referred to the Hermann material as type. Anderberg's choice therefore has priority.

Sphagnum alpinum Linnaeus, *Species Plantarum* 2: 1106. 1753.
"Habitat in Angliae summis alpium paludibus." RCN: 7987.
Type not relevant.
Current name: ***Campylopus flexuosus*** (Hedw.) Brid. (Dicranaceae).
Note: As this name appears to relate to a member of the Musci that does not belong to the Sphagnaceae, *S. alpinum* is a pre-Starting Point name and has no nomenclatural standing.

Sphagnum palustre Linnaeus, *Species Plantarum* 2: 1106. 1753.
"Habitat in Europae paludibus profundis sylvaticis." RCN: 7986.
Lectotype (Eddy in Jarvis & al., *Regnum Veg.* 127: 90. 1993): [icon] *"Sphagnum palustre molle deflexum, squamis cymbiformibus"* in Dillenius, Hist. Musc.: 240, t. 32, f. 1. 1741. – Voucher: Herb. Dillenius (OXF).

Generitype of *Sphagnum* Linnaeus (vide Andrews, *N. Amer. Fl.* 15: 3. 1913).
Current name: ***Sphagnum palustre*** L. (Sphagnaceae).

Spigelia anthelmia Linnaeus, *Species Plantarum* 1: 149. 1753.
"Habitat in Cajeuna, Brasilia." RCN: 1186.
Lectotype (Leeuwenberg in *Acta Bot. Neerl.* 10: 464. 1961): Herb. Linn. No. 210.2 (LINN).
Generitype of *Spigelia* Linnaeus.
Current name: ***Spigelia anthelmia*** L. (Strychnaceae).

Spigelia marilandica (Linnaeus) Linnaeus, *Systema Naturae*, ed. 12, 2: 734. 1767.
["Habitat in Virginia, Marilandia, Carolina."] Sp. Pl. 1: 175 (1753). RCN: 1187.
Basionym: *Lonicera marilandica* L. (1753).
Lectotype (Reveal & al. in *Huntia* 7: 230. 1987): *Clayton s.n.* (BM-000098044).
Current name: ***Spigelia marilandica*** (L.) L. (Strychnaceae).

Spilanthes acmella (Linnaeus) Linnaeus, *Systema Vegetabilium*, ed. 13: 610. 1774.
["Habitat in Zeylona."] Sp. Pl. 2: 901 (1753). RCN: 6013.
Basionym: *Verbesina acmella* L. (1753).
Lectotype (Koster & Philipson in *Blumea* 6: 349, f. 1. 1950): Herb. Hermann 2: 10, No. 309 (BM-000594573).
Current name: ***Blainvillea acmella*** (L.) Philipson (Asteraceae).

Spilanthes atriplicifolia (Linnaeus) Linnaeus, *Systema Naturae*, ed. 12, 3: 236. 1768.
["Habitat in America meridionali. Miller."] Cent. II Pl.: 30 (1756). RCN: 6014.
Basionym: *Bidens atriplicifolia* L. (1756).
Lectotype (Keil & Stuessy in *Syst. Bot.* 6: 269. 1981): Herb. Linn. No. 974.4 (LINN).
Current name: ***Isocarpha atriplicifolia*** (L.) DC. (Asteraceae).

Spilanthes oleracea Linnaeus, *Systema Naturae*, ed. 12, 2: 534. 1767.
RCN: 6016.
Lectotype (Jansen in *Syst. Bot. Monogr.* 8: 65. 1985): Herb. Linn. No. 974.5 (LINN).
Current name: ***Acmella oleracea*** (L.) R.K. Jansen (Asteraceae).

Spilanthes pseudoacmella (Linnaeus) Linnaeus, *Systema Vegetabilium*, ed. 13: 610. 1774.
RCN: 6012.
Basionym: *Verbesina pseudoacmella* L. (1753).
Lectotype (Koster & Philipson in *Blumea* 6: 349, f. 2. 1950): Herb. Hermann 3: 29, No. 308 (BM-000621911).
Current name: ***Eclipta prostrata*** (L.) L. (Asteraceae).

Spinacia fera Linnaeus, *Species Plantarum*, ed. 2, 2: 1456. 1763.
"Habitat in Sibira. Gmelin." RCN: 7428.
Type not designated.
Original material: *Gmelin*, Herb. Linn. No. 1174.2 (LINN).
Current name: ***Spinacia fera*** L. (Chenopodiaceae).

Spinacia oleracea Linnaeus, *Species Plantarum* 2: 1027. 1753.
"Habitat – – – –" RCN: 7427.
Lectotype (Hedge in Jarvis & al., *Regnum Veg.* 127: 90. 1993): Herb. Linn. No. 1174.1 (LINN).
Generitype of *Spinacia* Linnaeus.
Current name: ***Spinacia oleracea*** L. (Chenopodiaceae).

S

Spinifex squarrosus Linnaeus, *Mantissa Plantarum Altera*: 300. 1771.
"Habitat in Indiae orientalis arenosis maritimis." RCN: 7542.
Lectotype (Heyligers in Cafferty & al. in *Taxon* 49: 257. 2000): Herb.
   Linn. No. 1216.2 (LINN).
Generitype of *Spinifex* Linnaeus.
Current name: ***Spinifex littoreus*** (Burm. f.) Merr. (Poaceae).

Spiraea aruncus Linnaeus, *Species Plantarum* 1: 490. 1753.
"Habitat in Austriae, Alvorniae montanis." RCN: 3726.
Lectotype (Cullen in Cafferty & Jarvis in *Taxon* 51: 544. 2002): Herb.
   Clifford: 463, *Aruncus* 1 (BM-000647516).
Current name: ***Aruncus dioicus*** (Walter) Fernald (Rosaceae).

Spiraea chamaedryfolia Linnaeus, *Species Plantarum* 1: 489. 1753.
"Habitat in Sibiria. D. Gmelin." RCN: 3721.
Lectotype (Duvigneaud in *Lejeunia*, n.s., 76: 2, f. 1. 1975): Herb.
   Linn. No. 651.6 (LINN).
Current name: ***Spiraea chamaedryfolia*** L. (Rosaceae).

Spiraea crenata Linnaeus, *Species Plantarum* 1: 489. 1753.
"Habitat in Sibiria, Hispania." RCN: 3722.
Lectotype (Morales in Cafferty & Jarvis in *Taxon* 51: 544. 2002):
   Gerber, Herb. Linn. No. 651.8, upper middle specimen (LINN).
Current name: ***Spiraea crenata*** L. (Rosaceae).

Spiraea filipendula Linnaeus, *Species Plantarum* 1: 490. 1753.
"Habitat in Europae pascuis." RCN: 3727.
Lectotype (Jonsell & Jarvis in *Nordic J. Bot.* 22: 77. 2002): Herb.
   Linn. No. 651.19 (LINN).
Current name: ***Filipendula vulgaris*** Moench (Rosaceae).

Spiraea hypericifolia Linnaeus, *Species Plantarum* 1: 489. 1753.
"Habitat in Canada." RCN: 3720.
Lectotype (Purohit & Panigrahi, *Fam. Rosaceae India* 1: 110, pl. 32, f.
   1. 1991): Herb. Linn. No. 651.5 (LINN).
Current name: ***Spiraea hypericifolia*** L. (Rosaceae).

Spiraea laevigata Linnaeus, *Mantissa Plantarum Altera*: 244. 1771.
"Habitat in Sibiria. D. Laxman. Profess: Petrop. Ac. scient." RCN:
   3717.
Lectotype (Ebel in Cafferty & Jarvis in *Taxon* 51: 544. 2002): Herb.
   Linn. No. 651.1 (LINN).
Current name: ***Sibiraea laevigata*** (L.) Maxim. (Rosaceae).

Spiraea opulifolia Linnaeus, *Species Plantarum* 1: 489. 1753.
"Habitat in Virginia, Canada." RCN: 3724.
Lectotype (Wijnands, *Bot. Commelins*: 183. 1983): *Kalm*, Herb. Linn.
   No. 651.12 (LINN).
Current name: ***Physocarpus opulifolius*** (L.) Maxim. (Rosaceae).
Note: Oh (in *Taxon* 53: 212. 2004) found that *Physocarpus opulifolius*
   (L.) Maxim. (1879) is a later homonym of *P. opulifolius* Raf. (1838)
   and successfully proposed the conservation of the former in order to
   maintain its usage.

Spiraea palmata Linnaeus, *Systema Vegetabilium*, ed. 13: 393. 1774,
   nom. illeg.
"Habitat in Sibiria." RCN: 3729.
Replaced synonym: *Spiraea lobata* Jacq. (1770).
Type not designated.
Note: An illegitimate replacement name for *Spiraea lobata* Jacq.
   (1770). The application of the latter name appears to be uncertain.

Spiraea salicifolia Linnaeus, *Species Plantarum* 1: 489. 1753.
"Habitat in Sibiria, Tataria." RCN: 3718.
Lectotype (Silverside in Jarvis & al., *Regnum Veg.* 127: 90. 1993):
   Herb. Linn. No. 651.2 (LINN).

Generitype of *Spiraea* Linnaeus (vide Green, *Prop. Brit. Bot.*: 159.
   1929).
Current name: ***Spiraea salicifolia*** L. (Rosaceae).

Spiraea sorbifolia Linnaeus, *Species Plantarum* 1: 490. 1753.
"Habitat in Sibiriae uliginosis." RCN: 3725.
Lectotype (Cullen in Cafferty & Jarvis in *Taxon* 51: 544. 2002):
   Amman s.n., Herb. Linn. No. 651.14 (LINN).
Current name: ***Sorbaria sorbifolia*** (L.) A. Braun (Rosaceae).

Spiraea tomentosa Linnaeus, *Species Plantarum* 1: 489. 1753.
"Habitat in Philadelphia. Kalm." RCN: 3719.
Lectotype (Reveal in Cafferty & Jarvis in *Taxon* 51: 544. 2002): *Kalm*,
   Herb. Linn. No. 651.4 (LINN).
Current name: ***Spiraea tomentosa*** L. (Rosaceae).

Spiraea trifoliata Linnaeus, *Species Plantarum* 1: 490. 1753.
"Habitat in Virginia, Canada." RCN: 3730.
Lectotype (Reveal in Cafferty & Jarvis in *Taxon* 51: 544. 2002): *Kalm*,
   Herb. Linn. No. 651.24 (LINN).
Current name: ***Gillenia trifoliata*** (L.) Moench (Rosaceae).

Spiraea trilobata Linnaeus, *Mantissa Plantarum Altera*: 244. 1771.
"Habitat in Sibiria. D. Laxman." RCN: 3723.
Lectotype (Ebel in Cafferty & Jarvis in *Taxon* 51: 544. 2002): Herb.
   Linn. No. 651.11 (LINN).
Current name: ***Spiraea trilobata*** L. (Rosaceae).

Spiraea ulmaria Linnaeus, *Species Plantarum* 1: 490. 1753.
"Habitat in Europae pratis uliginosis, umbrosis." RCN: 3728.
Lectotype (Purohit & Panigrahi in *Bangladesh J. Bot.* 10: 95. 1981):
   Herb. Linn. No. 651.21 (LINN).
Current name: ***Filipendula ulmaria*** (L.) Maxim. (Rosaceae).

Spondias lutea Linnaeus, *Species Plantarum*, ed. 2, 1: 613. 1762, *nom.
   illeg.*
"Habitat in America meridionali." RCN: 3336.
Replaced synonym: *Spondias mombin* L. (1753).
Lectotype (Howard, *Fl. Lesser Antilles* 5: 101. 1989): [icon] *"Prunus
   americana"* in Merian, Metamorph. Insect. Surinam.: 13, t. 13.
   1705.
Current name: ***Spondias mombin*** L. (Anacardiaceae).
Note: As noted by Howard (*Fl. Lesser Antilles* 5 : 101. 1989), this is a
   superfluous name for the earlier *S. mombin* L. (1753).

Spondias mombin Linnaeus, *Species Plantarum* 1: 371. 1753.
"Habitat in Brasilia, Jamaica." RCN: 3336.
Replaced synonym of: *Spondias myrobalanus* L. (1759), *nom. illeg.*;
   Spondias lutea L. (1762), *nom. illeg.*
Lectotype (Howard, *Fl. Lesser Antilles* 5: 101. 1989): [icon] *"Prunus
   americana"* in Merian, Metamorph. Insect. Surinam.: 13, t. 13.
   1705 (see opposite, above left).
Generitype of *Spondias* Linnaeus.
Current name: ***Spondias mombin*** L. (Anacardiaceae).

Spondias myrobalanus Linnaeus, *Systema Naturae*, ed. 10, 2: 1036.
   1759, *nom. illeg.*
["Habitat in Brasilia, Jamaica."] Sp. Pl. 1: 371 (1753). RCN: 3336.
Replaced synonym: *Spondias mombin* L. (1753).
Lectotype (Howard, *Fl. Lesser Antilles* 5: 101. 1989): [icon] *"Prunus
   americana"* in Merian, Metamorph. Insect. Surinam.: 13, t. 13.
   1705.
Current name: ***Spondias mombin*** L. (Anacardiaceae).
Note: An illegitimate replacement name for the earlier *S. mombin*
   (1753). *Spondias myrobalanus* L. (*Syst. Nat.*, ed. 10, 2: 1036.

The lectotype of *Spondias mombin* L.

May–Jun 1759) is not homotypic with *S. myrobalanus* L. (*Fl. Jam.*: 16. Dec 1759). However, the latter, too, is illegitimate as it is a later homonym.

Spondias myrobalanus Linnaeus, *Flora Jamaicensis*: 16. 1759, *nom. illeg.*
"Habitat [in Jamaica.]"
Lectotype (Howard, *Fl. Lesser Antilles* 5: 103. 1989): [icon] *"Myrobalanus minor folio fraxini alato, fructu purpureo, ossiculo magno fibroso"* in Sloane, Voy. Jamaica 2: 126, t. 219, f. 3, 4, 5. 1725. – Typotype: Herb. Sloane 7: 66 (BM-SL).
Current name: ***Spondias purpurea*** L. (Anacardiaceae).
Note: Spondias myrobalanus L. (*Syst. Nat.*, ed. 10, 2: 1036. May–Jun 1759) is not homotypic with *S. myrobalanus* L. (*Fl. Jam.* 16. Dec 1759). However, the latter is illegitimate as it is a later homonym.

Spondias purpurea Linnaeus, *Species Plantarum*, ed. 2, 1: 613. 1762.
"Habitat in India occidentali." RCN: 3335.
Lectotype (Bornstein in Howard, *Fl. Lesser Antilles* 5: 103. 1989): [icon] *"Myrobalanus minor folio fraxini alato, fructu purpureo, ossiculo magno fibroso"* in Sloane, Voy. Jamaica 2: 126, t. 219, f. 3, 4, 5. 1725. – Typotype: Herb. Sloane 7: 66 (BM-SL).
Current name: ***Spondias purpurea*** L. (Anacardiaceae).

Stachys aethiopica Linnaeus, *Systema Naturae*, ed. 12, 2: 395; *Mantissa Plantarum*: 82. 1767.
"Habitat ad Cap. b. spei. DD. Royen." RCN: 4243.

Lectotype (Codd in Leistner, *Fl. Southern Africa* 28(4): 62. 1985): Herb. Linn. No. 736.13 (LINN).
Current name: ***Stachys aethiopica*** L. (Lamiaceae).

Stachys alpina Linnaeus, *Species Plantarum* 2: 581. 1753.
"Habitat in Germania, Helvetia." RCN: 4235.
Lectotype (Falciani in *Lagascalia* 19: 194. 1997): Herb. Linn. No. 736.3 (LINN).
Current name: ***Stachys alpina*** L. (Lamiaceae).

Stachys annua (Linnaeus) Linnaeus, *Species Plantarum*, ed. 2, 2: 813. 1763.
"Habitat in Germania, Helvetia, Gallia, ad agrorum margines." RCN: 4246.
Basionym: *Betonica annua* L. (1753).
Lectotype (Nelson in Jarvis & al. in *Taxon* 50: 510. 2001): Herb. Clifford: 310, *Stachys* 7, sheet A "annua" (BM-000646054).
Current name: ***Stachys annua*** (L.) L. (Lamiaceae).

Stachys arvensis (Linnaeus) Linnaeus, *Species Plantarum*, ed. 2, 2: 814. 1763.
"Habitat in Europae arvis." RCN: 4247.
Basionym: *Glechoma arvensis* L. (1753).
Lectotype (Turland in Jarvis & al. in *Taxon* 50: 511. 2001): Herb. Burser XIII: 63 (UPS).
Current name: ***Stachys arvensis*** (L.) L. (Lamiaceae).
Note: Scott (in Bosser & al., *Fl. Mascareignes* 139: 11. 1994) wrongly treated this as a new species (rather than a new combination) and incorrectly indicated a Mútis collection (736.21 LINN) as type.

Stachys cretica Linnaeus, *Species Plantarum* 2: 581. 1753.
"Habitat in Creta." RCN: 4237.
Lectotype (Turland in Jarvis & al. in *Taxon* 50: 520. 2001): [icon] *"Stachys folio obscure virenti, fl. roseo"* in Walther, Design. Pl.: 108, t. 19. 1735. – Epitype (Turland in Jarvis & al. in *Taxon* 50: 520. 2001): Greece. Crete, in dumosis m. Lassithi, Jun 1899, *Baldacci s.n.* (BM).
Current name: ***Stachys cretica*** L. (Lamiaceae).

Stachys germanica Linnaeus, *Species Plantarum* 2: 581. 1753.
"Habitat in Germania, Anglia, Gallia." RCN: 4236.
Lectotype (Falciani in *Lagascalia* 19: 201. 1997): Herb. Linn. No. 736.4 (LINN).
Current name: ***Stachys germanica*** L. (Lamiaceae).

Stachys glutinosa Linnaeus, *Species Plantarum* 2: 581. 1753.
"Habitat in Creta." RCN: 4238.
Lectotype (Nelson in Jarvis & al. in *Taxon* 50: 520. 2001): Herb. Clifford: 310, *Stachys* 9 (BM-000646057).
Current name: ***Stachys glutinosa*** L. (Lamiaceae).

Stachys hirta Linnaeus, *Species Plantarum*, ed. 2, 2: 813. 1763, *nom. illeg.*
"Habitat in Orientalis, Hispaniae, Italiae collibus." RCN: 4244.
Replaced synonym: *Galeopsis hirsuta* L. (1753).
Lectotype (Turland in Jarvis & al. in *Taxon* 50: 511. 2001): Herb. Linn. No. 736.16 (LINN).
Current name: ***Stachys ocymastrum*** (L.) Briq. (Lamiaceae).
Note: Galeopsis hirsuta was transferred to *Sideritis* in 1759 (as *S. ocymastrum* L. because of the existence of *Sideritis hirsuta* L. (1753)), and then appeared as *Stachys hirta* L. in 1763. The use of "hirta" may originally have been an error for "hirsuta" (as *G. hirsuta* is included in its synonymy), but as Linnaeus continued to use "hirta" in later works (Linnaeus 1767: 395; 1774: 447), *Stachys hirta* is treated as illegitimate.

S

Stachys orientalis Linnaeus, *Species Plantarum* 2: 582. 1753.
"Habitat in Oriente." RCN: 4240.
Type not designated.
Original material: none traced.
Current name: ***Stachys alpina*** L. (Lamiaceae).

Stachys palaestina Linnaeus, *Species Plantarum*, ed. 2, 2: 1674. 1763.
"Habitat in Palaestina. Arduini." RCN: 4241.
Lectotype (Hedge in Jarvis & al. in *Taxon* 50: 520. 2001): *Arduino s.n.*, Herb. Linn. No. 736.9 (LINN).
Current name: ***Stachys palaestina*** L. (Lamiaceae).

Stachys palustris Linnaeus, *Species Plantarum* 2: 580. 1753.
"Habitat in Europa ad ripas, inque cultis humidiusculis." RCN: 4243.
Lectotype (Hedge in Ali & Nasir, *Fl. Pakistan* 192: 187. 1990): Herb. Linn. No. 736.2 (LINN).
Current name: ***Stachys palustris*** L. (Lamiaceae).

Stachys recta Linnaeus, *Systema Naturae*, ed. 12, 2: 395; *Mantissa Plantarum*: 82. 1767.
"Habitat in Europae australi." RCN: 4245.
Type not designated.
Original material: none traced.
Current name: ***Stachys recta*** L. (Lamiaceae).

Stachys spinosa Linnaeus, *Species Plantarum* 2: 581. 1753.
"Habitat in occidentali Cretae." RCN: 4239.
Lectotype (Turland in Jarvis & al. in *Taxon* 50: 520. 2001): Herb. Clifford: 310, *Stachys* 8 (BM-000646056).
Current name: ***Stachys spinosa*** L. (Lamiaceae).

Stachys sylvatica Linnaeus, *Species Plantarum* 2: 580. 1753.
"Habitat in Europae nemoribus umbrosis." RCN: 4233.
Lectotype (Press in Jarvis in *Taxon* 41: 570. 1992): Herb. Clifford: 309, *Stachys* 1 (BM-000646043).
Generitype of *Stachys* Linnaeus.
Current name: ***Stachys sylvatica*** L. (Lamiaceae).
Note: Stachys sylvatica, with the type designated by Press, was proposed as conserved type of the genus by Jarvis (in *Taxon* 41: 570. 1992). However, the proposal was eventually ruled unnecessary by the General Committee (see Barrie, *l.c.* 55: 795–796. 2006 for a review of the history of this and related proposals).

Staehelina arborescens Linnaeus, *Systema Naturae*, ed. 12, 2: 538; *Mantissa Plantarum*: 111. 1767, *nom. illeg.*
"Habitat in Creta, insula stoechadum; in rupe Victoriae Galloprovinciae." RCN: 6080.
Replaced synonym: *Staehelina arborea* Schreb. (1766).
Type not designated.
Current name: ***Staehelina petiolata*** (L.) Hilliard & B.L. Burtt (Asteraceae).
Note: An illegitimate renaming of *Staehelina arborea* Schreber (*Icones et Descriptiones Plantarum Minus Cognitarum*: 1. 1766), which is cited by Linnaeus in the protologue.

Staehelina centauroides Linnaeus, *Species Plantarum* 2: 840. 1753.
"Habitat in Aethiopia." RCN: 6105.
Lectotype (Wijnands in *Taxon* 32: 302, f. 1. 1983): Herb. Clifford: 398, *Santolina* 6 (BM-000646973).
Current name: ***Athanasia crenata*** (L.) L. (Asteraceae).

Staehelina chamaepeuce (Linnaeus) Linnaeus, *Systema Naturae*, ed. 12, 2: 538. 1767.
RCN: 6082.
Basionym: *Serratula chamaepeuce* L. (1753).

Lectotype (Greuter in *Boissiera* 22: 105. 1973): [icon] *"Chamaepeuce"* in Alpino, Pl. Exot.: 77, 76. 1627 (see p. 105). – Epitype (Greuter in *Boissiera* 22: 105. 1973): Greece. Crete, Distr. Hagios Vasilis. "An Felsen ober Spili, 16.IV" Dörfler, Iter Creticum 1904, n. 1014 (G; iso- B, GB, Gr, M, PI, PR etc.).
Current name: ***Ptilostemon chamaepeuce*** (L.) Less. (Asteraceae).
Note: Greuter also designated a "standard specimen" in conjunction with the Alpino plate – similar to the epitype (Art. 9.7) of subsequent Codes. He publishes a photograph of the capitula of this material in his plate Ia.

Staehelina dubia Linnaeus, *Species Plantarum* 2: 840. 1753.
"Habitat in Hispania, G. Narbonensi." RCN: 6079.
Lectotype (Dittrich in Jarvis & al., *Regnum Veg.* 127: 90. 1993): Herb. Linn. No. 981.2 (LINN).
Generitype of *Staehelina* Linnaeus (vide Cassini, *Dict. Sci. Nat.* 47: 512. 1827).
Current name: ***Staehelina dubia*** L. (Asteraceae).

Staehelina fruticosa (Linnaeus) Linnaeus, *Systema Naturae*, ed. 12, 2: 538. 1767.
["Habitat in Creta, Oriente. Gerard."] Sp. Pl., ed. 2, 2: 1286 (1763). RCN: 6081.
Basionym: *Centaurea fruticosa* L. (1759).
Lectotype (Dittrich in *Boissiera* 51: 75. 1996): *Gérard 11*, Herb. Linn. No. 981.4 (LINN).
Current name: ***Hirtellina fruticosa*** (L.) Dittrich (Asteraceae).

Staehelina gnaphaloides Linnaeus, *Species Plantarum* 2: 840. 1753.
"Habitat in Aethiopia." RCN: 6078.
Lectotype (designated here by Nordenstam): Herb. Linn. No. 981.1 (LINN).
Current name: ***Syncarpha gnaphaloides*** (L.) DC. (Asteraceae).
Note: The lectotype is material that was originally in the Clifford herbarium.

Stapelia hirsuta Linnaeus, *Species Plantarum* 1: 217. 1753, *typ. cons.*
"Habitat ad Cap. b. Spei." RCN: 1791.
Lectotype (Brown in Thistleton-Dyer, *Fl. Cap.* 4(1): 939. 1909): Herb. Clifford: 77, *Stapelia* 2 (BM-000558154).
Generitype of *Stapelia* Linnaeus, *nom. cons.*
Current name: ***Stapelia hirsuta*** L. (Asclepiadaceae).
Note: Stapelia hirsuta, with the type designated by Brown, was proposed as conserved type of the genus by Jarvis (in *Taxon* 41: 570. 1992). This was approved by the Committee for Spermatophyta (in *Taxon* 44: 612. 1995) and ratified by the General Committee (in *Taxon* 48: 374. 1999). However, subsequent Codes do not list Herb. Clifford: 77, *Stapelia* 2 (BM) as the generitype, so the specimen remains a lectotype, rather than a conserved type.

Stapelia mamillaris Linnaeus, *Mantissa Plantarum Altera*: 216. 1771.
"Habitat ad Cap. b. spei." RCN: 1792.
Lectotype (Bruyns in *Bradleya* 1: 63. 1983): [icon] *"Stapelia aphyllos, ad nodos mammillaris, flosculo rubello, siliquis pendulis"* in Burman, Rar. Afric. Pl.: 27, t. 11. 1738.
Current name: ***Quaqua mamillaris*** (L.) Bruyns (Asclepiadaceae).

Stapelia variegata Linnaeus, *Species Plantarum* 1: 217. 1753.
"Habitat ad Cap. b. Spei." RCN: 1790.
Lectotype (Brown in Thistleton-Dyer, *Fl. Cap.* 4(1): 994. 1909): Herb. Linn. No. 311.1 (LINN).
Current name: ***Orbea variegata*** (L.) Haw. (Asclepiadaceae).

Staphylea pinnata Linnaeus, *Species Plantarum* 1: 270. 1753.
"Habitat in Europae australioris succulentis." RCN: 7421.

Lectotype (Peruzzi & al. in *Taxon* 53: 541. 2004): Herb. Clifford: 112, *Staphylea* 1, sheet D (BM-000558443).
Generitype of *Staphylea* Linnaeus (vide Hitchcock, *Prop. Brit. Bot.*: 142. 1929).
Current name: ***Staphylea pinnata*** L. (Staphyleaceae).

Staphylea trifolia Linnaeus, *Species Plantarum* 1: 270. 1753.
"Habitat in Virginia." RCN: 2148.
Lectotype (designated here by Reveal): Herb. Linn. No. 382.2 (LINN).
Current name: ***Staphylea trifolia*** L. (Staphyleaceae).

Statice armeria Linnaeus, *Species Plantarum* 1: 274. 1753.
"Habitat in Europae & Americae septentrionalis campis." RCN: 2186.
Lectotype (Lawrence in *Gentes Herb.* 4: 406. 1940): Herb. Linn. No. 395.1 (LINN).
Generitype of *Statice* Linnaeus, *nom. rej.* (vide Hitchcock, *Prop. Brit. Bot.*: 143. 1929).
Current name: ***Armeria vulgaris*** Willd. (Plumbaginaceae).
Note: Statice Linnaeus, *nom. rej.* in favour of *Armeria* Willd. Gibbons & Lousley (in *Watsonia* 4: 125. 1958) indicated a Clifford sheet as the type but their choice is pre-dated by that of Lawrence.

Statice aurea Linnaeus, *Species Plantarum* 1: 276. 1753.
"Habitat in Dauriae campis montosis." RCN: 2200.
Type not designated.
Original material: Herb. Linn. No. 395.19 (LINN); [icon] in Amman, Stirp. Rar. Ruth.: 100, t. 18, f. 2. 1739.
Current name: ***Limonium aureum*** (L.) Hill (Plumbaginaceae).

Statice cordata Linnaeus, *Species Plantarum* 1: 275. 1753.
"Habitat ad maris Mediterranei litora." RCN: 2188.
Type not designated.
Original material: Herb. Burser X: 115 (UPS); [icon] in Barrelier, Pl. Galliam: 66, t. 805. 1714.
Current name: ***Limonium cordatum*** (L.) Mill. (Plumbaginaceae).
Note: Erben (in *Mitt. Bot. Staatssamml. München* 14: 421. 1978) indicated 395.8 (LINN), an Allioni specimen, as type but it is a 1757 addition to the collection and cannot be original material for the name.

Statice echinus Linnaeus, *Species Plantarum* 1: 276. 1753, *nom. utique rej.*
"Habitat in Graeciae & Mediae desertis." RCN: 2194.
Lectotype (Meyer in *Haussknechtia* 3: 7. 1987): [icon] "*Limonium cespitosum, foliis aculeatis*" in Buxbaum, Pl. Minus Cognit. Cent. 2: 18, t. 10. 1728.
Current name: ***Acantholimon tenuiflorum*** Boiss. (Plumbaginaceae).

Statice echioides Linnaeus, *Species Plantarum* 1: 275. 1753.
"Habitat Monspelii." RCN: 2191.
Lectotype (Erben in *Mitt. Bot. Staatssamml. München* 14: 558. 1978): [icon] "*Limonium minus annuum bullatis foliis vel echioides*" in Magnol, Bot. Monspel.: 157, 156. 1676.
Current name: ***Limonium echioides*** (L.) Mill. (Plumbaginaceae).

Statice ferulacea Linnaeus, *Species Plantarum*, ed. 2, 1: 396. 1762.
"Habitat in Barbaria, Lusitania, Hispania. Alstromer." RCN: 2201.
Lectotype (Erben in *Mitt. Bot. Staatssamml. München* 14: 398. 1978): *Alströmer 34*, Herb. Linn. No. 395.20 (LINN).
Current name: ***Limonium ferulaceum*** (L.) Chaz. (Plumbaginaceae).

Statice flexuosa Linnaeus, *Species Plantarum* 1: 276. 1753.
"Habitat in Sibiria." RCN: 2195.
Type not designated.

Original material: Herb. Linn. No. 395.14 (LINN); [icon] in Gmelin, Fl. Sibirica 2: 217, t. 89, f. 1. 1752.
Current name: ***Limonium flexuosum*** (L.) Kuntze (Plumbaginaceae).

Statice incana Linnaeus, *Systema Naturae*, ed. 12, 2: 222; *Mantissa Plantarum*: 59. 1767.
"Habitat in Arabia. Forskåhl." RCN: 2188.
Type not designated.
Original material: Herb. Linn. No. 395.7 (LINN).
Current name: ***Goniolimon incanum*** (L.) Hepper (Plumbaginaceae).

Statice limonium Linnaeus, *Species Plantarum* 1: 274. 1753.
"Habitat in Europae & Virginiae maritimis." RCN: 2187.
Type not designated.
Original material: Herb. Linn. No. 395.3 (LINN); Herb. Burser X: 114 (UPS); Herb. Burser X: 113 (UPS); Herb. Clifford: 115, *Statice* 2, 12 sheets (BM); Herb. Burser X: 112 (UPS); *Clayton 573* (BM); [icon] in Boccone, Icon. Descr. Rar. Pl. Siciliae: 25, 26, t. 13, f. 3. 1674.
Current name: ***Limonium vulgare*** Mill. (Plumbaginaceae).

Statice minuta Linnaeus, *Systema Naturae*, ed. 12, 2: 223; *Mantissa Plantarum*: 59. 1767.
"Habitat ad Mare Mediterraneum." RCN: 2197.
Type not designated.
Original material: *Scopoli 63*, Herb. Linn. No. 395.16? (LINN); [icon] in Boccone, Icon. Descr. Rar. Pl. Siciliae: 64, t. 34. 1674; [icon] in Plukenet, Phytographia: t. 200, f. 5. 1692; Almag. Bot.: 221. 1696 – Voucher: Herb. Sloane 96: 149 (BM-SL); [icon] in Boccone, Icon. Descr. Rar. Pl. Siciliae: 26, 25, t. 13, f. 3. 1674.
Current name: ***Limonium minutum*** (L.) Chaz. (Plumbaginaceae).
Note: Erben (in *Mitt. Bot. Staatssamml. München* 14: 447. 1978; 27: 396. 1988) treated 395.16 (LINN) as the type. However, there seems little to link this Scopoli collection, received by Linnaeus around 1762–63, with the protologue apart from Linnaeus filius' determination. Erben (1988) excluded Linnaeus' cited synonyms and evidently uses the name in a sense entirely different from that employed by Pignatti (in Tutin & al., *Fl. Europaea* 3: 43. 1972), and previously (1978) by Erben himself. In 1988, he described *L. pseudominutum* Erben for that taxon.

Statice monopetala Linnaeus, *Species Plantarum* 1: 276. 1753.
"Habitat in Sicilia." RCN: 2199.
Type not designated.
Original material: Herb. Clifford: 116, *Statice* 3 (BM); [icon] in Boccone, Icon. Descr. Rar. Pl. Siciliae: 34, 32, 33, t. 16, f. 2, t. 17. 1674.
Current name: ***Limoniastrum monopetalum*** (L.) Boiss. (Plumbaginaceae).

Statice pruinosa Linnaeus, *Systema Naturae*, ed. 12, 2: 223; *Mantissa Plantarum*: 59. 1767.
"Habitat in Palaestina." RCN: 2202.
Type not designated.
Original material: *Hasselquist*, Herb. Linn. No. 395.32 (LINN); Herb. Linn. No. 133.3 (S).
Current name: ***Limonium pruinosum*** (L.) Kuntze (Plumbaginaceae).

Statice purpurata Linnaeus, *Systema Naturae*, ed. 12, 2: 223; *Mantissa Plantarum*: 59. 1767.
"Habitat ad Cap. b. spei." RCN: 2196.
Lectotype (Dyer in Dyer & al., *Fl. Southern Africa* 26: 23. 1963): Herb. Linn. No. 395.15 (LINN).
Current name: ***Limonium purpuratum*** (L.) L.H. Bailey (Plumbaginaceae).

S

Statice reticulata Linnaeus, *Species Plantarum* 1: 275. 1753.
"Habitat in Melita." RCN: 2190.
Type not designated.
Original material: Herb. Linn. No. 395.9 (LINN); [icon] in Plukenet, Phytographia: t. 42, f. 4. 1691; Almag. Bot.: 221. 1696; [icon] in Boccone, Icon. Descr. Rar. Pl. Siciliae: 82, 83, t. 44, f. L. 1674.
Current name: ***Limonium* sp.** (Plumbaginaceae).
Note: The application of this name appears uncertain – see Salmon (in *J. Bot.* 51: 95. 1913).

Statice sinuata Linnaeus, *Species Plantarum* 1: 276. 1753.
"Habitat in Sicilia, Palaestina, Africa." RCN: 2203.
Lectotype (Bokhari in Nasir & Ali, *Fl. W. Pakistan* 28: 9. 1972): Herb. Linn. No. 395.33 (LINN).
Current name: ***Limonium sinuatum*** (L.) Mill. (Plumbaginaceae).

Statice speciosa Linnaeus, *Species Plantarum* 1: 275. 1753.
"Habitat in Tataria." RCN: 2192.
Type not designated.
Original material: Herb. Linn. No. 395.11 (LINN); [icon] in Gmelin, Fl. Sibirica 2: 221, t. 91, f. 1. 1752.
Current name: ***Goniolimon speciosum*** (L.) Boiss. (Plumbaginaceae).

Statice suffruticosa Linnaeus, *Species Plantarum* 1: 276. 1753.
"Habitat in Sibiria. D. Gmelin." RCN: 2198.
Lectotype (Rechinger & Schiman-Czeika in Rechinger, *Fl. Iranica* 108: 11. 1974): *Gmelin s.n.*, Herb. Linn. No. 395.17 (LINN).
Current name: ***Limonium suffruticosum*** (L.) Kuntze (Plumbaginaceae).

Statice tatarica Linnaeus, *Species Plantarum* 1: 275. 1753.
"Habitat in Tataria." RCN: 2193.
Lectotype (designated here by Edmondson): *Amman, s.n.*, Herb. Linn. No. 395.12 (LINN).
Current name: ***Goniolimon tataricum*** (L.) Boiss. (Plumbaginaceae).

Stellaria arenaria Linnaeus, *Species Plantarum* 2: 1196. 1753.
"Habitat in Hispania." RCN: 3281.
Lectotype (López González in Cafferty & Jarvis in *Taxon* 53: 1053. 2004): Herb. Linn. No. 581.14 (LINN).
Current name: ***Arenaria hispanica*** Spreng. (Caryophyllaceae).

Stellaria biflora Linnaeus, *Species Plantarum* 1: 422. 1753.
"Habitat in Alpibus Lapponicis." RCN: 3280.
Lectotype (Jonsell & Jarvis in *Nordic J. Bot.* 14: 159. 1994): Herb. Linn. No. 584.11 (LINN).
Current name: ***Minuartia biflora*** (L.) Schinz & Thell. (Caryophyllaceae).

Stellaria cerastoides Linnaeus, *Species Plantarum* 1: 422. 1753.
"Habitat in Alpibus Lapponicis, Horto Dei monspeliensi." RCN: 3279.
Lectotype (Jonsell & Jarvis in *Nordic J. Bot.* 14: 159. 1994): Herb. Linn. No. 584.8 (LINN).
Current name: ***Cerastium cerastoides*** (L.) Britton (Caryophyllaceae).
Note: Möschl (in *Mem. Soc. Brot.* 17: 96. 1964, and later publications) indicated material in LINN as type but did not distinguish between sheets 584.8, 584.9 and 584.10 (LINN). As they are evidently not part of a single gathering, Art. 9.15 does not apply.

Stellaria dichotoma Linnaeus, *Species Plantarum* 1: 421. 1753.
"Habitat in Alpibus Helveticis, Sibiricis." RCN: 3275.
Lectotype (Lazkov in Cafferty & Jarvis in *Taxon* 53: 1053. 2004): *Amman s.n.*, Herb. Linn. No. 584.2 (LINN).
Current name: ***Stellaria dichotoma*** L. (Caryophyllaceae).

Stellaria graminea Linnaeus, *Species Plantarum* 1: 422. 1753.
"Habitat in siccis juniperetis sepibus tectis Europae." RCN: 3278.
Lectotype (Jonsell & Jarvis in *Nordic J. Bot.* 14: 159. 1994): Herb. Burser XI: 111 (UPS).
Current name: ***Stellaria graminea*** L. (Caryophyllaceae).

Stellaria holostea Linnaeus, *Species Plantarum* 1: 422. 1753.
"Habitat in Europae nemoribus." RCN: 3277.
Lectotype (Jonsell & Jarvis in Jarvis & al., *Regnum Veg.* 127: 91. 1993): Herb. Linn. No. 584.4 (LINN).
Generitype of *Stellaria* Linnaeus (vide Green, *Prop. Brit. Bot.*: 155. 1929).
Current name: ***Stellaria holostea*** L. (Caryophyllaceae).
Note: Jonsell & Jarvis (in *Nordic J. Bot.* 14: 159. 1994) added further comments on their 1993 type choice.

Stellaria nemorum Linnaeus, *Species Plantarum* 1: 421. 1753.
"Habitat in Europae nemorandibus." RCN: 3274.
Lectotype (Jonsell & Jarvis in *Nordic J. Bot.* 14: 159. 1994): Herb. Burser XIV(1): 69 (UPS).
Current name: ***Stellaria nemorum*** L. (Caryophyllaceae).

Stellaria radians Linnaeus, *Species Plantarum* 1: 422. 1753.
"Habitat in Sibiria." RCN: 3276.
Lectotype (Lazkov in Cafferty & Jarvis in *Taxon* 53: 1053. 2004): *Gmelin s.n.*, Herb. Linn. No. 584.3 (LINN).
Current name: ***Stellaria radians*** L. (Caryophyllaceae).

Stellera chamaejasme Linnaeus, *Species Plantarum* 1: 559. 1753.
"Habitat in Sibiria. D. Gmelin." RCN: 2838.
Lectotype (Kit Tan in Jarvis & al., *Regnum Veg.* 127: 91. 1993): [icon] "*Chamaeiasme radice Mandragorae*" in Amman, Stirp. Rar. Ruth.: 16, t. 2. 1739 (see p. 105).
Generitype of *Stellera* Linnaeus (vide Fasano in *Atti Reale Accad. Sci. Napoli* 1787: 245. 1788).
Current name: ***Stellera chamaejasme*** L. (Thymelaeaceae).

Stellera passerina Linnaeus, *Species Plantarum* 1: 559. 1753.
"Habitat in Europae arvis, campis, apricis, aridis." RCN: 2837.
Lectotype (Kit Tan in *Notes Roy. Bot. Gard. Edinburgh* 38: 237. 1980): Herb. Linn. No. 503.1 (LINN).
Current name: ***Thymelaea passerina*** (L.) Coss. & Germ. (Thymelaeaceae).

Stemodia maritima Linnaeus, *Systema Naturae*, ed. 10, 2: 1118. 1759.
["Habitat in Jamaica."] Sp. Pl., ed. 2, 2: 881 (1763). RCN: 4586.
Lectotype (Sutton in Jarvis & al., *Regnum Veg.* 127: 91. 1993): *Browne*, Herb. Linn. No. 797.1 (LINN).
Generitype of *Stemodia* Linnaeus, *nom. cons.*
Current name: ***Stemodia maritima*** L. (Scrophulariaceae).
Note: Stemodia Linnaeus, *nom. cons.* against *Stemodiacra* P. Browne. Turner & Cowan (in *Phytologia* 74: 90; 75: 305. 1993) incorrectly designated Houstoun material (BM) as lectotype. However, this is not original material for the name, and Sutton's type choice (of a Patrick Browne collection) is accepted here.

Sterculia balanghas Linnaeus, *Species Plantarum* 2: 1007. 1753.
"Habitat in India." RCN: 7301.
Lectotype (Verdcourt in Dassanayake & al., *Revised Handb. Fl. Ceylon* 9: 434. 1995): Herb. Hermann 2: 42, No. 350 (BM-000594604).
Current name: ***Sterculia balanghas*** L. (Sterculiaceae).
Note: Tantra (in *Pengum. Lemb. Lemb. Penelitian Kehut.* 102: 141. 1976) discussed the Hermann material and the Rheede plate, treating them both as the type.

Sterculia foetida Linnaeus, *Species Plantarum* 2: 1008. 1753.
"Habitat in India." RCN: 7302.
Lectotype (Tantra in *Pengum. Lemb. Lemb. Penelitian Kehut.* 102: 46. 1976): Herb. Linn. No. 1143.1 (LINN).
Generitype of *Sterculia* Linnaeus (vide Green, *Prop. Brit. Bot.*: 190. 1929).
Current name: ***Sterculia foetida*** L. (Sterculiaceae).

Steris javana Linnaeus, *Systema Naturae,* ed. 12, 2: 197; *Mantissa Plantarum*: 54. 1767.
"Habitat in India." RCN: 1836.
Neotype (Davenport in *Rhodora* 90: 198. 1988): Herb. Linn. No. 322.2 (LINN).
Generitype of *Steris* Linnaeus (1767), *nom. illeg.*, non Adans. (1763).
Current name: ***Hydrolea zeylanica*** (L.) Vahl (Hydrophyllaceae).
Note: From its annotations, it is difficult to see how 322.2 (LINN) could be accepted as original material for the name, but as no other original material appears to exist, Davenport's choice of this material as lectotype is accepted as a neotypification (under Art. 9.8).

Stewartia malacodendron Linnaeus, *Species Plantarum* 2: 698. 1753.
"Habitat in Virginia." RCN: 5109.

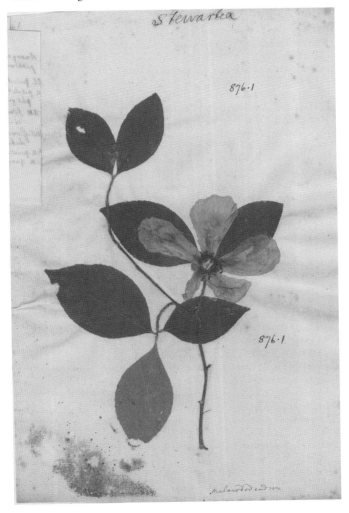

Lectotype (Spongberg in *J. Arnold Arbor.* 55: 194. 1974): *Clayton 734,* Herb. Linn. No. 876.1 (LINN; iso- BM).

Generitype of *Stewartia* Linnaeus.
Current name: ***Stewartia malacodendron*** L. (Theaceae).

Stilago bunius Linnaeus, *Systema Naturae,* ed. 12, 2: 597; *Mantissa Plantarum*: 122. 1767.
"Habitat in India." RCN: 6912.
Lectotype (Airy Shaw in *Kew Bull.* 35: 693. 1980): [icon] *"Bunius sativa"* in Rumphius, Herb. Amboin. 3: 204, t. 131. 1743.
Generitype of *Stilago* Linnaeus.
Current name: ***Antidesma bunius*** (L.) Spreng. (Euphorbiaceae).

Stilbe ericoides (Linnaeus) Linnaeus, *Mantissa Plantarum Altera*: 305. 1771.
"Habitat ad Cap. b. Spei." RCN: 7707.
Basionym: *Selago ericoides* L. (1767).
Type not designated.
Original material: as basionym.
Current name: ***Stilbe ericoides*** (L.) L. (Stilbaceae).

Stilbe pinastra (Linnaeus) Linnaeus, *Mantissa Plantarum Altera*: 305. 1771.
"Habitat ad Cap. b. spei." RCN: 7706.
Basionym: *Selago pinastra* L. (1759).
Type not designated.
Original material: as basionym.
Current name: ***Stilbe pinastra*** (L.) L. (Stilbaceae).
Note: Specific epithet spelled "prunastri" in the protologue.

Stillingia sylvatica Linnaeus, *Systema Naturae,* ed. 12, 2: 637; *Mantissa Plantarum*: 126. 1767.
"Habitat in Carolinae pinetis. D. Garden." RCN: 7306.
Lectotype (Reveal in Jarvis & al., *Regnum Veg.* 127: 91. 1993): *Garden,* Herb. Linn. No. 1147.1 (LINN).
Generitype of *Stillingia* Linnaeus.
Current name: ***Stillingia sylvatica*** L. (Euphorbiaceae).

Stipa arguens Linnaeus, *Species Plantarum,* ed. 2, 1: 117. 1762.
"Habitat in India." RCN: 662.
Lectotype (Merrill, *Interpret. Rumph. Herb. Amb.*: 89. 1917): Herb. Linn. No. 94.10 (LINN).
Current name: ***Themeda arguens*** (L.) Hack. (Poaceae).

Stipa aristella Linnaeus, *Systema Naturae,* ed. 12, 3: 229. 1768.
"Habitat Monspelii. Gouan." RCN: 658.
Lectotype (Vázquez & al. in *Anales Jard. Bot. Madrid* 52: 182. 1995): *Gouan 3,* Herb. Linn. No. 94.6 (LINN).
Current name: ***Achnatherum bromoides*** (L.) P. Beauv. (Poaceae).

Stipa avenacea Linnaeus, *Species Plantarum* 1: 78. 1753.
"Habitat in Virginia." RCN: 660.
Lectotype (Hitchcock in *Contr. U. S. Natl. Herb.* 12: 122. 1908): *Clayton 621,* Herb. Linn. No. 94.5 (LINN; iso- BM?, US, fragm.).
Current name: ***Piptochaetium avenaceum*** (L.) Parodi (Poaceae).
Note: Baum in *Canad. J. Bot.* 45: 1851. 1967) argued that Hitchcock's choice was flawed and that *Clayton 621* (BM) is the holotype. However, the material in LINN designated as type by Hitchcock is original material for the name, and his typification has priority.

Stipa capillata Linnaeus, *Species Plantarum,* ed. 2, 1: 116. 1762.
"Habitat in Germania, Gallia." RCN: 657.
Lectotype (Freitag in *Notes Roy. Bot. Gard. Edinburgh* 42: 453. 1985): Herb. Burser I: 127 (UPS).
Current name: ***Stipa capillata*** L. (Poaceae).
Note: See discussion by Vázquez & al. (in *Anales Jard. Bot. Madrid* 52: 181–182. 1995).

Stipa juncea Linnaeus, *Species Plantarum* 1: 78. 1753.
"Habitat in Helvetia, Gallia." RCN: 656.
Lectotype (Vázquez & al. in *Anales Jard. Bot. Madrid* 52: 179. 1995):
   Herb. Linn. No. 94.2 (LINN).
Current name: ***Stipa juncea*** L. (Poaceae).
Note: This name has often been treated as ambiguous (see discussion
   by Moraldo in *Webbia* 40: 227–228. 1986) and informally rejected
   in favour of e.g. *S. offneri* Breistr., *S. capillata* L., and *S. celakovskyi*
   Martinovský. See extensive discussion by the typifying authors who
   conclude that they prefer to typify the name in the sense of *S.
   celakovskyi* and to allow the Linnaean name to be applied in this
   sense.

Stipa membranacea Linnaeus, *Species Plantarum* 1: 560. 1753.
"Habitat in Hispania. Loefling." RCN: 661.
Lectotype (Stace & Cotton in *Watsonia* 11: 119. 1976): *Löfling s.n.*,
   Herb. Linn. No. 94.9 (LINN).
Current name: ***Vulpia membranacea*** (L.) Dumort. (Poaceae).
Note: Lambinon (in *Taxon* 30: 364. 1981) proposed the name for
   rejection but the proposal failed to gain the necessary majority and
   was not recommended by the Committee for Spermatophyta (in
   Taxon 35: 562. 1986).

Stipa pennata Linnaeus, *Species Plantarum* 1: 78. 1753.
"Habitat in Austria, Gallia." RCN: 655.
Lectotype (Freitag in *Notes Roy. Bot. Gard. Edinburgh* 42: 437. 1985):
   Herb. A. van Royen No. 900.320–437 (L).
Generitype of *Stipa* Linnaeus (vide Hitchcock, *Prop. Brit. Bot.*: 121.
   1929).
Current name: ***Stipa pennata*** L. (Poaceae).
Note: Although Mansfeld (in *Repert. Spec. Nov. Regni Veg.* 47: 268. 1939)
   interpreted the name via a cited Clusius plate, he did not appear to
   make a formal choice of type. Recognising that a number of taxa were
   included within Linnaeus' species concept, many authors (e.g. Scholz
   in *Willdenowia* 4: 304. 1968; Fuchs-Eckert in *Feddes Repert.* 90:
   535–538. 1980; Kerguélen in *Lejeunia* n.s., 10: 48. 1983) rejected
   the name as a *nomen ambiguum*. Martinovský & Skalický (in *Preslia*
   41: 330. 1969) had in the meantime designated Jussieu material,
   unseen by Linnaeus and not original material for the name, as
   lectotype. Meikle (*Fl. Cyprus* 2: 1793. 23 Apr 1985) indicated *Löfling
   54a* (94.1 LINN) as type, a collection already dismissed as conflicting
   with the protologue by earlier authors. This is fortunate as it is
   apparently identifiable as *S. pulcherrima* C. Koch. Later in the same
   year, Freitag (in *Notes Roy. Bot. Gard. Edinburgh* 42: 437–438. 1985)
   provided a further review, designated a van Royen collection as
   lectotype, and restored the name to use. He has subsequently been
   followed by authors such as Moraldo (in *Webbia* 20: 244. 1986) and
   Kerguélen & al. (in *Lejeunia* n.s., 120: 171. 1987).

Stipa spinifex Linnaeus, *Systema Naturae*, ed. 12, 2: 98; *Mantissa
   Plantarum*: 34. 1767.
"Habitat in Indiae arenosis maritimis." RCN: 663.
Lectotype (Heyligers in Cafferty & al. in *Taxon* 49: 257. 2000): [icon]
   "Cyperus littoreus echinato capite" in Rumphius, Herb. Amboin. 6: 6,
   t. 2, f. 2. 1750.
Current name: ***Spinifex littoreus*** (Burm. f.) Merr. (Poaceae).

Stipa tenacissima Linnaeus, *Centuria I Plantarum*: 6. 1755.
"Habitat in Hispaniae collibus sabulosis." RCN: 659.
Lectotype (Vázquez & al. in *Anales Jard. Bot. Madrid* 52: 184. 1995):
   Löfling 556b, Herb. Linn. No. 94.7, right specimen (LINN).
Current name: ***Macrochloa tenacissima*** (L.) Kunth (Poaceae).

Stoebe aethiopica Linnaeus, *Species Plantarum* 2: 831. 1753.
"Habitat in Aethiopia." RCN: 6725.

Lectotype (Anderberg in Jarvis & al., *Regnum Veg.* 127: 91. 1993):
   [icon] *"Eupatorioides Capensis capitatus"* in Petiver, Gazophyl. Nat.:
   13, t. 8, f. 1. 1702–1709.
Generitype of *Stoebe* Linnaeus.
Current name: ***Stoebe aethiopica*** L. (Asteraceae).

Stoebe gnaphaloides Linnaeus, *Systema Vegetabilium*, ed. 13: 664.
   1774, *nom. illeg.*
RCN: 6728.
Replaced synonym: *Gnaphalium niveum* L. (1753).
Type not designated.
Original material: as replaced synonym.
Current name: ***Helichrysum niveum*** (L.) Less. (Asteraceae).
Note: Although Hilliard & Burtt (in *Bot. J. Linn. Soc.* 82: 244, 259.
   262. 1981) indicated Plukenet material in Herb. Sloane 100: 24
   (BM-SL) as the lectotype of *Gnaphalium niveum* L. (the replaced
   synonym of *S. gnaphaloides*), this material was never seen by
   Linnaeus, is not associated with any Plukenet illustration, and is not
   original material for the earlier name.

Stoebe prostrata Linnaeus, *Mantissa Plantarum Altera*: 291. 1771.
"Habitat ad Cap. b. spei." RCN: 6727.
Lectotype (Koekemoer in Jarvis & Turland in *Taxon* 47: 368. 1998):
   Herb. Linn. No. 1048.3 (LINN).
Current name: ***Stoebe prostrata*** L. (Asteraceae).

Stratiotes alismoides Linnaeus, *Species Plantarum* 1: 535. 1753.
"Habitat in India." RCN: 3974.
Lectotype (designated here by Simpson): [icon] *"Ottel-ambel"* in
   Rheede, Hort. Malab. 11: 95, t. 46. 1692.
Current name: ***Ottelia alismoides*** (L.) Pers. (Hydrocharitaceae).
Note: Cook & Urmi-König (in *Aquatic Bot.* 20: 133. 1984) indicated
   703.2 (LINN) as type but this collection lacks the relevant *Species
   Plantarum* number (i.e. "2") and was a post-1753 addition to the
   herbarium, and is not original material for the name.

Stratiotes aloides Linnaeus, *Species Plantarum* 1: 535. 1753.
"Habitat in Europae septentrionalis aquis pigris." RCN: 3973.
Lectotype (Simpson in Jarvis & al., *Regnum Veg.* 127: 91. 1993):
   Herb. Burser XVI(1): 105 (UPS).
Generitype of *Stratiotes* Linnaeus.
Current name: ***Stratiotes aloides*** L. (Hydrocharitaceae).

Struthiola erecta Linnaeus, *Systema Naturae*, ed. 12, 2: 127; *Mantissa
   Plantarum*: 41. 1767, *nom. illeg.*
"Habitat ad Cap. b. spei." RCN: 1002.
Replaced synonym: *Passerina dodecandra* L. (1755).
Neotype (Rogers in Rogers & Spencer in *Taxon* 55: 487. 2006): South
   Africa. Western Cape Province, Caledon District, Cape Hangklip,
   near the hotel, 50m, 1 Oct 1956, *R. Dahlgren & B. Peterson 526*
   (MO-5033766).
Current name: ***Struthiola dodecandra*** (L.) Druce (Thymelaeaceae).
Note: A superfluous name for *Passerina dodecandra* L. (1755).

Struthiola virgata Linnaeus, *Systema Naturae*, ed. 12, 2: 127;
   Mantissa Plantarum: 41. 1767, *typ. cons.*
"Habitat ad Cap. b. Spei." RCN: 1001.
Lectotype (Rogers in Rogers & Spencer in *Taxon* 55: 488. 2006):
   Herb. Linn. No. 162.1 (LINN).
Generitype of *Struthiola* Linnaeus, *nom. cons.*
Current name: ***Struthiola ciliata*** (L.) Lam. (Thymelaeaceae).
Note: *Struthiola* Linnaeus, *nom. cons.* against *Belvala* Adans.

Strychnos colubrina Linnaeus, *Species Plantarum* 1: 189. 1753, *nom.
   utique rej.*

"Habitat in India." RCN: 1501.
Lectotype (Bisset & al. in *Lloydia* 36: 183. 1973): [icon] *"Modira-caniram"* in Rheede, Hort. Malab. 8: 47, t. 24. 1688.
Current name: ***Strychnos wallichiana*** Steud. ex A. DC. (Strychnaceae).

Strychnos nux-vomica Linnaeus, *Species Plantarum* 1: 189. 1753.
"Habitat in India." RCN: 1500.
Lectotype (Tirel-Roudet in Aubréville & Leroy, *Fl. Cambodge Laos Vietnam* 13: 41. 1972): [icon] *"Caniram"* in Rheede, Hort. Malab. 1: 67, t. 37. 1678.
Generitype of *Strychnos* Linnaeus (vide Hitchcock, *Prop. Brit. Bot.*: 133. 1929).
Current name: ***Strychnos nux-vomica*** L. (Strychnaceae).
Note: Bisset & al. (in *Lloydia* 36: 189. 1973) designated Herb. Hermann 4: 33, No. 91 (BM) as lectotype. However, this choice is pre-dated by that of Tirel-Roudet.

Styrax officinale Linnaeus, *Species Plantarum* 1: 444. 1753.
"Habitat in Syria, Judaea, Italia." RCN: 3119.
Lectotype (Barrie in Jarvis & al., *Regnum Veg.* 127: 92. 1993): Herb. Clifford: 187, *Styrax* 1 (BM-000628613).
Generitype of *Styrax* Linnaeus.
Current name: ***Styrax officinalis*** L. (Styracaceae).

Subularia aquatica Linnaeus, *Species Plantarum* 2: 642. 1753.
"Habitat in Europae borealis inundatis lacustribus fluviis." RCN: 4667.
Lectotype (Jonsell in Jarvis & al., *Regnum Veg.* 127: 92. 1993): Herb. Linn. No. 264.9 (S).
Generitype of *Subularia* Linnaeus.
Current name: ***Subularia aquatica*** L. (Brassicaceae).
Note: Mulligan & Calder (in *Rhodora* 66: 131. 1964) designated 822.1 (LINN) as lectotype, but this sheet lacks a *Species Plantarum* number (i.e. "1") and is a post-1753 addition to the herbarium. It is not original material for the name, and Jonsell therefore designated a sheet in S as lectotype.

Suriana maritima Linnaeus, *Species Plantarum* 1: 284. 1753.
"Habitat ad littora maris in Bermudis, Jamaica." RCN: 3366.
Lectotype (Basak in Jain & al. in *Fasc. Fl. India* 4: 17. 1980): [icon] *"Arbor. Americ. Salicis folio frondosa, Bermudensibus"* in Plukenet, Phytographia: t. 241, f. 5. 1692; Almag. Bot.: 44. 1696.
Generitype of *Suriana* Linnaeus.
Current name: ***Suriana maritima*** L. (Surianaceae).
Note: Malik (in Nasir & Ali, *Fl. Pakistan* 162: 7. 1984) chose the cited Sloane plate as lectotype but this choice is pre-dated by that of Basak.

Swertia corniculata Linnaeus, *Species Plantarum* 1: 227. 1753.
"Habitat in Sibiria, Gmelin; Canada, Kalm." RCN: 1854.
Type not designated.
Original material: *Gmelin*, Herb. Linn. No. 327.4 (LINN).
Current name: ***Halenia corniculata*** (L.) Cornaz (Gentianaceae).

Swertia dichotoma Linnaeus, *Species Plantarum* 1: 227. 1753.
"Habitat in Sibiria. D. Gmelin." RCN: 1857.
Type not designated.
Original material: *Gmelin*, Herb. Linn. No. 327.5 (LINN).
Current name: ***Anagallidium dichotomum*** (L.) Griseb. (Gentianaceae).

Swertia difformis Linnaeus, *Species Plantarum* 1: 226. 1753.
"Habitat in Virginia." RCN: 1855.

Lectotype (Blake in *Rhodora* 17: 51. 1915): *Clayton 171* (BM-000038852).
Current name: ***Sabatia difformis*** (L.) Druce (Gentianaceae).

Swertia perennis Linnaeus, *Species Plantarum* 1: 226. 1753.
"Habitat in Helvetia, Bavaria." RCN: 1854.
Lectotype (Barrie in Jarvis & al., *Regnum Veg.* 127: 92. 1993): Herb. Linn. No. 327.1 (LINN).
Generitype of *Swertia* Linnaeus (vide Hitchcock, *Prop. Brit. Bot.*: 138. 1929).
Current name: ***Swertia perennis*** L. (Gentianaceae).

Swertia rotata Linnaeus, *Species Plantarum* 1: 226. 1753.
"Habitat in Sibiria. D. Gmelin." RCN: 1855b.
Lectotype (Liu & Ho in *Acta Phytotax. Sinica* 30: 309. 1992): *Krascheninnikov*?, Herb. Linn. No. 327.3 (LINN).
Current name: ***Lomatogonium rotatum*** (L.) Fr. ex Fernald (Gentianaceae).

Symphytum officinale Linnaeus, *Species Plantarum* 1: 136. 1753.
"Habitat in Europae umbrosis subhumidis." RCN: 1099.
Lectotype (Gadella in *Ann. Missouri Bot. Gard.* 71: 1063. 1984): Herb. Linn. No. 185.1 (LINN).
Generitype of *Symphytum* Linnaeus (vide Hitchcock, *Prop. Brit. Bot.*: 128. 1929).
Current name: ***Symphytum officinale*** L. (Boraginaceae).

Symphytum orientale Linnaeus, *Species Plantarum* 1: 136. 1753.
"Habitat juxta Constantinopoli rivulos primo vere." RCN: 1099.
Lectotype (Kurtto in *Ann. Bot. Fenn.* 22: 330. 1985): [icon] *"Symphytum Constantinopolitanum, Borraginis folio & facie, flore albo"* in Buxbaum, Pl. Minus Cognit. Cent. 5: 36, t. 68. 1740.
Current name: ***Symphytum orientale*** L. (Boraginaceae).
Note: Stearn (in *Ann. Mus. Goulandris* 7: 177. 1986) subsequently made the same type choice as Kurtto. Bottega & Garbari (in *Webbia* 58: 264, f. 10. 2003) reproduce the type illustration.

Symphytum tuberosum Linnaeus, *Species Plantarum* 1: 136. 1753.
"Habitat in Germania australi." RCN: 1098.
Lectotype (Stearn in *Ann. Mus. Goulandris* 7: 177. 1985): Herb. Linn. No. 185.3 (LINN).
Current name: ***Symphytum tuberosum*** L. (Boraginaceae).

Syringa persica Linnaeus, *Species Plantarum* 1: 9. 1753.
"Habitat in Persia?" RCN: 59.
Type not designated.
Original material: Herb. Linn. No. 22.2 (LINN); Herb. Clifford: 6, *Syringa* 2 (BM).
Current name: ***Syringa × persica*** L. (Oleaceae).

Syringa persica Linnaeus var. **laciniata** Linnaeus, *Species Plantarum*, ed. 2, 1: 12. 1762.
RCN: 59.
Type not designated.
Original material: Herb. Linn. No. 22.4 (LINN); [icon] in Miller, Fig. Pl. Gard. Dict. 2: 110, t. 164, f. 2. 1757.
Current name: ***Syringa* sp.** (Oleaceae).
Note: The application of this name appears uncertain.

Syringa vulgaris Linnaeus, *Species Plantarum* 1: 9. 1753.
"Habitat versus Persiam." RCN: 58.
Lectotype (Green in Jarvis & al., *Regnum Veg.* 127: 92. 1993): Herb. Linn. No. 22.1 (LINN).
Generitype of *Syringa* Linnaeus (vide Hitchcock, *Prop. Brit. Bot.*: 116. 1929).
Current name: ***Syringa vulgaris*** L. (Oleaceae).

S

T

Tabernaemontana alternifolia Linnaeus, *Species Plantarum* 1: 211. 1753.
"Habitat in Malabaria." RCN: 1741.
Lectotype (Majumdar & Bakshi in *Taxon* 28: 353. 1979): [icon] *"Curutu-pala"* in Rheede, Hort. Malab. 1: 83, t. 46. 1678.
Current name: ***Tabernaemontana alternifolia*** L. (Apocynaceae).
Note: The type of this formerly little-used name is identifiable as material of the widespread *T. heyneana* Wall., and Middleton & Leeuwenberg (in *Taxon* 47: 481. 1998) therefore proposed *T. alternifolia* for rejection against *T. heyneana*. However, this was not recommended by the Committee for Spermatophyta (in *Taxon* 49: 272. 2000).

Tabernaemontana amsonia Linnaeus, *Species Plantarum,* ed. 2, 1: 308. 1762.
"Habitat in Virginia." RCN: 1742.
Type not designated.
Original material: Herb. Linn. No. 304.5 (LINN); *Clayton 306* (BM).
Current name: ***Amsonia tabernaemontana*** Walter (Apocynaceae).

Tabernaemontana citrifolia Linnaeus, *Species Plantarum* 1: 210. 1753.
"Habitat in utraque India." RCN: 1737.
Lectotype (Leeuwenberg in Jarvis & al., *Regnum Veg.* 127: 92. 1993): [icon] *"Tabernaemontana"* in Plumier, Nov. Pl. Amer.: 18, t. 30. 1703.
Generitype of *Tabernaemontana* Linnaeus (vide Hitchcock, *Prop. Brit. Bot.*: 136. 1929).
Current name: ***Tabernaemontana citrifolia*** L. (Apocynaceae).

Tabernaemontana echites Linnaeus, *Systema Naturae,* ed. 10, 2: 945. 1759.
["Habitat in Jamaica."]Sp. Pl., ed. 2, 1: 308 (1762). RCN: 1723.
Basionym of: *Cameraria echites* (L.) L. (Dec 1759).
Type not designated.
Original material: *Browne,* Herb. Linn. No. 304.4 (LINN); [icon] in Sloane, Voy. Jamaica 1: 207, t. 131, f. 2. 1707.
Current name: ***Echites umbellata*** Jacq. (Apocynaceae).

Tabernaemontana laurifolia Linnaeus, *Species Plantarum* 1: 210. 1753.
"Habitat in Jamaica ad ripas fluviorum." RCN: 1738.
Lectotype (Stearn in *J. Arnold Arbor.* 52: 616. 1971): [icon] *"Nerium arboreum folio latiore obtuso flore luteo minore"* in Sloane, Voy. Jamaica 2: 62, t. 186, f. 2. 1725. – Typotype: Herb. Sloane 6: 58 (BM-SL), see also p. 31 and above right.
Current name: ***Tabernaemontana laurifolia*** L. (Apocynaceae).

Tagetes erecta Linnaeus, *Species Plantarum* 2: 887. 1753.
"Habitat in Mexico." RCN: 6418.
Lectotype (Howard, *Fl. Lesser Antilles* 6: 601. 1989): Herb. Linn. No. 1009.3 (LINN).
Generitype of *Tagetes* Linnaeus (vide Green, *Prop. Brit. Bot.*: 182. 1929).
Current name: ***Tagetes erecta*** L. (Asteraceae).
Note: Tagetes patula L. was treated as the generitype by Rydberg (*N. Amer. Fl.* 34: 149. 1915; see McNeill & al. in *Taxon* 36: 386. 1987). However, under Art. 10.5, Ex. 7 (a voted example) of the Vienna Code, this is a type choice made under the American Code and is to be replaced under Art. 10.5b by Green's choice (*Prop. Brit. Bot.*: 182. 1929) of *T. erecta.*

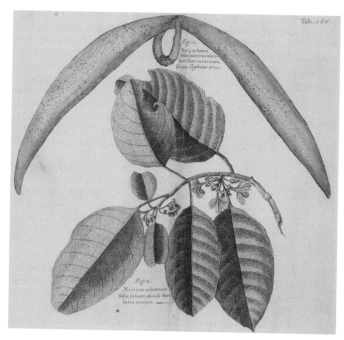

The lectotype of *Tabernaemontana laurifolia* L.

Grierson (in Dassanayake & Fosberg, *Revised Handb. Fl. Ceylon* 1: 234. 1980) indicated unspecified Clifford material as type, failing to distinguish between two relevant sheets there. As they do not appear to be part of a single gathering, Art. 9.15 does not apply, and Howard's choice of material in LINN as the type is accepted here.

Tagetes minuta Linnaeus, *Species Plantarum* 2: 887. 1753.
"Habitat in Chili." RCN: 6419.
Lectotype (Delgado Montaño in Jarvis & Turland in *Taxon* 47: 368. 1998): [icon] *"Tagetes multiflora, minuto flore albicante"* in Dillenius, Hort. Eltham. 2: 374, t. 280, f. 362. 1732.
Current name: ***Tagetes minuta*** L. (Asteraceae).
Note: Hind (in Bosser & al., *Fl. Mascareignes* 109: 224. 1993) indicated, though with doubt ("?"), Clifford material as type, but there is no relevant material preserved in the Clifford herbarium.

Tagetes patula Linnaeus, *Species Plantarum* 2: 887. 1753.
"Habitat in Mexico." RCN: 6417.
Lectotype (Hind in Jarvis & al., *Regnum Veg.* 127: 92. 1993): Herb. Linn. No. 1009.1 (LINN).
Current name: ***Tagetes patula*** L. (Asteraceae).
Note: Tagetes patula was treated as the generitype by Rydberg (*N. Amer. Fl.* 34: 149. 1915; see McNeill & al. in *Taxon* 36: 386. 1987). However, under Art. 10.5, Ex. 7 (a voted example) of the Vienna Code, this is a type choice made under the American Code and is to be replaced under Art. 10.5b by Green's choice (*Prop. Brit. Bot.*: 182. 1929) of *T. erecta* L.
Moore (in Fawcett & Rendle, *Fl. Jamaica* 7: 262. 1936) noted the existence of material in the Clifford herbarium but did not designate a type.

Tamarindus indica Linnaeus, *Species Plantarum* 1: 34. 1753.
"Habitat in India, America, Aegypto, Arabia." RCN: 271.

Lectotype (Jansen, *Spices, Condiments Med. Pl. Ethiopia*: 249. 1981): Herb. Linn. No. 49.2 (LINN).
Generitype of *Tamarindus* Linnaeus.
Current name: ***Tamarindus indica*** L. (Fabaceae: Caesalpinioideae).
Note: Fawcett & Rendle (*Fl. Jamaica* 4: 119. 1920), and a number of later authors, indicated unspecified material at LINN as the type, but failed to distinguish between sheets 49.1, 49.2 and 49.3. These are not part of the same gathering so Art. 9.15 does not apply. Larsen & Larsen (in Aubréville & Leroy, *Fl. Cambodge Laos Viêt-Nam* 18: 146. 1980) indicated 49.1 (LINN) as type but it lacks the *Species Plantarum* number (i.e. "1") and is not original material for the name. Jansen's choice, also made independently by Polhill (in Jarvis & al., *Regnum Veg.* 127: 92. 1993), is accepted here.

Tamarix gallica Linnaeus, *Species Plantarum* 1: 270. 1753.
"Habitat in Gallia, Hispania, Italia." RCN: 2149.
Lectotype (Baum, *Genus* Tamarix: 32. 1978): Herb. Clifford: 111, *Tamarix* 1 (BM-000558434).
Generitype of *Tamarix* Linnaeus (vide Hitchcock, *Prop. Brit. Bot.*: 142. 1929).
Current name: ***Tamarix gallica*** L. (Tamaricaceae).

Tamarix germanica Linnaeus, *Species Plantarum* 1: 271. 1753.
"Habitat in Germaniae locis inundatis." RCN: 2150.
Type not designated.
Original material: Herb. Clifford: 112, *Tamarix* 2, 2 sheets (BM); Herb. Linn. No. 383.2 (LINN); Herb. Burser XXV: 37 (UPS); [icon] in Plantin, Pl. Stirp. Icon. 2: 218. 1581.
Current name: ***Myricaria germanica*** (L.) Desv. (Tamaricaceae).

Tamus communis Linnaeus, *Species Plantarum* 2: 1028. 1753.
"Habitat in Europa australi." RCN: 7435.
Type not designated.
Original material: Herb. Linn. No. 1181.2 (LINN); Herb. Clifford: 458, *Tamus* 1 (BM); Herb. Burser XVII: 25 (UPS); Herb. Burser XVII: 26 (UPS); [icon] in Dodoëns, Stirp. Hist. Pempt., ed. 2: 400, 401. 1616.
Generitype of *Tamus* Linnaeus.
Current name: ***Dioscorea communis*** (L.) Caddick & Wilkin (Dioscoreaceae).
Note: Labani (in Jafri & El-Gadi, *Fl. Libya* 70: 2. 1980) indicated 1181.1 (LINN) as type. However, the material came from Brander and was not received by Linnaeus until 1756 so it cannot be original material for the name. Caddick & al. (in *Taxon* 51: 112. 2002) indicated "plate on Hort. Cliff. p. 458" as type but no illustration of this taxon appears to be figured in that work.

Tamus cretica Linnaeus, *Species Plantarum* 2: 1028. 1753.
"Habitat in Creta." RCN: 7436.
Neotype (Kit Tan in Davis, *Fl. Turkey* 8: 553. 1984): Herb. Tournefort No. 283 (P).
Current name: ***Dioscorea communis*** (L.) Caddick & Wilkin (Dioscoreaceae).
Note: Kit Tan cited Herb. Tournefort No. 283 (P) as an isotype. Although this collection was not studied by Linnaeus, in the absence of any original material for the name, Kit Tan's statement is accepted as a neotypification (Art. 9.8).

Tanacetum annuum Linnaeus, *Species Plantarum* 2: 844. 1753.
"Habitat in Hispania, Hetruria." RCN: 6119.
Lectotype (Humphries in Jarvis & Turland in *Taxon* 47: 368. 1998): Herb. Linn. No. 987.5 (LINN).
Current name: ***Tanacetum annuum*** L. (Asteraceae).

Tanacetum balsamita Linnaeus, *Species Plantarum* 2: 845. 1753.
"Habitat in Hetruria, Narbona." RCN: 6122.
Lectotype (Humphries in Jarvis & Turland in *Taxon* 47: 368. 1998): Herb. Clifford: 398, *Tanacetum* 1 (BM-000646976).
Current name: ***Tanacetum balsamita*** L. (Asteraceae).

Tanacetum cotuloides Linnaeus, *Mantissa Plantarum Altera*: 282. 1771.
"Habitat ad Cap. b. spei." RCN: 6118.
Lectotype (Humphries in Jarvis & Turland in *Taxon* 47: 368. 1998): Herb. Linn. No. 987.3 (LINN).
Current name: ***Hippia pilosa*** (P.J. Bergius) Druce (Asteraceae).

Tanacetum crithmifolium Linnaeus, *Species Plantarum* 2: 843. 1753.
"Habitat in Aethiopia." RCN: 6114.
Replaced synonym of: *Athanasia parviflora* L. (1774).
Lectotype (Wijnands, *Bot. Commelins*: 70. 1983): Herb. Linn. No. 986.17 (LINN).
Current name: ***Hymenolepis crithmifolia*** (L.) Greuter & al. (Asteraceae).
Note: Although the correct name for this species in *Athanasia* is *A. parviflora* L. (1774), the epithet "crithmifolia" being pre-occupied, the correct name in *Hymenolepis* is *H. crithmifolia* (L.) Greuter & al., as pointed out by Greuter & al. (in *Taxon* 54: 155. 2005).

Tanacetum frutescens Linnaeus, *Species Plantarum* 2: 844. 1753.
"Habitat in Aethiopia." RCN: 6701.
Basionym of: *Hippia frutescens* (L.) L. (1771); *Eriocephalus pectinifolius* L. (1767), *nom. illeg.*
Lectotype (Wijnands, *Bot. Commelins*: 77. 1983): Herb. Linn. No. 1039.3 (LINN).
Current name: ***Hippia frutescens*** (L.) L. (Asteraceae).

Tanacetum incanum Linnaeus, *Species Plantarum* 2: 844. 1753.
"Habitat in Oriente." RCN: 6117.
Lectotype (Ling in Jarvis & Turland in *Taxon* 47: 368. 1998): Herb. Clifford: 404, *Artemisia* 9 (BM-000647035).
Current name: ***Artemisia incana*** (L.) Druce (Asteraceae).
Note: Although Poljakov (in Schischkin & Bobrov, *Fl. U.R.S.S.* 26: 525. 1961; Shetler & Unumb, Engl. Ed.: 499. 2000) indicated unspecified material in Leningrad as type, this would in any case not have been seen by Linnaeus and would not be original material for the name.

Tanacetum monanthos Linnaeus, *Systema Naturae*, ed. 12, 2: 541; *Mantissa Plantarum*: 111. 1767.
"Habitat in Oriente. Forskåhl." RCN: 6120.
Lectotype (Humphries in *Bull. Brit. Mus. (Nat. Hist.), Bot.* 7: 116. 1979): Herb. Linn. No. 987.8 (LINN).
Current name: ***Anacyclus monanthos*** (L.) Thell. (Asteraceae).

Tanacetum sibiricum Linnaeus, *Species Plantarum* 2: 844. 1753.
"Habitat in Sibiria." RCN: 6116.
Lectotype (Tzvelev in Schischkin & Bobrov, *Fl. U.R.S.S.* 26: 418. 1961): [icon] *"Tanacetum foliis pinnatis multifidis, laciniis linearibus bifidus et trifidis"* in Gmelin, Fl. Sibirica 2: 134, t. 65, f. 2. 1752.
Current name: ***Filifolium sibiricum*** (L.) Kitam. (Asteraceae).
Note: Humphries (in *Taxon* 47: 368. 1998) designated Herb. Linn. 987.1 (LINN) as type, but this choice is pre-dated by that of Tzvelev, who formally chose Gmelin's plate as type.

Tanacetum suffruticosum Linnaeus, *Species Plantarum* 2: 843. 1753.
"Habitat in Aethiopia." RCN: 6115.
Replaced synonym of: *Cotula tanacetifolia* L. (1767), *nom. illeg.*

Lectotype (Wijnands, *Bot. Commelins*: 80. 1983): Herb. Linn. No. 987.11 (LINN).
Current name: ***Oncosiphon suffruticosum*** (L.) Källersjö (Asteraceae).

Tanacetum vulgare Linnaeus, *Species Plantarum* 2: 844. 1753.
"Habitat in Europae aggeribus." RCN: 6121.
Lectotype (Humphries in Jarvis & al., *Regnum Veg.* 127: 92. 1993): Herb. Clifford: 398, *Tanacetum* 3 (BM-000646978).
Generitype of *Tanacetum* Linnaeus (vide Green, *Prop. Brit. Bot.*: 180. 1929).
Current name: ***Tanacetum vulgare*** L. var. ***vulgare*** (Asteraceae).
Note: Although Dillon (in *Fieldiana, Bot.*, n.s., 7: 20. 1981) stated that an unspecified and unseen holotype was in BM, he gave no indication of what collection it might be.

Tanacetum vulgare Linnaeus var. **crispum** Linnaeus, *Species Plantarum* 2: 845. 1753.
RCN: 6121.
Lectotype (Humphries in Jarvis & Turland in *Taxon* 47: 368. 1998): Herb. Burser VII(1): 2 (UPS).
Current name: ***Tanacetum vulgare*** L. var. ***crispum*** L. (Asteraceae).

Tarchonanthus camphoratus Linnaeus, *Species Plantarum* 2: 842. 1753.
"Habitat in Aethiopia." RCN: 6095.
Lectotype (Anderberg in Jarvis & al., *Regnum Veg.* 127: 92. 1993): Herb. Clifford: 398, *Tarchonanthus* 1 (BM-000646983).
Generitype of *Tarchonanthus* Linnaeus.
Current name: ***Tarchonanthus camphoratus*** L. (Asteraceae).

Targionia hypophylla Linnaeus, *Species Plantarum* 2: 1136. 1753.
"Habitat in Italia, Hispania, Constantinopoli." RCN: 8139.
Type not designated.
Original material: Herb. Linn. No. 1268.1 (LINN); [icon] in Micheli, Nov. Pl. Gen.: 3, t. 3. 1729; [icon] in Colonna, Ekphr.: 331, 333. 1606; [icon] in Dillenius, Hist. Musc.: 532, t. 78, f. 9. 1741; [icon] in Buxbaum, Pl. Minus Cognit. Cent. 1: 41, t. 61, f. 4. 1728.
Generitype of *Targionia* Linnaeus.
Current name: ***Targionia hypophylla*** L. (Targioniaceae).
Note: See discussion by Isoviita (in *Acta Bot. Fenn.* 89: 8. 1970) and Grolle (in *Feddes Repert.* 87: 238. 1976).

Taxus baccata Linnaeus, *Species Plantarum* 2: 1040. 1753.
"Habitat in Europa, Canada." RCN: 7510.
Lectotype (Jonsell & Jarvis in Jarvis & al., *Regnum Veg.* 127: 93. 1993): Herb. Clifford: 464, *Taxus* 1 (BM-000647522).
Generitype of *Taxus* Linnaeus (vide Green, *Prop. Brit. Bot.*: 192. 1929).
Current name: ***Taxus baccata*** L. (Taxaceae).
Note: Jonsell & Jarvis (in *Nordic J. Bot.* 14: 150. 1994) gave an explanation of their earlier (1993) typification.

Taxus nucifera Linnaeus, *Species Plantarum* 2: 1040. 1753.
"Habitat in Japonia." RCN: 7512.
Lectotype (designated here by Farjon): [icon] *"Fi, vulgo Kaja. Taxus nucifera"* in Kaempfer, Amoen. Exot. Fasc.: 814, 815. 1712.
Current name: ***Torreya nucifera*** (L.) Siebold & Zucc. (Taxaceae).

Telephium imperati Linnaeus, *Species Plantarum* 1: 271. 1753.
"Habitat in Gallo-provincia." RCN: 2157.
Lectotype (Williams in *J. Bot.* 44: 293. 1906): Herb. Clifford: 73, *Telephium* 1 (BM-000558133).
Generitype of *Telephium* Linnaeus.
Current name: ***Telephium imperati*** L. (Caryophyllaceae).

Telephium oppositifolium Linnaeus, *Species Plantarum*, ed. 2, 1: 388. 1762.
"Habitat in Barbaria." RCN: 2158.
Type not designated.
Original material: [icon] in Shaw, Cat. Pl. Afr. As.: 46, f. 572. 1738.
Current name: ***Telephium imperati*** L. (Caryophyllaceae).
Note: Williams (in *J. Bot.* 44: 300. 1906) treated a Shaw specimen at OXF as the type specimen. However, this was never seen by Linnaeus and is not original material for the name.

Terminalia catappa Linnaeus, *Systema Naturae*, ed. 12, 2: 674; *Mantissa Plantarum*: 128. 1767.
"Habitat in India." RCN: 7625.
Lectotype (Byrnes in *Contr. Queensland Herb.* 20: 38. 1977): Herb. Linn. No. 1222.1 (LINN).
Generitype of *Terminalia* Linnaeus, *nom. cons.*
Current name: ***Terminalia catappa*** L. (Combretaceae).
Note: Terminalia Linnaeus, *nom. cons.* against *Bucida* L. and *Adamaram* Adans.
   Smith (in *Brittonia* 23: 405. 1971) regarded Exell (in *J. Bot.* 69: 125. 1931) as having typified the name by a sheet in LINN but Exell notes, in the context of establishing a generitype, that *T. catappa* is the only species represented in LINN.

Tetracera volubilis Linnaeus, *Species Plantarum* 1: 533. 1753, *nom. cons.*
"Habitat in Barbados, Vera Cruce, Marilandia." RCN: 3960.
Conserved type (Barrie & Todzia in *Taxon* 40: 652. 1991): Mexico. Veracruz, Zacuapan, Sulphur Spring, Dec 1906, *Purpus 2206* (F; iso- US).
Generitype of *Tetracera* Linnaeus.
Current name: ***Tetracera volubilis*** L. (Dilleniaceae).
Note: Barrie & Todzia (in *Taxon* 40: 652–655. 1991) provided an extensive review of this name along with their conservation proposal.

Tetragonia fruticosa Linnaeus, *Species Plantarum* 1: 480. 1753.
"Habitat in Aethiopia." RCN: 3666.
Lectotype (Adamson in *J. S. African Bot.* 21: 113. 1955): Herb. Linn. No. 648.1 (LINN).
Generitype of *Tetragonia* Linnaeus (vide Green, *Prop. Brit. Bot.*: 159. 1929).
Current name: ***Tetragonia fruticosa*** L. (Aizoaceae).

Tetragonia herbacea Linnaeus, *Species Plantarum* 1: 480. 1753.
"Habitat in Aethiopia." RCN: 3667.
Lectotype (Adamson in *J. S. African Bot.* 21: 140. 1955): [icon] *"Tetragonocarpus Afric. radice magna, crassa et carnosa"* in Commelin, Hort. Med. Amstelod. Pl. Rar. 2: 203, t. 102. 1701.
Current name: ***Tetragonia herbacea*** L. (Aizoaceae).

Tetragonotheca helianthoides Linnaeus, *Species Plantarum* 2: 903. 1753.
"Habitat in Virginia." RCN: 6655.
Replaced synonym of: *Polymnia tetragonotheca* L. (1767), *nom. illeg.*
Lectotype (Reveal in Jarvis & al., *Regnum Veg.* 127: 93. 1993): *Clayton 97* (BM-000051150).
Generitype of *Tetragonotheca* Linnaeus.
Current name: ***Tetragonotheca helianthoides*** L. (Asteraceae).
Note: Turner & Dawson (in *Sida* 8: 299. 1980) indicated that they had seen a photograph of "Gronovius 301", which they regarded as the type. However, *Gronovius 301* is associated with *Heuchera americana*, and there is no p. 301 in Gronovius' *Flora Virginica*. Reveal's choice of *Clayton 97* (BM) as type is accepted here.

Teucrium alpinum Linnaeus, *Systema Naturae,* ed. 10, 2: 1094. 1759.
RCN: 4123c.
Neotype (Navarro in Jarvis & al. in *Taxon* 50: 520. 2001): France. Marne: 22km before Châlons-sur-Marne on A4 [road] SE Reims, 1 Jul 1983, *Akeroyd & al. 3003* (BM-000576285).
Current name: ***Teucrium botrys*** L. (Lamiaceae).

Teucrium arduinoi Linnaeus, *Systema Naturae,* ed. 12, 2: 388; *Mantissa Plantarum:* 81. 1767.
"Habitat . ." RCN: 4136.
Lectotype (Turland in Jarvis & al. in *Taxon* 50: 720. 2001): *Arduino s.n.,* Herb. Linn. No. 722.18 (LINN).
Current name: ***Teucrium arduinoi*** L. (Lamiaceae).
Note: Specific epithet spelled "arduini" in the protologue.

Teucrium asiaticum Linnaeus, *Systema Naturae,* ed. 12, 2: 388; *Mantissa Plantarum:* 80. 1767.
"Habitat in India Orientali?" RCN: 4134.
Lectotype (Navarro in Jarvis & al. in *Taxon* 50: 520. 2001): Herb. Linn. No. 722.17 (LINN).
Current name: ***Teucrium asiaticum*** L. (Lamiaceae).
Note: Rosselló & Sáez (in *Collect. Bot.* 25: 104. 2000) incorrectly indicated 722.17 (LINN) as a syntype. As a syntype is not, by definition, the sole type of a name (unlike a holotype, lectotype or neotype), their statement is not accepted as correctable under Art. 9.8. Consequently, Navarro's choice of the same collection as lectotype is accepted here.

Teucrium botrys Linnaeus, *Species Plantarum* 2: 562. 1753.
"Habitat in Germaniae, Galliae, Helvetiae, Italiae apricis cultis." RCN: 4120.
Lectotype (Navarro & El Oualidi in *Acta Bot. Malac.* 22: 193. 1997): Herb. Linn. No. 722.3 (LINN).
Current name: ***Teucrium botrys*** L. (Lamiaceae).

Teucrium campanulatum Linnaeus, *Species Plantarum* 2: 562. 1753.
"Habitat in Oriente." RCN: 4118.
Neotype (Navarro & El Oualidi in *Acta Bot. Malac.* 22: 189. 1997): Algeria. Tiaret to Aflou, 10–15km S of Ain Dehleb, 1 Jun 1975, *Davis 58520* (BM; iso- E).
Current name: ***Teucrium campanulatum*** L. (Lamiaceae).

Teucrium canadense Linnaeus, *Species Plantarum* 2: 564. 1753.
"Habitat in Canada." RCN: 4137.
Lectotype (Reveal in Jarvis & al. in *Taxon* 50: 520. 2001): *Clayton 135* (BM-000038174).
Current name: ***Teucrium canadense*** L. (Lamiaceae).
Note: Epling (in *J. Bot.* 67: 6. 1929) described as "standard" a specimen in LINN, probably 722.19, which lacks a *Species Plantarum* number (i.e. "15"). He also noted the existence of a Clayton sheet which was later designated as the type by Reveal.

Teucrium capitatum Linnaeus, *Species Plantarum* 2: 566. 1753.
"Habitat in Hispania." RCN: 4150.
Lectotype (Rosúa & Navarro in *Taxon* 36: 469, f. 1. 1987): *Löfling 417a,* Herb. Linn. s.n. (SBT).
Current name: ***Teucrium capitatum*** L. (Lamiaceae).

Teucrium chamaedrys Linnaeus, *Species Plantarum* 2: 565. 1753.
"Habitat in Germania, Helvetia, Gallia." RCN: 4143.
Lectotype (Navarro & El Oualidi in *Acta Bot. Malac.* 22: 189. 1997): Herb. Linn. No. 722.26, central specimen (LINN).
Current name: ***Teucrium chamaedrys*** L. (Lamiaceae).

Teucrium chamaepitys Linnaeus, *Species Plantarum* 2: 562. 1753.
"Habitat in Creta." RCN: 4121.
Lectotype (Hedge in Jarvis & al. in *Taxon* 50: 520. 2001): Herb. Linn. No. 722.5 (LINN).
Current name: ***Ajuga chamaepitys*** (L.) Schreb. (Lamiaceae).

Teucrium creticum Linnaeus, *Species Plantarum* 2: 563. 1753.
"Habitat in Creta." RCN: 4128.
Lectotype (Ekim in Davis, *Fl. Turkey* 7: 56. 1982): Herb. Linn. No. 722.11 (LINN).
Current name: ***Teucrium creticum*** L. (Lamiaceae).

Teucrium flavum Linnaeus, *Species Plantarum* 2: 565. 1753.
"Habitat in Italia, Sicilia, Maltha, Hispania, Monspelii." RCN: 4145.
Lectotype (Siddiqi in Jafri & El-Gadi, *Fl. Libya* 118: 20. 1985): Herb. Linn. No. 722.30 (LINN).
Current name: ***Teucrium flavum*** L. (Lamiaceae).

Teucrium fruticans Linnaeus, *Species Plantarum* 2: 563. 1753.
"Habitat in Baeticae, Siciliae maritimis." RCN: 4126.
Lectotype (Siddiqi in Jafri & El-Gadi, *Fl. Libya* 118: 16. 1985): Herb. Linn. No. 722.10 (LINN).
Generitype of *Teucrium* Linnaeus (vide Green, *Prop. Brit. Bot.*: 164. 1929).
Current name: ***Teucrium fruticans*** L. (Lamiaceae).

Teucrium hircanicum Linnaeus, *Systema Naturae,* ed. 10, 2: 1095. 1759.
["Habitat in Hircania."] Sp. Pl., ed. 2, 2: 789 (1763). RCN: 4139.
Lectotype (Hedge in Jarvis & al. in *Taxon* 50: 521. 2001): Herb. Linn. No. 722.20 (LINN).
Current name: ***Teucrium hircanicum*** L. (Lamiaceae).

Teucrium iva Linnaeus, *Species Plantarum* 2: 563. 1753.
"Habitat in Lusitania, G. Narbonensi, Monspelii." RCN: 4124.
Lectotype (Siddiqi in Jafri & El-Gadi, *Fl. Libya* 118: 12. 1985): Herb. Linn. No. 722.8 (LINN).
Current name: ***Ajuga iva*** (L.) Schreb. (Lamiaceae).

Teucrium latifolium Linnaeus, *Species Plantarum* 2: 563. 1753.
"Habitat in regione Baetica." RCN: 4127.
Lectotype (Navarro & El Oualidi in *Acta Bot. Malac.* 22: 188. 1997): [icon] *"Teucrium fruticans Baeticum, minore folio"* in Dillenius, Hort. Eltham. 2: 379, t. 284, f. 367. 1732.
Current name: ***Teucrium fruticans*** L. (Lamiaceae).

Teucrium laxmannii Linnaeus, *Systema Vegetabilium,* ed. 13: 439. 1774.
"Habitat in Sibiria. D. Laxman." RCN: 4131.
Neotype (Navarro in Jarvis & al. in *Taxon* 50: 521. 2001): Moldova. Khotin district, Lipkany, Plants of Bessarabia 1898, *Keichel s.n.* (LE).
Current name: ***Ajuga laxmannii*** (L.) Benth. (Lamiaceae).
Note: Linnaeus evidently described this name based on Laxman material that is no longer extant, and Navarro therefore designated a neotype.

Teucrium lucidum Linnaeus, *Systema Naturae,* ed. 10, 2: 1095. 1759.
["Habitat in alpinis vallis Barsilionensis Sabaudiae; in monte Lachin Galloprovinciae. Gerard."] Sp. Pl., ed. 2, 2: 790 (1763). RCN: 4144.
Lectotype (Navarro in Jarvis & al. in *Taxon* 50: 521. 2001): Herb. Linn. No. 722.28, central specimen (LINN).
Current name: ***Teucrium lucidum*** L. (Lamiaceae).

T

Teucrium marum Linnaeus, *Species Plantarum* 2: 564. 1753.
"Habitat in regno Valentino." RCN: 4129.
Lectotype (Castroviejo & Bayón in *Anales Jard. Bot. Madrid* 47: 508. 1990): Herb. Linn. No. 722.12 (LINN).
Current name: *Teucrium marum* L. (Lamiaceae).

Teucrium massiliense Linnaeus, *Species Plantarum*, ed. 2, 2: 789. 1763.
"Habitat in Creta, Gallia australi: villa Franca." RCN: 4141.
Lectotype (Turland in Jarvis & al. in *Taxon* 50: 521. 2001): Herb. Linn. No. 722.23 (LINN).
Current name: *Teucrium massiliense* L. (Lamiaceae).

Teucrium mauritanum Linnaeus, *Species Plantarum* 2: 563. 1753.
"Habitat in Mauritania." RCN: 4125.
Lectotype (Navarro & El Oualidi in *Acta Bot. Malac.* 22: 189. 1997): [icon] *"Teucrium Delphinii folio, non ramosum"* in Shaw, Cat. Pl. Afr. As.: 46, f. 575. 1738 (see p. 159).
Current name: *Teucrium pseudochamaepitys* L. (Lamiaceae).

Teucrium montanum Linnaeus, *Species Plantarum* 2: 565. 1753.
"Habitat in siccis Germaniae, Monspelii, Genevae, Helvetiae, Parisiis." RCN: 4146.
Lectotype (Navarro in *Acta Bot. Malac.* 20: 235. 1995): Herb. Linn. No. 722.31, central specimen (LINN).
Current name: *Teucrium montanum* L. (Lamiaceae).

Teucrium mucronatum Linnaeus, *Species Plantarum* 2: 566. 1753.
"Habitat – – – –" RCN: 4153.
Lectotype (Navarro in Jarvis & al. in *Taxon* 50: 521. 2001): [icon] *"Scordium spinosum odoratum Annuum"* in Barrelier, Pl. Galliam: 33, t. 202. 1714. – Epitype (Navarro in Jarvis & al. in *Taxon* 50: 521. 2001): Spain. Sevilla. between Alcalá de Guadaira and Morón de la Frontera, 22 May 1981, *Fernández, Luque & Valdés 168.81* (BM-000576286; iso- ATH, B, BC, BCF, COI etc.).
Current name: *Teucrium spinosum* L. (Lamiaceae).

Teucrium multiflorum Linnaeus, *Species Plantarum* 2: 564. 1753.
"Habitat in Hispania." RCN: 4130.
Lectotype (Navarro in Jarvis & al. in *Taxon* 50: 521. 2001): Herb. Clifford: 303, *Teucrium 14* (BM-000628945).
Current name: *Teucrium chamaedrys* L. (Lamiaceae).

Teucrium nissolianum Linnaeus, *Species Plantarum* 2: 563. 1753.
"Habitat – – – –" RCN: 4122.
Lectotype (Navarro & El Oualidi in *Acta Bot. Malac.* 22: 188. 1997): Herb. Linn. No. 722.6 (LINN).
Current name: *Teucrium pseudochamaepitys* L. (Lamiaceae).

Teucrium orientale Linnaeus, *Species Plantarum* 2: 562. 1753.
"Habitat in Oriente." RCN: 4119.
Lectotype (Wijnands, *Bot. Commelins*: 119. 1983): Herb. Clifford: 301, *Teucrium 1* (BM-000628924).
Current name: *Teucrium orientale* L. (Lamiaceae).

Teucrium polium Linnaeus, *Species Plantarum* 2: 566. 1753.
"Habitat in Italia, Hispania, Lusitania, Narbonia." RCN: 4149.
Lectotype (Siddiqi in Jafri & El-Gadi, *Fl. Libya* 118: 25. 1985): Herb. Linn. No. 722.35 (LINN).
Current name: *Teucrium polium* L. (Lamiaceae).
Note: Hedge & Lamond (in *Notes Roy. Bot. Gard. Edinburgh* 28: 147. 1968) indicated unspecified material at LINN as type but did not distinguish between sheets 722.35 and 722.36 (which are evidently not part of a single gathering so Art. 9.15 does not apply). Navarro & Rosúa (in *Anales Jard. Bot. Madrid* 47: 35–41. 1989) provide an

extensive discussion and designate as lectotype a specimen (in M) sent by Linnaeus to Schreber. However, Siddiqi's type choice of 722.35 (LINN) has priority, and Navarro & El Oualidi (in *Acta Bot. Malac.* 22: 195. 1997) appear to have subsequently accepted this.

Teucrium pseudochamaepitys Linnaeus, *Species Plantarum* 2: 562. 1753.
"Habitat in Hispania." RCN: 4123b.
Lectotype (Navarro & El Oualidi in *Acta Bot. Malac.* 22: 189. 1997): Herb. Burser XIV(1): 62 (UPS).
Current name: *Teucrium pseudochamaepitys* L. (Lamiaceae).

Teucrium pumilum Linnaeus, *Centuria I Plantarum*: 15. 1755.
"Habitat in Hispania." RCN: 4151.
Lectotype (Navarro & Rosúa in *Candollea* 45: 588. 1990; Navarro in *Acta Bot. Malac.* 20: 243. 1995): *Löfling 419b*, Herb. Linn. No. 722.42, upper specimen (LINN).
Current name: *Teucrium pumilum* L. (Lamiaceae).
Note: Navarro (1995) restricted the original type choice made by Navarro & Rosúa (1990) to the upper specimen on sheet 722.42 (LINN).

Teucrium pyrenaicum Linnaeus, *Species Plantarum* 2: 566. 1753.
"Habitat in Pyrenaeis." RCN: 4148.
Lectotype (Navarro & Rosúa in *Candollea* 45: 587. 1990; Navarro in *Acta Bot. Malac.* 20: 212. 1995): Herb. Linn. No. 722.34, right specimen (LINN).
Current name: *Teucrium pyrenaicum* L. (Lamiaceae).
Note: Navarro (1995) restricted the original type choice made by Navarro & Rosúa (1990) to the right-hand specimen on sheet 722.34 (LINN).

Teucrium salicifolium Linnaeus, *Systema Naturae*, ed. 12, 2: 388; *Mantissa Plantarum*: 80. 1767.
"Habitat in Oriente." RCN: 4133.
Lectotype (Davis, *Fl. Turkey* 7: 46. 1982): *Schreber*, Herb. Linn. No. 722.15 (LINN).
Current name: *Ajuga salicifolia* (L.) Schreb. (Lamiaceae).

Teucrium scordium Linnaeus, *Species Plantarum* 2: 565. 1753.
"Habitat in Europae paludosis." RCN: 4142.
Lectotype (Navarro & El Oualidi in *Acta Bot. Malac.* 22: 192. 1997): Herb. Linn. No. 722.24 (LINN).
Current name: *Teucrium scordium* L. (Lamiaceae).
Note: Hedge & Lamond (in *Notes Roy. Bot. Gard. Edinburgh* 28: 146. 1968) indicated unspecified material at LINN as type but did not distinguish between sheets 722.24 and 722.25 (which are evidently not part of a single gathering so Art. 9.15 does not apply).

Teucrium scorodonia Linnaeus, *Species Plantarum* 2: 564. 1753.
"Habitat in arenosis editis Germaniae, Helvetiae, Galliae, Angliae, Belgii: in dunis praedii Hartcampi, beati quondam mihi Paradisi." RCN: 4140.
Lectotype (Navarro in Jarvis & al. in *Taxon* 50: 521. 2001): Herb. Linn. No. 722.21 (LINN).
Current name: *Teucrium scorodonia* L. (Lamiaceae).

Teucrium sibiricum Linnaeus, *Species Plantarum* 2: 564. 1753.
"Habitat in Sibiria." RCN: 4132.
Lectotype (Budantzev in Jarvis & al. in *Taxon* 50: 521. 2001): Herb. Linn. No. 722.13 (LINN), see opposite, above left.
Current name: *Nepeta ucranica* L. (Lamiaceae).

Teucrium spinosum Linnaeus, *Species Plantarum* 2: 566. 1753.
"Habitat in Lusitania." RCN: 4152.

The lectotype of *Teucrium sibiricum* L.

Lectotype (Navarro & El Oualidi in *Acta Bot. Malac.* 22: 193. 1997): Herb. Linn. No. 722.44, right specimen (LINN).
Current name: ***Teucrium spinosum*** L. (Lamiaceae).

Teucrium supinum Linnaeus, *Species Plantarum* 2: 566. 1753.
"Habitat in agro Viennensi." RCN: 4147.
Lectotype (Navarro in Jarvis & al. in *Taxon* 50: 521. 2001): Herb. Linn. No. 722.32 (LINN).
Current name: ***Teucrium montanum*** L. (Lamiaceae).

Teucrium virginicum Linnaeus, *Species Plantarum* 2: 564. 1753.
"Habitat in Virginia." RCN: 4138.
Type not designated.
Original material: none traced.
Current name: ***Teucrium canadense*** L. var. ***virginicum*** (L.) Eaton (Lamiaceae).
Note: There appears to be no extant original material for this name.

Thalia geniculata Linnaeus, *Species Plantarum* 2: 1193. 1753.
"Habitat in America." RCN: 16.
Lectotype (Andersson in *Nordic J. Bot.* 1: 55. 1981): [icon] *"Thalia"* in Plumier in Burman, Pl. Amer.: 98, t. 108, f. 1. 1757.
Generitype of *Thalia* Linnaeus.
Current name: ***Thalia geniculata*** L. (Marantaceae).

Thalictrum alpinum Linnaeus, *Species Plantarum* 1: 545. 1753.
"Habitat in Alpibus Lapponiae, Arvoniae." RCN: 4040.
Lectotype (Jonsell & Jarvis in *Nordic J. Bot.* 14: 162. 1994): Herb. Linn. No. 225 (LAPP).
Current name: ***Thalictrum alpinum*** L. (Ranunculaceae).

Thalictrum angustifolium Linnaeus, *Species Plantarum* 1: 546. 1753.
"Habitat in Germania rarius." RCN: 4048.
Lectotype (Hand in *Nordic J. Bot.* 20: 528. 2001 [2000]): Herb. Linn. No. 713.19 (LINN).
Current name: ***Thalictrum lucidum*** L. (Ranunculaceae).

Thalictrum aquilegiifolium Linnaeus, *Species Plantarum* 1: 547. 1753.
"Habitat in Scania, Helvetia." RCN: 4052.
Lectotype (Jonsell & Jarvis in Jonsell in *Nordic J. Bot.* 20: 520. 2001 [2000]): Herb. Clifford: 226, *Thalictrum* 1, sheet 3 (BM-000628861).
Current name: ***Thalictrum aquilegiifolium*** L. (Ranunculaceae).
Note: Specific epithet spelled "aquilegifolium" in the protologue.

Thalictrum contortum Linnaeus, *Species Plantarum* 1: 547. 1753.
"Habitat in Sibiria. G. Demidoff." RCN: 4053.
Lectotype (Hand in Jarvis & al. in *Taxon* 54: 470. 2005): Herb. Linn. No. 713.28 (LINN).
Current name: ***Thalictrum aquilegiifolium*** L. (Ranunculaceae).

Thalictrum cornuti Linnaeus, *Species Plantarum* 1: 545. 1753.
"Habitat in Canada." RCN: 4043.
Lectotype (Hand in Jarvis & al. in *Taxon* 54: 470. 2005): [icon] *"Thalictrum sem. triquetro foliis Aquilegiae"* in Morison, Pl. Hist. Univ. 3: 325, s. 9, t. 20, f. 15. 1699.
Current name: ***Thalictrum aquilegiifolium*** L. (Ranunculaceae).

Thalictrum dioicum Linnaeus, *Species Plantarum* 1: 545. 1753.
"Habitat in Canada. Kalm." RCN: 4044.
Lectotype (Boivin in *Rhodora* 46: 436. 1944): *Kalm*, Herb. Linn. No. 713.7 (LINN).
Current name: ***Thalictrum dioicum*** L. (Ranunculaceae).

Thalictrum flavum Linnaeus, *Species Plantarum* 1: 546. 1753.
"Habitat in Europae septentrionalioris subhumidis." RCN: 4049.
Lectotype (Sell in Jonsell & Jarvis in *Nordic J. Bot.* 14: 162. 1994): Herb. Clifford: 226, *Thalictrum* 2, sheet 6 (BM-000628865).
Current name: ***Thalictrum flavum*** L. (Ranunculaceae).

Thalictrum flavum Linnaeus var. **speciosum** Linnaeus, *Species Plantarum* 1: 546. 1753.
"Habitat in Hispania." RCN: 4049.
Lectotype (Hand, *Revis. Eur. Art.* Thalictrum *subsect.* Thalictrum: 255. 2001): *Löfling 403*, Herb. Linn. No. 713.22 (LINN).
Current name: ***Thalictrum speciosissimum*** Loefl. (Ranunculaceae).

Thalictrum foetidum Linnaeus, *Species Plantarum* 1: 545. 1753, *typ. cons.*
"Habitat Monspelii, inque Valletia, Helvetia." RCN: 4041.
Conserved type (Hand in *Taxon* 51: 199. 2002): Italy. Val d'Aosta. Clemenceau near Lignan, WSW of the village, rocks in gorge, ca. 1,650m, 23 Apr 1993. Cultivated at B; herbarium specimen preserved 10 Jun 1998, *R. Hand 933* (B; iso- BM, C, K).
Generitype of *Thalictrum* Linnaeus, *nom. cons.*
Current name: ***Thalictrum foetidum*** L. (Ranunculaceae).
Note: Thalictrum foetidum, with Herb. Clifford: 227, *Thalictrum* 5 (BM) there designated by Riedl, was proposed as conserved type of the genus by Jarvis (in *Taxon* 41: 574. 1992). Hand (*Revis. Eur. Art.*

Thalictrum *subsect.* Thalictrum: 135, 305. 2001) identified the proposed conserved type as *T. minus* L., not *T. foetidum* and, in the light of the disruption that this would cause were the original proposal to be approved, proposed (in *Taxon* 51: 199. 2002) *Hand 933*, from Italy, as *typ. cons. prop.* This was recommended by the Committee for Spermatophyta (in *Taxon* 53: 821. 2004). The original conservation proposal was eventually approved by the General Committee (see review of the history of this proposal by Barrie, *l.c.* 55: 795–796, 798. 2006) with the conserved type as proposed by Hand.

Thalictrum lucidum Linnaeus, *Species Plantarum* 1: 546. 1753.
"Habitat Parisiis & in Hispania." RCN: 4051.
Lectotype (Hand in *Nordic J. Bot.* 20: 528. 2001 [2000]): [icon] *"Thalictrum minus lucidum Libanotidis Coronariae foliis"* in Plukenet, Phytographia: t. 65, f. 5. 1691; Almag. Bot.: 363. 1696. – Voucher: Herb. Sloane 98: 88 (BM-SL). – Epitype (Hand in *Nordic J. Bot.* 20: 528. 2001): Hungary. Heves, E of Poroszló, riverine meadows along dam of Tisza reservoir, 6 Jun 1996, *Hand 1057a* (B).
Current name: ***Thalictrum lucidum*** L. (Ranunculaceae).

Thalictrum minus Linnaeus, *Species Plantarum* 1: 546. 1753.
"Habitat in Europae pratis." RCN: 4045.
Lectotype (Botschantzeva in *Bot. Zhurn.* 58: 1642. 1973): Herb. Linn. No. 713.12 (LINN).
Current name: ***Thalictrum minus*** L. (Ranunculaceae).

Thalictrum petaloideum Linnaeus, *Species Plantarum,* ed. 2, 1: 771. 1762.
"Habitat in Sibiria." RCN: 4054.
Neotype (Hand in Jarvis & al. in *Taxon* 54: 470. 2005): Herb. Linn. No. 713.30 (LINN).
Current name: ***Thalictrum petaloideum*** L. (Ranunculaceae).
Note: Specific epithet spelled "petalodeum" in the protologue.

Thalictrum purpurascens Linnaeus, *Species Plantarum* 1: 546. 1753.
"Habitat in Canada?" RCN: 4047.
Lectotype (Boivin in *Bull. Soc. Roy. Bot. Belgique* 88: 36. 1956): Herb. Linn. No. 713.14 (LINN).
Current name: ***Thalictrum minus*** L. (Ranunculaceae).
Note: See notes by Hand (*Revis. Eur. Art.* Thalictrum *subsect.* Thalictrum: 325. 2001).

Thalictrum sibiricum Linnaeus, *Species Plantarum* 1: 546. 1753.
"Habitat in Sibiria. D. Gmelin." RCN: 4046.
Lectotype (Hand in Jarvis & al. in *Taxon* 54: 470. 2005): Herb. Linn. No. 713.13 (LINN).
Current name: ***Thalictrum minus*** L. (Ranunculaceae).

Thalictrum simplex Linnaeus, *Flora Suecica,* ed. 2: 191. 1755.
"Habitat in Smolandia ad limites agrorum & in uliginosis cum Myrica." RCN: 4050.
Lectotype (Jonsell & Jarvis in *Nordic J. Bot.* 14: 162. 1994): *Lidbeck?,* Herb. Linn. No. 713.23 (LINN).
Current name: ***Thalictrum simplex*** L. (Ranunculaceae).

Thalictrum tuberosum Linnaeus, *Species Plantarum* 1: 545. 1753.
"Habitat in Hispania." RCN: 4042.
Lectotype (Hand in Jarvis & al. in *Taxon* 54: 471. 2005): Herb. Clifford: 226, *Thalictrum* 4 (BM-000628868).
Current name: ***Thalictrum tuberosum*** L. (Ranunculaceae).

Thapsia asclepium Linnaeus, *Species Plantarum* 1: 261. 1753.
"Habitat in Apulia." RCN: 2087.

Lectotype (Reduron & Watson in Jarvis & al. in *Taxon* 55: 215. 2006): [icon] *"Panax asclepium apulum"* in Colonna, Ekphr.: 87, 86. 1606.
Current name: ***Elaeoselinum asclepium*** (L.) Bertol. (Apiaceae).

Thapsia foetida Linnaeus, *Species Plantarum* 1: 261. 1753.
"Habitat in Hispania." RCN: 2086.
Lectotype (Watson in Jarvis & al. in *Taxon* 55: 215. 2006): Herb. Clifford: 105, *Thapsia* 2, sheet 4 (BM-000558374).
Current name: ***Elaeoselinum foetidum*** (L.) Boiss. (Apiaceae).

Thapsia garganica Linnaeus, *Systema Naturae,* ed. 12, 2: 216; *Mantissa Plantarum:* 57. 1767.
"Habitat in Barbaria, Gargano Apuliae. Gouan." RCN: 2088.
Lectotype (Jafri in Jafri & El-Gadi, *Fl. Libya* 117: 111. 1985): *Gouan s.n.,* Herb. Linn. No. 368.2 (LINN), see p. 208.
Current name: ***Thapsia garganica*** L. (Apiaceae).

Thapsia trifoliata Linnaeus, *Species Plantarum* 1: 262. 1753.
"Habitat in Virginia." RCN: 2089.
Lectotype (Fernald in *Rhodora* 41: 442. 1939): *Kalm,* Herb. Linn. No. 368.3 (LINN).
Current name: ***Thaspium trifoliatum*** (L.) A. Gray (Apiaceae).

Thapsia villosa Linnaeus, *Species Plantarum* 1: 261. 1753.
"Habitat in Hispania, Lusitania." RCN: 2085.
Lectotype (Reduron & Jarvis in Jarvis & al., *Regnum Veg.* 127: 93. 1993): Herb. Clifford: 105, *Thapsia* 1 (BM-000558373).
Generitype of *Thapsia* Linnaeus (vide Hitchcock, *Prop. Brit. Bot.*: 141. 1929).
Current name: ***Thapsia villosa*** L. (Apiaceae).

Thea bohea Linnaeus, *Species Plantarum,* ed. 2, 1: 734. 1762, *nom. illeg.*
"Habitat in Japonia, China." RCN: 3882.
Replaced synonym: *Thea sinensis* L. (1753).
Lectotype (Bartholomew in Jarvis & al., *Regnum Veg.* 127: 93. 1993): [icon] *"Tsja"* in Kaempfer, Amoen. Exot. Fasc.: 605, 606. 1712.
Current name: ***Camellia sinensis*** (L.) Kuntze (Theaceae).
Note: A superfluous name for *T. sinensis* L. (1753).

Thea sinensis Linnaeus, *Species Plantarum* 1: 515. 1753.
"Habitat in Japonia, China." RCN: 3882.
Replaced synonym of: *Thea bohea* L. (1762), *nom. illeg.*
Lectotype (Bartholomew in Jarvis & al., *Regnum Veg.* 127: 93. 1993): [icon] *"Tsja"* in Kaempfer, Amoen. Exot. Fasc.: 605, 606. 1712.
Generitype of *Thea* Linnaeus.
Current name: ***Camellia sinensis*** (L.) Kuntze (Theaceae).

Thea viridis Linnaeus, *Species Plantarum,* ed. 2, 1: 735. 1762.
"Habitat in China." RCN: 3883.
Type not designated.
Original material: *Gordon,* Herb. Linn. No. 685.3 (LINN); [icon] in Hill, Exot. Bot.: 22, t. 22. 1759.
Current name: ***Camellia sinensis*** (L.) Kuntze (Theaceae).

Theligonum cynocrambe Linnaeus, *Species Plantarum* 2: 993. 1753.
"Habitat in Italia, Monspelii." RCN: 7206.
Type not designated.
Original material: [icon] in Bauhin & Cherler, Hist. Pl. Univ. 3(2): 365. 1651; [icon] in Barrelier, Pl. Galliam: 115, t. 335. 1714; [icon] in Bauhin, Prodr. Theatri Bot.: 59. 1620.
Generitype of *Theligonum* Linnaeus.
Current name: ***Theligonum cynocrambe*** L. (Rubiaceae).
Note: Ali (in Ali & Jafri, *Fl. Libya* 8: 3. 1977) indicated 1126.1 (LINN) as type but the sheet lacks a *Species Plantarum* number (i.e.

"1") and is a post-1753 addition to the collection, and not original material for the name.

Theobroma augusta Linnaeus, *Systema Naturae*, ed. 12, 3: 233. 1768.
"Habitat in India orientali." RCN: 5724.
Type not designated.
Original material: none traced.
Current name: ***Ambroma augusta*** (L.) L. f. (Sterculiaceae).

Theobroma cacao Linnaeus, *Species Plantarum* 2: 782. 1753.
"Habitat in America meridionali, Antillis." RCN: 5722.
Lectotype (Dorr in Jarvis & al., *Regnum Veg.* 127: 93. 1993): [icon] *"Cacao"* in Sloane, Voy. Jamaica 2: 15, t. 160. 1725. – Typotype: Herb. Sloane 5: 59 (BM-SL).
Generitype of *Theobroma* Linnaeus (vide Green, *Prop. Brit. Bot.*: 177. 1929).
Current name: ***Theobroma cacao*** L. (Sterculiaceae).
Note: Cuatracasas (in *Contr. U.S. Natl. Herb.* 35: 385, 496, 508, 513. 1964) designated the flowers and leaves in Herb. Sloane 5: 59 (BM-SL) as lectotype, with a Tournefort illustration (not cited in Linnaeus' protologue) as a "Fruit-lectotype". As Linnaeus would not have seen the flowers themselves, they cannot be original material for the name. However, Dorr has formally designated Sloane's illustration as lectotype, with Sloane's material (the basis for the illustration) as typotype.

Theobroma guazuma Linnaeus, *Species Plantarum* 2: 782. 1753.
"Habitat in Jamaicae campestribus." RCN: 5723.
Lectotype (Cristóbal in *Bonplandia* 6: 190, f. 2. 1989): Herb. Clifford: 379, *Theobroma* 2 (BM).
Current name: ***Guazuma ulmifolia*** Lam. (Sterculiaceae).
Note: Freytag (in *Ceiba* 1: 220. 1951) and some later authors wrongly indicated as the type sheet 934.2 (LINN), a Mútis collection received long after 1753. Similarly, Verdcourt (in Dassanayake & al., *Revised Handb. Fl. Ceylon* 9 : 421. 1995) wrongly indicated 934.3 (LINN), a Patrick Browne collection not received by Linnaeus until 1758, as lectotype. Cristóbal's type choice is correct, though her treatment of the Clifford material as a neotype, rather than the lectotype, was noted and corrected by Fryxell (in McVaugh, *Fl. Novo-Galiciana* 3: 123. 2001).

Theophrasta americana Linnaeus, *Species Plantarum* 1: 149. 1753.
"Habitat in America aequinoctiali." RCN: 1185.
Lectotype (Ståhl in *Nordic J. Bot.* 7: 534. 1987): [icon] in Plumier, Codex Boerhaavianus (University Library, Groningen).
Generitype of *Theophrasta* Linnaeus.
Current name: ***Theophrasta americana*** L. (Theophrastaceae).

Thesium alpinum Linnaeus, *Species Plantarum* 1: 207. 1753.
"Habitat in Italiae alpibus." RCN: 1689.
Neotype (Miller in Jarvis & al., *Regnum Veg.* 127: 93. 1993): *Scopoli 41*, Herb. Linn. No. 292.5 (LINN).
Generitype of *Thesium* Linnaeus (vide Hitchcock, *Prop. Brit. Bot.*: 135. 1929).
Current name: ***Thesium alpinum*** L. (Santalaceae).

Thesium amplexicaule Linnaeus, *Mantissa Plantarum Altera*: 213. 1771.
"Habitat in Capitis b. spei montibus altis." RCN: 1698.
Type not designated.
Original material: none traced.
Current name: ***Thesium euphorbioides*** P.J. Bergius (Santalaceae).

Thesium capitatum Linnaeus, *Species Plantarum* 1: 207. 1753.
"Habitat in Aethiopia." RCN: 1683.

Type not designated.
Original material: [icon] in Burman, Rar. Afric. Pl.: 133, t. 48, f. 3. 1739.
Current name: ***Thesium capitatum*** L. (Santalaceae).

Thesium frisea Linnaeus, *Mantissa Plantarum Altera*: 213. 1771.
"Habitat ad Cap. b. spei. D. Koenig." RCN: 1690.
Type not designated.
Original material: *König s.n.*, Herb. Linn. No. 292.6 (LINN).
Current name: ***Thesium frisea*** L. (Santalaceae).

Thesium funale Linnaeus, *Systema Naturae*, ed. 10, 2: 944. 1759.
["Habitat ad Cap. b. spei."] Sp. Pl., ed. 2, 1: 302 (1762). RCN: 1692.
Type not designated.
Original material: Herb. Linn. No. 292.8 (LINN).
Current name: ***Thesium funale*** L. (Santalaceae).

Thesium linophyllon Linnaeus, *Species Plantarum* 1: 207. 1753.
"Habitat in Europae siccis montosis." RCN: 1688.
Type not designated.
Original material: Herb. Clifford: 41, *Thesium* 1 (BM); Herb. Burser XII: 27 (UPS); Herb. Linn. No. 292.1 (LINN); [icon] in Clusius, Rar. Pl. Hist. 1: 323, 324. 1601; [icon] in Daléchamps, Hist. General. Pl. 1: 491. 1587; [icon] in Morison, Pl. Hist. Univ. 3: 601, s. 15, t. 1, f. 3. 1699.
Current name: ***Thesium linophyllon*** L. (Santalaceae).

Thesium paniculatum Linnaeus, *Systema Naturae*, ed. 12, 2: 188; *Mantissa Plantarum*: 51. 1767.
"Habitat ad Cap. b. spei." RCN: 1697.
Type not designated.
Original material: Herb. Linn. No. 292.14 (LINN).
Current name: ***Thesium paniculatum*** L. (Santalaceae).

Thesium scabrum Linnaeus, *Species Plantarum*, ed. 2, 1: 302. 1762.
"Habitat ad Cap. b. spei." RCN: 1696.
Type not designated.
Original material: Herb. Linn. No. 292.13 (LINN); Herb. Linn. No. 292.12 (LINN).
Current name: ***Thesium scabrum*** L. (Santalaceae).

Thesium spicatum Linnaeus, *Mantissa Plantarum Altera*: 214. 1771.
"Habitat ad Cap. b. spei montibus." RCN: 1691.
Type not designated.
Original material: *Tulbagh 133*, Herb. Linn. No. 292.7 (LINN).
Current name: ***Thesium spicatum*** L. (Santalaceae).

Thesium umbellatum Linnaeus, *Species Plantarum* 1: 208. 1753.
"Habitat in Virginiae, Pensylvaniae pascuis siccis. Kalm." RCN: 1695.
Lectotype (Piehl in *Mem. Torrey Bot. Club* 22(1): 61. 1965): *Kalm*, Herb. Linn. No. 292.11 (LINN).
Current name: ***Comandra umbellata*** (L.) Nutt. (Santalaceae).

Thlaspi alliaceum Linnaeus, *Species Plantarum* 2: 646. 1753.
"Habitat in Europa australi." RCN: 4699.
Lectotype (Marhold & Mártonfi in *Novon* 11: 189, f. 1. 2001): [icon] *"Scorodothlaspi Ulyssis Aldroandi"* in Bauhin & Cherler, Hist. Pl. Univ. 2: 932. 1651.
Current name: ***Thlaspi alliaceum*** L. (Brassicaceae).
Note: A specimen in Herb. Aldrovandi (BOLO) was treated as the lectotype by Franchetti & al. (in Edwards & al., *Fl. Ethiopia Eritrea* 2(1): 135. 2000), but was not seen by Linnaeus and is not original material for the name. Meyer (in *Haussknechtia* 8: 27. 2001) designated a van Royen collection (901.257–174, L) as lectotype but this choice is pre-dated by that of Marhold & Mártonfi.

T

Thlaspi alpestre Linnaeus, *Species Plantarum*, ed. 2, 2: 903. 1763, *nom. illeg.*
"Habitat in Austria. Stamina flore longiora." RCN: 4705.
Lectotype (Marhold & Mártonfi in Cafferty & Jarvis in *Taxon* 51: 536. 2002): Herb. Linn. No. 825.14 (LINN).
Current name: ***Thlaspi caerulescens*** J. Presl & C. Presl (Brassicaceae).
Note: A later homonym of *T. alpestre* Jacq. (1762) and hence illegitimate. There has been some confusion in the way the Linnaean name has been either used or synonymised (see review by Kerguélen & al. in *Lejeunia* n.s., 120: 175. 1987), which was clarified by the typification made by Marhold & Mártonfi.

Thlaspi arvense Linnaeus, *Species Plantarum* 2: 646. 1753.
"Habitat in Europae agris." RCN: 4698.
Lectotype (Jafri in Nasir & Ali, *Fl. W. Pakistan* 55: 85. 1973): Herb. Linn. No. 825.2 (LINN).
Generitype of *Thlaspi* Linnaeus (vide Green, *Prop. Brit. Bot.*: 170. 1929).
Current name: ***Thlaspi arvense*** L. (Brassicaceae).

Thlaspi bursa-pastoris Linnaeus, *Species Plantarum* 2: 647. 1753.
"Habitat in Europae cultis ruderatis." RCN: 4706.
Lectotype (Fawcett & Rendle, *Fl. Jamaica* 3: 241. 1914): Herb. Linn. No. 825.15 (LINN).
Current name: ***Capsella bursa-pastoris*** (L.) Medik. (Brassicaceae).

Thlaspi campestre Linnaeus, *Species Plantarum* 2: 646. 1753.
"Habitat in Europae arvis, viis argillosis, apricis." RCN: 4702.
Type not designated.
Original material: Herb. Linn. No. 41 (SBT); Herb. Clifford: 330, *Thlaspi* 3, 2 sheets (BM); Herb. Linn. No. 267.3? (S); Herb. Linn. No. 825.8 (LINN); [icon] in Fuchs, Hist. Stirp.: 305, 306. 1542.
Current name: ***Lepidium campestre*** (L.) R. Br. (Brassicaceae).

Thlaspi hirsutum Linnaeus, *Flora Anglica*: 19. 1754, *orth. var.*
RCN: 4701.
Lectotype (López González in Cafferty & Jarvis in *Taxon* 51: 536. 2002): Herb. Linn. No. 825.7 (LINN).
Current name: ***Lepidium hirtum*** (L.) Sm. (Brassicaceae).
Note: Stearn (*Introd. Ray's Syn. Meth. Stirp. Brit.* (Ray Soc. ed.): 68. 1973) treats this as an orthographical error for *T. hirtum* L. (1753).

Thlaspi hirtum Linnaeus, *Species Plantarum* 2: 646. 1753.
"Habitat in Italia, Narbona." RCN: 4701.
Lectotype (López González in Cafferty & Jarvis in *Taxon* 51: 536. 2002): Herb. Linn. No. 825.7 (LINN).
Current name: ***Lepidium hirtum*** (L.) Sm. (Brassicaceae).

Thlaspi montanum Linnaeus, *Species Plantarum* 2: 647. 1753.
"Habitat in Helvetiae, Austriae, Italiae, Monspelii petrosis." RCN: 4703.
Lectotype (Marhold & Mártonfi in *Novon* 11: 189. 2001): Herb. Linn. No. 825.10 (LINN).
Current name: ***Thlaspi montanum*** L. (Brassicaceae).

Thlaspi peregrinum Linnaeus, *Species Plantarum* 2: 645. 1753.
"Habitat – – – –" RCN: 4697.
Lectotype (Hedge in Cafferty & Jarvis in *Taxon* 51: 536. 2002): Herb. Clifford: 330, *Thlaspi* 1 (BM-000646264).
Current name: ***Aethionema saxatile*** (L.) R. Br. (Brassicaceae).

Thlaspi perfoliatum Linnaeus, *Species Plantarum* 2: 646. 1753.
"Habitat in Germaniae, Helvetiae, Galliae apricis, agris." RCN: 4704.

Lectotype (Jafri in Nasir & Ali, *Fl. W. Pakistan* 55: 85. 1973): *Magnol*, Herb. Linn. No. 825.9 (LINN).
Current name: ***Microthlaspi perfoliatum*** (L.) F.K. Mey. (Brassicaceae).
Note: Meyer (in *Haussknechtia* 9: 17. 2003) independently chose the same type as Jafri, and (pp. 35–38) provided an extensive discussion, also reproducing the cited Clusius illustration (as Abb. 1).

Thlaspi saxatile Linnaeus, *Species Plantarum* 2: 646. 1753.
"Habitat in Italiae, G. Narbonensis, Provinciae saxosis." RCN: 4700.
Lectotype (Hedge in Cafferty & Jarvis in *Taxon* 51: 536. 2002): [icon] "*Lithothlaspi quartum carnoso rotundofolio*" in Colonna, Ekphr.: 279, 277 [lower fig.]. 1606. – Epitype (Hedge in Cafferty & Jarvis in *Taxon* 51: 536. 2002): Herb. Linn. No. 825.4 (LINN).
Current name: ***Aethionema saxatile*** (L.) R. Br. (Brassicaceae).

Thrianthema portulacastrum Linnaeus, *Flora Jamaicensis*: 14. 1759, *orth. var.*
["Habitat in Jamaica, Curassao."] Sp. Pl. 1: 223 (1753). RCN: 3134.
Lectotype (Jeffrey in *Kew Bull.* 14: 236. 1960): [icon] "*Portulaca Corassavica Capparidis folio*" in Hermann, Parad. Bat.: 213. 1698.
Current name: ***Trianthema portulacastrum*** L. (Aizoaceae).
Note: An orthographic variant of *Trianthema portulacastrum* L. (1753).

Thryallis brasiliensis Linnaeus, *Species Plantarum*, ed. 2, 1: 554. 1762.
"Habitat in Brasilia." RCN: 3051.

Type not designated.
Original material: [icon] in Marggraf, Hist. Rer. Nat. Bras.: 79. 1648
 – Typotype: Marggraf s.n. (C).
Generitype of *Thryallis* Linnaeus, *nom. rej.*
Current name: **Galphimia brasiliensis** (L.) Juss. (Malpighiaceae).
Note: Thryallis Linnaeus, *nom. rej.* in favour of *Thryallis* Mart.

Thuja aphylla Linnaeus, *Centuria I Plantarum*: 32. 1755.
"Habitat in Aegypto." RCN: 7252.
Lectotype (Burtt in *Kew Bull.* 9: 388. 1954): Herb. Linn. No. 1136.3
 (LINN).
Current name: **Tamarix aphylla** (L.) H. Karst. (Tamaricaceae).

Thuja cupressoides Linnaeus, *Systema Naturae,* ed. 12, 2: 633;
 Mantissa Plantarum: 125. 1767.
"Habitat ad Cap. b. spei." RCN: 7254.
Type not designated.
Original material: [icon] in Shaw, Cat. Pl. Afr. As.: 40, f. 188. 1738.
Current name: **Widdringtonia nodiflora** (L.) Powrie (Cupressaceae).
Note: Powrie (in *J. S. African Bot.* 38: 303. 1972) incorrectly treated
 this name as homotypic with *Brunia nodiflora* L. (1753), typified by
 material in the Clifford herbarium. *Thuja cupressoides* is an
 independent name and Farjon (*Monogr. Cupressaceae* Sciadopitys:
 471. 2005) indicated the cited Shaw plate as the holotype (which it
 is not). It may well be the obvious choice as lectotype, but because
 Farjon's statement was published after 1 Jan 2001, the omission of
 the phrase "designated here" or an equivalent (Art. 7.11) means that
 the choice is not effective.

Thuja occidentalis Linnaeus, *Species Plantarum* 2: 1002. 1753.
"Habitat in Canada, Sibiria." RCN: 7252.
Lectotype (Reveal in Jarvis & al., *Regnum Veg.* 127: 94. 1993): *Kalm,*
 Herb. Linn. No. 1136.1 (LINN).
Generitype of *Thuja* Linnaeus (vide Green, *Prop. Brit. Bot.*: 189.
 1929).
Current name: **Thuja occidentalis** L. (Cupressaceae).

Thuja orientalis Linnaeus, *Species Plantarum* 2: 1002. 1753.
"Habitat in China." RCN: 7253.
Lectotype (Nguyên Tiên Hiêp & Vidal in Morat, *Fl. Cambodge Laos
 Viêtnam* 28: 72. 1996): Herb. Linn. No. 1136.2 (LINN).
Current name: **Platycladus orientalis** (L.) Franco (Cupressaceae).

Thymbra spicata Linnaeus, *Species Plantarum* 2: 569. 1753.
"Habitat in Macedonia, Libano." RCN: 4163.
Lectotype (Morales & López González in Jarvis & al., *Regnum Veg.*
 127: 94. 1993): [icon] *"Thymum majus longifolium, Staechadis
 foliaceo capite purpurascente, pilosum"* in Plukenet, Phytographia: t.
 116, f. 5. 1691; Almag. Bot.: 368. 1696.
Generitype of *Thymbra* Linnaeus (vide Green, *Prop. Brit. Bot.*: 164.
 1929).
Current name: **Thymbra spicata** L. (Lamiaceae).
Note: Morales Valverde (in *Anales Jard. Bot. Madrid* 44: 371. 1987)
 designated 724.1 (LINN) as lectotype but the sheet lacks a *Species
 Plantarum* number and is a post-1753 addition to the herbarium,
 and not original material for the name.

Thymbra verticillata Linnaeus, *Species Plantarum* 2: 569. 1753.
"Habitat in Europa australi." RCN: 4164.
Lectotype (Morales in Jarvis & al. in *Taxon* 50: 521. 2001): Herb.
 Linn. No. 724.2 (LINN).
Current name: **Thymbra spicata** L. (Lamiaceae).
Note: Although Morales (in *Anales Jard. Bot. Madrid* 44: 373. 1987)
 noted the existence of the Linnaean material, he did not formally
 typify the name there.

Thymus acinos Linnaeus, *Species Plantarum* 2: 591. 1753.
"Habitat in Europae glareosis, cretaceis, siccis." RCN: 4301.
Lectotype (Morales in Jarvis & al. in *Taxon* 50: 522. 2001): Herb.
 Linn. No. 744.14 (LINN).
Current name: **Clinopodium acinos** (L.) Kuntze (Lamiaceae).

Thymus alpinus Linnaeus, *Species Plantarum* 2: 591. 1753.
"Habitat in Alpibus Helveticis, Austriacis, Monspelii. D. Rathgeb."
 RCN: 4302.
Lectotype (Morales in Jarvis & al. in *Taxon* 50: 522. 2001): Herb.
 Burser XII: 155 (UPS).
Current name: **Clinopodium alpinum** (L.) Kuntze (Lamiaceae).

Thymus cephalotos Linnaeus, *Species Plantarum* 2: 592. 1753.
"Habitat in Hispania, Lusitania." RCN: 4304.
Type not designated.
Original material: [icon] in Barrelier, Pl. Galliam: 28, t. 788. 1714;
 [icon] in Boccone, Mus. Piante Rar. Sicilia: 50, t. 43. 1697.
Current name: **Thymbra capitata** (L.) Cav. (Lamiaceae).
Note: The application of this name is uncertain. Morales (in *Ruizia* 3:
 179. 1986) designated Herb. Linn. 247.5 (S) as lectotype. However,
 this sheet lacks any Linnaean annotations and, as such, is not
 original material for the name and not eligible for designation as
 lectotype. Morales identified this specimen as *Thymbra capitata* (L.)
 Cav. and therefore placed *Thymus cephalotos* in its synonymy.
 Spanish authors have in the past used *Thymus cephalotos* in the
 sense of *T. moroderi* Pau ex Martínez (probably based on the
 identity of the Barrelier and Boccone synonyms) but Portuguese
 authors have also used the Linnaean name in the sense of what has
 recently been called *Thymus lotocephalos* G. López & Morales
 (1984).

Thymus mastichina (Linnaeus) Linnaeus, *Species Plantarum,* ed. 2, 2:
 827. 1763.
"Habitat in Hispaniae petrosis." RCN: 4306.
Basionym: *Satureja mastichina* L. (1753).
Lectotype (Morales in *Ruizia* 3: 151. 1986): Herb. Linn. No. 744.19,
 right specimen (LINN).
Current name: **Thymus mastichina** (L.) L. (Lamiaceae).

Thymus piperella Linnaeus, *Systema Naturae,* ed. 12, 2: 400.
 1767.
"Habitat in Hispania." RCN: 4303.
Lectotype (Morales in *Ruizia* 3: 174. 1986): Herb. Linn. No. 744.18,
 right specimen (LINN).
Current name: **Thymus piperella** L. (Lamiaceae).

Thymus pulegioides Linnaeus, *Species Plantarum* 2: 592. 1753.
"Habitat Monspelii. D. Sauvages." RCN: 171.
Replaced synonym of: *Cunila thymoides* L. (1762).
Lectotype (Ronniger in *Deutsche Heilpflanze* 10(5): 37. 1944): Herb.
 Linn. No. 38.5 (LINN).
Current name: **Thymus pulegioides** L. (Lamiaceae).

Thymus serpyllum Linnaeus, *Species Plantarum* 2: 590. 1753.
"Habitat in Europae aridis apricis." RCN: 4298.
Lectotype (Marhold & Mártonfi in *Bot. J. Linn. Soc.* 128: 273, f. 2.
 1998): Herb. Burser XII: 118 (UPS).
Current name: **Thymus serpyllum** L. (Lamiaceae).

Thymus villosus Linnaeus, *Species Plantarum* 2: 592. 1753.
"Habitat in Lusitania." RCN: 4305.
Neotype (Morales in *Ruizia* 3: 180. 1986): Herb. Tournefort No.
 1332, lower specimen (P-TOURN).
Current name: **Thymus villosus** L. (Lamiaceae).

T

Thymus virginicus Linnaeus, *Systema Vegetabilium*, ed. 13: 453. 1774, *nom. illeg.*
["Habitat in Virginia."] Sp. Pl. 2: 567 (1753). RCN: 4154.
Replaced synonym: *Satureja virginiana* L. (1753).
Type not designated.
Original material: as replaced synonym.
Current name: ***Pycnanthemum virginianum*** (L.) B.L. Rob. & Fernald (Lamiaceae).
Note: This name has been interpreted as an illegitimate renaming of *Satureja virginiana* L. (1753) in *Thymus*, the earlier binomial remaining untypified at present (see *S. virginiana* for more details).

Thymus vulgaris Linnaeus, *Species Plantarum* 2: 591. 1753.
"Habitat in G. Narbonensis, Hispaniae montosis saxosis." RCN: 4299.
Lectotype (Morales in *Ruizia* 3: 216. 1986): Herb. Burser XII: 101, lower left specimen (UPS).
Generitype of *Thymus* Linnaeus (vide Green, *Prop. Brit. Bot.*: 165. 1929).
Current name: ***Thymus vulgaris*** L. (Lamiaceae).
Note: Cramer (in Dassanayake & Fosberg, *Revised Handb. Fl. Ceylon* 3: 192. 1981) indicated 744.6 (LINN), a Löfling collection associated with *T. zygis* L., as type. Morales rejected this choice on the grounds of conflict with the protologue, designating Burser material as lectotype in its place.

Thymus zygis Linnaeus, *Species Plantarum* 2: 591. 1753.
"Habitat in Hispania." RCN: 4300.
Lectotype (Morales in *Ruizia* 3: 236. 1986): Herb. Linn. No. 744.6 (LINN).
Current name: ***Thymus zygis*** L. (Lamiaceae).

Tiarella cordifolia Linnaeus, *Species Plantarum* 1: 405. 1753.
"Habitat in America & Asia septentrionali." RCN: 3177.
Lectotype (Reveal in *Phytologia* 71: 480. 1991): Herb. Linn. No. 175.9 (S).
Generitype of *Tiarella* Linnaeus (vide Rafinesque, *Fl. Tell.* 2: 74. 1837).
Current name: ***Tiarella cordifolia*** L. (Saxifragaceae).

Tiarella trifoliata Linnaeus, *Species Plantarum* 1: 406. 1753.
"Habitat in Asia boreali. G. Demidoff." RCN: 3178.
Neotype (Reveal in *Phytologia* 71: 481. 1991): Alaska, Sitka, *Mertens s.n.* (BM).
Current name: ***Tiarella trifoliata*** L. (Saxifragaceae).

Tilia americana Linnaeus, *Species Plantarum* 1: 514. 1753.
"Habitat in Virginia Canada." RCN: 3871.
Neotype (Reveal & al. in *Huntia* 7: 237. 1987): Herb. Sherard No. 1095 (OXF).
Current name: ***Tilia americana*** L. (Tiliaceae).
Note: Reveal provides a review of the extensive literature on the interpretation of this name.

Tilia europaea Linnaeus, *Species Plantarum* 1: 514. 1753.
"Habitat in Europae pratis." RCN: 3870.
Lectotype (Pigott & Sell in Jarvis & al., *Regnum Veg.* 127: 94. 1993): Herb. Linn. No. 679.1 (LINN).
Generitype of *Tilia* Linnaeus (vide Green, *Prop. Brit. Bot.*: 161. 1929).
Current name: ***Tilia europaea*** L. (Tiliaceae).
Note: Pigott & Sell (in *Kew Bull.* 50: 135–139, f. 1. 1995) have provided a detailed discussion of their earlier (1993) formal choice of lectotype.

Tillaea aquatica Linnaeus, *Species Plantarum* 1: 128. 1753.
"Habitat in Europae inundatis." RCN: 1051.

Lectotype (Jonsell & Jarvis in *Nordic J. Bot.* 22: 72. 2002): Herb. Linn. No. 178.1 (LINN).
Current name: ***Crassula aquatica*** (L.) Schönl. (Crassulaceae).

Tillaea muscosa Linnaeus, *Species Plantarum* 1: 129. 1753.
"Habitat in Italiae, Siciliae, Galliae muscosis." RCN: 1052.
Lectotype (Bywater & Wickens in *Kew Bull.* 39: 726. 1984): Herb. Linn. No. 178.3 (LINN).
Generitype of *Tillaea* Linnaeus (vide Hitchcock, *Prop. Brit. Bot.*: 127. 1929).
Current name: ***Tillaea muscosa*** L. (Crassulaceae).

Tillaea rubra Linnaeus, *Species Plantarum* 1: 129. 1753.
"Habitat Monspelii inter muscos." RCN: 2254.
Lectotype ('t Hart & Jarvis in *Taxon* 42: 409. 1993): Herb. Linn. No. 400.23 (LINN).
Current name: ***Sedum caespitosum*** (Cav.) DC. (Crassulaceae).

Tillandsia lingulata Linnaeus, *Species Plantarum* 1: 286. 1753.
"Habitat in Americae meridionalis arboribus vetustis." RCN: 2274.
Lectotype (Gouda in Görts-van Rijn, *Fl. Guianas*, ser. A, 3: 21. 1987): [icon] *"Viscum cariophylloides maximum capitulis in summitate conglomeratis"* in Sloane, *Voy. Jamaica* 1: 189, t. 120. 1707. – Typotype: Herb. Sloane 3: 101 (BM-SL), see pp. 160–162.
Current name: ***Guzmania lingulata*** (L.) Mez (Bromeliaceae).
Note: Smith & Downs (in *Fl. Neotropica* 14: 1351. 1977) incorrectly treated material in the Sloane herbarium (BM) as the type, but this was not studied by Linnaeus and is not original material for the name.

Tillandsia monostachia (Linnaeus) Linnaeus, *Species Plantarum*, ed. 2, 1: 410. 1762.
"Habitat in America meridionali." RCN: 2278.
Basionym: *Renealmia monostachia* L. (1753).
Type not designated.
Original material: as basionym.
Current name: ***Guzmania monostachia*** (L.) Mez (Bromeliaceae).

Tillandsia paniculata (Linnaeus) Linnaeus, *Species Plantarum*, ed. 2, 1: 410. 1762.
"Habitat in America meridionali." RCN: 2276.
Basionym: *Renealmia paniculata* L. (1753).
Lectotype (Smith & Downs, *Fl. Neotropica* 14: 1018. 1977): [icon] *"Renalmia foliis brevissimis"* in Plumier in Burman, *Pl. Amer.*: 233, t. 237. 1760.
Current name: ***Tillandsia paniculata*** (L.) L. (Bromeliaceae).

Tillandsia polystachia (Linnaeus) Linnaeus, *Species Plantarum*, ed. 2, 1: 410. 1762.
"Habitat in America calidiore." RCN: 2277.
Basionym: *Renealmia polystachia* L. (1753).
Neotype (Smith & Downs, *Fl. Neotropica* 14: 924. 1977): *Plumier, s.n.* (P).
Current name: ***Tillandsia polystachia*** (L.) L. (Bromeliaceae).

Tillandsia recurvata (Linnaeus) Linnaeus, *Species Plantarum*, ed. 2, 1: 410. 1762.
"Habitat in Jamaicae arboribus." RCN: 2280.
Basionym: *Renealmia recurvata* L. (1753).
Type not designated.
Original material: as basionym.
Current name: ***Tillandsia recurvata*** (L.) L. (Bromeliaceae).

Tillandsia serrata Linnaeus, *Species Plantarum* 1: 286. 1753.
"Habitat in America meridionali." RCN: 2273.

Lectotype (Howard, *Fl. Lesser Antilles* 3: 406. 1979): [icon] *"Tillandsia foliis superne dentato-spinosis"* in Plumier in Burman, Pl. Amer.: 63, t. 75, f. 1. 1756.

Current name: ***Aechmea serrata*** (L.) Mez (Bromeliaceae).

Note: Smith & Downs (in *Fl. Neotropica* 14: 1901. 1979) treated an unpublished Plumier drawing at P as the type, but this was not studied by Linnaeus and is not original material for the name.

Tillandsia tenuifolia Linnaeus, *Species Plantarum* 1: 286. 1753.

"Habitat in Americae meridionalis arboribus." RCN: 2275.

Lectotype (Smith & Downs, *Fl. Neotropica* 14: 829. 1977): Herb. A. van Royen No. 893.318–85 (L).

Current name: ***Tillandsia tenuifolia*** L. (Bromeliaceae).

Tillandsia usneoides (Linnaeus) Linnaeus, *Species Plantarum,* ed. 2, 1: 411. 1762.

"Habitat in Virginiae, Jamaicae, Brasiliae arboribus." RCN: 2281.

Basionym: *Renealmia usneoides* L. (1753).

Lectotype (Gouda in Görts-van Rijn, *Fl. Guianas,* ser. A, 3: 68. 1987): Herb. Clifford: 129, *Renealmia* 1 (BM-000558543).

Current name: ***Tillandsia usneoides*** (L.) L. (Bromeliaceae).

Tillandsia utriculata Linnaeus, *Species Plantarum* 1: 286. 1753.

"Habitat in Americae meridionalis arboribus." RCN: 2272.

Neotype (Till in Jarvis & al., *Regnum Veg.* 127: 94. 1993): Jamaica. Middlesex County, St Ann Parish, Cole Gate about 4 miles south of Ocho Rios, 210m, 20 Aug 1992, *W. Till 9014* (WU; iso- BM, US).

Generitype of *Tillandsia* Linnaeus (vide Hitchcock, *Prop. Brit. Bot.*: 144. 1929).

Current name: ***Tillandsia utriculata*** L. (Bromeliaceae).

Note: Smith & Downs (in *Fl. Neotropica* 14: 972. 1977) indicated unspecified material in Herb. Sloane (BM-SL) as type. However, although Linnaeus referred to a Sloane polynomial in the protologue, it was (unusually) unaccompanied by an illustration. The material would not have been seen by Linnaeus and cannot be original material for the name, nor is there any other. Till therefore designated a neotype from Jamaica.

Tinus occidentalis Linnaeus, *Systema Naturae,* ed. 10, 2: 1010. 1759.

["Habitat in Jamaica."] Sp. Pl., ed. 2, 1: 530 (1762). RCN: 2923.

Type not designated.

Original material: [icon] in Browne, Civ. Nat. Hist. Jamaica: 214, t. 21, f. 1. 1756.

Generitype of *Tinus* Linnaeus.

Current name: ***Clethra occidentalis*** (L.) Kuntze (Clethraceae).

Toluifera balsamum Linnaeus, *Species Plantarum* 1: 384. 1753.

"Habitat in America prope Carthagenam." RCN: 3018.

Type not designated.

Original material: none traced.

Generitype of *Toluifera* Linnaeus, *nom. rej.*

Current name: ***Myroxylon balsamum*** (L.) Harms var. **balsamum** (Fabaceae: Faboideae).

Note: Toluifera Linnaeus, *nom. rej.* in favour of *Myroxylon* Linnaeus filius.

Although Dillon (in Dwyer & al. in *Ann. Missouri Bot. Gard.* 67: 736. 1980) indicated unseen material in BAS as type, and Rudd (in Dassanayake & Fosberg, *Revised Handb. Fl. Ceylon* 1: 432. 1980) did the same for unspecified material in L, there appears to be no extant original material for the name.

Tomex tomentosa Linnaeus, *Species Plantarum* 1: 118. 1753.

"Habitat in India." RCN: 972.

Basionym of: *Callicarpa tomentosa* (L.) L. (1774); *Callicarpa lanata* L. (1771), *nom. illeg.*

Lectotype (Trimen in *J. Linn. Soc., Bot.* 24: 136. 1887): Herb. Hermann 1: 64, No. 59 (BM-000594496).

Generitype of *Tomex* Linnaeus.

Current name: ***Callicarpa tomentosa*** (L.) L. (Verbenaceae).

Tordylium anthriscus Linnaeus, *Species Plantarum* 1: 240. 1753.

"Habitat in Europae septentrionalis arvis ruderatis." RCN: 1933.

Lectotype (Jury & al. in Jarvis & al. in *Taxon* 55: 215. 2006): Herb. Clifford: 90, *Tordylium* 5 (BM-000558245).

Current name: ***Torilis japonica*** (Houtt.) DC. (Apiaceae).

Tordylium apulum Linnaeus, *Species Plantarum* 1: 239. 1753.

"Habitat in Italiae, Apuliae incultis." RCN: 1931.

Lectotype (Jury & Al-Eisawi in *Bot. J. Linn. Soc.* 97: 393. 1988): Herb. Clifford: 90, *Tordylium* 3 (BM-000558242).

Current name: ***Tordylium apulum*** L. (Apiaceae).

Note: Jury & Al-Eisawi incorrectly indicated the Clifford sheet as a syntype (it was not an explicitly cited specimen), so under Art. 9.8, this is treated as correctable to lectotype.

Tordylium latifolium Linnaeus, *Species Plantarum* 1: 240. 1753.

"Habitat in Gallia, Italia." RCN: 1937.

Lectotype (Reduron & Jarvis in Jarvis & al. in *Taxon* 55: 215. 2006): Herb. Clifford: 91, *Caucalis* 1 (BM-000558247).

Current name: ***Turgenia latifolia*** (L.) Hoffm. (Apiaceae).

Tordylium maximum Linnaeus, *Species Plantarum* 1: 240. 1753.

"Habitat in Italiae ruderatis sepibus." RCN: 1932.

Lectotype (Al-Eisawi & Jury in Jarvis & al., *Regnum Veg.* 127: 94. 1993): Herb. Clifford: 90, *Tordylium* 4 (BM-000558244).

Generitype of *Tordylium* Linnaeus (vide Hitchcock, *Prop. Brit. Bot.*: 139. 1929).

Current name: ***Tordylium maximum*** L. (Apiaceae).

Note: Alavi (in Rechinger, *Fl. Iranica* 162: 465. 1987) indicated 337.4 (LINN) as type, but the sheet lacks the *Species Plantarum* number (i.e. "4") and was a post-1753 addition to the herbarium, and is not original material for the name.

Tordylium nodosum Linnaeus, *Species Plantarum* 1: 240. 1753.

"Habitat in Gallia, Italia ad vias." RCN: 1934.

Lectotype (Jafri in Jafri & El-Gadi, *Fl. Libya* 117: 116. 1985): Herb. Linn. No. 337.6 (LINN).

Current name: ***Torilis nodosa*** (L.) Gaertn. (Apiaceae).

Tordylium officinale Linnaeus, *Species Plantarum* 1: 239. 1753.

"Habitat in Narbona, Italia, Sicilia." RCN: 1929.

Lectotype (Al-Eisawi in Jarvis & al. in *Taxon* 55: 215. 2006): Herb. Linn. No. 337.2 (LINN).

Current name: ***Tordylium officinale*** L. (Apiaceae).

Tordylium peregrinum Linnaeus, *Systema Naturae,* ed. 12, 2: 204; *Mantissa Plantarum*: 55. 1767.

"Habitat in Oriente. D. Arduini." RCN: 1930.

Lectotype (Reduron & Jarvis in Jarvis & al. in *Taxon* 55: 215. 2006): *Arduino s.n.,* Herb. Linn. No. 337.3 (LINN).

Current name: ***Capnophyllum peregrinum*** (L.) Lange (Apiaceae).

Tordylium syriacum Linnaeus, *Species Plantarum* 1: 239. 1753.

"Habitat in Syria." RCN: 1928.

Lectotype (Al-Eisawi in Jarvis & al. in *Taxon* 55: 216. 2006): Herb. Linn. No. 337.1 (LINN).

Current name: ***Tordylium syriacum*** L. (Apiaceae).

Torenia asiatica Linnaeus, *Species Plantarum* 2: 619. 1753.

"Habitat in India. Toren." RCN: 4475.

T

Lectotype (Saldanha in *Bull. Bot. Surv. India* 8: 126. 1966): *Torén*, Herb. Linn. No. 770.1 (LINN).

Generitype of *Torenia* Linnaeus.

Current name: **Torenia asiatica** L. (Scrophulariaceae).

Note: The story of the discovery of this plant by Olof Torén and the questions raised about its provenance have been discussed by Torén (in *Svenska-Linné Sällsk. Årsskr.* 36: 17–56. 1954), who also illustrates the type specimen as Bild 24, Saldanha (in *Bull. Bot. Surv. India* 8: 126. 1966) and Burtt (in *Rheedea* 1: 5–7. 1991).

Tormentilla erecta Linnaeus, *Species Plantarum* 1: 500. 1753.

"Habitat in Europae pascuis siccis." RCN: 3802.

Lectotype (Soják in Jarvis & al., *Regnum Veg.* 127: 94. 1993): Herb. Linn. No. 656.1 (LINN).

Generitype of *Tormentilla* Linnaeus (vide Green, *Prop. Brit. Bot.*: 159. 1929).

Current name: **Potentilla erecta** (L.) Raeusch. (Rosaceae).

Tormentilla reptans Linnaeus, *Species Plantarum* 1: 500. 1753.

"Habitat in Anglia." RCN: 3803.

Lectotype (Rico & Martínez Ortega in Cafferty & Jarvis in *Taxon* 51: 544. 2002): [icon] *"Pentaphyllum reptans alatum foliis profundius serratis"* in Plot, Nat. Hist. Oxford-shire: 145, t. 9, f. 5. 1677.

Current name: **Potentilla reptans** L. (Rosaceae).

Tournefortia cymosa Linnaeus, *Species Plantarum*, ed. 2, 1: 202. 1762, *nom. illeg.*

"Habitat in Jamaica, praecedenti nimis affinis." RCN: 1137.

Replaced synonym: *Tournefortia glabra* L. (1753).

Lectotype (Miller in Cafferty & Jarvis in *Taxon* 53: 804. 2004): [icon] *"Heliotropii flore, frutex, folio, maximo, oblongo, acuminato, glabro"* in Sloane, Voy. Jamaica 2: 109, t. 212, f. 2. 1725. – Typotype: Herb. Sloane 7: 50 (BM-SL).

Current name: **Tournefortia glabra** L. (Boraginaceae).

Note: An illegitimate replacement name for *T. glabra* L. (1753).

Tournefortia foetida Linnaeus, *Flora Jamaicensis*: 13. 1759, *orth. var.* ["Habitat in Mexico, Jamaica."] Sp. Pl. 1: 140 (1753). RCN: 1135.

Lectotype (Lourteig in *Phytologia* 65: 388. 1988): [icon] *"Tournefortia foliis ovato-lanceolatis"* in Plumier in Burman, Pl. Amer.: 226, t. 230. 1760.

Current name: **Tournefortia foetidissima** L. (Boraginaceae).

Note: An orthographic variant of *T. foetidissima* L. (1753).

Tournefortia foetidissima Linnaeus, *Species Plantarum* 1: 140. 1753.

"Habitat in Mexico, Jamaica." RCN: 1135.

Lectotype (Lourteig in *Phytologia* 65: 388. 1988): [icon] *"Tournefortia foliis ovato-lanceolatis"* in Plumier in Burman, Pl. Amer.: 226, t. 230. 1760.

Current name: **Tournefortia foetidissima** L. (Boraginaceae).

Tournefortia glabra Linnaeus, *Species Plantarum* 1: 141. 1753.

"Habitat in Jamaica." RCN: 1137.

Replaced synonym of: *Tournefortia cymosa* L. (1762), *nom. illeg.*

Lectotype (Miller in Cafferty & Jarvis in *Taxon* 53: 804. 2004): [icon] *"Heliotropii flore, frutex, folio, maximo, oblongo, acuminato, glabro"* in Sloane, Voy. Jamaica 2: 109, t. 212, f. 2. 1725. – Typotype: Herb. Sloane 7: 50 (BM-SL).

Current name: **Tournefortia glabra** L. (Boraginaceae).

Tournefortia hirsutissima Linnaeus, *Species Plantarum* 1: 140. 1753, *typ. cons.*

"Habitat in America calidiore." RCN: 1133.

Conserved type (Johnston in *J. Arnold Arbor.* 30: 133. 1949): [icon] *"Tournefortia caule hirsuto"* in Plumier in Burman, Pl. Amer.: 226, t. 229. 1760.

Generitype of *Tournefortia* Linnaeus, *nom. cons.*

Current name: **Tournefortia hirsutissima** L. (Boraginaceae).

Note: Tournefortia hirsutissima, with the type designated by Johnston, was proposed as conserved type of the genus by Jarvis (in *Taxon* 41: 571. 1992). This was eventually approved by the General Committee (see review of the history of this proposal by Barrie, *l.c.* 55: 795–796. 2006).

Tournefortia humilis Linnaeus, *Species Plantarum* 1: 141. 1753.

"Habitat in America calida." RCN: 1136.

Lectotype (Miller in Cafferty & Jarvis in *Taxon* 53: 804. 2004): [icon] *"Tournefortia foliis lanceolatis"* in Plumier in Burman, Pl. Amer.: 224, t. 227, f. 2. 1760. – Epitype (Miller in Cafferty & Jarvis in *Taxon* 53: 804. 2004): Martinique. Casa Pilote, collines arides, Feb 1868, *L. Hahn 416* (BM).

Current name: **Heliotropium ternatum** Vahl (Boraginaceae).

Tournefortia serrata Linnaeus, *Species Plantarum* 1: 140. 1753.

"Habitat in America calidiore." RCN: 1132.

Type not designated.

Original material: [icon] in Plumier in Burman, Pl. Amer.: 224, t. 228, f. 1. 1760.

Note: The application of this name is uncertain. It is not in use and may be a candidate for rejection as the only original element, a Plumier plate, appears to be identifiable as *Cordia mirabiloides* (Jacq.) Roem. & Schult.

Tournefortia sibirica Linnaeus, *Species Plantarum* 1: 141. 1753.

"Habitat in Dauriae apricis glareosis aridis." RCN: 1131.

Basionym of: *Messersmidia argusia* L. (1762), *nom. illeg.*; *M. sibirica* (L.) L. (1771).

Lectotype (Majorov in Cafferty & Jarvis in *Taxon* 53: 804. 2004): *Gerber*, Herb. Linn. No. 192.1 (LINN).

Current name: **Argusia sibirica** (L.) Dandy (Boraginaceae).

Tournefortia suffruticosa Linnaeus, *Species Plantarum*, ed. 2, 1: 202. 1762.

"Habitat in Jamaica." RCN: 1138.

Lectotype (Miller in Cafferty & Jarvis in *Taxon* 53: 804. 2004): [icon] *"Thymeleae facie, frutex maritimus tetraspermos, flore tetrapetalo"* in Sloane, Voy. Jamaica 2: 29, t. 162, f. 4. 1725. – Typotype: Herb. Sloane 5: 105 (BM-SL).

Current name: **Suriana maritima** L. (Surianaceae).

Note: Published in 1762, although this name did appear in later editions of the *Systema Naturae* (e.g. ed. 12 in 1767), it was not taken up by other authors and does not appear to be in current use. The sole original element for the name, a Sloane illustration, is identifiable as *Suriana maritima* L. (and indeed this plate was cited by Linnaeus (1753: 284) as part of the protologue of that name). Typification of *T. suffruticosa* by Miller using this element resulted in it falling into the synonymy of the earlier *S. maritima* (Surianaceae).

Tournefortia volubilis Linnaeus, *Species Plantarum* 1: 140. 1753.

"Habitat in Jamaica, Mexico, arbores scandens." RCN: 1134.

Lectotype (Miller in Cafferty & Jarvis in *Taxon* 53: 804. 2004): [icon] *"Bryonia nigra fruticosa, racemi ramulis varie implicitis, atque caudae scorpionis instar in se contortis, baccis albis una vel altera nigra macula notatis"* in Sloane, Voy. Jamaica 1: 234, t. 143, f. 2. 1707. – Typotype: Herb. Sloane 4: 92 (BM-SL).

Current name: **Tournefortia volubilis** L. (Boraginaceae).

Tozzia alpina Linnaeus, *Species Plantarum* 2: 607. 1753.

"Habitat in Alpibus Helveticis, Austriacis, Italicis, Pyrenaeis, locis asperis, humidis." RCN: 4396.

Lectotype (Sutton in Jarvis & al., *Regnum Veg.* 127: 95. 1993): Herb. Linn. No. 762.1 (LINN).
Generitype of *Tozzia* Linnaeus.
Current name: ***Tozzia alpina*** L. (Scrophulariaceae).

Trachelium caeruleum Linnaeus, *Species Plantarum* 1: 171. 1753.
"Habitat in Italiae umbrosis." RCN: 1348.
Lectotype (Barrie in Jarvis & al., *Regnum Veg.* 127: 94. 1993): Herb. Clifford: 66, *Trachelium* 1 (BM-000558076).
Generitype of *Trachelium* Linnaeus.
Current name: ***Trachelium caeruleum*** L. (Campanulaceae).

Tradescantia axillaris (Linnaeus) Linnaeus, *Mantissa Plantarum Altera*: 321. 1771.
["Habitat in India."] Sp. Pl. 1: 42 (1753). RCN: 2288.
Basionym: *Commelina axillaris* L. (1753).
Lectotype (Faden in Dassanayake & Clayton, *Revised Handb. Fl. Ceylon* 14: 119. 2000): [icon] *"Ephemerum Phalangoides Maderaspatanum minimum, secundum caulem quasi ex utriculis floridium"* in Plukenet, Phytographia: t. 174, f. 3. 1692; Almag. Bot.: 135. 1696. – Voucher: Herb. Sloane 96: 16 (BM-SL).
Current name: ***Cyanotis axillaris*** (L.) Sweet (Commelinaceae).

Tradescantia cristata (Linnaeus) Linnaeus, *Systema Naturae*, ed. 12, 2: 233. 1767.
["Habitat in Zeylona."] Sp. Pl. 1: 42 (1753). RCN: 2289.
Basionym: *Commelina cristata* L. (1753).
Lectotype (Faden in Dassanayake & Clayton, *Revised Handb. Fl. Ceylon* 14: 123. 2000): Herb. Hermann 5: 152, No. 32 [icon] (BM).
Current name: ***Cyanotis cristata*** (L.) D. Don (Commelinaceae).

Tradescantia malabarica Linnaeus, *Species Plantarum*, ed. 2, 1: 412. 1762.
"Habitat in Malabaria." RCN: 2285.
Lectotype (Faden in Dassanayake & Clayton, *Revised Handb. Fl. Ceylon* 14: 145. 2000): [icon] *"Tali-pullu"* in Rheede, Hort. Malab. 9: 123, t. 63. 1689.
Current name: ***Murdannia nudiflora*** (L.) Brenan (Commelinaceae).

Tradescantia nervosa Linnaeus, *Mantissa Plantarum Altera*: 223. 1771.
"Habitat in Suratte? D. Mutis." RCN: 2286.
Type not designated.
Original material: *Mútis*, Herb. Linn. No. 406.3 (LINN).
Current name: ***Telipogon nervosus*** (L.) Druce (Orchidaceae).

Tradescantia papilionacea Linnaeus, *Systema Naturae*, ed. 12, 2: 233; *Mantissa Plantarum*: 61. 1767.
"Habitat in India. Burmann." RCN: 2290.
Lectotype (Rao in *Notes Roy. Bot. Gard. Edinburgh* 25: 185. 1964): Herb. Linn. No. 406.7 (LINN).
Current name: ***Cyanotis papilionacea*** (L.) Roem. & Schult. (Commelinaceae).

Tradescantia virginiana Linnaeus, *Species Plantarum* 1: 288. 1753.
"Habitat in Virginia." RCN: 2284.
Type not designated.
Original material: [icon] in Morison, Pl. Hist. Univ. 3: 606, s. 15, t. 2, f. 4. 1699.
Generitype of *Tradescantia* Linnaeus.
Current name: ***Tradescantia virginiana*** L. (Commelinaceae).
Note: This name presents particular difficulties because the original material, 406.1 (LINN) and Herb. Burser III: 104b (UPS), is identifiable as *Tradescantia ohiensis* Raf. As noted by Jarvis & al.

(*Regnum Veg.* 127: 6. 1993), their Linnaean Generic List was conceived as a possible "Names in Current Use" (NCU) List which, if the concept had been adopted, could have allowed types listed there some protection. With this in mind, Reveal there (p. 95) designated a neotype from Virginia. However, as the NCU proposals were not adopted, this neotypification is invalid, because original material is in existence. It appears that a conservation proposal is necessary if the application of *T. virginiana* is not to change.

Tragia chamaelea Linnaeus, *Species Plantarum* 2: 981. 1753.
"Habitat in India." RCN: 7106.
Lectotype (Esser in *Blumea* 44: 176. 1999): Herb. Hermann 4: 43, No. 335 (BM-000628196).
Current name: ***Microstachys chamaelea*** (L.) Müll. Arg. (Euphorbiaceae).
Note: Airy Shaw (in *Kew Bull.* 35: 686. 1980) indicated material in LINN (presumably sheet 1103.5) as type, but this reached Linnaeus long after 1753 and is not original material for the name.

Tragia involucrata Linnaeus, *Species Plantarum* 2: 980. 1753.
"Habitat in India." RCN: 7103.
Type not designated.
Original material: Herb. Hermann 2: 14 (BM); Herb. Hermann 2: 12 (BM); Herb. Hermann 3: 14 (BM); Herb. Hermann 2: 84 (BM); [icon] in Burman, Thes. Zeylan.: 202, t. 92. 1737; [icon] in Rheede, Hort. Malab. 2: 73, t. 39. 1679.
Current name: ***Tragia involucrata*** L. (Euphorbiaceae).

Tragia mercurialis Linnaeus, *Species Plantarum* 2: 980. 1753.
"Habitat in India." RCN: 7104.
Lectotype (Radcliffe-Smith in *Kew Bull.* 37: 425. 1982): [icon] *"Mercurialis Maderaspatensis tricoccos acetabulis destituta"* in Plukenet, Phytographia: t. 205, f. 4. 1692; Almag. Bot.: 248. 1696. – Typotype: Herb. Sloane 96: 187 (BM-SL).
Current name: ***Micrococca mercurialis*** (L.) Benth. (Euphorbiaceae).

Tragia scandens Linnaeus, *Herbarium Amboinense*: 18. 1754.
RCN: 7102.
Lectotype (Merrill, *Interpret. Rumph. Herb. Amb.*: 33, 365. 1917): [icon] *"Funis urens"* in Rumphius, Herb. Amboin. 5: 13, t. 9. 1747.
Current name: ***Tetracera scandens*** (L.) Merr. (Dilleniaceae).

Tragia urens Linnaeus, *Species Plantarum*, ed. 2, 2: 1391. 1763.
"Habitat in Virginia." RCN: 7105.
Type not designated.
Original material: [icon] in Plukenet, Phytographia: t. 107, f. 5. 1691; Almag. Bot.: 320. 1696.
Current name: ***Tragia urens*** L. (Euphorbiaceae).

Tragia volubilis Linnaeus, *Species Plantarum* 2: 980. 1753.
"Habitat in Jamaica." RCN: 7102.
Lectotype (Fawcett & Rendle, *Fl. Jamaica* 4: 305. 1920): Herb. Linn. No. 1103.1 (LINN).
Generitype of *Tragia* Linnaeus (vide Green, *Prop. Brit. Bot.*: 187. 1929).
Current name: ***Tragia volubilis*** L. (Euphorbiaceae).
Note: Some authors have treated either the cited Sloane illustration (e.g. Lourteig in *Bradea* 5: 352. 1990) or Sloane's material (e.g. Radcliffe-Smith in *Kew Bull.* 37: 690. 1983) as the type but Fawcett & Rendle's choice has priority.

Tragopogon asper Linnaeus, *Species Plantarum* 2: 790. 1753.
"Habitat Monspelii." RCN: 5786.
Type not designated.

T

Original material: none traced.
Current name: **Urospermum picroides** (L.) Scop. ex F.W. Schmidt
(Asteraceae).
Note: Specific epithet spelled "asperum" in the protologue.

Tragopogon crocifolius Linnaeus, *Systema Naturae*, ed. 10, 2: 1191.
1759.
["Habitat in Italia, Monspelii."] Sp. Pl. ed. 2, 2: 1110 (1763). RCN:
5782.
Lectotype (Díaz de la Guardia & Blanca in *Taxon* 41: 550. 1992):
Herb. Linn. No. 946.4 (LINN).
Current name: **Tragopogon crocifolius** L. (Asteraceae).
Note: Specific epithet spelled "crocifolium" in the protologue.

Tragopogon dalechampii Linnaeus, *Species Plantarum* 2: 790. 1753.
"Habitat in Hispania." RCN: 5784.
Type not designated.
Original material: Herb. Clifford: 382, *Tragopogon* 3, 2 sheets (BM);
Herb. Linn. No. 946.6 (LINN); [icon] in Clusius, Rar. Pl. Hist. 2:
143. 1601.
Current name: **Urospermum dalechampii** (L.) Desf. (Asteraceae).

Tragopogon dandelion (Linnaeus) Linnaeus, *Species Plantarum,* ed.
2, 2: 1111. 1763.
"Habitat in Virginia." RCN: 5787.
Basionym: *Leontodon dandelion* L. (1753).
Lectotype (Kim & Turner in *Brittonia* 44: 192. 1992): *Clayton 19 &
383*, Herb. Linn. No. 946.8 (LINN).
Current name: **Krigia dandelion** (L.) Nutt. (Asteraceae).

Tragopogon hybridus Linnaeus, *Species Plantarum* 2: 789. 1753.
"Habitat in Italia." RCN: 5776.
Lectotype (Díaz de la Guardia & Blanca in *Lazaroa* 9: 38. 1988
[1986]): Herb. Linn. No. 945.1 (LINN).
Current name: **Geropogon hybridus** (L.) Sch. Bip. (Asteraceae).
Note: Specific epithet spelled "hybridum" in the protologue.

Tragopogon lanatus (Linnaeus) Linnaeus, *Species Plantarum,* ed. 2, 2:
1111. 1763.
"Habitat in Oriente, Palaestina." RCN: 5776.
Basionym: *Leontodon lanatus* L. (1755).
Lectotype (Díaz de la Guardia & Blanca in *Taxon* 46: 761. 1997):
Hasselquist, Herb. Linn. No. 946.9 (LINN; iso- UPS-HASSELQ
678).
Current name: **Scorzonera lanata** (L.) O. Hoffm. (Asteraceae).
Note: Specific epithet spelled "lanatum" in the protologue.

Tragopogon orientalis Linnaeus, *Species Plantarum* 2: 789. 1753.
"Habitat in Oriente." RCN: 5780.
Lectotype (Díaz de la Guardia & Blanca in *Taxon* 41: 549. 1992):
Gerber, Herb. Linn. No. 946.2 (LINN).
Current name: **Tragopogon orientalis** L. (Asteraceae).
Note: Specific epithet spelled "orientale" in the protologue.

Tragopogon picroides Linnaeus, *Species Plantarum* 2: 790. 1753.
"Habitat in Creta, Monspelii." RCN: 5785.
Lectotype (Turland in Jarvis & Turland in *Taxon* 47: 369. 1998):
Herb. Clifford: 382, *Tragopogon* 2 (BM-000646822).
Current name: **Urospermum picroides** (L.) Scop. ex F.W. Schmidt
(Asteraceae).

Tragopogon porrifolius Linnaeus, *Species Plantarum* 2: 789. 1753.
"Habitat – – – –" RCN: 5781.
Lectotype (Díaz de la Guardia & Blanca in *Taxon* 41: 549. 1992):
Herb. Burser XV(2): 69, centre specimen (UPS).

Generitype of *Tragopogon* Linnaeus (vide Díaz de la Guardia & Blanca
in Jarvis & al., *Regnum Veg.* 127: 95. 1993).
Current name: **Tragopogon porrifolius** L. (Asteraceae).
Note: Specific epithet spelled "porrifolium" in the protologue.
Although *T. pratensis* L. has historically been treated as the
generitype (e.g. by Britton & Brown, *Ill. Fl. N.U.S.* ed. 2, 3: 313.
1913; Green, *Prop. Brit. Bot.*: 177. 1930), Díaz de la Guardia &
Blanca (in Jarvis & al., *Regnum Veg.* 127: 95. 1993) designated *T.
porrifolius* as type in its place. They rejected the earlier choice on the
grounds that *T. pratensis* has five involucral bracts, conflicting with
the eight described in Linnaeus' generic protologue.

Tragopogon pratensis Linnaeus, *Species Plantarum* 2: 789. 1753.
"Habitat in Europae pratis apricis." RCN: 5779.
Lectotype (Díaz de la Guardia & Blanca in *Taxon* 41: 548. 1992):
Herb. Burser XV(2): 63 (UPS).
Current name: **Tragopogon pratensis** L. subsp. **pratensis** (Asteraceae).
Note: Specific epithet spelled "pratense" in the protologue.
Although *T. pratensis* has historically been treated as the
generitype (e.g. by Britton & Brown, *Ill. Fl. N.U.S.* ed. 2, 3: 313.
1913; Green, *Prop. Brit. Bot.*: 177. 1930), Díaz de la Guardia &
Blanca in Jarvis & al., *Regnum Veg.* 127: 95 (1993) designated *T.
porrifolius* as type in its place. They rejected the earlier choice on the
grounds that *T. pratensis* has five involucral bracts, conflicting with
the eight described in Linnaeus' generic protologue.

Tragopogon villosus Linnaeus, *Species Plantarum*, ed. 2, 2: 1110.
1763.
"Habitat in Hispania." RCN: 5783.
Lectotype (Díaz de la Guardia & Blanca in *Taxon* 41: 548. 1992):
Herb. Linn. No. 946.5, left specimen (LINN).
Current name: **Tragopogon villosus** L. (Asteraceae).
Note: Specific epithet spelled "villosum" in the protologue.
Although the name is typified, it is treated by the authors of the
type choice as of uncertain application, "at least as far as the Iberian
peninsula is concerned". Blanca & Díaz de la Guardia (in *Anales
Jard. Bot. Madrid* 54: 360. 1996) reiterate this.

Tragopogon virginicus Linnaeus, *Species Plantarum* 2: 789. 1753.
"Habitat in Virginia, Canada. Kalm." RCN: 5789.
Lectotype (Kim & Turner in *Brittonia* 44: 193. 1992): *Kalm*, Herb.
Linn. No. 946.10 (LINN).
Current name: **Krigia biflora** (Walter) S.F. Blake var. **biflora**
(Asteraceae).

Trapa natans Linnaeus, *Species Plantarum* 1: 120. 1753.
"Habitat in Europae australis, Asiaeque stagnis limosis." RCN: 990.
Type not designated.
Original material: [icon] in Rheede, Hort. Malab. 11: 65, t. 33. 1692.
Generitype of *Trapa* Linnaeus.
Current name: **Trapa natans** L. (Trapaceae).
Note: Ghazanfar (in Nasir & Ali, *Fl. W. Pakistan* 97: 3. 1976)
indicated 158.1 (LINN) as type but this is unannotated by
Linnaeus, and sterile, and is not original material for the name.
Material in Herb. Clifford (BM) exists, as well as a Rheede
illustration, but both are sterile. Because of the importance of fruit
characters, Verdcourt in *Kew Bull.* 41: 448 (1986) therefore
designated a fruiting specimen (*Fiori 471*, K) as a neotype.
Although this is contrary to Art. 9.15, Verdcourt's neotype choice
could be corrected to an epitype (Art. 9.8) if one of the original
elements were to prove to be a suitable lectotype.

Tremella adnata Linnaeus, *Flora Suecica*, ed. 2: 430. 1755.
"Habitat supra rupes submarinas ad Küllen Scaniae." RCN: 8264.
Type not designated.

Original material: none traced.

Note: The application of this name appears to be uncertain (see Drouet & Daily in *Butler Univ. Bot. Stud.* 12: 167. 1956) and it may be a candidate for rejection.

Tremella auricula Linnaeus, *Species Plantarum* 2: 1157. 1753.
"Habitat ad Arbores putridas." RCN: 8502.
Basionym of: *Peziza auricula* (L.) L. (1767).
Type not designated.
Original material: [icon] in Clusius, Rar. Pl. Hist. 2: 276. 1601; [icon] in Micheli, Nov. Pl. Gen.: 124, t. 66, f. 1. 1729.
Current name: ***Auricularia auricula-judae*** (Fr.: Fr.) J. Schröt. (Auriculariaceae).

Tremella difformis Linnaeus, *Flora Suecica,* ed. 2: 429. 1755.
"Habitat in Confervis maris occidentalis frequens." RCN: 8261.
Neotype (Irvine in Spencer & al. in *Taxon,* in press): Denmark. Hirsholm (Kattegat), 30 Jun 1998, *B. Jensen 258* (BM-000774388).
Current name: ***Leathesia difformis*** (L.) Aresch. (Chordariaceae).

Tremella hemisphaerica Linnaeus, *Species Plantarum* 2: 1158. 1753.
"Habitat in Rupibus & Confervis submarinis." RCN: 8262.
Neotype (Irvine & Pentecost in Spencer & al. in *Taxon,* in press): Sweden. "Suecicae ad Varholmen prope Göteborg", Aug 1865, *A. Åkermark s.n.* (BM-000917717).
Current name: ***Rivularia atra*** Bornet & Flahault (Rivulariaceae).

Tremella juniperina Linnaeus, *Species Plantarum* 2: 1157. 1753.
"Habitat in Juniperetis primo vere." RCN: 8257.
Type not designated.
Original material: none traced.
Generitype of *Tremella* Linnaeus ex Arthur.
Current name: ***Gymnosporangium juniperinum*** (L.) Fr. (Pucciniaceae).
Note: Tremella Linnaeus ex Arthur (in *Proc. Indiana Acad. Sci.* 1900: 133. 1901 (non Persoon ex Saint Amans 1821 (nom. cons.), nec Persoon ex E.M. Fries 1822)).

Tremella lichenoides Linnaeus, *Species Plantarum* 2: 1157. 1753.
"Habitat in Muscis, locis umbrosis ad montes." RCN: 8259.
Lectotype (Jørgensen & al. in *Bot. J. Linn. Soc.* 115: 371, f. 67. 1994): Herb. Linn. No. 1276.9, lower specimen (LINN).
Current name: ***Leptogium lichenoides*** (L.) Zahlbr. (Collemataceae).

Tremella nostoc Linnaeus, *Species Plantarum* 2: 1157. 1753.
"Habitat in Pratis post pluvias." RCN: 8258.
Lectotype (Irvine & Pentecost in Spencer & al. in *Taxon,* in press): [icon] *"Tremella terrestris sinuosa, pinguis & fugax"* in Dillenius, Hist. Musc.: 52, t. 10, f. 14. 1741. – Voucher: Herb. Dillenius (OXF).
Current name: ***Nostoc commune*** Vaucher (Nostocaceae).
Note: In the absence of any material in LINN, Drouet (in *Beih. Nova Hedwigia* 57: 25. 1978) designated "Tremella terrestris sinuosa, pinguis & fugax" in Herb. Dillenius (OXF) as a neotype. However, the existence of original material for the name means that Drouet's neotype choice is contrary to Art. 9.11 (see Spencer & al. in *Taxon,* in press).

Tremella purpurea Linnaeus, *Species Plantarum* 2: 1158. 1753.
"Habitat in Arborum ramis moribundis & emortuis." RCN: 8263.
Type not designated.
Original material: [icon] in Dillenius, Hist. Musc.: 127, t. 18, f. 6. 1741.
Current name: ***Nectria cinnabarina*** (Tode: Fr.) Fr. (Nectriaceae).

Tremella verrucosa Linnaeus, *Species Plantarum* 2: 1158. 1753.
"Habitat supra Lapides in rivulis." RCN: 8260.
Lectotype (Irvine & Pentecost in Spencer & al. in *Taxon,* in press): [icon] *"Tremella fluviatilis gelatinosa & uterculosa"* in Dillenius, Hist. Musc.: 54, t. 10, f. 16. 1741. – Voucher: Herb. Dillenius (OXF).
Current name: ***Nostoc commune*** Vaucher (Nostocaceae).
Note: In the absence of any material in LINN, Drouet (in *Beih. Nova Hedwigia* 57: 26. 1978) designated material in Herb. Dillenius (OXF) as a neotype. However, the existence of original material for the name means that Drouet's neotype choice is contrary to Art. 9.11 (see Spencer & al. in *Taxon,* in press).

Trewia nudiflora Linnaeus, *Species Plantarum* 2: 1193. 1753.
"Habitat in Malabariae arenosis." RCN: 3862.
Lectotype (Radcliffe-Smith in Nasir & Ali, *Fl. Pakistan* 172: 57. 1986): [icon] *"Canschi"* in Rheede, Hort. Malab. 1: 76, t. 42. 1678.
Generitype of *Trewia* Linnaeus.
Current name: ***Trewia nudiflora*** L. (Euphorbiaceae).

Trianthema decandra Linnaeus, *Systema Naturae,* ed. 12, 2: 297; *Mantissa Plantarum*: 70. 1767.
"Habitat in India." RCN: 3136.
Lectotype (Melville in *Kew Bull.* 7: 263. 1952): Herb. Linn. No. 572.4 (LINN).
Current name: ***Zaleya decandra*** (L.) Burm. f. (Aizoaceae).

Trianthema monogyna Linnaeus, *Systema Naturae,* ed. 12, 2: 297; *Mantissa Plantarum*: 69. 1767, *nom. illeg.*
"Habitat in America calidiore." RCN: 3134.
Replaced synonym: *Trianthema portulacastrum* L. (1753).
Lectotype (Jeffrey in *Kew Bull.* 14: 236. 1960): [icon] *"Portulaca Corassavica Capparidis folio"* in Hermann, Parad. Bat.: 213. 1698.
Current name: ***Trianthema portulacastrum*** L. (Aizoaceae).
Note: A superfluous name for *T. portulacastrum* L. (1753).

Trianthema pentandra Linnaeus, *Systema Naturae,* ed. 12, 2: 297; *Mantissa Plantarum*: 70. 1767.
"Habitat in Arabia." RCN: 3135.
Lectotype (Melville in *Kew Bull.* 7: 264. 1952): Herb. Linn. No. 572.2 (LINN).
Current name: ***Zaleya pentandra*** (L.) C. Jeffrey (Aizoaceae).

Trianthema portulacastrum Linnaeus, *Species Plantarum* 1: 223. 1753.
"Habitat in Jamaica, Curassao." RCN: 3134.
Replaced synonym of: *Trianthema monogyna* L. (1767), *nom. illeg.*
Lectotype (Jeffrey in *Kew Bull.* 14: 236. 1960): [icon] *"Portulaca Corassavica Capparidis folio"* in Hermann, Parad. Bat.: 213. 1698.
Generitype of *Trianthema* Linnaeus.
Current name: ***Trianthema portulacastrum*** L. (Aizoaceae).
Note: Fawcett & Rendle (*Fl. Jamaica* 3: 167. 1914) stated: "Type in Herb. Mus. Brit." but gave no indication of what the material in question might be. Jeffrey's appears to be the first explicit type choice.

Tribulus cistoides Linnaeus, *Species Plantarum* 1: 387. 1753.
"Habitat in America calidiore." RCN: 3050.
Lectotype (Wijnands, *Bot. Commelins*: 203. 1983): [icon] *"Tribulus Terrestris Major Corassavicus"* in Hermann, Parad. Bat.: 236. 1698.
Current name: ***Tribulus cistoides*** L. (Zygophyllaceae).

Tribulus lanuginosus Linnaeus, *Species Plantarum* 1: 387. 1753.
"Habitat in Zeylona." RCN: 3048.
Lectotype (El Hadidi in Polhill, *Fl. Trop. E. Africa, Zygophyllaceae*: 8. 1985): Herb. Linn. No. 547.2 (LINN).
Current name: ***Tribulus terrestris*** L. (Zygophyllaceae).

T

Tribulus maximus Linnaeus, *Species Plantarum* 1: 386. 1753.
"Habitat in Jamaicae aridis." RCN: 3047.
Lectotype (Porter in *Contr. Gray Herb.* 198: 98. 1969): Herb. Clifford:
160, *Tribulus* 2 (BM-000558735).
Current name: ***Kallstroemia maxima*** (L.) Hook. & Arn.
(Zygophyllaceae).

Tribulus terrestris Linnaeus, *Species Plantarum* 1: 387. 1753.
"Habitat in Europa australi ad semitas." RCN: 3049.
Lectotype (Burtt in *Kew Bull.* 9: 398. 1954): Herb. Clifford: 160,
Tribulus 1 (BM-000558734).
Generitype of *Tribulus* Linnaeus (vide Hitchcock, *Prop. Brit. Bot.*:
153. 1929).
Current name: ***Tribulus terrestris*** L. (Zygophyllaceae).
Note: Schweickerdt (in *Bothalia* 3: 174. 1937) treated 547.4 (LINN)
as the type, but the sheet lacks a *Species Plantarum* number (i.e. "3")
and is a post-1753 addition to the herbarium, and not original
material for the name. El Hadidi (in Jarvis & al., *Regnum Veg.* 127:
95. 1993) independently designated the same type as Burtt.

Trichilia glabra Linnaeus, *Systema Naturae,* ed. 10, 2: 1020. 1759.
RCN: 3027.
Lectotype (Fawcett & Rendle, *Fl. Jamaica* 4: 212. 1920): *Browne,*
Herb. Linn. No. 541.1 (LINN).
Current name: ***Trichilia glabra*** L. (Meliaceae).

Trichilia guara (N.J. Jacquin) Linnaeus, *Species Plantarum,* ed. 2, 1:
551. 1762.
"Habitat in Brasilia aliisque indiae occidentalis." RCN: 7629.
Basionym: *Melia guara* Jacq. (1760).
Replaced synonym of: *Guarea trichilioides* L. (1771), *nom. illeg.*
Type not designated.
Current name: ***Guarea guidonia*** (L.) Sleumer (Meliaceae).

Trichilia hirta Linnaeus, *Systema Naturae,* ed. 10, 2: 1020. 1759.
["Habitat in Jamaica."] Sp. Pl., ed. 2, 1: 550 (1762). RCN: 3026.
Neotype (Pennington, *Fl. Neotropica* 28: 54. 1981): Jamaica. Herb.
Sloane 7: 30 (BM-SL).
Current name: ***Trichilia hirta*** L. (Meliaceae).

Trichilia trifolia Linnaeus, *Systema Naturae,* ed. 10, 2: 1020. 1759.
["Habitat in America meridionali."] Sp. Pl., ed. 2, 1: 551 (1762).
RCN: 3028.
Neotype (Pennington, *Fl. Neotropica* 28: 106. 1981): Venezuela. Sucre,
Cumaná, *Humboldt & Bonpland, s.n.* (P).
Current name: ***Trichilia trifolia*** L. (Meliaceae).

Trichomanes aculeatum Linnaeus, *Flora Jamaicensis*: 23. 1759, *nom.
nud.*
"Habitat [in Jamaica.]"
Type not relevant.

Trichomanes adiantoides Linnaeus, *Species Plantarum* 2: 1098. 1753.
"Habitat in India, Africa." RCN: 7950.
Type not designated.
Original material: Herb. Hermann 3: 47, No. 385 (BM); [icon] in
Burman, Thes. Zeylan.: 97, t. 43. 1737; [icon] in Plukenet,
Phytographia: 10, t. 123, f. 6. 1692; Almag. Bot.: 10. 1696 –
Typotype: Herb. Sloane 95: 16 (BM-SL).
Current name: ***Asplenium polyodon*** G. Forst. (Aspleniaceae).

Trichomanes canariense Linnaeus, *Species Plantarum* 2: 1099.
1753.
"Habitat in Canariis, Lusitania, ad latera montium." RCN: 7953.
Type not designated.

Original material: Herb. Linn. No. 1253.12? (LINN); Herb. Linn.
No. 1253.10 (LINN); [icon] in Plukenet, Phytographia: 156, t.
291, f. 2. 1694; Almag. Bot.: 156. 1696.
Current name: ***Davallia canariensis*** (L.) Sm. (Davalliaceae).
Note: Specific epithet spelled "canariensis" in the protologue.
Nooteboom (in *Blumea* 39: 176. 1994) indicated Löfling
material in LINN as the type. However, he did not distinguish
between sheets 1253.10 and 1253.12 (neither of which is, in any
case, from Löfling), and as they are evidently not part of a single
gathering, Art. 9.15 does not apply.

Trichomanes capillaceum Linnaeus, *Species Plantarum* 2: 1099.
1753.
"Habitat in America." RCN: 7954.
Lectotype (Proctor, *Ferns Jamaica*: 109. 1985): [icon] *"Adiantum
Capillaceum"* in Plumier, Traité Foug. Amér.: 83, t. 99, f. D. 1705.
Current name: ***Trichomanes capillaceum*** L. (Hymenophyllaceae).

Trichomanes capillare Linnaeus, *Flora Jamaicensis*: 23. 1759, *orth.
var.*
["Habitat in America."] Sp. Pl. 2: 1099 (1753). RCN: 7954.
Lectotype (Proctor, *Ferns Jamaica*: 109. 1985): [icon] *"Adiantum
Capillaceum"* in Plumier, Traité Foug. Amér.: 83, t. 99, f. D. 1705.
Current name: ***Trichomanes capillaceum*** L. (Hymenophyllaceae).
Note: An orthographic variant of *T. capillaceum* L. (1753).

Trichomanes chinense Linnaeus, *Species Plantarum* 2: 1099. 1753.
"Habitat in China. Osbeck." RCN: 7952.
Type not designated.
Original material: none traced.
Current name: ***Sphenomeris chinensis*** (L.) Maxon
(Dennstaedtiaceae).
Note: Specific epithet spelled "chinensis" in the protologue.
Fosberg (in *Taxon* 18: 596–598. 1969) and Kramer (in van
Steenis, *Fl. Malesiana*, ser. II, 1: 182. 1971) treat Osbeck material in
S as the type, but this collection has not been traced – see Hansen
& Fox Maule (in *Bot. J. Linn. Soc.* 67: 208. 1973).

Trichomanes crispum Linnaeus, *Species Plantarum* 2: 1097. 1753,
typ. cons.
"Habitat in Martinica." RCN: 7945.
Lectotype (Proctor in Howard, *Fl. Lesser Antilles* 2: 95. 1977): [icon]
"Polypodium crispum, caliciferum" in Plumier, Traité Foug. Amér.:
67, t. 86. 1705.
Generitype of *Trichomanes* Linnaeus, *nom. cons.*
Current name: ***Trichomanes crispum*** L. (Hymenophyllaceae).
Note: Trichomanes crispum, with the type designated by Proctor, was
proposed as conserved type of the genus by Jarvis (in *Taxon* 41: 571.
1992). The Committee for Pteridophyta (in *Taxon* 48: 133. 1999)
recommended conservation as proposed, and it was approved by the
General Committee (in *Taxon* 48: 377. 1999). However,
subsequent Codes have not listed the Plumier plate (proposed as the
generitype), so the plate is a lectotype, rather than a conserved type.

Trichomanes hirsutum Linnaeus, *Species Plantarum* 2: 1098. 1753.
"Habitat in America." RCN: 7947.
Lectotype (Morton in *Contr. U. S. Natl. Herb.* 29: 157, 173. 1947):
[icon] *"Filicula digitata"* in Plumier, Traité Foug. Amér.: 73, t. 50, f.
B. 1705.
Current name: ***Hymenophyllum hirsutum*** (L.) Sw.
(Hymenophyllaceae).

Trichomanes membranaceum Linnaeus, *Species Plantarum* 2: 1097.
1753.
"Habitat in America." RCN: 7944.

Lectotype (Proctor in Howard, *Fl. Lesser Antilles* 2: 83. 1977): Herb. Linn. No. 1253.1 (LINN).

Current name: ***Trichomanes membranaceum*** L. (Hymenophyllaceae).

Trichomanes membranoides Linnaeus, *Flora Jamaicensis*: 23. 1759, *orth. var.*

"Habitat [in Jamaica.]" RCN: 7944.

Lectotype (Proctor in Howard, *Fl. Lesser Antilles* 2: 83. 1977): Herb. Linn. No. 1253.1 (LINN).

Current name: ***Trichomanes membranaceum*** L. (Hymenophyllaceae).

Note: An orthographic variant of *T. membranaceum* L. (1753).

Trichomanes polypodioides Linnaeus, *Species Plantarum* 2: 1098. 1753.

"Habitat in India." RCN: 7946.

Neotype (Proctor in Howard, *Fl. Lesser Antilles* 2: 93. 1977): Montserrat. *Proctor 19068* (A; iso- US).

Current name: ***Trichomanes polypodioides*** L. (Hymenophyllaceae).

Trichomanes pyxidiferum Linnaeus, *Species Plantarum* 2: 1098. 1753.

"Habitat in America." RCN: 7948.

Lectotype (Proctor, *Ferns Jamaica*: 106. 1985): [icon] *"Filicula pyxidifera"* in Plumier, Traité Foug. Amér.: 74, t. 50, f. E. 1705.

Current name: ***Trichomanes pyxidiferum*** L. (Hymenophyllaceae).

Trichomanes scandens Linnaeus, *Species Plantarum* 2: 1098. 1753.

"Habitat in America." RCN: 7951.

Lectotype (Proctor, *Ferns Jamaica*: 104. 1985): [icon] *"Adiantum scandens ramosissimum laciniis retusis dissectum"* in Plumier, Traité Foug. Amér.: 76, t. 93. 1705.

Current name: ***Trichomanes scandens*** L. (Hymenophyllaceae).

Note: See discussion by Britton (in *Bull. Torrey Bot. Club* 29: 476. 1902), who observed that while "most authors have followed the English school in taking as the type the specimen in the Linnaean herbarium...the Germans have gone to the original plates cited by Linnaeus...and taken that as the type". However, no explicit choice appears to have been made before Proctor.

Trichomanes tunbrigense Linnaeus, *Species Plantarum* 2: 1098. 1753.

"Habitat in Anglia, Italia." RCN: 7949.

Type not designated.

Original material: Herb. Linn. No. 1253.4 (LINN); [icon] in Plukenet, Phytographia: 10, t. 3, f. 5, 6. 1691; Almag. Bot.: 10. 1696; [icon] in Boccone, Mus. Piante Rar. Sicilia: 24, t. 2. 1697.

Current name: ***Hymenophyllum tunbrigense*** (L.) Sm. (Hymenophyllaceae).

Note: Evans & Jermy (in *Brit. Fern Gaz.* 9: 84. 1962) stated that Linnaeus based his concept on an English plant (meaning 1253.5 LINN?), but Proctor (*Ferns Jamaica*: 90. 1985) noted that 1253.5 (LINN) was a post-1753 addition to the herbarium and so cannot be the type.

Trichosanthes amara Linnaeus, *Species Plantarum* 2: 1008. 1753.

"Habitat in Domingo." RCN: 7312.

Type not designated.

Original material: [icon] in Plumier, Descr. Pl. Amér.: 86, t. 100. 1693.

Current name: ***Trichosanthes amara*** L. (Cucurbitaceae).

Trichosanthes anguina Linnaeus, *Species Plantarum* 2: 1008. 1753.

"Habitat in China." RCN: 7309.

Lectotype (Jeffrey in Jarvis & al., *Regnum Veg.* 127: 95. 1993): [icon] *"Anguina Sinensis, flore albo, elegantissimo, capillamentis tenuissimis ornato, fructu longo intorto, sub initium ex albo, & viridi variegato, per maturitatem prorsus rubro"* in Micheli, Nov. Pl. Gen.: 12, t. 9. 1729 (see also p. 59).

Generitype of *Trichosanthes* Linnaeus (vide Green, *Prop. Brit. Bot.*: 190. 1929).

Current name: ***Trichosanthes cucumerina*** L. (Cucurbitaceae).

Note: Keraudren-Aymonin (in Aubréville & Leroy, *Fl. Cambodge Laos Viêt-Nam* 15: 90. 1975) indicated cultivated material (presumably sheet 1149.1) in LINN as type but it lacks a *Species Plantarum* number (i.e. "1") and is a later addition to the herbarium, and not original material for the name. Jeffrey (in *Kew Bull.* 34: 797. 1980) designated the polynomial from Linnaeus' *Hortus Cliffortianus* account as the lectotype, but this is contrary to Art. 8.1.

Trichosanthes anguria Linnaeus, *Mantissa Plantarum Altera*: 497. 1771, *orth. var.*

RCN: 7309.

Lectotype (Jeffrey in Jarvis & al., *Regnum Veg.* 127: 95. 1993): [icon] *"Anguina Sinensis, flore albo, elegantissimo, capillamentis tenuissimis ornato, fructu longo intorto, sub initium ex albo, & viridi variegato, per maturitatem prorsus rubro"* in Micheli, Nov. Pl. Gen.: 12, t. 9. 1729.

Current name: ***Trichosanthes cucumerina*** L. (Cucurbitaceae).

Note: An orthographic variant of *T. anguina* L. (1753).

Trichosanthes cucumerina Linnaeus, *Species Plantarum* 2: 1008. 1753.

"Habitat in India." RCN: 7311.
Lectotype (Keraudren-Aymonin in Aubréville & Leroy, *Fl. Cambodge Laos Viêt-Nam* 15: 91. 1975): [icon] *"Padavalam"* in Rheede, Hort. Malab. 8: 29, t. 15. 1688.
Current name: ***Trichosanthes cucumerina*** L. (Cucurbitaceae).

Trichosanthes nervifolia Linnaeus, *Species Plantarum* 2: 1008. 1753.
"Habitat in India." RCN: 7310.
Lectotype (Majumdar & Bakshi in *Taxon* 28: 354. 1979): [icon] *"Tota-piri"* in Rheede, Hort. Malab. 8: 33, t. 17. 1688.
Current name: ***Trichosanthes nervifolia*** L. (Cucurbitaceae).

Trichosanthes palmata Linnaeus, *Systema Naturae*, ed. 10, 2: 1278. 1759.
RCN: 7313.
Lectotype (Jeffrey in Stoffers & Lindeman, *Fl. Suriname* 5(1): 463. 1984): [icon] *"Trichosanthes foliis palmatis"* in Plumier in Burman, Pl. Amer.: 14, t. 24. 1755.
Current name: ***Ceratosanthes palmata*** (L.) Urb. (Cucurbitaceae).

Trichosanthes punctata (Linnaeus) Linnaeus, *Amoenitates Academicae* 3: 423. 1756.
"Habitat in India." RCN: 7434.
Basionym: *Bryonia punctata* L. (1753).
Lectotype (Wunderlin in Woodson & Schery in *Ann. Missouri Bot. Gard.* 65: 314. 1978): Herb. Linn. No. 1180.1 (LINN).
Current name: ***Fevillea cordifolia*** L. (Cucurbitaceae).

Trichostema brachiatum Linnaeus, *Species Plantarum* 2: 598. 1753.
"Habitat in America septentrionali." RCN: 4345.
Lectotype (Reveal in Jarvis & al. in *Taxon* 50: 520. 2001): [icon] *"Teucrium Virginicum, Origani folio"* in Dillenius, Hort. Eltham. 2: 380, t. 285, f. 369. 1732.
Current name: ***Isanthus brachiatus*** (L.) Britton & al. (Lamiaceae).
Note: Although Epling (in *J. Bot.* 67: 11. 1929) treated material in LINN as the "standard", this is not equivalent to a type statement (see Jarvis & al. in *Taxon* 50: 508. 2001).

Trichostema dichotomum Linnaeus, *Species Plantarum* 2: 598. 1753.
"Habitat in Virginia, Pensylvania." RCN: 4344.
Lectotype (Reveal & al. in *Huntia* 7: 216. 1987): Herb. Linn. No. 750.1 (LINN).
Generitype of *Trichostema* Linnaeus (vide Green, *Prop. Brit. Bot.*: 166. 1929).
Current name: ***Trichostema dichotomum*** L. (Lamiaceae).
Note: Although Epling (in *J. Bot.* 67: 10. 1929) treated a Clayton collection as the "standard", this is not equivalent to a type statement (see Jarvis & al. in *Taxon* 50: 508. 2001).

Tridax procumbens Linnaeus, *Species Plantarum* 2: 900. 1753.
"Habitat in Vera Cruce." RCN: 6510.
Lectotype (Powell in *Brittonia* 17: 80. 1965): *Houstoun*, Herb. Clifford: 418, *Tridax* 1 (BM-000647229).
Generitype of *Tridax* Linnaeus.
Current name: ***Tridax procumbens*** L. (Asteraceae).
Note: Although Brown (in *Trans. Linn. Soc. London* 12: 103. 1818) noted the absence of material in LINN and said that Clifford's specimen "is the only authority for the genus", this does not constitute formal typification.

Trientalis capensis Linnaeus, *Species Plantarum* 1: 344. 1753.
"Habitat ad Cap. b. spei." RCN: 2643.
Type not designated.
Original material: Herb. Linn. No. 474.3 (LINN); Herb. A. van Royen No. 901.187–245 (L).
Current name: ***Crassula capensis*** (L.) Baill. (Crassulaceae).

Trientalis europaea Linnaeus, *Species Plantarum* 1: 344. 1753.
"Habitat in Europae borealis sylvis & juniperetis." RCN: 2636.
Type not designated.
Original material: Herb. Linn. No. 153.7 (S); Herb. Linn. No. 474.1 (LINN); Herb. Burser X: 105 (UPS); Herb. Linn. No. 139 (LAPP); Herb. Burser X: 107, syntype (UPS).
Generitype of *Trientalis* Linnaeus (vide Hitchcock, *Prop. Brit. Bot.*: 149. 1929).
Current name: ***Trientalis europaea*** L. (Primulaceae).

Trifolium agrarium Linnaeus, *Species Plantarum* 2: 772. 1753, *nom. utique rej.*
"Habitat in Europae pratis." RCN: 5677.
Type not designated.
Original material: Herb. Burser XVIII(2): 22 (UPS); Herb. Linn. No. 930.57 (LINN); Herb. Clifford: 374, *Trifolium* 10, 3 sheets (BM); [icon] in Vaillant, Bot. Paris.: 196, t. 22, f. 3. 1727; [icon] in Dodoëns, Stirp. Hist. Pempt., ed. 2: 576. 1616.
Current name: ***Trifolium aureum*** Pollich (Fabaceae: Faboideae).

Trifolium alexandrinum Linnaeus, *Centuria I Plantarum*: 25. 1755.
"Habitat in Aegypto. D. Hasselquist." RCN: 5670.
Lectotype (Zohary in Davis, *Fl. Turkey* 3: 438. 1970): *Hasselquist*, Herb. Linn. No. 930.49 (LINN; iso- UPS-HASSELQ 623, 624).
Current name: ***Trifolium alexandrinum*** L. (Fabaceae: Faboideae).

Trifolium alpestre Linnaeus, *Species Plantarum*, ed. 2, 2: 1082. 1763.
"Habitat in Europa, etiam in Suecia." RCN: 5658.
Lectotype (Zohary in *Candollea* 27: 128. 1972): Herb. Linn. No. 930.28 (LINN).
Current name: ***Trifolium alpestre*** L. (Fabaceae: Faboideae).

Trifolium alpinum Linnaeus, *Species Plantarum* 2: 767. 1753.
"Habitat in Alpibus Italicis, Helveticis, Pyrenaeis, Baldo." RCN: 5651.
Lectotype (Lassen in Turland & Jarvis in *Taxon* 46: 481. 1997): Herb. Linn. No. 930.18 (LINN).
Current name: ***Trifolium alpinum*** L. (Fabaceae: Faboideae).
Note: Zohary & Heller (*Genus* Trifolium: 108. 1984) designated the specimen Herb. Clifford: 499, *Trifolium* 23 (BM) as the lectotype (indicating that they had seen the material), and were followed by Muñoz Rodríguez (in *Stud. Bot. Univ. Salamanca* 14: 60. 1995). However, as no such specimen can be traced, Lassen designated an alternative lectotype.

Trifolium angustifolium Linnaeus, *Species Plantarum* 2: 769. 1753.
"Habitat in G. Narbonensi, Italia." RCN: 5663.
Lectotype (Lassen in Turland & Jarvis in *Taxon* 46: 481. 1997): Herb. Clifford: 375, *Trifolium* 14, sheet 2 (BM-000646747).
Current name: ***Trifolium angustifolium*** L. (Fabaceae: Faboideae).
Note: Zohary (in *Candollea* 27: 149. 1972), followed by several later authors, indicated material in Herb. Clifford (BM) as the lectotype, but it is unclear which of two possible specimens was meant, only one of which supports current usage. Lassen therefore designated as lectotype the sheet supporting current usage.

Trifolium arvense Linnaeus, *Species Plantarum* 2: 769. 1753.
"Habitat in Europa, America septentrionali." RCN: 5664.
Lectotype (Zohary in *Candollea* 27: 146. 1972): Herb. Clifford: 374, *Trifolium* 13 (BM-000646746).
Current name: ***Trifolium arvense*** L. (Fabaceae: Faboideae).

Trifolium biflorum Linnaeus, *Species Plantarum* 2: 773. 1753.
"Habitat in Virginia, Canada." RCN: 5681.
Lectotype (Reveal & al. in *Huntia* 7: 212. 1987): *Kalm*, Herb. Linn. No. 930.67 (LINN).

Current name: **Stylosanthes biflora** (L.) Britton & al. (Fabaceae: Faboideae).

Trifolium caeruleum Linnaeus, *Species Plantarum* 2: 764. 1753.
"Habitat in Bohemia, Lybia." RCN: 5637.
Lectotype (Lassen in Turland & Jarvis in *Taxon* 46: 481. 1997): Herb. Linn. No. 930.1 (LINN).
Current name: **Trigonella caerulea** (L.) Ser. (Fabaceae: Faboideae).
Note: Specific epithet spelled "M. caerulea" ["M." for "Melilotus"] in the protologue. Later corrected to *T. caeruleum* in *Systema Naturae*, ed. 10, 2: 1176 (1759). As is established custom, the "Melilotus" is to be ignored (see Art. 23.8 and Ex. 19).

Trifolium cherleri Linnaeus, *Demonstr. Pl. Horto Upsaliensi*: 21. 1753.
["Habitat in Hispania."] Cent. I Pl.: 24–25 (1755). RCN: 5654.
Lectotype (Lassen in Turland & Jarvis in *Taxon* 46: 481. 1997): *Magnol*, Herb. Linn. No. 930.22 (LINN).
Current name: **Trifolium cherleri** L. (Fabaceae: Faboideae).

Trifolium clypeatum Linnaeus, *Species Plantarum* 2: 769. 1753.
"Habitat in Oriente." RCN: 5666.
Lectotype (Turland in *Bull. Nat. Hist. Mus. London, Bot.* 25: 155, f. 25. 1995): Herb. Linn. No. 930.41 (LINN).
Current name: **Trifolium clypeatum** L. (Fabaceae: Faboideae).

Trifolium comosum Linnaeus, *Species Plantarum* 2: 767. 1753.
"Habitat in America." RCN: 5650.
Lectotype (Vincent in Turland & Jarvis in *Taxon* 46: 481. 1997): Herb. A. van Royen No. 913.103–40 (L).
Current name: **Trifolium reflexum** L. (Fabaceae: Faboideae).

Trifolium corniculatum Linnaeus, *Species Plantarum* 2: 766. 1753.
"Habitat in Gargano, Apuliae." RCN: 5707.
Basionym of: *Trigonella corniculata* (L.) L. (1759).
Lectotype (Greuter in Greuter & Rechinger in *Boissiera* 13: 78. 1967): Herb. Linn. No. 932.8 (LINN).
Current name: **Trigonella corniculata** (L.) L. (Fabaceae: Faboideae).
Note: Specific epithet spelled "M. corniculata" ["M." for "Melilotus"] in the protologue. Later cited as "Trifolium corniculatum" in synonymy of *Trigonella corniculata*, *Systema Naturae*, ed. 10, 2: 1180 (1759). As is established custom, the "Melilotus" is to be ignored (see Art. 23.8 and Ex. 19).

Trifolium creticum Linnaeus, *Species Plantarum* 2: 765. 1753.
"Habitat in Creta." RCN: 5642.
Lectotype (Greuter in Greuter & Rechinger in *Boissiera* 13: 76. 1967): Herb. Linn. No. 930.7 (LINN).
Current name: **Melilotus creticus** (L.) Desr. (Fabaceae: Faboideae).
Note: Specific epithet spelled "M. cretica" ["M." for "Melilotus"] in the protologue. Later corrected to *T. creticum*, *Systema Naturae*, ed. 10, 2: 1176 (1759). As is established custom, the "Melilotus" is to be ignored (see Art. 23.8 and Ex. 19).

Trifolium filiforme Linnaeus, *Species Plantarum* 2: 773. 1753, *nom. utique rej.*
"Habitat in Anglia." RCN: 5680.
Type not designated.
Original material: Herb. Linn. No. 930.63 (LINN); Herb. Linn. No. 930.64 (LINN); [icon] in Morison, Pl. Hist. Univ. 2: 142, s. 2, t. 13, f. 2. 1680; [icon] in Ray, Syn. Meth. Stirp. Brit., ed. 3: 331, t. 14, f. 4. 1724.
Current name: **Trifolium micranthum** Viv. (Fabaceae: Faboideae).

Trifolium fragiferum Linnaeus, *Species Plantarum* 2: 772. 1753.
"Habitat in Suecia, Gallia, Anglia." RCN: 5675.
Lectotype (Zohary & Heller in *Israel J. Bot.* 19: 317. 1970): Herb. Linn. No. 930.54 (LINN).
Current name: **Trifolium fragiferum** L. (Fabaceae: Faboideae).

Trifolium fruticans Linnaeus, *Species Plantarum* 2: 770. 1753.
"Habitat in Aethiopia." RCN: 5621.
Replaced synonym of: *Ononis trifoliata* L. (1767), *nom. illeg.*
Lectotype (Stirton in *S. African J. Bot.* 52: 3. 1986): Herb. Clifford: 373, *Trifolium* 5 (BM-000646736).
Current name: **Otholobium fruticans** (L.) C.H. Stirt. (Fabaceae: Faboideae).
Note: Although Wijnands (*Bot. Commelins*: 166. 1983) stated that the Clifford material "probably could serve as the lectotype", this did not effect formal typification. Stirton subsequently made a formal type choice.

Trifolium globosum Linnaeus, *Species Plantarum* 2: 767. 1753.
"Habitat Monspelii." RCN: 5653.
Lectotype (Katznelson in *Israel J. Bot.* 14: 172. 1965): Herb. Clifford: 374, *Trifolium* 12 (BM-000646745).
Current name: **Trifolium globosum** L. (Fabaceae: Faboideae).

Trifolium glomeratum Linnaeus, *Species Plantarum* 2: 770. 1753.
"Habitat in Anglia." RCN: 5668.
Lectotype (Rudd in Dassanayake & Fosberg, *Revised Handb. Fl. Ceylon* 1: 454. 1980): Herb. Clifford: 373, *Trifolium* 3 (BM-000646734).
Current name: **Trifolium glomeratum** L. (Fabaceae: Faboideae).

Trifolium hybridum Linnaeus, *Species Plantarum* 2: 766. 1753.
"Habitat in Europae Cultis." RCN: 5648.
Lectotype (Zohary & Heller, *Genus* Trifolium: 145. 1984): Herb. Linn. No. 930.15 (LINN).
Current name: **Trifolium hybridum** L. (Fabaceae: Faboideae).
Note: Zohary & Heller give BM as the location of the lectotype, but it is clear from the cited sheet number that this is a simple error for LINN.

Trifolium incarnatum Linnaeus, *Species Plantarum* 2: 769. 1753.
"Habitat in Italia." RCN: 5661.
Lectotype (Zohary in *Candollea* 27: 131. 1972): Herb. Linn. No. 930.32 (LINN).
Current name: **Trifolium incarnatum** L. (Fabaceae: Faboideae).

Trifolium indicum Linnaeus, *Species Plantarum* 2: 765. 1753.
"Habitat in India, Africa." RCN: 5638.
Lectotype (Ali in Nasir & Ali, *Fl. W. Pakistan* 100: 309. 1977): Herb. Linn. No. 930.2 (LINN).
Current name: **Melilotus indicus** (L.) All. (Fabaceae: Faboideae).
Note: Specific epithet spelled "M. indica" ["M." for "Melilotus"] in the protologue. Later corrected to *T. indicum* in *Systema Naturae*, ed. 10, 2: 1176 (1759). As is established custom, the "Melilotus" is to be ignored (see Art. 23.8 and Ex. 19).

Trifolium italicum Linnaeus, *Species Plantarum* 2: 765. 1753.
"Habitat in Italia." RCN: 5641.
Lectotype (Jafri in Jafri & El-Gadi, *Fl. Libya* 86: 220. 1980): Herb. Linn. No. 930.6 (LINN).
Current name: **Melilotus italicus** (L.) Lam. (Fabaceae: Faboideae).
Note: Specific epithet spelled "M. italica" ["M." for "Melilotus"] in the protologue. Later corrected to *T. italicum* in *Systema Naturae*, ed. 10, 2: 1176 (1759). As is established custom, the "Melilotus" is to be ignored (see Art. 23.8 and Ex. 19).

T

Trifolium lappaceum Linnaeus, *Species Plantarum* 2: 768. 1753.
"Habitat Monspelii." RCN: 5655.
Type not designated.
Original material: none traced.
Current name: ***Trifolium lappaceum*** L. (Fabaceae: Faboideae).
Note: Many authors have followed Zohary (in *Candollea* 27: 144. 1972) in treating 930.28 (LINN) as the type. However, this sheet is not annotated in a way to link it to this name, and is indeed the lectotype of another species, *T. alpestre* L. Although it is possible that Zohary cited sheet 930.28 in error for 930.23 (apparently original material for this name), this cannot be safely assumed, and the name remains at present untypified.

Trifolium lupinaster Linnaeus, *Species Plantarum* 2: 766. 1753.
"Habitat in Sibiria." RCN: 5645.
Lectotype (Gillett in *Canad. J. Bot.* 50: 1985. 1972): Herb. Linn. No. 930.13 (LINN).
Current name: ***Trifolium lupinaster*** L. (Fabaceae: Faboideae).

Trifolium medium Linnaeus, *Amoenitates Academicae* 4: 105. 1759.
"Habitat [in Anglia.]" RCN: 5658.
Lectotype (Zohary in *Candollea* 27: 118. 1972): Herb. Linn. No. 930.27 (LINN).
Current name: ***Trifolium medium*** L. (Fabaceae: Faboideae).

Trifolium messanense Linnaeus, *Mantissa Plantarum Altera*: 275. 1771.
"Habitat in Sicilia. H.U." RCN: 5644.
Lectotype (Ali in Nasir & Ali, *Fl. W. Pakistan* 100: 308. 1977): *Jacquin 9*, Herb. Linn. No. 930.11 (LINN).
Current name: ***Melilotus siculus*** (Turra) B.D. Jacks. (Fabaceae: Faboideae).

Trifolium montanum Linnaeus, *Species Plantarum* 2: 770. 1753.
"Habitat in pratis siccis Europae septentrionalis." RCN: 5676.
Lectotype (Jonsell & Jarvis in *Nordic J. Bot.* 22: 78. 2002): Herb. Linn. No. 930.56 (LINN).
Current name: ***Trifolium montanum*** L. subsp. ***montanum*** (Fabaceae: Faboideae).
Note: Zohary & Heller (*Genus* Trifolium: 228. 1984) indicated 930.56 (LINN) only doubtfully as the type so they cannot be accepted as having made an effective choice. Jonsell & Jarvis therefore made a formal typification.
    Linnaeus erred in giving the same name to two different European species of *Trifolium* in *Species Plantarum* in 1753 (p. 770, No. 29 and p. 772, No. 37). Realising this, he renamed the latter *T. spadiceum* L. in 1755.

Trifolium montanum Linnaeus, *Species Plantarum* 2: 772. 1753.
"Habitat in Europae pratis siccis." RCN: 5678.
Replaced synonym of: *Trifolium spadiceum* L. (1755).
Lectotype (Zohary & Heller, *Genus* Trifolium: 328. 1984): Herb. Linn. No. 930.60 (LINN).
Current name: ***Trifolium spadiceum*** L. (Fabaceae: Faboideae).
Note: Linnaeus erred in giving the same name to two different European species of *Trifolium* in *Species Plantarum* in 1753 (p. 770, No. 29 and p. 772, No. 37). Realising this, he renamed this one *T. spadiceum* L. in 1755.

Trifolium ochroleucum Linnaeus, *Systema Naturae*, ed. 12, 3: 233. 1768, *nom. illeg.*
"Habitat in Anglia, Helvetia." RCN: 5662.
Lectotype (Lassen in Turland & Jarvis in *Taxon* 46: 481. 1997): *Latourette*, Herb. Linn. No. 930.35, left specimen (LINN), see p. 219.

Current name: ***Trifolium ochroleucon*** Huds. (Fabaceae: Faboideae).
Note: A later homonym of *Trifolium ochroleucon* Huds. (1762) and hence illegitimate.

Trifolium officinale Linnaeus, *Species Plantarum* 2: 765. 1753.
"Habitat in Europae campestribus." RCN: 5640.
Lectotype (Sales & Hedge in *Anales Jard. Bot. Madrid* 51: 173. 1993): Herb. Burser XVIII(2): 64 (UPS).
Current name: ***Melilotus officinalis*** (L.) Lam. (Fabaceae: Faboideae).
Note: Specific epithet spelled "M. officinalis" ["M." for "Melilotus"] in the protologue. Later corrected to *T. officinale* in *Systema Naturae*, ed. 10, 2: 1176 (1759). As is established custom, the "Melilotus" is to be ignored (see Art. 23.8 and Ex. 19).
    Jafri (in Jafri & El-Gadi, *Fl. Libya* 86: 220. 1980) treated Herb. Linn. No. 930.4 (LINN) as the type, but this sheet is annotated "polnicum 3" by Linnaeus and is not original material for *T. officinale.*

Trifolium ornithopodioides Linnaeus, *Species Plantarum* 2: 766. 1753.
"Habitat in Anglia, Gallia." RCN: 5643.
Lectotype (Zohary & Heller, *Genus* Trifolium: 68. 1984): Herb. Clifford: 376, *Medicago* 2 (BM-000646769).
Current name: ***Trifolium ornithopodioides*** L. (Fabaceae: Faboideae).
Note: Specific epithet spelled "M. ornithopodioides" ["M." for "Melilotus"] in the protologue. Later corrected to *T. ornithopodioides* in *Systema Naturae*, ed. 10, 2: 1176 (1759). As is established custom, the "Melilotus" is to be ignored (see Art. 23.8 and Ex. 19).

Trifolium polonicum Linnaeus, *Species Plantarum* 2: 765. 1753.
"Habitat in Polonia." RCN: 5639.
Lectotype (Lassen in Turland & Jarvis in *Taxon* 46: 481. 1997): Herb. Linn. No. 930.4 (LINN).
Current name: ***Melilotus polonicus*** (L.) Pall. (Fabaceae: Faboideae).
Note: Specific epithet spelled "M. polonica" ["M." for "Melilotus"] in the protologue. Later corrected to *T. polonicum* in *Systema Naturae*, ed. 10, 2: 1176 (1759). As is established custom, the "Melilotus" is to be ignored (see Art. 23.8 and Ex. 19).

Trifolium pratense Linnaeus, *Species Plantarum* 2: 768. 1753.
"Habitat in Europae graminosis." RCN: 5657.
Lectotype (Polhill in Jarvis & al., *Regnum Veg.* 127: 96. 1993): Herb. Clifford: 375, *Trifolium* 16, sheet A (BM-000646751).
Generitype of *Trifolium* Linnaeus (vide Green, *Prop. Brit. Bot.*: 177. 1929).
Current name: ***Trifolium pratense*** L. (Fabaceae: Faboideae).
Note: Zohary (in *Candollea* 27: 112. 1972) indicated Clifford material (BM) as the type, but did not distinguish between two sheets associated with this name (which are not part of the same gathering so Art. 9.15 does not apply). Polhill subsequently designated one of these sheets as lectotype.

Trifolium procumbens Linnaeus, *Species Plantarum* 2: 772. 1753, *nom. utique rej.*
"Habitat in Europae campestribus." RCN: 5679.
Type not designated.
Original material: Herb. Linn. No. 930.62 (LINN); Herb. Linn. No. 930.61 (LINN); [icon] in Ray, Syn. Meth. Stirp. Brit., ed. 3: 330, t. 14, f. 3. 1724.
Current name: ***Trifolium campestre*** Schreb. (Fabaceae: Faboideae).
Note: Stearn (in *Biol. J. Linn. Soc.* 5: 12. 1973), in an account of Linnaeus' Öland and Gotland journey of 1741, treated Hoburg in Gotland as the restricted type locality, noting the existence of

930.63 (LINN) which was annotated by Linnaeus as from Gotland. Stearn noted that the name had been treated as a *nomen ambiguum*, and Turland & al. (in *Taxon* 45: 551. 1996) subsequently successfully proposed the name for rejection.

Trifolium reflexum Linnaeus, *Species Plantarum* 2: 766. 1753.
"Habitat in Virginia." RCN: 5646.
Lectotype (Vincent in Turland & Jarvis in *Taxon* 46: 481. 1997): *Clayton 289* (BM-000051808).
Current name: ***Trifolium reflexum*** L. var. ***reflexum*** (Fabaceae: Faboideae).

Trifolium repens Linnaeus, *Species Plantarum* 2: 767. 1753.
"Habitat in Europae pascuis." RCN: 5649.
Lectotype (Fawcett & Rendle, *Fl. Jamaica* 4: 13. 1920): Herb. Linn. No. 930.16 (LINN).
Current name: ***Trifolium repens*** L. (Fabaceae: Faboideae).
Note: Although Fawcett & Rendle stated only "Type in Herb. Linn.", there is only one sheet associated with this name so it is accepted as the lectotype. Rudd (in Dassanayake & Fosberg, *Revised Handb. Fl. Ceylon* 1: 453. 1980) subsequently treated Herb. Clifford: 375, *Trifolium* 18 (BM) as type but this choice is pre-dated by that of Fawcett & Rendle.

Trifolium resupinatum Linnaeus, *Species Plantarum* 2: 771. 1753.
"Habitat in Anglia, Belgio." RCN: 5673.
Lectotype (Ali in Nasir & Ali, *Fl. W. Pakistan* 100: 286. 1977): Herb. Linn. No. 930.52 (LINN).
Current name: ***Trifolium resupinatum*** L. (Fabaceae: Faboideae).

Trifolium retusum Linnaeus, *Demonstr. Pl. Horto Upsaliensi*: 21. 1753.
"Habitat in Hispania. Loefl."
Lectotype (Lassen in Turland & Jarvis in *Taxon* 46: 481. 1997): Herb. Linn. No. 930.14 (LINN).
Current name: ***Trifolium retusum*** L. (Fabaceae: Faboideae).

Trifolium rubens Linnaeus, *Species Plantarum* 2: 768. 1753.
"Habitat in Italia, G. Narbonensi, Helvetia." RCN: 5656.
Lectotype (Lassen in Turland & Jarvis in *Taxon* 46: 481. 1997): Herb. Clifford: 375, *Trifolium* 15, sheet 3 (BM-000646749).
Current name: ***Trifolium rubens*** L. (Fabaceae: Faboideae).
Note: Zohary (in *Candollea* 27: 127. 1972) indicated a specimen in Herb. Clifford (BM) as the lectotype, but it is unclear which of the two relevant specimens was intended. Lassen's subsequent choice is of the collection that supports current usage.

Trifolium scabrum Linnaeus, *Species Plantarum* 2: 770. 1753.
"Habitat in Anglia, Gallia, Italia." RCN: 5667.
Lectotype (Lassen in Turland & Jarvis in *Taxon* 46: 482. 1997): Herb. Linn. No. 930.42 (LINN).
Current name: ***Trifolium scabrum*** L. (Fabaceae: Faboideae).
Note: Zohary (in *Candollea* 27: 137. 1972), followed by several later authors, treated unspecified material in Herb. Clifford (BM) as syntypes. However, the two sheets there associated with this name are not part of a single gathering (so Art. 9.15 does not apply), nor were they explicitly cited by Linnaeus (so they are not syntypes). Lassen's later choice of material in LINN as lectotype is therefore accepted here.

Trifolium spadiceum Linnaeus, *Flora Suecica*, ed. 2: 261. 1755.
"Habitat in pratis montosis cum praecedente ad Gottsundam Upsaliae & alibi rarius." RCN: 5678.
Replaced synonym: *Trifolium montanum* L. (1753: 772, No. 37, non 1753: 770, No. 29).

Lectotype (Zohary & Heller, *Genus* Trifolium: 328. 1984): Herb. Linn. No. 930.60 (LINN).
Current name: ***Trifolium spadiceum*** L. (Fabaceae: Faboideae).
Note: Linnaeus erred in giving the same name to two different European species of *Trifolium* in *Species Plantarum* in 1753 (p. 770, No. 29 and p. 772, No. 37). Realising this, he renamed the latter *T. spadiceum* L. in 1755.

Trifolium spumosum Linnaeus, *Species Plantarum* 2: 771. 1753.
"Habitat in Gallia, Italia, Apulia." RCN: 5672.
Lectotype (Zohary & Heller, *Genus* Trifolium: 274. 1984): Herb. Clifford: 274, *Trifolium* 7 (BM-000646738).
Current name: ***Trifolium spumosum*** L. (Fabaceae: Faboideae).

Trifolium squamosum Linnaeus, *Amoenitates Academicae* 4: 105. 1759.
Lectotype (Lassen in Turland & Jarvis in *Taxon* 46: 482. 1997): [icon] *"Trifolium stellatum glabrum"* in Plukenet, Phytographia: t. 113, f. 4. 1691; Almag. Bot.: 376. 1696. – Voucher: Herb. Sloane 83: 96 (BM-SL). – Epitype (Lassen in Turland & Jarvis in *Taxon* 46: 482. 1997): United Kingdom. Avon, in pratis humidis juxta ripam fluvii prope Sea Mills non procul oppido Clifton in comitatu Gloucestrensi, 15 Jun 1883, *Trifolium maritimum. James W. White s.n.* (LD).
Current name: ***Trifolium squamosum*** L. (Fabaceae: Faboideae).

Trifolium squarrosum Linnaeus, *Species Plantarum* 2: 768. 1753.
"Habitat in Hispania." RCN: 5660.
Lectotype (Zohary in *Candollea* 27: 256. 1972): *Magnol*, Herb. Linn. No. 930.31 (LINN).
Current name: ***Trifolium squarrosum*** L. (Fabaceae: Faboideae).

Trifolium stellatum Linnaeus, *Species Plantarum* 2: 769. 1753.
"Habitat in Sicilia, Italia, G. Narbonensi." RCN: 5665.
Lectotype (Lassen in Turland & Jarvis in *Taxon* 46: 482. 1997): Herb. Linn. No. 930.39 (LINN).
Current name: ***Trifolium stellatum*** L. (Fabaceae: Faboideae).
Note: Zohary (in *Candollea* 27: 130. 1972) treated material in Herb. Clifford (BM) as syntypes. However, the two sheets there associated with this name are not part of a single gathering (so Art. 9.15 does not apply), nor were they explicitly cited by Linnaeus (so they are not syntypes). Lassen's later choice of material in LINN as lectotype is therefore accepted here. See earlier comments on this name by Jarvis (in *Webbia* 45: 111–113. 1991).

Trifolium striatum Linnaeus, *Species Plantarum* 2: 770. 1753.
"Habitat in Germania, Gallia, Hispania." RCN: 5669.
Lectotype (Lassen in Turland & Jarvis in *Taxon* 46: 482. 1997): Herb. Linn. No. 930.47, right specimen (LINN).
Current name: ***Trifolium striatum*** L. (Fabaceae: Faboideae).
Note: Zohary (in *Candollea* 27: 133. 1972), indicated *Löfling 565*, Herb. Linn. 930.45 (LINN) as a syntype. As it was not explicitly cited in the protologue, this collection cannot be a syntype and Lassen, because of doubts over the precise date of receipt of this material by Linnaeus, designated another collection in LINN as the lectotype.

Trifolium strictum Linnaeus, *Centuria I Plantarum*: 24. 1755.
"Habitat in Italiae pratis, pascuis." RCN: 5647.
Lectotype (Lassen in Turland & Jarvis in *Taxon* 46: 482. 1997): [icon] *"Trifoliastrum pratense, annuum, erectum, minimum, foliis longis, angustis, pulchre venatis, ac tenuissime serratis, floribus albis, in capitulum sphaericum congestis, siliquis minimis, dispermis"* in Micheli, Nov. Pl. Gen.: 29, t. 25, f. 7. 1729.
Current name: ***Trifolium strictum*** L. (Fabaceae: Faboideae).

T

Trifolium subterraneum Linnaeus, *Species Plantarum* 2: 767. 1753.
"Habitat in Galliae, Italia." RCN: 5652.
Lectotype (Katznelson & Morley in *Israel J. Bot.* 14: 123. 1965):
Herb. Clifford: 374, *Trifolium* 11 (BM-000646744).
Current name: ***Trifolium subterraneum*** L. (Fabaceae: Faboideae).

Trifolium suffocatum Linnaeus, *Mantissa Plantarum Altera*: 276.
1771.
"Habitat in Siciliae arenosis." RCN: 5682.
Lectotype (Lassen in Turland & Jarvis in *Taxon* 46: 482. 1997): [icon]
"Trifolium suffocatum" in Jacquin, Hort. Bot. Vindob. 1: 24, t. 60.
1770.
Current name: ***Trifolium suffocatum*** Jacq. (Fabaceae: Faboideae).
Note: This name was published by Linnaeus but without reference to
Jacquin. However, in Linnaeus' own copy of *Mant. Pl. Alt.* at
LINN, there is a reference to Jacquin written in, and "Jacq. hort." is
cited by Linnaeus in a later account (in *Syst. Veg.*, ed. 13: 574.
1774). Jacquin (1770) included a description with his binomial,
adding "Linn. mant. part. 2.". The two names are clearly the same
and, since Jacquin published a year before Linnaeus, the name is
attributable to him.

Trifolium tomentosum Linnaeus, *Species Plantarum* 2: 771. 1753.
"Habitat in G. Narbonensi, Hispania, Lusitania, D. Sauvages.
Loefling." RCN: 5674.
Lectotype (Zohary & Heller in *Israel J. Bot.* 19: 327. 1970): [icon]
"Trifolium fragiferum tomentosum" in Magnol, Bot. Monspel.: 265,
264. 1676.
Current name: ***Trifolium tomentosum*** L. (Fabaceae: Faboideae).

Trifolium uniflorum Linnaeus, *Species Plantarum* 2: 771. 1753.
"Habitat in Creta." RCN: 5671.
Lectotype (Jafri in Jafri & El-Gadi, *Fl. Libya* 86: 227. 1980):
Hasselquist, Herb. Linn. No. 930.50 (LINN).
Current name: ***Trifolium uniflorum*** L. (Fabaceae: Faboideae).
Note: Trifolium uniflorum L., *Cent. I Pl.*: 24. 1755 ("Habitat in
Constantinopoli, inque Syria, Arabia, Judaea. Hasselquist.") may
appear to be a later homonym of *T. uniflorum* L. (1753), and hence
illegitimate, because the cited illustrations (two Buxbaum figures)
for the former name, and the places mentioned in the "Habitat"
statement, are incorporated into *T. uniflorum sensu* L. (1753) in the
account in *Sp. Pl.*, ed. 2, 2: 1085. 1763. However, the lectotype of
the 1753 name, LINN 930.50, bears the symbol associated with
Hasselquist's collections, and also has a label with "uniflorum"
written on it. Therefore it seems preferable to treat *T. uniflorum* L.
(1755) as a partially modified reuse of *T. uniflorum* (1753), rather
than as an illegitimate later homonym.

Triglochin bulbosa Linnaeus, *Mantissa Plantarum Altera*: 226.
1771.
"Habitat ad Cap. b. spei." RCN: 2609.
Lectotype (Obermeyer in Codd & al., *Fl. Southern Africa* 1: 93. 1966):
Herb. Linn. No. 466.3 (LINN).
Current name: ***Triglochin bulbosa*** L. (Juncaginaceae).
Note: Although the material indicated as type by Obermeyer is almost
certainly not original material for the name (it is annotated only by
Linnaeus filius), the absence of any other candidates means that it
can be treated as a neotype (under Art. 9.8).

Triglochin maritima Linnaeus, *Species Plantarum* 1: 339. 1753.
"Habitat in Europae maritimis." RCN: 2610.
Lectotype (Dandy in Rechinger, *Fl. Iranica* 78: 1. 1971): Herb. Linn.
No. 466.2 (LINN).
Current name: ***Triglochin maritima*** L. (Juncaginaceae).
Note: Specific epithet spelled "maritimum" in the protologue.

Triglochin palustris Linnaeus, *Species Plantarum* 1: 338. 1753.
"Habitat in Europae inundatis uliginosis." RCN: 2608.
Lectotype (Simpson in Jarvis & al., *Regnum Veg.* 127: 96. 1993):
Herb. Linn. No. 466.1 (LINN).
Generitype of *Triglochin* Linnaeus (vide Hitchcock, *Prop. Brit. Bot.*:
148. 1929).
Current name: ***Triglochin palustris*** L. (Juncaginaceae).
Note: Specific epithet spelled "palustre" in the protologue.

Trigonella corniculata (Linnaeus) Linnaeus, *Systema Naturae*, ed. 10,
2: 1180. 1759.
["Habitat in Europa australi."] Sp. Pl. ed. 2, 2: 1094 (1763). RCN:
5707.
Basionym: *Trifolium corniculatum* L. (1753).
Lectotype (Greuter in Greuter & Rechinger in *Boissiera* 13: 78. 1967):
Herb. Linn. No. 932.8 (LINN).
Current name: ***Trigonella corniculata*** (L.) L. (Fabaceae: Faboideae).

Trigonella foenum-graecum Linnaeus, *Species Plantarum* 2: 777.
1753.
"Habitat Monspelii." RCN: 5710.
Lectotype (Westphal, *Pulses Ethiopia, Taxon. Agric. Signif.*: 199, 202.
1974): Herb. Linn. No. 932.16 (LINN).
Generitype of *Trigonella* Linnaeus (vide Green, *Prop. Brit. Bot.*: 177.
1929).
Current name: ***Trigonella foenum-graecum*** L. (Fabaceae: Faboideae).

Trigonella foenum-graecum Linnaeus var. **sylvestris** Linnaeus,
Systema Naturae, ed. 10, 2: 1180. 1759.
RCN: 5710.
Lectotype (Lassen in Turland & Jarvis in *Taxon* 46: 482. 1997): Herb.
Linn. No. 932.17 (LINN).
Current name: ***Trigonella gladiata*** M. Bieb. (Fabaceae: Faboideae).

Trigonella hamosa Linnaeus, *Systema Naturae*, ed. 10, 2: 1180. 1759,
nom. utique rej.
["Habitat in Aegypto. Hasselquist."] Sp. Pl. ed. 2, 2: 1094 (1763).
RCN: 5705.
Lectotype (Lassen in *Taxon* 36: 478. 1987): *Hasselquist*, Herb. Linn.
No. 932.5 (LINN; iso- UPS-HASSELQ 580, 581).
Current name: ***Trigonella hierosolymitana*** Boiss. (Fabaceae:
Faboideae).

Trigonella indica Linnaeus, *Species Plantarum* 2: 778. 1753.
"Habitat in India." RCN: 5711.
Lectotype (Rudd in Dassanayake & Fosberg, *Revised Handb. Fl.
Ceylon* 7: 184. 1991): Herb. Hermann 3: 24, No. 285 (BM-
000621888).
Current name: ***Rothia indica*** (L.) Druce (Fabaceae: Faboideae).

Trigonella laciniata Linnaeus, *Species Plantarum*, ed. 2, 2: 1095.
1763.
"Habitat in Aegypto. Burmannus." RCN: 5709.
Lectotype (Lassen in Turland & Jarvis in *Taxon* 46: 482. 1997): Herb.
Linn. No. 932.15 (LINN).
Current name: ***Trigonella laciniata*** L. (Fabaceae: Faboideae).

Trigonella monspeliaca Linnaeus, *Species Plantarum* 2: 777. 1753.
"Habitat Monspelii." RCN: 5708.
Lectotype (Lassen in Turland & Jarvis in *Taxon* 46: 482. 1997): Herb.
Linn. No. 932.13, right specimen (LINN).
Current name: ***Medicago monspeliaca*** (L.) Trautv. (Fabaceae:
Faboideae).
Note: Ali (in Nasir & Ali, *Fl. W. Pakistan* 100: 292. 1977) and others
have treated Herb. Linn. No. 932.12 (LINN) as the lectotype, but

this cannot be regarded as relevant original material because it lacks Linnaeus' annotation with the *Species Plantarum* species number (in this case "5") and is a post-1753 addition to the collection and not original material for the name.

Trigonella platycarpos Linnaeus, *Species Plantarum* 2: 776. 1753.
"Habitat in Sibiria." RCN: 5703.
Lectotype (Lassen in Turland & Jarvis in *Taxon* 46: 483. 1997): Herb. Linn. No. 932.2 (LINN).
Current name: ***Medicago platycarpos*** (L.) Trautv. (Fabaceae: Faboideae).

Trigonella polyceratia Linnaeus, *Species Plantarum* 2: 777. 1753.
"Habitat in Hispania." RCN: 5704.
Lectotype (Lassen in Turland & Jarvis in *Taxon* 46: 483. 1997): Herb. Linn. No. 932.4 (LINN).
Current name: ***Medicago polyceratia*** (L.) Trautv. (Fabaceae: Faboideae).

Trigonella ruthenica Linnaeus, *Species Plantarum* 2: 776. 1753.
"Habitat in Sibiria." RCN: 5702.
Lectotype (Lassen in Turland & Jarvis in *Taxon* 46: 483. 1997): Herb. Linn. No. 932.1 (LINN).
Current name: ***Medicago ruthenica*** (L.) Trautv. (Fabaceae: Faboideae).

Trigonella spinosa Linnaeus, *Species Plantarum* 2: 777. 1753.
"Habitat in Creta." RCN: 5706.
Lectotype (Lassen in Turland & Jarvis in *Taxon* 46: 483. 1997): Herb. Linn. No. 932.7 (LINN).
Current name: ***Trigonella spinosa*** L. (Fabaceae: Faboideae).

Trilix lutea Linnaeus, *Mantissa Plantarum Altera*: 247. 1771.
"Habitat Carthagenae Americes." RCN: 3815.
Type not designated.
Original material: none traced.
Generitype of *Trilix* Linnaeus.
Current name: ***Prockia crucis*** L. (Flacourtiaceae).
Note: Sleumer (*Fl. Neotropica* 22: 68. 1980) indicated unseen Mútis material at MA as holotype. Such material would not have been seen by Linnaeus and would not be original material for the name. However, if this material exists (it is unclear from Sleumer's statement if he knew it to exist or if he merely hoped it might be found at MA), it should be accepted as a neotype in accordance with Art. 9.8.

Trillium cernuum Linnaeus, *Species Plantarum* 1: 339. 1753.
"Habitat in Carolina." RCN: 2617.
Lectotype (Gleason in *Bull. Torrey Bot. Club* 33: 390. 1906): Kalm, Herb. Linn. No. 469.1 (LINN; iso- UPS).
Generitype of *Trillium* Linnaeus (vide Hitchcock, *Prop. Brit. Bot.*: 148. 1929).
Current name: ***Trillium cernuum*** L. (Liliaceae/Trilliaceae).
Note: Although Rendle (in *J. Bot.* 39: 332. 1901) discussed the original elements for this name, including the Kalm specimen in LINN, he did not refer to any of them as the type. See Reveal (in *Phytologia* 72: 1. 1992) for a more recent review.

Trillium erectum Linnaeus, *Species Plantarum* 1: 340. 1753.
"Habitat in Virginia." RCN: 2618.
Lectotype (Reveal in *Phytologia* 72: 2. 1992): [icon] *"Solanum triphyllum Canadense"* in Cornut, Canad. Pl. Hist.: 166, 167. 1635 (see p. 123).
Current name: ***Trillium erectum*** L. (Liliaceae/Trilliaceae).

Trillium sessile Linnaeus, *Species Plantarum* 1: 340. 1753.
"Habitat in Virginia, Carolina." RCN: 2619.
Lectotype (Freeman in *Brittonia* 27: 11. 1975): *Clayton 856* (BM-000051758).
Current name: ***Trillium sessile*** L. (Liliaceae/Trilliaceae).
Note: See also review by Reveal (in *Phytologia* 72: 2. 1992).

Triopterys jamaicensis Linnaeus, *Species Plantarum* 1: 428. 1753.
"Habitat in America calidiore." RCN: 3329.
Lectotype (Anderson in Jarvis & al., *Regnum Veg.* 127: 96. 1993): Herb. Clifford: 169, *Triopteris* 1 (BM-000628499).
Generitype of *Triopterys* Linnaeus, *nom. & orth. cons.*
Current name: ***Triopterys jamaicensis*** L. (Malpighiaceae).

Triosteum angustifolium Linnaeus, *Species Plantarum* 1: 176. 1753.
"Habitat in Virginia." RCN: 1385.
Type not designated.
Original material: *Clayton 626* (BM); [icon] in Plukenet, Phytographia: t. 104, f. 2. 1691; Almag. Bot.: 287. 1696.
Current name: ***Triosteum angustifolium*** L. (Caprifoliaceae).

Triosteum perfoliatum Linnaeus, *Species Plantarum* 1: 176. 1753.
"Habitat in America septentrionali." RCN: 1384.
Lectotype (Reveal in Jarvis & al., *Regnum Veg.* 127: 96. 1993): [icon] *"Triosteospermum latiore folio, flore rutilo"* in Dillenius, Hort. Eltham. 2: 394, t. 293, f. 378. 1732.
Generitype of *Triosteum* Linnaeus (vide Hitchcock, *Prop. Brit. Bot.*: 131. 1929).
Current name: ***Triosteum perfoliatum*** L. (Caprifoliaceae).

Triplaris americana Linnaeus, *Systema Naturae,* ed. 10, 2: 881. 1759.
["Habitat in America meridionali."] Sp. Pl., ed. 2, 1: 130 (1762). RCN: 737.

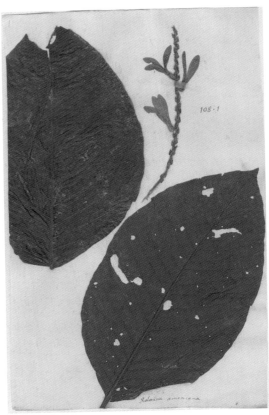

Lectotype (Dugand in *Caldasia* 8: 388. 1960): Herb. Linn. No. 108.1 (LINN), see p. 901.
Generitype of *Triplaris* Linnaeus.
Current name: **Triplaris americana** L. (Polygonaceae).

Tripsacum dactyloides (Linnaeus) Linnaeus, *Systema Naturae*, ed. 10, 2: 1261. 1759.
["Habitat in America."] Sp. Pl. 2: 972 (1753). RCN: 7050.
Basionym: *Coix dactyloides* L. (1753).
Lectotype (Hitchcock in *Contr. U. S. Natl. Herb.* 12: 124. 1908): Herb. Linn. No. 1097.1 (LINN).
Generitype of *Tripsacum* Linnaeus.
Current name: **Tripsacum dactyloides** (L.) L. (Poaceae).

Tripsacum hermaphrodita Linnaeus, *Systema Naturae*, ed. 10, 2: 1261. 1759.
["Habitat in Jamaica."] Sp. Pl., ed. 2, 2: 1379 (1763). RCN: 7051.
Lectotype (Davidse in Cafferty & al. in *Taxon* 49: 257. 2000): Herb. Linn. No. 1097.2 (LINN).
Current name: **Anthephora hermaphrodita** (L.) Kuntze (Poaceae).
Note: Judziewicz (in Görts-van Rijn, *Fl. Guianas*, ser. A, 8: 58. 1990) indicated 1097.2 (LINN) as a "possible holotype...not seen", which is inadequate as a type designation. However, this sheet appears to be the only extant original material for the name, and was formally chosen as the lectotype by Davidse.

Triticum aestivum Linnaeus, *Species Plantarum* 1: 85. 1753, *nom. cons.*
"Habitat – – – –" RCN: 718.
Lectotype (Bowden in *Canad. J. Bot.* 37: 674. 1959): Herb. Clifford: 24, *Triticum* 3 (BM-000557670).
Generitype of *Triticum* Linnaeus (vide Hitchcock in *Amer. J. Bot.* 10: 513. 1923).
Current name: **Triticum aestivum** L. (Poaceae).
Note: Triticum aestivum is conserved against *T. hybernum* L. (1753). Although the types of both names are listed in their Vienna Code entries (2006: 464), neither type is conserved.
    Hanelt & al. in *Taxon* 32: 492 (1983) provided a review of the typification of the name, and illustrated the type (as f. 1).

Triticum caninum Linnaeus, *Species Plantarum* 1: 86. 1753.
"Habitat in Europae sepibus." RCN: 704.
Basionym of: *Elymus caninus* (L.) L. (1755).
Lectotype (Cope & van Slageren in Cafferty & al. in *Taxon* 49: 258. 2000): Herb. Linn. No. 100.10 (LINN; iso- US, fragm.).
Current name: **Agropyron caninum** (L.) P. Beauv. (Poaceae).
Note: Although Kerguélen (in *Lejeunia*, n.s., 75: 252. 1975) stated "Type: ...LINN", this is not accepted as a formal typification, for the reasons explained by Cafferty & al. (in *Taxon* 49: 240. 2000).

Triticum compositum Linnaeus, *Systema Vegetabilium*, ed. 13: 108. 1774.
RCN: 720.
Neotype (Cope in Cafferty & al. in *Taxon* 49: 258. 2000): Cultivated. "*Triticum compositum* L. Introdotto nella coltura del basso Egitto", Herb. Figari (K; iso- FI).
Current name: **Gigachilon polonicum** (L.) Seidl subsp. **turgidum** (L.) Á. Löve (Poaceae).

Triticum hybernum Linnaeus, *Species Plantarum* 1: 86. 1753, *nom. rej.*
"Habitat – – – –" RCN: 719.
Lectotype (Hanelt & al. in *Taxon* 32: 496, f. 2. 1983): Herb. Clifford: 24, *Triticum* 2 (BM-000557669).
Current name: **Triticum aestivum** L. (Poaceae).

Note: Triticum hybernum is rejected in favour of *T. aestivum* L. (1753). Although the types of both names are listed in their Vienna Code entries (2006: 464), neither type is conserved.

Triticum junceum Linnaeus, *Centuria I Plantarum*: 6. 1755.
"Habitat in Helvetia, Oriente." RCN: 725.
Lectotype (Jarvie in *Nordic J. Bot.* 12: 167. 1992; Jarvie in Cafferty & al. in *Taxon* 49: 258. 2000): *Hasselquist*, Herb. Linn. No. 104.5 (LINN; iso- 104.6 LINN).
Current name: **Elytrigia juncea** (L.) Nevski (Poaceae).
Note: Löve (in *Feddes Repert.* 95: 476. 1984) stated "... quoad pl. lectotyp. Ab HASSELQUIST lectam", without indicating any sheet or location. Jarvie (in *Nordic J. Bot.* 12: 167. 1992) indicated material at LINN as type, but did not distinguish between sheets 104.5 and 104.6 (which might well be part of a single gathering). Jarvie subsequently restricted his earlier choice to one of them, in accordance with Art. 9.15.

Triticum maritimum Linnaeus, *Species Plantarum*, ed. 2, 1: 128. 1762.
"Habitat in Galliae & Angliae maritimis." RCN: 727.
Lectotype (Stace & Jarvis in *Bot. J. Linn. Soc.* 91: 441. 1985): *Alströmer 20*, Herb. Linn. No. 104.11 (LINN).
Current name: **Cutandia maritima** (L.) Barbey (Poaceae).
Note: Meikle (*Fl. Cyprus* 2: 1724. 23 Apr 1985) indicated unspecified material in LINN as type but did not distinguish between sheets 104.11, 104.12 and 104.13 (which are not part of a single gathering so Art. 9.15 does not apply). Stace & Jarvis' typification (in *Bot. J. Linn. Soc.* 91: 441. 11 Dec 1985) is more detailed than that of Stace (in Davis, *Fl. Turkey* 9: 468. Dec 1985), published in the same month but with the precise date unknown.

Triticum monococcum Linnaeus, *Species Plantarum* 1: 86. 1753.
"Habitat – – – –" RCN: 724.
Lectotype (Bowden in *Canad. J. Bot.* 37: 664. 1959): Herb. Linn. No. 104.4 (LINN).
Current name: **Triticum monococcum** L. (Poaceae).

Triticum polonicum Linnaeus, *Species Plantarum*, ed. 2, 1: 127. 1762.
"Habitat – – – –" RCN: 722.
Lectotype (Bowden in *Canad. J. Bot.* 37: 670. 1959): *Scheuchzer*, Herb. Linn. No. 104.3 (LINN), see p. 227.
Current name: **Gigachilon polonicum** (L.) Seidl subsp. **polonicum** (Poaceae).

Triticum repens Linnaeus, *Species Plantarum* 1: 86. 1753.
"Habitat in Europae cultis." RCN: 726.
Lectotype (Bowden in *Canad. J. Bot.* 43: 1431. 1965): Herb. Linn. No. 104.7 (LINN).
Current name: **Elytrigia repens** (L.) Nevski (Poaceae).

Triticum spelta Linnaeus, *Species Plantarum* 1: 86. 1753.
"Habitat – – –" RCN: 723.
Lectotype (Morrison in *Taxon* 47: 709. 1998): Herb. Linn. No. 104.1 (LINN).
Current name: **Triticum spelta** L. (Poaceae).

Triticum tenellum Linnaeus, *Systema Naturae*, ed. 10, 2: 880. 1759.
["Habitat Monspelii? Sauvages."] Sp. Pl. ed. 2, 1: 127 (1762). RCN: 728.
Neotype (Meikle, *Fl. Cyprus* 2: 1723. 1985): Herb. Linn. No. 104.14 (LINN).
Current name: **Micropyrum tenellum** (L.) Link (Poaceae).
Note: Specific epithet spelled "tenenellum" in *Sp. Pl.* ed. 2, 1: 127 (1763).

Although Meikle (*Fl. Cyprus* 2: 1723. 23 Apr 1985) indicated unspecified material in LINN as type, there is only one collection that can be associated with this name. Stace & Jarvis (in *Bot. J. Linn. Soc.* 91: 439. 11 Dec 1985) independently discussed and typified *T. tenellum*, concluding that the same Linnaean material should be a neotype, rather than a lectotype, because of the absence of any Linnaean annotation on the sheet. Neotypification is therefore attributed to Meikle (Art. 9.8).

Triticum turgidum Linnaeus, *Species Plantarum* 1: 86. 1753.
"Habitat – – – –" RCN: 721.
Lectotype (Morrison in *Taxon* 47: 707. 1998): Herb. A. van Royen No. 913.62–257 (L).
Current name: ***Gigachilon polonicum*** (L.) Seidl subsp. ***turgidum*** (L.) Á. Löve (Poaceae).
Note: Bowden (in *Canad. J. Bot.* 37: 669. 1959) designated 104.2 (LINN) as lectotype. However, Morrison (in *Taxon* 47: 705. 1998) has found that this material belongs not to *T. turgidum* but rather to *T. aestivum*. From the annotations, Morrison argues that 104.2 (LINN) was not original material for *T. turgidum* (but rather for *T. hybernum*) and rejects Bowden's typification, choosing a van Royen sheet as lectotype in its place.

Triticum unilaterale Linnaeus, *Systema Naturae*, ed. 12, 2: 102; *Mantissa Plantarum*: 35. 1767.
"Habitat in maritimis Italiae, Galliae australis." RCN: 729.
Lectotype (Stace & Jarvis in *Bot. J. Linn. Soc.* 91: 442. 1985): Herb. Linn. No. 104.15 (LINN).
Current name: ***Vulpia unilateralis*** (L.) Stace (Poaceae).

Triumfetta annua Linnaeus, *Systema Naturae*, ed. 12, 2: 327; *Mantissa Plantarum*: 73. 1767.
"Habitat in India orientali." RCN: 3453.
Lectotype (Wild in Leistner, *Fl. Southern Africa* 21(1): 25. 1984): [icon] "*Triumfetta foliis oblongo-ovatis obtuse serratis petiolis longissimis*" in Miller, Fig. Pl. Gard. Dict. 2: 199, t. 298. 1760.
Current name: ***Triumfetta annua*** L. (Tiliaceae).

Triumfetta bartramii Linnaeus, *Systema Naturae*, ed. 10, 2: 1044. 1759, *nom. illeg.*
["Habitat in India."] Sp. Pl., ed. 2, 1: 638 (1762). RCN: 3451.
Replaced synonym: *Bartramia indica* L. (1753).
Lectotype (Fawcett & Rendle, *Fl. Jamaica* 5: 82. 1926): Herb. Hermann 1: 44, No. 174 (BM-000621387).
Current name: ***Triumfetta rhomboidea*** Jacq. (Tiliaceae).
Note: As noted by Fosberg & Sachet (in *Smithsonian Contr. Bot.* 47: 36. 1981), this is a superfluous name for *Bartramia indica* L. (1753).

Triumfetta lappula Linnaeus, *Species Plantarum* 1: 444. 1753.
"Habitat in Jamaica, Brasilia, Bermudis." RCN: 3450.
Type not designated.
Original material: Herb. Clifford: 210, *Triumfetta* 1 (BM); Herb. Linn. No. 620.1 (LINN); [icon] in Plukenet, Phytographia: t. 245, f. 7. 1692; Almag. Bot.: 206. 1696.
Generitype of *Triumfetta* Linnaeus.
Current name: ***Triumfetta lappula*** L. (Tiliaceae).

Trollius asiaticus Linnaeus, *Species Plantarum* 1: 557. 1753.
"Habitat in Sibiria, Cappadocia." RCN: 4102.
Lectotype (Siplivinsky in *Novosti Sist. Vyssh. Rast.* 9: 168. 1972): *Gerber*, Herb. Linn. No. 716.2 (LINN).
Current name: ***Trollius asiaticus*** L. (Ranunculaceae).

Trollius europaeus Linnaeus, *Species Plantarum* 1: 556. 1753.
"Habitat in Alpibus & subalpinis Sueciae, Germaniae, Angliae." RCN: 4101.

Lectotype (Siplivinsky in *Novosti Sist. Vyssh. Rast.* 9: 165. 1972): Herb. Linn. No. 716.1 (LINN).
Generitype of *Trollius* Linnaeus.
Current name: ***Trollius europaeus*** L. (Ranunculaceae).
Note: Specific epithet spelled "europeus" in the protologue.
Jonsell & Jarvis (in Jarvis & al., *Regnum Veg.* 127: 96. 1993), with discussion in *Nordic J. Bot.* 14: 162 (1994), designated material in LINN as the lectotype, unaware of Siplivinsky's earlier type choice based on the same material.

Tropaeolum hybridum Linnaeus, *Systema Naturae*, ed. 12, 2: 263; *Mantissa Plantarum*: 64. 1767, *nom. illeg.*
"Habitat nullibi, enata Holmiae in Horto Ehrenreich, semine rarius propaganda planta. Hort. Upsal." RCN: 2646.
Replaced synonym: *Tropaeolum quinquelobum* P.J. Bergius (1765).
Lectotype (Sparre & Andersson in *Opera Bot.* 108: 67. 1991): Herb. Bergius (SBT).
Current name: ***Tropaeolum majus*** L. (Tropaeolaceae).
Note: As noted by Sparre (in *Bot. Not.* 118: 448. 1965), this is a superfluous name for *Tropaeolum quinquelobum* P.J. Bergius (1765).

Tropaeolum majus Linnaeus, *Species Plantarum* 1: 345; *Species Plantarum* 2: Errata. 1753.
"Habitat in Peru, unde in Europam venit 1684 cura Bewerningii." RCN: 2645.
Lectotype (Sparre in *Bot. Not.* 118: 448. 1965): Herb. Clifford: 143, *Tropaeolum* 1 (BM-000558602).
Generitype of *Tropaeolum* Linnaeus (vide Hitchcock, *Prop. Brit. Bot.*: 149. 1929).
Current name: ***Tropaeolum majus*** L. (Tropaeolaceae).
Note: See additional discussion by Sparre & Andersson (in *Opera Bot.* 108: 67. 1991).

Tropaeolum minus Linnaeus, *Species Plantarum* 1: 345; *Species Plantarum* 2: Errata. 1753.
"Habitat in Peru, Lima." RCN: 2644.
Lectotype (Sparre in *Bot. Not.* 118: 448. 1965): Herb. Burser XVII: 79 (UPS).
Current name: ***Tropaeolum minus*** L. (Tropaeolaceae).
Note: See additional discussion by Sparre & Andersson (in *Opera Bot.* 108: 64. 1991).

Tropaeolum peregrinum Linnaeus, *Species Plantarum* 1: 345. 1753.
"Habitat in Peru, nondum mihi visa in Europa." RCN: 2647.
Lectotype (Sparre in *Bot. Not.* 118: 449. 1965): [icon] "*Cardamindum quinquefido folio, vulgo Malla*" in Feuillée, J. Obs. 2: 756, t. 42. 1714.
Current name: ***Tropaeolum peregrinum*** L. (Tropaeolaceae).
Note: Sparre (in *Bot. Not.* 119: 338, f. 1. 1966) reproduces the lectotype figure.

Trophis americana Linnaeus, *Systema Naturae*, ed. 10, 2: 1289. 1759.
["Habitat in Jamaica."] Sp. Pl. ed. 2, 2: 1451 (1763). RCN: 7400.
Lectotype (Berg in Harling & Andersson, *Fl. Ecuador* 60: 18. 1998): [icon] "*Trophis foliis oblongo-ovatis glabris alternis, floribus masculinis spicatis ad alas*" in Browne, Civ. Nat. Hist. Jamaica: 357, t. 37, f. 1. 1756.
Current name: ***Trophis racemosa*** (L.) Urb. (Moraceae).

Tubularia acetabulum (Linnaeus) Linnaeus, *Systema Naturae*, ed. 12, 1(2): 1303. 1767.
Basionym: *Madrepora acetabulum* L. (1758).
Lectotype (John in Spencer & al. in *Taxon*, in press): [icon] "*Acetabulum*" in Tournefort, Inst. Rei Herb.: 569, t. 338. 1700.
Current name: ***Acetabularia acetabulum*** (L.) P.C. Silva (Dasycladaceae).

Tubularia fragilis (Linnaeus) Linnaeus, *Systema Naturae,* ed. 12, 1(2): 1302. 1767.
"Habitat in O. Americano."
Basionym: *Eschara fragilis* L. (1758).
Lectotype (Huisman & Townsend in *Bot. J. Linn. Soc.* 113: 100, f. 1. 1993): Herb. Linn. No. 1297.1, upper specimen (LINN).
Current name: ***Tricleocarpa fragilis*** (L.) Huisman & R.A. Towns. (Galaxauraceae).

Tulbaghia capensis Linnaeus, *Mantissa Plantarum Altera*: 223. 1771.
"Habitat ad Cap. b. spei." RCN: 2303.
Lectotype (Burbidge in *Notes Roy. Bot. Gard. Edinburgh* 36: 77, 84. 1978): Herb. Linn. No. 411.1 (LINN).
Generitype of *Tulbaghia* Linnaeus, *nom. & orth. cons.*
Current name: ***Tulbaghia capensis*** L. (Liliaceae/Alliaceae).
Note: Tulbaghia Linnaeus (1771), *nom. cons.* against *Tulbaghia* Heist. (1755).

Tulipa breyniana Linnaeus, *Species Plantarum* 1: 306. 1753.
"Habitat in Aethiopia." RCN: 2407.

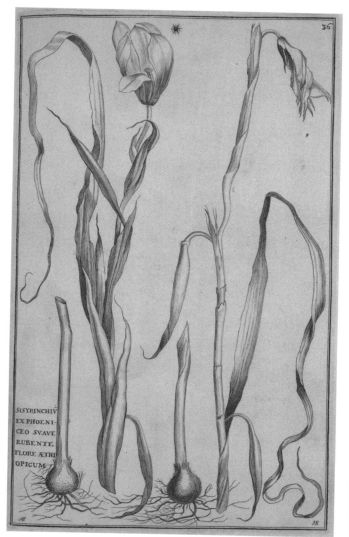

Lectotype (Lewis in *J. S. African Bot.* 7: 59. 1941): [icon] *"Sisyrinchium ex phoeniceo suave rubente flore Aethiopicum"* in Breyn, Exot. Pl. Cent.: 83, t. 36. 1678.

Current name: ***Homeria breyniana*** (L.) G.J. Lewis (Iridaceae).
Note: Lewis (in *J. S. African Bot.* 7: 59. 1941) formally chose the Breyn plate as the type, accepted it as belonging to what had been known as *Homeria collina* (Thunb.) Vent., and made the combination *H. breyniana* (L.) G.J. Lewis for it. However, other authors, notably Goldblatt (in *J. S. African Bot.* 39: 139, f. 2. 1982), have been less certain of the identity of the type and appear to have informally rejected the name in favour of *H. collina*.

Tulipa gesneriana Linnaeus, *Species Plantarum* 1: 306. 1753.
"Habitat in Cappadocia, unde in Europam 1559." RCN: 2406.
Lectotype (Dasgupta & Deb in *Candollea* 40: 158. 1985): Herb. Linn. No. 425.2 (LINN).
Generitype of *Tulipa* Linnaeus (vide Hitchcock, *Prop. Brit. Bot.*: 145. 1929).
Current name: ***Tulipa gesneriana*** L. (Liliaceae).

Tulipa sylvestris Linnaeus, *Species Plantarum* 1: 305. 1753.
"Habitat Monspelii, inque Apenninis, Lundini." RCN: 405.
Lectotype (van Raamsdonk in Wisskirchen in *Feddes Repert.* 108: 106. 1997): Herb. Linn. No. 425.1 (LINN).
Current name: ***Tulipa sylvestris*** L. (Liliaceae).

Turnera cistoides Linnaeus, *Species Plantarum*, ed. 2, 1: 387. 1762.
"Habitat in America meridionali, Jamaica, Surinami." RCN: 2156.
Lectotype (Arbo in *Ann. Missouri Bot. Gard.* 77: 350. 1990): *Rolander,* Herb. Linn. No. 384.6 (LINN).
Current name: ***Piriqueta cistoides*** (L.) Griseb. (Turneraceae).

Turnera pumilea Linnaeus, *Systema Naturae,* ed. 10, 2: 965. 1759.
["Habitat in Jamaica."] Sp. Pl., ed. 2, 1: 387 (1762). RCN: 2154.
Type not designated.
Original material: *Browne,* Herb. Linn. No. 384. 4 (LINN); [icon] in Sloane, Voy. Jamaica 1: 202, t. 127, f. 6. 1707.
Current name: ***Turnera pumilea*** L. (Turneraceae).

Turnera sidoides Linnaeus, *Systema Naturae,* ed. 12, 2: 220; *Mantissa Plantarum*: 58. 1767.
"Habitat in Brasilia. D. Arduini." RCN: 2155.
Lectotype (Arbo in *Candollea* 40: 184. 1985): Herb. Linn. No. 384.5 (LINN).
Current name: ***Turnera sidoides*** L. (Turneraceae).

Turnera ulmifolia Linnaeus, *Species Plantarum* 1: 271. 1753.
"Habitat in Jamaica & in America calidiore." RCN: 2153.
Lectotype (Stearn, *Introd. Linnaeus' Sp. Pl.* (Ray Soc. ed.): 47. 1957): [icon] *"Turnera e petiolo florens, foliis serratis"* in Linnaeus, Hort. Cliff.: 112, t. 10. 1738.
Generitype of *Turnera* Linnaeus.
Current name: ***Turnera ulmifolia*** L. (Turneraceae).

Turraea virens Linnaeus, *Mantissa Plantarum Altera*: 237. 1771.
"Habitat in India orientali. Koenig." RCN: 3029.
Lectotype (Mabberley & Cheek in *Taxon* 41: 544. 1992): *König s.n.,* Herb. Linn. No. 549.1 (LINN; iso- BM).
Generitype of *Turraea* Linnaeus.
Current name: ***Turraea virens*** L. (Meliaceae).

Turritis alpina Linnaeus, *Systema Naturae,* ed. 12, 2: 443. 1767.
RCN: 4847.
Lectotype (Al-Shehbaz & Turland in Cafferty & Jarvis in *Taxon* 51: 536. 2002): Herb. Linn. No. 843.3, right specimen (LINN).
Current name: ***Arabis hirsuta*** (L.) Scop. var. ***glaberrima*** Wahlenb. (Brassicaceae).

Turritis glabra Linnaeus, *Species Plantarum* 2: 666. 1753.
"Habitat in Europae pascuis siccis apricis." RCN: 4845.
Lectotype (Jafri in Nasir & Ali, *Fl. W. Pakistan* 55: 183. 1973; Talavera & Velayos in *Anales Jard. Bot. Madrid* 50: 147. 1992): Herb. Linn. No. 843.1, right specimen (LINN).
Generitype of *Turritis* Linnaeus (vide Green, *Prop. Brit. Bot.*: 171. 1929).
Current name: ***Turritis glabra*** L. (Brassicaceae).
Note: Jafri (in Nasir & Ali, *Fl. W. Pakistan* 55: 183. 1973) indicated 843.1 (LINN) as the type and Talavera & Velayos (in *Anales Jard. Bot. Madrid* 50: 14. 1992) restricted this choice to the right of the three specimens mounted on the sheet.

Turritis hirsuta Linnaeus, *Species Plantarum* 2: 666. 1753.
"Habitat in Sueciae, Germaniae, Angliae pascuis sylvaticis." RCN: 4846.
Lectotype (Titz in *Feddes Repert.* 87: 496. 1976): [icon] *"Erysimo similis hirsuta alba"* in Bauhin, Prodr. Theatri Bot.: 42. 1620.
Current name: ***Arabis hirsuta*** (L.) Scop. (Brassicaceae).

Tussilago alba Linnaeus, *Species Plantarum* 2: 866. 1753.
"Habitat in Europa." RCN: 6266.
Lectotype (Toman in *Folia Geobot. Phytotax.* 7: 385. 1972): Herb. Linn. No. 995.20 (LINN).
Current name: ***Petasites albus*** (L.) Gaertn. (Asteraceae).

Tussilago alpina Linnaeus, *Species Plantarum* 2: 865. 1753.
"Habitat in Alpibus Helvetiae, Austriae, Bohemiae." RCN: 6262.
Type not designated.
Original material: Herb. A. van Royen No. 900.337–75 (L); Herb. Burser X: 149 (UPS); Herb. Burser X: 148 (UPS); Herb. Clifford: 411, *Tussilago* 2 (BM); [icon] in Clusius, Rar. Pl. Hist. 2: 113. 1601; [icon] (var. β) in Clusius, Rar. Pl. Hist. 2: 113. 1601.
Current name: ***Homogyne alpina*** (L.) Cass. (Asteraceae).

Tussilago anandria Linnaeus, *Species Plantarum* 2: 865. 1753.
"Habitat in Sibiria." RCN: 6259.
Lectotype (Hansen in *Nordic J. Bot.* 8: 68. 1988): Herb. Linn. No. 995.1 (LINN).
Current name: ***Leibnitzia anandria*** (L.) Turcz. (Asteraceae).

Tussilago dentata Linnaeus, *Species Plantarum,* ed. 2, 2: 1213. 1763.
"Habitat in America." RCN: 6260.
Lectotype (Nesom in *Brittonia* 36: 397. 1984): [icon] *"Tussilago scapo nudo unifloro"* in Plumier in Burman, Pl. Amer.: 28, t. 40, f. 2. 1756.
Current name: ***Chaptalia dentata*** (L.) Cass. (Asteraceae).

Tussilago farfara Linnaeus, *Species Plantarum* 2: 865. 1753.
"Habitat in Europae argillosis subtus humidis." RCN: 6263.
Lectotype (Rechinger, *Fl. Iranica* 164: 44. 1989): Herb. Linn. No. 995.10 (LINN).
Generitype of *Tussilago* Linnaeus (vide Green, *Prop. Brit. Bot.*: 181. 1929).
Current name: ***Tussilago farfara*** L. (Asteraceae).

Tussilago frigida Linnaeus, *Species Plantarum* 2: 865. 1753.
"Habitat in Alpium Lapponiae, Helvetiae, Sibiriae convallibus." RCN: 6265.
Lectotype (Toman in *Folia Geobot. Phytotax.* 7: 389. 1972): Herb. Linn. No. 995.17 (LINN; iso- LAPP?).
Current name: ***Petasites frigidus*** (L.) Fr. (Asteraceae).

Tussilago hybrida Linnaeus, *Species Plantarum* 2: 866. 1753.
"Habitat in Germania, Hollandia." RCN: 6267.

Lectotype (Rechinger, *Fl. Iranica* 164: 43. 1989): Herb. Linn. No. 995.24 (LINN).
Current name: ***Petasites hybridus*** (L.) Gaertn. (Asteraceae).

Tussilago japonica Linnaeus, *Systema Naturae,* ed. 12, 2: 550; *Mantissa Plantarum*: 113. 1767.
"Habitat in Japonia." RCN: 6264.
Type not designated.
Original material: none traced.
Current name: ***Farfugium japonicum*** (L.) Kitam. (Asteraceae).
Note: Lawrence (in *Baileya* 5: 98. 1957) stated that Linnaeus knew this from a Japanese collection by Kleynhoff but did not designate a type.

Tussilago nutans Linnaeus, *Systema Naturae,* ed. 10, 2: 1214. 1759.
["Habitat in America."] Sp. Pl. ed. 2, 2: 1213 (1763). RCN: 6261.
Lectotype (Simpson in Woodson & Schery in *Ann. Missouri Bot. Gard.* 62: 1278. 1975): *Browne*, Herb. Linn. No. 995.5 (LINN).
Current name: ***Chaptalia nutans*** (L.) Pol. (Asteraceae).
Note: Moore (in Fawcett & Rendle, *Fl. Jamaica* 7: 280. 1936) noted the existence of 995.5 (LINN) but did not designate a type. The eventual type choice is discussed in more detail by Nesom (in *Phytologia* 78: 162. 1995).

Tussilago petasites Linnaeus, *Species Plantarum* 2: 866. 1753.
"Habitat in Europa temperatiore." RCN: 6268.
Type not designated.
Original material: Herb. Clifford: 411, *Tussilago* 3 (BM); Herb. Burser X: 150 (UPS); Herb. Linn. No. 995.28 (LINN); Herb. Linn. No. 995.29 (LINN); [icon] in Mattioli, Pl. Epit.: 592. 1586.
Current name: ***Petasites hybridus*** (L.) Gaertn. (Asteraceae).

Typha angustifolia Linnaeus, *Species Plantarum* 2: 971. 1753.
"Habitat in Europae paludibus." RCN: 7046.
Type not designated.
Original material: Herb. A. van Royen No. 908.251–1363? (L); [icon] in Morison, Pl. Hist. Univ. 3: 246, s. 8, t. 13, f. 2. 1699; [icon] in Fuchs, Hist. Stirp.: 822, 823. 1542.
Generitype of *Typha* Linnaeus (vide Green, *Prop. Brit. Bot.*: 187. 1929).
Current name: ***Typha angustifolia*** L. (Typhaceae).
Note: Typha latifolia L. was treated as the generitype by Wilson (*N. Amer. Fl.* 17: 3. 1909; see McNeill & al. in *Taxon* 36: 387. 1987). However, under Art. 10.5, Ex. 7 (a voted example) of the Vienna Code, this is a type choice made under the American Code and is to be replaced under Art. 10.5b by Green's choice (*Prop. Brit. Bot.*: 187. 1929) of *T. angustifolia.*
Guha & Mondal (in *J. Econ. Taxon. Bot.* 22: 519. 1998) indicated 1094.1 (LINN) as type but the sheet lacks a *Species Plantarum* number (i.e. "2") and was evidently a post-1753 addition to the herbarium, and hence not original material for the name.

Typha latifolia Linnaeus, *Species Plantarum* 2: 971. 1753.
"Habitat in paludibus Europae." RCN: 7045.
Type not designated.
Original material: [icon] in Morison, Pl. Hist. Univ. 3: 246, s. 8, t. 13, f. 1. 1699.
Current name: ***Typha latifolia*** L. (Typhaceae).
Note: Typha latifolia was treated as the generitype by Wilson (*N. Amer. Fl.* 17: 3. 1909; see McNeill & al. in *Taxon* 36: 387. 1987). However, under Art. 10.5, Ex. 7 (a voted example) of the Vienna Code, this is a type choice made under the American Code and is to be replaced under Art. 10.5b by Green's choice (*Prop. Brit. Bot.*: 187. 1929) of *T. angustifolia* L.

T

U

Ulex capensis Linnaeus, *Species Plantarum* 2: 741. 1753.
"Habitat in Aethiopia." RCN: 5244.
Type not designated.
Original material: [icon] in Plukenet, Phytographia: t. 185, f. 6. 1692; Almag. Bot.: 166. 1696; [icon] in Petiver, Gazophyl. Nat.: 9, t. 83, f. 9. 1709.
Current name: ***Nylandtia spinosa*** (L.) Dumort. (Polygalaceae).

Ulex europaeus Linnaeus, *Species Plantarum* 2: 741. 1753.
"Habitat in Anglia, Gallia, Brabantia." RCN: 5243.
Lectotype (D'Arcy in Woodson & Schery in *Ann. Missouri Bot. Gard.* 67: 789. 1980): Herb. Linn. No. 915.1 (LINN).
Generitype of *Ulex* Linnaeus (vide Green, *Prop. Brit. Bot.*: 175. 1929).
Current name: ***Ulex europaeus*** L. subsp. ***europaeus*** (Fabaceae: Faboideae).
Note: Although Fawcett & Rendle (*Fl. Jamaica* 4: 12. 1920) indicated the type was in LINN, they did not distinguish between several sheets there (evidently from more than one gathering so Art. 9.15 does not apply).

Ulmus americana Linnaeus, *Species Plantarum* 1: 226. 1753.
"Habitat in Virginia." RCN: 1846.
Lectotype (Seymour in *Rhodora* 54: 139. 1952): Herb. Linn. No. 321.3 (LINN).
Current name: ***Ulmus americana*** L. (Ulmaceae).

Ulmus campestris Linnaeus, *Species Plantarum* 1: 225. 1753.
"Habitat in Europa ad pagos." RCN: 1845.
Lectotype (Armstrong & Sell in *Bot. J. Linn. Soc.* 120: 42. 1996): Herb. Linn. No. 321.1 (LINN).
Generitype of *Ulmus* Linnaeus.
Current name: ***Ulmus scabra*** Mill. (Ulmaceae).
Note: The name has long been treated as a *nomen ambiguum*, and Armstrong & Sell indicated that they were proposing the name for formal rejection. However, no proposal appears to have been published.

Ulmus pumila Linnaeus, *Species Plantarum* 1: 226. 1753.
"Habitat in Sibiria." RCN: 1847.
Type not designated.
Original material: Herb. Linn. No. 111.19 (S); Herb. Linn. No. 321.4 (LINN).
Current name: ***Ulmus pumila*** L. (Ulmaceae).

Ulva compressa Linnaeus, *Species Plantarum* 2: 1163. 1753.
"Habitat in Europae mari & tectis maritimis." RCN: 8363.
Lectotype (Blomster & al. in *J. Phycol.* 34: 332, f. 50, 55–57. 1998): [icon] *"Tremella marina tenuissima & compressa"* in Dillenius, Hist. Musc.: 48, t. 9, f. 8. 1741. – Voucher: Herb. Dillenius (OXF).
Current name: ***Ulva compressa*** L. (Ulvaceae).

Ulva confervoides Linnaeus, *Species Plantarum* 2: 1163. 1753.
"Habitat in Mari." RCN: 8366.
Type not designated.
Original material: Herb. Linn. No. 1275.11 (LINN); Herb. Linn. No. 1275.12 (LINN); [icon] in Dillenius, Hist. Musc.: 34, t. 6, f. 39. 1741.
Current name: ***Ceramium virgatum*** Roth (Ceramiaceae).
Note: This name is a potential threat to the well-known names of several species of algae and is a candidate for rejection.

Ulva granulata Linnaeus, *Species Plantarum* 2: 1164. 1753.
"Habitat in Europa ad ripas fluviorum." RCN: 8374b.

Lectotype (Irvine in Spencer & al. in *Taxon*, in press): [icon] *"Tremella palustris, vesiculis sphaericis fungiformibus"* in Dillenius, Hist. Musc.: 55, t. 10, f. 17. 1741. – Voucher: Herb. Dillenius (OXF).
Current name: ***Botrydium granulatum*** (L.) Grev. (Botrydiaceae).
Note: Drouet & Daily (in *Butler Univ. Bot. Stud.* 12: 167. 1956) indicated unspecified material in LINN as the type, and Drouet (in *Beih. Nova Hedwigia* 57: 219. 1978) stated that the type was "Ulva granulata" in LINN. It is unclear which material was intended as the only sheet to carry this name (as an incidental, later annotation) is associated with *Tremella* rather than *Ulva* and is in any case unannotated by Linnaeus, and a post-1753 addition to the herbarium. It is not original material for the name.

Ulva intestinalis Linnaeus, *Species Plantarum* 2: 1163. 1753.
"Habitat in Mari." RCN: 8362.
Lectotype (Blomster & al. in *J. Phycol.* 34: 332, f. 49, 52–54. 1998): [icon] *"Tremella marina tubulosa, intestinorum figura"* in Dillenius, Hist. Musc.: 47, t. 9, f. 7. 1741. – Voucher: Herb. Dillenius (OXF).
Current name: ***Ulva intestinalis*** L. (Ulvaceae).

Ulva labyrinthiformis Linnaeus, *Species Plantarum*, ed. 2, 2: 1633. 1763.
"Habitat in Thermis Patavinis gradu caloris 49, pulchre arei incisa cum descriptione a Vandellio." RCN: 8371.
Lectotype (Pentecost in Spencer & al. in *Taxon*, in press): [icon] *"Ulva thermalis valvulosa, erecta simplex, capitulo subrotundo"* in Vandelli, Tract. Therm. Agri Patav.: 215, t. 2. 1761.
Current name: ***Spirulina labyrinthiformis*** Gomont (Spirulinaceae).
Note: Specific epithet spelled "labyrintiformis" in the protologue.
    This name relates to a member of the algae that has a post-1753 Starting Point (Nostocaceae Homocysteae – Art. 13.1(e) and which therefore has no nomenclatural standing (see Spencer & al. (in *Taxon*, in press).

Ulva lactuca Linnaeus, *Species Plantarum* 2: 1163. 1753, *typ. cons.*
"Habitat in Oceano." RCN: 8368.
Lectotype (Papenfuss in *J. Linn. Soc., Bot.* 56: 304, pl. 1, f. 10. 1960): Herb. Linn. No. 1275.24 (LINN).
Generitype of *Ulva* Linnaeus, *nom. cons.*
Current name: ***Ulva lactuca*** L. (Ulvaceae).

Ulva lanceolata Linnaeus, *Systema Naturae*, ed. 12, 2: 719. 1767.
"Habitat in Oceano." RCN: 8370.
Lectotype (Irvine in Spencer & al. in *Taxon*, in press): [icon] *"Tremella marina, Porri folio"* in Dillenius, Hist. Musc.: 46, t. 9, f. 5. 1741. – Voucher: Herb. Dillenius (OXF).
Current name: ***Ulva linza*** L. (Ulvaceae).

Ulva latissima Linnaeus, *Species Plantarum* 2: 1163. 1753.
"Habitat in Mari Europae." RCN: 8367.
Lectotype (Papenfuss in *J. Linn. Soc., Bot.* 56: 303. 1960): Herb. Linn. No. 1275.14 (LINN). – Epitype (Lane in Spencer & al. in *Taxon*, in press): United Kingdom. Cornwall, Looe, Hannafore Point, 24 Jul 2005, *J. Brodie* (BM-000893632).
Current name: ***Saccharina latissima*** (L.) C.E. Lane & al. (Laminariaceae).

Ulva linza Linnaeus, *Species Plantarum* 2: 1163. 1753.
"Habitat in Oceano." RCN: 3872.
Lectotype (Brodie & Irvine in Spencer & al. in *Taxon*, in press): [icon] *"Tremella marina fasciata"* in Dillenius, Hist. Musc.: 46, t. 9, f. 6. 1741. – Voucher: Herb. Dillenius (OXF).

Current name: *Ulva linza* L. (Ulvaceae).
Note: Although Hayden & al. (in *Europ. J. Phycol.* 38: 289. 2003) indicated the cited Dillenian figure as the lectotype (following a ms. note by Irvine) and material in Herb. Gronovius (OXF) as an epitype, this statement was published after 1 January 2001 and so the omission of the phrase "designated here" or an equivalent (Art. 7.11) means that it was not effective.

Ulva lumbricalis Linnaeus, *Mantissa Plantarum Altera*: 311. 1771.
"Habitat ad Cap. b. spei. Koenig. 40." RCN: 8364.
Lectotype (Irvine in Spencer & al. in *Taxon*, in press): *König s.n.*, Herb. Linn. No. 1275.2 (LINN).
Current name: **Champia lumbricalis** (L.) Desv. (Champiaceae).

Ulva papillosa Linnaeus, *Mantissa Plantarum Altera*: 311. 1771, *nom. illeg.*
"Habitat in Mari Aethiopico. Koenig. 41." RCN: 8369.
Replaced synonym: *Fucus muricatus* S.G. Gmel. (1768).
Lectotype (Irvine in Spencer & al. in *Taxon*, in press): [icon] *"Fucus muricatus"* in Gmelin, Hist. Fucorum: 111, t. 6, f. 4. 1768.
Current name: **Eucheuma denticulatum** (Burm. f.) Collins & Herv. (Solieriaceae).
Note: A superfluous name for *Fucus muricatus* S.G. Gmel. (1768) – see Spencer & al. (in *Taxon*, in press).

Ulva pavonica (Linnaeus) Linnaeus, *Systema Naturae*, ed. 12, 2: 719. 1767.
["Habitat in Mari Europae australis."] Sp. Pl. 2: 1162 (1753). RCN: 8360, 8296.
Basionym: *Fucus pavonicus* L. (1753).
Lectotype (De Clerck in Spencer & al. in *Taxon*, in press): Herb. Burser XX: 106 (UPS).
Current name: **Padina pavonica** (L.) J.V. Lamour. (Dictyotaceae).
Note: Specific epithet spelled "pavonia" in the protologue. This is an orthographic variant of "pavonica" – see discussion under *Fucus pavonius*.

Ulva pruniformis Linnaeus, *Species Plantarum* 2: 1164. 1753.
"Habitat in lacubus Sueciae, Borussiae." RCN: 8373.
Neotype (Drouet in *Beih. Nova Hedwigia* 57: 26. 1978): Germany. "In lacu qui Hollandermeer appellayur prope Jeveram, *G.H.B. Jürgens*, in Jürgens, Alg. Aquat. 15: 8 (1822), annotated by E. Bornet (PC).
Current name: **Nostoc commune** Vaucher (Nostocaceae).
Note: In the absence of any original material for the name, Drouet's indication of type material is accepted as a neotypification (Art. 9.8).

Ulva rugosa Linnaeus, *Mantissa Plantarum Altera*: 311. 1771.
"Habitat ad Cap. b. spei. Koenig. 39." RCN: 8365.
Type not designated.
Original material: Herb. Linn. No. 1275.9 (LINN); *König 39*, Herb. Linn. No. 1275.31, lower right specimen (LINN); *König s.n.*, Herb. Linn. No. 1275.8, left specimen (LINN).
Current name: **Splachnidium rugosum** (L.) Grev. (Splachnidiaceae).
Note: Unusually, there is a syntype (*König 39*, 1275.31 LINN) in existence for this name but, unfortunately, its identity does not correspond with the generally accepted usage of *S. rugosum* (L.) Grev. *Ulva rugosa* may therefore prove to be a candidate for conservation (see Spencer & al. in *Taxon*, in press).

Ulva umbilicalis Linnaeus, *Species Plantarum* 2: 1163. 1753.
"Habitat in Oceano." RCN: 8361.
Lectotype (Conway in *Brit. Phycol. Bull.* 2: 349, pl. I, f. 1. 1964): [icon] *"Tremella marina umbilicata"* in Dillenius, Hist. Musc.: 45, t. 8, f. 3. 1741. – Voucher: Herb. Dillenius (OXF).
Current name: **Porphyra umbilicalis** (L.) Kütz. (Bangiaceae).
Note: Conway, in typifying the name, also treated a specimen in the Dillenian *Synopsis* herbarium (OXF), illustrated as pl. 1, f. 2, as a typotype. However, John & al. (in *Bull. Brit. Mus. (Nat. Hist.), Bot.* 7: 77. 1979) disagreed that this was the basis for the illustration, arguing that a collection in the Sherard herbarium (OXF) is a better match for the figure.

Uniola bipinnata (Linnaeus) Linnaeus, *Species Plantarum,* ed. 2, 1: 104. 1762.
"Habitat in Aegypto. Hasselquist." RCN: 567.
Basionym: *Briza bipinnata* L. (1756).
Lectotype (Danin in Cafferty & al. in *Taxon* 49: 248. 2000): *Hasselquist*, Herb. Linn. No. 89.2 (LINN).
Current name: **Desmostachya bipinnata** (L.) Stapf (Poaceae).

Uniola mucronata Linnaeus, *Species Plantarum*, ed. 2, 1: 104. 1762.
"Habitat in India. Burmannus." RCN: 598.
Neotype (Renvoize in Cafferty & al. in *Taxon* 49: 258. 2000): Sri Lanka. Wilpatti National Park, 30 Dec 1968, *Fosberg & al. 50918* (K; iso- US).
Current name: **Halopyrum mucronatum** (L.) Stapf (Poaceae).

Uniola paniculata Linnaeus, *Species Plantarum* 1: 71. 1753.
"Habitat in Carolina." RCN: 596.
Lectotype (Hitchcock in *Contr. U. S. Natl. Herb.* 12: 121. 1908): Herb. Linn. No. 89.1 (LINN).
Generitype of *Uniola* Linnaeus (vide Hitchcock, *Prop. Brit. Bot.*: 120. 1929).
Current name: **Uniola paniculata** L. (Poaceae).

Uniola spicata Linnaeus, *Species Plantarum* 1: 71. 1753.
"Habitat in Americae borealis maritimis." RCN: 599.
Lectotype (Hitchcock in *Contr. U. S. Natl. Herb.* 12: 121. 1908): *Kalm*, Herb. Linn. No. 89.4 (LINN; iso- UPS-KALM 26).
Current name: **Distichlis spicata** (L.) Greene (Poaceae).
Note: Baum (in *Canad. J. Bot.* 45: 1848. 1967) argued that the Kalm collection, as it was not explicitly cited, cannot be the lectotype but should instead be treated as a neotype. However, it appears to have been original material for the name, and Hitchcock's type choice is therefore accepted here.

Unxia camphorata Linnaeus, *Plantae Surinamenses*: 14. 1775, *nom. inval.*
"Habitat [in Surinamo.]"
Type not relevant.
Current name: **Unxia camphorata** L. f. (Asteraceae).
Note: In *Plantae Surinamenses* (1775), *Unxia* was given no separate generic description and *U. camphorata* is therefore invalid. *Unxia* L. f., and its type *U. camphorata* L. f. were validly published only in *Suppl. Pl.*: 56, 368 (1782), as noted by Stuessy (in *Brittonia* 21: 316. 1969).

Urena lobata Linnaeus, *Species Plantarum* 2: 692. 1753.
"Habitat in China." RCN: 5070.
Lectotype (Borssum Waalkes in *Blumea* 14: 140. 1966): Herb. Linn. No. 873.1 (LINN).
Generitype of *Urena* Linnaeus (vide Green, *Prop. Brit. Bot.*: 173. 1929).
Current name: **Urena lobata** L. (Malvaceae).

Urena procumbens Linnaeus, *Species Plantarum* 2: 692. 1753.
"Habitat in China monticulis. Osbeck." RCN: 5073.
Lectotype (Hu, *Fl. China, Fam. 153 Malvaceae*: 78. 1955): Herb. Linn. No. 873.4, left specimen (LINN).
Current name: **Urena procumbens** L. (Malvaceae).
Note: See Hansen & Fox Maule (in *Bot. J. Linn. Soc.* 67: 208. 1973) who noted an Osbeck collection in SBT.

U

Urena sinuata Linnaeus, *Species Plantarum* 2: 692. 1753.
"Habitat in India." RCN: 5071.
Lectotype (Fawcett & Rendle, *Fl. Jamaica* 5: 127. 1926): Herb.
  Hermann 4: 34, No. 257 (BM-000621193).
Current name: ***Urena lobata*** L. subsp. ***sinuata*** (L.) Borss. Waalk.
  (Malvaceae).

Urena typhalaea Linnaeus, *Mantissa Plantarum Altera*: 258. 1771.
"Habitat in Surinamo, Jamaica." RCN: 5072.
Neotype (Areces & Fryxell, *Fl. Cuba*, in press): Jamaica. St Thomas
  Parish, along the Sulphur River above Bath Fountain, ca. 400ft, 25
  Jun 1968, *G.R. Proctor 28806* (LL; iso- NY, U).
Current name: ***Pavonia fruticosa*** (Mill.) Fawc. & Rendle
  (Malvaceae).

Urtica aestuans Linnaeus, *Flora Jamaicensis*: 21. 1759.
["Habitat Surinami."] Sp. Pl., ed. 2, 2: 1397 (1763). RCN: 7139.
Lectotype (de Rooij in Lanjouw & Stoffers, *Fl. Suriname* 5(1): 310.
  1975): Herb. Linn. No. 1111.14 (LINN).
Current name: ***Laportea aestuans*** (L.) Chew (Urticaceae).

Urtica alienata Linnaeus, *Systema Naturae*, ed. 12, 2: 622. 1767, *nom.
illeg.*
RCN: 7135.
Replaced synonym: *Parietaria zeylanica* L. (1753).
Lectotype (Wadhwa in Dassanayake & Clayton, *Revised Handb. Fl.
  Ceylon* 13: 269. 1999): Herb. Hermann 3: 5, No. 371 (BM-
  000621805).
Current name: ***Pouzolzia zeylanica*** (L.) Benn. (Urticaceae).
Note: A superfluous name for *Parietaria zeylanica* L. (1753).

Urtica baccifera Linnaeus, *Species Plantarum*, ed. 2, 2: 1398.
  1763.
"Habitat in America." RCN: 7145.
Lectotype (de Rooij in Lanjouw & Stoffers, *Fl. Suriname* 5(1): 302.
  1975): [icon] *"Urtica foliis alternis, cordatis"* in Plumier in Burman,
  Pl. Amer.: 259, t. 260. 1760.
Current name: ***Urera baccifera*** (L.) Gaudich. (Urticaceae).

Urtica balearica Linnaeus, *Amoenitates Academicae* 3: 46. 1756.
["Habitat in India."] Sp. Pl., ed. 2, 2: 1395 (1763). RCN: 7128.
Lectotype (Rosselló & Sáez in *Collect. Bot. (Barcelona)* 25: 174. 2000):
  Herb. Linn. No. 1111.9 (LINN), see above right.
Current name: ***Urtica pilulifera*** L. (Urticaceae).

Urtica canadensis Linnaeus, *Species Plantarum* 2: 985. 1753.
"Habitat in Canada, Sibiria." RCN: 7142.
Lectotype (Monro in Monro & Spencer in *Taxon* 54: 797. 2005):
  Herb. Clifford: 440, *Urtica* 5, sheet A (BM). – Epitype (Monro in
  Monro & Spencer in *Taxon* 54: 797. 2005): Canada. Ontario,
  Ottawa, Ex Herb. Geological Survey of Canada, 4 Aug 1894, *J.
  Macoum s.n.* (BM-000754949).
Current name: ***Laportea canadensis*** (L.) Wedd. (Urticaceae).

Urtica cannabina Linnaeus, *Species Plantarum* 2: 984. 1753.
"Habitat in Sibiria." RCN: 7134.
Lectotype (Geltman in *Novosti Sist. Vyssh. Rast.* 25: 78. 1988): Herb.
  Linn. No. 1111.10 (LINN).
Current name: ***Urtica cannabina*** L. (Urticaceae).

Urtica capitata Linnaeus, *Species Plantarum* 2: 985. 1753.
"Habitat in Canada. Kalm." RCN: 7140.
Lectotype (Wilmot-Dear & Friis in *Opera Bot.* 129: 18. 1996): *Kalm*,
  Herb. Linn. No. 1111.15, lower right specimen (LINN).
Current name: ***Boehmeria cylindrica*** (L.) Sw. (Urticaceae).

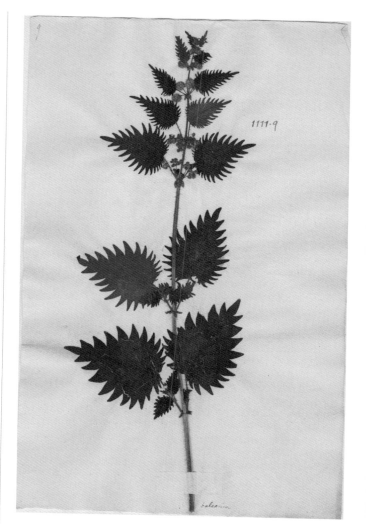

The lectotype of *Urtica balearica* L.

Urtica ciliaris Linnaeus, *Systema Naturae*, ed. 10, 2: 1266. 1759.
["Habitat in America."] Sp. Pl., ed. 2, 2: 1397 (1763). RCN: 7138.
Lectotype (Kellogg in Howard, *Fl. Lesser Antilles* 4: 87. 1988): [icon]
  "Urtica foliis ovatis, & ciliatis" in Plumier in Burman, Pl. Amer.:
  111, t.120, f. 2. 1757.
Current name: ***Pilea parietaria*** (L.) Blume (Urticaceae).

Urtica cylindrica Linnaeus, *Species Plantarum* 2: 984. 1753.
"Habitat in Jamaica, Virginia, Canada." RCN: 7136.
Lectotype (Wilmot-Dear & Friis in *Opera Bot.* 129: 18. 1996): Herb.
  Linn. No. 1111.12 (LINN).
Current name: ***Boehmeria cylindrica*** (L.) Sw. (Urticaceae).
Note: Wilmot-Dear & Friis discussed the original elements for the name,
  noting that 1111.12 (LINN) was designated as lectotype by
  Stuyveysant in 1984, in an unpublished M.Sc thesis. The latter cannot
  provide a valid typification but, as Wilmot-Dear & Friis evidently
  accept this sheet as the type, the choice is attributed to them.

Urtica dioica Linnaeus, *Species Plantarum* 2: 984. 1753.
"Habitat in Europae ruderatis." RCN: 7133.
Lectotype (Woodland in *Syst. Bot.* 7: 283. 1982): Herb. Linn. No.
  1111.8 (LINN).

Generitype of *Urtica* Linnaeus (vide Green, *Prop. Brit. Bot.*: 188. 1929).

Current name: ***Urtica dioica*** L. (Urticaceae).

Note: Ghafoor (in Jafri & El-Gadi, *Fl. Libya* 47: 15. 1977) indicated both 1111.7 and 1111.8 (LINN) as type but they are evidently not part of a single gathering, so Art. 9.15 does not apply. Similarly, Bhopal & Chaudhri (in *Pakistan Syst.* 1(2): 42. 1977) indicated unspecified material in LINN as the holotype but did not distinguish between these sheets.

Urtica divaricata Linnaeus, *Species Plantarum* 2: 985. 1753.

"Habitat in Virginia, Canada." RCN: 7141.

Lectotype (Monro in Monro & Spencer in *Taxon* 54: 797. 2005): *Kalm*, Herb. Linn. No. 1111.16 (LINN). – Epitype (Monro in Monro & Spencer in *Taxon* 54: 797. 2005): Canada. Quebec, 1926, Ex Herb. G.C. Brown, *Fr. Euphrosin s.n.* (BM-000754950).

Current name: ***Laportea canadensis*** (L.) Wedd. (Urticaceae).

Urtica dodartii Linnaeus, *Systema Naturae*, ed. 10, 2: 1265. 1759.

["Habitat – – – –"] Sp. Pl., ed. 2, 2: 1395 (1763). RCN: 7129.

Lectotype (Monro in Monro & Spencer in *Taxon* 54: 797. 2005): *Clayton 508*, Herb. Linn. No. 1111.2 (LINN).

Current name: ***Urtica pilulifera*** L. (Urticaceae).

Urtica grandifolia Linnaeus, *Systema Naturae*, ed. 10, 2: 1266. 1759.

["Habitat in Jamaica."] Sp. Pl., ed. 2, 2: 1396 (1763). RCN: 7131.

Lectotype (Monro in Monro & Spencer in *Taxon* 54: 797. 2005): *Browne?*, Herb. Linn. No. 1111.21 (LINN), see p. 168.

Current name: ***Pilea grandifolia*** (L.) Blume (Urticaceae).

Note: Although Fawcett & Rendle (*Fl. Jamaica* 3: 72. 1914) indicated material in BM as type, they did not specify what this was (though probably material in Herb. Sloane, unseen by Linnaeus and not original material for the name).

Urtica interrupta Linnaeus, *Species Plantarum* 2: 985. 1753.

"Habitat in India." RCN: 7143.

Lectotype (Chew in *Gard. Bull. Singapore* 25: 148. 1969): Herb. Hermann 3: 1, No. 336 (BM-000594643).

Current name: ***Laportea interrupta*** (L.) Chew (Urticaceae).

Urtica nivea Linnaeus, *Species Plantarum* 2: 985. 1753.

"Habitat in Chinae muris." RCN: 7144.

Lectotype (Ghafoor in Jafri & El-Gadi, *Fl. Libya* 47: 18. 1977): Herb. Linn. No. 1111.19 (LINN).

Current name: ***Boehmeria nivea*** (L.) Gaudich. (Urticaceae).

Urtica parietaria Linnaeus, *Species Plantarum* 2: 985. 1753.

"Habitat in Jamaica." RCN: 7137.

Lectotype (Kellogg in Howard, *Fl. Lesser Antilles* 4: 87. 1988): [icon] "*Parietaria foliis ex adverso nascentibus, urticae racemiferae flore*" in Sloane, Voy. Jamaica 1: 144, t. 93, f. 1. 1707. – Typotype: Herb. Sloane 2: 120 (BM-SL).

Current name: ***Pilea parietaria*** (L.) Blume (Urticaceae).

Note: Although Fawcett & Rendle (*Fl. Jamaica* 3: 65. 1914) indicated material in BM as type, they did not specify what this was (though probably material in Herb. Sloane, unseen by Linnaeus and not original material for the name).

Urtica pilulifera Linnaeus, *Species Plantarum* 2: 983. 1753.

"Habitat in Europa australi." RCN: 7127.

Lectotype (Monro in Monro & Spencer in *Taxon* 54: 797. 2005): Herb. Clifford: 440, *Urtica* 1 (BM-000647369).

Current name: ***Urtica pilulifera*** L. (Urticaceae).

Note: Although Bhopal & Chaudhri (in *Pakistan Syst.* 1(2): 42. 1977) indicated unspecified material in LINN as the holotype, the only

material there associated with this name (1111.1) lacks the relevant *Species Plantarum* number (i.e. "1") and was a post-1753 addition to the herbarium, and is not original material for the name.

Urtica pumila Linnaeus, *Species Plantarum* 2: 984. 1753.

"Habitat in Canada." RCN: 7130.

Lectotype (Monro in Monro & Spencer in *Taxon* 54: 797. 2005): *Kalm*, Herb. Linn. No. 1111.3 (LINN).

Current name: ***Pilea pumila*** (L.) A. Gray (Urticaceae).

Urtica urens Linnaeus, *Species Plantarum* 2: 984. 1753.

"Habitat in Europae cultis." RCN: 7132.

Lectotype (Ghafoor in Jafri & El-Gadi, *Fl. Libya* 47: 12. 1977): Herb. Linn. No. 1111.5 (LINN).

Current name: ***Urtica urens*** L. (Urticaceae).

Utricularia bifida Linnaeus, *Species Plantarum* 1: 18. 1753.

"Habitat in China. Osbeck." RCN: 150.

Lectotype (Taylor in *Kew Bull., Addit. Ser.* 14: 308. 1989): *Osbeck s.n.*, Herb. Linn. No. 34.7 (LINN).

Current name: ***Utricularia bifida*** L. (Lentibulariaceae).

Utricularia caerulea Linnaeus, *Species Plantarum* 1: 18. 1753.

"Habitat in Zeylona." RCN: 151.

Lectotype (Committee for Spermatophyta in *Taxon* 38: 302. 1989): Herb. Hermann 2: 13, No. 23 (BM-000621547).

Current name: ***Utricularia caerulea*** L. (Lentibulariaceae).

Note: Smith (in *Exot. Bot.* 2: 119–120. 1805) has been credited with the typification of the name, basing it on the Hermann element. However, as the name had also been interpreted via other, discordant elements, Bhattacharyya (in *Taxon* 35: 750. 1986) proposed the name for rejection. This was not approved by the Committee for Spermatophyta, who ruled (in *Taxon* 38: 302. 1989) that the Hermann element should be the type, and that the name should be used in the sense of this type. Taylor (in *Kew Bull., Addit. Ser.* 14: 192. 1989) gives a review.

Utricularia foliosa Linnaeus, *Species Plantarum* 1: 18. 1753.

"Habitat in Americes Gallia aequinoctiali." RCN: 145.

Lectotype (Taylor in *Kew Bull., Addit. Ser.* 14: 675. 1989): [icon] in Plumier, Codex Boerhaavianus (University Library, Groningen).

Current name: ***Utricularia foliosa*** L. (Lentibulariaceae).

Utricularia gibba Linnaeus, *Species Plantarum* 1: 18. 1753.

"Habitat in Virginia." RCN: 149.

Lectotype (Taylor in *Kew Bull.* 18: 197. 1964): *Clayton 515 & 517* (BM-000098329).

Current name: ***Utricularia gibba*** L. (Lentibulariaceae).

Utricularia minor Linnaeus, *Species Plantarum* 1: 18. 1753.

"Habitat in Europae fossis rarius." RCN: 147.

Lectotype (Casper in Rechinger, *Fl. Iranica* 58: 2. 1969): Herb. Linn. No. 34.3 (LINN).

Current name: ***Utricularia minor*** L. (Lentibulariaceae).

Utricularia subulata Linnaeus, *Species Plantarum* 1: 18. 1753.

"Habitat in Virginia." RCN: 148.

Lectotype (Taylor in *Kew Bull.* 18: 81. 1964): *Clayton 31* (BM-000032596).

Current name: ***Utricularia subulata*** L. (Lentibulariaceae).

Utricularia vulgaris Linnaeus, *Species Plantarum* 1: 18. 1753.

"Habitat in Europae fossis." RCN: 146.

Lectotype (Taylor in *Kew Bull.* 18: 171. 1964): Herb. Linn. No. 34.2 (LINN).

Generitype of *Utricularia* Linnaeus (vide Hitchcock, *Prop. Brit. Bot.*: 116. 1929).
Current name: ***Utricularia vulgaris*** L. (Lentibulariaceae).

Uvaria japonica Linnaeus, *Species Plantarum* 1: 536. 1753.
"Habitat in Japonia." RCN: 3988.
Lectotype (Smith in *Sargentia* 7: 181. 1947): [icon] *"Futo Kadsura"* in Kaempfer, Amoen. Exot. Fasc.: 476, 477. 1712.
Current name: ***Kadsura japonica*** (L.) Dunal (Schizandraceae).
Note: Saunders (in *Syst. Bot. Monogr.* 54: 64. 1998) also accepts Kaempfer's plate as the type, and reproduces it as his f. 1 (p. 5).

Uvaria zeylanica Linnaeus, *Species Plantarum* 1: 536. 1753.
"Habitat in India." RCN: 3987.
Lectotype (Huber in Dassanayake & Fosberg, *Revised Handb. Fl. Ceylon* 5: 17. 1985; Kessler in Jarvis & al., *Regnum Veg.* 127: 97. 1993): Herb. Hermann 5: 163, No. 224 [icon] (BM).
Generitype of *Uvaria* Linnaeus (vide Hutchinson in *Bull. Misc. Inform. Kew* 1923: 256. 1923).
Current name: ***Uvaria zeylanica*** L. (Annonaceae).
Note: Huber indicated material from several volumes of Herb. Hermann material (BM) as type. However, as it appears to have been part of a single gathering, his statement is accepted as the first typification (Art. 9.15), with the choice subsequently restricted by Kessler.

Uvularia amplexifolia Linnaeus, *Species Plantarum* 1: 304. 1753.
"Habitat in Bohemiae, Silesiae, Saxoniae, Delphinatus montibus." RCN: 2399.
Type not designated.
Original material: Herb. A. van Royen No. 913.62–465 (L); [icon] in Bauhin & Cherler, Hist. Pl. Univ. 3(2): 530. 1651; [icon] in Barrelier, Pl. Galliam: 58, t. 720. 1714; [icon] in Morison, Pl. Hist. Univ. 3: 537, s. 13, t. 4, f. 11. 1699; [icon] in Mattioli, Pl. Epit.: 936. 1586; [icon] in Clusius, Rar. Pl. Hist. 1: 276. 1601.
Current name: ***Streptopus amplexifolius*** (L.) DC. (Liliaceae/Convallariaceae).

Uvularia perfoliata Linnaeus, *Species Plantarum* 1: 304. 1753, *nom. cons.*
"Habitat in Virginia, Canada." RCN: 2400.
Conserved type (Reveal in *Taxon* 41: 586. 1992): *Clayton 258* (BM-000040316).
Generitype of *Uvularia* Linnaeus.
Current name: ***Uvularia perfoliata*** L. (Liliaceae/Colchicaceae).

Uvularia sessilifolia Linnaeus, *Species Plantarum* 1: 305. 1753.
"Habitat in Canada. Kalm." RCN: 2401.
Lectotype (Wilbur in *Rhodora* 65: 175. 1963): *Kalm*, Herb. Linn. No. 422.4 (LINN).
Current name: ***Uvularia sessilifolia*** L. (Liliaceae/Colchicaceae).

V

Vaccinium album Linnaeus, *Species Plantarum* 1: 350. 1753.
"Habitat in Pensylvania. Kalm." RCN: 2703.
Lectotype (Blake in *Rhodora* 16: 118. 1914): *Kalm*, Herb. Linn. No. 497.4 (LINN).
Current name: ***Symphoricarpos albus*** (L.) Blake (Caprifoliaceae).

Vaccinium arctostaphylos Linnaeus, *Species Plantarum* 1: 351. 1753.
"Habitat in Cappadocia." RCN: 2708.
Lectotype (Stevens in Davis, *Fl. Turkey* 6: 102. 1978): *Tournefort*, Herb. Linn. No. 497.14 (LINN).
Current name: ***Vaccinium arctostaphylos*** L. (Ericaceae).

Vaccinium corymbosum Linnaeus, *Species Plantarum* 1: 350. 1753.
"Habitat in America septentrionali. Kalm." RCN: 2705.
Lectotype (Vander Kloet in *Canad. J. Bot.* 58: 1196. 1980): *Kalm*, Herb. Linn. No. 497.6 (LINN).
Current name: ***Vaccinium corymbosum*** L. (Ericaceae).

Vaccinium frondosum Linnaeus, *Species Plantarum* 1: 351. 1753.
"Habitat in America septentrionali." RCN: 2706.
Lectotype (Vander Kloet in Cafferty & Jarvis in *Taxon* 51: 753. 2003 [2002]): *Kalm*, Herb. Linn. No. 497.8 (LINN).
Current name: ***Gaylussacia frondosa*** (L.) Torr. & A. Gray (Ericaceae).

Vaccinium hispidulum Linnaeus, *Species Plantarum* 1: 352. 1753.
"Habitat in Virginiae paludosis." RCN: 2711.
Lectotype (Vander Kloet in Cafferty & Jarvis in *Taxon* 51: 753. 2003 [2002]): *Kalm*, Herb. Linn. No. 497.20 (LINN).
Current name: ***Gaultheria hispidula*** (L.) Muhl. (Ericaceae).

Vaccinium ligustrinum Linnaeus, *Species Plantarum* 1: 351. 1753.
"Habitat in Pensylvania." RCN: 2707.
Lectotype (Judd in *J. Arnold Arbor.* 62: 189. 1981): *Kalm*, Herb. Linn. No. 497.11 (LINN).
Current name: ***Lyonia ligustrina*** (L.) DC. (Ericaceae).

Vaccinium mucronatum Linnaeus, *Species Plantarum* 1: 350. 1753.
"Habitat in America septentrionali. Kalm." RCN: 2704.
Lectotype (Powell & al. in *Kew Bull.* 55: 345. 2000): *Kalm*, Herb. Linn. No. 497.5 (LINN).
Current name: ***Ilex mucronata*** (L.) M. Powell & al. (Aquifoliaceae).

Vaccinium myrtillus Linnaeus, *Species Plantarum* 1: 349. 1753.
"Habitat in Europae borealis sylvis umbrosis." RCN: 2700.
Lectotype (Vander Kloet, *Genus* Vaccinium *N. America*: 130. 1988): Herb. Linn. No. 497.1 (LINN).
Current name: ***Vaccinium myrtillus*** L. (Ericaceae).
Note: See also Vander Kloet (in *Taxon* 38: 133. 1989).

Vaccinium oxycoccos Linnaeus, *Species Plantarum* 1: 351. 1753.
"Habitat in Europae paludibus sphagnoque repletis." RCN: 2710.
Lectotype (Vander Kloet in *Rhodora* 85: 35. 1983): Herb. Linn. No. 497.18 (LINN).
Current name: ***Vaccinium oxycoccus*** L. (Ericaceae).
Note: See also Vander Kloet (in *Taxon* 38: 131. 1989).

Vaccinium stamineum Linnaeus, *Species Plantarum* 1: 350. 1753.
"Habitat in America septentrionali." RCN: 2701.
Lectotype (Vander Kloet in *Taxon* 38: 131. 1989): *Kalm*, Herb. Linn. No. 497.2 (LINN).
Current name: ***Vaccinium stamineum*** L. (Ericaceae).

Note: Vander Kloet (*Genus* Vaccinium *N. America*: 91. 1988) stated that the type was a Kalm collection at LINN but did not make it clear whether he regarded 497.2 or 497.22, both of which he mentioned, as the type. The type choice therefore dates from 1989.

Vaccinium uliginosum Linnaeus, *Species Plantarum* 1: 350. 1753.
"Habitat in Sueciae borealibus & alpinis, uliginosis." RCN: 2702.
Lectotype (Vander Kloet in *Taxon* 30: 647. 1981): Herb. Linn. No. 497.3 (LINN).
Generitype of *Vaccinium* Linnaeus (vide Vander Kloet in *Taxon* 30: 647. 1981).
Current name: ***Vaccinium uliginosum*** L. (Ericaceae).
Note: Vaccinium uliginosum, with the type designated by Vander Kloet, was proposed as conserved type of the genus by Jarvis (in *Taxon* 41: 571. 1992). However, the proposal was eventually ruled unnecessary by the General Committee (see Barrie, *l.c.* 55: 795–796. 2006 for a review of the history of this and related proposals).

Vaccinium vitis-idaea Linnaeus, *Species Plantarum* 1: 351. 1753.
"Habitat in Europae frigidioros sylvis macris." RCN: 2709.
Lectotype (Vander Kloet, *Genus* Vaccinium *N. America*: 116. 1988): Herb. Linn. No. 497.17 (LINN).
Current name: ***Vaccinium vitis-idaea*** L. (Ericaceae).
Note: See also Vander Kloet (in *Taxon* 38: 131. 1989).

Valantia aparine Linnaeus, *Species Plantarum* 2: 1051. 1753.
"Habitat inter Germaniae, Galliae, Siciliae segetes." RCN: 7600.
Lectotype (Natali & Jeanmonod in Jeanmonod, *Compl. Prodr. Fl. Corse, Rubiaceae*: 152. 2000): Herb. Linn. No. 1219.6 (LINN).
Current name: ***Galium verrucosum*** Huds. (Rubiaceae).

Valantia articulata Linnaeus, *Species Plantarum* 2: 1052. 1753.
"Habitat in Aegypto, Syria." RCN: 7601.
Type not designated.
Original material: Herb. Linn. No. 1219.8 (LINN).
Current name: ***Valantia articulata*** L. (Rubiaceae).
Note: The collection (1219.10 LINN) which was designated as the type by Jelenevsky & Kuranova (in *Novosti Sist. Vyssh. Rast.* 32: 160. 2000) lacks the relevant *Species Plantarum* number (i.e. "3"), and is apparently a post-1753 addition to the collection, and not original material for the name.

Valantia cruciata Linnaeus, *Species Plantarum* 2: 1052. 1753.
"Habitat in Germania, Helvetia, Gallia." RCN: 7602.
Lectotype (Ehrendorfer in *Ann. Naturhist. Mus. Wien* 65: 16. 1962): Herb. Linn. No. 1219.11 (LINN).
Current name: ***Cruciata laevipes*** Opiz (Rubiaceae).

Valantia cucullaris Linnaeus, *Centuria I Plantarum*: 33. 1755.
"Habitat in Cappadociae & Arabiae montosis." RCN: 7599.
Lectotype (Jafri in Jafri & El-Gadi, *Fl. Libya* 65: 39. 1979): Herb. Linn. No. 1219.5 (LINN).
Current name: ***Callipeltis cucullaris*** (L.) Steven (Rubiaceae).

Valantia glabra Linnaeus, *Species Plantarum*, ed. 2, 2: 1491. 1763.
"Habitat in Austria, Italia." RCN: 7603.
Lectotype (Natali & Jeanmonod in Jeanmonod, *Compl. Prodr. Fl. Corse, Rubiaceae*: 20. 2000): Herb. Linn. No. 408.9 (S).
Current name: ***Cruciata glabra*** (L.) Ehrend. (Rubiaceae).

V

Valantia hispida Linnaeus, *Systema Naturae*, ed. 10, 2: 1307. 1759.
["Habitat in Europa australi."] Sp. Pl., ed. 2, 1: 1490 (1762). RCN: 7598.
Lectotype (Natali & Jeanmonod in Jeanmonod, *Compl. Prodr. Fl. Corse, Rubiaceae*: 184. 2000): Herb. Linn. No. 1219.3 (LINN).
Current name: *Valantia hispida* L. (Rubiaceae).

Valantia hypocarpia Linnaeus, *Systema Naturae*, ed. 10, 2: 1307. 1759.
["Habitat in Jamaica."] Sp. Pl., ed. 2, 1: 1491 (1762). RCN: 7604.
Lectotype (Dempster in *Allertonia* 5: 306. 1990): *Browne*, Herb. Linn. No. 1219.13 (LINN).
Current name: *Relbunium hypocarpium* (L.) Hemsl. (Rubiaceae).
Note: Ehrendorfer (in *Bot. Jahrb. Syst.* 76: 536. 1955) noted that the name was based on Browne's account but failed to trace any Browne specimen in LINN and therefore felt a neotype would be necessary. However, 1219.13 (LINN) is original material for the name.

Valantia muralis Linnaeus, *Species Plantarum* 2: 1051. 1753.
"Habitat in G. Narbonensis, Italiae muris." RCN: 7597.
Lectotype (Natali in Jarvis & al., *Regnum Veg.* 127: 97–98. 1993): Herb. Linn. No. 1219.2 (LINN).
Generitype of *Valantia* Linnaeus.
Current name: *Valantia muralis* L. (Rubiaceae).
Note: Jafri (in Jafri & El-Gadi, *Fl. Libya* 65: 9. 1979) indicated 1219.1 (LINN) as the type but this sheet lacks a *Species Plantarum* number (i.e. "1") and was a post-1753 addition to the herbarium, and not original material for the name.

Valeriana calcitrapae Linnaeus, *Species Plantarum* 1: 31. 1753.
"Habitat in Lusitania." RCN: 251.
Lectotype (Richardson in *Bot. J. Linn. Soc.* 71: 231. 1976): Herb. Linn. No. 48.3 (LINN).
Current name: *Centranthus calcitrapae* (L.) Dufr. (Valerianaceae).

Valeriana celtica Linnaeus, *Species Plantarum* 1: 32. 1753.
"Habitat in alpibus Helvetiae, Valesiae." RCN: 258.
Type not designated.
Original material: Herb. Burser VIII: 120 (UPS); Herb. Burser VIII: 121 (UPS); [icon] in Mattioli, *Pl. Epit.*: 14. 1586; [icon] in Bauhin & Cherler, *Hist. Pl. Univ.* 3(2): 205. 1651.
Current name: *Valeriana celtica* L. (Valerianaceae).

Valeriana chinensis Linnaeus, *Species Plantarum* 1: 33. 1753.
"Habitat in China. Osbeck." RCN: 264.
Lectotype (Nasir in Nasir & Ali, *Fl. W. Pakistan* 115: 12. 1977): Herb. Linn. No. 48.13 (LINN).
Current name: *Commicarpus chinensis* (L.) Heimerl (Nyctaginaceae).
Note: See Hansen & Fox Maule (in *Bot. J. Linn. Soc.* 67: 208. 1973) for comments on Osbeck material.

Valeriana cornucopiae Linnaeus, *Species Plantarum* 1: 31. 1753.
"Habitat in Americae, Mauritaniae, Siciliae, Hispaniae arvis." RCN: 252.
Lectotype (Alavi in Jafri & El-Gadi, *Fl. Libya* 46: 10. 1977): Herb. Linn. No. 48.4 (LINN).
Current name: *Fedia cornucopiae* (L.) Gaertn. (Valerianaceae).

Valeriana dioica Linnaeus, *Species Plantarum* 1: 31. 1753.
"Habitat in Europae campis uliginosis." RCN: 253.
Type not designated.
Original material: Herb. Burser VIII: 107 (UPS); Herb. Burser VIII: 113 (UPS); Herb. Clifford: 16, *Valeriana* 7 (BM); Herb. Linn. No. 48.5 (LINN).
Current name: *Valeriana dioica* L. (Valerianaceae).

Valeriana echinata Linnaeus, *Systema Naturae*, ed. 10, 2: 861. 1759.
["Habitat in Italia & Monspelii umbrosis. Sauvages."] Sp. Pl., ed. 2, 1: 47 (1762). RCN: 267.
Lectotype (Meikle, *Fl. Cyprus* 2: 845. 1985): Herb. Linn. No. 48.19 (LINN).
Current name: *Valerianella echinata* (L.) DC. (Valerianaceae).

Valeriana locusta Linnaeus, *Species Plantarum* 1: 33. 1753.
RCN: 265.
Neotype (Prakash in *J. Econ. Taxon. Bot., Addit. Ser.* 17: 56. 1999): Herb. Linn. No. 48.14 (LINN).
Current name: *Valerianella locusta* (L.) Laterr. (Valerianaceae).
Note: There appear to be no original elements for the name. Consequently, Prakash's statement is accepted as a neotypification under Art. 9.8. The homonym and var. *olitoria* are therefore homotypic, and synonymous, which accords with usage.

Valeriana locusta Linnaeus var. **coronata** Linnaeus, *Species Plantarum* 1: 34. 1753.
"Habitat in Lusitaniae arvis." RCN: 265.
Lectotype (Nasir in Nasir & Ali, *Fl. W. Pakistan* 101: 15. 1976): Herb. Linn. No. 48.16 (LINN).
Current name: *Valerianella coronata* (L.) DC. (Valerianaceae).

Valeriana locusta Linnaeus var. **dentata** Linnaeus, *Species Plantarum* 1: 34. 1753.
"Habitat in Europae australioris arvis." RCN: 265.
Lectotype (Nasir in Nasir & Ali, *Fl. W. Pakistan* 101: 17. 1976): *Löfling 26*, Herb. Linn. No. 48.18 (LINN).
Current name: *Valerianella dentata* (L.) Pollich (Valerianaceae).

Valeriana locusta Linnaeus var. **discoidea** Linnaeus, *Demonstr. Pl. Horto Upsaliensi*: 2. 1753.
RCN: 265.
Type not designated.
Original material: Herb. Linn. No. 48.17? (LINN); [icon] in Morison, *Pl. Hist. Univ.* 3: 104, s. 7, t. 16, f. 29. 1699.
Current name: *Valerianella discoidea* (L.) Loisel. (Valerianaceae).

Valeriana locusta Linnaeus var. **mutica** Linnaeus, *Species Plantarum*, ed. 2, 2: 1676. 1763.
RCN: 265.
Type not designated.
Original material: [icon] in Plantin, *Pl. Stirp. Icon.*: 716. 1581.
Current name: *Valerianella coronata* (L.) DC. (Valerianaceae).

Valeriana locusta Linnaeus var. **olitoria** Linnaeus, *Species Plantarum* 1: 33. 1753.
"Habitat in Europae arvis." RCN: 265.
Lectotype (Dyal in *Rhodora* 40: 191. 1938): Herb. Linn. No. 48.14 (LINN).
Current name: *Valerianella locusta* (L.) Laterr. (Valerianaceae).

Valeriana locusta Linnaeus var. **pumila** Linnaeus, *Systema Naturae*, ed. 12, 2: 73. 1767.
RCN: 265.
Type not designated.
Original material: [icon] in Plantin, *Pl. Stirp. Icon.*: 716. 1581.
Current name: *Valerianella pumila* (L.) DC. (Valerianaceae).

Valeriana locusta Linnaeus var. **radiata** Linnaeus, *Species Plantarum* 1: 34. 1753.
"Habitat in Marilandiae arvis." RCN: 265.
Lectotype (Reveal & al. in *Huntia* 7: 237. 1987): *Clayton 43* (BM-000042693).
Current name: *Valerianella radiata* (L.) Dufr. (Valerianaceae).

Valeriana locusta Linnaeus var. **vesicaria** Linnaeus, *Species Plantarum* 1: 33. 1753.
"Habitat in Cretae arvis." RCN: 265.
Lectotype (Alavi in Jafri & El-Gadi, *Fl. Libya* 46: 6. 1977): Herb. Linn. No. 48.15 (LINN).
Current name: *Valerianella vesicaria* (L.) Moench (Valerianaceae).

Valeriana mixta Linnaeus, *Species Plantarum* 1: 34. 1753.
"Habitat Monspelii." RCN: 266.
Type not designated.
Original material: [icon] in Morison, Pl. Umbell. Distrib. Nova: Elenchus t. 7, t. 1, f. 56, 57. 1672.
Current name: *Centranthus calcitrapae* (L.) Dufr. (Valerianaceae).
Note: See extensive discussion by Thiébaut (in Jeanmonod & Burdet, *Compl. Prodr. Fl. Corse, Valerianaceae*: 32–33. 1996), who says this is a mixture of *Centranthus calcitrapae* (L.) Dufr. and a *Valerianella* species, and argues that the name should be treated as ambiguous and should be rejected.

Valeriana montana Linnaeus, *Species Plantarum* 1: 32. 1753.
"Habitat in Helveticis, Rhaeticis, Pyrenaeis." RCN: 257.
Type not designated.
Original material: Herb. Burser VIII: 112 (UPS); Herb. Burser VIII: 122, syntype (UPS); Herb. Burser VIII: 111 (UPS); [icon] in Plukenet, Phytographia: t. 232, f. 2. 1692; Almag. Bot.: 380. 1696; [icon] in Bauhin, Prodr. Theatri Bot.: 87. 1620.
Current name: *Valeriana montana* L. (Valerianaceae).

Valeriana officinalis Linnaeus, *Species Plantarum* 1: 31. 1753.
"Habitat in Europae nemoribus paludosis." RCN: 254.
Lectotype (designated here by Kirschner): Herb. Burser VIII: 100 (UPS). – Epitype (designated here by Kirschner): Czech Republic. Southern Bohemia, Písek, along the railway between Razice and Herman, alt. 380m, 16 Aug 2006, *J. Kirschner & M. Soukup 1608* (PRA; iso- BM).
Generitype of *Valeriana* Linnaeus (vide Hitchcock, *Prop. Brit. Bot.*: 117. 1929).
Current name: *Valeriana officinalis* L. (Valerianaceae).
Note: Valeriana pyrenaica was treated as the generitype by Britton & Brown (*Ill. Fl. N. U. S.*, ed. 2, 3: 284. 1913; see McNeill & al. in *Taxon* 36: 387. 1987). However, under Art. 10.5, Ex. 7 (a voted example) of the Vienna Code, this is a type choice made under the American Code and is to be replaced under Art. 10.5b by Hitchcock's choice (*Prop. Brit. Bot.*: 117. 1929) of *V. officinalis* L. Grubov (in *Novosti Sist. Vyssh. Rast.* 33: 214. Mar 2001) stated "Type in London (LINN)". Only 48.6 (LINN) can be associated with this name, so this statement would otherwise be acceptable as a formal typification. However, the omission of "designated here" or an equivalent leaves this type choice contrary to Art. 7.11.

Valeriana phu Linnaeus, *Species Plantarum* 1: 32. 1753.
"Habitat in Alsatia." RCN: 255.
Type not designated.
Original material: Herb. Clifford: 16, *Valeriana* 6 (BM); Herb. Linn. No. 48.7 (LINN); Herb. Burser VIII: 97 (UPS).
Current name: *Valeriana phu* L. (Valerianaceae).

Valeriana pyrenaica Linnaeus, *Species Plantarum* 1: 33. 1753.
"Habitat in Pyrenaeis?" RCN: 262.
Lectotype (Barrie in Jarvis & al., *Regnum Veg.* 127: 98. 1993): Herb. Linn. No. 48.12 (LINN).
Current name: *Valeriana pyrenaica* L. (Valerianaceae).
Note: Valeriana pyrenaica was treated as the generitype by Britton & Brown (*Ill. Fl. N. U. S.*, ed. 2, 3: 284. 1913; see McNeill & al. in *Taxon* 36: 387. 1987). However, under Art. 10.5, Ex. 7 (a voted example) of the Vienna Code, this is a type choice made under the American Code and is to be replaced under Art. 10.5b by Hitchcock's choice (*Prop. Brit. Bot.*: 117. 1929) of *V. officinalis* L.

Valeriana rubra Linnaeus, *Species Plantarum* 1: 31. 1753.
"Habitat in Galliae, Helvetiae, Italiae ruderatis." RCN: 250.
Type not designated.
Original material: Herb. Clifford: 15, *Valeriana* 1 β (BM); Herb. Burser VIII: 114 (UPS); Herb. Clifford: 15, *Valeriana* 1 (BM); Herb. Clifford: 15, *Valeriana* 1 α (BM); [icon] in Clusius, Rar. Pl. Hist. 2: 56. 1601.
Current name: *Centranthus ruber* (L.) DC. (Valerianaceae).
Note: Richardson (in *Bot. J. Linn. Soc.* 71: 220. 1976) indicated unspecified material in BM as the type. Even if he intended Clifford material as the type choice, there are three sheets associated with this name so this cannot be accepted as a formal typification.

Valeriana saxatilis Linnaeus, *Species Plantarum* 1: 33. 1753.
"Habitat in alpibus Styriae, Austriae." RCN: 260.
Type not designated.
Original material: Herb. Burser VIII: 26, syntype (UPS).
Current name: *Valeriana saxatilis* L. (Valerianaceae).

Valeriana scandens Linnaeus, *Species Plantarum*, ed. 2, 1: 47. 1762.
"Habitat in Cumana." RCN: 263.
Neotype (Barrie in *Taxon* 38: 296. 1989): Venezuela. Distrito Federal: En sitios abrigados, de colonias de Barrancas, 3 Nov 1940, *F. Tamayo 1440* (US; iso- F, UC).
Current name: *Valeriana scandens* L. (Valerianaceae).

Valeriana sibirica Linnaeus, *Species Plantarum* 1: 34. 1753.
"Habitat in Sibiriae campis." RCN: 269.
Type not designated.
Original material: [icon] in Amman, Stirp. Rar. Ruth.: 18, t. 3. 1739.
Current name: *Patrinia sibirica* (L.) Juss. (Valerianaceae).
Note: Grubov (in *Novosti Sist. Vyssh. Rast.* 33: 217. Mar 2001) stated "Type in London (LINN)". Only 48.21 (LINN) can be associated with this name, but it appears to be a post-1753 addition to the collection and not original material for the name. In any case, the omission of "designated here" or an equivalent leaves this type choice contrary to Art. 7.11.

Valeriana tripteris Linnaeus, *Species Plantarum* 1: 32. 1753.
"Habitat in alpibus Helvetiae." RCN: 256.
Type not designated.
Original material: Herb. Linn. No. 48.8 (LINN); Herb. Burser VIII: 109 (UPS); Herb. Burser VIII: 110 (UPS); [icon] in Bauhin, Prodr. Theatri Bot.: 86. 1620; [icon] in Plukenet, Phytographia: t. 231, f. 7, 8. 1692; Almag. Bot.: 380. 1696.
Current name: *Valeriana tripteris* L. (Valerianaceae).

Valeriana tuberosa Linnaeus, *Species Plantarum* 1: 33. 1753.
"Habitat in Dalmatia, Sicilia, Galloprovincia." RCN: 259.
Type not designated.
Original material: Herb. Burser VIII: 119 (UPS); [icon] in Mattioli, Pl. Epit.: 16. 1586.
Current name: *Valeriana tuberosa* L. (Valerianaceae).

Vallisneria spiralis Linnaeus, *Species Plantarum* 2: 1015. 1753.
"Habitat in Pisae & Florentiae fossis." RCN: 7355.
Lectotype (Simpson in *Kew Bull.* 44: 456, f. 1. 1989): [icon] "*Vallisneria palustris, Algae folio, Italica, foliis in summitate denticulatis, flore purpurascente*" in Micheli, Nov. Pl. Gen.: 12, t. 10. 1729.
Generitype of *Vallisneria* Linnaeus.
Current name: *Vallisneria spiralis* L. (Hydrocharitaceae).

Vandellia diffusa Linnaeus, *Systema Naturae*, ed. 12, 2: 422; *Mantissa Plantarum*: 89. 1767.
"Habitat in Insula S. Thomae. D.D. Browne." RCN: 4585.
Lectotype (Edmondson in Davis, *Fl. Turkey* 6: 680. 1978): Herb. Linn. No. 795.3 (LINN).
Generitype of *Vandellia* Linnaeus.
Current name: **Lindernia diffusa** (L.) Wettst. (Scrophulariaceae).
Note: Lewis (in *Castanea* 65: 117. 2000) accepts 795.3 (LINN) as the lectotype but expressed doubts as to its identity.

Varneria augusta Linnaeus, *Amoenitates Academicae* 4: 136. 1759, *nom. inval.*
Type not relevant.
Current name: **Gardenia jasminoides** J. Ellis (Rubiaceae).
Note: This name is invalid because the genus *Varneria* was given no separate generic description. Under Art. 42.1, the names of a genus and a species may not be simultaneously validated by a reference to an earlier description or diagnosis, as occurred here. However, some authors (e.g. Merrill, *Interpret. Rumph. Herb. Amb.*: 486. 1917) have treated this as the basionym of *G. augusta* (L.) Merrill, wrongly interpreted as the correct name for the species otherwise known as *G. jasminoides* J. Ellis (1761).

Varronia bullata Linnaeus, *Systema Naturae*, ed. 10, 2: 916. 1759.
["Habitat in America."] Sp. Pl., ed. 2, 1: 276 (1762). RCN: 1533.
Lectotype (Gaviria in *Mitt. Bot. Staatssamml. München* 23: 187. 1987): [icon] *"Periclymenum rectum, salviae folio rugoso, majore, subrotundo, bullato"* in Sloane, Voy. Jamaica 2: 81, t. 195, f. 1. 1725. – Voucher: Herb. Sloane 6: 82 (BM-SL).
Current name: **Cordia bullata** (L.) Roem. & Schult. (Boraginaceae).

Varronia lineata Linnaeus, *Systema Naturae*, ed. 10, 2: 916. 1759, *nom. illeg.*
["Habitat in Jamaica."] Sp. Pl. 2: 628 (1753). RCN: 1532.
Replaced synonym: *Lantana corymbosa* L. (1753).
Lectotype (Johnston in *J. Arnold Arbor.* 30: 94. 1949): [icon] *"Ulmi angustifoliae facie Baccifera Jamaicensis foliis superne scabris, subtus villosis, floribus flavis perpusillis, fructu botryoide monospermo"* in Plukenet, Phytographia: t. 328, f. 5. 1694; Almag. Bot.: 393. 1696. – Typotype: Herb. Sloane 102: 132 (BM-SL).
Current name: **Cordia linnaei** Stearn (Boraginaceae).
Note: An illegitimate replacement name in *Varronia* for *Lantana corymbosa* L. (1753).

Vateria indica Linnaeus, *Species Plantarum* 1: 515. 1753.
"Habitat in India." RCN: 3878.
Lectotype (Meijer in *Ceylon J. Sci., Biol. Sci.* 10: 77. 1972): [icon] *"Paenoe"* in Rheede, Hort. Malab. 4: 33, t. 15. 1683.
Generitype of *Vateria* Linnaeus.
Current name: **Vateria indica** L. (Dipterocarpaceae).

Vatica chinensis Linnaeus, *Mantissa Plantarum Altera*: 242. 1771.
"Habitat in China." RCN: 3439.
Lectotype (Ashton in Jarvis & al., *Regnum Veg.* 127: 98. 1993): Herb. Linn. No. 614.1 (LINN).
Generitype of *Vatica* Linnaeus.
Current name: **Vatica chinensis** L. (Dipterocarpaceae).
Note: Meijer (in *Ceylon J. Sci., Biol. Sci.* 10: 77. 1972) stated "Vatica...is based on *Vatica chinensis* Linn., according to Ashton (msc) with as holotype a Hermann collection s.n. in the Linnaean herbarium (London)". There are two sheets in LINN associated with this name, neither apparently from Hermann. Ashton (in Dassanayake, *Revised Handb. Fl. Ceylon* 1(2): 196. 1977; in Dassanayake & Fosberg, *Revised Handb. Fl. Ceylon* 1: 422. 1980) subsequently published what Meijer had reported, followed by

Towary & Sarkar (in *J. Econ. Taxon. Bot.* 8: 420. 1986), who placed the material in L, rather than LINN. None of these statements distinguishes between 614.1 and 614.2 (LINN) so Ashton's 1993 explicit choice of 614.1 (LINN) as lectotype is accepted here.

Velezia rigida Linnaeus, *Species Plantarum* 1: 332. 1753.
"Habitat in Europa australi." RCN: 1853.
Lectotype (Strid in Cafferty & Jarvis in *Taxon* 53: 1053. 2004): *Löfling 307*, Herb. Linn. No. 326.1 (LINN).
Generitype of *Velezia* Linnaeus.
Current name: **Velezia rigida** L. (Caryophyllaceae).
Note: Although Ghazanfar & Nasir (in Nasir & Ali, *Fl. Pakistan* 175: 120. 1986) indicated material in LINN and UPS as syntypes (incorrectly, as neither collection was explicitly cited in the protologue), the specimens do not form part of a single collection (Art. 9.15) so their statement cannot be interpreted as a formal typification.

Vella annua Linnaeus, *Species Plantarum* 2: 641. 1753.
"Habitat in Hispania." RCN: 4663.
Lectotype (Rosselló in Cafferty & Jarvis in *Taxon* 51: 536. 2002): Herb. Clifford: 329, *Vella* 1 (BM-000646253).
Current name: **Carrichtera annua** (L.) DC. (Brassicaceae).

Vella pseudocytisus Linnaeus, *Species Plantarum* 2: 641. 1753.
"Habitat in Hispania circa oppidum Aranjuez. D. Minuart." RCN: 4664.
Lectotype (Gómez-Campo in Jarvis & al., *Regnum Veg.* 127: 98. 1993): [icon] *"Cytisi facie Alysson fruticans quorundam"* in Plantin, Pl. Stirp. Icon. 2: 49. 1581.
Generitype of *Vella* Linnaeus (vide de Candolle, *Syst. Nat.* 2: 640, 641. 1821).
Current name: **Vella pseudocytisus** L. (Brassicaceae).

Veratrum album Linnaeus, *Species Plantarum* 2: 1044. 1753.
"Habitat in Russiae, Sibiriae, Austriae, Helvetiae, Italiae, Graeciae montosis." RCN: 7539.
Lectotype (Mathew in Jarvis & al., *Regnum Veg.* 127: 98. 1993): *Gerber*, Herb. Linn. No. 1210.1 (LINN).
Generitype of *Veratrum* Linnaeus (vide Green, *Prop. Brit. Bot.*: 193. 1929).
Current name: **Veratrum album** L. (Liliaceae/Melanthiaceae).

Veratrum luteum Linnaeus, *Species Plantarum* 2: 1044. 1753.
"Habitat in Virginia, Canada." RCN: 7541.
Lectotype (designated here by Reveal): *Kalm*, Herb. Linn. No. 1210.3 (LINN).
Current name: **Chamaelirium luteum** (L.) A. Gray (Liliaceae/Melanthiaceae).

Veratrum nigrum Linnaeus, *Species Plantarum* 2: 1044. 1753.
"Habitat in Hungariae, Sibiriae apricis siccis." RCN: 7540.
Type not designated.
Original material: Herb. Burser X: 38 (UPS); *Gerber*, Herb. Linn. No. 1210.2? (LINN); [icon] in Morison, Pl. Hist. Univ. 3: 485, s. 12, t. 4, f. 2. 1699.
Current name: **Veratrum nigrum** L. (Liliaceae/Melanthiaceae).

Verbascum arcturus Linnaeus, *Species Plantarum* 1: 178. 1753.
"Habitat in Creta." RCN: 4497.
Lectotype (Turland in *Willdenowia* 36: 306, f. 3. 2006): Herb. Burser XIII: 130 (UPS).
Current name: **Verbascum arcturus** L. (Scrophulariaceae).

Verbascum blattaria Linnaeus, *Species Plantarum* 1: 178. 1753.
"Habitat in Europae australis locis argillaceis." RCN: 1412.

Lectotype (Huber-Morath in *Denkschr. Schweiz. Naturf. Ges.* 87: 143. 1971): Herb. Linn. No. 242.6 (LINN).
Current name: **Verbascum blattaria** L. (Scrophulariaceae).

Verbascum boerhavii Linnaeus, *Systema Naturae,* ed. 12, 2: 169; *Mantissa Plantarum*: 45. 1767.
"Habitat in Europa australi." RCN: 1407.
Type not designated.
Original material: Herb. Linn. No. 242.2 (LINN); [icon] in Miller, Fig. Pl. Gard. Dict. 2: 182, t. 273. 1758.
Current name: **Verbascum boerhavii** L. (Scrophulariaceae).
Note: Specific epithet spelled "boerhavi" in the protologue.

Verbascum lychnitis Linnaeus, *Species Plantarum* 1: 177. 1753.
"Habitat in Europae ruderatis cultis." RCN: 1409.
Lectotype (Fischer in *Feddes Repert.* 108: 115. 1997): Herb. Clifford: 54, *Verbascum* 2 (BM-000557980).
Current name: **Verbascum lychnitis** L. (Scrophulariaceae).

Verbascum myconi Linnaeus, *Species Plantarum* 1: 179. 1753.
"Habitat in Pyrenaeorum nemorosis." RCN: 1416.
Type not designated.
Original material: Herb. Linn. No. 242.9 (LINN).
Current name: **Ramonda myconi** (L.) Reichb. (Gesneriaceae).

Verbascum nigrum Linnaeus, *Species Plantarum* 1: 178. 1753.
"Habitat in Europa ad pagos, vias." RCN: 1410.
Lectotype (Fischer in Wisskirchen & Haeupler, *Standardliste Farn-Blütenpfl. Deutschl.*: 537. 1998): Herb. Clifford: 54, *Verbascum* 1 (BM-000557979).
Current name: **Verbascum nigrum** L. (Scrophulariaceae).

Verbascum osbeckii Linnaeus, *Species Plantarum* 1: 179. 1753.
"Habitat in Hispania. Osbeck." RCN: 1414.
Lectotype (Hansen & Hansen in *Lagascalia* 3: 184, f. 1, 2. 1973): *Osbeck s.n.*, Herb. Linn. No. 87.17 (S).
Current name: **Triguera osbeckii** (L.) Willk. (Solanaceae).

Verbascum phlomoides Linnaeus, *Species Plantarum* 2: 1194. 1753.
"Habitat in Europa australi. D. Monti." RCN: 1408.
Lectotype (Fischer in *Feddes Repert.* 108: 115. 1997): Herb. Burser XIII: 125 (UPS).
Current name: **Verbascum phlomoides** L. (Scrophulariaceae).

Verbascum phoeniceum Linnaeus, *Species Plantarum* 1: 178. 1753.
"Habitat in Europa australi, Bohemia, Lusitania inferiore." RCN: 1411.
Lectotype (Huber-Morath in *Denkschr. Schweiz. Naturf. Ges.* 87: 146. 1971): Herb. Linn. No. 242.5 (LINN).
Current name: **Verbascum phoeniceum** L. (Scrophulariaceae).

Verbascum sinuatum Linnaeus, *Species Plantarum* 1: 178. 1753.
"Habitat Monspelii, Florentiae." RCN: 1413.
Lectotype (Huber-Morath in *Denkschr. Schweiz. Naturf. Ges.* 87: 94. 1971): Herb. Linn. No. 242.7 (LINN).
Current name: **Verbascum sinuatum** L. (Scrophulariaceae).

Verbascum spinosum Linnaeus, *Centuria II Plantarum*: 10. 1756.
"Habitat in Creta." RCN: 1415.
Lectotype (Turland in *Bull. Nat. Hist. Mus. London, Bot.* 25: 134, f. 7. 1995): [icon] *"Leucoium Spinosum"* in Alpino, Pl. Exot.: 37, 36. 1627. – Epitype (Turland in *Bull. Nat. Hist. Mus. London, Bot.* 25: 134, f. 8. 1995): *Baldacci 241* (BM).
Current name: **Verbascum spinosum** L. (Scrophulariaceae).

Verbascum × thapsi Linnaeus, *Species Plantarum,* ed. 2, 2: 1669. 1763.
"Habitat in Europa rarius. Filius observabit." RCN: 1406.
Type not designated.
Original material: none traced.
Current name: **Verbascum sp.** (Scrophulariaceae).
Note: The precise application of this name appears uncertain. Linnaeus identified this as a hybrid between *V. lychnitis* L. and *V. thapsus* L.

Verbascum thapsoides Linnaeus, *Systema Naturae,* ed. 12, 2: 169. 1767.
RCN: 1405.
Type not designated.
Original material: none traced.
Current name: **Verbascum sp.** (Scrophulariaceae).
Note: The precise application of this name appears uncertain.

Verbascum thapsus Linnaeus, *Species Plantarum* 1: 177. 1753.
"Habitat in Europae glareosis sterilibus." RCN: 1404.
Lectotype (Huber-Morath in *Denkschr. Schweiz. Naturf. Ges.* 87: 43. 1971): Herb. Linn. No. 242.1 (LINN).
Generitype of *Verbascum* Linnaeus (vide Hitchcock, *Prop. Brit. Bot.*: 132. 1929).
Current name: **Verbascum thapsus** L. (Scrophulariaceae).
Note: Although Huber-Morath did not explicitly cite the sheet number of 242.1 (LINN), it is the only sheet there associated with this name and is accepted here as the lectotype.

Verbena bonariensis Linnaeus, *Species Plantarum* 1: 20. 1753.
"Habitat in agro Bonariensi." RCN: 160.
Lectotype (Moldenke in *Phytologia* 8: 252. 1962): Herb. Linn. No. 35.11 (LINN).
Current name: **Verbena bonariensis** L. (Verbenaceae).

Verbena carolina Linnaeus, *Systema Naturae,* ed. 10, 2: 852. 1759.
["Habitat in America septentrionali."] Sp. Pl., ed. 2, 1: 29 (1762). RCN: 162b.
Type not designated.
Original material: [icon] in Dillenius, Hort. Eltham. 2: 407, t. 301, f. 388. 1732.
Current name: **Verbena carolina** L. (Verbenaceae).
Note: Moldenke (in *Phytologia* 8: 495. 1963) designated 35.17 (LINN) as the type but this was a post-1759 addition to the herbarium, and is not original material for the name.

Verbena curassavica Linnaeus, *Species Plantarum* 1: 19. 1753.
"Habitat in Curassao Americes." RCN: 158.
Lectotype (Méndez Santos & Cafferty in *Taxon* 50: 1139. 2002 [2001]): [icon] *"Veronicae similis fruticosa Corassavica"* in Hermann, Parad. Bat.: 240. 1698.
Current name: **Tamonea curassavica** (L.) Pers. (Verbenaceae).

Verbena hastata Linnaeus, *Species Plantarum* 1: 20. 1753.
"Habitat in Canadae humidis." RCN: 161.
Type not designated.
Original material: Herb. A. van Royen No. 913.30–210 (L); Herb. Linn. No. 35.12 (LINN); Herb. A. van Royen No. 913.30–198 (L); [icon] in Hermann, Parad. Bat.: 242. 1698.
Current name: **Verbena hastata** L. (Verbenaceae).

Verbena indica Linnaeus, *Systema Naturae,* ed. 10, 2: 851. 1759.
["Habitat in Zeylona. Dav. Royen."] Sp. Pl., ed. 2, 1: 27 (1762). RCN: 153.
Lectotype (Moldenke & Moldenke in Dassanayake & Fosberg, *Revised Handb. Fl. Ceylon* 4: 266. 1983): Herb. Linn. No. 35.1 (LINN).

Current name: ***Stachytarpheta indica*** (L.) Vahl (Verbenaceae).
Note: See extensive discussion by Fernandes & Brenan (in *Bol. Soc. Brot.*, sér. 2, 57: 94. 1985).

Verbena jamaicensis Linnaeus, *Species Plantarum* 1: 19. 1753.
"Habitat in Jamaica & Carabaeis." RCN: 154.
Lectotype (Fernandes in *Bol. Soc. Brot.*, sér. 2, 57: 100. 1984): Herb. Linn. No. 7.13 (S).
Current name: ***Stachytarpheta jamaicensis*** (L.) Vahl (Verbenaceae).
Note: Moldenke & Moldenke (in Dassanayake & Fosberg, *Revised Handb. Fl. Ceylon* 4: 253. 1983) indicated 35.2 (LINN) as the type, but this is a Patrick Browne collection which was not received by Linnaeus until 1758 and cannot therefore be original material for this name.

Verbena lappulacea Linnaeus, *Species Plantarum* 1: 19. 1753.
"Habitat in Jamaica." RCN: 162.
Neotype (Howard, *Fl. Lesser Antilles* 6: 238. 1989): *Browne*, Herb. Linn. No. 35.5 (LINN).
Current name: ***Priva lappulacea*** (L.) Pers. (Verbenaceae).
Note: See Méndez Santos & Cafferty (in *Taxon* 50: 1139. 2002), who change Howard's stated lectotype choice to a neotype under Art. 9.8.

Verbena mexicana Linnaeus, *Species Plantarum* 1: 19. 1753.
"Habitat in Mexico." RCN: 156.
Lectotype (Willmann & al., *Fl. Valle Tehuacán-Cuicatlán* 27: 50. 2000): Herb. Linn. No. 35.4 (LINN).
Current name: ***Priva mexicana*** (L.) Pers. (Verbenaceae).

Verbena nodiflora Linnaeus, *Species Plantarum* 1: 20. 1753.
"Habitat in Virginia." RCN: 159.
Lectotype (Townsend in Davis, *Fl. Turkey* 7: 32. 1982): Herb. Clifford: 11, *Verbena* 3 (BM-000557561).
Current name: ***Phyla nodiflora*** (L.) Greene (Verbenaceae).

Verbena officinalis Linnaeus, *Species Plantarum* 1: 20. 1753.
"Habitat in Europae mediterraneae ruderatis." RCN: 164.
Lectotype (Verdcourt in Jarvis & al., *Regnum Veg.* 127: 98. 1993): Herb. Clifford: 11, *Verbena* 6, sheet 6 (BM-000557564).
Generitype of *Verbena* Linnaeus (vide Hitchcock, *Prop. Brit. Bot.*: 116. 1929).
Current name: ***Verbena officinalis*** L. (Verbenaceae).
Note: Jafri (in Nasir & Ali, *Fl. W. Pakistan* 77: 4. 1977), followed by a number of later authors, indicated 35.15 (LINN) as type. However, this sheet lacks the *Species Plantarum* number (i.e. "13") and is a post-1753 addition to the herbarium, and not original material for the name. Verdcourt's choice of a Clifford sheet as lectotype is followed here.

Verbena orubica Linnaeus, *Species Plantarum* 1: 18. 1753.
"Habitat in Oruba insula americes septentrionalis." RCN: 152.
Type not designated.
Original material: Herb. Clifford; 10, *Verbena* 1 (BM); [icon] in Plukenet, Phytographia: t. 228, f. 4. 1692; Almag. Bot.: 383. 1696; [icon] in Plukenet, Phytographia: t. 327, f. 7. 1694; Almag. Bot.: 383. 1696; [icon] in Ehret, Pl. Papil. Rar.: t. 5, f. 1. 1748.
Current name: ***Stachytarpheta orubica*** (L.) Vahl (Verbenaceae).
Note: Although Wijnands (*Bot. Commelins*: 201. 1983) provided an extensive discussion, he did not typify the name.

Verbena prismatica Linnaeus, *Species Plantarum* 1: 19. 1753.
"Habitat in Jamaica." RCN: 155.
Neotype (Moldenke in *Repert. Spec. Nov. Regni Veg.* 49: 98. 1940): *Browne*, Herb. Linn. No. 35.3 (LINN). – Epitype (Méndez Santos

& Cafferty in *Taxon* 50: 1140. 2002): Jamaica. St Andrew Parish, banks of Hope River bed E of University of West Indies campus just E of Kingston, 13 Jun 1963, *Crosby & al. 132* (US; iso- DUKE).
Current name: ***Bouchea prismatica*** (L.) Kuntze (Verbenaceae).
Note: See Méndez Santos & Cafferty (in *Taxon* 50: 1139. 2002) who change Moldenke's stated type choice to a neotype under Art. 9.8, and designate an epitype in its support.

Verbena spuria Linnaeus, *Species Plantarum* 1: 20. 1753.
"Habitat in Canada, Virginia." RCN: 163.
Type not designated.
Original material: none traced.
Current name: ***Verbena officinalis*** L. (Verbenaceae).

Verbena stoechadifolia Linnaeus, *Species Plantarum* 1: 19. 1753.
"Habitat in America Galliae aequinoctialis." RCN: 157.
Neotype (Méndez Santos & Cafferty in *Taxon* 50: 1140. 2002 [2001]): Herb. A. van Royen No. 913.13–121 (L).
Current name: ***Phyla stoechadifolia*** (L.) Small (Verbenaceae).

Verbena supina Linnaeus, *Species Plantarum* 1: 21. 1753.
"Habitat in Hispania." RCN: 165.
Lectotype (Moldenke in *Phytologia* 11: 255. 1965): *Löfling 16*, Herb. Linn. No. 9.1 (S).
Current name: ***Verbena supina*** L. (Verbenaceae).

Verbena urticifolia Linnaeus, *Species Plantarum* 1: 20. 1753.
"Habitat in Virginiae, Canadae aridis." RCN: 163.
Lectotype (Méndez Santos & Cafferty in *Taxon* 50: 1140. 2002 [2001]): Herb. Linn. No. 35.13 (LINN).
Current name: ***Verbena urticifolia*** L. (Verbenaceae).

Verbesina acmella Linnaeus, *Species Plantarum* 2: 901. 1753.
"Habitat in Zeylona." RCN: 6013.
Basionym of: *Spilanthes acmella* (L.) L. (1774).
Lectotype (Koster & Philipson in *Blumea* 6: 349, f. 1. 1950): Herb. Hermann 2: 10, No. 309 (BM-000594573).
Current name: ***Blainvillea acmella*** (L.) Philipson (Asteraceae).

Verbesina alata Linnaeus, *Species Plantarum* 2: 901. 1753, *typ. cons.*
"Habitat in Curassao, Surinamo." RCN: 6518.
Lectotype (Wijnands, *Bot. Commelins*: 86. 1983): Herb. Clifford: 411, *Verbesina* 1 (BM-000647141).
Generitype of *Verbesina* Linnaeus, *nom. cons.*
Current name: ***Verbesina alata*** L. var. ***alata*** (Asteraceae).
Note: The Clifford material was proposed as the conserved type by Jeffrey (in *Taxon* 41: 595. 1992), subsequently recommended by both the Committee for Spermatophyta (in *Taxon* 43: 276. 1994) and the General Committee (in *Taxon* 43: 281. 1994). Olsen (in *Brittonia* 38: 364. 1986) was credited as being the typifier by Jeffrey in his proposal. However, Wijnands had already made the same choice.

Verbesina alba Linnaeus, *Species Plantarum* 2: 902. 1753.
"Habitat in Virginia, Surinamo." RCN: 6513.
Basionym of: *Cotula alba* (L.) L. (1767); *Eclipta erecta* L. (1771), *nom. illeg.*
Lectotype (D'Arcy in Woodson & Schery in *Ann. Missouri Bot. Gard.* 62: 1102. 1975): Herb. Linn. No. 1020.1 (LINN).
Current name: ***Eclipta prostrata*** (L.) L. (Asteraceae).

Verbesina asteroides Linnaeus, *Species Plantarum* 2: 902. 1753.
"Habitat – – – –" RCN: 6511.
Neotype (Rommel in *Mitt. Bot. Staatssamml. München* 13: 596. 1977): Herb. Linn. No. 1023.1 (LINN).

Current name: **Amellus asteroides** (L.) Druce (Asteraceae).
Note: Rommel (in *Mitt. Bot. Staatssamml. München* 13: 596. 1977) indicated 1023.1 (LINN) as the lectotype but this collection is associated not with this name, but with *Amellus lychnites* L. (1759). However, in the absence of any original material for *V. asteroides*, Rommel's statement is treated as a correctable error, with 1023.1 (LINN) accepted as a neotype (rather than a lectotype) under Art. 9.8.

Verbesina biflora Linnaeus, *Species Plantarum*, ed. 2, 2: 1272. 1763.
"Habitat in India." RCN: 6523.
Lectotype (Wild in *Kirkia* 5: 4. 1965): Herb. Linn. No. 1021.4 (LINN).
Current name: **Melanthera biflora** (L.) Willd. (Asteraceae).

Verbesina calendulacea Linnaeus, *Species Plantarum* 2: 902. 1753.
"Habitat in Zeylona." RCN: 6524.
Lectotype (Grierson in Dassanayake & Fosberg, *Revised Handb. Fl. Ceylon* 1: 215. 1980; Pruski in *Novon* 6: 411. 1996): Herb. Hermann 1: 73, No. 311 (BM-000594505; iso- BM, Herb. Hermann 2: 16; 3: 21; 4: 43).
Current name: **Sphagneticola calendulacea** (L.) Pruski (Asteraceae).
Note: Grierson (in Dassanayake & Fosberg, *Revised Handb. Fl. Ceylon* 1: 215. 1980) indicated material in Herb. Hermann (BM) as type but did not distinguish between the various specimens scattered between four volumes. However, as these appear to be part of a single gathering, Art. 9.15 applies so Grierson is the original typifier, with Pruski subsequently restricting the earlier choice.

Verbesina chinensis Linnaeus, *Species Plantarum* 2: 901. 1753.
"Habitat in China. Osbeck." RCN: 6521.
Lectotype (Wild in *Kirkia* 4: 50. 1964): Herb. Linn. No. 1021.3 (LINN).
Current name: **Anisopappus chinensis** (L.) Hook. & Arn. (Asteraceae).

Verbesina fruticosa (Linnaeus) Linnaeus, *Systema Naturae,* ed. 10, 2: 1226. 1759.
RCN: 6526.
Basionym: *Bidens fruticosa* L. (1753).
Lectotype (D'Arcy in Woodson & Schery in *Ann. Missouri Bot. Gard.* 62: 1110. 1975): Herb. Clifford: 399, *Bidens* 3 (BM-000646989).
Current name: **Lasianthaea fruticosa** (L.) K.M. Becker (Asteraceae).

Verbesina lavenia Linnaeus, *Species Plantarum* 2: 902. 1753.
"Habitat in Zeylona." RCN: 6522.
Lectotype (Panigrahi in *Kew Bull.* 30: 647. 1976): [icon] *"Eupatoriophalacron Scrophulariae aquaticae foliis oppositis"* in Burman, Thes. Zeylan.: 95, t. 42. 1737 (see p. 113; above right).
Current name: **Adenostemma lavenia** (L.) Kuntze (Asteraceae).

Verbesina linifolia Linnaeus, *Systema Naturae,* ed. 10, 2: 1226. 1759.
["Habitat in America."] Sp. Pl., ed. 2, 2: 1250 (1763). RCN: 6519.
Lectotype (Keil in *Taxon* 34: 284. 1985): *Browne,* Herb. Linn. No. 1011.2 (LINN).
Current name: **Pectis linifolia** L. (Asteraceae).

Verbesina mutica Linnaeus, *Species Plantarum*, ed. 2, 2: 1273. 1763, *nom. illeg.*
"Habitat in America meridionali." RCN: 6487.
Replaced synonym: *Anthemis americana* L. (1753).
Lectotype (D'Arcy in Woodson & Schery in *Ann. Missouri Bot. Gard.* 62: 1184. 1975): Herb. Clifford: 414, *Buphthalmum* 5 (BM-000647176).
Current name: **Chrysanthellum americanum** (L.) Vatke (Asteraceae).

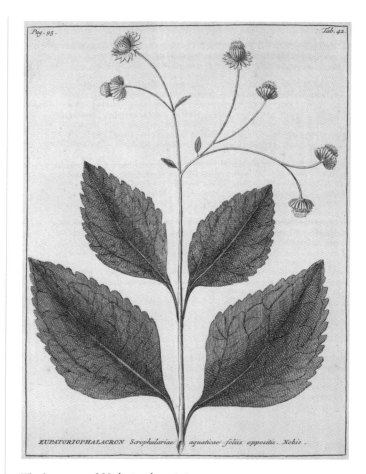

The lectotype of *Verbesina lavenia* L.

Verbesina nodiflora Linnaeus, *Centuria I Plantarum*: 28. 1755.
"Habitat in Caribaeis." RCN: 6525.
Type not designated.
Original material: Herb. Linn. No. 357.15? (S); Herb. Linn. No. 357.17 (S); [icon] in Sloane, Voy. Jamaica 1: 262, t. 154, f. 4. 1707; [icon] in Dillenius, Hort. Eltham. 1: 53, t. 45, f. 53. 1732.
Current name: **Synedrella nodiflora** (L.) Gaertn. (Asteraceae).
Note: Moore (in Fawcett & Rendle, *Fl. Jamaica* 7: 247. 1936) noted the existence of 1021.7 (LINN) but did not designate a type. Grierson (in Dassanayake & Fosberg, *Revised Handb. Fl. Ceylon* 1: 223. 1980) indicated unspecified material in Herb. Sloane (BM-SL), though with doubt ("?"), as type, but this would not have been seen by Linnaeus and is not original material for the name. Howard (*Fl. Lesser Antilles* 6: 600. 1989) indicated 1021.7 (LINN) as the type, but this is a Patrick Browne collection which Linnaeus did not acquire until 1758 and which cannot, therefore, be original material for a name published in 1755.

Verbesina prostrata Linnaeus, *Species Plantarum* 2: 902. 1753.
"Habitat in India." RCN: 6514.
Basionym of: *Cotula prostrata* (L.) L. (1767); *Eclipta prostrata* (L.) L. (1771).
Lectotype (Wijnands, *Bot. Commelins*: 74. 1983): [icon] *"Chrysanthemum Maderaspatanum, Menthae arvensis folio & facie, floribus bigemellis, ad foliorum alas, pediculis curtis"* in Plukenet, Phytographia: t. 118, f. 5. 1691; Almag. Bot.: 100. 1696. – Typotype: Herb. Sloane 94: 175 (BM-SL).

V

Current name: ***Eclipta prostrata*** (L.) L. (Asteraceae).
Note: D'Arcy (in *Ann. Missouri Bot. Gard.* 62: 1102. 1975) indicated 1020.4 or 1020.5 (LINN) as the type, presumably in error as both are associated with the name "Eclipta latifolia" rather than *V. prostrata*. Neither they, nor 1020.7 LINN, the post-1753 Patrick Browne collection treated as the lectotype by Kupicha (in Davis, *Fl. Turkey* 5: 46. 1975), are original material for the name. Grierson (in Dassanayake & Fosberg, *Revised Handb. Fl. Ceylon* 1: 212. 1980) treated material in Herb. Plukenet (BM-SL) as "type", but this would not have been seen by Linnaeus and is not original material either. Wijnands' 1983 choice of the Plukenet illustration as lectotype is therefore accepted here.

Verbesina pseudoacmella Linnaeus, *Species Plantarum* 2: 901. 1753.
"Habitat in Zeylona." RCN: 6012.
Basionym of: *Spilanthes pseudoacmella* (L.) L. (1774).
Lectotype (Koster & Philipson in *Blumea* 6: 349, f. 2. 1950): Herb. Hermann 3: 29, No. 308 (BM-000621911).
Current name: ***Eclipta prostrata*** (L.) L. (Asteraceae).

Verbesina virginica Linnaeus, *Species Plantarum* 2: 901. 1753.
"Habitat in Virginia." RCN: 6521.
Lectotype (Olsen in *Sida* 8: 132. 1979): *Clayton 166* (BM-000038850).
Current name: ***Verbesina virginica*** L. var. ***virginica*** (Asteraceae).

Veronica acinifolia Linnaeus, *Species Plantarum, ed. 2,* 1: 19. 1762.
"Habitat in Europa australi." RCN: 101.
Lectotype (Fischer in *Pl. Syst. Evol.* 120: 415. 1972): [icon] *"Veronica minor, annua, Clinopodii minoris folio"* in Vaillant, Bot. Paris.: 201, t. 33, f. 3. 1727.
Current name: ***Veronica acinifolia*** L. (Scrophulariaceae).

Veronica agrestis Linnaeus, *Species Plantarum* 1: 13. 1753.
"Habitat in Europae cultis, arvis." RCN: 95.
Lectotype (Martínez Ortega & al. in *Taxon* 51: 763. 2003 [2002]): Herb. Celsius 5: 780 (UPS).
Current name: ***Veronica agrestis*** L. (Scrophulariaceae).
Note: Fischer (in *Feddes Repert.* 108: 115. 1997) designated Herb. Linn. 26.58 (LINN) as lectotype, a specimen of *V. arvensis* which had already been formally designated as the type of the latter name. As none of the elements then thought to be original material for *V. agrestis* corresponded with the usage of the name, Martínez Ortega & al. (in *Taxon* 49: 99. 2000) proposed the name for conservation with a conserved type. However, further original material, from the Celsius herbarium in Uppsala, subsequently came to light. This material is identifiable as *V. agrestis* and Martínez Ortega & al. (in *Taxon* 51: 763. 2003) therefore rejected Fischer's type choice (Art. 9.17) in favour of a Celsius collection, and withdrew their proposal to reject the name.

Veronica alpina Linnaeus, *Species Plantarum* 1: 11. 1753.
"Habitat in alpibus Europae." RCN: 79.
Lectotype (Fischer in *Feddes Repert.* 108: 115. 1997): Herb. Linn. No. 26.26 (LINN).
Current name: ***Veronica alpina*** L. (Scrophulariaceae).

Veronica anagallis-aquatica Linnaeus, *Species Plantarum* 1: 12. 1753.
"Habitat in Europa ad fossas." RCN: 82.
Lectotype (Fischer in *Feddes Repert.* 108: 115. 1997): Herb. Linn. No. 5.7 (S).
Current name: ***Veronica anagallis-aquatica*** L. (Scrophulariaceae).
Note: Although Pennell (in *Acad. Nat. Sci. Philadelphia Monogr.* 1: 362. 1935) indicated 26.35 (LINN) as type, this sheet is annotated only by Ehrhart and is a post-1753 addition to the collection, and not original material for the name.

Veronica aphylla Linnaeus, *Species Plantarum* 1: 11. 1753.
"Habitat in alpibus Europae australioris." RCN: 76.
Lectotype (Fischer in *Feddes Repert.* 108: 115. 1997): Herb. Burser XIV(1): 48 (UPS).
Current name: ***Veronica aphylla*** L. (Scrophulariaceae).

Veronica arvensis Linnaeus, *Species Plantarum* 1: 13. 1753.
"Habitat in Europae arvis, cultis." RCN: 96.
Lectotype (Cramer in Dassanayake & Fosberg, *Revised Handb. Fl. Ceylon* 3: 438. 1981): Herb. Linn. No. 26.58 (LINN).
Current name: ***Veronica arvensis*** L. (Scrophulariaceae).

Veronica austriaca Linnaeus, *Systema Naturae,* ed. 10, 2: 849. 1759.
["Habitat in Austria."] Sp. Pl., ed. 2, 1: 16 (1762). RCN: 90.
Lectotype (Fischer in *Feddes Repert.* 108: 115. 1997): Herb. Linn. No. 26.47 (LINN).
Current name: ***Veronica austriaca*** L. (Scrophulariaceae).
Note: Soják (in *Cas. Nár. Muz. Praze, Rada Prír.* 152: 16, 24. 1983) noted three sheets in LINN from which a type should be selected, along with two further post-1753 sheets. However, he did not designate a type.

Veronica beccabunga Linnaeus, *Species Plantarum* 1: 12. 1753.
"Habitat in Europa ad rivulos." RCN: 81.
Lectotype (Fischer in *Feddes Repert.* 108: 116. 1997): Herb. Clifford: 8, *Veronica* 5 (BM-000557538).
Current name: ***Veronica beccabunga*** L. (Scrophulariaceae).
Note: Although Pennell (in *Acad. Nat. Sci. Philadelphia Monogr.* 1: 362. 1935) indicated what must be 26.34 (LINN) as type, this is a later specimen from Ehrhart, unannotated by Linnaeus, and not original material for the name.

Veronica bellidioides Linnaeus, *Species Plantarum* 1: 11. 1753.
"Habitat in Helvetia, Pyrenaeis." RCN: 77.
Lectotype (Fischer in *Feddes Repert.* 108: 116. 1997): Herb. Burser XIV(1): 27 (UPS).
Current name: ***Veronica bellidioides*** L. (Scrophulariaceae).

Veronica biloba Linnaeus, *Mantissa Plantarum Altera*: 172. 1771.
"Habitat inter Cappadociae segetes. D. Schreber." RCN: 94.
Lectotype (Martínez Ortega & al. in *Taxon* 50: 551. 2001): [icon] *"Veronica arvensis annua, Chamaedryos folio"* in Buxbaum, Pl. Minus Cognit. Cent. 1: 24, t. 36. 1728. – Epitype (Martínez Ortega & al. in *Taxon* 50: 551. 2001): Turkey. Kayseri, Erciyas Dag, 2,350m, 11 Jul 1977, *Sorger 77–38–21* (WU).
Current name: ***Veronica biloba*** L. (Scrophulariaceae).

Veronica bonarota Linnaeus, *Species Plantarum* 1: 11. 1753.
"Habitat in alpibus Italicis." RCN: 106.
Basionym of: *Paederota bonarota* (L.) L. (1762).
Lectotype (Sutton in Jarvis & al., *Regnum Veg.* 127: 72. 1993): Herb. Burser XIV(1): 46 (UPS).
Current name: ***Paederota bonarota*** (L.) L. (Scrophulariaceae).

Veronica chamaedrys Linnaeus, *Species Plantarum* 1: 13. 1753.
"Habitat in Europae pratis." RCN: 89.
Lectotype (Fischer in *Feddes Repert.* 108: 116. 1997): Herb. Clifford: 8, *Veronica* 7 (BM-000557541).
Current name: ***Veronica chamaedrys*** L. (Scrophulariaceae).
Note: Although Pennell (in *Acad. Nat. Sci. Philadelphia Monogr.* 1: 352. 1935) stated that the type was in LINN, he did not distinguish between sheets 26.43 and 26.44 (which are not part of a single gathering so Art. 9.15 does not apply). Fischer (in *Österr. Bot. Zeitschr.* 121: 75. 1973) regarded both sheets as comprising the type so this statement, too, does not result in a formal choice of type.

Veronica fruticulosa Linnaeus, *Species Plantarum,* ed. 2, 1: 15. 1762. "Habitat in Alpibus Austriae, Helvetiae, Pyrenaeis." RCN: 78.
Lectotype (Fischer in *Feddes Repert.* 108: 116. 1997): Scopoli *s.n.*, Herb. Linn. No. 26.24 (LINN).
Current name: ***Veronica fruticulosa*** L. (Scrophulariaceae).
Note: Linnaeus subsequently added *Veronica fruticans* Jacq. (in *Enum. Stirp. Vindob.*: 200. 1762) to the synonymy of his *V. fruticulosa* (in *Species Plantarum,* ed. 2, 2: 1676. 1763). See notes by Martínez Ortega & al. (in *Taxon* 50: 552. 2001).

Veronica hederifolia Linnaeus, *Species Plantarum* 1: 13. 1753. "Habitat in Europae ruderatis." RCN: 97.
Lectotype (Fischer in *Feddes Repert.* 108: 116. 1997): Herb. Clifford: 9, *Veronica* 10 (BM-000557548).
Current name: ***Veronica hederifolia*** L. (Scrophulariaceae).
Note: Specific epithet spelled "hederaefolia" in the protologue. Although Pennell (in *Acad. Nat. Sci. Philadelphia Monogr.* 1: 350. 1935) stated that the type was in LINN, he did not distinguish between sheets 26.60 and 26.61 (which are not part of a single gathering so Art. 9.15 does not apply).

Veronica hybrida Linnaeus, *Species Plantarum* 1: 11. 1753. "Habitat in Europa rarius." RCN: 73.
Lectotype (Trávníček in *Preslia* 70: 217. 1998): *Tessin?*, Herb. Linn. No. 26.14 (LINN), see p. 231.
Current name: ***Veronica spicata*** L. subsp. ***hybrida*** (L.) Gaudin (Scrophulariaceae).

Veronica incana Linnaeus, *Species Plantarum* 1: 10. 1753. "Habitat in Ucrania, Samara." RCN: 71.
Lectotype (Trávníček in *Preslia* 70: 196. 1998): Herb. Linn. No. 26.7, second specimen from the left (LINN).
Current name: ***Veronica incana*** L. (Scrophulariaceae).

Veronica latifolia Linnaeus, *Species Plantarum* 1: 13. 1753, *nom. utique rej. prop.*
"Habitat in Helvetia, Bithynia." RCN: 92.
Lectotype (Webb in Heywood in *Bot. J. Linn. Soc.* 65: 266. 1972): Herb. Linn. No. 26.52 (LINN).
Current name: ***Veronica teucrium*** L. (Scrophulariaceae).
Note: Smith (in Rees, *Cycl.* 37: Veronica No. 58. 1819) described a specimen in LINN of which Pennell (in *Rhodora* 23: 32. 1921) says "...the specimen of the Linnaean herbarium should stand as type". However, Smith's published account does not distinguish between sheets 26.52 and 26.53 (which are not part of a single gathering) so Pennell's statement, and a similar, later one (in *Acad. Nat. Sci. Philadelphia Monogr.* 1: 35. 1935) do not effect typification. Webb, in typifying the name, also informally rejected it as a *nomen ambiguum*. Martínez Ortega & al. (in *Taxon* 55: 538. 2006) subsequently made a formal proposal for the rejection of the name.

Veronica longifolia Linnaeus, *Species Plantarum* 1: 10. 1753. "Habitat in Tataria, Austria, Suecia." RCN: 70.
Lectotype (Fischer in *Feddes Repert.* 108: 114. 1997): Herb. Linn. No. 26.6 (LINN).
Current name: ***Veronica longifolia*** L. (Scrophulariaceae).
Note: See comments on the application of this name by Trávníček & al. (in *Folia Geobot.* 39: 177. 2005).

Veronica marilandica Linnaeus, *Species Plantarum* 1: 14. 1753. "Habitat in Virginia." RCN: 103.
Lectotype (Reveal & al. in *Huntia* 7: 237. 1987): *Clayton 226* (BM-000042220).
Current name: ***Polypremum procumbens*** L. (Loganiaceae/Buddlejaceae).

Veronica maritima Linnaeus, *Species Plantarum* 1: 10. 1753. "Habitat in maritimis Europae macris apricis." RCN: 69.
Lectotype (Fischer in *Feddes Repert.* 108: 114. 1997): Herb. Linn. No. 26.4 (LINN).
Current name: ***Veronica longifolia*** L. (Scrophulariaceae).
Note: See comments on the application of this name by Trávníček & al. (in *Folia Geobot.* 39: 177. 2005).

Veronica montana Linnaeus, *Centuria I Plantarum*: 3. 1755. "Habitat in montanis Mattesii Italiae & Greismari Germaniae umbrosis." RCN: 88.
Lectotype (Fischer in *Feddes Repert.* 108: 116. 1997): *Schreber*, Herb. Linn. No. 26.42 (LINN).
Current name: ***Veronica montana*** L. (Scrophulariaceae).

Veronica multifida Linnaeus, *Species Plantarum* 1: 13. 1753. "Habitat in Armenia, Iberiae graminosis." RCN: 91.
Lectotype (Martínez Ortega & al. in *Taxon* 47: 438. 1998): [icon] *"Veronica montana, folio vario"* in Buxbaum, Pl. Minus Cognit. Cent. 1: 24, t. 38. 1728. – Epitype (Martínez Ortega & al. in *Taxon* 47: 438. 1998): Turkey. Kastamonu, 1,100m, marly hills above town, 9 Jun 1954, *Davis & Polunin 21770* (BM; iso- K).
Current name: ***Veronica multifida*** L. (Scrophulariaceae).

Veronica officinalis Linnaeus, *Species Plantarum* 1: 11. 1753. "Habitat in Europae sylvestribus sterilibus." RCN: 75.
Lectotype (Sutton in Jarvis & al., *Regnum Veg.* 127: 98. 1993): Herb. Clifford: 8, *Veronica* 4 (BM-000557537).
Generitype of *Veronica* Linnaeus (vide Hitchcock, *Prop. Brit. Bot.*: 116. 1929).
Current name: ***Veronica officinalis*** L. (Scrophulariaceae).
Note: Pennell (in *Acad. Nat. Sci. Philadelphia Monogr.* 1: 352. 1935) stated that the type was in LINN but did not distinguish between sheets 26.19 and 26.20. As these two collections are not part of the same gathering, Art. 9.15 does not apply. Sutton subsequently designated a Clifford sheet as lectotype.

Veronica paniculata Linnaeus, *Systema Naturae,* ed. 10, 2: 849. 1759. ["Habitat in Tataria."] Sp. Pl., ed. 2, 1: 18 (1762). RCN: 93.
Lectotype (Fischer in *Feddes Repert.* 108: 114. 1997): Herb. Linn. No. 26.56 (LINN).
Current name: ***Veronica spuria*** L. (Scrophulariaceae).

Veronica pectinata Linnaeus, *Systema Naturae,* ed. 12, 2: 58; *Mantissa Plantarum*: 24. 1767.
"Habitat Constantinopoli." RCN: 87.
Lectotype (Martínez Ortega & al. in *Taxon* 50: 553. 2001): Herb. Linn. No. 26.41, central specimen (LINN).
Current name: ***Veronica pectinata*** L. (Scrophulariaceae).

Veronica peregrina Linnaeus, *Species Plantarum* 1: 14. 1753. "Habitat in Europae hortis, arvisque." RCN: 102.
Lectotype (Fischer in *Feddes Repert.* 108: 116. 1997): Herb. Linn. No. 26.67 (LINN).
Current name: ***Veronica peregrina*** L. (Scrophulariaceae).
Note: Although Pennell (in *Acad. Nat. Sci. Philadelphia Monogr.* 1: 337. 1935) stated that the type was in LINN, he did not distinguish between sheets 26.66 and 26.67 (which are not part of a single gathering so Art. 9.15 does not apply).

Veronica pilosa Linnaeus, *Species Plantarum,* ed. 2, 2: 1663. 1763. "Habitat in Austria." RCN: 85.
Lectotype (Martínez Ortega & al. in *Taxon* 50: 553. 2001): Herb. Burser XIV(1): 55 (UPS).
Current name: ***Veronica prostrata*** L. (Scrophulariaceae).

Note: Fischer (in *Österr. Bot. Zeitschr.* 122: 289. 1973) discussed the application of the name by a succession of authors but did not typify the name in the sense of Linnaeus.

Veronica pinnata Linnaeus, *Systema Naturae,* ed. 12, 2: 57; *Mantissa Plantarum*: 24. 1767.
"Habitat in Sibiria. Laxman." RCN: 74.
Type not designated.
Original material: none traced.
Current name: ***Veronica pinnata*** L. (Scrophulariaceae).
Note: Kosachev (in *Turczaninowia* 6(1): 31. 2003) indicated unspecified material in LINN as type, but the herbarium contains no original material for the name.

Veronica prostrata Linnaeus, *Species Plantarum,* ed. 2, 1: 17. 1762.
"Habitat in Germaniae, Italiae collibus." RCN: 86.
Lectotype (Fischer in *Feddes Repert.* 108: 116. 1997): Herb. Linn. No. 26.39 (LINN).
Current name: ***Veronica prostrata*** L. (Scrophulariaceae).

Veronica romana Linnaeus, *Species Plantarum* 1: 14. 1753.
"Habitat in Europae australioris agris." RCN: 100.
Lectotype (Martínez Ortega & al. in *Taxon* 50: 554. 2001): Herb. Linn. No. 26.65 (LINN).
Current name: ***Veronica peregrina*** L. (Scrophulariaceae).
Note: Pennell (in *Acad. Nat. Sci. Philadelphia Monogr.* 1: 337. 1935) stated that material in LINN was the basis for Linnaeus' diagnosis but he fell short of calling it the type.

Veronica scutellata Linnaeus, *Species Plantarum* 1: 12. 1753.
"Habitat in Europae inundatis." RCN: 83.
Lectotype (Fischer in *Feddes Repert.* 108: 116. 1997): Herb. Linn. No. 26.37 (LINN).
Current name: ***Veronica scutellata*** L. (Scrophulariaceae).

Veronica serpyllifolia Linnaeus, *Species Plantarum* 1: 12. 1753.
"Habitat in Europa & America septentrionali ad vias, agros." RCN: 80.
Lectotype (Cramer in Dassanayake & Fosberg, *Revised Handb. Fl. Ceylon* 3: 437. 1981): Herb. Linn. No. 26.30 (LINN).
Current name: ***Veronica serpyllifolia*** L. (Scrophulariaceae).
Note: Pennell (in *Acad. Nat. Sci. Philadelphia Monogr.* 1: 335. 1935) designated what he felt to be the more glabrous of the specimens in LINN as type. As it is difficult to be sure which collection was intended, Cramer's choice (which has been followed by later authors) is accepted here.

Veronica sibirica Linnaeus, *Species Plantarum,* ed. 2, 1: 12. 1762.
"Habitat in Dauria." RCN: 66.
Type not designated.
Original material: Herb. Linn. No. 26.1 (LINN); [icon] in Amman, Stirp. Rar. Ruth.: 20, t. 4. 1739.
Current name: ***Veronicastrum sibiricum*** (L.) Pennell (Scrophulariaceae).

Veronica spicata Linnaeus, *Species Plantarum* 1: 10. 1753.
"Habitat in Europae borealis campestris." RCN: 72.
Lectotype (Fischer in *Feddes Repert.* 108: 114. 1997): Herb. Linn. No. 26.10 (LINN).
Current name: ***Veronica spicata*** L. subsp. ***spicata*** L. (Scrophulariaceae).

Veronica spuria Linnaeus, *Species Plantarum* 1: 10. 1753.
"Habitat in Europa australiore, Sibiria." RCN: 68.
Type not designated.

Original material: Herb. Burser XIV(1): 16? (UPS); [icon] in Barrelier, Pl. Galliam: 17, t. 891. 1714.
Current name: ***Veronica spuria*** L. (Scrophulariaceae).
Note: Kosachev (in *Turczaninowia* 6(1): 16. 2003) indicated unspecified material in LINN as type but the herbarium contains no original material for the name.

Veronica teucrium Linnaeus, *Species Plantarum,* ed. 2, 1: 16. 1762.
"Habitat in Germania." RCN: 84.
Lectotype (Fischer in *Feddes Repert.* 108: 117. 1997): Herb. Burser XIV(1): 52 (UPS).
Current name: ***Veronica teucrium*** L. (Scrophulariaceae).

Veronica triphyllos Linnaeus, *Species Plantarum* 1: 14. 1753.
"Habitat in Europae agris." RCN: 98.
Lectotype (Fischer in *Feddes Repert.* 108: 117. 1997): Herb. Clifford: 9, *Veronica* 11 (BM-000557550).
Current name: ***Veronica triphyllos*** L. (Scrophulariaceae).

Veronica verna Linnaeus, *Species Plantarum* 1: 14. 1753.
"Habitat in Sueciae, Germaniae, Hispaniae aridis apricis." RCN: 99.
Lectotype (Fischer in *Feddes Repert.* 108: 117. 1997): Herb. Linn. No. 26.63 (LINN).
Current name: ***Veronica verna*** L. (Scrophulariaceae).

Veronica virginica Linnaeus, *Species Plantarum* 1: 9. 1753.
"Habitat in Virginia." RCN: 67.
Lectotype (Albach & al. in *Taxon* 53: 434, 436. 2004): Herb. Clifford: 7, *Veronica* 1, sheet 24 (BM-000557530).
Current name: ***Veronicastrum virginicum*** (L.) Farw. (Scrophulariaceae).

Viburnum acerifolium Linnaeus, *Species Plantarum* 1: 268. 1753.
"Habitat in Virginia." RCN: 2134.
Lectotype (Malécot in *Taxon* 51: 747. 2003 [2002]): *Kalm,* Herb. Linn. No. 379.7 (LINN).
Current name: ***Viburnum acerifolium*** L. (Caprifoliaceae).

Viburnum cassinoides Linnaeus, *Species Plantarum,* ed. 2, 1: 384. 1762.
"Habitat in America septentrionali." RCN: 2137.
Lectotype (Malécot in *Taxon* 51: 747. 2003 [2002]): *Kalm,* Herb. Linn. No. 379.12 (LINN).
Current name: ***Viburnum cassinoides*** L. (Caprifoliaceae).

Viburnum dentatum Linnaeus, *Species Plantarum* 1: 268. 1753.
"Habitat in Virginia." RCN: 2132.
Lectotype (Svenson in *Rhodora* 42: 1, pl. 585. 1940): *Miller,* Herb. Linn. No. 379.5 (LINN).
Current name: ***Viburnum dentatum*** L. (Caprifoliaceae).

Viburnum lantana Linnaeus, *Species Plantarum* 1: 268. 1753.
"Habitat in Europae australioris sepibus argillosis." RCN: 2133.
Lectotype (Press in *Taxon* 41: 572. 1992): Herb. Burser XXIII: 18 (UPS).
Generitype of *Viburnum* Linnaeus.
Current name: ***Viburnum lantana*** L. (Caprifoliaceae).
Note: Viburnum lantana, with the type designated by Press, was proposed as conserved type of the genus by Jarvis (in *Taxon* 41: 572. 1992). However, the proposal was eventually ruled unnecessary by the General Committee (see Barrie, *l.c.* 55: 795–796. 2006 for a review of the history of this and related proposals).

Viburnum lentago Linnaeus, *Species Plantarum* 1: 268. 1753.
"Habitat in Canada. Kalm." RCN: 2136.

Lectotype (Malécot in *Taxon* 51: 748. 2003 [2002]): *Kalm*, Herb. Linn. No. 379.10 (LINN).
Current name: ***Viburnum lentago*** L. (Caprifoliaceae).

Viburnum nudum Linnaeus, *Species Plantarum* 1: 268. 1753.
"Habitat in Virginia." RCN: 2130.
Lectotype (Malécot in *Taxon* 51: 748. 2003 [2002]): *Clayton 64* (BM-000042708).
Current name: ***Viburnum nudum*** L. (Caprifoliaceae).

Viburnum opulus Linnaeus, *Species Plantarum* 1: 268. 1753.
"Habitat in Europae pratis humidiusculis." RCN: 2135.
Lectotype (Malécot in *Taxon* 51: 748. 2003 [2002]): Herb. Clifford: 109, *Opulus* 1A (BM-000558413).
Current name: ***Viburnum opulus*** L. (Caprifoliaceae).

Viburnum opulus Linnaeus var. **roseum** Linnaeus, *Species Plantarum* 1: 268. 1753.
RCN: 2135.
Lectotype (Malécot in *Taxon* 51: 749. 2003 [2002]): Herb. Burser XXIV: 23 (UPS).
Current name: ***Viburnum opulus*** L. var. ***roseum*** L. (Caprifoliaceae).

Viburnum prunifolium Linnaeus, *Species Plantarum* 1: 268. 1753.
"Habitat in Virginia, Canada." RCN: 2131.
Lectotype (Malécot in *Taxon* 51: 749. 2003 [2002]): *Kalm*, Herb. Linn. No. 379.4 (LINN).
Current name: ***Viburnum prunifolium*** L. (Caprifoliaceae).

Viburnum tinus Linnaeus, *Species Plantarum* 1: 267. 1753.
"Habitat in Lusitania, Hispania, Italia." RCN: 2129.

Lectotype (Ali in Ali & Jafri, *Fl. Libya* 24: 3. 1977): Herb. Linn. No. 379.1 (LINN).
Current name: ***Viburnum tinus*** L. (Caprifoliaceae).

Vicia amphicarpa Linnaeus, *Species Plantarum*, ed. 2, 2: 1030. 1763.
RCN: 5387.
Lectotype (Romero Zarco in *Anales Jard. Bot. Madrid* 56: 178. 1998): [icon] *"An Theophrasti araco homoion?"* in Clusius, Exot. Libri: 87, 88. 1605.
Current name: ***Vicia sativa*** L. subsp. ***amphicarpa*** (L.) Batt. (Fabaceae: Faboideae).
Note: This binomial appears in a footnote at the end of an account of *Lathyrus amphicarpus* L., accompanied by a reference to a Clusius description and illustration. The binomial was previously attributed to Dorthes (in *J. Phys. Chim. Hist. Nat. Arts* 35: 131. 1789), but Romero Zarco has recently accepted Linnaeus' statement as valid publication of the name and also lectotypified *V. amphicarpa* L.

Vicia angustifolia Linnaeus, *Amoenitates Academicae* 4: 105. 1759.
Lectotype (Verdcourt in Milne-Redhead & Polhill, *Fl. Trop. E. Africa, Leguminosae* 4: 1069. 1971): England. Oxford, Shotover Hill. *Bobart s.n.* in Herb. Morison (OXF).
Current name: ***Vicia sativa*** L. subsp. ***nigra*** Ehrh. (Fabaceae: Faboideae).
Note: See Stearn (*Introd. Ray's Syn. Meth. Stirp. Brit.* (Ray Soc. ed.): 68. 1973). Linnaeus' name is validated solely by reference to Ray, and Verdcourt's chosen lectotype was selected from material cited by Ray.

Vicia benghalensis Linnaeus, *Species Plantarum* 2: 736. 1753.
"Habitat in Benghala." RCN: 5414.
Lectotype (Verdcourt in Milne-Redhead & Polhill, *Fl. Trop. E. Africa, Leguminosae* 4: 1073. 1971): Herb. Linn. No. 906.18 (LINN).
Current name: ***Vicia benghalensis*** L. (Fabaceae: Faboideae).
Note: Romero Zarco (in *Anales Jard. Bot. Madrid* 56: 178. 1998) designated the cited Hermann plate as lectotype but this choice is pre-dated by that of Verdcourt.

Vicia biennis Linnaeus, *Species Plantarum* 2: 736. 1753.
"Habitat in Sibiria." RCN: 5413.
Lectotype (Hanelt & Mettin in *Kulturpflanze* 10: 48, Abb. 1. 1962): Herb. Linn. No. 906.16 (LINN).
Current name: ***Vicia biennis*** L. (Fabaceae: Faboideae).

Vicia bithynica (Linnaeus) Linnaeus, *Systema Naturae*, ed. 10, 2: 1166. 1759.
["Habitat in Italiae, Bavariae, arvis."] Sp. Pl. 2: 731 (1753). RCN: 5421.
Basionym: *Lathyrus bithynicus* L. (1753).
Lectotype (Ali in *Bot. Not.* 120: 48. 1967): Herb. Linn. No. 906.19 (LINN).
Current name: ***Vicia bithynica*** (L.) L. (Fabaceae: Faboideae).

Vicia cassubica Linnaeus, *Species Plantarum* 2: 735. 1753.
"Habitat in Germania." RCN: 5409.
Lectotype (Jonsell & Jarvis in *Nordic J. Bot.* 22: 78. 2002): Herb. Clifford: 368, *Vicia* 1 (BM-000646679).
Current name: ***Vicia cassubica*** L. (Fabaceae: Faboideae).
Note: Stankevicz (in *Novosti Sist. Vyssh. Rast.* 18: 213. 1981) indicated 901.11 (LINN) as type. However, this sheet corresponds with *Glycine bituminosa* L., and is not original material for *V. cassubica*.

Vicia cracca Linnaeus, *Species Plantarum* 2: 735. 1753.
"Habitat in Europae pratis, agris." RCN: 5410.
Lectotype (Chrtková-Zertová in Rechinger, *Fl. Iranica* 140: 29. 1979): Herb. Clifford: 368, *Vicia* 2 (BM).
Current name: ***Vicia cracca*** L. (Fabaceae: Faboideae).

V

Vicia dumetorum Linnaeus, *Species Plantarum* 2: 734. 1753.
"Habitat in Thuringia, Gallia." RCN: 5407.
Lectotype (Lassen in Turland & Jarvis in *Taxon* 46: 483. 1997): Herb. Linn. No. 906.3 (LINN).
Current name: *Vicia dumetorum* L. (Fabaceae: Faboideae).

Vicia faba Linnaeus, *Species Plantarum* 2: 737. 1753.
"Habitat – – –" RCN: 5423.
Lectotype (Westphal, *Pulses Ethiopia, Taxon. Agric. Signif.*: 205. 1974): Herb. Linn. No. 906.34 (LINN).
Current name: *Vicia faba* L. (Fabaceae: Faboideae).

Vicia hybrida Linnaeus, *Species Plantarum* 2: 737. 1753.
"Habitat Monspelii, Massiliae." RCN: 5418.
Lectotype (Chrtková-Žertová in Rechinger, *Fl. Iranica* 140: 42. 1979): Herb. Linn. No. 906.27 (LINN).
Current name: *Vicia hybrida* L. (Fabaceae: Faboideae).

Vicia lathyroides Linnaeus, *Species Plantarum* 2: 736. 1753.
"Habitat in Scothia, Lusatia." RCN: 5416.
Lectotype (Lassen in Turland & Jarvis in *Taxon* 46: 483. 1997): Herb. Burser XIX: 97 (UPS).
Current name: *Vicia lathyroides* L. (Fabaceae: Faboideae).

Vicia lutea Linnaeus, *Species Plantarum* 2: 736. 1753.
"Habitat in Gallia." RCN: 5417.
Lectotype (Chrtková-Žertová in Rechinger, *Fl. Iranica* 140: 48. 1979): *Löfling 538*, Herb. Linn. No. 906.25 (LINN).
Current name: *Vicia lutea* L. (Fabaceae: Faboideae).

Vicia narbonensis Linnaeus, *Species Plantarum* 2: 737. 1753.
"Habitat in Gallia, Anglia." RCN: 5422.
Lectotype (Schäfer in *Kulturpflanze* 21: 246, Abb. 13. 1973): [icon] *"Vicia Narbonensis"* in Rivinus, Ordo Pl. Fl. Tetrapetal.: t. 57. 1691 (see p. 153).
Current name: *Vicia narbonensis* L. (Fabaceae: Faboideae).
Note: Ali (in *Bot. Not.* 120: 50. 1967) noted that 906.33 (LINN) conflicted with Linnaeus' diagnosis, and although other authors (e.g. Chrtková-Žertová in Rechinger, *Fl. Iranica* 140: 56. 1979) have treated Clifford material as the type, Schäfer's choice of the Rivinus plate pre-dates this.

Vicia nissoliana Linnaeus, *Species Plantarum* 2: 735. 1753.
"Habitat in Oriente." RCN: 5412.
Type not designated.
Original material: Herb. Linn. No. 906.15 (LINN).
Current name: *Vicia* sp. (Fabaceae: Faboideae).
Note: The application of this name appears uncertain.

Vicia onobrychioides Linnaeus, *Species Plantarum* 2: 735. 1753.
"Habitat in Gallia. D. Sauvages." RCN: 5411.
Lectotype (Lassen in Turland & Jarvis in *Taxon* 46: 483. 1997): *Magnol*, Herb. Linn. No. 906.14 (LINN), see p. 221.
Current name: *Vicia onobrychioides* L. (Fabaceae: Faboideae).

Vicia peregrina Linnaeus, *Species Plantarum* 2: 737. 1753.
"Habitat in Gallia. D. Sauvages." RCN: 5419.
Lectotype (Ali in Nasir & Ali, *Fl. W. Pakistan* 100: 270. 1977): *Magnol*, Herb. Linn. No. 906.28 (LINN).
Current name: *Vicia peregrina* L. (Fabaceae: Faboideae).

Vicia pisiformis Linnaeus, *Species Plantarum* 2: 734. 1753.
"Habitat in Pannoniae sylvis." RCN: 5406.
Lectotype (Jonsell & Jarvis in *Nordic J. Bot.* 22: 79. 2002): Herb. Clifford: 369, *Vicia* 8 (BM-000646691).
Current name: *Vicia pisiformis* L. (Fabaceae: Faboideae).

Vicia sativa Linnaeus, *Species Plantarum* 2: 736. 1753.
"Habitat inter Europae segetes hodie." RCN: 5415.
Lectotype (Fawcett & Rendle, *Fl. Jamaica* 4: 42. 1920): Herb. Linn. No. 906.20 (LINN).
Generitype of *Vicia* Linnaeus (vide Green, *Prop. Brit. Bot.*: 175. 1929).
Current name: *Vicia sativa* L. subsp. *sativa* (Fabaceae: Faboideae).
Note: Sheet 906.20 is the only one in LINN associated with this name so Fawcett & Rendle's type statement is accepted as the earliest.

Vicia sativa Linnaeus var. **angustifolia** Linnaeus, *Flora Suecica*, ed. 2: 255. 1755.
RCN: 5415.
Replaced synonym of: *Vicia sativa* L. var. *nigra* L. (1763), *nom. illeg.*
Lectotype (Lassen in Turland & Jarvis in *Taxon* 46: 483. 1997): [icon] *"Vicia angustifolia"* in Rivinus, Ordo Pl. Fl. Tetrapetal.: t. 55. 1691. – Epitype (Lassen in Turland & Jarvis in *Taxon* 46: 483. 1997): Sweden. Skåne: Tjörnarp sn 400m NO kvarnen, RUBIN 3D 2c 07 47, 10 Jun 1992, *S. Karlsson 921771* (LD).
Current name: *Vicia sativa* L. subsp. *nigra* Ehrh. (Fabaceae: Faboideae).
Note: Verdcourt (in Milne-Redhead & Polhill, *Fl. Trop. E. Africa, Leguminosae* 4: 1069. 1971) indicated a Haller specimen (P) as the lectotype. However, this cannot be regarded as relevant original material because Linnaeus is not known to have studied Haller's herbarium. *Vicia sativa* var. *nigra* is nomenclaturally superfluous under Arts 52.1 & 52.2, because Linnaeus included in its protologue all the material eligible as the lectotype of the earlier var. *angustifolia* (i.e. Rivinus' illustration). The current name, *V. sativa* subsp. *nigra* Ehrh., is therefore to be treated as a *nomen novum*, rather than a new combination, based on the same type as var. *nigra* (Art. 58.1).

Vicia sativa Linnaeus var. **nigra** Linnaeus, *Species Plantarum*, ed. 2, 2: 1037. 1763, *nom. illeg.*
RCN: 5415.
Replaced synonym: *Vicia sativa* var. *angustifolia* L. (1755).
Lectotype (Lassen in Turland & Jarvis in *Taxon* 46: 483. 1997): [icon] *"Vicia angustifolia"* in Rivinus, Ordo Pl. Fl. Tetrapetal.: t. 55. 1691. – Epitype (Lassen in Turland & Jarvis in *Taxon* 46: 483. 1997): Sweden. Skåne: Tjörnarp sn 400m NO kvarnen, RUBIN 3D 2c 07 47, 10 Jun 1992, *S. Karlsson 921771* (LD).
Current name: *Vicia sativa* L. subsp. *nigra* Ehrh. (Fabaceae: Faboideae).
Note: A superfluous name because Linnaeus included in the protologue all the elements eligible as the lectotype of the earlier var. *angustifolia* (Arts 52.1 & 52.2). Romero Zarco (in *Anales Jard. Bot. Madrid* 56: 179. 1998) appears to treat the name as legitimate, and also proposes a different lectotype.

Vicia sepium Linnaeus, *Species Plantarum* 2: 737. 1753.
"Habitat in Europae sepibus." RCN: 5420.
Lectotype (Ali in *Bot. Not.* 120: 49. 1967): Herb. Linn. No. 906.31 (LINN).
Current name: *Vicia sepium* L. (Fabaceae: Faboideae).

Vicia sylvatica Linnaeus, *Species Plantarum* 2: 734. 1753.
"Habitat in Sueciae, Germaniae, Galliae sylvis." RCN: 5408.
Lectotype (Jonsell & Jarvis in *Nordic J. Bot.* 22: 79. 2002): Herb. Linn. No. 906.4 (LINN).
Current name: *Vicia sylvatica* L. (Fabaceae: Faboideae).

Vinca lutea Linnaeus, *Centuria II Plantarum*: 12. 1756.
"Habitat in Carolina." RCN: 1713.

Lectotype (Dandy, *Sloane Herbarium*: 112. 1958): [icon] *"Apocynum scandens, Salicis folio, flore amplo pleno"* in Catesby, Nat. Hist. Carolina 2: 53, t. 53. 1736.
Current name: ***Pentalinon luteum*** (L.) B.F. Hansen & Wunderlin (Apocynaceae).

Vinca major Linnaeus, *Species Plantarum* 1: 209. 1753.
"Habitat in Gallia Narbonensi, Hispania." RCN: 1712.
Lectotype (Stearn in Taylor & Farnsworth, Vinca *Alkaloids*: 79. 1973): Herb. Linn. No. 299.3 (LINN).
Current name: ***Vinca major*** L. (Apocynaceae).
Note: Vinca major was treated as the generitype by Britton & Brown (*Ill. Fl. N. U. S.*, ed. 2, 3: 20. 1913). However, under Art. 10.5, Ex. 7 (a voted example) of the Vienna Code, this is a type choice made under the American Code and is to be replaced under Art. 10.5b by Hitchcock's choice (*Prop. Brit. Bot.*: 136. 1929) of *V. minor* L.

Vinca minor Linnaeus, *Species Plantarum* 1: 209. 1753.
"Habitat in Germania, Anglia, Gallia." RCN: 1711.
Lectotype (Stearn in Taylor & Farnsworth, Vinca *Alkaloids*: 47. 1973): Herb. Linn. No. 299.1 (LINN).
Generitype of *Vinca* Linnaeus.
Current name: ***Vinca minor*** L. (Apocynaceae).
Note: Vinca major L. was treated as the generitype by Britton & Brown (in *Ill. Fl. N. U. S.*, ed. 2, 3: 20. 1913). However, under Art. 10.5, Ex. 7 (a voted example) of the Vienna Code, this is a type choice made under the American Code and is to be replaced under Art. 10.5b by Hitchcock's choice (*Prop. Brit. Bot.*: 136. 1929) of *V. minor*.

Vinca rosea Linnaeus, *Systema Naturae*, ed. 10, 2: 944. 1759.
["Habitat in Madagascar, Java."] Sp. Pl., ed. 2, 1: 305 (1762). RCN: 1714.
Lectotype (Codd in Dyer & al., *Fl. Southern Africa* 26: 268. 1963): [icon] *"Vinca, foliis oblongo-ovatis integerrimis, tubo floris longissimo caule ramoso fruticoso"* in Miller, Fig. Pl. Gard. Dict. 2: 124, t. 186. 1757.
Current name: ***Catharanthus roseus*** (L.) G. Don (Apocynaceae).
Note: See Boiteau (in *Adansonia*, sér. 2, 12: 29–135. 1972) for a discussion on the earliest description and collection of this plant.

Viola arborea Linnaeus, *Systema Naturae*, ed. 10, 2: 1239. 1759.
"Habitat [in America.]" RCN: 6789.
Type not designated.
Original material: none traced.
Current name: ***Corynostylis arborea*** (L.) S.F. Blake (Violaceae).

Viola arborescens Linnaeus, *Species Plantarum* 2: 935. 1753.
"Habitat in Hispania." RCN: 6784.
Type not designated.
Original material: [icon] in Barrelier, Pl. Galliam: 77, t. 568. 1714.
Current name: ***Viola arborescens*** L. (Violaceae).
Note: See comments by Greuter (in Greuter & Rechinger, *Boissiera* 13: 58–59. 1967).

Viola biflora Linnaeus, *Species Plantarum* 2: 936. 1753.
"Habitat in Alpibus Lapponiae, Austriae, Helvetiae, Angliae." RCN: 6778.
Lectotype (Qaiser & Omer in Nasir & Ali, *Fl. Pakistan* 166: 20. 1984): Herb. Linn. No. 1052.16 (LINN).
Current name: ***Viola biflora*** L. (Violaceae).
Note: Banerjee & Pramanik (in Jain & al., *Fasc. Fl. India* 12: 17. 1982) indicated 1052.16 and 1052.17 (LINN) as type but as these collections are evidently not part of a single gathering, Art. 9.15 does not apply.

Viola calcarata Linnaeus, *Species Plantarum* 2: 935. 1753.
"Habitat in Pyrenaeis." RCN: 6782.
Type not designated.
Original material: Herb. Linn. No. 1052.23 (LINN); Herb. Burser XI: 6 (UPS); [icon] in Daléchamps, Hist. General. Pl. 2: 1204. 1586.
Current name: ***Viola calcarata*** L. (Violaceae).

Viola calceolaria Linnaeus, *Species Plantarum*, ed. 2, 2: 1327. 1763.
"Habitat in Cumana." RCN: 6787.
Type not designated.
Original material: none traced.
Current name: ***Hybanthus calceolaria*** (L.) Schulze-Menz (Violaceae).

Viola canadensis Linnaeus, *Species Plantarum* 2: 936. 1753.
"Habitat in Canada. Kalm." RCN: 6776.
Lectotype (Juel in *Rhodora* 33: 179. 1931): Herb. Burser XI: 8 (UPS).
Current name: ***Viola canadensis*** L. (Violaceae).

Viola canina Linnaeus, *Species Plantarum* 2: 935. 1753.
"Habitat in Europae apricis." RCN: 6773.
Lectotype (Nikitin in *Bot. Zhurn.* 80(7): 93. 1995): Herb. Linn. No. 277 (LAPP).
Current name: ***Viola canina*** L. (Violaceae).
Note: Jonsell & Jarvis (in *Nordic J. Bot.* 22: 81. 2002), unaware of Nikitin's earlier choice, designated Clifford material as lectotype. It seems possible that the Lapland type material is identifiable with ssp. *montana* (L.) Hartm. rather than the typical subspecies. If confirmed, this will prove nomenclaturally disruptive.

Viola cenisia Linnaeus, *Species Plantarum*, ed. 2, 2: 1325. 1763.
"Habitat in Cenesii alpinis Ronche dictis." RCN: 6775.
Type not designated.
Original material: [icon] in Allioni, Rar. Pedem. Stirp.: 14, t. 3, f. 4. 1755.
Current name: ***Viola cenisia*** L. (Violaceae).

Viola cornuta Linnaeus, *Species Plantarum*, ed. 2, 2: 1325. 1763.
"Habitat in Pyrenaeis." RCN: 6783.
Type not designated.
Original material: none traced.
Current name: ***Viola cornuta*** L. (Violaceae).

Viola diandra Linnaeus, *Systema Vegetabilium*, ed. 13: 669. 1774.
RCN: 6791.
Type not designated.
Original material: none traced.
Current name: ***Corynostylis diandra*** (L.) Spreng. (Violaceae).

Viola enneasperma Linnaeus, *Species Plantarum* 2: 937. 1753.
"Habitat in India." RCN: 6785.
Lectotype (Tennant in *Kew Bull.* 16: 432. 1963): Herb. Hermann 1: 19, No. 317 (BM-000594450).
Current name: ***Hybanthus enneaspermus*** (L.) F. Muell. (Violaceae).

Viola grandiflora Linnaeus, *Systema Naturae*, ed. 12, 2: 585; *Mantissa Plantarum*: 120. 1767.
"Habitat in Alpibus Helveticis, Pyrenaicis." RCN: 6781.
Type not designated.
Original material: Herb. Linn. No. 1052.22 (LINN); Herb. Burser XI: 10 (UPS); Herb. Burser XI: 13 (UPS); [icon] in Barrelier, Pl. Galliam: 77, t. 692. 1714; [icon] in Barrelier, Pl. Galliam: 77, t. 691. 1714.
Current name: ***Viola tricolor*** L. (Violaceae).

V

Viola hirta Linnaeus, *Species Plantarum* 2: 934. 1753.
"Habitat in Europae frigidioris nemoribus." RCN: 6770.
Lectotype (Haesler in *Mitt. Bot. Staatssamml. München* 18: 292.
  1982): [icon] *"Viola"* in Brunfels, Herbarum Vivae Eicones 1: 137,
  lower right fig. 1530 (see p. 111).
Current name: ***Viola hirta*** L. (Violaceae).

Viola hybanthus Linnaeus, *Species Plantarum*, ed. 2, 2: 1328. 1763,
  nom. illeg.
"Habitat in America meridionali." RCN: 6789.
Replaced synonym: *Hybanthus havanensis* Jacq. (1760).
Type not designated.
Current name: ***Hybanthus havanensis*** Jacq. (Violaceae).
Note: A superfluous name for *Hybanthus havanensis* Jacq. (*Enum. Syst.
  Pl.*: 2, 17. 1760), cited by Linnaeus in the protologue. *Calceolaria
  frutescens* Loefl. (*Iter Hispanicum*: 185. 1758), also cited by
  Linnaeus, appears to be a short polynomial, not a binomial.

Viola ipecacuanha Linnaeus, *Mantissa Plantarum Altera*: 484.
  1771.
RCN: 6790.
Type not designated.
Original material: none traced.
Current name: ***Hybanthus calceolaria*** (L.) Schulze-Menz (Violaceae).

Viola lanceolata Linnaeus, *Species Plantarum* 2: 934. 1753.
"Habitat in Canada, Sibiria." RCN: 6768.
Lectotype (designated here by Reveal): *Kalm*, Herb. Linn. No. 1052.4
  (LINN).
Current name: ***Viola lanceolata*** L. (Violaceae).

Viola mirabilis Linnaeus, *Species Plantarum* 2: 936. 1753.
"Habitat in Germaniae, Sueciae nemoribus." RCN: 6777.
Lectotype (Nikitin in *Novosti Sist. Vyssh. Rast.* 31: 217. 1998): Herb.
  Linn. No. 1052.15 (LINN).
Current name: ***Viola mirabilis*** L. (Violaceae).
Note: Jonsell & Jarvis (in *Nordic J. Bot.* 22: 82. 2002), unaware of
  Nikitin's earlier choice, independently chose the same lectotype.

Viola montana Linnaeus, *Species Plantarum* 2: 935. 1753.
"Habitat in Alpibus Lapponiae, Austriae, Baldo." RCN: 6774.
Lectotype (Nikitin in *Bot. Zhurn.* 73: 1536. 1988): Herb. Linn. No.
  1052.13 (LINN).
Current name: ***Viola montana*** L. (Violaceae).
Note: See Wilmott (in *J. Bot.* 54: 257–262. 1916) for a discussion of
  the status of this name. However, no explicit choice of type was
  made. Treated as a *nomen ambiguum* by some authors, it has also
  been applied by others to a taxon in the *V. canina* L. group.
  However, Nikitin's formal typification has made *V. montana* the
  earliest name for the taxon widely known as *V. elatior* Fr.

Viola odorata Linnaeus, *Species Plantarum* 2: 934. 1753.
"Habitat in Europae nemoribus." RCN: 6772.
Lectotype (Haesler in *Mitt. Bot. Staatssamml. München* 18: 294.
  1982): Herb. Burser XI: 1 (UPS).
Generitype of *Viola* Linnaeus (vide Green, *Prop. Brit. Bot.*: 184.
  1929).
Current name: ***Viola odorata*** L. (Violaceae).

Viola oppositifolia Linnaeus, *Species Plantarum*, ed. 2, 2: 1327.
  1763.
"Habitat in Cumana." RCN: 6788.
Type not designated.
Original material: none traced.
Current name: ***Hybanthus oppositifolius*** (L.) Taub. (Violaceae).

Viola palmata Linnaeus, *Species Plantarum* 2: 933. 1753.
"Habitat in Virginia." RCN: 6765.
Lectotype (McKinney in *Sida Bot. Misc.* 7: 12. 1992): Herb. Linn. No.
  1052.1 (LINN).
Current name: ***Viola palmata*** L. (Violaceae).
Note: See discussion on the application of this name by Gil-ad (in
  Boissiera 53: 93–95. 1997).

Viola palustris Linnaeus, *Species Plantarum* 2: 934. 1753.
"Habitat in Europae frigidioris paludibus." RCN: 6771.
Lectotype (Jonsell & Jarvis in *Nordic J. Bot.* 22: 82. 2002): Herb.
  Linn. No. 278 (LAPP).
Current name: ***Viola palustris*** L. (Violaceae).

Viola pedata Linnaeus, *Species Plantarum* 2: 933. 1753.
"Habitat in Virginia." RCN: 6766.
Lectotype (Reveal & al. in *Huntia* 7: 238. 1987): *Kalm*, Herb. Linn.
  No. 1052.2 (LINN).
Current name: ***Viola pedata*** L. (Violaceae).

Viola pinnata Linnaeus, *Species Plantarum* 2: 934. 1753.
"Habitat in Sibiria & Alpibus Europae." RCN: 6767.
Type not designated.
Original material: Herb. Linn. No. 1052.3 (LINN); [icon] in Bauhin
  & Cherler, Hist. Pl. Univ. 3(2): 544. 1651.
Current name: ***Viola pinnata*** L. (Violaceae).

Viola primulifolia Linnaeus, *Species Plantarum* 2: 934. 1753.
"Habitat in Sibiria, Virginia." RCN: 6769.
Lectotype (designated here by Reveal): *Clayton 470* (BM).
Current name: ***Viola primulifolia*** L. (Violaceae).

Viola suffruticosa Linnaeus, *Species Plantarum* 2: 937. 1753.
"Habitat in India." RCN: 6786.
Lectotype (Tennant in *Kew Bull.* 16: 432. 1963): Herb. Hermann 1:
  41, No. 318 (BM-000621376).
Current name: ***Hybanthus enneaspermus*** (L.) F. Muell. (Violaceae).

Viola tricolor Linnaeus, *Species Plantarum* 2: 935. 1753.
"Habitat in Europae cultis." RCN: 6780.
Lectotype (Banerjee & Pramanik in Jain & al. in *Fasc. Fl. India* 12: 36.
  1983): Herb. Linn. No. 1052.21 (LINN).
Current name: ***Viola tricolor*** L. (Violaceae).
Note: See discussion by Nauenburg (in *Willdenowia* 21: 52. 1991) who
  independently reached the same conclusion as Banerjee &
  Pramanik. A plate from Fuchs, cited by Linnaeus, is reproduced by
  Fuller (in *Pansies, Violas & Violettas*: 25. 1990).

Viola uniflora Linnaeus, *Species Plantarum* 2: 936. 1753.
"Habitat in Sibiria." RCN: 6779.
Type not designated.
Original material: Herb. Linn. No. 1052.18 (LINN); Herb. Linn. No.
  369.11 (S).
Current name: ***Viola uniflora*** L. (Violaceae).

Virecta virens Linnaeus, *Plantae Surinamenses*: 7. 1775, *nom. inval.*
"Habitat [in Surinamo.]" RCN: 1367.
Type not relevant.
Note: As the generic name was not validly published until 1782, this
  binomial is invalid.

Viscum album Linnaeus, *Species Plantarum* 2: 1023. 1753.
"Habitat in Europae arboribus, parasitica." RCN: 7402.
Lectotype (Bhopal & Chaudhri in *Pakistan Syst.* 1(2): 58. 1977):
  Herb. Linn. No. 1166.1 (LINN).

Generitype of *Viscum* Linnaeus (vide Green, *Prop. Brit. Bot.*: 191. 1929).
Current name: **Viscum album** L. (Loranthaceae).
Note: See also Jonsell & Jarvis (in *Nordic J. Bot.* 14: 153. 1994), who independently made the same choice of type.

Viscum opuntioides Linnaeus, *Species Plantarum* 2: 1023. 1753.
"Habitat in Jamaica, parasitica." RCN: 7405.
Type not designated.
Original material: Herb. Linn. No. 397.3 (S); [icon] in Sloane, Voy. Jamaica 2: 93, t. 201, f. 2. 1725 – Voucher: Herb. Sloane 6: 109 (BM-SL).
Current name: **Dendrophthora opuntioides** (L.) Eichl. (Loranthaceae).

Viscum purpureum Linnaeus, *Species Plantarum* 2: 1023. 1753.
"Habitat in Carolina, parasitica." RCN: 7404.
Lectotype (Dandy, *Sloane Herbarium*: 112. 1958): [icon] *"Viscum foliis latioribus; baccis purpureis pediculis incidentibus"* in Catesby, Nat. Hist. Carolina 2: 95, t. 95. 1743.
Current name: **Dendropemon purpureum** (L.) Krug & Urb. (Loranthaceae).

Viscum rubrum Linnaeus, *Species Plantarum* 2: 1023. 1753.
"Habitat in Carolina, parasitica." RCN: 7403.
Lectotype (Dandy, *Sloane Herbarium*: 112. 1958): [icon] *"Viscum foliis longioribus baccis rubris"* in Catesby, Nat. Hist. Carolina 2: 81, t. 81. 1743. – Voucher: Herb. Sloane 232: 2, n. 8 (BM-SL).
Current name: **Phoradendron rubrum** (L.) Griseb. (Loranthaceae).

Viscum terrestre Linnaeus, *Species Plantarum* 2: 1023. 1753.
"Habitat in Philadelphiae pratis subhumidis. Kalm. IX. 32." RCN: 7407.
Lectotype (designated here by Reveal): *Kalm, "IX. 32"*, Herb. Linn. No. 1166.11 (LINN).
Current name: **Lysimachia terrestris** (L.) Britton (Primulaceae).

Viscum verticillatum Linnaeus, *Species Plantarum* 2: 1023. 1753.
"Habitat in Jamaica, parasitica." RCN: 7406.
Lectotype (Nicolson & Jarvis in *Taxon* 33: 726. 1984): Herb. Linn. No. 1166.10 (LINN).
Current name: **Cissus verticillata** (L.) Nicolson & C.E. Jarvis (Vitaceae).

Vitex agnus-castus Linnaeus, *Species Plantarum* 2: 638. 1753.
"Habitat in Siciliae et Neapolis paludosis." RCN: 4637.
Lectotype (Moldenke in *Phytologia* 5: 170. 1955): Herb. Linn. No. 811.4 (LINN).
Generitype of *Vitex* Linnaeus (vide Green, *Prop. Brit. Bot.*: 170. 1929).
Current name: **Vitex agnus-castus** L. (Verbenaceae).

Vitex negundo Linnaeus, *Species Plantarum* 2: 638. 1753.
"Habitat in India." RCN: 4639.
Lectotype (Moldenke in *Phytologia* 5: 490. 1955): Herb. Linn. No. 811.8 (LINN).
Current name: **Vitex negundo** L. (Verbenaceae).
Note: Jafri & Ghafoor (in Nasir & Ali, *Fl. W. Pakistan* 77: 27. 1974) indicated 790.8 (LINN) as type but this collection is associated with *Buchnera* and is not original material for *V. negundo*.

Vitex pinnata Linnaeus, *Species Plantarum* 2: 638. 1753.
"Habitat in Zeylona." RCN: 4640.
Lectotype (Moldenke in *Phytologia* 6: 71. 1957): Herb. Hermann 1: 16, No. 415, lower left specimen (BM-000621283).
Current name: **Vitex pinnata** L. (Verbenaceae).

Vitex trifolia Linnaeus, *Species Plantarum* 2: 638. 1753.
"Habitat in India." RCN: 4638.
Lectotype (Moldenke & Moldenke in Dassanayake & Fosberg, *Revised Handb. Fl. Ceylon* 4: 378. 1983): Herb. Linn. No. 811.7 (LINN).
Current name: **Vitex trifolia** L. (Verbenaceae).
Note: Moldenke (in *Phytologia* 6: 171. 1958) discussed original material for the name but did not designate a type.

Vitis arborea Linnaeus, *Species Plantarum* 1: 203. 1753.
"Habitat in Carolina, Virginica." RCN: 1646.
Lectotype (designated here by Reveal): [icon] *"Frutex scandens Petroselini foliis Virginianus, claviculis donatus"* in Plukenet, Amalth. Bot.: t. 412, f. 2. 1705; Almag. Mant.: 85. 1700.
Current name: **Ampelopsis arborea** (L.) Koehne (Vitaceae).

Vitis heptaphylla Linnaeus, *Mantissa Plantarum Altera*: 212. 1771.
"Habitat in India orientali." RCN: 1645.
Lectotype (Frodin in *Bot. J. Linn. Soc.* 104: 314, f. 1. 1991): Herb. Linn. No. 281.10 (LINN).
Current name: **Schefflera heptaphylla** (L.) Frodin (Araliaceae).

Vitis indica Linnaeus, *Species Plantarum* 1: 202. 1753.
"Habitat in India." RCN: 1640.
Lectotype (Shetty & Singh in *Taxon* 37: 169. 1988): Herb. Hermann 1: 36, No. 99 (BM-000594467).
Current name: **Ampelocissus indica** (L.) Planch. (Vitaceae).

Vitis labrusca Linnaeus, *Species Plantarum* 1: 203. 1753.
"Habitat in America septentrionali." RCN: 1641.

Lectotype (Bailey in *Gentes Herb.* 3: 186. 1934): Herb. Linn. No. 281.5 (LINN), see p. 925.
Current name: ***Vitis labrusca*** L. (Vitaceae).
Note: See also Fernald (in *Rhodora* 42: 436, pl. 636, f. 1. 1940).

Vitis laciniosa Linnaeus, *Species Plantarum* 1: 203. 1753.
"Habitat – – – –" RCN: 1644.
Type not designated.
Original material: Herb. Linn. No. 281.6 (LINN); Herb. Clifford: 74, *Vitis* 2 (BM); [icon] in Bauhin & Cherler, Hist. Pl. Univ. 2: 73. 1651; [icon] in Cornut, Canad. Pl. Hist.: 182, 183. 1635.
Current name: ***Vitis vinifera*** L. (Vitaceae).

Vitis trifolia Linnaeus, *Species Plantarum* 1: 203. 1753.
"Habitat in India." RCN: 1643.
Neotype (Shetty & Singh in *Taxon* 37: 171. 1988): *Samuel Browne 67*, Herb. Sloane 165: 84 (BM-SL).
Current name: ***Cayratia trifolia*** (L.) Domin (Vitaceae).

Vitis vinifera Linnaeus, *Species Plantarum* 1: 202. 1753.
"Habitat in Orbis quatuor partibus temperatis." RCN: 1639.
Lectotype (Siddiqi in Jafri & El-Gadi, *Fl. Libya* 83: 2. 1980): Herb. Linn. No. 281.1 (LINN).
Generitype of *Vitis* Linnaeus (vide Hitchcock, *Prop. Brit. Bot.*: 135. 1929).
Current name: ***Vitis vinifera*** L. (Vitaceae).

Vitis vinifera Linnaeus var. **apyrena** Linnaeus, *Species Plantarum* 1: 202. 1753.
RCN: 1639.
Type not designated.
Original material: none traced.
Current name: ***Vitis vinifera*** L. (Vitaceae).

Vitis vulpina Linnaeus, *Species Plantarum* 1: 203. 1753.
"Habitat in Virginia." RCN: 1642.

Lectotype (Fernald in *Rhodora* 41: 433. 1939): *Kalm*, Herb. Linn. No. 281.7 (LINN).
Current name: ***Vitis vulpina*** L. (Vitaceae).
Note: See discussion by Bailey (*Evol. Native Fruits*: 103. 1898; in *Gentes Herb.* 3: 235. 1934) who, however, does not make an explicit choice of type.

Volkameria aculeata Linnaeus, *Species Plantarum* 2: 637. 1753.
"Habitat in Jamaica, Barbados." RCN: 4630.
Type not designated.
Original material: Herb. Linn. No. 809.2 (LINN); [icon] in Sloane, Voy. Jamaica 2: 25, t. 166, f. 2, 3. 1725 – Voucher: Herb. Sloane 5: 89 (BM-SL).
Generitype of *Volkameria* Linnaeus (vide Steudel, *Nom.*, ed. 2, 2: 779. 1841).
Current name: ***Clerodendrum aculeatum*** (L.) Schltr. (Verbenaceae).

Volkameria inermis Linnaeus, *Species Plantarum* 2: 637. 1753.
"Habitat in India." RCN: 4631.
Lectotype (Jafri in Nasir & Ali, *Fl. W. Pakistan* 77: 33. 1974): Herb. Linn. No. 809.3 (LINN).
Current name: ***Clerodendrum inerme*** (L.) Gaertn. (Verbenaceae).

Volkameria serrata Linnaeus, *Systema Naturae*, ed. 12, 2: 425; *Mantissa Plantarum*: 90. 1767.
"Habitat in India." RCN: 4632.
Lectotype (Moldenke & Moldenke in Dassanayake & Fosberg, *Revised Handb. Fl. Ceylon* 4: 418. 1983): Herb. Linn. No. 809.5 (LINN).
Current name: ***Rotheca serrata*** (L.) Steane & Mabb. (Lamiaceae).

Volvox globator Linnaeus, *Systema Naturae*, ed. 10, 1: 820. 1758.
"Habitat in Europae lacubus."
Lectotype (John in Spencer & al. in *Taxon*, in press): [icon] *"The Globe Animal"* in Baker, Employ. Microscope: 323, t. 12, f. 27. 1753.
Generitype of *Volvox* Linnaeus (vide Ehrenberg, *Infus.*: 72. 1838).
Current name: ***Volvox globator*** L. (Volvocaceae).

W

Wachendorfia umbellata Linnaeus, *Systema Vegetabilium,* ed. 13: 80. 1774, *nom. illeg.*

["Habitat ad Cap. b. spei."] Mant. Pl.: 27 (1767). RCN: 345.

Replaced synonym: *Ixia hirsuta* L. (1767).

Type not designated.

Original material: as replaced synonym.

Current name: ***Dilatris corymbosa*** P.J. Bergius (Haemodoraceae).

Waltheria americana Linnaeus, *Species Plantarum* 2: 673. 1753.

"Habitat in Bahama, Barbiches, Surinamo." RCN: 4911.

Lectotype (Verdoorn in *Bothalia* 13: 275. 1981): Herb. Linn. No. 852.1 (LINN).

Generitype of *Waltheria* Linnaeus (vide Green, *Prop. Brit. Bot.*: 172. 1929).

Current name: ***Waltheria indica*** L. (Sterculiaceae).

Note: St John (in *Phytologia* 33: 89–92. 1976) discussed the specimens in LINN, and stated that he had studied "the types of both of the Linnaean species". However, in this he did not distinguish between 852.1 and 852.2 (LINN), which are not part of a single gathering and so Art. 9.15 does not apply. Verdoorn's type choice appears to be the earliest.

Waltheria angustifolia Linnaeus, *Systema Naturae,* ed. 10, 2: 1140. 1759.

["Habitat in America."] Sp. Pl., ed. 2, 2: 941 (1763). RCN: 4912.

Type not designated.

Original material: Herb. Linn. No. 852.4 (LINN).

Current name: ***Waltheria indica*** L. (Sterculiaceae).

Waltheria indica Linnaeus, *Species Plantarum* 2: 673. 1753.

"Habitat in India." RCN: 4913.

Lectotype (Verdcourt in Dassanayake & al., *Revised Handb. Fl. Ceylon* 9: 418. 1995): Herb. Hermann 3: 5, No. 244 (BM-000621807).

Current name: ***Waltheria indica*** L. (Sterculiaceae).

Note: St John (in *Phytologia* 33: 89–92. 1976) appeared to regard 852.3 (LINN) as the type but this sheet lacks the relevant *Species Plantarum* number (i.e. "2") and was a post-1753 addition to the herbarium, and is not original material for the name. The same is

true of 852.2 (LINN), treated as the type by Verdoorn (in *Bothalia* 13: 275 1981), but not linked by Linnaeus with this name, and not original material for it.

Weinmannia pinnata Linnaeus, *Systema Naturae,* ed. 10, 2: 1005. 1759.

["Habitat in Jamaica."] Sp. Pl., ed. 2, 1: 515 (1762). RCN: 2850.

Lectotype (Harling in Harling & Andersson, *Fl. Ecuador* 61: 22. 1999): Herb. Linn. No. 508.1 (LINN).

Generitype of *Weinmannia* Linnaeus, *nom. cons.*

Current name: ***Weinmannia pinnata*** L. (Cunoniaceae).

Note: Weinmannia Linnaeus, *nom. cons.* against *Windmannia* P. Browne.

Willichia repens Linnaeus, *Mantissa Plantarum Altera*: 558. 1771.

"Habitat in Mexico." RCN: 276.

Lectotype (Hedberg in *Bot. Not.* 108: 175. 1955): *Mútis 62*, Herb. Linn. No. 475.4 (LINN).

Generitype of *Willichia* Linnaeus.

Current name: ***Sibthorpia repens*** (L.) Kuntze (Scrophulariaceae).

Note: Although there are some doubts as to whether the Mútis specimen was in Linnaeus' possession by 1771, there are no other original elements for the name. If this collection proves to be a post-1771 addition to the herbarium, it should be treated as a neotype (designated by Hedberg) in accordance with Art. 9.8. In any event, Hedberg's choice has priority over that of Hampshire (in Jarvis & al., *Regnum Veg.* 127: 99. 1993) who proposed a different neotype (*Stafford & al. 361*, BM) from Mexico.

Winterana canella Linnaeus, *Systema Naturae,* ed. 10, 2: 1045. 1759.

["Habitat in Jamaica, Barbados, Carolina."] Sp. Pl. 1: 371 (1753). RCN: 3446.

Replaced synonym: *Laurus winterana* L. (1753).

Type not designated.

Original material: as replaced synonym.

Generitype of *Winterana* Linnaeus.

Current name: ***Canella winterana*** (L.) Gaertn. (Canellaceae).

X

Xanthium orientale Linnaeus, *Species Plantarum*, ed. 2, 2: 1400. 1763. "Habitat in China, Japonia, Zeylona." RCN: 7155.
Lectotype (Jeanmonod in Gamisans & Jeanmonod, *Compl. Prodr. Fl. Corse, Asteraceae I*: 190. 1998): Herb. Linn. No. 1113.2 (LINN). – Epitype (Wisskirchen in Jarvis & Turland in *Taxon* 47: 369. 1998): France. Perigord, rechtes Ufer der Dordogne bei Bezenac, 14 Sep 1987, *Wisskirchen 230* (BM-000576318; iso- BOCH).
Current name: ***Xanthium orientale*** L. (Asteraceae).
Note: Löve & Dansereau (in *Canad. J. Bot.* 37: 174, f. 2. 1959) noted the material on sheet 1113.2 (LINN) as immature and evidently did not consider it as the type. However, Jeanmonod (in *Compl. Prodr. Fl. Corse, Asteraceae I*: 190. 1998) treated 1132.2 (LINN) as the type, citing Löve & Dansereau. This choice (before Mar 1998) pre-dates that of Wisskirchen (in *Taxon* 47: 369. May 1998) but the latter's additional choice of an epitype stands. See discussion of the complex by Jeanmonod (in *Candollea* 53: 446. 1998), who notes the epitype choice. Wisskirchen (*Standardliste Farn- Blütenpfl. Deutschl.*: 550 (1998) gives a further review.

Xanthium spinosum Linnaeus, *Species Plantarum* 2: 987. 1753. "Habitat in Lusitania." RCN: 7156.
Lectotype (Wijnands, *Bot. Commelins*: 87. 1983): Herb. Linn. No. 1113.3 (LINN).
Current name: ***Xanthium spinosum*** L. (Asteraceae).
Note: The type choice made by Wijnands (Sep 1983) narrowly pre-dates a different choice of Clifford material (BM) made by Alavi (in Jafri & El-Gadi, *Fl. Libya* 107: 123. Dec 1983).

Xanthium strumarium Linnaeus, *Species Plantarum* 2: 987. 1753. "Habitat in Europa, Canada, Virginia, Jamaica, Zeylona, Japonia." RCN: 7154.
Lectotype (Rechinger, *Fl. Iranica* 164: 39. 1989): Herb. Linn. No. 1113.1 (LINN).
Generitype of *Xanthium* Linnaeus (vide Green, *Prop. Brit. Bot.*: 188. 1929).
Current name: ***Xanthium strumarium*** L. var. ***strumarium*** (Asteraceae).
Note: Löve & Dansereau (in *Canad. J. Bot.* 37: 174. 1959) discussed the material in LINN, and illustrated sheet 1113.1 (as their f. 1). However, in their opinion this did "not represent a Linnaean type collection".

Xanthium strumosum Linnaeus, *Flora Anglica*: 24. 1754, *orth. var.* RCN: 7154.
Lectotype (Rechinger, *Fl. Iranica* 164: 39. 1989): Herb. Linn. No. 1113.1 (LINN).
Current name: ***Xanthium strumarium*** L. (Asteraceae).
Note: This is evidently an orthographic variant of *X. strumarium* L. (1753).

Xeranthemum annuum Linnaeus, *Species Plantarum* 2: 857. 1753. "Habitat in Austria." RCN: 6194.
Lectotype (Burtt in Jarvis & al., *Regnum Veg.* 127: 99. 1993): Herb. Clifford: 400, *Xeranthemum* 1, sheet 1 (BM-000646992).
Generitype of *Xeranthemum* Linnaeus (vide Green, *Prop. Brit. Bot.*: 181. 1929).
Current name: ***Xeranthemum annuum*** L. (Asteraceae).
Note: Hilliard & Burtt (in *Bot. J. Linn. Soc.* 82: 249. 1981) indicated material in the Clifford herbarium (BM) as type but did not distinguish between the two relevant sheets that are there. They are evidently not part of a single gathering so Art. 9.15 does not apply. Burtt subsequently designated one of the sheets as lectotype.

Xeranthemum annuum Linnaeus var. **inapertum** Linnaeus, *Species Plantarum* 2: 858. 1753.
"Habitat in Italia, Helvetia G. Narbonensi." RCN: 6194.
Lectotype (Hilliard & Burtt in *Bot. J. Linn. Soc.* 82: 254. 1981): *Löfling 621*, Herb. Linn. No. 990.2 (LINN).
Current name: ***Xeranthemum inapertum*** (L.) Mill. (Asteraceae).

Xeranthemum annuum Linnaeus var. **orientale** Linnaeus, *Species Plantarum* 2: 858. 1753.
RCN: 6194.
Neotype (Hilliard & Burtt in *Bot. J. Linn. Soc.* 82: 249. 1981): Herb. Tournefort No. 4768 (P-TOURN).
Current name: ***Chardinia orientalis*** (L.) Kuntze (Asteraceae).
Note: Although Linnaeus did not study Tournefort's herbarium, and the sheet indicated as the type by Hilliard & Burtt is not original material for the name, the absence of any original material means that Hilliard & Burtt's choice can be treated as a neotypification (under Art. 9.8).

Xeranthemum canescens Linnaeus, *Plantae Rariores Africanae*: 20. 1760.
["Habitat ad Cap. b. spei."] Sp. Pl., ed. 2, 2: 1202 (1763). RCN: 6198.
Lectotype (Hilliard & Burtt in *Bot. J. Linn. Soc.* 82: 249, 259. 1981): Herb. Burman, specimen illustrated in Burman, *Rar. Afr. Pl.*: t. 68, f. 1 (G).
Current name: ***Syncarpha canescens*** (L.) B. Nord. (Asteraceae).

Xeranthemum ciliatum Linnaeus, *Species Plantarum* 2: 859. 1753. "Habitat in Aethiopia." RCN: 6574.
Lectotype (Roessler in *Mitt. Bot. Staatssamml. München* 3: 304. 1959): [icon] "*Aster Africanus frutescens splendentibus parvis et reflexis foliis*" in Commelin, Hort. Med. Amstelod. Pl. Rar. 2: 55, t. 28. 1701.
Current name: ***Polyarrhena reflexa*** (L.) Cass. subsp. ***reflexa*** (Asteraceae).
Note: Wijnands (*Bot. Commelins*: 80. 1983) provides further information on the original material for this name.

Xeranthemum erucifolium Linnaeus, *Species Plantarum* 2: 858. 1753.
"Habitat in Tanain prope oppidum Cavilnense." RCN: 6637.
Replaced synonym of: *Centaurea radiata* L. (1767).
Type not designated.
Original material: [icon] in Gmelin, Fl. Sibirica 2: 108, t. 47, f. 1. 1752.
Current name: ***Klasea erucifolia*** (L.) Greuter & Wagenitz (Asteraceae).

Xeranthemum imbricatum Linnaeus, *Plantae Rariores Africanae*: 20. 1760.
["Habitat ad Cap. b. spei."] Sp. Pl., ed. 2, 2: 1202 (1763). RCN: 6199.
Lectotype (Hilliard & Burtt in *Bot. J. Linn. Soc.* 82: 250. 1981): [icon] "*Elichrysum foliis Thymi incanis dense stipatum, floribus singularibus amplis patentibus*" in Breyn, Prodr. Fasc. Rar. Pl.: 28, t. 18, f. 1. 1739.
Current name: ***Helichrysum aureum*** (Houtt.) Merr. (Asteraceae).

Xeranthemum paniculatum Linnaeus, *Species Plantarum* 2: 859. 1753.
"Habitat in Aethiopia." RCN: 6206.
Lectotype (Hilliard & Burtt in *Bot. J. Linn. Soc.* 82: 250, 258. 1981):

Herb. Burman, specimen illustrated in Burman, *Rar. Afr. Pl.*: t. 67, f. 1 (G).
Current name: **Syncarpha paniculata** (L.) B. Nord. (Asteraceae).
Note: Wijnands (*Bot. Commelins*: 77. 1983) provides further information on the original material for this name.

Xeranthemum proliferum Linnaeus, *Species Plantarum* 2: 858. 1753.
"Habitat in Aethiopia." RCN: 6197.
Lectotype (Hilliard & Burtt in *Bot. J. Linn. Soc.* 82: 250. 1981): [icon] *"Elichrysum, Abrotani foeminae foliis"* in Breyn, Prodr. Fasc. Rar. Pl.: 28, t. 17, f. 1. 1739.
Current name: **Phaenocoma prolifera** (L.) D. Don (Asteraceae).

Xeranthemum retortum Linnaeus, *Species Plantarum* 2: 858. 1753.
"Habitat in Aethiopia." RCN: 6200.
Lectotype (Hilliard & Burtt in *Bot. J. Linn. Soc.* 82: 251. 1981): Herb. Clifford: 400, *Xeranthemum* 2 (BM-000646995).
Current name: **Helichrysum retortum** (L.) Willd. (Asteraceae).

Xeranthemum sesamoides Linnaeus, *Species Plantarum* 2: 859. 1753.
"Habitat in Aethiopia." RCN: 6202.
Lectotype (Hilliard & Burtt in *Bot. J. Linn. Soc.* 82: 217, 251, 258. 1981): Herb. Burman, specimen illustrated in Burman, *Rar. Afr. Pl.*: t. 67, f. 2 (G).
Current name: **Edmondia sesamoides** (L.) Hilliard (Asteraceae).

Xeranthemum speciosissimum Linnaeus, *Species Plantarum* 2: 858, Add. 1753.
"Habitat in Aethiopia [in Addenda]." RCN: 6196.
Lectotype (designated here by Nordenstam): [icon] *"Xeranthemum, tomentosum, latifolium, flore maximo"* in Burman, Rar. Afric. Pl.: 178, t. 66, f. 2. 1739.
Current name: **Syncarpha speciosissima** (L.) B. Nord. (Asteraceae).
Note: Hilliard & Burtt (in *Bot. J. Linn. Soc.* 82: 251. 1981) designated 990.5 (LINN) as lectotype. However, it lacks the relevant *Species Plantarum* number (i.e. "4"), is a post-1753 addition to the collection, and is not original material for the name.

Xeranthemum spinosum Linnaeus, *Species Plantarum* 2: 859. 1753.
"Habitat in Aethiopia." RCN: 6201.
Lectotype (Hilliard & Burtt in Jarvis & Turland in *Taxon* 47: 369. 1998): [icon] *"Xeranthemum ramosum, foliolis simplicibus, capite spinoso"* in Burman, Rar. Afric. Pl.: 182, t. 67, f. 3. 1739.
Current name: **Dicoma spinosum** (L.) Druce (Asteraceae).
Note: Hilliard & Burtt (in *Bot. J. Linn. Soc.* 82: 256. 1981) reproduce the Burman type plate.

Xeranthemum staehelina Linnaeus, *Systema Naturae,* ed. 12, 2: 546. 1767.
"Habitat ad Cap. b. spei. Dav. Royen." RCN: 6204.
Lectotype (Hilliard & Burtt in *Bot. J. Linn. Soc.* 82: 251. 1981): Herb. A. van Royen No. 900.312–106 (L; iso- LINN).
Current name: **Syncarpha virgata** (L.) B. Nord. (Asteraceae).

Xeranthemum variegatum Linnaeus, *Systema Naturae,* ed. 12, 2: 546. 1767.
RCN: 6205.
Type not designated.
Original material: none traced.
Current name: **Syncarpha vestita** (L.) B. Nord. (Asteraceae).
Note: This is either a later usage, or a later homonym, of *X. variegatum* P.J. Bergius (1767). Linnaeus does not cite Bergius' account, but both names have a Ray reference in common in their synonymies. However, Bergius' name also has Breyn and Petiver illustrations cited in its synonymy, and its diagnosis is not identical to that used

by Linnaeus. It nevertheless seems unlikely that Bergius and Linnaeus would independently have chosen the same name for different taxa.

Xeranthemum vestitum Linnaeus, *Species Plantarum* 2: 858. 1753.
"Habitat in Aethiopia." RCN: 6195.
Lectotype (designated here by Nordenstam): [icon] *"Xeranthemum frutescens, lanuginosum, foliis longis, mollibus, flore argenteo, amplissimo"* in Burman, Rar. Afric. Pl.: 177, t. 66, f. 1. 1739.
Current name: **Syncarpha vestita** (L.) B. Nord. (Asteraceae).
Note: Hilliard & Burtt (in *Bot. J. Linn. Soc.* 82: 251, 254. 1981) designated 990.3 (LINN) as lectotype. However, it lacks the relevant *Species Plantarum* number (i.e. "3"), is a post-1753 addition to the collection, and is not original material for the name.

Ximenia aegyptiaca Linnaeus, *Species Plantarum* 2: 1194. 1753.
"Habitat in Aegypto." RCN: 2690.
Lectotype (Basak in Thothrathi in *Fasc. Fl. India* 4: 20. 1980; Sands in *Kew Bull.* 56: 51, 55. 2001): [icon] *"Agihalid"* in Alpino, De Plantis Aegypti: 38, 39, excl. fr. 1640. – Epitype (Sands in *Kew Bull.* 56: 51. 2001): Tanzania. Tanga Prov., Mombe Forest reserve, 29 Nov 1962, *Semsei 3580* (K).
Current name: **Balanites aegyptiaca** (L.) Delile (Zygophyllaceae/Balanitaceae).
Note: Sands restricted Basak's earlier type choice by excluding the fruits depicted by Alpino, and also designated an epitype.

Ximenia americana Linnaeus, *Species Plantarum* 2: 1193. 1753.
"Habitat in America." RCN: 2688.
Lectotype (Lucas in Milne-Redhead & Polhill, *Fl. Trop. E. Africa, Olacaceae*: 5. 1968): Herb. Clifford: 483, *Ximenia* 1 (BM-000647659).
Generitype of *Ximenia* Linnaeus.
Current name: **Ximenia americana** L. (Olacaceae).

Ximenia inermis Linnaeus, *Amoenitates Academicae* 5: 378. 1760.
["Habitat in Jamaica."] Sp. Pl., ed. 2, 1: 497 (1762). RCN: 2689.
Type not designated.
Original material: none traced.
Current name: **Ximenia americana** L. (Olacaceae).
Note: Sleumer (*Fl. Neotropica* 38: 90. 1984) claimed that this name is illegitimate as it is based on "Amyris? arborescens" P. Browne (1756) but as Browne did not use binomial nomenclature, *X. inermis* is not illegitimate.

Xylophylla latifolia Linnaeus, *Mantissa Plantarum Altera*: 221. 1771, *nom. illeg.*
"Habitat in America calidiore." RCN: 2152.
Replaced synonym: *Phyllanthus epiphyllanthus* L. (1753).
Lectotype (Webster in *J. Arnold Arbor.* 37: 2. 1956): Herb. Clifford: 439, *Phyllanthus* 1 (BM-000647366).
Current name: **Phyllanthus epiphyllanthus** L. (Euphorbiaceae).
Note: A superfluous name for *Phyllanthus epiphyllanthus* L. (1753).

Xylophylla longifolia Linnaeus, *Mantissa Plantarum Altera*: 221. 1771.
"Habitat in India orientali." RCN: 2151.
Lectotype (Stauffer in *Mitt. Bot. Mus. Univ. Zürich* 213: 222. 1959): [icon] *"Xylophyllos Ceramica"* in Rumphius, Herb. Amboin. Auct.: 19, t. 12. 1755. – Epitype (Stauffer in *Mitt. Bot. Mus. Univ. Zürich* 213: 222. 1959): Papua New Guinea. Morobe District, Wau, Karissa Creek, 25 Mar 1953, *B. W. Taylor 4780* (LAE; iso- A, BRI, BO, L).
Current name: **Exocarpos longifolius** (L.) Endl. (Santalaceae).

X

Note: There has been some confusion between this name and *Phyllanthus epiphyllanthus* L. However, Stauffer (in *Mitt. Bot. Mus. Univ. Zürich* 213: 221. 1959) provided a detailed treatment, and concluded that *E. longifolius* is the correct name for this taxon. He (p. 222) indicated Rumphius, Herb. Amboin. 7: t. 12 as the type, and also indicated a neotype from New Guinea. The Rumphius plate is original material for the name and is accepted as the lectotype, with Stauffer's neotype interpreted as an epitype under Art. 9.8.

Xylopia glabra Linnaeus, *Systema Naturae,* ed. 10, 2: 1250. 1759.
["Habitat in America."] Sp. Pl., ed. 2, 2: 1367 (1763). RCN: 6977.
Lectotype (designated here by Rainer): [icon] *"Xylopicron arbor Barbadensibus"* in Plukenet, Phytographia: t. 238, f. 4. 1692; Almag. Bot.: 395. 1696. – Typotype: Herb. Sloane 98: 117 (BM-SL).
Current name: ***Annona squamosa*** L. (Annonaceae).
Note: See Fawcett & Rendle (*Fl. Jamaica* 3: 199. 1914) who, however, did not make a formal choice of type.

Xylopia muricata Linnaeus, *Systema Naturae,* ed. 10, 2: 1250. 1759, *typ. cons.*
["Habitat in America."] Sp. Pl., ed. 2, 2: 1367 (1763). RCN: 6976.

Lectotype (Fawcett & Rendle, *Fl. Jamaica* 3: 200. 1914): *Browne,* Herb. Linn. No. 1077.1 (LINN).
Generitype of *Xylopia* Linnaeus, *nom. cons.*
Current name: ***Xylopia muricata*** L. (Annonaceae).
Note: Xylopia Linnaeus, *nom. cons.* against *Xylopricum* P. Browne.

Xylopia strigilata Linnaeus, *Flora Jamaicensis*: 20. 1759, *nom. nud.*
"Habitat [in Jamaica.]"
Type not relevant.

Xyris indica Linnaeus, *Species Plantarum* 1: 42. 1753.
"Habitat in Indiis." RCN: 358.
Lectotype (Hansen in Leroy, *Fl. Cambodge Laos Viêt-Nam* 20: 157. 1983): [icon] *"Kotsjiletti-pullu"* in Rheede, Hort. Malab. 9: 139, t. 71. 1689.
Generitype of *Xyris* Linnaeus.
Current name: ***Xyris indica*** L. (Xyridaceae).
Note: Rendle (in *J. Bot.* 37: 497–499. 1899) and Nilsson (in *Kongl. Svenska Vetensk. Acad. Handl.,* n.s., 24(14): 38. 1892) discussed the original elements for this name in some detail but did not choose a type for the Old World element to which this name has long been applied.

Y

Yucca aloifolia Linnaeus, *Species Plantarum* 1: 319. 1753.
"Habitat in Jamaica, Vera Cruce." RCN: 2508.
Lectotype (Wijnands, *Bot. Commelins*: 140. 1983): [icon] *"Yucca arborescens, foliis rigidioribus, rectis serratis"* in Dillenius, Hort. Eltham. 2: 435, t. 323. f. 416. 1732.
Generitype of *Yucca* Linnaeus (vide Hitchcock, *Prop. Brit. Bot.*: 146. 1929).
Current name: **Yucca aloifolia** L. (Agavaceae).

Yucca draconis Linnaeus, *Species Plantarum* 1: 319. 1753.
"Habitat in America." RCN: 2509.
Lectotype (Wijnands, *Bot. Commelins*: 141. 1983): [icon] *"Yucca draconis folio serrato, reflexo"* in Dillenius, Hort. Eltham. 2: 437, t. 324, f. 417. 1732.
Current name: **Yucca aloifolia** L. var. **draconis** (L.) Engelm. (Agavaceae).

Yucca filamentosa Linnaeus, *Species Plantarum* 1: 319. 1753.
"Habitat in Virginia." RCN: 2510.
Lectotype (Fernald in *Rhodora* 46: 8, pl. 8, f. 1. 1944): *Clayton 720* (BM-000051821).
Current name: **Yucca filamentosa** L. (Agavaceae).
Note: See discussion by Ward (in *Castanea* 71: 80. 2006).

Yucca gloriosa Linnaeus, *Species Plantarum* 1: 319. 1753.
"Habitat in Canada, Peru." RCN: 2507.
Type not designated.
Original material: Herb. Linn. No. 441.1 (LINN); Herb. Burser IV: 3 (UPS); Herb. Clifford: 130, *Yucca* 1 (BM); Herb. Linn. No. 441.2 (LINN); Herb. A. van Royen (L), see p. 8; [icon] in Barrelier, Pl. Galliam: 70, t. 1194. 1714.
Current name: **Yucca gloriosa** L. (Agavaceae).

Z

Zamia pumila Linnaeus, *Species Plantarum*, ed. 2, 2: 1659. 1763.
"Habitat in America meridionali." RCN: 7737.
Lectotype (Eckenwalder in *J. Arnold Arbor.* 61: 715. 1980): [icon]
"Palma Prunifera humilis non spinosa Insulae Hispaniolae, fructui jujubino similis, ossiculo triangulo" in Commelin, Hort. Med. Amstelod. Pl. Rar. 1: 111, t. 58. 1697.
Generitype of *Zamia* Linnaeus, *nom. cons.*
Current name: ***Zamia pumila*** L. (Zamiaceae).
Note: Zamia Linnaeus, *nom. cons.* against *Palma-filix* Adans.

Zannichellia palustris Linnaeus, *Species Plantarum* 2: 969. 1753.
"Habitat in Europae, Virginiae fossis, fluviis." RCN: 7027.
Lectotype (Obermeyer in Codd & al., *Fl. Southern Africa* 1: 77. 1966): Herb. Linn. No. 1085.1 (LINN).
Generitype of *Zannichellia* Linnaeus.
Current name: ***Zannichellia palustris*** L. (Zannichelliaceae).
Note: Most authors since Obermeyer have treated 1085.1 (LINN) as the type, although van Vierssen (in *Aquatic Bot.* 12: 125–126. 1982) indicated Herb. Burser X: 126 (UPS) as type (illustrating the fruits as f. 10) and has been followed by several later authors. However, Obermeyer's choice of type has priority.

Zanonia indica Linnaeus, *Systema Naturae*, ed. 10, 2: 1292. 1759.
["Habitat in Malabaria."] Sp. Pl., ed. 2, 2: 1457 (1763). RCN: 7432.
Lectotype (Keraudren-Aymonin in Aubréville & Leroy, *Fl. Cambodge Laos Viêt-Nam* 15: 18. 1975; Chakravarty in Jain & al. in *Fasc. Fl. India* 11: 126. 1982): [icon] *"Penar-valli mas"* in Rheede, Hort. Malab. 8: 39, t. 49. 1688.
Generitype of *Zanonia* Linaneus.
Current name: ***Zanonia indica*** L. (Cucurbitaceae).
Note: Although *Zanonia* dates from 1753, the account of this species (in *Sp. Pl.* 2: 1028) omitted any specific epithet, so *Z. indica* dates from 1759. Keraudren-Aymonin (in Aubréville & Leroy, *Fl. Cambodge Laos Viêt-Nam* 15: 18. 1975) indicated all three of the cited Rheede plates (t. 47–49) as type. This choice was restricted to t. 49 by Chakravarty, pre-dating that of Jeffrey (in *Regnum Veg.* 127: 100. 1993) who restricted it to t. 47.

Zanthoxylum clava-herculis Linnaeus, *Species Plantarum* 1: 270. 1753.
"Habitat in Jamaica, Carolina, Virginia." RCN: 7421.
Type not designated.
Original material: [icon] in Catesby, Nat. Hist. Carolina 1: 26, t. 26. 1730.
Generitype of *Zanthoxylum* Linnaeus (vide Hitchcock, *Prop. Brit. Bot.*: 142. 1929).
Current name: ***Zanthoxylum clava-herculis*** L. (Rutaceae).
Note: Porter (in *Brittonia* 28: 444. 1977) indicated Linnaeus' description from *Hortus Cliffortianus* (1738) as the type but this is contrary to Art. 8.1.

Zanthoxylum trifoliatum Linnaeus, *Species Plantarum* 1: 270. 1753.
"Habitat in China. Osbeck." RCN: 7422.
Type not designated.
Original material: *Osbeck 90*, Herb. Linn. No. 1171.5 (LINN).
Current name: ***Eleutherococcus trifoliatus*** (L.) S.Y. Hu (Araliaceae).
Note: See discussion of 1171.5 (LINN) by Hansen & Fox Maule (in *Bot. J. Linn. Soc.* 67: 205. 1973).

Zea mays Linnaeus, *Species Plantarum* 2: 971. 1753.
"Habitat in America." RCN: 7049.
Lectotype (Iltis & Doebley in *Amer. J. Bot.* 67: 1001. 1980): Herb. Linn. No. 1096.1 (LINN).
Generitype of *Zea* Linnaeus.
Current name: ***Zea mays*** L. (Poaceae).

Zinnia multiflora Linnaeus, *Species Plantarum*, ed. 2, 2: 1269. 1763.
"Habitat – – – – N. L. Burmannus." RCN: 6424.
Type not designated.
Original material: Herb. Linn. No. 353.5? (S); Herb. Linn. No. 1019.2? (LINN).
Current name: ***Zinnia peruviana*** L. (Asteraceae).
Note: Both Torres (in *Brittonia* 15: 12. 1963) and Hind (in Bosser & al., *Fl. Mascareignes* 109: 179. 1993) indicated some doubt ("?") as to whether 1019.2 (LINN) should be considered the type, possibly because Linnaeus wrote in his protologue "Semina hujus misit Burmannus, plantam non dum vidi".

Zinnia pauciflora Linnaeus, *Species Plantarum*, ed. 2, 2: 1269. 1763, *nom. illeg.*
"Habitat in Peru." RCN: 6423.
Replaced synonym: *Zinnia peruviana* L. (1759).
Lectotype (Jeffrey in Jarvis & al., *Regnum Veg.* 127: 100. 1993): [icon] *"Bidens calyce oblongo squamoso, seminibus radii corolla non decidua coronatis"* in Miller, Fig. Pl. Gard. Dict. 1: 43, t. 64. 1756.
Current name: ***Zinnia peruviana*** L. (Asteraceae).
Note: An illegitimate replacement name for *Z. peruviana* L. (1759); see Torres (in *Brittonia* 15: 14. 1963).

Zinnia peruviana Linnaeus, *Systema Naturae*, ed. 10, 2: 1221. 1759.
["Habitat in Peru."] Sp. Pl., ed. 2, 2: 1269 (1763). RCN: 6423.
Replaced synonym of: *Zinnia pauciflora* L. (1763), *nom. illeg.*
Lectotype (Jeffrey in Jarvis & al., *Regnum Veg.* 127: 100. 1993): [icon] *"Bidens calyce oblongo squamoso, seminibus radii corolla non decidua coronatis"* in Miller, Fig. Pl. Gard. Dict. 1: 43, t. 64. 1756 (right).
Generitype of *Zinnia* Linnaeus, *nom. cons.*
Current name: ***Zinnia peruviana*** L. (Asteraceae).
Note: Zinnia Linnaeus, *nom. cons.* against *Crassina* Scepin and *Lepia* Hill.
Zinnia peruviana L. is a new name, not a combination based on *Chrysogonum peruvianum* L. (1753).

Zizania aquatica Linnaeus, *Species Plantarum* 2: 991. 1753.
"Habitat in Jamaicae, Virginiae inundatis." RCN: 7191.
Lectotype (Reveal in *Phytologia* 72: 6. 1992): Herb. Linn. No. 1119.1 (LINN).
Generitype of *Zizania* Linnaeus (vide Green, *Prop. Brit. Bot.*: 188. 1929).
Current name: ***Zizania aquatica*** L. (Poaceae).
Note: Hitchcock (in *Contr. U. S. Natl. Herb.* 12: 124. 1908) and Fassett (in *Rhodora* 26: 153. 1924) each discussed original elements for this name and reached different conclusions as to its application, but without formally typifying the name. Reveal's formal typification appears to have clarified any remaining uncertainty.

Zizania palustris Linnaeus, *Mantissa Plantarum Altera*: 295. 1771.
"Habitat in Americae septentrionalis aquosis. H. U." RCN: 7192.
Neotype (Reveal in *Phytologia* 72: 7. 1992): Herb. Linn. No. 1119.2 (LINN).
Current name: ***Zizania palustris*** L. (Poaceae).

Zizania terrestris Linnaeus, *Species Plantarum* 2: 991. 1753.
"Habitat in Malabariae siccis." RCN: 7193.

The lectotype of *Zinnia peruviana* L.

Lectotype (Majumdar & Bakshi in *Taxon* 28: 354. 1979): [icon]
"*Katou-tsjolam*" in Rheede, Hort. Malab. 12: 113, t. 60. 1693.
Current name: ***Scleria terrestris*** (L.) Fassett (Cyperaceae).
Note: Although a number of earlier authors (e.g. Fassett in *Rhodora* 26:
159. 1924; Kern in *Adansonia*, sér. 2, 2: 101. 1962) have suggested
that the name may have been based on the Rheede illustration,
Majumdar & Bakshi appear to have been the first to explicitly treat
it as the type.

Ziziphora acinoides Linnaeus, *Species Plantarum* 1: 22. 1753.
"Habitat in Sibiria." RCN: 175.
Lectotype (López González & Bayer in *Acta Bot. Malac.* 13: 157.
1988): *Amman 24*, Herb. Linn. No. 39.4 (LINN).
Current name: ***Ziziphora acinoides*** L. (Lamiaceae).

Ziziphora capitata Linnaeus, *Species Plantarum* 1: 21. 1753.
"Habitat in Syria." RCN: 172.
Lectotype (López González & Bayer in *Acta Bot. Malac.* 13: 160.
1988): Herb. Linn. No. 39.1 (LINN).
Generitype of *Ziziphora* Linnaeus (vide Hitchcock in *Amer. J. Bot.* 10:
514. 1923).
Current name: ***Ziziphora capitata*** L. (Lamiaceae).

Ziziphora hispanica Linnaeus, *Centuria I Plantarum*: 3. 1755.
"Habitat in Hispania. Loefl. 441." RCN: 173.
Lectotype (López González & Bayer in *Acta Bot. Malac.* 13: 153.
1988): *Löfling 441*, Herb. Linn. No. 39.2 (LINN).
Current name: ***Ziziphora hispanica*** L. (Lamiaceae).

Ziziphora tenuior Linnaeus, *Species Plantarum* 1: 21. 1753.
"Habitat in Syria?" RCN: 174.
Lectotype (Davis in *Kew Bull.* 6: 120. 1951): Herb. Linn. No. 39.3
(LINN).
Current name: ***Ziziphora tenuior*** L. (Lamiaceae).

Zoegea leptaurea Linnaeus, *Systema Naturae*, ed. 12, 2: 571; *Mantissa
Plantarum*: 15, 117. 1767.
"Habitat in Aegypto? ex Horto Haffniensi. D. zoega." RCN: 6577.
Lectotype (Dittrich in Jarvis & al., *Regnum Veg.* 127: 100. 1993):
Herb. Linn. No. 1028.1 (LINN).
Generitype of *Zoegea* Linnaeus.
Current name: ***Zoegea leptaurea*** L. (Asteraceae).

Zostera marina Linnaeus, *Species Plantarum* 2: 968. 1753.
"Habitat in mari Balthico, Oceano." RCN: 7025.
Lectotype (designated here by Jonsell & Jarvis): [icon] "*Zostera*" in
Linnaeus, Wästgöta Resa: 166, t. 4. 1747.
Generitype of *Zostera* Linnaeus.
Current name: ***Zostera marina*** L. (Zosteraceae).

Zostera oceanica Linnaeus, *Systema Naturae*, ed. 12, 2: 605; *Mantissa
Plantarum*: 123. 1767.
"Habitat in Oceano." RCN: 7026.
Type not designated.
Original material: Herb. Burser XX: 82 (UPS); [icon] in Plantin, Pl.
Stirp. Icon. 2: 248. 1581.
Current name: ***Posidonia oceanica*** (L.) Delile (Posidoniaceae).

Zygophyllum aestuans Linnaeus, *Species Plantarum*, ed. 2, 1: 552.
1762.
"Habitat in Surinamo. Rolander; sed impubes periit." RCN: 3040.
Type not designated.
Original material: none traced.
Note: The application of this name is uncertain.

Zygophyllum album Linnaeus filius, *Dec. Prima Pl. Horti Upsal.*: 11.
1762.
Lectotype (El Hadidi in *Webbia* 33: 51. 1978): Herb. Linn. No. 544.2
(LINN).
Current name: ***Zygophyllum album*** L. f. (Zygophyllaceae).

Zygophyllum coccineum Linnaeus, *Species Plantarum* 1: 386. 1753.
"Habitat in Aethiopia." RCN: 3035.
Type not designated.
Original material: [icon] in Shaw, Cat. Pl. Afr. As.: 41, f. 231. 1738.
Current name: ***Zygophyllum coccineum*** L. (Zygophyllaceae).
Note: El Hadidi (in *Webbia* 33: 56. 1978) designated a Shaw specimen
from Memphis, Egypt (BM) as lectotype. However, this has not
been located in BM, and would not, in any case, have been seen by
Linnaeus so it is not original material for the name.

Zygophyllum fabago Linnaeus, *Species Plantarum* 1: 385. 1753.
"Habitat in Syria." RCN: 3034.
Lectotype (El Hadidi in Rechinger, *Fl. Iranica* 98: 26. 1972): Herb.
Linn. No. 544.1 (LINN).
Generitype of *Zygophyllum* Linnaeus (vide Hitchcock, *Prop. Brit. Bot.*:
153. 1929).
Current name: ***Zygophyllum fabago*** L. (Zygophyllaceae).

Zygophyllum fulvum Linnaeus, *Species Plantarum* 1: 386. 1753.
"Habitat in Aethiopia." RCN: 3038.
Basionym of: *Zygophyllum sessilifolium* var. *fulvum* (L.) L. (1762).
Type not designated.
Original material: [icon] in Burman, Rar. Afric. Pl.: 6, t. 3, f. 1. 1738.
Current name: ***Zygophyllum fulvum*** L. (Zygophyllaceae).

Zygophyllum morgsana Linnaeus, *Species Plantarum* 1: 385. 1753.
"Habitat in Aethiopia." RCN: 3037.
Type not designated.
Original material: Herb. Linn. No. 544.3 (LINN); [icon] in Dillenius, Hort. Eltham. 1: 142, t. 116, f. 141. 1732; [icon] in Plukenet, Amalth. Bot.: 173, t. 429, f. 4. 1705; [icon] in Burman, Rar. Afric. Pl.: 7, t. 3, f. 2. 1738.
Current name: ***Zygophyllum morgsana*** L. (Zygophyllaceae).
Note: Although Schreiber (in *Mitt. Bot. Staatssamml. München* 5: 92. 1963) indicated material in LINN as the type, no distinction was made between sheets 544.3 and 544.4 (which are evidently not part of a single gathering so Art. 9.15 does not apply).

Zygophyllum nitraria Linnaeus, *Demonstr. Pl. Horto Upsaliensi*: 11. 1753.
RCN: 3457.
Type not designated.
Original material: none traced.
Note: The application of this name appears uncertain.

Zygophyllum sessilifolium Linnaeus, *Species Plantarum* 1: 385. 1753.
"Habitat in Aethiopia." RCN: 3038.
Type not designated.
Original material: Herb. Clifford: 160, *Zygophyllum* 2 (BM); [icon] in Commelin, Hort. Med. Amstelaed. Pl. Rar.: 10, t. 10. 1706; [icon] in Burman, Rar. Afric. Pl.: 4, t. 2, f. 1. 1738; [icon] in Dillenius, Hort. Eltham. 1: 142, t. 116, f. 142. 1732.
Current name: ***Zygophyllum sessilifolium*** L. (Zygophyllaceae).
Note: Wijnands (*Bot. Commelins*: 204. 1983) indicated 544.5 (LINN) as type but this collection lacks the relevant *Species Plantarum* number (i.e. "3") and was a post-1753 addition to the herbarium, and is not original material for the name.

Zygophyllum sessilifolium Linnaeus var. **fulvum** (Linnaeus) Linnaeus, *Species Plantarum*, ed. 2, 1: 552. 1762.
["Habitat in Aethiopia."] Sp. Pl. 1: 386 (1753). RCN: 3038.
Basionym: *Zygophyllum fulvum* L. (1753).
Type not designated.
Original material: as basionym.
Current name: ***Zygophyllum fulvum*** L. (Zygophyllaceae).

Zygophyllum simplex Linnaeus, *Systema Naturae*, ed. 12, 2: 295; *Mantissa Plantarum*: 68. 1767.
"Habitat in Arabia. Forskåhl." RCN: 3033.
Type not designated.
Original material: none traced.
Current name: ***Zygophyllum simplex*** L. (Zygophyllaceae).
Note: Authors since Schreiber (in *Mitt. Bot. Staatssamml. München* 5: 100, 102. 1963) have referred to apparently unseen Forsskål material as the type but this has not been traced.

Zygophyllum spinosum Linnaeus, *Species Plantarum* 1: 386. 1753.
"Habitat in Aethiopia." RCN: 3039.
Type not designated.
Original material: [icon] in Burman, Rar. Afric. Pl.: 5, t. 2, f. 2. 1738.
Current name: ***Zygophyllum spinosum*** L. (Zygophyllaceae).

AUTHORS OF NEW TYPIFICATIONS

I am most grateful to the specialists, listed below, who have kindly contributed the new typifications that are published in this book.

Carlos Aedo, Real Jardín Botánico, Consejo Superior de Investigaciones Científicas, Pza. de Murillo, 2, 28014 Madrid, Spain.

Riccardo Baldini, Dipartimento di Biologia Vegetale, Università degli Studi, Via G. La Pira 4, I-50121, Firenze, Italy.

Peter Ball, Erindale College, University of Toronto, 3359 Mississauga Road, N. Mississauga, Ontario L5L 1C6, Canada.

Fred R. Barrie, Missouri Botanical Garden, P.O. Box 299, Saint Louis, Missouri 63166-0299, U.S.A.

Henk Beentje, Royal Botanic Gardens, Kew, Richmond, Surrey, TW9 3AE, U.K.

Irina Belyaeva, Royal Botanic Gardens, Kew, Richmond, Surrey, TW9 3AE, U.K.

Carles Benedí, Departament de Productes Naturals, Unitat de Botànica, Universitat de Barcelona, Avda. Joan XXIII s/n, E-08028 Barcelona, Spain.

Paul E. Berry, University of Michigan Herbarium, 3600 Varsity Drive, Ann Arbor, MI 48108-2287, USA.

Paola Bizzarri, via Cantagrilli 1, Montagnana Val di Pesa, I-50020 Firenze, Italy.

Stephen Blackmore, Royal Botanic Garden, Inverleith Row, Edinburgh, EH3 5LR, U.K.

Santiago Castroviejo, Real Jardín Botánico, Consejo Superior de Investigaciones Científicas, Pza. de Murillo, 2, 28014 Madrid, Spain.

Nicoletta Cellinese, Botany Division, Peabody Museum of Natural History, Yale University, 170 Whitney Avenue, P.O. Box 208118, New Haven, CT 06520-8118, U.S.A.

Arthur Chater, Windover, Penyrangor, Aberystwyth, Dyfed, SY23 1BJ, U.K.

Martin Cheek, Royal Botanic Gardens, Kew, Richmond, Surrey, TW9 3AE, U.K.

Jennifer Edmonds, University of Leeds, Louis Compton Miall Building, Leeds LS2 9JT, U.K.

John Edmondson, World Museum Liverpool, William Brown Street, Liverpool, L3 8EN, U.K.

Holger De Groot, Technische Universität Dresden, Institut für Botanik, 01062 Dresden, Germany.

Hans-Joachim Esser, Botanische Staatssammlung München, Menzinger Strasse 67, D-80638 München, Germany.

Aljos Farjon, Royal Botanic Gardens, Kew, Richmond, Surrey, TW9 3AE, U.K.

Chris Freeland, Missouri Botanical Garden, P.O. Box 299, Saint Louis, Missouri 63166-0299, U.S.A.

Helmut Freitag, Universität Gesamthochschule Kassel, Heinrich-Plett-Strasse 40, D-34132 Kassel, Germany.

Mercè Galbany-Casals, Departament de Productes Naturals, Unitat de Botànica, Universitat de Barcelona, Avda. Joan XXIII s/n, E-08028 Barcelona, Spain.

Roy Gereau, Missouri Botanical Garden, P.O. Box 299, Saint Louis, Missouri 63166-0299, U.S.A.

Heidrun Hartmann, Institut für Allgemeine Botanik, Ohnhorststrasse 18, D-22609 Hamburg, Germany.

Peter Hoch, Missouri Botanical Garden, P.O. Box 299, Saint Louis, Missouri 63166-0299, U.S.A.

Anton Hofreiter, Ludwig-Maximilians-Universität München, Fakultät für Biologie, Systematische Botanik, Menzinger Strasse 67, D-80638 München, Germany.

Bruce K. Holst, Center for Tropical Plant Science & Conservation, Marie Selby Botanical Gardens, 811 South Palm Ave, Sarasota, FL 34236-7726, U.S.A.

Bengt Jonsell, Konsumvägen 20 B, Uppsala SE-76545, Sweden.

Stephen Jury, Centre for Plant Diversity and Systematics, Plant Science Laboratories, University of Reading, Reading, RG6 6AS, U.K.

Deborah Katz-Downie, Department of Plant Biology, 239 Morrill Hall, 505 South Goodwin Avenue, University of Illinois at Urbana-Champaign, Urbana, Illinois 61801, U.S.A.

Jan Kirschner, Institute of Botany, Academy of Sciences, CZ-25243 Průhonice 1, Czech Republic.

Sandra Knapp, Department of Botany, Natural History Museum, Cromwell Road, London, SW7 5BD, U.K.

H. Walter Lack, Botanischer Garten und Botanisches Museum Berlin-Dahlem, Zentraleinrichtung der Freien Universität Berlin, Königin-Luise-Strasse 6-8, D-14195, Germany.

John McNeill, Royal Botanic Garden, Inverleith Row, Edinburgh, EH3 5LR, U.K.

Christoph Neinhuis, Technische Universität Dresden, Institut für Botanik, 01062 Dresden, Germany.

Dan Nicolson, Department of Systematic Biology-Botany, National Museum of Natural History, Smithsonian Institution, Washington D.C., 20013-7012, U.S.A.

Kevin C. Nixon, Bailey Hortorium Herbarium, Department of Plant Biology, Cornell University, 228 Plant Science Building, Ithaca, New York 14853, U.S.A.

Bertil Nordenstam, Swedish Museum of Natural History, P.O. Box 50007, S-104 05 Stockholm, Sweden.

Hideaki Ohba, University of Tokyo, 7-3-1 Hongo, Bunkyo-ku, Tokyo 113-0033, Japan.

E.G.H. Oliver, Department of Botany & Zoology, University of Stellenbosch, Private Bag X1, Matieland 7602, South Africa.

Sylvia Phillips, Royal Botanic Gardens, Kew, Richmond, Surrey, TW9 3AE, U.K.

Annalaura Pistarino, Museo Regionale di Scienze Naturali, via G. Giolitti 36, 10123 Torino, Italy.

Dieter Podlech, Botanische Staatssammlung München, Menzinger Straße 67, D-80638 München, Germany.

Chris Preston, Centre for Ecology and Hydrology, Monks Wood, Abbots Ripton, Huntingdon, Cambs PE28 2LS, U.K.

Heimo Rainer, Institut für Botanik, Universität Wien, Rennweg 14, A-1030 Wien, Austria.

Peter Raven, Missouri Botanical Garden, P.O. Box 299, Saint Louis, Missouri 63166-0299, U.S.A.

Jean-Pierre Reduron, 10, rue de l'Arsenal, 68100 Mulhouse, France.

James L. Reveal, 18625 Spring Canyon Road, Montrose, Colorado 81401, U.S.A.

Harold Robinson, Department of Systematic Biology-Botany, National Museum of Natural History, Smithsonian Institution, Washington D.C., 20013-7012, U.S.A.

Norman Robson, Department of Botany, Natural History Museum, Cromwell Road, London, SW7 5BD, U.K.

Llorenç Sáez, Departament de Biologia Animal, Unitat de Botànica, Universitat Autònoma de Barcelona, E-08193 Bellaterra, Barcelona, Spain.

John C. Semple, Department of Biology, University of Waterloo, Waterloo, ON N2L 3G1, Canada.

David Simpson, Royal Botanic Gardens, Kew, Richmond, Surrey, TW9 3AE, U.K.

George Staples, Bishop Museum, 1525 Bernice Street, Honolulu, Hawaii 96817-2704, U.S.A.

David A. Sutton, Department of Botany, Natural History Museum, Cromwell Road, London, SW7 5BD, U.K.

Edward E. Terrell, Department of Systematic Biology-Botany, National Museum of Natural History, Smithsonian Institution, Washington D.C., 20013-7012, U.S.A.

Nicholas Turland, Missouri Botanical Garden, P.O. Box 299, Saint Louis, Missouri 63166-0299, U.S.A.

Warren Wagner, Department of Systematic Biology-Botany, National Museum of Natural History, Smithsonian Institution, Washington D.C., 20013-7012, U.S.A.

Stefan Wanke, Technische Universität Dresden, Institut für Botanik, 01062 Dresden, Germany.

ACKNOWLEDGEMENTS

Order out of Chaos is the culmination of more than 20 years' work by a small team, of varying personnel based in London, in collaboration with not far short of a thousand botanists scattered throughout the world. It springs from the work of the Linnaean Plant Name Typification Project, which has been housed and supported by the Natural History Museum throughout this period, with additional funding provided by a range of different agencies, but most particularly by the Linnean Society of London.

This book would have been far more modest in scope were it not for the generosity of the Linnean Society of London in underwriting its production costs. During the year leading up to the production of this volume, the Society has also, through grant support, funded expert nomenclatural, database and editorial support by Katherine Challis, and project management, book production and picture research expertise from Leonie Berwick. I am particularly grateful to Gren Lucas, Gina Douglas, John Edmondson, Elaine Shaughnessy, Sandy Knapp and their colleagues at the Society for their long-term support.

Drawing, by Linnaeus, of *Dryas octopetala* L. in his Lapland journal

At the Natural History Museum, Trudy Brannan has supported the development of this book from the outset, and Pat Hart expertly photographed many hundreds of specimens, books, manuscripts and artefacts to provide most of the images that appear here. Others, chiefly of herbarium sheets, were scanned by Tania Durt. The majority of these images come either from the collections of the Natural History Museum or the Linnean Society, but I am also grateful to the Museum of Evolution, Uppsala (Mats Hjertson), the Swedish Museum of Natural History (Arne Anderberg), the Linnaeus Museum, Uppsala (Carl-Olof Jacobsen, Cecilia Bergström and Eva Björn), Statens Fastighetsverk, Stockholm (Lisbeth Söderhäll), the Museo di Storia Naturale, Firenze (Chiara Nepi), the Conservatoire et Jardin botaniques de la Ville de Genève (Daniel Jeanmonod) and the Nationaal Herbarium Nederland, Leiden (Gerard Thijsse) for their generosity in supplying the additional images used here.

Database support has been provided by Sharon Grant, and Nick Turland generously designed an output macro that saved many hours of manual editing. Steve Cafferty's liaising with many taxonomists has resulted in the many new typifications that are published here. Various parts of a draft of the opening chapters of this book were kindly (and carefully) scrutinised by Fred Barrie, Werner Greuter, Bengt Jonsell, H. Walter Lack, Sandy Knapp, John McNeill, Bob Press and Nick Turland, and David Mabberley in addition read the A–Z section of Chapter 7. Their contributions have done much to improve the accuracy of what appears here, but all omissions and errors are my own.

I have been privileged to work within a community of biologists between whom the sharing of expertise and information is freely and gladly undertaken, and without which this broader work could not have been achieved. The scale of this project, and the extended period over which it has taken place makes it impractical to mention all of these biologists by name, though many of them are listed in this book as typifiers of Linnaean names.

The Linnaean Plant Name Typification Project would never have been started without the efforts of William Stearn, Peter Green and John Cannon in obtaining an initial grant to the Linnean Society of London. Norman Robson guided my early attempts to grapple with matters Linnaean and he has always been available to advise on nomenclatural questions and, most significantly, on matters of Latin. Elizabeth Young, John Fiddean-Green, John Marsden and Adrian Thomas, successive Executive Secretaries at the Society have always been supportive, as have John Cannon, Stephen Blackmore, Richard Bateman and Johannes Vogel, Keepers of Botany at the Natural History Museum which has provided the core funding for the Project.

Generous grant support has been successively received from the Science and Engineering Research Council, the National Science Foundation (in association with Missouri Botanical Garden; thanks to Peter Raven, Jim Reveal and Porter P. Lowry), the Leverhulme Trust and, predominantly, the Linnean Society of London. This support has allowed the employment of a succession of Research Fellows who have included Fred Barrie, Dorothy Allan, Nick Turland, Nicoletta Cellinese, Laura Forrest, Steve Cafferty, Mark Spencer and Katherine Challis. Students have included Melanie Hyde, Emma Powell, Peter Brooks, Laurence Carvalho, John Pinel and Sarah Courtney.

Travel to study Linnaean-linked herbaria has been funded primarily by the Natural History Museum but also via grants from NATO and the British Council. Many colleagues have been generous in their time and hospitality during these visits. In Sweden, I am particularly grateful to Arne Anderberg, Kåre and Birgitta Bremer, Bengt and Lena Jonsell, Marie Källersjö, Per-Ola Karis, Jens Klackenburg, Roger Lundin, Roland Moberg and Mats Thulin, and in Finland, Ilkka Kukkonen. In the Netherlands, Willem Brandenburg, Peter Leenhouts, Toon Leeuwenberg, Emiel Oost, JeF Veldkamp and Onno Wijnands helped me a great deal, as did Alicia Lourteig and Porter P. Lowry in Paris. In Geneva, Andre Charpin was a generous host, as were Riccardo and Zita Baldini, Paola Bizzarri, Giovanni Cristofolini, Piero Cuccuini, Giuliana Forneris, Fabio Garbari, Guido Moggi, Enio Nardi, Chiara Nepi, Giorgio Padovani, Rodolfo Pichi-Sermolli, Annalaura Pistarino, Mauro Raffaelli and Annalisa Santangelo in Italy. In North America, I am grateful for the generous help and hospitality of Peter and Elinor Crane, Dan and Alice Nicolson, and Jim and Rose Reveal.

Lastly, I owe an enormous debt of gratitude to Fiona Wild who, over the last two years, has spent an inordinate amount of time reading both my original text and the subsequent proofs of *Order out of Chaos*. Without her help and moral support, I would have been unable to write this book.

PICTURE CREDITS

The Linnean Society of London and the Natural History Museum, London wish to thank the following institutions for their kind permission to use the images listed in the credits, and acknowledge the copyright thereof:

Museum of Evolution, Uppsala, Sweden
Swedish Museum of Natural History, Stockholm, Sweden
Linnaeus Museum, Uppsala, Sweden
Statens Fastighetsverk, Stockholm, Sweden
Museo di Storia Naturale, Florence, Italy
Nationaal Herbarium, Leiden, Netherlands
Conservatoire et Jardin botaniques de la Ville de Genève, Geneva, Switzerland
L'Institut de France, Paris, France

Endpapers: *front* –Linnaeus' annotations on the front endpapers of his own copy of *Species Plantarum*, ed. 2, vol. 1 (1762) and *back* – on the back endpapers of ed. 2, vol. 2 (1763) © The Linnean Society of London.

Linnean Society of London: ii, vi (and 597), ix, x, xi, 3, 4 (and 614), 5, 7, 8 (upper image), 28, 35, 43 (in margin), 45, 50, 52, 54, 63, 67, 72, 74 (and 815), 82, 91, 142, 167–170, 171 (left image), 172, 173, 187–190, 192–196, 198 (left image), 199–210, 213–215, 216 (upper left image), 217–223, 224 (right image), 225–235, 248 (and 408), 264, 269, 291, 295, 308, 314, 319, 323, 331, 340, 353, 363, 368, 383, 388, 397, 404, 408 (and 248), 417, 426, 441, 447, 464, 469, 477, 479, 483, 492, 505, 510, 525, 532, 540, 544, 552, 564, 571, 580, 597 (and vi), 614 (and 4), 624, 644, 654, 680, 683, 695, 699, 705, 712, 718, 723, 744, 748, 755, 773, 787, 790, 795, 806, 815 (and 74), 822, 831, 843, 848, 851, 856, 862, 867, 871, 875, 883, 886, 901, 908, 921, 925, 937

Natural History Museum, London: 2, 6, 9, 13 (and 375), 15, 18–23, 27, 29, 30–32, 38–40, 43 (lower image), 55, 59 (and 895), 66 (lower image), 68–70, 75, 79 (lower right image), 81, 84–89, 92, 93, 95, 96, 100, 101, 103–112, 113 (and 917), 114–142, 143 (lower image), 144–166, 179–181, 182 (left image), 183 (and 481), 198 (right image, also 448), 212, 249, 250, 253, 277, 297, 345, 359, 371, 375, 410, 432, 436, 448 (and 198), 454, 458, 475, 481 (and 183), 498, 518, 548 (and 165), 561, 578, 589, 593 (and 179), 606, 620, 633, 656, 668, 674, 690, 729, 735, 750, 764, 779, 806, 812, 839, 852, 878, 895 (and 59), 904, 917 (and 113), 933, 1017

Museum of Evolution, Uppsala, Sweden: 182 (right image), 184, 197, 216 (upper right and bottom centre images)

Swedish Museum of Natural History, Stockholm, Sweden: 80, 102, 174, 175

Linnaeus Museum, Uppsala, Sweden: 1

Statens Fastighetsverk, Stockholm, Sweden: 79 (upper and lower left images)

Museo di Storia Naturale, Florence, Italy: 143 (upper image)

Nationaal Herbarium, Leiden, Netherlands: 8 (lower image), 185, 247

Conservatoire et Jardin botaniques de la Ville de Genève, Geneva, Switzerland: 11, 224 (left image)

L'Institut de France, Paris, France: 66 (upper image), 171 (right image), 176

Charlie Jarvis: v

GENERAL INDEX

Two separate indices are provided here. The first is a General Index to people, places, events, institutions, publications, herbarium collections and concepts in taxonomy and nomenclature in the opening quarter of the book (i.e. the Introduction, Chapters 1–6 and the introductory parts of Chapter 7). Events in Linnaeus' life are indexed as is usually done in indices to biographies, i.e. as sub-entries in chronological order, under a main entry of "Linnaeus, Carl".

Page number references in *italic* refer to illustrations.

Dissertations prepared by Linnaeus and defended by his pupils are marked as "(diss.)", as some of the dissertations have titles identical to other publications (e.g. the dissertation *Herbarium Amboinense* (1754) and a six volume book of the same name published by Georg Eberhard Rumphius between 1741 and 1750).

A separate Index to Taxonomic Names follows this General Index.

*Stirpium rariorum in Imperio Rutheno sponte provenientium
    icones et descriptiones collectae ab Ioanne Ammano*
    (Ammanus) 105, *105, 619*
Stobaeus, Kilian 63
Stockholm
    Bergius Foundation 8, 26, 176, 192
    Linnaeus' residence 72
    Natural History Museum 1
    Celsius herbarium 184, 198
    Linnaean herbarium 172–176
Strand, B.J. 93
Stuttgart, Staatliches Museum für Naturkunde 26, 177
succulent plants 110
Suite…de plantes à fleurs composées (Vaillant) 165
superfluous names 61
Supplementum Plantarum (Linnaeus filius) 83, 101, 231
suppliers of specimens 33–34
Sur l'arbre du quinquina (Condamine) 123
Surian, herbarium 71
Svensk Flora (Linnaeus, ed. Broberg & al.) 93
Swartz, Olof 168, 178, 231
Swedish Museum of Natural History, Stockholm 8, 26
Swenska Wetenskaps Academiens Handlingar 84
Sydney Code 46
Sylva Hercynia, sive Catalogus plantarum (Thalius) 159
symbols 36, 176
    "aquatic" symbol 36
    annual symbol 34
    biennial symbol 34
    Browne herbarium symbol 229
    Gerber/western Asia symbol 206
    "good description" symbol 29
    Kalm herbarium symbol 215
    Kamchatka symbol 207
    Magnol herbarium symbol 221
    "Meliloti" symbol 36
    Near East (Hasselquist) symbol 209
    perennial symbol 34
    "poorly-known" symbol 29
    Siberia symbol 207
    "veneris" symbol 36
    woodiness symbol 34
synonyms, Linnaean 30
Synopsis Methodica Stirpium Britannicarum (Raius) 17, 92,
    151
syntypes 17–20, 37, 56–57, 61
Systema Naturae (Linnaeus) 1, 3
    and animal nomenclature 3
    descriptions 37
    diagnoses 25
    editions using binomial system 34

    ed. 1 68
    ed. 4 94
    ed. 10 78, 94–95, *95*
    ed. 12 80, 98–99
    ed. 13 101, 223
    Göttingen ed. 80
    and Gronovius 68
    protologues in 24–25
    species name positions 34
    – see also Opera Varia
Systema Vegetabilium (Linnaeus) 101, 223

Tärnström, Christopher 231
taxon 61
Taxonomic Literature (Stafleu & Cowan) 103
taxonomic system, Bauhin 107
Tessin, Carl Gustaf 72, 78, 231, *231*
Thal, Johannes (Thalius) 159
Theatri botanici…liber primus (Bauhinus, C.) 107–108, *107*
Theatrum botanicum (Parkinson) 145
Theodorus aus Bergzabern, Jacobus (Tabernaemontanus) 159
Thesaurus (Seba) 68
Thesaurus Zeylanicus (Burmannus, J.) 68, *68, 113*, 211, *917*
Thoüin, André 231
Thunberg, Carl Peter 231
    Florence specimens 178
    post-1753 material 80, 168
    Uppsala specimens 176
Tilli, Michelangelo 159
TL-2 103
Tokyo Code 9, 22, 48, 58
topotypes 24, 47, 61
Torén, Olof 194, 224, 231–232
Torneå 65
Torner, E. 94
Torsborgen 47
Tournefort, Joseph Pitton de 232
    herbarium 71, 232, 252
    plant classification 64
    publications 159–164
travel 208, 232
*Tractatus de filicibus Americanis (Traité des fougères de
    l'Amérique)* (Plumier) 150, *150*
Treschow, Hermann 211
Trew, Christopher Jacob 20, 164, 78, 79
Trimen 51
trinomials 92
Triumfetti, Giovanni Battista 164
trivial names 2, 34–36
Tulbagh, C. Rijk 232, *232*
    post-1753 material 168

TAXONOMIC INDEX

This taxonomic index includes references to all taxonomic names in the Introduction, Chapters 1–6 and the opening part of Chapter 7. For the A–Z section of Chapter 7, this Index also lists those current names that differ from the original Linnaean binomial for any individual record, as well as replaced synonyms which were not described by Linnaeus. However, as the Linnaean binomials in this section are arranged alphabetically, and are cross-referenced to related basionyms and replaced synonyms, they are not listed again here.

Page number references in *italic* refer to illustrations.

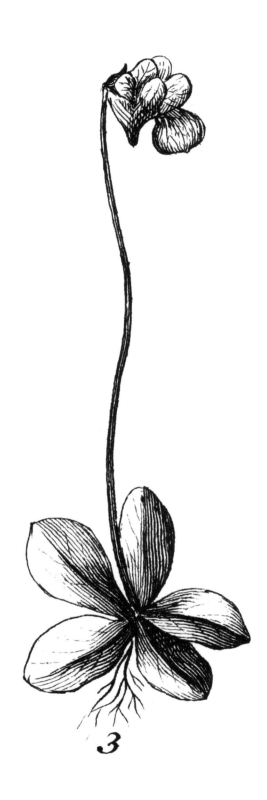

3

Allioni Stirpes rar. pedemontii Taur. 1755. 4to
       plantæ agri Nicein. Paris 1758. 8.
Brown Patr. Natural. hist. jamaica. Lond. 1756. fol.
Kramer Guil. Henr. Elenchus Austriæ inf. Wien 1756. 8.
Müller Joh. Gott. Species plant. dec. 1. Berlin 175.. fol.
Berg... G. P. Flora capensis Stoct. 1757. ol.
Ardoini Petr. observationes botanic. Ved 1759. et 1764.
Jacquin Nic. observ. botanica Wien 1764, 1767.
Meeze David Flora Topica France 1760. 8.
Gouthier Plantæ Avignon 1760. 8.
Micheli J. F. ficus in Italia Rom 1760. 12.
Oeder G. C. Flora danica Hafn. 1761. cc
Gerard Lud Flora Galloprovincialis Paris 1761.
Leysser F. W. Flora halensis Hall 1761.
Quer Jos. Flora hispanica Madrid 1762.
Sauvages Aug. Hortus Monspeliensis Monsp. 1762.
Hudson Guil. Flora anglica Lond. 1762.
Durande P. J. Transactio Lotharingiæ Lother 1766.
Gmelin Phil. Fr. Fasciculus pl. patriæ Tubing 1764
Martin Thom. plantæ cantabrigiensis Lond. 1763. 8.
Lyons Isr. Fasciculus pl. cantabrigiæ Lond. 1763
Schreber J. C. Gramina Lips. 1766.
Reygero Gottl. icones & desc. plant. Hall 1766. fol.
Batsch Ferd. Flora zeelandica Leiden 1764, 17..
     Ambrosinia Bonon 1763.
Carolo irritabilis flor. Florent 1764.
du Chesne Manuel de Botanique Paris 1764.
     Hist. fragariæ Paris 1766.
Wilke J. S. Flora gryphica Gryphy 1765
Wulf Aug. Flora borussica Regiom 1765
Lipp Fr. J. Culindus Botanicum Wien 1765
Gunner J. C. Flora norvegica Nidros 1766.
Rosier Damestr. elementos. botan. Lion 1766. 8.
Müller O. Fr. Flora indices danica Hafn. 1767.
Capeller M. A. desc. montes pilati Basil 1767.
Titius J. D. Systema pl. sexuale Viteb 1767.
Haller Hist. stirpium Helvetia Bern 1768. fol.